REASONING

This interdisciplinary work is a collection of major essays on reasoning: deductive, inductive, abductive, belief revision, defeasible (non-monotonic), cross cultural, conversational, and argumentative. They are each oriented toward contemporary empirical studies. The book focuses on foundational issues, including paradoxes, fallacies, and debates about the nature of rationality, the traditional modes of reasoning, as well as counterfactual and causal reasoning. It also includes chapters on the interface between reasoning and other forms of thought. In general, this last set of essays represents growth points in reasoning research, drawing connections to pragmatics, cross-cultural studies, emotion, and evolution.

Jonathan E. Adler is a professor of philosophy at Brooklyn College and the Graduate School, CUNY. His D. Phil. in philosophy is from Oxford University. His main areas of research and publication are epistemology, philosophy of psychology, informal logic, ethics, and philosophy of education. He is the author of *Belief's Own Ethics*.

Lance J. Rips is a professor of psychology at Northwestern University. He received his Ph.D. from the Psychology Department at Stanford University and has taught at the University of Chicago. He is on the editorial board of the journals *Cognition*, *Public Opinion Quarterly*, and *Informal Logic* and is the author of *The Psychology of Proof* and *The Psychology of Survey Response* (with Roger Tourangeau and Kenneth Rasinski).

REASONING

Studies of Human Inference and Its Foundations

Edited by

JONATHAN E. ADLER
Brooklyn College and the Graduate School, CUNY

and

LANCE J. RIPS
Northwestern University

CAMBRIDGE
UNIVERSITY PRESS

CAMBRIDGE UNIVERSITY PRESS
Cambridge, New York, Melbourne, Madrid, Cape Town, Singapore, São Paulo, Delhi

Cambridge University Press
32 Avenue of the Americas, New York, NY 10013-2473, USA

www.cambridge.org
Information on this title: www.cambridge.org/9780521612746

First published 2008

Printed in the United States of America

A catalog record for this publication is available from the British Library.

Library of Congress Cataloging in Publication Data
Reasoning : studies of human inference and its foundations / edited by
Jonathan E. Adler, Lance J. Rips.
p. cm.
Includes bibliographical references and index.
ISBN 978-0-521-84815-2 (hardback) – ISBN 978-0-521-61274-6 (pbk.)
1. Reasoning.   I. Adler, Jonathan Eric,   II. Rips, Lance J.   III. Title.
BC177.R4344   2008
160–dc22   2007038693

ISBN   978-0-521-84815-2 hardback
ISBN   978-0-521-61274-6 paperback

Contents

* Denotes contributions new to this volume.

v

Preface

This is a collection of essays on reasoning – deductive, inductive, abductive, belief-revision, defeasible, cross-cultural, conversational, argumentative – oriented toward contemporary empirical research. The study of reasoning is, of course, a major focus of investigation in both philosophy and psychology, and this volume attempts to combine these perspectives. Philosophy, especially logic and philosophy of science, inspired psychology's interest in deduction, induction, and other forms of inference. In the past thirty years, the focus of common interest has greatly enlarged to include causal reasoning, cross-cultural comparisons, moral reasoning, and argumentation. There is increasing attention to reasoning as a response to new information or change of belief (belief-revision or defeasible reasoning), which is a far-reaching concern in epistemology. These advances, along with the more than twenty-year debate on rationality, have made reasoning a focal point of cognitive science research and reflections.

Three additional paths also are now converging on reasoning as major research interests. The first is a focus on fallacious reasoning and its reduction through education, which usually goes under the banner of informal logic or critical thinking. Second, the development of pragmatics, particularly following Grice's foundational contribution, has given rise to fruitful applications to traditional reasoning tasks. A number of commentators in the rationality debate have suggested connections between performance on those tasks and conversational expectations. These suggestions are coming in for experimental testing and some corroboration. Third, and last, neuroimaging studies suggest that the contrasts between inductive and deductive reasoning, and, more surprisingly, between thinking about different ethical dilemmas, are realized by distinct areas of brain activity. This volume takes up these issues, along with the more traditional ones.

The idea for this volume began when Adler searched fruitlessly for a collection for a graduate seminar on reasoning. Rips could not do better, because existing anthologies on reasoning were quite out of date. We have tried to choose topics for this book to fill this gap, concentrating on central and emerging issues that are underrepresented elsewhere. We have largely avoided the topic of practical reasoning because it has been much less studied empirically, is more oriented toward philosophical issues, and is well represented in a recent collection (Millgram's *Varieties of Practical Reasoning*). Similarly, there are excellent collections of work in both decision making and analogical reasoning that allowed us to focus on other topics here.

We hope this volume will interest students of reasoning in philosophy, psychology, and cognitive science and that it will inspire the teaching of interdisciplinary courses on reasoning. Readers will, of course, find their way to those sections of the book most relevant to their interests, but we have planned the sequence of chapters to begin with foundational topics that may illuminate issues in the rest of the book. The introductory chapter and the essays in Part I provide (mostly philosophical) background on the general topic of reasoning and rationality. The remaining two parts of the book more evenly comingle work by psychologists and philosophers. Part II focuses on the traditional "ductions" – deduction, induction, abduction, and a few others – and Part III features new trends or less traditional topics, such as the relation of reasoning to pragmatics, cross-cultural research, modularity, and biology. Readers can concentrate on just the psychological or just the philosophical chapters in Parts II and III, but we sincerely hope they won't. Part of our own excitement in putting together this book came from juxtaposing work from these fields that we believe deserve closer linkage. To cite just one example, we think there is much to glean by reading Davidson and Williams on relativism alongside Burnett and Medin's and Nisbett, Peng, Choi, and Norenzayan's chapters on reasoning across cultures.

We have included previously published papers that we deem of special importance to ongoing work, but many of the chapters (labeled with asterisks in the Table of Contents) appear here for the first time. We feel especially fortunate in being able to persuade some of the leaders in the field to set out their points of view on earlier research and to comment on recent trends. Some of these new contributions are detailed summaries and updates of earlier research; others tackle new problems or outline newly emerging research domains. We thank these contributors for their patience during the preparation of this anthology. Our thanks to Blakely Phillips, as well, for her major assistance with the indexing. And special thanks to our families for not deserting us in what was an unexpectedly lengthy and complicated process.

List of Contributors

Jonathan E. Adler
Department of Philosophy
Brooklyn College and the Graduate School
CUNY
New York, NY

George Ainslie
Veterans Affairs Medical Center
Coatesville, PA
Temple University Medical School
Philadelphia, PA

Russell C. Burnett
Department of Psychology
Yale University
New Haven, CT

Stefano Cappa
Neurology Department
University of Brescia Medical School
Brescia, Italy

Susan Carey
Psychology Department
Harvard University
Cambridge, MA

Nick Chater
Department of Psychology
University College London
London, UK

Patricia W. Cheng
Psychology Department
University of California Los Angeles
Los Angeles, CA

Incheol Choi
Department of Psychology
Seoul National University, Korea
Seoul, Korea

L. Jonathan Cohen
Department of Philosophy
Oxford University
Oxford, UK

Leda Cosmides
Psychology Department
University of California Santa Barbara
Santa Barbara, CA

Donald Davidson
Department of Philosophy
University of California Berkeley
Berkeley, CA

Ronald de Sousa
Department of Philosophy
University of Toronto
Toronto, Canada

Renée Elio
Department of Computing Science
University of Alberta
Edmonton, Canada

Jon Elster
Departments of Philosophy and
    Political Science
Columbia University
New York, NY

Jonathan St. B. T. Evans
School of Psychology
University of Plymouth
Plymouth, UK

Ferruccio Fazio
Scientific Institute H. San Raffaele
University of Milan
Milan, Italy

Jerry A. Fodor
Department of Philosophy
Rutgers University
New Brunswick, NJ

Peter Gärdenfors
Department of Cognitive Science
Lund University Kunghuset
Lund, Sweden

Bart Geurts
Department of Philosophy
University of Nijmegen
Nijmegen, The Netherlands

Vittorio Girotto
University IUAV of Venice
Venice, Italy

Franco Grassi
Scientific Institute H. San Raffaele
University of Milan
Milan, Italy

H. Paul Grice
Department of Philosophy
University of California Berkeley
Berkeley, CA

Ulrike Hahn
School of Psychology
Cardiff University
Cardiff, UK

Jonathan Haidt
Department of Psychology
University of Virginia
Charlottesville, VA

Jamin Halberstadt
Department of Psychology
University of Otago
Dunedin, New Zealand

Gilbert Harman
Department of Philosophy
Princeton University
Princeton, NJ

Evan Heit
Department of Psychology
University of California
   Merced
Merced, CA

Denis J. Hilton
Department of Psychology
University of Toulouse
Toulouse, France

Keith J. Holyoak
Psychology Department
University of California
   Los Angeles
Los Angeles, CA

Philip N. Johnson-Laird
Department of Psychology
Princeton University
Princeton, NJ

Daniel Kahneman
Department of Psychology
Princeton University
Princeton, NJ

Deanna Kuhn
Teachers College
Columbia University
New York, NY

Henry E. Kyburg, Jr.
Departments of Computer
   Science and Philosophy
University of Rochester
Rochester, NY

Isaac Levi
Department of Philosophy
Columbia University
New York, NY

David Lewis
Department of Philosophy
Princeton University
Princeton, NJ

Alejandro López
USOLAB
Madrid, Spain

Ken I. Manktelow
Division of Psychology
University of Wolverhampton
Wolverhampton, UK

Douglas L. Medin
Department of Psychology
Northwestern University
Evanston, IL

Elijah Millgram
Department of Philosophy
University of Utah
Salt Lake City, UT

Richard E. Nisbett
Psychology Department
University of Michigan
Ann Arbor, MI

Ara Norenzayan
Department of Psychology
University of British Columbia
Vancouver, Canada

Mike Oaksford
Department of Psychology
Birkbeck College
London, UK

Daniel N. Osherson
Department of Psychology
Princeton University
Princeton, NJ

David E. Over
Department of Psychology
Durham University
Durham, UK

Francis Jeffry Pelletier
Department of Philosophy
Simon Fraser University
Burnaby
British Columbia
Canada

Kaiping Peng
Department of Psychology
University of California Berkeley
Berkeley, CA

Daniela Perani
Scientific Institute H. San Raffaele
University of Milan
Milan, Italy

John L. Pollock
Department of Philosophy
University of Arizona
Tucson, AZ

Lance J. Rips
Department of Psychology
Northwestern University
Evanston, IL

Hans Rott
Department of Philosophy
University of Regensburg
Regensburg, Germany

R. M. Sainsbury
Department of Philosophy
University of Texas
Austin, TX

Tatiana Schnur
Scientific Institute H. San Raffaele
University of Milan
Milan, Italy

Eldar Shafir
Department of Psychology
Princeton University
Princeton, NJ

Brian Skyrms
Department of Logic and
   Philosophy of Science
University of California, Irvine
Irvine, CA
Department of Philosophy
Stanford University
Stanford, CA

Steven A. Sloman
Department of Cognitive and
   Linguistic Sciences
Brown University
Providence, RI

Edward E. Smith
Department of Psychology
Columbia University
New York, NY

Elizabeth Spelke
Psychology Department
Harvard University
Cambridge, MA

Dan Sperber
Centre National de la
   Recherche Scientifique
Paris, France

Robert C. Stalnaker
Department of Philosophy
Massachusetts Institute of
   Technology
Cambridge, MA

Keith E. Stanovich
Department of Human Development
   and Applied Psychology
University of Toronto
Toronto, Canada

Keith Stenning
School of Informatics
University of Edinburgh
Edinburgh, Scotland

Paul Thagard
Computer Science
Philosophy, and Psychology
University of Waterloo
Ontario, Canada

John Tooby
Department of Anthropology
University of California
   Santa Barbara
Santa Barbara, CA

Stephen Edelston Toulmin
Department of International Relations
University of Southern
   California
Los Angeles, CA

Amos Tversky
Department of
   Psychology
Stanford University
Stanford, CA

Bas C. Van Fraassen
Department of Philosophy
Princeton University
Princeton, NJ

Michiel van Lambalgen
Department of Philosophy
University of Amsterdam
Amsterdam, The Netherlands

Carol A. Varey
Sauder School of Business
University of British Columbia
Vancouver, Canada

Achille C. Varzi
Department of Philosophy
Columbia University
New York, NY

Ormond Wilkie
Psychology Department
University of Michigan
Ann Arbor, MI

Bernard Williams
Department of Philosophy
Oxford University
Oxford, UK

Timothy D. Wilson
Department of Psychology
University of Virginia
Charlottesville, VA

Introduction: Philosophical Foundations

JONATHAN E. ADLER

1. Reasoned Transitions

Reasoning is a transition in thought, where some beliefs (or thoughts) provide the ground or reason for coming to another. From Jim's beliefs that

(1)   Either Bill receives an A or a B on the final.

and

(2)   Bill does not receive an A.

he infers that

(3)   Bill receives a B.

Assuming that Jim bases his inference on the deductive relation of (1) and (2) to (3), his conclusion is warranted, since the argument is valid. (1) and (2) implies (3), since it is not possible, as contradictory, for (1) and (2) to be true and (3) false. More formally, φ is a logical consequence of Γ if and only if there is no interpretation (model) in which all sentences of Γ are true but φ is false (Tarski 1983).

Although in reaching (3) Jim comes to a new belief, its information is already entailed by (1) and (2). Unlike deduction, an inductively good argument provides for new beliefs whose information is not already entailed by the beliefs from which it is inferred:

(4)   Bill brought his back pack to class every day of the semester.

So, [probably] (5) Bill will bring it to the next class.

The falsity of the conclusion (5) is compatible with the truth of the premises (4). The premises only render the truth of the conclusion more probable (than in their absence). Although this is a good inductive argument, the premises can be true and the conclusion false, so the argument is invalid.

Deductive validity is monotonic: A valid argument cannot be converted into an invalid argument by adding additional premises. But an inductively good argument is nonmonotonic: new premises alone can generate an argument that is not good. If I add to the argument from (4) to (5), a premise that

(4.1) Bill's back pack was stolen,

the conclusion no longer follows.

In either argument, there is a reasoned transition in thought. The person who draws the inference, takes the premises as his reasons to believe the conclusion (or, in the second case, to believe it probable.) By contrast, the transition in thought from the belief that

(6)   Joe's cousin drives a BMW.

to

(7)   I better call Fred.

is not reasoning because, let's suppose, (6) is merely a cue or stimulus or prompt for the thought that (7) to arise. (6) could not serve as the reason for accepting (believing) (7) as true, as (1) and (2) could for (3). (Another technical use of 'accepting' is for momentary purposes, as, say, when one accepts a supposition for a proof Stalnaker 1987).

Grice (2001) draws the connection between reasons and reasoning by noting that if reason is the faculty which "equips us to recognize and operate with *reasons*" then we should also think of it as the faculty which "empowers us to engage in *reasoning*." Elaborating, he writes

> if reasoning should be characterizable as the occurrence or production of a chain of inferences, and if such chains consist in (sequentially) arriving at conclusions which are derivable from some initial set of

premises. . . . of which, therefore, these premises are . . . reasons, the connection between the two ideas is not accidental. (5)

Grice's 'not accidental' is, presumably, a cautious expression for a conceptual dependence of reasoning on reasons.

Minimally, to have a reason is to have a favorable consideration. However, a reason to do something as in 'my reason to go to the ice cream store is get a sundae' serves to motivate action, whereas a reason to believe does not serve in a motivational role. You can be indifferent to the grade Bill receives, but not, presumably, to the ice cream sundae. Of course, reasons or evidence are typically uncovered through investigation, as when trying to determine the grade Bill receives. But then the motive to investigate obtains independent of the reason to believe. However, in other cases, and much more typically, we acquire evidence that a statement is true and then we come to believe that statement, like it or not. If you overhear Jim affirm (3) that Bill receives a B, then special circumstances aside (e.g., you do not trust Jim), you will come to the corresponding belief, even if you are indifferent to Bill's grade. There is no gap between judging that there are sufficient reasons to believe p true and judging (accepting) that p is true, nor between judging that p is true and believing it.

What is a favorable consideration? Is (1) and (2) a reason to believe (3) because they constitute a mental state or because they constitute facts which serves as the content of that state? If my wanting the sundae is my reason to go to the store, the mental state is the reason. If, instead, what I want to be the case – the fact that I buy apples – is my reason, it supports the truth of the belief's content that I go to the market. ("Belief" suffers a similar ambiguity. Does it refer to an attitude (believing) or to the content of that attitude? We assume that when disambiguation is needed, context will prove adequate.)

Is the reason (as a proposition) a consideration to hold a certain attitude – believing or desiring – or is it a consideration favoring the truth of the content of that attitude (Parfit 2001)? The mother who learns that her son survived a fire in school will be relieved by coming to the belief that he survived, which is then a reason – a consideration in favor – of her taking the attitude of believing it. But that value or utility to her of holding the belief is not a reason that renders it true that her son did survive. In general, it seems that the utility of believing a statement, since it is never a reason for the statement's truth,

can never serve as a proper reason to believe. Arguably, though, even if utilities can not bear on what to believe, they may enter with the question of whether to hold a belief rather than not to hold any (Nozick 1993 Ch. III).

2. Belief and Truth

Induction and deduction supply reasons to believe, since each seeks to preserve the truth of its premises, while extending them to new truths acquired as beliefs. Beliefs are the product of reasoning since belief aims at truth. The end result in belief explains why reasoning matters so profoundly to us. We care to get correct conclusions both intrinsically, since that is what having a belief claims, but also, and more obviously, extrinsically. Belief guides actions, and actions are expected to succeed (reach their goal) only if the beliefs that guide them are true. If you want an ice cream sundae immediately and you believe that the only near-by place to purchase one is on the corner of Broadway and 110th St., then you are expected to succeed (to satisfy your desire for the sundae) only if your belief as to its location is true.

Both forms of reasoning or inference aim to discern what is the case, and so aim, figuratively, for the mind to fit the world (e.g., that I come to believe that a sundae is produced at the store just because it is). By contrast, to desire the ice cream sundae, which specifies one's goal in action (to acquire and to eat the ice cream sundae), is to desire the world to conform to the mind. Beliefs and desires have opposite "directions of fit" (Anscombe 1957, Searle 1983).

The fundamental notion of belief is that of "believing that", a characteristic propositional attitude. If Jim believes that Mary is in Alaska, Jim believes the proposition Mary is in Alaska to be true. Propositions are the contents of sentences or statements as expressed on an occasion. The sentence 'I like Krispy Kreme donuts' cannot be true or false as it stands, since the 'I' has no definite reference. But, on an occasion of use, the fixed meaning of 'I' (and similarly for other indexicals like 'you' or 'now') will have their reference determined; the reference of 'I' is the speaker on that occasion (Kaplan 1989). When values for all indexical and similarly context-sensitive terms in an assertion are fixed, the statement expresses an abstract entity of a corresponding form, a proposition. (The prominent features of context are speaker, hearer, location, and time.)

What is it we are claiming of a proposition when we attribute to it truth or falsity? There does not seem to be any difference between

(8) John believes that the proposition that the nearest ice cream store is on Broadway and 110th St. is true.

and

(9) John believes that the nearest ice cream store is on Broadway and 110th St.

Both seem to say the same thing – to be true or false under the same circumstances – suggesting the generalization:

(T) The proposition that **p** is true if and only if **p**.

The left-hand side of (T) ("The proposition that **p** is true") speaks about a proposition. The right-hand side speaks about the world or a fact of the world namely, that the nearest ice cream store is on Broadway and 110th St. The circular appearance does not run deep.

If (T) is correct, there is no further problem about understanding truth than understanding the corresponding proposition. If you understand the proposition that the library is open on Saturday, no special difficulty attends to your understanding the proposition – that the library is open on Saturday – is true (Tarski 1983; Horwich 1990). However, the (T) equivalence does not tell you how to determine or verify or discover whether a proposition is true.

3. Theoretical and Practical Reasoning

Reasoning to how one should act can involve inductive and deductive transitions, but its aim or purpose is distinctive from reasoning whose endpoint is belief:

(10) I want an ice cream sundae.

(11) The closest ice cream store is on Broadway.

(12) There are no barriers to my going there.

So, (13) I should now go to the ice cream store on Broadway.

[Alternatively, (13) I shall/intend to now go ...]

(10)–(12) constitute good reasons for concluding (believing) that (13) is true. But the ultimate purpose of this reasoning is not to figure out what is the case. Reasoning whose endpoint is belief is referred to as *theoretical reasoning*. Rather, this reasoning (10)–(13) aims to figure out how one should act or *practical reasoning*. The goal is to figure out what one [I] should do (Millgram 2001). As indicated by the alternative reading, (13) should be viewed not just as a judgment as to what is best for me to do, but the actual intention to so act.

Theoretical reasoning aims to answer whether **p** is the case, not whether I ought to believe it, whereas practical reasoning is concerned to determine what I ought to do. The structure of theoretical reasoning is obscured if its conclusions are taken to be of the form 'I ought to believe **p**.' What it is best to do is that act which is better than all the alternatives, on the available reasons. But what one can or should believe is only what is genuinely worthy of belief, not what is currently better than the alternatives. (Think here of the difference between poker, where the best hand wins, and rummy, where only the right or proper hand can win Adler 2002).

The end or goal to which practical reasoning is directed is characteristically set by what one wants or desires, expressed in premise (10). (Not that any desire or want specifies a real end or goal – something that you aim to pursue or that even supplies a reason or motive to pursue. You may have a desire to humiliate yourself, which you neither value nor with which you identify.) Practical reasoning aims at figuring out how to go about satisfying a desire, if opportunity permits. When one's wants or desires set a genuine end or goal, motivation to act according to the conclusion's directive is built in. It is unremarkable self-interest to attempt to satisfy one's own ends.

Can one be motivated to act other than internally (from one's wants or desires)? The Humean 'internalist' answers 'no', whereas the Kantian and other 'externalists' answer 'yes.' (Williams this volume). Externalists hold that one can be motivated purely by recognition of a reason (belief) that a rule or principle or duty applies. So, for example, can a child be motivated to visit his grandmother without any desire to do so nor any threat of punishment? Can his recognition that visiting his grandmother is the right thing to do give him a reason to act accordingly, even if he has no internal – desire – motive to do so? Can reason alone, as a source of judgments of truth and falsity, be a source of reasons (motivation) to act?

With slight differences, the internalist answers "no" to these questions, holding that reason is inert. Reason (belief) is only able to guide one to those actions that are likely to satisfy the motivation that lies elsewhere (in one's desires or wants).

Are one's wants or desires the endpoint to fix one's goal or aims to which practical reasoning is directed? Internalists typically deny that one's ends (or goals) can be rationally altered except on the basis of further desires or wants. One methodological weakness in this instrumentalism is that one's desires are often too unspecific to fix any end. (Richardson 1994; Millgram this volume). Hardly anything is fixed by one's desire to be happily married (to whom?) or to get a good job (which one?). One's ends must be specified to serve as a guide to action, and the specification requires input from beliefs.

Similarly, one's plans need constant updating and modification as they begin to be executed (Bratman 1987). When you learn of a traffic jam further up on the highway, you turn off to the service road. In this way, you fill in your plans, not just modify them. One's plans direct one toward one's goal, but they do so in an open-ended way, leaving room to fill in details and for modifications, as more information is learned.

In theoretical reasoning, motivation is not an ingredient, which is another way to mark its "inertness." Once you judge a conclusion true, based on the reasoning, you thereby believe accordingly, idiosyncratic psychological barriers aside (e.g., distraction). Belief is in one way passive and not subject to choice: Think of all the beliefs you pick up on the way to your morning commuter train to which you are completely indifferent, for example, that your new neighbor is wearing a green jacket today. No motivation is necessary for belief to respond to a convincing argument. It is a heard contradiction, discussed further below, to affirm a statement of the form "p is true, but I don't believe it" ("Moore's Paradox").

The objective of theoretical reasoning is to relieve doubt or to satisfy curiosity or to diminish puzzlement by achieving corresponding beliefs, whereas the objective of practical reasoning is to secure the means to realize one's ends. Because practical reasoning is directed toward action it is overtly constrained by time and resources – its objective is to discover which option is best, all available things considered. But the objective of theoretical reasoning is not merely to discover what proposition (option) is best supported by one's available evidence, but what is correct (true). Consequently, to draw a conclusion in theoretical reasoning requires the claim not just that one's evidence is the total relevant evidence available, but that the evidence is

representative, rather than a skewed sample. It follows further that our limits in gathering and assessing evidence contours theoretical reasoning, but, like utilities, our limits cannot play an overt role in drawing a conclusion. You should not – and, perhaps, cannot – believe a conclusion because it is best supported by the evidence so far and that you do not have more time to examine further evidence. (The problems raised here are for assimilating theoretical to practical reasoning. For a discussion of the assimilation of practical to theoretical reasoning, see Velleman 2000.)

4. Theoretical Reasoning: Limits, Closure, and Belief-Revision

Our limits restrict the resources and time to devote to empirical search, testing, and inquiry, as well as to the inferences worth carrying out. The valid and sound argument from "Trump is rich" to "Trump is rich or cousin Harry is in Jamaica" yields no new worthwhile information. Endless such trivial consequences (e.g., p, p or q, p or q or r, ...; p, p & p, p & p & p ...)[1] can be so generated, which will just "clutter" one's memory as explicit beliefs (Harman 1986; Sperber and Wilson 1986). Also, if one "loses" or forgets the origination of the disjunctive belief in the belief that Trump is rich, one will mislead oneself on attending to it that one has special reason to believe Harry is in Jamaica or that it bears a significant connection to the other alternative that Trump is rich.

Theoretical reasoning involves revising beliefs we already hold. Rules of standard logic or implication, however, do not (Harman 1986). Jane believes that if she attends Yale, she'll become an atheist. She believes that she will attend Yale. If she reasons by the impeccable rule of Modus Ponens (MP: p and if p, q implies q), she concludes that she will become an atheist. But although she now has a reason to believe that conclusion, logic does not decide that she will or should believe it. Once Jane becomes aware of that conclusion, she also becomes aware of other beliefs, which deny that she will ever be an atheist. Instead of drawing the MP conclusion, Jane ceases to believe the conditional, which served as her main premise. Reasoning that results in modification of beliefs of one's own may be dubbed "self-reductios" (ad absurdum).

Examples such as the previous one show how from deduction we can learn something new about the content of our beliefs, even though, in a figurative way of speaking, deduction only renders explicit information already in the premises. Briefly, our beliefs are not closed under deduction. (Similar, but distinguishable, worries attend to the requirement that our beliefs at a given time be consistent. The worries are different for failures of closure or consistency that the agent does not recognize and those cases in which the agent does recognize the failure. The latter cases generate more forceful conceptual friction with the concept of belief. For recent treatment of these logical requirements on belief, see Christensen 2004.) One's beliefs are closed just in case if one believes p and p implies q, one believes q. None of us mortals have bodies of beliefs that are deductively, let alone inductively, closed. There are complex tautologies or logical equivalents to what we believe, which we will not believe and may even disbelieve. The failure of deductive closure for belief is a facet again of our limits, including our limited grasp of our own beliefs, our lack of omniscience, and our "inability" to perceive the future. If Socrates believes that no one does wrong knowingly, does Socrates believe that Richard Nixon did no wrong knowingly? (For examples and critical reflection's see Stalnaker 1987: Ch. 5.) Implications or deductions from one's beliefs can yield surprising conclusions. Well before the discovery of penicillin by Fleming, biologists knew that molds cause clear spots in bacteria cultures, and they knew that a clear spot indicates no bacterial growth. Yet, they did not come to realize, or even to hypothesize, that molds release an antibacterial agent. The observations did not render salient the disparate beliefs and place focus on them together (Cherniak 1986).

So, putting aside closure imposed as an idealization for specialized purposes (Hintikka 1962), one can believe, or even know, p, and p imply q, without believing or knowing q. Similarly, it can be the case that a = b and that one believes (and even knows) that a is F, without one believing that b is F, though the embedded argument is valid. So, for example, Lois Lane may know that

(14) Superman flies.

In the tale, it is true that

(15) Superman is Clark Kent.

But Lois Lane does not know (and actually believes false) that

(16) Clark Kent flies.

The fault lies with a lack of knowledge of the middle step – (15). Knowledge or belief is "opaque" – in "S believes that a is F" the position of "a" is not purely referential. (Opacity intrudes on what counts as a reason: If Lois Lane wants to marry only a man who flies, does she have reason to marry Clark Kent?) Consequently, substitution of arbitrary coreferential terms is not truth-preserving. Within the scope of Lois Lane's beliefs or knowledge, "Superman" in (14) does not simply refer to an object (Superman), but to that object as understood by Lois Lane. (The problem originates with Frege [1970]. An alternative account holds that the substitution does go through. The assumption as to how the person [Lois Lane] thinks of the name is only pragmatic. A parallel worry applies to the distinction between attributive and referential meanings of a term [Kripke 1977]. To appreciate this alternative reading substitute for the names a pure pointing device like "this" or "that.")

A much-discussed example takes the problem of closure a step further, because it holds that knowledge is not closed even when the person knows the "middle" step – the relevant implication (Dretske 1970; Nozick 1981). Assume that Tony is looking at an animal behind a cage marked "zebra," which looks like a zebra. Barring any weird circumstances, we would say that Tony knows that

(14) The animal I am looking at is a zebra.

Let's now grant that Tony also knows the implication that

(15) If the animal I am looking at is a zebra, then it is not a mule cleverly disguised to look like a zebra.

(14) and (15) imply

(16) The animal I am looking at is not a mule cleverly disguised to look like a zebra.

Still, we are reluctant to attribute knowledge of (16) to Tony. Those who oppose closure reason that Tony has never checked that the animal he is looking at is not such a cleverly disguised mule. Tony is simply looking at the animal from outside the cage. These theorists reject:

(Epistemic Closure EC) If X knows that p and X knows that p implies q, then X knows that q.

Arguably, this is the principle licensing Descartes' famed sceptical argument: If you know that you are in your office and you know

6 JONATHAN E. ADLER

that if you are in your office, you are not just *dreaming* it, then you know you are not just dreaming it. But you do not know that you are not dreaming it. So you do not know you are in your office.

The rejection of EC fits the previous zebra example, answers Descartes' sceptical argument, and it is explained as due to our not checking on all the implications of propositions that we know. The rejection also follows from analyzing knowledge as involving satisfaction of the following subjunctive or counterfactual conditional:

(Tracking Knowledge TK) Were *p* false, S would not believe *p*.

The most likely (or nearest) way for it to be false that you are in your office is for you to be somewhere else, like your kitchen. If so, you would clearly recognize where you were in the other room. Consequently, you would satisfy (TK), because you would not believe that you were in your office. (TK) does not then support (EC). (Contextualists, whose views we return to below, hold that you do know that you are not dreaming, when you are in an ordinary setting. However, when Descartes or a skeptic mentions the possibility that you are dreaming, they alter the context or standards for knowing. Only then you do not know that you are not dreaming. But, in that case and compatible with EC, you do not know that you are in your office either.)

Despite these advantages, the dominant view is that EC cannot be rejected, since deductive implication preserves truth. What better way to know the truth of a proposition but by deducing it from a proposition one does know? (For overview, see Luper 2006). Without pursuing this line, it's worth noting that sometimes (nontrivial) deductions seem not be a way to advance knowledge. From the evidence of (17),

(17) The Smiths are making an extravagant wedding for their daughter.,

(18) is concluded:

(18) The Smiths are wealthy.

From (18), (19) follows:

(19) In making the extravagant wedding, the Smiths are not just appearing to be wealthy.

Assume that you are in a discussion with someone who disputes whether the Smiths are really wealthy. Although (18) implies (19), it seems to

beg the question in this context to use (18) as a reason to believe (19). (17) can only provide evidence for (18) if (19) is assumed or presupposed. But (19) is in dispute. If it is presupposed in treating (17) as evidence for (18), then the warrant or support that (17) lends to (18) does not *transmit* to the conclusion (19) (Wright 2000).

5. Belief-Revision, Holism, and the Quine–Duhem Thesis

If a corpus of beliefs is not closed for the reasons suggested, it is likely to be inconsistent. If there are serious implications of one's beliefs that one fails to believe, one is likely to acquire the contrary of some of those beliefs without recognizing the incompatibility. Here's a very ordinary illustration of Lewis's:

I used to think that Nassau Street ran roughly east-west; that the railroad nearby ran roughly north-south; and that the two were roughly parallel. (1982, 436)

Once these beliefs are brought together with the evident tacit belief, Lewis recognizes that the set of beliefs {Nassau Street ran roughly east-west; the railroad nearby ran roughly north-south; Nassau Street and the railroad nearby are roughly parallel; if one path is east-west and another is north-south, they are not parallel} is inconsistent. They cannot be simultaneously true. Once Lewis recognizes the inconsistency, he can no longer hold on to all these beliefs ("I used to think..."). The question that he now confronts – the question of belief-revision – is how he should restore consistency.

Rejecting any one or more of the members of the inconsistent set will restore consistency. Quine (1980) argued that selection to restore consistency depends on extralogical considerations. He made these claims in developing his criticism of the "dogma of empiricism" that statements (hypotheses) can be tested in isolation. Instead, he put forth what is referred to as the "Quine–Duhem Thesis" (Duhem 1954) that hypotheses are never tested in isolation. Hypotheses (or theories) do not entail any observational predictions by themselves. To derive predictions that serve to test a hypothesis, assumptions are required that crucial terms are not empty and that conditions are normal. Newton's enormously successful theory of gravity and mechanics erred in its (pre-1846) prediction of the orbit of Uranus. But Uranus's deviation was treated as an anomaly, rather than a falsification, because the theory made substantial assumptions about the operative gravitational forces. In the discovery of Neptune, some of those assumptions were abandoned, rather than the Newtonian theory itself. In general, when a well-regarded hypothesis fails, we do not immediately conclude that the hypothesis is false, as the traditional view implies, rather than that some of the conditions assumed normal – the auxilliary assumptions – failed.

The hypothetico-deductive model incorporating the Quine–Duhem thesis is represented schematically as

H and Auxilliary Assumptions (AA) imply O.

If O, then (H and AA) are confirmed.

If not O, then (H or AA) fails.

The latter is the crucial result because consistency does not demand the falsity of H.

The problem of what extralogical principles to apply to belief-revision has generated numerous investigations and constructions of logics of belief revision (Hanson 2006; for an introduction to a computational approach to belief reasoning and revision, see Pollock and Cruz 1999: Ch. 7). A central proposal is that belief revision should be conservative. One revises one's beliefs so that rejection or modification is minimal. You all-out believe that Skinner wrote *Walden II* and that Chaucer wrote the *Canterbury Tales*. But if you discovered that one of these is wrong, you would sooner surrender one rather than both and the latter, rather than the former, which is attested to by a greater variety of good sources. To surrender the belief about Skinner's authorship would require surrendering – nonconservatively – much more information than surrendering the latter.

But conservatism cannot stand alone. Lewis cannot just decide to give up the belief that Nassau Street ran roughly east-west and keep the one that the railroad nearby ran roughly north-south, although that surrenders only one, rather than more, among equally contentful, incompatible, beliefs. Merely his deciding would not be a sufficient reason that the belief retained is true.

Other principles of belief revision include prominently simplicity and coherence. The more a belief coheres, fits, or is explanatorily connected, with others, the more resistant it should be to modification. But some conflictual beliefs may be surrendered (in strain with

conservatism) to increase coherence. You believe that ten-year-old Jim is in good health, that he will be in the tennis tournament tomorrow, and that he will meet you for lunch at noon. You learn that he is not at school today and that his mother is not at her office. You infer that Jim is sick. That best explains the latter two beliefs – unifies them in an explanatory nexus. But as a consequence you surrender other beliefs about Jim (e.g., that he will be at tennis practice later in the afternoon).

Coherence is an internal requirement on one's beliefs. But our belief corpus improves by external input, especially through our senses. The improvement is not just in the addition of new beliefs picked up as we navigate our environment. Perception and other sensory mechanisms provide for ongoing self-correction which is a hallmark of scientific method (Sellars 1963). If you believe that Lisa is in Alaska and you see her car at the local diner, you surrender – and so correct – your belief. Normally, beliefs operate as a filter on perceptual judgment. If Lisa drives a blue Ford and that was all that was in your perceptual field as you approached the diner, then if you noticed the car, you would not think of it as hers, given that you believe that she is in Alaska.

However, there must be limits to this filtering role, otherwise our beliefs would not be subject to correction. Once you see the car more closely, and observe the familiar dent on the hood, you are compelled to notice that it is Lisa's blue Ford. Your belief is revised. The new perceptual information nullifies your prior belief, evidence that perception can succeed as a self-corrective on reasoning only if it has some independence of operation from belief and reasoning (from one's "central systems," Fodor 1983).

If the formation of perceptual beliefs always had to be first checked (for veracity) by way of one's corpus of beliefs, it would be subject to the "dogmatism paradox." If you know that Lisa is in Alaska, why should you even acknowledge as putative undermining evidence that it is her car at the Brooklyn diner? Shouldn't you rather judge that, say, her husband must have taken her car, because, if you know that she is in Alaska, shouldn't you know that putative evidence against it must be mistaken or misleading? [Think of the tautology: $p{\rightarrow}((q{\rightarrow}{\sim}p) {\rightarrow} {\sim}q)$.]

However, there is something deviant about the conditional "If there is evidence against my knowledge (that Lisa is in Alaska), then that evidence is mistaken or misleading." It does not seem to be open to modus ponens, just as the following is not:

> If my wife cheated on me, I would never know. (Harman 1973; Ginet 1980; Stalnaker 1987)

Were I to discover that my wife cheated on me, I would reject the conditional (or its antecedent), rather than conclude that I would never know that she cheated on me. Similarly, the previous conditional of the dogmatism paradox is to be rejected when the undermining evidence is obtained, rather than rejecting the evidence as misleading or false.

6. Deductive Rules and Deviant Logics

Usually, of course, conclusions drawn from one's beliefs simply form new beliefs. But often conclusions are drawn that cast doubt back on the premises (beliefs) or the inferential transitions from which those conclusions are drawn.

In drawing out conclusions, what rules should be used? Although in the case of induction and especially deduction a core of rules and results are well established, disputes abound about their scope and other putative rules are flat-out contested. After considering some of these rules and disputes, we briefly turn to how the rules are to be justified and selected.

Standard or classical logic is first-order quantification or predicate logic – the logic of the truth-functions ("and," "or," "not," "if, then") and the quantifiers ("For every . . . ," "For at least one . . . ") The "first-order" implies that the variables of quantification take as values objects or individuals, not names, predicates, propositions, or properties. First-order logic (including identity) is sound: no proof (a syntactic notion) will take one from truths to falsehoods. Every proof corresponds to a valid argument, a semantic notion. But also and more distinctively, first-order logic is complete (every logical truth or valid argument is provable). Once second-order quantification is admitted, particularly to embrace set theory, the extended logic is no longer complete.

Unlike additions to standard logic, as in adding axioms for necessity and possibility to logic, deviant logics deny some basic logical law. Quine's "holism" opened a door to defend deviation from classical logic, which Quine (1970) attempted to quickly shut. The holistic assumption that justification for logical laws, like the justification of empirical claims, is sensitive to the whole body of beliefs provides an opening

for arguing that a logical law is to be rejected because removing it from one's corpus of beliefs increases coherence. But although Quine's opened this door as a theoretical possibility, he argued that the standard logical laws are too useful or indispensable to the progress of science for abandonment.

Additionally, Quine argued that when you try to deny a logical law like the law of non-contradiction (i.e., $\sim(p$ & $\sim p)$, your "&" and "$\sim$" no longer translate "and" and "not," as intended. These operators are fully specified by the truth-tables and the implied laws. They are defined implicitly by their roles in these assignments and laws. (However, we know that unless restraints are imposed on implicit definitions, specifically, that they introduce no new theorems ["conservative"], the introduction of new connectives can generate crazy rules, ones from which anything can be deduced; Prior 1960; Belnap 1962). If someone infers from an utterance of "A or B" to "A," we can be sure his "A or B" is not the English disjunction. The deviant logician's predicament is that "when he tries to deny the doctrine he only changes the subject" (Quine 1970), p. 81.

Quine's argument opposes the plausible claim that the denial of an operator in some inferential roles is compatible with its playing the appropriate roles in other inferences, sufficiently so as to remain a viable candidate for capturing the basic meaning. Even the denial that all contradictions are false, allows for preserving a good deal of classical logic with suitable adjustments. In classical logic, every sentence follows from a contradiction. However, this trivialization can be excised by denying the rules from p to $p \vee q$ (weakening); and from $p \vee q$ and $\sim p$ to q (disjunctive syllogism)). In the former case, the denial is independently motivated by the lack of relevance in subject matter of the premise to the disjunct q. With a number of other adjustments a major portion of basic logic remains in tact, and the resulting logical system can be sound and complete (Priest 1998).

Although most of the alleged examples of contradictions that are candidates for the ascription of truth are rarified, one of them is a resource from which a number of deviant logics draw strength, and it resonates with everyday reasoning. The resource is in the phenomena of vagueness. The vagueness of a term is that while it sorts objects into those to which the term applies and those to which it does not, it leaves undecided many objects. When a teenager's room has no clothes on the floor and dirty dishes have been removed, but it has not been dusted or swept, it is indeterminate, let's suppose, whether it is clean or not. A defender of the view that there can be true contradictions might say that the room is both clean and not clean. Others may deny the law of excluded middle: that either the room is clean or it is not clean.

A contextualist confronted by an assertion such as "John's room is clean" will respond that for everyday purposes, it is enough that his clothes are off the floor and that the dirty dishes have been removed. But if John develops asthma, you will not count the room as clean until a careful dusting is complete. The proposition expressed by the assertion is false in that context. Outside of any contextual specification, there is no assigning it a truth-value (or assigning it additional truth-values) (Lewis 1983). Contextualism explains how one utterance of "John's room is clean" can be true and another false, when there is no change in John's room. Because contextual variations include variations in the importance of the matter, contextualism also makes sense of why when you inquire as to the truth of a hypothesis, you are bound to investigate harder in one context (where the costs of error are greater) than in another.

Contextualism, however, is a minority view in how to handle the sceptical implications of vagueness that originates from the "sorites paradox." In its historical form, the sorites is presented as the "paradox of the heap" (Sainsbury 1988; this volume). If you have a heap of sand, and you subtract one grain, you still have a heap (one grain cannot make a significant difference). The judgment suggests a principle: if you now subtract one grain from the previous heap, you still have a heap. But repeated applications leaves you with a couple of grains that you are committed to taking to be a heap, even though they obviously do not make a heap.

Intuitionists respond that when there are too few grains in a pile to clearly be a heap and too many grains to clearly not be a heap, it is not true that either that pile is a heap or that it is not a heap, contrary to the law of excluded middle. And if it not clearly either, the failure to not be a heap does not imply that it is a heap, contrary to the law of double-negation.

The sorites is derivable via the impeccable principle of mathematical induction: R_0 is the base case with a certain property P (e.g., That large collection of grains of sand is a heap). And if R_n has P, there is some fraction of it (e.g., one grain of sand) such that if we decrease R_n by that amount, then what results – R_{n-1} – still is P (e.g.,

that 1-less grain collection is a heap). Then any lesser R_i has P (e.g., every collection of grains of sand less than the base case is a heap including a one-grain collection). Alternatively, the paradox can be presented simply as a string of MP arguments, each one yielding a decrement from the previous. Either way, the nonnoticeable difference for any sized heap – the decrement between R_n and R_{n-1} – becomes a marked difference after enough applications.

The sorites paradox is particularly wrenching because it seems to arise merely from the vagueness of terms, which holds of most terms. Most, if not all (nonartificial) terms leave undecided an unlimited range of cases for example, "blue," "happy," "short," "table," "flat," "rich," "child." At what moment does childhood end? The exception would be contrived cases where an exact specification is provided: We could define a U.S. adult citizen as rich* just in case his total wealth is $484,234.04 or higher. However, to attempt exact replacements for our vague terms would fail to preserve their value or usefulness. (On utility considerations for vagueness, see Parikh 1994.) The contrived precision would require a sharp break in judgments, where a gradation of responses is appropriate (between, e.g., a person who is rich and one who is very well off financially). The vagueness of a term reflects its "tolerance" for certain tiny alterations, which can mount up to significant alterations.

But is this insensitivity in the term or is it merely because of the limits of our discriminatory powers, which are foisted on to the term? "Epistemicists" favor the latter, which allows them to avoid offending against standard logic. They hold that there is an exact boundary for vague terms, but it is unknowable (Williamson 1994; Sorensen 2001). (The previous question suggests another: Is it reality – heaps themselves – that is vague or how we describe it, e.g., some collections of grains of sand are described as "heaps"?)

Among the numerous attempts to solve the problem the dominant view preserves almost all of standard logic, allowing only for truth-value gaps. A "supervaluationist" observes that within the indeterminate cases, we are free, as far as a consistent assignment of truth-values, to decide them as serves our purposes, as contextualists claim, too (Fine 1975). Some will treat a U.S. citizen with total wealth of $325,683.03 as rich and others not (for purposes of assigning, say, an estate tax), because this amount is clearly between the definitely not rich and the definitely rich. When we so decide cases we provide "sharpenings." However, on every sharpening "That citizen is either rich or not rich" will be true, so supervaluationists can accept the logical law of excluded middle (although neither disjunct may be definitely true). Consequently, on a supervaluationist view, a conditional sentence – the second step in the sorites paradox (e.g., if that citizen is rich with $325,683.03 then he is rich with $325,683.02) will not come out true for every sharpening of it. There is a sharpening under which the antecedent is true, but the consequent false, so that the conditional is false. Because supervaluationism does not reject logical laws and it does not require powers in our language that supercede our own, it has the advantage of providing for a conservative response to the sorites.

But is the supervaluationist right, to return to the earlier example, that "'either that room is clean or not" is definitely true, when the room is clearly a borderline case? Worries like this incline others, although far fewer, to take the route of treating the initial reaction that neither alternative is true at face value. We can say only that John's room is clean to a certain degree, or to a higher degree than others. The error on this probabilistic approach is to contrive to derive absolute judgments from matters of degree.

7. Ordinary Language Challenges to Logic and the Conversationalist Response

A very different source of doubts about logical reasoning as standard first-order logic derives from alleged deviations from ordinary language. Numerous patterns of inference of ordinary language, as well as straightforward readings of complex statements, prima facie do not obey the rules governing deductive logic or the logical operators. Some examples:

(20) John goes drinking and John gets arrested.

(21) John gets arrested and John goes drinking.

If "and" is the "&" of formal logic, it is symmetric, so (20) and (21) should be equivalent. Yet, they do not seem to mean the same, (21) does not follow from (20) (or conversely). Another:

(22) John will order either pasta or steak, but he orders pasta.

So (23) John does not order steak.

The inference seems valid, but fails on the truth-table analysis of "v" (inclusive "or"). Finally for an example using a conditional to which we devote the next section:

(24) If you tutor me in logic, I'll pay you $50.

So (25) if you don't tutor me, I won't.

The conclusion seems to follow. However, the straightforward translation of it into logic yields a fallacious form, one that appears valid, but that isn't.

One reaction to such discrepancies is: so much the worse for ordinary language. It requires formal regimentation to be a satisfactory medium of reasoned argument. The opposed reaction is: so much the worse for logic's claim to provide a systematic analysis of ordinary reasoning.

The most profound reaction is that of H. P. Grice's (1989). His account of conversational reasoning opposes both previous ones. Grice's claim is that the logic of ordinary language is already that of formal logic. However, we impose, without recognition of the imposition, assumptions or expectations on ordinary language because we treat the sentences as assertions or other contributions to a conversation. In (22)–(23), we assume that John could not order both pasta and steak, given our knowledge about eating. The inference from (20) to (21) (or their equivalents) stands. However, the speaker exploits the listing of conjuncts, which is mutual with the hearer, as implicating an ordering (in time). Grice's account explains these deviations without positing an ambiguity in the relevant logical constant (e.g., "and," "and then").

Conversation or social communicational exchanges are facilitated by shared or mutual assumptions that are not part of what is said or its logical implications, but which nevertheless are invited, given the common goals of the cooperative exchange. The fundamental "maxim" (and so expectation or presumption) is that the speaker intends to cooperate to advance the purposes of the conversational exchange. The Cooperative Principle (cp) includes subsidiary maxims. The speaker intends his contribution to be informative, warranted, relevant, and well formed (for brevity, style, politeness, and comprehension). This package of maxims under the cp Grice thought to be justified as principles for rational cooperative arrangements for beneficial ends (of transferring information).

What we mean to communicate typically goes beyond what is said, although calculated on the basis of what is said:

H (hearer): Are you going to Jeff's party?
S (speaker): I have an exam the next day.

S's stated response has nothing to do with H's question. But H presumes that S is following the cp, and that is best explained if S meant to communicate a negative answer, as well as supplying H with further information (as to her reason). S conversationally *implicates*, in Grice's term, that she will not attend. If, however, the assertion's only function was to yield this implicature, then the burden on the hearer of drawing the inference, and the risk that he would not succeed, is not worthwhile: Why not answer the question directly? Consequently, assuming that the cp is in force, the speaker must intend to communicate further thoughts (beliefs) – that the studying is his reason for not attending, and that the activities are incompatible. She efficiently conveys much more information than she would by a mere "no." (Optimization of costs and inferences is central to the pragmatics of Sperber and Wilson 1986).

The technical term "implicature" is meant to draw a comparison with logical implication, yet to distinguish them. The best, although still imperfect, test for implicatures, as contrasted to logical or semantical implications, is *cancellation*. This speaker could say without contradiction: "I have an exam on the next day, but maybe I'll go to the party anyhow." The second clause cancels the implicature of the first. In (20)–(21), the ordering is arguably not part of the meaning because we can append to either, without contradiction, a cancellation "...but maybe not in that order."

Cancellation provides a way to establish that the fundamental speech-act of assertion does not merely conversationally implicate that the speaker believes what he asserts. For, again, it is contradictory to assert any statement of the form "*p*, but I do not believe that *p*," which is the basic form of Moore's Paradox. The paradox is that this sentence is consistent: It can be raining (*p*), say, but I not believe it. Yet, it is inconsistent to assert. The impossibility of canceling the implicature leads Grice to explain the "heard" contradiction as stemming from assertion expressing belief, not merely implicating it.

Because the expectation generated by the maxims are mutually known to speakers and hearers, speakers can exploit them to communicate better. Speakers can overtly violate a maxim as with metaphor or irony. In Plato's *Euthyphro*, when Socrates tells Euthyphro "I should be your student, Euthyphro," what he asserted is recognized as blatantly unwarranted by his audience (and it is expected to be so recognized by the speaker), so that Socrates implicates the opposite.

Grice characterizes when *p* conversationally implicates *q* as follows:

> He [the speaker] has said that *p*; there is no reason to suppose that he is not observing the maxims, or at least the Cooperative Principle; he could not be doing this unless he thought that *q*; he knows (and knows that I know that he knows) that I can see that the supposition that he thinks that *q* is required... he intends me to think... that *q*; and so he has implicated that *q*. (31)

These chained inferences require the speaker to assume not just that the hearer knows the maxims under the cp, but that the hearer can work out or calculate the implicature, based on his presumption that the speaker complies with the cp.

Grice's essays on conversational implicatures have given rise to a vast amount of extremely fruitful research on pragmatics, spanning a number of disciplines.

8. Conditionals and Conversation

Of all the originally intended applications of Grice's pragmatics to ordinary language inference, the most promising and the most difficult is to the indicative conditional, such as "If John's car is in his driveway, then he is at home."[2] The wide disparities between the ordinary indicative conditional (If A, B) and the material conditional ($\supset$ or 'hook') of propositional logic are well known. Aside from the material conditional not requiring any overlap in content between antecedent (A) and consequent (B), counterintuitive results follow when the antecedent is false, because then the material conditional is true. (The only secure row in the truth-table for the material conditional is falsity, when antecedent is true and consequent false.) For one problem case: Assume it is false that Jones fails the final. Then it will be true for the material conditional that if Jones fails the final, she will be overjoyed (and also, of course, that if Jones fails the final, she will not be overjoyed).

Grice's suggestion for the alleged failings of the material conditional is that we confuse whether the conditional is true with whether it is assertible (without misleading). I know that if it is false that Jones fails the final, it would be misleading to assert the conditional. The conditional is noticeably weaker than the relevant information I could assert instead with no more burden on the hearer namely, Jones will not fail the final. (Compare to: either Jones does not fail the final or she will be overjoyed, which is logically equivalent to the material conditional). So the hearer will take the speaker to have (falsely) implicated that she does not know whether Jones fails the final. To explain away the irrelevance problem, a Gricean proposal is that asserting two sentences close to one another would be confusing (disorderly), unless they enjoy some common relation to the informational purposes of the exchange. In the case of the conditional, the relation would be some reason or ground (expressed in the antecedent) for the consequent.

Jackson (1987) developed a Gricean approach. With qualifications, the conditional is the material conditonal. But it is assertible only when the consequent remains highly probable (is "robust") in the event that the antecedent turns out to be true. That is, not only should the conditional be highly probable in itself, but it should also be highly probable *given* that the antecedent is true. The reason for this is that upon learning that the antecedent is true, we want to be able to proceed with such inferences as modus ponens, rather than having to withdraw the (material) conditional. Although it may be true that if Jones fails the final, she will be overjoyed, if it is true only because she will not fail, it is unassertible, since it is not robust with respect to its antecedent.

Grice's proposal, particularly as developed by Jackson, contains insights that all draw on. Tom believes that his son Joe will get his driver's license, regardless of whether he takes a driver's ed course. So it will be misleading for him to assert, even if circumstances are otherwise appropriate, "If Joe takes the driver's ed class, he will get his driver's license," although Tom does believe this. Still, the objections to the Gricean analysis are formidable for thought, not just its home territory of conversation. If you believe it is false that Jones fails the final, you may still disbelieve (and not just refrain from asserting) that if she fails, she will be overjoyed. Or, because the negation of a material conditional implies the antecedent and negation of the consequent, I will disbelieve (believe false) that if I get arrested tonight, I'll go dancing in the morning, while disbelieving, as well, that I will be arrested tonight.

A widely adopted proposal denies Grice's argument that the conditional is actually truth-functional. Instead, the "if" directs a supposition of the antecedent. (Bennett 2003 for a survey with references to the main contributors.) If, given that supposition, the consequent holds (or it is highly probable) within one's corpus of beliefs when the corpus is minimally altered to accommodate to the antecedent, the conditional is assertible. (An alternative formulation is via the similarity of possible worlds.) In short, the assertibility (warrant; acceptability) of "if A, B" equals that of pr(B/A), where this is the subjective conditional probability of B given A, determined in accord with the suggested procedure.

The 'suppositional' proposal follows upon the major discovery of Lewis's (1986b) that the simple equation of pr(A–>B) and pr(B/A) (when pr(A)>0) fails. Conditional probabilities cannot, without trivialization, be the probability of the truth of a (conditional) proposition. Consequently, one should not view "if A, B" as a truth-bearing proposition, but as an evaluative procedure whereby the proposition A is supposed and B is evaluated on that supposition. The result of that evaluation is not, however, a proposition that is probably true, when B is probably true, given A.

There have been extensive developments of this framework, and the discovery of a number of sticking points such as how to handle embedded conditionals and cases in which it seems that two persons could each have sufficient reasons to accept conflicting conditionals A–>B; A–>~B. (McGee 1985; Gibbard 1981)

9. Foundational Problems of Induction

Gricean implicatures are inductive inferences or inferences to the best explanation (what the speaker meant as the best explanation of why he asserted what he did). Aside from a dominant commitment to the probability calculus, there is no analogue for inductive logic of the basic laws or rules of first-order logic to which deviant inductive logics may dissent. Even so basic a rule as the "straight rule" (if m/n As are Bs infer that the probability that the next A will be a B is m/n) has been questioned (doesn't it matter under what conditions the As were discovered – a single or varied sample?).

Although it seems evident that positive inductive evidence for a hypothesis provides support for it, does that support actually provide reasons to believe that its claims will continue to hold (in the future)? A negative answer was offered by Hume, at the launching point for investigations of induction. Hume writes

> We have said, that all arguments concerning existence are founded on the relation of cause and effect; that our knowledge of that relation is derived entirely from experience; and that all our experimental conclusions proceed upon the supposition, that the future will be conformable to the past. To endeavour, therefore, the proof of this last supposition by probable arguments, or arguments regarding existence, must be evidently going in a circle, and taking that for granted, which is the very point in question. (Hume 1977: 23)

Nondemonstrative arguments about an unobserved (future) event only work if we assume that "the future will be conformable to the past," which is referred to as the assumption of the uniformity of nature (UN) – the future will be like the past (at least in respect of the regularity involved). So the argument should really be:

In the past, Fs have been followed by Gs (and never by non-Gs).

This present case is an F.

UN: Nature is uniform (at least in regard to Fs followed by Gs).

So, the present case of an F will be followed by a G.

The cogency of this argument turns on the uniformity supposition. Its defense can not be, again, by demonstrative argument, because it is possible that the future is not like the past in this or any other respect. The laws could break down. ("It's possible," in Hume's weak sense of possibility as logical consistency, that the sun does not rise tomorrow.) So then we need a parallel argument for uniformity:

In the past, nature has been uniform (at least in regard to Fs followed by Gs).

The present case is an instance of that uniformity (of an F).

So, the present case will be followed by a continuation of the uniformity (a G will follow).

Because the premises are all about the past and the conclusion is about the future, what is needed is a past-future linking assumption:

In the past, nature has been uniform (at least in regard to Fs followed by Gs).

The present case is an instance of that uniformity (of an F).

Nature is uniform (at least in regard to the uniformity of Fs followed by Gs).

So, the present case will be followed by a continuation of the uniformity (a G will follow).

But the premise affirmed is effectively the conclusion itself or a proposition that implies it. The reasoning is circular in a way that would be found for any inductive or nondemonstrative argument, since they all require the uniformity assumption.[3] In brief, even if induction has worked in the past to infer that it will continue to work in the future would itself presuppose the validity of inductive inference, which is what we were supposed to prove.

Karl Popper (1959) champions Hume's inductive scepticism, stressing that Hume's doubts or scepticism apply even if the inductive conclusion is to follow only with high probability. Deduction is really the only kind of reasoning. Even if no amount of evidence can increase the inductive probability of any statement, one negative instance is enough to falsify it conclusively.

Popper's falsificationism claims that scientists should aim only to falsify, not confirm, hypotheses and so they should express hypotheses in as strong a form as possible. Falsificationism runs up against many technical hurdles. Most relevant is a nontechnical problem. Because a strict falsificationist denies any inductive inference, he cannot make sense of the relation between finding positive evidence and rational increases in confidence.

Other responses to Hume's problem include the proposal to vindicate induction, showing that even if induction cannot be justified, it is the best or the only method that works if anything does (i.e., if nature is uniform) (Reichenbach 1961) and the "Oxford" position that it is a conceptual truth that an empirical statement is justified by positive evidence (Strawson 1952). The latter, however, seems to only push the problem back to determining what counts as positive evidence. Bayesian views, discussed below, hold that opinions or subjective judgments are free for the asking. Conformity with the axioms of probability is the only constraint. But with new evidence our confidence in those opinions and judgments, as hypotheses, are rationally alterable according to a probabilistic analogue of logical consistency and a rule for learning (or updating values). Together these equate the new probability with the old conditional probability of a hypothesis on that new evidence. The justification of inductive judgments should be viewed diachronically, not synchronically.

We know that overwhelmingly inductive inferences do work. They must or else our success in action, and that of other animals, makes no sense, since induction is our guide to forming expectations and to the future. This is not an answer to Hume's sceptical argument, but only a way to clarify its scope. Even if we cannot demonstrate that inductive arguments must be reliable, it is enough for our confidence in induction that it regularly succeeds. The possibility that the future is unlike the past is not often realized and the world is by-and-large lawful, even if neither observation can be massaged into a justification of induction.

10. Qualitative Confirmation and Its Paradoxes

Although Hume's analysis of induction is the background to the development of an inductive logic, its nearer roots are the project of articulating a logic of scientific method. The project takes off from the failure of Positivist or Logical Empiricist attempts to provide a criterion to demarcate science from metaphysics or nonsense, or, less tendentiously, nonscience. Because scientific hypotheses are typically in the form of generalizations – for example, "F = ma" – whose scope is unlimited, and because our evidence for any hypothesis at any time is finite, hypotheses could not be established deductively with premises that only report the evidence.

Our hypotheses are highly underdetermined by the evidence in their favor. Developing a confirmation theory or inductive logic was aimed at the fundamentals of epistemology – to provide standards of rational belief. Initially, the attempt was to propose and examine rules of qualitative confirmation, whose findings were expected to be incorporated into a quantitative account (Hempel 1965).

An attractive starting point is that a generalization of the form "All As are Bs" should be confirmed by all positive instances of it. So a basic rule would be:

(IC) A hypothesis is of the form "All As are Bs" is confirmed by any positive instance "Aa &Ba."[4]

A second principle is that logical equivalence preserves confirmation, which is recommended if logical equivalence, as mutual implication, is sameness of content:

(EQ) If H and H′ are logically equivalent, then if e confirms H, e confirms H′.

(For development and refinement, the classic is Hempel 1965)

However, a problem was quickly recognized, referred to as the "raven paradox." The hypothesis

All ravens are black

is logically equivalent to

All nonblack things are nonravens.

According to (IC), the latter hypothesis is confirmed by positive instances, which include blue shoes, a red jacket, yellow baskets, and the noncolorable number 33. So by (EQ) these each confirm H. The result is supposed to be paradoxical because IC and EQ are individually credible, yet they allow that finding a red jacket confirms that all ravens are black.

But is it a real paradox? The basic notion – confirmation itself – is not quantitative. Perhaps, the blue shoe does provide confirmation, only very little. Hempel also observed that simply to reject the EQ is questionable because hypotheses are involved in deductive arguments (for explanations and predictions), and validity does not vary with logically equivalent sentences.

The raven paradox has structural analogies with the Wason selection task – with "vowel" for "raven"; "consonant" for "black"; "even" for "nonraven"; and "odd" for "nonblack." The well-known findings are that to test the conditional "if there is a vowel on one side then there is an even number on the other" with cards A, D, 4, 7, subjects turn over the A card, but not the 7, and many the 4. The results, originally explained as a result of a bias in search for confirming (positive) to falsifying instances, provides insight into our response to the raven paradox: we think of looking for ravens to observe whether they are black, but not of looking for nonblack things to test for whether they are nonravens.

However, the analogy breaks down at two junctures: First, our response is presumably influenced by the background information of both the relative frequency of the different classes and of the underlying explanatory connections (a genetic account of the original hypothesis rings true, but not for the contrapositive one).

Second, in the Wason task, the pairs selected are the unusual ones for which the contradictory is as natural as the original – even-odd; vowel-consonant. But objects that are nonblack are not merely objects with colors other than black, but all manner of objects, like numbers, that could not have a color at all. The Wason task is the specialized one in which the contradictory of a natural category or predicate is itself natural.

Quine (1969) picked up on the unnaturalness of the negation of a natural class to propose that even if the two hypotheses are logically equivalent only the one with the predicate for the natural class is fit for confirmation or projection (to new cases). The notion of projectibility he drew from the far reaching ("grue") paradox of Goodman (1983). Goodman's target was a qualitative account of confirmation that attempts to model confirmation (or inductive) arguments on deductive arguments in which validity turns on their form, not their content.

The hypothesis that Goodman selected to formulate his 'grue' paradox is:

(Green) All emeralds are green.

He then offered a competing hypothesis:

(Grue) All emeralds are grue.

Something is grue, he proposed, if and only if either it is green and examined before 2050 or blue and examined after 2050. Now take any collection of positive instances of (Green) – for example, the finding of ten green emeralds each confirms, according to IC, (Green). But this same evidence will also be positive instances of (Grue), and so, by IC, confirm it. But this is the ruin of confirmation theory because (Green) and (Grue) compete (they disagree over the color of emeralds discovered after 2050), yet "grue" - type hypotheses can be manufactured for any hypothesis.

The analogy with the "curve fitters" problem is often made. Through any finite set of data points, an infinite number of functions can yield those data points. Which one should be preferred and why? If one of them is near enough a straight line, the others will appear as much more complex, if not bizarre. Still, does this basis for preference correspond to an objective feature of the world or of what we find simple?

Goodman's Paradox harmonizes with three other important theses about inference and reasoning, noted already: underdetermination, the Quine–Duhem thesis, and holism. Each of these theses, like Goodman's Paradox, are extensions of Hume's insight about induction that the evidence for a hypothesis, however strong, never implies that hypothesis. This much underdetermination is unremarkable. A slightly more exciting thesis is that for any positive evidence for a hypothesis, there are always other competing hypotheses compatible with that evidence. This is only slightly more exciting, because further evidence can be gathered, or tests constructed, to select among the hypotheses at the previous stage. A much stronger and very controversial thesis of underdetermination is that there are sets of hypotheses that are empirically equivalent (sharing the same observational consequences), so that despite their competing or conflicting, no evidence can select between them. Underdetermination has been urged against realist inferences from the confirmation of a scientific theory to either its truth or to the reference of the theoretical terms in it.

These neighboring problems lead to the question of what constraints can be applied to hypotheses so that evidence is a reliable basis to discriminate among hypotheses. In the case of Goodman's Paradox, a natural thought about "grue" is that it is artificially complex or contrived or that it predicts an arbitrary and radical change in color. Goodman anticipates this worry. He introduces another predicate "bleen": something is bleen if it is blue and examined before 2050 or green and examined after 2050. For a language with "grue" and "bleen" as primitive or simple as "green" and "blue" in our language, the latter appear complex "x is green if and only if x is grue and examined before 2050 or x is bleen and examined after 2050." From the point of view of that language, our green hypothesis is complex and it posits a radical change from objects that were grue up to 2050 to their becoming bleen after.

Goodman proposes that "green" is preferable to "grue" because it is projectible, and it is projectible because, in fact, it has been successfully used (projected) in our predictive practices. The solution, as resting projectibility on our successful habits of projection, has struck many as turning on too superficial or accidental a feature. But doubts about Goodman's solution are not doubts about his paradox as arguing for the need for prior restrictions on the predicates suitable for inductive inference and the confirmation of hypotheses, as well as the formulation of laws of nature.

11. Quantitative Induction and Confirmation

A dominant response to both paradoxes is to give up on qualitative confirmation for a quantitative approach through probability. The basic thought is that probability provides a measure of the degree of inductive support that evidence for a hypothesis transfers to it: If

$$pr(h \mid e\&b) > pr(h \mid b),$$

where b is the background or previous evidence and e is new evidence, then e is positive evidence or confirms h, and the difference between the two values is the degree of support or confirmation. (For alternative measures of degree of confirmation, see Fitelson 1999, 2003; Kyburg and Teng 2001; Tentori, Crupi, Bonini, and Osherson 2007.)

Because there are hugely many nonblack things, as well as nonravens, especially compared to the class of ravens and the class of black things, the antecedent probability of finding a nonraven among nonblack things is extremely high. Consequently, finding a nonblack nonraven little increases the probability that "All ravens are black." Understanding confirmation as above, the difference will be very small, the posterior probability becomes only slightly greater. In application to the "grue" paradox, since the prior probability assigned to "All emeralds are green" is significantly higher than to "All emeralds are grue," the former hypothesis is claimed to be much better supported by a collection of green emeralds than the latter by the same evidence described as grue emeralds. (Is this how the grue-bleen language speakers would describe the difference?)

Goodman originally directed his paradox against the earliest formulations of quantitative confirmation theory in the pioneering work of Carnap (1947; 1962) and Hempel (1965). Carnap began with the specification of a formal language over which a confirmation function was to be defined. Because there were no restrictions beyond coherence on the predicates, Carnap's formal language was ripe for the "grue" paradox, which demands such prior restrictions.

Carnap's simplest languages involved one-place predicates and names, and then a state-description is defined as the maximally consistent combination (via negation and conjunction) of all predicates and names.[5] Each state-description described a complete possible world. How should an initial probability distribution be set up among these possible worlds? Because there is no basis for taking one world as more likely than another before obtaining evidence, Carnap invoked something like a *principle of indifference* to justify assigning equal probabilities to each state-description. The arresting consequence was that learning from experience – a change in probability values with new evidence – was impossible. Consequently, Carnap proposed a set of inductive method determined by the continuum of ways to reject the assignment of equal weights to each state-description. Of these, one has the philosophical advantage that it is indifferent to bare differences between individuals, but not to kinds or properties. (See Kyburg and Teng 2001; for methods to assess these different inductive strategie's see Lewis 1971.) Carnap's plausible line of reasoning from the assignment of equal weights to state-descriptions converged on the implication of Hume's and Goodman's analyses that without prior favoring or biasing toward some "worlds" (state-descriptions) over others induction could not take place.

Conditionalization is the key principle for changing degrees of belief or learning from experience for Bayesians. Given a body of new evidence e, you should adjust your degree of belief in a hypothesis h so that it is now equal to what was (before learning the new evidence) the conditional probability of the hypothesis given the evidence. Conditionalization stipulates that

$$pr_{new}(h) = pr_{old}(h \mid e).$$

But how should you compute $pr_{old}(h \mid e)$? Bayesians take their name from Bayes's Theorem, an elementary consequence of the probability calculus. Bayesians claim that Bayes's Theorem and its role in conditionalization captures all or just about all that one requires for inductive or statistical inference, including that probabilities can be assigned to all statements. Bayesians have problems with assigning prior probabilities – what is the probability of Newton's second law before any evidence is in? If the probability is to be assigned objectively, it will have to rely on a principle of indifference. That principle runs into difficulties of conflicting representations of the set of statements to which one's ignorance is to translate into an equal distribution of probabilities. If wholly subjective, why should the assignments be accorded any respect (Sober 2005)?

In one form (where h and –h are the only two hypotheses) Bayes' Theorem states that:

$$pr(h \mid e) = \frac{pr(e \mid h)pr(h)}{pr(e \mid h)pr(h) + pr(e \mid -h)pr(-h)}$$

(Here as elsewhere, it is assumed that denominators do not equal 0.) Where there are n mutually exclusive and exhaustive hypotheses (h_i), the general formula is:

$$pr(h_j \mid e_j) = \frac{pr(e_j \mid h_j)pr(h_j)}{\sum_{i=1}^{n} pr(e_i \mid h_i)pr(h_i)}$$

The main components of Bayes's Thorem are the likelihood $pr(e \mid h)$ and the prior probability $pr(h)$. To know how likely it is that the evidence arose from h requires knowing not only of the connection between e and h, but also how antecedently likely it is that h is true. It is highly likely that if there is a snow storm in Miami that school will be canceled. Yet, the probability that the school was actually canceled because of a snow storm is still quite low. To derive the probability of h on e also requires evaluating the probability that h actually arose from e compared to the other possible hypotheses that might account for e (the denominator above).

Bayes's Theorem provides good explanations for intuitive judgments about induction such as the value of evidence that is surprising or diverse (Bovens and Hartmann 2003: Ch. 4). The posterior conditional probability of h on e, $pr(h \mid e)$, expresses how much more expected h is were e true. Assume that finding e is very unexpected (its prior probability is low) (e.g. Alfred E. Neumann receives an A in his logic final). However, were h true (e.g., he had a copy of the exam earlier), e would not be surprising. So pr(AEN gets an A | AEN has the exam in advance) is high. In that case, e greatly confirms h [i.e. pr(AEN has the exam | AEN gets an A) is also high]. (This pattern of reasoning is common in inference to the best explanation discussed in the next section.)

When we move from Bayes's Theorem to Bayesianism, which restricts probability to degrees of belief or subjective probabilities, we move from the taken-for-granted to the controversial. A major advantage claimed for Bayesianism is theoretical minimalism: No claims or assumptions are made as to the basis for the initial assignment of probabilities beyond what follows from one's degrees of belief (with prior probabilities, before any learning, problematically dependent on a principle of indifference, as noted earlier). The only demand on those degrees of belief is consistency or coherence.

The minimalism is one source of criticism: any assignment of probabilities is as good as any other provided only that they are coherent (i.e., conform to the axioms of probability). Conditionalization provides for the response that if individuals assign similar values to the likelihood and conditionalize, then with new information there will be convergence on assignments of probability. But only if there is uniformity in how to judge the new information as evidence. (Another problem is how to treat old evidence newly discovered to be implied by a long-standing hypothesis or theory, so that there is no change in the probability of the evidence; Glymour 1980.)

Bayesians tend to treat all learning from experience as changes in probability by conditionalization. The treatment is in opposition to construing theoretical reasoning as aiming at the all-out acceptance (or rejection) of a hypothesis as true, detaching it from its evidential base. The Bayesians worry that the detachment is in conflict with a recognition of our fallibility, discussed later, and related problems like the dogmatism paradox mentioned in Section 5 (Levi 1980; Jeffrey 1983; Kaplan 1996).

The possibility of detachment is one way to understand a difference between probability and inductive inference. Think of a simple inductive inference, for example, Alice is an academic whose library is filled with books on early American history, so she is [probably] a historian. Strong detachment marks the end of an inquiry. The judgment or hypothesis is separated from its evidential base with all-out acceptance. Detachment implies a claim that the evidence is sufficient or representative enough for drawing a conclusion, rather than just assigning a probability on that evidence. Detachment is a risk, requiring an underlying pattern or law or regularity that is indicated by the evidence. But without taking that risk, an inquiry would never terminate, so long as the evidence leaves open the possibility of error (i.e., does not establish the hypothesis as certainly correct). The underlying regularity allows for the detached judgment, since it allows us to project from, but to go well beyond, the evidence.

By contrast, consider a fair lottery with one thousand tickets of which you own one. The probability of your losing is very high: .999. It is reasonable to assume that this probability of your losing is higher than the probability that Alice is a historian, based on your knowledge and observation (maybe the library is simply an inheritance from her parents who bequeathed her the house?). Yet you cannot detach – all-out believe – that you will lose the lottery. Otherwise, purchasing a ticket would be worse than merely incurring a high negative expected utility. It would be to throw away money, since there is a cost without prospect of gain. Still, you can all-out believe or come to know that Alice is a historian. How come? The answer resides in the assumed underlying regularity or law in the historian case, but not for the lottery. Only the former then permits projection beyond the evidence.

An alternative explanation is that in the former case (that Alice is a historian) there is an implicit deductive argument, yielding a probability of 1, but not in the latter (that you will lose the lottery). However, even if the generalizations, regularities, and other assumptions, which underlie the inference, would, if stated explicitly, yield a deductive argument, it does not follow that the original argument is only an enthymeme for (i.e., an abbreviated version of) that deductive argument. The presumed generalization includes that conditions are normal and that in such conditions, if one is an academic and one's library is dominated by books in a certain field, then the field is one's profession. If the normalcy condition is understood to exclude all ways that the conclusion could be false, not already excluded by the explicit premise, we have a formula to convert any inductive argument into a deductive one (see Smith, Shafir, and Osherson 1993). But this does not explain the difference between the historian and the lottery arguments, any more than if we add a conditional whose antecedent is the conjunction of premises and the consequent is the conclusion, as a way to turn any argument into a modus ponens deductive one. For these additional assumptions, which are unnecessary for the high probability of the lottery cases, are themselves not backed by any grounds additional to the premises. The risk – that is, the inductive gap between premises and conclusion – is the same as the gap between premises and these assumptions. Nothing is advanced in the argument, but only in the recognition of its basis.

If there is all-out acceptance, how should it be based on probability? A simple proposal for

relating probability to acceptance (one that we have just implicitly rejected) is

(ACC) Acc(p) if and only if $pr(p \mid e) > r$, r is some suitably large value – certainly greater than .5.

But for acceptance (or detachment) more is needed. The evidence e must constitute representative evidence. Its weight of evidence – the proportion of the evidence – must be high or maximal (Keynes 1952, Cohen 1977).

Regardless of the value selected for r, Kyburg (1961) showed that a paradox follows if a conjunction principle holds:

(CR) $Acc(q_1), \ldots, Acc(q_n) ==> Acc(q_1 \& \ldots \& q_n).$

To make it clear that the "Lottery Paradox" is indifferent to values of r (less than 1), let's set the criterion very high, say, .95. Kyburg asks us to imagine that there is a fair lottery with one thousand tickets. You have one ticket t_{123}. The probability that you will lose the lottery with that ticket is .999, which exceeds the criterion. So, in accord with (ACC), you accept the statement that you will lose the lottery. But now for each of the other 999 tickets, the probability that each of them will lose is also .999. So each of these satisfies the condition for acceptance. Because, by (ACC) you accept, for each of the one thousand tickets, the statement that it will lose, (CR) tells us that the conjunction of those one thousand statements is likewise accepted. It follows that you have accepted that all the tickets will lose. But it is impossible for every ticket to lose, if it is a fair lottery.

Both (ACC) and (CR) have come in for rejection as a basis to resolve the lottery paradox. (CR) is disputed (and here is where the Bayesian attacks) because when probabilities are multiplied (in non-extreme cases), the result is necessarily a diminution in probability. (The probability of $q_1 \& \ldots \& q_{1000}$ will typically be far below the acceptance threshold, r.) However, if acceptance is all-out, the truth of a conjunction is logically equivalent to the truth of its individual conjuncts, and so (CR) seems another expression of the basic idea of acceptance. This defense of (CR) goes along with a challenge to (ACC): probability alone is never sufficient for acceptance. As noted earlier, in distinguishing the assignment of probability from genuine inference (and detachment), no one can all-out believe that they will lose a lottery with a single ticket in contrast to the more precise assignment of a high degree of belief. The contrast between the lottery case and genuine inductive inferences provides for an answer to the lottery paradox that is different from the one Bayesians offer, when they allow for acceptance at all (Kaplan 1996). What more than high probability (and high weight of evidence) is required for acceptance is a lingering question.

12. Inference to the Best Explanation

A natural form of inference is to infer the hypothesis that best explains the data. Sherlock Holmes infers that the owner of the dog committed the crime because this is the best explanation of why the dog did not bark when the crime was committed nearby. The data of the dog's not barking confirms the hypothesis that the owner committed the crime, and the hypothesis is introduced to explain why the dog did not bark. Inference and explanation implicate each other. Inference to the best explanation is at work where observable events, like John's rude behavior at a party, are explained by the hypothesis of an unobserved (and sometimes unobservable) cause (e.g., John was just fired from his job). (For criticisms, see van Fraassen 1980.)

Inference to the best explanation offers a promising approach to the confirmation paradoxes. The best explanation of why nonblack things are nonravens will *not* be that all ravens are black, or even that all nonblack things are nonravens. The finding of nonravens among nonblack things is best explained by the fact that nonblack things are just such a numerous and heterogeneous collection that it is unsurprising that we should find some, and so it calls for no further explanation. Similarly, that the observed emeralds have been green is well explained if all emeralds are green, which, as well, give us reason to expect the next observed emerald to be green. But the grueness of the observed emerald is not well explained by the hypothesis that all emeralds are grue, because that implies that unobserved emeralds will be blue. (For advances along these lines, see Jackson 1975; White 2005.)

Inference to the best explanation captures Peirce's (1931) "abduction," whereby plausibility accrues to a hypothesis – it is worth taking seriously. When you meet someone at a party who dresses in a similar slightly off-beat way of another acquaintance, you might think that they share political or cultural views. Although the off-beat dress is a reason to take seriously the hypothesis that the two share political or cultural views, it is hardly much of a reason to actually believe it. Suggestive or analogical reasons are important in view of the underdetermination problem of the unlimited number of hypotheses to fit any data, as well as the problem of coming up with credible hypotheses to explain complex data or observations.

Inference to the best explanation serves a stronger role as a form of eliminative inductive, whereby evidence is sought to select among rivals:

> one infers, from the premise that a given hypothesis would provide a "better" explanation for the evidence than would any other hypothesis, to the conclusion that the given hypothesis is true. (Harman 1965)

Inference to the best explanation is closest to causal explanation, where competitors are specified by contrasts – why p rather than q. When the bank robber Willie Sutton was asked why he robbed banks, he responded "Because that's where the money is." He construed the question as something such as "Why do you rob banks, rather than grocery stores?" Although having lots of money in an accessible location is only one cause for his robbing banks, it is the one that makes the distinctive difference between Sutton's robbing the bank and his robbing the grocery store. However, his questioners actually had in mind a different question, calling for an answer selected from a different contrast class ("rather than"): "Why do you rob banks rather than working a decent job?" (Garfinkel 1981).

If the best explanation is accepted as correct or even as worthy of investigation, it must at least provide a good explanation, not merely the best of a lousy lot. Criteria for the best explanation include that the hypothesis is simple, conservative, and unifying. However, the criteria should not include an explicitly truth relevant property such as high probability. That is the conclusion to be reached not assumed. The hypothesis that yields the most understanding must prove itself to be the likeliest (Lipton 2004).

Inference to the best explanation is at the center of the "miracle argument" from the success of science to a realist view of science, which hold that scientific theories are at least approximately true and that its theoretical terms genuinely refer, rather than merely serving as useful posits. The question is whether these realist claims are the best explanation for the success of science, whose success would otherwise be a "miracle" (a grand coincidence).

13. Foundational Justification: Coherence and Reflective Equilibrium

How at the most basic level should the putative rules or principles of logic (inductive, deductive, practical) be justified?

Earlier, we noted that Bayesianism's admirable minimalism invites the criticism that it allows one to believe almost anything, so long as one conforms to the axioms of probability. It is evident that logical consistency is much too weak a criterion for rational belief – the belief that Santa Claus brings presents or that there are an even number of stars are both logically consistent. But, recall, Bayesians have a distinctive consistency requirement – coherence – which they offer to justify the probability axioms as representations of degrees of belief and preferences, and this notion they think is sufficient (with conditionalization) to represent rational belief.

The coherence arguments for commitment to the probability calculus are known as "Dutch Book Arguments." These arguments claim that if your preferences or degrees of belief do not conform to the probability calculus then a set of bets (a "book") can be designed that you are committed to regarding individually as fair, because fitting your preferences. (For references and presentation, see Hacking 2001; van Fraassen, this volume.) The bets, however, guarantee that you cannot win or that you must lose. (Conversely, if your degrees of belief do conform to the probability axioms, no "book" can be made against you.) The argument requires an idealization away from influences on betting besides an interest in winning, like the pleasure of gambling. A more problematic assumption is that logical omniscience (deductive closure) is needed, because the probability of deductive truths must be assigned the value 1.

The "sure loss" or "Dutch Book" argument can be extended to justify a principle for changing one's degree of belief by conditionalization (see Section 11). Conditionalization, recall, assigns a new probability when evidence is obtained as the old conditional probability on that evidence:

$$pr_{new}(h) = pr_{old}(h \mid e).$$

(Teller 1973; Lewis 1999; for a more general form of conditionalization, see Jeffrey 1983).

If coherence is an extension of consistency, it provides a model for the justification of the axioms of probability as representing degrees of belief that is *a priori* (not dependent on experience or sense perception). It remains an open question as to how successful are the Dutch Book Arguments and how general a model for justifying principles they provide. They do not pretend to answer Hume's problem, but they do claim to mitigate it. A principle for learning from experience is justifiable as a way to protect against a self-defeating set of preferences or degrees of belief, even if it cannot guarantee success.

Can this model be generalized to justify rules of logic (inductive, deductive, practical)? A familiar problem is that consistency or coherence is too weak, since plausible rules that are incompatible with one another can form internally consistent systems. Once substantive principles are offered besides consistency, the evident problem is a version of Hume's circularity problem (see Section 9): To establish the rules of logic requires reasoning, and how can one reason without logic (Boghossian 2000)? However, certain kinds of circularity are not a failing or not a decisive one. Proofs of the soundness of a logical principle, like the rule of conjunction simplification ("p&q" implies "p"), use an analogue of that principle in the proof. But the analogue – the soundness proof – is not syntactic or at the object level, but at the meta-level or the semantics (Dummett 1978).

A traditional view is that logic is established *a priori*. We have already noted that the Dutch Book Arguments aspire to an a priori justification for inductive principles. But Dutch Book Arguments do not reach to the foundations, since they presuppose a particular view of consistency. For logic, one approach is to claim that from reflection on, or analysis of, concepts such as "if, then," we can validate laws like modus ponens. Reflection on the concept of negation is supposed to show that instances of the $p\&\sim p$ must be false. This view is an advance on the one that claims that we have an faculty of intuition to discern logical laws, which merely pushes the problem back to validating the faculty of intuition. A priori knowledge is knowledge that is not based on experience, and since on traditional views they are necessary truths, such knowledge is indefeasible (no empirical findings could count as evidence against a genuine logical law).

Strict empiricists – stricter even than Hume – are not satisfied with the claimed power of reflection. They attempt a straightforward a posteriori or inductive approach to logical laws as generalizations from observations of uniformly successful inferences. These laws are subject to hypothesis testing akin to any empirical claim (Mill 1963).

The strict empiricist approach is unpopular on Kantian grounds that observations or related evidential considerations can never establish the necessity of logical laws. An improvement over empiricism on this count is that with a logical law we cannot conceive of its failing. But what is the relation between conceivability or imaginability and real possibility (Yablo 1993)? As Putnam (1975) noted, our ability to conceive that water is not H_2O does not entail that it is really possible that water is not H_2O.

A more recent approach is to seek reflective equilibrium between principles (or rules) and judgments (or intuitions). Earlier, we noted how a soundness proof justifies a particular rule by showing that it generates only valid arguments. The semantic version of the rule is legitimate if its use is only to explain why the rule is endorsed. But for ultimate justification of a rule or principle, this explanation, which takes a lot of standard semantics for granted, is not sufficient. The justification of any set of principles eventually confronts two horns of an ancient dilemma. Either the justification process relies on further principles to justify others, which must finally be exhausted, and so return – circularly – to principles already used or, and this is the other horn, the process never exhausts itself. The process never stops. Each new principles requires a further and different principle to justify it in turn. There is an infinite regress, because these different principles must themselves be justified. The rules for, say, the derivation of excluded middle – that is, $p \vee \sim p$ – are justified by the truth-table for "$\sim$" and "$\vee$." But what justifies the truth-table (as corresponding to "not" and "or")?

Reflective equilibrium answers the latter horn by claiming that there is a starting point, rather than a regress, in the judgments of validity we already accept. It answers the former, circularity, horn by conceiving some circularities as an acceptable matter of accommodation or balance. In the richly suggestive passage that launched the reflective equilibrium model, Goodman explicitly compared the justification of inductive and deductive rules:

> How do we justify a *de*duction? Plainly, by showing that it conforms to the general rules of deductive inference.... Analogously, the basic task in justifying an inductive inference

is to show that it conforms to the general rules of *in*duction.

> ... Principles of deductive inference are justified by their conformity with accepted deductive practice.... Justification of general rules thus derives from judgments rejecting or accepting particular deductive inferences.
>
> This looks flagrantly circular.... But this circle is a virtuous one. The point is that rules and particular inferences alike are justified by being brought into agreement with each other. *A rule is amended if it yields an inference we are unwilling to accept; an inference is rejected if it violates a rule we are unwilling to amend.* The process of justification is the delicate one of making mutual adjustments between rules and accepted inferences; and in the agreement achieved lies the only justification needed for either. (Goodman 1965: 63–64)

Reflective equilibrium is intended as an alternative to a purely a priori justification of logical principles. Reflective equilibrium embraces neither a crude inductive justification (as just a generalization from successful instances) nor a "foundational" one, which treats some principles as sacrosanct.

In this respect, reflective equilibrium is closely aligned with coherentism in epistemology, the view that justification is holistic (Elgin 1996): A principle is justified to the extent that it coheres within one's corpus of beliefs. However, if the coherence is only within one's current corpus of beliefs, it is a narrow reflective equilibrium. It lacks the justificatory force of a wide reflective equilibrium, where one's judgments (intuitions) and principles are evaluated against alternatives principles and they are subjected to extended critical analysis. Although the approach was originally proposed as a guide to generating inductive rules, it has been invoked predominantly as the underlying model for theory construction in moral or political philosophy (Rawls 1971).

As a description of our actual practices in proposing or justifying rules, reflective equilibrium is on target. When it comes to the conditional, for instance, modus ponens and falsity when antecedent is true and consequent false are strong intuitions, with contraposition much less secure, and modus tollens in between. However, reflective equilibrium can provide little further substantive guidance. It does not specify how to balance among principles or judgments when they conflict. So it cannot settle serious disputes.

Recall that Goodman himself rejected an intuition about his "grue" paradox that most others took as a pillar.

What counts as an intuition anyway? Most of us deny the validity of disjunctive weakening (i.e., "p" implies "p v q") on initial presentation. But students are brought around by the truth-table analysis. Is the former the intuition or the latter, and how do we characterize the difference in a general way? (Is it to be assimilated to the difference between narrow and wide reflective equilibrium?) Systematization pressures intuitions. Given the interconnections that any logical system quickly establishes, principles and rules are not going to be readily adoptable or modifiable piecemeal to capture particular judgments or intuitions. Thus, to use the unintuitive rule of disjunctive weakening again, it follows almost immediately if the rules either of reductio ad absurdum or conditional proof are available.[6] Without further modification, to reject the former requires rejecting the latter. (Intuitionists and their sympathizers, however, treat the additional losses as a bargain.)

14. Paradoxes

Reflective equilibrium is a practical approach to the evaluation of reasoning principles, offering no latitude for sceptical doubts about the ultimate justification of our principles (or intuitions). A search for reflective equilibrium is impatient with paradoxes, like the sorites, because one option in the face of paradoxes is a sceptical or nihilist conclusion that certain basic concepts are ultimately incoherent, even if we seem to make intuitive sense in talking about them.

Paradoxes involve the derivation of either a contradictory or a starkly unacceptable conclusion, like that there are no heaps or rich people, from prima facie valid chains of reasoning, derived from apparently sound premises. A solution to a paradox would be to uncover an error either in the premises or in the reasoning. Difficulties in solving the paradoxes, particularly ancient ones like the sorites, raise sceptical prospects.

If not the sorites, then the Liar, is the paradox that has occasioned the most intense investigations. Tarski's equivalence condition earlier (see Section 2) was formulated in his response to the Liar Paradox:

(A) Sentence A is false.

From an intuitive assumption about any sentence, (A) is either true or false (or expresses a proposition that is either true or false). If it is true, what it claims is correct. But what it claims is that (A) is false, which is, effectively, "I am false." So, it's false. If, however, it is false, then what it claims is wrong. So it is true. In short: (A) is true if and only if (A) is false.

Like the sorites, the Liar Paradox encourages suspicion of bi-valence (the thought that every sentence is true or false), while supporting logics allowing for truth-value gaps, as well as gluts (more than two truth-values) However, if you think that this move alone will do the trick, out pops a "strengthened Liar"

(A′) Sentence A′ is not true.

One can claim that denying "Sentence A is false" does not necessarily imply that Sentence A is true. But this is no escape from the strengthened Liar, because even if "not true" is weaker than "false," as the strategy requires, the contradiction arises when we ask whether (A′) is true.

Focusing on a version like (A), Tarski thought the culprit is that "semantically closed languages" (i.e., those which contain their own truth predicate and a device – like naming – to denote each sentence) are inconsistent. In those languages, not every sentence can be assigned the value *true* or *false*. Part of Tarski's solution is to define truth only for open languages, establishing a hierarchy: truth for language L is defined in a higher (meta) language, which has the resources to pick out all the sentences of L. Tarski showed how to define truth for a language (in a metalanguage) by way of recursive definition. From a finite assignment of truth to atomic sentences, sentences of any complexity can be generated, for example, "A and B" is true if and only if "A" is true and "B" is true. (For critical discussion Field 1972; for applications to natural language Davidson 1984. Kripke (1975) contains both an example of consistent predications of truth that receive contradictory assignments in Tarski's hierarchy and an alternative way to define truth.)

One problem with Tarski's approach to our ordinary notion of truth is that we can understand sentences that predicate truth without any knowledge of their truth-level in his hierarchy. A suggestion here is that "true" is implicitly indexical, like "I" or "you," whose reference is determined within the context of utterance, although the meaning is constant (Kaplan 1989). Thus:

(A) Sentence A is not true₁

and

(A)   Sentence A is true$_{l+1}$

are not contradictory, anymore than "You are a lefty" and "You are a righty" affirmed of different people (Burge 1979).

A paradox of set theory, whose origin lies with Liar-like self-reference, was discovered by Russell – hence, "Russell's Paradox." Typically, members of a class, like members of the class of people, are not themselves classes and so they cannot be members of themselves. But some classes are: The class containing as members all classes that have more than five members. Russell asked a question that combined these: Is the class of all classes that are not members of themselves a member of itself? If so, then it meets the defining conditions that it is not a member of itself, so it is not a member of itself. But if it is not a member of itself, then it satisfies the condition, and so must be included as a member of the class of all classes that are not members of itself. In brief, the class of all classes that are members of themselves is a member of itself if and only if it isn't.

Even though Russell's Paradox is one of set-theory and the Liar one of semantics, they have striking similarilities, which led Russell to compare them. The contradiction yielded by either involves similar reasoning from respective self-referential questions. Both involve extremely plausible existence claims about the universal predication of their respective key notions (truth-value; membership) and invite similar hierarchical restrictions on that predication. The problem is not self-reference alone. Numerous self-referential statements are unproblematically true ("This sentence is in English") and others unproblematically false ("This sentence is in Russian"). Russell thought that the essential connection was, roughly, that a member of a totality is defined in terms of the totality (the Vicious Circle Principle).

A number of the central paradoxes share a feature close to the fault line that Russell proposed. These paradoxes claim the existence of a meaningful property or term to fit a specified general condition. The sorites requires that to every concept there is a determinate answer to whether the concept applies to an object or not. The very different "grue" paradox still has this feature: It casts doubt on the condition that to every predicate there corresponds a confirmable or projectible property. The Liar Paradox assumes the condition that to every grammatically well-formed sentence there is one of

two truth values. Russell's Paradox is sometimes illustrated by the Barber Paradox. In a town, where the barber shaves all and only those citizens who do not shave themselves, who shaves the barber? A Russell's Paradox-like contradiction follows. But the Barber is only a contradiction, no paradox. For no credible principle establishes that there is such a barber. Not so for Russell's Paradox. Russell originally directed his paradox to an explicit axiom of Frege's system, which implied the assumption tacitly made in constructing the paradox: To every coherent condition there is a set meeting exactly that condition.

The natural reaction to Russell's Paradox is to deny that the membership in the set of all sets that are not members of themselves is a coherent condition. But the denial does not sit well with much positive work in set theory and, specifically, if the restriction suggested is not qualified it undermines other fundamental results (e.g., Cantor's diagonal proof that the power set of a class has more members than the class, a proof that shares structural features with many paradoxes, including the Liar and Russell's).

15. The Preface Paradox, the First Person, and Fallibility

The Preface Paradox is a paradox of self-reflection that arises naturally from thoughts about one's fallibility. Its name derives from a typical disclaimer that occurs in prefaces to books (Makinson 1964). The author of a non-fictional work writes something intended to express modesty "Remaining errors in the book are my own." The author is justified in making this assertion. Given the numerous statements in the book, he is bound to have made some error. Assuming the author is conscientious, however, he believes each sentence he wrote and asserts them to be true. But it is impossible for each statement in the book to be true, if the preface is part of the book.

The bite of the Preface Paradox arises when we realize that fallibility about one's own beliefs is akin to the modesty expressed in the preface. In taking oneself to be fallible one appears to believe that "at least one of my beliefs is false." However, for each of one's beliefs, one does (trivially) believe it. But one's corpus of beliefs, including the belief in one's fallibility so expressed, is inconsistent. As standardly presented, the Preface Paradox has the form of "w-inconsistency." All instances of a generalization are true, but not the generalization itself.

Unlike other paradoxes, the dominant view is that the consequence of the Preface Paradox is acceptable. In maintaining this corpus, a fallible believer is "being rational though inconsistent" (Makinson 1964: 207).

But can we just resign ourselves to this consequence? The result would be a kind of complex Moore's Paradox: "p_1, p_2, ... p_n, [are each true] but I believe that not all of p_1, p_2, ... p_n [are true]," where among the p_i is the quoted sentence itself. A different way out is that even those who admit their fallibility do not really all-out believe that at least one their beliefs is false. Rather, they take it to be only extremely probable in parallel to the impossibility of all-out accepting that one will lose a fair lottery with a single ticket.

How should one factor into any of one's reasoning (inclusive of that reasoning) one's belief that one is fallible? Hume (1978) observed that if we incorporate into our judgments an evaluation of those judgments that represents our fallibility, a sceptical regress threatens. Hume writes:

> In every judgment, which we can form concerning probability, as well as concerning knowledge, we ought always to correct the first judgment, deriv'd from the nature of the object, by another judgment, deriv'd from the nature of the understanding. . . . In the man of the best sense and longest experience, this authority is never entire; since even such-a-one must be conscious of many errors in the past, and must still dread the like for the future. Here then rises a new species of probability to correct and regulate the first . . .
>
> Having thus found in every probability, beside the uncertainty inherent in the subject, a new uncertainty deriv'd from the weakness of that faculty, which judges, and having adjusted these two together, we are oblig'd by our reason to add a new doubt deriv'd from the possibility of error in the estimation we make of the truth and fidelity of our faculties. . . . But this decision, tho' it shou'd be favourable to our preceeding judgment, being founded only on probability, must weaken still further our first evidence, and must itself be weaken'd by a fourth doubt of the same kind, and so on *in infinitum*; till at last there remain nothing of the original probability. (182–183)

This argument is puzzling even aside from its skeptical end, because it seems only to require a recognition of one's fallibility and the willingness to take that into account to qualify one's judgment. However, once a judgment is made, it is made, and to do it over in light of one's fallibility is to just double-count. Moreover, why should the correction – representing one's fallibility – lessen the original probability, rather than raise it? After all, fallibility is about error, and one can err in either of two directions – overestimate, as well as underestimate. Fallibility bears on the weight of evidence, not its force. (In familiar psychological studies, subjects are asked, e.g., "Which is more populous city San Diego or Santa Fe?" After providing that answer, subjects are asked, "How confident are you in your prior judgment?" Hume's conflated question now is evident: "How probable do you now think it is that Santa Fe is larger than San Diego in light of your prior judgment of fairly high confidence in your even earlier judgment than Santa Fe is larger than San Diego?" [huh?].) Consequently, it does not make sense to calculate the probability of a judgment by an integration (via Bayes's Theorem) with the weight of evidence, where this is measured in Hume's terms, by one's estimate of one's degree of fallibility for the judgment at hand.

16. Fallacy and Charity

If the objections just given succeed, Hume's argument is fallacious. A fallacy is an argument that seems to be good, but which isn't (Hamblin 1970). One is falsely persuaded, unlike the case of crudely bad reasoning (e.g., If John is in Albany, he is in New York. So even if he isn't in Albany, he is in New York.).

The following is an example of a student committing a fallacy of denying the antecedent (i.e., "If p then q; not p; therefore, not q"):

(26) If I don't study, my dad won't let me go to the party.

So, (27) I'll study, then he has to let me go out.

More common and seductive are fallacies of scope:

(28) Necessarily, if Jeff is a teenager, he is under twenty.

(29) Jeff is a teenager.

So, (30) Necessarily, Jeff is under twenty [i.e., he cannot become an adult].

Or, (31) Alice does not believe that the library is open on Saturday.

So (32) Alice believes that the library is not open on Saturday.

But are these common fallacies? Would not anyone who reasons to (30), really mean that Jeff must be under twenty only given that he is a teenager? Assumptions about the necessity of human rationality have led to scepticism about whether people ever really commit fallacies or that there really are common fallacies. (A weaker reading is that the attribution of fallacies is never warranted. Problems with the former, which we concentrate on, apply to the latter.) The best defense of this conclusion is that when we understand the speech-acts of others, we must see them as rational, hence, we must interpret their assertions under a *principle of charity* (Davidson 1984). Think of the comprehension of metaphor or hyperbole or similar figurative speech, along lines already suggested by Gricean pragmatics (see Section 7). A recent newspaper column states "Bush is radioactive." If the political commentator who wrote it really believed that President Bush is subject to radioactive decay, he would have to be so bereft of rational thought that he would be unintelligible, including to himself. Instead, the striking falsity of a literal reading of that utterance is a signal to infer that the best explanation of what is meant is something different, for example, if a political leader associates closely with President Bush, the association immediately taints that leader. Now the speaker can be readily viewed as rational (Davidson 1984) and as speaking in accord with the cooperative principle (Grice 1989).

Because a fallacy is a serious failure of reasoning, the principle of charity, as well as the cp, are alleged to undermine a fallacy reading, especially, where an evident nonfallacious alternative is available. In (26)–(27), the first premise, although stated as a conditional, is reasonably meant as a biconditional and then the inference goes through.

Scepticism about the commission of fallacies is unwarranted. First, when someone commits a fallacy, the person need not, even cannot, recognize it as having a fallacious form (e.g., if A, B; so if not A, not B), let alone being a fallacy (which would be to commit a Moore's Paradox: "My argument establishes its conclusion, but the argument is fallacious"). Second, the principle of charity, assumptions of rationality, and the cooperative principle assume a background of mostly well-founded beliefs and good reasoning. One can commit many fallacies compatible with this assumption, because the "mostly"

is for a much larger reference class of beliefs and reasoning than the "many" (salient or prominent arguments). The former include such banalities as that: If today is Tuesday, I have class. Today is Tuesday, so I have class. Or, Jim is not in the classroom. So, Jim is somewhere else. You can easily understand and communicate with a person, who commits the above three fallacies, because his reasoning remains predominantly cogent.

In fact, one can readily explain on rational grounds why the above and other seductive fallacies are committed. It is easy enough to construct a reasonable path (from a misunderstanding of the law of large numbers) to the committing of a gambler's fallacy. Or, take (26)–(27). The student understands the relevant words and sentences he utters, which already presupposes a huge amount of rationality. (The student realizes that his father takes seriously that he should study, that this is a domain of his father's authority, and that his going to the party depends on his father's approval.) The student also understands that many times when he has done what the father regarded as his duty, the father allowed him to engage in a desired activity only when the duty was performed. Factor in to this attempt at rational explanation for fallacious thought normal human distraction and indifference, as well as our inclinations to impose contextually invited assumptions. It is not then at all uncharitable to ascribe to the student an inference on these occasions to the belief that whenever he fulfills a necessary condition for gaining his father's permission, he has thereby fulfilled a sufficient condition, although the student probably would not describe it in these ways (of "necessary" and "sufficient" conditions). Finally, a simple test applies. Would the student who reasons from (26) to (27) be surprised and taken aback, rather than hostile to an unfair accusation, by the following argument as paralleling his own in form and yet clearly (to his mind) fallacious?:

(33) If I don't study, I won't get into Yale.

So, (34) I'll study, then I must get into Yale.

17. Implicitness and Argument

These examples all illustrate one facilitator of fallacies, compatible with our rationality and basic reasoning competence. Much of our reasoning and particularly our ordinary arguments are tacit or implicit as compared to the reconstructions of those arguments, where missing or hidden assumptions are stated. The student would likely not endorse the abstract logical principle his argument assumes: if p, q. So, if not p, not q.

This observation provides no formula for eliminating common fallacies, because ordinary argument and reasoning cannot aspire to much explicitness. Implicitness is a barrier that can be overcome in specific cases, but it is ineliminable, for reasons of economy and limited grasp of our beliefs. Tacitness or implicitness is evident in the drawing of conversational implicatures, allowing communication of much information with brevity (see Section 7).

The extent of the implicitness even of deductive arguments is obscured when they are reconstructed so that the validity is exhibited in the logical form alone as with the opening example (1)–(3): Either p or q. Not p. So, q. There are valid arguments, whose validity does not reside in their logical form:

(35) John is taller than Jim.

So, (36) Jim is not taller than John.

The argument's validity pivots on the asymmetry of "is taller than." But asymmetry is clearly not a property of all relations or two-place predicates (cf., "as smart as"). To capture the validity of (35)–(36) by logical form, there would need to be a separate premise affirming the asymmetry of "is taller than."

In everyday reasoning rarely would such a premise be explicitly thought. If arguments or inferences are not valid by their logical form alone, then arguments such as (35)–(36) can be valid as they stand (Brandom 1994, Ch. 2; Thomson 1965). It is valid as a result of the content of its substantive or nonlogical vocabulary ("is taller than"), rather than only because of its logical form as with (1)–(3).

Accepting the validity of (35)–(36) as it stands is one way to introduce the implicit nature of much reasoning, though greatly understating it. The following would be quickly recognized as a good argument, although stating the assumptions informing it explicitly would be burdensome:

(37) North Korea successfully tested missiles today.

So, (38) the United States is going to call on the United Nations to impose sanctions.

The argument draws on the audience's vast background knowledge to efficiently – without stating – provide a bridge to the conclusion.

Although brevity and limited knowledge are fundamental reasons for an ineliminable implicitness of argument and reasoning, persuasion is aided by it. The one persuaded will supply without recognition the missing assumptions, and so he commits himself to them. The benefit to persuasion may not be intended, but simply a product of ignorance, because we often do not know what are the assumptions our arguments require. An argument that used to be found persuasive is

(39) Scientists discovered that the Morning Star and the Evening Star are Venus.

So, (40) it is a contingent matter that the Morning Star and the Evening Star are one and the same.

We now realize that the argument rests on an assumption:

If it is an empirical discovery that p (i.e., if from the point of view of the investigators, it might have turned out otherwise), it is contingent that p (i.e., p could actually turn out false).

Once the assumption is stated explicitly, it immediately appears suspect. Our missing the invalidity of the inference is evidence that until Kripke's (1980) discovery we did not even recognize that an assumption was made.

A conceptual basis for implicitness – in particular, that an argument cannot express as premises all the reasons logically involved in deriving its conclusions – is the moral of Lewis Carroll's (1895) parable "Achilles and the Tortoise." Achilles wants to show the Tortoise that anyone who accepts (41) and (42) must accept (43):

(41) Things that are equal to the same are equal to each other.

(42) The two sides of this Triangle are things that are equal to the same.

(43) The two sides of this Triangle are equal to each other.

The Tortoise accepts (41) and (42), but not (43). Achilles agrees that he must now show the Tortoise that

(44) If (41) and (42), then (43)

But what if the Tortoise responds that he accepts (41), (42), and (44), yet he still does not accept (43)? Then Achilles must show him, by parity,

(45) If (41) and (42) and (44), then (43).

Clearly, Achilles has been persuaded to enter an infinite regress. The moral of the story or one moral, anyway, is that Achilles should have balked at the first step: (41) and (42) already imply (43), so that no further premise is necessary to justify that inference. For the Tortoise to claim that he accepts the conditional (41), as well as (42), but that he does not accept (43) is to contradict himself (the validity of the inference is implicit in the meaning of the conditional). He is committed to (43), even if he lacks any specific belief in modus ponens as a valid argument form.

Despite the essential benefits to reasoning of implicitness, the reconstruction of arguments in which assumptions are stated and terms and statements are standardized is central for purposes of the critical analysis of arguments. By rendering these assumptions visible and as entering claims to truth, burdens of proof are imposed on the claimant. Explicitness renders bad reasoning and confabulation more difficult.

Explicitization is a natural consequence of argumentation as a dialectical exchange. Because argumentation is social – ideally, public – to engage in it is to impose a questioner or critic or interlocutor on oneself, and so a device of self-correction. If the interlocutor is not under the arguer's control, if he does not share the same biases as the arguer, he is thereby an obstacle to bending argument to favor the arguer's own position. Socratic questioning compels focus by interlocutors on crucial consequences or implications, keeping the dialectical exchange on target. Of course, explicitization can also add biased information. It can overload and distract one's thoughts. Interlocutors may be heavily self-selected. But these are interferences with argumentation, and our purpose here is to highlight its potential value functioning optimally for reasoning (Adler 2006).

Argumentation involves moving one's argument from its inchoate form to an articulate one. For complex arguments, argumentation almost certainly calls for written formulation, which is characterized by greater explicitness, since addressed to a more impersonal audience (than in casual thought or conversation). In articulate forms, the social activity of argumentation can become public, with unrestricted access. In argumentation, participants attempt to render explicit implicit assumptions, inferences, qualifications, and so on. Explicitization brings forth the basic structures or generalizations that constitute the underlying warrants for inferences. (On warrants, see Toulmin 1958: Ch. III; this volume) It facilitates reconstruction of the argument with variables, which encourages testing in disparate domains, through diverse substitutions for the variables.

18. Social Reasoning and Oneself Over Time

Argumentation is a form of social or dialectical exchange. In one form, close to Socratic dialogue, one agent acts as questioner of another's claim or thesis and elicits his reasons for that claim or thesis. The objective is to test whether that claim or thesis and the reasons for it are consistent, including with other claims (beliefs).

Besides its value for self-correction and learning, argumentation and social reasoning, more generally, foster coordination with others or oneself in the future and they exploit a division of epistemic or cognitive labor. In argumentation, we take turns as questioners and claimants (arguers) and by presenting arguments to others we automatically draw on information and skills that they have, which we do not.

Although we cannot draw on information that we will obtain only in the future, we can alter beliefs as new information comes in, which improves the beliefs of our later self. Recall that conditionalization is a primary mechanism for updating probabilities with new information, generating a rational connection between earlier and later stages of oneself (see Section 11). An analogue of conditionalization in practical reasoning does not appear as secure. Suppose the deterrence of a nuclear war is expected to succeed if the United States provides evidence that it will retaliate. Then the deterrence effect is a reason to intend to retaliate. However, this reason, though sufficient to justify the attitude, may not be a reason sufficient to render it true that one will retaliate. Were the deterrence to fail, it might be better to enter negotiation rather than engage in all-out nuclear retaliation (Gauthier 1986; Kavka 1983). The transition from the conditional intention to the all-out intention, when the condition is realized, ought not to be taken for granted. Is conditionalization subject to anything like this gap?

The gap involves how one's present self seeks to guide itself over time. The future self subject to the conditional intention does not regard itself as bound by it. Surely, I am not bound now to agree with what I regard as my earlier foolishness. (However, the earlier judgment could be a strategic one, adopted with the intention that one's later self should not be faithful to it.

More on this strategic explanation later.) Conditionalization seems applicable. I may recognize a continuous chain via conditionalization to my present position. But I may now regard the limited information and foolishness of my earlier self as implying that my past assignment of probabilities places no restrictions on my present self. I do not conditionalize from the position of (what I now believed are) earlier immature thoughts.

However, when we turn to our understanding of ourselves in the future – our future selves – a surprising principle has, like conditionalization, also been defended by a Dutch Book (or "sure loss") Argument. This is van Fraassen's "Reflection Principle," which says, informally, that if your probability now that A at some later time is r, then right now the probability that you assign to A should be r. More formally:

$$\mathrm{Pr}_t(A \mid \mathrm{pr}_{t+x}(A) = r) = r \text{ (van Fraassen 1984).}$$

The principle implies a commitment to consistency with one's later self, not merely an expectation that one's later self will be more informed or mature. The commitment holds even if one regards one's later self as subject to prejudices or biases (e.g., one's present youthful liberal self anticipates that with middle age one will become, unfortunately, less liberal and more politically conservative), unless one ceases to identify with one's later self.

This principle seems to say that I cannot regard my future self as foolish as I can my past self. Can't I, and if not, why? (It does not seem to be a Moore's Paradox to affirm "Taxes to support welfare is just, but I *will* (in my conservative middle age) not believe it.") (Bovens 1995) Is this a problem for the Reflection Principle? Alternatively, does it show that "sure loss" arguments, which turn on preferences as fixed only by one's judgments of what is likely, are not applicable to all-out beliefs or acceptance? All-out acceptance is responsive to our need to economize – to end inquiry in a finite amount of time, despite the possibility of acquiring further evidence.

The hold of my present self on my future self is central to practical reasoning – one's present self determines how one's future self should act. Once a goal or end is fixed for practical reasoning, though, what form do the conclusions take? When a student reasons about whether she should talk to a teacher to question a low grade, her conclusion is not merely that on the evidence, she should go to talk to him. That does not yet determine how she should act – perhaps,

she should find more evidence? Her conclusion is a commitment or intention to act accordingly – to speak to him (or not) – akin to all-out acceptance. Although sometimes practical reasoning does not reach a terminus and further inquiry is called for, the aim is a decision to act, when feasible.

A natural principle of rationality is that if I conclude that I ought to A (e.g., floss my teeth), all things considered, then I form the intention to A or I act to A. But this natural principle is one we often disobey. My concluding that I ought to floss tonight is a far cry from my deliberately forming the intention to floss. When I judge that I ought to floss all things considered (including my laziness and displeasure with flossing), but I do not intend to floss or I deliberately or intentionally do not floss, I suffer weakness of will or *akrasia*. Because weakness of will smacks of irrationality, perhaps the cases that seem to fit it are really ones where at the moment of action, I change my judgment to a denial that I ought to floss, rather than just relax in bed. Attributions of irrationality are hard to square with actions that appear to make sense. There is then a drive to avoid the attribution by redescribing what is going on as a change in judgment (a form of the "principle of charity"). Still, not all cases can be redescribed in this way. When I do not floss, I have not changed my mind that I am really better off not flossing. I suffer weakness of will, allowing laziness to thwart good judgment (Davidson 1980).

But there are some cases in which the conclusion of practical reasoning does not yield the corresponding intention or action, and there is no irrationality. A teenager reasons that because a teacher purposely embarrassed him in class, he should get even by puncturing the tire on the teacher's car. The student reaches this conclusion, yet when the moment of truth comes he does not act. Nevertheless, his weakness of will is not irrational, given the teenager's overall values, beliefs, and interests. His practical reasoning simply did not comprehend all his genuine reasons for actions in the circumstance, some of which provide forceful resistance to the teenager's proposed action.

What force is there then in speaking of commitments, decisions, or intentions, over and above (detached from) the relation of the evidence or reasons to the conclusions as to how one ought to act? In either case one ends inquiry with a judgment and sets up a barrier to reconsideration. When one commits oneself, however, one takes a stance that one will not act otherwise, regardless of what one learns in the interim except in extreme cases. That stance goes beyond merely drawing a conclusion as to how one should act. A promise is the most familiar example: If I promise to meet you for lunch next Tuesday and in the interim I receive another invitation, I will not accept it. Of course, if an emergency comes up in the interim, then I do legitimately break the engagement (Raz 1990).

When promising, as when one forms an intention or commitment, one's present self generates reasons that bind one's later self from acting otherwise. Given that one's later self will acquire further information, unavailable to one's present self, including detailed information about the current circumstances, how can it be rational to so bind oneself in the future? Answers to this question, which also go a good way to answering an analogous question for why we should ever adopt rules, center on coordination with oneself and with others and anticipated limits on rational judgment. If I decide that I will be in London in June, rather than merely regarding that as my best option so far, I can form plans around that trip (e.g., to purchase tickets to a London play). More important, if I commit myself to act in certain ways, others can coordinate their plans with me. We can arrange for a meeting on the presumption that we will all attend, which we could not do if inquiry or options remain open.

In binding one's future self, one forecloses one's later self from exercising its will. Most vividly and with highly variable success, we commit ourselves to diets that deny our later self from acting deliberately on its own. How is the binding to work, because at that later time, I can simply decide to follow my current judgment, rather than my past one?

One famous model for these problems is the tale of Ulysses and the Sirens (Elster 1984). Ulysses wants to hear the song of the Sirens, but he wants to avoid the dangerous madness that hearing their song is known to induce. His solution is to have his men tie him to the mast as they pass the Sirens' island, and to stuff their ears so that they can hear neither his cries for release nor, more importantly, the Sirens' song, as he can.

However, the irreversible binding is risky. What would happen if Ulysses' sailors spy a storm or an enemy ship, while he is bound? They acquire information unavailable to Ulysses' present deciding self. They need Ulysses' guidance, but only if the sailors release him, could he provide it. If the sailors follow the earlier command, it will be to the ship's detriment. Alter-

natively, the new determination counts as an emergency circumstance cuing them to release Ulysses and to unstuff their ears. But this alternative reintroduces a role for his sailors' judgment and thus the original problem of how to maintain the decision of the earlier self.

Irreversible or absolute binding does not, in fact, cover many realistic cases where the binding is porous (e.g., "controlled cheating" in diets: you can occasionally eat a sweet for dessert) and we add incentives to lessen the benefits of the immediate reward (e.g., if you lose a certain amount of weight, your family takes you on a vacation) (Ainslie 1992).

Commitments that are less binding than that of Ulysses are often made to avoid temptations that one judges overall worse for oneself. You purchase a subscription to the theater, even when you believe, let us assume, that you will have no problem purchasing a ticket for performances on the selected evenings. You do so because you value going to the theater and you know that your own laziness on the night of the performance will lead you just stay home and watch TV. The subscription pressures you to go because otherwise you will have wasted money, and so you are very likely, as you anticipate, to go to far more plays with the subscription than without it.

But wait: If on a given night, you genuinely prefer to stay home, why should it make any difference whether you have a subscription or not? The money is spent in any case, and since without the subscription you would not have gone, why should you allow the past to force you to do what you currently disprefer? Economists refer to these past investments as "sunk costs," and they recommend that we do not honor them. It is irrational to do so, if our only goal is to maximize profits. In that case, future return is all.

But is maximizing profit all? We value committing ourselves to a plan and sticking to it. For others to trust us, requires that when we enter a commitment to another – say to meet them for lunch – we honor it. In this way, one gains a reputation for trustworthiness, which invites others to continue to cooperate, an invitation that is foregone if one regularly subjects one's commitments to the test of better offers and future returns (Nozick 1993).

The honoring of commitments and the maintenance of trust are necessary for stable solutions in "Prisoner's Dilemma" (PD) situations. In a standard example, we agree to a long-distance trade – your $1,000 for my stereo – and we will realize the trade by your sending a check to me and my shipping the stereo to you. If the trade goes through, we are both better off, since I value your $1,000 more than my stereo and you value my stereo more than your $1,000.

There are, however, two contrary pulls: fear of being a sucker and the prospect of far greater gain. If you do not hold up your end of the bargain and I do, I am out a stereo without compensation; and if you hold up your end of the bargain, I realize far more if I do not send you my stereo. Now if the trade is made through any legal institution, like e-Bay, each participant has a legitimate fear of punishment if he reneges. However, the recourse to an external authority, which Hobbes took as the only way to resolve the dilemma, should be unnecessary. Isn't rationality enough to allow us to realize the mutual, if second-best, gain of cooperation?

The problem is represented vividly in the following matrix:

if you defect by taking an extra long shower, that will not be noticed, so you free-ride. As long as few of you defect, the community does stave off the drought. In fact, if few defect this is presumably better overall, because it is sufficient for conserving that most, not all, cooperate, even if the really cooperative result would be to rotate opportunities for longer showers. Free-riding will only succeed for you however if not only does it remain fairly secret that you defect, but it remains secret that any group or collection is free-riding. However, the pull toward free-riding is available to anyone who reasons as the defectors do. The conservation policy will then be undermined and all will be worse off.

The cooperative solution, whether in the two-person or the many-person PD, is a case where self-interest and ethics harmonize, giving a positive answer to the ancient question "Why

		You	
		Cooperate	Not Cooperate
Me	Cooperate	A. Me: + 100; You: + 100	B. Me: −100; You: + 200
	Not Cooperate	C. Me + 200; You: − 100	D. Me: 0; You: 0

Except in special cases, these numbers, which are to represent utilities, not monetary value, do not matter only the ordering:

For me: C>A>D>B
For you: B>A>D>C

Our best and worst outcomes are opposites; and our second and third best match. As a consequence there is a "Dominance" argument not to cooperate. From my point of view, C is better than A and D is better than B. Although the Dominance argument is strictly rational, its Achilles Heel is that if you reason as I do, we both wind up at D, which is worse for both than if we cooperated (A). These two opposed arguments – for and against cooperation – are what make the PD a dilemma.

The problem arises as well in many person PDs, for those who would "free ride" – gain the benefits of the cooperation of others without sharing the sacrifices. A large community is conserving water in order to avoid a drought. (Another obvious example is voting.) You know that most others will conserve, and that if most others do, there will be no need for rationing water, which will be far worse for all. Because there are so many persons who are involved,

should I be ethical?," treating cooperation as the ethical result. Cooperation benefits each cooperator. It's in their interest to do what is ethical. In a two-person PD, we are both better off cooperating than if, instead, neither of us do, both acting on behalf of immediate, rather than enlightened, self-interest.

Outside the bounds of an external authority, realizing the cooperative result depends on trusting other participants, which thereby leaves us vulnerable if another is untrustworthy or chooses to defect. In a repeated Prisoner's Dilemma, as with ongoing trades or meetings, there is much greater prospects for trust and so the cooperative option. We each know what the other did previously, giving each the power to retaliate or to defect on the next round. Each of us recognizes the benefits of maintaining our cooperative practice for which either one can opt out, as well as defect. The strategy that is overall most successful is "tit-for-tat." If you play tit-for-tat you start off by cooperating and continue to cooperate unless the other party defects. After which you defect in retaliations, but then return to cooperating, rather than holding a grudge. The strategy is simple and it is easy for others to recognize that you are playing it, which are among the main reasons for its success (Axelrod 1984).

The Prisoner's Dilemma in its one-shot form bears unexpected affinities to another dilemma that Nozick (1969) introduced: Newcomb's Problem. In Newcomb's Problem, the Superior Being, whose predictions have always come to pass over many trials, offers you a choice to be made one week later between taking the contents of Box 1, which contains 0 or $1,000,000 only or taking as well the contents of Box 2, which contains $1,000. If the Superior Being predicts that you will take the contents only of Box 1, he places $1,000,000 in it; otherwise, if he predicts that you will take the contents of both boxes, he does not put anything in Box 1, and you wind up with only $1,000. The argument to take only the contents of Box 1 is evident enough: you secure $1,000,000. The argument to take the contents of both boxes is also evident: Because the being has already placed the money in Box 1 or not, you have nothing to lose now – one week later – in taking the contents of both boxes.

In Newcomb's Problem, your action of selecting a box is causally independent of what the Superior Being does (assuming no reverse causal process). But there is a probabilistic dependence, since what you now do affects the probability of the reward that you will receive. (In the PD, the actions of each party is assumed causally and probabilistically independent of the other. Were there probabilistic dependence, the PD gives rise to a similar conflict.) Then there is a dominance argument to take both boxes:

		Superior Being	
		Predicts One	Predicts Take Both
You	Take One	$1 million	$0
	Take Two	$1 million + $1000	$1000

Taking the contents of both boxes dominates for you over just taking the contents of Box 1 (the box, which you cannot see into, that has $1 million or $0).

However, assuming that the probability of the Superior Being is very high (e.g., .95) and that your utility is roughly the same as the dollar rewards, you maximize expected utility by taking only Box 1:

EU(Box 1 only) = (1,000,000) (.95) + (0) (.05)
   = 950,000

EU(Box 1 and 2) = (1,001,000) (.05) + (1,000) (.95) = 51,000.

Another twist, which favors a two-box choice, is to limit the expected utilities to causal dependencies of the action taken and the results, which, again, is assumed not to operate backward in time. For a typical application: Assume that smoking and lung cancer have a genetic base, but that the only cause of lung cancer is genetic. Smoking and lung cancer remain probabilistically dependent. Then it would seem that one should not quit smoking to avoid lung cancer, assuming that smoking is pleasurable. Yet to do so does lower the probability that one has lung cancer (Gibbard and Harper 1978; Lewis 1986a; for a collection on the Newcomb Problem and the Prisoner's Dilemma with an excellent introduction, see Campbell and Sowden 1985; also Sainsbury 1988, this volume).

Earlier, we mentioned a strategy that you would like to adopt here. You would like to intend to take the contents of only Box 1, up to the moment when the Superior Being makes his prediction. But then, when your moment of decision comes (one week later), you actually do not follow through on that intention. You then take the contents of both boxes. You secure the prediction you seek from the Superior Being without the real commitment to it. However, this strategy confronts the obstacle that the Superior Being may see through your facade. So you have a new version of the old conflict: a dominance argument to take both boxes and an expected utility argument to take only the contents of the million dollar box. What should you do?

Notes

1   In this chapter, we use the symbols "&" (and), "v" (inclusive or), "~" (not), and "⊃" (the material conditional) was the meanings given in standard texts on classical logical logic.

2   A nice example to distinguish indicative from counterfactual (subjunctive) conditionals is from Adams 1970: on our current understanding, the indicative that if Oswald did not kill Kennedy, someone else did, is true, but the counterfactual that if Oswald hadn't killed Kennedy, someone else would have, is false.

3   On this reading, Hume's argument is a far-reaching scepticism:

> Even after the observation of the frequent or constant conjunction of objects, we have no reason to draw any inference concerning any object beyond those of which we have had experience. (1978: 139)

4   There are examples that violate IC e.g., the hypothesis is that ravens are under 5′ long, and you find a raven that is 4′10″. This and similar examples depend, however, on background

information, which the original presentation of confirmation theory attempts to abstract from.

5   For example, suppose that there are just two predicates in our universe, Red and Square, and just three names, Huey, Dewey, and Louie. Then a state description is an assignment of each predicate or its negation to each of the individuals. For example:

Square(Huey) & not-Red(Huey) & not-Square(Dewey) & not-Red(Dewey) & Square(Louie) & Red(Louie)

In general, if there are n logically independent predicates, then there are 2^n possible combinations of predicates that could be assigned to an individual. If there are m names, each of which could have any of the 2^n combinations, then there are $(2^n)^m$ state descriptions in all.

6   Here's a simple reductio proof: We're given p. Suppose, for the sake of the reductio, that $\sim(p \lor q)$. By DeMorgan's Law, this last sentence implies $\sim p \ \& \sim q$, from which $\sim p$ follows. But $\sim p$ contradicts the premise p. Hence, the assumption $\sim(p \lor q)$ is false, and $p \lor q$ is true.

7   Thanks to Lance Rips for his valuable comments.

References

Adams, E. (1970) "Subjunctive and Indicative Conditionals." *Foundations of Language* 6: 89–94.

Adler, J. (2002) "Akratic Believing?" *Philosophical Studies* 110: 1–27.

———. (2006) "Confidence in Argument." *Canadian Journal of Philosophy* 36: 225–258.

Ainslie, G. (1992) *Picoeconomics: The Strategic Interaction of Successive Motivational States within the Person* (Cambridge: Cambridge University Press).

Anscombe, G. E. M. (1957) *Intentions* (Oxford: Blackwell).

Axelrod, R. (1984) *The Evolution of Cooperation* (New York: Basic Books).

Belnap, N. (1962) "Tonk, Plonk and Plink." *Analysis* 22: 130–133.

Bennett, J. (2003) *A Philosophical Guide to Conditionals* (Oxford: Oxford University Press).

Boghossian, P. (2000) "Knowledge of Logic" in P. Boghossian and C. Peacocke, eds. *New Essays on the A Priori* (Oxford: Oxford University Press): 229–254.

Bovens, L. (1995) "'P and I Will Believe Not-P': Diachronic Constraints on Rational Belief." *Mind* 104: 737–760.

Bovens, L. and Hartmann, S. (2003) *Bayesian Epistemology* (Oxford: Oxford University Press).

Brandom, R. (1994) *Making It Explicit: Reasoning, Representing, and Discursive Commitment* (Cambridge: Harvard University Press).

Bratman, M. E. (1987) *Intentions, Plans, and Practical Reason* (Cambridge, MA: Harvard University Press).

Burge, T. (1979) "Semantic Paradoxes" *Journal of Philosophy* 76: 169–198.

Campbell, R. and Sowden, L., eds. (1985) *Paradoxes of Rationality and Cooperation.* (Vancouver: University of British Columbia Press).

Carnap, R. (1947) "On the Application of Inductive Logic." *Philosophy and Phenomenological Research* 8: 133–147.

———. (1962) *Logical Foundations of Probability* Second Edition (Chicago: University of Chicago Press).

Carrol, L. (1895) "What the Tortoise Said to Achilles," *Mind* 4: 278–280.

Cherniak, C. (1986) *Minimal Rationality* (Cambridge, MA: MIT Press).

Cohen, L. J. (1977) *The Probable and the Provable* (Oxford: Oxford University Press).

Christensen, D. (2004) *Putting Logic in its Place: Formal Constraints on Rational Belief* (Oxford: Oxford University Press).

Davidson, D. (1980) "How Is Weakness of Will Possible?" in his *Essays on Actions and Events* (Oxford: Oxford University Press): 21–42.

———. (1984) *Inquiries into Truth and Interpretation* (Oxford: Oxford University Press).

Dretske, F. (1970) "Epistemic Operators." *The Journal of Philosophy* 69: 1015–1016.

Duhem, P. (1954) *The Aim and Structure of Physical Theory* (Princeton, NJ: Princeton University Press).

Dummett, M. (1978) "The Justification of Deduction" in his *Truth and Other Enigmas* (Cambridge, MA: Harvard University Press): 290–318.

Elgin, C. Z. (1996) *Considered Judgment* (Princeton, NJ: Princeton University Press).

Elster, J. (1984) *Ulysses and the Sirens*, Second Edition (Cambridge: Cambridge University Press).

Field, H. (1972) "Tarski's Theory of Truth" *Journal of Philosophy* 69: 347–375.

Fine, K. 1975. "Vagueness, Truth and Logic." *Synthese* 30: 265–300.

Fitelson, B. (1999) "The Plurality of Bayesan Measures of Confirmation and the Problem of Measure Sensitivity." *Philosophy of Science* 66: 362–378.

———. (2003) "A Probabilistic Theory of Coherence." *Analysis* 63: 194–199.

Fodor, J. (1983) *Modularity of Mind* (Cambridge, MA: MIT Press).

Frege, G. (1970) "On Sense and Reference" in *Translations from the Philosophical Writings of Gottlob Frege* (Oxford: Blackwell): 56–78.

Garfinkel, A. (1981) *Forms of Explanation* (New Haven, CI: Yale University Press).

Gauthier, D. (1986) *Morals by Agreement* (Oxford: Oxford University Press).

Gibbard, A. (1981) "Two Recent Theories of Conditions" in Harper, W. L., Stalnaker, R. and Pearce G., eds. *Ifs* (Dordrecht: Reidel): 211–247.

Gibbard, A. and Harper, W. (1978) "Counterfactuals and Two Kinds of Expected Utility" in *Foundations and Applications of Decision Theory*, C. A. Hooker et al., eds. (Dordrecht: Reidel).

Ginet, Carl (1980) "Knowing Less by Knowing More." *Midwest Studies in Philosophy V 1980* (Minneapolis: University of Minnesota Press): 151–161.

Glymour, C. (1980) *Theory and Evidence* (Princeton, NJ: Princeton University Press).

Goodman, N. (1965) *Fact, Fiction, and Forecast* (Indiana: Bobbs-Merrill).

Goodman, N. (1983) *Fact, Fiction, and Forecast* (Cambridge, MA: Harvard University Press).

Grice, H. P. (1989) *Studies in the Way of Words* (Cambridge: Harvard University Press).

_____. (2001) *Aspects of Reason* R. Warner, ed. (Oxford: Oxford University Press).

Hacking, I. (2001) *An Introduction to Probability and Inductive Logic* (Cambridge: Cambridge University Press).

Hamblin, C. L. (1970) *Fallacies* (London: Methuen).

Hansson, S. O. (2006) "Logic of Belief Revision" in *The Stanford Encyclopedia of Philosophy* Edward N. Zalta (ed.), available at: http://plato.stanford.edu/archives/sum2006/entries/logic-belief-revision/.

Harman, G. (1973) *Thought* (Princeton, NJ: Princeton University Press).

_____. (1986) *Change in View: Principles of Reasoning* (Cambridge, MA: MIT Press).

Hempel, C. G. (1965) "Studies in the Logic of Confirmation" in his *Aspects of Scientific Explanation* (New York: The Free Press): 3–46.

Hintikka, J. (1962) *Knowledge and Belief* (Ithaca: Cornell University Press).

Horwich, P. (1990) *Truth* (Oxford: Blackwell).

Hume D. (1977) *An Enquiry Concerning Human Understanding*, E. Steinberg, ed. (Indianapolis: Hackett Publishing Co.).

_____. (1978) *A Treatise of Human Nature*, Second Edition, L. A. Selby-Bigge and P. H. Nidditch, eds. (Oxford: Oxford University Press).

Jackson, F. (1975) "'Grue.'" *Journal of Philosophy* 72: 113–131.

_____. (1987) *Conditionals* (Oxford: Blackwell).

Jeffrey, R. C. (1983) *The Logic of Decision*, Second Edition (Chicago: University of Chicago Press).

Kaplan, D. (1989) "Demonstratives" in J. Almog, J. Perry, and H. Wettstein, eds. *Themes from Kaplan* (Oxford: Oxford University Press): 481–563.

Kaplan, M. (1996) *Decision Theory as Philosophy* (Cambridge: Cambridge University Press).

Kavka, G. (1983) "The Toxin Puzzle." *Analysis* 43: 33–36.

Keynes, J. M. (1952) *A Treatise on Probability* (London: Macmillan).

Kripke, S. (1975) "Outline of a Theory of Truth." *Journal of Philosophy* 72: 690–716.

_____. (1977) "Speaker's Reference and Semantic Reference." *Midwest Studies in Philosophy* 2: 255–76.

_____. (1980) *Naming and Necessity* (Cambridge: Harvard University Press).

Kyburg, H. E. (1961) *Probability and the Logic of Rational Belief* (Middletown, CT: Wesleyan University Press).

Kyburg, H. E., and Teng, C. M. (2001) *Uncertain Inference* (Cambridge: Cambridge University Press).

Levi, Isaac. (1980) *The Enterprise of Knowledge* (Cambridge, MA: MIT Press).

Lewis, D. (1971) "Immodest Inductive Methods." *Philosophy of Science* 38: 54–63.

_____. (1982). "Logic for Equivocators" *Nous* XIV: 431–441.

_____. (1983) "Scorekeeping in a Language-Game" in his *Philosophical Papers: Vol. I* (Oxford: Oxford University Press): 233–249.

_____. (1986a) "Causal Decision Theory" (and "Postscript") in his *Philosophical Papers Vol. II* (Oxford: Oxford University Press): 305–339.

_____. (1986b) "Probabilities of Conditionals and Conditional Probabilities" (with postscript) in his *Philosophical Papers Vol. II* (Oxford: Oxford University Press): 133–156.

_____. (1999) "Why Conditionalize?" in his *Papers in Metaphysics and Epistemology* (Cambridge: Cambridge University Press): 403–407.

Lipton, P. (2004) *Inference to the Best Explanation*, Second Edition (London: Routledge).

Luper, S. (2006) "The Epistemic Closure Principle" in *The Stanford Encyclopedia of Philosophy* Edward N. Zalta (ed.), available at: http://plato.stanford.edu/archives/spr2006/entries/closure-epistemic/.

Makinson, D. C. (1964) "The Paradox of the Preface." *Analysis* 25 205–207.

McGee, V. (1985) "A Counterexample to Modus Ponens." *Journal of Philosophy* 82: 462–471.

Mill, J. S. (1963) "A System of Logic" in *Collected Works of John Stuart Mill Vol. 7–8* J. M. Robson, ed. (Toronto: University of Toronto Press).

Millgram, E. (2001) "Practical Reasoning: The Current State of Play" in his *Varieties of Practical Reasoning* (Cambridge, MA: The MIT Press): 1–26.

Nozick, R. (1969) "Newcomb's Problem and Two Principles of Choice" N. Rescher, ed. in *Essays in Honor of Carl G. Hempel*, (Dordrecht: Reidel)

_____. (1981) *Philosophical Explanations* (Cambridge, MA: Harvard University Press).

_____. (1993) *The Nature of Rationality* (Princeton, NJ: Princeton University Press).

Parfit, D. (2001) "Rationality and Reasons." *Proceedings of the Aristotelian Society Supplementary* LXXV 1: 195–216.

Parikh, R. (1994) "Vagueness and Utility: the Semantics of Common Nouns." *Linguistics and Philosophy* 17: 521–535.

Peirce, C. S. (1931) *Collected Papers* C. Hartshorne and P. Weiss, eds. (Cambridge, MA: Harvard University Press). Vol. 5: 180–189.

Pollock, J. L. and Cruz, J. (1999) *Contemporary Theories of Knowledge*, Second Edition (Lanham, MD: Rowman and Litlefield).

Popper, K. R. (1959) *The Logic of Scientific Discovery* (New York: Harper).

Priest, G. (1998) "What Is So Bad about Contradictions?" *Journal of Philosophy* 95: 410–426.

Prior, A. (1960) "The Runabout Inference-Ticket." *Analysis* 21: 38–39.

Putnam, H. (1975) "The Meaning of 'Meaning'" in his *Mind, Language and Reality Philosophical Papers Volume 2* (Cambridge: Cambridge University Press): 215–271.

Quine, W. V. O. (1980) "Two Dogmas of Empiricism" reprinted in *From a Logical Point of View*, Second Edition (Cambridge, MA: Harvard University Press): 20–46.

———. (1969) "Natural Kinds" in his *Ontological Relativity and Other Essays* (New York: Columbia University Press): 114–138.

———. (1970) *Philosophy of Logic* (Englewood Cliffs, NJ: Prentice Hall).

Rawls, J. (1971) *A Theory of Justice* (Cambridge: Harvard University Press).

Raz, J. (1990) *Practical Reason and Norms*, Second Edition (Princeton, NJ: Princeton University Press).

Reichenbach, H. (1961) *Experience and Prediction* (Chicago: University of Chicago Press).

Richardson, H. (1994) *Practical Reasoning About Final Ends* (Cambridge: Cambridge University Press).

Sainsbury, R. M. (1988) *Paradoxes* (Cambridge: Cambridge University Press).

Searle, J. *Intentionality* (Cambridge: Cambridge University Press, 1983).

Sellars, W. "Empiricism and the Philosophy of Mind" in his *Science, Perception and Reality* (London: Routledge & Kegan Paul, 1963): 127–196.

Smith, E. E., Shafir, E. and Osherson, D. (1993) "Similarity, Plausibility, and Judgments of Probability." *Cognition* 49: 67–96.

Sober, E. (2005) "Bayesianism – Its Scope and Limits" in R. Swinburne, ed. *Bayes's Theorem* (Oxford: Oxford University Press).

Sorensen, R. (2001) *Vagueness and Contradiction* (Oxford: Oxford University Press).

Sperber, D. and Wilson, D. (1986) *Relevance: Communication and Cognition* (Cambridge: Harvard University Press).

Stalnaker, R. C. (1987) *Inquiry* (Cambridge, MA: MIT Press).

Strawson, P. (1952) *Introduction to Logical Theory* (London: Methuen).

Tarksi, A. (1983) "The Concept of Truth in Formalized Languages" in his *Logic, Semantics, and Meta-Mathematics*, Second Edition, J. H. Woodger, trans.; J. Corcoran, ed. and intro. (Cambridge, UK: Hackett) 152–278.

Teller, P. (1973) "Conditionalization and Observation." *Synthese* 26: 218–258.

Tentori, K., Crupi, V., Bonini, N., & Osherson, D. (2007) "Comparison of confirmation measures." *Cognition* 107–119.

Thomson, J. J. (1965) "Reasons and Reasoning" in Max Black, ed. *Philosophy in America* (Ithaca: Cornell University Press): 282–303.

Toulmin, S. (1958) *The Uses of Argument* (Cambridge: Cambridge University Press).

van Fraassen, B. C. (1980) *The Scientific Image* (Oxford: Oxford University Press).

———. (1984) "Belief and the Will." *Journal of Philosophy* 81: 235–256.

Velleman, J. D. (2000) *The Possibility of Practical Reason* (Oxford: Oxford University Press).

White, R. (2005) "Explanation as a Guide to Induction." *Philosophers' Imprint*, available at: www.philosophersimprint.org/005002/, 5: 1–29.

Williams, B. A. O. (1973) "Internal and External Reasons" in his *Moral Luck* (Cambridge: Cambridge University Press).

Williamson, T. (1994) *Vagueness* (London: Routledge).

Wright, C. (2000) "Cogency and Question-Begging: Some Reflections on McKinsey's Paradox and Putnam's Proof." *Philosophical Issues 10 Skepticism*: 140–163.

Yablo, S. (1993) "Is Conceiveability a Guide to Possibility?" *Philosophy and Pheomenological Research* 53: 1–42.

Section 1: Some Philosophical Viewpoints

Chapter 1: Change in View: Principles of Reasoning

GILBERT HARMAN

BELIEF AND DEGREE OF BELIEF

Probabilistic Implication

We have a rule connecting implication and reasoning:

Principle of Immediate Implication That *P* is immediately implied by things one believes can be a reason to believe *P*.

Is there also a weaker probabilistic version of this rule?

Hypothetical Principle of Immediate Probabilistic Implication That *P* is obviously highly probable, given one's beliefs, can be a reason to believe *P*.

Suppose Mary purchases a ticket in the state lottery. Given her beliefs, it is obviously highly probable that her ticket will not be one of the winning tickets. Can she infer that her ticket will not win? Is she justified in believing her ticket is not one of the winning tickets?

Intuitions waver here. On the one hand, if Mary is justified in believing her ticket is not one of the winning tickets, how can she be justified in buying the ticket in the first place? Furthermore, it certainly seems wrong to say she can *know* that her ticket is not one of the winning tickets if it is really a fair lottery. On the other hand the probability that the ticket is not one of the winning tickets seems higher than the probability of other things we might easily say Mary knows. We ordinarily allow that Mary can come

to know various things by reading about them in the newspaper, even though we are aware that newspapers sometimes get even important stories wrong.

This issue is one that I will return to several times, but I want to begin by considering a suggestion which I think is mistaken, namely, that the trouble here comes from not seeing that belief is a matter of degree.

All-or-Nothing Belief

I have been supposing that for the theory of reasoning, explicit belief is an all-or-nothing matter. I have assumed that, as far as principles of reasoning are concerned, one either believes something explicitly or one does not; in other words an appropriate "representation" is either in one's "memory" or not. The principles of reasoning are principles for modifying such all-or-nothing representations.

This is not to deny that in some ways belief is a matter of degree. For one thing implicit belief is certainly a matter of degree, since it is a matter of how easily and automatically one can infer something from what one believes explicitly. Furthermore, explicit belief is a matter of degree in the sense that one believes some things more strongly than others. Sometimes one is only somewhat inclined to believe something, sometimes one is not sure what to believe, sometimes one is inclined to disbelieve something, sometimes one is quite confident something is not so, and so forth.

How should we account for the varying strengths of explicit beliefs? I am inclined to suppose that these varying strengths are implicit in a system of beliefs one accepts in a yes/no fashion. My guess is that they are to be explained as a kind of epiphenomenon resulting from the operation of rules of revision. For example, it may be that *P* is believed more strongly than *Q* if it would be harder to stop believing *P* than to stop believing *Q*, perhaps because it would require more of a revision of one's view to stop believing *P* than to stop believing *Q*.

In contrast to this, it might be suggested that principles of reasoning *should* be rules for modifying explicit *degrees of belief*. In this view, an account of reasoning should be embedded in a theory of subjective probability, for example, as developed by Jeffrey (1983), not that Jeffrey himself accepts this particular suggestion. In fact, this suggestion cannot really be carried out. People do not normally associate with their beliefs degrees of confidence of a sort they can use in reasoning. It is too complicated for them to do so. Degrees of belief are and have to be implicit rather than explicit, except for a few special cases of beliefs that are explicitly beliefs about probabilities.

Let me say why this is so. To begin with, Kyburg (1961) observes that the Immediate Implication and Inconsistency Principles would not be right even as approximations if belief were a matter of degree.

> *Immediate Implication Principle* The fact that one's view immediately implies *P* can be a reason to accept *P*.

> *Immediate Inconsistency Principle* Immediate logical inconsistency in one's view can be a reason to modify one's view.

Propositions that are individually highly probable can have an immediate implication that is not. The fact that one assigns a high probability to *P* and also to *if P then Q* is not a sufficient reason to assign a high probability to *Q*. Each premise of a valid argument might be probable even though the conclusion is improbable. Since one might assign a high degree of belief to various propositions without being committed to assigning a high degree of belief to a logical consequence of these propositions, Kyburg argues that the Logical Implication Principle is mistaken.

Similarly, each of an inconsistent set of beliefs might be highly probable. To take Kyburg's lottery example, it might be that the proposition, "one of the *N* tickets in this lottery is the winning ticket" is highly probable, and so is each proposition of the form, "ticket *i* is not the winning ticket," for each *i* between 1 and *N*. So one might believe each of these propositions to a high degree while recognizing that they are jointly inconsistent. Kyburg argues there is nothing wrong with this, so the Logical Inconsistency Principle is mistaken.

It is not just that these principles have exceptions. We have seen that they are defeasible and hold only other things being equal. But if belief were always a matter of degree the principles would not even hold in this way as defeasible principles. They would not hold at all.

It would be odd for someone to take this seriously in a routine matter. It is contrary to the way we normally think. Imagine arguing with such a person. You get him to believe certain premises and to appreciate that they imply your conclusion, but he is not persuaded to believe this conclusion, saying that, although you have persuaded him to assign a high probability to each of your premises, that is not enough to show he should assign a high probability to the conclusion! This is not the way people usually respond to arguments.

Or consider the following attitude toward contradiction. As Jack asserts several things, you observe that he has contradicted himself. His response is that he sees nothing wrong, since all the things he has asserted are highly probable. This is comprehensible, but it is again different from the normal way of doing things.

A normal reaction to someone's refusal to accept the conclusion of a clearly valid argument after he says he has been persuaded to accept the premises, if he gives Kyburg's reason, is to suppose that he does not really accept the premises after all, but only believes of each that it is probable. Similarly, we suppose that a person who says at least one ticket will win and also says of each ticket that it will not win does not really believe of each ticket that it will not win but merely believes of each ticket that it is unlikely that that ticket will win. We do not ordinarily think of this as like the case in which an author believes each of the things he or she says in a book he or she has written and also believes that, given human fallibility, at least one of the things he or she has said in the book must be false. Such a person is justified in having inconsistent beliefs, but that does not show that the Recognized Inconsistency Principle is incorrect. It only shows that the principle is defeasible.

Of course, to say one normally thinks of belief in an all-or-nothing way is not to deny one sometimes has beliefs about probabilities. More important, one often manifests a varying degree of confidence in this or that proposition as revealed in one's willingness to *act*, for example, to bet. But this does not show one normally or usually assigns *explicit* levels of confidence or probability to one's beliefs. The degree of confidence one has might be merely implicit in one's system of beliefs. Subjective probability theory can give an account of one's dispositions without being an account of the psychological reality underlying those dispositions.

It might be said one *ought* to operate using explicit degrees of belief. This would imply one should make much more use of probability theory than one does.

Similarly, it might be said that one's goals should be treated as matters of degree. Since different prospects are more or less desirable, one ought to assign them different degrees of "subjective utility." In acting, one should act so as to maximize expected utility.

I argue [in Chapter 9 of *Change in View*] that this is not right. But even if it were right, such an appeal to probability theory would not eliminate the need for reasoning in the sense of change in view. One's subjective probability assignments would never be complete. They would often have to be extended. To some extent they could be extended by means of the Principle of Immediate Implication by considering the immediate implications of one's current probability assignments and by allowing for clutter avoidance and other relevant considerations. Furthermore, there would also often be cases in which current subjective probability assignments would have to be changed, for example because they were not consistent with each other. The Principle of Immediate Inconsistency then has a role to play. And there are other cases in which one will want to modify such assignments, for example, when one discovers that a current theory would explain old evidence one had not realized it would explain (Glymour 1980, chap. 3). And whatever principles are developed for changing all-or-nothing belief will apply to changing degrees of belief, treating these as all-or-nothing beliefs about probabilities.

Conditionalization

Some probability theorists appear to deny these obvious points. They seem to suppose that reasoned revision is or ought always to be in accordance with a special principle of "conditionalization" that applies when one comes to treat evidence E as certain. The claim is that in such a case one is to modify one's other degrees of belief so that the new probability one assigns to any given proposition P is given by the following formula:

$$\text{new prob } (P) = \frac{\text{old prob } (P \& E)}{\text{old prob } (E)}$$

The quotient on the right-hand side is sometimes called the conditional probability of P given E, which is why the principle is called conditionalization.

R. C. Jeffrey (1983, chap. 11) shows how this formula can be generalized to allow for the case in which evidence propositions change in probability without becoming certain. Suppose that there are n relevant atomic evidence propositions $E_1, \ldots E_n$, so that there are 2^n strongest conjunctions C_i, each containing E_i, or its denial. Then the new probability one assigns to any given proposition P is the sum of all the quantities of the following form:

$$\text{new prob } (C_i) \times \frac{\text{old prob } (P \& C_i)}{\text{old prob}(C_i)}$$

So, let us consider the following hypothesis, which is widely accepted by subjective probability theorists:

Reasoning is conditionalization The updating of probabilities via conditionalization or generalized conditionalization is (or ought to be) the only principle of reasoned revision.

One way to argue for this is to try to show that various intuitively acceptable principles of reasoning from evidence can be accounted for if this hypothesis is accepted (e.g., Dorling 1972; Horwich 1982).

However, there is a problem with making extensive use of this method of updating. One can use conditionalization to get a new probability for P only if one has already assigned a prior probability not only to E but to P & E. If one is to be prepared for various possible conditionalizations, then for every proposition P one wants to update, one must already have assigned probabilities to various conjunctions of P together with one or more of the possible evidence propositions and/or their denials. Unhappily, this leads to a combinatorial explosion, since the number of such conjunctions is an exponential function of the number of possibly relevant evidence propositions. In other words, to be prepared for coming to accept or reject any of ten evidence propositions, one would have to record probabilities of over a thousand such conjunctions for each proposition one is interested in updating. To be prepared for twenty evidence propositions, one must record a million probabilities. For thirty evidence propositions, a billion probabilities are needed, and so forth.

Clearly, one could not represent all the needed conjunctions explicitly. One would have to represent them implicitly using some sort of general principle. Given such a general principle, one's total probability distribution would then be determined, by either (1) the total evidence one accepts as certain (using conditionalization) or (2) the various new probabilities assigned to the C_i, (using Jeffrey's generalization of conditionalization). But neither (1) nor (2) is feasible. Consider what is involved in each case.

The idea behind (1) is to represent the degrees of belief to which one is presently committed by means of some general principle, specifying an initial probability distribution, together with a list of all the evidence one has come to treat as certain. Such evidence will include all immediate perceptual evidence – how things look, sound, smell, etc., to one at this or that moment. One will have to remember all such evidence that has influenced one's present degrees of belief. But in fact one rarely remembers such evidence beyond the moment in which one possesses it (a point I return to [in the following part of this chapter]). So (1) is not a usable approach.

On the other hand, (2) requires that one keep track of one's current degree of belief in each of the relevant conjunctions C_i, of evidence propositions and/or their denials. These are things one does not have to be certain about, so the relevant propositions need not be for the most part about immediate perceptual experience, as in (1). So the objection that one hardly ever remembers such propositions does not apply to (2). But (2) is also unworkable, since the number of relevant conjunctions C_i is an exponential function of the number of atomic evidence propositions.

These objections assume one sticks with one's original general principle describing one's initial degrees of belief and records one's present degrees of belief by representing the new evidence accepted as certain or the new probabilities of the various conjunctions C_i.

Alternatively, one might try each time to find a new principle describing one's updated degrees of belief in a single general statement. But the problem of finding such a general principle is

intractable, and anyway there will normally be no simpler way to describe one's new probability distribution than the description envisioned in (1) or (2), so this will not normally be feasible either.

Doing extensive updating by conditionalization or generalized conditionalization would be too complicated in practice. Therefore one must follow other principles in revising one's views. It is *conceivable* that all or some of these principles might refer to strength or degree of belief and not just to whether one believes something in a yes/no fashion. But the actual principles we follow do not seem to be of that sort, and it is unclear how these principles might be modified to be sensitive to degree or strength of belief. In the rest of this book I assume that, as far as the principles of revision we follow are concerned, belief is an all-or-nothing matter. I assume that this is so because it is too complicated for mere finite beings to make extensive use of probabilities.

POSITIVE VERSUS NEGATIVE UNDERMINING

I now want to compare two competing theories of reasoned belief revision, which I will call the foundations theory and the coherence theory since they are similar to certain philosophical theories of justification sometimes called foundations and coherence theories (Sosa 1980; Pollock 1979). But the theories I am concerned with are not precisely the same as the corresponding philosophical theories of justification, which are not normally presented as theories of belief revision. Actually, I am not sure what these philosophical theories of "justification" are supposed to be concerned with. So, although I will be using the *term* "justification" in what follows, as well as the terms "coherence" and "foundations," I do not claim that my use of any of these terms is the same as its use in these theories of justification. I mean to be raising a new issue, not discussing an old one.

The key issue is whether one needs to keep track of one's original justifications for beliefs. What I am calling the *foundations* theory says yes; what I am calling the *coherence* theory says no.

The foundations theory holds that some of one's beliefs "depend on" others for their current justification; these other beliefs may depend on still others, until one gets to foundational beliefs that do not depend on any further beliefs for their justification. In this view reasoning or belief revision should consist, first, in subtracting any of one's beliefs that do not now have a satisfactory justification and, second, in adding new beliefs that either need no justification or are justified on the basis of other justified beliefs one has.

On the other hand, according to the coherence theory, it is not true that one's ongoing beliefs have or ought to have the sort of justificational structure required by the foundations theory. In this view ongoing beliefs do not usually require any justification. Justification is taken to be required only if one has a special reason to doubt a particular belief. Such a reason might consist in a conflicting belief or in the observation that one's beliefs could be made more "coherent," that is, more organized or simpler or less ad hoc, if the given belief were abandoned (and perhaps if certain other changes were made). According to the coherence theory, belief revision should involve minimal changes in one's beliefs in a way that sufficiently increases overall coherence.

In this chapter I elaborate these two theories in order to compare them with actual reasoning and intuitive judgments about such reasoning. It turns out that the theories are most easily distinguished by the conflicting advice they occasionally give concerning whether one should *give up* a belief P from which many other of one's beliefs have been inferred, when P's original justification has to be abandoned. Here a surprising contrast seems to emerge – "is" and "ought" seem to come apart. The foundations theory seems, at least at first, to be more in line with our intuitions about how people *ought* to revise their beliefs; the coherence theory is more in line with what people *actually do* in such situations. Intuition seems strongly to support the foundations theory over the coherence theory as an account of what one is *justified* in doing in such cases; but *in fact* one will tend to act as the coherence theory advises.

After I explain this I consider how this apparent discrepancy can be resolved. I conclude that the coherence theory is normatively correct after all, despite initial appearances.

The Foundations Theory of Belief Revision

The basic principle of the foundations theory, as I will interpret it, is that one must keep track of one's original reasons for one's beliefs, so that one's ongoing beliefs have a justificational struc-

ture, some beliefs serving as reasons or justifications for others. These justifying beliefs are more basic or fundamental for justification than the beliefs they justify.

The foundations theory rejects any principle of *conservatism*. In this view a proposition cannot acquire justification simply by being believed. The justification of a given belief cannot be, either in whole or in part, that one has that belief. For example, one's justification for believing something cannot be that one already believes it and that one's beliefs in this area are reliable.

Justifications are *prima facie* or defeasible. The foundations theory allows, indeed insists, that one can be justified in believing something P and then come to believe something else that undermines one's justification for believing P. In that case one should stop believing P, unless one has some further justification that is not undermined.

I say "unless one has some further justification," because in this view a belief can have more than one justification. To be justified, a belief must have *at least* one justification. That is, if a belief in P is to be justified, it is required either that P be a foundational belief whose intrinsic justification is not defeated or that there be at least one undefeated justification of P from other beliefs one is justified in believing. If one believes P and it happens that all one's justifications for believing P come to be defeated, one is no longer justified in continuing to believe P, and one should subtract P from one's beliefs.

Furthermore, and this is important, if one comes not to be justified in continuing to believe P in this way, then not only is it true that one must abandon belief in P but justifications one has for other beliefs are also affected if these justifications appeal to one's belief in P. Justifications appealing to P must be abandoned when P is abandoned. If that means further beliefs are left without justification, then these beliefs too must be dropped along with any justifications appealing to them. So there will be a chain reaction when one loses justification for a belief on which other beliefs depend for their justification. (This is worked out in more detail for an artificial intelligence system by Doyle (1979, 1980).)

Now, it is an important aspect of the foundations theory of reasoning that justifications cannot legitimately be circular. P cannot be part of the justification for Q while Q is part of the justification for P (unless one of these beliefs has a different justification that does not appeal to the other belief).

The foundations theory also disallows infinite justifications. It does not allow P to be justified by appeal to Q, which is justified by appeal to R, and so on forever. Since justification cannot be circular, justification must eventually end in beliefs that either need no justification or are justified but not by appeal to other beliefs. Let us say that such basic or foundational beliefs are intrinsically justified.

For my purposes it does not matter exactly which beliefs are taken to be intrinsically justified in this sense. Furthermore, I emphasize that the foundations theory allows for situations in which a basic belief has its intrinsic justification defeated by one or more other beliefs, just as it allows for situations in which the justification of one belief in terms of other beliefs is defeated by still other beliefs. As I am interpreting it, foundationalism is not committed to the *incorrigibility* of basic beliefs.

A belief is a basic belief if it has an intrinsic justification which does not appeal to other beliefs. A basic belief can also have one or more nonintrinsic justifications which do appeal to other beliefs. So, a basic belief can have its intrinsic justification defeated and still remain justified as long as it retains at least one justification that is not defeated.

The existence of basic beliefs follows from the restrictions against circular and infinite justifications. Infinite justifications are to be ruled out because a finite creature can have only a finite number of beliefs, or at least only a finite number of *explicit beliefs*, whose content is explicitly represented in the brain. What one is justified in believing either implicitly or explicitly depends entirely on what one is justified in believing explicitly. To consider whether one's implicit beliefs are justified is to consider whether one is justified in believing the explicit beliefs on which the implicit beliefs depend. A justification for a belief that appeals to other beliefs must always appeal to things one believes explicitly. Since one has only finitely many explicit beliefs, there are only finitely many beliefs that can be appealed to for purposes of justification, and so infinite justifications are ruled out.

The Coherence Theory of Belief Revision

The coherence theory is *conservative* in a way the foundations theory is not. The coherence theory supposes one's present beliefs are justified just as they are in the absence of special reasons to change them, where changes are allowed only to the extent that they yield sufficient increases in coherence. This is a striking difference from the foundations theory. The foundations theory says one is justified in continuing to believe something only if one has a special reason to continue to accept that belief, whereas the coherence theory says one is justified in continuing to believe something as long as one has no special reason to stop believing it.

According to the coherence theory, if one's beliefs are incoherent in some way, because of outright inconsistency or simple *ad hoc*ness, then one should try to make minimal changes in those beliefs in order to eliminate the incoherence. More generally, small changes in one's beliefs are justified to the extent these changes add to the coherence of one's beliefs.

For present purposes, I do not need to be too specific as to exactly what coherence involves, except to say it includes not only consistency but also a network of relations among one's beliefs, especially relations of implication and explanation.

It is important that coherence competes with conservatism. It is as if there were two aims or tendencies of reasoned revision, to maximize coherence and to minimize change. Both tendencies are important. Without conservatism a person would be led to reduce his or her beliefs to the single Parmenidean thought that all is one. Without the tendency toward coherence we would have what Peirce (1877) called the method of tenacity, in which one holds to one's initial convictions no matter what evidence may accumulate against them.

According to the coherence theory, the assessment of a challenged belief is always holistic. Whether such a belief is justified depends on how well it fits together with everything else one believes. If one's beliefs are coherent, they are mutually supporting. All one's beliefs are, in a sense, equally fundamental. In the coherence theory there are not the asymmetrical justification relations among one's ongoing beliefs that there are in the foundations theory. It can happen in the coherence theory that P is justified because of the way it coheres with Q and Q is justified because of the way it coheres with P. In the foundations theory, such a pattern of justification is ruled out by the restriction against circular justification. But there is nothing wrong with circular justification in the coherence theory, especially if the circle is a large one!

I turn now to testing the foundations and coherence theories against our intuitions about cases. This raises an apparent problem for the coherence theory.

An Objection to the Coherence Theory: Karen's Aptitude Test

Sometimes there clearly are asymmetrical justi-fication relations among one's beliefs.

Consider Karen, who has taken an aptitude test and has just been told her results show she has a considerable aptitude for science and music but little aptitude for history and philosophy. This news does not correlate perfectly with her previous grades. She had previously done well not only in physics, for which her aptitude scores are reported to be high, but also in history, for which her aptitude scores are reported to be low. Furthermore, she had previously done poorly not only in philosophy, for which her aptitude scores are reported to be low, but also in music, for which her aptitude scores are reported to be high.

After carefully thinking over these discrepan-cies, Karen concludes that her reported aptitude scores accurately reflect and are explained by her actual aptitudes; so she has an aptitude for sci-ence and music and no aptitude for history and philosophy; therefore her history course must have been an easy one, and also she did not work hard enough in the music course. She decides to take another music course and not to take any more history.

It seems quite clear that, in reaching these conclusions, Karen bases some of her beliefs on others. Her belief that the history course was easy depends for its justification on her belief that she has no aptitude for history, a belief which depends in turn for its justification on her belief that she got a low score in history on her aptitude test. There is no dependence in the other direction. For example, her belief about her aptitude test score in history is not based on her belief that she has no aptitude for history or on her belief that the history course was an easy one.

According to the coherence theory, the rele-vant relations here are merely *temporal* or *causal* relations. The coherence theory can agree that Karen's belief about the outcome of her apti-tude test precedes and is an important cause of her belief that the history course she took was an easy one. But the coherence theory denies that a relation of dependence or justification holds or ought to hold between these two beliefs as time goes by, once the new belief has been firmly accepted.

In order to test this, let me tell more of Karen's story. Some days later she is informed that the report about her aptitude scores was incorrect! The scores reported were those of someone else whose name was confused with hers. Unfortunately, her own scores have now been lost. How should Karen revise her views, given this new information?

The foundations theory says she should aban-don all beliefs whose justifications depend in part on her prior belief about her aptitude test scores. The only exception is for beliefs for which she can now find another and independent justifica-tion which does not depend on her belief about her aptitude test scores. She should continue to believe only those things she would have been justified in believing if she had never been given the false information about those scores. The foundations theory says this because it does not accept a principle of conservatism. The foun-dations theory does not allow that a belief can acquire justification simply by being believed.

Let us assume that, if Karen had not been given the false information about her apti-tude test scores, she could not have reasonably reached any of the conclusions she did reach about her aptitudes for physics, history, philoso-phy, and music; and let us also assume that with-out those beliefs Karen could not have reached any of her further conclusions about the courses she has already taken. Then, according to the foundations theory, Karen should abandon her beliefs about her relative aptitudes for these sub-jects, and she should give up her belief that the history course she took was easy as well as her belief that she did not work hard enough in the music course. She should also reconsider her decisions to take another course in music and not to take any more history courses.

The coherence theory does not automatically yield the same advice that the foundations the-ory gives about this case. Karen's new informa-tion does produce a loss of overall coherence in her beliefs, since she can no longer coher-ently suppose that her aptitudes for science, music, philosophy, and history are in any way responsible for the original report she received about the results of her aptitude test. She must abandon that particular supposition about the explanation of the original report of her scores. Still, there is considerable coherence among the beliefs she inferred from this false report. For example, there is a connection between her belief that she has little aptitude for history, her belief that her high grade in the history course was the result of the course's being an easy one, and her belief that she will not take any more courses in history. There are similar con-nections between her beliefs about her aptitudes for other subjects, how well she did in courses in those subjects, and her plans for the future in those areas. Let us suppose that from the original report Karen inferred a great many other things that I haven't mentioned; so there are many beliefs involved here. Abandoning all these beliefs is costly from the point of view of conservatism, which says to minimize change. Suppose that there are so many of these beliefs and that they are so connected with each other and with other things Karen believes that the coherence theory implies Karen should retain all these new beliefs even though she must give up her beliefs about the explanation of the report of her aptitude scores. (In fact, we do not really need to suppose these beliefs are intricately connected with each other or even that there are many of them, since in the coherence theory a belief *does* acquire justification simply by being believed.)

The foundations theory says Karen should give up all these beliefs, whereas the coherence theory says Karen should retain them. Which theory is right about what Karen ought to do? Almost everyone who has considered this issue sides with the foundations theory: Karen should not retain any beliefs she inferred from the false report of her aptitude test scores that she would not have been justified in believing in the absence of that false report. That does seem to be the intuitively right answer. The foundations theory is in accordance with our intuitions about what Karen *ought* to do in a case like this. The coherence theory is not.

Belief Perseverance

In fact, Karen would almost certainly keep her new beliefs! That is what people actually do in situations like this. Although the foundations theory seems to give intuitively satisfying advice about what Karen *ought* to do in such a situation, the coherence theory is more in accord with what people actually do.

To document the rather surprising facts here, let me quote at some length from a recent survey article (Ross and Anderson 1982, pp. 147–149), which speaks of

the dilemma of the social psychologist who has made use of deception in the course of an experiment and then seeks to debrief the subjects who had been the target of such deception. The psychologist reveals the totally contrived and inauthentic nature of the information presented presuming that

this debriefing will thereby eliminate any effects such information might have exerted upon the subjects' feelings or beliefs. Many professionals, however, have expressed public concern that such experimental deception may do great harm that is not fully undone by conventional debriefing procedures. . . .

Ross and Anderson go on to describe experiments designed to "explore" what they call "the phenomenon of belief perseverance in the face of evidential discrediting." In one experiment.

Subjects first received continuous false feedback as they performed a novel discrimination task (i.e., distinguishing authentic suicide notes from fictitious ones). . . . [Then each subject] received a standard debriefing session in which he learned that his putative outcome had been predetermined and that his feedback had been totally unrelated to actual performance. . . . [E]very subject was led to explicitly acknowledge his understanding of the nature and purpose of the experimental deception. Following this total discrediting of the original information, the subjects completed a dependent variable questionnaire dealing with [their] performance and abilities. The evidence for postdebriefing impression perseverance was unmistakable. . . . On virtually every measure . . . the totally discredited initial outcome manipulation produced significant "residual" effects upon [subjects'] . . . assessments. . . .

Follow-up experiments have since shown that a variety of unfounded personal impressions, once induced by experimental procedures, can survive a variety of total discrediting procedures. For example, Jennings, Lepper, and Ross . . . have demonstrated that subjects' impressions of their ability at interpersonal persuasion (having them succeed or fail to convince a confederate to donate blood) can persist after they have learned that the initial outcome was totally inauthentic. Similarly, . . . two related experiments have shown that students' erroneous impressions of their "logical problem solving abilities" (and their academic choices in a follow-up measure two months later) persevered even after they had learned that good or poor teaching procedures provided a totally sufficient explanation for the successes or failures that were the basis for such impressions.

. . . [Other] studies first manipulated and then attempted to undermine subjects' theories about the functional relationship between two measured variables: the adequacy of firefighters' professional performances and their prior scores on a paper and pencil test of risk performance.... [S]uch theories survived the revelations that the cases in question had been totally fictitious and the different subjects had, in fact, received opposite pairings of riskiness scores and job outcomes.... [O]ver 50% of the initial effect of the "case history" information remained after debriefing.

In summary, it is clear that beliefs can survive . . . the total destruction of their original evidential bases.

It is therefore quite likely that Karen will continue to believe many of the things she inferred from the false report of her aptitude test scores. She will continue to believe these things even after learning that the report was false.

The Habit Theory of Belief

Why is it so hard for subjects to be debriefed? Why do people retain conclusions they have drawn from evidence that is now discredited? One possibility is that belief is a kind of habit. This is an implication of behaviorism, the view that beliefs and other mental attitudes are habits of behavior. But the suggestion that beliefs are habits might be correct even apart from behaviorism. The relevant habits need not be overt behavioral habits. They might be habits of thought. Perhaps, to believe that P is to be disposed to *think* that P under certain conditions, to be disposed to use this thought as a premise or assumption in reasoning and in deciding what to do. Then, once a belief has become established, considerable effort might be needed to get rid of it, even if the believer should come to see that he or she ought to get rid of it, just as it is hard to get rid of other bad habits. One can't simply decide to get rid of a bad habit; one must take active steps to ensure that the habit does not reassert itself. Perhaps it is just as difficult to get rid of a bad belief.

Goldman (1978) mentions a related possibility, observing that Anderson and Bower (1973) treat coming to believe something as the establishing of connections, or "associative links," between relevant conceptual representations in the brain. Now, it may be that, once set up, such connections or links cannot easily be broken unless competing connections are set up that overwhelm the original ones. The easiest case

might be that in which one starts by believing P and then comes to believe *not P* by setting up stronger connections involving *not P* than those involved in believing P. It might be much harder simply to give up one's belief in P without substituting a contrary belief. According to this model of belief, in order to stop believing P, it would not be enough simply to notice passively that one's evidence for P had been discredited. One would have to take positive steps to counteract the associations that constitute one's belief in P. The difficulties in giving up a discredited belief would be similar in this view to the difficulties envisioned in the habit theory of belief.

But this explanation does not give a plausible account of the phenomenon of belief perseverance. Of course, there are cases in which one has to struggle in order to abandon a belief one takes to be discredited. One finds oneself coming back to thoughts one realizes one should no longer accept. There are such habits of thought, but this is not what is happening in the debriefing studies. Subjects in these studies are not struggling to abandon beliefs they see are discredited. On the contrary, the subjects do not see that the beliefs they have acquired have been discredited. They come up with all sorts of "rationalizations" (as we say) appealing to connections with other beliefs of a sort that the coherence theory, but not the foundations theory, might approve. So the correct explanation of belief perseverance in these studies is not that beliefs which have lost their evidential grounding are like bad habits.

Positive versus Negative Undermining

In fact, what the debriefing studies show is that people simply do not keep track of the justification relations among their beliefs. They continue to believe things after the evidence for them has been discredited because they do not realize what they are doing. They do not understand that the discredited evidence was the *sole* reason why they believe as they do. They do not see they would not have been justified in forming those beliefs in the absence of the now discredited evidence. They do not realize these beliefs have been undermined. It is this, rather than the difficulty of giving up bad habits, that is responsible for belief perseverance.

The foundations theory says people should keep track of their reasons for believing as they do and should stop believing anything that is not associated with adequate evidence. So the foundations theory implies that, if Karen has not kept track of her reason for believing her history course was an easy one, she should have abandoned her belief even before she was told about the mix-up with her aptitude test scores. This seems clearly wrong.

Furthermore, since people rarely keep track of their reasons, the theory implies that people are unjustified in almost all their beliefs. This is an absurd result! The foundations theory turns out not to be a plausible normative theory after all. So let us see whether we cannot defend the coherence theory as a normative theory.

We have already seen how the coherence theory can appeal to a nonholistic *causal* notion of local justification by means of a limited number of one's prior beliefs, namely, those prior beliefs that are most crucial to one's justification for adding the new belief. The coherence theory does not suppose there are *continuing* links of justification dependency that can be consulted when revising one's beliefs. But the theory can admit that Karen's coming to believe certain things depended on certain of her prior beliefs in a way that it did not depend on others, where this dependence represents a kind of local justification, even though in another respect whether Karen was justified in coming to believe those things depended on everything she then believed.

Given this point, I suggest the coherence theory can suppose it is incoherent to believe both *P* and also that all one's reasons for believing *P* relied crucially on false assumptions. Within the coherence theory, this implies, roughly, the following:

> *Principle of Positive Undermining* One should stop believing *P* whenever one positively believes one's reasons for believing *P* are no good.

This is only roughly right, since there is also the possibility that one should instead stop believing that one's reasons for *P* are no good, as well as the possibility that one cannot decide between that belief and *P*. In any event, I want to compare this rough statement of the principle with the corresponding principle in a foundations theory:

> *Principle of Negative Undermining* One should stop believing *P* whenever one does not associate one's belief in *P* with an adequate justification (either intrinsic or extrinsic).

The Principle of Positive Undermining is much more plausible than the Principle of Negative Undermining. The Principle of Negative Undermining implies that, as one loses track of the justifications of one's beliefs, one should give up

those beliefs. But, if one does not keep track of one's justifications for most of one's beliefs, as seems to be the case, then the Principle of Negative Undermining says that one should stop believing almost everything one believes, which is absurd. On the other hand the Principle of Positive Undermining does not have this absurd implication. The Principle of Positive Undermining does not suppose that the absence of a justification is a reason to stop believing something. It only supposes that one's belief in *P* is undermined by the *positive* belief that one's reasons for *P* are no good.

It is relevant that subjects *can* be successfully debriefed after experiments involving deception if they are made vividly aware of the phenomenon of belief perseverance, that is, if they are made vividly aware of the tendency for people to retain false beliefs after the evidence for them has been undercut, and if they are also made vividly aware of how this phenomenon has acted in their own case (Nisbett and Ross 1980, p. 177). It might be suggested that this shows that under ideal conditions people really do act in accordance with the foundations theory after all, so that the foundations theory *is* normatively correct as an account of how one ideally ought to revise one's beliefs. But in fact this further phenomenon seems clearly to support the coherence theory, with its Principle of Positive Undermining, and not the foundations theory, with its Principle of Negative Undermining. The so-called process debriefing cannot merely undermine the evidence for the conclusions subjects have reached but must also directly attack each of these conclusions themselves. Process debriefing works not just by getting subjects to give up beliefs that originally served as evidence for the conclusions they have reached but by getting them to accept certain further positive beliefs about their lack of good reasons for each of these conclusions.

What about Our Intuitions?

It may seem to fly in the face of common sense to suppose that the coherence theory is normatively correct in cases like this. Remember that, after carefully considering Karen's situation, almost everyone agrees she should give up all beliefs inferred from the original false report, except those beliefs which would have been justified apart from any appeal to evidence tainted by that false information. Almost everyone's judgment about what Karen ought to do coincides with what the foundations theory says she ought to do. Indeed, psychologists who have studied the phenomenon of belief perseverance in the face of debriefing consider it to be a paradigm of irrationality. How can these strong normative intuitions possibly be taken to be mistaken, as they must be if the coherence theory is to be accepted as normatively correct?

The answer is that, when people think about Karen's situation, they ignore the possibility that she may have failed to keep track of the justifications of her beliefs. They imagine Karen is or ought to be aware that she no longer has any good reasons for the beliefs she inferred from the false report. And, of course, this is to imagine that Karen is violating the Principle of Positive Undermining. It is hard to allow for the possibility that she may be violating not that principle but only the foundationalist's Principle of Negative Undermining.

Keeping Track of Justification

People do not seem to keep track of the justifications of their beliefs. If we try to suppose that people do keep track of their justifications, we would have to suppose that either they fail to notice when their justifications are undermined or they do notice but have great difficulty in abandoning the unjustified beliefs in the way a person has difficulty abandoning a bad habit. Neither possibility offers a plausible account of the phenomenon of belief perseverance.

It stretches credulity to suppose people always keep track of the sources of their beliefs but often fail to notice when these sources are undermined. That is like supposing people always remember everything that has ever happened to them but cannot always retrieve the stored information from memory. To say one remembers something is to say one has stored it in a way that normally allows it to be retrieved at will. Similarly, to say people keep track of the sources of their beliefs must be to say they can normally use this information when it is appropriate to do so.

I have already remarked that the other possibility seems equally incredible, namely, that people have trouble abandoning the undermined beliefs in the way they have trouble getting rid of bad habits. To repeat, participants in belief perseverance studies show no signs of knowing their beliefs are ungrounded. They do not act like people struggling with their beliefs as with bad habits. Again, I agree it sometimes happens that one keeps returning to thoughts after one has seen there can be no reason to accept those

thoughts. There are habits of thought that can be hard to get rid of. But that is not what is going on in the cases psychologists study under the name of belief perseverance.

This leaves the issue of whether one should *try* always to keep track of the local justifications of one's beliefs, even if, in fact, people do not seem to do this. I want to consider the possibility that there is a good reason for not keeping track of these justifications.

Clutter Avoidance Again

We have seen there is a practical reason to avoid too much clutter in one's beliefs. There is a limit to what one can remember, a limit to the number of things one can put into long-term storage, and a limit to what one can retrieve. It is important to save room for important things and not clutter one's mind with a lot of unimportant matters. This is an important reason why one does not try to believe all sorts of logical consequences of one's beliefs. One should not try to infer all one can from one's beliefs. One should try not to retain too much trivial information. Furthermore, one should try to store in long-term memory only the key matters that one will later need to recall. When one reaches a significant conclusion from one's other beliefs, one needs to remember the conclusion but does not normally need to remember all the intermediate steps involved in reaching that conclusion. Indeed, one should not try to remember those intermediate steps; one should try to avoid too much clutter in one's mind.

Similarly, even if much of one's knowledge of the world is inferred ultimately from what one believes oneself to be immediately perceiving at one or another time, one does not normally need to remember these original perceptual beliefs or many of the various intermediate conclusions drawn from them. It is enough to recall the more important of one's conclusions. This means one should not be disposed to try to keep track of the local justifications of one's beliefs. One could keep track of these justifications only by remembering an incredible number of mostly perceptual original premises, along with many, many intermediate steps which one does not want and has little need to remember. One will not want to link one's beliefs to such justifications because one will not in general want to try to retain the prior beliefs from which one reached one's current beliefs.

The practical reason for not keeping track of the justifications of one's beliefs is not as severe as the reason that prevents one from trying to operate purely probabilistically, using generalized conditionalization as one's only principle of reasoned revision. The problem is not that there would be a combinatorial explosion. Still, there are important practical constraints. It is more efficient not to try to retain these justifications and the accompanying justifying beliefs. This leaves more room in memory for important matters.

Bibliography

Anderson, J. R., and Bower, G. H. (1973). *Human Associative Memory* (Washington, D.C.: Winston).

Dorling, Jon (1972). "Bayesianism and the rationality of scientific inference," *British Journal for the Philosophy of Science* 23:181–190.

Doyle, Jon (1979). "A truth maintenance system," *Artificial Intelligence* 12:231–272.

Doyle, Jon (1980). "A Model for Deliberation, Action, and Introspection," MIT Artificial Intelligence Laboratory Technical Report 581.

Glymour, Clark (1980). *Theory and Evidence* (Princeton, N.J.: Princeton University Press).

Goldman, Alvin I. (1978). "Epistemology and the psychology of belief," *Monist* 61:525–535.

Horwich, Paul (1982). *Probability and Evidence* (Cambridge: Cambridge University Press).

Jeffrey, Richard C. (1983). *The Logic of Decision* (Chicago: University of Chicago Press).

Kyburg, Henry (1961). *Probability and the Logic of Rational Belief* (Middletown, Conn.: Wesleyan University Press).

Nisbett, Richard, and Ross, Lee (1980). *Human Inference: Strategies and Shortcomings of Social Judgement* (Englewood Cliffs, N.J.: Prentice-Hall).

Peirce, C. S. (1877). "The fixation of belief," *Popular Science Monthly* 12:1–15. Reprinted in *Philosophical Writings of Peirce*, Justice Buchler, ed. (New York: Dover, 1955), 5–22.

Pollock, John (1979). "A plethora of epistemological theories," in *Justification and Knowledge*, George Pappas, ed. (Dordrecht, Holland: Reidel), 93–114.

Ross, Lee, and Anderson, Craig A. (1982). "Shortcomings in the attribution process: On the origins and maintenance of erroneous social assessments," in *Judgement under Certainty: Heuristics and Biases*, Daniel Kahneman, Paul Slovic, and Amos Tversky, eds. (Cambridge: Cambridge University Press), 129–152.

Sosa, Ernest (1980). "The raft and the pyramid: Coherence versus foundations in the theory of knowledge," *Midwest Studies in Philosophy* 5:3–25.

Chapter 2: Belief and the Will

BAS C. VAN FRAASSEN

Can we rationally come to believe a proposition that is entailed neither by those we have believed heretofore nor by our previous opinions conjoined to the evidence before us? Discussing this question, William James quoted W. K. Clifford's statement (in "Ethics of Belief") that it is wrong always, everywhere, and for everyone to believe anything on insufficient evidence.[1] Arguing against this, James claimed that, in forming beliefs, we pursue two aims: to believe truth and to avoid error, and argued that the extent to which we pursue either at the cost of the other is a matter of choice: "he who says 'Better go without belief forever than believe a lie!' merely shows his own preponderant private horror of becoming a dupe. He may be critical of many of his desires and fears, but this fear he slavishly obeys . . . a certain lightness of heart seems healthier than this excessive nervousness [about error]. At any rate, it seems the fittest thing for the empiricist philosopher."[2]

In philosophy of science, until recently, something of this sort was regarded as part of the received view: general theories, such as Darwin's, Einstein's, or Bohr's, cannot be established on the basis of the evidence, but we may rationally come to believe that they are true. In addition, what we take as evidence itself is not indubitable, and we may later come to regard it as having been false. We regard ourselves as infallible neither with respect to what we take as evidence nor with respect to our extrapolation beyond the evidence, but neither do we think ourselves irrational for engaging in this cognitive enterprise.

The situation is prima facie not affected by the replacement of undogmatic, full belief by gradations of partial belief. Perhaps when I pro-

fess belief or acceptance, I merely indicate that the proposition seems highly likely to me. But the evidence at hand, especially if itself not fully believed, plus our opinions heretofore, generally does not entail a high probability of truth for general hypotheses or theories – especially not for the sort studied by scientists, which have empirical consequences for all past and future. Only recently have these views come under attack, by writers inspired by Bayesian foundations of statistics.

My strategy in this paper will be first to submit the traditional espistemological views to a critique along Bayesian lines (without claiming to be a Bayesian of any sort). Then I shall show the implications of that critique for those ways of changing one's opinions which Bayesians have generally admitted as rational. The result will be, I think, a puzzle for all concerned. Indeed, this puzzle suggests that we must obey a principle (which I shall call *Reflection*), going beyond the simple laws of probability, which looks prima facie quite unacceptable. I selected James's essay to introduce the topic because I wish to propose a solution to the puzzle along the broadly voluntarist lines of the views he defended. I hope that by consistently carrying through the voluntarist point of view we can, without sacrificing the theory of personal probability as a logic of epistemic judgment, nevertheless maintain the traditional epistemology.[3]

I. To Believe a Theory

Imagine that today I do not profess total certainty about whether the basic theory of evolution is true nor about whether I shall be sure of its truth next year. It does seem quite possible to

Reproduced with permission from van Fraassen, Bas (1984) Belief and the Will. *Journal of Philosophy*, 81, 235–256.

me that I shall become sure of its truth, but also, unfortunately, somewhat possible that I shall form this belief although it is in fact false. Does the state of opinion I have just described seem totally absurd or irrational to you? If not, this section may convince you otherwise.

The critique I am about to offer is along Bayesian lines, though not exactly standard ones, nor perhaps uncontroversial: I request the reader to bear with my rather informal and naive presentation here; in the next section I shall make the argument at once more general and more precise. As described, my present state of opinion is one of uncertainty. The degrees of uncertainty about the different propositions are not the same; it is common today to describe them in terms of subjective or personal probability.[4] In Bayesian eyes, personal probability is the guide to life. The simplest cases we find are in buying contracts, insurance policies, and wagers. Without going into the details, I shall take the following as paradigm: if a contract is worth 1 to me if A be the case, and nothing otherwise, then its present value for me equals my personal probability for A. More generally,

if it is worth z to me if A and nothing otherwise and if my personal probability that A is the case equals $P(A)$, then the value of this contract for me (fair in buying or selling) equals $zP(A)$.

That is all we shall need for our discussion.

So let H be the hypothesis under discussion – say, the theory of evolution – and let E be the proposition that Bas van Fraassen will fully believe that H (say, one year from today). For definiteness, suppose that $P(E)$ – my degree of belief that E will be the case – equals 0.4 and $P(\sim H\&E)$ – my degree of belief that I will mistakenly come to bestow full belief on H – equals 0.2. For now I shall assume that full belief entails personal probability equal to 1. The argument would go through for a degree very close to 1 as well, but I shall in any case consider more explicitly the case of non-full-belief formation below.

At this point we may introduce into the story a Dutch bookie.[5]

He elicits all the above information from me, and he decides on a secret strategy for betting with me. As a first step, he offers me three bets. I call him Dutch, because what he has offered me is what is called a *Dutch book*, a set of bets such that, no matter what happens, I will lose money. And the unfortunate fact is that each of the bets is fair, according to my own state of opinion.

Because I will describe his betting scheme in full generality in the next section. I ask the reader to consider the present figures only cursorily. The trick up his sleeve is that (a) if I do not come to fully believe H, I win only the second bet, and (b) if I do come to fully believe H, then I lose the second bet, but I also tell the bookie myself that I have lost the first bet as well. At this point he takes the second step in his strategy, which is in effect to buy back the ticket for the first bet, for a pittance. (He can do this by formally offering to buy from me a bet that H is false; since I am sure that H is true, any price at all for that new bet will be more than fair in my opinion.) In either case I will have a net loss.

Here are the bets: the first pays 1 if I come to believe H and H is really false – he asks 0.2 for it. The second will pay 0.5 if I do not come to believe H, and he asks me 0.3 for that one. The third pays 0.5 if I really do come to believe H; that one costs 0.2. All these prices are fair, given my state of opinion. (I leave out units of value; so they can be adjusted for inflation and the like.) None of the bets pay anything if they are not won. My total cost is 0.7 for all three.

On one scenario I do not embrace H; I win the second bet and lose the other two. On the other scenario I do embrace the hypothesis; now I lose the second bet, tell him myself that H is true, so I get nothing for the first bet (though I receive a pittance when I sell him back a bet on $\sim H$ for next to nothing), and I win the third. On either scenario I get at most a little more than 0.5, and I have a net loss. This bookie had a strategy which he knew beforehand would allow him to offer me only bets that would be fair by my lights, and yet necessarily give him a net profit. He devised this strategy without any special knowledge either of whether Darwin was right or of whether I would come to believe that hypothesis.

All this may look like so much *léger-de-main* at this point. Suppose for a moment, however, that I have not pulled any tricks. In that case whoever is as I described myself, hypothetically, at the beginning of this section, is in a state of opinion which the Bayesian calls incoherent (a polite word for irrational). Whether or not I actually bought the bets does not matter, of course: my incoherence consists in regarding them as fair.

Unhappy mortal! I found myself in this incoherence merely by contemplating that I could do what James said I could – without even actually deciding to believe Darwin's theories, or anything like it. Not only people so rash as actually to come to believe theories on less than totally compelling evidence, but anyone who does not, with Clifford, reject such a new belief as utterly irrational, is caught in the trap. Who, upon seeing this Bayesian refutation, does not immediately find himself in full flight from voluntarism and pragmatism, toward the imitation of Carnap's robot?

II. To Raise One's Opinion of a Matter of Fact

The preceding argument gives rise to three initial suspicions. The first is that bets cannot sensibly be made on propositions, like Darwin's hypothesis, which cannot be verified or falsified in a finite amount of time. The second is that it is irrational to become fully certain of any propositions except tautologies. The third suspicion one may have is that it is irrational to change one's mind in any way except by what the Bayesians call "conditionalization on one's evidence." [Roughly speaking, this means that one becomes fully certain of the proposition(s) one takes as evidence, and makes only the minimal adjustments to the rest of one's opinions needed to accommodate this new certainty. We may think of this as Clifford's position, updated to accommodate degrees of belief.] Note well that the second and third suspicion cannot be jointly entertained unless evidence is always tautological. So we must confront the second and third separately, but I think we can show the irrelevance of the first along the way. Later on we shall turn to still further suspicions, for example, about the suitability of one's own future opinions as a subject for prevision.

Before going on to examples, we should look at what exactly is involved in Dutch book arguments. In the simple or *synchronic* case, the bookie is able (without having knowledge superior to the agent's) to offer the agent several bets, which demonstrably have the following features: (a) each bet taken individually looks fair to the agent at this time, and (b) taken together the bets are such that, no matter what happens, the agent will suffer a net loss. The expression 'looks fair' is explicated by the Bayesians in terms of the agent's personal probability P and utility evaluations, following the paradigm that $zP(A)$ is the exact value of a bet on proposition A with payoff z. In the case described, the bets in question constitute a Dutch book, and the agent's vulnerability brands his state of opinion as *incoherent* (and indeed, it can be deduced that P violates the probability calculus).

In the *diachronic* case we should speak of a *Dutch strategy* rather than a Dutch book. The bookie is able (without superior knowledge of present or later circumstances) to devise a strategy for offering bets to the agent which is demonstrably to the agent's disadvantage. This strategy is demonstrably such that, under all eventualities, the agent will be offered bets with two features: (a) individually, each bet will look fair to the agent at the time of the offer, and (b) taken together, the bets offered will be such that, whatever happens, the agent will suffer a net loss. Let us emphasize especially that these features are demonstrable *beforehand*, without appeal to any but logical considerations, and the strategy's implementation requires no information inaccessible to the agent himself. The general conclusion must be that an agent vulnerable to such a Dutch strategy has an initial state of opinion or practice of changing his opinion, which together constitute a demonstrably bad guide to life. In this paper, success of the strategies discussed will be independent of the agent's practices for changing opinion, and hence any blame must attach to his initial state of opinion – his vulnerability reveals an initial incoherence.

It is now time to describe the exact betting strategy used by our Dutch bookie. We have two propositions, H (the hypothesis) and E, a proposition about the customer's future attitude to the hypothesis. The customer has degrees of belief $P(E)$ and $P(\sim H \& E)$, neither of which is 0 or 1. The three bets are:

(I)   The bet which pays 1 if $(\sim H \& E)$ and which costs $P(\sim H \& E)$

(II) The bet which pays x if $\sim E$ and which costs $xP(\sim E)$

(III) The bet which pays y if E and which costs $yP(E)$

Here the probability of $\sim E$ equals 1 minus the probability of E. The number x is the usual conditional probability of $\sim H$ given E; that is, $P(\sim H \& E) \div P(E)$. And finally y is x minus the subjective probability the customer will have for the hypothesis, when and if E becomes true. It helps to observe that I and II together form in effect a *conditional bet* on $\sim H$ on the supposition that E, which bears the cost x and has prize 1, with the guarantee of your money back should the supposition turn out to be false.[6] So the total cost of all the bets together must equal $x + yP(E)$.

Let us now consider an example in which all propositions will have their truth value settled by a certain definite time and in which it is not strictly implied that anyone is fully certain of the truth of any nontautology. Since we are now on the attack, the example should be made as simple and hygienic as possible. Let it be a race, at Hollywood Park, tomorrow at noon. The proposition H is that the horse Table Hands will run in that race and win it. The bookie now asks me seriously to consider the possibility that tomorrow morning, at 8 A.M., I shall consider fair a bet on this proposition at odds 2 to 1. I say I do not know if that will happen – my personal probability for that eventuality, call it E, is $P(E) = 0.4$. Next he elicits my opinion about how reliable I think I am as a handicapper of horses. What is my subjective probability that E will indeed be true but that the hypothesis that Table Hands will win, is false? Suppose I answer that this degree of belief of mine, $P(\sim H \& E)$, equals 0.3. The exact numbers do not matter here too much, except that they indicate a certain lack of confidence in my own handicapping skill. In this case they entail that my present conditional probability for Table Hands' winning, on the supposition that tomorrow morning I will have subjective probability 1/3 for it, is only 1/4. The calculation is simple.[7]

What the bookie does now, if I buy the bets, is also simple. He approaches me at 8 A.M. the next morning. If I do not consider odds of 2 to 1 on Table Hands fair, he pays me off on the second bet, but he has won (I) and (III). On the other hand, if I do call those odds fair, he first of all pays me for bet (III). But then he buys from me a bet, with prize 1, against Table Hands' winning, at my newly announced odds. The result of this is, of course, that whether or not Table Hands wins at noon, no money need change hands between us – he has, so to say, bought (I) back from me. So we can now tally up our prospective losses and gains, and again it turns out that I shall have been the loser come what may.[8]

I chose this example to disarm both the first two initial suppositions at once. For there is no implication, in the description of this case, that anyone ever raises the probability of any nontautology to *one* (though in that case the bookie is being quite agreeable about paying me off before he is totally certain that he has heard me correctly). On the other hand, every proposition becomes settled in a certain finite amount of time. The disaster – which consists of course in my present vulnerability to his strategy, not in any actual bets made or lost – happened again because I profess some doubts today about my judgment of tomorrow.

Let us therefore not think about gambling anymore, and turn to the scientist in his lair, Clifford's ideal who (according to James's quotation) "will guard the purity of his belief with a very fanaticism of jealous care, lest at any time it should rest on an unworthy object, and catch a stain which can never be wiped away" and who, therefore, never believes anything upon insufficient evidence (James, *op. cit.*, p. 92). He is then just like Carnap's robot: his senses bring him propositions that he takes as evidence, and his total response to this consists in *conditionalizing* his present state of opinion on these propositions.[9] To conditionalize on a proposition X taken as evidence means this: your odds for various eventualities on the supposition that X are still the same, but that supposition you now regard as certainly true.

Well suppose that e is the sort of proposition that I typically do take as evidence. We need not decide here exactly what sort that is. Perhaps it is the sort of report that comes from Mount Wilson observatory, after having been checked and verified numerous times. Or perhaps it is simple everyday propositions like "That rose is red" or "That is a rose." In any of these cases, the example is decided on the basis of perception. Now let me give the reins over to you, reader: do you think that I am infallible when it comes to perception? Do you think that I shall certainly not take a rose to be red if it is not? Or that a needle will never turn out to have been to the left of the number 7 on a dial, when I said it was to the right? All right, you have convinced me: my subjective probability that e is false, on the supposition that I shall take it as evidence, is not zero.

It is not difficult to see that, formally speaking, I am now in exactly the same position as I was when I thought that I might come to believe a false hypothesis of Darwin's. (Let E be the proposition that I shall take e as evidence, and H the hypothesis that e is true.) Merely by contemplating this eventuality and admitting that I am not sure it cannot happen, I imply that I regard as fair each of three bets which together form the basis for a Dutch strategy. Even if I insist that my epistemic life is lived in the Imitation of Carnap's Robot, mere admission of my fallibility, it seems, makes me diachronically incoherent.

III. Prevision of Our Own Previsions

When we begin to think about the laws and sources of our own epistemic judgments and states of opinion, we are automatically led to deal with them as facts in the world and to consider them in general: that is, with no regard to persons, treating others' no differently from our own. Yet a closer reading of the preceding arguments, once the initial suspicions have been disarmed, presents us with only two possible ways out. The first is that we should have no opinion at all concerning the reliability of our own future judgments; the second, to form as a matter of principle an exceptionally high opinion of their reliability in our own case.[10]

The first may claim precedent in the discussions of de Finetti and Savage themselves, rejecting the intelligibility of higher-order degrees of belief. Their reasons have been incisively criticized by Brian Skyrms.[11] As I shall explain later, I think there is something to the view that the statement that my opinion is such and such "is not a proposition." But we can, I think, quickly dismiss the simpler objections along this line. First of all, whatever is done by the person who says "It seems as likely to me as not that today will be rainy," we do have a proposition that is true if and only if he is at the moment in the psychological state of considering rain as likely as not, being as willing to bet on rain as on the toss of a coin, and so forth. Psychological studies of this subject are well known and we do not think them, surely, to be of an illusory or nonexistent phenomenon.

More important is the worry that, in asking us to consider our own states of opinion, we may be led into the vagaries and paradoxes of self-reference. It would be no surprise if the attempt to assign degrees of credence or credibility to self-referential statements generally were as beset with paradox as the attempt to assign them all truth values. But actually the puzzles or arguments I have presented do not presuppose that degrees of belief are accorded to self-referential statements at all. Suppose that "Cicero" and "D-Day" are context-independent rigid designators referring to a person and a time, respectively, and that p is a function defined on some set of propositions such that $p(A) = r$ if and only if Cicero has on D-Day subjective probability r for proposition A. For definiteness, suppose that the domain of p contains only propositions of an extremely simple sort, such as that Table Hands wins the race or that a certain coin lands heads up or that a certain rose is red. There can surely be no difficulty in anyone's having at any time a degree of belief for the proposition that $p(A) = r$. Hence Cicero may have exactly that the day before D-Day. In addition, there is (independent of these considerations) surely no prob-

lem about Cicero's being able to know that he is Cicero or to know that the day in question is in fact the day before D-Day. If there are difficulties with any of these suppositions, they must be deep skeptical problems concerning the very coherence (in the nontechnical sense) of the concept of subjective probability and the concept of knowledge about who we are and what time it is. This coherence is all our arguments required. At no point did we need to assume that anyone's degrees of belief were accorded to any but time and context-independent propositions.

We come therefore finally to the last way out, which is to say that all three examples were cases in which I made the agent out to be genuinely irrational. This could only be because in each case his degree of belief about what would happen, on the supposition that he would have a certain opinion about that in the future, differed from *that* opinion. The principle we are thereby led to postulate as a new requirement of rationality, in addition to the usual laws of probability calculation is this:

(Reflection) $P_t^a(A \mid p_{t+x}^a(A) = r) = r$

Here P_t^a is the agent a's credence function at time t, x is any nonnegative number, and $p_{t+x}^a(A) = r$ is the proposition that at time $t + x$, the agent a will bestow degree r of credence on the proposition A. To satisfy the principle, the agent's present subjective probability for proposition A, on the supposition that his subjective probability for this proposition will equal r at some later time, must equal this same number r. It is tempting to call this principle of reflection by some more memorable name, such as 'Self-confidence', 'Optimism', or perhaps 'EST', or even 'Self-deception', but I have chosen a more neutral name because I propose to examine, and indeed advocate, serious attempts to defend the principle.[12]

Since none of us is willing to adopt a similar principle governing our own opinion concerning the reliability of others' opinions – or the corollary that they will never take as evidence something that is in fact false – justification of this principle can follow no ordinary route! Indeed, it would seem that we already believe that most people whose credence function obeys this principle of Reflection are by that very fact mistaken about themselves.

At the same time we can give independent or indirect reasons to think that criteria of coherence, concerning degrees of belief that are guides for action, will require this Reflection principle for their satisfaction. To show this I must first briefly outline another justification for the additivity of synchronic degrees of belief, a sort of dual to the Dutch book argument.[13]

To explain the idea of *calibration*, consider a weather forecaster who says in the morning that the probability of rain equals 0.8. That day it either rains or does not. How good a forecaster is he? Clearly to evaluate him we must look at his performance over a longer period of time. Calibration is a measure of agreement between judgments and actual frequencies. Without going into detail, it is still easy to explain perfect calibration. This forecaster was perfectly calibrated over the past year, for example, if, for every number r, the proportion of rainy days among those days on which he announced probability r for rain, equalled r.

Although perfect calibration may not be a reasonable aim by itself, and hardly to be expected at the best of times, it certainly looks like a virtue. It would seem to be irrational to organize your degrees of belief in such a way as to ruin, a priori, the possibility of perfect calibration. A few qualifications must at once be introduced: this forecaster would not have been perfectly calibrated over the past year if he had announced irrational numbers, or even numbers not equal to some fraction of form $x/365$. So the only possibility that we should require him not to ruin beforehand is that of arbitrarily close approximation to perfect calibration if he were asked sufficiently often about events that he considers exactly similar to those he was actually asked about during the evaluation period. It can now be proved that satisfaction of this criterion of potential perfect calibration is exactly equivalent to satisfaction of the probability calculus (in exactly the same sense that this equivalence can be claimed for the criterion of invulnerability to Dutch books).

But it is easy to see what will happen if the evaluation is extended to the forecaster's opinions concerning the calibration of his own judgments. For suppose that he is actually perfectly calibrated in his judgments concerning rain over the next year. Then if he has made judgments to the effect that there will be a discrepancy between the actual frequencies and his announced probabilities, *those* judgements will not be perfectly calibrated. Hence by adding such a judgment as "The probability of rain on days on which I announce the probability of rain to be 0.8, equals 0.7" he would automatically ensure that the class of all his judgments was not perfectly calibrated on any possible scenario. Our criterion accordingly appears to require him to express perfect confidence in the calibration of his own judgments.

Dutch book considerations are of course more familiar; it is interesting to see that the principle of Reflection follows as an immediate corollary to this equivalent, less familiar criterion of coherence. It helps to dispel as vain the small hope that criteria of rationality of this general sort could be satisfied by anyone with doubts that violate Reflection. Yet – and here is the puzzle – we all begin with the intuition that such doubts are not of the radically skeptical kind, but reasonable and rightly common.

IV. Circumventing Moore's Paradox

The main purpose of this section will be to show that certain attempts to defend the principle of Reflection do not work. But at the same time I will attempt to show that even an agent adhering to that principle may have some way to express doubt about the reliability of his own future opinions. Hence the discussion will at least undermine one objection to the principle, even if it does not yet issue in a good defense.

The first proposal to defend (Reflection) is this: to announce my subjective conditional probability for X, on the supposition that Y, is simply to announce what my opinion concerning X would be, should I learn that Y. This thesis implies (Reflection) at once, but the thesis is quite untenable. Richmond Thomason once objected to a similar theory of what it was to believe a conditional, that he believed to be true the proposition that, if his wife were not faithful to him (she being so clever), he would believe that she was. If I go on to reflect on other examples, it is only because I wish to do more than defeat the proposal.[14]

Are there propositions that we must admit to be possibly true but could never believe? Hilary Putnam has argued this status for the proposition that we are brains in a vat, and Donald Davidson for the proposition that most of our beliefs are false. These are forms of general and radical skepticism. An older and simpler case is Moore's paradox: "There is a goldfinch in the garden and I do not believe that there is." This statement could of course be true (at the moment I do not believe that there is, yet there might be one) but I could not very well assert it, for this is not a proposition that I can believe. Note, however, that I have just stated parenthetically that, for all I know or believe, it may be true; so I clearly do not disbelieve it. It is also to be remarked that Moore's paradox does not presuppose that belief is a propositional attitude that we can have toward self-referential propositions. For if Cicero knows himself to be Cicero, he cannot believe that (there is a goldfinch and Cicero does not believe that there is). To consider a somewhat more general version, we must introduce the distinction between probabilities as gradations of belief and as degrees of objective chance.

This distinction is now commonly made, and several recent papers have been devoted to the principles governing their combination.[15] The minimal such principle looks formally similar to the synchronic version of (Reflection):

$$(\text{Miller}) = P_t(A \mid ch_t(A) = r) = r$$

so called because of its role in the (famous but fallacious) argument known as Miller's paradox.[16] To satisfy this principle, the agent's subjective probability for a proposition A, on the supposition that the objective chance that A equals r, must be equal to that same number r. Justification of this principle certainly rests on nontrivial assumptions about what we are like – namely, that we are temporal and finite beings, aware of our temporality and finitude. To see this we deduce that, for an agent whose epistemic history satisfies (Miller), perfect foreknowledge is incompatible with indeterminism. For suppose that such an agent had subjective probability P equalling 1 or 0 for every factual proposition, and indeed, 1 exactly if the proposition is true. Then there is, for each factual proposition A, a number r such that $ch_t(A) = r$ and $P_t(ch_t(A) = r) = 1$. Hence also $P_t(A) = r$, by (Miller); but then it follows that r is 0 or 1; so whether or not A will be the case is already determined with certainty by the facts at this time.[17]

If we add to (Miller) the synchronic – I should think, uncontroversial – part of (Reflection) we can now find a proposition which I can admit to be quite possibly true but which I know I could never fully believe. Suppose I have a coin in my hand which I am about to toss and I have picked it at random from a box that contained one fair coin and one magician's coin, the latter having a two-to-one chance of landing heads up. My present subjective probability for the coin in my hand to land heads up is, accordingly, the average of the two objective chances, $1/2(1/2 + 2/3) = 7/12$. So my present subjec-

tive probability for the proposition (the chance of heads equals 1/2 and my personal probability for it equals 7/12) equals 1/2. But of course I could never fully believe that conjunction; for, by (Miller), if I fully believed the first conjunct, my personal probability would automatically equal 1/2 too. [More rigorously: (Miller) and the synchronic ($x = 0$) part of (Reflection) together entail that if $P_t(ch_t(A) = r \& P_t(A) = s) = 1$ then $r = s$.]

So now we have found a proposition Y to which we can indeed assign a positive subjective probability, but which we cannot conditionalize on. Hence it is clear that $P(X \mid Y)$ is not to be thought of as the probability we would accord X should we learn that Y. The proposal for defending (Reflection) made at the beginning of this section has failed. But we have learned something useful. Even while adhering to (Reflection) we can to some extent express doubts about the correctness or reliability of our future opinions. For example, without violating (Reflection) I can say: "It does not seem unlikely to me that Table Hands' objective chance of winning tomorrow will be considerably less than my subjective probability for that event tomorrow morning."

Those who believe that we conditionalize on – hence raise to subjective certainty – propositions that we take as evidence, do not have this sort of consolation. For presumably we mean to take as evidence at $t + x$ only propositions A whose truth value becomes settled at or by that time, which implies that A is equivalent to $ch_{t+x}(A) = 1$. To say, therefore, that it is not totally unlikely that tomorrow morning I shall take A as evidence even though its chance is less than 1 is to violate (Reflection) by implication. A simple one-place probability function will never allow us to characterize the epistemic state of someone who says that he may become certain of a proposition but will not reject as absurd the possibility that future evidence will prove him wrong.[18] But it remains that in the preceding paragraphs we have seen considerable leeway for the person who wishes to be diachronically coherent and yet express doubt about the reliability of his future opinions considered as indicators of what will happen.

Leaving this (at least somewhat) happy digression, let us turn to another proposal to defend (Reflection). Could it not be entailed by some more general principle about conveyance of factual information? Perhaps it would not be rational to have a state of opinion that it was not rational to convey, in so many words, to a suitable audience. But suppose I were to tell you: "If I say tomorrow morning that it will rain, there will still be a 50/50 chance that it will not." You would certainly look at me askance and reply that, in that case, you might as well not listen to me tomorrow morning. But then my assertion just now has taken away all value from my words of tomorrow morning about rain. We can see this as pathological if we take the following point of view: my expressions of opinion make statements about my mental state and, more particularly, about the aspect of my mental state which is meant to be a reliable indicator of relevant facts outside it. The value of these descriptions of my mental state – whether in the terminology of belief or of subjective probability – to my audience lies exactly in the information thus conveyed indirectly about what it is meant to be a reliable indicator of. Hence I have made a statement that cancels the normal conversational force of my statements of that sort.

I do not think that these reflections are entirely without force or relevance to (Reflection), but, as they stand, the rationale is quite wrong, and they do not constitute a defense. There is some ambiguity in the common use of both 'say' and 'there is a chance.' The first can be used to mean "assert" in a sense that implies belief, or requires in some other way that the assertor believes what he asserts; and the terminology of chance is sometimes used simply to express degrees of credence. If we adopt these interpretations when reading the example, it certainly has something putatively wrong with it, but that something is exactly that it implies a violation of (Reflection). Hence it does not manage to point to a more general principle to help us. If on the other hand we understand 'say' as "utter the words" or 'chance' as "objective chance," we have merely a statement that expresses doubt about the reliability of either my mental states or feelings or my words as indicators of rain. Although it is true that the audience is thereafter well advised not to take my words or opinion into account when deciding about the need for umbrellas, no principles or conversational maxims have been contravened. Such statements about my reliability as indicator of rain need no more be logically odd or conversationally pathological than similar statements about the reliability of my watch. The audience is simply, in strict accordance with our conventions of conversational cooperation, advised to listen to the radio weather report (respectively, time signal) rather than to my guesses about this particular topic.

V. Voluntarism as Solution

for what else is it to believe but to assent to the truth of what is propounded? Consent being a matter of the will. . . .

St. Augustine,
On the Spirit and the Letter, 54

The problem raised by the apparent need for principle of Reflection is, it seems to me, one of interpretation. A tenable interpretation of personal probability must either sever the link between rationality and coherence or else entail that Reflection is a form of epistemic judgment to which we must assent. It seems to me that among the debris in the preceding section there are some usable materials for the construction of an interpretation of the latter sort. The interpretation will first of all consider how the probability calculus can be viewed as a logic of epistemic judgments, and then consider exactly what such judgments are.

Let us begin with two challenges, one very familiar, the other due to Gilbert Harman. The first is that we simply do not have such a finely graded state of opinion as numerically precise subjective probabilities require. This challenge is answered by the admission that our personal probabilities are to some extent vague. Rain tomorrow seems no less likely to me than a tossed coin's coming up heads four times in a row, no more likely than at least one of four tossed coins' coming up heads. My state of opinion is no more precise than this. Harman's challenge goes deeper. Since probabilities, unlike truth values, are not functional – $P(A\&B)$ is not a function of $P(A)$ and $P(B)$ –, storing the information contained in an assignment of probabilities to sentences of even a "small" simple language quickly gets beyond the storage capacity of the mind. With vague probabilities the information storage problem gets worse, because each sentence now has two numbers assigned – a lower and upper probability. To circumvent this information explosion we must characterize a person's opinions as consisting of some which are more or less directly accessible plus all those to which the former commit him, on pain of violation of some higher criteria of rationality to which he subscribes.

No one, we say, has numerically precise degrees of belief. But at a given time I may, more or less consciously or overtly, make or be committed to a number of judgments of such forms as: it seems likely to rain, it seems as likely as not to snow, it seems likely to me – supposing it rains – that it will be cold, and so forth. These judgments express my opinions on various matters of fact; let us call them *epistemic judgments*. A certain family of these, accordingly, characterize my present state of opinion; they are *mine*. Unless I am very opinionated, they are not many, and they leave gaps: they may for instance not include, either directly or by implication, any judgment nontrivially comparing in such terms as the above, rain and newspaper reports of murder, or Darwin's theories and Einstein's.

It will be clear how an assignment of numbers to propositions could in principle reflect these judgments, because we are all familiar with their counterparts in the terminology of subjective probability. A person has, in the technical sense, a *coherent* state of opinion only if there exists at least one probability function P such that $P(A) > P(B)$ if it seems more likely to him that A than that B, $P(A) \geq P(B)$ if it seems no less likely to him that A than that B, $P(A|C) > P(B|C)$ if on the supposition that C it seems more likely to him that A than that B, and so forth. Let us say that such a function P *satisfies* his judgments. The lack of precision and other gaps in his judgments entail now that, if any one probability function P satisfies his judgments, then so do a number of others. The class of all that do, we may call the *representor* for his state of opinion. Unless that representation contains only a single function, we also say that his degrees of belief, or subjective probabilities, are to some extent vague or indeterminate.[19]

We can now introduce a quite exact concept of implication among epistemic judgments for coherent states of opinion: if all probability functions satisfying each of a class X of judgments also satisfy judgment J, then (and only then) does X *coherently entail* J. It is exactly in such a case, when a person overtly makes all the judgments in X, that we say that he is also committed to J, on pain of incoherence.

Obviously a coherent state of opinion can be re-expressed in judgments formulated in the language of vague probability theory. "My subjective probability for A is no less than x, no greater than y" characterizes my state of opinion correctly if and only if, for every member P of my representor, $x \leq P(A) \leq y$. Similarly for subjective conditional probability, subjective odds, and subjective expectation. We see, therefore, that

subjective-probability talk is merely the formulation, in sophisticated and flexible language, of judgments that have exactly the same status as, and indeed are entailed by, the epistemic judgments with which we began our discussion – for coherent states of opinion.

Therefore we must now look closely at exactly what an epistemic judgment is. Suppose I express my opinion as follows: "It seems more likely to me – supposing that it stays this cold – that it will snow than that it will rain." What exactly have I just done? One answer, the answer I wish to dispute, is that I have just made an autobiographical statement, describing my own psychological state.[20] Certainly, if you hear me say the above, you will be able to infer something about my psychological state, and perhaps this fact even provided the motive for my utterance. But that is very different from saying that what I did was to make an autobiographical statement of fact. (I belabor the point only because John Austin is not generally discussed in writings on subjective probability.) Consider this story: yesterday morning I said to you "I promise you a horse by nightfall." This morning you point out that I have not got you a horse, and you accuse me of the heinous immorality of breaking my promise. Not at all, I say, I am guilty only of the lesser sin of lying; what I said yesterday morning was only a false autobiographical statement, for I was not in fact promising you a horse.

The sentence "I promised you a horse yesterday" is clearly a statement of fact, the fact that became true yesterday when I made the promise (perhaps by saying "I promise you a horse"). I wish to make the same sort of distinction with respect to the terminology of personal probability. In the preceding sections I already introduced a symbolic distinction, with the capital and lower-case distinction in $P(p_t(A) = r) = s$. If I were to say that, I would be expressing my opinion concerning a factual proposition about what my opinion was (is, will be) at time t. As analogue, consider "I promise you that I will not make you any promises concerning future dividends until I have carefully looked into the chances of success."

I do not mean that to express an opinion is to make a promise. The latter is a sort of ceremony in which I take upon myself, bring into being, an obligation to someone else. Two other alternatives suggest themselves: to express my opinion is to express my feelings, or it is to express an intention or commitment. There is something to be said for the first. A promise properly made will *follow* the agent's realization that he is willing, and able, to enter the corresponding contract or obligation. But expressing one's feelings generally involves, and may be the only means for, exploration of those feelings – I know that I feel strongly about this subject, but I don't know what I feel until I begin to talk or act or paint or write, and I discover almost as much about what I feel as the onlooker does. In this respect expressing one's opinions is often less like promising and more like emotive expression. But in this respect, expression of intentions is often the same. A difference is that, both in the case of opinion and of intention, and not in the case of feeling, the act of expression does not typically turn from genuine expression into something else, if one deliberately repeats the act.

Suppose, for example, that I have looked at my calibration score, found that I have generally overestimated the chances of rain, and now have exactly the same feelings on the question of rain as I did yesterday. Then my judgment about rain will now be different from what it was yesterday, for this judgment does not have the function of merely expressing my feelings – properly made, formulating my judgment follows deliberation.

It seems then that, of the alternatives examined, epistemic judgments are most like expressions of intention. I may express an intention either by simply stating the outcome of what I have decided upon ("You will be my successor") or by choosing a form of words traditionally suited to such expression ("You shall be my successor"). In either case, it is conveyed that I have made a decision, have formed an intention, am committed to a certain stance or program or course of action. There is no direct obligation to anyone else to fulfill this intention, but I have, as it were, entered a contract with myself. If I express this intention to an audience, then, just as in the case of a promise, I invite them to rely on my integrity and to feel assured that they now have knowledge of a major consideration in all my subsequent deliberation and courses of action. In this respect, expressing a considered judgment is similar.

Returning now to the principle (Reflection), consider the following analogies. I say, "I promise you a horse," and you ask, "And what are the chances that you'll get me one"? I say, "I am starting a diet today," and you ask, "And how likely is it that you won't overeat tomorrow? In both cases, the *first* reply I must give is "You heard me"! To express anything but a full commitment to stand behind my promises and intentions, is to undermine my own status as a person of integrity and, hence, my entire activity of avowal. This applies equally in the case of conditional questions. "If you promise to marry me, will you actually do it"? "If you decide to join our crusade, will you really participate"? In the first instance these questions are not invitations to an academic discussion of the objective chances, but challenges or probes of one's avowed intentions and commitments. It is confusing that the same words can be used for either purpose – not confusing in actual dialogue where contextual factors disambiguate, but confusing in written discussion.

Avowal, qua avowal, has its own constraints, which affect the logic of expressions of avowal. In none of the above cases do we have a simple way of characterizing what it is to be "false" to one's commitment. Having made a promise, I also have some obligation to prevent circumstances that would make it impossible to keep the promise. Having decided on a program of regular exercise, I have obliged myself to some extent to prevent travel arrangements, hangovers, lack of proper clothes and shoes, and so forth, that would interfere. It may not be easy for the onlooker, or even for me, to allocate blame or to decide whether I was false to myself or merely a victim of circumstances. In the same way, if I express my opinion, I invite the world to rely on my integrity and to infer from this what advice to myself and anyone else in like circumstances, concerning the carrying of umbrellas, purchase of insurance policies, entering wagers, I would presently consider the best. Only in clinically hygienic cases would it be uncontroversially clear whether or not I really stood behind my expressed opinion. But that is so in the case of any expression of commitment or intention.

I conclude that my integrity, qua judging agent, requires that, if I am presently asked to express my opinion about whether *A* will come true, on the supposition that I will think it likely tomorrow morning, I must stand by my own cognitive *engagement* as much as I must stand by my own expressions of commitment of any sort. I can rationally and objectively discuss the possibility of a discrepancy between objective chance and my previsions. But I can no more say that I regard *A* as unlikely on the supposition that tomorrow morning I shall express my high expectation of *A*, than I can today make the same statement on the supposition that tomorrow morning I shall promise to bring it about that *A*. To do so would mean that I am now less than fully committed (a) to giving due regard to the felicity conditions for this act, or (b) to standing by the commitments I shall overtly enter.

VI. Traditional Epistemology Revised

This paper began with a statement of what I regard as a traditional epistemological view in philosophy of science: that we may rationally decide or come to believe propositions, hypotheses, theories which are not entailed by (and which we ourselves do not regard as being made certain by) the evidence at hand. In addition – still spelling out this view – evidence itself is only the body of propositions that we have taken as evidence, and what we take to be evidence on a particular occasion may in fact be false. The refutation, along familiar Bayesian lines, was quick and sure and deadly: anyone who even regards himself as not totally unlikely to do what this view calls rational, is diachronically incoherent: vulnerable in that he implicitly regards as fair, disastrous combinations of wagers.

But then we also saw that the refutation is blocked by adherence to a principle, which goes well beyond the probability calculus, but which is equally required for the diachronic coherence of agents that Bayesian writers regard as rational. So the refutation is no refutation: we need not stop at conditionalization on the evidence on pain of incoherence, as long as we adhere to this principle, which even the strict conditionalizer himself (and also the less committal observer described by Jeffrey) needs equally badly. Of course, the more improbable the proposition we decide to believe, or equivalently, the more we raise our credence in an uncertain proposition, the more risk we take. But that is merely a matter of degree, and there is no violation of coherence or any other criterion of rationality. Any accusation of epistemic extravagance is in any case to be met, by Jamesian and Bayesian alike, with the cool judgment "My credence that A is true, on the supposition that tomorrow I shall accord it credence to degree r, equals r." We can put the matter in either of two ways, depending on how we value the epithet of "Bayesian." Either that non-Bayesian epistemic behavior is defensible by exactly the same defense needed for Bayesian behavior; or, if you like, that apparently non-Bayesian behavior described by James and other traditional epistemologists turns out to be, after all, entirely acceptable as far as Bayesian standards go. It may be a bit scary to think that

such leaps of faith as James described in "The Will to Believe" or St. Augustine in "On Belief in Things Unseen" – he included his own belief in the existence of the Ocean – are not ruled out by the Bayesian's standards of coherence. But it is also a welcome thought, if we regard considerations of coherence as eminently rational, yet hope to find room for independence and enterprise in forming our world picture.

But then there is still the matter of the defense of the defense. I have argued that it is in fact indefensible if we regard the epistemic judgment – whether formulated in probabilistic or more qualitative terms – as a statement of autobiographical fact. The principle (Reflection) can be defended, namely as a form of commitment to stand behind one's own commitments, if we give a different, voluntarist interpretation of epistemic judgment. I call it "voluntarist," because it makes judgment in general, and subjective probability in particular, a matter of cognitive commitment, intention, *engagement*. Belief is a matter of the will.

Notes

1 "The Will to Believe." Page references will be to his *Essays in Pragmatism* (New York: Hafner, 1948).

2 *Op. cit.* p. 100. Note that on the next page James grants that scientists doing science proceed as Clifford has it. This concession may have been for the sake of argument (for compare the skepticism about the reach of science on pages 23, 25 and 38), rather than a genuine subscription to the objectivity of strict induction from the evidence. Recent philosophy of science has in any case not been so sanguine.

3 James's view may be attacked on the flank by arguing that belief is not a matter of the will at all, not under voluntary control. Voluntarism with respect to belief is usually attacked in its naive versions and defended in more sophisticated formulation; I will of course not suggest that we can believe just any proposition at will. Cf. James. *op. cit.* p. 90; Barbara Winters, "Believing at Will," *Journal of Philosophy*, LXXVI; 5 (May 1979): 243–256; and Robert Holyer, "Belief and Will Revisited," *Dialogue*, XXII, 2 (June 1983: 273–290).

4 Some common objections, such as that we do not have numerically precise degrees of certainty and uncertainty, are I think, easily met (see, further, Section V-below). But if the reader is willing to conclude that it is the idea of subjective probability that is at fault, he does not need my present defense of traditional epistemology.

5 This term is a reference to the so-called "Dutch book theorem." The usual or synchronic Dutch book argument establishes the obedience of degrees of belief to the probability calculus as a criterion of rationality ("coherence") for one's state of opinion at a single time. The betting scheme I am about to describe is part of David Lewis's diachronic Dutch book argument to justify conditionalization as the correct rule for transforming prior into posterior degrees of belief [see P. Teller, "Conditionalization, Observation, and Change of Preference" in W. L. Harper and C. A. Hooker, *Foundations of Probability Theory*, vol. (Boston: Reidel, 1976)]. Bayes himself had given a similar argument, and a more sophisticated theorem has been proved by Glen Shafer; see his "Bayes' Two Arguments for Conditioning," *Annals of Statistics*, x (1982): 1075–1089, and "A Subjective Approach to Conditional Probability," *Journal of Philosophical Logic*, XII, 3 (November 1983): 453–466.

6 To see what the total cost is of I and II together, calculate

$$P(\sim H \& E) + xP(\sim E) = P(\sim H \mid E)P(E) + xP(\sim E)$$
$$= x(P(E)) + P(\sim E)) = x$$

7 E implies that my probability for H tomorrow morning will be 1/3, and so my probability for $\sim H$ then is 2/3. We have $x = 0.3/0.4 = 3/4$ and $y = x - 2/3 = 1/12$. The costs of the bets are 0.3 for (I), $x(1 - P(E) = (3/4)(0.6) = 0.45$ for bet (II), and $yP(E) = (1/12)(0.4) = (1/30)$ for (III), for a total cost of $(3/4) + (1/30)$.

8 From footnote 7 we know that the initial total cost was $(3/4) + (1/30)$. If E is false, I collect only $x = (3/4)$. If E is true, I collect 1/12 on the third bet, but then I receive in addition only what I then consider a fair price for the bet against Table Hands' winning, namely 2/3; so my total return equals 3/4 again.

9 When conditionalized on A, the function P becomes the function P' such that $P'(X) = P(X \mid A) = P(X \& A) / P(A)$ for all propositions X. This can be done only if $P(A)$ is not zero.

10 A third possibility was advocated in discussion by David Lewis: that the standard of rationality exemplified by Dutch-book Invulnerability applies to a certain sort of ideally rational agent, who not only believes himself to be, but is, infallible with respect to perception, and which we explicitly realize ourselves not to be. But this leaves us still with the task of constructing an epistemological theory that does apply to our own case.

11 "Higher Order Degrees of Belief" in D. H. Mellor, ed. *Prospects for Pragmatism: Essays in Honour of F. P. Ramsey* (New York: Cambridge, 1980), pp. 109–137, and Appendix 2 of his *Causal Necessity* (New Haven, Conn.: Yale, 1980).

12 In Skyrm's article the synchronic form $(x = 0)$ is advocated; the discussion contains diachronic examples as well, but they concern the supposition that the agent *learns* his posterior credence, whereupon the synchronic form applies.

13 See my "Calibration: A Frequentist Justification of Personal Probability," in L. Laudan and R. Cohen, eds., *Philosophy, Physics, Psychoanalysis* (Boston: Reidel, 1983). Please note well that calibration by itself is not a good scoring rule, and the criterion explained below does not entail that better calibration is always better *tout court*.

14 It would not help to say that $P(A|B)$ is the probability that A would have for me if B were to become my total new evidence, just because that would tell us nothing about what $P(A|B)$ is when B is not the sort of proposition that could be one's total new evidence. Instead I interpret conditional probability in a way that has no logical connection with learning. To say that $P(A) = 2/3$ is to say that, to me, A is twice as likely to be the case as not – this re-expresses the opinion in terms of personal odds for A as against $\sim A$. Similarly, $P(A|B) = 2/3$ expresses my personal odds for $(A\&B)$ as against $(\sim A\&B)$.

15 See my "A Temporal Framework for Conditionals and Chance," *Philosophical Review*, LXXXIX, 1 (January 1980), 91–108, and reprinted in W. L. Harper, *Ifs* (Boston: Reidel, 1981); and David Lewis, "A Subjectivist's Guide to Objective Chance," *ibid.*, pp. 267–298.

16 See Richard Jeffrey's review of articles by David Miller et al., *Journal of Symbolic Logic*, xxxv, 1 (March 1970): 124–127.

17 If we generalize (Miller) to $P_t(A \mid \text{ch}_{t+x}(A) = r) = r$, then we can derive the stronger result that if the truth value of A becomes settled at time $t + x$ [this truth value then equals $\text{ch}_{t+x}(A)$, and must be 0 or 1], the agent cannot at t believe with certainty that the present chance of A is something different from 0 or 1 if he also believes that A will be true (respectively false) at its settling time ("there are no crystal balls").

18 This is not meant as an argument against conditionalization as a rational procedure; more sophisticated machinery than single one-place probability functions can be explored. This problem of how to represent certainty without dogmatism, which I shall not go into further here, is broached in Isaac Levi, *The Enterprise of Knowledge* (Cambridge, Mass.: MIT Press, 1980). It is not a problem if full certainty is not rational.

19 This emphasis on vagueness, and this sort of way to represent it, is especially to be found in Isaac Levi's and Richard Jeffrey's writings. For more technical details see also my "Rational Belief and Probability Kinematics," *Philosophy of Science*, XLVII, 2 (June 1980): 165–187.

20 It is never easy to gauge one's agreement with other writers, but I think that in this I side with de Finetti – see p. 189 of his *Probability, Induction and Statistics* (New York: Wiley, 1972) – against Ramsey – see "Truth and Probability" in his *Foundations of Mathematics and Other Essays* (New York: Humanities Press, 1950). I would also like to refer to Stuart Hampshire's discussions of the connections between intention and knowledge or belief, in his *Freedom of the Individual* (Princeton, N.J.: University Press, 1975). Let me emphasize, however, with reference to the examples used here, that I regard acceptance of scientific theories as involving both more and less than belief; see my *The Scientific Image* (New York: Oxford, 1980), pp. 12/3, 80–83, 198–200.

Chapter 3: Internal and External Reasons

BERNARD WILLIAMS

Sentences of the forms 'A has a reason to ϕ' or 'There is a reason for A to ϕ' (where 'ϕ' stands in for some verb of action) seem on the face of it to have two different sorts of interpretation. On the first, the truth of the sentence implies, very roughly, that A has some motive which will be served or furthered by his ϕ-ing, and if this turns out not to be so the sentence is false: there is a condition relating to the agent's aims, and if this is not satisfied it is not true to say, on this interpretation, that he has a reason to ϕ. On the second interpretation, there is no such condition, and the reason–sentence will not be falsified by the absence of an appropriate motive. I shall call the first the 'internal', the second the 'external', interpretation. (Given two such interpretations, and the two forms of sentence quoted, it is reasonable to suppose that the first sentence more naturally collects the internal interpretation, and the second the external, but it would be wrong to suggest that either form of words admits only one of the interpretations.)

I shall also for convenience refer sometimes to 'internal reasons' and 'external reasons', as I do in the title, but this is to be taken only as a convenience. It is a matter for investigation whether there are two sorts of reasons for action, as opposed to two sorts of statements about people's reasons for action. Indeed, as we shall eventually see, even the interpretation in one of the cases is problematical.

I shall consider first the internal interpretation, and how far it can be taken. I shall then consider, more sceptically, what might be involved in an external interpretation. I shall end with some very brief remarks connecting all this with the issue of public goods and free–riders.

The simplest model for the internal interpretation would be this: A has a reason to ϕ iff A has some desire the satisfaction of which will be served by his ϕ-ing. Alternatively, we might say... some desire, the satisfaction of which A believes will be served by his ϕ-ing; this difference will concern us later. Such a model is sometimes ascribed to Hume, but since in fact Hume's own views are more complex than this, we might call it *the sub-Humean model*. The sub-Humean model is certainly too simple. My aim will be, by addition and revision, to work it up into something more adequate. In the course of trying to do this, I shall assemble four propositions which seem to me to be true of internal reason statements.

Basically, and by definition, any model for the internal interpretation must display a relativity of the reason statement to the agent's *subjective motivational set*, which I shall call the agent's *S*. The contents of *S* we shall come to, but we can say:

(i) An internal reason statement is falsified by the absence of some appropriate element from *S*.

The simplest sub-Humean model claims that any element in *S* gives rise to an internal reason. But there are grounds for denying this, not because of regrettable, imprudent, or deviant elements in *S* – they raise different sorts of issues – but because of elements in *S* based on false belief.

The agent believes that this stuff is gin, when it is in fact petrol. He wants a gin and tonic. Has he reason, or a reason, to mix this stuff with tonic and drink it? There are two ways here (as suggested already by the two alternatives for formulating the sub-Humean model). On the one hand, it is just very odd to say that he has a reason to drink this stuff, and natural to say that he has no reason to drink it, although he thinks that he has. On the other hand, if he does drink it, we not only have an explanation of his doing so (a reason why he did it), but we have such an explanation which is of the reason-for-action form. This explanatory dimension is very important, and we shall come back to it more than once. If there are reasons for action, it must be that people sometimes act for those reasons, and if they do, their reasons must figure in some correct explanation of their action (it does not follow that they must figure in all correct explanations of their action). The difference between false and true beliefs on the agent's part cannot alter the *form* of the explanation which will be appropriate to his action. This consideration might move us to ignore the intuition which we noticed before, and lead us just to legislate that in the case of the agent who wants gin, he has a reason to drink this stuff which is petrol.

I do not think, however, that we should do this. It looks in the wrong direction, by implying in effect that the internal reason conception is concerned only with explanation, and not at all with the agent's rationality, and this may help to motivate a search for other sorts of reason which are connected with his rationality. But the internal reasons conception is concerned with the agent's rationality. What we can correctly ascribe to him in a third-personal internal reason statement is also what he can ascribe to himself as a result of deliberation, as we shall see. So I think that we should rather say:

(ii)   A member of S, D, will not give A a reason for ϕ-ing if either the existence of D is dependent on false belief, or A's belief in the relevance of ϕ-ing to the satisfaction of D is false.

(This double formulation can be illustrated from the gin/petrol case: D can be taken in the first way as the desire to drink what is in this bottle, and in the second way as the desire to drink gin.) It will, all the same, be true that if he does ϕ in these circumstances, there was not only a reason why he ϕ-ed, but also that that displays him as, relative to his false belief, acting rationally.

We can note the epistemic consequence:

(iii)   a.   A may falsely believe an internal reason statement about himself, and (we can add)

b.   A may not know some true internal reason statement about himself.

(b) comes from two different sources. One is that A may be ignorant of some fact such that if he did know it he would, in virtue of some element in S, be disposed to ϕ: we can say that he has a reason to ϕ, though he does not know it. For it to be the case that he actually has such a reason, however, it seems that the relevance of the unknown fact to his actions has to be fairly close and immediate; otherwise one merely says that A would have a reason to ϕ if he knew the fact. I shall not pursue the question of the conditions for saying the one thing or the other, but it must be closely connected with the question of when the ignorance forms part of the explanation of what A actually does.

The second source of (iii) is that A may be ignorant of some element in S. But we should notice that an unknown element in S, D, will provide a reason for A to ϕ only if ϕ-ing is rationally related to D; that is to say, roughly, a project to ϕ could be the answer to a deliberative question formed in part by D. If D is unknown to A because it is in the unconscious, it may well not satisfy this condition, although of course it may provide the reason why he ϕ's, that is, may explain or help to explain his ϕ-ing. In such cases, the ϕ-ing may be related to D only symbolically.

I have already said that

(iv)   internal reason statements can be discovered in deliberative reasoning.

It is worth remarking the point, already implicit, that an internal reason statement does not apply only to that action which is the uniquely preferred result of the deliberation. '*A* has reason to ϕ' does not mean 'the action which A has overall, all-in, reason to do is ϕ-ing'. He can have reason to do a lot of things which he has other and stronger reasons not to do.

The sub-Humean model supposes that ϕ-ing has to be related to some element in S as causal means to end (unless, perhaps, it is straightforwardly the carrying out of a desire which is itself that element in S). But this is only one case: indeed, the mere discovery that some course of action is the causal means to an end is not in itself a piece of practical reasoning.[1] A clear example of practical reasoning is that leading to the conclusion that one has reason to ϕ because ϕ-ing would be the most convenient, economical, pleasant, and so on way of satisfying some element in S, and this of course is controlled by other elements in S, if not necessarily in a very clear or determinate way. But there are much wider possibilities for deliberation, such as: thinking how the satisfaction of elements in S can be combined, e.g. by time-ordering; where there is some irresoluble conflict among the elements of S, considering which one attaches most weight to (which, importantly, does not imply that there is some one commodity of which they provide varying amounts); or, again, finding constitutive solutions, such as deciding what would make for an entertaining evening, granted that one wants entertainment.

As a result of such processes an agent can come to see that he has reason to do something which he did not see he had reason to do at all. In this way, the deliberative process can add new actions for which there are internal reasons, just as it can also add new internal reasons for given actions. The deliberative process can also subtract elements from S. Reflection may lead the agent to see that some belief is false, and hence to realise that he has in fact no reason to do something he thought he had reason to do. More subtly, he may think he has reason to promote some development because he has not exercised his imagination enough about what it would be like if it came about. In his unaided deliberative reason, or encouraged by the persuasions of others, he may come to have some more concrete sense of what would be involved, and lose his desire for it, just as, positively, the imagination can create new possibilities and new desires. (These are important possibilities for politics as well as for individual action.)

We should not, then, think of S as statically given. The processes of deliberation can have all sorts of effect on S, and this is a fact which a theory of internal reasons should be very happy to accommodate. So also it should be more liberal than some theorists have been about the possible elements in S. I have discussed S primarily in terms of desires, and this term can be used, formally, for all elements in S. But this terminology may make one forget that S can contain such things as dispositions of evaluation, patterns of emotional reaction, personal loyalties, and various projects, as they may be abstractly called, embodying commitments of the agent. Above all, there is of course no supposition that the desires or projects of an agent have to be egoistic; he will, one hopes, have non-egoistic projects of various kinds, and these equally can provide internal reasons for action.

There is a further question, however, about the contents of S: whether it should be taken, consistently with the general idea of internal reasons, as containing *needs*. It is certainly quite natural to say that A has a reason to pursue X, just on the ground that he needs X, but will this naturally follow in a theory of internal reasons? There is a special problem about this only if it is possible for the agent to be unmotivated to pursue what he needs; I shall not try to discuss here the nature of needs, but I take it that insofar as there are determinately recognisable needs, there can be an agent who lacks any interest in getting what he indeed needs. I take it, further, that that lack of interest can remain after deliberation, and, also that it would be wrong to say that such a lack of interest must always rest on false belief. (Insofar as it does rest on false belief, then we can accommodate it under (ii), in the way already discussed.)

If an agent really is uninterested in pursuing what he needs; and this is not the product of false belief; and he could not reach any such motive from motives he has by the kind of deliberative processes we have discussed; then I think we do have to say that in the internal sense he indeed has no reason to pursue these things. In saying this, however, we have to bear in mind how strong these assumptions are, and how seldom we are likely to think that we know them to be true. When we say that a person has reason to take medicine which he needs, although he consistently and persuasively denies any interest in preserving his health, we may well still be speaking in the internal sense, with the thought that really at some level he *must* want to be well.

However, if we become clear that we have no such thought, and persist in saying that the person has this reason, then we must be speaking in another sense, and this is the external sense. People do say things that ask to be taken in the external interpretation. In James' story of Owen Wingrave, from which Britten made an opera, Owen's family urge on him the necessity and importance of his joining the army, since all his male ancestors were soldiers, and family pride requires him to do the same. Owen Wingrave has no motivation to join the army at all, and all his desires lead in another direction: he hates everything about military life and what it means. His family might have expressed themselves by saying that *there was a reason for Owen to join the army*. Knowing that there was nothing in Owen's S which would lead, through deliberative reasoning, to his doing this would not make them withdraw the claim or admit that they made it under a misapprehension. They mean it in an external sense. What is that sense?

A preliminary point is that this is not the same question as that of the status of a supposed categorical imperative, in the Kantian sense of an 'ought' which applies to an agent independently of what the agent happens to want: or rather, it is not undoubtedly the same question. First, a categorical imperative has often been taken, as by Kant, to be necessarily an imperative of morality, but external reason statements do not necessarily relate to morality. Second, it remains an obscure issue what the relation is between 'there is a reason for A to . . .' and 'A ought to . . .' Some philosophers take them to be equivalent, and under that view the question of external reasons of course comes much closer to the question of a categorical imperative. However, I shall not make any assumption about such an equivalence, and shall not further discuss 'ought'.[2]

In considering what an external reason statement might mean, we have to remember again the dimension of possible explanation, a consideration which applies to any reason for action. If something can be a reason for action, then it could be someone's reason for acting on a particular occasion, and it would then figure in an explanation of that action. Now no external reason statement could *by itself* offer an explanation of anyone's action. Even if it were true (whatever that might turn out to mean) that there was a reason for Owen to join the army, that fact by itself would never explain anything that Owen did, not even his joining the army. For if it was true at all, it was true when Owen was not motivated to join the army. The whole point of external reason statements is that they can be true independently of the agent's motivations. But nothing can explain an agent's (intentional) actions except something that motivates him so to act. So something else is needed besides the truth of the external reason statement to explain action, some psychological link; and that psychological link would seem to be belief. A's believing an external reason statement about himself may help to explain his action.

External reason statements have been introduced merely in the general form 'there is a reason for A to . . .', but we now need to go beyond that form, to specific statements of reasons. No doubt there are some cases of an agent's φ-ing because he believes that there is a reason for him to φ, while he does not have any belief about what that reason is. They would be cases of his relying on some authority whom he trusts, or, again, of his recalling that he did know of some reason for his φ-ing, but his not being able to remember what it was. In these respects, reasons for action are like reasons for belief. But, as with reasons for belief, they are evidently secondary cases. The basic case must be that in which A φ's, not because he believes only that there is some reason or other for him to φ, but because he believes of some determinate consideration that it constitutes a reason for him to φ. Thus, Owen Wingrave might come to join the army because (now) he believes that it is a reason for him to do so that his family has a tradition of military honour.

Does believing that a particular consideration is a reason to act in a particular way provide, or indeed constitute, a motivation to act? If it does not, then we are no further on. Let us grant that it does – this claim indeed seems plausible, so long at least as the connexion between such beliefs and the disposition to act is not tightened to that unnecessary degree which excludes *akrasia*. The claim is in fact *so* plausible, that this agent, with this belief, appears to be one about whom, now, an *internal* reason statement could truly be made: he is one with an appropriate motivation in his S. A man who does believe that considerations of family honour constitute reasons for action is a man with a certain disposition to action, and also dispositions of approval, sentiment, emotional reaction, and so forth.

Now it does not follow from this that there is nothing in external reason statements. What does follow is that their content is not going to be revealed by considering merely the state of one who believes such a statement, nor how that state explains action, for that state is merely the state with regard to which an internal reason statement could truly be made. Rather, the content of the external type of statement will have to be revealed by considering what it is to *come to believe* such a statement – it is there, if at all, that their peculiarity will have to emerge.

We will take the case (we have implicitly been doing so already) in which an external reason statement is made about someone who, like Owen Wingrave, is not already motivated in the required way, and so is someone about whom an internal statement could not also be truly made. (Since the difference between external and internal statements turns on the implications accepted by the speaker, external statements can of course be made about agents who are already motivated; but that is not the interesting case.) The agent does not presently believe the external statement. If he comes to believe it, he will be motivated to act; so coming to believe it must, essentially, involve acquiring a new motivation. How can that be?

This is closely related to an old question, of how 'reason can give rise to a motivation', a question which has famously received from Hume a negative answer. But in that form, the question is itself unclear, and is unclearly related to the argument – for of course reason, that is to say, rational processes, can give rise to new motivations, as we have seen in the account of deliberation. Moreover, the traditional way of putting the issue also (I shall suggest) picks up an onus of proof about what is to count as a 'purely rational process' which not only should it not pick up, but which properly belongs with the critic who wants to oppose Hume's general conclusion and to make a lot out of external reason statements – someone I shall call 'the external reasons theorist'.

The basic point lies in recognising that the external reasons theorist must conceive *in a special way* the connexion between acquiring a motivation and coming to believe the reason statement. For of course there are various means by which the agent could come to have the motivation and also to believe the reason statement, but which are the wrong kind of means to interest the external reasons theorist. Owen might be so persuaded by his family's moving rhetoric that he acquired both the motivation and the belief. But this excludes an element which the external reasons theorist essentially wants, that the agent should acquire the motivation *because* he comes to believe the reason statement, and that he should do the latter, moreover, because, in some way, he is considering the matter aright. If the theorist is to hold on to these conditions, he will, I think, have to make the condition under which the agent appropriately comes to have the motivation something like this, that he should deliberate correctly; and the external reasons statement itself will have to be taken as roughly equivalent to, or at least as entailing, the claim that if the agent rationally deliberated, then, whatever motivations he originally had, he would come to be motivated to φ.

But if this is correct, there does indeed seem great force in Hume's basic point, and it is very plausible to suppose that all external reason statements are false. For, *ex hypothesi*, there is no motivation for the agent to deliberate *from*, to reach this new motivation. Given the agent's earlier existing motivations, and this new motivation, what has to hold for external reason statements to be true, on this line of interpretation, is that the new motivation could be in some way rationally arrived at, granted the earlier motiva-

tions. Yet at the same time it must not bear to the earlier motivations the kind of rational relation which we considered in the earlier discussion of deliberation – for in that case an internal reason statement would have been true in the first place. I see no reason to suppose that these conditions could possibly be met.

It might be said that the force of an external reason statement can be explained in the following way. Such a statement implies that a rational agent would be motivated to act appropriately, and it can carry this implication, because a rational agent is precisely one who has a general disposition in his S to do what (he believes) there is reason for him to do. So when he comes to believe that there is reason for him to φ, he is motivated to φ, even though, before, he neither had a motive to φ, nor any motive related to φ-ing in one of the ways considered in the account of deliberation.

But this reply merely puts off the problem. It reapplies the desire and belief model (roughly speaking) of explanation to the actions in question, but using a desire and a belief the content of which are in question. *What* is it that one comes to believe when he comes to believe that there is reason for him to φ, if it is not the proposition, or something that entails the proposition, that if he deliberated rationally, he would be motivated to act appropriately? We were asking how any true proposition could have that content; it cannot help, in answering that, to appeal to a supposed desire which is activated by a belief which has that very content.

These arguments about what it is to accept an external reason statement involve some idea of what is possible under the account of deliberation already given, and what is excluded by that account. But here it may be objected that the account of deliberation is very vague, and has for instance allowed the use of the imagination to extend or restrict the contents of the agent's S. But if that is so, then it is unclear what the limits are to what an agent might arrive at by rational deliberation from his existing S.

It *is* unclear, and I regard it as a basically desirable feature of a theory of practical reasoning that it should preserve and account for that unclarity. There is an essential indeterminacy in what can be counted a rational deliberative process. Practical reasoning is a heuristic process, and an imaginative one, and there are no fixed boundaries on the continuum from rational thought to inspiration and conversion. To someone who thinks that reasons for action are basically to be understood in terms of the internal reasons model, this is not a difficulty. There is indeed a vagueness about 'A has reason to φ', in the internal sense, insofar as the deliberative processes which could lead from A's present S to his being motivated to φ may be more or less ambitiously conceived. But this is no embarrassment to those who take as basic the internal conception of reasons for action. It merely shows that there is a wider range of states, and a less determinate one, than one might have supposed, which can be counted as A's having a reason to φ.

It is the external reasons theorist who faces a problem at this point. There are of course many things that a speaker may say to one who is not disposed to φ when the speaker thinks that he should be, as that he is inconsiderate, or cruel, or selfish, or imprudent; or that things, and he, would be a lot nicer if he were so motivated. Any of these can be sensible things to say. But one who makes a great deal out of putting the criticism in the form of an external reason statement seems concerned to say that what is particularly wrong with the agent is that he is *irrational*. It is this theorist who particularly needs to make this charge precise: in particular, because he wants any rational agent, as such, to acknowledge the requirement to do the thing in question.

Owen Wingrave's family may not have expressed themselves in terms of 'reasons', but, as we imagined, they could have used the external reasons formulation. This fact itself provides some difficulty for the external reasons theorist. This theorist, who sees the truth of an external reason statement as potentially grounding a charge of irrationality against the agent who ignores it, might well want to say that if the Wingraves put their complaints against Owen in this form, they would very probably be claiming something which, in this particular case, was false. What the theorist would have a harder time showing would be that the words used by the Wingraves *meant* something different from what they mean when they are, as he supposes, truly uttered. But what they mean when uttered by the Wingraves is almost certainly *not* that rational deliberation would get Owen to be motivated to join the army – which is (very roughly) the meaning or implication we have found for them, if they are to bear the kind of weight such theorists wish to give them.

The sort of considerations offered here strongly suggest to me that external reason statements, when definitely isolated as such, are false, or incoherent, or really something else misleadingly expressed. It is in fact harder to isolate them in people's speech than the introduction of them at the beginning of this chapter suggested. Those who use these words often seem, rather, to be entertaining an optimistic internal reason claim, but sometimes the statement is indeed offered as standing definitely outside the agent's S and what he might derive from it in rational deliberation, and then there is, I suggest, a great unclarity about what is meant. Sometimes it is little more than that things would be better if the agent so acted. But the formulation in terms of reasons does have an effect, particularly in its suggestion that the agent is being irrational, and this suggestion, once the basis of an internal reason claim has been clearly laid aside, is bluff. If this is so, the only real claims about reasons for action will be internal claims.

A problem which has been thought to lie very close to the present subject is that of public goods and free riders, which concerns the situation (very roughly) in which each person has egoistic reason to want a certain good provided, but at the same time each has egoistic reason not to take part in providing it. I shall not attempt any discussion of this problem, but it may be helpful, simply in order to make clear my own view of reasons for action and to bring out contrasts with some other views, if I end by setting out a list of questions which bear on the problem, together with the answers that would be given to them by one who thinks (to put it cursorily) that the only rationality of action is the rationality of internal reasons.

1. Can we define notions of rationality which are not purely egoistic?
    Yes.

2. Can we define notions of rationality which are not purely means–end?
    Yes.

3. Can we define a notion of rationality where the action rational for A is in no way relative to A's existing motivations?
    No.

4. Can we show that a person who only has egoistic motivations is irrational in not pursuing non-egoistic ends?
    Not necessarily, though we may be able to in special cases. (The trouble with the egoistic person is not characteristically irrationality.)

Let there be some good, G, and a set of persons, P, such that each member of P has egoistic reason to want G provided, but delivering G requires action C, which involves costs, by each of some proper subset of P; and let A be a member of P: then

5. Has A egoistic reason to do C if he is reasonably sure either that too few members of P will do C for G to be provided, or that enough other members of P will do C, so that G will be provided?

    No.

6. Are there any circumstances of this kind in which A can have egoistic reason to do C?

    Yes, in those cases in which reaching the critical number of those doing C is sensitive to his doing C, or he has reason to think this.

7. Are there any motivations which would make it rational for A to do C, even though not in the situation just referred to?

    Yes, if he is not purely egoistic: many. For instance, there are expressive motivations – appropriate e.g. in the celebrated voting case.[3] There are also motivations which derive from the sense of fairness. This can precisely transcend the dilemma of 'either useless or unnecessary', by the form of argument 'somebody, but no reason to omit any particular body, so everybody'.

8. Is it irrational for an agent to have such motivations?

    In any sense in which the question is intelligible, no.

9. Is it rational for society to bring people up with these sorts of motivations?

    Insofar as the question is intelligible, yes. And certainly we have reason to encourage people to have these dispositions – e.g. in virtue of possessing them ourselves.

I confess that I cannot see any other major questions which, at this level of generality, bear on these issues. All these questions have clear answers which are entirely compatible with a conception of practical rationality in terms of internal reasons for action, and are also, it seems to me, entirely reasonable answers.

Notes

1   A point made by Aurel Kolnai: see his 'Deliberation is of Ends', in *Ethics, Value and Reality* (London and Indianapolis, 1978). See also David Wiggins, 'Deliberation and Practical Reason', PAS, LXXVI (1975–6); reprinted in part in *Practical Reasoning*, ed. J. Raz (Oxford, 1978).

2   It is discussed in chapter 9 of *Moral Luck*.

3   A well-known treatment is by M. Olson Jr. *The Logic of Collective Action* (Cambridge, Mass., 1965). On expressive motivations in this connexion, see S. I. Benn, 'Rationality and Political Behaviour', in S. I. Benn and G. W. Mortimore, eds., *Rationality and the Social Sciences* (London, 1976). On the point about fairness, which follows in the text, there is of course a very great deal more to be said: for instance, about how members of a group can, compatibly with fairness, converge on strategies more efficient than everyone's doing C (such as people taking turns).

Chapter 4: Paradoxes

R. M. SAINSBURY

ACTING RATIONALLY

1. Newcomb's Paradox

You are confronted with a choice. There are two boxes before you, *A* and *B*. You may either open both boxes, or else just open *B*. You may keep what is inside any box you open, but you may not keep what is inside any box you do not open. The background is this.

A very powerful being, who has been invariably accurate in his predictions about your behavior in the past, has already acted in the following way:

He has put $1,000 in box *A*.

If he has predicted that you will open just box *B*, he has in addition put $1,000,000 in box *B*.

If he has predicted that you will open both boxes, he has put nothing in box *B*.

The paradox consists in the fact that there appears to be a decisive argument for the view that the most rational thing to do is to open both boxes; and also a decisive argument for the view that the most rational thing to do is to open just box *B*. The arguments commend incompatible courses of action: If you take both boxes, you cannot also take just box *B*. Putting the arguments together entails the overall conclusion that taking both boxes is the most rational thing and also not the most rational thing. This is unacceptable, yet the arguments from which it derives are apparently acceptable.

The argument for opening both boxes goes like this. The powerful being – let us call him the Predictor – has already acted. Either he has put money in both boxes or he has put money in just box *A*. In the first case, by opening both boxes you will win $1,001,000. In the second case, by opening both boxes you will at least win $1,000, which is better than nothing. By contrast, if you were to open just box *B*, you would win just $1,000,000 on the first assumption (i.e., that the Predictor has put money in both boxes) and nothing on the second assumption (i.e., that the Predictor has put money just in box *A*). In either case, you would be $1,000 worse off than had you opened both boxes. So opening both boxes is the best thing to do.

The argument for opening just box *B* goes as follows. Since the Predictor has always been right in his previous predictions, you have every reason for thinking that he will be right in this one. So you have every reason to think that if you were to open both boxes, the Predictor would have predicted this and so would have left box *B* empty. So you have every reason to think that it would not be best to open both boxes. Likewise, you have every reason to think that if you choose to open just box *B*, the Predictor will have predicted this, and so will have put $1,000,000 inside. Imagine a third party, who knows all the facts. He will bet heavily that if you open just box *B* you will win $1,000,000. He will bet heavily that if you open both boxes you will get only $1,000. You have to agree that his bets are rational. So it must be rational for you to open just box *B*.

This paradox has been used to compare two different principles for determining how it is rational to act. One principle is this: You should act so as to maximize the benefit you can expect

---

Reproduced with permission from Sainsbury, R. M. (1988) *Paradoxes* (chapters 3 and 4). Cambridge, UK: Cambridge University Press.

from your action. In stating this principle, "benefit" is usually replaced by the technical term "utility." Part of the point of the technical term is to break any supposed connection between rationality and selfishness or lack of moral fiber. A benefit or "utility" consists in any situation that you want to obtain. If you are altruistic, you may desire someone else's welfare, and then an improvement in his welfare will count as a utility to you. If you want to do what is morally right, an action will attract utility simply by being in conformity with what, in your eyes, morality requires, even if from other points of view, say the purely material one, the consequences of the action are not beneficial to you.

There is obviously something appealing in the principle that it is rational to act so as to *maximize expected utility* – MEU for short. Consider gambling: The bigger the prize in the lottery, the more money it is rational to pay for a ticket, everything else being equal; the larger the number of tickets, the less money it is rational to pay. The MEU principle tells you to weigh both these factors. If there are 100 tickets and there is just one prize of $1,000, then you will think that you are doing well if you can buy a ticket for less than $10. (For consider: If you could buy them *all* for less than $10 each, then you could be certain of gaining $1,000 for an expenditure of less than $1,000.) If the tickets cost more than $10, you may have to think of the lottery as a way of raising money for a charity that you wish to support, if you are to buy a ticket.

Such an example contains a number of quite unrealistic assumptions. Some of these are inessential, but at least one is essential if the MEU principle is to compare any possible pair of actions for their degree of rationality. This is the supposition that utilities and probabilities can be measured.[1,2,3] If they can, then we can simply compute which of the actions open to us have greatest expected utility: We multiply the measure of utility by the measure of the probability of that utility accruing. Suppose that there are two lotteries, one as described above, with 1,000 tickets at $1 and a single $1,000 prize, and another with 99 tickets at $10 and a single $999 prize. The MEU principle tells you to prefer buying tickets in the second lottery rather than the first. For the first, the expected utility is the chance you think you have of winning, $\frac{1}{100}$, multiplied by the utility of the win, which can be represented as 1,000; so the expected utility is 10. For the second, it is $\frac{1}{99} \times 999 = 10.09$ (approximately).

	the Predictor has not put money in B	the Predictor has put money in B
you open $A + B$	$1,000	$1,001,000
you open just B	$ 0	$1,000,000

Figure 1. Newcomb's Paradox.

The MEU principle does not commend you to buy a ticket in either lottery. There may well be (and one would hope that there in fact were) many alternative ways of spending your money with expected utilities higher than those associated with either lottery. The principle only tells you that *if* you are going to buy a ticket for either, it should be for the second.[4]

The notion of utility was introduced in terms of what upshot an agent wants. What someone wants sometimes means what he or she wants all things considered. If I decide to go to the dentist, then typically I want to go – that is, want to go all things considered. However, what a person wants can also mean anything to which he attaches some positive value. In this sense, it is true of me, when I freely and willingly go to the dentist, that I want not to go: Not going has the positive value of sparing time and present discomfort. If I go, it is because this want is trumped by another: I want to avoid decay, and for the sake of that benefit I am prepared to put up with the loss of time and the discomfort. The appropriate connection between utility and wanting should exploit not what an agent wants overall, but rather that to which he attaches any positive value.

The situation that gives rise to Newcomb's Paradox can be represented as shown in Figure 1. The expected utility of opening both boxes is calculated as follows. By the background of the problem, you regard it as very likely that the Predictor will have correctly predicted your choice. Hence if you open both boxes you must think that it is very likely that the Predictor will have predicted this and so will have put no money in box B. So the expected utility is some high ratio, call it h, measuring the likelihood of this outcome, multiplied by 1,000, measuring the utility. Analogously, the expected utility for you of opening just box B is the same high ratio, measuring the likelihood of the Predictor having correctly predicted that this is what you would do, and so having put $1,000,000 in box B, multiplied by 1,000,000, measuring the utility of that outcome. Since, whatever exactly h may be, $1,000 \times h$ is much less than $1,000,000 \times h$, MEU commends opening just box B.[5]

The MEU principle underwrites the argument for opening just box B. To resolve the paradox, however, one would need to show what was wrong with the other argument, the argument for opening both boxes. Those who are persuaded that it is rational to open both boxes will regard the fact that the MEU principle delivers the contrary recommendation as a refutation of the principle.

One attractive feature of MEU is that it is a quite general, and independently attractive, principle. Are there any other principles of rational action that are also attractive, yet that deliver a different recommendation? There are. One example is the so-called *dominance principle* – DP for short.

According to DP, it is rational to perform in action α if it satisfies the following two conditions:

(a) Whatever else may happen, doing α will result in your being no worse off than doing any of the other things open to you.

(b) There is at least one possible outcome in which your having done α makes you better off than you would have been had you done any of the other things open to you.

DP has commonsensical appeal. If you follow it you will act in such a way that nothing else you could do would have resulted in your faring better, except by running the risk of your faring worse.

Figure 1 shows that opening both boxes satisfies DP, and that opening only box B does not. Whatever the Predictor has done, you are better off opening both boxes than opening just one. In either case, you stand to gain an extra $1,000 as compared with the other course of action open to you. Hence DP and MEU conflict: They commend opposite courses of action.

One way to diagnose Newcomb's Paradox is precisely as the manifestation of this conflict of principle. The constructive task is then to explain how the principles are to be restricted in such a way that they cease to conflict, while retaining whatever element of truth they contain.

How is the Predictor so good at predicting? Suppose it worked like this. Your choice would cause the Predictor to have made the correct prediction of it. To take this alleged possibility seriously, we have to take seriously the possibility of

"backward causation": that is, a later event (here your choice) causing an earlier one (here the Predictor's prediction). Let us for the moment take this in our stride. If one knew that this was how things worked, surely there could not be two views about what it would be rational to do. One should open just box B, for this would cause the Predictor to predict that this is what one would do, which would lead to his putting $1,000,000 in box B. Not making this choice, by contrast, would lead to his not putting the $1,000,000 in box B. Clearly it would be crazy not to choose to open just box B.

The original case was, perhaps, underdescribed. Perhaps it did allow for the possibility (if there is such a possibility) of backward causation. To prevent confusion, let us stipulate that the *original case* is one that excludes backward causation. It is instructive, however, to consider this *other* case, where there is supposed to be backward causation. Perhaps the attraction of opening just box B in the original case sprang from thinking of it as the backward causation case. More generally, perhaps the paradox strikes us as paradoxical only to the extent that we confuse the original case with the backward causation case. To the extent that we think of the case as involving backward causation, we are tempted by MEU. To the extent that we think of it as excluding backward causation we are tempted by DP. What strikes us as conflicting views of the same case are really views of different cases.

In the original case, one might suppose that the Predictor bases his decision on general laws, together with particular past facts. These might all be physical, or they might be psychological: For example, the laws might be laws of psychology, and the particular facts might concern your personality. There is no question of backward causation. Then the basis for the prediction consists in facts that lie in the past. Rejecting backward causation, this means that nothing you can now do can affect the basis for the prediction. Hence nothing you now do can make any difference to whether there is or is not money in box B. So you should open both boxes.

There is a complicating factor: Suppose that determinism is true. Suppose, in particular, that the psychological laws, together with data about your character up to the time at which the Predictor made his prediction, determine how you will now act, in the sense of making it impossible for you to do anything other than what, in fact, you will do. This may totally undermine the idea of rational decision, and so make the whole question of what is best to do one that cannot arise. In short, there is a case for saying that if there were such a Predictor, then there could be no question about which choice is rational. I shall ignore this case, and argue that it is rational to open both boxes. Those who are moved by it could read my conclusion as hypothetical: If we can make sense of rationality at all in the Newcomb situation, then the rational thing is to open both boxes.[6]

In defending this conclusion, I need to consider whether, as claimed earlier, it is rational for the onlookers to bet heavily on the following two conditionals:

(a)   if you select both boxes, box B will be empty.

(b)   if you select just box B, it will contain $1,000,000.

If they are rational, the onlookers will bet in accordance with their expectations. Their expectations are the same as yours. They have very strong reason to believe the two conditionals, given the Predictor's past successes. How can this be reconciled with my claim that if the Predictor bases his prediction on past evidence, then it is rational to open both boxes? If it is rational for the onlookers to expect the conditionals to be true, it must be rational for you to expect the same. However, it seems, you have a *choice* about which conditional will count. It is rational, surely, to make the second conditional count, and you can do this by opening just box B. How can one reconcile the rationality of belief in the conditionals with the rationality of opening both boxes?

Let us look more closely at the basis of the rationality of belief in the conditionals. We can do this by looking at it from the point of view of the onlookers. They reason as follows. The Predictor has always been right in the past. Since he has already filled the boxes, his prediction is based on knowing some past facts about you and your circumstances, and applying some generalizations. Our best evidence for what he has predicted is what you choose to do. This is why we believe the conditionals. Your opening just box B is evidence that the Predictor has predicted this and, hence, by the way the problem is set up, is evidence that he has filled box B with $1,000,000. Likewise for the other possibility.

The rationality of these beliefs does not entail the rationality of opening just box B. This is most easily seen if we switch to the subject's point of view: to *your* point of view, as we are pretending.

The Predictor makes his choice on the basis of past facts about you, together with some generalizations. To simplify, let us say that there are two relevant possible facts about what sort of person you were at the time the Predictor made his prediction: Either you were a one-boxer – that is, a person disposed to open just box B – or you were a two-boxer – that is, a person disposed to open both boxes. Now if you find a tendency to open both boxes well up in you, that is bad news.[7] It is evidence that you are now a two-boxer and, all other things being equal, is thereby evidence that you were a two-boxer at the time when the Predictor made his decision. Hence it is evidence that he will have predicted that you will open both boxes, and so it is evidence that there will be no money in the B box. However, there is no point in trying to extirpate this disposition, and it would be a confusion to think that you could make any difference to the situation by resisting it. There is no point trying to extirpate it *now*, since either the Predictor has made his prediction on the basis of perceiving such a disposition in you or he has not; and getting rid of it now, supposing it has been perceived, is closing the stable door after the horse has bolted. It would be a confusion to think that anything you can now do can make any difference as to whether or not you were a two-boxer at the time the Predictor made his prediction. If you found in yourself an inclination to open just box B, that would be good news, for analogous reasons; but it is an inclination that it would be more prudent to resist. By resisting it and opening both boxes, you cannot make the money that you can reasonably presume is already in the B box go away, and you will gain the extra $1,000 in the A box.

Here is an objection. If this is where the reasoning were to end, would not a really good Predictor have predicted this, and therefore have ensured that there is nothing in box B? Furthermore, had you taken the reasoning through a further twist, using the fact just mentioned as a reason for in the end taking just box B, the Predictor would have predicted this too, and so would have filled box B. So is not this what you should do?

However, the original difficulty remains and cannot be overcome. No matter what twists and turns of reasoning you go in for now, you cannot affect what the Predictor has already done. Even if you could make yourself now into a one-boxer, it would not help. What mattered was whether you were a one-boxer, or a person likely to become a one-boxer, at the time when the Predictor made his prediction. You cannot change the past.[8,9]

We have said that the Predictor has *always* been right in the past.[10] Let us imagine, in particular, that he has always been right about Newcomb problems. We shall suppose that each person is confronted with the problem only once in his life (there is no second chance), and that the Predictor has never been wrong: That is, never has a two-boxer found anything in box *B*, and never has a one-boxer found box *B* empty. Most of your friends have already had the chance. The one-boxers among them are now millionaires. You wish above all things that you were a millionaire like them, and now your chance has come: You are faced with the Newcomb problem. Is it not true that all you have to do is choose just box *B*? Is that not a sure-fire way to riches? So how could it be rational to refuse it?

So far, this raises no new considerations: The two-boxer's reply still stands. However, I have put the matter this way in order to add the following twist. Being of good two-box views, you think that the Predictor is, for some crazy reason, simply rewarding irrationality: He makes one-boxers rich, and one-boxers are irrational. Still, if you want to be rich above all things, then is not the *rational* thing to do to join the irrational people in opening just box *B*? Sir John Harington (1561–1612) wrote that

> Treason doth never prosper; what's the reason?
> Why, if it prosper, none dare call it treason.

Likewise, if "irrationality" pays, then it is not irrationality at all! You want to be rich like your millionaire friends, and if you think as they do you will be. It is rational to adapt means to ends, so it is rational to think the way they think.

This suggestion can be represented as involving two main points. The first is that one might reasonably want to be a different sort of person from the sort one is: here, a less rational sort. Some people committed to lucidity and truth as values find this suggestion unpalatable.[11] However, a second point is needed: that if it is reasonable to want to be a different sort of person, then it is reasonable, even as things are, to act as that other sort of person would have acted. The second point is what secures the passage from envying the one-boxers to the claim that it would be rational to follow their lead. Once clearly stated, this second point can be seen to be incorrect: Given that you are not a "natural" one-boxer, given that you are persuaded by the

argument for two-boxing, nothing can as things stand make it *rational* for you to one-box.[12]

A clear perception of the advantages of being a one-boxer cannot give you a *reason* for becoming one – even if that were in your power. An atheist might clearly perceive the comfort to be derived from theism, but this does not give him or her a *reason* for believing that God exists. The light of reason cannot direct one toward what one perceives as irrational. To adopt a position one regards as irrational one needs to rely on something other than reason: drugs, fasting, chanting, dancing, or whatever.

This way of dealing with the paradox takes no account of the two principles, MEU and DP. Is either to be accepted? MEU cannot be correct, since it commends taking just box *B*. DP cannot be correct since, in the other version of the paradox, in which backward causation was admitted, DP wrongly commended taking both boxes.[13,14] However, we may be able to see why the principles let us down when they did, and this may lead to ways of suitably restricting them.

In the backward causation case, it is no accident that DP gives the wrong result. It has no means of taking into account the fact that your choice will affect what is in the boxes, by affecting the Predictor. More generally, it gives the wrong result because it makes no provision for the ways in which one's acting can affect the probabilities of outcomes. The backward causation case alone shows that DP cannot serve as it stands as a correct principle of rational action: It cannot be rational to act in such a way as to cause a diminution in the likelihood of someone else doing something that would increase one's benefits.

Equally, it is no accident that MEU gives the right result for the backward causation case. The rationale of MEU is given by the thought that it is rational to act in ways one takes to be likely to *promote* one's benefits. In the backward causation case, one has reason to believe that how one acts will affect one's benefits by affecting the Predictor's decision. In this case, the conditional probabilities reflect the probability of one's action genuinely promoting one rather than another outcome.

By contrast, in the original case, this does not hold. The conditional probabilities obtain, but in a way that fails to reflect the underlying rationale of the MEU. The probability that if you open both boxes, box *B* will be empty is indeed high; but it is not high because your opening both boxes will have any causal role in bringing it about that box *B* is empty. The right restriction on MEU, so far as Newcomb's Paradox goes, is that one should act on the principle only when the conditional probabilities reflect what one believes one's actions will *produce*.[15]

We have seen that DP is not an acceptable principle of rational action, since it takes no account of conditional probabilities. This fact explains why it happens to give the right result in the original case. Here, because the probabilities are irrelevant, in that they do not reflect the likely effects of the possible actions, it is right to ignore them. So far as this case goes, the appropriate restriction on DP is that it can be used only when there is no relevant difference in the probability of the various possible outcomes.

Though these considerations explain away Newcomb's Paradox, they leave a great deal of work to be done within the wider task of understanding the nature of rational action. A first point to consider would be whether the modified versions of MEU and DP are *consistent*: whether, that is, they would deliver the same account for all cases of how it is rational to act.[16] One would have to go on to ask whether they are *correct*: whether either delivers for all cases a correct account of how it is rational to act. It is unlikely that any such simple principles would be adequate to this task. Indeed, many philosophers are skeptical concerning many of the notions upon which this discussion has been based. It is not at all plausible to think that the values that are at issue in deciding what to do are measurable in the way that has been presupposed. It would be important to consider whether any substantive principles of rationality can be formulated that do not rest on this supposition. A wider issue is whether we have any right to a supposedly objective, culture-independent notion of rationality as a scale against which any action at all can be measured. Perhaps there are species of rationality, or perhaps rationality is simply one value among others. In the next section, I consider one alleged threat to the coherence of the notion of rationality.

2. The Prisoner's Dilemma

You and I have been arrested for drug running and placed in separate cells. Each of us learns, through his own attorney, that the district attorney has resolved as follows (and we have every reason to trust this information):

1. If we both remain silent, the district attorney will have to drop the drug-running charge for lack of evidence, and will

	you confess	*you don't confess*
I confess	<5,5>	<0,10>
I don't confess	<10,0>	<1,1>

Figure 2. The Prisoner's Dilemma.

instead charge us with the much more minor offense of possessing dangerous weapons: We would then each get a year in jail.

2. If we both confess, we shall both get five years in jail.

3. If one remains silent and the other confesses, the one who confesses will get off scot-free (for turning State's evidence), and the other will go to jail for ten years.

4. The other prisoner is also being told all of (1)–(3).

    How is it rational to act? We build into the story the following further features:

5. Each is concerned only with getting the smallest sentence for himself.

6. Neither has any information about the likely behavior of the other, except that (5) holds of him and that he is a rational agent.

There is an obvious line of reasoning in favor of confessing. It is simply that whatever you do, I shall do better to confess. For if you remain silent and I confess, I shall get what I most want, no sentence at all; whereas if you confess, then I shall do much better by confessing too (five years) than by remaining silent (ten years). We can represent the situation by Figure 2, and the reasoning in favor of confessing is the familiar dominance principle (DP).

In the figure <0,10> represents the fact that on this option I go to prison for zero years, and you go for ten years; and so on. The smaller the number on my (left) side of the pair, the better I am pleased. It is easy to see that confessing dominates silence: Confessing, as compared to silence, saves me five needless years if you confess, and one if you do not.

Since you and I are in relevantly similar positions, and [by (6)] we are both rational, presumably we shall reason in the same way, and thus perform the same action. So if it is rational for me to confess, it is rational for you to do likewise; but then we shall each go to prison for five years. If we both remain silent, we would go to prison for only one year each. By acting supposedly rationally, we shall, it seems, secure for ourselves an outcome that is worse for both of us than what we could achieve.

On this view, rational action in some circumstances leads to worse outcomes than other courses of action. Even if this is depressing, it is not as it stands paradoxical: We all know that irrational gambles can succeed. What is arguably paradoxical is that the case is one in which the failure of rationality to produce the best results is not a matter of some chance intervention, but is a predictable and inevitable consequence of so-called rational reasoning. How, in that case, can it be rational to be "rational"?[17] The allegedly unacceptable consequence of the apparently acceptable reasoning is that rational action can be seen in advance to make a worse outcome highly likely.

If this is a paradox, then the correct response, I believe, is to deny that the consequence is really unacceptable. The unacceptability is supposed to consist in the fact that if we were both to act in a certain way, we would be better off than if each were to follow the supposed dictates of rationality. Hence rationality is not the *best* guide to how to act, in that acting in the other way would lead to a better outcome for both. The trouble with this suggestion is that any guide to action has to be available to the agent's decision-making processes. To be guided by the thought that we would both be better off if both remained silent than if both confessed, I would need to know that you would remain silent. What it is rational to do must be relative to what we know. If we are ignorant, then of course acting rationally may not lead us to the best upshot. Here, the ignorance of each concerns what the other will do; and this, rather than some defect in rationality, is what yields the less than optimal upshot.

However, we are now close to a paradox of a different sort. I have said that there is a compelling argument for the rationality of confessing. However, it appears that there is also a strong case for the rationality of remaining silent. If this case is good, then two apparently acceptable arguments lead to conclusions that, taken together, are unacceptable.

The argument for silence goes like this. We both know we are rational agents, because that is built into the story. We therefore know that any reason one of us has for acting will apply to the other. Hence we know that we shall do the same thing. There are two courses of action that count as doing the same thing: both confessing or both remaining silent. Of these, the latter is preferable for both of us. So of the available courses of action, it is obvious which each of us must rationally prefer: remaining silent. This, then, is the rational choice.

This argument invites a revenge. Suppose silence is the rational choice, and that I know it is. Then, in knowing that you are rational, I know that it is the choice you will make. So I know that you will remain silent. However, in that case it must be rational for me to confess, thus securing my preferred outcome: getting off scot-free. On the other hand, I know that you can reason like this too; therefore you, if rational, will not keep silent. In that case it is again – but more urgently – rational for me to confess. The way of silence is unstable. Thus the hypothesis that keeping silent is the rational choice is refuted.

This shows that the Prisoner's Dilemma does not really entail an unacceptable conclusion concerning rationality. We should not, however, be content with simply showing this: We should see how the case connects with the principles of rational action already discussed.

The MEU principle, as stated in Section 1, claimed that the rational act was whatever maximized expected utility, where this was to be understood in terms of two factors; the desirability of a certain outcome and its probability, conditional upon the performance of a given act. In connection with Newcomb's Paradox, I originally said that the relevant probabilities were

(a)   the probability of there being $1,000,000 in box *B*, *given that* I choose to open both boxes, and

(b)   the probabilty of there being $1,000,000 in box *B*, *given that* I choose to open just box *B*.

In the discussion, I claimed that these are not the right probabilities to consider in those cases in which these conditional probabilities do not reflect the tendency of my action to *produce* the outcome in question. So what are the right probabilties to consider? One suggestion is that they are

(a′)   the probability of my bringing it about that there will be $1,000,000 in box *B* by choosing both boxes, and

(b′)   the probability of my bringing it about that there will be $1,000,000 in box *B* by choosing one box.

Both of these probabilities are 0. If we stipulate that anything known to be true anyway (having a probability of 1, regardless of my action) is something that *anything* I do counts as bringing about, then opening box *A* has an expected utility equal to the utility of $1,000, and opening only box *B* has an expected utility of 0. The version of MEU that considers the probabilities (a′) and (b′), rather than (a) and (b). supports two-boxing.

Let us apply the contrast between these two versions of MEU to the Prisoner's Dilemma, starting with the original version. The probability of you confessing, given that I confess, is high and equal to the probability of you remaining silent, given that I remain silent. Moreover, the probability of you confessing, given that I remain silent, is low, and so is the probability of the converse. These conditional probabilities follow from my knowledge, built in to the example, that you and I will reason in similar ways, since we are both rational.[18] With suitable utilities, there will be versions of the dilemma in which MEU, in its original form, designates silence as the rational course of action.[19]

In its modifed form, MEU was to take into account the probability of an action *producing* the relevant outcome. Since that probability is by stipulation 0 in the present case, because each of us makes his decision before knowing what the other has decided, the modified MEU does not give us any guidance: All the expected utilities, understood in this way, are the same. However, this fact would be a telling reason for applying DP: If you have no idea what outcomes your actions will bring about, choose that action that will make things better for you whatever the other person does.

It has been suggested that Newcomb's Paradox is simply a version of the Prisoner's Dilemma. In Newcomb's Paradox, the crucial matter – whether or not there is anything in box *B* – is one of match: The money is in the box if and only if my action matches the "prediction." It does not matter whether the "prediction" occurs before or after the act of choice; what matters is that the act of choice should have no effect on the content of the prediction. Likewise, match is of the essence in the Prisoner's Dilemma: Knowing that we are both rational, I expect my action to match yours, just as I expect the prediction to match my choice. Moreover, just as I cannot affect the prediction, so I cannot affect your choice. Figure 3 sets out the similarities.

In a nutshell, the two arguments we have considered are these:

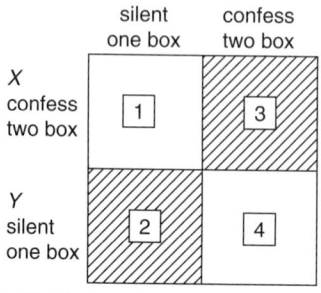

Figure 3. Similarities between Newcomb's Paradox and the Prisoner's Dilemma. I have to choose whether to do X (confess, take both boxes) or Y (remain silent, take just one box). The column indicates what the other character in the story may do: The other prisoner remains silent or confesses; the Predictor predicts that I shall one-box or else that I shall two-box. My preferences among the outcomes, from best to worst, are in this order: 1,2,3,4. The "matching possibilities" are shaded: The other prisoner does what I do, the Predictor predicts correctly. I know that my choice cannot affect whether or not a match will occur. I know that a match is much more likely than a mismatch.

A.   Do X, since you are better off, whatever the other does, than you would be if you were to do Y: 1 is better than 2, and 3 is better than 4.

B.   Do Y, since match is the most likely kind of outcome, and of these 2 is better than 3.

If this analogy is correct, then one has *consistent* views on the problems only if one is either a two-boxer and a believer in confessing, or else a one-boxer and a believer in silence. My view is the first.

The Prisoner's Dilemma is a simplified version of a well-known conflict: If our cooperating means each of us forgoing something that he (or she) would otherwise have preferred, then cooperation appears not to be in my best interests. What serves my purposes best is to secure cooperation from you, while not being cooperative in return. In the Prisoner's Dilemma, what would be best for me is that you remain silent, perhaps under the influence of persuasion, threats, or promises from me, while I, perhaps reneging on undertakings to you, confess. If the first view is correct, and X-ing is the rational thing to do, then if we both pursue our interests rationally, we shall end up serving these interests less well then we might. This is not really unacceptable, for it is true; but it may seem depressing.

In the case we have considered, there is just a single situation requiring a decision. Suppose instead that we are confronted with a "multiple Prisoner's Dilemma": Suppose that there are a series of choices, and that we each know this – in particular, we each know that this is not the last time we shall be playing the game with each other – and that we also know that the other will remember, and no doubt be guided by, what has happened on previous occasions. There is an argument to the effect that this new situation would push me in the direction of silence. Suppose you get the idea that I am the sort of person who generally confesses. Then I know that this will make you confess too, to protect yourself from the disasterous consequences of silence, and the overall result will be less than the best for me, time after time. So I have an interest in getting you to believe that I am the sort of person who generally remains silent. One way I can propagate this view is by in fact remaining silent. (We all know, from our knowledge of used car salesmen and politicians, that this is not the only way to try to achieve this kind of effect.) I also know that you will follow the same policy. So in this situation the cooperative policy of silence would appear to be the rational one.[20]

There is fascinating evidence that this is not far from the truth. In some computer simulations of Prisoner's Dilemma situations, the following strategy did better than any other: Start by remaining silent; thereafter do what the other player did during the previous round. In suitable circumstances, this will lead to a situation of stable cooperation. Since the multiple Prisoner's Dilemma corresponds more closely to more of real life than the single case, it may be that the upshot of the discussion ought not to be so depressing: Perhaps rational self-interest is not doomed to lead to a nonoptimal outcome. However, the main point that I have been concerned to establish is that the paradoxical appearance of the Prisoner's Dilemma, like that of Newcomb's Paradox, can be resolved.

BELIEVING RATIONALLY

This part of this chapter concerns problems about what it is to have knowledge or rational belief. It is in two main sections: The first, called "Paradoxes of Confirmation," is about two paradoxes that might be called "philosophers' paradoxes." Let me explain.

Most of the paradoxes in this book are quite straightforward to state. Seeing what is paradoxical about them does not require any special knowledge – you do not have to be a games theorist or a statistician to see what is paradoxical about Newcomb's Paradox or the Prisoner's Dilemma, nor do you have to be a physicist or sportsman to see what is paradoxical about Zeno's paradoxes. By contrast, the paradoxes of confirmation arise, and can only be understood, in the context of a specifically philosophical project. Therefore these paradoxes need some background (Section 1.1) before being introduced (in Section 1.2 and 1.3). The background section sets out the nature of the project within which the paradoxes arise.

The second main section of the chapter concerns the paradox of the Unexpected Examination. Although it is hard to resolve, it is easy enough to state. This paradox has been used to cast doubt on intuitively natural principles about rational belief and knowledge.

1. Paradoxes of Confirmation

1.1. Background

We all believe that there is a firm distinction between strong, good, or reliable evidence on the one hand, and weak, bad, or unreliable evidence on the other. If a stranger at the racetrack tells you that Wolf-face will win the next race, and you have no other relevant information, you would be a fool to bet heavily on Wolf-face. The evidence that he will win is extremely thin. However, had the trainer given you the same tip, that would have provided you with much stronger evidence. It would be stronger still if you knew that the trainer was a crook who believed that you were on to him, and if you also knew that he thought a good tip would buy you off.

Most of our actions are guided by scarcely conscious assessments of how good our evidence is for certain of our beliefs. When we choose what film to see or what restaurant to patronize we are often guided by past experience: by whether the director or actors have good track records, or whether the restaurant has produced good food in the past. We are also guided by what other people say: We weigh their testimony, trusting some – good reviewers, or people we know to be good judges of food – more than others. In such everyday cases, our assessment of the quality of the evidence is pretty rough and ready: We recognize good judges and bad judges, good signs and bad signs; but we never normally ask ourselves what *constitutes* a good judge or a good sign.

The philosophical project within which the paradoxes of Section 1 arise is to state general principles determining what counts as good evidence. Such principles sometimes surface outside philosophy departments. In law courts, for example, explicit categorizations of the evidence ("circumstantial," "inadmissible") are used to grade it; and in scientific investigations, in particular those involving certain kinds of numerically structured data, there are elaborate and sophisticated statistical theories bearing on the question of the extent to which data support a hypothesis.

The branch of philosophy in which philosophers have tried to articulate general principles determining the quality of evidence is called "confirmation theory." These attempts have given rise to surprising paradoxes. Understanding them will lead to a better idea of the nature of evidence.

If a body of propositions constitutes *some* evidence (however slight) for a hypothesis, let us say that these propositions *confirm* the hypothesis. From this starting point one might hope to develop an account of what one should believe. For example, one might think that one ought to believe, of all the relevant hypotheses that one can conceive, that which is best confirmed by all of one's data. Be that as it may, there are problems enough even with the starting point, let alone what one might develop from it.

A very natural thought is that the following principle will play some fundamental role in an account of confirmation:

G1. A generalization is confirmed by any of its instances.

Here are some examples of generalizations:

1. All emeralds are green.

2. Whenever the price of cocaine falls, its consumption rises.

3. Everyone I have spoken to this morning thinks that the Democrats will win the next election.

4. All AIDS victims have such-and-such a chromosome.

G1 asserts that these propositions are confirmed by their instances – that is, respectively, by this, that, or the other emerald being green; by cases in which the price of cocaine falls and its consumption increases; by the fact that I spoke to Mary this morning, and she thinks that the Democrats will win; and by the fact that Frank, who has AIDS, also has this chromosome. Notice that G1 does not assert, crazily, that an instance can *establish* a generalization, A single instance can *confirm*, according to G1, but obviously that does not settle the matter. A single instance does not even show that it is rational to believe the hypothesis, let alone that it is true.

I have spoken both of objects (like emeralds) and of facts (like the fact that Frank has AIDS and also this chromosome) as instances of generalizations, and I shall continue to do so. However, on state occasions I shall say that an instance of a generalization is itself a proposition. When the generalization has the form

All *A*'s are *B*'s,

an *instance* of it is any proposition of the form

This *A* is a *B*.

Thus

This emerald is green

is an instance of

All emeralds are green.

A *counterinstance* of a generalization "All *A*'s are *B*'s" is a proposition of the form

This *A* is not a *B*.

So

This emerald is not green

is a counterinstance of "All emeralds are green." Just as we may, on nonstate occasions, speak of green emeralds as instances of this latter proposition, so we can speak of nongreen emeralds as counter-instances of it.

The opposite of confirmation is *disconfirmation*. A hypothesis is disconfirmed by propositions that tend to show it to be false. An extreme case is *falsification:* A generalization is falsified by any counterinstance of it.

The principle G1 is to be understood to mean that any proposition that is an instance of a generalization confirms that generalization. It is not always clear how this is meant to link up with the notion of good evidence. Obviously, one AIDS victim with a certain chromosome does not alone constitute good evidence for the hypothesis that all AIDS victims have it; but perhaps a large number of instances, and no counterinstances, do add up to good evidence.

If so, we shall think of each instance as making a positive contribution to this good evidence, and this is what people have in mind by the notion of confirmation. G1 does not say, absurdly, that an instance of a generalization would, in and of itself, give us good reason to believe that generalization. Rather, it says that an instance makes a positive contribution, however slight, and however liable to be outweighed by other factors, toward constituting good evidence. The idea is that if we know of an instance of a generalization, we have taken one small step toward having good evidence for that generalization, even though other things we know may undermine this evidence. Indeed, our other knowledge might include a counterinstance of that same generalization.

The quality of evidence is a matter of degree: Some evidence is stronger, other evidence weaker. One way we might try to build toward this from the idea of confirmation, together with G1, is by saying that your evidence for a generalization is stronger the more instances of it your total body of knowledge contains – provided that it contains no counterinstances. However, one must beware of supposing that it is at all easy to arrive at a correct account. The following shows that what has just been suggested is indeed wrong. One could well have come across many instances, and no counterinstances, of the generalization

All places fail to contain my spectacles

(one has searched high and low without success); yet one would be quite right to be certain that this generalization is false.

The appeal of G1 comes in part from the thought that *extrapolation* is reasonable. If all the things of kind *A* that you have examined have also been of kind *B*, then you have some reason to extrapolate to the hypothesis that all things of kind *A* are of kind *B*. Of course, the evidence may be slight, and it may be outweighed by other evidence.

We are not usually interested in confirmation (in the technical sense used here) in cases of generalizations such as "Everyone I met this morning said that the Democrats would win." If I had met a reasonably small number of people, I might say in the afternoon: "I don't need evidence – I already *know* that it's true." The idea is that my own experience already determines the truth of the generalization. The contrast is with generalizations such as "Whenever the price of cocaine falls, its consumption increases." You may know

that this has held so far, but this does not settle that the proposition is true, for it speaks to future cases as well as past ones. This is the sort of generalization for which we feel we need evidence: a generalization not all of whose instances one has encountered.[21]

Inductive reasoning, as philosophers call it, consists in arguing from evidence or data to hypotheses not entailed by these data. One traditional philosophical problem has been to justify this process: to show that it is at least sometimes legitimate to "go beyond the data." Let us call this the problem of *justification*. Another philosophical problem is this: to give a general account of the kinds of inductive reasoning we *take* to be legitimate (without necessarily pronouncing on whether or not they are really legitimate). Let us call this the problem of *characterization*. We take it that it is legitimate to argue from the fact that the sun has risen every day so far to the conclusion that it will, probably, rise every day in the future; or, at least, to the conclusion that it will, probably, rise tomorrow. By contrast, we do not think that it is legitimate to argue from these same data to the conclusion that the sun will sometime cease to rise, or to the conclusion that it will not rise tomorrow.[22] The problem of characterization is to give an illuminating general account of the features of evidence that make us count it as *good* evidence, as a legitimate basis for the hypothesis in question.

An initial answer to the problem of characterization is that inductive reasoning is generally taken to be legitimate when it is a case of extrapolation: when one reasons on the assumption that what one has not experienced will resemble what one has. G1 is connected with this initial suggestion, for it specifies a way of extrapolating.

These problems of induction are akin to problems already encountered. Earlier, we asked, "Under what conditions are data good evidence for a hypothesis?" If we can answer this question in some illuminating way (and not merely by saying, for example, "When they are"), we shall thereby be close to having solved the problem of justification – for we shall then be close to showing that it *is* sometimes legitimate to go beyond the data.[23] Moreover, if we could answer the question "Under what conditions are data *taken to be* good evidence for a hypothesis?" we would have answered the problem of characterization.

We shall be concerned only with the characterization problem: not the question of whether there is any genuinely legitimate inductive reasoning, but rather the question of what sort of inductive reasoning we (rightly or wrongly) take to be legitimate. Though this seems the easier problem, attempts to answer it lead quickly to contradictions.

1.2. *The Paradox of the Ravens*

Despite the initial appeal of G1, it leads, in conjunction with other apparently innocuous principles, to a paradox discovered by Carl Hempel [1945], and now generally known as the Paradox of the Ravens.

In order to derive the paradoxical consequence, we need just one other principle:

E1. If two hypotheses can be known *a priori* to be equivalent, then any data that confirm one confirm the other.

This needs some explanation.[24] Something can be known *a priori* if it can be known without any appeal to experience. For example, one does not have to conduct any kind of social survey to discover that all women are women: Indeed, one could not discover this by a survey. What can be known *a priori* can be known simply on the basis of reflection and reasoning.

Two hypotheses are equivalent just on condition that if either one is true, so is the other, and if either one is false, so is the other. E1 asks us to consider cases in which two hypotheses can be known *a priori* to be equivalent. An example would be the hypotheses

R1. All ravens are black

and

There are no ravens that are not black

and also

R2. Everything nonblack is a nonraven.

Any two of these three hypotheses are equivalent, and this can be shown simply by reflection, without appeal to experience; so the equivalence can be known *a priori*. For example, suppose R1 is true: All ravens are black. Then, clearly, any nonblack thing is not a raven, or, as R2 puts it, is a nonraven. So if R1 is true, so is R2. Now suppose that R1 is false; then some ravens are not black. However, this means that some things that are not black are ravens, so R2 is false, too. Thus R1 and R2 are equivalent, and this can be known *a priori*.[25]

We can now show how the Paradox of the Ravens is derived from G1 and E1. By G1, R2

is confirmed by its instances – for example, by a white shoe, or (using the state-occasion notion of an instance) by, for example:

P1. This nonblack (in fact, white) thing is a nonraven (in fact, a shoe).

Instance P1 confirms R2, but R2 can be known *a priori* to be equivalent to R1. So, by E1, P1 confirms R1, "All ravens are black." This, on the face of it, is absurd. Data relevant to whether or not all ravens are black must be data about ravens. The color of shoes can have no bearing whatsoever on the matter. Thus G1 and E1 – apparently acceptable principles – lead to the apparently unacceptable conclusion that a white shoe confirms the hypothesis that all ravens are black. This, finally, is our paradox.

The principles of reasoning involved do not appear to be open to challenge, so there are three possible responses:

(a) to say that the apparently paradoxical conclusion is, after all, acceptable;

(b) to deny E1; or

(c) to deny G1.

Hempel himself makes the first of these responses. One could argue for it as follows. First, we must bear in mind that "confirm" is being used in a technical way. It does not follow from the supposition that a white shoe *confirms* that all ravens are black that observing a white shoe puts you in a position reasonably to believe that all ravens are black. Second, there are cases in which it seems quite natural, or at least much less absurd, to allow that P1 confirms that all ravens are black – that is, that P1 could make a positive contribution to some good evidence for the hypothesis. Suppose that we are on an ornithological field trip. We have seen several black ravens in the trees and formulate the hypothesis that all ravens are black. We then catch sight of something white in a topmost branch. For a moment we tremble for the hypothesis, fearing a counterinstance – fearing, that is, that we have found a white raven. A closer look reveals that it is a shoe. In this situation, we are more likely to agree that a white shoe confirms the hypothesis. Hempel tells a similar story for a more realistic case. Investigating the hypothesis that all sodium salts burn yellow, we come across something that does not burn yellow. When we discover that the object is a lump of ice, we regard the experiment as having confirmed the hypothesis.

The first point appeals to the idea that some complicated story must be told in order to link confirmation to having good reason to believe. Furthermore, in the telling, it will be apparent why observing white shoes, despite their confirmatory character with respect to the hypothesis that all ravens are black, does not normally contribute to giving one good reason to believe the hypothesis. We cannot assess the suggestion until we know the details of this story.

The second of these points emphasizes that confirmation, as we normally think of it, is not an absolute notion but is relative to what background information we possess. Making this point leaves unstarted the task of specifying how the technical notion of confirmation – which, so far, has been taken as absolute – should be modified so as to take account of this relativity.

Perhaps these points can be developed so as to justify the first response, (a); but I shall now turn to the other possible responses.

Response (b) is to deny E1. For example, one might simply insist that anything that confirms a generalization must be an instance of it. This avoids the paradox and is inconsistent with E1, but it is very hard to justify. For example, suppose that we are investigating an outbreak of Legionnaires' disease. Our hypothesis is that the source of the infection was the water at St. George's school, consumed by all the children who attended last week. Will only an instance of the generalization "All pupils attending St. George's last week contracted Legionnaires' disease" confirm it? Imagine that we find some St. George's children who are free from the disease, but that it then turns out they they missed school last week. We would normally count this as evidence in favor of our hypothesis – some potential and highly relevant counterinstances have been eliminated – and yet these children are not instances of the hypothesis.

There is a more general argument against the rejection of E1. Suppose we find some data that confirm two hypotheses, H1 and H2. It is standard practice to reason as follows: H3 is a consequence of H1 and H2, so to the extent that H1 and H2 are confirmed, so is H3. For example, if we had data that confirmed both the hypothesis that all anorexics are zinc-deficient and the hypothesis that everyone who is zinc-deficient is zinc-intolerant, the data would surely confirm the hypothesis that all anorexics are zinc-intolerant. However, if we allow that data confirm the *a priori* knowable consequences of hypotheses they confirm, we have in effect allowed E1.[26]

The third possible response to the paradox is to reject G1. This is both the most popular response, and also, I believe, the correct one. The Paradox of the Ravens already gives us some reason to reject it, if the other responses are unsatisfactory. The paradox of "grue," to be considered in the next section, gives a decisive reason for rejecting it. Moreover, there are quite straightforward counterexamples to it. Consider, for example, the hypothesis that all snakes inhabit regions other than Ireland. According to G1, a snake found outside Ireland confirms the hypothesis; but however we pile up the instances, we get no evidence for the hypothesis. Quite the contrary: The more widespread we find the distribution of snakes to be, the more unlikely it becomes that Ireland is snakefree. A non-Irish snake does not confirm the hypothesis, since it makes no positive contribution to the evidence in favor of the hypothesis, and may even count against it.

Rejecting G1 resolves the paradox, but it leaves us in a rather unsatisfactory position regarding confirmation: We have made very little progress toward uncovering the principles that underlie our discrimination between good and bad evidence. The next paradox brings to light more difficulties in the path of this project.

1.3. "Grue"

According to G1, green emeralds confirm the hypothesis that all emeralds are green. Now consider the predicate "grue," invented by Nelson Goodman [1955] with an eye to showing the inadequacy of G1. The meaning of "grue" ensures, by stipulation, that a thing x counts as *grue* if and only if it meets either of the following conditions:

Gr1. x is green and has been examined, or
Gr2. x is blue and has not been examined.[27]

The class of grue things is thus, by definition, made up of just the examined green things together with the unexamined blue things. All examined emeralds, being all of them green, count as grue, by Gr1. It follows from G1 that the hypothesis that all emeralds are grue is confirmed by our data: Every emerald we have examined is a confirming instance because it was green. This is absurd. If the hypothesis that all emeralds are grue is true, then unexamined emeralds (supposing that there are any) are blue. This we all believe is false, and certainly not confirmed by our data. G1 must be rejected.[28]

What is paradoxical is that a seeming truth, G1, leads, by apparently correct reasoning, to a seeming falsehood: that our data concerning emeralds confirm the hypothesis that they are all grue.[29] The paradox relates to the problem of *characterization* – of saying what kinds of evidence we take to be good, or what sorts of inductive argument we take to be legitimate – because we need to say what makes us treat green and grue differently. G1 does not discriminate the cases.

Notice that the conclusion is unacceptable even if we recall that "confirms" is being used in a technical sense: It is not equivalent to "gives us good reason to believe," but means only something like "would make a positive contribution to a good reason for believing." It strikes us as unacceptable to suppose that an examined green emerald makes any contribution at all to giving a good reason for supposing that all emeralds are grue.[30]

We have already seen in connection with the ravens (section 1.2) that there is a case for rejecting G1; that case is, of course, strengthened by the present Grue Paradox. If we reject G1, then the paradox is, for the moment, resolved, for we shall have said that an apparently acceptable premise is not really acceptable. However, what can we put in its place? It would seem that something like G1 must be true. Is there an appropriate modification? If not, then the Grue Paradox remains unresolved; for to say that there is no appropriate modification of G1 is to say that there are no principles governing what makes a body of data confirm a hypothesis. This seems as unacceptable as the view that green emeralds confirm the hypothesis that all emeralds are grue.

Several suggestions have been made. Most of them can be seen as falling into one of two patterns:

1. The blame is placed on the word "grue," which is said to be of a particularly nasty kind, rather than on the structure of G1. All we need is a general principle for excluding the *grue*some words, and G1 will be acceptable for the remainder.

2. The blame is placed not so much on "grue" as on the attempt to formulate a principle, like G1, that takes no account at all of *background information* – information that is always in play in any real-life case of evidence or confirmation.

If we try the first response, the difficulty is to say exactly what is nasty about "grue." It is not enough to say that "grue" is an invented word, rather than one that occurs naturally in our language. Scientists often have to invent words (like "electron") or use old words in new ways (like "mass"), but it would be extravagant to infer that these new or newly used words cannot figure in confirmable generalizations.

It is more appealing to say that what is wrong with "grue" is that it implicitly mentions a specific time in its definition. Its definition appeals to what has *already* been examined, and this refers to the time at which the definition is made. In this respect, "grue" and "green" differ sharply, for there is no *verbal* definition of "green" at all, and so it is not the case that the definition of "green" involves reference to a particular time.

However, if we were to restrict G1 to generalizations in which there is no reference to a time, we would make it too restrictive. For example, the generalization "In Tudor times, most agricultural innovations were made in the north of the country" is one that could be confirmed or disconfirmed on the pattern of G1. In addition, G1 would not be restrictive enough. The structure of the Grue Paradox is preserved if we can find a way of picking out just the emeralds we have already examined. We might do this by giving each one a name, e_1, e_2, . . . ; or it might be that all and only the emeralds so far examined have come from a certain emerald mine (now exhausted); or something of the kind. Then we could define a predicate equivalent to "grue" without mentioning a time: In the one case we could say that it is to apply to any of e_1, e_2, . . . just on condition that that thing is green, and to anything else just in case it is blue; in the other case we could say that it is to apply to everything taken from a certain mine just on condition that it is green, and to anything else just on condition that it is blue. Therefore it is not of the essence of the paradox that the definition of "grue" mentions a time.

There are other ways of trying to say what is nasty about "grue." Goodman's own attempt has at least superficial similarities to one I rejected earlier. He says that what is wrong with "grue" is that it is not "well-entrenched"; that is, the class of entities to which it applies is a class that has not been alluded to much – indeed, at all – in the making of predictions. To treat being poorly entrenched as sufficient for being incapable of figuring in confirmable generalizations seems to put an intolerable block on scientific innovativeness. Though Goodman is well aware of this problem, there is room for doubt about whether he deals with it successfully.[31]

I now want to consider a response of the other kind I mentioned: not restricting G1 by limiting it to generalizations that do not contain words sharing the supposed nasty features of "grue," whatever these features may be; but rather restricting G1 by appeal to background information. Intuitively, what is wrong with supposing that our information about examined emeralds gives us any reason for thinking that all emeralds are grue is that we know that the examined ones are grue only in virtue of having been examined. We do not believe that our examining the emeralds had any "real" effect on them. We believe that if they had not been examined they would not have been grue. What makes it so absurd to suppose, on the basis of our data, that all emeralds are grue is that we know that the unexamined ones lack the property in virtue of which the examined ones *are* grue: namely, having been examined. An initial attempt to formulate this thought might look like this:

G2. A hypothesis "All *F*'s are *G*'s" is confirmed by its instances if and only if there is no property *H* such that the *F*'s in the data are *H*, and if they had not been *H*, they would not have been *G*.[32]

We might try to support G2 by applying this to the following case, which in some respects looks similar to the grue emeralds. Suppose that we are gathering evidence about the color of lobsters, but unfortunately we have access only to boiled ones. All the lobsters in our sample are pink. Moreover, we know that the lobsters in the sample are pink only in virtue of having been boiled. Then it would be absurd for us to think that our sample confirms the hypothesis that all lobsters are pink. Here the hypothesis is "All lobsters (*F*) are pink (*G*)," and *H* is the property of having been boiled. Because the lobsters in the sample are boiled, and had they not been boiled would not have been pink, the data do not meet the condition imposed by G2 for confirming the hypothesis.

The lobster case brings to light a difficulty, or series of difficulties, connected with G2. We start to uncover them if we ask: How do we know that the lobsters in the sample would not have been pink had they not been boiled? It would seem that if we know this, then we know that some lobsters are not pink at all times, and thus we are in a position to know that the hypothesis is false.

This shows that we can explain, without appealing to G2, why the evidence for the hypothesis that all lobsters are pink was deficient. A body of evidence fails to confirm any hypothesis to which it contains a counterinstance. However, the case in addition brings to

light something more fundamental: that G2, as it stands, does not require our *body of data* to contain the proposition that there is no *H* such that the examined *F*'s would not have been *G* had they not been *H*. It requires only that this proposition be true. What would be relevant to G2 would thus be a variant of the lobster case in which all observed lobsters are pink, but we, the observers, do not realize that they are pink only because they have been boiled. G2 does *not rule* that, in this state of ignorance, our data confirm the generalization that all lobsters are pink.[33] Is this acceptable?

This raises an important issue. If it sounds wrong to say that the person who has observed only pink lobsters, and who knows nothing of the connection between boiling and color (and perhaps does not even know that the sample lobsters have been boiled), lacks data that would confirm the hypothesis that all lobsters are pink, this is because we intuitively feel that evidence should be *transparent*. By this I mean that we intuitively feel that if a body of data is evidence for a hypothesis, then we ought to be able to tell that this is so merely by examining the data and the hypothesis: One ought, in other words, to be able to tell that this is so a *priori*. This intuitive feeling might be supported by the following argument. Suppose that no evidence is, in this sense, transparent. Then, a claim to the effect that a body of data *D* confirms a hypothesis *H* will itself be a hypothesis needing confirmation. We shall need to cast around for data to confirm, or disconfirm, the hypothesis that *D* confirms *H*. It looks as if we are set on an infinite regress, and that we could never have any reason to suppose that anything confirms anything unless evidence is transparent.

Not all evidence is transparent. Spots can confirm the hypothesis that the patient has measles, but one needs medical knowledge to recognize that the data, the spots, are thus related to the hypothesis: One needs to know that only people, or most people, with spots of this kind have measles. In other words, it is clear that in many cases the evidence is not transparent. In any case, the most the argument of the preceding paragraph could show is that *some* evidence needs to be transparent, since this is all that is needed to block the alleged regress.

If we feel that some evidence should be transparent, we shall surely feel that an example is the limiting case in which everything that *can* be included among the data *has* been included. In this case, we shall feel that one ought to be able to tell *a priori*, without further investigation, which hypotheses these data confirm. However, this is not guaranteed by G2, for two reasons.

First, for some hypotheses, "All *F*'s are *G*'s," our data may include plenty of instances and no counterinstances but fail to contain either the proposition "There is no *H* such that all examined *F*'s are *H* and would not have been *G* had they not been *H*" or its negation. In this case, if G2 is true, we could not tell *a priori* whether our data confirm the hypothesis, since we could not tell whether the condition it places on the instances of the hypothesis obtains or not.

Second, it is a debatable question whether this condition *could* properly be included among our data. One might hold that all data must, in the end, be observations, and that a condition such as "There is no *H* such that all examined *F*'s are *H* and would not have been *G* had they not been *H*" is not something immediately available to observation, and so cannot be a datum.

These objections point in controversial directions. The second objection presupposes a form of *foundationalism*, which is highly controversial. Perhaps, contrary to the presupposition, there is nothing in the intrinsic nature of a proposition that qualifies it as a datum; thus, on occasion, the counterfactual condition could count as a datum. If this is allowed, then we could envisage a variant of G2 that meets the first of the two objections.

G3. A hypothesis "All *F*'s are *G*'s" is confirmed by a body of data containing its instances if and only if the data also contain the proposition "There is no such property *H* such that the *F*'s in the data are *H*, and if they had not been *H*, they would not have been *G*."

Like G2, this does not rule that "All emeralds are grue" is confirmed by its instances, if we can allow that our data contain the proposition "There is a property, namely *being examined*, such that the emeralds in the data have been examined, and had they not been examined, they would not have been grue." It has the further merit of being consistent with transparency: Whether or not a body of data confirms a hypothesis depends only on the body and the hypothesis themselves, and not on other, perhaps inaccessible, facts. However, it has the apparently dubious feature that smaller bodies of data can confirm more than can larger bodies.

To see how this works, imagine two people, both confronted with pink boiled lobsters, and both concerned to consider the question of whether their data confirm "All lobsters are pink." One person does not realize that all the lobsters he has seen have been boiled, or else does not realize that boiling them affects their color. If G3 is correct, that person's data do confirm the hypothesis "All lobsters are pink." The other person, by contrast, knows that the lobsters would not have been pink had they not been boiled. G3 does not entail that that person's data confirm the hypothesis that all lobsters are pink. If you know more, your data may confirm less.

This feature is one that should come as no surprise. A body of data full of instances of a generalization, and containing no counter-instances, may confirm the generalization, though the same body enriched by a counterinstance would not. Still, G3 needs refinement. For one thing, it still leads, in conjunction with E1, to the Ravens Paradox.[34] For another thing, we need to relax it a little, as the following example shows.

Suppose you find, year after year, that although all the other vegetables in your garden are attacked by pests, your leeks are always pest-free. Would it be reasonable to conclude that leeks are immune to pests? Let us suppose that you know no proposition to the effect that your leeks would not have been healthy had they not possessed some property *P*. According to G3, the hypothesis that all leeks are immune to pests is confirmed by your data; but I think that we should not, in fact, put much confidence in the hypothesis, given the data. Even if one knows no proposition of the relevant kind, one may strongly suspect that *there is* one, even though one does not know it. One knows in a general way that susceptibility to pests is likely to be affected by such factors as the nature of the soil, how strongly the plant grows, and what other vegetation is around. Even though your data do not include a proposition that selects a factor that explains the pest-free quality of your leeks, you might well believe that *there* is a proposition of this kind. If so, you should not put much faith in the hypothesis that all leeks, including those grown in very different conditions, are immune to pests.

If it is to deliver the results we want in such cases, the proviso in G3 must be understood in such a way that:

(a) The data must not contain even the proposition that *there is* a proposition to the effect that the *F*'s are *G* only in virtue of being *H*; and

(b) The background information in general, and this in particular, do not have to be *known* or be *certain*.

All other things being equal, the fact that we think it quite *likely* that there are conditions under which leeks suffer from pests is enough to diminish, or even perhaps cancel, the confirmatory impact of our pest-free leeks. I shall assume that these modifications to G3 have been made.

G3 entails that the hypothesis that all emeralds are grue *is* confirmed by the data consisting just of propositions of the form "This is an emerald," "This has been examined," and so on; but it does not entail that this hypothesis is confirmed by the body of data, including background information, that we in fact possess. That body of data includes the proposition that the examined emeralds would not have been grue had they not been examined; that is, it includes a proposition of the form "There is a property H (*having been examined*) such that the emeralds would not have been grue had they not had *H*."

The Grue Paradox has been held to have more distant ramifications. To gesture toward these, let us consider a corollary that Goodman stresses:

Regularities are where you find them, and you can find them anywhere.

The old idea – found, for example, in Hume – was that the reasoning from experience that we take to be legitimate is that in which we extrapolate regularities obtaining within our experience to portions of the world that lie outside our experience. One thing that Goodman's "grue" shows is that this is, at best, a highly incomplete account. The question is: What is to count as a regularity? The regular connection between being an emerald and being green? *And* the regular connection between being an emerald and being grue? Our original problem reemerges in this form: Either we can give no account of what a regularity is, in which case the account that uses the notion is useless; or else we give an account of regularity that includes the undesirable emerald – grue regularity as well as the desirable emerald – green one.

This relatively narrow point about confirmation suggests a deeper metaphysical one: that whether a series of events counts as a regularity depends upon how we choose to describe it. This has suggested to some a quite thoroughgoing conventionalism, according to which there is no separating how the world is in itself from the conventions we bring to bear in describing and classifying it. To others, it has had the effect of deepening their skepticism about the legitimacy of inductive reasoning. If there are endless regularities that we could have extrapolated, what makes it rational to pick on the ones we in fact do? It is bad enough having to justify extrapolating a regularity, but it is worse when one must, in addition, justify selecting one rather than any of the countless other regularities in the data to extrapolate. To yet others, the Grue Paradox has suggested that there is something quite undetermined, at least at the individual level, about our concepts. Wittgenstein asked us to consider someone who, having added 2 to numbers all the way up to 1,000, continues this way – 1,004, 1,008, . . . – and yet protests that he is "going on in the same way." We could define a gruelike operator "+*" as follows: $x +^* 2 = x + 2$, if $x < 1,000$; otherwise $x +^* 2 = x + 4$. It has been suggested that there are no facts, or at least no individual facts, that make it true of us that we use concepts like *green* and + rather than concepts like *grue* and $+^*$.

The impact of grue thus goes well beyond the problems of finding a nonparadoxical account of our notion of confirmation.

2. The Unexpected Examination

The teacher tells the class that sometime during the next week she will give an examination. She will not say on which day for, she says, she wants it to be a surprise. On the face of it, there is no reason why the teacher, despite having made this announcement, should not be able to do exactly what she has announced: give the class an unexpected examination. It will not be totally unexpected, since the class will know, or at least have good reason to believe, that it will occur sometime during the next week. However, surely it could be unexpected in this sense: that on the morning of the day on which it is given, the class will have no good reason to believe that it will occur on *that* day, even though they knew, or had good reason to believe, the teacher's announcement. Cannot the teacher achieve this aim by, say, giving the examination on Wednesday?

The class reasons as follows. Let us suppose that the teacher will carry out her threat, in both its parts: That is, she will give an examination, and it will be unexpected. Then the teacher cannot give the examination on Friday (assuming this to be the last possible day of the week); for, by the time Friday morning arrives, and we know that all the previous days have been examination-free, we would have every reason to expect the examination to occur on Friday. So leaving the examination until Friday is inconsistent with giving an *unexpected* examination. For similar reasons, the examination cannot be held on Thursday. Given our previous conclusion that it cannot be delayed until Friday, we would know, when Thursday morning came, and the previous days had been examination-free, that it would have to be held on Thursday. So if it were held on Thursday, it would not be unexpected. Thus it cannot be held on Thursday. Similar reasoning supposedly shows that there is no day of the week on which it can be held, and so supposedly shows that the supposition that the teacher can carry out her threat must be rejected. This is paradoxical, for it seems plain that the teacher *can* carry out her threat.

Something must be wrong with the way in which the class reasoned; but what?

The class's argument falls into two parts: One applies to whether there can be an unexpected examination on the last day, Friday; the other takes forward the negative conclusion on this issue, and purports to extend it to the other days.

Let us begin by looking more closely at the first part. On Friday morning, the possibilities can be divided up as follows:

(a)   The examination will take place on Friday and the class will expect this.

(b)   The examination will take place on Friday and the class will not expect this.

(c)   The examination will not take place on Friday and the class will expect this.

(d)   The examination will not take place on Friday and the class will not expect this.

When we speak of the class's expectations, we mean their rational or well-grounded ones. It is not to the point that they may have expectations to which they are not entitled, or lack expectations to which they are entitled. For example, it is not to the point that the class might irrationally (without entitlement or justification) believe that the examination would take on Wednesday. Even if it then did take place on Wednesday, this would not show that the teacher's announcement was false, for she said that the class would have *no good reason* to believe it would occur when it did.

The overall structure of the class's argument is meant to be a *reductio ad absurdum*: They take as a supposition that the teacher's announce-

ment is true, then aim to show that this leads to a contradiction, and hence that the supposition must be rejected. In this first part of the argument, the supposition is used to show that the examination cannot occur on Friday. This is extended to every day of the week in the second part of the argument, so that, in the end, the supposition is rejected. Thus the teacher's announcement is disproved.

Given that the examination has not occurred on the previous days, at most possibility (b) is consistent with the truth of the teacher's announcement. The class's argument aims to show that (b) is not a real possibility.

The idea is that the class can infer that if the examination occurs on Friday, then the announcement is false, contrary to the supposition. The inference is based on the consideration that the class will know that Friday is the last possible day for the examination. So, given the supposition that the teacher's announcement is true, they would expect the examination, were it to occur on Friday; but this is inconsistent with the truth of the announcement. If we hold on to the supposition, the examination cannot take place on Friday.

That this argument is not straightforward can be brought out by the following. Imagine yourself in the class, and it is Friday morning. There is surely a real question, which you may well feel that you do not know how to answer: Has the teacher forgotten or changed her mind, or will the examination indeed take place that day? It would seem that this doubt is enough to ensure that if it does take place that day, it will be unexpected: The class was not entitled to expect it.

The class's argument is meant to circumvent this difficulty by using the truth of the teacher's announcement as a supposition – one that, in the end, is going to be rejected. Given this supposition, the class on Friday morning can rule out the nonoccurrence of the examination. On the other hand, it can also rule out its occurrence – and this is what is meant to show that, if the supposition is true, the examination cannot occur on Friday.

However, it is a mistake to think that the supposition merely of the *truth* of the teacher's announcement will do the required work. To see this, imagine ourselves once more among the class on Friday morning. Suppose that the teacher's announcement is true but that we do not know or even believe this. Then we may not believe that the examination will occur. This is enough to make the truth of the announcement possible: If the examination does occur, we shall not have expected it. This shows a fallacy in the reasoning as so far presented. Merely supposing, for *reductio*, that the teacher's announcement is true is not enough to establish that the examination will not be held on Friday. At that point in the argument, we need as a supposition that we *know* that the teacher's announcement is true.[35]

If we are to have a paradoxical argument worth discussing, we need to make some changes. There are various ways in which one could do this; I shall consider two. The details are quite complicated: To make the discussion manageable, we shall soon need to use some abbreviations.

One modification we could make is to leave the announcement unchanged but alter the structure of the argument. Instead of taking the announcement itself as our supposition, we shall suppose that the class *knows* the truth of the announcement. This supposition is refutable, on Friday, by the considerations outlined. If on Friday we know that the announcement is true, we know that the examination will occur on Friday. If we know that the examination will occur on Friday, the announcement is not true. If the announcement is not true, then we do not know that it is true. The supposition that we know that it is true entails its own falsehood, and so can be rejected. Applying similar reasoning to the other days of the week, the upshot would be that the class can show that it cannot *know* that the announcement is true. This may seem paradoxical: Intuitively, we want to say that we knew, from the announcement, that there would be an examination sometime, though we did not know when, and so it was unexpected.

An alternative modification involves changing the announcement to include the fact that the class will not know, on the basis of the announcement, that the examination will take place on the day that it does. In a way that can only be made clear by some abbreviations, this will give us a valid argument for the conclusion that the announcement is false. If this is paradoxical, it is because it seems intuitively obvious that such an announcement could be true.

Let us call the original version of the argument OV, the first proposed modified version MV1, and the second propose modified version MV2. Since the number of days of the week is irrelevant, let us simplify by supposing that there are just two possible examination days, Monday or Tuesday. For OV and MV1, I shall abbreviate the announcement as:

A1. I shall give you an examination on either Monday or Tuesday, and you will not know – or have good reason to believe – on the morning of the examination that it will occur that day.

The other abbreviations are as follows:

M for "the examination occurs on Monday";

T for "the examination occurs on Tuesday";

$K_M(\dots)$ for "the class knows on Monday morning that..."; and

$K_T(\dots)$ for "the class knows on Tuesday morning that...."[36]

We can express A1 symbolically as:

$$([M \text{ and not-}K_M(M)] \text{ or } [T \text{ and not-}K_T(T)]) \text{ and not both M and T.}$$

(That is, either there will be an examination on Monday and the class does not know this on Monday morning, or there will be an examination on Tuesday and the class does not know this on Tuesday morning; and there will be an examination on at most one morning.)[37]

OV can be represented as follows:

1. Suppose A1.
   2. Suppose not-M
      3. $K_T(\text{not-M})$ [from 2 + memory]
      4. If not-M, T.   [by the definition of A1]
      5. $K_T(T)$ [from 3 + 4]
      6. If $K_T(T)$ and not-M, then not-A1   [by the definition of A1]
      7. not-A1   [from 2, 5, + 6]
   8. So, still supposing A1, we must conclude that M (and so not-T)
   9. $K_M(M)$ [from 8 + A1]
   10. If $K_M(M)$ and not-T, then not-A1   [definition of A1]
   11. not-A1   [from 8, 9, + 10]
12. not-A1   [from 1 + 11]

The overall shape of the argument is *reductio ad absurdum:* One makes an assumption in order to show that it leads to a contradiction and so must be rejected. In the present case, the supposition of A1 is supposed to lead eventually to the conclusion that A1 is false. (Indentation is used to show that – and how – some steps of the argument occur within the scope of a supposition.)[38] It seems that we intuitively hold that A1 can be true; and that clash constitutes the paradox.

OV suffers from the defect that no adequate justification is provided for step (5). The idea is meant to be this: If A1 is true, then the examination must occur on Tuesday if it does not occur on Monday; so if we knew the examination did not occur on Monday, we would know that it would occur on Tuesday. However, this is not a sound inference: We would also need to *know* that the examination must occur on Tuesday if it does not occur on Monday.[39]

MV1 can be represented as follows:

1. Suppose $K(A1)$
   2. Suppose not-M
      3. K_T(not-M)   [from 2 and memory]
      4. If not-M, T   [by the definition of A1]
      5. K_T(If not-M, T)   [by supposition 1]
      6. K_T(T)   [from 3 + 5]
      7. If K_T(T), then not-A1   [definition of A1]
      8. If not-A1, then not-$K(A1)$ [only the truth is known]
      9. If K_T(T) then not-$K(A1)$ [from 7 + 8]
  10. So, given $K(A1)$, we must conclude that M (and so not-T)
  11. K_M(M)   [from 10][40]
  12. If K_M(M) and M, then not-A1   [definition of A1]
  13. not-A1   [from 10, 11, + 12]
  14. If not-A1, then not-$K(A1)$ [only the truth is known]
  15. not-$K(A1)$ [from 13 + 14]
16. not-$K(A1)$ [from 1 + 15]

Even if MV1 is valid (and footnote 40 gives a reason for doubt on this point), it is questionable whether there is anything paradoxical in this conclusion. To have a paradox, we would need also to have an argument for the conclusion that $K(A1)$. Perhaps it is just intuitively obvious that $K(A1)$, given, if you like, the class's knowledge of the teacher's unimpeachable reputation for veracity and constancy of purpose; but suppose someone failed to share this intuition?

If not-$K(A1)$, then it is very easy for A1 to be true: The class will not on the basis of A1 have any expectations, since the students can establish that they cannot know A1. This gives the teacher plenty of scope for surprising them.

However, the class can also go through the reasoning of the preceding paragraph: "Our proof that A1 cannot be known shows us how easy it is for A1 to be true. If it *can* be true, then, given the teacher's proven veracity and determination, we have every reason to believe that it *is* true." If the class is led by this consideration to believe the announcement, then there is a case for thinking that their belief amounts to knowledge. So it seems that *if* the argument is valid, we have a paradox.[41]

MV2 requires a different announcement:

A2.   Either [M and not-K_M(If A2, then M)] or [T and not-K_T (If A2, then T)].

(That is, the examination will take place on Monday or Tuesday, but you will not know on the basis of this announcement which day it will be.) Notice that A2 differs from A1 in a striking respect: The specification of A2 refers to A2 itself; in other words, A2 is a *self-referential* announcement.

MV2 can be represented as follows:

1. Suppose A2
   2. Suppose not-M
      3. K_T(not-M)   [from (2) + memory]
      4. K_T(If not-M, then if A2, then T)   [the class understands A2]
      5. K_T(If A2, then T)   [from 3 + 4]
      6. not-A2   [from 2 + 5]
   7. M   [from 1, 2, + 6]
   8. If A2, then M   [summarizing 1–7]
   9. K_M(If A2, then M)   [the proved is known]
  10. If K_M(If A2, then M), then if A2, then not-M   [from definition of A2]
  11. If A2, then not-M   [from 9 + 10]
12. not-A2   [from 8 + 11]

MV2 purports to prove that A2 is not true. This is paradoxical only if we have some good reason to think that it is, or could be, true. We seem to have some reason: Have we not all been exposed to such threats of unexpected examinations? The form of A2 admittedly has the self-referential feature already noticed, but it is not clear that this should make any difference. When the teacher says that the examination is to be unexpected, what is clearly intended is that it be unexpected on any basis, including on the basis of this present announcement. So the intuitions that told us that A1 could be true, and could be known, should also tell us that A2 could be true. However, intuition may be less than wholly confident when faced with the validity of MV2.

Using a self-referential type of announcement, one can construct a further announcement, call it A3, that is certainly paradoxical. It has come to be called the Knower Paradox:[42]

A3.   K(not-A3).

(That is, A3 is as follows: "The class knows that this very announcement is false.")

We can represent the argument that establishes both A3 and not-A3 as follows-call it MV3:

1. Suppose A3
   2. K(not-A3)   [definition of A3]
   3. not-A3   [what is known is true]
4. If A3, then not-A3   [summarizing 1–3]
5. not-A3   [from 4]
6. not-K(not-A3)   [from 5 + definition of A3]
7. K(not-A3)   [5 + what is proved is known]

Lines (6) and (7) are contradictory.

In view of this result, we must examine carefully (a) the nature of the announcement and (b) the epistemic principles – the principles involving the nature of knowledge – used to reach the paradoxical conclusion. If there is anything wrong with the principles, then we may have to revise our views about the earlier arguments, for they, too, rest on these principles.

(a) It is important to see that we cannot satisfy ourselves merely by saying that A3 is contradictory. A contradiction is false, whereas A3, if the argument MV3 is sound, is demonstrably true [see line (7)]. More hopeful would be to say that A3 is *unintelligible*, perhaps in part because of its self-referentiality. What, we might ask, does it

say? What is it that it claims cannot be known? If we say it claims that it itself cannot be known, we seem to be grappling in thin air rather than genuinely answering the question.

Some of this doubt might be removed by changing the example. Suppose now that we have two teachers, X and Y. X says "What Y will say next is something you can know to be false." Y then says "What X has just said is true." It looks as though we have to count both utterances as intelligible, since in other contexts they certainly would have been intelligible, and even in this context we can understand X's without knowing what Y will say, and can understand Y's without knowing what X has said. However, in the context Y's announcement appears to be equivalent to A3. We could argue informally for the contradiction like this. Suppose Y is true (let X and Y now also abbreviate the respective teachers' remarks). Then X is true, so you can know Y to be false, so it is false. So the supposition that Y is true leads to the conclusion that it is false. Hence we can conclude that it is false [cf. MV3(5)]. Hence we can conclude that *we can know Y to be false*. However, if Y is false, then X is false; i.e., *we cannot know Y to be false*. So it seems we have an argument that has the essential features of A3, but that is not open to the charge that the announcement is unintelligible.[43]

(b) Let us isolate the epistemic principles concerning knowledge appealed to in MV3. There are three: The first – call it EK1 – is what licenses the move from (2) to (3) in MV3. In its most general form it is that what is known is true. We could write it:

EK1.   If K(φ), then φ.

The other point at which appeal to epistemic principles is made is the move at (7) from (5). It cannot be true that anything that is provable on the basis of no matter what assumptions is knowable. Given as assumption that $5 > 7$, I could perhaps prove that $5 > 6$, but obviously I could not *know* this. So the principle that we need at this point is that anything proved from known assumptions (or from no assumptions) is known.[44] We could write this as:

EK2.   If C is provable from $(P_1, \ldots, P_n)$ and K$(P_1, \ldots, P_n)$, then K(C).

What assumptions (corresponding to P_1, etc.) are in play in the move from (5) to (7)? Just one: EK1. So, in order to apply EK2, we need to add:

EK3.   K(EK1).

Are these three principles plausible? Expressed informally they are the following:

EK1. What is known is true.
EK2. What is provable from things known is known.
EK3. It is known that what is known is true.

The first principle has sometimes been doubted on the grounds that, for example, people once knew that whales were fish; but this doubt is dispelled by the reflection that the correct account of the matter is that people *thought* they knew this, although they really did not. How could they have known it if it is not even true?

EK2 does not hold generally: We do not know all the infinitely many things that could be proved from what we know; we do not even believe all these things, if only because it would be beyond our powers to bring them all to mind. However, this implausible aspect of EK2 is not required for the paradox, which only needs this much narrower claim: that at least one person who has constructed a correct proof of not-A3 from a known premise knows that not-A3.

The third principle cannot be seriously questioned, once we have granted the first. So the only doubt about the premises attaches to EK2. We could circumvent this by using an even weaker and very hard to controvert principle: What is provable from something known is *capable* of being known by a fully rational subject. With appropriate modifications to A3, we shall be able to prove a contradiction from principles that appear indubitable, together with the admission of the intelligibility of the teacher's announcement.[45]

It is very hard to know what to make of this paradox. One promising suggestion sees a similarity between it and the Liar Paradox (see Section 5.2 [of author's book *Paradoxes*]). Knowledge quite clearly involves the notion of truth, and the Liar Paradox shows that this notion can lead to paradox. So perhaps what is at fault in the concept of knowledge is the concept of truth it contains, as displayed in EK1; and perhaps the remedy consists in applying to knowledge whatever nonparadoxical elaboration of the notion of truth we can extract from consideration of the Liar Paradox.

The suggestion cannot be quite right for the following reason. Unlike knowledge, belief does not entail truth; yet a paradox rather like the Knower – we could call it the Believer – can be constructed in terms just of belief. Consider the following:

B_1. α does not believe what B_1 says.[46]

Question: Does α believe B_1, or not? If α does believe B_1, then he can see that he is believing something false. There is no gap between seeing that something is false and not believing it, so if α believes B_1, he does not believe it. Equally, however, if α does not believe B_1, then he can see that B_1 is true. There is no gap between seeing that something is true and believing it, so if α does not believe B_1 he believes it. The paradox depends on at least two assumptions:

1. that α *can* see that, if he believes B_1, it is false, and if he does not believe it, it is true;

2. that what α can see he *will* see.

Neither assumption would be capable of true generalization. For (1) to hold of α requires, among other things, that he be able to see that he is α. One could arguably envisage this not being true, if α had an unusually low level of self-awareness. For (2) to hold of α requires a positive level of intellectual energy: One does not always take advantage of one's epistemic opportunities. However, we have a paradox if we can make the following highly plausible assumption: that there is at least one person with the self-awareness and energy required to make (1) and (2) true of him (or her).

We can represent the argument to the contradiction, and the assumptions upon which it depends, in a manner analogous to the representation of the Knower Paradox.[47] We abbreviate "α believes that ( )" as "B( )"; then $B_1 = \text{not-}B(B_1)$.

1. Suppose $B(B_1)$
2. If $B(B_1)$, then $B[B(B_1)]$ [self-awareness]
3. $B[B(B_1)]$ [from 1 + 2]
4. B [If B_1, then not-$B(B_1)$]   [α understands B_1]
5. If $B[B(B_1)]$, then not-$B[\text{not-}B(B_1)]$ [rationality]
6. not-$B[\text{not-}B(B_1)]$ [from 3 + 5]
7. not-$B(B_1)$ [4, 6, + closure]
8. If $B(B_1)$, then not-$B(B_1)$ [summarizing 1–7]
9. not-$B(B_1)$ [from 8]
10. $B[\text{not-}B(B_1)]$.   [from 9 + self-awareness]
11. $B(B_1)$ [from 10 + definition of B_1]

The unconditionally derived lines (9) and (11) are contradictory.

Let us examine the assumptions upon which the argument depends. The first principle to be used is what I have called "self-awareness." In its most general form it could be represented as follows:

EB1. If B(φ), then B[B (φ)].

This is not very plausible. If it were true, then having one belief, say φ, would involve having infinitely many: that you believe that φ, that you believe you believe that φ, and so on. However, all that is required for the paradox are two instances of EB1: that if α believes B_1, under circumstances that can be as favorable as you like to self-awareness, then he will believe he does so; and if α does not believe B_1, then he will believe he does not. It seems impossible to deny that there could be a person of whom this is true.

The second assumption is that α understands B_1 and therefore realizes (and so believes), from the definition of B_1, that if B_1, then not-B(B_1). Again, it seems impossible to deny that there could be a person who has this belief.

Next comes the principle called rationality. A generalization would be the following:

EB2. If B(φ) then not-B(not-φ).

Put so generally, this is not plausible, since people in fact have contradictory beliefs without realizing it; but we need only impute a fairly modest degree of rationality to α in order for the premise needed at line (5) to obtain.

A generalization of the closure principle is this:

EB3. If B(if φ, then ψ) and B(not-ψ), then B(not-φ).

For normal persons, this is not a plausible principle: We do not believe all the consequences of things we believe. However, it again seems easy to imagine that α verifies the particular case of the principle needed in the above argument.

Let us step back. A suggestion was that the Knower Paradox should be treated like the Liar Paradox, on the grounds that knowledge entails truth, and the Liar Paradox shows that the notion of truth requires special treatment. The point of introducing the Believer Paradox was to challenge this suggestion. Belief does not entail truth, yet belief gives rise to a paradox quite similar to the Knower.

The conclusion is that the reason given for treating the Knower and the Liar in similar ways is deficient.

Notes

1 Q: Suppose that on Monday you are penniless and starving, but that on Tuesday you win $1,000,000 in a betting pool. Do you think that the number 5 can be used to measure the utility of $5 to you on each of these days?

2 Q: Suppose you have four courses of action open to you, (a)–(d), associated with rewards as follows: (a) $1, (b) $6, (c) $10,000, (d) $10,005. Do you think that the number 5 can be used to measure both the difference between the utilities of (a) and (b) and the difference between the utilities of (c) and (d)?

3 Q: Discuss the following view:

Although people want things other than money, we can nevertheless measure how much they want things in numerical terms, by finding out how much they would be willing to pay, supposing, perhaps *per impossibile*, that what they want could be bought. If a man says he wants a happy love affair, we can measure the utility of this upshot to him by finding out how much money he would be willing to give up to get what he wants. Would he give up his car? His house? His job? All that is needed is the ability to imagine things being other than they are: to imagine that things that in fact cannot be bought can be bought.

4 Q: Could the MEU principle register a general dislike of gambling, as opposed to other ways of spending money? If so, how?

5 In more detail, the expected utility of an action is calculated as follows. First, you determine the possible outcomes O_i. Each is associated with a probability, conditional upon doing A, and a utility. The expected utility of an *outcome*, relative to an action A, is the product of its utility and its probability given A. The expected utility of an action A is the sum of the expected utilities of its outcomes relative to A:

$$EU(A) = [\text{prob}(O_1/A)U(O_1)] + [\text{prob}(O_2/A)U(O_2)] + \cdots$$

Here $EU(A)$ stands for the expected utility of A, prob(O_i/A) for the probability of outcome O_i given A, and $U(O_i)$ for the utility of that outcome. Applied to Newcomb's paradox, using B for the action of opening only box B, and $A\&B$ for the action of opening both boxes, we have:

$$EU(B) = [\text{prob}(B \text{ is empty}/B)U(B \text{ is empty})] + [\text{prob}(B \text{ is full}/B)U(B \text{ is full})]$$
$$= (1 - h)0 + h\,1,000,000.$$
$$EU(A\&B) = [\text{prob}(B \text{ is empty}/A\&B) \times U(B \text{ is empty and } A \text{ is full})] + [\text{prob}(B \text{ is full}/A\&B) \times U(B \text{ is full and } A \text{ is full})]$$
$$= h1,000 + [(1 - h)1,001,000].$$

Setting $h = 0.9$ makes $EU(B) = 900,000$ and $EU(A\&B) = 101,100$, giving a nearly ninefold advantage to taking just box B.

Here I have taken for granted the notion of the probability an agent associates with an upshot. How is this probability determined, and how analyzed? My own preference is for the pioneering account in Ramsey [1926]. However, the reader should consult Jeffrey [1965]; and, for wider applications of probability, Kyburg [1961] and Levi [1967].

6 If you think that the arguments for one-boxing and for two-boxing are equally compelling, then you could see this as refuting the story (as in the case of the Barber). That is, you could see the unacceptable consequence as showing that there could not be a being capable of predicting free choices. For this line, see Schlesinger [1974]. See also a critical discussion by Benditt and Ross [1976], which makes some important distinctions.

7 Q: How would you respond to the following argument?

It would come as wonderful news to learn that I am one-boxer, for then I will be able to infer that I will soon be rich. However, I can give myself that news simply by deciding to be a one-boxer. So this is what I should decide to do.

8 Q: We have envisaged the choice before you being a once-in-a-lifetime chance. However, suppose you know that you were going to be allowed to make this choice once a week for the rest of your life, and suppose the facts about the Predictor remain the same. What is the most rational policy to pursue?

9 Q: Consider a variant of the problem – let us call it the "sequential Newcomb." The difference is that you are allowed to make your choice in two stages: You can elect to open box B, reserving your choice about box A until you find out what is in box B. Suppose you open B and there is nothing inside. Should you elect also to open A? Suppose you open B and there is $1,000,000 inside. Should you elect also to open A? Do your answers have any implications for the original Newcomb?

10 Q: Consider a variant in which he has *mostly* been right in the past. Would this make any difference to the argument? Try working out what the MEU commends if we set the probability of the Predictor being right at 0.6.

11 Q: What are your own views on this point? Some people say that they wish they could believe in life after death. If this wish involves wishing that they could cease to be moved by the evidence *against* life after death, it is an example of the sort of desire whose reasonableness or rationality is in question.

12 Human frailty being what it is, no doubt social pressures would, in the envisaged circumstances, make one-boxers of all but the stoutest of us. This does not touch the question of what the *rational* course of action in such circumstances would be.

13 Q: Consider some familiar gambling game (e.g., roulette or poker). Can DP be used to say which bets in your selected game are rational? Assume that the only aim is to win as much money as possible.

14 Q: Israel is wondering whether to withdraw from territories it occupies. Egypt is wondering whether or not to go to war with Israel. From Israel's point of view, the utilities are as follows:

	Egypt declares war	Egypt does not declare war
Israel withdraws	0	2
Israel remains	1	3

Show how this example can be used to demonstrate that DP does not always give correct results. (See Bar-Hillel and Margalit [1972]).

15 One could capture this by saying that the relevant probability, for a correct MEU, is not the conditional probability of an outcome upon an action, but rather the unconditional probability of a statement of the form "If I were to act thus, this would be the outcome." This so-called counterfactual conditional requires for its truth something approaching the relation between act and upshot mentioned in the text: The act should *produce* the upshot. Compare Gibbard and Harper [1978].

16 Q: How would you respond to the following argument?

The dominance principle DP cannot conflict with the MEU principle, if by this is meant that there is a situation in which an action with maximum expected utility would fail to be preferred by the dominance principle. For any upshot, the probability of its occurring is the same regardless of the action, so the only relevant fact, for each upshot, is the utility. So MEU and DP cannot diverge. The table makes this plain:

	P_1	$P2$
A_1	5	2
A_2	4	2

A_1 and A_2 are actions open to you. The possible outcomes are P_1 and P_2. If you do A_1 and P_1 is the outcome, your utility is measured by the number 5. Likewise for the other cells in the table. The dominance principle commends A_1 in preference to A_2. The MEU either does likewise or else is indifferent between A_1 and A_2 and in either case the principles do not conflict. To show this, let us call the agent's probabilities of P_1 and P_2 respectively π_1 and π_2. We do not know what these values are, but we can be sure that $5 \times \pi_1$ is greater than $4 \times \pi_1$, and that $2 \times \pi_2$

is not greater than $2 \times \pi_2$. So MEU must either commend A_1 or else be neutral.

17 Compare: How could it be rational to be a two-boxer, if being a one-boxer would ensure that one would be a millionaire?

18 Q: Clarify the assumption behind the remark that if two people are rational, then for any problem both will reason about it in similar ways. Is the assumption justifiable?

19 Q: Using the numbers in the table in the text as the utilities of the various outcomes (prefix each with a minus sign to show that the outcomes are mostly undesirable), how could you assign conditional probabilities (using numbers between 0 and 1) in such a way as to make the expected utility of silence higher than that of confession? [For details, you may find it useful to refer to footnote 5 above.] Your assignment will justify the sentence in the text.

20 Q: Suppose, however, that all parties know in advance how many times they will be in this situation – fifty times, say. How would you state the case for the view that the most rational policy is always to confess?

21 Q: There are generalizations of which one could not be sure that one had encountered all the instances. What are some examples?

22 Q: Victims of the so-called Monte Carlo fallacy dispute this. They hold that the longer the run of successive reds on a fair roulette wheel the *less* likely it is that red will come up on the next spin. What, if anything, is wrong with this view? Is there anything right about it?

23 Q: How might answering this question fail to show that inductive reasoning is sometimes legitimate, and thus fail to be a complete answer to the problem of justification?

24 I should note a departure from Hempel's formulation – and his is the formulation used in almost all discussions. The equivalence relation he uses is that of *logical* equivalence, not *a priori* equivalence. Two proportions are logically equivalent just on condition that some system of formal logical has a theorem saying that either both propositions are true, or else both are false. Thus "Tom is a bachelor" and "Tom is a bachelor or the earth is round or not-round" are logically equivalent, but "Tom is a bachelor" and "Tom is an unmarried man" are not logically equivalent (though they can be known a priori to be equivalent). The intuitive motivation for the equivalence principle is this, in my view: If P and Q are in the appropriate sense equivalent, then if we can find evidence supporting P, we need no further empirical data to see that Q is thereby supported to the same extent. If this motivation is accepted, it seems clear that the appropriate equivalence relation is wider than logical equivalence, and is precisely, a priori equivalence.

25 The proof of equivalence may seem incomplete: The definition of equivalence also required that if R2 is true, so is R1, and if R2 is false, so is R1; yet these issues were not explicitly addressed. However, classical logic has it that, for any propositions P and Q, the truth of
  If P is false, then Q is false
ensures the truth of
  if Q is true, then P is true.
Likewise classical logic has it that the truth of
  If P is true, then Q is true
ensures the truth of
  If Q is false, then P is false.
Given these implications of classical logic, what is said in the text *does* establish the equivalence of R1 and R2.

26 Q: How does this follow?

27 There has been controversy about how Goodman defines "grue." He writes that "grue" is to be introduced so that:
  it applies to all things examined before t just in case they are green but to other things just in case they are blue.(1955, p. 74)
The time t is arbitrary, and was introduced on Goodman's previous page. In giving my account, I have imagined ourselves being at that time. For discussion of some alternative interpretations, see Jackson [1975].

28 Goodman [1955]. p. 74:
  although we are well aware which of the two incompatible predictions [sic., "All emeralds subsequently examined will be green," "All emeralds subsequently examined will be grue"] is genuinely confirmed, they are equally well confirmed according to our definition [of confirmation – a definition close to G1].

29 Q: An alternative presentation of the paradox identifies the apparently unacceptable conclusion as being that the same body of data can confirm the *inconsistent* hypotheses that all emeralds are green and that all emeralds are grue. Is it unthinkable that a body of data should confirm inconsistent hypotheses?

30 We could rework the paradox using "gives good reason to believe" rather than "confirms." Our observations of emeralds, we suppose, give us good reason to believe that all emeralds are green. "Parity of reasoning" seems to require that our observations of emeralds also give us good reason to believe that they are all grue. If we tried to identify what this parity of reasoning consisted in, we would no doubt finger G1 or some very similar principle.

31 For his discussion of the problem, see Goodman [1955], esp. p. 97ff. Goodman's theory of entrenchment is more sophisticated than my very brief mention of it would suggest.

32 Cf. Jackson [1975]. It is no doubt true that Goodman's overall project would preclude him from accepting this version of G2 because it contains a subjunctive conditional ("If it had not been that . . . , it would not have been that . . . ").

However, the current project is simply to address what I have called the problem of characterization (section 1.1), and it is unclear that any prohibition upon the use of subjunctive conditionals attends this project.

33 Q: How would G2 need to be modified for it to rule that, in this variant lobster case, our data do *not confirm* the generalization?

34 Q: How can one "prove" the Ravens Paradox using G3 rather than G1?

35 This point is made by Quine [1953].

36 I offer no view about whether believing or knowing are to be properly represented by an operator or by a predicate. Those who prefer the operator treatment will have to read "A1," as it occurs in the formal argument, as short for "A1 is true." Those who prefer the predicate treatment will have to read various expressions within the scope of K as names of (equiform) expressions, rather than as expressions in use. It may be worth reminding those familiar with these matters that Montague and Kaplan [1960] present the paradox using the predicate treatment to avert the suspicion that operators are to blame (see p. 272). Asher and Kamp [1986] take the Knower Paradox (discussed later in this section) to bear essentially on the question of what is the appropriate account of propositional attitude constructions.

37 Q: Would it be better to have A1 abbreviate the following? (M or T) and not-K_M(M) and not-K_T(T)?

38 I hope that the intended structure of the argument will be self-explanatory, but some observations may be useful for those unused to seeing arguments presented in this sort of way. What is the difference between lines (7), (11), and (12)? Each has the same conclusion, but it has been reached from different suppositions. At (7), as the extra indent shows, the argument claims that we have reached *not-A1* on the basis of supposing that A1 is true and that not-M is true. This would mean that we have reached a contradiction: Since anything entails itself, the supposition of both A1 and not-M leads to the contradiction that A1 and not-A1. We must therefore reject at least one of these. Line (8) claims that if we hold on to A1, we must reject not-M (equivalently, T). At line (11), *not-A1* depends only on the supposition of A1 itself. In other words, at this point we have shown that A1 entails its own negation. This is enough to show that, on the basis of *no* suppositions at all, we can infer the falsehood of A1, since anything entailing its own negation is false, and this is what (12), by having *no* indent, expresses.

39 Q: Does this criticism also apply to (9)?

40 The argument is suspect at this point. We have supposedly proved M [at (10)] on the basis of K(A1). It is quite plausible to hold that this

means that we can know the corresponding conditional, viz.:
If K(A1), then M.
However, to obtain K_M(M) from K[If K(A1), then M] would appear to require as a premise not merely K(A1), but K[K(A1)]. We should avoid obtaining the latter by the dubious schema:
If K(φ), then K[K(φ)].
However, it could be argued that, in the envisaged case, K(A1) would ensure K[K(A1)]: Nothing relevant to whether the class knows A1 would be unknown to it. Q: Why is this last principle—if K(φ), then K[K(ϕ)]—dubious?

41 Once one starts thinking about knowledge, one can rather easily convince oneself that there is less of it than one might have thought. So I would not be surprised if someone were to say, "We could not *know* that the teacher would carry out her threat, however reliable we knew her to have been in the past. The most we would be entitled to is the justified belief that she would."

   Q: Rework MV1 in terms of justified belief rather than knowledge. (You will probably find you have to make an inference from "It was rational for the class to believe the teacher's announcement when it was made" to "It would be rational for the class to believe the teacher's announcement on the morning of the last day, if the exam had not yet been given.") (Is this inference sound? Is the parallel inference in the case of knowledge sound? At what points was it assumed in the arguments displayed above?

42 Cf. Montague and Kaplan [1960]. A similar paradox is in Buridan's Sophism 13; see Hughes [1982].

43 Compare a similar line of argument in Burge [1978], p. 30.

44 Compare with the principle sometimes called "epistemic closure":
If K(if φ, then Ψ) and K(φ), then K(Ψ).
Q: Is EK2 is entailed by the closure principle? Does the converse entailment hold?

45 Q: Provide the modified A3 (call it A4) and the appropriate argument, setting out the epistemic principles in detail.

46 A version of the Believer analogous to the "What I am now saying is false" version of the Liar would be as follows:
The person now reading this sentence does not believe what it says.

47 For a different version of the argument, see Burge [1978], esp. p. 29.

References

Asher, Nicholas M., and Kamp, Johan A. W. [1986] "The knower paradox and representational theories of the attitudes." In J. Halpern, ed. *Theoretical Aspects of Reasoning about Knowledge*. Morgan Kaufman, New York, pp. 131–148.

Bar-Hillel, Maya, and Margalit, Avishai [1972] "Newcomb's paradox revisited." *British Journal for Philosophy of Science* 23: 295–304.

Benditt, T. M., and Ross, David J. [1976] "Newcomb's paradox." *British Journal for the Philosophy of Science* 27: 161–4.

Burge, Tyler [1978] "Buridan and epistemic paradox." *Philosophical Studies* 34: 21–35.

Gibbard, A., and Harper, W. L. [1978] "Counterfactuals and two kinds of expected utility." In C. A. Hooker, J. J. Leach, and E. F. McClennen, eds. *Foundations and Applications of Decision Theory*, vol. 1. Reidel, Dordrecht, pp. 125–162.

Goodman, Nelson [1955] *Fact, Fiction and Forecast*. Harvard University Press, Cambridge, MA.; 2nd ed., Bobbs-Merrill, Indianapolis, 1965.

Hempel, Carl [1945] *Aspects of Scientific Explanation and Other Essays in the Philosophy of Science*. The Free Press, New York. Reprint ed., 1965.

Hughes, G. E., ed. and trans. [1982] *John Buridan on Self-Reference*. Cambridge University Press, Cambridge & New York. This work by Buridan was originally entitled *Sophismata*.

Jackson, Frank [1975] "Grue." *Journal of Philosophy* 72: 113–131.

Jeffrey, Richard C. [1965] *The Logic of Decision*. McGraw-Hill, New York.

Kyburg, Henry [1961] *Probability and the Logic of Rational Belief*. Wesleyan University Press, Middletown, CT.

Levi, Isaac [1967] *Gambling with Truth*. RKP, London.

Montague, Richard, and Kaplan, David [1960] "A paradox regained." *Notre Dame Journal of Formal Logic* 1: 79–90.

Nozick, R. [1969] "Newcomb's problem and two principles of choice." In Nicholas Rescher, ed. *Essays in Honor of Carl G. Hempel*. Reidel, Dordrecht.

Quine, Willard van O. [1953] "On a so-called paradox." *Mind* 62: 65–67.

Ramsey, Frank P. [1926] "The foundations of mathematics." Reprinted in D. H. Mellor, ed. *Foundations*. Humanities Press, Atlantic Highlands, NJ. 1978, pp. 152–212.

Schlesinger, G. [1974] "The unpredictability of free choice." *British Journal for the Philosophy of Science* 25: 209–221.

Section 2: Fallacies and Rationality

Chapter 5: When Rationality Fails

JON ELSTER

1. Introduction

There are two ways in which theories can fail to explain: through indeterminacy and through inadequacy. A theory is indeterminate when and to the extent that it fails to yield unique predictions. It is inadequate when its predictions fail. Of these, the second is the more serious problem. A theory may be less than fully determinate and yet have explanatory power if it excludes at least one abstractly possible event or state of affairs. To yield a determinate prediction, it must then be supplemented by other considerations. The theory is weak, but not useless. It is in more serious trouble if an event or state of affairs that actually materializes is among those excluded by the theory. In saying this, I am not espousing naïve falsificationism, but simply making the common-sense observation that it is worse for a theory to predict wrongly than to predict weakly but truthfully.[1] In the former case it must be replaced or modified, not supplemented.

My concern here is not with scientific theories in general, but with failures of rational-choice theory. As argued below, rational-choice theory is first and foremost a normative theory and only secondarily an explanatory approach. It tells people how to act and predicts that they will act in the way it tells them to. To the extent that it fails to give unambiguous prescriptions, it is indeterminate. To the extent that people fail to follow its prescriptions – to the extent, that is, that they behave irrationally – the theory is inadequate. In this book as a whole, the emphasis is on the indeterminacy of rational-choice theory.[2] The inadequacy of the theory is also a constant theme, closely intertwined with that of indeterminacy. I argue, in fact, that failure to recognize the indeterminacy of rational-choice theory can lead to irrational behaviour.

Let me sketch, as a foil to the later discussion, how the problems of indeterminacy and inadequacy arise in another normative domain – the theory of distributive justice. My point of departure will be John Rawls's view that theories of distributive justice are constrained by data, namely people's intuitions about particular moral problems.[3] Any theory of justice can be judged, therefore, by the criteria of determinacy and adequacy. A theory of justice is determinate if it allows us to tell, at least in principle, how a given allocation problem should be resolved.[4] It is adequate if its prescriptions about particular cases correspond to our considered intuitions about these cases. In addition, of course, the theory must be independently plausible – that is, correspond to some general moral principle that can be defended in abstraction from particular cases.

Among the major theories of justice, utilitarianism and Robert Nozick's theory are intended to be determinate. Rawls's theory is explicitly not advanced with this intention. It is concerned only with the justice of the basic structure of society,[5] not with justice in particular contexts such as the allocation of scarce medical resources or the selection of soldiers for military service. For such problems, the theory has to be supplemented by local principles. I believe, although the argument cannot be made here,[6] that none of the major theories is adequate. Each yields consequences that are strongly counterintuitive,[7] even when we allow intuitions to be refined and modified pari passu with the construction of the theory. They stand in need of being replaced rather than supplemented.

These remarks are also relevant to the methodology of rational choice. Like the theory of justice, the theory of rational choice is constrained at both ends. On the one hand, the notion of rationality has to be independently plausible as a normative account of human behaviour. On the other hand, it has to yield prescriptions about particular cases that fit our preanalytical notions about what is rational in such cases. As in the case of justice, these notions are somewhat elastic. As we construct a theory of what is rational, some intuitions about what is rational in particular contexts may change. In particular, theory may force determinacy on our intuitions in situations where initially they were indeterminate. The theoretical notion of an equilibrium, for instance, can serve as a guide to intuition and action when otherwise we would not know what to think or to do. Other, more recalcitrant intuitions can force us to modify the theory.[8]

In what follows, I first set out the bare bones of rational-choice theory (2), including a discussion of whether desires can be rational. I then consider failures of rationality that are due to a lack of determinacy (3) and go on to discuss failures due to a lack of adequacy (4). In the final section (5), I briefly discuss how rationality can be supplemented or replaced by other guides to action. In chapter IV of *Solomonic Judgements*, the same issues are examined with respect to political choices.

2. Rational Action

As I said, rational-choice theory is first and foremost normative.[9] It tells us what we ought to do in order to achieve our aims as well as possible. It does not, in the standard version, tell us what our aims ought to be. (Some nonstandard comments on this problem are offered later.) From the normative account, we can derive an explanatory theory by assuming that people are rational in the normatively appropriate sense. The privileged, but not exclusive status of this assumption is discussed in 5.

The central explananda of rational-choice theory are *actions*. To explain an action, we must first verify that it stands in an optimizing relationship to the desires and beliefs of the agent. The action should be the best way of satisfying the agent's desires, given his beliefs. Moreover, we must demand that these desires and beliefs be themselves rational. At the very least, they

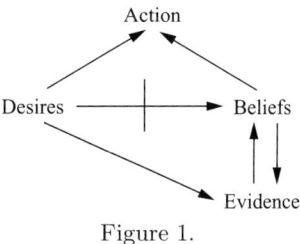

Figure 1.

must be internally consistent. With respect to beliefs, we must also impose a more substantive requirement of rationality: they should be optimally related to the evidence available to the agent. (The substantive rationality of desires is discussed later.) In forming their beliefs, the agents should consider all and only the relevant evidence, with no element being unduly weighted. As a logical extension of this requirement, we also demand that the collection of evidence itself be subject to the canons of rationality. The efficacy of action may be destroyed both by the gathering of too little evidence and by the gathering of too much. The optimal amount of evidence is determined partly by our desires: more important decisions make it rational to collect more evidence. It is determined partly by our prior beliefs about the likely cost, quality and relevance of various types of evidence. Schematically, these relations can be represented as in Figure 1.

Rational action, then, involves three optimizing operations: finding the best action, for given beliefs and desires; forming the best-grounded belief, for given evidence; and collecting the right amount of evidence, for given desires and prior beliefs. Here, desires are the unmoved movers, reflecting Hume's dictum that 'reason is, and ought only to be the slave of the passions'.[10] Hume did not mean that reason ought to obey every whim and fancy of the passions. In particular, he would not have endorsed the direct shaping of reason by passion found in wishful thinking, illustrated by the blocked arrow in the diagram. To serve his master well, a slave must have some independence of execution; beliefs born of passion serve passion badly.[11]

It follows from this sketch that rational-choice theory can go wrong at three levels, and that in each case the failure may be due either to indeterminacy or to irrationality. There may not exist a uniquely optimal action, belief or amount of evidence. Or people may fail to carry out the action, form the belief or collect the evidence as rationality requires them to do. Such failures of rationality are discussed in 3 and 4. Here I want to consider whether one can impose substantive rationality conditions on the desires of the agent.[12] The first idea that comes to mind is that it is rational to have the desires and emotions having which tends to make one happy. The proposal, however, turns out to be flawed.

To have a strong desire for something that is manifestly out of reach can make one desperately unhappy. Sometimes it seems natural to say that desires such as this are irrational. A person with moderate means who is tormented by desires for expensive luxury goods might well be called irrational. But we would not usually say that a person who lives in a totalitarian regime is irrational if he does not get rid of the desires for freedom that makes him deeply miserable.[13] Human beings are more than happiness machines:

Example 1. Psychiatric treatment of Soviet dissidents. The Serbsky Institute for Forensic Psychiatry in Moscow has become notorious for its treatment of political dissidents as mentally ill. 'Some psychiatrists have buttressed their argument about the dissenter's poor adaptation by pointing to the tenacity with which he acts out his beliefs despite the odds. . . . The dissenter does indeed operate in dangerous territory; the reaction of the regime is often harsh. But he is fully aware of the risks inherent in his non-conformist behaviour; his moral integrity compels him to take them. Some dissenters have parried the psychiatrists on this point by asking whether Lenin and his colleagues were "poorly adapted" when, in their struggle against the tsarist regime, they were constantly subject to harassment and arrest'.[14]

If anything, it is the conformist – the happy slave – rather than the dissident who appears to be irrational. Unconscious adaptation to the inevitable is a heteronomous mechanism, while rational desires must be autonomous.[15] One cannot be rational if one is the plaything of psychic processes that, unbeknownst to oneself, shape one's desires and values. This preanalytical idea is at least as strong as the intuition that rational desires are desires having which one is happy. Sometimes the two ideas point in the same direction. People who always most want what they cannot get are neither autonomous nor happy. People who adapt to their environment by a process of conscious character planning are both autonomous and happy.[16] At other times, as with the unconscious conformist and the autonomous dissident, the two ideas

diverge. Tocqueville captures this ambiguity of conformism when he asks, 'Should I call it a blessing of God, or a last malediction of His anger, this disposition of the soul that makes men insensible to extreme misery and often even gives them a sort of depraved taste for the cause of their afflictions?'[17]

Could one entertain a similar proposal with respect to belief rationality? Could one argue, that is, that it is rational to have the beliefs having which one tends to be happy? In general, we would expect that one's happiness is best promoted by having beliefs which are well grounded in the evidence, since these are by definition the beliefs most likely to be true. Successful action requires correct factual beliefs. Yet in special cases this connection fails. To keep away from dangerous substances it may be necessary to have an exaggerated notion about the dangers of drug abuse.[18] High levels of motivation and achievement often require an unrealistically positive self-image, whereas people with more accurate self-perceptions tend to lose the motivations to go on with the business of living. They are sadder, but wiser:[19]

Example 2. Stability of marriage. 'Expectations about divorce are partly self-fulfilling because a higher expected probability of divorce reduces investments in specific capital and thereby raises the actual probability'.[20] 'It is far from clear that a bride and a groom would be well advised to believe, on their wedding day, that the probability of their divorce is as high as ·40'.[21] The low-probability expectations of divorce are only partly self-fulfilling. Our misplaced confidence in ourselves motivates us to achievements that make it somewhat less misplaced, but still less than fully justified.

A belief which is unjustified and indeed false may well be instrumentally useful, but it seems odd to call it rational. Rationality, as usually understood, is a variety of intentionally. For something to be rational, it has to be within the scope of conscious, deliberate action or reflection. Useful false beliefs obtain by fluke, not by conscious reflection upon the evidence. Although one cannot in the short run choose one's desires or one's emotional patterns, one can over time shape and bend them to some extent. Beliefs, by contrast, resist manipulation for instrumental purposes. Believing at will, for the sake of the good consequences of having the belief, is a self-defeating enterprise because one cannot – conceptually cannot – at one and the same time believe something and believe that the belief has been adopted on noncognitive grounds.[22] It is easy, therefore, to understand why exhortations to self-esteem, propagated by manuals on self-help therapy, have very limited success.[23]

3. Indeterminacy

To explain and predict events or states of affairs, a theory must have determinate implications about what will happen under given initial conditions. Ideally, the implications should be not only determinate, but unique. Among all possible events or states, exactly one should be singled out by the theory. Outside quantum mechanics, this is the explanatory ideal of science. A theory which does not yield unique predictions is incomplete. It may still, of course, be vastly superior to there being no theory at all. It can be very valuable to know that certain things will *not* happen. Also, for practical purposes it may not matter much which of the events consistent with the theory is actually realized. This said, the prospect of unique prediction dominates and guides scientific work.

In economics, and increasingly in the other social sciences, the neoclassical theory of choice holds out the promise of uniqueness. By its relentless insistence that all behavior is maximizing, it can draw on a basic mathematical theorem which says that every well-behaved function has exactly one maximum in a well-behaved set.[24] Moreover, in economic contexts many functions and sets are well behaved in the relevant sense. For the consumer, there is usually exactly one consumption bundle that maximizes utility within the set of purchases that satisfy his budget constraint. For the producer, there is exactly one combination of the factors of production which maximizes profit per unit of output.

Here I discuss a variety of circumstances under which rational-choice theory fails to yield unique predictions. There may be *several* options which are equally and maximally good. More important, there may be *no* option with the property that it is at least as good as any other.

The problem of multiple optima is, with one notable exception, relatively trivial. It arises when the agent is indifferent between two or more alternatives, each of which is deemed superior to all others. In such cases, rational-choice theory must be supplemented by other approaches to predict which of the equi-optimal alternatives will actually be chosen or 'picked'.[25]

If they are very similar to one another, it is not important to be able to make this prediction. Nobody cares which of two apparently identical soup cans on the supermarket shelf is chosen. If the options differ from one another in offsetting ways, as when a consumer is indifferent between two cars with different strengths and weaknesses, the choice is more consequential. The car dealers will certainly care about the choice. I believe, however, that most cases of this kind are better described by saying that the consumer is unable to rank and compare the options (as discussed later). If he really were indifferent, a reduction of one dollar in the price of one car should induce a clear preference, but I do not believe it usually would.

The exception referred to is game theory, in which multiple optima abound. In noncooperative games with solutions in mixed strategies, it can be shown that an agent will always be indifferent between the strategy prescribed to him by the solution and any other linear combination of the pure strategies that enter into the solution, always assuming that the other players stick to their solution behaviour. John Harsanyi argues that the lack of a good reason for the agent to conform to the solution in such cases is a flaw in game theory as traditionally conceived. In his substitute solution concept, only 'centroid' or equiprobabilistic mixed strategies are allowed. This proposal reflects the idea that when there are several optima, one is chosen at random by 'what amounts to an unconscious chance mechanism inside [the agent's] nervous system'.[26] Here rational choice is supplemented by a purely causal mechanism. I have more to say about randomized strategies in II.3 of *Solomonic Judgements*.

Nonexistence of rational choice is a more serious difficulty than nonunicity. The problem arises at all three levels distinguished earlier: when gathering evidence, when deriving beliefs from the given evidence, and when deriving an action from the given beliefs and desires. I shall consider them in the reverse order.

If the agent has an incomplete preference ordering, that is, is unable to compare and rank all the options in his feasible set, there may be no action which is optimal.[27] It would be misleading to say that the agent is irrational: having complete preferences is no part of what it means to be rational. On the contrary, to insist that preferences must be complete and all pairs of alternatives be comparable can be a form of hyperrationality – that is, of irrationality. Other forms of hyperrationality are considered in 4.

Example 3. Choice of career. 'Life is not long, and too much of it must not pass in idle deliberation how it shall be spent: deliberation, which those who begin it by prudence, and continue it with subtlety, must, after long expence of thought, conclude by chance. To prefer one future mode of life to another, upon just reasons, requires faculties which it has not pleased our Creator to give to us'.[28] Suppose that I am about to choose between going to law school or to a school of forestry – a choice not simply of career but of lifestyle. I am attracted to both professions, but I cannot rank and compare them.[29] If I had tried both for a lifetime, I might be able to make an informed choice between them. As it is, I know too little about them to make a rational decision. What often happens in such cases is that peripheral considerations move to the center. In my ignorance about the first decimal – whether my life will go better as a lawyer or as a forester – I look to the second decimal. Perhaps I opt for law school because that will make it easier for me to visit my parents on weekends. This way of deciding is as good as any – but it is not one that can be underwritten by rational choice as superior to, say, just tossing a coin.

The nonexistence of an optimal action can also arise because of peculiar features of the feasible set. In planning models with infinite horizons and no time discounting, one can run into the paradox that 'there is always an incentive to postpone consumption: on the other hand postponing consumption for ever is clearly not optimal'.[30] While a theoretical possibility, this problem is not central to actual decision making. By contrast, the difficulties stemming from incomplete preferences are real and important. In addition to the problem of intrapersonal comparisons of welfare referred to in Example 3, the difficulty of making interpersonal comparisons can prevent us from ranking the options, if the ranking takes account of the welfare others derive from them.[31]

At the next level, nonexistence of an optimal belief can arise in two ways: because of uncertainty and because of strategic interaction. 'Uncertainty' here means radical ignorance, the lack of ability to assign numerical probabilities to the possible outcomes associated with the various options. If such assignments are possible, we face a problem of decision making under risk, in which the rational decision rule – to maximize expected utility – can be counted on to yield

an optimal choice. Farmers deciding on a crop mix or doctors deciding whether to operate act under risk. They can rely on well-defined probabilities derived from past frequencies. Stock market speculators, soldiers and others who have to act in novel situations cannot rely on frequencies. If they have sufficient information and good judgement, they may be able to make good probability estimates to feed into the expected utility calculus. If they have little information or poor judgement, rationality requires them to abstain from forming and acting upon such estimates. To attempt to do so would, for them, be a form of hyperrationality.

Example 4. Nuclear waste. 'Different geological mechanisms may be capable of generating the release of radioactive waste in the environment. Among these are groundwater flow, faulting, diapirism, erosion, fall of meteorites, magma intrusion, and modification of the drainage level of water. An approach to geological confinement is often sought by trying to quantify the probability of occurrence of any of these events and their nuisance value to man. Then, by combining these probabilities and nuisance values, one tries to assess the safety coefficient of the repository and to compare it to the accepted safety coefficient for present risks. This approach does not seem realistic to us *because basically the earth's development has not been a random phenomenon* (possibly apart from the fall of meteorites) and no geologist can seriously give reasonable figures for these probabilities'.[32] Here is a case in which objective probabilities and judgemental, subjective probabilities are equally out of reach.

When the situation is recognized as one of uncertainty, rational-choice theory is limited, but not powerless. Sometimes we are able to dismiss an option in the presence of another that, regardless of which state of the world obtains, has better consequences. Having done this, however, we are often left with several options for each of which there is some state in which it has better consequences than one of the others. Decision theory tells us that in choosing among these we are allowed to take account only of the best and the worst consequences of each action.[33] This may also narrow the field a bit, but often more than one option will be left. In choosing among these, one may adopt the rule of thumb to choose the option with the best worst-consequences (maximin), but there are no grounds for saying that this is more rational than to choose the option with best-consequences (maximax). To illustrate, consider the following matrix of outcomes as dependent on actions and states:

	S_1	S_2	S_3
A_1	3	4	5
A_2	1	2	8
A_3	2	0	7
A_4	0	0	6

Outcome A_4 can be excluded from consideration since under any state of affairs it yields worse consequences than A_2. Among the remaining, A_3 can also be excluded since both its best consequence and its worst consequence are worse than those of A_2. Of the remaining, maximin reasoning would make us prefer A_1 over A_2, while maximax would lead to the opposite choice. Psychological theories may be able to explain which choice will be made, but rational-choice theory, by itself, is indeterminate.

A special case arises when we have to choose among several scientific theories. Let us assume that each theory assigns numerical probabilities to the events that can occur, but that the choice of one theory rather than another is a matter of uncertainty. Controversies about the effect of CO_2 release in the atmosphere are of this kind. As shown by Jørgen Aasness and Aanund Hylland in unpublished work, this kind of theoretical uncertainty is less devastating than total ignorance, since we can use the content of the theories even if we do not know which of them is correct. If we can assume that one of them is correct, many abstractly possible states of affairs can be excluded and the optimal decision may differ from what it would have been had there been no restrictions on what could happen.

To illustrate the point, assume that we have to choose between acts A_1 and A_2. There are two theories T_1 and T_2. According T_1, state S_1 occurs with probability 1/3 and state S_2 with probability 2/3. According to T_2, state S_3 is certain to occur. The act–state matrix is the following:

	S_1	S_2	S_3
A_1	12	0	6
A_2	3	15	5

The best and worst outcomes of A_1 are, respectively, 12 and 0; those of A_2, 15 and 3. Define now X as the set of all triples $(\frac{2}{3} \cdot b, \frac{1}{3} \cdot b, 1 - b)$, where b ranges from 0 to 1. X is a subset of the set Y of all triples $(p_1, p_2, 1 - p_1 - p_2)$, with p_1 and p_2 ranging from 0 to 1. Y can be understood as the set of all abstractly possible probability vectors for the states S_i, whereas X is the restricted set that incorporates the information provided by the two theories. The standard theory of choice under uncertainty, defined over the full set Y, says that A_2 should be chosen, since it has a better best-consequence and a better worst-consequence than A_1. On the restricted set, however, A_1 is the best choice. It has a utility of $2b + 6$, whereas A_2 yields only $2b + 5$.

. . . . . .

Consider next strategic interaction as an obstacle to rational-belief formation. Often, rational choice requires beliefs about choices to be made by other people. These beliefs, to be rational, must take account of the fact that these others are similarly forming beliefs about oneself and about each other. Sometimes, these beliefs are indeterminate, when the situation has multiple equilibria with different winners and losers. The games of Chicken and Battle of the Sexes are well-known examples. Each of these games has two equilibria, each of which is better for both players than the worst outcome and preferred by one party to the other equilibrium. In the absence of enforcement or commitment devices, there is no way in which a player can form a rational belief about what the other will do.[34]

Example 5. Rational expectations. To make decisions about consumption and investment, economic agents must form expectations about the future state of the economy. According to an earlier view, these are 'adaptive expectations', or extrapolations from current and past states. This view is unsatisfactory, because it assumes that people react mechanically without using all the information available to them. For instance, following the quadrupling of oil prices in 1973, we would expect expectations to change more radically and rapidly than what would be predicted by the theory of adaptive expectations. The theory of rational expectations, which emerged as a dominant paradigm in the 1970s, assumes that people are forward looking, not backward looking, when forming their expectations and that, moreover, they make the best use of the information available to them. Essentially, people predict the future development of the economy using a correct economic model. Since expectations are part of the model, rational expectations must be self-fulfilling. The problem[35] is that often there are several sets of expectations about the economy that, if held by everybody, would be self-fulfilling. In the absence of government intervention to eliminate some of the equilibria, rational agents will not be able to form mutually supporting, self-fulfilling expectations.

Uncertainty and strategic interaction, taken separately, create problems for rational belief formation. When both are present, they wreak havoc. In planning for war, generals are hindered both by uncertainty about whether their sophisticated systems will work and by strategic complexities. The old dictum – Don't base your plans on the enemy's intentions but on his capabilities – no longer applies, if it ever did, since generals are equally uncertain about the effectiveness of the weapons of the enemy (and about the degree of uncertainly among the generals on the other side).

Example 6. Explaining investment. 'The outstanding fact is the extreme precariousness of the basis of knowledge on which our estimates of prospective yield will have to be made. Our knowledge of the factors which will govern the yield of an investment some years hence is usually very slight and often negligible. If we speak frankly, we have to admit that our basis of knowledge for estimating the yield ten years hence of a railway, a copper mine, a textile factory, the goodwill of a patent medicine, an Atlantic liner, a building in the city of London amounts to little and sometimes to nothing; or even five years hence'.[36] For the special case of investment in research and innovation, this lack of foreknowledge decomposes into the elements of uncertainty and strategic interaction. On the one hand, the outcome of innovative activities is inherently uncertain. One may strike gold, or find nothing. As Humphrey Lyttelton is reported to have said, 'If I knew where jazz was going I'd be there already'. But suppose one could know how the chance of finding gold is related to the amount one has invested. Under the 'winner-take-all' system of modern industry, it also matters whether one finds it before others do. If other firms invest massively, the chances that a given firm will be first past the post may be too small to make the investment worth while. If other firms do not invest, the chances are much higher.

But if it is true of each firm that it should invest if and only if others do not, it has no basis for anticipating what others will do.[37] Entrepreneurs might as well follow Keynes's advice and be guided by their 'animal spirits'.

Finally, determinacy problems arise with respect to the optimal amount of information one should collect before forming an opinion. Information is useful, but costly to acquire. Ideally, the rational agent would strike a balance between these two considerations: he would acquire information up to the point at which the marginal cost of acquiring information equaled its expected marginal value. In some areas of decision making these calculations can be carried out with great accuracy. Thus 'To detect intestinal cancer, it has become common to perform a series of six inexpensive tests ('guaiacs') on a person's stool. The benefits of the first two tests are significant. However, when calculations are done for each of the last four tests to determine the costs of detecting a case of cancer (not even curing it), the costs are discovered to be $49 150, $469 534, $4 724 695 and $47 107 214, respectively. To some these calculations suggest that the routine should be reduced, say to a three-guaiac test'.[38]

Sometimes it is impossible to estimate the marginal cost and benefit of information. Consider a general in the midst of battle who does not know the exact disposition of the enemy troops. The value of more information, while potentially great, cannot be ascertained. Determining the expected value would require a highly implausible ability to form numerical probability estimates concerning the possible enemy positions. (Indeterminacy of rational belief due to strategic interaction is important here.) The costs of acquiring information are equally elusive. The opportunity costs might be enormous, if the time spent gathering information offered the enemy a chance to attack or to prepare his defence, or they might be quite trivial. Under such circumstances, one might as well follow Napoleon's maxim 'On s'engage et puis on voit'.

In between these extremes – medical diagnosis and the conduct of battle – fall most everyday situations. The observations that a rational person should make 'greater investment in information when undertaking major than minor decisions',[39] while true, does not help him to decide *how* much to invest. That decision requires estimates about the probable costs and benefits of the search for information. Search theories of unemployment, for instance, assume that the unemployed worker knows the distribution of job offers or at least the general shape of the distribution. Using this knowledge, he can calculate the optimal time spent searching for well-paid jobs. This argument is of dubious value. The doctor carrying out a medical diagnosis finds himself *many* times in the *same situation*. Most persons are unemployed only once or, if more than once, under widely diverging circumstances. They have no way of learning by experience what the job distribution looks like. To be sure, they know something about the job market, but there is no reason to think that they can piece together their bits of information to a reliable subjective distribution.[40] Similar arguments apply to many consumer decisions, like the purchase of a car or an apartment. People know that it makes sense to spend some time searching and that it would be pointless to search forever, but between these lower and upper limits there is usually an interval of indeterminacy.

4. Irrationality

In this section I survey some main varieties of irrationality, including, as a special case, hyperrationality. The latter notion is defined as *the failure to recognize the failure* of rational-choice theory to yield unique prescriptions or predictions. As in Kant's critique, the first task of reason is to recognize its own limitations and draw the boundaries within which it can operate. The irrational belief in the omnipotence of reason is what I call hyperrationality.

Failures to conform to well-defined prescriptions of rational-choice theory arise at all three levels distinguished in Figure 1. Consider first how actions can fail to relate optimally to given desires and beliefs. The paradigm case is weakness of will, characterized by the following features. (a) There is a prima facie judgement that X is good. (b) There is a prima facie judgement that Y is good. (c) There is an all-things-considered judgement that X is better than Y. (d) There is the fact that Y is chosen. Often, X is an act that is in the long-term interest of a person or corresponds to his moral will, whereas Y is a short-term impulse or a self-interested desire. There is no conceptual link, however, between weakness of will, myopia and selfishness.[41]

Example 7. Neo-Freudianism. Freud depicted two forms of human irrationality: being under the sway of the pleasure-seeking id and being dominated by the rigid, compulsive superego. As bearer of the rational will, the ego is engaged in a two-front war against these two enemies. The nature of the id, ego and superego in Freud's theory is somewhat unclear. Are they separate homunculi, each with a will of its own and capable of engaging in strategic interaction with the others?[42] Or, more soberly, are they conflicting tendencies of one and the same subject? In his recent reinterpretation of Freud's trichotomy, George Ainslie has clarified the matter.[43] The ego's struggle with the id is interpreted in terms of time preference functions with the peculiar feature that a larger delayed reward which is preferred to a small early reward when they are both in the distant future becomes less preferred when the time for choice approaches. (Think of a person who makes an appointment with his dentist and then cancels it the day before.) To avoid such weak-willed behaviour, the ego can ally itself with the future, for if the situation can be expected to recur, *bunching* of all the small rewards and of all the large rewards makes it easier to choose the latter. By its rigid, uncompromising character, however, bunching may be as crippling to rationality as the problem it was supposed to resolve. If the ego abdicates its will to get rid of the id, it substitutes one form of weakness of will for another. Even when the person sees that it makes sense to give himself a break, he cannot bring himself to do so.

There is another set of cases in which desires and beliefs can fail to bring about the end for which they provide reasons. They have been referred to as 'excess of will',[44] although they are not in any sense the contrary of weakness of will. Assume that if I do X, I shall bring about Y, which is what I most desire. Moreover, I am able to do X, in the straightforward sense in which I am able to raise my arm. The snag, however, is that X will bring about Y only if I do X without the intention to bring about Y. Doing X for the purpose of bringing about Y will not succeed. Examples of X and Y could be: drinking hot tea at bedtime and falling asleep; working hard and forgetting a humiliating experience; looking at erotic pictures and becoming sexually aroused; joining a political movement and achieving self-respect.[45] Further examples are discussed at more length below.

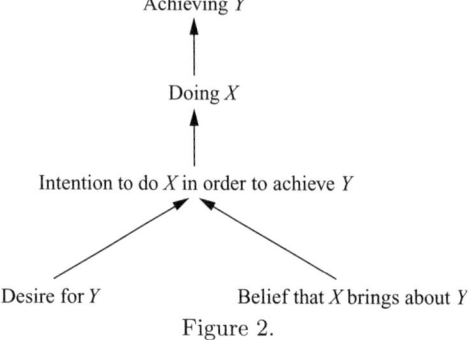

Figure 2.

It might appear that someone who does X to achieve Y acts rationally. He is doing what he believes is (let us assume) the best way of getting what he most desires. This would be true if the situation conformed to the standard scheme of action, depicted in Figure 2.

The scheme goes from beliefs and desires through the intention to the action and finally to the outcome of the action. There is no guarantee, of course, that the intended outcome will occur. The belief that X brings about Y could be mistaken. Extraneous factors might intervene. Actions that fail to bring about their intended outcomes for such reasons are not irrational. They fail, as it were, honourably. Matters stand differently when the failure is intrinsic to the action, as when the very intention to do X for the sake of Y interferes with the efficacy of X to bring about Y. This nonstandard scheme is shown in Figure 3.

Example 8. Don't wait for return of husband. This was the heading of a column in the *Miami Herald* (April 1987), in which Howard Halpern, a psychologist in private practice in New York City, answered the following question: 'I am a 57-year-old woman whose husband of 36 years has decided to live alone. We've sold our house and are living in separate dwellings. He speaks of "hope" and

"working things out", while happily living the single life. I am unable to get on with my life in such an independent manner. We've had a great deal of joint and individual therapy, but it has not restored our relationship. We've lived together for a few months in the past two years. Each time I thought we would get back together, but then he would leave again. Is there something I should be doing besides waiting?' Mr Halpern answered, 'When you use the word "waiting", I get the impression that you have put your life on hold until your husband's hoped-for return. It is time to stop waiting. By that I don't mean you should make your separation legal – I'm not suggesting any action in particular. I think you must accept your situation as real, understand that your husband may not return and refuse to let your life be dependent on his decision. You have already made efforts to get him to return. Now you must pay attention to your own life and outline your own goals. Focusing on yourself may make you more appealing to him, but that is not the reason to do it. You must do it for yourself'. It is hard to think of advice that would be more misguided. The remark that focusing on herself might make her more appealing to him, while obviously intended to motivate her efforts, is sure to ruin their effect.

Consider next the varieties of irrationality that arise at the level of beliefs and desires. These can be subverted and distorted by causal forces in two main ways: by drives and motivations or by inadequate cognitive processing. Since the end result can be a motivational state (a desire) or a cognitive one (a belief), we have four categories, which I now proceed to illustrate.

The Motivational Basis of Motivations

By this phrase, I do not have in mind conscious character planning, the shaping of preferences by metapreferences. Rather it refers to nonconscious motivational mechanisms that shape our desires 'behind our back'. The best known is what Festinger called 'cognitive dissonance reduction', the natural tendency of the mind to rearrange its desires and beliefs so as to reduce the tension created by high valuations of objects believed to be unattainable or low valuations of objects believed to be inescapable.[46] Also, being faced, like Buridan's ass, with two objects that appear equally attractive creates a form of

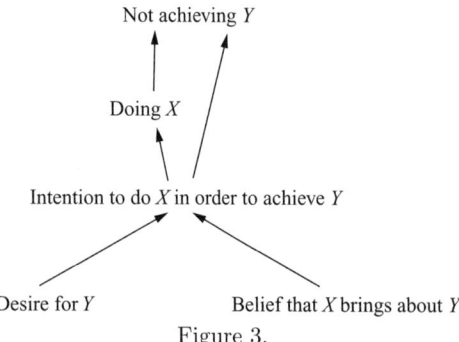

Figure 3.

cognitive dissonance extensively discussed in chapter II of *Solomonic Judgements*.

Some applications of dissonance theory focus on the adjustments of beliefs, while others emphasize the motivated change in evaluations.

Example 9. The Hungarian black market.[47] One mechanism of dissonance reduction is 'I paid a lot for it, so it must be good'. A Hungarian coffee shop begins to offer high-quality coffee to customers who are willing to pay a bit extra. Since the shop has a limited quota of coffee beans, each customer who pays the high price creates an externality for the customers who pay the official price. The official cups of coffee being increasingly diluted, more and more customers are willing to pay the premium. Yet, as more and more do so, the quality of black-market coffee approaches the initial quality of the ordinary coffee. In the end, everybody pays the higher price for coffee of ordinary quality. It would appear, therefore, that everybody has lost, in a standard *n*-person Prisoner's Dilemma. The twist to the story is that because of cognitive dissonance nobody experiences any subjective loss. Since everyone is paying more for the coffee, it must be better than it used to be. The Prisoner's Dilemma yields a Pareto improvement: the shop keeper gains more and the customers are happy.

It is not obvious that desires shaped by dissonance reduction are, ipso facto, irrational. They do, after all, make people happier. Desires shaped by dissonance-increasing mechanisms are more obviously irrational. Many people, for instance, have a preference for novelty that gets them into trouble:

Example 10. What father does is always right. In H. C. Andersen's story of this name, a farmer goes to the market in the morning to sell or exchange his horse. First, he meets a man with a cow, which he likes so much that he exchanges it for the horse. In successive transactions, the cow is then exchanged for a sheep, the sheep for a goose, the goose for a hen and, finally, the hen for a sack, of rotten apples. The farmer's road to ruin is paved with stepwise improvements.[48] (Actually he is not ruined, because a pair of English tourists make and lose a bet that his wife will be angry with him when he comes back with the apples.) Although the story does not say so, it is likely that the farmer would have refused to exchange his horse for a sack full of rotten apples. Curiosity and the thirst for novelty are triggered by options which are neither too similar nor too dissimilar from the current state.[49] In Johannes V. Jensen's story of the same name – a take-off on Andersen's classic tale – the farmer goes to the market with a set of rotten apples.[50] By a series of lucky accidents, he comes back with a horse. When he tells his wife about the deals, she manages to see each of them in an unfavourable light. Although the story is not fully clear on this point, it appears that she even thought a horse for a sack of apples a bad deal. Thus her perverse attitude can probably be explained by her belief that her husband cannot do anything right, not by an inherent conservatism that would be the converse of a preference for novelty. If the latter was the case, she would probably prefer the end state over the initial state, while being opposed to each of the intermediate steps.

The Motivational Basis of Cognitions

Dissonance reduction can also take the form of belief adjustment. Workers who take jobs in unsafe industries alter their estimated probabilities of accidents.[51] As a result, when safety equipment becomes available, they may choose not to purchase it. Here, as in other cases, misformation of private beliefs (or preferences) creates a case for government intervention.[52] In addition to direct motivational interference with the cognition, there can be indirect interference with the evidence on which cognition is based. People who dread having a dangerous disease put off seeing the doctor. People who fear they might be gaining weight avoid stepping on the scales.

Belief-oriented dissonance reduction is a form of wishful thinking. To the extent that it makes one feel happy, it might be thought to be a good thing. Usually, however, the pleasure of wishful thinking is of brief duration, like the warmth provided by pissing in one's pants. *Acting* on beliefs formed in this way can be disastrous and is likely to force a change in the beliefs. When action is not called for, the wishful beliefs can be more stable. The 'just-world' theory, for instance, suggests that people adjust their beliefs about guilt and responsibility so as to preserve their belief that the world is fundamentally just.[53] The best-known example is the 'blame the victim' syndrome, further discussed in II.8 *Solomonic Judgements*. While it would be perverse to say that blaming the victim is rational, it can certainly contribute to one's peace of mind.

Some forms of motivated belief formation do not even have that effect. The congenital pessimist, who systematically believes that the world is as he would *not* like it to be, creates dissonance instead of reducing it. Dissonance reduction, while a threat to autonomy and rationality, is at least intelligible in terms of the 'wirings of the pleasure machine', as Amos Tversky has put it. Dissonance production indicates that the wires have been crossed and that something is radically wrong.

The Cognitive Basis of Motivations

Under this heading fall the violations of expected utility theory that have been extensively studied over the past decade or so.[54] An important example is 'framing', that is, preference reversal induced by redescription of the choice situation.[55] People who would abstain from buying credit cards if firms impose a 3 per cent surcharge on card users may be less deterred if firms offer a 3 per cent discount on cash purchases.[56] Time preferences can be manipulated by presenting the difference between present and future consumption as a delay premium or as a speed-up cost.[57] These are examples in which the reference points or frames are imposed from the outside. A more intriguing problem arises if we ask about the principles that regulate spontaneous choice of frames.[58] It has been suggested that people choose the frame that induces the choice that makes them happy,[59] but it is far from obvious that nonconscious motivational mechanisms are capable of operating in this indirect manner.

Another set of deviations from expected utility theory arises because people do not treat known probabilities as the theory tells them to. (The problem comes on the top of their difficulties in estimating unknown probabilities.) Thus 'low probabilities are over-weighted, moderate and high probabilities are underweighted, and the latter effect is more pronounced than the former'.[60] In other words, people exaggerate the difference between impossible events and low-probability events and, especially, between near-certain and certain events. Attitudes towards nuclear accidents and other great disasters may, for this reason, include elements of irrationality. The point is *not* that it is irrational to feel anxiety at the prospect of a low-probability nuclear accident. What is irrational is that this attitude, when combined with other attitudes that may also appear unobjectionable in isolation, can be made to yield inconsistent choices. 'It is not easy

to determine whether people value the elimination of risk too much or the reduction of risk too little. The contrasting attitudes to the two [logically equivalent] forms of protective action, however, are difficult to justify on normative grounds'.[61]

The Cognitive Basis of Cognitions

There is by now a massive body of evidence showing how belief formation can fail because people rely on misleading heuristic principles or, more simply, ignore basic facts about statistical inference.[62] Securities and futures markets seem excessively sensitive to current information.[63] Baseball trainers who notice that last season's star is not living up to his past performance are rapid to conclude that he has been spoilt by success, ignoring the statistical principle that, on the average, an outstanding performance is likely to be followed by one closer to average ('regression to the mean').[64] 'Labeling' theorists of mental illness cite as evidence for their theory the fact that the longer people have been in mental hospitals, the less likely they are to get well, ignoring the alternative explanation that the probabilities of getting well may differ across people but be constant over time.[65]

> *Example 11. Calvinism.* The previous two examples turn upon a confusion between causal and noncausal interpretation of the facts. Max Weber's interpretation of the affinity between Calvinism and economic activity invokes a similar tendency to infuse diagnostic facts with causal value. "Thus, however useless good works might be as a means of attaining salvation, for even the elect remain beings of the flesh, and everything they do falls infinitely short of divine standards, nevertheless, they are indispensable as a sign of election. They are the technical means, not of purchasing salvation, but of getting rid of the fear of damnation'.[66] It has been argued that the mechanism invoked here is motivational, a form of dissonance reduction.[67] It could, however, be a purely cognitive tendency to confuse diagnostic and causal efficacy. When people ask themselves, 'If not now, when?' and 'If not me, who?' they commit similar fallacies, albeit very useful ones.[68] People who open only one box in Newcomb's Problem do the same.[69]

I conclude this section with a few remarks about hyperrationality. Since the concept is discussed extensively in later chapters of *Solomonic*

Judgements, especially in II.3 and II.8, I content myself here with a brief enumeration of some main varieties. (a) Sometimes people attempt to eliminate uncertainty of beliefs or incompleteness of preferences, although the choice situation is essentially indeterminate. It is always possible to devise questions that will force a person to reveal his preferences or subjective probabilities, but often there is no reason to believe in the robustness of the results. If the outcome depends on the procedures of elicitation, there is nothing 'out there' which is captured by the questions. (b) Sometimes people look to the second decimal when they are ignorant about the first. In some contexts, this method of problem solving is as good as any other. In others, it can be very wasteful, if people differ in their assessment of the second decimal and spend resources arguing about it. (c) Sometimes people will reframe an indeterminate decision problem so as to make it appear determinate. If one option stands out along one dimension, that dimension may take on increased importance so as to make the choice an easier one. (d) Sometimes people seek out what is rational to do in any given situation instead of looking for more general rules that cover many similar cases. Focusing on rules rather than acts can economize on costs of decision (see Chapter III of *Solomonic Judgements*) and also have superior incentive effects.[70] (e) Sometimes people ignore the costs of decision making. They search for the solution that would have been best if found instantaneously and costlessly, ignoring the fact that the search itself has costs that may detract from optimality.

5. Alternatives to Rationality

In light of earlier sections, several questions arise. How serious are these failures of rational-choice theory? Is there any reason to think that the theory has a privileged status in the study of human action? What are the alternative accounts that could supplement or replace the theory?

The failures of indeterminacy appear to me to be quite serious. One way of assessing the power of the theory is to distinguish choice situations by two criteria: the importance of the problem and the number of agents involved. 'Small' problems, that is, problems in which the options do not differ much in value from one another, do not lend themselves to the rational approach. Either the options are equally good or it is not clear that it would pay to find out which is the better, or pay to find out whether it will pay to find out. 'Large' problems,[71] in which the choice

can be expected to have wide-ranging consequences, also tend to fall outside the scope of the theory. Preference rankings over big chunks of life tend to be incomplete, and subjective probabilities over events in the distant future tend to be unreliable. The theory is more powerful when applied to medium-sized problems like the purchase of a car or a house, but even here the question of optimal search is largely indeterminate.

Other things being equal, decision problems with one agent or with many agents are more likely to yield determinate solutions than problems with a small number of agents. By definition, one-agent problems have no strategic indeterminacy. With many sellers and many buyers, competition forces a unique set of equilibrium prices. With one seller and one buyer, there is often a large range of mutually acceptable outcomes and much indeterminacy concerning which outcome will be realized.[72] A rough conclusion is that rational-choice theory is applicable mainly to one-agent and many-agent problems of intermediate size. Although precise quantification is impossible, indeterminacy is not a marginal problem that can be assimilated to 'friction' or 'noise'.

The factual importance of irrationality does not lend itself to a similarly systematic analysis. The central issue is whether people deal irrationally with important problems. The issue cannot be studied experimentally, since limitations on funding rarely allow stakes to be high enough and subjects to be numerous enough to get reliable results.[73] Introspection, casual observation, historical case studies and novels suggest that irrationality is quite widespread. Drug abuse is perhaps the most striking evidence. More generally, the widespread inability to be properly swayed by future consequences of present action points to a serious deficit in rationality.[74] Studies of 'group think'[75] suggest that political and military decisions are often made in disregard of the evidence. The motivated ignorance of the Holocaust is a massive example of irrational belief formation.[76] The vast sales of self-therapy manuals suggest that many people believe that they can talk themselves into self-confidence and self-respect. I could go on enumerating cases, but they would not add much to the general idea. Irrationality is neither marginal nor omnipresent.

Although indeterminacy and irrationality are widespread, they do not affect the normative privilege of rationality. First and foremost, rationality is privileged because we want to be rational.[77] We take little pride in our occasional or frequent irrationality, although sometimes it has to be accepted as the price we pay for other things we value. In our dealings with people, we are compelled to treat them as, by and large, rational. Communication and discussion rest on the tacit premise that each interlocutor believes in the rationality of the others, since otherwise there would be no point to the exchange.[78] To understand others, we must assume that, by and large, they have rational desires and beliefs and act rationally upon them. If a person says that he wants X and yet deliberately refrains from using the means that he knows to be the most conducive to X, we usually conclude not that he is irrational but that he does not really want X. Sometimes, of course, we may conclude that irrationality offers the best explanation of a given kind of behaviour, but even then most of the evidence about the agent that goes into that conclusion is formed on the assumption that he is, by and large, rational.[79]

The explanatory privilege of rationality rests on two grounds. As just observed, rationality is presupposed by any competing theory of motivation, whereas rationality itself does not presuppose anything else. On grounds of parsimony, therefore, we should begin by assuming nothing but rationality.[80] Also, while rationality may have its problems, the opposition is in even worse shape. The dictum that you cannot beat something with nothing applies here, with some modifications. As will be clear from what I shall say about the alternatives to rational-choice theory, they are more than nothing, but they do not quite amount to something either.

Herbert Simon's theory of satisficing is intended to supplement rational-choice theory when it is indeterminate.[81] It has been applied to technical change,[82] consumer choice,[83] and numerous other problems. The strength and main weakness of the theory are its realism. On the one hand, it is true and important that many people are happy once their aspiration level has been reached. They stop searching once they have found something that is good enough. On the other hand, there is to my knowledge no robust explanation of why people have the aspiration levels they do, nor of why they use the particular search rules they do. The theory describes behaviour, but does not really explain it. Now, one might say that a similar criticism applies to rational-choice theory, which does not, after all, explain why people have the preferences they do. The hypothesis that people behave rationally is nevertheless simpler, more general and more powerful than the assumption that they are guided by their aspiration levels. In the theory of the firm, for instance, rational-choice theory needs only one assumption, namely that the firm maximizes profits. Satisficing theory needs many assumptions, stipulating one aspiration level for each of the many subroutines of the firm and, when that level is not attained, one search mechanism for each routine.

Simon's theory, and other theories in the same vein,[84] are intended to *supplement* rational-choice theory, both as a guide to and as an explanation of action. They are rarely intended to *replace* the rationality assumption. Proponents of these alternatives usually grant that rational-choice theory has substantial explanatory power in the absence of uncertainty, but add that most real-life decision making is characterized by a high degree of uncertainty that is costly or impossible to resolve. This is also the point of departure of the theory offered by Isaac Levi to guide and explain decision making under value conflicts and uncertainty.[85] Under conditions of unresolved value conflict, he recommends that we use lexicographically secondary values to decide among the options that are 'admissible' according to the primary, conflicting values, an admissible option being one that is optimal according to one of these values (or to some weighted average of them). Under conditions of uncertainty, he similarly recommends the use of *security* and *deferability* to supplement the expected-value criterion. Levi also argues that many apparent violations of rationality can be understood by assuming that the agents are acting in accordance with his prescriptions. Their choices reflect reasonable ways of coping with unresolved value conflicts and uncertainty rather than cognitive illusions of the kind discussed above.[86] Levi does not try, however, to account for all the apparent violations of expected utility theory.

Other theories, offered squarely as alternatives to rational-choice theory, aim to explain what they admit to be violations of rationality. They can be classified, very roughly, into psychological, biological and sociological alternatives to the economic approach to behaviour.

Psychological theories attempt to explain the observed violations of expected utility theory referred to earlier by providing an account that (a) is simple and intuitively plausible, (b) explains all observed deviations from expected utility theory and (c) predicts no unobserved deviations. Attempts to achieve this goal include prospect theory,[87] generalized expected utility theory[88] and regret theory.[89] This is a field where nonexperts should tread warily, and I abstain from evaluating the various proposals, beyond making the presumably uncontroversial remark that only prospect theory appears to be capable of explaining framing phenomena. I note later, however, an apparent example of irrationality through framing that is more plausibly explained by a sociological alternative to rational-choice theory.

Biological alternatives take off from findings about animal behaviour. Animals can be constrained to choose between two responses, each of which has a particular reward schedule. In variable-ratio (VR) schedules we set up a constant probability of reward for each response. The one-armed bandit of the Las Vegas variety illustrates this reward schedule. It is a mechanism with no memory: if we hit the jackpot on one occasion, we are just as likely to hit it again the next time. In variable-interval (VI) schedules we set up a mechanism with memory, so that each unrewarded response increases the probability that the next response will be rewarded. In each period the experimenter uses a chance device, with constant probabilities, to decide whether food is to be made available. Once it has been made available, it stays available. The animal does not know, however, whether it is available. To find out, and to get the food, it must make the appropriate response.

The central question is whether animals allocate their attention optimally between the two responses, that is, whether they act to maximize their rewards. Faced with the choice between two VR schedules, animals often do the rational thing and allocate all their attention to the response with the highest probability of reward. Sometimes, however, they commit 'gambler's fallacy' of distributing the stakes in proportion to the odds. With two VI schedules, the findings are also ambiguous. In a VI-VR schedule, animals usually do not optimize. Instead of equalizing the marginal return of the two responses, as rationality would require them to do, they equalize the average return. They forget, as it were, that most of the VI rewards come from a few responses, and that it is not really profitable to pay attention to this schedule beyond visiting it from time to time to collect any reward that might have come due after its last visit.

Richard Herrnstein argues that the principle of equalizing average returns ('the matching law') is a more fundamental principle than utility maximization.[90] In addition to explaining allocation of behaviour across schedules, it can explain the allocation over time. Specifically, the matching law predicts that time discounting will be steeper than the exponential discount functions usually stipulated by economists. Although the empirical verdict is not yet in, there is evidence that much animal and human discounting is nonexponential.[91] On the other hand, the matching law explains only the most naïve forms of human behaviour. People can use conscious thought processes to analyse the structure of the choice situation. Unlike animals, they are not restricted to myopic learning. The matching law may describe 'prerational' behaviour, but it is powerless to explain more sophisticated choice processes.

A sociological alternative to the economic approach is the theory of social norms.[92] I define social norms mainly by their non-outcome-oriented character. Whereas rationality tells people, 'If you want Y, do X', many social norms simply say, 'Do X'. Some social norms are hypothetical, but they make the action contingent on past behaviour of oneself or others, not on future goals. These norms say, 'If others do Y, do X' or 'If you have done Y, do X'. The norms are *social* if they satisfy two further conditions: they are shared with other members of the community and they are in part enforced by sanctions provided by others.

Here are some examples of social norms, chosen with a view to the contrast with rational action: (a) the norm of voting is very strong in Western democracies. It accounts for most voting in national elections.[93] Selfish voters have virtually nothing to gain from voting, while the costs are non-negligible. Altruistic voters might find voting rational, were it not for problems of strategic interaction. Altruistic voting is a game with multiple equilibria, in each of which most but not all voters go to the polls.[94] (b) The norm of vengeance practised in many traditional societies is triggered by an earlier offence, not motivated by future rewards. Indeed, from the future-oriented point of view vengeance is point-less at best, suicidal at worst. (c) In most Western societies there is a norm against walking up to someone in a cinema queue and asking to buy his place. The norm is puzzling, as nobody would lose and some could gain from the transaction. (d) Norms of dress and etiquette do not seem to serve any ulterior purpose, unlike for instance traffic rules that serve to prevent accidents.

Consider finally an example that could be explained both in terms of framing and in terms of social norms. Consider a suburban community where all houses have small lawns of the same size.[95] Suppose a houseowner is willing to pay his neighbour's son ten dollars to mow his lawn, but not more. He would rather spend half an hour mowing the lawn himself than pay eleven dollars to have someone else do it. Imagine now that the same person is offered twenty dollars to mow the lawn of another neighbour. It is easy to imagine that he would refuse, probably with some indignation. But this has an appearance of irrationality. By turning down the offer of having his neighbour's son mow his lawn for eleven dollars, he implies that half an hour of his time is worth at most eleven dollars. By turning down the offer to mow the other neighbour's lawn for twenty dollars, he implies that it is worth at least twenty dollars. But it cannot both be worth less than eleven and more than twenty dollars.

The explanation in terms of framing suggests[96] that people evaluate losses and gains forgone differently. Credit card companies exploit this difference when they insist that stores advertise cash discounts rather than credit card surcharges. The credit card holder is affected less by the lost chance of getting the cash discount than by the extra cost of paying with the card. Similarly, the houseowner is affected more by the out-of-pocket expenses that he would incur by paying someone to mow his lawn than by the loss of a windfall income. But this cannot be the full story, because it does not explain why the houseowner should be indignant at the proposal. Part of the explanation must be that he does not think of himself as the kind of person who mows other people's lawns for money. It *isn't done*, to use a revealing phrase that often accompanies social norms.

Economists often argue that norms can be reduced to individual rationality. One version of the reductionist claim is that norms are 'nothing but' raw material for strategic manipulation; that people invoke norms to rationalize their self-interest while not believing in them. But this is absurd: if nobody believed in the norms, there would be nothing to manipulate.[97] A more serious reductionist argument proceeds from the fact that norms are maintained by sanctions. Suppose I face the choice between taking revenge for the murder of my cousin and not doing anything. The cost of revenge is that I might in turn be the target of countervengeance. The cost of not doing

anything is that my family and friends are certain to desert me, leaving me out on my own, defencelessly exposed to predators. A cost–benefit analysis is likely to tell me that revenge is the rational choice. More generally, norm-guided behaviour is supported by the threat of sanctions that make it rational to obey the norm.

Against this argument, each of the following objections is a sufficient refutation. First, sometimes norms are followed in the absence of any observers who could sanction violations. Many people vote even when nobody would notice if they did not. Second, we have to ask why anyone would want to impose the sanctions. Perhaps they follow a metanorm to sanction people who violate first-order norms, but then we have to ask whether it is rational to follow that norm. In the regress that now arises, there must come a point at which the cost of expressing disapproval is less than the cost of receiving disapproval for not expressing it, since the former cost is approximately constant while the second goes rapidly to zero. The chain of norms must have an unmoved mover, to which the rationalist reduction does not apply.

Among the alternatives to rational-choice theory, the (as yet undeveloped) theory of social norms holds out most promise. It is radically different from rational-choice theory, whereas the other alternatives are largely variations on the same consequentialist theme. They are different species of the same genus, whereas the theory of norms is of a different genus altogether. Other species of that genus might include the theory of neurotic behaviour, which is similarly rigid, mechanical and nonconsequentialist. Eventually, the goal of the social sciences must be to construct the family comprising both genera – to understand outcome-oriented motivations and nonconsequentialist ones as elements in a general theory of action. As long as this task is not accomplished, rational-choice theory will probably remain privileged, by virtue of the simplicity and power of the maximizing assumption. And in the event that it should one day be accomplished, rationality would still retain its privilege as a normative account of action.

Notes

1   The Popperian view that it is better to predict strongly than weakly, because strong predictions are more likely to be falsified and therefore more surprising if not falsified, is quite consistent with this assertion. Popper was concerned with the

ex ante choice of research strategy, whereas I am here discussing ex post properties of predictions.

2 In Elster (1983a, 1984), the emphasis is mainly on cases of inadequacy.

3 Rawls (1971), pp. 19–20.

4 In practice, there are many obstacles to determinacy. Some theories require information about preferences and productive capacities that may be impossible to collect, if only because people may not find it in their interest to reveal them. Others require irretrievable information about events in the distant past or about hypothetical events that would have ensued if these past events had been different.

5 Rawls (1971), p. 8.

6 This is largely a euphemism for 'I don't yet have it'.

7 Yaari and Bar-Hillel (1984); Frohlich, Oppenheimer and Eavey (1987).

8 For an example, see Elster (1984), p. 121, n. 17. A recent debate of similar issues is Binmore (1987).

9 The following draws heavily on Elster (1983a), ch. 1, and Elster (1986a).

10 Hume (1739), p. 415.

11 Veyne (1976), p. 667.

12 I discuss this question in Elster (1983a, secs. I.4 and III.4). For the closely related question of whether it makes sense to assess emotional reactions as rational or irrational, see Elster (1985a).

13 We might want to say that, however, if his desire for freedom is caused by the fact that he does not have it. For a brief discussion of such 'counteradaptive preferences' see Elster (1983a), pp. 111–12.

14 Bloch and Reddaway (1978), p. 255.

15 Elster (1983a), ch. 3.

16 Ibid., pp. 117–19.

17 Tocqueville (1969), p. 317.

18 Winston (1980).

19 Lewinsohn et al. (1980); see also Alloy and Abrahamson (1979) and, for a discussion of their findings, Elster (1985a).

20 Becker (1981), p. 224.

21 Nisbett and Ross (1981), p. 271.

22 For this argument, see Williams (1973) and Elster (1984), sec. II.3. A recent challenge by Cook (1987) places too much weight on a (hypothetical) example in which the belief adopted at will is also the one that is better grounded in the evidence. A nonhypothetical example of a decision to adopt an unfounded belief would have been more convincing.

23 Quattrone and Tversky (1986), p. 48.

24 Technically, the function may be continuous and the set be compact and convex.

25 Ullmann-Margalit and Morgenbesser (1977).

26 Harsanyi (1977a), p. 114.

27 A special and important case is that of moral conflict, discussed in Levi (1986).

28 J. Boswell, *The Life of Samuel Johnson*, A. D. 1766 (Aetat 57), a letter from Johnson to Boswell dated 21 August 1766. I owe this reference to John Broome.

29 If I know myself well, I may be able to predict that whatever I do I shall end up preferring the occupation I choose, or perhaps the one that I do not choose, but this is not to know which choice will make me more happy.

30 Heal (1973), p. 300.

31 Sen and Williams (1982), p. 17.

32 De Marsily et al. (1977), p. 521. Italics added.

33 Luce and Raiffa (1957), p. 296; Arrow and Hurwicz (1971). Other proposals are discussed in 1.5.

34 At least this holds for the symmetric version of these games. With asymmetries, tacit bargaining may lead the parties to converge to the equilibrium that favours the party who is least worried by the prospect of the worst outcome. The weak may accept a legal regime that favours the strong because, unlike the strong, they cannot survive in the state of nature.

35 Actually, one of the many problems that beset rational-expectations theory. For a survey, see Begg (1982), pp. 61–70.

36 Keynes (1936), pp. 149–50.

37 Dasgupta and Stiglitz (1980).

38 Menzel (1983), p. 6. The marginal value of the information is controversial, since it depends on an assessment of the value of life.

39 Becker (1976), p. 7.

40 On the general point, see Tversky and Kahneman (1974); Lichtenstein, Fischhoff and Phillips (1982). For a devastating criticism of optimal search theories, see Hey (1981).

41 Elster (1985b).

42 Kolm (1980), pp. 302–11.

43 Ainslie (1982, 1984, 1986).

44 Farber (1976).

45 These examples and many others are extensively discussed in Elster (1985a), ch. 2.

46 Festinger (1957, 1964); Wicklund and Brehm (1976). Economic applications include Akerlof and Dickens (1982) and Schlicht (1984).

47 The example draws upon Galasi and Kertesi (1987).

48 von Weizsäcker (1971) offers a formal model of this process.

49 Middleton (1986).

50 I am indebted to Hilde Sejersted for bringing this story to my attention.

51 This example is taken from Akerlof and Dickens (1982). This otherwise excellent article is marred by the idea that people can choose their own beliefs so that, for instance, they can weigh the psychic benefits of believing that their job is safe against the cost of increased chances of accidents. Although I am sure that both the costs and the benefits of dissonance reduction influence

the extent to which it occurs, I do not think they do so by virtue of conscious comparison since, as argued above, beliefs cannot be deliberately chosen.

52 Sunstein (1986) has a general discussion of such cases.
53 Lerner and Miller (1978).
54 A recent summary is Machina (1987).
55 Tversky and Kahneman (1981).
56 Thaler (1980).
57 Loewenstein (1987).
58 Fischhoff (1983).
59 Machina (1987), p. 146.
60 Tversky and Kahneman (1981), p. 454.
61 Ibid., p. 456.
62 Good summaries are Nisbett and Ross (1981) and Kahneman, Slovic and Tversky, eds. (1982).
63 Arrow (1982).
64 Nisbett and Ross (1981), p. 164, referring to 'the sophomore slump'.
65 Gullestad and Tschudi (1982).
66 Weber (1985), p. 115.
67 Barry (1978), p. 41.
68 See Quattrone and Tversky (1986) for the latter fallacy and Elster (1985b) for a discussion of the former.
69 For exposition and discussion of this problem, see the articles collected in Campbell and Sowden, eds. (1985). A perfect illustration is a circular letter issued by English Baptists around 1770: 'Every soul that comes to Christ to be saved . . . is to be encouraged. . . . The coming soul need not fear that he is not elected, for none but such would be willing to come' (Thompson 1968, p. 38).
70 In addition, focusing on rules can protect one against weakness of will.
71 See Ullmann-Margalit (1985) for an analysis of 'big decisions' which nicely complements the analysis of 'small-decisions' in Ullmann-Margalit and Morgenbesser (1977).
72 Although noncooperative bargaining theory has done much to force determinacy in such problems (Rubinstein 1982), it is mainly of use in two-person contexts. Three-person bargaining problems remain largely indeterminate even in the noncooperative approach (Sutton 1986).
73 To get around this problem it has been suggested that in Third World countries experiments be conducted in which five- or ten-dollar rewards represent high stakes. To get around any ethical problems, all subjects could receive the maximal reward when the experiment was completed, even though told beforehand that they would get it only if they performed well. For reasons explained in Barry (1986), severe ethical problems would still remain.
74 Against those who say that discounting the future only shows a 'taste for the present' and

that *de gustibus non est disputandum*, I would reply, first, that much time discounting is inconsistent (Elster 1985b) and, second, that even consistent time discounting beyond what is justified by mortality tables is a failure of rationality.
75 Janis (1972).
76 Laqueur (1980).
77 Føllesdal (1982).
78 Midgaard (1980); Habermas (1982).
79 Davidson (1980).
80 The situation is somewhat similar to the privileged status of the assumption of selfishness. We can consistently imagine a world in which everybody behaves selfishly all the time, but not a world in which everybody behaves altruistically all the time, because altruism presupposes some nonaltruistic pleasures that the altruist can promote.
81 I disregard the interpretation of satisficing as maximizing under constraints on information-processing capacities. Limited calculating ability is only one obstacle to first-best rationality. A more important obstacle, in my view, is our inherently limited knowledge about the value of information. Also, people with severely limited cognitive capacities may not be able to understand their limits and hence are not, subjectively, constrained by them.
82 Nelson and Winter (1982).
83 Hey (1981, 1982).
84 Notably Heiner (1983, 1988).
85 Levi (1974, 1986).
86 Levi (1986), p. 33, shows that a perfectly sensible way of handling unresolved value conflicts can lead to violation of Sen's 'property alpha', which says that if *a* is chosen in the set (*a*,*b*), *b* should never be chosen in a larger set (*a*, *b*, *c*). Similarly he argues (Levi 1986, ch. 7) that the Ellsberg and Allais paradoxes of choice under risk can be handled without imputing irrationality to the agents who make these apparently inconsistent decisions.
87 Kahneman and Tversky (1979); Tversky and Kahneman (1987).
88 Machina (1983).
89 Loomes and Sugden (1982).
90 Herrnstein and Vaughan (1980); Vaughan and Herrnstein (1987); Herrnstein (1988). A cautiously optimizing approach to animal behaviour is that of Staddon (1983, 1987).
91 Ainslie (1975, 1982, 1984, 1986).
92 I discuss this theory at some length in a companion volume (Elster 1989) to the present book, and the following account must be read only as a sketch of that more extended argument.
93 Barry (1979a), pp. 17–18; Wolfinger and Rosenstone (1980), p. 8 and passim.
94 For the reasoning behind this statement, see Oliver, Marwell and Teixeira (1985) or cases B, D and E in Schelling (1978), p. 220.

95 I am indebted to Amos Tversky for suggesting this to me as an example of social norms.
96 Thaler (1980), p. 43.
97 Edgerton (1985), p. 3.

References

Ainslie, G. (1975). Specious reward. *Psychological Bulletin* 82: 463–96.
_____. (1982). A behavioral economic approach to the defense mechanisms: Freud's energy theory revisited. *Social Science Information* 21: 735–79.
_____. (1984). Behavioral economics II: Motivated involuntary behavior. *Social Science Information* 23: 247–74.
_____. (1986). Beyond microeconomics. In J. Elster (ed.), *The multiple self*, pp. 133–76. Cambridge University Press.
Akerlof, G. and Dickens, W. T. (1982). The economic consequences of cognitive dissonance. *American Economic Review* 72: 307–19.
Arrow, K. and Hurwicz, L. (1971). An optimality criterion for decision-making under uncertainty. In C. F. Carter and J. L. Ford (eds.), *Uncertainty and expectation in economics*, pp. 1–11. Clifton, N.J.: Kelley.
Barry, B. (1978). Comment. In S. Benn et al., *Political participation*, pp. 37–48. Canberra: Australian National University Press.
_____. (1979a). *Sociologists, economists and democracy*, 2d ed. University of Chicago Press.
_____. (1986). Lady Chatterley's lover and doctor Fischer's bomb party. In J. Elster and A. Hylland (eds.), *Foundations of social choice theory*, pp. 11–44. Cambridge University Press.
Becker, G. (1976). *The economic approach to human behavior*. University of Chicago Press.
_____. (1981). *A treatise on the family*. Cambridge, Mass.: Harvard University Press.
Begg, D. K. H. (1982). *The rational expectations revolution in macroeconomics*. Oxford: Allan.
Binmore, K. (1987). Remodeled rational players. *Economics and Philosophy* 3: 179–214.
Bloch, S. and Reddaway, P. (1978). *Russia's political hospitals*. London: Futura Books.
Campbell, R. and Sowden L. (eds.) (1985). *Paradoxes of rationality and cooperation*. Vancouver: University of British Columbia Press.
Cook, J. T. (1987). Deciding to believe without self-deception. *Journal of Philosophy* 84: 441–6.
Dasgupta, P. and Stiglitz, J. (1980). Uncertainty, industrial structure, and the speed of R&D. *Bell Journal of Economics* 11: 1–28.
Davidson, D. (1980). *Essays on actions and events*. New York: Oxford University Press.
De Marsily, G. De et al. (1977). Nuclear waste disposal: Can the geologist guarantee isolation? *Science* 197: 519–27.

Edgerton, R. B. (1985). *Rules, exceptions and social order*. Berkeley and Los Angeles: University of California Press.
Elster, J. (1983a). *Sour Grapes*. Cambridge University Press.
_____. (1984). *Ulysses and the sirens*, rev. ed. Cambridge University Press.
_____. (1985a). Sadder but wiser? Rationality and the emotions. *Social Science Information* 24: 375–406.
_____. (1985b). Weakness of will and the free-rider problem. *Economics and Philosophy* 1: 231–65.
_____. (1986a). Introduction to J. Elster (ed.), *Rational choice*, pp. 1–33. Oxford: Blackwell Publisher.
_____. (1989). *The cement of society*. Cambridge University Press.
Festinger, L. (1957). *A theory of cognitive dissonance*. Stanford, Calif.: Stanford University Press.
_____. (1964). *Conflict, decision and dissonance*. Stanford, Calif.: Stanford University Press.
Fischhoff, B. (1983). Predicting frames. *Journal of Experimental Psychology: Learning, Memory and Cognition* 9: 103–16.
Føllesdal, D. (1982). The status of rationality assumptions in interpretation and in the explanation of action. *Dialectica* 36: 301–16.
Frohlich, N., Oppenheimer, J. and Eavey, C. (1987). Laboratory results on Rawls's distributive justice. *British Journal of Political Economy* 17: 1–21.
Galasi, P. and Kertesi, G. (1987). *The spread of bribery in a Soviet-type economy* (unpublished manuscript).
Gullestad, S. and Tschudi, F. (1982). Labeling theories of mental illness. *Psychiatry and Social Sciences* 2: 213–26.
Habermas, J. (1982). *Zur Theorie des kommunikativen Handelns*. Frankfurt a.M.: Suhrkamp.
Heal, G. (1973). *The theory of economic planning*. Amsterdam: North-Holland.
Heiner, R. (1983). The origin of predictable behavior. *American Economic Review* 83: 560–95.
_____. (1988). The necessity of imperfect decision. *Journal of Economic Behavior and Organization* 10: 29–55.
Herrnstein, R. (1988). A behavioral alternative to utility maximization. In S. Maital (ed.), *Applied behavioral economics*, pp. 3–60. New York: New York University Press.
Herrnstein, R. and Vaughan, W. (1980). Melioration and behavioral allocation. In J. E. R. Staddon (ed.), *Limits to action: The allocation of individual behavior*, pp. 143–76. New York: Academic Press.
Hey, J. D. (1981). Are optimal search rules reasonable? *Journal of Economic Behavior and Organization* 2: 47–70.
_____. (1982). Search for rules of search. *Journal of Economic Behavior and Organization* 3: 65–82.

Hume, D. (1739). *A treatise of human nature*, ed. Selby-Bigge. New York: Oxford University Press 1960.

Janis, I. (1972). *Victims of group-think* Boston: Houghton Mifflin.

Kahneman, D. and Tversky, A. (1979). Prospect theory. *Econometrica* 47: 263–91.

Kahneman, D., Slovic, P. and Tversky, A. (eds.) (1982). *Judgment under uncertainty*. Cambridge University Press.

Keynes, J. (1936). *The general theory of employment, interest and money*. London: Macmillan Press.

Lacqueur, W. (1980). *The terrible secret*. Boston: Little, Brown.

Lerner, M. J. and Miller, D. T. (1978). Just world research and the attribution process. *Psychological Bulletin* 85: 1030–51.

Levi, I. (1974). On indeterminate probabilities. *Journal of Philosophy* 71: 391–418.

———. (1986) *Hard choices*. Cambridge University Press.

Lichtenstein, S., Fischhoff, B. and Phillips, L. D. (1982). Calibration of probabilities: The state of the art to 1980. In D. Kahneman, P. Slovic, and A. Tversky (eds.), *Judgment under uncertainty*, pp. 306–34. Cambridge University Press.

Loewenstein, G. (1987). Frames of mind in intertemporal choice. *Management Science* 34: 200–14.

Loomes, G. and Sugden, R. (1982). Regret theory. *Economic Journal* 92: 805–24.

Luce, R. D. and Raiffa, H. (1957). *Games and decisions*. New York: Wiley.

Machina, M. (1983). Generalized expected utility analysis and the nature of observed violations of the independence axiom. In B. T. Stigum and F. Wenstøp (eds.), *Foundations of utility and risk theory with applications*, pp. 263–93. Dordrecht: Reidel.

———. (1987). Choice under uncertainty. *Journal of Economic Perspectives* 1(1): 121–54.

Menzel, P. T. (1983). *Medical costs, moral choices*. New Haven, Conn.: Yale University Press.

Middleton, E. (1986). Some testable implications of a preference for subjective novelty. *Kyklos* 39: 397–418.

Midgaard, K. (1980). On the significance of language and a richer concept of rationality. In L. Lewin and E. Vedung (eds.), *Politics as rational action*, pp. 83–97. Dordrecht: Reidel.

Nelson, R. and Winter, S. (1982). *An evolutionary theory of economic change*. Cambridge, Mass.: Harvard University Press.

Nisbett, R. and Ross, L. (1981). *Human inference: Strategies and shortcomings of social judgment*. Englewood Cliffs, N.J.: Prentice Hall.

Oliver, P., Marwell, G. and Teixeira, R. (1985). A theory of the critical mass. I. Interdependence, group heterogeneity and the production of collective action. *American Journal of Sociology* 91: 522–56.

Quattrone, G. and Tversky, A. (1986). Self-deception and the voter's illusion. In J. Elster (ed.), *The multiple self*, pp. 35–58. Cambridge University Press.

Rawls, J. (1971). *A theory of justice*. Cambridge, Mass.: Harvard University Press.

Rubinstein, A. (1982). Perfect equilibrium in a bargaining model. *Econometrica* 50: 97–109.

Schelling, T. C. (1978). *Micromotives and macrobehavior*. New York: Norton.

Sen, A. and Williams, B. A. O. (1982). Introduction to A. Sen and B. A. O. Williams (eds.), *Utilitarianism and beyond*, pp. 1–22. Cambridge University Press.

Staddon, J. E. R. (1983). *Adaptive behavior and learning*. Cambridge University Press.

———. (1987). Optimality theory and behavior. In J. Dupre (ed.), *The latest on the best*, pp. 179–98. Cambridge, Mass.: MIT Press.

Sunstein, C. (1986). Legal interference with private preferences. *University of Chicago Law Review* 53: 1129–74.

Sutton, J. (1986). Non-cooperative bargaining theory: An introduction. *Review of Economic Studies* 53: 709–24.

Thaler, R. (1980). Towards a positive theory of consumer choice. *Journal of Economic Behavior and Organization* 1: 39–60.

Thompson, E. P. (1968). *The making of the English working class*. Harmondsworth. Penguin Books.

Tocqueville, A. de (1969). *Democracy in America*. New York: Anchor Books.

Tversky, A. and Kahneman, D. (1974). Judgment under uncertainty. *Science* 185: 1124–30.

———— (1981). The framing of decisions and the psychology of choice. *Science* 211: 453–58.

———. (1987). Rational choice and the framing of decisions. In R. M. Hogarth and M. W. Reder (eds.), *Rational choice*, pp. 67–94. University of Chicago Press.

Ullmann-Margalit, E. (1985). Opting: The case of 'big' decisions (unpublished manuscript).

Ullmann-Margalit, E. and Morgenbesser, S. (1977). Picking and choosing. *Social Research* 44: 757–85.

Vaughan, W. and Herrnstein, R. (1987). Stability, melioration, and natural selection. In L. Green and J. Kagel (eds.), *Advances in behavioral economics*, vol. 1, pp. 185–215. Norwood, N.J.: Ablex.

Veyne, P. (1976). *Le pain et le cirque*. Paris: Editions du Seuil.

Weber, M. (1985). *The Protestant ethic and the spirit of capitalism*. New York: Scribner.

von Weizsäcker, C. C. (1971). Notes on endogenous change of tastes. *Journal of Economic Theory* 3: 345–72.

Wicklund, R. and Brehm, J. (1976). *Perspectives on cognitive dissonance*. Hillsdale, N.J.: Erlbaum.

Williams, B. A. O. (1973). Deciding to believe. In *Problems of the self*, pp. 136–41. Cambridge University Press.

Winston, G. (1980). Addiction and backsliding: A theory of compulsive consumption. *Journal of Economic Behavior and Organization* 1: 295–324.

Wolfinger, R. E. and Ronsenstone, S. J. (1980). *Who votes?* New Haven, Conn.: Yale University Press.

Yaari, M. and Bar-Hillel, M. (1984). On dividing justly. *Social Choice and Welfare* I: 1–25.

Chapter 6: Extensional Versus Intuitive Reasoning: The Conjunction Fallacy in Probability Judgment

AMOS TVERSKY AND DANIEL KAHNEMAN

Uncertainty is an unavoidable aspect of the human condition. Many significant choices must be based on beliefs about the likelihood of such uncertain events as the guilt of a defendant, the result of an election, the future value of the dollar, the outcome of a medical operation, or the response of a friend. Because we normally do not have adequate formal models for computing the probabilities of such events, intuitive judgment is often the only practical method for assessing uncertainty.

The question of how lay people and experts evaluate the probabilities of uncertain events has attracted considerable research interest in the last decade (see, e.g., Einhorn & Hogarth, 1981; Kahneman, Slovic, & Tversky, 1982; Nisbett & Ross, 1980). Much of this research has compared intuitive inferences and probability judgments to the rules of statistics and the laws of probability. The student of judgment uses the probability calculus as a standard of comparison much as a student of perception might compare the perceived sizes of objects to their physical sizes. Unlike the correct size of objects, however, the "correct" probability of events is not easily defined. Because individuals who have different knowledge or who hold different beliefs must be allowed to assign different probabilities to the same event, no single value can be correct for all people. Furthermore, a correct probability cannot always be determined even for a single person. Outside the domain of random sampling, probability theory does not determine the probabilities of uncertain events – it merely imposes constraints on the relations among them. For

example, if A is more probable than B, then the complement of A must be less probable than the complement of B.

The laws of probability derive from extensional considerations. A probability measure is defined on a family of events and each event is construed as a set of possibilities, such as the three ways of getting a 10 on a throw of a pair of dice. The probability of an event equals the sum of the probabilities of its disjoint outcomes. Probability theory has traditionally been used to analyze repetitive chance processes, but the theory has also been applied to essentially unique events where probability is not reducible to the relative frequency of "favorable" outcomes. The probability that the man who sits next to you on the plane is unmarried equals the probability that he is a bachelor plus the probability that he is either divorced or widowed. Additivity applies even when probability does not have a frequentistic interpretation and when the elementary events are not equiprobable.

The simplest and most fundamental qualitative law of probability is the extension rule: If the extension of A includes the extension of B (i.e., A ⊃ B) then $P(A) \geq P(B)$. Because the set of possibilities associated with a conjunction A&B is included in the set of possibilities associated with B, the same principle can also be expressed by the conjunction rule $P(A\&B) \leq P(B)$: A conjunction cannot be more probable than one of its constituents. This rule holds regardless of whether A and B are independent and is valid for any probability assignment on the same sample space. Furthermore, it applies not

Reproduced with permission from Tversky, A., and Kahneman, D. (1983) Extensional versus intuitive reasoning: The conjunction fallacy in probability judgment. *Psychological Review*, 90, 293–315.

only to the standard probability calculus but also to nonstandard models such as upper and lower probability (Dempster, 1967; Suppes, 1975), belief function (Shafer, 1976), Baconian probability (Cohen, 1977), rational belief (Kyburg, 1983), and possibility theory (Zadeh, 1978).

In contrast to formal theories of belief, intuitive judgments of probability are generally not extensional. People do not normally analyze daily events into exhaustive lists of possibilities or evaluate compound probabilities by aggregating elementary ones. Instead, they commonly use a limited number of heuristics, such as representativeness and availability (Kahneman et al., 1982). Our conception of judgmental heuristics is based on *natural assessments* that are routinely carried out as part of the perception of events and the comprehension of messages. Such natural assessments include computations of similarity and representativeness, attributions of causality, and evaluations of the availability of associations and exemplars. These assessments, we propose, are performed even in the absence of a specific task set, although their results are used to meet task demands as they arise. For example, the mere mention of "horror movies" activates instances of horror movies and evokes an assessment of their availability. Similarly, the statement that Woody Allen's aunt had hoped that he would be a dentist elicits a comparison of the character to the stereotype and an assessment of representativeness. It is presumably the mismatch between Woody Allen's personality and our stereotype of a dentist that makes the thought mildly amusing. Although these assessments are not tied to the estimation of frequency or probability, they are likely to play a dominant role when such judgments are required. The availability of horror movies may be used to answer the question, "What proportion of the movies produced last year were horror movies?", and representativeness may control the judgment that a particular boy is more likely to be an actor than a dentist.

The term *judgmental heuristic* refers to a strategy – whether deliberate or not – that relies on a natural assessment to produce an estimation or a prediction. One of the manifestations of a heuristic is the relative neglect of other considerations. For example, the resemblance of a child to various professional stereotypes may be given too much weight in predicting future vocational choice, at the expense of other pertinent data such as the base-rate frequencies of occupations. Hence, the use of judgmental heuristics gives rise to predictable biases. Natural assess-

ments can affect judgments in other ways, for which the term *heuristic* is less apt. First, people sometimes misinterpret their task and fail to distinguish the required judgment from the natural assessment that the problem evokes. Second, the natural assessment may act as an anchor to which the required judgment is assimilated, even when the judge does not intend to use the one to estimate the other.

Previous discussions of errors of judgment have focused on deliberate strategies and on misinterpretations of tasks. The present treatment calls special attention to the processes of anchoring and assimilation, which are often neither deliberate nor conscious. An example from perception may be instructive: If two objects in a picture of a three-dimensional scene have the same picture size, the one that appears more distant is not only seen as "really" larger but also as larger in the picture. The natural computation of real size evidently influences the (less natural) judgment of picture size, although observers are unlikely to confuse the two values or to use the former to estimate the latter.

The natural assessments of representativeness and availability do not conform to the extensional logic of probability theory. In particular, a conjunction can be more representative than one of its constituents, and instances of a specific category can be easier to retrieve than instances of a more inclusive category. The following demonstration illustrates the point. When they were given 60 sec to list seven-letter words of a specified form, students at the University of British Columbia (UBC) produced many more words of the form _ _ _ _ ing than of the form _ _ _ _ _ n _, although the latter class includes the former. The average numbers of words produced in the two conditions were 6.4 and 2.9, respectively, $t(44) = 4.70$, $p < .01$. In this test of availability, the increased efficacy of memory search suffices to offset the reduced extension of the target class.

Our treatment of the availability heuristic (Tversky & Kahneman, 1973) suggests that the differential availability of *ing* words and of _ n _ words should be reflected in judgments of frequency. The following questions test this prediction.

In four pages of a novel (about 2,000 words), how many words would you expect to find that have the form _ _ _ _ ing (seven-letter words that end with "ing")? Indicate your best estimate by circling one of the values below:

0   1–2   3–4   5–7   8–10   11–15   16+.

A second version of the question requested estimates for words of the form _ _ _ _ _ n _. The median estimates were 13.4 for *ing* words ($n = 52$), and 4.7 for _ n _ words ($n = 53$, $p < .01$, by median test), contrary to the extension rule. Similar results were obtained for the comparison of words of the form _ _ _ _ _ *ly* with words of the form _ _ _ _ _ *l* _; the median estimates were 8.8 and 4.4, respectively.

This example illustrates the structure of the studies reported in this article. We constructed problems in which a reduction of extension was associated with an increase in availability or representativeness, and we tested the conjunction rule in judgments of frequency or probability. In the next section we discuss the representativeness heuristic and contrast it with the conjunction rule in the context of person perception. The third section describes conjunction fallacies in medical prognoses, sports forecasting, and choice among bets. In the fourth section we investigate probability judgments for conjunctions of causes and effects and describe conjunction errors in scenarios of future events. Manipulations that enable respondents to resist the conjunction fallacy are explored in the fifth section, and the implications of the results are discussed in the last section.

Representative Conjunctions

Modern research on categorization of objects and events (Mervis & Rosch, 1983; Rosch, 1978; Smith & Medin, 1981) has shown that information is commonly stored and processed in relation to mental models, such as prototypes and schemata. It is therefore natural and economical for the probability of an event to be evaluated by the degree to which that event is representative of an appropriate mental model (Kahneman & Tversky, 1972, 1973; Tversky & Kahneman, 1971, 1982). Because many of the results reported here are attributed to this heuristic, we first briefly analyze the concept of representativeness and illustrate its role in probability judgment.

Representativeness is an assessment of the degree of correspondence between a sample and a population, an instance and a category, an act and an actor or, more generally, between an outcome and a model. The model may refer to a person, a coin, or the world economy, and the respective outcomes could be marital status, a sequence of heads and tails, or the current price of gold. Representativeness can be investigated empirically by asking people, for example, which

of two sequences of heads and tails is more representative of a fair coin or which of two professions is more representative of a given personality. This relation differs from other notions of proximity in that it is distinctly directional. It is natural to describe a sample as more or less representative of its parent population or a species (e.g., robin, penguin) as more or less representative of a superordinate category (e.g., bird). It is awkward to describe a population as representative of a sample or a category as representative of an instance.

When the model and the outcomes are described in the same terms, representativeness is reducible to similarity. Because a sample and a population, for example, can be described by the same attributes (e.g., central tendency and variability), the sample appears representative if its salient statistics match the corresponding parameters of the population. In the same manner, a person seems representative of a social group if his or her personality resembles the stereotypical member of that group. Representativeness, however, is not always reducible to similarity; it can also reflect causal and correlational beliefs (see, e.g., Chapman & Chapman, 1967; Jennings, Amabile, & Ross, 1982; Nisbett & Ross, 1980). A particular act (e.g., suicide) is representative of a person because we attribute to the actor a disposition to commit the act, not because the act resembles the person. Thus, an outcome is representative of a model if the salient features match or if the model has a propensity to produce the outcome.

Representativeness tends to covary with frequency: Common instances and frequent events are generally more representative than unusual instances and rare events. The representative summer day is warm and sunny, the representative American family has two children, and the representative height of an adult male is about 5 feet 10 inches. However, there are notable circumstances where representativeness is at variance with both actual and perceived frequency. First, a highly specific outcome can be representative but infrequent. Consider a numerical variable, such as weight, that has a unimodal frequency distribution in a given population. A narrow interval near the mode of the distribution is generally more representative of the population than a wider interval near the tail. For example, 68% of a group of Stanford University undergraduates ($N = 105$) stated that it is more representative for a female Stanford student "to weigh between 124 and 125 pounds" than "to weigh more than 135 pounds".

On the other hand, 78% of a different group ($N = 102$) stated that among female Stanford students there are more "women who weigh more than 135 pounds" than "women who weigh between 124 and 125 pounds." Thus, the narrow modal interval (124–125 pounds) was judged to be more representative but less frequent than the broad tail interval (above 135 pounds).

Second, an attribute is representative of a class if it is very diagnostic, that is, if the relative frequency of this attribute is much higher in that class than in a relevant reference class. For example, 65% of the subjects ($N = 105$) stated that it is more representative for a Hollywood actress "to be divorced more than 4 times" than "to vote Democratic." Multiple divorce is diagnostic of Hollywood actresses because it is part of the stereotype that the incidence of divorce is higher among Hollywood actresses than among other women. However, 83% of a different group ($N = 102$) stated that, among Hollywood actresses, there are more "women who vote Democratic" than "women who are divorced more than 4 times." Thus, the more diagnostic attribute was judged to be more representative but less frequent than an attribute (voting Democratic) of lower diagnosticity. Third, an unrepresentative instance of a category can be fairly representative of a superordinate category. For example, chicken is a worse exemplar of a bird than of an animal, and rice is an unrepresentative vegetable, although it is a representative food.

The preceding observations indicate that representativeness is nonextensional: It is not determined by frequency, and it is not bound by class inclusion. Consequently, the test of the conjunction rule in probability judgments offers the sharpest contrast between the extensional logic of probability theory and the psychological principles of representativeness. Our first set of studies of the conjunction rule were conducted in 1974, using occupation and political affiliation as target attributes to be predicted singly or in conjunction from brief personality sketches (see Tversky & Kahneman, 1982, for a brief summary). The studies described in the present section replicate and extend our earlier work. We used the following personality sketches of two fictitious individuals, Bill and Linda, followed by a set of occupations and avocations associated with each of them.

Bill is 34 years old. He is intelligent, but unimaginative, compulsive, and generally lifeless. In school, he was strong in mathe-matics but weak in social studies and humanities.

Bill is a physician who plays poker for a hobby.
Bill is an architect.
Bill is an accountant. (A)
Bill plays jazz for a hobby. (J)
Bill surfs for a hobby.
Bill is a reporter.
Bill is an accountant who plays jazz for a hobby. (A&J)
Bill climbs mountains for a hobby.

Linda is 31 years old, single, outspoken, and very bright. She majored in philosophy. As a student, she was deeply concerned with issues of discrimination and social justice, and also participated in anti-nuclear demonstrations.

Linda is a teacher in elementary school.
Linda works in a bookstore and takes Yoga classes.
Linda is active in the feminist movement. (F)
Linda is a psychiatric social worker.
Linda is a member of the League of Women Voters.
Linda is a bank teller. (T)
Linda is an insurance salesperson.
Linda is a bank teller and is active in the feminist movement. (T&F)

As the reader has probably guessed, the description of Bill was constructed to be representative of an accountant (A) and unrepresentative of a person who plays jazz for a hobby (J). The description of Linda was constructed to be representative of an active feminist (F) and unrepresentative of a bank teller (T). We also expected the ratings of representativeness to be higher for the classes defined by a conjunction of attributes (A&J for Bill, T&F for Linda) than for the less representative constituent of each conjunction (J and T, respectively).

A group of 88 undergraduates at UBC ranked the eight statements associated with each description by "the degree to which Bill (Linda) resembles the typical member of that class." The results confirmed our expectations. The percentages of respondents who displayed the predicted order (A > A & J > J for Bill; F > T & F > T for Linda) were 87% and 85%, respectively. This finding is neither surprising nor objectionable. If, like similarity and prototypicality, representativeness depends on both common and distinctive features (Tversky, 1977), it should be enhanced by the addition of shared features. Adding eyebrows to a schematic face makes it

Table 1: Tests of the Conjunction Rule in Likelihood Rankings

Subjects	Problem	Direct Test				Indirect Test		
		V	R(A & B)	R(B)	N	R(A & B)	R(B)	Total N
Naive	Bill	92	2.5	4.5	94	2.3	4.5	88
	Linda	89	3.3	4.4	88	3.3	4.4	86
Informed	Bill	86	2.6	4.5	56	2.4	4.2	56
	Linda	90	3.0	4.3	53	2.9	3.9	55
Sophisticated	Bill	83	2.6	4.7	32	2.5	4.6	32
	Linda	85	3.2	4.3	32	3.1	4.3	32

Note. V = percentage of violations of the conjunction rule; R (A & B) and R (B) = mean rank assigned to A & B and to B, respectively; N = number of subjects in the direct test; Total N = total number of subjects in the indirect test, who were about equally divided between the two groups.

more similar to another schematic face with eyebrows (Gati & Tversky, 1982). Analogously, the addition of feminism to the profession of bank teller improves the match of Linda's current activities to her personality. More surprising and less acceptable is the finding that the great majority of subjects also rank the conjunctions (A & J and T & F) as more *probable* than their less representative constituents (J and T). The following sections describe and analyze this phenomenon.

Indirect and Subtle Tests

Experimental tests of the conjunction rule can be divided into three types: *indirect tests, direct-subtle tests,* and *direct-transparent tests.* In the indirect tests, one group of subjects evaluates the probability of the conjunction, and another group of subjects evaluates the probability of its constituents. No subject is required to compare a conjunction (e.g., "Linda is a bank teller and a feminist") to its constituents. In the direct-subtle tests, subjects compare the conjunction to its less representative constituent, but the inclusion relation between the events it not emphasized. In the direct-transparent tests, the subjects evaluate or compare the probabilities of the conjunction and its constituent in a format that highlights the relation between them.

The three experimental procedures investigate different hypotheses. The indirect procedure tests whether probability judgments conform to the conjunction rule; the direct-subtle procedure tests whether people will take advantage of an opportunity to compare the critical events; the direct-transparent procedure tests whether people will obey the conjunction rule when they are compelled to compare the critical events. This sequence of tests also describes the

course of our investigation, which began with the observation of violations of the conjunction rule in indirect tests and proceeded – to our increasing surprise – to the finding of stubborn failures of that rule in several direct-transparent tests.

Three groups of respondents took part in the main study. The statistically *naive* group consisted of undergraduate students at Stanford University and UBC who had no background in probability or statistics. The *informed* group consisted of first-year graduate students in psychology and in education and of medical students at Stanford who were all familiar with the basic concepts of probability after one or more courses in statistics. The *sophisticated* group consisted of doctoral students in the decision science program of the Stanford Business School who had taken several advanced courses in probability, statistics, and decision theory.

Subjects in the main study received one problem (either Bill or Linda) first in the format of a direct test. They were asked to rank all eight statements associated with that problem (including the conjunction, its separate constituents, and five filler items) according to their probability, using 1 for the most probable and 8 for the least probable. The subjects then received the remaining problem in the format of an indirect test in which the list of alternatives included either the conjunction or its separate constituents. The same five filler items were used in both the direct and the indirect versions of each problem.

Table 1 presents the average ranks (R) of the conjunction R(A & B) and of its less representative constituents R(B), relative to the set of five filler items. The percentage of violations of the conjunction rule in the direct test is denoted by

V. The results can be summarized as follows: (a) the conjunction is ranked higher than its less likely constituents in all 12 comparisons, (b) there is no consistent difference between the ranks of the alternatives in the direct and indirect tests, (c) the overall incidence of violations of the conjunction rule in direct tests is 88%, which virtually coincides with the incidence of the corresponding pattern in judgments of representativeness, and (d) there is no effect of statistical sophistication in either indirect or direct tests.

The violation of the conjunction rule in a direct comparison of B to A & B is called the *conjunction fallacy*. Violations inferred from between-subjects comparisons are called *conjunction errors*. Perhaps the most surprising aspect of Table 1 is the lack of any difference between indirect and direct tests. We had expected the conjunction to be judged more probable than the less likely of its constituents in an indirect test, in accord with the pattern observed in judgments of representativeness. However, we also expected that even naive respondents would notice the repetition of some attributes, alone and in conjunction with others, and that they would then apply the conjunction rule and rank the conjunction below its constituents. This expectation was violated, not only by statistically naive undergraduates but even by highly sophisticated respondents. In both direct and indirect tests, the subjects apparently ranked the outcomes by the degree to which Bill (or Linda) matched the respective stereotypes. The correlation between the mean ranks of probability and representativeness was .96 for Bill and .98 for Linda. Does the conjunction rule hold when the relation of inclusion is made highly transparent? The studies described in the next section abandon all subtlety in an effort to compel the subjects to detect and appreciate the inclusion relation between the target events.

Transparent Tests

This section describes a series of increasingly desperate manipulations designed to induce subjects to obey the conjunction rule. We first presented the description of Linda to a group of 142 undergraduates at UBC and asked them to check which of two alternatives was more probable:

Linda is a bank teller. (T)

Linda is a bank teller and is active in the feminist movement. (T&F)

The order of alternatives was inverted for one half of the subjects, but this manipulation had no effect. Overall, 85% of respondents indicated that T&F was more probable than T, in a flagrant violation of the conjunction rule.

Surprised by the finding, we searched for alternative interpretations of the subjects' responses. Perhaps the subjects found the question too trivial to be taken literally and consequently interpreted the inclusive statement T as T & not-F; that is, "Linda is a bank teller and is *not* a feminist." In such a reading, of course, the observed judgments would not violate the conjunction rule. To test this interpretation, we asked a new group of subjects ($N = 119$) to assess the probability of T and of T & F on a 9-point scale ranging from 1 (extremely unlikely) to 9 (extremely likely). Because it is sensible to rate probabilities even when one of the events includes the other, there was no reason for respondents to interpret T as T & not-F. The pattern of responses obtained with the new version was the same as before. The mean ratings of probability were 3.5 for T and 5.6 for T & F, and 82% of subjects assigned a higher rating to T & F than they did to T.

Although subjects do not spontaneously apply the conjunction rule, perhaps they can recognize its validity. We presented another group of UBC undergraduates with the description of Linda followed by the two statements, T and T & F, and asked them to indicate which of the following two arguments they found more convincing.

> Argument 1. Linda is more likely to be a bank teller than she is to be a feminist bank teller, because every feminist bank teller is a bank teller, but some women bank tellers are not feminists, and Linda could be one of them.

> Argument 2. Linda is more likely to be a feminist bank teller than she is likely to be a bank teller, because she resembles an active feminist more than she resembles a bank teller.

The majority of subjects (65%, n = 58) chose the invalid resemblance argument (Argument 2) over the valid extensional argument (Argument 1). Thus, a deliberate attempt to induce a reflective attitude did not eliminate the appeal of the representativeness heuristic.

We made a further effort to clarify the inclusive nature of the event T by representing it as a disjunction. (Note that the conjunction rule can also be expressed as a disjunction rule P (A or B) ≥ P(B).) The description of Linda was used again, with a 9-point rating scale for judgments of probability, but the statement T was replaced by

> Linda is a bank teller whether or not she is active in the feminist movement. (T*)

This formulation emphasizes the inclusion of T & F in T. Despite the transparent relation between the statements, the mean ratings of likelihood were 5.1 for T & F and 3.8 for T* $p < .01$, by t test). Furthermore, 57% of the subjects (n = 75) committed the conjunction fallacy by rating T & F higher than T*, and only 16% gave a lower rating to T & F than to T*.

The violations of the conjunction rule in direct comparisons of T & F to T* are remarkable because the extension of "Linda is a bank teller whether or not she is active in the feminist movement" clearly includes the extension of "Linda is a bank teller and is active in the feminist movement." Many subjects evidently failed to draw extensional inferences from the phrase "whether or not," which may have been taken to indicate a weak disposition. This interpretation was supported by a between-subjects comparison, in which different subjects evaluated T, T*, and T & F on a 9-point scale after evaluating the common filler statement, "Linda is a psychiatric social worker." The average ratings were 3.3 for T, 3.9 for T*, and 4.5 for T & F, with each mean significantly different from both others. The statements T and T* are of course extensionally equivalent, but they are assigned different probabilities. Because feminism fits Linda, the mere mention of this attribute makes T* more likely than T, and a definite commitment to it makes the probability of T & F even higher!

Modest success in loosening the grip of the conjunction fallacy was achieved by asking subjects to choose whether to bet on T or on T & F. The subjects were given Linda's description, with the following instruction:

> If you could win $10 by betting on an event, which of the following would you choose to bet on? (Check one)

The percentage of violations of the conjunction rule in this task was "only" 56% (n = 60), much too high for comfort but substantially lower than the typical value for comparisons of the two events in terms of probability. We conjecture that the betting context draws attention to the conditions in which one bet pays off whereas the other does not, allowing some subjects to discover that a bet on T dominates a bet on T & F.

The respondents in the studies described in this section were statistically naive undergraduates at UBC. Does statistical education eradicate the fallacy? To answer this question, 64 graduate students of social sciences at the University of California, Berkeley and at Stanford University, all with credit for several statistics courses, were given the rating-scale version of the direct test of the conjunction rule for the Linda problem. For the first time in this series of studies, the mean rating for T & F (3.5) was lower than the rating assigned to T (3.8), and only 36% of respondents committed the fallacy. Thus, statistical sophistication produced a majority who conformed to the conjunction rule in a transparent test, although the incidence of violations was fairly high even in this group of intelligent and sophisticated respondents.

Elsewhere (Kahneman & Tversky, 1982a), we distinguished between positive and negative accounts of judgments and preferences that violate normative rules. A positive account focuses on the factors that produce a particular response; a negative account seeks to explain why the correct response was not made. The positive analysis of the Bill and Linda problems invokes the representativeness heuristic. The stubborn persistence of the conjunction fallacy in highly transparent problems, however, lends special interest to the characteristic question of a negative analysis: Why do intelligent and reasonably well-educated people fail to recognize the applicability of the conjunction rule in transparent problems? Postexperimental interviews and class discussions with many subjects shed some light on this question. Naive as well as sophisticated subjects generally noticed the nesting of the target events in the direct-transparent test, but the naive, unlike the sophisticated, did not appreciate its significance for probability assessment. On the other hand, most naive subjects did not attempt to defend their responses. As one subject said after acknowledging the validity of the conjunction rule, "I thought you only asked for my opinion."

The inverviews and the results of the direct transparent tests indicate that naive subjects do not spontaneously treat the conjunction rule as decisive. Their attitude is reminiscent of children's responses in a Piagetian experiment. The child in the preconservation stage is not altogether blind to arguments based on conservation of volume and typically expects quantity to be conserved (Bruner, 1966). What the child fails to see is that the conservation argument is decisive and should overrule the perceptual impression that the tall container holds more water than the short one. Similarly, naive subjects generally endorse the conjunction rule in the abstract, but their application of this rule to the Linda problem is blocked by the compelling impression that T & F is more representative of her than T is. In this context, the adult subjects reason as if they had not reached the stage of formal operations. A full understanding of a principle of physics, logic, or statistics requires knowledge of the conditions under which it prevails over conflicting arguments, such as the height of the liquid in a container or the representativeness of an outcome. The recognition of the decisive nature of rules distinguishes different developmental stages in studies of conservation; it also distinguishes different levels of statistical sophistication in the present series of studies.

More Representative Conjunctions

The preceding studies revealed massive violations of the conjunction rule in the domain of person perception and social stereotypes. Does the conjunction rule fare better in other areas of judgment? Does it hold when the uncertainty regarding the target events is attributed to chance rather than to partial ignorance? Does expertise in the relevant subject matter protect against the conjunction fallacy? Do financial incentives help respondents see the light? The following studies were designed to answer these questions.

Medical Judgment

In this study we asked practicing physicians to make intuitive predictions on the basis of clinical evidence.[1] We chose to study medical judgment because physicians possess expert knowledge and because intuitive judgments often play an important role in medical decision making. Two groups of physicians took part in the study. The first group consisted of 37 internists from the greater Boston area who were taking a postgraduate course at Harvard University. The second group consisted of 66 internists with admitting privileges in the New England Medical Center. They were given problems of the following type:

A 55-year-old woman had pulmonary embolism documented angiographically 10 days after a cholecystectomy.

Please rank order the following in terms of the probability that they will be among the conditions and experienced by the patient (use 1 for the most likely and 6 for the least likely). Naturally, the patient could experience more than one of these conditions.

dyspnea and hemiparesis (A & B)	syncope and tachycardia hemiparesis (B)
calf pain	hemoptysis
pleuritic chest pain	

The symptoms listed for each problem included one, denoted B, which was judged by our consulting physicians to be nonrepresentative of the patient's condition, and the conjunction of B with another highly representative symptom denoted Λ. In the above example of pulmonary embolism (blood clots in the lung), dyspnea (shortness of breath) is a typical symptom, whereas hemiparesis (partial paralysis) is very atypical. Each participant first received three (or two) problems in the indirect format, where the list included either B or the conjunction A & B, but not both, followed by two (or three) problems in the direct format illustrated above. The design was balanced so that each problem appeared about an equal number of times in each format. An independent group of 32 physicians from Stanford University were asked to rank each list of symptoms "by the degree to which they are representative of the clinical condition of the patient."

The design was essentially the same as in the Bill and Linda study. The results of the two experiments were also very similar. The correlation between mean ratings by probability and by representativeness exceeded .95 in all five problems. For every one of the five problems, the conjunction of an unlikely symptom with a likely one was judged more probable than the less likely constituent. The ranking of symptoms was the same in direct and indirect tests: The overall mean ranks of A & B and of B, respectively, were 2.7 and 4.6 in the direct tests and 2.8 and 4.3 in the indirect tests. The incidence of violations of the conjunction rule in direct tests ranged from 73% to 100%, with an average of 91%. Evidently, substantive expertise does not displace representativeness and does not prevent conjunction errors.

Can the results be interpreted without imputing to these experts a consistent violation of the conjunction rule? The instructions used in the present study were especially designed to eliminate the interpretation of Symptom B as an exhaustive description of the relevant facts, which would imply the absence of Symptom A. Participants were instructed to rank symptoms in terms of the probability "that they will be among the conditions experienced by the patient." They were also reminded that "the patient could experience more than one of these conditions." To test the effect of these instructions, the following question was included at the end of the questionnaire:

In assessing the probability that the patient described has a particular symptom X, did you assume that (check one)
X is the *only* symptom experienced by the patient?
X is *among* the symptoms experienced by the patient?

Sixty of the 62 physicians who were asked this question checked the second answer, rejecting an interpretation of events that could have justified an apparent violation of the conjunction rule.

An additional group of 24 physicians, mostly residents at Stanford Hospital, participated in a group discussion in which they were confronted with their conjunction fallacies in the same questionnaire. The respondents did not defend their answers, although some references were made to "the nature of clinical experience." Most participants appeared surprised and dismayed to have made an elementary error of reasoning. Because the conjunction fallacy is easy to expose, people who committed it are left with the feeling that they should have known better.

Predicting Wimbledon

The uncertainty encountered in the previous studies regarding the prognosis of a patient or the occupation of a person is normally attributed to incomplete knowledge rather than to the operation of a chance process. Recent studies of inductive reasoning about daily events, conducted by Nisbett, Krantz, Jepson, and Kunda (1981), indicated that statistical principles (e.g., the law of large numbers) are commonly applied in domains such as sports and gambling, which include a random element. The next two studies test the conjunction rule in predictions of the outcomes of a sports event and of a game of chance, where the random aspect of the process is particularly salient.

A group of 93 subjects, recruited through an advertisement in the University of Oregon newspaper, were presented with the following problem in October 1980:

Suppose Bjorn Borg reaches the Wimbledon finals in 1981. Please rank order the following outcomes from most to least likely.
A. Borg will win the match (1.7)
B. Borg will lose the first set (2.7)
C. Borg will lose the first set but win the match (2.2)
D. Borg will win the first set but lose the match (3.5)

The average rank of each outcome (1 = most probable, 2 = second most probable, etc.) is given in parentheses. The outcomes were chosen to represent different levels of strength for the player, Borg, with A indicating the highest strength; C, a rather lower level because it indicates a weakness in the first set; B, lower still because it only mentions this weakness; and D, lowest of all.

After winning his fifth Wimbledon title in 1980, Borg seemed extremely strong. Consequently, we hypothesized that Outcome C would be judged more probable than Outcome B, contrary to the conjunction rule, because C represents a better performance for Borg than does B. The mean rankings indicate that this hypothesis was confirmed; 72% of the respondents assigned a higher rank to C than to B, violating the conjunction rule in a direct test.

Is it possible that the subjects interpreted the target events in a nonextensional manner that could justify or explain the observed ranking? It is well known that connectives (e.g., *and, or, if*) are often used in ordinary language in ways that depart from their logical definitions. Perhaps the respondents interpreted the conjunction (A and B) as a disjunction (A or B), an implication (A implies B), or a conditional statement (A if B). Alternatively, the event B could be interpreted in the presence of the conjunction as B and not A. To investigate these possibilities, we presented to another group of 56 naive subjects at Stanford University the hypothetical results of the relevant tennis match, coded as sequences of wins and losses. For example, the sequence LWWLW denotes a five-set match in which Borg lost (L) the first and the third sets but won (W) the other sets and the match. For each sequence the subjects were asked to examine the four target events of the original Borg problem and to indicate, by marking + or −, whether the given sequence was consistent or inconsistent with each of the events.

With very few exceptions, all of the subjects marked the sequences according to the standard (extensional) interpretation of the target events. A sequence was judged consistent with the conjunction "Borg will lose the first set but win the match" when both constituents were satisfied (e.g., LWWLW) but not when either one or both constituents failed. Evidently, these subjects did not interpret the conjunction as an implication, a conditional statement, or a disjunction. Furthermore, both LWWLW and LWLWL were judged consistent with the inclusive event "Borg will lose the first set," contrary to the hypothesis that the inclusive event B is understood in the context of the other events as "Borg will lose the first set and the match." The classification of sequences therefore indicated little or no ambiguity regarding the extension of the target events. In particular, all sequences that were classified as instances of B&A were also classified as instances of B, but some sequences that were classified as instances of B were judged inconsistent with B&A, in accord with the standard interpretation in which the conjunction rule should be satisfied.

Another possible interpretation of the conjunction error maintains that instead of assessing the probability $P(B/E)$ of Hypothesis B (e.g., that Linda is a bank teller) in light of evidence E (Linda's personality), subjects assess the inverse probability $P(E/B)$ of the evidence given the hypothesis in question. Because $P(E/A \& B)$ may well exceed $P(E/B)$, the subjects' responses could be justified under this interpretation. Whatever plausibility this account may have in the case of Linda, it is surely inapplicable to the present study where it makes no sense to assess the conditional probability that Borg will reach the finals given the outcome of the final match.

Risky Choice

If the conjunction fallacy cannot be justified by a reinterpretation of the target events, can it be rationalized by a nonstandard conception of probability? On this hypothesis, representativeness is treated as a legitimate nonextensional interpretation of probability rather than as a fallible heuristic. The conjunction fallacy, then, may be viewed as a misunderstanding regarding the meaning of the word *probability*. To investigate this hypothesis we tested the conjunction rule in the following decision problem, which

provides an incentive to choose the most probable event, although the word *probability* is not mentioned.

Consider a regular six-sided die with four green faces and two red faces. The die will be rolled 20 times and the sequence of greens (G) and reds (R) will be recorded. You are asked to select one sequence, from a set of three, and you will win $25 if the sequence you chose appears on successive rolls of the die. Please check the sequence of greens and reds on which you prefer to bet.

   (a) RGRRR
   (b) GRGRRR
   (c) GRRRRR

Note that Sequence 1 can be obtained from Sequence 2 by deleting the first G. By the conjunction rule, therefore, Sequence 1 must be more probable than Sequence 2. Note also that all three sequences are rather unrepresentative of the die because they contain more Rs than Gs. However, Sequence 2 appears to be an improvement over Sequence 1 because it contains a higher proportion of the more likely color. A group of 50 respondents were asked to rank the events by the degree to which they are representative of the die; 88% ranked Sequence 2 highest and Sequence 3 lowest. Thus, Sequence 2 is favored by representativeness, although it is dominated by Sequence 1.

A total of 260 students at UBC and Stanford University were given the choice version of the problem. There were no significant differences between the populations, and their results were pooled. The subjects were run in groups of 30 to 50 in a classroom setting. About one half of the subjects ($N = 125$) actually played the gamble with real payoffs. The choice was hypothetical for the other subjects. The percentages of subjects who chose the dominated option of Sequence 2 were 65% with real payoffs and 62% in the hypothetical format. Only 2% of the subjects in both groups chose Sequence 3.

To facilitate the discovery of the relation between the two critical sequences, we presented a new group of 59 subjects with a (hypothetical) choice problem in which Sequence 2 was replaced by RGRRRG. This new sequence was preferred over Sequence 1, RGRRR, by 63% of the respondents, although the first five elements of the two sequences were identical. These results suggest that subjects coded each sequence in terms of the proportion of Gs and Rs and ranked the sequences by the discrepancy between the proportions in the two sequences (1/5 and 1/3) and the expected value of 2/3.

It is apparent from these results that conjunction errors are not restricted to misunderstandings of the word *probability*. Our subjects followed the representativeness heuristic even when the word was not mentioned and even in choices involving substantial payoffs. The results further show that the conjunction fallacy is not restricted to esoteric interpretations of the connective *and*, because that connective was also absent from the problem. The present test of the conjunction rule was direct, in the sense defined earlier, because the subjects were required to compare two events, one of which included the other. However, informal interviews with some of the respondents suggest that the test was subtle: The relation of inclusion between Sequences 1 and 2 was apparently noted by only a few of the subjects. Evidently, people are not attuned to the detection of nesting among events, even when these relations are clearly displayed.

Suppose that the relation of dominance between Sequences 1 and 2 is called to the subjects' attention. Do they immediately appreciate its force and treat it as a decisive argument for Sequence 1? The original choice problem (without Sequence 3) was presented to a new group of 88 subjects at Stanford University. These subjects, however, were not asked to select the sequence on which they preferred to bet but only to indicate which of the following two arguments, if any, they found correct.

Argument 1: The first sequence (RGRRR) is more probable than the second (GRGRRR) because the second sequence is the same as the first with an additional G at the beginning. Hence, every time the second sequence occurs, the first sequence must also occur. Consequently, you can win on the first and lose on the second, but you can never win on the second and lose on the first.

Argument 2: The second sequence (GRGRRR) is more probable than the first (RGRRR) because the proportions of R and G in the second sequence are closer than those of the first sequence to the expected proportions of R and G for a die with four green and two red faces.

Most of the subjects (76%) chose the valid extensional argument over an argument that formu-

lates the intuition of representativeness. Recall that a similar argument in the case of Linda was much less effective in combating the conjunction fallacy. The success of the present manipulation can be attributed to the combination of a chance setup and a gambling task, which promotes extensional reasoning by emphasizing the conditions under which the bets will pay off.

Fallacies and Misunderstandings

We have described violations of the conjunction rule in direct tests as a fallacy. The term *fallacy* is used here as a psychological hypothesis, not as an evaluative epithet. A judgment is appropriately labeled a fallacy when most of the people who make it are disposed, after suitable explanation, to accept the following propositions: (a) They made a nontrivial error, which they would probably have repeated in similar problems, (b) the error was conceptual, not merely verbal or technical, and (c) they *should* have known the correct answer or a procedure to find it. Alternatively, the same judgment could be described as a failure of communication if the subject misunderstands the question or if the experimenter misinterprets the answer. Subjects who have erred because of a misunderstanding are likely to reject the propositions listed above and to claim (as students often do after an examination) that they knew the correct answer all along, and that their error, if any, was verbal or technical rather than conceptual.

A psychological analysis should apply interpretive charity and should avoid treating genuine misunderstandings as if they were fallacies. It should also avoid the temptation to rationalize any error of judgment by ad hoc interpretations that the respondents themselves would not endorse. The dividing line between fallacies and misunderstandings, however, is not always clear. In one of our earlier studies, for example, most respondents stated that a particular description is more likely to belong to a physical education teacher than to a teacher. Strictly speaking, the latter category includes the former, but it could be argued that *teacher* was understood in this problem in a sense that excludes physical education teacher, much as *animal* is often used in a sense that excludes insects. Hence, it was unclear whether the apparent violation of the extension rule in this problem should be described as a fallacy or as a misunderstanding. A special effort was made in the present studies to avoid ambiguity by defining the critical event

THE M → A
PARADIGM

THE A → B
PARADIGM

Figure 1. Schematic representation of two experimental paradigms used to test the conjunction rule. (Solid and broken arrows denote strong positive and negative association, respectively, between the model M, the basic target B, and the added target A.)

as an intersection of well-defined classes, such as bank tellers and feminists. The comments of the respondents in postexperimental discussions supported the conclusion that the observed violations of the conjunction rule in direct tests are genuine fallacies, not just misunderstandings.

Causal Conjunctions

The problems discussed in previous sections included three elements: a causal model M (Linda's personality); a basic target event B, which is unrepresentative of M (she is a bank teller); and an added event A, which is highly representative of the model M (she is a feminist). In these problems, the model M is positively associated with A and is negatively associated with B. This structure, called the M → A paradigm, is depicted on the left-hand side of Figure 1. We found that when the sketch of Linda's personality was omitted and she was identified merely as a "31-year-old woman," almost all respondents obeyed the conjunction rule and ranked the conjunction (bank teller and active feminist) as less probable than its constituents. The conjunction error in the original problem is therefore attributable to the relation between M and A, not to the relation between A and B.

The conjunction fallacy was common in the Linda problem despite the fact that the stereotypes of bank teller and feminist are mildly incompatible. When the constituents of a conjunction are highly incompatible, the incidence of conjunction errors is greatly reduced. For example, the conjunction "Bill is bored by music and plays jazz for a hobby" was judged as less probable (and less representative) than its constituents, although "bored by music" was

preceived as a probable (and representative) attribute of Bill. Quite reasonably, the incompatibility of the two attributes reduced the judged probability of their conjunction.

The effect of compatibility on the evaluation of conjunctions is not limited to near contradictions. For instance, it is more representative (as well as more probable) for a student to be in the upper half of the class in both mathematics and physics or to be in the lower half of the class in both fields than to be in the upper half in one field and in the lower half in the other. Such observations imply that the judged probability (or representativeness) of a conjunction cannot be computed as a function (e.g., product, sum, minimum, weighted average) of the scale values of its constituents. This conclusion excludes a large class of formal models that ignore the relation between the constituents of a conjunction. The viability of such models of conjunctive concepts has generated a spirited debate (Jones, 1982; Osherson & Smith, 1981, 1982; Zadeh, 1982; Lakoff, Note 1).

The preceding discussion suggests a new formal structure, called the A → B paradigm, which is depicted on the right-hand side of Figure 1. Conjunction errors occur in the A → B paradigm because of the direct connection between A and B, although the added event, A, is not particularly representative of the model, M. In this section of the article we investigate problems in which the added event, A, provides a plausible cause or motive for the occurrence of B. Our hypothesis is that the strength of the causal link, which has been shown in previous work to bias judgments of conditional probability (Tversky & Kahneman, 1980), will also bias judgments of the probability of conjunctions (see Beyth-Marom, Note 2). Just as the thought of a personality and a social stereotype naturally evokes an assessment of their similarity, the thought of an effect and a possible cause evokes an assessment of causal impact (Ajzen, 1977). The natural assessment of propensity is expected to bias the evaluation of probability.

To illustrate this bias in the A → B paradigm consider the following problem, which was presented to 115 undergraduates at Stanford University and UBC:

A health survey was conducted in a representative sample of adult males in British Columbia of all ages and occupations.

Mr. F. was included in the sample. He was selected by chance from the list of participants.

Which of the following statements is more probable? (check one)

Mr. F. has had one or more heart attacks.

Mr. F. has had one or more heart attacks and he is over 55 years old.

This seemingly transparent problem elicited a substantial proportion (58%) of conjunction errors among statistically naive respondents. To test the hypothesis that these errors are produced by the causal (or correlational) link between advanced age and heart attacks, rather than by a weighted average of the component probabilities, we removed this link by uncoupling the target events without changing their marginal probabilities.

A health survey was conducted in a representative sample of adult males in British Columbia of all ages and occupations.

Mr. F. and Mr. G. were both included in the sample. They were unrelated and were selected by chance from the list of participants.

Which of the following statements is more probable? (check one)

Mr. F. has had one or more heart attacks.

Mr. F has had one or more heart attacks and Mr. G. is over 55 year old.

Assigning the critical attributes to two independent individuals eliminates in effect the A → B connection by making the events (conditionally) independent. Accordingly, the incidence of conjunction errors dropped to 29% ($N = 90$). The A → B paradigm can give rise to dual conjunction errors where A & B is perceived as more probable than each of its constituents, as illustrated in the next problem.

Peter is a junior in college who is training to run the mile in a regional meet. In his best race, earlier this season, Peter ran the mile in 4:06 min. Please rank the following outcomes from most to least probable.

Peter will run the mile under 4:06 min.

Peter will run the mile under 4 min.

Peter will run the second half-mile under 1:55 min.

Peter will run the second half-mile under 1:55 min, and will complete the mile under 4 min.

Peter will run the first half-mile under 2:05 min.

The critical event (a sub-1:55 minute second half *and* a sub-4 minute mile) is clearly defined as a conjunction and not as a conditional. Nevertheless, 76% of a group of undergraduate students from Stanford University ($N = 96$) ranked it above one of its constituents, and 48% of the subjects ranked it above both constituents. The natural assessment of the relation between the constituents apparently contaminated the evaluation of their conjunction. In contrast, no one violated the extension rule by ranking the second outcome (a sub-4 minute mile) above the first (a sub-4:06 minute mile). The preceding results indicate that the judged probability of a conjunction cannot be explained by an averaging model because in such a model P(A & B) lies between P(A) and P(B). An averaging process, however, may be responsible for some conjunction errors, particularly when the constituent probabilities are given in a numerical form.

Motives and Crimes

A conjunction error in a motive-action schema is illustrated by the following problem – one of several of the same general type administered to a group of 171 students at UBC:

John P. is a meek man, 42 years old, married with two children. His neighbors describe him as mild-mannered, but somewhat secretive. He owns an import–export company based in New York City, and he travels frequently to Europe and the Far East. Mr. P. was convicted once for smuggling precious stones and metals (including uranium) and received a suspended sentence of 6 months in jail and a large fine.

Mr. P. is currently under police investigation.

Please rank the following statements by the probability that they will be among the conclusions of the investigation. Remember that other possibilities exist and that more than one statement may be true. Use 1 for the most probable statement, 2 for the second, etc.

Mr. P. is a child molester.

Mr. P. is involved in espionage and the sale of secret documents.

Mr. P. is a drug addict.

Mr. P. killed one of his employees.

One half of the subjects ($n = 86$) ranked the events above. Other subjects ($n = 85$) ranked a modified list of possibilities in which the last event was replaced by

Mr. P. killed one of his employees to prevent him from talking to the police.

Although the addition of a possible motive clearly reduces the extension of the event (Mr. P. might have killed his employee for other reasons, such as revenge or self-defense), we hypothesized that the mention of a plausible but nonobvious motive would increase the perceived likelihood of the event. The data confirmed this expectation. The mean rank of the conjunction was 2.90, whereas the mean rank of the inclusive statement was 3.17 ($p < .05$, by t test). Furthermore, 50% of the respondents ranked the conjunction as more likely than the event that Mr. P. was a drug addict, but only 23% ranked the more inclusive target event as more likely than drug addiction. We have found in other problems of the same type that the mention of a cause or motive tends to increase the judged probability of an action when the suggested motive (a) offers a reasonable explanation of the target event, (b) appears fairly likely on its own, (c) is nonobvious, in the sense that it does not immediately come to mind when the outcome is mentioned.

We have observed conjunction errors in other judgments involving criminal acts in both the A → B and the M → A paradigms. For example, the hypothesis that a policeman described as violence prone was involved in the heroin trade was ranked less likely (relative to a standard comparison set) than a conjunction of allegations – that he is involved in the heroin trade and that he recently assaulted a suspect. In that example, the assault was not causally linked to the involvement in drugs, but it made the combined allegation more representative of the suspect's disposition. The implications of the psychology of judgment to the evaluation of legal evidence deserve careful study because the outcomes of many trials depend on the ability of a judge or a jury to make intuitive judgments on the basis of partial and fallible data (see Rubinstein, 1979; Saks & Kidd, 1981).

Forecasts and Scenarios

The construction and evaluation of scenarios of future events are not only a favorite pastime of reporters, analysts, and news watchers. Scenarios are often used in the context of planning, and their plausibility influences significant decisions. Scenarios for the past are also important in many contexts, including criminal law and the writing of history. It is of interest, then, to evaluate whether the forecasting or reconstruction of real-life events is subject to conjunction errors. Our analysis suggests that a scenario that includes a possible cause and an outcome could appear more probable than the outcome on its own. We tested this hypothesis in two populations: statistically naive students and professional forecasters.

A sample of 245 UBC undergraduates were requested in April 1982 to evaluate the probability of occurrence of several events in 1983. A 9-point scale was used, defined by the following categories: less than .01%, .1%, .5%, 1%, 2%, 5%, 10%, 25%, and 50% or more. Each problem was presented to different subjects in two versions: one that included only the basic outcome and another that included a more detailed scenario leading to the same outcome. For example, one half of the subjects evaluated the probability of

a massive flood somewhere in North America in 1983, in which more than 1000 people drown.

The other half of the subjects evaluated the probability of

an earthquake in California sometime in 1983, causing a flood in which more than 1000 people drown.

The estimates of the conjunction (earthquake and flood) were significantly higher than the estimates of the flood ($p < .01$, by a Mann-Whitney test). The respective geometric means were 3.1% and 2.2%. Thus, a reminder that a devastating flood could be caused by the anticipated California earthquake made the conjunction of an earthquake and a flood appear more probable than a flood. The same pattern was observed in other problems.

The subjects in the second part of the study were 115 participants in the Second International Congress on Forecasting held in Istanbul, Turkey, in July 1982. Most of the subjects were professional analysts, employed by industry, universities, or research institutes. They were professionally involved in forecasting and planning, and many had used scenarios in their work. The research design and the response scales were the same as before. One group of forecasters evaluated the probability of

a complete suspension of diplomatic relations between the USA and the Soviet Union, sometime in 1983.

The other respondents evaluated the probability of the same outcome embedded in the following scenario:

> a Russian invasion of Poland, and a complete suspension of diplomatic relations between the USA and the Soviet Union, sometime in 1983.

Although *suspension* is necessarily more probable than *invasion and suspension*, a Russian invasion of Poland offered a plausible scenario leading to the breakdown of diplomatic relations between the superpowers. As expected, the estimates of probability were low for both problems but significantly higher for the conjunction *invasion and suspension* than for *suspension* ($p < .01$, by a Mann–Whitney test). The geometric means of estimates were .47% and .14%, respectively. A similar effect was observed in the comparison of the following outcomes:

> a 30% drop in the consumption of oil in the US in 1983.

> a dramatic increase in oil prices and a 30% drop in the consumption of oil in the US in 1983.

The geometric means of the estimated probability of the first and the second outcomes, respectively, were .22% and .36%. We speculate that the effect is smaller in this problem (although still statistically significant) because the basic target event (a large drop in oil consumption) makes the added event (a dramatic increase in oil prices) highly available, even when the latter is not mentioned.

Conjunctions involving hypothetical causes are particularly prone to error because it is more natural to assess the probability of the effect given the cause than the joint probability of the effect and the cause. We do not suggest that subjects deliberately adopt this interpretation; rather we propose that the higher conditional estimate serves as an anchor that makes the conjunction appear more probable.

Attempts to forecast events such as a major nuclear accident in the United States or an Islamic revolution in Saudi Arabia typically involve the construction and evaluation of scenarios. Similarly, a plausible story of how the victim might have been killed by someone other than the defendant may convince a jury of the existence of reasonable doubt. Scenarios can usefully serve to stimulate the imagination, to establish the feasibility of outcomes, or to set bounds on judged probabilities (Kirkwood &

Pollock, 1982; Zentner, 1982). However, the use of scenarios as a prime instrument for the assessment of probabilities can be highly misleading. First, this procedure favors a conjunctive outcome produced by a sequence of likely steps (e.g., the successful execution of a plan) over an equally probable disjunctive outcome (e.g., the failure of a careful plan), which can occur in many unlikely ways (Bar-Hillel, 1973; Tversky & Kahneman, 1973). Second, the use of scenarios to assess probability is especially vulnerable to conjunction errors. A detailed scenario consisting of causally linked and representative events may appear more probable than a subset of these events (Slovic, Fischhoff, & Lichtenstein, 1976). This effect contributes to the appeal of scenarios and to the illusory insight that they often provide. The attorney who fills in guesses regarding unknown facts, such as motive or mode of operation, may strengthen a case by improving its coherence, although such additions can only lower probability. Similarly, a political analyst can improve scenarios by adding plausible causes and representative consequences. As Pooh-Bah in the *Mikado* explains, such additions provide "corroborative details intended to give artistic verisimilitude to an otherwise bald and unconvincing narrative."

Extensional Cues

The numerous conjunction errors reported in this article illustrate people's affinity for non-extensional reasoning. It is nonetheless obvious that people can understand and apply the extension rule. What cues elicit extensional considerations and what factors promote conformity to the conjunction rule? In this section we focus on a single estimation problem and report several manipulations that induce extensional reasoning and reduce the incidence of the conjunction fallacy. The participants in the studies described in this section were statistically naive students at UBC. Mean estimates are given in parentheses.

> A health survey was conducted in a sample of adult males in British Columbia, of all ages and occupations. Please give your best estimate of the following values:
>
> What percentage of the men surveyed have had one or more heart attacks? (18%)
>
> What percentage of the men surveyed both are over 55 years old and have had one or more heart attacks? (30%)

This version of the health-survey problem produced a substantial number of conjunction errors among statistically naive respondents: 65% of the respondents ($N = 147$) assigned a strictly higher estimate to the second question than to the first.[2] Reversing the order of the constituents did not significantly affect the results.

The observed violations of the conjunction rule in estimates of relative frequency are attributed to the A → B paradigm. We propose that the probability of the conjunction is biased toward the natural assessment of the strength of the causal or statistical link between age and heart attacks. Although the statement of the question appears unambiguous, we considered the hypothesis that the respondents who committed the fallacy had actually interpreted the second question as a request to assess a conditional probability. A new group of UBC undergraduates received the same problem, with the second question amended as follows:

> Among the men surveyed who are over 55 years old, what percentage have had one or more heart attacks?

The mean estimate was 59% ($N = 55$). This value is significantly higher than the mean of the estimates of the conjunction (45%) given by those subjects who had committed the fallacy in the original problem. Subjects who violate the conjunction rule therefore do not simply substitute the conditional $P(\text{B/A})$ for the conjunction $P(\text{A \& B})$.

A seemingly inconsequential change in the problem helps many respondents avoid the conjunction fallacy. A new group of subjects ($N = 159$) were given the original questions but were also asked to assess the "percentage of the men surveyed who are over 55 years old" prior to assessing the conjunction. This manipulation reduced the incidence of conjunction error from 65% to 31%. It appears that many subjects were appropriately cued by the requirement to assess the relative frequency of both classes before assessing the relative frequency of their intersection.

The following formulation also facilitates extensional reasoning:

> A health survey was conducted in a sample of 100 adult males in British Columbia, of all ages and occupations. Please give your best estimate of the following values:
> How many of the 100 participants have had one or more heart attacks?

> How many of the 100 participants both are over 55 years old and have had one or more heart attacks?

The incidence of the conjunction fallacy was only 25% in this version ($N = 117$). Evidently, an explicit reference to the number of individual cases encourages subjects to set up a representation of the problems in which class inclusion is readily perceived and appreciated. We have replicated this effect in several other problems of the same general type. The rate of errors was further reduced to a record 11% for a group ($N = 360$) who also estimated the number of participants over 55 years of age prior to the estimation of the conjunctive category. The present findings agree with the results of Beyth-Marom (Note 2), who observed higher estimates for conjunctions in judgments of probability than in assessments of frequency.

The results of this section show that nonextensional reasoning sometimes prevails even in simple estimates of relative frequency in which the extension of the target event and the meaning of the scale are completely unambiguous. On the other hand, we found that the replacement of percentages by frequencies and the request to assess both constituent categories markedly reduced the incidence of the conjunction fallacy. It appears that extensional considerations are readily brought to mind by seemingly inconsequential cues. A contrast worthy of note exists between the effectiveness of extensional cues in the health-survey problem and the relative inefficacy of the methods used to combat the conjunction fallacy in the Linda problem (argument, betting, "whether or not"). The force of the conjunction rule is more readily appreciated when the conjunctions are defined by the intersection of concrete classes than by a combination of properties. Although classes and properties are equivalent from a logical standpoint, they give rise to different mental representations in which different relations and rules are transparent. The formal equivalence of properties to classes is apparently not programmed into the lay mind.

Discussion

In the course of this project we studied the extension rule in a variety of domains; we tested more than 3,000 subjects on dozens of problems, and we examined numerous variations of these problems. The results reported in this article constitute a representative though not exhaustive summary of this work.

The data revealed widespread violations of the extension rule by naive and sophisticated subjects in both indirect and direct tests. These results were interpreted within the framework of judgmental heuristics. We proposed that a judgment of probability or frequency is commonly biased toward the natural assessment that the problem evokes. Thus, the request to estimate the frequency of a class elicits a search for exemplars, the task of predicting vocational choice from a personality sketch evokes a comparison of features, and a question about the co-occurrence of events induces an assessment of their causal connection. These assessments are not constrained by the extension rule. Although an arbitrary reduction in the extension of an event typically reduces its availability, representativeness, or causal coherence, there are numerous occasions in which these assessments are higher for the restricted than for the inclusive event. Natural assessments can bias probability judgment in three ways: The respondents (a) may use a natural assessment deliberately as a strategy of estimation, (b) may be primed or anchored by it, or (c) may fail to appreciate the difference between the natural and the required assessments.

Logic Versus Intuition

The conjunction error demonstrates with exceptional clarity the contrast between the extensional logic that underlies most formal conceptions of probability and the natural assessments that govern many judgments and beliefs. However, probability judgments are not always dominated by nonextensional heuristics. Rudiments of probability theory have become part of the culture, and even statistically naive adults can enumerate possibilities and calculate odds in simple games of chance (Edwards, 1975). Furthermore, some real-life contexts encourage the decomposition of events. The chances of a team to reach the playoffs, for example, may be evaluated as follows: "Our team will make it if we beat team B, which we should be able to do since we have a better defense, or if team B loses to both C and D, which is unlikely since neither one has a strong offense." In this example, the target event (reaching the playoffs) is decomposed into more elementary possibilities that are evaluated in an intuitive manner.

Judgments of probability vary in the degree to which they follow a decompositional or a holistic approach and in the degree to which the assessment and the aggregation of probabilities

are analytic or intuitive (see, e.g., Hammond & Brehmer, 1973). At one extreme there are questions (e.g., What are the chances of beating a given hand in poker?) that can be answered by calculating the relative frequency of "favorable" outcomes. Such an analysis possesses all the features associated with an extensional approach: It is decompositional, frequentistic, and algorithmic. At the other extreme, there are questions (e.g., What is the probability that the witness is telling the truth?) that are normally evaluated in a holistic, singular, and intuitive manner (Kahneman & Tversky, 1982b). Decomposition and calculation provide some protection against conjunction errors and other biases, but the intuitive element cannot be entirely eliminated from probability judgments outside the domain of random sampling.

A direct test of the conjunction rule pits an intuitive impression against a basic law of probability. The outcome of the conflict is determined by the nature of the evidence, the formulation of the question, the transparency of the event structure, the appeal of the heuristic, and the sophistication of the respondents. Whether people obey the conjunction rule in any particular direct test depends on the balance of these factors. For example, we found it difficult to induce naive subjects to apply the conjunction rule in the Linda problem, but minor variations in the health-survey question had a marked effect on conjunction errors. This conclusion is consistent with the results of Nisbett et al. (1981), who showed that lay people can apply certain statistical principles (e.g., the law of large numbers) to everyday problems and that the accessibility of these principles varied with the content of the problem and increased significantly with the sophistication of the respondents. We found, however, that sophisticated and naive respondents answered the Linda problem similarly in indirect tests and only parted company in the most transparent versions of the problem. These observations suggest that statistical sophistication did not alter intuitions of representativeness, although it enabled the respondents to recognize in direct tests the decisive force of the extension rule.

Judgment problems in real life do not usually present themselves in the format of a within-subjects design or of a direct test of the laws of probability. Consequently, subjects' performance in a between-subjects test may offer a more realistic view of everyday reasoning. In the indirect test it is very difficult even for a sophisticated judge to ensure that an event has no subset that would appear more probable than it does and no superset that would appear less probable. The satisfaction of the extension rule could be ensured, without direct comparisons of A & B to B, if all events in the relevant ensemble were expressed as disjoint unions of elementary possibilities. In many practical contexts, however, such analysis is not feasible. The physician, judge, political analyst, or entrepreneur typically focuses on a critical target event and is rarely prompted to discover potential violations of the extension rule.

Studies of reasoning and problem solving have shown that people often fail to understand or apply an abstract logical principle even when they can use it properly in concrete familiar contexts. Johnson-Laird and Wason (1977), for example, showed that people who err in the verification of *if then* statements in an abstract format often succeed when the problem evokes a familiar schema. The present results exhibit the opposite pattern: People generally accept the conjunction rule in its abstract form (B is more probable than A & B) but defy it in concrete examples, such as the Linda and Bill problems, where the rule conflicts with an intuitive impression.

The violations of the conjunction rule were not only prevalent in our research, they were also sizable. For example, subjects' estimates of the frequency of seven-letter words ending with *ing* were three times as high as their estimates of the frequency of seven letter words ending with _ n_. A correction by a factor of three is the smallest change that would eliminate the inconsistency between the two estimates. However, the subjects surely know that there are many _ n _ words that are not *ing* words (e.g., *present, content*). If they believe, for example, that only one half of the _ n _ words end with *ing*, then a 6:1 adjustment would be required to make the entire system coherent. The ordinal nature of most of our experiments did not permit an estimate of the adjustment factor required for coherence. Nevertheless, the size of the effect was often considerable. In the rating-scale version of the Linda problem, for example, there was little overlap between the distributions of ratings for T & F and for T. Our problems, of course, were constructed to elicit conjunction errors, and they do not provide an unbiased estimate of the prevalence of these errors. Note, however, that the conjunction error is only a symptom of a more general phenomenon: People tend to overestimate the probabilities of representative (or available) events and/or underestimate the probabili-

ties of less representative events. The violation of the conjunction rule demonstrates this tendency even when the "true" probabilities are unknown or unknowable. The basic phenomenon may be considerably more common than the extreme symptom by which it was illustrated.

Previous studies of the subjective probability of conjunctions (e.g., Bar-Hillel, 1973; Cohen & Hansel, 1957; Goldsmith, 1978; Wyer, 1976; Beyth-Marom, Note 2) focused primarily on testing the multiplicative rule $P(A \& B) = P(B)P(A/B)$. This rule is strictly stronger than the conjunction rule; it also requires cardinal rather than ordinal assessments of probability. The results showed that people generally overestimate the probability of conjunctions in the sense that $P(A \& B) > P(B)P(A/B)$. Some investigators, notably Wyer and Beyth-Marom, also reported data that are inconsistent with the conjunction rule.

Conversing Under Uncertainty

The representativeness heuristic generally favors outcomes that make good stories or good hypotheses. The conjunction *feminist bank teller* is a better hypothesis about Linda than *bank teller*, and the scenario of a Russian invasion of Poland followed by a diplomatic crisis makes a better story than simply *diplomatic crisis*. The notion of a good story can be illuminated by extending the Gricean concept of cooperativeness (Grice, 1975) to conversations under uncertainty. The standard analysis of conversation rules assumes that the speaker knows the truth. The maxim of quality enjoins him or her to say only the truth. The maxim of quantity enjoins the speaker to say all of it, subject to the maxim of relevance, which restricts the message to what the listener needs to know. What rules of cooperativeness apply to an uncertain speaker, that is, one who is uncertain of the truth? Such a speaker can guarantee absolute quality only for tautological statements (e.g., "Inflation will continue so long as prices rise"), which are unlikely to earn high marks as contributions to the conversation. A useful contribution must convey the speaker's relevant beliefs even if they are not certain. The rules of cooperativeness for an uncertain speaker must therefore allow for a trade-off of quality and quantity in the evaluation of messages. The expected value of a message can be defined by its information value if it is true, weighted by the probability that it is true. An uncertain speaker may wish to follow the maxim of value: Select the message that has the highest expected value.

The expected value of a message can sometimes be improved by increasing its content, although its probability is thereby reduced. The statement "Inflation will be in the range of 6% to 9% by the end of the year" may be a more valuable forecast than "Inflation will be in the range of 3% to 12%," although the latter is more likely to be confirmed. A good forecast is a compromise between a point estimate, which is sure to be wrong, and a 99.9% credible interval, which is often too broad. The selection of hypotheses in science is subject to the same trade-off: A hypothesis must risk refutation to be valuable, but its value declines if refutation is nearly certain. Good hypotheses balance informativeness against probable truth (Good, 1971). A similar compromise obtains in the structure of natural categories. The basic level category *dog* is much more informative than the more inclusive category *animal* and only slightly less informative than the narrower category *beagle*. Basic level categories have a privileged position in language and thought, presumably because they offer an optimal combination of scope and content (Rosch, 1978). Categorization under uncertainty is a case in point. A moving object dimly seen in the dark may be appropriately labeled *dog*, where the subordinate *beagle* would be rash and the superordinate *animal* far too conservative.

Consider the task of ranking possible answers to the question, "What do you think Linda is up to these days?" The maxim of value could justify a preference for T & F over T in this task, because the added attribute *feminist* considerably enriches the description of Linda's current activities, at an acceptable cost in probable truth. Thus, the analysis of conversation under uncertainty identifies a pertinent question that is legitimately answered by ranking the conjunction above its constituent. We do not believe, however, that the maxim of value provides a fully satisfactory account of the conjunction fallacy. First, it is unlikely that our respondents interpret the request to rank statements by their probability as a request to rank them by their expected (informational) value. Second, conjunction fallacies have been observed in numerical estimates and in choices of bets, to which the conversational analysis simply does not apply. Nevertheless, the preference for statements of high expected (informational) value could hinder the appreciation of the extension rule. As we suggested in the discussion of the interaction of picture size and real size, the answer to a question can be biased by the availability of an answer to a cognate question – even when the respondent is well aware of the distinction between them.

The same analysis applies to other conceptual neighbors of probability. The concept of surprise is a case in point. Although surprise is closely tied to expectations, it does not follow the laws of probability (Kahneman & Tversky, 1982b). For example, the message that a tennis champion lost the first set of a match is more surprising than the message that she lost the first set but won the match, and a sequence of four consecutive heads in a coin toss is more surprising than four heads followed by two tails. It would be patently absurd, however, to bet on the less surprising event in each of these pairs. Our discussions with subjects provided no indication that they interpreted the instruction to judge probability as an instruction to evaluate surprise. Furthermore, the surprise interpretation does not apply to the conjunction fallacy observed in judgments of frequency. We conclude that surprise and informational value do not properly explain the conjunction fallacy, although they may well contribute to the ease with which it is induced and to the difficulty of eliminating it.

Cognitive Illusions

Our studies of inductive reasoning have focused on systematic errors because they are diagnostic of the heuristics that generally govern judgment and inference. In the words of Helmholtz (1881/1903), "It is just those cases that are not in accordance with reality which are particularly instructive for discovering the laws of the processes by which normal perception originates." The focus on bias and illusion is a research strategy that exploits human error, although it neither assumes nor entails that people are perceptually or cognitively inept. Helmholtz's position implies that perception is not usefully analyzed into a normal process that produces accurate percepts and a distorting process that produces errors and illusions. In cognition, as in perception, the same mechanisms produce both valid and invalid judgments. Indeed, the evidence does not seem to support a "truth plus error" model, which assumes a coherent system of beliefs that is perturbed by various sources of distortion and error. Hence, we do not share Dennis Lindley's optimistic opinion that "inside every incoherent person there is a coherent one trying to get out" (Lindley, Note 3), and we suspect that incoherence is more than skin deep (Tversky & Kahneman, 1981).

It is instructive to compare a structure of beliefs about a domain (e.g., the political future of Central America) to the perception of a scene (e.g., the view of Yosemite Valley from Glacier Point). We have argued that intuitive judgments of all relevant marginal, conjunctive, and conditional probabilities are not likely to be coherent, that is, to satisfy the constraints of probability theory. Similarly, estimates of distances and angles in the scene are unlikely to satisfy the laws of geometry. For example, there may be pairs of political events for which $P(A)$ is judged greater than $P(B)$ but $P(A/B)$ is judged less than $P(B/A)$ – see Tversky and Kahneman (1980). Analogously, the scene may contain a triangle ABC for which the A angle appears greater than the B angle, although the BC distance appears to be smaller than the AC distance.

The violations of the qualitative laws of geometry and probability in judgments of distance and likelihood have significant implications for the interpretation and use of these judgments. Incoherence sharply restricts the inferences that can be drawn from subjective estimates. The judged ordering of the sides of a triangle cannot be inferred from the judged ordering of its angles, and the ordering of marginal probabilities cannot be deduced from the ordering of the respective conditionals. The results of the present study show that it is even unsafe to assume that $P(B)$ is bounded by $P(A \& B)$. Furthermore, a system of judgments that does not obey the conjunction rule cannot be expected to obey more complicated principles that presuppose this rule, such as Bayesian updating, external calibration, and the maximization of expected utility. The presence of bias and incoherence does not diminish the normative force of these principles, but it reduces their usefulness as descriptions of behavior and hinders their prescriptive applications. Indeed, the elicitation of unbiased judgments and the reconciliation of incoherent assessments pose serious problems that presently have no satisfactory solution (Lindley, Tversky, & Brown, 1979; Shafer & Tversky, Note 4).

The issue of coherence has loomed larger in the study of preference and belief than in the study of perception. Judgments of distance and angle can readily be compared to objective reality and can be replaced by objective measurements when accuracy matters. In contrast, objective measurements of probability are often unavailable, and most significant choices under risk require an intuitive evaluation of probability. In the absence of an objective criterion of validity, the normative theory of judgment under uncertainty has treated the coherence of belief as the touchstone of human rationality. Coherence has also been assumed in many descriptive analyses in psychology, economics, and other social sciences. This assumption is attractive because the strong normative appeal of the laws of probability makes violations appear implausible. Our studies of the conjunction rule show that normatively inspired theories that assume coherence are descriptively inadequate, whereas psychological analyses that ignore the appeal of normative rules are, at best, incomplete. A comprehensive account of human judgment must reflect the tension between compelling logical rules and seductive nonextensional intuitions.

Notes

1 We are grateful to Barbara J. McNeil, Harvard Medical School, Stephen G. Pauker, Tufts University School of Medicine, and Edward Baer, Stanford Medical School, for their help in the construction of the clinical problems and in the collection of the data.

2 The incidence of the conjunction fallacy was considerably lower (28%) for a group of advanced undergraduates at Stanford University ($N = 62$) who had completed one or more courses in statistics.

Reference Notes

1. Lakoff, G. Categories and cognitive models (Cognitive Science Report No. 2). Berkeley: University of California, 1982.
2. Beyth-Marom, R. The subjective probability of conjunctions (Decision Research Report No. 81–12). Eugene, Oregon: Decision Research, 1981.
3. Lindley, Dennis, Personal communication, 1980.
4. Shafer, G., & Tversky, A. Weighing evidence: The design and comparisons of probability thought experiments. Unpublished manuscript, Stanford University, 1983.

References

Ajzen, I. Intuitive theories of events and the effects of baserate information on prediction. Journal of Personality and Social Psychology, 1977, 35, 303–314.

Bar-Hillel. M. On the subjective probability of compound events. Organizational Behavior and Human Performance, 1973, 9, 396–406.

Bruner, J. S. On the conservation of liquids. In J. S. Bruner, R. R. Olver, & P. M. Greenfield, et al. (Eds.), Studies in cognitive growth. New York: Wiley, 1966.

Chapman, L. J., & Chapman, J. P. Genesis of popular but erroneous psychodiagnostic observations. *Journal of Abnormal Psychology*, 1967, *73*, 193–204.

Cohen, J., & Hansel, C. M. The nature of decision in gambling: Equivalence of single and compound subjective probabilities. *Acta Psychologica*, 1957, *13*, 357–370.

Cohen, L. J. *The probable and the provable.* Oxford, England: Clarendon Press, 1977.

Dempster, A. P. Upper and lower probabilities induced by a multivalued mapping. *Annals of Mathematical Statistics*, 1967, *38*, 325–339.

Edwards, W. Comment. *Journal of the American Statistical Association*, 1975, *70*, 291–293.

Einhorn, H. J., & Hogarth, R. M. Behavioral decision theory: Processes of judgment and choice. *Annual Review of Psychology*, 1981, *32*, 53–88.

Gati, I., & Tversky, A. Representations of qualitative and quantitative dimensions. *Journal of Experimental Psychology: Human Perception and Performance*, 1982, *8*, 325–340.

Goldsmith, R. W. Assessing probabilities of compound events in a judicial context. *Scandinavian Journal of Psychology*, 1978, *19*, 103–110.

Good, I. J. The probabilistic explication of information, evidence, surprise, causality, explanation, and utility. In V. P. Godambe & D. A. Sprott (Eds.), *Foundations of statistical inference: Proceedings on the foundations of statistical inference.* Toronto, Ontario, Canada: Holt, Rinehart & Winston, 1971.

Grice, H. P. Logic and conversation. In G. Harman & D. Davidson (Eds.), *The logic of grammar.* Encino, Calif.: Dickinson, 1975.

Hammond, K. R., & Brehmer, B. Quasi-rationality and distrust: Implications for international conflict. In L. Rappoport & D. A. Summers (Eds.), *Human judgment and social interaction.* New York: Holt, Rinehart & Winston, 1973.

Helmholtz, H. von. *Popular lectures on scientific subjects* (E. Atkinson, trans.). New York: Green, 1903. (Originally published, 1881.)

Jennings, D., Amabile, T., & Ross, L. Informal covariation asessment. In D. Kahneman, P. Slovic, & A. Tversky (Eds.), *Judgment under uncertainty: Heuristics and biases.* New York: Cambridge University Press, 1982.

Johnson-Laird, P. N., & Wason, P. C. A theoretical analysis of insight into a reasoning task. In P. N. Johnson-Laird & P. C. Wason (Eds.), *Thinking.* Cambridge, England: Cambridge University Press, 1977.

Jones, G. V. Stacks not fuzzy sets: An ordinal basis for prototype theory of concepts. *Cognition*, 1982, *12*, 281–290.

Kahneman, D., Slovic, P., & Tversky, A. (Eds.) *Judgment under uncertainty: Heuristics and biases.* New York: Cambridge University Press, 1982.

Kahneman, D., & Tversky, A. Subjective probability: A judgment of representativeness. *Cognitive Psychology*, 1972, *3*, 430–454.

Kahneman, D., & Tversky, A. On the psychology of prediction. *Psychological Review*, 1973, *80*, 237–251.

Kahneman, D., & Tversky, A. On the study of statistical intuitions. *Cognition*, 1982, *11*, 123–141. (a)

Kahneman, D., & Tversky, A. Variants of uncertainty. *Cognition*, 1982, *11*, 143–157. (b)

Kirkwood, C. W., & Pollock, S. M. Multiple attribute scenarios, bounded probabilities, and threats of nuclear theft. *Futures*, 1982, *14*, 545–553.

Kyburg, H. E. Rational belief. *The Behavioral and Brain Sciences*, 1983, *6*, 231–73.

Lindley, D. V., Tversky, A., & Brown, R. V. On the reconciliation of probability assessments. *Journal of the Royal Statistical Society*, 1979, *142*, 146–180.

Mervis, C. B., & Rosch, E. Categorization of natural objects. *Annual Review of Psychology*, 1981, *32*, 89–115.

Nisbett, R. E., Krantz, D. H., Jepson, C., & Kunda, Z. The use of statistical heuristics in everyday inductive reasoning. *Psychological Review*, 1983, *90*, 339–363.

Nisbett, R., & Ross, L. *Human inference: Strategies and shortcomings of social judgment.* Englewood Cliffs, N.J.: Prentice-Hall, 1980.

Osherson, D. N., & Smith, E. E. On the adequacy of prototype theory as a theory of concepts. *Cognition*, 1981, *9*, 35–38.

Osherson, D. N., & Smith, E. E. Gradeness and conceptual combination. *Cognition*, 1982, *12*, 299–318.

Rosch, E. Principles of categorization. In E. Rosch & B. B. Lloyd (Eds.), *Cognition and categorization.* Hillsdale, N.J.: Erlbaum, 1978.

Rubinstein, A. False probabilistic arguments vs. faulty intuition. *Israel Law Review*, 1979, *14*, 247–254.

Saks, M. J., & Kidd, R. F. Human information processing and adjudication: Trials by heuristics. *Law & Society Review*, 1981, *15*, 123–160.

Shafer, G. *A mathematical theory of evidence.* Princeton, N.J.: Princeton University Press, 1976.

Slovic, P., Fischhoff, B., & Lichtenstein, S. Cognitive processes and societal risk taking. In J. S. Carroll & J. W. Payne (Eds.), *Cognition and social behavior.* Potomac, Md.: Erlbaum, 1976.

Smith, E. E., & Medin, D. L. *Categories and concepts.* Cambridge, Mass.: Harvard University Press, 1981.

Suppes, P. Approximate probability and expectation of gambles. *Erkenntnis*, 1975, *9*, 153–161.

Tversky, A. Features of similarity. *Psychological Review*, 1977, 84, 327–352.

Tversky, A., & Kahneman, D. Belief in the law of small numbers. *Psychological Bulletin*, 1971, *76*, 105–110.

Tversky, A., & Kahneman, D. Availability: A heuristic for judging frequency and probability. *Cognitive Psychology*, 1973, *5*, 207–232.

Tversky, A., & Kahneman, D. Causal schemas in judgements under uncertainty. In M. Fishbein (Ed.), *Progress in social psychology*. Hillsdale, N.J.: Erlbaum, 1980.

Tversky, A., & Kahneman, D. The framing of decisions and the psychology of choice. *Science*, 1981, *211*, 453–458.

Tversky, A., & Kahneman, D. Judgments of and by representativeness. In D. Kahneman, P. Slovic, & A. Tversky (Eds.), *Judgment under uncertainty:*

Heuristics and biases. New York: Cambridge University Press, 1982.

Wyer, R. S., Jr. An investigation of the relations among probability estimates. *Organizational Behavior and Human Performance*, 1976, *15*, 1–18.

Zadeh, L. A. Fuzzy sets as a basis for a theory of possibility. *Fuzzy Sets and Systems*, 1978, *1*, 3–28.

Zadeh, L. A. A note on prototype theory and fuzzy sets. *Cognition*, 1982, *12*, 291–297.

Zentner, R. D. Scenarios, past, present and future. *Long Range Planning*, 1982, *15*, 12–20.

Chapter 7: Can Human Irrationality Be Experimentally Demonstrated?

L. JONATHAN COHEN

Introduction

The experimental study of human rationality – that is, of validity in deductive or probabilistic reasoning – has become entangled during the past decade or so in a web of paradox. On the one hand, reputable investigators tell us that "certain psychological discoveries have bleak implications for human rationality" (Nisbett & Borgida 1975), or that "for anyone who would wish to view man as a reasonable intuitive statistician, such results are discouraging" (Kahneman & Tversky 1972b) or that "people systematically violate principles of decision-making when judging probabilities, making predictions, or otherwise attempting to cope with probabilistic tasks" and they "lack the correct programs for many important judgmental tasks" (Slovic, Fischhoff & Lichtenstein 1976). On the other hand, those investigators are reminded that people could not even drive automobiles unless they could assess uncertainties fairly accurately (Edwards 1975). The ordinary person is claimed to be prone to serious and systematic error in deductive reasoning, in judging probabilities, in correcting his biases, and in many other activities. Yet, from this apparently unpromising material – indeed, from the very same students who are the typical subjects of cognitive psychologists' experiments – sufficient cadres are recruited to maintain the sophisticated institutions of modern civilisation. Earlier decades, in an era of greater optimism, may well have overestimated the natural reasoning powers of human beings. But

there seems now to be a risk of underestimating them.

What is needed here is a conceptual framework within which to think coherently about problems of cognitive rationality and the relevant experimental data, and the object of the present paper is to sketch such a framework. For this purpose it is necessary first of all to examine the credentials of those normative theories by reference to which investigators may legitimately evaluate the rationality or irrationality of a native subject's inference or probability judgment. Such a normative theory, I shall argue, is itself acceptable for the purpose only so far as it accords, at crucial points, with the evidence of untutored intuition. This thesis was also argued long ago by Goodman (1954, pp. 66–67). But the argument needs to be expanded and fortified against more recent opposition. What then follows from the thesis is that ordinary human reasoning – by which I mean the reasoning of adults who have not been systematically educated in any branch of logic or probability theory – cannot be held to be faultily programmed: it sets its own standards. Of course, various kinds of mistakes are frequently made in human reasoning, both by laboratory subjects and in ordinary life. But in all such cases some malfunction of an information-processing mechanism has to be inferred, and its explanation sought. In other words, the nature of the problem constrains us to a competence-performance distinction. Our fellow humans have to be attributed a competence for reasoning validly, and this provides the

Reproduced with permission from Cohen, L. J. (1981) Can human Irrationality be experimentally demonstrated?
Behavioral and Brain Sciences, 4, 317–370.

backcloth against which we can study defects in their actual performance. That is the theme to be argued in the first part of the paper.

At the same time, allegations of defects in performance need to be carefully scrutinised. Some of these allegations are correct and important. But others seem to arise from a misapplication or misconception of the relevant standards of rationality by which the experimentally revealed phenomena should be judged, even when those phenomena themselves are quite robust and incontestable. The second part of the paper will therefore suggest four categories to which a critical assessment of existing allegations of performance defects might appropriately assign them.

In sum, those who once tended to exaggerate human reasoning powers may be construed as having concentrated thcir attention too much on the facts of competence, while those who have more recently tended to underestimate these powers have concentrated their attention too much on the facts of performance, and in some cases have judged these facts too harshly.

I. The Argument for Rational Competence

1. Intuitions as the Basis of Normative Criteria for the Evaluation of Deductions

Investigators who wish to evaluate the validity of their subjects' deductions would turn naturally to some educationally well regarded textbook of formal logic, such as Quine (1952), Copi (1954). or Lemmon (1965). The assumption would be that all and only the rules of inference that are given or derivable in those systems of so-called natural deduction are valid principles of deducibility, so far as deducibility hinges on the interplay of the logical particles "not," "and," "or," "if," "some," and "every" (or their equivalents in French, German, or any other language). But how can an assumption of this kind be defended? I shall argue that at a crucial point it has to rely on ordinary people's intuitions of deducibility.

Note, however, that the term "intuition" here is not being used in the sense of Spinoza (1914), Bergson (1903), or Husserl (1911). It does not describe a cognitive act that is somehow superior to sensory perception. Nor, on the other hand, does it refer merely to hunches that are subsequently checkable by sensory perception or by calculation. Nor does this kind of intuition entail introspection,[1] since it may just be implicit in a spoken judgment. Its closest analogue is an intuition of grammatical well-formedness. In short, an intuition that p is here just an immediate and untutored inclination, without evidence or inference, to judge that p.

To avoid any reliance on intuition in that sense, it would be necessary to show that the assumption in question (about the nature of deducibility) is defensible within some well-recognised system of scientific procedure. Transcendental (that is, Kantian) arguments are obviously too controversial for the purpose. So either this procedure has to be empirically based and inductive, or it has to depend on some appropriate metamathematical theorem. But, as it turns out, neither of these strategies can wholly succeed: at crucial nodes an appeal to ordinary people's intuition is indispensable.

The empirical-inductive strategy offers us an account of logic (as in Stich 1975) in which it is viewed as an adjunct to science in general rather than, like geometry, an adjunct to physics in particular: Such an applied logic is understood as the combination of a formal system with appropriate interpretative rules; and it is to be tested, we are told, by assessing the explanatory and predictive power of the total theory that results from meshing it with the theories of the several sciences. In this way, it seems, what are accepted as logical truths turn out just to constitute one type of component in the total holistic system of what is accepted as scientific truth. They seem as much beholden to experiment and observation for the warranty as are any other scientific discoveries.

However, this kind of hard-line positivism comes up against some serious difficulties, which preclude it from supplying an intuition-free validation of deductive logic. First, certain regulative principles for theory construction, such as ideals of comprehensiveness, consistency, and simplicity, have in any case to be granted a priori status, so that in the defence of this status at least some principles of reasoning may be conceded an intuitive warranty. Second, much of the reasoning for which we need a logically articulate reconstruction does not take place in science at all but in law or administration, and is concerned not with what is in fact the case but with what ought to be. Third, the same logical principles have to be applied within each piece of scientific reasoning about the relative merits of two or more hypotheses, so that if ever any hypothesis has to be given up in the face of adverse experience it is always a factual, rather than a logical, one. For example, we cannot claim, as does

Reichenbach (1944), that quantum physics constitutes a restriction on the range of application of classical two-valued logic as well as of classical mechanics because it is only in accordance with shared logical principles that it would be fair to elicit and compare the differing experimental conseqences of classical mechanics and quantum theory.[2] Hence, so far as we treat the totality of acceptable scientific hypotheses as constituting a single holistic system, we also need a single set of logical principles. Fourth, logically true statements are statements that are true in all logically possible worlds, and the evidence of happenings in the actual world must thus fall far short of establishing them.

Moreover, so far as the epistemology of a particular discipline is obligated to endorse the criteria of evaluation that are generally accepted in practice by reputable investigators in the field, it is certainly the appeal to intuitions that deserves endorsement for applied logic rather than the empirical-inductive strategy. Applied logicians make no attempt at all to test out the theories empirically within the context of a project to the holistic systematisation of all knowledge. On all the issues that are much discussed – issues about modality (for example, Quine 1960), subjunctive conditionals (Lewis 1973), indirect discourse (Carnap 1947), relative identity (Griffin 1977), proper names (Kripke 1972), adverbs (Davidson 1966), and so on – an implied or explicit appeal to intuition provides some of the vital premises for the applied logician's argument.

Nor are the prospects for a metamathematical justification of applied logic any better than those for an empirical-inductive one. Any system in which rules of derivation are specified in formal terms is said to be "sound" if under some interpretation for the formalism of the system it can be proved that from true premises these rules lead only to true conclusions. So it might seem as though, by thus using a semantic definition of logical consequence to check on a syntactic one, the rationality of a set of inferential rules could be established by experts in a metamathematical proof, without any recourse to intuitions other than those involved in the perception of the proof (Dummett 1978). But, though such a strategy has an agreeably professional appeal, it does not come to grips with the whole of the underlying epistemological problem. No reason is provided for supposing that the deductive liaisons of the logical particles of natural language can be mapped onto those of the connectives and quantifiers in the normal system that is proved to be sound.

For example, in any natural deduction system for the classical calculus of propositions the formula

$$((A \to B)\&(C \to D))$$

(or a notational variant) can constitute a premise from which

$$((A \to D)\text{V}(C \to B))$$

(or a notational variant) is derivable. And under the interpretation that Russell (1919) proposed for this calculus, a derivation could turn into an inference from

> If John's automobile is a Mini, John is poor, and if John's automobile is a Rolls, John is rich

to

> Either, if John's automobile is a Mini, John is rich, or, if John's automobile is a Rolls, John is poor

which would obviously be invalid. But what makes this invalidity obvious? The fact is that our own intuitions about the legitimate deductive liaisons of the logical particles (for example, the intuition that from the conditional "If John's automobile is a Mini, John is rich," we should be able to deduce the existence of a connection between antecedent and consequent that is independent of truth values) combine with our empirical knowledge of automobile costs to make it easy to imagine situations in which (3) is true and (4) is false. So though the propositional calculus is demonstrably sound, it resists Russell's interpretation as a logic of everyday reasoning in which conditional sentences may have a role, because it cannot capture intuitions like those on the basis of which we judge an inference from (3) to (4) to be invalid.[3] Admittedly, those intuitions might be said just to concern the *meanings* of the logical particles "if," "and," and "or," and there is nothing particularly remarkable, it might be objected, about the fact that one has to understand the meaning of an utterance to be able to appraise its validity. But the relevant point is that knowing the meanings of "if," "and," and "or" is indistinguishable from knowing, in principle, their legitimate deductive liaisons. So we cannot avoid appealing to intuitions of inferential validity in order to determine the claim of an interpreted formal system to constitute a theory of deducibility for everyday reasoning.

In other words, the problem of justification takes two rather different forms in regard to theories of deducibility. On the one hand, there is the issue of the theory's soundness, on the other, the issue of its application. Intuitions of inferential validity supply data in relation to the latter issue, not the former. But these intuitions are nevertheless an indispensable type of evidence for any theory of deducibility in everyday reasoning. Unless we assume appropriate intuitions to be correct, we cannot take the normative theory of everyday reasoning that they support to be correct. No doubt two different people, or the same people on two different occasions, may sometimes have apparently conflicting intuitions. But such an apparent conflict always demands resolution. The people involved might come to recognise some tacit misunderstanding about the terms of the problem, so that there is no real conflict; or they might repudiate a previously robust intuition, perhaps as a result of becoming aware that an otherwise preferred solution has unacceptable implications; or they might conclude that different idiolects or conceptions of deducibility are at issue.[4]

2. Intuitions as the Basis of Normative Criteria for the Evaluation of Probability Judgments

The position in regard to normative theories of probabilistic reasoning is rather analogous. We can take the mathematical calculus of chance, as axiomatised by Kolmogorov (1950), Reichenbach (1949), or Popper (1959a), to be a formal system that is open to semantical interpretation as a theory of the constraints that probability judgments of certain kinds *ought* to place on one another. But to just what kinds of probability judgment does the theory apply? This question has been much discussed. For example, proofs or arguments are available (Ramsey 1931; de Finetti 1931) to show that where probabilities are measured by betting quotients within a suitably coherent system of wagers their system conforms to the calculus of chance. A similar conformity has been demonstrated by Reichenbach (1949) and von Mises (1957) for the conception of probability as a relative frequency; by Carnap (1950) for the conception of probability as a type of logical relation that varies in strength along a spectrum that extends from contradiction at one extreme to entailment at the other; by Popper (1959b, 1968) and Mellor (1971) for the conception of probability as a causal propensity – a causally rooted tendency – and so on.

But none of those proofs or arguments establishes which conceptions of probability are operative – and under what conditions – in the everyday reasoning of lay adults, such as are the typical subjects of experiments carried out by cognitive psychologists. That is to say, it is one thing to establish one or more probabilistic interpretations for the calculus of chance, and quite another to show that the resultant theory applies to some or all of the probability judgments that are made in everyday reasoning. In order to discover what criteria of probability are appropriate for the evaluation of lay reasoning we have to investigate what judgments of probability are intuitively acceptable to lay adults and what rational constraints these judgments are supposed to place on one another. We have to select the conception or conceptions of probability in terms of which the most coherent account of lay judgments can be given, rather than evaluate those judgments by some single independently established standard.

The importance of this selection should not be underestimated. There are at least four ways in which it can make a lot of difference.

First, where probabilities are measured by betting quotients or construed as logical relations, we have to say – properly speaking – that they are functions of propositions; where they are relative frequencies they are functions of sets; and where they are causal propensities, they are functions of properties (Cohen 1977b). Such categories of functions differ considerably in regard to their appropriateness for the evaluation of definite singular instances, as has often been pointed out (see Reichenbach 1949, pp. 376–77; Carnap 1950, pp. 226–28; Nagel 1939, pp. 60–75). They differ also in regard to their appropriateness for counterfactual inference (Cohen 1977b, pp. 306–9).

Second, where a probability is measured by a betting quotient, its statement is normally treated as an assertion about the strength of the speaker's belief in the outcome. Such a subjective fact is logically quite consistent with another speaker's having a different strength of belief in relation to the same issue. So when two people measure the probability of the same outcome subjectively by different betting quotients, they are not contradicting one another, whereas assertions of different relative frequencies, different logical relations, or different causal propensities would be logically inconsistent if they concerned the same issue.

Third, different probability functions may legitimately be assigned different values in relation to the same situation of uncertainty. Carnap, for example, demonstrated the existence of a nondenumerably infinite number of different measures for his logical relation type of probability; the odds that are taken as appropriate to betting on a particular outcome on a given occasion need not correspond with the actual frequency of such outcomes in the relevant population; and the high frequency of B's among A's may be due to a series of coincidences, so that as a measure of causal propensity $p(B \mid A)$ [i.e., $p(B$ given $A)] = p(B)$ even though as a measure of relative frequency $p(B \mid A) > p(B)$. There is no mathematically demonstrable reason, therefore, why people should not in fact use different measures of probability for different situations or purposes, just as traders sometimes find it worthwhile to measure quantities of apples by weight and sometimes by number.

Fourth, if one or more semantic characterisations of probability are possible (as distinct from an implicit definition in terms of a set of mathematical axioms), then one might even need other formal systems than the calculus of chance to represent the syntax of some semantically defined categories of probability judgments other than the four already mentioned. The mathematics of probability may have no more reached its apogee in the work of Kolmogorov, than the mathematics of space did in that of Euclid. Nonclassical theories of probability may turn out to have an interest analogous to that of non-Euclidean geometries.

3. The Systematisation of Normative Intuitions

It has been argued so far that any normative analysis of everyday reasoning – any statement that such and such lay judgments of deducibility or probability are correct, or incorrect, as the case may be – must in the end rely for its defence on the evidence of relevant intuitions. You cannot dodge this by an appeal to textbooks of logic or statistics. Of course, on any issue that can be settled empirically we naturally treat intuitions only as hunches that either will be confirmed by favourable observation or will give way to counter-observations. And in some area, such as the grammar of natural language, the question whether ultimate data are observational or intuitive or both is currently controversial: compare Chomsky (1965) and Sampson (1975). But on indisputably normative issues – on issues about how people *may* or *ought to* think or behave as distinct from how they *do* – we cannot expect a major point at stake to be settled by observation. Here, if our aim is

to build up a comprehensive system of theory, it is prudent to check our general hypotheses against intuitions in concrete individual cases – though in order to avoid an obvious risk of bias, these must always be the intuitions of those who are not theorists themselves. For example, the practice of the courts provides much evidence for a theory of lay intuitions about probability in forensic reasoning (Cohen 1977b), but writers on this subject should not invoke their own intuitions.

Normative theories are subject to the usual inductive criteria. They are better supported if they apply to a wider rather than a narrower range of significantly different kinds of intuitive inference or judgment, just as the more comprehensively explanatory theories have greater merit in natural science. But there would obviously be a point at which even the mere process of putting problems to a person in varied contexts, in order to extract his intuitions, could reasonably be taken to cross over into a procedure for changing his normative outlook instead of just recording it. Thus recent writers on ethics (for example, Rawls 1972; Daniels 1979, 1980) have distinguished between the narrow reflective equilibrium that is constituted by coherent reconstruction of a person's existing moral principles, where only an occasional intuition is repudiated (for the sake of consistency), and the wide reflective equilibrium that is obtained when a person chooses between his existing moral principles and proposed alternatives, on the basis of sociological, historical, economic, psychological, or other considerations that may weigh with him. In matters of deducibility or probability the analogue of this philosophical choice would occur in the process of education research, or philosophising whereby hitherto uncommitted students are sometimes transformed into the thoroughgoing Quineians, say, or Bayesians, or Popperians so that they come to adopt substantially different conceptions of deducibility or probability from those once operating in their untutored judgments. But the normative theories that are at issue in the present context require a narrow, not a wide, reflective equilibrium. The judgments of everyday reasoning must be evaluated in their own terms and by their own standards.

4. The Derivation of an Account of Human Competence in Deductive or Probabilistic Reasoning

If a physicist observes the position of the needle on a certain dial under chosen experimental conditions, then the datum to be explained is the position of the needle, not the fact that someone observes it. The event observed, not the act of observing it, is what is relevant. Otherwise optics (and perhaps acoustics) would be all the science that there is. Analogously, the datum that the moralist has to take into account is the rightness or wrongness of a particular action, not the deliverance of conscience that pronounces it right or wrong; and the logician's datum is the validity or invalidity of a particular inference, not the intuition that assures us of it. So enquiry into the norms of everyday reasoning no more aims at a theory *about* intuitions than physics or chemistry aims at a theory *about* observations. Epistemology does not dominate ontology here. And fortunately it is not necessary for present purposes to determine what exactly the study of moral value, probability, or deducibility has as its proper subject matter. For example, an applied logician's proper aim may be to limn the formal consequences of linguistic definitions (Ayer 1946), the most general features of reality (Quine 1960), or the structure of ideally rational belief systems (Ellis 1979). But, whatever the ontological concern of applied logicians, they have to draw their evidential data from intuitions in concrete, individual cases; and the same is true for investigations into the norms of everyday probabilistic reasoning.

It follows that for every such normative theory, which determines how it is proper to act or reason, there is room to construct a factual theory that does take intuitions as its subject matter. This factual theory will describe or predict the intuitive judgments that formulate the data for the corresponding normative theory. It will be a psychological theory, not a logical or ethical one. It will describe a competence that normal human beings have – an ability, uniformly operative under ideal conditions and often under others, to form intuitive judgments about particular instances of right or wrong, deducibility or nondeducibility, probability or improbability. This factual theory of competence will be just as idealised as the normative theory from which it derives. And though it is a contribution to the psychology of cognition it is a by-product of the logical or philosophical analysis of norms rather than something that experimentally oriented psychologists need to devote effort to constructing. It is not only all the theory of competence that is needed in its area. It is also all that is possible, since a different competence, if it actually existed, would just generate evidence that called for a revision of the corresponding normative theory.

In other words, where you accept that a normative theory has to be based ultimately on the data of human intuition, you are committed to the acceptance of human rationality as a matter of fact in that area, in the sense that it must be correct to ascribe to normal humans beings a cognitive competence – however often faulted in performance – that corresponds point by point with the normative theory. Of course, it would be different if you believed in some other source of normative authority. If, for instance, you believe in a divinely revealed ethics, you are entitled to think that some people's competence for moral judgment may fall short of correct moral ideals: you could consistently invoke some doctrine of original sin to account for the systematic failure of untaught intuition to accord with the correct norms of moral judgment. But, if you claim no special revelation in ethics, you will have to take intuitive judgments as your basis, and then people's competence for moral judgment – as distinct, of course, from their actual performance in this – cannot be faulted. Analogously, if you claim no special revelation in matters of logic or probability, you will have to be content there too to accept the inherent rationality of your fellow adults.

To ascribe a cognitive competence, in this sense, within a given community is to characterise the content of a culturally or genetically inherited ability which, under ideal conditions, every member of the community would exercise in appropriate circumstances. It states what people can do, rather than what they will do, much as the characterisation of a linguistic competence can be taken to describe what it is that native speakers must be assumed capable of recognising about the structure of morphophonemic strings (Chomsky 1965) rather than what they do actually recognise. The fact is that conditions are rarely, if ever, ideal for the exercise of such a competence. Just as passion or self-interest may warp our moral discernment, or memory limitations may restrict the length of the sentences we utter, so too a variety of factors may interfere with the excercise of a competence for deductive or probabilistic reasoning. A local unsuitability of childhood environment may inhibit the maturation of innate ability, education (that is, education in subjects other than logic and probability theory) may fail to make the most of it, individual disabilities or normal memory limitations may set limits to what even the best environment and education can achieve, and various motivational and other factors may operate to induce malfunctions of the relevant information processing mechanisms. To suppose that all normal adults are able to reason deductively is certainly not to suppose that they will never err in their judgments of logical validity, and still less that they will in practice execute any particular finite chain of reasoning that is called for, however complex it may be, just so long as it is licensed by intuitively evident rules of natural deduction. In practice, our rationality is "bounded" (Simon 1957, pp. 198–202). We are all able to walk, if in normal health, but it does not follow that we can all walk on a tight rope, or for a thousand miles without stopping, or that none of us ever stumbles. It is here that the issues arise that will be discussed in the second part of this paper.

In short, accounts of human competence can be read off from the appropriate normative theories, so far as they are based on the evidence of intuitions; accounts of actual performance under different conditions are to be obtained by experiment and observation; and hypotheses about the structure and operation of human information-processing mechanisms must then be tested against the facts of competence and performance that it is their task to explain. The structure of design of such a mechanism must account for the relevant competence, but its operation must be subject to various causes of malfunction that will account for the flaws found in actual performance.

One may be tempted to ask: "How do we know that any intuition of the relevant kind is veridical?" But to ask for knowledge here is to ask for what is in principle impossible, at least in the sense in which knowledge is something like justified true belief, and where there is no alternative to invoking intuition, since an intuitive judgment that p essentially lacks any external ground to justify accepting that p. The best that normative theorists can hope for in this field (and also what they need to achieve), if they do not claim any special revelation, is that the contents of all relevant intuitions – suitably sifted or qualified, if necessary – can be made to corroborate one another by being exhibited as the consequences of a consistent and relatively simple set of rules or axioms that also sanctions other intuitively acceptable, but previously unremarked, patterns of reasoning. The inductive principle of mutual corroboration here is analogous to that operative in natural science, as Bacon long ago pointed out in regard to normative theories of ethics or jurisprudence (Kocher 1957; cf. Cohen 1970).

It would be different if we were evaluating the cognitive competence of some other species, or even of human children. We should be free to find their intuitive efforts at probabilistic reasoning, for example, or their moral sensitivity, to be rather inferior by the standard of our own norms. But we cannot attribute inferior rationality to those who are themselves among the canonical arbiters of rationality. Nothing can count as an error of reasoning among our fellow adults unless even the author of the error would, under ideal conditions, agree that it is an error.

Other arguments about rationality do not concern us here: It is true that, even where animals, children, or Martians are concerned, there are limits to the extent to which we can impute irrationality. As has been well remarked (Dennett 1979, p. 11), if the ascription of a belief or desire to a mouse is to have any predictive power, the mouse must be supposed to follow the rules of logic insofar as it acts in accordance with its beliefs and desires. But this is not to suppose that the mouse has any great powers of ratiocination. Equally (Quine 1960) we have to impute a familiar logicality to others if we are to suppose that we understand when they say: different logics for my idiolect and yours are not coherently supposable. But there is always the possibility that we understand less than we think we do and that some imputations of logicality are therefore not defensible on this score. Again, evolutionary pressure in the long run eliminates any species that is not sufficiently well equipped to surmount threats to its biological needs. But evolutionary considerations are better fitted to put an explanatory gloss on the extinction of a species after this event has already occurred than to predict the precise level of rationality that is required for this or that species' continued survival within its present environment.

What I have been arguing is that normative criteria for ordinary human reasoning rely for their substantiation on a procedure analogous to what is called "boot strapping" in artificial intelligence (see Dawes & Corrigan 1974). The intuitions of ordinary people are the basis for constructing a coherent system of rules and principles by which those same people can, if they so choose, reason much more extensively and accurately than they would otherwise do.[5] Consequently these ordinary people cannot be regarded as intrinsically irrational in regard to any such cognitive activity. An investigator who wanted to make out a serious case for deep-level human irrationality in this area might be tempted to operate with normative criteria that were the product of philosophical argument for some appropriately wide reflective equilibrium and consequently differed from the narrow, bootstrapping, reflective equilibrium which merely reconciles intuitions. But any kind of scientific or mathematical reasoning to which such criteria directly apply has a specialised and technically regimented quality that makes it difficult or impracticable for those who have not been trained appropriately. For example, it may involve deduction within an artificial language system, or employ relatively sophisticated concepts of statistical theory. Hence the investigator's experiments would founder in characteristic indeterminacy. They would constitute an accurate test of their subjects' competence for reasoning only to the extent that these subjects were not ordinary people but specially trained experts. So the results of the test might reveal how good was the training or how effective were the procedures for selecting people to be trained; they would tell us nothing about the rationality or irrationality of untrained people. Though a person may well acquire a wide reflective equilibrium with regard to ethical issues that is inconsistent with a previously existing narrow reflective equilibrium, there is no possibility of an analogous inconsistency with regard to deducibility or probability. In the case of deducibility, narrow reflective equilibrium remains the ultimate framework of argument about the merits of other deductive systems, and in the case of probability, we are merely replacing some modes of measuring uncertainty by others.

II. Four Categories of Research into Defects of Cognitive Rationality

The past decade or so has seen the growth of a vast literature of psychological research into replicable defects of human reasoning. Often investigators are content just to argue for the existence of such defects and to suggest explanations. But sometimes they also claim justification for extensive criticisms of human rationality. Several convenient reviews of this literature are already available (for example, Slovic, Fischhoff & Lichtenstein 1977; Nisbett & Ross 1980; Einhorn & Hogarth 1981), and I do not aim to produce another here. Rather, the purpose of the second part of the paper is to establish four categories, into one or the other of which, on close assessment, any item in this literature may be seen capable of being assigned without "bleak implications for human rationality," once an account of the normative criteria for ordinary human

reasoning is agreed to entail an ascription of the corresponding competence to ordinary human adults (as argued in part I). For reasons that will emerge in the sequel, these four categories of research activity are appropriately entitled "Studies of cognitive illusions," "Tests of intelligence or education," "Misapplications of appropriate normative theory," and "Applications of inappropriate normative theory." Examples will be furnished for each category. It will be assumed in every case that the phenomena reported are replicable, and that no technical faults occur in the presentation of the data, such as miscalculations of statistical significance: if the examples furnished here are in fact faulty, others are easily found. The issues raised here do not concern the robustness of the phenomena, solely their interpretation.

The categorisation is intended to be an exhaustive one, not in the sense that every item in the literature is actually assigned to one of the four categories but that in principle it could be. Claims that human reasoning tends to be invalid in certain circumstances are either correct or incorrect. The correct claims relate either to fallacies that, on reflection, everyone would admit to be such, as in studies of cognitive illusions, or to fallacies that require some more elaborate mode of demonstration as in tests of intelligence or education; the incorrect claims result either from misapplications of appropriate normative theory or from applications of inappropriate normative theory.

1. Studies of Cognitive Illusions

In view of what has been argued above about ordinary people's competence for deductive and probabilistic reasoning, there is a prima facie presumption, in regard to any experimental data in this area, that they can be explained as a manifestation of some such competence, even though the details of the explanation may not be easy to fill in. Where no explanation of this kind is available, one possibility is that experimenters have created a cognitive illusion. They have manipulated the circumstances of a situation in such a way that subjects are induced to indulge in a form of reasoning that on a few moments' prompted reflection they would be willing to admit is invalid.

A very good example of this is the familiar four-card problem (Wason 1966). The subjects are presented with four laboratory cards showing, respectively, 'A,' 'D,' '4,' and '7,' and know from previous experience that every card, of which these are a subset, has a letter on one side and a number on the other. They are then given this rule about the four cards in front of them: "If a card has a vowel on one side, then it has an even number on the other side." Next they are told: "Your task is to say which of the cards you need to turn over in order to find out whether the rule is true or false." The most frequent answers are "A and 4" and "only A," which are both wrong, while the right answer "A and 7" is given spontaneously by very few subjects.

Wason and his colleagues, in attempting to account for these data (see Johnson-Laird & Wason 1970), interpret the error as a bias towards seeking verification rather than falsification in testing the rule. But if that were the nature of the error one would expect "D" to show up in the answer like "4" does, since the contrapositive equivalent of the rule is, "If a card does not have an even number on one side, it does not have a vowel on the other." Perhaps it will be said that this is simply owing to a failure to grasp the equivalence of contrapositives here. But such a failure would account also for the absence of "7" from most answers, without the need to suppose that in testing a conditional rule subjects do anything other than check, in each case in which the antecedent holds true, whether the consequent does also: this is because the presence of "4" in many answers may then be put down to the prevalence of inference from an utterance that is of the form "if p then q" to an utterance that is of the form "if q then p" – a prevalence for which there is independent evidence (see II.3 in regard to the fallacy of illicit conversion). I shall assume, therefore, that the subjects' specific error here is best interpreted as a failure to apply the law of contraposition. What then causes that failure?

It would be wrong to conclude that the deductive competence of most logically untutored subjects does not embrace the law of contraposition. A subsequent experiment (Wason & Shapiro 1971) has been claimed to show that if the four cards are those related to a more concrete rule, namely, "Every time I go to Manchester, I go by train," then substantially more subjects are successful. Even better results were obtained (Johnson-Laird, Legrenzi & Sonino Legrenzi 1972) when the rule was, "If a letter is sealed, then it has a fivepenny stamp on it" and the laboratory cards were replaced by (sealed or unsealed, stamped or unstamped) envelopes.

Further experimentation (Van Duyne 1974, 1976) has also been claimed to show that degrees of realism in fact affect performance in a continuous, linear way. However, it looks as though we need to distinguish here between two different ways in which realism may be increased. One is by writing descriptive words or sentences on the cards, instead of just letters and numerals, and altering the rule accordingly: the other is by using real objects (envelopes) instead of cards. The results of Manktelow and Evans (1979) suggest that when realism is increased in the former manner the fallacy still occurs. But those results do not weaken the finding that when real objects replace cards the fallacy hardly ever occurs. It seems, therefore, that experimenters' power to generate an illusion here depends on the relative unfamiliarity and artificiality of their apparatus. In their familiar concrete concerns human beings show themselves well able to apply the law of contraposition to appropriate problems. Faced instead with a situation in which the items against which a conditional rule is to be checked are things (cards bearing letters, numerals, words, sentences, geometrical diagrams, and the like) that echo the symbolism in which the conditional rule itself is formulated, subjects' reasoning tends to be led astray in the "matching bias" to which Manktelow and Evans have traced the fallacy.

The point of describing experimental effects like Wason's as cognitive illusions is to invoke the analogy with visual illusions: it is in no way intended to derogate from their importance, nor to suggest that if the circumstances that cause the illusion occur naturally (as distinct from being the result of an experimenter's contrivance) then the illusion will not occur.[6] The discovery of any such effect in human performance generates a significant piece of evidence about the way in which the underlying information-processing mechanism operates. The findings about the four-card problem may legitimately be said (Johnson-Laird & Wason 1977) to support the view (Piaget 1972) that most people manage to apply their logical competence without ever formulating it expressly at a level of generality sufficient for it to be readily applicable to wholly unfamiliar tasks. People will distinguish form from content in their reasoning, or extrapolate accurately from one content to another, only to the extent that similarity of form is accompanied by some rough equality of vital interest. So subjects who reason fallaciously about the four-card problem need not be supposed to lack the correct deductive "program." Indeed, none of the experimenters in the area suggests this. The subjects merely fail to recognise the similarity of their task to those familiar issues in which they have profited by using the deductive procedure of contraposition. As a result, either that procedure receives no input or its output is deleted, and the behaviour of the subjects manifests a matching bias.

Analogously, other experimental data show, it has been argued (Wason 1960, 1968), that in an abstract task, like hypothesising about the rule that generates a given series of numbers, most people are unable to use the procedure of proving a hypothesis by eliminating alternatives to it.[7] They tend to seek confirmatory evidence for their favoured hypothesis rather than disconfirmatory evidence for alternatives to it. In addition, they often do not relinquish hypotheses that have been shown to be false. Nor is people's eliminative performance substantially better when confronted with a computer-screen simulation of a simple mechanical problem (Mynatt, Doherty & Tweney 1977). Yet it hardly needs an experiment to show that most people are quite capable of using eliminative procedures correctly when dealing with real objects – not simulated ones – in familiar everyday situations: if the soap is not in the basin, we reason, it must be in the bath; if one's caller has not come by automobile, he must have walked; and so on. So it is not that ordinary people lack competence for the kind of deductive inference that moves from "p or q" and "not-p" to "q," which is essential to all such eliminative reasoning. It seems rather that in normal investigative situations the disjunctive premise for this pattern of reasoning is supplied by previous experience, and in an artificial or unfamiliar situation we lack the relevant kind of previous experience to supply the input. To build up that experience some pursuit of confirmatory (as distinct from disconfirmatory or eliminative) strategies would not be unreasonable, as is recognised by Mynatt, Doherty, and Tweney (1978, p. 405); and retention of a falsified hypothesis would even be desirable if it explained quite a lot of the evidence and no unfalsified hypothesis were available that had as good explanatory value. So too the sharply falsificationist model of scientific progress that was originally offered by Popper (1959a) has rightly met with substantial criticism from other historians and philosophers of science (for example, Swinburne 1964; Lakatos 1970).

Again, it may seem puzzling that subjects seem unable to judge correctly in the laboratory that some event is controlled by another, or is independent of it, as the case may be, and yet the very same subjects gets along all right most of the time in their everyday life (Jenkins & Ward 1965). But the puzzle may be lessened by considering some of the ways in which their expert mental tasks are not representative of the normal conditions for such judgments: checkups are excluded, temporal variations are absent, the output considered unnaturally discrete, the response has to be a relatively hurried one, and so on.

Experimenters need to devise a great variety of experiments involving such cognitive illusions in order to test out theories about how human beings in fact perform, or fail to perform, the various acts of reasoning for which they apparently possess a competence. But one should recognise these experiments for what they are, and not conceive of the illusions that they generate as some kind of positive, though fallacious, heuristic that is employed by the subjects. Consider for example, the supposed heuristic of availability (Tversky & Kahneman 1973). A person is said to employ this heuristic whenever he estimates frequency or probability by the ease with which instances or associations are brought to mind. For example, if student subjects, when asked in the laboratory, erroneously judge English words beginning with re to be more frequent than words ending with re, they are diagnosed to have employed the heuristic of availability because the former words are more easily brought to mind than the latter. But a heuristic is a way of finding something out that one does not already have at the front of one's mind. The availability illusion consists instead in relying on data that one already has at the front of one's mind. There is a lot of evidence most people are too slow to change certain kinds of beliefs (Ross & Lepper, 1980). But no one thinks that this evidence establishes a "conservatism heuristic," rather than that it just manifests the influence of factors which make for belief inertia. Analogously, if the argument for rational competence (in part I) is accepted, the "availability" results must be interpreted to have shown, not that the subjects are estimating the frequency or probability of an x by reference to the availability of an x, but that they are doing this by reference to those x's that happen to be available. The subjects are not to be construed as operating on the evidently wild assumption that frequency can safely be taken to equal availability. Rather, where A is the available population, they are to be construed as operating on the not so evidently wild assumption that frequency can safely be taken to equal frequency in A, which is a very different matter.

In other words, to be entitled to recognise an error in subjects' reasoning here, we have to attribute to them a conception of the frequency or probability of an x, $p(x)$, such that it is incorrect to infer $p(x) = n$, where x's are y's, from $p(x \mid y)$ [$p(x$ given $y)$] $= n$, unless the y's are a suitably representative sample of the total population. So we thereby (see part I) also attribute to them competence to avoid those incorrect inferences. It follows that their probability-estimating mechanism must be supposed to include some such procedure as: check whether available evidence constitutes a fair sample in relevant respects, and, if not, seek evidence that is of the missing kind or kinds. What happens is just that the operation of this procedure tends to be obstructed by factors like the recency or emotional salience of the existing evidential input, by the existence of competing claims for computing time, or by a preference for least effort. Cognitive illusions, in the laboratory or in real life, depend on the power of such factors to hold subjects back, under the pressure of interrogation, from obtaining an appropriate additional input to their information-processing operation, just as when a visual conjurer relies at a crucial moment on his own speed of action, and on the visual inattentiveness of those who are watching, to hold the latter back from obtaining an appropriate additional input to their visual information-processing operation.

Another procedure referred to in the literature as a "heuristic" is the method of anchoring and adjustment, whereby a natural starting point or anchor is used as a first approximation to the required judgment of frequency, probability, expected value, and so on, and is then adjusted to accommodate the implications of additional information. Tversky and Kahneman (1974) have shown the existence of a tendency for adjustments to be insufficient: subjects with high starting points end up with higher estimates than those with lower ones. This tendency has also been noted (Lichtenstein & Slovic 1973) in an experiment with people who were gambling in a Las Vegas casino. Even there, an element of conjuring was present, in that the game that was played was specially designed for the purpose. But it would obviously be implausible to

suppose that any kind of cognitive illusion occurs only when the circumstances that cause it are deliberately contrived: conjuring is not the only source of visual illusions either.

A somewhat similar phenomenon has been demonstrated in relation to hindsight (Fischhoff 1975): judges with knowledge of the outcome tend to overestimate the probability that they would have declared prior to the event. This is like starting with an anchor at 100% probability and adjusting to allow, not for more information, but for less, that is, for ignorance of the actual outcome.

However, unlike in the case of the supposed heuristic of availability, there is nothing intrinsically fallacious in the procedure of anchoring and adjustment. It is a perfectly legitimate heuristic if correctly operated. What goes wrong is just that the effects of recency or salience are generally too strong to permit correct operation. Thus, Slovic et al. (1976) are right to point out that bias from anchoring, like that from availability, is congruent with the hypothesis that human reasoners resemble computers that have the right programs and just cannot execute them properly. But Slovic et al. also claim that there are certain other errors prevalent in probabilistic reasoning, concerned with sampling and prior probabilities that are not congruent with this hypothesis, and we shall see shortly that the latter claim cannot be sustained.

2. Tests of Intelligence or Education

A second category of research activity found in the literature concerns ignorance, not illusion. It demonstrates a lack of mathematical or scientific expertise.

A lack of mathematical expertise here amounts to an ignorance of principles that not everyone can be expected to acknowledge readily, still less to elicit spontaneously from their relevant competence. Possession of a competence for deductive or probabilistic reasoning entails the possession of a mechanism that must include not only certain basic procedures, corresponding to a set of axioms or primitive rules for the normative system concerned, but also a method of generating additional procedures, corresponding to the proof of theorems or derived rules in that normative system. But the actual operation of this method, beyond its simplest forms, may require skills that are relatively rare, just as a particular talent is required for the discovery of proofs in logic or mathematics wherever no mechanical decision procedure is known. In the latter case what are needed in an outstanding degree are such capacities as those for discerning shared structure in superficially different materials, for memorising complex relationships, and the like – in other words, whatever promotes the proposal of worthwhile hypotheses in the trial-and-error search for appropriate connexions. Correspondingly, only people with those skills in an outstanding degree can be expected to generate interesting new procedures for eliciting deductive consequences or estimating probabilities. Only they will be able to supply spontaneously the input, in terms of perceived similarities and the like that will enable the method of generating additional procedures to operate fruitfully. Others will have to learn these proofs or derivations, or acquire the additional procedures, at second hand. Education must supplement innate intelligence, where intelligence is understood not as the competence that everyone has but as the level of those skills that are required to supply the novel input essential for the discovery of proofs. So experiment in this area may be able to show us the limits of ordinary people's intelligence, in the appropriate sense, or the extent to which subjects have profited from logical or mathematical education. But it cannot demonstrate an erroneous competence.

For example, it required the genius of a great mathematician (Bernoulli 1713) to discover and prove that, if you estimate the probability of a certain characteristic's incidence in a population from its frequency in a sample, then the probability of your estimate's being correct, within a specifiable interval of approximation, will vary with the size of the sample. So it is easily understandable that psychological experiment finds a tendency among ordinary people, untutored in statistical theory, to be ignorant of this principle and its applications (Tversky & Kahneman 1971). No doubt equally cogent experiments could be designed to establish the fact that those untutored in Euclidean geometry are still ignorant of the fact that the square on the longest side of a right-angled triangle is equal in area to the sum of the squares on the other two sides, since it required another outstanding mathematician, Pythagoras, to discover a proof of this fact. Again, it is said (Tversky & Kahneman 1971, p. 109) that at a meeting of mathematical psychologists and at a general session of the American Psychological Association the typical respondent attached excessive significance to inferences from relatively small samples. But what this adds to the previous finding is just a

reason for reassessing the extent or success of the education that the respondents had in fact undergone. And the same holds true in relation to those who are supposed to have some statistical training but still fail to recognise new examples of regression to the mean for what they are (Kahneman & Tversky 1973).

Not all errors of estimation that are due to ignorance arise from subjects' deficiencies in mathematical expertise. Some arise instead from subjects' deficiencies in scientific (for example, psychological) expertise. For example, there is a good deal of evidence (reviewed in Slovic et al. 1977, pp. 5–6) that people are often overconfident in their second-order estimates of the accuracy of their own primary estimates. What happens here is that they are unaware of the various ways in which the information-processing mechanism that generates the primary estimates may be affected by performance error. However, this is scarcely surprising, since the facts about those patterns of error are being discovered only gradually and only by difficult (and sometimes controversial) research. No doubt it would be salutary if all nonpsychologists were taught every such fact that has been properly established. But all that is discovered, when their ignorance of such a fact is discovered, is a gap in their education.

3. Misapplications of Appropriate Normative Theory

We have been concerned so far with genuine fallacies, to which experiments reveal that people are prone because of either illusion or ignorance. However the literature also contains several examples of more questionable claims that a common fallacy exists. These are situations in which the experimental data may be explained as a direct manifestation of the relevant competence without any need to suppose an error in performance. Such claims arise either through a misapplication of the appropriate normative theory or through an application of an inappropriate one.

One particularly instructive example of the former kind relates to the alleged prevalence of the fallacy of illicit conversion, and, in particular, of inference from a proposition of the form "if p then q" to one of the form "if q then p." Intellectuals have remarked for over two millennia (Hamblin 1970) on the tendency of their inferiors to commit this fallacy, and in recent years it too has been a topic for psychological investigation (Wason & Johnson-Laird 1972). The investigators conclude that, in situations in which subjects are apparently prone to illicit conversion of conditionals, "this is not because the subjects possess faulty rules of inference but because they sometimes make unwarranted interpretations of conditional statements" (p. 65). The subjects are claimed to treat these conditionals as if they were statements of causal connexion which allow one to infer from effect to cause as well as from cause to effect.

But it is not clear that the subjects must in fact be supposed even to be making an unwarranted interpretation. We have to bear in mind here that the principles of a normative theory, such as one that systematises criteria for deducibility, inevitably involve abstraction and idealisation (see Part I, Section 3). So what are to be taken as the actual, concrete premises that are represented by the initial formulas in a primitive or derived rule for natural deduction, when such rules are taken to be the norms relevant to some actual sequence of human reasoning? The mere sentences uttered do not normally constitute all of the premises conveyed by the total act of communication, since we are presumptively entitled to take the latter as including also any judgments that are implied by the act of uttering those sentences in the contextual circumstances. For example, as far as human conversation is governed by rules of relevance, brevity, informativeness, and so on, as required by the purpose in hand (Grice 1975),[8] the information provided by the utterance of a solitary conditional sentence – if p then q – may be presumed, unless there are specific indications to the contrary, to be all that is required in the circumstances to satisfy the interest either of someone who wants to know what is also true if the antecedent of the conditional is true, or of someone who wants to know the conditions under which the consequent of the conditional sentence is true. In the former case ("If you interrupt him now, he'll be cross") the conditional is convertible because its utterance would normally be pointless unless "if not-p then not-q" were also true and "if not p then not-q" is formally equivalent to the converse of "if p, then q." In the other case ("If you give him a tip, he'll let you in") the conditional is convertible because its solitary utterance may be presumed to state the only condition under which the consequent is true.

Hence if we consider the total content of the message communicated, rather than just the conditional sentence that is uttered, it would not be fallacious or unwarranted for subjects to presume, unless there are specific indications to the contrary, that the converse of the condi-

tional is implicit in the message, and the convertibility of causal conditionals is just a special form of this. A psychological experimenter who wishes to exclude the legitimacy of presuming the converse in such a case must contrive suitable instructions to his subjects and teach them how to distinguish between the implications of a sentence uttered and the implications of its utterance. But how could we judge the suitability of such instructions without taking into account the extent of their success in averting inferences to the converse? In other words, a tendency to commit the fallacy of illicit conversion in everyday life is demonstrable only on the basis of an unrealistic assumption – namely, that when a normative theory is invoked for the evaluation of commonsense reasoning its criteria should be applied to nothing but the linguistic forms that are actually uttered.

Another line of research activity (see, for example, Wagenaar 1972) in which appropriate norms seem to be sometimes misapplied is in studies of judgments of randomness. Results over quite a variety of tests seem to confirm the hypothesis that subjects who are attempting to behave randomly will produce series that have too many alternations and too few repetitions. But as has been well pointed out (Lopes 1980), a series may have randomness with respect to its atomic or elementary events, while still possessing molecular units, such as groups of ten consecutive atomic events, that do not exhibit randomness. Or randomness may be achieved for a certain category of molecular events, at the cost of sacrificing randomness with respect to elementary events. Unless this distinction between different kinds of randomness is clearly presented to the subjects, they are not in a position to know what kind is being sought by the experimenters. And again it is not easy to see how the subjects' apparent failure to produce correct judgments of randomness should not be regarded as simply a measure of the aptness of their instructions.

A different way in which an appropriate normative theory may be misapplied was instantiated in the course of an attempt to show that, as compared with their treatment of predictive evidence, people are prone to "a major underestimation of the impact" of diagnostic evidence "which could have severe consequences in the intuitive assessment of legal, medical, or scientific evidence" (Tversky & Kahneman 1977, p. 186). Subjects were given two sets of questions that were regarded by the experimenters as similar in relevant structure. But in fact the predictive set concerned conditional probabili- ties, as in – for one instance – "The chance of death from heart failure is 45% among males with congenital high blood pressure," while the diagnostic set concerned unconditional ones, as in "The radiologist who examined Bill's X-ray estimated the chance of a malignancy to be 45%," and this difference sufficed to account quite rationally for differences in the numerical answers to the two sets of questions (see Cohen 1979, pp. 403–5). Moreover, when the dissimi- larity of structure was remedied, the alleged phe- nomenon of diagnostic underestimation failed to emerge. Other results that appear to evince this phenomenon have to be discounted for different reasons (Cohen 1979, pp. 401–3). But the fail- ure to distinguish appropriately here between conditional and unconditional probabilities is a good example of how the appearance of a fallacy in subjects' reasoning may be generated by a slip in the application of the appropriate probabilis- tic analysis,[9] since within normative probability theory the distinction between conditional and unconditional probabilities is well established.

Even the so-called gambler's fallacy, or "fal- lacy of the maturity of chances," which is some- times referred to in the literature on cogni- tive irrationality (Tversky & Kahneman 1974; Hogarth 1975), comes under some suspicion. More empirical work seems necessary here, but there are at least three possible approaches to the phenomenon that call into question its interpre- tation as a fallacy of probabilistic reasoning.

If some people believe that after a long run of heads the probability of tails on the next toss will be greater than $\frac{1}{2}$, then one possibil- ity is that they should be interpreted as believ- ing thereby in a spirit of distributive justice that regulates the whole cosmos with a policy that ensures ever-increasing probabilities of a trend- reversing intervention whenever identical out- comes begin to succeed one another within an otherwise chance set-up. On this construal, a gambler's metaphysical belief may be at fault, but not the rationality of his reasoning from it. However, such an interpretation needs indepen- dent evidence to support the attribution of belief in the particular case. Otherwise it is open to the charge of being culpably ad hoc, if not of merely repeating what is to be explained within the explanation.

Second, we may need to distinguish here between two rather different probabilities, either of which might be a matter for estima- tion. Is the gambler supposed to be estimating, in relation to the next toss of a fair coin, the

probability of a tails outcome within a space that consists of the two alternative outcomes: heads and tails? Or is the probability in mind, at the nth toss of a fair coin, that of having at least one tails outcome within any space that con- sists of n outcomes? Whereas the correct figure for the former would be $\frac{1}{2}$, the correct figure for the latter would get greater and greater than $\frac{1}{2}$ as n itself increases beyond 1, in accordance with Bernoulli's theorem. To ascertain clearly and unmistakably which of the two probabilities is being estimated it would be necessary to ques- tion the gambler in a way that would tend to dis- courage any incorrect estimate, since in order to convey the exact meaning of a particular type of probability assignment (or, indeed, of any other type of statement), one needs to state the con- ditions under which such a judgment is true. So we are left with a characteristic indeterminacy here. Any attempt to extract an exact answer from the gambler would transform the situation in a way that would tend to disconfirm the occur- rence of fallacious reasoning, and to the extent that the situation was not so transformed, the exact nature of the situation would remain in doubt. But it remains an open question, in view of what was said earlier about ordinary people's ignorance of Bernoulli's theorem, whether ordi- nary gamblers may legitimately be expected to be aware of its implications.

Finally, it may be that the matter at issue needs to be regarded more as a pragmatic than as a cognitive phenomenon. In the long run a gambler could integrate the so-called fallacy into a winning strategy against any opponent who always insists on even odds but is willing to play as long as the gambler wants: the gambler has only to continue increasing the stakes suffi- ciently at each toss until tails actually comes up. But, of course, such a strategy could be executed only within the limits of any restriction that is imposed on the stakes either by the opponent or by the gambler's resources, just as any intel- lectual competence is subject to limitations in actual performance.

4. Applications of Inappropriate Normative Theory

There is a tendency for some investigators of irrationality to proceed as if all questions about appropriate norms have already been settled and the questions that remain open concern only the extent of actual conformity to these norms. It is as if existing textbooks of logic or statistics had some kind of canonical authority. But in fact many important normative issues are still controversial. For example, it seemed at one time that at least the Frege-Russell logic of quantification had become a universally received doctrine. But its closeness of fit for the appraisal of natural-language reasoning is now under a powerful challenge (Sommers 1981) from work that exploits hitherto undiscovered ways of developing the Aristotelian tradition. Again, it seemed at one time to be generally agreed – and accepted by psychological investigators of decision making (see Slovic et al. 1977) – that the rational way to base action on estimates of chance was to follow the rule: "Rank possible courses of action according to their conditional subjective estimations of utility." But this rule has been seriously challenged in recent years because it seems not to take proper account of the difference between actions as symptoms, and actions as causes, of states of affairs that we act to promote or avert (Jeffrey 1980).

Great care has certainly to be taken also in selecting the normative criteria by which the correctness of subjects' probability judgments is assessed. In one experiment, for example, subjects were told that in a certain town blue and green cabs operate in a ratio of 85 to 15, respectively. A witness identifies a cab in a crash as green, and the court is told that in the relevant light conditions he can distinguish blue cabs from green ones in 80% of cases. The subjects were then asked: what is the probability (expressed as a percentage) that the cab involved in the accident was blue? The median estimated probability was .2, and investigators (Kahneman & Tversky 1972a) claim that this shows the prevalence of serious error, because it implies a failure to take base rates (that is, prior probabilities) into account. Kahneman and Tversky commented: "Much as we would like to, we have no reason to believe that the typical juror does not evaluate evidence in this fashion." Lyon and Slovic (1976) have confirmed the robustness of the phenomenon, which is impervious to variations in the topic, numerical details, and sequential formulation of the story told to the subjects (with the proviso that blue and green cabs were present in equal numbers during the tests on the witness). And they complain that "since the world operates according to Bayes's theorem, experience should confirm the importance of base rates" despite the apparent failure of subjects to recognize that it does so.

At best, these experiments would constitute a test of their subjects' intelligence or education, since the ordinary person might no more be expected to generate Bayes's theorem spontaneously than Bernoulli's. But in fact it is doubtful whether the subjects have made any kind of mathematical error at all. The experimenters seem to be reasoning as follows. In the long run, they say to themselves, the witness may be expected to make 68% correct identifications of a cab as blue ($^4/_5 \times 85\%$), 3% incorrect identifications of a cab as blue ($^1/_5 \times 15\%$), 12% correct identifications of a cab as green ($^4/_5 \times 15\%$), and 17% incorrect identifications as green ($^1/_5 \times 85\%$). Therefore he will altogether make 29% identifications as green, and the fraction of them that will be incorrect is $^{17}/_{29}$. Consequently, according to the way in which the experimenters seem to be reasoning, the probability that the cab involved in the accident was blue is $^{17}/_{29}$, not $^1/_5$.

But this last step is a questionable one. The ratio $^{17}/_{29}$ is the value of the conditional probability that a cab colour identification by the witness is incorrect, on the condition that it is an identification as green. Jurors, however, or people thinking of themselves as jurors, ought not to rely on that probability if they can avoid doing so, since reliance on it assumes the issue before the court to concern a long run of cab-colour identification problems – whereas in fact it concerns just one problem of this type. Jurors here are occupied, strictly speaking, just with the probability that the cab actually involved in the accident was blue, on the condition that the witness said it was green. And the latter probability is equivalent in the circumstances to the probability that a statement to the effect that the cab actually involved in the accident was green, is false, on the condition that the statement is made by the witness. If the jurors know that only 20% of the witness's statements about cab colours are false, they rightly estimate the probability at issue as $^1/_5$, without any transgression of Bayes's law. The fact that cab colours actually vary according to an $^{85}/_{15}$ ratio is strictly irrelevant to this estimate, because it neither raises nor lowers the probability of a specific cab-colour identification being correct on the condition that it is an identification by the witness. A probability that holds uniformly for each of a class of events because it is based on causal properties, such as the physiology of vision, cannot be altered by facts, such as chance distributions, that have no causal efficacy in the individual events. For example, if the green cab company suddenly increased the size of its fleet relative to that of the blue company, the accuracy of the witness's vision would not be affected, and the credibility of his testimony would therefore remain precisely the same in any particular case of the relevant kind.

The same point can be put another way by emphasising the difference between probability functions that measure relative frequencies and probability functions that measure causal propensities (see Part I, Section 2 of this chapter). Propensity-type probabilities may be *estimated from* frequencies in appropriate samples (as with the witness's reliability), but what is actually evaluated is something different: a propensity, not a frequency. And propensity-type probabilities can be derived for individual events because they are predictable distributively. So it is natural to suppose that this is the kind of probability with which a jury is properly concerned, whereas the mere relative frequency of blue and green cabs is an accidentally accumulated characteristic of the town's cab population, considered collectively, and does not generate any causal propensity for the particular cab in the accident. Of course, if no testimony is mentioned and subjects know nothing except the relative frequency of the differently coloured cabs, then no causal propensity is at issue and the only basis for estimating the required probability is indeed the relative frequency. And this is in fact the kind of estimate that the investigators have then found to occur under experimental conditions (Lyon & Slovic 1976, p. 294).

The issue here is an important one since it has many ramifications. If the investigators had been right to impugn the rationality of common-sense judgments in the above example, it would have certainly been difficult to defend the continued use of lay juries. Consider too what you yourself would decide in the following circumstances. You are suffering from a disease that, according to your manifest symptoms, is either A or B. For a variety of demographic reasons disease A happens to be nineteen times as common as B. The two diseases are equally fatal if untreated, but it is dangerous to combine the respectively appropriate treatments. Your physician orders a certain test which, through the operation of a fairly well understood causal process, always gives a unique diagnosis in such cases, and this diagnosis has been tried out on equal numbers of A- and B-patients and is known to be correct on 80% of those occasions. The tests report that you are suffering from disease B. Should you nevertheless opt for the treatment appropriate to A, on the supposition (reached by calculating as the experimenters did) that the probability of your suffering from A is $19/23$? Or should you opt for the treatment appropriate to B, on the supposition (reached by calculating as the subjects did) that the probability of your suffering from B is $4/5$? It is the former option that would be the irrational one for you, qua patient, not the latter; and in a rather comparable experimental situation (Hammerton 1973) subjects tended in fact to judge the matter along just those lines. Indeed, on the other view, which is the one espoused in the literature, it would be a waste of time and money even to carry out the tests, since whatever *their* results, the base rates would still compel a more than $4/5$ probability in favour of disease A. So the literature under criticism is propagating an analysis that could increase the number of deaths from a rare disease of this kind.

Admittedly, the standard statistical method would be to take the prior frequency into account here, and this would be absolutely right if what was wanted was a probability for any patient considered not as a concrete particular person, not even as a randomly selected particular person, but simply as an instance of a long run of patients. The administrator who wants to secure a high rate of diagnostic success for his hospital at minimal cost would be right to seek to maximise just that probability, and therefore to dispense altogether with the tests. But a patient is concerned with success in his own particular case, not with stochastic success for the system. So he needs to evaluate a propensity-type probability, not a frequency-type one, and the standard statistical method would then be inappropriate. Note, however, that the causal propensity analysis does not involve any repudiation of Bayes's theorem. It is just that the prior probabilities have to be appropriate ones, and there is no information about you personally that establishes a greater predisposition in your case to disease A than to disease B. We have to suppose equal predispositions here, unless told that the probability of A is greater (or less) than that of B among people who share all your relevant characteristics, such as age, medical history, blood group, and so on. An analogous supposition has to be made about the cab colours, unless we are told that because of faulty maintenance, say, the probability of a blue cab's being involved in accidents that share all the relevant characteristics of the present one, such as poor braking, worn tires, and the like, is greater (or less) than that of a green cab's being involved. Similarly, in a criminal law court the object is to do justice in each individual case, without taking a defendant's past criminal record, if he has one, into account. But it is easy enough to imagine analogous cases in which a shoplifter, say, would escape conviction on the basis of probabilistic testimony about identification, if the relative frequency of honest shoppers could be cited in his defence! Or consider an example very like that cited by Todhunter (1949/1865, p. 400) in connection with the danger of applying the standard statistical method – which he traces to Condorcet – indiscriminately. A witness of 99.9% reliability asserts that the number of the single ticket drawn in a lottery of 10,000 tickets was, say, 297: ought we really to reject that proposition just because of the size of the lottery?

The difference between frequency probability and propensity probability is a difference between two functions that both satisfy the formal axioms of the classical calculus of chance. The two functions differ in their semantics, that is, with regard to the nature x and y must have, and the relation they must bear to one another, when, for a particular n, it is true that $p(x|y) = n$. But both functions have the same logical syntax; that is, each satisfies a multiplicational law for conjunction, a complementational law for negation, and so on. Nevertheless (as remarked above) it should by no means be taken for granted that all valid types of probability judgment in everyday reasoning can be modeled by functions that share this syntax.

For example, it has been held (Kahneman & Tversky 1972b, 1973, 1974; Tversky & Kahneman 1974) that intuitive judgments of probability are biased towards predicting that outcomes will be similar to the evidence afforded by typical cases. It is claimed that people use a representativeness heuristic as a rough-and-ready, though often misleading, guide in their probabilistic reasoning. But the validity of this claim depends on the assumption that such a judgment about degree of representativeness has to be interpreted as a means towards drawing some conclusion about probability in a sense of that term that conforms to the classical calculus of chance. If instead we abandon that assumption, we can avoid imputing any fallacies here. We can suppose that the judgment of representativeness leads to a conclusion about probability in a sense in which an inference from representativeness to probability is always quite legitimate – albeit a sense that conforms to principles different from those derivable within the calculus of chance. In fact, these principles can be shown to be implicit in the logic of controlled experiment, which was first developed by Francis Bacon (Cohen 1979). Bacon, in the preface to his *Novum Organum*, described the

central concern of his own enquiry in just the same terms as Bernoulli (1713, p. 211) described his, namely, the determination of "degrees of certainty." But Bacon's method defines a different concept of probability from Bernoulli's (Cohen 1980b). Hume (1739) called it "probability arising from analogy," and he wrote:

> Without some degree of resemblance, as well as union, 'tis impossible there can be any reasoning; but as this resemblance admits of many different degrees, the reasoning becomes proportionally more or less firm and certain. An experiment loses of its force, when transfer'd to instances, which are not exactly resembling; tho' 'tis evident it may still retain as much as may be the foundation of probability, as long as there is any resemblance remaining.

When all this is made precise and its implications are developed systematically, one can show that, in appropriate contexts, concern with representativeness is not a potentially fallacious heuristic but rather a quite reliable, albeit somewhat crude, mode of commonsense reasoning under conditions of uncertainty (Cohen 1979, 1980d). It appears otherwise only if evaluated against a type of normative theory that is inappropriate in the circumstances (though admirably appropriate in many other circumstances).

Conclusion

The upshot of all this may be summarised as follows. No doubt ordinary people often err in their reasoning, and such a mistake begins to be of scientific interest when it can be shown to instantiate some regular pattern of performance error. However, nothing in the existing literature on cognitive reasoning, or in any possible future results of human experimental enquiry could have bleak implications for human rationality, in the sense of implications that establish a faulty competence. At best, experimenters in this area may hope to discover revealing patterns of illusion. Often they will only be testing subjects' intelligence or education. At worst they risk imputing fallacies where none exist.

Notes

1   The same is true for intuitions of grammaticalness, pace Sampson (1975).
2   This issue is too complex to be treated adequately here; for a useful review; see Haack (1974).

3   I leave open here the much discussed question whether (Lewis and Langford 1959), Anderson and Belnap, 1974, or some other system provides a better fitting logic of everyday reasoning.

4   For example, the intuition that B is deducible from A whenever A-and-not-B is inconsistent (Lewis & Langford 1959) clashes with the intuition that one may not deduce every proposition from an inconsistent one (Anderson & Belnap 1974). So, though consistency is normally an overriding ideal for theory construction, one cannot treat the demand for it as the only foundation needed for a theory of deducibility: other intuitions, too, have to be taken into account.

5   Cf. how, in a maximally specific case, the systematic model of a clinician's judgmental strategies may be a better predictor than the clinician's own judgment (Goldberg 1970).

6   The analogy with perceptual illusion (such as the Muller & Lyer) was also drawn by Chapman and Chapman (1967, p. 194) in their interpretation of the partly experimental and partly real-life data about erroneous use of Draw-a-Person tests in psychiatric diagnosis. Both here and in their work on the psychodiagnostic use of Rorschach cards (1969) they traced the source of illusory correlations to a powerful bias by verbal association, since subjects with no clinical experience all tended to make the same erroneous correlations as many clinicians.

7   Apparently none of Wason's subjects objected, as would have been justified, that no finite number of questions and answers, whether falsificatory or verificatory, could prove such a hypothesis correct.

8   I take Grice to have established the mental or social reality of some such rules. In the logical context, however he does not use them, as I do, to explain the alleged prevalence of the fallacy of illicit conversion. Instead he tries to use them to explain away the apparent inappropriateness of a truth functional logic for the analysis of deductive reasoning a natural language, and in this he attempts an impossible task (see Cohen 1971; 1977a).

9   This has now been acknowledged by its authors (Kahneman & Tversky 1979).

References

Anderson, A. R. & Belnapr N. D. (1974) *Entailment: The logic of relevance and necessity*. Vol. 1. Princeton: Princeton University Press.

Ayer, A. J. (1946) *Language, truth and logic*. (London: Gollancz).

Bergson, H. (1903) *Introduction a la métaphysique*. (Paris: A. Bourgeois Cahiers de la quinzaine).

Bernoulli, J. (1713) *Ars conjectandi*. Basle.

Carnap, R. (1947) *Meaning and necessity*. (Chicago: University of Chicago Press).

_____. (1950) *Logical foundations of probability*. (Chicago: University of Chicago Press).

Chapman, L. J. & Chapman, J. P. (1967) "Genesis of popular but erroneous psychodiagnostic observations." *Journal of Abnormal Psychology* 72 (3): 193–204.

_____. (1969) "Illusory correlation as an obstacle to the use of valid psychodiagnostic signs." *Journal of Abnormal Psychology* 74 (3): 271–80.

Chomsky, N. (1965) *Aspects of the theory of syntax*. Cambridge, Mass.: MIT Press.

Cohen, L. J. (1970) *The implications of induction*. (London: Methuen).

_____. (1971) "Some remarks on Grice's views about the logical particles of natural language." In: *Pragmatics of natural language*, ed. Y. Bar-Hillel. (Dordrecht: Reidel.)

_____. (1977a) "Can the conversationalist hypothesis be defended?" *Philosophical Studies* 31: 81–90.

_____. (1977b) *The probable and the provable*. (Oxford: Oxford University Press).

_____. (1979) "On the psychology of prediction: Whose is the fallacy?" *Cognition* 7: 385–407.

_____. (1980b) "Some historical remarks on the Baconian conception of probability." *Journal of the History of Ideas* 41: 219–31.

_____. (1980d) "Whose is the fallacy? A rejoinder to Daniel Kahneman and Amos Tversky." *Cognition* 8: 89–92.

Copi, I. M. (1954) *Symbolic logic*. (New York: Macmillan).

Daniels, N. (1979) "Wide reflective equilibrium and theory acceptance in ethics." *Journal of Philosophy* 76: 256–82.

_____. (1980) "On some methods of ethics and linguistics." *Philosophical Studies* 37: 21–36.

Davidson, D. (1966) "The logical form of action sentences." In: *The logic of decision and action*, ed. N. Rescher. (Pittsburgh: University of Pittsburgh Press).

Dawes, B. M. & Corrigan, B. (1974) "Linear models in decision making." *Psychological Bulletin* 81: 95–106.

de Finetti, B. (1931) Sul significato soggettivo della probabilita. *Fundamenta mathematicae* 17: 298–329.

Dennett, D. C. (1979) *Brainstorms*. (Hassocks: Harvester.)

Dummett, M. (1978) "The justification of deduction." In: *Truth and other enigmas*, ed. M. Dummett. (London: Duckworth).

Edwards, W. (1975) "Comment." *Journal of the American Statistical Association* 70: 291–93.

Einhorn, H. J. & Hogarth, R. M. (1981) "Behavioral decision theory: Processes of judgment and choice." *Annual Review of Psychology*, 32: 53–88.

Ellis, B. (1979) *Rational belief systems*. (Oxford: Blackwell.)

Fischhoff, B. (1975) "Hindsight ≠ foresight: The effect of outcome knowledge on judgment under uncertainty." *Journal of Experimental Psychology: Human Perception and Performance* 1: 288–99.

Goldberg, L. R. (1970) "Man versus model of man: A rationale, plus some evidence, for a method of improving on clinical inferences." *Psychological Bulletin* 73(6): 422–32.

Goodman, N. (1954) *Fact, fiction, and forecast.* (London: Athlone).

———. (1979) *Fact, fiction, and forecast.* 3rd ed. (Indianapolis: Hackett).

Grice, H. P. (1975) "Logic and conversation." In: *The logic of grammar,* ed. D. Davidson and G. Harman. (Encino, Calif.: Dickenson).

Griffin, N. (1977) *Relative identity.* (Oxford: Oxford University Press).

Haack, S. (1974) *Deviant logic.* (Cambridge: Cambridge University Press).

Hamblin, C. L. (1970) *Fallacies.* (London: Methuen).

Hammerton, M. (1973) "A case of radical probability estimation." *Journal of Experimental Psychology* 101: 252–54.

Hogarth, B. M. (1975) "Cognitive processes and the assessment of subjective probability distributions." *Journal of the American Statistical Association* 70: 271–89.

Hume, D. (1739) *A treatise of human nature.* (London: John Noon).

Husserl, E. (1911) "Philosophie als strenge Wissenschaft." *Logos* 1: 289–341.

Jeffrey, R. C. (1980) "How is it reasonable to base preferences on estimates of chance?" In: *Science, belief and behaviour,* ed. D. H. Mellor. (Cambridge: Cambridge University Press).

Jenkins, H. M. & Ward, W. C. (1965) "Judgment of contingency between responses and outcomes." *Psychological Monographs: General and Applied* 79, whole no. 594.

Johnson-Laird, P. N., Legrenzi, P., & Sonino Legrenzi, H. (1972) "Reasoning and a sense of reality." *British Journal of Psychology* 63: 395–400.

Johnson-Laird, P. N. & Wason, P. C. (1970) "A theoretical analysis of insight into a reasoning task." *Cognitive Psychology* 1: 134–48.

———. (1977) "Postscript." In: *Thinking: Readings in Cognitive Science,* ed. P. N. Johnson-Laird & P. C. Wason. (Cambridge: Cambridge University Press).

Kahneman, D. & Tversky, A. (1972a) "On the psychology of prediction." *Oregon Research Institute Research Bulletin* 12, whole no. 4.

———. (1972b) "Subjective probability: A judgment of representativeness." *Cognitive Psychology* 3: 430–54.

———. (1973) "On the psychology of prediction." *Psychological Review* 80: 237–51.

———. (1974) "Subjective probability: A judgment of representativeness." In: *The concept of probability in psychological experiments,* ed. C. A. S. Stael von Holstein. (Dordrecht: Reidel.)

———. (1979) "On the interpretation of intuitive probability: A reply to Jonathan Cohen." *Cognition* 7: 409–11.

Kocher, P. H. (1957) "Francis Bacon on the science of jurisprudence." *Journal of the History of Ideas* 18: 3–26.

Kolmogorov, A. (1950) *Foundations of probability.* (New York: Chelsea).

Kripke, S. (1972) "Naming and necessity." In: *Semantics of natural language,* ed. D. Davidson and G. Harman. (Dordrecht: Reidel).

Lakatos, I. (1970) "Falsificationism and the methodology of scientific research programs." In: *Criticism and the growth of knowledge,* ed. I. Lakatos and A. E. Musgrave. (Amsterdam: North Holland).

Lemmon, E. J. (1965) *Beginning logic.* (London: Nelson).

Lewis, D. (1973) *Counterfactuals.* (Oxford: Blackwell).

Lichtenstein, S. & Slovic, P. (1973) "Response-induced reversals of preference in gambling: An extended replication in Las Vegas." *Journal of Experimental Psychology* 101: 16–20.

Lopes, L. L. (1980) "Doing the impossible: A note on induction and the experience of randomness." Paper presented at 18th Bayesian Research Conference, Los Angeles, Calif.

Lyon, D. & Slovic, P. (1976) "Dominance of accuracy information and neglect of base rates in probability estimation." *Acta Psychologica* 40: 287–98.

Manktelow, K. I. & Evans, J. St. B. T. (1979) "Facilitation of reasoning by realism: Effect or non-effect." *British Journal of Psychology* 70: 477–88.

Mellor, D. H. (1971) *The matter of chance.* (Cambridge: Cambridge University Press).

Mynatt, C. B., Doherty, M. E. & Tweney, R. D. (1977) "Confirmation bias in a simulated research environment: An experimental study of scientific inference." *Quarterly Journal of Experimental Psychology* 29: 85–95.

———. (1978) "Consequences of confirmation and disconfirmation in a simulated research environment." *Quarterly Journal of Experimental Psychology* 30: 395–406.

Nagel, E. (1939) "Principles of the theory of probability." *International Encyclopaedia of Unified Science,* vol. 1, no. 6. (Chicago: University of Chicago Press).

Nisbett, R. E. & Borgida, E. (1975) "Attribution and the psychology of predictions." *Journal of Personality and Social Psychology* 32: 932–43.

Nisbett, R. E. & Ross, L. (1980) *Human inference: Strategies and shortcomings of social judgment.* (Englewood Cliffs: Prentice-Hall).

Piaget, J. (1972) *The principles of genetic epistemology.* (London: Routledge and Kegan Paul).

Popper, K R. (1959a) *The logic of scientific discovery*. (London: Hutchinson).

_____. (1959b) "The propensity interpretation of probability." *British Journal for Philosophy of Science* 10: 25–42.

_____. (1968) "On the rules of detachment and so-called inductive logic." In: *The problem of inductive logic*, ed. I. Lakatos. (Amsterdam: North Holland).

Quine, W. V. O. (1952) *Methods of logic*. (London: Routledge and Kegan Paul).

_____. (1960) *Word and object*. (Cambridge, Mass.: MIT Press).

Ramsey, F. P. (1931) *The foundations of mathematics*. (London: Routledge and Kegan Paul).

Rawls, J. (1972) *A theory of justice* (Oxford: Oxford University Press).

Reichenbach, H. (1944) *Philosophic foundations of quantum mechanics*. (Berkeley: University of California Press).

_____. (1949) *The theory of probability*. (Berkeley: University of California Press.)

Ross, L. & Lepper, M. B. (1980) "The perseverance of beliefs: Empirical and normative considerations." In: *New directions for methodology of behavioral science: Fallible judgment in behavioral research*, ed. R. A. Shweder & D. Fiske. (San Francisco: Jossey-Bass).

Russell, B. (1919) *Introduction to mathematical philosophy*. (London: Allen & Unwin).

Sampson, C. K. (1975) *The form of language*. (London: Weidenfeld & Nicolson).

Simon, H. A. (1957) *Models of man*. (New York: John Wiley).

Slovic, P., Fischhoff, B. & Lichtenstein, S. (1976) "Cognitive processes and societal risk taking." In: *Cognition and social behavior*, ed. J. S. Carroll & J. W. Payne. (Hillsdale, N. J.: Erlbaum).

_____. (1977) "Behavioral decision theory." *Annual Review of Psychology* 28: 1–39.

Sommers, F. (1981) *The logic of natural language*. (Oxford: Oxford University Press).

Spinoza, B. de. (1914) *Opera*. (Hague: Nijhoff).

Stich, S. P. (1975) Logical form and natural language. *Philosophical Studies* 28: 397–418.

Swinburne, R. C. (1964) "Falsifiability of scientific theories." *Mind* 73: 434–36.

Todhunter, I. (1949) *A history of the mathematical theory of probability from the time of Pascal to that of Laplace*. Reprint of 1865 edition. (New York: Chelsea).

Tversky, A. & Kahneman, D. (1971) 'The belief in the "law of small numbers."' *Psychological Bulletin* 76: 105–10.

_____. (1973) "Availability: A heuristic for judging frequency and probability." *Cognitive Psychology* 5: 207–32.

_____. (1974) "Judgment under uncertainty: Heuristics and biases." *Science* 125: 1124–31.

_____. (1977) "Causal thinking in judgment under uncertainty." In: *Basic problems in methodology and linguistics*, ed. R. Butts & J. Hintikka. (Dordrecht: Reidel).

Van Duyne, P. C. (1974) "Realism and linguistic complexity." *British Journal of Psychology* 65: 59–67.

_____. (1976) "Necessity and contingency in reasoning." *Acta Psychologica* 40: 85–101.

von Mises, K. (1957) *Probability, statistics and truth*. (London: Allen & Unwin).

Wagenaar, W. A. (1972) "Generation of random sequences by human subjects: A critical survey of literature." *Psychological Bulletin* 77: 65–72.

Wason, P. C. (1960) "On the failure to eliminate hypothesis in a conceptual task." *Quarterly Journal of Experimental Psychology* 12: 129–40.

_____. (1966) "Reasoning." In: *New horizons in psychology*, vol. 1, ed. B. Foss. (Hammondsworth: Penguin).

_____. (1968) "Reasoning about a rule." *Quarterly Journal of Experimental Psychology* 20: 273–81.

Wason, P. and Johnson-Laird, P. N. (1972) *Psychology of reasoning: Structure and content*. (London: Ratsford).

Wason, P. C. & Shapiro, D. (1971) "Natural and contrived experience in a reasoning problem." *Quarterly Journal of Experimental Psychology* 23: 63–71.

Chapter 8: Breakdown of Will

GEORGE AINSLIE

1. Introduction

There have been plenty of books and articles that describe how irrational we are – in consuming drugs and alcohol and cigarettes, in gambling, in forming destructive relationships, in failing to carry out our own plans, even in boring ourselves and procrastinating. The paradoxes of how people knowingly choose things they'll regret don't need rehashing. Examples of self-defeating behaviors abound. Theories about how this could be are almost as plentiful, with every discipline that studies the problem represented by several. However, the proliferation of theories in psychology, philosophy, economics, and the other behavioral sciences is best understood as a sign that no one has gotten to the heart of the matter.

These theories almost never mention failures of will.[1] This is just not a concept that behavioral scientists used much in the twentieth century. Some writers have even proposed that there's no such thing as a "will," that the word refers only to someone's disposition to choose. Still, the word crops up a lot in everyday speech, especially as part of "willpower," something that people still buy books to increase.

It's widely perceived that some factor transforms motivation from a simple reflection of the incentives we face to a process that is somehow *ours*, that perhaps even becomes *us* – some factor that lies at the very core of choice-making. We often refer to it as our will, the faculty by which we impose some overriding value of ours on the array of pressures and temptations that seem extrinsic. People usually ascribe control of temptation to the power of will and the unpredictability of this control to the freedom of will.

Unfortunately, there has been no way to talk about such a faculty in the language of science, that is, in a way that relates it to simpler or better-understood elements. Without addressing this factor, science paints a stilted picture of human experience in general. However, quantitative motivational research has produced a distinctly new finding that promises to account for the phenomenon of will – with elements that are already familiar to behavioral science. That, in a sentence, is the topic of this book.

1.1. A Brief History of Self-Defeating Behavior

A lot has been said about the will since the classical Greeks wrote about why people don't – or shouldn't – follow their spontaneous inclinations. Plato quoted Socrates describing what can go wrong when people weigh their future options:

> Do not the same magnitudes appear larger to your sight when near, and smaller when at a distance? . . . Is not [the power of appearance] that deceiving art which makes us wander up and down and take the things at one time of which we repent at another? . . . Men err in their choice of pleasures and pains, that is, in their choice of good and evil, from defect of . . . that particular knowledge that is called measuring.

Aristotle gave this disorder a name, *akrasia*, "weakness of will."[2] Thus a human faculty, not called will until later, was defined by the situation in which it failed.

Normally, a person was said to follow "reason," to weigh her options in proportion to their real importance; but sometimes an option seemed to loom too large, a process called "passion." Passion was the enemy of reason. As this dichotomy evolved, it began to define a functional anatomy of the self. Reason was the major part of your real identity; passion was something that *came over you* – the term was often contrasted with "action," something you *do*.[3]

The self used reason to defend itself from passions and, if successful, developed a "disposition" to behave temperately. Reason and a temperate disposition were the good guys; passion and *akrasia* were the bad guys, perhaps the *other* guys. The Roman physician Galen said that their relationship was that of a man to an animal: "Irascible" passions could be tamed, but "concupiscible" passions (appetites, like sex and gluttony) were too wild and could be controlled only by starving them.[4]

The Judeo-Christian theological view of "weakness of the flesh" developed in parallel with the Greek rationalist one. A noteworthy difference was that the theological view made reason somewhat external to the self, and passion more internal. Reason was the word of God, and a function called will was, to a large extent, supplied by God's grace. Passion was sin, a relentless part of man's identity since Adam's fall; but passion was sometimes augmented by external possession in the form of demons. The self swayed between reason and passion, hoping, in its reflective moments at least, that God would win:

I do not even acknowledge my own actions as mine, for what I do is not what I want to do, but what I detest. But if what I do is against my will, it means that I agree with the law and hold it to be admirable. But as things are, it is no longer I who perform the action, but sin that lodges in me ... the good which I want to do, I fail to do; but what I do is the wrong which is against my will; and if what I do is against my will, clearly it is no longer I who am the agent, but sin that has its lodging in me. I discover this principle, then: that when I want to do the right, only the wrong is within my reach. In my inmost self I delight in the law of God, but perceive that there is in my bodily members a different law, fighting against the law that my reason approves and making me a prisoner under the law that is in my members, the law of sin.[5]

The assertion that the individual will had somewhat more power than this, and thus might not depend on the grace of God, was rejected as one of the great heresies, Pelagianism.[6]

Other philosophies and religions have all included major analyses of the passions. They also discuss how to avoid them. Buddhism, for instance, concerns itself with emancipation from "the bond of worldly passions" and describes five strategies of purification, essentially: having clear ideas, avoiding sensual desires by mind control, restricting objects to their natural uses, "endurance," and watching out for temptations in advance. However, the ways that non-Western religions enumerate causes of and solutions to self-defeating behaviors seem a jumble from any operational viewpoint of trying to maximize a good.

Despite all the attention paid, not many really new ideas about self-control have appeared over the years, even in the great cultural exchanges that brought the whole world into communication. One significant advance was Francis Bacon's realization that reason didn't have its own force, but had to get its way by playing one passion against another: It had to

set affection against affection and to master one by another: even as we use to hunt beast with beast.... For as in the government of states it is sometimes necessary to bridle one faction with another, so it is in the government within.[7]

The implication was that passion and reason might be just different patterns in the same system. Furthermore, they might be connected not by cognition but by some internal economic process, in which reason had to find the wherewithal to motivate its plans.

Another new idea was the Victorian discovery that the will could be analyzed into specific properties that might respond to strengthening exercises. We'll look at these in detail later (Section 3.1.4 of this chapter).

Even as some nineteenth-century authors were dissecting the will, others began to get suspicious of it. Observers had long known that the will could get bogged down in minutiae, a problem that medieval scholastics called a "scrupulous conscience."[8] In early Victorian times Soren Kierkegaard warned of a more general but insidious affliction that seemed to come from the very success of willpower in controlling passion – a loss of what the existential school of philosophy, Kierkegaard's heirs, came to call "authenticity." The existentialists said that authenticity comes from a responsiveness to the immediacy of experience, a responsiveness that is lost when people govern themselves according to preconceived "cognitive maps."[9]

At the turn of the twentieth century, Freud described a division of motivational processes into those that serve long-range goals (the "reality principle") and those that serve short-range ones (the "pleasure principle"). But the long-term processes are always distorted by an alien influence, "introjected" from parents, making them rigid. Freud rarely used the word "will," and used it trivially when he did; but his farsighted processes and the "superego" that made them rigid would have been recognizable to his audience as components of will and willpower.[10]

Interest in the will grew steadily until about the time of World War I. After that the concept of will suddenly became highly unfashionable, even distasteful – as if people blamed it for their countries' steadfastness in commanding millions of soldiers to face murderous fire and perhaps for the fortitude that led the soldiers to obey. Whatever the reason, the twentieth century saw our concepts of impulsiveness and self-control become diffuse. We continued to analyze reason in the form of utility theory, which defined that perfect rationalist, Economic Man. Passion and *akrasia*, however, are another story entirely, as are any devices that might be needed to overcome them. Explanations of them are ad hoc and higgledy-piggledy.

Willpower had become a popular Victorian virtue without any examination of where it came from. When it became tainted there was no agreed-upon way to analyze what was wrong, or what alternatives there might be, or even precisely what function it was supposed to perform.

1.2. How to Study Self-Defeating Behavior

Something is obviously wrong or at least incomplete about the way we've understood *akrasia* and self-control. I believe that new findings make it possible to say a lot about the will and the reasons why it succeeds and fails where it does; but first, we have to look at what's already been said. Behavioral scientists still study weakness and strength of will, although usually without those specific concepts in their minds – sometimes without even the concept of motivation. But these scientists don't talk to most of their colleagues. Like so many fields where people are probing a mystery, decision science has split into schools whose members agree within their groups on certain assumptions and ways of doing research. Reading other schools' writings means forgoing the shorthand you've become adept at

in your own school, not to mention the confidence that what you write yourself will have a willing audience. Mostly, we don't bother.

But these schools have separately discovered many different tools to work on the will problem. Before we start work, we need to look at the available methods. Here's an informal list of the schools that have studied will-related decisions:

Behaviorism is the school that has designed most of the systematic experiments on utility theory. The behaviorists have made especially good use of animal models. Lower animals are different from people, of course, but their subcortical brain structures are similar, including the systems that govern motivation, and this similarity is reflected in a similar response to most (but not all) schedules of reward. For instance, animals can become addicted to all the substances that affect people. Based on their ability to judge how rich different sources of reward are, animals often seem to be more rational than people.[11]

The neurologist Paul MacLean once observed that the human cortex rides on lower brain functions like a man riding a horse. Although we can't use animals to study some higher functions – wit, irony, or self-consciousness, for instance – we can use them to study the horse we all ride. And when a mental process can be demonstrated in animals – like a conflict between motives at successive times – it spares us speculation about subtle causes like quirks of culture.

However, the careful experiments that the behaviorists do have been overshadowed by their righteousness about method. To the average educated person, a behaviorist is somebody who believes that the mind doesn't exist, and that people's behavior can be accounted for entirely by the observable stimuli that impinge on them. Even the academic community tired of this brand of logical positivism and stripped the behavioral school of most of its glory. As a source of carefully controlled data, however, it remains unsurpassed, and its data are the starting place of this book.

Cognitive psychology, often as applied to social psychology, is currently the most widespread approach to both research and theory dealing with irrational behavior. It generally has high standards of experimental proof and has described many examples of maladaptive behavior. However, its theorists seem to have gone out of their way to avoid dealing with the process of motivation, seeing it as at most some kind of internal communication that a higher judge – the irreducible person – can and often should disregard. Thus its theories of irrationality have been restricted to finding errors of perception or logic.

Economics is the field that deals with rational decision-making in the real world. In modern times it has embraced the assumptions of utility theory, as characterized by Paul Samuelson: "The view that consumers maximize utility is not merely a law of economics, it is a law of logic itself." Gary Becker showed that economic concepts could handle even nonmonetary incentives like drug highs and the risk of jail.[12]

However, economists have made some unrealistic assumptions about decisions: that they're all deliberate, that they're based only on external goods (as opposed to rewards that you might generate in your own head), and that they're naturally stable in the absence of new information. Since this stability should make decisions consistent, economic theories have attributed irrationality only to inadequate information or steep discounting of the future, explanations that are both inadequate, as we'll see.

Philosophy of mind looks at model-making itself, and has pioneered thought experiments whereby every reader can test a particular theory.[13] However, it has stayed within the conventional assumptions of a unitary self – unitary in the sense of not housing contradictory or unconscious elements. If anything should allow exploration of a more molecular model of the self, it should be thought experiments; but the seeming paradoxes that some have demonstrated have not led analysis beyond standard utility theory. They remain paradoxical.

Psychoanalysis was the first major attempt to confront self-contradictory behaviors with utility analysis. As an explorer of scientifically virgin territory, Freud sketched out several different models – one based on motivation ("libido"), one based on consciousness, one based on organization ("id," "ego," "superego"), and so on. But he didn't work out how the various models got along with each other. Without the discipline of either controlled observation or conceptual parsimony, psychoanalysis grew overinclusive, until it resembled the polytheisms from which it drew some of its observations.

Oversold in the middle third of the twentieth century, psychoanalysis has lately been the target of vigorous attacks aimed at its standards of observation and proof. The essayist Frederick Crews concluded that

the designer of psychoanalysis was at bottom a visionary but endlessly calculating artist, engaged in casting himself as the hero of a multivolume fictional opus that is part epic, part detective story, and part satire on human self-interestedness and animality.[14]

It hasn't been fashionable to ask whether even a fictional opus that once had such immense popularity among intelligent people may offer insights worth keeping.

Actually, Freud brought together a lot of previous work that describes disunity of the self, and this has gone into limbo with him.[15] Worse, people who have found his answers wrong or incomplete have stopped asking his questions, and these questions have to be in the forefront of any attempt to explain impulsiveness and impulse control: Is all behavior motivated? How can someone obey internally contradictory motives? How can you hide information from yourself? How can self-control sometimes make you worse off? On many questions I'll start with Freud's ideas – because, in my view, after modern criticism tackled the ball carrier, no one ever picked up the ball.

Bargaining research, a new discipline, has used elementary games to see how small groups of competing agents can reach stable relationships. It is especially suggestive when it shows how such a group can reach stable decisions that are not in all or any member's best interest. However, until now, bargaining research has not seemed applicable to conflict within the individual because of the supposed unity of the person. Given a rationale for disunity, we'll find it useful.

Chaos theory, an even newer theory of analysis, has been applied to other subjects – the weather, for instance – to explore how outcomes may depend on a recursive feedback system. It has also shown how such a system may lead to similar patterns at different levels of magnification and even to the growth of the different levels themselves. So far chaos theory has lacked any important motivational example. However, the fundamental unpredictability of the human will, which has defied attempts to explain it by antecedent causes, makes it look like some of the natural phenomena where the chaos approach has proven useful. As we find recursive processes in the will, chaos theory will become relevant.

Sociobiology has studied competition among populations of reward-seeking organisms, so it has developed concepts that might be useful for populations of behaviors – the range of behaviors that an organism tries out – as well. Behaviorists have proposed that reinforcement acts on behaviors the way natural selective factors act on organisms.[16] This suggests some way that sociobiological theory might apply to conflicting motives.

Neurophysiology has produced increasingly precise findings on brain mechanisms, including those that create motivation. It's possible to see, for instance, exactly where and by what neurotransmitters cocaine rewards the behaviors that obtain it;[17] but pinpointing the transmitters doesn't explain how a conflict between alternative rewards gets resolved or why it fails to get resolved in some cases. It may be, for instance, that some alcoholics have inherited settings in their reward mechanisms that make alcohol more rewarding for them than for most people; but this doesn't tell us why many alcoholics are conflicted about their drinking – why they often decide not to drink despite the intensity of this reward and, having decided this, why they sometimes fail to carry out their own decision. Neurobiology will be useful here mainly as a check on reality, as a body of findings with which any motivational theory must at least be consistent.

Theology shouldn't be disregarded. It has studied a part of our decision-making experience that seems to lie outside the will and has been least influenced by the lure of utility theory. Despite its own theory that its insights come mystically, by faith, revelation, or some such nonempirical route, theology actually demands that its tenets ring true to experience. Sin, for instance, seems synonymous with the self-defeating behaviors that the more scientific disciplines have talked about; the debates that have occurred over the power of the individual will to overcome sin have appealed to what is, in effect, clinical experience. But what this inspirational approach has gained in sensitivity it has lost in testability, and it becomes arbitrary when it tries to nail down its insights in a systematic way. Like psychoanalysis, it will be a source more of questions than of answers. But the questions are important ones.

Finally, any explanation of *akrasia* has to be at least compatible with *subjective experience* and might well find evidence there. Some behavioral scientists sniff at experiential evidence as "folk psychology" and warn of the days when psychologists tried to gather data using trained introspectors. While common sense is suggestive at best and, as theory, almost always inconsistent and ad hoc, it is by far the largest body of human observations. Useful samples of common experience appear in the writings of the pre-experimental (Victorian) psychologists and of later clinicians who have interviewed patients, as well as in those works of fiction that have rung

true with generations of readers. Jon Elster has been especially insightful in sorting the pieces of our written heritage by their motivational implications.[18]

1.2.1. MY APPROACH TO THE PROBLEM

So how should we assemble a working tool kit from all of these methods? I'll suggest one way, obviously not the only one possible. But as far as I can tell, it's the only proposal so far that reconciles the familiar paradoxes of motivation with basic research.

I warn the reader in advance that this approach is *reductionistic*. That is, I assume that every change in thinking, feeling, wanting, planning, and so on, has a physical basis in the nerve cells of the brain, which in turn depend on chemical changes within the cells, and so on. I'm not saying that thinking and feeling are best studied by studying the chemistry of cells – only that all explanations of behavior should at least be consistent with what's known in the physical and biological sciences.

Nonreductionistic (and antireductionistic) theories have been created for a reason, of course. In the past, reductionistic theories ignored causes that were hard to observe or to imagine – that is, too hidden or complex or internally fed back – like cognitions, or intuitions, or will. "Scientific" explanations therefore made people seem like robots.[19]

By the same token, my proposals are *deterministic*. Aside from some irrelevant arguments about whether the movements of subatomic particles are strictly determined, the physical sciences assume that all things that happen are shaped completely by prior causes, which have causes in turn. I do, too. I don't mean that these causes can be found. Some are probably too hidden or complex or internally fed back ever to be useful for practical prediction; but again, explanations of behavior should never depend on some uncaused or otherwise imponderable factor.

Students of human behavior often rebel against reductionism and determinism in favor of holistic, humanistic approaches so that science can still examine feelings, not to mention the many other private subtleties that can be introspected but not tested. However, I'll argue that these subtleties – among them self-deception, self-control and its loss, self-esteem and its loss, and freedom of will itself – are completely consistent with a reductionistic theory of choice.

So please don't be put off by my warning. The humanist reader will find protection, even ammunition, in the model of choice I'm going to propose.

1.3. Summary

The human bent for defeating our own plans has puzzled writers since antiquity. From Plato's idea that the better part of the self – reason – could be overwhelmed by passion, there evolved the concept of a faculty, will, that lent reason the kind of force that could confront passion and defeat it. The construct of the will and its power became unfashionable in twentieth-century science, but the puzzle of self-defeating behavior – what Aristotle called *akrasia* – and its sometime control has not been solved. With the help of new experimental findings and conceptual tools from several different disciplines, it will be possible to form a hypothesis about the nature of will that does not violate the conventions of science as we know it.

2. The Warp in How We Evaluate the Future

If the headache would only precede the intoxication, alcoholism would be a virtue.
                                   Samuel Butler

Lore abounds not only about how people mistrust their own future preferences, but how they sometimes engage in strategic planning to outsmart the future selves that will have these preferences. Here is Ulysses facing the Sirens or Coleridge moving in with his doctor to be protected from his opium habit. We know that the stakes in this intertemporal game sometimes reach tragic proportions. Yet we can't reconcile this game with utility theory's basic meat-and-potatoes notion that people try to maximize their prospects. The irony of smart people doing stupid things – or having to outsmart themselves in order not to – appears in literature again and again, but without an explanation.

This quandary may have been one reason for the popularity of cognitive explanations, which at least stay close to intuition. The problem hasn't undermined utility theorists, but it has cramped their style. They go from success to success in areas like finance and sociobiology, where tough competition selects strongly for individuals who function like calculating machines. However, their attempts to explain self-defeating choice on a rational basis have been unconvincing; the most notable has been the effort by economists Gary Becker and Kevin

Murphy to show how a person who sharply devalues the future might maximize her prospective pleasure by addictive behavior. Their proposal is basically that devaluation of the future leads to addictive behaviors, which further increase this devaluation. They suggest no rationale for fearing future choices, much less for trying to restrain them.[20] Utility theorists have mostly stayed away from the subject. Some writers have thrown up their hands altogether by concluding that there are options that, although substitutable for one another, can't be weighed against each other.[21] While science stands by, mystified, people keep wrecking their own lives.

2.1. The Hyperbolic Curve that Discounts Future Events

Another solution to the self-harm puzzle has always been logically possible, but utility theorists and cognitivists alike keep ruling it out, perhaps because its implications would require the rethinking of basic assumptions about rationality: People indeed maximize their prospective rewards, but they discount their prospects using a different formula from the one that's obviously rational. It will take a little arithmetic to illustrate this possibility clearly.

Few utility theorists question the assumption that people discount future utility the way banks do: by subtracting a constant proportion of the utility there would be at any given delay for every additional unit of delay. If a new car delivered today would be worth $10,000 to me and my discount "rate" is 20% a year, then the prospect of guaranteed delivery today of the same car would have been worth $8,000 to me a year ago, $6,400 two years ago, and so on (disregarding inflation, which merely subtracts another fixed percentage per unit of time).

Utility theory operates the same way for reward itself, although it has to use a fanciful unit of measure like the "utile." If drinking a bottle of whisky is worth 100 utiles to me right now and my discount rate for drinking is 20% per day, the prospect of today's drinking would have been worth 80 utiles to me yesterday, 64 utiles the day before, and so on. Furthermore, if the drinking has a cost of 120 utiles that has to be paid the day after in the form of a hangover, reproaches from my family, and so on, and I discount these at the same rate, the net utility of drinking today will be 100 – (120 × 80%, or 96), or 4 utiles. So I should decide to drink. If I foresaw this episode from a day away, the net value would have been $(100 \times 80\%) - (120 \times 80\% \times 80\%)$, viz., $80 - 76.8$, or 3.2 utiles. At that point I would still have decided to drink.

The arithmetic is simple. You just multiply each discounted value on any day by 80% for each anticipated day of further delay and find the difference: 3.2 utiles for one day in advance, 2.56 utiles for two days in advance, and so on. The discounting method can be summarized for delays of any length by the formula

Value = "Objective" value
$$\times\ (1 - \text{Discount rate})^{\text{Delay}}$$

This discount function is called "exponential" because it calculates value by an exponential, or power, function of the discount rate.[22]

With exponential discounting, the difference in the utility of drinking in our example gradually gets smaller, but the important thing is that it never goes negative or even gets to zero. If I'd choose to drink when the opportunity was right at hand, I'd also choose to drink when it was a week or a year away. If I'd choose not to drink from the vantage point of some delay – if, say, my discount rate were just 10% – then I'd still choose not to drink when the opportunity was immediately at hand, as well as at all other distances. (The net value of drinking would be −8 utiles at no delay, −7.2 utiles one day in advance, −6.48 at two days, and so on.)

This arithmetic seems to describe the consistency many people show toward large purchases – bankers, at least, and others who decide "rationally"; but it misses the mark for drinkers, or at least for people whose drinking is serious enough to involve hangovers and reproaches from their families. People who are strongly drawn to drinking – or taking drugs, or gambling, or kleptomania, or any other thrills of the kind that people later regret – typically experience swings of preference between indulging their habit and giving it up. And the swings are often influenced by how close an opportunity for indulgence is. People trying to control a bad habit tend to keep a distance between themselves and opportunity – avoid the streets where their favorite bars are located and similar strategies.[23]

Faced with this instability of choice – economists have taken to calling it "dynamic inconsistency," but it amounts just to a temporary preference for the poorer alternative – writers have come up with various fudge factors to make it fit the principle that people strictly maximize their exponentially discounted prospects for reward

(see the introduction to this chapter). The most obvious suggestion is that people discount different kinds of reward at different rates. If I discount drinking by 40% per day but discount not having a hangover the day after (worth 120 utiles) by 20%, then the net utility of an immediate drinking bout would be $100 - (120 \times 80\%)$, or 4 utiles; but its net utility a day in advance would be $(100 \times 60\%) - (120 \times 80\% \times 80\%)$, $60 - 76.8$ or -16.8 utiles. I would drink if the chance were at hand but not if it were delayed.

The trouble with this solution is that many cases of temporary preference involve the same kind of reward on both sides of the choice; a difference in discount rate for different kinds of reward can't be a factor. The punishment for gambling to win money is to lose money. Likewise, people in experiments do things like choosing a shorter period of relief from noxious noise over a longer but later period of relief from the same noise if and only if the shorter, earlier period is imminent. It makes no sense to hypothesize that the earlier relief is discounted at 40% but the later relief of the same kind is discounted at 20%.

Long ago philosophers noted that avarice was a bad habit partly because it was self-defeating – that impatience for riches usually made people poorer in the long run.[24] If the basic reward-weighing mechanism is the same among all the higher animals – the same assumption that lets us study addictive drugs in rats, for instance – we can see this self-defeating phenomenon clearly in quantitative experiments. For instance, pigeons will choose a shorter, earlier access to grain over a later, larger one when the shorter one is immediate and not when it's delayed; and some of them will actually peck a colored key in advance to prevent themselves from later getting offered a differently colored key that produces the smaller reward – showing that in some way the pigeons themselves are responding to their own tendency to choose the smaller, earlier reward as a problem.[25]

In light of such findings, it's not enough to say that the kinds of things that reward impulses are discounted more steeply than the kinds of things that reward rational choices. Exponential discounting can't account for temporary preferences in knowing subjects. On the other hand, any kind of nonexponential discounting should lead to maladaptive behavior.

The main theoretical rival to the exponential curve is *hyperbolic* – more bowed than an exponential curve; when goods at both very short and very long delays would be valued the same as

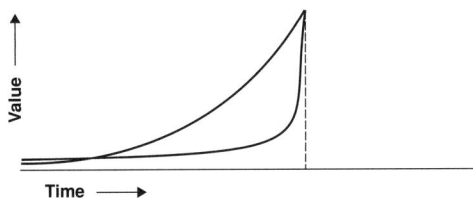

Figure 1. An exponential discount curve and a hyperbolic (more bowed) curve from the same reward. As time passes (rightward along the horizontal axis), the motivational impact – the *value* – of her goals gets closer to its undiscounted size, which is depicted by the vertical line.

with exponential discounting, goods in between would be valued less[26] (Figure 1). If people devalue future goods proportionately to their delay, their discount curve will be hyperbolic.

The greater bowing means that if a hyperbolic discounter engaged in trade with someone who used an exponential curve, she'd soon be relieved of her money. Ms. Exponential could buy Ms. Hyperbolic's winter coat cheaply every spring, for instance, because the distance to the next winter would depress Ms. H's valuation of it more than Ms. E's. Ms. E could then sell the coat back to Ms. H every fall when the approach of winter sent Ms. H's valuation of it into a high spike. Because of this mathematical pattern, only an exponential discount curve will protect a person against exploitation by somebody else who uses an exponential curve.[27] Thus exponential curves seem not only rational, in the sense that they're consistent, but also adaptive. At first glance, it looks as if natural selection should have weeded out any organism that didn't discount the future exponentially.

Nevertheless, there's more and more evidence that people's natural discount curve is not only nonexponential, but specifically hyperbolic. The simplest sign is that such curves cross if they're from alternative rewards available at different times.

The experiment used to test whether a subject's discount curves cross is simple: You offer subjects a choice between a small reward at delay D versus a larger reward of the same kind that will be available at that delay plus a constant lag, L. A subject gets the small reward at delay D from the moment she chooses or the larger reward at delay D + L. If she discounts the choices according to conventional theory, her curves will stay proportional to each other (Figure 2A). If she chooses the larger reward when D is long but switches to the smaller reward as D

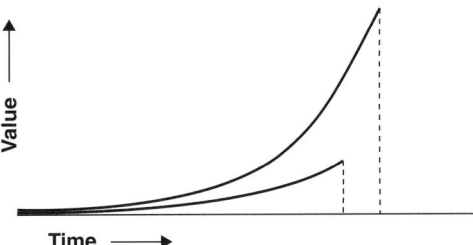

Figure 2A. Conventional (exponential) discount curves from two rewards of different sizes available at different times. In the experimental design described in the text, the delay D is the distance between when the subject chooses and when the earlier and later rewards will be available, and the lag L is the distance between when the earlier and later rewards will be available, shown by the vertical lines. At every point at which the subject might evaluate them, their values stay proportional to their objective sizes.

gets shorter, she's showing the temporary preference effect that implies a discount curve more bowed than an exponential one (Figure 2B).

This research strategy has one potential problem: If people really discount the future with highly bowed curves that cross, then when D is long they'll be motivated not only to choose the later, larger reward but somehow to forestall the change of choice that occurs as D gets shorter. Like the pigeons that learned to peck the colored key to forestall the tempting, other-colored key, subjects might have learned ways to make up for this tendency. Otherwise, they'll have been at risk of exploitation by other people who have learned these ways – as in the overcoat example. An experiment like this might not uncover their natural, spontaneous preferences, but only those that they had been educated

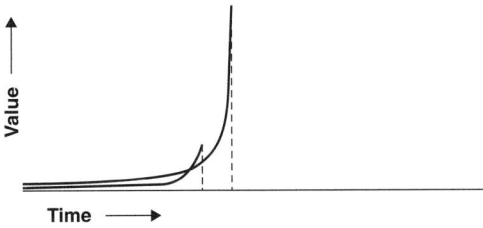

Figure 2B. Hyperbolic discount curves from two rewards of different sizes available at different times. The smaller reward is temporarily preferred for a period before it is available, as shown by the portion of its curve that projects above that from the later, larger reward.

to express. This kind of learned compensation might be a serious obstacle to observation.

The best way around this obstacle should be to use the kind of reward that the subject experiences ("consumes") on delivery and also the kinds that don't lend themselves to mental arithmetic. When experimenters have used this kind of reward, people have shown a persistent tendency to reverse their preferences as D changes, evidence that their basic discount curves cross and are thus more hyperbolic than exponential: People exposed to noxious noise and given a choice between shorter, earlier periods of relief and longer, more delayed periods choose the shorter periods when D is small and the longer periods when D is long. College students show the same pattern when choosing between periods of access to video games. Retarded adolescents show it in choosing between amounts of food. Certainly at the gut level, people's discount curves cross.[28]

Furthermore, it turns out that whatever method people may have learned in order to compensate for hyperbolic discounting, it doesn't spoil temporary preference experiments. Even money, the archetypical token reward – "token" in the sense that it has its effect only by letting subjects buy other rewards later, and invites the counting and comparing of alternatives – turns out sometimes to be chosen differently, depending on D. If I ask a roomful of people to imagine that they've won a contest and can choose between a certified check for $100 that they can cash immediately and a postdated certified check for $200 that they can't cash for three years, more than half of the people usually say they would rather have the $100 now. If I then ask what about $100 in six years versus $200 in nine years, virtually everyone picks the $200. But this is the same choice seen at six years' greater distance.

This is an experiment you can perform for yourself. I recommend it as a way of getting direct experience with this unexpected warp in people's outlook. You might want to confront the people you ask with the fact that they've changed their preference on the basis of their vantage point, and ask how they explain it. Answers involving inflation or uncertainty about getting the later amount obviously make no sense, since the lag between the alternatives is the same in both examples. Some subjects have suggested that the promise of immediate money has a sensory (sensuous?) quality that money at any delay doesn't have, and other subjects say that the three-year lag doesn't seem as

long when postponed; neither of these explanations is inconsistent with the notion of a high spike of value at short delays. The one explanation that might preserve exponential discounting is that a student expects to graduate within the next three years, and thus thinks she needs the money significantly more right now than she will at three, six, or nine years. However, getting the temporary preference effect doesn't depend on having young and perhaps temporarily poor subjects or, for that matter, on making the smaller value of D zero. Various groups of subjects have shown the change of preference over a range of D values. Some excellent recent work has made it possible to describe the exact shape of subjects' discount curve in similar amount-versus-delay experiments.[29] It's clearly hyperbolic for all age groups, although older subjects discount the future less steeply than younger ones, introverts less steeply than extroverts, and ordinary adults less steeply than heroin addicts or even smokers.[30]

Subjects working for actual cash don't always show the temporary preference effect. The factors that determine whether they'll show it or not have just begun to be explored, but the early findings are revealing: For instance, when subjects had to choose between amounts of money such that choice A produced a conspicuously larger reward than choice B, but choice A led to poorer subsequent payoffs for both choices, the outcome depended on an important detail of the design: Where choice of a larger amount reduced the *amounts* to choose between on subsequent turns, most subjects soon discovered the strategy of picking the smaller amount in the current choice so as to have better choices later. However, where choosing the larger amount led to greater *delay* before subsequent choices, thus reducing total income in trials of fixed duration, subjects tended to keep picking the larger amounts and getting smaller subsequent returns. They were lured into what the experimenters called "melioration," taking what by itself seems the best choice without considering the bigger picture. Amounts are well defined and obvious, lending themselves to conscious scrutiny; delays are vague unless you specifically count the seconds. As we might expect, when the experimenters pointed out to their subjects the greater delay that came from choosing the larger reward, these subjects, too, started choosing the smaller one.[31]

Hyperbolic discounting is even more evident in lower animals, which shows that it isn't some quirk of human culture. In scores of experiments, animals have always chosen rewards in inverse proportion to their delays – and, similarly, punishments in direct proportion. Animals also do what crossing discount curves predict: In amount-versus-delay experiments they choose the smaller, earlier reward when D is short and the larger, later reward when D is long. It was the consistency of animal findings that led Herrnstein nearly forty years ago to propose a universal law of choice, which he called the "matching law": that rewards tend to be chosen in direct proportion to their size and frequency of occurrence and in inverse proportion to their delay. Many researchers have since offered variations to fine-tune the matching law to describe individual differences in impatience, but the best seems to be one of the simplest:[32]

$$\text{Value} = \text{Amount}/(\text{Constant}_1 + (\text{Constant}_2 \times \text{Delay}))$$

In practice the constants seem to stay close to 1.0 which simplifies the equation still further. When I discuss the likely consequences of hyperbolic discounting, I'll be using this formula.

2.2. Implications of Hyperbolic Discounting

Does this apparent universality of hyperbolic discounting mean that utility theorists through the ages have been wrong – that philosophers and bankers and welfare economists should have been calculating the worth of goods using the deeply bowed curves of Figure 2B? This can't be true either. We saw in the overcoat example that exponential discounting is better than hyperbolic discounting, in the sense that exponential discounters win out in competition with hyperbolic discounters.

The conventional answer would almost certainly be that since only exponential curves produce consistent preferences, they're the ones that are objectively rational, and that people should learn to correct their spontaneous valuations to fit them. After all, science has long known that the intensity of many other subjective experiences is described by hyperbolic curves and that people can learn to correct such impressions. It soon becomes second nature to a child that the telephone pole down the street is as tall as the one nearby, even though it forms a smaller image on her retina. Even where spontaneous impressions are misleading, you learn to trust instruments for measuring objective size – light by your camera's light meter, distance to travel by an odometer or map, and so on – without feeling that you're wrestling with some inner resistance. You develop "object constancy." Can't people learn to value reward in proportion to its objective amount, just as we learn to gauge objective brightness and distance?

That's what conventional utility theory calls for; but despite data from your clocks and calendars, such an adjustment seems to occur irregularly, sometimes not at all. It usually takes some kind of effort (willpower again) to evaluate a smaller present satisfaction as less desirable than a greater one in the future. This is where the analogy of delay to other sensory impressions like length breaks down: You may move through time toward a goal just as you move through space toward a building, and the matching law formula describing your spontaneous valuation of a goal is indeed close to the formula for the retinal height of the building.[33] But the building doesn't seem to get larger as it gets closer, whereas the goal often seems to get more valuable. Insofar as you fail to make the correction in value that corresponds to your correction of retinal height, poorer goals that are close can loom larger than better distant goals. Although people develop some faculty for utility constancy, it takes effort and remains tenuous.

These observations provide additional help with the question we discussed earlier: Which is more basic, cognitive or motivational evaluation? If cognitive judgments ultimately control choice, it should make no difference whether you're estimating the size of a building or a reward; either way, an evaluation with full knowledge should parallel the objective size of the objects in question, and any choices that depend on this evaluation should follow without further effort. If hedonistic effects are primary, however, the two cases will differ: A larger image on the retina doesn't of itself pull a person one way or another and thus doesn't resist cognitive transformation. But if reward is the fundamental selective force of choice, then however you perceive or categorize it, you're still acted upon by its direct influence. You should often prefer lesser alternatives during the period when they're imminent; and this is just what the foregoing research describes. Thus experience suggests that there's a raw process of reward that constitutes the active determinant of value. While it can be perceived abstractly, it doesn't occur differently because of this abstraction.

In the following comparison of lines, the second one continues to look longer, even after we've measured them and found that they are the same length:

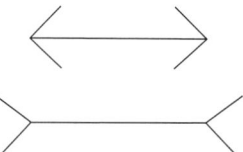

In the same way, knowing that, all things considered, eating another dessert or putting off going to the dentist will make me less happy in the long run doesn't of itself reduce my urge to do these things. Still, any sensible person would argue that we learn not to do them – most of the time, anyway. Doesn't this mean that we've learned to change our discount curves?

Yes and no. If we infer someone's curve from her expressed preferences, then as she gets older and wiser, we'll see her apparent curve get shallower and less bowed; often we'll see her act exactly as if she discounted future goods exponentially at the rate of inflation plus 3% or so a year. But as we've seen, there will be situations where she'll be both more impatient and more inconsistent than that. These are signs of the persistence of another curve – one that is both steeper and has a tendency to cause reversals of preference. The banker–like curve seems to represent an added accomplishment, not a fundamental change.

This is what we should expect. If a person could learn to change the discount curve she was born with, there would always be a strong incentive to do so as much as possible: If some distant prospect – a Christmas present, say – was worth only 3 utiles to you now, but by some trick you could make it worth 5 utiles, you could make yourself 2 utiles richer just by doing this trick. If you could act directly on your discount curves, you could coin reward for yourself, so to speak. We'd expect everyone to exploit this trick all the time, as much as they could. If it was the kind of trick you had to keep doing, it would be like candy or a tranquilizer, something you did *instead* of getting impatient. If it was the kind of trick you could do once and for all, then your impulsive urges to drink or smoke or spend should just disappear. The point is that we study people – and animals, for that matter – after whatever curve–flattening they're capable of should have already happened. The hyperbola we detect is what has survived this learning. The trick of behaving as if your curve were exponential has to be an effortful, sometime thing, not a modification your basic curve.

Of course, nature doesn't always put things together in the simplest way. The widespread appearance of hyperbolic discounting may not mean that it's a universal form, the underlying pattern from which all other valuation patterns are derived. The appearance of hyperbolic discounting in some situations and exponential discounting in others may turn out to have an explanation now hidden from us. But theories should always start in the simplest way. Let's assume that the ubiquitous hyperbola is the basic discount curve – that our basic instinct is to evaluate future events by dividing their amount by their delay – and see where its implications lead us.

2.2.1. HOW UTILITY THEORY CAN PREDICT INCONSISTENCY

The most basic implication is that you'll tend to prefer smaller, earlier rewards to larger, later ones temporarily, during the time that they're imminent. Then the obvious task is to find out what kind of effort could sometimes make your expressed preferences look exponential. Hyperbolic discounting is a shock for utility theory. Suddenly the pavement moves beneath our feet, and we have to take the simple concept of maximizing expected reward not as a description of basic human nature but just as a norm that we try to implement. Only if a person is lucky or skillful can she achieve such consistency in the face of this screwball valuation system.

The good news is that hyperbolic discounting, and its consequent temporary preferences, will let utility theory move beyond its stalemate with cognitivism. Let's return to the problems that the two approaches have had in explaining *akrasia*. In cognitive models the person ultimately stands outside of her emotions – emotions being the closest cognitivist equivalent of motivation – and says, "This experience is misleading. I'll select my behavior instead on the basis of accurate calculations of its value." The trouble is that there's a lot of leeway in the calculation process, as cognitive research itself has shown; when someone has a choice among different ways of calculating value, how does she choose the one she'll use? To be sure, everyone has had the experience of mistrusting an emotion, or even disowning it. We inhibit an emotion sometimes or "nurse" one. To some extent we can indeed mold the influence that in turn molds us. But when I stand outside of my emotions, what am I standing on? In other words, what determines my choice of cognitions?

The argument between the cognitive and utilitarian schools has been about whether choice is fundamentally determined by some kind of internal marketplace, or else by a planned economy, in effect an internal bureaucracy of principles and logic. The conventional view of a person's self-command structure is definitely bureaucratic, on the model of a corporation or an army, where superior agents simply pass commands down to inferior ones. However, closer examination of corporations and armies has shown that despite the establishment of hierarchical command structures, they remain marketplaces where officers must motivate rather than simply ordering behaviors.[34] Sheer instructions aren't enough to control someone's behavior, as bureaucrats have discovered again and again; any system that tries to govern behavior by regulations develops an underground economy of motives – of favors and obstructions, and hiding places from supervisory procedures – that ultimately determines what gets done.[35]

Utility theory says that the experience of reward is the fundamental selective factor for behaviors, so that you can't stand outside of that experience and choose dispassionately among rewards. You might as well say, "The thermometer tells me not to feel cold, so I won't." The utilitarians' problem has been that they've assumed a person's evaluation of rewards (or emotions) to be exponentially discounted, and hence consistent over time; as a result, utility theory hasn't been able to account for self-defeating choices, or for the various kinds of uniquely human effort that we call forth to avoid them. If we simply maximize our prospective reward, what use do we have for self-control? What role is there for a will, either strong or free?

My argument is that exchanging hyperbolic discounting for the exponential kind in the reward-maximizing process supplies utility theory with its missing element. Utility theory can now explain the seductiveness of self-defeating choices; and the assumption that a person has to strictly maximize her expected, discounted reward explains why she doesn't automatically learn to be objective, the way she does with sizes and distances. Reward has its effect directly, and intellectual adjustment takes place only tangentially. With hyperbolic instead of exponential discounting, utility theory now says that people will naturally go for smaller, earlier over larger, later rewards. We're unable *not* to choose the reward that looms largest when discounted to the moment of choice. *Akrasia* is just maximizing expected reward, discounted in highly bowed curves.

2.2.2. THE SELF AS A POPULATION

Hyperbolic discounting shifts the main problem for utility theory. We're no longer at a loss to explain shortsighted choices. Now we have to account for how people learn the adaptive controls that let them behave like bankers. How does an internal marketplace that disproportionately values immediate rewards grow into what can be mistaken for either the reasoning self of the cognitivists or the long-range reward maximizer of conventional utilitarians?

We can no longer regard people as having unitary preferences. Rather, people may have a variety of contradictory preferences that become dominant at different points because of their timing. The orderly internal marketplace pictured by conventional utility theory[36] becomes a complicated free-for-all, where to prevail an option not only has to promise more than its competitors, but also act strategically to keep the competitors from turning the tables later on. The behaviors that are shaped by the competing rewards must deal not only with obstacles to getting their reward if chosen, but also with the danger of being un-chosen in favor of imminent alternatives.

How does a marketplace of hyperbolically discounted choices ever come to look like a single individual? If I discount future reward hyperbolically, and make whatever choices maximize my discounted prospective reward at the moment I make them, then my choices won't consistently follow the same set of goals over time, the way they would if I were ruled either by reason or by exponentially discounted passion. If I'm a susceptible person and I'm close to a bottle of whisky or a box of chocolates, or perhaps a provocation to rage or panic, I'll value these options differently than when I'm far away from them. Often I'll choose in the opposite direction when I'm close and when I'm distant, which means I'll regularly do things at one time and undo them at another. Obviously if what I do in a particular situation regularly gets undone later, I'll learn to stop doing it in the first place – but not out of agreement with the later self that undoes it, only out of realism. I'll keep trying to find ways to get what I want from this particular vantage point, things that won't get undone, and take precautions against a future self that will try to undo them. In this way I'll be like a group of people rather than a single individual; often these people will be as different as Jekyll and Hyde.

An agent who discounts reward hyperbolically is not the straightforward value estimator that an exponential discounter is supposed to be. Rather, it is a succession of estimators whose conclusions differ; as time elapses, these estimators shift their relationship with one another between cooperation on a common goal and competition for mutually exclusive goals. Ulysses planning for the Sirens must treat Ulysses hearing them as a separate person, to be influenced if possible and forestalled if not.

To take an everyday example: You may hate to go to bed at a prudent hour, even though you hate even worse getting up in the morning without enough sleep. Your mind this morning curses your mind of last night and tries to forestall your expected mind of tonight, but runs up against the effect of hyperbolic discount curves: Your mind holds a population of reward-seeking processes that have grown to survive in contradiction to each other, and that endure despite each other. You keep on staying up late when the chance is at hand and the morning is far away – unless you can do something to bring the incentives to sleep, which are larger in the long run, to bear on your evening self.

What can you do? If a person is a population of processes that have grown in the same mind through the selective action of reward, what factors, if any, impose unity on this population? For single moments we can model unity easily. The process by which diverse needs interact to produce a single decision doesn't have to be different from the process that motivates a social group to reach agreement.

Separate individuals can have widely diverse interests that conflict with the interests of others, because they have separate organs for reward that can act differently at the same time. One person can be tearful while her neighbor is rapturously happy, or seek out parties while her neighbor avoids them, without there being any necessary confrontation between these opposite choices. What coordinates diverse interests in separate people is limitation of resources. If there's only one room to sit in, the sad person and the happy one will have to see each other, and each will have to deal with the other's effect on her own mood. If they're roommates, they'll have to decide whether or not to use the room for a party that evening. It seems reasonable to suppose that analogous constraints impose at least some unity on the competing processes within the individual person, but that this unity is incomplete insofar as contradictory goals can coexist.

There may or may not be separate neural centers for different kinds of reward. As we've discussed, there's evidence that the reward process is at least concentrated in specific location(s) rather than diffused throughout the brain.[37] The question doesn't matter much when you have only one set of limbs – or, more to the point, a finite channel of attention that has to direct those limbs. There may be a lot of people or part-people in your mind, but they're all constrained to coordinate what they do by the fact of being permanent roommates. If a given behavior can be influenced by more than one center, these centers must compete for the exercise of this influence, and whatever process governs this competition will act in effect like a single comprehensive reward center.[38] Insofar as one behavior can be replaced by another, it has to compete with the other for expression, and this competition operates as a single reward clearinghouse for all substitutable behaviors – all behaviors among which a person can choose. This is the constraint that unifies a person's behavior at any given moment.

Integration over time is more difficult. Any explanation has to account for our observations not only of unity but also of varying degrees of disunity, ranging from preference reversals in "normal" people to Jeckylls and Hydes. The key factor is doubtless the highly concave shape of the discount curves in Figure 2B, which limits what the market of choice can do to unify a person's purposes over time. Ulysses' wish to sail home and his wish to hear the Sirens will be integrated only for individual moments; this piecemeal integration will make different options dominant, depending on when the choice occurs. There will be a regular conflict between the mental operations that win out when the lure of the Sirens' song is dominant and those that win out when the prospect of finishing the journey is dominant.

You could call the mental operations selected for by a particular kind of reward the person's "interest" in that reward. Interests within the person should be very similar to interests within a social group, those factions that are rewarded by ("have an interest in") the goal that names them (e.g., "the petroleum interest," "the arts interest"). Since a person's purposes should be coherent except where conflicting rewards dominate at successive times, it makes sense to name an interest only in cases of conflict. I wouldn't be said to have separate chocolate and vanilla ice cream interests, even though they're often alternatives, because at the time when I prefer chocolate I don't increase my prospective reward by forestalling a possible switch to vanilla. But I may have an ice cream interest and a diet interest, such that each increases the prospective reward in its own time range by reducing the likelihood of the other's dominance. Put another way, I don't increase my prospective reward in either the long or short range by defending my choice of chocolate against the possibility that I may change to vanilla; but I increase my prospective long–range reward by defending my diet against ice cream, and I increase my prospective short-range reward by finding evasions of my diet for the sake of ice cream. Whichever faction promises the greatest discounted reward at a given moment gets to decide my move at that moment; the sequence of moves over time determines which faction ultimately gets its way.

Where alternative rewards are available at different times, each will build its own interest, and one interest will be able to forestall the other only if it can leave some enduring commitment that will prevent the other reward from becoming dominant: If my diet interest can arrange for me not to get too close to ice cream, the discounted prospect of ice cream may never rise above the discounted prospect of the rewards for dieting, and the diet interest will effectively have won. However, whenever the value of ice cream spikes above that of dieting, the ice cream interest may undo the effect of many days of restraint. The ultimate determinant of a person's choice is not her simple preference, any more than the determinant of whether a closely contested piece of legislation becomes law is simple voting strength in the legislature; in both processes, strategy is all.

This process – power bargaining made necessary by finite means of expression – may be all that unifies a person. Philosophers and psychologists are used to speaking about an organ of unification called the "self" that can variously "be" autonomous, divided, individuated, fragile, well-bounded, and so on,[39] but this organ doesn't have to exist as such. The factor that impels toward unity the various behavioral tendencies that grow from a person's rewards may be the realization that they are, in effect, locked up in a room together.

If this room is divided, so that only some of the person's learned processes ever have access to particular resources for expression, she starts to behave like two people. This actually happened when neurosurgeons developed an operation for epilepsy that cut the main connection between the cerebral hemispheres, the corpus callosum. The right half of the brain controlled the left hand and the left half, the right hand; if the two halves were fed information separately, they sometimes fought over a decision to the extent that one hand restrained the other by the wrist. Conversely, when convention or necessity makes two people act in concert over long periods – for example, in some identical twinships and some marriages – the site of the marketplace seems to shift somewhat from the individual to the pair. But where in the pair? Here the choice-maker is clearly not an organ but a process, something in the empathic engagement between the two twins; and if that is true for the pair, why not for the individual or the neurosurgeon's half-individual? The constraint of limited resources for expression may be all that impels a person toward selfhood; and the success of her currently dominant interests in bargaining with interests that will be dominant in the future may be what determines the kind of unity her self will have.[40]

Are ordinary people really populations of interests rather than something more solid? It's disturbing to think of yourself as so fluid, so potentially unstable, held together only by the shifting influence of available rewards. It's like being told that atoms are mostly empty and wondering how they can bear weight. Yet the bargaining of interests in a society can produce highly stable institutions; perhaps that's also true of the internal interests created by a person's rewards. Shortly we'll look at the patterns of choice that hyperbolic discounters would be likely to follow, and see if these patterns look like familiar properties of personality.

Of the basic discounting phenomenon there can no longer be much doubt. Remarkably, hyperbolic discounting seems to occur over all observable time ranges. Subjects choosing between hypothetical amounts of money at delays of years show it as much as those choosing between differences in food, or comfort, or direct brain stimulation, over periods of seconds. Economist Charles Harvey has pointed out that the most long-range planning that ever occurs – choices to preserve the environment or leave money to grandchildren – follows a hyperbolic discount pattern rather than the exponential one that the planners themselves sometimes claim to be using. He points out that exponential discounting of goals decades away at even moderate rates would make them relatively worthless in a competitive economy; it's only the comparatively high tails of hyperbolic curves that could make us concern ourselves with the distant future at all. Accordingly, respondents to a random household survey on the hypothetical value of saving lives 25, 50, and 100 years from the present demonstrated that "if [exponential] discount rates are computed under the assumption that they vary with time, the mean annual discount rate is 7% today and 0% in 100 years."[41] That is, the more delayed an option is, the less discounted it is, just the pattern that hyperbolic discounting predicts.

Economists David Laibson and Christopher Harris have recently modeled people's lifetime saving/spending patterns with hyperbolic curves, and have found that they predict many observed behaviors that exponential curves don't. For instance, hyperbolic curves make a preference for illiquid savings rational – such savings serve as commitments – and thus can explain why people borrow on credit cards at 18% to avoid dipping into savings that are earning far less (see Section 6.2).[42]

2.3. The Adaptiveness of Hyperbolic Discounting

If our basic discount curve has been hyperbolic, then the biggest job of civilization must have been to change people's spontaneous choice into something that produces fewer internal conflicts and reversals of preference. Before assuming that this has been the case, we should ask an obvious question: How could such a curve, with such potential to put an individual at a competitive disadvantage, survive the process of natural selection?

Sociobiologists, who used to believe that animals maximize their expected intake of resources over time, have now also done experiments demonstrating the hyperbolic shape of the basic discount curve.[43] However, despite their interest in evolution, these authors haven't tried to reconcile this finding with survival of the fittest. I'll suggest two ways that highly bowed discount curves could have survived natural selection. They could have preserved genes at the expense of the individual, or they could have been a harmless by-product until too recently to have affected evolution. Arguments about evolutionary fitness can aim only for plausibility, not proof. Take your pick.

1. The evolution of species occurs through the survival of genes, not of individuals. There are many familiar cases where an individual organism must sacrifice itself to maximize survival of its genes. Maybe hyperbolic discounting is a way to get an animal to do that: The anger that makes an animal fight to defend its young probably isn't much different from the anger that recruiting sergeants exploit in wartime, and neither is in the individual's own long-range interest. If cool reason prevailed, the animal would survive more often and the gene-bearing offspring less often. Similarly, bearing young is probably never in an animal's selfish interest. Of course, it may be that many human mothers in previous centuries accepted the roughly 15% risk of eventual death in childbirth out of altruism, or from cultural pressures that made the alternatives worse, but impulsive romances must have made a big contribution too. Even in modern times,

> [C]ourtship leads to romantic love, a temporary suspension of reason, in which the couple is conveyed by the most compelling of short-term rewards, into marriage, a commitment with a lifetime horizon.[44]

The mechanism by which individuals come to reduce their rational utility for the sake of a larger group has been controversial even since Erasmus first praised the seeming folly of having children or going into politics.[45] Hyperbolic discounting is one candidate.

2. It's also possible that hyperbolic discounting has been carried along as a hitherto harmless by-product of vertebrates' basic perceptual tooling. All higher animals get sensory impressions in proportion to the *change* in level of stimulation, rather than perceiving its absolute level. The same perceptual processes that make you sense a change in light or temperature proportionately to its previous intensity may prepare you to evaluate delays the same way. This wouldn't have been a great problem for animals that couldn't change the environments in which they evolved. Where survival has demanded foresighted behavior – sleep at a certain time, or hoarding of food or mating in a certain season – instinctual mechanisms have evolved to convert such long-range interests into short-range rewards. The animal experiences an immediate appetite to sleep or hoard or mate, and there's no intertemporal conflict unless a devious experimenter creates one.

By contrast, people have learned to manipulate both their environment and their instinctual appetites. We learn to divorce sleep from darkness, to cultivate appetites for hoarding what we don't need, to mate without reproducing, indeed to obtain many of the rewards of mating vicariously, through fiction or fantasy, and in general to cultivate motives that overwhelm the incentives of nature. We've also changed our environments radically from the ones in which we evolved. We've increasingly taken our long-range plans into our own hands, and are threatened to the same extent by the operation of our hyperbolic discount functions. As we overcome the historical limitations imposed by poverty and primitive technology, the scope of the decisions governed directly by these discount functions becomes broader. Evolution hasn't had time to respond to these, if indeed it has mechanisms available. It's unlikely that modern humans will ever grow wheels instead of feet, for instance, adaptive as that might be.[46]

Thus there's good reason to believe – and nothing to keep us from believing – that the human race evolved with a very regular but deeply bowed discount curve for evaluating the future. That hypothesis can explain a lot about why people defeat their own plans so relentlessly. However, it raises more questions than it answers. How do people become consistent choice makers? How do painful options interact with pleasurable ones? Why do we often choose according to logical categories? How do "higher" mental functions fit in?

The answers will come by deducing how a bent for temporary preference can be expected to create a marketplace of choice within the individual, the behavior of which depends on strategy rather than the simple value comparisons depicted by exponential curves. For that reason, I've suggested that this approach represents the most microscopic application of economic thinking – micromicroeconomics, perhaps, or picoeconomics.[47]

2.4. Summary

There is extensive evidence that both people and lower animals spontaneously value future events in inverse proportion to their expected delays. The resulting hyperbolic discount curve is seen over all time ranges, from seconds to decades. Because a hyperbolic curve is more bowed than the exponential curve that most utility theories go by, it describes a preference pattern that these theories would call irrational: It predicts temporary preferences for the poorer but earlier of two alternative goals during the time right before the poorer goal becomes available. Regular temporary preferences, in turn, predict that a population of conflicting interests will grow and survive within the individual, sometimes leading to choices that are self-defeating in the long run. A self that is a marketplace for such interests differs radically from the conventional image, and needs exploring in detail.

3. The Elementary Interaction of Interests

I have described a model of learned interests that compete freely on the basis of the time frames over which their rewards are preferred. The most important implication of such a model is an incentive within each interest to learn strategic behaviors that forestall competing interests.

If a person is a population of these kinds of roommates, each clamoring to control the use of the room, how does she make decisions? An interest can't eliminate a competitor simply by providing more reward than the other does, either at one time or on the average, since the competitor might undo the first choice when it became dominant at a particular time in the future. On the other hand, to continue to exist, each interest has to be the highest bidder at some time or it will extinguish; to achieve this, each may have to constrain others and can't be too constrained by them. Just because an interest is dominant at one moment in time doesn't mean it will get its intended reward; while an interest is dominant it has to forestall conflicting interests long enough to realize the reward on which it's based.

3.1. How One Interest Binds Another

For long-range interests, this usually means committing the person not to give in to short-range interests that might become dominant in the future. Long-range interests don't usually conflict with each other, except in the trivial sense of being close choices, because the effect of distant rewards tends to be proportional to their "objective" size; the less well rewarded of two equally long-range interests tends not to survive, but there is no time when this interest includes an incentive to resist this fate, that is, no time when such resistance would increase your prospective discounted reward. I won't be examining this kind of choice-making.

For short-range interests, survival usually means evading commitments. However, short-range interests are also served by committing you not to act on other, incompatible short-range interests; and sometimes they can even commit you to disobey long-range interests. While on an eating binge, you avoid information about calories that might remind you of a diet, for instance, and you're incidentally forestalled from giving in to temptations that aren't compatible with absorption in eating, like having a sexual adventure.

There seem to be four kinds of tactics an interest can employ to commit future choice.

3.1.1. EXTRAPSYCHIC COMMITMENT

You can make it physically impossible to choose a future alternative or arrange for additional outside incentives that will influence a future self. Most examples involve a long-range interest controlling a shorter-range one.

Both the problem and the solution are basic. They're not the results of sophisticated human cognition. They can be shown to exist in birds: As I described earlier, pigeons can learn to peck a key, the only effect of which is to commit them to wait for a later, larger food reward.[48]

Examples of this elementary tactic persist in modern times. Many authors return to Ulysses' problem. The economist Robert Strotz, for instance, pointed out that apparently rational consumers pay to have their future range of choice narrowed. Movie stars pay financial managers to keep them from spending their own money, and many people used to put money in Christmas Club accounts that didn't pay interest in order to give themselves an extra incentive to save money. Jon Elster named a book after Ulysses' problem.[49]

Addiction therapists have been especially interested in disulfiram, a drug that changes the metabolism of alcohol so that drinking leads to nausea or even violent sickness. Disulfiram seemed to be a perfect solution to the temporary preference problem, but its results have been disappointing, probably because addictions can have some strategic value for long-range interests; we discuss these in Chapter 9 [of *Breakdown of Will*].[50]

Some self-control devices make sense even in a world of purely exponential discounting – for instance, diet pills that act by reducing a person's appetite. If a rational planner decides that she ought to eat less, it's certainly easier if she can arrange not to be hungry. But devices that tie you to the figurative mast don't act by spoiling your appetite – for drinking or spending money, for instance. They keep you from acting when your appetite is strong. Such a plan makes no sense for conventional utility theory, which has people maximizing their prospects consistently over time. Hyperbolic discounting predicts a market for exactly this kind of commitment; and, as we saw, even pigeons will sometimes work to get it.

The availability and usefulness of physical committing devices are obviously limited. Even if you can get someone to hold your money until a certain time arrives, you may find that you

really need it in the meantime. For that reason – or just because of the change of preference you originally foresaw – you may find yourself spending a lot of energy undoing the same plan you set up – for instance, by finding a way to borrow against your expectations of getting your money when your commitment has expired.

More often people find other people to influence them. We join groups that seem to be doing what we want to do – Weight Watchers or Alcoholics Anonymous, or a fitness club or even a discussion group. We may just let a friend know that changing a certain behavior is important for us, so that the friend will be disappointed if we don't actually change it. The tactic is to put your reputation in a community at stake. It was described by the sociologist Howard Becker as cultivating other people's respect or love so that this forms a "side bet," an additional incentive to avoid the impulses that these people would disapprove of.[51]

Social side bets are much more flexible than physical commitments, but they, too, are limited. For instance, they're useless against concealable impulses and against any impulse of which other people don't happen to disapprove; they would actually be counterproductive against an impulse to buy popularity. Furthermore, vulnerability to social influence has costs, especially in a cosmopolitan society, which multiplies a person's chances of meeting predators who would exploit this vulnerability. Despite these problems, it's a major strategy for people with strong social motivations. Carol Gilligan suggests that it may be more important in women than in men, a possibility I'll talk more about later.[52]

Short-range interests may use extrapsychic committing tactics against longer-range interests, too, but most examples are trivial. Getting drunk means that you can't be sober for a while, but there isn't much to say about this kind of commitment.

3.1.2. MANIPULATION OF ATTENTION

You can try to avoid information that would change your mind. If you already know that a seductive reward is available, you can try to avoid thinking about it: "If you speak of the Devil, he'll appear." This is the advice that was most respected in our culture before Freud pointed out the bad side effects of repression. A typical example appears in an early-twentieth-century book called *Right and Wrong Thinking and Their Results*, which advised the reader to "avoid discordant thoughts," by distraction if possible and if necessary by "the rule at Donnybrook Fair: 'whenever you see a head, hit it.' The least is not too small to be terminated if it is wrong." Behavioral writers even today advocate "stimulus control" as a useful way of avoiding impulses. It's a large part of what psychologists Janet Metcalfe and Walter Mischel suggest that people use to control passion. Even economists have begun to consider the "value of ignorance (in the form of not acquiring [even] free information)" for this purpose.[53]

Attentional tactics seem to be especially effective against very-short-range urges that require only a moment of attention to become dominant. In a previous chapter [of *Breakdown of Will*], I mentioned examples of structuring people's attention as a way of controlling dental or obstetrical pain. Similarly, I've known patients who have told of "fighting off" panic attacks, dissociative episodes, and even epileptic seizures by vigorously directing their minds away from the feeling that these events were about to occur.

There are obviously occasions when a blind eye at the right time keeps you from giving in to an urge. The trouble is that short-range interests may actually make more effective use of attention control than long-range interests can. When it's in your long-range interest not to realize that a temptation is available, it's also in your short-range interest not to get information on the long-range consequences of giving in. In the competition between long- and short-range interests, attention control is a two-edged sword. In fact, much of the psychotherapy developed by Freud and his followers involved teaching patients to catch themselves using suppression (deliberate avoidance of a thought), repression (unconscious but still goal-directed avoidance of a thought), and denial (avoidance of the implications of a thought). If a person could just avoid fooling herself, Freud thought, she would be simply rational.

Many writers besides the psychoanalysts have described how wishful thinking undermines people's long-range plans. Examples date back to Aristotle, who said that desire had the same effect on belief as being drunk, an observation often reported by people who have suffered lapses while trying to give up bad habits.[54] Motivated changes of perception are yet another phenomenon that makes no sense in a scheme where people discount the future exponentially.

Given temporary preference for present comfort, it isn't hard to picture a mechanism for repression. Many ways have been described

whereby selective attention can systematically distort the information you collect. Experiments have shown that we tend to label our memories with their emotional meanings and retrieve them by these labels. What comes to mind first when I see someone walking toward me isn't her name or where I saw her last, but a sense of whether I'd like to see more of her or avoid her. The same is true of a book on the shelf or a place I have a chance to visit. If that first sense spells trouble, it's easy enough to steer in another direction without ever going into why I want to or whether I have an obligation not to do so. Economist Matthew Rabin has described how self-serving moral reasoning can occur in just such an unconscious way.[55]

3.1.3. PREPARATION OF EMOTION

You can cultivate or inhibit the motivational processes that have intrinsic momentum – generally the emotions. These processes can change how the expectation of reward influences your choice, at least in the near future. Once your appetite for a particular satisfaction is aroused, it has a committing effect that lasts for a while. It increases the rewarding power of its objects and may arouse distaste for things that interfere with it. The dessert cart comes, and suddenly the appeal of desserts is greater than it was. Or your anger is provoked, and suddenly it looms larger than the motives that had been present, possibly even including personal safety. Or you start to caress on a date, and sexuality looms in the same way, just as dating manuals for teenagers have always warned.[56]

In a previous chapter [of *Breakdown of Will*], I described examples where people learned not to have appetites when the rewards on which they were based were certain not to occur or when punishment for them would occur. If this behavior were based on a fear of temptation, it would be an example of preparation of emotion. In fact, when someone is worried that her emotionality makes her vulnerable to other people's influence, she may learn to almost never entertain emotion, thus developing the alexithymia that I mentioned earlier. In a laboratory setting, children as young as five who are given the choice between a better, later food and a less preferred, earlier one can learn to guide their thoughts so as to avoid appetite and thus wait for the better, later food.[57]

These are forms of the impulse-controlling technique that the psychoanalysts call "isolation of affect." It requires single-minded consistency to work. Emotionality and other appetites have a relentless tendency to arise when there's even the slightest chance that they'll be rewarded, though some more so than others – remember Galen's observation that anger could be tamed like a horse, but that the "concupiscible" power (sexual desire) was like a wild boar or goat that had to be controlled by starvation (Section 1.1).

The psychoanalysts also describe cultivation of an emotion to forestall the development of a contrary one – "reaction formation" or "reversal of affect." If I were afraid I'd hate my mother, I might look for things to love about her; or if I thought my soft heart got me into trouble, I might look for ways to see people as my enemies. Again, the analysts only publicized what earlier writers had noticed. I've already quoted Francis Bacon, who wrote with approval about setting "affection against affection and to master one by another: even as we use to hunt beast with beast" (Section 1.1). In the eighteenth century this tactic was sometimes held out as the only practical committing device: The philosopher David Hume said, "Nothing can oppose or retard the impulse of passion but a contrary impulse."[58]

The short-range committing effect of emotion can serve both short- and long-range interests, just as external commitments and attention controls can. A long-range interest may cultivate emotions in order to achieve bravery or virtue, but it's at least as common that someone seeks refuge in a passion so as not to listen to reason.

3.1.4. PERSONAL RULES

You can make a resolution. This may be the most common way that people deal with temporary preferences but also the most mysterious. What is there about "making a resolution" that adds anything to your power to resist changing motivation? This is just the will, the concept that Gilbert Ryle analyzed and found superfluous, and that conventional utility theorists like Gary Becker leave no place for.

Conventional utility theory doesn't suggest any role for a will – but of course, it doesn't recognize a temporary preference problem to begin with. Because of its assumption that people discount the future exponentially, it confounds two distinct meanings of will: a hypothetical element needed in dualistic philosophies to connect mind and body, as in "I willed my arm to move," and the faculty for resisting temptation that's commonly called willpower. If discounting is exponential, resisting temptation is a function just as superfluous as connecting mind and body; we'd be right to dispense with both.

By contrast, hyperbolic discounting can be expected to produce temporary preferences, which will in turn motivate the three committing tactics I've just talked about. The question now is whether these three tactics can account for the experience of willing things.

Most people I've talked with don't report using any of these devices while resisting temptation. When they've given up smoking or climbed out of debt, they mostly say they "just did it." Words like "willpower," "character," "intention," and "resolve" are often applied, but they don't suggest how people actually resist a temporary preference.[59] Some writers have described specific properties, however.

The most robust idea is that will comes from turning individual choices into a matter of principle. As early as the fourth century B.C., Aristotle proposed this idea (referring to dispositions to choose as "opinions"): "We may also look to the cause of incontinence [*akrasia*] scientifically in this way: One opinion is universal, the other concerns particulars. . . ." Galen said that passion was best controlled not by looking at individual opportunities but by following the general principles of reason; he noticed that impulse control was a skill that suffered disproportionately from failure to use it, and that habitual disuse made it especially hard for a person "to remove the defilement of the passions from his soul."

By Victorian times, the list of the properties of willpower had grown. The will was said to:

- come into play as "a new force distinct from the impulses primarily engaged";
- "throw in its strength on the weaker side . . . to neutralize the preponderance of certain agreeable sensations";
- "unite . . . particular actions . . . under a common rule," so that "they are viewed as members of a class of actions subserving one comprehensive end";
- be strengthened by repetition;
- be exquisitely vulnerable to nonrepetition, so that "every gain on the wrong side undoes the effect of many conquests on the right"; and
- involve no repression or diversion of attention, so that "both alternatives are steadily held in view."[60]

The property that stands out in this list is still Aristotle's universality: to unite particular actions under a common rule. Similarly, two researchers from the behavioral school have explored the idea that self-control requires a subject to think in terms of broad categories of choice rather than just seeing the particular choices at hand. Gene Heyman has found that pigeons can learn to make choices in an "overall" context instead of a "local" one if they are rewarded for following a cue telling them when they are doing this; they do not learn without this extra reward, however.[61] Howard Rachlin has said that self-control comes from choosing "patterns" of behavior over time rather than individual "acts." The latter is "molecular" and myopic, the former "molar," that is, global, an overview, based on a series of elements taken as a whole. In an experiment he did with Eric Siegel, pigeons made an impulsive choice significantly less often when 30 previous nonimpulsive choices were required than when the choice stood by itself.[62] These experiments don't model will specifically; but they do suggest that choosing categorically can partially undo the effects of hyperbolic discounting, even where the complexities of human culture aren't a factor.

Even cognitively oriented writers have noted the value of choosing in categories. Baumeister and Heatherton, for instance, speak of the need for "transcendence," which is "a matter of focusing awareness beyond the immediate stimuli," so that these stimuli are seen "in the context of more distal concerns." Similarly, some philosophers of mind have recognized the importance of making "a present choice in favor of a valued sequence of future actions or a valued policy to act in certain ways on certain occasions" in order to achieve "intention stability."[63]

There remains the question of how these categories of choice arise and what makes them recruit extra motivation. Baumeister and Heatherton imagine an ability characterized only as "one's strength to override the unwanted thought, feeling, or impulse." The philosopher Edward McClennen attributes "resolute choice" to "a sense of commitment to a plan initiated by [a prior] self." Using a more complex model, philosopher Michael Bratman argues that it is "rational to follow through with [a prior] plan in those circumstances for which one specifically planned" despite a current change of preference, not because of a commitment, but because of "a planning agent's concern with how she will see her present decision at plan's end." Both philosophers are describing a conflict of impulse and plan, but neither addresses the motivational dimension of the conflict.

Even Rachlin, a "radical" behaviorist, assumes that the necessary categories are intrinsically stable – that patterns of choice naturally hold together like the notes of a symphony, so that, once you're aware of the pattern, you'll be motivated not to break it up. For instance, if you see the pattern of "a healthy breakfast" as consisting of juice, cereal, a bran muffin, and skim milk, the reason you don't substitute apple pie for the bran muffin is that it would break up the pattern, just as not hearing the last notes of a symphony would spoil the experience of hearing the symphony. Likewise, a controlled drinker doesn't drink too much because it would spoil a pattern of temperance.[64]

There's something appealing about this viewpoint, and yet it doesn't ring entirely true. How do patterns like healthy breakfasts and temperance get decided on in the first place? And is it really true that we forgo the apple pie for the sake of consistency per se? Especially in potential addictions like overeating and drinking alcohol, people report that their urge is to break the patterns, not preserve them. Sticking to them feels effortful – quite the opposite of the case of listening to a symphony, where breaking away in the middle is what takes effort. What enforces a diet or a resolution?

Basic utility theory can provide an answer, but only if the form of the discount curve is hyperbolic. Assuming only that the discounted rewarding impacts of successive events add together, we can see that series of rewards will be chosen more in proportion to their objective sizes than will single rewards. The property of additivity hasn't been studied much, but a few experiments suggest that the hyperbolically discounted effects of each reward in a series simply add, at least in pigeons and rats.[65] Since this is also the simplest assumption, I'll adopt it from here on.

Consider a series of larger, later rewards and their smaller, earlier alternatives – for instance, philosopher Bratman's example of a pianist who throws his nightly performance off by drinking wine beforehand:[66] At a distance the pianist prefers to abstain and perform well, but every night at dinnertime he changes his preference to drinking the wine. However, as Figure 3A suggests, even at dinnertime he may prefer the prospect of abstaining every night to the prospect of drinking every night for the foreseeable future: The incentives for choosing between these categories of reward will be the summed expected values of the series of rewards. The incentives for choosing just for one night will be the curves from a lone pair, as we saw in Figure 2B.

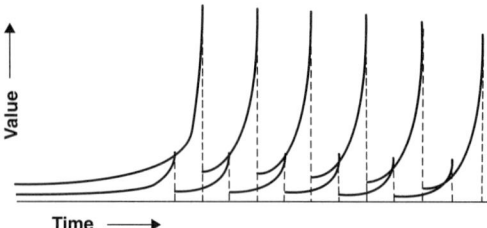

Figure 3A. Summed hyperbolic curves form a series of larger-later rewards and a series of smaller-earlier alternatives. At the beginning of the series, the period of temporary preference for the series of smaller rewards is about zero. The curves from just the final pair of rewards are the same as in Figure 2B.

In the schoonerlike picture of the summed discount curves from series of rewards, the "sails" get gradually lower as the choice point moves later in the series, for they comprise a decreasing number of curves added together. The last pair of sails are the same as a lone pair. If the series has no foreseeable end, which is the case for most real-life categories, the sails may be added forward to some kind of time horizon that stays a constant distance ahead, so that the height of the summed rewards stays roughly constant. In any case, summation of a series of rewards makes the first few sails higher than the sail drawn on a lone pair of rewards would be.

More importantly, the delayed rewards add roughly in proportion to their objective sizes, so that when their aggregate height is added in, the first sail in the series of smaller rewards doesn't protrude as high above the first sail in the series of larger rewards as it does in a solitary pair; with series of some amounts at some delays, the earliest sail doesn't protrude above its larger, later alternative at all. That would mean that when the pianist chooses categorically, he would always prefer to abstain, even at dinnertime. The choice of a whole series of rewards will be influenced by the rewards expected after the most immediate pair, and for all the subsequent pairs the discounted value of the larger, later alternatives is greater than that of the smaller, earlier ones. Only the nearest choice in a series is dominated by the smaller, immediate reward – although the nearest choice will obviously carry more weight than any single one of the later choices.

Two recent experiments confirm that choosing between whole series of small, early versus large, late pairs increases the preference for the large, late alternatives. Psychologists Kris Kirby

and Barbarose Guastello found that undergraduates who preferred the small, early amount of money when choosing between one pair at a time regularly switched to preferring the large, late amount when choosing between series of five payoffs to be delivered at weekly intervals. The same switch occurred when amounts of pizza were offered rather than money. Similarly, psychologist John Monterosso and I have observed that rats choosing between squirts of sucrose prefer the shorter, earlier of a single pair of squirts but a series of three longer, later squirts over a series of three shorter, earlier alternatives.[67] The finding in rats suggests that the bundling effect comes from a basic property of the discount curves rather than from some cultural norm.

This property has to be a highly concave shape, such as that of hyperbolas. Exponential discount curves from a single pair stay proportional, and adding the whole series together doesn't change their relative heights (Figure 3B). Thus, bundling choices together wouldn't affect the direction of preference if discount curves were exponential rather than hyperbolic. The fact that hyperbolic discounting predicts the often-described – and now experimentally observed – increase in patience for bundled rewards seems to confirm that we're on the right track: The strategic implications of these curves may be central to whatever rationality human choice-making can achieve.[68]

3.1.4.1. Bundling Rewards that Extend Over Time. Most choices in real life aren't between brief moments of different intensity, but

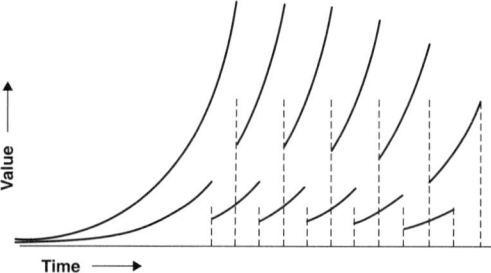

Figure 3B. Summed exponential curves from the two series of rewards shown in Figure 3A. Summing doesn't change their relative heights. (This would also be true if the curves were so steep that the smaller, earlier rewards were preferred; but in that case, summing would add little to their total height anyway, because the tails of exponential curves are so low.)

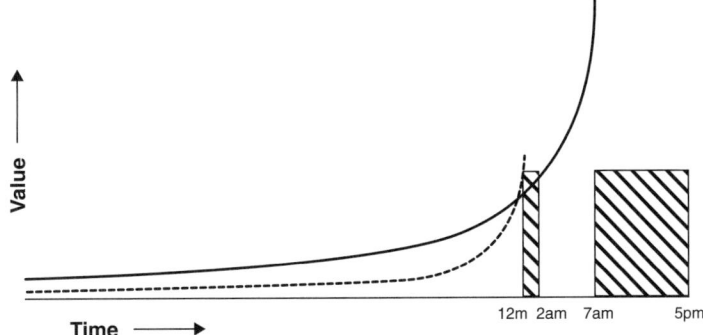

Figure 4A. Curves that are the aggregate of hyperbolic discount curves from each moment of time during continuing rewards – staying up from midnight to 2 A.M. versus feeling rested from 7 A.M. to 5 P.M.

between extended experiences – the pleasure of a binge versus feeling fit and having intact prospects the next Monday, a venting of rage versus keeping a job and friends. Often the difference isn't between intensities of satisfaction-per-minute, but between different durations of comparable satisfactions. The pleasure of staying up for a couple of hours after midnight may be the same as the differential pleasure of not being tired the next day, but the latter pleasure lasts all day. However, if successive rewards are additive, it's easy to convert durations to total amounts. For instance, if you value the fun of staying up at one unit per minute and expect to lose one unit per minute of comfort from when you get up at seven the next morning until you leave work at 5 P.M., your discount curves from a day's aggregation of these rewards will look like those in Figure 4A.[69]

If you face a similar choice nightly and can make your choice for a long series of future nights at once (say 10), your incentives will be described by the curves in Figure 4B.[70] As with more discrete moments of reward, bundling these experiences into series moves your incentives toward the larger, later rewards.

So choosing behaviors in whole categories will lead to less impulsiveness, just as the philosophers have said. Here, then, is a fourth strategy to defend your long-range interest: the *personal rule* to behave alike toward all the members of a category. It's the equivalent of the philosopher Immanuel Kant's "categorical imperative": to make all choices as if they were to define universal rules. Similarly, it echoes the psychologist Lawrence Kohlberg's sixth and highest principle of moral reasoning: deciding according to principle.[71]

3.2. The Will's Achilles Heel

The trouble is that this insight about choosing categorically doesn't eliminate the attraction of small, immediate rewards; it offers only a

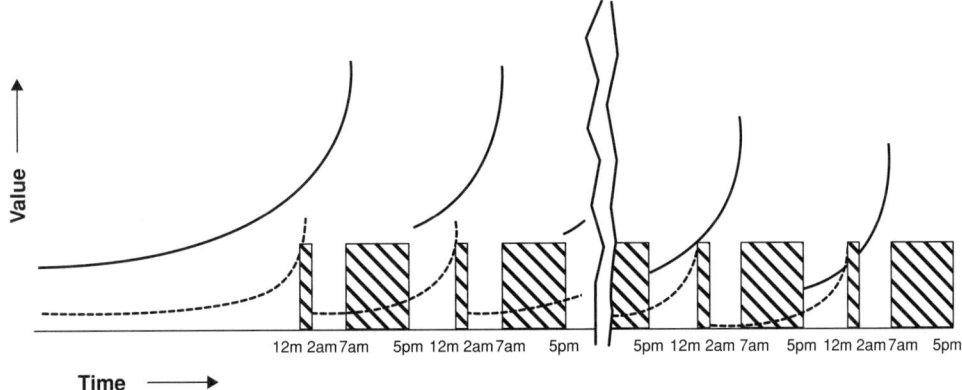

Figure 4B. Summed curves from ten pairs of the rewards depicted in Figure 4A. The effect of summation is the same as from the point rewards in Figure 3B.

discipline that a long-range interest would benefit from at the expense of short-range interests *if only the person were consistently motivated to follow it*. So far I've described no reason why, when an inferior reward is immediately available, a pigeon or person shouldn't take it. When Rachlin and Siegel (Section 3.1.4) introduced a signal to remind their pigeons of the immediate availability of single rewards, the birds' apparent discounting shifted back from the exponential toward the hyperbolic.

People have more brainpower than pigeons and can probably perceive greater series of rewards, but short-range interests as well as long-range ones can use their enhanced reasoning skills. The bad news is that knowing the power of categorical decision making isn't enough. There's persistent pressure to backslide even after you've learned about molar or overall bookkeeping.

Ganging up on a short-range interest isn't the same thing as killing it. While acting in this interest, you're still motivated to learn anything that can evade the "universal principle" that dominates it. A quick mind can put together rules in any number of ways, so finding evasions is also easy. The trick is to differentiate between the choice at hand and the set of choices that are bound together by a rule. Just as the will is well described in history, so is our readiness to evade it. When William James wrote his pioneering analysis of "effort of will," he pointed out how a person's "anti-impulsive conceptions" – that is, her molar conceptions à la Rachlin – are vulnerable to exceptions:

> How many excuses does the drunkard find when each new temptation comes! It is a new brand of liquor which the interests of intellectual culture in such matters oblige him to test; moreover it is poured out and it is a sin to waste it; or others are drinking and it would be churlishness to refuse; or it is but to enable him to sleep, or just to get through this job of work; or it isn't drinking, it is because he feels so cold; or it is Christmas day; or it is a means of stimulating him to make a more powerful resolution in favor of abstinence than any he has hitherto made; or it is just this once, and once doesn't count, etc., etc., *ad libitum* – it is, in fact, anything you like except *being a drunkard*.[72]

Even Aristotle went on in his description of "universal" and "particular" interpretations

of choice to describe an ongoing competition between them.[73]

Thus people who have learned a "higher" or "richer" principle of choice aren't thereby freed from temptation. We aren't very old before our razor-sharp wits discover a perverse truth: If behaving according to categorical principles promises more discounted, expected reward than making an isolated choice does, then making an isolated choice now and acting by rule in the future promises still more.

The problem is that there are many possible ways to define global categories. The ice cream at hand may violate one diet but not another; and even if it's so outrageously rich as to violate all conceivable diets, there's apt to be a circumstance that makes the present moment an exception, just as with James's drunkard: It's Thanksgiving dinner or my birthday, or a host has taken special trouble to get it, or I have cause to celebrate or to console myself just today, and so on. The molar principle that offers an exception *just this once* will be rewarded more than the one that doesn't, for it produces an aggregation of rewards, as shown in Figures 3 and 4, for all but the first larger, later rewards *and* the spike of reward at hand.

The tough question is not how molar bookkeeping recruits motivational support for long-range interests, but how this process defends itself from short-range interests, sometimes unsuccessfully. Acting in my long-range interest, how do I keep a short-range interest from repeatedly proposing an exception to my rule "just this once?"

Simple intuition offers the answer: Excuses that are too blatant lower my expectation of following the amended principle. I may be able to go off my diet on Thanksgiving without reducing my belief that I'll stick to it at other times; but if I try proposing other holidays, I'll probably notice that I'm starting down a slippery slope. The ability to take a drink at New Years or go off the diet on Thanksgiving provides flexibility to a potentially rigid commitment to a concrete rule; but the same principle that keeps Thanksgiving from setting a precedent might also work for my birthday and, with decreasing credibility, for the Fourth of July, St. Patrick's Day, Labor Day, Arbor Day, St. Swithin's Day, and Just This Once. This kind of logic can degrade a personal rule without my ever breaking it. Once I expect myself to find an exception whenever the urge is strong, I no longer have the credible prospect of the whole series of later, larger rewards – the cumulative benefits of my diet – available to choose.

In this way, hyperbolic discount curves make self-control a matter of self-prediction. This effect will be especially noticeable where self-control is tenuous. The hyperbolic discounter can't simply estimate whether she's better off dieting or eating spontaneously and then following the best course, the way an exponential discounter could. Even if she plans to eat less from a perspective of distance, she won't know whether or not she'll regularly prefer to eat ad lib when she's hungry. If she expects to eat ad lib, her long-range perspective will be useless to her unless she can use one of the first three kinds of commitments I described earlier – not a rich selection.

But what if she makes a new resolution to "decide according to principle" – to go on a diet – and starts off expecting to stick to it in the future if she sticks to it now? This condition may be enough to motivate sticking to it, but only insofar as she thinks it will be both necessary and enough. If she then violates the diet and loses faith in it, her principle will magically stop being enough. Personal rules are a *recursive* mechanism; they continually take their own pulse, and if they feel it falter, that very fact will cause further faltering.

Thus deciding according to molar principles is not a matter of making dispassionate judgments, but of defending one way of counting your prospects against alternative ways that are also strongly motivated. Your motivation to stick to a principle is not pure a priori reason – reason is not motivation – but the saving of your expectation of continuing to stick to it. It's the internal equivalent of the "self-enforcing contracts" made by traders who'll be dealing with each other for a long time, contracts that let them do business on the strength of handshakes.[74] This recursive process of staking the credibility of a resolution on each occasion when it's tested gives your resolve momentum over successive times. The ongoing temptation to commit a wrong act that will set a damaging precedent – and the ever-present anxiety that this may happen – is probably what makes this strategy of self-control feel effortful. It separates *intentions* from plain *expectations* and force of will from force of habit.

This model proceeds from hyperbolic discounting with almost no extra assumptions – only rough additiveness – and predicts credible weapons for either side in the closely fought contests that seem to occur as people make decisions

about self-control: Long-range interests define principles, and short-range interests find exceptions.

3.3. *Summary*

An interest that has survived in someone's internal marketplace must have included ways to forestall incompatible interests, at least well enough to sometimes get the reward it's based on. This need accounts for the examples of self-committing tactics that have long puzzled utility theorists. Three kinds are straightforward: finding constraints or influences outside of your psyche, sometimes physical devices like pills, but more often the opinion of other people; manipulating your attention, as in the Freudian defense mechanisms of suppression, repression, and denial; and preparing your emotions, as in the defense mechanisms of isolation and reversal of affect. A fourth tactic, willpower, seems to be at once the strongest and most versatile, but has hitherto been mysterious.

Hyperbolic discount curves from series of choices increase the preference for larger but later rewards when they're added together, which suggests a solution to the mystery: The device of choosing according to principle, which has been advocated since Aristotle's day, groups your choices into just such series. Principles of choice, or "personal rules," represent self-enforcing contracts with your future motivational states; such contracts depend on your seeing each current choice as a precedent that predicts how you're apt to choose among similar options in the future. Short-range interests evade personal rules by proposing exceptions that might keep the present case from setting a precedent. The will is a recursive process that bets the expected value of your future self-control against each of your successive temptations.

Notes

1   For instance, Baumeister & Heatherton (1996), Becker & Murphy (1988), Polivy (1998), Rachlin (1995a).

2   Plato's *Protagoras* (sections 356–357) in Jowett's translation (1892/1937). His theories and Aristotle's are thoroughly discussed in Charlton (1988, pp. 13–59).

3   Averill (1988).

4   Galen (1963, p. 47); This man-vs.-animal figure has also had a long life.

5   Romans 7:15–23.

6   Mourant (1967).

7   Quoted by Hirschman (1977, p. 22).

8   Vanderveldt & Odenwald (1952); Ricoeur (1971).

9   Kobasa & Maddi (1983); Perls et al. (1958).

10 Freud's two principles (1911, p. 223); superego (1923).

11 Comparative response to schedules of reward: Madden et al. (1998). Animal models of addiction are reviewed in Altman et al. (1996). Behaviorally, pigeons detect and respond to tiny changes in frequencies of electric shock even when these are not signaled by cues (Herrnstein, 1969). Human obtuseness to reward is especially conspicuous in children from ages 6 to 12, perhaps because this is when they first begin to override their feelings with preconceptions of the world (Sonuga-Barke et al., 1989).

12 Samuelson (1976); Becker (1976).

13 Sorensen (1992).

14 Crews (1995 p. 12).

15 See the many sources reviewed in Ellenberger (1970).

16 Vaughan & Herrnstein (1987).

17 Gardner (1997).

18 In this book I'll refer most often to his work on emotion (1999b).

19 For example, just 10 years ago a prominent behaviorist, Howard Rachlin, proposed that pain shouldn't be regarded as a subjective experience, but just as a behavior to get external rewards. These rewards might be anything from avoiding injury to getting sympathy, but they could never be something that occurred entirely within the person's mind (1985).

20 Becker & Murphy (1988).

21 "Some sets of commodities are simply incomparable or incommensurable" (Schwartz, 1986); see also Allison (1981), Taylor (1982).

22 An outcome that loses 20% of its value for every unit of time it is delayed is worth $(1.00 - .20)^1$, or .80 of its value, at 1 unit of delay, $(1.00 - .20)^2$, or .64 of its value, at 2 units of delay, $(1.00 - .20)^{10}$, or .107 at 10 units, .0000000002 at 100 units, and so on.

23 For most people, the availability of a good excuse is even more important; but we'll have to figure out why anybody would need to give an excuse to *herself* before talking about that.

24 Hume quoted in Hirschman (1977, p. 25); Senault (1649, p. C1).

25 Ainslie & Herrnstein (1981); Ainslie (1974).

26 The simplest hyperbola is:

Value = Objective value / Delay

However, this formula could probably never describe a natural process, since it would make value infinite at zero delay. A hyperbolic formula that makes "objective" value equal to discounted value at zero delay is:

Value = Objective value/(1 + Delay)

A value would fall to $1.00/(1 + 1)$, or .50 of what it would be if immediate at 1 unit of delay, $1.00/(1 + 2)$, or .33, at 2 units, and $1.00/(1 + 10)$, or .09, at 10 units of delay, but would still be worth $1.00/(1 + 100)$, or .01 at 100 units, compared to the .000030 predicted by the exponential formula at 10%. This formula still allows for no differences in discount "rate," or impatience, among different people, a rigidity that will need correcting.

27 And among exponential discounters, those who discount at a lower rate will accumulate money faster than those who discount at a higher rate. In that case, however, the high disounter wouldn't mind this prospect, since she devalues the future, just as Becker and Murphy's rational addict doesn't regret her addiction.

28 Noise: Solnick et al. (1980); Navarick (1982). Video games: Millar & Navarick, 1984. Food: Ragotzy et al. (1988).

29 Green et al. (1981); Kirby & Herrnstein (1995); Ostaszewski (1996); Kirby (1997); Madden et al. (1997); Richards et al. (1999); Vuchinich & Simpson (1998).

30 That is, older subjects have a smaller Constant$_2$ in the general discount equation ([see below]; Ainslie & Haendel, 1983; Green et al., 1981; Kirby & Herrnstein. 1995), as do introverts (Ostaszewski, 1996), nonaddicts (Kirby et al., 1999), and nonsmokers (Bickel et al., 1999).

31 Herrnstein et al. (1993). These findings are consistent with an earlier description of the factors that make human subjects respond differently than animals in some experimental designs (Mawhinney, 1982).

32 Generalized from Mazur (1987). I compare the possible formulas in Ainslie (1992, pp. 63–76). Constant$_1$ keeps the value from going to infinity when a reward is immediate; Constant$_2$ describes how steeply a subject discounts the future.

33 $Y = 1/X$, where Y is the magnitude in question and X is the distance to the building or goal.

34 Brunsson (1985), Chapters 1 and 2; Brennan & Tullock (1982, p. 226).

35 The classical work is by Max Weber (1925/1964).

36 Navon and Gopher (1979).

37 Olds (1992). Because of neurophysiological findings, it has been suggested that "hot" and "cool" (= passionate and reasonable) choice-making systems may be based on information processed in the amygdala and hippocampus, respectively, with the implication that the resulting motives are also in separate systems (Metcalfe & Jacobs, 1998; Metcalfe & Mischel, 1990).

38 Conversely, however concentrated the reward process is within one location, it must still have

separate components, ultimately neurons, that compete for control of whatever output pathway it has. Localization will always be relative.

39 E.g., Klein (1989).

40 Cognitive psychologist Julius Kuhl and his colleagues have suggested what is in effect a population model of the person, in which one part sometimes controls others like a dictator but does better exercising "democratic leadership" (Kuhl, 1994). In this model a function called "autonomy" ("the holistic integrated functioning through which action is centrally regulated") "stabilizes and boosts autonomy and action, for example, by facilitating the identification and efficient expression of goals . . . and shielding such goals from competing impulses" (Ryan et al., 1997). However, they don't say why this stabilization, or shielding, should be needed, and imply that one faction's attempt to control others is a cause rather than a response to conflict between them.

41 Cropper et al. (1991); Harvey (1994). Among other consequences, this unifomity over scale makes preference reversal a candidate for being analyzed as a fractal in chaos theory (see Gleick, 1987).

42 Laibson (1997); Harris & Laibson (1999). Their "quasi-hyperbolic function saptures the qualitative property that discount rates decline (weakly) with horizon length" (1999, p. 2), and is adapted from the formula that Phelps and Pollack originally developed to describe the value of property transferred between generations (1968).

43 Foraging theory has always assumed that natural selection has shaped animals' choices to maximize aggregate net energy gain (Krebs, 1978; Maynard Smith, 1978); its proponents haven't examined the discounting process until recently. When they've done so, they've found that animals will regularly choose poorer, imminently available prey over better, delayed alternatives to the detriment of overall foraging efficiency (Kagel et al., 1986; Lea, 1979; Snyderman, 1983).

44 Offer (in 2006) The Challenge of Affluence: Prosperity and Well-Being in the United States and Britain since 1945, p. 11.

45 Erasmus (1509/1983).

46 See Simon (1983).

47 First in 1986; see also Ainslie (1992).

48 Ainslie (1974); see Section 2.1.

49 Strotz (1956) acknowledged that the problem implied a nonexponential discount curve but didn't suggest a hyperbola; Elster (1979).

50 Azrin et al. (1982); Fuller & Roth (1979).

51 Becker (1960).

52 Gilligan (1977).

53 Right thinking: Crane (1905, p. 115); stimulus control: Kanfer (1975, pp. 309–355);

Goldiamond (1965); Metcalfe & Mischel (1999); value of ignorance: Carillo (1999).

54 Freud (1926/1956); Aristotle's Nichomachean Ethics 1147b9–15; lapses in smokers: Sjoberg & Johnson (1978).

55 Labeling by emotional salience: Zajonc (1980); calling up memories by category: Shiffrin & Schneider (1977); self-serving ethics: Rabin (1995).

56 The momentum of an appetite – a positive feedback effect that leads to potentiation rather than satiation – is what has made conditioning theories of temporary preference so attractive. These include the latest incarnation of the passion/reason model, Metcalfe and Mischel's "hot/cool system analysis" (1999). I discuss this phenomenon at length in Ainslie (1999b).

57 Alexithymia: Nemiah (1977). This is the opposite of cultivating your vulnerability to influence, one of the extrapsychic committing devices. The fact that a person may see either one as serving her long-range interest doubtless comes from the fact that vulnerability to influence is a two-edged sword. Children: Mischel & Mischel (1983).

58 Bacon quoted in Hirschman (1977, p. 22); David Hume quoted in Hirschman (1977, pp. 24–25). Economist Robert Frank gives several examples of emotions that seem to serve as self-control devices (1988, pp. 81–84).

59 Psychologist Julius Kuhl (1996) proposes a similar list of "self-regulatory . . . mechanisms and strategies," but without extrapsychic examples: "attention control," "emotion and activation control," and what sound like aspects of will – "motivation control," "goal maintenance," and "impulse control."

Each of Jon Elster's "devices for precommitment" is also an example or a subset of one of these tactics. He divides extrapsychic devices into "eliminating options," "imposing costs," "setting up rewards," "creating delays," and "changing preferences [i.e., early avoidance]." Attention control is "inducing ignorance," and preparation of emotion is "inducing passion." As I'm about to argue, "investing in bargaining power [i.e., maintaining your credibility]" is part of the mechanism of will, but Elster separates it from my core mechanism for will, bundling of choices, which he calls "bunching" and lists as an "alternative to precommitment" (2000, pp. 6, 84–86). Similarly, I believe that all of his reasons for precommitment ("overcome passion," "overcome self-interest," "overcome hyperbolic discounting," "overcome strategic time inconsistency," and "neutralize or prevent preference change") are ultimately motivated by one reason: the problem of hyperbolic discounting; however, he believes that passion, at least, is not an example of that problem (see Ainslie. 1999b; Elster, 1999).

60 Aristotle, *Nichomachean Ethics*, 1147a24–28; Galen (1963, p. 44); new force, throw strength on weaker side, unite actions, strengthened by repetition: Sully (1884, pp. 631, 663, 669); vulnerable to nonrepetition: Bain (1859/1886, p. 440); held steadily in view: James (1890, p. 534).

61 Heyman (1996); Heyman & Tanz (1995).

62 Rachlin (1995a); Siegel & Rachlin (1996).

63 Baumeister & Heatherton (1996); philosophers: Bratman (quoted) (1999, pp. 50–56); McClennen (1990, pp. 157–161); others discussed in Bratman (1999, pp. 69–73).

64 Rachlin (1995a, 1995b).

65 Mazur (1986) reported that pigeons choosing between a single food reward and a series of more delayed rewards decide as if they simply added each amount divided by its delay, thus confirming less precise findings by McDiarmid and Rilling (1965).

66 Bratman (1999, pp. 35–57).

67 Making choices in the context of similar future choices can increase self-control: Kirby & Guastello (2000); bundling choices into series makes rats switch their preference from smaller, earlier to larger, later sucrose rewards: Ainslie & Monterosso (2000). In the latter experiment, rats given the choice between .4 second access to sugar water immediately and .6 second access at a 3.0 second delay regularly chose the immediate reward; they regularly chose a series of three .6 second rewards over a series of .4 second alternatives 3.0 seconds earlier, even though the first .4 second reward was immediate.

68 The bundling and other phenomena that follow from hyperbolic discounting are also consistent with the hyperboloid curves that some economists have adopted for their tractability (see note 42). Roland Benabou and Jean Tirole have derived most of the properties of personal rules from such curves (2000).

69 At midnight the value of staying up will be

$$V_{up} = \sum_{i=0.5\to1.5} 60/(1+i) = 64$$

and the differential value of feeling rested at work will be

$$V_{bed} = \sum_{i=7.5\to16.5} 60/(1+i) = 49$$

Given only this choice, you'll probably stay up and suffer the next day.

70 The values of your alternatives are:

$$V_{up} = \left(\sum_{i=.5\to1.5} 60/(1+i)\right) + \left(\sum_{i=24.5\to25.5} 60/(1+i)\right)$$
$$+ \left(\sum_{i=48.5\to49.5} 60/(1+i)\right) + \ldots$$
$$+ \left(\sum_{i=216.5\to217.5} 60/(1+i)\right) = 78$$

for staying up on the next 10 nights vs.

$$V_{bed} = \left(\sum_{i=7.5\to16.5} 60/(1+i)\right)$$
$$+ \left(\sum_{i=31.5\to40.5} 60/(1+i)\right) + \ldots$$
$$+ \left(\sum_{i=223.5\to232.5} 60/(1+i)\right) = 105$$

for going to bed.

71 Kant (1793/1960, pp. 15–49); Kohlberg (1963).

72 James (1890, p. 565).

73 He also illustrated the difficulty of making sense of this competition without a rationale for temporary preference. When he tried to specify the details, he got hopelessly tangled:

> One opinion is universal, the other concerns particulars, things about which perception has the deciding say. When one [opinion] arises from them the soul must, in the one case, affirm the conclusion, in cases to do with doing, act at once ... When, therefore, on the one hand there is the universal [opinion] forbidding to taste, and on the other, [the opinion] that everything sweet is pleasant, and this is pleasant (and it is this opinion which operates), and desire happens to be present, the one says to avoid this but desire drives; for it has the power to move each of the parts [of the body]. So it turns out that the man who acts akratically does so under the influence in a way of reason and of opinion, opinion, however, which is not opposed in itself to the right principle – it is the desire, not the opinion, which is opposed to that – but opposed incidentally. (*Nichomachean Ethics*, 1147a24-bl7).

74 Self-enforcing contracts are described by Macaulay (1963), and by Klein and Leffler (1981), and analyzed in terms of game theory by Stähler (1998). Howard Rachlin (1995b) incorrectly ascribes the active ingredient in the picoeconomic theory of will to "the law of exercise," an old behaviorist term for force of habit.

References

Agarwal, D. P. and Goedde, H. W. (1989) Human aldehyde dehydrogenases: Their role in alcoholism. *Alcohol* 6, 517–523.

Ainslie, G. (1970) Experiment described by Howard Rachlin in his *Introduction to Modern Behaviorism*. San Francisco: Freeman, pp. 186–188.

Ainslie, G. (1974) Impulse control in pigeons. *Journal of the Experimental Analysis of Behavior* 21, 485–489.

Ainslie, G. (1986) Beyond microeconomics: Conflict among interest in a multiple self as a determinant of value. In J. Elster (ed.), *The Multiple*

Self. Cambridge: Cambridge University Press, pp. 133–175.

Ainslie, G. (1992) *Picoeconomics: The Strategic Interaction of Successive Motivational States within the Person*. Cambridge: Cambridge University Press.

Ainslie, G. (1999b) The intuitive explanation of passionate mistakes, and why it's not adequate. In J. Elster (ed.), *Addiction: Entries and Exits*. New York: Sage, pp. 209–238.

Ainslie, G. and Herrnstein, R. (1981) Preference reversal and delayed reinforcement. *Animal Learning and Behavior* 9, 476–482.

Ainslie, G. and Monterosso, J. (2000) Building choices into series makes rats switch preference from the smaller-earlier to larger-later sucrose rewards. Unpublished manuscript.

Allison, J. (1981) Economics and operant conditioning. In P. Harzen and M. D. Zeiler (eds.), *Predictability, Correlation, and Contiguity*. New York: Wiley, pp. 321–353.

Altman J., Everitt, B. J., Glautier, S., Markou, A., Nutt, J., Oretti, R., Phillips, G. D., and Robbins T. W. (1996) The biological, social and clinical bases of drug addiction: Commentary and debate. *Psychopharmacology* 125, 285–345.

Aristotle (1984) *The Complete Works of Aristotle*. J. Barnes (ed.). Princeton, NJ: Princeton University Press.

Averill, J. R. (1988) Disorders of emotion. *Journal of Social and Clinical Psychology* 6, 247–268.

Azrin, N. H., Nunn, R., and Frantz-Renshaw, S. (1982) Habit reversal vs. negative practice of self-destructive oral habit (biting, chewing, or licking of lips, cheeks, tongue, or palate). *Journal of Behavior Therapy in Experimental Psychiatry* 13, 49–54.

Baumeister, R. F. and Heatherton, T. (1996) Self-regulation failure: An overview. *Psychological Inquiry* 7, 1–15.

Becker, G. S. (1976) *The Economic Approach to Human Behavior*. Chicago: Chicago University Press.

Becker, G. S. and Murphy, K. (1988) A theory of rational addiction. *Journal of Political Economy* 96, 675–700.

Becker, H. S. (1960) Notes on the concept of commitment. *American Journal of Sociology* 66, 32–40.

Benabou, R. and Tirole, J. (2000) Personal rules. Paper delivered at the ECARES-CEPR Conference on Psychology and Economics, Brussels, June 9–11.

Bickel, W. K., Odum, A. L., and Madden, G. J. (1999) Impulsivity and cigarette smoking: Delay discounting in current, never, and ex-smokers. *Psychopharmacology* 146, 447–454.

Boring, E. G. (1950) *A History of Experimental Psychology*. New York: Appleton Century-Crofts.

Bratman, M. E. (1999) *Faces of Intention: Selected Essays on Intention and Agency*. Cambridge: Cambridge University Press.

Brennan, G. and Tullock, G. (1982) An economic theory of military tactics: Methodological individualism at war. *Journal of Economic Behavior and Organization* 3, 225–242.

Brunner, D. and Gibbon, J. (1995) Value of food aggregates: Parallel versus serial discounting. *Animal Behavior* 50, 1627–1634.

Brunsson, N. (1985) *The Irrational Organization*. Stockholm: Stockholm School of Economics.

Carrillo, J. D. (1999) Self-control, moderate consumption, and craving. Unpublished manuscript. Universite Libre de Bruxelles.

Case, D. (1997) Why the delay-of-reinforcement gradient is hyperbolic. Paper presented at the 20th Annual Conference of the Society for the Quantitative Analysis of Behavior, Chicago, May 22.

Charlton, W. (1988) *Weakness of the Will*. Oxford: Blackwell.

Crane, A. M. (1905) *Right and Wrong Thinking and Their Results*. Boston: Lathrop.

Crews, F. (1995) *The Memory Wars: Freud Legacy in Dispute*. New York: New York Review of Books.

Cropper, M. L., Aydede, S. K., and Portney, P. R. (1991) Discounting human lives. *American Journal of Agricultural Economics* 73, 1410–1415.

DeVilliers, P. and Herrnstein, R. (1976) Toward a law of response strength. *Psychological Bulletin* 83, 1131–1153.

Ellenberger, H. F. (1970) *The Discovery of the Unconscious*. New York: Basic Books.

Elster, J. (1979) *Ulysses and the Sirens: Studies in Rationality and Irrationality*. Cambridge: Cambridge University Press.

Elster, J. (1999) *Strong Feelings: Emotion; Addiction, and Human Behavior*. Cambridge, MA: MIT Press.

Elster, J. (2000) *Ulysses Unbound*. Cambridge: Cambridge University Press.

Erasmus, D. (1509/1983) *The Praise of Folly*. Leonard F. Dean (ed.). Putney, VT: Hendricks House.

Freud, S. (1895/1956) *Project for a Scientific Psychology*. In J. Strachey and A. Freud (eds.), *The Standard Edition of the Complete Psychological Works of Sigmund Freud*. London: Hogarth Vol. I.

Freud, S. (1911) Ibid., vol. 12. *Formulations on the Two Principles of Mental Functioning*.

Freud, S. (1923) Ibid., vol. 19. *The Ego and the Id*.

Freud, S. (1926/1956) Ibid., vol. 20. *Inhibitions, Symptoms, and Anxiety*.

Frijda, N. H. (1986) *The Emotions*. Cambridge: Cambridge University Press.

Fuller, R. K. and Roth, H. P. (1979) Disulfiram for the treatment of alcoholism. *Annals of Internal Medicine* 90, 901–904.

Galen (1963) *Galen on the Passions and Errors of the Soul*. P. W. Harkins (trans.). Columbus, OH: Ohio State University Press.

Gardner, E. L. (1997) Brain reward mechanisms. In J. H. Lowinson, P. Ruiz, R. B. Millman, and J. G. Langrod (eds.), *Substance Abuse: A Comprehensive Textbook* (3d ed.). Baltimore: Williams & Wilkins, pp. 51–85.

Gilligan, C. (1977) In a different voice: Womens' conceptions of self and morality. *Harvard Educational Review* 47, 481–517.

Gleick, J. (1987) *Chaos: Making a New Science*. New York: Viking Penguin.

Goldiamond, I. (1965) Self-control procedures in personal behavior problems. *Psychological Reports* 17, 851–868.

Goldsmith, H. H., Buss, K. A., and Lemery, K. S. (1997) Toddler and childhood temperament: Expanded content, stronger genetic evidence, new evidence for the importance of environment. *Developmental Psychology* 33, 891–905.

Grace, R. C. (1994) A contextual model of concurrent chains choice. *Journal of the Experimental Analysis of Behavior* 61, 113–129.

Green, L., Fisher, E. B., Jr., Perlow, S., and Sherman, L. (1981) Preference reversal and self-control: Choice as a function of reward amount and delay. *Behaviour Analysis Letters* 1, 43–51.

Hampton, C. (1976) *Savages*. London: Samuel French.

Harris, C. and Laibson, D. (1999) Dynamic choices of hyperbolic consumers. Paper Presented at the GREMAQ/CEPR Conference on Economics and Psychology, Toulouse, France, June 19.

Harvey, C. M. (1994) The reasonableness of non-constant discounting. *Journal of Public Economics* 53, 31–51.

Herrnstein, R. J. (1961) Relative and absolute strengths of response as a function of frequency of reinforcement. *Journal of the Experimental Analysis of Behavior* 4, 267–272.

Herrnstein, R. J. (1969) Method and theory in the study of avoidance. *Psychological Review* 76, 49–69.

Herrnstein, R. J. (1997) *The Matching Law: Papers in Psychology and Economics*. H. Rachlin and D. I. Laibson (eds.). New York: Sage.

Herrnstein, R. J., Loewenstein, G., Prelec, D., and Vaughan, W., Jr. (1993) Utility maximization and melioration: Internalities in individual choice. *Journal of Behavioral Decision Making* 6, 149–185.

Heyman, G. M. (1996) Resolving the contradictions of addiction. *Behavioral and Brain Sciences* 19, 561–610.

Heyman, G. M. and Tanz, L. (1995) How to teach a pigeon to maximize overall reinforcement rate. *Journal of the Experimental Analysis of Behavior* 64, 277–297.

Hirschman, A. (1977) *The Passions and the Interests*. Princeton, NJ: Princeton University Press.

James. W. (1890) *Principles of Psychology*. New York: Holt.

Kagel, J. H., Green, L., and Caraco, T. (1986) When foragers discount the future: Constraint or adaptation? *Animal Behavior* 34, 271–283.

Kanfer, F. H. (1975) Self-management methods. In F. Kanfer and A. Goldstein (eds.), *Helping People Change*. Elmsford, NY: Pergamon, pp. 283–345.

Kant, I. (1793/1960) *Religion Within the Limits of Reason Alone*. T. Green and H. Hucken (trans.). New York: Harper and Row, pp. 15–49.

Kirby, K. N. (1997) Bidding on the future: Evidence against normative discounting of delayed rewards. *Journal of Experimental Psychology: General* 126, 54–70.

Kirby, K. N. and Guastello, B. (2000) Making choices in the context of similar, future choices can increase self-control. Unpublished manuscript.

Kirby, K. N. and Herrnstein, R. J. (1995) Preference reversals due to myopic discounting of delayed reward. *Psychological Science* 6, 83–89.

Kirby, K. N., Petry, N. M., and Bickel, W. K. (1999) Heroin addicts have higher discount rates for delayed rewards than non-drug-using controls. *Journal of Experimental Psychology: General* 128, 78–87.

Klein, B. and Leffler, K. B. (1981) The role of market forces in assuring contractual performance. *Journal of Political Economy* 89, 615–640.

Klein, R. (1989) Introduction to the disorders of the self. In J. F. Masterson and R. Klein (eds.), *Psychotherapy of the Disorders of the Self*. New York: Brunner/ Mazel.

Kohlberg, L. (1963) The development of children's orientations toward a moral order: I. Sequence in the development of moral thought. *Vita Humana* 6, 11–33.

Kuhl, J. (1994) Motivation and volition. In G. d'Ydewalle, P. Bertelson, and P. Eelen (eds.), *International Perspectives on Psychological Science*, vol. 2. Hillsdale, NJ: Erlbaum, pp. 311–340.

Kuhl, J. (1996) Who controls whom when "I control myself"? *Psychological Inquiry* 7, 61–68.

Kyokai, B. D. (1996) *The Teaching of Buddha: The Way of Practice* (893rd ed.). Tokyo: Kosaido Printing Co.

Laibson, D. (1997) Golden eggs and hyperbolic discounting. *Quarterly Journal of Economics* 62, 443–479.

Lassers, E. and Nordan, R. (1978) Separation-individuation of an identical twin. *Adolescent Psychiatry* 6, 469–479.

Lea, S. E. G. (1979) Foraging and reinforcement schedules in the pigeon. *Animal Behavior* 27, 875–886.

Macaulay, S. (1963) Non-contractual relations in business: A preliminary study. *American Sociological Review* 28, 55–67.

Madden, G. J., Chase, P. N., and Joyce, J. H. (1998) Making sense of sensitivity in the human operant literature. *Behavior Analyst* 21, 1–12.

Madden, G. J., Petry, N. M., Badger, G. J., and Bickel, W. K. (1997) Impulsive and self-control choices in opioid-dependent patients and non-drug-using control patients: Drug and monetary rewards. *Experimental and Clinical Psychopharmacology* 5, 256–262.

Mawhinney, T. C. (1982) Maximizing versus matching in people versus pigeons. *Psychological Reports* 50, 267–281.

Maynard Smith, J. (1978) Optimization theory in evolution. *Annual Review of Ecology and Systematics* 9, 31–56.

Mazur, J. E. (1986) Choice between single and multiple delayed reinforcers. *Journal of the Experimental Analysis of Behavior* 46, 67–77.

Mazur, J. E. (1987) An adjusting procedure for studying delayed reinforcement. In M. L. Commons, J. E. Mazur, J. A. Nevin, and H. Rachlin (eds.), *Quantitative Analyses of Behavior V: The Effect of Delay and of Intervening Events on Reinforcement Value*. Hillsdale, NJ: Erlbaum, pp. 55–73.

Mazur, J. E. (1997) Choice, delay, probability, and conditioned reinforcement. *Animal Learning and Behavior* 25, 131–147.

Mazur, J. E. and Logue, A. W. (1978) Choice in a self-control paradigm: Effects of a fading procedure. *Journal of the Experimental Analysis of Behavior* 30, 11–17.

McClennen, E. F. (1990) *Rationality and Dynamic Choice*. New York: Cambridge University Press.

McDiarmid, C. G. and Riling, M. E. (1965) Reinforcement delay and reinforcement rate as determinants of schedule preference. *Psychonomic Science* 2, 195–196.

Metcalfe, J. and Jacobs, W. (1998) Emotional memory: The effects of stress on "cool" and "hot" memory systems. In D. L. Medin (ed.), *The Psychology of Learning and Motivation, Vol. 38: Advances in Research and Theory*. San Diego, CA: Academic Press, pp. 187–222.

Millar, A. and Navarick, D. J. (1984) Self-control and choice in humans: Effects of video game playing as a positive reinforcer. *Learning and Motivation* 15, 203–218.

Mischel, H. N. and Mischel, W. (1983) The development of children's knowledge of self-control strategies. *Child Development* 54, 603–619.

Mourant, J. A. (1967) Pelagius and Pelagianism. In P. Edwards (ed.), *The Encyclopedia of Philosophy*, vol. 6. New York: Macmillan, pp. 78–79.

Navarick, D. J. (1982) Negative reinforcement and choice in humans. *Learning and Motivation* 13, 361–377.

Navon, D. and Gopher, D. (1979) On the economy of the human-processing system. *Psychological Review* 86, 214–255.

Nemiah, J. C. (1977) Alexithymia: Theoretical considerations. *Psychotherapy and Psychosomatics* 28, 199–206.

Offer, A. (1995) Going to war in 1914: A matter of honor? *Politics and Society* 23, 213–240.

———. (2006) The challenge of Affluence: Self-Control and Well-Being the United States (Oxford: Oxford University Press)

Olds, J. (1992) Mapping the mind onto the brain. In Frederick G. Worden and J. P. Swazey (eds.), *The Neurosciences: Paths of Discovery*. Boston: Birkhaeuser, pp. 375–400.

Ostaszewski, P. (1996) The relation between temperament and rate of temporal discounting. *European Journal of Personality* 10, 161–172.

Phelps, E. S. and Pollack, R. A. (1968) On second-best national saving and game-equilibrium growth. *Review of Economic Studies* 35, 185–199.

Plato (1892) *The Dialogues of Plato*. B. Jowett (trans.). New York: Random House, vol. 1. (See also Jowett, 1892/1937.)

Polivy, J. (1998) The effects of behavioral inhibition: Integrating internal cues, cognition, behavior, and affect. *Psychological Inquiry* 9, 181–204.

Rabin, M. (1995) Moral preferences, moral constraints, and self-serving biases. Working Paper 95-241, Department of Economics, University of California at Berkeley.

Rachlin, H. (1985) Pain and behavior. *Behavioral and Brain Sciences* 8, 43–83.

Rachlin, H. (1995a) Self-control: Beyond commitment. *Behavioral and Brain Sciences* 18, 109–159.

Rachlin, H. (1995b) Behavioral economics without anomalies. *Journal of the Experimental Analysis of Behavior* 64, 396–404.

Ragotzy, S. P., Blakely, E., and Poling, A. (1988) Self-control in mentally retarded adolescents: Choice as a function of amount and delay of reinforcement. *Journal of the Experimental Analysis of Behavior* 49, 191–199.

Richards, J. B., Zhang, L., Mitchell, S. H., and deWit, H. (1999) Delay or probability discounting in a model of impulsive behavior: Effect of alcohol. *Journal of the Experimental Analysis of Behavior* 71, 121–143.

Ricoeur, P. (1971) Guilt, ethics, and religion. In J. Meta (ed.), *Moral Evil Under Challenge*. New York: Herder and Herder.

Ryan, R. M., Kuhl, J., and Deci, E. L. (1997) Nature and autonomy: An organizational view of social and neurobiological aspects of self-regulation in behavior and development. *Development and Psychopathology* 9, 701–728.

Samuelson, P. (1976) *Economics* (10th ed.). New York: McGraw-Hill.

Schwartz, B. (1986) *The Battle for Human Nature: Science, Morality and Modern Life*. New York: Norton.

Shiffrin, R. M. and Schneider, W. (1977) Controlled and automatic human information processing: II. Perceptual learning, automatic attending, and a general theory. *Psychological Review* 84, 127–190.

Shull, R., Spear, D., and Bryson, A. (1981) Delay or rate of food delivery as a determiner of response rate. *Journal of the Experimental Analysis of Behavior* 35, 129–143.

Siegel, E. and Rachlin, H. (1996) Soft commitment: Self-control achieved by response persistence. *Journal of the Experimental Analysis of Behavior* 64, 117–128.

Simon, H. (1983) *Reason in Human Affairs*. Stanford, CA: Stanford University Press.

Simon, J. L. (1995) Interpersonal allocation continuous with intertemporal allocation: Binding commitments, pledges, and bequests. *Rationality and Society* 7, 367–430.

Sjoberg, L. and Johnson, T. (1978) Trying to give up smoking: A study of volitional breakdowns. *Addictive Behaviors* 3, 149–167.

Skog, O.-J. (1999) Rationality, irrationality, and addiction. In J. Elster and O.-J. Skog (eds.), *Getting Hooked: Rationality and Addiction*. Cambridge: Cambridge University Press.

Snyderman, M. (1983) Optimal prey selection: Partial selection, delay of reinforcement and self-control. *Behavioral Analysis Letters* 3, 131–147.

Solnick, J., Kaimenberg, C., Eckerman, D., and Wailer, M. (1980) An experimental analysis of impulsivity and impulse control in humans. *Learning and Motivation* 2, 61–77.

Sonuga-Barke, E. J. S., Lea, S. E. G., and Webley, P. (1989) Children's choice: Sensitivity to changes in reinforcer density. *Journal of the Experimental Analysis of Behavior* 51, 185–197.

Sorensen, R. A. (1992) *Thought Experiments*. New York: Oxford University Press.

Spealman, R. (1979) Behavior maintained by termination of a schedule of self-administered cocaine. *Science* 204, 1231–1233.

Sperry, R. W. (1984) Consciousness, personal identity and the divided brain. *Neuropsychologia* 22, 661–673.

Stahler, F. (1998) *Economic Games and Strategic Behavior: Theory and Application*. Cheltenham, UK: Elgar.

Stevenson, M. K. (1986) A discounting model for decisions with delayed positive or negative outcomes. *Journal of Experimental Psychology: General* 115, 131–154.

Strotz, R. H. (1956) Myopia and inconsistency in dynamic utility maximization. *Review of Economic Studies* 23, 166–180.

Sully, J. (1884) *Outlines of psychology*. New York: Appleton.

Sunstein, C. R. (1995) Problems with rules. *California Law Review* 83, 953–1030.

Szekely, J. (1980) *Twins on Twins*. New York: Potter. (Probably indexed under its photographers, Kathryn Abbe and Frances Gill.)

Taylor, C. (1982) The diversity of goods. In A. Sen and B. Williams (eds.), *Utilitarianism and Beyond*. Cambridge and London: Cambridge University Press, pp. 129–144.

Vanderveldt, J. H. and Odenwald, R. P. (1952) *Psychiatry and Catholicism*. New York: McGraw-Hill.

Vaughan, W., Jr. and Herrnstein, R. J. (1987) Stability, melioration, and natural selection. In L. Green and J. H. Kagel (eds.), *Advances in Behavioral Economics*, vol. 1. Norwood, NJ: Ablex, pp. 185–215.

Vuchinich, R. E. and Simpson, C. A. (1998) Hyperbolic temporal discounting in social drinkers and problem drinkers. *Experimental and Clinical Psychopharmacology* 6, 292–305.

Weber, M. (1925/1964) *The Theory of Social and Economic Organization*. New York: Free Press.

Zajonc, R. B. (1980) Feeling and thinking: Preferences need no inferences. *American Psychologist* 35, 151–175.

PART II: MODES OF REASONING

Section 3: Deductive Reasoning

Chapter 9: Logical Approaches to Human Deductive Reasoning[1]

LANCE J. RIPS

The idea that formal logic bears a close relationship to human reasoning is extremely controversial within cognitive science. For example, Wason and Johnson-Laird (1972: 245) concluded their influential study of reasoning by stating that "only gradually did we realize first that there was no existing formal calculus which correctly modeled our subjects' inferences, and second that no purely formal system would succeed." This kind of opposition is based on evidence that subjects' judgments about an argument sometimes depart from the answer that the experimenter derived by translating the argument into some system of logic and assessing its correctness within that system. The strength of this evidence, however, clearly depends on the system the investigator uses. If the investigator's conception is too narrow, what is classified as nonlogical behavior may turn out logical after all. To evaluate the evidence, we need some clear idea of what logic has to offer.

Most cognitive theories that contain a logic-like component (e.g., Braine 1978; Johnson-Laird 1975; Osherson 1974, 1975, 1976; Rips 1983) are based on the notion of proof, particularly the "natural deduction" proofs originally devised by Gentzen (1935/1969) and Jaskowski (1934). The basic notion is familiar to anyone who has taken a high school mathematics course: If you want to know whether a particular argument is deductively correct, you can find out by taking its premises as given and then trying to derive its conclusion by applying a specified set of rules. If a proof or a derivation is possible, then the argument is deductively correct; the conclusion is *deducible* from the premises. We also can say, by extension, that the argument as a whole is deducible. The left column of Table 1 summarizes this terminology.

Contemporary logical theory supplements the notions of formal proof and deducibility with a twin "semantic" system whose central concepts are the truth of a sentence and the validity of an argument (Tarski 1936/1956). In the semantic system the deductive correctness of an argument is a matter of the relationship between the truth of the premises and the truth of the conclusion. In particular, an argument is deductively correct if and only if the conclusion is true in all states of affairs in which the premises are true. In this case, the conclusion is *(semantically) entailed* by the premises, and the entire argument is *valid*, as shown in the right column in Table 1. (We also can speak of a single sentence as valid if it is true in all states of affairs. This is, of course, a stronger notion of semantic correctness for a sentence than the simple truth of a sentence in the *actual* state of affairs; it is the difference between *Insects have six legs*, which is true in our present state but false in a logically possible state in which they have eight, and *Six is less than eight*, which is true in all possible states.)

Reproduced with permission from Rips, L. (1994) *The Psychology of Proof* (chapters 2, 4, and 5). Cambridge, MA: MIT Press.

Table 1: Summary of Logical Terminology

	Proof Theory	*Semantics*
Correctness of the relation of the conclusion to the premises	deducibility (= conclusion provable from the premises)	semantic entailment (= conclusion true in all states of affairs in which the premises are true)
Correctness of an argument	deducibility	validity

In this dual setup, then, we have two criteria of deductive correctness: deducibility and validity. We might hope that these two criteria coincide in confirming exactly the same set of arguments. For simple logical systems – for example, classical sentential and predicate logic – they do coincide; such systems are said to be *complete*. In these systems, it doesn't matter which criterion we use, as long as all we are interested in is determining which arguments are the correct ones. However, there are three reasons for keeping both criteria in mind. First, the proof-theoretic description is computationally relevant: The description contains rules that yield a finite proof of a deducible argument. By contrast, the semantic description is computationally independent, since the criterion it gives for validity does not depend on there being any finite procedure for assessing it. Second, there are more complex logical systems in which the criteria *don't* coincide – incomplete systems in which some entailments are not deducible. Third, according to an intriguing theory put forth by Johnson-Laird (e.g., 1983; Johnson-Laird and Byrne 1991), it is the semantic rather than the proof-theoretic criterion that is important in human reasoning (contrary to the other cognitive theories cited earlier).

Of course, changing the deduction rules of a logical system (or changing the way in which truth is assigned to propositions) can alter which arguments are deemed deductively correct. Logicians and philosophers of logic have in fact proposed a variety of plausible systems that differ in the elements of natural language that come in for formal treatment, and in the analysis that they give these elements. Current logics are available for concepts such as knowledge and belief, temporal precedence and succession, causality, obligation and permission, and logical necessity and possibility. For each of these concepts, there are alternative logics differing in exactly which arguments are deductively correct. Psychologists have almost completely overlooked this variety, tacitly assuming a single standard of deductive correctness. This means that,

when subjects' judgments have failed to conform to the standard, psychologists have been too ready to label them illogical, or, at least, to assume that logic is of no help in understanding them.

Formal Proof

At the most general level, a formal proof is a finite sequence of sentences $(s_1, s_2, \ldots, s_k)$ in which each sentence is either a premise, an axiom of the logical system, or a sentence that follows from preceding sentences by one of the system's rules. An argument is deducible in the system if there is a proof whose final sentence, s_k, is the conclusion of the argument. For example, consider a system that includes modus ponens among its inference rules. Modus ponens stipulates that the sentence Q follows from sentences of the form IF P THEN Q and P. Thus, (1) is deducible in this system.

(1) IF Calvin deposits 50 cents THEN Calvin will get a coke.

Calvin deposits 50 cents.

Calvin will get a coke.

The proof consists simply of the sequence of three sentences in the order listed above, since (a) each sentence in the sequence either is a premise or follows from preceding sentences by modus ponens and (b) the final sentence is the conclusion of the argument. (Capital letters are used for *IF* and *THEN* to mark the fact that these words are parts of the proof system and are not necessarily equivalent in meaning or force to English *if . . . then . . .*).

In this stripped-down system, we also could prove the deducibility of (2).

(2) IF Calvin deposits 50 cents THEN Calvin gets a coke.

IF Calvin gets a coke THEN Calvin will buy a burger.

Calvin deposits 50 cents.

Calvin will buy a burger.

In this case, a proof involves two applications of modus ponens, as (3) shows.

(3) a. IF Calvin deposits 50 cents THEN Calvin gets a coke. — Premise
    b. Calvin deposits 50 cents. — Premise
    c. Calvin gets a coke. — Modus ponens
    d. IF Calvin gets a coke THEN Calvin will buy a burger. — Premise
    e. Calvin will buy a burger. — Modus ponens

Sentences (3a), (3b), and (3d) are premises of argument (2), and sentences (3c) and (3e) are derived by modus ponens from preceding ones.

To prove a more diverse set of arguments, we will clearly need greater deductive power. We can get it, within this framework, by introducing axioms or additional inference rules. An *axiomatic* (or *logistic*) proof system contains a set of axioms and usually has modus ponens as its only rule. *Natural-deduction* systems contain several distinct inference rules and eliminate axioms. The two kinds of system can be equivalent in proving exactly the same set of theorems, but they possess rival advantages and disadvantages in other respects. On the one hand, axiomatic systems sometimes have an advantage over natural-deduction systems when we must derive characteristics *about* the proof system itself (though natural-deduction systems have interesting metatheoretic properties of their own – see Fine 1985a, 1985b; Gentzen 1935/1969; Prawitz 1965; Ungar 1992). On the other hand, it is usually easier to prove theorems *within* a natural-deduction system, and consequently most elementary textbooks on logic make use of natural deduction as a main proof method (e.g., Copi 1954; Thomason 1970). For the same reason, natural deduction has been the method of choice in psychological models, and I'll concentrate on versions of natural deduction systems here.

Natural-deduction methods simplify proofs by permitting us to make other temporary assumptions or suppositions. As an example of how suppositions can simplify a proof, consider the argument in (4):

(4) IF Calvin deposits 50 cents THEN Calvin gets a coke.

Calvin does not get a coke.
_____
Calvin does not deposit 50 cents.

An informal justification of (4) might look like this:

(5) a. According to the first premise, if Calvin deposits 50 cents then Calvin gets a coke.
    b. Suppose, contrary to the conclusion, that Calvin *does* deposit 50 cents.
    c. Then (by modus ponens), Calvin would get a coke.
    d. But the second premise tells us that Calvin does not get a coke.
    e. Hence, Calvin must not have deposited 50 cents.

This justification embodies a typical *reductio ad absurdum* (or NOT Introduction) pattern: In (5b) we assume temporarily the opposite of the conclusion we wish to prove and then show that this leads to contradictory information. Because the supposition could not hold, the conclusion itself must follow from the premises. In other words, (5) tacitly appeals to an inference rule stating that if a supposition leads to a pair of contradictory sentences then the negation of that supposition must follow. This *reductio* rule, together with modus ponens, is sufficient to show that (4) is deducible.

Natural-deduction systems formalize this method of making suppositions in the service of a proof. Within these systems, we can introduce suppositions freely as lines of a proof in order to draw further inferences from them. Before the proof is complete, however, we must apply a rule that resolves or "discharges" the supposition, because the conclusion of the proof must depend on the premises alone and not on any of the arbitrary assumptions we have made along the way. In (5), for example, the supposition made in line b is resolved when we conclude that the supposition could not in fact hold (because of the contradiction).

To state this a bit more systematically, we can use the term *domain* to refer to a designated set of lines of the proof that are associated with a supposition. Then no supposition (apart from the premises) can include the conclusion of the proof in its domain. In (5) the domain of the premises comprises lines a, d, and e, and the domain of the supposition in line b is just lines b and c. Figure 1 illustrates these domains. In the figure, solid lines indicate which sentences are used in deducing others (e.g., line c is deduced by modus ponens from lines a and b), and dashed lines indicate the scope of the domains. The premises in lines a and d are connected by dashed

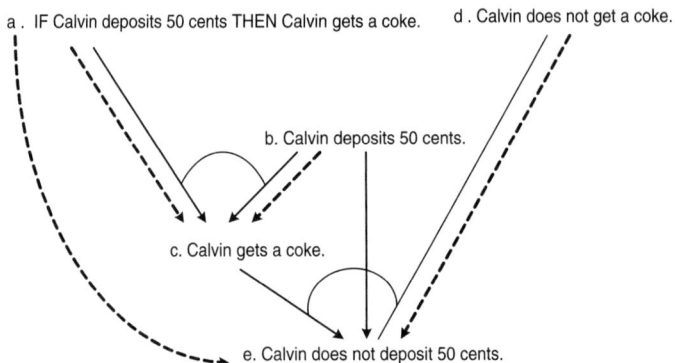

Figure 1. A proof diagram for the argument:

IF Calvin deposits 50 cents THEN Calvin gets a coke.

Calvin does not get a coke.

Calvin does not deposit 50 cents.

lines to the conclusion e, and the supposition in line b is connected by a dashed line to c. One domain can be subordinated to another: The domain of b and c is a subdomain of the premises' domain. A sentence can be said to *hold* in the domain in which it appears, and this means that deduction rules that apply to the domain can use it freely. In the systems for classical sentential and predicate logic, sentences also hold in all subdomains of their domain. According to this system, for example, line a holds throughout the proof, including the subdomain. (Of course, line c holds only in the subdomain.) Other logical systems, however, place special restrictions on which sentences hold in subdomains.

Search

Blindly applying logical rules is a poor strategy for even simple deduction problems. As long as the rules are stated in the unconstrained form of most elementary logic textbooks, they will not automatically lead to a proof in an acceptable amount of time. Because some rules produce infinite sets of irrelevant sentences, finding a short proof by randomly applying rules would be a matter of sheer luck. If deductive reasoning is anything like a practical process, then there must be better ways to direct the search for a proof. The constraints on proofs that investigators in computer science have found differ in how encompassing they are. At one extreme, there are general methods that are applicable to all proof-finding situations; at the other, there are special-purpose heuristics that take advantage of particular types of rules or lines in the

proof. It turns out that the heuristics are more important for psychological purposes.

One innovation due to Newell, Shaw, and Simon (1957) was to apply the system's proof rules in a backward direction. The idea was to keep the rules aimed in the right direction by applying them only when needed to prove the conclusion. Applied in this way, modus ponens takes a conclusion Q as input and checks for a corresponding assertion *IF P THEN Q;* if such an assertion is available, the rule then tries to prove P. If it succeeds, then Q must follow. In this case, P serves as a *subgoal* for Q. I will call these goal-to-subgoal procedures *backward rules.* We can contrast these with *forward rules* that operate in the more typical premise-to-conclusion direction. As a forward rule, modus ponens takes as input the sentences P and *IF P THEN* Q, and it adds the sentence Q to the proof.

It is easy to see that certain deduction rules will work in a reasonable way only in the backward direction. For example, the natural deduction rule called AND Introduction enables the conclusion P AND Q to be added to a proof whenever the proof already contains P and Q separately. There is no doubt about the validity of this inference, but applying it in the forward direction yields infinitely many new sentences, most of which will be irrelevant to the proof at hand. From P and Q, we can derive P AND Q; from P and P AND Q, we can then derive P AND (P AND Q); from P and P AND (P AND Q), we can derive P AND (P AND (P AND Q)); and so on, mindlessly. Limiting AND Introduction to use as a backward rule reigns in this unlimited productivity.

Other rules, however, can apply in the forward direction without the same runaway consequences. Modus ponens, for example, applies just once to sentences of the form *P* and *IF P THEN Q* to yield the result *Q*. Because modus ponens does not apply to its own output, it will yield just a single new sentence for each pair of input sentences (provided that we have a way to ensure that it doesn't repeatedly apply to the same pair). Thus, we can use modus ponens in a forward direction as soon as its input conditions are met. Having a forward rule like this, however, doesn't preclude having a backward version, too. In the context of certain proof systems, it is sensible to include backward modus ponens, in addition to the forward version just described. There may be situations, for instance, where the system needs to prove Q, has *IF P THEN Q* as an assertion, but does not yet have *P*. In this case, it may be necessary to propose *P* as a subgoal in order to finish the proof.

A Theory for Sentential Reasoning

The rest of this chapter outlines a theory for sentential reasoning along natural-deduction lines and demonstrates that the theory can explain data from a reasoning experiment in which subjects evaluated the deducibility of arguments.

The central notion in the theory will be that of a mental proof. I assume that when people confront a problem that calls for deduction they attempt to solve it by generating in working memory a set of sentences linking the premises or givens of the problem to the conclusion or solution. Each link in this network embodies an inference rule that the individual recognizes as intuitively sound and that provides some control on search. Taken together, this network of sentences then provides a bridge between the premises and the conclusion that explains why the conclusion follows. Of course, people are not always successful in producing a mental proof of this sort. They may not possess or may not be able to apply an inference rule that is crucial for a particular proof. Resource limitations – for example, capacity restrictions in working memory – may keep them from completing a proof. They may even possess nonstandard rules of inference that lead them to conclusions not sanctioned in classical predicate logic. Nevertheless, the claim is that people will at least *attempt* a mental proof during their problem-solving process.

In this chapter I explore the idea of mental proof by asking how *sentential* proofs are produced. But of course this is only one of the challenges that a theory of deduction faces. We don't want to stop with sentential reasoning, because much of deduction's power depends on its ability to bind variables. Although developing a full theory of quantificational reasoning is beyond the scope of this chapter, interested readers can find such an extension in Rips (1994, 1999, 2000).

Overview of the Core Theory

The basic inference system consists of a set of deduction rules that construct mental proofs in the system's working memory. If we present the system with an argument to evaluate, the system will use those rules in an attempt to construct an internal proof of the conclusion from the premises. If we present the system with a group of premises and ask for entailments of those premises, the system will use the rules to generate proofs of possible conclusions. The model comes up with a proof by first storing the input premises (and conclusion, if any) in working memory. The rules then scan these memory contents to determine whether any inferences are possible. If so, the model adds the newly deduced sentences to memory, scans the updated configuration, makes further deductions, and so on, until a proof has been found or no more rules apply. Thus, the inference routines carry out much of the work in the basic system, deciding when deductions are possible, adding propositions to working memory, and keeping the procedure moving toward a solution. In what follows, I will refer to the system as PSYCOP (short for Psychology of Proof). The system was implemented as a PROLOG program for personal computers.

PSYCOP's strategy in evaluating arguments is to work from the outside in, using forward rules to draw implications from the premises and using backward rules to create subgoals based on the conclusion. The forward rules operate in a breadth-first way, and create a web of new assertions. The backward rules operate depth-first: PSYCOP pursues a given chain of backward reasoning until it finds assertions that satisfy the required subgoals or until it runs out of backward rules to apply. In the first case, the proof is complete, because there is a logical pathway that connects the premises to the conclusion. In the second case, PSYCOP must backtrack to an earlier choice point where some alternative sub-goal presented itself and try to satisfy it instead. If all the subgoals fail, PSYCOP gives up. In situations in which PSYCOP is expected to produce conclusions rather than to evaluate them, it can use only its forward rules to complete the task, because there is no conclusion-goal to trigger the backward rules.

Assumptions about Memory

The PSYCOP model possesses a standard memory architecture that is divided into long-term and working-memory components. The two systems are similar in structure, the main difference between them being working memory's smaller capacity. Both memory systems contain internal sentences connected by labeled links, as in earlier memory models proposed by Anderson (1983), Collins and Loftus (1975), and others. We can examine the main features of both memory systems by returning to the proof in Figure 1.

The links connecting memory sentences are probably of a large variety of types, but there are two that are especially relevant to the deduction process. Let us call them *deduction links* and *dependency links*. The deduction links – represented as solid arrows in the figure – run from memory sentences to any other sentences that they immediately entail. In Figure 1, for example, there are deduction links that connect the sentences *IF Calvin deposits 50 cents THEN Calvin gets a coke* and *Calvin deposits 50 cents* to the sentence *Calvin gets a coke*, indicating that PSYCOP deduced the latter sentence from the two former sentences in a single inference step. Each deduction link is the product of a particular rule (modus ponens, in this example). In cases like this, two sentences combine to produce a third. To indicate that sentences like these are jointly responsible for an inference, I use an arc to connect the deduction links emanating from them, as in Figure 1. Thus, deduction links give us a record of the individual steps in a derivation, each link (or set of arc-connected links) corresponding to the application of a single deduction rule.

The dependency links in memory (dashed lines) represent the way the sentences depend on premises or suppositions in the mental proof. As we've already noted, the dependency link from sentence b to c in Figure 1 represents the fact that c belongs to supposition b's domain. This is important because subdomain sentences like c usually do not hold in their superdomains, and

confusion about a sentence's domain can lead to logical inconsistencies.

We assume, of course, that working memory has a limited capacity. If mental proofs exceed this capacity, a person will usually have to recompute and recode information in order to avoid making mistakes. This is in line with demonstrations by Hitch and Baddeley (1976) and by Gilhooly, Logie, Wetherick, and Wynn (1993) that a working-memory load from an unrelated task can produce errors on deduction problems.

Assumptions about Inference Rules

Exactly which inferences are immediate or primitive is an empirical matter, and so it is not possible to enumerate them before the evidence is in. Nevertheless, theoretical considerations and previous experiments suggest some plausible candidates for rules to add to PSYCOP's repertoire. Table 2 lists some of the ones that are needed to prove the arguments from an experiment on reasoning, to be reported in the next section. The rules appear in Table 2 in their conventional argument form (on the left side of the table) and then in the form of inference routines (on the right). These rules come from the theories of Braine, Reiser, and Rumain (1984), Johnson-Laird (1975), Osherson (1975), Rips (1983), Sperber and Wilson (1986), and others. (Not all rules from these sources necessarily appear in the table. The names given these rules are not standard ones in all cases, but they may help in keeping the rules in mind.)

Many of the inference patterns embodied in the rules of Table 2 could be derived in alternative ways. For example, we can capture Disjunctive Modus Ponens – the inference from *IF P OR Q THEN R* and *P* to *R* – by means of the regular modus ponens rule (IF Elimination) together with OR Introduction. Psychologically, however, Disjunctive Modus Ponens appears simpler than OR Introduction. In research to be discussed later, I estimated the probability that subjects correctly applied each of these rules when it was appropriate for them to do so in evaluating a sample of sentential arguments. According to this measure, subjects applied the Disjunctive Modus Ponens rule on 100 percent of relevant trials, but applied OR Introduction on only 20 percent. If these estimates are correct, the subjects could not have been using OR Introduction to achieve the effect of Disjunctive Modus Ponens. Thus, it seems reasonable to

Table 2: Examples of PSYCOP's Inference Routines

Forward Rules:

Forward IF Elimination

IF P THEN Q
P

Q

(a) If a sentence of the form IF P THEN Q holds in some domain D,
(b) and P holds in D.
(c) and Q does not yet hold in D,
(d) then add Q to D.

Forward DeMorgan (NOT over AND)

NOT(P AND Q)

(NOT P) OR (NOT Q)

(a) If a sentence of the form NOT (P AND Q) holds in some domain D,
(b) and (NOT P) OR (NOT Q) does not yet hold in D,
(c) then add (NOT P) OR (NOT Q) to D.

Forward Disjunctive Syllogism

P OR Q
NOT Q

P

(a) If a sentence of the form P OR Q holds in some domain D,
(b)   then if NOT P holds in D and Q does not yet hold in D,
(c)   then add Q to D.
(d)   Else, if NOT Q holds in D and P does not yet hold in D,
(e)   then add P to D.

Forward Disjunctive Modus Ponens

IF P OR Q THEN R
P

R

(a) If a sentence of the form IF P OR Q THEN R holds in some domain D,
(b) and P or Q also holds in D,
(c) and R does not yet hold in D,
(d) then add R to D.

Forward AND Elimination

P AND Q

P

(a) If a sentence of the form P AND Q holds in some domain D,
(b) then if P does not yet hold in D,
(c)   then add P to D,
(d) and if Q does not yet hold in D,
(e)   then add Q to D.

Backward Rules:

Backward IF Elimination

IF P THEN Q
P

Q

(a) Set D to domain of current goal.
(b) Set Q to current goal.
(c) If the sentence IF P THEN Q holds in D,
(d) and D does not yet contain subgoal P,
(e) then add P to the list of subgoals.

Backward DeMorgan (NOT over AND)

NOT(P AND Q)

(NOT P) OR (NOT Q)

(a) Set D to domain of current goal.
(b) If current goal is of the form (NOT P) OR (NOT Q),
(c) and NOT (P AND Q) is a subformula of a sentence that holds in D,
(d) then add NOT(P AND Q) to the list of subgoals.

Backward Disjunctive Syllogism

P OR Q
NOT Q

P

(a) Set D to domain of current goal.
(b) Set Q to current goal.
(c) If a sentence of the form P OR Q or Q OR P holds in D,
(d) and NOT P is a subformula of a sentence that holds in D,
(e) and D does not yet contain the subgoal NOT P,
(f) then add NOT P to the list of subgoals.

(continued)

193

Table 2 (*continued*)

Backward Rules:

Backward Disjunctive Modus Ponens

IF P OR Q THEN R
P

R

(a) Set D to domain of current goal.
(b) Set R to current goal.
(c) If the sentence IF P OR Q THEN R holds in D,
(d) and D does not yet contain the subgoal P,
(e) then add P to the list of subgoals.
(f) If the subgoal in (e) fails,
(g) and D does not yet contain the subgoal Q,
(h) then add Q to the list of subgoals.

Backward AND Elimination

P AND Q

P

(a) Set D to domain of current goal.
(b) Set P to current goal.
(c) If the sentence P AND Q is a subformula of a sentence that holds in D,
(d) and D does not yet contain the subgoal P AND Q,
(e) add P AND Q to the list of subgoals.
(f) If the subgoal in (e) fails,
(g) and the sentence Q AND P is a subformula of a sentence that holds in D,
(h) and D does not yet contain the subgoal Q AND P,
(i) then add Q AND P to the list of subgoals.

Backward AND Introduction

P
Q

P AND Q

(a) Set D to domain of current goal.
(b) If current goal is of the form P AND Q,
(c) and D does not yet contain the subgoal P,
(d) then add the subgoal of proving P in D to the list of subgoals.
(e) If the subgoal in (d) succeeds,
(f) and D does not yet contain the subgoal Q,
(g) then add the subgoal of proving Q in D to the list of subgoals.

Backward OR Introduction

P

P OR Q

(a) Set D to domain of current goal.
(b) If current goal is of the form P OR Q,
(c) and D does not yet contain the subgoal P,
(d) then add the subgoal of proving P in D to the list of subgoals.
(e) If the subgoal in (d) fails,
(f) and D does not yet contain subgoal Q,
(g) then add the subgoal of proving Q in D to the list of subgoals.

Backward NOT Introduction

+P
.

.
Q AND (NOT Q)

NOT P

(a) Set D to domain of current goal.
(b) If current goal is of the form NOT P,
(c) and P is a subformula of the premises or conclusion,
(d) and Q is an atomic subformula of the premises or conclusion,
(e) and neither D nor its superdomains nor its immediate subdomains contain suppositions P and subgoal Q AND (NOT Q),
(f) then set up a subdomain of D, D′, with supposition P,
(g) and add the subgoal of proving Q AND (NOT Q) in D′ to the list of subgoals.

Backward OR Elimination

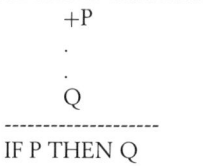

          (a) Set D to domain of current goal.
          (b) Set R to current goal.
          (c) If a sentence of the form P OR Q holds in D,
          (d) and both P and Q are subformulas or negations of subformulas of the
               premises or conclusion,
          (e) and R is a subformula or negation of a subformula of the premises or
               conclusion,
          (f) and neither D nor its superdomains nor its immediate subdomains
               contain supposition P and subgoal R,
          (g) and neither D not its superdomains nor its immediate subdomains
               contain supposition Q and subgoal R,
          (h) then set up a subdomain of D, D′, with supposition P,
          (i) and add the subgoal of proving R in D′ to the list of subgoals.
          (j) If the subgoal in (i) succeeds,
          (k) then set up another subdomain of D, D, with supposition Q,
          (l) and add the subgoal of proving R in D to the list of subgoals.

Backward IF Introduction

          +P
           .
           .
           Q

    IF P THEN Q

          (a) Set D to domain of current goal.
          (b) If current goal is of the form IF P THEN Q,
          (c) and neither D nor its superdomains not any of its immediate
               subdomains contain supposition P and subgoal Q,
          (d) and IF P THEN Q is a subformula of the premises or conclusion,
          (e) then set up a domain of D, D′, with supposition P,
          (f) and add the subgoal of proving Q in D′ to the list of subgoals.

suppose that Disjunctive Modus Ponens functions as a primitive inference rule on its own, despite its logical redundancy. Braine et al. (1984) and Sperber and Wilson (1986) present further reasons for favoring Disjunctive Modus Ponens as a primitive.

Psychological models of deduction differ in which rules they consider to be the primitive ones. These differences are not merely notational, since some arguments are provable in one system but not in others. But the choice of rules is not the most important point of comparison between models. This is because most investigators have been cautious about claiming that the particular rules incorporated in their models exhaust the primitive ones. (The work by Braine 1978 and Braine et al. 1984 is an exception.) The usual claim (Osherson 1975; Rips 1983) is that the incorporated rules are a subset of the primitive ones. It is also worth noting that the evidence on the status of a rule is sometimes ambiguous, particularly if primitive rules can vary in how easy they are to deploy. It is not always clear, for example, whether subjects are proving a given argument by means of two very efficient primitives or by means of one more global but not-so-efficient primitive. The problem becomes even more complex if we allow for individual differences and for the learning or the compiling of new primitive rules. For these reasons, it seems wise to concentrate on other criteria in compar-

ing and evaluating deduction systems. In developing PSYCOP, I have tried to include most of the rules that earlier models have taken as primitive, so the model's current repertoire is fairly large. (See Rips 1994 for the full set of rules.)

Notice that the backward rules in Table 2 are stated in a way that appears much less general than their usual formulation in logic texts. One reason for this is that many of these rules can lead to infinite backward searches unless they are constrained. Take the case of the rule called AND Elimination, which allows us to deduce P (or Q) from the sentence P AND Q. If we use AND Elimination backward on goal P to produce subgoal P AND Q, then we should be able to use it again on P AND Q to obtain the subgoal (P AND Q) AND R, and so on. Perhaps the most reasonable solution, under these circumstances, is to restrict the rules so that no subgoal can be produced that isn't already a "part" of the current set of assertions. To pin down this notion of part more precisely, let us use the term *subformula* to denote any consecutive string of symbols in a sentence (including the entire sentence) that would also qualify as a grammatical sentence on its own. Thus, *Calvin gets a coke AND Calvin buys a burger* is a subformula of *IF Calvin deposits 50 cents THEN (Calvin gets a coke AND Calvin buys a burger)*, but *(Calvin gets a coke AND Calvin buys a burger) AND Calvin deposits 50 cents* is not. The restriction in question prohibits a rule from pursuing a subgoal that is more complex than the premises or conclusion of the problem it is working on.

Assumptions about Control

The rules in Table 2 leave room for some further decisions about the order in which PSYCOP should deploy them. We need to specify, for example, when PSYCOP should apply forward rules and when backward rules, as well as which rules in each class it should try first. In making these choices, we need to consider the internal characteristics of the rules. Clearly, PSYCOP can apply its forward rules in a nearly automatic way, because their self-constraining nature requires little external monitoring and will never lead to infinite forward searches. It therefore seems reasonable to activate them as soon as possible whenever a triggering assertion appears in the database. Backward rules, however, present more of a control problem. Although the constraints we have placed on the backward rules keep them from producing infinite loops, they nevertheless have the potential to produce extremely inefficient searches. This means that we might want to adopt a flexible approach to using these rules, allowing the system to profit from heuristic advice about which subgoals to follow up.

Currently, when PSYCOP has to evaluate an argument it begins by applying its forward rules to the premises until no new inferences are forthcoming. It then considers the conclusion of the argument, checking to see whether the conclusion is already among the assertions. If so, the proof is complete; if not, it will treat the conclusion as a goal and attempt to apply one of the backward rules. PSYCOP tests each of the backward rules to see if it is appropriate in this situation, and it does this in an order that is initially determined by the complexity of the backward rules. The idea is that simple rules should be tried first, since less work will have been lost if these rules turn out to lead to dead ends. PSYCOP prefers backward rules that can be satisfied by a single subgoal and that do not require new subdomains; thus, it tries Backward IF Elimination and similar rules first. If none of these rules is applicable, it next tries Backward AND Introduction, which requires two subgoals to be satisfied but which does not use subdomains. Finally, it will resort to the subdomain-creating rules IF Introduction, OR Elimination, and NOT Introduction.

Once a backward rule has been activated and has produced a subgoal, PSYCOP checks whether the new subgoal matches an assertion. If not, PSYCOP places the subgoal on an agenda, reruns the forward rules in case some assertions were added, and repeats its cycle. In principle, PSYCOP could try the subgoals on the agenda in any order – for instance, according to a heuristic measure of how "easy" these subgoals seem. In the absence of other instructions, however, it will follow a depth-first search; that is, it first tries to fulfill the conclusion-goal, then a subgoal to the conclusion that a backward rule has proposed, then a sub-subgoal to the first subgoal, and so on. If it reaches a subgoal to which no backward rules apply, it backtracks to the preceding subgoal and tries to fulfill it another way via a different backward rule. There is also a provision in PSYCOP for a bound on the depth of its search, limiting the length of a chain of subgoals to some fixed number. Finally, PSYCOP halts with a proof if it has found assertions to fulfill all the subgoals along some path to the conclusion. It halts with no proof if it can complete none of the subgoal paths.

An Example

As an example of how the system operates, consider (6) – a simple argument that it can evaluate using the rules in Table 2.

(6)   IF Betty is in Little Rock THEN Ellen is in Hammond.

Phoebe is in Tucson AND Sandra is in Memphis.

IF Betty is in Little Rock THEN (Ellen is in Hammond AND Sandra is in Memphis).

At the start of this problem, working memory will contain just these three sentences, as shown in Figure 2a. The conclusion appears with a question mark to indicate its status as a goal, and the premises end with periods to show that they are assertions. To begin, PSYCOP notices that the second premise is a conjunction and is therefore subject to Forward AND Elimination. Applying this rule creates two new sentences, *Phoebe is in Tucson* and *Sandra is in Memphis*, which it stores in working memory (Figure 2b).

At this stage of the proof no other forward rules apply, but it is possible to begin some work in the backward direction. Since the conclusion (and goal) of the argument is a conditional, Backward IF Introduction is appropriate here. According to this rule (Table 2), we

a.

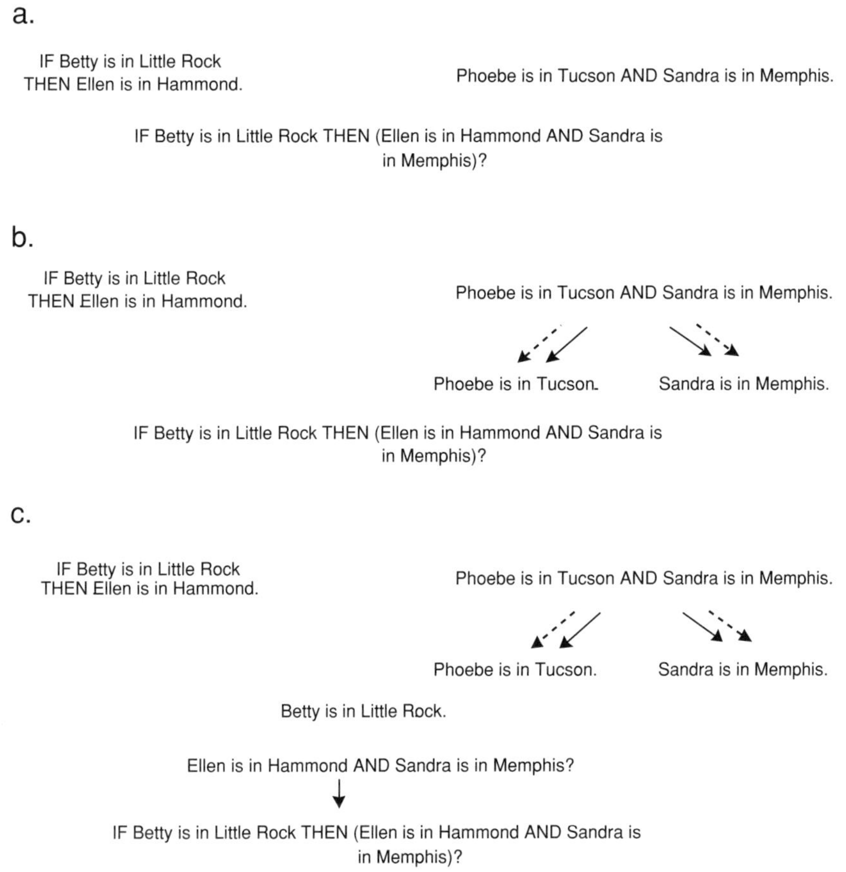

IF Betty is in Little Rock
THEN Ellen is in Hammond.   Phoebe is in Tucson AND Sandra is in Memphis.

IF Betty is in Little Rock THEN (Ellen is in Hammond AND Sandra is
in Memphis)?

b.

IF Betty is in Little Rock
THEN Ellen is in Hammond.   Phoebe is in Tucson AND Sandra is in Memphis.

Phoebe is in Tucson.   Sandra is in Memphis.

IF Betty is in Little Rock THEN (Ellen is in Hammond AND Sandra is
in Memphis)?

c.

IF Betty is in Little Rock
THEN Ellen is in Hammond.   Phoebe is in Tucson AND Sandra is in Memphis.

Phoebe is in Tucson.   Sandra is in Memphis.

Betty is in Little Rock.

Ellen is in Hammond AND Sandra is in Memphis?

IF Betty is in Little Rock THEN (Ellen is in Hammond AND Sandra is
in Memphis)?

Figure 2. PSYCOP's proof of the argument:

IF Betty is in Little Rock THEN Ellen is in Hammond.

Phoebe is in Tucson AND Sandra is in Memphis.

IF Betty is in Little Rock THEN (Ellen is in Hammond AND Sandra is in Memphis).

should try to deduce the conclusion by setting up a new subdomain whose supposition is *Betty is in Little Rock* (the antecedent of the conditional conclusion) and attempting to prove *Ellen is in Hammond AND Sandra is in Memphis* in that subdomain. Figure 2c shows this supposition and the resulting subgoal in the developing memory structure. (The structure represents subdomains by means of the pattern of dashed arrows, as mentioned earlier.) Because we are now assuming both *Betty is in Little Rock* and *IF Betty is in Little Rock THEN Ellen is in Hammond*, the forward IF Elimination (i.e., modus ponens) rule will automatically deduce *Ellen is in Hammond* (Figure 2d). However, we must still satisfy the subgoal of proving *Ellen is in Hammond AND Sandra is in Memphis*. The relevant rule is, of course, Backward AND Introduction, which advises us to set up subgoals corresponding to the two halves of this conjunction. The first of

these, *Ellen is in Hammond*, is easy to fulfill, since it matches the assertion that we have just produced. (Double lines are used in the figure to represent the match between assertion and subgoal.) The second subgoal can also be fulfilled by an earlier assertion. Satisfying these two subgoals satisfies the conjunction, and this in turn satisfies the main goal of the problem. Thus, Figure 2e is a complete proof of argument (6).

PSYCOP's core system fulfills some of the criteria for an adequate deduction theory in psychology. Even with the limited rule set in Table 2, PSYCOP can prove an infinite set of theorems in sentential logic. Of course, we also need to be careful that the model isn't too productive, generating irrelevant inferences when it should be focusing more narrowly on the task at hand. The combination of forward and backward rules, however, helps eliminate irrelevancies while ensuring that the model will be able

d.

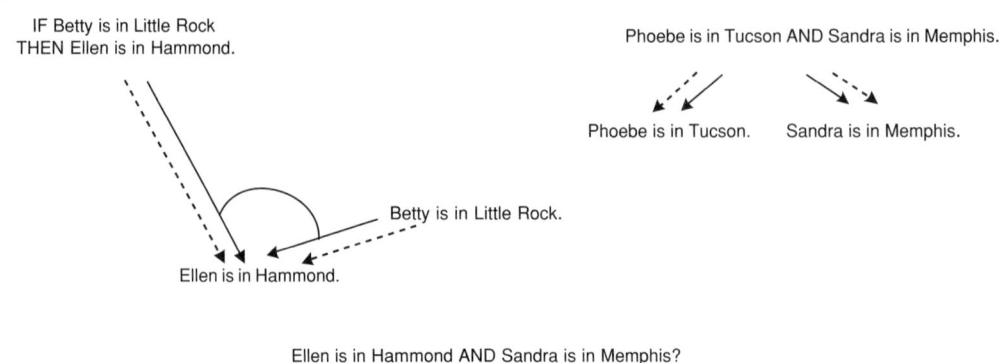

e.

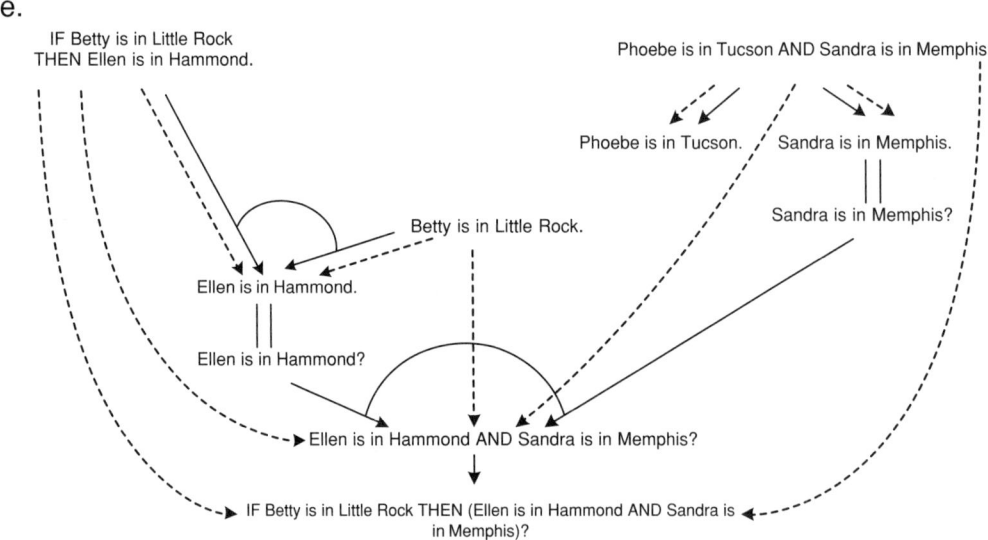

Figure 2 (*continued*)

to derive needed sentences. Rules such as IF Introduction also allow PSYCOP to manipulate suppositions in order to advance its proof of complex arguments. This characteristic matches subjects' use of suppositions. In Figure 2, for instance, the system used the supposition *Betty is in Little Rock* as a crucial element in the proof. The memory links shown in the figure provide a way of keeping track of these suppositions and the sentences that depend on them.

Empirical Findings

The traditional experiment in the psychology of reasoning is one in which subjects study a set of arguments and decide which of them are valid. This paradigm dates at least as far back as Storring's (1908) experiments. In view of this long history, it might be useful to show that the model can predict these results. In order to conduct such a test, I assembled the 32 problems listed in Table 3. (The table uses "&" for AND, "v" for OR, "-" for NOT, and "→" for IF...THEN.) These problems are all deducible in classical sentential logic. The critical rules for these problems are IF Elimination, IF Introduction, DeMorgan (NOT over AND), Disjunctive Syllogism, Disjunctive Modus Ponens, AND Elimination, AND Introduction, OR Introduction, NOT Introduction, and OR Elimination. Although the experiment does not test the full range of PSYCOP's inference skills, it does test

Table 3: Percentage of Correct "Valid" Responses from Experiment (Observed) and Predictions from the PSYCOP Model

	Argument	Observed	Predicted		Argument	Observed	Predicted
A	$\dfrac{(p \vee q) \,\&-p}{q \vee r}$	33.3	33.3	R	$\dfrac{p \to r}{(p \,\& q)-r}$	58.3	69.1
B	$\dfrac{\begin{array}{c}s\\ p \vee q\end{array}}{-p \to (q \,\& s)}$	66.7	70.2	S	$\dfrac{\begin{array}{c}s\\ p \to r\end{array}}{p \to (r \,\& s)}$	75.0	70.9
C	$\dfrac{\begin{array}{c}p \to -(q \,\& r)\\ (-q \vee -r) \to -p\end{array}}{-p}$	16.7	32.4	T	$\dfrac{p \vee q}{-p \to (q \vee r)}$	33.3	32.2
D	$\dfrac{\begin{array}{c}--p\\ -(p \,\& q)\end{array}}{-q \vee r}$	22.2	30.6	U	$\dfrac{\begin{array}{c}p\\ (p \vee q) \to r\\ r \to s\end{array}}{s \vee t}$	38.9	33.9
E	$\dfrac{(p \vee r) \to q}{(p \vee q) \to q}$	83.3	79.9	V	$\dfrac{p \,\& q}{q \,\& (p \vee r)}$	47.2	37.6
F	$\dfrac{-p \,\& q}{q \,\&-(p \,\& r)}$	41.7	40.5	W	$\dfrac{\begin{array}{c}-(p \,\& q)\\ (-p \vee -q) \to -r\end{array}}{-(r \,\& s)}$	23.0	35.5
G	$\dfrac{\begin{array}{c}(p \vee q) \to -r\\ r \vee s\end{array}}{p \to s}$	61.1	70.2	X	$\dfrac{\begin{array}{c}(p \vee s) \to r\\ s\end{array}}{-(r \to -s)}$	50.0	36.1
H	$\dfrac{(p \to q) \,\& (p \,\& r)}{q \,\& r}$	80.6	76.6	Y	$\dfrac{p \to -q}{p \to -(q \,\& r)}$	36.1	33.9
I	$\dfrac{\begin{array}{c}(p \vee q) \to -s\\ s\end{array}}{-p \,\& s}$	55.6	41.2	Z	$\dfrac{\begin{array}{c}-(p \,\& q) \,\& r\\ (-p \vee -q) \to s\end{array}}{s}$	66.7	73.9
J	$\dfrac{q}{p \to ((p \,\& q) \vee r)}$	33.3	36.0	A′	$\dfrac{(p \vee q) \to (r \,\& s)}{p \to r}$	91.7	86.9
K	$\dfrac{\begin{array}{c}(p \vee -q) \to -p\\ p \vee -q)\end{array}}{-(q \,\& r)}$	22.2	35.6	B′	$\dfrac{\begin{array}{c}-r\\ q \vee r\end{array}}{r \to --q}$	36.1	38.7
L	$\dfrac{(p \vee q) \to -(r \,\& s)}{(p \to (-r \vee -s)}$	75.0	70.4	C′	$\dfrac{\begin{array}{c}-(p \,\& q)\\ --q\end{array}}{-p \,\&-(p \,\& q)}$	72.2	62.2
M	$\dfrac{\begin{array}{c}-p\\ q\end{array}}{-(p \,\& r) \,\& (q \vee s)}$	22.2	26.4	D′	$\dfrac{(p \vee q) \,\& ((r \vee s) \to -p)}{q}\ ,\ r$	83.3	75.8
N	$\dfrac{(p \vee r) \to -s}{p \to -(s \,\& t)}$	50.0	38.1	E′	$\dfrac{\begin{array}{c}p \vee s\\ (p \vee r \to s)\end{array}}{s \vee t}$	26.1	36.0
O	$\dfrac{\begin{array}{c}-(p \,\& q)\\ (-p \vee -q) \to r\end{array}}{-(p \,\& q) \,\& r}$	77.8	75.8	F′	$\dfrac{\begin{array}{c}t\\ -(r \,\& s)\end{array}}{((-r \vee -s) \,\& t) \vee u}$	36.1	33.8
P	$\dfrac{(q \vee r) \,\& s}{-q \to r}$	69.4	68.5				
Q	$\dfrac{\begin{array}{c}p\\ (p \vee q) \to -r\end{array}}{p \&-(r \,\& s)}$	33.3	40.5				

an important subset. The arguments were constructed so that each could be proved by means of three rules selected from the above list. In addition to these deducible arguments, there were also thirty-two nondeducible ones, created by recombining the premises and conclusions of the first set. Finally, forty filler arguments were added to the ensemble; most of these were simple deducible problems.

The subjects in this study saw the arguments in a single randomized list. For each argument, they were to circle the phrase "necessarily true" beneath the problem if the conclusion had to be true whenever the premises were true, and the phrase "not necessarily true" otherwise. Subjects responded to each problem in this way even if they had to guess. For half of the subjects, the arguments appeared in instantiations having to do with the location of people in cities. For example, argument E in Table 3 would have looked like (7).

(7)   If Judy is in Albany or Barbara is in Detroit, then Janice is in Los Angeles.
       _____
       If Judy is in Albany or Janice is in Los Angeles, then Janice is in Los Angeles.

The remaining subjects saw the same problems rephrased in terms of the actions of hypothetical machines. Thus, for these subjects, the sample argument appeared in the following guise:

(8)   If the light goes on or the piston expands, then the wheel turns.
       _____
       If the light goes on or the wheel turns, then the wheel turns.

The subjects in both groups were students or nonstudents of approximately the same age. None of them had taken a formal course in logic.

According to our theory, subjects should correctly respond that the conclusion of such an argument is necessarily true if they can construct a mental proof of that conclusion, and success in doing so will obviously depend on whether they can muster all the inference rules needed to complete the proof. As a working assumption, we will suppose that errors on these problems are due to a failure to apply the rules. The failure may be due to retrieval difficulties, slips in carrying out the steps of the rule, failure to recognize the rule as applicable in the current context, or other factors. In general, we can think of each rule R_i as associated with a probability

p_i that the rule will be available on a given trial. This means that there will be some occasions on which R_i would be useful in completing a proof but is not available to the subject. On these occasions, the subject will have to search for an alternative proof that uses rules other than R_i. (Such alternatives are sometimes possible because of the redundancy of the system.) If no such alternative exists, we will assume that the subject either guesses at the answer (with probability p_g) or simply responds incorrectly that the conclusion does not necessarily follow (with probability $1 - p_g$). For example, when all the rules listed above are available, the model will prove (7) or (8) using a combination of IF Introduction, OR Elimination, and Disjunctive Modus Ponens. If these rules are available with probabilities p_1, p_2, and p_3, respectively, then (assuming independence) the probability of a correct "necessarily true" response might be (9), where the first term is the probability of a correct mental proof and the second term reflects a correct guess after failure to find the proof.

(9)   P("necessarily") = $p_1 p_2 p_3 + 0.5 p_g (1 - p_1 p_2 p_3)$,

This equation is not quite right, however, because the model can still find a proof of these arguments even if Disjunctive Modus Ponens is missing. OR Introduction and IF Elimination can combine to fill the same role played by the unavailable rule. (All the remaining rules are necessary for the problem, since omitting them keeps the model from producing any proof at all.) To correct for this alternative derivation, we must add some new terms to the equation. If p_4 is the probability that IF Elimination is available and p_5 is the probability that OR Introduction is available, then the proper expression is (10).

(10)   P("necessarily") = $p_1 p_2 p_3 + (1 - p_3)$ $p_1 p_2 p_4 p_5 + 0.5 p_g [1 - p_1 p_2 p_3 - (1 - p_3)$ $p_1 p_2 p_4 p_5]$

The first term is again the probability of finding a proof by the original method, the second term is the probability of finding the alternative proof, and the third is the probability of a correct guess.

To derive predictions from the model, then, we need two pieces of information about each of the arguments in Table 3: the rules that are used in a proof of that argument, and the probability that each of these rules will be available. We can obtain the first type of information by simulation, giving the model the argument and inspecting the proof to find which rules it employs. These rules can then be omitted (singly and in combination) to determine whether there are alternative proofs. The process is then repeated until no new proofs are forthcoming. This simulation allows us to formulate an equation like (10) for each of the arguments. The rule availabilities can be estimated by treating them as parameters when fitting the resulting equations to the data.

Table 3 gives the obtained and predicted percentages of correct "necessarily true" responses for the critical deducible problems. An analysis of variance of the data turned up no effect of the problem content (people in locations vs. machine actions) and no interaction of this factor with scores on the individual problems. Hence, the data from the two groups of subjects are combined in the table. The overall rate of correct responses is fairly low (50.6%), although there is obviously a very wide range across individual problems – from 16.7 percent correct on the hardest problem to 91.7 percent correct on the easiest. The percentage of incorrect "necessarily true" responses to the nondeducible problems (i.e., false alarms) was 22.9 percent. Thus, despite the low hit rate, subjects were distinguishing the deducible from the nondeducible items. In experiments like this one involving choice of alternative responses, the absolute response rate depends not only on subjects' accuracy but also on the criterion they adopt for a "necessarily true" response. Cautious subjects, for example, are likely to give somewhat low rates of positive responses, even though they are able to discriminate correct from incorrect arguments with reasonable accuracy. In accounting for these results, we therefore need to concentrate on the relative scores across the set of problems.[2]

The predicted scores in the table are the result of fitting equations similar to (10) to the data. The full model requires a large number of availability parameters, since we need a distinct parameter for each inference rule. To reduce this number somewhat, we have collapsed forward and backward versions of a given rule, using the same parameter for both members of a pair. For example, the same parameter represented the availability of backward and forward IF Elimination. We also set the guessing parameter, p_g, using the data from the nondeducible problems: If subjects respond "necessarily true" to these nondeducible items only because of bad guesses, then the guessing rate (after fail-

Table 4: Parameter Estimates for the Model as Applied to the Argument-Evaluation Experiment

Rule	Estimate
Disjunctive Modus Ponens	1.000
AND Introduction	1.000
AND Elimination	0.963
IF Introduction	0.861
OR Elimination	0.858
IF Elimination	0.723
DeMorgan (NOT over AND)	0.715
Disjunctive Syllogism	0.713
NOT Introduction	0.238
OR Introduction	0.197

ure to find a proof) should be twice this value, or 45.8 percent. (This is not the overall probability of guessing; it is the conditional probability of guessing rather than saying "not necessarily true" given that no proof was forthcoming.) These economy moves still leave ten parameters, but there are twenty-one remaining degrees of freedom for a test of the model.[3]

Although the fit of the model is difficult to summarize because of the varied nature of the problems, Table 3 shows that the predictions are reasonably accurate. The correlation between predicted and observed scores, 0.93, yields a significant proportion of variance accounted for when tested against the Problem x Subject interaction from an analysis of variance: $F(10,1054) = 26.43$, $p < 0.01$. The residual variance is fairly small, but it is also significant because of the large number of residual degrees of freedom: $F(21, 1054) = 1.88$, $p < 0.05$. The parameter estimates are those in Table 4. For the most part, these parameters are what we might expect on the basis of the intuitive nature of the rules. The easiest rules are those that seem obviously correct, including AND Introduction, AND Elimination, and Disjunctive Modus Ponens. The most difficult rule is OR Introduction, which allows us to deduce sentences of the form P OR Q from P. Many subjects apparently fail to apply this rule, probably for pragmatic reasons (Grice 1989; Gazdar 1979; McCawley 1981; Pelletier 1977): The conclusion of such an inference contains information that may seem to be irrelevant to the premise on which it is based and thus to violate conversational conventions.[4] (For more empirical evidence on the difficulty of OR Introduction, see Rips and Conrad 1983.)

One puzzling aspect of these estimates is the very low availability for NOT Introduction versus the relatively high availabilities for OR Elimination and IF Introduction. The routines for these rules in Table 2 make them seem about equally complex: All three are backward rules that involve subdomains. So why should NOT Introduction be so much harder to apply? The difficulty might be explained as an artifact of the particular sample of problems, but in fact we can also find evidence for such difficulty in other paradigms (see Rips 1994: Ch. 5). Evidently, the reductio strategy of assuming the opposite of what one wants to prove is not an obvious move for subjects who haven't had extensive mathematics training. A plausible guess is that this difficulty is related to the conceptual distance between the main goal of proving *NOT P* and the subgoal of proving a contradiction *Q* and *NOT Q* on the basis of *P.* By contrast, OR Elimination and IF Introduction seem more direct, more intimately tied to the goals and assertions that trigger them.

One way to see what the model buys us is to compare the fits just mentioned against what we can obtain using other possible measures of problem difficulty. We might expect, for example, that the greater the number of premises in an argument, the more difficult that argument would be to evaluate. Similarly, the greater the number of atomic sentences in the argument, the harder it should be. For instance, argument F' in Table 3 contains four types of atomic sentences (*r, s, t,* and *u*), and seven atomic sentence tokens or occurrences. It should therefore be more difficult than B', which contains only two atomic sentence types and five tokens. In general, however, these measures of surface complexity fail to provide a good account of the data. The correlation between the percentage of correct responses and the number of premises is -0.23, and the correlations with number of types and tokens of atoms are -0.04 and 0.10, respectively. This suggests that the true difficulty of the arguments is associated with the inference patterns they display, where these patterns are close to those specified in PSYCOP.

Summary

One way to think about the theory developed here is as a merger of two main ideas about the human nature of deductive reasoning. One of these ideas is that reasoning involves the ability to make suppositions or assumptions – that is, to entertain propositions temporarily in order to trace their consequences. This idea comes from formal natural-deduction systems in logic, but it is clearly psychological at root. Nothing about deduction *per se* forces suppositions on us, since there are perfectly good deduction systems that do without them; we could start with a set of axioms and derive all the same theorems. But human styles of reasoning aren't like that, as both Gentzen and Jaskowski observed. We tend to assume propositions for the sake of the argument in order to focus our efforts in exploring what follows.

The second of the key ideas is that reasoning includes subgoals. People are able to adopt on a temporary basis the desire to prove some proposition in order to achieve a further conclusion. This idea seems more mundane than the one about suppositions, because we are accustomed to the use of subgoals in cognitive and computer science. Even the simplest AI programs use subgoaling to reduce the amount of search. But, again, deduction itself doesn't require subgoals. Even natural-deduction systems, as logic textbooks formulate them, don't have subgoals. Instead instructors in elementary logic have to provide informal hints about strategies for applying the rules, generally in the form of advice about working backward from the conclusion to more easily achievable lemmas. If these subordinate conclusions don't pan out, we can abandon them for others that may prove more successful. Our theory gives this purposefulness a status equal to that of suppositions.

Although I have borrowed suppositions from logic and subgoals from computer science, these concepts are closely interrelated. Suppositions are roughly like provisional beliefs, and subgoals roughly like provisional desires. In something like the way beliefs and desires about external states guide external actions, provisional beliefs and desires guide internal action in reasoning. According to the current theory, what gives human reasoning its characteristic tempo is the way these suppositions and subgoals coordinate: Can we show that some sentence C follows from another sentence *P*? Well, C would follow if we can show that C' follows from *P'*; so let's assume *P'* for now and try to find out whether C' holds; and so on. From one perspective, this sequence helps to simplify the problem at hand by lemma-izing it into manageable parts. But reasoning of this type also presupposes some fairly sophisticated cognitive apparatus for keeping track of the nesting of suppositions within suppositions and sub-subgoals en route to subgoals.

In the present theory, most of the responsibility for handling suppositions and subgoals devolves on the deduction rules. The rules in the model are a conservative choice of principles that seem psychologically (although not always logically) primitive. Research in this area should consider expanding this set of principles, and perhaps amending the current set, to achieve better coverage of the logical resources of natural language (see, e.g., Dowty 1993). But the present rules seem to provide a good starting point.

Notes

1   This chapter is a slightly modified excerpt from Rips (1994: Chs. 2–5).

2   For this reason, it is unwarranted to conclude from a low score on a given problem that subjects weren't engaged in reasoning about the problem. In this vein, Braine et al. (1984: 360) point to problem B in Table 3 as one in which "the conclusion seems to follow transparently from the premises," and state that the subjects' score on this item (66.7 percent "necessarily true" responses) "suggests that the experiment often failed to engage the reasoning procedure of subjects." It is unclear what rationale Braine et al. are applying in judging that this argument "transparently follows." The basic point, however, is that it is impossible to determine the extent to which subjects were engaged in reasoning from an absolute score without also knowing the response criterion the subjects were adopting. Fred Conrad and I (Rips and Conrad 1983) have replicated the experiment described here and found higher absolute scores (62% vs. 51% of subjects judged the classically valid arguments "necessarily true") but a very similar pattern of scores across problems.

3   Another method for estimating parameters is to include in the stimulus set an argument that turns on a single rule. The percentage of correct answers for that argument is then the estimate for that rule's availability (Braine et al. 1984; Osherson 1974, 1975, 1976). One difficulty with this procedure, for our theory, is that some of the rules, such as IF Introduction and NOT Introduction, can't be the sole rule used in the proof of an argument. Thus, the alternative method gives us no estimates for these items. Second, use of simple arguments to estimate parameters may sometimes spuriously inflate the fit of the theory. This is because the premise or the conclusion of a single-rule argument will often share the syntactic structure of the premise or conclusion of the argument that the investigator is trying to predict, especially when the proof is short. Hence, any difficulties associated with comprehending the syntax will increase the correlation with the arguments' scores.

4   This pattern of parameter values explains some observations about this experiment that Johnson-Laird, Byrne, and Schaeken (1992) have made. The low availabilities for OR Introduction and NOT Introduction mean that the model predicts a fairly low proportion of "necessarily true" responses on arguments that involve these rules and a fairly high proportion on arguments that don't. Johnson-Laird et al. also claim that the scores for the problems in Table 3 depend on whether or not the arguments "maintain the semantic information of the premises." By the amount of "semantic information," Johnson-Laird et al. mean the percentage of possible states of affairs that the premises eliminate. A possible state of affairs is, in turn, determined by an assignment of truth or falsity to each of the atomic sentences that appear in the argument (Johnson-Laird 1983: 36; Johnson-Laird et al. 1992: 423). For example, consider the simple argument:

$$\frac{p \text{ AND } q}{q}$$

Because this argument contains just two atomic sentence types, the four possible states of affairs are one in which p is true and q is true, one in which p is true and q is false, one in which p is false and q is true, and one in which p is false and q is false. (Thus, the states of affairs are equivalent to the horizontal lines of a standard truth table for the argument.) In the sample argument, the premise rules out all but one of these states of affairs (the one in which p is true and q is true). However, the conclusion rules out only two states of affairs (the ones in which p is false). Of course, in any valid argument the conclusion must be true in all states of affairs in which the premises are true, and this means that the amount of semantic information conveyed by the premise must be greater than or equal to the amount conveyed by the conclusion. Johnson-Laird (1983) talks of an argument "maintaining semantic information" if the premises and conclusion have the same amount of semantic information, and "throwing away semantic information" if the conclusion contains less semantic information than the premises. Thus, the argument above throws away semantic information.

According to Johnson-Laird et al. (1992: 428), "to throw away semantic information is to violate one of the fundamental principles of human deductive competence, and so we can predict that performance with these problems should be poorer." They then report a test comparing sixteen arguments in Table 3 that purportedly maintain semantic information with sixteen arguments that don't. However,

Johnson-Laird et al. apparently miscalculated the amount of semantic information in these arguments; according to the criterion of Johnson-Laird (1983), only three of the thirty-two arguments (C, O, and X) maintain semantic information. The percentage of "necessarily true" responses for these problems was 48.2 percent, nearly the same as the percentage for the entire problem set (50.6%). Instead, Johnson-Laird et al. seem to have decided which arguments maintained semantic information according to whether the conclusion contains an atomic sentence token that does not appear in the premises. (E.g., the conclusion of Argument A contains an *r* that does not appear in the premises.) Adding atomic sentences to the conclusion, however, is not the only way of reducing semantic information, as we have already seen with respect to the sample argument above.

In short, contrary to Johnson-Laird et al., there is no evidence from these data that "throwing away semantic information" hurts subjects' performance. What does seem to cause difficulty is the presence of atomic sentences in the conclusion that did not appear in the premises and may therefore seem irrelevant to those premises. This may be traced in turn to rules like OR Introduction (*P*; Therefore, *P OR Q*) that add sentences in this way.

References

Anderson, J. R. (1983). *The architecture of cognition*. Cambridge, MA: Harvard University Press.

Braine, M. D. S. (1978). On the relation between the natural logic of reasoning and standard logic. *Psychological Review, 85*, 1–21.

Braine, M. D. S., Reiser, B. J., and Rumain, B. (1984). Some empirical justification for a theory of natural propositional reasoning. *Psychology of Learning and Motivation, 18*, 313–371. Orlando, FL: Academic Press.

Collins, A. M., and Loftus, E. F. (1975). A spreading activation theory of semantic precessing. *Psychological Review, 13*, 1–50.

Copi, I. M. (1954). *Symbolic logic*. New York: Macmillan.

Dowty, D. R. (1993). *Categorial grammar, reasoning, and cognition*. Paper presented at the 29th regional meeting of the Chicago Linguistics Society.

Fine, K. (1985a). Natural deduction and arbitrary objects. *Journal of Philosophical Logic, 14*, 57–107.

Fine, K. (1985b). *Reasoning with arbitrary objects*. Oxford: Blackwells.

Gazdar, G. (1979). *Pragmatics*. New York: Academic Press.

Gentzen, G. (1969). Investigations into logical deduction. In M. E. Szabo (ed.), *The collected papers of Gerhard Gentzen*. Amsterdam: North Holland. (Originally published 1935)

Gilhooly, K. J., Logie, R. H., Wetherick, N. E., and Wynn, V. (1993). Working memory and strategies in syllogistic reasoning task. *Memory and Cognition, 21*, 115–124.

Grice, H. P. (1989). *Studies in the way of words*. Cambridge, MA: Harvard University Press.

Hitch, G. J., & Baddeley, A. D. (1976). Verbal reasoning and working memory. *Quarterly Journal of Experimental Psychology, 28*, 603–621.

Jaskowski, S. (1934). On the rules of supposition in formal logic. *Studia Logica, 1*, 5–32.

Johnson-Laird, P. N. (1975). Models of deduction. In R. J. Falmagne (ed.), *Reasoning: Representation and process in children and adults*. Hillsdale, NJ: Erlbaum.

Johnson-Laird, P. N. (1983). *Mental models*. Cambridge, MA: Harvard University Press.

Johnson-Laird, P. N., & Byrne, R. M. J. (1991). *Deduction*. Hillsdale, NJ: Erlbaum.

Johnson-Laird, P. N., Byrne, R. M. J., & Schaeken, W. (1992). Propositional reasoning by model. *Psychological Review, 96*, 658–673.

McCawley, J. D. (1981). *Everything linguists have always wanted to know about logic but were ashamed to ask*. Chicago: University of Chicago Press.

Newell, A., Shaw, J. C., & Simon, H. A. (1957). Empirical explorations with the Logic Theory Machine. In *Proceedings of the Joint Computer Conference*.

Osherson, D. N. (1974). *Logical abilities in children*, vol. 2. Hillsdale, NJ: Erlbaum.

Osherson D. N. (1975). *Logical abilities in children*, vol. 3. Hillsdale, NJ: Erlbaum.

Osherson D. N. (1976). *Logical abilities in children*, vol. 4. Hillsdale, NJ: Erlbaum.

Pelletier, F. J. (1977). Or. *Theoretical linguistics, 4*, 61–74.

Prawitz, D. (1965). *Natural deduction: A proof-theoretical study*. Stockholm: Almqvist and Wiksell.

Rips, L. J. (1983). Cognitive processes in propositional reasoning. *Psychological Review, 90*, 38–71.

Rips, L. J. (1994). *The psychology of proof: Deduction in human thinking*. Cambridge, MA: MIT Press.

Rips, L. J. (1999). Human modes of quantificational reasoning. In S. B. Cooper & J. K. Truss (Eds.), *Models and computability*. Cambridge, England: Cambridge University Press.

Rips, L. J. (2000). The cognitive nature of instantiation. *Journal of Memory and Language, 43*, 20–43.

Rips, L. J., & Conrad, F. G. (1983). Individual differences in deduction. *Cognition and Brain Theory, 6*, 259–285.

Sperber, D., & Wilson, D. (1986). *Relevance*. Cambridge, MA: Harvard University Press.

Störring, G. (1908). Experimentelle Untersuchungen über einfache Schlussprozesse. *Archiv für die Gesamte Psychologie, 11*, 1–127.

Tarski, A. (1956). On the concept of truth in formalized languages. In *Logic, semantics, metamathematics.* Oxford: Oxford University Press. (Originally published 1936)

Thomason, R. H. (1970). *Symbolic logic.* New York: Macmillan.

Ungar, A. M. (1992). *Normalization, cut-elimination, and the theory of proofs.* Stanford, CA: CSLI.

Wason, P. C., & Johnson-Laird, P. N. (1972). *The psychology of reasoning.* Cambridge, MA: Harvard University Press.

Chapter 10: Mental Models and Deductive Reasoning

PHILIP N. JOHNSON-LAIRD

How do people reason? The view that I learned at my mother's knee was that they rely on logic. During the 1960s and 1970s when the study of thinking had become respectable again after the Dark Ages of Behaviorism, psychologists – including the present author – took this view for granted. The idea that logic provided the norms of reasoning can be traced back to the rise of modern logic, and was defended in the nineteenth century by both Boole (1854) and Mill (1874). In the twentieth century, the Swiss psychologist, Jean Piaget, and his colleagues argued that the construction of a formal logic in the mind was the last great step in children's intellectual development, and that it occurred at about the age of twelve (see, e.g., Inhelder and Piaget, 1958). And so thirty years ago the task for psychologists appeared to be to determine which particular formal logic was laid down in the mind and which particular rules of inference were used in its mental formulation. That, at least, was how several like-minded authors conceived their research (see, e.g., Osherson 1974–1976; Johnson-Laird 1975; Braine 1978; Rips 1983). In the parallel "universe" of artificial intelligence, researchers were similarly developing computer programs that proved theorems relying on formal rules of inference (e.g., Bledsoe 1977). The main skeptics were those engaged in trying to analyze everyday arguments. They discovered that it was extraordinarily difficult to translate such arguments into formal logic. As a result, many of them abandoned logic as a method of analysis (see, e.g., Toulmin 1958; Scriven 1976), and later they went on to found a pedagogical society, AILACT (Association for Informal Logic and Critical Thinking), in which they advocated a variety of other methods of analysis.

The event that woke me from my dogmatic slumbers was the late Peter Wason's discovery of the effects of content on his "selection" task. In the abstract version of the task (Wason 1966), the experimenter lays down four cards in front of you, such as: A, B, 2, 3. You know that each card has a number on one side and a letter on the other side. Your task is to select just those cards to turn over that are relevant to determining whether a general claim is true or false. The general claim in one version of the task is:

If a card has an "A" on one side then it has a "2" on the other side.

Like all the studies described in the present article, the experiment tested "naïve" individuals – I use the term, not to impugn their intelligence, but merely to mean that they had received no training in logic. In the selection task, they tended to choose the A card, and sometimes the 2 card. But, they rarely chose the 3 card. You can grasp the need to do so if you think about the consequences of turning over the A card. If a 3 is on its other side, the general claim is false. By parity of argument, if you turn over the 3 card and find an A on its other side, the general claim is also false. Hence, you do need to select the 3 card. If you select the 2 card, then nothing on its other side can show that the general claim is false, unless you take the claim to mean: if and *only if* a card has an "A" on one side then it has a "2" on its other side. In this case, however, you ought to select all four cards.

The selection task was inspired by Popper's philosophy of science. He had argued that what divides science from nonscience is "falsifiability": a scientific hypothesis is one that in principle observations could show to be false (Popper 1959). Any hypothesis that could not be refuted in this way is outside the borders of science. What Wason discovered is that individuals unfamiliar with logic or with Popper's idea have a perverse propensity *not* to try to falsify general claims. The failure was embarrassing to

Piagetians, because Piaget had argued that once children attain the level of "formal operations" – the level corresponding to the acquisition of logic – they would check the truth of conditionals of the form, *If A then B*, by searching for counterexamples of the form: *A and not-B*. But, the participants signally failed to reason in this way: the 3 card corresponds to not-B, and they did not select it. For anyone who had studied logic, this error of omission was puzzling. And so Wason and I embarked on a three-year research program, helped by a graduate, Diana Shapiro, to try to understand what was going on.

Why don't individuals select that 3 card? There were many possibilities. The experimental procedure might somehow mislead them. Psychological experiments are social interactions in a microcosm, and sensitive to all sorts of unforeseen factors. The participants may construe the task in ways quite different from what the experimenter has in mind. The psychologist may use inappropriate materials or procedures, or fail to control the experiment properly. The instructions explain the task, but the participants also think for themselves. This point became vivid to me when I read a participant the instructions, and he then said, "Yes, but what do you *really* want me to do?" We tried all sorts of experimental manipulations in order to elicit a correct performance. We changed the form of the rule; we put all the information on one side of a card; we gave participants brief "intellectual psychotherapy." None of these manipulations did much good (see Wason and Johnson-Laird 1972).

Wason then suggested changing the *content* of the cards and the claim. Perhaps because my head was still stuffed with formal logic, I thought that this manipulation was crazy (although I didn't say so). Wason and Shapiro went ahead with the experiment. They used a general claim with an underlying conditional meaning:

Every time I go to Manchester I travel by train

and four cards about journeys, with a destination on one side and a mode of transport on the other side: Manchester, Leeds, train, car. The participants were now much more likely to realize that a journey by *car* (the *not-B* case) was pertinent to the truth or falsity of the claim, and to select this card. If the destination on the other side was Manchester, then the claim was false (Wason and Shapiro 1971). It is hard to convey the stunning nature of this result at the time. A change in content alone had a striking effect on reasoning, even though the two sorts of contents were identical in formal structure. Paolo and Maria

Legrenzi and I carried out a similar experiment using a regulation about the postage required on sealed envelopes. The same robust change in performance occurred, and it did not transfer to the abstract version of the task (Johnson-Laird, Legrenzi, and Sonino Legrenzi 1972).

The true reason for the difference in performance between abstract and concrete selection tasks remains a matter of controversy, and several hypotheses purport to explain it (e.g., Cheng and Holyoak 1985; Cosmides 1989; Johnson-Laird and Byrne 1991; Oaksford and Chater 1998; see also the chapters in this volume by Fodor and by Sperber). But, at the time, the phenomenon convinced several psychologists that formal logic could not explain human reasoning. Formal logic, by definition, is concerned solely with the logical form of assertions, not their content. Yet, the selection task showed that content mattered just as much as form in reasoning (Wason and Johnson-Laird 1972).

The search for an alternative theory took some time, but it led to the topic of the present chapter, the theory of mental models or the "model theory" for short. The chapter begins with an outline of this theory. It examines in some detail the theory's account of negation, and of how one model is conjoined with another. Unlike logic, the interpretation of sentences in daily life is often modulated by knowledge, both a knowledge of what is being referred to and general knowledge. The chapter explains these phenomena, and their consequences on reasoning. It considers how individuals develop strategies for reasoning with particular sorts of problem. And, finally, it draws some general morals about reasoning.

The Mental Model Theory

The mental model theory has various antecedents of which the most important is the use of models in logic to provide a systematic method for the interpretation of assertions in logical calculi. However, this article is concerned, not with the history of the theory (for that, see Johnson-Laird 2004), but with its current formulation. This section accordingly outlines its main principles. Its fundamental assumption is that reasoning is about possibilities. When we read a description of a situation, we try to envisage the alternative possibilities with which the description is compatible. If someone tell us:

My house is in the middle of the street,

we construct a mental model of a single possibility. The proposition could be true in infinitely many ways (as model theory in logic recognizes), but we cannot hold in mind such an infinitude. So, strictly speaking, our mental model of the situation captures what is common to this swarm of possibilities, namely, that the speaker's house is (roughly) in the middle of the street rather than toward one end or the other. The sort of diagram that we might draw to convey this proposition is along the following lines:

House House Speaker's house House House

It has an interesting property, which the great nineteenth-century philosopher and logician Charles Sanders Peirce called "iconicity" (see, e.g., Peirce, 1931–1958, Vol. 4, paragraph 433). He meant that the structure of such a diagram is the same as the structure of what it represents, and so the parts of the diagram map onto the parts of the scene, and the relations among the parts of the diagram are the same as the relations among the parts of the scene. Mental models are similarly as iconic as possible. An iconic representation, as Peirce (Vol. 2, para. 279, and Vol. 4, para. 530) pointed out, has the advantage that it can yield a conclusion that was not asserted by any of the premises used in its construction. As a simple example, consider the following premises:

The cup is on the right of the saucer.

The spoon is on the left of the saucer.

An iconic diagram of the possibility compatible with these premises is as follows:

spoon   saucer   cup

where the left-to-right axis in the diagram corresponds to the left-to-right axis of the scene. The diagram shows that the cup is on the right of the spoon, and this conclusion follows from the premises, but it was not asserted in them. The inferential system must work according to the principle that in such cases the axes have a spatial interpretation. Various ways exist to keep track of this information, but no one knows which way the human system uses. In contrast, the use of formal logic calls for a single noniconic notation for all inferences, additional premises about the logical properties of the spatial terms, and the use of formal rules of inference.

We have difficulty in thinking about more than one possibility at a time. Working memory, which holds models in mind while we cogitate, is limited in its capacity (see, e.g., Baddeley 1986).

Hence, we much prefer to consider just a single possibility at a time, and a sure way to get us to make mistakes is to overload us with alternative possibilities. The word "or" in English is an excellent device for causing us problems, as several experiments have shown (Bauer and Johnson-Laird 1993). The logical meaning of "or" in an assertion, such as:

The broadcast is on network TV or it's on the radio, or both

conveys three different possibilities, and individuals can readily list them, as I have done here in abbreviated form on separate horizontal lines:

network TV
                    radio
network TV   radio

Reasoning becomes very difficult if we have to juggle such possibilities in our minds. Hence, if, in addition, we receive a second premise:

The broadcast isn't on the radio or it's on cable TV, or both.

we have to consider the different possibilities compatible with both the first premise and this new one. That's difficult, and few of us can cope with the task.

One way to carry out the task of multiplying possibilities – a method used in a program that I wrote – is, first, to flesh out the possibilities to make them fully explicit. The two premises are:

1.   The broadcast is on network TV or it's on the radio, or both.

2.   The broadcast isn't on the radio or it's on cable TV, or both.

These premises are compatible with the following two sets of possibilities respectively:

1.   network TV   not radio
       not network TV   radio
          network TV   radio

and:

2.   not radio   not cable TV
         radio   cable TV
      not radio   cable TV

Two simple procedures multiply the two sets of possibilities in order to yield those that are compatible with both premises. The first procedure is used when one possibility, such as: *not on radio*, is incompatible with another, such as: *on radio* (see procedure 2 in Table 1). Their conjunction yields the null model, which is a special model, akin to the empty set, that represents impossibilities. The second procedure is that if one possibility is consistent with another, their conjunction combines the information in both of them without redundancy (see procedure 3 in Table 1).

The two procedures can be applied to the two sets of models above. The three possibilities for the first premise have to be multiplied by three possibilities for the second premise, that is, a total of nine conjunctions. The conjunction of the first possibility for the first premise with the first possibility for the second premise:

network TV   not radio

and:

not radio   not cable TV

is consistent, and yields the following possibility:

network TV   not radio   not cable TV

The conjunction of the first possibility for the first premise with the second possibility for the second premise is inconsistent – one asserts that the broadcast wasn't on radio and the other asserts that it was – and so the conjunction yields the null model. The nine conjunctions yield the following possibilities, where I have omitted the null models because they represent impossibilities:

network TV	not radio	not cable TV
network TV	not radio	cable TV
not network TV	radio	cable TV
network TV	radio	cable TV

These possibilities support various conclusions, notably:

The broadcast is on network TV or it's on cable TV, or both.

This conclusion holds for all the possibilities compatible with the premises, and so, as logicians say, it is *valid*, that is, it must be true given that the premises are true.

Naïve individuals are most unlikely to make inferences in this way. The method is a good one, but it is too demanding on working memory. One assumption of the model theory is accordingly the principle of *truth*: mental models represent

sent clauses in the premises, affirmative or negative, only when they are true, and not when they are false (Johnson-Laird and Savary 1999). As an example, consider again the disjunction:

The broadcast isn't on the radio or it's on cable TV.

Its three fully explicit models are shown earlier. But, its mental models depend on the principle of truth, and so each of its two clauses (the broadcast isn't on radio, it's on cable TV) is represented in a possibility only when it is true. Hence, the disjunction has the mental models:

not radio	
	cable TV
not radio	cable TV

In the model of the first possibility, for example, the second clause of the disjunction is false, and so it isn't represented in the model.

Readers sometimes assume that mental models merely represent whatever clauses occur in assertions, and do not represent what is not explicitly mentioned in assertions. But, if that were so, then assertions containing the two clauses here would have the same mental models regardless of whether the sentential connective interrelating them was "if," "and," or "or." The right way to think of the principle of truth is therefore that mental models represent only those states of affairs that are possible given an assertion, and that within each of these possibilities they represent a clause in the assertion, whether it is affirmative or negative, only if it is true in that possibility. (Table 1 spells out explicitly just how such a system can work.) Individuals may make a mental footnote about what is false in a possibility, and, if they retain it, then they can try to flesh out mental models into fully explicit models. Mental models lighten the load on working memory, because they represent less information. But, as we'll see, they have some unexpected and unfortunate consequences.

Even with mental models, we may not try to multiply out the possibilities. The model theory allows that we can develop a variety of strategies for reasoning, which I describe presently. One strategy is to make a supposition – for the sake of inference, we assume that a particular proposition holds. The previous premises are:

The broadcast is on network TV or it's on the radio, or both.

The broadcast isn't on the radio or it's on cable TV, or both.

Hence, we might think to ourselves: suppose that the broadcast isn't on network TV. We can try to combine a model of this possibility with the first mental model of the first premise, but there's an inconsistency. We can combine it with the second model, which yields the possibility that the broadcast is on the radio. So, if the broadcast isn't on network TV, then it's on the radio. We can combine the model of this possibility with the models of the second premise, and it is compatible with only one of them: the broadcast is on cable TV. It follows that if the broadcast isn't on network TV, then it's on cable TV. A moment's thought should convince you that this claim is equivalent to the disjunctive conclusion, which I proved earlier: The broadcast is on network TV or it's on cable TV.

One problematical connective is the conditional: "if." An assertion such as:

If the broadcast isn't on network TV, then it's on cable TV

is compatible with the possibility:

not network TV   cable TV

But, suppose that the broadcast *is* on network TV, what does the conditional assert then? The answer, which is borne out by psychology evidence, is that it allows that the broadcast may, or may not, be on cable TV (see, e.g., Barrouillet, Grosset, and Leças 2000). The conditional is accordingly compatible with three possibilities:

not network TV   cable TV
    network TV   not cable TV
    network TV   cable TV

These possibilities are the same as those for the disjunction:

The broadcast is on network TV or it's on cable TV, or both.

This fact explains the ability of individuals to paraphrase conditionals as disjunctions and vice versa (Ormerod and Richardson 2003).

When individuals reason from conditionals, they normally rely on mental models, and the theory postulates that the mental models of conditionals represent the initial possibility but use a wholly implicit model (shown as an ellipsis here) to represent the possibilities in which the antecedent clause (the if-clause) is false:

not network TV   cable TV.

        . . .

One consequence of these models is that inferences of the sort known as "modus ponens" are easy:

If the broadcast isn't on network TV, then it's on cable TV.

The broadcast isn't on network TV.

Therefore, it's on cable TV.

In contrast, inferences of the sort known as "modus tollens" are difficult:

If the broadcast isn't on network TV, then it's on cable TV.

The broadcast isn't on cable TV.

Therefore, it's on network TV.

To make this inference, reasoners have either to flesh out their mental models into fully explicit models, or to use some other strategy such as the suppositional one.

An inference can fail to be valid in two different ways. One way is for its conclusion to be inconsistent with the premises. Consider this putative inference:

The broadcast is on network TV or it's on the radio, or both.

The broadcast isn't on the radio or it's on cable TV, or both.

Therefore, the broadcast is neither on network TV nor on cable TV.

This conclusion corresponds to the possibility:

not network TV   not cable TV

And this possibility is inconsistent with each of the four possibilities compatible with the two premises (shown earlier). Hence, the conclusion, far from following from the premises, contradicts them.

Another way in which an inference can be invalid is if its conclusion fails to follow from the premises, though it is consistent with them. Consider this putative conclusion from the previous premises:

The broadcast is on network TV and it is on cable TV.

This conclusion is compatible with the premises: it corresponds to the second and fourth possibilities listed above. So, how can we discover that it is invalid? If we use formal rules of inference, one method is to show that no proof yields the conclusion from the premises. Such a method would be exhausting, and would predict that the task of establishing invalidity would be interminable. Reasoning with mental models, in contrast, allows us a much simpler method. We merely find a *counterexample* to the conclusion, where a counterexample is a possibility consistent with the premises but inconsistent with the conclusion (Johnson-Laird and Hasson 2003). Such a counterexample to the previous conclusion is, for example:

network TV   not cable TV

So much for the general principles of the model theory. In order to explain a crucial prediction, the next section details the procedures for constructing mental models.

The Procedures for Negation and Conjunction

When individuals draw conclusions from a set of premises, they envisage possibilities compatible with the premises. They can cope with this task for two or three possibilities (García-Madruga, Moreno, Carriedo, Gutiérrez, and Johnson-Laird 2001), but the task gets progressively harder when the number of possibilities increases beyond this point (Bauer and Johnson-Laird 1993). But, what are the procedures for combining possibilities? The answer is that they depend on negation and conjunction.

A problem that is harder than it seems at first is to list the possibilities given the following assertion:

It is not the case that both Pat is here and Viv is here.

The task isn't trivial, because we don't have the answer in memory: we have to work it out. And how do we that? First, we have to work out what the unnegated proposition means:

Both Pat is here and Viv is here.

It allows just one possibility, which I'll abbreviate as:

Pat   Viv

The negative proposition rules out this possibility to leave its complement, that is, all the other possibilities. The first one that we're likely to think of is the mirror image of the possibility above in which neither Pat nor Viv is here:

not Pat   not Viv

Some individuals go no further, but others are likely to realize that there are two other possibilities, in which one or other of the two individuals isn't here. Hence, the proposition as a whole is compatible with three possibilities:

not Pat   not Viv
not Pat   Viv
    Pat   not Viv

In general, the way to interpret a negative proposition is to take the propositions that occur within the negation, and to work out all the possible combinations of them and their negations. One removes from these combinations those that are compatible with the unnegated proposition, and the remaining possibilities are those for the negative proposition. No wonder that people do not cope very well with the task of listing the possibilities compatible with negative assertions (Barres and Johnson-Laird 2003). They tend to be better at negating a disjunction than a conjunction, perhaps because the former yields fewer models than the latter. They often assume that the negation of a complex proposition consists solely of a conjunction of the negations of each of its constituent propositions.

A disjunction of alternative possibilities can be represented as a list of alternative models. To combine two such sets of models according to any logical relation between them calls only for negation, which I've described, and logical conjunction. When individuals interpret a set of premises, their task is to construct a model of an initial clause or premise, and then to update this model from the remaining information in the premises. Table 1 summarizes the procedures for conjoining one model with another, and it illustrates them for the conjunction of the premises:

If Pat is here then Viv is here.

Mo is here or else Pat is here, but not both.

Before you read Table 1, you might like to think for a moment what possibilities are compatible with the two premises. Most people think that there are two: Pat and Viv are here, or else Mo is here.

The procedures in Table 1 apply to both mental models and fully explicit models. In both cases, the core of the interpretative process is the conjunction of one model with another. Although the mental models of the preceding premises yield a valid conclusion (see Table 1), they omit a possibility compatible with the

Table 1: The Procedures for Conjoining Sets of Models Illustrated with an Example

---

The premises:

> If Pat is here then Viv is here.
> Mo is here or else Pat is here, but not both.

The first premise has the mental models:

> Pat   Viv
>
>   . . .

The second premise has the mental models:

> Mo
>   Pat

The procedures:

Procedure 1 (which applies only to mental models): The conjunction of two mental models, such as: A B, and B, depends on the set of models from which the second model of B alone is drawn. If A occurs in one of these models, then its absence in the current model is treated as its negation. The conjunction is in effect a contradiction: A B, and not-A B. If A does not occur in the set of models from which B is drawn, then its absence does not yield a contradiction. Hence, the four conjunctions from the models yield the following equivalences:

Pat Viv *and* Mo	is equivalent to:	Pat Viv *and* Mo not-Pat
. . . *and* Pat	is equivalent to:	not-Pat . . . *and* Pat
Pat Viv *and* Pat	is equivalent to:	Pat Viv *and* Pat Viv
. . . *and* Mo	is equivalent to:	Mo . . . *and* Mo

Procedure 2. The conjunction of a pair of models containing respectively a proposition and its negation yield the *null* model, which represents contradictions:

Pat Viv   *and* Mo not-Pat *yield* nil.
not-Pat . . . *and* Pat   *yield* nil.

Procedure 3. The conjunction of a pair of models that do not contain a contradiction yields a model containing all the elements of both models (except that explicit content replaces implicit content):

Pat Viv *and* Pat Viv *yield* Pat Viv
Mo . . . *and* Mo   *yield* Mo

Procedure 4. The conjunction of a pair of models in which at least one of them is the null model yields the null model, for example:

Pat Viv *and* nil   *yield* nil.

The results:

The conjunction of the two sets of mental models above yields:

> Pat   Viv
>   Mo

These models support the valid conclusion:

Pat and Viv are here, or else Mo is here.

---

premises. The conjunction of fully explicit models shows that a third possibility is:

not Pat   Viv   Mo

The same conclusion as the one in Table 1 still follows, but reasoners who rely on mental models will fail to envisage this possibility. They should think that it is impossible for both Viv and Mo to be here. This prediction is typical of the model theory.

Mental models are based on the principle of truth, and, as I mentioned, they yield a crucial prediction, which I illustrate in two contrasting inferences. The first is:

Either Jane is kneeling by the fire and she is looking at the TV or else Mark is standing at the window and he is peering into the garden.

Jane is kneeling by the fire.

Does it follow that she is looking at the TV?

Most people say: "yes." The second inference has the same initial premise, but it is followed instead by the categorical assertion:

Jane is not kneeling by the fire.

and the question is:

Does it follow that Mark is standing by the window?

Again, most individuals say: "yes." Let's see what the theory predicts.

The first premise in both inferences is an exclusive disjunction of two conjunctions. The theory predicts that individuals should rely on mental models, and use the procedures in Table 1. Hence, they should use the meaning of the first conjunction, Jane is kneeling by the fire and she is looking at TV, to build a mental model representing this possibility, which I abbreviate as follows:

Jane: kneeling looking

They should build an analogous model of the second conjunction:

Mark: standing peering

These two models must now be combined according to the exclusive disjunction in the premises. An exclusive disjunction of the form, *either A or else B*, has two mental models, which represent its clauses only in the possibilities in which they are true. Hence, the exclusive disjunction as a whole has the mental models:

Jane: kneeling looking

Mark: standing peering

In the first inference, the categorical premise is:

Jane is kneeling by the fire

According to Table 1, its conjunction with the preceding models of the disjunction yields:

Jane: kneeling looking

And so individuals should respond: yes, Jane is looking at the TV. This analysis may strike you as glaringly obvious.

In fact, the inference is a fallacy. The principle of truth postulates that individuals normally represent what is true in possibilities, but not what is false. When I first wrote a computer program to simulate the theory, and inspected its output, I thought that there was an error in the program. I searched for this "bug" for half a day, before

I discovered that the program was correct, and the error was in my thinking. What the program revealed is that for some inferences a discrepancy occurs between mental models and fully explicit models. The theory accordingly predicts that individuals should reason in a systematically fallacious way for these inferences. In some cases, the fallacies are so compelling that they resemble cognitive illusions, and so my colleagues and I refer to them as "illusory" inferences.

If you succumbed to the illusion, then you are in the company of Clare Walsh and myself. We worked with the inferences above for two days, in designing an experiment on another topic, before we realized that we were making an illusory inference, and that was *after* the discovery of other sorts of illusion. The fully explicit models of the disjunctive premise reveal the correct conclusion. The disjunction has six fully explicit models, because when one conjunction is true, the other conjunction is false, and you will remember that there are three possibilities compatible with the falsity of a conjunction. So, suppose that Mark is standing at the window and peering into the garden, then Jane can be kneeling provided that she isn't looking at the TV. This possibility is a counterexample to the illusory inference.

The second problem had the categorical premise that Jane is not kneeling by the fire, and posed the question of whether it followed that Mark is standing by the window. Most people respond "yes," which is a conclusion supported by the mental models shown above. This inference *is* valid. Walsh and I carried out an experiment examining a series of illusory inferences and control problems of this sort. The participants were much more likely to respond correctly to the control problems (78% correct) than to the illusory problems (10% correct), and all but one of participants showed this difference (Walsh and Johnson-Laird 2004). Analogous illusions occur in many other domains – from reasoning about probabilities to reasoning about whether a set of assertions is consistent (for a review, see Johnson-Laird 2006). Certain logical systems can be formulated so that they yield the same valid deductions whether they are based on models or on formal rules (Jeffrey 1981). The same principle holds for psychological theories based on mental models or on formal rules (Stenning and Yule 1997). But, because the theories differ in the procedures they use, a way to distinguish between them empirically is, for example, in the systematic errors that they predict. Illusory inferences are accordingly a

214 PHILIP N. JOHNSON-LAIRD

crucial test for mental models, because no other current theory including those based on formal rules predicts them.

Semantic and Pragmatic Modulations and Their Effects on Inference

The picture of reasoning that you are likely to have developed from the theory so far is a logical one. We use premises to construct mental models, which are sometimes fleshed out into fully explicit models. If we reason with fully explicit models and make no mistakes, then our reasoning is logical. Unfortunately, our capacity to hold information in working memory is limited, and so we tend to reason with mental models, which represent only what is true, and which can accordingly lead us to make illusory inferences. Nevertheless, it may seem that our method of reasoning is logical, and so you might suppose that the logic and psychology of reasoning are quite similar. In fact, another gap exists between them. What causes this divergence is that when human beings reason, they take their knowledge into account. As a result, they often go beyond the explicit information given to them, and take a step into inductive reasoning (as knowledge is fallible).

Suppose that the following claim is true:

Ed played soccer or he played some game.

If you learn that Ed didn't play soccer, you can infer that at least he played some game. The procedures that I have described yield this inference. Its formal pattern is valid in logic, and at first sight it seems to be valid in life – to the point that when theorists postulate formal rules (see, e.g., Johnson-Laird 1975; Rips 1994), they include a rule of the form:

A or B.

Not A.

Therefore, B.

Consider the premise again:

Ed played soccer or he played some game.

And suppose that you learn:

Ed didn't play any game.

This fact denies the second clause of the premise, and so you should infer:

He played soccer.

This inference also follows from a formal rule for disjunction. Yet, the inference is absurd. No one in her right mind (apart from a logician) would draw it. The reason is obvious. You know that soccer is a game. That's part of the *meaning* of the word "soccer." So, if Ed didn't play any game, he can't have played soccer.

Your knowledge of the meaning of the word, "soccer," blocks the construction of a possibility in the interpretation of the assertion. And so the assertion is compatible with just two possibilities. In one of them, Ed played soccer; and in the other, he played a game. So, either way, he played a game, and the possibility that knowledge blocks is the one in which Ed played soccer but didn't play a game. The second premise asserts that Ed didn't play a game, and so it eliminates both possibilities. The second premise contradicts the first, and individuals tend to infer:

Ed didn't play soccer

This analysis shows that the meaning of a word can modulate the interpretation of a sentential connective.

General knowledge and knowledge of the context can produce yield similar pragmatic modulations. Consider this inference, for example:

If Pat entered the elevator then Viv got out one floor up.

Pat entered on the second floor.

Therefore, Viv got out on the third floor.

You envisage a possibility in which Pat entered the elevator on the second floor, Viv was already in it, the two of them traveled up together to the next floor up, the third floor, and then Viv got out. You infer this sequence of events from your knowledge of how elevators work. In such cases, pragmatic modulation adds information about temporal and spatial relations between the events referred to in a conditional (Johnson-Laird and Byrne 2002).

Another effect of knowledge is to lead individuals to flesh out mental models into fully explicit models. Given the assertion:

Either the roulette wheel comes up red or else Viv is bankrupt

you are likely to envisage two possibilities. In one, the wheel does come up red and Viv isn't bankrupt; in the other, the wheel doesn't come up red, and as a result Viv loses all her money and goes bankrupt:

Wheel: red	Viv: not bankrupt
not red	bankrupt

You are likely to represent both possibilities in a fully explicit way, unlike your interpretation of disjunctions that do not engage your knowledge, such as: "Either there is a triangle or else there is a circle, but not both." Your knowledge overrides the principle of truth, and you think about both possibilities in full.

Modulation can help or hinder reasoning. These effects have been demonstrated in studies in which the participants make the same form of inference with different contents (e.g., Johnson-Laird and Byrne 2002). Assertions such as: *Pat is in Rio or she is in Norway*, elicit knowledge that one person cannot be in two places at the same time, and so the truth of the first clause implies the falsity of the second clause. In an unpublished experiment carried out in collaboration with Tom Ormerod, participants were accordingly faster and more accurate in drawing conditional conclusions from such disjunctions than from those with neutral contents, such as *Pat is in Rio or Viv is in Norway*. Neutral contents in turn led to faster and to a greater number of valid inferences than contents, such as: *Pat is in Rio or she is in Brazil*, for which, contrary to the disjunctive form of the assertion, the truth of the first clause implies the truth of the second clause.

Experiments with conditionals have also corroborated the same effects on reasoning from conditional premises (Johnson-Laird and Byrne 2002). Conditionals describing spatial inclusions enhanced modus tollens. For example, the premises:

If Bill is in Rio de Janeiro then he is in Brazil.

Bill is not in Brazil.

readily yielded the conclusion:

Bill is not in Rio de Janeiro

Reasoners knew that Rio de Janeiro is in Brazil, and so if Bill is not in Brazil then he cannot be in Rio. In contrast, spatial exclusions inhibited modus tollens. For example, given the premises:

If Bill is in Brazil then he is not in Rio de Janeiro.

Bill is in Rio de Janeiro.

reasoners tended to balk at the conclusion:

Bill is not in Brazil.

They knew that if Bill is in Rio then he must be in Brazil. The participants in the experiment drew twice as many modus tollens inferences from the spatial inclusions than from the spatial exclusions.

Most theories of reasoning allow for pragmatic effects, and the semantic and pragmatic modulation of mental models explains how these effects occur according to the model theory. It may be possible to explain them without recourse to models in, say, a framework based on formal rules of inference. However, as Byrne and I argued, the potential for meaning and knowledge to modulate the interpretation of connectives means that the system for interpreting sentences must always be on the lookout for such effects. It must always examine the meaning and reference of clauses to check whether they and the knowledge that they elicit modulate interpretation. This step must occur even for examples that turn out to receive a logical interpretation. The system for interpreting sentential connectives cannot work in the "truth functional" way that logic works, taking into account only the truth values of clauses (see, e.g., Jeffrey 1981). It must take meaning, reference, and knowledge into account. That is why the process of interpretation is never purely logical. The fact that modulation can add spatial and temporal relations between the events described in a sentence means that sentences of a given form, such as conditionals or disjunctions, have an indefinite number of different interpretations and cannot be interpreted as truth functions – an implication that has eluded some commentators on the model theory (pace Evans, Over, and Handley 2005).

The Development of Strategies for Reasoning

You might suppose that individuals are equipped with a single deterministic strategy for reasoning, which unwinds like clockwork. But, over the years, psychologists have discovered various embarrassments for this view. The order of the premises, for instance, has robust effects on inferences from conditional premises. It is easier to make a modus tollens inference when the categorical premise is presented before the conditional than vice versa – presumably the categorical can immediately block the representation of the otherwise salient case in which the antecedent is true (Girotto, Mazzocco, and Tasso 1997). Such effects seem inconsistent with a single inferential strategy. Perhaps the principal reason for postulating a single strategy, however, is that studies were often insensitive to strategy. They used no more than two premises; they recorded only the conclusions that the participants drew and perhaps how long it took them to draw them. Such data cannot reveal how the participants reached their conclusions. In contrast, studies with three of four premises, even though the inferences were easy to make, revealed that individuals spontaneously developed a variety of strategies.

Consider, for instance, the following problem from a study of strategies (Van der Henst, Yang, and Johnson-Laird 2002):

There is a red marble in the box if and only if there is a brown marble in the box.

Either there is a brown marble in the box or else there is a gray marble in the box, but not both.

There is a gray marble in the box if and only if there is a black marble in the box.

Does it follow that: If there is not a red marble in the box then there is a black marble in the box?

When most individuals encounter such a problem for the first time, they are nonplussed for a moment. Gradually, however, they work out its solution. The problem is, in fact, so easy that they almost always get it right. Over the course of a few problems of a similar sort, they develop a strategy, and different individuals develop different strategies. An obvious corollary is equally important. Individuals do not come to the psychological laboratory already armed with strategies for these sorts of inferences.

The correct answer to the preceding problem is: yes, if there isn't a red marble in the box then there is a black marble. As you think about the problem, you will see what is meant by a strategy, which my colleagues and I define as follows:

A *strategy* in reasoning is a systematic sequence of elementary steps that an individual follows in making an inference.

When you learn long multiplication, you learn a strategy, but it is a deterministic one. Each juncture leads to just one next step. When you develop a strategy for reasoning, however, it doesn't fix the sequence of steps in such a rigid

way. Each step in a strategy is a *tactic*. The procedures underlying a tactic are seldom, if ever, available to consciousness. You can't introspect on what enables you to combine two premises to draw a conclusion (see Table 1). But, individuals do report the particular tactical steps that they make when they carry out inferences such as the one above.

In the study from which the preceding example was taken (Van der Henst et al. 2002), the premises of each problem were compatible with just two possibilities, and half of them were presented with a valid conclusion and half of them were presented with an invalid conclusion. The participants had to think aloud as they reasoned, and they were allowed to use paper and pencil. A video camera was above them and focused down on the desk at which they sat. The participants occasionally made uninterpretable remarks, and they also made false starts that petered out. But, everyone correctly evaluated every problem, and it was clear what strategies they had used for nearly every problem. Sometimes they changed from one strategy to another in the middle of a problem. Overall in this experiment and subsequent ones, the participants developed five distinct strategies, which I will outline.

1. Integrated diagrams. This strategy relies on the construction of a single diagram that integrates all the information from the premises, very much along the lines of a set of mental models of the premises. With the problem above, a participant read the first premise aloud: "There's a red marble if and only if there's a brown marble," and made an immediate inference, "If brown then red." He then drew a simple diagram of this conclusion, where the arrow presumably denoted the conditional relation:

brown → red

He read the second premise aloud, "Brown or else gray," and added an element to his diagram to represent an alternative possibility:

gray

brown → red

His performance on earlier problems showed that he represented separate possibilities on separate lines. He read the third premise: "There's a gray marble if and only if there's a black marble," inferred: "If gray then black," and added a new referent to his diagram:

gray → black

brown → red

The diagram supports the conclusion: if not red then black, which he accepted. He then checked the inference, working through the premises again, and comparing them with his diagram of the two possibilities. His protocol allowed us to identify his strategy and its component tactics. But, he said nothing along the following lines, "my aim is to build a single diagram based on all the premises from which I can check whether the conclusion follows." And, as one would expect, he said nothing about the procedures underlying the tactical steps. Some participants who used this strategy drew a vertical line down the page and wrote down the colors of the marbles in the two possibilities on either side of it. Others, as in the preceding protocol, arranged the possibilities horizontally. One participant merely drew circles around the terms in the premises themselves to pick out one of the two possibilities. A telltale sign of the integrated diagram strategy is that the participants work through the premises in the order in which they are stated, and they include in their diagrams information from premises that are irrelevant to evaluating the conclusion.

2. The step strategy. The participants follow up step by step the consequences of a single possibility. If a problem includes a premise that makes a categorical assertion, then they may follow up its consequences. Otherwise, they make a supposition, that is, an assumption, to start the strategy rolling. Here's an example. The premises were as follows in abbreviation:

A pink if and only if a black.

Either a black or else a gray.

A gray if and only if a blue.

Does it follow that: If not a pink then a blue?

The participant began by reading each premise aloud, and then said: "Assuming we have no pink," which is a supposition corresponding to the "if" clause of the conclusion. The participant repeated: "There is no pink," and crossed out the word "pink" in the first premise. The participant inferred: "So there is no black," thereby drawing the first of a series of conclusions concerning a single possibility. The participant crossed out the word "black" in the first and second premises, and drew another conclusion: "There is gray," circling the word "gray" in the third premise. The participant drew another conclusion: "There is blue." Finally, the participant said, "Yes," to accept the conclusion, adding, "not pink and blue," and reiterated the imprimatur, "yes."

The participants did not always use suppositions correctly. Given, say, a conclusion to evaluate, such as:

If not a red then a black

they sometimes made the supposition:

Suppose there's a black.

and were able to infer that there is not a red. They then responded that the conditional followed from the premises. They may have made the correct response, but they haven't truly shown than that the conditional follows from the premises. A conditional allows that the "then" clause can be true even when the "if" clause is false, and so the right way to proceed is to make a supposition of the "if" clause and to show that it leads to the truth of the "then" clause.

One variant of the step strategy was sophisticated. A few participants made a supposition of a *counterexample* to a conclusion, and then used the step strategy to pursue its consequences. For instance, given the problem:

Either a red or else a blue.

Either a blue or else a gray.

A gray if and only if a white.

Does it follow that: A red if and only if a white?

one participant reasoned as follows:

Assuming red and not white. [a counterexample to the conclusion]

Then not gray. [from the supposition and the third premise]

Then not red. [from the previous step and the second and first premises]

No, it is impossible to get from red to not red.

The main diagnostic signs of the step strategy are that reasoners start by stating a supposition or a categorical premise, and then infer a series of simple categorical conclusions, each concerning a single possibility. In cases where an inference yields more than one model, the conclusion often has a modal qualification, for example, "possibly, there isn't a black marble," and any subsequent conclusions are themselves modal in the same way.

3. The compound strategy. Reasoners drew a compound conclusion from a pair of compound premises, where "compound" means that a sentence contains a connective. They sometimes made the inferences from diagrams of the premises. They expressed the conclusion either

verbally or by drawing a new diagram, or both. By combining the conclusion with a new compound, they drew another compound conclusion, and so on, until they finally reached the answer to the question. Here's an example based on the premises:

A white if and only if a blue.

If a blue then a pink.

Either a pink or else a brown.

Does it follow that: a white or a brown?

The participant read aloud all the premises, and then drew a diagram to represent the first premise:

blue → white

The participant read the second premise again, wrote it down, and drew a conclusion (which was invalid) from these two premises:

If there's a pink then there's a white

The participant drew a diagram to represent this conclusion:

pink → white

From this conclusion and the third premise, the participant inferred:

If there's a brown then there isn't a white

Finally, from this conclusion, the participant inferred the answer to the question:

Either there's a brown or else a white.

In the compound strategy, one premise is used to construct models, and the other premise is used to update them. The combination of two compound premises can put a heavy load on working memory, especially when both premises have multiple models, and so it is not surprising that individuals sometimes draw a modal conclusion about only one possibility.

4. The chain strategy. This strategy was totally unexpected, and no mention of it appears to be in either the psychological or logical literature. The reasoner constructs a chain of conditionals leading from one clause in a conditional conclusion to the other clause. This "chain" strategy resembles the step strategy, but has two crucial differences. First, reasoners do not announce that they are making a supposition. Indeed, they are not making a supposition, because they do not draw any intermediate conclusions. Second, they convert any premise that is not a conditional into

a conditional, either verbally or in a diagram. These conversions include cases where a biconditional, such as:

There's a gray if and only if there's a red

is transformed into a conditional, such as:

If there isn't gray then there isn't a red.

The reasoner's aim is to ensure that the "then" clause in one conditional matches the "if" clause of the next conditional. A participant using this strategy began by drawing a separate diagram for each premise in the problem. The premises were depicted as I have shown in this statement of the problem:

A gray if and only if a red.   r → g
Either a red or else a white.   r × w
A white if and only if a blue.   b → w

Does it follow that: If not a gray then a blue?

The participant, pointing at each diagram in turn, then said:

If not gray then not red.

If not red then white.

White comes from blue.

Yes.

The final "yes" was to acknowledge that the conclusion followed from the premises. This "chain" strategy is correct provided that reasoners construct a chain leading from the "if" clause of the conclusion to its "then" clause. However, reasoners often worked incorrectly in the opposite direction. It is easier to make inferences from conditionals than from disjunctions, because conditionals have only one explicit mental model whereas disjunctions have at least two explicit mental models. Hence, the model theory predicts that chains of conditionals are much more likely than chains of disjunctions. Indeed, my colleagues and I have never observed anyone who developed a strategy in which the premises are converted into a chain of disjunctions.

5. The concatenation strategy. This strategy occurred only occasionally. The participants concatenated two or more premises in order to form an intermediate conclusion. They usually went on to use some other strategy, but sometimes they formulated their own conclusion by concatenating all the premises, and this conclusion was then used as the premise for an immediate inference yielding the required conclusion.

For example, one participant argued from the premises:

A white and a blue.

A blue if and only if a black.

A black if and only if a red.

to the concatenation:

A white and a blue if and only if a black

and thence to the further concatenation:

A white and a blue if and only if a black if and
    only if a red.

At this point, the participant made an immediate inference to the required conclusion:

A white and a red.

The strategy accordingly depends on concatenating at least two premises into a single conclusion, and then either drawing such a conclusion, or else evaluating a given conclusion, if necessary by an immediate inference. The telltale sign of the strategy is that the participants join together premises and their connectives to form a single conclusion.

You might suppose the strategy depends on a formal procedure. On the contrary, it depends critically on mental models of possibilities. To see why, consider premises of the form:

A if and only if B.

Either B or else C.

C if and only if D.

where A, B, C, D, refer to the presence of different colored marbles in the box. Five different concatenated conclusions are possible, depending on the placing of the parentheses, for example:

A if and only if (B or else (C if and only if D))

((A if and only if B) or else C) if and only if D.

You might wonder which of them follows validly from the premises. In fact, none of them does. Four participants in one of our experiments used the concatenation strategy with these premises (see Van der Henst et al. 2002), and each of them spontaneously constructed this conclusion:

(A if and only if B) or else (C if and only if D).

It is the only concatenation out of the five possibilities that has the same mental models as those of the premises:

A   B
        C   D

But, the conclusion is invalid, because its fully explicit models do not correspond to the mental models of the premises. Ten participants out of the twenty in this experiment used the concatenation strategy. On 82 percent of occasions, the resulting conclusions were compatible with the mental models of the premises, and nine of the ten participants concatenated more conclusions of this sort than not. Van der Henst and his colleagues accordingly concluded that concatenation depends on mental models.

Depending on the particulars of the experimental procedure, variation occurs in the frequencies with which the participants develop the different strategies. For example, when they have to formulate their own conclusions, they tend not to use the chain strategy. Conversely, the concatenation strategy is more frequent when they do have to formulate their own conclusions. The most frequent strategy in both cases, however, was the integrated diagram strategy. Participants mix strategies, and switch from one to another. Sometimes a switch occurs in the middle of a problem; sometimes from one problem to the next. There are no fixed sequences of steps that anyone invariably followed. Likewise, although the problems are all within the scope of sentential reasoning, the participants quite often went beyond its scope to draw intermediate conclusions about possibilities. Regardless of strategy, as a further experiment showed, problems that yield only one mental model are easier than those that yield two mental models, which in turn are easier than those that yield three mental models (Van der Henst et al. 2002).

The variety of strategies is not unique to reasoning on the basis of sentential connectives. It occurs when individuals reason about the relations between relations (Goodwin and Johnson-Laird 2005a, 2005b), and when they reason with quantifiers such as "all" and "some" (Bucciarelli and Johnson-Laird 1999). It also occurs when they have to refute invalid conclusions based on sentential connectives. Given a conclusion that is consistent with the premises but that does not follow from them of necessity, their most frequent strategy is to try to construct a counterexample (Johnson-Laird and Hasson 2003). With a conclusion that is not even consistent with the premises, the same studies showed that individuals tend to detect the inconsistency, that is, they grasp that the conclusion is impossible given the premises.

Conclusions

This article has outlined the model theory's account of deductive reasoning. Its main principles are:

1. Reasoning is based on models of possibilities, and each mental model represents what is common to a possibility.

2. As far as possible, a mental model is iconic: its structure represents the structure of the possibility that its represents.

3. Human reasoners tend to think about possibilities one model at a time.

4. Reasoning can proceed by conjoining the possibilities compatible with the different premises, but conjunctions of inconsistent models yield the null model.

5. Mental models are based on the principle of truth: they represent clauses in the premises only when they are true in possibilities. If individuals retain mental footnotes about what is false then they can flesh out mental models into fully explicit models representing both what is true and what is false.

6. Semantic and pragmatic modulation affect the interpretation of connectives so they cannot be treated as strictly truth-functional.

7. Individuals develop different strategies for reasoning, for example, they may use integrated diagrams to represent multiple possibilities, make steps from a single possibility, or think of a possibility that serves as a counterexample to a putative conclusion.

The theory has been applied to most domains of reasoning. They include reasoning with temporal relations (e.g., Schaeken, Johnson-Laird, and d'Ydewalle 1996), spatial relations (e.g., Vanderendonck, Dierckx, and De Vooght 2004), and other relations (e.g., Carreiras and Santamaría 1997). It also has been applied to counterfactual reasoning (Byrne 2005), causal reasoning (Goldvarg and Johnson-Laird 2001), deontic reasoning (Bucciarelli and Johnson-Laird 2005), reasoning from suppositions (Byrne and Handley 1997), and reasoning about probabilities (e.g., Johnson-Laird, Legrenzi, Girotto, Legrenzi, and Caverni 1999). Recently, it has

begun to be extended to inductive reasoning, especially the sorts that occur in problem solving (Lee and Johnson-Laird 2005a), in the revision of beliefs in the face of inconsistency (Johnson-Laird, Legrenzi, Girotto, and Legrenzi 2000), in diagnoses (Goodwin and Johnson-Laird 2005c), and in the reverse engineering of simple systems (Lee and Johnson-Laird 2005b).

The chapter began with the effects of content on the selection task. Their discovery motivated the development of the model theory, and so you may be curious about what the theory has to say about the selection task. It postulates that individuals rely on mental models of abstract claims, such as, "If a card has an 'A' on one side then it has a '2' on the other side." They think of the salient possibility represented in the one explicit mental model:

A   2

and they choose the "A" card, and sometimes the innocuous "2" card, too. To make the correct selections, they need to overrule the principle of truth in order to envisage a *counterexample* to the conditional:

A   not 2

and then to choose the corresponding cards: A and 3. Most people fail. Any manipulation that makes counterexamples more salient, including the use of sensible contents or claims about what is permissible, yields an improvement in performance (see Johnson-Laird 2001).

At the heart of the model theory is the assumption that individuals who have had no training in logic are able to make deductions. The theory does not abandon logic entirely (pace, e.g., Toulmin 1958). Mental models relate to the model theory of logic, and to the logical principle that an inference is valid if there are no counterexamples to its conclusion. Individuals accordingly reason by constructing mental models of possibilities. These models are parsimonious in that they represent what is true, not what is false. The advantage is that individuals are able to make inferences that depend on more than one possibility. The disadvantage is that mental models can mislead individuals into thinking that they have grasped possibilities that in fact are beyond them.

Acknowledgments

The theory of mental models has developed as a result of the work of many researchers; see the Webpage maintained by Ruth Byrne and her colleagues: http://www.tcd.ie/Psychology/Ruth_Byrne/mental_models/.

I am grateful to these researchers for their help over the years. I am also grateful to the editors of this volume for their invitation to contribute this chapter, and for their helpful comments on an initial draft. The research was made possible in part by a grant from the National Science Foundation (Number 0076287) to study strategies in reasoning.

References

Baddeley, A. D. (1986) *Working Memory*. Oxford: Clarendon Press.

Barres, P., and Johnson-Laird, P. N. (2003) On imagining what is true (and what is false). *Thinking & Reasoning*, 9, 1–42.

Barrouillet, P., Grosset, N., and Leças, J. F. (2000) Conditional reasoning by mental models: Chronometric and developmental evidence. *Cognition*, 75, 237–266.

Bauer, M. I., and Johnson-Laird, P. N. (1993) How diagrams can improve reasoning. *Psychological Science*, 4, 372–378.

Bledsoe, W. W. (1977) Non-resolution theorem proving. *Artificial Intelligence*, 9, 1–35.

Boole, G. (1854) *An Investigation of the Laws of Thought on Which are Founded the Mathematical Theories of Logic and Probabilities*. London: Macmillan.

Braine, M. D. S. (1978) On the relation between the natural logic of reasoning and standard logic. *Psychological Review*, 85, 1–21.

Bucciarelli, M., and Johnson-Laird, P. N. (1999) Strategies in syllogistic reasoning. *Cognitive Science*, 23, 247–303.

Bucciarelli, M., and Johnson-Laird, P. N. (2005) Naïve deontics: A theory of meaning, representation, and reasoning. *Cognitive Psychology*, 50, 159–193.

Byrne, R. M. J. (2005) *The Rational Imagination: How People Create Alternatives to Reality*. Cambridge, MA: MIT Press.

Byrne, R. M. J., and Handley, S. J. (1997) Reasoning strategies for suppositional deductions. *Cognition*, 62, 1–49.

Carreiras, M., and Santamaría, C. (1997) Reasoning about relations: Spatial and nonspatial problems. *Thinking & Reasoning*, 3, 191–208.

Cheng, P., and Holyoak, K. J. (1985) Pragmatic reasoning schemas. *Cognitive Psychology*, 17, 391–416.

Cosmides, L. (1989) The logic of social exchange: Has natural selection shaped how humans reason? *Cognition*, 31, 187–276.

Evans, J.St.B.T., Over, D. E., and Handley, S. J. (2005) Suppositions, extensionality, and conditionals: A critique of the mental model theory of Johnson-Laird & Byrne (2002). *Psychological Review*, 112, 1040–1052.

García-Madruga, J. A., Moreno, S., Carriedo, N., Gutiérrez, F., and Johnson-Laird, P. N. (2001) Are conjunctive inferences easier than disjunctive inferences? A comparison of rules and models. *Quarterly Journal of Experimental Psychology*, 54A, 613–632.

Girotto, V., Mazzocco, A., and Tasso. A. (1997) The effect of premise order in conditional reasoning: A test of the mental model theory. *Cognition*, 63, 1–28.

Goldvarg, Y., and Johnson-Laird, P. N. (2001) Naïve causality: A mental model theory of causal meaning and reasoning. *Cognitive Science*, 25, 565–610.

Goodwin, G., and Johnson-Laird, P. N. (2005a) Reasoning about relations. *Psychological Review*, 112, 468–493.

Goodwin, G., and Johnson-Laird, P. N. (2005b) Reasoning about the relations between relations. *Quarterly Journal of Experimental Psychology*, 59, 1–23.

Goodwin, G., and Johnson-Laird, P. N. (2005c) Diagnosis of ambiguous faults in simple networks. *Proceeding of the Twenty-Seventh Annual Conference of the Cognitive Science Society*. Stresa, Italy. Mahwah, NJ: Erlbaum. 791–796.

Inhelder, B., and Piaget, J. (1958) *The Growth of Logical Thinking from Childhood to Adolescence*. London: Routledge & Kegan Paul.

Jeffrey, R. (1981) *Formal Logic: Its Scope and Limits*. Second edition. New York: McGraw-Hill.

Johnson-Laird, P. N. (1975) Models of deduction. In Falmagne, R. J. (Ed.) *Reasoning: Representation and Process in Children and Adults*. Hillsdale, NJ: Erlbaum. pp. 7–54.

Johnson-Laird, P. N. (2001) Mental models and deduction. *Trends in Cognitive Science*, 5, 434–442.

Johnson-Laird, P. N. (2004) The history of mental models. In Manktelow, K., and Chung, M. C. (Eds.) *Psychology of Reasoning: Theoretical and Historical Perspectives*. New York: Psychology Press. pp. 179–212.

Johnson-Laird P. N. (2006) Mental models, sentential reasoning, and illusory inferences. In Held, C., Knauff, M. and Vosgerau, G. (Eds.) *Mental Models: A Conception in the Intersection of Cognitive Psychology, Neuroscience and Philosophy*. Berlin: Elsevier. pp. 27–52.

Johnson-Laird, P. N., and Byrne, R. M. J. (1991) *Deduction*. Hillsdale, NJ: Erlbaum.

Johnson-Laird, P. N., and Byrne, R. M. J. (2002) Conditionals: A theory of meaning, pragmatics, and inference. *Psychological Review*, 109, 646–678.

Johnson-Laird, P. N., and Hasson, U. (2003) Counterexamples in sentential reasoning. *Memory & Cognition*, 31, 1105–1113.

Johnson-Laird, P. N., Legrenzi, P., Girotto, P., and Legrenzi, M. S. (2000) Illusions in reasoning about consistency. *Science*, 288, 531–532.

Johnson-Laird, P. N., Legrenzi, P., Girotto, V., Legrenzi, M., and Caverni, J-P. (1999) Naive probability: A mental model theory of extensional reasoning. *Psychological Review*, 106, 62–88.

Johnson-Laird, Legrenzi, P., and Sonino Legrenzi, M. (1972) Reasoning and a sense of reality. *British Journal of Psychology*, 63, 395–400.

Johnson-Laird, P. N., and Savary, F. (1999) Illusory inferences: A novel class of erroneous deductions. *Cognition*, 71, 191–229.

Lee, N. G. L., and Johnson-Laird, P. N. (2005a) Strategies in problem solving. Under submission.

Lee, N. G. L., and Johnson-Laird, P. N. (2005b) Synthetic reasoning and the reverse engineering of Boolean circuits. *Proceeding of the Twenty-Seventh Annual Conference of the Cognitive Science Society*. Stresa, Italy. Mahwah, NJ: Erlbaum. 1260–1265.

Manktelow, K. I. and Over, D. E. (1995) Deontic reasoning. In Newstead, S. E., and Evans, J.St.B. T. (Eds.) *Perspectives on Thinking and Reasoning: Essays in Honour of Peter Wason*. Mahwah, NJ: Erlbaum. pp. 91–114.

Mill, J. S. (1874) *A System of Logic, Ratiocinative and Inductive: Being a Connected View of the Principles of Evidence and the Methods of Scientific Evidence*. Eighth edition. New York: Harper. (First edition published 1843.)

Oaksford, M., and Chater, N. (1998) A revised rational analysis of the selection task: Exceptions and sequential sampling. In Oaksford, M. and Chater, N. (Eds.) *Rational Models of Cognition*. Oxford: Oxford University Press.

Ormerod, T. C., and Richardson, J. (2003) On the generation and evaluation of inferences from single premises. *Memory & Cognition*, 31, 467–478.

Osherson, D. N. (1974–6) *Logical Abilities in Children*, Vols. 1–4. Hillsdale, NJ: Erlbaum.

Peirce, C. S. (1931–1958) *Collected Papers of Charles Sanders Peirce*. 8 vols. Hartshorne, C., Weiss, P., and Burks, A. (Eds.) Cambridge, MA: Harvard University Press.

Popper, K. (1959) *The Logic of Scientific Discovery*. London: Hutchinson.

Rips, L. J. (1983). Cognitive processes in propositional reasoning. *Psychological Review*, 90, 38–71.

Rips, L. (1994) *The Psychology of Proof*. Cambridge, MA: MIT Press.

Schaeken, W. S., Johnson-Laird, P. N., d'Ydewalle, G. (1996) Mental models and temporal reasoning. *Cognition*, 60, 205–234.

Scriven, M. (1976) *Reasoning*. New York: McGraw-Hill.

Stenning, K., and Yule, P. (1997) Image and language in human reasoning: A syllogistic illustration. *Cognitive Psychology*, 34, 109–159.

Toulmin, S. E. (1958) *The Uses of Argument*. Cambridge: Cambridge University Press.

Van der Henst, J.-B., Yang, Y., and Johnson-Laird, P. N. (2002) Strategies in sentential reasoning. *Cognitive Science*, 26, 425–468.

Vandierendonck, A., Dierckx, V., and De Vooght, G. (2004) Mental model construction in linear reasoning: Evidence for the construction of initial annotated models. *Quarterly Journal of Experimental Psychology*, 57A, 1369–1391.

Walsh, C., and Johnson-Laird, P. N. (2004) Co-reference and reasoning. *Memory & Cognition*, 32, 96–106.

Wason, P. C. (1966) Reasoning. In Foss, B. M. (Ed.) *New Horizons in Psychology*. Harmondsworth, Middx: Penguin.

Wason, P. C., and Johnson-Laird, P. N. (1972) *The Psychology of Deduction: Structure and Content*. Cambridge, MA: Harvard University Press. London: Batsford.

Wason, P. C., and Shapiro, D. (1971) Natural and contrived experience in a reasoning problem. *Quarterly Journal of Experimental Psychology*, 23, 63–71.

Chapter 11: Interpretation, Representation, and Deductive Reasoning

KEITH STENNING AND MICHIEL VAN LAMBALGEN

A View with no Room

Is the psychology of deduction about the few well-known laboratory tasks in which subjects are presented with logical puzzles and asked to solve them: the selection task, syllogisms, the suppression task, conditional reasoning, . . . ? And if our capacity of deduction is not just for performing these tasks, what is it for? What everyday functions does it serve? How are theoretical analyses of deductive performance in these laboratory tasks related to analyses of other cognitive functions?

From the position of being absolutely central in the cognitive revolution, which was founded on conceptions of reasoning, computation and the analysis of language, the psychology of deduction has gone to being the deadbeat of cognitive psychology, pursued in a ghetto, surrounded by widespread scepticism as to whether human reasoning really happens outside the academy. "Isn't what we *really* do decision?" we increasingly often hear. Many eminent psychology departments do not teach courses on reasoning. Imagine such a psychology department (or indeed any psychology department) not teaching any courses on perception. Even where they do teach reasoning they are more likely to be focused on analogical reasoning, thought of as a kind of reasoning at the opposite end of some dimension of certainty from deduction.

We believe that the reason for this ghettoisation can be traced to a series of assumptions which we will consider shortly. We will argue that the way out of the ghetto is to drop these assumptions, none of which bears scrutiny anyway. It is then possible to give an account of the relation between the abstracted laboratory tasks and the real life reasoning which was

the original goal. Dropping these assumptions not only reconnects the laboratory to the wild, but also reconnects formal to empirical contributions.

Within the ghetto, the issue with the highest visibility has been about the nature of the mental representations underlying deduction – is it "rules" or is it "models." There has been almost universal acceptance that the goal of the field is the characterisation of "the fundamental human (deductive) reasoning mechanism," and that it must work on one or the other of these two kinds of representation. Yet there are good formal reasons for doubting whether these kinds of representations can be discriminated on the basis of data of the kind offered – data simply about input premises and output conclusions. And if this really is the most important issue, why aren't data about representations sought – data about working memory for "models" or "cases," for example? The empirical investigations seem ill-fitted to the purported theoretical goal.

Along with confidence that there is a single fundamental human reasoning mechanism, goes confidence that classical logic is the unchallenged arbiter of correct reasoning, although classical logic is often simultaneously rejected as a useful guide to mental representation or process. It is assumed that the classical logical form of the materials used in the experiments lies very near to their surface without any substantial interpretative process. This idea of interpretation as the superficial translation of natural language into logical form, carries over into neglect of the processes whereby artificial logical languages are interpreted – assigned a mapping onto the world. Natural languages do not come with this mapping in anything like the detail required for discourse interpretation – artificial languages still less so – witness the flourishing industry of trying to explain how it is done.

Even if classical logic were the only logic involved in peoples' reasoning in these tasks (and it clearly isn't), why do we not hear about its interpretative apparatus, but only its proof-theoretical machinery of derivation-rule applications in proof? This field sees itself as studying *representations*. We believe it is chiefly studying the outcomes and processes of *interpretation*. Of course, these are both rich and slippery concepts, which will repay some introduction.

Representational systems can be studied at the level of specifying *what* information is represented, and what is abstracted away from – the functional "input-output" level of analysis Marr called the "computational" level. This is the level that logical analysis generally addresses. At this level many of the studies in the field do contribute to the study of representations. But at this level there are simple theorems showing that for the range of materials concerned, these studies cannot discriminate between rules and models treatments. This level is crucial for the foundations of cognitive analyses – get the wrong analysis and all more detailed work is doomed to bark up the wrong tree. But what psychologists generally intend when they make representational claims is not at this level – it is at the level of the *implementation* of systems. In fact, this word is often a useful way of distinguishing this level of representational concern. This level is concerned with how the abstract structures of informational analysis – discourses, sentences, models, proofs – are implemented, both in the world and in the mind. Is there something like a diagram, or like a text implemented in the mind? Or on the paper the subject is using? Here one is concerned with memory, both long-term and working memory, with modalities (visuo-spatial, phonetic, orthographic, ...), with the environment (as it functions representationally), and eventually with the brain – all the paraphernalia of psychological analysis. Here differences may certainly be expected between how the information specified in sentences and the information specified in models gets implemented. But remarkably little study has been aimed at this level until very recently, and much of what has been aimed at it has been based on dubious informational-level analyses.

Interpretation also gets used at several levels. The interpretation of a representational system is an abstract analysis of a mapping from abstract representations (a language, a diagrammatic system, ...) to things in the world – shoes, ships, sealing wax.[1]

From a logical perspective, the most active and interesting part of this mapping is not the very general concerns about how natural language lexical items such as "shoe" map on to shoes past, present, and future, but the much more local issues about just exactly which shoes are "in play" in the current fragment of discourse – perhaps just the ones in the hall cupboard, or the ones Shoe Co. plans to make in the United Kingdom next year. At this level an interpretation of a language is a purely informational structure. But, of course, just like representations, interpretations also have more concrete implementations. Especially when we pay this very local attention to how interpretations become constructed during discourses, interpretation is also a process. Processes of interpretation may be thought of at the abstract informational level at which one characterises *what* choices of mapping are possible and what choices are actually made, or at the concrete implementational level where one gives cognitive accounts of particular mental processes that implement these choices.

This might all seem very academic and irrelevant to psychological analysis, but it is exactly such processes which we believe are the dominant processes observed in the experiments in the psychology of deductive reasoning. These processes come very near to the surface when we engage subjects in "socratic dialogues" about their reasoning in these tasks (for extended quoted examples, see Stenning and van Lambalgen [2004]). Interpretations, even at this abstract informational level, also become much more obviously "psychological" when logical analysis shows that interpretations have to include the *goals* of reasoning as well as the propositions involved. Earlier, we used the contrast between interpretation and reasoning to complain that interpretation had been rather neglected in this field, but this terminology can be confusing. Taken as a process, interpretation involves a kind of reasoning, and at least some examples of that kind of reasoning can be given an abstract informational analysis in terms of logics. These are the logics that we will chiefly be concerned with here. Defeasible reasoning *to* interpretations can be given models based on nonmonotonic logics.

Bringing interpretation center-stage, and modeling particular examples in logical (informational) systems, invites the accusation of regress. The new nonmonotonic logic is a language (a representational system) and so it has a semantics – a mapping of sentences onto worlds – and can be given proof theoretical apparatus such as inference rules. Reasoning to an interpretation of the original object-language being interpreted, will have to be implemented in the mind somehow, but there will now have to be a process of interpretation of this new nonmonotonic logic – and so on. We believe that this regress in fact grounds out – it is a virtuous regress – and that one of the great insights offered is that the nonmonotonic logic is a crucial part of an implementational account of how languages are grounded and given content. This must remain a promissary note, though we believe the neural implementation of a particular nonmonotonic logic in Section 3.2.1 goes some way to suggesting how this grounding might go.

Perhaps it is possible to forestall at least one misunderstanding about this regress. The implementation of reasoning about what interpretation to adopt for a discourse, does not itself have to be a cogitative process. All the psychological indications are that subjects who have not studied logic to some depth have very little access to the interpretative decisions they make, and that they are often triggered by superficial analyses of problems based on habits of understanding developed over very extensive practise with our mother tongue. In Subsection 4.1, we suggest that these implemented logics of interpretation may correspond to an important part of "System 1" processes as invoked by Evans (2003). Neither the fact there is a logic of interpretation, nor the assumption that it is really implemented in our minds, need necessarily lead to a regress of cogitation. This warning we hope at least makes it clear that we take the process of interpretation very seriously, both at an informational level (reasoning to as opposed to reasoning from) and at a concrete implementational level (as a real-time process in the mind).

In summary, interpretation sometimes contrasts with reasoning and sometimes with representation. Interpretation and representation are both susceptible to informational-level and implementational-level analyses. Our complaint about the field of the psychology of reasoning can be summarised by saying that it has pretty much ignored interpretation (save for some small details within classical logic), and that it has confused informational and implementational issues about representation.

Rehearsing these relations between interpretation, reasoning and representation should not lead us to forget that there are those with much more radical rejections of this entire machinery. Recently, there have been rejections of the appropriateness of logical deductive models of reasoning in favour of inductive information gain models, which turn reasoning into decision. But even those who have departed from accepting classical logic as the relevant competence model (Oaksford and Chater 1994), have continued to accept that it makes sense to treat all subjects as "trying to do the same thing" and so the goal might be described as changing to that of characterising the "fundamental human information gain mechanism." But as Stenning and van Lambalgen (2005) argue even this apparently radical move to a completely different competence model, still smuggles classical logic in at the back door.

The dissatisfactions of the ghetto have led even some prominent community members to depart entirely, claiming that once the ecological context of real life is considered seriously, what we find are decision processes, not reasoning processes, and that fast and frugal heuristics without any reference to competence models can replace logic, probability and all other cumbersome systems of reasoning. Reasoning is the idle pastime of the academy, but not the bread-and-butter of the real world.

We believe that the route out of this ghetto lies in taking interpretation seriously. In fact we believe that the mental processes mainly evoked by the laboratory tasks mentioned are interpretative processes – the processes of reasoning to interpretations. Modern logic provides a rich landscape of possibilities and we believe the empirical evidence is that subjects are engaged in setting a series of parameters in this space in order to formalise their understanding of what it is they are being asked to do. The evidence is that in these abstracted and unnatural settings student subjects are error-prone – so rich interpretation does not mean infallible reasoning. However, recasting the phenomena as interpretative provides a bridge between the laboratory and the wild. Laboratory tasks force interpretation in a vacuum, and the scattering that results can tell us much about what happens at more normal pressures. Furthermore, the wild, at least in "developed" societies with extended formal schooling, is full of tasks that are abstracted in ways rather closely related to the laboratory tasks, which were, after all, originally collected or adapted from various teaching sources. The nature of this bridge is then a good guide to the tasks in the wild, which most bring reasoning into play.

An immediate corollary of the formal stance of taking the multiplicity of interpretations seriously is the empirical consequence of needing to take individual differences seriously. Subjects do different things in the experiments, and this has so far been treated as simply stringing them out along a dimension of intelligence. They are all deemed to be trying to do the same thing, but succeeding or failing in different degrees. If there are many interpretations and each poses a qualitatively different task, then subjects are not even trying to do the same thing (at least at any finer grain than "understand what the hell they are being asked to do"), and suddenly the data and the theoretical demands become far richer. And most important of all, the working relation between formalisation and experiment changes entirely. Taking interpretation seriously and separating semantic from representational issues offers a room with a view quite panoramic enough to serve as foundations for human cognition.

The plan of the paper is as follows. We begin by illustrating the improvements in empirical understanding which can be purchased in the analysis of the laboratory tasks by taking them as being dominantly about reasoning *to* interpretations. We then present a sketch of the reconceptualisation of logical form which is involved in taking interpretation seriously – that is, of the landscape of many logical systems related by different kinds of parameter settings that characterise discourses' syntactic and semantic properties and their concepts of validity (or reasoning goals). This sets the scene for recasting the debate about the nature of the representations underlying reasoning. We will argue that the rules/models debate is conceptually ill-posed, and this has led to a mismatch between theoretical presentation and empirical investigation, and to the failures of empirical analysis illustrated in Section 2.1.

The following section introduces closed world reasoning, a variety of nonmonotonic logic. These logics can, for example, be used to analyze the suppression task and to show how the reasoning to an interpretation can be implemented in neural networks. The implementability is crucially dependent on the defeasibility of the semantics. Choosing these logics over classical logic as a basis for cognitive modeling hugely narrows the gap between formal competence model and psychological process account. So nonmonotonic logics offer a variety of precise and general accounts of interpretation. Although we will not expand on this

issue here, these logics provide another illustration of how existing psychological data mainly fails to bear on issues of representation. Stenning and van Lambalgen (2006) describe how nonmonotonic systems show the same representational indeterminacy between rules and models accounts. Just as with the classical cases considered in the rules/models debate, it is possible to conceive of these nonmonotonic systems as being represented and processed in several different modes. So by giving a nonmonotonic logical account of the interpretation of materials in these reasoning tasks we are *not* taking the "mental logic" side of the debate, nor the other. Specifying the logic does not settle how it is to be represented, and even when we give a particular neural implementation in Section 3.2.1 all that it shows is how implementations of sentences work together with implementations of models in computing consequence of discourses. To resolve representational issues one has to study how representations are implemented. The psychological study of these representations has hardly begun.

The paper ends with consideration of the resulting reconnection of the study of interpretation and reasoning to other cognitive fields. Where might reasoning to and form interpretations be most evident in the wild? What can logical and psychological theories of interpretation and reasoning contribute to these fields? What can it gain from them? And how are formal and empirical researchers to work together to study them?

2. Taking Interpretation Seriously

2.1. *Empirical Illustrations*

2.1.1. SELECTION TASK

Wason's 1968 selection task presents subjects with a rule. They have to select cases (cards) in order to make judgements, either about the cases' compliance or about the truth of the rule itself. This task provides a fascinating study of the problem of interpreting material into one of several logics, and the problems encountered in doing this in a context which obscures or removes the normal cues on which this choice of interpretation depends. Versions of the task compare the rules "If a card has a vowel on one side, it has an even number on the other" (the so-called abstract task) with "If a drinker's drink is alcoholic, then they must be over 18 years of age" (the so-called thematic task). The content of the latter rule is sufficient to cue subjects from the populations tested to adopt a deontic interpretation. The semantic consequence of this interpretation is that the task cannot be to test the truth of the rule since deontic rules don't have truth values. Indeed, the instructions in this latter task are to test the compliance of drinkers, given their drinks and ages. Such an interpretation leads to very simple reasoning in the selection task because this semantic relation between rule and case (unlike truth) is one-to-one. There are therefore no contingencies between choices of cards (whether one drinker violates the rule has no bearing on whether any other drinker does). Stenning and van Lambalgen (2004) use these semantic observations to make predictions about problems which will show up in the content of socratic dialogues about the task. The abstract task of judging truth of a descriptive rule is essentially in conflict with most subjects' initial interpretations of the rule. Stenning and van Lambalgen (2004) use their semantic observations to design several novel versions of the task and make and test predictions about them.

The interpretation of the abstract task is far more complex, even though the task is, of course, as concrete as it is possible to be. The root of the problem is that subjects' habitual interpretation of descriptive natural language conditionals, especially ones described as "rules," is as law-like conditionals robust to exceptions. Armed with this interpretation, subjects face an immediate impasse – they have no basis for telling exceptions (which still allow the rule to be true) from counterexamples (which reveal its falsehood). Notoriously, no test of a finite sample of cases will establish truth of such conditionals. It is true that Wason's instructions are that the conditional applies to only these four cards, but this merely conflicts with subjects' notions of what a rule is. One might object that if robust interpretation is subjects' problem, then they should object to the experimenter that the task is impossible. We would not expect this kind of response on the grounds of subjects' tendency to compliance (and, it must be said, lack of opportunity), and because they are neither conceptually well aware of the structure of their interpretations, nor in possession of a vocabulary for expressing their problems. The 'conjunctive rule' condition of Stenning and van Lambalgen (2004) provides vivid illustration of the tendency to comply by choosing some cards, even when the rule is blatantly false on the evidence before turning any cards.

Besides the problem of robustness to exceptions, once the task is about the truth of rules, rather than the compliance of single cases, this creates extra difficulties. The semantic relation is not one-to-one any more – several cases may need to be examined, and a judgement is only possible on the basis of the configuration of results (as Wason argues). So, in general, *sets of* cards are required to test truth, and this raises the problem of contingency of choice. If I choose this card and find it does not fit the rule, then that may affect whether I need to turn other cards. The vernacular relation of truth is, unlike the deontic relation which can be assessed a case-at-a-time, better seen as a whole family of relations: a card complying with a descriptive rule is a very different relation from the relation of a card making a rule true, and this ambiguity is predicted, and observed, to cause problems both in dialogues and in experiments.

For example, a two-rule version of the task was designed. This task presented two conditionals, one of which subjects are instructed is true and the other false, and their task is to choose cards to decide which rule is which. The rules were of the form: (1) if P then Q, and (2) If not P then Q. Here turning the false-consequent card alone is sufficient to guarantee a resolution. However, in socratic dialogues in this task, several subjects turned the true consequent card (Q), which turned out to comply with both rules, and then complained that this *showed that both rules are true* and the experiment was therefore flawed. Here is a confusion between the card complying with a rule, and a card showing that the rule is true. Our interpretation of the dialogues is supported by the fact that this impasse often precipitated insight into the contrast between these two meanings of "true," and into the task in general.

How does this approach explain the patterns of card choice in the task? Our most general claim is that none of the combinations of cards chosen is sufficient to fix the subjects' reasons for choice. In particular, the modal P, Q choice can be arrived at for several reasons, and only dialogue evidence is rich enough to start to isolate specific reasons. Table 3 in Stenning and van Lambalgen (2008) attempts to give some impression of the complexities involved.

This semantic analysis integrates accounts of a wide range of observations from the large number of versions of this task which have been run over the last thirty-five years. Many of the observed phenomena were known in the literature (many to Wason himself in the earliest days of his experiment) but remained unconnected. For example, Wason (1987) himself observed that subjects struggled with the contingencies of response involved in having to make all one's choices without any feedback. Wason and Green (1984) showed that a "reduced array" version of the task in which only the true-consequent and false-consequent cards were offered induced subjects to choose the false consequent over the true consequent they typically chose in the full array task. Of course, this reduction of array eliminates the contingency problem arising from this descriptive interpretation. Wason and Johnson-Laird's (1970) own investigations revealed subjects who realised that a 7 card with an A on the back *would* fail to fit the rule, but still refused to choose to turn it, as one might expect it the subjects problem is that nonfitting cases could be exceptions or counterexamples and it is not possible to tell which. Gigerenzer and Hug (1992) showed that when a rule which would standardly be interpreted as deontic was combined with task instructions to test whether it or an alternative were "in force" (i.e., to test the truth of a *description* of the rule in force), the task reverted to performance similar to that in descriptive tasks. Although others (Manktelow and Over 1990; Oaksford and Chater 1994; Fodor 2000) had pointed out that the drinking age task was deontic, and Cheng and Holyoak (1985) had proposed what was essentially an informal fragment of deontic logic in their account of "pragmatic reasoning schemas," no one had previously drawn out the semantic consequences of this interpretation in the context of a case selection task.

As mentioned earlier, the semantically based account makes new predictions such as those tested in the new two-rule task. This task is of considerably greater complexity than the single rule versions but it backgrounds the problem of robust interpretation. This deflection of the problems of robustness produced six times as many classically correct solutions as the corresponding single rule task, despite its added complexity, and even though subjects had to suppress the temptation to turn the ever attractive true consequent, and turn only the false-consequent card. A second prediction of problems induced by the contingency between the feedback from turn and the necessity for further turns was tested by simple instructions to "make your choices before any feedback." This quadrupled the classically correct responding in the single rule task by eliminating the contingency problems. Even more basically, the semantic analysis predicted that many of subjects' problems should not be limited to conditional

rules but should apply equally well to conjunctive ones, and indeed it was shown that a conjunctive rule "The cards have vowels on one side and even numbers on the other" produces almost exactly the same performance as the conditional rule. One factor which arises here from novel conflicts with the instructions (classically correct choice is to refuse to turn any cards) is the possibility of interpreting the conjunctive rule deontically. But it had also been known at least since Fillenbaum (1978) that conjunctive interpretations of natural language conditionals are common.

Revisiting the old experiments which were supposed to have revealed content effects on identical logical forms reveals that these effects are mediated through contents' influence on the choice of deontic vs. descriptive interpretations. For example, Johnson-Laird et al. (1972) showed that a rule based on a U.K. postal regulation familiar to their subjects facilitated classical performance, but the same materials failed to influence U.S. subjects unfamiliar with the regulation (Griggs and Cox 1982). This was interpreted as a familiarity effect. Reexamination of the materials shows that the rule was stated indicatively: "If a letter has a second class stamp, it is left unsealed." So U.K. subjects familiar with the rule interpret it deontically; U.S. subjects with no cue that the rule is a deontic regulation suffer all the problems just listed with the interpretation of descriptive conditionals.

The two rules: "If a card has a vowel on one side, it has an even number on the other" and "If a drinker's drink is alcoholic, then they must be over 18 years of age," as interpreted in the experimental settings, are of quite different logical forms and the subjects' judgments can be largely predicted by which logical form is adopted. A single generalization captures almost all the variance in the very large number of experiments in the literature: if interpretation is deontic, the task will yield Wason's "competence response"; if the task is interpreted descriptively, it will yield the scattering of interpretations outlined earlier and the card choices Wason originally observed. This generalization was missed by all the theoretical accounts: mental models, matching theory, evolutionary psychology, relevance theory, and information gain. The phenomena observed are driven by interpretational processes. None of the theories took the phenomena to be primarily interpretative phenomena. All assume classical logic as providing the only possible interpretation and seek to explain what are, on this interpretation, baffling observations.

2.1.2. SUPPRESSION TASK

Byrne's 1989 task develops syllogism about content and form, inherited from the study of the selection task, into an argument about mental representations – rules versus models. When subjects are presented with the modus ponens premises "If she has an essay she studies late in the library. She has an essay," they almost universally draw the conclusion that she studies late. When instead they are presented with the same premises *plus* the premise: "If the library is open she studies late in the library," about half of them withdraw the inference. Analogously, many subjects presented with "If she has an essay to write, she studies late in the library. She doesn't have an essay to write" draw the (classically invalid) conclusion "She doesn't study late in the library." When instead they are presented with these premises plus "If she has a textbook to read, she studies late in the library," then again many who did draw the inference withdraw it. Byrne concludes that inference rules cannot be used to explain the initial performances since they evidently cannot explain the subsequent withdrawal of inferences. Rules, if they are to be invoked, must be invoked universally and uniformly. So much the worse for mental logics – so mental models are the underlying representations, concludes Byrne.

While the selection task is, we have argued, a disguised interpretation task, here the task is much more obviously interpretative. Subjects are presented with mini-discourses, and a large proportion of them experience enough tension in the materials to make some accommodation, which is evidenced in their withdrawal of inferences, as they seek to find the intended model, using whatever knowledge or guesswork comes to hand. Once one enters into dialogue with subjects engaged in this task, it is even more evident that tensions are experienced even when inferences are not withdrawn. Stenning and van Lambalgen (2005) show that in the nonmonotonic logic appropriate to this interpretative process, on at least one plausible interpretation, modus ponens does not apply to the triple-premise discourses. This then explains the withdrawal of the inferences by substantial numbers of subjects. The experiment does not bear on a choice between rules and models. Funnily enough, this nonmonotonic logic is in fact the logic one requires to capture the subjects' likely initial interpretation of the lawlike robust conditional rules in the selection task. We will see more of this logic later when we discuss discourse semantics and representational issues.

In taking her experiment to be about representation by models or rules, Byrne misses several important issues: First, the difference between reasoning *to* an interpretation and reasoning *from* an interpretation. Classical logic, which she assumes is the only relevant logic, is clearly only relevant to reasoning from interpretations. One possibility is that mental models theory is being extended to encompass a theory of this defeasible interpretational process. But mental models theory was developed as a theory of classical reasoning *from* interpretations (in the syllogism). If it is now to be taken to be a model of defeasible reasoning it had better be compared to logics of defeasible reasoning, not classical logic. And if it is being extended, then we need to be told when it is doing the one thing and when the other. Unfortunately what we find is simultaneous claims for both within the compass of the same paper:

> According to the model theory of deduction, people make inferences according to the semantic principle that a conclusion is valid if there are no counterexamples to it. (Byrne et al. 1999: 350)[2]

The explanation attempts to stay with a classical concept of validity and, in a roundabout way, to retain classical logic's interpretation of the conditional as material implication as the "basic" meaning of conditionals. It therefore comes as something of a surprise to see that the penultimate section of Byrne et al. (1999) is entitled *"Suppression and the nonmonotonicity or defeasibility of inferences,"* where it is claimed that "the model theory attempts to provide an account of one sort of nonmonotonic reasoning, undoing default assumptions..." (Byrne et al. 1999: 370; see Stenning and van Lambalgen 2005: 930 for fuller analysis of this equivocation).

But perhaps more seriously still for a psychological theory, Byrne's account of the suppression task ignores most of the data. What, for example, are the other half of the subjects doing who don't "suppress" the modus ponens inference after the second conditional is presented? A moment's thought suggests that there are several interpretations of the materials which are quite consistent with continuing to draw the inference. For example, the "suppression" interpretation interprets the second conditional as a kind of "repair" on the part of the speaker – a weakening of the originally strong claim, perhaps after remembering, say, that it's a bank holiday. There is an equally good interpretation which treats the speaker as *strengthening* the original claim – "In fact she's such a diligent student, she'll be in the library whether she has an essay or not." Lechler (2004) conducts an exploration of the range of interpretations that subjects do in fact develop, and indeed this strengthening class is common. Yet another possibility is a presuppositional interpretation (i.e., presupposing that the library is open) which is clear evidence that non-suppression is consistent with a nonmonotonic nonclassical reading. Later we present a formal analysis which relates some of these different interpretations.

Individual differences as diagnosed by interpretation have received some attention in the psychological literature. For example, Stanovich (1999) presents evidence that the 5 percent of student subjects in the selection task who choose the cards Wason claims are "correct," show significantly higher SAT scores than the rest of the subjects. Our theory proposes many possible interpretations in both the selection and suppression tasks, and so if one assumed these are all equally good fits to the information the subject is presented with, Stanovich's results would be hard to explain. We do not make this assumption. The small minority of students getting Wason's answer are clearly more adept at finding the interpretation intended amongst all the conflicting information Wason supplied. Because this task of understanding the strange instructions of professors is very close to many of the problems set in school, we would expect correlation with SAT scores. Stenning (2002) presents evidence that one mechanism by which real logic courses can improve general reasoning skills is through increasing flexibility of interpretation.

If mental models theory is really about the process of interpretation, why so little empirical curiosity about the range of interpretations people actually adopt? Empirical curiosity is the victim of the focus on the representational issue of models versus rules which the data cannot decide. Because there is obviously interpretative variety, the data of individual differences should become primary. It is not that all subjects are trying to do the same thing, and merely succeeding or failing to different degrees. If subjects have different interpretations, then we need to be able to characterise them. We might want a principled theory of why some interpretations are more sustainable than others, but we can't get such a theory until we acknowledge interpretational variety. Muddling together the pro-

cesses of reasoning to and reasoning from interpretations has the consequence of obscuring the needed empirical insights.

2.1.3. IMMEDIATE INFERENCE AND THE SYLLOGISM

The syllogism, for the logic teacher, and perhaps for the psychological experimenter, is a fragment of classical monadic predicate logic, usually with some existence assumptions thrown in. This interpretation does not extend to the majority of experimental subjects. Newstead (1989–1995) was among the first to systematically study subjects' interpretations of syllogistic quantifiers using what he called the "immediate inference" task. His goal was to reconcile interpretation with reasoning, which was known to be extremely prone to error by the standards of classical interpretation.

In the immediate inference task, subjects were asked to assume that, say, "All A are B" and then asked whether it followed that, say, "All B are A" must be true, false, or could be either.[3] This pattern of presenting a single premise and asking about a targeted conclusion was then repeated for all combinations of quantifiers and subject/predicate inversions. Newstead showed that a healthy majority of subjects did not even approximate a classical logical interpretation of the quantifiers, many drawing patterns of Gricean implicature feature such as, for example, concluding "Some A are not B" from the assumption that "Some A are B" (Grice 1975). Many other nonclassical patterns of inference appear in his data and were known from earlier data, notably "illicit conversion" (responding "true" to the example with "all" above). In this literature, illicit conversion is simply defined as a syntactic pattern observed in the data, and no semantic rationale for this behaviour is supplied.

Despite extended analysis, Newstead failed to find any systematic relation between subjects' patterns of interpretation in this task, and their subsequent syllogistic reasoning – drawing conclusions from pairs of the same premises. Roberts et al. (2001) extended this approach and claimed to rule out Gricean models of interpretation in syllogistic reasoning. Their best fitting models involved "illicit conversion."

But taking a broader perspective, "illicit conversion" and Gricean implicature are closely related patterns of credulous reasoning. Illicit conversion is what is called in AI "closed-world reasoning." For example, given only the information that "if it's an A then it's a B," closed-world reasoning on this single rule permits the conclusion that the only way something can get to be a B is if it is an A – the illicit conversion pattern. This inference is closely related to Grice's Maxim of Quantity which generates the implicatures illustrated earlier. The Maxim enjoins speakers to "say enough and not too much." Closed-world reasoning results from the assumption that the specification of the world we have been given is all that we are reasoning about. One might observe that relations between the Gricean account and closed world reasoning are already complicated. One might argue that the speaker's decision to say "All As are Bs" instead of "As and Bs are the same" enough to generate the implicature that not all Bs are As? However, if this were so it is too strong, and indeed Grice's theory has much room for wriggle. "As and Bs are the same" has interpretations which such a speaker might not want to suggest, and there is also the issue of economy of expression. Grice's theory is notoriously hard to turn into a processing model and was not intended as such. The important point here is that Grice's theory and closed-world-reasoning are overlapping accounts of credulous interpretation, and this connection has either not been made or explicitly denied in this literature.

So we can define a more general approach to discourse interpretation as *credulous* discourse processing. A hearer attempts to construct the speaker's "intended model" of the discourse, using whatever general and contextual knowledge can be brought to bear and assuming that the speaker is cooperative (the suppression task discourses quoted above are good examples). Credulous processing goes "beyond the information given" in that, for example, it draws implicatures based on surmises about the speaker's intentions, and retrieves relevant general knowledge from databases of conditionals in long-term memory (Stenning and van Lambalgen (2005).

Once a broader view of the semantic/pragmatic theories is adopted, the data takes on a different caste. Stenning and Cox (2006) show that Newstead's operationalisation of Gricean implicature is too narrow. It operationalises Gricean implicature in terms of a couple of implicatures and neglects the reasons why these implicatures might sometimes be suppressed. It also misses the close affinity to illicit conversion, seeing conversion as an unrelated arbitrary pattern of reasoning. Finally, Roberts *et al.* misin-

terpret Grice's pragmatics as licensing fixed patterns of reasoning regardless of the pragmatic circumstance. The latter point can be illustrated with an example.

Roberts et al.'s (p. 174) considers the syllogism *All B are A. Some C are B*, and observes that with Gricean interpretations it may either get encoded with set A identical to set C, or with the two sets partially overlapping. They then argue that "with the outcome sets made explicit, a problem for anyone adopting these interpretations becomes apparent. Gricean interpretations affect not only the *encoding* of a problem, but also its *decoding* of the final outcomes so that conclusions can be generated . . . The [Gricean] assumption of the mutual exclusivity of *some* and *all* during encoding will result in a contradiction on decoding."

But this argument supposes that the hearer treats the "output models" of the interpretation process like models of classical logical conclusions, true in all models of the premises, and that now, from the point of view all speaker concluding from this construction. *Some A are B* is inconsistent with *All A are B* – not merely that it would be misleadingly uninformative to say the former when the latter is true in the intended model. In Grice's theory, the aim of processing determines the semantics of the representations and in giving a competence model, one should not forget this and return to a classical interpretation in midstream. The credulous process which Grice described is defeasible and therefore non-monotonic. Inferences that might be made at the end of premise one may not be made after premise two. The construal of the task and the interpretation mechanism are perfectly homogeneous across tasks, though they have the effect that implicatures arising at one point may get canceled at another.

These theoretical insights suggest empirical questions. By adopting a more exploratory approach to immediate inference data, Stenning and Cox show that there are broad patterns interpretable along two dimensions – whether the subject's interpretation is credulous or sceptical (classical), and whether subject/predicate conversion is involved in the inference. Conversion, it turns out, is not merely of interest when it is "illicit." A hitherto unnoticed subgroup of subjects refuse to draw subject/predicate inverted conclusions, even when they are classically valid (e.g., given "Some A are B" they refuse to infer that "Some B are A"). Interestingly, the subgroup who show this pattern are disjoint from the subgroup who illicitly convert the "all" example.

Superficially, this observation that drawing implicatures is at least somewhat independent from drawing illicit conversions is at odds with the observation that both are credulous patterns of reasoning. If a subject is credulous in one pattern, why not the other? Well, they may both be credulous patterns but there are psychologically important differences. The relevant kind of closed-world reasoning is a kind of "backward" reasoning from result to initial conditions. From the truth of a consequent, and the absence of other conditionals with that consequent, an inference is made to the truth of its antecedent. Gricean quantifier implicatures of the kind illustrated here are forward reasoning guided by the grammatical organisation of the discourse. As we shall now see, the empirical evidence is that these two aspects of credulous reasoning are differentially adopted by different subjects and in different tasks. Here we will not dwell on the subclassification of credulous reasoning but rather note the empirical evidence is that further logical work remains to be done to understand why this should be.

And at a surface level, subject/predicate inversion in the simple existentially quantified sentences such as "Some A are B" operates as a form of information packaging – structural variation which leaves truth conditions unchanged. Information packaging is a vital part of credulous discourse processing, guiding the hearer's focus of attention toward identification of the "intended" model. Much of the difficulties students have learning elementary classical logic is with learning to put aside thesis focusing of credulous discourse. So, although "Some A are B" is true just whenever "Some B are A," the conditions under which a cooperative speaker would choose to utter the one are different from the conditions that would lead to the other choice.

Stenning and Cox (2006), armed with their two-dimensional analysis of immediate inference data, show that it is then possible to predict aspects of several subgroups of subjects' reasoning in the syllogistic task. Indeed, so large are the differences between these subgroups' performances that it is possible to find subgroups of syllogisms for which subgroups of subjects defy most of the powerful generalisations in the literature derived from analysing group data without regard to individual differences. The search of the 'fundamental human reasoning mechanism' has produced models that may not fit any of the subjects' actual mental processes.

Stenning and Cox (2006) incorporate their newly characterised individual difference dimensions into Stenning and Yule's 1997 "source-premise identification model" of conclusion term order through the different heuristics which subjects employ to identify the source-premises on which they construct their discourse representations. The model reveals several novel phenomena in this much studied domain. For example, the subgroup of subjects who refuse the "some" inference quoted above are saved from making many classically illegitimate inferences by the information packaging of the premises. In contrast, there is a subgroup of subjects who not only draw the "forward" Gricean implicatures from "Some A are B" to "Some A are not B," but are equally happy to draw the inverted implicature "Some B are not A." Stenning and Yule's 1997 original development of the source-founding model had already disposed of mental model theory's claims to be able to predict conclusion term-order in syllogistic reasoning on the basis of the FIFO (first-in-first-out) properties of working memory. They showed that far from having to arrange the three terms with the middle-term (B) in between A and C so that it could be "canceled," in fact subjects' commonest arrangement of terms in their working memory is with B initial (see Cooper 2002: 170 ff. for computational modeling of the source-founding model). Besides the observations, it is odd that a model-based theory should plump for such a syntactically dependent "cancellation" mechanism.

The search for the fundamental human reasoning mechanism through these three tasks – selection, suppression, and syllogism – has employed narrow hypothesis testing methodology rather than an exploratory convergent-evidence approach. It has ignored the support available from modern logical, semantic and pragmatic methods, and instead targeted its criticism of logic on inappropriate classical logic which it has still not eradicated from its normative pronouncements. Rejecting logic has led only to attempts to reinvent it and produced some strange hard-to-interpret systems. Wanting to focus on grand representational issues has led to missing the most important empirical generalisations which are about the semantics of alternative interpretations. Later we will show that mistaking representation for interpretation has also mangled the study of representations. With this much empirical motivation, in the next section we turn to a sketch of the concept of logic which has lain not far submerged beneath these empirical analyses.

2.2. *Formal Consequences of an Interpretative Stance*

2.2.1. THE MANY LANGUAGES OF THOUGHT

In the psychology of reasoning literature one commonly finds a picture of reasoning as proceeding according to preestablished logical laws, which can be applied by anybody in any circumstances whatsoever.

It would not do to blame the psychologists alone for this, because it is a picture frequently promulgated in the philosophical literature. To take just one example, we see Ryle (*Dilemmas*, 1954) characterising logical constants (for example *all, some, not, and, or, if*) as being indifferent to subject matter, or *topic neutral*. Characterisations such as this are related to a superficial reading of the classical definition of validity, say for a syllogism such as

All *A* are *B*.

All *B* are *C*.

Therefore, all *A* are *C*.

The validity of this schema is taken to mean something like "whatever you substitute for *A*, *B* and *C*, if the premises are true for the substitution, then so is the conclusion." Analyzing an argument thus consists of finding the topic-neutral expressions (the logical constants), replacing the topic-dependent expressions by variables, and checking whether a substitution that verifies the premises also verifies the conclusion. If so, one knows that the argument is correct for the particular substitution one is interested in.

This *schematic* character of inference patterns is identified with the "domain-independence" or "topic-neutrality" of logic generally, and many take it to be the principal interest of logic that its laws seem independent of subject matter. In fact, however, logic is very much domain-dependent in the sense that the relevant schemata (i.e., logical forms) depend on the domain in which one reasons, *with what purpose*. We therefore view reasoning as consisting of two stages: first one has to establish the domain about which one reasons and its formal properties (what we will call "reasoning to an interpretation") and only after this initial step has been taken can one's reasoning be guided by formal laws (what we will call "reasoning *from* an interpretation").

2.2.2. REASONING TO AN INTERPRETATION AS PARAMETER SETTING

Let us first be slightly more specific about what is involved in formalising a domain. It is very hard to pin down the notion of domain itself; for now, we restrict ourselves to listing some examples that will be treated in this chapter: actions, plans and causality; contracts; norms; other people's beliefs; mathematical objects; natural laws. Formally, a domain is described by a set of mathematical representations, called structures, of the main ingredients of the domain, together with a formal language to talk and reason about these structures; the latter require a definition of how the formal language is interpreted on the relevant set of structures. This notion of structure is extremely general, and instead of being more precise at this point, we refer the reader to the different examples that will be given below.

The reader may wonder why language should be relative to a domain: isn't there a single language – our natural language – which we use to talk and reason about everything? A moment's reflection shows however that it is not useful to have a single language (*with a single semantics*) for talking about everything. Even though we use natural language to reason about both legal laws and scientific laws, the semantic structures of these domains are radically different. Hence it is best to keep these languages distinct: there are many "languages of thought" instead of Fodor's monolith. This reflects a different (and, as we believe, more useful) conception of language, as consisting not only of symbolic expressions, but as a set of symbolic expressions together with a semantics.

Thus far, what is proposed here is analogous to the approach to logic known as "model theoretic logics" (see Barwise and Feferman 1985). However, we also want to formally incorporate the *purpose* for which we reason, and this often involves taking into account the definition of logical consequence. A good illustration of this is furnished by legal reasoning in the courtroom, of which the following is a concrete example (simplified from a case which recently gained notoriety in The Netherlands). A nurse is indicted for murdering several terminally ill patients, who all died during her shifts. No forensic evidence for foul play is found, but the public prosecutor argues that the nurse must have caused the deaths, because she was the only one present at the time of all the deaths. This is an example of "plausible" or "credulous" reasoning: an inference is drawn on the basis of data gathered and plausible causal relationships. This can be viewed as an inference where the premises are interpreted on a very restricted class of models, namely models in which no "mysterious" events happen, neither divine intervention nor unknown intruders.

The defence countered the prosecutor's argument with an instance of "skeptical" reasoning, by arguing that the cause of death might as well have been malfunctioning of the morphine pumps, and contacted the manufacturer to see whether morphine pumps had had to be recalled because of malfunctioning – which indeed turned out be the case. The move of the defense can be viewed as enlarging the class of models considered, thus getting closer to the standard notion of logical consequence where one considers all models of the premises instead of a restricted class.

The approach to logic which we would like to advocate views logics from the point of view of possible syntactic and semantic choices, or what we will call parameter settings. This metaphor should not be taken too literally: we do not claim that a logic can be seen as a point in a well-behaved many-dimensional space. The use of the term "parameter" here is analogous to that in generative linguistics, where "Universal Grammar" is thought to give rise to concrete grammars by fixing parameters such as word order. The set of parameters characterizing a logic can be divided in three subsets

1.   choice of a formal language

2.   choice of a semantics for the formal language

3.   choice of a definition of valid arguments in the language

Different choices may be appropriate in different domains – a domain gives rise to a semantics (that is, a notion of structure), and in principle each domain comes with its own language. We claim that subjects in reasoning tasks such as the ones discussed above are mostly engaged in a process of interpretation, of the verbal material *and* of the task, and that this process can be viewed as the imposition of logical form, in the sense just defined. The reader may balk at this: Surely a reasoner does not literally choose a formal language? Although it certainly true that reasoners do not have the terminology of the logical theories, and their choice of interpretation is made in context and without much awareness of the reasons applied or the decisions taken, there is nevertheless good evidence that

they do make these decisions. For example, some subjects in the selection task allow true conditionals to have exceptions, others do not. The latter operate with a representation of the conditional as of the form[4] $p \rightarrow q$ (i.e., featuring the atoms p, q only); the former operate with a more elaborate syntactic representation, something of the form $p \wedge \neg e \rightarrow q$, where e is an atom denoting an exceptional situation. Analogously for the other parameters: the claim is that a theory of the phenomena observed must have recourse to these notions. Educationally, and psychologically, the process of gaining more explicit control over adoption of interpretations is an important one which we address below.

It is, in particular, subjects' interpretation of the task that has an important influence on the assignment of logical form. This can be seen very clearly in the suppression task, repeated here for convenience: "If she has an essay she studies late in the library. If the library is open she studies late in the library. She has an essay." Here the subject may view the task as trying to make the implied speaker's utterances consistent (the "credulous stance"), or she may adopt the "skeptical stance" by interpreting the second conditional as refuting the first. The skeptical stance leads to the adoption of classical logic as the logical form: the subject considers the first conditional to be a proposal for a universal generalization which is falsified by a situation in which the protagonist has an essay while the library is closed. In the credulous stance, the first conditional is not abandoned but modified. However, even within the credulous stance there are several possibilities; the subject may view the second conditional as a weakening or on the contrary as a strengthening of the original claim. In the first case, the subject chooses a representation for the conditional which allows exceptions, such as $p \wedge \neg e \rightarrow q$ (as in the selection task), together with a clause saying that closure of the library ('c') constitutes an exception e. Nonmonotonic logic then allows one to infer the weaker rule $p \wedge \neg c \rightarrow q$, from which nothing follows given p only. Here we have a case of a parameter-setting which differs from classical logic in all parameters. If the subject views the second conditional as a strengthening, this can be represented by the same form of nonmonotonic reasoning, this time applied to the second conditional, given formally by $r \wedge \neg \acute{e} \rightarrow q$, where $\acute{e}$ again denotes an exceptional circumstance, this time relevant to the second conditional. It might be thought for instance that not having an essay counts as such an exception $\acute{e}$, but the "strengthening interpretation" says that there are in effect no exceptions: that's how diligent the student is. This is again a difference in logical form: strengthening affects the formal representation of the second conditional, while weakening influences that of the first.

A final remark for those who are still sceptical about the use of a logical form featuring a non-monotonic consequence relation. Such a logical form comes naturally to subjects because they are used to it as speakers of natural language. If one views language understanding as the construction of discourse models (Kamp and Reyle [1993]), then one must allow that these models may have to be revised completely as new information is coming in. This can be illustrated by means of the two sentences (1a) and (1b) (adapted from Asher and Lascarides 2003; for related examples, see van Lambalgen and Hamm 2004).

(1) a. Max fell. John pushed him.
     b. Max fell. John pushed him over the edge of the abyss to dispose of the corpse.

World knowledge applied to (1a) leads to the computation of an event structure in which the pushing precedes the falling. However, (1b) conjures up a scenario in which John shoots Max causing the latter to fall, after which he is shoved over the edge. We perform such recomputations of the event order effortlessly[5] all the time, and it is not particularly bold to suggest that subjects applies these skills to reasoning tasks.

3. Representational Issues

In Section 2.1, we argued that both models- and rules-based theories missed empirical generalizations in interpreting the experimental data in three central paradigms used in the psychology of deductive reasoning. What is it about the theories that led to this outcome? In Section 2, we argued that one problem was mistaking reasoning *to* interpretations for reasoning *from* them. But it was also caused by a general tendency to conflate logical/semantic issues with representational/implementational ones, and it is to this problem we turn now. We begin by clarifying the levels distinction and its bearing on the inadequacy of the kind of data which has dominated the field, for resolving representational issues. We propose nonmonotonic logics give a better fit to informational analyses of subjects' actual understandings of these tasks, but choosing these

logics over classical logics does not resolve representational/implementational issues.

In fact, one might suppose that nothing changed with respect to the representational issues with this shift in logic. That would be a mistake. Although the early forms of nonmonotonic logic (Reiter 1980; McCarthy 1980) developed bad reputations for intractability of reasoning, the newer systems derived from logic programming proposed here are radically more tractable than classical logic. This has immediate consequences for representation. Sets of premises have single preferred models which can be identified with "intended" models in credulous discourse processing. The gap between semantics and psychology closes up. At the end of the section, we show how this means that these logics can be interpreted in neural networks, or alternatively as rules in production system architectures such as ACT-R (Anderson and Lebiere 1998: Ch. 12). Thus, the shift in logical framework shows how real representational questions can be approached, at least in computational analysis if not yet in experimental analysis. We end the section with some speculations about how these computational treatments offer possibilities of bridging the gap to more psychologically conventional studies of memory.

3.1. Models and Rules – Some Formal Concepts

A semantic (model-theoretic) level and a syntactic (proof-theoretic) level are easily distinguished in logical systems. At the more fundamental semantic level, logics employ an apparatus of interpretation (a mapping of nonlinguistic elements of the world onto a vocabulary of the language studied). The interpretations (models) that figure are *not* implementations (or representations), and this semantic level of logic is *not* a mode of implementation (representation). Models are abstract specifications of mappings – the information would need to be implemented in some mode before any computations could be performed. At this level, specifying models specifies *what* information is to be implemented, but not *how* any implementations or computations on them are to be performed.

One source of confusion is that the logical use of "model" often inverts the everyday sense. Whereas we generally think of representational elements (such as the cardboard model of the house we are building) as being a model of the real-world nonrepresentational thing (the house), in logic this relation gets inverted.

Because logic is focused on representing languages, the nonrepresentational world that the language is about becomes the "model" for the language. A still further source of confusion is that much of the technical logical apparatus of modern logic was developed for dealing with worlds which really are abstract – mathematical worlds. Our only access to these worlds is via representation systems and calculations in them. Here the grounding onto the world all too easily becomes backgrounded to the point of disappearance.

Needless to say, models in this logical sense can be represented by (sets of) sentences in a language, by diagrams (at least in some cases where the models are sufficiently simple), and by other means as well. Psychologically what is important about these abstract mappings is that there is evidence that some sorts of natural language discourse processing are strongly organized around them (e.g., for some early observations: Bransford et al. 1972; Craik 1967; Stenning 1978). Just as Chomsky showed that sentences had to be regarded as abstract hierarchical structures without which theories of language knowledge and processing were impossible, so a number of authors in the early 1970s showed that the abstract objects logicians call models are also essential players in theories of discourse semantics (Kamp 1981). Just as psycholinguistics has studied how the abstract objects which are sentences are implemented in the mind, so the business of psychological studies of reasoning is to explain the implementation of abstract models in the mind, and, of course, the interplay between implementations of sentences and implementations of models. Just as with implementing sentences (e.g., working memory implementations are different from long term memory implementations), so multiple kinds of implementation are to be expected for models.

Moving to the syntactic level, what is known as a proof theory provides a set of rules (or axioms) which are designed to capture the semantically valid inferences embodied in the chosen notion of logical consequence. If the rules can be shown to not produce any non-consequences, then they are sound. If they can generate all the semantic consequences, then the rule system is complete. Although many systems of interest to mathematicians are provably incomplete (there are semantic consequences not computable within the rule system), for the systems studied by psychologists of reasoning, incompleteness is not an operative issue. Rules are a way of capturing the underlying semantic consequences. To make a computational process out of such a rule system one still requires a theorem prover which chooses which rule to apply at any given point in a derivation, either heuristically or algorithmically. So, from a logical point of view, it is very natural to think of the syntactic level as the level at which computational processes of reasoning go on, and if modeling mental processes is the goal, this object-language level is a natural place to begin, though it is as well to remember that "proof theories" can be given for nonsentential reasoning as well as sentential (for some diagrammatic examples, see Stenning 2002).

There is, however, another possibility – and that is to compute consequences "directly" at a model-theoretic level. An example would be reasoning by model generation and model checking. At first sight, this might appear to be what mental models theory proposes for mental processes. For example, the syllogism is treated by giving model-construction and model-checking algorithms. But the directness is a bit of an illusion. Reasoning meta-linguistically over models, without object-language sentential rules of inference, still has to go on in some meta-language and with regard to some representation of the models involved. Such meta-logical reasoning is generally presented in English as the meta-language, but for a computational account, the meta-language is generally set-theory – the need is to talk of sets of models involved in consequence relations.

If the processes of reasoning about models in this meta-language is to be proposed as an analogue for the mental processes of subjects, then the meta-language comes center-stage. What are the inference rules of this language which constitute reasoning? How are the models reasoned over represented? What is *the meta-language's* proof-theory? What is the theorem prover for this language? How are all these abstractions implemented? When pressed along these lines, Johnson-Laird falls back on his implementation of the theory in a computer program written in LISP. Perhaps we should construe LISP as the meta-language? But this won't help. LISP is sufficiently powerful to express any kind of reasoning procedure over syllogistic models. The program is only substantive if the program uses a constrained set of model-generating and model-checking procedures. We have argued elsewhere that mental models theory is not consistent in its specification of constraints (Stenning and van Lambalgen 2008).

The various expositions of mental models theory are both incomplete (in the nontechnical sense) and inconsistent the one with the other. If we attempt to understand the notations offered as embodying mental models theory we should be clear that what we are doing is giving an account of the proof-theory of the mental-models "language," although we should also be clear that we are given to start from is a formalism with no better than an intuitive treatment of its own semantics. Far from studying "directly semantic" reasoning over models we are at two steps removed from any grounded semantic study.

In this connection it is worth observing that one of the central motivations of mental models theory was always to explain the "content dependence" of reasoning which it claimed to be observed in the selection task. We have seen in Section 2.1 that the effects of content in that task are best understood as the effects of content on the selection of differently formalised interpretations. However, a further problem with mental models theory is that it is formulated in terms of formal manipulations of token letters in some implicit meta-language and this does not address content effects. This reasoning by manipulating model-representations is formal, even if not fully formalized. So mental models theory's appeals to "direct semantic processing" fail to engage with content. In contrast, the implementation of a default logic given in Subsection 3.2.1 provides an account of the grounding of interpretation in the content encoded in a database of conditionals in long-term memory.

So we have argued that models as abstractions are essential to psychological theory (at an informational level) because model theory (in the logical sense) is essential to giving accounts of discourse meanings, and psychology needs the concepts of logic for foundations for its theories as much as logic does. What about representations of models implementing mental structures and computational processes: Either external representations such as maybe diagrams or internal (mental) representations of models? Is there some useful employment for implementations of models at this computational level? Well, the first thing to be said is that we should expect in general that there will be lots of different implementations of models – in languages, in diagrams,. . . . Looking at external representation examples which are easier to lay hands on, there are obviously linguistic and diagrammatic representations of models, and other kinds besides. But is there some kind of implementation of

models which is particularly closely related to abstract-level models?

Stenning (2002) develops a theory of a subclass of "directly" interpreted diagrammatic representations which are, (in their primitive form) rather close to representing single logical models. The technical definition of directness involved here is "lacking an abstract syntax interpolated between representation and represented." Direct representations are contrasted with "indirectly interpreted representations" which require an interpolated "abstract syntax" – natural and artificial sentential languages being the obvious examples.

For example, Euler diagrams, suitably interpreted, are shown to provide a well-specified, directly interpreted, analogue of mental models notation for syllogisms. This direct mode of representation has interesting consequences for processing. Once dealing with explicit external direct representations such as diagrams it is possible to contrast their behavior with external linguistic representations – written language. Empirical studies show that subjects are differentially affected by learning from explicit external representations. Here is palpably representational evidence suggestive that nonsentential representations of models are psychologically active in at least some subjects some of the time.

What are we to make of the large body of "mental models" experiments which study subjects' solutions to linguistically presented deductive puzzles and claim thereby to show that the fundamental human deductive reasoning mechanism uses model-like rather than sentence-like representations (Johnson-Laird and Byrne 1991)? At the most general level, we know from completeness proofs, that any inference in expressed in models-style will correspond to an inference in a sentential-rule system. But this is a weak kind of correspondence – there might in principle be little correspondence in complexity of these inferences (supposing we had an arguably appropriate measure of complexity). However, there are much stronger correspondences between the mental models representational apparatus and natural deduction sentential rules systems (Stenning and Yule 1997). Mental models derivations correspond to a style of proof known as "proof by cases" in natural deduction systems. There is not just weak input-output correspondence, but operation by operation correspondence. The psychological literature has assumed that in comparing complexity of derivations, number of inference rule applications is the relevant metric. But the correspondence between proof-by-cases and mental models shows that if the metric chosen is number of cases, then the data offered cannot discriminate. There is no principled reason why the mental implementation of proof-by-cases should not implement the representation of cases is such a way as to yield this results (for a proposal along these lines, see Stenning and Oberlander 1994).

One might argue that even so, mental models experiments provide richer data through error-patterns, reaction times, and so on. But exploiting this richness requires a specification of the kinds of corruption of memory representations that occur, and this kind of representational detail is just what is missing from mental models theory. To make claims about representation one has to study representations, and input-output functions from sentences to sentences are not enough. We shall see presently that where serious study of representations has been undertaken, the evidence is that both model-like and sentence-like representations appear to be involved and that differences between subjects are cognitively important – there is no evidence for a single fundamental human deductive reasoning mechanism. This empirical evidence is supported by the computational account given below of neurally implemented default logics. In those implementations there are simultaneously representations of (sets of) sentences (as network structures) and representations of models (as activated subsets of nodes in the networks), And the database of conditionals in default systems really does connect episodes of reasoning to content.

In summary, we agree with mental models theory that the logician's concept of model provides a specification of information which is clearly important for accounts of psychological processing. A psychology based on the abstract object of the sentence alone is not going to be able to give useful accounts of the meaning of natural languages, and meaning dominates human processing. But the kinds of evidence required to show how models are represented has not been forthcoming from mental models theorists. In the next section, we turn to more formal studies of discourse meaning which implicate abstract models in human processing.

3.2. Really Representational Questions

The tasks discussed in Section 2.1 have been used to make representational claims. in particular to argue against mental rules and for mental models. We have seen that the arguments proffered are not convincing, but it is of course an extremely interesting question whether reasoning experiments together with sound logical theorising can yield information about representations. Here we put forward a proposal for one set of mental representations which could underly performance in the suppression task – a neural network implementation.

To position this proposal with regard ro the rest of the chapter, what we will specify is a network which has been constructed as a result of interpreting an example discourse from the suppression task. So we assume that the subject has decided that the appropriate task is credulous interpretation of this discourse and has set the requisite logical parameters according to the prescriptions of our particular default logic. We do not provide a model of the process of construction of the network, some of which will be taken from structures already existing in long-term memory, and some of which will be new, perhaps in working memory, although for more discussion of that problem, see Stenning and van Lambalgen (2008: Ch. 8). The resulting network fragment will, given as its inputs any set of valuations (in the three-valued semantics) of the relevant atomic propositions from the discourse, compute the "intended model." So the network represents a mapping from a set of valuations onto particular discourse models. Needless to say, all the usual questions about how the propositions represented in the network are grounded to their real-world content remain unanswered, as they do in mental models and mental logic theories. There are also of course interesting questions about how the novel episodic features of the discourse (perhaps that the student in the library is called Ermintrude) is related to the representation of the long-term general knowledge about libraries, essays, students, and closing, and so on. These questions will not be pursued here.

3.2.1. NETWORK IMPLEMENTATIONS

We have seen that reasoning performance on the suppression task can be explained logically in a defeasible logic operating on conditionals of the form $p \land \neg ab \to q$, in words: "if p and nothing exceptional occurs, then also q." The various answers can be explained as different manipulations on e. For example, if a subject "suppresses" the modus ponens inference this can be viewed as the addition of a rule $c \to ab$, where c denotes closure of the library, and applying closed world reasoning to get $c \leftrightarrow ab$, whence $p \land \neg c \to q$ – from which q does not follow given only p.

Now let us look more carefully at the computations that are taking place here, starting from the task materials. There are two steps to be distinguished:

1.   coding the materials into rules, and

2.   the computation showing that q does not follow.

For both steps, the particular logical form of the task materials turns out to be essential. Suppose that indeed the materials are represented as rules $p \wedge \neg ab \to q$ and $c \to ab$. Logic has much to say about rules of this form, characterised by the fact that the consequent is atomic, in particular about their semantics. In general, that is, starting from an arbitrary set of propositional formulas, it is impossible to compute models of this set efficiently, as a consequence of the P = NP problem. The situation is different for rules of this special form. These rules form part of so-called *logic programs*, whose models can be computed in a time linear in the size of the input.

Of especial relevance is the observation that there is a strong connection between logic programs and recurrent neural networks (see Hölldobler and Kalinke 1994, and for an extension to closed world reasoning, see Stenning and van Lambalgen 2005). To each logic program one can associate a recurrent neural network in such a way that models of the program (which are abstract entities) are represented by stable states of the network (which in principle can be realised physically). This takes care of (2): the stable state of the neural network associated to the suppression task (via a suitable logic program) is such that q is not activated.

The network implementation makes a representational choice – the models-mode. But unlike mental models theory it comes with a very specific account of how the language is incorporated into the network. The main issue to be discussed here is the representation of conditionals as links in a network, that is, (1). We will indicate briefly how such links may be set up in working memory, following the highly suggestive treatment in a series of papers by von der Malsburg starting with 1981 (see von der Malsburg 2003 for a recent summary), some of which were written in collaboration with Bienenstock. Bienenstock and von der Malsburg (1987), von der Malsburg and Bienenstock (1987), von der Malsburg (1988) and with Willshaw von der Malsburg and Willshaw (1977), Willshaw and von der Malsburg (1976, 1979), von der Malsburg and Willshaw (1981). These authors

observed that, apart from the "permanent" connection strengths between nodes created during storage in declarative memory, one also needs variable connection strengths, which vary on the psychological time scale of large fractions of a second. More formally, let the synaptic connection between brain cells i and j be characterised by a strength w_{ij}. It is postulated that the weight w_{ij} of an excitatory synapse depends on two variables with different time scale of behaviour, a_{ij} and s_{ij}. The set $\{s_{ij}\}$ constitutes the permanent network structure. Its modification (synaptic plasticity) is slow and is the basis for long-term memory. The new dynamic variable a_{ij} termed the *state of activation of* the synapse ij (as distinct from the activation of the cell), changes on a fast time scale (fractions of a second) in response to the correlation between the signals of cells i and j. These changes may be viewed as subserving working memory. The overall weight of a connection w_{ij} is then a function of the s_{ij} and the a_{ij}, for instance via the simple rule $w_{ij} = a_{ij}s_{ij}$.

If we apply the ideas just outlined to our representation of the suppression task, we get something like the following. Declarative memory, usually modeled by some kind of spreading activation network, contains units representing the "concept library," with links to units representing concepts such as "open," "study," "essay," and "book." These concepts may combine into propositions. Neurally, one may view an atomic proposition ("the library is open") as a single unit (say U_p) which is activated when the units for the constitutive concepts ("library," "open") are activated; for example, because mutual reinforcement of the units for "library" and "open" makes their combined weighted output exceed the threshold of U_p. Two propositional units p, q ("the library is open," "she will study late in the library") can be combined into a conditional by the activation of a further link from p to q.

All these links can be viewed at two time scales. At large time scales the links are connections laid down in declarative memory; these links have positive (although small) weights and correspond to the $\{s_{ij}\}$ in the above description. At small time scales, links may become temporarily reinforced by sensory input, through an increase of the $\{a_{ij}\}$. For example, upon being presented with the conditional "if she has an essay, she will study late in the library" ($p \wedge \neg ab \to q$), the link from p to q via ab in Figure 1 becomes temporarily reinforced by synaptic modulation, and thus forms a fast functional link. As a result, the system of units and links

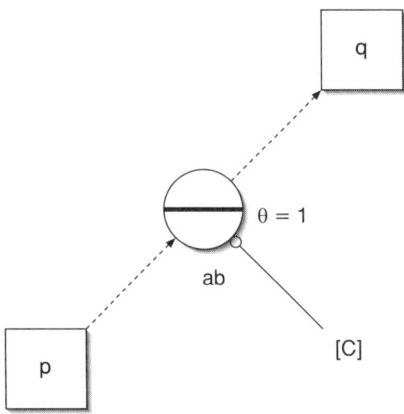

Figure 1. A hidden layer of abnormalities.

thereby becomes part of working memory, forming a network like the ones studied above, where the $\{w_{ij}\}$ are a function of the $\{a_{ij}\}$ and the $\{a_{ij}\}$. Working memory then computes the stable state of the network, and the state of the output node is passed on to the language production system.

As a further refinement we may incorporate abnormalities in the neural representations of rules, as illustrated in Figure 1. As we have seen, abnormalities play a special role as inhibitors in rules. They may inhibit an inference, and they also may inhibit actions. Abnormalities in rules are furthermore special in that they need not occur in the overt linguistic representation of a rule. They may, however, be activated, or suppressed, by material which is overtly represented. We therefore prefer to represent abnormalities as a hidden layer in the network and hypothesize that normally this layer is present in all networks representing condition – action rules. We hypothesize that this hidden layer is responsible for the possibility of flexible planning.

Consider a conditional like $p \wedge \neg\, ab \to q$ together with a further determination of the abnormality as $\neg\tau \to ab$. The effect of the abnormality is captured by an ANDNOT unit, which has two incoming links, one excitatory (for the left argument of ANDNOT) and one inhibitory (for the right argument), and threshold 1. The p unit is connected to the excitatory channel, and the $\neg\tau$ unit to the inhibitory channel (see Figure 1). If ab is not connected to an atom (i.e., if there is no condition of the form $C \to ab$), the inhibitory channel never fires.

It should be noted once again that this result very much depends on the logic adopted here – logic programs governed by closed-world reason-

ing – and would not hold for classical logic. The computational properties of this logic are highly suggestive as candidates for "System 1 processes" much discussed in dual process theories of reasoning (Evans 2003):

> System 1 is … a form of universal cognition shared between animals and humans. It is actually not a single system but a set of subsystems that operate with some autonomy. System 1 includes instinctive behaviours that are innately programmed and would include any innate input modules of the kind proposed by Fodor. … The System 1 processes that are most often described, however, are those that are formed by associate learning of the kind produced by neural networks. … System 1 processes are rapid, parallel and automatic in nature; only their final product is posted in consciousness (Evans 2003: 454).

In these theories, logical reasoning is considered to belong to "System 2" which is "slow and sequential in nature and makes use of the central working memory system" (Evans 2003: 454).

Our proposals certainly challenge the idea that fast and automatic processes are thereby not logical processes, thus drawing a different boundary between System 1 and System 2 processes. It depends on the logic whether it allows fast automatic processing or not. Classical logic can be viewed as a conscious repair process: the subject observes the output of the automatic reasoning process, reflects on it and decides to incorporate more models, thereby perhaps invalidating a conclusion.

4. Peering over the Ghetto Walls

This last section will conclude the paper by surveying the view from the edifice so far constructed. What connections to the rest of cognitive science are prominent from this viewpoint? What in the wild brings out interpretation and reasoning? We have argued that much of the psychology of reasoning is about interpretation, and that we should reinterpret an important subset of System 1 processes as defeasible reasoning to interpretations.

The nonmonotonic logics advocated here for modeling defeasible credulous interpretation processes are also known as "planning logics." This association by label to planning is important but possibly obscure. We perhaps tend to think first of conscious deliberate planning – a form of problem solving – rather than the sort of effortless automatic planning involved in say planning motor actions. The connection between planning and System 1 is through the latter kind of planning, though relations to the former deliberate kind are important in considering relations between System 1 and System 2.

The fundamental logical connection of interpretation to planning is its defeasibility. When we plan (deliberately or automatically) we plan in virtue of our best guess about the world in which we will have to execute our plan. We may plan for what to do if we miss the bus, but we don't plan for what to do if the bus doesn't come because the gravitational constant changes, even though that is a logical possibility. If we used classical logic throughout our planning we would have to consider all logically possible worlds, or at least make explicit exactly what range of worlds we consider. This necessity is what gives rise to the notorious frame problem in AI.

With this association of planning in mind, we will begin by discussing what our account of System 1 processes reveals about the connections of the psychology of reasoning to other areas of cognition, then ask how how System 2 processes manifest themselves, and finally how the two kinds of processes are related.

4.1. System 1 Processes

As we saw in implementing a particular version of planning logic in Subsection 3.2.1, a single model of the discourse was maintained at every point of its development. Maintaining a single model of our best guess about the current situation and its relevance to current goals is a very much more plausible biological function than reasoning about all logically possible models of our current assumptions. As we also saw, along with biological plausibility of function came efficiency of computation – the model is derived from the representation of the assumptions in linear time. Focusing on biologically plausible automatic planning is helpful in connecting this approach to other cognitive processes.[6]

On the account of the nature of System 1 processes as defeasible reasoning to an interpretation, they have of course already received considerable attention in a range of psychological literatures. Closest to reasoning is the psycholinguistics literature (Gernsbacher 1994). Here the whole enterprise is to ask how subjects defeasibly derive interpretations for discourses, and the story ends with successful interpretation. Because the problem is of such practical concern, there is very considerable study how how this

process of interpretation can be implemented in computers.

Psycholinguistics has recently branched out beyond the interpretation of purely linguistic input to treat situations in which visual perception of the nonlinguistic world goes on in parallel with linguistic interpretation of relevant utterances (Tanenhaus et al. 1995). Indications are that linguistic and nonlinguistic interpretation is about as integrated as it is possible to be. Visual evidence can be used "immediately" to resolve linguistic choices in interpretation. This should serve to remind us that defeasible processes modeled by planning logics are not particularly linguistic. Perception is a process of interpretation, and a good part of psycholinguistics is just about the perception of language. The production side of psycholinguistics is about action and the planning of action. Perception produces interpretations and action acts upon them.

When thinking of what planning logic might reconnect us to, one should not, of course, neglect work more explicitly about planning itself. Conscious deliberate planning has been studied in normal subjects in the context of problem solving, and indeed it is strange that this literature is regarded as so separate from the psychology of reasoning literature. When Newell and Simon's 1972 subjects have to solve a tower of Hanoi problem, reasoning seems to be what is called for. This, at first experience, evokes System 2 planning. But the surprising outcome of Simon and Newell's empirical studies and theoretical conclusions was that expertise resulted in System 2 processes "going underground" and being compiled into System 1 skills. The expert chess player or doctor has, to a large extent automated the planning process and indeed may have done so to the extent that the skill is no longer accessible to reflective analysis – a hallmark of System 1 processes. This change was indeed conceptualized by Simon and Newell as the acquisition of very large databases of "productions" – conditional default rules.

This same turn toward the study of learning and acquisition of reasoning skills has not happened in the psychology of reasoning. As long as the goal is characterisation of the fundamental human reasoning mechanism, learning, acquisition, and even skill are deemed irrelevant, and as processes which are "educational," rather than part of the nature of human cognition in the wild. Stenning (2002) shows how differences between subjects' reasoning and learning can be explained in terms of their representational strategies, developed by slow deliberate System 2 learning. Representational differences are just as relevant to the study of System 1 processes as to System 2. Indeed, representational variety can be studied as a real empirical issue here. It is a fine irony that professors should come to the view that conceptual learning is not a part of human nature, but merely a cultural oddity.

The other considerable literature growing out of planning is the neuropsychological literature on executive function. Lots of categories of patient have planning problems, often to do with inhibiting prepotent responses, managing goals and subgoals, and so forth. This literature straddles automatic and deliberative planning and control. Perhaps the moral of this literature of most current relevance here is that although human System 1 processes include our biological heritage from nonhuman cognition, System 1 is also distinctively changed in humans. Our System 1 not only keeps a model of our best interpretation of our current real-world circumstances but also can maintain a model of our best interpretation of, at the other extreme, a completely fictional discourse where relation to the real worlds is totally unspecified. It is understanding such fictional discourses in the laboratory that provides the data that we began by discussing. Studies of the evolution of human language and cognitive skills also exploit this relation between planning and language skills (Arbib and Rizzolatti 1997; Greenfield 1991; Steedman 2002).

One thing that is special about interpreting discourse (as opposed to present perceptual circumstances) is that it requires reasoning about others' intentions and meanings. One sees this made concrete in pragmatic frameworks such as Grice's where credulous interpretation of discourse involves assumptions of cooperativeness, knowledge, and ignorance, for example. The "theory of mind" reasoning that has been studied in the developmental literature provides further examples. Stenning and van Lambalgen (2006) sketch a treatment of the reasoning about beliefs in "false belief" tasks in default logic. The key idea here is to analyze communications, perceptions, and beliefs, as causes and consequences of a specific kind, and the reasoning as a variety of causal reasoning.

Mention of Grice raises questions about how the proposed approach is related to pragmatic theories such as Grice's and Sperber and Wilson's Relevance Theory, and what general effects it has on the boundary between pragmatics and semantics. To take the second question first, it is clear that the boundary does shift. Default logic makes at least some pragmatic implicatures in Grice's theory into logical inferences in its new semantics. Whether all of pragmatics would become incorporated in a more extensive development of the approach remains to be seen, but we have our doubts. However, this preference for giving precise fully formalized accounts of limited phenomena, over giving extremely generalized accounts such as Grice's or Relevance Theory is an important methodological preference. An good example of our reason for this preference can be seen in the analysis of the selection task. Sperber has written at some length on how pragmatic phenomena explain observations in the selection task, but without ever observing that the contrast between deontic and descriptive semantics is sufficient to derive the vast majority of the differences in his own examples. So while we agree with the general thrust of his conclusion that subjects are able interpreters rather than logical dunces, it appears that Relevance Theory is couched at such an abstract level that it misses the crucial detail here.

Finally, in this survey of System 1 cognition from the perspective of planning, we should note that planning also brings motivation and emotion into the cognitive picture. We plan with respect to goals, and those goals induce subgoals and sub-subgoals as we negotiate the obstacles to achieving our desires. Even if motivation and emotion don't always seem the most obvious destinations of a logic-based cognition, Damasio (1994) made a forceful argument that without motivation to reason, precious little rationality is likely, and he has made a plausible case for a class of patients with intact reasoning capacities but malfunctioning motivation. Gambling paradigms reveal their deficits as aberrant utility functions which unreasonably discount the future in their planning.

In summary, we need an account of how human System 1 processes evolved and develop, so that nonmonotonic logics appear in human cognition implemented in such a way they can deliver interpretations of situations other than the here-and-now. It is hard to see how a creature could evolve human abilities for entertaining System 1 interpretations of circumstances at some remove from its present circumstances, without also evolving some System 2 processes for managing and repairing interpretations. And without the former capacities, human language would not be possible – languages of fixed interpretation would not be natural languages. This account also needs to be augmented by an account of how System 2 processes are related to System 1, and where they happen outside the lab. The key proposal here is that the former grow out of repair processes called into action when System 1 breaks down and no intended model is therefore available.

The reader might be puzzled at this association between breakdown in defeasible interpretations and resort to different kinds of reasoning. Were not defeasible systems designed precisely for tackling the problems of apparent contradictions arising in interpretation? To take the classic example, when we infer that Tweety can fly from the premise that Tweety is a bird, and later we find out that Tweety is a penguin, we are faced with a conflict. The defeasibility of the logic was designed to model precisely this kind of accommodation by withdrawal of the inference. The default logic proposed here is similar in that it will resolve such conflicts automatically – when the library turns out to be closed, it drops the inference that our heroine will be inside. But this does not mean that *all* conflicts are resolvable, and so we assume that whatever default system is considered makes a demarcation between conflicts that can be automatically resolved, and those which will require a change of machinery. While trying to forstall misunderstandings, it's important to note that the particular defeasible logics proposed here as models of System I reasoning contrast with the early defeasible logics in being highly tractable, and this is what makes them interesting candidates for System 1 processes.

4.2. System 2 Processes

Breakdown of mutual interpretation in credulous processing interrupts a discourse if the hearer's interpretation yields an interpretational impasse. Here, however much the hearer is willing in general to accept the speaker's assertions, a contradiction or other divergence of new utterances from the hearer's model of the speaker's intentions to this point, means that no model can be found, and no model means no "intended model." The hearer now has to engage in repair, and may interrupt the speaker to find out how to repair understanding. Such repair of contradiction may be based on interludes of skeptical reasoning *from* interpretations (or broken attempts

at interpretation), embedded in credulous reasoning *to* interpretations.

On this story, classical logic is a good account of some reasoning that does occur in the wild under particular circumstances – the circumstances of "adversarial" communication. The credulous interpretation of discourse assumes a certain asymmetry of authority between speaker and hearer. The hearer accepts that speaker's authority for the truth of the discourse, at least for the purposes of the current episode of communication. The purest case is where a speaker tells a novel fictional story to the hearer who patently accepts he has no grounds for disagreement. But as we have just seen, this acceptance of asymmetry of authority breaks down when contradiction is encountered and can only be restored by repair. The discourses of adversarial communication are cases where breakdown of mutual interpretation is much wider spread. In the discourse of argument, participants consider themselves to have equal authority for assertions, and a disagreement about what is true.

In full-fledged argument, the parties may be unwilling to accept offered repairs. They may explore for reinterpretations of the assumptions on which they can agree, or they may resort to less communicative tactics. Here it is plausible that the logic governing the derivations from assumptions is classical – demanding that conclusions be true in all logically possible interpretations of the assumptions. Here is what lies behind Ryle's 1954 statement:

There arises, I suppose, a special pressure upon language to provide idioms of the [logical] kind, when a society reaches the stage where many matters of interest and importance to everyone have to be settled or decided by special kinds of talk. I mean, for example, when offenders have to be tried and convicted or acquitted; when treaties and contracts have to be entered into and observed or enforced; when witnesses have to be cross-examined; when legislators have to draft practicable measures and defend them against critics; when private rights and public duties have to be precisely fixed; when complicated commercial arrangements have to be made; when teachers have to set tests to their pupils; and [...] when theorists have to consider in detail the strengths and weaknesses of their own and one another's theories.

One of the hallmarks of formal adversarial communication is that reasoning is intended to proceed from the explicit assumptions negotiated to obtain – the "admissible evidence" as written down. Introduction of extraneous assumptions not formally entered in the record is strictly impermissible. This making explicit of what is assumed for reasoning classically from interpretations contrasts with the vagueness of what long-term knowledge is in play in defeasible reasoning *to* interpretations. This difference in demarcation is reflected in the relations between long-term and working memory in the network implementation of our nonmonotonic logic.

In adversarial communication, reasoning is not defeasible, at least when the rules are followed literally, and finding some interpretation which makes the premises true and the opponent's desired conclusion false is sufficient to defeat it. What combination of classical or defeasible logics provides the best model of how real legal and parliamentary practise works is a complex question, but an albeit highly idealized core of adversarial legal reasoning arguably provides one model for classical logical reasoning in the wild. The study of adversarial reasoning played an important part in the emergence of logical theory in classical Athens. A purer example of adversarial communication involving sceptical classical reasoning is the discourse of mathematical proof – another Athenian preoccupation. Yet another example of adversarial communication is argument about the correct interpretation of religious texts – the context which seems to have been particularly important in the emergence of Indian logical theory. Of course, we assume that capacities for sceptical reasoning preceded these developments of theories about the conduct of sceptical reasoning.

One might ask whether breakdown of automatic System I interpretation processes always leads to a resort to sceptical reasoning and classical logic. There are two other possibilities and we believe these are open empirical questions worth exploration. The first is that the stalled interpreter might resort to more powerful, and perhaps more effortfull, but nevertheless defeasible systems. The second is that she might resort to sceptical reasoning in some monotonic system other than classical logic. The reader familiar with the analysis of real argument will be aware that it is often proposed that defeasible logics are the right framework for this (Chesnevar et al. 2000). On our view this would be because most real arguments (e.g., legal argument) involve a considerable component of mutual interpretation to identify what premises are shared and which at variance. These processes would be best modeled defeasibly. So our claimed association between sceptical reasoning and monotonic logic is intended only to apply to the portions of argument in which reasoning is *from* an interpretation.

The relation between adversarial communication and logic was traditionally very much the focus of late secondary and tertiary education, at least of the élites who were trained for performance in lawcourt and parliament (and later scientific laboratory). We have already made reference to legal reasoning in Subsection 2.2.2. The tasks of the psychology of reasoning are directly taken from, or derived by small extensions from, the curriculum of this tradition of education (Stenning 2002).

It would be a great mistake to assume that such discourse is limited to court and parliament, or to professional practise. Conceptual learning in educational dialogue has many of the same features. Teacher and student start out, by definition, conceptually misaligned – teacher knows some concepts that student doesn't. The abstract concepts of secondary and tertiary education are not teachable by ostension, and require teaching indirectly through rehearsal of their axioms and applications of those axioms in argument. For example, to teach a student to differentiate the physical concepts of amount, weight, density, volume and mass it is no good pointing at an instance of one, because any instance of one is an instance of all the others. Instead, one has to rehearse the transformations which leave them invariant and the ones that change them. For example, compression changes density and volume but not weight or mass. Going to the moon changes weight but not mass. (Stenning 1998 discusses the close analogy between learning abstract physical concepts and learning logical concepts such as truth, validity, consequence, inference rule, . . .). The part that multiple representations play in teaching these abstract subjects points from a different perspective to the same centrality of interpretation in mental life. Multiple representational systems (languages, diagrammatic systems, multimedia animations, . . .) mean multiple interpretations and that there is an ever present task of selecting between interpretations/representations or constructing new ones. The empirical literature which has studied the effects of multiple representations (reviewed in this reference) attests to the cognitive costs as well as the benefits of learning new interpretations.

Although such teaching dialogue is superficially highly asymmetrical in authority (teacher is boss), teacher's aim should be to hand over authority for inference to student. By the end of successful teaching, the student commands the authority which is provided by the inference patterns from the newly learned concepts, and appreciates *why* these inferences are true, without recourse to the argument from authority that "teacher said so." The successful student can now convict the teacher of mistakes in reasoning. Of course, there may be ways of acquiring these adversarial discourse skills outside of formal educational circumstances. For example, Bernstein's 1971 theory of different familial discourse styles ("extended" and "restricted" codes) could be construed as a proposal along such lines.

This literature is focused on the effects of different "representational surfaces" (various diagrams, new terminology, alternative descriptions, ...) on conceptual learning. As such it emphasizes the other 'face' of interpretation than the one that we have been mainly concerned with here. For example, all these different surfaces may be all mapped onto, say, a classical logical interpretation. Even our brief earlier discussion showed that formally these "faces" of interpretation are not entirely separable. For example, choosing a nonmonotonic logic over a classical logic (a semantic choice) changed the syntactic characterization (the surface) of the conditional from the syntax of material implication to a noniterable syntax for defaults. Changes in representational surface are just as important as changes in underlying semantics. Both are needed to give a rounded account of conceptualization and its part in learning, and both can have profound effects on the tractability of reasoning. Again, assuming a single fundamental human deductive reasoning mechanism has ensured that this aspect of reasoning has not been studied under the heading of reasoning.

On this account, classical deductive reasoning is important not because an implementation of it is the "universal deductive reasoning mechanism," but, rather, because classical reasoning is important for aligning and repairing mutual interpretation across some gulf of understanding or agreement, and that learning more explicit control over System 2 processes, and their relation to System 1 processes, can have a large impact on many students' interpretation, learning and reasoning processes. The skills of skeptical reasoning are then one extremely important set of concepts and skills for learning to learn.

The Relation Between System 1 and System 2

If the skills required for reasoning in something approaching classical logic are acquired or honed in this kind of education, are the mental processes acquired, implementations of patterns of reasoning explicitly taught – implementation of a novel formalism of "Ps and Qs," or mnemonics for valid syllogisms, say – or are they somehow implementations founded on new strategic uses of existing defeasible machinery? For example, one might think of the grasp of classical logical discourse as growing out of more and more extended episodes of repair of credulous discourse. Certainly the traditional teaching of logic focused on teaching students the skill of detecting equivocations in arguments – cases in which the same word is used in different interpretations. There are several well-known empirical studies of logic teaching which show little transfer to general reasoning ability (Cheng et al. 1986; Lehman et al. 1988). However, Stenning (2002) reviews these studies as seeking transfer at inappropriate levels, and presents empirical evidence from real classroom logic learning that it can transfer if the teaching objective is transfer at plausible levels. It isn't new inference rules (MP, MT, etc.) that transfer (perhaps because these rules aren't new, being shared with defeasible logics), but the much more general semantic skills of insulating the "admissible evidence" (current assumptions) from "general knowledge" and exploring all interpretations rather than just the most plausible ones, along with a much more explicit grasp of (and terminology for) discussing the contrasts between credulous and sceptical stances. Not to speak of the need to unlearn the influences of the information packaging of natural languages designed to focus the credulous interpreter's understanding on the intended model.

There is an issue whether adversarial discourse can best be modelled as alternations between nonmonotonic logics and classical logic, or whether they are better modeled entirely within a nonmonotonic framework as an enlargement of the set of models considered, is one that will not be resolved here. Much of this issue hangs on the degree to which assumptions are made explicit in the process (thus cutting down on the number of models a classical approach needs to consider), or remain implicit although now mutual.

Stenning's study of logic learning arose out of comparisons between diagrammatic and linguistic presentations of classical logic in teaching reasoning skills. Like Amarel's work cited earlier, it focuses on the importance of representation and *re*representation in human problem solving and learning. Its slogan is "Human reasoning proceeds by finding an interpretation in which the problem at hand is trivial to solve – if it can't find one, then it gives up." This does not cover *all* human reasoning, but outside of professional practises it covers a surprisingly large proportion. Rerepresentation is a form of reinterpretation which has not been studied in the psychology of reasoning. If the goal is to characterize the "fundamental human reasoning mechanism," and that is to be done by plumping for rules or models, then rerepresentation is not an issue that can be studied.

The educational process of *learning* to reason classically correctly in their laboratory tasks has not been seen as within the psychology of reasoning's remit. This can only be because the field does not believe that learning logic is something that goes on in the wild, or has much impact on what goes on in the wild. In turn, this relies on the idea that classical logic is just an empty formalism unrelated to "natural behavior." On our view, the skills of the sceptical stance which can be enhanced by logic learning are central to conceptual learning (a central preoccupation of the academic bit of the wild which we happen to inhabit) and are in the curriculum precisely for the help they offer those destined for some of the wildest parts of the wild where disagreement is the main business.

System 1 and System 2 processes work together from early on in human development. System 1 processes are rather direct implementations of a range of nonmonotonic logics. System 2 processes start as repair processes when System 1 meets an impasse. The great variety of logics available for interpreting tasks has been our focus here. This variety comes with variety in linguistic conceptualizations and in diagrammatic systems. Another aspect of interpretation is choosing between these alternative surfaces which we have said little about here. System 1 and System 2 interact to create this wealth of alternative systems. Cognitive development and learning stocks this representational supermarket, and teaches intelligent consumption. This is a rather different picture of reasoning than the

Fodorian one in which sentences in the already (presumably classically) interpreted language of thought are spat out of the encapsulated perception modules into the reasoning mill to grind out the inferences of mental life.

Notes

1. There are, of course deep issues about what worlds are for this purpose. Shoes and ships may be less fraught than sets, numbers, possibilities . . . This is especially so when our discourse turns to discussion of representations themselves, as ours so often must. But these problems are not the ones that most afflict cognitive analyses of reasoning, and it is important to keep in mind that semantics is a mapping onto things – not just some new language.
2. In principle, a counterexample is different from an exception: the former falsifies a rule, the latter does not. It seems however that Byrne et al. reinterpret counterexamples as exceptions, as the next quotations indicate.
3. These inferences are "immediate" only in the sense that they involve single premises – not necessarily in the logical sense of being derived by single rule-applications.
4. We use $\rightarrow$ for implication, $\wedge$ for conjunction, and $\neg$ for negation.
5. ERP studies indicate that this inference is not quite literally effortless (Baggio et al. Submitted).
6. In this connection, it should be noted, planning logics are also used in robotics for planning motor actions (Shanahan 2000).

References

J. R. Anderson and C. Lebiere. *The atomic components of thought*. Mahwah, NJ: Lawrence Erlbaum, 1998.

M. A. Arbib and G. Rizzolatti. Neural expectations: A possible evolutionary path from manual skills to language. *Communication and Cognition*, 29: 393–424, 1997.

N. Asher and A. Lascarides. *Logics of conversation*. Cambridge: Cambridge University Press, 2003.

G. Baggio, M. van Lambalgen, and P. Hagoort. Computing and recomputing discourse models: An ERP study of the semantics of temporal connectives. *Journal of Memory and Language*, Submitted.

J. Barwise and S. Feferman, editors. *Model-theoretic logics*. New York: Springer-Verlag, 1985.

B. Bernstein. *Class, codes and control: Vol. 1, Theoretical studies towards a sociology of language*. London: Routledge and Kegan Paul, 1971.

E. Bienenstock and C. von der Malsburg. A neural network for invariant pattern recognition. *Europhysics Letters*, 4(1):121–126, 1987.

J. D. Bransford, J. R. Banks, and J. J. Franks. Sentence memory: A constructive versus an interpretive approach. *Cognitive Psychology*, 3:193–209, 1972.

R. M. J. Byrne. Suppressing valid inferences with conditionals. *Cognition*, 31:61–83, 1989.

R. M. J. Byrne, O. Espino, and C. Santamaria. Counterexamples and the supression of inferences. *Journal of Memory and Language*, 40:347–373, 1999.

P. Cheng and K. Holyoak. Pragmatic reasoning schemas. *Cognitive Psychology*, 14, 1985.

P. Cheng, K. Holyoak, R. E. Nisbett, and L. Oliver. Pragmatic versus syntactic approaches to training deductive reasoning. *Cognitive Psychology*, 18: 293–328, 1986.

C. Chesnevar, G. Maguitman, and R. Loui. Logical models of argument. *ACM Computing Surveys*, 32:337–383, 2000.

R. P. Cooper. *Modelling high-level cognitive processes*. Erlbaum, Mahwah, NJ, 2002.

K. J. W. Craik. *The nature of explanation*. Cambridge: Cambridge University Press, 1967.

A. R. Damasio. *Descartes' error: Emotion, reason and the human brain*. New York: Putnam, 1994.

J.St.B. T. Evans. In two minds: Dual-process accounts of reasoning. *TRENDS in Cognitive Sciences*, 7(10):454–459, 2003.

S. I. Fillenbaum. How to do some things with if. In Cotton and Klatzky, editors, *Semantic 'factors' in cognition*. Hillsdale NJ: Lawrence Erlbaum Associates, 1978.

J. A. Fodor. *The mind doesn't work that way*. Cambridge, MA: MIT Press, 2000. In appendix.

M. A. Gernsbacher. *Handbook of psycholinguistics*. New York: Academic Press, 1994.

G. Gigerenzer and K. Hug. Domain-specific reasoning: Social contracts, cheating, and perspective change. *Cognition*, 43:127–171, 1992.

P. M. Greenfield. Language, tools and the brain: The ontogeny and phylogeny of hierarchically organized sequential behavior. *Behavioral and brain sciences*, 14:531–595, 1991.

H. P. Grice. Logic and conversation. In P. Cole and J. Morgan, editors, *Syntax and semantics Vol 3: Speech acts*. London: Academic Press, 1975.

R. A. Griggs and J. R. Cox. The elusive thematic-materials effect in Wason's selection task. *British Journal of Psychology*, 73:407–420, 1982.

S. Hölldobler and Y. Kalinke. Towards a massively parallel computational model of logic programming. In *Proceedings ECAI94 Workshop on combining symbolic and connectionist processing*, 68–77. ECAI, 1994.

P. N. Johnson-Laird and R. M. Byrne. *Deduction*. Hove, Sussex: Lawrence Erlbaum Associates, 1991.

P. N. Johnson-Laird, P. Legrenzi, and M. S. Legrenzi. Reasoning and a sense of reality. *British Journal of Psychology*, 63:395–, 1972.

H. Kamp. A theory of truth and semantic representation. In J. Groenendijk, T. Janssen, and M. Stokhof, editors, *Formal methods in the study of language*. Amsterdam: Mathematical Centre Tracts 135, Amsterdam, 277–322, 1981.

H. Kamp and U. Reyle. *From Discourse to Logic, Introduction to Modeltheoretic Semantics of Natural Language, Formal Logic and Discourse Representation Theory, Part 1*, volume 42 of *Studies in Linguistics and Philosophy*. Dordrecht: Kluwer Academic Publishers, 1993.

A. Lechler. Interpretation of conditionals in the suppression task. M.Sc. thesis, HCRC, University of Edinburgh, 2004.

D. Lehman, R. Lempert, and R. Nisbett. The effects of graduate training on reasoning: Formal discipline and thinking about everyday life events. *American Psychologist*, 431–442, 1988.

K. Manktelow and D. Over. *Inference and understanding: A philosophical perspective*. London: Routledge, 1990.

J. McCarthy. Circumscription – a form of non-monotonic reasoning. *Artficial Intelligence*, 13:27–39, 1980.

A. Newell and H. Simon. *Human problem solving*. Englewood Cliffs, NJ: Prentice Hall, 1972.

S. Newstead. Interpretational errors in syllogistic reasoning. *Journal of Memory and Language*, 28:78–91, 1989.

S. Newstead. Gricean implicatures and syllogistic reasoning. *Journal of Memory and Language*, 34:644–664, 1995.

M. R. Oaksford and N. C. Chater. A rational analysis of the selection task as optimal data selection. *Psychological Review*, 101:608–631, 1994.

R. Reiter. A logic for default reasoning. *Artificial Intelligence*, 13:81–132, 1980.

M. Roberts, S. Newstead, and R. A. Griggs. Quantifier interpretation and syllogistic reasoning. *Thinking and Reasoning*, 7(2):173–204, 2001.

G. Ryle. *Dilemmas*. Cambridge University Press: Cambridge, 1954.

M. Shanahan. Reinventing shakey. In J. Minker, editor, *Logic-based artificial intelligence*. Dordrecht: Kluwer, 2000.

K. E. Stanovich. *Who is rational? Studies of individual differences in reasoning*. Mahwah, NJ: Lawrence Erlbaum, 1999.

M. Steedman. Plans, affordances and combinatory grammar. *Linguistics and Philosophy*, 25(5–6): 725–753, 2002.

K. Stenning. Anaphora as an approach to pragmatics. In M. Halle, J. Bresnan, and G. A. Miller, editors, *Linguistic theory and psychological reality*. MIT Press, 1978.

K. Stenning. Representation and conceptualisation in educational communication. In M. van Someren, P. Reimann, E. Boshuizen, and T. de Jong, editors, *Learning with multiple representations*, Advances in Learning and Instruction, chapter 16, pages 321–334. Amsterdam: Elsevier, 1998.

K. Stenning. *Seeing reason. Image and language in learning to think.* Oxford: Oxford University Press, 2002.

K. Stenning and R. Cox. Rethinking deductive tasks: Relating interpretation and reasoning through individual differences. *Quarterly Journal of Experimental Psychology*, 59:1454–1483, 2006.

K. Stenning and J. Oberlander. Spatial inclusion as an analogy for set membership: A case study of analogy at work. In K. Holyoak and J. Barnden, editors, *Analogical connections, volume 2 of Advances in connectionist and neural computation theory,* chapter 9, pages 446–486. Hillsdale, NJ: Erlbaum, 1994.

K. Stenning and M. van Lambalgen. *Human reasoning and cognitive science.* Cambridge, MA: MIT Press, 2008.

K. Stenning and M. van Lambalgen. A little logic goes a long way: Basing experiment on semantic theory in the cognitive science of conditional reasoning. *Cognitive Science*, 28(4):481–530, 2004.

K. Stenning and M. van Lambalgen. Semantic interpretation as reasoning in nonmonotonic logic: The real meaning of the suppression task. *Cognitive Science*, 29(6):919–960, 2005.

K. Stenning and M. van Lambalgen. Explaining the domain generality of human cognition. In M. Roberts, editor, *Integrating the Mind*, chapter 8, pages 179–209, Psychology Press, Hove, Sussex, 2006.

K. Stenning and P. Yule. Image and language in human reasoning: A syllogistic illustration. *Cognitive Psychology*, 34:109–159, 1997.

M. Tanenhaus, M. Spivey-Knowlton, K. Eberhard, and J. Sedivy. Integration of visual and linguistic information in spoken language comprehension. *Science*, 268:632–634, 1995.

M. van Lambalgen and F. Hamm. *The proper treatment of events.* Blackwell, Oxford and Boston, 2004.

C. von der Malsburg. The correlation theory of brain function. Internal Report 81–2, Dept. of Neurobiology, Max-Planck-Institute for Biophysical Chemistry, Goettingen, Germany, 1981. Reprinted in: E. Domany, J. L. van Hemmen and K. Schulten (eds.) *Models of neural networks II,* Springer Verlag, 1994.

C. von der Malsburg. Pattern recognition by labeled graph matching. *Neural Networks*, Berlin, 1:141–148, 1988.

C. von der Malsburg. The dynamic link architecture. In M. A. Arbib, editor, *The handbook of brain theory and neural networks.* Cambridge, MA: MIT Press, 2003. 2nd edition.

C. von der Malsburg and E. Bienenstock. A neural network for the retrieval of superimposed connection patterns. *Europhysics Letters*, 3(11):1243–1249, 1987.

C. von der Malsburg and D. Willshaw. Co-operativity and the brain. *Trends in Neurosciences*, 4(4):80–83, 1981.

C. von der Malsburg and D. J. Willshaw. How to label nerve cells so that they can interconnect in an ordered fashion. *Proc. Nat. Acad. Sci. U.S.A.*, 74:5176–5178, 1977.

P. C. Wason. Reasoning about a rule. *Quarterly Journal of Experimental Psychology*, 20:273–281, 1968.

P. C. Wason. Problem solving. In R. L. Gregory, editor, *The Oxford Companion to the Mind*, pages 641–644. Oxford: Oxford University Press, 1987.

P. C. Wason and D. W. Green. Reasoning and mental representation. *Quarterly Journal of Experimental Psychology*, 36A:598–611, 1984.

P. C. Wason and P. N. Johnson-Laird. A conflict between selecting and evaluating information in an inferential task. *British Journal of Psychology*, 61(4):509–515, 1970.

D. J. Willshaw and C. von der Malsburg. How patterned neural connections can be set up by self-organization. *Proceedings Royal Society of London*, B194:431–445, 1976.

D. J. Willshaw and C. von der Malsburg. A marker induction mechanism for the establishment of ordered neural mappings: Its application to the retinotectal problem. *Philosophical Transactions of Royal Society of London*, B287:203–243, 1979.

Chapter 12: Reasoning with Quantifiers

BART GEURTS

1. Introduction

In logic, inference and interpretation are always closely tied together. Consider, for example, the standard inference rules associated with conjunctive sentences:

$$\frac{\varphi \,\&\, \psi}{\varphi} \qquad \frac{\varphi \,\&\, \psi}{\psi} \qquad \textit{\&-exploitation}$$

$$\frac{\varphi}{\dfrac{\psi}{\varphi \,\&\, \psi}} \qquad \textit{\&-introduction}$$

&-introduction allows a sentence of the form "φ & ψ" to be derived whenever φ and ψ are given, and &-exploitation licenses the derivation of either conjunct of "φ & ψ". Of course, this is what one should expect in view of the meaning of "&", which is that "φ & ψ" is false unless φ is true and ψ is true. In logic, the search for a system of inference is usually guided by a (possibly informal) construal of a set of logical constants, and inference rules are judged by the constraints they impose on the interpretation of such logical vocabulary as they involve. Not that such customs are particularly remarkable, for there clearly must be an intimate connection between the meaning of an expression and valid arguments which make essential use of that expression. What is remarkable is that such connections have not played an equally central part in the psychological study of deductive reasoning, and especially of syllogistic reasoning.

In the past two or three decades, the semantics of natural language has come into its own, and quantification may have received more attention than any other semantic topic. During the same period, the psychological study of deduction made great advances, too, and one of *its* central topics is syllogistic inference, which is just a restricted form of reasoning with quantifiers. Strangely enough, these two enterprises have remained disconnected so far. All current approaches to syllogistic reasoning are based on first-order mental representations, which encode quantified statements in terms of individuals. Such representations are unsuitable for dealing with many quantified statements (e.g., "Most A are B", "At least three A are B", etc.), but semanticists have developed a general framework which overcomes these problems, and it will be argued that this framework should be adopted in the psychology of reasoning, too.

The plan for this paper is as follows. I start out with a survey of the central facts concerning syllogistic reasoning, and then go on to discuss the main approaches to deductive inference, arguing that each is flawed in the same way: they all employ representational schemes that are inadequate in principle for dealing with natural-language quantification, and in this sense they are all *ad hoc*. I then turn to the interpretation of quantified expressions, and sketch the outlines of a general framework for dealing with quantification that is widely accepted in the field of natural-language semantics. Research within this framework has shown that certain logical properties are especially important to natural systems of quantification, and I contend that the very same properties go a long way to explain the peculiarities of syllogistic reasoning.

It bears emphasizing, perhaps, that the general view on syllogistic reasoning adopted here is not original with me. Indeed, the key ideas

Reproduced with permission from Geurts, B. (2003) Reasoning with quantifiers. *Cognition*, 86, 223–251.

have a venerable ancestry and can be traced back in part to medieval times and partly to the founder of syllogistic logic, Aristotle. More recent developments in semantic theory have systematized these ideas and incorporated them in a much broader framework. Therefore, my objective is a modest one: to show that this view on quantification is relevant to the *psychology* of syllogistic inference, too.

2. Syllogistic Reasoning

The syllogistic language is confined to four sentence types, or "moods":

> All A are B : universal affirmative (A)
> Some A are B : particular affirmative (I)
> No A are B : universal negative (E)
> Some A are not B : particular negative (O)

Although the scholastic labels A, I, E, O, (from Latin "AffIrmo" and "nEgO") have all but ceased to be mnemonic, they are still widely used, and I will use them here, too. Most psychological studies on syllogistic reasoning have adopted the traditional definition according to which there are four classes of syllogisms, called "figures", which are determined by the arrangement of terms in the arguments' premisses; the order of the terms in the conclusion is always the same:[1]

Figure 1	Figure 2	Figure 3	Figure 4
B C	C B	B C	C B
A B	A B	B A	B A
A C	A C	A C	A C

Following standard practice, I will sometimes identify syllogisms by their moods and figures. Thus, "AE4O" stands for the syllogism of the fourth figure whose premisses are of type A and E, in that order, and whose conclusion is of type O; that is:

> All C are B
> AE4O: No B are A
> —————————
> Some A are not C

There are 256 syllogistic arguments altogether, 24 of which are valid according to the canons of traditional syllogistic logic. Of these 24, only 15 are valid in modern predicate logic. The difference lies in the interpretation of the universal quantifiers "all" and "no". In predicate logic, sentences of the form "All A are B" or "No

A are B" are vacuously true if the set of As is empty, and therefore the following inferences are not valid in predicate logic:

All A are B	No A are B
Some A are B	Some A are not B

Intuitively, these inferences appear to be valid, however, and they are accepted as such by traditional logicians; therefore, for example, syllogism AE4O (displayed above) is valid in traditional logic but not in predicate logic. It is the traditional notion of validity that is adopted in the psychological literature, and I will do so, too.[2] Hence, by default I will use the term "validity" to denote traditional validity.

Experimental investigations in syllogistic reasoning have explored a number of paradigms. In most cases, subjects were given two premisses and then asked either to choose from a list of possible conclusions (e.g., Dickstein, 1978, 1981) or simply to say what, if anything, followed from the premisses; the latter format has always been used by Johnson-Laird and his associates. Relatively few researchers (including Rips, 1994) have used evaluation tasks, asking subjects to decide whether a given argument was valid or not. By and large, these various paradigms yield the same results, but there are some differences, too, as we will presently see.

Chater and Oaksford (1999) compared five experimental studies that used the full set of 256 syllogisms: two by Dickstein (1978), two by Johnson-Laird and Steedman (1978), and one by Johnson-Laird and Bara (1984). Chater and Oaksford found that the results of these experiments are very similar, and that differences in design appear to have had little effect. In fact, the weakest correlation they observed was not between Dickstein's multiple-choice studies and Johnson-Laird's production studies, but between the two experiments by Johnson-Laird and Steedman (1978), which adopted the same paradigm. Chater and Oaksford computed the average number of times (weighted by sample size) each conclusion was drawn in the five studies just listed; their data are reproduced in Table 1.[3] None of the studies collated by Chater and Oaksford used an evaluation paradigm, but their figures are very much in agreement with those of Rips (1994), who did. There are just two salient exceptions: for the valid AAI syllogisms Rips obtained much higher scores than one should expect on the basis of Chater and Oaksford's meta-analysis, and the same holds for the valid AEO and EAO syllogisms. Almost

Table 1: Percentage of Times Each Syllogistic Conclusion was Endorsed According to the Meta-Analysis by Chater and Oaksford (1999)[a]

Premisses & Figure	Conclusion				Premisses & Figure	Conclusion				Premisses & Figure	Conclusion			
	A	I	E	O		A	I	E	O		A	I	E	O
AA1	90	5	0	0	AO1	1	6	1	57	IO1	3	4	1	30
AA2	58	8	1	1	AO2	0	6	3	67	IO2	1	5	4	37
AA3	57	29	0	0	AO3	0	10	0	66	IO3	0	9	1	29
AA4	75	16	1	1	AO4	0	5	3	72	IO4	0	5	1	44
AI1	0	92	3	3	OA1	0	3	3	68	OI1	4	6	0	35
AI2	0	57	3	11	OA2	0	11	5	56	OI2	0	8	3	35
AI3	1	89	1	3	OA3	0	15	3	69	OI3	1	9	1	31
AI4	0	71	0	1	OA4	1	3	6	27	OI4	3	8	2	29
IA1	0	72	0	6	II1	0	41	3	4	EE1	0	1	34	1
IA2	13	49	3	12	II2	1	42	3	3	EE2	3	3	14	3
IA3	2	85	1	4	II3	0	24	3	1	EE3	0	0	18	3
IA4	0	91	1	1	II4	0	42	0	1	EE4	0	3	31	1
AE1	0	3	59	6	IE1	1	1	22	16	EO1	1	8	8	23
AE2	0	0	88	1	IE2	0	0	39	30	EO2	0	13	7	11
AE3	0	1	61	13	IE3	0	1	30	33	EO3	0	0	9	28
AE4	0	3	87	2	IE4	0	1	28	44	EO4	0	5	8	12
EA1	0	1	87	3	EI1	0	5	15	66	OE1	1	0	14	5
EA2	0	0	89	3	EI2	1	1	21	52	OE2	0	8	11	16
EA3	0	0	64	22	EI3	0	6	15	48	OE3	0	5	12	18
EA4	1	3	61	8	EI4	0	2	32	27	OE4	0	19	9	14
										OO1	1	8	1	22
										OO2	0	16	5	10
										OO3	1	6	0	15
										OO4	1	4	1	25

A = all	E = no
I = some	O = some . . . not

[a] All figures have been rounded to the nearest integer; valid conclusions are shaded. Whenever two conclusions in the same row are valid, only the first one is valid in predicate logic.

certainly, these discrepancies are due to the fact that in an evaluation task alternative inferences never have to compete with each other: the paradigm allows subjects to endorse several conclusions for the same pair of premisses. By contrast, in the multiple-choice and production paradigms, a subject who judges AA4A to be valid (which it isn't) is thereby prevented from endorsing AA4I (which is valid). Furthermore, production and multiple-choice tasks may be more susceptible to interference from response factors (see below). So all things considered, the evaluation paradigm may be more suitable for gauging reasoning capabilities. In practice, however, this consideration is of minor importance, since all paradigms paint the same general picture.

Turning to the main trends in the data of Table 1, it is evident that logical validity is a major factor in determining performance on syllogistic tasks. To begin with, the most widely endorsed syllogisms tend to be valid. According to Chater and Oaksford's data, valid syllogisms are endorsed 51% of the time on average; invalid syllogisms, 11% of the time. Seventeen valid syllogisms score above the upper quartile point ($P_{0.75} = 16.5$), and the remaining seven are presumably undervalued because they are in competition with more popular syllogisms. In Rips' data the effect of validity is even clearer, for his first 22 syllogisms are all valid. Furthermore, high-frequency errors tend to occur in the vicinity of valid argument forms. For example, of the four AAA syllogisms, only one is valid (i.e., AA1A), and it is typically recognized as such; in fact, it is one of the easiest syllogisms. But the invalid AAA arguments appear to share in this popularity, and are endorsed well above average. Other clusters of arguments for which this holds are AII, IAI, AEE, EAE, AOO, and OAO. The upshot of these observations is that people are rather good at syllogistic reasoning: not only are valid arguments very often recognized as such, but when invalid arguments are considered to be valid, they are often identical, *modulo* figure, to valid arguments.

Of the four syllogistic sentence types, two license *conversion* whilst the other two do not; whereas it follows from "Some A are B" and "No A are B" that "Some B are A" and "No B are A", respectively, conversion is illegitimate in the case of "All A are B" and "Some A are not B". There are 256 pairs of syllogisms that are identical up to conversion which is to say that they can be made to coincide by applying conversion to one of the premisses. For example, EA1E and EA2E are a conversion pair, because conversion applied to the first premiss of one yields the other:

	No B are C			No C are B
EA1E:	All A are B		EA2E:	All A are B
	No A are C			No A are C

From a logical point of view, one would expect people to perform the same on the members of a conversion pair, and this expectation is not disappointed: for the set of pairs $\langle \varphi, \psi \rangle$ which are intertranslatable by means of conversion alone, the correlation between the φs and the ψs is quite good ($r = 0.93$).[4] This observation lends additional credit to the notion that many of the errors in syllogistic reasoning are caused by *illicit* conversion. This idea, which goes back to Wilkins (1928) and has since been supported by many researchers, comes in a variety of incarnations, the most promising of which is that people have a certain tendency to infer "All B are A" from "All A are B", and likewise (though less importantly) "Some B are not A" from "Some A are not B". Illicit conversion accounts in large part for the errors made in syllogistic reasoning. In Chater and Oaksford's data, the 16 most frequently occurring erroneous inferences (endorsed 49–75% of the time) are all attributable to illicit conversion.

There is also independent evidence that people make conversion errors. In an experimental task with single-premiss arguments, about one-third of the participants will incorrectly convert "all" propositions, and for "some not" propositions about two-thirds will endorse conversion (Newstead & Griggs, 1983); performance on this task correlates with errors predicted by illicit conversion in syllogistic tasks (Newstead & Griggs, 1983). Further evidence for illicit conversion is the finding by Dickstein (1981) that more elaborate clarification of a syllogistic task substantially improves performance, but in a selective way: clarification is significantly less effective with conversion errors. Dickstein suggests that illicit conversion can be accounted for

by a general preference for symmetric relations, as demonstrated, for example, by Tsai (1977), and this explanation accords with the observation made above about the importance of *licit* conversion in syllogistic reasoning.

It has often been suggested that figure is a major factor affecting the difficulty of syllogistic arguments. Proponents of this view typically hold that syllogisms in figure 1 are the easiest, those in figure 4 are the hardest, while figures 1 and 3 lie in between (e.g. Evans, Newstead, & Byrne, 1993). Such claims are not entirely without foundation, but it is doubtful that they bear much weight. To begin with, we don't find straightforward empirical support for the proposition that easier syllogisms tend to be in the lower figures. Amongst the ten easiest syllogisms in Table 1, figures 2 and 4 are represented twice each, while figures 1 and 3 are represented three times each, which indicates already that the figural effect, such as it is, is not a particularly strong one. Furthermore, it is unlikely that a figural effect could be particularly forceful in view of the fact that syllogisms which are conversion pairs tend to evoke similar responses; as we have just seen any two syllogisms that are identical up to conversion tend to be equally difficult, though conversion always entails a change in figure.

Dickstein (1978) observed that quite a few of the early reports on figural effects were flawed for various methodological reasons, but chiefly because they confounded potential figural effects with the effects of other variables, such as validity and illicit conversion (cf. also Rips, 1994). Dickstein argued that when all these factors are taken into account, only 12 argument forms remain that are suitable for testing the effects of figure. From an experiment with this restricted sample, he inferred that "figure is a significant determinant of performance *within a specific subset of syllogisms*" (p. 80, emphasis added). The tacit implication is that, when all proper precautions have been taken, it cannot be established that figure is a major factor in syllogistic reasoning.

Rather more impressive results have been reported by Johnson-Laird and his associates who showed that premisses of the form AB-BC encouraged subjects to produce AC conclusions, while premisses of the form BA-CB inclined them more towards CA conclusions; the other two ways of arranging terms in the premisses caused no clear preferences (Johnson-Laird & Bara, 1984; Johnson-Laird & Steedman, 1978). Johnson-Laird et al. attribute these results to two factors: the fact that they adopt a production paradigm, which forces subjects to formulate their own conclusions, and, relatedly, the fact that subjects are allowed to draw AC as well CA conclusions, which effectively doubles the standard set of syllogisms from 256 to 512.[5] However, a study by Wetherick and Gilhooly (1990), which had the same enlarged set of syllogisms but used a multiple-choice test instead of a production design, failed to replicate Johnson-Laird et al.'s findings, so it seems rather likely that it is the change of paradigm alone that is crucial.

It has often been suggested that figural effects are linguistic in origin (e.g., Rips, 1994; Wetherick & Gilhooly, 1990). The pattern found by Johnson-Laird et al. is that there is a preference for co-opting the subject of one of the premises to fill the same grammatical slot in the conclusion. Given that the middle term (i.e., B) cannot figure in the conclusion, this simple rule predicts a preference for AC conclusions for figure 1 syllogisms, a preference for CA conclusions for figure 4 syllogisms, and no distinct preferences otherwise: in figure 2, the A and C terms both act as subject in one of the premises, and in figure 3 neither of them do. The rationale behind the subject rule is obviously pragmatic. An argument is just a special kind of discourse, and one of the main structural principles underlying natural discourse is topic continuity: you keep talking about Fred, say, until other topics become more urgent, and whatever is the topic of conversation will tend to act as grammatical subject; that is what subjects are for, pragmatically speaking. This line of thinking explains why figural effects are so much stronger in production experiments than in other designs: a subject who has to formulate his own conclusion perforce relies more on his linguistic competence than one who just has to say yes or no, or choose from a list of alternatives. However, this account also implies that figural effects tell us little about deductive reasoning *per se*.

To sum up the main findings of our brief empirical survey, we have seen that validity is one of the main factors shaping performance in syllogistic tasks, and that a good deal of the errors in syllogistic reasoning are due to illicit conversion of A ("all") and O ("some . . . not") propositions. Conversion is central in a more general way, too, since syllogisms that are conversion pairs strongly tend to elicit equivalent responses. Finally, I considered so-called "figural effects", arguing that they are less substantial than they have been claimed to be, and suggest-

ing that such directionality effects as have been demonstrated are plausibly viewed as being linguistic not inferential in nature.

Although in its long history psychological research on syllogistic reasoning has accumulated a rich supply of experimental results, it must be noted that in a way its empirical base is rather narrow. Syllogistic logic covers only a fragment of predicate logic, and even predicate logic falls short of the plethora of deductive arguments expressible in natural language. Hence, there are ample opportunities for varying experimental materials, yet these opportunities have barely been explored. As far as I am aware, there have been no studies on cardinal quantifiers like "five", "at least six", "at most seven", etc., no studies on the role of negation in syllogistic reasoning, almost no studies on arguments with multiple quantifiers or relational predicates, and so on. Inevitably, this preoccupation with a handful of argument schemas demands its toll; for, as will be shown in the next section, *no* current theory can deal with certain extensions of the syllogistic language, some of which are downright trivial.

3. Psychological Theories of Syllogistic Reasoning

Over the years, many theories about syllogistic reasoning have been proposed, the large majority of which fall into one of three families: logic-based approaches, mental-model theories, and heuristic theories. The theory to be presented below belongs to the first family. Existing accounts in the logic-based tradition are mostly based on natural deduction, which is a species of proof theory developed by Jakowski and Gentzen in the 1930s.[6] The inference rules for "&" cited in Section 1 are natural-deduction rules. The inference rules for the quantifiers are in the same format, as the following definitions for the universal quantifier illustrate; here "$\varphi[a/x]$" denotes the result of replacing all free occurrences of x in φ with the individual constant a:

$$\frac{\forall x \varphi}{\varphi[a/x]} \ \forall\text{-exploitation} \qquad \frac{\varphi[a/x]}{\forall x \varphi} \ \forall\text{-introduction}$$

The basic idea is straightforward: if $\forall x \varphi$ is given one may derive $\varphi[a/x]$, for any individual constant a. Conversely, if we have $\varphi[a/x]$, and a was chosen arbitrarily, then we may conclude $\forall x \varphi$.[7]

Here is an example of a proof that involves both
∀-rules and both &-rules:

[1] ∀x [Px & Qx]   *premiss*
[2] Pa & Qa   *∀-exploitation applied to* [1]
[3] Pa   *&-exploitation applied to* [2]
[4] Qa   *&-exploitation applied to* [2]
[5] Qa & Pa   *&-introduction applied to* [3]
                             and [4]
[6] ∀x[Qx & Px]   *∀-introduction applied to* [5]

In words: since "Px & Qx" holds for all individuals
x, the same must be true for an arbitrary individual
a, and as "Pa & Qa" is true, Pa and Qa are
true, as well; therefore, "Qa & Pa" is true, and
since *a* was chosen arbitrarily, this holds for all
individuals, and therefore "∀x[Qx & Px]" cannot fail to be true. This proof illustrates how,
in order to arrive at a quantified conclusion, we
have to reason about arbitrary *individuals*. This
setup leads to implausible consequences. Intuitively, one is inclined to say that "∀x[Qx & Px]"
follows directly from "∀x[Px & Qx]" by trans-
position of the conjuncts. But in standard systems of natural deduction, this cannot be proved
directly, since the proof has to go via arbitrary
individuals. The problem is quite general, and
affects syllogistic arguments, too. Consider, for
example, the archetypical syllogism known since
medieval times as "Barbara":

            All B are C
AA1A: All A are B
            All A are C

As this is one of the easiest syllogisms, one should
expect the conclusion to follow more or less
immediately, but a standard proof will take no
less than seven steps. In an attempt to remedy
this type of problem, psychologists working with
natural deduction have introduced further rules
of inference, which enable the reasoner to make
inferential shortcuts. For example, Rips (1994)
postulates, in effect, that Barbara *is* a rule of
inference, which means, of course, that the argument above becomes provable in one step.

From a logical point of view, such shortcut rules are simply pointless, since they don't
enhance the system's logical power; they merely
help to shorten some of the proofs. From a psychological viewpoint, however, this strategy is
more objectionable. On the one hand, it is blatantly stipulative. Rips' system, for example, predicts purely by fiat that AA1A and EA1E are
easy, which of course diminishes the theory's

explanatory potential. On the other hand, the
introduction of shortcut rules raises the question of how deduction skills could ever develop.
Consider the quantified version of "mental logic"
by Braine (1998), which has no less than a dozen
rules for reasoning with "all". The system is
highly redundant, and its redundancy has to be
of just the right sort: practically any other collection of shortcut rules would yield different predictions about the relative difficulty of deductive arguments. How might such a system be
acquired? On what grounds does a child "decide"
that AA1A is easier than most other syllogisms,
and therefore merits a special shortcut rule? Or,
if mental logic is innate, why did Mother Nature
fit us with *this* particular set of rules? Such questions are never easy, to be sure, but theories such
as Braine's and Rips' add a whole new dimension
to what is already a hairy issue, simply because
it is unclear why any cognitive system should be
redundant in one particular way, as opposed to
(literally) infinitely many others.

Logic-based approaches to deduction tend to
be more powerful than others in that they generalize more easily beyond syllogistic argument
forms. Since natural deduction was designed as a
method of proof for full predicate logic, systems
based on this method have the logical resources
for dealing with propositions containing multiple quantifiers and many-place predicates. Yet,
such systems have their limitations, too, especially if we want to use them as psychological
models. To begin with, some quantifiers, such
as "most" and "at least half of" aren't expressible
in standard predicate logic at all. The reason for
this, informally speaking, is that they refer to
sets, not individuals. For example, "At least half
of the foresters are vegetarians" states that the
set of foresters who are vegetarians is not smaller
than the set of foresters who aren't. Since predicate logic only allows for talk about individuals,
it is not expressive enough for representing such
sentences. By the same token, any system of
inference that deals with quantifiers in terms of
arbitrary individuals cannot handle arguments
like the following, if Q is replaced with "most",
say:

All Vegetarians are teetotallers
Q foresters are vegetarians

Q foresters are teetotallers

Intuitively, it doesn't make much of a difference
if Q stands for "all" or "most", and experimental
evidence confirms this impression (Oaksford &

Chater, 2001). However, even if it is granted that they are adequate for "all" and other universal quantifiers, current logic-based theories cannot be extended in a straightforward way to deal with "most" and its kin.

Even if a quantifier is expressible in predicate logic, the representations involved may be ill-suited for psychological purposes. Consider, for example, how "At least two foresters are teetotallers" goes over into predicate logic:

$$\exists x \exists y [x \neq y \ \& \ \text{forester}(x) \ \& \ \text{teetotaller}(x)$$
$$\& \ \text{forester}(y) \ \& \ \text{teetotaller}(y)]$$

Since predicate logic doesn't offer the means for talking about sets, a rather cumbersome representation is called for: we have to introduce two individual variables and ensure that their values are distinct and that both stand for a forester as well as a teetotaller. The complexity of this representation is proportional to the rank of the cardinal that needs to be represented: "At least n A are B" requires n variables and $0 + \cdots + n - 1$ clauses of the form $x \neq y$. This peculiarity makes predicate logic an unlikely vehicle for reasoning with cardinal numbers. It entails, for example, that if we replace the Q in the argument above with "some" or "at least twenty", the former argument should be much easier than the latter. This is intuitively false, and the intuition is corroborated by experimental evidence (see Section 5 below).

I have argued that the mental representations used by logic-based theories of reasoning are unsatisfactory. They are incapable of capturing even the simplest non-standard quantifiers, the hurdle being that in predicate logic we cannot speak and reason about sets. This is what renders it flatly impossible to represent proportional quantifiers, such as "most" and "at least half of", and it is for the same reason that the predicate-logical way of dealing with cardinals yields representations that, though logically impeccable, are inadequate from a psychological point of view. And it is not only logic-based approaches that suffer from these problems: all extant theories of reasoning run into the same sort of trouble. To illustrate this, I will briefly discuss Johnson-Laird's mental-model framework and the probabilistic treatment of quantification proposed by Chater and Oaksford.

In the theory of mental models developed by Johnson-Laird et al. over the past two decades, quantified propositions are represented directly in terms of arbitrary individuals. For example,

Table 2: Representation and Integration According to the Theory of Mental Models

	Mental Model		
1st premise: "All A are B"	[a]	b	
	[a]	b	
2nd premise: "All B are C"		[b]	c
		[b]	c
Integrated model of the two premises	[a]	[b]	c
	[a]	[b]	c
Extended model, i.e. counterexample against "All C are A"	[a]	[b]	c
	[a]	[b]	c
			c

in the Bucciarelli and Johnson-Laird (1999) version of the theory, processing the premises of AA1A (in non-canonical order) results in the suite of mental models shown in Table 2. Every line in a mental model represents an individual, so for the first premise we have two individuals, which have the same properties, A and B. The second premise gives rise to a similar model, which merges with the first so as to produce an integrated representation of the two premises. This representation is a partial one; further information may be added, though not all possible extensions are allowed, with square brackets signalling that the property in question is "exhaustively represented". Once the argument's premises have been encoded, preliminary conclusions can be formulated. In the case at hand, the integrated model verifies "All A are C" as well as "All C are A", but as these conclusions are based on a partial model they are not necessarily valid, and have to be tested. This is done by trying to refute each of the preliminary conclusions by a counterexample: an extended model in which the premises are still true but the conclusion is false. Such a counterexample can be found for "All C are A" (as shown in the last row of Table 2) but not for "All A are C", so only the latter survives and is spelled out as the final conclusion.

One of the things critics of mental-model theory have complained about is that it is not quite clear what it *is*, not only because the theory has gone through so many revisions, but because its key tenets remain somewhat underspecified. Usually, a version of the mental-model theory comes with one or more computer implementations and a description of what these programs do, but in general this does not suffice to pin down exactly what mental models are. To illustrate, while the first model in Table 2 is said to represent the proposition "All A are B", we are also told that the model in the third row verifies the proposition "All C are A". The former claim suggests that individuals representing the subject term must be enclosed in square brackets, to encode that its representation is exhaustive; the latter suggests that this is not necessary. It is only because mental models lack an explicit semantics that such inconsistencies tend to go unnoticed.

Or consider the sentence "Two A are B". How can we represent this in a mental model? One might think that the first model of Table 2 is a plausible candidate, but this cannot be right, for two reasons at least. First, this model already represents the interpretation of "All A are B", which is patently not synonymous with "Two A are B". Secondly, if it takes two individuals to represent "two", then presumably it takes sixty individuals to represent "sixty", which gets us back to the same problem we discussed in connection with predicate-logical representations of cardinalities. This is not a coincidence, of course, since predicate logic and mental-model theory are both individual-based systems, which forswear reference to entities other than individuals. It is for this reason that the two accounts get into the same trouble with non-standard quantifiers.[8]

A rather different way of dealing with quantification is Chater and Oaksford's probabilistic semantics, which underlies their "probability heuristics model" of syllogistic reasoning (Chater & Oaksford, 1999; Oaksford & Chater, 2001). According to Chater and Oaksford, humans are geared towards reasoning with uncertainty; we were designed by evolution to reason not logically but probabilistically, hence it is quite reasonable to ask for a probabilistic interpretation of quantified expressions. And for some quantifiers at least such an interpretation is easy enough to provide. Thus, "All A are B" means, probabilistically speaking, that $P(B \mid A) = 1$, i.e., the conditional probability of B given A equals 1. Similarly, "No A are B" conveys that $P(B \mid A) = 0$, and "Some A are B" that $P(B \mid A) > 0$. As a matter of elementary probability theory, the conditional probabilities of the premises of a syllogism will occasionally restrict the conditional probability of the conclusion, and whenever this happens, "logical" inferences can be drawn (shudder quotes are called for here, because the probabilistic account implies that there is nothing logical about such inferences). For example,

if the conditional probability of the conclusion is 1, a proposition with "all" can be inferred.

One virtue of the probabilistic approach is that it affords a representation of proportional quantifiers, such as "most": according to Chater and Oaksford's definition, "Most A are B" means that $P(B \mid A)$ is high though less than 1. In this respect, a probabilistic semantics is more expressive than the approaches we have considered before, but it is still not expressive enough. In general, propositions involving cardinal quantifiers cannot be translated into a probabilistic format. For example, if it is given that "Two A are B", we do not know what $P(B \mid A)$ is unless it is also known how many As there are. It might be proposed, therefore, that "Two A are B" means that $P(B \mid A) = 2/\text{card}(A)$ (where "card(A)" stands for the cardinality of the set of As). Thus, if there are five vegetarians altogether, "Two vegetarians are liberals" means that there is a 0.4 probability that a given vegetarian is a liberal. This proposal is up to a number of problems, the most obvious one being that it suffices for "Two vegetarians are liberals" to be true that there are two liberal vegetarians; the grand total of vegetarians is irrelevant. In brief, going probabilistic is tantamount to claiming that *all* quantifiers are proportional, which is unintuitive for some (like "some") and demonstrably false for others (like the cardinals).

In the foregoing we have looked at each of the main approaches to deductive reasoning, and found that they all lack the expressive power for dealing with some quantifiers that would appear to be quite innocuous. I have focused my attention on cardinal expressions because they are common, simple, and yet manage to create problems of principle for all current theories. However, the trouble is not restricted to one or two types of quantifier; it is symptomatic of a much deeper problem, which is that all approaches to syllogistic reasoning are *ad hoc* from the vantage point of language understanding. It is a truism that solving a syllogistic task begins with an exercise in interpretation: how are the premises (and, in some paradigms, the conclusion) to be construed? The range of possible answers to this question is restricted by what is known about the interpretation of quantified sentences, obviously, and as quantification happens to be one of the central topics in the field of natural-language semantics, one might expect semantic theorizing to have had at least some impact on psychological accounts of syllogistic reasoning. As it turns out, however, any such expectations will be disappointed: thus far the impact has been practically nil.

And it is not as if the semantic theory hadn't made any progress on the subject of quantification. On the contrary, it is widely agreed that the past two decades have taught us a great deal about this topic, and there is even a broad consensus on what is the best general framework for dealing with quantified expressions. In the following I will argue that this framework goes a long way to explain how people reason with quantifiers.

The plan for the remainder of this paper is as follows. Since my central claim is that a psychological account of syllogistic reasoning presupposes an adequate theory of interpretation, I start out by discussing the general framework for treating quantification that semanticists have settled on. Research within this framework has shown that there are certain logical properties that are especially relevant to natural-language quantifiers, and I present an inference system that capitalizes on these properties. The resulting model of syllogistic reasoning is motivated almost entirely by semantical considerations. It is therefore not *ad hoc* in the way current theories of syllogistic reasoning are nor does it share their representational shortcomings.

4. Interpreting Quantifier Expressions

In the field of natural-language semantics, expressions like "all", "most", "some", etc. are analyzed as denoting relations between sets, or generalized quantifiers.[9] Thus, "All A are B" is taken to mean that the set of As is a subset of the set of Bs, while "No A are B" asserts that the intersection between the As and the Bs is empty. Formally, if we render "Q A are B" as "Q(A, B)", and use $\|X\|$ to refer to the extension of a term (i.e., the set of all Xs), "all" and "no" are interpreted as follows:[10]

all (A, B) is true iff $\|A\| \subseteq \|B\|$
no (A, B) is true iff $\|A\| \cap \|B\| = \emptyset$

This style of interpretation extends in a natural way to other quantifying expressions. For example, "Some A are B" means that the intersection between the As and the Bs is nonempty:

some (A, B) is true iff $\|A\| \cap \|B\| \neq \emptyset$

"Three A are B" means that the cardinality of the intersection between the As and the Bs equals three:

three (A, B) is true iff $card(\|A\| \cap \|B\|) = 3$

Quantifiers like "most", "many", and "few" are more challenging, because they are vague and perhaps ambiguous, to boot. This is just to say, however, that they spell trouble for *any* semantic analysis. But the general kind of meaning they convey can be captured in the present framework without further ado. For example, to a first approximation at least "Most A are B" means that the majority of the As are B, i.e., that there are more As that are B than As that aren't:

most (A, B) is true iff $card(\|A\| \cap \|B\|) >$
    $card(\|A\| - \|B\|)$

One of the reasons why predicate logic is inadequate as a semantics for natural language is that it cannot express this kind of meaning, which *essentially* involves reference to sets.

Viewing quantifiers as relations between sets means that we can try and capture semantic distinctions and similarities amongst quantifying expressions in terms of properties of relations. There are various such properties that have proved to be especially relevant to natural-language quantification, two of which I want to single out here, viz. symmetry and monotonicity. According to the definitions just given, some quantifiers are symmetric while others are not. For example, "some", "no", and "three" are symmetric; "all" and "most" are not. Hence, it follows from the definitions above that the following propositions must be valid:

If some lawyers are crooks then some crooks are lawyers.
If no lawyers are crooks then no crooks are lawyers.
If three lawyers are crooks then three crooks are lawyers.

This prediction is confirmed by speakers' intuitions. The following, on the other hand, should not be valid:

If all lawyers are crooks then all crooks are lawyers.
If most lawyers are crooks then most crooks are lawyers.

This prediction, too, appears to be correct. Non-symmetric quantifiers are universal (English "all", "every", and "each") or proportional, like "most" and "half of the". The distinction between symmetric and non-symmetric quantifiers has been shown to manifest itself in several ways, the best-known of which is that in many

Table 3: Monotonicity Profiles of Some Quantifiers, with Diagnostic Tests

	Validity Test for A-Position	*Validity Test for B-Position*
all(A⁻, B⁺)	If all pachyderms are pink, then all elephants are pink.	If all elephants are navy blue, then all elephants are blue.
some(A⁺, B⁺)	If some elephants are pink, then some pachyderms are pink.	If some elephants are navy blue, then some elephants are blue.
some(A⁺, B⁻)	If some elephants are not pink, then some pachyderms are not pink.	It some elephants are not blue, then some elephants are not navy blue.
no(A⁻, B⁻)	If no pachyderms are pink, then no elephants are pink.	If no elephants are blue, then no elephants are navy blue.
at-least-three(A⁺, B⁺)	If at least three elephants are pink, then at least three pachyderms are pink.	If at least three elephants are navy blue, then at least three elephants are blue.
at-most-three(A⁻, B⁻)	If at most three pachyderms are pink, then at most three elephants are pink.	If at most three elephants are blue, then at most three elephants are navy blue.

languages, including English, existential *there*-sentences only admit symmetric quantifiers:

There are {some, no, three, *all, *most} lawyers on the beach.

The distinction between symmetric and non-symmetric quantifiers is also implicated in the interpretation of donkey sentences,[11] for example, and it plays an important role in the acquisition of quantifying expressions. It is well-known that young children tend to have difficulties interpreting propositions like "All the boys are kissing a girl", as uttered of a scene with, say, three boys kissing one girl each plus one further girl who isn't kissed by anyone. Children are prone to believe that the sentence is false in such a situation, but they never make analogous mistakes with symmetric quantifiers. Furthermore, it has been shown that previous exposure to sentences with symmetric quantifiers has an adverse effect on children's performance with non-symmetric quantifiers, though not vice versa.[12] It appears, therefore, that symmetry is a key element in the acquisition of quantification, too.

Another property (or rather, family of properties) that looms large in the semantic literature is monotonicity. Like symmetry, this notion is not restricted to quantifiers, and I will introduce it with the help of a non-quantified example:

Fred's tie is navy blue.

Fred's tie is blue.

Since "navy blue" entails "blue" (the latter predicate applies to everything of which the former holds), the first sentence entails the second. The position occupied by "navy blue" in the first sentence is *upward entailing* (or monotone increasing), which is to say that truth will be preserved if "navy blue" is replaced with a term it entails. Similarly, it follows from "Fred's tie isn't blue" that "Fred's tie isn't navy blue". The position occupied by "blue" in the first sentence is *downward entailing* (or monotone decreasing), which is to say that truth will be preserved if "blue" is replaced with a term it is entailed by (negation reverses monotonicity). Monotonicity is a very broad concept: in principle, any linguistic position may be upward or downward entailing, or neither (non-monotone). In particular, each quantifier has its own monotonicity profile. Consider, for example, the following proposition:

If all pachyderms are navy blue, then:

(a) all pachyderms are blue, and

(b) all elephants are navy blue.

Since everything that is navy blue is blue, (a) implies that the second argument position of "all" is upward entailing; and as "elephant" entails "pachyderm", (b) implies that the first argument position is downward entailing. Using a plus sign for upward entailing and a minus sign for downward entailing positions, we can summarize the monotonicity profile of "all" thus: all(A⁻, B⁺). Table 3 gives the monotonicity profiles of the syllogistic moods and two sentence schemas with cardinal quantifiers.

Note that "exactly three" is non-monotone in both of its argument positions. The following propositions, neither of which is valid, illustrate this for the first argument position:

If exactly three pachyderms are blue, then exactly three elephants are blue.

If exactly three elephants are blue, then exactly three pachyderms are blue.

The following proposition, on the other hand, *is* valid:

If three elephants are blue, then some elephants are blue.

This is because the position occupied by the quantifier "three" *itself* is upward entailing, and "three" entails "some"; it follows from the definitions given above that, for any pair of predicates A, B, if "three(A, B)" is true, then "some(A, B)" is true, as well. More generally, if we have a sentence of the form "Q(A, B)", then the position occupied by Q is upward entailing; that is to say, this property holds irrespective of the quantified expression replacing Q.

It was already mentioned in passing that negative expressions reverse monotonicity: upward becomes downward, and vice versa. For example, if "all(A$^-$, B$^+$)" occurs within the scope of a negation operator, we get "not all(A$^+$, B$^-$)", as witness the following, which are both valid:

If not all elephants are blue, then not all pachyderms are blue.

If not all elephants are blue, then not all elephants are navy blue.

There is one syllogistic mood which involves explicit negation, namely "some(A, not B)", whose monotonicity profile is: "some(A$^+$, not(B$^-$)$^+$)". Note that the position within the scope of the negation operator is downward entailing, while the argument position as such, now occupied by a negated predicate, remains upward entailing.

Monotonicity has been shown to be involved in various semantic phenomena, including donkey sentences, the semantics of temporal connectives, co-ordination, and polarity; here I will briefly illustrate the latter two. Compare the following propositions, both of which are valid:

If at least five lawyers sang *and* danced, then at least five lawyers sang and at least five lawyers danced.

If at most five lawyers sang *or* danced, then at most five lawyers sang and at most five lawyers danced.

More generally, for some Qs, we may infer from Q(A, B and C) that Q(A, B) and Q(A, C), while for other Qs, the same conclusion may be drawn from Q(A, B or C). The former pattern holds for quantifiers that are upward entailing in their second argument position, and the latter holds for quantifiers that are downward entailing in that position. Since the predicate "sing and dance" entails "sing" as well as "dance", each of which entails "sing or dance", and "at least five" and "at most five" are, respectively, upward and downward entailing in their second argument, the facts observed above follow from the monotonicity properties of the quantifiers "at least five" and "at most five".

All languages have negative polarity items, which are so-called because they typically occur within the scope of a negative expression, and are banned from positive environments. English negative polarity items are "any" and "ever", for example:

Wilma $\left\{ \begin{array}{l} \text{*has} \\ \text{doesn't have} \end{array} \right\}$ any luck.

$\left\{ \begin{array}{l} \text{*Someone} \\ \text{No one} \end{array} \right\}$ has any luck.

On closer inspection, it turns out that negative polarity items do not necessarily require a negative environment, though there certainly are constraints on where they may occur, as witness:

If Wilma has any luck, she will pass the exam.

*If Wilma passes the exam, she must have any luck.

Everyone who has any luck will pass the exam.

*Everyone who passes the exam must have any luck.

The generalization is that negative polarity items may only occur in downward entailing positions. In effect, a negative polarity item serves to *signal* that the environment in which it occurs is downward entailing, which goes to show that monotonicity is of some importance to languages and their speakers (Ladusaw, 1979, 1996).

The purpose of the foregoing survey was to explain why semanticists count symmetry and monotonicity among the most important properties of natural-language quantifiers. Assuming that they are right about this, it is not unreasonable to hypothesize that these properties play a role in reasoning with quantifiers, as well. I will now try to show that this hypothesis is a fertile one.

5. A Monotonicity-Based Model of Reasoning with Quantifiers

In this section I present a very simple logic which builds on the observations made in the foregoing. In this logic all valid classical syllogisms are provable, but it goes far beyond traditional syllogistic logic in that it renders many other arguments valid, as well. The logic has three rules of inference, which follow directly from the interpretation of the quantifiers and negation. The logic's workhorse is monotonicity, which turns out to be implicated in every valid syllogistic argument. Once this logic is in place, it is not very difficult to produce a processing model that accounts for the data reviewed in Section 2.[13,14]

To begin with, we need a formal syntax for our representation language, which is not too hard to provide, because the syntax of syllogistic logic is so simple. Matters are complicated slightly because we need a representation in which upward and downward entailing positions are made explicit, but this, too, is fairly straightforward:[15]

Vocabulary:

▪ basic terms: A, B, C, . . .
▪ quantifiers: all, some, no
▪ a special two-place predicate: $\Rightarrow$
▪ diacritical signs and brackets: $^+$, $^-$,), (

Syntax:

▪ If α is a basic term, then α^+ and $(\text{not } \alpha^-)^+$ are positive terms and α^- and $(\text{not } \alpha^+)^-$ are negative terms.
▪ If α is a negative term and β is a positive term, then $\text{all}^+(\alpha, \beta)$ is a sentence.
▪ If α and β are positive terms, then $\text{some}^+(\alpha, \beta)$ is a sentence.
▪ If α and β are negative terms, then $\text{no}^+(\alpha, \beta)$ is a sentence.
▪ If α and β are both either terms or quantifiers, then $\alpha \Rightarrow \beta$ is a sentence.

These rules generate the kind of strings we have been using already, like "$\text{all}^+(A^-, B^+)$", "$\text{some}^+(A^+, (\text{not } B^-)^+)$", and so forth. Since the position of negation is not restricted to the second term, this syntax also produces strings like "$\text{all}^+((\text{not } A^+)^-, B^+)$", for which there is no use in a syllogistic logic, but which will not be in the way, either. Other strings that aren't part of tra-

ditional logic, but are essential to ours, are of the form "$\alpha \Rightarrow \beta$", where α and β are either terms or quantifiers; this proposition may be read as "α implies β". If A and B are terms, then "A $\Rightarrow$ B" means that all As are Bs. Hence, "A $\Rightarrow$ B" and "all(A, B)" are synonymous, and will accordingly be treated as notational variants. Implication is not restricted to terms; quantifiers may imply each other, too. For example, in traditional syllogistic logic (though not in predicate logic) "all" implies "some", which is rendered in the present notation as "all $\Rightarrow$ some".

These syntactic rules define the official language of our logic. In practice, however, we will drop the brackets enclosing negated terms, as well as all diacritics save for the ones required by the occasion. Thus, whenever a diacritical plus or minus appears it flags a position that is actually used in a proof.

Our chief rule of inference is the following:

$$
\begin{array}{ll}
\alpha \Rightarrow \beta & \beta \Rightarrow \alpha \\
\dots \alpha^+ \dots & \dots \alpha^- \dots \\
\overline{\quad\quad\quad} & \overline{\quad\quad\quad} \\
\dots \beta^+ \dots & \dots \beta^- \dots \quad \text{MON}
\end{array}
$$

In words: any expression α occurring in an upward entailing position may be replaced with any expression β that is implied by α, and any expression α occurring in a downward entailing position may be replaced with any expression β that implies α.

Our second rule of inference is based on symmetry, and its application is therefore restricted to symmetric quantifiers; it is the conversion rule used already by Aristotle:

$$
\begin{array}{ll}
Q(A, B) & \\
\overline{\quad\quad\quad} & \\
Q(B, A) & \text{CONV} \quad\quad (Q = \text{"some" or "no"})
\end{array}
$$

Without further provisions, MON and CONV suffice to prove 11 syllogistic arguments valid in predicate logic. In all cases the conclusion is derivable in one or two steps, using either MON alone or MON and CONV. The following proof of AE4E is as complex as it gets:

[1] all(C, B)   *premiss*
[2] no(B$^-$, A)   *premiss*
———————
[3] no(C, A)   MON *applied to* [1] *and* [2]
[4] no(A, C)   CONV *applied to* [3]

Here MON applies to an argument, but the rule is not restricted to any particular category of expression, and may affect negated terms, too, as in the following proof of AO2O:

[1] all(C, B)   *premiss*
[2] some(A, not B⁻)   *premiss*
_____
[3] some(A, not C)   MON *applied to* [1] *and* [2]

The remaining valid syllogisms cannot be obtained with MON and CONV alone. This is partly due to the fact that MON is as yet restricted in its application to terms, but we also need one further rule:

no(A, B)
_____
all(A, not B)   NO/ALL-NOT

Like the conversion rule, this one follows directly from the meanings of the quantifiers involved. As it turns out, the effect of the NO/ALL-NOT rule will always be to feed into the MON rule. With our new rule, we can prove all 15 syllogisms that are valid in standard predicate logic. The following proof, of syllogism EI3O, uses all rules introduced thus far:

[1] no(B, C)   *premiss*
[2] some(B, A)   *premiss*
_____
[3] some(A, B⁺)   CONV *applied to* [2]
[4] all(B, not C)   NO/ALL-NOT *applied to* [1]
[5] some(A, not C)   MON *applied to* [3] *and* [4]

This is a relatively long proof, but then the syllogism is not an easy one.

The remaining syllogisms are not valid in standard predicate logic, because they require the presupposition that "all" and "no" range over non-empty domains of quantification. Slightly more accurately: traditional logic has it that "all(A, B)" and "no(A, B)" entail that there are As. In terms of generalized quantifier theory, this is to say that these quantifiers are construed as follows:

all(A, B) is true iff $\|A\| \neq \emptyset$ and $\|A\| \subseteq \|B\|$
no(A, B) is true iff $\|A\| \neq \emptyset$ and $\|A\| \cap \|B\| = \emptyset$

There is a simple way of capturing this presupposition in our system, namely by adding the following axiom, which just says that "all" implies "some":

all ⇒ some   ALL/SOME

Again, this addition is licensed directly by the interpretation of the quantifiers involved (as construed in traditional logic), and as with the

NO/ALL-NOT rule, the main function of ALL/SOME will be to feed into the MON rule. With this new axiom, "some(A, B)" can be derived from "all(A, B)", courtesy of the MON rule, and "some(A, not B)" becomes derivable from "no(A, B)", because NO/ALL-NOT gives us "all(A, not B)", from which "some(A, not B)" follows through MON. The following proof of syllogism EA2O illustrates the use of ALL/SOME:

[1] no(C, B⁻)   *premiss*
[2] all(A, B)   *premiss*
_____
[3] no(C, A)   MON *applied to* [1] and [2]
[4] no(A, C)   CONV *applied to* [3]
[5] all⁺(A, not C)   NO/ALL-NOT *applied to* [4]
[6] some(A, not C)   MON *applied to* [5] and
                       ALL/SOME

Thus, all valid arguments can be accounted for with a handful of inference rules that follow directly from the semantics of the logical vocabulary of syllogistic logic: "all", "some", "no", and "not".

What remains to be shown is how this logic can be embedded in a processing model. In principle, there are many ways of doing this, but for current purposes it will suffice to show that even a crude processing model can produce reasonable predictions. Let us assume, therefore, that inference rules are applied in a breadth-first fashion until the right sort of conclusion is found or no new inferences can be made. What the "right sort of conclusion" is depends on the task. In an evaluation paradigm, it is the conclusion specified by the experimenter, or its negation; in a multiple-choice paradigm, any one of the given conclusions is of the right sort; and in a production paradigm, any sentence of the syllogistic language is of the right sort.[16] Since inference rules are applied breadth-first, the system is guaranteed to find a minimal proof that isn't longer than any other proof (if a proof exists, that is). In many cases, there will be more than one minimal proof of a valid syllogism, but these will only differ in the order in which inference steps are made: the rules will be the same, and so will the number of inferences.[17]

As is common in logic-based accounts, I take it that the complexity of a syllogism is determined chiefly by the number of inference steps needed to get from the premises to the conclusion. In the present case, this is to say that the length of any minimal proof is the main predictor. But there is another factor, as well, viz. grammatical structure. It is a well-established fact

Table 4: Predicted Difficulty of Valid Syllogisms According to the Model Described in the Text, Compared with Chater and Oaksford's Scores (in Parentheses)

AA1A	80	(90)	OA3O	70	(69)	EA1O	40	(3)
EA1E	80	(87)	AO2O	70	(67)	EA2O	40	(3)
EA2E	80	(89)	EI1O	60	(66)	EA3O	40	(22)
AE2E	80	(88)	EI2O	60	(52)	EA4O	40	(8)
AE4E	80	(87)	EI3O	60	(48)	AE2O	40	(1)
IA3I	80	(85)	EI4O	60	(27)	AE4O	40	(2)
IA4I	80	(91)	AA1I	60	(5)			
AI1I	80	(92)	AA3I	60	(29)			
AI3I	80	(89)	AA4I	60	(16)			

that more syntactic structure makes a sentence harder to process, and as deduction tasks always involve sentence processing, it doesn't come as a surprise that grammatical complexity plays a role in reasoning, too. Grammatically speaking, three quarters of all syllogistic propositions have the same structure: "Q A are B". However, O-propositions have the form "Some A are not B", and should therefore be harder to process than propositions in the other moods.

Putting these considerations together, I propose the following model. Our abstract reasoner starts out with a budget of 100 units, which are used to pay for inferences and grammatical complexity, according to the following rules:[18]

- For every use of MON, subtract 20 units.
- For every use of NO/ALL-NOT, subtract 10 units.
- If a proof contains an O-proposition, subtract 10 units.

For reasons discussed in Section 2, I assume that CONV is for free. That the NO/ALL-NOT rule is cheaper than MON is plausible, too, because the latter rule combines information from two propositions, whilst the former merely maps one proposition onto another. Table 4 shows the predicted difficulty of all valid syllogisms alongside the scores of Chater and Oaksford's meta-study (cf. Table 1). The correlation between the two is good ($r = 0.93$).

We now have a monotonicity-based model which accounts quite well for people's performance on valid syllogisms, which was one of our main objectives, because validity is the major factor in syllogistic reasoning, as I argued in Section 2. In the same section, we saw that many errors in syllogistic reasoning can be put down to illicit conversion of propositions with "all" and "some . . . not". This is something that is easily incorporated in our model. We only need to extend CONV so that it applies not only to propositions with "some" and "no" but also to propositions with "all" or "some . . . not". However, we still want to differentiate between licit and illicit conversion, because the latter is less common than the former. Therefore, we assume that, unlike its legal counterpart, illicit conversion is not for free: it costs 20 units. Even with illicit conversion, most syllogisms remain unprovable, and we simply assume that an unprovable syllogism sets the reasoner back by 80 units, which is the price of the most difficult argument that does have a proof (with illicit conversion).[19] This model makes quite reasonable predictions for the complete set of syllogisms, with $r = 0.83$, and if we set aside the syllogisms which are probably under-valued by Chater and Oaksford's figures because, in the experiments analyzed by Chater and Oaksford, they had to compete with other syllogisms, then $r = 0.88$.

The main virtue that I claim for my account is that it extends in a natural way beyond the confines of traditional syllogistic logic. For example, it is a trivial exercise to incorporate cardinal quantifiers, like "at least n". From a semantical point of view, "at least n" is of the same type as "some": both are symmetric quantifiers that are upward entailing in both of their argument positions. The proposed account predicts, therefore, that arguments with "at least n" will be equally complex as corresponding arguments with "some", regardless the size of n.

Ceteris paribus, I would predict that "at most n" affects the complexity of an argument in the same measure as "at least n" does, for the following reason. The main difference between "some" and "no" is that whereas the former is upward entailing the latter is downward entailing in both of its argument positions. Therefore, whenever we have commensurable arguments with "some" and "no", they should be equally complex. This prediction is borne out by the data (see the Chater and Oaksford (1999) figures for AEE/EAE and AII/IAI arguments). Moreover, "at most n" is of the same semantic type as "no": they are both symmetric quantifiers that are downward entailing in both argument positions. Hence, by transitivity, "at least n", and "at most n" should be equally difficult.

However, all things are not equal: considerations extraneous to the proposed model suggest that "at most n" may be more difficult than "at least n". There is a wealth of linguistic and psychological evidence which shows that in pairs like "tall–short", "many–few", "happy–unhappy", etc., the first member, which is in a sense the positive one, enjoys a privileged status (see Horn, 1989, for a survey). Linguistically, the negative form is marked, which means that it does not figure in all environments that admit its positive counterpart. For example, one normally would ask, "How tall is Fred?", not "How short is he?". Psychologically, negative expressions take longer to process, cause more errors, and are harder to retain than positive ones. Now, it seems likely that "at least n-at most n" will follow the pattern of "tall–short", "many–few", and "happy–unhappy", and if it does, arguments with "at most n" will be more difficult than arguments with "at least n", presumably because the representation of "at most n" contains a negative element: "At most n A are B" is represented as "Not more than n A are B". In terms of our semantic framework, this means that we must not interpret "at most n" directly:

at-most-n(A, B) is true iff card($\|A \cap B\|$) $\leq n$

Instead, "at most n" is interpreted as the negation of "more than n":

more-than-n(A, B) is true iff card($\|A \cap B\|$) $> n$

From a logical point of view, these interpretations are equivalent ("at-most-n(A, B)" and "not more-than-n(A, B)" always have the same truth value), but linguistically as well as psychologically they are different.

To summarize: I predict that "at least n" is of the same complexity level as "some", for any n, whereas "at most n" is more difficult. In order to test these predictions, I conducted an experiment in which subjects were presented with syllogistic arguments involving (the Dutch equivalents of) "some", "at least n", and "at most n", where n was an integer between 20 and 30 (the variation was used as a precaution against inter-

ference between tasks). The terms of each syllogism were randomly selected from a small collection of nouns like "forester", "communist", "poet", and so on. For each quantifier Q, there were four arguments to be assessed:

Figure 1	Figure 2	Figure 3	Figure 4
All B are C	All C are B	All B are C	All C are B
Q A are B	Q A are B	Q B are A	Q B are A
Q A are C	Q A are C	Q A are C	Q A are C

Note that the arguments in figures 1 and 3 are valid if the B-positions in "Q A are B" and "Q B are A" are upward entailing, and invalid otherwise; similarly, the arguments in figures 2 and 4 are valid if the B-positions in "Q A are B" and "Q B are A" are downward entailing, and invalid otherwise. With three quantifiers and four argument schemata, there were 12 syllogistic arguments altogether, which were alternated with one-premiss arguments like the following:

At least 24 communists own a blue bicycle.

At least 24 communists own a bicycle.

Note that this is a monotonicity argument, too, though it should be easier than the corresponding figure 1 syllogism, because it is shorter.

Since I had to make do without the usual experimental facilities, I cajoled 23 friends and relations into taking the test. All participants were native speakers of Dutch with an academic degree in psychology or linguistics, but no previous exposure to logic.

The results of the experiment are presented in Table 5.[20] To analyze these data, a repeated measures ANOVA was conducted with three within-subject factors: quantifier ("at least", "at most", "some"), argument length (one or two premisses), and validity (valid or invalid). This yielded main effects for quantifier ($F(2, 44) = 14.533$, $P < 0.001$) and argument length ($F(1, 22) = 12.517$, $P < 0.002$), but not for validity. There were interactions between quantifier and argument length ($F(2, 44) = 6.466$, $P < 0.009$) and quantifier and validity ($F(2, 44) = 4.926$, $P < 0.018$). Further analysis of these two interactive effects tied them to arguments featuring "at most"; in both cases there were significant differences between arguments with "at most" and "some" (quantifier/argument length: $P < 0.010$; quantifier/validity: $P < 0.033$) and between arguments with "at most" and "at least" (quantifier/argument length: $P < 0.017$; quantifier/

Table 5: Percentage of Correct Responses in the Experiment Described in the Text, with Standard Deviations in Parentheses

	1 Premiss	2 Premisses	Valid	Invalid	All
At least	97 (9)	92 (14)	96 (10)	93 (14)	95 (8)
Some	95 (11)	90 (12)	93 (14)	91 (14)	92 (8)
At most	89 (15)	67 (24)	70 (21)	87 (22)	78 (15)

validity: $P < 0.016$). There were no significant differences between "at least" and "some". In order to determine if any of the differences between arguments with the same quantifier were significant, t-tests were conducted with quantifier and argument length and quantifier and validity as factors. These tests, too, attained significance only for arguments with "at most": $t = 3.792$ ($P < 0.001$, two-tailed) and $t = -2.577$ ($P < 0.017$, two-tailed), respectively.

These results are consistent with our main predictions: that there is no relevant difference between "some" and "at least", and that arguments with "at most" are more difficult. But at the same time they cloud the picture somewhat, because it turns out that the strictly additive measure of complexity that underlies our model is not quite adequate. It is not as if *any* argument with "at most" is harder than parallel arguments with "some" or "at least"; rather, it is valid and/or two-premiss arguments with "at most" that are more difficult than others. This, however, is a concern not only for the present proposal but for all current theories of deductive reasoning.

Of the two interactions found in this study, the one between quantifier type and validity is the most troubling, in my view. Earlier on in this chapter I argued that valid arguments tend to be easier than invalid ones (see Section 2), and now we find that some valid arguments are harder than their invalid counterparts. This need not be a contradiction, of course, but I do believe that there is a serious problem lurking here. It is that thus far we lack a good understanding of why people reject some arguments as "not valid" or maintain that "nothing follows" from a given set of premises. If someone says that a conclusion φ does not follow, it may be either because he has a proof of "not φ" or because he doesn't know how to prove φ. These are quite different things, obviously, but the evaluation task used in our experiment doesn't distinguish between the two. Other experimental techniques are more discriminating in this respect, but even the paradigms which allow

subjects to say that "nothing follows" are relatively crude instruments because there is likely to be more than one possible reason why someone should think that "nothing follows"; for example, he may judge that a given conclusion, though correct, is pointless or odd.[21] In brief, this is a topic that calls for more, and better, experimentation.

6. Concluding Remarks

One popular way of characterizing logical inference is that a conclusion φ follows logically from a set of premises $\psi_1 \ldots \psi_n$ if the *meanings* of φ and $\psi_1 \ldots \psi_n$ alone guarantee that φ is true if $\psi_1 \ldots \psi_n$ are. It is not the facts but the meanings of its component propositions that render an argument valid or invalid. Hence, in order to understand logical inference we must understand how arguments are interpreted: no inference without interpretation. I have endeavoured to demonstrate that this slogan applies with a vengeance to syllogistic reasoning.

The main virtues of the model I have presented are the following. First and most importantly, my account is based on a system of inference that is independently motivated by the meaning of its logical vocabulary: "all", "no", "some", and "not". Second and relatedly, this system can be extended in a straightforward and principled way not only to the non-classical quantifiers but across the board. Third, the model predicts a complexity ranking that fits well with the experimental data. Fourthly, the current proposal is simpler than any other theory that covers the same ground, including "fast and frugal" heuristic models of syllogistic reasoning like Chater and Oaksford's.

Methodological considerations aside, the key element in my proposal, which distinguishes it from all previous accounts in the psychological literature, is that it drops the assumption that syllogistic reasoning is always in terms of *individuals*. Generalized-quantifier theory leads us to expect that reasoning with quantifiers is done in terms of *sets* instead, and I have tried to show that a processing model based on this assumption can be quite successful.

Logic-based approaches to deduction have been criticized on a number of counts. There is a popular view that ordinary folk are bad at logical reasoning, and that, consequently, it is a priori unlikely that they employ anything like a mental logic. A related argument, advanced by Chater and Oaksford (Chater & Oaksford, 1999; Oaksford & Chater, 2001), among others, is that everyday reasoning is not logical, so that whatever it is people do when they solve deduction tasks cannot be logic. Arguments along these lines invariably rely on carefully selected evidence. To a large extent, the rumour that people aren't good at logic is based on experimental data on conditional reasoning. In particular, it has been demonstrated again and again that subjects fail in large numbers on certain versions of the Wason task. But then conditionals rank high among the more controversial topics in semantics and the philosophy of language; at present, it is simply unclear what their logic *is*, and therefore we lack a sound normative theory against which subjects' performance can be assessed. Moreover, even if it had been established that performance on *some* conditional-reasoning tasks is poor from a logical point of view, there are scores of logical inferences that people are quite good at, like the following, for example:

The butler and the chauffeur have an alibi.

The chauffeur has an alibi.

I take it to be self-evident that very few people will have problems with this, and the experimental work of Braine, Reiser, and Rumain (1984) proves, if proof is required, that there are lots of arguments like this. Such bread-and-butter inferences tend to pass unnoticed, but we are making them all the time, and it would be far-fetched to deny that they are logical inferences, pure and simple.

Another objection against logic-based accounts of reasoning has been made by evolutionary psychologists (e.g., Cosmides, 1989; Cosmides & Tooby, 1992; Gigerenzer & Hug, 1992). Logic-based theories, so the criticism goes, assume that we have a mental logic which is a domain-independent instrument for reasoning about anything that happens to arouse our interest. But how did we acquire this general-purpose tool? There is precious little evidence that our parents teach us how to reason, nor is it clear how evolution could have hit upon such a device. It seems rather likely that Mother Nature equipped us with specialized modules for reasoning about physical objects, social relationships, snakes and spiders, and so forth, but it is utterly mysterious how a full-blown logical faculty could be the outcome of natural selection. I sympathize with this line of argument, and have used it myself to criticize previous logic-based theories of reasoning (Section 3). However, this criticism takes for granted a view on mental logic that I believe is wrong. Though it may be that some elementary notions of logic are innate, mental logic must not be conceived of as an autonomous module of the mind. As I have said a number of times already, and as I have illustrated in the foregoing with syllogistic reasoning, there has to be an intimate connection between the meaning of an expression and valid arguments which make essential use of that expression. Mental logic is largely a concomitant of our linguistic prowess, and though it is still a matter of controversy where *that* came from, nobody will doubt that we *have* it.

Notes

1   Sometimes, in the psychological literature, the premises trade places, and conclusions of the form "C A" are admitted, as well; such variations can affect the outcome of an experiment, as we will see below.

2   However, this is not to say that I endorse the traditional notion of validity wholesale. Researchers in semantics and pragmatics generally agree that a universal quantifier *presupposes* that its domain is non-empty, and presupposition is not the same as logical consequence (see, for example, Geurts, 1999; Horn, 1989). Strictly speaking, therefore, the nine syllogisms that separate the two notions of validity have a different status, because they are contingent upon the presuppositions of "all" and "no". And this distinction is relevant from a psychological point of view, too, since the 15 syllogisms valid in predicate logic are easier than the ones that are valid in traditional logic only.

3   Not shown in Table 1 is the percentage of times subjects concluded that "nothing follows" from a given pair of premises. Such non-propositional conclusions (as they have been called) raise some highly problematic issues, but as far as I can tell none of these has any bearing on the principal tenets of this paper.

4 As is customary in set theory, I count φ, ψ and ψ, φ as two pairs. If they are counted as one, the number of conversion pairs is halved, and we are faced with the question of what is supposed to correlate with what. This question is a delicate one, because the members of a conversion pair are connected by a symmetry relation, and there is no principled criterion for separating between the factors of the correlation. However, I expect that in practice this would not matter very much, because some random separations I tried out yielded scores that didn't deviate too much from the one quoted in the text.

5 Note that allowing AC as well as CA conclusions yields the same collection of syllogisms as allowing the order of the premises to vary.

6 Sundholm (1983) gives a nice introduction, to natural deduction, and compares it to older Frege-Hilbert style systems.

7 To say that *a* was chosen arbitrarily means that *a* may neither occur in φ nor in the premises (if any) from which φ was derived.

8 Johnson-Laird, Byrne, and Tabossi (1989: 672) remark in passing that "[t]he model-based theory is readily extendible to deal with non-standard quantification" (cf. also Johnson-Laird, 1983: 443). In view of the considerations adduced in the foregoing, however, such claims must be wrong.

9 The concept of generalized quantifier was introduced by Mostowski in 1957, and imported into natural-language semantics by Barwise and Cooper (1981), whose article remains one of the best introductions to the subject. Generalized quantifiers may be viewed not only as relations between sets, as I do here, but also as functions from sets to families of sets. From a logical point of view, one perspective is as good as the other, but the former is more natural and more adequate from a processing perspective.

10 In these definitions I adopt the truth-conditional stance on meaning, and explicate the meaning of a sentence by specifying the circumstances under which it is true ("iff" is an abbreviation of "if and only if"). Readers not familiar with truth-conditional semantics can take "is true iff" as synonymous with "means that".

11 Donkey sentences are so-called after the classic example of Geach (1962), "Every farmer who owns a donkey beats it." See Kanazawa (1994) and Geurts (2002) for more recent discussion.

12 Smith (1979, 1980). See Drozd (2001) and Geurts (2001) for discussion of symmetry in the context of language acquisition.

13 I am by no means the first to observe the importance of monotonicity to syllogistic reasoning. Indeed, it may be argued that the concept is implicit in the traditional *dictum de omni* and

the notion of so-called distributed occurrence of terms. The most thorough discussion of the role monotonicity plays in syllogistic inference is by Sánchez Valencia (1991).

14 A caveat: my main concern in this paper is with the representations used in reasoning with quantifiers. The processing model presented below is my official proposal, to be sure, but whatever interest it has lies chiefly in the rules and representations it employs. I have nothing new to say about reasoning errors, and nothing at all about reasoning strategies. Concerning the latter point, I consider it quite likely that people employ different types of reasoning strategies, which may involve different types of representation (as, for example, Ford, 1995, has argued), but in this paper I confine my attention to one particular type.

15 For monotonicity marking in less trivial languages, see Sánchez Valencia (1991) and Dowty (1994).

16 More sophisticated models can be obtained by refining the notion of "right sort of conclusion", which is somewhat simplistic as it stands. Such refinements should account for the fact that we prefer to draw conclusions that are non-trivial and relevant to our current purposes – which may be rather a tall order.

17 As the number of valid syllogisms is quite small, this can easily be proved by enumeration of alternatives.

18 Of course, this talk of "reasoning budgets" is merely a picturesque alternative to the common procedure of assigning numerical weights to inference rules. It must be admitted that it is not entirely clear what such weights stand for. The basic idea surely is that weights represent processing effort, but this notion is inappropriate if we allow for illicit inference rules. I will not attempt to sort out this matter here.

19 This is admittedly stipulative, but it is not entirely arbitrary because it means, in the present model, that the reasoning system begins to falter after four or five inference steps – which seems quite reasonable to me. Still, this is a matter that calls for a more refined treatment.

20 I am indebted to Frans van der Slik for carrying out the analyses reported in the following and helping me interpret the results.

21 A case in point is the well-known fact that the seemingly trivial step from "It is raining" to "It is raining or snowing" is actually quite hard to take, though it doesn't seem right to say that the inference is especially complex; it is just *odd* that someone should want to draw this conclusion. Some researchers have, implicitly or explicitly, rejected this diagnosis. Thus, Braine, Reiser, and Rumain (1984) set up their "mental logic" in such a way that it is very hard to derive "φ or ψ" from φ alone. However, this also makes

the following argument virtually impossible to prove:

$$\frac{\varphi \quad \text{If } \varphi \text{ or } \psi, \text{ then } \chi}{\chi}$$

Subjects typically find it very easy to see that this is valid, and therefore Braine et al. have no choice but to stipulate that this is a valid pattern of inference. I have criticized such manoeuvres in Section 3, and argued that they should be avoided at all costs. There is quite a bit more to say about this matter, but I will not say it here.

References

Barwise, J., & Cooper, R. (1981). Generalized quantifiers and natural language. *Linguistics and Philosophy, 4*, 159–219.

Braine, M. D. S. (1998). Steps towards a mental-predicate logic. In M. D. S. Braine & D. P. O'Brien (Eds.), *Mental logic* (pp. 273–331). Mahwah, NJ: Lawrence Erlbaum Associates.

Braine, M. D. S., Reiser, B. J., & Rumain, B. (1984). Some empirical justification for a theory of natural propositional logic. In G. H. Bower (Ed.), *The psychology of learning and motivation*. New York: Academic Press.

Bucciarelli, M., & Johnson-Laird, P. N. (1999). Strategies in syllogistic reasoning. *Cognitive Science, 23*, 247–303.

Chater, N., & Oaksford, M. (1999). The probability heuristics model of syllogistic reasoning. *Cognitive Psychology, 38*, 191–258.

Cosmides, L. (1989). The logic of social exchange: has natural selection shaped how humans reason? Studies with the Wason selection task. *Cognition, 31*, 187–276.

Cosmides, L., & Tooby, J. (1992). Cognitive adaptations for social exchange. In J. H. Barkow, L. Cosmides & J. Tooby (Eds.), *The adapted mind: evolutionary psychology and the generation of culture* (pp. 163–228). Oxford: Oxford University Press.

Dickstein, L. S. (1978). The effect of figure on syllogistic reasoning. *Memory and Cognition, 6*, 76–83.

Dickstein, L. S. (1981). Conversion and possibility in syllogistic reasoning. *Bulletin of the Psychonomic Society, 18*, 229–232.

Dowty, D. (1994). The role of negative polarity and concord marking in natural language reasoning. In M. Harvey & L. Santelmann (Eds.), *Proceedings from semantics and linguistic theory IV* (pp. 114–144). Ithaca, NY: Cornell University Press.

Drozd, K. F. (2001). Children's weak interpretations of universally quantified questions. In M. Bowerman & S. C. Levinson (Eds.), *Language acquisition and conceptual development* (pp. 340–376). Cambridge University Press: Cambridge.

Evans, J. St. B. T., Newstead, S. E., & Byrne, R. M. J. (1993). *Human reasoning: the psychology of deduction*, Hove: Lawrence Erlbaum.

Ford, M. (1995). Two modes of mental representation and problem solution in syllogistic reasoning. *Cognition, 54*, 1–71.

Geach, P. T. (1962). *Reference and generality*. Ithaca, NY: Cornell University Press.

Geurts, B. (1999). *Presuppositions and pronouns*. Oxford: Elsevier.

Geurts, B. (2001). *Quantifying kids*. Unpublished manuscript.

Geurts, B. (2002). Donkey business. *Linguistics and Philosophy, 25*, 129–156.

Gigerenzer, G., & Hug, K. (1992). Domain-specific reasoning: social contracts, cheating and perspective change. *Cognition, 43*, 127–171.

Horn, L. R. (1989). *A natural history of negation*. Chicago, IL: Chicago University Press.

Johnson-Laird, P. N. (1983). *Mental models*. Cambridge: Cambridge University Press.

Johnson-Laird, P. N., & Bara, B. G. (1984). Syllogistic inference. *Cognition, 16*, 1–61.

Johnson-Laird, P. N., Byrne, R. M. J., & Tabossi, P. (1989). Reasoning by model: the case of multiple quantification. *Psychological Review, 96*, 658–673.

Johnson-Laird, P. N., & Steedman, M. (1978). The psychology of syllogisms. *Cognitive Psychology, 10*, 64–99.

Kanazawa, M. (1994). Weak vs. strong readings of donkey sentences and monotonicity inference in a dynamic setting. *Linguistics and Philosophy, 17*, 109–158.

Ladusaw, W. A. (1979). *Polarity sensitivity as inherent scope relations*. PhD dissertation, University of Texas at Austin, Austin, TX.

Ladusaw, W. A. (1996). Negation and polarity items. In S. Lappin (Ed.), *The handbook of contemporary semantic theory* (pp. 321–341). Oxford: Blackwell.

Newstead, S. E., & Griggs, R. A. (1983). Drawing inferences from quantified statements: a study of the square of oppositions. *Journal of Verbal Learning and Verbal Behavior, 22*, 535–546.

Oaksford, M., & Chater, N. (2001). The probabilistic approach to human reasoning. *Trends in Cognitive Sciences, 5*, 349–357.

Rips. L. J. (1994). *The psychology of proof: deductive reasoning in human thinking*. Cambridge, MA: MIT Press.

Sánchez Valencia, V. M. (1991). *Studies on natural logic and categorial grammar*. Doctoral dissertation, University of Amsterdam, Amsterdam.

Smith, C. L. (1979). Children's understanding of natural language hierarchies. *Journal of Experimental Child Psychology, 27*, 437–458.

Smith, C. L. (1980). Quantifiers and question answering in young children. *Journal of Experimental Child Psychology, 30*, 191–205.

Sundholm, G. (1983). Systems of deduction. In D. Gabbay & F. Guenthner (Eds.), *Handbook of philosophical logic* (pp. 133–188). Vol. 1. Dordrecht: Reidel.

Tsai, Y. (1977). Symmetry and transitivity assumptions about a nonspecified logical relation. *Quarterly Journal of Experimental Psychology, 29*, 677–684.

Wetherick, N. E., & Gilhooly, K. J. (1990). Syllogistic reasoning: effects of premiss order. In K. J. Gilhooly, M. T. G. Keane, R. H. Logie & G. Erdos (Eds.), *Lines of thinking: reflections on the psychology of thought* (pp. 99–108). Vol. 1. Chichester: Wiley.

Wilkins, M. C. (1928). The effect of changed material on ability to do formal syllogistic reasoning. *Archives of Psychology, 16*, 1–83.

Chapter 13: The Problem of Deduction

ROBERT C. STALNAKER

Our main concern is not with the explanation of rational action generally but with the particular cluster of rational activities which are directed toward answering the questions about the way the world is. Engaging in inquiry is of course itself a form of rational behavior and the pragmatic picture implies that such behavior should be explained according to the same belief-desire pattern as the naive, unreflective behavior of dogs and children. But in order to treat the special problems that arise in explaining those actions which explicitly concern the evaluation and modification of the agent's beliefs, we need a more specialized apparatus designed to describe that specific kind of activity. We need to be able to talk about an agent's beliefs about his beliefs, about the form in which his beliefs are expressed, and about the ways in which his beliefs may change in response to his experience.

The concept of *acceptance* will be a central concept in the account of inquiry developed here. Acceptance, as I shall use this term, is a broader concept than belief; it is a generic propositional attitude concept with such notions as presupposing, presuming, postulating, positing, assuming and supposing as well as believing falling under it. Acceptance is a technical term: claims I make about acceptance are not intended as part of an analysis of a term from common usage. But I do want to claim that this technical term picks out a natural class of propositional attitudes about which one can usefully generalize. Belief is obviously the most fundamental acceptance concept, but various methodological postures that one may take toward a proposition in the course of an inquiry or conversation are sufficiently like belief in some respects to justify treating them together with it.

To accept a proposition is to treat it as a true proposition in one way or another – to ignore, for the moment at least, the possibility that it is false. One may do this for different reasons, more or less tentatively, more or less self-consciously, with more or less justification, and with more or less feeling of commitment. As a rough criterion, one may say that a propositional attitude concept is an acceptance concept if the attitude is said to be *correct* whenever the proposition is true. Belief is an acceptance concept because a correct belief is a true belief. Correct here contrasts with justified. To say that a belief was correct is not to say it was adequately supported; to say that an assumption was correct is to say nothing about whether the assumption should have been made. Correct beliefs, assumptions, suppositions and presumptions are beliefs, assumptions, suppositions and presumptions the contents of which are true. A correct desire or hope, however, is not one that will in fact be satisfied, nor is a judgment that P is highly probable said to be correct because P turns out to be true. Thus this criterion distinguishes acceptance concepts from so-called pro attitudes like wishes and wants, from mixed emotive-cognitive attitudes like hope and fear, and from attitudes of partial belief or acceptance as represented by subjective probabilities.

Within this class of propositional attitudes there is considerable diversity. To accept a proposition is to act, in certain respects, as if one believed it, but there are several ways in which acceptance, in the intended sense, may differ from belief, and in which acceptance concepts may differ from each other. First, acceptance may have a social dimension. In a cooperative inquiry, a dialogue or a debate, what *we* accept

Reproduced with permission from Stalnaker, R. C. (1984) *Inquiry* (chapter 5) Cambridge, MA: MIT Press.

may be more important than what *I* accept. It is our common beliefs and assumptions, or what we take to be our common beliefs and assumptions, that will set the boundaries of our discussion and determine its direction. No matter how convinced you are that something is true, if it is what I am disputing, then you beg the question by accepting it in the context of our argument.[1]

Second, acceptance may be more passive or more active. As noted in [chapter 4 of *Inquiry*], some propositions may be taken for granted or presupposed by a person only because the possibility of their being false has never occurred to him, while others are explicitly accepted after reflection or investigation. Some people may be reluctant to apply the term "belief" to tacit presuppositions, but they are among the propositions accepted.

Third, a person may accept a proposition for the moment without the expectation that he will continue to accept it for very long. If a person expects a particular one of his *beliefs* to be overturned, he has already begun to lose it, but an assumption he makes may be quite explicitly temporary, and he may presume that something is true even when expecting to be contradicted.

Fourth, what a person accepts can be compartmentalized in a way in which what he believes cannot be. A person may accept something in one context, while rejecting it or suspending judgment in another. There need be no conflict that must be resolved when the difference is noticed, and he need not change his mind when he moves from one context to the other. But something is wrong if I have separate incompatible sets of beliefs for different circumstances. I cannot reasonably believe what I disbelieved yesterday without thinking that yesterday's belief was mistaken.

Finally, acceptance may be the product of methodological decision rather than subjective commitment. One may accept something for the sake of the argument, although one cannot believe things for this reason. The judge may direct the members of the jury to accept something, although he cannot reasonably direct them to believe it. In these ways, acceptance may diverge from belief, although belief is a kind of acceptance.

Ignoring for the moment the important differences between different kinds of acceptance, think of an inquirer as a person in an initial *acceptance state* preparing to perform some actions which are intended to lead to a change in that state. Following the strategy discussed in [chapter 4 of *Inquiry*], I will define an acceptance state not as a set of propositions accepted, but as a nonempty set of possible situations – the possibilities that remain open for an agent in the acceptance state. The set of propositions accepted contain just those propositions that are true in all of these possible situations. This way of defining belief and acceptance states has the advantages previously discussed: it imposes on the set of propositions accepted a structure that is motivated by the pragmatic-causal picture; it allows for a natural account of unconscious beliefs, tacit presuppositions and enthymematic reasoning. But it has the disagreeable consequence that the set of propositions accepted relative to an acceptance state is always consistent and deductively closed, which seems to imply that an inquirer never has inconsistent beliefs and always accepts all the consequences of any set of propositions every member of which he accepts. And this consequence is not just a rationality condition imposed on a set of propositions accepted, but a condition that follows from the definition of an acceptance state. So one cannot soften the disagreeable consequence by calling it an ideal which ordinary acceptance states strive for. If acceptance is to be defined in this way then acceptance states, however far from the ideal, must meet the consistency and closure conditions. Thus the model of acceptance that I will develop faces the problem of deduction in a particularly acute form.

To discuss the problem of deduction, I will distinguish three deductive conditions on the set of propositions determined by an acceptance state, all of which must hold if acceptance states are to be defined in terms of possible situations in the way I have suggested. Then I will argue that each of the conditions, applied to belief, is motivated by the pragmatic picture. Finally, I will try to show how they can be reconciled with the phenomena. The three conditions are as follows:

1. If P is a member of a set of accepted propositions, and P entails Q, then Q is a member of that set.

2. If P and Q are each members of a set of accepted propositions, then $P\&Q$ is a member of that set.

3. If P is a member of a set of accepted propositions, then not-P is not a member of that set.

Beliefs, according to the pragmatic picture, are conditional dispositions to act. A rational agent is, in general and by definition, disposed to act appropriately, where what is appropriate is defined relative to his beliefs and desires. To say that an agent believes that P is to say something like this: the actions that are appropriate for that agent – those he is disposed to perform – are those that will tend to serve his interests and desires in situations in which P is true. But this is not quite right for the following reason: it would be too strong to require that appropriate actions tend to serve the agent's ends in *any* possible situation in which one of his individual beliefs is true. Suppose I believe, as I do, that someone will be elected President of the United States in 1988. One way in which that proposition could be realized is for *me* to be the one elected, but I know that that is not the way my belief will come true. For my actions to be appropriate, given that I have this belief, it is surely not required that I take account of that possibility, since it is excluded by other of my beliefs. The actions that are appropriate for an agent who believes that P depend not only on what he wants but also on what else he believes. So it is necessary to define appropriateness relative to a total set of beliefs, or a belief state. And all that matters about such a belief state, as far as the appropriateness of actions or the agent's dispositions to act are concerned, are the entailments of the belief state. So there is no basis, on the dispositional account, for excluding from the set of an agent's beliefs any propositions that are entailed by his beliefs. That is, there is no basis, given the pragmatic account of belief, for defining the set of propositions believed, relative to a belief state, in a way that conflicts with the first deductive condition.

If one accepts this, then the argument for the second deductive condition is straightforward. If a person is in a belief state that entails both P and Q, then he is in a belief state that entails the conjunction of P and Q. If a person is, in general, disposed to act in ways that would tend to be successful if P (together with his other beliefs) were true and is also disposed to act in ways that would be successful if Q (together with his other beliefs) were true, then he is disposed to act in ways that would be successful if P&Q (together with his other beliefs) were true. But while the second deductive condition is a reasonable one, given the pragmatic account, to impose on the propositions determined by a belief state, it is not a reasonable condition to impose on the totality of an agent's beliefs. It is compatible with the pragmatic account that the rational dispositions that a person has at one time should arise from several different belief states. A person may be disposed, in one kind of context, or with respect to one kind of action, to behave in ways that are correctly explained by one belief state, and at the same time be disposed in another kind of context or with respect to another kind of action to behave in ways that would be explained by a different belief state. This need not be a matter of shifting from one state to another or vacillating between states; the agent might, at the same time, be in two stable belief states, be in two different dispositional states which are displayed in different kinds of situations. If what it means to say that an agent believes that P at a certain time is that some one of the belief states the agent is in at that time entails that P, then even if every set of propositions defined by a belief state conforms to the second deductive condition, the total set of propositions believed by an agent might not conform to that condition.[2]

The same distinction can be made with respect to the third deductive condition – the consistency condition. Applied to the set of propositions determined by a single belief state, it must hold. This is clear since the only set of propositions conforming to the first two conditions but violating the third is the set of all propositions, and no belief state in which all propositions were believed could distinguish any actions as appropriate or inappropriate. But if an agent can be in distinct belief states at the same time in the way suggested above, then there is no reason why these belief states cannot be incompatible. In such a case an agent would believe both a proposition and its contradictory, but would not therefore believe everything. It would still be possible in such a situation to explain the agent's actions as rational actions according to the usual pattern.

I noted above, in distinguishing belief from acceptance in general, that acceptance may be compartmentalized in a way that belief cannot. Now I am suggesting that an agent may at one time be in separate, even incompatible belief states. But there is no conflict here. The earlier point was not that an agent's beliefs *are* always integrated into a single state, but rather that they ought to be. A person's beliefs are defective if they do not fit together into a single coherent system. An agent who recognizes the consequences of the conjunction of separate beliefs must either accept the consequences or abandon one of the original beliefs. An agent who discovers a conflict between his separate beliefs must modify them in some way. One cannot agree to disagree with oneself.

There are, then, two ways in which the second and third deductive conditions apply to belief. First, they are *defining* conditions of the concept of a belief state. Second, they are *rationality* conditions on the set of all beliefs that an agent has at one time. They are rationality conditions on an agent's beliefs because, ideally, an agent's beliefs should be integrated into a single system.

In calling the closure and consistency conditions rationality conditions, I do not mean to imply that an agent whose beliefs fail to conform to them is irrational but only that his beliefs diverge from an ideal of perfect rationality. The ideal is perhaps one that is never met, but that is an imperfection in rational agents, not in the model of rationality. The fact that the ideal is unrealistic does not threaten the adequacy of the theory because one can still use the theory to describe coherently the dispositions of agents whose beliefs diverge from the ideal, and to explain their actions as rational actions.

I also want to emphasize that it is not implied that conforming to the rationality conditions is an easy or a mechanical task. If the contents of beliefs were like sentences and belief were something like assent, then it would be a simple matter of noting and remembering what one is doing to put a belief that *P* and a belief that *Q* together into a belief that *P&Q*. But on our account, beliefs are behavioral dispositions. Separate belief states are dispositions which are displayed in different kinds of situations. To integrate such belief states is to change one's dispositions so that the actions one is disposed to perform in the two kinds of situations are appropriate relative to the same belief state – the same conception of the way the world is. To change one's rational dispositions in this way may require only a routine calculation, or it may be a challenging and creative intellectual task. It is this kind of task, I want to suggest, that deductive inquiry is designed to accomplish.

There are two complementary parts to the strategy I am suggesting for treating the problem of deduction. The first, discussed at the end of [chapter 4 of *Inquiry*], begins with the observation that it may be a nontrivial problem to see what proposition is expressed by a given sentence. The apparent failure to see that a proposition is necessarily true, or that propositions are necessarily equivalent, is to be explained as the failure to see what propositions are expressed by the expressions in question. Relative to any propositional expression one can determine two propositions: there is the proposition that is

expressed, according to the standard rules, and there is the proposition that relates the expression to what it expresses. If sentence *s* expresses (according to the standard rules) proposition *P*, then the second proposition in question is the proposition that *s* expresses *P*. In cases of ignorance of necessity and equivalence, I am suggesting, it is the second proposition that is the object of doubt and investigation.

The second part of the strategy begins with the observation that it may be a nontrivial problem to put separate beliefs together into a single coherent system of belief. All of my actions may be rational in that they are directed toward desired ends and guided by coherent conceptions of the way things are even if there is no single conception of the way things are that guides them all. There may be propositions which I would believe if I put together my separate systems of belief, but which, as things stand, hold in none of them. These are the propositions whose truth might be discovered by a purely deductive inquiry.

Is this a plausible strategy for explaining deduction? Given the very general conception of content and information that we are using, I think it can be seen as a natural, even inevitable, strategy. There are two questions posed by the problem of deduction: first, what is the nature of the information conveyed in a statement about deductive relationships? Second, how do we acquire this information? The first part of the strategy responds to the first question; the second part responds to the second question.

According to the conception of content that lies behind the possible worlds analysis of propositions and propositional attitudes, content requires contingency. To learn something, to acquire information, is to rule out possibilities. To understand the information conveyed in a communication is to know what possibilities would be excluded by its truth. Now if one asks, what real possibilities are excluded when one learns that a necessary truth is true, the answer is clear: they will not normally be situations in which extralinguistic facts are different than they actually are, but they will be possible situations where the rules for determining the truth value of the statement yield a different result from the result they actually yield.

For some examples of necessary truths, pointing this out would be sufficient to reconcile necessity with the possibility of ignorance. If someone is ignorant of the fact that all ophthamologists are eye doctors, this is probably because he is ignorant of the meaning of one of the words in that statement. The relevant possible situations which his knowledge fails to exclude are ones in which the *sentence* "all ophthamologists are eye doctors" means something different from what it actually means. If a person is ignorant of the fact that Hesperus is Phosphorus, it is because his knowledge fails to exclude a possible situation in which, because causal connections between names and objects are different, one of those names refers to a different planet, and so the statement, "Hesperus is Phosphorus" says something different than it actually says. In both of these cases, there is clearly a piece of factual information which the person ignorant of the truth of a necessary truth is missing. Empirical inquiry, about language or about astronomy, is what is needed to straighten the situation out. But in the case of ignorance of mathematical truths and deductive relationships, there are no such pieces of missing factual information in terms of which the ignorance can be explained, and that is why, even given the answer to the first question, there remains a puzzle about the second. Deductive inquiry is concerned neither with lexicography nor with causal connections between names and things in the world. The information which one receives when one learns about deductive relationships does not seem to come from outside of oneself at all. It seems to be information which, in some sense, one has had all along. What one does is to transform it into a usable form, and that, it seems plausible to suppose, is a matter of putting it together with the rest of one's information.

If this conception of deductive inquiry is to fit the facts, then even to account for straightforward mechanical deductive problems one will have to postulate a large number of concurrent but separate belief states. According to the pragmatic picture, many separate belief states means many separate dispositions, each with its own domain of display. This can be plausible only where there is a natural way to match up separate beliefs with actions – where there is some basis independent of what the agent happens to do for saying which of his many belief states is relevant to explaining which of his actions. If the belief that P is to be kept distinct from the belief that Q, there must be some actions appropriate to the belief that P and some actions appropriate to the belief that Q which are different from the actions that are appropriate to the belief that $P\&Q$. This is, I think, exactly the situation in mathematics. The answer to the first question about deductive knowledge suggested that the subject matter of mathematical propositions is notation or structures exhibited in notation. The actions that are made appropriate by belief in distinctively mathematical propositions are actions of manipulating notation: calculating in particular ways and making moves in the construction of proofs. Because mathematical beliefs concern expressions, it is easy to find actions that manifest belief in particular propositions without manifesting belief in other stronger propositions which have them as consequences. To take a simple case of calculation, a person may display his belief that four plus three equals seven by performing certain operations on numerals that contain four and three as digits – for example by writing down "7" as the first step in adding sixty-four to twenty-three. A person who is competent at doing sums but not particularly quick or intuitive could manifest his separate beliefs that four plus three equals seven and that six plus two equals eight in calculating the sum of sixty-four and twenty-three, but he would show that before doing the calculation, he did not have the belief that sixty-four plus twenty-three is eighty-seven. That last belief results only after the two simpler arithmetic beliefs were put together against a background of more general beliefs and presuppositions about arithmetic operations.[3]

The thesis that acquiring deductive knowledge is putting one's separate belief states together will not, by itself, throw much light on the process of deductive inquiry. It says nothing about how one goes about answering questions about deductive relationships; the focus is not on the means of deductive inquiry, but on its end, and even the end is described only in very abstract terms. But our concern is not with the special features of deductive inquiry. The problem this thesis is intended to solve is the problem of finding a way to describe deductive inquiry as a special case of inquiry in general, a way which brings out the common features which the search for mathematical knowledge shares with the search for knowledge about the world. We need a framework in which one can give analyses of such concepts as knowledge, explanation, inference, and justification which allows for their application to both mathematics and empirical investigation.

The goal of inquiry, in both cases, is the acquisition of knowledge, and this is most naturally thought of as the receiving of information from outside. The simple conception of the inquirer adjusting his beliefs in response to new data, or filling in further details in his picture of the world as a result of interaction with it obviously fits empirical contexts more comfortably than mathematical ones. But the account of deduction as the integration of the separate belief states of a single agent provides a way to apply this conception to deductive inquiry as well. Inquiry in general is a matter of adjusting one's beliefs in response to new information, but in the case of deductive inquiry, the information that initiates the change is new, not to the agent, but only to one of his belief states. By dividing the agent into separate centers of rationality, we make it possible to see the processing of the information an agent already has as a phenomenon with the same structure as the reception of new information.

Whether this kind of account of deduction will work remains to be seen. One needs to look carefully at more detailed and challenging examples of mathematical questions, and at particular problems in the epistemology of mathematics. But I will assume that it gives us a way around the problem of deductive ignorance and inquiry – that it at least shows that the existence of deductive ignorance and inquiry is not an immediate refutation of the assumptions I am making about propositions, propositional attitudes, and inquiry.

Even if the deductive constraints on acceptance can be reconciled with the existence of deductive inquiry in the way I have suggested, there are other objections to them which must be answered. First, there are apparent counterexamples to the first deductive condition – that a person accepts any proposition that is entailed by any single proposition that he accepts. It is not obvious how the suggestion that a person's beliefs can be divided among separate belief states is relevant to explaining counterexamples to this principle. Second, there are examples and arguments that purport to show that the deductive principles are not acceptable even as rationality conditions. Sometimes, it has been suggested, one may reasonably accept each member of a set of propositions while not accepting their conjunction, even when one sees all the relevant deductive connections. I will discuss several such examples, some of them familiar in the literature, and try to show how the deductive constraints on acceptance can be defended against them.

I will begin with two counterexamples to the first deductive condition, as applied to belief. (1) William III of England believed, in 1700, that England could avoid a war with France. But avoiding a war with France entails avoiding a nuclear war with France. Did William III believe

England could avoid a nuclear war? It would surely be strange to say that he did. (2) The absentminded detective believes that the butler did it. There is no direct evidence of his guilt, but the detective has made what he thought was an exhaustive list of the possible suspects, investigated them one by one, and eliminated everyone except the butler. The problem is that he completely forgot about the chauffeur, who had both motive and opportunity. Would it be correct to say that the detective believes that the chauffeur did not do it? He does believe that no one other than the butler did it – that was essential to his reasoning – and this entails that the chauffeur did not do it. But it would be misleading to say that the detective had this belief, since that seems to suggest that the chauffeur was one of the suspects eliminated from his list.

Even if it is strange or misleading, I am not sure whether it would be literally incorrect to say that William III and the absentminded detective had these beliefs. It is not that the king was in doubt about nuclear war or that the detective suspended judgment on the chauffeur's guilt. If these propositions were not believed, they were at least tacitly presupposed, and so they were propositions which were accepted in some sense. One way or another, the king and the detective ignored the possibility that the propositions in question were false. So the examples do not threaten the principle that one must *accept* the deductive consequences of any proposition one accepts, even if they do refute the principle as applied to a more specific kind of acceptance such as belief. The examples do not suggest that acceptance states should be defined in a different way, but at most that different acceptance concepts may be used to categorize the propositions entailed by a single acceptance state.

Perhaps for it to be true that x believes that P, it is necessary that x understand the proposition that P, or that x have entertained the proposition that P. If so, then it is too simple to identify the propositions believed with the entailments of a belief state. One would have to say that the beliefs were the entailments of a belief state which met certain further conditions. One might, for example, define the *active* beliefs of an agent as those propositions which are entailed by a belief state, but not entailed by the weaker acceptance state which determines the tacit presuppositions. This would ensure that an agent's beliefs would include only propositions which distinguish between possibilities that he recognizes.

Compare some other propositional attitudes where it is clearer that this kind of move is necessary. The first analogy is with wanting. If a rational man *wants* it to be the case that *P*, and recognizes that *P* entails *Q*, must he want it to be the case that *Q*? If wanting it to be the case that *P* is wanting one of the possible worlds in which *P* is true to be the actual world, then it would seem that the consequence condition should hold for wanting. One cannot rationally want *P* to be true without *Q*, since that is a logical impossibility, and there are no possible worlds, desirable or undesirable, in which logical impossibilities are realized. But there are persuasive counterexamples to the consequence condition on rational wants. Suppose I am sick. I want to get well. But getting well entails having been sick, and I do not want to have been sick. Suppose there was a murder. I want to know who committed the murder. But my knowing who committed the murder entails that the murder was committed, and I never wanted the murder to have been committed. One can reconcile these examples with a qualified consequence condition by noting that wanting something is preferring it to certain relevant alternatives, the relevant alternatives being those possibilities that the agent believes will be realized if he does not get what he wants. Some propositions which are entailed by propositions that one wants to be true in this sense are also entailed by the relevant alternatives. It is not that I want these propositions to be true – it is just that I accept that they will be true whether I get what I want or not. Given that there was a murder, I would rather know who committed it than not know. The question of whether or not I look with favor on the fact that there was a murder – whether I am glad that it happened or wish that it had not – does not arise in that context. To raise *that* question, one needs to expand the set of relevant alternatives, to compare the actual situation with possible situations in which the murder never took place.

The qualified consequence condition for rational wants motivated by these considerations is this: the propositions one wants to be true (relative to a set of relevant alternative possibilities) includes all the consequences of any proposition one wants to be true *which distinguish between the relevant alternatives*.

The second analogy is with epistemic concepts such as knowledge and justified belief. Suppose all justification is local in the sense that it takes place against a background of beliefs and presuppositions which themselves need not be justified, at least in that context. Then justi-fied belief, and perhaps knowledge, will conform only to a qualified consequence condition such as the one discussed above for rational wants. Here is an example, taken from an article by Fred Dretske, which tends to support such a conclusion. You are at the zoo next to the zebra cage with your son. The zebras are in plain view and the sign on the cage says "zebra." Your son asks you what they are, and you tell him. Do you *know* that they are zebras? Of course. But that they are zebras entails that they are not mules cleverly disguised by the zoo authorities to look like zebras. Do you know that they are not mules cleverly disguised in this way? Dretske suggests that you do not. The hypothesis that they are mules may not be very plausible; it is surely reasonable to ignore the possibility that they are. But you must admit that if they were disguised mules, things would look exactly as they in fact look. The kinds of reasons you have for ignoring this hypothesis – general considerations of plausibility – do not seem sufficient to give you knowledge.[4]

The example is, of course, a typical Cartesian skeptic's example. Given the assumption that a person knows all the known consequences of anything known, the example supports the conclusion that you do not *really* know that the animals you see are zebras. But Dretske suggests abandoning the consequence condition instead of the knowledge claim. This is not the place to discuss the adequacy of this response to the skeptic. The point I want to make here is just that this kind of context-dependent conception of justification and knowledge which rejects the consequence condition for propositions known or justifiably believed is compatible with the possible worlds analysis of states of knowledge and belief. In fact, the possible worlds framework allows for a natural formulation of such a conception.

Let me now consider some examples and arguments, drawn from the work of Henry Kyburg, which go against the second deductive condition, the conjunction principle. First, the notorious lottery paradox. I have ticket number seven in a fair lottery with a million tickets. "Consider the hypothesis 'ticket number seven will not win . . .' There is only one chance in a million that the hypothesis is false. Surely . . . this is reason enough to accept the hypothesis." The same reasoning applies to each of the other tickets, and so I should accept every hypothesis of the form "ticket *i* will not win." But I cannot consistently accept the conjunction of all these hypotheses since I know that some ticket will win.[5]

The weak point in this argument, I think, is the assumption that a probability of .999999 is sufficient for acceptance. Why should a probability of .999999 be a reason for doing anything more than believing the hypothesis to degree .999999? The practical difference between accepting a hypothesis and believing it to degree $1 - \epsilon$ may, in some cases, become negligible as ϵ diminishes, but there does seem to be a significant difference in this case. If the price of the ticket is low enough, and the value of the prize is great enough, it is rational for me to buy a ticket even if I will benefit from the purchase only if I win. But my purchase is rational, on this assumption, only if I leave open the possibility that I might win. The day that the winning ticket is announced, I learn that ticket number seven did not win. My attitude toward the hypothesis that ticket seven would not win changes. I do not come to accept that a proposition I already accepted was true – that would be no change at all. Rather, I learn that a hypothesis I was almost sure of is indeed true.

One could easily enough define a concept of acceptance which identified it with a high subjective or epistemic probability (probability greater than some specified number between one-half and one), but it is not clear what the point of doing so would be. Once a subjective or epistemic probability value is assigned to a proposition, there is nothing more to be said about its epistemic status. Bayesian decision theory gives a complete account of how probability values, including high ones, ought to guide behavior, in both the context of inquiry and the application of belief outside of this context. So what could be the point of selecting an interval near the top of the probability scale and conferring on the propositions whose probability falls in that interval the honorific title "accepted"? Unless acceptance has some consequences, unless the way one classifies the propositions as accepted, rejected, or judgment suspended makes a difference to how the agent behaves, or ought to behave, it is difficult to see how the concept of acceptance can have the interest and importance for inquiry that it seems to have.

If the conjunction principle governs the concept of acceptance, then it is clear that one can say something, at least, about the consequences of acceptance: to accept a proposition is to permit oneself to put that proposition together with any others that one accepts, and draw any consequences that may follow. Reasoning in this way

from accepted premises to their deductive consequences (P, also Q, therefore R) does seem perfectly straightforward. Someone may object to one of the premises, or to the validity of the argument, but one could not intelligibly agree that the premises are each acceptable and the argument valid, while objecting to the acceptability of the conclusion. But given a probabilistic rule of acceptance (accept P if and only if the probability of P is at least as great as some fixed number between one-half and one), just knowing that P has the status *accepted* would give you no license to put it together with anything else. One would have to know, among other things, the probability on which the proposition achieved that status.

Another paradox, closely related to the lottery paradox, is the paradox of the preface. In the preface to his historical narrative, the author admits that he has undoubtedly made some mistakes – that some of the statements he made in his narrative are false. He is not confessing to insincerity – he continues to *believe* everything he wrote – he is just confessing to fallibility. It does not take excessive modesty to believe that *some* of one's many beliefs or sincere assertions are false. This is only reasonable. Yet to believe this is to believe each member of a set of propositions that are recognized to be inconsistent. If these propositions were conjoined and their consequences accepted, the result would be to accept the truth of every proposition.

The paradox of the preface and the lottery paradox are alike in that both may be used to support the conclusion that a person may sometimes be justified in accepting all the members of a recognizably inconsistent set of propositions. But the two paradoxes are different in at least one important respect. The assumption that high probability is sufficient for acceptance is essential to the argument of the lottery paradox. One response to that paradox – the one I endorsed – is to reject that assumption. But the paradox of the preface does not depend on that assumption and cannot be answered in the same way. It cannot plausibly be denied that the author *accepts* the truth of each of the statements made in his narrative, nor can it be denied that he accepts that at least one of those statements is false. But it also seems plausible to say that the author accepts, or at least commits himself to, any conjunction of the statements in the narrative. In presenting his narrative, the author is aiming at a coherent total story. It is, in fact, a methodological constraint on a historian's construction of his narrative (as on a scientist's interpretation of his results) that the propositions he accepts fit together into a coherent story. Unless one can freely conjoin propositions, it is difficult to see how considerations of coherence can play the methodological role which they obviously play in inductive procedure.

So the historian does not intend his confession of fallibility to prevent the reader from putting together the different statements made in telling his story. He intends only that the reader recognize that the story as a whole is undoubtedly wrong in some of its details. But the fact remains that the author denies in his preface something that is entailed by what he asserts in his narrative, and the reader is obviously not supposed to conjoin these contradictory accepted propositions. So I agree with Kyburg in rejecting a global conjunction rule for accepted propositions, even as a rationality condition. This is not because high probability is sufficient for acceptance; it is rather because sometimes it is reasonable to *accept* something that one knows or believes is false.

When is it reasonable to accept something one believes is false? When one believes that it is *essentially* true, or close to the truth – as close as one can get, or as close as one needs to get for the purposes at hand. It is not obvious how one judges a false proposition, or a whole story, to be roughly or essentially correct, or even what one is judging when one does, but it is obvious that people do make such judgments and that they play a role in their decisions about what to accept. Sometimes these decisions are based on practical considerations. Accepting a certain false proposition may greatly simplify an inquiry, or even make possible an inquiry not otherwise possible, while at the same time it is known that the difference between what is accepted and the truth will have no significant effect on the answer to the particular question being asked. When a scientist makes idealizing assumptions, he is accepting something for this kind of reason. Particles or planets may be treated as point masses, the atmosphere may be assumed to be a vacuum, consumers or governments may be thought of as rational. Of course in other inquiries these same assumptions might greatly distort the results, but the scientist might be in a position to know that in his inquiry they would not. The scientist does not, of course, *believe* the propositions he accepts, but he acts, in a limited context, as if he believed them in order to further his inquiry.

Even if an inquiry has no practical motivation – even if one's aim is just to tell a story right – a divergence between acceptance and belief may be reasonable. The historian in the example believes that his narrative is *mostly* right, and the doubts he does have about it are based on general considerations of fallibility. What more effective way does he have to say just what he is *sure* of than to tell the story as best he can, and then add, in the preface, that it is probably only roughly true. Here his motive for accepting what he does not believe is that doing so is an efficient means of telling what he does believe.

I am suggesting that one may accept, for various reasons, what one does not believe, but one may not, of course, believe what one does not believe or reasonably believe what one believes is false. The explanation of the preface phenomenon that I am suggesting requires that we say that the historian does not, without qualification, *believe* that the story he accepts is correct; nor does he believe, without qualification, all of the individual statements he makes in telling the story. We must say this to reconcile the phenomenon with a conjunction condition as a rationality condition for belief. But isn't this what we do want to say? The historian, when he wrote his preface, was not just making some additional statements for the reader to believe along with those in his narrative; he was taking something back. It is a conjunction condition for belief, together with a consistency condition, which explains why the reader takes the preface as a hedge or a qualification to the text.

Kyburg has a more general reason for rejecting the conjunction principle as a rationality condition on belief: he believes that it leads to a distorted picture of the process of inductive inquiry. He points out that any system of acceptance rules that includes the strong deductive conditions will require that there be "essentially only *one* hypothesis that we may induce from given evidence. Anything else we are allowed to induce will turn out to be merely an implicate of the evidence and that one strongest hypothesis."[6] "This approach . . . suggests that as scientists or even as people we do not induce hypothesis by hypothesis, but that induction consists in principle of inducing at each stage of inquiry . . . a single monumentally complex conjunctive statement."[7] "It is preposterous to suppose that all our inductive knowledge has to be embodiable in a single fat statement."[8]

Kyburg is of course right that if rational belief conforms to the strong deductive conditions, then an ideal state of rational belief could be represented by a single proposition – a proposition that is itself believed and which entails all propositions believed by someone in that ideal state. It is because of this fact that it is possible to represent any belief state meeting the strong deductive conditions by a single set of possible worlds. But is this so preposterous? Some of the things Kyburg says make this consequence seem more implausible than it is.

First, Kyburg's remarks suggest that he has a linguistic picture of the objects of propositional attitudes in mind. The strongest accepted proposition is described as a "monumentally complex conjunctive statement." But on the possible worlds conception of proposition, the complexity of a statement is in the means of representing a proposition and not in the proposition itself. And the fatter the statement, the thinner the proposition, since a proposition is defined by the possible worlds in which it is true. Some of Kyburg's reservations about the consequences of the conjunction principle may derive from questionable assumptions about the structure of propositions.

Second, it must be kept in mind that a global conjunction rule is a rationality condition for belief, which means that conjunction or integration of separate beliefs is an ideal that believers aim at rather than a feature essential to the set of a person's beliefs. It may be preposterous to suppose that anyone's inductive knowledge or beliefs actually do get embodied in a single very fat (or very thin) proposition, but that by itself does not threaten the normative force of the ideal.

Third, while it is true that any state of belief which conforms to the conjunction principle *can* be represented by a single strongest proposition, it does not follow from this that that representation has any special methodological status. Despite Kyburg's claims to the contrary, the conjunction principle does not prevent people from inducing hypothesis by hypothesis, or require them to reevaluate all of their beliefs every time they receive a new piece of evidence. The description of a rational change of belief as the replacement of one fat conjunctive hypothesis with a different one may seem to suggest that every belief change must be a scientific revolution, but if it does so, then it is a misleading description. Nothing implied by the conjunction principle says that one can't replace one fat conjunctive hypothesis with another one simply by tinkering with one of the conjuncts. Nothing

implied by the conjunction principle requires one to ignore the fact that some propositions have nothing to do with one another. Where the evidence for or against one proposition is irrelevant to another and where the actions to which the truth or falsity of the one proposition is relevant are distinct from the actions to which the truth or falsity of the other are relevant, then believing the conjunction of the two propositions is no different from believing them separately. To recognize their independence *is* to conjoin or integrate them in the only way that is required.

Still, I think there is a real problem which Kyburg is pointing to, not a problem with the conjunction principle but a limitation of the possible worlds representation of a belief or acceptance state. The problem can be most clearly seen by considering how one might represent a change in what one accepts – a change brought about by a discovery of information that conflicts with something that one initially accepts. If a belief state is represented by a set of possible situations, then in the case of this kind of change the initial belief state and the new one must be represented by disjoint sets of possibilities. The two sets will have no possibilities in common, even if the change of belief is, intuitively, a very small one. At this level of abstraction, there is no difference between a discovery that one was mistaken about some small isolated factual detail and a scientific revolution or global conversion. In both cases, *all* of the possibilities compatible with one's initial belief state are incompatible with the new one. But surely an adequate account of inquiry must account for such extreme differences.

It might seem that a representation of a belief state as a list of sentence-like propositions would more easily and naturally account for what is preserved in a belief change, and for the difference between minor and major belief changes. And so in terms of such a representation, it might be easier to state and defend rules for revising belief in response to discoveries that conflict with one's initial beliefs, or at least to put constraints on such rules. The following kind of rule of revision, for example, might seem initially plausible: add the new information to the list of propositions believed that constitutes one's initial belief state, and then delete from the list the items which are incompatible with the new information. But there are well-known problems here. There will not, in general, be a unique consistent revision of the list, since the new information may require the deletion of one of a set of items without requiring the deletion of any particular one of them. And one cannot adequately compare the magnitude of a belief change simply by counting the propositions changed, since there will be logical and conceptual relations between them. A list of propositions believed will not be a list of independent pieces of information.

A simple abstract example will illustrate the problem. Suppose two agents, George and Harry, both begin by believing both P and Q, and then discover that P is false. George rejects Q along with P, while Harry retains his belief in Q. Isn't it obvious that George's beliefs change more than Harry's? Not necessarily, for P and Q won't be George and Harry's only initial beliefs. If they recognize the obvious consequences of their beliefs, then both of them will also believe, for example, $P \vee \sim Q$. Harry, to remain consistent, must give up this belief when he learns that P is false, while George need not. Each must choose between his belief that Q and his belief that $P \vee \sim Q$, and it is not obvious that one change is more minimal than the other.

This may seem artificial. One might argue that Q is more basic than $P \vee \sim Q$. The latter is believed only because P is believed, while the former is believed independently. But this may or may not be true. One cannot infer from the logical complexity of $P \vee \sim Q$ that belief in it is epistemically dependent on its parts. If George has some independent reason to believe $P \vee \sim Q$ then it will seem perfectly reasonable to take it, together with the new information that P is false as a reason for rejecting Q.

A belief change in response to conflicting information will always force one to choose between alternative revisions, none of which can be seen, on logical grounds alone, to be preferable to the others. The choice will depend on assumptions about epistemic and causal dependence and independence, on the reasons one has for one's beliefs as well as on the beliefs themselves. Whether we represent belief states by lists of sentences or by sets of possible worlds, we will need to impose additional structure on our notion of a belief state before we can say very much about the way beliefs change or ought to change in response to new information.

The abstract example we used above is reminiscent of the examples used by Nelson Goodman to refute various proposed analyses of counterfactual conditionals.[9] The problem of belief change in response to conflicting information is closely related to Goodman's problem; a solu-

tion to one is likely to come together with a solution to the other. It was the main negative lesson of Goodman's early paper on counterfactuals that one cannot analyze this kind of statement using only logical relations such as logical independence, compatibility and entailment, together with unproblematic factual assumptions. Some additional, more substantive relations between propositions were needed. The possible worlds analysis of propositions – an analysis Goodman would have no use for – is obviously not the source of Goodman's problem, or of the related problem about belief change. What this analysis does is to make the problems manifest by representing propositions in terms of their minimal logical structure, thereby removing the illusion that we have some account of the structure of possibilities and of the intuitive notions of dependence and independence, similarity and difference between possibilities, which a solution to the problems will require.

The abstract possible worlds framework treats possible worlds as unstructured points. This is not, of course, because the theory makes a claim that possible worlds are some kind of simple unstructured object, but because the theory seeks to capture what is essential and common to a diverse range of applications. The structure of possibilities may be very different from one context to another, but in any interesting context possible situations will be quite complex, and the way we represent and express propositions as well as the way we respond to new information will depend on the structure of the possible worlds in terms of which the propositions and propositional attitudes states are defined. Possible worlds will normally have spatiotemporal structure, domains of individuals instantiating properties and standing in relations to each other. The facts and states of affairs that constitute a possible world may be more or less independent of each other. In terms of the structure of a possible world, one might characterize various relations of similarity and difference between possible worlds, and in terms of such relations one might say more about rational belief change and more generally about the process of inquiry.

Let me conclude by describing the picture of inquiry that has emerged from our discussion so far. A state of belief is most perspicuously represented, not by a set of sentences or propositions believed, but by the set of possibilities recognized as ways the world may be. Propositions believed, relative to such a belief state, are propositions true in all possible situations in the set. There is nothing essentially linguistic about belief, according to this picture, although the subject matter of belief may be linguistic expressions, or conceptual structures that essentially involve language, and this may be true even when it is not evident from the surface forms of belief attributions.

The beliefs of a perfectly rational intelligence could be represented by a single belief state of this kind – one coherent conception of the way the world is represented by one set of alternative possibilities. But the beliefs of mere mortals will require a more complicated representation. Mortals may be in many belief states at once, represented by separate spaces of possibilities. The integration of such separate belief states may in some cases be a simple matter of putting two and two together, but it may also be a task that requires nontrivial computation or creative activity. Deductive inquiry, I suggested, is inquiry which is designed to accomplish such tasks.

Belief is not the only attitude that is relevant to the cognitive situation of inquirers. Inquirers make posits, presumptions, assumptions and presuppositions as well. These methodological attitudes may diverge from belief in various ways, giving rise to additional complexity in a representation of an epistemic situation. But, I suggested, the cluster of propositional attitudes which were grouped together under the label *acceptance* share a common structure with belief.

Inquiry is the process of changing such acceptance states, either by interaction with the world or by interaction between different acceptance states. Methodological policies are policies constraining such changes. To have a framework for describing methodological policy, we might assume that acceptance states have two components: a set of alternative possibilities representing the inquirer's current conception of the way the world is, and a change function representing his disposition to change what he accepts in response to new information. This function will take propositions (the potential new information) into new acceptance states. It seems plausible to assume that when the new information is compatible with everything initially accepted, then the new acceptance state will be the intersection of the new information with the initial state. But where the new information conflicts with something initially believed, the new acceptance state will be a disjoint set of possible situations. No constraints can be put on such changes without adding further structure to our representation of an inquirer's epistemic situation, or to our representation of the possible situations.

One should expect the two components of an acceptance state to interact: our current conception of the way the world is constrains our dispositions to change our beliefs in response to new evidence, and those dispositions may contribute to the formation of concepts in terms of which we describe the world.

Notes

1 I discuss a notion of presupposition which is a social acceptance concept of this kind in Stalnaker (1974). For discussions of closely related notions of mutual knowledge and common knowledge, see D. Lewis (1969) and Schiffer (1972).
2 David Lewis discusses a theory for representing fragmented states of belief, as he calls them, in D. Lewis (1982).
3 There will inevitably be a certain arbitrariness in drawing the line between the propositions an agent believes "straightaway" and those he is disposed to come to believe after perfunctory calculation. Where one draws this line will depend in part on what one is interested in explaining.
4 The example comes from Drestke (1970), 1015–1016. See also Dretske (1981), 123–134. For an interesting discussion of Dretske's example and argument, see Stine (1976).
5 Kyburg (1970), 56.
6 Ibid., 74.
7 Ibid., 76. This remark was made about two particular systems, one developed by Jaakko Hintikka and Risto Hilpinen and the other by Keith Lehrer, but Kyburg says that "any global system in which the conjunction principle is satisfied will suffer from these shortcomings" (ibid., 76).
8 Ibid., 77.
9 Goodman (1947), which is also chapter 1 of Goodman (1955).

References

Dretske, Fred I. (1970). "Epistemic Operators," *Journal of Philosophy*, 67, 1007–1023.
Dretske, Fred I. (1981). *Knowledge and the Flow of Information*. Cambridge, Mass.: Bradford Books, MIT Press.
Goodman, Nelson (1947). "The Problem of Counterfactual Conditionals," *Journal of Philosophy*, 44, 113–128. Reprinted in Goodman (1955), 3–27.

Goodman, Nelson (1955). *Fact, Fiction and Forecast.* Cambridge, Mass.: Harvard University Press,

Kyburg, Henry F. (1970). "Conjunctivitis," in Marshall Swain, ed., *Induction, Acceptance and Rational Belief*, 55–82, Dordrecht: Reidel.

Lewis, David (1969). *Convention.* Cambridge, Mass.: Harvard University Press.

Lewis, David (1982). "Logic for Equivocators," *Nous*, 16, 431–441.

Schiffer, Stephen (1972). *Meaning.* Oxford: Oxford University Press.

Stalnaker, Robert (1974). "Pragmatic Presuppositions," in Milton Munitz and Peter Unger, eds., *Semantics and Philosophy*, 197–214. New York: New York University Press.

Stine, Gail (1976). "Skepticism, Relevant Alternatives, and Deductive Closure," *Philosophical Studies*, 29, 249–261.

Section 4: Induction

Chapter 14: Patterns, Rules, and Inferences

ACHILLE C. VARZI

Introduction

Some of our reasoning is strictly *deductive*; we conclude that the available evidence supports a certain claim as a matter of logical necessity. For example, the following reasoning is deductive, since it is not possible for the conclusion to be false if both premises are true.

(1)   Every *F* is *G*, and *x* is *F*. Therefore, *x* is *G*.

Often, however, we are not in a position to produce a deductive argument; often we can only establish that the evidence supports the conclusion to a high degree of probability. Such *inductive* reasoning, as it is normally called, is in turn divisible into two types, according to whether or not it presupposes that the universe or some relevant aspect of it is law-like, or rule-governed. Reasoning that does not require this presupposition may be classified as *statistical*, since the evidence described by the premises supports the conclusion for purely mathematical reasons. For example, the following inductive reasoning is statistical:

(2)   Almost every *F* is *G*, and *x* is *F*. Therefore, *x* is *G*.

Here it is rational to reach the conclusion even though it does not follow as a matter of logical necessity, for the probability of *x*'s being *G* is, given the facts, much higher than the probability of *x*'s not being *G* (other things being equal). The second type of inductive reasoning is generally classified as *Humean*, after the philosopher who first studied it thoroughly, and corresponds to those arguments that do require the presupposition of law-likeness. The following is an example:

(3)   Every *F* previously observed was *G*, and *x* is *F*. Therefore, *x* is *G*.

Again, the conclusion does not follow as a matter of logical necessity, so the argument is not deductive. Yet the available evidence gives excellent reasons to believe in the conclusion rather than in its negation. Unless the relationship between being *F* and being *G* is random, the evidence strongly suggests the existence of a law to the effect that *every F is G*.

Humean arguments are of great practical utility, since we often need to reach conclusions and make decisions on the basis of evidence that is neither conclusive (thus preventing us from reasoning deductively) nor complete (preventing us from reasoning statistically). The presupposition of law-likeness, however, plays a crucial and controversial role, and figuring out exactly what role it plays is no straightforward business.

The Game of the Rule

Consider the following familiar game. X thinks of a certain sequence (say, a sequence of numbers) and Y must figure out what the sequence is. To get started, X gives an initial fragment of the sequence. Y must look at it carefully and, on the basis of what she sees, she must try and figure out how the sequence continues. Which is to say: she must figure out the underlying pattern, uncover the rule by means of which the sequence is generated. For example, let us focus on (infinite) number sequences. If X's initial segment looks like this:

(A)   1, 3, 5, 7, 9, 11, . . .

then Y is likely to come up with a quick and reasonable guess: The sequence must consist of the positive odd integers, in their natural order. If the initial segment looks like this:

(B)   1, 2, 3, 5, 7, 11, . . .

then, again, Y may easily figure out how to continue – hence the rule by means of which the sequence is generated: This is the ordered sequence of the prime numbers, that is, the positive integers that do not have any other integer factors except for 1 and themselves. If Y guesses the rule within the allotted time, she wins the game. Otherwise X wins.

Now, some cases are more challenging than others, of course, and this is where the game gets interesting. For instance, consider the segment

(C) 1, 3, 6, 10, 15, 21, 28, . . .

This is the beginning of the sequence of the so-called triangular numbers, namely, those numbers that equal the sum of consecutive integers beginning with 1. More precisely, the rule underlying this sequence is that the nth element, S_n, is the sum of the first n positive integers:

(C*) $S_n = 1 + 2 + 3 + \cdots + n$.

(For example, the fourth triangular number is $10 = 1 + 2 + 3 + 4$.) One may want to run a test and see how people actually perform, but a good guess would be that in this case it takes more thinking to figure out the solution. Y might even object that she has never heard of the triangular numbers – whereas she had heard of even and prime integers – so how could she figure out the rule? Still, X may just answer that one need not *know* what a triangular number is in order to see the pattern. With some patience, Y could still figure out that the sequence obeys the rule defined in (C*). Or she could figure out the rule under a different, more intuitive description. For example, Y might realize that the numbers in the sequence correspond to the different ways in which we can form a triangular array of dots, or bowling pins, or billiard balls, as in the following diagram:

| 1 | 3 | 6 | 10 | 15 | 21 | 28 |

So Y could describe the sequence in terms of this intuition:

(C)** S_{n+1} = the smallest number of dots (pins, balls) that are needed to form a triangular array of size greater than S_n, starting from $S_1 = 1$.

(This is actually why these numbers are called *triangular*, in analogy with the *square* numbers,

which correspond to the different ways in which we can form a square array of dots.) How one comes up with the rule and how one describes it – X may insist – is not important in order to win the game. It is only important in a derivative sense, namely insofar as it makes the game playable by people with different backgrounds. The game is interesting precisely because the mental process whereby the rule is uncovered may involve different sorts of cognitive insight.

In fact, it is worth noting that although in these examples the rule by means of which the sequence is generated is essentially determined by its number-theoretic properties, it need not be so in general, even if the sequence consists of numbers. For instance, suppose X offers the following segment:

(D) 1, 22, 333, 4444, 55555, . . .

This is the beginning of an obvious sequence and, as it turns out, there is a mathematical key to this sequence, corresponding to the equation

(D*) $S_n = n \cdot \dfrac{(10^n - 1)}{9}$

But of course Y is more likely to describe the sequence on the basis of a different criterion, which reads the rule directly off the visual pattern exhibited by its elements:

1	One 1
22	Two 2s
333	Three 3s
4444	Four 4s
55555	Five 5s
⋮	⋮

In that case, Y's rule would not be (D*) but, rather, something like this:

(D)** S_n = the string consisting of the number n repeated n times.

X himself, in giving the initial segment, may have thought of the sequence in terms of (D**), not (D*), so the fact that there is a number-theoretic description of this sequence is entirely irrelevant. And in some cases there is no number-theoretic description at all, as in

(E) 1, 3, 4, 5, 7, 8, 9, 12, 14, 17, 18, . . .

Here X may be thinking of a rule that can be defined with reference to a linguistic property and that concerns the numerals, not the numbers:

(E*) S_n = the nth integer whose name in English has an even number of vowels.

A favorite example of this sort is actually one that does not depend on purely linguistic considerations, just as it does not depend on purely arithmetical considerations, and is due to the American mathematician John Conway:[1]

(F) 1, 11, 21, 1211, 111221, 312211, 13112221, ...

Is there a rule behind this sequence? If we look for a purely arithmetical or linguistic key, we won't find any. We must look at the sequence from a different perspective. Exactly what perspectives one may consider is of course hard to tell. But if we start reading the sequence aloud we might get a clue. Let's not read it like this:

1	One
11	Eleven
21	Twenty-one
1211	One thousand, two hundred, eleven
111221	One hundred eleven thousand, two hundred, twenty-one
312211	Three hundred twelve thousand, two hundred, eleven
13112221	Thirteen million, one hundred twelve thousand, ...
⋮	⋮

Let us read it like this:

1	1
11	One 1
21	Two 1s
1211	One 2 and one 1
111221	One 1, one 2, and two 1s
312211	Three 1s, two 2s, and one 1
13112221	One 3, one 1, two 2s, and two 1s
⋮	⋮

Then we suddenly realize what is going on: this is a "self-describing" sequence. It begins with 1 and then goes on to describe itself, in the sense that each subsequent term gives an "audioactive" description of its predecessor. The rule can be put thus, where '$d_i|r_i$' designates the string obtained by repeating r_i times the digit d_i:

(F*) If S_n is the string $d_1|r_1 \ldots d_k|r_k$ ($d_i \neq d_{i+1}$ for all $i < k$), then S_{n+1} is the string $r_1 d_1 \ldots r_k d_k$, starting with $S_1 = 1$.

The Rules of the Game

So much for this familiar game. It takes a moment now to realize that the game is a good model of what goes on when we engage in Humean inductive reasoning. For the game of the rule is a familiar one, not only insofar as it is often played for fun, or for pedagogical purposes (elementary school teachers often rely on it to explain – for instance – certain basic arithmetical concepts and operations); it is also familiar precisely because we find ourselves playing it all the time in our daily interactions with the world around us. We are constantly trying to figure out the rules or laws that govern the natural world, or the social world, or the stock market. We look at the facts and we try to figure out the underlying pattern, so as to predict what will happen next, exactly as we try to figure out the pattern of a sequence of numbers on the basis of an initial segment. We look at our history so far – that's the initial segment – and we try to figure out the underlying rationale, so as to know what to expect next. It may sound metaphorical, but it wouldn't be so far-fetched to claim that science as a whole is engaged in a game of this sort. Every F observed thus far is G (every number in the visible portion of the sequence is prime, for instance), so we think that there is a lawlike connection between being F and being G: we think that being F goes hand in hand with being G and we conclude that the next F in the sequence must be G, too. That is precisely the idea behind Humean inductive reasoning. And there are researchers who would claim that being able to reason that way – to play such a game – is a distinctive trait of rational behavior. Douglas Hofstadter and his research group, for instance, believe that this trait is close to the core – if not *the* core – of human intelligence, and that designing computer programs capable of playing the game of the rule is the deepest and most fascinating challenge that so-called artificial intelligence must face.[2]

To fully appreciate the import of these claims, however, it is important that we now be explicit about a few things that we have so far been taking for granted. There are, in fact, two crucial implicit assumptions that must be satisfied in order for the game to be played correctly – two tacit Rules (with the capital "R") that the players must observe.

The first tacit Rule is that the initial segment by means of which the sequence is introduced should provide enough information for Y to figure out the solution. For instance, with

(G)   1, 11, . . .

rather than (F) as the sole piece of evidence, Y would hardly come up with the Conway sequence, simply because this initial segment is compatible with many other, more plausible solutions. The sequence could in fact continue in several ways, each of which corresponds to a different solution that "fits the data" equally well insofar as the data are fixed by (G). For example, it could continue in any of the following three ways:

(G$_a$)   1, 11, 121, 1331, 14641, 161051, . . .
(G$_b$)   1, 11, 111, 1111, 11111, 111111, . . .
(G$_c$)   1, 11, 1, 11, 1, 11, 1, 11, 1, 11, . . .

and each way would correspond to a completely different rule:

(G$^*_a$) $S_n = 11^{(n-1)}$
(G$^*_b$) $S_n = 1|n$
(G$^*_b$) $S_n = 1$ if n is odd, and $S_n = 11$ if n is even.

There are obviously lots of possibilities, and for this reason Y would be entitled to complain if all X gave her as a starter was just the small bit in (G). For the problem is not merely that one can come up with different answers; we have already seen that sometimes the same sequence can be generated or described in accordance with more than one rule, as with (D*) and (D**). The problem is that in the present case the different answers would not be equivalent: They would describe different sequences, not the same sequence in different ways.

So this is the first tacit Rule of the game, which we can approximately formulate as follows:

R1   *The initial segment must uniquely identify the sequence.*

The interesting question, of course, is whether this Rule can be successfully implemented, or even whether it can be implemented at all. We shall come back to this question shortly. First let us mention the second tacit Rule of the game, which is equally important. This second Rule says that the sequence in question cannot be a *random* sequence. For example, it would be strange if X said that the sequence in (G) continued thus:

(G$_d$)   1, 11, 3, 4, 5, 10, 7, 8, 9, 9, 10, 12, 12, . . .

It would be strange because, on the face of it, this sequence appears to continue in a totally arbitrary fashion and there seems to be no way of subsuming it under a rule, hence no way for Y – or for anybody – to describe the sequence other than by laying out each term that compose it, one after the other. For the same reason, of course, it would be strange if Y insisted that (G$_d$) is on equal footing with (G$_a$)–(G$_c$). For (G$_a$)–(G$_c$) do exhibit a pattern, or so it seems, whether (G$_d$) does not. So, as a first approximation, the second Rule of the game can be put as follows:

R2   *The sequence must not be random, i.e., it must be rule-governed.*

In a way, R2 follows from R1. For if a sequence were random, then certainly *no* proper initial segment could uniquely identify it. Hence, by contraposition, if there is a proper initial segment that uniquely identifies the sequence, as per R1, the sequence cannot be random. In fact, this is how randomness is often defined, at least since the pioneering work of Ray Solomonoff, Andrei Kolmogorov, and Gregory Chaitin in the mid-1960s: a sequence is random if it cannot be described more efficiently than by laying out the whole sequence itself.[3] However, as we said, R1 may not be entirely in order as it stands, so it is convenient to formulate R2 independently. And again, we shall come back shortly to the important question – whether this second Rule can be properly implemented, or taken for granted. Right now the point is just that R1 and R2 are standardly assumed to hold whenever two players engage in a game of this sort, for otherwise there is no way one can succeed in guessing the sequence.

Too Good to Be True

So, are R1 and R2 in order? Not quite, unfortunately. Let us begin with R1. On closer look, this rule turns out to be just as crucial as it is unsatifiable – upsetting as this might sound to the players of the game. Let us first illustrate this negative fact with reference to the sort of cases that we have considered so far; then we may turn to generalizations.

Consider again the example with which we began – the sequence corresponding to the segment

(A)   1, 3, 5, 7, 9, 11, . . .

Surely we can all see a pattern here: the odd numbers. But how do we know that this is *the* pattern? How does Y know that this is the sequence X had in mind? Y doesn't know it. She sees that every number in (A) is odd, and she sees that no odd number is missing, and since she is assuming that this initial segment uniquely characterizes the whole sequence, she concludes that the dots must be filled in by the odd numbers. That is, she concludes that the underlying rule must be this:

(A*) $S_n = 2n - 1$

Strictly speaking, however, she doesn't *know* that this is the rule any more than she knows the truth of any generalization based on a limited amount of data. The generalization is justified precisely because she is assuming that R1 is being observed. But how can that be right? How can the initial segment by means of which the sequence is introduced provide *enough information* for anybody to figure out the solution and continue the sequence by filling in the dots accordingly? As Wittgenstein famously put it: "Whence comes the idea that the beginning of a series is a visible section of rails invisibly laid to infinity?"[4]

Suppose Y says that the sequence in question consists of the odd numbers and X says: "No, it doesn't. It consists of the odd digits repeated once, then repeated twice, then repeated three times, and so on. Here is what it would look like if I continued a little longer:

(A′) 1, 3, 5, 7, 9, 11, 33, 55, 77, 99, 111, ...

If you want me to be more precise, I can even spell out the rule in mathematic terms:

(A**) $S_n = 2_n - 1$ mod 10, repeated $(2n$ div 10) + 1 times,

where mod is the function that returns the remainder of the division (of the first argument by the second) and div the function that returns the division without the remainder." Is Y entitled to complain?

In a way she is: If *that* is the rule X had in mind, then X did not comply to R1 because (A) does not amount to a uniquely identifying segment. In particular, it does not uniquely identify the sequence described in (A**), for the dots can be filled in in conformity to that rule as also in conformity to the rule that Y originally suggested, (A*). Of course, this means that (A) does not uniquely identify the sequence of the odd numbers, either, so Y's complaint is self-defeating. But never mind that. It is a fact that relative to (A**) – the rule that X had in mind

and that B was supposed to figure out – the segment in (A) is not informative enough, just as the short segment in (G) would not have been informative enough to identify the rule of the Conway sequence, (F*). So Y's complaint is right on the mark.

By contrast, what is X to make of this complaint? *What* would count as an appropriate, uniquely identifying segment for the rule he had in mind? Suppose X gives the longer segment in (A′) rather than (A). Would that be enough? It would not. It would be enough to rule out the hypothesis that his sequence consists of the odd integers. But many other sequences would still be compatible with that initial segment. The sequence might continue in conformity to the pattern X actually has in mind, but it might also continue according to a different pattern. For example, the sequence could consist of the perfect palindromic odds, that is, those numbers that consist exclusively of odd digits and that are the same when written forward or backward. All the numbers in (A′) are perfect palindromic odds. But whereas X's sequence would continue thus:

(A′_a) ..., 333, 555, 777, 999, 1111, ...

the rest of the sequence of the palindromic odds would contain several additional, intermediate elements:

(A′_b) ..., 131, 151, 171, 191, 313, 333, ...

Needless to say, even (A′_a) would be ambiguous as an input for guessing X's rule, for one may still think of different ways of continuing the series. The more we go on – the longer the initial segment is – the more the alternatives look convoluted and, in some way, "unnatural." But this is precisely the point. It is not R1 by itself that imposes a plausible constraint on the game, for R1 can *never* be satisfied: any finite segment can be continued in an infinite number of ways, just as any line-segment drawn on a sheet of paper can be extended in an infinite number of ways. Rather, the constraint comes from R1 together with the additional implicit assumption that the sequence in question must be a "natural" sequence. And sad as it might sound, it is a fact that what looks "natural" to Y may very well not coincide with what looks "natural" to X – and vice versa.

It takes a moment now to realize how important this is when it comes to playing the game for real – when the player to issue the initial segment is not just someone like us but the world itself.

A sequence of observed events may suggest that a certain pattern is in place and we – playing the role of player Y – eventually come to think of that pattern as revealing a corresponding law of nature. But this is not to say that the observed events uniquely identify that law. And if the next observed event is not what we expected, we can hardly voice a complaint on the grounds that the resulting sequence looks "unnatural." We must simply admit that we were wrong, and learn to live with the possibility that our next guess will be off the mark, too. Such is the limit of our inductive practices, when they are not merely statistical but strictly Humean.[5]

Let us now look at our second meta-Rule, R2. Indeed, it might be thought that this is precisely the point where R2 enters the picture. This second Rule says that the sequence to be guessed must not be random, that is, it must be rule-governed. And for all that has been said so far, the fact that any initial segment can be continued in many different ways does not mean that it can be continued in many *rule-governed* ways. The segment in (A) can, as also the longer segment in (A′). But perhaps a sufficiently longer segment could be provided that will admit *only one* rule-governed extension. If so, then the impasse that we have just reached in connection with R1 would dissolve as soon as we plug in R2: it would be possible to uniquely identify a sequence by means of an initial segment (a sufficiently long one) on account of the fact that all the alternative ways of continuing the sequence would qualify as random and would therefore be unacceptable by R2. In fact that is precisely the intended role of this second Rule: earlier we said that R2 follows from R1, but now we see that R1 is empty unless some further constraint is added – and R2 provides such a constraint.

Unfortunately, R2 turns out to be just as useless as R1. There are two ways of making the point. The first way goes back at least as far as Leibniz, who in the *Discourse of Metaphysics* addressed the question of whether and how one could discriminate a world in which science applies from one in which it does not.[6] Imagine – he said – that someone jots down a quantity of ink spots upon a sheet of paper helter skelter ("as do those who exercise the ridiculous art of Geomancy"). Regardless of the particular configuration that we get, Leibniz claimed that there will always be a continuous function whose graph passes through this finite set of points, a "geometrical line whose concept shall be uniform and constant that is, in accordance with a certain formula." As far as we can tell, the

existence of such a function was purely conjectured by Leibniz, but today we know that he was absolutely right. Many good ways to construct a function that does the job are now known. For example, so-called Lagrangian polynomial interpolation will do.[7] This is the sort of function that is implemented in most computer graphics programs: We click the mouse on each spot as we go over them, and the function returns a normalized curve that connects them all – like this:

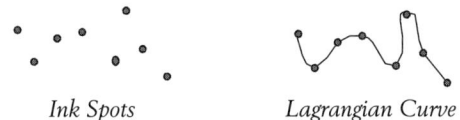

Ink Spots   *Lagrangian Curve*

Now, if we take it that the existence of a suitable function is an indication of the fact that the pattern is not random, then it follows that no such pattern is random. And since it is plausible to suppose that every finite sequence can be represented by a corresponding pattern of ink spots, it follows that *no* finite sequence whatsoever is random. So here is the problem: when playing the game of the rule, there is no way X can provide an initial segment that is "sufficiently long" to admit of only one rule-governed extension. *Any* finite extension of any initial segment, no matter how long, will be nonrandom. Which is to say that R2 does not impose any restriction of the desired sort, leaving R1 in the trashcan.

The second way of making the point is this. Suppose we rely on a more austere definition of randomness. Indeed, suppose we stick to the definition of randomness mentioned earlier, which today is widely accepted: a sequence is random if (and only if) it cannot be described more efficiently than by giving the whole sequence itself. In other words, although every sequence can be described by *some* function – as Leibniz pointed out – in some cases the function in question is too complex to do the job efficiently, and we can take that to be a sign of randomness. If we stick to this definition, then we can be assured that *there are* random sequences, so the above problem does not arise. This is obvious for infinite sequences, since the total number of such sequences is uncountable, whereas there are only countably many efficient, finite descriptions. But it is easy to prove that there are also infinitely many random sequences of finite length, at least if the language in which the sequences are coded is the same as the language available to describe them. (Regardless of the alphabet, the number of sequences consisting of n symbols is always greater than the number of all sequences consisting of fewer symbols, hence greater than the number of all descriptions of length less than n.[8]) Does this help?

Unfortunately, it doesn't. The problem is not that this more austere definition of randomness depends on a notion of "efficient" description that appears to be vague. We could make that more precise. Rather, the problem is that this more austere notion of randomness turns out to be *undecidable*. That is, it can be proved that there exists no effective decision procedure (intuitively: no procedure that can be implemented as a computer program) that will always deliver a definite answer to every question of the form: Is this a random sequence?[9] Sometimes we can deliver a negative answer. The sequence of the odd numbers, for example, or even a reasonably long finite initial segment thereof, is not random because we can efficiently describe it by means of a rule such as (A^*). Ditto for the sequence of the repeated odds, the sequence of the palindromic odds, and many other sequences considered earlier. However, *in general* we may not be in a position to determine whether a given sequence (finite or infinite) is random. All we can say, if we cannot come up with a corresponding rule, is that the sequence is random *to the best of our knowledge* – and that is not enough. For example, at first sight the initial segment of the Conway sequence given in

(F)   1, 11, 21, 1211, 111221, 312211, 13112221, . . .

looks pretty random. Y might have tried to come up with an algorithm to describe it and she might have failed. So Y might have been inclined to conclude that the segment is the beginning of a random sequence, when in fact it isn't. Likewise for (G_d): we have said that the series

(G_d)   1, 11, 3, 4, 5, 10, 7, 8, 9, 9, 10, 12, 12, . . .

looks random, but who knows – maybe one can come up with a way of describing it that does the job. This is particularly pressing in view of the fact that there are many ways of describing a sequence: as we have seen, the description need not be number-theoretic, and it need not be in the format that comes to us most naturally. That is the lesson of the Conway sequence. (In fact, coming to think of it, even (G_d) may very well be the beginning of a nonrandom sequence. The rule

(G^*_d) $S_n = n$ if the English name for this integer has an even number of vowels, otherwise $S_n = (n \bmod 5) + 9$

fits the data perfectly well . . .)

Now, why is this a problem? After all, Y knows that X *is not* thinking of a random sequence, at least if X is playing in accordance with R2, so Y knows that the sequence she has to guess *does* admit of a suitable description. Well, the problem is that Y cannot do much of this piece of knowledge. She knows that X is not thinking of a random sequence, but she doesn't know what this amounts to. Y doesn't know what sequences are ruled out because she doesn't have any effective procedure for telling what are the good candidates. She might believe that a certain way of continuing the initial segment is out because she might not be able to bring it under a rule – but she might just be wrong. Y might just be incapable of seeing the underlying pattern, so she might treat that as a random sequence when in fact it isn't. It might be precisely the sequence X is thinking about.

So here is the picture in a nutshell. If we stick to a generic notion of randomness as lawlessness, no sequence is random and R2 is perfectly useless. If, by contrast, we stick to the more austere definition of randomness as incompressibility, then there are random sequences and R2 is fine as a matter of principle. Yet it is still useless when it comes to matters of practice. We may fully convince ourselves *that* a given sequence complies with the no-randomness requirement. But we may not be in a position to determine with certainty *whether* a given sequence complies with it.

Playing the Game for Real

So what are we left with? The "game of the rule" – it turns out – cannot be safely played. But why should that be a worry? After all, there are many other games that we can play, so why bother?

Well, there are indeed many other games we can safely play, but, as we have already pointed out, this one is a game that we cannot dismiss so easily. The game of the rule is a game that *we play all the time*, whenever we engage in Humean inductive reasoning. We play it whenever we try to figure out the mechanisms of the world we live in, the laws of nature and the laws of society. We don't play it with number sequences but with the sequences of events that make up our history, when we try to make sense of them and see where they are leading to. And to say that this game cannot be played safely is not to say that we can stop playing it altogether.

At this point we have come to full circle and our story becomes a familiar one in the philosophy of science. Some think that the sort of skepticism that we have illustrated must be taken very seriously. For all we know, the world might not even be *trying* to play the game in accordance with R1 and R2, in which case our Humean inductive practices would just rest on a false presupposition. But even if the world were trying to play by the rules – even if the events with which we have to deal were fully in agreement with the presupposition of lawlikeness – the fact that randomness phenomena cannot be effectively identified would be enough to justify a merely pragmatic attitude toward the endeavors of science. There is no way we can hope to "break the code." We can only hope to play the game in such a way that *we* find satisfaction in the laws that we envision, just as we find satisfaction in the social and political laws with which we try to regiment our daily interactions with our peers. Others feel differently. Not only do they think that we should play the game on the assumption that the world is issuing its challenges in compliance with R1 and R2; they also believe that we should not give up our hopes to get things right. After all, when we play the game for fun, we often win. We often succeed in uncovering the hidden pattern in spite of the difficulties that have been mentioned. Even if the initial segment that we are given does not uniquely identify the intended sequence, and even if we are not in a position to keep randomness under control, we often hit the correct rule because the other options are just too far-fetched to deserve serious consideration. So why not suppose that the same can happen when we play the game with the world of nature? All we have to do is to make sure that the world and we are on the same wavelengths, so to say – that what looks natural or far-fetched to us is indeed natural or far-fetched *simpliciter*. The history of science shows that sometimes we make mistakes, but that has never blocked scientists from pursuing their research with increased determination. On the contrary, the general thought has been that we can learn from such mistakes, and that we are getting closer and closer to winning the game at the next try.

This is no place to dwell upon this controversial dialectics. We may choose our party as we see fit. But the underlying predicament is something that can be best appreciated once we begin to see this familiar dialectics from the standpoint we have been suggesting here. For, on the one hand, we should not overlook one important sense in which playing the game with the world of nature may be easier than playing it *inter nos*. When both X and Y are people like us, each will try to win the game; in particular, X will try to issue his challenge in such a way as to make it difficult for Y to come up with the right guess – he will make every effort to design a rule that would be very hard, if not impossible, to discover in real time. By contrast, there is no reason to suppose that this is how the world out there issues its challenges. The world is not an intentional agent and does not care about "beating" us in the game, or so we may assume. In this sense, the practice of scientific induction need not be as hard as playing the game of the rule against a clever opponent trying to be smarter than we are, and the thought that we should try to be on the same wavelengths as the world is all but unreasonable. (That was indeed the main rationale behind Keynes's principle of "limited variety," a principle whose roots can be traced back to the philosophy of Francis Bacon:[10] An object of inductive inference should not be infinitely complex, nor determined by an infinite number of generators, and if we are assuming that the world is playing by the rules, we may well suppose that it is playing according to this additional principle, too.) On the other hand, there is also an important sense in which playing the game with the world of nature is not as easy as playing it *inter nos*. When we play, one player gives the beginning of the sequence and the other must figure out the rest. That may be tough, for the reasons that we have seen, but at least the input is clear – the first player is giving it explicitly. When we play with the world, by contrast, we must be careful. Not any series of events is on equal footing. We may witness the rising of the sun every morning and take that as an input for a law that we may reasonably formulate as a Humean inductive generalization. We might even think that it's worth looking at the series of events that we get by tossing a coin, for it might not be a random sequence after all. But when we zap channels during a commercial break, for example, the series of events that follow one another on our TV screen is not worth looking at. When we check the sky every time we hiccup, the series of events that we thereby collect is not worth any serious study. This is not to say that such series are random; there might even be a pattern, surprising as that might be. ("Every time I watch the Yankees, they lose.") It's just that such series are not interesting. They don't count, so to speak. And they don't count because they would be there *even if it turned out that we live in a totally deterministic world*, a world where nothing is random and everything happens for a reason. To put it briefly, when we play with the world we have got to figure out *which* sequences to consider before we can start figuring out *what* they are, for the world does not tell us that. The world does not issue its challenges as explicitly as people do when they play with one another.

Now, precisely this is the main difficulty with Humean inductive reasoning. We can live with randomness and we can live with the fact that randomness is undecidable. Science has learned to cope with that, one way or the other. We can even assume that the world – unlike clever human players – has no interest in *beating* us. But we must be careful because our cognitive makeup is such that we constantly look for patterns and trends even where there may be none. And there may be none, not because we may be dealing with random sequences, but because maybe there is no sequence to deal with. Maybe we are just exercising "the ridiculous art of Geomancy," as Leibniz put it, and that's not a way to play the game. For in the end, when it comes to playing the game for real, the one tacit Rule that we can *never* rely on is also the most obvious and important of all:

R3   *The initial segment of the sequence must be given explicitly.*

Notes

1   J. H. Conway, "The Weird and Wonderful Chemistry of Audioactive Decay," *Eureka* 46 (1986): 5–16.
2   Hofstadter's views and early results in this area are documented in his book *Fluid Concepts and Creative Analogies*, New York: Basic Books, 1995.
3   The seminal works are R. J. Solomonoff, "A Formal Theory of Inductive Inference. Part I," *Information and Control* 7 (1964): 224–254; A. Kolmogorov, "Three Approaches to the Quantitative Definition of Information," *Problems of Information Transmission* 1 (1965): 1–17; G. J. Chaitin, "On the Length of Programs for Computing Finite Binary Sequences: Statistical Considerations," *Journal of the ACM* 16 (1969): 145–159.
4   L. Wittgenstein, *Philosophische Untersuchungen/Philosophical Investigations*, ed. by G. E. M. Anscombe and R. Rhees, with an Eng. trans. by G. E. M. Anscombe, Oxford: Basil Blackwell, 1953, Sec. 218.
5   D. Hume, *Enquiries Concerning Human Understanding*, Sec. IV. The connection between Wittgenstein's views on rule following and Hume's skepticism has been made explicit by S. A. Kripke in his book, *Wittgenstein on Rules and Private Language*, Cambridge (MA): Harvard University Press, 1982.
6   G. W. Leibniz, *Discourse of Metaphysics*, Sec. VI.
7   See, for instance, H. Jeffreys and B. S. Jeffreys, *Methods of Mathematical Physics*, Cambridge: Cambridge University Press, 1983, §9.011. (The label comes from the Italian mathematician Joseph-Louis Lagrange, who discovered the method over a century after Leibniz's conjecture.)
8   If the alphabet contains $k > 1$ symbols, the number of all sequences consisting of n symbols from the alphabet is k^n, which is greater than $k^1 + k^2 + \cdots + k^{n-1}$ for all $n \geq 1$. Of course, if we only allow for certain sequences, i.e., if the sequences are coded in a language (say, the numerals) of lesser expressive power than the language available to describe them (say, English plus the language of number theory), then the result may not hold.
9   See, e.g., G. J. Chaitin, *Information, Randomness and Incompleteness*, Singapore; World Scientific, 1987.
10 See J. M. Keynes, *A Treatise on Probability*; New York: Macmillan, 1921, Ch. 22. Compare the beginning of Bacon's *Magna Instauratio* and Book II of his *New Organon*.

Chapter 15: Inductive Logic and Inductive Reasoning

HENRY E. KYBURG, JR. [†]

In days of yore, logic was neatly divided into two parts, *Deductive Logic* and *Inductive Logic* (Mill 1949/1843). The two parts were often taught as parts of a single course. Inductive logic has faded away, and now the very term has acquired a slightly antiquated patina. It has also acquired a number of quite specific modern meanings.

One very narrow and very specific meaning is that inductive inference is the inference from a set of observations or observation sentences (crow #1 is black; crow #2 is black; ...; crow #n is black) to their universal generalization (all crows are black). There is not much *logic* here, but there is a big problem: to determine when, if ever, such an inference is "justified."

A somewhat less ambitious construal of "induction" is as the inference from a statistical sample to a statistical generalization, or an approximate statistical generalization: from "51% of the first 10,000 tosses of this coin yielded heads," to "Roughly half of the tosses of the coin will, in the long run, yield heads." So construed (as by Baird 1992), the line between the logic of induction and the mathematics of statistics is a bit vague. This has been of little help to inductive logic, since the *logic* of statistical inference has itself been controversial.

Another way of looking at induction is as a part of logic proper. This approach takes as its guiding insight that while in the case of valid deductive inference *every* model of the premises is a model of the conclusion, in the case of valid inductive inference we should ask that *most* of the models of the premises (the statements expressing the evidence) are models of

the conclusion. The problem, of course, is how to count models in any reasonably complex language (Carnap 1950, 1991). There are an infinite number of ways of constructing models of even quite simple languages.

What most writers have focused on, at least as a long term ideal goal, is the development of standards for scientific inference. As observed by C. D. Broad (1930) (among others), much of actual scientific inference is straightforwardly deductive in character. We know that if one sample of a compound melts at *t* degrees centigrade under standard conditions, *all* samples of that compound will. We may agrue that if one sample of compound *X* melts at 34°C, then *all* samples of compound *X* melt at 34°C, and thus obtain the universal statement concerning all samples from the observation concerning one sample. Generalizing, even on the basis of one instance, may be valid, given the right premises.

Of course, this does not mean that no uncertainty is involved. The form of the *argument* is deductive, to be sure, but there is uncertainty involved in the specific claim that *this* sample melts at *t* degrees centigrade (all measurement admits of error) and there may be uncertainty about the universal generalization that if one sample melts at *t* then all do.

In the past, many writers, recognizing that the conclusion of an inductive inference is generally not certain, have focused on the idea that the conclusion of an inductive inference may yet be *probable*. This is helpful only if we understand probability, and probability itself has been controversial; several different interpretations of probability have been offered, not all of which are of relevance to induction.

As a branch of mathematics, there is nothing mysterious about probability. Probability is defined on an algebra of *sets*; it is *nonnegative* with a maximum value of 1; and it is *additive*,

[†] We regret that Henry E. Kyburg, Jr., died during the publication of this book. The editors are grateful for his contribution to this volume and, more generally, to the study of inductive inference and non-monotonic reasoning.

which just means that if *A* and *B* are disjoint sets, the probability of their union is the sum of their probabilities.

But this is not what we want to know. We want to know what those sets *are* for which probability is defined. We want to know where the *values* of those probabilities *come from*. We want to know how these matters are related to knowledge or rational belief. In short, we want to how probability fits into logic, and to explore that question we need to reflect on the foundations of logic itself.

1. Logic

The first paragraph of George Boole's *Laws of Thought* [Boole 1854, p.1.) focuses on this general question; it reads:

> The design of the following treatise is to investigate the fundamental laws of those operations of the mind by which reasoning is performed; to give expression to them in the symbolical language of a Calculus, and upon this foundation to establish the science of Logic and construct its method; to make that method itself the basis of a general method for the application of the mathematical doctrine of Probabilities; and, finally, to collect from the various elements of truth brought to view in the course of these inquiries some probable intimations concerning the nature and constitution of the human mind.

This certainly seems to have powerful psychological overtones, to say the least. Frege took it so, writing (1950/1893: p xv):

> The ambiguity of the word "law" is fatal here. In one sense it states what is, in the other it prescribes what should be. Only in the latter sense can the laws of logic be called the laws of thought.... But the expression "law of thought" tempts us into viewing these laws as governing thinking in the same way as the laws of nature govern events in the external world. They can then be nothing other than psychological laws, since thinking is a mental process. And if logic were concerned with these psychological laws then it would be part of psychology.... I understand by logical laws not psychological laws of *holding true* but laws of *being true*.

In a recent article, Gil Harman argues that logic is a theory of "what follows from what" and not a theory of reasoning. On this ground, he writes (Harman and Kulkarni 2006):

> ... to call deductive rules "rules of inference" is a real fallacy, not just a terminological matter. It lies behind attempts to develop relevance logics or inductive logics that are thought better at capturing ordinary reasoning than classical deductive logic does, as if deductive logic offers a partial theory of ordinary logic.

The first thing to observe is that things are not, of course, this simple. Boole distinguishes between the "general laws of Nature," which are "never wholly divested" of "the character of probability," and the "laws of mind" in which the general truth is seen with certainty in the single instance.

Whence comes the power of that single clearly understood instance? Boole does not explain, and to my mind commits here an epistemological blunder. But although that reflects his conviction that logic is not an empirical science, not even an empirical science of the mind, it does not mean that logic is not about the mind in some sense. If it is not "descriptive" in the sense of empirical science, it bears some other relation to the mind.

What springs to mind, of course, is exactly the normative relation that Frege sought. Logic is not the theory of how we *do* reason, but the theory of how we *ought* to reason. But this seems almost as silly as the descriptive claim would be: surely it is not intended that we should *reason* in accord with some particular system of logic! We are not being exhorted to construct *proofs* in our minds, that is sequences of formulas each of which is either a premise or is inferred from earlier formulas by a permissible rule of inference. (And if that were the case, which formal system would we be supposed to follow?)

No, logic is not a prescription for psychological health. Is it that what must be intended is that our reasonings should admit of translation into proofs in a system of logic? But the notion of translation is a loose one, as Quine has pointed out (1960). Since most of our reasonings are enthymemes, it would seem that by choosing appropriate premises any reasoning could be warranted.

Here's another idea. Some of our reasoning, especially in mathematics, does seem to have the structure of a proof outline. This is particularly the case when we are doodling around with pen and paper trying to figure out how a proof could go. We think of, or perhaps even write down, a few of the significant high points of the proof. We may write down some of the premises of the proof. At some point, if we are lucky, we *see* how the proof goes. We *see* how the conclusion follows from the premises. For many of us this is sufficient to establish the entailment from premises to conclusion. (There are also the intellectually insecure, like me, who often want to see a detailed proof!)

One thing that logic can do is to help us fill in the valleys between the peaks of such a proof sketch. What is the point of that? Well, if the idea of a logical argument is to be fully persuasive, a formal proof surely suffices. But generally a formal proof is overkill. If we are facing an interlocutor of good will, something between a very brief proof sketch and a formal proof will suffice. All this takes the *point* of logic to be to show that conclusion C *follows from* premises $P_1, P_2, \ldots, P_n$, when it does. To this extent, Harman's idea seems to be vindicated: logic concerns what follows from what.

Of course there are other things that first order logic is good for. Sometimes I am my own interlocutor: I am concerned to really persuade myself that the conclusion follows from the premises. Sometimes I am constructing a proof for fun. It is often said that studying logic and constructing proofs is good training for the mind. (I have no very firm opinion one way or the other on this!)

There is nothing much about *thinking* or *reasoning* in any of this, with the possible exception of training in thinking. Yet there is the relativization to human abilities in the actual use of logic: We do not invent logic, unmotivated, out of whole cloth. We begin with an idea, presumably parasitic on ordinary language, of what follows from what. With the idea of formal proof, the role of human abilities is minimized; but we must still recognize that the antecedent of line four is the same as line three.

2. Variations on Classical Logic

Let us refer to classical first order logic as the system H. There are, of course, may variations. First, there are weaker systems: intuitionistic logic, constructive logic. These do not concern us in the present context, but stronger systems do. For example, the logic of strict implication, modal logic, and relevance logic were proposed to capture certain aspects of human reasoning and argument (concerning, for example, counterfactuals) that escaped the constraints of system H. These systems include new connectives (for example, $>$ and $\diamond$) and new axioms. They

are nevertheless classical in the sense that they include classical logic.

In relatively recent years (the last twenty or twenty-five) we have seen the introduction of nonmonotonic logics and probabilistic logics. These are often intended to play the role of inductive logic. These, too, are essentially classical. For example, in Reiter's default logic, *default rules* are added to the system (Reiter 1980). A default rule has the form: $\alpha : \beta_1, \ldots, \beta_n/\theta$. The intent is that if none of the formulas $\beta_1, \ldots, \beta_n$ hold in the set of accepted formulas, then the formula θ may be accepted "by default." Thus we start with a set W of statements, and take the corresponding *extension* to be the deductively closed fixed point yielded by W and the set of default rules. There may be no extension, and there may be more than one. The classical example is to take W to be the single sentence "Tweety is a bird," and D to be the single rule "Tweety is a bird": "Tweety can fly." / "Tweety can fly." We can believe "Tweety can fly." But we may consistently add "Tweety is a penguin" and "No penguins can fly" to W, and we will no longer be able to apply the default rule, and so no longer justified in believing that Tweety can fly.

Autoepistemic logic (Moore 1985) is another nonmonotonic formalism. It is quite easily represented as a modal logic, and provides a natural link between default logic and the various modal logics (Lewis 1918), with "□" interpreted as "knows that".

The idea behind this, and other AI formalisms for nonmonotonic logic, is to capture "common sense" reasoning. "If I know that Tweety is a bird, other things being equal, I know that Tweety can fly" (Reiter 1980). "If I had an older brother, I would know it" (Moore 1985). It is common sense that if all the crows I have seen are black, then it is reasonable for me to believe that crows are black. Of course, there are various ways of interpreting the vague phrase "common sense" and, in consequence, various formalisms for nonmonotonic logic. In many cases, the result of the application of the rules of inductive logic is a deductively closed set of statements – that is, a set of statements deductively closed in the sense of classical first order logic.

What is of interest from a foundational point of view is that the goal of these formalisms is the *representation* of nonmonotonic or inductive or commonsense reasoning. "Representation" is an ambiguous expression in this context. We could represent the psychological process that commonsense reasoners go through with varying degrees of accuracy and varying degrees of normativity. By this I mean that the subject, the model, of the activity we are seeking to represent is the reasoning of an educated, intelligent, native speaker of our language – probably male, probably trained (or overtrained) in classical logic. Such reasoning, of course, is precisely the reasoning that we – you and I – take intuitively to be rational. Guess why! On the other hand (is it really other?) the system we come up with (whatever it is) we will defend as *normative*: the inductive conclusions supported by our systems are the ones that an agent, having the evidence he has, *ought* to accept.

We encounter another difficulty. What is "the evidence" that the agent has? It is all very well to symbolize the evidence with the single letter "*E*," but if the point is to rationalize, or even represent the relation between evidence and hypothesis this is not much help. Furthermore, the single letter is ordinarily taken to represent the *conjunction* of all the evidence the agent has. But it is at least open to argument whether or not the set of sentences accepted, or accepted as evidence, if these are not the same thing, should be closed under conjunction. I have argued (Kyburg 1997) that if there is a small chance of error in each of the two acceptable statements, then there may be a greater chance of error in their conjunction. We will return to this issue in the find section of this essay.

In short, even if we could settle on one of these formalisms as the right way to approach nonmonotonic logic, there seem to be insuperable difficulties lying in the way of applying it to anything more than the simplest toy Tweety model. There is the problem of representing the evidence in such a way that it can be agreed to (or argued over); and, even more serious in the light of the difficulty with the evidence, there is the question of how the system can both be interpreted in terms of representation and normativity. How do we resolve the tension between what people actually do, what people think it is intuitively correct to do, and what people really ought to do?

3. Probabilism

Another approach to uncertain inference that has been getting a lot of press in recent years is Probabilism. I wouldn't presume to define probabilism – I'm not even sure it should be capitalized – but the basic idea is that we replace qualitative all-or-none belief by *degrees* of belief, and we are to modify our degrees of belief in the light of new evidence by conditioning on

that evidence. This approach is called "Probabilism" because *degrees* of *belief* are to satisfy the probability axioms, and conditioning is to satisfy the relation imposed by the condition that the degree of belief in a conjunction is to be the product of the degree of belief in one conjunct multiplied by the conditional degree of belief in the other conjunct, *given* the first conjunct.

(There has been some misguided discussion of how you "define" conditional probability in such a way that the probability of the condition may be zero. The simple answer is that you don't. Conditional probability has never legitimately been defined in this way. Furthermore, all sensible formalizations of probability, including Kolmogorov's, have taken conditional probability as primitive. The idea of "defining" conditional probability as a quotient is a red herring.)

It is sometimes said that probability is nonmonotonic. This seems wrong, since, as was pointed out even by Keynes (1952), conditioning does not give you a new probability, but makes a different probability relevant. If $P(S \mid B) = 0.5$, where B is our background knowledge, and we learn T, then what is relevant is $P(S \mid B \land T) = 0.8$; but that does not make $P(S \mid B) = 0.5$ *wrong*. New information does not undermine an old probability nonmonotonically; it makes a new probability more interesting.

Naturally, the idea of connecting the logic of conditionals with conditional probability has occurred to more than one person (Adams 1975; Pearl 2000; McGee 1989). There are difficulties (Lewis 1981; Suppes 1962), but they can be seen as challenges. The upshot is that this is an extremely rich general area of logical research. There seem to be no bounds on the systems that people can come up with. At the very least, this is evidence of the unbounded ingenuity and creativeness of human beings.

How does all this ingenuity bear on inductive logic? It depends, of course, on what we want inductive logic to do. If we want it to represent inductive reasoning, or rational inductive reasoning, we must somehow settle the interplay between the normative and descriptive aspects of "representation" we have in mind. It is surely not the case that any formalism that has been proposed has been proposed as a serious description of the actual workings of the human mind. The most ardent probabilist would not suggest that any actual human being had degrees of belief satisfying the axioms of the probability calculus, much less that they were updated by conditioning. By contrast, patent failures of coherence – for example, that an agent takes it to be more probable that Linda is a liberal banker than that she is a banker – are to be "corrected." Note that the direction of correction is open: the agent may increase his belief that Linda is a banker, or decrease his belief that Linda is a liberal banker. If I don't like the result of conditioning S on E, I can change the prior probability either of $S \land E$ or of E.

Representation is anyway only part of the story. If logic is to be a theory of what follows from what, or of what is evidence for what, then we must develop a standard, a criterion, and we must also develop a means of applying it. In the first order deductive realm, we must adopt a classical, or an intuitionistic, or a minimalist standard; and we must also develop a way of knowing when that standard is met. There are two things that this can mean: We might ask for a decision procedure: given a set of formulas and a formula, this would be a procedure that would tell us if the formula followed from the set of formulas. Or we could (as we must in first-order logic) settle for the the idea of *proof* – that is, a sequence of formulas each of which is one of the premises (the set of formulas) or is derivable from earlier formulas in the sequence by a rule of the logic. The existence of a proof of S from premises $P_1, \ldots, P_n$ *guarantees* that S follows from $P_1, \ldots, P_n$ in first-order logic, and S follows from (is entailed by) $P_1, \ldots, P_n$ guarantees that a proof exists, though it does not tell us how to construct it.

One difficulty we face in the case of inductive argument is that the set of sentences that yields our conclusion must be very large – it must comprise everything we know. This is a burden for nonmonotonic logic as well as for inductive logic. In both cases, we must allow that a conclusion S is supported by a set of evidence statements $\mathcal{E}$, but is not supported by a more inclusive set of evidence statements $\mathcal{E}'$. Both probabilists and logicians fudge this problem: the former write B for "background knowledge," the latter write "F" for the set of accepted facts. It is easy to write B or F to stand for the evidence, but if we are either to represent realistic idealizations or apply the theory normatively, we need some way of unpacking the contents of $\mathcal{E}$.

As we remarked earlier, nobody ever thought that humans should, or could, reason in the form of proofs. The idea of a proof is that it definitively establishes that the conclusion follows from the premises. The role of ordinary "deductive" argument is to provide enough hints to show that a proof exists. Similarly "reasoning" could be construed as a psychological process of casting about for potential arguments. To the extent that reasoning is successful in coming up with arguments to which there correspond actual proofs, it accomplishes its task. Therein lies the normative dimension of deductive logic.

Something similar could be said about uncertain reasoning, but there are important differences. The most important difference is that while a deductive argument depends on an explicit (usually short) list of premises, an inductive argument depends on "all" our background knowledge. This is a consequence of the nonmonotonicity of inductive argument; new information can always undermine an inductive conclusion. As a consequence, the background knowledge B or the facts F do not easily admit of explicit listing, as do the premises of a deductive argument. But we must be able to say something about what is there.

Another significant difference is that there is nothing corresponding to "proof" for inductive arguments. We shall have more to say about this later.

A third difference (hardly unexpected) is that if S is provable from $P_1, \ldots, P_n$ then S is true in every model of $P_1, \ldots, P_n$, while if S is inferrible from the set of evidence statements $\mathcal{E}$, we can at best argue that S is true in *almost all* the models of every maximal consistent subset of $\mathcal{E}$. We shall say then that S is supported by $\mathcal{E}$ with maximum error ϵ, where "almost all" corresponds to $1 - \epsilon$.

Is it possible to develop an inductive logic that respects these differences, and that serves the same function as deductive logic in providing a framework in which people can come to agreement about whether S is supported by $\mathcal{E}$ with maximum error ϵ?

4. Probability

Like many other writers, we will take probability to be central to induction. More specifically, we shall interpret "S is supported by $\mathcal{E}$ with maximum error ϵ" as "The lower bound of the evidential probability of S relative to $\mathcal{E}$ is at least $1 - \epsilon$." Because there are many "interpretations" of probability floating around, we shall say *evidential probability* (Kyburg and Teng 2001) to signal our interpretation.

Just as modus ponens may be taken as the sole form of deductive inference (Quine 1951), so direct inference may be taken as the sole form of inductive inference. Direct inference is the form of inference that proceeds from knowledge of relative frequency, and of membership in a reference class, to probability (Broad 1968). For example, if you know that about a third of the freshman women are anorexic, and that Jane is a freshman woman, then there is an argument that the probability that Jane is anorexic is about a third. Of course there are other considerations. Jane is a college woman, and maybe you know that only between 10 percent and 14 percent of college women are anorexic. For that matter, you may know Jane personally, and know that she is fat and jolly.

It has been argued by some that conditioning is the basic form of inductive inference. But the inference from $P(H)$ and $P(H \wedge E)$ to $P(H|E)$ is not inductive at all, since $P(H|E)$ is just the quotient of the first two probabilities. Furthermore, conditional probabilities – $P(H|E)$ – can like any other proabilities be based on our knowledge of frequencies.

Direct inference is unlike modus ponens, however, since the probability to which it leads is only a *possible* conclusion. As in the example, many of these conclusions may conflict. We face the problem of sorting out and combining the various possible inferences.

To put the matter explicitly, to compute the probability of a statement S, relative to a body of evidence $\mathcal{E}$, we look at a set of triples of sentences. (In what follows, we use Greek τ and ρ for predicates, Greek α for a term; we enclose formulas, say $\ulcorner \rho(\alpha) \urcorner$, in corners to indicate that we are referring to unspecified sentences of our object language.) The triples that concern us are the triples $\ulcorner \tau(\alpha) \urcorner$, $\ulcorner \rho(\alpha) \urcorner$, and $\ulcorner \%x(\tau(x),\ \rho(x),p,\ q) \urcorner$ such that $\ulcorner S \leftrightarrow \tau(\alpha) \urcorner$ is in $\mathcal{E}$, $\ulcorner \rho(\alpha) \urcorner$ is in $\mathcal{E}$, and the statistical statement $\ulcorner \%x(\tau(x),\ \rho(x),p,\ q) \urcorner$ (read "The proportion of items satisfying the reference formula ρ that also satisfy the target formula τ lies between the explicitly given rationals p and q") is in $\mathcal{E}$ where τ is a suitable target formula and ρ is a suitable reference formula.[1] Note that α may represent a tuple of terms, and x a tuple of variables.

The point of the rules is to allow us to focus on the *relevant* parts of our statistical knowledge. To this end, we want to disregard some of the triples of sentences. We say that two statistical statements $\%x(\tau(x),\rho(x),p,q)$ and $\%x(\tau'(x),\rho'(x),p',q')$ *conflict* just in case neither $[p,\ q] \subseteq [p',q']$ nor $[p',\ q'] \subseteq [p,q]$ holds. Thus $[0.3,\ 0.5]$ and $[0.4,\ 0.7]$ conflict, as do $[0.1,\ 0.5]$ and $[0.8,\ 1.0]$, but $[0.5,\ 0.6]$ and $[0.4,\ 0.6]$ do not, nor do $[0.0,\ 1.0]$ and $[0.5,\ 0.5]$ conflict.

We apply the following rules sequentially:

1. If two statistical statements differ and the first is based on a marginal distribution, while the second is based on the full joint distribution, bracket the first. This gives conditional probabilities pride of place *when they conflict with the equivalent unconditional probabilities*.

    Example: Suppose we have thirty black and thirty white balls in a collection C. The relative frequency of black balls among balls in C is 0.5, and this could serve as a probability that a specific ball a in C is black. But if the members of C are divided into three urns, one of which contains twelve black balls and twenty-eight white balls, and two of which each contain nine black balls, and one white ball, then if a is selected by a procedure that consists of (1) selecting an urn, and (2) selecting a ball from that urn, the relative frequency of black balls is $1/3(12/40) + 1/3(9/10) + 1/3(9/10) = 0.70$, and this is the appropriate probability that a, known to be selected in this way, is black. Note that it is based on relative frequencies. The marginal distribution is given by 30 black balls out of sixty; the full distribution reflects the division of the balls into the urns, and the distribution of colors in each urn.

	urn 1	urn 2	urn 3	
black	12	9	9	30
white	28	1	1	30
	40	10	10	60

2. If two statistical statements differ and the second employs a reference formula that logically entails the reference formula employed by the first, bracket the first. This embodies the well-known principle of *specificity*.

    Example: Suppose you want the probability that Jane, the college freshman of our previous example, is anorexic. You know that she is a college woman, and that between 10 percent and 14 percent of college women are anorexic; but you also know that she is a freshman, and that about a third of freshman women are anorexic. These two potential direct inferences conflict. Specificity directs us to ignore the broad class in favor of the more specific class.

Those statistical statements we are not licensed to bracket we will call *relevant*. A smallest set of statistical statements that contains every relevant statistical statement that *differs* from a statement in it will be said to be *closed under difference*.

3. The probability of S is the shortest cover of any non-empty set of relevant statistical statements closed under difference; alternatively it is the intersection of all such covers.

    Example: Suppose the intervals mentioned in the set of relevant statements are [0.20,0.30], [0.25,0.35], [0.22,0.37], [0.40,0.45], [0.20,0.80], [0.10,0.90], [0.10,0.70]. There are three sets that are closed under difference: {[0.20,0.30], [0.25,0.35], [0.22,0.37], [0.40,0.45]}, {[0.20,0.80], [0.10,0.70]}, and {[0.10, 0.90]}. The first set contains an interval that is included in another interval, and the third set is a singleton. The probability is [0.20,0.45].

We note that probability is interval valued; it is a function from sentences S and sets of sets of evidential statements $\mathcal{E}$, to subintervals of [0,1]. If S is a finite set of statements and $\mathcal{E}$ a set of evidence statements, then there exists a classical probability function P whose domain includes S such that for every $S \in S$, $P(S) \in \text{Prob}(S,\mathcal{E})$. Note that it need *not* be the case that for every S and T in S there is a classical probability function P such that $P(S|T) \in \text{Prob}(S,\mathcal{E} \cup \{T\})$. Bayesian conditioning need not be reflected in evidential probability.

We can show that probability is sound, in the sense that if $\text{Prob}(S,\mathcal{E}) = [p,q]$, then the proportion of models in which S is true, among models of maximal consistent subsets of $\mathcal{E}$ lies between p and q. Note also that $\mathcal{E}$ is not assumed to be deductively closed, or even consistent. We do assume that $\mathcal{E}$ is closed under singular consequence – that is, that if S is in $\mathcal{E}$ and $S \vdash T$, then T is in $\mathcal{E}$. This is a consequence of probabilistic induction, as we shall see.

5. Induction

The idea we take as basic for inductive logic is that we can inductively infer S from $\mathcal{E}$ just in case the chance of our being in error is less than ϵ. We seek truth, else we would not infer at all; but we also seek to control error. We cannot ensure the truth of our inferences; we can ensure that

errors are rare. High probability does so. If the probability of S is high (its lower bound is greater than $1 - \epsilon$), then the proportion of models of our data in which S fails to hold is less than ϵ.

But can this be made to work? Can we show that in a state of empirical ignorance, empirical data can render statistical generalizations highly probable? The answer is "yes."

First, we note that some statistical generalizations are true a priori. Consider the set of satisfiers of the formula "$A(x)$." We suppose that there is a large number of these things. Some of them, say an unknown proportion r, also satisfy the formula "$B(x)$". Chebycheff's inequality – an elementary theorem of probability theory – says that the frequency with which a quantity (such as F, the relative frequency of B's in a sample of n A's) will differ from its expectation by more than k times its standard deviation, is less than $1/k^2$. We do not know the value of r, but we know that the standard deviation of F, which is $\sqrt{r(1-r)/n}$, cannot be greater than $1/2\sqrt{n}$, whatever r may be. We also know that the expectation of F is r. In English: it is a priori that the relative frequency of n membered samples in which F *differs* by more than $k/2\sqrt{n}$ from the relative frequency r in the original population is less than $1/k^2$. Let $nA(x)$ denote the set of n-membered samples of A's, and $F(x) \pm k/2\sqrt{n}$ denote the set of samples that contain a proportion of B's differing from r by less than $k/2\sqrt{n}$. Then we have as an a priori truth in our body of knowledge $\mathcal{E}$ the statistical statement, $\%x(F(x) \pm k/2\sqrt{n}, nA(x), 1 - 1/k^2, 1.0)$ Indeed, we have such a statement for any n and any k. Our body of a priori knowledge is full of a priori statistical statements!

Now we must show that this statistical knowledge can confer a high probability on a statement of the form $\ulcorner\%x(B(x), A(x), p, q)\urcorner$. Let us suppose that $\mathcal{E}$, in addition to the a priori information just indicated, contains the report of a sample of 10,000 A's, of which 3,812 were B's. We will show that the probability of "$\%x(B(x),A(x), 0.3312, 0.4312)$" is at least [0.99,1.0]. (By "at least [0.99,1.0]", I mean a subinterval of [0.99,1.0].) Note first that the standard deviation of the frequency F of B's among A's in a sample, though it depends on the value of r (the overall relative frequency of B's among A's), must be less than $1/2\sqrt{1/n} = .005$. By Chebycheff's inequality the fraction of samples of 10,000 that fail to exhibit a value of F within 10 standard deviations of r (the mean of F is r), is less than $1/(10^2)$. Thus we have in $\mathcal{E}$ (since it is true a priori) $\%x(|F(x) - r| > 0.05,$

$A^{10,000}$, .00, .01). We are supposing that the only sample we have is the sample s of 10,000 A's. Since we know, in $\mathcal{E}$, that 3,812 members of the sample are B's, we know $F(s) = 0.3812$ and therefore we know the biconditional $|0.3812 - r| \leq 0.05 \leftrightarrow \%x(B(x),A(x),0.3312,0.4312)$.

Thus, we have the three ingredients for the probability statement we are after:

1. $|F(s) - r| \leq 0.05 \leftrightarrow \%x(B(x), A(x), 0.3312, 0.4312)$

2. $\%x(|F(x) - r| \leq 0.05, A^{10,000}, 0.99, 1.0)$

3. $s \in A^{10,000}$

We still need to consider the three rules.

Do we know of a reference formula, target formula, and statistical statement that would lead us to bracket $\%x[|F(x) - r| > 0.05, A^{10,000}, 0.99,1.0)$ on the basis of conditioning? Here is one difference between inductive logic and deductive logic. To know that there is no such triple of formulas entailed by $\mathcal{E}$ is to survey the entailments of $\mathcal{E}$ exhaustively. But there are certain natural questions that can be raised.

One possible reference formula would be that generated by background knowledge concerning the source of A. For example if the set of A's were selected from a *set of sets* in each of which we know the distribution of B's, this could trigger rule 1. (For example, A might be the set of balls in a bag, and the bag might be selected from a *set* of bags, containing a known distribution of the proportion of B's in each bag.) That is to say, we might know a prior distribution over r, the relative frequency in A. This is the classical Bayesian case. We could condition on the *distribution* of values of r. But we have supposed ourselves to have only the sampling knowledge in $\mathcal{E}$; were we to have knowledge of a prior distribution for r we could infer a posterior distribution on the basis of the sample by conditioning. (Note that this boils down to direct inference concerning the selection of a population and then of a sample from that population.)

Here is another alternative: if our knowledge is as described, then we also know of a sample of 6,000 A's, *none* of which are B's. Let this sample be s'. $F(s') = 1$, so we have, by a parallel argument:

1. $(F(s') - 0.6688 \leq r \leq F(s') - 0.5688) \leftrightarrow \%x(B(x), A(x), 0.3312, 0.4312)$

2. $\%x((F(x) - 0.6688 \leq r \leq F(x) - 0.5688), A^{6,000}, 0.0, 0.0)$, or

$\%x(r + 0.5688) \leq F(x) \leq r + 0.6688), A^{6,000}, 0.0, 0.0)$

3. $s' \in A^{6,000}$

The proportion of 6,000-member subsets of A that have the property in question is not *exactly* 0, of course, but as close as makes no difference. In any event, we clearly have conflict. What allows us to retain an inference based on s and to reject an inference based on s'?

Answer: Rule 1 and our initial triple of sentences. The set $A^{6,000} \times A^{4,000}$ is the same as, or has the same statistics as the set $A^{10,000}$. That generates a triple that conflicts with the statistics of 6,000-member samples and leads to the bracketing of the corresponding statistical statement, which corresponds to a marginal distribution in the product space $A^{6,000} \times A^{4,000}$.

Of course, if we also had knowledge of a larger sample than s – a supersample of s – things would be different, just as they would be different if we had knowledge of a prior distribution for r. But, by assumption, we don't.

Do we know of a reference class that would lead us to bracket $\%x(|F(x) - r| \leq 0.05, A^{10,000}, 0.99,1.0)$ on the basis of Rule 2, specificity? That would require our knowing of a *subset* of $A^{10,000}$ within which $|F(x) - r| \leq 0.05$ would be true with a *differing* relative frequency. In real life we might well know of such a subset to which we know that s belongs. We might know that s was obtained by a procedure that was biased against the selection of B's, and thus that s was a member of a subset of $R^{10,000}$ in which the relative frequency of samples satisfying $|F(x) - r| \leq 0.05$ is much lower than it is in $A^{10,000}$ in general. But to know this is already to have general empirical knowledge. We have supposed that this is not the case in our example.

Finally, do we know of a set of reference classes closed under difference whose cover is properly contained in $[0.99, 1.0]$? I suspect we do, since Chebycheff's inequality is a very rough one: We can probably find a higher lower bound on the frequency of representative samples. Or, equivalently, we could tighten the notion of representativeness and achieve the same lower bound of 0.99. But this is not to the point here. Our object here was simply to show that induction in the most simple-minded sense can be justified probabilistically.

6. Inductive Logic

It is important to note that on the our view, the conclusion of an inductive argument is, just like the conclusion of a deductive argument, *accepted*: It is a sentence that "follows from" a set of sentences $\mathcal{E}$ that we accept as evidence, in the sense that it is almost always true when sentences of $\mathcal{E}$ are true. That is why the inference is nonmonotonic or inductive. The conclusion is not, as Carnap (1950) proposed, a sentence asserting a probability. We inductively conclude "S," not "probably S," and certainly not the Carnapian, "The probability of S, relative to total evidence $\mathcal{E}$ is p." This latter form of conclusion, as Keynes (1952) observed, is not *corrected* by additional evidence $\mathcal{E}'$; it is simply replaced by "The probability of S, relative to $\mathcal{E} \cup \mathcal{E}'$ is q." The Carnapian inference is monotonic.

If inductive conclusions are to be accepted, as we suggest, however, we must immediately face the question of how a rejection level ϵ is to be chosen. But this is a question that is faced by researchers all the time, and is answered, somewhat arbitrarily, by the conventions of the trade. Psychologists are often willing to reject null hypotheses at the 0.05 or 0.02 level; in the physical sciences one supposes that measurements are not more than two and a half standard deviations in error. Engineers deal with factors of safety of two to ten, which can also be translated into probabilities of error. Some very tentative systematic ideas relating the acceptable level of error to what might be generally at stake were advanced in Kyburg (1988), but a lot more thought could be devoted to this question. The question is answered in practice but not in theory.

Furthermore, if statements are accepted on the basis of their low likelihood of error, the set of accepted conclusions will not be closed under conjunction, and thus not deductively closed (Kyburg 1997). The chance that S is in error may be less than ϵ and the chance that T is in error may be less than ϵ, while the chance that $S \wedge T$ is in error may be greater than ϵ so that the conjunction may not be accepted. Of course, this is a marginal phenomenon – there are many cases in which conjunctions are acceptable. Thus (to use the time-worn lottery once again) if our level of rejection is 0.001, in a million ticket lottery we will be able to accept the conjunction of up to a thousand "ticket i will not win" statements, and therefore also the logical consequences of such sets of statements.

Now of course that holds for the conjunction of *any* thousand such statements, so we have the lottery problem all over again: the set of acceptable statements is inconsistent. This should not

be surprising for inductive conclusions. In those disciplines in which the null hypothesis of "no effect" is tested at the 0.05 level, we reject each hypothesis rejected at this level, and simultaneously accept that in the long run one out of twenty of such hypotheses are true. Similarly, in physical measurement we may decide that one chance in a hundred of being in error is tolerable risk, and so accept that the true measure of a quantity is in an interval of 2.5 standard deviations about the observed value. But we also know, within the same margin of error, that at least one of five hundred measurements will be in error by *more* than 2.5 standard deviations. Put explicitly: the agent should believe that *each* of the next five hundred measurements is correct within 2.5 standard deviations, and the agent should believe that at least one of these measurements is not correct within 2.5 standard deviations.

There is no explosive problem here. It is true that the set of accepted statements *entails* all statements, because it is inconsistent. But "$1 = 0$", though it is entailed by the set of accepted statements is not itself one: Its probability is 0 and does not exceed $1 - \epsilon$. We would only face a deductive explosion if we took the set of accepted statements to be deductively closed, or, what is the same thing, closed under conjunction (Kyburg 1970).

This raises the question of what logical structure there is in the set of accepted statements. We can show that if $S \vdash T$, $\text{Prob}(S, \mathcal{E}) \subset [1 - \epsilon, 1]$, then $\text{Prob}(T, \mathcal{E}) \subset [1 - \epsilon, 1]$. Thus if S is acceptable and S entails T, then T is acceptable. Anything entailed by any statement accepted at a certain level is acceptable at that level. If a conjunction a thousand conjuncts long is acceptable, anything entailed by that conjunction is acceptable.

Let us turn our attention to $\mathcal{E}$, the set of statements relative to which we perform our inductive inferences. We note that since probabilities are based on statements of long run frequency (though not to be identified with them!), $\mathcal{E}$ will have to include such statements. Some such statements, as we have seen, are true a priori: Any (approximately) normally distributed quantity will deviate from its mean by more than 2.5 standard deviations no more than 1 percent of the time; the proportion of hundred member samples of A's that differ in their fraction of B's from the set of all A's by as much as 0.30 ($\geq$ six standard deviations) is less than 1/36 (using Chebycheff's inequality and the fact that the standard deviation of the relative frequency is less than 1/20). But of course most of the probabilities that interest us are based on *empirical* frequencies that are known in $\mathcal{E}$ – that is, they are based on induction!

That means that $\mathcal{E}$ itself should include statements only supported with high probability (or bearing low risk of error) relative to some *other* body of evidence $\mathcal{E}'$, which in turn includes only statements with an even lower risk of error. Note that $\mathcal{E}$ may contain observation statements that, according to $\mathcal{E}'$ have low probability of error, as well as empirical statistical generalizations based on $\mathcal{E}'$; there need be no foundation of incorrigible observation statements.

This is not a problem for *induction*, which concerns the rational acceptance of statements that run low risk of error, relative to a set of statements accepted as evidence, although it may be a problem for general epistemology. What concerns us here is not general epistemology, but the structure of $\mathcal{E}$ and the fact that it has the same open structure as the set of inductive conclusions we infer from it on the basis of their high probability or low chance of error relative to $\mathcal{E}$. Although $\mathcal{E}$ clearly contains an infinite number of statements (in virtue of the fact that it contains all the entailments of any statement in it), it seems reasonable to suppose that it admits of a finite basis, that is, a finite set of statements from which all and only statements in $\mathcal{E}$ follow. So as a basis for inductive conclusions having a probability of error of less than ϵ we take as evidence a set of statements $\mathcal{E}$ that

1.   Are more reliable than $1 - \delta$, where $\delta < \epsilon$;
2.   Has a finite basis;
3.   May be inconsistent;
4.   Are expressed in our first order language $\mathcal{L}$.

How does the logic of induction we have outlined stack up against first-order logic? As we observed, first-order logic does not represent how people should think deductively, or even how they should argue deductively, but, rather, through its formal notion of proof, first-order logic serves as a gold standard for the resolution of disagreements or doubts about what entails what, about what follows from what. Although there is more than one first-order logic, in most contexts the variants come to the same thing. Similarly, inductive logic is not "inductive" because it reflects how people think, but because

it concerns what is *evidence* for what, just as deductive logic concerns what *follows* from what.

But there is one big difference between deductive logic and inductive logic. If there is a proof that C follows from $P_1, \ldots, P_n$ it can ordinarily be rendered short and perspicuous. Such a proof depends only on the sentences $P_1, \ldots, P_n$. In contrast, when we say that $P_1, \ldots, P_n$ provides *evidence* for C, citing $P_1, \ldots, P_n$ explicitly, we mean that it does so *in the context of everything else we know*, $\mathcal{E}$. Since an addition to our total evidence $\mathcal{E}$ can undermine the relation of evidence, the evidential relation depends on what we don't know as well as on what we know, or, put otherwise, in depends on *all* we know. That is why the inductive evidential relation is nonmonotonic, while the entailment relation is not.

Note that there is no algorithm for producing a proof (when one exists) in deductive logic. Inductive logic is no worse off in this regard. The difficulty in inductive logic is caused by the fact that the "premises" of an inductive argument consist of everything we know, and, more seriously, on the fact that an inductive argument depends on entailments of what we know.

The biggest problem is managing $\mathcal{E}$. Earlier I pointed out that writing "B" for background knowledge doesn't help us in resolving disagreements about what is evidence for what. Writing "$\mathcal{E}$" is no more help. What we need to do is to represent $\mathcal{E}$ explicitly. Of course you can't "write down everything you know." But in a scientific context, by and large, most of what differentiates your body of knowledge from mine is irrelevant to the support provided C by $P_1, \ldots, P_n$. It does not seem unreasonable to ask that a basis for $\mathcal{E}$ be provided.

Furthermore, inductive support is measured by evidential probability, and all probabilities come from constructions of direct inference. Thus within this formalization, to establish the probability of S, we are looking for triples of formulas:

$$\ulcorner S \leftrightarrow T(a) \urcorner, \ulcorner \%(T(x), R(x), p, q) \urcorner, \text{and } \ulcorner R(a) \urcorner$$

implied by the $\mathcal{E}$. This requires first, as we have said, that the body of knowledge $\mathcal{E}$ have a basis, and second, that we have some way of telling when a triple of sentences is entailed by sentences of $\mathcal{E}$. In the case of deductive logic we can manage without a procedure for finding proofs: When a proof of S from $A_1, \ldots, A_2$ is needed, we can depend on ingenuity to come up with one. Once we have one it is checkable, and it remains valid whatever we add to the premises $A_1, \ldots, A_2$. In principle, it becomes part of our social store of data.

In contrast, even checking an inductive argument from $\mathcal{E}$ to S requires a complete survey of the consequences of $\mathcal{E}$; and given a valid inductive argument yielding $\mathrm{Prob}(S, \mathcal{E}) = [p, q]$, that argument may be undermined by additions to $\mathcal{E}$. This is unavoidable. It is just what it *means* for an argument to be inductive.

Note

1   The requirement of "suitability" has been with us since Kyburg (1961), in one form or another. In a number of places, random quantities, functions from objects in the domain to real numbers, are also taken account of explicitly. Both classes of formulas were intended to be given, recursively, as part of the specification of the language.

References

Ernest W. Adams. *The Logic of Conditionals*. Reidel, Dordrecht, 1975.

Davis Baird. *Inductive Logic: Probability and Statistics*. Prentice-Hall, Englewood Cliffs, NJ, 1992.

George Boole. *An Investigation into the Laws of Thought*. Dover Publications, New York, 1854 (orig).

C. D. Broad. The principles of demonstrative induction. *Mind*, 39:302–317; 426–439, 1930.

C. D. Broad. *Induction, Probability and Causation: Selected Papers*. Humanities Press, New York, 1968.

Rudolf Carnap. *The Logical Foundations of Probability*. Chicago: University of Chicago Press, 1950.

Rudolf Carnap. A basic system of inductive logic, part i. In Richard Jeffrey and Rudolf Carnap, editors, *Studies in Inductive Logic and Probability*, pages 33–165. University of California, Berkley, 1971.

Gottlob Frege. *The Foundations of Arithmetic*. Basil Blackwell, Oxford, 1950 (1893).

Harman Gilbert and Sanjeev Kulkarni. The problem of induction. *Philosophy and Phenomenological Research*, 72:559–75.

John Maynard Keynes. *A Treatise on Probability*. Macmillan and Co., London, 1952.

Henry E. Kyburg, Jr. and Choh Man Teng. *Uncertain Inference*. Cambridge University Press, New York, 2001.

Henry E. Kyburg, Jr. *Probability and the Logic of Rational Belief*. Wesleyan University Press, Middletown, CT, 1961.

Henry E. Kyburg, Jr. Conjunctivitis. In Marshall Swain, editor, *Induction, Acceptance and Rational Belief*, volume 5, pages 55–82. Reidel, Dordrecht, 1970.

Henry E. Kyburg, Jr. Full belief. *Theory and Decision*, 25:137–162, 1988.

Henry E. Kyburg, Jr. The rule of adjunction and reasonable inference. *Journal of Philosophy*, 94:109–125, 1997.

Clarence Irving Lewis. *A Survey of Symbolic Logic*. University of California Press, Berkeley, 1918.

David Lewis. Probabilities of conditionals and conditional probability. In W. Harper, R. Stalnaker, and G. Pearce, editors, *Ifs*, pages 129–147. Reidel, Dordrecht, 1981.

Vann McGee. Conditional probabilities and compounds of conditionals. *The Philosophical Review*, 48:485–541, 1989.

John Stuart Mill. *A System of Logic*. Longmans Greene and Co., London, 1949, 1843.

Robert C. Moore. Semantical considerations on nonmonotonic logic. *Artificial Intelligence*, 25:75–94, 1985.

Judea Pearl. *Causality*. Cambridge University Press, New York, 2000.

W. V. O. Quine. *Mathematical Logic*. Harvard University Press, Cambridge, MA, 1951.

W. V. O. Quine. *Word and Object*. John Wiley and Sons, New York, 1960.

Raymond Reiter. A logic for default reasoning. *Artificial Intelligence*, 13:81–132, 1980.

Patrick Suppes. Subjective probability as a measure of a non-measurable set. In Suppes, Nagel and Tarski, editors, *Logic, Methodology and Philosophy of Science*, pages 319–329. University of California Press, Berkeley, 1962.

Chapter 16: Reasoning in Conceptual Spaces

PETER GÄRDENFORS

1. Three Levels of Modeling Reasoning

Processes of reasoning have been at the heart of analysis in analytic philosophy, artificial intelligence (AI) and in the early development of cognitive science. In these traditions, reasoning has been modeled as operations on propositions that are expressed by symbolic structures. I will call this approach the *symbolic paradigm*.

The central tenet of the symbolic paradigm is that representing and processing information essentially consists of *symbol manipulation* according to explicit *rules*. For example, Pylyshyn (1984: 29) writes: "[T]o be in a certain representational state is to have a certain symbolic expression in some part of memory." The symbols can be concatenated to form expressions in a *language of thought* (Fodor 1975), which is sometimes called Mentalese. The content of a sentence in Mentalese is a belief or a thought of an agent. The different beliefs in the cognitive states of a person are connected via their *logical* or *inferential relations*. Thus, the manipulations of symbols are performed without considering the semantic content of the symbols. In applications within AI, first-order logic has been the dominating inferential system (or some related programming version of it, such as Prolog). But in other areas more general forms of inference, like those provided by inductive logic or decision theory, have been utilized.

The symbols are used for modeling logical inferences and the expressions represent *propositions*, which stand in various *logical relations* to each other. Information processing involves above all *computations* of logical consequences. Here I am referring to the traditional sequential kind of computer programs with "explicit" symbol representations and not to connectionist systems (see later), which may use "intrinsic" representations (compare Palmer 1978).

In brief, a cognitive agent is seen as a kind of logic machine that operates on sentences from some formal language. The following quotation from Fodor (1981: 230) is a typical formulation of the symbolic paradigm:

> Insofar as we think of mental processes as computational (hence as formal operations defined on representations), it will be natural to take the mind to be, inter alia, a kind of computer. That is, we will think of the mind as carrying out whatever symbol manipulations are constitutive of the hypothesized computational processes. To a first approximation, we may thus construe mental operations as pretty directly analogous to those of a Turing machine.

The main methodological point of this chapter is to argue that, despite the dominance of the symbolic paradigm, *reasoning can be described on different cognitive levels* and that these levels bring out other aspects of the reasoning process (Gärdenfors 1994). Reasoning is not done by symbols alone. For instance, consider how to analyze animal reasoning. Because it is likely that human is the only species that can productively use symbols, it would follow that other forms of animal reasoning fall outside the symbolic paradigm.

There are areas where the symbolic approach to reasoning has led to problems. Maybe the most pressing concerns the attempts to explain inductive inferences. The most ambitious project of analyzing induction during the previous century has been that of the logical positivists. Inductive inferences were important for them, since such inferences were necessary for their verificationist aims. The basic objects of study for them were sentences in some more or less regimented language. However, it became apparent that the methodology of the positivists led to serious problems in relation to induction. The most famous ones are Hempel's (1965) "paradox of confirmation" and Goodman's (1955) "riddle of induction." These problems will be presented and discussed in Section 6.

I shall describe two other levels of cognitive modeling: the *conceptual* and the *subconceptual*. The subconceptual level corresponds to what has often been called the subsymbolic (Smolensky 1988). During the last decades this level has been implemented in *connectionist* systems, also known as parallel distributed processes (Rumelhart and McClelland 1986). Connectionist systems, often called *artificial neuron networks*, consist of large numbers of simple but highly interconnected units ("neurons"). The units process information in *parallel* (in contrast to most symbolic models where the processing is serial). There is no central control unit for the network, but all neurons "act" as individual processors. Processes of "reasoning" in such a system are modeled by the dynamics of the activities of the artificial neurons. In many cases, it can be said that a "conclusion" is reached when the network stabilizes in some equilibrium state (see Balkenius and Gärdenfors 1991 for an analysis of nonmonotonic reasoning by artificial neuron networks in these terms).

In addition to the symbolic and the subconceptual levels, I shall present a middle level of describing reasoning – the conceptual level, based on geometric structures in conceptual spaces. My focus will be on how models on this level can be used to understand *reasoning about concepts*, in particular inductive and nonmonotonic reasoning.[1] I shall argue that these processes are described more accurately on the conceptual level.

Apart from the implications for philosophical and psychological research, models of inductive and nonmonotonic reasoning have applications within several practical areas involving computerized management of concepts. In particular, the recent attempts to create a "Semantic Web" would benefit from such models (Gärdenfors 2004). I shall return to this topic in the concluding section.

The crucial question for my task is how concepts should be modeled. On the symbolic level, basic concepts are not modeled, but just *named* by the elementary symbols. Then names of more complex concepts are constructed by compositions, logical or syntactical, of the simple names. And when it comes to connectionist systems,

concepts are often represented *implicitly* in such systems. The primary motivation for introducing a conceptual level is to provide tools for *explicit* representations of basic concepts and their roles in reasoning. It is natural to view the conceptual level as being between the symbolic and the subconceptual levels in its cognitive granularity.

My main modeling tool will be *conceptual spaces* that employ geometric structures rather than symbols or associations. Information is represented by points, vectors and regions in dimensional spaces. On the basis of these structures, reasoning with concepts can be described in a natural way in terms of distances in a space. The framework of this chapter follows the theory presented in my book *Conceptual Spaces: The Geometry of Thought* (Gärdenfors 2000). As we shall see, this kind of model will help clarify the relationship between inductive and nonmonotonic reasoning. Before presenting the conceptual level, I will give some motivations for studying inductive and nonmonotonic reasoning.

2. Three Ways of Describing an Observation

To illustrate the relevance of the three levels of modeling reasoning, let us look at the notion of an *observation* as it is used in inductive reasoning. It is commonplace that induction is going from single observations to generalizations. But this statement loses its air of triviality if one takes seriously the question of *what* an observation is. It is surprising that this question has received very little attention within the philosophy of science.[2] I want to argue that there is no unique way of characterizing an observation. Indeed, I shall distinguish three levels of accounting for observations corresponding to the three levels of modeling described in the introduction (or, since all levels may be adopted at the same time, they may as well be called perspectives):

1. *The symbolic level*: This way of viewing observations consists of describing them in some specified language. The language is assumed to be equipped with a fixed set of primitive predicates and the denotations of these predicates are taken to be known. An observation is a particular type of *statement* (proposition). The observational statements are supposed to be furnished to the reasoner by incorrigible perceptual mechanisms.

2. *The conceptual level*: On this level observations are not defined in relation to

some language but characterized in terms of some underlying conceptual space. The conceptual space, which is more or less connected to perceptual mechanisms, consists of a number of "quality dimensions" (these will be described later). Using the notion of conceptual spaces, an observation can be defined as *an assignment to an object of a location in a conceptual space*. For example, the observation that is described on the symbolic level as "x is red" is expressed on the conceptual level by assigning x a point in color space. On this level, induction is seen as closely related to *concept formation*. According to the conceptual perspective, inductive inferences show prototype effects, in contrast to the symbolic perspective that operates on Aristotelian concepts (cf. Smith and Medin 1981).[3]

3. *The subconceptual level*: In the most basic sense an observation is what is received by our sensory organs. In this sense, an observation can be identified with what is received by a set of *receptors*. For human beings and other animals these inputs are provided by the sensory receptors, but one can also talk of a machine making observations of this kind via some measuring instruments serving as receptors. Actually, this is what happens in modern science. Many "observations" never pass a human eye or ear, but are transmitted directly from the measuring devices to a computational database that is then used to evaluate the experiment.

The receptors provide "raw" data in the sense that the information is not assumed to be processed in any way, neither in a conceptual space, nor in the form of some linguistic expression. The observations are thus described as occurring before conceptualization. The inductive process is seen as establishing connections between various types of inputs. One currently popular way of modeling this kind of process is by using artificial neuron networks.

One objective of this chapter is to argue that depending on which approach to observations is adopted, thoroughly different considerations about inductive inferences will come into focus.[4] In my opinion there is a multitude of aspects of inductive reasoning and not something that can be identified as *the* problem of induction. The upshot is that there is no canonical way of studying induction. What is judged to be the salient features of the inductive process depends to a large extent on *what* an observation is considered to be and thus on what cognitive level the process is modeled.

3. Nonmonotonic Reasoning

Concepts play an important role in the generation of *inferences*. As Holland et al. (1986: 180) put it: "To know that an instance is a member of a natural category is to have an entry point into an elaborate default hierarchy that provides a wealth of expectations about the instance." In this section, I will argue that what has been called *nonmonotonic reasoning* is tightly connected to this role of concepts. As I shall argue in Section 7, this form of reasoning is best described on the conceptual level instead of on the symbolic level that has been dominating in the literature.

The deductive reasoning of traditional logic is *monotonic* in the sense that when a proposition A can be inferred from a set S of sentences, then A can be inferred from any set that contains S. However, everyday reasoning, which in general is based on assumptions about what is "normally" the case, is often nonmonotonic. For example, if I learn that Gonzo is a bird, then with the aid of the presumption that birds normally fly, I conclude that Gonzo flies. But if I obtain the additional information that Gonzo is an emu, this conclusion is no longer drawn.

Nonmonotonic reasoning has become a central topic within AI.[5] However, most of the research efforts have been concentrated on finding the appropriate *logical rules* that govern nonmonotonic reasoning. This means that a symbolic representation of the relevant knowledge is already presumed. However, I believe that in order to understand nonmonotonic reasoning one must go below the symbolic level of representation. Strangely enough, the relationship between induction and nonmonotonic reasoning does not seem to have been investigated.

The basic idea of nonmonotonic inferences is that when more information is obtained about an object, some inferences that were earlier reasonable are no longer so. An important point that is often overlooked is that information about an object may be of two kinds: *propositional* and *conceptual*. When the new information is propositional, one learns new *facts* about the object, for example, that x is an emu. When the new information is conceptual, one *categorizes* the object in a new way, for example, x is *seen as* an emu instead of as just a bird. It is important to notice that describing information as propositional or as conceptual does not mean that these kinds of information are in conflict with one another. On the contrary, they should be seen as different *perspectives* on how information is described.

The theory of nonmonotonic reasoning has focused on propositions; hence it has been seen as a nonmonotonic *logic*. However, in the examples discussed in the literature, the great majority derives from the nonmonotonicity of *concepts*. For example, the *default rules* studied by Reiter (1980) and his followers have been conceived of as inference rules, although a more natural interpretation of "defaults" is to view them as *relations between concepts*. For instance, when something is categorized as a fruit, it will also, by default, be categorized as sweet, even though it is well known that the category contains many exceptions that are not sweet.

It may be argued that there is no harm done in focusing on the symbolic perspective of nonmonotonicity since information about categorization can be quite naturally transferred to propositional information: categorizing x as an emu, for example, can be expressed by the proposition "x is an emu." However, this transformation into the symbolic form tends to suppress the internal *structure* of concepts. Once one formalizes categorizations of objects by *predicates* in a first order language, there is a strong tendency to view the predicates as primitive atomic notions and to forget that there are rich relations between concepts that disappear when put into standard logical formalism.

Indeed, in the symbolic paradigm, the fact that the concept of an emu is a subcategory of "bird" is represented by an explicit axiom in the form of a universal sentence "for all x, if x is emu, then x is a bird." However, if the geometrical structure of concepts, as it is given in a conceptual space, were built into the predicates of the language themselves, such an axiom would be totally redundant because the region representing emus is a subregion of the one representing birds. As we shall see, the inclusion relations between the regions and their domains will, in a sense, become *analytic* in a conceptual space.

To be sure, there is in the literature one well-known theory of nonmonotonic inferences that focuses on conceptual relations, namely *inheritance networks* (see, for example, Touretsky 1986 and Makinson and Schlechta 1991). However, in the theory of inheritance networks, concepts are represented by (nonstructured) *points* without any structure, and their relations by two kinds of links: "is-a" and "is-not-a." Since these links say nothing about the structure of concepts, this form of representation is far too meager to handle the relations between concepts that are exploited in inferences, monotonic as well as nonmonotonic. In contrast, I submit that a theory of conceptual structure is necessary in order to understand different kinds of nonmonotonic inferences involving concepts.

As a challenge to any theory about nonmonotonic inferences, I would like to point out the following nonmonotonic aspects of reasoning about concepts:

(a) Change from a General Category to a Subordinate

This is the most well known nonmonotonic aspect of concepts. When we shift from applying a "basic" category (a term borrowed from prototype theory) like *bird* to an object x, to applying a "subordinate" category like *emu*, we often give up some of the (default) properties associated with the basic category: a bird is normally small and sings and flies, while an emu has none of these properties.

(b) Contrast Classes

In standard uses of first order logic, *combinations* of concepts are expressed by *conjunctions* of predicates. However, there are many different combinations of concepts that cannot be analyzed in this manner. As a matter of fact, nonmonotonicity is ubiquitous in concept combinations. For example, even though "Zinfandel" is a subcategory of "wine" and "wine" is a subcategory of "object," "white Zinfandel" is not a subcategory of "white wine" (it is a rosé wine) and "white wine" is not a subcategory of "white objects" (it is light yellow).

For another example, consider the seemingly innocent concept *red*. In the *Advanced Learner's Dictionary of Current English*, it is defined as "of the colour of fresh blood, rubies, human lips, the tongue, maple leaves in the autumn, post-office pillar boxes in Gt. Brit." This definition fits very well with letting *red* correspond to the normal region of the color space (see Section 4). Now consider *red* in the following combinations:

- Red book
- Red wine
- Red hair
- Red skin
- Red soil
- Redwood

Figure 1. Cuplike objects (From Labov 1973).

In the first example, *red* corresponds to the dictionary definition, and it can be combined with *book* in a straightforward extensional way that is expressed by a conjunction of predicates in first-order logic. In contrast, *red* would denote *purple* when predicated of wine, *copper* when used about hair, *tawny* when of skin, and *pinkish brown* when of wood. Thus the class of objects that the concept is applied to, the so-called *contrast class*, changes the meaning of *red* in a nonmonotonic fashion (Broström 1994).

(c) Metaphors

Even more drastic combination effects occur in metaphorical uses of concepts. For example, when we talk about a *red newspaper*, we do not expect it to be printed on red paper, only to express a certain political viewpoint. And in everyday metaphors such as the "legs" of a table, the "hands" of a clock, the "mouth" of a river,

we do not think of tables, clocks and rivers as having bodies. The kind of conceptual change involved in a metaphor corresponds to a *revision* of the concept, and thus the inferences involved in metaphorical uses of concepts parallels *belief revisions* that are modeled in propositional systems (Gärdenfors 1988; for a comparison between nonmonotonic inferences and belief revision, see Gärdenfors and Makinson 1994).

Metaphors are notoriously difficult to handle within the symbolic paradigm, since it is assumed that the reference of a predicate is fixed in advance. In most logical theories, these linguistic figures have thus been treated as deviant phenomena and have been ignored or incorporated via special stylistic rules.

(d) Context Effects

Combinations of concepts can result in nonmonotonic effects as exemplified by contrast

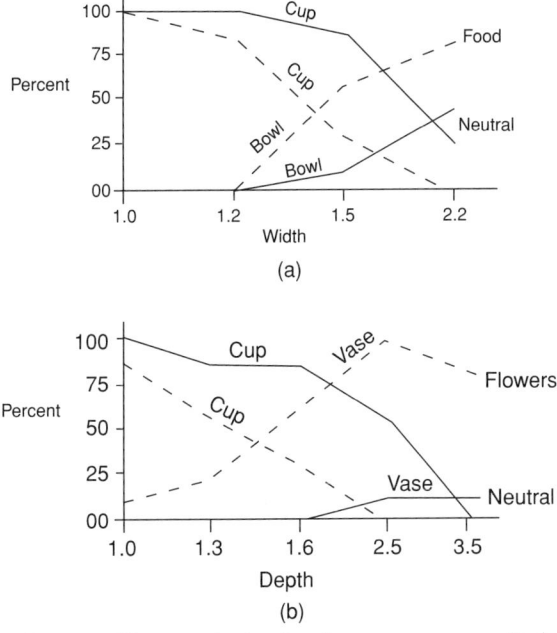

Figure 2. Context effects on the borders between concepts (Labov 1973).

classes and metaphors. Sometimes the mere *context* in which a concept is used may trigger different *associations* that lead to nonmonotonic inferences. Barsalou (1987: 106) gives the following example: "When *animals* is processed in the context of milking, *cow* and *goat* are more typical than *horse* and *mule*. But when *animals* is processed in the context of riding, *horse* and *mule* are more typical than *cow* and *goat*."

Another example of how the context affects the application of concepts is the following, due to Labov (1973). He showed subjects pictures of objects like those in Figure 1 in order to determine how the variations in shape influence the names the subjects use. But he also wanted to see whether the *functions* of the objects also influences naming.[6] In the "neutral" context, subjects were asked to imagine the object in someone's hand. In a "food" context, they were asked to imagine the object filled with mashed potatoes; and in a "flowers" context, they were told to imagine the object with cut flowers in it.

Figure 2 shows the results, when the *width* of objects 1 to 4 (Figure 2a) and *depth* of objects 1 and 5 to 9 (Figure 2b) varied as is represented on the horizontal axes. The vertical axis represents the percentage of subjects that named the object with a particular word. As can be seen, the names for the objects were heavily influenced by the imagined context.

This example shows that even if the "core" or "prototype" of two concepts like *cup* and *bowl*

remain unchanged, the context may change the *border* between the concepts. Such a change may clearly have nonmonotonic effects on the reasoning involving the concepts.

I have here presented four different kinds of nonmonotonic aspects of reasoning with concepts. It should be obvious that these aspects are interrelated. However, in the literature, the focus has almost exclusively been on what happens when one changes from a general category to a subordinate. I submit that other aspects are equally important and in need of a systematic explanation. Furthermore, the relation to inductive reasoning has been neglected. In the following two sections, I will outline a theory that I believe can shed light on all of the nonmonotonic aspects of concepts discussed here.

4. Conceptual Spaces as a Representational Framework

As a framework for a geometric structure used in describing the cognitive level of reasoning, I have proposed (Gärdenfors 1990a, 1990b, 1992, 2000) the notion of a *conceptual space*. Conceptual spaces represent information by *geometric* structures rather than by symbols. Information is represented by points (standing for individuals or objects), and regions (standing for properties and relations) in dimensional spaces. A great deal of the structure of concepts, for example similarity relations, can be modeled in a natural way by exploiting *distances* in the space.

A conceptual space consists of a number of *quality dimensions*. Examples of such dimensions are: color, pitch, temperature, weight, and the three ordinary spatial dimensions. I have chosen these dimensions because they are closely connected to what is produced by our sensory receptors (Schiffman 1982). However, there are also quality dimensions that are of an abstract nonsensory character.

The primary role of the dimensions is to represent various "qualities" of objects in different *domains*. Since the notion of a domain is central to my analysis, it should be given a more precise meaning. To do this, I rely on the notions of separable and integral dimensions taken from cognitive psychology (see, e.g., Garner 1974; Maddox 1992; Melara 1992). Certain quality dimensions are *integral* in the sense that one cannot assign an object a value on one dimension without giving it a value on the other. For example, an object cannot be given a hue, without also giving it a brightness value. Or the pitch of a sound always goes along with a loudness. Dimensions that are not integral are said to be *separable*, as for example the size and hue dimensions. Using this distinction, the notion of a *domain* can now be defined as a set of integral dimensions that are separable from all other dimensions.

The domains form the framework used to assign *properties* to objects and to specify *relations* between them (see next section). The dimensions are taken to be independent of symbolic representations in the sense that we can represent the qualities of objects, for example by vectors, without presuming an explicit language in which these qualities are expressed.

The notion of a dimension should be understood literally. It is assumed that each of the quality dimensions is endowed with certain *topological* or *metric* structures. As a first example, I will take the dimension of *time*. In science, time is a one-dimensional structure that is isomorphic to the line of real numbers. If *now* is seen as the zero point on the line, the future corresponds to the infinite positive real line and the past to the infinite negative line. This representation of time is not universal, but is to some extent culturally dependent, so that other cultures have a different time dimension as a part of their cognitive structure. There is thus no unique way of choosing a dimension to represent a particular quality, but in general one has a wide array of possibilities.

In order to separate different uses of quality dimensions, it is important to introduce a distinction between a *psychological* and a *scientific* interpretation. The psychological interpretation concerns how humans (or other organisms) structure their perceptions. The scientific interpretation, by contrast, deals with how different dimensions are presented within a scientific theory. The distinction is relevant when the dimensions are seen as cognitive entities, in which case their topological or metric structure should not be determined by scientific theories, which attempt at giving a "realistic" description of the world, but by *psychophysical* measurements that determine the structure of how our perceptions are represented.

A paradigmatic example of a domain involves *color*. In brief, our cognitive representation of color can be described by three dimensions. The first dimension is *hue*, which is represented by the familiar *color circle*. The topological structure of this dimension is thus different from the quality dimensions representing time or weight which are isomorphic to the real line. One way of illustrating the differences in topology is by noting that we can talk about psychologically *complementary* colors, that is, colors that lie *opposite* to each other on the color circle. In contrast it is *not meaningful* to talk about two points of time or two weights being "opposite" to each other.

The second psychological dimension of color is *saturation*, which ranges from grey (zero color intensity) to increasingly greater intensities. This dimension is isomorphic to an interval of the real line. The third dimension is *brightness*, which varies from white to black and is thus a linear dimension with end points. Together, these three dimensions, one with circular structure and two with linear, constitute the color space which is a subspace of our perceptual conceptual space.

This space is often illustrated by the so-called *color spindle* (see Figure 3). Brightness is shown on the vertical axis. Saturation is represented as the distance from the center of the spindle towards its perimeter. Hue, finally, is represented by the positions along the perimeter of the central circle.

It is impossible to provide a complete list of the quality dimensions involved in the conceptual spaces of humans. Some of the dimensions seem to be *innate* and to some extent hardwired in our nervous system, as for example color, pitch, and probably also ordinary space. Other dimensions are presumably *learned*. Learning

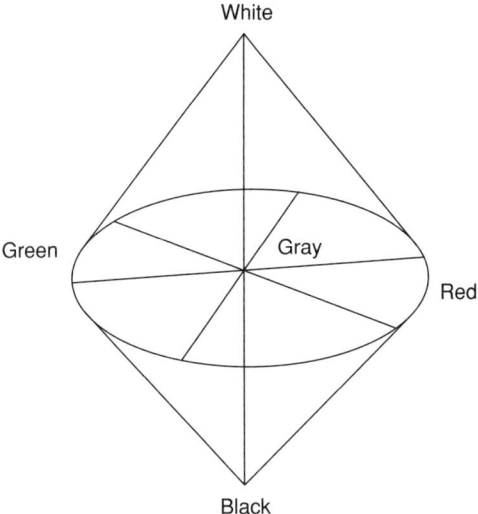

White

Green

Gray

Red

Black

Figure 3. The color spindle.

new concepts often involves expanding one's conceptual space with new quality dimensions. *Functional* properties used for describing artifacts may be an example here. Even if we do not know much about the topological structures of these dimensions, it is quite obvious that there is some such nontrivial structure (see the analyses of functional representation in Vaina 1983 and Gärdenfors 2007). Still other dimensions may be *culturally* dependent. Finally, some quality dimensions are introduced by *science*.

5. Characterizing Concepts

The theory of conceptual spaces will now be used to provide a definition of properties and concepts. In my technical use a property is a concept that concerns only one domain of quality dimensions, while a concept in general connects several kinds of dimensions. I propose the following criterion (Gärdenfors 1990b, 1992, 2000) where the topological characteristics of the quality dimensions are utilized to introduce a spatial structure for properties:

> *Criterion P*: A *natural property* is a convex region in some domain.

The motivation for the criterion is that if some objects which are located at v_1 and v_2 in relation to some quality dimension (or several dimensions) are both examples of the property C, then any object that is located between v_1 and v_2 on the quality dimension(s) will also be an example of C. Criterion P presumes that the notion of

betweenness is meaningful for the relevant quality dimensions. This is, however, a rather weak assumption which demands very little of the underlying geometrical structure. (For a different proposal based on topological properties, see Mormann 1993).

Further motivation for criterion P comes from recent results by Jäger and van Rooij (2007) concerning the emergence of a common semantics in a community. They show that if two persons communicate about a common metric conceptual space, for example the color space, using a finite number of expressions, the most efficient communication results if both of them use the expressions to refer to a set of prototypes in the space and then partition the space according to the so-called Voronoi tessellation. It is well known that such a tessellation always results in convex regions (see Gärdenfors 2000: Sec. 3.9).

Criterion P does not presume that one can identify sharp borders between concepts, but it can also be applied to *fuzzy* concepts or concepts that are defined by *probabilistic* criteria. What convexity requires is that if two object locations v_1 and v_2 both satisfy a certain membership criterion, e.g., has a certain degree or probability of membership, then all objects between v_1 and v_2 also satisfy the criterion.

Most properties expressed by simple words in natural languages seem to be natural properties in the sense specified here. For instance, I conjecture that all *color terms* in natural languages express natural properties with respect to the psychological representation of the three color dimensions. It is well known that different languages carve up the color circle in different ways, but all carvings seems to be done in terms of convex sets (see Berlin and Kay 1969).

Properties, as defined by criterion P, form a special case of *concepts*. I define this distinction by saying that a property is based on a *single* domain, while a concept may be based on *several* domains. The distinction between properties and concepts has been obliterated in the symbolic as well as connectionist representations that have dominated the discussion in the cognitive sciences. In particular, both properties and concepts are represented by *predicates* in first order languages.

The predicates of a first order language correspond to several different grammatical categories in a natural language, most importantly those of adjectives, nouns and verbs. The main semantic difference between adjectives and nouns, on the one hand, is that adjectives like "red," "tall," and "round" normally refer to a single domain and thus represent properties, whereas nouns such as "dog," "apple," and "town" normally contain information about several domains and thus represent concepts. Verbs, on the other hand, are characterized by their temporal structure, that is, they essentially involve the time dimension (see Langacker 1987 for conceptual representations of verbs). Using conceptual spaces, one can thus express the fundamental semantic differences between the most important grammatical categories. First order languages do not seem to be sufficiently rich to make these distinctions in a systematic manner.

Let us now focus on the differences between single-domain properties and multi-domain concepts. As a paradigm example of a concept that is represented in several domains, consider "apple" (compare Smith et al. 1988). The first problem when representing a concept is to decide which are the relevant domains. When we encounter apples as children, the first domains that we learn about are presumably color, shape, texture and taste. Later, we learn about apples as (biological) fruits, about their nutritional value, and possibly about some further dimensions. It should be noted that I do not require that a concept should be associated with a closed set of domains. On the contrary, this set may be expanded as one learns about further aspects of a concept.

The next problem is to determine the geometric structure of the domains. Taste space can presumably be represented by the four dimensions sweet, sour, salty, and bitter, and the color domain by hue, saturation, and brightness. Other domains are trickier: it is difficult to say much about, for example, the topological structure of "fruit space." Some ideas about how "shape space" should be modeled have been discussed in, for example, Marr and Nishihara (1978) and Gärdenfors (1990b, 2000). Instead of giving a detailed presentation of the geometric structures of the different domains, let me represent the "apple" regions verbally as follows:

Dimension	Region
Color	Red-yellow-orange
Shape	Roundish
Texture	Smooth
Taste	Regions of the sweet and sour dimensions
Fruit	Specification of seed structure, flesh and peel type, etc.
Nutrition	Values of sugar content, vitamins, fibers, etc.

When several domains are involved in a representation, some principle for how the different domains are to be *weighed* together must be assumed. These weights influence the distances in the conceptual space. The relative weights of the domains depend on the *context* in which the concept is used. Hence, I assume that in addition to the regions associated with each domain, the concept representation contains information about the *prominence* of the different domains. The prominence values of different domains determine which *associations* can be made and thus which *inferences* can be triggered by a particular use of a concept. The prominence values can change with the context, and with the knowledge and interests of the user. For example, if you are eating an apple, its taste will be more prominent than if you are using an apple as a ball when playing with an infant, which would make the shape domain particularly prominent.

Concepts are not just bundles of properties. The proposed representation for a concept also includes an account of the *correlations* between the regions from different domains that are associated with the concept. In the "apple" example there is a very strong (positive) correlation between the sweetness in the taste domain and the sugar content in the nutrition domain and a weaker correlation between the color red and a sweet taste.

These considerations of prominence and correlations motivate the following definition of concept representation:

> *Criterion* C: A *natural concept* is represented as a set of convex regions in a number of domains together with a prominence assignment to the domains and information about how the regions in different domains are correlated.

Concerning human abilities to detect clusters of properties, it turns out that we are, in general, extremely poor at performing *abstract* correlation assessment tasks (Nisbett and Ross 1980; Kornblith 1993: 96–100). However, work by Billman (1983) and Billman and Knutson (1996) indicates that humans are quite good at detecting correlations that cluster *several dimensions*, in spite of our limitations in detecting isolated correlations between variables. A plausible explanation of this phenomenon is that our perceptions of "natural" concepts (according to Criterion C) do show correlations along multiple dimensions, and, as a result of natural selection, we have developed a competence to detect such clustered correlations.[7] In brief, we are better at learning concepts than learning scattered cor-relations between properties. In line with this, Holland et al. (1986: 183–184) formulate the hypothesis that the *basic level* categories of pro-totype theory (Rosch 1975, 1978) are character-ized by distinctive clusters of correlated prop-erties. If valid, this hypothesis would provide a potent underpinning for that part of prototype theory.

In this analysis of concepts I have tried to bring in elements from other theories in psy-chology and linguistics. Some related ideas can be found in, among others, Barsalou (1992), Holmqvist (1993), Langacker (1987: 154–166), and Smith et al. (1988). The main difference between these theories and the one presented here is that I put greater emphasis on the geome-trical structure of the concept representations, in particular via the requirement of representing by convex regions of quality dimensions. As will be seen in the following sections, these structures are crucial for the analysis of the inductive and nonmonotonic reasoning processes.

6. Induction in Conceptual Spaces

One of the most impressive features of human reasoning is our ability to perform *inductive inferences*. Without any perceived effort, we are prepared, sometimes with overwhelming confi-dence, to generalize from a very limited num-ber of observations. These inferences concern connections between properties from different domains.

However, we do not perform inductive infer-ences in an arbitrary manner. Peirce (1932: 476) notes that there are certain forms of *constraints* that delimit the vast class of possible inferences. As he puts it:

Nature is a far vaster and less clearly arranged repertory of facts than a census report; and if men had not come to it with special aptitudes for guessing right, it may well be doubted whether in the ten or twenty thousand years that they may have existed their greatest mind would have attained the amount of knowledge which is actually possessed by the lowest idiot. But, in point of fact, not man merely, but all animals derive by inheritance (presumably by natural selection) two classes of ideas which adapt them to their environ-ment. In the first place, they all have from birth some notions, however crude and con-crete, of force, matter, space, and time; and, in the next place, they have some notion of

what sort of objects their fellow-beings are, and how they will act on given occasions.

Here, Peirce hints at an *evolutionary* explana-tion of why "the human intellect is peculiarly adapted to the comprehension of the laws and facts of nature" (1932: 474). In Quine's (1969: 125) words: "To trust induction as a way of access to the truths of nature . . . is to suppose, more nearly, that our quality space matches that of cosmos."

In this section, I shall use conceptual spaces to develop a theory of constraints for inductive reasoning. I shall focus on the problem of *pro-jectibility*, that is, the problem of which proper-ties and concepts may be used in induction.

6.1. Observation Statements and the Riddles of Induction

The most ambitious project of analyzing induc-tive inferences during the previous century has been that of the logical positivists. According to their program, the basic objects of scientific inquiry are sentences or statements in some for-mal or natural language. As mentioned in Sec-tion 2, the observational statements are taken to be provided by incorrigible perceptual mecha-nisms.

Ideally, the scientific language is a version of first order logic where a designated subset of the atomic predicates represent observational prop-erties and relations. These observational pred-icates are taken to be primitive notions. This means that when it comes to inductive reason-ing, all observational predicates are treated in the same way. For example, Carnap (1950: Sec. 18B) requires that the primitive predicates of a language be logically independent of each other. The advantage of this, from the point of view of the positivists, is that induction then becomes amenable to logical analysis, which, in the purist form, is the only tool admitted.

However, it became apparent that the metho-dology of the positivists led to serious problems for their analysis of induction. The most famous ones are Goodman's (1955) "riddle of induction" and Hempel's (1965) "paradox of confirmation." To see the problems for the symbolic paradigm, I will give brief recapitulations of these para-doxes.

Hempel's paradox of confirmation deals with the problem of what observations would count as inductive support for a general law. Sup-pose we are interested in a law of the form (x) $(Rx \rightarrow Bx)$ (for example, "all ravens are black").

The most obvious confirming instances are sentences of the form Ra & Ba (black ravens). However, the general law is logically equivalent to (x) (¬Bx → ¬Rx). For symmetry reasons, the observations confirming this law are of the form ¬Ba & ¬Ra (nonblack nonravens). But if this is true, we can confirm the law that all ravens are black by gathering green apples, blue suede shoes, and red herrings. This is obviously counterintuitive.

Goodman's puzzle starts from the universal sentence that all emeralds (examined up to 1999) are green. The property "grue" is defined as something that is green before the year 2000 and blue after the beginning of year 2000. Similarly, "bleen" means blue before 2000 and green thereafter. According to the definition, all emeralds examined up to 1999 have been grue. So why should we not expect that the inductive inference that all emeralds are grue is as valid as the seemingly more natural inference that all emeralds are green?

Note that it does not help to say that "green" is a *simpler* predicate than "grue" because it does not involve any reference to a particular point of time. It is true that "grue" can be defined in terms of "green" and "blue" and a time reference, but it is equally true that "green" can be defined as "grue before the year 2000 and bleen thereafter." So from a purely logical point of view, "green" and "grue" are perfectly symmetrical as predicates. And the logical point of view is the only one that counts within the methodology of orthodox logical positivism, which is based on symbolic representations. However, as Goodman and Hempel have shown, such a purist position results in paradoxes concerning induction.

One conclusion to be drawn from these paradoxes is that the symbolic level is not sufficient for a complete understanding of inductive reasoning. What is needed is a *nonlogical* way of distinguishing the predicates that may be used in inductive inferences from those that may not. There are several suggestions for such a distinction in the literature. One idea is that some predicates denote "natural kinds" or "natural properties" while others don't, and it is only the former that may be used in inductive reasoning. Natural kinds are normally interpreted realistically, following the Aristotelian tradition, and thus assumed to represent something that exists in the world independently of human cognition. However, when it comes to inductive *inferences* it is not sufficient that the properties exist out there somewhere, but we must be able to represent the natural kinds in our minds, if they

are to be used in planning and decision making. In other words, what is needed to understand induction, as performed by humans, is an analysis of natural properties on the conceptual level.

6.2. *Induction and Natural Concepts*

Let us approach the problem by considering how observations are identified on the conceptual level. As discussed in Section 2, an observation can be defined as an assignment to an object of a location in a conceptual space. For example, the observation that is described on the symbolic level as "x is yellow" is represented on the conceptual level by assigning x a point in the yellow region of color space. Since natural languages only divide the color domain into a finite number of categories the information contained in the statements that x is yellow is much less precise than the information furnished by assigning x a location in color space. In this sense, the conceptual level allows much richer instruments for representing observations than the symbolic level.

Let us have a look at how Goodman's predicate "grue" can be modeled in a conceptual space. Given the standard representations of colors as presented in Section 4, "green" and "blue" are natural properties according to Criterion P, while "grue" and "bleen" are not. "Grue" presumes two dimensions, color and time, for its description.

To model the predicate, we can consider the cylindrical space that is generated by taking the Cartesian product of the time dimension and the hue dimension (the color circle). This cylinder is depicted in Figure 4. In this space, "grue" and "bleen" would not represent convex regions, but rather be discontinuous at the point on the time dimension representing the year 2000. In contrast "blue" and "green" would still correspond to convex regions.

Mormann (1993: 230–231) suggests a slightly different solution to Goodman's riddle. The underlying conceptual space is again the "time-color" cylinder of Figure 4. Simplifying Mormann's construction a bit, a closed set is a region A × B (a Cartesian product) where A is a segment of the time dimension and B a segment of the color circle. In a sense, the closed sets are all the "rectangles" of the time-color cylinder. Mormann proposes the criterion that a natural property on the time-color cylinder is such a closed set. On this criterion, "green" and "blue"

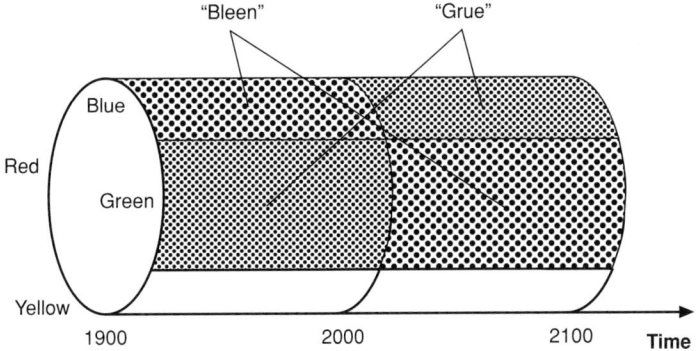

Figure 4. The time-color cylinder.

are again natural properties, while "grue" and "bleen" are not.

Carnap (1971: 70–76) excludes Goodman-type predicates by distinguishing between "locational" and "nonlocational" attributes. "Grue" denotes a locational attribute since it refers to a particular temporal location. However, Carnap's solution seems rather ad hoc since it does not explain, for example, why a nonlocational predicate like "green or orange" is not regarded as projectible.

Let us take a brief look at the concepts that occur in Hempel's (1965) paradox of confirmation. As a matter of fact, "nonblack" corresponds to a convex region of the color space since any color between two nonblack colors is also nonblack. I have no firm intuitions on whether "nonblack" is projectible or not. "All nonblack bodies reflect some light" seems to be a completely acceptable generalization. However, the concept "nonraven" would be difficult to count as a natural property according to Criterion P of Section 5. The class of all objects that are nonravens belong to many unrelated domains. Hence, it would be extremely tricky to specify the associated regions in a way that satisfies Criterion P. Even if "nonraven" is restricted to the domain of birds, it depends on the structure of this domain, which to a large extent is unknown, whether "nonraven" corresponds to a convex region.

Even if both F and G denote natural properties, the disjunction "F or G" need not denote a natural property (in concordance with this, learning such a non-natural disjunctive property can only be achieved by learning each of the disjuncts); and if F is a natural property, but G is not, then "F and G" need not be a natural property. However, if both F and G are natural properties, the conjunction "F and G" will also be nat-

ural, since the intersection of two convex regions is again convex.

In line with this, Nolan (1994: 134–137) points out that grue-like predicates cannot be *learned* in the normal way of learning a language. This idea fits well with my emphasis on natural properties. Given a conceptual space, it is much easier to learn a predicate that corresponds to a natural region of the space, than learning something that corresponds to an irregular subset of the space.

The upshot is that Criterion P is proposed as a solution to the problem of projectibility in induction. It provides a way of delimiting the class of properties that can function in inductive reasoning. It should be noted that Criterion P depends on the geometric structure of the conceptual spaces because it involves the notion of convexity, and hence the criterion cannot be expressed on the symbolic level. On the conceptual level of representation, inductive reasoning then consists in finding the relevant connections between natural properties in different domains.

Followers of Goodman could argue that even if predicates like "grue" and its ilk do not correspond to natural properties in our standard conceptual space, it is conceivable that such predicates would correspond to natural properties in some other conceptual space, where, consequently, our predicates "green" and "blue" would denote nonnatural properties. In other words, what counts as a natural property is dependent on the underlying conceptual space. This form of relativism in handled in Gärdenfors (1993) with the aid of evolutionary considerations. In brief, the structure of our conceptual space has been molded by the environment we live in.

Furthermore, a consequence of the analysis presented here that if we assume that the meanings of the predicates are determined by a mapping into a conceptual space S, Criterion P and the topological structure of different quality dimensions entail that certain statements will become *analytically true*. For example it follows from the linear structure of the length dimension that comparative relations like "earlier than" are *transitive*. This is thus an analytic feature of such a relation (*analytic-in-S*, that is). Similarly, it is analytic that everything that is green is colored (since "green" refers to a region of the color space) and that nothing is both green and blue. Analytic-in-S is thus defined on the basis of the topological and geometrical structure of the conceptual space S. However, different conceptual spaces will yield different notions of analyticity, which leads to a form of relativism that would be foreign to a classical notion of analyticity.

Category-Based Induction

A different tradition of investigating inductions involving concepts rather than properties concerns so-called *categorical inductive inferences* (see, e.g., Osherson et al. 1990; Sloman 1993; Heit 2000; Rips 2001). Osherson et al. (1990) studied two types of inductive arguments: general, where the conclusion concerns a class that is superordinate to those of the premises, and specific, where the class of the conclusion is on the same categorical level as the premises. An example of a general argument is the following:

Grizzly bears love onions
Polar bears love onions
_____
All bears love onions

And an example of a specific argument is:

Robins use serotonin as a neurotransmitter
Bluejays use serotonin as a neurotransmitter
_____
Geese use serotonin as a neurotransmitter

Osherson et al. (1990) investigated thirteen qualitative patterns concerning how subjects judge the confirmation strength of such inductive arguments. For example, the inference

Robins use serotonin as a neurotransmitter
Bluejays use serotonin as a neurotransmitter
_____
Sparrows use serotonin as a neurotransmitter

was considered stronger than the inference

Robins use serotonin as a neurotransmitter
Bluejays use serotonin as a neurotransmitter
_____
Geese use serotonin as a neurotransmitter

The underlying reason is that robins and bluejays resemble sparrows more than they resemble geese. Relations of similarity are thus important for our judgments of the validity of inductive inferences.

Osherson et al. present different kinds of empirical evidence to support the patterns of confirmation that they have identified. The model they put forward claims that the confirmation assigned to categorical inductive inferences "varies directly with the following two variables: a = the degree to which the premise categories resemble the conclusion category; and b = the degree to which the premise categories resemble the members of the lowest level category that includes both the premise and conclusion categories" (1990: 189–190).

This model is challenged by Sloman (1993). Instead of a category-based model, he proposes a feature-based one. Every category in the inductive arguments is described by a vector of real number from the [0,1] interval. Sloman calls each coordinate of the vector a "feature," but in the present context they may as well be called dimensions. He says that these features "represent a large number of interdependent perceptual and abstract attributes. In general, these values may depend on the context in which categories are presented" (1993: 237).

To explain the patterns of confirmation that were investigated by Osherson et al. (1990), Sloman (1993) develops a connectionist model. Using this model, he is able to explain ten of the previous patterns and three new ones, not treated by Osherson et al. He also presents empirical support for the new patterns. According to Sloman's model, the strength of an inductive argument can be determined as the proportion of features in the conclusion category that are also included in the premise categories. In the simplest case there is only one premise "All Ps are Q" and a conclusion of the form "All Cs are Q." The premise category P can be represented by a vector $F(P)$ of feature values and the conclusion category C by a corresponding vector $F(C)$. In the single-premise case of Sloman's model, the strength of the inductive argument is measured by the value $F(P) \cdot F(C)/|F(C)|^2$, where $F(P) \cdot F(C)$ can be seen as a measure of the overlap of the features of P and C and $|F(C)|^2$ a measure of the magnitude of the conclusion category vector.[8] The strength of the inductive argument is thus measured as the *similarity* between the premise and the conclusion category. Hence, Sloman's connectionist model could be replaced by a similarity measure in a conceptual

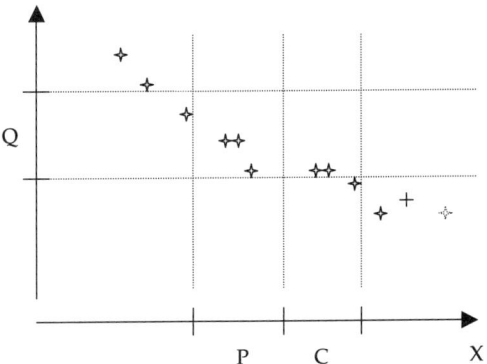

Figure 5. Projections of properties onto domains.

space covering the dimensions of the feature vector.

The results concerning category-based induction show that humans have powerful abilities to handle multiple correlations between different domains, which accords with the discussion at the end of Section 5 (Heit 2000). In the theory of conceptual spaces, this kind of inductive process corresponds to determining *mappings* between the different domains of a space. Using such a mapping, one can then determine correlations between the regions of different domains, by looking at the *projections* of objects onto the domains. Since all objects in Figure 5 that are projected onto the P-region in dimension X are projected onto the Q-region of the dimension Y, "all Ps are Q" is valid. Now if property C on the X dimension is close to (similar to) P, then it is likely that all Cs are Q too.

7. Nonmonotonic Reasoning with Concepts

In this section, the theory of conceptual spaces will be applied to outline explanations for the different kinds of nonmonotonic features of concepts that were presented in Section 3. In the concluding section, I shall then point out some relations between inductive and nonmonotonic reasoning.

(a) *Change from General Category to Subordinate*

A first observation is that describing properties as convex regions of conceptual spaces fits very well with the so-called *prototype theory* of categorization developed by Rosch and her collaborators (Rosch 1975, 1978; Mervis and Rosch 1981; Lakoff 1987). The main idea of prototype theory is that, within a category of objects, certain members are judged to be more representative of the category than others. For example robins are judged to be more representative of the category *bird* than are ravens, penguins and emus; and desk chairs are more typical instances of the category *chair* than rocking chairs, deck chairs, and beanbags. The most representative members of a category are called *prototypical* members. It is well known that some properties, like *red* and *bald* have no sharp boundaries and for these it is perhaps not surprising that one finds prototypical effects. However, these effects have been found for most properties including those with comparatively clear boundaries like *bird* and *chair*.

If concepts are described as convex regions of a conceptual space, prototype effects of reasoning are indeed to be expected. In a convex region one can describe positions as being more or less *central*. For example, if color concepts are identified with convex subsets of the color space, the central points of these regions would be the most prototypical examples of the color.

Subordinate concepts may move away from the prototypes of the general concept and thus result in atypical properties. Here the representation of concepts as convex regions in a conceptual space may be useful. If the first thing I ever hear about the individual Gonzo is that it is a bird, I will naturally locate it in the conceptual space as a more or less prototypical bird, that is, at the center of the region representing birds. (The relevant conceptual space may be something like a many-dimensional hierarchical space of coordinates in the style of Marr and Nishihara 1978.) And in that area of the conceptual space, birds do fly, that is, almost all individuals located there also have the ability to fly. However, if I then learn that Gonzo is an emu, I must *revise* my earlier concept location and put Gonzo in the emu region, which is a subset of the bird region but presumably lies at the outskirts of that region. And in the emu region of the conceptual space almost none of the individuals fly. This form of reasoning can thus be described as a *relocation* of an object in a conceptual space.

This simple example only hints at how the *correlation* between different parts of a region representing a property and regions representing other properties can be used in understanding nonmonotonic reasoning. For this analysis, the spatial structure of properties is essential. Such correlations will only be formulated in an *ad hoc* manner if a propositional representation of information is used where the spatial structure cannot be utilized.

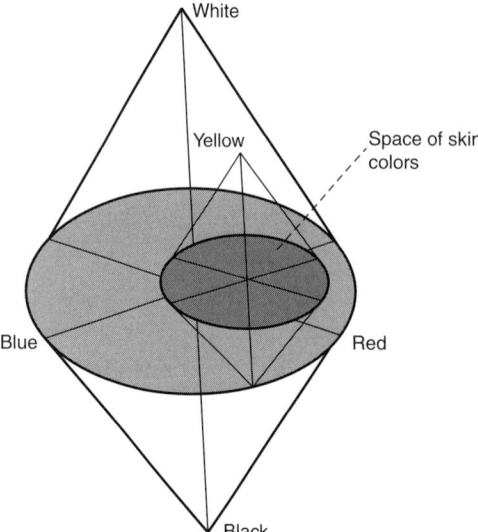

White
Yellow
Space of skin colors
Blue
Red
Black

Figure 6. The subspace of skin colors embedded in the full color spindle.

(b) Contrast Classes

I have proposed that properties correspond to connected regions of a conceptual space. However, as was noticed in Section 3, a word like "red" has many uses that can result in nonmonotonic inferences: red book, red wine, red hair, red skin, red soil, redwood, etc. "Red book" accords with the dictionary definition, but the other uses don't fit with the standard color region assigned to red. How can we then explain that the same word is used in so many different contexts?

I don't see how this phenomenon can be analyzed in a simple way using the symbolic or subconceptual approaches. However, the idea of a contrast class can quite easily be given a general interpretation with the aid of conceptual spaces. For each domain, for example skin colors, we can map out the class of possible colors on the color spindle. This mapping will determine a subset of the full color space. The shape of this subset may be rather irregular. However, if the subset is embedded in a space with the *same dimensional structure* as the full space we obtain a picture that looks like Figure 6.

In this smaller spindle, the color words are then used in the same way as in the full space, even if the hues of the color in the smaller space don't match the hues of the complete space. Thus, *white* is used about the lightest forms of skin, even though white skin is pinkish, *black* refers to the darkest form of skin, even though black skin is brown, and so on. The embeddings into smaller conceptual spaces will natu-

rally result in nonmonotonic effects. For example, from the fact that x is a white wine, one cannot conclude that x is a white object, even though *person* is subordinate to *object*. This analysis of contrast classes is presented in greater detail in Gärdenfors (2000).

(c) Metaphors

Metaphors have been notoriously difficult to handle within traditional semantic theories, let alone first order logic. In contrast, they are given key positions within cognitive semantics. Not only poetic metaphors but also everyday "dead" metaphors are seen as central semantic features and are given systematic analyses. One of the first works in this area was Lakoff and Johnson (1980).

In Gärdenfors (2000), I have proposed an analysis of metaphors within the theory of conceptual spaces. The core hypothesis is that *a metaphor expresses a similarity in topological or metrical structure between different quality dimensions*. A concept that corresponds to a particular structure in one quality dimension can be used as a metaphor to express a similar structure about another dimension. In this way one can account for how a metaphor can *transfer knowledge* about one conceptual dimension to another.

As a simple example, let us consider the expression "the peak of a career." The literal meaning of *peak* refers to a structure in physical space, namely the vertically highest point in a horizontally extended (large) object, typically a mountain. This structure thus presumes two spatial dimensions, one horizontal and one vertical (see Figure 7a).

A career is an abstract entity without location in space. So how can a career have a *peak*? I submit that when we metaphorically talk about the peak of a career the same geometrical structure is applied to a two-dimensional space that consists of the *time* dimension (of the career) and a dimension of *social status* (see Figure 7b). The latter dimension is normally conceived of as being vertical: we talk about somebody having a "higher" rank, "climbing" in the hierarchy, and so on (see Lakoff and Johnson 1980).

It can now be seen that the role of different contrast classes for the same concept, as described earlier, is closely related to that of metaphorical uses of a word. A metaphor expresses a similarity in topological or geometrical structure between *different* quality dimensions. Now, in the case of contrast classes, one set of dimensions is not really mapped onto a

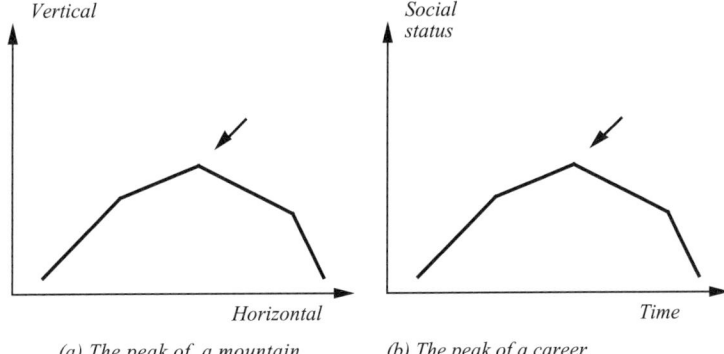

(a) The peak of a mountain   *(b) The peak of a career*

Figure 7. The literal and a metaphorical meaning of "peak."

different set, but it is mapped onto a *subspace* of itself retaining the same topological structure.

(d) Context Effects

The main effect of applying a concept in a particular context is that certain dimensions of the concept are put into focus by the context. In relation to the model given in the previous section, this means that the context determines the *relative saliency* of the dimensions. For example, in a context of moving furniture, the weight dimension becomes highly salient. Hence, the concept *piano* may lead to an inference of *heavy*. In contrast, in a context of musical instruments, the weight dimension is much less salient and an application of the concept *piano* will probably not become associated with *heavy* (Barclay et al. 1974).

Another effect of changes in context is that change in saliency of certain dimensions may result in a shift of the *borders* between different concepts. As was seen in Section 3, once the functionality was put in focus in Labov's study of the concept *cup*, the border between *cup* and *bowl* changed considerably. Such changes of borders naturally lead to nonmonotonic effects when the concepts are applied in different contexts.

As a matter of fact, also the nonmonotonic effects of contrast classes discussed above can be seen as a context effect. By introducing a concept like *skin* or *wine*, a context is set up in which the contrast class of the objects falling under the concept is focused. Hence it is quite natural that the application of, for example, color concepts become restricted to the contrast class.

When analyzed on the symbolic level, nonmonotonic reasoning has concerned the class of logical *rules* that are valid (Gabbay et al.

1993; Gärdenfors and Makinson 1994). However, when transformed into representations in conceptual spaces one finds several different kinds of processes that produce nonmonotonic features when described symbolically. The conclusion is that nonmonotonic inferences cannot be seen as a unified type of reasoning, but must be broken down into different kinds of processes, as has been argued in this section.

Fodor (1998) criticizes the use of conceptual spaces (vector spaces) to model concepts where "the similarity between your concepts and mine is expressed by the positions in our respective spaces" (1998: 33). He continues:

> Suppose, in particular that it is constitutive of the difference between our NIXON concepts that you think Nixon was even more of a crook than I do. Once again, a robust notion of content identity is presupposed since each of our spaces is required to have a dimension that expresses crookedness; a fortiori, both are required to have dimensions which express degrees of the *very same property*. [. . .] You and I can argue about whether Nixon was merely crooked or very crooked only if the concept of *being crooked* is one that we have in common. (Fodor 1998: 33–34, italics in original)

First of all it should be noticed that Fodor here uses "concept" to denote also what I would classify as individuals (Nixon) and dimensions (crookedness), which complicates the picture. I believe that distinguishing between individuals, properties, concepts and dimensions, as is done in the theory of conceptual spaces, helps in clearing up a lot of meta-conceptual confusion.

Secondly, on my account it is possible to have the same concepts even if we do not have the same underlying dimensions. It is sufficient that our conceptual spaces partition the world in the same way. Let me give a slightly artificial example to show this: Suppose my classification of *rectangles* is based on the dimensions "length" and "width," while yours is based on "area" and "side proportion." So I represent a particular rectangle by the vector <6,3> while you represent the same rectangle as <18,2>. Even though we use different "properties" in Fodor's sense to classify and identify rectangles, we will nevertheless be in perfect agreement in our communication about the objects. Thus, in contrast to what Fodor claims, the "Publicity constraint" that he puts forward does not entail that we have to sort the world according to identical diemensions.

Thirdly, Fodor also argues that vector space based concepts cannot account for the compositionality of concepts. The best way of countering his argument is to present such an account, which I do in Gärdenfors (2000: Sec. 4.4). The role of contrast classes as discussed above is a special case of this theory.

8. Conclusion

The aim of this chapter has been to present various aspects of inductive and nonmonotonic reasoning about concepts. I have distinguished between three levels of representing reasoning and outlined a theory of conceptual spaces as a tool for representing reasoning on the conceptual level. The theory emphasizes *topological* and *geometrical* structures rather than logical and symbolic. The theory of conceptual spaces provides a viable framework for analyzing various aspects of reasoning about concepts. In particular, it can be used to explain different kinds of inductive and nonmonotonic reasoning. I have aimed at showing that the theory provides better and richer tools for this purpose than do symbolic or connectionist models.

The theory also allows us to elucidate the relationship between inductive and nonmonotonic reasoning. As I have argued in Section 6, inductive reasoning concerns *establishing* the correlations between properties from different domains that are part of concept representations. And in Section 7, I have shown that nonmonotonic reasoning concerns *using* such correlations for various kinds of default conclusions. Thus both types of reasoning processes depend on correlations between properties in different domains. Such correlations also form the basis for our *expectations*. There is much more to learn

about how humans discover such correlations in their inductive reasoning and in what way the correlations are exploited in everyday reasoning, nonmonotonic or not. Nevertheless, I believe that describing these processes on the conceptual level is helpful in bringing out the relations between these kinds of reasoning.

However, the geometric models used in the descriptions of conceptual spaces can also be used in technical applications of reasoning. In particular, the efforts to develop a Semantic Web would benefit from using representations on the conceptual level as I have argued in Gärdenfors (2004). The program I propose there involves a radical shift in focus of what meta-data should be added to the Web. In the current Semantic Web, the information mainly concerns taxonomies and inference rules that are expressed by symbolic information. If conceptual spaces are used as a foundational methodology, the focus will be on describing *domain structures*. This involves, above all, specifying the geometric and topological structure of the domains. Describing domains will require a different programming methodology compared to what exists in the current web languages. Once the relevant information about domain structure and concepts becomes available, the taxonomies that have been in focus of the current Semantic Web will emerge from the domain structure and the symbolic inference mechanism will become more or less superfluous. The type of representing information suggested by conceptual spaces require computations involving vectors, using reasoning based on similarities, rather than inference mechanisms based on tree searching in a rule-based symbolic approach.

Notes

1 Some aspects of reasoning about categories are presented in Gärdenfors and Williams (2001).
2 One notable exception is Shapere (1982).
3 For a presentation of the theory of prototypes, see, for example, Rosch (1975, 1978), Mervis and Rosch (1981), Lakoff (1987).
4 I cannot talk about three ways of *describing* observations, because the very notion of "describing" presumes the linguistic level.
5 See Gabbay et al. (1993) for a survey of some of the research areas. In Balkenius and Gärdenfors (1991), nonmonotonic reasoning is connected to representations in artificial neuron networks and in Gärdenfors and Makinson (1994), it is connected to expectation structures.
6 For an analysis of functional aspects of concepts see Gärdenfors (2007).

7   Garcia and Koelling (1966) showed that rats can quickly learn correlations between domains (as, for example, a particular kind of food and sickness) if the connection between the domains has some *ecological validity*. Without such a correlation the rats perform very poorly. Presumably, similar mechanisms operate in humans.

8   $F(P) \cdot F(C)$ is the *inner product* of the two vectors, defined as $\sum_i F(P)_i \cdot F(C)_i$ and $|F(C)|^2$ is the inner product of $F(C)$ with itself, defined as $\sum_i F(P)_i^2$.

References

C. Balkenius and P. Gärdenfors (1991): "Nonmonotonic inferences in neural networks," in *Principles of Knowledge Representation and Reasoning: Proceedings of the Second International Conference*, J. A. Allen, R. Fikes and E. Sandewall, eds., Morgan Kaufmann, San Mateo, CA, 32–39.

J. R. Barclay, J. D. Bransford, J. J. Franks, N. S. McCarrell and K. Nitsch (1974): "Comprehension and semantic flexibility," *Journal of Verbal Learning and Verbal Behavior 13*, 471–481.

L. W. Barsalou (1987): "The instability of graded structure: Implications for the nature of concepts," in *Concepts and Conceptual Development*, U. Neisser, ed., Cambridge University Press, Cambridge, 101–140.

L. W. Barsalou (1992): "Flexibility, structure, and linguistic vagary in concepts: Manifestations of a compositional system of perceptual symbols," in *Theories of Memory*, A. F. Collins, S. E. Gathercole, M. A. Conway, and P. E. Morris, eds., Lawrence Erlbaum Associates, Hillsdale, NJ, 29–89.

B. Berlin and P. Kay (1969): *Basic Color Terms: Their Universality and Evolution*. University of California Press: Berkeley, CA.

D. O. Billman (1983): *Procedures for Learning Syntactic Structure: A Model and West with Artificial Grammars*, doctoral dissertation, University of Michigan.

D. O. Billman and J. Knutson (1996): "Unsupervised concept learning and value systematicity: A complex whole aids learning the parts," *Journal of Experimental Psychology: Learning, Memory and Cognition 22*, 458–475.

S. Broström (1994): *The Role of Metaphor in Cognitive Semantics*, Lund University Cognitive Studies 31, Lund.

R. Carnap (1950): *Logical Foundations of Probability*, Chicago University Press, Chicago.

R. Carnap (1971): "A basic system of inductive logic, Part 1," in Carnap, R. and Jeffrey, R. C., eds., *Studies in Inductive Logics and Probability, Vol. 1*, University of California Press, Berkeley, CA, 35–165.

J. A. Fodor (1975): *The Language of Thought*, Harvard University Press, Cambridge, MA.

J. A. Fodor (1981): *Representations*, MIT Press, Cambridge, MA.

J. A. Fodor (1998): *Concepts: Where Cognitive Science Went Wrong*, Clarendon Press, Oxford.

D. Gabbay, C. J. Hogger, and J. A. Robinson, eds. (1993): *Handbook of Logic in Artificial Intelligence and Logic Programming, Volume III: Non-Monotonic and Uncertain Reasoning*, Oxford University Press, Oxford.

J. Garcia and R. A. Koelling (1966): "Relation of cue to consequences in avoidance learning," *Psychonomic Science 4*, 123–124.

P. Gärdenfors (1988): *Knowledge in Flux*, MIT Press, Cambridge, MA.

P. Gärdenfors (1990a): "Induction, conceptual spaces and AI," *Philosophy of Science 57*, 78–95.

P. Gärdenfors (1990b): "Frameworks for properties: Possible worlds vs. conceptual spaces," in *Language, Knowledge and Intentionality*, L. Haaparanta, M. Kusch, and I. Niiniluoto, eds. (*Acta Philosophica Fennica, 49*), 383–407.

P. Gärdenfors (1992): "A geometric model of concept formation," in *Information Modelling and Knowledge Bases III*, S. Ohsuga et al., eds., IOS Press, Amsterdam, 1–16.

P. Gärdenfors (1993): "Induction and the evolution of conceptual spaces," in *Charles S. Peirce and the Philosophy of Science*, E. C. Moore, ed., The University of Alabama Press, Tuscaloosa, 72–88.

P. Gärdenfors (1994): "Three levels of inductive inference," in *Logic, Methodology, and Philosophy of Science IX*, D. Prawitz, B. Skyrms and D. Westersthl, eds., Elsevier Science, Amsterdam, 427–449.

P. Gärdenfors (2000): *Conceptual Spaces: The Geometry of Thought*, Cambridge, MA, MIT Press.

P. Gärdenfors (2004): "How to make the Semantic Web more semantic," pp. 19–36 in *Formal Ontology in Information Systems*, ed. by A. C. Varzi and L. Vieu, IOS Press.

P. Gärdenfors (2007): "Representing actions and functional properties in conceptual spaces," in *Body, Language and Mind*, T. Ziemke and J. Zlatev, eds., Benjamins, Amsterdam, 167–195.

P. Gärdenfors and D. Makinson (1994): "Nonmonotonic inference based on expectations," *Artificial Intelligence 65*, 197–245.

P. Gärdenfors and M.-A. Williams (2001): "Reasoning about categories in conceptual spaces," *Proceedings of IJCAI 2001*, Morgan Kaufmann, Palo Alto, 385–392.

W. R. Garner (1974): *The Processing of Information and Structure*, Erlbaum, Potomac, MD.

N. Goodman (1955): *Fact, Fiction, and Forecast*, Harvard University Press, Cambridge, MA.

E. Heit (2000): "Properties of inductive reasoning," *Psychonomic Bulletin and Review 7*, 569–592.

C. G. Hempel (1965): *Aspects of Scientific Explanation, and Other Essays in the Philosophy of Science*, Free Press, New York.

J. H. Holland, K. J. Holyoak, R. E. Nisbett and P. R. Thagard (1986): *Induction: Processes of Inference, Learning, and Discovery*, MIT Press, Cambridge, MA.

K. Holmqvist (1993): *Implementing Cognitive Semantics*, Lund University Cognitive Studies 17, Lund.

G. Jäger and R. van Rooij (2007): "Language structure: Psychological and social constraints," *Synthese 159*, 99–130.

H. Kornblith (1993): *Inductive Inference and Its Natural Ground: An Essay in Naturalistic Epistemology*, MIT Press, Cambridge, MA.

W. Labov (1973): "The boundaries of words and their meanings," in *New Ways of Analyzing Variation in English*, J. Fishman, ed., Georgetown University Press, Washington, DC, 340–373.

G. Lakoff (1987): *Women, Fire, and Dangerous Things*, University of Chicago Press, Chicago.

G. Lakoff and M. Johnson (1980): *Metaphors We Live By*, University of Chicago Press, Chicago.

R. W. Langacker (1987): *Foundations of Cognitive Grammar, Vol. 1*, Stanford University Press, Stanford, CA.

W. T. Maddox (1992): "Perceptual and decisional separability," in *Multidimensional Models of Perception and Cognition*, G. F. Ashby, ed., Lawrence Erlbaum Associates, Hillsdale, NJ, 147–180.

D. Makinson and K. Schlechta (1991): "Floating conclusions and zombie paths: Two deep difficulties in the 'directly skeptical' approach to defeasible inheritance nets," *Artificial Intelligence 48*, 199–209.

D. Marr and H. K. Nishihara (1978): "Representation and recognition of the spatial organization of three-dimensional shapes," *Proceedings of the Royal Society in London, B 200*, 269–294.

R. D. Melara (1992): "The concept of perceptual similarity: From psychophysics to cognitive psychology," in D. Algom, editor, *Psychophysical Approaches to Cognition*, Elsevier, Amsterdam, 1992, 303–388.

C. Mervis and E. Rosch (1981): "Categorization of natural objects," *Annual Review of Psychology 32*, 89–115.

T. Mormann (1993): "Natural predicates and the topological structure of conceptual spaces," *Synthese 95*, 219–240.

R. E. Nisbett and L. Ross (1980): *Human Inference: Strategies and Shortcomings of Social Judgement*, Prentice-Hall, Englewood Cliffs, NJ.

R. Nolan (1994): *Cognitive Practices: Human Language and Human Knowledge*, Blackwell, Oxford.

D. N. Osherson, E. E. Smith, O. Wilkie, A. López, and E. Shafir (1990): "Category-based induction," *Psychological Review 97*, 185–200.

S. E. Palmer (1978): "Fundamental aspects of cognitive representation," in *Cognition and Categorization*, E. Rosch and B. B. Lloyd, eds., Lawrence Erlbaum Associates, Hillsdale, NJ, 259–303.

C. S. Peirce (1932): *Collected Pappers of Charles Sanders Peirce, volume II, Elements of Logic*. C. Hartshorne and P. Weiss, eds., Harvard University Press, Cambridge, MA.

Z. Pylyshyn (1984): *Computation and Cognition*, MIT Press, Cambridge, MA.

W. v. O. Quine (1969): "Natural kinds," in *Ontological Relativity and Other Essays*, Columbia University Press, New York, 114–138.

R. Reiter (1980): "A logic for default reasoning," *Artificial Intelligence 13*, 81–132.

L. Rips (2001): "Necessity and natural categories," *Psychological Bulletin 127*, 827–852.

E. Rosch (1975): "Cognitive representations of semantic categories," *Journal of Experimental Psychology: General 104*, 192–233.

E. Rosch (1978): "Prototype classification and logical classification: The two systems," in *New Trends in Cognitive Representation: Challenges to Piaget's Theory*, E. Scholnik, ed., Lawrence Erlbaum Associates, Hillsdale, NJ, 73–86.

D. E. Rumelhart and J. L. McClelland (1986): *Parallel Distributed Processing*, Vols. 1 and 2, MIT Press, Cambridge, MA.

H. R. Schiffman (1982): *Sensation and Perception*, 2nd ed., John Wiley and Sons, New York.

D. Shapere (1982): "The concept of observation in science and philosophy," *Philosophy of Science 49*, 485–525.

S. A. Sloman (1993): "Feature-based induction," *Cognitive Psychology 25*, 231–280.

E. E. Smith and D. L. Medin (1981): *Categories and Concepts*, Harvard University Press, Cambridge, MA.

E. E. Smith, D. N. Osherson, L. J. Rips, and M. Keane (1988): "Combining prototypes: A selective modification model," *Cognitive Science 12*, 485–527.

P. Smolensky (1988): "On the proper treatment of connectionism," *Behavioral and Brain Sciences 11*, 1–23.

D. S. Touretsky (1986): *The Mathematics of Inheritance Systems*, Morgan Kaufmann, Los Altos, CA.

L. Vaina (1983): "From shapes and movements to objects and actions," *Synthese 54*, 3–36.

Chapter 17: Category-Based Induction

DANIEL N. OSHERSON, EDWARD E. SMITH, ORMOND WILKIE, ALEJANDRO LÓPEZ, AND ELDAR SHAFIR

The Problem of Argument Strength

Fundamental to human thought is the confirmation relation, joining sentences $P_1 \ldots P_n$ to another sentence C just in case belief in the former leads to belief in the latter. Theories of confirmation may be cast in the terminology of argument strength, because $P_1 \ldots P_n$ confirm C only to the extent that $P_1 \ldots P_n/C$ is a strong argument. We here advance a partial theory of argument strength, hence of confirmation.

To begin, it will be useful to review the terminology of argument strength. By an *argument* is meant a finite list of sentences, the last of which is called the *conclusion* and the others its *premises*. Schematic arguments are written in the form $P_1 \ldots P_n/C$, whereas real arguments are written vertically, as in the following examples:

Grizzly bears love onions.
Polar bears love onions.

All bears love onions. (1)

Owls prey on small rodents. (2)

Rattlesnakes prey on small rodents.

An argument A is said to be *strong* for a person S just in case S's believing A's premises causes S to believe A's conclusion. Mere belief in the conclusion of an argument (independently of its premises) is not sufficient for argument strength. For this reason, Argument 1 is stronger than Argument 2 for most people, even though the conclusion of Argument 2 is usually considered more probable than that of Argument 1. An extended discussion of the concept of argument

strength is provided in Osherson, Smith, and Shafir (1986). It will be convenient to qualify an argument as strong, without reference to a particular person S, whenever the argument is strong for most people in a target population (e.g., American college students). We also say that $P_1 \ldots P_n$ confirm C if $P_1 \ldots P_n/C$ is strong.

An illuminating characterization of argument strength would represent a long step toward a theory of belief fixation and revision. Unfortunately, no general theory is yet in sight, and even partial theories are often open to elementary counterexamples (see Osherson et al., 1986). This article offers a hypothesis about the strength of a restricted set of arguments, exemplified by Arguments 1 and 2. The premises and conclusions of such arguments attribute a fixed property (e.g., *preys on small rodents*) to one or more categories (e.g., OWL and RATTLESNAKE).[1] The present study focuses on the role of categories in confirmation; the role of properties is not systematically investigated. In this sense, the model we advance concerns induction that is category based.

Category-based induction was first examined by Rips (1975). He studied the strength of single-premise arguments involving categories such as RABBIT and MOUSE, or EAGLE and BLUE-JAY. The present investigation builds on one of the models that Rips discusses and applies it to a larger class of arguments.

Our discussion proceeds as follows. After defining the class of arguments to be considered in this article, and introducing some relevant terminology, we document a set of 13 qualitative phenomena that must be deduced by any

Reproduced with permission from Osherson, D. N., Smith, E. E., Wilkie, O., López, A., and Shafir, E. (1990) Category-based induction. *Psychological Review*, 97, 185–200.

adequate theory of argument strength. Our own theory is then presented and shown to account for all of the phenomena. Next, we describe several experiments designed to test the theory quantitatively. Refinements and alternatives to the theory are discussed in the final section.

Arguments To Be Considered

An argument is called *categorical* just in case its premises and conclusion have the logical form *all members of X have property Y*, where X is a (psychologically) simple category like FALCON, VEHICLE, or MAMMAL, and, Y remains fixed across premises and conclusion. Arguments 1 and 2 are categorical in this sense. The arguments discussed in this article are all categorical.

The property ascribed to the categories figuring in Argument 1 is *loves onions*. Subjects are likely to have prior beliefs about the kinds of animals that love onions, as well as prior beliefs about properties that are correlated with this one, such as *eats a wide variety of fruits and vegetables*. Beliefs such as these can be expected to weigh heavily on argument strength, defeating our goal of focusing on the role of categories in the transmission of belief from premises to conclusions. For this reason, the arguments to be examined all involve predicates about which subjects in our experiments have few beliefs, such as *requires biotin for hemoglobin synthesis*. Such predicates are called *blank*. Although blank predicates are recognizably scientific in character (in the latter case, biological), they are unlikely to evoke beliefs that cause one argument to have more strength than another.

In summary, the theories discussed below bear on categorical arguments involving natural kinds and blank predicates. An example of such an argument is

Mosquitoes use the neurotransmitter Dihedron.
Ants use the neurotransmitter Dihedron.

Bees use the neurotransmitter Dihedron.

$$(3)$$

Henceforth, the term *argument* is to be understood in the foregoing sense.

Terminology and Notation

We assume that subjects (and experimenters) largely agree with each other about facts related to the hierarchical level of natural-kind concepts. To illustrate, wide agreement is presupposed about the following judgments:

1. FALCON and PELICAN are at the same hierarchical level;

2. BIRD is one level above both FALCON and PELICAN; and

3. ANIMAL is one level above BIRD.

We cannot presuppose universal agreement about such levels. For example, some subjects might take BIRD-OF-PREY to be one level above EAGLE, whereas others (who make fewer distinctions) might take BIRD to be one level above EAGLE. This kind of individual difference about fine-grained categories will be harmless in what follows. It is sufficient that agreement exists about salient categories such as EAGLE, BIRD, and ANIMAL.

Recall that all premises and conclusions to be discussed have the form *all members of X have property Y*. Given such a premise P or conclusion C, we denote the category that figures in P or C by CAT(P) or CAT(C). Thus, if P is the first premise of Argument 1 above, then CAT(P) = GRIZZLY BEAR. If C is the conclusion of Argument 3, then CAT(C) = BEE.

Let Argument $A = P_1 \ldots P_n/C$ be given. A is called *general* if CAT(P_1) \ldots CAT(P_n) are all properly included in CAT(C). For example, Argument 1 is general. A is called *specific* if any category that properly includes one of CAT(P_1) \ldots CAT(P_n), CAT(C) also properly includes the others. For example, Argument 3 is specific. By this definition, no argument is both general and specific. A is called *mixed* if A is neither general nor specific. The following argument is mixed:

Flamingoes require titanium for normal muscle development.
Mice require titanium for normal muscle development.

All mammals require titanium for normal muscle development.

$$(4)$$

Argument 4 is not general because FLAMINGO is not included in MAMMAL. It is not specific because BIRD properly includes FLAMINGO but not MOUSE or MAMMAL. Argument 2 is also mixed.

Phenomena

General Remarks

Even within the restricted class of arguments at issue in this article, a variety of phenomena can be discerned that must be accounted for by any adequate theory of category-based induction. Each phenomenon signals the importance of a given variable in argument strength when other variables are held more or less constant. The phenomena should thus be conceived as tendencies rather than strict laws determining confirmation. We now present 13 such phenomena and illustrate each with a contrasting pair of arguments. The first argument in each pair is claimed to be stronger than the second, in conformity with the phenomenon that the pair illustrates. At the end of this section, we describe a study that empirically documents all of these claims about relative argument strength.

Phenomena Concerning General Arguments

Let general argument $P_1 \ldots P_n/C$ be given.

PHENOMENON 1 (PREMISE TYPICALITY)

The more representative or typical $\text{CAT}(P_1) \ldots \text{CAT}(P_n)$ are of $\text{CAT}(C)$, the more $P_1 \ldots P_n$ confirm C. Because robins are more typical than penguins of BIRD, this phenomenon is illustrated by the following pair of arguments:

Robins have a higher potassium concentration in their blood than humans.

All birds have a higher potassium concentration in their blood than humans.

(5a)

Penguins have a higher potassium concentration in their blood than humans.

All birds have a higher potassium concentration in their blood than humans.

(5b)

The foregoing arguments have single premises. Multiple-premise illustrations of the same point are easy to construct. A premise typicality effect for social categories has been reported by Rothbart and Lewis (1988, see also Collins and Michalski 1989).

PHENOMENON 2 (PREMISE DIVERSITY)

The less similar $\text{CAT}(P_1) \ldots \text{CAT}(P_n)$ are among themselves, the more $P_1 \ldots P_n$ confirm C. Thus, since hippos and hamsters differ from each other more than do hippos and rhinos, the following arguments illustrate the premise diversity phenomenon:

Hippopotamuses have a higher sodium concentration in their blood than humans.

Hamsters have a higher sodium concentration in their blood than humans.

All mammals have a higher sodium concentration in their blood than humans.

(6a)

Hippopotamuses have a higher sodium concentration in their blood than humans.

Rhinoceroses have a higher sodium concentration in their blood than humans.

All mammals have a higher sodium concentration in their blood than humans.

(6b)

Observe that Argument 6a is stronger than Argument 6b even though hamsters are less typical than rhinoceroses of MAMMAL. Thus, the greater diversity of the premise categories in Argument 6a outweighs the greater typicality of the premise categories in Argument 6b.

PHENOMENON 3 (CONCLUSION SPECIFICITY)

The more specific is $\text{CAT}(C)$, the more C is confirmed by $P_1 \ldots P_n$. Thus, because BIRDS is a more specific category than ANIMAL, this phenomenon is illustrated by the following pair of arguments:

Bluejays require Vitamin K for the liver to function.

Falcons require Vitamin K for the liver to function.

All birds require Vitamin K for the liver to function.

(7a)

Bluejays require Vitamin K for the liver to function.

Falcons require Vitamin K for the liver to function.

All animals require Vitamin K for the liver to function.

(7b)

A phenomenon related to conclusion specificity is reported by Gelman (1988, p. 78) in a developmental study.

PHENOMENON 4 (PREMISE MONOTONICITY)

For general arguments, more inclusive sets of premises yield more strength than less inclusive sets. The following pair of arguments illustrates this kind of monotonicity:

Hawks have sesamoid bones.
Sparrows have sesamoid bones.
Eagles have sesamoid bones.
_____
All birds have sesamoid bones.

(8a)

Sparrows have sesamoid bones.
Eagles have sesamoid bones.
_____
All birds have sesamoid bones.

(8b)

Premise monotonicity has been investigated by Carey (1985).

Phenomena Concerning Specific Arguments

Let specific argument $P_1 \ldots P_n/C$ be given.

PHENOMENON 5 (PREMISE–CONCLUSION SIMILARITY)

The more similar $\text{CAT}(P_1) \ldots \text{CAT}(P_n)$ are to $\text{CAT}(C)$, the more $P_1 \ldots P_n$ confirm C. Because robins and bluejays resemble sparrows more than they resemble geese, this phenomenon is illustrated by the following pair of arguments:

Robins use serotonin as a neurotransmitter.
Bluejays use serotonin as a neurotransmitter.
_____
Sparrows use serotonin as a neurotransmitter.

(9a)

Robins use serotonin as a neurotransmitter.
Bluejays use serotonin as a neurotransmitter.
_____
Geese use serotonin as a neurotransmitter.

(9b)

The present phenomenon was originally reported by Rips (1975) for single-premise arguments (see also Collins and Michalski 1989).

PHENOMENON 6 (PREMISE DIVERSITY)

The less similar $\text{CAT}(P_1) \ldots \text{CAT}(P_n)$ are among themselves, the more $P_1 \ldots P_n$ confirm C. Illustration is provided by the following pair inasmuch as lions are less similar to giraffes than than they are to tigers.

Lions use norepinephrine as a neurotransmitter.
Giraffes use norepinephrine as a neurotransmitter.
_____
Rabbits use norepinephrine as a neurotransmitter.

(10a)

Lions use norepinephrine as a neurotransmitter.
Tigers use norepinephrine as a neurotransmitter.
_____
Rabbits use norepinephrine as a neurotransmitter.

(10b)

Phenomenon 6 corresponds to Phenomenon 2 for general arguments. Observe that Argument 10a is stronger than Argument 10b even though giraffes resemble rabbits no more than do tigers.

PHENOMENON 7 (PREMISE MONOTONICITY)

More inclusive sets of premises yield more strength than less inclusive sets, provided that the new premise is drawn from the lowest level category that includes the old premises and conclusion. The following pair of arguments illustrates this kind of monotonicity.

Foxes use Vitamin K to produce clotting agents in their blood.
Pigs use Vitamin K to produce clotting agents in their blood.
Wolves use Vitamin K to produce clotting agents in their blood.
_____
Gorillas use Vitamin K to produce clotting agents in their blood.

(11a)

Pigs use Vitamin K to produce clotting agents in their blood.
Wolves use Vitamin K to produce clotting agents in their blood.
_____
Gorillas use Vitamin K to produce clotting agents in their blood.

(11b)

PHENOMENON 8 (PREMISE–CONCLUSION ASYMMETRY)

Single-premise arguments are not symmetric, in the sense that P/C may not have the same strength as C/P. This kind of asymmetry is illustrated by the following pair of arguments:

Mice have a lower body temperature at infancy than at maturity.
_____
Bats have a lower body temperature at infancy than at maturity.

(12a)

Bats have a lower body temperature at infancy than at maturity.
_____
Mice have a lower body temperature at infancy than at maturity.

(12b)

Premise–conclusion asymmetry was first discussed by Rips (1975).

Phenomena Concerning Mixed Arguments

PHENOMENON 9 (NONMONOTONICITY, GENERAL)

Some general arguments can be made weaker by adding a premise that converts them into mixed arguments. This kind of nonmonotonicity is illustrated by the following contrast:

Crows secrete uric acid crystals.
Peacocks secrete uric acid crystals.
$\overline{\text{All birds secrete uric acid crystals.}}$ (13a)

Crows secrete uric acid crystals.
Peacocks secrete uric acid crystals.
Rabbits secrete uric acid crystals.
$\overline{\text{All birds secrete uric acid crystals.}}$ (13b)

PHENOMENON 10 (NONMONOTONICITY, SPECIFIC)

Some specific arguments can be made weaker by adding a premise that converts them into mixed arguments. This kind of nonmonotonicity is illustrated as follows.

Flies require trace amounts of magnesium for reproduction.
$\overline{\hspace{3cm}}$
Bees require trace amounts of magnesium for reproduction. (14a)

Flies require trace amounts of magnesium for reproduction.
Orangutans require trace amounts of magnesium for reproduction.
$\overline{\hspace{3cm}}$
Bees require trace amounts of magnesium for reproduction. (14b)

A Phenomenon Involving Both General and Specific Arguments

PHENOMENON 11 (INCLUSION FALLACY)

A specific argument can sometimes be made stronger by increasing the generality of its conclusion. Because BIRD includes OSTRICH, this phenomenon is illustrated as follows:

Robins have an ulnar artery.
$\overline{\text{Birds have an ulnar artery.}}$ (15a)

Robins have an ulnar artery.
$\overline{\text{Ostriches have an ulnar artery.}}$ (15b)

The choice of Argument 15a as stronger than Argument 15b is counternormative and may be termed an *inclusion fallacy*. For discussion and analysis of inclusion fallacies in another context, see Shafir, Smith, and Osherson (in press).

Two Limiting-Case Phenomena

The last two phenomena to be discussed have an evident character, and no data are needed for their documentation.

PHENOMENON 12 (PREMISE–CONCLUSION IDENTITY)

Any argument of the form Q/Q is perfectly strong. One such argument is as follows:

Pelicans have property Y.
$\overline{\text{Pelicans have property Y.}}$ (16)

PHENOMENON 13 (PREMISE–CONCLUSION INCLUSION)

Suppose that statements P and C are such that the conclusion category is included in the premise category. Then the argument P/C is perfectly strong. For example:

All animals have property Y.
$\overline{\text{All birds have property Y.}}$ (17)

Table 1 summarizes all 13 phenomena.

Empirical Documentation of Phenomena 1–11

Two studies were performed to empirically document Phenomena 1–11. In Study 1, subjects were presented a 12-page booklet. The first page contained instructions, and each of the following pages contained one of the contrasting pairs of arguments used above to illustrate Phenomena 1–11. The instructions were as follows:

> We are interested in how people evaluate arguments. On each page of your booklet there will be two arguments labeled "a" and "b." Each will contain one, two, or three statements separated from a conclusion by a line. Assume that the statements above the line are facts, and choose the argument whose facts provide a better reason for believing its conclusion. These are subjective judgments; there are no right or wrong answers.

On each subsequent page, the contrasting pair of arguments was arranged vertically; across all subjects each argument appeared equally

Table 1: Summary of the 13 Phenomena

Phenomenon	Stronger Argument (Version a)	Weaker Argument (Version b)
General arguments		
1. Premise Typicality	ROBIN/BIRD [73]	PENGUIN/BIRD [7]
2. Premise Diversity	HIPPO, HAMSTER/MAMMAL [59]	HIPPO, RHINO/MAMMAL [21]
3. Conclusion Specificity	BLUEJAY, FALCON/BIRD [75]	BLUEJAY, FALCON/ANIMAL [5]
4. Premise Monotonicity	HAWK, SPARROW/EAGLE/BIRD [75]	SPARROW/EAGLE/BIRD [5]
Specific arguments		
5. Premise–Conclusion Similarity	ROBIN, BLUEJAY/SPARROW [76]	ROBIN, BLUEJAY/GOOSE [4]
6. Premise Diversity	LION, GIRAFFE/RABBIT [52]	LION, TIGER/RABBIT [28]
7. Premise Monotonicity	FOX, PIG/WOLF/GORILLA [66]	PIG, WOLF/GORILLA [14]
8. Premise–Conclusion Asymmetry	MICE/BAT [41] (40)	BAT/MICE [39] (20)
Mixed arguments		
9. Nonmonotonicity, General	CROW, PEACOCK/BIRD [68]	CROW, PEACOCK/RABBIT/ BIRD [12]
10. Nonmonotonicity, Specific	FLY/BEE [51]	FLY, ORANGUTAN/BEE [29]
General and specific arguments		
11. Inclusion Fallacy	ROBIN/BIRD [52]	ROBIN/OSTRICH [28]
Limiting-case arguments		
12. Premise–Conclusion Identity	PELICAN/PELICAN	
13. Premise–Conclusion Inclusion	ANIMAL/BIRD	

Note. Number of subjects in Study 1 preferring each argument is given in brackets.
Entries in parentheses are results of Study 2.

often in the upper and lower positions. The order of the argument pairs was randomized anew for each subject. The subjects were 80 University of Michigan undergraduates who were paid for their participation and tested in groups of 20.

The results of Study 1 are presented in Table 1. For each contrasting pair, the number of subjects choosing a given argument is shown in brackets next to the argument. In all cases but one, the majority choice is overwhelmingly for the argument we claimed in the preceding section to be stronger (these differences are significant at the .01 level by a two-tailed sign test). The sole exception is Phenomenon 8, premise–conclusion asymmetry, in which there is roughly an equal preference for the two contrasting arguments.

Postexperimental comments by some subjects suggested that the arguments constituting Phenomenon 8 were treated differently than other arguments. Because the arguments MOUSE/BAT and BAT/MOUSE contain identical statements, subjects apparently reasoned that there could be no difference in strength between them. This metacognitive strategy may have obscured the underlying difference in strength in which we are interested.

To respond to the foregoing difficulty, Study 2 was performed. Subjects were presented with

a four-page booklet in which the first page contained instructions and each of the three test pages contained a contrasting pair of arguments. One contrasting pair was that used above to illustrate premise–conclusion asymmetry (Phenomenon 8) (viz., MOUSE/BAT versus BAT/MOUSE). The other two pairs were fillers. The instructions were designed to suppress the metacognitive strategy. They were the same as the instructions of Study 1, except that the last sentence was replaced by

Although the two arguments in a pair may sometimes seem very similar, there is always a difference in how much reason the facts of an argument give to believe its conclusion. However small this difference may be, we would like you to indicate for which argument the facts provide a better reason to believe the conclusion.

As before, each argument in a pair appeared equally often in the upper and lower positions, and the order of arguments was varied across subjects. The subjects were 60 University of Michigan undergraduates, paid for their participation and tested in groups of 20. None had participated in Study 1.

Most subjects preferred the MOUSE/BAT argument to the BAT/MOUSE argument. The difference, 40 versus 20, is significant at the .01 level by a sign test (two-tailed).

Replications

We have replicated the foregoing results – including the preference for MOUSE/BAT over BAT/MOUSE – in several studies using sets of argument pairs that overlap those described earlier. In addition, we have documented the phenomena with an alternative methodology, as follows. Forty University of Michigan undergraduates were given 24 arguments in individually randomized order. They were asked to estimate the probability of each conclusion on the assumption that the respective premises were true. Twenty-two of the arguments corresponded to the 11 contrasts of Phenomena 1–11. Illustrating with nonmonotonicity, general (Phenomenon 9), 2 of the arguments were as follows:

Terriers secrete uric acid crystals.

All canines secrete uric acid crystals.   (18a)

Terriers secrete uric acid crystals.
Mustangs secrete uric acid crystals.

All canines secrete uric acid crystals.   (18b)

Twenty-four of the 40 subjects assigned a higher conditional probability to Argument 18a than to Argument 18b; 10 showed the reverse judgment, and 6 assigned the same conditional probability to each conclusion. This bias in favor of nonmonotonicity is significant by a sign test ($p < .01$, one-tailed). The other phenomena tested in the original experiments have been similarly replicated except for premise–conclusion asymmetry, which was tested without special instructions and yielded only a nonsignificant difference in the predicted direction.

Theory

Two Variables in Confirmation

The theory developed below claims that confirmation varies directly with the following two variables: a = the degree to which the premise categories resemble the conclusion category; and b = the degree to which the premise categories resemble members of the lowest-level category that includes both the premise and conclusion categories. These variables can be illustrated with Argument 9b, in which the premise categories are ROBIN and BLUEJAY and in which the conclusion category is GOOSE. Variable a corresponds to the similarity between robins and bluejays on the one hand, and geese on the other. Regarding variable b, observe that BIRD is the lowest-level category that includes ROBIN, BLUEJAY, and GOOSE. Hence, b corresponds to the similarity between robins and bluejays on the one hand, and all birds on the other. This variable is intended to capture the following kind of reasoning:

> "Since robins and bluejays have the property, it may be the case that all birds have the property. Geese are birds. So maybe geese have the property too."

Although we do not claim that such reasoning is consciously produced by the typical subject, we do claim that it represents a thought process that is central to inductive judgment (see also Carey 1985).

Rips (1975) has already proposed that variables a and b are fundamental to category-based induction. Our goal is to formulate this idea in a way that applies to a broader set of arguments than the single-premise, specific arguments considered by Rips. We show that the resulting model is consistent with all 13 phenomena discussed above and provides a reasonable fit of quantitative data described later.

Extended Similarity Functions

Both variables a and b invoke similarity as the underlying mechanism of confirmation judgment. Accordingly, our model rests on an extended notion of similarity. For a given subject S, we suppose the existence of a function SIM, defined on any pair of elements that are at the same hierarchical level within some natural category. Pairs of this kind include (BEE, MOSQUITO), (APPLE, WATERMELON), and (FALCON, CHIMPANZEE) – the last pair consists of elements at the same hierarchical level within the category ANIMAL. Given such a pair (k, g), $\text{SIM}_s(k; g)$ is assumed to return a real number between 0 and 1 that reflects the similarity that S perceives between k and g, where values near 0 and 1 represent low and high similarity, respectively. Although $\text{SIM}_s(k; g)$ need not always equal $\text{SIM}_s(g; k)$ (see Tversky 1977), symmetry does seem to be approximately true for the stimuli that figure in our discussion.

The SIM function is directly relevant only to single-premise, specific arguments P/C. For such arguments, $\text{SIM}_s(\text{CAT}(P); \text{CAT}(C))$ represents the similarity between the categories in P and C. To be relevant to multiple-premise arguments, both general and specific, we extend the domain of the SIM function as follows. Let $k_1 \ldots k_n$, g be elements that are at the same hierarchical level within some natural category. We define $\text{SIM}_s(k_1 \ldots k_n;\ g)$ to be the maximum of $\{\text{SIM}_s(k_1;\ g) \ldots \text{SIM}_s(k_n;\ g)\}$. In words, $\text{SIM}_s(k_1 \ldots k_n;\ g)$ is the greatest similarity that S perceives between g and some one of $k_1 \ldots k_n$. To illustrate, if S's intuitions conform to ours, $\text{SIM}_s(\text{robin}, \text{crow}; \text{sparrow}) = \text{SIM}_s(\text{robin}; \text{sparrow})$. When $n = 1$, the extended SIM function reduces to the original one.[2]

The foregoing use of the MAX function can be motivated by the following considerations about similarity and confirmation. Consider the argument

---

Rhinos have BCC in their blood.

Antelopes have BCC in their blood.   (19)

Although not exceptionally strong, Argument 19 has nonnegligible strength, partly because of the similarity of RHINO to ANTELOPE. The same remarks apply to

---

Elephants have BCC in their blood.

Antelopes have BCC in their blood.   (20)

However, combining the two premises, as in

Rhinos have BCC in their blood.
Elephants have BCC in their blood.

Antelopes have BCC in their blood.   (21)

---

yields an argument that seems to be only slightly stronger than Argument 19 or 20, not twice as strong. The similarity of premise categories to conclusion categories thus appears not to summate when overall confirmation is mentally computed. This lack of additivity cannot be due to a mechanism that averages the similarity of premises to conclusion because averaging is inconsistent with premise monotonicity for specific arguments (see Phenomenon 7). In particular, since elephants resemble antelopes more than do monkeys, an averaging mechanism would render the single-premise Argument 20 stronger than

---

Elephants have BCC in their blood.
Monkeys have BCC in their blood.

Antelopes have BCC in their blood.   (22)

But Argument 22 is clearly stronger than is Argument 20.

These considerations point to a maximizing principle in computing the similarity of multiple premises to a specific conclusion. With regard to Arguments 19–21, such a principle allows the similarity of RHINO to ANTELOPE to be eclipsed by the greater similarity of ELEPHANT to ANTELOPE (or vice versa, if RHINO is more similar to ANTELOPE than is ELEPHANT), which explains why Argument 21 is not twice as strong as Argument 19.

A theory based on maximization must also account for the greater strength of Argument 22 compared with 20. Our theory achieves this, not by considering the additional similarity of MONKEY to ANTELOPE, but by considering the greater "coverage" of the category MAMMAL by the set {ELEPHANT, MONKEY} than by {ELEPHANT}. In the same way, the somewhat greater coverage by {RHINO, ELEPHANT} compared to {ELEPHANT} of the category MAMMAL accounts for the somewhat greater strength of Argument 21 compared with 20. The need to formalize this notion of coverage leads us to a second extension of the SIM function.

We extend the SIM function so that it applies to tuples of the form $(k_1 \ldots k_n;\ G)$, where $k_1 \ldots k_n$ are at the same hierarchical level of some natural category, and G is at a higher level. In this case, we define $\text{SIM}_s(k_1 \ldots k_n;\ G)$ to be the average of

$$\{\text{SIM}_s(k_1 \ldots k_n; g) \mid S \text{ believes that } g \text{ is at the same level as } k_1 \ldots k_n \text{ and that } g \text{ belongs to } G\}.$$

In words, $\text{SIM}_s(k_1 \ldots k_n;\ G)$ is the average similarity that S perceives between $k_1 \ldots k_n$ and members of G at the level of $k_1 \ldots k_n$. To illustrate, suppose that all the songbirds that S can think of appear in the list: ROBIN, SPARROW, FINCH, CARDINAL, BLUEJAY, ORIOLE. Then, SIM_s(CARDINAL, SPARROW; SONGBIRD) is the average of

$\text{MAX}\{\text{SIM}_s(\text{CARDINAL; ROBIN}),\ \text{SIM}_s(\text{SPARROW; ROBIN})\}$

$\text{MAX}\{\text{SIM}_s(\text{CARDINAL; SPARROW}),\ \text{SIM}_s(\text{SPARROW; SPARROW})\}$

$\text{MAX}\{\text{SIM}_s(\text{CARDINAL; FINCH}),\ \text{SIM}_s(\text{SPARROW; FINCH})\}$

$\text{MAX}\{\text{SIM}_s(\text{CARDINAL; CARDINAL}),\ \text{SIM}_s(\text{SPARROW; CARDINAL})\}$

$\text{MAX}\{\text{SIM}_s(\text{CARDINAL; BLUEJAY}),\ \text{SIM}_s(\text{SPARROW; BLUEJAY})\}$

$\text{MAX}\{\text{SIM}_s(\text{CARDINAL; ORIOLE}),\ \text{SIM}_s(\text{SPARROW; ORIOLE})\}$

If we make the further supposition that S's intuitions are like our own, $\mathrm{SIM_s}$(CARDINAL, SPARROW; SONGBIRD) equals the average of

$\mathrm{SIM_s}$(SPARROW; ROBIN)

$\mathrm{SIM_s}$(SPARROW; SPARROW)

$\mathrm{SIM_s}$(SPARROW; FINCH)

$\mathrm{SIM_s}$(CARDINAL; CARDINAL)

$\mathrm{SIM_s}$(CARDINAL; BLUEJAY)

$\mathrm{SIM_s}$(CARDINAL; ORIOLE).

As a second illustration, $\mathrm{SIM_s}$(RABBIT; MAMMAL) equals the average of $\mathrm{SIM_s}$(RABBIT; ELEPHANT), $\mathrm{SIM_s}$(RABBIT; MOUSE), and so forth. $\mathrm{SIM_s}$(RABBIT; PACHYDERM) does not figure in this average because PACHYDERM is not at the same level as RABBIT.[3]

It may be helpful to provide an intuitive interpretation of such expressions as $\mathrm{SIM_s}$(CARDINAL, SPARROW; SONGBIRD). $\mathrm{SIM_s}$ returns a high value on (CARDINAL, SPARROW; SONGBIRD) to the extent that every songbird (retrieved by S) is similar to either cardinals or sparrows or both. Conversely, the value is low if there are many songbirds that are similar to neither cardinals nor sparrows. Thinking of similarity (solely as an aid to intuition) as a decreasing function of metric distance in a space of instances, $\mathrm{SIM_s}$(CARDINAL, SPARROW; SONGBIRD) is large to the extent that the set {CARDINAL, SPARROW} "covers" the space of songbirds, in the sense that every songbird is near some member of {CARDINAL, SPARROW}.

Finally, it is worth pointing out that we could not properly reconstruct the coverage conception if we had earlier defined $\mathrm{SIM_s}(k_1 \ldots k_n; g)$ to be the sum rather than the maximum of $\{\mathrm{SIM_s}(k_1; g) \ldots \mathrm{SIM_s}(k_n; g)\}$. To see this, consider a seven-member category $\Gamma = \{A, B, C, D, E, F, G\}$, the similarities of which are represented (inversely) by linear distance in the following diagram:

AB   CDE   FG

Intuitively, {B, D, F} covers Γ better than {C, D, E} does. This intuition conforms to the MAX-version of $\mathrm{SIM_s}(k_1 \ldots k_n; g)$ because every member of Γ is near some member of {B, D, F}, whereas some members of Γ – namely, A, B, F, and G – are far from every member of {C, D, E}. That is, $\mathrm{SIM_s}$(B, D, F; Γ) > $\mathrm{SIM_s}$(C, D, E; Γ). However, the intution that {B, D, F} covers Γ better than does {C, D, E} is violated if $\mathrm{SIM_s}(k_1 \ldots k_n; g)$ is computed as SUM$\{\mathrm{SIM_s}(k_1; g) \ldots \mathrm{SIM_s}(k_n; g)\}$. For, by measuring distances in

the diagram the reader can verify that if the SUM version is used, the average of $\{\mathrm{SIM_s}(C, D, E; \gamma)|$ $\gamma \in \Gamma\}$ exceeds the average of $\{\mathrm{SIM_s}(B, D, F; \gamma)|$ $\gamma \in \Gamma\}$. Thus, the sum version of $\mathrm{SIM_s}(k_1 \ldots k_n;$ $g)$ counterintuitively declares {C, D, E} to provide better coverage of Γ than does {B, D, F}. The same counterintuitive result is obtained if an average version of $\mathrm{SIM_s}(k_1 \ldots k_n; g)$ is used.

The Model

Our model is formulated with the help of the following notation. Given a list $k_1 \ldots k_m$ of categories, we denote by $[k_1 \ldots k_m]$ the lowest level category K such that each of $k_1 \ldots k_m$ is a subset of K. For example:

1. [TROUT, SHARK] = FISH;

2. [RABBIT, ELEPHANT] = MAMMAL;

3. [LION, SALMON] = ANIMAL;

4. [PORCUPINE, MAMMAL] = MAMMAL;

5. [HORNET, COW, ANIMAL] = ANIMAL.

The similarity–coverage model of argument strength: For every person S there is a positive constant $\alpha \in (0, 1)$ such that for all arguments $A = P_1 \ldots P_n/C$, the strength of A for S is given by

$$\alpha \mathrm{SIM_s}(\mathrm{CAT}(P_1) \ldots \mathrm{CAT}(P_n); \mathrm{CAT}(C))$$
$$+ (1 - \alpha)\mathrm{SIM_s}(\mathrm{CAT}(P_1) \ldots \mathrm{CAT}(P_n);$$
$$[\mathrm{CAT}(P_1) \cdots \mathrm{CAT}(P_n), \mathrm{CAT}(C)]).$$

Thus, the model allows for individual differences in the relative importance attributed to similarity and coverage in argument strength. Such differences are represented by the parameter α. In contrast, for any given subject it is assumed that a single value of α applies to all arguments evaluated in a given context.

To illustrate the model, consider the argument

Beavers require oxydilic acid for good digestion.
Raccoons require oxydilic acid for good digestion.
_____
Bears require oxydilic acid for good digestion.

(23)

According to the model, the strength of Argument 23 for a given subject S is a weighted sum of terms a and b, where

a = $\mathrm{SIM_s}$(BEAVER, RACCOON; BEAR) and

b = $\mathrm{SIM_s}$(BEAVER, RACCOON; [BEAVER, RACCOON, BEAR]).

Table 2: Summary of the Similarity–Coverage Model

Theoretical Concept	Explanation
$\text{SIM}_s(k; g)$, where k is at the same hierarchical level as g	Similarity according to S of k to g
$\text{SIM}_s(k_1 \ldots k_n; g)$, where $k_1 \ldots k_n$ are at the same hierarchical level as g	Maximum $\{\text{SIM}_s(k_1; g) \mid i \leq n\}$
$\text{SIM}_s(k_1 \ldots k_n; G)$, where $k_1 \ldots k_n$ are at the same hierarchical level and G is at a higher level	Average $\{\text{SIM}_s(k_1 \ldots k_n; g) \mid g \in G\}$ (= average $\{\text{maximum } \{\text{SIM}_s(k_i; g) \mid i \leq n\} \mid g \in G\}$)
$[k_1 \ldots k_n]$	Lowest level category G such that each of $k_1 \ldots k_n$ is a subset of G
$\text{CAT}(P)$, $\text{CAT}(C)$	Category terms figuring in premise or conclusion
Strength of $P_1 \ldots P_n/C = \alpha \text{SIM}_s(\text{CAT}(P_1) \ldots \text{CAT}(P_n); \text{CAT}(C))$ $+ (1 - \alpha)\text{SIM}_s(\text{CAT}(P_1) \ldots \text{CAT}(P_n); [\text{CAT}(P_1) \ldots \text{CAT}(P_n), \text{CAT}(C)])$	

Term a is the greater of $\text{SIM}_s(\text{BEAVER; BEAR})$ and $\text{SIM}_s(\text{RACCOON; BEAR})$. By the definition of the bracket notation (i.e., the lowest level category that includes the bracketed categories), [BEAVER, RACCOON, BEAR] = MAMMAL, so Term b amounts to $\text{SIM}_s(\text{BEAVER, RACCOON; MAMMAL})$. This term represents the coverage of MAMMAL by BEAVER and RACCOON, that is, the average of $\text{MAX}\{\text{SIM}_s(\text{BEAVER; } m), \text{SIM}_s(\text{RACCOON; } m)\}$ across all mammals m known to S.

Now consider the related argument

Beavers require oxydilic acid for good digestion.
Raccoons require oxydilic acid for good digestion.

All mammals require oxydilic acid for good digestion.

(24)

According to the model, the strength of Argument 24 for a given subject S is given by the sum of a and b, where

a = $\alpha \text{SIM}_s(\text{BEAVER, RACCOON; MAMMAL})$ and

b = $(1 - \alpha)\text{SIM}_s(\text{BEAVER, RACCOON; [BEAVER, RACCOON, MAMMAL]})$.

By the definition of the bracket notation, [BEAVER, RACCOON, MAMMAL] = MAMMAL, so b may be rewritten as

b' = $(1 - \alpha)\text{SIM}_s(\text{BEAVER, RACCOON; MAMMAL})$.

The sum of a and b' is $\text{SIM}_s(\text{BEAVER, RACCOON; MAMMAL})$, regardless of the value of the parameter α. Consequently, according to the model, the strength of Argument 24 for S depends only on the coverage of MAMMAL by {BEAVER, RACCOON}.

The last example motivates the additive form of our model. It is intuitively plausible that the strength of Argument 24 depends only on the sole variable of coverage. This dependency is deduced by adding terms of the form αX and $(1 - \alpha)X$, where X is the coverage variable. We note as well that the additive combination of similarity and coverage is the simplest hypothesis for a model that invokes both variables. Support for the additive form of the model thus provides better confirmation for its underlying idea (stated in the *Two Variables in Confirmation* section above) than would support for a version of the model that relies on more complicated mechanisms.

Table 2 summarizes the concepts figuring in the similarity coverage model.

The Phenomena Revisited

Given plausible assumptions about the SIM_s function, the similarity–coverage model predicts the 13 phenomena discussed earlier. In this sense, the phenomena provide qualitative support for the model. For each phenomenon we repeat its description, and then apply the similarity–coverage model to the contrasting arguments that were used as illustration. See Table 1 for a synopsis of relevant arguments.

Phenomena Concerning General Arguments

PHENOMENON 1 (PREMISE TYPICALITY)

The more representative or typical $\text{CAT}(P_1)$ $\ldots \text{CAT}(P_n)$ are of $\text{CAT}(C)$, the more $P_1 \ldots P_n$ confirm C. According to the model, for a given person S, the strengths of Arguments 5a and 5b are given by

$\alpha \text{SIM}_s(\text{ROBIN; BIRD})$

$+ (1 - \alpha) \text{SIM}_s(\text{ROBIN; [ROBIN, BIRD]})$

and

$$\alpha \text{SIM}_s \text{ (PENGUIN; BIRD)}$$
$$+ (1 - \alpha) \text{SIM}_s(\text{PENGUIN}; [\text{PENGUIN, BIRD}]),$$

respectively. Because [ROBIN, BIRD] = [PENGUIN, BIRD] = BIRD, the foregoing expressions reduce to SIM_s (ROBIN; BIRD) and SIM_s(PENGUIN; BIRD), respectively. SIM_s(ROBIN; BIRD) equals the average similarity of robins to other birds, whereas SIM_s (PENGUIN; BIRD) equals the average similarity of penguins to other birds. It is reasonable to suppose that for a majority of subjects, the former value is greater than the latter, which yields the greater strength of Argument 5a compared with Argument 5b. More generally, the average similarity of an instance to the members of a given category is known as the *typicality* of that instance in the given category (Smith and Medin 1981; Tversky 1977), and the model thus predicts greater strength for general arguments the premises of which are typical rather than atypical (other factors held constant). This generalization captures Phenomenon 1.[4]

PHENOMENON 2 (PREMISE DIVERSITY)

The less similar $\text{CAT}(P_1) \ldots \text{CAT}(P_n)$ are among themselves, the more $P_1 \ldots P_n$ confirm C. According to the model, for a given person S, the strengths of Arguments 6a and 6b are given by

$$\alpha \text{SIM}_s(\text{HIPPO, HAMSTER; MAMMAL})$$
$$+ (1 - \alpha)\text{SIM}_s(\text{HIPPO, HAMSTER};$$
$$[\text{HIPPO, HAMSTER, MAMMAL}])$$

and

$$\alpha \text{SIM}_s(\text{HIPPO, RHINO; MAMMAL})$$
$$+ (1 - \alpha) \text{SIM}_s(\text{HIPPO, RHINO};$$
$$[\text{HIPPO, RHINO, MAMMAL}]),$$

respectively. Because [HIPPO, HAMSTER, MAMMAL] = [HIPPO, RHINO, MAMMAL] = MAMMAL, these expressions reduce to SIM_s(HIPPO, HAMSTER; MAMMAL) and SIM_s(HIPPO, RHINO; MAMMAL), respectively. To see that for most persons S, SIM_s (HIPPO, HAMSTER; MAMMAL) is likely to be greater than SIM_s(HIPPO, RHINO; MAMMAL), it suffices to observe that

1. For many $k \in$ MAMMAL (e.g., LION, ELEPHANT, HORSE), SIM_s(HIPPO, HAMSTER; k) $\approx$ SIM_s(HIPPO, RHINO; k) because most everything that resembles rhinoceroses resembles hippopotamuses as well. (The

use of the MAX interpretation of SIM_s is crucial here.)

2. For no $k \in$ MAMMAL does SIM_s(HIPPO, RHINO; k) exceed SIM_s-(HIPPO, HAMSTER; k) by much because no mammal resembles rhinoceroses much more than it resembles hippopotamuses; and

3. For some $k \in$ MAMMAL (e.g., MOUSE, SQUIRREL, CHIPMUNK), SIM_s(HIPPO, HAMSTER; k) appreciably exceeds SIM_s(HIPPO, RHINO; k) because these mammals resemble hamsters more than they resemble rhinoceroses.

These facts yield the greater strength of Argument 6a compared with Argument 6b, in conformity with Phenomenon 2.

PHENOMENON 3 (CONCLUSION SPECIFICITY)

The more specific is CAT(C), the more C is confirmed by $P_1 \ldots P_n$. According to the model, the strengths of Arguments 7a and 7b reduce to SIM_s(BLUEJAY, FALCON; BIRD) and SIM_s(BLUEJAY, FALCON; ANIMAL), respectively. The greater homogeneity of BIRD compared to ANIMAL implies that {BLUEJAY, FALCON} covers the former better than the latter. This implies that Argument 7a is stronger than Argument 7b, in conformity with Phenomenon 3.

PHENOMENON 4 (PREMISE MONOTONICITY)

For general arguments, more inclusive sets of premises yield more strength than less inclusive sets. Similarly to before, the model implies that the strengths of 8a and 8b boil down to SIM_s(HAWK, SPARROW, EAGLE; BIRD) and SIM_s(SPARROW, EAGLE; BIRD), respectively. Obviously, {HAWK, SPARROW, EAGLE) covers BIRD better than {SPARROW, EAGLE} does. This implies that Argument 8a is stronger than Argument 8b, as required by Phenomenon 4.

Phenomena Concerning Specific Arguments

PHENOMENON 5 (PREMISE–CONCLUSION SIMILARITY)

The more similar $\text{CAT}(P_1) \ldots \text{CAT}(P_n)$ are to CAT(C), the more $P_1 \ldots P_n$ confirm C. According to the model, for a given person S, the strengths of Arguments 9a and 9b are given by

$$\alpha \text{SIM}_s(\text{ROBIN, BLUEJAY; SPARROW})$$
$$+ (1 - \alpha)\text{SIM}_s(\text{ROBIN, BLUEJAY};$$
$$[\text{ROBIN, BLUEJAY, SPARROW}])$$

and

αSIM$_s$(ROBIN, BLUEJAY; GOOSE)

   $+ (1 - \alpha)$SIM$_s$(ROBIN, BLUEJAY;

     [ROBIN, BLUEJAY, GOOSE]),

respectively. Because [ROBIN, BLUEJAY, SPARROW] = [ROBIN, BLUEJAY, GOOSE] = BIRD, these expressions reduce to

αSIM$_s$(ROBIN, BLUEJAY; SPARROW)

   $+ (1 - \alpha)$SIM$_s$(ROBIN, BLUEJAY; BIRD)

and

αSIM$_s$(ROBIN, BLUEJAY; GOOSE)

   $+ (1 - \alpha)$SIM$_s$(ROBIN, BLUEJAY; BIRD),

respectively. Because the two $(1 - \alpha)$ terms are identical, Argument 9a is predicted to be stronger than Argument 9b if SIM$_s$(ROBIN, BLUEJAY; SPARROW) > SIM$_s$(ROBIN, BLUEJAY; GOOSE). Surely this is the case for most subjects. Phenomenon 5 is thereby captured.[5]

PHENOMENON 6 (PREMISE DIVERSITY)

   The less similar CAT (P_1) ... CAT (P_n) are among themselves, the more $P_1 ... P_n$ confirm C. According to the model, for a given person S, the strengths of Arguments 10a and 10b are given by

αSIM$_s$(LION, GIRAFFE; RABBIT)

   $+ (1 - \alpha)$SIM$_s$(LION, GIRAFFE;

     [LION, GIRAFFE, RABBIT])

and

αSIM$_s$(LION, TIGER; RABBIT)

   $+ (1 - \alpha)$SIM$_s$(LION, TIGER;

     [LION, TIGER, RABBIT]),

respectively. Because [LION, GIRAFFE, RABBIT] = [LION, TIGER, RABBIT] = MAMMAL, these expressions reduce to

αSIM$_s$(LION, GIRAFFE; RABBIT)

   $+ (1 - \alpha)$SIM$_s$(LION, GIRAFFE; MAMMAL)

and

αSIM$_s$(LION, TIGER; RABBIT)]

   $+ (1 - \alpha)$ SIM$_s$(LION, TIGER; MAMMAL),

respectively. Because SIM$_s$(LION; RABBIT) is likely to be no smaller than either SIM$_s$(TIGER; RABBIT) or SIM$_s$(GIRAFFE; RABBIT), it follows (via the MAX interpretation of SIM$_s$) that SIM$_s$(LION, GIRAFFE; RABBIT) is no smaller than SIM$_s$(LION,

TIGER; RABBIT) for most persons S. On the other hand, it is clear that {LION, GIRAFFE} covers MAMMAL better than {LION, TIGER} does. Under the assumptions of the model, these facts imply that Argument 10a is stronger than 10b, in conformity with Phenomenon 6.

PHENOMENON 7 (PREMISE MONOTONICITY)

   More inclusive sets of premises yield more strength than less inclusive sets, provided that the new premise is drawn from the lowest level category that includes the old premises and conclusion. According to the model, for a given person S, the strengths of Arguments 11a and 11b are given by

αSIM$_s$(FOX, PIG, WOLF; GORILLA)

   $+ (1 - \alpha)$SIM$_s$(FOX, PIG, WOLF;

     [FOX, PIG, WOLF, GORILLA])

and

αSIM$_s$(PIG, WOLF; GORILLA)

   $+ (1 - \alpha)$SIM$_s$(PIG, WOLF;

     [PIG, WOLF, GORILLA]),

respectively. Because [FOX, PIG, WOLF, GORILLA] = [PIG, WOLF, GORILLA] = MAMMAL, these expressions reduce to

αSIM$_s$(FOX, PIG, WOLF; GORILLA)

   $+ (1 - \alpha)$SIM$_s$(FOX, PIG, WOLF; MAMMAL)

and

αSIM$_s$(PIG, WOLF; GORILLA)

   $+ (1 - a)$SIM$_s$(PIG, WOLF; MAMMAL),

respectively. By the MAX interpretation of SIM$_s$, SIM$_s$(FOX, PIG, WOLF; GORILLA) is at least as great as SIM$_s$(PIG, WOLF; GORILLA). Also by MAX, {FOX, PIG, WOLF} covers MAMMAL better than {PIG, WOLF} does. Argument 11a is thereby predicted to be stronger than Argument 11b, in conformity with Phenomenon 7.

PHENOMENON 8 (PREMISE-CONCLUSION ASYMMETRY)

   Single-premise arguments are not symmetric, in the sense that P/C may not have the same strength as C/P. According to the model, for a given person S, the strengths of Arguments 12a and 12b are given by

αSIM$_s$(MOUSE; BAT)

   $+ (1 - \alpha)$SIM$_s$(MOUSE; [MOUSE, BAT])

and

$\alpha \text{SIM}_s(\text{BAT; MOUSE})$
  $+ (1 - \alpha)\text{SIM}_s(\text{BAT; [BAT; MOUSE]}),$

respectively. Because [MOUSE, BAT] = [BAT, MOUSE] = MAMMAL, these expressions reduce to

$\alpha \text{SIM}_s(\text{MOUSE; BAT})$
  $+ (1 - \alpha)\text{SIM}_s(\text{MOUSE; MAMMAL})$

and

$\alpha \text{SIM}_s(\text{BAT; MOUSE})$
  $+ (1 - \alpha)\text{SIM}_s(\text{BAT; MAMMAL}),$

respectively. It may be assumed that $\text{SIM}_s(\text{BAT; MOUSE})$ is roughly equal to $\text{SIM}_s(\text{MOUSE; BAT})$. On the other hand, the average similarity of mice to other mammals is greater than that of bats to other mammals. Hence, $\text{SIM}_s(\text{MOUSE; MAMMAL}) > \text{SIM}_s(\text{BAT; MAMMAL})$. Putting these facts together yields greater predicted strength for Argument 12a than for 12b, in line with Phenomenon 8. The foregoing derivation also reveals the following prediction of the similarity–coverage model: For a specific argument P/C to exhibit asymmetry, CAT(P) and CAT(C) must differ in typicality.

Phenomena Concerning Mixed Arguments

PHENOMENON 9 (NONMONOTONICITY, GENERAL)

Some general arguments can be made weaker by adding a premise that converts them into mixed arguments. According to the model, for a given person S, the strengths of Arguments 13a and 13b are given by

$\alpha \text{SIM}_s(\text{CROW, PEACOCK; BIRD})$
  $+ (1 - \alpha)\,\text{SIM}_s(\text{CROW, PEACOCK;}$
    $[\text{CROW, PEACOCK, BIRD}])$

and

$\alpha \text{SIM}_s(\text{CROW, PEACOCK, RABBIT; BIRD})$
  $+ (1 - \alpha)\text{SIM}_s(\text{CROW, PEACOCK, RABBIT;}$
    $[\text{CROW, PEACOCK, RABBIT, BIRD}]),$

respectively. Because [CROW, PEACOCK, BIRD] = BIRD and [CROW, PEACOCK, RABBIT, BIRD] = ANIMAL, these expressions reduce to

$\alpha \text{SIM}_s(\text{CROW, PEACOCK; BIRD})$
  $+ (1 - \alpha)\,\text{SIM}_s(\text{CROW, PEACOCK; BIRD})$

and

$\alpha \text{SIM}_s(\text{CROW, PEACOCK, RABBIT; BIRD}) + (1 - \alpha)$
  $\times \text{SIM}_s(\text{CROW, PEACOCK, RABBIT; ANIMAL}),$

respectively. Regarding α-terms, {CROW, PEACOCK} probably covers BIRD as well as {CROW, PEACOCK, RABBIT} does. Regarding $(1 - \alpha)$-terms, {CROW, PEACOCK} covers BIRD better than {CROW, PEACOCK, RABBIT} covers ANIMAL, in view of the greater variability among animals compared to the subset birds. Under the assumptions of the model, these facts imply that Argument 13a is stronger than 13b, as specified by Phenomenon 9.

PHENOMENON 10 (NONMONOTONICITY, SPECIFIC)

Some specific arguments can be made weaker by adding a premise that converts them into mixed arguments. According to the model, for a given person S, the strengths of Arguments 14a and 14b are given by

$\alpha \text{SIM}_s(\text{FLY; BEE}) + (1 - \alpha)\text{SIM}_s(\text{FLY; [FLY, BEE]})$

and

$\alpha \text{SIM}_s(\text{FLY, ORANGUTAN; BEE})$
  $+ (1 - \alpha)\text{SIM}_s(\text{FLY, ORANGUTAN;}$
    $[\text{FLY, ORANGUTAN, BEE}]),$

respectively. Because [FLY, BEE] = INSECT and [FLY, ORANGUTAN, BEE] = ANIMAL, these expressions reduce to

$\alpha \text{SIM}_s(\text{FLY; BEE}) + (1 - \alpha)\text{SIM}_s(\text{FLY; INSECT})$

and

$\alpha \text{SIM}_s(\text{FLY, ORANGUTAN; BEE})$
  $+ (1 - \alpha)\text{SIM}_s(\text{FLY, ORANGUTAN; ANIMAL}),$

respectively. Regarding α-terms, $\text{SIM}_s(\text{FLY; BEE}) > \text{SIM}_s(\text{ORANGUTAN; BEE})$ and, consequently, $\text{SIM}_s(\text{FLY; BEE}) = \text{SIM}_s(\text{FLY, ORANGUTAN; BEE})$. Regarding $(1 - \alpha)$-terms, {FLY} covers INSECT better than {FLY, ORANGUTAN} covers the varied category ANIMAL. The model thus implies that Argument 14a is stronger than Argument 14b, in conformity with Phenomenon 10.[6]

A Phenomenon Involving Both General and Specific Arguments

PHENOMENON 11 (INCLUSION FALLACY)

A specific argument can sometimes be made stronger by increasing the generality of its conclusion. The model implies that for a given person S, the strengths of Arguments 15a and 15b are given by

$$\alpha SIM_s(\text{ROBIN; BIRD})$$
$$+ (1 - \alpha)SIM_s(\text{ROBIN; [ROBIN, BIRD]})$$

and

$$\alpha SIM_s(\text{ROBIN; OSTRICH})$$
$$+ (1 - \alpha)SIM_s(\text{ROBIN; [ROBIN, OSTRICH]}),$$

respectively. Because [ROBIN, BIRD] = [ROBIN, OSTRICH] = BIRD, these expressions reduce to

$$\alpha SIM_s(\text{ROBIN; BIRD}) + (1 - \alpha)SIM_s(\text{ROBIN; BIRD})$$

and

$$\alpha SIM_s(\text{ROBIN; OSTRICH})$$
$$+ (1 - \alpha)SIM_s(\text{ROBIN; BIRD}),$$

respectively. The $1 - \alpha$ terms are identical. Regarding the α-terms, $SIM_s(\text{ROBIN; BIRD})$ represents the average similarity of robins to other birds, including songbirds like sparrows, cardinals, and orioles. Because this average is partially weighted by the similar songbirds, SIM_s (ROBIN; BIRD) exceeds $SIM_s(\text{ROBIN; OSTRICH})$, since ostriches are highly dissimilar to robins. Phenomenon 11 follows. The foregoing derivation also reveals the following prediction of the similarity–coverage model: Arguments P/C and P/C' – with $\text{CAT}(C') \in \text{CAT}(C)$ – can give rise to the inclusion–fallacy phenomenon only if $\text{CAT}(C')$ is an atypical member of $\text{CAT}(C)$.

Two Limiting-Case Phenomena

PHENOMENON 12 (PREMISE–CONCLUSION IDENTITY)

Any argument of the form Q/Q is perfectly strong. According to the model, for a given person S, the strength of Argument 16 is given by

$$\alpha SIM_s(\text{PELICAN; PELICAN})$$
$$+ (1 - \alpha)SIM_s(\text{PELICAN; [PELICAN, PELICAN]}).$$

Because [PELICAN, PELICAN] = PELICAN, this expression reduces to $SIM_s(\text{PELICAN; PELICAN})$. It is safe to assume that subjects perceive the similarity of pelicans to themselves to be extremely high, thereby accounting for the extreme strength of Argument 16. If we assume that $SIM_s(\text{PELICAN; PELICAN})$ is in fact the maximal value 1, then Argument 16 is predicted to be perfectly strong.

PHENOMENON 13 (PREMISE–CONCLUSION INCLUSION)

Suppose that statements P and C are such that the conclusion category is included in the premise category. Then the argument P/C is perfectly strong. We must explain why Argument 17 is at least as strong as any other argument. Let $k_1 \ldots k_n$ be all the animals known to S. Then, according to the model, $SIM_s(\text{ANIMAL; BIRD})$ equals the average of

$$\{SIM_s(k_1 \ldots k_n; g) \mid S \text{ believes that } g \text{ is a bird}\}$$

Because birds are animals, this expression is the average of terms of the form $SIM_s(x; x)$. Such an average may be assumed to equal 1, and Phenomenon 13 is explained thereby.[7]

A Related Finding

Gelman and Markman (1986) documented a pattern of inference in young children and adults that may be illustrated as follows. Subjects were told that a pictured flamingo had a right aortic arch, whereas a pictured bat had a left aortic arch. They were then shown a pictured blackbird that resembled the bat in appearance more than it did the flamingo. Subjects nonetheless attributed the flamingolike, right aortic arch to blackbirds rather than the batlike, left aortic arch. Gelman and Markman concluded that category membership rather than similarity governs these kinds of inferences in both young children and adults.

We may represent the Gelman–Markman finding in terms of the strengths of the following arguments.

Flamingos have a right aortic arch.	
Blackbirds have a right aortic arch.	(25a)

Bats have a left aortic arch.	
Blackbirds have a left aortic arch.	(25b)

According to the similarity–coverage model, for a given person S, the strengths of Arguments 25a and 25b are given by

$$\alpha SIM_s(\text{FLAMINGO; BLACKBIRD}) + (1 - \alpha)$$
$$\times SIM_s(\text{FLAMINGO; [FLAMINGO, BLACKBIRD]})$$

and

$$\alpha SIM_s(\text{BAT; BLACKBIRD})$$
$$+ (1 - \alpha)SIM_s(\text{BAT; [BAT, BLACKBIRD]}),$$

respectively. Because [FLAMINGO, BLACKBIRD] = BIRD and [BAT, BLACKBIRD] = ANIMAL, these expressions reduce to

$$\alpha \mathrm{SIM_s}(\text{FLAMINGO; BLACKBIRD})$$
$$+ (1 - \alpha)\mathrm{SIM_s}(\text{FLAMINGO; BIRD})$$

and

$$\alpha \mathrm{SIM_s}(\text{BAT; BLACKBIRD})$$
$$+ (1 - \alpha)\mathrm{SIM_s}(\text{BAT; ANIMAL})),$$

respectively. Regarding the α-terms, $\mathrm{SIM_s}$ (FLAMINGO; BLACKBIRD) < $\mathrm{SIM_s}$(BAT, BLACKBIRD). Regarding the $(1 - \alpha)$-terms, because {FLAMINGO} covers BIRD better than {BAT} covers the varied category ANIMAL, $\mathrm{SIM_s}$(FLAMINGO; BIRD) > $\mathrm{SIM_s}$(BAT; ANIMAL). As a consequence, Argument 25 will be judged stronger than Argument 25b if: (1) α is not too large, and (2) the coverage advantage of Argument 25a is not greatly outweighed by the similarity advantage of Argument 25b. We find these latter two assumptions reasonable, and thus believe that the Gelman–Markman finding is explainable in the context of the similarity–coverage model.

Quantitative Test of the Model

We performed 12 experiments designed to obtain quantitative data bearing on the similarity–coverage model. In an initial study, subjects rated the similarity of pairs of mammals in order for us to empirically estimate the SIM function underlying the model. From the approximated SIM function, predictions were derived about the relative strength of an extensive set of arguments. The predictions were then tested against ratings of argument strength provided by an independent group of subjects. The following is a condensed description of these experiments. A full report is available in Smith, Wilkie, López, and Osherson (1989).

Initial Similarity Study

Seven of the experiments were based on the category MAMMAL and the following base set of instances:

HORSE, COW, CHIMP, GORILLA, MOUSE, SQUIRREL, DOLPHIN, SEAL, ELEPHANT, RHINO.   (26)

An initial study was performed to obtain similarity judgments for all 45 pairs of distinct mammals drawn from this set. Each pair was printed on a separate card, and 40 subjects rank ordered all 45 cards in terms of "how similar the mammals appearing on each card are" (no ties allowed). The mean rank of each pair was divided by 45 to obtain a similarity scale between 0 and 1 (1 for perfect similarity, 0 for perfect dissimilarity). In addition, each identity pair (e.g., (HORSE, HORSE)) was assigned a score of 1. Table 3 records these similarity scores.

We used these pairwise similarity scores to approximate $\mathrm{SIM_s}(k; g)$ for each subject S and each pair of instances k, g drawn from the base set shown earlier. Averaging over subjects yields a composite similarity function defined over pairs of instances. This composite function will be denoted by SIM (without subscript), and represents the similarity intuitions of the average subject.

SIM may be extended via the MAX principle discussed earlier so that $\mathrm{SIM}(k_1 \ldots k_n; g)$ is defined for any choice of instances $k_1 \ldots k_n$; g. However, we have no direct estimate of $\mathrm{SIM}(k_1 \ldots k_n; G)$, where G is the given, natural kind category and $k_1 \ldots k_n$ are instances of G drawn from the base set. This is because calculation of $\mathrm{SIM}(k_1 \ldots k_n; G)$ presupposes the value of $\mathrm{SIM}(k_1 \ldots k_n; g)$ for all $g \in G$ that are retrieved by S, and not all of these g figure among the base set of instances (e.g., MOOSE is an instance of MAMMAL retrievable by most subjects, but does not figure in our base set for MAMMAL). An approximation to $\mathrm{SIM}(k_1 \ldots k_n; G)$ is therefore necessary. For this purpose, we have replaced G by its base set of instances. For example, to compute SIM(SQUIRREL, HORSE; MAMMAL), we computed SIM(SQUIRREL, HORSE: G'), where $G' = \{$HORSE, COW, CHIMPANZEE, GORILLA, MOUSE, SQUIRREL, DOLPHIN, SEAL, ELEPHANT, RHINO$\}$. This approximation is crude, but it represents in straightforward fashion the larger set of computations entailed by the model.

Finally, we consider the exact form of the predictions to be tested in the experiments. For a given argument A, the predictor variable of the model has the form $\alpha X_A + (1 - \alpha) Y_A$, where X_A is the model's similarity term for A and Y_A is its coverage term for A. Both of these terms are empirically estimated from ratings of similarity. Likewise, the predicted variable is estimated from ratings of argument strength. The two rating procedures cannot, however, be relied on to provide identical scales for the two types of judgment. As a result, we take the model to be supported by any observed linear relation between predictor and predicted variables; that is, we test the prediction that for some choice of the

Table 3: Similarity Scores for Pairs of Mammals

Mammals		Score	Mammals		Score
HORSE	COW	.93	CHIMP	RHINO	.48
HORSE	CHIMP	.60	GORILLA	MOUSE	.37
HORSE	GORILLA	.62	GORILLA	SQUIRREL	.48
HORSE	MOUSE	.50	GORILLA	DOLPHIN	.39
HORSE	SQUIRREL	.54	GORILLA	SEAL	.34
HORSE	DOLPHIN	.33	GORILLA	ELEPHANT	.65
HORSE	SEAL	.37	GORILLA	RHINO	.65
HORSE	ELEPHANT	.80	MOUSE	SQUIRREL	.94
HORSE	RHINO	.74	MOUSE	DOLPHIN	.17
COW	CHIMP	.55	MOUSE	SEAL	.25
COW	GORILLA	.59	MOUSE	ELEPHANT	.35
COW	MOUSE	.48	MOUSE	RHINO	.36
COW	SQUIRREL	.49	SQUIRREL	DOLPHIN	.18
COW	DOLPHIN	.26	SQUIRREL	SEAL	.27
COW	SEAL	.38	SQUIRREL	ELEPHANT	.41
COW	ELEPHANT	.79	SQUIRREL	RHINO	.35
COW	RHINO	.79	DOLPHIN	SEAL	.92
CHIMP	GORILLA	.97	DOLPHIN	ELEPHANT	.29
CHIMP	MOUSE	.51	DOLPHIN	RHINO	.26
CHIMP	SQUIRREL	.56	SEAL	ELEPHANT	.36
CHIMP	DOLPHIN	.50	SEAL	RHINO	.32
CHIMP	SEAL	.45	ELEPHANT	RHINO	.92
CHIMP	ELEPHANT	.53			

parameter α, constants c and d, and for all arguments A, the empirically determined strength of A equals $c[\alpha X_A + (1 - \alpha)Y_A] + d$. This latter predictor has the form $aX_A + bY_A + d$, so the model predicts a high, multiple correlation between: (1) the empirically obtained estimates of argument strength and (2) approximations to the similarity and coverage variables figuring in the model. Since the similarity–coverage model makes no claims about the average value of the parameter α in the sample of subjects participating in our studies, we leave the a, b, and d coefficients as free parameters.

Confirmation Studies

Separate groups of 20 subjects ranked the strength of arguments based on the instances in the base set. For example, one group ranked 45 arguments of the form

X requires biotin for hemoglobin synthesis.
Y requires biotin for hemoglobin synthesis.
Z requires biotin for hemoglobin synthesis.
_____
All mammals require biotin for hemoglobin synthesis.

where X, Y, and Z are distinct mammals drawn from the base set, and different arguments contain distinct trios of mammals in their premises. Together, there are 120 such premise-triples, and 45 were randomly generated to create the 45 arguments. These premise-triples are presented in Table 4.

Four sets of 45 cards were prepared, corresponding to the 45 arguments generated for the experiment. The names of the three mammals figuring in the premises were printed near the top of each card. The four sets differed in the order in which the mammals on a card appeared; four different random patterns were used. The following instructions were used:

We are frequently called upon to make judgments of the likelihood of something being true on the basis of limited information. Consider the following statement:

All mammals require biotin for hemoglobin synthesis.

How likely would you think that this statement is true if you knew, say, that all coyotes required biotin for hemoglobin synthesis? Would your opinion change if, instead of

Table 4: Confirmation Scores for Three-Premise, General Arguments

Mammals			Score	Mammals			Score
HORSE	COW	MOUSE	.33	COW	SEAL	ELEPHANT	.47
HORSE	COW	SEAL	.39	COW	ELEPHANT	RHINO	.14
HORSE	COW	RHINO	.17	CHIMP	GORILLA	SQUIRREL	.30
HORSE	CHIMP	SQUIRREL	.55	CHIMP	GORILLA	DOLPHIN	.31
HORSE	CHIMP	SEAL	.75	CHIMP	GORILLA	SEAL	.30
HORSE	GORILLA	SQUIRREL	.64	CHIMP	SQUIRREL	DOLPHIN	.80
HORSE	GORILLA	DOLPHIN	.73	CHIMP	SQUIRREL	ELEPHANT	.62
HORSE	MOUSE	SQUIRREL	.28	CHIMP	SQUIRREL	RHINO	.61
HORSE	MOUSE	SEAL	.69	CHIMP	DOLPHIN	ELEPHANT	.72
HORSE	MOUSE	RHINO	.42	GORILLA	MOUSE	SEAL	.82
HORSE	SQUIRREL	SEAL	.63	GORILLA	MOUSE	ELEPHANT	.58
HORSE	SQUIRREL	ELEPHANT	.47	GORILLA	SQUIRREL	DOLPHIN	.80
HORSE	DOLPHIN	SEAL	.27	GORILLA	SEAL	ELEPHANT	.60
HORSE	DOLPHIN	ELEPHANT	.49	GORILLA	ELEPHANT	RHINO	.26
COW	CHIMP	DOLPHIN	.76	MOUSE	SQUIRREL	SEAL	.35
COW	CHIMP	SEAL	.70	MOUSE	DOLPHIN	SEAL	.32
COW	CHIMP	ELEPHANT	.40	MOUSE	SEAL	ELEPHANT	.70
COW	MOUSE	SEAL	.68	MOUSE	SEAL	RHINO	.65
COW	MOUSE	RHINO	.40	MOUSE	ELEPHANT	RHINO	.31
COW	SQUIRREL	DOLPHIN	.76	SQUIRREL	DOLPHIN	SEAL	.30
COW	SQUIRREL	RHINO	.36	SQUIRREL	DOLPHIN	RHINO	.68
COW	DOLPHIN	ELEPHANT	.48	SQUIRREL	SEAL	RHINO	.62
COW	DOLPHIN	RHINO	.49				

coyotes, you knew the statement to be true of moles, or anteaters?

In this task you will be helping us to find out more about this type of reasoning. You will be handed a set of 45 cards. On each card will be written the name of the three mammals. For each card, you are to accept it as given that the mammals listed require biotin for hemoglobin synthesis. On the basis of this evidence, you are to determine how likely it is that all mammals require biotin for hemoglobin synthesis. Each card is to be evaluated entirely independently of the others.

Some of the mammals may seem to provide stronger evidence than others. Your task is to arrange the 45 cards in order of increasing strength of evidence.

The mechanics of a ranking procedure were then explained, and it was made explicit that no ties in the ranking were permitted.

The ranks assigned by the 20 subjects were averaged and divided by 45. Each argument thus received an "obtained confirmation score," namely, a number between 0 and 1, where 1 represents *high* assessed confirmation and 0 repre-

sents *low* assessed confirmation. These obtained confirmation scores are presented in Table 4.

Consider now the predicted confirmation scores. According to the similarity–coverage model, the strength of each of the arguments is given by

$$\alpha \text{SIM}(X, Y, Z; \text{MAMMAL})$$
$$+ (1 - \alpha)\text{SIM}(X, Y, Z; [X, Y, Z, \text{MAMMAL}]).$$

Because X, Y, and Z are mammals, $[X, Y, Z, \text{MAMMAL}] = \text{MAMMAL}$, so the foregoing expression reduces to $\text{SIM}(X, Y, Z; \text{MAMMAL})$. For each triple X, Y, Z of mammals figuring in the experiment, an approximation to $\text{SIM}(X, Y, Z; \text{MAMMAL})$ was computed by first determining the maximum similarity of each mammal in the base set to X, Y, Z, and then taking the average of these maximum similarities. The correlation between predicted confirmation scores and obtained confirmation scores is .87 ($N = 45$, $p < .01$).

A replication of the previous study was performed with new subjects using all 45 arguments based on 2 distinct mammals from the base set. The resulting correlation between obtained and predicted confirmation scores was .63 ($N = 45$, $p < .01$). Another replication used all one-premise arguments derived from the base

Table 5: Confirmation Scores for Two-Premise Specific
Arguments (Horse, Experiment 4)

Mammals		Score	Mammals		Score
COW	CHIMP	.79	GORILLA	SEAL	.41
COW	GORILLA	.75	GORILLA	ELEPHANT	.61
COW	MOUSE	.74	GORILLA	RHINO	.63
COW	SQUIRREL	.72	MOUSE	SQUIRREL	.17
COW	DOLPHIN	.73	MOUSE	DOLPHIN	.28
COW	SEAL	.73	MOUSE	SEAL	.25
COW	ELEPHANT	.75	MOUSE	ELEPHANT	.58
COW	RHINO	.77	MOUSE	RHINO	.62
CHIMP	GORILLA	.23	SQUIRREL	DOLPHIN	.32
CHIMP	MOUSE	.42	SQUIRREL	SEAL	.26
CHIMP	SQUIRREL	.40	SQUIRREL	ELEPHANT	.54
CHIMP	DOLPHIN	.40	SQUIRREL	RHINO	.61
CHIMP	SEAL	.43	DOLPHIN	SEAL	.06
CHIMP	ELEPHANT	.59	DOLPHIN	ELEPHANT	.54
CHIMP	RHINO	.64	DOLPHIN	RHINO	.54
GORILLA	MOUSE	.48	SEAL	ELEPHANT	.51
GORILLA	SQUIRREL	.47	SEAL	RHINO	.56
GORILLA	DOLPHIN	.38	ELEPHANT	RHINO	.57

set and gave a correlation of .75 ($N = 10$, $p < .01$).

The foregoing experiments provide evidence for the predictive value of the coverage variable of the similarity–coverage model. To evaluate the role of the similarity variable, a second series of studies was performed with specific conclusions. For example, 20 new subjects rated all 36 possible arguments of the form

X requires biotin for hemoglobin synthesis.
Y requires biotin for hemoglobin synthesis.
___
Horses require biotin for hemoglobin synthesis.

where X and Y are distinct mammals drawn from the base set, neither of them HORSE, and different arguments contain distinct pairs of mammals in their premises. As before, the ranks assigned by the 20 subjects to the 36 arguments were averaged and divided by 36. Table 5 presents these mean ranks.

According to the similarity–coverage model, the strength of each argument is given by

αSIM(X, Y; HORSE)
     $+ (1 - \alpha)$SIM(X, Y; [X, Y, HORSE]).

Because X and Y are mammals, [X, Y, HORSE] = MAMMAL, so the foregoing expression reduces to

αSIM(X, Y; HORSE)
     $+ (1 - \alpha)$SIM(X, Y; MAMMAL).

For each pair X, Y of mammals figuring in the experiment, the value of SIM(X, Y; HORSE) was taken directly from the data of the initial similarity study (using the MAX interpretation of SIM(X, Y; HORSE)). Regarding the second term, an approximation to SIM(X, Y; MAMMAL) was computed as described above. The similarity–coverage model implies that these two predictor variables should predict the obtained confirmation scores up to linearity. In fact, the multiple correlation coefficient between the latter two variables and the obtained confirmation scores is .96 ($N = 45$, $p < .01$).

Can the data be used to provide evidence for both similarity and coverage variables in the strength of specific arguments, that is, is there evidence for both SIM(X, Y; HORSE) and SIM(X, Y; MAMMAL) in an argument of form X, Y/HORSE? A natural way to test for the effect of these variables would be to compute the partial correlation between each predictor variable and the obtained confirmation score with the effects of the other predictor variable partialled out. Unfortunately, the interpretation of such an analysis is clouded by the fact that the similarity and coverage variables rely on overlapping facts about SIM. In particular, a high value of SIM(X, Y; HORSE) increases the value of SIM(X, Y; MAMMAL). For this reason, instead of partial correlations, we have computed nonpartial, Pearson coefficients between obtained confirmation and each predictor variable taken alone. The correlation between obtained confirmation scores and the similarity variables SIM(X, Y; HORSE) is .95 ($N = 45$, $p < .01$). The correlation between obtained confirmation scores and the coverage variable SIM(X, Y; MAMMAL) is .67 ($N = 45$, $p < .01$). These two coefficients are significantly different ($p < .01$).

The foregoing results suggest that maximum similarity to HORSE is sufficient to account for the obtained confirmation scores. This fact should not be taken to support the view that the strength of specific arguments depends only on the similarity of the premise categories to the conclusion category. Such a hypothesis is contradicted by qualitative phenomena discussed earlier (e.g., premise diversity for specific arguments, see Phenomenon 6).

The foregoing study was replicated three times using different mammals for the conclusion category, and different numbers of premises. The obtained correlations between predicted and observed confirmation scores were all .94 or better.

Other Replications

As a check on the robustness of the preceding findings, five additional studies were performed. Each study involved one or more of the following changes compared to the seven original studies. First, instead of ranking arguments, subjects rated the probability of an argument's conclusion assuming the truth of its premises; in addition, different blank properties were used for every argument. Second, subjects were native French or Spanish speakers, working with translated materials. Third, the category INSECT was used in place of MAMMAL. All correlations in these studies between predicted and observed confirmation scores were significant at the .01 level, with a median correlation of .88. See Smith et al. (1989) for details.

Discussion

The conjunction of qualitative and quantitative evidence discussed in previous sections provides reason to believe that the two terms of the similarity–coverage model reflect genuine psychological processes that are central to confirmation. The model nonetheless remains underdetermined by the data considered in this article. In this section, we take up several proposals for theoretical refinement or amendment.

Weighting of Instances by Availability

Different members of the same category are often differentially available to a person S, even if S can recognize all of them as members of the category. For example, robins may be more accessible than turtledoves in S's memory as members of the category BIRD. To represent such differential availability, the present version of the similarity–coverage model requires refinement. One way to achieve this is to incorporate relative availability in the computation of coverage. Specifically, for members $k_1 \ldots k_n$ of category G, SIM($k_1 \ldots k_n$; G) can be redefined so that the maximum similarity of $k_1 \ldots k_n$ to $g \in$ G is weighted by the availability of g to S.

Although weighting by availability does not affect the model's ability to deduce the 13 qualitative phenomena, it could conceivably improve predictive accuracy in the experiments reported. Accordingly, we examined several principled bases – all derived from rated typicality – for assigning relative availability to the mammals figuring in the experiments. None of these revisions of the model resulted in better overall predictive accuracy. This lack of improvement is probably due to low variability in availability among the mammals used; all were highly typical, and no doubt became even more available by virtue of their continued use in a given experiment.

MAX Versus SUM in SIM($k_1 \ldots k_n$; g)

Consider a specific argument P_1, P_2/C. In computing the overall similarity of CAT(P_1), CAT(P_2) to CAT(C), the similarity–coverage model employs a MAX function over the similarities of CAT(P_1) to CAT(C) and CAT(P_2) to CAT(C). Use of maximization was motivated by the observation that the strength of P_1, P_2/C seems not to be the sum of the strengths of P_1/C and P_2/C.

MAX is an extreme example of a nonadditive function, and it is possible that subjects use a function somewhere between MAX and SUM. Indeed, a more elaborate form of the similarity–coverage model might be equipped with another parameter that reflects an individual subject's position in the MAX to SUM continuum. Given this new parameter value β, the model would define $\text{SIM}_s(k_1 \ldots k_n; g)$ to be

$$\beta \text{MAX}\{\text{SIM}_s(k_1, g) \ldots \text{SIM}_s(k_n, g)\}$$
$$+ (1 - \beta)\text{SUM}\{\text{SIM}_s(k_1, g) \ldots \text{SIM}_s(k_n, g)\}.$$

This parameterized SIM function could then be incorporated into the similarity–coverage model as before, the resulting model having two parameters instead of one.

Diversity Versus Coverage

Philosophers of science underscore the usefulness of diversified data in testing scientific theories. Intuitively, there are fewer plausible alternatives to a theory that predicts phenomena of different sorts compared to one the predictions of which are always of the same kind. (For discussion, see Horwich 1982.) Given subject S and argument $P_1 \ldots P_n/C$, the closest variable to diversity in the present model is the coverage by $\{CAT(P_1) \ldots CAT(P_n)\}$ of the lowest level category that includes the premise and conclusion categories.

What is the relation between diversity in the philosopher's sense, and coverage in the present sense? To answer this question, it is necessary to assign a precise meaning to the diversity concept. Given subject S and set K of instances, we define $DIV_s(K)$ – the diversity of K (for S) – to be

$$SUM\{1 - SIM_s(k_1; k_2) \mid k_1, k_2 \in K\},$$

that is, the sum of the dissimilarities between members of K. Given sets K and G, we define the "diversity of K compared to G (for S)" to be $DIV_s(K)$ divided by $DIV_s(G)$. This latter quotient is denoted by $DIV_s(K; G)$. Observe that if either K or G have less than two members, then $DIV_s(K; G)$ is not defined.

Now let a subject S, a category G, and two instances k_1, k_2 be given. Then, $SIM_s(k_1, k_2; G)$ is the coverage of $\{k_1, k_2\}$ in G, and $DIV_s(\{k_1, k_2\}; G)$ is the diversity of $\{k_1, k_2\}$ compared with G. These two terms may differ considerably. For example, if k_1, k_2 represent highly dissimilar but very eccentric instances of G (e.g., whales and bats in the category MAMMAL), then $DIV_s(\{k_1, k_2\}; G)$ may be comparatively high but $SIM_s(k_1, k_2; G)$ may be comparatively low. We may use the similarity data of Table 3 to empirically contrast coverage and diversity. Taking G to be the base set of mammals, we calculated $SIM(k_1, k_2; G)$ and $DIV(\{k_1, k_2\}; G)$ over all 45 pairs k_1, k_2 of instances drawn from this set. The correlation of these two variables is only .55.

In terms of the DIV function, the philosopher's intuition about diversity may be stated as the following theory about general arguments involving more than one premise.

The diversity model for general arguments: For every person S and every general argument $A = P_1 \ldots P_n/C$ in which $n \geq 2$, the strength of A for S is given by

$$DIV_s(\{CAT(P_1) \cdots CAT(P_n)\}; CAT(C))$$

The reader can verify that the diversity model is compatible with those qualitative phenomena that bear on general arguments having more than one premise, namely, premise diversity, conclusion specificity, and premise monotonicity (Phenomena 2–4). We do not believe, however, that the diversity model is an accurate portrayal of the strength of general arguments. First, the model provides no account of single-premise, general arguments (because individual premises manifest no diversity). As a consequence, incorporating diversity into a more complete theory of category-based induction requires positing separate psychological mechanisms for single- versus multiple-premise arguments. Special provision would also be necessary for mixed arguments, for in such arguments confirmation can decrease rather than increase as premises become more dissimilar (cf. Phenomenon 9, nonmonotonicity, general). In contrast, the similarity–coverage model relies on a single (albeit extended) similarity function, and it applies uniformly to arguments of any number of premises, be they specific, mixed, or general. It may turn out that multiple, independent mechanisms underlie human inductive judgment, even for the restricted class of arguments at issue in this article. But complex models should not be favored over simple ones until required by recalcitrant data.

Also, there is a datum that seems to favor the coverage approach to general arguments over the diversity approach. There are general arguments $P_1, P_2/C$ and $Q_1, Q_2/C$ such that the diversity of $\{Q_1, Q_2\}$ exceeds that of $\{P_1, P_2\}$, but $P_1, P_2/C$ is stronger than $Q_1, Q_2/C$. To provide an example of such a pair of arguments, we note that $\{PELICAN, ALBATROSS\}$ is at least as diverse as $\{ROBIN, SPARROW\}$. The same experimental procedure used to verify the 11 qualitative phenomena also yields the following contrast.

Robins have a choroid membrane in their eyes.
Sparrows have a choroid membrane in their eyes.

All birds have a choroid membrane in their eyes.

(27a)

Pelicans have a choroid membrane in their eyes.
Albatrosses have a choroid membrane in their eyes.

All birds have a choroid membrane in their eyes.

(27b)

The diversity model is incompatible with this result. In contrast, the similarity–coverage model provides the following explanation for it. According to the model, for a given person S, the strengths of Arguments 27a and 27b are given by:

$$\alpha \text{SIM}_s(\text{ROBIN, SPARROW; BIRD})$$
$$+ (1 - \alpha)\text{SIM}_s(\text{ROBIN, SPARROW;}$$
$$[\text{ROBIN, SPARROW, BIRD}])$$

and

$$\alpha \text{SIM}_s(\text{PELICAN, ALBATROSS; BIRD})$$
$$+ (1 - \alpha)\text{SIM}_s(\text{PELICAN, ALBATROSS;}$$
$$[\text{PELICAN, ALBATROSS, BIRD}]),$$

respectively. Because [ROBIN, SPARROW, BIRD] = [PELICAN, ALBATROSS; BIRD] = BIRD, these expressions reduce to $\text{SIM}_s(\text{ROBIN, SPARROW; BIRD})$ and $\text{SIM}_s(\text{PELICAN, ALBATROSS; BIRD})$, respectively. These latter terms represent the coverage by {ROBIN, SPARROW} of BIRD, and the coverage by {PELICAN, ALBATROSS} of BIRD, respectively. $\text{SIM}_s(\text{ROBIN, SPARROW; BIRD})$ equals the average of $\text{MAX}\{\text{SIM}_s(\text{ROBIN; } b), \text{SIM}_s(\text{SPARROW; } b)\}$ over all birds b known to S. $\text{SIM}_s(\text{PELICAN, ALBATROSS; BIRD})$ equals the average of MAX $\{\text{SIM}_s(\text{PELICAN; } b), \text{SIM}_s(\text{ALBATROSS; } b)\}$ over all such birds b. It is obvious that for most subjects S, the former average is greater than the latter, because most birds known to S are small, sing, and so forth. The greater strength of Argument 27a compared to 27b is thereby deduced.

The Multiplicity of Categories in Confirmation Judgment

The similarity–coverage model assumes the existence of a preestablished hierarchy of categories that classify the instances figuring in an argument. The success of the model in predicting the qualitative phenomena discussed earlier testifies to the approximate soundness of the model's assumption. Greater predictive accuracy nonetheless requires supplementary principles to describe the variety of categories that subjects may create "on line" when reasoning about argument strength (cf. Barsalou 1983; Kahne-

man and Miller 1986). Thus, the following argument may give rise to the covering category SMALL ANIMAL in the minds of many subjects, despite the absence of this category from their prestored list of animal classes.

Hummingbirds require Vitamin L for carbohydrate breakdown.
Minnows require Vitamin L for carbohydrate breakdown.

Titmice require Vitamin L for carbohydrate breakdown.

The mental origin of such categories in reasoning about argument strength remains a central problem in the study of confirmation.

Notes

1   We use capitals to denote categories. Properties are italicized.
2   Outside the context of confirmation judgment, subjects may rate the similarity of a set to an object by averaging rather than by taking MAX. The present definition of $\text{SIM}_s(k_1 \ldots k_n; g)$ is not intended to apply outside the domain of confirmation.
3   Our present definition of $\text{SIM}_s(k_1 \ldots k_n; G)$ does not correctly apply to cases like SIM_s (EAST-MEXICAN-CHIHUAHUA; MAMMAL) because hardly any members of MAMMAL are at the same level as the very specific category EAST-MEXICAN-CHIHUAHUA. Such cases can be handled by a slight reformulation of our definitions. We do not pause for the details, however, because they are not relevant to the arguments considered in this article.
4   A spatial interpretation of similarity helps in understanding why central birds such as robins have greater average similarity to other birds than do peripheral birds such as penguins. Consider again the linearly arranged category Γ from the Extended Similarity Functions section. The reader can verify that the average distance between the peripheral member B and the rest of Γ is greater than the average distance between the central member D and the rest of Γ.
5   For some subjects, [ROBIN, BLUEJAY, SPARROW] may equal SONGBIRD rather than BIRD. Because {ROBIN, BLUEJAY} covers SONGBIRD even better than it covers BIRD, the model predicts such subjects to prefer Arguments 9a to 9b even more strongly than subjects for which [ROBIN, BLUEJAY, SPARROW] = BIRD.
6   It has been suggested to us that Argument 14b is weaker than Argument 14a because the former contains a pragmatic violation. Specifically, the violation is said to consist in the

fact that the orangutan premise of Argument 14b appears irrelevant to the conclusion, inasmuch as orangutans and bees belong to such different categories. Against this interpretation we may report that 64 of 100 Chilean undergraduates judged Argument 14c, below, to be stronger than Argument 14a, even though more of its premises violate the alleged pragmatic constraint.

Flies require trace amounts of magnesium for reproduction.

Orangutans require trace amounts of magnesium for reproduction.

Salmon require trace amounts of magnesium for reproduction.

Hawks require trace amounts of magnesium for reproduction.

Jellyfish require trace amounts of magnesium for reproduction.

Rattlesnakes require trace amounts of magnesium for reproduction.

Bees require trace amounts of magnesium for reproduction.

(14c)

We leave it to the reader to deduce from the similarity–coverage model the greater strength of Argument 14c compared with Argument 14a.

7   We note that this derivation rests on a questionable assumption, namely that a category such as ANIMAL can be mentally construed as a set of instances.

References

Barsalou, L. (1983). Ad hoc categories. *Memory & Cognition. 11*, 211–227.

Carey, S. (1985). *Conceptual change in childhood.* Cambridge, MA: MIT Press.

Collins, A., & Michalski, R. (1989). The logic of plausible reasoning: A core theory. *Cognitive Science. 13*, 1–50.

Gelman, S. (1988). The development of induction within natural kind and artefact categories. *Cognitive Psychology. 20*, 65–95.

Gelman, S., & Markman, E. (1986). Categories and induction in young children. *Cognition. 23*, 183–209.

Horwich, P. (1982). *Probability and evidence.* Cambridge, England: Cambridge University Press.

Kahneman, D., & Miller, D. (1986). Norm theory: Comparing reality to its alternatives. *Psychological Review. 93*, 136–153.

Osherson, D., Smith, E., & Shafir, E. (1986). Some origins of belief. *Cognition. 24*, 197–224.

Rips, L. (1975). Inductive judgments about natural categories. *Journal of Verbal Learning and Verbal Behavior. 14*, 665–681.

Rothbart, S., & Lewis, P. (1988). Inferring category attributes from exemplar attributes. *Journal of Personality and Social Psychology. 55*, 861–872.

Shafir, E., Smith, E. E., & Osherson, D. (in press). Typicality and reasoning fallacies. *Memory & Cognition.*

Smith, E. E., & Medin, D. (1981). *Categories and concepts.* Cambridge, MA: Harvard University Press.

Smith, E., Wilkie, O., López, A., & Osherson, D. (1989). *Test of a confirmation model* (Occasional Paper). Cambridge: Massachusetts Institute of Technology.

Tversky, A. (1977). Features of similarity. *Psychological Review. 84*, 327–352.

Chapter 18: When Explanations Compete: The Role of Explanatory Coherence on Judgments of Likelihood

STEVEN A. SLOMAN

Introduction

One way to decide whether a proposition is likely to be true is by considering why it might be true. We generate explanations and evaluate their plausibility. If the only available means of evaluating our explanations is in turn to explain them, then we are in danger of an infinite regress which leaves us uncertain as to the truth of the original proposition. But often some other means is available. We can evaluate our explanations by appealing to logic, authority, general knowledge or episodic memory. For example, to establish belief in the proposition

(A) Experienced car mechanics earn in the top quartile of incomes in the United States.

we might generate the explanation that they charge exorbitant and unnecessary labor costs which we can confirm from our own experience. This would increase the subjective likelihood of the proposition.

In the case of inductive inference, where we're deciding whether a proposition (a conclusion) is likely on the basis of knowledge that one or more related propositions (premises) are true, we must often consider not only why the conclusion might hold, but also why the premises do hold, and, most importantly, what implications our explanation for the premises has for the conclusion. One context in which this occurs is when we're reasoning by analogy. For example, consider the proposition concerning car mechanics above given the new information that

(B) Experienced electricians tend to earn in the top quartile of incomes in the United States.

A reasonable strategy would be to try to explain why both electricians and car mechanics would be in such income brackets and then decide whether the explanation for electricians is relevant to car mechanics. We can distinguish two cases. Either the explanations will be the same, if, for example, we ascribe both propositions to our belief that all skilled manual laborers earn that kind of money, or the explanations will be different, as they would be if we attribute the fact about electricians to their skill but we attribute the suggestion about car mechanics to their greed.

If the explanations are identical, we would expect the premise to increase belief in the conclusion. Because we know the premise to be true, any plausible explanation for it gains credibility. This form of reasoning is commonly called *abduction* and can be traced to the philosopher Charles Peirce (Ketner, 1992). Because our explanation has gained credibility, and because it also applies to the conclusion, our belief in the conclusion should increase. In short, a fact which increases the credibility of our explanation for an uncertain proposition should increase the subjective likelihood of that proposition. In other words, the conditional subjective likelihood of proposition A given proposition B, $Pr\{A|B\}$, should be greater than the unconditional subjective likelihood of proposition A, $Pr\{A\}$.

But what if our explanations for the premise and conclusion are different? How do people treat the evidential relation between propositions that they attribute to different causes? One reasonable strategy would be to treat the two propositions as separate and unrelated such that the given proposition does not influence willingness to confirm the other. If we believe that electricians earn as much money as they do because they are skilled and that car mechanics earn money for entirely different reasons, knowledge about electricians might have no bearing on our beliefs concerning the earning potential of car mechanics. If so, $Pr\{A \mid B\}$ should be equal to $Pr\{A\}$. Alternatively, if simply increasing the probability of the value of a property like earned income – by attributing it to electricians – increases the subjective likelihood that that property value will apply to other professions, regardless of our explanations for the propositions, then B should increase belief in A; $Pr\{A \mid B\}$ should again be greater than $Pr\{A\}$.

Explanation Discounting

Finally, different explanations might compete with each other. People may have a tendency to consider only one explanation for a property. The mere presence of an alternative explanation may cause discounting of others. A proposition B that provided a different explanation for the property could reduce confidence in the original explanation for proposition A and thereby decrease A's subjective likelihood. This reduction in confidence could arise in one or both of two ways. The alternative explanation could have its effect directly on the assessment of plausibility. The presence of an alternative could reduce the credibility of the original explanation. Another possibility is that the alternative explanation could reduce the likelihood of generating the original explanation. The presence of an alternative could inhibit the construction or retrieval of other, potentially more convincing explanations. Even if only one of these effects occurs, a proposition would *reduce* belief in another proposition whose explanation is different; $Pr\{A \mid B\}$ would be less than $Pr\{A\}$.

In sum, given an argument with premise B and conclusion A and taking Pr to be a particular person's subjective scale of probability, I hypothesize that $Pr\{A \mid B\} > Pr\{A\}$ if and only if A and B have the same explanation for that person and $Pr\{A \mid B\} < Pr\{A\}$ if and only if that person would explain A and B differently. The hypothesis pertains to the class of arguments in which

a single property is predicated of two categories, one in the premise and the other in the conclusion. To make the hypothesis viable, certain cases must be eliminated. In particular, the hypothesis does not apply to arguments in which premise and conclusion describe or imply competing outcomes or states of affairs. Consider the argument

Car mechanics claim to be the highest paid manual laborers.

Therefore, skilled electricians claim to be the highest paid manual laborers.

If we explain these statements in the same way, for example by attributing both claims to the two groups' willingness to work hard, then the premise would probably reduce belief in the conclusion because only one claim can be true (car mechanics and skilled electricians cannot both be the highest paid manual laborers). On the other hand, if we explain these statements differently, then the premise could increase belief in the conclusion. For example, if we explain the premise by appealing to a belief that car mechanics are habitual liars but explain the conclusion by attributing it to our belief that skilled electricians work hard, then the premise would be likely to increase belief in the conclusion because, by implying that the car mechanics' claim is false, it reduces the competition skilled electricians have to the title "highest paid manual laborer". Other exceptions to the hypothesis may also exist.

A variety of evidence is consistent with the hypothesis that a premise will decrease the judged probability of a conclusion when the two statements have different explanations. Indeed, the hypothesis is related to Kelley's (1973) discounting principle which states that the role of a given cause in producing a given effect is discounted if other plausible causes are also present (p. 113). The attribution of cause is one form of explanation. Kelley's principle summarizes the results of a number of studies in which subjects evoke compliance from either a lower- or higher-status target person. Subjects are less likely to attribute the lower-status target person's behavior to internal as opposed to external factors than the higher-status person's (although an overall bias to make internal attributions has also been observed; e.g., Ginzel, Jones, & Swann, 1987). The suggestion is that people will discount certain causes, like helpfulness, if other plausible ones, like desire-to-please, are available. As these studies show, such a heuristic can provide a rational solution to an attribution problem.

Shaklee and Fischhoff (1982) elaborated on this principle by showing that people use a "truncated search" strategy when determining the causes of an event with multiple possible causes. Subjects who knew that a cause was involved in an event chose to learn additional details about the cause rather than learn about other possible causes. They not only discounted alternative causes, they didn't even want to learn more about them. Knowledge of the relevance of one cause inhibited interest in others.

Finally, evidence suggesting the explanation discounting hypothesis comes from research concerning the psychological strength of arguments containing unfamiliar predicates – predicates which subjects cannot reason about or explain, such as "require trace amounts of magnesium for reproduction". Using such arguments, Osherson, Smith, Wilkie, Lopez, and Shafir (1990) demonstrated a phenomenon that they called nonmonotonicity. They asked people to choose the stronger of the following two arguments; that is, to choose the argument whose conclusion was made more likely by the premises:

(C)   *Flies require trace amounts of magnesium for reproduction.*

   Therefore, bees require trace amounts of magnesium for reproduction.

(D)   *Flies require trace amounts of magnesium for reproduction.*
   Orangutans require trace amounts of magnesium for reproduction.

   Therefore, bees require trace amounts of magnesium for reproduction.

Most subjects chose argument C. Adding the premise concerning orangutans to the argument concerning flies and bees actually reduced argument strength. I have suggested (Sloman, 1993) that the strength of such arguments is proportional to feature coverage – the extent to which the features of the premises *cover* those of the conclusion. I have also suggested that the cause of the nonmonotonicity phenomenon is that incompatible premise features compete and inhibit one another, which reduces their coverage of the features of the conclusion. We may have a bias to put greater weight on features that are common to all premises. Because orangutans and flies share few features, the distinctive fea-

tures of orangutans may inhibit those of flies. And because orangutans share few features with bees as well, whereas flies share many, some of those inhibited features will likely be common to flies and bees. Orangutans would reduce the weight of features shared by premises and conclusion without contributing to feature coverage.

What is meant by "feature" in this context? One interpretation is that a feature is a pointer to an explanation; each premise feature can be associated with an explanation for why the predicate applies to that premise category. Under this interpretation, my hypothesis amounts to the claim that explanations compete with and inhibit each other. In the nonmonotonicity example, all the competition happens to take place amongst alternative explanations for the premises. If the principle of explanation discounting holds, then it should apply more generally. Alternative explanations suggested by the premise should also have the effect of reducing the credibility of a conclusion for which a different explanation is readily available.

In sum, three ideas converge to suggest the operation of an explanation discounting principle: Kelley's (1973) suggestion of a discounting principle, Shaklee and Fischhoff's (1982) demonstration of the truncated search strategy in causal attribution, and the explanation for the nonmonotonicity phenomenon offered by Sloman (1993). I now report two experiments that test whether this principle operates when people are making inductive inferences concerning meaningful properties.

Experiment 1

I test the hypothesis that explanations compete with each other by comparing the difference between judgements of the probability of a conclusion when presented alone and the conditional probability of the conclusion given some fact, that is, a premise, under two conditions: either the premise and conclusion have the same explanation or they have different explanations. Consider the following argument:

(E)   *Many ex-cons are hired as bodyguards.*

   Many war veterans are hired as bodyguards.

If both these statements are true, they are likely true for the same reason, namely that both ex-cons and war veterans tend to be tough and experienced fighters. But the statements of the next argument have different explanations:

(F)   *Many ex-cons are unemployed.*

       Many war veterans are unemployed.

The reason the premise may be true is that ex-cons are often considered untrustworthy. However, the reasons for the conclusion are that war veterans sometimes suffer psychological trauma or that they're social outcasts. Explanation discounting would predict that the conditional probability judgement in the first case, where premise and conclusion explanations are the same, should be greater than the raw conclusion probability judgements. In the second case, where explanations are different, they should be lower.

Method

Sixteen category pairs were chosen. Each pair was used to construct two arguments: one whose premise and conclusion explanations were expected to be the same, and one whose explanations were expected to be different. Arguments were constructed by choosing two predicates: one for the argument in the Same condition and the other for the argument in the Different condition. Twenty Brown University undergraduates, paid for their participation, were tested on each of the resulting 32 arguments. Each subject completed four questionnaires that asked them to, respectively, judge the probability of each premise, judge the probability of each conclusion, judge the conditional probability of each conclusion given its corresponding premise, and provide an explanation for each premise and each conclusion. These explanations were collected in order to verify that explanations were the same for Same-condition arguments and different otherwise.

All subjects first completed the premise probability judgement task. They were shown a scale, from 0 to 1.0 in increments of 0.1, that was labeled "very unlikely" under 0, "completely unsure" under 0.5 and "very likely" under 1.0. They were also shown two examples of statements, unrelated to any of the arguments, with different probabilities filled in and justified. They were instructed to write a number from 0 to 1.0 beside each statement that indicated the likelihood that the statement was true. One group consisting of half the subjects next judged the conditional probabilities and a second group

Table 1: Conclusion and Conditional Likelihood Estimates in Experiment 1 as a Function of Relation Between Explanations

Judgement Task	Premise and Conclusion Explanations	
	Same	*Different*
Pr{Conclusion}	0.62	0.54
Pr{Conclusion/Premise}	0.66	0.47
Pr{C | P} – Pr{C}	0.041	−0.071

consisting of the other half judged the conclusion probabilities. In the third phase, the two groups switched tasks. Instructions for the conclusion task were identical to those for the premise task except that no examples were provided. When conclusions were rated second, subjects were requested to ignore the facts from the preceding section. For the conditional ratings, subjects were again shown a scale and asked to rate the probability of the conclusion taking into account the fact that precedes it, whether the fact seems true or not. Each premise was preceded by "Fact:" in bold lettering and each conclusion by "Conclusion:", also in bold format. An example was provided. Finally, each subject provided the most plausible explanation of each statement of each argument as they could. Two example explanations of one sentence each were presented. Subjects were encouraged to be brief. Completing the four tasks took about an hour per subject.

Two orders of items were used. The first consisted of a random order of Same and Different arguments under the constraint that an equal number of Same and Different arguments appeared in the first and second halves of the list. The second order was identical except that the order of the two list halves was reversed. Each order was given to half of each group of subjects. The same order was used for each task. Each subject saw the premises, the conclusions, the arguments and the statements to explain in the order given by the arguments from which they came.

Results and Discussion

As predicted, the difference between conditional and conclusion probabilities was positive for Same-condition arguments and negative for Different-condition arguments, as shown in Table 1. The premise increased subjects' willingness to affirm the conclusion when both statements of the arguments had the same explanation. For example, they judged the probability that *many war veterans are hired as bodyguards* to be higher when told that *many ex-cons are hired as bodyguards* than when they were not told anything about ex-cons. Furthermore, the premise decreased subjects' willingness to affirm the conclusion when statements had different explanations. The conditional probability that *many war veterans are unemployed* given that many ex-cons are was judged lower than the unconditional probability of war veterans exhibiting the property. This pattern is corroborated by a repeated-measures analysis of variance whose factors were judgement task (conclusion vs. conditional probability) and type of explanation (same or different). Conclusion and conditional probability judgements were not significantly different, $F(1, 19) < 1$. Judgements in the Different condition were significantly lower than those in the Same condition, $F(1, 19) = 68.80$; $p < .0001$, partly because, as expected, conditionals were lower in the Different condition and partly because, by chance, conclusion probabilities were also lower. Most importantly, the interaction between the two variables was significant, $F(1, 19) = 14.29$; $p < .01$. As described above, premises had opposite effects in the two conditions. The analysis across items showed an identical pattern. Furthermore, premises had a significantly positive effect in the Same condition, $t(19) = 2.22$; $p < .05$, and a significantly negative effect in the Different condition, $t(19) = -2.16$; $p < .05$.

The analyses just described collapse over the order in which subjects made the probability judgements and are therefore all within-subjects. However, if we consider only those judgements that were made prior to (and are therefore uncontaminated by) conclusion judgements and those conclusion judgements that were made prior to (and are therefore uncontaminated by) conditionals, an identical pattern of means is observed. Because these two types of judgements were made first by different groups of subjects, this comparison is between-subjects. The difference in the Same condition increased to 0.075 and the difference in the Different condition increased to −0.063.

Were our intuitions about whether explanations would be the same or different correct? We answered this question by rating subjects' explanations. We categorized as either same or different each pair of explanations (from phase 4 of the experiment) provided by each subject that corresponded to the premise and conclusion of each argument. We thus had 20 ratings of expla-

nation sameness, one from each subject, for each argument. We then asked a naive judge to make these ratings. The judge was instructed to rate the explanations as the same if they had substantially the same content, that is, if a naive person given one explanation would treat it as synonymous with the other. She agreed with 84% of our judgements. The discrepant cases were given to a second naive judge, who made a final decision.

Analysis of these judgements shows that explanations tended to be more different than we had expected. Only 60% of explanations in the Same condition were actually the same whereas 91% in the Different condition were actually different. Most importantly, however, if we condition probability judgements on whether explanations were actually the same or different, we obtain an identical pattern of results to that reported above.

Moreover, the number of explanations consistent with our expectations helps to predict the magnitude of the effect we see across items. If we consider only those items that we expected to have the same explanation, the correlation between the number of times they actually had the same explanation and the difference between the conditional and conclusion probability judgments was .43. In contrast, if we consider only those items for which we expected explanations to be different, the number of actually different explanations helped to predict when we would expect a large negative difference, the correlation being −.21. The magnitude of this correlation is fairly low because of range attenuation; the number of actually different explanations was usually very close to 20.

The mean premise probability judgements were 0.60 in the Same condition and 0.63 in the Different condition. Their difference is marginally significant, $t(19) = 2.07$, $.05 < p < .10$, although probably not meaningful. The differential effect of the premise on belief in the conclusion in the two conditions is not easily attributed to differences in either premise or conclusion probabilities because of the double dissociation observed: the premise has a positive effect in one condition but a negative effect in the other. In any case, these attributions are ruled out by the next experiment.

Experiment 2

Because different arguments were used in the Same and Different conditions of Experiment 1 (although categories were held constant), the logical possibility exists that the effects we observed were the result of our particular choices of premises and conclusions. Perhaps, purely by chance and not because of their underlying explanations, we chose premises in the Same condition that had a positive influence on their conclusions and premises in the Different condition that had a negative influence. Experiment 2 both tests this possibility and attempts to replicate the results of Experiment 1.

To test whether the chosen premises were responsible for the observed interaction, we reversed the condition of each premise. Each premise that was in the Same condition was associated with a new conclusion that we expected would have a different explanation, and each Different-condition premise was associated with a new conclusion that we expected would have the same explanation. The prediction is identical to that above: premises should have a positive effect in the Same condition and a negative effect in the Different condition. Changing the arguments in this way also tests whether the results of Experiment 1 were due to our particular choice of conclusions in that Experiment 2 involves a new set of conclusions.

Method

The method of Experiment 2 was identical to that of Experiment 1 except that a different set of arguments was used. We again tested 20 Brown University undergraduates. The premises in the Same condition were identical to those that appeared in Experiment 1's Different condition and those in the Different condition appeared in the previous experiment's Same condition. New conclusions were constructed to make the explanations for the premise and conclusions the same or different, as desired. For example, consider argument E above from the Same condition. We changed the conclusion category so that the new argument read

(G)   *Many ex-cons are hired as bodyguards.*

Many bachelors are hired as bodyguards.

Now the explanation for the conclusion will probably be different from that of the premise. Instead of having to do with toughness, it will reflect that bachelors have no attachments and therefore nothing to lose. Similarly, Different-condition argument F above was changed to read

(H)   *Many ex-cons are unemployed.*

Many people with bad credit histories are unemployed.

Table 2: Conclusion and Conditional Likelihood Estimates in Experiment 2 as a Function of Relation Between Explanations

Judgement Task	Premise and Conclusion Explanations	
	Same	Different
Pr{Conclusion}	0.50	0.58
Pr{Conclusion/Premise}	0.61	0.49
Pr{C|P} – Pr{C}	0.11	−0.098

Now both statements are likely to have the same explanation; namely, that those people tend to be treated as bad risks.

Results and Discussion

The results replicated those of Experiment 1 closely except that the difference between the Same and Different conditions was more pronounced. Again as predicted, the difference between conditional and conclusion probabilities was positive for Same-condition arguments and negative for Different-condition arguments, as shown in Table 2. A two-factor repeated-measures analysis of variance across subjects again confirms the reported pattern. This time neither the main effect of judgement task nor of type of explanation was significant, both $Fs < 1$, but the interaction was highly significant, $F(1, 19) = 30.30$; $p < .0001$. The F-ratios across items were substantially similar. The effect of the premise was significantly positive in the Same condition, $t(19) = 5.43$; $p < .001$, and significantly negative in the Different condition, $t(19) = -3.13$; $p < .01$. If we consider only those conditional judgements that were made prior to conclusion judgements and conclusion judgements that were made prior to conditionals – a between-subjects comparison – the pattern of means is identical. The difference in the Same condition increases to 0.14 and in the Different condition to −0.090.

We used subjects' explanations to evaluate whether explanations were actually the same or different in a manner identical to that used in Experiment 1. This time the first naive judge agreed with 90% of our initial judgements. We again overestimated our subjects' tendency to provide the same explanation for two statements although this time we were more accurate. Sixty-eight percent of explanations in the Same condition were actually the same, 85% in the Different condition were actually different.

Again, conditioning probability judgements on whether explanations were actually the same or different makes no substantial difference to the effects we observe.

The number of explanations consistent with our expectations provides an even better prediction of the magnitude of our effect across items relative to Experiment 1. For items that we expected to have the same explanation, the correlation between the number of times they actually had the same explanation and the difference between the conditional and conclusion probability judgements was .54, whereas for items for which we expected explanations to be different, the correlation between the number of actually different explanations and the probability differences was −.51.

The mean premise probability judgements were 0.59 in the Same condition and 0.56 in the Different condition. The difference is not significant, $t(19) = 1.09$, n.s. Because no difference was observed and because the order of means is opposite to that of Experiment 1, the differential effect of the premise cannot be attributed to its probability. Analogously, because the order of conclusion probability means was opposite to that of Experiment 1, the effects of the premise cannot be attributed to their relative order.

General Discussion

Two experiments have shown that categorical facts in the context of arguments will tend to increase the subjective likelihood of other categorical statements if their explanations are consistent. They will tend to decrease the subjective likelihood of other statements if their explanations are different. Because all categories and predicates appeared in both explanation conditions, the differential effect of the premises is not due to peculiarities of the statements chosen. These results support the explanation discounting principle, which assumes that the likelihood of a statement is often derived by evaluating the plausibility of its explanation, and posits that people will tend to focus on a single explanation such that alternative explanations compete and inhibit one another.

The results that I have reported cannot be dismissed by attributing to subjects a misunderstanding of the conditional probability rating task. One might argue that, instead of rating the conditional probability of the conclusion given the premise – which combines prior belief in the conclusion with the belief transmitted by the premise – subjects are evaluating the

strength of the argument – which factors out prior belief and reflects only the belief transmitted by the premise. On this view, subjects' relatively low conditional likelihood judgements may simply reflect their belief that arguments in which premise and conclusion have different explanations are weak. This interpretation is unsatisfactory both for empirical and conceptual reasons. First, the correlation between conclusion and conditional probabilities was 0.53 in Experiment 1 and 0.44 in Experiment 2 ($ps <$ .001). Such high correlations would be expected on the assumption that subjects were doing what they were asked to do – namely, rate the likelihood of the conclusion given all available evidence. If subjects were actually rating argument strength, the correlation should not differ from 0. More fundamentally, this hypothesis sheds no light on the central question under scrutiny: how are people influenced by the relation between the explanations of a premise and a conclusion when generalizing a property? It simply rephrases the question in terms of the determinants of argument strength.

One implication of my hypothesis is that two statements should have symmetric effects on each other. Given statements A and B whose explanations are different, $Pr(A \mid B) < Pr(A)$ if and only if $Pr(B \mid A) < Pr(B)$. Likewise, given statements A′ and B′ whose explanations are the same, $Pr(A' \mid B') > Pr(A')$ if and only if $Pr(B' \mid A') > Pr(B')$. My hypothesis thus predicts a property of subjective probability scales that also happens to obtain for probability scales that satisfy the axioms of standard probability theory.

I have suggested two mechanisms that could be responsible for the effects we observe when the explanation of the premise is not consistent with that of the conclusion. First, the presence of the premise explanation could cause subjects to discount their explanation for the conclusion by making them aware that alternative explanations are available. Second, the presence of the premise explanation could inhibit subjects from constructing or retrieving an alternative and more plausible explanation for the conclusion when they are evaluating its likelihood by causing them to perseverate on their explanation for the premise. I do not propose to attempt to distinguish these two hypotheses, not only because both probably capture some aspect of subjects' reasoning, but also because the proposals may not be distinguishable after sufficient elaboration. To illustrate, consider a model of likelihood assessment that states that the credibility of a statement is proportional to the success of a process which attempts to construct an explanation for the statement that is maximally consistent with one's knowledge and beliefs. Furthermore, the process is competitive in the sense that propositions that cohere with the emerging explanation become more active and those that are incoherent are inhibited so that only a small set of propositions come out as "winners". A natural representation for the plausibility of an explanation in this model would be its degree of activation after a winner has been chosen. Similarly, a natural representation of the degree to which an explanation has been constructed or retrieved in this model would also be its degree of activation. So, by this model, the two hypotheses would be indistinguishable because they would both be represented by the same theoretical construct.

The decisive role played by the explanation of an event in providing a sense of certainty in an outcome is now well established (Sloman, 1990). For example, Koriat, Lichtenstein, and Fischhoff (1980) were able to reduce subjects' probability judgements concerning their answers to general knowledge questions by having them generate reasons contradicting their answers. Indeed, counterexplanation techniques have proved to be one of the few successful methods for reducing certain forms of bias in confidence judgements, such as the confirmation bias (Lord, Lepper, & Preston, 1984) and the hindsight bias (Slovic & Fischhoff, 1977). Ross, Lepper, Strack, and Steinmetz (1977) had subjects explain events in the lives of two psychiatric patients. They then informed subjects that the events were fictitious. Despite this discreditation of the evidence, subjects rated the likelihood of the event higher than did a group who had not generated an explanation. Apparently, explaining an event can be sufficiently convincing to make belief in it independent of data.

Pennington and Hastie (1988) argue that decision-making is "explanation based" (see also Wilson, Dunn, Kraft, & Lisle, 1989). They presented evidence to subjects in a mock courtroom situation either in chronological order, in which subjects were able to construct a story of the event in question, or in random (witness) order. Subjects were swayed more by evidence presented in story order than in witness order. Again, construction of a single coherent explanation for an event made it more credible, which is consistent with the present result that making different explanations simultaneously available

reduced confidence. People try to generate an internally consistent organizational structure to evaluate the likelihood of an event in a way that can override the desire to be as complete as possible in the consideration of alternatives. Explanation discounting may be less a product of an active competitive process than a side-effect of our tendency to try to capture relevant information in one coherent package. The very act of constructing an explanation may cause us to neglect others.

The notion of "explanation" is not unambiguous and a complete analysis is not yet available. One illustrative attribute of an explanation is that it must not presuppose the statement that it is explaining (see Osherson, Smith, & Shafir, 1986, for a fuller discussion of related issues). At minimum, a convincing explanation can be characterized as one which reduces a statement to others which can be independently confirmed through some form of logic, memory, or appeal to authority.

The experiments that I describe do not distinguish explanations that are inconsistent from those that are merely different. I have shown that, under the present conditions, $Pr(A \mid B) < Pr(A)$ if and only if A and B are related through the sharing of a predicate (and possibly otherwise related) and they have different explanations. The effect may have emerged because subjects treated the explanations as inconsistent. The possibility remains open that statements which are completely unrelated and have different explanations will not influence each other, $Pr(A \mid B) = Pr(A)$.

Variations of the conditional probability rating task employed in this research have been used to study the process of inductive inference in both children (e.g., Carey, 1985) and adults (e.g., Rips, 1975). This work has demonstrated a variety of systematicities in the inductive process, most of which are summarized by the dozen phenomena described by Osherson et al. (1990) and Sloman (1993) concerning judgements of the strength of arguments that use statements with unfamiliar predicates. An example phenomenon is nonmonotonicity, described above, which states that adding a premise will sometimes decrease the strength of an argument.

The work has also spawned a variety of theories of the process of inductive inference, including two computational models (Osherson et al., 1990; Sloman, 1993). Osherson et al. explain the nonmonotonicity phenomenon by positing that people consider a higher-level, inclusive category which they draw from a stable category hierarchy when judging argument strength. Their model predicts nonmonotonicities whenever the additional premise category is not included in the higher-level category under consideration because people then have to consider an even higher-level, more inclusive category. This rule has some exceptions. See Osherson et al. (1990). In Experiment 1 of this paper, arguments in both the Same and Different conditions used the same categories. Therefore, cases in which the premise reduced confidence in the conclusion cannot be attributed to a change in the inclusive category under consideration. Apparently, we cannot always appeal to category-inclusion hierarchies to understand the conditions under which premises make a conclusion seem less plausible.

An alternative hypothesis, implemented in the feature-based model of Sloman (1993), is that the strength of an argument is directly related to feature coverage – the proportion of the conclusion category's features or attributes that it shares with the premise categories. The model is implemented as a simple connectionist network that takes advantage of the automatic generalization properties of distributed representations so that the links between categories and the predicate in the premises will automatically transfer to the conclusion by way of common features. As stated, this model has no way of accounting for nonmonotonicities. However, I explain them in Sloman (1993), as described above, by essentially invoking the principle of explanation discounting and discuss one of several ways to implement it in the model.

People's tendency to discount explanations when alternatives are available is an effective strategy for reducing uncertainty in a variety of situations. For example, we saw above how it helped to elucidate the motivation behind a person's behavior. When you ask someone over whom you have power to do you a favor, a reasonable conclusion is that their agreement to do so does not imply that they are intrinsically helpful. Similarly, if Alaska's leading cause of death were pneumonia, we could reasonably increase our degree of belief that pneumonia is associated with a cold climate, which in turn would make it less likely that Mexico's leading cause of death is pneumonia. However, an unrestrained use of such a strategy can also lead us astray. We found that the claim that many furniture movers have bad backs made subjects less

likely to believe that many secretaries have bad backs. The explanation discounting hypothesis explains this on the basis of the fact that secretaries will have bad backs from sitting over a desk for too long whereas furniture movers will have bad backs as a result of heavy lifting. If the hypothesis is right, then the different explanations compete and inhibit one another. But should they? Presumably humans can have bad backs for several reasons. The mere fact that heavy lifting can cause back problems should have no bearing on whether sitting too long at a desk can also cause back problems. Our hesitancy to consider multiple explanations for a property can lead us to underestimate the likelihood of propositions that can be true for multiple reasons.

References

Carey, S. (1985). *Conceptual change in childhood*. Cambridge: MIT Press.

Ginzel, L. E., Jones, E. E., & Swann, W. B., Jr. (1987). How "naive" is the naive attributor? Discounting and augmentation in attitude attribution. *Social Cognition*, 5, 108–130.

Kelley, H. H. (1973). The processes of causal attribution. *American Psychologist*, 28, 107–127.

Ketner, K. L. (Ed.) (1992). *Reasoning and the logic of things: The Cambridge Conferences Lectures of 1898, Charles Sanders Peirce*. Cambridge, MA: Harvard University Press.

Koriat, A., Lichtenstein, S., & Fischhoff, B. (1980). Reasons for confidence. *Journal of Experimental Psychology: Human Learning and Memory*, 6, 107–118.

Lord, C. G., Lepper, M. R., & Preston, E. (1984). Considering the opposite: A corrective strategy for social judgment. *Journal of Personality and Social Psychology*, 47, 1231–1243.

Osherson, D., Smith, E. E., & Shafir, E. (1986). Some origins of belief. *Cognition*, 24, 197–224.

Osherson, D., Smith, E. E., Wilkie, O., López, A., & Shafir, E. (1990). Category-based induction. *Psychological Review*, 97, 185–200.

Pennington, N., & Hastie, R. (1988). Explanation-based decision making: Effects of memory structure on judgment. *Journal of Experimental Psychology: Learning, Memory, and Cognition*, 14, 521–533.

Rips, L. (1975). Inductive judgments about natural categories. *Journal of Verbal Learning and Verbal Behavior*, 14, 665–681.

Ross, L., Lepper, M. R., Strack, F., & Steinmetz, J. (1977). Social explanation and social expectation: Effects of real and hypothetical explanations on subjective likelihood. *Journal of Personality and Social Psychology, 35,* 817–829.

Shaklee, H., & Fischhoff, B. (1982). Strategies of information search in causal analysis. *Memory & Cognition, 10,* 520–530.

Sloman, S. A. (1990). *Persistence in memory and judgment: Part-set inhibition and primacy.* Unpublished doctoral dissertation, Stanford University.

Sloman, S. A. (1993). Feature-based induction. *Cognitive Psychology, 25,* 231–280.

Slovic, P., & Fischhoff, B. (1977). On the psychology of experimental surprises. *Journal of Experimental Psychology: Human Perception and Performance, 3,* 544–551.

Wilson, T. D., Dunn, D. S., Kraft, D., & Lisle, D. J. (1989). Introspection, attitude change, and attitude-behavior consistency: The disruptive effects of explaining why we feel the way we do. In L. Berkowitz (Ed.), *Advances in Experimental Social Psychology* (Vol. 22, pp. 287–343). New York: Academic Press.

Chapter 19: Properties of Inductive Reasoning

EVAN HEIT

Imagine that during an evening while you are out at the theater, your home is broken into and several personal items are stolen. This sudden event, in addition to having practical and possibly emotional consequences, is going to lead to changes in your beliefs and predictions about the future. Whereas you may have previously thought that your home was secure, you may now believe, on the basis of this one event, that it is rather likely that your home will be burgled again.

In the terms of inductive reasoning, you may well see similarities between one case – your home on this particular evening – and future cases – that is, your home on other, future evenings – leading you to project a predicate – being burgled – from the one case to the others. Of course, carrying out this sort of inductive reasoning would be more complicated, because there are the many past cases of evenings on which your home has not been burgled, and these cases too seem to have implications for the future. In addition, other information may be useful, such as whether or not nearby homes have been burgled recently. It seems that due to the similarity in location, knowing the history of other homes would help you to predict the safety of your own home.

This paper addresses how people project information from known cases to the unknown. The aim is to integrate the findings from a large number of psychological studies conducted over the past 25 years, on adults as well as children. From a tradition starting with Rips (1975), psychological experiments on inductive reasoning have typically addressed how people make inferences about predicates or properties of things such as animals – for example, about whether

a dog is susceptable to a particular kind of disease – rather than idiosyncratic events such as home burglaries. One reason for the extensive study of reasoning using animal categories rather than individual personal events is that we have a rich and well-documented categorical structure for representing animals and other living things.

It is possible to think of many cognitive activities as containing an element of inductive reasoning, using the known to predict the unknown; such activities range from problem solving to social interaction to motor control. However, this paper will focus on a narrower range of phenomena, concerning how people evaluate inductive arguments such as the following example:

Goldfish thrive in sunlight

Tunas thrive in sunlight.

The information above the line is taken as a premise that is assumed to be true; the task is to evaluate the likelihood or strength of the conclusion, below the line. There are several possible variants of this task. For example, the premise and conclusion could be presented as sentences or in pictures. There could be more than one premise. In addition, information in the premises could be provided for a category, such as all goldfish, or for an individual, such as one particular fish. Likewise, the conclusion could refer to a category or a specific individual. Finally, there are several ways to collect judgments about the conclusion; one could, for example, require responses on a scale of probability or inductive strength, or forced-choice judgments, in which subjects must choose between different

Reproduced with permission from Heit, E. (2000) Properties of inductive reasoning. *Psychonomic Bulletin & Review*, 7, 569–592.

conclusions. Indeed, some studies could be described as collecting behavioral judgments rather than asking questions. For example, in some infant studies, induction is measured in terms of what action the child performs with a particular toy. Generally speaking, not all the results reported in this paper have been documented for all the different task variants, because researchers have typically assumed that the different variants address the same underlying processing. However, when systematic differences between different task versions have been reported, these will be highlighted.

This paper is intended to answer a number of questions about inductive reasoning, using the current findings from psychological research. The first three questions are factual and empirical, concerning how people respond to various kinds of inductive arguments. First, what makes a case generalizable? That is, when does an observation that something has a certain property promote the inference that something else has that property? Second, what makes a set of cases generalizable? The evidence shows that simply putting together a list of the most convincing, or induction-promoting, cases does not necessarily lead to the strongest possible ensemble of cases. The interesting result is that sometimes a set of individually weak cases can make a strong case together. Third, what makes a property projectable? That is, when we observe an object with various properties, which properties of the object are more likely to be projected to another case or inferred than others? Many psychological studies of inductive reasoning have addressed more than one of these questions. Therefore, different facets of the results of these studies will be described at different points in this paper.

The final question to be addressed is as follows: What are the psychological models of inductive reasoning? In the fourth main section of this paper, formal models of inductive reasoning will be discussed. Rather than present all of these accounts in detail, these accounts will be described just in terms of how they address the results covered by the first three questions. In Table 1, the touchstone results from psychological experiments on inductive reasoning will be listed, and the models of induction will be assessed against this list.

However, before proceeding with this review of psychological work on inductive reasoning, it is worth acknowledging that the study of induction has a longer history in other fields such as philosophy. Perhaps the best-known analysis

Table 1: Touchstone Results in Inductive Reasoning

Inferences From Single Cases
1. Similarity between premise and conclusion categories promotes induction.
2. Typicality of the premise category promotes induction. (No corresponding findings for the conclusion category.)
3. Homogeneity of the conclusion category promotes induction. (No corresponding findings for the premise category.)

Inferences From Multiple Cases
4. Greater number of observations, or premises, promotes induction (although the evidence is weak for children).
5. Greater diversity of observations, or premises, promotes induction (although the evidence is mixed for children, and too much diversity may not help even for adults).

Influence of Properties
6. There is widespread evidence that people draw inferences differently depending on the property being projected (found in adults and children).
7. Some properties are idiosyncratic or transient, with a narrow scope for inferences, whereas other properties are more broadly projected.
8. The assessment of similarity between categories in an argument depends on the property being projected.

from philosophy is Hume's (1748/1988) argument against the logical justification of induction. Hume argued that, unlike deductive inference, there is no basis for establishing the validity of a method for drawing inductive inferences. Although psychological work on induction has not directly addressed this traditional problem of induction, psychological research does paint a somewhat more optimistic picture, emphasizing how inductive reasoning is widespread in human thought and how people perform this reasoning very systematically. Psychological research has uncovered a rich and interesting set of phenomena that reveal much about cognitive processes. Furthermore, although they fall short of a complete logical justification for induction, some psychological accounts have addressed whether people's patterns of inductive reasoning do meet basic cognitive goals and to what extent people are subject to fallacies or internal contradictions. As the psychological phenomena are reviewed in this paper, when there have been related philosophical analyses these will be presented as well.

What Makes a Good Case?

The first issue to be addressed is why do we more readily draw inferences from some cases than others? For example, hearing about a burglary 2 miles away normally would have more effect than a burglary 100 miles away, on inferences about the security of one's own home. In fact, the notion of proximity is central to understanding induction, because similarity between cases has been found to be one of the main determinants of inductive strength. Actually, in this section, two questions will be covered. First, what is it about a premise category that promotes inferences to a conclusion category? Second, what makes a conclusion category itself seem like a good target for inferences? All of the results in this section will refer to situations where there is a single premise provided, because there is a well-established set of central phenomena for single-premise arguments. In the next section of this paper, inferences using multiple premises will be considered.

Initial Adult Studies

The seminal study of inductive reasoning was that of Rips (1975). This work looked at how adults project properties of one category of animals to another. Subjects were told to assume that on a small island, it had been discovered that all members of a particular species (of birds or mammals) had a new type of contagious disease. Then the subjects judged for various other species what proportion would also have the disease. For example, if all rabbits had this disease, what proportion of dogs would have it? Rips used a variety of animal categories in the premise and conclusion roles, with the categories having a known similarity structure derived using multidimensional scaling techniques. It was found that two factors consistently promoted inferences from a premise category to a conclusion category.

First, similarity between premises and conclusions promoted strong inferences. For example, subjects made stronger inferences from rabbits to dogs than from rabbits to bears. Second, the typicality of the premise, with respect to its superordinate category, was critical in promoting inferences. (Typicality of *rabbit*, for example, would be measured in terms of its distance from the representation of its superordinate, *mammal*, in a multidimensional scaling solution.) The result was that more typical premise

categories led to stronger inferences than did atypical premise categories. For example, with the bird stimuli, having *bluejay* as a premise category led to stronger inferences overall than did having *goose* as a premise category. Using multiple regression analyses, Rips (1975) found distinct contributions of premise–conclusion similarity and premise typicality. Interestingly, there was no evidence for a role of conclusion typicality. For example, all other things being equal, people would be as willing to draw a conclusion about a bluejay or about a goose, despite the difference in typicality of these two categories. It is important to keep these three findings in mind, because they recur in many subsequent studies of inductive reasoning – namely, that premise–conclusion similarity and premise typicality promote induction, but that typicality of the conclusion category does not seem to affect inductive strength.

Chronologically speaking, the next major study in this paradigm was done by Nisbett, Krantz, Jepson, and Kunda (1983), who also asked subjects to draw inferences about items (animals, people, and objects) found on a remote island. For example, subjects were told to imagine that one member of the Barratos tribe was observed to be obese, and they estimated the proportion of all members of this group that would be obese. Likewise, the subjects were told that one sample of the substance "floridium" was observed to conduct electricity, and they estimated the proportion of all members of this set that would conduct electricity. There were several interesting findings from the Nisbett et al. study, but for our present purposes the most relevant is that the subjects were very sensitive to perceived variability of the conclusion category. For a variable category such as Barratos people (and their potential obesity), the subjects were rather unwilling to make strong inferences about other Barratos, after just one case. But for a homogenous category such as floridium samples, the subjects were willing to generalize the observation of electrical conductance to most or all of the population.

This result, that subjects were more willing to draw inferences about homogenous conclusion categories, makes a striking comparison to the results of Rips (1975). Whereas Rips found that typicality of the conclusion did not affect inductive strength, the results of Nisbett et al. (1983) results show that conclusion categories do matter, at least in terms of their variability. The criteria for what makes a good premise category are different than the criteria for what makes a good conclusion category.

Studies with Children on Use of Shared Category Membership

The Rips (1975) task has been adapted for testing with children, first by Carey (1985). There are a number of important reasons to study inductive reasoning in children. Such studies could show how inductive abilities develop, perhaps guiding or constraining accounts of fully developed, adult inductive reasoning. In comparing two models that equally account for adult data, if one model can also give an explanation of the course of development, then that model ought to be favored. Also, the performance of children on induction tasks can help the researcher determine what children know about a particular domain. For example, a pattern of age-related changes in reasoning about animals could reflect the growth of children's knowledge or theories about living things. Of course, with these different reasons for studying the development of induction, there is always the challenge of whether to attribute a change in performance to development of reasoning processes or development of knowledge.

Carey (1985) used an induction task with pictures of humans, animals, plants, and other things. Children, as young as age 4, were shown a picture of a premise item, such as a picture of a person, and told that it had some property, such as that of having a spleen inside.[1] Then the child was shown several pictures of other things, such as dogs, bees, and flowers, and was asked whether each also had the same property – for example, that of having a spleen. A number of results showed what makes a good case, from the point of view of young children. For children of age 6 and under, information about persons, as premises, tended to promote strong inductions. For example, when told that a person had a spleen, children were inclined to judge that dogs and bees had spleens as well. On the other hand, other animals did not make good cases, or were considered weak premises. For example, projection from dogs to humans was much weaker than projection from humans to dogs. This result maps well onto the finding of typicality effects by Rips (1975), given the assumption that children consider humans to be very typical animals.

Some of the other results from Carey (1985) also map well onto past results, in particular that similarity effects were also found. A fact about humans was projected most strongly to other mammals, then to other animals such as birds and bees, and progressively less to plants and inanimate objects. Children as young as age 4 showed this pattern, but the steepness of the generalization gradient was greater in older children, suggesting greater sensitivity to similarity between categories.

On their own, these results from Carey (1985) would perhaps be described best as resulting from a change in knowledge rather than a change in processing. That is, as children get older, they lessen their use of humans as a prototype, and they increase the steepness of their generalization gradient when using information about similarity between various animals, plants, and inanimate objects. These changes could well reflect a maturing conception of things in the living world, and an increasing differentiation between various categories, rather than changes in how inductive reasoning is actually performed. However, this issue will be revisited as other results are described.

Chronologically, the Carey (1985) study was followed by several studies by Gelman and colleagues (Gelman 1988; Gelman and Coley 1990; Gelman and Markman 1986; Gelman and O'Reilly 1988). In these experiments, similar procedures to Carey's were used, with children being told a property of some animal or object in a picture and then judging whether or not other animals or objects would also have this property. Gelman and Markman tested children as young as age 4, with the particular aim of looking at the nature of similarity effects. Although Carey did find similarity effects in young children, there are various ways in which animals and other things could be considered similar, and it is important to understand what kind of conception of similarity is guiding inductive inferences. Gelman and Markman contrasted similarity based on perceptual appearances with similarity based on underlying shared category membership. For example, a blackbird and a bat may look fairly similar, whereas a blackbird and a flamingo may not appear too similar, but the latter two share many internal characteristics because they are both birds. Using questions about unfamiliar internal properties, Gelman and Markman found that young children preferred to project between pairs of items with shared category membership, even when the members of the pair were less similar on the surface than those of some other pair. Therefore it was concluded that children used a fairly sophisticated conception of similarity to guide inductive reasoning, with deeper similarities such as category membership overriding more superficial similarities.

Gelman (1988) examined inductive reasoning at different levels of a taxonomic hierarchy (cf. Rosch, Mervis, Gray, Johnson, and Boyes-Braem 1976). For example, given the premise that a daffodil has some novel property, children were asked whether the property would be true of another daffodil (same subordinate level category), a rose (same basic level category), a houseplant (same superordinate level category), and a bowl (unrelated category). Children as young as age 4 showed a generalization gradient that was similar to that for the results of Carey (1985), with the most projections within the subordinate level, and decreasing projections at higher levels of the taxonomy. Gelman pointed out that the results could reflect not only similarity-based reasoning but also sensitivity to category variability or homogeneity (as in Nisbett et al. 1983), with lower level categories being more homogenous. Indeed in some cases adult judgments of category homogeneity were significantly correlated with likelihood of children's inferences to that category. In a second study done by Gelman (1988), children were asked to generate their own familiar properties for the premise category and were then asked to judge whether this property held for the various conclusion categories as well. It was found that judgments about familiar properties followed the same patterns as did judgments about novel properties, suggesting that subjects might make inferences about novel properties by considering the distribution of known properties (see Heit 1998).

As in Gelman's (1988) experiments, Gelman and O'Reilly (1988) looked at inductive reasoning at different points in a taxonomic hierarchy, but the focus was at higher or more superordinate levels of the taxonomy. Again, the pattern of results consisted in a decreasing likelihood of inferences at progressively higher taxonomic levels. This study also showed that children were equally willing to make inferences to typical superordinate category members and atypical superordinate category members, as in Rips (1975).

Gelman and Coley (1990) tried to extend the main results from older children to 2-year-olds, using a somewhat simpler procedure. The key findings were that children were able to use shared category membership to guide inferences, even when it conflicted with surface similarity, and that, again, the typicality of conclusion categories did not affect induction. In a useful control condition, it was found that the sharing of

a category label, such as "bird," was critical to obtaining these results. Shared transient properties, such as "wet," did not serve as a reliable basis for induction.

At this point, it is worth mentioning parenthetically that despite this evidence for shared category membership as a basis for induction, in preference to perceptual similarity and other shared attributes, there is indeed evidence that perceptual similarity and other shared attributes do have some role in promoting inductive reasoning. That is, if two things look alike, you may still want to project a property from one to another on this basis, despite different category membership. In studies with children (as young as age 3) and adults, Florian (1994) found effects of perceptual similarity and shared attributes on induction, beyond effects of category membership. (See also Loose and Mareschal 1999.)

Keeping with the progression of finding category membership as a basis for induction at increasingly younger ages, it is interesting to consider the relevant studies done with infants. Children as young as 3 or 4 years have shown a rather sophisticated use of similarity and category membership to guide induction. How well does this ability extend to even younger children? Again, induction tasks with infants could reflect their inductive reasoning abilities as well as their knowledge base for a particular domain of categories. Baldwin, Markman, and Melartin (1993) examined inductive inference in infants between 9 and 14 months of age, using an exploratory play task. The children learned, after a brief exposure of 30 seconds about a property of a novel toy – for example, that a can would make a wailing sound when squeezed. The test was whether children would expect another toy of similar appearance to have this property as well. Children played for a longer time with a second object that did not have the target property (e.g., a can that did not wail) in comparison with appropriate control conditions, suggesting that the infants had inferred that the second toy would be like the first toy and were surprised that it did not have the same property. This study showed that some of the inductive ability in older children is also present with infants, but it was not designed to look at whether or not children use a taxonomy of categories to support induction.

Mandler and McDonough (1996) also looked at induction with infants, but focused more on use of established taxonomies of categories. They looked especially at the use of the superordinates *animal* and *vehicle*. The infants were taught an action to perform on an object, such as giving a (toy) dog a drink; then they were tested on whether this action was generalized to other objects in the same superordinate category (e.g., a rabbit) and the other superordinate category (e.g., a bus). The children's pattern of play respected the boundaries of superordinate categories, with actions taught on one animal being extended to other animals but not to other vehicles, and likewise actions taught on one vehicle extended to other vehicles but not animals. However, there was not evidence for much sensitivity to distinctions within the superordinate category. That is, infants did not project more between similar items (e.g., *dog* and *rabbit*) than between dissimilar items (e.g., *dog* and *fish*), as long as all items were in the same superordinate category. There are a number of ways to conceive of this result. As in Gelman and Markman (1986), it shows the primacy of shared (superordinate) category membership. Unlike Gelman (1988), Mandler and McDonough (1996) did not address shared subordinate or basic level category membership, so it is difficult to say whether inductions would have been even stronger with subordinate or basic level categories than with superordinate categories (but see Mandler and McDonough 2000). Would the inferences have been even stronger from one kind of dog to another? Finally, the dissimilar conclusion categories in Mandler and McDonough (1996) tended to be atypical of the superordinate category (e.g., fish are less typical animals than are rabbits), so the lack of distinctions among various conclusion categories within a particular superordinate category could be taken as a replication of the finding that conclusion typicality does not affect induction (Carey 1985; Gelman and O'Reilly 1988; Rips 1975).

Perhaps the best way to summarize the Baldwin et al. (1993) and Mandler and McDonough (1996) studies is that they documented an important subset of the known results for older children, using ordinary infant behaviors (playing with toys) as a means of measuring induction rather than other forms of the task which would require explicit judgments.

Further Phenomena Involving Typicality, Similarity, and Specificity

One of the advantages of studying induction in adults rather than children is that it is possible to present a greater number of problems in one session and potentially address a greater range of phenomena. Indeed, Osherson, Smith, Wilkie, López, and Shafir (1990) have made a substantial and influential contribution to the study of inductive reasoning by documenting a set of important phenomena (see also Osherson, Stern, Wilkie, Stob, and Smith 1991). Several of these phenomena involve reasoning from just a single premise category, whereas the remainder involve multiple premises and will be described in a later section of this paper. The experiments of Osherson et al. (1990) involved giving subjects pairs of inductive arguments such as the following:

Robins use serotonin as a neurotransmitter
———————————————————————————
Sparrows use serotonin as a neurotransmitter

and

Robins use serotonin as a neurotransmitter
———————————————————————————
Geese use serotonin as a neurotransmitter.

Subjects would tend to choose the first argument as stronger than the second, illustrating the premise–conclusion similarity phenomenon (reported by Rips 1975, and subsequently others). In addition, Osherson et al. (1990) documented the premise typicality effect, reported by Rips and others. As an extension of this result, Osherson et al. (1990) described the premise–conclusion asymmetry phenomenon; for example, the argument from robins to geese above would be stronger than the reversed argument, from geese to robins (see also Carey 1985, for an example of asymmetry). This phenomenon follows from the premise typicality effect, because whenever an argument has a premise category more typical than its conclusion category, the reversed argument should be weaker than the original argument.

Next, Osherson et al. (1990) documented the conclusion specificity phenomenon. It was found that arguments with a more specific conclusion category, such as *bird*, were considered stronger than arguments with a more general conclusion category, such as *animal*. This result makes sense from a logical perspective, in that more evidence should be needed to support a more sweeping conclusion about a relatively superordinate category, in comparison with a narrow conclusion about a more subordinate category. (See also McDonald, Samuels, and Rispoli 1996, for correlational evidence that over a range of arguments, scope of conclusion category is one of three good predictors of inductive strength.) This phenomenon can also be tied to the Nisbett et al. (1983) result showing that people make stronger inferences about more homogenous categories. In general, superordinate categories should be more variable than their subordinate categories, because the superordinate includes its own subordinates.

One of the important contributions of Osherson et al. (1990) was that they began to show where people's inductive inferences diverge from normative patterns. Rather than take the Humean approach of addressing whether induction can be justified, Osherson et al. (1990) aimed to show examples in which people's inductive inferences were clearly not justified – for example, because they violated axioms of probability. One relevant phenomenon is the inclusion fallacy, illustrated in the following arguments:

Robins secrete uric acid crystals

All birds secrete uric acid crystals

and

Robins secrete uric acid crystals

Ostriches secrete uric acid crystals.

People choose the first argument as stronger than the second, even though the first conclusion logically implies the second. Because the second conclusion is implied by the first conclusion, the probability of the second conclusion should not be lower than the probability of the first conclusion. The inclusion fallacy seems to reflect the use of similarity between the premise and conclusion in making judgments. If the representations of *robin* and *bird* are quite similar (due to the typicality of *robin*), but *ostrich* has a quite different representation than *robin*, then the second argument could seem weaker than the first. However, it should be noted that the more general result is the conclusion specificity phenomenon, in which arguments with more specific conclusion categories are considered stronger. The inclusion fallacy would seem to apply only in cases such as the example above involving a pair of category members, one very typical, such as *robin*, and one atypical, such as *ostrich*.

Also, using picture versions of the Osherson et al. (1990) tasks, López, Gelman, Gutheil, and Smith (1992) found evidence for a number of the Osherson et al. (1990) single-premise phenomena with children ranging from ages 5 to 9. In addition to typicality effects, López et al. (1992) found conclusion specificity effects; for example, inferences were weaker for a conclusion about animals and plants than for a conclusion about just animals. This result, again, can be taken as support for the Nisbett et al. (1983) findings of poor generalization to variable categories, here with young children. Likewise, the López et al. (1992) result converges nicely with the Gelman (1988) and Gelman and O'Reilly (1988) results that children draw strong inferences between items that are both members of a relatively specific, subordinate category.

Furthermore, Sloman (1993, 1998) extended the findings of the inclusion fallacy by demonstrating another phenomenon, inclusion similarity. As in the inclusion fallacy, the inclusion similarity phenomenon shows an effect of similarity between premise and conclusion categories, in an apparently nonnormative way. However, Sloman reported these effects even more dramatically, for deductively valid, perfectly strong arguments. Subjects found arguments of the form Animals/Mammals (i.e., with *animal* as the premise category and *mammal* as the conclusion category) stronger than arguments like Animals/Reptiles. Notably, both of these arguments are equally, and perfectly, valid. That is, anything true of all animals must necessarily be true of all mammals and all reptiles as well. However, an argument such as Animals/Reptiles may get a low strength rating because of relatively low similarity between the respective representations of *animal* and *reptile*.

Sloman (1998) documented a related phenomenon, called *premise specificity*, which also shows compellingly the influences of similarity on people's evaluations of inductive arguments. This phenomenon is well illustrated by the following example: People will prefer an argument with the form Birds/Sparrows over an argument with the form Animals/Sparrows. As in the inclusion similarity phenomenon, each argument is perfectly valid – there is no difference in the probability of the conclusion for one argument versus the other. Still, subjects describe the first argument, with a narrow premise category, as being stronger than the second, with a broad premise category. Sloman (1998) reported that the inclusion similarity and premise specificity findings were fairly robust over variations in procedure, but it is possible to prevent subjects from drawing such fallacious inferences by making the category inclusion relations explicit – for example, by reminding subjects that all sparrows are animals. It is also interesting to compare the premise specificity phenomenon with the conclusion specificity phenomenon

(Osherson et al. 1990), in which people draw stronger inferences about a narrower conclusion, such as *bird* in comparison with *animal*. In contrast, conclusion specificity does seem to be compatible with axioms of probability theory.

Effects of Expertise on Induction

Developmental research on induction is important because, potentially, both knowledge and cognitive capacities are changing as children get older, allowing researchers to collect a very rich set of data. However, as mentioned, it can be difficult to attribute a developmental change uniquely to a change in knowledge or a change in cognitive mechanism. At the other end of the developmental continuum, adults are acquiring expertise on various topics suited to their living conditions or working needs. Although adults with different areas of expertise, or from different cultures, could possibly differ in terms of cognitive processing, it is plausible to attribute expertise differences in inductive reasoning largely to differences in knowledge. A recent, exciting trend consists of research on experts' inductive reasoning, going beyond past studies which had mainly looked at reasoning in American college students and American children. Coley, Medin, and Atran (1997) and López, Atran, Coley, Medin, and Smith (1997) studied inductive reasoning by Itzaj Mayans in the rainforest of Guatemala, people with great expertise regarding local plants and animals. Medin, Lynch, Coley, and Atran (1997) looked at inductive reasoning about categories of plants, by various kinds of tree experts.

Coley et al. (1997) looked at inductive reasoning at different levels of the taxonomic hierarchy of animals and plants. The purpose of this work was to see whether some taxonomic level is "privileged" or specially favored for inductive inferences, and whether this privileged level varies on the basis of expertise. For example, subjects were told to assume that all black vultures (a subspecies) are susceptible to a particular disease and were asked the likelihood that all vultures (a species, or strictly speaking a folk-generic category) would be susceptible to this disease. Coley et al. (1997) tested various premise–conclusion pairs, including the pairings of varietal and subspecies, subspecies and species, subspecies and lifeform (e.g., birds), species and lifeform, and lifeform and kingdom (e.g., animals). The key result, for both Itzaj and American college students, was that there was a sharp drop in strength of inferences when

conclusion categories were beyond the species level. That is, inferences regarding subspecies and species conclusion categories were quite strong, whereas inferences regarding the lifeform and kingdom level were much weaker. Coley et al. (1997) interpreted this result as showing that the species level is privileged, in that it is the broadest taxonomic level that supports strong inferences. However, specificity of the premise category did not seem to have much effect on induction, to the extent that Coley et al. (1997) compared premise categories at different taxonomic levels.

This study can be tied to a number of past results. First, the general result of weaker inferences for broader or more variable conclusion categories recapitulates the findings of Nisbett et al. (1983) and more recently the conclusion specificity phenomenon in Osherson et al. (1990) and López et al. (1992). Also there is some similarity between the study of Coley et al. (1997) and the work done by Carey as well as Gelman and colleagues, showing weaker inferences to the extent that the category encompassing the premise and conclusion items is more general or superordinate. However, the specific finding of Coley et al. (1997), that the species level is privileged, would not necessarily be predicted on the basis of past work. Indeed, it is surprising that the same level of privileged inference was found for the Itzaj and American college students, considering the knowledge differences – the far greater daily experience of plants and animals among the Itzaj. Coley et al. (1997) suggested that beliefs about categories' usefulness for induction could go beyond actually known facts and experiences. For example, American college students could simply have a belief that different species of animals have their own characteristic anatomies, diseases, and so forth, without any more specific knowledge to this effect (see also Heit 1998, Shipley 1993), so someone could treat a particular level as being privileged without detailed knowledge to support this distinction.

López et al. (1997) also compared induction by the Itzaj and by American college students and, in contrast to Coley et al. (1997), found more widespread influences of knowledge on patterns of inductive reasoning. They examined similarity and typicality effects and found that the patterns of inductions differed between the two cultures in cases where their category representations diverged. For example, the Itzaj reported foxes as being more similar to cats than to dogs, whereas American students stated that foxes are more similar to dogs. This pattern was reflected by choices in a task where subjects saw pairs of inductive arguments. Itzaj subjects stated that arguments of the form Foxes/Cats were stronger, whereas Americans stated that those of the form Foxes/Dogs were stronger. Although Coley et al. (1997) did not find cross-cultural differences in the privileged level of conclusion categories, it is clear from López et al. (1997) that indeed there are some cultural, or knowledge-derived, differences.

Further evidence for effects of knowledge on induction comes from Medin et al. (1997), who looked at inferences about plant categories for three kinds of (American) tree experts: taxonomists, landscapers, and tree maintenance workers. Medin et al. were mainly interested in effects of similarity or shared category membership, for groups that differed among themselves regarding preferred taxonomic membership and, on occasion, differed with regard to standard scientific taxonomies. For example, on a free sorting task, landscapers and maintenance workers tended to organize tree species in terms of their shape or utility for various landscaping tasks. Medin et al. (1997) devised questions on a test of inductive reasoning that pitted scientific matches against alternative, functional category structures. For example, two tree species might be distant in terms of the scientific taxonomy, but they could both be useful for providing shade. The test items for the inductive inferences used biological properties concerning reproduction, disease, or physiology. It was found that taxonomists (not surprisingly) sorted trees on the basis of scientific taxonomy and likewise favored inductive arguments between categories that were close in the scientific taxonomy. Maintenance workers seemed to favor a more functional category organization for both sorting and reasoning. Landscapers seemed to be more flexible and possibly more conversant with multiple category structures; they tended to prefer functional organization for sorting but their biological inferences reflected knowledge of the scientific taxonomy. In sum, these three groups of experts generally showed the similarity effects that have been documented in other populations, but the groups' knowledge about trees mediated these similarity effects. (See also Proffitt, Coley, and Medin 2000.)

Discussion

The study of inductive arguments with a single premise category has produced a number of interesting and consistent results. What promotes an inference from one case to another? The three key factors that promote inductive inferences are similarity between premise and conclusion category (in terms of a taxonomic hierarchy rather than superficial similarities), typicality of the premise category, and homogeneity of the conclusion category. Returning to the example at the start of this paper, how would these variables affect inferences about home burglaries? Similar cases should promote inference, so a burglary that is particularly near your home, or a recent burglary as opposed to one from the distant past, should increase the perceived risk for your own home. In addition, typicality of the given case should affect inferences, beyond any given effect of similarity. For example, if your neighborhood consists mainly of houses, a burglary in a houseboat should not generalize well to burglaries in other homes. The relation between houses and houseboats could well be asymmetrical, reflecting this difference in typicality. That is, characteristics of houses may seem to generalize to characteristics of houseboats better than characteristics of houseboats would generalize to those of houses. Finally, variability of the conclusion category should lead to weaker inferences. For example, a home that is sequentially occupied by different people with different habits and different possessions and is sometimes completely unoccupied would be relatively difficult to make predictions about, compared with a more stable conclusion item.

These three results have ties to past philosophical work on induction. Similarity effects, or the idea that seeing some commonalties between two items should promote the inference of further commonalties, has been a longstanding position in philosophy (see, e.g., Mill 1874). However, Goodman (1972) has argued that similarity itself may not be a primitive notion; for example, the features that are used to assess similarity can be context dependent (see Hahn and Chater 1997, and Medin, Goldstone, and Gentner 1993, for reviews of related psychological results). Likewise, Gelman and Markman (1986) made an important distinction between inductions based on internal similarity and those based on external, perceptual similarity. This issue will be returned to in the third section, which describes results in which the use of similarity depends on the property being projected.

Furthermore, Shipley (1993) has applied Goodman's (1955) work on induction to several results in psychology. The idea that some categories, such as more typical categories, are particularly good for promoting inferences, in part because of their past frequency of use, is related to Goodman's (1955) idea of entrenchment of predicates, with some predicates (or categories) promoting inferences more than others. However, this analysis does not explain why entrenchment, or typicality, of premise categories matters but typicality of conclusion categories does not. Again, the point could be made that typicality is not a primitive concept any more than similarity, and there could be several determinants of typicality such as frequency of use, centrality, similarity to other category members, and nearness to an ideal (cf. Barsalou 1985).

Finally, the use of beliefs about variability of conclusion categories, or beliefs that some taxonomic level may be privileged for induction, is tied to Goodman's (1955) concept of overhypotheses. Overhypotheses are general beliefs that guide inference, without necessarily having much specific content. For example, a person can believe that samples of a particular kind of metal will be homogenous in terms of whether they conduct electricity, without any more specific knowledge of whether this kind of metal does in fact conduct electricity. The sensitivity to conclusion variability in Nisbett et al. (1983) can be explained in terms of use of overhypotheses about different kinds of categories (metals, people, etc.).

To conclude, it is interesting to note the results that have not been reported. For example, there have been no reports to date of independent effects of the typicality of the conclusion category as opposed to the premise category. Indeed, it would seem useful for any account of induction to address why conclusion typicality does *not* matter, even as it explains why premise typicality does matter. Another nonresult relates to the homogeneity or variability of a premise category. It is clear that conclusion homogeneity promotes inferences, but no studies have directly addressed the effects of homogeneity of a single premise category. (Sloman's, 1998, premise specificity effect comes the closest, but this result seems to have depended heavily on similarity between the premise and conclusion categories, rather than on the homogeneity of the premise category.) This issue may be somewhat easier to study with multiple premise categories, because the diversity within, say, a pair of premise categories can be manipulated easily by choosing similar versus different pairings. The next section will address

premise diversity as well as several other important results that have been obtained by studying induction with multiple categories.

What Makes a Good Set of Cases?

When people try to make an inference about some object or event, they are typically faced with a great deal of information. Rather than just one past case being available or relevant, in many realistic situations there will be an extensive set of cases that could be relied on. How do people draw inductive inferences from multiple cases? What makes a set of cases or precedents seem strong, compelling, or useful for promoting inferences? One factor is numerosity. For example, the more homes that have been broken into on your street, the greater the perceived risk for your own home. However, one of the fascinating characteristics of human inductive inference is that people do not simply add up evidence from individual cases. That is, putting together two cases that are strong on their own does not necessarily lead to an even stronger argument based on both cases. In the first part of this section, the evidence for when numerosity does increase inductive strength will be covered, then the evidence for more complex and subtle phenomena, dependent on the diversity and variability of cases rather than their numerosity, will be reviewed.

Number of Cases

In their study involving inferences about people and objects on an island, Nisbett et al. (1983) systematically varied the given number of observations. For example, subjects were told that one, three, or twenty obese members of the Barratos group had been observed and were asked what proportion of all Barratos are obese. In general, inferences were stronger with increased sample size. However, this effect interacted with homogeneity of the conclusion category. If the conclusion category was perceived as very homogenous (e.g., floridium samples with respect to electrical conductivity), then just one case was enough for subjects to generalize to the whole population (or nearly 100%). Therefore there was something of a ceiling effect, and increases in sample size did not always lead to higher estimates.

Osherson et al. (1990) referred to the sample size effect as *premise monotonicity* – namely, a monotonic relation between the number of premise categories in an inductive argument and rated inductive strength. Although they found interesting exceptions to this phenomenon, to be described shortly, the overall trend supported this generalization. Likewise, McDonald et al. (1996) measured inductive strength for a variety of arguments and found that the number of premise categories in the argument was one of the reliable predictors of strength.

Not only does sample size or number of premise categories serve as a robust determinant of inductive strength in adults, but in some cases children's inductive inferences appear to be sensitive to sample size. In particular, both López et al. (1992) and Gutheil and Gelman (1997) found some evidence for sample size effects in 9-year-olds. López et al. (1992) used a picture version of the Osherson et al. (1990) task, and found that 9-year-olds favored an argument of the form Raccoon, Leopard, Skunk, Tiger, Giraffe/Animal over the form Skunk, Tiger, Giraffe/Animal. More premise categories led to greater inductive strength. However, the sample size effect was not entirely robust, even in 9-year-olds. Children of this age did not show sample size effects for similar arguments with a more specific conclusion category – that is, *bear* rather than *animal*. López et al. (1992) interpreted this difference between more general and more specific conclusion categories in terms of the account proposed by Osherson et al. (1990). According to Osherson et al. (1990), evaluating an argument with a specific conclusion category such as *bear* would require the generation of a superordinate category, such as *animal* or *mammal*. Therefore the arguments with a specific conclusion would require more cognitive processing and hence would be more difficult overall, masking any sensitivity to sample size. In contrast, López et al. (1992) failed to find any sensitivity to sample size among 5-year-olds for both general and specific arguments, even in a task in which the experimenter counted the number of premise categories for the child. At present, there seems to be no evidence that children younger than 9 use sample size evidence in inductive reasoning, although it is tempting to imagine that sample size is such a central element of reasoning that in the future procedures might be devised to find sensitivity in younger children.

Gutheil and Gelman (1997) also looked at sample size effects in 9-year-olds. As in López et al. (1992), there was actually mixed evidence, with the children failing to show sensitivity to sample size in some cases. Gutheil and Gelman used a similar procedure to that of López et al. (1992), describing hidden properties of animals, but with categories at a somewhat lower taxonomic level. All of the premise items were in the same basic level category (e.g., they were all frogs). On the basis of past work (e.g., Gelman and O'Reilly 1988) showing that children's inferences are stronger at lower taxonomic levels, it was hoped that the sample size effect would be more evident at lower levels. Gutheil and Gelman used a specific conclusion (e.g., a picture of another frog), and in their first attempt they did not find sample size effects in 9-year-olds, essentially replicating López et al. (1992). In a second study, however, they simplified the task by not showing the picture of the conclusion item but simply describing it. Here, Gutheil and Gelman found sample size effects – namely, stronger inferences based on five premise items as opposed to one premise item.

Diversity of Cases

Although sheer numerosity of cases does have some effect on induction, there is also substantial evidence that variability or diversity of cases affects inductive strength. Intuitively, repeating the same evidence, or highly similar pieces of evidence, again and again should not be much more convincing than just giving the evidence once. On the other hand, if different kinds of converging evidence come from different sources, then potentially a stronger or broader case can be made. This result, that more variable observations promote broader or stronger generalizations, is now considered a truism in areas of research near to induction, such as categorization (e.g., Fried and Holyoak 1984; Homa and Vosburgh 1976; Posner and Keele 1968).

The first study of diversity-based reasoning in induction was a developmental one by Carey (1985), comparing 6-year-olds and adults. Carey looked at patterns of inductive projection, given the premises that two diverse animals, dogs and bees, have some biological property. The purpose of this study was to see whether subjects would reason that "if two such disparate animals as dogs and bees" had this property then "all complex animals must" (p. 141). Indeed, adults made broad inferences to all animals, extending the property not only to things that were close to the premises (other mammals and insects) but also to other members of the *animal* category (such as birds and worms). In contrast, the children seemed to treat each premise separately;

they drew inferences to close matches such as other mammals and insects, but they did not use the diversity information to draw a more general conclusion about animals. Therefore, in this first attempt there was evidence for effects of diversity in adults but not children. However, Carey was simultaneously interested in development of reasoning as well as development of the *animal* concept. The nonappearance of the diversity effect in children could have been due to an undeveloped *animal* concept in 6-year-olds, rather than different or incomplete processing.

In a follow-up study, Carey (1985) looked at diversity effects based on the concept *living thing* rather than *animal*. The most relevant result was that subjects were taught a biological fact either about dogs and bees or about dogs and flowers, with the latter being even more diverse than the former. Given a fact about dogs and flowers, children did tend to generalize fairly broadly, suggesting that children may have some sensitivity to diversity of premise categories. However, if anything, they tended to overgeneralize, extending the property not only to other living things but often to inanimate objects as well. Therefore Carey concluded that 6-year-old children did not quite have a developed *living thing* concept serving as the basis for induction. Still, there was suggestive evidence for the impact of diversity of premise categories in this study.

Continuing along this line of research that looks for diversity effects in children, López et al. (1992) found limited evidence for 9-year-olds and no evidence for 5-year-olds. For the 5-year-olds, choices in a picture-based task did not show any sensitivity to diversity of premise categories, even when the diversity was explicitly mentioned by the experimenter. However, 9-year-olds did show sensitivity to diversity of premises, but only for arguments with a general conclusion category such as *animal* rather than a specific conclusion category such as *kangaroo*. Again, López et al. (1992) explained this result in terms of arguments with specific conclusion categories' requiring more stages of cognitive processing than are needed for arguments with general conclusion categories.

Gutheil and Gelman (1997) attempted to find evidence of diversity-based reasoning for specific conclusions in 9-year-olds, using category members at lower taxonomic levels, which would presumably enhance reasoning. However, like López et al. (1992), Gutheil and Gelman did not find diversity effects in 9-year-olds, although

in a control condition with adults, there was robust evidence for diversity effects.

More recently, however, Heit and Hahn (1999) reported diversity effects in children younger than 9 years, in experiments with pictures of people and everyday objects as stimuli rather than animals with hidden properties. For example, children were shown a diverse set of dolls (a china doll, a stuffed doll, and a Cabbage Patch doll), all being played with by a girl named Jane. Also children were shown a nondiverse set: three pictures of Barbie dolls, being played with by Danielle. The critical test item was another kind of doll, a baby doll, and the question was, Who would like to play with this doll? In another stimulus condition, there was a diverse set of hats worn by one person, and a nondiverse set worn by another person, and again, the critical question was whether another hat would belong to the person with diverse hats or the person with nondiverse hats. For 74% of these critical test items, children 5 to 8 years of age made the diverse choice rather than the nondiverse choice. It seems from the Heit and Hahn experiments that children can follow the diversity principle at some level. However, it will take further work to establish the critical differences that led the past studies not to find diversity effects in children.

Indeed for adults, or at least American college students, there has been considerable evidence for diversity-based reasoning. Osherson et al. (1990) documented diversity effects in adults, for written arguments with general as well as specific conclusion categories. López (1995) devised a stricter test of diversity-based reasoning, in which people chose premise categories rather than simply evaluate arguments given a set of premises. In other words, would people's choices of premises reveal that they valued diverse evidence? Subjects were given a fact about one mammal category, and they were asked to evaluate whether all mammals had this property. In aid of this task, the subjects were allowed to test one other category of mammals. For example, subjects would be told that lions had some property, and then they were asked whether they would test leopards or goats as well. The result was that subjects consistently preferred to test the more dissimilar item (e.g., goats rather than leopards). It appears on the basis of López that for inductive arguments about animals, subjects do make robust use of diversity in not only evaluating evidence but also seeking evidence. (See also Spellman, López, and Smith 1999, for a comparison with other reasoning tasks involving evidence selection.)

Do adults in other cultures show evidence of diversity-based reasoning? One might think that, just as diversity effects are age-dependent, they might also depend on knowledge or cultural experience. Choi, Nisbett, and Smith (1997) reported diversity effects in Korean university students, for both animal categories and categories of people. However, in their study of Itzaj adults in Guatemala, López et al. (1997) did not find evidence for diversity-based reasoning, using arguments with various categories of living things and questions about disease transmission. Indeed, sometimes Itzaj subjects reliably chose arguments with homogenous premise categories over arguments with diverse categories. (See also Coley, Medin, Proffitt, Lynch, and Atran 1999.) From the subjects' explanations, it seems that they were using other knowledge about disease transmission that conflicted with diversity-based reasoning. For example, given a nondiverse argument, that two similar kinds of tall palm trees could get a certain disease, one subject claimed that it would be easy for the shorter kinds of palm trees, below, to get the disease as well. This issue, of how knowledge about properties guides induction beyond the structural effects of the categories themselves, will be discussed extensively in the next section on what makes a good property for induction. It does appear that the appearance of diversity may depend on relevant supporting knowledge's being accessed. In a follow-up study, López et al. (1997) found that the Itzaj did show diversity-based reasoning effects in some contexts. For example, Itzaj subjects were told to imagine buying several bags of corn. The question was whether it would be better to inspect two corn cobs from one bag, or one corn cob from each of two different bags. (See Nagel 1939, p. 72, for a related example.) The subjects tended to prefer the latter, more diverse choice. This important result suggests, following Carey (1985), that diversity-based reasoning depends not only on processing but on knowledge.

Exceptions to Diversity Effects

The lack of diversity effects found in the Itzaj people suggests that there may well be other systematic responses to diverse information, and that in some cases diverse premise categories may not lead to a very convincing argument. In their influential work, Osherson et al. (1990) documented situations in which more diverse premise categories actually led to weaker inferences, referring to these as *nonmonotonicity effects*. For example, consider the following pair of arguments:

Flies require trace amounts of magnesium for reproduction

Bees require trace amounts of magnesium for reproduction

and

Flies require trace amounts of magnesium for reproduction

Orangutans require trace amounts of magnesium for reproduction

Bees require trace amounts of magnesium for reproduction.

Adult subjects tended to judge the first argument as stronger than the second, in apparent contradiction to both the sample size and diversity phenomena. According to Osherson et al. (1990), the reason why the second argument seems weaker is that it brings to mind a broader superordinate context, animals rather than insects. Whereas flies are highly typical insects, in the context of animals, flies are much less typical and orangutans are not prototypical either. Hence the second argument would be weaker because of lower typicality of premise categories.

Sloman (1993) reported a related violation of diversity, referred to as the *feature exclusion effect*. It was found that most subjects found an argument of the form Foxes, Deer/Weasels to be stronger than an argument of the form Foxes, Rhinos/Weasels, despite the greater diversity of the latter set of premises. According to Sloman (1993), the reason for this result was that rhinos and weasels have so few features in common (i.e., they are so dissimilar) that adding information about rhinos to a statement about foxes just does not warrant any further conclusions about weasels.

Finally, it is useful to mention that this nonmonotonicity effect has been replicated with Korean undergraduates (Choi et al. 1997), and furthermore that López et al. (1992) found some evidence for nonmonotonicity effects in 5-year-olds and even more consistent evidence with 9-year-olds. Perhaps the best conclusion to be drawn from nonmonotonicity effects as well as feature exclusion effects is that although diverse premises promote induction, too much diversity can actually hurt rather than help.

Discussion

When multiple premises are used to evaluate an inductive argument, the associated phenomena are rather interesting and varied. The key results can be summarized in terms of two main findings as well as the exceptions to these findings. The main findings are, again, that higher numbers of premise categories, as well as diversity of premise categories, promote inferences. The sample size effect seems to be robust, although its empirical status could be clarified for children of age 9 and younger. The diversity effect seems to be less robust, in that there are cultural or knowledge-based differences as well as a number of negative results with children. Some of the negative findings with respect to sample size and diversity seem consistent enough to treat as phenomena in their own right – for example, nonmonotonicity effects (Osherson et al. 1990) and feature exclusion effects (Sloman 1993).

Because the results are particularly variable for diversity effects, it is useful to systematically enumerate why in a particular situation a person, whether child or adult, may not show diversity-based reasoning (see Coley et al. 1999 for a further discussion). This question is especially interesting, considering that it seems normative to draw stronger inferences from more diverse observations. This claim has been made by philosophers such as Nagel (1939) in the context of probability theory and Hempel (1966) in the context of scientific inference from experiments (see also Bacon 1620/1898; Heit 1998; López 1995). Note that the point of these claims was not to provide a complete justification for inductive inference, but rather to argue that diverse evidence may be more likely to satisfy particular goals. For example, Hempel claimed that conducting diverse experiments is compatible with a falsifying strategy in testing a scientific theory, compared with conducting a series of similar experiments.

One class of explanation for a lack of diversity effects, say in children, would consist of processing differences. For example, López et al. (1992) suggested, following the model of Osherson et al. (1990), that adults carry out a two-stage procedure in assessing inductive strength, assessing premise-to-conclusion similarity as well as the diversity of the premise categories (or how well they cover a generated superordinate). The lack of diversity effects in children could be due to an abbreviated procedure in which they complete the first stage but not the second. Processing explanations bring up the question of whether processing in children is truly different from adult processing, or simply more fragile. Perhaps under the right conditions – for example, with simple materials that minimize task demands – children could show the same processing as do adults.

Another class of explanation comprises knowledge differences, which was highlighted by the cross-cultural studies of López et al. (1997), who showed domain differences in diversity for Itzaj adults in Guatemala. Likewise, Carey (1985) treated the diversity task as a measure of the maturity of various concepts such as *living thing* and *animal*.

Finally, it is possible that when a group of subjects, say children, fail to show diversity effects, they do so because there is a mixture of systematic responses. For example, about half of the time the children might be showing diversity effects, whereas for various reasons the other half of the time they could be doing something else systematically, such as being affected by the feature exclusion effect. Indeed, there are borderline results in both López et al. (1992) and Gutheil and Gelman (1997) that are opposite to diversity, suggesting the possibility that children were systematically doing something different rather than simply guessing. For a particular nonfinding of diversity, explanations due to missing processing mechanisms, performance difficulties, knowledge effects, or other systematic effects would all be possible. It is suggested that a future goal of studies on diversity should be not only to document when diversity-based reasoning does and does not occur, but to specifically aim at distinguishing among different explanations for its nonoccurrence.

As mentioned in the section on single-premise arguments, the studies of premise diversity effects facilitate the comparison with studies on conclusion variability (e.g., Nisbett et al. 1983). Whereas having a variable or broad conclusion category leads to weaker inferences, it now seems that having a variable or broad set of premise categories generally leads to stronger inferences (at least in American adults). It seems that people are concerned about breadth of categories for both premises and conclusions of inductive arguments, but breadth of premises leads to the opposite result of breadth of the conclusion category. It would be very interesting for models of induction to address directly why this variable has different effects for premise categories and conclusion categories.

In conclusion, to return to the example of homes and burglaries, it is useful to consider what would make a set of cases likely to promote inferences about another burglary. The effect of sample size has an intuitive effect; the more burglaries on your street, the higher your perceived risk. Can diversity effects be tied to the home burglary example? Perhaps. Say that it is the first of February. If there were a dozen burglaries on your street last year, one in each month, that may seem to indicate a fair risk for your own home. On the other hand, what if there were a dozen burglaries, all taking place on Christmas Eve? This situation would involve more recent events, but they seem to form a localized or restricted cluster. The other situation, with a greater diversity of burglary occasions over the span of a year, all more distant from the present date, might promote a stronger inference about the present situation.

What Makes a Good Property?

So far, this review has focused on the effects of categories on induction; that is, what makes a set of categories promote inductive inference? This emphasis has followed the historical emphasis of the field; for example, three of the most influential studies of induction (Carey 1985; Osherson et al. 1990; Rips 1975) also focused on categories. However, properties or predicates also have a crucial role in inductive reasoning – the end part of a statement, such as *thrives in sunlight* or *secretes uric acid crystals*, has considerable effects on how people respond to inductive arguments. In the example of homes, it makes intuitive sense that different predicates will have different patterns of projection. For example, if your neighbor's home is burglarized, the perceived risk for your own home seems greater. The proximity between the two homes promotes this inference. However, if your neighbor's home is painted blue, that does not seem to increase the risk that your own home will be painted blue. For this predicate, proximity does not have much predictive value. In this section, several ways that properties matter will be reviewed. A number of past results on property effects can be described as relating to the scope of the property. For example, house color is a stable or consistent property for one house, but it tends to vary more within a group of nearby houses. Other property effects could be attributed to differing use of similarity informa-

tion for different properties. In many past studies already reviewed, subjects have seemed to reason about biological properties of animals in terms of some notion of internal similarity – projecting, for example, more readily from horses to cows rather than to lizards. But for other properties, such as house burglaries, the relevant measure of similarity might be physical proximity. Finally, a number of other ways that the content of properties influences inductive reasoning will be reviewed.

Scope of Properties

The Nisbett et al. (1983) study is a good first illustration of how knowledge about the scope of a property affects inductive inference. As already reviewed, seeing that just one member of the Barratos group is obese does not seem to promote the inference that other people in this group will be obese. Obesity seems to be more of an individual characteristic rather than a group characteristic. On the other hand, Nisbett et al. found that people make stronger inferences for the same category but another property, skin color. Here, seeing the skin color of just one Barratos promotes inferences about other members of this group, on the assumption that members of the same ethnic group will likely have some shared physical characteristics. In another study with adults, Gutheil and Gelman (1997) reported property effects like those found by Nisbett et al., but for a wider range of properties. In the terminology of Goodman (1955), it appears that some properties are more projectable than others.

This use of knowledge about scope of properties is not limited to adults but is clearly evident in young children as well. For example, Gelman (1988) compared stable, internal properties with more transient or idiosyncratic properties, in reasoning tasks performed by children as young as age 4. For projectable properties such as *has pectin inside*, children's inferences showed similarity effects, reflecting the taxonomic hierarchy of categories. But for properties such as *has a little scratch on it*, children showed chance patterns of reasoning, indicating that for properties with an idiosyncratic scope, they did not have a systematic basis of projection. (Also, see Springer 1992 for similar results, in which children used kinship information to project biological properties, but projected idiosyncratic properties at a chance level.)

Young children's reasoning about the scope of properties is surprisingly sophisticated. A study by Macario, Shipley, and Billman (1990) showed rather subtle use of information about property variability by 4-year-olds. In particular, children were able to use the variability of one property to infer the variability of another property. The task was to learn about groups of objects that were preferred by one puppet or another. For example, children would see that the objects in one group all were blue and that a contrast category had one red member. Then the children were presented with a set of transfer items for classification, and on the basis of these choices it appeared they had inferred that the contrast category's other members would all be red. Likewise, after seeing that one category's members varied in shape, children inferred that the contrast category's members would also vary in shape. As in Nisbett et al. (1983), it was demonstrated that children would more readily base their inferences on a homogenous property as opposed to a property that varied across category members. But in addition it was shown that children could infer the variability or scope of a property in a sensible and productive manner.

More recently, Waxman, Lynch, Casey, and Baer (1997) have looked at knowledge about scope of properties for real animal categories. In an initial experiment, Waxman et al. found that given a property of, say, a collie, young children tended to extend this property to other members of the same subordinate category (other collies) as well as other members of the same basic level category (other dogs). As in Macario et al. (1990), the question was whether children could learn about scope of properties, and in particular whether they would infer that some properties were distinctive for different subordinate categories, but homogenous within each subordinate. Children were taught facts about two subcategories, such as that one breed of dog was used to find birds and another breed of dog was used to pull sleds. Then the children were taught that a dog of a third kind had another characteristic, such as that of being used to help take care of sheep. Finally, the children were tested on whether this third characteristic would extend to a variety of dogs and other animals. Unlike in the initial experiment, when this training was provided the children tended to restrict the scope of their inferences to the original subordinate category. With a small amount of training, 4-year-old children were able to learn about the scope of a property and use this information in a consistent way.

It seems that even infants show evidence for increasing sophistication about the scope of properties. Mandler and McDonough (1998) used an imitation task to compare 14-month-olds and 20-month-olds on inferences with properties that would have a scope at the basic level of categorization (e.g., chewing on bones would apply to dogs but not other animals such as birds). It was found that the 14-month-olds were willing to project properties rather widely, such as projecting bone-chewing to birds, but that the 20-month-olds were more restricted in the breadth of their generalizations, suggesting that they were sensitive to the scope of these properties.

Properties and Similarity

Although it might seem from the previous section that some properties have a wide scope for projection whereas other properties are simply idiosyncratic and harder to project, the picture is actually more complicated and more interesting. Depending on the argument – that is, depending on the categories in an inductive argument – a particular property may be projectable, nonprojectable, or somewhere in between. Consider the following example, from Heit and Rubinstein (1994). For a typical blank anatomical property, such as *has a liver with two chambers*, people will make stronger inferences from chickens to hawks than from tigers to hawks. Because chickens and hawks are from the same biological category and share many internal properties, people are quite willing to project a novel anatomical property from one bird to another. But since tigers and hawks differ in terms of many known internal biological properties, it seems less likely that a novel anatomical property will project from one to the other. This result illustrates the priority of biological categories that has been observed in induction (e.g., Carey 1985; Gelman 1988). However, now consider the behavioral property *prefers to feed at night*. Heit and Rubinstein found that inferences for behavioral properties concerning feeding and predation were weaker between the categories *chicken* and *hawk* than between the categories *tiger* and *hawk* – the opposite of the result for anatomical properties. Here, it seems that despite the considerable biological differences between tigers and hawks, people were influenced by the known similarities between these two animals in terms of predatory behavior, thus making strong inferences about a novel behavioral property. In comparison, chickens and hawks differ in terms of predatory behavior (with chickens tending to be pacifists), so that people were less willing to project a novel behavioral property between these two animals. Together, these results suggest that each property is more projectable for a different pair of animals. (Also see Choi et al. 1997 for a comparison between anatomical and behavioral properties.) It is not simply the case that some properties are always more projectable than other properties. Instead, there was a crossover interaction pattern between properties and premise–conclusion matches.

Recently, Ross and Murphy (1999) have also provided evidence for the flexibility of people's reasoning about different kinds of properties. Ross and Murphy's interest was the domain of foods, which perhaps in comparison with other domains such as the animal kingdom leads more readily to cross-classification. For example, a bagel can be considered as part of the breads category (a taxonomic organization) or as a breakfast food (a script-based organization). (See also Murphy and Ross 1999.) Ross and Murphy compared two kinds of properties: biochemical properties and situational properties relating to how a food might be used. It was found that for biochemical properties, subjects preferred inferences based on taxonomic matches, whereas for situational properties, subjects preferred script-based matches. Just as in Heit and Rubinstein (1994), any account of induction that does not take into account the property being projected could not account for these results. In particular, inductive inference cannot be reduced to simply assessing the similarity between premise and conclusion categories, unless a flexible conception of similarity is allowed, in which similarity depends on the property being projected. For example, inferences about behavioral or situational properties might lead to behavioral or situational features being emphasized in similarity computations. Smith, Shafir, and Osherson (1993) referred to such an effect as *feature potentiation* (and see Heit 1997 for a review of related work). However, this term in itself does not give an account of how the process would take place. It seems likely that feature potentiation would rely on other mechanisms of memory (of which inferences have been successful in the past) as well as explanatory reasoning (about which features might be useful).

There is also some evidence that this kind of property effect occurs in children's reasoning as well. Gelman and Markman (1986) provided children with a property for one item (e.g., a blackbird) and then asked them whether the property would be true for a perceptually similar item (e.g., a bat) or an item that was a taxonomic match but less similar perceptually (e.g., a flamingo). It was found that for biological properties (e.g., referring to eating habits), the children preferred the taxonomic match, but that for perceptual properties (e.g., texture), they were at chance level or in some cases they showed a tendency to choose the perceptual match, suggesting that different features might have been potentiated for perceptual inferences.

Using a somewhat different task, Kalish and Gelman (1992) have looked at property inferences based on novel combined categories, such as *glass scissors*. Children were given facts about one of these categories, such as *used for partitioning* (a functional property) or *will get fractured if put in really cold water* (a dispositional property). The subjects were asked whether these properties would be true of other items as well, such as metal scissors and a glass bottle. The children (age 4) preferred matches in terms of object kind (e.g., both scissors) when projecting a novel functional property, but they preferred matches in terms of composition (e.g., both glass) when projecting a novel dispositional property, showing an impressive degree of sophistication about inferences.

Moving to even younger ages, Mandler and McDonough (1996, 1998) reported sensitivity to different kinds of properties for infants. Using a task in which 14-month-old children imitated actions performed on various objects, they found that the children were sensitive to the difference between animal actions (e.g., giving a drink) and vehicle actions (e.g., opening with a key). The children were less likely to repeat animal actions performed on a vehicle or vehicle actions performed on an animal than they were to repeat actions that matched the items. Again, there was evidence that quite young children are sensitive to the idea that there are different kinds of properties, with differing relevant criteria for projecting these properties. At no point during the course of their development has it been demonstrated that children treat all properties as the same – the default seems to be to show property effects of some kind.

Other Property Effects

In addition to the property effects just reviewed, researchers have documented a number of other interesting phenomena deriving from the content of properties. The diversity of these phenomena attests to the importance and prevalence of property effects, touching on several aspects of inductive reasoning. What these phenomena have in common, however, is that they all point to the limitations of similarity as a basis for inductive inference. Smith et al. (1993; see also Osherson, Smith, Myers, Shafir, and Stob 1994) provided an important example in which inferences go in the opposite direction of what overall similarity would predict. Consider the following two arguments:

Poodles can bite through barbed wire

German shepherds can bite through barbed wire

and

Dobermans can bite through barbed wire

German shepherds can bite through barbed wire.

Clearly there is greater similarity between Dobermans and German shepherds than there is between poodles and German shepherds. Yet people find the first argument stronger than the second. An informal way to justify this reasoning is that if poodles, a rather weak and tame kind of dog, can bite through barbed wire, then obviously German shepherds, which are much stronger and more ferocious, must be able to bite through barbed wire as well. This property, *can bite through barbed wire*, seems to depend on the magnitude of other dimensions such as strength and ferocity. Again, informally, it seems that subjects are trying to explain how the various animals could bite through barbed wire, in terms of known facts about these animals.

However, this result could be explained alternatively in terms of the diversity effect, on the assumption that in addition to the premises provided to subjects, people use their own prior knowledge to create additional, hidden premises. For example, people might already believe that another large, ferocious kind of dog, such as a Rottweiler, can bite through wire. This belief could serve as a hidden premise that would affect judgments about the conclusion. In this situation, supplying the premise that poodles can bite though barbed wire would lead to a diverse range of premise categories, Rottweilers and poodles. In contrast, supplying the premise that Dobermans can bite through barbed wired would represent a fairly narrow set of premises, Rottweilers and Dobermans. Hence, following the already established diversity effect, the premise with poodles should lead to a stronger conclusion.

Sloman (1994, 1997) has investigated the role of explanations in inductive reasoning more directly. Sloman has concluded that people are highly sensitive to the content of properties being projected, coming up with an explanation of the manifested property as a means of assessing inductive strength. An argument will be strong to the extent that premise and conclusion statements have the same explanations. For example, consider the following.

Many ex-cons are hired as bodyguards

Many war veterans are hired as bodyguards

and

Many ex-cons are unemployed

Many war veterans are unemployed.

According to Sloman (1994), the first argument is strong because both statements have the same explanation – namely, that ex-convicts and war veterans are hired as bodyguards because in both cases they are tough and experienced fighters. The second argument is weaker because the two statements would have different explanations – namely, that ex-convicts might be unemployed for different reasons than war veterans. (Sloman, 1997, investigated this phenomenon further, distinguishing between unrelated explanations and conflicting explanations.) As in the Smith et al. (1993) results, and for that matter the results of Heit and Rubinstein (1994) and Ross and Murphy (1999), it seems that inductive inference with meaningful properties critically depends on determining which known characteristics of the categories are causally related to or predictive of the property to be projected. Indeed, when Lassaline (1996) made various causal relations explicit to subjects, she found that they were particularly sensitive to causal relations between characteristics of the premise category and the property to be projected. (See also Hadjichristidis, Sloman, Stevenson, and Over 1999, and Wu and Gentner 1998).

Finally, as possibly converging evidence for the role of explanations, McDonald et al. (1996) found that number of conclusions suggested by a set of premises was negatively correlated with perceived inductive strength. Perhaps when a set of premises all have the same explanation, it leads to a single, clear, and strong conclusion, but when there are multiple conclusions it is reflective of conflicting possible explanations, and thus any particular inference will be weak.

Discussion

The main conclusion from this section is that properties matter, a great deal! In addition to factors such as similarity between premise and conclusion categories, and typicality and diversity of premise categories, the content of the property being projected from premise to conclusion has a central role in inductive inference. Perhaps most dramatically, idiosyncratic properties such as being obese or having a scratch do not lead to widespread, systematic inferences. In addition, Smith et al. (1993) showed that for some properties, similarity between premise and conclusion categories is negatively correlated with inductive strength, although this result could also be explained in terms of diversity. To account for other results (e.g., those of Heit and Rubinstein 1994), one must assume that different kinds of similarity would be used for inferences about different properties, fitting with Goodman's (1972) points about the flexibility of similarity. Sensitivity to different kinds of properties has been observed in young children and even infants. If one thing is clear, it is that any complete account of inductive reasoning needs to address property effects. Many valuable and systematic results, reviewed in the first two sections of this paper, have been obtained from studies in which properties were not varied systematically, but it seems that these studies were looking at only a restricted range of human abilities. Just as it is possible to learn more about the cognitive processes underlying induction by using arguments with multiple premises rather than a single premise, it is possible to learn yet more about induction by comparing performance with different properties.

In all three sections of this paper so far, a few themes have emerged repeatedly. One is that, as Goodman (1955) noted, categories and properties vary in terms of their entrenchment. Some categories and some properties seem to be more suitable for inductive reasoning than others. Although Goodman referred to this issue as a "riddle," it seems that humans are rather systematic in terms of what they treat as more or less entrenched; typical categories, for example, tend to be good for induction whereas transient properties tend to be bad for induction. Another theme is that for categories as well as properties, there is a sense that scope or variability is critical to induction. A varied set of premise categories will promote induction, but it is easier to draw an inference about a narrow conclusion category than about a broad conclusion category. Properties in an inductive argument seem to have a breadth or scope of their own, with some properties being restricted to a particular place or time and other properties seeming to generalize easily to many cases. Even 4-year-old children seem to have a sophisticated awareness about the scope of properties (Waxman et al. 1997). The final theme is that similarity is a crucial concept. Just as similarity between premise and conclusion categories promotes induction, dissimilarity within a set of premise categories also promotes induction. (Indeed, the diversity effect can be thought of as a kind of similarity effect. Because similar categories are expected to share properties, learning that two diverse categories share a property seems more surprising or informative than learning that two similar categories share a property.) Even typicality effects can be explained in terms of similarity, because a category's typicality is highly correlated with its similarity to the representation of its superordinate.

The property effects described here are interesting because they place limits on the use of similarity as an account for inductive inference: Different measures of similarity would be needed for different properties, and in some cases, it is clear that other constructs such as explanations are needed in order to account for human inference. Sloman (1994, 1997) explicitly investigated explanation-based reasoning in induction, and the other studies on property effects (e.g., Heit and Rubinstein 1994, and Smith et al. 1993) also point, indirectly, to reasoning processes beyond straightforward assessment of similarity.

How Do Psychological Models of Induction Address These Results?

Now that these main results in inductive reasoning have been presented (see Table 1 for a list of key results), it is time to move to the models of induction that have been developed by psychologists. Choosing these models for presentation requires some degree of focus. After all, any theoretical account or explanation of inductive reasoning could be considered a model in some sense. However, for comparability, the focus will be on formal models that are either mathematical or computational descriptions. Also, this section will focus on whether the various models can account for the main results, rather than provide complete presentations of the models themselves (for which the reader is referred to the original sources).

Rips (1975)

Chronologically speaking, the first formal model of induction was that of Rips (1975). This modeling effort was performed by deriving multidimensional scaling solutions for different categories of animals, so that similarity and typicality measures could be derived from the animals' positions on a scaling solution. Then Rips applied a set of multiple regression equations to look at various predictors of inductive strength, such as premise–conclusion similarity, premise typicality, and conclusion typicality. The resulting regression model, which included the first two predictors, can account for some of the main results with adult subjects and single-premise arguments – namely, similarity and premise typicality effects.

Potentially, this model could also be applied to some of the developmental trends that have been reviewed, with the assumption that adults and children of different ages would have different multidimensional representations of their knowledge of animals. For example, some of the differences in projection for children and adults reported by Carey (1985) could be explained in terms of *human* being more typical (or central) for children than for adults. Likewise the greater sensitivity to similarity for older children could be captured in terms of greater differentiation in the multidimensional representation for older children, or a greater coefficient for similarity in the regression equation. In principle, this model could be applied to expertise differences as well; the cultural differences found by López et al. (1997), for example, could again be explained in terms of different representations of animal categories being used by American college students and Itzaj subjects.

To evaluate whether this model can account for differences due to development and expertise, it would be necessary to perform multidimensional scaling for the relevant subject population. The model predicts that inductive judgments will be strongly related to these derived similarity measures. However, Medin et al. (1997) did find some dissociations between similarity judgments and inductive judgments for different kinds of tree experts, so the model would have some trouble with these results. Likewise, the results that showed people overriding similarity (e.g., those in Lassaline 1996 and Smith et al. 1993), would be out of bounds for this model.

Without further assumptions, the model does not seem to be sensitive to property effects.

For example, Heit and Rubinstein (1994) and Ross and Murphy (1999) showed that different measures of similarity were used for predicting different properties. But if the Rips (1975) model relies on a fixed multidimensional scaling solution, then it would predict the same use of similarity information for different properties. In addition, the model does not really address the difference between projectable and nonprojectable properties, or why permanent characteristics seem to project better than idiosyncratic properties.

Which other results can the Rips (1975) model not address? This model was aimed only at single-premise arguments, so it does not address any of the phenomena with multiple-premise categories. Also, the model does not account for one of the most basic results with single-premise arguments – namely, that specificity or homogeneity of the conclusion category promotes induction (Nisbett et al. 1983; Osherson et al. 1990). This model derives its predictions from points represented in multidimensional space. If, for example, *robins* and *birds* are located very near each other in conceptual space because of their similar representations, then the regression model will make similar predictions for inferences about these two categories. In contrast, people will make weaker inferences about the more general category, *birds*. More generally, the model does not make a distinction between categories and individuals. For example, an individual robin would have about the same multidimensional representation as would the *robin* category. Therefore, the model can be applied equally well to reasoning about individuals and about categories, but the model cannot account for any systematic differences that might be found.

Finally, the Rips (1975) model was used to make one of the important discoveries in this area, that typicality of the conclusion category does not affect inductive strength. However, the model itself does not give an explanation as to why conclusion typicality has no effect. Table 1 shows that the Rips model makes a good start toward addressing Results 1 and 2 and could even account for some group differences such as developmental or expert–novice differences. Otherwise the model does not address these results. Out of fairness, though, it must be said that this model was the first formal psychological account in this area, and it predates most of the results in the table! The Rips model, as will be seen, was influential for subsequent modeling work.

Osherson et al. (1990)

The next model of induction, that of Osherson et al. (1990), simultaneously takes a major qualitative leap beyond the Rips (1975) model, now addressing multiple-premise arguments, while at the same time including the Rips model as a special case for single-premise arguments. Just as the Rips model used similarity and typicality as predictors, the Osherson et al. (1990) model has two main components. The first component assesses the similarity between the premise categories and the conclusion category. However, the similarity measure is derived from overlap in a featural representation, rather than from a multidimensional scaling solution. The model can be applied to individuals or to categories, as long as as they can be described in terms of feature sets. The second component measures how well the premise categories cover the superordinate category that includes all the categories mentioned in an argument. For single-premise arguments, coverage more or less reduces to typicality, but for multiple-premise arguments, coverage gives something closer to a measure of diversity. Coverage is best explained in terms of a series of examples (although Osherson et al. do give a computational formulation):

Squirrels have property X
_____
Cows have property X (A)

Cows have property X
_____
Squirrels have property X (B)

Cows have property X
_____
Tunas have property X (C)

Dogs have property X
Cats have property X
_____
Cows have property X (D)

Dogs have property X
Elephants have property X
_____
Cows have property X (E)

Dogs have property X
Elephants have property X
_____
Roses have property X. (F)

For Arguments A and B, the lowest level superordinate that includes all the categories is *mammal*. Coverage is assessed in terms of the average similarity of the premise category to members of the superordinate. To the extent that cows are more typical mammals than squirrels are, and therefore more similar to other kinds of mammals, Argument B will have greater coverage than Argument A. This is how the model addresses typicality effects. Next, consider Argument C. The lowest level superordinate including all the categories would be *animal* rather than *mammal*. On average, cows are less similar to various kinds of animals, in comparison with the similarity between cows and just mammals. Therefore, Argument C has worse coverage than Argument B does.

The remaining arguments have multiple premises. In assessing similarity between members of the superordinate category and the multiple premises, only the maximum similarity for any one premise category is considered. So, for Argument D, small mammals tend to be similar to dogs and cats, and large mammals tend not to be similar to dogs and cats. So including *cat* as a premise category does not add much information beyond just having *dog* as a premise category alone. In contrast, for Argument E, some mammals are similar to dogs and other mammals are similar to elephants. Therefore, the *elephant* premise adds information, and the coverage for Argument E is greater than that for Argument D. In this way, the model of Osherson et al. (1990) addresses diversity effects, to the extent that greater coverage is correlated with greater diversity. Finally, the model addresses some exceptions to diversity. For example, in Argument F, the inclusive superordinate category would be *living things* rather than *mammals*. In terms of this much wider category, dogs and elephants do not provide particularly good coverage. Hence there would not be much of a diversity effect for Argument F.

The Osherson et al. (1990) model can address all the single-premise phenomena listed above for the Rips (1975) model, and likewise has many of the same limitations, such as not really addressing property effects at all. But in addition the model can address conclusion specificity to some extent. For example, the model can predict stronger inferences with *bird* as a conclusion category rather than *animal*, to the extent that *animal* suggests a broader superordinate category and a lower measure of coverage for the premise category or categories. With a similar rationale, the model might be applied to the conclusion variability results of Nisbett et al. (1983). For example, a narrow category such as "floridium samples" might be easier to cover than a broader category such as "people in the Barratos tribe." However, further investigation would be needed to see whether the model can address the whole pattern of results. In addition, the model as formulated would not make different predictions for obesity versus skin color of the Barratos. In sum, further assumptions would be needed for this model to fully address the effects of homogeneity of the conclusion category.

Another characteristic of the Osherson et al. (1990) model is that it depends on people generating a useful superordinate to include all the categories presented in an argument. Potentially, different people might generate different superordinates. Indeed, López et al. (1992) suggested that there could be developmental changes in the ability to generate superordinates, so that children might show more adult-like patterns of reasoning when a superordinate is provided, in comparison with situations where they need to generate their own superordinate. This issue of having to generate a superordinate is also implicit in the Rips (1975) model, where typicality assessments must be made relative to some superordinate category.

The Osherson et al. (1990) model is particularly useful for addressing multiple-premise arguments. The second, coverage-based component is valuable for explaining sample size and diversity effects, and some of the exceptions. It is also appealing to explain any lack of sample size and diversity effects in young children as being due to an underdeveloped mechanism for assessing coverage. More generally, one of the advantages of the Osherson et al. (1990) model over the Rips (1975) model is that it seems to give more of a mechanistic explanation rather than simply provide a means for fitting data. Also, particularly for multiple-premise arguments, the Osherson et al. (1990) model is complex enough and well-specified enough to predict a rich and interesting set of phenomena, profitably addressed by Osherson et al. (1990) themselves.

The Osherson et al. (1990) model gives an account of the first two results in Table 1 and addresses Result 3 to some extent. By assuming that different groups of people, such as children and adults, have different featural representations, the model could account for some group differences in these basic results. The coverage component allows the model to account for sample size and diversity effects, Results 4 and 5. Without further assumptions, the model does not address the remaining results, concerning property effects.

Sloman (1993)

This model was implemented as a connectionist network, and perhaps its most important difference from the Osherson et al. (1990) model is that it relies solely on feature overlap without a second mechanism assessing coverage of a superordinate category. Indeed, the Sloman model is especially valuable because it shows how much can be accomplished without this second mechanism, bringing into focus what the second mechanism might actually contribute. The Sloman (1993) model can account for many of the same phenomena as can the Osherson et al. (1990) model, and it likewise has many of the same limitations, so mainly the differences will be covered here. In brief, the way this model works is that premises of an argument are encoded by training the connectionist network to learn associations between input nodes representing the features of the premise categories and an output node for the property to be considered. Then the model is tested by presenting the features of the conclusion category and measuring the activation of the same output node. The model accounts for similarity effects, because training and testing on similar input vectors will lead to strong outputs during testing. The model accounts for diversity effects, because training on a diverse set of categories will tend to strengthen a greater number of connections than will training on a narrow range of categories. It would be interesting to see whether the Sloman model could address the apparent developmental changes in diversity effects that can be accounted for rather naturally by the Osherson et al. (1990) model.

The treatment of typicality effects is somewhat less straightforward. Although Rips (1975) found a distinctive contribution of premise typicality beyond similarity, and, more generally, typicality effects have been one of the most robust findings in inductive reasoning, the Sloman (1993) model does not always predict typicality effects. For arguments with general conclusion categories, for example, an argument such as Cows/Mammals being stronger than Squirrels/Mammals, the model would account for any typicality effect in terms of feature overlap. That is, *cows* would be more typical of *mammal* as well as being more similar to the representation of *mammal*, and hence the first argument would be stronger. Although the model does predict some premise–conclusion asymmetries (p. 256), it does not predict an independent effect of premise typicality on arguments with specific conclusion categories (e.g., *dog* rather than *mammal*) – that is, independent of any effect of feature overlap or representation of the conclusion category. More precisely, imagine that category A is more typical than category B, but that these two categories have equal feature overlap to category C. On the basis of the results from Rips (1975), we would expect an argument with the form A/C to be stronger than B/C, but this model would not predict any difference between the two arguments. Indeed, the model seems to predict independent effects of typicality of the conclusion category, a result that has not been reported elsewhere.

One of the advantages of the reliance on feature overlap by the Sloman (1993) model is that it can readily account for nonnormative human results that seem to be heavily influenced by similarity, such as the inclusion fallacy and the inclusion similarity effect. An example of the inclusion similarity effect is that the argument Animals/Mammals seems stronger than Animals/Reptiles, despite the two arguments being equally valid. The Sloman model accounts for this result readily in terms of greater feature overlap between animals and mammals, whereas the Osherson et al. (1990) model predicts that the two arguments would be equally (and perfectly) strong.

Again, in terms of Table 1, the Sloman (1993) model addresses similarity effects, and to an incomplete extent, typicality effects. Like the Osherson et al. (1990) model, the Sloman model can address some effects of different taxonomic levels of the conclusion category, partly addressing Result 3, but it is not clear whether it fully addresses the effects of conclusion variability as described by Nisbett et al. (1983). The model gives a good account for Results 4 and 5, going beyond the Osherson et al. model in terms of explaining some exceptions to diversity effects. Like the previous two models, without further assumptions the Sloman model does not address property effects, Results 6, 7, and 8.

Smith et al. (1993)

Unlike the previous three models which did not really address property effects, the "gap" model of Smith et al. (1993) was explicitly intended to address some of the effects of properties on induction. To illustrate this model, it is best to refer to the example in which the premise that poodles can bite through wire is considered stronger than the premise that German shepherds can bite through wire, for the conclusion that Dobermans can bite through wire. According to the gap model, the first step is that the property *biting through wire* potentiates a set of relevant features or dimensions (e.g., size and strength) and a criterion is set for possessing this property (e.g., a minimum size and strength necessary). Then the premise category is compared with this criterion. In the case of poodles biting through wire, the criterion for the property *biting through wire* would be lowered because there is a large gap between previous beliefs about poodles and what has been expected about biting through wire. The result is that Dobermans biting through wire becomes more plausible, owing to a lowered criterion. In comparison, given the premise about German shepherds, the gap would be so small that beliefs would not change much. This premise would not really lead to changes in the plausibility of the conclusion.

Perhaps what is most appealing about the gap model is that it explicitly includes a stage for potentiating features that are relevant to inferences about a particular property. Unlike in the three previous models, there is no default assumption that different properties will be treated the same. Still, the model does not provide an account of the feature potentiation process, but simply assumes that it would be there. The gap model does include a similarity component as well. Thus the model could account for basic similarity effects, and to an initial extent addresses results such as those of Heit and Robinstein (1994), who found use of different similarity measures for different properties. However, it is not obvious how the model would capture differences between projectable and nonprojectable properties – that is, why some properties are not projected at all or are just projected randomly. Furthermore, the model does not seem to address typicality effects. Even so, the model does allow for multiple-premise categories to be combined and explains sample size effects, but it is unclear whether the model would account for diversity effects or nonmonotonicity effects (see Smith et al. 1993, p. 84).

In sum, in several ways the gap model is an important advance over the Osherson et al. (1990) model, but in other ways the model is somewhat simplified and some key phenomena are left out. In terms of Table 1, the model addresses Results 1, 4, 6, and 8.

Table 2: Sample Application of the Bayesian Model

Hypothesis	Range	Degree of Prior Belief $P(H_i)$	$P(D \mid H_i)$	Posterior Belief $P(H_i \mid D)$
1	**Cow→ True** **Sheep→ True**	.70	1	.93
2	**Cow→ True** Sheep → False	.05	1	.07
3	Cow → False **Sheep→ True**	.05	0	.00
4	Cow → False Sheep → False	.20	0	.00

Note – Cases in which the property is true for a category are in boldface.

Heit (1998)

The final model to be discussed is the Bayesian model proposed by Heit (1998). The Bayesian model differs somewhat from the other models in that it perhaps is less of a processing-level account. This model was intended to be a computational-level analysis of what, given certain assumptions, would be normative for inductive inferences. The Bayesian model is an attempt to address normative issues in the spirit of Anderson's (1990) rational analysis of cognition. That is, after specifying the goals of a system, the optimal computational means for attaining these goals are considered. Note that the Bayesian model is by no means an attempt to provide logical justification for inductive inferences or to explain why induction is successful in the real world. It is simply an analysis of the steps that could be taken in a probability estimation task.

According to the Bayesian model, evaluating an inductive argument is conceived of as learning about a property, in particular learning for which categories the property is true or false. For example, in argument

Cows can get disease X
_____
Sheep can get disease X,

the goal is to learn which animals can get this disease and which animals cannot. The model assumes that for a novel property such as the one in this example, people would rely on prior knowledge about familiar properties in order to derive a set of hypotheses about what the novel property might be like. For example, people know some facts that are true of all mammals, including cows and sheep, but they also know some facts that are true just of cows and likewise some facts that are true just of sheep. The

question is, Which of these known kinds of properties does the novel property *can get disease* X resemble most? Is it a cow-and-sheep property, a cow-only property, or a sheep-only property? To answer this question, the Bayesian model treats the premise or premises in an inductive argument as evidence, which is used to revise beliefs about the prior hypotheses according to Bayes's theorem. Once these beliefs have been revised, the plausibility of the conclusion is estimated.

It will be helpful to present more details of the model in the context of this example. People know quite a few properties of animals, but these known properties must fall into four types: properties that are true of cows and sheep, properties that are true of cows but not sheep, properties that are true of sheep but not cows, and properties that are not true of either cows or sheep. These four types of known properties can serve as four hypotheses when one is reasoning about novel properties, because any new property must also be one of these four types. These four types of properties are listed in Table 2, with cases in which the property is true for a category shown in boldface for emphasis.

As is shown in Table 2, a person would have prior beliefs about these hypotheses. For example, the value of .70 for Hypothesis 1 represents the belief that there is a 70% chance that a new property would be true of both cows and sheep. This high value could reflect the high degree of similarity between cows and sheep and that people know many other animal properties that are true of both cows and sheep. (The particular numbers are used only for illustration at this point.) However, the person might see a 5% chance that a new property would be true of cows and not sheep, a 5% chance that a new property would be true of sheep and not cows, and a 20% chance that the property is true of neither category. Note that because the four hypotheses are exhaustive and mutually exclusive, their corresponding prior beliefs add up to 1.

This table describes prior beliefs not only about the four hypotheses but also about the two categories. If we combine Hypotheses 1 and 2, it appears that the person believes that there is a 75% chance that cows would have the new property; likewise, if we combine Hypotheses 1 and 3, the person believes that there is a 75% chance that sheep have the new property.

The next step is to combine these prior beliefs with new evidence, using Bayes's theorem. The given premise, *Cows have Property P*, is used to update beliefs about the four hypotheses, so that a better evaluation of the conclusion, *Sheep have Property P*, may be achieved. When we apply Bayes's theorem (Equation 1), the premise is treated as the data, D. The prior degree of belief in each hypothesis is indicated by $P(H_i)$. (Note that there are four hypotheses, so $n = 4$ here.) The task is to estimate $P(H_i \mid D)$ – that is, the posterior degree of belief in each hypothesis, given the data.

$$P(H_i \mid D) = \frac{P(H_i)P(D \mid H_i)}{\sum_{j=1}^{n} P(H_j)P(D \mid H_j)} \qquad (1)$$

In Table 2, the calculations are shown for all four hypotheses, given the data that *Cows have Property P*. The calculation of $P(D \mid H_i)$ is quite easy. Under Hypotheses 1 and 2, cows have the property in question, so obtaining the data (that cows have the property) has a probability of 1. But under Hypotheses 3 and 4, cows do not have the property, so the probability of obtaining the data must be 0 under these hypotheses. The final column, indicating the posterior beliefs in the four types of properties, has been calculated with Equation 1. Notably, Hypothesis 1, that cows and sheep have the property, and Hypothesis 2, that just cows have the property, have been strengthened. The two remaining hypotheses have been eliminated from contention, because they are inconsistent with the data or premise that cows have the property.

Finally, the values in Table 2 may be used to evaluate the conclusion, that sheep have Property P. The degree of belief in this conclusion is simply the sum of the posterior beliefs for Hypotheses 1 and 3, or .93. Recall that before the introduction of evidence that cows have the property, the prior belief that sheep have the property was only .75. Thus, the premise that cows have the property led to an increase in the belief that horses have the property.

This illustration raises the important issue of how the prior beliefs, such as the numbers in the third column of Table 2, might be derived. Are the exact values of the priors important? These questions are fundamental issues for Bayesian statistics (see, e.g., Box and Tiao 1973; Raiffa and Schlaifer 1961; see also Heit and Bott 2000). For the purposes of Heit (1998), it was assumed that the priors would be determined by the number of known properties of each type that are brought to mind in the context of evaluating the inductive argument. It might be said that the prior beliefs for new properties are estimated with the use of something like an availability heuristic (Tversky and Kahneman 1973) based on known properties. The basic idea is that when reasoning about novel animal properties, people would retrieve a set of familiar animal properties from memory. Then they would count up how many known properties are consistent with each of the four properties – for example, how many known properties of animals are true of both cows and horses. The priors in Tables 2, for example, are consistent with the idea that 20 known properties are brought to mind: 14 of Type 1, 1 of Type 2, 1 of Type 3, and 4 of Type 4.

In addition, Heit (1998) argued that the exact values for the prior beliefs are not critical in many cases. For instance, in the present example, the initial degree of belief in Hypothesis Type 4, that neither cows nor horses have the property, was not at all important. The posterior belief in Hypothesis 1, $P(H_1 \mid D)$, can be calculated simply from the prior beliefs in Hypotheses 1 and 2, $P(H_1 \mid D) = P(H_1) / [P(H_1) + P(H_2)]$, or $.93 = .70 / (.70 + .05)$. The posterior belief in Hypothesis 1 would be the same regardless of the value of $P(H_4)$, as long as $P(H_1)$ and $P(H_2)$ maintain the same ratio to each other.

The Bayesian model addresses many of the key phenomena reviewed in this paper. For example, the model predicts similarity effects, because novel properties would be assumed to follow the same distributions as would familiar properties. The argument Cows/Sheep seems strong, because many known properties are true of both categories. In contrast, Hedgehogs/Sheep seems weaker, because prior knowledge indicates that there are fewer properties in common for these two categories. The Bayesian model also addresses typicality effects, under the assumption that according to prior beliefs, atypical categories such as *hedgehog* would have a number of idiosyncratic features. Hence a premise asserting a novel property about hedgehogs would suggest that this property is likewise idiosyncratic and not to be widely projected. In contrast, prior beliefs about typical categories would indicate that they have many features in common with other categories, and hence a novel property of a typical category should generalize well to other categories. (In comparison with the Sloman 1993 model, the Bayesian model predicts an independent influence of premise typicality, rather than conclusion typicality, beyond feature overlap.)

The Bayesian model also addresses diversity effects, with a rationale similar to that for typicality effects. An argument with two similar premise categories, such as *cows* and *horses*, could bring to mind a lot of idiosyncratic properties that are true just of large farm animals. Therefore a novel property of cows and horses might seem idiosyncratic as well. In contrast, an argument with two diverse premise categories, such as *cows* and *hedgehogs*, could not bring to mind familiar idiosyncratic properties that are true of just these two animals. Instead, the prior hypotheses would be derived from known properties that are true of all mammals or all animals. Hence a novel property of cows and hedgehogs should generalize fairly broadly. This is a quite strong prediction of the Bayesian model, and it is not yet clear how the model would account for any lack of diversity in children. Likewise, it would take further investigation to see whether the Bayesian model would apply to other exceptions to diversity such as the nonmonotonicity effect reported by Osherson et al. (1990) as well as other nonnormative results such as the inclusion fallacy (Osherson et al. 1990) and the inclusion similarity effect (Sloman 1993, 1998). It could be the case that the Bayesian model has difficulty explaining these nonnormative results. On the other hand, to the extent that people can rely on different priors for answering different questions, the apparent inconsistencies in reasoning might be due to the knowledge that is retrieved for answering particular questions rather than the reasoning process itself.

The Bayesian model can address conclusion homogeneity effects, as in Nisbett et al. (1983). For example, Nisbett et al. found that after a single observation, people were fairly willing to generalize that all floridium samples conduct electricity. The result can be explained in terms of people's initially entertaining two hypotheses: All floridium samples do not conduct electricity, and all floridium samples do conduct electricity. Observing just a single sample of floridium that conducts electricity fits with the second hypothesis and rules out the first hypothesis; hence a strong generalization proceeds rapidly. In contrast, the result for Barratos and obesity was that seeing just one obese Barratos did not promote strong inferences about the whole group. In this case, people might entertain a whole distribution of prior hypotheses – for example, 0% of Barratos are obese, 1% are obese, 2% are obese, . . . , 50% are obese, 51% are obese, . . . , 99% are obese, 100% are obese. Observing one obese Barratos would rule out the 0% hypothesis, and it might cast doubt on the 1% hypothesis; but it would not license the strong inference that all Barratos are obese.

In a similar way, an idiosyncratic property such as *has a scratch on it* could lead people to entertain a diffuse set of prior hypotheses, so that a single observation would not lead to strong inferences. More generally, because the essence of the Bayesian model is that it derives inferences based on prior knowledge of familiar properties, it should be highly sensitive to content effects such as property differences and effects of expertise. The key idea is that the novel property in an argument serves as a cue for retrieving familiar properties. Most psychology experiments on inductive reasoning have used novel properties that sounded at least vaguely biological or internal. In addition, people may retrieve familiar biological properties as a default, for animal categories. So unless the novel property suggests otherwise, people would tend to rely on distributional information about known biological properties.

To give another example, when reasoning about the anatomical and behavioral properties in Heit and Rubinstein (1994), subjects could have drawn on different priors for the two kinds of properties. As in many other experiments, reasoning about anatomical properties led people to rely on prior knowledge about familiar anatomical properties. In contrast, when reasoning about a behavioral property such as *prefers to feed at night*, the prior hypotheses could be drawn from knowledge about familiar behavioral properties. These priors would tend to promote inferences between animals such as hawks and tigers that are similar behaviorally rather than anatomically.

To conclude, the Bayesian model has the potential to address all of the phenomena listed in Table 1. However, the main drawback of this model is that it has not been fully tested. Heit (1998) presented illustrations of how the model might account for a variety of phenomena, but the model has not been directly applied to human data. To test the Bayesian model properly, it would be necessary to collect data about people's beliefs about a large number of familiar properties and then use these data to predict judgments about novel properties. Of course, the other models also depend on collected data such as property listings or similarity ratings, in order to generate predictions. One difference is that the Bayesian model can also respond to beliefs about hidden essences (cf. Medin and Ortony 1989); for example, the belief that all pieces of limestone have got something unique and distinctive in common, even if one cannot specify exactly what that is. These beliefs might not be easily measured from property listings. Still, the Bayesian model does begin to address a broader range of phenomena than those addressed by the other models.

Discussion

To some extent, there has been a developmental trend among psychological models of induction, with more recent models not surprisingly taking on a wider range of results. Still, perhaps what all the models have in common is more important than their differences, with some notion of similarity (in terms of feature overlap or proximity in multidimensional space) and some notion of diversity (in terms of category coverage or feature overlap) driving many of the predictions. Given the commonalties among all the models, the main value of the Bayesian analyses by Heit (1998) may be that they highlight the normative basis for the models' predictions. Although it does not address property effects, the Osherson et al. (1990) model has been most influential because it does bring together a lot of phenomena and make interesting predictions of further results.

If one can project from past trends, future models of induction may address content and property effects to a further extent, in light of results showing effects of expertise on induction and widespread property effects even with very young children. Certainly, the wide range of phenomena addressed by the Heit (1998) model, even at an initial stage, should encourage future models to go further. Ideally, future models will give a better process-level account of what Smith et al. (1993) referred to as *feature potentiation* – that is, selecting features that are relevant to a particular inference. Also, to the extent that induction involves explanatory or causal reasoning as suggested by the studies of Sloman (1994) and others, it must be admitted that none of the existing models gives a satisfying account of explanatory reasoning.

Conclusion: Future Directions for Empirical Research

Although much progress has been made in empirical work on inductive reasoning in the past 25 years, by reading between the lines in this review one can see areas of incompleteness that might be profitably investigated in future studies. Perhaps the clearest way to look at inductive reasoning is to do so in terms of the various phenomena, such as typicality effects and diversity effects, that appear in Table 1. As one considers these results, it is natural to be interested in whether they appear in different groups of people, such as children or adults, and Western cultures or non-Western or traditional cultures. Work that addresses such questions is well under way, although there are still many interesting questions to be addressed, such as why diversity-based reasoning seems to be harder to find in some groups.

Another way to think about induction is to do so in terms of the various tasks and responses that would require inductive reasoning. For example, in the experiments described in this review researchers have used response measures such as probability judgments, judgments of inductive strength, forced-choice predictions, and behaviors such as how an infant plays with a toy. The tasks varied in another important way as well. In some experiments, the premises gave information about individuals (e.g., a particular bird has some property) and in other experiments, the premises gave information about categories (e.g., a kind of bird has some property). Possibly there was even some ambiguity in some experiments whether the premises referred to individuals or categories. This problem could particularly come up when premises are presented in picture form, if it is unclear whether a picture of some individual is meant to stand for a class of items. It would be important to establish whether the various phenomena of inductive reasoning, listed in Table 1, do appear for different versions of the task. For example, all of the models of induction described here can apparently be applied to inferences about individuals or categories. Systematic research could potentially show differences in reasoning about individuals as opposed to categories, and these differences might or might not correspond to the models' predictions.

A related issue is how well the laboratory-based tasks reported here match up to inductive reasoning as manifested by everyday judgments and decisions. How well do the phenomena reviewed here correspond to everyday reasoning? It is hoped that most of the key results in Table 1 would occur outside of the laboratory as well. Perhaps the more contentious results would be the fallacies reported by Osherson et al. (1990) and Sloman (1993, 1998), in which people violate basic laws of probability. It would be valuable to study whether these reasoning fallacies are robust enough to appear in the real world and in everyday choices, or whether they are dependent on the characteristics of experimental settings and survey methodology.

Still another way to think about the phenomena of inductive reasoning is to consider whether they might be different for various domains of knowledge or different kinds of categories – for example, natural kinds, artifacts, social categories, event categories, ad hoc categories (Barsalou 1983). Again, this is an intriguing possibility that would need to be investigated more systematically in future research. Some studies have been done with different kinds of categories, but the majority of published experiments have used animal categories (and animals' biological properties). Although there could be many reasons for this focus on categories of animals, the risk remains that the results might be different in other domains or with other kinds of categories. It is unclear whether the emphasis on animal categories in published papers simply reflects the choices of experimenters in creating stimuli, or whether there is some nonpublication bias because experiments with other stimuli did not yield interpretable results.

Therefore, after 25 years of psychological research on inductive reasoning, it is time both to acknowledge the extensive progress that has been made, especially in terms of the regularities that have been documented, and to acknowledge that future empirical work needs to be more ambitious, ideally guided by more ambitious models as well.

Note

1   Quite a few studies, including parts of Carey (1985), have looked at attribution tasks rather than projection tasks. In an attribution task, the subject, typically a child, states whether some familiar item has some familiar property, such as whether dogs sleep. The contribution of inductive reasoning to attribution tasks is unclear, because in many cases the subject would be able to answer on the basis of established knowledge or observations without a major role for inductive inference. Therefore, this paper will focus on projection tasks, which involve unfamiliar categories and/or properties.

References

Anderson, J. R. (1990). *The adaptive character of thought*. Hillsdale, NJ: Erlbaum.

Bacon, F. (1898). *Novum organum*. London: George Bell and Sons. (Original work published 1620).

Baldwin, D. A., Markman, E. M., & Melartin, R. L. (1993). Infants' ability to draw inferences about nonobvious object properties: Evidence from exploratory play. *Child Development*, **64**, 711–728.

Barsalou, L. W. (1983). Ad hoc categories. *Memory & Cognition*, **11**, 211–227.

Barsalou, L. W. (1985). Ideals, central tendency, and frequency of instantiation as determinants of graded structure in categories. *Journal of Experimental Psychology: Learning, Memory, & Cognition*, **11**, 629–654.

Box, G. E. P., & Tiao, G. C. (1973). *Bayesian inference in statistical analysis*. London: Addison-Wesley.

Carey, S. (1985). *Conceptual change in childhood*. Cambridge, MA: MIT Press, Bradford Books.

Choi, I., Nisbett, R. E., & Smith, E. E. (1997). Culture, category salience, and inductive reasoning. *Cognition*, **65**, 15–32.

Coley, J. D., Medin, D. L., & Atran, S. (1997). Does rank have its privilege? Inductive inferences within folkbiological taxonomies. *Cognition*, **64**, 73–112.

Coley, J. D., Medin, D. L., Proffitt, J. B., Lynch, E. B., & Atran, S. (1999). Inductive reasoning in folkbiological thought. In D. L. Medin & S. Atran (Eds.), *Folkbiology* (pp. 205–232). Cambridge, MA: MIT Press.

Florian, J. E. (1994). Stripes do not a zebra make, or do they: Conceptual and perceptual information in inductive inference. *Developmental Psychology*, **30**, 88–101.

Fried, L. S., & Holyoak, K. J. (1984). Induction of category distributions: A framework for classification learning. *Journal of Experimental Psychology: Learning, Memory, & Cognition*, **10**, 234–257.

Gelman, S. A. (1988). The development of induction within natural kind and artifact categories. *Cognitive Psychology*, **20**, 65–95.

Gelman, S. A., & Coley, J. D. (1990). The importance of knowing a dodo is a bird: Categories and inferences in 2-year-old children. *Developmental Psychology*, **26**, 796–804.

Gelman, S. A., & Markman, E. M. (1986). Categories and induction in young children. *Cognition*, **23**, 183–209.

Gelman, S. A., & O'Reilly, A. W. (1988). Children's inductive inferences within superordinate categories: The role of language and category structure. *Child Development*, **59**, 876–887.

Goodman, N. (1955). *Fact, fiction, and forecast.* Cambridge, MA: Harvard University Press.

Goodman, N. (1972). *Problems and projects.* Indianapolis: Bobbs-Merrill.

Gutheil, G., & Gelman, S. A. (1997). Children's use of sample size and diversity information within basic-level categories. *Journal of Experimental Child Psychology*, **64**, 159–174.

Hadjichristidis, D., Sloman, S. A., Stevenson, R. J., & Over, D. E. (1999). Centrality and property induction. In *Proceedings of the Twenty-First Annual Conference of the Cognitive Science Society* (p. 795). Mahwah, NJ: Erlbaum.

Hahn, U., & Chater, N. (1997). Concepts and similarity. In K. Lamberts & D. Shanks (Eds.), *Knowledge, concepts, and categories* (pp. 43–92). London: Psychology Press.

Heit, E. (1997). Knowledge and concept learning. In K. Lamberts & D. Shanks (Eds.), *Knowledge, concepts, and categories* (pp. 7–41). London: Psychology Press.

Heit, E. (1998). A Bayesian analysis of some forms of inductive reasoning. In M. Oaksford & N. Chater (Eds.), *Rational models of cognition* (pp. 248–274). Oxford: Oxford University Press.

Heit, E., & Bott, L. (2000). Knowledge selection in category learning. In D. L. Medin (Ed.), *The psychology of learning and motivation* (Vol. 39, pp. 163–199). San Diego: Academic Press.

Heit, E., & Hahn, U. (1999). Diversity-based reasoning in children age 5 to 8. In *Proceedings of the Twenty-First Annual Conference of the Cognitive Science Society* (pp. 212–217). Mahwah, NJ: Erlbaum.

Heit, E., & Rubinstein, J. (1994). Similarity and property effects in inductive reasoning. *Journal of Experimental Psychology: Learning, Memory, & Cognition*, **20**, 411–422.

Hempel, C. G. (1966). *Philosophy of natural science.* Englewood Cliffs, NJ: Prentice Hall.

Homa, D., & Vosburgh, R. (1976). Category breadth and the abstraction of prototypical information. *Journal of Experimental Psychology: Human Learning & Memory*, **2**, 322–330.

Hume, D. (1988). *An enquiry concerning human understanding.* La Salle, IL: Open Court. (Original work published 1748).

Kalish, C. W., & Gelman, S. A. (1992). On wooden pillows: Multiple classifications and children's category-based inductions. *Child Development*, **63**, 1536–1557.

Lassaline, M. E. (1996). Structural alignment in induction and similarity. *Journal of Experimental Psychology: Learning, Memory, & Cognition*, **22**, 754–770.

Loose, J. J., & Mareschal, D. (1999). Inductive reasoning revisited: Children's reliance on category labels and appearances. In *Proceedings of the Twenty-First Annual Conference of the Cogni-* tive Science Society (pp. 320–325). Mahwah, NJ: Erlbaum.

López, A. (1995). The diversity principle in the testing of arguments. *Memory & Cognition*, **23**, 374–382.

López, A., Atran, S., Coley, J. D., Medin, D. L., & Smith, E. E. (1997). The tree of life: Universal and cultural features of folkbiological taxonomies and inductions. *Cognitive Psychology*, **32**, 251–295.

López, A., Gelman, S. A., Gutheil, G., & Smith, E. E. (1992). The development of category-based induction. *Child Development*, **63**, 1070–1090.

Macario, J. F., Shipley, E. F., & Billman, D. O. (1990). Induction from a single instance: Formation of a novel category. *Journal of Experimental Child Psychology*, **50**, 179–199.

Mandler, J. M., & McDonough, L. (1996). Drinking and driving don't mix: Inductive generalization in infancy. *Cognition*, **59**, 307–335.

Mandler, J. M., & McDonough, L. (1998). Studies in inductive inference in infancy. *Cognitive Psychology*, **37**, 60–96.

Mandler, J. M., & McDonough, L. (2000). Advancing downward to the basic level. *Journal of Cognition & Development*, **1**, 379–403.

McDonald, J., Samuels, M., & Rispoli, J. (1996). A hypothesis assessment model of categorical argument strength. *Cognition*, **59**, 199–217.

Medin, D. L., Goldstone, R. L., & Gentner, D. (1993). Respects for similarity. *Psychological Review*, **100**, 254–278.

Medin, D. L., Lynch, E. B., Coley, J. D., & Atran, S. (1997). Categorization and reasoning among tree experts: Do all roads lead to Rome? *Cognitive Psychology*, **32**, 49–96.

Medin, D. L., & Ortony, A. (1989). Psychological essentialism. In S. Vosniadou & A. Ortony (Eds.), *Similarity and analogical reasoning* (pp. 179–195). Cambridge: Cambridge University Press.

Mill, J. S. (1874). *A system of logic.* New York: Harper.

Murphy, G. L., & Ross, B. H. (1999). Induction with cross-classified categories. *Memory & Cognition*, **27**, 1024–1041.

Nagel, E. (1939). *Principles of the theory of probability.* Chicago: University of Chicago Press.

Nisbett, R. E., Krantz, D. H., Jepson, C., & Kunda, Z. (1983). The use of statistical heuristics in everyday inductive reasoning. *Psychological Review*, **90**, 339–363.

Osherson, D. N., Smith, E. E., Myers, T. S., Shafir, E., & Stob, M. (1994). Extrapolating human probability judgment. *Theory & Decision*, **36**, 103–129.

Osherson, D. N., Smith, E. E., Wilkie, O., López, A., & Shafir, E. (1990). Category-based induction. *Psychological Review*, **97**, 185–200.

Osherson, D. N., Stern, J., Wilkie, O., Stob, M., & Smith, E. E. (1991). Default probability. *Cognitive Science*, **15**, 251–269.

Posner, M. I., & Keele, S. W. (1968). On the genesis of abstract ideas. *Journal of Experimental Psychology*, **77**, 353–363.

Proffitt, J. B., Coley, J. L., & Medin, D. L. (2000). Expertise and category-based induction. *Journal of Experimental Psychology: Learning, Memory, & Cognition*, **26**, 811–828.

Raiffa, H., & Schlaifer, R. (1961). *Applied statistical decision theory*. Boston: Harvard University, Graduate School of Business Administration.

Rips, L. J. (1975). Inductive judgments about natural categories. *Journal of Verbal Learning & Verbal Behavior*, **14**, 665–681.

Rosch, E., Mervis, C. G., Gray, W. D., Johnson, D. M., & Boyes-Braem, P. (1976). Basic objects in natural categories. *Cognitive Psychology*, **8**, 382–439.

Ross, B. H., & Murphy, G. L. (1999). Food for thought: Cross-classification and category organization in a complex real-world domain. *Cognitive Psychology*, **38**, 495–553.

Shipley, E. F. (1993). Categories, hierarchies, and induction. In D. L. Medin (Ed.), *The psychology of learning and motivation* (Vol. 30, pp. 265–301). San Diego: Academic Press.

Sloman, S. A. (1993). Feature-based induction. *Cognitive Psychology*, **25**, 231–280.

Sloman, S. A. (1994). When explanations compete: The role of explanatory coherence on judgments of likelihood. *Cognition*, **52**, 1–21.

Sloman, S. A. (1997). Explanatory coherence and the induction of properties. *Thinking & Reasoning*, **2**, 81–110.

Sloman, S. A. (1998). Categorical inference is not a tree: The myth of inheritance hierarchies. *Cognitive Psychology*, **35**, 1–33.

Smith, E. E., Shafir, E., & Osherson, D. (1993). Similarity, plausibility, and judgments of probability. *Cognition*, **49**, 67–96.

Spellman, B. A., López, A., & Smith, E. E. (1999). Hypothesis testing: Strategy selection for generalising versus limiting hypotheses. *Thinking & Reasoning*, **5**, 67–91.

Springer, K. (1992). Children's awareness of the biological implications of kinship. *Child Development*, **63**, 950–959.

Tversky, A., & Kahneman, D. (1973). Availability: A heuristic for judging frequency and probability. *Cognitive Psychology*, **5**, 207–232.

Waxman, S. R., Lynch, E. B., Casey, K. L., & Baer, L. (1997). Setters and samoyeds: The emergence of subordinate level categories as a basis for inductive inference in preschool-age children. *Developmental Psychology*, **33**, 1074–1090.

Wu, M., & Gentner, D. (1998). Structure in category-based induction. In *Proceedings of the Twentieth Annual Conference of the Cognitive Science Society* (pp. 1154–1158). Mahwah, NJ: Erlbaum.

Section 5: Dual and Integrative Approaches

Chapter 20: Human Reasoning and Argumentation: The Probabilistic Approach

MIKE OAKSFORD, NICK CHATER, AND ULRIKE HAHN

When compared to standard logic, research in the psychology of deductive reasoning has found that people make large and systematic (i.e., non-random) errors (Manktelow 1999), which suggests that humans may be irrational (Stein 1996; Stich 1985). However, the probabilistic approach argues against this interpretation. Rather than view this behaviour as errorful, it is argued that performance may have been compared to the wrong normative standard. When compared to probability theory rather than logic, participants' reasoning may be seen in a more positive light.

The probabilistic approach contrasts with mental logic (e.g., Rips 1994) and mental model theories (e.g. Johnson-Laird and Byrne 1991) which both argue that systematic deviations from logic represent unavoidable performance errors. In both theories working memory limitations restrict people's reasoning abilities. These approaches are hard to reconcile with the high error rates seen in some tasks, for example, up to 96 percent in Wason's selection task, and the fact that everyday thought and action seems to be highly successful. How can this success be understood if peoples' reasoning system is prone to so much error? The probabilistic approach resolves this problem by adopting a different normative theory (Oaksford and Chater 1998b; Stanovich and West 2000) and by considering the role of the environment in reasoning (Anderson 1990, 1991; Chater and Oaksford 1999b; Oaksford and Chater 1998a).

The goal of this chapter is to review recent primarily empirical developments[1] in the probabilistic approach to explaining the core tasks in the area, conditional inference, data selection in the Wason selection task, and syllogistic reasoning. We also look at how the probabilistic approach has been generalised to *argumentation*, that is, the process of persuading others of a, possibly controversial, standpoint, which is arguably the more general human activity of which deductive reasoning is but a part. We first provide an overview of our approach which links the three areas of reasoning we look at and which addresses some of the standard criticisms.

Overview

We look first at conditional inference, i.e., inferences involving the expression *if . . . then*. In psychological experiments on conditional inference, participants are provided with a conditional premise, for example, *if something is a bird then it flies*, and a categorical premise, for example, *Tweety is a bird*. They are often told to assume that the premises are true. On this assumption, they are then asked whether *Tweety flies* can be inferred from the premises. This inference is the logically valid inference form of *modus ponens* (MP). So, if they reason logically, they should endorse this inference. When simple alphanumeric stimuli are used (*if A then 2, A, therefore 2?*), participants typically endorse this inference, but when everyday materials are used, like in our example, they tend to endorse it less. Moreover, even with alphanumeric stimuli, people endorse another logically valid inference, *modus tollens* (MT, categorical premise: *Tweety does not fly*, conclusion: *Tweety is not a bird*) far less than MP.

According to the probabilistic approach these findings relate to the fact that inferences involving everyday conditionals are *defeasible*, i.e., adding premises can lose conclusions. So if you then learn that *Tweety is an Ostrich* the MP inference above is *defeated*, that is, adding a premise has lost a conclusion (this behaviour is called *non-monotonicity*). There are a variety of logical proposals to get around this problem but none appear to succeed (see Chater and Oaksford 1993; Oaksford and Chater 1991, 1992, 1993, 1995, 1998b). However, probability theory simply *is* non-monotonic and so handles cases like these with ease, that is, the probability that birds fly is high ($P(flies(x) \mid bird(x)) = .9$) but the probability of a bird flying given that it is also an ostrich is near 0 ($P(flies(x) \mid bird(x), ostrich(x)) \approx 0$). Treating conditionals as expressing conditional probabilities was proposed in philosophy by Adams (1966, 1975, 1998), and has been used in artificial intelligence by Pearl (1988, 2000).

As we have just indicated, the primary motivation for the probabilistic approach is that the introduction of probabilities provides a potential solution to the problem of non-monotonicity in real human reasoning. Our original critiques of *logicist* cognitive science (Chater and Oaksford 1990; Oaksford and Chater 1991) in general and of *logicist* psychological theories of human reasoning in particular (Chater and Oaksford, 1993; Oaksford and Chater 1993, 1995, 1998) focussed on the inability of accounts, like those proposed by Fodor (1987) and by mental logics and mental models theories, to deal with non-monotonicity. Subsequent research within the probabilistic approach has been aimed at showing how probability theory, which deals with this problem head-on, may also provide better accounts of human reasoning data and may also preserve human rationality. In artificial intelligence, probability theory (Pearl 1988, 2000) or other uncertainty formalisms (see Prakken and Vreeswijk 2002, for a recent overview) have become the dominant approach to providing practical systems that deal with defeasibility. Providing practical artificial reasoning systems that deal with the computational problems surrounding defeasible inference requires something like probability theory. Our hunch is that natural reasoning systems have evolved a similar solution.

Our approach to the other areas of human reasoning that we discuss in this chapter follows on directly from adopting the conditional probability interpretation of the conditional (Adams 1998; Bennett 2003). In the Wason selection task (Wason 1966, 1968), participants must select the best types of evidence to determine whether a conditional rule is true or false. This task is interpreted as selecting the evidence that best distinguishes a conditional hypothesis, *if p then q*, where $P(q \mid p)$ is high and in particular higher than $P(q)$, from a foil hypothesis where $P(q \mid p) = P(q)$. The evidence that best distinguishes these possibilities turns out to depend on the priors $P(p)$ and $P(q)$. If these are low, what Oaksford and Chater (1994) called "the rarity assumption," then the theory of *optimal data selection* predicts the empirically observed pattern of evidence selection, which can not therefore be regarded as irrational.

In syllogistic reasoning, people must draw conclusions from two *quantified* premises, for example, *All beekeepers are artists, Some beekeepers are chemists*, therefore, *Some artists are chemists*. The probabilistic analysis of these inferences starts from the observation that many conditionals in natural language are implicitly quantified. So the logical form of *birds fly* could be *for all x if x is a bird then x flies*. Chater and Oaksford (1999), therefore, interpreted the quantifier in *all p are q* to mean that $P(q \mid p) = 1$. They then provided interpretations based on conditional probability for the other quantified statements, for example, *some p are q* means $P(q \mid p) > 0$. This approach importantly allowed interpretations for quantifiers that had not been used in reasoning experiments. For example, the case where $P(q \mid p)$ is high but less than 1, provides the interpretation for *most p are q*. *Most birds fly* seems to be the most appropriate interpretation of *birds fly* but one that is unavailable in standard logic. Using these interpretations of the quantifiers allows the *probabilistic validity* of syllogistic inferences to be defined including those involving *generalized* quantifiers (Barwise and Cooper 1981) like *most* and *few*. Moreover, a simple set of probabilistic heuristics can be described that reliably identifies the *p*-valid conclusion if there is one.

We have seen how a simple interpretation of the conditional as conditional probability runs through our whole approach to human reasoning. This approach might be characterised as arguing that although people are poor at logical reasoning they are nonetheless good at probabilistic reasoning. However, this claim seems to be at odds with established results apparently showing that people are also very poor probabilistic reasoners (e.g., Tversky and Kahneman 1974; Kahneman, Slovic and Tversky 1982). For example, people seem to be insensitive to base rates, that is, in applying Bayes's theorem people often provide estimates of posterior probabilities that seem to reflect only the likelihoods and not the priors. People also seem to be overconfident in their probability judgements, that is, they do not seem to be well calibrated to the actual frequencies of events in the world. Moreover, people also seem prone to the conjunction fallacy. That is, they violate the probabilistic law that the joint probability of any two events can not be greater than either individual event, i.e., $P(A) \geq P(A, B) \leq P(B)$.

There are several points to make here. Our accounts of human reasoning are framed at the computational level, that is, they characterise what is being computed not how (although we do provide a process account in terms of *probabilistic heuristics* for syllogistic reasoning). That people's behaviour well approximates the norms provided by these models, which are thereby descriptively adequate, does not necessarily mean that people are doing complex probabilistic computations in their heads. As Oaksford and Chater (1994) argued, people could approximate these norms using a small set of hard wired heuristics (Gigerenzer and Goldstein 1996). To the extent that this is the case we would expect people to be relatively insensitive to probabilistic manipulations (see Oaksford et al. 1997). However, as we will see, people are sensitive to a variety of probabilistic manipulations in these tasks. Consequently it would appear that people may be performing some forms of rudimentary probabilistic calculations. Again these may bear no direct relation to the explicit manipulation of probability values using the rules of probability theory represented in our model. However, if people are responding appropriately to probabilistic manipulations then this behaviour does seem inconsistent with their systematically falling into error on probabilisitic reasoning tasks.

But there are good reasons to suspect that Kahneman and Tversky's assessment of people's probabilistic reasoning abilities was premature (McKenzie 2005). According to recent analyses many of the apparent errors and biases observed in probabilistic reasoning are a consequence of presenting the probabilistic information in an unnatural format (Gigerenzer and Hoffrage 1995). Most often in experiments of this type people are given the probabilistic information in terms of explicit probability statements or percentages, for example, .05 or 5 percent. However, Gigerenzer and Hoffrage (1995)

argue that this is unnatural given the normal sampling situation where we build up frequency information as a result of multiple encounters with objects and events. What you discover by such a process is, for example, that something like ninety-five out of the one hundred ravens you have examined are black. A wide variety of replications of Kahneman and Tversky's original experiments now show that when a frequency format is used to express the probabilities, far fewer deviations from probability theory are observed.

Moreover, there are many recent (Bovens and Hartmann 2003; and indeed older, e.g., Birnbaum 1983) normative analyses showing that apparent deviations from normative probability can be readily explained without recourse to inaccurate heuristics. In particular, Bovens and Hartmann (2003) have recently shown that by construing the information in the conjunction problem as deriving from more or less reliable witnesses a Bayesian network can be constructed in which it is possible for the probability of the report of a joint event to be more likely than a report of one of the conjuncts. For example, given the background information in the Linda problem, she is more likely to be active in the feminist movement than a bank teller. Under these conditions, one is more likely to believe a witness who tells you that Linda is active in the feminist movement and a bank teller than one who only tells you that Linda is a bank teller. If people construe the conjunction task in this way, they need be doing nothing irrational.

We have dealt here with perhaps the most obvious objection to a probabilistic approach to human reasoning. However, we do not want to pretend that the probabilistic approach is without problems. Many issues are discussed in Oaksford and Chater (1998: 279–291) and they mainly involve how probabilities are assigned to whole bodies of knowledge and how changes are tracked through such large knowledge bases. These are profound problems but we are optimistic that recent research into Bayes nets that introduce structure, via strong independence assumptions, into such knowledge bases may resolve some of these issues. Moreover, the move to probabilistic and related approaches in artificial intelligence has been motivated by even more profound problems for the logicist approach (Chater and Oaksford 1990; Oaksford and Chater 1991, 1993, 1995, 1998). Again, our hunch is that the natural reasoning system has evolved a similar solution.

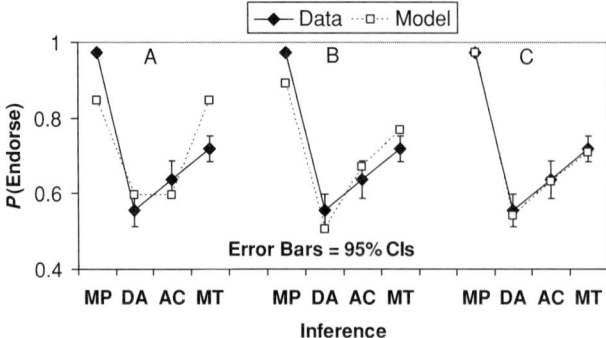

Figure 1. The probability that each inference is endorsed showing the fits of standard logic (Panel A), the conditional probability model (Panel B), and the revised probability model (Panel C) to the data from Schroyens and Schaeken's (2003) meta-analysis.

We now turn to each of the three domains of reasoning research before showing how the probabilistic approach may also apply to the more general human activity of argumentation.

Conditional Inference

The conditional inference task involves presenting participants with a conditional premise, *if p then q* ($p \rightarrow q$), and one of four categorical premises, p, $\neg p$, q, or $\neg q$. If people interpret the everyday conditional of natural language ("$\rightarrow$") as the material conditional of standard logic ("$\supset$"), then they should endorse the logical rules of inference, *modus ponens* ("MP") and *modus tollens* ("MT"):

$$\text{MP} \quad \frac{p \supset q, p}{\therefore q} \qquad \text{MT} \quad \frac{p \supset q, \neg q}{\therefore \neg p} \qquad (1)$$

These inference schemata read that if the propositions above the line are true, then it can be inferred that the propositions below the line are true. Moreover, they should *not* endorse the logical fallacies of *denying the antecedent* ("DA") and *affirming the consequent* ("AC"):

$$\text{DA} \quad \frac{p \supset q, \neg p}{\therefore \neg q} \qquad \text{AC} \quad \frac{p \supset q, q}{\therefore p} \qquad (2)$$

So logically participants should endorse MP and MT equally and they should refuse to endorse DA or AC. However, they endorse MP significantly more than MT and they endorse DA and AC at levels significantly above zero. Figure 1, Panel A, shows the results of a recent meta-analysis of conditional inference (Schroyens and Schaeken 2003) together with the best fits obtainable by standard logic (for how this fit was

obtained, see Oaksford and Chater 2003a). In the next section we outline the theory of conditional inference developed in the probabilistic approach.

Theory

Following other researchers in this area (e.g., Anderson 1995; Chan and Chua 1994; George 1997, 1999; Liu 2003; Liu, Lo, and Wu 1996; Politzer 2005; Stevenson and Over 1995), we proposed a model of conditional reasoning based on conditional probability (Oaksford and Chater 2003a, 2003b, 2003c, 2003d; Oaksford, Chater, and Larkin 2000). The probability of the conditional, $P(p \rightarrow q)$, is the conditional probability, $P(q \mid p)$. This is what Edgington (1991) calls *The Equation*. The greater the probability of the conclusion given the premises the more it should be endorsed. The constraints on conditional inference were specified in a 2×2 contingency table as in Oaksford and Chater (1998c). A notational variant of this table is shown in Table 1, in which $a = P(q \mid p)$, $b = P(p)$, and $c = P(q)$.[2]

Oaksford et al. (2000) derived conditional probabilities of the conclusion for each inference MP, MT, AC, and DA. Oaksford and Chater (2007, 2008) recently showed that this account of conditional inference is equivalent to the *dynamic* approach to conditional inference in *probability logic* (Adams 1998). From this perspective, conditionals allow people to update their beliefs (prior probability distributions) given new information. So if a high probability is assigned to *if x is a bird, x flys*, then on acquiring the new information that *Tweety is a bird*, one's degree of belief in *Tweety flys* should be revised to one's degree of belief in *Tweety flys given Tweety is a bird*, i.e., one's degree of belief in the conditional. So using P_0

Table 1: The Contingency Table for a Conditional Rule If *p* Then *q*, Where There is a Dependency Between the *p* and *q* that May Admit Exceptions, $a = P(q \mid p)$, $b = P(p)$, and $c = P(q)$

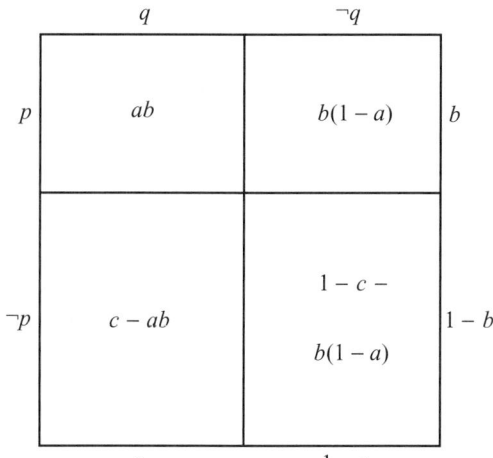

	q	¬*q*	
p	ab	$b(1 - a)$	b
¬*p*	$c - ab$	$1 - c - b(1 - a)$	$1 - b$
	c	$1 - c$	

to indicate *prior* degree of belief and P_1 to indicate *posterior* degree of belief, then:

$$P_1(q) = P_0(q \mid p), \quad \text{when } P_1(p) = 1. \tag{3}$$

Thus according to this account, the probability with which someone should endorse the MP inference is the conditional probability, exactly as in Oaksford et al. (2000).

However, as Oaksford and Chater (2007, 2008) pointed out there is a problem with

extending this account to MT, DA and AC (Sober 2002). The appropriate conditional probabilities for the categorical premise of these inferences to conditionalize on are $P(\neg p \mid \neg q)$, $P(\neg q \mid \neg p)$, and $P(p \mid q)$ respectively. However, the premises of MT and the fallacies do not entail values for these conditional probabilities (Sober 2002, 2004; Wagner 2004). Oaksford et al. (2000) suggested that people had prior knowledge of the marginals, $P(p)$ and $P(q)$, which together with $P(q \mid p)$ do entail appropriate values (see, Wagner [2004] for a similar approach):

$$\text{MP} \quad P_1(q) = P_0(q \mid p) = a \tag{4}$$

$$\text{DA} \quad P_1(\neg q) = P_0(\neg q \mid \neg p) = \frac{1 - c - (1 - a)b}{1 - b} \tag{5}$$

$$\text{AC} \quad P_1(p) = P_0(p \mid q) = \frac{ab}{c} \tag{6}$$

$$\text{MT} \quad P_1(\neg p) = P_0(\neg p \mid \neg q) = \frac{1 - c - (1 - a)b}{1 - c} \tag{7}$$

Equations (4) to (7) show the posterior probabilities of the conclusion of each inference assuming the posterior probability of the categorical premise is 1. The behavior of this account is shown in Figure 2. By using Jeffrey conditionalization, these cases can be readily generalized to when the probability of the categorical premise

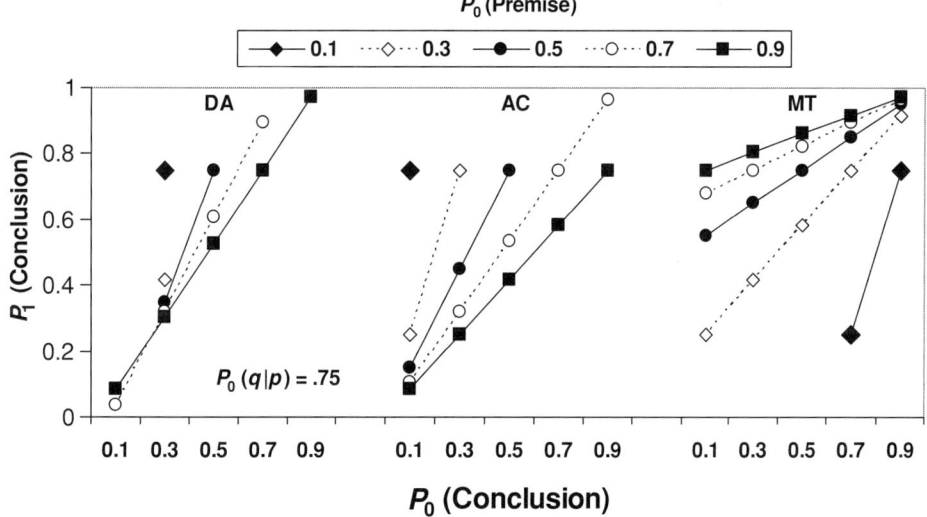

Figure 2. How the probability that a conclusion should be drawn varies as a function of the prior probabilities of the categorical premise and conclusion for DA, for AC, and for MT.

is less than 1. For example, for MP:

$$P_1(q) = P_0(q \mid p)P_1(p) + P_0(q \mid \neg p)P_1(\neg p). \quad (8)$$

An important constraint on Jeffrey conditionalization is the *rigidity condition:*

Rigidity Condition: $P_1(q \mid p) = P_0(q \mid p)$ (9)

That is, discovering the posterior probability of the categorical premise does not alter the estimate of the probability of the conditional. The possible effects of the failure of rigidity can be illustrated using a concrete example, that is, what happens if you believe that *if you turn the key (p) the car starts (q)* and that on this occasion *the car didn't start.* There would seem to be little reason to expect the car to start unless one was reasonably confident that the key had been turned. Put another way, the assertion of the categorical premise of MT only seems to be informative against a background where the car was expected to start. Normally this is only a reasonable expectation if it is known that the key has been turned. So this seems like a case in which rigidity might be violated. That is, the effect of a failure of rigidity is to suggest the possibility of a counterexample to the conditional, that is, the categorical premise of MT suggests a case where the key has been turned but the car has not started $(p, \neg q)$.

Oaksford and Chater (2007, 2008) suggested that because rigidity violations indicated the possibility of a counterexample, people adjust $P_0(q \mid p)$ to a revised value, $P_0^R(q \mid p)$, by Bayesian revision, assuming a model where turning keys and cars starting are independent as a foil hypothesis (Oaksford and Chater 1994, 1996, 2003e).[3] This adjustment means that the value of the conditional probability used to calculate the posterior probabilities for DA, AC, and MT is lower than for MP. As we now see, Oaksford (2005) showed how this revision provided a much better account of the baseline rates of endorsement for the conditional inferences investigated in the psychology of reasoning. In the next section, we outline some of the evidence that this account can explain.

The Evidence

In this section, we first discuss the *inferential asymmetries* in the base-line results. We then discuss the recent evidence on the probability of the conditional before returning to the older data on *negative conclusion bias* and *suppression effects.*

THE INFERENTIAL ASYMMETRIES

Oaksford and Chater (2007, 2008) observed that the first hurdles any account of conditional inference must get over are the empirical asymmetries observed between MP and MT, that is, MP is endorsed more than MT, and between DA and AC, AC is endorsed more than DA (see Figure 1). Figure 1 Panel B shows the fit of the original Oaksford et al. (2000) model. It is clear that it *underestimates* the magnitude of the MP–MT asymmetry and *overestimates* the magnitude of the DA–AC asymmetry. This fact has recently been used to argue against Oaksford et al.'s (2000) probabilistic approach (Evans and Over 2004; Schroyens and Schaeken 2003).

Oaksford and Chater (2003b) showed that the original model, despite its limitations, did not provide significantly worse fits to the data than other theories like mental models (Johnson-Laird and Byrne 1991, 2002) or mental logic (e.g., Rips 1994). Consequently, there is no need to invoke processing limitations at the algorithmic level like those invoked by these theories to explain the mismatch between the data and the computational level theory they adopt for this task, that is, standard logic. Oaksford and Chater (2003a, 2003b) suggested that concentrating on the algorithmic level may lead to better fits.

Schroyens and Schaeken (2003) provided an alternative mental models account, in which people seek for counterexamples from long term memory to putative conclusions suggested by their initial mental models. They showed that a parameterised version of this model provided better fits to the data in Figure 1 than Oaksford et al.'s (2000) model. The parameters of this model corresponded to the probabilities of retrieving the p and $\neg q$, $\neg p$ and q, and the $\neg p$ and $\neg q$ cases from long term memory. Oaksford and Chater (2003a) argued that there were several conceptual problems with this account. For example, Schroyens and Schaeken suggested that it may be consistent with a probabilistic construal of rationality. This might be true if the three parameters of their model corresponded to the joint probabilities, $P(p,\neg q)$, $P(\neg p,q)$ and $P(\neg p,\neg q)$. However, the best fit values of their parameters summed to greater than 1, implying that $P(p,q) < 0$. Thus, their account is forced to attribute people with probabilistically inconsistent beliefs. Moreover, Oaksford and Chater (2003c) showed that when fitted to data where probabilities are explicitly manipulated (Oaksford et al. 2000), Schroyens and Schaeken's model provided worse fits than the original conditional probability model.

However, the magnitude of the inferential asymmetries observed in the conditional inference task remained unexplained. Oaksford and Chater's (2007, 2008) invocation of rigidity violations may explain the magnitude of these asymmetries at the computational level. Rigidity violations suggest a lower revised value for the conditional probability, that is, $P_0^R (q \mid p)$. It is this lower value that is used to estimate the relevant conditional probabilities for the categorical premises of DA, AC, and MT to conditionalize on. Oaksford and Chater (2007, 2008) fitted a model to the same data in Figure 1, where a lower value was used (but which had the same number of free parameters) and the fits were significantly better (see Figure 1, Panel C). The relationship between the revised value, $P_0^R (q \mid p)$, and $P_0(q \mid p)$ was also consistent with Bayesian revision on one counterexample. These results seem to show that the magnitude of the MP–MT asymmetry can also be explained from a Bayesian perspective.

EVIDENCE FOR "THE EQUATION"

Recent evidence shows that people do regard the probability of a conditional to be the conditional probability (i.e., *The Equation* [Edgington 1991; see also Bennett 2003]) as the probabilistic account presupposes (Evans et al. 2003; Oberauer and Wilhlem 2003; Over et al. 2005). We focus on Evans et al. (2003), who assessed people's probabilistic interpretations of conditional rules and their contrapositives (*if ¬q then ¬p*). They tested three possibilities. First, material implication predicts that the probability of a conditional should be $1 - P(p, \neg q)$, that is, 1 minus the probability of finding a falsifying case. Second, the conditional probability account predicts that the probability of a conditional should be $P(q \mid p)$. Finally, in the defective truth table account (Johnson-Laird and Tagart 1969), where false antecedent cases are irrelevant, the probability of a conditional should be the joint probability, $P(p, q)$. According to material implication, conditionals and their contrapositives should be endorsed equally because they are logically equivalent. Consequently, there should be a strong correlation between ratings of how likely the conditional and its contrapositive are to be true. However, according to the conditional probability account,

$P(q \mid p)$ and $P(\neg p \mid \neg q)$ can differ considerably and would not be expected to reveal a perfect correlation.

Evans et al. (2003) varied $P(q \mid p)$, $P(\neg q \mid p)$ and $P(\neg p)$ by describing the distribution of cards in packs of varying sizes. For example, given a conditional *if the card is yellow then it has a circle printed on it*, participants could be told that there are four yellow circles, one yellow diamond, sixteen red circles and sixteen red diamonds (Oaksford et al. [2000] used similar manipulations).[4] So $P(q \mid p) = .8, P(\neg q \mid p) = .2$ and $P(\neg p) = 32/3$. On material implication, increases in $P(\neg p)$ should increase ratings of P(*if the card is yellow then it has a circle printed on it*); according to conditional probability, they should be independent of $P(\neg p)$; and according to conjunction interpretation, they should decrease with increases in $P(\neg p)$. The evidence supported conditional probability with some evidence for a joint probability interpretation.

Recently, Over et al. (2005) replicated these findings for everyday conditionals pretested for $P(p)$ and $P(q)$ as in Oaksford, Chater, and Grainger (1999) and Oaksford et al. (2000: Exp. 3). They also found that for these conditionals the conjunctive interpretation was not adopted by a significant proportion of participants unlike in Evans et al. (2003). Consequently, the conjunctive interpretation is probably an artefact of unrealistic stimuli. Similar results have been found by Oberauer and Wilhelm (2003). Moreover, Ohm and Thompson (in press) also have shown that people's inferential behaviour corresponds closely to the probabilistic approaches predictions given their conditional probability interpretations.

Oberauer, Weidenfeld, and Hörnig (2004) had participants learn about the probabilities of the antecedent and consequent of a conditional but observed no effects on the conditional inference task. This result is not consistent with the large range of probabilistic effects in conditional inference (Chan and Chua 1994; George 1997, 1999; Liu 2003; Liu, Lo, and Wu 1996; Ohm and Thompson in press; Stevenson and Over 1995). It also appears inconsistent with these authors' own findings on the probability of the conditional (Oberauer and Wilhlem 2003). Unless, that is, people's probabilistic interpretation of the conditional has absolutely no consequences for their inferential behaviour.

NEGATIVE CONCLUSION BIAS

The behaviour of the model shown in Figure 2 explains *negative conclusion bias*, which arises in *Evans' negations paradigm* (Evans 1977; Evans, Clibbens, and Rood 1995; Evans and Handley 1999). Here negations are used in the antecedents and consequents of the rules to create four task rules (A: Affirmative; N: Negative): *if p then q* (AA), *if p then ¬q* (AN), *if ¬p then q* (NA), and *if ¬p then ¬q* (NN). This manipulation means that half the conclusions of any inference, MP, DA, AC, or MT, will be affirmative and half of them will be negative. *Negative conclusion bias* is observed when participants endorse more inferences with a negative conclusion than with an affirmative conclusion. Negated categories have a higher probability than their affirmative counterparts, for example, $P(x$ is a dog$) < P(x$ is not a dog$)$ (Oaksford and Stenning 1992; Oaksford and Chater 1994). Consequently if a conclusion is negated then it corresponds to a high probability conclusion. The probability of the conclusion is on the x-axis in Figure 2. It is clear that as this probability increases so the probability with which the model predicts an inference should be endorsed also increases.

This account was confirmed by Oaksford et al. (2000) who varied the probabilities of the antecedents, $P(p)$, and consequents, $P(q)$, to produce four variants analogous to those in the negations paradigm but with high probabilities in place of negations. The four rules were (L: low probability; H: high probability), LL, LH, HL, and HH corresponded to the AA, AN, NA, and NN rules respectively. Oaksford et al. (2000) observed a significant high probability conclusion effect directly analogous to negative conclusion bias (see also Schroyens, Schaeken, Fias, and d'Ydewalle 2000; Schroyens, Verschueren, Schaeken, and d'Ydewalle 2000).

SUPPRESSION EFFECTS

Suppression effects occur when further information reduces the degree to which an inference is endorsed. For example, if someone is told that *if the key is turned the car starts* and that *the key is turned*, they are likely to infer that *the car starts* by MP. However, if they are also told that *if the petrol tank is not empty the car starts*, then they are less likely to endorse this conclusion because the car may not start if the petrol tank is empty (Byrne 1989). The petrol tank being empty provides an *exception* to the rule. These cases have been called "additional antecedents." Their presence suppresses the valid inferences MP and MT (Byrne 1989). These effects are predicted by the probabilistic model. Additional antecedents increase the probability of $P(p, \neg q)$ cases and so reduce the conditional probability, $P(q \mid p)$,

and hence the probability of drawing the MP inference. The model predicts a similar effect for MT which is also observed. More counterintuitively the model predicts that decrease in $P(q \mid p)$ should also decrease endorsements of DA and AC (Oaksford and Chater 2003d), and this effect has been observed (George 1997). Oaksford and Chater (2003d) also discuss a variety of other suppression effects consistent with the conditional probability model (e.g., Chan and Chua 1994; Cummins 1995; Cummins, Lubarts, Alksnis, and Rist 1991; George 1997; Liu, Wo, and Wu 1996; Stevenson and Over 1995; Thompson 1994; Thompson and Mann 1995). Bonnefon and Hilton (2004; see also Bonnefon 2004) also report results on the suppression effect that they argue are best explained by the probabilistic approach.

Further Theoretical Issues

We conclude this section on conditional inference by addressing three further theoretical issues that have arisen in the recent literature on conditional inference surrounding the probabilistic approach. First, we look at the theoretical differences between the probabilistic approach and recent accounts of conditional reasoning that preserve the logical approach but supplement it with a search for counterexamples in long-term memory. Second, we look at Liu's (2003) recent *two-step conditionalisation* model and whether it differs significantly from the account in (4)–(7) above. Finally, we suggest the future direction of conditional reasoning research, in particular at the algorithmic level.

LOGIC AND LONG-TERM MEMORY SEARCH

The definition of conditional probability in Adams's (1998) account and Oaksford et al.'s (2000) is based on the subjective definition provided by the Ramsey Test (Ramsey 1990, originally 1931; see footnote 1). That is, the antecedent is added to one's stock of beliefs, appropriate revisions are made, and the resulting degree of belief in the consequent is the conditional probability. The Ramsey test clearly relies on an account of how knowledge is stored and accessed. Oaksford and Chater (2003a; see also Sellen, Oaksford, and Gray 2005) observed that this reliance means that the probabilistic approach to the MP–MT and DA–AC asymmetries is very similar to some other approaches (Markovits and Barrouillet 2002; Markovits and Quinn 2002; Markovits, Fleury, Quinn, and Venet 1998; Quinn and Markovits 1998; Quinn and Markovits 2002; Schroyens, Schaeken, and d'Ydewalle 2001a, 2001b). These approaches suggest that people search long-term memory for counterexamples and if they find them they reduce the ratings they assign to an inference or do not endorse it at all. According to Oaksford and Chater's (2007, 2008) account, counterexamples are often suggested to DA, AC, and MT inferences because of possible rigidity violations (Sobel 2004). This results in revising the conditional probability for these inferences. One difference is that the probabilistic approach provides a normatively consistent account of what people do when they consider a counterexample, that is, they revise down $P(q \mid p)$ by Bayesian revision. As we now show, these other approaches seem to encounter all the problems of defeasible inference that motivated our original adoption of probability theory.

The problem centers on the continued adherence of these approaches to a truth functional view of the conditional. People are proposed to initially interpret the conditional as true, that is, they must assume there can be no counterexamples. On this assumption, they draw the appropriate logical inference. According to the extension of mental models theory, proposed by Schroyens and Schaeken (2003), people then search for counterexamples to the conclusion and conclude the conditional is false if they find one. So given the nonlogical axiom, *if x is a bird, x flys*, and the claim that *Tweety is a bird*, it is concluded validly that *Tweety can fly*, but when the proposition that *Tweety is an ostrich* is retrieved it is concluded that *if x is a bird, x flys* is false (presumably because it is also known that *if x is an ostrich, x can not fly*). This argument has the form of a logically acceptable *reductio ad absurdum* of this conditional claim. However, it has the unacceptable consequence that most conditional knowledge is strictly false because it is defeasible.

This consequence is unproblematic from a probabilistic point of view because probability theory is *non-monotonic* (see *Introduction*) and hence on this view most conditional knowledge, while highly probable, is strictly false. However, it means that people can not have a deductive reasoning system of the kind proposed by mental models. Schroyens and Schaeken (2003) do not say what they think happens to the proposition that *if x is a bird, x flys* when people infer that it is false. There are two options: Retain it as an axiom or expunge it from long-term memory. Only the latter option is logically consistent because if it is nonetheless retained as an axiom, then contradictions will result. For example, on subsequently learning that *Chirpy is a bird and an ostrich*, the axioms about birds and ostriches above lead to the conclusion that *Chirpy can fly and Chirpy can not fly*, that is, a logical contradiction. To avoid this situation, the conditional claim needs to be expunged from long-term memory. But then this very useful generalization is no longer available to draw reasonable inferences about the world!

TWO-STEP CONDITIONALISATION

Liu, Wo, and Wu (1996; see also Liu 2003) presented participants with two conditions. In one participants might be asked, *if I tell you this is a rock, would you infer it is hard* (a *reduced* problem), which contains no conditional premise. In another condition they would be asked, *if I tell you that if something is a rock it is hard and that this is a rock, would you infer that it is hard* (a *complete* problem). The pattern of results was very similar. So even without a conditional premise, as long as the materials can access appropriate world knowledge, performance is very much the same. However, while the general pattern of responding is unchanged, adding the conditional premise leads to systematic increases in the endorsement of the inferences. This could be because people engage a logical reasoning mechanism when explicit premises are provided.

However, Liu (2003) favors a probabilistic interpretation involving two steps of conditionalisation. So, for MP, people first update their probability that q is true by conditionalising on the truth of p, that is, the categorical premise, to arrive at $P(q \mid p)$. This is what Liu (2003) calls the "proportionality hypothesis," which he attributes to Oaksford et al. (2000). According to this hypothesis, people disregard the conditional premise. In the second step of conditionalization, people take the conditional premise into account to evaluate $P(q \mid p, if\ p\ then\ q)$. This second step explains the differences observed between the two conditions of Liu's (2003) experiments.

A problem for two-step conditionalisation is that the second step seems redundant. The first step conditionalises on the categorical premise. To do this an estimate of $P(q \mid p)$ is derived from long-term memory for world knowledge for $P(p) = 1$ to conditionalise on. By the Ramsey test this is estimated by adding p to world knowledge, adjusting, and reading off the degree of belief in q. But then the second step is redundant. The second premise is *if p then q* and $P(if\ p\ then\ q) = P(q \mid p)$, which must be estimated *in exactly the same way as in the first step*. So it seems unlikely that the second-step conditionalisation could alter the results of the first step.

Pragmatically it could be that the act of asserting the conditional for a complete problem provides further evidence that p is sufficient for q, that is, $P(q \mid p)$ is higher than just considering one's own world knowledge would suggest.[5] However, this would seem to violate the constraints on Jeffrey conditionalization, which works by keeping the relationships between cells in the joint probability distribution constant, that is, the conditional probabilities do not change. As we have seen, this is called the rigidity condition in Jeffrey conditionalization, that is, $P_0(q \mid p) = P_1(q \mid p)$. Liu's second step argues that conditionalizing on the conditional premise leads to an increase in this conditional probability, that is, $P_2(q \mid p) > P_1(q \mid p)$. But by Jeffrey conditionalization these should remain the same, that is, $P_0(q \mid p) = P_1(q \mid p) = P_2(q \mid p)$.

It seems that the only effect the assertion of the conditional premise could have is to provide additional *evidence* that q and p are related which increases the assessment of $P_2(q \mid p)$ *because people now know more than they did before*, although this violates the rigidity condition. That is, Liu's (2003) second step can not be described as just another application of Jeffrey conditionalization. We therefore see no advantage in Liu's (2003) two-step approach. Our original account (Oaksford et al. 2000) did not disregard the conditional premise but assumed that people conditionalize on it (see (4)–(7) above). Consequently, people were assumed to take the extra knowledge, that in this context the conditional premise is asserted into account and therefore $P(q \mid p)$ is higher than their prior world knowledge would predict. When reduced problems are presented participants are not provided with the extra knowledge that the dependency described in the conditional rule holds in this context.

FUTURE DIRECTIONS: THE RAMSEY TEST

The analysis provided here and by probability logic (e.g., Adams 1998) shows that the principle effort in the psychology of conditional inference should be directed at delineating the cognitive processes underlying the Ramsey test. Our best philosophical understanding of conditional probability is given by this test which essentially invokes a currently unarticulated mental process (Bennett 2003). Moreover, recent appeals to the Ramsey test (Evans and Over 2004) treat it as a primitive mental operation and deal only with the mental representations that may result from having performed one.

In contrast, Oaksford (2004) presented an algorithmic account of conditional inference

based on the probability conditional using a simple constraint satisfaction neural network (McClelland 1998; Rumelhart, Smolensky, McClelland, and Hinton 1986). In such a framework, performing a Ramsey test amounts to clamping on (or off) the node corresponding to the categorical premise and reading off the activation level of the node corresponding to the conclusion. As the Ramsey test requires, this process is *conservative*, that is, it involves minimal changes, as all the connection weights remain the same. Given certain constraints (McClelland 1998), for MP this operation corresponds to computing the real posterior probability, that is, $P_0(q \mid p,K)$, where K stands for the other knowledge embedded in the connections between nodes. K will also include $P_0(p)$ and $P_0(q)$ which are represented as bias terms.

This framework also may capture the contrast between MP and MT. For MP people may simply perform the Ramsey test without considering other possibilities. However, as it has been argued, the conditions under which the categorical premise of MT can be asserted suggests a counterexample. Consequently, people may not just clamp off the q-node to perform the Ramsey test but may also consider the possibility where the q-node is clamped off and the p-node is clamped on. This can lead to updating of the connection weight by local learning (which would need to be reversible as people are only *supposing*, after all).[6] The q-node is then clamped off and the posterior probability, $P_0(\neg p \mid \neg q, K)$ (with the revised $P_0(q \mid p,K)$), read off. The results of these operations would also need to be stored in working memory, perhaps as "mental models." While the constraints that guarantee this probabilistic interpretation of the network's operation may be unrealistic (McClleland 1998), this seems at least a promising avenue to pursue to provide an algorithmic level account of inference based on probability logic and the Ramsey test.

This account of the Ramsey test suggests that future theorising in the psychology of reasoning must address the storage and representation of world knowledge and how this interacts with reasoning process, a point made many times before (Oaksford and Chater 1991, 1993, 1998a). However, with the advent of probabilistic approaches with their emphasis on the Ramsey test (see also Evans and Over 2004) and the interpretation of neural networks as Bayesian statistical analyzers (McClelland 1998), how this can be achieved is perhaps clearer than it once was.

Data Selection

The probabilistic approach was originally applied to Wason's (1968) selection task, where participants must select cards to find out whether a rule, e.g., *if there is an A on one side (p) there is a 2 on the other side (q)*, is true or false (Oaksford and Chater 1994, 1996). That is, they must select the data most relevant to judging this hypothesis. Participants see four cards, one with A showing (*p*), one with K (¬*p*), one with 2 (*q*) and one with 7 (¬*q*). They are then told to select only those they must turn. Logically participants should select only the *p* and ¬*q* cards. However, Figure 4, Panel A (Data), shows the results of a meta-analysis of selection task results (Oaksford and Chater 1994) showing clearly that the logical response does not occur. People generally select the *p* card alone of the more commonly the *p* and the *q* card.

This task was originally introduced into the literature as a task involving scientific inference to establish the truth of a general hypothesis (Wason and Johnson-Laird 1972). More recently, some authors have assumed that it is a purely deductive task. By assuming that that rule only applies to the four cards and not the unlimited domains of a scientific hypothesis (*all ravens are black* applies to all swans that have, do, and will exist), a purely deductive solution to this task is possible (e.g., Feeney and Handley 2000; Feeney, Handley, and Kentridge 2003; Handley, Feeney, and Harper 2002). Oaksford and Chater (1994, 1996, 1998c, 2003e) treated the task as it was originally introduced, as one of scientific hypothesis testing and their approach was in the spirit of recent Bayesian accounts of scientific inference in the philosophy of science (Earman 1992; Howson and Urbach 1989). As in the section on conditional inference, we first introduce the theory and then consider the evidence.

Theory

In the *information gain or optimal data selection* model[6], people are assumed to select evidence (i.e., turn cards) to determine whether *q* depends on *p*, as in Table 1 in the section on conditional inference (the *dependence hypothesis*, H_D), or whether *p* and *q* are statistically independent (the independence hypothesis, H_I). Participants are looking for evidence that provides the most discrimination between these two hypotheses. Initially participants are maximally uncertain about which is true, that is, the prior

probabilities of H_D and H_I are .5. Participants' goal is to select evidence (turn cards) that would be expected to produce the greatest reduction in this uncertainty. This involves calculating the posterior probabilities of the hypotheses, H_D or H_I, being true given some evidence. These probabilities are calculated using Bayes' theorem which requires information about prior probabilities ($P(H_D) = P(H_I) = .5$) and the likelihoods of evidence given a hypothesis, e.g., the probability of finding an A when turning the 2 card assuming H_D ($P[A \mid 2, H_D]$). These likelihoods can be calculated directly from the contingency tables for each hypothesis: for H_D, Table 1, and for H_I, the independence model where the cell values are simply the products of the marginals. The expected reduction in uncertainty by turning any of the four cards can then be calculated.

A brief more formal explication can be presented by exploiting the equivalence between expected information gain and *mutual information* (Cover and Thomas 1991) noted by Oaksford and Chater (1996) and Hattori (2002). Hattori (1999, 2002) also proposed a logistic selection tendency function that maps this quantity into a probability that a card will be selected. Below we show the equation for the probability of checking ravens to assess their colour (i.e., turning the *p* card).

$$P(p \text{ card}) = \frac{1}{1 + e^{-2.37 + 9.06M(p)}}, \qquad (10)$$

$$\text{where} \quad M(p) = \frac{I(p)}{\sum_i I(x_i)}, \qquad (11)$$

$$\text{and} \quad I(p) = \sum_{ij} P(q_i, H_j \mid p) \log_2$$

$$\left(\frac{P(q_i, H_j \mid p)}{P(q_i \mid p)P(H_j \mid p)} \right) \qquad (12)$$

(10) is the selection tendency function. The parameters 2.37 and 9.06 were derived from Hattori (1999). They provide the best fit between the expected information gains and the probability of selecting a card in a meta-analysis of past data. In (11) x_i ranges over the four cards in the task. $M(p)$ is consequently the proportion of the overall information gain available represented by checking a raven for its colour (i.e., turning the *p* card). (12) is the equation for expected mutual information. In (12) q_i ranges over the possible other sides of the *p* card, for example, whether a raven is black or some other colour, and H_j ranges over the two possible

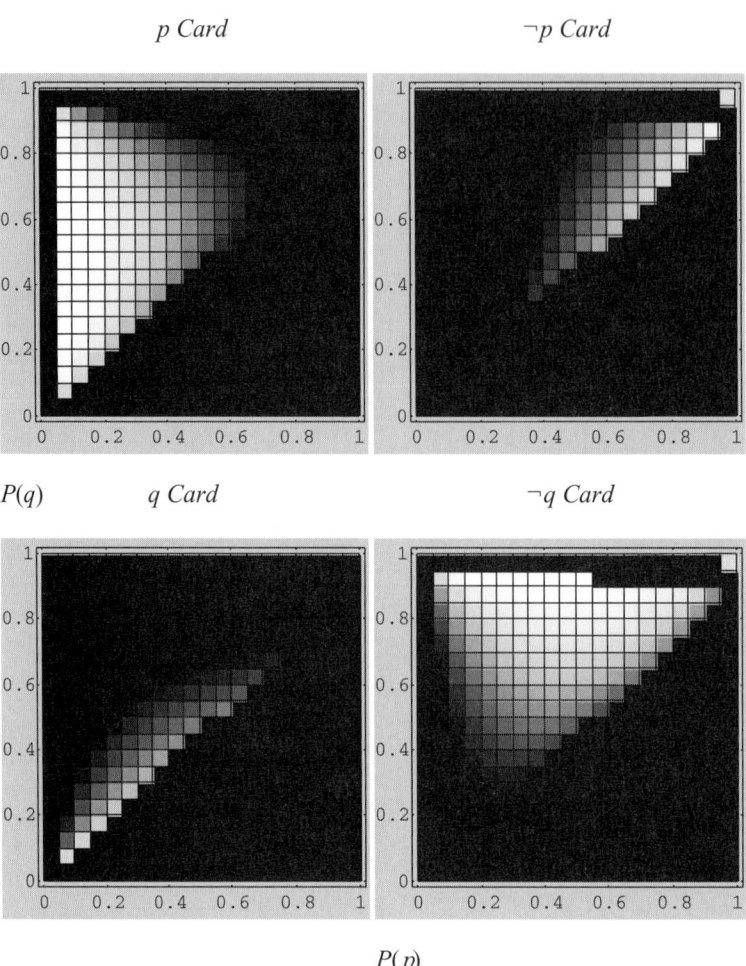

Figure 3. The probabilities with which a card should be selected as a function of the probabilities of the antecedent ($P(p)$, x-axes) and the consequent ($P(q)$, y-axes) according to the revised information gain model. The lighter the region, the greater the probability that a card should be selected. These probabilities were calculated by transforming the information gains using a logistic selection tendency function. The prior probabilities ($P(M_I)$ and $P(M_D)$) were set to .5 and the exceptions parameter (ε) was set to .1. Points in the lower triangular region in black violate the assumptions of the dependence model that $P(q) > P(p)\,P(q\,|\,p)$.

hypotheses, H_D and H_I. With some rearrangement, the probabilities in (12) can all be calculated from Table 1 and the corresponding independence model.

We show the behaviour of the revised model in Figure 3. Each panel represents a card using a density plot with the probability of the antecedent ($P(p)$) on the x-axis and the probability of the consequent ($P(q)$) on the y-axis. The third dimension, shown by shading, corresponds to the probability that the card should be selected, $P(T_x)$; the lighter the shading the higher the probability that a card should be

selected. As in Oaksford and Chater's (1994) original model, the prior probabilities do not affect the ordering over the probabilities with which each card should be selected. So the prior probabilities were set to the same value, that is, $P(H_D) = P(H_I) = .5$. $P(q\,|\,p)$ was set to .9. Points in the lower triangular region in black violate the assumption of the dependence model that $P(q) > P(q\,|\,p)P(p)$. As Figure 3 shows, when the marginal probabilities $P(p)$ and $P(q)$ are small (the "rarity assumption"), the p and the q cards are expected to provide the greatest reduction in uncertainty about which hypothesis was

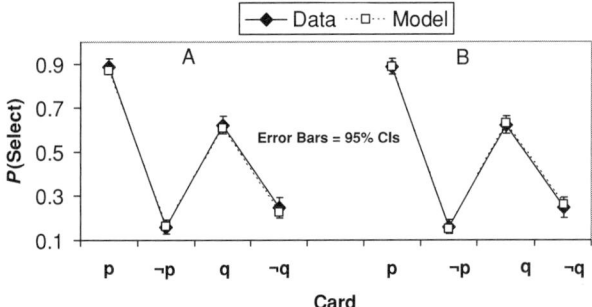

Figure 4. The probability that each card is selected in the standard selection task showing the fit of the optimal data selection model (Panel A) and mental models (Panel B).

true. Consequently, the selection of cards apparently demonstrating human irrationality may reflect a rational data selection strategy. Indeed in an environment where most properties are rare, this may be the optimal strategy (but see Klauer 1999; Laming 1996; Chater and Oaksford 1999c; see Oaksford and Chater 1996, for a reply).

The Evidence

Oaksford and Chater (1994) showed how the original model was consistent with a range of previously observed results. We will not review all this material again but concentrate in this section on briefly surveying the more recent evidence for the information gain or optimal data selection model.[7]

BASE-LINE RESULTS

The base-line results are shown in Figure 4 (data). Oaksford and Chater (2003e) fitted the model in (10)–(12) to these results. Figure 4, Panel A (Model) shows that the fit to the data was very good. Oaksford and Chater (2003e) also fitted the mental models theory to these data and the fits are shown in Panel B. The fits look comparable. However, the predicted values are means calculated from individual fits to the thirty-four studies in the meta-analysis. In fact, the mental models account was rejected as a model of these data as overall, that is, across all studies, it produced a significantly poorer fit than a saturated model.

Across the studies in Oaksford and Chater's (1994) meta-analysis, the mean value of the probability of the p card, $P(p)$, was .22 (SE = .019) and the mean value of the probability of the q card, $P(q)$, was .27 (SE = .022). These values were very close to the expected prior probability of a cause (.25) and of an effect (.27) found by Anderson (1990) when modeling

causal estimation tasks (Schustack and Stemberg 1981). It would seem that participants bring very similar prior expectations to bear in both tasks. This suggests that in the selection task, people by default adopt values for the probability of the antecedent and consequent which are analogous to their knowledge and causes and effects.

MATCHING BIAS

Evans' negations paradigm, which we met in the discussion of conditional inference, was originally used in the selection task (Evans and Lynch 1973). Exactly the same four rules are used – AA, AN, NA, and NN. Rules with a negated consequent: *if p, then ¬q*, and *if ¬p, then ¬q* produce selections more consistent with falsification (Evans 1983, 1984, 1989; Evans and Lynch 1973). Participants select more consequent cards that can make the rule false (i.e., false consequent, or FC, cards) than consequent cards that can make it true (i.e., true consequent, or TC, cards). For example, for the *if p, then ¬q* rule participants select the *q* card (FC). Evans (e.g., 1998) explains this finding by people "matching," that is, they display a *matching bias*. Participants ignore the negations and match the items named in the rule to the corresponding cards. Thus, no sudden insight into logic is required to explain why, for example, people select the falsifying *q* card for the *if p, then ¬q* rule. The cards that falsify or confirm vary between rules. So the convention has been adopted of referring to the cards using the labels: true antecedent (TA), false antecedent (FA), true consequent (TC) and false consequent (FC). For example, for the *if ¬p, then ¬q* rule, TA is the ¬p card, FA is the p card, TC is the ¬q card, and FC is the q card.

As for the conditional inference, Oaksford and Chater (1994; see also Oaksford

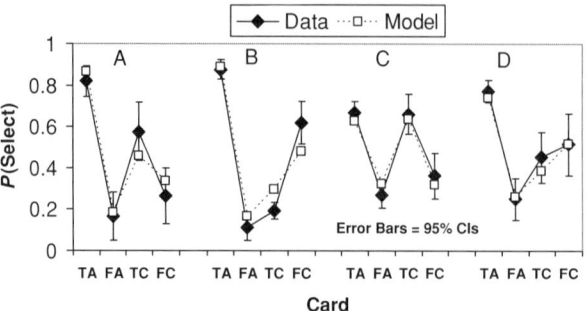

Figure 5. The probability that each card is selected in the negations paradigm selection task showing the fit of the optimal data selection model for, *if p then q* (Panel A), *if p then not-q* (Panel B), *if not-p then q* (Panel C), and *if not-p then not-q* (Panel D).

2002a) argued that these effects can be rationally explained by negations defining higher probability contrast classes (Oaksford and Stenning 1992). Recently, Oaksford and Chater (2003e) fitted the information gain model to a meta-analysis of results on the negations paradigm selection task and the fits are shown in Figure 5. They also fitted a mental models account of these results and found very similar fits. However, as Oaksford and Chater (2003b) argued, the information gain model explains why people behave as they do. In their normal environment where properties are rare, selecting confirming evidence is more likely to be informative. However, they are also sensitive to the fact that negations define higher probability contrast sets which alters the probabilities of the antecedent and consequent. So despite the change in logical status people are always looking for the rare evidence, that is, the p and q cards.

Yama (2001) pitted the matching bias explanation against the contrast class approach. He did this by using rules like *if p then q* and *if p then ¬q* where the q category was binary and related to the blood types, Rh+ and Rh−. People were told that one of these categories, Rh−, was rare. Therefore, by the contrast class account the rule *if p then ¬Rh+* should lead to selecting the rare Rh− card but according to matching they should select the Rh+ card: In four experiments, the predictions of optimal data selection *and* matching were confirmed, although as Oaksford (2002) argued there was most support for optimal data selection. In a recent experiment Oaksford and Moussakowski (2004) replicated Yama's (2001) Experiment 4, which provides most evidence for the matching account, but used a *natural sampling* method (see later) to convey the probability information. In this

experiment, the detailed predictions of the optimal data selection and contrast class account were strongly confirmed. Moreover, the model provided good fits to the data.

EVIDENCE FOR THE RARITY ASSUMPTION

The rarity assumption is a key element in the rational explanation of the selection task. Recently, it has been shown that rarity is the default when people are testing (Anderson and Sheu 1995; McKenzie and Mikklesen 2000) or framing hypotheses (McKenzie, Ferreira, Mikkelsen, McDermott, and Skrable 2001). McKenzie and Mikkelsen (2000) showed that people regard rare evidence as more relevant to supporting a hypothesis than common evidence. So for example, logically both black ravens and non-black non-ravens (e.g., pink flamingos) confirm the hypothesis that *if it's a raven, then it's black*. However, people regard black ravens as more supportive of this hypothesis (see also Oaksford and Chater 1996). Moreover, rare observations were often selected even when they were not mentioned in the hypothesis.

It could be argued that people are simply matching the salient named items (see Evans 1998). However, McKenzie et al. (2001) showed that hypotheses are normally phrased in terms of rare events so that such a matching strategy is invariably the rational thing to do. They showed participants data about a group of students' SAT scores and whether these students were admitted to a select university. Only one student was admitted and this was the only student with a high SAT score. When asked to fill in a sentence frame describing this situation, "If___, then___," participants strongly preferred the phrasing "if applicants have high SAT scores, they will be accepted" over "if applicants have low SAT scores, they will be rejected" even though both are equally legitimate ways to complete the statement. Crucially, when given the information that most students were accepted, and that few applicants had low SAT scores, this finding reversed, that is, they now preferred the second phrasing. In both cases, participants preferred to frame a hypothesis in terms of rare rather than common events. In sum, the rarity assumption not only makes conceptual sense of the literature in the philosophy of science (see Mackie 1963; Oaksford and Chater 1996), it is also a part of people's normal expectations about the hypotheses they formulate and test about their everyday world.

EVIDENCE FOR INFORMATION GAIN

As Evans and Over (1996) pointed out there are many different measures of the informativeness of data to test a hypothesis other than information gain. Oaksford and Chater (1996) argued that information gain seemed to have some nice properties not shared with measures like diagnosticity; for example, it does not go to infinity as a type of evidence becomes unlikely and it extends naturally to the case in which there are more than two competing hypotheses. Recently, Nelson (2005) has tested a variety of putative data selection norms that have been appealed to in the psychological literature, including Bayesian diagnosticity (Evans and Over 1996; McKenzie and Mikkelsen in press), information gain (mutual information) (Oaksford and Chater 1994, 1996, 2003e; Hattori 2002), Kullback-Liebler distance (Klauer 1999; Oaksford and Chater 1996), probability gain (error minimization) (Baron 1981, 1985), and impact (absolute change) (Nickerson 1996).

Nelson used a combination of computer simulation and experiment to assess the theoretical and empirical adequacy of these norms. First, he showed that they disagree on the best data to select under certain circumstances. For example, diagnosticity differs from all the other sampling norms when the probabilities of evidence are very low and so diagnosticity approaches infinity. Nelson then took a range of cases where the norms differ on the ordering in the informativeness of data and conducted an experiment to see what order people would adopt. He found the strongest correlations with information gain (.78) and probability gain (.69) which is the same as impact (Nickerson 1996). Correlations with diagnosticity ($-.22$) and log diagnosticity ($-.41$) were actually *negative*, strongly contradicting the view

that people's data selection behaviour can be modelled using these norms, *pace*, for example, Evans and Over (1996). The agreement between information gain and impact mirrored Oaksford, Chater, and Grainger's (1999) experimental results on the selection task, which failed to discriminate between these measures while being able to reject the alternative measures proposed by Evans and Over (1996) and Klauer (1999).

MANIPULATING PROBABILITIES

Just as for conditional inference, the main prediction of the information gain model is that systematically varying $P(p)$ and $P(q)$ should also alter people's data selection behaviour in a way that mirrors the effects of negations. There has now accumulated a substantial body of evidence showing that probability manipulations do indeed have the predicted effects in the selection task (Green and Over 1997, 1998, 2000; Green, Over, and Pyne 1997; Hattori 1999, 2002; Kirby 1994; Oaksford, Chater, and Grainger 1999; Oaksford, Chater, Grainger, and Larkin 1997; Oaksford and Moussakowski 2003; Oaksford and Wakefield 2004; Yama 2001). This evidence is discussed in detail in Oaksford and Chater (2003e) and seems to support the view expressed by Green and Over (2000; 66) that "...no account of the selection task is sufficiently general if it cannot take account of the set size of p and the set size of q or the probability judgements which reflect these." That is, any explanation of the selection task must take a probabilistic approach like that embodied in the information gain model or the other probabilistic approaches to data selection suggested in the literature (Evans and Over 1996; Klauer 1999; Nickerson 1996; but see Nelson 2005).

However, there has been some evidence cited as being inconsistent with the optimal data selection account. Some of this evidence shows that more logiclike performance can arise without varying probabilities (Almor and Sloman 1996; Gebauer and Laming 1997; Moshman and Geil 1998; Osman and Laming 2001). Other evidence apparently reveals an effect not predicted by optimal data selection (Hardman 1998; Feeney and Handley 2000). Oaksford and Chater (1996) addressed some of these results. For example, the logical responses in Almor and Sloman (1996) occurred for rules expressing analytic truths, for example, "if a large object is stored then a large container must be used," for which evidence is irrelevant. It is part of the meaning of "large object" that if it is stored, a large container must be used.[8] As this has to be true there is no uncertainty to be reduced, so the optimal data selection account cannot apply. Oaksford and Chater (2003e) discuss most of the other cases and make similar observations.

Other experiments have attempted to explicitly manipulate probabilities and have failed to find effects (Feeney, Handley, and Kentridge 2003; Handley, Feeney, and Harper 2002; Oberauer, Wilhelm, and Diaz 1999; Oberauer, Weidenfeld, and Hörnig 2004). We outline several reasons why these data do not significantly challenge the optimal selection model.

First, and perhaps most important, these apparent failures to replicate have to confront the accumulated evidence, listed earlier, showing that probabilistic manipulations do affect data selection performance on Wason's task. Against this background, it is difficult to interpret failures to replicate like Oberauer, Wilhelm, and Diaz (1999), and Oberauer, Weidenfeld, and Hörnig (2004). Moreover, in none of these papers is a systematic attempt to explain away the experiments showing successful probability manipulations. It is all too easy not to find effects if your hypothesis is that they should not occur.

Second, Feeney and Handley's (2000) original experiments were only inconsistent with the original model presented in Oaksford and Chater (1994) in which the $\neg p$ card was always uninformative. However, Oaksford (2002b) showed that this card can be informative using the contingency table in Table 1 (introduced by Oaksford et al. 2000) and that this model provides very good fits to Feeney and Handley's (2000). Similarly, when Oaksford and Chater (2003e) fitted the model to the data from Oberauer et al.'s (1999) Experiment 1 they actually found very good fits.

Third, Handley et al. (2002) repeated these experiments and also manipulated $P(q)$. Feeney et al. (2003) also fitted the optimal data selection model to these data and showed poor fits. However, by the same standards adopted in Oaksford and Chater (2003e), the model could not be rejected for thirteen out of the eighteen conditions in Handley et al. (2002). Although when participants' estimates of $P(q)$ were used rather than allowing this to be a free parameter, the model could be rejected for all eighteen conditions. But as Oaksford and Wakefield (2003) and Over et al. (2005) have observed, estimates such as these need to be obtained more indirectly.

Fourth, Feeney and colleagues do not show that their own theory provided better fits to the data. This runs counter to the standard logic of model fitting: the idea is to do better than the competition. Our original model fitting exercise responded to an explicit claim that optimal data selection couldn't explain Feeney and Handley's (2000) data and showed that it could. However, as they are advocating an alternative model, the burden of proof is on them to show that their model provides better fits.[9]

Fifth, there is recent evidence contradicting Feeney et al.'s main claim that variations in $\neg p$ card selections supports deductive processing in the selection task (Lucas and Ball 2005). They argue that this card is selected when participants assume a bi-conditional interpretation and infer there is $\neg q$ on the other side. So given the rule *if A then 2* participants who turn the *L* card infer that the hidden face is, for example, a 7. However, they are then told that *if L then 2*, and now they tend not to turn this card because they now know that there is very likely to be a 2 on the other side, that is, they now know that the presence of an A is not necessary for there to be a 2 on the other side. This explanation means that people select this card because they contemplate that the hidden side should be a number that does not match the number in the rule, that is, a number other than 2. However, using protocol analysis, Lucas and Ball (2005) found that for all selected cards the hidden sides participants mention match those stated in the rule. So rather than consider the 7 on the hidden face, as Feeney and Handley (2000; Handley et al. 2002; Feeney et al. 2003) predict, they consider the 2. Lucas and Ball (2005) observe that this "secondary matching" effect (Wason and Evans 1975) is inconsistent with Feeney and Handley (2000), but that it is consistent with the optimal data selection model because it predicts that people should seek the rare cases, which are always the matching cases.

Finally, it would be premature to speculate further on what Feeney and colleagues' experiments reveal about human reasoning, partly because some of the probability manipulations also seemed to be particularly weak. This was also a criticism made by Oaksford and Wakefield (2003) of some experiments reported by Oberauer, Wilhelm, and Diaz (1999). Oaksford and Wakefield (2003; see also Oaksford and Moussakowski 2004) used the same materials as Oberauer et al.'s (1999) Experiment 3 but provided probability information via "natural sampling," which should lead to a stronger probability manipulation (Gigerenzer and Hoffrage,

1995). Participants were shown forty cards one at a time. The proportion of p, $\neg p$, q, and $\neg q$ cards reflected the probability information. Strong probability effects were observed. Probability estimates were also obtained from participants *indirectly*. They classified fifty cards "drawn" from the pack into the four possible card types: p and q, p and $\neg q$, $\neg p$ and q, and $\neg p$ and $\neg q$ (see also Over et al. 2005). These were used to provide parameter free fits to the selection task data, which were very good. The indirect estimates overestimated the low probabilities and underestimated the high probabilities mirroring a π-function (Kahneman and Tversky 1979) relating the experimentally given probabilities to the best-fit estimates. Critically, Oaksford and Wakefield (2003) confirmed a unique prediction of the model that for the HH rule in this experiment, the $\neg p$ card should be selected more than the q card.[10]

Syllogistic Reasoning

The probabilistic approach has also been extended to syllogistic reasoning, for example, *Some of the artists are beekeepers*, *All the beekeepers are chemists*, therefore, *Some of the artists are chemists*. As before, we start with the theory which Chater and Oaksford (1999) called the *probability heuristics model* (PHM).

Theory

In the probability heuristics model (Chater and Oaksford, 1999a), PHM, the probabilistic interpretation of conditionals is extended to quantified claims: *All*, *Some*, *None*, and *Some . . . not*. In Table 1, if there are no exceptions, then the probability of the consequent given the antecedent, ($P[q\,|\,p]$), is 1. The conditional and the universal quantifier *All* have the same underlying logical form: $\forall x (if\ P(x)\ then\ Q(x))$. Consequently, universal claims such *All Ps are Qs*, were interpreted as asserting that the probability of the predicate term (Q) given the subject term (P) is 1, that is, $P(Q\,|\,P) = 1$. Probabilistic meanings for the other quantifiers are then easily defined: *None*, $P(Q\,|\,P) = 0$; *Some*, $P(Q\,|\,P) > 0$; *Some . . . not*, $P(Q\,|\,P) < 1$. Given these probabilistic interpretations it is possible to prove what conclusions follow probabilistically for all sixty-four syllogisms (i.e., which syllogisms are "p-valid").

Moreover, given these interpretations and again making the rarity assumption (see earlier, on the selection task), the quantifiers can be ordered in terms of how *informative* they are: *All* > *Some* > *None* > *Some . . . not*. A quantified statement is informative to extent that it is surprising, that is, its probability is low. Basic level natural language categories usually only refer to a small subset of objects. So if two predicates were selected at random it is rarely the case that they cross classify an object. For example, "table" and "toupees" never apply to the same object. Consequently the statement most likely to be true of an object given two randomly selected predicates X and Y is that *No X are Y*. The rarest case is when *All X are Y*, which is therefore the most informative. Moreover as long as the probability of *No X are Y* is less than .5, *Some . . . not* is the least informative.

A simple set of heuristics defined over the informativeness of the premises can successfully predict the p-valid conclusion if there is one.

There are three generation heuristics in the PHM:

(G1) The *min*-heuristic: Choose the quantifier of the conclusion to be the same as the quantifier in the least informative premise (the *min-premise*).

The most informative conclusions that can validly follow almost always follow this rule. Some conclusions probabilistically entail ("p-entail") other conclusions. For example, if *All X are Y*, then it is probable that *Some X are Y* (this will follow as long as there are some *X*s). Thus the second heuristic is:

(G2) *P*-entailments: The next most preferred conclusion will be the p-entailment of the conclusion predicted by the *min*-heuristic (the "*min*-conclusion").

Heuristics (G1) and (G2) specify the quantifier of the conclusion. The third heuristic, the *attachment*-heuristic, specifies the order of end terms in the conclusion:

(G3) *Attachment*-heuristic: If just one of the possible conclusion subject noun phrases matches the subject noun phrase of just one premise, then the conclusion has that subject noun phrase[1].

Where subject noun is: *All X*, *All Z*, *Some X*, *Some Z*, etc. Crucially, *Some X are not Z* and *Some X are Z* have the *same* subject noun phrase "*Some X*." We illustrate these heuristics with an example (where "_" stands as a place holder for a subject of predicate term in the mental representation of the putative conclusion):

All Y are X   (*min*-premise)
Some Z are Y   (*max*-premise)
Some _ are _   (by *min*)
Some Z are X   (by *attachment*)
Some _ are not _   (by *p*-entailment)
Some Z are not X   (by *attachment*)

By the *min*-heuristic, the conclusion is *Some*. The *min*-premise has an end term (Z) as its subject. Therefore, by *attachment*, the conclusion will have Z as its subject term, and the form *Some Z are X*. The *p*-entailment of the *min*-conclusion is *Some Z are not X* which is predicted to be the next most endorsed conclusion.

G1–G3 generate syllogistic conclusions. It is assumed that people are rarely able to test these conclusions for *p*-validity (or, for that matter, logical validity). However, it is argued that people employ two test heuristics that provide a fast and frugal estimate of how likely the conclusion generated by G1–G3 is to be informative and *p*-valid (Chater and Oaksford 1999a):

(T1) The *max*-heuristic: Be confident in the conclusion generated by G1–G3 in proportion to the informativeness of the most informative premise (the *max*-premise).
(T2) The *Some...not*-heuristic: Avoid producing or accepting *Some...not* conclusions, because they are so uninformative relative to other conclusions.

The most important heuristic is the *min*-heuristic, which states that the conclusion will have the form of the least informative premise. So for example, a *p*-valid syllogism such as, *All B are A, Some B are not C*, yields the conclusion *Some A are not C*. This simple heuristic captures the form of the conclusion for most *p*-valid syllogisms. Moreover, if over-generalised to the invalid syllogisms, the conclusions it suggests match the empirical data very well.

The most important feature of PHM is that it can generalise to syllogisms containing quantifiers such as *Most* and *Few* that have no logical interpretation. In terms of Table 1 these quantifiers are used when there are some (*Most*) or many (*Few*) exceptions. So the meaning of *Most* is: $1 - \Delta < P(Q|P) < 1$, and the meaning of *Few* is: $0 < P(Q|P) < \Delta$, where Δ is small. These interpretations lead to the following order of informativeness: $All > Most > Few > Some > None > Some...not$. Consequently,

PHM uniquely makes predictions for the 144 syllogisms that are produced when *Most* and *Few* are combined with the standard logical quantifiers. Chater and Oaksford (1999) showed that these heuristics pick out the *p*-valid conclusions for these new syllogisms, and they report experiments confirming the predictions of PHM when *Most* and *Few* are used in syllogistic arguments.

The Evidence

For syllogisms, the base-line results are provided by the previous research carried out with the standard logical quantifiers, *All, Some, Some-not*, and *None*. We discuss these data first before moving on to how the model generalises to *Most* and *Few*. We then look at work on informativeness orders (Oaksford, Roberts, and Chater 2002) and other data PMH can explain on strong and weak possible conclusions. As before we discuss other data claimed to be inconsistent with the model.

BASE-LINE DATA

Table 2 shows the results of a meta-analysis showing the weighted average of correct responses to the logically valid syllogisms in all the studies using all sixty-four syllogisms that had been published up until then (Dickstein 1978; Johnson-Laird and Bara 1984; Johnson-Laird and Steedman 1978). The pairs, for example, (X,Z), in the syllogistic premises are ordered to show their status as the subject (first) or the predicate (second) term. The logically valid conclusion and the number of mental models required to reach that conclusion are also shown.

These data reveal how the heuristics of PHM can explain the data. Note that all the syllogisms above the double line are drawn more often than all those below it (with one exception). Moreover, all the syllogisms above the single line are drawn more often than all of those below it. All the syllogisms above the double line conform perfectly to the *min*-heuristic (G1), those below, although not violating the *min*-heuristic (the conclusion is *less* informative than the *min*-conclusion), do not conform to it. All those syllogisms that are below the single line only have a very uninformative *Some...not* conclusion (T2) and interestingly this conclusion is drawn only as often as None which is the *min*-conclusion. Moreover, *Some...not* is a *p*-entailment of *None* (G2). Finally, all those syllogisms above the double line also have very informative *max*-premises (T1). Thus it would seem that

Table 2: Meta-Analysis of the Logically Valid Syllogisms Showing the Form of the Conclusion, the Number of Mental Models Needed to Reach that Conclusion, and the Percentage of Times the Valid Conclusion was Drawn in Each of the Five Experiments Analyzed by Chater and Oaksford (1995)

Syllogism	Conc.	MMs	Mean
All(Y,X), All(Z,Y)	All	1	89.87
All(X,Y), All(Y,Z)	All	1	75.32
All(Y,X), Some(Z,Y)	Some	1	86.71
Some(Y,X), All(Y,Z)	Some	1	87.97
All(Y,X), Some(Y,Z)	Some	1	88.61
Some(X,Y), All(Y,Z)	Some	1	86.71
No(Y,X), All(Z,Y)	No	1	92.41
All(X,Y), No(Z,Y)	No	1	84.81
No(X,Y), All(Z,Y)	No	1	88.61
All(X,Y), No(Y,Z)	No	1	91.14
All(X,Y), Some...not(Z,Y)	Some...not	2	67.09
Some...not(X,Y), All(Z,Y)	Some...not	2	56.33
All(Y,X), Some...not(Y,Z)	Some...not	2	66.46
Some...not(Y,X), All(Y,Z)	Some...not	2	68.99
Some(Y,X), No(Z,Y)	Some...not	3	16.46
No(Y,X), Some(Z,Y)	Some...not	3	66.46
Some(X,Y), No(Z,Y)	Some...not	3	30.38
No(X,Y), Some(Z,Y)	Some...not	3	51.90
Some(Y,X), No(Y,Z)	Some...not	3	32.91
No(Y,X), Some(Y,Z)	Some...not	3	48.10
Some(X,Y), No(Y,Z)	Some...not	3	44.30
No(X,Y), Some(Y,Z)	Some...not	3	26.58

Note. The means in the final column are weighted by sample size.

a set of very simple heuristics defined over the informativeness of the premises can explain the differences in performance for the logically valid syllogisms.

GENERALISED QUANTIFIERS

Chater and Oaksford also conducted two experiments where they introduced the generalised quantifiers Most and Few into syllogistic arguments with the other logical quantifiers. In their Experiment 1 they used the quantifiers, All, Most, Few, and Some...not and in their Experiment 2 they used the quantifiers, Most, Few, Some, and None. No other theory of syllogistic reasoning task performance makes any predictions for the extra 80 syllogisms introduced by this manipulation. However, PHM predicts business as usual, that is, given the informational ordering, All > Most > Few > Some > None > Some...not, participants should simply apply the heuristics as we have seen they do for the logical quantifiers. The results of Chater and Oaksford (1999) confirmed these predictions. For each syllogism type the modal response is that predicted by the min-heuristic and the next

most frequent response is its p-entailment(s). So for example, for All-Few the modal response was Few and the next most frequent response was Some...not. Moreover, for All...Some...not, the weak p-entailments[11] of Some...not, most and few, are both endorsed more frequently than All. This pattern confirms the predictions of PHM's probabilistic semantics for the generalised quantifiers. These experiments show that PHM applies successfully across all 144 possible syllogisms involving the quantifiers, All, Most, Few, Some, None, Some...not (although not with all possible conclusion types). The uniform pattern in these data across the generalized and the standard logical quantifiers challenges other theories of syllogistic reasoning, which currently apply only to the logical quantifiers, to generalize to these data.

INFORMATIVENESS ORDERS

Some of the results of Chater and Oaksford's (1999) experiments were unexpected from the perspective of their theory. In particular the results seemed to question a core assumption of the model concerning the ordering in the informativeness of the quantifiers. For example, for *Few-Some...not* (*Some...not-Few*) syllogisms, the *min*-heuristic predicts a *Some...not* conclusion. However, in Chater and Oaksford's Experiment 1 there was no significant difference in mean percentage endorsements of *Few* and *Some...not*, although they were both endorsed significantly more often than the other possible response. Moreover, for *Few-Some* (*Some-Few*) syllogisms, the *min*-heuristic predicts a *Some* conclusion. However, in Chater and Oaksford's Experiment 2 there was no significant difference in mean percentage endorsements of *Few* and *Some*, although they were both endorsed significantly more often than the other possible response options. These results suggest that in Chater and Oaksford's Experiment 1, *Few* was regarded as having the same informativeness as *Some...not*, whereas in their Experiment 2, *Few* was regarded as having the same informativeness as *Some*.

Oaksford, Roberts, and Chater (2002) address this apparent discrepancy. By appeal to the pragmatics literature (Moxey and Sanford 1987, 1993), they argued that *few* is ambiguous and that given the different range of quantifiers available in each of the experiments in Chater and Oaksford (1999) a different interpretation would have dominated in each experiment. Oaksford et al. (2002) conducted a series of experiments to see if under the probabilistic interpretations assigned to each version of *few* they could emulate Chater and Oaksford's (1999) results. Their experiments permitted them to calculate the informativeness of each quantifier for each participant, so they could compare the informativeness of the two versions of *few* with *some* and *some-not*. Under the appropriate interpretation one version of *few* did not differ significantly from *some* and the other did not differ significantly from *some-not*. Consequently, some minor revision of the model is required to take into account the two possible interpretations of *few* but this serves only to improve the fit to the data.

STRONG AND WEAK POSSIBLE CONCLUSIONS

The *min*-heuristic captures the novel distinction between strong and weak possible conclusions (Evans, Handley, Harper, and Johnson-Laird 1999). Take the syllogism *All Y are X, Some Z are Y*. The conclusion *Some Z are X*, follows *necessarily* from these premises; *No Z are X*, is *impossible*; but *Some Z are not X* and *All Z are X* are *possible*. Some possible conclusions are endorsed as strongly as necessary conclusions (e.g., *Some Z are not X*) and some are endorsed as weakly as impossible conclusions (e.g., *All Z are X*). Possible strong conclusions all conform to the *min*-heuristic, that is, they either match the *min*-premise or are less informative than the *min*-premise. Possible weak conclusions all violate the *min*-heuristic (bar one), that is, they have conclusions that are more informative than the *min*-premise. Mental models theory may explain this result. Strong possible conclusions are licensed in the initial model but not in subsequent models. Weak possible conclusions are licensed only in noninitial models. This means that the conclusions recommended by the *min*-heuristic correspond to those licensed by initial mental models. This is an interesting coincidence as neither theory was constructed with the distinction between strong and weak possible conclusions in mind. However, it is unclear why mental models licences these initial models. The only suggestion is that it is an "emergent property" of the computer program embodying the mental models theory. But no account of the principles underlying initial model construction that can explain why this property emerges has been forthcoming.

ALTERNATIVE CONCLUSIONS

In a series of experiments designed to test the claim that syllogism difficulty is determined by the number of alternative mental models constructed, Newstead, Handley, and Buck (1999) found evidence consistent with PHM. Participants were asked to indicate the alternative conclusions they considered for different syllogisms or were asked to draw diagrams consistent with the premises. According to mental models theory more alternative conclusions and more diagrams should be produced for multiple model syllogisms than for single model syllogisms. However, Newstead et al. found no relationship between the number of models a syllogism requires for its solution and the number of conclusions or diagrams participants produced. This is consistent with PHM where it is argued that test procedures are rarely invoked. In all Newstead et al.'s experiments, participants' responses also agreed with those predicted by the *min*- and *attachment*-heuristics. Furthermore, according to PHM there should be no differences in task difficulty dependent on figure, a prediction that is inconsistent with mental models theory. Consistent with PHM, in two of Newstead's et al.'s experiments where figure was an independent variable, they found no effect of figure on syllogism difficulty. As they point out, their findings clearly favour PHM over mental models.

However, Newstead et al. (1999) argue that some other aspects of their results sit less well with PHM. We look at what we consider the most important here and refer the reader to Oaksford and Chater (in press) for further discussion. Newstead et al. argue that PHM predicts that people would consider more conclusions when they are less confident in the *min*-conclusion. Consequently, they argue there should be a linear trend in the number of alternative conclusions considered such that *All* < *Some* < *Some-not* ≈ *None*. However, they found no such result. We are unsure how Newstead et al. derived this prediction. The only way that PHM allows alternative conclusions to be generated is via *p*-entailments. However, in modelling the data from their meta-analysis, Chater and Oaksford (1999) argued that *p*-entailments were endorsed in a fixed proportion across all syllogisms. In their meta-analysis, this proportion was .09. Thus, for each *max*-premise type, PHM predicts one conclusion predicted by the *min*-heuristic to be considered plus this small proportion of *p*-entailments, leading to approximately 1.09 conclusions considered. For *All* *max*-premise type syllogisms Newstead et al. observed an average of 1.05 and for the other *max*-premise type syllogisms they observed an average of 1.13. Thus their findings seem completely consistent with PHM.

WORKING MEMORY AND SYLLOGISTIC REASONING

Copeland and Radvanksy (2004) have recently observed that there have been few experiments directly relating memory span measures to syllogistic reasoning performance. They therefore took a variety of working memory span measures and then had participants perform a computerised version of the standard syllogistic reasoning task. They also compared the predictions of the mental models theory and PHM. PHM makes similar predictions to mental models theory because it too can account for the difference in accuracy on the 1-, 2-, and 3-model syllogisms. Getting the valid conclusion requires the use of different numbers of heuristics. For 1-model syllogisms, just the *min*-heuristic and attachment is required. For 2-model syllogisms, the *min*-heuristic, attachment and the *Some . . . not*-heuristic are invoked (because the conclusion is always *some . . . not*, so the *some . . . not*-heuristic is invoked, leading to fewer correct selections).[12] For 3-model syllo-

logisms, a *p*-entailment has to be drawn, the *min*-heuristic and attachment applied and the *some-not*-heuristic invoked. Thus, for 1-model syllogisms two heuristics are invoked, for 2-model syllogisms three are invoked, and for 3-model syllogisms four are invoked. The generation heuristics operate over a mental representation of the premises to generate a conclusion, the test heuristics determine confidence that will be related to RTs. The more mental operations that need to be performed the more complex the inference. People with high IQs are likely to be better at more complex processes and WM span and IQ are highly correlated. Thus, it seems that the analyses in terms of the number mental models are consistent with PHM.

Consistent with this analysis Copeland and Radvansky (2004) found significant correlations between working memory span and strategy use for both mental models and PHM. Moreover there were no differences between mental models and PHM on the percentage of responses made that agreed with the predictions of each model. Consequently, although these data did not discriminate between theories, they confirmed the predictions that each theory independently makes for the complexity of syllogistic reasoning and its relation to working memory span.

ACTIVATION OF END TERMS

As with conditional inference and data selection, there have also been some work that it is claimed is not consistent with PHM. Here we consider some experiments by Espino, Santamaria, and Garcia-Madruga (2000). They reported the results of studies investigating the time to respond to a probe word that has or has not occurred in the premises of a syllogistic argument. They derived predictions from mental models theory that they compared to the predictions of the other leading theories in this area including PHM. In their Experiments 2 to 5, they claimed to have found conclusive evidence for the mental models account of syllogistic reasoning and against all these contenders.

We focus on one of their results (more discussion can be found in Oaksford 2001). In their Experiments 2 to 4, Espino et al. found that for Figure 4 syllogisms (e.g., *All the X are Y, All the Y are Z*) responses were faster when the end term Z was used as the probe than when the end term X was used as the probe. However, this reversed for Figure 1 syllogisms (e.g., *All the Y are X, All the Z are Y*). Espino et al. argued that this finding is consistent with mental models theory because the end term responded to the fastest is the last item in the mental model. In theories of language comprehension, the last mentioned item in an integrated representation of a multiclausal sentence is the most active because this item is where further information must be attached. Espino et al. argued that PHM makes the opposite prediction because the *attachment*-heuristic, determining the order of end terms in the conclusion, must attach to the end term in subject position, that is, X for Figure 4 and Z for Figure 1.

Espino et al. assumed that the heuristics of PHM are applied to the premises during the comprehension stage. The heuristics of PHM operate over representations of the premises (see Chater and Oaksford 1999a: 236) to build a representation of the conclusion. For example, take the Figure 4 syllogism, All the X are Y, All the Y are Z, the *min*-heuristic selects the frame "All _ are _" as the form of the conclusion with place holders for the end terms. The *attachment*-heuristic selects the subject term of the *min*-premise (as long as it is an end term) as the subject term of the conclusion: All X are _. This representation is incomplete. The final operation is to place the other end term in the remaining place holder: All X are Z. That is, the last item to enter the representation in Figure 4 is Z. Consequently, consistent with existing accounts of language comprehension, PHM makes exactly the same predictions as mental models. Therefore, PHM is consistent with Espino et al.'s most robust finding.

DISPELLING THE ATMOSPHERE EFFECT

Shaw and Johnson-Laird (1998) provide evidence and arguments that they take to conclusively dispel accounts of syllogistic reasoning like PHM which argue that the conclusion will be affected by the surface form of the premises. The first such account was called the "atmosphere effect," which has two parts. First, if one or both premises are negative (*None* or *Some . . . not*), the conclusion should be negative, otherwise it is positive (*All* or *Some*). Second, if one or both premises are particular (*Some* or *Some . . . not*), then the conclusion will be particular, otherwise it is universal (*All* or *None*).

Shaw and Johnson-Laird (1998) argue that some conclusions do not fit any form of the atmosphere effect. For example, in Johnson-Laird and Steedman (1978), the most frequent response to the *All-None*[3] syllogism was *Some X are not Z*. This conclusion does not violate the *min*-heuristic because this conclusion is less

informative than the *min*-conclusion (*None*). This point is an example of picking the result to suit the argument. Although *Some . . . not* was the most frequent response to this syllogism in Johnson-Laird and Steedman (1978), in Chater and Oaksford's (1999) meta-analysis (which included this study), the *None* conclusion, licensed by the *min*-heuristic, was endorsed by 61.39% of participants versus only 13.29% who endorsed *Some . . . not*. Consequently, this finding does not question PHM.

Shaw and Johnson-Laird also argued that for every syllogism there is a conclusion that is consistent with atmosphere and so, counter-evidentially, there should be no "no valid conclusion" responses. However, according to the *max*-heuristic, this response will be more likely as the informativeness of the *max*-premise decreases. So PHM does predict "no valid conclusion" responses. Shaw and Johnson-Laird also report an experiment on multiply quantified sentences apparently showing that responses matching one of the premises reduce for multiple model syllogisms. They argue that an initial model is always generated where a conclusion can be read off that matches one of the premises, that is, there is a conclusion consistent with the *min*-heuristic. This conclusion can not be refuted in one-model syllogisms but it can be in multiple model syllogisms where people can seek alternative models. However, the balance of evidence (Evans et al. 1999; Klauer, Musch, and Naumer 2000; Newstead et al. 1999; Schroyens, Schaeken, Fias, and d'Ydewalle 2000) indicates that people rarely construct more than one model, which renders this explanation improbable. PHM explains these results in terms of multiple model syllogisms leading to less informative conclusions, and consequently an increase in no valid conclusion responses. In sum, Shaw and Johnson-Laird's attempt to dispel the atmosphere hypothesis may succeed but it does nothing to dispel PHM.

Argumentation and the Fallacies

Reasoning typically takes place in the service of argumentation, i.e., the attempt to persuade yourself or others of a particular, perhaps controversial, position (van Eemeren and Grootendorst 1992). Argumentation is the overarching human activity that studies of deductive reasoning, inductive reasoning, judgment and decision making are really required to explain. So one might attempt to persuade someone else to accept a controversial standpoint p by trying to persuade them that p is actually a logical consequence of their prior beliefs or current commitments; or that p has strong inductive support; or, where p is an action, that p will help to achieve their current goals. By extending the probabilistic approach to at least some aspects of argumentation, we hope to show that it can generalize beyond the narrow confines of most current psychology of reasoning to the real human activity of which deduction, induction and decision making are but a small part.

Fallacies, or arguments that seem correct but aren't, for example, DA and AC, have been a longstanding focus of debate. Catalogues of reasoning and argumentation fallacies originate with Aristotle and populate books on logic and informal reasoning to this day. The classic tool brought to the analysis of fallacies such as the argument from ignorance is formal logic and it is widely acknowledged to have failed in providing a satisfactory account. Testament to this is the fact that fallacies figure in logic textbooks under the header of "informal reasoning fallacies" (see, e.g., Hamblin 1970) – an acknowledgment of the inability to provide a sufficient formal logical treatment. In particular, logical accounts have proved unable to capture the seeming exceptions to fallacies that arise with simple changes in content that leave the structure of the argument unaffected. This suggests that either it is not formal aspects of fallacies that make them fallacious, or else that the relevant formal aspects are not being tapped into by classical logics.

Oaksford and Hahn (2004; see also Hahn and Oaksford; 2006, 2007; Hahn, Oaksford, and Bayinder 2005; Hahn, Oaksford, and Corner 2005) provide evidence of such variation and put forward an alternative, Bayesian account: Individual arguments are composed of a conclusion and premises expressing evidence for that conclusion. Both conclusion and premises have associated probabilities which are viewed as expressions of subjective degrees of belief. Bayes' theorem then provides an update rule for the degree of belief associated with the conclusion in light of the evidence. *Argument strength*, then, on this account is a function of the degree of prior conviction, the probability of evidence, and the relationship between the claim and the evidence, in particular how much more likely the evidence would be if the claim were true. That is, different instances of argumentative fallacies may vary in argument strength conceived of as the probability of the conclusion given the premises. Oaksford and Hahn (2007) also show how the concept of argument strength in argumentation is related to the probabilistic analysis of the conditional (see above) and recent discussion in Rips (2001). We now illustrate this approach by appeal to a particular informal reasoning fallacy: the argument from ignorance.

Theory: The Argument from Ignorance

A classic informal argument fallacy, which dates back to John Locke, is the so-called argument from ignorance, or *argumentum ad ignorantiam*.

Ghosts exist, because nobody has proven that
    they don't.   (13)

This argument does indeed seem weak. One would hesitate in positing the existence of all manner of things whose non-existence simply had not been proven, whether these be UFOs or flying pigs with purple stripes. However, is it really the general structure of this argument that makes it weak, and if so what aspect of it is responsible? Other arguments from negative evidence are routine in scientific and everyday discourse and seem perfectly acceptable:

This drug is safe, because no-one has found any
    toxic effects.   (14)

Should all arguments from negative evidence be avoided, or can a systematic difference between the two examples be recognized and explained?

A Bayesian account can capture the difference between (13) and (14) as we show below. Moreover, it can capture the difference between positive and negative evidence which allows one to capture the intuition that the positive argument (15) is stronger than the negative argument (16):[13]

Drug A is toxic because a toxic effect was
    observed (positive argument)   (15)

Drug A is not toxic because no toxic effects
    were observed (negative argument, i.e.,
    the argument from ignorance).   (16)

Although (16), too, can be acceptable where a legitimate test has been performed, that is,

If drug A were toxic, it would produce toxic
    effects in legitimate tests.

Drug A has not produced toxic effects in such
    tests

Therefore, A is not toxic

Demonstrating the relevance of Bayesian inference for negative vs. positive arguments involves defining the conditions for a legitimate test. Let e stand for an experiment in which a toxic effect is observed and $\neg e$ stands for an experiment where a toxic effect is not observed; likewise let T stand for the hypothesis that the drug produces a toxic effect and $\neg T$ stand for the alternative hypothesis that the drug does not produce toxic effects. The strength of the argument from ignorance is given by the conditional probability that the hypothesis, T, is false given that a negative test result, $\neg e$, is found, $P(\neg T \mid \neg e)$. This probability is referred to as negative test validity. The strength of the argument we wish to compare with the argument from ignorance is given by positive test validity, that is, the probability that the hypothesis, T, is true given that a positive test result, e, is found, $P(T \mid e)$. These probabilities can be calculated from the sensitivity ($P(e \mid T)$) and the selectivity ($P(\neg e \mid \neg T)$) of the test and the prior belief that T is true ($P(T)$) using Bayes's theorem. Let n denote sensitivity, that is, $n = P(e \mid T)$, l denote selectivity, that is, $l = P(\neg e \mid \neg T)$, and h denote the prior probability of drug A being toxic, that is, $h = P(T)$, then,

$$p(T \mid e) = \frac{nh}{nh + (1 - l)(1 - h)} \qquad (17)$$

$$p(\neg T \mid \neg e) = \frac{l(1 - h)}{l(1 - h) + (1 - n)h} \qquad (18)$$

Sensitivity corresponds to the "hit rate" of the test and 1 minus the selectivity corresponds to the "false positive rate."

Positive test validity is greater than negative test validity as long as the following inequality holds:

$$h^2(n - n^2) > (1 - h)^2(l - l^2) \qquad (19)$$

Assuming maximal uncertainty about the toxicity of drug A, that is, $P(T) = .5 = h$, this means that positive test validity, $P(T \mid e)$, is greater than negative test validity, $P(\neg T \mid \neg e)$, when selectivity (l) is higher than sensitivity. As Oaksford and Hahn (2004) argue this is often a condition met in practice for a variety of clinical and psychological tests. Therefore, in a variety of settings, positive arguments are stronger than negative arguments.

The Evidence

Oaksford and Hahn (2004) also provide experimental evidence to the effect that positive arguments such as (15) are indeed viewed as more convincing than their negative counterparts under the conditions just described. The evidence from their experiment further shows that people are sensitive to manipulations in the amount of evidence (one versus fifty studies or tests) as predicted by the account. Finally, participants' in their experiment displayed sensitivity to the degree of prior belief a character in a dialogue initially displayed toward the conclusion as the Bayesian account predicts. This finding captures the "audience dependence" of argumentation assumed in the rhetorical research tradition (e.g., Perelman and Olbrechts-Tyteca 1969).

Hahn, Oaksford, and Bayindir (2005) generalized this account to other versions of the argument from ignorance and addressed an outstanding problem. The ghosts example (20) differs from Oaksford and Hahn's (2004) experimental materials in one, possibly important way. The argument for ghosts not only involves negative evidence, but also a flip in polarity between evidence and conclusion: Negative evidence is provided to support the *positive* existence of something. In other words, the inference is of the form:

not proven (*not* exist) → exist   (20)

as opposed to merely:

not proven (exist) → *not* exist   (21)

The examples in Oaksford and Hahn (2004) have the structure in (21) not the structure in (20). But it may be the opposite polarity case (20) that constitutes the true fallacy of the argument from ignorance.

Classical logic licenses an inference from *not*(*not p*) to *p*, but not the inference underlying (20) which might be rendered as:

not says (*not p*) → ?   (22)

This is because when one has not said "*not p*," one can either have said "*p*" or not spoken about "*p*" at all. For example, in an argument one might defend oneself with the claim "I didn't say you were rude," which could be true either because one had specifically claimed the opposite or because one had not mentioned rudeness at all. So maybe nothing at all can be inferred in such cases?

Hahn, Oaksford, and Bayindir (2005) established that (22) can be a strong argument by using a form of the argument from ignorance based on *epistemic closure* which is related to the negation as failure procedure in artificial intelligence (Clark 1978). The case can be made with an informal example: imagine your work colleagues are having a staff picnic. You ask the picnic organizing whether your colleague Smith is coming and receive the reply that "Smith hasn't said that he's not coming." Should this allow you to infer that he is in fact coming, or has he simply failed to send the required reply by e-mail? Your confidence that Smith will be attending will vary depending on the number of people that have replied. If you are told that no one has replied so far, assuming Smith's attendance seems premature; if by contrast you are told that everyone has replied, you would be assured of his presence. In between these two extremes your degree of confidence will be scaled: the more people have replied the more confident you will be. In other words, the epistemic closure of the database in question (the e-mail inbox of the organizer) can vary from no closure whatsoever to complete closure, giving rise to corresponding changes in the probability that *not says* (*not p*) does in fact suggest that *p*.

Hahn, Oaksford, and Bayindir's (2005) experiments confirmed that people are sensitive to variations in the epistemic closure of a database and that this affects their willingness to endorse argument like (22). Moreover, they found that arguments like (22) can be regarded as stronger than the standard negative evidence case (21). Therefore, as our example suggested, there would seem to be nothing in the structure of arguments like the Ghosts example that make them inherently unacceptable.

The real reasons why negative evidence on ghosts is weak, that is, why (13) is a weaker argument than (14), are the lack of sensitivity (ability to detect ghosts) of our tests as well as our low prior belief in their existence, that is, (13) is weak because of the probabilistic factors that affect the strength of the argument. Hahn and Oaksford (2006, 2007) have shown how this account generalises to other inferential fallacies, such as *circularity* and the *slippery slope* argument.

In summary, in this section we have shown how the concept of argument strength can resolve the problem of why some instances of informal argument fallacies nonetheless seem like perfectly acceptable arguments that should rationally persuade an audience of the conclusion.

Conclusion

In this chapter, we have reviewed the evidence that has recently accumulated for the probabilistic approach to human reasoning. Across the three core areas of the psychology of deductive reasoning there is now considerable support for the view that people utilise probabilistic strategies to draw reasonable inferences about the uncertain world in which they live. We have also replied to occasional critiques of the probabilistic approach and shown how it can be extended to argumentation, which is the more general human activity of which deductive reasoning is but a small part. This review shows that a probabilistic approach to human reasoning (Oaksford and Chater 1994, 1996, 1998, 2001) may be able to explain the seeming paradox of why such a successful organism occasionally seems so irrational in the laboratory: The wrong normative standard has been applied.

Notes

1   For a more detailed look at the some of the theoretical and conceptual issues surrounding this approach see, Oaksford and Hahn (2007) and Oaksford and Chater (2007).

2   According to Adams (1998) probability logic, indicative conditionals of natural language are not candidates for truth or falsity (see Oaksford and Hahn 2007 for more discussion). Consequently standard rules that apply to the material conditional, such as when *if p then q is true, then* $P(q \mid p) = 1$, do not apply to the indicative conditional of everyday language. It also means that rules like transitivity do not generally apply, that is, *if p then q, if q then r, therefore, if p then r*. However, as Pearl (1988: 493–497) observes, if the conditional probabilities associated with these conditionals are sufficiently extreme, then transitivity may hold to an approximation (assuming also that the transitive chain is not too long).

3   On Adams (1998) account and that endorsed here (see also Evans and Over 2004), the meaning of the conditional probability is given by the Ramsey (1990, originally 1931) test, in which people *suppose* the antecedent of a conditional to be true, adjust their other beliefs accordingly, and read off their new degree of belief in the consequent. That people only *suppose* the antecedent to be true is important and implies that the cognitive system can undo any revisions made and crucially does not cause people to act on a supposition in the way they would act on a belief: For example, no action is required to avoid death on *supposing* I am on the deck of the *Titanic* as it sinks but if I believed this I would have to take action and would probably need the help of a mental health professional.

4   One might argue that these materials produce a binary situation, for example, a card that is not yellow is definitively red. This could lead to

affirmative re-interpretations of negated cases, that is, for the contrapositives. This distinction is known to affect people's interpretation of conditionals (see Oaksford 2002; Oaksford and Stenning 1992; Schroyens et al. 2000). However, these results have been replicated with everyday materials (Over et al. 2003).

5   On this account, the probability of tacit conditionals, that is, ones that are not explicitly asserted but that are implicit in a text (spoken or written), would be assigned a probability based on prior knowledge. For example, suppose you hear someone state that "So Arsenal will win tonight" (Arsenal is a U.K. football club) in response to their interlocutor just saying "It will rain tonight." The truth of the first person's utterance depends on the truth of the tacit conditional, "if it rains, Arsenal win." Having no other information to go on you would probably only assign this conditional a probability at chance levels. However, if someone actually asserted this conditional, it seems that to obey pragmatic rules of conversation, they may have some concrete evidence for this assertion and so on the basis of the assertion alone it would make sense to assign a higher probability to this conditional.

6   This is again a *conservative* option as it only requires altering a single weight. However, it does imply the existence of a control mechanism capable of holding all else constant while this one weight is adjusted, that is, neural network learning algorithms where the weights are learned from repeated presentations of whole patterns over the network are not being invoked.

7   We also do not discuss the probabilistic decision theoretic account that Oaksford and Chater (1994) supplied for *deontic* versions of the selection task. Many of the predictions of this account have recently been confirmed by Perham and Oaksford (2005).

8   One might object that large objects might be folded, disassembled and so on. This point is well taken but it simply reflects the ambiguity in the philosophical literature over the term "analytic." The classic example of an analytic claim is that "bachelor" means "unmarried man." This claim could be expressed as a meaning potulate *if someone is a bachelor then they are an unmarried man.* But there are counterexamples, as just here. For example, someone who has a bachelor's degree is not necessarily an unmarried man. Our view in these cases is that the distinction is a matter of degree, that is, the probability of the consequent given the antecedent is so high that there is only an infinitesimal chance that the antecedent is not accompanied by the consequent.

9   Given Feeney and colleagues manipulations it is also difficult to determine how to appropriately parameterise the mental models theory, to

which they appeal, to derive quantitative fits. In these cases mental models "wins by vagueness." That is, the representations it proposes are claimed to explain some qualitative feature of the evidence but it is impossible to quantatively assess whether this is actually the case.

10   Oaksford and Chater (1995) explain the relationship between Sperber, Cara, and Girotto's (1995) relevance account and the ODS model.

11   *Weak p*-entailments are where the overlap on the probability interval is not one of perfect inclusion. So, for example, *Some* is a strong *p*-entailment of *Most* because the interval $[1-\Delta, 1)$ is included in the interval $(0, 1)$. However, *Most* is only a weak *p*-entailment of *Some* because while the converse incluson is not true the intervals overlap to an extent depending on Δ.

12   It could be questioned how the *some…not*-heuristic can lead to better performance. The reason is that many invalid syllogisms can potentially lead to this conclusion via the *min*-heuristic or *p*-entailments and, consequently, a general heuristic against endorsing such conclusions does help discriminate valid from invalid syllogisms in general.

13   One might argue that (15) and (16) are problematic because replacing "not toxic" with "safe" would alter the status of these arguments. This is not the case because we do not have a concept of a "safe effect." The *tests* are tests for *toxic* effects. So (16) could be rephrased as, "Drug A is safe because no toxic effects were observed," but not as, "Drug A is safe because *safe* effects were observed." As the observation of toxic effects is driving these distinctions, what "safe" means in this context must be defined in terms of toxicity in order to define the relevant probabilities.

References

Adams, E. W. (1966). Probability and the logic of conditionals. In J. Hintikka and P. Suppes (Eds.) *Aspects of inductive logic.* Amsterdam: North Holland.

Adams, E. W. (1975). *The logic of conditionals: An application of probability theory to deductive logic.* Dordrecht: Reidel.

Adams, E. W. (1998). *A primer of probability logic.* Stanford, CA: CSLI Publications.

Almor, A., and Sloman, S. A. (1996). Is deontic reasoning special? *Psychological Review, 103,* 374–380.

Anderson, J. R. (1990). *The adaptive character of thought.* Hillsdale, NJ: LEA.

Anderson, J. R. (1991). Is human cognition adaptive? *Behavioral and Brain Sciences, 14,* 471–517.

Anderson, J. R. (1995). *Cognitive psychology and its implications.* New York: W. H. Freeman and Company.

Anderson, J. R., and Sheu, C. F. (1995). Causal inferences as perceptual judgments. *Memory & Cognition, 23,* 510–524.

Baron, J. (1981). *An analysis of confirmation bias.* Paper presented at 1981 Psychonomic Society meeting.

Baron, J. (1985). *Rationality and Intelligence.* Cambridge: Cambridge University Press.

Bennett, J. (2003). *A philosophical guide to conditionals.* Oxford: Oxford University Press.

Bonnefon, J.-F. (2004). Reinstatement, floating conclusions, and the credulity of mental model reasoning. *Cognitive Science, 28,* 621–631.

Bonnefon, J. F., and Hilton, D. J. (2004). Consequential conditionals: Invited and suppressed inferences from valued outcomes. *Journal of Experimental Psychology: Learning, Memory, and Cognition, 30,* 28–37.

Bovens, L., and Hartmann, S. (2003). *Bayesian epistemology.* Oxford: Oxford University Press.

Braine, M. D. S., and O'Brien, D. P. (1998). *Mental logic.* London: Lawrence Erlbaum.

Byrne, R. M. J. (1989). Suppressing valid inferences with conditionals. *Cognition, 31,* 1–21.

Chan, D., and Chua, F. (1994). Suppression of valid inferences: Syntactic views, mental models, and relative salience. *Cognition, 53,* 217–238.

Chater, N., and Oaksford, M. (1993). Logicism, mental models and everyday reasoning. *Mind and Language, 8,* 72–89.

Chater, N., and Oaksford, M. (1999a). The probability heuristics model of syllogistic reasoning. *Cognitive Psychology, 38,* 191–258.

Chater, N., and Oaksford, M. (1999b). Ten years of the rational analysis of cognition. *Trends in Cognitive Sciences, 3,* 57–65.

Chater, N., and Oaksford, M. (1999c). Information gain vs. decision-theoretic approaches to data selection: Response to Klauer. *Psychological Review, 106,* 223–227.

Clark, K. L. (1978). Negation as failure. In H. Gallaire and J. Minker (Eds.), *Logic and databases* (pp. 293–322). New York: Plenum Press.

Copeland, D. E., and Radvansky, G. A. (2004). Working memory and syllogistic reasoning. *Quarterly Journal of Experimental Psychology, 57A,* 1437–1457.

Cover, T. M., and Thomas, J. A. (1991). *Elements of information theory.* New York: John Wiley and Sons.

Cummins, D. D. (1995). Naïve theories and causal deduction. *Memory & Cognition, 23,* 646–658.

Cummins, D. D., Lubart, T., Alksnis, O., and Rist, R. (1991). Conditional reasoning and causation. *Memory & Cognition, 19,* 274–282.

Dickstein, L. S. (1978). The effect of figure on syllogistic reasoning. *Memory and Cognition, 6,* 76–83.

Earman, J. (1992). *Bayes or bust?* Cambridge, MA: MIT Press.

Edgington, D. (1991). The matter of the missing matter of fact. *Proceedings of the Aristotelian Society, Suppl. Vol. 65,* 185–209.

Eemeren, F. H. van, and Grootendorst, R. (1992). *Argumentation, communication, and fallacies.* Hillsdale, NJ: Lawrence Erlbaum.

Espino, O., Santamaria, C., and Garcia-Madruga, J. A. (2000). Activation of end-terms in syllogistic reasoning. *Thinking and Reasoning, 6,* 67–89.

Evans, J. St. B. T. (1977). Linguistic factors in reasoning. *Quarterly Journal of Experimental Psychology, 29,* 297–306.

Evans, J. St. B. T. (1983). Linguistic determinants of bias in conditional reasoning. *Quarterly Journal of Experimental Psychology, 35,* 635–644.

Evans, J. St. B. T. (1984). Heuristic and analytic processes in reasoning. *British Journal of Psychology, 75,* 451–468.

Evans, J. St. B. T. (1989). *Bias in human reasoning: Causes and consequences.* Hillsdale, NJ: Erlbaum.

Evans, J. St. B. T. (1998). Matching bias in conditional reasoning: Do we understand it after 25 years? *Thinking and Reasoning, 4,* 45–82.

Evans, J. St. B. T., Clibbens, J., and Rood, B. (1995). Bias in conditional inference: Implications for mental models and mental logic. *Quarterly Journal of Experimental Psychology, 48A,* 644–670.

Evans, J. St. B. T., and Handley, S. J. (1999). The role of negation in conditional inference. *Quarterly Journal of Experimental Psychology, 52,* 739–770.

Evans, J. St. B. T., Handley, S. J., Harper, C. N. J., and Johnson-Laird, P. N. (1999). Reasoning about necessity and possibility: A test of the mental model theory of deduction. *Journal of Experimental Psychology: Learning, Memory, and Cognition, 25,* 1495–1513.

Evans, J. St. B. T., Handley, S. J., and Over, D. E. (2003). Conditionals and conditional probability. *Journal of Experimental Psychology: Learning, Memory, & Cognition, 29,* 321–335.

Evans, J. St. B. T., and Lynch, J. S. (1973). Matching bias in the selection task. *British Journal of Psychology, 64,* 391–397.

Evans, J. St. B. T., Newstead, S. E., and Byrne, R. M. J. (1993). *Human Reasoning.* Hillsdale, N.J.: Lawrence Erlbaum Associates.

Evans, J. St. B. T., and Over, D. E. (1996). Rationality in the selection task: Epistemic utility versus uncertainty reduction. *Psychological Review, 103,* 356–363.

Evans, J. St. B. T., and Over, D. (1996). *Rationality and reasoning.* Hove, Sussex: Psychology Press.

Evans, J. St. B. T., and Over, D. E. (2004). *If.* Oxford: Oxford University Press.

Feeney, A., and Handley, S. J. (2000). The suppression of *q* card selections: Evidence for deductive inference in Wason's selection task. *Quarterly Journal of Experimental Psychology, 53,* 1224–1242.

Feeney, A., Handley, S. J., and Kentridge, R. (2003). Deciding between accounts of the selection task: A reply to Oaksford (2002). *Quarterly Journal of Experimental Psychology, 56*, 1079–1088.

Fodor, J. A. (1987). *Psychosemantics: The problem of meaning in the philosophy of mind.* Cambridge, MA: MIT Press.

Gebauer, G., and Laming, D. (1997). Rational choices in Wason's selection task. *Psychological Research, 60*, 284–293.

George, C. (1997). Reasoning from uncertain premises. *Thinking and Reasoning, 3*, 161–190.

George, C. (1999). Evaluation of the plausibility of a conclusion from several arguments with uncertain premises. *Thinking and Reasoning, 5*, 245–281.

Green, D. W., and Over, D. E. (1997). Causal inference, contingency tables and the selection task. *Current Psychology of Cognition, 16*, 459–487.

Green, D. W., and Over, D. E. (1998). Reaching a decision: A reply to Oaksford. *Thinking and Reasoning, 4*, 231–248.

Green, D. W., and Over, D. E. (2000). Decision theoretical effects in testing a causal conditional. *Current Psychology of Cognition, 19*, 51–68.

Green, D. W., Over, D. E., and Pyne, R. A. (1997). Probability and choice in the selection task. *Thinking and Reasoning, 3*, 209–236.

Hahn, U., and Oaksford, M. (2006). A Bayesian approach to informal argument fallacies. *Synthese,152*, 207–236.

Hahn, U., and Oaksford, M. (2007). The rationality of informal argumentation: A Bayesion approach to reasoning fallacies. *Psychological Review, 114*, 704–732.

Hahn, U., Oaksford, M., and Bayindir, H. (2005). How convinced should we be by negative evidence? In B. Bara, L. Barsalou, and M. Bucciarelli (Eds.), *Proceedings of the 27th Annual Conference of the Cognitive Science Society* (pp. 887–892), Mahwah, N.J.: Lawrence Erlbaum Associates.

Hahn, U., Oaksford, M., and Corner, A. (2005). Circular arguments, begging the question and the formalization of argument strength. In A. Russell, T. Honkela, K. Lagus, and M. Pöllä (Eds.), *Proceedings of AMKLC'05, International Symposium on Adaptive Models of Knowledge, Language and Cognition* (pp. 34–40), Espoo, Finland, June 2005.

Hamblin, C. L. (1970). *Fallacies.* London: Methuen.

Handley, S. J., Feeney, A., and Harper, C. (2002). Alternative antecedents, probabilities, and the suppression of inference in Wason's selection task. *Quarterly Journal of Experimental Psychology, 55*, 799–818.

Hardman, D. (1998). Does reasoning occur on the selection task: A comparison of relevance-based theories. *Thinking and Reasoning, 4*, 353–376.

Hattori, M. (1999). The effects of probabilistic information in Wason's selection task: An analysis of strategy based on the ODS model. *Procceedings of the 16th Annual Meeting of the Japanese Cognitive Science Society, 16*, 623–626.

Hattori, M. (2002). A quantitative model of optimal data selection in Wason's selection task. *Quarterly Journal of Experimental Psychology, 55A*, 1241–1272.

Howson, C., and Urbach, P. (1989). *Scientific reasoning: The Bayesian approach.* La Salle, IL: Open Court.

Johnson-Laird, P. N., and Bara, B. G. (1984). Syllogistic inference. *Cognition, 16*, 1–62.

Johnson-Laird, P. N., and Byrne, R. M. J. (1991). *Deduction.* Hillsdale, NJ: Erlbaum.

Johnson-Laird, P. N., and Byrne, R. M. J. (2002). Conditionals: A theory of meaning, pragmatics, and inference. *Psychological Review, 109*, 646–678.

Johnson-Laird, P. N., and Steedman, M. (1978). The psychology of syllogisms. *Cognitive Psychology, 10*, 64–99.

Johnson-Laird, P. N., and Tagart, J. (1969). How implication is understood. *American Journal of Psychology, 82*, 367–373.

Klauer, K. C. (1999). On the normative justification for information gain in Wason's selection task. *Psychological Review, 106*, 215–222.

Klauer, K. C., Musch, J., and Naumer, B. (2000). On belief bias in syllogistic reasoning. *Psychological Review, 107*, 852–894.

Laming, D. (1996). On the analysis of irrational data selection: A critique of Oaksford and Chater (1994). *Psychological Review, 103*, 364–373.

Liu, I. M. (2003). Conditional reasoning and conditionalisation. *Journal of Experimental Psychology: Learning, Memory & Cognition, 29*, 694–709.

Liu, I., Lo, K., and Wu, J. (1996). A probabilistic interpretation of "If-then." *Quarterly Journal of Experimental Psychology, 49A*, 828–844.

Lucas, E. J., and Ball, L. J. (2005). Think-aloud protocols and the selection task: Evidence for relevance effects and rationalisation processes. *Thinking and Reasoning, 11*, 35–66.

Mackie, J. L. (1963). The paradox of confirmation. *British Journal for the Philosophy of Science, 38*, 265–277.

Manktelow, K. (1999). *Reasoning and thinking.* Hove, Sussex: Psychology Press.

Manktelow, K. I., Sutherland, E. J., and Over, D. E. (1995). Probabilistic factors in deontic reasoning. *Thinking and Reasoning, 1*, 201–220.

Markovits, H., and Barrouillet, P. (2002). The development of conditional reasoning: A mental model account. *Developmental Review, 22*, 5–36.

Markovits, H., Fleury, M.-L., Quinn, S., and Venet, M. (1998). The development of conditional reasoning and the structure of semantic memory. *Child Development, 64*, 742–755.

Markovits, H., and Quinn, S. (2002). Efficiency of retrieval correlates with "logical" reasoning from causal conditional premises. *Memory and Cognition, 30,* 696–706.

McClelland, J. L. (1998). Connectionist models and Bayesian inference. In M. Oaksford and N. Chater (Eds.), *Rational models of cognition* (pp. 21–53). Oxford: Oxford University Press.

McKenzie, C. R. M., and Mikkelsen, L. A. (2000). The psychological side of Hempel's paradox of confirmation. *Psychonomic Bulletin & Review, 7,* 360–366.

McKenzie, C. R. M., and Mikkelsen, L. A. (in press). A Bayesian view of covariation assessment. *Cognitive Psychology.*

McKenzie, C. R. M., Ferreira, V. S., Mikkelsen, L. A., McDermott, K. J., and Skrable, R. P. (2001). Do conditional statements target rare events? *Organizational Behavior & Human Decision Processes, 85,* 291–309.

McKenzie, C. R. M. (2005). Judgment and decision making. In K. Lamberts and R. L. Goldstone (Eds.), Handbook of cognition (pp. 321–338). London: Sage.

Moshman, D., and Geil M. (1998). Collaborative reasoning: Evidence for collective rationality. *Thinking and Reasoning, 4,* 231–248.

Moxey, L., and Sanford, A. (1987). Quantifiers and focus. *Journal of Semantics, 5,* 189–206.

Moxey, L., and Sanford, A. (1993). *Communicating quantities.* Hove, England: Erlbaum.

Nelson, J. (in press). Finding useful questions: On Bayesian diagnosticity, probability, impact, and information gain. *Psychological Review.*

Newstead, S. E., Handley, S. J., and Buck, E. (1999). Falsifying mental models: Testing the predictions of theories of syllogistic reasoning. *Memory & Cognition, 27,* 344–354.

Nickerson, R. S. (1996). Hempel's paradox and Wason's selection task: Logical and psychological puzzles of confirmation. *Thinking and Reasoning, 2,* 1–32.

Oaksford, M. (2001). Language processing, activation and reasoning: A reply to Espino, Santamaria & Garcia-Madruga. *Thinking & Reasoning, 7,* 205–208.

Oaksford, M. (2002a). Contrast classes and matching bias as explanations of the effects of negation on conditional reasoning. *Thinking & Reasoning, 8,* 135–151.

Oaksford, M. (2002b). Predicting the results of reasoning experiments: Reply to Feeney and Handley. *Quarterly Journal of Experimental Psychology, 55A,* 793–798.

Oaksford, M. (2004, August). *Conditional inference and constraint satisfaction: Reconciling probabilistic and mental models approaches?* Paper presented at the 5th International Conference on Thinking, University of Leuven, Leuven, Belgium.

Oaksford, M., and Chater, N. (1991). Against logicist cognitive science. *Mind & Language, 6,* 1–38.

Oaksford, M., and Chater, N. (1992). Bounded rationality in taking risks and drawing inferences. *Theory & Psychology, 2,* 225–230.

Oaksford, M., and Chater, N. (1993). Reasoning theories and bounded rationality. In K. I. Manktelow, and D. E. Over (Eds.), *Rationality* (pp. 31–60). London: Routledge.

Oaksford, M., and Chater, N. (1994). A rational analysis of the selection task as optimal data selection. *Psychological Review, 101,* 608–631.

Oaksford, M., and Chater, N. (1995). Theories of reasoning and the computational explanation of everyday inference. *Thinking and Reasoning, 1,* 121–152.

Oaksford, M., and Chater, N. (1995). Information gain explains relevance which explains the selection task. *Cognition, 57,* 97–108.

Oaksford, M., and Chater, N. (1996). Rational explanation of the selection task. *Psychological Review, 103,* 381–391.

Oaksford, M., and Chater, N. (1998a) (Eds.). *Rational models of cognition.* Oxford: Oxford University Press.

Oaksford, M., and Chater, N. (1998b). *Rationality in an uncertain world: Essays on the cognitive science of human reasoning.* Hove, Sussex: Psychology Press.

Oaksford, M., and Chater, N. (1998c). A revised rational analysis of the selection task: Exceptions and sequential sampling. In M. Oaksford, and N. Chater (Eds.), *Rational models of cognition* (pp. 372–398). Oxford: Oxford University Press.

Oaksford, M., and Chater, N. (2001). The probabilistic approach to human reasoning. *Trends in Cognitive Sciences, 5,* 349–357.

Oaksford, M., and Chater, N. (2003a). Computational levels and conditional reasoning: Reply to Schroyens and Schaeken (2003). *Journal of Experimental Psychology: Learning, Memory & Cognition, 29,* 150–156.

Oaksford, M., and Chater, N. (2003b). Conditional probability and the cognitive science of conditional reasoning. *Mind & Language, 18,* 359–379.

Oaksford, M., and Chater, N. (2003c). Modeling probabilistic effects in conditional inference: Validating search or conditional probability? *Revista Psychologica, 32,* 217–242.

Oaksford, M., and Chater, N. (2003d). Probabilities and pragmatics in conditional inference: Suppression and order effects. In D. Hardman, and L. Macchi (Eds.), *Thinking: Psychological perspectives on reasoning, judgment and decision making* (pp. 95–122). Chichester, UK: John Wiley & Sons.

Oaksford, M., and Chater, N. (2003e). Optimal data selection: Revision, review and reevaluation. *Psychonomic Bulletin & Review, 10,* 289–318.

Oaksford, M., and Chater, N. (2007). *Bayesion rationality: The probabilistic approach to human reasoning.* Oxford: Oxford University Press.

Oaksford, M., and Chater, N. (2008). Probability logic and the modus ponens – modus tollens asymmetry in conditional inference. In Chater, N., & Oaksford, M. (Eds.), The Probabilistic mind (pp. 97–120). Oxford, UK: Oxford University Press..

Oaksford, M., Chater, N., and Grainger, B. (1999). Probabilistic effects in data selection. Thinking and Reasoning, 5, 193–243.

Oaksford, M., Chater, N., Grainger, B., and Larkin, J. (1997). Optimal data selection in the reduced array selection task (RAST). Journal of Experimental Psychology: Learning, Memory and Cognition, 23, 441–458.

Oaksford, M., Chater, N., and Larkin, J. (2000). Probabilities and polarity biases in conditional inference. Journal of Experimental Psychology: Learning, Memory & Cognition, 26, 883–899.

Oaksford, M., and Hahn, U. (2004). A Bayesian approach to the argument from ignorance. Canadian Journal of Experimental Psychology, 58, 75–85.

Oaksford, M., and Hahn, U. (2007). Induction, deduction and argument strength in human reasoning and argumentation. In A. Feeney, and E. Heit (Eds.), Inductive Reasoning (pp. 269–301), Cambridge: Cambridge University Press.

Oaksford, M., and Moussakowski, M. (2004). Negations and natural sampling in data selection: Ecological vs. heuristic explanations of matching bias. Memory & Cognition, 32, 570–581.

Oaksford, M., Roberts, L., and Chater, N. (2002). Relative informativeness of quantifiers used in syllogistic reasoning. Memory & Cognition, 30, 138–149.

Oaksford, M., and Stenning, K. (1992). Reasoning with conditionals containing negated constituents. Journal of Experimental Psychology: Learning, Memory & Cognition, 18, 835–854.

Oaksford, M., and Wakefield, M. (2003). Data selection and natural sampling: Probabilities do matter. Memory & Cognition, 31, 143–154.

Oberauer, K., and Wilhelm, O. (2003). The meaning of conditionals: Conditional probabilities, mental models, and personal utilities. Journal of Experimental Psychology: Learning, Memory, & Cognition, 29, 321–335.

Oberauer, K., Weidenfeld, A., Hörnig, R. (2004). Logical reasoning and probabilities: A comprehensive test of Oaksford and Chater (2001). Psychonomic Bulletin and Review, 11, 521–527.

Oberauer, K., Wilhelm, O., & Dias, R., R. (1999). Bayesian rationality for the Wason selection task? A test of optimal data selection theory. Thinking and Reasoning, 5, 115–144.

Ohm, E., and Thompson, V. (in press). Conditional probability and pragmatic conditionals: Truth, reasoning and behavioural effectiveness. Thinking and Reasoning.

Over, D. E., Hadjichristidis, C., Evans, J. St. B. T., Handley, S. J., and Sloman, S. A. (2005). The probability of ordinary indicative conditionals. Manuscript submitted for publication.

Osman, M., and Laming D. (2001). Misinterpretation of conditional statements in Wason's selection task. Psychological Research, 65, 128–144.

Pearl, J. (1988). Probabilistic reasoning in intelligent systems. San Mateo, CA: Morgan Kaufman.

Pearl, J. (2000). Causality. Cambridge: Cambridge University Press.

Perelman, C., and Olbrechts-Tyteca, L. (1969). The new rhetoric: A treatise on argumentation. Notre Dame, IN: University of Notre Dame Press.

Perham, N., and Oaksford, M. (2005). Deontic reasoning with emotional content: Evolutionary psychology or decision theory? Cognitive Science, 29, 681–718.

Politzer, G. (2005). Uncertainty and the suppression of inferences. Thinking and Reasoning, 11, 5–34.

Prakken, H., and Vreeswijk, G. A. W. (2002). Logics for defeasible argumentation. In D. M. Gabbay, and F. Guenthner (Eds.), Handbook of Philosophical Logic, 2nd edition, Vol. 4 (pp. 219–318). Dordrecht: Kluwer Academic Publishers.

Quinn, S., and Markovits, H. (1998). Conditional reasoning, causality, and the structure of semantic memory: Strength of association as a predictive factor for content effects. Cognition, 68, B93–B101.

Quinn, S., and Markovits, H. (2002). Conditional reasoning with causal premises: Evidence for a retrieval model. Thinking and Reasoning, 8, 179–191.

Ramsey, F. P. (1990). General propositions and causality. In D. H. Mellor (Ed.), Philosophical Papers of F. P. Ramsey (pp. 145–163). Cambridge: Cambridge University Press. (Originally published in 1931).

Rips, L. J. (1994). The psychology of proof. Cambridge, MA: MIT Press.

Rips, L. J. (2001). Two kinds of reasoning. Psychological Science, 12, 129–134.

Rumelhart, D. E., Smolensky, P., McClelland, J. L., and Hinton, G. E. (1986). Schemata and sequential thought processes in PDP models. In McClelland, J. L., and Rumelhart, D. E. (Eds.), Parallel distributed processing: Explorations in the microstructure of cognition, Vol. 2: Psychological and biological processes (Chapter 14, pp. 7–57). Cambridge, MA: MIT Press.

Schroyens, W., and Schaeken, W. (2003). A critique of Oaksford, Chater, and Larkin's (2000) conditional probability model of conditional reasoning. Journal of Experimental Psychology: Learning, Memory & Cognition, 29, 140–149.

Schroyens, W., Schaeken, W., Fias, W., and d'Ydewalle, G. (2000). Heuristic and analytic processes in conditional reasoning with negatives. *Journal of Experimental Psychology: Learning, Memory & Cognition, 26,* 1713–1734.

Schroyens, W., Schaeken, W., and d'Ydewalle, G. (2001a). The processing of negations in conditional reasoning: A meta-analytic case study in mental model and/or mental logic theory. *Thinking and Reasoning, 7,* 121–172.

Schroyens, W., Schaeken, W., and d'Ydewalle, G. (2001b). *A meta-analytic review of conditional reasoning by model and/pr rule: Mental models theory revised.* Manuscript submitted for publication. Available at: http://www.psy.kuleuven.ac.be/~walters/cognition.pdf.

Schroyens, W., Verschueren, N., Schaeken, W., and d'Ydewalle, G. (2000). Conditional reasoning with negations: Implicit and explicit affirmation or denial and the role of contrast classes. *Thinking & Reasoning, 6,* 221–251.

Schustack, M. W., and Sternberg, R. J. (1981). Evaluation of evidence in causal inference. *Journal of Epxerimental Psychology: General, 110,* 101–120.

Sellen, J. L., Oaksford, M., and Gray, N. S. (2005). Schizotypy and conditional inference. *Schizophrenia Bulletin, 31,* 105–116.

Shaw, V. F., and Johnson-Laird, P. N. (1998). Dispelling the 'atmosphere' effect in reasoning. In A. C. Quelhas, and F. Pereira (Eds.), *Cognition and Context* (Special issue of *Analise Psicologia*) (pp. 169–199). Lisbon, Portugal: Instituto Superior De Psicologia Aplicada.

Sobel, J. H. (2004). *Probable modus ponens and modus tollens, and updating on uncertain evidence.* Unpublished Manuscript, Department of Philosophy, University of Toronto at Scarborough. Available at: www.scar.toronto.ca/~sobel/ConfDisconf.pdf.

Sober, E. (2002). Intelligent design and probability reasoning. *International Journal for Philosophy of Religion, 52,* 65–80.

Sperber, D., Cara, F., and Girotto, V. (1995). Relevance explains the selection task. *Cognition, 57,* 31–95.

Stanovich, K. E., and West, R. F. (2000). Individual differences in reasoning: Implications for the rationality debate. *Behavioral & Brain Sciences, 23,* 645–726.

Stein, E. (1996). *Without good reason.* Oxford: Oxford University Press.

Stevenson, R. J., and Over, D. E. (1995). Deduction from uncertain premises. *Quarterly Journal of Experimental Psychology, 48A,* 613–643.

Stich, S. (1985). Could man be an irrational animal? *Synthese, 64,* 115–135.

Thompson, V. A. (1994). Interpretational factors in conditional reasoning. *Memory and Cognition, 22,* 742–758.

Thompson, V. A., and Mann, J. M. (1995). Perceived necessity explains the dissociation between logic and meaning: The case of "Only if". *Journal of Experimental Psychology: Learning, Memory & Cognition, 21,* 1554–1567.

Wagner, C. G. (2004). *Modus tollens* probabilized. *British Journal for Philosophy of Science, 55,* 747–753.

Wason, P. C. (1968). Reasoning about a rule. *Quarterly Journal of Experimental Psychology, 20,* 273–281.

Wason, P. C., and Johnson-Laird, P. N. (1972). *Psychology of reasoning: Structure and content.* Cambridge, MA: Harvard University Press.

Yama, H. (2001). Matching versus optimal data selection in the Wason selection task. *Thinking and Reasoning, 7,* 295–311.

Chapter 21: Individual Differences in Reasoning and the Algorithmic/Intentional Level Distinction in Cognitive Science

KEITH E. STANOVICH

When a layperson thinks of individual differences in reasoning they think of IQ tests. It is quite natural that this is their primary associate, because IQ tests are among the most publicized products of psychological research. This association is not entirely inaccurate either, because intelligence – as measured using IQ-like instruments – is correlated with performance on a host of reasoning tasks (Ackerman, Kyllonen, and Roberts 1999; Carroll 1993; Hunt 1999; Lohman 2000; Lubinski 2004; Rips and Conrad 1983; Sternberg 1977, 1985). Nonetheless, a major theme of this chapter will be that certain very important classes of individual differences in thinking are ignored if only intelligence-related variance is the primary focus. A number of these ignored classes of individual differences are those relating to rational thought.

In this chapter, I will argue that intelligence-related individual differences in thinking are largely the result of differences at the algorithmic level of cognitive control. Intelligence tests thus largely fail to tap processes at the intentional level of control. Because understanding rational behavior necessitates understanding processes operating at both levels, an exclusive focus on intelligence-related individual differences will tend to obscure important differences in human thinking.

This argument obviously depends strongly on differentiating the algorithmic from the intentional level of analysis. Therefore, in the next section I will outline the sources that I rely on for this conceptual distinction and how I will utilize the distinction to provide a framework for thinking about individual differences in reasoning.

Levels of Analysis in Cognitive Science

Levels of analysis in cognitive theory have been discussed by numerous theorists (Anderson 1990, 1991; Bermudez 2001; Davies 2000; Dennett 1978, 1987; Horgan and Tienson 1993; Levelt 1995; Marr 1982; Newell 1982, 1990; Oaksford and Chater 1995; Pylyshyn 1984; A. Sloman 1993; Sterelny 1990, 2001). For example, Anderson (1990) defines four levels of theorizing in cognitive science. At bottom is a biological level that is inaccessible to cognitive theorizing. Just above is an implementation level which is basically a comprehensible shorthand approximation to the biological. Next comes the so-called algorithmic level which is concerned with the computational processes and information processing operations necessary to carry out a task. The cognitive psychologist works largely at this level by showing that human performance can be explained by positing certain information processing mechanisms in the brain (input coding mechanisms, perceptual registration mechanisms, short- and long-term-memory storage systems, etc.). For example, a simple letter pronunciation task might entail encoding the letter, storing it in short-term memory, comparing it with information stored in long-term memory, if a match occurs making a response decision, and then executing a motor response.

Finally, in Anderson's (1990) scheme, there is the rational level where the issues of biological constitution and algorithmic processing sequence are set aside and predictions are made by attempting to provide a specification of the *goals* of the system's computations (*what the*

Table 1: Different Levels of Cognitive Theory as Characterized by Several Investigators and in This Chapter

Anderson	Marr	Newell	Dennett	This Chapter
Rational Level	Computational Level	Knowledge Level	Intentional Stance	Intentional Level
Algorithmic Level	Representation and Algorithm	Program Symbol Level	Design Stance	Algorithmic Level
Implementation Level		Register Transfer Level		
Biological Level	Hardware Implementation	Device	Physical Stance	Biological Level

system is attempting to compute and *why*) and its knowledge structure. The rational level of analysis is concerned with the goals of the system, beliefs relevant to those goals, and the choice of action that is rational given the system's goals and beliefs (Bratman, Israel, and Pollack 1991; Dennett 1987; Newell 1982, 1990; Pollock 1995).

Many similar taxonomies exist in the literature (Sterelny 1990: 46, warns of the "bewildering variety of terms" used to describe these levels of analysis). Indeed, Anderson's (1990) draws heavily on the work of Marr (1982) and Newell (1982). Table 1 presents the alternative, but similar, schemes of Anderson (1990), Marr (1982), Newell (1982), Dennett (1987), and a compromise scheme that I used in a 1999 volume (Stanovich 1999) and that will be used in this chapter. The first level of analysis is termed the biological level in my taxonomy because I will be largely concerned with human information processing rather than computational devices in general. My scheme follows Marr (1982) and Dennett (1987) in collapsing Anderson's algorithmic and implementation levels into one because for the purposes of the present discussion the distinction between these two levels is not important. This second level is termed algorithmic – a term that is relatively uncontroversial.

In contrast, the proper term for the third level is variable and controversial. Borrowing from Dennett (1987), I have termed this level of analysis the intentional level for the following reasons. First, Anderson (1990) has argued that Marr's (1982) terminology is confusing and inapt because "his level of computational theory is not really about computation but rather about the goals of the computation. His basic point is that one should state these goals and understand their implications before one worries about their

computation, which is really the concern of the lower levels of his theory" (p. 6). Dennett (1987) makes the same critique of Marr's terminology by noting that "the highest level, which he misleadingly calls computational, is in fact not at all concerned with computational processes but strictly (and more abstractly) with the question of what function the system in question is serving" (pp. 74–75). The term chosen by Newell (1982) – the knowledge level – is equally inapt in not signaling that this level is concerned with action selection based on expected goal attainment in light of current beliefs. Instead, I have adapted Dennett's terminology and referred to this level as the intentional level of analysis.

Although Sterelny (1990: 45) argues that this level of analysis is not necessarily tied to an intentional psychology, it is an important part of my usage that I *do* want to conjoin the two. So, in the present case, the term is apt. Importantly, intentional level states in my framework have more conceptual reality than in Dennett's view where they are imputed by someone taking an intentional stance toward another organism. The view taken here is more like that of Newell (1982) than that of Dennett. In discussing the differences between their two positions, Newell (1982) notes that Dennett "does not, as noted, assign reality to the different system levels, but keeps them in the eye of the beholder" (p. 123; see Brook and Ross 2002; Elton 2003; Mirolli 2002; Ross 2000, for discussions of the complexities in Dennett's evolving position; and Davies 2000 for a discussion of personal and subpersonal constructs).

Intentional-level processes would, in my view, be exemplified in models such as A. Sloman's (1993) where desires function as control states that can produce behavior either directly or through a complex control hierarchy by changing intermediate desire-states. He views dispositions (high-level attitudes, ideals, and personality traits) as long-term desire states that "work through a control hierarchy, for instance, by changing other desire-like states rather than triggering behaviour" (p. 85). For the purposes of the present discussion, intentional-level psychological constructs consist of control states that regulate behavior at a high level of generality, epistemic dispositions that likewise operate very indirectly to alter information pickup tendencies, and cognitive regulatory systems that alter thresholds for things such as belief consistency checks. Importantly, these high-level control states and epistemic dispositions implicate issues of rationality (both practical and theoretical rationality).

To summarize, each level of analysis in cognitive theory frames a somewhat different issue. At the algorithmic level, the key issue is one of computational efficiency, and at the biological level the paramount issue is whether the physical mechanism has the potential to instantiate certain complex algorithms. In contrast, it is at the intentional level that issues of rationality arise.

Intelligence, Rationality, and Levels of Analysis

Work in the psychology of individual differences has long recognized a distinction between cognitive capacities (intelligence) and thinking dispositions (e.g., Baron 1985; Ennis 1987; Moshman 1994; Nickerson 2004; Norris 1992; Perkins 1995; Sinatra and Pintrich 2003; Sternberg 1997, 2003). It is important to realize that the psychological constructs identified by this distinction exist at different conceptual levels in cognitive theory: Measures of cognitive capacities primarily index individual differences at the algorithmic level and measures of thinking dispositions largely index individual differences at the intentional level. For example, cognitive psychologists have focused on the type of algorithmic-level cognitive capacities that underlie traditional psychometric intelligence: perceptual speed, discrimination accuracy, working memory capacity, goal maintenance, and the efficiency of the retrieval of information stored in long-term memory (Ackerman et al. 1999; Carpenter, Just, and Shell 1990; Deary 2000; Hunt 1987, 1999; Kane and Engle 2002; Lohman 2000; Sternberg 1977, 1985, 2000).

In contrast to cognitive psychologists, who have focused largely on cognitive capacities, personality psychologists have focused on thinking dispositions and cognitive styles. Generally, thinking dispositions are seen as more malleable than cognitive capacities: "Although you cannot improve working memory by instruction, you can tell someone to spend more time on problems before she gives up, and if she is so inclined, she can do what you say" (Baron 1985: 15). The important point for the argument of this chapter is that thinking dispositions, as studied by psychologists, are largely intentional-level constructs. For example, many concern beliefs, belief structure, and, importantly, attitudes toward forming and changing beliefs. Other cognitive styles that have been identified in the literature concern a person's goals and goal hierarchy.

I will focus in this chapter on thinking dispositions and cognitive styles that operate to foster reasoning and rational thinking. That is, although cognitive styles relevant to many aspects of personality have been studied (Austin and Deary 2002; Matthews and Deary 1998; McCrae and Costa 1997), the focus here is on those that relate most closely to human rationality – those that relate to the adequacy of belief formation and decision making, things like "the disposition to weigh new evidence against a favored belief heavily (or lightly), the disposition to spend a great deal of time (or very little) on a problem before giving up, or the disposition to weigh heavily the opinions of others in forming one's own" (Baron 1985: 15).

These, then, are the distinctions to be used in my subsequent discussion. Individual differences in omnibus measures of cognitive capacities such as intelligence tests will be understood as primarily indexing individual differences in the efficiency of processing at the algorithmic level. In contrast, thinking dispositions as traditionally studied in psychology (e.g., Cacioppo, Petty, Feinstein, and Jarvis 1996; Klaczynski, Gordon, and Fauth 1997; Kruglanski and Webster 1996; Schommer-Aikins 2004; Sinatra and Pintrich 2003; Stanovich 2002, 2008; Sternberg 1997, 2003) index individual differences at the intentional level of analysis. Thinking disposition measures are telling us about the individual's goals and epistemic values – and they are indexing broad tendencies of pragmatic and epistemic self-regulation.

These distinctions capture the important sense in which rationality is a more encompassing construct than intelligence. The reason is that rationality is an organismic-level concept. It concerns the actions of an entity in its environment that serve its goals. It concerns both levels of analysis – the algorithmic and the intentional level. To be rational, an organism must have well-calibrated beliefs (intentional level) and must act appropriately on those beliefs to achieve its goals (intentional level). The organism must, of course, have the algorithmic-level machinery that enables it to carry out the actions and to process the environment in a way that enables the correct beliefs to be fixed.

Thus, individual differences in rational thought and action can arise because of individual differences in intelligence (an algorithmic-level construct) or because of individual differences in thinking dispositions (an intentional-level construct). To put it simply, the concept of rationality encompasses two things (thinking dispositions and algorithmic-level capacity) whereas the concept of intelligence – at least as it is commonly operationalized – is largely confined to algorithmic-level capacity.[1] As long as variation in thinking dispositions is not perfectly correlated with intelligence, then there is the statistical possibility of dissociations between rationality and intelligence. As will be discussed later, there is in fact a considerable amount of evidence indicating that individual differences in thinking dispositions are substantially dissociated from intelligence.

What Intelligence Tests Leave Out and Why

The tasks on tests of cognitive capacities (intelligence tests or other aptitude measures) are often quite similar to those on tests of critical thinking (in the educational literature, the term critical thinking is often used to cover tasks and mental operations that a cognitive scientist would term indicators of rational thought). An outsider to psychometrics or cognitive science might deem the classification of tasks into one category or the other somewhat arbitrary. In fact, it is far from arbitrary and actually reflects a distinction that is important from the standpoint of both the field of psychometrics and the field of cognitive science.

Psychometricians have long distinguished typical performance situations from optimal (sometimes termed maximal) performance situations (Ackerman 1994, 1996; Ackerman and Heggestad 1997; Cronbach 1949; Matthews, Zeidner, and Roberts 2002). Typical performance situations are unconstrained in that no overt instructions to maximize performance are given, and the task interpretation is determined to some extent by the participant. In contrast, optimal performance situations are those where the task interpretation is determined externally (not left to the participant), the participant is instructed to maximize performance, and is told how to do so. All tests of intelligence or cognitive aptitude are optimal performance assessments, whereas measures of critical or rational thinking are often assessed under typical performance conditions.

Using the terminology for cognitive levels introduced previously, a way to capture this difference in the language of cognitive science is to say that tests of intelligence are constrained at the intentional level (an attempt is made to specify the task demands so explicitly that variation in intentional level thinking dispositions are minimally influential). In contrast, tests of critical or rational thinking are not constrained at the intentional level (or at least are much less constrained). Tasks of the latter but not the former type allow high-level personal goals and their regulation to become implicated in performance, as well as tendencies to change beliefs in the face of contrary evidence (or tendencies to exhaustively or nonexhaustively think through problem possibilities).

Consider the type of syllogistic reasoning item usually examined by cognitive psychologists studying belief bias effects:

Premise 1: All living things need water

Premise 2: Roses need water

Therefore, Roses are living things

Approximately 70 percent of the university students who have been given this problem incorrectly think that the conclusion is valid (Markovits and Nantel 1989; Sá, West, and Stanovich 1999; Stanovich and West 1998c). That the believability of the conclusion is interfering with the assessment of logical validity is clear from the fact that virtually all of the same students correctly judge the following structurally similar syllogism to be invalid:

Premise 1: All insects need oxygen

Premise 2: Mice need oxygen

Therefore, Mice are insects

A substantial number of people deeming the "rose" syllogism valid now switch and call the "mice" syllogism invalid. What is happening here has been studied extensively by investigators who have examined belief bias effects (e.g., Dias, Roazzi, and Harris 2005; Evans 2002; Evans, Barston, and Pollard 1983; Evans and Feeney

2004; Goel and Dolan 2003; Nickerson 1998; Simoneau and Markovits 2003; Stanovich and West 1997). Prior belief in the conclusion is becoming implicated in the judgment of logical validity.

The important point for the present discussion is that it would not be surprising to see an item such as the "rose" syllogism (that is, an item that pitted prior belief against logical validity) on a critical thinking test. Such tests measure performance under typical conditions, do not constrain intentional-level thinking dispositions, and in fact attempt to probe and assess the nature of such cognitive tendencies to bias judgments in the direction of prior belief or to trump prior belief with new evidence. Thus, for example, an exercise on the *Watson-Glaser Critical Thinking Appraisal* (Watson and Glaser 1980) requires that respondents reason regarding the proposition: Groups in this country who are opposed to some of our government's policies should be permitted unrestricted freedom of press and speech. Obviously, this is an issue on which prior opinion might be strong. However, to do well on a test such as this, one has to set aside prior opinion because one must evaluate whether arguments relevant to the proposition are strong or weak. When such tests are well designed, strong and weak arguments are presented supporting both the "pro" side of the proposition and the "anti" side of the proposition. Regardless of prior opinion, on some items the respondent is presented with a conflict between prior opinion and argument strength. Thus, the respondent must regulate how much to weigh the structure of the argument versus the prior belief. The test directly taps intentional-level epistemic regulation.

In using items with such content, critical thinking tests such as the Watson-Glaser create (even if the instructions attempt to disambiguate) ambiguity about what feature of the problem to rely on – ambiguity that is resolved differently by individuals with different epistemic dispositions. The point is that on an intelligence test, there would be no epistemic ambiguity created in the first place. Such tests attempt to constrain intentional-level functioning in order to isolate processing abilities at the algorithmic level of analysis. It is the efficiency of computational abilities under optimal (not typical) conditions that is the focus of IQ tests. Variation in intentional-level thinking dispositions would contaminate this algorithmic-level assessment.[2] Thus, you will not find an item like the "rose" syllogism on an intelligence test

(or any aptitude measure or cognitive capacity measure). If syllogistic reasoning abilities are to be assessed, the content of the syllogism will be stripped (all As are Bs, etc.) or unfamiliar content will be used, such as this example with the same form as the "rose" syllogism:

Premise 1: All animals of the hudon class are ferocious

Premise 2: Wampets are ferocious

Therefore, Wampets are animals of the hudon class

Items like this strip away the belief bias component and thus eliminate the intentional-level conflict between epistemic tendencies to preserve logical validity and the tendency to project prior knowledge. They constrain the intentional level and thus are candidates for the measurement of algorithmic-level computational capacities.

The Key Algorithmic-Level Operation Behind Psychometric g

Although tests of intelligence leave out critical intentional-level factors, they do in fact assess a mental capacity that is of considerable importance for rational thought. For decades psychologists have searched for the common mental operation(s) underlying the positive correlations (psychometric g) among algorithmic-level cognitive measures (Deary 2000; Sternberg and Grigorenko 2002). Only recently has there been some convergence on what this factor is and why it is important for human functioning. That extremely important mental operation is the decoupling of cognitive representations. My conception of cognitive decoupling relies on a synthesis of two literatures in cognitive science – the literature on the evolution and development of mental representations and the literature on individual differences in cognitive control and executive function.

Cognitive decoupling supports one of our most important mental functions: hypothetical thinking. Hypothetical reasoning involves representing possible states of the world rather than actual states of affairs and it is involved in myriad reasoning tasks, from deductive reasoning, to decision making, to scientific thinking (Carruthers, Stich, and Siegal 2002; Currie and Ravenscroft 2002; Evans and Over 1999, 2004; Nichols and Stich 2003; Sterelny 2001). For example, deductive reasoning involves hypotheticality when the premises are not things the individual knows but instead assumptions about the world; utilitarian or consequentialist decision making involves representing possible future states of the world (necessarily not actual states) so that optimal actions can be chosen; and alternative hypotheses in scientific thinking are imagined causes from which consequences can be deduced for testing.

In order to reason hypothetically, a person must be able to represent a belief as separate from the world it is representing. It is decoupling ability that allows us to mark a belief as a hypothetical state of the world rather than a real one, an ability that has been stressed by numerous cognitive theorists (e.g., Carruthers 2002; Cosmides and Tooby 2000; Dienes and Perner 1999; Evans and Over 2004; Geary 2005; Glenberg 1997; Jackendoff 1996; Leslie 1987; Lillard 2001; Nichols and Stich 2003; Perner 1991; Povinelli and Giambrone 2001; Stanovich 2004). Decoupling skills prevent our representations of the real world from becoming confused with representations of imaginary situations that we create on a temporary basis in order predict the effects of future actions or think about causal models of the world that are different from those we currently hold. Dienes and Perner (1999) emphasize the importance of the mental separation between facts in one's knowledge base from one's attitude toward those facts for cognitive control. For example, when considering an alternative goal state different from the current goal state, one needs to be able to represent both and not confuse which is which. This is an exercise in cognitive control, and thus it is not surprising that decoupling skill has been linked to issues of executive functioning (Dempster and Corkill 1999; Duncan, Emslie, Williams, Johnson, and Freer 1996; Handley, Capon, Beveridge, Dennis, and Evans 2004; Harnishfeger and Bjorklund 1994; Markovits and Doyon 2004; Moutier, Angeard, and Houde 2002; Muller, Zelazo, Hood, Leone, and Rohrer 2004; Norman and Shallice 1986; Simoneau and Markovits 2003; Zelazo 2004).

Language provides the discrete representational medium that greatly enables decoupling and thus allows hypotheticality to flourish as a culturally acquired mode of thought (Evans and Over 2004; Jackendoff 1996; Povinelli and Bering 2002; Povinelli and Giambrone 2001; Tomasello 1999). For example, hypothetical thought involves representing assumptions, and linguistic forms such as conditionals provide a medium for such representations. Increases in representational complexity, and the con-

comitant increase in decoupling potential, are greatly fostered by the acquisition of language. Tacit learning can take place without decoupling, but explicit learning is dependent on it. This is why intelligence is such a good correlate of explicit learning but not tacit learning (Reber, Walkenfeld, and Hernstadt 1991; Sternberg 2003; Wagner 2002; Wagner and Sternberg 1985).

Decoupling skills vary in their recursiveness and complexity. The skills discussed thus far are those that are necessary for creating what Perner (1991) calls secondary representations – the decoupled representations that are the multiple models of the world that enable hypothetical thought. At a certain level of development, decoupling becomes used for so-called meta-representation – thinking about thinking itself (there are many subtleties surrounding the concept of meta-representation; see Dennett 1984; Nichols and Stich 2003; Perner 1991; Sperber 2000; Sterelny 2003; Suddendorf and Whiten 2001; Whiten 2001). Meta-representation – the representation of one's own representations – is what enables the self-critical stances that are a unique aspect of human cognition (Dennett 1984, 1996; Frankfurt 1971; Stanovich 2004; Tomasello 1999). We form beliefs about how well we are forming beliefs, just as we have desires about our desires, and possess the ability to desire to desire differently. Decoupling processes enable one to distance oneself from one's own tendencies to represent the world so that they can be reflected on and potentially improved.

The ability to distance ourselves from thoughts and try them out internally as models of the world makes human beings the supreme hypothesis testers in the animal kingdom and variation in this ability is a contributor to individual differences in assessed intelligence. This is because decoupling – outside of certain domains such as behavioral prediction (so-called theory of mind) – is a cognitively demanding operation. It now appears that perhaps the key operation underlying intelligence is the ability to maintain decoupling among representations while carrying out mental simulation.[3] This is becoming clear from converging work on executive function (Baddeley 1992; Baddeley, Chincotta, and Adlam 2001; Duncan et al. 2000; Fuster 1990; Gernsbacher and Faust 1991; Goldman-Rakic 1992; Gray, Chabris, and Braver 2003; Hasher, Zacks, and May 1999; Kane 2003; Kane and Engle 2002; Salthouse, Atkinson, and Berish 2003) and working memory (Colom,

Rebollo, Palacios, Juan-Espinosa, and Kyllonen 2004; Conway, Cowan, Bunting, Therriault, and Minkoff 2002; Conway, Kane, and Engle 2003; Engle 2002; Engle, Tuholski, Laughlin, and Conway 1999; Kane, Bleckley, Conway, and Engle 2001; Kane and Engle 2003; Kane, Hambrick, Tuholski, Wilhelm, Payne, and Engle 2004; Sub et al. 2002). First, there is a startling degree of overlap in individual differences on working memory tasks and individual differences in measures of fluid intelligence. Second, it is becoming clear that working memory tasks are only incidentally about memory. Or, as Engle (2002) puts it, "WM capacity is just as important in retention of a single representation, such as the representation of a goal or of the status of a changing variable, as it is in determining how many representations can be maintained. WM capacity is not directly about memory – it is about using attention to maintain or suppress information. WM capacity is about memory only indirectly. Greater WM capacity does mean that more items can be maintained as active, but this is a result of greater ability to control attention, not a larger memory store" (p. 20).

Engle (2002) goes on to review evidence indicating that working memory tasks really tap the preservation of internal representations in the presence of distraction or, as I have termed it – the ability to decouple a secondary representation (or meta-representation) from a primary representation and manipulate the former. For example, he describes an experiment using the so-called antisaccade task. Subjects must look at the middle of a computer screen and respond to a target stimulus that will appear on the left or right of the screen. Before the target appears, a cue is flashed on the opposite side of the screen. Subjects must resist the attention-capturing cue and respond to the target on the opposite side when it appears. Subjects scoring low on working memory tasks were more likely to make an eye movement (saccade) in the direction of the distracting cue than were subjects who scored high on working memory task.

That the antisaccade task has very little to do with memory is an indication of why investigators have reconceptualized the individual difference variables that working memory tasks are tapping. Individual differences on such tasks are now described with a variety of different terms (attentional control, resistance to distraction, executive control), but the critical operation needed to succeed in them – and the reason they are the prime indicator of fluid intelligence – is that they reflect the ability to sustain decoupled representations. Such decoupling is an important aspect of behavioral control that is related to rationality, as will be discussed below.

Why Intelligence Correlates with Reasoning Tasks

Given the previous discussion, it is no surprise that intelligence should correlate with performance on a variety of constrained reasoning tasks (that is, tasks that constrain the operation of the intentional level of processing). Virtually all of the higher-level constrained reasoning tasks in the literature require the respondent to construct hypothetical models of situations and mentally manipulate these models; in short, to run mental simulations while maintaining decoupled representations. That this critical mental operation underlies psychometric g explains why general intelligence (or intelligence proxies, such as working memory measures, see Colom et al. 2004) correlates robustly with a variety of reasoning tasks such as deductive reasoning, performance on analogies tasks, syllogistic reasoning, matrix completion, and spatial reasoning (see Bara, Bucciarelli, and Johnson-Laird 1995; Copeland and Radvansky 2004; Gilhooly 2004; Hambrich and Engle 2003; Handley et al. 2004; Lohman 2000; Rips 1994; Rips and Conrad 1983; Stanovich and West 1998c; Sternberg 1977; Verschueren, Schaeken, and D'Ydewalle 2005).

A more difficult theoretical challenge is presented by data on unconstrained reasoning tasks. Here there is more to explain, because it has been found that intelligence sometimes correlates with unconstrained reasoning tasks and sometimes it does not. My theoretical explanation for these on-again, off-again correlations makes use of a dual-process theory of cognition, of which there are many in the literature (I listed twenty-two such theories in a recent book, and that was not an exhaustive list; for reviews, see Evans 2003; Feldman Barrett, Tugade, and Engle 2004; Kahneman and Frederick 2002, 2005; Osman 2004; S. Sloman 2002; Stanovich 1999, 2004). Briefly, these models distinguish between autonomous processing and nonautonomous processing.

There are many different autonomous systems in the brain, and to signal this plurality I have suggested the acronym TASS (for The Autonomous Set of Systems, see Stanovich 2004). These processes are termed autonomous because: (1) their execution is rapid, (2) their execution is mandatory when the triggering stimuli are encountered, (3) they do not put a heavy load on central processing capacity, (4) they are not dependent on input from high-level control systems, and (5) they can operate in parallel. Included in TASS are processes of implicit learning, overlearned associations practiced to automaticity, processes of behavioral regulation by the emotions, and the encapsulated modules for solving specific adaptive problems that have been posited by the evolutionary psychologists (on the types of processes in TASS, see Atran 1998; Carruthers 2002; Cosmides and Tooby 1992; Evans 2003; Mithen 1996; Pinker 1997; Sperber 1994; Stanovich 2004).

The nonautonomous system(s) – sometimes going under the name of analytic processing – have the contrasting set of properties. Analytic cognitive processes are serial (as opposed to parallel), rule-based, often language-based, and computationally expensive. The analytic system is the one responsible for the decoupled cognitive simulation abilities discussed previously.[4] It can create temporary models of the world – for example, by retrieving goals and beliefs from long-term memory as well as stored procedures for operating on the goals and beliefs and testing the outcomes of imaginary actions (see Currie and Ravenscroft 2002; Nichols and Stich 2003; Perner 1991).

An important function of the decoupling system is that it can override responses primed by an autonomous system by taking early representations triggered by TASS offline and substituting better responses that have survived the cognitive selection process of simulation (McClure, Laibson, Loewenstein, and Cohen 2004; Nichols and Stich 2003). It is the necessity of the operation of this override function that determines whether an unconstrained rational thinking task will show correlations with general intelligence. For example, many unconstrained thinking tasks are tasks in which the optimal responses determined by TASS and by the analytic system are designed to be different (assuming, in the latter case, that the analytic system is actually engaged to run a simulation). I have argued (Stanovich 1999; Stanovich and West 2000) that is just such situations that will generate significant correlations between intelligence and task performance.[5] This correlation might arise for two reasons. First, some subjects are more likely to operate entirely with TASS systems and these are more likely to be the low IQ subjects. Second, even within the sample of subjects experiencing response conflict,[6] it is assumed that the subjects of higher intelligence will be more likely

to resolve the conflict in favor of the response generated by the analytic system.

Many tasks in the heuristics and biases literature are of the type that create such significant correlations, because many were specifically constructed[7] so as to pit a TASS subsystem against the analytic system (Kahneman and Frederick 2002, 2005; Kahneman and Tversky 1996). A classic example is presented in a problem that is famous in the literature of cognitive psychology, the so-called Linda problem (Tversky and Kahneman 1983):

> Linda is 31 years old, single, outspoken, and very bright. She majored in philosophy. As a student, she was deeply concerned with issues of discrimination and social justice, and also participated in anti-nuclear demonstrations. Please rank the following statements by their probability, using 1 for the most probable and 8 for the least probable.
> a. Linda is a teacher in an elementary school ___
> b. Linda works in a bookstore and takes Yoga classes ___
> c. Linda is active in the feminist movement ___
> d. Linda is a psychiatric social worker ___
> e. Linda is a member of the League of Women Voters ___
> f. Linda is a bank teller ___
> g. Linda is an insurance salesperson ___
> h. Linda is a bank teller and is active in the feminist movement ___

Because alternative h is the conjunction of alternatives c and f, the probability of h cannot be higher than that of either c or f. Yet 85 percent of the participants in Tversky and Kahneman's (1983) study (and in dozens of replications) rated alternative h as more probable than f, thus displaying what is termed a conjunction fallacy. Tversky and Kahneman (1983) argued that logical reasoning (analytic system processing) on the problem is overwhelmed by a TASS heuristic based on so-called representativeness.[8] Representativeness primes answers to problems based on an assessment of similarity (a feminist bank teller seems to overlap more with the description of Linda than does the alternative "bank teller"). Of course, logic dictates that the subset (feminist bank teller), superset (bank teller) relationship should trump assessments of representativeness when judgments of probability are at issue.

S. Sloman (1996) views the Linda Problem as the quintessence of dual-process conflict. He quotes Stephen Gould's introspection that

"I know the [conjunction] is least probable, yet a little homunculus in my head continues to jump up and down, shouting at me – 'but she can't be a bank teller; read the description'" (Gould 1991: 469). According to Sloman (1996), the associative system responds to the similarity in the conjunction; whereas the rule-based system engages probabilistic concepts which dictate that bank teller is more probable. Thus, in the Linda problem, we have a case of a TASS response tendency (a similarity-based judgment of representativeness) being pitted against an analytic system response tendency (the logic of subset/superset relations). As Kahneman and Tversky (1996) note, "the within-subjects design addresses the question of how the conflict between the heuristic and the rule is resolved" (p. 587).

That 85 percent of respondents answer the Linda conjunction problem incorrectly indicates that, for most people, analytic processes are not very firmly in control of their judgments. Nevertheless, because a TASS-override is necessary for normative responding, it might be expected that making the normative response would be associated with more algorithmic computational capacity, and this is indeed the case. In one study (Stanovich and West 1998b), we examined the performance of 150 subjects on the Linda Problem. Consistent with the results of previous experiments on this problem (Tversky and Kahneman 1983), 80.7 percent of our sample displayed the conjunction fallacy – they rated the feminist bank teller alternative as more probable than the bank teller alternative. However, the mean SAT score of the 121 subjects who committed the conjunction fallacy was 82 points *lower* than the mean score of the 29 who avoided the fallacy. This difference was highly significant and it translated into an effect size of .746 (which Rosenthal and Rosnow, 1991, classify as large).[9]

Similar results obtain with other tasks from the heuristics and bias literature that pit TASS-processes against analytic reasoning. For example, consider the experiments conducted by Seymour Epstein and colleagues (Denes-Raj and Epstein 1994; Kirkpatrick and Epstein 1992; Pacini and Epstein 1999a, 1999b). Participants in these experiments were presented with two bowls of jelly beans. In the first were nine white jelly beans and one red jelly bean. In the second were ninety-two white jelly beans and eight red. A random draw was to be made from one of the two bowls and if the red jelly bean was picked, the participant would receive a dollar.

The participant could choose which bowl to draw from. Although the two bowls clearly represent a 10 percent and an 8 percent chance of winning a dollar, many participants chose the one-hundred bean jar, thus reducing their chance of winning.[10] Although most were aware that the large bowl was statistically a worse bet, that bowl also contained more enticing winning beans – the eight red ones. Many could not resist trying the bowl with more winners despite some knowledge of its poorer probability. That many participants were aware of the poorer probability but could, nonetheless, not resist picking the large bowl is indicated by comments from some of them such as the following: "I picked the ones with more red jelly beans because it looked like there were more ways to get a winner, even though I knew there were also more whites, and that the percents were against me" (Denes-Raj and Epstein 1994: 823). In short, the simpler TASS tendency to respond to the absolute number of winners trumps the more analytic process of calculating a ratio for a surprising number of participants. Nevertheless, parallel to our findings with the Linda conjunction task, my research group (e.g., Kokis, Macpherson, Toplak, West, and Stanovich 2002) has found that making the normative higher percentage response in the Epstein task is positively correlated with cognitive ability.

There are many more examples from the heuristics and biases literature that display the same pattern (see Stanovich and West 2000; West and Stanovich 2003). For example, the avoidance of the belief bias effect in syllogistic reasoning discussed previously is correlated with cognitive ability (Evans and Perry 1995; Handley et al. 2004; Markovits and Doyon 2004; Newstead, Handley, Harley, Wright, and Farrelly 2004; Sá et al. 1999) as is normatively correct responding on the Wason four-card selection task (DeShon, Smith, Chan, and Schmitt 1998; Stanovich and West, 1998a; Valentine 1975; but see Newstead et al. 2004). These situations are cognitively quite varied, and it is more likely than not that they are not of the same cognitive or neurophysiological class. Their only commonality may be the status of these tasks as presenting situations where a TASS response, if not overcome, will lead to an nonoptimal outcome.

For all categories of suboptimal TASS priming, successful override is achieved only through the coordinated operation of intentional-level functioning (recognizing the need for override of TASS processes) and algorithmic-level functioning (carrying out the cognitive decoupling operations necessary to cancel the TASS-primed response). Because measures of intelligence or cognitive ability tap primarily individual differences in the latter, conceptually, there is room for individual differences in intentional-level thinking dispositions to predict differences in unconstrained reasoning tasks.[11] In the remainder of this chapter, I will illustrate how evidence supports the existence of such an association, and I will explore the philosophical implications of the existence of variance on unconstrained reasoning tasks that can be predicted by measures other than intelligence.

Thinking Dispositions as Predictors of Performance on Unconstrained Reasoning Tasks

In light of the emphasis in the critical thinking literature on the importance of evaluating arguments independently of prior belief (e.g., Nickerson 1998; Paul 1984, 1987; Perkins 1995), it is noteworthy that there are increasing indications in the research literature that individual differences in this skill can be predicted by thinking dispositions even after differences in general cognitive ability have been partialled out. For example, Schommer (1990) found that a measure of the disposition to believe in certain knowledge predicted the tendency to draw one-sided conclusions from ambiguous evidence even after verbal ability was controlled. Kardash and Scholes (1996) found that the tendency to properly draw inconclusive inferences from mixed evidence was related to belief in certain knowledge and to a measure of need for cognition (Cacioppo et al. 1996). Furthermore, these relationships were not mediated by verbal ability because a vocabulary measure was essentially unrelated to evidence evaluation. Likewise, Klaczynski (1997; see also Klaczynski and Gordon 1996; Klaczynski et al. 1997; Klaczynski and Lavallee 2005; Klaczynski and Robinson 2000) found that the degree to which participants criticized belief-inconsistent evidence more than belief-consistent evidence was unrelated to cognitive ability.

Results from my own laboratory have converged with those of Schommer (1990) and Kardash and Scholes (1996) in indicating that thinking dispositions can predict argument evaluation skill once cognitive ability is partialled out. We have developed an argument evaluation task in which we derive an index of the degree to which argument evaluation is associated with argument quality independent of prior

belief (see Stanovich and West 1997, 1998c; Sá et al. 1999). We have consistently found that, even after controlling for cognitive ability, individual differences on our index of argument-driven processing can be predicted by measures of dogmatism and absolutism (Rokeach 1960), categorical thinking (Epstein and Meier 1989), openness (Costa and McCrae 1992), flexible thinking (Stanovich and West 1997), belief identification (Sá et al. 1999), counterfactual thinking, superstitious thinking (Stanovich 1989; Tobacyk and Milford 1983), and actively open-minded thinking (Sá, Kelley, Ho, and Stanovich 2005; Stanovich and West 1997).

These findings support a conceptualization of human cognition that emphasizes the potential separability of cognitive capacities and thinking styles/dispositions as predictors of reasoning skill. Such a separation in psychological constructs makes sense if indeed they do map on to different levels of analysis in cognitive theory. I proposed earlier that variation in cognitive ability indexes individual differences in the efficiency of processing at the algorithmic level. In contrast, thinking dispositions index individual differences at the intentional level. They are telling us about the individual's goals and epistemic values. For example, consider an individual who scores high on our measures of actively open-minded thinking and low on measures of dogmatism and absolutism – a person who agrees with statements such as "People should always take into consideration evidence that goes against their beliefs" and who disagrees with statements such as "No one can talk me out of something I know is right." Such a response pattern is indicating that this person values belief change in order to get closer to the truth. This individual is signaling that they value being an accurate *belief forming system* more than they value holding on to the beliefs they currently have (see Cederblom 1989 for an insightful discussion of this distinction and our scale based on this notion in Sá et al. 1999).

In contrast, consider a person scoring low on actively open-minded thinking measures and high on measures of absolutism and categorical thinking – a person who disagrees with statements such as "A person should always consider new possibilities" and who agrees with statements such as "There are a number of people I have come to hate because of the things they stand for." Such a response pattern is indicating that retaining current beliefs is an important goal for this person. This individual is signaling that they value highly the beliefs they currently have and that they put a very small premium on mechanisms that might improve belief accuracy (but that involve belief change). In short, thinking dispositions of this type provide information about epistemic goals at the intentional level of analysis. Within such a conceptualization, we can perhaps better understand why such thinking dispositions predict additional variance in argument evaluation even after cognitive ability is partialled out. This result may be indicating that to understand variation in reasoning in such a task we need to examine more than just differences at the algorithmic level (computational capacity) – we must know something about the epistemic goals of the reasoners.

Thus, performance on tasks requiring reasoning about previously held beliefs, while certainly somewhat dependent on the cognitive capacity of the subject, also depends on the balance of epistemic goals held by the reasoners. The instructions for many tasks which require reasoning in the face of belief bias (e.g., Baron 1995; Evans, Newstead, Allen, and Pollard 1994; Handley et al. 2004; Oakhill, Johnson-Laird, and Garnham 1989; Stanovich and West 1997) dictate that prior belief be totally discounted in evaluating the argument. But individuals may differ in their willingness as well as their ability to adapt to such instructions. Some individuals may put a low priority on allocating computational capacity to evaluate the argument. Instead, for them, capacity is engaged to assess whether the conclusion is compatible with prior beliefs (Evans, Barston, and Pollard 1983; Evans et al. 1994). Other individuals – of equal cognitive ability – may marshal their cognitive resources to decouple argument evaluation from their prior beliefs as the instructions demand. These individuals may easily engage in such a processing strategy because it does not conflict with their epistemic goals. Tasks unconstrained at the intentional level are the type of tasks able to detect such individual differences. Tasks constrained at the intentional level, such as IQ tests, are largely unable to detect these differences.

Thus, to fully understand variation in evidence evaluation performance, we need to consider variation at the intentional level as well as at the algorithmic level of cognitive analysis. Indeed, this seems to be true for other tasks in the heuristics and biases literature as well. For example, we have linked various measures of thinking dispositions to statistical reasoning tasks of various types (Kokis et al. 2002; Stanovich 1999; Stanovich and West 1998c, 1999, 2000). One such task derives from the work of Nisbett and Ross (1980), who studied the tendency of human judgment to be overly influenced by vivid but unrepresentative personal and testimonial evidence and to be underinfluenced by more representative and diagnostic statistical evidence. Studying the variation in this response tendency is important because Griffin and Tversky (1992) argue that "the tendency to prefer an individual or 'inside' view rather than a statistical or 'outside' view represents one of the major departures of intuitive judgment from normative theory" (pp. 431–432). The quintessential problem (see Fong, Krantz, and Nisbett 1986) involves choosing between contradictory car purchase recommendations – one from a large-sample survey of car buyers and the other the heartfelt and emotional testimony of a single friend. Fong et al. (1986) and Jepson, Krantz, and Nisbett (1983) have studied a variety of such problems and we have examined a number of them in our own research. We have consistently found that, even though these problems are presented to participants as having no right or wrong answers, dispositions toward actively open-minded thinking are consistently associated with reliance on the statistical evidence rather than the testimonial evidence. Furthermore, this association remains even after cognitive ability has been controlled.

We have examined a variety of other critical and rational thinking tasks and have consistently found the same pattern. For example, we have examined the phenomenon of outcome bias in decision evaluation (Baron and Hershey 1988) – the tendency to rate decision quality according to the outcome of the decision even when the outcome provides no cues to the information available to the decision maker. We again found that the ability to avoid outcome bias was associated with dispositions toward actively open-minded thinking and that this tendency was not due solely to differences in cognitive ability. Similar results were found for a variety of other hypothesis testing and reasoning tasks (Kokis et al. 2002; Stanovich 1999, 2004; Stanovich and West 1998c, 2000; Toplak and Stanovich 2002). I have argued elsewhere that the thinking dispositions that serve as good independent predictors in these studies tend to be those that reflect a tendency toward cognition decontextualization – the tendency to strip unnecessary context from problems (Stanovich 2003, 2004). Such dispositions serve to counter one aspect of what I have termed the fundamental computational bias of human cognition. That aspect is the tendency to contextualize a problem with as much prior knowledge as is easily accessible. This fundamental computational bias was useful in our evolutionary history, but modern bureaucratic societies often require that this bias be overridden. Many tasks in the heuristics and biases literature tap the ease with which we recognize this necessity.

In summary, throughout several of our studies, normative responding on a variety of problems from the heuristics and biases literature was moderately correlated with cognitive ability. Nevertheless, the magnitude of the associations with cognitive ability left considerable room for the possibility that the remaining reliable variance might indicate that there are systematic variation in intentional-level psychology. It was rarely the case that once capacity limitations had been controlled, the remaining variations from normative responding were unpredictable (which would have indicated that the residual variance consisted largely of random error). In several studies, we have shown that there was significant covariance among the scores from a variety of tasks in the heuristics and biases literature after they had been residualized on measures of cognitive ability (Stanovich 1999; see also Parker and Fischhoff 2005). And, as I have just reviewed, the residual variance (after partialling cognitive ability) also was systematically associated with questionnaire responses that were conceptualized as intentional-level styles relating to epistemic regulation. Both of these findings are indications that the residual variance is systematic.

Why Intentional-Level Individual Differences Are Controversial

In this chapter, it has been proposed that thinking dispositions should be distinguished from cognitive capacities because the two constructs are at different levels of analysis in cognitive theory and do separate explanatory work. This distinction motivates interest in a consistent empirical finding in the literature reviewed in the last section: that thinking dispositions can predict performance on reasoning and rational thinking tasks even after individual differences in measures of general cognitive ability have been partialled out. Finding systematic variance in intentional-level functioning that is not explained by computational capacity has implications for what has been termed the great rationality debate in cognitive science – a debate that has generated an enormous literature and a high degree of contention (e.g., Adler 1991, 1998;

Cohen 1981; Evans and Over 1996; Gigerenzer 1996; Johnson-Laird 1999; Kahneman and Frederick 2005; Kahneman and Tversky 1996, 2000; Kuhberger 2002; Lopes 1991; Manktelow 2004; Margolis 1987; Over 2002; Samuels and Stich 2004; Samuels, Stich, and Bishop 2002; Shafir and LeBoeuf 2002, 2005; Stanovich 1999, 2004; Stein 1996; Tetlock and Mellers 2002).

This debate has pitted the heuristics and bias researchers and their claims of empirically demonstrated irrational behavior against a host of so-called Panglossian positions that argue against the possibility of actual (as opposed to apparent) variation in the optimality of intentional-level functioning (for extensive discussions of these various positions, see Samuels and Stich 2004; Stanovich 1999, 2004; Stein 1996). None of these Panglossian positions has difficulty with the finding of zero-order correlations between performance on heuristics and biases tasks and intelligence as long as intelligence is viewed as a proxy for algorithmic-level computational capacity. This is because theorists on all sides of the rationality debate take seriously the stricture that to characterize a suboptimal behavior as irrational, it must be the case that the normative model is computable in the cognitive mechanism under study (Cherniak 1986; Stich 1990). The intelligence correlations might simply be reflecting the fact that variability in performance on tasks from the heuristics and bias literature may be just a combination of varying computational limitations and random error. Such a view is undermined, however, by findings indicating that there is systematic variability in responding over and above that accounted for by intelligence. That there is systematic variability remaining necessarily means that at least some individuals are characterized by intentional-level functioning that is less than optimal.

The systematic variance in intentional-level function isolated in the experiments reviewed here has perhaps not received sufficient attention because of the heavy reliance on the competence/performance distinction in philosophical treatments of rational thought. In such views, all of the important psychological mechanisms are allocated to the competence side of the dichotomy. For example, Rescher (1988) argues that "to construe the data of these interesting experimental studies [of probabilistic reasoning] to mean that people are systematically programmed to fallacious processes of reasoning – rather than merely that they are inclined to a variety of (occasionally questionable) substantive suppositions – is a very questionable step. . . . While all (normal) people are to be credited with the capacity to reason, they frequently do not exercise it well" (p. 196). There are two parts to Rescher's (1988) point here: the "systematically programmed" part and the "inclination toward questionable suppositions" part. As Rips (1994) notes, such views frame the rationality debate in terms of "whether incorrect reasoning is a 'systematically programmed' part of thinking [or] just a peccadillo" (p. 394).

Rescher's (1988) focus is on the issue of how humans are "systematically programmed." It seems that "inclinations toward questionable suppositions" are only of interest to those in these philosophical debates as mechanisms that allow one to drive a wedge between competence and performance – thus maintaining a theory of near-optimal human rational competence in the face of a host of responses that seemingly defy explanation in terms of standard normative models. For example, like Rescher, Cohen (1982) argues that there really are only two factors affecting performance on rational thinking tasks: "normatively correct mechanisms on the one side, and adventitious causes of error on the other" (p. 252). Not surprisingly given such a conceptualization, the processes contributing to error ("adventitious causes") are of little interest to Cohen (1981, 1982). On this view, human performance arises from an intrinsic human competence that is impeccably rational, but responses occasionally deviate from normative correctness due to inattention, memory lapses, lack of motivation, and other fluctuating but basically unimportant causes (e.g., "performance" errors). There is nothing in such a view that would motivate any interest in patterns of errors or individual differences in such errors because it is strongly implied that the errors are random. It is just this assumption that is challenged by the research reviewed in this chapter. Beyond variation in computational capacity, there is systematic variance in human intentional psychology – in high-level control states that are related to epistemic and practical rationality.

One of the purposes of the present chapter is to reverse the figure and ground in the rationality debate, which has tended to be dominated by the particular way that philosophers frame the competence/performance distinction. From a psychological standpoint, there may be important implications in precisely the aspects of performance that have been backgrounded in this controversy ("adventitious causes," "peccadillos"). That is, whatever the outcome of the disputes about how humans are "systematically programmed," variation in the "inclination toward questionable suppositions" is of psychological interest as a topic of study in its own right (see Margolis 1987). The experiments discussed in this chapter provide at least tentative indications that the "inclination toward questionable suppositions" has some degree of domain generality and that it is predicted by thinking dispositions that concern the epistemic and pragmatic goals of the individual and that are part of people's intentional-level psychology.

Consider that the search for counterexamples or alternative theories is the key to normative thinking in domains as varied as decision making, logical reasoning, practical reasoning, and scientific thinking (Carruthers, Stich, and Siegal 2002; Evans 2005; Evans and Over 1999, 2004; Johnson-Laird 1999, 2005; Kahneman and Miller 1986; Rips 1994; Roese 1997; Tor and Bazerman 2003). Many models of thinking in these domains have not historically been focused on individual differences and thus have not emphasized the fact that there may be systematic control features that determine the extent of the search for alternatives and counterexamples – and that there may be predictable variance in these higher-level control functions. I would argue that the work reviewed above on epistemically related cognitive dispositions may in fact be reflecting just such higher-level control features. Individual differences in the extensiveness of the search for alternative models could arise from a variety of cognitive factors that may be far from "adventitious" – factors such as dispositions toward premature closure, cognitive confidence, reflectivity, dispositions toward confirmation bias, ideational generativity, and so on.

I argued previously that this panoply of thinking dispositions is particularly related to the cognitive decontextualization that commonly results when TASS processes are overridden by the analytic system. The decontextualized nature of many normative responses is a feature that is actually emphasized by many *critics* of the heuristics and biases literature who, nevertheless, fail to see it as implying a research program for differential psychology. For example, if to contextualize a problem is the natural and nearly universal reasoning style of human beings (what I have called the fundamental computational bias, see Stanovich 2003, 2004), then it is not surprising that many people respond incorrectly when attempting a psychological task that is explicitly designed to require a decontextualized reasoning style (contrary-to-fact syllogisms, argument evaluation, etc.). But the fact that some people *do* give the decontextualized response means that at least some people have available a larger repertoire of reasoning styles (they can flexibly reason so as to override the fundamental computational bias if the situation requires).

For example, Rescher (1988) defends responses that exhibit the gambler's fallacy on the grounds that people assume a model of saturation that is valid in other domains (e.g., food ingestion, sleep) and that "the issue may well be one of a mistaken factual supposition rather than one of fallacious reasoning" (pp. 195–196) and he stresses the enthymematic character of much human reasoning. But, again, the fact remains that many people do *not* reason enthymematically in this or other reasoning problems and instead give the normative response. This implies that at least some people have available a larger repertoire of reasoning styles (they can flexibly reason enthymematically and nonenthymematically as the task requires). Or, at the very least, it means that certain people are more easily shifted out of their natural enthymematic reasoning style. Research reviewed here would support the conclusion that having such thinking tendencies can improve performance on many reasoning and decision making tasks regardless of the level of a person's algorithmic-level capacity (intelligence). This is one important implication of the fact that intentional-level cognitive constructs are independent predictors of reasoning skill.

Notes

1   My use of the algorithmic/intentional distinction here parallels somewhat the way that Bermudez (2001) has characterized the difference between neuropsychological disorders and psychiatric disorders. Most neuropsychological disorders (unilateral neglect, agnosias, etc.) involve impairment restricted to algorithmic-level functioning (most often in a modular component of the autonomous set of systems, see discussion later). Bermudez (2001) notes that they are traditionally explained by recourse to subpersonal functions. Psychiatric disorders (particularly those such as delusions), in contrast, implicate intentional-level functioning. Bermudez (2001) argues that the "impairments in which they manifest themselves are of the sort that would standardly be explained at the personal level, rather than at the subpersonal level. In the terms of Fodor's dichotomy, psychiatric disorders seem to be disorders of central process-

ing rather than peripheral modules. . . . Many of the symptoms of psychiatric disorders involve impairments of rationality – and consequently that the norms of rationality must be taken to play a vital role in the understanding of psychiatric disorders" (pp. 460, 461).

2   I do not wish to argue that intelligence tests are entirely successful in this respect – that they entirely eliminate intentional-level factors; only that the constructors of the tests *attempt* to do so. Additionally, it is certainly the case that some higher-level strategic control is exercised on intelligence test items, but this tends to be a type of micro-level control rather than the activation of macro-strategies that are engaged by critical thinking tests. For example, on multiple-choice IQ-test items, the respondent is certainly engaging in a variety of control processes such as suppressing responses to identified distractor items. Nonetheless, if the test is properly designed, they are not engaging in the type of macro-level strategizing that is common on critical thinking tests – for example, deciding how to construe the task or how to allocate effort across differing construals.

3   More technically, it is probably a key correlate of fluid intelligence and not crystallized intelligence. The term fluid intelligence refers to one of the major two factors underlying intelligence in the so-called Cattell/Horn/Carroll theory of intelligence – as close as there is to a consensus view in the field of intelligence research (Carroll 1993; Cattell 1963, 1998; Daniel 2000; Geary 2005; Horn and Cattell 1967; Horn and Noll 1997; McGrew 1997; McGrew and Woodcock 2001; Taub and McGrew 2004). Sometimes called the theory of fluid and crystallized intelligence (symbolized Gf-Gc theory), this theory posits that tests of mental ability tap a small number of broad factors, of which two are dominant. Fluid intelligence (Gf) reflects reasoning abilities operating across of variety of domains – including novel ones. It is measured by tasks such as figural analogies, Raven Matrices, and series completion. Crystallized intelligence (Gc) reflects declarative knowledge acquired from acculturated learning experiences. It is measured by vocabulary tasks, verbal comprehension, and general knowledge measures. Ackerman (1996) discusses how the two dominant factors in the Cattell/Horn/Carroll theory reflect a long history of considering two aspects of intelligence: intelligence-as-process (Gf) and intelligence-as-knowledge (Gc).

4   My view of individual differences in this type of cognitive decoupling as the key operation assessed by measures of intelligence was anticipated by Thurstone (1927), who also stressed that decoupling is related to inhibition of automatic responses: "Intelligence is therefore the capacity of abstraction, which is an inhibitory

process. In the intelligent moment the impulse is inhibited while it is still only partially specified, while it is still only loosely organized.... The trial-and-error choice and elimination, in intelligent conduct, is carried out with alternatives that are so incomplete and so loosely organized that they point only toward types of behaviour without specifying the behaviour in detail" (p. 159).

5   This is because intelligence indexes differences in analytic system processing but not the algorithmic-level processes in TASS – primarily because individual differences in the latter are severely restricted (Anderson 1992, 1998; Baron-Cohen 1995; Reber 1992, 1993; Reber, Walkenfeld, and Hernstadt 1991; Saffran, Aslin, and Newport 1996; Vinter and Detable 2003; Vinter and Perruchet 2000; Zacks, Hasher, and Sanft 1982).

6   The conflict need not always be conscious, although dual-process conflict will be especially strong when it is (see S. Sloman 1996).

7   Note that in the vast majority of cases, the response primed by TASS will coincide with that determined by the analytic system – that is, in most cases, TASS does in fact prime the rational response. The minority of instances in which it does not may be situations of some import, however (see Stanovich 1999, 2004).

8   Current understanding of representativeness interprets it as a form of attribute substitution (see Kahneman and Frederick, 2002). Other TASS heuristics have been proposed as the cause of the conjunction error in this problem – many involving conversational assumptions that are automatically applied to the problem (on this by now quite large literature, see Adler 1984, 1991; Dulany and Hilton 1991; Girotto 2004; Hilton 1995; Mellers, Hertwig, and Kahneman 2001; Politzer and Macchi 2000; Politzer and Noveck 1991; Slugoski and Wilson 1998).

9   As mentioned previously, this correlation with intelligence might arise for two reasons. First, some subjects may operate solely on the basis of representativeness and these are more likely to be the low IQ subjects. Secondly, even within the sample of subjects who experienced conflict between representativeness and the subset/superset relationship, the subjects of higher intelligence might have been more likely to resolve the conflict in favor of the latter.

10   The Epstein results are not inconsistent with the findings of Fetherstonhaugh, Slovic, Johnson, and Friedrich (1997) that people's willingness to intervene to save lives was more determined by the proportion of lives saved than by the absolute number. The vividness that is the common cause of the normatively inappropriate response patterns in the two experimental situations operates differently in the two cases.

Stimulus situations in this experimental area are subtley and importantly different (see also Yamagishi 1997). Which aspect of the situation will dominate because of vividness depends greatly on the comparative aspects of the experimental situation (see Slovic, Finucane, Peters, and MacGregor 2002).

11   There is a slightly different way of stating these two conclusions that might clarify the model I am developing here. First, there is a correlation between intelligence and performance on these tasks because once the need for override is recognized, the probability of carrying out the sustained decoupling required by override is higher for those with more algorithmic-level cognitive capacity. Nevertheless, the correlation is substantially less than perfect because the mere cognitive capacity for decoupling is alone not enough – the need for override must be recognized, and this depends on intentional-level thinking dispositions of the type discussed in the next section.

References

Ackerman, P. L. (1994). Intelligence, attention, and learning: Maximal and typical performance. In D. K. Detterman (Ed.), *Current topics in human intelligence (Vol. 4)* (pp. 1–27). Norwood, NJ: Ablex.

Ackerman, P. L. (1996). A theory of adult development: Process, personality, interests, and knowledge. *Intelligence, 22,* 227–257.

Ackerman, P. L., & Heggestad, E. D. (1997). Intelligence, personality, and interests: Evidence for overlapping traits. *Psychological Bulletin, 121,* 219–245.

Ackerman, P. L., Kyllonen, P., and Roberts, R. (Eds.) (1999). *The future of learning and individual differences research: Processes, traits, and content.* Washington, DC: American Psychological Association.

Adler, J. E. (1984). Abstraction is uncooperative. *Journal for the Theory of Social Behaviour, 14,* 165–181.

Adler, J. E. (1991). An optimist's pessimism: Conversation and conjunctions. In E. Eells & T. Maruszewski (Eds.), *Probability and rationality: Studies on L. Jonathan Cohen's philosophy of science* (pp. 251–282). Amsterdam: Editions Rodopi.

Adler, J. E. (1998). Rationality of belief. In E. Craig (Ed.), *Routledge encyclopedia of philosophy* (pp. 86–90). London: Routledge.

Anderson, J. R. (1990). *The adaptive character of thought.* Hillsdale, NJ: Erlbaum.

Anderson, J. R. (1991). Is human cognition adaptive? *Behavioral and Brain Sciences, 14,* 471–517.

Anderson, M. (1992). *Intelligence and development: A cognitive theory*. Oxford: Basil Blackwell.

Anderson, M. (1998). Mental retardation, general intelligence, and modularity. *Learning and Individual Differences, 10,* 159–178.

Atran, S. (1998). Folk biology and the anthropology of science: Cognitive universals and cultural particulars. *Behavioral and Brain Sciences, 21,* 547–609.

Austin, E. J., and Deary, I. J. (2002). Personality dispositions. In R. J. Sternberg (Ed.), *Why smart people can be so stupid* (pp. 187–211). New Haven, CT: Yale University Press.

Baddeley, A. D. (1992). Working memory. *Science, 255,* 556–559.

Baddeley, A., Chincotta, D., and Adlam, A. (2001). Working memory and the control of action: Evidence from task switching. *Journal of Experimental Psychology: General, 130,* 641–657.

Bara, B. G., Bucciarelli, M., and Johnson-Laird, P. N. (1995). Development of syllogistic reasoning. *American Journal of Psychology, 108,* 157–193.

Baron, J. (1985). *Rationality and intelligence.* Cambridge: Cambridge University Press.

Baron, J. (1995). Myside bias in thinking about abortion. *Thinking and Reasoning, 1,* 221–235.

Baron, J., and Hershey, J. C. (1988). Outcome bias in decision evaluation. *Journal of Personality and Social Psychology, 54,* 569–579.

Baron-Cohen, S. (1995). *Mindblindness: An essay on autism and theory of mind.* Cambridge, MA: MIT Press.

Bermudez, J. L. (2001). Normativity and rationality in delusional psychiatric disorders. *Mind & Language, 16,* 457–493.

Bratman, M. E., Israel, D. J., & Pollack, M. E. (1991). Plans and resource-bounded practical reasoning. In J. Cummins & J. Pollock (Eds.), *Philosophy and AI: Essays at the interface* (pp. 7–22). Cambridge, MA: MIT Press.

Brook, A., & Ross, D. (2002). Dennett's position in the intellectual world. In A. Brook & D. Ross (Eds.), *Daniel Dennett* (pp. 3–37). Cambridge: Cambridge University Press.

Buss, D. M. (1991). Evolutionary personality psychology. *Annual Review of Psychology, 42,* 459–491.

Cacioppo, J. T., Petty, R. E., Feinstein, J., & Jarvis, W. (1996). Dispositional differences in cognitive motivation: The life and times of individuals varying in need for cognition. *Psychological Bulletin, 119,* 197–253.

Carpenter, P. A., Just, M. A., & Shell, P. (1990). What one intelligence test measures: A theoretical account of the processing in the Raven Progressive Matrices Test. *Psychological Review, 97,* 404–431.

Carroll, J. B. (1993). *Human cognitive abilities: A survey of factor-analytic studies.* Cambridge: Cambridge University Press.

Carroll, J. B. (1997). Psychometrics, intelligence, and public perception. *Intelligence, 24,* 25–52.

Carruthers, P. (2002). The cognitive functions of language. *Behavioral and Brain Sciences, 25,* 657–726.

Carruthers, P., Stich, S., & Siegal, M. (Eds.). (2002). *The cognitive basis of science.* Cambridge: Cambridge University Press.

Cattell, R. B. (1963). Theory for fluid and crystallized intelligence: A critical experiment. *Journal of Educational Psychology, 54,* 1–22.

Cattell, R. B. (1998). Where is intelligence? Some answers from the triadic theory. In J. J. McArdle & R. W. Woodcock (Eds.), *Human cognitive abilities in theory and practice* (pp. 29–38). Mahwah, NJ: Erlbaum.

Cederblom, J. (1989). Willingness to reason and the identification of the self. In E. Maimon, D. Nodine, & O'Conner (Eds.), *Thinking, reasoning, and writing* (pp. 147–159). New York: Longman.

Cherniak, C. (1986). *Minimal rationality.* Cambridge, MA: MIT Press.

Cohen, L. J. (1981). Can human irrationality be experimentally demonstrated? *Behavioral and Brain Sciences, 4,* 317–370.

Cohen, L. J. (1982). Are people programmed to commit fallacies? Further thoughts about the interpretation of experimental data on probability judgment. *Journal for the Theory of Social Behavior, 12,* 251–274.

Colom, R., Rebollo, I., Palacios, A., Juan-Espinosa, M., & Kyllonen, P. C. (2004). Working memory is (almost) perfectly predicted by g. *Intelligence, 32,* 277–296.

Conway, A. R. A., Cowan, N., Bunting, M. F., Therriault, D. J., & Minkoff, S. R. B. (2002). A latent variable analysis of working memory capacity, short-term memory capacity, processing speed, and general fluid intelligence. *Intelligence, 30,* 163–183.

Conway, A. R. A., Kane, M. J., & Engle, R. W. (2003). Working memory capacity and its relation to general intelligence. *Trends in Cognitive Science, 7,* 547–552.

Copeland, D. E., & Radvansky, G. A. (2004). Working memory and syllogistic reasoning. *Quarterly Journal of Experimental Psychology, 57A,* 1437–1457.

Cosmides, L., & Tooby, J. (1992). Cognitive adaptations for social exchange. In J. Barkow, L. Cosmides, & J. Tooby (Eds.), *The adapted mind* (pp. 163–228). New York: Oxford University Press.

Cosmides, L., & Tooby, J. (2000). Consider the source: The evolution of adaptations for decoupling and metarepresentation. In D. Sperber (Ed.), *Metarepresentations: A multidisciplinary perspective* (pp. 53–115). Oxford: Oxford University Press.

Costa, P. T., & McCrae, R. R. (1992). *Revised NEO personality inventory*. Odessa, FL: Psychological Assessment Resources.

Cronbach, L. J. (1949). *Essentials of psychological testing*. New York: Harper.

Currie, G., & Ravenscroft, I. (2002). *Recreative minds*. Oxford: Oxford University Press.

Daniel, M. H. (2000). Interpretation of intelligence test scores. In R. J. Sternberg (Ed.), *Handbook of intelligence* (pp. 477–491). Cambridge, MA: Cambridge University Press.

Davies, M. (2000). Interaction without reduction: The relationship between personal and subpersonal levels of description. *Mind & Society, 1*, 87–105.

Deary, I. J. (2000). *Looking down on human intelligence: From psychometrics to the brain*. Oxford: Oxford University Press.

Denes-Raj, V., & Epstein, S. (1994). Conflict between intuitive and rational processing: When people behave against their better judgment. *Journal of Personality and Social Psychology, 66*, 819–829.

Dennett, D. C. (1978). *Brainstorms: Philosophical essays on mind and psychology*. Cambridge, MA: MIT Press.

Dennett, D. C. (1984). *Elbow room: The varieties of free will worth wanting*. Cambridge, MA: MIT Press.

Dennett, D. (1987). *The intentional stance*. Cambridge, MA: MIT Press.

Dennett, D. C. (1996). *Kinds of minds: Toward an understanding of consciousness*. New York: Basic Books.

DeShon, R. P., Smith, M. R., Chan, D., & Schmitt, N. (1998). Can racial differences in cognitive test performance be reduced by presenting problems in a social context? *Journal of Applied Psychology, 83*, 438–451.

Dias, M., Roazzi, A., & Harris, P. L. (2005). Reasoning from unfamiliar premises: A study with unschooled adults. *Psychological Science, 16*, 550–554.

Dienes, Z., & Perner, J. (1999). A theory of implicit and explicit knowledge. *Behavioral and Brain Sciences, 22*, 735–808.

Dulany, D. E., & Hilton, D. J. (1991). Conversational implicature, conscious representation, and the conjunction fallacy. *Social Cognition, 9*, 85–110.

Duncan, J., Emslie, H., Williams, P., Johnson, R., & Freer, C. (1996). Intelligence and the frontal lobe: The organization of goal-directed behavior. *Cognitive Psychology, 30*, 257–303.

Elton, M. (2003). *Daniel Dennett: Reconciling science and our self-conception*. Cambridge, UK: Polity Press.

Engle, R. W. (2002). Working memory capacity as executive attention. *Current Directions in Psychological Science, 11*, 19–23.

Engle, R. W., Tuholski, S. W., Laughlin, J. E., & Conway, A. R. A. (1999). Working memory, short-term memory, and general fluid intelligence: A latent-variable approach. *Journal of Experimental Psychology: General, 128*, 309–331.

Epstein, S., & Meier, P. (1989). Constructive thinking: A broad coping variable with specific components. *Journal of Personality and Social Psychology, 57*, 332–350.

Evans, J. St. B. T. (2002). The influence of prior belief on scientific thinking. In P. Carruthers, S. Stich, & M. Siegal (Eds.), *The cognitive basis of science* (pp. 193–210). Cambridge: Cambridge University Press.

Evans, J. St. B. T. (2003). In two minds: Dual-process accounts of reasoning. *Trends in Cognitive Sciences, 7*, 454–459.

Evans, J. St. B. T. (2005). Deductive reasoning. In K. J. Holyoak & R. G. Morrison (Eds.), *The Cambridge handbook of thinking and reasoning* (pp. 169–184). New York: Cambridge University Press.

Evans, J. St. B. T., Barston, J., & Pollard, P. (1983). On the conflict between logic and belief in syllogistic reasoning. *Memory & Cognition, 11*, 295–306.

Evans, J. St. B. T., & Feeney, A. (2004). The role of prior belief in reasoning. In J. P. Leighton & R. J. Sternberg (Eds.), *The nature of reasoning* (pp. 78–102). Cambridge: Cambridge University Press.

Evans, J. St. B. T., Newstead, S., Allen, J., & Pollard, P. (1994). Debiasing by instruction: The case of belief bias. *European Journal of Cognitive Psychology, 6*, 263–285.

Evans, J. St. B. T., & Over, D. E. (1996). *Rationality and reasoning*. Hove, England: Psychology Press.

Evans, J. St. B. T., & Over, D. E. (1999). Explicit representations in hypothetical thinking. *Behavioral and Brain Sciences, 22*, 763–764.

Evans, J. St. B. T., & Over, D. E. (2004). *If*. Oxford: Oxford University Press.

Evans, J. St. B. T., & Perry, T. (1995). Belief bias in children's reasoning. *Cahiers de Psychologie Cognitive, 14*, 103–115.

Feldman Barrett, L., Tugade, M. M., & Engle, R. W. (2004). Individual differences in working memory capacity and dual-process theories of the mind. *Psychological Bulletin, 130*, 553–573.

Fetherstonhaugh, D., Slovic, P., Johnson, S. M., & Friedrich, J. (1997). Insensitivity to the value of human life: A study of psychophysical numbing. *Journal of Risk and Uncertainty, 14*, 282–300.

Fong, G. T., Krantz, D. H., & Nisbett, R. E. (1986). The effects of statistical training on thinking about everyday problems. *Cognitive Psychology, 18*, 253–292.

Frankfurt, H. (1971). Freedom of the will and the concept of a person. *Journal of Philosophy, 68*, 5–20.

Fuster, J. M. (1990). Prefrontal cortex and the bridging of temporal gaps in the perception-action cycle. In A. Diamond (Ed.), *The development and neural bases of higher cognitive functions* (pp. 318–336). New York: New York Academy of Sciences.

Geary, D. C. (2005). *The origin of the mind: Evolution of brain, cognition, and general intelligence.* Washington, DC: American Psychological Association.

Gernsbacher, M. A., & Faust, M. E. (1991). The mechanism of suppression: A component of general comprehension skill. *Journal of Experimental Psychology: Learning, Memory, and Cognition, 17,* 245–262.

Gigerenzer, G. (1996). On narrow norms and vague heuristics: A reply to Kahneman and Tversky (1996). *Psychological Review, 103,* 592–596.

Gilhooly, K. J. (2004). Working memory and reasoning. In J. P. Leighton & R. J. Sternberg (Eds.), *The nature of reasoning* (pp. 49–77). Cambridge: Cambridge University Press.

Gilovich, T. (1991). *How we know what isn't so.* New York: Free Press.

Girotto, V. (2004). Task understanding. In J. P. Leighton & R. J. Sternberg (Eds.), *The nature of reasoning* (pp. 103–125). Cambridge: Cambridge University Press.

Glenberg, A. M. (1997). What memory is for. *Behavioral and Brain Sciences, 20,* 1–55.

Goel, V., & Dolan, R. J. (2003). Explaining modulation of reasoning by belief. *Cognition, 87,* B11–B22.

Goldman-Rakic, P. S. (1992). Working memory and the mind. *Scientific American, 267,* 111–117.

Gould, S. J. (1991). *Bully for the Brontosaurus.* New York: Norton.

Gray, J. R., Chabris, C. F., & Braver, T. S. (2003). Neural mechanisms of general fluid intelligence. *Nature Neuroscience, 6,* 316–322.

Griffin, D., & Tversky, A. (1992). The weighing of evidence and the determinants of confidence. *Cognitive Psychology, 24,* 411–435.

Hambrich, D. Z., & Engle, R. W. (2003). The role of working memory in problem solving. In J. E. Davidson & R. J. Sternberg (Eds.), *The psychology of problem solving* (pp. 176–206). Cambridge: Cambridge University Press.

Handley, S. J., Capon, A., Beveridge, M., Dennis, I., & Evans, J. St. B. T. (2004). Working memory, inhibitory control and the development of children's reasoning. *Thinking and Reasoning, 10,* 175–195.

Hasher, L., Zacks, R. T., & May, C. P. (1999). Inhibitory control, circadian arousal, and age. In D. Gopher & A. Koriat (Eds.), *Attention & Performance XVII, Cognitive Regulation of Performance: Interaction of Theory and Application* (pp. 653–675). Cambridge, MA: MIT Press.

Hilton, D. J. (1995). The social context of reasoning: Conversational inference and rational judgment. *Psychological Bulletin, 118,* 248–271.

Horgan, T., & Tienson, J. (1993). Levels of description in nonclassical cognitive science. In C. Hookway & D. Peterson (Eds.), *Philosophy and cognitive science* (pp. 159–188). Cambridge: Cambridge University Press.

Horn, J. L., & Cattell, R. B. (1967). Age differences in fluid and crystallized intelligence. *Acta Psychologica, 26,* 1–23.

Horn, J. L., & Noll, J. (1997). Human cognitive capabilities: Gf-Gc theory. In D. Flanagan, J. Genshaft, & P. Harrison (Eds.), *Contemporary intellectual assessment: Theories, tests, and issues* (pp. 53–91). New York: Guilford Press.

Hunt, E. (1987). The next word on verbal ability. In P. A. Vernon (Ed.), *Speed of information-processing and intelligence* (pp. 347–392). Norwood, NJ: Ablex.

Hunt, E. (1999). Intelligence and human resources: Past, present, and future. In P. Ackerman, P. Kyllonen, & R. Richards (Eds.), *Learning and individual differences: Process, trait, and content determinants* (pp. 3–28). Washington, DC: American Psychological Association.

Jackendoff, R. (1996). How language helps us think. *Pragmatics and Cognition, 4,* 1–34.

Jepson, C., Krantz, D., & Nisbett, R. (1983). Inductive reasoning: Competence or skill? *Behavioral and Brain Sciences, 6,* 494–501.

Johnson-Laird, P. N. (1999). Deductive reasoning. *Annual Review of Psychology, 50,* 109–135.

Johnson-Laird, P. N. (2005). Mental models and thought. In K. J. Holyoak & R. G. Morrison (Eds.), *The Cambridge handbook of thinking and reasoning* (pp. 185–208). New York: Cambridge University Press.

Kahneman, D., & Frederick, S. (2002). Representativeness revisited: Attribute substitution in intuitive judgment. In T. Gilovich, D. Griffin, & D. Kahneman (Eds.), *Heuristics and biases: The psychology of intuitive judgment* (pp. 49–81). New York: Cambridge University Press.

Kahneman, D., & Frederick, S. (2005). A model of heuristic judgment. In K. J. Holyoak & R. G. Morrison (Eds.), *The Cambridge handbook of thinking and reasoning* (pp. 267–293). New York: Cambridge University Press.

Kahneman, D., & Miller, D. T. (1986). Norm theory: Comparing reality to its alternatives. *Psychological Review, 93,* 136–153.

Kahneman, D., & Tversky, A. (1996). On the reality of cognitive illusions. *Psychological Review, 103,* 582–591.

Kahneman, D., & Tversky, A. (Eds.). (2000). *Choices, values, and frames.* Cambridge: Cambridge University Press.

Kane, M. J. (2003). The intelligent brain in conflict. *Trends in Cognitive Sciences, 7,* 375–377.

Kane, M. J., Bleckley, M., Conway, A., & Engle, R. W. (2001). A controlled-attention view of WM capacity. *Journal of Experimental Psychology: General, 130,* 169–183.

Kane, M. J., & Engle, R. W. (2002). The role of prefrontal cortex working-memory capacity, executive attention, and general fluid intelligence: An individual-differences perspective. *Psychonomic Bulletin and Review, 9,* 637–671.

Kane, M. J., & Engle, R. W. (2003). Working-memory capacity and the control of attention: The contributions of goal neglect, response competition, and task set to Stroop interference. *Journal of Experimental Psychology: General, 132,* 47–70.

Kane, M. J., Hambrick, D. Z., Tuholski, S. W., Wilhelm, O., Payne, T., & Engle, R. W. (2004). The generality of working memory capacity: A latent-variable approach to verbal and visuospatial memory span and reasoning. *Journal of Experimental Psychology: General, 133,* 189–217.

Kardash, C. M., & Scholes, R. J. (1996). Effects of pre-existing beliefs, epistemological beliefs, and need for cognition on interpretation of controversial issues. *Journal of Educational Psychology, 88,* 260–271.

Kirkpatrick, L., & Epstein, S. (1992). Cognitive-experiential self-theory and subjective probability: Evidence for two conceptual systems. *Journal of Personality and Social Psychology, 63,* 534–544.

Klaczynski, P. A. (1997). Bias in adolescents' everyday reasoning and its relationship with intellectual ability, personal theories, and self-serving motivation. *Developmental Psychology, 33,* 273–283.

Klaczynski, P. A., & Gordon, D. H. (1996). Self-serving influences on adolescents' evaluations of belief-relevant evidence. *Journal of Experimental Child Psychology, 62,* 317–339.

Klaczynski, P. A., Gordon, D. H., & Fauth, J. (1997). Goal-oriented critical reasoning and individual differences in critical reasoning biases. *Journal of Educational Psychology, 89,* 470–485.

Klaczynski, P. A., & Lavallee, K. L. (2005). Domain-specific identity, epistemic regulation, and intellectual ability as predictors of belief-based reasoning: A dual-process perspective. *Journal of Experimental Child Psychology.*

Klaczynski, P. A., & Robinson, B. (2000). Personal theories, intellectual ability, and epistemological beliefs: Adult age differences in everyday reasoning tasks. *Psychology and Aging, 15,* 400–416.

Kokis, J, Macpherson, R., Toplak, M., West, R. F., & Stanovich, K. E. (2002). Heuristic and analytic processing: Age trends and associations with cognitive ability and cognitive styles. *Journal of Experimental Child Psychology, 83,* 26–52.

Kruglanski, A. W., & Webster, D. M. (1996). Motivated closing the mind: "Seizing" and "freezing". *Psychological Review, 103,* 263–283.

Kuhberger, A. (2002). The rationality of risky decisions: A changing message. *Theory & Psychology, 12,* 427–452.

Leslie, A. M. (1987). Pretense and representation: The origins of "Theory of Mind." *Psychological Review, 94,* 412–426.

Levelt, W. (1995). Chapters of psychology. In R. L. Solso & D. W. Massaro (Eds.), *The science of the mind: 2001 and beyond* (pp. 184–202). New York: Oxford University Press.

Lillard, A. (2001). Pretend play as twin Earth: A social-cognitive analysis. *Developmental Review, 21,* 495–531.

Lohman, D. F. (2000). Complex information processing and intelligence. In R. J. Sternberg (Ed.), *Handbook of intelligence* (pp. 285–340). Cambridge: Cambridge University Press.

Lopes, L. (1991). The rhetoric of irrationality. *Theory & Psychology, 1,* 65–82.

Lubinski, D. (2004). Introduction to the special section on cognitive abilities: 100 years after Spearman's (1904) "General Intelligence, Objectively Determined and Measured." *Journal of Personality and Social Psychology, 86,* 96–111.

Manktelow, K. I. (2004). Reasoning and rationality: The pure and the practical. In K. I. Manktelow & M. C. Chung (Eds.), *Psychology of reasoning: Theoretical and historical perspectives* (pp. 157–177). Hove, England: Psychology Press.

Margolis, H. (1987). *Patterns, thinking, and cognition.* Chicago: University of Chicago Press.

Markovits, H., & Doyon, C. (2004). Information processing and reasoning with premises that are empirically false: Interference, working memory, and processing speed. *Memory & Cognition, 32,* 592–601.

Markovits, H., & Nantel, G. (1989). The belief-bias effect in the production and evaluation of logical conclusions. *Memory & Cognition, 17,* 11–17.

Marr, D. (1982). *Vision.* San Francisco: W. H. Freeman.

Matthews, G., & Deary, I. J. (1998). *Personality traits.* Cambridge: Cambridge University Press.

Matthews, G., Zeidner, M., & Roberts, R. D. (2002). *Emotional intelligence: Science & myth.* Cambridge, MA: MIT Press.

McClure, S. M., Laibson, D. I., Loewenstein, G., & Cohen, J. D. (2004). Separate neural systems value immediate and delayed monetary rewards. *Science, 306,* 503–507.

McCrae, R. R., & Costa, P. T. (1997). Personality trait structure as a human universal. *American Psychologist, 52,* 509–516.

McGrew, K. S. (1997). Analysis of major intelligence batteries according to a proposed comprehensive Gf-Gc framework. In D. Flanagan, J. Genshaft, & P. Harrison (Eds.), *Contemporary intellectual assessment: Theories, tests, and issues* (pp. 151–180). New York: Guilford Press.

McGrew, K. S., & Woodcock, R. W. (2001). *Technical Manual. Woodcock-Johnson III.* Itasca, IL: Riverside Publishing.

Mellers, B., Hertwig, R., & Kahneman, D. (2001). Do frequency representations eliminate conjunction effects? An exercise in adversarial collaboration. *Psychological Science, 12,* 269–275.

Mirolli, M. (2002). A naturalistic perspective on intentionality: Interview with Daniel Dennett. *Mind & Society, 3,* 1–12.

Mithen, S. (1996). *The prehistory of mind: The cognitive origins of art and science.* London: Thames and Hudson.

Moshman, D. (1994). Reasoning, metareasoning, and the promotion of rationality. In A. Demetriou & A. Efklides (Eds.), *Intelligence, mind, and reasoning: Structure and development* (pp. 135–150). Amsterdam: Elsevier.

Moutier, S., Angeard, N., & Houde, O. (2002). Deductive reasoning and matching-bias inhibition training: Evidence from a debiasing paradigm. *Thinking and Reasoning, 8,* 205–224.

Muller, U., Zelazo, P. D., Hood, S., Leone, T., & Rohrer, L. (2004). Interference control in a new rule use task: Age-related changes, labeling, and attention. *Child Development, 75,* 1594–1609.

Newell, A. (1982). The knowledge level. *Artificial Intelligence, 18,* 87–127.

Newell, A. (1990). *Unified theories of cognition.* Cambridge, MA: Harvard University Press.

Newstead, S. E., Handley, S. J., Harley, C., Wright, H., & Farrelly, D. (2004). Individual differences in deductive reasoning. *Quarterly Journal of Experimental Psychology, 57A,* 33–60.

Nichols, S., & Stich, S. P. (2003). *Mindreading: An integrated account of pretence, self-awareness, and understanding other minds.* Oxford: Oxford University Press.

Nickerson, R. S. (1998). Confirmation bias: A ubiquitous phenomenon in many guises. *Review of General Psychology, 2,* 175–220.

Nickerson, R. S. (2004). Teaching reasoning. In J. P. Leighton & R. J. Sternberg (Eds.), *The nature of reasoning* (pp. 410–442). Cambridge: Cambridge University Press.

Nisbett, L., & Ross, L. (1980). *Human inference: Strategies and shortcomings of social judgment.* Englewood Cliffs, NJ: Prentice Hall.

Norris, S. P. (1992). Testing for the disposition to think critically. *Informal Logic, 14,* 157–164.

Oakhill, J., Johnson-Laird, P. N., & Garnham, A. (1989). Believability and syllogistic reasoning. *Cognition, 31,* 117–140.

Oaksford, M., & Chater, N. (1995). Theories of reasoning and the computational explanation of everyday inference. *Thinking and Reasoning, 1,* 121–152.

Osman, M. (2004). An evaluation of dual-process theories of reasoning. *Psychonomic Bulletin and Review, 11,* 988–1010.

Over, D. E. (2002). The rationality of evolutionary psychology. In J. L. Bermudez & A. Millar (Eds.), *Reason and nature: Essays in the theory of rationality* (pp. 187–207). Oxford: Oxford University Press.

Pacini, R., & Epstein, S. (1999a). The interaction of three facets of concrete thinking in a game of chance. *Thinking and Reasoning, 5,* 303–325.

Pacini, R., & Epstein, S. (1999b). The relation of rational and experiential information processing styles to personality, basic beliefs, and the ratio-bias phenomenon. *Journal of Personality and Social Psychology, 76,* 972–987.

Parker, A. M., & Fischhoff, B. (2005). Decision-making competence: External validation through an individual differences approach. *Journal of Behavioral Decision Making, 18,* 1–27.

Paul, R. W. (1984). Critical thinking: Fundamental to education for a free society. *Educational Leadership, 42*(1), 4–14.

Paul, R. W. (1987). Critical thinking and the critical person. In D. N. Perkins, J. Lockhead, & J. Bishop (Eds.), *Thinking: The second international conference* (pp. 373–403). Hillsdale, NJ: Erlbaum.

Perkins, D. N. (1995). *Outsmarting IQ: The emerging science of learnable intelligence.* New York: Free Press.

Perner, J. (1991). *Understanding the representational mind.* Cambridge, MA: MIT Press.

Pinker, S. (1997). *How the mind works.* New York: Norton.

Politzer, G., & Macchi, L. (2000). Reasoning and pragmatics. *Mind & Society, 1,* 73–93.

Politzer, G., & Noveck, I. A. (1991). Are conjunction rule violations the result of conversational rule violations? *Journal of Psycholinguistic Research, 20,* 83–103.

Pollock, J. L. (1995). *Cognitive carpentry: A blueprint for how to build a person.* Cambridge, MA: MIT Press.

Povinelli, D. J., & Bering, J. M. (2002). The mentality of apes revisited. *Current Directions in Psychological Science, 11*(4), 115–119.

Povinelli, D. J., & Giambrone, S. (2001). Reasoning about beliefs: A human specialization? *Child Development, 72,* 691–695.

Pylyshyn, Z. (1984). *Computation and cognition.* Cambridge, MA: MIT Press.

Reber, A. S. (1992). The cognitive unconscious: An evolutionary perspective. *Consciousness and Cognition, 1,* 93–133.

Reber, A. S. (1993). *Implicit learning and tacit knowledge.* New York: Oxford University Press.

Reber, A. S., Walkenfeld, F. F., & Hernstadt, R. (1991). Implicit and explicit learning: Individual differences and IQ. *Journal of Experimental Psychology: Learning, Memory, and Cognition, 17,* 888–896.

Rescher, N. (1988). *Rationality: A philosophical inquiry into the nature and rationale of reason.* Oxford: Oxford University Press.

Rips, L. J. (1994). *The psychology of proof.* Cambridge, MA: MIT Press.

Rips, L. J., & Conrad, F. G. (1983). Individual differences in deduction. *Cognition and Brain Theory, 6,* 259–285.

Roese, N. (1997). Counterfactual thinking. *Psychological Bulletin, 121,* 131–148.

Rokeach, M. (1960). *The open and closed mind.* New York: Basic Books.

Ross, R. (2000). Introduction: The Dennettian stance. In R. Ross, A. Brook, & D. Thompson (Eds.), *Dennett's philosophy: A comprehensive assessment* (pp. 1–26). Cambridge, MA: MIT Press.

Sá, W., Kelley, C., Ho, C., & Stanovich, K. E. (2005). Thinking about personal theories: Individual differences in the coordination of theory and evidence. *Personality and Individual Differences, 38,* 1149–1161.

Sá, W., West, R. F., & Stanovich, K. E. (1999). The domain specificity and generality of belief bias: Searching for a generalizable critical thinking skill. *Journal of Educational Psychology, 91,* 497–510.

Saffran, J. R., Aslin, R. N., & Newport, E. L. (1996). Statistical learning by 8-month-old infants. *Science, 274,* 1926–1928.

Saks, M., & Kidd, R. (1980–1981). Human information processing and adjudication: Trial by heuristics. *Law and Society Review, 15,* 123–160.

Salthouse, T. A., Atkinson, T. M., & Berish, D. E. (2003). Executive functioning as a potential mediator of age-related cognitive decline in normal adults. *Journal of Experimental Psychology: General, 132,* 566–594.

Samuels, R., & Stich, S. P. (2004). Rationality and psychology. In A. R. Mele & P. Rawling (Eds.), *The Oxford handbook of rationality* (pp. 279–300). Oxford: Oxford University Press.

Samuels, R., Stich, S. P., & Bishop, M. (2002). Ending the rationality wars: How to make disputes about human rationality disappear. In R. Elio (Ed.), *Common sense, reasoning and rationality* (pp. 236–268). New York: Oxford University Press.

Scheffler, I. (1991). *In praise of the cognitive emotions.* New York: Routledge.

Schoenfeld, A. H. (1983). Beyond the purely cognitive: Belief systems, social cognitions, and metacognitions as driving forces in intellectual performance. *Cognitive Science, 7,* 329–363.

Schommer, M. (1990). Effects of beliefs about the nature of knowledge on comprehension. *Journal of Educational Psychology, 82,* 498–504.

Schommer-Aikins, M. (2004). Explaining the epistemological belief system: Introducing the embedded systemic model and coordinated research approach. *Educational Psychologist, 39,* 19–30.

Shafir, E., & LeBoeuf, R. A. (2002). Rationality. *Annual Review of Psychology, 53,* 491–517.

Shafir, E., & LeBoeuf, R. A. (2005). Decision making. In K. J. Holyoak & R. G. Morrison (Eds.), *The Cambridge handbook of thinking and reasoning* (pp. 243–265). New York: Cambridge University Press.

Simoneau, M., & Markovits, H. (2003). Reasoning with premises that are not empirically true: Evidence for the role of inhibition and retrieval. *Developmental Psychology, 39,* 964–975.

Sinatra, G. M., & Pintrich, P. R. (Eds.). (2003). *Intentional conceptual change.* Mahwah, NJ: Erlbaum.

Sloman, A. (1993). The mind as a control system. In C. Hookway & D. Peterson (Eds.), *Philosophy and cognitive science* (pp. 69–110). Cambridge: Cambridge University Press.

Sloman, S. A. (1996). The empirical case for two systems of reasoning. *Psychological Bulletin, 119,* 3–22.

Sloman, S. A. (2002). Two systems of reasoning. In T. Gilovich, D. Griffin, & D. Kahneman (Eds.), *Heuristics and biases: The psychology of intuitive judgment* (pp. 379–396). New York: Cambridge University Press.

Slovic, P., Finucane, M. L., Peters, E., & MacGregor, D. G. (2002). The affect heuristic. In T. Gilovich, D. Griffin, & D. Kahneman (Eds.), *Heuristics and biases: The psychology of intuitive judgment* (pp. 397–420). New York: Cambridge University Press.

Sperber, D. (1994). The modularity of thought and the epidemiology of representations. In L. A. Hirschfeld & S. A. Gelman (Eds.), *Mapping the mind: Domain specificity in cognition and culture* (pp. 39–67). Cambridge: Cambridge University Press.

Sperber, D. (2000). Metarepresentations in evolutionary perspective. In D. Sperber (Ed.), *Metarepresentations: A Multidisciplinary Perspective* (pp. 117–137). Oxford: Oxford University Press.

Stanovich, K. E. (1989). Implicit philosophies of mind: The dualism scale and its relationships with religiosity and belief in extrasensory perception. *Journal of Psychology, 123,* 5–23.

Stanovich, K. E. (1999). *Who is rational? Studies of individual differences in reasoning.* Mahwah, NJ: Erlbaum.

Stanovich, K. E. (2002). Rationality, intelligence, and levels of analysis in cognitive science: Is dysrationalia possible? In R. J. Sternberg (Ed.), *Why smart people can be so stupid* (pp. 124–158). New Haven, CT: Yale University Press.

Stanovich, K. E. (2003). The fundamental computational biases of human cognition: Heuristics that (sometimes) impair decision making and problem solving. In J. E. Davidson & R. J. Sternberg (Eds.), *The psychology of problem solving* (pp. 291–342). New York: Cambridge University Press.

Stanovich, K. E. (2004). *The robot's rebellion: Finding meaning in the age of Darwin*. Chicago: University of Chicago Press.

Stanovich, K. E. (2008). What IQ tests miss: The cognitive science of rational and irrational thinking. New Haven, CT: Yale University Press.

Stanovich, K. E., & West, R. F. (1997). Reasoning independently of prior belief and individual differences in actively open-minded thinking. *Journal of Educational Psychology, 89,* 342–357.

Stanovich, K. E., & West, R. F. (1998a). Cognitive ability and variation in selection task performance. *Thinking and Reasoning, 4,* 193–230.

Stanovich, K. E., & West, R. F. (1998b). Individual differences in framing and conjunction effects. *Thinking and Reasoning, 4,* 289–317.

Stanovich, K. E., & West, R. F. (1998c). Individual differences in rational thought. *Journal of Experimental Psychology: General, 127,* 161–188.

Stanovich, K. E., & West, R. F. (1999). Discrepancies between normative and descriptive models of decision making and the understanding/acceptance principle. *Cognitive Psychology, 38,* 349–385.

Stanovich, K. E., & West, R. F. (2000). Individual differences in reasoning: Implications for the rationality debate? *Behavioral and Brain Sciences, 23,* 645–726.

Stein, E. (1996). *Without good reason: The rationality debate in philosophy and cognitive science*. Oxford: Oxford University Press.

Sterelny, K. (1990). *The representational theory of mind: An introduction*. Oxford: Basil Blackwell.

Sterelny, K. (2001). *The evolution of agency and other essays*. Cambridge: Cambridge University Press.

Sterelny, K. (2003). *Thought in a hostile world: The evolution of human cognition*. Malden, MA: Blackwell Publishing.

Sternberg, R. J. (1977). *Intelligence, information processing, and analogical reasoning*. Hillsdale, NJ: Lawrence Erlbaum.

Sternberg, R. J. (1985). *Beyond IQ: A triarchic theory of human intelligence*. Cambridge: Cambridge University Press.

Sternberg, R. J. (1997). *Thinking styles*. Cambridge: Cambridge University Press.

Sternberg, R. J. (Ed.). (2000). *Handbook of intelligence*. New York: Cambridge University Press.

Sternberg, R. J. (2003). *Wisdom, intelligence, and creativity synthesized*. Cambridge: Cambridge University Press.

Sternberg, R. J., & Grigorenko, E. L. (Eds.). (2002). *The general factor of intelligence: How general is it?* Mahwah, NJ: Lawrence Erlbaum Associates.

Stich, S. P. (1990). *The fragmentation of reason*. Cambridge, MA: MIT Press.

Sub, H.-M., Oberauer, K., Wittmann, W. W., Wilhelm, O., & Schulze, R. (2002). Working-memory capacity explains reasoning ability – and a little bit more. *Intelligence, 30,* 261–288.

Suddendorf, T., & Whiten, A. (2001). Mental evolution and development: Evidence for secondary representation in children, great apes, and other animals. *Psychological Bulletin, 127,* 629–650.

Taub, G. E., & McGrew, K. S. (2004). A confirmatory factor analysis of Cattell-Horn-Carroll theory and cross-age invariance of the Woodcock-Johnson tests of cognitive abilities III. *School Psychology Quarterly, 19,* 72–87.

Tetlock, P. E., & Mellers, B. A. (2002). The great rationality debate. *Psychological Science, 13,* 94–99.

Thurstone, L. L. (1927). *The nature of intelligence*. New York: Harcourt, Brace and Company.

Tobacyk, J., & Milford, G. (1983). Belief in paranormal phenomena. *Journal of Personality and Social Psychology, 44,* 1029–1037.

Tomasello, M. (1999). *The cultural origins of human cognition*. Cambridge, MA: Harvard University Press.

Toplak, M., & Stanovich, K. E. (2002). The domain specificity and generality of disjunctive reasoning: Searching for a generalizable critical thinking skill. *Journal of Educational Psychology, 94,* 197–209.

Tor, A., & Bazerman, M. H. (2003). Focusing failures in competitive environments: Explaining decision errors in the Monty Hall game, the Acquiring a Company problem, and multiparty ultimatums. *Journal of Behavioral Decision Making, 16,* 353–374.

Tversky, A., & Kahneman, D. (1983). Extensional versus intuitive reasoning: The conjunction fallacy in probability judgment. *Psychological Review, 90,* 293–315.

Valentine, E. R. (1975). Performance on two reasoning tasks in relation to intelligence, divergence and interference proneness: Content and context effects in reasoning. *British Journal of Educational Psychology, 45,* 198–205.

Verschueren, N., Schaeken, W., & D'Ydewalle, G. (2005). Everyday conditional reasoning: A working memory-dependent tradeoff between counterexample and likelihood use. *Memory & Cognition, 33,* 107–119.

Vinter, A., & Detable, C. (2003). Implicit learning in children and adolescents with mental retardation. *American Journal of Mental Retardation, 108,* 94–107.

Vinter, A., & Perruchet, P. (2000). Implicit learning in children is not related to age: Evidence from drawing behavior. *Child Development, 71,* 1223–1240.

Wagner, R. K. (2002). Smart people doing dumb things: The case of managerial incompetence. In R. J. Sternberg (Ed.), *Why smart people can be so stupid* (pp. 42–63). New Haven, CT: Yale University Press.

Wagner, R. K., & Sternberg, R. J. (1985). Practical intelligence in real-world pursuits: The role of tacit knowledge. *Journal of Personality and Social Psychology, 49*, 436–458.

Watson, G., & Glaser, E. M. (1980). *Watson-Glaser critical thinking appraisal*. New York: Psychological Corporation.

West, R. F., & Stanovich, K. E. (2003). Is probability matching smart? Associations between probabilistic choices and cognitive ability. *Memory & Cognition, 31*, 243–251.

Whiten, A. (2001). Meta-representation and secondary representation. *Trends in Cognitive Sciences, 5*, 378.

Yamagishi, K. (1997). When a 12.86% mortality is more dangerous than 24.14%: Implications for risk communication. *Applied Cognitive Psychology, 11*, 495–506.

Zacks, R. T., Hasher, L., & Sanft, H. (1982). Automatic encoding of event frequency: Further findings. *Journal of Experimental Psychology: Learning, Memory, and Cognition, 8*, 106–116.

Chapter 22: Reasoning, Decision Making, and Rationality

JONATHAN ST. B. T. EVANS, DAVID E. OVER, AND KEN I. MANKTELOW

Introduction

The psychological fields of reasoning and of decision making are reported in different literatures, mostly by different authors and with little cross-reference. Is this just a matter of research traditions, or are the cognitive processes involved fundamentally different? On the face of it, a reasoning task is significantly different from a decision task. In the study of deductive reasoning, for example, subjects may be presented with the premises of some argument and asked whether or not a conclusion follows. For example, a subject may be asked to evaluate a syllogism such as

No A are B

Some B are not C

Therefore, some C are not A

and to indicate whether or not the conclusion follows. This is presumed to involve a process of reasoning from the premises which may or may not support the conclusion. If the subject has *deductive competence* – discussed below – it should be possible for him or her to solve the problem set without further information. In this sense, deductive reasoning tasks can be viewed as a special case of well-defined problem-solving tasks, whose main purpose is to investigate people's ability to understand and apply logical principles.

Decision-making tasks, on the other hand, involve choices between actions and normally involve commitment to particular acts at one point in time, whose consequences will only later be apparent. A simple example might be decid-ing whether or not to place a bet on a horse. One might think that a "good" decision is one that works out, that is, placing the bet on a horse who wins, or withholding on one who loses, but it is not that simple. Because real-world events are uncertain, good and bad decisions must be judged on their theoretical merits, not on their outcomes (see von Winterfeldt and Edwards 1986). The standard normative principle is that of *subjective expected utility* (SEU). Subjects are assumed to make the choice that maximizes the expression $\Sigma s_i U_i$, where s represents the subjective probability of an outcome associated with a choice and U represents its utility, that is, subjective value or pay-off to the decision maker. Hence an objectively good decision is one which would pay off best on average if the decision could be made under the same circumstances a large number of times.

Both reasoning and decision-making literatures involve assessing people's actions against normative theories of "correct" behavior but in so doing they imply different notions of rationality. In one case it is apparently rational to reason logically, and in the other case it is rational to achieve maximization of expected utility. This distinction is discussed in the following section and we believe it is critical to understanding the relation between the two fields. Leaving this aside for the moment, it is clear that both reasoning and decision tasks involve high-level thought processes. On further reflection it is apparent that reasoning tasks usually involve making decisions, and that choosing between actions often requires one to make inferences. In real-world situations the distinction between reasoning and decision making is blurred.

Reproduced with permission from Evans, J. St. B. T., Over, D. E., and Manktelow, K. I. (1993) Reasoning, decision making, and rationality. *Cognition*, 49, 165–187.

Decision making, or at least rational decision making, usually involves *forecasting*. That is to say, one action is preferred to another because the chooser believes that he or she would rather live in the slightly different world that will exist when this action is taken. But what does forecasting consist of, if not reasoning? Consider the situation of a school leaver deciding which university to apply to for degree study. A number of factors will influence such a decision, including the academic merits of the courses offered and the advantages and disadvantages of different geographical locations. In reading prospectuses of different universities the chooser is trying to infer which course he or she will most benefit from. The sophisticated chooser will make allowances for the promotional techniques and biases in the literature read – this too is reasoning.

If we look at deductive reasoning in the laboratory, we find that the great majority of tasks given to subjects involve decision making (see the reviews of Evans 1982; Evans, Newstead, and Byrne, 1993). Subjects are asked whether a given conclusion follows or not, or which of a list of conclusions is the best candidate, or on the famous Wason selection task (of which more later) which of several cards should be turned over. (Researchers who ask subjects simply to generate inferences are in the minority, but see Johnson-Laird and Byrne 1991, for good examples.) These decisions have a goal structure, albeit one that is often implicit. If the subjects are trying to find the logically correct answer it is because the instructions have motivated them to do precisely that, or because they do not wish to look foolish, or because they want to enhance their self-esteem.

It is difficult to think of cases in the real world when we make inferences *except* to make a decision or achieve a goal of some kind. The apparent exception is that of inferences drawn in order to enhance our knowledge or revise our beliefs in some way. However, maintenance of coherent and accurate belief systems is fundamental to our survival and achievement of goals in the real world and is clearly motivated in its own right. Hence some of our goals are *epistemic* or knowledge serving.

In the following section we lay out our thoughts about rationality in reasoning and decision making and relate this to the distinction between theoretical and practical inference. We argue that the separation of the psychology of reasoning from that of decision making is primarily due to emphasis on the study of logical

competence and theoretical reasoning, and that more attention to practical reasoning will not only develop the link with the study of decision making but also enhance the ecological validity of reasoning research. To illustrate our arguments we present discussions of two major areas within the psychology of deductive reasoning – belief bias in syllogistic inference and deontic reasoning on the Wason selection task – whose findings are interpreted within the framework proposed. Finally, we present a critical examination of the value of decision theory as a criterion for rational choice and reasoning.

Rationality and Practical Inference

Evans (1993) has argued that the debate about rationality in human reasoning and decision making is confused by two different, but implicit definitions of rationality. These can be defined as follows:

rationality₁ (rationality of purpose): reasoning in a way which helps one to achieve one's goals;

rationality₂ (rationality of process): reasoning in a way which conforms to a supposedly appropriate normative system such as formal logic.

In the classical decision-making literature (e.g., Savage 1954) the primary definition of rationality has been an idealized version of rationality₁: A rational person is believed to be one who chooses in such a way as to maximize his or her SEU. (We shall, however, later question the adequacy of decision theory defining rational choice.) In the literature on deductive reasoning, however, the rationality argument has focused on the concept of *logicality*, that is, validity or deductive correctness in reasoning, with the consequent adoption of the rationality₂ concept. There is, of course, a further implicit assumption, namely that rationality₂ serves rationality₁: in particular that logical reasoning will lead to the achievement of goals. This idea resembles Dennett's (e.g. 1978) "argument from natural selection" which is criticized by Stich (1985; see also Manktelow and Over 1987).

Leading researchers continue to equate rationality with deductive competence, as the following quotations from three very recent sources illustrate:

At the heart of rationality is the capacity to make valid deductions. (Johnson-Laird 1993, p. 2)

The concept of rationality assumes that people can engage in abstract deductive arguments and derive valid conclusions from a set of premises. (Stevenson 1993)

The classical Greek view of human nature included a rationality that allows for logical reasoning. My colleagues and I have argued elsewhere... that we have no adequate reason to abandon this view, and that this rationality includes a mental logic that accounts for our basic logical intuitions. (O'Brien 1993)

However, it is true that in addition to the current authors (Evans 1993; Over and Manktelow 1993) others have started to adopt a rationality$_1$ perspective in the study of reasoning. For example:

...what counts as human rationality: reasoning processes that embody content-independent formal rules, such as propositional logic, or reasoning processes that are well designed for solving important adaptive problems, such as social contents or social regulations? (Gigerenzer and Hug 1992, p. 129)

Many authors have argued that we should regard rationality as axiomatic (e.g., Cohen 1981; Dennett 1978). Humans are the most intelligent species on earth and have evolved into creatures extraordinarily capable of flexible response to their environment. Our ability to solve problems and to achieve goals is self-evident. The present authors accept this premise with two important reservations: (1) Rationality is only axiomatic in the sense of rationality$_1$, not rationality$_2$; and (2) the rationality we hold is highly *bounded* by cognitive constraints. Our position is thus similar to the argument for bounded rationality proposed by Newell and Simon (e.g., 1972): We assume that people try to achieve goals, and when they fail it is indicative of limitations in their processing capacity or ability. Due to cognitive limitations we also propose that goals are more likely to be achieved by *satisficing*, that is, finding an adequate solution, rather than by optimizing or maximizing utility across all possible choices and outcomes as proposed in classical decision theory. (For a philosophical treatment of satisficing, see Slote 1989.)

Recently, there has been increasing interest in a type of thinking in which the relation between

reasoning and decision making, and between rationality$_1$ and rationality$_2$, has been brought into sharp focus. This is the type actually known in philosophy as practical reasoning, and distinguished from so-called theoretical reasoning, the center of so much earlier psychological research. (See Audi 1989, on the history of the philosophical study of practical reasoning, which goes back to Aristotle.) People use practical reasoning to try to achieve their goals in the actions they perform, and when they do this in the right way, they display rationality$_1$. They use so-called theoretical reasoning to try to acquire true beliefs about matters of fact, and they have rationality$_2$ when they do this in the right way.

Theoretical reasoning, despite its name, does not have to be about scientifically theoretical entities, like subatomic particles, but may concern ordinary material objects, like cats and mats. You are engaged in theoretical reasoning if you are just trying to discover whether the cat is on the mat; you are engaged in practical reasoning if you are trying to decide whether you should kick the cat off your new mat. You have to have some basic ability to do theoretical reasoning, otherwise you would not know, for one thing, what is presupposed by your practical reasoning: that the cat is on your new mat. Only a quite bounded or limited logical ability is necessary to acquire such knowledge, and not even a much more sophisticated ability at deductive logic would be sufficient for it. Inductive inferences are also necessary, in general, to acquire empirical knowledge.

It is our purpose in this paper to concentrate on rationality$_1$ and practical reasoning. Before doing so, however, a little more must be said about the nature of rationality$_2$ and theoretical reasoning. We concede that the literature on deductive reasoning does contain evidence of deductive competence and that is one aspect of the evidence that theories of reasoning must explain (see Evans 1991). However, we also believe that an undue emphasis on rationality$_2$ and the belief in the logicality = rationality equation has not only dominated theoretical effort in the psychology of reasoning but has also led to widespread misinterpretation of much of the data which demonstrate "biases" and content effects. Detailed arguments against the "rationality = logicality" thesis are presented by Evans (1993) and will not be repeated here. Reinterpretation of literature in terms of practical reasoning will, however, be offered in the review sections of this paper.

The Belief Bias Effect in Syllogistic Reasoning

Real-life reasoning is not, in general, well modeled by laboratory reasoning tasks. In everyday life we do not reason in order to be logical, but are logical (when we are) in order to achieve our goals. We often do not restrict ourselves to information given in premises, and frequently go beyond any information we have in inductive reasoning. Rational$_1$ reasoning in the real world means that it is applied to the achievement of a practical goal, or the selection of a decision, and that as much relevant knowledge as possible is retrieved and applied to the problem at hand. It is in this context that laboratory studies must be interpreted. If logical errors occur then we must ask first whether these result from processes which would be adaptive (i.e., goal-fulfilling) in application to real-world problems. Only if the answer to this is negative is it sensible to consider what the "errors" tell us about the cognitive constraints on human inference.

We illustrate the problem of illogicality in experimental studies of reasoning by reference to the belief bias effect in deductive reasoning – a phenomenon which appears on first inspection to render people inherently irrational. First, we will present a brief review of the recent research findings in this area and then we will offer an interpretation of the effect in the context of the current argument. In a typical deductive reasoning task, subjects are presented with the premises of an argument and asked whether a particular conclusion follows logically from them. Alternative procedures involve asking subjects to choose from a list of putative conclusions or asking them to generate a conclusion of their own. With the first method, belief bias consists in tending to endorse conclusions which are *a priori* believable as valid and those which are unbelievable as invalid, regardless of the logic of the problem.

Belief Bias: The Phenomena

The belief bias effect was first reported by Wilkins (1928) and replicated a number of times during the following 30 years or so. Unfortunately, a number of these studies were marred by methodological errors (see Evans 1982, pp. 107–111; Revlin, Leirer, Yopp, and Yopp 1980). Paradoxically, recent interest in the phenomenon was revived by Revlin et al. (1980), whose motivation was apparently to discredit the belief bias effect. In particular they argued that subjects

might be converting premises, for example, reading "All A are B" as "All B are A." In their own experiments, with new controls, they did produce significant, if small, effects of belief bias which they play down in discussion. Revlin et al. asked subjects to choose from a list of conclusions which leads to problems of interpretation as to what is the correct answer and may have led them to underestimate the size of the bias.

Evans, Barston, and Pollard (1983) used carefully constructed syllogisms whose premises were logically unaffected by conversion, and presented a single conclusion for evaluation. Instructions to subjects included the following sentences, intended explicitly to preclude the use of prior beliefs about the problem material:

> You should answer the question on the assumption that the two statements are, in fact, true. If you judge that the conclusion necessarily follows from the statements, you should answer "yes" otherwise "no".

An example of an invalid syllogism with a believable conclusion used by Evans et al. is the following:

No addictive things are inexpensive

Some cigarettes are inexpensive

Therefore, some addictive things are not cigarettes

By reordering the words, the same logical form can produce a syllogism with an unbelievable conclusion as follows:

No cigarettes are inexpensive

Some addictive things are inexpensive

Therefore, some cigarettes are not addictive

If the terms in the conclusion are reordered without altering the premises then the argument is valid. Thus it is possible to construct four classes of syllogism: valid–believable, valid–unbelievable, invalid–believable, and invalid–unbelievable. In spite of the use of explicit deductive reasoning instructions and an intelligent undergraduate student population, massive effects of belief bias were observed. The basic acceptance rate of conclusions in these four categories observed by Evans et al. is shown in Table 1. There are three substantial and highly significant effects: (1) Subjects endorse more conclusions which are logically valid than invalid; (2) subjects endorse more conclusions which are believable than unbelievable; and

Table 1: Percentage Conclusions Accepted by Subjects in the Study of Evans, Barston and Pollard (1983) Averaged Over Three Experiments

	Believable	*Unbelievable*
Valid	89	56
Invalid	71	10

(3) logic and belief interact in their effect on subjects' choices. The latter finding reflects the fact that the belief bias effect is much larger for invalid syllogisms.

Subsequent research has been mostly theory driven. Evans et al. (1983) favored an account of the findings which was later named as the selective scrutiny model (see Barston 1986; Evans 1989). The other major account is based upon the mental models theory of reasoning (Johnson-Laird 1983; Johnson-Laird and Byrne 1991) and was first developed by Oakhill and Johnson-Laird (1985). The selective scrutiny model assumes that subjects first evaluate the believability of the conclusion. If it is believable, they usually accept it without an attempt to assess the logic of the syllogisms. If it is unbelievable, then they are more likely to check the logic. This predicts the interaction shown in Table 1 due to the "selective scrutiny" of arguments with unbelievable conclusions.

Evidence in favor of the selective scrutiny model is provided first by verbal protocol analyses reported by Evans et al. (1983). They found that subjects who referred only to the conclusion showed most belief bias, while those who referred to the premises and then the conclusion showed the least belief bias. Intermediate levels were associated with subjects who referred to the premises *after* reference to the conclusion. Hence, belief bias was associated with conclusion rather than premise-based reasoning. A second source of evidence was that of Evans and Pollard (1990), who predicted and found that increasing the logical complexity of the problems – and hence the overall error rate – did *not* increase the size of the belief bias effect. This surprising finding is predicted on the grounds that in the selective scrutiny model belief bias occurs prior to an attempt at reasoning. Hence, any subsequent failures in reasoning due to logical complexity will add only random error.

The mental model theory of deductive reasoning (see Johnson-Laird and Byrne 1991) assumes that subjects attempt to build models

compatible with the premises from which putative conclusions are formed. Invalid conclusions are generally avoided by searching for counter-examples, that is, by attempting to generate models compatible with premises but incompatible with the putative conclusions. Oakhill and Johnson-Laird (1985) argued that where putative conclusions are believable subjects may neglect the third stage of seeking counter-examples. This would lead to precisely the high acceptance of invalid–believable conclusions which is typical of findings in the area (see Table 1). While a kind of selective scrutiny argument itself, the mental model account differs from the proposals of Evans et al. (1983) in assuming that some reasoning always occurs prior to the influence of belief.

A variety of types of evidence have been claimed in favor of the mental models account. Oakhill and Johnson-Laird (1985) and Oakhill, Johnson-Laird, and Garnham (1989) have shown that subjects may be biased in favor of *producing* believable conclusions when given only the premises of the argument, hence showing that the effect is not simply due to the evaluation of presented conclusions. However, Oakhill et al. (1989) also found that subjects may withhold unbelievable conclusions on one-model valid problems, where no counter-examples exist, and are only able to offer an ad hoc account in terms of "conclusion filtering." In fact, there are several sources of evidence demonstrating a negative belief bias, that is, preference for neutral over unbelievable conclusions (Evans and Perry 1990; Evans and Pollard 1990; Newstead, Pollard, Evans, and Allen 1992) which present theoretical problems for both accounts considered here.

A recent paper by Newstead et al. (1992) reports five new experiments which fail to support the original selective scrutiny model and which provide evidence for a modified mental model account. One new finding reported (Experiments 1 and 2) was that little belief bias occurs, and the belief by logic interaction disappears, when the invalid syllogisms used have conclusions which are determinately *false* rather than indeterminate as in the Evans et al. (1983) study. This cannot be explained on the assumption that belief bias precedes an attempt at reasoning. However, the mental model account proposes that initial modeling and formation of a putative conclusion precede the influence of belief. In these cases a believable–invalid conclusion could not survive the initial stage since *no* model of the premises will permit it. Another finding reported (Experiment 5) was that the belief by logic interaction was removed by elaborated instructions emphasizing logical necessity, which would presumably discourage premature conclusions and stimulate a search for counter-examples. (For discussion of this paper, and a reply, see Oakhill and Garnham 1993; Newstead and Evans 1993).

Is Belief Bias Rational₁?

Now what should we make of these findings in terms of our argument for rationality$_1$ in human reasoning? These findings do appear to provide evidence of highly irrational reasoning. In the Evans et al. study, for example, subjects were told to base their reasoning only on the information presented and to endorse only conclusions which necessarily followed from the premises. Despite the fact that subjects *can* figure out the logic – as the large effect of validity shows – they were nonetheless quite unable to ignore the believability of the conclusions. Can the belief bias effect be explained within the notion of bounded rationality$_1$ presented earlier? We believe it can. First, we have to recognize that mechanisms of reasoning have evolved to facilitate the achievement of goals in the real world rather than to solve problems in the psychological laboratory. Second, we have to be sensitive to relevant cognitive constraints.

The first question, then, is whether belief bias effects could result from a normally adaptive process. Both major theoretical accounts considered above involve the notion of selective scrutiny. Only conclusions which are *unbelievable* to the reasoner appear likely to get a full process of logical evaluation. Other invalid conclusions are often accepted unless they are incompatible with the premises or unless elaborated instructions are provided. In general, both believable and even neutral conclusions tend to be accepted without adequate search for counter-examples.

Why would it be adaptive to reason only selectively and more so when the argument goes against rather than for one's beliefs? The maintenance of a large and stable set of beliefs is essential for intelligent behavior, since this forms the basis for any actions which one may take to achieve one's goals. When arguments are encountered which support existing beliefs, the evidence suggests that we do not examine them closely. This is surely rational$_1$ since (1) it is advantageous to maintain beliefs unless there is good reason to revise them, and (2) the processing effort required constantly to question the evidence of current beliefs would be enormous. The situation when confronted with argument or evidence for a statement which contradicts one's beliefs is quite different. To accept such an argument uncritically would be damaging to the individual since this would introduce a contradiction and disrupt the internal consistency of their belief system. Hence, it is quite rational that such arguments should be subjected to the closest possible scrutiny and refuted if at all possible.

A distinct but related phenomenon to belief bias is that of confirmation bias, although some controversy surrounds the evidence claimed for the phenomenon (see Evans 1989; Klayman and Ha 1987). Confirmation bias consists of a tendency to seek out evidence which confirms rather than contradicts current beliefs and thus runs counter to the rational$_2$ falsification model of science espoused by the philosopher Karl Popper (1959, 1962). The two phenomena together constitute belief-maintaining biases which are often portrayed as evidence of high irrationality in human reasoning. However, Baron (1985) in discussing possible causes of belief-preserving biases offers an argument related to our above comment on belief bias:

> "...when beliefs are integrated with each other, so that each provides support (evidence) for the others, a change in one belief might weaken others as well. If we are also motivated to have consistent beliefs, such a change might require reevaluation of other beliefs than the one under attack at the moment. Such reevaluation will require thinking, which has a cost. Thus, revision of a single belief might lead either to inconsistency or to further thinking, both undesirable consequences, although perhaps not equally undesirable for all people. (pp. 165–166)"

The problem with viewing confirmation bias as evidence of irrationality is first that this is based upon rationality$_2$, and second that it regards any act of confirmation as illogical. Beliefs that hold on most occasions and which maintain consistency with other beliefs may benefit the individual, even though occasional exceptions show them to be strictly false.

Consider the example of falsifying evidence in scientific research. Reading the arguments of some psychologists discussing belief and confirmation biases, you would think that abandonment of a theory was required by a single failed prediction. These psychologists are apparently presupposing quite a naive Popperian scientific methodology, which has been heavily criticized by philosophers of science in recent years, in large part for rejecting any notion of confirmation or inductive reasoning (Earman 1992; Howson and Urbach 1989). A prediction is usually inferred, not from a theory on its own, but from the theory along with an indefinite number of background beliefs, for example, about the conditions under which the experiment is conducted, and the reliability of the experimental equipment. It is also rare for the prediction to be certain given all these beliefs or hypotheses. For these reasons, it can be far from certain that there is a serious problem at the heart of a previously well-confirmed theory when there has been a failed prediction.

In this section we have offered an interpretation of one of the most reliable biases in the experimental literature on reasoning which is compatible with our notion of rationality₁ in reasoning. We now turn to another area of the experimental literature on deductive reasoning in order to discuss recent work on reasoning with deontic conditionals. This work, we believe, directly demonstrates the decision-making nature of subjects' inferences using laboratory tasks.

Deontic Reasoning

The primary purpose of most of our ordinary reasoning is to help us make good decisions, so that we can have reasonable success in achieving our goals. This point was brought out clearly by Grice (1975), who noted that efficient communication has to be a goal-directed process, in which the participants must infer each other's purposes and then make appropriate decisions about their own speech acts and other actions. Similarly, the purpose of reasoning is best served by drawing inferences from *all* our beliefs, not just from an artificially restricted set of premises, as in most psychological experiments on reasoning.

On this basis, we should also expect people to display rationality₁ in experiments calling for something like ordinary practical reasoning, which is aimed at realistic goals and not at abstract theoretical ones. Striking results of changing the nature of experimental reasoning tasks in this way can be observed in the recent history of work on the Wason selection task. The developments in question have focused selection task research on a type of *deontic* reasoning which is directly and immediately practi-

cal. The object of deontic reasoning is to infer what actions ought to be taken, or may be taken, and it calls for cognitions of probability, utility, and social perspective – aspects of thought which hitherto were the prime concern of research on decision making. Thus in deontic-reasoning research we have a premier case of cross-pollination between the two fields of reasoning and decision making.

The Indicative and Deontic Selection Tasks

As many readers will be aware, a typical selection task experiment involves presenting a conditional sentence of the form *if p then q* with four cards, each of which has a *p* or *not-p* value one one side and a *q* or *not-q* value on the other (see Evans et al. 1993, Chapter 4, for a comprehensive review of work on this problem). In the standard – what we describe as *indicative* – form of the selection task, the conditional is couched in abstract materials (e.g., "If there is an A on one side of a card then there is a 3 on the other"), and the subject is asked to decide which cards would need to be turned over in order to decide *whether the conditional is true or false*. The correct answer is *p* and *not-q* since only the combination of these two values on the same cards could disprove the conditional. However, typically fewer than 10% of intelligent adult subjects give the correct response when the task is presented in this way: Most often they say *p* and *q* or just *p*. In recent times most researchers' attention has been concentrated on facilitating the production of the logically warranted response by changing the content and context in which the problem is presented. Many of these involve a *deontic* version of the task in which subjects decide which cards will tell if a *rule has been followed or violated*, as opposed to deciding whether it is true or false.

For the purposes of the present discussion, the crucial development was the use of a generalized deontic context by Cheng and Holyoak (1985). To explain why the use of such a context has the effect of facilitating the "correct" response, Cheng and Holyoak introduced the theory of *pragmatic reasoning schemas*. It is held that in situations clearly perceived by the reasoner as deontic (in their research, they referred specifically to situations of *permission* and *obligation*, though there are some problems with their definition of these terms; see Manktelow and Over 1991), a set of generalized production rules was activated in which the relation between preconditions and actions was specified. Mapping these to the specific task content would deliver the appropriate selections.

For example, a version which reliably facilitates performance is that of the drinking age rule (Griggs and Cox 1982). Subjects are asked to imagine that they are police officers checking whether the rule "If a person is drinking beer then that person must be over 19 years of age" has been violated, by inspecting cards which have a beverage on one side and the age of the drinker on the other. Most subjects correctly turn over "beer" (*p*) and an age under 19 years (*not-q*). This is attributed by Cheng and Holyoak to use of a permission schema in which the rule is mapped to "If you perform an action (*in this case drinking beer*) then you must fulfil a precondition (*in this case being over 19 years of age*)."

This theory has led to an upsurge in research on deontic reasoning and has dominated the explanations of its findings, but it has not gone unchallenged. Its two principal competitors are the theory of mental models (derived from Johnson-Laird and Byrne 1991) and the social contract theory of Cosmides (1989). We shall defer discussion of the former for the moment, and pause briefly on the latter before looking in detail at some of the most recent work. Cosmides' theory has sustained serious criticism, making it no longer tenable in its original form (see, e.g., Cheng and Holyoak 1989; Manktelow and Over 1987, 1991). However, it is of singular importance in one respect: its emphasis on benefits and cost in the explanatory framework. Cosmides' theory holds that the essence of the kinds of deontic thinking explored by reasoning researchers, for example permissions, lies in social exchange; this in turn boils down to an implicit or explicit contract held by its parties, that *if you take a benefit then you pay a cost*. Human life would be impossible without an innate understanding of this contract, says Cosmides, which entails an immediate ability to detect its violation: instances of people taking a benefit without paying a cost, or *cheaters* as she calls them.

Recent Studies of Deontic Reasoning

Recent experimental work has enlarged our understanding of the nature of deontic reasoning, and enabled us to look not only at the particular issue of explaining what goes on in selection tasks of this type, but also at the implications of these findings for theory and for the relation between reasoning and decision making. Let us take these issues in turn.

Gigerenzer and Hug (1992), for example, distinguish between two core components of Cosmides' theory: social contracts and cheating. They found that casting a task in social contract form was not sufficient to produce facilitation of the *p, not-q* response. This only occurred when a cheating context was specified. When the cheating conditions are clearly set out, this form of deontic reasoning becomes very straightforward, as Light, Girotto, and Legrenzi (1990) found: Children of 12 or younger are adept at such reasoning tasks. Detection of the violation of a clearly specified deontic rule such as a permission (Gigerenzer and Hug 1992; Manktelow and Over 1991), promise (Light et al. 1990), obligation (Gigerenzer and Hug 1992), or warning (Politzer and Nguyen-Xuan 1992) has been demonstrated to be a natural cognitive process by these studies.

Such research has also elucidated the role of social cognition in this form of practical thought. All the studies just cited have pointed out the role of two fundamental parties in deontic reasoning: the one who lays down the rule, and the one whose behavior is its target, termed the *agent* and the *actor*, respectively, by Manktelow and Over (1991). These authors have shown that violations of a rule such as permission can be performed by either party and in more than one way. Take the use of a standard conditional permission rule, *if you do p then you may do q*, which in many contexts pragmatically implies that the only way you get permission to do *q* is by doing *p*. Subjects readily understand that, in realistic contexts of this general type, the actor goes wrong by doing *q* without fulfilling *p*, while the agent goes wrong by not allowing the actor to do *q* although *p* has been fulfilled, or by allowing *q* without *p* being fulfilled. Note that these are not all cases of someone being *cheated*, but they are all cases in which someone suffers a cost because of the failure to conform to the rule, or what is pragmatically conveyed by its use, in a realistic context. Permission has, as Gigerenzer and Hug term it, *bilateral* options for violation; some deontic relations are *unilateral* in that they can generally only be violated by the agent (e.g., in the case of promises) or the actor (in the case of obligations).

These observations have forced a reconsideration of the traditional facilitation effect in selection task research, and consequently to an appreciation of the relation between what has always been seen as a reasoning task and its role in explaining decision making, hence to the relation between rationality₁ and rationality₂, as set out above.

As we saw, the idea of the facilitation effect arises from the original use of the selection task in research on theoretical reasoning, using indicative conditionals, for which a correct response has generally been taken to be to select the *p* and *not-q* cards. The recent studies outlined above have shown that it is routinely possible to elicit high rates of *not-p, q* selections in certain well-defined contexts. For instance, Manktelow and Over (1991) used a permission rule, "If you spend more than £100 then you may take a free gift"; subjects were readily cued to select the *not-p, q* combination (spent less than £100, took the gift) when the scenario referred to a store giving out more than it should, or customers taking more than they were entitled to (see also Politzer and Nguyen-Xuan 1992, who independently used similar materials and reported similar effects). It is clear then that what is being facilitated here is not something corresponding to the truth conditions of the material conditional.

A Rational₁ Interpretation of Deontic Reasoning

The notion of testing the truth conditions of a conditional does not apply to deontic reasoning at all. In the experiments discussed above, people are not being asked to test the truth of rules, but are being asked to detect violations (a form of action) of rules whose truth status is not in question. This leads to further questions: What counts as a correct response in this case? What counts as a true deontic rule?

The first question leads us to focus again on the relation between reasoning and decision making, and between rationality₁ and rationality₂. As Light et al. (1990) put it, responses in deontic selection tasks should be judged as correct if they lead to the detection of the possible violators, independent of the values that the corresponding cases would have under a formal heading. Detecting violation is an important practical matter. If we could not do this, we would fail to achieve many of our prudential, social, and moral goals.

As for the truth of deontic rules, this gives us reason to part from the schema theories (derived from Cheng and Holyoak, which most current theorists adhere to) on the grounds that the theory of pragmatic reasoning schemas is a non-semantic production rule theory: It contains no component which could specify why a deontic utterance should be made or accepted in the first place, or when it would be felicitous to do so. We have put forward elsewhere an alternative based on the theory of mental models (see Manktelow and Over 1991; and Over and Manktelow 1993, for details) which addresses this and other points. It is based on the semantic notion of modeling the state of affairs specified by the particular deontic context and content, and the notion of preference between these states.

Suppose that a mother is trying to decide whether to let her son go out to play. She might think that he is likely to get into trouble if he goes out, and in that case, she will prefer him to stay in. She will then announce her decision by saying, "You must stay in," which places her son under an obligation. Another possibility is that she is indifferent to whether he goes out or not, and she might even prefer him to go out (where he will not be under her feet). Expressing a permission, she will consequently say, "You may go out." A slightly more complex case would be one in which she is indifferent to whether her son goes out provided that he satisfies some condition which she has as a goal, say, that of getting his room tidy. She will now utter a conditional permission, that is, a deontic conditional like "If you tidy your room, you may go out."

The mother will consider the above conditional permission true just in case she is indifferent to whether her son goes out, or even prefers her son to go out, given that he tidies his room. If he does do that, he will give his mother something which has utility for her, a tidy room, in exchange for achieving a goal which has utility for him, going out. Notice that this concept of truth for deliberative deontic statements is a subjective one, and indeed depends on the decision theoretic notion of preference, and also that of subjective probability (which we shall discuss below). If the mother foresaw more likely benefit, or less likely cost, in her son staying in than going out after he tidied his room, she would not assert the conditional permission as true. Note also that we are using these terms in a technical sense. To say that a tidy room has more utility for the mother than an untidy one is just to say that she prefers the former to the latter. To say that her son going out is a benefit for the mother, or a cost, is just to say that she prefers the former to the present state of affairs which the son is in, or vice versa.

From the son's perspective, he has to grasp the social context in which he finds himself. His mother has power or authority over him, and can give him benefits or extract costs from him. She is in a position to make obligation or permission statements which he must take account of if he is to achieve his goals. To do that, he must also understand the essentially pragmatic notion of a violation of a rule. He would generally infer pragmatically, from his mother's utterance of the conditional permission, that the only way he could get permission to go out would be by tidying his room. But the mother might add that the son may go out if he does the washing up (or anything else constructive), and then he might adjust his pragmatic inferences accordingly. Moreover, if the house catches fire, he needs to know that he will not violate his mother's rules, along with her presupposed qualifying conditions and underlying goals to do with his safety, if he rushes out without tidying his room or doing the washing up. In technical terms, his deontic reasoning, at least about violations, has to be nonmonotonic, and be highly sensitive to context, implicated and presupposed information, and the way benefits and costs for himself and his mother change with changing circumstances.

The evidence we have reviewed implies that subjects can identify themselves with a perspective like that of the son's and make rational$_1$ decisions from it. The subjects, acting as the son, decide to pick just those cards which might reveal a violation by the mother. This violation would be one in which the son suffered a cost because he tidied his room, but his mother did not allow him to attain his goal of going out. It is important for the son to uncover such cases to help him prevent them in the future, by not believing his mother's promises. It could be said that, in this simple case, subjects are acting in a way that would enable them to maximize subjective expected utility from the perspective they adopt. But that does mean that subjects would always act so as to meet such an ideal standard in any deontic reasoning task.

There is, in fact, already some evidence (in Manktelow and Over 1990) that subjects do far less well in a deontic selection task when violating a rule would bring less benefit than conforming to it, rather than a strict loss from a neutral position, such as might result from being punished by an authority. Classical normative decision theory does not distinguish between benefits and costs in a way which would justify this. Some descriptive decision theories, however, do predict special sensitivity to costs, such as the seminal prospect theory of Kahneman and Tversky (1979) with its notion of a reference point, below which one thinks of oneself as suffering a loss. It can also be argued that, if one's present position is reasonably satisfactory, then being especially sensitive to possible losses is a good, rational$_1$, satisficing strategy. (See Kahneman and Varey 1991 for recent work on loss aversion, and a discussion of its possible long-term benefits.)

Decision Theory and Rationality

The deontic reasoning we have discussed is practical reasoning, in which we try to infer which actions we ought to perform or may perform. We have suggested that people try to determine whether to accept or assert deontic rules by considering which states of affairs they prefer to others. After doing this, they can use these rules efficiently to infer what they should or may do in appropriate contexts, as these arise in ordinary affairs. This view sees a deep link between deontic reasoning and decision making, in which preference is the basic notion. But as we have also said, classical decision theory lays down the normative SEU principle, according to which rational action is a matter of maximizing expected utility in one's choices, and this should not be the standard of what it is to have rationality$_1$. We have followed Simon (e.g., 1957, 1983) in rejecting this standard and in speaking instead of bounded rationality. Put in the simplest way, the essential point is (as philosophers say) that *ought* implies *can*; in other words, if we are serious in holding that people ought to conform to some standard, then they should be able to conform to it. But people are often unable to conform to the absolute ideal of classical decision theory, and so it cannot always be the case that they ought to do this.

One particular limitation of classical decision theory we must continue to stress, because this has received so little comment in the psychological literature, is its failure to account for, or take proper account of, people's practical reasoning. Classical decision theory presupposes that people can express their preferences, and that these can be measured in some way, but obviously people's preferences are not always given merely by their basic drives and immediate desires. Preferences are often inferred in sometimes quite complex deontic reasoning, employing perhaps many prudential, social, or moral rules. We must have some account of these inferred preferences in decision making; and yet at the same time, we cannot idealistically assume that people have been able to perform all relevant deontic inferences when they express preferences after some actual deontic reasoning in the real world.

Depending on the circumstances, we might be able to set a reasonable standard for the number and type of deontic inferences people can be expected to perform, if they have rationality₁. We could not necessarily require them to perform all relevant deontic inferences, from the rules they accept, and so maximize their subjective expected utility, where this is defined by the ideal preferences they would have if they had the time and mental power to perform all these inferences. This is just to say that we could only require some degree of bounded rationality₁ of them.

Another limitation of classical decision making shows in the standard it sets for probability judgments. It requires that these judgments conform to the principles of the abstract mathematical theory of probability: the probability calculus. We do need good probability judgments in practical reasoning. One option is not necessarily better than another because it may lead to the more highly desired outcome or goal; it can all depend on how probable the different outcomes are. There are powerful arguments for holding that probability judgments should ideally conform to the probability calculus (Howson and Urbach 1989). None of us, however, can ensure that we conform to the theory's principles in all cases. This is well illustrated by the fact that the probability calculus requires that all logical truths be assigned a probability of 1, although there is in general no effective way of deciding whether or not a proposition is a logical truth.

The probability calculus also requires that the probability of the conclusion of a valid inference given its premises to be 1. But asking people what follows from given premises, which they are in effect to take as certain and definitely not to supplement with anything else they believe, is an unnatural request in itself. People, quite rightly for ordinary decision making, are generally concerned with what follows from their relevant beliefs, and they do not necessarily take even these as certain. For a belief bias effect to limit seriously people's rationality₁ it would have to be the case that people often fail to achieve their ordinary goals because they are too confident, or not confident enough, in the conclusions they infer from their beliefs, whether they think of these as certain or uncertain. Note that the uncertainty of a belief is 1 minus its subjective probability, and that the degree of uncertainty of a conclusion validly inferred from

uncertain beliefs should not exceed the sum of their uncertainties, according to a basic principle of rationality₂ (Adams 1975; Edgington 1992). The research we reviewed above on belief bias effects in deductive reasoning does not show that people often depart from this principle in their actual decision making (though see Tversky and Kahneman 1983 on the conjunction fallacy), nor that if they do in some cases, they often fail to achieve their goals as a result.

So far we have spoken of what people's confidence in the conclusion of a deductive inference should be just given specific premises, which are either to be thought of as certain, or as expressing beliefs which may not be certain. However, degrees of confidence are usually discussed in the body of research on probability judgments and decision making, which unfortunately, as we say, has been seen as distinct from the work on deductive reasoning until recently. In the former body of research, people are said to be overconfident, or underconfident, about some proposition depending on whether the subjective probability they ascribe to it is greater than, or less than, its objective probability, which is usually measured or estimated by the frequency with which events occur in the real world. For example, we may think it highly likely to be sunny on days when it is, in fact, objectively unlikely to be sunny. This difference should show up in a tendency for us to be wrong in our forecasting of sunny days, and we are said to be overconfident that it will be sunny on one of these days. On the other hand, if our subjective confidence that it will be sunny more or less matches the objective probability that it will be, then we are said to be well calibrated on this matter.

Whether people are generally well calibrated obviously has something to do with their rationality, and there is a vigorous debate in progress about the extent to which people are sometimes underconfident and sometimes overconfident, the possible reasons for this, and how far it affects their rationality. (See particularly Gigerenzer, Hoffrage, and Kleinbölting 1991 and Griffin and Tversky 1992.) We can only make some brief points here about this issue and rationality₁.

The abstract principles of the probability calculus do not themselves specify how the subjective and objective notions of probability should be related to each other. This relation has to be covered by some further rule or rules, such as the main one proposed and discussed by a number of philosophers, usually called the principal principle. (For more on this, and the philosophical issues it raises which we cannot go into here, see Lewis 1981; Howson and Urbach 1989; and Earman 1992.) Suppose we are sure that there is a low (alternatively middling or high) objective probability that it will be sunny on a certain type of day, say, just characterized by the fact that the barometer is falling (steady or rising). Then according to a version of the principal principle, our subjective confidence that it will be sunny on a particular day of just that type should be equally low (middling or high). There are reasons for holding that it is rational$_1$ to conform to this principle generally, though perhaps not invariably, as we will shortly illustrate. However, the problem with testing whether subjects conform to this principle is, again, that it is difficult to be sure that subjects are restricting themselves to just the information they are strictly given by the experimenters, say, that the day is to be characterized by the fact that the barometer is falling and in no other way. This is particularly a problem if we move away from rather abstract questions about matters distant from real life, such as ones about colored balls in urns, to more realistic ones, to which further information may be relevant, including perhaps what might be pragmatically inferred from the experimental context.

It is very important to note the research which has increasingly found evidence that subjects can sometimes be good at reasoning about objective frequencies (see Cosmides and Tooby 1996; Gigerenzer et al. 1991; Tversky and Kahneman 1983; but note also Griffin & Tversky 1992). This is something that they would have to be fairly competent at in order to have a reasonable chance of achieving some of their goals in ordinary affairs. But it is striking that there is sometimes quite a difference, displayed in this research, between what subjects say about the subjective probability of a single case and about the frequency with which something will happen in cases of that type. We would show this difference if we expressed great confidence that it would be sunny on a particular day, yet were also sure that it rained on most days like that. Thus we would appear to violate the principal principle, and this could limit our ability to achieve some of our ordinary goals. If we observe the frequency with which it rains under certain conditions, but do not adjust our degree of belief appropriately to this, then we could tend to get wet when we want to be dry. We would also be in trouble if we did not match our subjective probability judgments about how trustworthy some-

one was to the frequency with which he broke promises to us.

Our arguments for rationality$_1$ by no means imply the extremely strong conclusion that people are always well calibrated and conform to the principal principle in ordinary affairs. We would not even make this claim, on simple evolutionary grounds, about people living under primitive conditions. No doubt pregnancy is very risky indeed under such conditions, and so it might be adaptive under those conditions to be *overconfident* about one's chances of safely producing healthy offspring. It is at least as hard to argue that being well calibrated about the risks of pregnancy would have led to greater reproductive success than being overconfident.

However that may be, research so far conducted has not shown that there is a widespread tendency to violate the principal principle in ordinary decision making, nor that when it is sometimes violated there, people invariably fail to achieve their goals as a result. Sometimes being overconfident in the technical sense could help to achieve one's goals, by increasing self-confidence in the ordinary sense and keeping doubts from one's mind. A woman who is overconfident about herself having a healthy baby, even though she knows the objective frequency of complications in pregnancy, may be helped by her positive attitude. Griffin and Tversky (1992) rightly give examples in which overconfidence is more of a cost than a benefit, but then we would not claim that people are never irrational$_1$ in particular cases, as there are cognitive constraints to take into account. These can exist alongside a general tendency for human beings to achieve a reasonable number of their goals, which they would have to do to survive any length of time, let alone to create complex societies and advanced technologies.

Conclusions

The notion of rationality which really matters to people is rationality$_1$. People in general do have this to a fair degree, as they do tend to be reasonably good at achieving most of their goals. This is obvious enough, as long as we do not make the mistake of thinking of goals only as grand, distant ends which take special ability or luck to achieve, like becoming a millionaire. We should be impressed enough that people are able to achieve more "mundane" goals, such as all those involved in learning a language, contributing to a cooperative group like a family, and generally finding one's way in the world. We cannot yet build intelligent machines which can do any of these things; it is much easier to program them to do formal logic. In experimental set-ups, people do sometimes depart from the normative principles of logic, the probability calculus, and decision theory. But this in itself does not demonstrate that they have pervasive biases and are generally irrational[1].

In fact, people sometimes achieve a goal in part because they do *not* try to maximize utility (in the technical sense) or hold coherent and consistent beliefs. With bounded capacities and limited time, people would sometimes miss the chance to achieve a reasonably satisfying goal if they paused to wonder whether their preference relation or their beliefs satisfied abstract normative principles. They can sometimes save precious time by accepting a plausible conclusion without examining closely the logic of its argument, or by being very vague about their preferences.

Of course, to say that people have a reasonable degree of rationality[1] is not to say that this can never be profitably improved. Our natural capacity for practical reasoning originally evolved under very different conditions from some of those in which we find ourselves today. In a technological society, having the means to be extremely precise, for example, about profits and losses can be important. Even quite artificial experiments may reveal bounds on our reasoning abilities which sometimes need to be overcome for achieving certain goals. We should thus study when and how logic, statistics, and decision theory can increase rationality[1] (see Evans 1989). But equally we should remember that normative research, particularly on practical reasoning, is far from an end. Probably the only way to obtain agreed normative principles for this is to study ever more closely the often highly efficient nature of ordinary goal-directed reasoning.

References

Adams, E. (1975). *The logic of conditionals: An application of probability to deductive logic*. Dordrecht: Reidel.

Audi, R. (1989). *Practical reasoning*. London: Routledge.

Baron, J. (1985). *Rationality and intelligence*. Cambridge, UK: Cambridge University Press.

Barston, J. L. (1986). *An investigation into belief biases in reasoning*. Unpublished Ph.D. thesis, University of Plymouth.

Cheng, P. W., & Holyoak, K. J. (1985). Pragmatic reasoning schemas. *Cognitive Psychology, 17*, 391–416.

Cheng, P. W., & Holyoak, K. J. (1989). On the natural selection of reasoning theories. *Cognition, 33*, 285–313.

Cohen, L. J. (1981). Can human irrationality be experimentally demonstrated? *Behavioural and Brain Sciences, 4*, 317–370.

Cosmides, L. (1989). The logic of social exchange: Has natural selection shaped how humans reason? Studies with the Wason selection task. *Cognition, 33*, 187–276.

Cosmides, L., & Tooby, J. (1996). Are humans good intuitive statisticians after all? Rethinking some conclusions from the literature on judgement under uncertainty. *Cognition, 58*, 1–73.

Dennett, D. C. (1978). *Brainstorms*. Cited by Stich, S. P. (1985). Could man be an irrational animal? *Synthese, 64*, 115–135.

Earman, J. (1992). *Bayes or bust: A critical examination of Bayesian confirmation theory*. Cambridge, MA: MIT Press.

Edgington, D. (1992). Validity, uncertainty and vagueness. *Analysis, 52*, 193–204.

Evans, J. St. B. T. (1989). *Bias in reasoning: Causes and consequences*. Hove, UK: Erlbaum.

Evans, J. St. B. T. (1991). Theories of human reasoning: The fragmented state of the art. *Theory and Psychology, 1*, 83–105.

Evans, J. St. B. T. (1992). *The psychology of deductive reasoning*. London: Routledge & Kegan Paul.

Evans, J. St. B. T. (1993). Bias and rationality. In K. I. Manktelow & D. E. Over (Eds.), *Rationality*. London: Routledge.

Evans, J. St. B. T., Barston, J. L., & Pollard, P. (1983). On the conflict between logic and belief in syllogistic reasoning. *Memory & Cognition, 11*, 295–306.

Evans, J. St. B. T., Newstead, S. E., & Byrne, R. M. J. (1993). *Human reasoning: The psychology of deduction*. Hove, UK: Erlbaum.

Evans, J. St. B. T., & Perry, T. (1990). *Belief bias in children's reasoning*. Unpublished manuscript, University of Plymouth.

Evans, J. St. B. T., & Pollard, P. (1990). Belief bias and problem complexity in deductive reasoning. In J. P. Caverni, J. M. Fabre, & M. Gonzales (Eds.), *Cognitive biases*. Amsterdam: North-Holland.

Gigerenzer, G., Hoffrage, U., & Kleinbölting, H. (1991). Probabilistic mental models: A Brunswikian theory of confidence. *Psychological Review, 98*, 506–528.

Gigerenzer, G., & Hug, K. (1992). Domain-specific reasoning: social contracts, cheating, and perspective change. *Cognition, 43*, 127–171.

Grice, H. P. (1975). Logic and conversation. In P. Cole & J. P. Morgan (Eds.), *Syntax and semantics. Vol 3: Speech acts*. New York: Seminar Press.

Griffin, D., & Tversky, A. (1992). The weighing of evidence and the determinants of confidence. *Cognitive Psychology, 24*, 411–435.

Griggs, R. A., & Cox, J. R. (1982). The elusive thematic-materials effect in Wason's selection task. *British Journal of Psychology, 73*, 407–420.

Howson, C., & Urbach, P. (1989). *Scientific reasoning: The Bayesian approach*. La Salle, IL: Open Court.

Johnson-Laird, P. N. (1983). *Mental models*. Cambridge, UK: Cambridge University Press.

Johnson-Laird, P. N. (1993). *Human and machine thinking*. Hillsdale, NJ: Erlbaum.

Johnson-Laird, P. N., & Byrne, R. M. J. (1991). *Deduction*. Hove, UK: Erlbaum.

Kahneman, D., & Tversky, A. (1979). Prospect theory: An analysis of decision under risk. *Econometrica, 47*, 263–291.

Kahneman, D., & Varey, C. (1991). Notes on the psychology of utility. In J. Elster & J. Roemer (Eds.), *Interpersonal comparisons of well-being*. Cambridge, UK: Cambridge University Press.

Klayman, J., & Ha, Y.-W. (1987). Confirmation, disconfirmation and information in hypotheses testing. *Psychological Review, 94*, 211–228.

Lewis, D. (1981). A subjectivist's guide to objective chance. In R. Jeffrey (Ed.), *Studies in inductive logic and probability*. Los Angeles: University of California Press.

Light, P. H., Girotto, V., & Legrenzi, P. (1990). Children's reasoning on conditional promises and permissions. *Cognitive Development, 5*, 369–383.

Manktelow, K. I., & Over, D. E. (1987). Reasoning and rationality. *Mind and Language, 2*, 199–219.

Manktelow, K. I., & Over, D. E. (1990). Deontic thought and the selection task. In K. Gilhooly, M. Keane, R. Logie & G. Erdos (Eds.), *Lines of thinking: Reflections on the psychology of thought* (Vol. 1). Chichester: Wiley.

Manktelow, K. I., & Over, D. E. (1991). Social roles and utilities in reasoning with deontic conditionals. *Cognition, 43*, 183–188.

Newell, A., & Simon, H. A. (1972). *Human problem solving*. Englewood Cliffs, NJ: Prentice-Hall.

Newstead, S. E., & Evans, J. St. B. T. (1993). Mental models as an explanation of belief bias effects in syllogistic reasoning. *Cognition, 45*, 93–97.

Newstead, S. E., Pollard, P., Evans, J. St. B. T., & Allen, J. (1992). The source of belief bias in syllogistic reasoning. *Cognition, 45*, 257–284.

Oakhill, J., & Garnham, A. (1993). On theories of belief bias in syllogistic reasoning. *Cognition, 46*, 87–92.

Oakhill, J., & Johnson-Laird, P. N. (1985). The effect of belief on the spontaneous production of syllogistic conclusions. *Quarterly Journal of Experimental Psychology, 37A*, 553–570.

Oakhill, J., Johnson-Laird, P. N., & Garnham, A. (1989). Believability and syllogistic reasoning. *Cognition, 31*, 117–140.

Oaksford, M., & Chater, N. (1992). Bounded rationality in taking risks and drawing inferences. *Theory and Psychology, 2*, 225–230.

O'Brien, D. P. (1993). Mental logic and irrationality: We can put a man on the moon, so why can't we solve those logical reasoning problems. In K. I. Manktelow & D. E. Over (Eds.), *Rationality*. London: Routledge.

Over, D. E., & Manktelow, K. I. (1993). Rationality, utility, and deontic reasoning. In K. I. Manktelow & D. E. Over (Eds.), *Rationality*. London: Routledge.

Politzer, G., & Nguyen-Xuan, A. (1992). Reasoning about conditional promises and warnings: Darwinian algorithms, mental models, relevance judgements or pragmatic schemas? *Quarterly Journal of Experimental Psychology, 44A*, 401–421.

Popper, K. R. (1959). *The logic of scientific discovery*. London: Hutchinson.

Popper, K. R. (1962). *Conjectures and refutations*. London: Hutchinson.

Revlin, R., Leirer, V., Yopp, H. & Yopp, R. (1980). The belief bias effect in formal reasoning: The influence of knowledge on logic. *Memory & Cognition, 8*, 584–592.

Savage, L. (1954). *The foundations of statistics*. New York: Wiley.

Simon, H. (1957). *Models of man: Social and rational*. New York: Wiley.

Simon, H. (1983). *Reason in human affairs*. Stanford: Stanford University Press.

Slote, M. (1989). *Beyond optimizing*. Cambridge, MA: Harvard University Press.

Stevenson, R. J. (1993). Rationality and reality. In K. I. Manktelow & D. E. Over (Eds.), *Rationality*. London: Routledge.

Stich, S. P. (1985). Could man be an irrational animal? *Synthese, 64*, 115–135.

Tversky, A., & Kahneman, D. (1983). Extensional versus intuitive reasoning: The conjunction fallacy in probability judgment. *Psychological Review, 90*, 293–315.

von Winterfeldt, D., & Edwards, W. (1986). *Decision analysis and behavioural research*. Cambridge, UK: Cambridge University Press.

Wilkins, M. C. (1928). The effect of changed material on the ability to do formal syllogistic reasoning. *Archives of Psychology*, No. 102.

Section 6: Abduction and Belief Change

Chapter 23: Defeasible Reasoning

JOHN L. POLLOCK

The Inadequacy of Deductive Reasoning

There was a long tradition in philosophy according to which good reasoning had to be deductively valid. However, that tradition began to be questioned in the 1960s, and is now thoroughly discredited. What caused its downfall was the recognition that many familiar kinds of reasoning are not deductively valid, but clearly confer justification on their conclusions. Here are some simple examples:

PERCEPTION

Most of our knowledge of the world derives from some form of perception. But clearly, perception is fallible. For instance, I may believe that the wall is gray on the basis of its looking gray to me. But it may actually be white, and it only looks gray because it is dimly illuminated. In this example, my evidence (the wall's looking gray) makes it reasonable for me to conclude that the wall is gray, but further evidence could force me to retract that conclusion.[1] Such a conclusion is said to be justified *defeasibly*, and the considerations that would make it unjustified are *defeaters*.

INDUCTION

There is one kind of reasoning that few ever supposed to be deductive, but it was often conveniently ignored when claiming that good reasoning had to be deductive. This is inductive reasoning, where we generalize from a restricted sample to an unrestrictedly general conclusion. For example, having observed a number of mammals and noted that they were all warm-blooded, biologists concluded that all mammals are warm-blooded. Hume's concern with induction was just that it is not deductive. He should have taken that as an indication that good reasoning need not be deductive, instead of taking that as a reason for worrying about whether it is reasonable to use induction.

PROBABILISTIC REASONING

We make essential use of probabilities in reasoning about our place in the world. Most of the generalizations that are justified inductively are probabilistic generalizations rather than exceptionless generalizations. For example, I believe that objects usually (with high probability) fall to the ground when released, but I do not believe that this will happen invariably. They might, for example, be hoisted aloft by a tornado. Still, we want to use these generalizations to predict what is going to happen to us. Because things usually fall to the ground when released, I confidently expect my keys to do so when I drop them. I am surely justified in this belief, although it is only based upon a probabilistic generalization. Because it is based on a probabilistic generalization, it is not a deductive consequence of my reasons for holding it. They make the conclusion reasonable, but I might have to retract it in the face of further information. The form of reasoning involved here is sometimes called *the statistical syllogism* (Pollock 1990), and has roughly the following form:

> From "This is an *A* and the probability of an *A* being a *B* is high," infer defeasibly, "This is a *B*."

TEMPORAL PROJECTION

Suppose we are standing in a courtyard between two clock towers, and I ask you whether the clocks agree. You look at one, noting that it reads "2:45," and then you turn to the other and note that it reads "2:45," so you report that they do. But note that you are making an assumption. You could not look at the two clocks at the same instant, so you are assuming that the time reported by the first clock did not change dramatically in the short interval it took you to turn and look at the second clock. Of course,

451

there is no logical guarantee that this is so. Things change.

Our perceptual access to the world is a kind of sampling of bits and pieces at diverse times, and to put the samples together into a coherent picture of the world we must assume that things do not change too rapidly. We have to make a defeasible assumption of stability over times. It might be supposed that we can rely upon induction to discover what properties are stable. We certainly use induction to fine-tune our assumption of stability, but induction cannot provide the origin of that assumption. The difficulty is that to confirm inductively that a property tends to be stable, we must observe that objects possessing it tend to continue to possess it over time, but to do that we must reidentify those objects over time. We do the latter in part in terms of what properties the objects have. For example, if my chair and desk could somehow exchange shapes, locations, colors, and so forth, while I am not watching them, then when I see them next I will reidentify them incorrectly. So the ability to reidentify objects requires that I assume that most of their more salient properties tend to be stable. If I had to confirm that inductively, I would have to be able to reidentify objects without regard to their properties, but that is impossible. Thus a defeasible presumption of stability must be a primitive part of our reasoning about the world.[2] A principle to the effect that one can reasonably believe that something remains true if it was true earlier is a principle of *temporal projection*.

The preceding examples make it clear that we rely heavily on defeasible reasoning for our everyday cognition about the world. The same considerations that mandate our use of defeasible reasoning make it likely that no sophisticated cognizer operating in a somewhat unpredictable environment could get by without defeasible reasoning. The philosophical problem is to understand how defeasible reasoning works.

A Very Brief History

In philosophy, the study of defeasible reasoning began with Hart's (1948) introduction of the term "defeasible" in the philosophy of law. Chisholm (1957) was the first epistemologist to use the term, taking it from Hart. He was followed by Toulmin (1958), Chisholm (1966), Pollock (1967, 1970, 1971, 1974), Rescher (1977), and then a number of authors. The philosophical work tended to look only casually at the logical structure of defeasible reasoning,

making some simple observations about how it works, and then using it as a tool in analyzing various kinds of philosophically problematic reasoning. Thus, for example, Pollock (1971, 1974) proposed to solve the problem of perception by positing a defeasible reason of the form:

> "*x* looks *R* to me" is a defeasible reason for me to believe "*x* is *R*" (for appropriate *R*).

Without knowing about the philosophical literature on defeasible reasoning, researchers in artificial intelligence (AI) rediscovered the concept (under the label "nonmonotonic logic") in the early 1980s (Reiter 1980; McCarthy 1980; McDermott and Doyle 1980). They were led to it by their attempts to solve the "frame problem," which I will discuss in detail in the section below "Illustration: The Frame Problem." Because they were interested in implementing reasoning in AI systems, they gave much more attention to the details of how defeasible reasoning works than philosophers had.[3] Unfortunately, their lack of philosophical training led AI researchers to produce accounts that were mathematically sophisticated but epistemologically naïve. Their theories could not possibly be right as accounts of human cognition, because they could not accommodate the varieties of defeasible reasoning humans actually employ. Although there is still a burgeoning industry in AI studying nonmonotonic logic, this shortcoming tends to remain to this day. I will give a few examples of this below.

There are still a number of competing views on the nature and structure of defeasible reasoning. What follows will be a (no doubt biased) account presenting my own views on the matter.

Defeasible Reasons and Defeaters

Defeasible reasoning is a form of reasoning. Reasoning proceeds by constructing arguments for conclusions, and the individual inferences making up the arguments are licensed by what we might call *reason schemes*. In philosophy, it is customary to think of arguments as linear sequences of propositions, with each member of the sequence being either a premise or the conclusion of an inference (in accordance with some reason scheme) from earlier propositions in the sequence. However, this representation of arguments is an artifact of the way we write them. In many cases the ordering of the elements of the sequence is irrelevant to the structure of the argument. For instance, consider an argument that proceeds by giving a subargument for

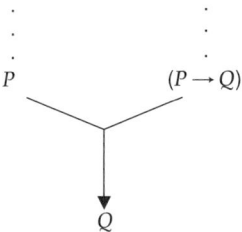

P and an unrelated subargument for $(P \rightarrow Q)$,

Figure 1. An inference graph.

P and an unrelated subargument for $(P \rightarrow Q)$, and then finishes by inferring Q by modus ponens. We might diagram this argument as in Figure 1. The ordering of the elements of the two subarguments with respect to each other is irrelevant. If we write the argument for Q as a linear sequence of propositions, we must order the elements of the subarguments with respect to each other, thus introducing artificial structure in the representation. For many purposes it is better to represent the argument graphically. Such a graph is an *inference graph*. The compound arrows linking elements of the inference graph represent the application of reason schemes.

In deductive reasoning, the reason schemes employed are deductive inference rules. What distinguishes deductive reasoning from reasoning more generally is that the reasoning is not defeasible. More precisely, given a deductive argument for a conclusion, you cannot rationally deny the conclusion without denying one or more of the premises. In contrast, consider an inductive argument. Suppose we observe a number of swans and they are all white. This gives us a reason for thinking that all swans are white. If we subsequently journey to Australia and observe a black swan, we must retract that conclusion. But notice that this does not give us a reason for retracting any of the premises. It is still reasonable to believe that each of the initially observed swans is white. What distinguishes defeasible arguments from deductive arguments is that *the addition* of information can mandate the retraction of the conclusion of a defeasible argument without mandating the retraction of any of the earlier conclusions from which the retracted conclusion was inferred. By contrast, you cannot retract the conclusion of a deductive argument without also retracting some of the premises from which it was inferred.

REBUTTING DEFEATERS

Information that can mandate the retraction of the conclusion of a defeasible argument constitutes a *defeater* for the argument. There are two kinds of defeaters. The simplest are *rebutting*

defeaters, which attack an argument by attacking its conclusion. In the inductive example concerning white swans, what defeated the argument was the discovery of a black swan, and the reason that was a defeater is that it entails the negation of the conclusion, that is, it entails that not all swans are black. More generally, a rebutting defeater could be any reason for denying the conclusion (deductive or defeasible). For instance, I might be informed by Herbert, an ornithologist, that not all swans are white. People do not always speak truly, so the fact that he tells me this does not entail that it is true that not all swans are white. Nevertheless, because Herbert is an ornithologist, his telling me that gives me a defeasible reason for thinking that not all swans are white, so it is a rebutting defeater.

UNDERCUTTING DEFEATERS

Not all defeaters are rebutting defeaters. Suppose Simon, whom I regard as very reliable, tells me, "Don't believe Herbert. He is incompetent." That Herbert told me that not all swans are white gives me a reason for believing that not all swans are white, but Simon's remarks about Herbert give me a reason for withdrawing my belief, and they do so without either (1) making me doubt that Herbert said what I took him to say or (2) giving me a reason for thinking it false that not all swans are white. Even if Herbert is incompetent, he might have accidentally gotten it right that not all swans are white. Thus Simon's remarks constitute a defeater, but not a rebutting defeater. This is an example of an *undercutting defeater*.

The difference between rebutting defeaters and undercutting defeaters is that rebutting defeaters attack the conclusion of a defeasible inference, while undercutting defeaters attack the defeasible inference itself, without doing so by giving us a reason for thinking it has a false conclusion. We can think of an undercutting defeater as a reason for thinking that it is false that the premises of the inference would not be true unless the conclusion were true. More simply, we can think of it as giving us a reason for believing that (under the present circumstances) the truth of the premises does not guarantee the truth of the conclusion. It will be convenient to symbolize this as "*premises ⊗ conclusion.*"

It is useful to expand our graphical representation of reasoning by including defeat relations. Thus we might represent the preceding example as in Figure 2. Here I have drawn the defeat relations using thick arrows. The rebutting defeater is represented by an arrow from the defeater

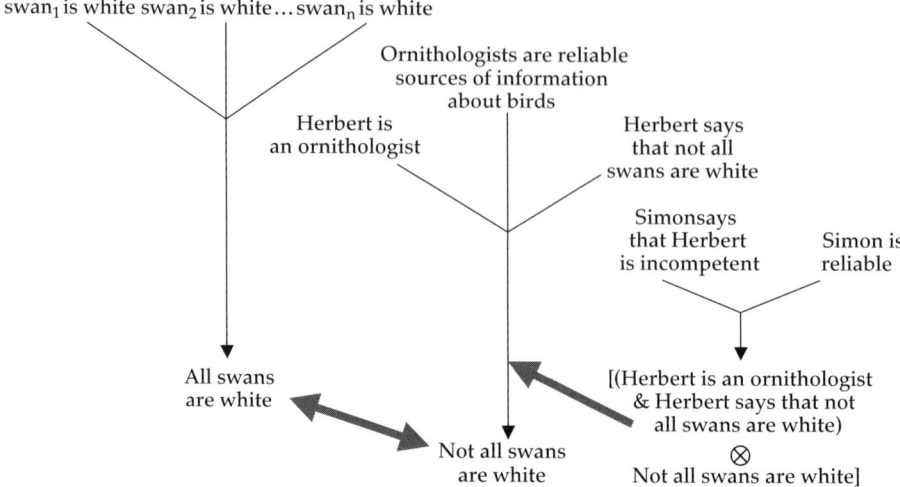

swan₁ is white   swan₂ is white ... swanₙ is white

Figure 2. Inference graph with defeat.

to the conclusion it attacks, because a rebutting defeater is a defeater for every defeasible inference having that conclusion. The undercutting defeater is represented by an arrow from the defeater to the inference (represented by a compound arrow) that it attacks. Note that the rebutting defeat is symmetrical, but undercutting defeat is not.

We can usefully distinguish between two concepts of a reason. In the preceding example, "Not all swans are white" is inferred from three premises. If we understand the reliability premise as being about probabilities, this can be seen to be an instance of the aforementioned statistical syllogism. But notice that it would also be natural to report more simply that our reason for thinking that not all swans are white is that Herbert says they aren't, ignoring the first two premises. That both ways of talking are natural suggests distinguishing between "full reason schemes" and "enthymatic reason schemes." In enthymatic reason schemes, we drop some of the premises that can be regarded as background information, just as we do in an enthymatic argument. For the purpose of understanding how reasoning works, it is best to avoid appeal to enthymatic reason schemes and express our reason schemes in full detail.

Semantics for Defeasible Reasoning

We can combine all of a cognizer's reasoning into a single inference graph and regard that as a representation of those aspects of his cognitive state that pertain to reasoning. The hardest problem in a theory of defeasible reasoning is to give a precise account of how the structure of the cognizer's inference graph determines what he should believe. Such an account is called a "semantics" for defeasible reasoning, although it is not a semantics in the same sense as, for example, a semantics for first-order logic. If a cognizer reasoned only deductively, it would be easy to provide an account of what he should believe. In that case, a cognizer should believe all and only the conclusions of his arguments (assuming that the premises are somehow initially justified). However, if an agent reasons defeasibly, then the conclusions of some of his arguments may be defeaters for other arguments, and so he should not believe the conclusions of all of them. For example, in Figure 2, the cognizer first concludes "All swans are white." Then he constructs an argument for a defeater for the first argument, at which point it would no longer be reasonable to believe its conclusion. But then he constructs a third argument supporting a defeater for the second (defeating) argument, and that should reinstate the first argument.

Obviously, the relationships between interacting arguments can be very complex. We want a general account of how it is determined which conclusions should be believed, or to use philosophical parlance, which conclusions are "justified" and which are not. This distinction enforces a further distinction between beliefs and conclusions. When a cognizer constructs an argument, he entertains the conclusion and he entertains the propositions comprising the intervening steps, but he need not believe them. Constructing arguments is one thing. Deciding which conclusions to accept is another. What we want is a criterion which, when applied to the inference graph, determines which conclusions are defeated and which are not, i.e., a criterion that determines the *defeat statuses* of the conclusions. The conclusions that ought to be believed are those that are undefeated.

One complication is that a conclusion can be supported by multiple arguments. In that case, it is the arguments themselves to which we must first attach defeat statuses. Then a conclusion is undefeated if it is supported by at least one undefeated argument. The only exception to this rule is "initial nodes," which (from the perspective of the inference graph) are simply "given" as premises. Initial nodes are unsupported by arguments, but are taken to be undefeated. Ultimately, we want to use this machinery to model rational cognition. In that case, all that can be regarded as "given" is perceptual input (construed broadly to include such modes of perception as proprioception, introspection, etc.), in which case it may be inaccurate to take the initial nodes to encode propositions. It is probably better to regard them as encoding percepts.[4]

It is in the computation of defeat statuses that different theories of defeasible reasoning differ. It might seem that this should be simple. The following four principles seem reasonable:

(1) A conclusion is undefeated (relative to an inference graph) if either it is an initial node or it is supported by at least one undefeated argument in the inference graph.

(2) An argument is undefeated if every inference in the argument is undefeated.

(3) If an inference graph contains an undefeated argument supporting a defeater for an inference used in one of its arguments A, then A is defeated.

(4) If an inference graph contains no undefeated arguments supporting defeaters for inferences used in one of its arguments A, then A is undefeated.

It might be supposed that we can apply these four principles recursively to compute the defeat status of any conclusion. For instance, in Figure 2, by principle (4), the third argument is undefeated because there are no defeating arguments for any of its inferences and hence no undefeated defeating arguments. Then by prin-

Figure 3. Collective defeat.

ciple (3), the second argument is defeated. Then by principle (4), the first argument is undefeated. Finally, by principle (1), the conclusion "All swans are white" is undefeated.

COLLECTIVE DEFEAT

Unfortunately, there are inference graphs that resist such a simple treatment. For example, consider the inference graph of Figure 2 without the third argument. The structure of this case can be diagrammed more simply as in Figure 3, where the dashed arrows indicate defeasible inference. Here we have no arguments lacking defeating arguments, so there is no way for the recursion to get started.

Figure 3 is an example of what is called "collective defeat," where we have a set of two or more arguments and each argument in the set is defeated by some other argument in the set. What should we believe in such a case? Consider a simple example. Suppose we are in a closed and windowless room, and Jones, whom we regard as reliable, enters the room and tells us it is raining outside. Then we have a reason for believing it is raining. But Jones is followed by Smith, whom we also regard as reliable, and Smith tells us it is not raining. Then we have arguments for both "It is raining" and "It is not raining," as in Figure 3. What should we believe? It seems clear that in the absence of any other information, we should not form a belief about the weather. We should withhold belief, which is to treat both arguments as defeated. But this means that in cases of collective defeat, an argument is defeated even though its defeating arguments are also defeated.

Cases of collective defeat violate principle (4). For example, in Figure 3, both R and ~R should be defeated, but neither has an undefeated defeater.

Cases of collective defeat are encountered fairly often. An example of some philosophical interest is the *lottery paradox* (Kyburg 1961). Suppose you hold a ticket in a fair lottery consisting of one million tickets. It occurs to you that the probability of any particular ticket being drawn is one in a million, and so in accordance with the statistical syllogism you can conclude defeasibly that your ticket will not be drawn.

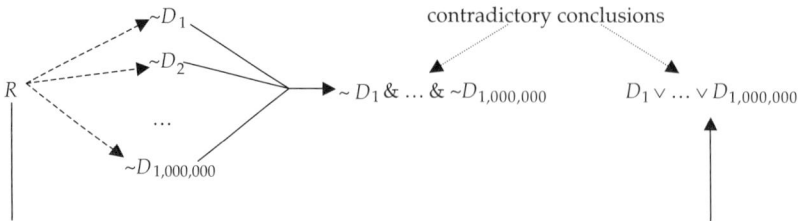

Figure 4. The lottery paradox.

Should you throw it away? Presumably not, because that probability is the same for every ticket in the lottery. Thus you get an equally good argument for each ticket that it will not be drawn. However, you are given that the lottery is fair, which means in part that some ticket will be drawn. So you have an inconsistent set of conclusions, viz., for each ticket n you have the conclusion $\sim D_n$ that it will not be drawn, but you also have the conclusion that some one of them will be drawn. This generates a case of collective defeat. The lottery paradox can be diagrammed initially as in Figure 4, where R is the description of the lottery.

This can be redrawn as a case of collective defeat by noticing that the set of conclusions $\sim D_1, \sim D_2, \ldots, \sim D_{1,000,000}, D_1 \vee \ldots \vee D_{1,000,000}$ is logically inconsistent. As a result, each subset of the form

$$\sim D_1, \sim D_2, \ldots, \sim D_{i-1}, \sim D_{i+1}, \ldots, \sim D_{1,000,000},$$
$$D_1 \vee \ldots \vee D_{1,000,000}$$

entails the negation of the remaining member, that is, entails D_i, so from each such subset of conclusions in the graph we can get an argument for the corresponding D_i, and that is a rebutting defeater for the argument to $\sim D_i$. More simply, pick one ticket. I have reason to think that it will lose. But I also have a reason to think it will *win* because I have reason to think that all the others will lose, and I know that one has to win. This yields the inference graph of Figure 5. Thus for each conclusion $\sim D_i$ we can derive the rebutting defeater D_i from the other conclusions $\sim D_i$, and hence we have a case of collective defeat.

Accordingly, given a theory of defeasible reasoning that can handle inference graphs with collective defeat, the lottery paradox is resolved by observing that we should not conclude of any ticket that it will not be drawn. (Of course, we can still conclude that it is highly unlikely that it will be drawn, but that yields no inconsistency.)

SELF-DEFEAT

Most theories of defeasible reasoning have some mechanism or other that enables them to get collective defeat right. But there is another kind of case they often have trouble with. This concerns "self-defeating arguments" that support defeaters for themselves. Figure 6 is a simple example of a self-defeating argument. In this example, it seems clear that Q should be defeated. If Q were undefeated, then R would be undefeated, because there is no defeater for the inference from Q to R, and then $(P \otimes Q)$ would be undefeated because it is inferred deductively from R. But if $(P \otimes Q)$ is undefeated, Q must be defeated instead of undefeated. Thus Q has to be regarded as defeated. It seems to follow that R and hence $(P \otimes Q)$ are also defeated. If principle (4) above were correct (we have already seen that it is not), then it would follow that Q is undefeated rather than defeated. This is another example in which principle (4) fails.

Although all standard theories of defeasible reasoning can handle simple cases of collective defeat, many of them have more trouble with self-defeat. For example, Reiter's (1980) default logic has been quite popular in AI, but it is unable to distinguish between the status of P

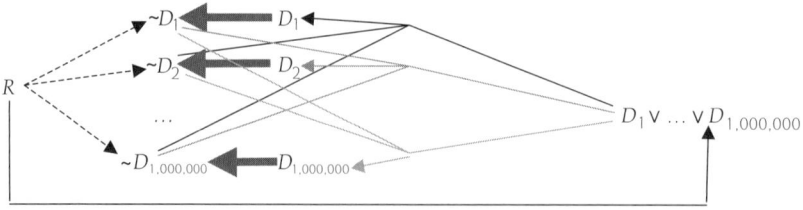

Figure 5. The lottery paradox as a case of collective defeat.

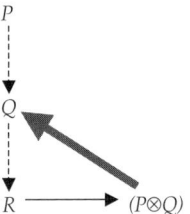

Figure 6. A self-defeating argument.

(which ought to be undefeated) and Q, R, and $(P \otimes Q)$ in Figure 6, so it must either rule them all defeated or all undefeated. But either conclusion is unacceptable.[5]

Even if a theory can handle both collective defeat and simple cases of self-defeat, it may not be able to handle combinations of the two. For example, the original semantics that I proposed for defeasible reasoning in Pollock (1986) got all of the above examples right, but it could not handle the example of Figure 7. This results from extending the inference graph for the lottery paradox by noting two things. First, we typically have only a defeasible reason P for believing the description R of the lottery. For example, we may read it in the newspaper. Second, we can combine the arguments for the individual $\sim D_i$s to obtain an argument for $\sim D_1 \& \ldots \& \sim D_{1,000,000}$, and that yields an argument for $\sim R$ (because R entails $D_1 \vee \ldots \vee D_{1,000,000}$). Thus, the argument from P is self-defeating. I call this "the lottery paradox paradox" (Pollock 1991).

If we distill the self-defeating subargument involving R out of Figure 7, we get the inference graph of Figure 8. This has essentially the same structure as Figure 4, so if we give it the same treatment we should end up concluding that we are not justified in believing R. That is, we should not believe the description of the lottery we get from the newspaper report. But that is clearly wrong — of course we should believe

it. Apparently the other parts of the inference graph change its structure in ways that alter the way the defeat statuses are computed.

The lottery paradox paradox is a counterexample to the semantics for defeasible reasoning that I proposed in Pollock (1986). Other theories also have trouble with it. For example, simple versions of circumscription (McCarthy 1980) pronounce R defeated when it should not be.[6] However, in Pollock (1995) I proposed a semantics that yields the intuitively correct answers in all of these examples.

My (1995) semantics turns on principles (1)–(4). We cannot apply them recursively to compute defeat statuses because they do not uniquely determine candidate defeat statuses. For example, in Figure 3, there are two different ways of assigning defeat statuses to the conclusions making up the inference graph in such a way that principles (1)–(4) are satisfied. This is diagrammed in Figure 9, where "+" indicates an assignment of "undefeated" and "−" indicates an assignment of "defeated." The conclusions and arguments that we want to regard as undefeated simpliciter are those that are assigned "+" by all of the ways of assigning defeat statuses consistent with (1)–(4).

The lottery paradox works similarly. For each i, there is a way of assigning defeat statuses according to which $\sim D_i$ is assigned "−," but for all $j \neq i$, $\sim D_i$ is assigned "+." Again, the conclusions that are intuitively undefeated are those that are always assigned "+."

If we turn to the lottery paradox paradox, the same thing holds. There are the same 1,000,000 assignments of defeat statuses, but now for every one of them $\sim D_i \& \ldots \& \sim D_{1,000,000}$ is assigned "−," and hence "$\sim R$" is assigned "−" and "R" is assigned "+." Thus, we get the desired result that we are justified in believing the description of the lottery, but we are not justified in believing that any particular ticket will not be drawn.

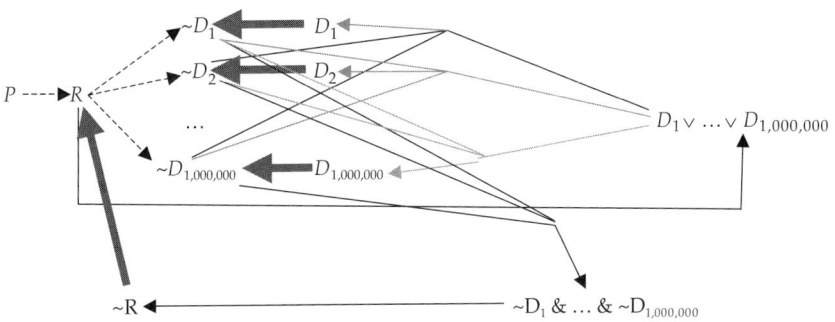

Figure 7. The lottery paradox paradox.

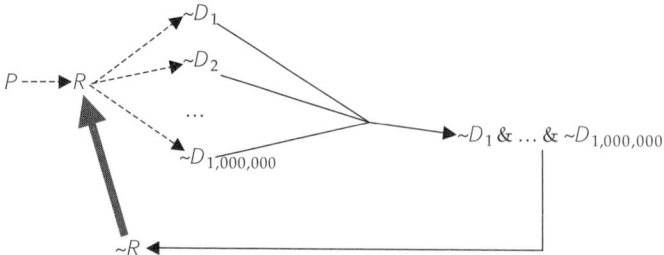

Figure 8. The self-defeating argument embedded in the lottery paradox paradox.

However, when we turn to the simpler case of self-defeat in Figure 6, things become more complicated. There is no way to assign defeat statuses consistent with principles (1)–(4). By (1), P must be assigned "+," which is unproblematic. But there is no way to assign a defeat status to Q. Suppose we assign "+." Then we must assign "+" to R and to $(P \otimes Q)$. Then we would have to assign "−" to Q, contrary to our original assignment. If instead we assign "−" to Q, then we must assign "−" to R and to $(P \otimes Q)$. Then we would have to assign "+" to Q, again contrary to our original assignment. So in this example there can be at most a partial assignment of defeat statuses consistent with (1)–(4). However, it remains true that the intuitively undefeated conclusions are those that are assigned "+" in all partial status assignments that assign statuses to as many conclusions as possible. Let us define:

A *partial status assignment* is an assignment of defeat statuses ("+" or "−") to a subset of the conclusions and arguments of an inference graph in a manner consistent with principles (1)–(4). A *status assignment* is a maximal partial status assignment, i.e., a partial status assignment that cannot be extended to further conclusions or arguments and remain consistent with principles (1)–(4).

My (1995) proposal was then:

The Defeat Status of an Argument
An argument is undefeated (relative to an inference graph) if every step of the argument is assigned "+" by every status assignment for that inference graph.

It would be natural to propose:

A conclusion is undefeated (relative to an inference graph) if it is assigned "+" by every status assignment for that inference graph.

Indeed, this works in all the preceding examples, but that is only because, in those examples, there are no conclusions supported by multiple arguments.[7] To see that this does not work in general, consider the case of collective defeat diagrammed in Figure 10. Once again, there are two status assignments. One assigns "+" to R, S, and $(S \vee T)$, and "−" to $\sim R$ and T. The other assigns "−" to R and S and "+" to $\sim R$, T, and $(S \vee T)$. On both assignments, $(S \vee T)$ is assigned "+." However, there is no argument supporting $(S \vee T)$ all of whose inferences are undefeated relative to both assignments, so there is no undefeated argument supporting $(S \vee T)$. If we regard $(S \vee T)$ as undefeated, then we are denying principle (1), according to which a non-initial node is only undefeated if it is supported by an undefeated argument. However, it seems that principle (1) ought to be true, so instead of the preceding I proposed:

The Defeat Status of a Conclusion
A conclusion is undefeated if it is supported by an undefeated argument.

This is my (1995) semantics. Its justification is that it seems to give the right answer in all those cases in which it is intuitively clear what the right answer is. This semantics has been implemented

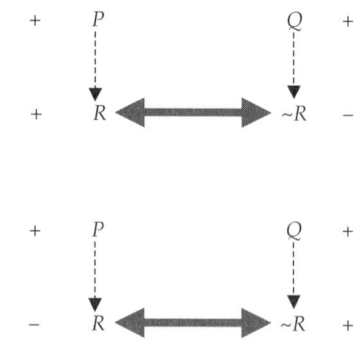

Figure 9. Two ways of assigning defeat statuses.

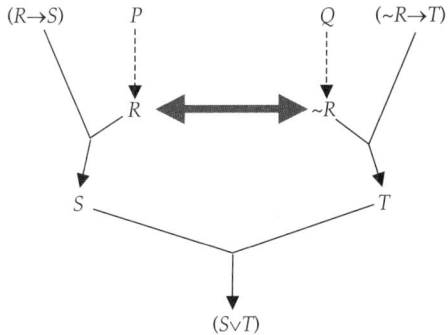

Figure 10. Collective defeat with multiple arguments.

in the OSCAR architecture.[8] This is an AI system that constitutes an architecture for cognitive agents, and among other things it is a general-purpose defeasible reasoner.

Although this semantics is fairly successful, it leaves at least one important question unaddressed. Reasons have strengths. Not all reasons are equally good, and this should affect the adjudication of defeat statuses. For example, if I regard Jones as significantly more reliable than Smith, then if Jones tells me it is raining and Smith says it is not, it seems I should believe Jones. In other words, this case of collective defeat is resolved by taking account of the different strengths of the arguments for the conflicting conclusions. An adequate semantics for defeasible reasoning must take account of differences in degree of justification. The preceding semantics only works correctly in cases in which all reasons are equally good. In my (1995) I extended the above semantics to deal with reason strengths, but I am now convinced that the (1995) proposal was not correct. I tried again in my (2002), and that semantics or a minor variation of it may be correct, but I have not yet implemented it in OSCAR. There are currently no other proposals in the AI or philosophical literature for how to perform defeasible reasoning with varying degrees of justification.

Defeasible Reasoning versus Bayesian Epistemology

There is another approach to nondeductive belief maintenance. This is *Bayesian epistemology*, which supposes that degrees of justification work like probabilities and hence conflicts can be resolved within the probability calculus. Bayesians propose that updating one's beliefs in the face of new information proceeds by conditioning the probabilities of the beliefs on the new information. Conditional probabilities are similar to defeasible reasons in that conditioning on additional information can lower the probability. That is, $prob(P/Q\&R)$ can be lower than $prob(P/Q)$. So it appears that Bayesian epistemology can handle the same phenomena that gave rise to theories of defeasible reasoning.

There is a huge literature on Bayesian epistemology, but I can only make some brief remarks here.[9] One of the most important differences between theories of defeasible reasoning and Bayesian approaches is that the former accommodate ordinary reasoning – either deductive or defeasible – as a way of deriving new justified beliefs from previously justified beliefs, but the latter do not. For example, theories of defeasible reasoning agree that if the cognizer is initially justified in believing P and $(P \rightarrow Q)$, and infers Q from those two premises, then in the absence of a reason for disbelieving Q, the cognizer becomes justified in believing Q. (Given a reason for $\sim Q$, the argument might instead require the cognizer to give up one of the premises.) By contrast, Bayesian epistemology makes even deductive reasoning problematic, for reasons I will now explain.

The simplest argument against Bayesian epistemology is that it would make it impossible for a conclusion to be justified on the basis of a deductive argument from multiple uncertain premises. This is because, if degrees of justification work like probabilities, then when you combine premises, the degree of justification decreases. Suppose you have one hundred independent premises, each with a degree of justification of .99. If Bayesian epistemology is correct, then by the probability calculus, the degree of justification of the conjunction will be only .37, so we could never be justified in using these one hundred premises conjointly in drawing a conclusion. But this flies in the face of common sense. For example, consider an opinion pollster surveying people about which of two products they prefer. She surveys one hundred people, collecting from each the verbal expression of an opinion of the form "I prefer x to y." She summarizes her data by saying, "I surveyed one hundred people, and seventy-nine of them reported preferring A to B." This conclusion follows deductively from her accumulated data. But each piece of data of the form "Person S reported preferring x to y" is something she believes with less than certainty – we are supposing she believes it with a degree of justification of .99. Then if degrees of justification work like probabilities, her degree of justification for thinking that she has surveyed one hundred people and seventy-nine of them reported preferring A to B would be at most .37, and hence she would not be justified in drawing that conclusion. Surely this is wrong.

Consider another example — counting apples in a barrel. Let us suppose you are a very meticulous counter. You examine each apple carefully as you remove it from the barrel, ascertaining that it is indeed an apple, and you then carefully jot down a mark to count the apple so that when you are finished you can read off the result as a number. Let us suppose you are virtually certain you have not lost count (your degree of justification in that is .999), so the only source of uncertainty is in your judgments that the individual objects counted are apples. Suppose you count n apples, judging each to be an apple with a degree of justification j. If degrees of justification work like probabilities, the probability calculus reveals that your degree of justification for believing that there are at least r $(r \leq n)$ apples in the barrel will be

$$\sum_{i=r}^{i=r} j^r \, (1-r)^{n-1} \frac{n!}{r!(n-i)!}.$$

For example, if you count one hundred apples in the barrel, being justified to degree .95 in believing that each object counted is an apple, then your degree of justification for believing that there are one hundred apples in the barrel is only .006. Your degree of justification for believing that there are at least ninety-six apples in the barrel is only .258. You have to drop all the way down to the judgment that there are at least ninety-five apples in the barrel before you get a degree of justification greater than .5. If you want a degree of justification of at least .95 for your judgment of the number of apples in the barrel, the best you can do is conclude that there are at least ninety-one. On this account, you cannot even count apples in a barrel. Similarly, if you have six daughters, and your degree of justification for believing of each that she is indeed one of your daughters is .95, then all you can be justified in believing to degree .95 is that you have at least five daughters. Surely this is ridiculous.

Still, there are philosophers (e.g., Kyburg 1970) who have been willing to bite the bullet and deny that deductive reasoning from justified premises conveys justification to the conclusion. We can make a distinction between two kinds of deductive inference rules. Let us say that a rule is *probabilistically valid* if it follows from the probability calculus that the conclusion is at least as probable as the least probable premise. For instance, *simplification* and *addition* are probabilistically valid:

Simplification: $(P \,\&\, Q) \vdash P$

Addition: $P \vdash (P \vee Q)$.

But not all familiar inference rules are probabilistically valid. For example, it is widely recognized that *adjunction* is not:

Adjunction: $P, Q \vdash (P \,\&\, Q)$.

In general, prob($P \,\&\, Q$) can have any value between 0 and the minimum of prob(P) and prob(Q). Because of this, Kyburg claims that it is a fallacy to reason using adjunction. He calls this fallacy "conjunctivitis." For those who are persuaded by these considerations, the view would be that we are only allowed to reason "blindly," without explicitly computing probabilities (or degrees of justification) as we go along, when the rules of inference we use are probabilistically valid. In all other cases, we must compute the probability of the conclusion to verify that it is still sufficiently probable to be believable. Bayesian epistemology is committed to this view. If degrees of justification satisfy the probability calculus, then without computing probabilities we can only be confident that a deductive argument takes us from justified premises to a justified conclusion if all of the inferences are probabilistically valid.

Which deductive inference rules are probabilistically valid? It is easily shown that any valid deductive inference rule proceeding from a single premise is probabilistically valid. By contrast, some rules proceeding from multiple premises are not. For example, *adjunction* is not. Are there others? People are generally amazed to discover that *no* deductive inference rule that proceeds from multiple premises essentially (that is not still valid if you delete an unnecessary premise) is probabilistically valid. They all go the way of adjunction. For instance, *modus ponens* and *modus tollens* are not probabilistically valid. Probabilistic validity is the exception rather than the rule.

The upshot of this is that if Bayesian epistemology is correct, there will be hardly any deductive reasoning from warranted premises that we can do blindly and still be confident that our conclusions are warranted. Blind deductive reasoning can play very little role in epistemic cognition. Epistemic cognition must instead take the degrees of justification of the premises of an inference and compute a new degree of justification for the conclusion in accordance with the probability calculus.

This might not seem so bad until we realize that it is impossible to do. The difficulty is that the probability calculus does not really enable us to compute most probabilities. In general, all the probability calculus does is impose upper and lower bounds on probabilities. For instance, given degrees of justification for P and Q, there is no way we can compute a degree of justification for $(P \& Q)$ just on the basis of the probability calculus. It is consistent with the probability calculus for the degree of justification of $(P \& Q)$ to be anything from $\text{prob}(P) + \text{prob}(Q) - 1$ (or 0 if $\text{prob}(P) + \text{prob}(Q) - 1 < 0$) to the minimum of the degrees of justification of P and Q individually. There is in general no way to compute $\text{prob}(P \& Q)$ just on the basis of logical form. The value of $\text{prob}(P \& Q)$ is normally a substantive fact about P and Q, and it must be obtained by some method other than mathematical computation in the probability calculus.

These observations lead to a general, and I think insurmountable, difficulty for Bayesian epistemology. Bayesian epistemology claims we must compute degrees of justification as we go along in order to decide whether to accept the conclusions of our reasoning. If conditional degrees of justification conform to the probability calculus, they will generally be idiosyncratic, depending upon the particular propositions involved. That is, they cannot be computed from anything else. If they cannot be computed, they must be stored innately. This, however, creates a combinatorial nightmare. As Gilbert Harman (1973) observed years ago, given a set of just 300 beliefs, the number of probabilities of single beliefs conditional on conjunctions of beliefs in the set is 2^{300}. This is approximately 10^{90}. To appreciate what an immense number this is, a recent estimate of the number of elementary particles in the universe was 10^{78}. So Bayesian epistemology would require the cognizer to store twelve orders of magnitude more primitive probabilities than the number of elementary particles in the universe. This is computationally impossible. Thus Bayesian epistemology would make reasoning impossible.

The upshot of this is that if Bayesian epistemology were correct, we could not acquire new justified beliefs by reasoning from previously justified beliefs. However, reasoning is an essential part of epistemic cognition. Without reasoning, all we could know is that our current environment looks and feels various ways to us. It is reasoning that allows us to extend this very impoverished perceptual knowledge to a coherent picture of the world. So Bayesian epistemology cannot be correct. Cognition requires a different kind of mechanism for updating beliefs in the face of new information. That is what defeasible reasoning purports to provide.

Reasoning Defeasibly

Above I discussed how to determine what a cognizer ought to believe given what arguments he has constructed. But a theory of rational cognition must also address the question of how the cognizer should go about constructing arguments. In this connection, one can ask how human reasoning works, which is a psychological question, but one can also ask more generally how we can evaluate an arbitrary system of reasoning. For a cognizer that performed only deductive reasoning, we would presumably want to require that the reasoning be consistent, and we would probably want it to be deductively complete in the sense that the system of reasoning is in principle capable of deriving any deductive consequence of the cognizer's beliefs. But for a cognizer that reasons defeasibly, things are more complicated.

There are many systems of automated deductive reasoning in AI. If we focus on reasoners that perform reasoning in the predicate calculus (first-order logic), they are generally sound and complete. In other words, they will produce all and only conclusions that follow deductively from whatever premises we give the system. It is natural to suppose that defeasible reasoners should behave similarly. But what is it for them to behave similarly? We need an analogue of deductive validity for defeasible reasoning.

Let us say that a conclusion is *justified* for a cognizer if it is undefeated relative to the inference graph that encodes all of his reasoning to date. However, for any sophisticated cognizer, reasoning is a nonterminating process. This is true even if the cognizer performs only deductive reasoning in the predicate calculus. However much reasoning the cognizer does, there will always be more that could be done. As a cognizer's inference graph expands, the cognizer may discover not only arguments for new conclusions, but also arguments for defeaters for earlier conclusions. The result is that a previously undefeated conclusion may become defeated just as a result of the cognizer's performing more reasoning, without any addition to the set of initial nodes from which he is reasoning. This indicates that there are two kinds of defeasibility that we should clearly distinguish. By definition, defeasible reasoning is *synchronically defeasible*, in the sense that the addition of new information (new initial nodes) can lead previously undefeated conclusions to become defeated. Human reasoning is also *diachronically defeasible*, in the sense that performing additional reasoning without adding any new information can change the defeat statuses of conclusions.

A cognizer's inference graph consists of all the reasoning it has so far performed. But we can also consider the idealized inference graph consisting of all the reasoning that could be performed given the cognizer's current initial nodes. Let us say that a proposition (it may not yet be a conclusion) *is warranted* for the cognizer if it is undefeated relative to this idealized inference graph. So warrant is justification in the limit. The set of warranted propositions is, in effect, the target at which defeasible reasoning aims.

Analogous to requiring a deductive reasoner to be sound and complete, we might require a defeasible reasoner to produce all and only warranted conclusions. This is precisely the requirement that has generally been imposed on automated defeasible reasoners in AI. However, for reasons that have been well known since 1980, no defeasible reasoner capable of performing sophisticated reasoning (e.g., reasoning that includes deductive reasoning in the predicate calculus) can satisfy this requirement. It is *mathematically impossible*. I will explain.

For the predicate calculus, it is possible to build an automated reasoner that draws all and only valid conclusions because the set of valid conclusions is *recursively enumerable*. A recursively enumerable set is one for which there is a mechanical procedure (an algorithm) for systematically generating all the members of the set in such a way that no nonmembers are ever generated by the procedure. Proof procedures for the predicate calculus are such procedures, and hence the completeness theorem for the predicate calculus tells us that the set of valid formulas is recursively enumerable. Automated theorem provers for the predicate calculus take advantage of this by implementing such a mechanical procedure.

When we turn to defeasible reasoning, nothing similar is possible. This is because, as Reiter (1980) and Israel (1980) observed, the set of warranted conclusions will not generally be recursively enumerable. Suppose, for instance, that we have a defeasible reasoner that uses a first-order language (i.e., the language contains the quantifiers and connectives of the predicate calculus). Suppose it makes a defeasible inference to a conclusion P. A necessary condition for P to be warranted is that $\sim P$ not be a theorem of the predicate calculus, for if $\sim P$ were a theorem, that would constitute defeat. If the system had to wait until it has determined that P is not defeated before adding it to its set of beliefs, it might have to wait forever. The difficulty is that, by Church's theorem, the set of nontheorems of the predicate calculus is not recursively enumerable. Thus there is no mechanical procedure for verifying that $\sim P$ is not a theorem. If it isn't then no matter what algorithms the reasoner employs, it may never discover that fact, and so it will never be in a position to affirm P.

This is a mathematical constraint on any system of defeasible reasoning. If it waits to affirm a conclusion until it has determined conclusively that the conclusion is undefeated, there will be many warranted conclusions that it will never be in a position to affirm, so it will not produce all warranted conclusions. By contrast, if it does not wait, then it will sometimes get things wrong and affirm conclusions that are justified given the current stage of its reasoning but not warranted.

All automated defeasible reasoners except OSCAR are crippled by this problem. Because they assume that a defeasible reasoner should work like a deductive reasoner, and produce all and only warranted conclusions, they restrict themselves to reasoning in very impoverished languages in which both the set of deductively valid formulas and the set of deductively invalid formulas are recursively enumerable. Technically, these are languages that are *decidable*. Unfortunately, only very weak and inexpressive languages are decidable. Thus with the exception of OSCAR, all automated defeasible reasoners tend to work only in the propositional calculus or some even less expressive subset of it.

Obviously, humans are not so constrained. How do humans avoid this difficulty? They do so by *reasoning defeasibly*. In other words, they draw conclusions with the expectation that they will occasionally have to retract them later. They don't wait for an absolute guarantee of warrant. After all, we draw conclusions in order to help us decide how to act. But we cannot wait for the end of a nonterminating process before deciding how to act. Decisions have to be based on what we currently believe, on our justified beliefs, not on the ideal set of warranted propositions. Any sophisticated defeasible reasoner must work similarly. OSCAR does the same thing humans do here. That is, OSCAR draws conclusions on the basis of its current reasoning, and when it has to decide how to act it bases its decision on its current beliefs, but as both reasoning and the input of new information proceed, it may have to withdraw some of its beliefs. This means that, occasionally, it will have acted in ways it would not have acted had it had time to do more reasoning. But that does not show that there is something wrong with OSCAR, or that OSCAR is behaving irrationally. It is just a fact of life that cognizers, human or otherwise, will make mistakes as a result of not knowing certain things that would have helped. Some of these mistakes will result from the cognizer not having acquired relevant information perceptually, but other mistakes will result from the cognizer not having time to do enough reasoning. This is just the way cognition works, and it is unrealistic to suppose we could completely avoid either source of mistakes through clever engineering.

Illustration: The Frame Problem

In philosophy, most work on defeasible reasoning has been aimed at using it as a tool for the analysis of philosophically interesting kinds of reasoning — mainly in epistemology but also in the philosophy of law. In AI, on the other hand, the investigation of defeasible reasoning was motivated by the desire to build implemented systems that could solve certain kinds of problems. One problem of interest to both philosophers and AI researchers is the *frame problem*, so I will use it as an illustration of the importance of understanding defeasible reasoning in order to understand how rational cognition works.

What Is the Frame Problem?

There is a great deal of confusion about just what the frame problem is, so I will begin with a brief history. The frame problem arose initially in AI planning theory. Planning theory is concerned with the construction of automated systems that will produce plans for the achievement of specified goals. In order to construct a plan, an agent must be able to predict the outcomes of the var-

ious actions that a plan might prescribe. For this purpose, let us suppose the agent has all the general background knowledge it might need. Consider a very simple planning problem. The agent is standing in the middle of a room, and the light is off. The light switch is by the door. The agent wants the light to be on. The obvious plan for achieving this goal is to walk to the vicinity of the light switch and activate the switch. *We human beings* can see immediately that, barring unforeseen difficulties, this is a good plan for achieving the goal. If an artificial agent is to be able to see this as well, it must be able to infer that the execution of this plan will, barring unforeseen difficulties, achieve the goal. The reasoning required seems easy. First, the switch is observed to be in position S. Our background knowledge allows us to infer that if we walk toward position S, we will shortly be in that vicinity. Second, our background knowledge allows us to infer that when we are in the vicinity of the switch, we can activate it. Third, it informs us that when we activate the switch, the light will come on. It may seem that this information is all that is required to conclude that if the plan is executed then the light will come on. But, in fact, one more premise is required. We know that the switch is initially in position S. However, for the plan to work, we must know that the switch will still be in position S when we get there. In other words, we have to know that walking to position S does not change the position of the switch. This, of course, is something that we do know, but what this example illustrates is that reasoning about what will change if an action is performed or some other event occurs generally presupposes knowing that various things will not change.

Early attempts in AI to model reasoning about change tried to do so deductively by formulating axioms describing the environment in which the planner was operating and then using those axioms to deduce the outcomes of executing proposed plans. The preceding example illustrates that among the axioms describing the environment there must be both causal axioms about the effects of various actions or events under specified circumstances, and a number of axioms about what does not change when actions are performed or events occur under specified circumstances. The latter axioms were called *frame axioms*.[10] In our simple example, we can just add a frame axiom to the effect that the switch will still be in position S if the agent walks to that position, and then the requisite reasoning can be performed. However, in pursuing this approach, it soon became apparent that more complicated situations required vastly more (and more complicated) frame axioms. A favorite example of early AI researchers was the Blocks World, in which children's building blocks are scattered about and piled on top of each other in various configurations, and the planning problem is to move them around and pile them up in a way that results in the blocks being arranged in some desired order. If we make the world sufficiently simple, then we can indeed axiomatize it and reason about it deductively. But if we imagine a world whose possibilities include all the things that can happen to blocks in the real world, this approach becomes totally impractical. For instance, moving a block does not normally change its color. But it might if, for example, an open can of paint is balanced precariously atop the block. If we try to apply the axiomatic approach to real-world situations, we encounter three problems. First, in most cases we will be unable to even formulate a suitable set of axioms that does justice to the true complexity of the situation. But, second, even if we could, we would find it necessary to construct an immense number of extraordinarily complex frame axioms. And, third, if we then fed these axioms to an automated reasoner and set it the task of deducing the outcomes of a plan, the reasoner would be forced to expend most of its resources reasoning about what does not change rather than what does change, and it would quickly bog down and be unable to draw the desired conclusions about the effects of executing the plan.[11]

The upshot of this is that in realistically complicated situations, axiomatizing the situation and reasoning about it deductively is made unmanageable by the proliferation and complexity of frame axioms. What became known as the *frame problem* is the problem of reorganizing reasoning about change so that reasoning about nonchanges can be done efficiently.[12]

Unfortunately, some philosophers have confused the frame problem with other rather distantly related problems, and this has confused its discussion in philosophy and cognitive science. For example, Fodor (2001) takes the frame problem to be the general problem of how to reason efficiently against the background of a large database of information. That is indeed a problem, but a solution to it would not tell us how to reason about change.

The frame problem arose in AI, and it has often gone unappreciated that it is equally a problem for human epistemology. Humans can perform the requisite reasoning, so they instantiate a solution to the frame problem. However, it is not obvious how they do it, any more than it is obvious how they perform inductive reasoning, probabilistic reasoning, or any other epistemologically problematic species of reasoning. Describing such reasoning is a task for epistemology. Furthermore, it seems quite likely that the best way to solve the frame problem for artificial rational agents is to figure out how it is solved in human reasoning and then implement that solution in artificial agents. Thus, the epistemological problem and the AI engineering problem become essentially the same problem.

The frame problem arose in the context of an attempt to reason about persistence and change deductively. That may seem naive in contemporary epistemology, where it is now generally agreed that most of our reasoning is defeasible, but it should be borne in mind that at the time this work was taking place (the late 1960s), philosophy itself was just beginning to appreciate the necessity for nondeductive reasoning, and at that time the predominant view was still that good arguments must be deductively valid. Thirty-five years later, nobody believes that. Some kind of defeasible reasoning is recognized as the norm, with deductive reasoning being the exception. To what extent does the frame problem depend upon its deductivist origins?

This same question occurred to AI researchers. Several authors proposed eliminating frame axioms altogether by reasoning about change defeasibly and adopting some sort of defeasible inference scheme to the effect that it is reasonable to believe that something doesn't change unless you are forced to conclude otherwise.[13] This is what I called "temporal projection" in Section 1. Implementing temporal projection was the original motivation in AI for research on defeasible reasoning and nonmonotonic logic.[14] Let us consider how temporal projection can be formulated using the system of defeasible reasoning discussed above. Then I will return to its use in the frame problem.

Temporal Projection

In the first section I argued that in order for cognition to work a cognitive agent must have a built-in presumption that the objects tend to have their properties stably. In other words, that an object has a property at one time gives us a defeasible reason for expecting that it will still have that property at a later time. The built-in epistemic arsenal of a rational agent must include reason-schemes of the following sort for at least some choices of P:

(1) If $t_0 < t_1$, believing P-at-t_0 is a defeasible reason for the agent to believe P-at-t_1.

Some such principle as (1) is of crucial importance in enabling an agent to combine the results of different perceptual samplings of the world into unified conclusions about the world. Without this, the agent would be stuck in separate time-slices of the world with no way to bridge the boundaries epistemically.

Principle (1) amounts to a presumption that P's being true is a stable property of a time. A stable property is one for which the probability is high that if it is possessed at one time, it will continue to be possessed at a later time. Let ρ be the probability that P will hold at time $t + 1$ given that it holds at time t. I will not prove this here, but assuming independence, it follows that the probability that P will hold at time $(t + \Delta t)$ given that it holds at time t is $\frac{1}{2}(2\rho - 1)^{\Delta t} + \frac{1}{2}$. In other words, the strength of the presumption that a stable property will continue to hold over time decays toward .5 as the time interval increases. In a system of defeasible reasoning that accommodates varying degrees of justification, this should be built into the principles of temporal projection by making the strength of the reason a monotonic decreasing function of Δt. However, I will not discuss this further here.

Temporal Projectibiity

Principle (1) is not yet an adequate formulation of temporal projection. It takes little reflection to see that there must be some restrictions on what propositions P it applies to. For example, knowing that it is now 3 PM does not give me a defeasible reason for thinking it will still be 3 PM in an hour. Surprisingly, it turns out that certain kinds of logical composition also create problems in connection with Principle (1). For example, we must in general be barred from applying temporal projection to disjunctions. This is illustrated by Figure 11. Let P and Q be unrelated propositions. In the inference-graph of Figure 11, the thin solid arrows symbolize deductive inferences. In this inference graph, the conclusion Q-at-t_2 is undefeated, but this is

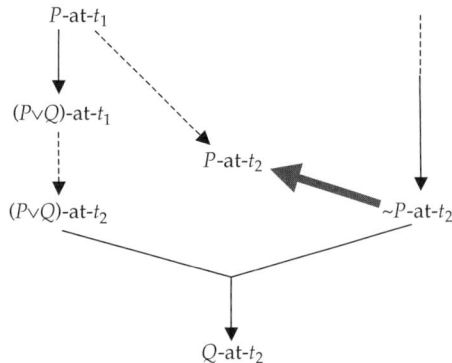

Figure 11. Temporal projection with disjunctions.

unreasonable. Q-at-t_2 is inferred from $(P \vee Q)$-at-t_2. $(P \vee Q)$ is expected to be true at t_2 only because it was true at t_1, and it was only true at t_1 because P was true at t_1. This makes it reasonable to believe $(P \vee Q)$-at-t_2 only insofar as it is reasonable to believe P-at-t_2, but the latter is defeated.

Just to have a label for the propositions to which temporal projection can be properly applied, let us say they are *temporally projectible*. The principle of temporal projection can then be formulated as follows:

Temporal Projection

   If P is temporally projectible, then believing P-at-t is a defeasible reason for the agent to believe P-at-$(t + \Delta t)$, the strength of the reason being a monotonic decreasing function of Δt.

However, we still need an account of temporal projectibility. That is hard to come by. It seems that the ascriptions of "simple" properties to objects will generally be projectible. For instance, "x is red" would seem to be temporally projectible. When we turn to logical compounds, it is easily proven that conjunctions of temporally projectible propositions are temporally projectible (Pollock 1998). But, as we have seen, disjunctions of temporally projectible propositions need not be temporally projectible. It follows from these two results that negations of temporally projectible propositions need not be temporally projectible. It is interesting to note that these observations about the "logic" of temporal projectibility are parallel to similar observations about the familiar projectibility constraint required for inductive reasoning (Pollock 1990), although the concepts are different. For one

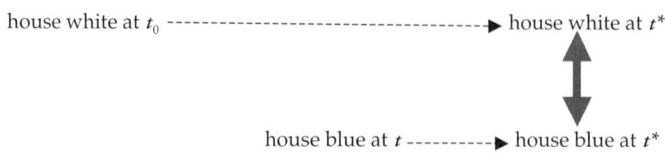

Figure 12. Conflicting temporal projections.

thing, inductive projectibility pertains to properties, whereas temporal projectibility pertains to propositions. It is, at this time, an unsolved problem just how to characterize the set of temporally projectible propositions.[15]

Temporal projection is based on an *a priori* presumption of stability for temporally projectible properties. However, it must be possible to override or modify the presumption by discovering that the probability of P's being true at time $t + 1$ given that P is true at time t is not high. This requires the following undercutting defeater:

Probabilistic Defeat for Temporal Projection
    "The probability of P-at-$(t + 1)$ given P-at-t is not high" is an undercutting defeater for temporal projection.

There is a second kind of defeater for temporal projection. Suppose we know that P is true at time t_0 but false at a later time t_1. We want to know whether P is true at a still later time t_2. The presumption should be that it is not. For instance, if my neighbor's house was white, but he painted it blue yesterday, then I would expect it to be blue tomorrow — not white. However, temporal projection gives us reasons for thinking that it is both white and blue, and these conclusions defeat each other collectively, as in Figure 12.

What is happening here is that temporal projection proceeds on the assumption that if something is true at t_0 then it is true not just at a later time t^*, but throughout the interval from t_0 to t^*. Thus knowing that it is false at some time t between t_0 and t^* should constitute an undercutting defeater for the temporal projection:

Discontinuity Defeat for Temporal Projection
    If $t_0 < t < t^*$, "$\sim P$-at-t" is an undercutting defeater for the inference by temporal projection from "P-at-t_0" to "P-at-t^*."

Incorporating this defeater into Figure 12 yields Figure 13. Applying the OSCAR semantics to this inference graph, there is just one status assignment, as indicated in the figure. In it, the undercutting defeater is undefeated, and hence "the house is white at t^*" is defeated, leaving "the house is blue at t^*" undefeated.

Reasoning about Change

Now let us return to the frame problem and the problem of how to predict changes caused either by our own actions or by extraneous events. To reason about change, we must be able to reason about what does not change, and it was proposed by several authors that the best way to do that is with a defeasible inference scheme to the effect that it is reasonable to believe that something does not change unless you are forced to conclude otherwise. The temporal projection principles defended above can be regarded as a precise formulation of the defeasible inference schemes sought. Unfortunately, these principles do not solve the frame problem. Steve Hanks and Drew McDermott (1986) were the first to observe that even with defeasible principles of persistence, a reasoner will often be unable to determine what changes and what does not. They illustrated this with what has become known as "the Yale shooting problem." Suppose (simplistically) that there is a causal law dictating that if the trigger is pulled on a loaded gun that is pointed at someone, that person will shortly be dead.

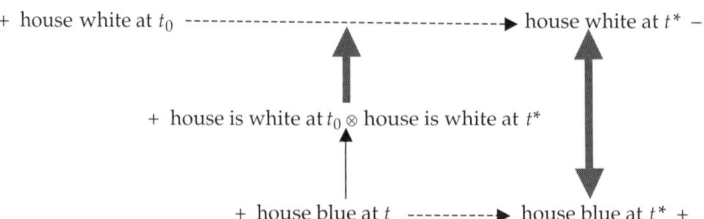

Figure 13. Conflicting temporal projections.

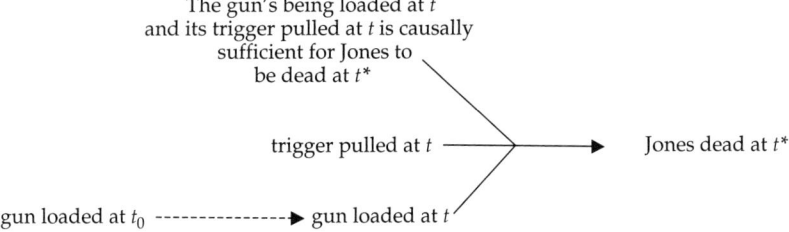

Figure 14. Yale shooting scenario.

Suppose we have a gun that is now loaded. It is then pointed at Jones and the trigger is pulled. It seems we should conclude that Jones will soon be dead. Notice, however, that when firing a gun, you cannot check that it is loaded at the same instant you fire it. You must first check that it is loaded, then point it and pull the trigger. Here you assume that the gun remains loaded until you fire it, and it seems that this is justified by temporal projection. Thus we can reason as in Figure 14.

But as Hanks and McDermott observed, there is a problem. We know that Jones is alive at some time t_{00} earlier than t, so it seems we can also use temporal projection to infer that he will still be alive at t^*. Given the causal premise and given that the trigger was pulled at t, it follows that the gun was not loaded at t. This gives us a complicated case of collective defeat, as diagrammed in Figure 15. (I have drawn one set of inference links in gray just to make the graph easier to read.) In terms of the OSCAR semantics, there are two status assignments, one in which "Jones is alive at t^*" is defeated and one in which it is undefeated.

The general form of this problem is common to cases of causal reasoning. We know that some proposition P is true at an initial time t_0. We know that action A is performed at a subsequent time t, and we know that if P is still true at t then Q will become true at a later time t^*. We want to infer defeasibly that P will still be true at t, and hence that Q will become true at t^*. This is the intuitively correct conclusion to draw. But temporal projection gives us a reason for thinking that because $\sim Q$ is true initially it will remain true at t^*, and hence P was not true at t after all. The problem is to understand what principles of reasoning enable us to draw the desired conclusion and avoid the collective defeat.

When we reason about causal mechanisms, we think of the world as "unfolding" temporally, and changes only occur when they are forced to occur by what has already happened. In our example, when A is performed, nothing has yet happened to force a change in P, so we conclude defeasibly that P remains true. But given the truth of P, we can then deduce that at a slightly later time, Q will become true. Thus when causal mechanisms force there to be a change, we conclude defeasibly that the change occurs in the later states rather than the earlier states. This seems to be part of what we mean by describing something as a causal mechanism. Causal mechanisms are systems that force changes, where "force" is to be understood in the context of

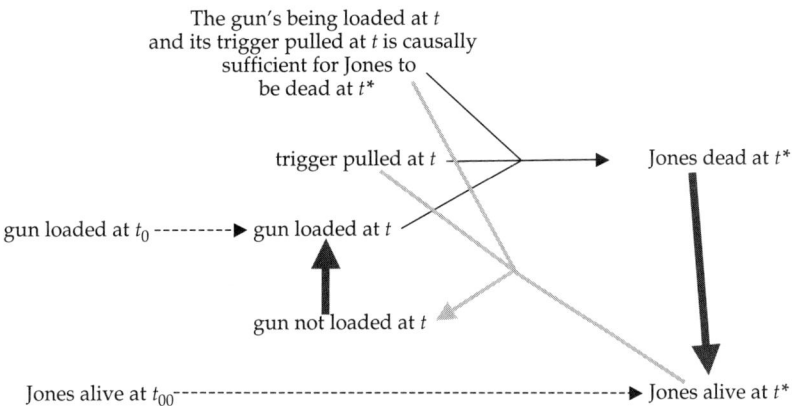

Figure 15. Yale shooting problem.

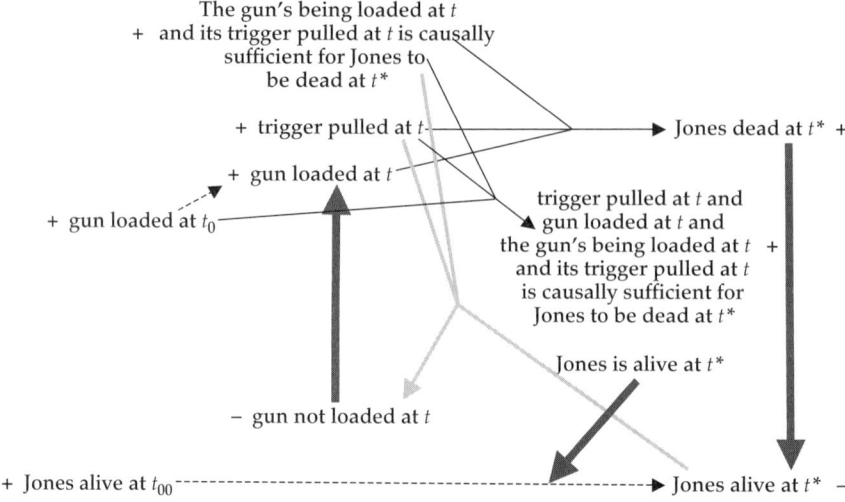

Figure 16. The solved Yale shooting problem.

temporal unfolding.[16] More precisely, when two temporal projections conflict because of a negative causal connection between their conclusions, the projection to the conclusion about the earlier time takes precedence over the later projection. In other words, given the causal connection, the earlier temporal projection provides a defeater for the later one. This can be captured as follows:

Causal Undercutting
If $t_0 < t < t^*$ and $t_{00} < t^*$, "P-at-t_0 and A-at-t and $[(P$-at-t & A-at-$t)$ is causally sufficient for Q at t^*]" is an undercutting defeater for the inference by temporal projection from "$\sim Q$-at-t_{00}" to "$\sim Q$-at-t^*."

Incorporating this undercutting defeater into Figure 15 gives us Figure 16. If we apply the OSCAR semantics to this inference graph, we find that there is just one status assignment, and in that status assignment the undercutting defeater is undefeated, and hence the temporal projection is defeated, so the conclusion that Jones is dead at t^* is undefeated.

Technically, what makes this solution work is that the undercutting defeater is inferred from the premise of the earlier temporal projection (in this case, "The gun is loaded at t_0"), not from the conclusion of that projection. If we redraw the inference graph so that it is inferred instead from the conclusion, we get another case of collective defeat. However, it must be borne in mind that it is the initial temporal projection to which we are giving precedence, and not just its premise. This is supposed to be a way of adjudicating between conflicting temporal projections, so it cannot just

be the premise of the earlier temporal projection that is relevant. This observation can be captured by appealing to the fact that undercutting defeaters are reasons for conclusions of the form $(P \otimes Q)$, and as such they can be defeasible. In the case of causal undercutting, anything that defeats the earlier temporal projection should defeat the application of causal undercutting, thus reinstating the later temporal projection. For example, if we examined the gun at t_0 and determined it was loaded, but then checked again before firing and the second time we looked it was not loaded, this defeats the temporal projection to the conclusion that the gun was loaded when fired. This is what I earlier called "a discontinuity defeater." In general, any defeater for the earlier temporal projection must also be a defeater for causal undercutting. We have noted two such defeaters, so we should have:

Discontinuity Defeat for Causal Undercutting
If $t_0 < t_1 < t$, "$\sim P$-at-t_1" is an undercutting defeater for an application of causal undercutting.

Probabilistic Defeat for Causal Undercutting
"The probability of P-at-$(t + 1)$ given P-at-t is not high" is an undercutting defeater for an application of causal undercutting.

Thus, the Yale shooting problem is solved. The same epistemic machinery that solves this problem seems to handle causal reasoning in general. It is not quite right to describe this as a solution to the frame problem, because the frame problem arose on the assumption that all good reasoning is deductive. The frame problem was the problem of how to handle causal reasoning given that assumption. Once we embrace defeasible reasoning, the original frame problem goes away. There is no reason to think we should be able to handle causal reasoning in a purely deductive way. However, the problem has a residue, namely, that of giving an account of how causal reasoning works. That is the problem I have tried to solve here. The solution has two parts – temporal projection and causal undercutting.

In closing, it is worth noting that this reasoning is easily implemented in OSCAR. I invite the reader to download the OSCAR code from the OSCAR Web site[17] and try it out on other problems.

Conclusions

The assumption that good reasoning must be deductively valid is seen to be wrong when we look carefully at the kinds of reasoning a sophisticated cognizer must be able to do. Defeasible reasoning is the norm, and deductive reasoning is the exception. Defeasible reasoning differs from deductive reasoning in that the reason-schemes employed in defeasible reasoning can have defeaters. A cognizer may produce a number of arguments, some of which defeat others. A semantics for defeasible reasoning aims to tell us how it is determined which of those arguments are defeated and which are undefeated. A cognizer's justified beliefs are then those that are supported by his undefeated arguments. I described the OSCAR semantics for defeasible reasoning, and illustrated its application with a discussion of the frame problem.

Notes

1   One might question whether this is really a case of reasoning. See Pollock and Oved (2006) for a more extensive discussion of this example.

2   This argument is from Chapter 6 of Pollock (1974).

3   I believe that I developed the first formal semantics for defeasible reasoning in 1979, but I did not initially publish it because, being ignorant of AI, I did not think anyone would be interested. That semantics was finally published in Pollock (1986).

4   See Pollock (1998) and Pollock and Oved (2006) for a fuller discussion of this.

5   Technically, default logic has the consequence that there are no "extensions" for this default theory.

6   There are many forms of circumscription, and by using what are essentially ad hoc priori-

tization rules it may be possible to get the right answer in Figure 7. Because the moves required are ad hoc, I don't think this shows anything.

7   This observation is due to Makinson and Schlechta (1991).

8   The OSCAR architecture is described in my (1995). For up-to-date information on OSCAR, see the OSCAR Web site at http://oscarhome. soc-sci.arizona.edu/ftp/OSCAR-web-page/ OSCAR.html.

9   See Pollock (2006) for a more extensive discussion.

10   McCarthy and Hayes (1969).

11   On this last point, the reader who lacks experience with automated reasoners will have to take my word, but this is a point about which no AI practitioner would disagree.

12   McCarthy and Hayes (1969).

13   Sandewall (1972), McDermott (1982), McCarthy (1986).

14   For example, see the collection of papers in Ginsberg (1987).

15   This problem is equally unsolved for inductive projectibility. A useful survey of literature on inductive projectibility can be found in Stalker (1994).

16   This intuition is reminiscent of Shoham's (1987) "logic of chronological ignorance," although unlike Shoham, I propose to capture the intuition without modifying the structure of the system of defeasible reasoning. This is also related to the proposal of Gelfond and Lifschitz (1993) and to the notion of progressing a database discussed in Lin and Reiter (1994, 1995). This same idea underlies my analysis of counterfactual conditionals in Pollock (1979) and (1984).

17   http://oscarhome.soc-sci.arizona.edu/ftp/ OSCAR-web-page/OSCAR.html.

References

Chisholm, Roderick 1957 *Perceiving*. Ithaca, NY: Cornell University Press.

Chisholm, Roderick 1966 *Theory of Knowledge*, Englewood Cliffs, NJ: PrenticeHall.

Fodor, Jerry 2001 *The Mind Doesn't Work That Way*, Cambridge, MA: MIT Press.

Gelfond, Michael, and Lifschitz, Vladimir 1993 "Representing action and change by logic programs," *Journal of Logic Programming* 17, 301–322.

Ginsberg, Matt 1987 *Readings in Nonmonotonic Reasoning*. Los Altos, CA: Morgan Kaufman.

Hanks, Steve, and McDermott, Drew 1987 "Nonmonotonic logic and temporal projection," *Artificial Intelligence*, 33, 379–412

Harman, Gilbert 1973 *Thought*. Princeton, NJ: Princeton University Press.

Hart, H. L. A. 1948 "The ascription of responsibility and rights," *Proceedings of the Aristotelian Society*, 1948–9.

Israel, David 1980 "What's wrong with non-monotonic logic?" *Proceedings of the First Annual National Conference on Artificial Intelligence*, 99–101.

Kyburg, Henry, Jr. 1961 *Probability and the Logic of Rational Belief*. Middletown, CT: Wesleyan University Press.

Kyburg, Henry, Jr. 1970 "Conjunctivitis," Marshall Swain (ed.), *Induction, Accveptance, and Rational Belief*. Dordrecht, D. Reidel.

Lin, Fangzhen, and Reiter, Raymond 1994 "How to progress a database (and why) I. Logical foundations." In *Proceedings of the Fourth International Conference on Principles of Knowledge Representation (KR '94)*. 425–436.

Lin, Fangzhen, and Reiter, Raymond 1995 "How to progress a database II: The STRIPS connection." *IJCAI-95*. 2001–2007.

Makinson, D., and Schlechta, K. 1991 "Floating conclusions and zombie paths: Two deep difficulties in the 'directly skeptical' approach to inheritance nets" *Artificial Intelligence* 48, 199–209.

McCarthy, John 1980 "Circumscription – A form of non-monotonic reasoning," *Artificial Intelligence* 13, 27–39, 171–172.

McCarthy, John 1986 "Applications of circumscription to formalizing common sense knowledge." *Artificial Intelligence* 26, 89–116.

McCarthy, John, and Hayes, Patrick 1969 "Some philosophical problems from the standpoint of artificial intelligence." In B. Metzer & D. Michie (eds.), *Machine Intelligence 4*. Edinburgh: Edinburgh University Press.

McDermott, Drew 1982 "A temporal logic for reasoning about processes and plans," *Cognitive Science* 6, 101–155.

McDermott, D., and Doyle, Jon, 1980 "Non-monotonic logic I," *Artificial Intelligence* 13: 41–72.

Pollock, John 1967 "Criteria and our knowledge of the material world," *The Philosophical Review*, 76, 28–60.

Pollock, John 1970 "The structure of epistemic justification," *American Philosophical Quarterly*, monograph series 4: 62–78.

Pollock, John 1971 "Perceptual knowledge," *Philosophical Review*, 80, 287–319.

Pollock, John 1974 *Knowledge and Justification*, Princeton University Press.

Pollock, John 1979 *Subjunctive Reasoning*, D. Reidel.

Pollock, John 1984 *The Foundations of Philosophical Semantics*, Princeton University Press.

Pollock, John 1986 *Contemporary Theories of Knowledge*, Rowman and Littlefield.

Pollock, John 1990 *Nomic Probability and the Foundations of Induction*, Oxford University Press.

Pollock, John 1991 "Self-defeating arguments," *Minds and Machines* 1, 367–392.

Pollock, John 1995 *Cognitive Carpentry*, MIT Press.

Pollock, John 1997 "Reasoning about change and persistence: a solution to the frame problem," *Nous* 31, 143–169.

Pollock, John 1998 "Perceiving and reasoning about a changing world," *Computational Intelligence*, 14, 498–562.

Pollock, John 2002 "Defeasible reasoning with variable degrees of justification," *Artificial Intelligence* 133, 233–282.

Pollock, John 2006 *Thinking about Acting: Logical Foundations for Rational Decision Making*. New York, Oxford.

Pollock, John and Oved, Iris, 2006 "Vision, knowledge, and the mystery link." In *Philosophical Perspectives* 19.

Reiter, Raymond 1980 "A logic for default reasoning," *Artificial Intelligence* 13, 81–132.

Rescher, Nicholas 1977 *Dialectics*, Albany: SUNY Albany Press.

Sandewall, Erik 1972 "An approach to the frame problem and its implementation." In B. Metzer and D. Michie (eds.), *Machine Intelligence 7*. Edinburgh: Edinburgh University Press.

Shoham, Yoav 1987 *Reasoning about Change*. Cambridge, MA: MIT Press.

Stalker, Douglas 1994 *Grue: The New Riddle of Induction*. Chicago: Open Court.

Toulmin, Stephen 1958 *The Place of Reason in Ethics*, Cambridge, MA: MIT Press.

Chapter 24: Explanatory Coherence

PAUL THAGARD

1. Introduction

Why did the oxygen theory of combustion super-sede the phlogiston theory? Why is Darwin's theory of evolution by natural selection superior to creationism? How can a jury in a murder trial decide between conflicting views of what happened? This target article develops a theory of explanatory coherence that applies to the evaluation of competing hypotheses in cases such as these. The theory is implemented in a connectionist computer program with many interesting properties.

The problem of inference to explanatory hypotheses has a long history in philosophy and a much shorter one in psychology and artificial intelligence (AI). Scientists and philosophers have long considered the evaluation of theories on the basis of their explanatory power. In the late nineteenth century, Peirce discussed two forms of inference to explanatory hypotheses: *hypothesis*, which involved the acceptance of hypotheses, and *abduction*, which involved merely the initial formation of hypotheses (Peirce 1931–1958; Thagard 1988a). Researchers in artificial intelligence and some philosophers have used the term "abduction" to refer to both the formation and the evaluation of hypotheses. AI work on this kind of inference has concerned such diverse topics as medical diagnosis (Josephson et al. 1987; Pople 1977; Reggia et al. 1983) and natural language interpretation (Charniak and McDermott 1985; Hobbs et al. 1988). In philosophy, the acceptance of explanatory hypotheses is usually called *inference to the best explanation* (Harman 1973, 1986). In social psychology, attribution theory considers how people in everyday life form hypotheses to explain events (Fiske and Taylor 1984). Recently, Pennington and Hastie (1986, 1987) have proposed that much of jury decision making can be best understood in terms of explanatory coherence. For example, to gain a conviction of first degree murder, the prosecution must convince the jury that the accused had a preformed intention to kill the victim. Pennington and Hastie argue that whether the jury will believe this depends on the explanatory coherence of the prosecution's story compared to the story presented by the defense.

Actual cases of scientific and legal reasoning suggest a variety of factors that go into determining the explanatory coherence of a hypothesis. How much does the hypothesis explain? Are its explanations economical? Is the hypothesis similar to ones that explain similar phenomena? Is there an explanation of why the hypothesis might be true? In legal reasoning, the question of explaining the hypothesis usually concerns motives: If we are trying to explain the evidence by supposing that the accused murdered the victim, we will find the supposition more plausible if we can think of reasons why the accused was motivated to kill the victim. Finally, on all these dimensions, how does the hypothesis compare against alternative hypotheses?

This paper presents a theory of explanatory coherence that is intended to account for a wide range of explanatory inferences. I shall propose seven principles of explanatory coherence that encompass the considerations just described and that suffice to make judgments of explanatory coherence. Their sufficiency is shown by the implementation of the theory in a connectionist computer program called ECHO that has been applied to more than a dozen complex cases of scientific and legal reasoning. My account of

Reproduced with permission from Thagard, P. (1989). Explanatory coherence. *Behavioral and Brain Sciences* 12, 435–467.

explanatory coherence thus has three parts: the statement of a theory, the description of an algorithm, and applications to diverse examples that show the feasibility of the algorithm and help to demonstrate the power of the theory (cf. Marr 1982). Finally, I shall discuss the implications of the theory for AI, psychology, and philosophy.

2. A Theory of Explanatory Coherence

2.1. Coherence and Explanation

Before presenting the theory, it will be useful to make some general points about the concepts of coherence and explanation, although it should be made clear that this paper does not purport to give a general account of either concept. The question of the nature of explanation is extremely difficult, and controversial. Philosophers disagree about whether explanation is primarily deductive (Hempel 1965), statistical (Salmon 1970), causal (Salmon 1984), linguistic (Achinstein 1983), or pragmatic (van Fraassen 1980). In AI, explanation is sometimes thought of as deduction (Mitchell et al. 1986) and sometimes as pattern instantiation (Schank 1986). This paper does not pretend to offer a theory of explanation, but is compatible with any of the foregoing accounts (except van Fraassen's, which is intended to make explanation irrelevant to questions of acceptability and truth).

Nor does this paper give a general account of coherence. There are various notions of coherence in the literatures of different fields. We can distinguish at least the following:

Deductive coherence depends on relations of logical consistency and entailment among members of a set of propositions.

Probabilistic coherence depends on a set of propositions having probability assignments consistent with the axioms of probability.

Semantic coherence depends on propositions having similar meanings. Bonjour (1985) provides an interesting survey of philosophical ideas about coherence. Here, I am only offering a theory of *explanatory* coherence.

Explanatory coherence can be understood in several different ways, as

(a) a relation between two propositions,

(b) a property of a whole set of related propositions, or

(c) a property of a single proposition.

I claim that (a) is fundamental, with (b) depending on (a), and (c) depending on (b). That is, explanatory coherence is primarily a relation between two propositions, but we can speak derivatively of the explanatory coherence of a set of propositions as determined by their pairwise coherence, and we can speak derivatively of the explanatory coherence of a single proposition with respect to a set of propositions whose coherence has been established. A major requirement of an account of explanatory coherence is that it shows how it is possible to move from (a) to (b) to (c); algorithms for doing so are presented as part of the computational model described below.

Because the notion of the explanatory coherence of an individual proposition is so derivative and depends on a specification of the set of propositions with which it is supposed to cohere, I shall from now on avoid treating coherence as a property of individual propositions. Instead, we can speak of the *acceptability* of a proposition, which depends on but is detachable from the explanatory coherence of the set of propositions to which it belongs. We should accept propositions that are coherent with our other beliefs, reject propositions that are incoherent with our other beliefs, and be neutral toward propositions that are neither coherent nor incoherent. Acceptability has finer gradations than just acceptance, rejection, and neutrality, however: The greater the coherence of a proposition with other propositions, the greater its acceptability.

In ordinary language, to cohere is to hold together, and explanatory coherence is a holding together because of explanatory relations. We can, accordingly, start with a vague characterization:

Propositions P and Q cohere if there is some explanatory relation between them.

To fill this statement out, we must specify what the explanatory relation might be. I see four possibilities:

(1) P is part of the explanation of Q.

(2) Q is part of the explanation of P.

(3) P and Q are together part of the explanation of some R.

(4) P and Q are analogous in the explanations they respectively give of some R and S.

This characterization leaves open the possibility that two propositions can cohere for nonexplanatory reasons: deductive, probabilistic, or semantic. Explanation is thus sufficient but not necessary for coherence. I have taken "explanation" and "explain" as primitives, while asserting that a relation of explanatory coherence holds between P and Q if and only if one or more of (1)–(4) is true. *Incoherence* between two propositions occurs if they contradict each other or if they offer explanations that background knowledge suggests are incompatible.

The psychological relevance of explanatory coherence comes from the following general predictions concerning the acceptance of individual propositions:

If a proposition is highly coherent with the beliefs of a person, then the person will believe the proposition with a high degree of confidence.

If a proposition is incoherent with the beliefs of a person, then the person will not believe the proposition. The applicability of this to several areas of psychological experimentation is discussed in section 9.

2.2. Principles of Explanatory Coherence

I now propose seven principles that establish relations of explanatory coherence and make possible an assessment of the global coherence of an explanatory system S. S consists of propositions P, Q, and $P_1 \ldots P_n$. Local coherence is a relation between two propositions. I coin the term "incohere" to mean more than just that two propositions do not cohere: To incohere is to *resist* holding together. The principles are as follows:

Principle 1. Symmetry.

(a)   If P and Q cohere, then Q and P cohere.

(b)   If P and Q incohere, then Q and P incohere.

Principle 2. Explanation.

If $P_1 \ldots P_m$ explain Q, then:

(a)   For each P_i in $P_1 \ldots P_m$, P_i and Q cohere.

(b)   For each P_i and P_j in $P_1 \ldots P_m$, P_i and P_j cohere.

(c)   In (a) and (b), the degree of coherence is inversely proportional to the number of propositions $P_1 \ldots P_m$.

Principle 3. Analogy.

(a)   If P_1 explains Q_1, P_2 explains Q_2, P_1 is analogous to P_2, and Q_1 is analogous to

Q_2, then P_1 and P_2 cohere, and Q_1 and Q_2 cohere.

(b)   If P_1 explains Q_1, P_2 explains Q_2, Q_1 is analogous to Q_2, but P_1 is disanalogous to P_2, then P_1 and P_2 incohere.

Principle 4. Data Priority.

Propositions that describe the results of observation have a degree of acceptability on their own.

Principle 5. Contradiction.

If P contradicts Q, then P and Q incohere.

Principle 6. Acceptability.

(a)   The acceptability of a proposition P in a system S depends on its coherence with the proposition in S.

(b)   If many results of relevant experimental observations are unexplained, then the acceptability of a proposition P that explains only a few of them is reduced.

Principle 7. System Coherence.

The global explanatory coherence of a system S of propositions is a function of the pairwise local coherence of those propositions.

2.3. Discussion of the Principles

Principle 1, Symmetry, asserts that pairwise coherence and incoherence are symmetric relations, in keeping with the everyday sense of coherence as holding together. The coherence of two propositions is thus very different from the nonsymmetric relations of entailment and conditional probability. Typically, P entails Q without Q entailing P, and the conditional probability of P given Q is different from the probability of Q given P. But if P and Q hold together, so do Q and P. The use of a symmetrical relation has advantages that will become clearer in the discussion of the connectionist implementation below.

Principle 2, Explanation, is by far the most important for assessing explanatory coherence, because it establishes most of the coherence relations. Part (a) is the most obvious: If a hypothesis P is part of the explanation of a piece of evidence Q, then P and Q cohere. Moreover, if a hypothesis P_2 is explained by another hypothesis P_1, then P_1 and P_2 cohere. Part (a) presupposes that explanation is a more restrictive relation than deductive implication, because otherwise we could prove that any two propositions cohere; for unless we use a relevance logic (Anderson and Belnap 1975), P_1 and the contradiction P_2 & not-P_2 imply any Q, so it would follow that P_1 coheres with Q. It follows from Principle 2(a), in conjunction with Principle 6, that the more a hypothesis explains, the more coherent and hence acceptable it is. Thus, this principle subsumes the criterion of explanatory breadth (which Whewell 1967 called "consilience") that I have elsewhere claimed to be the most important for selecting the best explanation (Thagard 1978, 1988a).

Whereas part (a) of Principle 2 says that what explains coheres with what is explained, part (b) states that two propositions cohere if together they provide an explanation. Behind part (b) is the Duhem–Quine idea that the evaluation of a hypothesis depends partly on the other hypotheses with which it furnishes explanations (Duhem 1954; Quine 1961; see Section 10.1). I call two hypotheses that are used together in an explanation "cohypotheses." Again I assume that explanation is more restrictive than implication; otherwise it would follow that any proposition that explained something was coherent with every other proposition, because if P_1 implies Q, then so does P_1 & P_2. But any scientist who maintained at a conference that the theory of general relativity and today's baseball scores together explain the motion of planets would be laughed off the podium. Principle 2 is intended to apply to explanations and hypotheses actually proposed by scientists.

Part (c) of Principle 2 embodies the claim that if numerous propositions are needed to furnish an explanation, then the coherence of the explaining propositions with each other and with what is explained is thereby diminished. Scientists tend to be skeptical of hypotheses that require myriad *ad hoc* assumptions in their explanations. There is nothing wrong in principle in having explanations that draw on many assumptions, but we should prefer theories that generate explanations using a unified core of hypotheses. I have elsewhere contended that the notion of *simplicity* most appropriate for scientific theory choice is a comparative one preferring theories that make fewer special assumptions (Thagard 1978, 1988a). Principles 2(b) and 2(c) together subsume this criterion. I shall not attempt further to characterize "degree of coherence" here, but the connectionist algorithm described below provides a natural interpretation. Many other notions of simplicity have been proposed (e.g., Foster and Martin 1966; Harman et al. 1988), but

none is so directly relevant to considerations of explanatory coherence as the one embodied in Principle 2.

The third criterion for the best explanation in my earlier account was analogy, and this is subsumed in Principle 3. There is controversy about whether analogy is of more than heuristic use, but scientists such as Darwin have used analogies to defend their theories; his argument for evolution by natural selection is analyzed below. Principle 3(a) does not say simply that any two analogous propositions cohere. There must be an explanatory analogy, with two analogous propositions occurring in explanations of two other propositions that are analogous to each other. Recent computational models of analogical mapping and retrieval show how such correspondences can be noticed (Holyoak and Thagard 1989; Thagard et al. 1989). Principle 3(b) says that when similar phenomena are explained by dissimilar hypotheses, the hypotheses incohere. Although the use of such disanalogies is not as common as the use of analogies, it was important in the reasoning that led Einstein (1952) to the special theory of relativity: He was bothered by asymmetries in the way Maxwell's electrodynamics treated the case of (1) a magnet in motion and a conductor at rest quite differently from the case of (2) a magnet at rest and a conductor in motion.

Principle 4, Data Priority, stands much in need of elucidation and defense. In saying that a proposition describing the results of observation has a degree of acceptability on its own, I am not suggesting that it is indubitable, but only that it can stand on its own more successfully than can a hypothesis whose sole justification is what it explains. A proposition Q may have some independent acceptability and still end up not accepted, if it is only coherent with propositions that are themselves not acceptable.

From the point of view of explanatory coherence alone, we should not take propositions based on observation as independently acceptable without any explanatory relations to other propositions. As Bonjour (1985) argues, the coherence of such propositions is of a nonexplanatory kind, based on background knowledge that observations of certain sorts are very likely to be true. From past experience, we know that our observations are very likely to be true, so we should believe them unless there is substantial reason not to. Similarly, at a very different level, we have some confidence in the reliability of descriptions of experimental results in carefully refereed scientific journals. Section 10.4 relates the question of data priority to current philosophical disputes about justification.

Principle 5, Contradiction, is straightforward. By "contradictory" here I mean not just syntactic contradictions like P & not-P, but also semantic contradictions such as "This ball is black all over" and "This ball is white all over." In scientific cases, contradiction becomes important when incompatible hypotheses compete to explain the same evidence. Not all competing hypotheses incohere, however, because many phenomena have multiple causes. For example, explanations of why someone has certain medical symptoms may involve hypotheses that the patient has various diseases, and it is possible that more than one disease is present. Competing hypotheses incohere if they are contradictory or if they are framed as offering *the* most likely cause of a phenomenon. In the latter case, we get a kind of pragmatic contradictoriness: Two hypotheses may not be syntactically or semantically contradictory, yet scientists will view them as contradictory because of background beliefs suggesting that only one of the hypotheses is acceptable. For example, in the debate over dinosaur extinction (Thagard 1988b), scientists generally treat as contradictory the following hypotheses:

(1) Dinosaurs became extinct because of a meteorite collision.

(2) Dinosaurs became extinct because the sea level fell.

Logically, (1) and (2) could both be true, but scientists treat them as conflicting explanations, possibly because there are no explanatory relations between them and their conjunction is unlikely.

The relation "cohere" is not transitive. If P_1 and P_2 together explain Q, while P_1 and P_3 together explain not-Q, then P_1 coheres with both Q and not-Q, which incohere. Such cases do occur in science. Let P_1 be the gas law that volume is proportional to temperature, P_2 a proposition describing the drop in temperature of a particular sample of gas, P_3 a proposition describing the rise in temperature of the sample, and Q a proposition about increases in the sample's volume. Then P_1 and P_2 together explain a decrease in the volume, while P_1 and P_3 explain an increase.

Principle 6, Acceptability, proposes in part (a) that we can make sense of the overall coherence of a proposition in an explanatory system just from the pairwise coherence relations established by Principles 1–5. If we have a hypothesis P that coheres with evidence Q by virtue of explaining it, but incoheres with another contradictory hypothesis, should we accept P? To decide, we cannot merely count the number of propositions with which P coheres and incoheres, because the acceptability of P depends in part on the acceptability of those propositions themselves. We need a dynamic and parallel method of deriving general coherence from particular coherence relations; such a method is provided by the connectionist program described below.

Principle 6(b), reducing the acceptability of a hypothesis when much of the relevant evidence is unexplained by any hypothesis, is intended to handle cases where the best available hypothesis is still not very good, in that it accounts for only a fraction of the available evidence. Consider, for example, a theory in economics that could explain the stock market crashes of 1929 and 1987 but that had nothing to say about myriad other similar economic events. Even if the theory gave the best available account of the two crashes, we would not be willing to elevate it to an accepted part of general economic theory. What does "relevant" mean here? [See BBS multiple book review of Sperber and Wilson's *Relevance*, BBS 10(4) 1987.] As a first approximation, we can say that a piece of evidence is *directly* relevant to a hypothesis if the evidence is explained by it or by one of its competitors. We can then add that a piece of evidence is relevant if it is directly relevant or if it is similar to evidence that is relevant, where similarity is a matter of dealing with phenomena of the same kind. Thus, a theory of the business cycle that applies to the stock market crashes of 1929 and 1987 should also have something to say about nineteenth-century crashes and major business downturns in the twentieth century.

The final principle, System Coherence, proposes that we can have some global measure of the coherence of a whole system of propositions. Principles 1–5 imply that, other things being equal, a system S will tend to have more global coherence than another if

(1) S has more data in it;

(2) S has more internal explanatory links between propositions that cohere because of explanations and analogies; and

(3) S succeeds in separating coherent subsystems of propositions from conflicting subsystems.

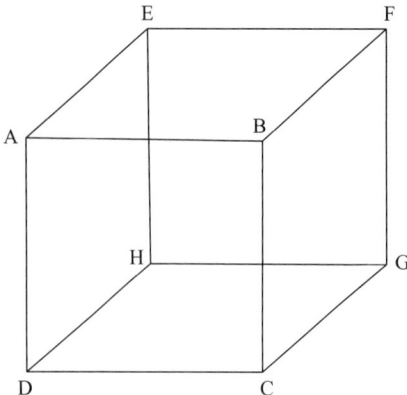

Figure 1. The Necker cube. Either ABCD or EFGH can be perceived as the front.

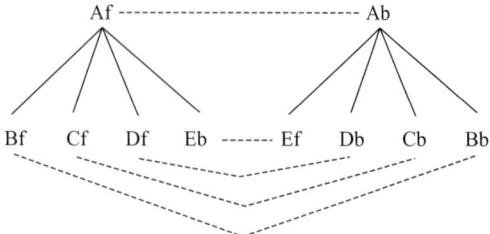

Figure 2. A connectionist network for interpreting the cube. Af is a unit representing the hypothesis that A is at the front, whereas Ab represents the hypothesis that A is at the back. Solid lines represent excitatory links; dotted lines represent inhibitory links.

The connectionist algorithm described below comes with a natural measure of global system coherence. It also indicates how different priorities can be given to the different principles.

3. Connectionist Models

To introduce connectionist techniques, I shall briefly describe the popular example of how a network can be used to understand the Necker cube phenomenon (see, e.g., Feldman and Ballard 1982; Rumelhart et al. 1986). Figure 1 contains a reversing cube: By changing our focus of attention, we are able to see as the front either face ABCD or face EFGH. The cube is perceived holistically, in that we are incapable of seeing corner A at the front without seeing corners B, C, and D at the front as well.

We can easily construct a simple network with the desired holistic property using *units*, crudely analogous to neurons, connected by links. Let Af be a unit that represents the hypothesis that corner A is at the front, while Ab represents the hypothesis that corner A is at the back. Similarly, we construct units Bf, Bb, Cf, Cb, Df, Db, Ef, Eb, Ff, Fb, Gf, Gb, Hf, and Hb. These units are not independent of each other. To signify that A cannot be both at the front and at the back, we construct an *inhibitory* link between the units Af and Ab, with similar links inhibiting Bf and Bb, and so on. Because corners A, B, C, and D go together, we construct *excitatory* links between each pair of Af, Bf, Cf, and Df, and between each pair of Ab, Bb, Cb, and Db. Analogous inhibitory and excitatory links are then set up for E, F, G, and H. In addition, we need inhibitory links between Af and Ef, Bf and Ff, and so on. Part of the resulting network is depicted in Figure 2. I have used solid lines

to indicate excitatory links, and dotted lines to indicate inhibitory links.

Units can have varying degrees of *activation*. Suppose that our attention is focused on corner A, which we assume to be at the front, so that unit Af is activated. Then by virtue of the excitatory links from Af to Bf, Cf, and Df, these units will be activated. The inhibitory links from Af to Ab and Ef will cause those units to be deactivated. In turn, the excitatory links from Ab to Bb, Cb, and Db will deactivate them. Thus activation will spread through the network until all the units corresponding to the view that A, B, C, and D are at the front are activated, while all the units corresponding to the view that E, F, G, and H are at the front are deactivated.

Goldman has pointed out some of the attractive epistemological properties of this sort of network (Goldman 1986: Ch. 15; see also Thagard 1989). A proposition, represented by a unit, is accepted if it is part of the best competing coalition of units and its rivals are rejected. Uncertainty consists in the absence of a clear-cut winner. Goldman argues that the connectionist view that has units representing propositions settling into either on or off states is more psychologically plausible and epistemologically appealing than the Bayesian picture that assigns probabilities to propositions.

4. ECHO

4.1. The Program

Let us now look at ECHO, a computer program written in Common LISP that is a straightforward application of connectionist algorithms to the problem of explanatory coherence. In ECHO, propositions representing hypotheses and results of observation are represented by units. Whenever Principles 1–5 state that two propositions cohere, an excitatory link between them is established. If two propositions incohere, an inhibitory link between them is established. In ECHO, these links are symmetric, as Principle 1 suggests: The weight from unit 1 to unit 2 is the same as the weight from unit 2 to unit 1. Principle 2(c) says that the larger the number of propositions used in an explanation, the smaller the degree of coherence between each pair of propositions. ECHO therefore counts the propositions that do the explaining and proportionately lowers the weight of the excitatory links between units representing coherent propositions.

Principle 4, Data Priority, is implemented by links to each data unit from a special evidence unit that always has activation 1, giving each unit some acceptability on its own. When the network is run, activation spreads from the special unit to the data units, and then to the units representing explanatory hypotheses. The extent of data priority – the presumed acceptability of data propositions – depends on the weight of the link between the special unit and the data units. The higher this weight, the more immune the data units become to deactivation by other units. Units that have inhibitory links between them because they represent contradictory hypotheses have to compete with each other for the activation spreading from the data units: The activation of one of these units will tend to suppress the activation of the other. Excitatory links have positive weights; best performance occurs with weights around .05. Inhibitory links have negative weights; best performance occurs with weights around −.2. The activation of units ranges between 1 and −1; positive activation can be interpreted as acceptance of the proposition represented by the unit, negative activation as rejection, and activation close to 0 as neutrality. The relation between acceptability and probability is discussed in Section 10.2.

To summarize how ECHO implements the principles of explanatory coherence, we can list key terms from the principles with the corresponding terms from ECHO:

Proposition: Unit

Coherence: Excitatory link, with positive weight

Incoherence: Inhibitory link, with negative weight

Data priority: Excitatory link from special unit

Acceptability: Activation

System coherence: See the function H defined in Section 4.9 below.

The following are some examples of the LISP formulas that constitute ECHO's inputs (I omit LISP quote symbols; see Tables 1–4 for actual input):

1. (EXPLAIN (H1 H2) E1)

2. (EXPLAIN (H1 H2 H3) E2)

3. (ANALOGOUS (H5 H6) (E5 E6))

4. (DATA (E1 E2 E5 E6))

5. (CONTRADICT H1 H4)

Formula 1 says that hypotheses H1 and H2 together explain evidence E1. As suggested by the second principle of explanatory coherence proposed above, formula 1 sets up three excitatory links, between units representing H1 and E1, H2 and E1, and H1 and H2.[1] Formula 2 sets up six such links, between each of the hypotheses and the evidence, and between each pair of hypotheses, but the weight on the links will be less than those established by formula 1, because there are more cohypotheses. In accord with Principle 3(a), Analogy, formula 3 produces excitatory links between H5 and H6, and between E5 and E6, if previous input has established that H5 explains E5 and H6 explains E6. Formula 4 is used to apply Principle 4, Data Priority, setting up explanation-independent excitatory links to each data unit from a special evidence unit. Finally, formula 5 sets up an inhibitory link between the contradictory hypotheses H1 and H4, as prescribed by Principle 5. A full specification of ECHO's inputs and algorithms is provided in the Appendix.

Input to ECHO can optionally reflect the fact that not all data and explanations are of equal merit. For example, a data statement can have the form

(DATA (E1 (E 2.8))).

This formula sets up the standard link from the special unit to E1, but interprets the ".8" as indicating that E2 is not as reliable a piece of evidence as E1. Hence, the weight from the special unit to E2 is only .8 as strong as the weight from the special unit to E1. Similarly, explain statements take an optimal numerical parameter, as in

(EXPLAIN (H1) E 1.9).

The additional parameter, .9, indicates some weakness in the quality of the explanation and results in a lower than standard weight on the excitatory link between H1 and E1. In ECHO's applications to date, the additional parameters for data and explanation quality have not been used, because it is difficult to establish them objectively from the texts we have been using to generate ECHO's inputs. But it is important that ECHO has the capacity to make use of judgments of data and explanation quality when these are available.

Program runs show that the networks thus established have numerous desirable properties. Other things being equal, activation accrues to units corresponding to hypotheses that explain more, provide simpler explanations, and are analogous to other explanatory hypotheses. The considerations of explanatory breadth, simplicity, and analogy are smoothly integrated. The networks are holistic, in that the activation of every unit can potentially have an effect on every other unit linked to it by a path, however lengthy. Nevertheless, the activation of a unit is directly affected only by those units to which it is linked. Although complexes of coherent propositions are evaluated together, different hypotheses in a complex can finish with different activations, depending on their particular coherence relations. The symmetry of excitatory links means that active units tend to bring up the activation of units with which they are linked, whereas units whose activation sinks below 0 tend to bring down the activation of units to which they are linked. Data units are given priority, but can nevertheless be deactivated if they are linked to units that become deactivated. So long as excitation is not set too high (see Section 12.2), the networks set up by ECHO are stable: In most of them, all units reach asymptotic activation levels after fewer than 100 cycles of updating. The most complex network implemented so far, comparing the explanatory power of Copernicus's heliocentric theory with Ptolemy's geocentric one, requires about 210 cycles before its more than 150 units have all settled. To illustrate ECHO's capabilities, I shall describe some very simple tests that illustrate its ability to handle considerations of explanatory breadth, simplicity, and analogy. Later sections on scientific and legal reasoning provide more complex and realistic examples.

4.2. Explanatory Breadth

We should normally prefer a hypothesis that explains more than alternative hypotheses. If hypothesis H1 explains two pieces of evidence, whereas H2 explains only one, then H1 should be preferred to H2. Here are four formulas

given together to ECHO as input:

(EXPLAIN (H1) E1)
(EXPLAIN (H1) E2)
(EXPLAIN (H2) E2)
(CONTRADICT (H1 H2))
(DATA (E1 E2))

These formulas generate the network pictured in Figure 3, with excitatory links corresponding to coherence represented by solid lines, and with inhibitory links corresponding to incoherence represented by dotted lines. Activation flows from the special unit, whose activation is clamped at 1, to the evidence units, and then to the hypothesis units, which inhibit each other. Because H1 explains more than its competitor H2, H1 becomes active, settling with activation above 0, while H2 is deactivated, settling with activation below 0. (See Section 4.10 for a discussion of the parameters that affect the runs, and the Appendix for sensitivity analyses.) Notice that although the links in ECHO are symmetric, in keeping with the symmetry of the coherence relation, the flow of activation is not, because evidence units get activation first and then pass it along to what explains them.

ECHO's networks have interesting dynamic properties. What happens if new data come in after the network has settled? When ECHO is given the further information that H2 explains additional data E3, E4, and E5, then the network resettles into a reversed state in which H2 is activated and H1 is deactivated. However, if the additional information is only that H2 explains E2, or only that H2 explains E3, then ECHO does not resettle into a state in which H1 and H2

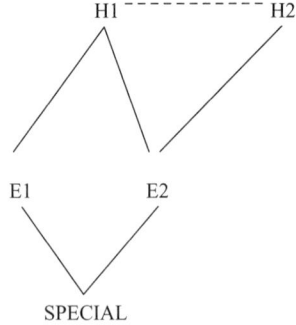

SPECIAL

Figure 3. Explanatory breadth. As in Figure 2, solid lines represent excitatory links, whereas dotted line represents inhibitory links. Evidence units E1 and E2 are linked to the special unit. The result of running this network is that H1 defeats H2.

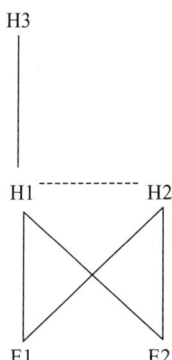

Figure 4. Being explained. H1 defeats H2 because it is explained by H3.

get equal activation. (It does give H1 and H2 equal activation if the input says that they have equal explanatory power from the start.) Thus ECHO displays a kind of conservatism also seen in human scientists. See the discussion of conservatism in Section 10.4.

4.3. Being Explained

Section 4.2 showed how Principle 2(a) leads ECHO to prefer a hypothesis that explains more than its competitors. The same principle also implies greater coherence, other things being equal, for a hypothesis that is explained. Consider the following input:

(EXPLAIN (H1) E1)

(EXPLAIN (H1) E2)

(EXPLAIN (H2) E1)

(EXPLAIN (H2) E2)

(EXPLAIN (H3) H1)

(CONTRADICT H1 H2)

(DATA (E1 E2))

Figure 4 depicts the network constructed using this input. Here, and in all subsequent figures, the special evidence unit is not shown. In Figure 4, H1 and H2 have the same explanatory breadth, but ECHO activates H1 and deactivates H2 because H1 is explained by H3. ECHO thus gives more activation to a hypothesis that is explained than to a contradictory one that is not explained. If the above formulas did not include a CONTRADICT statement, then no inhibitory links would be formed, so that all units would asymptote with positive activation. Because of the decay parameter, activation is still less than 1: See the equations in the Appendix.

4.4. Refutation

According to Popper (1959), the hallmark of science is not the acceptance of explanatory theories but the rejection of falsified ones. Take the simplest case where a hypothesis H1 explains (predicts) some piece of "negative evidence" NE1, which contradicts data E1. Then E1 becomes active, deactivating NE1 and hence H1. Such straightforward refutations, however, are rare in science. Scientists do not typically give up a promising theory just because it has some empirical problems, and neither does ECHO. If, in addition to explaining NE1, H1 explains some positive pieces of evidence, E2 and E3, then ECHO does not deactivate it. However, an alternative hypothesis H2 that also explains E2 and E3 is preferred to H1, which loses because of NE1. Rejection in science is usually a complex process involving competing hypotheses, not a simple matter of falsification (Lakatos 1970; Thagard 1988a: Ch. 9; Section 10.1 below).

4.5. Unification

The impact of explanatory breadth, being explained, and refutation all arise from Principle 2(a), which says that hypotheses cohere with what they explain. According to Principle 2(b), cohypotheses that explain together cohere with each other. Thus, if H1 and H2 together explain evidence E, then H1 and H2 are linked. This gives ECHO a preference for unified explanations, ones that use a common set of hypotheses rather than having special hypotheses for each piece of evidence explained. Consider this input, which generates the network shown in Figure 5:

(EXPLAIN (H1 A1) E1)

(EXPLAIN (H1 A2) E2)

(EXPLAIN (H2 A3) E1)

(EXPLAIN (H2 A3) E2)

(CONTRADICT H1 H2)

(DATA (E1 E2))

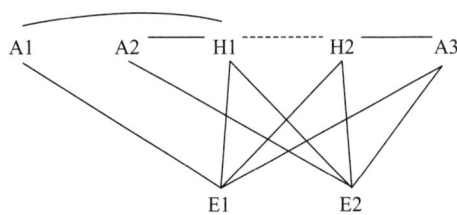

Figure 5. Unification. H2 defeats H1 because it gives a more unified explanation of the evidence.

Although H1 and H2 both explain E1 and E2, the explanation by H2 is more unified in that it uses A3 in both cases. Hence ECHO forms a stronger link between H2 and A3 than it does between H1 and A1 or A2, so H2 becomes activated and H1 is deactivated. The explanations by H2 are not simpler than those by H1, in the sense of Principle 2(c), because both involve two hypotheses. ECHO's preference for H2 over H1 thus depends on the coherence of H2 with its auxiliary hypothesis and the evidence being greater than the coherence of H1 with its auxiliary hypotheses and the evidence. One might argue that the coherence between cohypotheses should be less than the coherence of a hypothesis with what it explains; ECHO contains a parameter that can allow the weights between cohypothesis units to be less than the weight between a hypothesis unit and an evidence unit.

4.6. Simplicity

According to Principle 2(c), the degree of coherence of a hypothesis with what it explains and with its cohypotheses is inversely proportional to the number of cohypotheses. An example of ECHO's preference for simple hypotheses derives from the input:

(EXPLAIN (H1) E1)

(EXPLAIN (H2 H3) E1)

(CONTRADICT H1 H2)

(DATA (E1))

Here H1 is preferred to H2 and H3 because it accomplishes the explanation with no cohypotheses. The generated network is shown in Figure 6.

Principle 2(c) is important for dealing with *ad hoc* hypotheses that are introduced only to save a hypothesis from refutation. Suppose that H1 is in danger of refutation because it explains negative evidence NE1, which contradicts evidence E1. One might try to save H1 by concocting an auxiliary hypothesis, H2, which together with H1 would explain E1. Such maneuvers are common in science: Nineteenth-century physicists did not abandon Newtonian mechanics because it gave false predictions concerning the motion of Uranus; instead, they hypothesized the existence of another planet, Neptune, to explain the discrepancies. Neptune, of course, was eventually observed, but we need to be able to discount auxiliary hypotheses that do not contribute to any additional explanations. Because the expla-

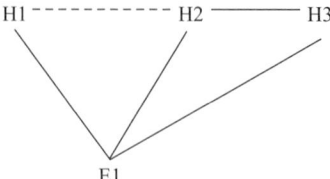

Figure 6. Simplicity. H1 defeats H2 because it gives a simpler explanation of the evidence.

nation of E1 by H1 and H2 is less simple than the explanation of NE1 by H1, the *ad hoc* maneuver does not succeed in saving H1 from deactivation.

4.7. Analogy

According to Principle 3(a), analogous hypotheses that explain analogous evidence are coherent with each other. Figure 7 shows relations of analogy, derived from the input:

(EXPLAIN (H1) E1)

(EXPLAIN (H2) E1)

(EXPLAIN (H3) H3)

(ANALOGOUS (H2 H3) (E1 E3))

(CONTRADICT H1 H2)

(DATA (E1 E3))

The analogical links corresponding to the coherence relations required by Principle 3 are shown by wavy lines. Running this example leads to activation of H2 and deactivation of its rival, H1. Figures 3–7 show consilience, simplicity, and analogy operating independently of each other, but in realistic examples these criteria can all operate simultaneously through activation adjustment. Thus ECHO shows how criteria such as explanatory breadth, simplicity, and analogy can be integrated. My most recent account of inference to the best explanation (Thagard 1988a) included a computational model that

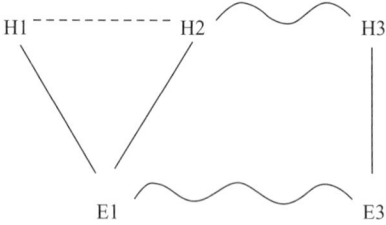

Figure 7. Analogy. The wavy lines indicate excitatory links based on analogies. H2 defeats H1 because the explanation it gives is analogous to the explanation afforded by H3.

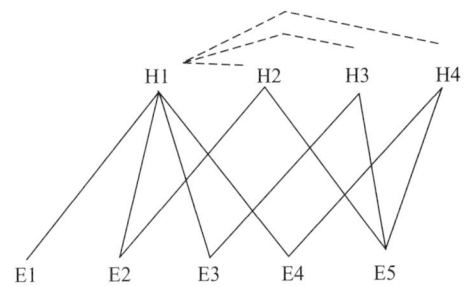

Figure 8. Downplaying of evidence. E5 is deactivated, even though it is an evidence unit, because it coheres only with inferior hypotheses.

integrated breadth and simplicity but left open the question of how to tie in analogy. Principle 3 and ECHO show how analogy can participate with consilience and simplicity in contributing explanatory power.

4.8. Evidence

Principle 4 asserts that data get priority by virtue of their independent coherence. But it should nevertheless be possible for a data unit to be deactivated. We see this both in the everyday practice of experimenters, in which it is often necessary to discard some of the data because they are deemed unreliable (Hedges 1987), and in the history of science where evidence for a discarded theory sometimes falls into neglect (Laudan 1976). Figure 8, which derives from the following input, shows how this might happen.

(EXPLAIN (H1) E1)
(EXPLAIN (H2) E2)
(EXPLAIN (H1) E3)
(EXPLAIN (H1) E4)
(EXPLAIN (H2) E2)
(EXPLAIN (H2) E5)
(EXPLAIN (H3) E3)
(EXPLAIN (H3) E5)
(EXPLAIN (H4) E4)
(EXPLAIN (H4) E5)
(CONTRADICT H1 H2)
(CONTRADICT H1 H3)
(CONTRADICT H1 H4)

These inputs lead to the deactivation of E5, dragged down by the deactivation of the inferior hypotheses H3, H4, and H5. Because E5 coheres only with propositions that are themselves unac-

ceptable, it becomes unacceptable too. Because H1 has four excitatory links, it easily deactivates the other three hypotheses, and their negative activation brings down the initially positive activation of E5 into the negative range.

Principle 6(b) also concerns evidence, undermining the acceptability of hypotheses that explain only a small part of the relevant data. Accordingly, ECHO automatically increases the value of a decay parameter in proportion to the ratio of unexplained evidence to explained evidence (see Appendix). A hypothesis that explains only a fraction of the relevant evidence will thus decay toward the beginning activation level of 0 rather than become activated.

4.9. Acceptability and System Coherence

If ECHO is taken as an algorithmic implementation of the first five principles of explanatory coherence, then it validates Principle 6, Acceptability, for it shows that holistic judgments of the acceptability of a proposition can be based solely on pairwise relations of coherence. A unit achieves a stable activation level merely by considering the activation of units to which it is linked and the weights on those links. Asymptotic activation values greater than 0 signify acceptance of the proposition represented by the unit, whereas negative values signify rejection.

ECHO also validates Principle 7, System Coherence, because we can borrow from connectionist models a measure H of the global coherence of a whole system of propositions at time t:

$$H(t) = \Sigma_i \Sigma_j w_{ij} a_i(t) a_j(t). \tag{1}$$

In this equation, w_{ij} is the weight from unit i to unit j, and $a_i(t)$ is the activation of unit i at time t. This measure or its inverse has been variously called the "goodness," "energy," or "harmony" of the network (Rumelhart et al. 1986, vol. 2, p. 13). For historical reasons, I prefer a variant of the last term with the alternative spelling "harmany" (Harman 1973). Thus ECHO stands for "Explanatory Coherence by Harmany Optimization."

Equation 1 says that to calculate the harmany of the network, we consider each pair of units a_i and a_j that are linked with weight w_{ij}. Harmany increases, for example, when two units with high activation have a link between them with high weight, or when a unit with high activation and a unit with negative activation have between them a link with negative weight. In ECHO the harmany of a system of propositions increases, other things being equal, with increases in the number of data units, the number of links, and the number of cycles to update activations to bring them more in line with the weights.

4.10. Parameters

The simulations just described depend on program parameters that give ECHO numerous degrees of freedom, some of which are epistemologically interesting. In the example in Section 4.2 (Figure 3), the relation between excitatory weights and inhibitory weights is crucial. If inhibition is low compared to excitation, then ECHO will activate both H1 and H2, because the excitation that H2 gets from E1 will overcome the inhibition it gets from H1. Let the *tolerance* of the system be the absolute value of the ratio of excitatory weight to inhibitory weight. With high tolerance, the system will entertain competing hypotheses. With low tolerance, winning hypotheses deactivate the losers. Typically, ECHO is run with excitatory weights set at .05 and inhibition at −.2, so tolerance is .25. If tolerance is high, ECHO can settle into a state where two contradictory hypotheses are both activated. ECHO performs well using a wide range of parameters (see the sensitivity analyses in the Appendix).

Other parameters establish the relative importance of simplicity and analogy. If H1 explains E1 by itself, then the excitatory link between H1 and E1 has the default weight .05. But if H1 and H2 together explain E1, then the weight of the links is set at the default value divided by 2, the number of cohypotheses, leaving it at .025. If we want to change the importance of simplicity as incorporated in Principle 2(c), however, then we can raise the number of cohypotheses to an exponent that represents the *simplicity impact* of the system. Equation 3 for doing this is given in the algorithm section of the Appendix. The greater the simplicity impact, the more weights will be diminished by having more cohypotheses. Similarly, the weights established by analogy can be affected by a factor representing *analogy impact*. If this is 1, then the links connecting analogous hypotheses are just as strong as those set up by simple explanations, and analogy can have a very large effect. If, on the other hand, analogy impact is set at 0, then analogy has no effect.

Another important parameter of the system is decay rate, represented by θ (see equation 4 in

the Appendix). We can term this the *skepticism* of the system, because the higher it is, the more excitation from data will be needed to activate hypotheses. If skepticism is very high, then *no* hypotheses will be activated. Whereas tolerance reflects ECHO's view of contradictory hypotheses, skepticism determines its treatment of all hypotheses. Principle 6(b) can be interpreted as saying that if there is much unexplained evidence, then ECHO's skepticism level is raised.

Finally, we can vary the priority of the data by adjusting the weights to the data units from the special unit. *Data excitation* is a value from 0 to 1 that provides these weights. To reflect the scientific practice of not treating all data equally seriously, it is also possible to set the weights and initial activations for each data unit separately. If data excitation is set low, then, contrary to Section 4.2, new evidence for a rejected hypothesis will not lead to its adoption. If data excitation is high, then, contrary to Section 4.8, evidence that supports only a bad hypothesis will not be thrown out.

With so many degrees of freedom, which are typical of connectionist models, one might question the value of simulations, as it might seem that any desired behavior whatsoever could be obtained. However, if a fixed set of default parameters applies to a large range of cases, then the arbitrariness is much diminished. In *all* the computer runs reported in this paper, ECHO has had excitation at .05, inhibition at −.2 (so tolerance is .25), data excitation at .1., decay (skepticism) at .05, simplicity impact at 1, and analogy impact at 1. As reported in the Appendix in the section on sensitivity analyses, there is nothing special about the default values of the parameters: ECHO works over a wide range of values. In a full simulation of a scientist's cognitive processes, we could imagine better values being *learned*. Many connectionist models do not take weights as given, but instead adjust them as the result of experience. Similarly, we can imagine that part of a scientist's training entails learning how seriously to take data, analogy, simplicity, and so on. Most scientists get their training not merely by reading and experimenting on their own but also by working closely with scientists already established in their field; hence, a scientist can pick up the relevant values from advisors. In ECHO they are set by the programmer, but it should be possible to extend the program to allow training from examples.

The examples described in this section are trivial and show merely that ECHO has some desired properties. I shall now show that ECHO

Table 1: Input Propositions for Lavoisier (1862) Example

Evidence

(proposition 'E1	"In combustion, heat and light are given off.")
(proposition 'E2	"Inflammability is transmittable from one body to another.")
(proposition 'E3	"Combusion only occurs in the presence of pure air.")
(proposition 'E4	"Increase in weight of a burned body is exactly equal to weight of air absorbed.")
(proposition 'E5	"Metals undergo calcination.")
(proposition 'E6	"In calcination, bodies increase weight.")
(proposition 'E7	"In calcination, volume of air diminishes.")
(proposition 'E8	"In reduction, effervescence appears.")

Oxygen hypotheses

(proposition 'OH1	"Pure air contains oxygen principle.")
(proposition 'OH2	"Pure air contains matter of fire and heat.")
(proposition 'OH3	"In combustion, oxygen from the air combines with the burning body.")
(proposition 'OH4	"Oxygen has weight.")
(proposition 'OH5	"In calcination, metals add oxygen to become calxes.")
(proposition 'OH6	"In reduction, oxygen is given off.")

Phlogiston hypotheses

(proposition 'PH1	"Combustible bodies contain phlogiston.")
(proposition 'PH2	"Combustible bodies contain matter of heat.")
(proposition 'PH3	"In combustion, phlogiston is given off.")
(proposition 'PH4	"Phlogiston can pass from one body to another.")
(proposition 'PH5	"Metals contain phlogiston.")
(proposition 'PH6	"In calcination, phlogiston is given off.")

can handle some much more substantial examples from the history of science and from recent legal deliberations.

5. Applications of ECHO to Scientific Reasoning

Theories in the philosophy of science, including computational ones, should be evaluated with respect to important cases from the history of science. To show the historical application of the theory of explanatory coherence, I shall discuss two important cases of arguments concerning the best explanation: Lavoisier's argument for his oxygen theory against the phlogiston theory, and Darwin's argument for evolution by natural selection. ECHO has also been applied to the following:

Contemporary debates about why the dinosaurs became extinct (Thagard 1988b);

Arguments by Wegener and his critics for and against continental drift (Thagard and Nowak 1988; 1990);

Psychological experiments on how beginning students learn physics (Ranney and Thagard 1988); and

Copernicus's case against Ptolemaic astronomy (Nowak and Thagard 1992).

Additional applications are currently under development.

5.1. Lavoisier

In the middle of the eighteenth century, the dominant theory in chemistry was the phlogiston theory of Stahl, which provided explanations of important phenomena of combustion, respiration, and calcination (what we would now call oxidation). According to the phlogiston theory, combustion takes place when phlogiston in burning bodies is given off. In the 1770s, Lavoisier developed the alternative theory that combustion takes place when burning bodies combine with oxygen from the air (for an outline of the conceptual development of his theory, see Thagard 1990). More than ten years after he first suspected the inadequacy of the phlogiston theory, Lavoisier mounted a full-blown attack on it in a paper called "Réflexions sur le Phlogistique" (Lavoisier 1862).

Tables 1 and 2 present the input given to ECHO to represent Lavoisier's argument in his 1783 polemic against phlogiston. Table 1 shows the eight propositions used to represent the evidence to be explained and the twelve used to represent the competing theories. The evidence concerns different properties of combustion and calcination, while there are two sets

Table 2: Input Explanations and Contradictions in Lavoisier (1862) Example

Oxygen explanations
  (explain '(OH1 OH2 OH3) 'E1)
  (explain '(OH1 OH3) 'E3)
  (explain '(OH1 OH3 OH4) 'E4)
  (explain '(OH1 OH5) 'E5)
  (explain '(OH1 OH4 OH5) 'E6)
  (explain '(OH1 OH5) 'E7)
  (explain '(OH1 OH6) 'E8)

Phlogiston explanations
  (explain '(PH1 PH2 PH3) 'E1)
  (explain '(PH1 PH3 PH4) 'E2)
  (explain '(PH5 PH6) 'E5)

Contradictions
  (contradict 'PH3 'OH3)
  (contradict 'PH6 'OH5)

Data
  (data '(E1 E2 E3 E4 E5 E6 E7 E8))

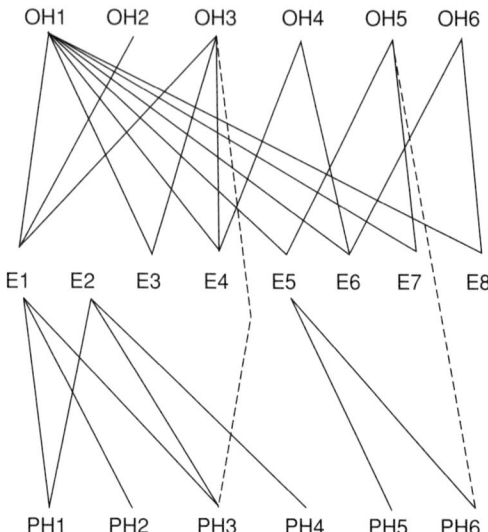

Figure 9. Network representing Lavoisier's (1862) argument. E1–E8 are evidence units. OH1–OH6 are units representing hypotheses of the oxygen theory; PH1–PH6 represent the phlogiston hypotheses. Solid lines are excitatory links; dotted lines are inhibitory.

of hypotheses representing the oxygen and phlogiston theories, respectively. These propositions do not capture Lavoisier's argument completely but do recapitulate its major points. (In a slightly more complicated simulation not presented here, I have encoded the attempt by the phlogiston theory to explain the increase in weight in combustion and calcination by the supposition that phlogiston has negative weight; Lavoisier argues that this supposition renders the phlogiston theory internally contradictory, because phlogiston theorists sometimes assumed that phlogiston has positive weight.)

Table 2 shows the part of the input that sets up the network used to make a judgment of explanatory coherence. The "explain" statements are based directly on Lavoisier's own assertions about what is explained by the phlogiston theory and the oxygen theory. The "contradict" statements reflect my judgment of which of the oxygen hypotheses conflict directly with which of the phlogiston hypotheses.

These explanations and contradictions generate the network partially portrayed in Figure 9. Excitatory links, indicating that two propositions cohere, are represented by solid lines. Inhibitory links are represented by dotted lines. All the oxygen hypotheses are arranged along the top line and all the phlogiston hypotheses along the bottom, with the evidence in the middle. Omitted from the figure for the sake of legibility are the excitatory links among the hypotheses of the two theories and the links between the evidence units and the special unit. In addition to its displayed links to evidence, OH1 has excitatory links to OH2, OH3, OH4, OH5, and OH6. The link between OH1 and OH3 is particularly strong, because these two hypotheses participate in three explanations together. Figure 10, produced by a graphics program that runs with ECHO, displays the links to OH3, with excitatory links shown by thick lines and the inhibitory link with PH3 shown by a thin line. The numbers on the lines indicate the weights of the links rounded to three decimal places: In accord with Principle 2(c), weights are different from the default weight of .05 whenever multiple hypotheses are used in an explanation. If the hypotheses participate in only one explanation, then the weight between them is equal to the default excitation divided by the number of hypotheses; but weights are additive, so that the weight is increased if two hypotheses participate in more than one explanation. For example, the link between OH3 and E1 has the weight .017 (.0166666 rounded), because the explanation of E1 by OH3 required two additional hypotheses. The weight between OH3 and OH1 is .058 (.025 + .0166666 + .0166666), because the two of them alone explain E3, and together they explain E1 and E4 along with a third hypothesis in each case. OH1 and OH3 are thus

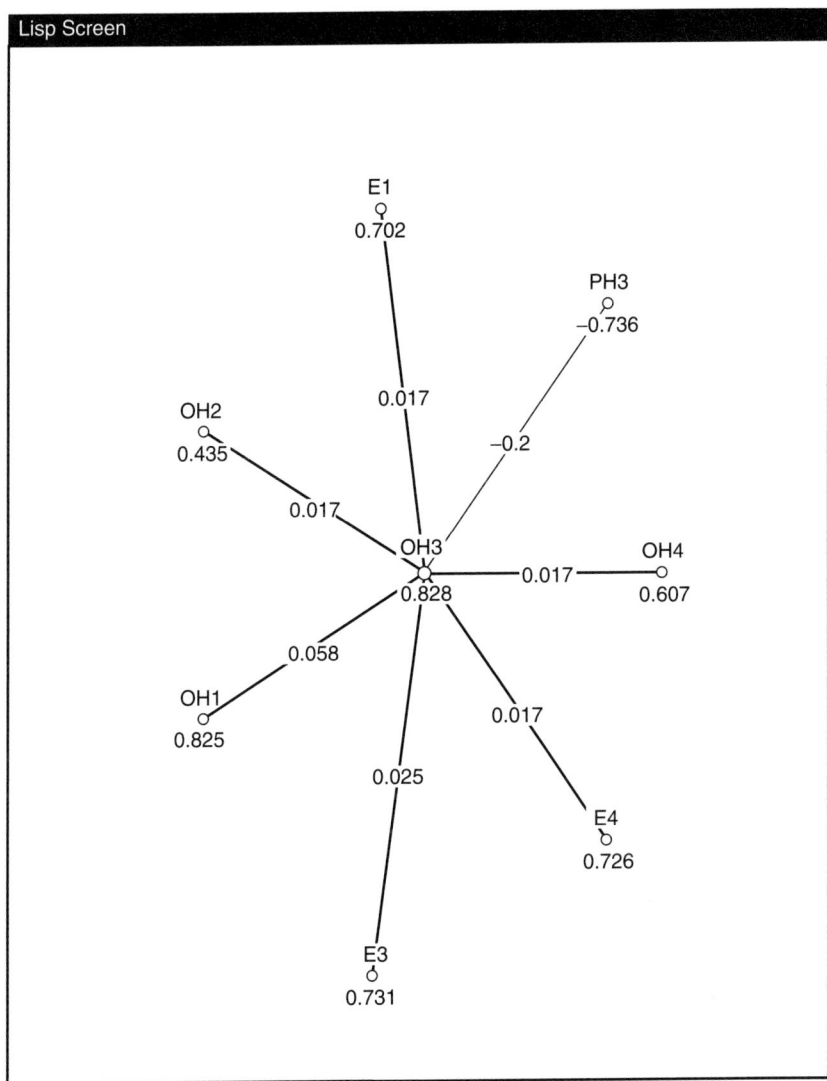

Figure 10. Connectivity of oxygen theory unit OH3. The numbers under the units are their activation values after the unit has settled. Thick lines indicate excitatory links; thin line indicates inhibitory link. Numbers on the lines indicate the weights on the links.

highly coherent with each other by virtue of being used together in multiple explanations.

The numbers beneath the names in Figure 10 indicate the final activation of the named units, rounded to three decimal places. When ECHO runs this network, starting with all hypotheses at activation .01, it quickly favors the oxygen hypotheses, giving them activations greater than 0. In contrast, all the phlogiston hypotheses become deactivated. The activation history of the propositions is shown in Figure 11, which charts activation as a function of the number of cycles of updating. Figure 11 shows graphs,

produced automatically during the run of the program, of the activations of all the units over the 107 cycles it takes them to reach asymptote. In each graph, the horizontal line indicates the starting activation of 0 and the y axis shows activation values ranging between 1 and −1. Notice that the oxygen hypotheses OH1–OH6 rise steadily to their asymptotic activations, while PH3 and PH6, which directly contradict oxygen hypotheses, sink to activation levels well below 0. The other phlogiston hypotheses that are not directly contradicted by oxygen hypotheses start out with positive activation but are

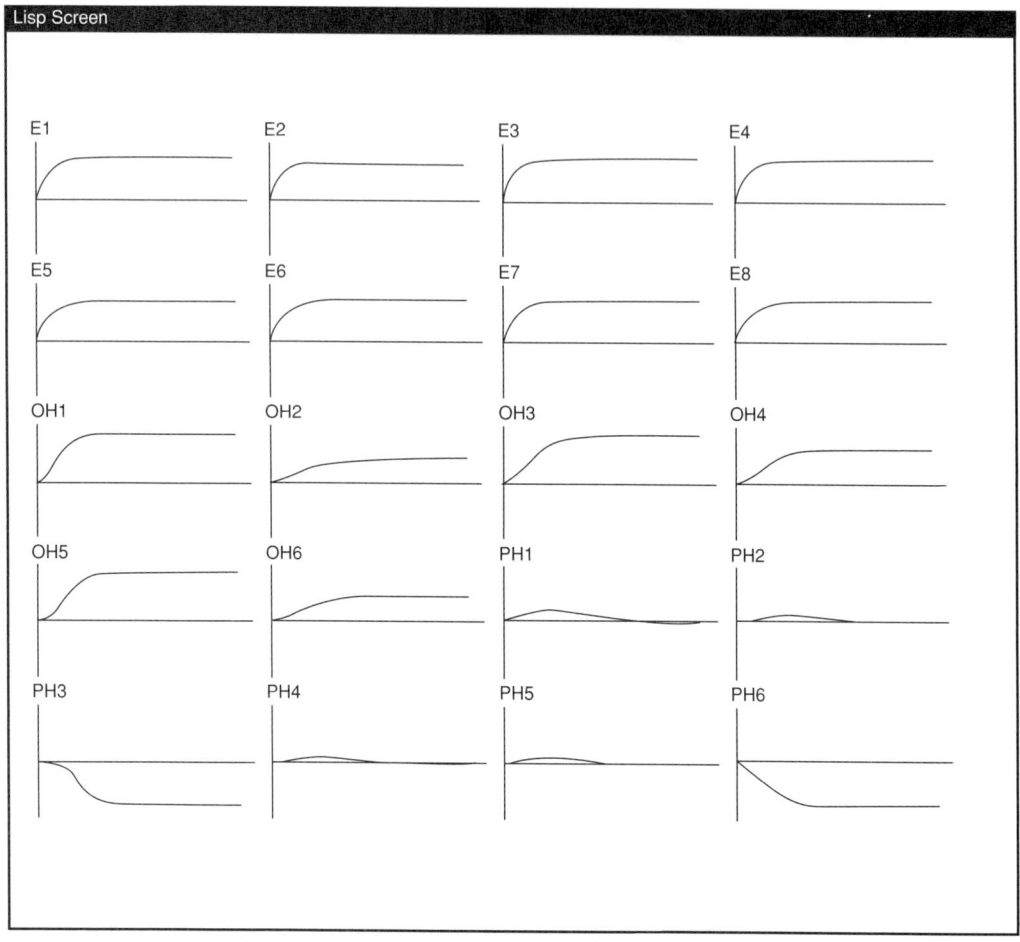

Figure 11. Activation history of Lavoisier (1862) network. Each graph shows the activation of a unit over 107 cycles of updating, on a scale of −1 to 1, with the horizontal line indicating the initial activation of 0.

dragged down toward 0 through their links with their deactivated cohypotheses. Thus the phlogiston theory fails as a whole.

This run of ECHO is biased toward the oxygen theory because it was based on an analysis of Lavoisier's argument. We would get a different network if ECHO were used to model critics of Lavoisier such as Kirwan (1789/1968), who defended a variant of the phlogiston theory. By the late 1790s, the vast majority of chemists and physicists, including Kirwan, had accepted Lavoisier's arguments and rejected the phlogiston theory, a turnaround contrary to the suggestion of Kuhn (1970) that scientific revolutions occur only when proponents of an old paradigm die off.

Lavoisier's argument represents a relatively simple application of ECHO, showing two sets of hypotheses competing to explain the evi-

dence. But more complex explanatory relations can also be important. Sometimes a hypothesis that explains the evidence is itself explained by another hypothesis. Depending on the warrant for the higher-level hypothesis, this extra explanatory layer can increase acceptability: A hypothesis gains from being explained as well as by explaining the evidence. The Lavoisier example does not exhibit this kind of coherence, because neither Lavoisier nor the phlogiston theorists attempted to explain their hypotheses using higher-level hypotheses; nor does the example display the role that analogy can play in explanatory coherence.

5.2. Darwin

Both these aspects – coherence based on being explained and on analogy – were important in

Table 3: Explanations and Contradictions for Darwin (1962) Example

Darwin's evidence
(proposition 'E1	"The fossil record contains few transitional forms.")
(proposition 'E2	"Animals have complex organs.")
(proposition 'E3	"Animals have instincts.")
(proposition 'E4	"Species when crossed become sterile.")
(proposition 'E5	"Species become extinct.")
(proposition 'E6	"Once extinct, species do not reappear.")
(proposition 'E7	"Forms of life change almost simultaneously around the world.")
(proposition 'E8	"Extinct species are similar to each other and to living forms.")
(proposition 'E9	"Barriers separate similar species.")
(proposition 'E10	"Related species are concentrated in the same areas.")
(proposition 'E11	"Oceanic islands have few inhabitants, often of peculiar species.")
(proposition 'E12	"Species show systematic affinities.")
(proposition 'E13	"Different species share similar morphology.")
(proposition 'E14	"The embryos of different species are similar.")
(proposition 'E15	"Animals have rudimentary and atrophied organs.")

Darwin's main hypotheses
(proposition 'DH1	"Organic beings are in a struggle for existence.")
(proposition 'DH2	"Organic beings undergo natural selection.")
(proposition 'DH3	"Species of organic beings have evolved.")

Darwin's auxiliary hypotheses
(proposition 'DH4	"The geological record is very imperfect.")
(proposition 'DH5	"There are transitional forms of complex organs.")
(proposition 'DH6	"Mental qualities vary and are inherited.")

Darwin's facts
(proposition 'DF1	"Domestic animals undergo variation.")
(proposition 'DF2	"Breeders select desired features of animals.")
(proposition 'DF3	"Domestic varieties are developed.")
(proposition 'DF4	"Organic beings in nature undergo variation.")
(proposition 'DF5	"Organic beings increase in population at a high rate.")
(proposition 'DF6	"The sustenance available to organic beings does not increase at a high rate.")
(proposition 'DF7	"Embryos of different domestic varieties are similar.")

Creationist hypothesis
| (proposition 'CH1 | "Species were separately created by God.") |

Darwin's argument for his theory of evolution by natural selection (Darwin 1962). His two most important hypotheses were:

DH2 – Organic beings undergo natural selection.

DH3 – Species of organic beings have evolved.

These hypotheses together enabled him to explain a host of facts, from the geographical distribution of similar species to the existence of vestigial organs. Darwin's argument was explicitly comparative: There are numerous places in the *Origin* where he points to phenomena that his theory explains but that are inexplicable on the generally accepted rival hypothesis that species were separately created by God.

Darwin's two main hypotheses were not simply cohypotheses, however, for he also used DH2 to explain DH3! That is, natural selection explains why species evolve: If populations of animals vary, and natural selection picks out those with features well adapted to particular environments, then new species will arise. Moreover, he offers a Malthusian explanation for why natural selection occurs as the result of the geometrical rate of population growth contrasted with the arithmetical rate of increase in land and food. Thus Malthusian principles explain why natural selection takes place, which explains why evolution occurs, and natural selection and evolution together explain a host of facts better than the competing creation hypothesis does.

The full picture is even more complicated than this, for Darwin frequently cites the analogy between artificial and natural selection as evidence for his theory. He contends that just as farmers are able to develop new breeds of domesticated animals, so natural selection has produced new species. He uses this analogy not simply to defend natural selection, but also to help in the explanations of the evidence: Particular explanations using natural selection incorporate the analogy with artificial selection. Finally, to complete the picture of explanatory coherence that the Darwin example offers, we must consider the alternative theological explanations that were accepted by even the best scientists before Darwin proposed his theory.

Analysis of *On the origin of species* suggests the 15 evidence statements shown in Table 3. Statements E1-E4 occur in Darwin's discussion of objections to his theory; the others are from the later chapters where he argues positively for his theory. Table 3 also shows Darwin's main hypotheses. DH2 and DH3 are the core of the theory of evolution by natural selection, providing explanations of its main evidence, E5–E15. DH4–DH6 are auxiliary hypotheses that Darwin uses in resisting objections based on E1–E3. He considers the objection concerning the absence of transitional forms to be particularly serious, but explains it away by saying that the geological record is so imperfect that we should not expect to find fossil evidence of the many intermediate species his theory requires. Darwin's explanations also use a variety of facts he defends with empirical arguments that would complicate the current picture too much to present here. Hence, I will treat them (DF1–DF7) simply as pieces of evidence that do not need explanatory support. The creationist opposition frequently mentioned by Darwin is represented by the single hypothesis that species were separately created by God.

Table 4 shows the explanation and contradiction statements that ECHO uses to set up its network, which is partially displayed in Figure 12. Notice the hierarchy of explanations, with the high rate of population increase explaining the struggle for existence, which explains natural selection, which explains evolution. Natural selection and evolution together explain many pieces of evidence. The final component of Darwin's argument is the analogy between natural and artificial selection. The wavy lines represent excitatory links based on analogy. Just as breeders' actions explain the development of domestic varieties, so natural selection explains the evolution of species. At another level, Darwin sees an embryological analogy. The embryos of different

Table 4: Explanations and Contradictions for Darwin Example

Darwin's explanations
(a) of natural selection and evolution
(explain '(DF5 DF6) 'DH1)
(explain '(DH1 DF4) 'DH2)
(explain '(DH2) 'DH3)

(b) of potential counterevidence
(explain '(DH2 DH3 DH4) 'E1)
(explain '(DH2 DH3 DH5) 'E2)
(explain '(DH2 DH3 DH6) 'E3)

(c) of diverse evidence
(explain '(DH2) 'E5)
(explain '(DH2 DH3) 'E6)
(explain '(DH2 DH3) 'E7)
(explain '(DH2 DH3) 'E8)
(explain '(DH2 DH3) 'E9)
(explain '(DH2 DH3) 'E10)
(explain '(DH2 DH3) 'E12)
(explain '(DH2 DH3) 'E13)
(explain '(DH2 DH3) 'E14)
(explain '(DH2 DH3) 'E15)

Darwin's analogies
(explain '(DF2) 'DF3)
(explain '(DF2) 'DF7)
(analogous '(DF2 DH2) '(DF3 DH3))
(analogous '(DF2 DH2) '(DF7 E14))

Creationist explanations
(explain '(CH1) 'E1)
(explain '(CH1) 'E2)
(explain '(CH1) 'E3)
(explain '(CH1) 'E4)

Contradiction
(contradict 'CH1 'DH3)

Data
(data '(E1 E2 E3 E4 E5 E6 E7 E8 E9 E10 E11
    E12 E13 E14 E15))
(data '(DF1 DF2 DF3 DF4 DF5 DF6 DF7))

domestic varieties are quite similar to each other, which is explained by the fact that breeders do not select for properties of embryos. Similarly, nature does not select for most properties of embryos, which explains the many similarities between embryos of different species.

Darwin's discussion of objections suggests that he thought creationism could naturally explain the absence of transitional forms and the existence of complex organs and instincts. Darwin's argument was challenged in many ways, but based on his own view of the relevant explanatory relations, at least, the theory of evolution by natural selection is far more coherent

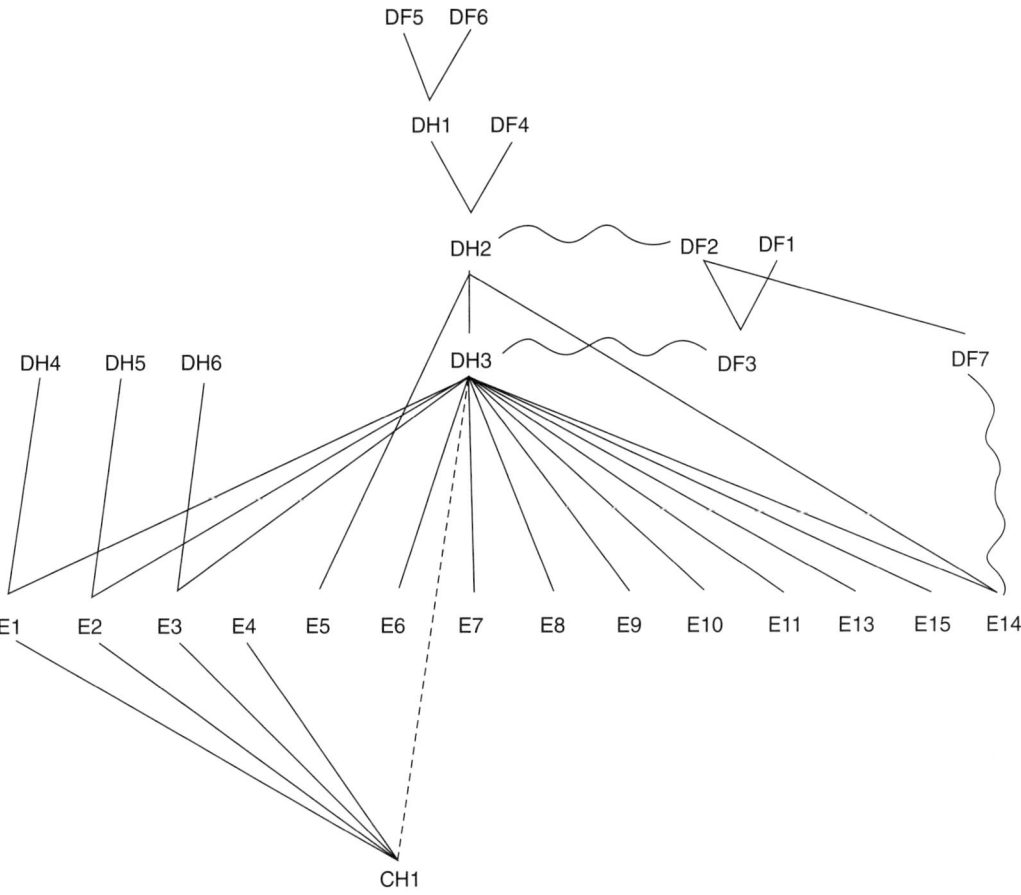

Figure 12. Network representing Darwin's (1962) argument. E1–E15 are evidence units. DH2 represents natural selection, and DH3 represents evolution of species. These defeat CH1, which represents the hypothesis that species were independently created. Solid lines are excitatory links; dotted line is inhibitory.

than the creation hypothesis. Creationists, of course, would marshal different arguments.

For clarity, Figure 12 omits the links from DH2 to all the evidence propositions besides E5, and the links from DH2 and DH3 to DH4, DH5, and DH6. Figure 13 shows the actual connectivity of DH3. Running ECHO to adjust the network to maximize harmany produces the expected result: Darwin's hypotheses are all activated, whereas the creation hypothesis is deactivated. In particular, the hypothesis DH3 – that species evolved – reaches an asymptote at .921, while the creation hypothesis, CH1, declines to −.491. DH3 accrues activation in three ways. It gains activation from above, from being explained by natural selection, which is derived from the struggle for existence, and from below, by virtue of the many pieces of evidence

it helps to explain. In addition, it receives activation by virtue of the sideways, analogy-based links with explanations using artificial selection. Figure 14 graphs the activation histories of most of the units over the 70 cycles it takes them to settle. Note that the creationist hypothesis, CH1, initially gets activation by virtue of what it explains, but is driven down by the rise of DH3, which contradicts it.

The Lavoisier and Darwin examples show that ECHO can handle very complex examples of actual scientific reasoning. One might object that in basing ECHO analyses on written texts, I have been modeling the rhetoric of the scientists, not their cognitive processes. Presumably, however, there is some correlation between what we write and what we think. ECHO could be equally well applied to explanatory relations

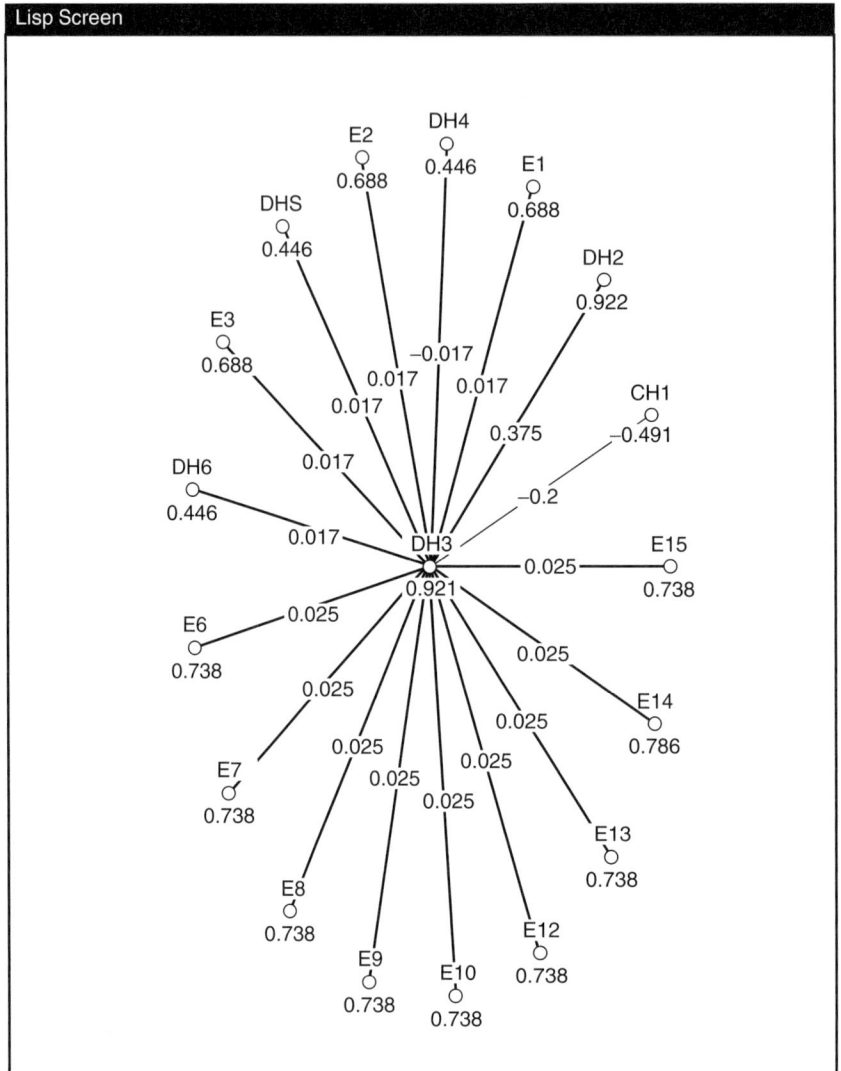

Figure 13. Connectivity of unit DH3 in the Darwin network. The numbers under the units are their activation values after the unit has settled. Thick lines indicate excitatory links; thin line indicates inhibitory link. Numbers on the lines indicate the weights on the links.

that were asserted in the heat of verbal debate among scientists. Ranney and Thagard (1988) describe ECHO's simulation of naive subjects learning physics, where the inputs to ECHO were based on verbal protocols.

6. Applications of ECHO to Legal Reasoning

Explanatory coherence is also important for some kinds of legal reasoning. Most discussions of legal reasoning concern either deductive inference, in which legal principles, rules, or statutes are applied to particular cases, or analogical inference, in which past cases are used as prece-

dents to suggest a decision in a current case (Carter 1984; Gardner 1987; Golding 1984). Recently, however, some attention has been paid to the role of explanatory inferences in legal reasoning (Hanen 1987; Pennington and Hastie 1986, 1987). These researchers are concerned primarily with inferences made by juries about factual, rather than legal, questions. In murder trials, for example, juries can be called upon to infer what happened, choosing between contradictory accounts provided by the prosecution and the defense. To get a conviction on a first-degree murder charge, the prosecution must show (1) that the accused killed the victim and (2) that the accused did so with a previously

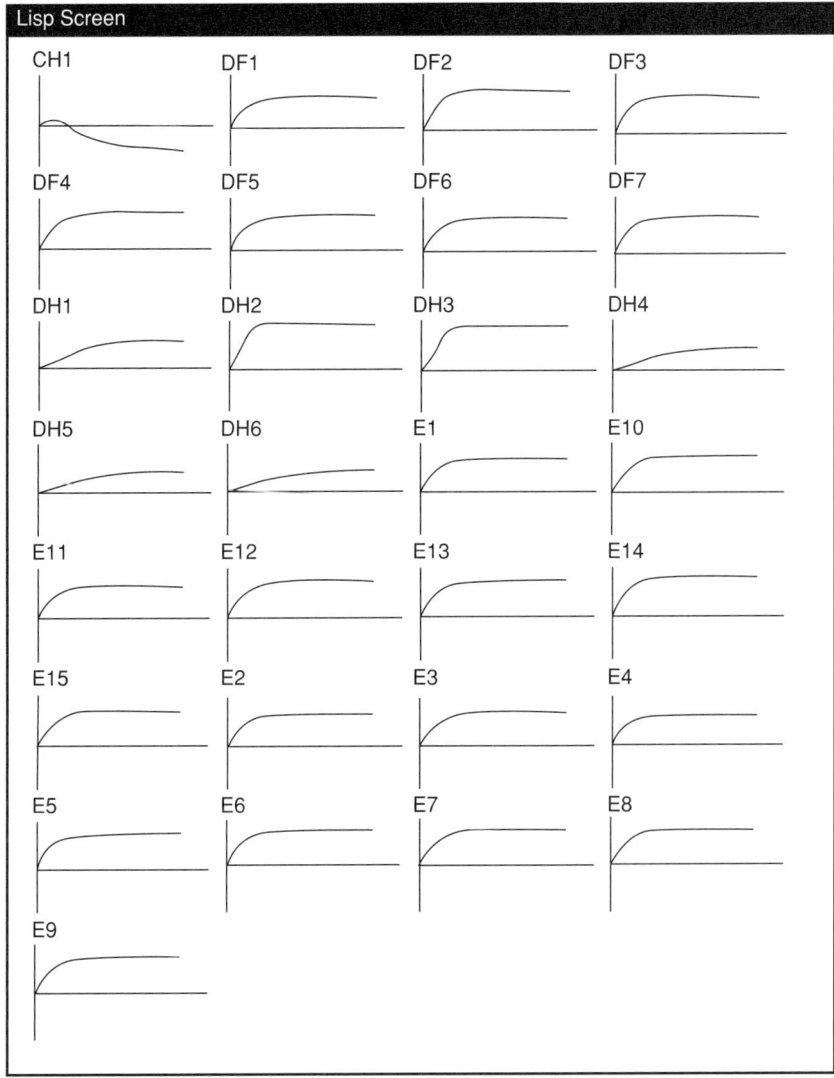

Figure 14. Activation history of the Darwin network. Each graph shows the activation of a unit over 49 cycles of updating, on a scale of −1 to 1, with the horizontal line indicating the initial activation of 0.

formed purpose in mind. The first proposition must account for much of the evidence; the second provides one possible explanation of the first. The defense may try to defend alternative hypotheses, such as that someone else killed the victim or that the accused acted in self-defense and therefore is innocent, or that the accused acted in the heat of the moment and is therefore guilty only of manslaughter. The defense need not provide an alternative explanation of the killing, but may undermine the explanatory coherence of the prosecution's account by providing alternative interpretations of key testimony. For example, in the Peyer murder trial discussed below, the defense tried to discredit two impor-

tant witnesses for the prosecution who had come forward just before the trial (a year after the killing) by saying that they were merely seeking publicity and had not seen what they claimed.

In terms of my theory of explanatory coherence and ECHO, we can think of the prosecution and defense as advocating incompatible ways of explaining the evidence. But, as in scientific reasoning, explanatory inference in the legal domain is not simply a matter of counting which of two hypotheses explains the most pieces of evidence. More complicated organizations of hypotheses and evidence will often arise. The hypothesis that the accused intended to kill the victim will be more plausible if we can

Table 5: Input Propositions for Chambers Case

Evidence
- (proposition 'E0   "L died.")
- (proposition 'E1   "L had wounds on her neck.")
- (proposition 'E2   "L said she liked sex with C.")
- (proposition 'E3   "L's blouse was around her neck.")
- (proposition 'E4   "L's panties were not found near her.")
- (proposition 'NE4   "L's panties were found near her.")
- (proposition 'E5   "The police were careless about evidence.")
- (proposition 'E6   "C lied to L's friend about not having seen L.")
- (proposition 'E7   "C had scratches on his face and cuts on his hands.")
- (proposition 'E8   "C had a broken hand.")
- (proposition 'E9   "The skin on C's hand was not broken.")
- (proposition 'NE9   "The skin on C's hand was broken.")
- (proposition 'E10   "L's left eye was swollen and her mouth was cut.")
- (proposition 'E11   "L's face was dirty.")
- (proposition 'E12   "L had pinpoint hemorrhages in eye tissue.")
- (proposition 'E13   "L's neck had severe hemorrhages.")
- (proposition 'E14   "Bloodstains of C's type were found on L's jacket.")
- (proposition 'E15   "C's fingers were bitten.")
- (proposition 'E16   "C's video said he had hit her once.")

Hypotheses that Chambers is guilty
- (proposition 'G1   "C strangled L.")
- (proposition 'G2   "C and L struggled.")
- (proposition 'G3   "C lied about what happened.")
- (proposition 'G4   "L's neck was held for at least 20 seconds.")
- (proposition 'G5   "C broke his hand punching L.")
- (proposition 'G6   "C intended to kill L.")
- (proposition 'G7   "C intended to hurt L but not kill her.")

Hypotheses that Chambers is innocent
- (proposition 'I1   "C killed L with a single blow.")
- (proposition 'I2   "The marks on L's neck were a scrape from C's watchband.")
- (proposition 'I3   "L was having sadistic sex with C.")
- (proposition 'I4   "L squeezed C's testicles.")
- (proposition 'I5   "The police moved L's panties.")
- (proposition 'I6   "C broke his hand falling on a rock.")
- (proposition 'I7   "C threw L over his shoulder.")
- (proposition 'I8   "C's blow triggered carotid sinus reflex.")

Note: L is Jennifer Levin; C is Robert Chambers.
Source: Data gathered from daily reports in the *New York Times* over a three-month period in 1988; see also Taubman (1988).

explain why the accused had it in for the victim, say, because of a previous altercation. Analogy can also play a role: Pennington and Hastie (1986, p. 254) report that jurors sometimes evaluate the plausibility of explanations by considering how *they* would act in analogous situations. For example, a juror might reason, "If the victim had done to me what he did to the accused, then I would be angry and would want to get back at him, so maybe the accused did intend to kill the victim." Explanatory inferences can also be relevant to evaluating the testimony of a witness. If a witness who was a good friend of the accused says they were together at the time of the murder, the jury has to decide whether

the best explanation of the witness's utterance is that (1) the witness really believed it or (2) the witness was lying to protect the accused.

The plausibility of a theory of explanatory coherence for legal reasoning depends on its application to real cases. ECHO has been used to model reasoning in two recent murder trials: the "preppy" murder trial in which Robert Chambers was accused of murdering Jennifer Levin in New York City and the San Diego trial in which Craig Peyer was accused of murdering Cara Knott. In both cases, there were no witnesses to the killing, so the juries had to infer on the basis of circumstantial evidence what actually happened.

Table 6: Explanations and Contradictions in Chambers Example

Data
    (data '(E0 E1 E2 E3 E4 E5 E6 E7 E8 E9 E10
        E11 E12 E13 E14 E15 E16))

Contradictions
    (contradict 'G1 'I1)
    (contradict 'G4 'I1)
    (contradict 'G5 'I6)
    (contradict 'G1 'I2)
    (contradict 'G2 'I3)
    (contradict 'G6 'G7)
    (contradict 'E4 'NE4)
    (contradict 'E9 'NE9)

Explanations supporting Chambers's innocence
    (explain '(I1 I8) 'E0)
    (explain '(I2) 'E1)
    (explain '(I3) 'I4)
    (explain '(I4) 'I1)
    (explain '(I3 I5) 'E4)
    (explain '(I6) 'E8)
    (explain '(I6) 'NE9)
    (explain '(I7) 'E12)
    (explain '(I3) 'E15)
    (explain '(I1) 'E16)

Explanations supporting Chambers's guilt
    (explain '(G2) 'G1)
    (explain '(G2) 'E3)
    (explain '(G2) 'E4)
    (explain '(G2) 'E7)
    (explain '(G2) 'E12)
    (explain '(G1) 'G4)
    (explain '(G1) 'E0)
    (explain '(G1) 'E1)
    (explain '(G2) 'E10)
    (explain '(G2) 'E11)
    (explain '(G4) 'E13)
    (explain '(G2) 'E14)
    (explain '(G2) 'E15)
    (explain '(G5) 'E8)
    (explain '(G5) 'E9)
    (explain '(G3) 'E16)
    (explain '(G3) 'E6)
    (explain '(G6) 'G1)
    (explain '(G7) 'G1)
    (explain '(G2) 'G7)

6.1. Chambers

On August 26, 1986, Robert Chambers, by his own admission, killed Jennifer Levin in Central Park after the two had left a bar together. He maintained, however, that the killing was accidental, occurring when he struck her by reflex when she hurt him during rough sex. The prosecution maintained, in contrast, that he had killed her intentionally during a violent struggle. The trial took place in the first three months of 1988 and was extensively reported in the press. The following ECHO analysis is based on daily reports in the *New York Times* that described the major testimony and arguments. This information is, of course, not nearly as complete as that presented in the courtroom itself, but it suffices for displaying the structure of a very complex explanatory inference (see also Taubman 1988).

The input to ECHO is shown in Tables 5 and 6. G1–G7 are hypotheses used by the prosecution to argue for Chambers's guilt, whereas I1–I8 present a very different explanatory account that supports his innocence. Figure 15 shows part of the network produced by this input, with excitatory links shown by solid lines and inhibitory ones shown by dotted lines (NE4 and NE9 are omitted to relieve crowding). The evidence propositions E0–E16 are indicated by number alone. Notice the layers of explanations: I3 explains I4, which explains I1, which explains E4. The prosecution's case does a better job of explaining the physical evidence using hypotheses concerning a struggle and a strangling. I have included two units, G6 and G7, to represent the question of Chambers's intent, which is crucial for deciding whether he is guilty of second-degree murder (he intended to kill her) or manslaughter (he intended merely to hurt her).

Running the network produces a clear win for G1, the main hypothesis implying Chambers's guilt. Figure 16 shows the links to G1 and the asymptotic activation of the units linked to it. Figure 17 displays the activation histories of all the units over 80 cycles. In the actual trial, the jury never got a chance to finish deciding the second-degree murder charge because a manslaughter plea-bargain was arranged during their deliberations. One important aspect that is not directly displayed in this simulation is the notion of determining guilt "beyond a reasonable doubt." Perhaps hypotheses concerning innocence should receive special activation so that hypotheses concerning guilt have to be very well supported to overcome them. Alternatively, we could require a high tolerance level so that guilt hypotheses would only be able to deactivate innocence hypotheses that were markedly inferior.

6.2. Peyer

Let us now consider another recent trial, where the evidence was less conclusive. Cara Knott was killed on December 27, 1986, and Craig Peyer,

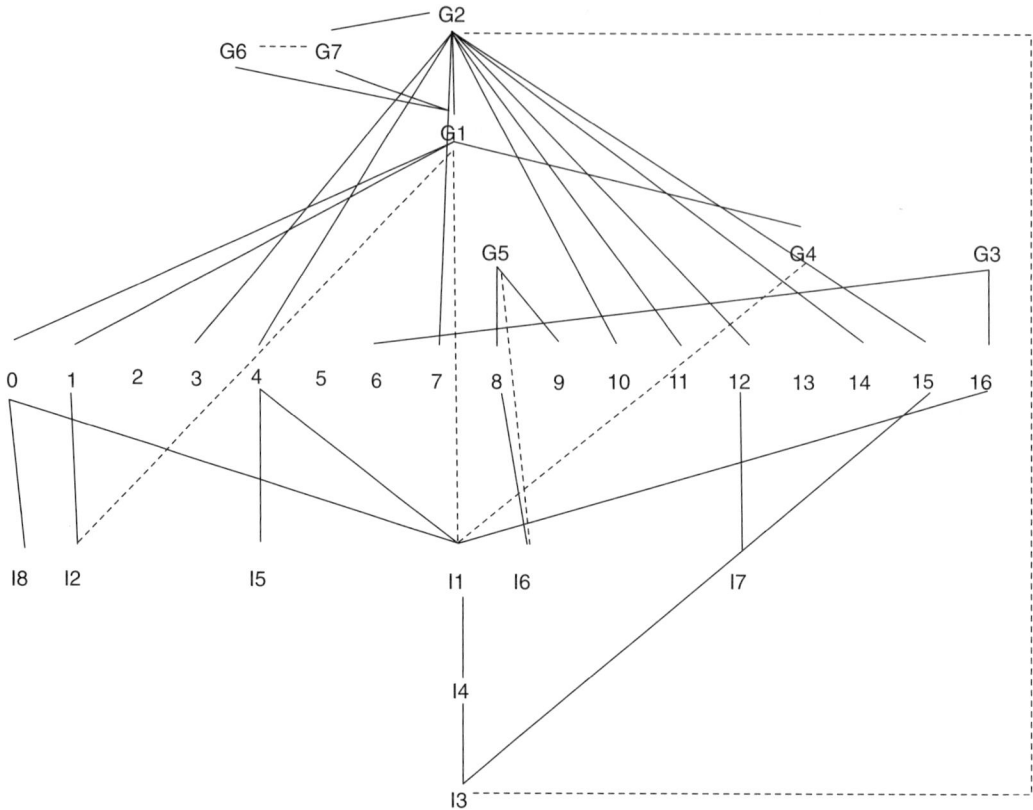

Figure 15. Network representing the Chambers trial. 1–16 are evidence units. G1–G7 represent hypotheses concerning Chambers's guilt; I1–I8 represent his innocence. Solid lines are excitatory links; dotted lines are inhibitory.

a veteran California Highway Patrolman, was accused. Twenty-two women, young and attractive like the victim, testified that they had been pulled over by Peyer for extended personal conversations near the stretch of road where Knott's body was found. The trial in San Diego ended February 27, 1988, and ECHO analysis is based on very extensive coverage (two full pages) that appeared the next day in the *San Diego Union* and the *San Diego Tribune*.

Tables 7 and 8 show the inputs to ECHO representing the evidence, hypotheses, and explanatory and contradictory statements in the Peyer trial. As in the Chambers representation, the G propositions are hypotheses concerning Peyer's guilt, whereas the I propositions concern his innocence. The prosecution can be understood as arguing that the hypothesis that Peyer killed Knott is the best explanation of the evidence, whereas the defense contends that the evidence does not support that claim beyond a reasonable doubt. Figure 18 shows the network ECHO sets up using the input given to it. Figure 19 shows

the connectivity of the unit G1 along with the asymptotic activation of units linked to it, and Figure 20 graphs the activation histories of most of the units, omitting E1 and E2 for lack of space.

Peyer's trial ended in a hung jury, with seven jurors arguing for conviction on the second-degree murder charge and five arguing against it; the case is being retried. Figure 20 shows that ECHO finds more explanatory coherence in the guilt hypotheses than in the innocence hypotheses, although the activation of some of the I units shows that, in part, the defense had a more convincing case. Why, then, were some jurors reluctant to convict? It could, in part, be the question of establishing guilt beyond a reasonable doubt. The sensitivity analyses reported in the Appendix (see Table 11) show that ECHO rejects the hypothesis of Peyer's innocence much less strongly than it rejects the hypothesis of Chambers's innocence. With greater tolerance accruing from somewhat higher excitation or lower inhibition, the unit representing Peyer's innocence is not deactivated.

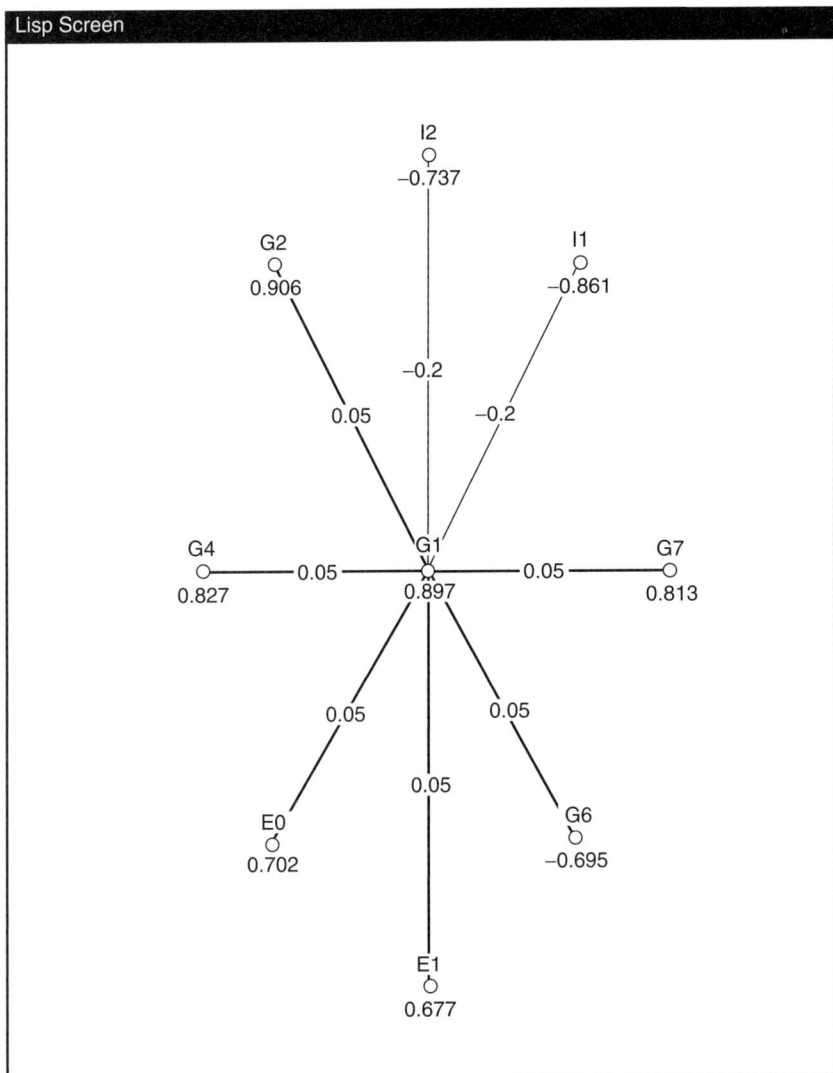

Figure 16. Connectivity of the unit G1, representing the claim that Chambers strangled Levin. The numbers under the units are their activation values after the unit has settled. Thick lines indicate excitatory links; thin lines indicate inhibitory links. Numbers on the lines indicate the weights on the links.

It is also possible that matters extraneous to explanatory coherence were playing the key role in convincing some of the jurors against conviction. One juror was quoted as saying that a California Highway Patrolman with 13 years of service could never have committed a murder. This line of reasoning is represented partially by I8, which in the above simulation is swamped by G1, but a juror could give E17 (Peyer's spotless record) such a high priority that I8 could defeat G1. The simulation here is not claimed to handle all the factors that doubtless go into real jurors' decisions: "I could tell he was lying because he

had shifty eyes," "The defense lawyer was such a nice man," "If he wasn't guilty of this, he was guilty of something else just as bad," and so on. But ECHO successfully handles a large part of the evidence and hypotheses in these two complex cases of legal reasoning.

7. Limitations of ECHO

It is important to appreciate what ECHO cannot do as well as what it can. The major current limitation of ECHO is that the input propositions, explanation statements, and contradiction

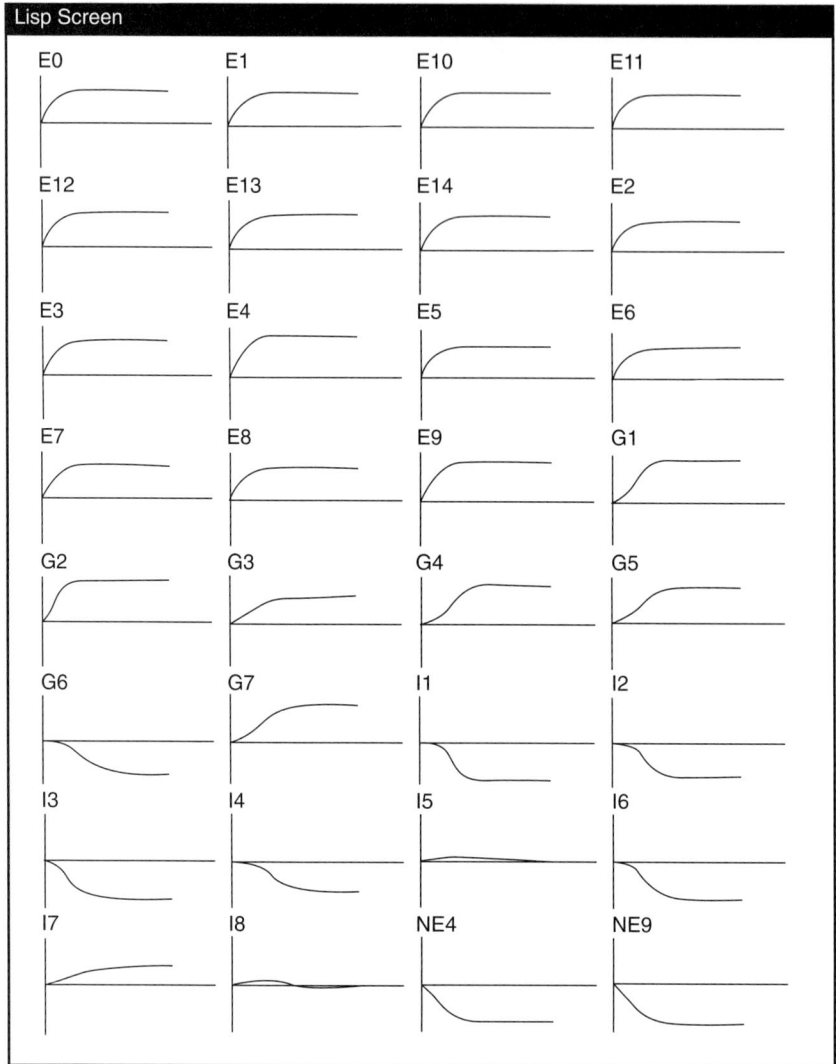

Figure 17. Activation history of the Chambers network. Each graph shows the activation of a unit over 59 cycles of updating, on a scale of −1 to 1, with the horizontal line indicating the initial activation of 0.

statements are constructed by the programmer. How arbitrary are these encodings? Several different people have successfully done ECHO analyses, on more than a dozen disparate cases. In all four of the examples presented in this paper, virtually no adjustment of input was required to produce the described runs. We have not yet done the experiment of having several people analyze the same case and assessing the intercoder reliability, however. We can nevertheless maintain that the representations are not arbitrary thought experiments, because they are derived from scientific texts, newspaper reports of trials, and subject protocols.

ECHO's scope is not universal: Not every case of reasoning can be analyzed for ECHO's application. In doing our analyses, we try to restrict the EXPLAIN statements to cases where there is a causal relation. A research assistant attempted to use ECHO to analyze arguments in this journal for and against parapsychology (Rao and Palmer 1987; Alcock 1987), but concluded that ECHO was not appropriate. This debate largely concerns the reliability of parapsychological experiments, and ECHO is not a data analyzer. ECHO would be appropriate for this case only if there were a general parapsychological theory whose explanatory coherence could be evaluated. The

Table 7: Input Propositions for the Peyer Example

Evidence
(proposition 'E1	"Knott's body and car were found on a frontage road near I-15.")
(proposition 'E2	"22 young women reported being talked to at length by Peyer after being stopped near where Knott's body was found.")
(proposition 'E3	"Calderwood said that he saw a patrol car pull over a Volkswagon like Knott's near I-15.")
(proposition 'E4	"Calderwood came forward only at the trial.")
(proposition 'E5	"Calderwood changed his story several times.")
(proposition 'E6	"6 fibers found on Knott's body matched Peyer's uniform.")
(proposition 'E7	"Ogilvie said Peyer quizzed her about the case and acted strangely.")
(proposition 'E8	"Dotson said Olgivie is a liar.")
(proposition 'E9	"Anderson and Schwartz saw scratches on Peyer's face the night of the killing.")
(proposition 'E10	"Martin said she saw Peyer pull Knott's Volkswagon over.")
(proposition 'E11	"Martin came forward only just before the trial.")
(proposition 'E12	"Anderson says she saw Peyer wipe off his nightstick in his trunk.")
(proposition 'E13	"Anderson did not say anything about the nightstick when she was first interrogated.")
(proposition 'E14	"Bloodstains found on Knott's clothes matched Peyer's blood.")
(proposition 'E15	"12,800 other San Diegans had blood matching that on Knott's clothes.")
(proposition 'E16	"A shabby hitchhiker was lunging at cars near the I-15 entrance.")
(proposition 'E17	"Peyer had a spotless record with the California Highway Patrol.")

Hypotheses that Peyer is guilty
(proposition 'G1	"Peyer killed Knott.")
(proposition 'G2	"Knott scratched Peyer's face.")
(proposition 'G3	"Fibers from Peyer's uniform were transferred to Knott.")
(proposition 'G4	"Peyer pulled Knott over.")
(proposition 'G5	"Calderwood was reluctant to come forward because he wanted to protect his family from publicity.")
(proposition 'G6	"Peyer liked to pull over young women.")
(proposition 'G7	"Peyer had a bloody nightstick.")
(proposition 'G8	"Anderson was having personal problems when first interrogated.")

Hypotheses that Peyer is innocent
(proposition 'I1	"Someone other than Peyer killed Knott.")
(proposition 'I2	"Calderwood made his story up.")
(proposition 'I3	"The 6 fibers floated around in the police evidence room.")
(proposition 'I4	"Ogilvie lied.")
(proposition 'I4A	"Ogilvie is a liar.")
(proposition 'I5	"Peyer's scratches came from a fence.")
(proposition 'I6	"Martin lied.")
(proposition 'I7	"Anderson was mistaken about the nightstick.")
(proposition 'I8	"Peyer is a good man.")

Source: Analysis based on coverage by the *San Diego Union* and *San Diego Tribune* on February 28, 1988.

general conclusion of Rao and Palmer is that parapsychological experiments are not explainable with current science, but that conclusion is not in itself an explanation of the experiments.

From a logical point of view, the analysis of explanatory relations is easily trivialized. The explanations of E1 and E2 by hypotheses H1 and H2 together can be collapsed logically by conjoining E1 and E2 into E3, and H1 and H2 into H3, so that we are left with only the boring explanation of E3 by H3. Fortunately, in real disputes in law and the history of science,

such trivializations do not occur. We can easily get the appropriate level of detail by attending to the claims that scientists and lawyers make about the explanatory power of their theories. Lavoisier and the phlogiston theorists operated at roughly the same level of detail. In analyzing texts to assess explanatory coherence, I recommend the following maxim:

Detail Maxim.

In analyzing the propositions and explanatory relations relevant to evaluating competing

Table 8: Explanations and Contradictions in the Peyer Example

The case for Peyer's guilt
  (explain '(G1) 'G2)
  (explain '(G1) 'G3)
  (explain '(G1) 'G7)
  (explain '(G1) 'E1)
  (explain '(G6) 'E2)
  (explain '(G4) 'E3)
  (explain '(G5) 'E4)
  (explain '(G3) 'E6)
  (explain '(G1) 'E7)
  (explain '(G2) 'E9)
  (explain '(G1) 'E10)
  (explain '(G7) 'E12)
  (explain '(G8) 'E13)
  (explain '(G1) 'E14)

The case for Peyer's innocence
  (explain '(I1) 'E1)
  (explain '(I2) 'E4)
  (explain '(I2) 'E5)
  (explain '(I3) 'E6)
  (explain '(I4) 'E7)
  (explain '(I4A) 'E8)
  (explain '(I4A) 'I4)
  (explain '(I5) 'E9)
  (explain '(I6) 'E10)
  (explain '(I6) 'E11)
  (explain '(I7) 'E12)
  (explain '(I7) 'E13)
  (explain '(I1 E15) 'E14)
  (explain '(I1) 'E16)
  (explain '(I8) 'E17)

Contradictions
  (contradict 'G1 'I1)
  (contradict 'G5 'I2)
  (contradict 'G7 'I7)
  (contradict 'G1 'I8)
  (contradict 'G2 'I5)
  (contradict 'G3 'I3)

Data
  (data '(E1 E2 E3 E4 E5 E6 E7 E8 E9 E10 E11
  E12 E13 E14 E15 E16 E17))

theories, go into as much detail as is needed to distinguish the explanatory claims of the theories from each other, and be careful to analyze all theories at the *same* level of detail.

Following this maxim removes much of the apparent arbitrariness inherent in trying to adjudicate among theories.

Ideally, we would want to automate the production of the input to ECHO. This could be done either in a natural language system capable of detecting explanatory arguments (cf. Cohen

1983) or, more easily, in an integrated system of scientific reasoning that formed explanatory hypotheses which could then be passed to ECHO for evaluation. PI (which is short for "processes of induction" and is pronounced "pie") is a crude version of such a system (Thagard 1988a). In PI, it is possible to represent hypotheses like those in the scientific examples discussed above using rules. One of Lavoisier's principles might be translated into the rule:

> If x is combustible and x combines with oxygen, then x bums.

Like other rule-based systems, PI can use such rules to make inferences. Given a set of such rules, PI can be set the task of explaining other rules representing the evidence. While PI runs, it is possible to keep track of which rules were used in explaining which pieces of evidence. Thus explanation from this computational point of view is a process of derivation that can be inspected to determine what was actually used in deriving what. Tracing back to which hypotheses were used in deriving which evidence could generate the EXPLAIN formulas that are input for ECHO. Because PI does not have the rules of inference that permit logicians to concoct nonexplanatory deductions – for example, to infer (A or B) from A – we can identify what hypotheses played a role in explaining what pieces of evidence. Putting together all the rules to make up Lavoisier's theory and furnish explanations is a daunting task, because his writings and my summary for ECHO omit much background knowledge that would have to be dredged up and included if the derivations were to look complete. But AI models of problem solving and learning such as PI provide at least a glimpse of how explanations can be noticed. Falkenhainer and Rajamoney (1988) describe a system that combines hypothesis formation by analogy with hypothesis evaluation by experimental design, so eventually it should be possible to integrate ECHO with a system that generates explanations and provides its input automatically.

ECHO is a very natural way of implementing the proposed theory of explanatory coherence, but one might argue for the construction of a nonconnectionist coherence model. Perhaps it could be based on simple rules such as the following:

(1)   If a proposition is a piece of evidence, then accept it.

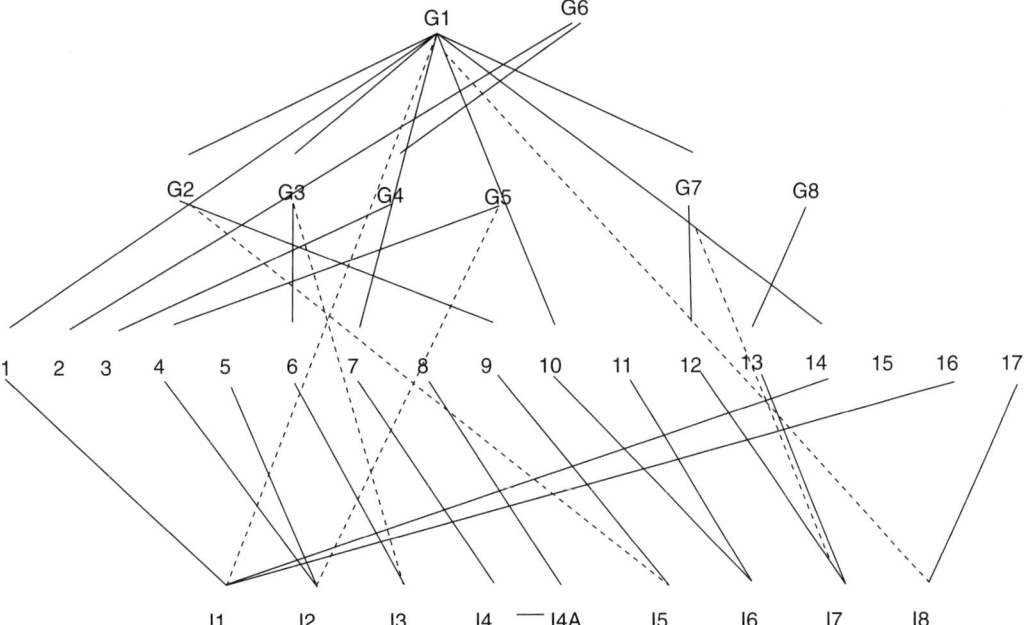

Figure 18. Network representing the Peyer trial. 1–17 are evidence units. G1–G8 represent hypotheses concerning Peyer's guilt; I1–I8 concern his innocence. Solid lines are excitatory links; dotted lines are inhibitory.

(2) If a proposition contradicts an accepted proposition, then reject it.

(3) Of two contradictory hypotheses, accept the one that coheres (by virtue of explanatory and analogical relations) with more accepted propositions and has fewer cohypotheses.

(4) If a proposition does not contradict any other propositions, accept it if it coheres with more accepted propositions than rejected ones.

Analysis suggests that an implementation of such rules could be a fair approximation to ECHO for many cases, but would lack several advantages that derive from ECHO's connectionist algorithms. First, rules such as (1) and (2) are much too categorical. ECHO is capable of rejecting a piece of evidence if it coheres only with a very inferior theory (Section 4.8), just as scientists sometimes throw out data. Similarly, a hypothesis should not be rejected just because it makes a false prediction, because additional assumptions may enable it to explain the evidence and explain away the negative result. Second, the rule-based implementation would be very sensitive to the order of application of rules, requir-

ing that the four rules stated above be applied in approximately the order given. Moreover, if a hypothesis is contradicted by two other propositions, it will be important to evaluate the other propositions first so that together they can count against the given hypothesis, otherwise it might be accepted and then knock them out one at a time. ECHO's parallelism enables it to evaluate all propositions simultaneously, so these undesirable order effects do not arise. Third, rules (3) and (4) above should not operate in isolation from one another: In our simulation of Wegener's argument for continental drift (Thagard and Nowak 1988), units representing the views that Wegener rejects become deactivated because of a *combination* of being contradicted and being coherent with rejected propositions. Fourth, the rule-based system's use of the binary categories of acceptance and rejection will prevent it from having the sensitivity of ECHO in indicating *degrees* of acceptance and rejection by degrees of activation. Fifth, the rule-based system does not come with a metric for system coherence (Section 4.9). Thus, although ECHO is not the only possible means for computing coherence, its connectionist algorithms give it many natural advantages over alternative approaches.

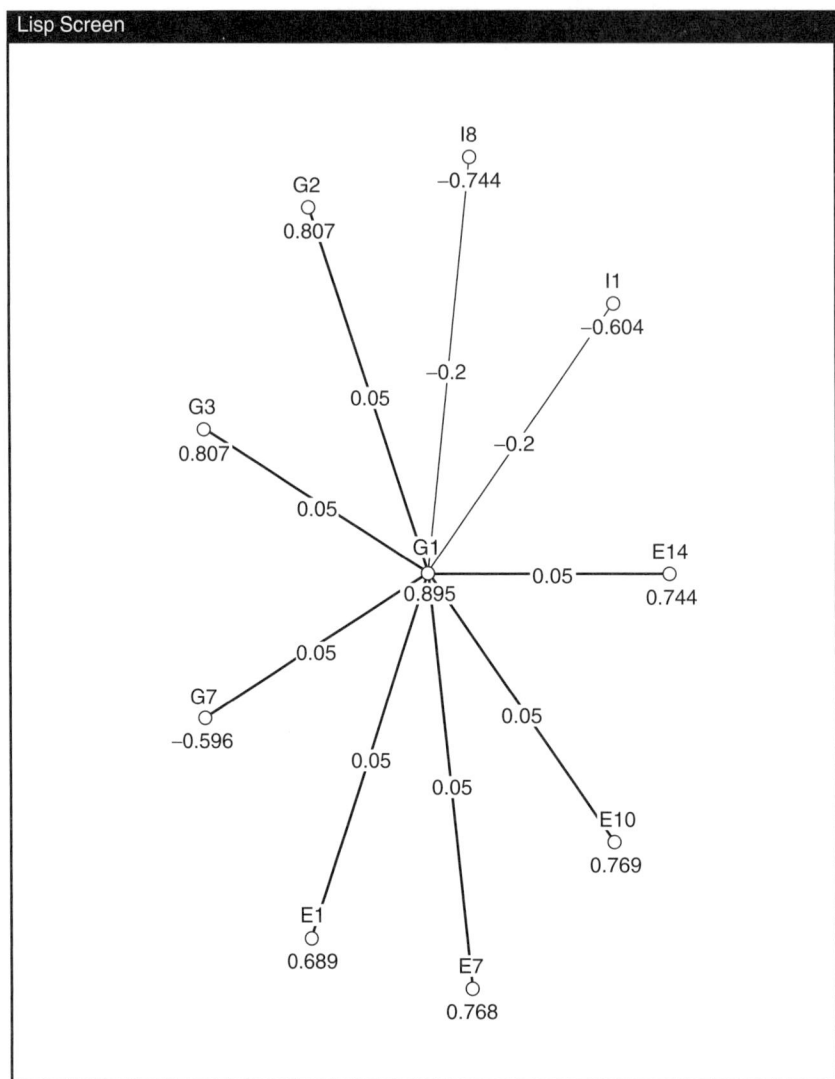

Figure 19. Connectivity of the unit G1, representing Peyer's guilt. The numbers under the units are their activation values after the unit has settled. Thick lines indicate excitatory links; thin lines indicate inhibitory links. Numbers on the lines indicate the weights on the links.

Finally, as an implementation of a theory of explanatory coherence, ECHO is only as good as the principles in that theory. The seven principles of explanatory coherence seem now to be complete enough to characterize a wide range of cases of hypothesis evaluation, but they are themselves hypotheses and therefore subject to revision.

research in the areas of artificial intelligence, cognitive psychology, and philosophy. Like the evaluation of scientific theories, the evaluation of philosophical and computational theories is a comparative matter. While discussing the computational, psychological, and philosophical significance of the approach proposed here, I shall compare it with similar research in these fields.

8. Implications for Artificial Intelligence

The theory of explanatory coherence and its implementation in ECHO have implications for

8.1. *Connectionism*

Very recently, other researchers have also suggested connectionist models for the evaluation of

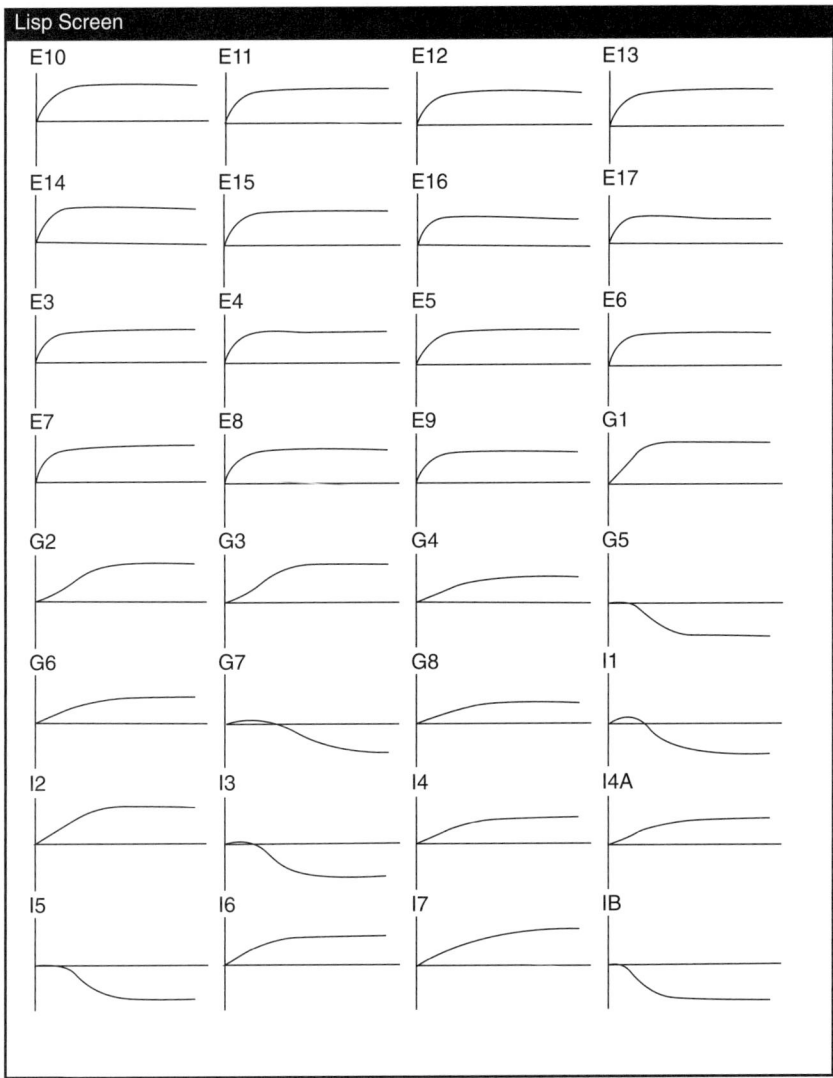

Figure 20. Activation history of the Peyer network. Each graph shows the activation of a unit over 54 cycles of updating, on a scale of −1 to 1, with the horizontal line indicating the initial activation of 0.

explanatory hypotheses. Peng and Reggia (1989) describe a connectionist model for diagnostic problem solving. Theoretically, it differs from my proposal mostly in that it does not use constraints involving simplicity (in the sense indicated by Principle 2[c]), analogy, and the desirability of a hypothesis being explained as well as explaining. Their implementation differs from ECHO most strikingly in that it does not use inhibitory links between units representing incompatible hypotheses, but instead has nodes competing for activation from the output of a source node. Goel et al. (1988) propose an architecture that chooses the best explanation by con-

sidering explanatory coverage of data, number of hypotheses, and prior plausibility of hypotheses. ECHO uses the first two of these criteria, but not the third, because in the domains to which it has been applied, plausibility appears to be determined by explanatory coherence alone.

Parallel constraint satisfaction models somewhat similar to ECHO have been proposed for other phenomena: analogical mapping (Holyoak and Thagard 1989), analog retrieval (Thagard et al. 1989), discourse processing (Kintsch 1988), and word pronunciation retrieval (Lehnert 1987). (See also surveys by Feldman and Ballard 1982 and Rumelhart et al. 1986.) These systems differ from Boltzmann machines and back-propagation networks (Rumelhart et al. 1986) in that they do not adjust weights while the network is running, only activations.

ECHO's connectionist character may prompt immediate boos or cheers from different partisan quarters. Currently, debate rages in cognitive science concerning competing methodologies. We can distinguish at least the following approaches to understanding the nature of mind and intelligence:

(1)   Straight neuroscience, studying neurons or sections of the brain

(2)   Computational models of actual neurons in the brain

(3)   Connectionist models using distributed representations, so that a concept or hypothesis is a pattern of activation over multiple units

(4)   Connectionist models using localist representations, in which a single unit represents a concept or proposition

(5)   Traditional artificial intelligence models using data structures such as frames and production rules

(6)   Psychological experiments

(7)   Mathematical analysis

(8)   Theoretical speculation

ECHO falls into (4), but I reject as *methodological imperialism* the opinion that other approaches are not worth pursuing as well. In the current neonatal state of cognitive science, restrictions on ways to study the mind are clearly premature. By pursuing all eight strategies, we can hope to learn more about how to investigate the nature of mind. As suggested by my juxtaposition of PI and ECHO in Section 7, I see no great incompatibility between connectionist systems and traditional symbolic AI. Much is to be gained from developing hybrid systems that exploit the strengths of both research programs (Hendler 1987; Lehnert 1987).

Despite ECHO's parallelism, and use of a vague neural metaphor of connections, I have not listed neural plausibility as one of its advantages, because current knowledge does not allow any sensible mapping from nodes of ECHO representing propositions to anything in the brain. For the same reason, I have not used the term "neural net." Parallelism has its advantages independent of the brain analogy (Thagard 1986).

8.2. Probabilistic Networks

The account of explanatory coherence I have given bears some similarity to Pearl's (1986, 1987) work on belief networks. Pearl also represents propositions as nodes linked by inferential dependencies and uses a parallel algorithm to update numerical values assigned to the nodes. The major difference between ECHO and Pearl's networks, however, is that he construes numerical values as the *probabilities* of the propositions, and weights between nodes as conditional probabilities. Thus, in contrast to links established by coherence relations, Pearl's links are asymmetric, because in general the probability of P given Q is not equal to the probability of Q given P.

Although Pearl's probabilistic approach appears promising for domains such as medical diagnosis where we can empirically obtain frequencies of co-occurrence of diseases and symptoms and thus generate reasonable conditional probabilities, it does not seem applicable to the cases of explanatory coherence I have been considering. What, for example, is the conditional probability of burned objects gaining in weight given the hypothesis that oxygen is combined with them? It would be 1 if the hypothesis entailed the evidence, but it does so only with the aid of the additional hypothesis that oxygen has weight, and some unstated background assumption about conservation of weight. To calculate the conditional probability, then, we need to be able to calculate the conjunctive probability that oxygen has weight and that oxygen combines with burning objects, but these propositions are dependent to an unknown degree. Moreover, what is the probability that the evidence is correct? In contrast to the difficulty of assigning probabilities to these propositions, the coherence relations established by my principles are easily seen directly in arguments used by scientists in their published writings. When frequencies are available because of empirical studies, probabilistic belief networks can be much more finely tuned than my coherence networks, but they are ill-suited for the kinds of nonstatistical theory evaluation that abounds in much of science and everyday life.

One clear advantage to the probabilistic approach is that the properties of probabilities are naturally understood using the axioms of probability and their natural interpretation in terms of games of chance. Acceptability, as indicated in ECHO by activation levels, has no such precise interpretation. (See Section 10.2 for further discussion of probability versus accept-ability.)

8.3. Explanation-Based Learning

In machine learning, a rapidly growing part of AI, the term "explanation-based" is used to distinguish cases of knowledge-intensive learning from cases of simple learning from examples (see, for example, DeJong and Mooney 1986). Rajamoney and DeJong (1988) discuss the problem of "multiple explanations" and describe a program that does simulated experiments to select an explanatory account. This program is Popperian in spirit, in that the experiments concerning electricity and heat flow serve to refute all but one of the competing hypotheses. (Science is rarely so neat; see Sections 4.4 and 10.4.) Systems that deal with more complex theories than those occurring in Rajamoney and DeJong's system will need a more comparative method of choosing among multiple explanations such as that found in ECHO.

Recently, there has been growing attention in AI to "abduction," construed as the construction and selection of competing explanatory hypotheses. (Peirce applied "abduction" only to hypothesis formation, but the term is used in many quarters to apply to hypothesis evaluation as well.) Abduction has been investigated in the domains of medical diagnosis (Josephson et al. 1987; Pople 1977; Reggia et al. 1983), natural language understanding (Hobbs et al. 1988), and folk psychology (O'Rorke et al. 1988). My account shares with these models the aim of finding the most comprehensive explanation, but it differs in both theory and implementation. The biggest theoretical difference is that my principles of explanatory coherence also favor hypotheses that are explained and fare well on considerations of simplicity and analogy. Leake (1988) describes a program for evaluating individual explanations, a problem different from selecting a hypothesis on the basis of how well it explains a wide range of evidence.

9. Implications for Psychology

The theory of explanatory coherence described here is intended to describe approximately the way people reason concerning explanatory hypotheses (see Section 10.5 for further discussion of the descriptive *and* normative character of the theory). The psychological relevance of explanatory coherence is evident in at least three important areas of psychological research: attri-bution theory, discourse processing, and conceptual change. After sketching how explanatory coherence is germane to these topics, I shall illustrate the testability of the ECHO model.

9.1. Attribution

Because the inferences that people make about themselves and others generally depend on causal theories, social psychology is a very rich domain for a theory of explanatory coherence, and *attribution theory* has been a major focus of research for several decades. Research on attribution "deals with how the social perceiver uses information in the social environment to yield causal explanations for events" (Fiske and Taylor 1984, p. 21). Much of the theorizing about attribution can be understood in terms of explanatory coherence. For example, we can interpret the *correspondent inference theory* of Jones and Davis (1965) as saying that we accept hypotheses about the dispositional attributes of other people on the basis of the hypotheses providing coherent explanations of their behavior. Jones and Davis's discussion of the *analysis of noncommon effects* can be understood as saying that we infer that someone has one of a set of intentions because that intention explains some aspects of their behavior that the other intentions do not. Our inferences about other people's dispositions will also depend on the available alternative explanations of their behavior, such as coercion, social desirability, social role, and prior expectations. Explanatory coherence theory does not address the question of how people form these kinds of hypotheses, but it does show how people can select from among the hypotheses they have formed. I conjecture that if cases of attributional inferences were analyzed in sufficient detail to bring out the relevant data and hypotheses, preferences for situational or dispositional explanations would follow from the nature of the explanatory networks.

As we saw in the preppy murder trial, jurors often have to infer the intentions of witnesses and of the accused. Pennington and Hastie (1986, 1987) have interpreted the results of their experiments on juror decision making by hypothesizing that jurors make judgments based on considerations of explanatory coherence; their cases look ripe for ECHO analysis. Of course, ECHO does not model all the kinds of reasoning involved in these experiments. In particular, it does not model how the jurors process the statements about evidence and combine them into explanatory stories. But it does give an account of how jurors choose between stories on the basis of their explanatory coherence.

9.2. *Discourse Processing*

The problem of recognizing intention in utterances can be understood in terms of explanatory coherence.[2] Clark and Lucy (1975) advocated a stage model of comprehension, according to which a literal meaning for an utterance is calculated before any nonliteral meanings are considered. In contrast, Gibbs (1984) and others have argued that hearers are able to understand that "Can you pass the salt?" is a request, without first interpreting it as a question. In explanatory coherence terms, we can think of competing hypotheses – that the utterance is a request and that it is a question – as simultaneously being evaluated with respect to what they explain and how they themselves are explained. To take an extreme example, the utterance might even be construed as an insult if it was expressed in a nasty tone of voice and if we had reason to believe that the utterer wanted to be insulting. Parallel evaluation of the different explanations of the utterance results in an appropriate interpretation of it.

Trabasso et al. (1984) have argued that causal cohesiveness is very important for story comprehension. They analyze stories in terms of networks of causally related propositions that are similar to ECHO's explanatory networks except that there are no links indicating contradictions. Comprehension differs from theory evaluation in lacking easily identified alternatives competing for acceptance. Still, it is possible that some mechanism similar to ECHO's way of activating a subset of mutually coherent propositions may be involved in reaching a satisfactory understanding of a story. Text comprehension obviously involves many processes besides inferences about causal or explanatory coherence, but ECHO-like operation may nevertheless contribute to the necessary task of appreciating the causal cohesiveness of a story.

9.3. *Belief Revision and Conceptual Change*

Ranney and Thagard (1988) describe the use of ECHO to model the inferences made by naive subjects learning elementary physics by using feedback provided on a computer display (Ranney 1987). Subjects were asked to predict the motion of several projectiles and then to explain these predictions. Analyses of verbal protocol data indicate that subjects sometimes underwent dramatic belief revisions while offering predictions or receiving empirical feedback. ECHO was applied to two particularly interesting cases of belief revision with propositions and explanatory relations based on the verbal protocols. The simulations captured well the dynamics of belief change as new evidence was added to shift the explanatory coherence of the set of propositions.

The theory of explanatory coherence sketched here has the capacity to explain major conceptual changes such as those that have been hypothesized to occur in scientific revolutions (Kuhn 1970; Thagard, 1990) and in children (Carey 1985). Because ECHO evaluates a whole network of hypotheses simultaneously, it is capable, when new data are added, of shifting from a state in which one set of hypotheses is accepted to a state in which an opposing set is accepted. This shift is analogous to the Gestalt switch described in Section 3, except that scientists rarely shift back to a rejected view. Developmental psychologists have speculated about the existence of some kind of "transition mechanism" that could shift a child forward from a primitive conceptual scheme to an advanced one. We currently have insufficient experimental data and theoretical understanding to know whether knowledge development in children has the somewhat precipitous nature attributed to scientific revolutions, but if children do undergo dramatic changes in conceptual systems because they have acquired a more coherent way of understanding their worlds, then ECHO may be very useful for modeling the transition.

9.4. *Testability*

So far, my discussion of the psychological relevance of ECHO has been merely suggestive, showing that explanatory coherence judgments may be plausibly considered to contribute to important kinds of inferential behavior. A defense of ECHO as a psychological model, however, will require controlled experiments that provide a much finer-grained evaluation of the theory of explanatory coherence. Fortunately, there appears to be great potential for testing explanatory coherence theory and the ECHO model by comparing the performance of human subjects with ECHO-based predictions about qualitative and quantitative features of the acceptance and rejection of hypotheses. Michael Ranney and I are planning several studies in which subjects will be given textual descriptions of scientific and legal debates. We want to determine whether, when ECHO is run with inputs derived from subjects' own analyses of debates, the analyses predict their conclusions. We also want to determine whether manipulating textual descriptions of evidence, explanations, and contradictory hypotheses will affect the confidence that subjects have in different hypotheses in a way that resembles how manipulations affect ECHO's activation levels. It will also be interesting to find out whether important transitional points in the amount of evidence and explanation that tend to tip ECHO's activations over to new sets of accepted beliefs correspond to major shifts in subjects' beliefs at the same points. Such transitions, in both subjects and ECHO, are described in Ranney and Thagard (1988).

The methodology here is to use ECHO to test the psychological validity of the theory of explanatory coherence embodied in the seven principles in Section 2.2. These principles in themselves are too general to have direct experimental consequences, but their implementation in ECHO makes possible very detailed predictions about the conclusions people will reach and the relative degree of confidence they will have in those conclusions. Merely proposing experiments does not, of course, show the psychological validity of the theory or the model, but it does show their joint testability. The theory of explanatory coherence presented in this paper has been well explored computationally, but I hope the above section shows that it is also suggestive psychologically.

10. Implications for Philosophy

In philosophy, a theory of explanatory coherence is potentially relevant to metaphysics, epistemology, and the philosophy of science. In metaphysics, a coherence theory of truth, according to which a proposition is said to be true if it is part of a fully coherent set, has been advocated by idealist philosophers such as Bradley and Rescher (Bradley 1914; Rescher 1973; see also Cohen 1978). In epistemology, the view that justified reasoning involves the best total explanatory account has been urged by Harman (1973, 1986) and contested by Goldman (1986) and Lehrer (1974). The theory of explanatory coherence in this paper is not aimed primarily at questions of truth or justification, but rather at the philosophy of science and of law, illuminating the kinds of reasoning used to justify the acceptance and rejection of scientific and legal hypotheses. The account of explanatory coherence offered here is as compatible with a correspondence theory of truth – according to which the truth of a proposition depends on its relation to an independent reality – as it is with a theory that attempts to define truth in terms of coherence.

10.1. Holism

A major concern in epistemology and philosophy of science concerns whether inference is holistic. According to Quine (1961, p. 41), "our statements about the external world face the tribunal of sense experience not individually but only as a corporate body." In a similar vein, Harman (1973, p. 159) writes that "inductive inference must be assessed with respect to everything one believes." Behind these holistic views is the antifoundationalist assumption that it is impossible to provide isolated justifications for isolated parts of our system of beliefs. Quine's position is based on his rejection of the analytic–synthetic distinction and on the view of Duhem (1954) that deducing an observation statement from a hypothesis always involves a complex of other hypotheses, so that no hypothesis can be evaluated in isolation. Because predictions are usually obtained from sets of hypotheses, observations that contradict the predictions do not provide grounds for rejecting any particular hypothesis, only for concluding that there is at least one false hypothesis. Harman argues that reasoning is inference to the best explanation, which includes both inference to hypotheses that explain the evidence and inference to what is explained. Inferential holism is therefore suggested by the following considerations:

(1) Hypotheses cannot be refuted and confirmed in isolation.

(2) Hypothesis evaluation must take into account the total sum of relevant evidence.

(3) The acceptability of a proposition is a function not only of what it explains but also of its being explained.

Unfortunately, holism brings many problems with it. Hegel (1967, p. 81) said that "the true is the whole," but he insisted that it should not be taken to be a crude, undifferentiated whole. If sets of hypotheses must be evaluated together, and everything is potentially relevant to everything else, how can we make a reasonable judgment about which hypotheses to maintain and which to reject? Kuhn's (1970) influential account of theory change as shifts in whole paradigms has been taken by some to imply that there is no rationality in science. Fodor (1983) has concluded from Quinean holism not only that philosophers have failed to provide a reasonable account of scientific confirmation, but even that cognitive science is unlikely ever to provide an account of such central psychological processes as hypothesis selection and problem solving (see Holland et al. 1986: Ch. 11, for a rebuttal).

My theory of explanatory coherence and its implementation in ECHO are holistic in that the acceptability of a hypothesis potentially depends on its relation to a whole complex of hypotheses and data. But there is nothing mystical about how ECHO uses pairwise relations of local coherence to come up with global coherence judgments. Although evidence units can be deactivated, just as data are sometimes ignored in scientific practice, the evidence principle gives some priority to the results of observation.

Although ECHO does not exhibit simplistic Popperian falsification, it need not succumb to the various strategies that can be used to save a hypothesis from refutation. The strongest direct evidence *against* a hypothesis is pointing out that it has implications that contradict what has been observed. One way of saving the hypothesis from an objection of this sort is to use an auxiliary hypothesis to explain away the negative evidence. Section 4.6 showed how simplicity considerations can prevent this strategem from working. Another way of saving a hypothesis in the face of negative evidence is to modify its cohypotheses. As Duhem and Quine pointed out, if H1 and H2 together imply some NE1 that contradicts a datum E1, then logic alone does not tell whether to reject H1, H2, or both. In ECHO, which hypotheses are deactivated depends on other relations of explanatory coherence. If H1 contributes to fewer explanations than H2, or if H1 contradicts another highly explanatory hypothesis, H3, then H1 will be more likely to be deactivated than H2.

Although ECHO makes it possible for a set of hypotheses to be accepted or rejected as a whole, it also admits the possibility of more piecemeal revision. Perrin (1988, p. 115) reports that the conversion of phlogiston theorists to the oxygen theory sometimes took several years, with the converts gradually accepting more and more of Lavoisier's views. ECHO's networks such as the oxygen–phlogiston one shown in Figure 9 do not connect everything to everything else. Explanatory relations may produce relatively isolated packets of coherent hypotheses and evidence;

these may sometimes be accepted or rejected independent of the larger theory.

10.2. Probability

My account of theory evaluation contrasts sharply with probabilistic accounts of confirmation that have been influential in philosophy since Carnap (1950). Salmon (1966), for example, advocates the use of Bayes's theorem for theory evaluation, which, if P(H,E) stands for the probability of H given E, can be written as:

$$P(H, E) = \frac{P(H)P(E, H)}{P(E)} \tag{2}$$

Consider what would be involved in trying to apply this to Lavoisier's argument against the phlogiston theory. We would have to take each hypothesis separately and calculate its probability given the evidence, but it is totally obscure how this could be done. Subjective probabilities understood as degrees of belief make sense in contexts where we can imagine people betting on expected outcomes, but scientific theory evaluation is not such a context. How could we take into account that alternative explanations are also being offered by the phlogiston theory? The issue is simplified somewhat if we consider only likelihood ratios for the oxygen and phlogiston theories – that is, the ratio of P(E, oxygen) to P(E, phlogiston) – but we still have the problem of dealing with the probability of the conjunction of a number of oxygen hypotheses whose degree of dependence is indeterminate. As I argued in Section 8.2, probabilities have marginal relevance to qualitative explanatory inferences in science and law.

My account of coherence based on explanation contrasts markedly with probabilistic accounts. A set of propositions, S, is probabilistically coherent if there is a real-valued function that gives an assignment of values to the propositions consistent with the axioms of probability (Levi 1980). This constraint is very different from the ones governing explanatory coherence that ECHO shows to be sufficient for accepting and rejecting hypotheses. The real numbers that are degrees of activation of propositions in ECHO are clearly not probabilities, because they range from 1 to −1, like the certainty factors in the AI expert system MYCIN (Buchanan and Shortliffe 1984). Note that two contradictory propositions can both have activation greater than 0, if neither is substantially more coherent with the evidence than the other.

Probabilities, ranging from 0 to 1, are often interpreted as degrees of belief, but this interpretation obscures the natural distinction between acceptance and rejection, belief and disbelief. I do not just have low confidence in the proposition that the configuration of the stars and planets at birth affects human personality; I reject it as false. One advantage of probability theory, however, is that it provides rules for calculating the probabilities of conjunctions and disjunctions. In contrast, the acceptability (in my sense) of "P and Q" and "P or Q" is not defined, because such composite propositions do not, in general, figure in explanations. One can concoct cases of disjunctive explanations ("He said he was flying in from either New York or Philadelphia, and the weather is very bad in both places, so that explains why he's delayed"), but I have never encountered one in a scientific or legal context. Explanations depending on conjunctions of cohypotheses are common, but ECHO has no need to calculate the acceptability of "P and Q," because relations of explanatory coherence tell you all you need to know about P and Q individually. The apparent advantage of probability theory is much weakened in practice by the fact that the calculation of conjunctive and disjunctive probabilities requires knowledge of the extent to which the two propositions are independent of each other. Such information is easily gained when one is dealing with games of chance and in other cases where frequencies are available, but it is hard to come by in cases of scientific and legal reasoning: For Lavoisier, what was the conditional probability of OH1 (pure air contains oxygen principle) given OH2 (pure air contains matter of fire and heat)?

10.3. Confirmation Theory

My view of theory evaluation based on explanatory coherence can also be contrasted with confirmation theory, according to which a hypothesis is confirmed by observed instances (Glymour 1980; Hempel 1965). The cases I discussed in detail in this paper are typical, I would argue, of the general practice in scientific argumentation that theories are not justified on the basis of particular observations that can be derived from them. Rather, observations are collected together into generalizations. These generalizations are sometimes rough, describing mere tendencies. In this process, particular observations can be tossed out as faulty or irrelevant. Theory evaluation starts with the explanation of the generalizations, not with particular observations.

Lavoisier, for example, did not defend his theory by pointing to particular confirming observations such as his measurements indicating that a sample of burned phosphorus gained weight on a particular day in 1772. Rather, his central claim in defense of his theory is that it explains why objects in general gain weight when burned. Qualitative confirmation theory also does not in itself suggest how simplicity, analogy, competition, and being explained can play a role in theory evaluation.

10.4. Explanationism and Conservatism

Now let me turn to a brief discussion of philosophical views that are much closer to my account of explanatory coherence. My discussion of hypotheses is compatible with the "explanationism" of Harman (1986) and Lycan (1988). Unlike them, however, I am not trying to give a general account of epistemic justification: I hold that there are other legitimate forms of inference besides inference to the best explanation. The principle of data priority assumes that results of observation start with a degree of acceptability that derives from their having been achieved by methods that lead reliably to true beliefs. This justification is closer to the "reliabilism" of Goldman (1986), a position which has problems, however, in justifying the acceptance of hypotheses (Thagard, 1989). My own view of justification is that explanation and truth are both epistemic goals that need to be taken into account as part of a larger process of justifying inferential strategies (Thagard 1988a: Ch. 7).

The other major difference I have with Harman and Lycan is that they both advocate conservatism as a supplement to considerations of explanatory coherence. Harman says we should try to maximize explanatory coherence while minimizing change. I view conservatism as a consequence of explanatory coherence, not as a separate factor in brief revision. In ECHO, we get a kind of conservatism about new evidence, as I showed in Section 4.2. For ECHO, new evidence that does not cohere with what has been accepted is not treated equally with old evidence. In addition to conservatism about new evidence, there is a kind of conceptual conservatism inherent in any cognitive system: If an alternative theory requires a network of concepts which differs from my own, then I cannot evaluate the new system until I have effortfully acquired that system of concepts (Thagard 1990). Hence, an existing set of views will be conservatively favored until the alternative is fully developed.

The conservatism favored by Harman and Lycan seems most plausible, not for actual scientific cases, but for imagined ones in which a trivial variant of an accepted theory appears as an alternative. Suppose H1 gets high activation as the best explanation of E1 and E2, and then H2 is proposed to explain them both. If H1 and H2 are contradictory, then ECHO readjusts activation so that H1 and H2 are virtually at the same level. What if H2 is just a trivial variant of H1? Then H2 does not really contradict H1, so they can both be highly active without any problem. One might worry that the system will quickly be cluttered with trivial variants, but in a full computational system, that would be taken care of by having pragmatic constraints on what hypotheses are generated (Holland et al. 1986).

As a final comparison, consider the complementary views on explanatory unification of Kitcher (1981). He describes how powerful theories such as Darwin's and Newton's provide unification by applying similar *patterns* of explanation to various phenomena. That this should contribute to explanatory coherence is a consequence of my theory, for if H1, H2, and H3 are all used to explain the evidence, we get the result not just that each coheres with the evidence, but also that they cohere with each other. Moreover, degrees of coherence are cumulative, so that the more two hypotheses participate in explaining different pieces of evidence, the more they cohere with each other. (See the simple example in Section 4.5.)

The major philosophical weakness of my account of explanatory coherence concerns the nature of explanation. This paper has bypassed the crucial question of what explanation is. Fortunately, to apply the principles of explanatory coherence and to generate input for ECHO, it is not necessary to have an exact analysis of the nature of explanation. We can take for granted the explanatory relations described by scientists such as Lavoisier and Darwin, or we can get an approximation using a computational system such as PI, as described in Section 7. For an outline of what a computational account of explanation might look like, see Thagard (1988a: Ch. 3).

10.5. The Descriptive and the Normative

Philosophy differs from psychology primarily in its concern with normative matters – how people *ought* to reason rather than how they do reason. For some philosophers, any analysis that smacks of psychology has disqualified itself as epistemology. From this perspective, one faces the dichotomy: Is my theory of explanatory coherence normative or is it merely descriptive? In accord with Goldman (1986) and Harman (1986), I reject this rigid dichotomy, maintaining that descriptive matters are highly relevant to normative issues (see Thagard 1988a: Ch. 7). The seven principles of explanatory coherence are intended to capture both what people generally do and what they ought to do. By no means do they constitute a full theory of rationality. There are undoubtedly cases where people deviate from explanatory coherence – for example, preferring a hypothesis because it makes them happy rather than because of the evidence for it (Kunda 1987). Racial or other types of prejudice may prevent jurors from taking a piece of evidence seriously. Various other biases (Nisbett and Ross 1980) may intrude to throw off considerations of explanatory coherence. Much psychological experimentation and modeling is needed to show when people's reasoning can be accounted for in terms of explanatory coherence and when it is affected by other factors. This work can go hand in hand with refinements in the normative aspects of the theory.

11. Conclusion

I conclude with a brief survey of the chief accomplishments of the theory of explanatory coherence offered here.

First, it fits directly with the actual arguments of scientists such as Lavoisier and Darwin who explicitly discuss what competing theories explain. There is no need to postulate probabilities or contrive deductive relations. The theory and ECHO have engendered a far more detailed analysis of these arguments than is typically given by proponents of other accounts. Using the same principles, it applies to important cases of legal reasoning as well.

Second, unlike most accounts of theory evaluation, this view based on explanatory coherence is inherently comparative. If two hypotheses contradict each other, they incohere, so the subsystems of propositions to which they belong will compete with each other. As ECHO shows, successful subsystems of hypotheses and evidence can emerge gracefully from local judgments of explanatory coherence.

Third, the theory of explanatory coherence permits a smooth integration of diverse criteria such as explanatory breadth, simplicity, and analogy. ECHO's connectionist algorithm shows the computability of coherence relations. The success of the program is best attributed to the usefulness of connectionist architectures for achieving parallel constraint satisfaction, and to the fact that the problem inherent in inference to the best explanation is the need to satisfy multiple constraints simultaneously. Not all computational problems are best approached this way, but parallel constraint satisfaction has proven to be very powerful for other problems as well – for example, analogical mapping (Holyoak and Thagard 1989).

Finally, my theory surmounts the problem of holism. The principles of explanatory coherence establish pairwise relations of coherence between propositions in an explanatory system. Thanks to ECHO, we know that there is an efficient algorithm for adjusting a system of propositions to turn coherence relations into judgments of acceptability. The algorithm allows every proposition to influence every other one, because there is typically a path of links between any two units, but the influences are set up systematically to reflect explanatory relations. Theory assessment is done as a whole, but a theory does not have to be rejected or accepted as a whole. Those hypotheses that participate in many explanations will be much more coherent with the evidence, and with each other, and will therefore be harder to reject. More peripheral hypotheses may be deactivated even if the rest of the theory they are linked to wins. We thus get a holistic account of inference that can nevertheless differentiate between strong and weak hypotheses. Although our hypotheses face evidence only as a corporate body, evidence and relations of explanatory coherence suffice to separate good hypotheses from bad.

12. Appendix

Technical Details of ECHO

For those interested in a more technical description of how ECHO works, this appendix outlines its principle algorithms and describes sensitivity analyses that have been done to determine the effects of the various parameters on ECHO's performance.

12.1. ALGORITHMS

As I described in Section 4.1, ECHO takes as input PROPOSITION, EXPLAIN, CONTRADICT, and DATA statements. The basic data structures in ECHO are LISP atoms that imple-

Table 9: Algorithms for Processing Input to ECHO

1. Input: (PROPOSITION NAME SENTENCE)
   Create a unit called NAME and an index for it. Store SENTENCE with NAME.
2. Input: (EXPLAIN LIST-OF-PROPOSITIONS PROPOSITION)
   Make excitatory links[a] between each member of LIST-OF-PROPOSITIONS and PROPOSITIONS.
   Make excitatory links[a] between each pair of LIST-OF-PROPOSITIONS.
   Record what explains what.
3. Input: (CONTRADICT PROPOSITON-1 PROPOSITION-2)
   Make an inhibitory link between PROPOSITION-1 and PROPOSITION-2.
4. Input: (DATA LIST-OF-PROPOSITIONS)
   For each member of LIST-OF-PROPOSITIONS, create an excitatory link from the special evidence unit with the weight equal to the data excitation parameter, unless the member is itself a list of the form (PROPOSITION WEIGHT). In this case, the weight of the excitatory link between the special unit and PROPOSITION is WEIGHT.
   If there are unexplained data propositions, increase the decay rate parameter by multiplying it by the ratio of the total number of evidence propositions to the number of explained evidence propositions.

[a] The weights on these links are determined by equation 3 given in the text. Weights are additive: If more than one EXPLAIN statement creates a link between two proposition units, then the weight on the link is the sum of the weights suggested by both statements.

ment units with property lists that contain information about connections and the weights of the links between units. Table 9 describes the effects of the four main kinds of input statements. All are very straightforward, although the EXPLAIN statements require a calculation of the weights on the excitatory links. The equation for this is:

$$weight(P,Q) = default\ weight/$$
$$(number\ of\ cohypotheses\ of\ P)^{(simplicity\ impact)} \quad (3)$$

Here simplicity impact is an exponent, so that increasing it lowers the weight even more, putting a still greater penalty on the use of multiple assumptions in an explanation. In practice, however, I have not found any examples where it was interesting to set simplicity impact at a value other than 1.

Table 10: Algorithms for Network Operation

1. Running the network:
   Set all unit activations to an initial starting value (typically .01), except that the special evidence unit is clamped at 1.
   Update activations in accordance with (2) below.
   If no unit has changed activation more than a specified amount (usually .001), or if a specified number of cycles of updating have occurred, then stop.
   Print out the activation values of all units.
2. Synchronous activation updating at each cycle:
   For each unit u, calculate the new activation u in accord with equations 3 and 4 in the text, considering the old activation of each unit u' linked to u.
   Set the activation of u to the new activation.

After input has been used to set up the network, the network is run in cycles that synchronously update all the units. The basic algorithm for this is shown in Table 10. For each unit j, the activation a_j, ranging from -1 to 1, is a continuous function of the activation of all the units linked to it, with each unit's contribution depending on the weight w_{ij} of the link from unit i to unit j. The activation of a unit j is updated using the following equation:

$$a_j(t+1) = a_j(t)(1-\theta)$$
$$+ \begin{cases} net_j(max - a_j(t)) & \text{if } net_j > 0 \\ net_j(a_j(t) - min) & otherwise \end{cases}$$
$$(4)$$

Here θ is a decay parameter that decrements each unit at every cycle, min is minimum activation (-1), max is maximum activation (1), and net_j is the net input to a unit. This is defined by

$$net_j = \Sigma_j w_{ij} a_i(t) \qquad (5)$$

Repeated updating cycles result in some units becoming activated (getting activation > 0) while others become deactivated (activation < 0).

12.2. SENSITIVITY ANALYSES

Multiple connected localist networks sometimes exhibit instability, failing to settle into stable activation patterns because complexes of mutually excitatory units produce activation oscillations. As Figures 11, 14, 17, and 20 suggest, ECHO's networks are generally stable, usually requiring fewer than 100 units of updating for all units to reach asymptotic levels. Pearl (1987) devotes considerable effort to rearranging probabilistic networks so that they will be singly connected and hence stable. Fortunately, the networks set up by ECHO in accord with the theory of explanatory coherence do not require any alteration to settle into stable activations. Whereas a probabilistic network may need links specifying the conditional probabilities of p given q, q given r, r given s, and s given p, such cyclic paths rarely arise in ECHO because the "explain" relation sets up hierarchies of units rather than cycles. ECHO undergoes activation oscillations only when the excitation parameter is high relative to inhibition, for example, in the Chambers case, if excitation has a value of .17 instead of .05. ECHO is efficient: In each of the four major examples, a complete run, including network creation and settling, takes less than a minute of cpu time on a Sun 3/75 workstation. Because networks with hundreds more units and thousands more links than ECHO's networks have run successfully in ACME, a similar program that does analogical mapping (Holyoak & Thagard, 1989), I see no problem in scaling ECHO up to run on much larger examples.

Table 11 shows, for each major example, the size of the networks created and the number of cycles of activation updating it takes for them to settle using the default parameter values of .05 for excitation, $-.2$ for inhibition, .1 for data excitation, and .05 for decay. Experiments have shown that ECHO exhibits the behavior described in the text over a wide range of values for these parameters. For example, in the Lavoisier example, no important differences in the results occur if the decay, excitation, inhibition, and

Table 11: Network Information for Four Major Examples

	Units	Links	Cycles to Settle	Excitation Ceiling	Inhibition Floor
Lavoisier	20	49	107	.13	$-.18$
Darwin	29	70	49	.06	$-.16$
Chambers	34	59	63	.17	$-.07$
Peyer	34	54	78	.08	$-.13$

data excitation parameters are all halved or doubled. In general, lowering positive parameters and making inhibition closer to 0 tends to prolong settling time. Increasing decay tends to flatten the activation curves, both positive and negative, keeping them closer to 0. Increasing data excitation leads evidence units to have higher asymptotic activation. Varying excitation and inhibition systematically reveals that there is a critical value for each. If excitation is high relative to inhibition, then the system shows much "tolerance" and does not deactivate inferior hypotheses. Table 11 lists excitation ceilings and inhibition floors for the four major examples. The excitation ceilings are the maximum values that excitation can have without activating units representing inferior hypotheses; inhibition here is constant at the default value of $-.2$. The excitation values at which networks become unstable are well above these ceilings. The inhibition floors are the minimum values that inhibition must have without failing to deactivate units representing inferior hypotheses; excitation here is constant at the default value of .05. The excitation ceiling and the inhibition floor indicate the most important respects in which quantitative parameter changes in ECHO have qualitative effects. Keep in mind that the excitation ceilings and inhibition floors listed in Table 11 are based on a fixed value for, respectively, inhibition and excitation. Varying these values will produce different floors and ceilings, so that the range of possible parameter values is much larger than Table 11 portrays.

Notes

1 From here on, I shall be less careful about distinguishing between units and the propositions they represent.
2 I owe this suggestion to Daniel Kimberg.

References

Achinstein, P. (1983) *The nature of explanation.* Oxford: Oxford University Press.

Alcock, J. E. (1987) Parapsychology: Science of the anomalous or search for the soul? *Behavioral and Brain Sciences* 10:553–65.

Anderson, A. & Belnap, N. (1975) *Entailment.* Princeton: Princeton University Press.

Bartlett, F. (1958) *Thinking: An experimental and social study.* New York: Allen and Unwin.

Bonjour, L. (1985) *The structure of empirical knowledge.* Cambridge: Harvard University Press.

Bradley, F. H. (1914) *Essays on truth and reality.* Oxford: Clarendon Press.

Buchanan, B. & Shortliffe, E., eds. (1984) *Rule-based expert systems.* Upper Saddle River, NJ: Addison Wesley.

Carey, S. (1985) *Conceptual change in childhood.* Cambridge: MIT Press.

Carnap, R. (1950) *Logical foundations of probability.* Chicago: University of Chicago Press.

Carter, L. (1984) *Reason in law.* Little, Brown: London.

Charniak, E. & McDermott, D. (1985) *Introduction to artificial intelligence.* Upper Saddle River, NJ: Addison-Wesley.

Clark, H. & Lucy, P. (1975) Understanding what is meant from what is said: A study in conversationally conveyed requests. *Journal of Verbal Learning and Verbal Behavior* 14:56–72.

Cohen, L. J. (1978) The coherence theory of truth. *Philosophical Studies* 34:351–60.

Cohen R. (1983) *A computational model for the analysis of arguments.* Technical report CSRG-151. Department of Computer Science. University of Toronto.

Darwin, C. (1962) *On the origin of species* (text of sixth edition of 1872). New York: Macmillan.

Dejong, G. & Mooney, R. (1986) Explanation-based learning: An alternative view. *Machine Learning* 1:145–76.

Duhem, P. (1954) The aim and structure of physical theory, trans. P. Wiener (first published 1914). Princeton: Princeton University Press.

Einstein, A. (1952) On the electrodynamics of moving bodies. In: *The principle of relativity,* ed. H. A. Lorentz, A. Einstein, H. Minkowski & H. Weyl. Dover (originally published in 1905). Long Island, New York.

Falkenhainer, B. & Rajamoney, S. (1988) The interdependencies of theory formation, revision, and experimentation. In: *Proceedings of the Fifth International Conference on Machine Learning,* ed. J. Laird. Burlington, MA: Morgan Kaufmann.

Feldman, J. & Ballard, D. (1982) Connectionist models and their properties. *Cognitive Science* 6:205–54.

Fiske, S. & Taylor, S. (1984) *Social cognition.* New York: Random House.

Fodor, J. (1983) *The modularity of mind.* Cambridge: MIT Press.

Foster, M. & Martin, eds. (1966) *Probability, confirmation, and simplicity.* New York: Odyssey Press.

Gardner, A. (1987) *An artificial intelligence approach to legal reasoning.* Cambridge: MIT Press/Bradford Books.

Gibbs, H. (1984) Literal meaning and psychological theory. *Cognitive Science* 8:275–304.

Glymour, C. (1980) *Theory and evidence.* Princeton: Princeton University Press.

Goel, A., Ramaiiujam, J., & Sadayappan, P. (1988) Towards a neural architecture for abductive reasoning. *Proceedings of the Second IEEE International Conference on Neural Networks,* vol. 1, San Diego.

Golding, M. (1984) *Legal reasoning.* New York: Knopf.

Goldman, A. (1986) *Epistemology and cognition.* Cambridge: Harvard University Press.

Grossberg, S., ed. (1988) *Neural networks and natural intelligence.* Cambridge: MIT Press.

Hanen, M. (1987) *Unpublished manuscript.* University of Calgary.

Harman, G. (1973) *Thought.* Princeton: Princeton University Press.

Harman, G. (1986) *Change in view: Principles of reasoning.* Cambridge: MIT Press/Bradford Books.

Harman, C., Ranney, M., Salem, K., Doring, F., Epstein, J. & Jaworksa, A. (1988) A theory of simplicity. *Proceedings of the Tenth Annual Conference of the Cognitive Science Society.* Hills Vale, NJ: Erlbaum.

Hedges, L. (1987) How hard is hard science, how soft is soft science? *American Psychologist* 42: 443–55.

Hegel, C. (1967) *The phenomenology of mind,* trans. J. Baillie (first published 1807). New York: Harper & Row.

Hempel, C. (1965) *Aspects of scientific explanation.* New York: Free Press.

Hendler, J. (1987) Marker-passing and microfeatures. *Proceedings of the Tenth International Joint Conference on Artificial intelligence.* Burlington, MA: Morgan Kaufmann.

Hobbs, J., Stickel, M., Martin, P. & Edwards, D. (1988) Interpretation as abduction. *Proceedings of the 26th Annual Meeting of the Association for Computational Linguistics.*

Holland, J., Holyoak, K., Nisbett, H. & Thagard, P. (1986) *Induction: Processes of inference, learning, and discovery.* Cambridge: MIT Press/Bradford Books.

Holyoak, K. & Thagard, P. (1989) Analogical mapping by constraint satisfaction, *Cognitive Science* 13:295–355.

Jones, E. & Davis, K. (1965) From acts to dispositions: The attribution process in person perception. In: *Advances in experimental social psychology,* vol. 2, ed. L. Berkowitz. New York: Academic Press.

Josephson, J., Chandrasekaran, B., Smith, J. & Tanner, M. (1987) A mechanism for forming composite explanatory hypotheses. *IEEE Transactions on Systems, Man, and Cybernetics* 17: 445–54.

Kintsch, W. (1988) The role of knowledge in discourse comprehension: A construction-integration model. *Psychological Review* 95:163–82.

Kirwan, R. (1789/1968) *An essay on phlogiston and the constitution of acids* (new impression of second English edition). London: Cass.

Kitcher, P. (1981) Explanatory unification. *Philosophy of Science* 48:507–31.

Kuhn, T. S. (1970) *Structure of scientific revolutions* (2nd ed., first published 1962). University of Chicago: Chicago Press.

Kunda, Z. (1987) Motivation and inference: Self-serving generation and evaluation of causal theories. *Journal of Personality and Social Psychology* 53:636–47.

Lakatos, I. (1970) Falsification and the methodology of scientific research programs. In: *Criticism and the growth of knowledge,* ed. I. Lakatos & A. Musgrave. Cambridge: Cambridge University Press.

Laudan, L. (1976) Two dogmas of methodology. *Philosophy of Science* 43:585–97.

Lavoisicr, A. (1862) *Oeuvres* (6 vols.). Paris: Imprimerie Imperiale.

Leake, D. (1988) Evaluating explanations. *Proceedings of the Seventh National Conference on Artificial Intelligence.* Burlington MA: Morgan Kaufmann.

Lehnert, W. (1987) Case-based problem solving with a large knowledge base of learned cases. *Proceedings of the Sixth National Conference on Artificial Intelligence.* Burlington MA: Morgan Kaufmann.

Lehrer, K. (1974) *Knowledge.* Oxford: Clarendon Press.

Levi, L. (1980) *The enterprise of knowledge.* Cambridge: MIT Press.

Lycan, W. (1988) *Judgment and justification.* Cambridge: Cambridge University Press.

Marr, D. (1982) *Vision.* San Francisco CA: Freeman.

Mitchell, T., Keller, R. & Kedar-Cabrelli, S. (1986) Explanation-based generalization: A unifying view. *Machine Learning* 1: 47–80.

Nisbett, R. E. & Ross, L. (1980) *Human inference: Strategies and shortcomings of social judgement.* Englewood Cliffs, NJ: Prentice-Hall.

Nowak, C. & Thagard, P. (1992) Copernicus, Newton, and explanatory coherence. *Minnesota Studies in the Philosophy of Science* 15:274–309.

O'Rorke, P., Aba, D. & Sage, S. (1988) A deductive-nomological model of abduction with learning. Unpublished manuscript. University of California at Irvine.

Pearl, J. (1986) Fusion, propagation, and structuring us belief networks. *Artificial Intelligence* 29:241–88.

Pearl, J. (1987) Distributed revision of composite beliefs. *Artificial Intelligence* 33:173–215.

Peirce, C. S. (1931–1958) *Collected papers* (8 vols.), ed. C. Hartshorne, P. Weiss & A. Burks. Cambridge: Harvard University Press.

Peng, Y. & Reggia, J. (1989) A connectionist model for diagnostic problem solving. *IEEE Transactions on Systems, Man and Cybernetics* 19: 285–298.

Pennington, N. & Hastic, R. (1986) Evidence evaluation in complex decision making. *Journal of Personality and Social Psychology* 51:242–58.

Pennington, N. & Hastic, R. (1987) Explanation-based decision making. *Proceedings of the Ninth Annual Meeting of the Cognitive Science Society.*

Perrin, C. (1988) The chemical revolution: Shifts in guiding assumptions. In: *Scrutinizing science: Empirical studies of scientific change*, ed. A. Donovan, L. Laudan & R. Laudan. Dordrecht: Kluwer.

Pople, H. (1977) The formation of composite hypotheses in diagnostic problem solving. In: *Proceedings of the Fifth International Joint Conference on Artificial Intelligence*. Burlington MA: Morgan Kaufmann.

Popper, K. (1959) *The logic of scientific discovery*. United Kingdom: Hutchinson.

Quine, W. V. (1961) *From a logical point of view* (2nd ed New York: Harper Torch-books.)

Rajamoney, S. & DeJong, C. (1988) Active explanation reduction: An approach to the multiple explanations problem. In: *Proceedings of the Fifth International Conference on Machine Learning*, ed. J. Laird. Burlington MA: Morgan Kanfmann.

Ranney, M. (1987) Changing naive conceptions of motion. Doctoral dissertation, Learning, Research, and Development Center, University of Pittsburgh.

Ranney, M. & Thagard, P. (1988) Explanatory coherence and belief revision in naive physics. *Proceedings of the Tenth Annual Conference of the Cognitive Science Society*.

Rao, K. R. & Palmer, J. (1987) The anomaly called psi: Recent research and criticism, *Behavioral and Brain Sciences* 10:539–51.

Reggia, J., Nan, D. & Wang, P. (1983) Diagnostic expert systems based on a set covering model *International Journal of Man-Machine Studies* 19:437–60.

Rescher, N. (1973) *The coherence theory of truth*. Oxford: Clarendon Press.

Rumelhart, D. E., McClelland, J. R. & the PDP Research Group (1986) *Parallel distributed processing: Explorations in the microstructure of cognition*, 2 vol Cambridge: MIT Press.

Salmon, W. (1966) *The foundations of scientific inference*. Pittsburgh: University of Pittsburgh Press.

Salmon, W. (1970) Statistical explanation. In: *The nature and function of scientific theories*, ad. R. Colodny. Pittsburgh: University of Pittsburgh Press.

Salmon, W. (1984) *Scientific explanation and the causal structure of the world*. Princeton Hills Vale, NJ: Princeton University Press.

Schank, R. (1986) *Explanation patterns*. New York: Erlbaum.

Taubman, B. (1988) *The preppy murder trial*. St. Martin's Press.

Thagard, P. (1978) The best explanation: Criteria for theory choice. *Journal of Philosophy* 75:76–92.

Thagard, P. (1986) Parallel computation and the mind-body problem. *Cognitive Science* 10:301–18.

Thagard, P. (1988a) *Computational philosophy of science*. Cambridge: MIT Press/Bradford Books.

Thagard, P. (1988b) The dinosaur debate: Application of a connectionist model of theory evaluation. Unpublished manuscript, Princeton University.

Thagard, P. (1989) Connectionism and epistemology: Goldman on winner-take-all networks. *Philosophia* 19: 189–196.

Thagard, P. (1990) The conceptual structure of the chemical revolution. *Philosophy of Science* 57: 183–209.

Thagard, P., Holyoak, K., Nelson, C. & Gochfeld, D. (1989) Analogical retrieval by constraint satisfaction. Unpublished manuscript, Princeton University.

Thagard, P. & Nowak, C. (1988) The explanatory coherence of continental drift. In: *PSA 1988*, vol. 1, ad. A. Fine & J. Leplin. Philosophy of Science Association.

Thagard, P. & Nowak, C. (1990) The conceptual structure of the geological revolution. In: *Computational models of discovery and theory formation*, ad. J. Shrager & P. Langley. San Mateo, CA: Morgan Kaufman, 27–72.

Trabasso, T., Sacco, T. & van dan Broek, P. (1984) Causal cohesion and story coherence. In: *Learning and comprehension of texts*, ed. H. Mandl, N. Stein & T. Trabasso. Hillsdale, NJ: Erlbaum: 83–111.

van Fraassen, B. (1980) The Scientific Image. Oxford: Clarendon Press.

Wald, J., Farach M., Tagamets, M. & Reggia, J. (1989) Generating plausible diagnostic hypotheses with self-processing causal networks *Journal of Experimental and Theoretical Artificial Intelligence* 1:91–112.

Chapter 25: Belief Revision

HANS ROTT

1. Introduction

The terms "belief revision" and "belief change" refer to the change of a system of beliefs or opinions in response to new information, in particular to information that is inconsistent with this system. In the 1960s and 1970s, works of Isaac Levi, William Harper, and Brian Ellis prepared the ground for systematic studies of belief change processes. In the 1980s, a seminal research paradigm of belief revision was established by Carlos Alchourrón, Peter Gärdenfors, and David Makinson (also known as "AGM") who discovered a common structure in the logic of normative systems and of the logic of counterfactual conditionals – areas which turned out to be structurally related and were merged into the field of belief change (also known as "theory change"). The AGM paradigm is a classic by now that has in many ways been extended and revised. Still almost all new theories that are being proposed today define themselves in relation to the basic ideas of AGM.

Belief revision theories are different from descriptive psychological investigations or investigations of theory dynamics as conducted in the philosophy of science in that they provide abstract logical postulates for rational revision processes, as well as construction recipes for belief changes on the basis of certain revision-guiding structures. At present, research in belief revision is an interdisciplinary undertaking in logic, philosophy, computer science, and, to a lesser extent, in economics and cognitive science. Belief revision theories are often assigned to the field of "knowledge representation" in computer science, and are presented as theories about "knowledge change," but this terminology is misleading because knowledge has to be true and justified, and neither truth nor justification are topics discussed at any depth in the belief revision literature. In terms originating with Plato, belief revision theories deal with the dynamics of *doxastic* rather than epistemic states.

The problem of belief revision is best illustrated by an example. Suppose you believe that

(1) David is excellent in teaching. t

(2) David has a paper in the p
     Journal of Philosophy.

(3) If David has a paper in the $p \to r$
     Journal of Philosophy he is
     excellent in research.

(4) If David is excellent in $r \wedge t \to j$
     research and teaching, he will
     get the job.

Like any person capable of good reasoning, you conclude from these premises that

(5) David will get the job. j

From the point of view of belief revision theories, it is not necessary that you actually perform the requisite reasoning and draw this conclusion in such a way that (5) becomes an occurrent belief. It is sufficient that you can be *ascribed* the belief that j, or that you are *committed* to believing j on the basis of premises (1) to (4). Now suppose that at a certain point you learn, from a perfectly reliable source, that David has not in fact got the job. This is a surprise to you that manifests itself in a contradiction between the new information $\neg j$ and your old premises (1) to (4). Thinking about the matter, you realize that given your initial premises, logic in a way compelled you to believe j. Since you have now found out that j is not true after all and you want to add $\neg j$ to your stock of beliefs, there are only two options. Either your logical reasoning that delivered the conclusion j was faulty, or (at least) one of the premises (1)–(4) was wrong. The answer typically given by belief revision theories is that classical logic is correct. So, assuming you want to accept the new piece of information $\neg j$, logic enforces that you give up (at least) one of the premises. Logic, however, is completely silent about *which* of the premises to give up. Something else has to step in that provides you with guidance how to proceed. The theme of belief revision theories is to find out what this "something else" is, and how it helps you to resolve such problems in the transformation of belief states or doxastic states.[1]

In order to accommodate the new information $\neg j$ and to avoid that your beliefs become inconsistent, you need to *revise* your belief base. Some of the original premises must be *retracted*. In general one does not want to give up all of one's beliefs, since this would mean an unnecessary loss of valuable information, but when giving up the belief j, you have to decide which of the reasons for holding j to retain and which to retract. You have to *choose* between retracting $r \wedge t \rightarrow j$, t, $p \rightarrow r$, or p. For instance, you may come to decide that you were too optimistic in endorsing $r \wedge t \rightarrow j$. Excellent research and teaching may not be sufficient to secure David a job.

The process of belief revision is nontrivial precisely because purely logical considerations alone do not tell us which of the beliefs to give up. What makes the task more difficult is that beliefs have logical consequences. When giving up a belief one has to decide as well which of its consequences to retain and which to retract. For example, one of the logical consequences of $r \wedge t \rightarrow j$ is

If David is excellent in research $\qquad r \wedge t \wedge i \rightarrow j$
and teaching and fluent in
Italian, he will get the job.

Should you keep this or some similar beliefs, if you decide to retract $r \wedge t \rightarrow j$ in the situation just described? How is the answer to this question to be decided?

2. The Representation of Belief

Any theory of the formation and transformation of belief states consists of (1) a static part describing the belief states that a person can be in and (2) a dynamic part describing how belief states change in response to external input. The static picture constrains the dynamic picture.

Any mechanism for belief revision is sensitive to the formalism chosen for the representation of belief states. We need to be precise about the items we are talking about before we can say how these items are to be changed, so we need to decide how to represent beliefs (what a person believes) and belief states (the mental states that believers are in).

The models we shall consider are all qualitative in the sense that they do not make use of any numbers. In qualitative theories, belief states don't carry numerical information, and reasoners accept new incoming information without numerical qualification. No numbers represent degrees of "certainty," "security," "plausibility," and so on, and belief is always plain belief, so these models tend to be rather crude. In quantitative theories, by contrast, reasoners do not, or in any case do not have to, accept new information *simpliciter*, but can accept them with a certain degree of certainty or plausibility.[2]

The best known quantitative modeling of belief is the probabilistic one. But there are other numerical methods of belief change using so-called *qualitative ("Baconian") probabilities* or *ranking functions* (Rescher 1976; Cohen 1977; Spohn 1988; Dubois and Prade 1988; Goldszmidt and Pearl 1992; all foreshadowed by Shackle 1949). Quantitative approaches are more expressive than qualitative methods. They provide representations of degrees of belief and, using arithmetic operations, of independence relations between beliefs. This additional expressive power of quantitative approaches is a substantial advantage, but it cannot be denied that there is a price to be paid for it: Often it is not clear where the numbers come from and what they are supposed to mean. While in probability theory numerical values are often considered to be explicable in terms of betting quotients, the precise meaning of the numbers in ranking functions remains largely unelucidated. Moreover, real as opposed to ideally rational persons are notoriously bad at reasoning with probabilities, so while working with numbers helps us to come to terms with many challenging modeling tasks, it is based on parameters the meaning of which is not fully understood and puts very heavy demands on a person's reasoning capabilities.

Belief revision theories have traditionally been *sentential* or *propositional* in the sense that beliefs are represented as sentences or propositions (with sentential structure). One must first fix an appropriate *language* in which to formulate the beliefs. Belief revision theories typically work with a language L closed under applications of the Boolean operators of negation, conjunction, disjunction, and implication. We will use lowercase letters p, q, and so on as atomic sentences from L, and capital letters A, B, C, etc., as variables standing for sentences in L.

A sentence A expresses a given proposition if and only if A is true in exactly that set of possible worlds that represents this proposition. Aside from technical details, possible worlds models for belief change are very similar to linguistic models of belief change, since the latter usually stipulate that different sentences that are logically equivalent should be treated alike. We will neglect technical problems concerning possibly indefinable infinite sets of possible worlds in this article.

In modern epistemology there is an important contrast between foundationalist and coherentist theories of the justification of belief. Although belief revision theories developed independently from philosophical discussions surrounding the concept of knowledge, this contrast is mirrored in belief revision theories. Foundationalists in belief revision assume that there is a set of foundational beliefs that are somehow given (*data* in the literal sense of the Latin word) and may be thought of as directly, noninferentially justified. All other beliefs are justified only in so far as they can be derived in a noncircular (well-founded) way from the stock of foundational beliefs. In more formal terms, such theories presume that there is a belief base H of distinguished sentences. Foundationalists in epistemology typically take simple perceptual beliefs as foundational and sometimes claim that they are infallible. Foundationalists in belief revision leave it completely open what the foundationalist beliefs are about, whether they are true or even infallibly true.

Any arbitrary set H of sentences in L can serve as a *belief base*. No restrictions whatsoever are imposed by belief revision theories on the structure or contents of *basic beliefs*. The elements of a belief base do not have to be true, let alone infallibly true. Basic beliefs are just given, they are *data* in the literal sense of the Latin word.

In the introductory example we began by focusing on a small set of basic beliefs, but then we saw that we have to take care of all their logical consequences as well. The basic beliefs are conceived as being directly justified, but there are other beliefs that arise as consequences from more basic beliefs and have no independent standing. Hence, another factor to be decided in a formal modeling of belief states is what logic governs the language that is used for expressing the beliefs. Let Cn be a *logic* or *consequence operation* that assigns to any set H of sentences the set $Cn(H)$ of all logical consequences of H. It is commonly assumed that Cn includes classical propositional logic, and is in general quite close to it.[3]

We call H a base for the belief set K if and only if $K = Cn(H)$. *Belief sets* are sets K of sentences in L that are closed under Cn, i.e., for which $K = Cn(K)$. Belief sets are *theories* in the logician's sense. The interpretation of such a belief set is that it contains all the sentences that are accepted by a person in a given belief state. If A is an element of K, then A is *accepted in K*. If the negation $\neg A$ is an element of K, then A is *rejected in K*. Of course, in general there are also sentences A that are neither accepted nor rejected, but on which the reasoner suspends judgment. In such a case, neither A nor $\neg A$ is in K (cf. Quine and Ullian 1978: 12, on the distinction between disbelief and nonbelief). A belief set can thus be seen as a theory that is a partial description of the world.

A belief derived from a belief base is justified by those elements of the base that are used in the derivation of the belief in question.[4] As already mentioned, modelings using belief bases may be regarded as belonging to the epistemological *foundations theories*, according to which propositions should not be accepted as beliefs unless they are positively justified. In foundations theories, reasoners must keep track of the justifications for their beliefs. In contrast, *coherence theories* hold that one track of the pedigrees of one's beliefs. The focus is instead on the logical or inferential structure of the beliefs – what matters for the rationality of a belief is how it coheres with the other beliefs that are accepted in the current state, and ultimately how all of one's beliefs fit together. For the coherentist, there is no designated set of basic beliefs. All beliefs depend in some way on there being certain other beliefs that support them.

Which model is the better one as a representation of doxastic states, that using belief bases or that using full belief sets? There is no general answer to this question. As models of explicit (active, occurrent) belief, bases are psychologically more realistic since they are usually finite entities. On the other hand, changes of belief sets rather than bases represent what an ideal reasoner would do when forced to reorganize his beliefs. Belief set dynamics offers a competence model that helps us to understand what people ought to do ideally if they were not bounded by limited logical or computational reasoning capabilities. It is sometimes said that the requirement of logical closure is too extreme an idealization to merit serious consideration. But there are interpretations that make good sense of it: A belief set may be taken to represent the set of beliefs *ascribed* to a reasoner, or the set of beliefs a reasoner *is committed* to.

Another important point is neutral with respect to the particular kind of representation one chooses for beliefs and belief states: Any systematic theory of belief revision should obey the following *Principle of Categorial Matching* (Gärdenfors and Rott 1995):

(PCM)   The representation of a belief state after a belief change has taken place should be of the same format as the representation of the belief state before the change.

In the early belief revision theories of the 1980s, belief sets tended to be identified with belief states, but as we shall see from Section 7 on, richer and more elaborate entities were introduced as representations of belief states later in the development of the research paradigm initiated by AGM.

3. Kinds of Belief Change

We saw that if belief states are represented by sets of sentences, there can only be three "degrees of belief." A sentence can be accepted, rejected, or neither (then it is a nonbelief, on which the reasoner suspends judgment). We distinguish two basic types of belief change: A sentence A can be *inserted* into a belief set (turned into a belief) or *deleted* from a belief set (turned into a nonbelief). In established terminology, the former is called a *revision* by A, denoted $K*A$, and the latter a *contraction* with respect to A, denoted $K \dot{-} A$.

The term "revision" is actually used in three different senses in the literature: In its widest meaning, "belief revision" is synonymous with "belief change" and refers to any operation of transforming belief states. In a second, narrower meaning, "revision" refers to the problem of introducing a new piece of information (expressed by a sentence A) into a belief state, irrespective of the sentence's status in the prior belief state. In its third and narrowest meaning, "revision" refers to the special case where the new information is inconsistent with the prior belief set, that is, where a disbelief is turned into a belief. Such *belief-contravening revisions* are usually taken to be much more interest-

ing than the consistent case in which revisions (in the second sense) are usually identified with expansions. An *expansion* $K + A$ of a belief set K by a new piece of information A is simply formed by set-theoretic addition and subsequent logical closure: $K + A = Cn(K \cup \{A\})$. An expansion thus defined is closed under logical consequences, and it is consistent as long as A is consistent with K. However, according to the classical rule of *Ex falso quodlibet*, a single inconsistency entails any arbitrary sentence, so the expansion operation is useless for the belief-contravening case. There is only one inconsistent set closed under Cn if Cn is a standard consequence operation, and this is the set of *all* sentences in the language. Gärdenfors once called this set "epistemic hell." If a reasoner wants to preserve the consistency of his or her belief set, the inclusion of a belief-contravening piece of information requires choices for retractions that cannot be made on the basis of set theory and logic alone. We shall use the term "revision" in its second meaning in what follows.

Expansion is defined solely in logical and set theoretical terms. It is not possible to give a similarly explicit definition of revisions and contractions. The specific problems of belief revision were illustrated in our introductory example. From a logical point of view, we had several ways of constructing the revision when accommodating $\neg j$. There is no purely logical reason for making one choice rather than another among the sentences to be retracted. One has to rely on additional information concerning these sentences. What is needed is a well-defined method for constructing the revision by new information that takes into account a number of coherence constraints (see Section 4). Such a method is represented formally by a *revision function* $*$ associated with a belief set K that takes sentences A and returns as values the revised belief sets $K*A$.[5]

The contraction process faces parallel problems. Let us return to our initial example and consider the belief set K containing the sentences t, p, $p \rightarrow r$, $t \wedge r \rightarrow j$ together with all their logical consequences (among which is j). Suppose that we want to contract K with respect to j. Of course, j must be deleted from K when forming $K \dot{-} j$, but at least one of the sentences t, p, $p \rightarrow r$, or $t \wedge r \rightarrow j$ must be given up as well in order to be able to maintain deductive closure. Again there is no purely logical reason for making one choice rather than another. Deleting j from our belief set poses quite the same problems as adding $\neg j$ to it.

We have now formed an idea that the problem of belief revision (by ¬ *j*) is closely related to the problem of belief contraction (with respect to *j*). In parallel with revision functions one can introduce the concept of a *contraction function* ÷ associated with a belief set *K* that takes sentences *A* and returns as values the contracted belief sets *K*÷*A*. While for belief-contravening revision the problem of maintaining consistency is most palpable, in belief contraction there is no problem with consistency: Shrinking one's set of beliefs can never introduce an inconsistency. Instead the problem of logical closure makes itself felt rather acutely. Just removing the target sentence from a belief set is not enough; one has to make sure that this sentence cannot be re-derived from other sentences that have remained in the belief set. The common denominator to the questions raised by revision and contraction is that a corpus of beliefs is not viewed merely as a collection of atomic items, but rather as a collection of sentences from which other sentences can be derived. The interaction between an updated "database" and its derived consequences is the ultimate source of the problem of belief change. In Section 6, we shall give a more formal presentation showing how closely the problems of revision and contraction are related.

4. Coherence Constraints for Belief Revision

Rational believers should be coherent – both coherent in their beliefs at a given point of time and coherent in the ways they change their beliefs. We can distinguish three quite different interpretations of this general maxim of coherence:

- ▪ a static notion of coherence encoding the idea of a reflective equilibrium
- ▪ a dynamic notion of coherence entailing a principle of minimal change
- ▪ a dispositional notion of coherence characterizing stable preferences across different potential belief changes

The static notion of coherence refers to the set or system of beliefs held by (or ascribed to) a person at a certain point of time.[6] A minimal notion of coherence is consistency. Since one of two contradictory sentences is bound to be false and we aim at truth in our beliefs, we will want to avoid holding contradictory beliefs. Consistency is perhaps *the* major driving force of belief revision theories.[7] A more demanding idea of static

coherence is that the set of beliefs should be logically closed, that is, form a belief set in the technical sense introduced above. Consistency and closure both refer to the logic *Cn* that governs the language used by the reasoner.

The dynamic notion of coherence refers to a sequence of doxastic states, where the transition from a state to its successor state is brought about by a single application of some belief change operation. Dynamic coherence says that the whole sequence should somehow "make sense." There should not be too many and too drastic disruptions. If the sequence were too erratic, we would have problems to ascribe any meaning to the individual stages. As a kind of corollary for pairs of successive belief states, consider the changes occasioned by some new piece of input perturbing as it were the static coherence of the prior state. In such cases, dynamic coherence requires that the changes be as small as permitted by the input. The information captured in the prior beliefs should not be abandoned beyond necessity. Dynamic coherence implies a principle of conservatism or, in different terms, of informational economy, minimal change, minimum mutilation (Quine) or cognitive inertia.

The notion of dispositional coherence refers to various potential transitions from a given doxastic state to possible successor states. It compares the believer's disposition to respond to different inputs, in particular to pieces of information of related syntactic structure or logical strength. As we shall see, a typical constraint relates the change by a conjunction to the changes by the conjoined sentences taken one by one. In the introductory example, we found that the problem of revision involves a choice which of the previous beliefs (whether basic or derived) to retract. Since logic alone is silent about this matter, an important methodological problem of belief revision is to isolate extralogical factors that determine the relevant choices. It has turned out that dispositional coherence in belief revision is closely related to the coherence of choices as studied in rational choice theory. Constraints for rational choices have been brought to bear on the choices involved in syntactic or semantic constructions for belief revision processes, and were shown to be 'translatable' into rationality postulates for belief revision (Lindström 1991; Rott 1993, 2001; Schlechta 1997; Lehmann 2001).

While static coherence is basically a logical notion, dynamic and dispositional coherence are notions relating to two different concepts of economic behavior.[8] The dynamic notion says that the amount of information lost in a belief change should be kept minimal. This principle has been advertised as one of the principal driving forces of belief revision theories by many researchers. It is, however, controversial whether this is an accurate description of the ideas that the formalisms developed in belief revision theory actually encode (Rott 2000). Dispositional coherence can be interpreted as referring to the sort of rational choice as captured in the theories championed by leading economists Paul Samuelson, Kenneth Arrow, Amartya Sen, and others.

5. Different Modes of Belief Change

Foundations and coherence theories of belief (Section 2) have different implications for what should count as rational *changes* of belief systems. According to the foundations theory, belief revision should see to it that all beliefs that do not have a satisfactory justification any more are given up, while propositions that have become justified are added to the stock of beliefs. Harman (1986: 39) suggests the following principle:

Principle of Negative Undermining: One should stop believing A whenever one does not associate one's belief in A with an adequate justification (either intrinsic or extrinsic). (Variable renamed)

Thus, if a belief state is revised so that a certain belief is lost, all beliefs that depend on it for their justification should be given up in the revised state, too. According to the coherence theory, in contrast, belief revision should primarily see to it that the requirements of coherence are obeyed. The following general principle that is again due to Harman is characteristic of coherentism:

Principle of Positive Undermining: One should stop believing A whenever one positively believes one's reasons for believing A are no good. (Variable renamed)

Coherentists think that there is no *Letztbegründung* and that all justification is ultimately coherence-based. Coherence tends to keep beliefs in place, so there must be some positive reason for giving up a sentence, not just a loss of justification.

Evidently, foundations and coherence theories of belief revision are based on conflicting ideas of what constitutes a rational change of belief. Without taking sides in this matter, let us keep in mind that it is an important methodological decision how to conceptualize the relation

between the basic (or explicit) beliefs and the beliefs that can be inferred from these (derived or implicit beliefs). One has to decide whether the former should be given a privileged status in comparison to "merely" derived beliefs, or whether the pedigree of a belief should be considered irrelevant for its fate in processes of belief revision.

From the standpoint of a foundationalist epistemology, every belief set K (or every more complex belief state) is regarded as generated from a belief base H which is associated with the belief set. The belief set K is labeled as it were with its pedigree H. Belief sets are less structured than belief bases, and the correspondence between belief sets and belief bases is one–many. Two different bases H and H' may well generate the same belief set K, so presumably the result of a revision of K by A is different depending on whether K is generated from H or H'. Instead of defining revision and contraction functions on belief sets, foundationalists suggest that these functions should operate on the bases of belief sets (or of belief states), or at least with essential reference to their bases. Such functions are called *base revisions* and *base contractions*, respectively. It is then plausible to assume that a revision of a belief set K is derived from a revision of its belief base H, followed by a process of drawing inferences from the (revised) belief base:

$$K * A = Inf(H * A)$$

Here $H * A$ and $K * A$ denote the revisions of the base and theory, respectively, by the new information A. *Inf* stands for some inference operation, which may be a standard consequence operation *Cn* but may also be of a much more sophisticated, perhaps paraconsistent and nonmonotonic kind.[9] In this model, the belief base H is not taken to be a mere axiomatization of the theory K. H carries important information in its syntactic structure (and, possibly, in a prioritization of its elements[10]) that plays a crucial role in potential or actual revisions of K. For instance, two sentences A and B taken together have the same logical power as the conjunction $A \wedge B$. But if A and B are individual elements of a belief base, the withdrawal of A will not result in a withdrawal of B, whereas if the belief base instead contains the conjunction $A \wedge B$, A cannot be canceled without canceling B. In the term "$Inf(H * A)$," the asterisk "*" stands for a *revision operation* on the base level, "*Inf*" for a *reflection operation* taking the reasoner from the base level to the theory level.

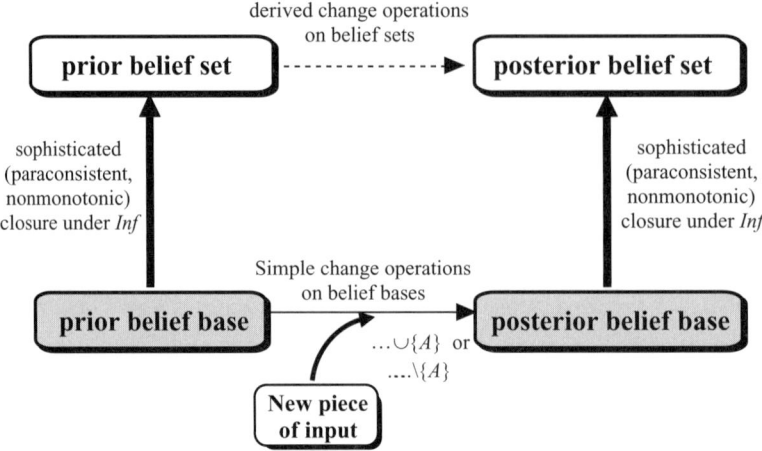

Figure 1. The immediate mode of belief revision (foundationalist perspective).

We are now in a position to distinguish two essentially different modes of performing belief changes that are suggested by the foundationalism–coherentism distinction. As foundational theories regard belief sets as generated from basic beliefs, they suggest a *direct* or *immediate* mode of belief change. In this mode, elements of belief bases are just inserted and deleted, without respect for any coherence constraints. The trivial change operations of insertion and deletion are subsequently followed by a sophisticated reflection process in which the reasoner draws inferences from the revised belief base (see Fig. 1). In a sense, the immediate mode reduces the dynamics of belief to the statics of inference relations: Revision is simple, reflection is difficult.

In contrast, the coherence view of belief states makes sense only if completed by a *logic-constrained* mode of revision. In this mode, the static or logical coherence constraints are taken as constraints controlling the very process of belief change, so that the change operations

themselves will become definitely nontrivial. In reward for these pains, the method may make use of a standard propositional logic as the inference operation (roughly, $Inf = Cn$). The reflection process reduces to the closing of the posterior set of beliefs under logical consequences. Whereas immediate belief change operates on belief bases that are not required to be logically closed, logic-constrained belief change operates on the level of belief sets, that is, on statically coherent theories (see Fig. 2). In this mode of belief change, revision is difficult, reflection is simple. This idea is most prominently instantiated by the original AGM model.[11]

Roughly speaking, immediate belief change allows the reasoner to forget the old belief *set* (or the old belief *state*) while logic-constrained belief change allows him or her to forget the old inputs (and also the old belief base).

In general, one can say that there is a trade-off here: The more challenging the task of drawing inferences from the belief base (the task of reflection, without external input) is, the easier

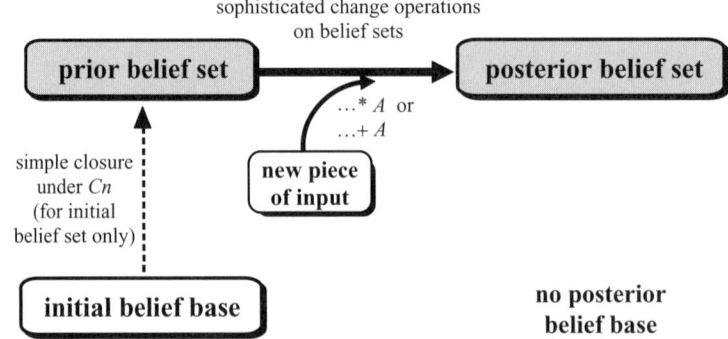

Figure 2. The logic-constrained mode of belief revision (coherentist perspective).

is the task of accommodating the input (the task of revision, of the transformation of the set of beliefs in response to some input). If one uses classical logic in the transition from a belief base to the belief set, the revision process has to take over the task of maintaining consistency. However, if some sort of paraconsistent inference operation is used in the transition from belief base to the theory, the revision process may well be allowed to introduce some "local" inconsistencies into the belief base.

6. Two Strategies for Characterizing Rational Changes of Belief

We have been dealing with very general considerations so far. When tackling belief revision in more concrete detail, two general strategies are viable. First, one can set out to make a list of desiderata that an appropriate belief revision function should fulfill. Our standards for revision and contraction functions can be laid down in various *rationality postulates*, which are typically given in the form of set-theoretic relationships. Second, one will ultimately want to present *explicit constructions* for rational changes of belief. The solution to the problem of belief revision will not be complete unless we know how to define and compute appropriate revision and contraction functions for a given belief state. We shall see that the classic constructions of belief change all make essential use of doxastic preference relations (or similar structures usable for making the necessary choices).

6.1. The Postulates Strategy

In their seminal paper, Alchourrón, Gärdenfors, and Makinson (1985) proposed a set of general *postulates* (now usually called the *AGM postulates*) for the rational revision of belief sets:

(∗1) $K*A$ is closed under Cn (*closure*)

(∗2) $A \in K*A$ (*success*)

(∗3) $K*A \subseteq K+A$ (*expansion 1*)

(∗4) If $\neg A \notin K$, then $K+A$ (*expansion 2*)
      $\subseteq K*A$

(∗5) If A is consistent, so is   (*consistency*)
      $K*A$

(∗6) If $Cn(A) = Cn(B)$,   (*extensionality*)
      then $K*A = K*B$

(∗7) $K*(A \wedge B) \subseteq (K*A)+B$ (*conjunction 1*)

(∗8) If $\neg B \notin K*A$, then   (*conjunction 2*)
      $(K*A) + B \subseteq K*(A \wedge B)$ or *rational*
      monotonicity)

We have already commented on the ideas behind closure (∗1), success (∗2) and consistency (∗5). Extensionality (∗6) says that it is the content of a new piece of information that matters, not its syntactic surface structure. The expansion postulates (∗3) and (∗4) jointly say that in the case where the new piece of information A is consistent with the belief set K, the revision is formed by set-theoretically adding A and then taking the logical closure. These are the only AGM postulates encoding the idea of minimal change. The conjunction postulates (∗7) and (∗8) compare revisions of K by a conjunction $A \wedge B$ with revisions by the first conjunct A. They state that whenever B is consistent with $K*A$, $K*(A \wedge B)$ can be identified with the expansion of $K*A$ by B.

Isaac Levi advanced the thesis that any rational belief revision occasioned by a new piece of information A is decomposable into two successive steps, namely, an elimination of the negation of A (a *contraction* with respect to $\neg A$), followed by an expansion by A (which produces no inconsistency, thanks to the previous contraction step). This suggestion, which is in accordance with the intuitive discussion of our introductory example, has become known as the *Levi identity*:

(L) $K*A = (K \dot{-} \neg A) + A$

Many authors have endorsed this suggestion and sought to reduce the problem of belief revision to the problem of withdrawing a belief from a belief set. They focused on postulates and methods of constructing belief contractions. But there is also an equation-defining contraction in terms of revision. This is the so-called *Harper identity*, which is in a rather precise sense the converse for the Levi identity:

(H) $K \dot{-} A = K \cap K * \neg A$

The contraction of a belief set K with respect to A is thus defined as that part of K that would survive K's revision by $\neg A$. Given the equations (L) and (H), the following set of *AGM postulates* for the rational contraction of belief sets has turned out to be equivalent to the set of postulates for belief revision:

(÷1) $K \dot{-} A$ is closed under Cn (*closure*)

(÷2) $K \dot{-} A \subseteq K$ (*inclusion*)

($\dot{-}$3) If $A \notin K$, then $K \dot{-} A = K$ (*vacuity*)

($\dot{-}$4) If $A \notin Cn(\emptyset)$, then $A \notin$ (*success*)
       $K \dot{-} A$

($\dot{-}$5) $K \subseteq (K \dot{-} A) + A$ (*recovery*)

($\dot{-}$6) If $Cn(A) = Cn(B)$, then (*extensionality*)
       $K \dot{-} A = K \dot{-} B$

($\dot{-}$7) $K \dot{-} A \cap K \dot{-} B \subseteq$ (*conjunction 1*)
       $K \dot{-} (A \wedge B)$

($\dot{-}$8) If $A \notin K \dot{-} (A \wedge B)$, then (*conjunction 2*)
       $K \dot{-} (A \wedge B) \subseteq K \dot{-} A$

Postulate ($\dot{-}$1) requires that the contraction of a belief set results in a belief set again. ($\dot{-}$2) says that a contraction produces a subset of the original belief set, and ($\dot{-}$3) says that this is a proper subset only if the sentence to be contracted is actually contained in the original set. The success postulate ($\dot{-}$4) requires that the sentence A to be eliminated is in fact excluded from the contracted belief set, unless A is a logical truth. The recovery postulate ($\dot{-}$5) says that one can undo contractions in the sense that contracting by A and subsequently adding A back again does not lose any prior beliefs. ($\dot{-}$6) states that it is the content of the sentence to be withdrawn that matters, not its syntactic surface structure. The conjunction postulates ($\dot{-}$7) and ($\dot{-}$8) compare contractions of K with respect to a conjunction $A \wedge B$ with contractions with respect to the conjuncts A and B. They state that any sentence that is contained both in the contraction of K with respect to A and in the contraction of K with respect to B is contained in the contraction of K with respect to $A \wedge B$. As a kind of converse, if the contraction with respect to $A \wedge B$ eliminates A, then any sentence contained in the contraction with respect to $A \wedge B$ is also contained in the contraction with respect to A. The idea of postulates ($\dot{-}$7) and ($\dot{-}$8) can be understood if one calls to mind that eliminating $A \wedge B$ in effect means eliminating A or eliminating B (or eliminating both).

The first six AGM postulates for revisions and contractions have been called the *basic* postulates, the last two *supplementary* postulates. It seems fair to say, however, that much of the power of, and of the interest in, AGM belief revision theory is due just to the latter pair of postulates. As we shall see in the next section, they entail that belief change operations are (or can be construed as being) guided by some well-behaved doxastic preference relation. In many contexts, however, postulates ($*$7) and ($*$8), and

correspondingly postulates ($\dot{-}$7) and ($\dot{-}$8), have turned out to be too strong. Interesting weakenings, for example, are the following:

($*$7c) If $B \in K * A$, then (*cut*)
       $K * (A \wedge B) \subseteq K * A$

($*$8c) If $B \in K * A$, then $K * A$ (*cautious
       $\subseteq K * (A \wedge B)$ monotonicity*)

($\dot{-}$7c) If $B \in K \dot{-} (A \wedge B)$, then
       $K \dot{-} A \subseteq K \dot{-} (A \wedge B)$

($\dot{-}$8c) If $B \in K \dot{-} (A \wedge B)$, then
       $K \dot{-} (A \wedge B) \subseteq K \dot{-} A$

The "c" in the names of these conditions means "cumulative," due to the fact that there are corresponding postulates for nonmonotonic logics that are characteristic of *cumulative reasoning* (cf. Section 9.3). Given the basic postulates, ($*$7c) and ($*$8c) taken together are equivalent to the following condition:

($*$R) If $A \in K * B$ and (*reciprocity* or
       $B \in K * A$, then   *Stalnaker*
       $K * A = K * B$ *property*)

The reciprocity condition says that if each of two sentences is believed after revision of K by the other, then these sentences lead to identical revisions of the belief set K. The corresponding condition for belief contractions is somewhat less intuitive:

($\dot{-}$R) If $A \rightarrow B \in K \dot{-} B$ and $B \rightarrow A \in K \dot{-} A$, then
       $K \dot{-} A = K \dot{-} B$

6.2. The Constructive Strategy

Logical postulates are not sufficient to determine a particular revision or contraction of K with respect to some proposition A, and this is just as it should be. For instance, if a person wants to contract successfully the belief set $K = Cn(\{p, p \rightarrow q\})$ with respect to q, he or she has to make a choice whether to give up p or to give up $p \rightarrow q$, and it is not a matter of logic or rationality which of these possibilities is to be preferred. The construction of contractions and revisions has to draw on extralogical factors such as a preference relation over the elements of K or over (some of) the subsets of K. In some constructions, the syntactic structure of the base for K is itself taken to encode such preferences (Lewis 1981; Nebel 1989, 1992). Since the 1990s, most researchers have assumed that these extralogical factors belong to, or can even be identified with, the reasoner's doxastic state. It may also be argued that external, objective criteria (like objective probability, informational content, truthlikeness, objective similarity between possible worlds) should play the key role in fixing such revision-guiding structures.[12] The crucial difference is that for models based on some objective standard, there is only one rational way to revise a given belief set in response to an input, while for subjectivists two persons with identical belief sets may well decide to choose different revisions in the face of the same input, and this is precisely because their personal belief states are different.

In the classic AGM paradigm of the 1980s, three standard methods were developed for the construction of the contraction $K \dot{-} A$ of a belief set K with respect to a sentence A.[13] The first method defines $K \dot{-} A$ as the intersection of the "best" maximal subsets of K not implying A, where what is best is determined by a doxastic preference relation (*partial meet contraction*). This method was later shown to be intimately related to a semantic modeling using possible worlds (Grove 1988, after Lewis 1973). Here $K \dot{-} A$ is defined as the set of sentences in K that are true in all maximally "plausible" worlds that do not satisfy A, where what is most plausible is determined by a system of spheres of possible worlds centered around the worlds satisfying K.[14] The second method keeps in $K \dot{-} A$ precisely those propositions of K that are "safe" in all minimal subsets of K that imply A, where again what is safe is determined by a doxastic preference relation (*safe contraction*). The third method keeps in $K \dot{-} A$, roughly speaking, those propositions that are doxastically "well-entrenched," where entrenchment relations are yet another kind of doxastic preferences (*entrenchment-based contraction*). Importantly, the doxastic preference relations used in each of these constructions are independent of the particular sentence to be contracted.

Having presented both postulates and constructions for belief change functions, it is natural to ask whether the two strategies can be connected in an enlightening way. The answer is "yes." Assuming that doxastic preferences meet a number of formal requirements (including transitivity and completeness), AGM and their followers were able to prove various *representation theorems* to the effect that a contraction operation for a belief set K satisfies the AGM postulates for contraction if and only if it can be (re-) constructed by any of the standard construction recipes. Revisions are taken care of with the help of the Levi identity. As a corollary, the three standard methods are thereby proven equivalent. This is an indirect method of proving equivalence, but there are also direct mappings linking the various sorts of doxastic preference relations used in partial meet contraction, safety relations, and entrenchment relations in such a way that preference relations mapped onto one another lead to the same belief change functions.[15]

The concept of entrenchment is particularly interesting because it has several quite diverse interpretations. Suppose that a belief set K is generated from a preordered belief base H, i.e., that $K = Cn(H)$, and there is a reflexive and transitive preference relation (i.e., a preorder) $\leq$ on H specifying the importance or certainty of the basic beliefs. Then an element A of K can be called more entrenched than another element B of K if there is a subset of H implying A the $\leq$-weakest element of which is $\leq$-stronger than the $\leq$-weakest element of any subset of H that implies B. This is a *positive* concept of entrenchment, saying intuitively that there is a more certain way of obtaining A than of obtaining B. But an alternative concept makes equally good sense. The idea is that an element A of K can be called more entrenched than another element B of K if for every subset H_1 of H not implying A there is another subset H_2 of H not implying B which is "better" than H_1 in the following sense: There is an element of H lost in H_1 but not in H_2 which is $\leq$-stronger than any element of H lost in H_2 but not in H_1. This is a *negative* concept of entrenchment, saying intuitively that there are less costly ways of getting rid of B than there are ways of getting rid of A. It can be shown that negative entrenchment is a refinement of positive entrenchment. Negative entrenchment introduces incomparabilities, while all beliefs are comparable in terms of the less discriminating positive entrenchment relation. Yet another, much more general but less constructive interpretation is to consider entrenchment as a *revealed preference relation* that can be abstracted from binary choices between beliefs: A is more entrenched in K than B if the contraction of K with respect to $A \wedge B$ (which, as noted earlier, comes down to the contraction of K with respect to at least one of A and B) contains A but does not contain B. Clearly, this idea is reconstructive rather than constructive, since it presumes that a method of belief contraction is already given. But it captures the meaning of the term "entrenchment" very well, and it does not presuppose that the belief set K is generated from a particular (prioritized) belief base H.

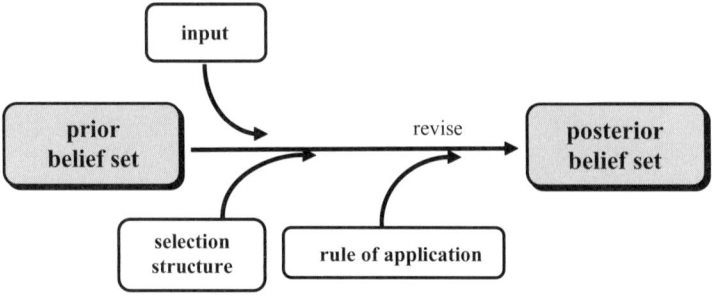

Figure 3. Elements of AGM-style theories of belief change.

While the idea of informational economy has played a rather modest role in AGM-style theorizing of belief revision, economical ideas have always formed an essential part of belief revision theories through the systematic study of the structure and application of preference relations to cognitive choice problems. Varying (usually weakening) the formal requirements for the relevant preference relations results in variations (usually weakenings) of the seventh and eighth AGM postulates. As already mentioned, the full set of AGM postulates is rather strong. Some natural relaxations of the requirements for preference relations (including the renunciation of completeness) lead to the postulates (∗7c) and (∗8c) mentioned in the last section. One can indeed show that insights gained in rational choice theory over the last four or five decades can be applied in quite a straightforward way to choice problems involved in belief change processes – choices concerning least plausible sentences or concerning most plausible possible worlds (Rott 2001). Seen from this perspective, the problem of belief revision is just an instantiation of the general problem of rational choice, with some additional constraints set up by the background logic Cn. While the formation and transformation of belief sets or theories would usually be classed as a problem of theoretical reason, the making of choices belongs to the realm of practical reason. The observation that from a purely formal point of view, the former falls under the latter is indeed a surprising result. However, the interpretation of this observation is far from clear. Should we take the use of choice functions as indicating that believers are free to decide to believe or not to believe a proposition according to their preferences (*doxastic voluntarism*)? Are they free to adopt the doxastic preferences as they wish? Or are such choices predetermined in a way similar to the choices of chess computers that are bound

to make the moves they evaluate as best in a perfectly deterministic and mechanical way? We have to leave these questions open here, but it is worth pointing out that only part of the problem of belief change, namely, the dispositional coherence part of the classic AGM theory, is within the reach of rational choice theory. As we shall see in Sections 8 and 9, this theory needs itself to be extended and revised in various ways. Rational choice theory cannot be brought to bear, for instance, on the problem of iterated belief change that goes well beyond AGM.

7. An Abstract View of the Elements of Belief Change

The problem of iterated belief change requires us to take a more abstract point of view. Belief change theories deal with the transformation of belief states (doxastic states) in response to incoming information. We have seen that we need more than just logical and set-theoretical means to tackle this task. In the beginning of belief revision theory as represented by the classic AGM framework, the following elements were involved in a single transition episode (see Fig. 3):

- a prior belief set
- a piece of input
- a selection structure
- a rule of how to apply the selection structure
- a posterior belief set

The belief state of a person was identified by AGM (more implicitly than explicitly) with his or her belief set, and accordingly, the revision functions operated on the belief sets. The selection structure, typically some preference relation or choice function, was *used*, but it never took center stage as an object of the discussion. This theory was formally beautiful, but it

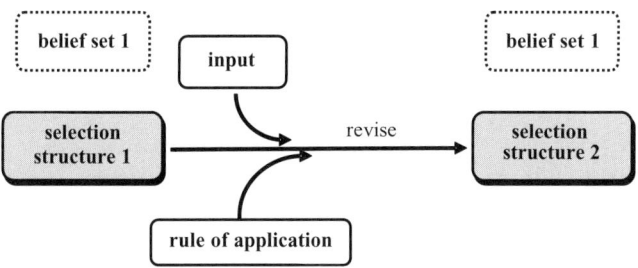

Figure 4. Elements of theories of iterated belief change.

remained silent about the question where the selection structure comes from. It was unclear whether the selection structure was conceived as an objective feature of the world, to be understood either on a priori or on empirical grounds, or whether it formed part of the reasoner's subjective belief state.[16] Support for the latter interpretation can be found in the fact that it was often assumed that the selection structure somehow "fits" the belief set. To see what is meant by that, one must know that for each selection structure there is a consistent belief set that can be retrieved from it. In the possible worlds modeling, for instance, the belief set of a person is determined by the set of sentences satisfied in all maximally plausible worlds according to the person's system of spheres. In the entrenchment modeling, it is determined as the set of sentences that are more than minimally entrenched according to his or her doxastic preferences. If a person's beliefs are exactly the ones associated with the person's doxastic preferences, the latter *fit* his or her belief set.

A few years after the AGM program had been started, changes of *belief bases* were suggested as an alternative, possibly more realistic model for human belief change (Nebel 1989, 1992; Fuhrmann 1991; Hansson 1991). It is important to see that belief bases can function as selection structures. First, the belief set can be retrieved from the belief base, by processing the latter with the help of a more or less sophisticated inference operation (we mentioned non-standard, paraconsistent, and nonmonotonic logics). Second, the relevant change functions operate on the belief base level rather than on the belief set level (cf. Section 5). Third, belief bases may themselves come with a preference relation, often called the prioritization of the elements of the base, and in such cases one needs to devise inference processes that respect and exploit the priorities as well as the syntactic structures of the basic beliefs. Depending on the inference oper-

ation applied, generating a belief set from the belief base can be, but need not be, a highly demanding task.

With the benefit of hindsight, one can interpret theories of belief base change as suggesting that belief bases should be regarded as more adequate representations of belief states than belief sets. Bases possess more structure than belief sets. The insight that belief states are more than just belief sets, however, gained wide currency only when the problem of *iteration* was attacked systematically in the 1990s. In order to be prepared for repeated belief changes, a reasoner needs not only a revised belief set after each step in the sequence, but also a new revision-guiding selection structure. Two ways of solving this problem are possible. One can either take the concept of belief state as primitive (Darwiche and Pearl 1997) and *assign* a belief set and a selection structure to a given belief state, or one can take the view that belief states can be *identified* with, or simply *are*, selection structures. This, I think, is the view implicit in most works on iterated belief revision, and the picture that emerges is shown in Fig. 4.

Here revision functions do not operate on the belief sets any more, but on selection structures, and this is what makes iterations possible in the first place. From such structures, we have already seen, belief sets can readily be retrieved. Preference relations are the paradigmatic selection structures. A variety of change functions on preference relations have been proposed in the literature (more on this in Section 8).

Recently, a further generalization of this picture has been developed in the field of *belief merging* (also known as *belief fusion*). The inputs of qualitative belief change processes have quite long been thought of as purely propositional in nature. But there is no reason to restrict inputs to such a format. Inputs may be much more finely structured than that. In fact, the input can even be a full selection structure, so that the prior

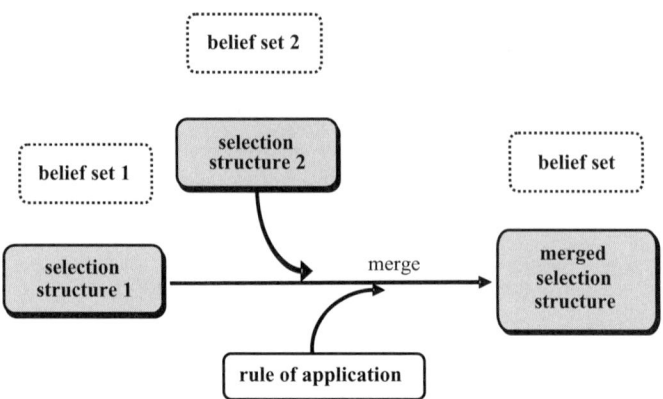

Figure 5. Elements of theories of belief merging for two reasoners.

belief state and the input have precisely the same format. This kind of input can most naturally be taken to be the belief state of another reasoner. The picture that surfaces for the two-person case is shown in Fig. 5.

Having gone that far, it is a small step to the merging of the belief states of any (finite) number of reasoners. Ordinary revision by a propositional input can in this model be mimicked by the merging with a very coarse-grained selection structure (e.g., by a system of spheres of possible worlds, or an entrenchment relation, with only two or three levels). The idea of belief merging is an important advancement of the theory of belief revision.

8. Iterated Changes of Belief

There is an almost universal consensus about how to use selection structures in one-step belief revision. If these structures satisfy the formal properties required by AGM, then the solution to the problem of belief change in response to a single piece of input is the AGM solution.[17] Iterated belief change, or equivalently, the change of selection-structures, however, exhibits substantial ambiguities (Darwiche and Pearl 1994, 1997). Even within the narrow confines of the technical framework of classic revision (no numbers, only propositional inputs), there are quite a few models that have been proposed.[18] I shall focus on four particularly important ones, taking the terminology from Rott (2003b). These models usually confirm the application of the AGM postulates to one-step belief change, but they also have at least one additional rule taking care of iterations.

The first method uses one and the same selection structure for all possible belief sets (the method is surveyed in Areces and Becher 2001). As this selection structure in general does not fit the reasoner's current belief set, it cannot represent his or her belief state, but is *external* to it. In contrast, the other three methods may be interpreted as identifying the belief state with the selection structure. The second method is *radical* in that the input is given uncompromising priority over the previous beliefs; any world or situation that does not satisfy the input is considered maximally implausible after the revision (Segerberg 1998; Friedman and Halpern 1999). The third method, in contrast to the second one, is maximally *conservative*; the selection structure is changed so that the input just gets accepted, but the changes made are absolutely minimal, and as a consequence the newly acquired information is very easily lost in further belief changes (Boutilier 1993, 1996). The fourth method is *moderate* in that it opts for an intermediate way between the second and the third methods; it recommends giving high priority to the incoming information, but it does not wipe out all plausibility distinctions between worlds or situations not complying with it (Nayak 1994; Nayak, Pagnucco, and Peppas 2003).

Each of these methods can be axiomatically characterized by a single axiom taking care of the iteration case. In the following axioms, the belief set K should be taken to be a fixed starting point.[19]

External revision (invariable selection structure with associated belief set F)[20]

$$(K*A)*B = \begin{cases} (K*A) + B & \text{if B is consistent} \\ & \text{with } K*A \\ F*B & \text{otherwise} \end{cases}$$

Radical reversion

$$(K*A)*B = K*(A \wedge B)$$

Conservative revision

$$(K*A)*B = \begin{cases} (K*A) + B & \text{if } B \text{ is consistent} \\ & \text{with } K*A \\ K*B & \text{otherwise} \end{cases}$$

Moderate revision

$$(K*A)*B = \begin{cases} K*(A \wedge B) & \text{if } B \text{ is consistent} \\ & \text{with } A \\ K*B & \text{otherwise} \end{cases}$$

All of these methods are well-defined independently of the presence of the seventh and eighth AGM axioms, that is, whether the reasoner's dispositions for one-step belief change are coherent or not (Rott 2003b). The belief set resulting from any finite number of revision steps can be generated inductively by repeated applications of the respective axiom. We can see that according to each method, two revision steps can be reduced to one-step revision, usually by means of some characteristic case distinction.[21] Radical revision is the only method that has no case distinction, and it leads to the inconsistent belief set as soon as the incoming information happens to be contradictory.[22] The lower lines of the other three methods indicate that earlier evidence is prone to be forgotten if inconsistencies with later evidence arise. Moderate revision appears to be the most reasonable method, because it forgets A only if B is inconsistent with A, and an inconsistency of B with A is much less likely to arise than an inconsistency of B with the full belief set $K*A$.

Summing up, we have seen that there are a number of competing models for iterated belief change, each of which appears to be adequate for some purposes. But it is not difficult to come up with examples showing that each of these methods has its drawbacks. At the time of writing, no-one has put forward a *methodology* that would tell us when to use which method or combination of methods.[23] Which of all these methods makes sense for which kinds of applications or contexts? And the same questions that we asked about the selection structures a few pages ago, can now be raised about the rules for changing selection structures: Where do they come from? Should we think of them as forming a part of the reasoner's belief state, of another compartment of the reasoner's mind, or are they external, subject to objective criteria and constraints? How do

we, and how should we, go about selecting the rules for changing selection structures?

9. Further Developments

9.1. *Variants and Extensions of Belief Revision*

The field of belief revision has widened considerably since the time of the classic AGM model. There have been numerous interesting developments of which we briefly mention only three and present a fourth one in slightly more detail. All of these extensions capture AGM-style belief revision as a limiting case; none of them is reducible to the classic AGM belief change theory.

Multiple revisions are occasioned by sets of sentences that have to be accepted or to be withdrawn simultaneously (Fuhrmann and Hansson 1994; Zhang and Foo 2001). In *nonprioritized belief revision*, reasoners do not invariably incorporate the new information, but first decide in the light of (a designated part of) his or her current belief state whether or not a belief change should take place at all (Hansson 1997; Chopra, Ghose, and Meyer 2003). *Two-dimensional belief revision* is a method that changes beliefs in response to imperatives of the form "Accept A with a degree of plausibility that at least equals that of B" (Cantwell 1997; Fermé and Rott 2004; Rott 2007). Put differently, one can say that this belief change operation takes two arguments, an *input sentence A* and a *reference sentence B*, or that the input is of the form "$B \leq A$." This method of changing belief states has both characteristics of belief revision (with respect to the input sentence) and characteristics of belief contraction (with respect to the reference sentence). Two-dimensional belief revision is much more flexible than the methods of iterated belief revision mentioned in Section 8. For instance, beliefs can be *lowered* and non-beliefs can be *raised* in doxastic status while still remaining beliefs and non-beliefs, respectively.

9.2. *Updates*

An important distinction arising already on the level of ordinary one-step belief change is marked by Katsuno and Mendelzon's (1992) terminological distinction between *revisions* and *updates*. Revisions are prompted by new information about a ("static") world that has not changed, while updates are prompted by information about changes in the ("dynamic") world. The difference comes out best by a possible worlds representation of the case where the new piece of information A is consistent with the belief set K. Revisions by A make a person eliminate from the set of worlds he or she deems possible those worlds that do not satisfy A. If you learn that David is the head of the department, with the understanding that this has been the case for a while, then you just cut off all possible worlds in which someone else is head of the department (this was already recommended by AGM). In contrast, if you learn that David is head of the department with the understanding that he has just been appointed head of the department, then you keep all your possible worlds and continue as it were every single one of them by letting David become head of the department there. So an update by A makes a person consider, for each world he or she deems possible, how the world would develop if A were brought about in this world. A formal mark of such updates is that they violate postulate (∗4) and instead satisfy the following monotonicity condition

(∗Ml) If $K_1 \subseteq K_2$, then   (∗-monotonicity
        $K_1 * A \subseteq K_2 * A$.   left)

(∗Ml) is a paradigmatic nontheorem of classic AGM-style belief revision (see Gärdenfors 1988: Ch. 7).

9.3. *Default Inferences as Expectation Revision*

Given the information that Tweety is a bird (A), your belief set will typically include that Tweety can fly, but given the information that Tweety is a penguin (B), which of course implies that Tweety is a bird, you will *not* believe that Tweety can fly (but instead believe that Tweety cannot fly). Thus belief revision theories characteristically fail to validate the following monotonicity principle

(∗Mr) If $A \in Cn(B)$, then   (∗-monotonicity
        $K * A \subseteq K * B$.   right)

The fact that belief revision theories violate (∗Mr) indicates that they can serve to model patterns of *defeasible* or *nonmonotonic reasoning*. It has been one of the most important insights of logic-based AI research of the past twenty-five years that for the basic inference patterns used in commonsense reasoning, an extension of the set of premises not only *gains*, but often *loses*

some conclusions that were drawn on the basis of the smaller premise set (Ginsberg 1987; Gabbay, Hogger, and Robinson 1994). You lose your belief in Tweety's ability to fly after gaining the new information that Tweety is a penguin. If you don't know that a particular bird doesn't fly, you take it that it flies. Everyday reasoning thus does not conform to (all) the rules of classical logic. The *argument from ignorance* or *appeal to ignorance* that has traditionally been dismissed as fallacious turns out to be, if judiciously employed, a useful and powerful scheme of ordinary reasoning. Inference operations *Inf* allowing for such nonmonotonic phenomena violate the following central rule of ordinary (Tarskian) logics

(M)   If $H \subseteq H'$, then   (*Inf-monotonicity*)
        $Inf(H) \subseteq Inf(H')$.

Makinson and Gärdenfors (1991) and Gärdenfors and Makinson (1994) proposed that the set of defeasible consequences $Inf(H)$ of a finite set of premises $H = \{A_1, \dots, A_n\}$ should be regarded as the theory that results from the revision of some set of *background assumptions*, *defaults*, or *expectations* E by the conjunction of the premise set H. They suggested the following identity

(I) $Inf(H) = E * (A_1 \wedge \dots \wedge A_n)$

For the inference relation *Inf* thus defined, adding information can defeat previously drawn conclusions, as we see when we enlarge the singleton premise set containing only 'Tweety is a bird' (A_1) with the sentence "Tweety is a penguin" (A_2). Given our expectations, the input A_1 makes us conclude that Tweety can fly, whereas the input A_2 (which, given our background theory, is equivalent with $A_1 \wedge A_2$) will make us draw the opposite conclusion.

Defeasible or nonmonotonic inference operations are quite irregular as compared to Tarskian logics. The failure of (M) is indeed incisive. However, commonsense reasoning nevertheless appears to leave intact quite a number of important classical inference patterns (Gabbay 1985; Kraus, Lehmann, and Magidor 1990; Makinson 1994, 2005). In the following, we identify finite premise sets with the conjunction of their elements and apply *Inf* to single sentences only. An inference relation is called *cumulative* if it satisfies the following six conditions:

Reflexivity $A \in Inf(A)$

Left Logical   If $Cn(A) = Cn(B)$, then
Equivalence $Inf(A) = Inf(B)$

Right Weakening	If $B \in Inf(A)$ and $C \in Cn(B)$, then $C \in Inf(A)$
And	If $B \in Inf(A)$ and $C \in Inf(A)$, then $B \wedge C \in Inf(A)$
Cut	If $B \in Inf(A)$, then $Inf(A \wedge B) \subseteq Inf(A)$
Cautious Monotonicity	If $B \in Inf(A)$, then $Inf(A) \subseteq Inf(A \wedge B)$

A cumulative inference relation Inf is *preferential* if it also satisfies the rule Or; it is *rational*, if it in addition satisfies Or and Rational Monotonicity:

Or	$Inf(A) \cap Inf(B) \subseteq Inf(A \vee B)$
Rational Monotonicity	If $\neg B \notin Inf(A)$, then $Inf(A) \subseteq Inf(A \wedge B)$

Makinson and Gärdenfors proved the following results. If a revision function * satisfies the AGM postulates (*1)–(*8), then the inference operation *Inf* generated by equation (I) has all the properties required of a rational inference relation. And conversely, for any rational inference operation *Inf*, there is a set E and a revision function * satisfying (*1)–(*8) such that *Inf* can be represented by equation (I). Similar correspondence theorems were shown for cumulative reasoning and the set consisting of (*1)–(*6) plus (*7c) and (*8c), and also for preferential reasoning and the set (*1)–(*7) plus (*8c). The expectation set E implicit in an inference operation *Inf* can be defined as $Inf(\text{TAUT})$, where TAUT is an arbitrary tautology. Results such as these suggest that belief change and defeasible reasoning are just "two sides of the same coin" (Gärdenfors).

9.4. Belief Merging

Arguably the most important of the recent developments is the field of *belief merging* or *belief fusion* that is concerned with the rational aggregation of two or more belief states (Baral et al. 1991, 1992; Revesz 1993, 1997; Nayak 1994; Liberatore and Schaerf 1997; Konieczny and Pino-Pérez 1998, 2002). In many versions, negotiation procedures or aggregation processes similar to those known from social choice theory find application in belief merging.

As our prime example, we present the axioms for *merging with integrity constraints* introduced by Konieczny and Pino-Pérez (2002). Following these authors, we use a finitary language, so that a belief set K can be represented by a single sen-

tence, viz., the conjunction of representatives of the equivalence classes of K under Cn. With a slight abuse of notation, we identify belief sets with the sentences representing them in the following. Let K_i be the belief set of reasoner i. A *belief profile P* is a multiset of (finitary) belief sets $[K_1, \ldots, K_n]$.[24]

While belief merging should be thought of as primarily combining belief states of several agents, room is also made for propositional "inputs" in the original AGM sense. This is what Konieczny and Pino-Pérez call "constraints," with the formal idea that any resulting belief set must contain the specified constraint. This is an analogue to the AGM postulate of "success." Now we are ready for the official definition. An operator * taking pairs consisting of a belief profile and a single sentence (representing an "integrity constraint" or, in our terminology, an "input"[25]) and returning belief sets is an operator of merging with constraints if and only if it satisfies the following postulates:

(KP0) $A \in [K_1, \ldots, K_n]*A$

(KP1) If A is consistent, so is $[K_1, \ldots, K_n]*A$

(KP2) If $K_1, \ldots, K_n$ are jointly consistent with A, then $[K_1, \ldots, K_n]*A = Cn(K_1 \wedge \ldots \wedge K_n \wedge A)$

(KP3) If $[K_1, \ldots, K_n]$ and $[K'_1, \ldots, K'_n]$ are member-wise equivalent under Cn and if $Cn(A) = Cn(A')$, then $[K_1, \ldots, K_n]*A = [K'_1, \ldots, K'_n]*A'$.

(KP4) If $A \in K \cap K'$ and $[K, K']*A$ is consistent with K, then $[K, K']*A$ is also consistent with K'.

(KP5) $[K_1, \ldots, K_n, K'_1, \ldots, K'_m]*A \subseteq Cn([K_1, \ldots, K_n]*A \cup [K'_1, \ldots, K'_m]*A)$

(KP6) If $[K_1, \ldots, K_n]*A$ is consistent with $[K'_1, \ldots, K'_m]*A$, then $[K_1, \ldots, K_n]*A \subseteq [K_1, \ldots, K_n, K'_1, \ldots, K'_m]*A$

(KP7) $[K_1, \ldots, K_n]*(A \wedge B) \subseteq ([K_1, \ldots, K_n]*A) + B)$

(KP8) If $[K_1, \ldots, K_n]*A$ is consistent with B, then $([K_1, \ldots, K_n]*A) + B \subseteq [K_1, \ldots, K_n]*(A \wedge B)$

Intuitively, $[K_1, \ldots, K_n]*A$ is the belief set that results from merging the beliefs of n reasoners under the constraint that A be accepted. Belief merging is an important generalization of the classic belief revision paradigm. An *AGM-style revision* is obtained from it by taking $n = 1$. An operator of *pure merging* (without "input" or "integrity constraint") can be defined by fixing a tautology as input. Postulates (KP1)–(KP3), (KP7), and (KP8) are easily recognized as counterparts to AGM postulates. Merging proper is dealt with by postulates (KP4)–(KP6). Postulate (KP4) is a fairness condition saying that if the constraint is satisfied by the belief sets of two players, the merging of both belief sets should not result in a belief set consistent with one but inconsistent with the other. Postulates (KP5) and (KP6) say, roughly, that if the constraint is fixed and no intermediate inconsistency arises, the merging of a belief profile of size $n + m$ can be achieved by merging subprofiles of size n and size m separately, and then taking the union of the two results and closing under logical consequences. Konieczny and Pino-Pérez show that the merging postulates can be modified or supplemented in a wide variety of interesting ways. They also provide a constructive approach by giving appropriate representation theorems for the basic as well as the modified and supplemented models.[26]

10. Concluding Remarks

After a quarter of a century's work, the field of belief revision is well established today. Some may say that the magic that dwells in each beginning has vanished, but a sizable bulk of knowledge has been accumulated, and important new developments have been initiated, particularly in iterated belief change and belief merging. Research in belief revision originally started out in philosophy and is now most actively pursued in computer science, but it is still an essentially interdisciplinary undertaking. On the one hand, for instance, there are difficult technical problems best addressed by mathematicians; on the other hand, psychologists have become interested because they are looking for clear-cut models of some interesting cognitive processes. There are certainly countless exciting things to explore. One of the tasks ahead is to develop a methodology for when to apply which of the many models on offer. Belief revision theory should be useful after all. Another task is to close the gap between idealized models of perfectly rational reasoners and the actual facts about the limited computational and logical capacities of human beings. Whether we view it from a normative or an empirical perspective, the formation and transformation of beliefs is a problem that raises

its head just about everywhere, and it will stay with us as an object of scientific theorizing for a long time to come.

Acknowledgments

I would like to thank Jonathan Adler, Guido Löhrer, Patrick Peindl, Matthias Söllner, and, in particular, Ralf Busse for valuable comments on an earlier version of this paper.

Notes

1   The terms "belief state" and "doxastic state" are used as synonyms throughout this paper.

2   In probability theory, plain conditionalization (which assigns probability 1 to new evidence) may be replaced by Jeffrey conditionalization with a certain parameter α which specifies the posterior probability of the new evidence at any arbitrary value between 0 and 1 (cf. Jeffrey 1965): $P_{A,\alpha}(B) = \alpha \cdot (P(A \wedge B)/P(A)) + (1 - \alpha) \cdot (P(\neg A \wedge B)/P(\neg A))$. In Spohn's (1988) model of ordinal conditional functions (now often called "ranking functions," Goldszmidt and Pearl 1992), beliefs are fully accepted, but inputs are accompanied by a value α of certainty as well: $\kappa_{A,\alpha}(B) = \min\{\kappa(A \wedge B) - \kappa(A), \alpha + \kappa(\neg A \wedge B) - \kappa(\neg A)\}$. Note that in these theories the input proposition *can* and *must* be qualified by a number that specifies the new proposition's degree of certainty or plausibility.

3   More precisely, the logic Cn is usually supposed to be *Tarskian*, that is, reflexive ($H \subseteq Cn(H)$), monotonic (if $H \subseteq H'$, then $Cn(H) \subseteq Cn(H')$), idempotent ($Cn(Cn(H)) \subseteq Cn(H)$), and compact (if $A \in Cn(H)$, then $A \in Cn(H')$ for some finite $H' \subseteq H$).

4   Being derived from a belief base through the application of Cn is only a very crude notion of justification. For more interesting ideas about justification in belief change, see Haas (2005).

5   Many authors present revision functions as two-place functions taking a pair of a belief set and a sentence and returning a new belief set. This way of putting things appears misleading to me, since one and the same belief set may be associated with different belief revision strategies, so * as acting on pairs ⟨K,A⟩ cannot be function in the K argument. This issue is a delicate one. For more details, see Rott (1999).

6   The term "static" is not meant to deny that the drawing of inferences is a process that takes time. I use the term here just to indicate that no input coming from the external world disturbs the belief state. Changes of the latter kind are "dynamic" phenomena in my terminology.

7   The consistency requirement can be seen as marking off the enterprise of belief revision from that of paraconsistent logic, which shares the aim

of explicating rational deliberation in the face of contradictory information. A logic or inference operation is paraconsistent if it does not satisfy the classical rule of *Ex falso quodlibet*, that is, if not everything is derivable from a classically inconsistent set of premises (Priest, Routley, and Norman 1989).

8   See Rott (2003a). An important way of deriving recipes for belief revision from decision-theoretic principles has been vigorously advocated by Isaac Levi (1991, 2004).

9   For paraconsistency, see footnote 7; for non-monotonicity, see Section 9.3.

10 A prioritization of a belief base is a preorder, that is, a transitive and connected relation, that reflects the priorities, or the degrees of importance, of the elements of the base.

11 I have been neglecting here an important mode located 'between' the direct mode and the logic-constrained mode. The change operation may be applied on belief bases and respect consistency, that is, the first half of static coherence, while ignoring the second half, closure. In this mode, revision is difficult and reflection may be performed with the simple logic $Inf = Cn$ (for a comprehensive and detailed treatment of various ways to implement this mode, see Hansson 1999). Thus the dichotomy between foundationalism and coherentism is not identical with that between the immediate and the direct mode. The foundationalist approach (change operations on belief bases rather than theories) is compatible with both the immediate mode and the logic-constrained mode. The coherence approach makes sense only if combined with the logic-constrained mode of belief revision.

12 See for instance Schlechta (1991), Hansson (1991), Katsuno and Mendelzon (1991), and Koncieczny and Pino-Pérez (2002). In computer science, the most common way of measuring distances between possible worlds (or models) is to set-theoretically compare or to count the atoms on which two worlds differ (the so-called Hamming distance). This concept of distance is independent of the belief state of the reasoner. Clearly, such ideas do not achieve full objectivity, since distances thus conceived are dependent on the language used to describe the world.

13 For more detailed overviews, see Gärdenfors (1988), Gärdenfors and Rott (1995), and Hansson (1999).

14 A system of spheres of possible worlds is equivalent to a complete preorder on the set of possible worlds – yet another closely related semantic modeling influential in belief revision theory (Katsuno and Mendelzon 1991).

15 For further discussion of the two strategies cf. Makinson (1985). More material about a great variety of representation theorems can be found in Gärdenfors (1988), Hansson (1999), Bochman (2001), and Rott (2001).

16 We shall soon encounter the surprising idea that a selection structure may also be (part of) the input.

17 Even though the AGM solution was more or less universally acclaimed, there were some significant discussions concerning most notably "updates" (see Section 9.2) and "withdrawals" (Pagnucco and Rott 1999; Levi 2004) of belief.

18 See Konieczny and Pino-Pérez (2000), Rott (2003b), and von Ditmarsch (2005).

19 Alternatively, the symbol K may be taken to stand, by abuse of notation, for a full belief *state* rather than a belief *set*. Compare Darwiche and Pearl (1997).

20 We should emphasize here that not all methods that may justly be called "external" validate this axiom scheme. Methods based on global (i.e., belief-state independent) similarities or distances between possible worlds are external, but their logical behavior is very different (more complicated and more interesting) in that they do take the current belief set into account in the case of a belief-contravening revision step. See Lehmann, Magidor, and Schlechta (2001).

21 This is true on the level of *belief sets*, but not on the level of *belief states* (selection structures).

22 There is a slightly less radical version of this operation that puts $(K*A)*B = K*(A \wedge B)$ if B is consistent with A, and $(K*A)*B = Cn(B)$ otherwise.

23 Notice that we need to provide for a mix of methods anyway, since in repeated belief changes reasoners are likely to encounter problems of contraction as well as revision.

24 Multisets are collections of objects at a level of abstraction between sets and sequences. The number of occurrences of the members in a multiset matters, but their order doesn't. For example, $[K, K, K']$ is identical with $[K, K', K]$, but different from $[K, K']$. In order to ensure continuity with our presentation, I have adapted Konieczny and Pino-Pérez's terminology. We call belief set what they call belief base, and we call belief profile what they call belief set. I have also adapted the notation of Konieczny and Pino-Pérez for easy comprehension in the context of this paper. Where they write $\Delta_A(P)$, I write $[K_1, \ldots, K_n]*A$.

25 Here the cautionary remark of footnote 5 does not apply because Konieczny and Pino-Pérez deliberately employ similarity relations that are external to the reasoner's belief states.

26 Konieczny and Pino-Pérez make use of a preorder semantics in the style of Katsuno-Mendelzon; cf. footnote 14.

References

Alchourrón, Carlos, Peter Gärdenfors, and David Makinson, On the Logic of Theory Change: Partial Meet Contraction and Revision Functions,

Journal of Symbolic Logic 50 (1985), 510–530.

Areces, Carlos, and Veronica Becher, Iterable AGM Functions, in Mary-Anne Williams and Hans Rott (eds.), *Frontiers of Belief Revision*, Dordrecht, Kluwer 2001, pp. 261–277.

Baral, Chitta, Sarit Kraus and Jack Minker, Combining multiple knowledge bases, *IEEE Transactions on Knowledge and Data Engineering* 3 (1991), 208–220.

Baral, Chitta, Sarit Kraus, Jack Minker and V. S. Subrahmanian, Combining multiple knowledge bases consisting of first order theories, *Computational Intelligence* 8 (1992), 45–71.

Bochman, Alexander, *A Logical Theory of Nonmonotonic Inference and Belief Change*, Berlin, Springer 2001.

Boutilier, Craig, Revision Sequences and Nested Conditionals, in R. Bajcsy (ed.), *IJCAI-93 – Proceedings of the Thirteenth International Joint Conference on Artificial Intelligence*, San Mateo, CA: Morgan Kaufmann 1993, 519– 525.

Boutilier, Craig, Iterated Revision and Minimal Change of Conditional Beliefs, *Journal of Philosophical Logic* 25 (1996), 263–305.

Cantwell, John, On the Logic of Small Changes in Hypertheories, *Theoria* 63 (1997), 54–89.

Chopra, Samir, Aditya Ghose and Thomas Meyer, Non-prioritised Ranked Belief Change, *Journal of Philosophical Logic* 32 (2003), 417–443.

Cohen, L. Jonathan, *The Probable and the Provable*, Clarendon Press, Oxford 1977.

Darwiche, Adnan, and Judea Pearl, On the Logic of Iterated Belief Revision, in Ronald Fagin, ed., *TARK '94 – Proceedings of the Fifth Conference on Theoretical Aspects of Reasoning About Knowledge*, Pacific Grove, CA: Morgan Kaufmann 1994, 5–23.

Darwiche, Adnan, and Judea Pearl, On the Logic of Iterated Belief Revision, *Artificial Intelligence* 89 (1997), 1–29.

Dubois, Didier, and Henri Prade, *Possibility Theory. An Approach to the Computerized Processing of Uncertainty*, New York, Plenum Press 1988.

Ellis, Brian, *Rational Belief Systems*, Oxford 1979.

Fermé, Eduardo, and Hans Rott, Revision by Comparison, *Artificial Intelligence* 157 (2004), 5–47.

Friedman, Nir, and Joseyph Y. Halpern, Belief Revision: A Critique, *Journal of Logic, Language and Information* 8 (1999), 401–420.

Fuhrmann, André, Theory Contraction Through Base Contraction, *Journal of Philosophical Logic* 20 (1991), 175–203.

Fuhrmann, André, *An Essay on Contraction*, Stanford, CA: CSLI Publications 1997.

Fuhrmann, André, and Sven Ove Hansson, A Survey of Multiple Contractions, *Journal of Logic, Language and Information* 3 (1994), 39–76.

Fuhrmann, André, and Michael Morreau (eds.), *The Logic of Theory Change*, Berlin, Springer 1991.

Fuhrmann, André, and Hans Rott (eds.), *Logic, Action, and Information. Essays on Logic in Philosophy and Artificial Intelligence*, Berlin/New York 1995.

Gabbay, Dov M., Theoretical Foundations for Nonmonotonic Reasoning in Expert Systems, in Krzysztof Apt (ed.), *Logics and Models of Concurrent Systems*, Berlin, Springer 1985, 439–457.

Gabbay, D. M., C. J. Hogger and J. A. Robinson (eds.), *Handbook of Logic in Artificial Intelligence and Logic Programming*, Volume III: Nonmonotonic Reasoning and Uncertain Reasoning, Oxford: Oxford University Press 1994.

Gabbay, D. M., C. J. Hogger and J. A. Robinson (eds.), *Handbook of Logic in Artificial Intelligence and Logic Programming*, Volume IV: Epistemic and Temporal Reasoning, Oxford: Oxford University Press 1995.

Gabbay, Dov, and Philippe Smets (eds.), Belief Change, Vol. III of the *Handbook of Defeasible Reasoning and Uncertainty Management Systems*, Dordrecht, Kluwer 1998.

Gärdenfors, Peter, *Knowledge in Flux. Modeling the Dynamics of Epistemic States*, Cambridge, MA: MIT Press 1988.

Gärdenfors, Peter (ed.), *Belief Revision*, Cambridge, Cambridge University Press 1992.

Gärdenfors, Peter, and David Makinson, Revisions of Knowledge Systems Using Epistemic Entrenchment, in: *Proceedings of the Second Conference on Theoretical Aspects of Reasoning about Knowledge*, M. Vardi (ed.), Los Altos, CA: Morgan Kaufmann 1988, 83–95.

Gärdenfors, Peter, and David Makinson, Nonmonotonic Inference Based on Expectations, *Artificial Intelligence* 65 (1994), 197–245.

Gärdenfors, Peter, and Hans Rott, Belief Revision, in: D. M. Gabbay, C. J. Hogger and J. A. Robinson (eds.), *Handbook of Logic in Artificial Intelligence and Logic Programming*, Volume IV: Epistemic and Temporal Reasoning, Oxford: Oxford University Press 1995, 35–132.

Ginsberg, Matthew L. (ed.), *Readings in Nonmonotonic Reasoning*, Los Altos, CA: Morgan Kaufmann 1987.

Goldszmidt, Moisés, and Judea Pearl, Rank-Based Systems: A Simple Approach to Belief Revision, Belief Update, and Reasoning About Evidence and Actions, in: *Proceedings of the Third International Conference on Principles of Knowledge Representation and Reasoning*, Cambridge, MA: Morgan Kaufmann 1992, 661–672.

Grove, Adam, Two Modellings for Theory Change, *Journal of Philosophical Logic* 17 (1988), 157–70.

Haas, Gordian, *Revision und Rechtfertigung. Eine Theorie der Theorieänderung*, Synchron Wissenschaftsverlag der Autoren, Heidelberg, Synchron Wissenschaftsverlag der Autoren 2005.

Hansson, Sven Ove, *Belief Base Dynamics*, Ph.D. thesis, Uppsala University, Uppsala 1991.

Hansson, Sven Ove, *A Textbook of Belief Dynamics: Theory Change and Database Updating*, Dordrecht Kluwer 1999.

Hansson, Sven Ove (ed.), Non-Prioritized Belief Revision, special issue of *Theoria* 63 (1997).

Harman, Gilbert, *Change in View*, Cambridge, MA, MIT Press 1986.

Jeffrey, Richard C., *The Logic of Decision*, New York, McGraw-Hill 1965: second edition Chicago, University of Chicago Press 1983.

Katsuno, Hirofumi, and Alberto O. Mendelzon, Propositional Knowledge Base Revision and Minimal Change, *Artificial Intelligence* 52 (1991), 263–294.

Katsuno, Hirofumi, and Alberto O. Mendelzon, On the Difference Between Updating a Knowledge Base and Revising It, in: Peter Gärdenfors (ed.), *Belief Revision*, Cambridge, Cambridge University Press 1992, 183–203.

Konieczny, Sébastien, and Ramón Pino-Pérez, On the Logic of Merging, in: *Proceedings of the Sixth International Conference on Principles of Knowledge Representation and Reasoning (KR'98)*, San Francisco, CA: Morgan Kaufmann 1998, 488–498.

Konieczny, Sébastien, and Ramón Pino-Pérez, A Framework for Iterated Revision, *Journal of Applied Non-Classical Logics* 10 (2000), 339–367.

Konieczny, Sébastien, and Ramón Pino-Pérez, Merging Information Under Constraints: A Qualitative Framework, *Journal of Logic and Computation* 12 (2002), 773–808.

Kraus, Sarit, Daniel Lehmann and Menachem Magidor, Nonmonotonic Reasoning, Preferential Models and Cumulative Logics, *Artificial Intelligence* 44 (1990), 167–207.

Lehmann, Daniel, Menachem Magidor and Karl Schlechta, Distance Semantics for Belief Revision, *Journal of Symbolic Logic* 66 (2001), 295–317.

Lehmann, Daniel, Nonmonotonic Logics and Semantics, *Journal of Logic and Computation* 11 (2001), 229–256.

Levi, Isaac, Subjunctives, Dispositions and Chances, *Synthese*, Oxford, Blackwell 34 (1977), 423–455.

Levi, Isaac, *The Fixation of Belief and Its Undoing*, Cambridge, Cambridge University Press 1991.

Levi, Isaac, *Mild Contraction. Evaluating Loss of Information Due to Loss of Belief*, Oxford, Oxford University Press 2004.

Lewis, David, Ordering Semantics and Premise Semantics for Counterfactuals. *Journal of Philosoponical Logic* 19 (1981), 217–234.

Liberatore, Paolo, and Marco Schaerf, Arbitration (Or How To Merge Knowledge Bases), *IEEE Transactions on Knowledge and Data Engineering* 10 (1998), 76–90.

Lindström, Sten, *A Semantic Approach to Nonmonotonic Reasoning. Inference Operations and Choice*, Department of Philosophy, Uppsala Prints and Preprints in Philosophy 1991:6, University of Uppsala 1991.

Makinson, David, How to Give It Up: A Survey of Some Formal Aspects of the Logic of Theory Change, *Synthese* 62 (1985), 347–363.

Makinson, David, General Patterns in Nonmonotonic Reasoning, in D. M. Gabbay, C. J. Hogger and J. A. Robinson (eds.), *Handbook of Logic in Artificial Intelligence and Logic Programming*, Vol. III: Nonmonotonic Reasoning and Uncertain Reasoning, Oxford: Oxford University Press 1994, 35–110.

Makinson, David, *Bridges from Classical to Nonmonotonic Logic*, London, King's College Publications 2005.

Makinson, David, and Peter Gärdenfors, Relations Between the Logic of Theory Change and Nonmonotonic Logic, in André Fuhrmann and Michael Morreau (eds.), *The Logic of Theory Change*, Springer LNAI 465, Berlin, Springer 1991, pp. 185–205.

Nayak, Abhaya, Iterated Belief Change Based on Epistemic Entrenchment, *Erkenntnis* 41 (1994), 353–390.

Nayak, Abhaya, Maurice Pagnucco and Pavlos Peppas, Dynamic Belief Revision Operations, *Artificial Intelligence* 146 (2003), 193–228.

Nebel, Bernhard, A Knowledge Level Analysis of Belief Revision, in Ronald Brachman, Hector Levesque and Ray Reiter (eds.), *Proceedings of the 1st International Conference on Principles of Knowledge Representation and Reasoning*, San Mateo, CA: Morgan Kaufmann. 1989, pp. 301–311.

Nebel, Bernhard, Syntax-based Approaches to Belief Revision, in: Peter Gärdenfors (ed.), *Belief Revision*, Cambridge, Cambridge University Press 1992, 52–88.

Pagnucco, Maurice, and Hans Rott, Severe Withdrawal (and Recovery), *Journal of Philosophical Logic* 28 (1999), 501–547 (corrected reprint in the *JPL* issue of February 2000).

Priest, Graham, Richard Routley and Jean Norman (eds.), *Paraconsistent Logic – Essays on the Inconsistent*, Munich, Philosophia Verlag 1989.

Quine, Willard V. O., and Joseph S. Ullian, *The Web of Belief*, second edition, New York, Random House 1978.

Rescher, Nicholas, *Plausible Reasoning*, Assen, Amsterdam van, Gorcum 1976.

Revesz, Peter, On the Semantics of Theory Change: Arbitration Between Old and New Information, *Proceedings of the Twelfth ACM SICACT-SIGMOD-SIGART Symposium on Principles of Databases*, 1993, 71–92.

Revesz, Peter, On the Semantics of Arbitration, *International Journal of Algebra and Computation* 7 (1997), 133–160.

Rott, Hans, Belief Contraction in the Context of the General Theory of Rational Choice, *Journal of Symbolic Logic* 58 (1993), 1426–1450.

Rott, Hans, Coherence and Conservatism in the Dynamics of Belief. Part I: Finding the Right Framework, *Erkenntnis* 50 (1999), 387–412.

Rott, Hans, Two Dogmas of Belief Revision, *Journal of Philosophy* 97 (2000), 503–522.

Rott, Hans, *Change, Choice and Inference*, Oxford, Oxford University Press 2001.

Rott, Hans, Economics and Economy in the Theory of Belief Revision, in Vincent Hendricks, Klaus Jørgensen and Stig Pedersen (eds.), *Knowledge Contributors*, Dordrecht: Dordrecht, Kluwer 2003a, 57–86.

Rott, Hans, Coherence and Conservatism in the Dynamics of Belief. Part II: Iterated Belief Change Without Dispositional Coherence, *Journal of Logic and Computation* 13 (2003b), 111–145.

Rott, Hans, Bounded Revision: Two-Dimensional Belief Change Between Conservatism and Moderation, in Toni Rønnow-Rasmussen, Björn Petersson, Jonas Josefsson and Dan Egonsson (eds.), *Hommage à Wlodek. Philosophical Papers Dedicated to Wlodek Rabinowicz*, Lund 2007: available at: http://www.fil.lu.se/hommageawlodek/site/papper/RottHans.pdf.

Schlechta, Karl, Some results on theory revision, in André Fuhrmann and Michael Morreau (eds.), *The Logic of Theory Change*, LNAI 465, Berlin, Springer 1991, pp. 72–92.

Schlechta, Karl, *Nonmonotonic Logics – Basic Concepts, Results, and Techniques*, LNAI 1187, Berlin, Springer 1997.

Segerberg, Krister, Irrevocable Belief Revision in Dynamic Doxastic Logic, *Notre Dame Journal of Formal Logic* 39 (1998), 287–306;

Shackle, George L. S., *Expectation in Economics*, Cambridge, Cambridge University Press 1949, second edition 1952.

Spohn, Wolfgang, Ordinal Conditional Functions: A Dynamic Theory of Epistemic States, in: W. L. Harper and B. Skyrms (eds.), *Causation in Decision, Belief Change, and Statistics*, Vol. 2, Dordrecht, Reidel 1988, 105–134.

Van Ditmarsch, Hans, Prolegomena to Dynamic Logic for Belief Revision, *Synthese 147 (2005), 229–275 (Knowledge, Rationality and Action*, pp. 41–87) 2005.

Williams, Mary-Anne, and Hans Rott (eds.), *Frontiers in Belief Revision*, Dordrecht, Kluwer 2001.

Zhang, Dongmo, and Norman Foo, Infinitary Belief Revision, *Journal of Philosophical Logic* 30 (2001), 525–570.

Chapter 26: Belief, Doubt, and Evidentialism

ISAAC LEVI

The Main Task of Epistemology: Justifying Changes in Full Belief

I would bet my bottom dollar that William Henry Seward was Secretary of State in the Cabinets of Presidents Abraham Lincoln and Andrew Johnson. I am equally confident that while holding that office under Johnson he negotiated the purchase of Alaska by the United States of America from Russia. I am sure that the purchase was in 1867 give or take a year or so. (I am fairly confident that the year was 1867 but not absolutely certain.) However, I am absolutely certain that Seward had his permanent residence in Auburn, New York, for most of his life.

Confident assertion of matters of fact strikes many as out of place. Epistemic modesty requires that I refrain from expressions of absolute certainty not only about the date of the purchase of Alaska but concerning all the other claims made in the previous paragraph.

A public claim of absolute certainty even when one is sincere in the claim is not the way to win friends and influence people. But champions of epistemic modesty are concerned with more than conversational etiquette or political correctness. Not only should we avoid *expressing* absolute certainty, we should not *be* absolutely certain about questions of fact.

Many philosophers would concede that we should all be certain about the truth of the theses of logic and, perhaps, concerning other theses lurking in the cores of our conceptual frameworks. Questions of logic ought to be non-controversial although even the principle of non-contradiction has been challenged. But disagreements over issues of fact are different. Some may disagree with my convictions about Seward. Others may never have heard of Seward or the alleged folly of purchasing Alaska. And others

may never have heard of Auburn, New York. There may, for all I know, be someone who is familiar with Seward's achievements but who is convinced that Seward is alive or who at least surmises that he still lives. What entitles anyone to absolute certainty that Seward lived in Auburn in the face of the circumstance that for one reason or another others doubt this?

The question concedes that seeking to justify one's convictions to those who already share them is as pointless as preaching to the converted. It presupposes, however, that to be entitled to absolute certainty, one should be in a position to justify one's convictions to others when they disagree. The presupposition is absurd on its face.

What is required of X in order for X to justify X's conviction that *h* to Y? One possibility is that X is obliged to show that X acquired X's full belief that *h* from previously held beliefs in a justifiable manner. But why should X be required to display the pedigree of X's conviction to Y in order to be entitled to absolute certainty that *h*? Even if Y acknowledges that X successfully justified adding belief that *h* to X's original belief state, Y may not recognize that as a legitimate reason to withdraw dissent from X's belief that *h* and be justified in thinking so. The disagreement between X and Y might persist.

Let the demand on X be to show that Y is justified in modifying Y's beliefs so as to come into accord with X's beliefs. No doubt we often seek to resolve our disagreements with others. If I try to convince someone else to become certain that Seward lived in Auburn, I might try to justify my view to that person by appealing to premises that my interlocutor endorses and new information the interlocutor acknowledges to be reliable (perhaps a respected history of the Republican Party).

Nonetheless, I am not obliged to convince everyone who disagrees with me upon demand. To be required to do so would be an excessive form of intellectual tyranny. No dictate of reason demands it of me. No special epistemological obligation calls for it.

Sometimes, of course, I do have a duty to justify my opinions to those who disagree with me. A wide variety of personal, moral, political, economic considerations may require my undertaking joint ventures with others. In the context of such collaborations, I may owe it to others to justify some of my convictions to them. But the notion that I am under some obligation to justify my views to others whenever the request for such justification is made is not supportable by any moral, political, or other value commitment I am prepared to accept.

Even when I think it desirable to justify my convictions to others, I do not need to justify my current full beliefs to myself. Asking whether I am entitled to be absolutely certain that Seward lived in Auburn given that I fully believe this to be so is incoherent. For me to ask is for me to seek information I already have. To ask is to acknowledge as a serious possibility that Seward did not live in Auburn when I have already ruled out that logical possibility as a serious possibility.[1]

Of course, I may not have ruled out this logical possibility. In that case, I do not fully believe that Seward lived in Auburn. In such a condition of doubt, my concern would be whether I can justify to myself *changing* from a position of suspense as to the location of Seward's permanent residence to full belief. But such justification aims at warranting a change in my state of full belief. It does not aim at warranting any of my current beliefs (i.e., it does not seek to justify any of the consequences of my initial state of full belief).

There do, however, appear to be counterinstances to this claim. For example, someone may ask me whether Seward lived near Lake Owasco, and I might express some doubt even though I am on record that Auburn is a small city on Lake Owasco in upstate New York. According to the argument I have given, the doubt I express presupposes that I fail to believe that Seward lived near Lake Owasco. So when someone points out to me that the truth of this proposition is a logical consequence of what I already believe, the demonstration justifies me in coming to believe that proposition. Yet, it may well be argued that I already do believe the proposition so that the justification is a justification of a current belief.

Moreover, the situation illustrates the possibility of doubting current full beliefs.

The counterinstance is specious. I am, in the example, *committed* to fully believing all the implications of my full beliefs; but the obstacles to logical omniscience preclude my fulfilling my commitments. We should distinguish between believing that Seward lived near Lake Owasco as a doxastic commitment and believing that Seward lived near Owasco as a fulfillment of that commitment. I may have the doxastic commitment and fail to fulfill it.

The doubt I express may be due to my failure to put two and two together – that is, to recognize the logical consequences of my full beliefs. This failure may be a symptom of computational incompetence or it may be a failure to recognize that I believe both that Seward lived in Auburn and that Auburn is a small city near Lake Owasco in upstate New York. Either way, the doubt in this case is a symptom of my failure to fulfill my doxastic commitments. I am committed to ruling out as impossible the logical possibility that Seward did not live near Lake Owasco. That is to say I am committed to fully believing that Seward did live near Owasco, and deducing this latter claim from the full beliefs I explicitly avow shows this to be so. In this sense, justifying current full beliefs may be saved from utter absurdity. The justification is not of my current doxastic commitment that Seward lived near Lake Owasco. It is rather a justification for some verbal, behavioral, or psychological affirmation on the grounds that it fulfills the doxastic commitment. Such justification interprets verbal, behavioral, or psychological activities as fulfilling doxastic commitments successfully. The kind of justification of core relevance to epistemology ought to be justification of change in doxastic commitment. Psychology ought to be focused on the extent to which agents fulfill such commitments.[2]

I call inquirer X's state K of doxastic commitment at a given time t, X's *state of full belief* at t. K belongs to a set K of *potential states of full belief*. The elements of K are states that at t X could have been in or could entertain being in. X's conceptual framework at t is constituted by the set of such potential states and constitutes a Boolean algebra (closed under meets and joins of sets of arbitrary cardinality up to the cardinality of the set K). Such an algebra K induces a partial ordering on the potential states from the strongest potential state to weaker ones. This partial ordering is a consequence relation. Potential state K′ is a consequence of potential state K if and only if K is stronger than or relieves doubt more than K'.

The set of consequences of K is the set of full beliefs to which an agent in state K is committed (Levi 1991: Ch. 1). Thus a state of full belief K is representable by the set of full beliefs to which the agent in that state is committed. Agent X in state K is committed to judging each member of this belief set true and the complements of the members of this set false. K is X's standard for judging truth.

Each potential state K in K divides the elements of K into those that have the complement K^c of K as consequence and those that do not. Elements of the first set are seriously impossible according to K and the other set is the set of serious possibilities. In this formal sense, each potential state K in K is capable of serving as a *standard for serious possibility*.[3] A potential state K is X's standard for serious possibility at a given time if and only if at t, X is committed to judging all and only those elements of K to be seriously impossible that are impossible according to K and the remainder to be seriously possible.

If X is in state K, X is committed to dividing K into three parts: those potential states whose complements are impossible according to K, those potential states that are impossible according to K, and those potential states that are serious possibilities and whose complements are serious possibilities.

The first set is the set of full beliefs, and the second is the set fully believed to be false. The potential states in the third category are held in suspense. X is uncertain as to their truth or falsity and may make fine-grained distinctions among these potential states with respect to how certain or uncertain X is.

Consider, for example, judgments of subjective probability. The inquiring agent X is committed to assigning credal probabilities to all potential states in K no matter what state K of full belief X is in. However, the consequences of K (the full beliefs) are all assigned credal probability 1 and their complements credal probability 0. No fine graining occurs. The potential states that are serious possibilities according to K and their complements are assigned credal probabilities ranging from 0 to 1 inclusive.[4]

It is clear that inquirers who adopt states of credal probability judgment are committed to standards for serious possibility and, hence, to states of full belief.

The same is true of inquirers who register some sort of uncertainty by measures of degrees of disbelief (potential surprise) and belief satis-fying the formalism invented by G. L. S. Shackle (1949, 1962) and reinvented by many others (for example, L. J. Cohen 1977 when he introduced "Baconian probability"). According to this formalism, a member of the third category (those potential states that are serious possibilities according to K and whose complements are also serious possibilities and are potential answers to a given question) carry a degree of belief equal to the degree of disbelief in their negation. The degree of belief in a conjunction is the minimum of the degree of belief in a conjunct. Given a set of exclusive and exhaustive potential states according to K each consistent with K, at least one of the complements carries a 0 degree of belief and all complements may do so. Full beliefs carry a maximum degree of belief and their complements carry a maximum degree of disbelief (we assume that there is a maximum that we stipulate to be 1).

We often claim that an inquirer is justified in adding belief that *h* to the initial state of full belief K, if the degree of belief that *h according to* K is sufficiently high. There has been a widespread tendency to think that "degree of belief" here means "credal probability" – even though this view leads to changing to inconsistent belief states. I have argued in many places that satisficing notions of degree of belief ought to satisfy Shackle's requirements that avoid such predicaments.[5]

Degrees of belief and disbelief as evaluated using Shackle measures presupposes, like probabilistic degrees of belief, a distinction between serious possibility and impossibility and, hence, a standard for serious possibility or state of full belief and thus a set of full beliefs to which the inquirer is committed at time t. Moreover, the use of such measures of belief and disbelief as satisficing measures presupposes that states of full belief may be changed legitimately by "expansion" through adding potential states consistent with K that carry sufficiently high degrees of belief.

In sum, states of full belief as standards for serious possibility are presupposed by judgments of uncertainty of the sort represented by states of credal probability judgment, by judgments of degree of belief and disbelief in the satisficing Shackle sense and, indeed, by many other candidate ways of representing uncertainty.

In addition, the use of some of these measures (e.g. satisficing measures) presupposes that states of full belief or standards for serious possibility are subject to legitimate modification through inquiry. The notion that we can dispense with full belief or absolute certainty except for logical, *a priori*, or conceptual truth is quite unwarranted.

To the contrary, the main preoccupation of epistemology ought to be with giving an account of prescriptions for X's justifying changes in X's state of full belief to X. The question of justifying X's current beliefs to others or to X ought to be ignored.

Evidentialism

Jonathan Adler (2002) shares with me the view that we are often warranted in coming to full belief and that full belief is corrigible. We also agree that if X fully believes that h, X is committed to judging that h is true.

Adler insists, however, that there must be a "link" between the "belief's claim of truth" and the "condition of the truth of the belief." That link is the "evidence" for X's belief that h.

According to Adler, X must have evidence for X's belief that h simultaneously with X's full belief. Otherwise, the link that entitles X to judge that h is true is absent. Need for such a link is a "crucial premise of any argument for evidentialism" (2002, p. 5). Evidentialism is the following view: "Our degree of belief must match our degree of evidential support since only the evidence can secure the claim to truth of belief" (2002, p. 2), and to fully believe that p, one must have adequate reasons that p (2002, p. 5).

To my way of thinking, evidentialism concerning degrees of belief and full belief are both incoherent. The remainder of this essay will be given over to elaborating on the untenability of both types of evidentialism.

Evidentialism Concerning Degrees of Belief

If Adler's crucial premise of any argument for evidentialism is to be entertained, full belief that h and degree of belief that h must both have truth conditions and so be true or false. Moreover, full belief that h and degree of belief that h must be true or false in a sense in which it can matter to the inquirer whether the inquirer's beliefs and degrees of belief are true or false.

I take it that avoiding false full beliefs is a desideratum that rational inquirers may pursue. I myself think that this desideratum should be a mandatory constituent of the goals of efforts to change full beliefs. It is enough for our purposes to take for granted that full beliefs are true or false in a sense that can matter to the inquirer.

Degrees of belief are a different matter. If X believes that h to degree r short of absolute certainty, X is committed to judging that h might be true and h might be false. That is to say, X makes that judgment in a context where the truth of h hangs in suspense.

X may well be *entertaining* the question as to whether h is true or false, but X is not judging that h is true or that h is false. So X cannot make a false judgment as to whether h is true or false, and he cannot make a true one either.

For example, I am in doubt as to how far Skaneateles is from Auburn. I have some confidence that it is about seven miles distant from the center of Auburn but not complete confidence. Suppose it is ten miles distant. Since I did not judge it true that the distance was seven miles, I cannot be charged with error.

Ramsey insisted that the axioms of the calculus of probabilities could not be a "logic of truth" for probability because probability judgments (as judgments of degree of belief or partial belief) lack truth-values (Ramsey 1991). Savage offered a decisive argument for maintaining that one could not assign credal probabilities other than 0 or 1 to credal probabilities and, in this sense, could not be "unsure" about credal probabilities (Savage 1954). So either credal probability judgments would have to be logical or conceptually necessary truths or lack truth-values. The former alternative is untenable. Even if there were a standard method for assigning degrees of credal probability given the available evidence, X's degree of probabilistic belief that Michael Bloomberg will be elected to a second term as Mayor of New York being equal to some value r is not a necessary truth. The handwriting is on the wall.

Perhaps, degrees of belief are not such "Pascalian" probabilities but are "Baconian" as Cohen maintained where Baconian probabilities are Shackle's degrees of belief. Savage's argument is thus evaded. Even so, the conclusion stands. According to Shackle-based degrees of belief, the higher the degree of boldness required for adding h to one's stock of full beliefs, the lower the degree of belief prior to adding h. The degree of boldness is itself an expression of the trade-off between the credal probability that h and the value of the information provided by full belief that h (Levi 1967: Ch. 8, 1984, 1996: 6.6, 6.7, 6.9, 2004: 3.6). Neither of the components in this trade-off carries a truth-value, nor does the weighing of the components in the trade-off. The judgment that the degree of belief that h has reached a given threshold is made prior to changing one's state of full belief when h is judged to be possibly false. That judgment lacks a truth-value just as the judgment that the credal probability that h is such and such regardless of the truth-value of h itself.

The two leading candidates for attitudes characterized as degrees of belief – degrees of credal or belief probability and degrees of belief in the sense of Shackle – characterize attitudes that are neither true nor false in a sense in which it makes sense to be concerned to avoid false belief in fixing such beliefs.

Thus, even though Adler thinks that the easiest part of the case for evidentialism concerns degrees of belief, there is no claim of truth in such cases. There are no truth conditions for such judgments. Hence, there is no need for a "link" between a nonexistent claim and a nonexistent truth condition. Adler has failed to make his case even in the easiest part.

Yet, I think we would be overhasty to dismiss evidentialism in the spirit if not the letter of Adler's thesis. As Adler himself seems to acknowledge, there could be reasons for belief that are not evidential in his sense because they are not reasons for the truth of the belief. Agents may have reason to believe various claims because doing so promotes their emotional stability, and they are good reasons, let us suppose, for the promotion of such stability. Adler would insist, however, that they are not relevant to the truth-value of the claims in question. If our concern is exclusively with forming true beliefs, emotional stability is no reason for belief. Only reasons that promote the quest for true beliefs qualify as evidence. Perhaps, evidentialism is supportable by an appeal to the aims of efforts to fix beliefs rather than to some missing links between truth claims that are often nonexistent and correspondingly dubious truth conditions.

Judgments of credal probability or belief probability are used to evaluate the expected values of gambles where payoffs depend on which of a set of rival hypotheses is true. Credal probability is well adapted to articulate assessments of risk of error in fixing belief. If we are concerned to minimize risk of error, assessments of risk of error should be controlled by evidence – that is, by X's stock of full beliefs without suggesting that the evidence supply a link between a claim of truth and a truth condition.

To put the demand more formally, we may require X to be committed to a method of assigning credal states to potential states of full belief in K representable by a function C: K->B from

K to the set B of potential credal states where a credal state determined by consistent potential state K is itself representable by a set B of conditional probability functions $p(y/x)$ where x is consistent with K.

In the past it has been widely taken for granted that the set B is a singleton so that credal probability judgments are numerically determinate. Carnap called the function C a confirmation function (1950) or, when emphasizing that it represented the commitment of an agent, a credibility function (1960). I call it a confirmational commitment (Levi 1980). Carnap among many others thought that there ought to be a standard confirmational commitment to which all agents ought to subscribe. He thought it ought to be numerically determinate. I think that confirmational commitments, like states of full belief, are subject to reasoned change. I also think that the revisability of confirmational commitments calls for abandonment of the view that the credal state B determined by the state of full belief K (Levi 1974, 1980, 1984: Ch. 11) should be a singleton. I shall not elaborate on this issue here.

Those who favor a standard confirmational commitment advocate a fairly strong form of evidentialism even if they do not always feel obliged to establish a "link" between claims of truth and truth conditions. As already indicated, this form of evidentialism seems as unacceptable as one that seeks the sort of "link" required by Adler.

There remains the weaker version of evidentialism with respect to degree of belief construed as degree of credal probability. According to this version, credal probability judgments may be indeterminate and confirmational commitments revisable. This form of evidentialism seems tolerable.

Full Belief as a Simplifying Device

Adler also claims that full belief, as a matter of conceptual necessity, ought to be determined by evidence or by "reasons" for the truth of the target beliefs. It is incoherent, according to Adler, for X to declare, "p but I lack evidence that p." He thinks he can parlay an alleged consensus among those who reflect on this point into a case for "evidentialism."[6]

Full belief that h, according to Adler (2002), ends inquiry as to its truth. On this we agree, but according to Adler, it thereby conserves resources and time (p. 232). In a footnote, Adler writes: "Because full belief reflects a demand on us to economize, betting behavior poorly captures the logic of full belief" (p. 325). Full belief, so it appears, is made necessary because various social, psychological, and physical constraints preclude expression of complex views in terms of degrees of belief. You must express your views often in terms of full beliefs.

> The unavoidability is never a barrier to responding to reasons. One can try to negotiate the constraints. One must express one's opinions, but if one's views are very complex, one seeks forums that tolerate more expansive and nuanced argument. My claim is that one cannot regularly opt out when one does not find such sophisticated forums. The strength of this "cannot" is the strength of demands on us to participate in many social, intellectual practices, and of our impotence to shape them. (Adler 2002: 215)

Full belief is necessitated, according to Adler, by the need to express opinions of some complexity in contexts where relatively little sophistication is tolerated. We must avoid the impression of being "flip floppers" like John Kerry if we want to get elected President. If I understand Adler correctly, X has adequate evidence to fully believe that h only if X's evidence warrants a degree of belief that h that is sufficiently high. By degree of belief, Adler appears not to mean credal or subjective probability. According to Adler's discussion of the paradoxes of the preface and the lottery, high credal probability is not sufficient to warrant full belief (Adler 2002: Ch. 7). I conjecture on purely circumstantial evidence that he thinks of the degree of belief as something like Cohen's Baconian probability or, with greater historical accuracy, Shackle's measure of degree of belief.

To my way of thinking, full belief is no mere concession to coarse-grained thinking. Anyone who is fortunate enough to formulate nuanced views in a forum that tolerates complexity and invokes judgments of subjective probability (whether numerically determinate or not), degrees of confidence exhibiting the structures introduced originally by G. L. S. Shackle or other such modes of assessment *presupposes* a distinction between serious possibility and impossibility and, as a consequence, embraces a state of full belief.

If X is not so fortunate and is obliged to formulate views in a more coarse-grained manner, X's coarse-grained judgment that p may express belief that p in some qualitative sense distinct from full belief. Insofar as the belief that p that is based on "adequate evidence" (that is, on suffi-

ciently strong evidence) is a coarse-grained simplification of the degree of belief appropriate to that degree of evidential support, the serious possibility ∼p acknowledged by the standard for serious possibility K is not ruled out. The qualitative sense of belief may correspond to mere belief as conceived in Levi (1967) or plain belief as in Spohn (1988). It is not to be confused with full belief.

Perhaps, the evidence in the initial state of full belief warrants changing the standard for serious possibility so that $\sim p$ is ruled out as a serious possibility. Then X is committed to a new state of full belief whether X reasons with the booboisie or with the sophisticated. There is nothing coarse-grained or simplifying about it.

Full Belief and Modified Evidentialism

Full belief is thus quite commonplace just as Adler maintains. But X's current state of full belief (i.e., X's standard for serious possibility) is not justified by reasons for its truth as Adler's evidentialism maintains. There is no serious possibility according to X's first personal point of view that X's state of full belief contains error. There is no room for doubt concerning its truth in the sense where doubting that h is equivalent to suspending judgment between h and $\sim h$. Where there is no doubt in this sense, there is no point in marshaling reasons for believing that h.[7]

X should, so I claim, require justification for ceasing to doubt that h given that X initially doubts it and for coming to doubt it given that X fully believes that h. So it might be thought that there is room for a modification of Adler's evidentialism in these cases. Justification of change in state of full belief or standard for serious possibility is, according to the modified evidentialism, justification for the change based exclusively on the initial state of full belief (which constitutes the evidence available to the inquirer prior to the change.

Even this modified evidentialism will not work. In cases where doubt in the sense of suspense is present, justifying coming to full belief that h (expanding K so that h is a consequence) by appeal to reasons or evidence does not secure a link between the claim that h is true and truth conditions for the claim. Matters are even worse in cases of ceasing to fully believe that h (contracting K so that h is no longer a consequence).

In inquiry, so I think the common feature of the diverse goals of efforts to remove doubts in various inquiries ought to be to avoid error and to acquire valuable new information. The goal here is constituted as the aggregation of two distinct desiderata: Coming to full belief that the information is true relieves doubt present according to K. It also incurs a risk of error as judged according to K. In order to justify expanding the initial state of full belief K by adding h and its consequences and thus coming to full belief that h, it is necessary to show that the information thereby obtained (the relief from doubt thus achieved) compensates for the risk of error incurred *as evaluated relative to the initial state of full belief* K when $\sim h$ is judged a serious possibility.

From X's point of view prior to expansion by adding h, the truth conditions for h can be specified by X's state of full belief K. That is to say, in seeking to avoid error, X is seeking to avoid adding a false belief by adding h to K, and this will happen if and only if the truth conditions for h on the assumption that K and its consequences are true fail to be satisfied. In this sense, K is the "link" between the claim that h is true in the sense of the coming to full belief that h and the truth conditions for h. Otherwise, I am not sure what Adler means by such a link. In this sense, the "evidence" as link is just K and its consequences.

On this construal, the risk of error incurred by adding h to K may reasonably be taken to mean credal probability of error. If the credal probability that h is determined by K as it would be if X endorsed a confirmational commitment specifying for each consistent K in K the credal state X should adopt, we might say that the evidence determines the risk of error. Hence if the sole reason for adding h to K were the risk of error incurred, the reason would satisfy Adler's evidentialist requirements as I understand them.

But X's reason for expanding K by adding h is not determined by the risk of error alone. As James rightly pointed out in criticizing Clifford (and as Popper reminded us)[8], focusing exclusively on risk of error argues for refusing to expand K at all. One needs, in addition, an incentive to risk error. In inquiry, that incentive is to relieve doubt by acquiring information of value. Now the value of information or relief from doubt is *not* determined by K alone – that is, by the link between the claim that h and the truth conditions for h.

Assessments of informational value are subject to some constraints. Stronger potential states of full belief carry more informational value than weaker ones. Hence, in seeking valuable information, inquirer X should never assess the *informational value* of a weaker potential state as greater than that of a stronger one. Sometimes the additional information carried by a stronger answer to a question is not worth anything given the demands of the question so the stronger may carry the same informational value as the weaker one. But insofar as the inquirer is concerned to maximize informational value, the inquirer should never rank a weaker potential answer over a stronger one.

Subject to this *weak positive monotonicity* constraint, there may be many ways to extend the partial ordering with respect to strength to obtain a weak ordering with respect to informational value. Considerations of simplicity, explanatory and predictive power, and other allegedly scientific or epistemic virtues are often invoked in order to complete the ordering. Whether these modes of assessment are or are not free of appeal to moral, political, economic, aesthetic, or religious values and whether or not other ways of completing the ordering that are more explicit in invoking such nonscientific or epistemic values are invoked, as long as positive weak monotonicity (and some other restrictions) is observed, the evaluation may serve as an assessment of informational value representing the incentive for risking error (Levi 2004: 80–86).

Given the assessment of risk of error and the assessment of informational value, the evaluation of *expected epistemic utility* of potential answers to a question is represented by a trade-off or balance between risk of error and informational value. The more the balance in favor of informational value, the bolder and less cautious the inquirer X. The best of the available answers is one that is optimal according to this evaluation of expected epistemic utility. The reason for adopting that answer is that it is the best and its optimality is a function of two components: risk of error and informational value as balanced by the boldness exercised by the inquirer.

The answer that is recommended is the expansion of K by adding some potential state of full belief or "doxastic proposition" that h and its consequences. The answer can also be characterized as the set of doxastic propositions that are warranted at a sufficiently low degree of boldness or sufficiently high degree of Baconian probability or degree of belief. To this extent, the reasons for fully believing the members of the set appear to have the properties that I think Adler intends them to have, but the evidence in the initial state K of full belief alone does not qualify as the reasons.

Thus, X may have a reason for expanding K by adding h, but the reason is not evidence for h in what I take to be Adler's sense. To be sure, one component of X's reason may be evidence in Adler's sense, but Adler is simply mistaken in maintaining that, all things considered, the reason for coming to believe that h is the reason for the truth of h. One dimension (risk of error) of the reason for coming to such belief is relevant to the truth of h. However, there is another dimension (informational value) that is not relevant in this way.

In this discussion, I have focused on reasons for expanding K. Recall, however, that K is a state of doxastic commitment. If h expresses a potential state that is a consequence of K, one might say that K is a reason for h in something akin to Adler's sense of a link between the coming to believe that h and its truth conditions. In this sense, deductive or logical reasons may be alleged to be reasons in Adler's sense, but, of course, they are not reasons for changing doxastic commitments.

Crucial Experiments and Tacit Confirmation

Adler may or may not be prepared to endorse my distinction between doxastic commitment and doxastic performance (I suspect not); but he does appear to think that he is demanding evidence for coming to believe and current belief that is not merely deductive and, hence, is, on my account, reason for changing doxastic commitment.

His most explicit discussion of this matter surfaces in his discussion of empirical support by tacit confirmation for background belief (Adler 2002: 6.2). According to the famous argument of Duhem, there is no crucial experiment for a hypothesis H. Suppose an allegedly crucial experiment is run and it yields datum e. If H&A entails e, where A is a set of so called "auxiliary assumptions," e confirms H if e is true. ~e disconfirms H and, indeed, falsifies it. Duhem and Quine insist that this is wrong. The experiment is not crucial in the way described because, in the face of ~e, A could be disconfirmed or falsified just as much as H. As Adler reports, it is now claimed that if ~e obtains, either H or A is disconfirmed.

Adler insists, however, that if this is so, then when e is true, *both* H and A are confirmed – H explicitly and A tacitly.

Adler is right to complain about the asymmetry in the treatment of auxiliary assump-

tions in confirmation and disconfirmation in the Duhem–Quine account. He is wrong in the way he seeks to address the asymmetry. There are three cases to consider.

Case 1: The initial state of full belief K implies A. Both H and ~H are consistent with K and, hence, serious possibilities. X conducts a test of the conjecture that H is true. If e is observed, H is confirmed. Since A is already fully believed, its truth is settled. There is no question about confirming or testing it. A is neither tacitly confirmed nor disconfirmed by e. If ~e is observed, H is falsified. Once more the truth of A is settled. Once more there is neither tacit confirmation nor disconfirmation for A. The asymmetry between H and A in this case is entirely legitimate. X is absolutely certain that A is true whereas H is a hypothesis subject to test. *Pace* Duhem, in such a situation, the test is a crucial experiment.

Case 2: Both H and A are hypotheses as is their conjunction H&A. All three potential states of full belief might be false according to X in state K. If e is observed, H&A gains confirmation. If ~e is observed, H&A is falsified. Neither H nor A is falsified. Neither H nor A alone is confirmed either explicitly or tacitly by e. H&A is confirmed. (I am using what I take to be Adler's standards for confirmation here.)

Case 3: Both H and A are implied by the initial state K. No experiment is run to test them since there is no point in doing so. However, an experiment is run for some other purpose (e.g., classroom demonstration) that yields e if H&A is true. Thus, Michelson's initial application of the interferometer was to establish that the velocity of the earth in the Ether could be measured. Michelson was not attempting to test the claim that the Ether existed, the classical mechanics, or electrodynamics. There can be no increase in confirmation for H&A since it is settled. Suppose ~e is observed. This constitutes an example of inadvertent expansion into inconsistency. (Thus, Michelson was committed to the view that his measurements would not yield a null result. Inadvertent expansion into inconsistency is as Gärdenfors put it, expansion into "epistemic hell." X must beat a retreat. See Levi 1991: 4.1 and 4.8; Olsson 2003; Levi 2003).

In retreating from inconsistency, X may call H&A into question by removing it from the full beliefs, may call e into question, or may do both. (All of the above were seriously pursued investigations after Michelson's initial null results).

Removing H&A while retaining e amounts, so I have proposed elsewhere, to contracting the original K (before inconsistency) by removing H&A and then expanding the result by adding e.

Calling e into question is (roughly) equivalent to remaining with K.

Doing both is (roughly) equivalent to contracting the original K by removing H&A.

I have urged elsewhere that one should assess the losses of valuable information incurred by the first two. If one incurs a greater loss in informational value than the other, the one that minimizes such loss should be chosen. If they both incur equal loss or if they are noncomparable, the contraction calling both H&A and e into question should be chosen.

These appraisals require a determination of the best contraction removing H&A from K. In particular, should H alone be removed, A alone, or both? Making these assessments calls for distinguishing between full beliefs relative to K with respect of vulnerability to being given up (degree of incorrigibility or degree of entrenchment). I contend that since both A and H are maximally certain, there can be no difference between them either in probabilistic or Shackle degree of belief. They are both maximally and absolutely certain. The difference in vulnerability to being given up depends exclusively on loss of informational value, and this has nothing to do with conditions of truth or evidential support in what seems to be Adler's official understanding of evidential support.

Without going into details, I suggest that if the first two options incur substantially equal losses in informational value, the third option should be deployed. Otherwise adopt one of the other options depending on which incurs the smallest loss in informational value.

To complete the third case, suppose that either the first or third option is deployed. H&A must then cease being fully believed. Which should be given up: H, A, or both? Once more the decisive factor is loss of informational value.

Now the important point to emphasize here relevant to Adler's discussion is that nowhere is there anything like tacit confirmation. Only conjectures subject to real and living doubt can be subject to confirmation and disconfirmation by testing. Full beliefs are always absolutely certain and perfectly free of all doubt.

Nonetheless, distinctions can be made between full beliefs in a state of full belief K. In removing H&A from K+e in Case 3, even though H and A are both equally and maximally certain according to K, they could differ with respect to the loss of informational value one or the other would incur in contraction, and it is loss of informational value that controls the relative vulnerability of these items to removal in contracting H&A.

Change of state of full belief in contraction, as in expansion, may be justified by reasons, but, as in the case of expansion, the reasons cannot be evidential reasons in Adler's sense. The relative losses of informational value H and A have little bearing on their truth-values as judged according to state of full belief K from which they are to be removed. According to K, both H and A are absolutely certainly true. In this respect, there is nothing to differentiate them from one another.

I have argued elsewhere (Levi 1991, 2004) that the evaluation of candidate contractions from K removing some doxastic proposition *h* ought to minimize *damped* informational value where such assessment of informational value obeys not only weak positive monotonicity but also constraints imposing the formal structure of Shackle measures on such appraisals. However, what, according to Shackle's intention was a degree of belief no longer is comes with this interpretation. It is now construed as an assessment of loss of informational value.

The two uses cannot, however, be identified. Shackle measures as degrees of belief are a function of two components, probability of truth and informational value in an undamped sense. Shackle measures, as measures of loss of informational value, are a function of undamped informational value where undamped informational value is converted to damped informational in a certain way. Probability of truth plays no role.

Many authors who have deployed Shackle-type measures (e.g., Gärdenfors and Makinson 1993; Spohn 1988) have recognized both uses of such measures but have sought to integrate them into a single measure. These authors want to avoid, however, changes in standards for serious possibility – or, at least, so it appears to me. Spohn, in particular, is quite clear that there should be no change in states of full belief. All changes in belief in a qualitative sense are changes in "plain" belief. X plainly believes that *h* if and only if X believes that *h* to some positive degree (in the Shackle sense). Plain belief is not the standard for serious possibility, which on Spohn's account does not change. Items that are consequences of the state of plain belief can differ from one another with respect to the degree of belief one has in their truth, and these differences will have a bearing, according to Spohn, on the vulnerability of these items to being given up under pressure.

There ought to be no dispute as to whether there is an intelligible notion of plain belief. When engaged in an inquiry aimed at determining how K ought to be expanded in order to answer a given question, the plain beliefs turn out to be the doxastic propositions that should be added if the inquirer is maximally bold. Of course, this characterization is one that Spohn could not endorse as giving important use to plain belief since it focuses on the topic of changing standards for serious possibility – something on which Spohn looks askance. My point is merely to note that for those who recognize the importance of justifying changes in states of full belief, plain belief can be acknowledged as intelligible and potentially useful.

Is Full Belief Compatible with Doubt?

Adler apparently does not want to follow the approach favored by Spohn. He does seem to think that full beliefs are modifiable. He wants to insist that full beliefs are judged as certain as certain can be. On these points he and I are on the same side in opposition to Mill. And it appears that in this respect, *all* full beliefs endorsed by X at time t are on the same footing.

Adler, however, wants to insist, in agreement with Mill, on the *fallibility* of belief and here Adler means full belief (2002: 256). Now my terminological practice has been to take fallibility of belief to mean possibility of falsehood. I claim that from X's point of view, there is no serious possibility that X's full beliefs are false. I have called this view "epistemological infallibilism" or infallibilism of the present. I do not think that Adler differs from me on this score. He uses "fallibilism" to mean something different from what I mean.

One possible meaning could be what I have called "corrigibilism" or vulnerability to being modified either by expansion or contraction. In the case of vulnerability to contraction, I have acknowledged that distinctions may be drawn between full beliefs or certainties with respect to losses of valuable information incurred by giving them as reflected in degrees of entrenchment or incorrigibility. This acknowledgment of corrigibilism, however, will not suffice, however, to justify giving a hearing to dissenting opinions. For one needs in addition to show that one is indeed justified in contracting one's state of full belief to give a hearing to the dissent. This is in my view often feasible, but the reasons that justify are not evidence in Adler's sense.

Now Adler wants to follow Mill in defending the giving of a hearing to dissenting views. He wants to do so even when we are absolutely certain that they are false. But he does not want to admit that what is absolutely certain might be false. So he draws a distinction between certainty (and probability), on the one hand, and confidence, on the other. We may be absolutely certain that h but less than maximally confident that h. We may have doubts. We can thus acknowledge a kind of fallibility. We can distinguish between certainties with respect to levels of confidence or doubtworthiness.

Adler is emphatic that this recognition of fallibility or presence of doubt that h is not evidence or reason to give up full belief that h. In contrast to my view, he does seem to think that sometimes inquirers have evidential reasons for contracting states of full belief. Insofar as I understand him, Adler thinks that in the case where X observes ~e when already fully believing that H&A, H&A has to be given up for evidential reasons. This is far from obvious both in scientific practice and according to common sense. Even if e is retained but H&A abandoned (which is not going to be always the appropriate recommendation), I fail to see how reason for this recommendation has anything to do with the truth or probability of truth of anything.

Even conceding this to him, Adler is silent as to how H&A is to be given up. Should H alone be given up? Should A alone be abandoned? Should X cease to be certain of both? Above all, do the reasons that support one recommendation rather than the other constitute evidence related to truth conditions for truth claims? The remarks made by Adler related to these matters fail to sustain his evidentialist position. For example, sometimes X should give up a proposition because, if the costs of error (or the value of being correct) are altered, the standards for adequate evidence for full belief are altered. Not only do I disagree with views that insist that one should give up full beliefs because the pedigree of their acquisition has been jeopardized, but even from Adler's point of view, the kind of reason he is talking about cannot be evidential. The account of contraction based on loss of informational value incurred in contraction furnishes a systematic response to these questions. Of course, it abandons evidentialism.

In any case, Adler insists that the presence of reasonable doubt or the acknowledgment of fallibility provides no evidential reasons for contraction. I am not interested in a word battle concerning what "fallible" and "doubt" mean although I remain perfectly content with my own usage. What is critical here is what function the fallibility of full belief and compatibility of full belief and doubt serves in deliberation and inquiry according to Adler's view.

It appears that the important function is that it allows X, who is absolutely certain that h, to engage in serious critical reflection as to whether h is true or false while certain that h. It requires X to give a hearing to the dissenter who proclaims $\sim h$ just as Mill seems to suggest. This stance is explicitly directed at claims I have made to the effect that, in order to subject a proposition h to critical scrutiny and test, it should cease being a certainty or settled assumption and become a hypothesis (p. 280). And in a discussion of Berlin's treatment of Mill's argument (Levi 1997: Ch. 12), I insisted that according a dissenter the respect of giving a serious hearing to the dissenter's view calls for opening up one's mind or contraction. Such a contraction needs to be justified. That is to say, the dissenter's view needs to earn the hearing.

Adler mounts an intricate and, to my way of thinking, unconvincing argument in support of his view that full belief and doubt are compatible. He begins by taking note of the paradox of ideal evidence arguments purporting to show that we need, in addition to the probability on the evidence, some indicator of how confident we are in the evidential backing for the probability judgment. (Ideas of this sort have been discussed by many authors, including Peirce and Keynes.) Probability is not full belief as Adler acknowledges, but Adler seeks to piggyback on the weight of argument versus balance of argument contrast found in Keynes to support his view that full beliefs come with varying levels of confidence. Adler then invokes the idea that full belief is, nonetheless, fallible – an idea that he makes intelligible by insisting that full belief is compatible with doubt – and a model of why base rates may be neglected and a few examples that he invokes as an intuition pump – one that does not touch me but which it would take much too long a time to discuss in detail.

I confess that my own usage of fallibilism is only one of many usages that could be derived from plain speech. But if full belief is the standard for serious possibility, doubt is incompatible with full belief. Adler seems to agree that full belief is the standard for serious possibility. Yet doubt is not ruled out. I think here that Adler

has stretched the meaning of doubt beyond anything that presystematic practice warrants, but whether I am right or wrong, as long as full belief is the standard for serious possibility, X cannot coherently subject h to critical scrutiny and test to check on the truth value of h unless X regards both h and $\sim h$ as serious possibilities. If initially X fully believes that h, X needs to contract.

Can X examine reasons for ceasing to fully believe that h where X already fully believes that h? Sometimes X may suppose that some proposition g is true *for the sake of the argument* and explore the ramifications of such a supposition for explaining some phenomenon. Given the initial state K, g is incompatible with h so that the supposition is belief contravening. The suppositional reflection yields the result that g has considerable virtue as an explanatory proposition. This does not itself alter X's full belief that g is false. However, recognition of this explanatory virtue could be a good reason (albeit not an evidential reason) to contract K in order to give g a hearing by conducting tests that, if successful, would render a verdict between h and g. That is to say, the nonevidential reason is a reason for coming to doubt that h is true not in the for-the-sake-of-the-argument fantasy but genuinely.

I have focused on the nonevidential status of reasons for contraction in these last remarks because the main burden of Adler's remarkable claims about belief and doubt seem to be addressed to sustaining evidentialism in the context of contraction, but evidentialism fares no better in the context of expansion than in the context of contraction as I have also argued. To resist evidentialism, however, is not to resist avoidance of error (and, hence, truth) as a desideratum in inquiry. It is to resist the thesis that it is the sole desideratum.

Finally, to maintain that the goals with respect to which changes in belief are justified are multidimensional and appeal not only to considerations of truth-value and risk of error but also to nonevidential considerations does not imply that the goals of inquiry are reducible to practical, moral, economic, political, aesthetic goals and values. The quest for knowledge ought, in my view, to promote the realization of certain special kinds of goals – in brief, the acquisition of new, error-free, and valuable information. Practical, moral, economic, political, aesthetic, and so goals often contribute to the determination of the value of information acquired. Neither avoidance of error, nor the acquisition of new, valuable information, nor the balance between the two is reducible to practical values in the vulgar sense just indicated. All of this is achievable without advocating evidentialism in Adler's conceptual sense or in any other.

Notes

1   Of course, the question asked must be posed as a sincere demand for information. It cannot be an invitation to a "paper doubt" of the sort that Peirce charged Descartes with posing. Had I initially been absolutely certain that Seward lived in Auburn and subsequently asked the question, I would have changed from certainty to doubt. The doubt would qualify as a paper doubt if I had not been justified in ceasing to be certain that Seward lived in Auburn.

2   Both epistemology and psychology thus have ineliminably normative components. They differ in the tasks they undertake to perform. We should avoid psychologizing epistemology or epistemologizing psychology by conflating the two tasks. See Levi 1991: Ch. 2, 1997: Ch. 1, and 2002 for further discussion of the commitment–performance distinction.

3   In Levi 1980: I.2 (and in publications dating back to the early 1970s), I took X's state of knowledge to be X's standard for serious possibility. I continue to think that the most useful definition of "X knows that h" is that X fully and truly believes that h. From X's current point of view, X's current state of knowledge and current state of full belief coincide. In later publications, I began speaking of state of certainty or full belief in order to avoid becoming engaged in tedious word battles. Analyzing the verb "to know" ought not to preoccupy epistemology. Accounting for conditions under which changes in states of full belief are and are not justified should.

4   Potential states that are serious possibilities according to K may be assigned 0 probability. Thus judgments of credal probability alone cannot distinguish between serious possibility and impossibility in those cases. The standard for serious possibility must be invoked. One might consider invoking judgments of conditional credal probability to do the job. $p(x/y) = r$ where r is some standard real value presupposes that y is consistent with K and thus a serious possibility according to K. That is to say, this is so when conditional probability is taken as primitive rather than unconditional probability and the multiplication theorem is taken as axiomatic. This is the practice of H. Jeffreys (1957, 1961), B. de Finetti (1972), Dubins (1975: 96), and I. Levi (1980), all of whom avoid assuming countable additivity. One might seek to derive the standard for serious possibility from the agent's state of credal probability judgment (credal state) by determining the set of elements of K that must be in the domain of definition of the permissible probability function of the credal state. An effort to do this based on an idea of van Fraassen's is developed by H. Arló Costa (2001).

5   For recent statements of this view, see Levi 1996: Ch. 8, 2002. Earlier statements are found in Levi 1966, 1967, and 1984: Ch. 14, where a comparison with L. J. Cohen's conception of Baconian probability in Cohen 1977 is undertaken.

6   When I sincerely assert that p, I am expressing my full belief that p. There is no serious possibility that ~p. No evidence I currently have can support what is already settled. No evidence I currently have could undermine it. Of course, my full belief that p could be counted as evidence I have that p, but it is not evidence in the sense that evidence is used to settle what is unsettled. In that sense, to declare that I lack evidence for my full belief is pointless. Hence, the declaration is strange but not paradoxical. It is surely not inconsistent. Adler compares "p but I lack evidence that p" to the more familiar saying and disbelieving paradox of G. E. Moore "p but I do not believe it" (Adler, 2002: Ch. 1.2 and Ch. 7.2). He claims that the Moore sentence is "heard" as inconsistent even though it is perfectly consistent. He argues that what is inconsistent is the claim that I know both that p but I do not believe that p. If the Moorean sentence were inconsistent, its negation "p ⊃ I believe that p" would be necessarily true. This is absurd. I may claim that whatever I fully believe is true but not the converse. What Adler has shown via his transparency assumption is that I cannot coherently believe or know "p ⊃ I believe that p" to be false. But I can coherently fail to believe it to be true. It is judged negatively but not positively valid in doxastic logic. (See Levi 1997: Ch. 3, Sec. 7 for more on this point.) Even if one conceded (as I do not) that "p but I lack evidence for p" is conceptually incoherent, it would not follow that one should embrace "p ⊃ I have evidence for p." Still if Adler were right about the analogy with the saying and disbelieving case, agent X would be incoherent if X believed one extralogical p true and also believed that X lacked evidence for it. Adler seems enthusiastically convinced he is right. It seems clear to me that he is mistaken. Indeed, for reasons explained above, if I fully believe that p, I cannot coherently claim to have evidence for p in the sense that evidence settles the unsettled. I might marshall reasons why you should come to believe that p or why I was justified in coming to believe that p in the first place, but I am not incoherent if I lack reasons of this kind even if I have no real and living doubt as to the truth of p.

7   Doubt that h sometimes means failure to believe – that is, either suspense or belief that

~h, and sometimes it may mean full belief that h is false. The presence of doubt in either of these senses is not sufficient to motivate inquiry. If the agent fails to be in suspense (fails to be uncertain) as to whether h is true or false, either the agent fully believes that h or fully believes that ~h. There is no real and living doubt motivating efforts to eliminate the doubt by finding reasons to come to full belief that h or full belief that ~h. The presence of doubt as I shall use understand it is in the sense of suspense.

8 See also Levi (1967).

References

Adler, J. (2002), *Belief's Own Ethics,*" Cambridge, MA: MIT Press.

Arló Costa, H. (2001), "Bayesian Epistemology and Epistemic Conditionals," *The Journal of Philosophy* 98, 555–593.

Carnap, R. (1950), *Logical Foundations of Probability*, Chicago: University of Chicago Press, second rev. ed. 1962.

Carnap, R. (1960), "The Aim of Inductive Logic," *Logic, Methodology and Philosophy of Science* ed. by E. Nagel, A. Tarski, P. Suppes, Stanford, CA: Stanford University Press.

Cohen, L. J. (1977), *The Probable and the Provable*, Oxford: Oxford University Press.

De Finetti, B. (1972), "On the Axiomatization of Probability Theory," *Probability, Induction and Statistics*, New York: Wiley.

Dubins, L. H. (1975), "Finitely Additive Conditional Probabilities, Conglomerability and Disintegrations," *The Annals of Probability*, 3, 89–99.

Gärdenfors, P. and Makinson, D. (1993), "Nonmonotonic Inference based on Expectations,: *Artificial Intelligence* 65, 197–246.

Jeffreys, H. (1957), *Scientific Inference* second ed., Cambridge: Cambridge University Press.

Jeffreys, H. (1961), *Theory of Probability* third ed., London: Oxford University Press.

Levi, I. (1966), "On Potential Surprise," *Ratio* v.8, 107–129.

Levi, I. (1967), *Gambling with Truth*, Cambridge, MA: MIT Press.

Levi, I. (1974), "On Indeterminate Probabilities," *Journal of Philosophy*, v.71, pp. 391–418.

Levi, I. (1980), *The Enterprise of Knowledge*, Cambridge, MA: Cambridge University Press.

Levi, I. (1984), *Decisions and Revisions*, Cambridge: Cambridge University Press.

Levi, I. (1991), *The Fixation of Belief and Its Undoing*, Cambridge: Cambridge University Press.

Levi, I. (1996), *For the Sake of the Argument*, Cambridge: Cambridge University Press.

Levi, I. (1997), *The Covenant of Reason*, Cambridge: Cambridge University Press.

Levi, I. (2002), "Commitment and Change of View," *Reason and Nature* edited by J. Bermudez and A. Millar, Oxford: Oxford University Press.

Levi, I. (2003), "Contracting from Epistemic Hell is Routine," *Synthese* 145, 141–164.

Levi, I. (2004), *Mild Contraction*, Oxford: Oxford University Press.

Olsson, E. (2003), "Avoiding Epistemic Hell: Levi on Pragmatism and Inconsistency," *Synthese* 145, 119–140.

Ramsey, F. P. (1990), *Philosophical Papers* ed. by D. H. Mellor, Cambridge: Cambridge University Press.

Savage, L. J. (1954), *The Foundations of Statistics*, New York: Wiley, second rev. ed. New York: Dover (1972).

Shackle, G. L. S. (1949), *Expectations in Economics* Cambridge: Cambridge University Press. Second rev. edition (1952).

Shackle, G. L. S. (1962), *Decision, Order and Time*, Cambridge: Cambridge University Press. Second ed. 1969.

Spohn, W. (1988), "A General non-probabilistic Theory of Inductive Reasoning," *Causation in Decision, Belief Change and Statistics*, ed. by W. Harper and B. Skyrms, Dordrecht: Reidel, 105–134.

Van Fraassen, B. (1995), "Fine Grained Opinion, Probability, and the Logic of Full Belief," *Journal of Philosophical Logic* 24, 345–377.

Chapter 27: Reflections on Conscious Reflection: Mechanisms of Impairment by Reasons Analysis

JAMIN HALBERSTADT AND TIMOTHY D. WILSON

Western culture has an ambivalent relationship with rationality, displaying a reverence for reasoning, objective evidence, and science, accompanied by a strong suspicion of them. Individuals respect logic and rationality, but often only when there are consistent with their intuition, and a common lay belief is that some, even most, judgments are best made on the basis of one's "gut feelings."

Is analytic thought good or bad? Perhaps not surprisingly, the answer lies in the theoretical expanse between these extremes. Researchers have become increasingly interested in this expanse, concluding that people are right to trust their intuitions under (at least) some circumstances. Studies of nonconscious judgments, automatic evaluations, and functional heuristics, for example, all show that people can and do make good decisions based on quick, unanalyzed responses (Bargh and Chartrand 1999; Damasio 1994; Dijksterhuis 2004; Gigerenzer 2000; LeDoux 1996; Wilson 2002). But it is also clear that people should not always trust their intuitions, which can be contaminated by unwanted or invalid information, often in ways in which people are unaware, as shown by research on the misuse of heuristics, biased information processing, and automatic prejudice (Devine 1989; Gilovich, Griffin, and Kahneman 2002; Greenwald and Banaji 1995; Nisbett and Ross 1980; Tversky and Kahneman 1974; Wilson and Brekke 1994).

In this chapter, we explore how conscious reflection has been operationalized and studied in the context of both preferences (e.g., for a particular sports team) and predictions (e.g., of whether that sports team will win its next game). In both cases conscious reflection makes judg-

ments worse, at least under some circumstances. But while substantial progress has been made in explaining the effects of reflection on preferences, how reflection reduces the accuracy of judgments relative to objective criteria poses an important theoretical puzzle. In the second half of the chapter, we speculate about a novel solution to this puzzle, reporting data to suggest that when people engage in conscious reflection they make relatively poor use of subjective experience, which can be a surprisingly valid cue to many objective decision criteria. Our proposal has implications for the integration of research on conscious reflection, as well as practical implications for when intuition can be trusted.

Effects of Conscious Reflection on Attitudes

Wilson and his colleagues have established that analyzing the reasons for one's attitude can change it (see Wilson, Dunn, Kraft, and Lisle 1989 for a review). In one study typical of the paradigm, college students evaluated two types of posters: reproductions of Impressionist paintings and contemporary, humorous posters, such as a photograph of a kitten perched on a rope with the caption, "Gimme a Break" (Wilson, Lisle, Schooler, Hodges, Klaaren, and LaFleur 1993). Half of the participants were asked to write down, privately and anonymously, why they felt the way they did about each poster, whereas control participants completed a filler task. Everyone then rated their liking for each poster and chose one poster to take home.

Control participants showed a strong preference for the Impressionist posters, giving these the highest ratings and overwhelmingly choosing one of them to take home. The people who analyzed reasons (hereafter "reasoners"), however, found it easiest to verbalize negative features of the Impressionist posters and positive features of the humorous ones. For example, many people focused on the colors of the Impressionist paintings, which were not entirely pleasing (e.g., "The green part in the middle of the Monet seems dull and dreary"). The reasons they found easiest to verbalize about the humorous posters were more positive (e.g., "I like the bright blue background, and I like the kitten's patchworky colors"). And, they based their preferences and choices on their reasons: They gave the humorous posters more positive ratings than did control participants, and they were significantly more likely to choose one of these posters to take home. The same reasons-based attitude change has been demonstrated with numerous other attitude objects, including soft drinks (Wilson and Dunn 1986), strawberry jams (Wilson and Schooler 1991), political candidates (Wilson, Kraft, and Dunn 1989), and romantic partners (Wilson and Kraft 1993). Such effects are not due to cognitive load or interference associated with the reasoning process, because participants who reason about *other* topics (such as their college major) fail to show attitude change. Nor do they appear to be the result of demand characteristics or self-presentational concerns (see Wilson et al. 1989 for a discussion of these issues).

Just because reasoners changed their attitudes, of course, does not necessarily mean that their attitudes were inferior in any way. One might even argue that a reasoned attitude is likely to be more stable or predictive of later behavior. However, research suggests that attitude change caused by analyzing reasons is unlikely to be particularly long-lasting. (Indeed, it would be rather surprising if a permanent change in people's attitudes could be brought about simply by asking them to explain why they felt the way they did.) After the passage of time, the reasons people brought to mind are less likely to be accessible in memory, and people are likely to revert to their chronic attitudes, those that come to mind without any conscious reflection.

One consequence of the temporary nature of reasons-induced attitude change is that attitudes expressed right after analyzing reasons will be worse predictors of people's later behavior than are unanalyzed reasons (Millar and Tesser 1986; Wilson, Bybee, Dunn, Hyman, and Rotondo 1984; for a review, see Wilson et al. 1989). A

second is that people will be prone to regret choices they make immediately after analyzing reasons, because their attitudes later revert to their chronic, unanalyzed preferences. Wilson et al. (1993) found support for this prediction in the poster study discussed earlier. They telephoned participants a few weeks after the study and asked them several questions about their current liking for the poster they chose to take home (e.g., how much they liked it, whether they still had it, whether they had hung it up on their wall). As predicted, people who analyzed reasons were less pleased with their choice of poster than people who did not.

It has also been proposed that reasoners' attitudes are not only relatively poor predictors of behavior and judgment satisfaction, but also that they are in some sense objectively inferior to nonreasoned ones. Wilson and Schooler (1991: Study 1), for example, compared participants' preferences for five brands of strawberry jam to the preferences of trained sensory experts. As predicted, people who first analyzed the reasons for their preferences reported attitudes that corresponded less with expert opinion than people who did not analyze reasons. Wilson and Schooler (1991: Study 2) similarly showed that attitudes toward psychology courses were impaired relative to a different type of expert – students who had actually taken the courses (a finding replicated by Halberstadt and Green 2004). And in perhaps the most face-valid demonstration of attitudinal impairment, Halberstadt and Green (2004) found that reasoners' evaluations of Olympic dives corresponded less well to the scores the dives received by the Olympic judges.

Halberstadt and Levine (1999) even demonstrated reasons-based impairment of judgments relative to an indisputably objective criterion for accuracy, the factual outcome of basketball games. In that study two samples of self-described "basketball experts" (students at Indiana University) predicted the outcomes of eight games prior to the third ("Sweet Sixteen") round of the National Collegiate Athletic Association (NCAA) Division I basketball tournament. Half of the participants, before making their predictions, listed reasons why they thought each team would do well or poorly in the tournament; the other half were told explicitly not to analyze their reasons and to make their judgments based on their "first instinct." As predicted (yet nevertheless surprisingly given the legendary unpredictability of the NCAA tournament), reasoners'

predictions were less accurate than nonreasoners', in terms of the proportion of outcomes correctly predicted, expert opinion (the Las Vegas
betting lines), and the margin of victory of those
games (see also Reifman, Larrick, Crandall, and
Fein 1996).

Mechanisms of Reasons-Based Interference

In the research on attitudinal analysis, thinking
about reasons is believed to lead to a change
in the information on which people base their
attitudes, a process we refer to as "information shift." Specifically, thinking about reasons
triggers three processes that lead to attitude
change. First, when queried about the reasons
for their attitude people construct their reasons online, either because they never knew the
actual causes of their attitudes (Bargh and Chartrand 1999; Nisbett and Wilson 1977b; Wegner 2002; Wilson 2002), or because they once
knew but later forgot. Indeed, research shows
that there is often little relationship between
people's memory for the attributes of a stimulus and their evaluation of that stimulus. That
is, people often form evaluations online as they
encode information about a stimulus, but are
unable to recall exactly what attributes of the
stimulus influenced their judgment (Hastie and
Park 1986). In any case, we believe that, when
asked to give reasons, people engage in a constructive process, whereby they infer their reasons, based on what sounds plausible, what is
accessible in memory, and what is easy to verbalize (Gazzaniga and LeDoux 1978; Hirstein
2005; Nisbett and Wilson 1977b). When people
in the Wilson et al. (1993) study generated reasons for why they liked or disliked the posters,
for example, it is unlikely that they were fully
aware of the exact reasons for their preferences,
causing them to construct reasons.

Second, the reasons people generate often
imply a somewhat different attitude than the
one people held before they thought about reasons. It might seem that people would attempt to
justify their initial attitude, focusing only on reasons that are consistent with it. If people are not
completely aware of why they love their spouse,
for example, it seems unlikely that they would
generate a list of reasons why they dislike him
or her. We acknowledge that such a justification
process can occur, whereby reasons that are consistent with an attitude are more accessible than
reasons that are inconsistent with it. Our point is
that there is there is room for slippage, whereby

the valence of reasons that are accessible, plausible, and easy to verbalize do not completely
match the valence of people's initial attitude.
People may not generate reasons why they hate
their spouse, but if they just had an argument
about whose turn it was to cook dinner, some
negative thoughts might be accessible and find
their way into their reasons.

Reasons also can have a different valence than
people's attitude because of cultural teachings
about why people feel the way they do. In Western cultures, there is a bias toward giving rational attributes of the attitude object as reasons
for liking or disliking it, even when attitudes
are caused by other factors. In the hundreds
of reasons we have coded over the years, by
far the majority of them are of this type, such
as, "We get along well because we have common friends and enjoy many of the same activities," "I like this puzzle because it had a logical answer," "I don't like this painting because
the flowers look like they're dying." In contrast,
there is ample evidence that attitudes are often
caused by factors other than rational cognitions
about the attributes of the attitude object, such
as mere exposure (Zajonc 1968), classical conditioning (Cacioppo, Marshall-Goodell, Tassinary,
and Petty 1992; Staats and Staats 1958), operant conditioning (Insko and Cialdini 1971), halo
effects (Nisbett and Wilson 1977a), and attitudes stemming from people's core values such
as their religious beliefs or the beliefs of their
parents (Ellsworth and Ross 1983; Herek 1986;
Rokeach 1973; Sears 1983). When people in our
studies are asked to think about reasons, they
rarely mention such factors.

Several studies have found support for the
idea that people's reasons do not entirely match
their initial attitudes. In these studies people
report their attitudes at Time 1, and then, at
some later time, they think about why they
feel the way they do about the attitude object.
Typically, we find that the correlation between
the valence of people's reasons and their initial attitude is significant, which is consistent
with the idea that people do not bring to mind
reasons that radically conflict with their initial
attitude. The correlations are sufficiently low,
however, to suggest that people often generate reasons that do not completely match the
valence of their initial attitudes. For example,
Wilson and Kraft (1993) asked people involved
in steady dating relationships to rate how happy
they were with their relationship. Then, on four
separate occasions, people wrote down why their

relationship was going the way it was. The correlation between the valence of the reasons people listed and their initial attitudes ranged from −.03 to .24, with an average of .10.

The third part of the information shift account is that people adopt the attitude implied by their reasons, much like a self-perception effect (Bem 1972), in part because they are unaware of their unawareness about the causes of their attitudes. They believe that the reasons they generate are accurate, a phenomenon that Wilson (2002) called the illusion of authenticity. For example, in our studies, almost no one has said, "I don't know" when asked for their reasons, even when they were assured that no one would ever look at what they wrote. Thus, people seem to have a fair degree of confidence that they know at least some of the reasons for their feelings – despite evidence that such reasons can be inaccurate.

Evidence for this part of the process has been obtained in studies in which researchers subtly influenced the kinds of reasons people would generate (Salancik 1974; Seligman, Fazio, and Zanna 1980). Seligman et al., for example, asked participants involved in romantic relationships one of two questions about why they were dating their partner. "I go out with this person *because I . . .*" or, "I go out with this person *in order to . . .*" The former question was designed to elicit reasons that were primarily internal (i.e., having to do with one's own feelings and commitment), while the latter question was designed to elicit reasons that were primarily external (i.e., having to do with factors other than love and commitment, such as the desire to impress one's friends). As predicted, participants seemed not to have realized that they had generated a biased set of reasons and adopted the attitude implied by their reasons. That is, subjects who answered the "because I" question reported significantly more love and expressed more of an intention to marry their partners than did subjects who answered the "in order to" question. Similarly, participants in reasons analysis studies often come up with biased samples of reasons, even without help from wily experimenters, and base their attitudes on these reasons. Consistent with this conclusion, the reasons that participants generate typically have a somewhat different valence than their initial attitude (as noted earlier), and the attitude they report after generating reasons is highly correlated with their reasons. For example, Wilson and Schooler (1991) found a correlation of .92 between the valence of people's reasons and their subsequent attitudes toward the posters.

More direct evidence for the hypothesis that people infer their attitudes from their reasons was obtained by Wilson, Hodges, and LaFleur (1995), who manipulated the valence of reasons that were accessible to people when they analyzed reasons. Participants read a list of positive, negative, and neutral behaviors that were performed by a target person and formed an initial impression of her. To manipulate whether the positive or negative behaviors were most accessible in memory, the researchers showed participants either the positive or negative behaviors again (participants expected to see all the behaviors again but the slide projector "malfunctioned" after only the positive or negative ones were repeated). After a delay, half of the participants listed reasons why they liked or disliked the target person, whereas half did not. All participants then rated how much they liked her.

The accessibility manipulation was successful; when the positive behaviors were repeated people were most likely to recall these behaviors, and when the negative behaviors were repeated people were most likely to recall these behaviors. Importantly, when people did *not* analyze reasons, the memory manipulation had no effect on their liking for the target person. Because people had already formed an impression of the target, showing them either the positive or negative behaviors did not change these impressions. When people analyzed the reasons for their impressions, however, they were influenced by the memory manipulation. Consistent with our hypothesis that people infer their attitudes from their reasons, subjects in the reasons condition reported significantly more liking for the target person when positive behaviors had been repeated than when negative behaviors had been repeated (see Figure 1).

These results are compatible with self-perception theory (Bem 1972), which argues that people often infer their attitudes from their behavior, but also extend the theory into new terrain. According to self-perception theory people infer their attitudes from external behavior that is observable by other people. In fact, a central tenet of the theory is that people are often in a functionally identical position to outside observers in knowing how they feel, because both actors and observers infer attitudes from the actor's overt behavior. Wilson et al. found

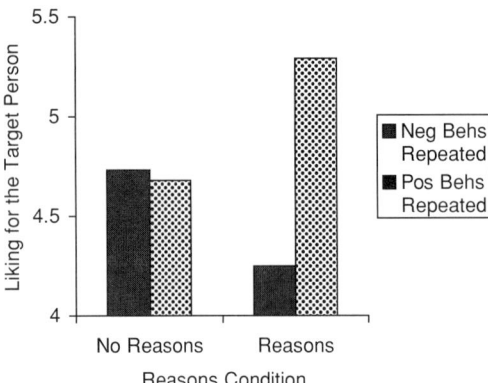

Figure 1. Liking for the target person: Study 1. The higher the rating, the greater the reported liking. *From*: Wilson T. D. (1995) *Journal of Personality and Social Psychology*, 69(1), 16–28.

that people also inferred their attitudes from *internal* cues, namely the nature of the thoughts that were accessible when they analyzed reasons – a self-perception process whereby people are not in a functionally identical position as outside observers, because they are inferring their attitudes from privileged information (their reasons).

Research on analyzing reasons also suggests that any situational factors that enhance the salience of particular reasons are likely to influence analyzed attitudes. This conclusion has particularly important implications for decision making in groups, where other people may provide novel reasons or enhance the plausibility of existing reasons for an individual's attitude. Such a mechanism, in different theoretical terms, has in fact been implicated in the group polarization effect, in which group members contribute confirmatory but unique information that pushes the group toward more extreme attitudes and decisions (Burnstein and Vinokur 1977). Thus, when the social setting serves to enhance the salience of reasons unrepresentative of individuals' attitudes, they may precipitate attitude change, at least when individuals are in an analytic frame of mind.

The Puzzle of the Quality of Objective Judgments

Although the information shift account of reasons analysis – a sometimes-unfortunate conjunction of memory-and based processing a biased subset of available information – provides a plausible mechanism of attitude change per se, it may not provide a complete explanation of all

reasoning phenomena, particularly the impairment of objective judgment quality and predictive accuracy. Specifically, it is not clear why information that is accessible, plausible, and easy to verbalize should happen to be less reliable than the information used under normal (nonreasoning) conditions. For the information shift account to explain impairment in basketball predictions, for example, it must account for why the reasons made hyperaccessible by analytic thought are worse cues than those used by people who do not analyze reasons. There is reason to believe, we suggest, that people naturally use cues and heuristics that often lead to accurate judgments, and that analyzing reasons reduces their use of these cues.

Affect Heuristics

We speculate that subjective feeling states, including both generalized affective experiences such as familiarity and fluency, as well as discrete emotional responses such as anger and fear, can serve as simple but highly predictive cues of even complex predictions and decisions. Gigerenzer, Todd et al. (1999), for example, have argued that many judgments can be approximated surprisingly well using stimulus recognition, that is, by simply choosing an alternative that is recognized over one that is not. This strategy, which Gigerenzer et al. (1999) call the "recognition heuristic" is effective when the criterion on which the stimuli are being judged covaries with the likelihood of stimulus exposure. For example, Goldstein and Gigerenzer (2002) asked Americans and Germans to judge the larger of pairs of German cities. By choosing the cities they recognized, the American participants performed better on this task than did German students, despite having less knowledge about the cities (the converse effect was found for judgments of American cities). Choosing recognized cities worked in this specific domain because, it turns out, the larger a city is, the more likely it is to be recognized, and only American students, who recognized some but not all of the cities, had this heuristic at their disposal.

More generally, whenever stimulus familiarity, which is the basis of recognition judgments, covaries via any mechanism with a criterion of interest, the former can in principle be used to directly and accurately infer the latter. Consider, for example, how we might reinterpret Halberstadt and Levine's (1999) basketball data in terms of a "familiarity heuristic." Although familiarity data were unfortunately not collected in that study, several proxies for familiarity can be used to explore the plausibility of an affective interference account. For example, the recency with which a team had appeared in the NCAA tournament should be related both to the subjective familiarity of a team (via extensive media coverage of the tournament), as well as to performance in the tournament in immediately subsequent years. Halberstadt and Catty (2005) discovered that if, for games in which only one team had appeared in the previous year's tournament, a person always bet on that team, and guessed on the remaining games, he could achieve 68.8 percent accuracy, approximately equal to nonreasoners' performance (70.4% vs. reasoners' 65.2%) in Halberstadt and Levine's original study. Similarly, Ayton and Onkal (1997, cited in Goldstein and Gigerenzer 2002) found that Turkish participants predicted the correct outcomes of British soccer matches 63 percent of the time by relying on their recognition of British cities (after which the soccer teams are named), a performance which almost equaled that of British participants (66%) who knew far more about the teams.

Furthermore, although familiarity has been extensively researched and linked to a number of important social psychological judgments (and errors), such as fame (Jacoby, Kelley, Brown, and Jasechko 1989), attractiveness (Halberstadt and Rhodes 2000; Halberstadt, Rhodes, and Catty 2003), liking (Zajonc 1968), and prototypicality (Franks and Bransford 1971; Gordon and Holyoak 1983; Halberstadt et al. 2003), in principle, any feeling state could become associated with any objective state of the world. Damasio's (1994) "somatic marker" hypothesis in fact explicitly assumes that valuable outcomes are associated with measurable physiological tags, which are used unconsciously to make good decisions in normal individuals. In a provocative illustration of the use and importance of somatic markers, Bechara, Damasio, Tranel, and Damasio (1997) found that normal participants chose the more advantageous of two bets, and showed corresponding physiological responses, before they could explicitly state the reasons for their choice. Participants with damage to their ventromedial prefrontal cortex (where emotional responses are stored and linked to declarative knowledge) showed neither anticipatory responses nor the adaptive decisions, even after they were able to state the differences between the bets. In general, prefrontal damage has been associated with impaired decision making and moral rea-

soning, in theory because individuals with this damage cannot access the somatic information that points toward adaptive responses. A number of other researchers have also proposed that positive emotional responses are used to infer judgments either directly or in the context of other cognitions. (e.g., Forgas 1995; Halberstadt and Badland 2005; Martin, Ward, Achee, and Wyer 1993; Monin 2003; Schwarz and Clore 1983, Slovic, Finucane, Peters, and MacGregor 2002).

Relatedly, perceptual and cognitive fluency – the ease with which a stimulus can be perceived and categorized – can potentially serve as a valid proxy for a variety of judgments. Winkielman and his colleagues have demonstrated a relationship between processing ease and positive affect, due either to the inherently positive nature of the feeling of successful comprehension and categorization, or due to the association that fluency has with positive cognitive assessments, such as the judgment that a stimulus is safe. Manipulations that facilitate stimulus processing, such as preceding the presentation of a stimulus with its outline (Reber, Winkielman, and Schwarz 1998) or a category-related priming word (2003, cited in Reber, Schwarz, and Winkielman 2004) increase liking judgments for the stimulus, as well as psychophysiological expressions of positive affect (2001). At the same time, fluency has been linked to a number of important social judgments, such as artistic pleasure (Leder, Belke, Oeberst, and Augustin 2004; Reber et al. 2004) and prototypicality (Winkielman, Halberstadt Fazendeiro, and Catty, 2006). Reber et al. (2004), for example, argue that many of the features of "beautiful" stimuli (clarity, simplicity, good form, familiarity, etc.) are empirically or theoretically associated with fluency. Indeed, Halberstadt and Hooton (in press) recently found that the speed with which a painting can be identified as a particular artist's work predicts liking for the painting.

Other, more discrete and basic emotional responses could also serve as valid cues to social judgments, such as of trustworthiness, safety, and threat. Just as behavioural implications of a stimulus (its "affordances") can theoretically be extracted directly from the rich information present in natural environmental covariation (MacArthur and Baron 1983), at least some social judgments may be inherent in the judgment targets themselves, and conveyed via reliable covariation with the particular feeling states they elicit. Thus, to the extent

Figure 2. Examples of violent offenders used in Halberstadt and Ngu (2005).

trustworthy people make us feel trusting, safe people make us feel safe, and unhappy people make us feel unhappy, we can accurately estimate these objective social realities directly from the corresponding feeling states. In a recent study in our laboratory, for example, participants were presented with a series of actual police "mug shots" of men, half of whom had been arrested for violent crimes (e.g., murder and serious assault) and the other half for nonviolent crimes (e.g., drunk driving and drug possession). Examples appear in Figure 2. Participants judged both the likelihood that each man was a violent offender (a task they can normally perform above chance; Memon, Vrij, and Bull 2003; Ruffman, personal communication 2005), as well as how threatened each man made them *feel*. Participants judged the violent offenders both as more violent and as more threatening than the nonviolent offenders and, more intriguingly, the latter judgments predicted (Halberstadt and Ngu, 2005) over 90 percent of the variance in the former. Although preliminary, these results suggest that social perceivers could rely on the natural correlation between their feelings and a person's dangerousness to assess the objective risk of a social interaction.

People's ability to exploit the correlations between feeling states and the stimuli that elicit them may partially account for the accuracy of "thin slice" judgments of personality (Ambady and Rosenthal 1992, 1993). Ambady and Rosenthal (1992), for example, found that undergraduates' ratings of teachers on fourteen dimensions of competency, such as empathy and supportiveness, correlated well with their "real" competen-

cies (i.e., student ratings at the end of the term), even when the former were based on silent video clips as short as 2s. What makes this finding so surprising, of course, is that it seems unlikely that teachers will display behavior representative or predictive of their performance in a short video clip, and indeed the researchers ruled out a number of simple nonverbal behaviours, such as head nodding and fidgeting, as judgment cues. However, even 2s slices of behavior can produce brief emotional responses in the perceiver, and if these responses correlate with the competency dimensions judged by others, the responses can be used to make direct and accurate inferences.

Reasoning and Affect Heuristics

Thus, affect heuristics – domain-specific relationships between feeling states and objective states of the world – can be a powerful and direct means of making accurate judgments. Such a mechanism is further implicated in reasons analysis effects because, we argue, reasoners are less likely than nonreasoners to access and use their subjective experiences appropriately. As already noted, historically the vast majority of information brought to mind by reasoners has been "cognitive," that is, rational arguments that do not invoke or reference affective experiences. One possible explanation of this bias involves relatively trivial semantic and conversational norms: People report cognitive reasons because they believe that the term "reasons" refers to such. Indeed "reason" means both "explanation" and "the human capacity for logic and rational thought," so it is plausible that people generally limit their "reasons" to those that can be logically and rationally justified. Even if people accept the validity of noncognitive reasons, cultural norms, particularly in the context of a scientific experiment, may prevent them from verbalizing those reasons. As noted, Western culture scorns decision-making based on illogical or emotional arguments, so individuals may be reluctant to report such factors when queried, or may themselves view them as implausible causes of their judgments.

Even if reasoners are willing to offer their subjective experiences as causes of their judgments, they may be unable to do so, for several reasons. First, such experiences may simply be too difficult to put into words. Although humans do have an enormous vocabulary of terms for their feeling states, this is not to say that they can precisely and accurately map those terms on to their own experience. Melcher and Schooler (1996), for example, argued that limitations on individuals' knowledge and language use could account for impaired memory following verbalization (a manipulation closely related to reasons analysis). The researchers found that participants with moderate knowledge of wine, whose vocabulary was inadequate relative to their perceptual and aesthetic experiences, who described the taste of wines remembered them less well than controls who did not verbalize. Importantly, such "verbal overshadowing" did not occur in either wine experts or wine novices, both of whose language and experience are likely to be more equally matched. Thus, both inadequate introspective ability to distinguish subjective experiences, as well as limited language to represent those experiences, are likely to limit reports of emotional responses in analyses of judgments.

Complicating matters further is that analytic thought, and reasons analysis in particular, is effortful, and effort itself is associated with affect. Research on "cognitive fluency," the effort involved in apprehending and categorizing a stimulus, demonstrates the relationship between processing ease (usually operationalized as forced choice categorization speed) and positive affect.

Although there are no studies examining the effort associated with reasons analysis per se, related studies on the subjective experience of retrieval (e.g., Schwarz 1998; Winkielman and Schwarz 2001) illustrate the informational value and use of processing ease in judgment. Winkielman and Schwarz (2001), for example, manipulated the difficulty of retrieving childhood memories (by asking participants to recall either four or twelve such memories), as well as the meaning of that difficulty (by suggesting that either positive or negative events tend to be forgotten). Participants believing in positive amnesia judged their childhood as more happy after the difficult task of recalling twelve events, than after the easy task of recalling four events. The reverse was true for participants believing in negative amnesia. Similarly, participants who find the experience of reasons analysis difficult or unpleasant are liable to use that subjective information in conjunction with their other beliefs to formulate a judgment. Indeed research on "need for cognition," the individual difference variable associated with reasons analysis, assumes that analytic processing is inherently effortful, but not necessarily unpleasant (items on the Need for Cognition scale include "Thinking is not my idea of fun" as well as "I prefer my life to be filled with puzzles that I must solve"). In any case it is clear that the cognitive effort involved in reasons analysis will produce affect that could obscure the detection of other judgment-relevant subjective responses.

Finally, reasoners may be impaired at identifying emotional responses in particular because, even with the proper skills and language, language and reasoning may be cognitively or neurologically incompatible with emotion perception. Recent research and theorizing (e.g., Halberstadt 2003, 2005; Schooler 2002) suggests that verbal processes may be incompatible with "configural" stimuli – stimuli that are processed as nondecomposable wholes rather than individual parts. Schooler and his colleagues have repeatedly shown that verbalization impairs recognition memory for configural stimuli, including faces (e.g., Dodson, Johnson, and Schooler 1997; Fallshore and Schooler 1995; Schooler and Engstler-Schooler 1990), facial expressions (Halberstadt 2005), colors (Schooler and Engstler-Schooler 1990), voices (Perfect, Hunt, and Harris 2002), wines (Melcher and Schooler 1995), music (Houser, Fiore, and Schooler 1996), and visual forms (Brandimonte, Schooler, and Gabbino 1997). These and other findings have led to the suggestion that language use produces a shift away from configural processing, speculatively related to the disparate brain regions controlling the two, which impairs the encoding and retrieval of configural stimuli (Schooler 2002).

Therefore, the featural processing shift associated with explicit analysis will interfere with the perception of a multidimensional feeling state if it is normally fused as a unitary subjective experience.

Empirical Studies

Thus, affect heuristics can in principle provide an account of reasons-based judgment impairment by assuming that quality is sometimes strongly predicted by the perceiver's subjective experience, and that subjective experience is in turn less likely to be used effectively in analytic conditions. To test the plausibility of this account empirically, Halberstadt and Catty (2005) examined reasoned judgments in a new domain, music popularity, for which they believed a high-valid affect heuristic – subjective familiarity – would be available. That is, a song's objective popularity (as quantified by its position on a national "top singles" list compiled based on sales and airplay) is likely to be strongly predicted by its subjective familiarity, in this case via the overwhelming media exposure popular songs receive. To test this assumption, Halberstadt and Catty asked participants to judge their subjective familiarity with songs that had appeared in either a high or low position on the New Zealand Top Singles List, emphasizing that they should assess their subjective *feeling* of familiarity, as opposed to whether they believed they had heard the songs before. As predicted, the more familiar a song felt, the more popular it had actually been ($r = .79$), and the more popular it was judged to be ($r = .73$).

Thus, subjective feelings of familiarity are a strongly predictive cue to the objective criterion of music popularity. However if, as argued above, reasons analysis interferes with either the assessment or use of this subjective experience, then it should decrease the correlation between familiarity and popularity judgments and, depending on just how good a cue familiarity is relative to other, more cognitive factors, it should decrease the accuracy of judgments. As an initial test of this hypothesis, Halberstadt and Catty asked participants to judge the more popular of pairs of songs that differed in their objective popularity. Ostensibly to help them with their decision making, half of the participants, while listening to short excerpts from each song, were told to "think about and analyze *why* one song might have been more or less popu-

lar than the other" (emphasis in original instructions), and to type into the computer at least two of those reasons. As in the pretest, subjective familiarity (measured later in the experiment) was associated with both perceived and actual popularity. Preliminary analyses indicated that participants chose the more familiar song of a pair as the more popular one 83 percent of the time and, because familiarity and popularity are indeed related, their choice was correct 76 percent of the time. Unexpectedly, however, reasoners did not differ from controls on either of these measures.

Further analysis of the data, however, revealed an important moderating variable. Although familiarity was predictive of popularity overall, it was not equally predictive for every participant. For whatever reasons – perhaps exposure to or liking for pop music – participants' "familiarity validity" (effectively, a participant's theoretical accuracy assuming consistent use of the familiarity heuristic) ranged from .43 to .92 (chance accuracy = .5). In other words, familiarity was useless for some participants and a near-perfect cue for others. As illustrated in Figure 3, reasoning impaired familiarity use and judgment accuracy only for participants with relatively high familiarity validity. Thus, the hypothesis that reasoning interferes with the use of affect heuristics was confirmed, but with an important, and (in retrospect) obvious, caveat: such impairment is only evidenced when subjective experience is indeed a good cue to judgment. When reasoning decreases use of a subjective feeling that was poorly predictive of the judgment criterion, the judgment is likely to remain unchanged, or even to improve, depending on value of the alternative information used. That is, when other cues exist that are highly predictive of the criterion, then reasoning could be beneficial by decreasing reliance on the (less valid) subjective information. Thus the affect heuristics account acknowledges that reasoning is sometimes beneficial, and in principle provides an algorithm for predicting when it will be: specifically, when subjective responses are both heavily weighted in a particular (nonanalyzed) judgment, and at the same time poorly predictive of its criterion.

Of course being essentially correlational, this study on its own is insufficient to show that participants chose the more familiar songs *because* they were familiar. Familiar songs may have differed from unfamiliar songs along other dimensions that could have served as cues to accurate

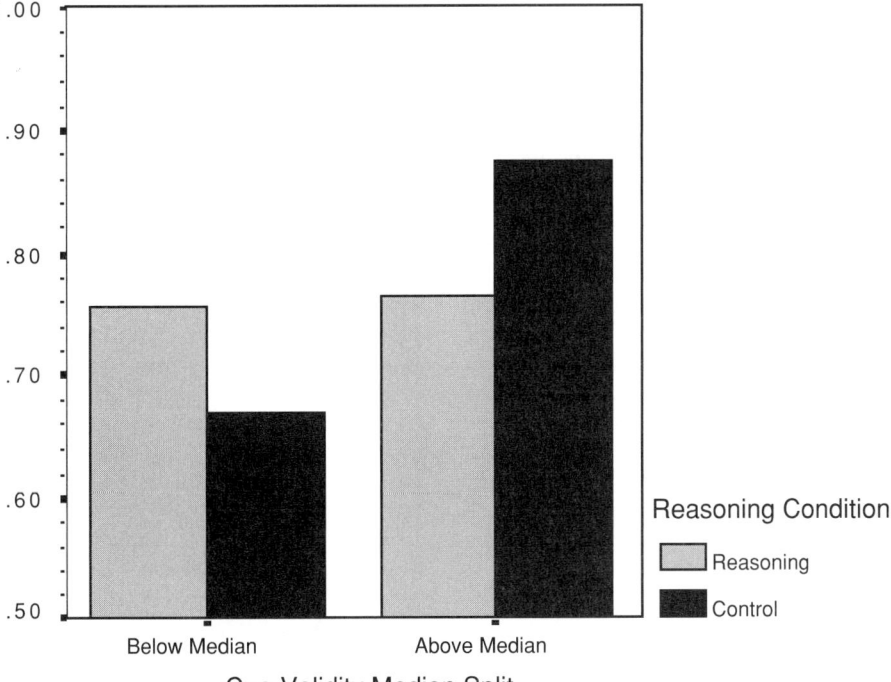

Figure 3. Percent of correct popularity judgments as a function of reasoning condition and cue validity.

judgments. In another study, however, Halber-stadt and Catty (in press) manipulated the famil-iarity of a new set of "songs" (actually brief, novel bass solos downloaded from the Internet) by pre-senting some of them earlier in the study. Again, participants judged which of two solos was more popular (according to a supposed Internet rat-ing system). Each pair of solos consisted of one familiar (i.e., previously heard) solo and one unfamiliar (never before heard) solo. And again, results indicated that participants who first ana-lyzed and recorded the reasons for their judg-ments before making them were less likely to choose previously encountered solos as more popular.

Halberstadt and Catty's studies thus pro-vide the first direct evidence for changes in the use of subjective experience following analytic thought, and thereby a plausible link between reasons analysis and objective decision quality. Participants who analysed their reasons were less likely to choose subjectively familiar songs as more popular. Unfortunately, the state of the world was such that, at least for many partici-pants, the subjectively familiar songs *were* more popular, and their inability or unwillingness to rely on their feelings of familiarity impaired their judgments.

When Will Reasoning Impair Judgment?

In sum, we have speculated that some judg-ments can and will be made using affect heuris-tics – that is, using feeling states that are directly predictive of the criterion of interest – and in these cases reasons analysis can produce objec-tively worse judgments by interfering with the use of the critical feeling states. We consider this account to be an extension of the information shift account offered for reasons-based attitude change. The latter proposes that reasoners fre-quently bring to mind information that is not representative of the real reasons for their atti-tude. The temporarily changed attitudes that result can be nonetheless damaging when sub-jectively poor (i.e., dissatisfying) decisions are made under their influence, but it is not clear why either the attitudes or the judgments should be worse relative to objective quality criteria. The affect heuristics account fills this theoretical gap by suggesting that people often make quick unanalyzed judgments on the basis of valid sub-jective responses and proposing several mech-anisms by which analytic thought will partic-ularly underweight such information. Together, the two accounts provide a more complete pic-ture of the process of analytic impairment, and suggest different conditions under which analytic thought will be most risky. We explore some of these conditions next.

VALIDITY

Whether analyzing reasons impairs objective judgments depends on whether the affective heuristic is a valid cue to the decision criterion. If it is not strongly predictive of the criterion, or is less predictive than the information brought to mind and used during reasons analysis, then its disruption will have either no effect or will improve judgment. Furthermore, even when valid information is accessible, reasoners may fail to use it if it seems implausible. The same is true of the information shift account: If the actual causes of attitudes are implausible, then people who analyze reasons will overlook these factors and focus on other reasons, often resulting in attitude change.

EXPERTISE

Expertise is a particularly interesting variable because there are suggestions of contradictory effects in the literatures on attitudes and judgment. A number of studies on attitude change and attitude-behavior consistency have concluded that experts are relatively immune to the effects of reasons analysis. For example, Wilson, Kraft, and Dunn (1989: Study 2) found that reasoning only changed attitudes toward political candidates among participants who were relatively unfamiliar with them. Knowledge had a similar moderating effect in Wilson et al.'s (1993) poster study discussed earlier, as well as in several other studies (see Table 1). By contrast, Halberstadt and Levine (1999), who explicitly recruited knowledgeable participants for their study, proposed that their effects might be more pronounced among experts.

This apparent contradiction, however, may be due to confounding two different kinds of expertise. One sense of expertise involves simply having more knowledge about a judgment domain, including facts about the decision options as well as about one's own responses to them. However, another dimension of expertise is the ability to use one's knowledge effectively. Although we believe that expertise in both senses will buffer an individual against the biasing effects of reasons analysis, the fact that they can emerge independently complicates any simple relationship between expertise and judgment, and requires that we consider their effects in turn.

The bulk of research on reasons analysis has treated expertise as factual knowledge. A number of studies have found that people who are knowledgeable about a topic are less susceptible to attitude change after analyzing reasons. For example, Wilson et al. (1989: Study 2) asked college students to rate their attitudes toward several candidates for president, early in the 1988 U.S. presidential race (before the major parties selected their candidates). Participants also rated how familiar they were with the candidates. Several weeks later they took part in an ostensibly unrelated laboratory experiment, in which half of the participants listed their reasons, privately and anonymously, as to why they liked or disliked six of the candidates. The other participants completed a filler task. All participants then rated their attitudes toward the candidates again. The standard effect of analyzing reasons was found among people who were relatively unknowledgeable: People who analyzed reasons changed their attitudes significantly more than those who did not. However, analyzing reasons had no significant effects on the attitudes of knowledgeable people. Knowledge had a similar moderating effect in the Wilson et al. (1993) poster study discussed earlier, as well as in several other studies (see Table 1).

There are a variety of possibilities as to why knowledgeable people are immune to reasons-based attitude change. Knowledgeable people may simply have stronger attitudes that are less likely to change in response to any manipulation, including introspecting about reasons. We suspect, however, that the answer lies in the conditions we have discussed that must be met for analyzing reasons to change people's attitudes: People have to bring to mind reasons that are of a different valence than their initial attitude, and they have to infer that these reasons reflect their current attitude. Do knowledgeable people bring to mind reasons that are more consistent with their attitudes, do they prevent themselves from basing their attitudes on their reasons, or both? To answer this question, we examined the reasons that knowledgeable and unknowledgeable people gave in the studies listed in Table 1. There was no evidence that knowledgeable people were less likely to base their attitudes on their reasons. Averaging across the five studies, the correlation between reasons and subsequently reported attitudes was no lower among knowledgeable than unknowledgeable people; in fact, it was slightly (albeit nonsignificantly)

Table 1: Studies Finding That Knowledge Moderates the Effects of Analyzing Reasons on Attitudes

Study	Attitude Object	Measure of Expertise/ Knowledge	Results
Wilson et al. (1984: Study 3)	Dating relationships	Length of relationship	Analyzing reasons lowered attitude-behavior consistency for low knowledge group, no effects in high knowledge group.
Wilson, Kraft, and Dunn (1989: Study 1)	Candidates for 1984 U.S. presidential election	Knowledge test	Analyzing reasons lowered attitude-behavior consistency for low knowledge group, no effects in high knowledge group.
Wilson, Kraft, and Dunn (1989: Study 2)	Candidates for 1988 U.S. presidential election	Self-reported familiarity with the candidates	Analyzing reasons produced attitude change in low knowledge group, not in high knowledge group.
Wilson et al. (1993)	Art posters	Number of art courses taken in high school and college	Analyzing reasons produced (a) attitude change and (b) reduced satisfaction with choice of poster in low knowledge but not high knowledge group.
Erber, Hodges, and Wilson (1995)	Ronald Reagan	Self-reported knowledge	Analyzing reasons more likely to produce attitude change among people low in knowledge (trend).

higher among knowledgeable people, $M = .87$ versus .75.

In contrast, knowledgeable people were less likely to bring to mind reasons that conflicted with their initial attitude. In two of the studies listed in Table 1, people's initial attitudes were measured before they analyzed reasons attitudes (Erber, Hodges, and Wilson 1995; Wilson et al. 1989: Study 1), and the correlation between these initial attitudes and the valence of the reasons they subsequently listed were higher among knowledgeable people. Averaging across studies, the correlation between reasons and initial attitudes was .87 among knowledgeable people and .65 among unknowledgeable people, $z = 2.34$, $p < .05$. Thus, knowledgeable people appear to be immune to the effects of analyzing reasons because they are less likely to generate reasons that conflict with their initial attitudes.

We should note that the reason for this difference is not entirely clear. There are at least two possibilities: First, knowledgeable people might have so much experience with the attitude object that they know more why they feel the way they do, whereas unknowledgeable people may be less aware of their reasons and

thus generate plausible-sounding causes, some of which are of a different valence than their initial attitude. Or, knowledgeable people may be no more aware of the actual causes of their attitudes than unknowledgeable people, but might be more likely to generate reasons that are consistent with their initial attitude. They might, for example, have more of a vested interest in their attitude (Crano 1995), or a better developed schema or knowledge-structure (Lusk and Judd 1988), leading to the construction of reasons that conform to their attitudes. In support of this latter possibility, we found that the reasons reported by knowledgeable people were of greater evaluative consistency than the reasons reported by unknowledgeable people. That is, in the five studies in Table 1, knowledgeable people were significantly more likely to report reasons of a consistent valence, whereas unknowledgeable people were more likely to report a mixture of positive and negative reasons (see Lusk and Judd 1988 for a similar result). The more knowledgeable people become about a topic the more they might organize their knowledge around a consistent evaluation, such that when they think about reasons, they focus on reasons that are consistent with this evaluation.

The second dimension of expertise, the ability to use one's knowledge effectively, also may moderate the effects of analyzing reasons. From the perspective of the information shift account, experts might be better able to identify the real reasons underlying their attitude, thereby avoiding the first condition necessary for introspection to cause attitude change (bringing to mind inaccurate or incomplete reasons). More intriguingly, experts might be able to recognize when the reasons they generate are not representative of their feelings, thereby avoiding the second condition necessary for introspection to cause attitude change (the inference that one's reasons reflect one's attitude). The latter is similar to Salthouse's (1991) conception of expertise as the circumvention of limitations on human information processing. "Experts" and "novices" alike would be unable to identify all of the causes of their attitudes via introspection, but only experts would recognize this limitation and overcome it by short-circuiting the self-perception process (inferring one's attitude from one's reasons) that normally occurs. Similarly, from the perspective of the affect heuristics account, experts may have learned to identify and use particular feeling states and the covariations between their feeling states and judgment criteria. In fact, participants in Halberstadt and Catty's research showed some proficiency in using their feeling states strategically; participants whose subjective familiarity was more weakly predictive of popularity were less likely to use familiarity to make their judgments. Because familiarity validity and use are theoretically independent, this difference suggests that participants may have moderated their use of familiarity to maximize its effectiveness (although any strategic use of familiarity was unconscious; a follow-up study revealed that participants had no explicit knowledge of the validity of their subjective cues).

Some social psychological theories have posited a general tendency to focus on oneself and to recognize one's abilities, traits, and feelings. Self-awareness theory (Carver and Scheier 1981; Duval and Wicklund 1972) argues that people cannot simultaneously focus inward on themselves and outward on the environment, and thus alternate between these two types of "awarenesses." Furthermore, the theory argues that there are individual differences in the amount of time people spend focusing on themselves (Fenigstein, Scheier, and Buss 1975). Some people are chronically high in "private self-

consciousness," in that they are more likely to endorse questionnaire items such as, "I reflect about myself a lot" (Fenigstein et al. 1975: 524). Furthermore, there is some evidence that people high in private self-consciousness make more accurate reports about their traits and abilities (e.g., Scheier, Buss, and Buss 1978).

It might seem that people high in private self-consciousness would also be more accurate at detecting the reasons for their attitudes, due to repeated practice. We are, however, dubious about such claims. Our hunch is that detecting the reasons for our feelings and attitudes is not a skill that improves with practice (Wilson 2002). The human mind seems to be constructed in such a way that a great deal of information processing occurs outside of awareness, and trying to improve the accuracy of introspection about reasons may be as difficult as trying to improve the accuracy of introspection about the digestive system. Some evidence consistent with this view can be found in the use of introspection as a method by early experimental psychologists such as Titchener and Wundt. Accurate introspection about the contents of the mind required practice, they reasoned; it was a skill that could be obtained. According to Boring (1953), Wundt gave his participants ten thousand practice trials before they were considered to be "good" introspectionists. And yet, even with this amazing amount of practice, the introspectionist method failed, largely because of the failure of one person's introspections to reliably match another's.

We have examined the question of individual differences in the accuracy of introspection in some of our studies, by including a few relevant personality measures. In the Wilson et al. (1993) poster study, for example, many of our participants had completed the Fenigstein et al. (1975) self-consciousness inventory during an earlier mass testing session. We examined whether any of the components of this measure – private self-consciousness, public self-consciousness, and social anxiety – moderated the effects of analyzing reasons, and found that they did not. In another study (Hodges and Wilson 1994), scores were available on another measure that might reflect expertise in introspection, Leary, Shepperd, McNeil, Jenkins, and Barnes's (1986) construct of "objectivism." This measure assesses the extent to which people base their judgments and decisions on introspections about empirical information versus subjective and intuitive considerations (e.g., one item states, "After I make a decision, it is often difficult for me to give logical reasons for it"; Leary et al. 1986: 34). Interestingly, this measure had no significant moderating effects on the tendency for analyzing reasons to change people's attitudes.

We do not mean to suggest that there are no individual differences that moderate the effects of analyzing reasons. There are other reasonable candidates that we have not examined, such as Cacioppo and Petty's (1982) measure of the need for cognition and Hansell, Mechanic, and Brondolo's (1986) measure of introspectiveness. Another possible individual difference is the extent to which people are able to deduce the reasons for their attitudes from observations of their own behavior. Even if people do not have direct access to their reasons, they can sometimes infer reasons from careful observations of the co-occurence of their preferences and the conditions that precede them (Wilson and Stone 1985). For example, after many observations a person might accurately infer that he or she prefers romantic partners who are independent and nurturing, even if this person was previously unaware of these influences. Conceivably there are individuals who are better at this sort of deduction than others.

Summary and Conclusions

Several lines of research have implicated analytic thought in attitude change, attitude-behavior inconsistency, subjectively poorer attitude judgments and behavioral predictions, and impairment of objectively verifiable judgments. Previous research and theory have produced a plausible model of thought-induced attitude change, what we termed the "information shift account," in which reasoners overweight salient, plausible, and easily verbalized information, to the exclusion of other factors on which their "real" attitude is based. On its own, however, this account is less plausible as an explanation of how reasons analysis can produce objectively worse judgments.

In this chapter, we have reviewed research on information shift and proposed a supplementary account to bridge the gap between reasoning-driven biases in information accessibility and judgment quality. In many domains, quality outcomes are associated with subjective experiences – particularly familiarity and positive affect, but potentially more specific and basic emotional responses as well – either as evolved psychological mechanisms or as fortuitous environmental covariations. In these cases, people can and do rely primarily or exclusively on their subjective feeling states as heuristics for quality judgments, and analyzing reasons can impair judgment by obscuring the nature or magnitude of the critical feeling states.

References

Ambady, N., and Rosenthal, R. (1992). Thin slices of expressive behavior as predictors of interpersonal consequences: A meta-analysis. *Psychological Bulletin*, 111, 256–274.

Ambady, N., and Rosenthal, R. (1993). Half a minute: Predicting teacher evaluations from thin slices of nonverbal behavior and physical attractiveness. *Journal of Personality and Social Psychology*, 64, 431–441.

Bargh, J. A., and Chartrand, T. L. (1999). The unbearable automaticity of being. *American Psychologist*, 54, 462–479.

Bechara, A., Damasio, H., Tranel, D., and Damasio, A. R. (1997). Deciding advantageously before knowing advantageous strategy. *Science*, 275, 1293–1295.

Bem, D. J. (1972). Self-perception theory. In L. Berkowitz (Ed.), *Advances in Experimental Social Psychology* (Vol. 6, pp. 1–62). New York: Academic Press.

Boring, E. G. (1953). A history of introspection. *Psychological Bulletin*, 50, 169–189.

Brandimonte, Maria A., Schooler, J. W., and Gabbino, P. (1997). Attenuating verbal overshadowing through color retrieval cues. *Journal of Experimental Psychology: Learning, Memory, and Cognition*, 23, 915–931.

Burnstein, E., and Vinokur, A. (1977). Persuasive argumentation and social comparison as determinants of attitude polarization. *Journal of Experimental Social Psychology*, 13, 315–332.

Cacioppo, J. T. Marshall-Goodell, B. S., Tassinary, L. G., and Petty, R. E. (1992). Rudimentary determinants of attitudes: Classical conditioning is more effective when prior knowledge about the attitude stimulus is low than high. *Journal of Experimental Social Psychology*, 28, 207–233.

Cacioppo, J. T., and Petty, R. E. (1982). The need for cognition. *Journal of Personality and Social Psychology*, 42, 116–131.

Carver, C. S., and Scheier, M. F. (1981). *Attention and self-regulation: A control-theory approach to human behavior*. New York: Springer-Verlag.

Crano, W. D. (1995). Attitude strength and vested interest. In R. E. Petty and J. A. Krosnick (Eds.), *Attitude strength: Antecedents and consequences* (p. 2). Hillsdale, NJ: Lawrence Erlbaum Associates.

Damasio, A. (1994). *Descarte's error: Emotion, reason, and the human brain*. New York: Grosset/Putnam.

Devine, P. G. (1989). Stereotypes and prejudice: Their automatic and controlled components. *Journal of Personality and Social Psychology*, 56, 680–690.

Dijksterhuis, A. (2004). Think different: The merits of unconscious thought in preference development and decision making. *Journal of Personality and Social Psychology*, 87, 586–598.

Dodson, C. S., Johnson, M. K., and Schooler, J. W. (1997). The verbal overshadowing effect: Why descriptions impair face recognition. *Memory and Cognition*, 25, 129–139.

Duval, S., and Wicklund, R. A. (1972). *A theory of objective self-awareness*. New York: Academic Press.

Ellsworth, P. C., and Ross, L. (1983). Public opinion and capital punishment: A close examination of the views of abolitionists and retentionists. *Crime and Delinquency*, 29, 116–169.

Erber, M. W., Hodges, S. D., and Wilson, T. D. (1995). Attitude strength, attitude stability, and the effects of analyzing reasons. In R. E. Petty and J. A. Krosnick (Eds.), *Attitude strength: Antecedents and consequences* (p. 2). Hillsdale, NJ: Lawrence Erlbaum Associates.

Fallshore, M., and Schooler, J. W. (1995). The verbal vulnerability of perceptual expertise. *Journal of Experimental Psychology: Learning, Memory, and Cognition*, 21, 1608–1623.

Fenigstein, A., Scheier, M. F., and Buss, A. H. (1975). Public and private self-consciousness: Assessment and theory. *Journal of Consulting and Clinical Psychology*, 43, 522–527.

Forgas, J. P. (1995). Mood and judgment: The affect infusion model (AIM). *Psychological Bulletin*, 117, 39–66.

Franks, J. J., and Bransford, J. D. (1971). Abstraction of visual patterns. *Journal of Experimental Psychology*, 90, 65–74.

Gazzaniga, M. S., and LeDoux, J. E. (1978). *The integrated mind*. New York: Plenum Press.

Gigerenzer, G. (2000). *Adaptive thinking: Rationality in the real world*. London: Oxford University Press.

Gigerenzer, G., Todd, P. M., and the ABC Research Group (1999). *Simple heuristics that make us smart*. New York: Oxford University Press.

Gilovich, T., and Griffin, D. (2002). Introduction – Heuristics and biases, then and now. In T. Gilovich, D. Griffin, and D. Kahneman (eds.), *Heuristics and biases: The psychology of intuitive judgment* (pp. 1–18). New York: Cambridge University Press.

Gilovich, T., Griffin, D., and Kahneman, D. (Eds.) (2002). *Heuristics and biases: The psychology of intuitive judgment*. New York: Cambridge University Press.

Goldstein, D. G., and Gigerenzer, G. (2002). Models of ecological rationality: The recognition heuristic. *Psychological Review*, 109, 75–90.

Gordon, P. C., and Holyoak, K. J. (1983). Implicit learning and generalization of the "mere exposure" effect. *Journal of Personality and Social Psychology*, 45, 492–500.

Greenwald, A. G., and Banaji, M. R. (1995). Implicit social cognition: Attitudes, self-esteem, and stereotypes. *Psychological Review*, 102, 4–27.

Halberstadt, J. B. (2003). The paradox of emotion attribution: Explanation biases perceptual memory for emotional expressions. *Current Directions in Psychological Science*, 12, 197–201.

Halberstadt, J. (2005). Featural shift in explanation-biased memory for emotional faces. *Journal of Personality and Social Psychology*, 88, 38–49.

Halberstadt, J. B., and Catty, S. (2005, July). Use and disruption of simple heuristics in intuitive judgments. Paper presented at the 14th General Meeting of the European Association of Experimental Social Psychology, Wurtzburg, Germany.

Halberstadt, S. B., and Catty, S. (in press). Analytic thought disrupt, familiarity-based decision making. *Social Cognition*.

Halberstadt, J. B., and Green J. (2004). Explicit reasoning impairs judgments of Olympic dives. *Australian Journal of Psychology*, 56 (Suppl), 116.

Halberstadt, J. B., and Hooton, K. (in press). The affect desruption hypothesis: The effect of analytic thought on the fluency and appeal of art. *Cognition: Emotion*.

Halberstadt, J. B., and Levine, G. L. (1999). Effects of reasons analysis on the accuracy of predicting basketball games. *Journal of Applied Social Psychology*, 29, 517–530.

Halberstadt S. B. and Ngu P. (2005). Use of threat cues in judgments of objective danger. Unpublished data, University of Otago.

Halberstadt, J. B., and Rhodes, G. (2000). The attractiveness of non-face averages: Implications for an evolutionary explanation of the attractiveness of average faces. *Psychological Science*, 11, 289–293.

Halberstadt, J. B., Rhodes, G., and Catty, S. (2003). Subjective and objective familiarity as explanations for the attraction to average faces. In F. Columbus (Ed.), *Advances in psychology research: Vol. 22* (pp. 35–50). Hauppauge, NY: Nova Science Publishers, Inc.

Hansell, S., Mechanic, D., and Brondolo, E. (1986). Introspectiveness and adolescent development. *Journal of Youth and Adolescence*, 15, 115–132.

Hastie, R., and Park, B. (1986). The relationship between memory and judgment depends on whether the judgment task is memory-based or on-line. *Psychological Review*, 93, 258–268.

Herek, G. (1986). The instrumentality of ideologies: Toward a neofunctional theory of attitudes. *Journal of Social Issues*, 42, 99–114.

Hirstein, W. (2005). *Brain fiction: Self-deception and the riddle of confabulation*. Cambridge, MA: MIT Press.

Hodges, S. D., and Wilson, T. D. (1994). Effects of analyzing reasons on attitude change: The moderating role of attitude accessibility. *Social Cognition*, 11, 353–366.

Houser, T., Fiore, S. M., and Schooler, J. W. (1996). Verbal overshadowing of music memory: What happens when you describe that tune? Unpublished manuscript, University of Pittsburgh, Learning Research and Development Center.

Insko, C. A., and Cialdini, C. A. (1971). *Interpersonal influence in a controlled setting: The verbal reinforcement of attitude*. New York: General Learning Press.

Jacoby, L. L., Lindsay, S. D., and Toth, J. P. (1992). Unconscious influences revealed: Attention, awareness, and control. *American Psychologist*, 47, 802–809.

Lane, S. M., and Schooler, J. W. (2004). Skimming the surface: Verbal overshadowing of analogical recall. *Psychological Science*, 15, 715–719.

Leary, M. R., Shepperd, J. A., McNeil, M. S., Jenkins, T. B., and Barnes, B. D. (1986). Objectivism in information utilization: Theory and measurement. *Journal of Personality Assessment*, 50, 32–43.

Leder, H., Belke, B., Oeberst, A., and Augustin, D. (2004). A model of aesthetic appreciation and aesthetic judgments. *British Journal of Psychology*, 95, 489–508.

LeDoux, J. (1996). *The emotional brain: The mysterious underpinnings of emotional life*. New York: Simon & Schuster.

Lusk, C. M., and Judd, C. M. (1988). Political expertise and the structural mediators of candidate evaluations. *Journal of Experimental Social Psychology*, 24, 105–126.

MacArthur, L. Z., and Baron, R. (1983). Toward an ecological theory of social perception. *Psychological Review*, 90, 215–238.

Martin, L. L., Ward, D. W., Achee, J. W., and Wyer, R. S. (1993). Mood as input: People have to interpret the motivational implications of their moods. *Journal of Personality and Social Psychology*, 64, 317–326.

Melcher, J. M., and Schooler, J. W. (1996). The misremembrance of wines past: Verbal and perceptual expertise differentially mediate verbal over-shadowing of taste memory. *Journal of Memory and Language*, 35, 231–245.

Memon, A., Vrij, A., and Bull, R. (2003). *Psychology and law: Truthfulness, accuracy and credibility*. West Sussex: John Wiley & Sons Ltd.

Millar, M. G., and Tesser, A. (1986). Effects of affective and cognitive focus on the attitude-behavior relationship. *Journal of Personality and Social Psychology*, 51, 270–276.

Monin, B. (2003). The warm glow heuristic: When liking leads to familiarity. *Journal of Personality and Social Psychology*, 58, 1035–1048.

Nisbett, R. E., and Ross, L. (1980). *Human inference: Strategies and shortcomings of human judgment*. Englewood Cliffs, NJ: Prentice Hall.

Nisbett, R. E., and Wilson, T. D. (1977a). The halo effect: Evidence for unconscious alteration of judgments. *Journal of Personality and Social Psychology*, 35, 250–256.

Nisbett, R. E., and Wilson, T. D. (1977b). Telling more than we can know: Verbal reports on mental processes. *Psychological Review*, 84, 231–259.

Perfect, T. J., Hunt, L. J., and Harris, C. M. (2002). Verbal overshadowing in voice recognition. *Applied Cognitive Psychology*, 16, 973–980.

Reber, R., Schwarz, N., and Winkielman, P. (2004). Processing fluency and aesthetic pleasure: Is beauty in the perceiver's processing experience? *Personality and Social Psychology Review*, 8, 364–382.

Reber, R., Winkielman, P., and Schwarz, N. (1998). Effects of perceptual fluency on affective judgments. *Psychological Science*, 9, 45–48.

Reifman, A. S., Larrick, R. P., Crandall, C. S., and Fein, S. (1996). Predicting sporting events: Accuracy as a function of reasons analysis, expertise, and task difficulty. Unpublished manuscript, Research Institute on Addictions, Buffalo, NY.

Rokeach, M. (1973). *The nature of human values*. New York: The Free Press.

Salancik, G. R. (1974). Inference of one's attitude from behavior recalled under linguistically manipulated cognitive sets. *Journal of Experimental Social Psychology*, 10, 415–427.

Salthouse, T. A. (1991). Expertise as the circumvention of human processing limitations. In K. A. Ericsson and J. Smith (Eds.), *Toward a general theory of expertise: Prospects and limits* (pp. 286–300). New York: Cambridge University Press.

Scheier, M. F., Buss, A. F., and Buss, D. M. (1978). Self-consciousness, self-report of aggressiveness, and aggression. *Journal of Research in Personality*, 12, 133–140.

Schooler, J. W. (2002). Verbal overshadowing produces a transfer inappropriate processing shift. *Applied Cognitive Psychology*, 16, 989–997.

Schooler, J. W., and Engstler-Schooler, T. Y. (1990). Verbal overshadowing of visual memories: Some things are better left unsaid. *Cognitive Psychology*, 17, 36–71.

Schooler, J. W., Ryan, R. S., and Reder, L. (1996). The costs and benefits of verbally rehearsing memory for faces. In D. Herrmann, M. Johnson, C. McEvoy, C. Hertzog, and P. Hertel (Eds.), *Basic and applied memory: New findings* (pp. 51–65). Hillsdale, NJ: Lawrence Erlbaum.

Schwarz, N. (1998). Accessible content and accessibility experiences: The interplay of declarative and experiential information in judgment. *Personality and Social Psychology Review*, 2, 87–99.

Schwarz, N., and Clore, G. L. (1983). Mood, misattribution, and judgements of well-being: Informative and directive functions of affective states. *Journal of Personality and Social Psychology*, 45, 513–523.

Sears, D. O. (1983). The persistence of early political predispositions: The roles of attitude object and life stage. In L. Wheeler and P. Shaver (Eds.), *Review of personality and social psychology* (Vol. 4, pp. 79–116). Beverly Hills, CA: Sage.

Seligman, C., Fazio, R. H., and Zanna, M. P. (1980). Effects of salience of extrinsic rewards on liking and loving. *Journal of Personality and Social Psychology*, 38, 453–460.

Slovic, P., Finucane, M., Peters, E., and MacGregor, D. G. (2002). The affect heuristic. In T. Gilovich, D. Griffin, et al. (Eds.), *Heuristics and biases: The psychology of intuitive judgment.* (pp. 397–420). New York: Cambridge University Press.

Staats, A. W., and Staats, C. K. (1958). Attitudes established by classical conditioning. *Journal of Abnormal and Social Psychology*, 57, 37–40.

Tversky, A., and Kahneman, D. (1974). Judgment under uncertainty: Heuristics and biases. *Science*, 185, 1124–1131.

Wegner, D. M. (2002). *The illusion of conscious will.* Cambridge, MA: Cambridge University Press.

Wilson, T. D., and Brekke, N. (1994). Mental contamination and mental correction: Unwanted influences on judgments and evaluations. *Psychological Bulletin*, 116, 117–142.

Wilson, T. D., Bybee, J. A., Dunn, D. S., Hyman, D. B., and Rotondo, J. A. (1984). Effects of analyzing reasons on attitude-behavior consistency. *Journal of Personality and Social Psychology*, 47, 5–16.

Wilson, T. D., and Dunn, D. S. (1986). Effects of introspection on attitude-behavior consistency: Analyzing reasons versus focusing on feelings. *Journal of Experimental Social Psychology*, 22, 249–263.

Wilson, T. D., Dunn, D. S., Kraft, D., and Lisle, D. J. (1989). Introspection, attitude change, and attitude-behavior consistency: The disrup-

tive effects of explaining why we feel the way we do. In L. Berkowitz (Ed.), *Advances in experimental social psychology* (Vol. 22, pp. 287–343). Orlando, FL: Academic Press.

Wilson, T. D., and Hodges, S. D. (1992). Attitudes as temporary constructions. In A. Tesser and L. Martin (Eds.), *The construction of social judgment* (pp. 37–65). Hillsdale, NJ: Erlbaum.

Wilson, T. D., Hodges, S. D., and LaFleur, S. J. (1995). Effects of introspecting about reasons: Inferring attitudes from accessible thoughts. *Journal of Personality and Social Psychology*, 69, 16–28.

Wilson, T. D., and Kraft, D. (1993). Why do I love thee?: Effects of repeated introspections about a dating relationship on attitudes toward the relationship. *Personality and Social Psychology Bulletin*, 19, 409–418.

Wilson, T. D., Kraft, D., and Dunn, D. S. (1989). The disruptive effects of explaining attitudes: The moderating effect of knowledge about the attitude object. *Journal of Experimental Social Psychology*, 25, 379–400.

Wilson, T. D., and LaFleur, S. J. (1995). Knowing what you'll do: Effects of analyzing reasons on self-prediction. *Journal of Personality and Social Psychology*, 68, 21–35.

Wilson, T. D., LaFleur, S. J., and Anderson, D. E. (1996). The validity and consequences of verbal reports about attitudes. In N. Schwarz and S. Sudman (Eds.), *Answering questions: Methodology for determining cognitive and communicative processes in survey research* (pp. 91–114). San Francisco: Jossey-Bass.

Wilson, T. D., Lisle, D., Schooler, J., Hodges, S. D., Klaaren, K. J., and LaFleur, S. J. (1993). Introspecting about reasons can reduce post-choice satisfaction. *Personality and Social Psychology Bulletin*, 19, 331–339.

Wilson, T. D., and Schooler, J. (1991). Thinking too much: Introspection can reduce the quality of preferences and decisions. *Journal of Personality and Social Psychology*, 60, 181–192.

Wilson, T. D., and Stone, J. I. (1985). Limitations of self-knowledge: More on telling more than we can know. In P. Shaver (Ed.), *Review of personality and social psychology* (Vol. 6, pp. 167–183). Beverly Hills, CA: Sage.

Winkielman, P., and Cacioppo, J. T. (2001). Mind at ease puts a smile on the face: Psychophysiological evidence that processing facilitation increases positive affect. *Journal of Personality and Social Psychology*, 81, 989–1000.

Winkielman, P., Halberstadt, J. B., Fazendeiro, T. and Catty, S. (2006). Prototypes are attractive because they are easy on the mind. *Psychological Science*, 17, 799–806.

Winkielman, P., and Schwarz, N. (2001). How pleasant was your childhood? Beliefs about memory shape inferences from experienced difficulty of recall. *Psychological Science*, 12, 176–177.

Winkielman, P., Schwarz, N., Fazendeiro, T., and Reber, R. (2003). The hedonic marking of processing fluency: Implications for evaluative judgment. In J. Musch and K. C. Klauer (Eds.), *The Psychology of evaluation: Affective processes in cognition and emotion* (pp. 189–217). Mahwah, NJ: Lawrence Erlbaum.

Zajonc, R. B. (1968). Attitudinal effects of mere exposure. *Journal of Personality and Social Psychology Monograph*, 9, 1–28.

Zajonc, R. B. (1980). Feeling and thinking: Preferences need no inferences. *American Psychologist*, 35, 151–175.

Chapter 28: Belief Change as Propositional Update

RENÉE ELIO AND FRANCIS JEFFRY PELLETIER

Introduction

Suppose you need to send an express courier package to a colleague who is away at a conference. You believe that whenever she is in New York City and the New York Rangers are playing a home game, she stays at the Westin Mid-Manhattan Hotel. You also believe that she is in New York City this weekend and that the Rangers are playing this weekend as well. You call up the Westin Mid-Manhattan Hotel and you find out that she isn't there. Something doesn't fit. What do you believe now? Well, assuming that you accept the hotel's word that she isn't there, there are various (logically consistent) ways to reconcile the contradiction between what you used to believe and this new information. First, you could believe that she is in New York City and that the Rangers are indeed playing, but disbelieve the conditional that says whenever both of these are true, then she stays at the Westin Mid-Manhattan Hotel. Alternatively, you could continue to believe the conditional, but decide that either she isn't in New York this weekend or that the Rangers aren't playing a home game (or possibly both). Which do you choose as your new set of beliefs?

Belief change – the process by which a rational agent makes the transition from one belief state to another – is an important component for most intelligent activity done by epistemic agents, both human and artificial. When such agents learn new things about the world, they sometimes come to recognize that new information extends or conflicts with their existing belief state. In the latter case, rational reasoners would identify which of the old and new beliefs clash to create the inconsistency, decide whether in

fact to accept the new information, and, if that is the choice, to eliminate certain old beliefs in favor of the new information. Alternatively, new information may not create any inconsistency with old information at all. In this case, the reasoner can simply add the new information to the current set of beliefs, along with whatever additional consequences this might entail.

Although this is an intuitively attractive picture, the principles behind belief-state change are neither well-understood nor agreed-upon. Belief revision has been studied from a formal perspective in the artificial intelligence (AI) and philosophy literatures and from an empirical perspective in the psychology and management-science literatures. One of the practical motivations for AI's concern with belief revision, as portrayed in our opening scenario, is the development of knowledge bases as a kind of intelligent database: one enters information into the knowledge base and the knowledge base itself constructs and stores the consequences of this information – a process which is non-monotonic in nature (i.e., accepted consequences of previously believed information may be abandoned). More generally, the current belief state of any artificial agent may be contradicted either when the world itself changes (an aspect of the so-called frame problem) or when an agent's knowledge about a static world simply increases. Katsuno and Mendelson (1991) distinguish between these two cases, calling the former belief *update* and latter belief *revision*. Although much of the AI belief revision work focuses on formalizing competence theories of update and revision, prescriptive principles for how artificial agents "should" resolve conflict in

Reproduced with permission from Elio, R., and Pelletier, F. J. (1997) Belief change as propositional update. *Cognitive Science*, 21, 419–460.

the belief revision case – where there is a need to contract the set of accepted propositions in order to resolve a recognized contradiction – are far from settled. From the perspective of human reasoning, we see an important interplay between issues of belief revision and deductive reasoning, particularly in terms of the kind of representational assumptions made about how a belief state should be modeled. But while human performance on classical deductive problems has been extensively studied, both Rips (1994, p. 299) and Harman (1986, p. 7) have noted the need for descriptive data and theories on how people resolve inconsistency when new information about a static world is presented. The studies we present in this article are concerned exactly with this issue.

We make two simplifications in our portrayal of belief revision and the paradigm we used to investigate it. The first concerns what we refer to as "beliefs." Here, beliefs are sentences that people are told to accept as true, in the context of resolving some (subsequent) contradiction arising from new information that is provided. Now, being told to accept something as true is not necessarily the same as believing it to be true. The contradictions we introduce in our paradigm are not probes into a person's preexisting belief system (e.g., as in social cognition investigations of attitude change; see Petty, Priester, & Wegener, 1994) or of a person's hypotheses that are acquired over time via direct interactions with the world. The second simplification we make is treating beliefs as propositions that are believed either to be true or to be false (or, sometimes, that have a belief status of "uncertain"). This idealization characterizes the perspective of AI researchers who are interested in showing how classical deductive reasoning is related to belief revision. We will call this perspective "classical belief revision," to distinguish it from other frameworks, including one direction in formal studies of defeasible reasoning, that map statistical or probabilistic information about a proposition into a degrees of belief in that proposition (Kyburg, 1983, 1994; Pearl, 1988; Pollock, 1990; Bacchus, Grove, Halpern, & Koller, 1992). Both classical belief revision and defeasible reasoning are concerned with non-monotonicity and it is possible to view belief revision as driving defeasible reasoning or vice versa (Gärdenfors, 1990a; Makinson & Gärdenfors, 1991).

This alternative formalization of beliefs and belief change in terms of probabilistic or statistical information have analogies in certain empirical investigations as well. A primary concern in the management-science literature, for example, is to understand what factors influence a shift in the degree of belief in a particular proposition of interest. These factors include information framing (e.g., Ashton & Ashton, 1990; Shields, Solomon, & Waller, 1987) and agreement with prior beliefs and expectations (e.g., Koehler, 1993). Carlson and Dulany (1988) have proposed a model of belief revision about causal hypotheses from circumstantial evidence, in which the level of certainty in a causal hypothesis depends in part on the level of certainty the reasoner ascribes to circumstantial evidence supporting it. In Thagard's (1989) computer model of explanatory coherence, propositions have levels of activation that roughly correspond to acceptance levels; such a model has been applied to accounts of scientific reasoning and to belief revision as evidenced in protocols of subjects performing elementary physics (Ranney & Thagard, 1988).

Notwithstanding these alternative ways to conceptualize belief states, we believe that the issues investigated under our simplifications are relevant to these other perspectives. Belief revision as a deliberate act by an agent must be driven by something, and that driving force must include the detection of a conflict (defined logically or otherwise) within the belief state. The problem of explicitly "expunging" or contracting of beliefs, after having noticed a conflict, has been acknowledged within some degree-of-belief frameworks (e.g., Kyburg, 1983, 1994). As soon as one attempts to define notions like "acceptance" or "full commitment to" within a degrees-of-belief framework, for the purpose of making a decision or taking an action, then new information can introduce conflict with existing accepted information. Hence, the issue still remains as to which prior belief or assumption an agent continues to believe (or to increase the degree of belief in) and which the agent decides to abandon (or decrease the degree of belief in).[1]

Belief revision has also been studied as something that does not occur when it "should." That is, there is considerable evidence indicating that people are in general very reluctant to change their current belief sets in the face of evidence that indicates those beliefs are unjustified; and that they are much more likely to reject, ignore, or reinterpret the new information which conflicts with their current beliefs rather than attempt to add it to their beliefs and make the necessary adjustments (Edwards, 1968; Einhorn & Hogarth, 1978; Ross & Lepper, 1980; Lepper, Ross, & Lau, 1986; Hoenkamp, 1988). Although it is true that there are occasions in which people fail to revise their beliefs or refuse to accept new information, and there are theories offered as accounts of that reluctance, our starting point in these investigations assumes that any inertia against changing a belief set has been overcome.

Given our simplifications for the representation of belief states, the specific issue that concerns us can be easily stated. It is the question of which belief(s) out of some initial set is (are) abandoned when new, contradictory information must be integrated. The matters we consider in this study relate to certain formal notions that have been central to (what we have called) the classical AI belief revision perspective. These notions are epistemic entrenchment (whether some forms or types of information are less readily abandoned to resolve contradiction) and minimal change. It is not possible to consider these ideas without considering the fundamental choice that theories make in modeling a belief state either as a set of formulae or as a set of models. The implications of choosing one framework or another are crucial to operationalizing ideas like epistemic entrenchment. We review these two alternative positions on modeling belief states, and their relation to theories of human deduction, in the next section.

On Modeling Belief States and Deduction

Classical Models of Belief Revision

Alchourrón, Gärdenfors, and Makinson (1985; henceforth, "AGM") proposed a set of "rationality postulates" as a competence specification of what rational belief change should be. Many of these ideas are intrinsically important to thinking about human belief revision as we are studying it here, so we borrow some key distinctions from that literature in setting the stage for our studies.

There are two predominant camps in how belief states are modeled within what we earlier defined as the classical belief revision community: "syntactic-based theories" *v.* "model-based theories." The majority of the work in either of these camps follow the idealizations we outlined above: that beliefs are propositional in nature, that the status of a belief is "believed true," "believed false," or "uncertain," and that logical inconsistency is to be avoided within the agent's chosen belief state.

The difference between the syntactic and model approaches can be seen by example. Consider what might be in a belief state of an agent told: *All of Kim's cars are made in the US; this (some particular) car is made in Germany*. The syntax-based theories take the position that what is stored in the agent's belief state are the two *formulas* mentioned (plus whatever background information the agent already had . . . also stored as a set of formulas). Since beliefs are just formulas, doing a logical inference amounts to performing some further mental activity on these formulas. This further activity would generate a *different* belief state from the initial one. And so there is no guarantee that the agent will perform *any* logical inferencing to generate new beliefs. For instance, there is no guarantee that this agent will use the background information it may have that Germany is a different country than the US and that cars made in the one are not made in the other to infer that this car is not made in the US. Even if it does perform this inference, there is no guarantee that it will make the further inference that the car is not owned by Kim. In this conception, two beliefs are different when and only when they are expressed by two syntactically distinct formulas.

In contrast to this, the model-based theories identify a belief state with a *model* – an interpretation of the world which would make a group of beliefs be true. In the above example of Kim's cars, a model-based theory would identify the agent's belief state with those models of the world in which all of Kim's cars are made in the US and where furthermore some particular car is made in Germany. Assuming the agent's background beliefs include that Germany is a different country than the US and that cars made in the one are not made in the other, the set of background models that can accommodate such situations in the world are merged with those describing the two stated beliefs and the output is a model (or models) in which Kim's cars are made in the US, and this car is made in Germany, and hence this car is not made in the US, and hence this car is not owned by Kim. All this sort of "inferencing" is done already in the very *description* of the belief state. The fact that the belief state is a model of the world described by the sentences guarantees that all logical consequences of these sentences will be represented, for otherwise it couldn't be a model of those sentences.

One common way of putting the difference is to say that the syntax-based approach is committed only to *explicit beliefs* as defining a belief state, whereas a model-based approach is committed to defining a belief state in terms not only of explicit beliefs but also of the implicit beliefs that are entailed by the explicit ones.

Both approaches involve a certain amount of theoretical idealization. Under the model-based view, the very definition of an agent's belief state already embodies finding the models that perfectly suit it, and this in effect means that all the logical conclusions of any explicit beliefs are included. Within the syntactic framework, there is an assumption that only "obvious" or "minimal" conclusions are drawn, but how these are recognized as such goes unspecified. Secondly, it is not clear how syntactic-based theories detect arbitrary logical contradictions beyond ones that can be immediately spotted by a syntactic pattern-match, such as "p and ∼p," since beliefs are represented as strings of symbols and not models of the world being described.[2]

A third conception of belief states – which could be seen as an intermediate stance between the syntactic and the model-based approaches – might be called a "theory-based" theory of beliefs. Here a belief state is identified with a *theory*, which is taken to be a set of sentences, as the syntactic-based theories hold. However, this set is the infinite set of all the logical consequences of the explicit beliefs.[3] This is the approach advocated in the original work done by AGM (1985). It too is obviously an idealization, for taken to the extreme, it would require a person's mind (or an agent's memory) to be infinite in order to hold a belief. Although theory-based theories are like syntax-based theories in containing formulas (and unlike model-based theories in this regard), they differ from syntax-based theories in obeying a principle called "The Irrelevance of Syntax": if two formulas are logically equivalent, then adding one of them to a belief state will yield the same result as adding the other, since the set of their logical consequences is the same. This principle is obeyed by both the theory-based and the model-based theories, and has been vigorously defended (AGM, 1985; Dalal, 1986; Yates 1990; Katsuno & Mendelson, 1991) on the grounds that all that is relevant to belief change is how the world is, or would be, if the beliefs were true.

Many of the concepts and distinctions mentioned above as characterizing classical AI belief revision also apply to other belief revision frameworks. Computational frameworks in which propositions are represented as nodes in some kind of belief network (e.g., Pearl, 1988; Thagard, 1989) are syntactic, because any semantic contradiction between two nodes is merely reflected by the names of the links chosen to join the nodes in the network. Methods proposed by Halpern (1990) and Bacchus et al. (1992) for deriving degrees of belief from statistical information are model-based approaches: the degree of belief in a sentence stems from the probability of the set of worlds in which the sentence is true. Kyburg's theory of rational belief (1983, 1994), in which levels of acceptance are also derived from probabilities, falls into what we have called the "theory theory" category. He models beliefs as a set of (first-order logic) sentences but then requires the set to obey the irrelevance of syntax principle: if two sentences have the same truth value in belief set, then their probabilities are also equivalent within that set. So we see that, although the classical belief revision approach comes from a milieu where performance criteria are not explicitly considered, the sorts of distinctions made within these classical belief revision frameworks can elucidate the representational assumptions of other approaches as well.

Performance Theories of Human Deduction

Harman (1986) has argued that the principles guiding belief revision are not the rules of deductive logic. Certainly, any principles that can dictate which of several different belief state changes to select are outside the scope of deductive inference rules. Any characterization of belief revision must first make some commitment to how a belief state is represented; as the formal theories we outlined above illustrate, making (or not making) inferences is crucial to how the belief revision process is to be conceptualized. Certainly, the ability to recognize inconsistency is a necessary step towards deliberate belief revision, and that step may involve some aspects of what has been studied and modeled as deductive reasoning. Hence, it seems that theories about how people draw inferences from propositional knowledge will be crucially related to the transition from one belief state to another, if only because those inferences may define the content of the belief states themselves.

Generally speaking, the theories of human deductive reasoning have split along a dimension that is similar to, but not identical with, the syntactic v. model-theoretic distinction in AI. On the one hand, mental-model theories of the type proposed by Johnson-Laird and colleagues (Johnson-Laird, Byrne, & Schaeken, 1992; Johnson-Laird & Byrne, 1991) hold that a person reasons from particular semantic interpretations (models) of sentences such as $p \rightarrow q$ and either p or q.[4] In this framework, a reasoner identifies or validates a particular conclusion by manipulating and comparing these models.

On the other hand, proof-theoretic approaches (Rips, 1983 1994; Braine & O'Brian, 1991) propose that people possess general inference rules and follow a kind of natural deduction strategy to derive conclusions from a set of premises. Like the different kinds of belief revision theories in AI, these different psychological accounts of human deduction offer distinct representational assumptions about the constituent parts that are said to define a belief state. But unlike the AI belief revision theories, psychological theories must make a commitment to a plausible process account of how a person generates and operates upon these different representations.

Neither mental-model nor proof-theoretic accounts of deduction were initially developed for belief revision as we have portrayed it here; nor have there been, as yet, extensions designed to accommodate aspects of this phenomenon. However, we consider some of their basic assumptions in the discussion of our tasks and results, and so here we briefly summarize the mental-models framework proposed by Johnson-Laird and colleagues and the proof-theoretic model proposed by Rips (1994).

If we apply a state-space abstraction to mental models frameworks and to proof-theoretic frameworks, the main distinction between proof theoretic and model-based theories of human deduction can be summarized as differences in what defines a state and what constitutes the operators that make transitions from one state to another. In a proof-theoretic system like the one proposed by Rips (1994), a state is a partial proof and the operators are a set of inference rules (a subset of the classical logic inference rules). These operators extend a proof (and hence move the system from one state to the next) by following a natural deduction-like strategy, with heuristics that order their application within this general control strategy. The goal can be viewed as a state (or a path to a state) which includes a given conclusion as an outcome of a proof (hence validating it) or includes a statement not already specified in the problem's premises (drawing a new conclusion). In the mental-models theory, a state contains one or more interpretations of the sentence set, i.e., tokens with specific truth values that correspond to some situation in the world. Operators retrieve models of sentences and move the system to new states that constitute candidate models of the world. More specifically, the mental models framework assumes there are particular models that are initially associated with particular sentence forms (conditionals, disjuncts, and so forth), with other models of these forms sometimes held in abeyance until there is a need to consider them. A conclusion is any truth condition that is not explicitly stated in the sentence set, but which must hold given a consistent interpretation of the sentence set. Hence, the goal state can be seen as one in which such a truth condition is identified. Thus, the proof-theoretic theory of human deduction can be seen as a search for alternative inference rules to apply to a sentence set in order to extend a proof, whereas the mental-models theory can be seen as a search for alternative interpretations of a sentence set, from which a novel truth condition can be identified or validated.

It is important to be clear not only about the similarities but also about the differences between the classical, competence belief-revision theories and the psychological performance theories of human deduction. What the mental-models theory shares with the formal model-based belief revision theories is the essential idea that the states being operated upon are models. These models capture the meaning of the connectives as a function of the possible truth values for individual atomic parts that the connectives combine. However, there are three key differences between these two types of model theories. First, although the irrelevance-of-syntax principle is a distinguishing feature of formal models of belief revision in AI, it does not distinguish between mental-models and proof-theoretic models of human deductive reasoning, both of which offer alternative accounts of the pervasive finding that syntactic form does influence how people reason about problems that are otherwise logically equivalent. Second, in the mental-models theory, the models of $p \rightarrow q$ are generated in a serial, as-needed basis, depending on whether a conclusion is revealed or validated by the initial interpretation (and it is the order in which such models are generated that plays in the mental model's account of the effect of syntactic form on deductive reasoning). The AI model-based belief revision frameworks do not make any such process assumptions, except in their idealization that all models are available as the belief state. Third, the mental-models framework may be considered closer to what we have called the "theory theory" classical belief-revision framework, than to the pure model framework, because separate models of each sentence are produced and operated upon.

What a psychological proof-theoretic framework of deduction shares with its formal AI syntactic-based counterparts is a commitment to apply deductively sound inference rules to sentences. But unlike the syntactic-based competence theories of belief revision, psychological proof-theoretic models of deduction do not presume that a person has a representation of every deductive rule of inference and they may presume there is some heuristic ordering of the available rules; these differences are relevant to how a proof-theoretic perspective models the relative difficulties that people have with certain forms of deductive problems. Further, some of the undesirable aspects of syntactic competence models, such as uncontrolled deductive closure in searching for contradictions, are avoided in proof-theoretic performance models (e.g., Rips, 1994) by explicitly positing that the reasoner's current goals and subgoals are what direct and control the application of inference rules.

Minimal Change and Epistemic Entrenchment

A basic assumption behind most AI theories of belief revision (e.g., the AGM postulates) and some philosophical accounts (e.g., Harman, 1986) is that an agent should maintain as much as possible of the earlier belief state while nonetheless accommodating the new information. But it is not completely clear what such a minimal change is. First, there is the problem in defining a metric for computing amounts of change. Often, this relies on counting the number of propositions whose truth value would change in one kind of revision versus another. The revision that leaves the belief state "closest" to the original one is to be preferred. But as we next illustrate, how such a definition of closeness works depends on whether one takes a syntactic or model-based approach.

As an example of the differences that can evolve, consider our earlier story about your New York–visiting colleague. Let n stand for she-is-in-New-York, r stand for Rangers-are-playing, and w stand for she-stays-at-the-Westin. Symbolically, your initial beliefs were [n & $r \rightarrow w$, n, r], from which you deduced w. But then you found out $\sim w$. In a model-based approach, the unique model describing your initial belief set (unique, at least, if we attend only to n, r, and w) is: n is true, r is true, w is true. Then you discover that the model is incorrect because w is false. The minimal change you could make is merely to alter w's truth value, and so your resulting belief states is: n is true, r is true, w is false. In a syntax-based approach, you would instead keep track of the ways that as many as possible of the

three initial sentences remain true when you add $\sim w$ to them. There are three such ways: $S_1 = [n$ & $r \rightarrow w$, n, $\sim r$, $\sim w]$, $S_2 = [n$ & $r \rightarrow w$, $\sim n$, r, $\sim w]$, $S_3 = [\sim(n$ & $r \rightarrow w)$, n, r, $\sim w]$.[5] Now consider what common sentences follow from each of S_1, S_2, and S_3, and the answer is that the consequences of [$\sim w$, $n \vee r$] will describe them. Note that this is different from the version given as a model-theoretic solution. In the syntactic case, only one of n and r need remain true, whereas in the model-based belief revision version, both need to remain true.

The notion of "epistemic entrenchment" in the belief revision literature (Gärdenfors, 1984, 1988; Gärdenfors & Makinson, 1988; Willard & Yuan, 1990; Nebel, 1991) has been introduced as a way to impose a preference ordering on the possible changes. Formally, epistemic entrenchment is a total pre-ordering relation on all the sentences of the language, and this ordering obeys certain postulates within the AGM framework. Less formally, epistemic entrenchment can be viewed as deeming some sentences as "more useful" in that they have greater explanatory power and hence are more deserving of entrenchment than other sentences; and in cases where there are multiple ways of minimizing a change to a new belief state, these priority schemes will dictate which way is chosen. Now, the general issue of whether some types of knowledge (e.g., sensory observations v. reasoned conclusions) should be a priori more epistemically privileged than other types of knowledge has occupied much of philosophy throughout its history. One particular, more modest, contrast is between what might be called statements about data v. statements about higher-order regularities. From one perspective, it can seem that conditional statements should enjoy a greater entrenchment in the face of conflicting evidence because they either express semantic constraints about the world or express an important predictive regularity that might be the result of some long-standing and reliable inductive process. As an example of this sort of perspective, one can point to scientific theorizing that is based on statistical analysis, where one rejects "outlying" data as unimportant, if other regularities characterize most of the remaining data. In doing so, we give priority to the regularity over (some of) the data. Certain approaches to database consistency (e.g., Elmasri & Navathe, 1994, pp. 143–151) and some syntactic theories of belief revision (e.g., Foo & Rao, 1988; Willard & Yuan, 1990) advocate the entrenchment of the conditional form $p \rightarrow q$ over non-conditional (ground) forms. For database consistency, a relation like $p \rightarrow q$ can be said to represent a semantic integrity constraint, as in "If x is y's manager, then x's salary is higher than y's salary." For classical belief revision theories, the intuition driving the idea of entrenching $p \rightarrow q$ over other types of sentences is not because material implication per se is important, but because "lawlike relations" are often expressed in sentences of this form. For example, Foo and Rao (1988) assign the highest epistemic entrenchment to physical laws, which may be especially effective in reasoning about how a dynamic world can change (e.g., the belief update, rather than revision, problem).

But there is another perspective that would propose exactly the opposite intuitions about entrenchment: what should have priority are observations, data, or direct evidence. These are the types of statements which are fundamental and about which we can be most certain. Any kind of semantic regularities expressed in conditional form are merely hypotheses or data-summarizing statements that should be abandoned (or at least suspected) when inferences predicted from them are not upheld by direct evidence. This sentiment for data priority seems plausible in the context of hypothesis evaluation (e.g., Thagard, 1989) as it did to some involved in the "logical construction of the world" (e.g., Russell, 1918; Wittgenstein, 1922).

In sum, we note that these alternative intuitions about entrenching conditionals *v.* nonconditionals are more or less readily accommodated, depending on the representation of belief states. It is easy to use the form of a sentence as a trigger for entrenchment principles, if one has a syntactic stance; but if a reasoner works with models of the world, then this sort of entrenchment is not as easily supported (unless sentences are individually modeled and knowledge of "form" is somehow retained). By first understanding the principles that actually guide belief revision in people, we are in a better position to formulate what kinds of representations would enable those principles to operate in a cognitive system.

Overview of Experiments

So far, we have touched upon a number of broad theoretical issues that bear on belief revision, at least when this is characterized as a deliberate decision to remove some proposition(s) that had been accepted as true, in order to resolve a contradiction noted in the belief set. Although our longer-term interest is to better understand

what plausible principles might define epistemic entrenchment, our immediate interest in the present studies was first to acquire some baseline data on what belief revision choices people make in relatively content-free tasks and to tie these results to models of deduction. To do this, we consider the simple task of choosing to abandon a conditional sentence *v.* a non-conditional, ground sentence as a way to resolve a logical contradiction. This decision corresponds to the example dilemma we presented at the start of this article. The initial belief state, defined by a conditional and a ground sentence, can be expanded by the application of a deductive inference rule. In our paradigm, it is this resulting inferred belief that is subsequently contradicted. Because we know that human deduction is influenced by the particular form of the inference rule used (cf. Evans, Newstead, & Byrne, 1993), we are secondarily interested in whether the inference rule used in defining the initial belief set impacts a subsequent belief revision rule. While these particular experiments are not designed to discriminate between proof theoretic or mental-models theories of deduction, such evidence is relevant to expanding either of these performance models of human reasoning to embrace aspects of resolving contradiction. The final two studies examine more directly various of the alternative model-theoretic definitions of minimal change, and investigate whether minimal change – by any of these definitions – is a principle for human belief revision. This organization notwithstanding, we note that these issues – the syntactic versus model-theoretic distinction, epistemic entrenchment, and minimal change – are tightly interwoven and each experiment bears on each of them in some way.

Entrenchment of Conditionals

In the first three experiments we report, we used two problem types that differed in whether the initial belief state included a conclusion drawn by the application of a modus ponens inference rule or by the application of a modus tollens inference rule. Modus ponens is the inference rule that from *If p then q*, and furthermore p, then infer q. The modus ponens belief set consisted of a conditional, a ground sentence that was the conditional's antecedent, and the derived consequent. Modus tollens is the rule that from *If p then q*, and furthermore $\sim q$, infer $\sim p$. The initial modus tollens belief set consisted of a conditional, a ground sentence that was the negation of its consequent, and the derived negation of the

Table 1: Definitions of Initial Belief States and Revision Alternatives for Experiment 1's Problem Set

Problem Type		Revision Alternatives
Modus Ponens		
Initial SS:	$p \rightarrow q$, p, q	1. $p \rightarrow q$, $\sim$p, $\sim$q
Expansion:	$\sim$q	2. $\sim(p \rightarrow q)$, $\sim$q, ?p
		3. $\sim(p \rightarrow q)$ p, $\sim$q
Modus Tollens		
Initial SS:	$p \rightarrow q$, $\sim$q, $\sim$p	1. $p \rightarrow q$, p, q
Expansion:	p	2. $\sim(p \rightarrow q)$, p, ?q
		3. $\sim(p \rightarrow q)$, p, ?q

Note. SS means sentence set. Expansion means the expansion information. ? means uncertain.

antecedent. We introduced contradiction with the initial belief state by providing new information – the expansion information – which contradicted whatever the derived conclusion was. In the modus ponens case, the expansion was $\sim$q. In the modus tollens case, the expansion was p.[6]

We defined belief-change problems, using these well-studied problem types, both to provide a baseline for understanding the role of syntactic form in belief-change problems, and to make contact with existing data and theories about human performance on these classic deductive forms in a different problem context. If a conditional enjoys some kind of entrenchment by virtue of its syntactic form, people should prefer a revision that retained the conditional but reversed the truth status of the ground sentence that permitted the (subsequently contradicted) inferred sentence. A related question is whether this belief revision choice is made differently, depending on whether the belief state consisted of a modus ponens or modus tollens inference. From an AI model-theoretic viewpoint, modus ponens and modus tollens are just two different sides of the same coin: they differ only in their syntactic expression. Classical AI model-theoretic approaches would consider a revision that denied the conditional to be a more minimal change.[7] From a psychological viewpoint, it is well documented (e.g., see the survey by Evans, Newstead, & Byrne, 1993) that people find making a modus tollens inference more difficult than making a modus ponens inference. In this work, we did not want this feature of reasoning to come into play. Therefore, we provided the inferences explicitly in defining the initial belief set, and then asked whether the deductive rule used to derive them affects the belief revision choice.

The existing literature on human reasoning performance also indicates an influence of domain-specific content on the kinds of inferences that people are able or likely to draw. To account for these effect, theories have proposed the use of abstract reasoning schemas (Cheng & Holyoak, 1989; Cheng, Holyoak, Nisbett, & Oliver, 1993) and a reasoning by analogy approach (Cox & Griggs, 1982). For these initial investigations of belief-revision choices, we were not interested in investigating the direct applicability of these theoretical distinctions to the issue of belief-revision, but rather considered the general empirical findings that people reason differently with familiar topics than they sometimes do when given problems involving abstract symbols and terms. If belief revision is viewed less as a decision task driven by notions like minimal change and more as a problem of creating consistent explanations of past and current data, then we might expect the pattern of revision choices to be different when the problem content is more "real-worldly" than abstract. So, these experiments used both abstract problems (containing letters and nonsense syllables to stand for antecedents and consequents) and equivalent versions using natural language formats.

Experiment 1

Method

PROBLEM SET

Table 1 gives the schematic versions of the two problem types used in this experiment. Each problem consisted of an initial sentence set, expansion information, and then three alternative revision choices. The initial sentence set was labeled "the well-established knowledge at time 1." The expansion information was introduced with the phrase, "By time 2, knowledge had increased to include the following."[8] Each revision alternative was called a "theory" and consisted of statements labeled "Believe," "Disbelieve," or "Undecided About." A theory could have statements of all these types, or of just some of these types. The task for subjects was to choose one of the alternative revision theories as their preferred belief state change.

For the modus ponens and modus tollens problems, the original sentence set included a conditional of the form $p \rightarrow q$ and either the antecedent p or the negated consequent $\sim q$, respectively. In both cases, the derived inferences were included in the initial set (q for modus ponens, $\sim p$ for modus tollens). The expansion information for both problems contradicted the derived inference and this was explicitly noted to subjects in the presentation of the problem. Revision choices 1 and 3 offered two different logically consistent ways to reconcile this: deny the conditional (choice 3) or retain the conditional but reverse the truth status of the ground sentence that permitted the inference (choice 1). Revision choice 2 was included to provide a choice that was non-minimal by almost any standard: it included the expansion information, denied the conditional, and labeled the ground sentence that permitted the inference to be made as "uncertain" (signified by a ? in Table 1). Note that all revision alternatives indicated that the expansion information must be believed.

Problems had one of two presentation forms: a symbolic form, using letters and nonsense syllables, and a science-fiction form. An "outer space exploration" cover story was used to introduce the science-fiction forms. Here is an example of how a modus tollens problem appeared in the science fiction condition:

On Monday, you know the following are true:

If an ancient ruin has a protective force field, then it is inhabited by the aliens called Pylons.

The tallest ancient ruin is not inhabited by Pylons.

Therefore, the tallest ancient ruin does not have a protective force field.

On Tuesday, you then learn:

The tallest ancient ruin does have a protective force field.

The Tuesday information conflicts with what was known to be true on Monday. Which of the following do you think should be believed at this point?

A corresponding symbol version of this problem was: *If Lex's have a P, then they also have an R. Max is a Lex that has a P. Therefore, Max has an R.* The expansion information was *Max does not have an R.*

DESIGN

All subjects solved both modus ponens and modus tollens problem types. Presentation form (symbolic *v.* science-fiction) was a between-subjects factor. The science-fiction cover stories used several different clauses to instantiate the problems. The clauses used for each problem type are shown in Appendix A.

SUBJECTS

One-hundred twenty subjects from the University of Alberta Psychology Department subject pool participated in the study. Equal numbers of subjects were randomly assigned to the symbol and science fiction conditions.

PROCEDURE

The modus ponens and modus tollens belief problems appeared as part of a larger set of belief revision problems. The order of revision alternatives for each problem was counterbalanced across subjects. Below are excerpts from the instructions, to clarify how we presented this task to our subjects:

... The first part of the problem gives an initial set of knowledge that was true and well-established at time 1 (that is, some point in time). There were no mistakes at that time. The second part of the problem presents additional knowledge about the world that has come to light at time 2 (some later time). This knowledge is also true and well-established.... The world is still the same but what has happened is that knowledge about the world has increased.... After the additional knowledge is presented, the problem gives two or more possible "theories" that reconcile the initial knowledge and the additional knowledge.... Your task is to consider the time 1 and time 2 knowledge, and then select the theory that you think is the best way to reconcile all the knowledge.

Results

Each subject contributed one revision-type choice for each of the two problem types. This

Table 2: Percentage of Subjects Choosing Each Revision Alternative, Experiment 1

| | Problem Type | | | | | |
| | Modus Ponens | | | Modus Tollens | | |
Revision Alternative	Symbol	SciFi	Mean	Symbol	SciFi	Mean
1. disbelieve ground sentence	.25	.14	.20	.33	.17	.25
2. disbelieve conditional, uncertain about ground sentence	.38	.29	.34	.38	.54	.46
3. disbelieve conditional	.37	.58	.48	.28	.29	.29

gives us frequency data for how often each revision choice was selected, as a function of two variables: problem form (modus ponens v. modus tollens) and presentation form (science-fiction v. symbolic). Table 2 presents this data as the percentages of subjects choosing a particular revision choice.

From the schematic versions of the problems in Table 1, it is clear that the three belief revision alternatives for the modus ponens (MP) and modus tollens (MT) problems have a certain symmetry, even though the actual details of each revision are necessarily different. In Table 2's presentation of the data, we re-label these revision alternatives in a more general form that reflects this symmetry. For both problem types, revision choice 1 retains the conditional but reverses the truth status for the ground sentence that was the other initial belief. (For the MP problem, the expansion was $\sim q$, so p was the initial ground sentence. For the MT problem, the expansion mentioned p; so $\sim q$ was the initial ground sentence.) In revision choice 2, the conditional is disbelieved and the ground sentence is uncertain. Under revision choice 3, the conditional is disbelieved and the ground sentence retains whatever truth value it had initially.

In general, subjects preferred revisions in which the $p \rightarrow q$ rule was disbelieved (revisions 2 and 3). Collapsing across presentation condition, the clearest difference between the MP and MT belief-change problems concerned which of these two rule-denial revisions subjects preferred: on MP problems, the preferred belief change saw subjects preferring simply to disbelieve only the rule; on MT problems, the preferred revision was to disbelieve the rule and to regard the initial ground sentence, $\sim q$, as uncertain.

To analyze this frequency data, one could create a set of two-way tables for each level of each variable of interest to assess whether the distribution of frequencies is different, and com-

pute a chi-square test of independence for each sub-table; however, this does not provide estimates of the effects of variables on each other. Loglinear models are useful for uncovering the relationships between a dependent variable and multiple independent variables for frequency data. A likelihood-ratio chi-square can be used to test how well a particular model's prediction of cell frequencies matches the observed cell frequencies.

We can first ask whether the three revision alternatives were selected with equal probability, when collapsed across all conditions. The observed percentages of 22.2%, 39.9%, and 37.9% for revision choices 1, 2, and 3, respectively, were significantly different from the expected percentages ($\chi^2 = 13.27$, $df = 2$, $p = .001$). By examining the residuals, we can identify patterns of deviation from the model. The two deviations in this case were the percentage of revision 1 and revision 2 choices.

To test whether revision choice is independent of problem type and presentation mode, we fit a model that included simple main effects for each factor, but no interaction terms. The chi-square value indicates that such an independence model does not fit the data well $\chi^2 = 15.33$, $p = .004$, $df = 4$). Models that included only one interaction term for revision by problem type, or only one for revision by presentation mode, were also poor fits to the observed data ($\chi^2 = 12.02$ and 10.52, respectively, df's $= 4$, p's $< .05$). The simplest model whose predicted frequencies were not significantly different from observed frequencies included both a revision by problem type and a revision by presentation-mode interaction term ($\chi^2 = 3.18$, $df = 2$, $p = .203$).[9]

The means in Table 2 indicate that the pattern of difference between MP and MT choices is primarily due to differences in responses on the science-fiction problems. Fifty-eight percent of the science-fiction condition subjects chose to

Table 3: Percentage of Subjects Choosing Each Response Alternatives, Experiment 2

	Problem	
Revision Choice	Modus Ponens	Modus Tollens
1. disbelieve ground sentence	.23	.26
2. disbelieve conditional; ground sentence uncertain	.12	.16
3. disbelieve conditional	.35	.12
4. disbelieve both conditional and ground sentence	.14	.02
5. both conditional and ground sentence uncertain	.16	.44

disbelieve $p \rightarrow q$ on modus ponens belief states, while only 29% did so in the modus tollens case. The most frequently chosen revision (54%) for a science fiction MT belief-revision was a non-minimal change: disbelieving $p \rightarrow q$ and changing q's initial truth status from false to uncertain. Only 29% of the subjects choose this revision on the modus ponens belief state.

Experiment 2

In Experiment 1, subjects may have been evaluating merely whether each revision option was logically consistent, independently of what the initial sentence set and expansion information was. Only two of the revisions alternatives offered minimal-changes to the initial sentence set, and this might have accounted for the close pattern of responses between symbolic-form MT and MP problems. Asking subjects to generate, rather than select, a revision would most directly address this possibility, but for these studies, we decided to retain the selection paradigm and to increase the alternatives. For Experiment 2, we included an extra non-minimal change revision and a revision in which the sentences were logically inconsistent.

Method

PROBLEM SET AND DESIGN

Table 3 presents the response alternatives for the modus ponens and modus tollens problems used in Experiment 2. The first three response choices were the same as those used in Experiment 1. The fourth choice denies both the rule and changes the original truth status of the initial ground sentence. This is a non-minimal change and results in an inconsistent set of sentences as well. The fifth revision choice labels both the conditional and the ground sentences from the initial belief set as uncertain. These changes too are non-minimal, but the final belief set is logically consistent.

Subjects and Procedure

Forty-three subjects participated as part of a course requirement for an introductory psychology course. All subjects solved both MP and MT problems, as part of a larger set of belief-revision problems. Only symbolic forms of the problems were used in this follow-up experiment. The instructions were the same as those used for Experiment 1.

Results

The percentage of subjects choosing each revision choice are also given in Table 3. There is some consistency in the patterns of responses across both Experiments 1 and 2. The frequency of revisions in which the initial ground sentence's truth value was changed (revision choice 1) was still relatively low (about 25%) on both problem types, as we had found in Experiment 1. About 33% of the subjects opted simply to disbelieve the conditional (revision 3) on the MP problem (as they had in Experiment 1). However, on the MT problem, changing both the conditional and the initial ground sentence to uncertain (revision 5) accounted for most of the choices. A chi-square computed on the revision-choice by problem-type frequency table confirmed there was a different pattern of revision choices for these modus ponens and modus tollens problems ($\chi^2 = 15.33$, $df = 4$, $p = .004$).

Experiment 3

In the first experiments, we explicitly included the derived consequences in the modus ponens and modus tollens problems. In Experiment 3, we tested whether or not this inclusion of consequences as explicit elements of the initial belief set (versus allowing the subjects to draw their own conclusions) would affect revision choice. Consider, for example, problem type 1 in Table 4. This problem's initial belief set supports

Table 4: Templates for Experiment 3 Problem Types

Problem Type 1
  Initial Sentence Set   m & d → g, m, d
                        [Therefore, g]
          Expansion   ~g
  Revision Alternatives   1. ~[m & d → g], m, d
                        2. m & d → g, (~m & d) or (m & ~d) or (~m & ~d)

Problem Type 2
  Initial Sentence Set   c → h, h → m, c.
                        [Therefore, h and m]
          Expansion   ~h
  Revision Alternatives   1. h → m, ~[c → h], c, ?m
                        2. h → m, c → h, ~c, ?m
                        3. h → m, ~[c → h], c, m
                        4. h → m, c → h, ~c, m

Note. Bracketed consequences appeared in the initial sentence set for "consequences given" condition and were omitted in the "no consequences given" condition. All response choices included the expansion sentence as part of the revision description. See text for percentages of subjects choosing each option.

a simple modus ponens inference from a conditional $m \& d \to g$ and the ground sentences m and d to generate the conclusion g. As in the previous experiments, there were two logically consistent ways to reconcile the $\sim g$ expansion information: deny the conditional or deny one or more of the ground sentences that comprise the conditional's antecedent. The two revision choices reflect these two choices. Alternative 1 disbelieves the conditional and retains belief in the ground sentences; alternative 2 retains belief in the conditional and calls into question one or both of the ground sentences.

Whether or not the initial sentence set includes derived consequences can have more profound implications when the initial belief set supports a chain of inferences. Consider problem type 2 in Table 4, in which the initial belief state is $[c \to h, h \to m; c]$ and the expansion information is $[\sim h]$. One conclusion supported in the initial belief set is h. And this is in conflict with the expansion information. There are two ways to resolve this conflict: deny the conditional $c \to h$, arriving at the final belief set of $[c, h \to m, \sim h]$. Or deny c and retain the conditional $c \to h$, to obtain, the revised belief set $[c \to h, h \to m, \sim c, \sim h]$. Note that m cannot be inferred from either of these two revised belief states, but note also that it was a consequence of the initial belief set. Should we continue to believe in m? We can do that only if we believed in m in the first place, that is, if we drew m as a logical consequence of the first set of sentences. Otherwise, its status would be uncertain – neither believed nor disbelieved. Belief revision alternatives were

provided for both these possibilities, and this was investigated both in the case where logical consequences of beliefs were explicitly included in the initial belief set (as in Experiments 1 and 2) and also without explicit inclusion.

A second factor we considered in this followup was whether the conditional sentences in the initial belief set were propositional sentences or were universally quantified sentences. The belief revision problem hinges on the reconciliation of conflicting information, but how that reconciliation proceeds may depend on whether it contradicts what is believed about a class (hence, is a factor relevant to predicate logic), versus what is believed about an individual (and hence is a feature of propositional logic). Therefore, we manipulated whether the initial belief set was specified by universally quantified sentences or propositional sentences for each of the problems studied in Experiment 3.

Method

PROBLEM SET AND DESIGN

The schematic versions of the two problem types given in Table 4 were used to create eight different problems. Two factors were crossed for both problem types 1 and 2. The first factor was whether the minimal logical consequences of the initial sentence set were explicitly given as part of the initial belief set. In Table 4, the bracketed ground sentences were either explicitly listed as part of the initial belief set in the consequences-given condition or were omitted in the no-consequences given condition.

The second factor, sentence-form, was whether the belief set was based only on propositional sentences, or concerned sentences about universally quantified arguments. Thus, one propositional form of a conditional was *If Carol is in Chicago, then she stays at the Hilton Hotel*, while the universally quantified form was *Whenever any manager from your company is in Chicago, s/he stays at the Hilton Hotel*. The associated ground sentences in each case referenced a particular individual. For the propositional example, the sentence instantiating the antecedent was *You know that Carol is in Chicago*. For the universally quantified condition, it was *You know that Carol, one of the company managers, is in Chicago*.

For problem type 1, the revision choices were either to disbelieve the conditional (revision alternative 1) or to disbelieve one or both of the initial ground sentences (revision alternative 2). The same distinction holds for problem type 2, which had four revision alternatives: alternatives 1 and 3 involved denying the conditional $c \rightarrow h$, while revision choices 2 and 4 retained the conditional and instead changed c to $\sim c$. The other key distinction in problem type 2's revision alternatives concerned the status of m, which was the chained inference that the initial belief set supports. Revision choices 1 and 2 labeled m as uncertain; revision alternatives choices 3 and 4 retained m as a belief.

All of the problems were presented in natural language formats. The following text illustrates how Problem Type 1 appeared in the consequences given – propositional condition:

Suppose you are reviewing the procedures for the Photography Club at a nearby university, and you know that the following principle holds:

If the Photography Club receives funding from student fees and it also charges membership dues, then it admits non-student members.

You further know that the Photography Club does receive funding from student fees. It also charges membership dues. So you conclude it admits non-student members.

You ask the Photography Club for a copy of its by-laws and you discover

The Photography Club does not admit non-student members – all members must be registered students.

SUBJECTS AND PROCEDURE

Thirty-five University of Alberta students served as subjects, to fulfill a course requirement for experiment participation. Problems were presented in booklet form, which included other belief-revision problems as fillers. All subjects solved all four versions of both problem types 1 and 2: no consequence – propositional, consequences given – propositional, no consequences – quantified, consequences given – quantified. There were six pseudo – random orders for the problems within the booklet; within each order, the four versions of any given problem were separated by at least two other problems of a different type. The order of response alternatives for each problem was also randomized.

Results

For problem type 1, revision choice 1 (disbelieving the conditional; see Table 4) accounted for 82% of the revision choices. This is consistent with the pattern of choices in Experiment 1's results on science-fiction problems, and this preference to disbelieve the conditional was not affected by whether or not the modus tollens inference was explicitly listed in the initial sentence set nor by the use of propositional v. universally quantified sentences. In terms of the first factor, we note that people generally find modus ponens an easy inference to make, and these results confirm that the general preference to disbelieve the conditional does not rest on whether the contradicted inference is explicitly provided. Concerning propositional v. universally quantified sentences, we observe that it is difficult to construct if $p \rightarrow q$ sentences that are not, somehow, interpretable as universally quantified over time. Thus, even sentences like *If Carol is in Chicago, then Carol is at the Hilton*, may be interpreted as *For all times when Carol is in Chicago,* ... There seems to be little in the line of systematic, empirical study of the effect of propositional v. single quantifier v. multiple quantifier logic upon people's reasoning (although both Rips, 1994, Chapts. 6 and 7, and Johnson-Laird & Byrne, 1991, Chapts. 6 and 7, address this issue in their respective computational frameworks). Nonetheless, it seems clearly to be an important issue for studies that place an emphasis upon recognition of contradictions, since the impact of contradictory information upon "rules" is different in these different realms.

There was also no impact of either the consequences-given or the sentence-form factor on the patterns of revision choices for problem type 2, in which the initial belief set contained an intermediate conclusion h and then a chained conclusion m, that depended on h, and where expansion information contradicted h. The percentage of revision choice 1 (denying the conditional $c \to h$) accounted for 52% of the choices; choice 2 (denying the ground sentence c) accounted for 29% of the choices. In both these cases, the status of m, the chained inference that depended on h, was labeled uncertain. Revision alternatives 3 and 4, which were analogous to alternatives 1 and 2 except that they retained belief in m, accounted for 14% and 5%, respectively, of the remaining choices. The preference to change m's truth status from true to uncertain rather than retain it as true is interesting: it is an additional change to the initial belief state beyond what is necessary to resolve the contradiction. Perhaps people's revision strategy is guided more by the recognition that a belief depends on another than upon minimizing the number of truth values that change from one state to the next.

Discussion

In Experiments 1–3, we aimed to identify what kinds of revision choices subjects would make in symbolic and non-symbolic types of problems, with the former providing some kind of baseline for whether a conditional statement enjoys some level of entrenchment merely as a function of its syntactic form. Our second concern was to assess whether belief revision choices were affected by the composition of an initial belief set, i.e., whether it was defined through the use of the conditional in a modus ponens or modus tollens inference. This offers us a bridge between belief revision (as a task of making a deliberate change in what is to be "believed" in the face of contradictory information) and the data and theories on deductive reasoning.

There was no evidence that people preferred to entrench the conditional on these tasks. In the choices we gave subjects, there was one way to continue to believe the conditional and two ways to disbelieve it. If people were equally likely to retain the conditional as they were to abandon it, we might expect 50% of the choices falling into the keep-the-conditional revision, with the two ways to disbelieve it each garnering 25% of the choices. On the symbolic problems in

Experiments 1 and 2, the frequency of retaining the conditional after the expansion information was only about 25% on both modus ponens and modus tollens problems; it was even lower on the natural language problems.

Although subjects' preference was to abandon belief in the conditional, the way in which this occurred on modus ponens and modus tollens problems was slightly different. On modus ponens problems, subjects disbelieved the conditional but continued to believe the ground sentence as it was specified in the initial belief set. On modus tollens problems, subjects tended towards more "uncertainty" in the new belief state: either denying the conditional and deciding the ground sentence was uncertain (Experiment 1) or labeling both as uncertain when that was an option (Experiment 2). These tendencies on modus tollens problems could be interpreted as conservative revision decisions, since neither the initial conditional nor the initial ground sentence is explicitly denied; on the other hand, they correspond to maximal changes because the truth values of both initial beliefs are altered. We leave further discussion of entrenchment issues to the "General Discussion."

It is natural at this point to consider the relationship between this belief-change task and standard deduction, and to ask whether this task and its results can be understood as a deduction task in some other guise. In next sections, we present two reasons we think it is not. First, we consider the task demands and results for the modus ponens and modus tollens belief revision problems, and then briefly outline results we have obtained on belief expansion problems that did not involve a contradiction.

The Task Demands of the Modus Ponens and Modus Tollens Belief-Revision Problems

We can neutrally rephrase the modus ponens belief-change problem that subjects faced as "Make sense of $[p \to q, p, q] + [\sim q]$," where the first sentence set represents the initial belief set and the second signifies the expansion information. Since subjects had to accept the expansion information, what we call the modus ponens problem thus becomes "Make sense of $[p \to q, p, \sim q]$, such that $\sim q$ is retained." Similarly, the modus tollens problem is "Make sense of $[p \to q, \sim q, p]$, such that p is retained." Because these two problems are semantically equivalent, the forms in the set of propositions to be considered are the same and the models of these sentence sets are the same. The difference lies only in the nature of the derivation in the initial sentence set, and the corresponding constraint on what must be retained after the revision.

What we have called the modus ponens belief revision problem could be construed as a modus tollens deduction problem, if subjects consider only the conditional in combination with the expansion information: "Given $[p \rightarrow q] + [\sim q]$, what can I derive?" The invited modus tollens inference is $\sim p$. If they derived this, they could at least consider retaining the conditional and changing p to $\sim p$ in their belief-state change. The trouble that modus tollens inferences present for people could in this way explain the observed prevalence of abandoning the conditional on modus ponens belief revision problems to achieve a consistent belief set.

Applying this same perspective on the task to the modus tollens problem, we would see the modus tollens belief revision problem becoming an modus ponens deduction problem, if only the conditional and the expansion information are considered: "Given $[p \rightarrow q] + [p]$, what can I derive?" People have little difficulty with modus ponens and under this analysis, it would be an "easy inference" to conclude q, and so be led to reverse the truth status of $\sim q$ as the belief change. But the majority of subjects did not do this – on these problems as well, they disbelieved the conditional. Therefore, it does not seem that our general pattern of disbelieving the conditional in belief revision can be reduced to, and accounted for by the nature of the difficulties in making certain types of standard deductive inferences.

It is possible that subjects did not accept the modus tollens belief set as consistent in the first place. (People have difficulty both in generating modus tollens inferences and in validating them when they are provided [cf. Evans, Newstead, & Byrne, 1993, p. 36].) So perhaps this could be used to account for why there was high percentage of "everything but the expansion information is uncertain" revisions on modus tollens problems in Experiment 2. However, this does not account for why, on these modus tollens problems, subjects would not simply focus on both the conditional and the expansion information, and then draw an modus ponens inference – that would lead to reversing the truth status of the initial ground sentence, as opposed to what they in fact did.

Deductive Reasoning and Belief-State Expansions

The second reason we believe these tasks are not reducible to equivalent deductive reasoning problem stems from results we obtained on other belief-state expansion problems, in the expansion information did not contradict the initial belief set (Elio & Pelletier, 1994). These problems used two different but logically equivalent forms of a biconditional: (*p if and only if q*) and $((p \ \& \ q) \vee (\sim p \ \& \ \sim q))$. The expansion information was sometimes p and at other times $\sim p$. Unlike the belief revision problems, these problems have a deductively "correct" answer: given $p \rightarrow q$ (in either form) as an initial belief, with the sentence p as the expansion, it logically follows that q should be asserted and made part of the belief state. (And if $\sim q$ is the expansion, then $\sim p$ should be believed). If we view the biconditional-plus-expansion information problems as biconditional modus ponens (or biconditional modus tollens) problems, then we would expect that subjects presented with our biconditional and disjunctive belief expansion problems should behave like the subjects given biconditional and disjunctive deductive problems in other studies. Yet we found that subjects asserted q on the *p if and only if q* form of our biconditionals much less frequently (about 72%) than typically reported for these problems presented as standard deduction tasks (e.g., 98% accuracy in Johnson-Laird et al., 1992). And fully 56% of subjects given the biconditional in disjunctive form followed by the belief expansion p did not augment their belief set with q, when the problem was presented with a science-fiction cover story. Instead, they decided q was uncertain and that the biconditional itself was uncertain or unbelievable.

In sum, we believe that the task of belief revision, even in the relatively constrained way we have defined it here, does not simply unpack into deductive reasoning, particularly when natural-language formats are used for the problem. That is, subjects may not integrate information arriving across time (e.g., learning "later" that p holds true) into a belief set in the same way as information known to be true at the same time ("From *If p is now true, then q is also true*, and furthermore *p is now true*, what follows?"). It may be that the belief revision task invites the reasoner to make certain assumptions about evidence that is not explicitly included in the initial or subsequent information; it may also be that couching the task as changes in beliefs invites a more conservative strategy than what characterizes people's choices on formal logic problems.

On Models of Belief States and Deduction

The experiments we designed do not speak to whether belief states are best modeled as sets of sentences or sets of models. However, we can observe the following. First, AI competence models are typically not concerned with human performance, yet they sometimes appeal to human rationality to justify their particular perspective. For example, a syntax-based competence model proponent may point to the fact that a model-based perspective involves an infinite number of models, when taken to the extreme, and because that is so clearly beyond the capability of human cognition, such modeling cannot be appropriate. That syntax-proponent might also observe that a model-theoretic competence framework could never model differences in human reasoning with modus ponens and modus tollens, since modus ponens and modus tollens are indistinguishable from the perspective of formal model theories. Further, our finding that people seem to prefer to abandon the conditional is problematic for model-theoretic frameworks, unless they retain some mapping between each sentence and the model which that sentence generates. But there are also difficulties for a syntactic-based perspective. A model-theoretic proponent might say that it is only via models of the actual world that the meaning of the sentences has any reality. And it is unclear that the syntactic form of sentences per se should be a primary tag for guiding belief revision decisions. Indeed, our finding that people were more willing to abandon the conditional on natural language problems than on symbolic problems suggests that there are other, non-syntactic considerations at play that may serve as pragmatic belief revision principles. We return to this issue in the "General Discussion."

The belief revision results we obtained do not speak directly to performance theories of human deduction, but there are some important observations we can make here as well. First, the Johnson-Laird mental models framework could possibly accommodate the general preference to deny the conditional, by the preference ordering it puts on models that different types of sentences generate. The mental model of $p \rightarrow q$

is "$[p\ q]\ldots$," where $[p\ q]$ represents the initial explicit model, in which both p and q are true, and the ellipsis "$\ldots$" represents that there are additional models of this sentence (corresponding to possible models in which p is not true; Johnson-Laird, Byrne, and Schaeken, 1992). For our modus ponens problem, the initial sentence set is $p \rightarrow q$, p, and $\therefore q$. Let C indicate models of the conditional, and S to indicate models of ground sentences in the initial belief set. Hence, the initial modus ponens model set would be C: $[p\ q]\ldots$, S: $[p]$, S:$[q]$, respectively. Note that the models for the ground sentences are consistent with what the mental models theory proposes as the initial explicit model for the conditional. The modus ponens expansion information is $\sim q$ and we denote its model as E:$[\sim q]$. Suppose a subject compares the expansion model E:$[\sim q]$, which must be retained in any revision, to each of the models from the initial set. The expansion model would eliminate the model S:$[q]$, be silent on the model S:$[p]$, and eliminate the model C:$[p\ q]$ of the conditional. By this process, the preferred revision choice should be to deny this model of the conditional and the retain the ground sentence p. In fact, this choice accounted for 75% of the modus ponens revisions in Experiment 1 and about 60% in Experiment 2. By the same general reasoning, the mental-models approach would find itself predicting a preponderance of conditional denials for modus tollens problems. While we did find this is true in general, there would have to be some further account for people's greater tendency to decide the conditionals are uncertain (rather than false) on modus tollens problems than on modus ponens problems.

From a proof-theoretic perspective, Rips (1994, pp. 58–62) directly considers the problem of belief revision as the issue of which of several premises to abandon in the face of contradiction, acknowledging that deduction rules cannot alone "solve" the belief revision problem. He discusses a multi-layer approach, in which the principles governing belief revision decisions are themselves "logic-based processing rules" that co-exist with the deduction rules that he proposes as components of reasoning and problem-solving. Thus, a proof-theoretic approach might be extended to deal with our belief revision results by having an explicit higher-level rule that, when contradiction is recognized, indicates the action of disbelieving a conditional form when it is one of the premises. But even without an appeal to this approach, it is possible to consider a proof-theoretic account of our results, as we did for the mental-models perspective, using Rips' (1994) framework. Recall again the above perspective that portrayed the modus ponens belief-revision problem as boiling down to "Given $[p \rightarrow q, p] + [\sim q]$ and the constraint that $\sim q$ must be retained as a belief, what can you prove?" One can imagine that a subject formulates two competing sets of premises. One set is $[p \rightarrow q, \sim q]$, to which a modus tollens rule could apply. But there is no direct modus tollens rule in Rips' theory (the modus tollens inference is accomplished through the application of two other inference rules), thus accounting for the notion that modus tollens proof for $\sim p$ is difficult and may halt. On the other hand, there is a readily available inference rule (so-called and introduction) that can apply to the other combination of premises $[p, \sim q]$ to yield $[p \ and \sim q]$. From this perspective, subjects might reach a state that they can more easily recognize as valid and that may be why they prefer a revision in which these sentences are retained and the conditional is disbelieved. On the modus tollens problem, we can characterize the belief revision dilemma as "Given $[p \rightarrow q, \sim q] + [p]$ and the constraint that p must be retained, what can you prove?" The modus ponens rule is readily available according to Rips' theory, and so the premise combination $[p \rightarrow q, p]$ easily yields q. Just as easily, the other combination of premises $[\sim q, p]$ yields $[p \ and \sim q]$. The greater tendency to prefer revisions that label the conditional (and the ground sentence) "uncertain" in the modus tollens belief-revision case relative to the modus ponens belief-revision case may reflect subjects' ability to prove something from both combinations of premises (as we have stated them) and their appreciation that they have no reason to prefer the premises of one proof over the other in these simple problems.

Our goal in considering how two contrasting perspectives of deductive reasoning might accommodate our results was not to support one over the other. The accounts we sketched above are offered as speculations on how each perspective might be extended into the realm of belief revision, given their representation and processing assumptions about deductive reasoning. Such extensions are an important component for an integrated theory of reasoning and required much more consideration than we have briefly allowed here.

Models and Minimal Change

As we noted earlier, one of the desiderata of the classical AI belief-revision perspective is that an agent should make a minimal change to its initial belief set, when resolving any conflict that results from new information. Within a syntactic approach, the definition of change is computed from the number of formulas retained from one belief state to another, there are not many different ways to compute this number, since the formulas are fixed. The primary issue is whether or not the set of formula is closed, i.e., includes all consequences of the initially specified set of sentences. When the set of formulas is not closed, making a formula become part of the explicit belief set is regarded as more of a change than having it be in the implicit beliefs.

Within a model-theoretic approach, it turns out there is more than one way to compute what a minimal change might be, even for the simplest problems. In this section, we present the gist of some alternative computational definitions of minimal change. None of these approaches were devised as psychological models of how humans might manipulate alternative models in the face of conflicting information. And while the ways the algorithms that compute minimal change might not be psychologically plausible, the final change that each one deems minimal often corresponds to an intuitively reasonable way of integrating both the old and new belief information. We provide simple algorithmic interpretations of each of these minimal change definitions in Table 5 and highlight the functional effects of computing minimal change according to one algorithm or another.

A straightforward way to quantify the degree of change is to count the number of propositions whose truth values change if one model (e.g., expansion information) is integrated with another model (e.g., the initial belief set). The tricky part comes when there is more than one model of the initial belief set, or of the expansion information, or both. Clearly, there will be more than one possible interpretation for a sentence set whenever there is an explicit uncertainty. By explicit uncertainty, we mean a belief sentence that directly mentions that the truth status of some proposition is either true or false. Hence, in the sentence set $(p, q \vee \sim q)$, q is explicitly uncertain, so there are two models of this sentence set: $[p \sim q], [p \ q]$. Suppose, however, that the initial sentence set were "Either p and q are true at the same time, or they are false at the

Table 5: Algorithms for Minimal Change

Algorithm

Algorithm D
D1 For each model of the expansion information do
       D1.1 For each model of the initial belief set do
            Find and save the differences.
       D1.2 From the set of differences, identify the smallest change. Put this smallest change and
            the expansion model responsible for it on the candidate stack.
D2 From the candidate stack, chose as the new belief state the expansion model that is responsible for
    the smallest of all the minimal changes saved from D1.2. If there is more than one, use their
    disjunction

Algorithm W
W1 For each model of the belief set do
       W1.1 For each model of expansion do
            Find and save the propositions that must change
       W1.2 Retain just the minimal set of propositions that must change for this pairing of an
            belief set model and an expansion model
W2 Take the union of all proposition sets identified in W1.2 and remove them from the initial belief set
W3 Identify the set of remaining KB propositions with known (certain) truth values. If this set is empty,
    then the new belief set is the expansion information. Otherwise, the new belief set is the
    conjunction of the old KB propositions with the expansion information

Algorithm B
B1 For each model of the initial belief set do
       B1.1 For each model of the expansion do
            Find the differences and save them
       B1.2 From the set of differences, identify the minimal change and put the expansion model
            responsible for it on the candidate stack
B2 Combine all models of expansion information on the candidate stack to determine the new belief
    state.

Algorithm S
S1 For each model of the initial belief set
            For each model of the expansion, stack the differences between them.
S2 From the set of differences, eliminate non-minimal changes
S3 Combine all models of expansion information on the candidate stack to determine the new belief
    state.

same time" and that the expansion information is "p is false, q is true, and furthermore r is true." The initial belief state has two models, [$p q$], [$\sim p \sim q$], and both p and q are explicitly uncertain. The proposition r was not in either of the initial models of the world. But clearly, its truth status (along with every other possible sentence) in the initial belief set was, in hindsight, uncertain. This is what we call implicit uncertainty, and all the algorithms in Table 5 construct different models of the initial belief set to accommodate the implicit uncertainty about r just as if it were explicitly uncertain in the first place. Thus, the computations for minimal change for this problem would begin with these models of the initial belief set [$pq\sim r$], [pqr], [$\sim p\sim q\sim r$], and [$\sim p\sim q\sim r$]. As we shall see in the first example below, this same approach of creating extra mod-els also applies when a sentence that is present in the initial belief set is not mentioned the expansion information.

One approach to determining a minimal change is to choose a model of the expansion sentences that is the minimal distance from some model of the initial belief set. Suppose an initial belief is "Either p, q, r, s are all true at the same time, or they are all false at the same time." So there are two different models of this initial belief: [$p\ q\ r\ s$] and [$\sim p\ \sim q\ \sim r\ \sim s$]. Expansion information such as "p is true s is false, and r is false" contradicts this initial belief state and furthermore does not mention anything about q. There are then two models of the expansion, one in which q is true [$p\ q\ \sim r\ \sim s$] and one in which it is false [$p\ \sim q\ \sim r\ \sim s$]. The latter model of the expansion is "close" to the second model (disjunct) of the initial belief set and is indeed "closer" than either expansion model is to the first model of the initial belief set. By this reasoning, a new belief state that represents a minimal change on the initial state is $[p \sim q \sim r \sim s]$). This is the gist of the minimal change approach proposed by Dalal (1988) and summarized as Algorithm D in Table 5. More formally, Dalal's revision of a belief set by an expansion sentence is a set of minimal models where (a) each member of this set satisfies the expansion information, and (b) there is no other model of the initial belief set that also satisfies the expansion information and differs from any model of initial belief set by fewer atoms than the set of minimal models. The revision results in the set of all these minimal models. Thus, Dalal's algorithm settles on one model of the expansion information, if possible, and in doing so, can be viewed as retroactively settling on one particular model of the initial belief set.

An alternative intuition would hold that: only informative (non-tautological) initial beliefs can be used to choose among multiple interpretations of the expansion information, if they exist. This is one way to interpret an algorithm proposed by Weber (1986). Simply put, Weber's algorithm first identifies the initially believed sentences that must take on whatever truth values are specified for them in the expansion. For the same example in the preceding paragraph, this set would contain the sentences p, r, and s, because they each have a specific value they are required to take, according to the new information. These sentences are then eliminated from the initial belief set to identify what (if any) informative sentences propositions might be retained from the initial belief set. Subtracting p, r, and s from the initial belief set $\{[p\,q\,r\,s], [\sim p \sim q \sim r \sim s]\}$ leaves $[q \vee \sim q]$, which is a tautology, and by Weber's algorithm, leaves no (informative) proposition. (Had there been some other sentence which was in both of the initial models, it would have then been assigned to the revised belief state.) The algorithm then conjoins these two components: the truth values of p, r, and s as determined by the expansion information $[p \sim r \sim s]$ and whatever can be retained with certainty from the initial belief set, which here is the empty model [ ]. Whereas Dalal's revision for this problem would be $[p \sim r \sim s \sim q]$, Weber's minimal revision would be $[p \sim r \sim s]$, with q implicitly uncertain by virtue of its absence from the model. A simple algorithm that corresponds to this approach is given as Algorithm W in Table 5.

Borgida (1985) proposes an algorithm that is similar to Dalal's, but produces what might be considered a more conservative belief-state change. Essentially, each expansion model is compared to each initial belief-set model: the expansion model that produces a minimal change for a particular initial-belief interpretation is remembered. All these expansions that are minimal with respect to some model of the initial belief set are then used to define the new belief set. An algorithm that captures this approach is given as Algorithm B in Table 5. Consider a case where there is more than one interpretation of the initial belief set. If $[p\,q \sim s]$ is the initial belief set, and $[\sim p \sim q\,r \sim s]$ and $[\sim p \sim q \sim r\,s]$ are two models of the expansion information, then two models of the initial belief set are considered: the first contains r and second contains $\sim r$. Both interpretations of the expansion information define a minimal change with one of the interpretations of the initial belief set (the first expansion disjunct with the first interpretation of the belief set, and the second expansion disjunct with the second interpretation of the belief set). Thus, both $[\sim p \sim q\,r \sim s]$ and $[\sim p \sim q \sim r\,s]$ are on the stack after step B1.2. Since neither of these is minimal with respect to the other, the final belief set consists of guaranteed truth values for those propositions on which the interpretations agree and uncertain truth values for propositions on which they disagree, yielding a final belief state of $[\sim p \sim q\,\{r \sim s \vee \sim r s\}]$. Algorithm B differs from Algorithm D in that each model of the initial belief set identifies, in Algorithm B, what model of the expansion information would result in a minimal change (by number of propositions changed). Once one of the expansion models is identified as minimal with respect to a particular model of the initial belief set, there is no further check of whether one change is more or less minimal than some other combination of initial-belief interpretation and expansion-interpretation (as Algorithm D does on step D2). This can be viewed as a more conservative belief-state change, because there isn't the possibility of settling on one particular model of the initial belief state.

Satoh (1988) proposed belief revision operator that is a less-restricted version of Borgida's revision operator, when applied to the propositional case. The feature that makes it less restricted is illustrated in Algorithm S, which is identical to Algorithm B, except that step B1.2 in Algorithm B occurs outside the first control loop as step S2 in Algorithm S. Functionally, this difference means that there is no pruning of non-minimal changes with respect to a particular belief-set model (as on Step 1.2 in Algorithm B). Instead, the entire set is saved until step S2, which removes any change that subsumes another change. After S2, all changes that remain are minimal. Step S3 then finds a model of the expansion that is consistent with the minimal set of necessary changes. Put more intuitively, this algorithm crosses all interpretations of the initial belief set and all interpretations of the expansion set to create the model set from which a minimal change is computed. The functional effect is that, when there is just one model of the initial belief set, that model may "choose" the closest interpretation of the expansion information; when there is just a single version of the expansion information, that model may "choose" among alternative models of the initial information. Only the latter may occur under the Borgida algorithm.

We are not interested so much in the means by which these alternative model-based revision frameworks define minimal change, as we are in the way they capture alternative intuitions about manipulating multiple models. In Algorithm D, the way that minimal change is computed can have the effect of "selecting" one of multiple interpretations of the initial belief set. The effect of Algorithm B is to retain multiple models in the new belief set when there are multiple models of the expansion information. Algorithm S will compute a new belief state with multiple models, when multiple models exist in both the initial and expansion information; but it can use a single model of either to produce a single model of the new belief set. Finally, Algorithm W uses the expansion information to define what can be believed with certainty; other belief-set sentences not mentioned in the expansion information may decide between multiple interpretations of the expansion information, but only if their truth value was known with certainty in the first place (i.e., was true in every model or false in every model of the initial belief state).

There are plausible elements in each of these approaches for principles that might dictate how people deal with multiple interpretations of information when resolving inconsistencies. Our interest was whether which, if any, of them, corresponded to how people integrate multiple models in a belief revision task. As the reader might surmise, for any particular problem, some or all of the methods could yield the same final belief set. It is possible, however, to define a set of problems for which a pattern of responses would distinguish among these alternative approaches. We developed such a problem set to obtain data on whether people follow a minimal change principle, as defined by any of these approaches. The revision problems were very simple: there were either one or two models of the initial belief set and either one or two models of the expansion information. The problem sets were designed to distinguish among the four model-based minimal change frameworks described above.

Experiment 4

Method

PROBLEM SET

Table 6 gives the problem set used for Experiments 4 and 5. The first five problems in this table were used only in Experiment 4; problem 6 was added for Experiment 5. For economy of space, we write sentence letters adjacent to one another to mean 'and'. Thus, the problem 1 notation $(pqrs) \vee (\sim p \sim q \sim r \sim s)$ means "Either p, q, r, and s are each true at the same time or else they are each false at the same time."

The subscripts for the revision choices in Table 6 correspond to the particular model-theoretic definition of minimal change: D for Algorithm D, W for Algorithm W, and so forth. Experiment 4 offered subjects two revision choices for Problems 1–5 (of Table 6); these each corresponded to one or more of the four definitions of minimal change we outlined in the previous section. It can be seen that each of the four algorithms selects a different set of answers across these five problems: Algorithm D selects answers <1,1,1,1,1> for its five answers; Algorithm B selects answers <2,2,2,1,1>; Algorithm S selects answers <2,2,1,1,2>; and Algorithm W selects answers <2,2,2,2,2>.

DESIGN

Problem type was a within-subjects factor; all subjects solved all five problems. As in Experiment 1, presentation form (symbolic v. science-fiction stories) was manipulated as a between-subjects factor. Appendix B shows how the initial-belief sentences and the expansion sentences were phrased in the symbolic condition; the revision alternatives were phrased in a similar manner. Different letters were used in each of the problems that the subjects actually solved. The five different science-fiction cover stories were paired with the problems in six different ways.

Table 6: Problems and Percentage of Subjects Choosing Each Revision Alternative, Experiments 4 and 5

Problem			Revision Alternative	Experiment 4	Experiment 5
1	Initial:	(pqrs) or (~p~q~r~s)	1. p ~q ~r ~s$_D$	.06	.07
	Expansion:	p~r~s	2. p ~r ~s ?q$_{B, S, W}$	.94	.58
			3. p q ~r ~s		.05
			4. p ?q ?r ?s		.30
2	Initial:	(pqrs) or (~p~q~r~s)	1. p ~q ~r ~s$_D$	.11	.07
	Expansion:	(~p~qrs) or (p~q~r~s)	2. (~p~qrs) or (p~q~r~s)$_{B, S, W}$	.89	.21
			3. ~p ~q r s		.35
			4. ~q ?p ?r ?s		.37
3	Initial:	pq~s	1. ~p ~q r ~s$_{D, S, W}$	.22	.20
	Expansion:	(~p~q) & [(r~s) or (~rs)]	2. (~p~q) & [(r~s) or (~rs)]$_B$	.78	.43
			3. ~p ~q ~r s		.0
			4. ~p ~q ?r ?s		.37
4	Initial:	pq	1. p or q, not both$_{D, B, S}$	.12	.07
	Expansion:	~p or ~q or (~p~q)	2. ~p or ~q or (~p~q)$_W$	.88	.30
			3. ~p ~q		.12
			4. ?p ?q		.51
5	Initial:	pqr	1. ~p q r$_{D, B}$	.10	.21
	Expansion:	(~pqr) or (p~q~r)	2. (~p q r) or (p ~q ~r)$_{S, W}$	.90	.26
			3. p ~q ~r		.07
			4. ?p ?q ?r		.46
6	Initial:	~p~q~r	1. p ~q ~r$_{D, B}$		.07
	Expansion:	(~pqr) or (p~q~r)	2. (~p q r) or (p ~q ~r)$_{S, W}$		.30
			3. ~p q r		.23
			4. ?p ?q ?r		.40

Note. 'Initial' means initial sentence set, 'Expansion' means expansion information.

SUBJECTS AND PROCEDURE

The same 120 subjects who participated in Experiment 1 provided the data presented here as Experiment 4. Sixty subjects were assigned to the symbolic condition and sixty were assigned to the science-fiction condition. Equal numbers of subjects received the six different assignments of science-fiction cover stories to problems. No science-fiction cover story appeared more than once in any subject's problem booklet. Other details about the procedure and instructions were as described for Experiment 1.

Results

Unlike the modus ponens and modus tollens belief revision problems, there was no significant effect for the symbolic versus science-fiction manipulation on these problems. Table 6 presents the percentage of subjects choosing each possible revision choice, collapsed across presentation condition. The only planned comparisons concerning these data were within-problem differences, i.e., whether one revision choice was preferred significantly more often than another. Within each problem, there is a clear preference for one revision over the other: subjects chose revisions that most closely matched the form of the expansion information. We also tabulated the number of subjects whose response pattern across problems matched the particular pattern associated with each revision algorithm described in Table 5. Virtually no subjects matched a particular response pattern for all five problems.

Experiment 5

A concern about these data is that subjects were not following any particular model of change at all, but simply using the expansion sentence to define the new belief set. This could mean that they viewed the problem as an update, rather than a revision, problem (i.e., the world has moved to a new state defined by the expansion and there is no reason to maintain anything from the initial belief state), or it could mean that they were simply not engaged in the task. Since the same subjects generated distinct problem-specific patterns of responses in Experiment 1, we do not believe the latter possibility holds.

In Experiment 5, we included two additional response alternatives for each problem in order to test whether subjects continued just to adopt the expansion information (which might be the simplest interpretation of the results). Revision choice 3 was a non-minimal change model that was consistent with some interpretation of the expansion information. Revision choice 4 included only those sentences whose truth values were not contradicted within the expansion information or between some model of the initial sentences and the expansion. Basically, revision choice 4 offered the minimal number of sentences that could be known with certainty and made all other conflicts between truth values become "uncertain."

We also added Problem 6, which was isomorphic in form to Problem 5, except that the initial belief set consisted of all negated sentences rather than of all positive sentences. If subjects have a bias for models that consist primarily of non-negated sentences, then they should prefer such "positive" models regardless of whether they are minimal change models. Problems 5 and 6 differed only in whether the sentences in the initial set were all true or all false. Note the symmetry between revision choices 1 and 3 for these problems: the revision $[\sim pqr]$, with one negated sentence, is a minimal change model for Problem 5 but a non-minimal change model for Problem 6. Conversely, $[p\sim q\sim r]$ is the minimal change model for Problem 6 and a non-minimal change model for Problem 5. If subjects are biased towards revisions that maximize non-negated sentences, then there should be an interaction between the form of the initial belief set and the revision selected. Finally, we stressed in the instructions that both the initial and subsequent information should be considered before determining what should or should not be believed, just in case subjects believed that the expansion information should replace the initial belief set.

Method

Forty-three subjects solved problems 1–6 from Table 6 in random order. Since Experiment 4 had shown no effect for symbolic v. science-fiction presentation, the problems were presented in symbolic form only and the response alternatives appeared in different random orders for each subject.

Results and Discussion

The percentages of subjects choosing each revision choice in Experiment 5 are given in Table 6. As in Experiment 4, Experiment 5's subjects did not consistently obey any particular pattern of minimal change. First, it is striking that revision choice 1 was never the most preferred revision – it is the syntactically simplest way of specifying a model that accommodates the expansion sentence and corresponds to Algorithm D, which has an intuitively simple notion of minimal change. The second feature of the results concerns the relative percentages of revision 2 (in which the new belief state is simply the adoption of the new information) and revision 4. While revision choice 2 was the clear preference in Experiment 4, it was no longer the clear favorite here. Generally speaking, if subjects were given the option of tagging certain sentences as "uncertain" (revision 4), they gravitated to this choice over a revision that more precisely (and more accurately) specifies the uncertainty as multiple models (revision 2). One conjecture is that subjects elect to use revision 4 as short-hand way of expressing the uncertainty entailed in having multiple models of the world. That is, they may see "p and q are both uncertain" as equivalent to $(p\sim q) \vee (\sim pq)$, although, of course, it is not. It is unclear whether subjects appreciate the 'loss of information' inherent in such a presumption of equivalence.

Problems 5 and 6 were of particular interest, because they differed only in whether the initial belief set consisted of positive or negated sentences; the expansion information was the same. The set of revision alternatives was also identical. As with the other problems, the most preferred revision choice (about 40%) was to declare all sentences uncertain, when their truth value differed in two different models of the expansion information (and subjects did not merely adopt the multiple model described by the expansion information as the new belief state, as they had in Experiment 4). However, if we restrict our attention just to the percentage of revision 1 and revision 3 choices in these problems, we see that about the same number of subjects (20%) chose the revision $\sim pqr$ when it served as minimal change revision 1 for problem 5 and also when it was the non-minimal revision 2 for Problem 6. Conversely, only 7% of the subjects chose $p{\sim}q{\sim}r$ when it was the non-minimal revision 1 for Problem 5, but also only 7% chose it when it was (the minimal change) revision 3 for Problem 5. A chi-square computed on the response-choice by problem type (Problem 5 v. Problem 6) frequency table was marginally significant ($\chi^2 = 7.52$, $df = 3$, $p = .057$). These results suggest that there may be a bias against revisions that have more negated beliefs than non-negated beliefs in them. There is some suggestion of this in problem 2 as well, in which 35% of the subjects choose a non-minimal change revision (revision 3) than either of the two minimal change revisions (revisions 1 and 2). Such a finding itself is certainly consistent with body of evidence indicating that reasoning about negated sentences pose more difficulties for subjects (see, e.g., Evans, Newstead & Byrne, 1993, on "negated conclusions"); hence, people may prefer to entertain models of situations that contain fewer negations, when possible. This possibility of a bias against models with negations needs further, systematic study. In sum, Experiments 4 and 5 suggest that subjects are not following any single model-based minimal change metric and do not integrate the expansion information wholeheartedly. Despite the availability of choices that could be selected via a matching procedure between disjuncts appearing in the initial and new information (revision 1 across all problems), our subjects seem to prefer belief states that consist of single models and models with non-negated beliefs, when possible.

General Discussion

We can summarize the main findings from this study as follows. First, to resolve the inconsistency that new information creates with an existing belief set that consists of ground sentences (p, q) and conditional sentences ($p \rightarrow q$), the preferred revision was to disbelieve the conditional rather than alter the truth status of the ground sentence. This preference was even stronger on problems using science-fiction or familiar topic cover stories than it was using symbolic formulas. Second, there were some differences in revision choices depending on whether the initial belief set was constructed by using a modus tollens or modus ponens inference. Subjects more often changed the truth status of the initial ground sentence (and the conditional, when there was that option) to "uncertain" on the modus tollens problems than they did on the modus ponens problems. Third, we observed that the patterns of revision choices on the simple problems we investigated does not depend on whether or not the (modus ponens) inference was explicitly listed in the initial belief set or whether subjects were left to perform the inference themselves. Fourth, we note that the patterns of revision did not change when the initial belief state was constructed from purely propositional reasoning or used universally quantified inferences. Fifth, we discovered that when an implied conclusion of the initial belief set itself gives rise to yet another conclusion, and when the first of these conclusions is contradicted by the expansion information, then the status of the second conclusion is regarded as "uncertain."

Finally, we investigated alternative model-theoretic definitions of minimal change. We found that subjects did not adhere to any of these particular prescriptions, some of which (e.g., Algorithm D) can be construed as a fairly straightforward matching strategy between a model in the initial information and a model of the expansion information. Even when the initial belief state had only one model, subjects did not use it to chose among alternative models of (uncertain) expansion information; and even when there was only a single model of expansion information, subjects did not use this to chose among alternative models of an (uncertain) initial belief state. And while a disjunction of multiple models can specify how the truth value of one sentence co-varies with another's, our subjects did not prefer such multiple-model specifications of a belief state as a way to represent uncertainty. They instead chose single-model revisions that retained only those sentences that had an unambiguous truth value across the initial and expansion information, and labeled all other sentences as uncertain (even though this results in a loss of information). There is a possibility as well that people prefer revisions that contain positive rather than negated sentences; this requires further study. In the remainder of this section, we consider these results for notions of epistemic entrenchment and minimal change.

On Epistemic Entrenchment

The rationale behind a notion like epistemic entrenchment is that, practically, an agent may need to choose among alternative ways to change its beliefs, and intuitively, there will be better reasons to chose one kind of change over another. These better reasons are realized as a preference to retain or discard some types of knowledge over another; the issue is what those epistemically based principles of entrenchment are or ought to be. As we noted in the introduction, some theorists have argued that conditional statements like $p \rightarrow q$ may warrant, a priori, a higher degree of entrenchment than some other sentence types, not because there is something to be preferred about material implications, but because that form often signals "law-like" or predictive relations that have explanatory power. And law-like relations, because of their explanatory power, should be retained over other types of knowledge when computing a new belief state.

We did not find evidence for this kind of entrenchment as a descriptive principle of human belief revision in the tasks we studied. In general, the frequency of continuing to believe the conditional was lower than what might be expected by chance, and lower still on natural language problems. Finding that belief-revision choices changed when the problems involved non-abstract topics is not surprising, for there are many results in the deductive problem solving literature indicating that real-world scenarios influence deductive inferences, serving either to elicit, according to some theories, general pragmatic reasoning schemas (e.g., Cheng & Holyoak, 1989) or, according to other interpretations, specific analogous cases (Cox & Griggs, 1982). On the other hand, there was no domain-specific knowledge subjects could bring to bear about a science-fiction world. Indeed, the clauses used to make science-fiction sentences are not unlike those used by Cheng and Nisbett (1993) as "arbitrary" stimuli to investigate causal interpretations of conditionals. Nonetheless it is clear that subjects revised and expanded non-symbolic belief sets differently than they did symbolic belief sets.

Subjects may have interpreted the science-fiction conditional relations as predictive, or possibly causal, relations. The instructions that set up the science-fiction problems enjoined subject to imagine that information about an alien world was being relayed from an scientific investigative team. This may have prompted a theory-formation perspective, based on the assumption that even alien worlds are governed by regularities. The generation of, and belief in, these regularities depends on observations. The initial belief set had such a regularity in it (the conditional), plus a "direct observation" sentence. When the expansion information indicated that the inference from these two was contradicted,

the "denial" of the conditional is one way of asserting that the regularity it expresses, as specified, does not hold, *in this particular case*. Cheng and Nisbett (1993) found that a causal interpretation of *if p, then q* invokes assumptions of contingency, namely, that the probability of q's occurrence is greater in the presence of p than in the absence of p. Subjects may have viewed the (contradictory) expansion information in the modus ponens and modus tollens problems as calling this contingency into question. Such a perspective only makes sense when the problems are not manipulations of arbitrary symbols, and is consistent with our finding a higher rate of rule denials on non-abstract problems than on symbolic problems.

When ground statements of p and q are viewed as observations about some world, $p \rightarrow q$ can be interpreted as a theory, or summarizing statement, about how the truth values of these observations are related. This is, essentially, a model-theoretic viewpoint: an expression such as $p \rightarrow q$ is shorthand for how the truth values of p and q occur in the world. Taking this understanding of conditionals, the preference of our subjects to deny the conditional as a way of resolving contradiction can be interpreted as a preference to retain the truth value of "data" (the ground sentences) and deny the particular interdependence that is asserted to hold between them. This seems rational from an empiricist viewpoint: the "regularities" are nothing more than a way of summarizing the data. So, for a through-and-through empiricist, it is not even consistent to uphold a "law" in the face of recalcitrant data. Such a perspective puts a different light on the observation that people did not make the "easy" modus ponens inference from the expansion information combined with a modus tollens belief set: to have opted for this revision would have required changing the truth values of observational data. While doing so may be a plausible alternative when problems involve meaningless symbols, it may not not seem rational alternative when working with information that is interpretable as observational data.

The idea that data enjoy a priority over regularities has been offered as a belief revision principle in other frameworks (Thagard, 1989; Harman, 1986) particularly when regularities are (merely) hypotheses under consideration to explain or systematize observed facts. There is a natural role, then, for induction mechanisms in specifying the process of belief revision, once the conditional "regularity" is chosen by the agent as suspect. We note that the classical AI belief revision community presents the belief revision problem as denying previously believed sentences, including conditionals. But replacing $p \rightarrow q$ with $(p \;\&\; r) \rightarrow q$ or $(p \;\&\; \sim s) \rightarrow q$ are equally good ways to deny $p \rightarrow q$. In such a case, the conditional regularity can either be "patched" or demoted to the status of default rule ("Most of the time, $p \rightarrow q$, except when r holds"). In our view, this method of denying a conditional as belief revision choice seems to be preferable to merely lowering a degree of belief in the conditional, for the latter leaves the agent is no wiser about when to apply such a rule, only wiser that it should be less confident about the rule. This approach is being pursued in some classical approaches to belief revision (e.g., Ghose, Hadjinian, Sattar, You, & Goebel, 1993) and in explanation-based learning approaches to theory revision in the machine learning community, where the inability of a domain theory to explain some data causes changes to the domain theory rules (Ourston & Mooney, 1990; Richards & Mooney, 1995).

While some aspects of the belief revision process can be viewed as inductive processes searching for a better account of some data, we note that such a perspective itself does provide principles for guiding such a process when there are alternative ways to reconcile a contradiction. Specifically, we don't *always* believe the data at the expense of a regularity or contingency that we currently believe holds in the world. As we noted in the introduction, there are intuitions opposite to those that would deny or change a regularity to accommodate data: Kyburg's (1983) belief framework includes a place for both measurement error and the knowledge that some types of observations are more prone to error than others. Thagard (1989) offers an explanatory coherence metric by which data can be discounted, if they cohere with hypotheses which themselves are poor accounts of a larger data set. Carlson and Dulany's (1988) model of reasoning with circumstantial evidence includes parameters for degrees of subjective belief in the evidence. So the broader questions for epistemic entrenchment might be to ask what kinds of data and what kinds of regularities are more differentially entrenched in the face of contradiction than others.

On our simple belief revision tasks, we found some baseline results that suggest a tendency to abandon the conditional. But it has long been recognized by researchers in both linguistics and human deduction that the *if p then q* form is used

to express a broad range of different types of information, e.g., scientific laws, statistical relationships, causal relations, promises, and intentions ("If it doesn't rain tomorrow, we will play golf"). More recent studies (Elio, 1997), using both the revision-choice task described here as well as a degree-of-belief rating task, have found that different types of knowledge expressed in conditional form-e.g., causal relations, promises, and definitions-appear differentially entrenched in the face of contradictory evidence. Elio (1997) discusses these results within a possible-worlds framework, in which epistemic entrenchment is not a guide for, but rather a descriptor of, the belief revision outcome. This possible-worlds interpretation also ties certain features of the belief-revision task investigated here to probabilistic aspects of deductive reasoning, in which the reasoner may not accord full belief in the premises from which some conclusion is based (e.g., George, 1995; Stevenson & Over, 1995).

On Multiple Models and Minimal Change

One clear result we obtained is that people retain uncertainty in their revised belief states – they did not use single models of the new information to chose among alternative interpretations of the initial information, or conversely, in the tasks we gave them (e.g., they did not follow Algorithm D). Further, they tended to select revisions that include more uncertainty than is logically defensible, opting for "p is uncertain and so is q" as often or more frequently than "p is true and q is false, or else p is false and q is true." It seems clear that people could recognize (were it pointed out to them) that the former is less informative than the latter about possible combinations of p and q's truth values, but our subjects chose it anyway. One way to view the results we obtained is to say that many of our subjects preferred revisions which were not minimal with respect to what was changed, but were instead minimal with respect to what they believed to hold true without doubt when both the initial and expansion information were considered jointly. It certainly seems more difficult to work with a "world" specification like $\{[\sim p \sim q\; r\; s]$ or $[p\; \sim q\; \sim r \sim s]\}$ than it is with one that says "q is false and I'm not sure about anything else," even though (from a logical point of view) the former specification contains much more information than the latter.

What we learned from our initial investigations on minimal change problems may have less to do with the metrics of minimal change and more to do with issues of how people manipulate multiple models of the world. Rips' (1989) work on the knights-and-knaves problem also highlights the difficulty that people have in exploring and keeping track of multiple models. In that task, the supposition that one character is a liar defines one model, being a truth-teller defines another model, and each of these might in turn branch into other models. Even working such a problem out on paper presented difficulties for subjects, Rips reported. Yet in real life, we can certainly reason about vastly different hypothetical worlds that could be viewed as being equivalent to disjunctions of complex sentence sets. Unlike the arbitrary problems give to our subjects or even the knights-and-knaves problems, alternative hypothetical worlds about real-world topics may have some "explanatory glue" that holds together the particular contingencies, and no others, among the truth values of the independent beliefs. The question is whether for more real-world situations, are people better able to retain and integrate the interdependencies among truth values in multiple models?

Alternative Representations of Belief States

Representing a belief state as a set of sentences or even as a set of models is a simplification. We believe that number of important issues arise from this simple conceptualization and this study offers data on some of those issues. We noted alternative approaches to modeling belief states in the introduction, specifically those that use probabilistic information and degrees of belief. But there are two other perspectives that have long been considered from a philosophical viewpoint: the foundationalist view and the coherentist view. The foundationalist view (Swain, 1979; Moser, 1985, 1989; Alston, 1993) distinguishes between beliefs that are accepted without justification and those that depend on the prior acceptance of others. Such a distinction is used in truth-maintenance systems (e.g., Doyle, 1979; deKleer, 1986) for keeping track of dependencies among beliefs and to prefer the retraction of the latter ("assumptions") over the former ("premises") when contradictions are caused by new information. Pollock's (1987) defeasible reasoning theory defines a wider class of distinctions (e.g., "warrants" and "undercutters") and such distinctions can also be used to define normative foundationalist models of belief revision. The coherentist view (Quine

& Ullian, 1978; BonJour, 1985; Harman, 1986) does not consider some beliefs as more fundamental than others, but rather emphasizes the extent to which an entire set of beliefs "coheres." One set of beliefs can be preferable to another if it has a higher coherence, however defined. Thagard's (1989) theory of explanatory coherence is an instance of this perspective and operational definitions of coherence can, in such a framework, be a means of implementing belief revision principles (Thagard, 1992). Pollock (1979) gives a whole range of epistemological theories that span the spectrum between foundationalist and coherentist.

It has been argued (e.g., Harman, 1986; Gärdenfors, 1990b; Doyle, 1992; Nebel, 1992) that the original AGM account of belief revision, as well as model-based versions of it, are coherentist in nature. Harman and Gärdenfors go so far as to say that a foundationalist approach to belief revision (as advocated, e.g., by Doyle, 1979; Fuhrmann, 1991; Nebel, 1991) is at odds with observed psychological behavior, particularly concerning people's ability to recall the initial justifications for their current beliefs. More marshaling of this and other experimental evidence (including the type we have reported in this article) could be a reasonable first step towards an experimentally justified account of how human belief structures are organized; and with this is perhaps an account of how belief structures of non-human agents could best be constructed.

Finally, we note that it remains a difficult matter to examine "real beliefs" and their revision in the laboratory (as opposed to the task of choosing among sentences to be accepted as true); the paradigm of direct experimentation with some micro-world, which has been used to study theory development, is one direction that can prove fruitful (e.g., Ranney & Thagard, 1988). However, conceptualizing a belief state merely as a set of beliefs can still afford, we think, some insight into the pragmatic considerations people make in resolving contradiction.

Future Work

There are many issues raised in these investigations that warrant further study; we have touched upon some of them throughout our discussions. The possibility of bias against changing negated beliefs to non-negated ones, or in preferring revisions with non-negated sentences, needs systematic study. We used a selection paradigm throughout this study and it is important to establish whether similar results hold when subjects generate their new belief state. A more difficult issue is whether there are different patterns of belief revision depending on whether the belief set is one a person induces themselves or whether it is given to them. In the former case, one can speculate that a person has expended some cognitive effort to derive a belief, and a by-product of that effort may create the kind of coherentist structure that is more resistant to the abandonment of some beliefs in the face of contradictory information. This kind of perspective can be applied to an early study by Wason (1977) on self-contradiction. He found that subjects given the selection task were quite reluctant to change their conclusions about how to validate a rule, even when they were shown that such conclusions were contradicted by the facts of the task. Yet on a different sort of task, he found that subjects can recognize and correct invalid inferences about the form of a rule they are actively trying to identify from a data set, when the data set leads them to valid inferences that contradict the invalid ones they make. If recognizing a contradiction depends on the demands that a task imposes on a reasoner, then this might elucidate how premises are formulated and how inferences are validated; in the belief revision scenarios we used in this study, the contradiction occurs not because of the reasoner's inferencing process, but because additional information about the world indicates that one of initially accepted premises must be suspect. The recognition and resolution of contradiction is important to general theories of human reasoning that employ deduction, induction, and belief revision. How general performance models of deductive and inductive reasoning can embrace belief revision decisions is an important open issue.

Appendix A: Clauses Used for Science-Fiction Stimuli, Experiment 1

Subjects received one of the three possible science-fiction versions of the modus ponens and modus tollens rules, given below. Each version was used equally often across subjects.

Modus Ponens Rules

> If a Partiplod hibernates during the day, then it is a meat eater.

> If a cave has a Pheek in it, then that cave has underground water.

> If a ping burrows underground, then it has a hard protective shell.

Modus Tollens Rules

> If Gargons live on the planet's moon, then Gargons favor interplanetary cooperation.

> If an ancient ruin has a force field surrounding it, then it is inhabited by aliens called Pylons.

> If a Gael has cambrian ears (sensitive to high-frequency sounds), then that Gael also has tentacles.

Appendix B: Phrasing of Problems in the Symbolic Condition for Experiments 4 and 5

Problem	Initial Belief Set	Expansion
1	Either A, B, C, and D are all true, or none of them are true.	A is true. C is true. C is false.
2	Either A, B, C, and D are all true, or none of them are true.	B is false. Exactly one of these is true, but no one knows for sure which one: • A is true, and C and D are both false. • A is false, and C and D are both true.
3	A is true. B is true. D is true.	A is false. B is false. Either C is true or D is true, but not both of them.
4	A is true. B is true.	At least one of A and B is false, and possibly both of them are.
5	A is true. B is true. C is true.	Either A is false and B and C are both true, or A is true and B and C are both false. No one knows for sure which it is.
6	A is false. B is false. C is false.	Either A is true and B and C are both false, or A is false and B and C are both true. No one knows for sure which it is.

Notes

1 We note, however, that not all proponents of probabilistic frameworks concur that acceptance is a required notion. Cheeseman (1988) and Doyle (1989), for example, argue that acceptance is really a mixture of two distinct components: the theory of degree of belief together with a theory of action. The latter theory uses degrees of belief plus a theory of utility to produce a notion of deciding to act in a particular circumstance. Jeffrey (1965) also proposes a framework that avoids an acceptance-based account of belief.

2 Most syntax-based approaches put into their definitions of belief revision that the set of all logical consequences is computed for the original belief state in order to determine the contradictions. But only changes to this original "base" belief set are considered in constructing the new belief state. One intuition behind this variety of belief revision is that certain beliefs (the ones in the "base") are more fundamental than other beliefs, and any change in belief states should be made to the implicit beliefs first and only to the base if absolutely required. This view has relations to the foundationalist conception of belief states that we return to in our general discussion.

3 Some works, e.g., Fagin, Ullman, and Vardi (1986), use the term "theory" to include both what we call a syntax-based approach and what we call a theory-based approach. When they want to distinguish the two, they call the latter a "closed theory."

4 We aim to carefully distinguish our remarks about model-theoretic competence frameworks, as proposed by what we have been calling the classical AI belief revision community, from remarks concerning model-theoretic performance frameworks of human deduction, such as the mental-models theory. It is proper to talk of "models" in the context of either framework. Context will normally convey which framework we intend, but we use the terms "formal AI models" or "mental models" when it is necessary.

5 The explicit inclusion of $\sim r$ in S_1 and $\sim n$ in S_2 is, by some accounts, an extra inference step beyond what is necessary to incorporate $\sim w$, since they could be considered as implicit beliefs rather than explicit beliefs; this could be accommodated simply by dropping any mention of r and n from S_1 and S_2, respectively.

6 The actual problems used in these first experiments were really quantified versions of modus ponens and modus tollens. Our modus ponens problem type is more accurately paraphrased as: from *For any x, if p holds of x, then q holds of x*, and furthermore *p holds of a*, we can infer *q holds of a*. Similar remarks can be made for our modus tollens.

7 The reason is this. In a model approach, the initial belief state is the model [*p is true, q is true*]. When this is revised with $\sim q$, thereby forcing the change from *q's* being true to *q's* being false in the model, we are left with the model [*p is true, q is false*]. Such a model has zero changes, other than the one forced by the expansion information; and in this model $p \rightarrow q$ is false. In order to make this conditional be true, a change to the model that was not otherwise forced by the revision information would be required, to make *p* be false. (Similar remarks hold for the modus tollens case.) Thus model theories of belief revision will deny the conditional in such problems.

8 We used the term "knowledge" rather than "belief" in instructions to subjects, because we wanted them to accord full acceptance to them prior to considering how they might resolve subsequent contradiction. The use of "knowledge" here, as something that could subsequently change in truth value, is nonstandard from a philosophical perspective, although common in the AI community. Although these instructions may have appeared inconsistent to a subject sensitive to such subtle distinctions, subsequent studies in which we called the initial belief set as "things believed to be true" have not impacted the type of results we report here.

9 The loglinear model for this data is $\ln(F_{ijk}) = \mu + \lambda\rho_i + \lambda pres_j + \lambda prob_k + \lambda\rho_i pres_j + \lambda\rho_i prob_k + \lambda pres_j prob_k$ where F_{ijk} is the observed frequency in the cell, $\lambda\rho_i$ is the effect of the ith response alternative, $\lambda pres_j$ is the effect of the jth presentation-form category, $\lambda\pi\rho o\beta_k$ is the effect of the kth problem-type category, and the remaining terms are two-way interactions among these. The equivalent "logit" model, in which response is identified as the dependent variable, has terms for response, response by presentation mode, and response by problem type; it yields identical chi-square values. Loglinear and logit procedures from SPSS version 5.0 were used for these analyses. Chi-squares computed on several two-way frequency tables are consistent with the loglinear analyses and the conclusions presented in the text. The effect of symbol *v.* science-fiction presentation approached significance on both MP and on MT problems, when chi-squares were computed for separate two-dimensional frequency tables ($\chi^2 = 5.65$ and 4.87, $p = .059$ and .087, $df = 2$ in both cases).

References

Alchourrón, C., Gärdenfors, P., and Makinson, D. (1985). On the logic of theory change: Partial meet contraction and revision functions. *Journal of Symbolic Logic, 50,* 510–530.

Alston, W. (1993). *The reliability of sense perception.* Ithaca, NY: Cornell University Press.

Ashton, R., and Ashton, A. (1990). Evidence-responsiveness in professional judgment: Effects of positive vs. negative evidence and presentation mode. *Organizational Behavior and Human Decision Processes, 46,* 1–19.

Bacchus, F., Grove, A., Halpern, J. Y., and Koller, D. (1992). From statistics to belief. In *Proceedings of the Tenth National Conference on Artificial Intelligence* (pp. 602–608). Cambridge, MA: MIT Press.

BonJour, L. (1985). *The structure of empirical knowledge.* Cambridge, MA: Harvard University Press.

Borgida, A. (1985). Language features for flexible handling of exceptions in information. *Systems ACM Transactions on Database Systems, 10,* 563–603.

Braine, M. D. S., and O'Brian, D. P. (1991). A theory of If: A lexical entry, reasoning program, and pragmatic principles. *Psychological Review, 98,* 182–203.

Carlson, R. A., and Dulany, D. E. (1988). Diagnostic reasoning with circumstantial evidence. *Cognitive Psychology, 20,* 463–492.

Cheeseman, P. (1988). Inquiry into computer understanding. *Computational Intelligence, 4,* 58–66.

Cheng, P. W., and Holyoak, K. J. (1989). On the natural selection of reasoning theories. *Cognition, 33,* 285–314.

Cheng, P. W., Holyoak, K. J., Nisbett, R. E., and Oliver, L. (1993). Pragmatic versus syntactic approaches to training deductive reasoning. *Cognitive Psychology, 18,* 293–328.

Cheng, P. W., and Nisbett, R. E. (1993). Pragmatic constraints on causal deduction. In R. E. Nisbett (Ed.), *Rules for reasoning.* Hillsdale, NJ: Lawrence Erlbaum.

Cox, J. R., and Griggs, R. A. (1982). The effects of experience on performance in Wason's selection task. *Memory & Cognition, 10,* 496–502.

deKleer, J. (1986). An assumption-based TMS. *Artifictal Intelligence, 28,* 127–162.

Dalal, M. (1988). Investigations into a theory of knowledge base revision: Preliminary report. *Proceedings of the Seventh American Association for Artificial Intelligence* (pp. 475–479).

Doyle, J. (1979). A truth maintenance system. *Artificial Intelligence, 12,* 231–272.

Doyle, J. (1989). Constructional belief and rational representation. *Computational Intelligence, 5,* 1–11.

Doyle, J. (1992). Reason maintenance and belief revision: Foundations vs. coherence theories. In P. Gärdenfors (Ed.), *Belief revision,* pp. 29–51. Cambridge: Cambridge University Press.

Edwards, W. (1968). Conservatism in human information processing. In B. Kleinmuntz (Ed.), *Formal representation of human judgment.* NewYork: Holt Rinehart & Winston.

Einhorn, H., and Hogarth, R. (1978). Confidence in judgment: Persistence in the illusion of validity. *Psychological Review, 85,* 395–416.

Elio, R. (1997). What to believe when inferences are contradicted: The impact of knowledge type and inference rule. In *Proceedings of the Nineteenth Annual Conference of the Cognitive Science Society.* Hillsdate, NJ: Lawrence Erlbaum.

Elio, R., and Pelletier, F. J. (1994). The effect of syntactic form on simple belief revisions and updates. In *Proceedings of the 16th Annual Conference of the Cognitive Science Society* (pp. 260–265). Hillsdale, NJ: Lawrence Erlbaum.

Elmasri, R., and Navathe, S. (1994). *Fundamentals of database systems,* 2nd Edition. Redwood City, CA: Benjamin/Cummins.

Evans, J. St. B. T., Newstead, S. E., and Byrne, R. M. J. (1993). *Human reasoning.* Hillsdale, NJ: Lawrence Erlbaum.

Fagin, R., Ullman, J., and Vardi, M. (1986). Updating logical databases. *Advances in Computing Research, 3,* 1–18.

Foo, N. Y., and Rao, A. S. (1988). *Belief revision is a microworld* (Tech. Rep. No. 325). Sydney: University of Sidney, Basser Department of Computer Science.

Fuhrmann, A. (1991). Theory contraction through base contraction. *Journal of Philosophical Logic, 20,* 175–203.

Gärdenfors, P. (1984). Epistemic importance and minimal changes of belief. *Australasian Journal of Philosophy, 62,* 137–157.

Gärdenfors, P. (1988). *Knowledge in flux: Modeling the dynamics of epistemic states.* Cambridge. MA: MIT Press.

Gärdenfors, P. (1990a). Belief revision and non-monotonic logic: Two sides of the same coin? In L. Aiello (Ed.), *Proceedings of the Ninth European Conference on Artificial Intelligence.* Stockholm, pp. 768–773.

Gärdenfors, P. (1990b). The dynamics of belief systems: Foundations vs. coherence theories. *Revue Internationale de Philosophie, 172,* 24–46.

Gärdenfors, P., and Makinson, D. (1988). Revisions of knowledge systems using epistemic entrenchment. In *Proceedings of the Second Conference on Theoretical Aspects of Reasoning about Knowledge* (pp. 83–95). Los Altos, CA.: Morgan Kaufmann.

George, C. (1995). The endorsement of the premises: Assumption-based or belief-based reasoning. *British Journal of Psychology, 86,* 93–111.

Ghose, A. K., Hadjinian, P. O., Sattar, A., You, J., and Goebel, R. (1993). Iterated belief change: A preliminary report. In *Proceedings of the Sixth Australian Conference on AI.* Melbourne, pp. 39–44.

Halpern, J. Y. (1990). An analysis of first-order logics of probability. *Artificial Intelligence, 46,* 311–350.

Harman, G. (1986). *Change in view.* Cambridge, MA: MIT Press.

Hoenkamp, E. (1988). An analysis of psychological experiments on non-monotonic reasoning. *Proceedings of the Seventh Biennial Conference of the Canadian Society for the Computational Study of Intelligence,* pp. 115–117.

Jeffrey, R. C. (1965). *The logic of decision.* New York: McGraw Hill.

Johnson-Laird, P. N., and Byrne, R. M. J. (1991). *Deduction.* Hillsdale, NJ: Lawrence Erlbaum.

Johnson-Laird, P. N., Byrne, R. M. J., and Schaeken, W. (1992). Propositional reasoning by model. *Psychological Review, 99,* 418–439.

Katsuno, H., and Mendelson, A. (1991). Propositional knowledge base revision and minimal change. *Artificial Intelligence, 52,* 263–294.

Koehler, J. J. (1993). The influence of prior beliefs on scientific judgments of evidence quality. *Organizational Behavior and Human Decision Processes, 56,* 28–55.

Kyburg, H. E., Jr. (1983). Rational belief. *Brain and Behavioral Sciences, 6,* 231–273.

Kyburg, H. E., Jr. (1994). Believing on the basis of evidence. *Computational Intelligence, 10,* 3–20.

Lepper, M. R., Ross, L., and Lau, R. R. (1986). Persistence of inaccurate beliefs about the self: Perseverance effects in the classroom. *Journal of Personality and Social Psychology, 50,* 482–491.

Makinson, D., and Gärdenfors, P. (1991). Relations between the logic of theory change and nonmonotonic logic. In A. Fuhrmann and M. Morreau (Eds.), *The logic of theory change.* Vol. 465 of Lecture Notes in Computer Science. Berlin: Springer-Verlag.

Moser, P. (1985). *Empirical justification.* Dordrecht: D. Reidel.

Moser, P. (1989). *Knowledge and evidence.* Cambridge: Cambridge University Press.

Nebel, B. (1991). Belief revision and default reasoning: Syntax-based approaches. In *Proceedings of the Second Conference on Knowledge Representation* (pp. 417–428). San Mateo, CA.: Morgan Kaufmann.

Nebel, B. (1992). Syntax based approaches to belief revision. In P. Gärdenfors (Ed.), *Belief revision* (pp. 52–88). Cambridge: Cambridge University Press.

Ourston, D., and Mooney, R. J. (1990). Changing the rules: A comprehensive approach to theory refinement. In *Proceedings of the Eighth National Conference on Artificial Intelligence* (pp. 815–820). Cambridge, MA: MIT Press.

Pearl, J. (1988). Fusion, propagation, and structuring in belief networks. *Artificial Intelligence, 29,* 241–288.

Petty, R. E., Priester, J. R., and Wegener, D. T. (1994). Cognitive processes in attitude change. In R. S. Wyer and T. K. Srull (Eds.), *Handbook of social cognition.* Volume 2: Applications (pp. 69–142). Hillsdale, NJ: Lawrence Erlbaum.

Pollock, J. L. (1979). A plethora of epistemological theories. In G. S. Pappas (Ed.), *Justification and knowledge: New studies in epistemology* (pp. 93–113). Boston: D. Reidel.

Pollock, J. L. (1987). Defeasible reasoning. *Cognitive Science, 11,* 481–518.

Pollock, J. L. (1990). *Nomic probabilities and the foundations of induction.* Oxford: Oxford University Press.

Quine, W., and Ullian, J. (1978). *The web of belief.* New York: Random House.

Ranney, M., and Thagard, P. (1988). Explanatory coherence and belief revision in naive physics. In *Proceedings of the Tenth Annual Conference of the Cognitive Science Society* (pp. 426–432). Hillsdale, NJ: Lawrence Erlbaum.

Richards, B. L., and Mooney, R. J. (1995). Automated refinement of first-order horn-clause domain theories. *Machine Learning, 19,* 95–131.

Rips, L. J. (1983). Cognitive processes in propositional reasoning. *Psychological Review, 90,* 38–71.

Rips, L. J. (1989). The psychology of knights and knaves. *Cognition, 31,* 85–116.

Rips, L. J. (1994). *The psychology of proof.* Cambridge, MA: MIT Press.

Ross, L., and M. Lepper (1980). The perseverance of beliefs: Empirical and normative considerations. In R. Shweder (Ed.), *Fallible judgment in behavioral research.* San Francisco: Jossey-Bass.

Russell, B. (1918). The philosophy of logical atomism. Reprinted in R. Marsh (Ed.), *Logic and knowledge.* New York: Allen and Unwin, 1956.

Satoh, K. (1988). Nonmonotonic reasoning by minimal belief revision. In *Proceedings of the International Conference on Fifth Generation Computer Systems* (pp. 455–462). ICOT: Tokyo.

Shields, M. D., Solomon, I., and Waller, W. S. (1987). Effects of alternative sample space representations on the accuracy of auditors' uncertainty judgments. *Accounting, Organizations, and Society, 12,* 375–385.

Stevenson, R. J., and Over, D. E. (1995). Deduction from uncertain premises. *Quarterly Journal of Experimental Psychology, 484,* 613–643.

Swain, M. (1979). Justification and the basis of belief. In G. S. Pappas (Ed.), *Justification and knowledge: New studies in epistemology.* Boston: D. Reidel.

Thagard, P. (1989). Explanatory coherence. *Behavioral and Brain Sciences, 12,* 435–502.

Thagard, P. (1992). Computing coherence. In R. Giere (Ed.) *Cognitive models of science.* Minneapolis: University of Minnesota Press.

Wason, P. (1977). Self-contradictions. In P. Johnson-Laird and P. Wason (Eds.), *Thinking: Readings in cognitive science* (pp. 113–128). Cambridge: Cambridge University Press.

Weber, A. (1986). Updating propositional formulas. In *Proceedings of the First Conference on Expert Database Systems* (pp. 487–500).

Willard, L., and Yuan, L. (1990). The revised Gärdenfors postulates and update semantics. In S. Abiteboul and P. Konellakis (Eds.), *Proceed-ings of the International Conference on Database Theory* (pp. 409–421). Volume 470 of Lecture Notes in Computer Science. Berlin: Springer. Verlag.

Wittgenstein, L. (1922). *Tractatus logico-Philoso-phicus*. London: Routledge & Kegan Paul.

Yates, J. F. (1990). *Judgment and decision making*. Englewood Cliffs, NJ: Prentice Hall.

Section 7: Causal and Counterfactual Reasoning

Chapter 29: Causal Thinking

LANCE J. RIPS[1]

One damn thing leads to another. I forget to open the garage door this morning, back my car into the door, and splinter it. The actions we perform cause other events – my backing up causes the splintering. But events of other kinds – non-actions – have their effects, too. With no help from me, last night's storm caused a branch to fall from a tree, putting a hole in my roof.

Much as we might like to forget them, we often keep track of events like these and the causes that unite them. Although we might not have predicted these events, we can remember and reconstruct part of the causal sequences after they occur. In retelling the events of last summer, for example, we tend to relate the events in forward causal order, starting, say, at the beginning of our trip to Virginia in May and proceeding chronologically. If we want to mention other kinds of events from the same period, such as our summer work experiences, we may start again at the beginning of the summer, moving along the events in a parallel causal stream (Barsalou 1988). We also remember fictional stories in terms of the causal changes that compose their main plot line, remembering less about events falling on deadend side plots (Trabasso and Sperry 1985). We sometimes attribute causal powers to concrete objects as well as to events, but we can understand this sort of talk as an abbreviation for event causation. If Fred caused the glass to break that's because one of Fred's actions – maybe his dropping it – caused the breaking. I'll take event causation as basic in this article on the strength of such paraphrases.

We remember causes and effects for event types as well as for event tokens. Ramming heavy objects into more fragile ones typically causes the fragile items damage; repeating phone numbers four or five times typically causes us to remember them for awhile. Negotiating routine events (e.g., Schank and Abelson 1977), con-structing explanations (e.g., Lewis 1986), and making predictions all require memory for causal relations among event categories. Causal gener-alities underlie our concepts of natural kinds, like daisies and diamonds (e.g., Ahn and Kim 2000; Barton and Komatsu 1989; Gelman and Wellman 1991; Keil 1989; Rehder and Hastie 2001; Rips 1989, 2001) and support our con-cepts of artifacts like pianos or prisms. Our knowledge of how beliefs and desires cause actions in other people props up our own social activities (e.g., Wellman 1990).

The importance of causality is no news. Nei-ther are the psychological facts that we attribute causes to events, remember the causes later, and reason about them – although, as usual, con-troversy surrounds the details of these mental activities. Recently, though, psychologists seem to be converging on a framework for causal knowledge, prompted by earlier work in com-puter science and philosophy. Rhetorical pres-sure seems to be rising to new levels among cognitive psychologists working in this area: For example, "until recently no one has been able to frame the problem [of causality]; the discussion of causality was largely based on a framework developed in the eighteenth cen-tury. But that's changed. Great new ideas about how to represent causal systems and how to learn and reason about them have been devel-oped by philosophers, statisticians, and com-puter scientists" (Sloman 2005: vii). And at a psychological level, "we argue that these kinds of representations [of children's knowledge of causal structure] and learning mechanisms can be perspicuously understood in terms of the normative mathematical formalism of directed graphical causal models, more commonly known as Bayes nets.... This formalism provides a natural way of representing causal structure, and it provides powerful tools for accurate prediction and effective intervention" (Gopnik et al. 2004: 4).

It's a little unfair to catch these authors in mid rhetorical flight. But the claims for these formalisms do provoke questions about how far they take us beyond the simple conclusions I've already mentioned. Kids and adults learn, remember, and apply causal facts. As a card-carrying CP (i.e., cognitive psychology) member, I believe that kids and adults therefore mentally represent these facts. But what's new here that further illuminates cognitive theorizing? Here's the gloomy picture: The new methods are at heart data-analytic procedures for summarizing or approximating a bunch of correlations. In this respect, they're a bit like factor analysis and a whole lot like structural equation modeling. (If you think it surprising that psychologists should seize on a statistical procedure as a model for ordinary causal thinking, consider that another prominent theory in this area is Kelley's [1967] ANOVA model; see the section on *Causation from Correlation*, and Gigerenzer 1991.) The idea that people use these methods to induce and represent causality flies in the face of evidence suggesting that people aren't much good at normatively correct statistical computations of this sort (e.g., Tversky and Kahneman 1980). Offhand, it's much more likely that what people have are fragmentary and error-prone representations of what causes what.

The rosier picture is the one about "great new ideas."

The jury is still out, and I won't be resolving this issue here. But sorting out the claims for the new causal representations highlights some important questions about the nature of causal thinking.

How Are Causal Relations Given to Us?

Here's a sketch of how a CD player works (according to Macaulay 1988): A motor rotates a spindle that rotates the CD. As the CD turns, a laser sends a beam of light through a set of mirrors and lenses onto the CD's surface. The light beam lands on a track composed of reflecting and nonreflecting segments that have been burned onto the CD. The reflecting segments bounce the light beam back to a photodiode that registers a digital "on" signal; the nonreflecting segments don't bounce the light back and represent an "off" signal. The pattern of digital signals

is then converted into a stereo electrical signal for playback.

You could remember this information in something like the form I just gave you – an unexciting little narrative about CD players. But the new psychological approach to causal knowledge favors directed graphs like Figure 1 as mental representations – "causal maps" of the environment (Gopnik et al. 2004). This graph contains nodes that stand for event types (e.g., the CD player's motor rotating or not rotating, the CD turning or not turning) and directed links that stand for causal connections between these events (the motor rotating causes the CD's turning; the laser producing a beam and the mirror-lens assembly focusing the beam jointly cause the beam to hit the CD's surface). Of course, no one disputes the fact that people can remember some of the information these diagrams embody. Although people can be over-confident about their knowledge of mechanical devices like this one (Rozenblit and Keil 2002), they're nevertheless capable of learning, say, that the CD player's motor causes the CD to turn. What's not so clear is how they acquire this cause-effect information, how they put the component facts together, and how they make inferences from such facts. In this section, we'll consider the acquisition problem, deferring issues of representation and inference till the second part of this chapter.

Causation in Perception

You're not likely to get much of the information in Figure 1 by passively observing a CD player, unless you already know about the nature of similar devices. But sometimes you do get an impression of cause from seeing objects move. Repeated sightings of an event of type E_1 followed by an event of type E_2 may provide evidence that E_1 causes E_2. Rather weak evidence, but evidence nonetheless. When we later see an example of the same sequence, we can infer the causal link. But psychologists sometimes claim there is a more intimate perception of cause in which an observer directly experiences one event causing another.

PERCEPTUAL STUDIES

In a famous series of demonstrations, Michotte (1963) rigged a display in which a square appeared to move toward a second square and to stop abruptly when they touched. If the second square then began to move within a fixed

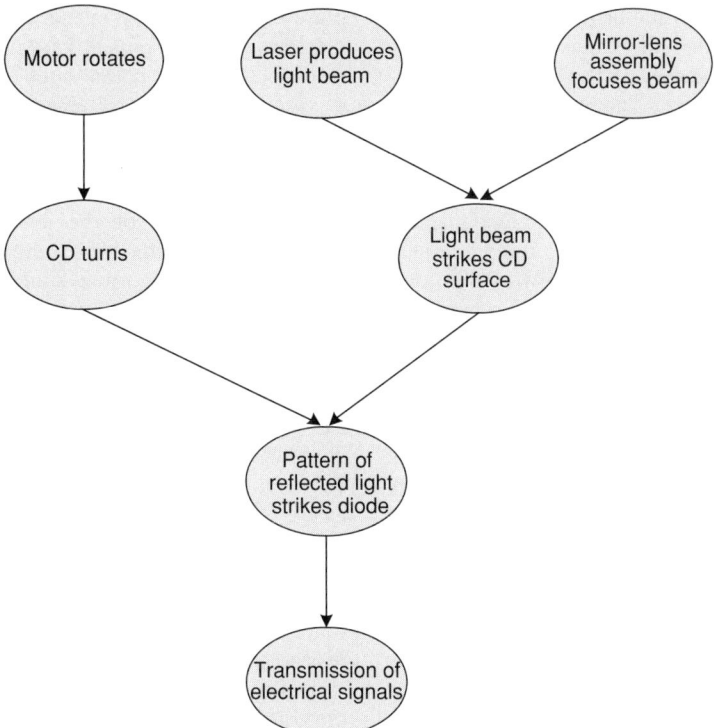

Figure 1. A directed graph representing the operation of a CD player, based on text by Macaulay (1988).

interval of the touching and at a speed similar to that of the first square, observers reported the first square causing the second to move, *launching* it.

Michotte's extensive experiments aimed to isolate the purely perceptual conditions that produce this immediate impression of causality, but there's a paradoxical quality to his efforts. The first square in the display doesn't actually cause the second to move. The displays showed 2-D projections of simple geometrical forms whose movements could be carefully controlled behind the scenes. (In those days before lab computers, Michotte engagingly created his displays using striped disks rotating behind slits or using pairs of moving slide projectors.) The goal was therefore not to determine when people correctly detect causal relations in their environment but instead to uncover the cues that lead them to report causality.[2] Michotte himself discusses a number of situations in which people report one event causing another, even though the interaction is physically unlikely or impossible. In one such case, a square A moves at 30 cm/s and comes into contact with another square B, which is already moving at 15 cm/s. If

A comes to a halt and B moves off at a *slower* pace than before (7.5 cm/s), observers report a causal effect. "Such cases are particularly interesting in that they show that causal impressions arise as soon as the psychological conditions of structural organization are fulfilled, and indeed that they can arise even in situations where we know from past experience that a causal impression is a downright impossibility" (Michotte 1963: 71). Michotte's project attempted to explain these causal impressions in noncausal terms: His descriptions of the crucial stimulus conditions don't presuppose one object causally influencing another. He believed that people's impression of causality arises as their perceptual systems try to resolve a conflict (e.g., in the launching event) between the initial view of the first square moving and the second square stationary and the final view of the first square stationary and the second moving. The resolution is to see the movement of the first object extending to the second, which Michotte called "ampliation of the movement" (which, I hope, sounds better in French).

Michotte (1963: 351–352) believed that this resolution "enables us to understand why, when such a structure is established, participants can communicate adequately what they perceive only by saying that they *see* the [initially moving] object make the second go forward." Why? The obvious answer would be that this perceptual situation is one that real objects produce when they undergo causal interactions. The resolution that takes place in the experimental displays reminds the observers, perhaps unconsciously, of what happens when they view causal comings and goings in the ordinary environment, and they therefore interpret it the same way. But this answer is one Michotte rejects, since he consistently denies that the launching effect is due to acquired knowledge. This is why physically impossible cases, like the one described in the previous paragraph, are important to him: They seem to rule out the possibility that observers are making an inference to causality based on experience.

The easiest way to understand Michotte's theory (though not in terms he used) is as the claim that people have a built-in causality detector that is triggered by the conditions he attempted to describe. Since the detector is presumably innate, its operations don't depend on learning from previous experience. Moreover, the detector responds reliably but not perfectly. Toads dart at insects in their visual fields but can be tricked into darting at moving black-on-white or white-on-black spots, according to the old ethology chestnut (e.g., Ewert 1974). In the same way, whenever the movement of an object "extends" to a second, people receive the impression of causality, whether or not the first object actually causes the second to move.

But this approach, like some moving spots, is hard to swallow. Although Michotte stressed that observers spontaneously report the events in causal language – for example, that "the first square pushed the second" – the impression of causality doesn't seem as immediate or automatic as typical perceptual illusions. We can't help but see the apparent difference in line length in the Muller-Lyer illusion or the apparently bent lines in the Poggendorf and Hering figures (see, e.g., Gregory 1978, for illustrations of these). And toads, so far as we know, can't help unleash their tongues at moving specks. But Michotte's demonstrations allow more interpretative leeway.

Suppose Michotte was right that people possess an innate detector of some sort that's broad enough to be triggered by the displays his participants report as causal. The detector, of course, produces false positive responses to some displays that are in fact noncausal (e.g., Michotte's displays), and it produces false negative or nonresponses to some causal ones (e.g., reflections of electromagnetic rays in an invisible part of the spectrum). So what the detector detects is not (all or only) causal interactions but perhaps something more like abrupt transitions or discontinuities in the speed of two visible objects at the point at which they meet. This would include both the normal launching cases and the causally unlikely or impossible ones, such as slowing on impact. Nor do we ultimately take the output of the detector as indicating the presence of a causal interaction. In the case of Michotte's demos, for example, we conclude that no real causal interaction takes place between the squares, at least when we become aware of what's going on behind the smoke and mirrors. The issue of whether we *see* causality in the displays, then, is whether there's an intermediate stage between the detector and our ultimate judgment, a stage that is both relevantly perceptual and also carries with it a causal verdict. Because these two requirements pull in opposite directions, the claim that we can see causality is unstable.

Here's an analogy that may help highlight the issue. People viewing a cartoon car, like the ones in the Disney film *Cars*, immediately "see" the cartoon as a car (and report it as a car), despite the fact that it is physically impossible for cars to talk, to possess eyes and mouths, and to move in the flexible way that cartoon cars do. Although I don't recommend it, you could probably spend your career pinning down the parameter space (e.g., length-to-width ratios) within which this impression of carness occurs. But there isn't enough evolutionary time since the invention of cars in the 19th century for us to have evolved innate car detectors. The fact that we immediately recognize cartoons as cars even when they possess physically impossible properties can't be evidence for innate car perception. Michotte's evidence seems no stronger as support for innate cause detection. Although it's an empirical issue, I'm willing to bet that the impression of carness generated by the cartoon cars is at least as robust as the impression of causality generated by launching displays.

Causality is an inherently abstract relation – one that holds not only between moving physical objects but also between subatomic particles, galaxies, and lots in the middle – and this abstractness makes it difficult to come up with a plausible theory that would have us perceiving it directly, as opposed to inferring it from more concrete perceived information.[3] There's no clear way to defeat the idea that "when we consider these objects with the utmost attention, we find only that the one body approaches the other; and the motion of it precedes that of the other without any sensible interval" (Hume 1739/1967: 77).

DISSOCIATION BETWEEN PERCEIVED AND INFERRED CAUSALITY

More recent evidence suggests that people's judgments about perceived causality are independent of some of the inferences they make about cause. Investigators have taken these dissociations to suggest that Michotte (1963) was right that perceived causality is an innate module. One such study (Roser, Fugelsang, Dunbar, Corballis, and Gazzaniga 2005) employed two split-brain patients, presenting causal tasks to the patients' right or left hemispheres. In one task, the patients saw Michotte-type launching events that varied in the spatial gap between the two objects at the moment the second object began to move and, also, the time-delay between the point at which the first object stopped and the second object began moving. Both spatial gaps and time delays tend to weaken the impression of perceived causality in normal participants. And so they did in the split-brain patients, but with an important qualification. The patients had to choose whether the first object appeared to cause the second to move or whether the second object moved on its own, and their positive "cause" judgments were more frequent when there was no delay and no gap. This difference appeared, however, only when the patients' right hemisphere processed the display. Left-hemisphere processing showed no difference between conditions. A second task asked the same split-brain patients to solve a problem in which they had to use the statistical co-occurrence between visually presented events to decide which of two switches caused a light to come on. Patients were more often correct in this task when the displays presented the information to their left hemispheres than when they presented it to their right hemispheres.

Split-brain patients may process causal information in atypical ways, but investigators have found similar dissociations with normal participants. Schlottmann and Shanks (1992, Experiment 2) varied the temporal gap within launching events (as in Roser et al. 2005) and also the contingency that existed across trials between whether the first object moved and whether the second object moved. On some

series of trials, the first object's moving was necessary and sufficient for the second object to move; on others, the second object could move independently of the first. Participants made two types of judgments on separate trials within these series: how convincing a particular collision appeared and whether the collisions were necessary for the second object to move. Schlottmann and Shanks found an effect of delay but no effect of contingency on judgments of the display's convincingness. Judgments of necessity, however, showed a big effect of contingency and a much smaller effect of delay.

These dissociations suggest – what should become clear in the course of this chapter – that causal thinking is not of one piece. Some causal judgments depend vitally on detailed perceptual processing, while others depend more heavily on schemas, rules, probabilities, and other higher-order factors. What's not so clear is whether the dissociations also clinch the case for a perceptual causality detector. The right hemispheres of Roser et al.'s (2005) split-brain patients could assess the quality of launching events even though they were unable to evaluate the impact of statistical independencies. But this leaves a lot of room for the influence of other sorts of inference or association on judgments about launching. Suppose, for example, that launching judgments depend on whether observers are reminded of real-world interactions of similar objects. Unless the right hemisphere is unable to process these reminders, inference could still influence decisions about launchings. Similarly, Schlottmann and Shanks's (1992) finding shows that observers can ignore long-run probabilities in assessing the convincingness of a particular collision, but not that they ignore prior knowledge of analogous physical interactions.

STUDIES OF INFANTS

Developmental studies might also yield evidence relevant to Michotte's claim, since if the ability to recognize cause is innate, we should find infants able to discriminate causal from non-causal situations. The evidence here suggests that by about six or seven months, infants are surprised by events that violate certain causal regularities (Kotovsky and Baillargeon 2000; Leslie 1984; Leslie and Keeble 1987; Oakes 1994). In one such study, for example, Kotovsky and Baillargeon first showed seven-month-olds static displays containing a cylinder and a toy bug, either with a thin barrier separating them (no-contact

No-contact Condition   Contact Condition
Familiarization Displays   Familiarization Displays

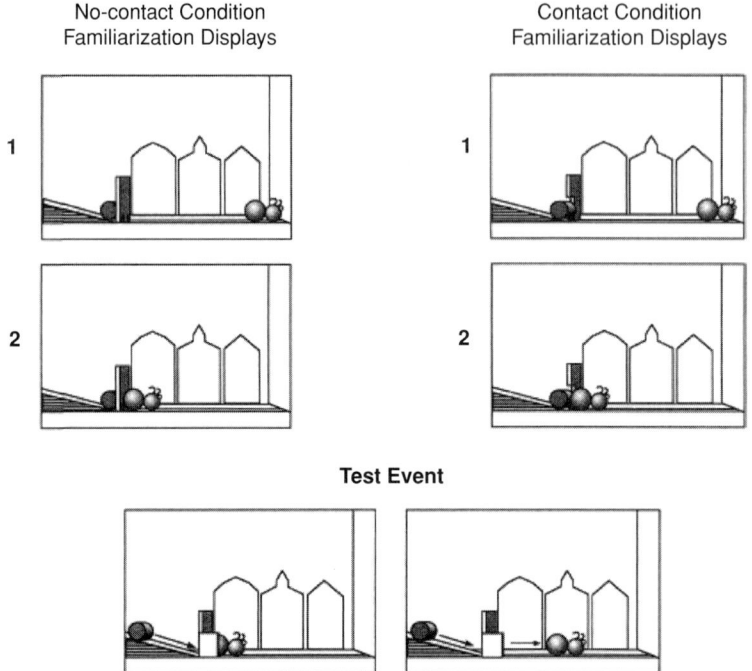

Figure 2. Familiarization and test conditions from Kotovsky and Baillargeon (2000).

condition) or with a partial barrier that did not separate them (contact condition). Figure 2 displays these two conditions at the left and right, respectively. A screen then hid the position that contained the barrier or partial barrier. In the experiment's test phase, the infants saw the cylinder roll down a ramp and go behind the screen, as shown at the bottom of Figure 2. The screen hid what would be the point of impact, but if the bug moved as if the cylinder had struck it, the infants looked longer in the no-contact than in the contact condition. If the bug failed to move, infants showed the opposite pattern of looking.

At seven months,[4] then, infants appear to discriminate some cases in which simple launching events will and won't occur, but should we take this as evidence for innate perception of causality? Unfortunately, there seems to be no evidence that would allows us to compare directly the class of interactions that Michotte's participants report as causal with the class that infants react to. It would be useful to know, in particular, whether the "impossible" displays that Michotte's observers report as causal are also ones to which infants give special attention. What we do know, however, is that infants take longer than seven months to recognize causal interactions even slightly more complex than simple launching. For example, at seven months

they fail to understand situations in which one object causes another to move in a path other than dead ahead, situations that adults report as causal (Oakes, 1994).

If the classes of interactions that adults and infants perceive as causal are not coextensive, this weakens the evidence for innate, modular perception of causality. You could maintain that the perceptual impression of causality changes with experience from an innate starting point of very simple causal percepts, such as dead on launchings, but this opens the door to objections to the very idea of directly perceiving cause. If learning can influence what we see as a causal interaction, then it seems likely that top-down factors – beliefs and expectations – can affect these impressions. Perhaps the learning in question is extremely local and low level. But if not – if observers' impressions of cause change because of general learning mechanisms – then this suggests that the impressions are a matter of inference rather than direct perception. Much the same can be said about evidence that seven-month-olds' reaction to launching events depends on whether the objects are animate or inanimate (Kotovsky and Baillargeon 2000). The animacy distinction presumably depends on higher-level factors, not just on the spatiotemporal parameters Michotte isolated (see Saxe and Carey 2006 for a review).

Of course, uncertainty about the evidence for direct perception of causality needn't affect the claim that the concept of causality is innate (see the section on causal primitives later in this chapter). Children may have such a concept but be initially unsure exactly what sorts of perceptual data provide evidence it applies. Moreover, nonperceptual, as well as perceptual, data may trigger such a concept; in fact, most theories of causality in psychology have avoided tying cause to specifically perceptual information. These theories take seriously the other aspect of Hume's (1739/1967) view, trying to account for judgments of causality in terms of our experience of the co-occurrence of events. Does recent research shed any light on this possibility?

Causation from Correlation

Even if we can literally perceive causality in some situations, we have to resort to indirect methods in others. A careful look at a CD player's innards can't disclose the causal link between the reflected pattern of light and the transmission of sound signals at the bottom of Figure 1. We may see the reflected light and hear the resulting sound, but we don't have perceptual access to the connection between them. Similarly, we can't see atmospheric pressure influencing the boiling point of a liquid or a virus producing a flu symptom or other people's beliefs motivating their actions. Experiments in science would be unnecessary if all we had to do to isolate a causal mechanism is look.

Scientists, of course, aren't the only ones in need of hidden causal facts. We need to predict how others will behave if we want to enlist them in moving a sofa. We need to know what buttons to press if we want to make a cell phone call or record an opera broadcast or adjust the drying cycle to keep from scorching our socks. We need to know which foods are likely to trigger our allergy, which windows are best for which plants, which greetings will produce another greeting versus a stunned silence or a slap in the face. We can sometimes rely on experts to tell us about the hidden causes. Allergists are often good on allergies, botanists on plants, and Miss Manners on manners. But sometimes we have to proceed on our own, and the question is how ordinary people cope with the task of recognizing causal relationships when they can't look them up. The answer that psychologists have usually given to this question is that people operate from bottom up, observing the temporal co-occurrence

of events and making an inductive inference to a causal connection. They might passively register the presence or absence of a potential cause and its effects or they may actively intervene, pressing some buttons to see what happens. In either case, they decide whether a cause-effect link is present on the basis of these results. This section considers the more passive route to discovering causes, and the next section looks at the more active one.

CAUSE, CONTRAST, CORRELATION

If we suspect event type C causes event type E, we should expect to find E present when C is present and E absent when C is absent. This correlation might not be inevitable even if C really is a cause of E. Perhaps E has an alternative cause C'; so E could appear without C. Or perhaps C is only a contributing cause, requiring C″ in order to produce E; then C could appear without E. But if we can sidestep these possibilities or are willing to define *cause* in a way that eliminates them, then a correlation between C and E may provide evidence of a causal relation. Codifying this idea, Mill (1874) proposed a series of well-known rules or canons for isolating the cause (or effect) of a phenomenon. The best known of these canons are the method of agreement and the method of difference. Suppose you're looking for the cause of event type E. To proceed by the method of agreement, you should find a set of situations in which E occurs. If cause C also occurs in all these situations but no other potential cause does, then C causes E. To use the method of difference, which Mill regarded as more definitive, you should find two situations that hold constant all but one potential cause, C, of E. If E is present when C is present, and E is absent when C is absent, then C causes E.

Psychologists have mostly followed Mill's canons in their textbooks and courses on scientific methods.[5] If you're a victim of one of those courses, you won't find it surprising that psychological theories of how nonscientists go about determining cause-effect relations reflect the same notions:

> The inference as to where to locate the dispositional properties responsible for the effect is made by interpreting the raw data ... in the context of subsidiary information from experiment-like variations of conditions. A naïve version of J. S. Mills' method of difference provides the basic analytic tool. The effect is attributed to that condition which is present when the effect is present and which

Table 1: Two Contrasts for Assessing the Presence of a Causal Relation

a.

	This Occasion		Other Occasions	
	Calvin	Other People	Calvin	Other People
tango	1	0	1	0
other dances	1	0	1	0

b.

	This Occasion		Other Occasions	
	Calvin	Other People	Calvin	Other People
tango	1	1	1	1
other dances	0	0	0	0

1's indicate that a person likes a particular dance on a given occasion; 0's indicate not liking to dance.

is absent when the effect is absent. (Kelley 1967: 194)

As an example (similar to one from Cheng and Novick 1990), suppose you know that Calvin danced the tango last Thursday. To find out the cause of this event, you need to examine potential causes that the outcome suggests: Maybe it was a disposition of Calvin's, maybe it was the tango, maybe it was something about this particular occasion. To figure out which of these potential causes was at work, you mentally design a study in which the three causes are factors. The design will look something like what's in Table 1. The 1's in the cells stand for somebody dancing on a particular occasion, and the 0's stand not dancing. If the pattern of data looks like what's in Table 1a, we have an effect for the person but no effects for either the occasion or the type of dance; so we might conclude that the reason Calvin danced the tango on this occasion is that he just likes dancing. By contrast, if the data come out in the form of Table 1b, where Calvin and others don't do other kinds of dancing, but everyone dances the tango, we might conclude that it was the tango that caused Calvin's dancing.

Kelley's (1967) ANOVA (analysis of variance) theory aimed to explain how individuals determine whether their reaction to an external object is due to the object itself (e.g., the tango) or to their own subjective response, and the theory focused on people, objects, times, and "modalities" (different ways of interacting with the entity) as potential factors. Cheng and Novick (1990, 1992) advocated a somewhat

more flexible approach in which people choose to consider a set of potential factors on pragmatic grounds: "Contrasts are assumed to be computed for attended dimensions that are present in the event to be explained" (1990: 551). According to this theory, people also determine causation relative to a particular sample of situations, a "focal set," rather than to a universal set. Within these situations, people calculate causal effectiveness in terms of the difference between the probability of the effect when the potential cause is present and the probability of the effect when the same potential cause is absent:

(1) $\Delta P = \text{Prob(effect} \mid \text{factor)} - \text{Prob(effect} \mid \sim\text{factor)},$

where $Prob$(effect | factor) is the conditional probability of the effect given the presence of the potential causal factor and $Prob$(effect | ~factor) is the conditional probability of the effect given the absence of the same factor. When this difference, ΔP, is positive, the factor is a contributory cause of the effect; when it's negative, the factor is an inhibitory cause; and when it's zero, the factor is not a cause. Cheng and Novick also distinguish causes (contributory or inhibitory) from "enabling conditions" – factors whose ΔP is undefined within the focal set of situations (because they are constantly present or constantly absent) but that have nonzero ΔP in some other focal set.

We can illustrate some of these distinctions in the Table 1 results. In Table 1a, $\Delta P = 1$ for Calvin versus other people, but 0 for the object and occasions factors. So something about

Calvin is a contributory cause of his dancing the tango at that time, and the tango and the occasion are noncauses. In the Table 1b data, the object (dance) factor has a ΔP of 1, whereas the person and occasion factors have ΔP's of 0; so the tango causes the event. Reversing the 0's and 1's in Table 1b, so that Calvin and others never dance the tango but always dance other dances, will produce a ΔP of -1. In this case, the tango is an inhibitory cause. A factor – perhaps, music – that is present in all the situations in the focal set considered here would be an enabling condition if it turned out to have a positive ΔP in a larger sample of situations in which it was present in some and absent in others. The results in Table 1 are all-or-none, but the ΔP measure obviously generalizes to situations in which the effect can occur within each cell sometimes but not always.

Related notions about cause derive from work on associative learning. Creatures learning that, say, a shock often follows a tone are remembering contingency information about the tone and shock (or the pain or fear that the shock creates – sorry, animal lovers, but these aren't my experiments). A number of researchers have proposed that this primitive form of association might provide the basis for humans' causal judgments (e.g., Shanks and Dickinson 1987; Wasserman, Kao, Van Hamme, Katagiri, and Young 1996). Data and models for such learning suggest that this process may be more complex than a simple calculation of ΔP over all trials. In particular, the associative strength between a specific cue (e.g., tone) and an unconditioned stimulus (shock) depends on the associative strength of other cues (lights, shapes, colors, etc.) that happen to be in play. The associative strength for a particular cue is smaller, for example, if the environment already contains stronger cues for the same effect. If these associative theories are correct models for judgments about a specific potential cause, then such judgments should depend on interactions with other potential causes, not just on "main effect" differences like those of the ANOVA model or ΔP. Evidence for these interactions in causal judgments appears in a number of studies (e.g., Chapman and Robbins 1990; Shanks and Dickinson 1987).[6] However, ΔP-based theories can handle some of these results if participants compute ΔP while holding other confounded factors constant (a conditional ΔP, see Cheng 1997; Spellman 1996). Also, under certain conditions (e.g., only one potential cause present), associative theories sometimes reduce to ΔP (Chapman and Robbins 1990; Cheng 1997).[7] Because both associative and statistical

models make use of the same bottom-up frequency information, we consider them together here (see the section on Power for more on interactions).

LOTS OF CORRELATIONS

The same textbooks on methodology that extol Mill's canons of causal inference also insist that a correlation between two variables can't prove that one causes the other. Because Mill's methods, the ANOVA theory, ΔP, associative theories, and their variants all work along correlational lines, how can they provide convincing evidence for causation?[8] If these methods yield a positive result, there's always the possibility that some unknown factor confounds the relation between the identified cause and its effect. Maybe Calvin's love of dancing didn't cause his dancing the tango Thursday, but instead the cause was his girlfriend's insistence that he dance every dance on every occasion (in the Table 1a example). If these methods yield a negative result for some putative cause, there's always the possibility that some unknown factor is suppressing the first. The tango's special allure might surface if Calvin and his girlfriend hadn't crowded other couples off the dance floor. If we can't identify a cause (due to possible confounding) and we can't eliminate a potential cause (because of possible suppression), how can we make any progress with these correlational methods? Of course, the ANOVA theory and the ΔP theory (unlike Mill's methods) are intended as models of ordinary people's causal reckoning, and ordinary people may not consider confoundings or suppressors. Superstitious behavior may attest to their unconcern about spurious causes and noncauses, as might the need for the textbook warnings about these weak inferences. Even children, however, can reject confoundings under favorable conditions (Gopnik et al. 2004; Koslowski 1996: Ch. 6). So we seem to need an explanation for how people can go beyond correlation in their search for causes.

Although a single contrast or correlation between factors may not be convincing evidence, multiple correlations may sometimes reveal more about the causal set up. To see why this is so, let's go back to the CD diagram in Figure 1. Both the rotating motor and the laser beam influence the final transmission of electrical signals. So we would expect both the rotation of the motor and the presence of the laser beam to be correlated with the transmission. The correlation between the motor and the light beam, however, should be zero, provided no further factors outside the diagram influence both of them. (If there is a power switch, for example, that controls both the motor and the laser, then, of course, there will be such a correlation. So imagine there are separate controls for present purposes.) Similarly, the diagram predicts that if we can hold constant the state of some of the variables in Figure 1, the correlation among other variables should go to zero. For instance, although there should be a correlation between whether the CD is rotating and transmission of signals, we should be able to break the correlation by observing only those situations in which the intermediate variable, the light striking the diode is constant For instance, when light is not striking the diode, there should be no correlation between the rotating and the transmission. The causal relations among the different parts of the diagram put restrictions on what is correlated with what. Working backward from the pattern of correlations, then, we may be able to discern which causal relations are consistent with these correlations and which are not. For example, the presence of a correlation between the rotation and the light beam would be a reason to think that the causal arrows in Figure 1 are incorrect. Statistical techniques like path analysis and structural equation modeling exploit systems of correlations in this way to test theories about the causal connections (e.g., Asher 1983; Klem 1995; Loehlin 1992).

There are limits to these methods, however, that are similar to those we noted in connection with single correlations (Cliff 1983). In the first place, there may still be confounding causes that are not among the factors considered in the analysis. In the setup of Figure 1, for example, we should observe a correlation between the light striking the diode and the transmission of signals, but there is no guarantee, based on correlations alone, that this is due to the direct effect of the diode on the signals (as the figure suggests). Rather, the correlation could be due to the effect of some third, confounding variable on both the diode and the signal. The same is obviously true for the rest of the direct connections that appear in the graph. Each direct connection is subject to exactly the same uncertainty about confoundings that we faced with single correlations. Second, the pattern of correlations can drastically underdetermine the causal structure. Consider, for example, a completely arbitrary set of correlations among four variables A, B, C, and D. The causal connections in Figure 3a (i.e., A has a direct causal effect on B, C, and D; B has a direct effect on C and D; and C has

a direct effect on D) will be perfectly consistent with those correlations, whatever they happen to be. For example, a path analysis based on these connections will *exactly* predict the arbitrary correlations. Moreover, so will any of the other twenty-three models in which the position of the variables in this structure is permuted – for instance, the one in Figure 3b in which D directly causes C, B, and A; C directly causes B and A; and B directly causes A. These are *fully recursive* models in path-analysis terminology, and they always fit the data perfectly. Additional information beyond the correlations would be necessary to discriminate among these sets of possible causal connections (Klem 1995; see also Pearl 2000 for a discussion of Markov equivalent causal structures).

CAUSAL MECHANISMS AND SCHEMAS

To compound these difficulties for the bottom-up, correlation-to-causation approach, the causal environment typically contains an enormous number of factors that could produce a given effect. Calvin, the tango, or the occasion may produce events that cause his dancing the tango on Thursday, but these factors are cover terms that contain many different potential causes: They serve as causal superordinate categories. Not all of Calvin's dispositions would plausibly cause him to dance, but this still leaves a seemingly unlimited number to choose from. Is the cause his showmanship, his athleticism, his musical talents, his religious fervor, his distaste of being a wallflower, his fear of letting down his girlfriend, . . . ? Moreover, we needn't stop at people, objects, and occasions, as we've already noted. Maybe it's his girlfriend's demands, maybe it's bribery by the DJ, maybe it's cosmic rays, maybe it's his therapist's hypnotic suggestion, maybe it's a disease (like St. Vitus dance), and so on. Since there is no end to the possibilities, there is no way to determine for each of them whether it is the cause, making a purely bottom-up approach completely hopeless.

We should again distinguish the plight of the scientist from the task of describing laypeople's causal search. Laypeople may take into account only a handful of potential causes and test each for a correlation with the effect. Although such a procedure might not be normatively correct, it may nevertheless be the recipe people follow in everyday life. But even if people use correlations over a restricted set of factors, an explanation of their causal reasoning would then also have to include an account at how they arrive at the restricted set. The factors they test are the factors

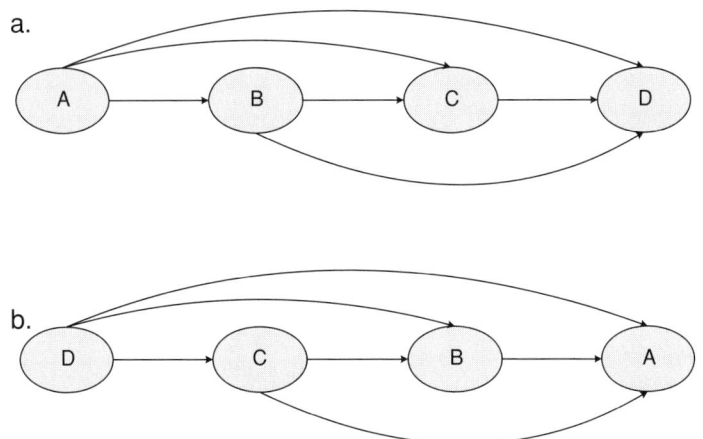

Figure 3. A hypothetical causal model for four variables in original form (a) and permuted form (b).

they attend to, of course, but what determines what they attend to? People's causal thinking often aims at explaining some phenomenon, where what needs explaining may be a function of what seems unusual or abnormal within a specific context (Einhorn and Hogarth 1986; Hilton 1988; Kahneman and Miller 1986). The explanation process itself depends on broadly pragmatic factors, such as the explainers' interest or point of view, the contrast class of explanations they have in mind, the intended audience for the explanation, and the availability of evidence, among others (Brem and Rips 2000; Hilton 1990; Lewis 1986; van Fraassen 1980). The same goes for determining "the cause" of a phenomenon, which is a disguised way of asking for the main cause or most important cause.

Evidence supports the notion that people's search for causes relies on information other than correlation. Ahn, Kalish, Medin, and Gelman (1995) asked participants what kinds of evidence they needed to determine the cause of an event like the one about Calvin. (Ahn et al. used some of the stimulus materials from Cheng and Novick 1990.) For example, participants had to write down questions that they would like to have answered in order to figure out the cause of (in this case) Calvin's *not* dancing the tango on this occasion. Ahn et al. predicted that if the participants were following the ANOVA or Cheng-Novick ΔP theory, they should be seeking information that fills out the rest of the design matrix in Table 1 – the kind of information they could use to compute experimental contrasts or ΔP. Did other people dance the tango? Did Calvin dance other kinds of dances?

Did Calvin dance the tango on other occasions? And so forth. What Ahn et al. found, though, is that participants asked these sorts of questions only about 10 percent of the time. Instead, participants asked what Ahn et al. call "hypothesis-testing" questions, which were about specific explanatory factors not explicitly mentioned in the description of the event. Participants asked whether Calvin had a sore foot or whether he ever learned the tango, and about similar sorts of common-sense causal factors. These hypothesis-testing questions showed up on approximately 65 percent of trials. Ahn et al. concluded that when people try to explain an event, they look for some sort of mechanism or process that could plausibly cause it. They have a set of these potential mechanisms available in memory, and they trot them out when they're trying to discover a cause.

People may also infer correlational information from their causal beliefs rather than the other way round. Psychologists have known since Chapman and Chapman's (1967; Chapman 1967) initial work on illusory correlations that causal expectancies can affect estimates of correlations (for reviews, see Alloy and Tabachnik 1984; Busemeyer 1991; Nisbett and Ross 1980). For example, both clinicians and laypeople overestimate the correlation between diagnostic categories (e.g., paranoia) and certain test results (e.g., unusual eye shapes in patients' drawings). This is probably because the judges' causal theories dictate a relation between the category and the result – paranoia causes patients to be especially aware of the way people look at them or of their own glances at others – since the true correlation is negligible.

Similarly, Tversky and Kahneman's (1980) experiments on causal schemas show that causal theories can dictate estimates of conditional probabilities. Participants in one experiment were asked to choose among the following options:

Which of the following events is more probable?

(a)   That a girl has blue eyes if her mother has blue eyes.

(b)   That a mother has blue eyes if her daughter has blue eyes.

(c)   The two events are equally probable.

The converse conditional probabilities in (a) and (b) are necessarily equal, according to Bayes Theorem, provided that the (marginal or unconditional) probability of being a blue-eyed mother is the same as being a blue-eyed daughter. (A follow-up experiment verified that most participants think this equality holds.) The results showed that 45 percent of participants correctly chose option (c). The remaining participants, however, chose (a) much more often than (b): 42 percent versus 13 percent. According to Tversky and Kahneman's interpretation, these judgments are biased by the belief that it's the mother who is causally responsible for the daughter's eye color rather than the reverse. This causal asymmetry induces an incorrect impression of an asymmetry in the conditional probabilities.

Finally, Waldmann and his colleagues have shown that people's judgment about a cause can depend on causal background beliefs, even when correlational information is constant (Waldmann 1996). Consider, for example, the fictitious data in Table 2, which exhibits the relation between whether certain fruit has been irradiated and the fruit's quality in two samples, A and B. Summed over the samples, the quality of fruit is positively related to irradiation; ΔP is positive when irradiation is the factor and quality the effect. Within each sample, however, the effect reverses. Both ΔP's are negative when calculated within sample, as shown in the bottom row of the table. This situation is an example of what's known as *Simpson's paradox*: When the number of cases in the cells is unequal, the size and even the direction of contingency statistics can depend on how the population is partitioned.[9] In Table 2, people should judge irradiation to be positively related to quality if they base their decision on the entire sample, but should make

Table 2: Contingency Information from Waldmann and Hagmayer (2001)

	Sample A	Sample B	Total
Irradiated	16/36	0/4	16/40
Not irradiated	3/4	5/36	8/40
ΔP	−.31	−.14	+.20

The first two rows indicate what fraction of a group of fruit was good as a function of whether the fruit was irradiated or not and whether it was from sample A or sample B. The top number in each fraction is the number of good fruit and the bottom number is the total number tested in that condition. Bottom row shows ΔP [i.e., Prob(Good | Irradiation) − Prob(Good-No Irradiation)] for the entire population and for each sample separately.

the opposite judgment if they attend to samples A and B separately. Waldmann and Hagmayer (2001: Experiment 1) manipulated participants' assumptions about the causal import of the sample by informing them in one condition that sample A consisted of one type of tropical fruit and sample B consisted of a different type. In a second condition, participants learned that A and B were samples randomly assigned to two different investigators. Participants in both conditions, however, saw the same list of 80 cases (distributed as in Table 2) that identified the sample (A or B) and, for each piece of fruit, its treatment (irradiated or not) and its outcome (good or bad quality). All participants then rated how strongly irradiation affected the fruits' quality. Although correlational information was constant for the two conditions, participants rated irradiation as negatively affecting quality when the samples were causally relevant (types of fruit) but positively affecting quality when the samples were irrelevant (different investigators).

Given these findings, there is little chance that people construct judgments of cause from bottom up, except under the most antiseptic conditions. Naturally, this doesn't mean that contingencies, associations, and correlations are irrelevant to people's assessment of cause, but the role they play must be a piece of a much larger picture.

POWER

As a step toward a more theory-based view of cause, we might analyze observed contingencies as due to two components: the mere presence or absence of the cause and the tendency or power of this cause to produce the effect (Cheng 1997; Novick and Cheng 2004). The cause can't bring about the effect, of course, unless it's present. But even if it is present, the cause may be co-opted by other causes or may be too weak to produce the effect in question. Ordinarily, we can observe whether or not the cause is present, at least in the types of experiments we have been discussing, but the cause's power is unobservable. In this vein, Novick and Cheng (2004: 455) claim that "previous accounts, however, are *purely covariational* in that they do not consider the possible existence of unobservable causal structures to arrive at their output. In contrast, our theory explicitly incorporates into its inference procedure the possible existence of *distal* causal structures: Structures in the world that exist independently of one's observations" (emphasis in the original). On this theory, you can detect the nature of these distal structures only under special circumstances. When these special assumptions are met, the distal causal power isn't exactly an ANOVA contrast or ΔP, but it looks much like a normalized ΔP.

To derive the power of a cause C, suppose first that C is present in the environment. Then the effect, E, will occur in two cases: (a) C produces E (with probability p_c), or (b) other alternative causes, collectively designated A, occur in the same environment and produce E (with probability $\text{Prob}(A \mid C) \cdot p_a$). Thus, the probability of E when C is present is:

(2) $\text{Prob}(E \mid C) = p_c + \text{Prob}(A \mid C) \cdot p_a - p_c \cdot \text{Prob}(A \mid C) \cdot p_a.$

The final term in (2) (after the minus sign) ensures that we count only once the case in which C and A both produce E. When C is absent, only the alternative causes A can bring about E. So the probability of E given that C is not present is:

(3) $\text{Prob}(E \mid \sim C) = \text{Prob}(A \mid \sim C) \cdot p_a.$

Substituting these expressions in Equation (1), above, we get:

(4) $\Delta P = [p_c + \text{Prob}(A \mid C) \cdot p_a - p_c \cdot \text{Prob}(A \mid C) \cdot p_a] - [\text{Prob}(A \mid \sim C) \cdot p_a].$

Solving (4) for p_c yields the following expression for the causal power of C:

(5) $p_c = \dfrac{\Delta P - [\text{Prob}(A \mid C) - \text{Prob}(A \mid \sim C)]p_a}{1 - \text{Prob}(A \mid C)p_a}.$

In the special case in which causes A and C occur independently (so that $\text{Prob}(A \mid C) =$

$\text{Prob}(A \mid \sim C) = \text{Prob}(A)$), then Equation (5) reduces to:

(6) $p_c = \dfrac{\Delta P}{1 - \text{Prob}(A)p_a}$

$= \dfrac{\Delta P}{1 - \text{Prob}(E \mid \sim C)}$

The last expression follows since, by Equation (3), $\text{Prob}(E \mid \sim C)$ is equal to $\text{Prob}(A) \cdot p_a$ when A and C are independent. The interpretation of (6) may be clearer if you recall that ΔP is itself equal to $\text{Prob}(E \mid C) - \text{Prob}(E \mid \sim C)$. In other words, p_c is roughly the amount that C contributes to producing E relative to the maximal amount that it could contribute. Thus, p_c, unlike ΔP, is immune to ceiling effects – situations in which E already occurs frequently in the absence of C – except in the extreme case in which $\text{Prob}(E \mid \sim C) = 1$, where p_c is undefined. (To see this, suppose $\text{Prob}(E \mid C) = .95$ and $\text{Prob}(E \mid \sim C) = .90$. Then $\Delta P = .05$, a seemingly small effect for C because both $\text{Prob}(E \mid C)$ and $\text{Prob}(E \mid \sim C)$ are high. But $p_c = .50$, a much larger effect because of the correction.) The formulas in (5) and (6) define contributory causal power, but analogous ones are available for inhibitory causal power (see Cheng 1997).

Does the power statistic, p_c, correspond to people's concept of a distal cause, as Novick and Cheng (2004) claim? Why shouldn't we consider it just another estimate of the likelihood that a particular cause will produce an effect – ΔP corrected for ceiling effects? The Cheng-Novick set-up portrays causation as a two-step affair. If we want to predict whether C causes E, we need to know both the likelihood that C is present and also the likelihood that C will produce E. But granting this framework, we may have some options in interpreting the latter likelihood. One issue might be whether people think that "distal power" is a probabilistic matter, as Luhmann and Ahn (2005) argue. Setting aside subatomic physics, which is outside the ken of ordinary thinking about ordinary causal interactions, people may believe that causal power is an all-or-none affair: Something either is a cause or isn't; it's not a cause with power .3 or .6. Of course, there might be reasons why a potential cause doesn't run its course, such as the failure of intermediate steps. For example, a drunk driver might have caused an accident if his car hadn't been equipped with antilock brakes. But do we want to say that the causal power of the drunk driving was some number between 0 and 1?[10] There are also cases in which a potential cause doesn't succeed in producing its effect for reasons that we simply don't know. If we're in the dark about why a cause doesn't always produce an effect, we might want to attach a probability to it. As Cheng and Novick (2005: 703) acknowledge, "A probabilistic causal power need not indicate any violation of the power PC assumptions even for a reasoner who believes in causal determinism.... A probabilistic causal power might instead reflect the reasoner's imperfect representation of this cause." But this isn't consistent with Novick and Cheng's distal causal power idea. Our lack of knowledge isn't an intermediate degree of distal causal power: It's a proximal matter of our beliefs. Probabilistic beliefs about causes aren't beliefs about probabilistic causes.

Novick and Cheng are likely right that people believe that there are causes in the world and that these causes have power to produce certain effects. What's in question is whether you can model these powers as probabilities in a way that doesn't sacrifice basic intuitions about causality, which for ordinary events might be necessarily all-or-none (Luhmann and Ahn 2005) and inherently mechanistic ("intrinsically generative," in White's 2005 terms). It is possible for power proponents to retreat to the position that causal power describes an idealized, normatively correct measure that actual causal judgments merely approach. After all, distal causal powers, like distal properties and objects, are the sorts of things we infer rather than directly apprehend. However, the causal power formulas in (5) and (6), and their variants for inhibitory and interactive cases, don't necessarily yield normatively correct estimates. Like other measures of causal effectiveness – main effect contrasts, ΔP, path analysis coefficients, and similar measures estimated directly from co-occurrence data – the power formulas don't always yield a normatively correct result. Glymour observes (2001: 87) that there "is an obvious reason why [the power method] will not be reliable: unobserved common causes. We have seen that the estimation methods [for generative and preventive powers] are generally insufficient when there are unobserved common causes at work, and often we have no idea before we begin inquiry whether such factors are operating." If we already know the structure of the causal environment, we can safely use power-like calculations to estimate the strength of particular pathways, and in this context, power may be a normative ideal. But this presupposes some way other than power to arrive at the correct structure.

Causation from Intervention

We're finally in a position to return to the claims at the beginning of this article about "great new ideas" for representing causation. One of these ideas is the use of multiple correlations or contingencies, as in the path-analysis theories we glimpsed in the previous section. Perhaps people represent a causal system as a graph connecting causes to effects, along the lines of Figures 1 and 3. These graphs embody statistical relations – the pattern of conditional probabilities among the depicted events – that put constraints on what can be a cause of what effect. At a psychological level, we might encode this pattern of contingencies and then find the best graph – or at least a good graph – that fits them. The resulting structure is our subjective theory or causal model of the reigning causal forces. You could complain that this isn't exactly a new idea, deriving as it does from data-analytic work by Wright in the 1920s (see Wright 1960 for a recap; see also Simon 1953). But perhaps it's an innovation to take such diagrams seriously as mental representations, mental causal maps. Further elaborations may constitute genuine advances. Let's see what these could be.

We noted that graphical representations of multiple-correlation systems are open to problems of confounding and underdetermination. The very same pattern of correlations and partial correlations can be equally consistent with very different causal graphs, as the Figure 3 example illustrates. Faced with this kind of causal indeterminacy, though, scientists don't always throw up their hands. They can sometimes bring experiments to bear in selecting among the alternative causal possibilities. In the case of Figure 3, for example, imagine an experiment in which a scientist explicitly manipulates factor A to change its value. You'd expect this experiment also to change the value of B in the set up of Figure 3a but not in that of Figure 3b. Intuitively, this is because manipulating a factor can have only forward influence on its effects, not backward influence on its causes. So intervention can discriminate the two causal frameworks. Of course, we can sometimes make the same discovery without getting our hands dirty if we know the time at which the factors change their values, since causes don't follow their effects in time. In the world of Figure 3a, observing a change in A should be followed by observing a change in B, but this is not the case in Figure 3b.

Manipulating factors, however, has an advantage that goes beyond merely clarifying temporal relationships. By changing the value of a factor, we can often remove the influence of other factors that typically covary with it, isolating the former from confoundings. If we're interested, for example, in whether listening to Mozart improves students' math scores, we could randomly assign one set of students to listen to fifteen minutes of Mozart and another to fifteen minutes of silence before a math test. In doing so, we're removing the influence of intelligence, social class, and other background factors that could affect both a tendency to listen to Mozart and to do well on math tests. In the graph of Figure 3a, suppose factor A is the social class of students' families, B is intelligence, C is listening to Mozart, and D is test performance. Then the manipulation just described deletes the links from social class and intelligence to Mozart listening. In the experiment we're contemplating, students with more intelligence are no more likely to listen to Mozart than those with low intelligence. If we still find an effect of listening on test scores, this can assure us that Mozart listening affects the scores apart from the influence of the two background variables. This advantage for manipulating is due at least in part to the fact that intervention places additional constraints on the statistical relations among the variables (Pearl 2000). If we manipulate Mozart listening as just described, we're essentially creating a new graphical structure – Figure 3a minus the arrows from social class and intelligence to Mozart listening – and we're demanding that the correlations change in a way that conforms to this remodeling.

Recent evidence suggests that adults, children, and even rats are sometimes aware of the benefits of explicitly manipulating variables in learning a causal structure (Blaisdell, Sawa, Leising, and Waldmann 2006; Gopnik et al. 2004; Lagnado and Sloman 2005; Steyvers, Tenenbaum, Wagenmakers, and Blum 2003). For example, Gopnik et al. (2004) report an experiment in which four-year-olds observed a stage containing two "puppets" (simple rods with differently colored balls attached). The experimenter could move the puppets in two ways: either out of the view of the children (by reaching under the stage) or in their view (by pulling them up and down). The experimenter told the children that one of the puppets was special in that this puppet could make the other move. The children's task was to decide which was special – say, the yellow or the green one. Children first saw the yellow and green puppets moving together as the result of the exper-

imenter's concealed action. They then observed the experimenter explicitly pulling up the yellow puppet while the green puppet remained stationary. Under these conditions, 78 percent of the children could identify the green puppet as the special one. Because a child saw the experimenter manipulate the yellow puppet without any effect on the green one, he or she could reason that the yellow puppet couldn't have been responsible for their initial joint movement and, thus, that the green puppet must be the cause. Purely association-based or correlation-based theories have trouble accounting for results like these, since such models don't distinguish between event changes that result from interventions and those that result from noninterventions.

In more complex situations (and with college-age participants), however, the advantage for interventions is not as clear-cut (Lagnado and Sloman 2005; Steyvers et al. 2003). According to Lagnado and Sloman, any benefit for intervention in their experiments seems due to the simple temporal consequences mentioned earlier (that interventions must precede their effects) rather than to the statistical independencies that interventions create. Steyvers et al. (2003: Experiment 2) presented ten observational trials about a three-variable system. They then allowed participants a single intervention, followed by an additional ten trials based on that intervention. (No explicit temporal information was available during the observation or intervention trials.) Participants' ability to identify the correct causal structure increased from 18 percent before intervention to 34 percent after (chance was 5.6 percent); however, ideal use of the intervention in this experiment should have led to 100 percent accuracy.[11] This suggests that when the environment is simple (as in Gopnik et al. 2004) and people know there are only a small number of potential causal alternatives (e.g., X causes Y vs. Y causes X), they can use facts about interventions to test which alternative is correct. When the number of alternatives is larger, hypothesis testing isn't as easy, and the participants are less able to use the difference between observations and interventions to determine the causal arrangement. Investigators have also looked at participants' ability to use a previously learned causal structure to make predictions based on observations or interventions, and we will consider the results of these experiments in the section on reasoning later in this article. The present point is that the intervention/observation difference is not very robust when people must go from data to causal structure.

Perhaps one reason why people don't always pick up on interventions is that – as every experimentalist knows – interventions don't guarantee freedom from confounding. The literature on causal nets sometimes suggests that intervening entails only removing causal connections – links from the immediate causes of the variable that's being manipulated (i.e., the independent variable). But manipulations typically insert a new cause into the situation that substitutes for the old one in controlling the independent variable, and sometimes the new cause comes along with extraneous connections of its own. Take the example of the Mozart effect. Randomizing participants to conditions removes the influence of intelligence and other participant-centered factors. But placing participants in a control group that has to experience fifteen minutes of silence may have an aversive effect that could lower test scores to a greater extent than would merely not listening to Mozart (see Schellenberg 2005). Figuring out the right manipulation isn't always an easy matter. Ambiguity about the possible effects of an intervention may lead participants to back off from using such cues during causal learning. Of course, you can define "intervention" as a manipulation that does not affect any variable other than the one intervened on (Gopnik et al. 2004; Hausman and Woodward 1999), but this is not much help to the working scientist or layperson, who often doesn't have advance knowledge of possible side effects of the manipulation.[12]

Reasoning from Causal Theories

We've just looked at the possibility that people discover causal relations by noticing the patterning of events in their surroundings. That method is problematic for both theoretical and empirical reasons. Theoretically, there is no limit on the number or complexity of potential causal relationships, and correlation is often unable to decide among these rival causal set ups. Empirically, there is no compelling evidence that people have hard-wired cause detectors, so people probably don't automatically derive causal facts from event perception. Moreover, our ability to infer cause from event co-occurrence seems to rely heavily on higher-level beliefs about what sorts of events can cause others, on beliefs about how events interact mechanistically, and on pragmatic pressures concerning what needs

to be explained. To make matters worse, knowledge about cause sometimes colors our knowledge about co-occurrence frequency or correlation.

The classic alternative strategy for deriving causal knowledge is a form of inference to the best explanation (Harman 1965). We can start with theories about the potential causes of some phenomenon and then check to see which theory best predicts the data. The theory that provides the best fit is the one that gives the right causal picture. Of course, this form of inference doesn't give us certainty about our causal conclusions, since it depends on the range of alternatives we've considered, on the validity of the tests we've performed, and on the goodness of the data we've collected. But *no* method yields certainty about such matters. What could give us a better idea about correct causal relations than the best explanation that exploits them? This approach reserves a place for observational data, but the place is at the receiving end of a causal theory rather than at its source.

This top-down strategy, however, yields a host of further psychological problems. We still need to know the source of our theories or hypotheses if they don't arise purely from observation. We also need to consider how people use causal theories to make the sorts of predictions that hypothesis testing depends on. In this last respect, the causal schemas or Bayes nets that we looked at earlier can be helpful. We noted that people don't always accurately construct such schemas from data, even when they're allowed to manipulate relevant variables. Nevertheless, once people settle on such a representation, it may guide them to conclusions that correctly follow.

Representing Causal Information: Causal Principles and Causal Theories

If we don't get causal information from innate perceptual cause detectors or from pure associative/correlational information, what's left?

CAUSAL PRIMITIVES

According to one top-down theory of causality, we have, perhaps innately, certain primitive causal concepts or principles that we bring to bear on the events we observe or talk about, primitives that lend the events a causal interpretation. Perhaps there is a single primitive causal relation, $cause(x, y)$, that we combine with other concepts to produce more complex and specific causal descriptions (e.g., Dowty 1979; McCawley 1968; Parsons 1990). Thus, we might mentally represent the sentence in (7a) as (7b):

(7) a. John paints a picture
     b. cause (John paints, become (a picture exists))

Or perhaps there are several primitive causal relations or subtypes that vary in ways that distinguish among causing, enabling, and preventing, among others (e.g., Jackendoff 1990; Schank and Riesbeck 1981; Talmy 1988; Wolff, Klettke, Ventura, and Song 2005; see also Tufte 2006 for related conclusions about causal graphs).

I suggested earlier that there was no strong evidence to support the view that people have innate cause detectors in perception, but this is consistent with the possibility of innate causal concepts. The difficulty for the perceptual view is that scenes that are supposed to trigger causal impressions automatically can usually be interpreted noncausally. But this Humean way of thinking about the perceptual demonstrations is exactly what we should expect if our interpretation of the scenes depends on how we apply our causal concepts. Having an innate concept of cause doesn't mean that external stimuli can force us to apply it. But having an innate (perceptual) cause detector – an input module in Fodor's (1983) sense – presumably does.

Of course, the existence of these concepts doesn't mean that perceptual or contingency information plays no role in our judgments about causality, and it doesn't mean that babies appear on the scene already knowing everything about causation that adults do. Percepts and contingencies can provide evidence about what we should investigate to uncover possible causal connections; however, they don't ordinarily provide a direct route to such connections. Similarly, having a causal concept may be necessary in understanding causal systems, but exactly what causes what in a particular physical setting often requires further learning. Knowing that events can be connected causally doesn't automatically tell us, for example, how chemical reactions take place or how astronomical objects interact; it simply gives us one of the ingredients or building blocks. Infants may have some domain-specific theories in areas such as psychology (Carey 1985), biology (Atran 1998), or physics (Spelke, Breinlinger, Macomber, and Jacobson 1992) that provide more specific information about causal relations in these areas, but

even initial theories obviously undergo elaborations with experience and schooling, perhaps quite radical ones.

The existence of conceptually primitive causal concepts goes along with the idea that babies come equipped with the notions that events have causes, that the causes precede their effects, and that the causes bring about the effects in a mechanistic way. Bullock, Gelman, and Baillargeon (1982) propose principles along these lines – their Determinism, Priority, and Mechanism principles – and they suggest that children's and adults' later understanding of cause builds on these principles by adding information both about specific types of causal relations and about which environmental cues are most important when events interact. Preschoolers do not understand that rainbows are caused by scattering light, but they know that rainbows have some preceding mechanistic cause or other.

CAUSAL SCHEMAS

Many cognitive theories suggest that people maintain unified representations of causal systems. If the system is the CD player in Figure 1, then memory for this information would include the individual causal relations (corresponding to the arrows in the figure) together with some larger structure that specifies how they fit together. Some theories represent the structure in terms of propositions, as in (7b), with further embedding for more complex situations (e.g., Gentner 1983); other theories employ more diagrammatic representations, similar to Figure 1 itself. The unified representations in either case may speed search for the included facts, make the included information less susceptible to interference, and highlight certain inferences. Of course, a commitment to a unified representation still leaves room for some flexibility in the representation's abstractness and completeness. It's possible that causal schemas are relatively sparse, even for familiar causal systems (Rozenblit and Keil 2002), and they may sometimes amount to little more than top-level heuristics, such as "more effort yields more results" (diSessa 2000).

As cognitive representations, causal schemas don't necessarily carry explicit information about the statistical relations among the included events. It seems possible that people could possess a schema similar to that of Figure 1 and still fail to notice the implications it has for statistical dependencies and independencies, such as the ones we considered earlier (see the section *Causation from Correlation*). What sets Bayes nets apart from other causal schemas in psychology is their tight connection to statistical matters. Bayes nets depend essentially for their construction on a property called the (Parental) Markov condition (Pearl 2000; Spirtes, Glymour, and Scheines 2000). This is the principle that conditioning on the states of the immediate causes (the "parents") of a variable renders that variable statistically independent of all other variables in the net, except for those it causes (its "descendants"). Because the Markov principle is what determines whether a Bayes net contains or omits a link, the plausibility of Bayes nets as a psychological representation depends on the Markov condition. In the case of the CD player in Figure 1, holding constant whether the light strikes the diode will make the transmission of electrical signals independent of the rest of the variables in the figure. In the next section, we examine the empirical status of this assumption: Do people who know the causal connections in a system obey the Markov principle? In the meantime, we consider some theoretical issues that surround Bayes nets as cognitive schemas.

CAUSAL BAYESIAN NETWORKS AND FUNCTIONAL CAUSAL MODELS AS CAUSAL SCHEMAS

Although psychologists commonly cite Pearl (2000) as a source for the theory of Bayes nets, they gloss over the fact that Pearl presents three different versions of the theory that provide successively more complex accounts of causality. These versions of Bayes nets seem to correspond to stages in the theory's evolution, with later versions placing more constraints on the representation. What Pearl refers to as "Bayesian networks" are directed graphs of variables and links that respect the Markov principle we just reviewed. What Bayesian networks depict are the pattern of statistical dependencies and independencies among a set of variables. If a set of variables X is statistically independent of another set Y given Z, then the graph displays these independencies (the graph is a *D-map* in Pearl's 1988 terminology). Conversely, if the graph displays X as independent of Y given Z, then the probability distribution contains this independency (the graph is an *I-map*). For reasons mentioned in connection with Figure 3, however, Bayesian networks do "not necessarily imply causation" (Pearl 2000: 21), since several different networks can be equally consistent with the pattern of statistical dependencies and independencies in a data set.

To overcome this indeterminacy problem, Pearl moves to a reformulated representation called "causal Bayesian networks." These networks have the same form as ordinary Bayes nets. They are still directed acyclic graphs (i.e., ones with no loops from a variable to itself), such as those in Figures 1 and 3. But causal Bayesian networks also embody constraints about interventions. These networks are answerable not just to the statistical dependencies inherent in the full graph of variables and links, but also to the statistical dependencies in the subgraphs you get when you manipulate or intervene on the variables. Within this theory, intervening on a variable means severing the connections from its parent variables and setting its value to a constant. For example, we could intervene on the "CD turns" variable in Figure 1 by disconnecting the CD holder from the motor and manually rotating it. Causal Bayes networks help eliminate the indeterminacy problem by requiring the representation to reflect all the new statistical relations that these interventions imply.

In the last part of Chapter 1 and in Chapter 7 of his book, Pearl (2000) moves to a third kind of representation: "functional causal models." At first glance, there doesn't seem to be much difference between causal Bayesian networks and functional causal models, and this might make Pearl's claims about the latter models surprising. Functional causal models are given by a set of equations of a particular type that have the form in (8):

$$(8) \quad x_i = f_i(pa_i, u_i), \quad i = 1, 2, \ldots, n.$$

Each of these equations specifies the value of one of the variables x_i on the basis of the immediate (parent) causes of that variable, pa_i, and an additional set of variables representing other unknown factors, u_i, that also affect x_i. In the case of Figure 1, for example, we can think of the node labeled CD turns as having the value 0 if the CD is not turning and 1 if it is turning. That is, $x_{CD} = 0$ means the CD is not turning and $x_{CD} = 1$ means that it is. This value will be determined by a function like that in (8), f_{CD}, that will depend on the value of the parent variable (whether the motor is turning) and of a variable u_{CD} (not shown in Figure 1) representing other unknown factors. Pearl considers a special case of this representation, called "Markovian causal models," in which the graph is acyclic and the u terms are independent of each other, and he proves that Markovian causal models are consistent with exactly the same joint probability distributions as the corresponding causal Bayes nets. "In all probabilistic applications of Bayesian networks . . . we can use an equivalent functional model as specified in [(8)], and we can regard functional models as just another way of encoding joint distribution functions" (Pearl 2000: 31).

So what's the advantage to functional causal models that we didn't already have with causal Bayesian nets? (From now on, let's call these "causal models" and "causal nets" for short.) We noticed in discussing causal nets that the definition of these nets was given, not in terms of causal mechanisms, but in terms of probabilities. A causal net is just a Bayesian network that captures additional probability distributions, namely, the ones we get by intervening on variables. With (Markovian) causal models, we are starting in the opposite direction, beginning with functions that completely determine the states of the variables rather than beginning with probabilities. This seems consistent with the lessons of the first half of this article. As Pearl (2000: 31) puts it, ". . . agents who choose to organize their knowledge using Markovian causal models can make reliable assertions about conditional independence relations without assessing numerical probabilities – a common ability among humanoids and a useful feature for inference." Everything operates in a deterministic way in causal models, with any uncertainty confined to our lack of knowledge about the values of the u_i's. Moreover, the system's equations in (8) are not just arbitrary functions that happen to give the correct x_i values for cases we've observed. They reflect the actual causal determinants of the system, with pa_i and u_i being the true causes of x_i.

Pearl is explicit about the fact that an important benefit of causal models over causal networks is that the models deal correctly with counterfactual conditionals – statements of the form "If X had happened, then Y would have happened," like *If Fred had taken the trouble to fix his brakes, he wouldn't have had an accident*. It's been recognized at least since Goodman (1955) that there's a close connection between counterfactuals and causation. The truth of many counterfactual conditionals seems to depend on causal laws that dictate the behavior of events. These laws hold not just in our current state of affairs, but also in alternative states that differ from ours but still obey the laws in question. It's reasonable to think that the sentence about Fred is true or false because of the causal laws governing mechanical devices like brakes. If causal schemas are records of our understanding of causal laws, then they should enable us

to make judgments about counterfactual conditionals. Pearl is clearly right that if causal models support counterfactuals, then this gives them a leg up on ordinary causal nets. But in order to do this, the functions in (8) have to mirror these causal laws and must be constant over all causally possible situations. Pearl outlines a specific procedure that is supposed to answer counterfactual questions ("Would Y have happened if X had happened?") using causal models, and we'll look at the psychological plausibility of this hypothesis in more detail in discussing causal reasoning. It's clear, though, that knowledge of causal laws (from the f_i's) and knowledge of the input states of the system (from the u_i's) ought to give us what we need to simulate how the system will work in all the eventualities it represents, including counterfactual ones.

The direction of explanation that Pearl's analysis takes is from causality (as given by the causal functions in (8)) to counterfactuals. At first glance, though, the opposite strategy may also seem possible. Some philosophical analyses of causation – prominently, David Lewis's (1973) – interpret causation in terms of counterfactuals. If event e would not have happened had c not happened, then e causally depends on c, according to this analysis. Psychologists have occasionally followed this lead, deciding whether one event in a story causes a second according to whether people are willing to say that the second would not have happened if the first hadn't happened (Trabasso and van den Broek 1985). Lewis's theory of counterfactuals, however, depends on similarity among possible worlds, where similarity can, in turn, depend on causal laws. The counterfactual "If c had not happened then e would not have happened" is true just in case there is a world in which neither c nor e happens that is closer to the actual world than any world where c doesn't happen but e does. And whether one world is closer to the actual world than another depends at least in part on whether the causal laws of the actual world are preserved in the alternative. Lewis didn't intend his analysis to eliminate causal laws but to provide a new way of exploiting them in dealing with relations between individual events.[13] So even if we adopt Lewis's theory, we still need the causal principles that the f_i's embody (see the papers in Collins, Hall, and Paul 2004 for more recent work on the counterfactual analysis of cause).

Another possible complaint about causal models as psychological representations is that they don't come with enough structure to explain how people are able to learn them (Tenenbaum, Griffiths, and Niyogi, in press). In figuring out how a device like a CD player works, we don't start out considering all potential networks that connect the key events or variables in the system. Instead, we take seriously only those networks that conform to our prior knowledge of what general classes of events can be causes for others. Because lasers are unlikely to turn motors, we don't waste time testing (or at least we give low weight to) causal models that incorporate such a link. According to Tenenbaum et al., people use higher-level theories to determine which network structures are possible, and this restricts the space of hypotheses they take into account. This objection seems right, since we do sometimes possess high-level knowledge (e.g., that diseases cause symptoms or that beliefs and desires cause actions) that shapes lower-level theories. Moreover, higher-level knowledge about causal laws seems necessary, given the restrictions on the f_i functions that we've just discussed. But even in Tenenbaum et al.'s more elaborate hierarchy, causal models are at center-stage, mediating higher-level theory and data. This leaves us with an empirical issue: Assuming the causal models are possible psychological representations, how well do they explain people's ability to reason from their causal beliefs?

Causal Reasoning

The phrase *causal reasoning* could potentially apply to nearly any type of causal thinking, including the types of causal attribution that we considered in the first part of this chapter. The issue there was how we reason *to* causal beliefs from data or other noncausal sources. Our considerations so far suggest that there may be relatively little reliable reasoning of this sort without a healthy dose of top-down causal information already in place. But how well are we able to exploit this top-down information? Once we know a batch of causal relations, how do we use them in drawing further conclusions?

CAUSAL INTERPRETATIONS OF INDICATIVE CONDITIONALS

Cognitive psychology has tip-toed up to the issue of how we reason from causal beliefs. A number of experiments have attempted to demonstrate that inferences from conditional sentences – ones of the form *If p then q* – can depend on whether the content of the conditionals suggests a causal relation (e.g., Cum-

mins, Lubart, Alksnis, and Rist 1991; Staudenmayer 1975; Thompson 1994). The conditionals in these experiments are indicatives, such as *If the car is out of gas, then it stalls*, rather than the counterfactual (or subjunctive) conditionals mentioned in the previous section (*If X had happened, then Y would have happened*). Because indicatives are less obviously tied to causal relationships than counterfactuals, people may reason with such conditionals in a way that does not depend on causal content.

What the results of these studies show, however, is that causal content affects people's inferences. For example, Thompson (1994) compared arguments like the ones in (9) to see how likely her participants were to say that the conclusion logically followed:

(9) a. If butter is heated, then it melts.
         The butter has melted.
         Was the butter heated?
     b. If the car is out of gas, then it stalls.
         The car has stalled.
         Is the car out of gas?

Arguments (9a) and (9b) share the same form in that both have the structure: *If p then q; q; p?* So if participants attend only to this form in deciding about the arguments, they should respond in the same way to each. However, people's beliefs about cars include the fact that running out of gas is just one thing that could cause a car to stall, whereas their beliefs about butter include the fact that heating butter is virtually the only way to get it to melt. If people lean on these beliefs in determining whether the conclusions logically follow, they should be more likely to endorse the argument in (9a) than the one in (9b), and indeed they do. The difference in acceptance rates is about forty percentage points. It is possible to argue about the role played by causal information versus more abstract logical information in experiments like these, and other aspects of the data show that participants aren't simply throwing away the *if...then* format in favor of their causal beliefs. For our purposes, however, the question is what such experiments can tell us about the nature of those causal principles.

Thompson (1994) and others view these results as due to people's knowledge of necessary and sufficient conditions (see also Ahn and Graham 1999). Heating butter is both necessary and sufficient for its melting, whereas running out of gas is sufficient but not necessary for a car stalling. Thus, given that the butter was melted, it was probably heated; but given the car has stalled, it may not be out of gas. The same point is sometimes made in terms of "alternative" causes or "additional" causes (e.g., Byrne 1989; Byrne, Espino, and Santamaria 1999; Cummins et al. 1991; De Neys, Schaeken, and d'Ydewalle 2003; Markovits 1984). An alternative cause is one that, independently of the stated cause (e.g., running out of gas), is able to bring about the effect, and an additional cause is one that must be conjoined with the stated cause in order for the effect to occur. The explanation of the difference between (9a) and (9b) is therefore that participants know of no alternative causes for the conditional in (9a) that would block the inference, but they do know of alternatives for the conditional in (9b) – perhaps an overheated engine or a broken fuel pump. Giving participants further premises or reminders that explicitly mention alternative or additional causes also affects the conclusions they're willing to draw (Byrne 1989; Byrne et al. 1999; De Neys et al. 2003; Hilton, Jaspars, and Clarke 1990).

The more general framing in terms of necessary and sufficient conditions, though, raises the issue of whether the experiments are tapping reasoning with specifically causal relations or with more abstract knowledge. Some of the same experiments cited earlier (Ahn and Graham 1999; Thompson 1994) demonstrate similar effects with conditionals that are about noncausal relations (e.g., conditional permissions such as *If the licensing board grants them a license, then a restaurant is allowed to sell liquor*). Likewise, you can interpret the results as due to participants' use of conditional probabilities (Evans and Over 2004; Oaksford and Chater 2003). According to Oaksford and Chater (2003), for example, people's response to the question in (9a) depends on the conditional probability that butter is heated given that it is melted, and the response to (9b) reflects the conditional probability that the car is out of gas given that it has stalled. Since the first of these is likely to be greater than the second, participants should tend to answer "yes" more often for (9a) than (9b). According to both the necessity/sufficiency and the probabilistic theories, people's beliefs about causation informs the way they represent these problems, but their reasoning is carried out over representations that don't distinguish causes from other relations.

REASONING WITH CAUSAL VERSUS INDICATIVE CONDITIONAL STATEMENTS

We may be able to get a more direct view of how people reason about causes by look-

ing at experiments that give participants statements containing the word *cause* or its derivatives. A number of studies have found that people make different inferences from statements of the form *p causes q* (or *q causally depends on p*) than from ones of the form *If p then q* (Rips 1983; Sloman and Lagnado 2005; Staudenmayer 1975). For example, Staudenmayer (1975) observed that participants were more likely to interpret explicit causal statements as implying a two-way, if-and-only-if, connection. For example, *Turning the switch on causes the light to go on* was more likely than *If the switch is turned on then the light goes on* to entail that the light goes on if and only if the switch is turned on. Many causal setups, however, don't lend themselves to such an interpretation. *My turning on the switch causes the light to go on* is a case in point, since the light's going on could be caused by someone else's turning. Staudenmayer included examples like these, in which the cause is not necessary for the effect. But if causal statements don't force an if-and-only-if interpretation, why the difference between causals and conditionals in the results? It seems possible that *cause* allows more freedom of interpretation than *if*. Although a two-way interpretation is possible for both *if* and *cause* in some situations (for pragmatic or other reasons), people may be more cautious about adopting it in the case of *if*.

In another respect, however, *cause* is more selective than *if*. Consider the arguments in (10):

(10) a. If the gear turns then the light flashes.
The bell rings.
Therefore, if the gear turns then both the light flashes and the bell rings.

b. The light flashing causally depends on the gear turning.
The bell rings.
Therefore, both the light flashing and the bell ringing causally depend on the gear turning.

The conclusion of (10a) seems to follow, since the conditionals are understood as statements about an existing state of affairs. The gear's turning means that the light will flash, and since the turning presumably won't affect the bell's ringing, then if the turning occurs, so will the flashing and the ringing. Argument (10a) is valid in classical propositional logic, reading *if* as the truth functional connective "⊃" and *and* as "&." There are many reasons to question whether natural language *if* is equivalent to ⊃ (see Bennett 2003 for a thorough review); but even if we treat the *if*'s in (10a) as expressing probabilistic or default relations – for example, that the conditional probability of the flashing is high given the turning, or that the turning occurs when the flashing does, all else being equal – the inference in (10a) still seems a strong one. Not so (10b). Intuitively, the conclusion asserts a causal connection between the gear's turning and the bell's ringing that goes beyond anything asserted in (10b)'s premises. In line with this impression, I found that, although 60.2 percent of participants agreed that the conclusion of arguments like (10a) had to be true whenever the premises were true, only 31.0 percent agreed to the conclusion of items like (10b) (Rips 1983). (The relatively low overall percentage of responses is probably due to the fact that the full data set included several arguments with more complex structures than that of (10).)

These differences between *cause* and *if* reflect fundamental differences in their meaning. There are disputes about the correct formal semantics for conditional sentences (see Bennett 2003). But it is plausible to think that people evaluate them by temporarily supposing that the *if*-part (antecedent) of the sentence is true and then assessing the *then*-part (consequent) in that supposed situation (Ramsey 1929/1990; Stalnaker 1968).[14] In these terms, *if* relates the current situation to a similar one (or similar ones) in which the antecedent holds. Conditionals can thus depend on circumstances that may not be a direct effect of the antecedent but simply carry over from the actual situation to the supposed one. This explains why we tend to judge that the conclusion of (10a) follows: Although the gear's turning doesn't cause the bell's ringing, nevertheless, the ringing occurs in the situation in which the gear turns. *Cause*, however, is not a sentence connective, but a predicate that connects terms for events. In order to create parallel structures between conditionals and causals in these experiments, investigators have to rephrase the antecedent and consequent as nominals (e.g., *the gear turns* in (10a) becomes *the gear turning* in (10b)), but the nominals still refer to events. Whether a causal sentence is true depends on exactly how these events are connected and not on what other circumstances may happen to hold in a situation in which the cause takes place. In this respect, causal sentences depend on the specifics of the cause-effect relation, just as ordinary predicates like *kiss* or *kick* do. Whether *John kisses Mary* is true depends on whether the appropriate relation holds between John and Mary, and whether the

gear's turning causes both the light's flashing and the bell's ringing likewise depends on whether the right causal connection holds between these events. The conclusion of (10b) fails to follow from the premises, since the premises entail no such connection.

This point about the difference between conditionals and causals may be an obvious one, but analyses of *cause* can sometimes obscure it. For example, some formal treatments of action, like McCarthy and Hayes's (1969) situation calculus, represent these actions (a type of cause) as a function from a situation that obtains before the action to one that obtains after it. But although we may be able to think of both *if* and *cause* as types of functions, the truth of a causal depends more intimately on the way in which the resulting state of affairs is brought about. We judge that "if c occurs then e occurs" on the basis of whether e holds in the situations that we get by supposing c is true, but this is not enough to support the assertion that "c causes e." Similarly, there are causal modal logics (e.g., Burks 1977) that represent the causal necessity or possibility of conditionals. Such logics, for example, can symbolize sentences of the type "It is causally necessary that if c occurs then e occurs," with the interpretation that "If c occurs then e occurs" in all possible worlds that retain the actual world's causal laws. However, causally necessary conditionals aren't equivalent to causals. It is causally necessary that if $5 + 7 = 12$ then $5 + 8 = 13$, since $5 + 7 = 12$ and $5 + 8 = 13$ are true in all possible worlds, including the causally necessary ones. But $5 + 7 = 12$ doesn't cause $5 + 8 = 13$ (or anything else, for that matter), since arithmetic facts don't have causal properties.

The experiments just mentioned provide evidence that people distinguish causal sentences from indicative conditional ones, even when the conditionals have causal content. The experiments have less to say, however, about the nature of causal reasoning itself. We'd like to know in more detail how accurately people recognize inferences that follow directly from causal relations. Two possibilities present themselves, both based on our earlier discussion of causal models. First, people who know the causal facts about a system should follow the causal Markov principle in estimating probabilities of the events these models encode. Second, people's predictions about the system's behavior should respect differences between interventions and observations. We'll see that although the evidence for the first of these predictions is weak, evidence for the second is more robust.

REASONING FROM CAUSAL MODELS: THE CAUSAL MARKOV PRINCIPLE

We've seen that Bayesian causal models (Pearl 2000) provide an explicit representation of cause-effect relations, and they include normative constraints that should govern causal reasoning. In particular, causal models obey the causal Markov principle, which provides their structural basis and mirrors statistical dependencies. We can therefore get a closer look at causal reasoning by teaching people causal connections that compose such a model and checking whether they follow the Markov principle in drawing inferences from it.

In a pioneering study of this kind, Rehder and Burnett (2005) taught participants explicit causal relations about fictional categories, such as Lake Victoria shrimp or Neptune computers. For example, participants might be told that Victoria shrimp tend to have a high quantity of ACh neurotransmitter, a long-lasting flight response, an accelerated sleep cycle, and a high body weight. The participants learned that about 75 percent of category members have each of these features. They also learned the causal relations among these features, both verbally and in an explicit diagram. For example, these participants might learn the "common cause" pattern in Figure 4a, in which high levels of ACh neurotransmitter in Lake Victoria shrimp cause a long-lasting flight response, an accelerated sleep cycle, and a high body weight. Rehder and Burnett then tested the participants by giving them descriptions of a category member with an unknown feature and asking them to rate how likely the category member was to have that feature. How likely is it, for instance, that a Victoria shrimp with high ACh, a long flight response, but no accelerated sleep cycle, also has high body weight?

The interesting predictions concern the causal Markov condition: Conditioning on the states of the parent variables renders a child variable statistically independent of all other variables, except its descendants. In the case of the Figure 4a example, if we know whether a Lake Victoria shrimp has high (or low) ACh, then the values of the lower-level features – flight response and body weight, for example – will be statistically independent of each other. If we're trying to predict whether a shrimp has high body weight, it should matter a lot whether it has high or low ACh levels. But as long as we know its ACh level, we needn't worry about whether it has any of the sister features (a long flight response or an accelerated sleep cycle), since these are not descendants of body weight. It shouldn't matter how many of these sister features the shrimp has, given that it has high (low) ACh.

What Rehder and Burnett (2005) found, however, is that participants systematically violated the Markov principle. Participants' estimates of the probability that a Lake Victoria shrimp has high body weight correctly depended on whether they were told it had high levels of ACh. But these estimates also increased if the shrimp had a long flight response and an accelerated sleep cycle, even when participants knew the state of the ACh level. (See Rehder 2006; Waldmann and Hagmayer 2005: Experiment 3, for evidence of similar violations in the case of causal systems other than categories.) Rehder and Burnett's participants had learned the common-cause structure in Figure 4a, which depicts the causal model, and the Markov principle is the central ingredient in defining the model. So why do participants flagrantly disregard the principle?

Rehder and Burnett propose that participants were indeed using causal nets, but nets with a configuration that differed from the one they learned. According to this theory, the participants were assuming that there is an additional hidden node representing the category member's underlying mechanisms. The network in Figure 4b illustrates this structure, containing the new hidden mechanism node with direct connections to all the observed nodes. According to Rehder and Burnett (2005: 37), "to the extent that an exemplar has most or all of the category's characteristic features, it also will be considered a *well functioning* category member. That is, the many characteristic features are taken as a sign that the exemplar's underlying causal mechanisms functioned (and/or are continuing to function) properly or normally for members of that kind. And if the exemplar's underlying mechanisms are operating normally, then they are likely to have produced a characteristic value on the unobserved dimension." Because participants obviously aren't told the state of the hidden mechanism, the sister nodes at the bottom of the figure are no longer statistically independent. Thus, participants' tendency to rely on these sister nodes no longer violates the Markov principle. Rehder and Burnett show in further experiments that this hidden-mechanism theory also predicts the results from experiments using different network structures – for example, a net consisting of a single chain of variables and a "common effect" net with multiple causes

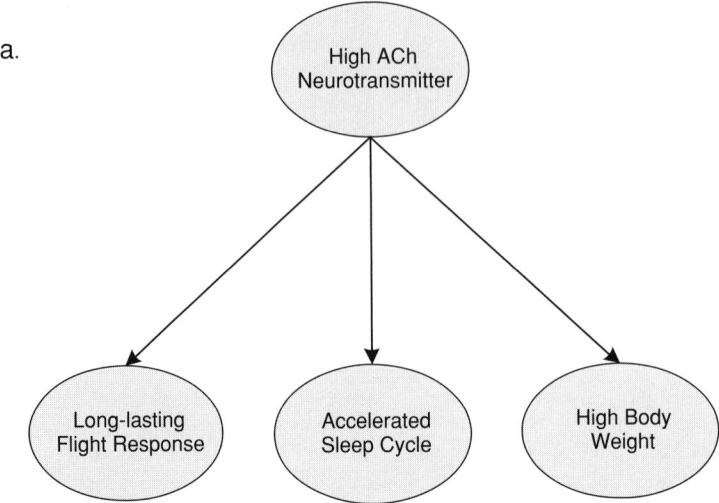

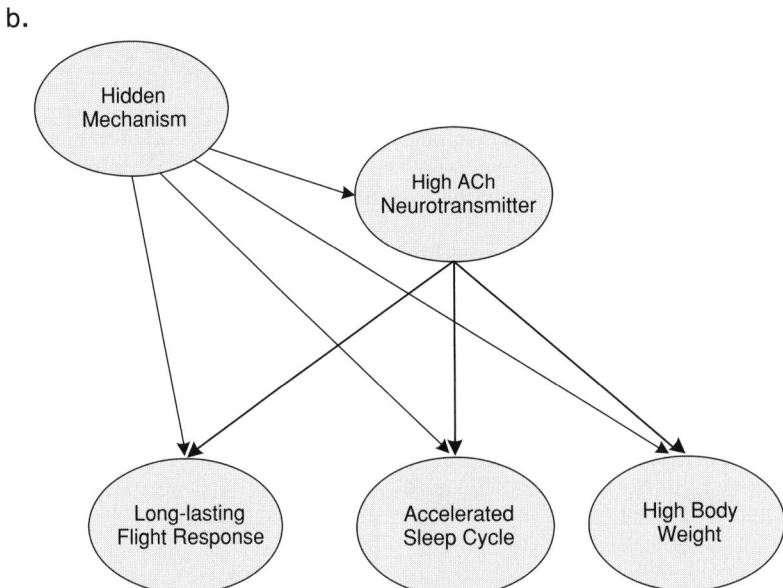

Figure 4. An example of the common cause condition from Rehder and Burnett (2005: Experiment 1). (a) The network participants learned, and (b) a possible alternative network to explain the empirical findings.

for a single effect. For the latter networks, the underlying mechanism idea seems quite plausible, and the theory is consistent with models of causal centrality and psychological essentialism (e.g., Ahn et al. 1995). Participants may suspect that a natural kind or complex artifact is likely to have some central cause or causes that hold the object together, an assumption that's in line with essentialist theories of categories (e.g., Gelman 2003; Medin and Ortony 1989). As Hausman and Woodward (1999) note, applications of the causal Markov principle have to ensure that all relevant variables are included in the model, that the causal system is analyzed at the right level, and that the included variables are not logically or definitionally related.

For common cause structures such as Figure 4a, however, why would participants go to the trouble of positing an extra hidden mechanism when they already have an explicit common cause? Rehder and Burnett (2005: Experiment 2) also found the same pattern of results – violations of the Markov constraint – when participants were taught a common cause structure like Figure 4a for a nonsense category, daxes, whose features were arbitrarily labeled A, B, C, and D. Even if hidden mechanisms are reasonable for shrimp and computers, where you might suppose there are underlying causes in addition to those taught in the experiment, it is harder to understand why you would posit them for an obviously fictitious category. Why would participants believe there are hidden mechanisms governing well-functioning daxes? You would at least expect some decrease in the non-independence effect when the category gives participants less reason to suppose that an underlying mechanism is at work. But there doesn't seem to be much, if any, difference in the extent of the violations for daxes versus known kinds and artifacts. Although it's possible that participants were positing hidden mechanisms, a simpler alternative might be that they were reasoning in a more primitive way. Perhaps they were assuming that the dominant values of a category's features tend to cluster together, without worry too much about the exact causal set up. Participants may have been short-cutting the Bayes net circuitry, relying instead on the belief that the more typical Lake Victoria shrimp features an item has, the more likely it is to have other Lake Victoria shrimp features. Ditto for daxes. Participants weren't completely ignoring the causal structure, since they recognized the role of direct causes. But they may have given little thought to implications for the indirectly connected variables.

REASONING FROM CAUSAL MODELS: OBSERVATION VERSUS INTERVENTION

In discussing whether people are able to infer causal nets from data (see *Causation from Intervention*), we found only limited support for the idea that people can exploit interventions in order to figure out the correct causal system. Although people use interventions within very simple systems, their ability to do so seems to fall off rapidly with even moderately complex networks. This difficulty may reflect general information-processing limits, since the number of possible causal nets (acyclic directed graphs) increases exponentially with the number of variables (see Rips and Conrad 1989). A more sensitive test of people's understanding of the intervention/observation difference is simply to

give people the relevant causal relations and see whether they can predict the effects of intervening on a variable versus observing its values.

Two series of experiments provide support for sensitivity to interventions. Sloman and Lagnado (2005: Experiment 6, p. 26) gave one group of participants the problem in (11):

(11) All rocket ships have two components, A and B. Movement of Component A causes Component B to move. In other word, if A, then B. Both are moving. Suppose Component B were prevented from moving, would Component A still be moving?

A second group received the same problem, except that the final question was changed to *Suppose Component B were observed not to be moving, would Component A still be moving?* If an external process explicitly manipulates a variable – in this case, prevents Component B from moving – the internal causal connections to that variable are no longer in force, and we can't reliably use them to predict the state of the cause (Component A). By contrast, if normal internal causes are intact – if B is merely observed not to be moving – then the state of the effect provides diagnostic information about the cause. In line with this difference, 85 percent of participants responded "yes" to the intervention question, but only 22 percent did so for the observation question. A slightly more complicated problem, involving a chain of three variables instead of two, produced a similar difference between intervention questions and observation questions (Sloman and Lagnado 2005: Experiment 2). Waldmann and Hagmayer (2005: Experiment 1) also found an observation/intervention difference, using more complex five-variable systems that they presented to participants in both verbal and graphical formats.

It may seem odd, at first glance, that causal nets (or models) make correct empirical predictions in the case of the intervention/observation difference but largely incorrect predictions in the case of the causal Markov principle. This divergence might be due to differences between studies, but in fact, both results have appeared within the same experiment (Waldmann and Hagmayer 2005: Experiment 3). On second thought, though, there is no reason why these principles should necessarily hang together. We associate both the observation/intervention distinction and the Markov principle with causal nets because causal modelers have given clear formal treatments for both. And the Markov principle, in particular, does seem tightly connected to causal nets because of the role it plays in their construction. But causal nets aren't the only way to formulate knowledge about interventions. The basic idea that you can't use the state of a manipulated variable to make inferences about its normal causes may simply be a piece of commonsense knowledge that's independent of the specific representation it gets in causal nets and models.[15] Evidence for correct understanding of interventions is support for correct causal reasoning but not necessarily support for causal nets.

REASONING FROM CAUSAL MODELS: COUNTERFACTUALS AND CAUSE

There's one more piece of the causal net puzzle we need to consider. We've noticed substantive differences, both theoretical and empirical, between indicative conditional sentences and related causal sentences, as in (10a) and (10b). We've also noticed a much closer conceptual link between counterfactual conditionals and causals (see *Causal Bayesian Networks and Functional Causal Models as Causal Schemas*). Pearl's (2000) move from causal nets to causal models, in particular, was due to the fact that causal models give a better formulation of counterfactual questions. Causal models, but not causal nets, can tell us whether a different effect would have occurred if a cause had taken a value other than its actual one. Do causal models correctly predict people's reasoning with counterfactuals?

To handle counterfactual statements within the causal-model framework, we need a set of structural equations, like those in (8), that specify the state of each variable in terms of the state of both its parents and of uncorrelated background factors or error terms. In the simplest possible case, consider a two-variable system, such as that in (11). We can assume for the sake of this example that the all variables are dichotomous, either on or off, which we will code as 1 or 0. We can then specify the f functions like this:

(12)   a. $f_A(u_A) = u_A$
         b. $f_B(A, u_B) = A * u_B$,

where A is the variable for Component A, and B for Component B. In other words, Component A will operate $(A = 1)$ provided that the error variable, u_A, has the value 1, and Component B will operate $(B = 1)$ provided both that its error variable, u_B, is 1 and that Component A is operating as well.

To determine the answer to a counterfactual question in this case – for example, *Suppose Component B were not operating, would Component A still operate?* – we follow a series of three steps, according to Pearl (2000: Theorem 7.1.7): We first update the probability of the background u variables, given the current evidence about the actual state of affairs. If we assume that the two components are operating in the actual state, as in (11), then $u_A = u_B = 1$. Second, we modify the causal model for an intervention on the event mentioned in the antecedent of the counterfactual. For the sample question just mentioned, we modify Component B in the usual way by orphaning B from its parent A and setting its value to a constant, while also keeping the u variables constant. This entails changing the equation in (12b) to:

(12)   b'. $f_B(u_B) = 0$,

since the antecedent states that Component B is not operating. Finally, to determine whether Component A would still operate, we compute its probability (i.e., the value of f_A) in the modified model, using the updated probabilities of the background variables. Since we have $u_A = 1$, the equation in (12a) gives us a positive answer.

According to the causal model framework, the answer to our sample counterfactual question should be exactly the same as what we would get if the question had directly mentioned the manipulation of Component B. For example, we should also get a "yes" to the question: *Suppose Component B were prevented from operating, would Component A still operate?* This question is also counterfactual and differs from the first one only in making the intervention explicit. Sloman and Lagnado's (2005) Experiment 5 directly compared answers to straight counterfactuals and prevention counterfactuals, but found a reliable difference between them (68% of participants answered "yes" to the straight counterfactual and 89% "yes" to the prevention counterfactual). A similar difference appeared for scenarios describing a slightly more complicated three-variable system (Sloman and Lagnado 2005: Experiment 2). One group of participants rated the answer to a straight counterfactual (e.g., *What is the probability that A would have happened if B had not happened?*), while a second group rated an explicit prevention counterfactual (*Someone intervened directly on B, preventing it from happening. What is the probability that A would have happened?*). The average probability rating for the straight counterfactual was 3.2 on a 1–5 response scale (1 = very low, 5 = very high probability), whereas the average was 3.9 for the prevention version. Although

Sloman and Lagnado don't compare these means statistically, they do report that the first was not significantly higher than the scale midpoint (3.0), whereas the second was significantly higher than the midpoint.

Because counterfactuals were the main reason for introducing causal models (as an alternative to causal nets), it's important to see why these predictions fail. It is possible that participants are behaving in nonnormative ways in the experiments just cited, but we should also consider the possibility that the procedure itself gives an incorrect account of how counterfactuals should be understood. One thing that seems clear is that Pearl's (2000) procedure can't evaluate all reasonable counterfactuals. As he points out, the procedure is useless with "backtracking" counterfactuals that hypothesize what would have happened prior to a supposed event. For example, Sentence (13) posits an event – getting an F in a course – and gives an earlier event as a probable cause:

(13) If Fred had gotten an F in Theoretical Billiards in June, then it would have had to have been the case that he had forgotten to do his homework during the entire month of May.

Backtracking counterfactuals are sometimes clumsy to express because of tense shifts and modality, but there is no reason to think they are incoherent or uninformative. However, we would be unable to understand or evaluate backtracking counterfactuals if we had to sever the effect from its normal parent causes, since it's precisely the cause that is in question. Backtracking counterfactuals take the proposition expressed in the antecedent of the counterfactual as diagnostic of the proposition in the consequent.

Perhaps we should follow Pearl (2000) in setting aside backtracking counterfactuals and taking his procedure as a proposal about forward counterfactuals only. However, even forward counterfactuals may depend on how the hypothetical cause was brought about. Imagine that Fred's F could have been the result of two possible causes: his failure to do his homework or negligence on the part of his instructor. Then our evaluation of the truth of the forward counterfactual in (14) will depend on which of these causes we believe is the correct one:

(14) If Fred had gotten an F in the course, his instructor would have been disciplined.

As it actually happened, Fred finished his homework, his instructor was diligent, and Fred got a C. If we hold background variables constant, snip the relevant causal connections (between Fred's homework and his grade and between the instructor's behavior and his grade), and then set the grade to F, how do we determine whether the counterfactual is true or false? Intuitively, our judgment about the sentence would seem to depend on the likelihood that Fred did his homework. On one hand, if he's a marginal student, then the cause of his F is probably his own doing, and it's unlikely that the instructor will be disciplined. On the other hand, if Fred is a model student, then it may be more likely that the cause of the F was the instructor's negligence. The problem is that cutting the connection between the state of Fred's homework and his course grade renders the probability of these variables independent, and this means that the probability that his instructor will be disciplined is also independent of the homework.

The motive for cutting causal ties to the past is clear. In a deterministic system, such as those conforming to (8), no change to the actual event can occur without some alteration to its causes. To envision Fred receiving an F rather than a C, we have to envision a world in which some of the causes that produced his grade are no longer in force. We must also construct this alteration leaving as much as possible of the causal fabric of the world intact, since arbitrary changes to preceding causes give us no way to determine whether a counterfactual sentence is true or false. But although some minimal break with the past is necessary, it isn't always correct to make this break by causally isolating the event mentioned in the antecedent of the counterfactual. As the examples in (13) and (14) show, we may have to trace back to some of the causes of the antecedent event in order to see which of them is most likely to have produced the alteration. Determining which of the preceding causes must be changed may depend on which is most mutable (Kahneman and Miller 1986), as well as which is powerful enough to bring about the new effect.[16]

These reflections may help explain the differences between straight counterfactuals and prevention counterfactuals in Sloman and Lagnado's (2005) experiments. Prevention counterfactuals require explicit manipulation of the event that the antecedent of the conditionals describes. The scenario in (11) suggests that if someone had prevented Component B from operating, the intervention occurred directly at

B (perhaps by disrupting its internal mechanism). But the straight counterfactual (i.e., *Suppose Component B were not operating, would Component A still operate?*) allows more room for interpretation. We're free to imagine different ways for B to have stopped operating, some of which might plausibly involve the failure of A. Although it might seem that a world in which both A and B fail is causally more distant from the actual workaday world than one in which only B fails, this depends on details that the scenario in (11) does not supply. Stopping B by direct action on B may be more disruptive than stopping B by stopping A. There is simply no way to tell. This ambiguity is related to one we have met before in our study of causal models (in the section *Causation from Intervention*). We noted that intervening on an event means more than removing an old cause. It also entails substituting a new cause, and the way in which the intervener does this can have important consequences for what follows in the world of the intervention. The present point is that if all we know is that some event has changed from the actual situation to a counterfactual one, we have an even larger choice of mechanisms for understanding that change.

The difficulty with Pearl's (2000) account of counterfactuals doesn't mean we necessarily have to give up causal models. There may be other theories of counterfactuals based on causal schemas that provide better approaches to cases such as (13)–(14).[17] Nevertheless, people's representations of causal models are necessarily incomplete depictions of event interactions, since any event has a causal history stretching back over enormous temporal distances. We can indicate our ignorance about these prehistories by including explicit representations of uncertainty, such as Pearl's *u* variables. But part of our causal reasoning consists in filling in some of these missing pieces, for example, in considering what sort of disturbance or manipulation could have brought about a hypothetical event. Severing preexisting connections in a model often won't be enough to explain these circumstances, since they may involve bringing in new mechanisms that we hadn't previously represented as parts of the model.

Concluding Comments

Causal theorizing must be essential, both in everyday thinking and scientific endeavors, but it is unclear how people accomplish it. The implication of the first part of this paper is that we probably don't do such thinking by strictly bottom-up observation. We can interpret simple displays of colliding geometric shapes as instances of pushings, pullings, and other causal events. Similarly, we can interpret other swarming movements of geometrical shapes as instances of actions – for example, chasings, catchings, and fightings, as Heider and Simmel (1944) demonstrated. But we can also take a more analytical attitude to these displays, interpreting these movements as no more than approachings, touchings, and departings with no implication that one shape caused the other to move. There is no evidence to suggest that the causal interpretations are hardwired or impenetrable in the way standard perceptual illusions often are. The evidence is consistent with the idea that we see these demos as causal, but probably only in the way that we see certain visual arrays as cows or toasters. This suggestion is reinforced by the fact that, although seven-month-old infants may register some of these animations as special, others that adults report as causal are not distinctive for these infants. Of course, doubts about innate perceptual causality detectors needn't extend to doubts about innate causal concepts, but it seems likely that causal concepts, innate or learned, must have sources that aren't purely perceptual.

Are the sources of causality co-occurrence frequencies? Here there are both empirical and conceptual difficulties. On the empirical side, people are obviously limited in which potential causes they can test using frequency-based methods, and there is no theory of how they search through the space of these causes. Moreover, even when an experimenter tells participants about the relevant candidates and provides the relevant frequencies, the participants appear guided by prior hypotheses in their evaluation of the data. Theoretically, the frequency-based or correlation-based methods – main effect contrasts, ΔP, conditional ΔP, Rescorla-Wagner strength, power, and path coefficients – all give incorrect answers in certain causal environments, especially when there are hidden confounding factors. Explicit manipulation or intervention can remove some of the ambiguities by eliminating the confoundings, just as in scientific experiments, but current research suggests that people are often unable to make use of such information, except in very simple settings. The empirical results are generally in line with the conclusions of Waldmann (1996) and others that people pursue knowledge of cause in a largely top-down fashion. The theoretical results are in line with the conclusion that this might be the correct way for them to pursue it.

A top-down approach implies that people begin with hypotheses when they assess or reason about cause. But this leaves plenty of room for variation. Causal hypotheses could be anything from fragmented bits of information about a system to highly integrated and consistent theories. It's clear that people can reason with causal information and that this reasoning differs (sometimes appropriately) from what they do with similar indicative conditionals. It also seems likely that people's causal knowledge of a situation is not entirely isolated into units at the grain of individual atomic propositions (e.g., Rumelhart 1975). It is very unclear, though, what else we can say about such representations.

Bayes nets present one way of representing causal information in schematic form, and these nets provide many advantages in understanding causal situations, especially in the context of data-mining and analysis. They provide a way to factor a situation into statistically independent parts, and they therefore clarify the kinds of conclusions that we can draw from specific observations and experiments. In particular, they delimit the cases in which traditional statistical methods, such as regression or factor analysis, are likely to lead to the right results. Should we also take Bayes nets to be the mental representations that people ordinarily use to store causal facts in memory? Bayes nets go beyond a vague commitment to causal schemas in this respect, since they embody strong assumptions about the relation between the causal links in the model and statistical regularities, and they generate predictions about how people could reason about interventions and counterfactuals. They may well be consistent with the way people learn about new causal situations, though they may require additional constraints or heuristics to achieve this. In simple cases that include a small number of variables, they produce correct predictions for both children's and adults' reasoning. There seems little doubt, for example, that people observe the distinction between observation and intervention that Bayes nets embody.

On the other side of the balance, there is very little evidence that people observe the causal Markov condition, the key ingredient in Bayes net's construction. All versions of Bayes nets tie the presence and absence of causal links to the presence and absence of statistical dependencies in the data. But participants' reasoning with causal information doesn't always agree with predictions based on these dependencies. Although we can interpret the results of these experiments on the assumption that the participants are reasoning with Bayes nets that are different from the ones they are taught, there is currently little positive evidence that the Markov principle constrains people's causal reasoning. And without the Markov principle, we're back to a position not much different from ideas about cognitive schemas, models, scripts, frames, or theories that preceded Bayes nets.

Bayes nets are also oddly inarticulate as cognitive representations. Proponents of Bayes nets have generally been uninterested in the way in which people express causal regularities, presumably because people's talk about cause is filtered through pragmatic channels, obscuring their underlying beliefs. But, although this can be true, it's also the case that people's causal reasoning depends on whether a cause or set of causes is necessary or sufficient, as the literature on causal conditionals attests. Likewise, reasoning depends on the differences between independent ("alternative") and interactive ("additional") causes. While we can derive information of this sort from the underlying conditional probabilities that Bayes nets capture, we can't get them from the graphs themselves. Two arrows running into an effect could equally represent two independent, individually sufficient causes of that effect or two causes that are only jointly sufficient. The same is true for contributory versus inhibitory causes. In addition, people make a wealth of adverbial distinctions in the way that causation comes about. They distinguish, for example, between pushings, shovings, and thrustings in ways that don't seem recoverable from the bare networks or even from their underlying conditional probabilities or functional equations. These limits on expressibility may not be fundamental ones, but they do lessen the appeal of Bayes nets as cognitive maps of our causal environment.

To accord with the facts about human causal thinking, we need a representation that's less nerdy – less tied to statistical dependencies and more discursive. This doesn't mean that we should jettison Bayes nets' insights, especially insights into the differences between intervention and observation. But it does suggest that we should be looking for a representation that better highlights people's talents in describing and reasoning about causation and downplays ties to purely quantitative phenomena.

Notes

1 I'm grateful to Jonathan Adler, Russell Burnett, Douglas Medin, Brian Scholl, and to undergraduate and graduate students in courses on causal reasoning at Northwestern for comments on this paper.

2 Michotte (1963) is inconsistent on how to understand these reports. On the one hand, he emphasizes the phenomenal character of the observers' experiences: "Now the responses in these conditions given by the subjects always relate, of course, to the physical 'world'. . . But the physical 'world' in question here is no longer the world of physical *science*, as revealed by measuring instruments; it is *the world of things, as it appears to the subject* on simple inspection, his 'phenomenal world', disclosed in this case by the indications which he gives as a human 'recording instrument'. Thus, when he says that A 'pulls B' or 'pushes B', he is referring to an event occurring in a world which appears as external to him, an event of which he thinks himself simply a witness and which he is merely describing" (p. 306). But one page later, on the other hand, Michotte retreats to a position in which statements about what an observer sees are no more than abbreviations for what the observer reports: "Throughout this book there often occur expressions such as 'what the subject sees', or 'the impression received by the subject', and so on. These expressions are clearly only abbreviations, and are used to make the text less cumbersome. They in fact refer to the subjects' verbal responses and they therefore mean 'what the subject says or asserts that he sees' or 'that of which the subject says or asserts that he has an impression', and so on" (p. 307, note 5, emphasis in the original in both these passages).

3 Fodor (2003: Ch. 3) argues that even if observers directly perceive an event in the display, it's likely to be a lower-level one like square *x* pushing another *y* (which is indeed what observers report, according to Michotte) rather than square *x* causing *y* to move. There's no reason to think, according to Fodor, that perceiving an event like a pushing entails perceiving the causing. Although *x pushes y* may imply *x causes y to move*, we may get the causing from the pushing by inference rather than by direct perception. This distinction may seem unimportant to investigators, who may be satisfied that at least one type of causal interaction (pushing or launching) is directly perceived, but it is a reminder that the conclusions about direct perception have limited scope.

4 There is some debate about the exact age at which infants are first able to perceive causal interactions as such. See Cohen and Oakes (1993) for the view that infants don't fully grasp the launching interactions as causal until seven to ten months. The exact age, however, is not crucial for the issues addressed here, though the extent to which infants' recognition of causal interactions changes with experience is important. What's of interest in the present context is that infants appear to recognize oblique launching events later than linear ones.

5 For example, according to a methodology textbook by Pelham and Blanton (2003), "Most researchers who wish to understand causality rely heavily on the framework proposed by the 19th-century philosopher John Stuart Mill" (p. 63). Similarly, Cook and Campbell (1979) note, "A careful reading of chapters 3 through 7 will reveal how often a modified form of Mill's canons is used to rule out identified threats to valid inference" (p. 19). Or, in more detail, "The conditions necessary for arriving at explanations were set forth in the nineteenth century by the philosopher John Stuart Mill. . . . Mill argued that causation can be inferred if some result, X, follows an event, A, if X and A vary together and if it can be shown that event A produces result X. For these conditions to be met, what Mill called the **joint method of agreement and difference** must be used. In the joint method, if A occurs then so will X, and if A does not occur, then neither will X" (Elmes, Kantowitz, and Roediger 1999: 103, emphasis in the original). The joint method is the third of Mill's canons, which he regarded as superior to the method of agreement but inferior to the method of difference.

6 There is also a normative problem with ΔP (as Cheng 1997 argues). Since ΔP does not take into account the presence of other causes, it can yield a misleading index of the strength of any particular cause. For example, if other causes usually bring about the effect, then ΔP for the target cause will be systematically too small. In general, measures of causal strength run into normative difficulties by ignoring the structure of the causal system (e.g., the possible presence of confounding factors). Glymour (2001) shows that this problem affects not only ΔP but also conditional ΔP, Rescorla-Wagner strength, power, multiple regression coefficients, and others.

7 Chapman and Robbins (1990) and Cheng (1997) prove that under simplifying assumptions Rescorla and Wagner's (1972) theory of associative conditioning reduces to ΔP. (In general, however, the equivalence does *not* hold; see Glymour 2001 citing earlier work by Danks.) A prominent member of my own faculty once declared that no graduate student from our cognitive program should get a Ph.D. without

having studied the Rescorla-Wagner model. So here's the idea: Suppose that a creature is learning a relation between a set of conditioned stimuli $C_1, C_2, \ldots, C_n$ (e.g., lights, tones, etc.) and an unconditioned stimulus U_j (e.g., shock). Then the change to the associative strength, ΔV_i, of a particular stimulus C_i on any trial is a function of the difference between the asymptotic level of strength that's possible for the unconditioned stimulus and the sum of associative strengths for all the conditioned stimuli:

$$\Delta V_i = \alpha_i \beta_j (\lambda_j - \Sigma V_k),$$

where α_i is the salience of cue C_i, β_j is the learning rate for U_j ($0 \leq \alpha, \beta \leq 1$), λ_j is the asymptotic level of strength possible for U_j, and the sum is over all cues in $C_1, C_2, \ldots, C_n$ present on the trial. The asymptote λ will have a high value (> 0) when the unconditioned stimulus is present and a low value (perhaps 0) when it is absent on a trial. No change occurs to the strength of C_i if it is not present on a trial ($\Delta V_i = 0$). The important thing to notice is that the change in strength for an individual cue depends on the strength of all others present. See Shanks and Dickinson (1987) for a discussion of the Rescorla-Wagner theory and other learning models as applied to causal judgments.

8   Psychologists tend to see ANOVA methods as superior to correlational ones in isolating the cause of some phenomenon. But as far as the statistics goes, there's no important difference between them, since ANOVA is a special case of multiple correlation/regression. The perceived difference between them is due to the fact that psychologists use ANOVA to analyze designed experiments but use correlations to analyze observational ones. Manipulation does have advantages over passive observation for reasons discussed in the following section.

9   "Simpson's paradox" is not a true paradox but an algebraic consequence of the fact that the difference between each of two proportions $a/b - c/d$ and $e/f - g/h$ can be positive (negative) while the aggregate difference $(a + e)/(b + f) - (c + g)/(d + h)$ can be negative (positive), as the numbers in Table 2 illustrate. Simpson (1951: 240) pointed out that this leaves "considerable scope for paradox and error" in how we interpret the two-way interaction between the remaining factors (i.e., the two that don't define the partition between a-d and e-h). For example, should we say that irradiation is positively or negatively related to the quality of fruit in Table 2?

10 These cases also may violate assumptions necessary in deriving p_c and, if so, lie outside the domain of the power theory (see Luhmann and Ahn 2005).

11 It's also difficult to tell how much of the improvement after interventions in Stevyers et al. (2003) is due to the extra trials rather than to the interventions themselves. That is, part of participants' increased ability to identify the correct causal structure may have been the result of a larger amount of data and not to interventions per se.

12 A variation on an example of Sloman's (2005: 57–59) illustrates the same ambiguity. Suppose peptic ulcers result either from bacterial infections of a certain sort or from taking too many aspirin and similar drugs. Peptic ulcers, in turn, cause burning pains in the gut. In this situation, we may be able to intervene on someone's ulcer by administering a drug – Grandma's special formula, in Sloman's example – that cures the ulcer and thereby relieves the pain. But what should we conclude about whether the bacteria or the aspirin continue to be present after the intervention? The natural thing to say is that this depends on how Grandma's formula works. If it acts as a kind of barrier that protects the stomach lining, then perhaps the presence of the bacteria or the aspirin is unchanged. But if it works by destroying the bacteria and neutralizing the aspirin, then, of course, neither will exist after the intervention. Sloman is careful to stipulate that Grandma's special formula "goes directly to the ulcer, by-passing all normal causal pathways, and heals it every time." But how often do we know in the case of actual interventions that they route around all normal causal channels? Isn't the more usual case one where the intervention disrupts some causal paths but not others and where it may be unclear how far upstream in the causal chain the intervention takes place?

13 The old way involved deducing causal relations between individual events from general "covering" laws plus particular statements of fact (see Hempel 1965).

14 Of course, a suppositional theory needs to be worked out more carefully than can be done here. In particular, the supposition can't be such as to block all modus tollens arguments that entail the falsity of the conditional's antecedent. For a recent attempt to construct such a theory, see Evans and Over (2004).

15 This isn't to say there is no relation between the causal Markov condition and the idea of intervention. Hausman and Woodward (1999: 553) argue that "the independent disruptability of each mechanism turns out to be the flip side of the probabilistic independence of each variable conditional on its direct causes from everything other than its effects." But their argument requires a number of strong assumptions (each variable in the Bayes net must have unobserved causes and these unobserved causes can affect only one variable) that may not always be true of the representations people have of causal systems. See Cartwright (2001) for a

general critique of the causal Markov condition, and Cartwright (2002) for a specific critique of Hausman and Woodward's "flip side" claim.

16 Morteza Dehghani and Rumen Iliev have suggested factors like these in conversation.

17 In one promising account, Hiddleston (2005) proposes a causal network theory of counterfactuals that improves on Pearl (2000). Given a causal network with variables A and C, we can evaluate the truth of the counterfactual *If A = a then C = c* by considering all minimally different assignments of values to variables in the network such that A = a. If C = c is true in all these minimal assignments, then so is *If A = a then C = c*. As assignment is minimally different, roughly speaking, if (a) it has as few variables as possible whose value is different from that in the actual situation but all of whose parents have the same values, and (b) among the variables that are not effects of A, it has as many variables as possible whose values are the same as in the actual situation and all of whose parents are also the same. As Hiddleston notes, this theory allows for backtracking counterfactuals such as (13). It is unclear, however, whether this theory can capture people's intuitions about the truth of (13)–(14) and their kin. Assume a model in which turning in homework and instructor diligence are both causes of getting a grade and in which instructor diligence and the grade cause discipline of the instructor. Then there are at least two minimal models of (13)–(14) in which Fred gets an F: In one of them, Fred does his homework, the instructor is negligent, Fred gets an F, and the instructor is disciplined. In the other, Fred forgets his homework, the instructor is diligent, Fred gets an F, and the instructor is not disciplined. Since Fred does his homework in one of these models but not in the other, (13) is false, according to the theory. Similarly, for (14). As already noted, however, people's judgment of (13)–(14) may depend on how easily they can imagine the change to Fred's grade being brought about by lack of homework versus instructor negligence.

References

Ahn, W.-K., and Graham, L. M. (1999). The impact of necessity and sufficiency in the Wason four-card selection task. *Psychological Science, 10,* 237–242.

Ahn, W.-K., Kalish, C. W., Medin, D. L., and Gelman, S. A. (1995). The role of covariation versus mechanism information in causal attribution. *Cognition, 54,* 299–352.

Ahn, W.-K., and Kim, N. (2000). The causal status effect in categorization: An overview. *Psychology of Learning and Motivation, 40,* 23–65.

Alloy, L. B., and Tabachnik, N. (1984). Assessment of covariation by humans and animals. *Psychological Review, 91,* 112–148.

Asher, H. B. (1983). *Causal modeling* (2nd ed.). Newbury Park, CA: Sage.

Atran, S. (1998). Folk biology and the anthropology of science: Cognitive universals and cultural particulars. *Behavioral and Brain Sciences, 21,* 547–609.

Barsalou, L. W. (1988). The content and organization of autobiographical memories. In U. Neisser & E. Winograd (Eds.), *Remembering reconsidered* (pp. 193–243). Cambridge: Cambridge University Press.

Barton, M. E., and Komatsu, L. K. (1989). Defining features of natural kinds and artifacts. *Journal of Psycholinguistic Research, 18,* 433–447.

Bennett, J. (2003). *A philosophical guide to conditionals.* Oxford: Oxford University Press.

Blaisdell, A. P., Sawa, K., Leising, K. J., and Waldmann, M. R. (2006). Causal reasoning in rats. *Science, 311,* 1020–1022.

Brem, S. K., and Rips, L. J. (2000). Evidence and explanation in informal argument. *Cognitive Science, 24,* 573–604.

Bullock, M., Gelman, R., and Baillargeon, R. (1982). The development of causal reasoning. In W. J. Friedman (Ed.), *The developmental psychology of time* (pp. 209–254). New York: Academic Press.

Burks, A. W. (1977). *Chance, cause, reason.* Chicago: University of Chicago Press.

Busemeyer, J. R. (1991). Intuitive statistical estimation. In N. H. Anderson (Ed.), *Contributions to information integration theory* (Vol. 1, pp. 187–215). Hillsdale, NJ: Erlbaum.

Byrne, R. M. (1989). Suppressing valid inferences with conditionals. *Cognition, 31,* 61–83.

Byrne, R. M. J., Espino, O., and Santamaria, C. (1999). Counterexamples and the suppression of inferences. *Journal of Memory and Language, 40,* 347–373.

Carey, S. (1985). *Conceptual change in childhood.* Cambridge, MA: MIT Press.

Cartwright, N. (2001). What is wrong with Bayes nets? *Monist, 84,* 242–264.

Cartwright, N. (2002). Against modularity, the causal Markov condition, and any link between the two. *British Journal for the Philosophy of Science, 53,* 411–453.

Chapman, G. B., and Robbins, S. J. (1990). Cue interaction in human contingency judgment. *Memory & Cognition, 18,* 537–545.

Chapman, L. J. (1967). Illusory correlation in observational report. *Journal of Verbal Learning and Verbal Behavior, 6,* 151–155.

Chapman, L. J., and Chapman, J. P. (1967). Genesis of popular but erroneous psychodiagnostic observations. *Journal of Abnormal Psychology, 72,* 193–204.

Cheng, P. W. (1997). From covariation to causation: A causal power theory. *Psychological Review, 104,* 367–405.

Cheng, P. W., and Novick, L. R. (1990). A probabilistic contrast model of causal induction. *Journal of Personality and Social Psychology, 58,* 545–567.

Cheng, P. W., and Novick, L. R. (1992). Covariation in natural causal induction. *Psychological Review, 99,* 365–382.

Cheng, P. W., and Novick, L. R. (2005). Constraints and nonconstraints in causal learning. *Psychological Review, 112,* 694–707.

Cliff, N. (1983). Some cautions concerning the application of causal modeling methods. *Multivariate Behavior Research, 18,* 115–128.

Cohen, L. B., and Oakes, L. M. (1993). How infants perceive a simple causal event. *Developmental Psychology, 29,* 421–433.

Collins, J., Hall, N., and Paul, L. A. (2004). *Causation and counterfactuals.* Cambridge, MA: MIT Press.

Cook, T. D., and Campbell, D. T. (1979). *Quasi-experimentation.* Chicago: Rand-McNally.

Cummins, D. D., Lubart, T., Alksnis, O., and Rist, R. (1991). Conditional reasoning and causation. *Memory & Cognition, 19,* 274–282.

De Neys, W., Schaeken, W., and d'Ydewalle, G. (2003). Inference suppression and semantic memory retrieval: Every counterexample counts. *Memory & Cognition, 31,* 581–595.

diSessa, A. A. (2000). *Changing minds: Computers, learning, and literacy.* Cambridge, MA: MIT Press.

Dowty, D. R. (1979). *Word meaning and Montague grammar.* Dordrecht, Holland: Reidel.

Einhorn, H. J., and Hogarth, R. M. (1986). Judging probable cause. *Psychological Bulletin, 99,* 3–19.

Elmes, D. G., Kantowitz, B. H., and Roediger, H. L., III. (1999). *Research methods in psychology.* Pacific Grove, CA: Brooks/Cole.

Evans, J. S. B. T., and Over, D. (2004). *If.* Oxford: Oxford University Press.

Ewert, J.-P. (1974). The neural basis of visually guided behavior. *Scientific American, 230,* 34–42.

Fodor, J. A. (1983). *Modularity of mind: An essay on faculty psychology.* Cambridge, MA: MIT Press.

Fodor, J. A. (2003). *Hume variations.* Oxford: Oxford University Press.

Gelman, S. A. (2003). *The essential child: Origins of essentialism in everyday thought.* Oxford, UK: Oxford University Press.

Gelman, S. A., and Wellman, H. M. (1991). Insides and essences: Early understanding of the nonobvious. *Cognition, 38,* 213–244.

Gentner, D. (1983). Structure mapping: A theoretical framework for analogy. *Cognitive Science, 7,* 155–170.

Gigerenzer, G. (1991). From tools to theories: A heuristic of discovery in cognitive psychology. *Psychological Review, 98,* 254–267.

Glymour, C. (2001). *The mind's arrows: Bayes nets and graphical causal models in psychology.* Cambridge, MA: MIT Press.

Goodman, N. (1955). *Fact, fiction, and forecast.* Cambridge, MA: Bobbs-Merrill.

Gopnik, A., Glymour, C., Sobel, D. M., Schulz, L., Kushnir, T., and Danks, D. (2004). A theory of causal learning in children: Causal maps and Bayes nets. *Psychological Review, 111,* 3–32.

Gregory, R. L. (1978). *Eye and brain* (3rd ed.). New York: McGraw-Hill.

Harman, G. H. (1965). The inference to the best explanation. *Philosophical Review, 74,* 88–95.

Hausman, D. M., and Woodward, J. (1999). Independence, invariance, and the causal Markov condition. *British Journal for the Philosophy of Science, 50,* 521–583.

Heider, F., and Simmel, M. (1944). An experimental study of apparent behavior. *American Journal of Psychology, 57,* 243–259.

Hempel, C. G. (1965). *Aspects of scientific explanations.* New York: Free Press.

Hiddleston, E. (2005). A causal theory of counterfactuals. *Nous, 39,* 632–657.

Hilton, D. J. (1988). Logic and causal attribution. In D. J. Hilton (Ed.), *Contemporary science and natural explanation: Commonsense conceptions of causality* (pp. 33–65). New York: New York University Press.

Hilton, D. J. (1990). Conversational processes and causal explanation. *Psychological Bulletin, 107,* 65–81.

Hilton, D. J., Jaspars, J. M. F., and Clarke, D. D. (1990). Pragmatic conditional reasoning. *Journal of Pragmatics, 14,* 791–812.

Hume, D. (1967). *A treatise of human nature* (L. A. Selby-Bigge, Ed.). Oxford: Oxford University Press. (Original work published 1739.)

Jackendoff, R. (1990). *Semantic structures.* Cambridge, MA: MIT Press.

Kahneman, D., and Miller, D. T. (1986). Norm theory: Comparing reality to its alternatives. *Psychological Review, 93,* 136–153.

Keil, F. C. (1989). *Concepts, kinds, and cognitive development.* Cambridge, MA: MIT Press.

Kelley, H. H. (1967). Attribution theory in social psychology. In D. Levine (Ed.), *Nebraska symposium on motivation* (Vol. 15, pp. 192–241). Lincoln: University of Nebraska Press.

Klem, L. (1995). Path analysis. In L. G. Grimm and P. R. Yarnold (Eds.), *Reading and understanding multivariate statistics* (pp. 65–97). Washington, DC: American Psychological Association.

Koslowski, B. (1996). *Theory and evidence: The development of scientific reasoning.* Cambridge, MA: MIT Press.

Kotovsky, L., and Baillargeon, R. (2000). Reasoning about collisions involving inert objects in 7.5-month-old infants. *Developmental Science, 3,* 344–359.

Lagnado, D. A., and Sloman, S. (2005). The advantage of timely intervention. *Journal of Experimental Psychology: Learning, Memory, and Cognition, 30*, 856–876.

Leslie, A. M. (1984). Spatiotemporal continuity and the perception of causality in infants. *Perception, 13*, 287–305.

Leslie, A. M., and Keeble, S. (1987). Do six-month-olds perceive causality? *Cognition, 25*, 265–288.

Lewis, D. (1973). Causation. *Journal of Philosophy, 70*, 556–567.

Lewis, D. (1986). Causal explanation. In *Philosophical papers* (Vol. 2, pp. 214–240). Oxford: Oxford University Press.

Loehlin, J. C. (1992). *Latent variable models: An introduction to factor, path, and structural analysis* (2nd ed.). Hillsdale, NJ: Erlbaum.

Luhmann, C. C., and Ahn, W.-K. (2005). The meaning and computation of causal power: Comment on Cheng (1997) and Novick and Cheng (2004). *Psychological Review, 112*, 685–693.

Macaulay, D. (1988). *The way things work.* Boston: Houghton Mifflin.

Markovits, H. (1984). Awareness of the "possible" as a mediator of formal thinking in conditional reasoning problems. *British Journal of Psychology, 75*, 367–376.

McCarthy, J., and Hayes, P. (1969). Some philosophical problems from the standpoint of artificial intelligence. In B. Meltzer & D. Michie (Eds.), *Machine intelligence 4* (pp. 463–502). Edinburgh: Edinburgh University Press.

McCawley, J. D. (1968). Lexical insertion in a transformational grammar without deep structure. In *Papers from the 4th regional meeting, Chicago Linguistics Society* (pp. 71–80). Chicago: Chicago Linguistics Society.

Medin, D. L., and Ortony, A. (1989). Psychological essentialism. In S. Vosniadou and A. Ortony (Eds.), *Similarity and analogical reasoning* (pp. 179–195). Cambridge: Cambridge University Press.

Michotte, A. (1963). *The perception of causality.* New York: Basic Books.

Mill, J. S. (1874). *A system of logic* (8th ed.). New York: Harper & Brothers.

Nisbett, R. L., & Ross, L. (1980). *Human inference.* Englewood Cliffs, NJ: Prentice Hall.

Novick, L. R., and Cheng, P. W. (2004). Assessing interactive causal power. *Psychological Review, 111*, 455–485.

Oakes, L. M. (1994). The development of infants' use of continuity cues in their perception of causality. *Developmental Psychology, 30*, 869–879.

Oaksford, M., & Chater, N. (2003). Conditional probability and the cognitive science of conditional reasoning. *Mind and Language, 18*, 359–379.

Parsons, T. (1990). *Events in the semantics of English: a study in subatomic semantics.* Cambridge, MA: MIT Press.

Pearl, J. (1988). *Probabilistic reasoning in intelligent systems.* San Mateo, CA: Morgan Kaufmann.

Pearl, J. (2000). *Causality.* Cambridge: Cambridge University Press.

Pelham, B. W., and Blanton, H. (2003). *Conducting research in psychology* (2nd ed). Belmont, CA: Wadsworth/Thomson.

Ramsey, F. P. (1990). General propositions and causality. In D. H. Mellor (Ed.), *Philosophical papers* (pp. 145–163). Cambridge: Cambridge University Press. (Original work published 1929.)

Rehder, B. (2006). Human deviations from normative causal reasoning. *Proceedings of the Cognitive Science Society* (p. 2596). Mahwah, NJ: Erlbaum.

Rehder, B., and Burnett, R. C. (2005). Feature inference and the causal structure of categories. *Cognitive Psychology, 50*, 264–314.

Rehder, B., and Hastie, R. (2001). Causal knowledge and categories: The effects of causal beliefs on categorization, induction, and similarity. *Journal of Experimental Psychology: General, 130*, 323–360.

Rescorla, R. A., and Wagner, A. R. (1972). A theory of Pavlovian conditioning: Variations in the effectiveness of reinforcement and nonreinforcement. In A. H. Black and W. F. Prokasy (Eds.), *Classical conditioning II: Current research and theory.* New York: Appleton-Century Crofts.

Rips, L. J. (1983). Cognitive processes in propositional reasoning. *Psychological Review, 90*, 38–71.

Rips, L. J. (1989). Similarity, typicality, and categorization. In S. Vosniadou and A. Ortony (Eds.), *Similarity and analogical reasoning* (pp. 21–59). Cambridge: Cambridge University Press.

Rips, L. J. (2001). Necessity and natural categories. *Psychological Bulletin, 127*, 827–852.

Rips, L. J., and Conrad, F. G. (1989). Folk psychology of mental activities. *Psychological Review, 96*, 187–207.

Roser, M. E., Fugelsang, J. A., Dunbar, K. A., Corballis, P. M., and Gazzaniga, M. S. (2005). Dissociating processes supporting causal perception and causal inference in the brain. *Neuropsychology, 19*, 591–602.

Rozenblit, L., and Keil, F. (2002). The misunderstood limits of folk science: An illusion of explanatory depth. *Cognitive Science, 26*, 521–562.

Rumelhart, D. E. (1975). Notes on a schema for stories. In D. G. Bobrow and A. Collins (Eds.), *Representation and understanding* (pp. 211–236). New York: Academic Press.

Saxe, R., and Carey, S. (2006). The perception of causality in infancy. *Acta Psychologica, 123*, 144–165.

Schank, R. A., and Abelson, R. P. (1977). *Scripts, plans, goals, and understanding.* Hillsdale, NJ: Erlbaum.

Schank, R. A., & Riesbeck, C. K. (1981). *Inside computer understanding.* Hillsdale, NJ: Erlbaum.

Schellenberg, E. G. (2005). Music and cognitive abilities. *Current Directions in Psychological Science, 14*, 317–320.

Schlottmann, A., and Shanks, D. (1992). Evidence for a distinction between judged and perceived causality. *Quarterly Journal of Experimental Psychology, 44A*, 321–342.

Shanks, D. R., and Dickinson, A. (1987). Associative accounts of causality judgment. *Psychology of Learning and Motivation, 21*, 229–261.

Simon, H. A. (1953). Causal ordering and identifiability. In W. C. Hood and T. C. Koopmans (Eds.), *Studies in econometric method* (pp. 49–74). New York: Wiley.

Simpson, E. H. (1951). The interpretation of interaction in contingency tables. *Journal of the Royal Statistical Society, Series B, 13*, 238–241.

Sloman, S. (2005). *Causal models: How people think about the world and its alternatives.* Oxford: Oxford University Press.

Sloman, S. A., and Lagnado, D. A. (2005). Do we "do"? *Cognitive Science, 29*, 5–39.

Smith, R. H., Hilton, D. J., Kim, S. H., and Garonzik, R. (1992). Knowledge-based causal inference: Norms and the usefulness of distinctiveness. *British Journal of Social Psychology, 31*, 239–248.

Spelke, E. S., Breinlinger, K., Macomber, J., and Jacobson, K. (1992). Origins of knowledge. *Psychological Review, 99*, 605–632.

Spellman, B. A. (1996). Conditionalizing causality. *Psychology of Learning and Motivation, 34*, 167–206.

Spirtes, P., Glymour, C., and Scheines, R. (2000). *Causation, prediction, and search* (2nd ed.). Cambridge, MA: MIT Press.

Stalnaker, R. C. (1968). A theory of conditionals. In N. Rescher (Ed.), *Studies in logical theory* (pp. 98–112). Oxford: Blackwell.

Staudenmayer, H. (1975). Understanding conditional reasoning with meaningful propositions. In R. J. Falmagne (Ed.), *Reasoning: representation and process in children and adults* (pp. 55–79). Hillsdale, NJ: Erlbaum.

Steyvers, M., Tenenbaum, J. B., Wagenmakers, E., and Blum, B. (2003). Inferring causal networks from observation and interventions. *Cognitive Science, 27*, 453–489.

Talmy, L. (1988). Force dynamics in language and cognition. *Cognitive Science, 12*, 49–100.

Tenenbaum, J. B., Griffiths, T. L., and Niyogi, S. (in press). Intuitive theories as grammars for causal inference. In A. Gopnik and L. Schulz (Eds.), *Causal learning: Psychology, philosophy, and computation.* Oxford: Oxford University Press.

Thompson, V. A. (1994). Interpretational factors in conditional reasoning. *Memory & Cognition, 22*, 742–758.

Trabasso, T., & Sperry, L. (1985). Causal relatedness and importance of story events. *Journal of Memory and Language, 24*, 595–611.

Trabasso, T., and Van den Broek, P. (1985). Causal thinking and the representation of narrative events. *Journal of Memory and Language, 24*, 612–630.

Tufte, E. (2006). *Beautiful evidence.* Cheshire, CT: Graphics Press.

Tversky, A., and Kahneman, D. (1980). Causal schemas in judgment under uncertainty. In M. Fishbein (Ed.), *Progress in social psychology* (pp. 49–72). Hillsdale, NJ: Erlbaum.

Van Fraassen, B. C. (1980). *The scientific image.* Oxford: Oxford University Press.

Waldmann, M. R. (1996). Knowledge-based causal induction. *Psychology of Learning and Motivation, 34*, 47–88.

Waldmann, M. R., and Hagmayer, Y. (2001). Estimating causal strength: The role of structural knowledge and processing effort. *Cognition, 82*, 27–58.

Waldmann, M. R., and Hagmayer, Y. (2005). Seeing versus doing: two modes of accessing causal knowledge. *Journal of Experimental Psychology: Learning, Memory, and Cognition, 31*, 216–227.

Wasserman, E. A., Kao, S. F., Van Hamme, L. J., Katagiri, M., and Young, M. E. (1996). Causation and association. *Psychology of Learning and Motivation, 34*, 207–264.

Wellman, H. M. (1990). *The child's theory of mind.* Cambridge, MA: MIT Press.

White, P. A. (2005). The power PC theory and causal powers: Comments on Cheng (1997) and Novick and Cheng (2004). *Psychological Review, 112*, 675–684.

Wolff, P., Klettke, B., Ventura, T., & Song, G. (2005). Expressing causation in English and other languages. In W.-K. Ahn, R. L. Goldstone, B. C. Love, A. B. Markman, and P. Wolff (Eds.), *Categorization inside and outside the laboratory* (pp. 29–48). Washington, DC: American Psychological Association.

Wright, S. (1960). Path coefficients and path regressions: alternative or complementary concepts. *Biometrics, 16*, 189–202.

Chapter 30: Causation

DAVID LEWIS

Hume defined causation twice over. He wrote "we may define a cause to be *an object followed by another, and where all the objects, similar to the first, are followed by objects similar to the second. Or, in other words, where, if the first object had not been, the second never had existed.*"[1]

Descendants of Hume's first definition still dominate the philosophy of causation: a causal succession is supposed to be a succession that instantiates a regularity. To be sure, there have been improvements. Nowadays we try to distinguish the regularities that count – the "causal laws" – from mere accidental regularities of succession. We subsume causes and effects under regularities by means of descriptions they satisfy, not by overall similarity. And we allow a cause to be only one indispensable part, not the whole, of the total situation that is followed by the effect in accordance with a law. In present-day regularity analyses, a cause is defined (roughly) as any member of any minimal set of actual conditions that are jointly sufficient, given the laws, for the existence of the effect.

More precisely, let C be the proposition that *c* exists (or occurs) and let E be the proposition that *e* exists. Then *c* causes *e*, according to a typical regularity analysis,[2] iff (1) C and E are true; and (2) for some nonempty set $\mathcal{L}$ of true law-propositions and some set $\mathcal{F}$ of true propositions of particular fact, $\mathcal{L}$ and $\mathcal{F}$ jointly imply $C \supset E$, although $\mathcal{L}$ and $\mathcal{F}$ jointly do not imply E and $\mathcal{F}$ alone does not imply $C \supset E$.[3]

Much needs doing, and much has been done, to turn definitions like this one into defensible analyses. Many problems have been overcome. Others remain: in particular, regularity analyses tend to confuse causation itself with various other causal relations. If *c* belongs to a minimal set of conditions jointly sufficient for *e*, given the laws, then *c* may well be a genuine cause of *e*. But *c* might rather be an effect of *e*: one which could not, given the laws and some of the actual circumstances, have occurred otherwise than by being caused by *e*. Or *c* might be an epiphenomenon of the causal history of *e*: a more or less inefficacious effect of some genuine cause of *e*. Or *c* might be a preempted potential cause of *e*: something that did not cause *e*, but that would have done so in the absence of whatever really did cause *e*.

It remains to be seen whether any regularity analysis can succeed in distinguishing genuine causes from effects, epiphenomena, and preempted potential causes – and whether it can succeed without falling victim to worse problems, without piling on the epicycles, and without departing from the fundamental idea that causation is instantiation of regularities. I have no proof that regularity analyses are beyond repair, nor any space to review the repairs that have been tried. Suffice it to say that the prospects look dark. I think it is time to give up and try something else.

A promising alternative is not far to seek. Hume's "other words" – that if the cause had not been, the effect never had existed – are no mere restatement of his first definition. They propose something altogether different: a counterfactual analysis of causation.

The proposal has not been well received. True, we do know that causation has something or other to do with counterfactuals. We think of a cause as something that makes a difference, and the difference it makes must be a difference from

Reproduced with permission from Lewis, D. (1973) Causation. *Journal of Philosophy*, 73, 556–567.

what would have happened without it. Had it been absent, its effects – some of them, at least, and usually all – would have been absent as well. Yet it is one thing to mention these platitudes now and again, and another thing to rest an analysis on them. That has not seemed worthwhile.[4] We have learned all too well that counterfactuals are ill understood, wherefore it did not seem that much understanding could be gained by using them to analyze causation or anything else. Pending a better understanding of counterfactuals, moreover, we had no way to fight seeming counterexamples to a counterfactual analysis.

But counterfactuals need not remain ill understood, I claim, unless we cling to false preconceptions about what it would be like to understand them. Must an adequate understanding make no reference to unactualized possibilities? Must it assign sharply determinate truth conditions? Must it connect counterfactuals rigidly to covering laws? Then none will be forthcoming. So much the worse for those standards of adequacy. Why not take counterfactuals at face value: as statements about possible alternatives to the actual situation, somewhat vaguely specified, in which the actual laws may or may not remain intact? There are now several such treatments of counterfactuals, differing only in details.[5] If they are right, then sound foundations have been laid for analyses that use counterfactuals.

In this chapter, I shall state a counterfactual analysis, not very different from Hume's second definition, of some sorts of causation. Then I shall try to show how this analysis works to distinguish genuine causes from effects, epiphenomena, and preempted potential causes.

My discussion will be incomplete in at least four ways. Explicit preliminary settings-aside may prevent confusion.

1. I shall confine myself to causation among *events*, in the everyday sense of the word: flashes, battles, conversations, impacts, strolls, deaths, touchdowns, falls, kisses, and the like. Not that events are the only things that can cause or be caused; but I have no full list of the others, and no good umbrella-term to cover them all.

2. My analysis is meant to apply to causation in particular cases. It is not an analysis of causal generalizations. Presumably those are quantified statements involving causation among particular events (or non-

events), but it turns out not to be easy to match up the causal generalizations of natural language with the available quantified forms. A sentence of the form "C-events cause E-events," for instance, can mean any of

(a) For some c in C and some e in E, c causes e.

(b) For every e in E, there is some c in C such that c causes e.

(c) For every c in C, there is some e in E such that c causes e, not to mention further ambiguities. Worse still, 'Only C-events cause E-events' ought to mean

(d) For every c, if there is some e in E such that c causes e, then c is in C.

if 'only' has its usual-meaning. But no; it unambiguously means (b) instead! These problems are not about causation, but about our idioms of quantification.

3. We sometimes single out one among all the causes of some event and call it "the" cause, as if there were no others. Or we single out a few as the "causes," calling the rest mere "causal factors" or "causal conditions." Or we speak of the "decisive" or "real" or "principal" cause. We may select the abnormal or extraordinary causes, or those under human control, or those we deem good or bad, or just those we want to talk about. I have nothing to say about these principles of invidious discrimination.[6] I am concerned with the prior question of what it is to be one of the causes (unselectively speaking). My analysis is meant to capture a broad and nondiscriminatory concept of causation.

4. I shall be content, for now, if I can give an analysis of causation that works properly under determinism. By determinism I do not mean any thesis of universal causation, or universal predictability-in-principle, but rather this: the prevailing laws of nature are such that there do not exist any two possible worlds which are exactly alike up to some time, which differ thereafter, and in which those laws are never violated. Perhaps by ignoring indeterminism, I squander the most striking advantage of a counterfactual analysis over a regularity analysis: that it allows undetermined events to be caused.[7] I fear, however, that my present analysis cannot yet

cope with all varieties of causation under indeterminism. The needed repair would take us too far into disputed questions about the foundations of probability.

Comparative Similarity

To begin, I take as primitive a relation of *comparative overall* similarity among possible worlds. We may say that one world is *closer to actuality* than another if the first resembles our actual world more than the second does, taking account of all the respects of similarity and difference and balancing them off one against another.

(More generally, an arbitrary world w can play the role of our actual world. In speaking of our actual world without knowing just which world is ours, I am in effect generalizing over all worlds. We really need a three-place relation: world w_1 is closer to world w than world w_2 is. I shall henceforth leave this generality tacit.)

I have not said just how to balance the respects of comparison against each other, so I have not said just what our relation of comparative similarity is to be. Not for nothing did I call it primitive. But I have said what *sort* of relation it is, and we are familiar with relations of that sort. We do make judgments of comparative overall similarity – of people, for instance – by balancing off many respects of similarity and difference. Often our mutual expectations about the weighting factors are definite and accurate enough to permit communication. I shall have more to say later about the way the balance must go in particular cases to make my analysis work. But the vagueness of overall similarity will not be entirely resolved. Nor should it be. The vagueness of similarity does infect causation, and no correct analysis can deny it.

The respects of similarity and difference that enter into the overall similarity of worlds are many and varied. In particular, similarities in matters of particular fact trade off against similarities of law. The prevailing laws of nature are important to the character of a world; so similarities of law are weighty. Weighty, but not sacred. We should not take it for granted that a world that conforms perfectly to our actual laws is *ipso facto* closer to actuality than any world where those laws are violated in any way at all. It depends on the nature and extent of the violation, on the place of the violated laws in the total system of laws of nature, and on the countervailing similarities and differences in other respects. Likewise, similarities or differences of particular fact may be more or less weighty, depending on their nature and extent. Comprehensive and exact similarities of particular fact throughout large spatiotemporal regions seem to have special weight. It may be worth a small miracle to prolong or expand a region of perfect match.

Our relation of comparative similarity should meet two formal constraints. (1) It should be a weak ordering of the worlds: an ordering in which ties are permitted, but any two worlds are comparable. (2) Our actual world should be closest to actuality; resembling itself more than any other world resembles it. We do *not* impose the further constraint that for any set A of worlds there is a unique closest A-world, or even a set of A-worlds tied for closest. Why not an infinite sequence of closer and closer A-worlds, but no closest?

Counterfactuals and Counterfactual Dependence

Given any two propositions A and C, we have their *counterfactual* $A \,\square\!\!\rightarrow C$: the proposition that if A were true, then C would also be true. The operation $\square\!\!\rightarrow$ is defined by a rule of truth, as follows. $A \,\square\!\!\rightarrow C$ is true (at a world w) iff either (1) there are no possible A-worlds (in which case $A \,\square\!\!\rightarrow C$ *is vacuous*), or (2) some A-world where C holds is closer (to w) than is any A-world where C does not hold. In other words, a counterfactual is nonvacuously true iff it takes less of a departure from actuality to make the consequent true along with the antecedent than it does to make the antecedent true without the consequent.

We did not assume that there must always be one or more closest A-worlds. But if there are, we can simplify: $A \,\square\!\!\rightarrow C$ is nonvacuously true iff C holds at all the closest A-worlds.

We have not presupposed that A is false. If A is true, then our actual world is the closest A-world, so $A \,\square\!\!\rightarrow C$ is true iff C is. Hence $A \,\square\!\!\rightarrow C$ implies the material conditional $A \supset C$; and A and C jointly imply $A \,\square\!\!\rightarrow C$.

Let A_1, A_2, ... be a family of possible propositions, no two of which are compossible; let C_1, C_2, ... be another such family (of equal size). Then if all the counterfactuals $A_1 \,\square\!\!\rightarrow C_1$, $A_2 \,\square\!\!\rightarrow C_2$, ... between corresponding propositions in the two families are true, we shall say that the *C's depend counterfactually* on the *A's*. We can say it like this in ordinary language: whether C_1 or C_2 or ... depends (counterfactually) on whether A_1 or A_2 or ....

Counterfactual dependence between large families of alternatives is characteristic of processes of measurement, perception, or control. Let R_1, R_2, ... be propositions specifying the alternative readings of a certain barometer at a certain time. Let P_1, P_2, ... specify the corresponding pressures of the surrounding air. Then, if the barometer is working properly to measure the pressure, the R's must depend counterfactually on the P's. As we say it: the reading depends on the pressure. Likewise, if I am seeing at a certain time, then my visual impressions must depend counterfactually, over a wide range of alternative possibilities, on the scene before my eyes. And if I am in control over what happens in some respect, then there must be a double counterfactual dependence, again over some fairly wide range of alternatives. The outcome depends on what I do, and that in turn depends on which outcome I want.[8]

Causal Dependence among Events

If a family C_1, C_2, ... depends counterfactually on a family A_1, A_2, ... in the sense just explained, we will ordinarily be willing to speak also of causal dependence. We say, for instance, that the barometer reading depends causally on the pressure, that my visual impressions depend causally on the scene before my eyes, or that the outcome of something under my control depends causally on what I do. But there are exceptions. Let G_1, G_2, ... be alternative possible laws of gravitation, differing in the value of some numerical constant. Let M_1, M_2, ... be suitable alternative laws of planetary motion. Then the M's may depend counterfactually on the G's, but we would not call this dependence causal. Such exceptions as this, however, do not involve any sort of dependence among distinct particular events. The hope remains that causal dependence among events, at least, may be analyzed simply as counterfactual dependence.

We have spoken thus far of counterfactual dependence among propositions, not among events. Whatever particular events may be, presumably they are not propositions. But that is no problem, since they can at least be paired with propositions. To any possible event e, there corresponds the proposition $O(e)$ that holds at all and only those worlds where e occurs. This $O(e)$ is the proposition that e occurs.[9] (If no two events occur at exactly the same worlds – if, that is, there are no absolutely necessary connections between distinct events – we may add that this correspondence of events and propositions is one to one.) Counterfactual dependence among events is simply counterfactual dependence among the corresponding propositions.

Let c_1, c_2, ... and e_1, e_2, ... be distinct possible events such that no two of the c's and no two of the e's are compossible. Then I say that the family e_1, e_2, ... of events *depends causally* on the family c_1, c_2, ... iff the family $O(e_1)$, $O(e_2)$, ... of propositions depends counterfactually on the family $O(c_1)$, $O(c_2)$, ... As we say it: whether e_1 or e_2 or ... occurs depends on whether c_1 or c_2 or ... occurs.

We can also define a relation of dependence among single events rather than families. Let c and e be two distinct possible particular events. Then e *depends causally* on c iff the family $O(e)$, $\sim O(e)$ depends counterfactually on the family $O(c)$, $\sim O(c)$. As we say it: whether e occurs or not depends on whether c occurs or not. The dependence consists in the truth of two counterfactuals: $O(c) \,\square\!\!\rightarrow O(e)$ and $\sim O(c) \,\square\!\!\rightarrow \sim O(e)$. There are two cases. If c and e do not actually occur, then the second counterfactual is automatically true because its antecedent and consequent are true: so e depends causally on c iff the first counterfactual holds. That is, iff e would have occurred if c had occurred. But if c and e are actual events, then it is the first counterfactual that is automatically true. Then e depends causally on c iff, if c had not been, e never had existed. I take Hume's second definition as my definition not of causation itself, but of causal dependence among actual events.

Causation

Causal dependence among actual events implies causation. If c and e are two actual events such that e would not have occurred without c, then c is a cause of e. But I reject the converse. Causation must always be transitive; causal dependence may not be; so there can be causation without causal dependence. Let c, d, and e be three actual events such that d would not have occurred without c and e would not have occurred without d. Then c is a cause of e even if e would still have occurred (otherwise caused) without c.

We extend causal dependence to a transitive relation in the usual way. Let c, d, e, ... be a finite sequence of actual particular events such that d depends causally on c, e on d, and so on throughout. Then this sequence is a *causal chain*. Finally, one event is a *cause* of another iff there exists a causal chain leading from the first to the second. This completes my counterfactual analysis of causation.

Counterfactual versus Nomic Dependence

It is essential to distinguish counterfactual and causal dependence from what I shall call *nomic dependence*. The family C_1, C_2, ... of propositions depends nomically on the family A_1, A_2, ... iff there are a nonempty set $\mathcal{L}$ of true law-propositions and a set $\mathcal{F}$ of true propositions of particular fact such that $\mathcal{L}$ and $\mathcal{F}$ jointly imply (but $\mathcal{F}$ alone does not imply) all the material conditionals $A_1 \supset C_1$, $A_2 \supset C_2$, ... between the corresponding propositions in the two families. (Recall that these same material conditionals are implied by the counterfactuals that would comprise a counterfactual dependence.) We shall say also that the nomic dependence holds *in virtue of* the premise sets $\mathcal{L}$ and $\mathcal{F}$.

Nomic and counterfactual dependence are related as follows. Say that a proposition B is *counterfactually independent* of the family A_1, A_2, ... of alternatives iff B would hold no matter which of the A's were true – that is, iff the counterfactuals $A_1 \,\square\!\!\rightarrow B$, $A_2 \,\square\!\!\rightarrow B$, ... all hold. If the C's depend nomically on the A's in virtue of the premise sets $\mathcal{L}$ and $\mathcal{F}$ and if in addition (all members of) $\mathcal{L}$ and $\mathcal{F}$ are counterfactually independent of the A's, then it follows that the C's depend counterfactually on the A's. In that case, we may regard the nomic dependence in virtue of $\mathcal{L}$ and $\mathcal{F}$ as explaining the counterfactual dependence. Often, perhaps always, counterfactual dependences may be thus explained. But the requirement of counterfactual independence is indispensable. Unless $\mathcal{L}$ and $\mathcal{F}$ meet that requirement, nomic dependence in virtue of $\mathcal{L}$ and $\mathcal{F}$ does not imply counterfactual dependence, and, if there is counterfactual dependence anyway, does not explain it.

Nomic dependence is reversible, in the following sense. If the family C_1, C_2, ... depends nomically on the family A_1, A_2, ... in virtue of $\mathcal{L}$ and $\mathcal{F}$, then also A_1, A_2, ... depends nomically on the family AC_1, AC_2, ..., in virtue of $\mathcal{L}$ and $\mathcal{F}$, where A is the disjunction $A_1 \vee A_2 \vee \ldots$. Is counterfactual dependence likewise reversible? That does not follow. For, even if $\mathcal{L}$ and $\mathcal{F}$ are independent of A_1, A_2, ... and hence establish the counterfactual dependence of the C's on the A's, still they may fail to be independent of AC_1, AC_2, ..., and hence may fail to establish the reverse counterfactual dependence of the A's on the AC's. Irreversible counterfactual dependence is shown below: @ is our actual world, the dots are the other worlds, and distance on the page represents similarity "distance."

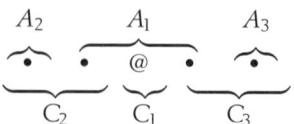

The counterfactuals $A_1 \,\square\!\!\rightarrow C_1$, $A_2 \,\square\!\!\rightarrow C_2$, and $A_3 \,\square\!\!\rightarrow C_3$ hold at the actual world; wherefore the C's depend on the A's. But we do not have the reverse dependence of the A's on the AC's, since instead of the needed $AC_2 \,\square\!\!\rightarrow A_2$ and $AC_3 \,\square\!\!\rightarrow A_3$ we have $AC_2 \,\square\!\!\rightarrow A_1$ and $AC_3 \,\square\!\!\rightarrow A_1$.

Just such irreversibility is commonplace. The barometer reading depends counterfactually on the pressure – that is as clear-cut as counterfactuals ever get – but does the pressure depend counterfactually on the reading? If the reading had been higher, would the pressure have been higher? Or would the barometer have been malfunctioning? The second sounds better: a higher reading would have been an incorrect reading. To be sure, there are actual laws and circumstances that imply and explain the actual accuracy of the barometer, but these are no more sacred than the actual laws and circumstances that imply and explain the actual pressure. Less sacred, in fact. When something must give way to permit a higher reading, we find it less of a departure from actuality to hold the pressure fixed and sacrifice the accuracy, rather than vice versa. It is not hard to see why. The barometer, being more localized and more delicate than the weather, is more vulnerable to slight departures from actuality.[10]

We can now explain why regularity analyses of causation (among events, under determinism) work as well as they do. Suppose that event c causes event e according to the sample regularity analysis that I gave at the beginning of this chapter, in virtue of premise sets $\mathcal{L}$ and $\mathcal{F}$. It follows that $\mathcal{L}$, $\mathcal{F}$, and $\sim O(c)$ jointly do not imply $O(e)$. Strengthen this: suppose further that they do imply $\sim O(e)$. If so, the family $O(e)$, $\sim O(e)$, depends nomically on the family $O(c)$, $\sim O(c)$ in virtue of $\mathcal{L}$ and $\mathcal{F}$. Add one more supposition: that $\mathcal{L}$ and $\mathcal{F}$ are counterfactually independent of $O(c)$, $\sim O(c)$. Then it follows according to my counterfactual analysis that e depends counterfactually and causally on c, and hence that c causes e. If I am right, the regularity analysis gives conditions that are almost but not quite sufficient for explicable causal dependence. That is not quite the same thing as causation; but causation without causal dependence is scarce, and if there is inexplicable causal dependence we are (understandably!) unaware of it.[11]

Effects and Epiphenomena

I return now to the problems I raised against regularity analyses, hoping to show that my counterfactual analysis can overcome them.

The *problem of effects*, as it confronts a counterfactual analysis, is as follows. Suppose that c causes a subsequent event e, and that e does not also cause c. (I do not rule out closed causal loops a priori, but this case is not to be one.) Suppose further that, given the laws and some of the actual circumstances, c could not have failed to cause e. It seems to follow that if the effect e had not occurred, then its cause c would not have occurred. We have a spurious reverse causal dependence of c on e, contradicting our supposition that e did not cause c.

The *problem of epiphenomena*, for a counterfactual analysis, is similar. Suppose that e is an epiphenomenal effect of a genuine cause c of an effect f. That is, c causes first e and then f, but e does not cause f. Suppose further that, given the laws and some of the actual circumstances, c could not have failed to cause e; and that, given the laws and others of the circumstances, f could not have been caused otherwise than by c. It seems to follow that if the epiphenomenon e had not occurred, then its cause c would not have occurred and the further effect f of that same cause would not have occurred either. We have a spurious causal dependence of f on e, contradicting our supposition that e did not cause f.

One might be tempted to solve the problem of effects by brute force: insert into the analysis a stipulation that a cause must always precede its effect (and perhaps a parallel stipulation for causal dependence). I reject this solution. (1) It is worthless against the closely related problem of epiphenomena, since the epiphenomenon e does precede its spurious effect f. (2) It rejects a priori certain legitimate physical hypotheses that posit backward or simultaneous causation. (3) It trivializes any theory that seeks to define the forward direction of time as the predominant direction of causation.

The proper solution to both problems, I think, is flatly to deny the counterfactuals that cause the trouble. If e had been absent, it is not that c would have been absent (and with it f, in the second case). Rather, c would have occurred just as it did but would have failed to cause e. It is less of a departure from actuality to get rid of e by holding c fixed and giving up some or other of the laws and circumstances in virtue of which c could not have failed to cause e, rather than to hold those laws and circumstances fixed and get rid of e by going back and abolishing its cause c. (In the second case, it would of course be pointless not to hold f fixed along with c.) The causal dependence of e on c is the same sort of irreversible counterfactual dependence that we have considered already.

To get rid of an actual event e with the least overall departure from actuality, it will normally be best not to diverge at all from the actual course of events until just before the time of e. The longer we wait, the more we prolong the spatiotemporal region of perfect match between our actual world and the selected alternative. Why diverge sooner rather than later? Not to avoid violations of laws of nature. Under determinism *any* divergence, soon or late, requires some violation of the actual laws. If the laws were held sacred, there would be no way to get rid of e without changing all of the past; and nothing guarantees that the change could be kept negligible except in the recent past. That would mean that if the present were ever so slightly different, then all of the past would have been different – which is absurd. So the laws are not sacred. Violation of laws is a matter of degree. Until we get up to the time immediately before e is to occur, there is no general reason why a later divergence to avert e should need a more severe violation than an earlier one. Perhaps there are special reasons in special cases – but then these may be cases of backward causal dependence.

Preemption

Suppose that c_1 occurs and causes e; and that c_2 also occurs and does not cause e, but would have caused e if c_1 had been absent. Thus c_2 is a potential alternate cause of e, but is preempted by the actual cause c_1. We may say that c_1 and c_2 overdetermine e, but they do so asymmetrically.[12] In virtue of what difference does c_1 but not c_2 cause e?

As far as causal dependence goes, there is no difference: e depends neither on c_1 nor on c_2. If either one had not occurred, the other would have sufficed to cause e. So the difference must be that, thanks to c_1, there is no causal chain from c_2 to e; whereas there is a causal chain of two or more steps from c_1 to e. Assume for simplicity that two steps are enough. Then e depends causally on some intermediate event d, and d in turn depends on c_1. Causal dependence is here intransitive: c_1 causes e via d even though e would still have occurred without c_1.

So far, so good. It remains only to deal with the objection that e does *not* depend causally on d, because if d had been absent then c_1 would have been absent and c_2, no longer preempted, would have caused e. We may reply by denying the claim that if d had been absent then c_1 would have been absent. That is the very same sort of spurious reverse dependence of cause on effect that we have just rejected in simpler cases. I rather claim that if d had been absent, c_1 would somehow have failed to cause d. But c_1 would still have been there to interfere with c_2, so e would not have occurred.

Notes

1 *An Enquiry concerning Human Understanding*, Section VII.
2 Not one that has been proposed by any actual author in just this form, so far as I know.
3 I identify a *proposition*, as is becoming usual, with the set of possible worlds where it is true. It is not a linguistic entity. Truth-functional operations on propositions are the appropriate Boolean operations on sets of worlds; logical relations among propositions are relations of inclusion, overlap, etc. among sets. A sentence of a language *expresses* a proposition iff the sentence and the proposition are true at exactly the same worlds. No ordinary language will provide sentences to express all propositions; there will not be enough sentences to go around.
4 One exception: Aardon Lyon, "Causality," *British Journal for Philosophy of Science*, XVIII, 1 (May 1967): 1–20.
5 See, for instance, Robert Stalnaker, "A Theory of Conditionals," in Nicholas Rescher, ed., *Studies in Logical Theory* (Oxford: Blackwell, 1968); and my *Counterfactuals* (Oxford: Blackwell, 1973).
6 Except that Morton G. White's discussion of causal selection, in *Foundations of Historical Knowledge* (New York: Harper & Row, 1965), pp. 105–181, would meet my needs, despite the fact that it is based on a regularity analysis.
7 That this ought to be allowed is argued in G. E. M. Anscombe, *Causality and Determination: An Inaugural Lecture* (Cambridge: University Press, 1971); and in Fred Dretske and Aaron Snyder, "Causal Irregularity," *Philosophy of Science*, XXXIX, 1 (March 1972): 69–71.
8 Analyses in terms of counterfactual dependence are found in two papers of Alvin I. Goldman: "Toward a Theory of Social Power," *Philosophical Studies*, XXIII (1972): 221–268; and "Discrimination and Perceptual Knowledge," presented at the 1972 Chapel Hill Colloquium.
9 Beware: if we refer to a particular event e by means of some description that e satisfies, then we must take care not to confuse $O(e)$, the proposition that e itself occurs, with the different proposition that some event or other occurs which satisfies the description. It is a contingent matter, in general, what events satisfy what descriptions. Let e be the death of Socrates – the death he actually died, to be distinguished from all the different deaths he might have died instead. Suppose that Socrates had fled, only to be eaten by a lion. Then e would not have occurred, and $O(e)$ would have been false; but a different event would have satisfied the description 'the death of Socrates' that I used to refer to e. Or suppose that Socrates had lived and died just as he actually did, and afterward was resurrected and killed again and resurrected again, and finally became immortal. Then no event would have satisfied the description. (Even if the temporary deaths are real deaths, neither of the two can be *the* death.) But e would have occurred, and $O(e)$ would have been true. Call a description of an event e rigid iff (1) nothing but e could possibly satisfy it, and (2) e could not possibly occur without satisfy it. I have claimed that even such commonplace descriptions as 'the death of Socrates' are nonrigid, and in fact I think that rigid descriptions of events are hard to find. That would be a problem for anyone who needed to associate with every possible event e a sentence $\phi(e)$ true at all and only those worlds where e occurs. But we need no such sentences – only propositions, which may or may not have expressions in our language.
10 Granted, there are contexts or changes of wording that would incline us the other way. For some reason, "If the reading had been higher, that would have been because the pressure was higher" invites my assent more than "If the reading had been higher, the pressure would have been higher." The counterfactuals from readings to pressures are much less clear-cut than those from pressures to readings. But it is enough that some legitimate resolutions of vagueness give an irreversible dependence of readings on pressures. Those are the resolutions we want at present, even if they are not favored in all contexts.
11 I am not here proposing a repaired regularity analysis. The repaired analysis would gratuitously rule out inexplicable causal dependence, which seems bad. Nor would it be squarely in the tradition of regularity analyses any more. Too much else would have been added.
12 I shall not discuss symmetrical cases of overdetermination, in which two overdetermining factors have equal claim to count as causes. For me these are useless as test cases because I lack firm naive opinions about them.

Chapter 31: Propensities and Counterfactuals: The Loser That Almost Won

DANIEL KAHNEMAN AND CAROL A. VAREY

The question of how people think of things that could have happened but did not has attracted increasing interest among psychologists in recent years (J. T. Johnson, 1986; Kahneman & Miller, 1986; Kahneman & Tversky, 1982a; Landman, 1987; D. T. Miller, Turnbull, & MacFarland, 1990; Wells & Gavanski, 1989; Wells, Taylor, & Turtle, 1987). As philosophers have long known, the study of counterfactuals cannot be separated from a conception of causality, and an understanding of causality requires a conception of possibility and conditional probability. Counterfactual assertions rest on causal beliefs, and causal attributions invoke counterfactual beliefs, for example, about what would have happened in the absence of a putative cause. Some counterfactual assertions assign degrees of probability or plausibility to unrealized outcomes, many causal beliefs are probabilistic, and judgments of probability often draw on impressions of causal tendencies or propensities. The present article is concerned with a psychological analysis of this nexus of issues.

Our study began with an attempt to understand the psychology of assertions of the form "X almost happened," which we call *close counterfactuals*. An important characteristic of such assertions is that they are not expressed as a conditional with a specified antecedent, as counterfactual conditionals are. The close counterfactual does not invoke an alternative possible world, but states a fact about the history of this world – namely, that things were close to turning out differently than they did.

Our approach combines some elementary phenomenological observations and an equally elementary linguistic inquiry into the conditions under which close counterfactual assertions are appropriate. The genre is not unknown in psychology: Heider (1958) and Schank and Abelson (1977), in particular, have successfully carried out ambitious exercises in this vein. Studies of what people mean when they say that "John went to the restaurant" or when they use the words *can* and *try* have contributed significantly to an understanding of how people think about events and actions. In this article, we examine the use of the word *almost* in a speculative attempt to explore how people think about counterfactuals, probability, and causation.[1] The present analysis is restricted to cases in which "X almost happened" implies that X could have happened. We ignore figurative uses of *almost* in which it is used to denote "coming close" without implication of possibility, as in "at that bend the train almost touches the embankment." We also restrict our discussion of *almost* to cases in which either the actual outcome or the close counterfactual is an achievement (see Lyons, 1977; G. A. Miller & Johnson-Laird, 1976; Vendler, 1967) – a change of state that occurs at a particular moment, usually as the culmination of a longer causal episode. We analyze the beliefs that a speaker expresses by the assertion that an individual almost died, or almost missed a deadline, and examine what such beliefs imply to us about the cognitive representation of uncertain events and of causal propensities.

Reproduced with permission from Kahneman, D., and Varey, C. A. (1990) Propensities and counterfactuals: The loser that almost won. *Journal of Personality and Social Psychology*, 59, 1101–1110.

This article develops the following ideas: (a) Counterfactuals, causes, and (some) probabilities are treated as facts about the world, not as constructions of the mind. (b) The absence of perfect hindsight indicates that people attribute inherent uncertainty to causal systems – what happened is not treated as necessary or inevitable. (c) The perception and representation of causal episodes is organized around possible outcomes of the episode. (d) Probabilities of outcomes can be assessed on the basis of advance knowledge (dispositions) or of cues gained from the causal episode itself (propensities). The distinction is critical to the use of *almost*, which requires the attribution of a strong propensity to the counterfactual outcome. (e) Cues to propensity are the temporal or causal proximity of the focal outcome and indications of rapid progress through a causal script. (f) A general schema of causal forces competing over time is applicable to many achievement contexts. (g) There are characteristic differences between a psychological and a philosophical approach to the analysis of probability, causality, and counterfactuals.

The Counterfactual Stance

The statement "X almost happened" implies several ancillary beliefs. It commits the speaker to the belief that another observer with the same information would agree with the counterfactual assertion, as would be the case with public, objective facts. The close counterfactual also implies that X could have happened, denying the necessity or inevitability of what actually happened and implicitly denying the deterministic character of the situation. We examine these beliefs in the following sections.

Objective Reference

By definition, counterfactual statements refer to events that did not, in fact, occur. However, there is a compelling intuition that some counterfactuals are treated as having an objective character, not as mere mental constructions. Refuting the possible-worlds analysis of counterfactuals, Goodman (1983) put the point strongly: "We have come to think of the actual as one among many possible worlds. We need to repaint that picture. All possible worlds lie within the actual one" (p. 57). In ascribing objective status to counterfactuals, we intend to contrast the attitude toward these objects of thought from the attitude toward imaginings, fantasies, and desires, which are normally tagged as subjec-

tive (M. K. Johnson, 1988). The discrimination of what actually happened from what almost did is, of course, essential in the monitoring of reality – the counterfactual event is not perceived as real, but it is not treated as subjective. The "fact" is that the outcome truly is close, or is not close, independently of anyone's beliefs.

The distinction between beliefs that have objective or subjective status recalls an earlier discussion of alternative cognitive representations of probability (Kahneman & Tversky, 1982b). Two main interpretations of that notion were identified, which respectively assign it subjective or objective status. In the subjective interpretation, which is standard in Bayesian philosophy, a probability judgment describes the subject's degree of belief in a proposition. "The probability that the Nile is longer than the Amazon is p" is usually understood as describing the speaker's beliefs, not as a fact about these rivers. The attribution of subjective status to a belief is often marked by the possessive pronoun: "My probability that the Nile is longer than the Amazon..." is more natural than "the probability that the Nile...." In contrast, the probability that a thumbtack will land on its point if tossed and the probability that Team A will defeat Team B are normally understood as descriptions of the causal dispositions of the thumbtack or of the competing teams. A speaker who wishes to indicate a subjective interpretation of probability will use the possessive pronoun: "My probability that Team A will win is..." acknowledges the possibility of valid alternatives, a stance that is not usually adopted in factual statements.

The two types of representation of uncertainty are most clearly distinguished when the uncertainty is removed. The possessive pronoun is then obligatory if the probability has subjective status. "The probability that the Nile is longer than the Amazon was..." is simply anomalous. In contrast, it is reasonable to maintain that the probability that the thumbtack would land on its point was .55 even when it is known that it did not do so on a particular instance. More interestingly, the statement that "the probability that Team A would win was high..." is acceptable even if that team is known to have lost. The statement of past probability need not refer to anyone's beliefs at the time of the episode. The statement could be made, for example, by a speaker who learned, after the game had ended, that a player of Team B had undertaken to throw the game if he had an opportunity to do so. As this example illustrates, current knowledge of the relevant causal factors may allow a speaker to say retrospectively that an event that did not take place had high probability – and as a special and rather extreme case to assert that the event almost occurred.

Although in this article we often appeal to the reader's intuitions in the expectation that they match ours, we also tested some of our conclusions by collecting judgments of appropriateness from native speakers of English. Subjects were recruited on the Berkeley campus by a poster offering students a small payment in return for a completed questionnaire. Respondents were given instructions and several questions as illustrated by the examples below.

In the following questions you are asked to rate statements on a scale from "appropriate" to "very peculiar." One or more statements are presented for each question. You are to rate whether the statement in italics is appropriate, given the information in the rest of the question.

1. *Tom almost died* but in fact he was never in real danger.

    Appropriate   Somewhat   Very
    7%   peculiar 27% peculiar 66%
                                 $(n = 29)^2$

2. *Everyone thought Phil almost died* but in fact he was never in real danger.

    Appropriate 69%   Very peculiar 10%
                       $(n = 29)$

3. The autopsy showed that when he was a child, Sid had suffered from a rare childhood disease. The pathologist said that if the disease had lasted a few days longer, it would have killed him. No one knew about it at the time; they thought he had a mild case of measles. *Sid almost died as a child from that rare disease.*

    Appropriate 61%   Very peculiar 0%
                       $(n = 18)$

These examples illustrate that the close counterfactual has the status of a historical fact. As is generally true when such facts are asserted, everything known to the speaker at the time of the utterance can be relevant, but the beliefs of observers of the actual event are not. As shown by Example 2, the objective status of close counterfactuals allows them to be believed erroneously. Indeed, counterfactuals can be faked. Professional wrestlers on television have perfected the art of appearing almost to kill one another, but they avoided regulation by

demonstrating that their occupation is actually quite safe.

Like counterfactuals and (some) probabilities, causal attributions are also treated as objective facts about the world. This is true of causality directly observed, as in the perception of a collision and in Michotte's (1946) demonstrations of launching. It is also true of the more abstract causes that are judged to raise the (objective) probabilities of events or, in some contexts, render them inevitable (Mackie, 1974). The counterfactual assertion that an effect would not have occurred in the absence of the cause, the sine qua non condition of necessity, has the same objective character.

Inherent Uncertainty

The frequent mentions of counterfactual possibilities in everyday discourse demonstrate a prevailing intuition that things could have been different, and in some cases almost were. This intuition commits the speaker to a particular set of beliefs about causality. Specifically, X is neither necessary nor inevitable if it can properly be said that Y almost happened instead of it. Naive intuitions are evidently not dominated by a pervasive belief in strict determinism. Kvart (1986) reached a similar conclusion in his discussion of counterfactual conditionals.

There is an intriguing tension between the intuition that things could have been otherwise and the well-known hindsight effect, in which the inevitability of events that actually took place tends to be exaggerated. The evidence is compelling that retrospective assessments of the probability of events are affected by knowledge of whether or not these events have taken place (Fischhoff, 1975, 1982). The term *creeping determinism* has been used in this context. Two distinct forms of hindsight effects are associated, respectively, with subjective and objective interpretations of probability. The most common test of hindsight effects requires the retrieval of a past state of belief: "What was your probability at the end of 1988 that the Berlin Wall would be opened within a year?" A hindsight bias is revealed in such questions by a tendency to exaggerate the past subjective probabilities of whatever is now known to be true. An example of an objective hindsight question could be "In the light of current knowledge, what was the probability in 1988 that the Berlin Wall would be opened within a year?" A discrepancy between prospective and retrospective probabilities is typically observed in tests of objective as well as subjective hindsight (Fischhoff, 1975).

Unlike the subjective case, hindsight with an objective interpretation of probability is not necessarily a mistake. It is entirely reasonable for an observer to make inferences about a causal system from the knowledge that it produced a particular outcome. Indeed, what is most puzzling in this context is the limited extent of creeping determinism in retrospective evaluations of outcomes.

Of course, not all causal systems are uncertain. As illustrated by most people's attitudes toward the mechanical and electronic devices that surround them, a belief in strict determinism does not require much understanding of how the system works; it cannot be ignorance about the causal system that precludes determinism about close counterfactuals. It is an important fact about causal reasoning that a sense of the necessity of consequences is often absent. In particular, there is no sense of necessity or inevitability in considering games of chance, many contests and competitions, some physical systems (e.g., weather and chance devices), or intentional actions.

The Representation of Causal Episodes

The idea that perceived goals serve to organize the representation of action and imbue events with meaning was articulated by Heider (1958), and is at the core of the more recent treatments of scripts and story grammars (Black & Bower, 1979; Kintsch & van Dijk, 1978; Rumelhart, 1977; Schank, 1975; Trabasso, Secco, & van den Broek, 1984) and treatments of decision making and causal reasoning that rely on a story-based account (Pennington & Hastie, 1988; Read, 1987). Our conception of causal episodes generalizes this idea to achievements. The class of achievements contains the outcomes of intentional action but is much richer: Dying from a disease, a river overflowing its bank, and the Dow–Jones index rising 1,000 points in a year are all achievements. Many achievements are associated with particular causal scripts. The representation of an episode as an instantiation of a causal script is therefore organized in terms of its possible *focal outcomes*, and attention to different achievements will alter the representation. The storm that could fill the reservoirs could also ruin the cherry crop, and its representation will be different if attention is directed to one of these outcomes rather than the other.

To illustrate the function of focal outcomes, we introduce a thought experiment to which we shall repeatedly return. Imagine observing a sequence of red and blue balls as they are drawn from an urn, or the representation of such a process on a computer screen. Note the potent effects of an intention to watch for a particular outcome, such as the color that is most frequent after eleven draws, or an excess of four red balls or six blue balls – whichever happens first. Although these focal outcomes are not goals, they serve the same function in organizing the impression of the sequence. Most important, watching the same sequence with different outcomes in mind alters the experience. Although our thought experiment involves real-time observation and uncertainty, neither of these elements is essential: A designated outcome will affect the interpretation of a story, and the effect is not reduced when thinking of an episode whose outcome is already known.

The probability of the focal outcome may fluctuate in the course of a causal episode. Changes of probability are always involved in close counterfactuals: Perhaps the most compelling intuition about the statement "X almost happened" is that the probability of X must have been quite high at some point before it dropped – all the way to zero if another outcome eventually terminated the episode.[3]

There are several reasons for probability changing in the course of an episode. We turn again to the urn example to illustrate two types of probability change. If there was initial uncertainty about the composition of the urn, beliefs about the urn will change to accommodate observed events – by Bayes's rule for an ideal observer – and the probability of the focal outcome will change accordingly. In addition, the actual probability of the focal outcome also changes *because* of the intervening events. Every red ball drawn makes it more probable that the aggregate outcome will be an excess of red over blue balls. The probability of the focal outcomes will change, more or less regularly and perhaps with large fluctuations, until a decisive event brings about an outcome that terminates the episode. Note that this situation can support a close counterfactual: It is easy to imagine a sequence of draws of which it can appropriately be said that the focal outcome almost occurred (red almost won), or almost did not.

The same types of changes of probability will also be found in observing (or hearing about) a storm that could cause a flood or a couple deciding on a joint future. The events that constitute the episode reveal the strength of an underlying causal process, and also contribute to bring about or retard the outcome. They also indicate possible changes in the causal system – changes that could be modeled by an urn whose composition is modified after each draw, perhaps in response to the draw.

Propensities and Dispositions

The discussion so far has been in terms of "objective" probabilities – in the chance example these are probabilities that could be computed precisely, given some initial beliefs about the composition of the urn. It is evident from this example that an account of *almost* in terms of probability has some appeal: The probability of the counterfactual outcome must have been high at some point. It turns out, however, that an account that relies exclusively on objective probabilities will not work. Some aspects of the puzzle to be solved are illustrated by the following examples:

4. Mark tried to register for the chess tournament. Because of a problem in mailing the form he missed the registration deadline by one day. Mark is a much stronger player than all the participants in the tournament. *Mark almost won the tournament.*

   Appropriate 0%   Very peculiar 97%
   ($n = 33$)

5. At the end of a long game of chance, John could have won the whole pot if a die that he rolled showed a six. The die that he rolled was loaded to show six 80% of the time. John rolled it and it showed a two. *The die almost showed six.*

   Appropriate 0%   Very peculiar 77%
   ($n = 31$)

6. At the end of a long game of chance, John could have won the whole pot if a die that he rolled showed a six. The die that he rolled was loaded to show six 80% of the time. John rolled it and it showed a two. *John almost won the whole pot.*

   Appropriate 43%   Very peculiar 20%
   ($n = 31$)

The close counterfactual is decisively rejected in Examples 4 and 5 but not in Example 6, although the prior probability of the focal outcome was high in all cases. Before it was rolled, the probability of the die showing six was .80

in Examples 5 and 6, and the prior probability of Mark winning the tournament was also high, though unspecified. Despite this, the intuition that *almost* is inappropriate in the first two examples is so strong that they seem almost absurd. A strong belief in the counterfactual conditional "Mark would have won if he had played" is not sufficient to support the close counterfactual "Mark almost won," even if it is also accepted that he almost played in the tournament. Why is this the case? And what else is required for the close counterfactual to be appropriate?

The answer to the first question is that the close counterfactual is never appropriate if it is only supported by indications of likelihood or causal force that were available before the onset of the relevant causal episode. Achievements, such as winning a tournament, getting married, or a die showing six, are associated with causal scripts that usually have a definite starting point: when play begins, when the couple start dating, when the die is rolled. Probabilities can be assigned to possible outcomes of a causal process before it is initiated: Mark may be a rated player, the couple could appear severely mismatched, the die could be loaded. We shall refer to the cognitive representation of such prior probabilities as the (perceived) *disposition* of a causal system to yield particular outcomes. Examples 4 and 5 show that dispositions, however strong, do not suffice to support the assertion of a close counterfactual.

A close counterfactual must be supported by the evidence of event cues, as these accumulate in the course of the causal episode. We use the term *propensity* for what is learned about the probability of an outcome from observing event cues or from hearing about them. Mark had a disposition to win his chess tournament and probably would have won it if he had registered, but the causal episode for his victory never began, and there was therefore no opportunity to establish a propensity for that outcome. The standard example of propensity in a chance event is the cinematic cliché of the roulette wheel that slows down as it approaches a critical number, slows down even more, leans against the spring, then finally trips it and stops on a neighboring number. To be described as almost showing six, a die must display a propensity to stop its roll in that position.

The contrasting responses to Examples 5 and 6 illustrate the need to distinguish propensity from probability. We suppose that our respondents would have assigned a probability of .8 both to the die showing six and to John winning the whole pot. However, the propensities of the two outcomes clearly differ. Example 6 illustrates a common structure in which one achievement (the die showing six) is nested inside another (John winning the pot). Because the focal outcome of winning the pot invokes a more inclusive causal episode that had begun long before the critical play, John can be said to have had a propensity to win, even if it is not established that the die had a propensity to show six. Thus, although the two statements have the same probability before the throw, the differential effects of propensity and disposition allow "John almost won" to be appropriate although "the die almost showed six" is not.

We should now review the rather subtle relations among the concepts of disposition, propensity, and probability, as they are used in this article. Disposition has been defined as the cognitive representation of the probability of a focal outcome, before the beginning of the relevant causal episode. A disposition can be assessed either prospectively or in hindsight, depending on whether or not the outcome is known. Disposition is a psychological construct, not a logical or mathematical one, and in view of what is known about intuitive judgment there is little reason to expect dispositions to obey the standard axioms of probability (Kahneman, Slovic, & Tversky, 1982). Dispositions represent knowledge about the particular causal system that will (or will not) produce the focal outcome of current concern. Dispositions are inferred from the base rates of outcomes previously produced by that system (Mark has won most of his tournaments) or from structural knowledge that supports causal inferences (the die was loaded in a particular fashion). Thus, the concept of disposition has causal as well as statistical implications.

Our concept of propensity is even more imbued with causal content. Event cues reveal the causal system in action. They indicate advance toward the focal outcome, or regression away from it. They suggest changes in the momentary state of the causal system – changes that may be real or illusory, as when a player is seen to have a "hot hand" (Gilovich, Vallone, & Tversky, 1985). Perhaps most important, propensities depend on the proximity of the outcome, on the possibility of quickly achieving a decisive advance to it. In sharp contrast to probability, the propensities for all competing outcomes of a process may be low early in a causal episode, and more than one propensity can be high at once when the end is close. These ideas are elaborated in subsequent sections.

Our main interest in the remainder of this article is to use close counterfactuals to learn about propensity. We consider propensity to be a dimension of the experience and cognitive representation of events, just as pitch is a dimension of auditory experience. There should be no presuppositions about the determinants of propensity; in particular, propensity could reflect causality as well as probability, just as pitch depends on both the frequency and the intensity of sound. To anchor this speculative analysis in observables, we assume that the appropriateness of *almost*, in its literal meaning, provides a usable indication of high propensity.

Disposition Neglect

Dispositions and propensities are differentially susceptible to revision in hindsight. Consider two cases in which the observer of the last lap of a footrace might assign a high probability of victory to a particular runner: (a) a runner who is in contention and is known to have a strong finish, or (b) a runner who has been catching up rapidly with the leader. The real-time expectations are equally strong in both cases, we assume, but they are based on different cues – dispositional knowledge in (a) and event cues in (b). Now imagine that the two runners both fail to win, by the same amount: The first did not show a strong finish and the second never quite caught up. Note that it will not do to say of the runner who usually has a strong finish that he or she almost won the race with a strong finish, if in fact he or she showed no evidence of talent on that particular occasion. The close counterfactual that the loser almost won is more applicable to (a) than to (b), although a counterfactual conditional could be appropriate in (a). The general hypothesis is that dispositional expectations that are not confirmed by event cues become irrelevant in hindsight.

The differential weighting of event cues and dispositional expectations in retrospective judgments will be called *disposition neglect*; the effect bears an intriguing resemblance to the relative neglect of base-rate information that has been observed in some prospective judgments. For example, the judged probability that a short personality sketch describes a lawyer rather than an engineer is not much affected by the proportion of engineers and lawyers in the sample from which it was drawn. The information about the individual case largely supersedes the information about the base rate instead of combining with it according to Bayes's rule (Kahneman &

Tversky, 1973). Similarly, Ajzen (1977) found that people predicting exam success for a student based their predictions on a descriptive sketch and gave little weight to the information that the student was drawn at random from a set selected by a researcher to include 75% failures. As Ajzen observed, however, the neglected base rate in these examples is merely statistical. There is no causal connection between the composition of the student sample and the factors that would make a particular student succeed or fail. The situation changes when such a causal connection is provided: The information that 75% of students taking the test failed it leads readily to the inference that the test was a difficult one, and the information has much more impact on the judgment of the probable success of an individual (Ajzen, 1977). There have been other demonstrations of the general principle that causally relevant base-rate information will not be neglected (Gigerenzer, Hell, & Blank, 1988; Tversky & Kahneman, 1980, 1982; see also Bar-Hillel, 1990, for a discussion of these issues).

Ajzen's (1977) experiment demonstrated that dispositional information tends to dominate statistical base rates, and that dispositional information from two sources (the difficulty of the exam and the student's ability) tends to be integrated. A variation of this experiment would demonstrate disposition neglect: Evidence that a student is extremely able does not support the inference that the student almost passed an exam that he failed, nor does the knowledge that a test was very hard support the conclusion that a student who passed almost failed it. In assessing close counterfactuals, event cues dominate causal base rates and other dispositional information.

The neglect of statistical base rates leads to violations of Bayes's rule in prospective judgments. The neglect of dispositional expectations in hindsight is not necessarily an error, but the psychology of the two effects may well reflect a single general principle. In both cases, the data that bear most directly on the causal forces at work in the individual case have the greatest impact.

Correlates of Propensity

In this section, we develop the concept of propensity by examining two of its close correlates: shrinking distance and increasing impact. The role of distance and motion in the close counterfactual is evident in the near syn-onymy of "X almost happened," "X nearly happened," and "X was close to happening." These expressions invoke a rich metaphor in which an extended causal process is represented as movement in space (e.g., see the "source–path–goal" kinesthetic image schema analyzed in Lakoff, 1987; the various "journey" metaphors in Lakoff & Johnson, 1980; and the force and space images in Talmy, 1981, 1983). This metaphor imposes a metric of causal distance between situations and suggests the closest approach to an outcome as a measure of its propensity. The second correlate of increasing propensity is an escalation in the apparent causal significance of events as the outcome is approached.

Causal Proximity

The present analysis has emphasized causal processes that extend over time, but close counterfactuals can be asserted on the basis of a measure of proximity or similarity even when the process is instantaneous. For example, the statement "The house was almost struck by lightning" is appropriate when lightning struck nearby. The actual outcome is the only event cue in such cases, and it induces a gradient of propensity in its spatial and temporal vicinity. From the fact that lightning struck in a particular place at a particular time, a propensity is inferred to strike in neighboring places, and at about the same time. Similarly, it is appropriate to say that Tom almost got six sixes in rolling dice if he got five sixes and a two. Indeed, it would be even more appropriate to say that Tom almost got six sixes if he rolled five sixes and a five.

Scripts for achievements often specify a series of landmarks that provide a provisional metric of proximity to the outcome. Getting a wedding license, for example, is one of the last landmarks in the script for marriage. It will usually be appropriate to say of a couple that came that far but did not marry that they almost got married. However, although high propensity for an outcome can be inferred from the near completion of the script for that outcome, such inferences are tentative and dependent on default assumptions about the causal system. Thus, it is not correct to say of a tethered mountain climber who falls that he or she "almost fell to the bottom of the cliff," or even was close to doing so, although the script for a fall to the bottom was almost completely satisfied. Nor will it be correct to say that Tom almost rolled six sixes if one of the dice has been altered to make that outcome impossible. The propensity for a counterfactual outcome cannot be reduced to a superficial assessment of the similarity of the actual episode to the completed script for that outcome.

Intentions can contribute to an impression of propensity. For example, it is more appropriate to say that the escaping murderer was almost killed by a shot that went six inches above his or her head if the shot was intended to kill than if it was intended to warn. Intentions do not suffice, however, when there are significant obstacles to be overcome. For an individual to "consider doing X" is sometimes sufficient to support the inference that the individual "almost did X," but not always. Selected examples follow:

7. Martin considered getting married to Meg. *Martin almost married Meg.*

    Appropriate 14%   Very peculiar 34%
    ($n = 29$)

8. Neil considered not getting married to Amanda. *Neil almost didn't marry Amanda.*

    Appropriate 62%   Very peculiar 19%
    ($n = 32$)

9. Fred considered stealing his child's savings. *Fred almost stole his child's savings.*

    Appropriate 30%   Very peculiar 15%
    ($n = 75$)

10. Ned considered breaking into a bank vault. *Ned almost broke into a bank vault.*

    Appropriate 18%   Very peculiar 44%
    ($n = 75$)

Mere consideration of a marriage is not sufficient (at least in this culture) to support the assertion that the marriage almost took place. The situation is somewhat different in Example 8, because either party (again in this culture) has the power single-handedly to put a stop to plans to marry. Responses to Examples 9 and 10 show that subjects are sensitive to the fact that much more remains to be done, beyond mere consideration, for the project of breaking into a bank vault than for stealing one's child's savings.

Decisiveness

Many outcomes are produced by a conjunction of events, all contributing to making the outcome necessary. It is useful to distinguish two privileged roles of events in multiple causation: *Critical events* are those that initiate a causal episode, potentiate subsequent causal events, or both; *decisive events* are those that rule out all alternatives, and ensure (or almost ensure) a particular outcome. The special role of critical events that initiate coherent causal episodes has been confirmed in studies of blame (J. T. Johnson, Ogawa, Delforge, & Early, 1989) and studies or mental simulations that "undo" outcomes (Wells et al., 1987). The person who starts a quarrel will get much of the blame for its consequences. However, the decisive and irreversible events that terminate causal episodes are also important, especially when the events in the causal sequence are not themselves causally related (D. T. Miller & Gunasegaram, 1990). Hart and Honore (1959) proposed that a cause is found by "tracing back" from the effect to the nearest plausible candidate in the causal chain. They also discussed the legal doctrine of the last clear chance: The last person who had a good chance to avoid harm is alone held responsible (see also Wells & Gavanski, 1989). The responsible individual is the one whose actions cannot be reversed by anyone else. The same intuition shows up in the context of blackjack; many players believe that the player on the seventh box, who receives cards immediately prior to the dealer's draw that all players are trying to beat, determines the outcomes for all players (Keren & Wagenaar, 1985). By the time the cards are dealt, the sequence of cards is fixed, though unknown, and the seventh player, by refusal or acceptance of a card, decisively determines its allocation.

It is instructive to analyze decisiveness in terms of probability. Consider an urn game that ends whenever the excess of balls of one color reaches a critical value. Suppose the prior probability of red being the "winning" color is high, because there are more red than blue balls in the urn. Now imagine another scenario, which involves a balanced urn and a majority of red balls in early draws. When the objective probabilities of a red victory are matched in these two scenarios, the probabilities of two more specific events will be higher in the case favored by event cues: (a) the probability of the outcome occurring *soon*, and (b) the probability that the current lead will be preserved until the end of the game. We suggest that impressions of propensity are related to the probability of the next favorable event being decisive, and of current progress not being reversed before the outcome is reached.

The intuition that causal impact increases in the course of the episode is especially compelling when the episode terminates at a fixed time. Obviously, the probability that a team that leads by a touchdown will win the ball game must increase as time remaining to play diminishes. A score that changes the lead is accordingly perceived as more likely to be decisive if it comes late rather than early in the game. Correspondingly, the close counterfactual is most compelling if the propensity for the unrealized outcome peaked late in the causal episode. An early event may support a counterfactual such as "Team A could have won if Fred had not missed that touchdown in the first quarter," but the description "Team A almost won" is much more convincing if the missed touchdown happened in the closing minutes of the game.

Propensities for all outcomes will be weak in the early phases of a causal episode, if no decisive advantage can be gained at that time. Early in a football game, neither team has a strong propensity to win, although one of them may have a strong disposition to do so. Later on, propensities to win will be attributed to a team to the extent that it already has, or appears on its way to achieving, a lead that is likely to be maintained to the end. Toward the end of the game, a team with a large lead has an overwhelming propensity to win, and both teams have a significant propensity if the game is close. On the usual interpretation of probability, of course, the sums of the probabilities of victory for the two teams (barring ties) should add to one at all stages of the game. A formal representation of propensities should incorporate the attribute of noncomplementarity, which is admissible in some nonstandard models of probability (Shafer, 1976).

Competitive Causation

The psychological concept of propensity that was introduced in the preceding section has a dual meaning as a probabilistic and as a causal notion. We have interpreted propensity as an intuitive assessment of the current probability of the focal outcome based on event cues, and also as an assessment of the current probability of particular cases of the focal outcome – for example, the event of this outcome occurring soon. But the term *propensity* was chosen because it also denotes a direct expression of causal force – *Webster's Dictionary* defines propensity as "an urgent and often intense natural inclination." Urgency and intensity are not part of the meaning of probability in theoretical discourse. We suggest, however, that these dynamic features are important aspects of the cognitive representation of many causal processes, including, in particular, the processes that have achievements as outcomes.

The probabilistic and the causal aspects of propensity suggest different representations of the relation between the alternative outcomes of a causal process. In the language of probability, this relation is expressed by complementarity: Changes in the probability of the focal outcome are mirrored by compensating changes in the aggregate probability of other outcomes. In the language of causal dynamics, the relation between alternative outcomes is best described as competition and conflict. The competition metaphor is evident in many phrases chosen to describe episodes and their outcomes (e.g., "They had to admit defeat and gave up hope of beating the deadline" or "The Harvard job offer won out"). A competitive model of causation is particularly appealing for close counterfactuals, where the strongest propensity is associated first with one outcome, then with another – suggesting a shifting balance between variable opposing forces.

A schema of competing and interacting propensities is most obviously applicable to athletic contests, from which several of our examples have been drawn, but is not restricted to these situations. Displays of the chance games that we have discussed invite a competitive interpretation, much as the figures in the famous Heider and Simmel (1944) animation evoke impressions of intentionality and meaningful interaction. We propose the general hypothesis that the competitive schema is commonly evoked by situations in which the focal outcome is an achievement. These include such varied cases as the making of a difficult individual decision, the vicissitudes of a couple that may or may not break up or get married, the struggle of a firm threatened with bankruptcy, the story of a life-threatening illness, the construction of a building under time constraints, and the wrecking of a building by a tropical storm. Each of these situations is defined by one or more focal achievements. Causal episodes that produce such achievements, or fail to produce them, are naturally described as a struggle of conflicting and variable forces favoring alternative outcomes, or in some cases as a struggle between a single variable force and a series of obstacles.

The notion of conflict between opposing forces is not new to psychological analyses of causality, at least in the context of explaining action. Lewin (1936) introduced motion in a force field as a model of action under conflict. His theory influenced Heider's subsequent analysis of the naive theory of action, in which action is the resultant of the effective personal force and the effective environmental force (Heider, 1958). Both models explain action as a vectorial combination of forces. Lewin's famous theory of conflict also incorporated a dynamic element: The forces acting on the individual change predictably as the individual moves toward sources of attraction or away from aversive states. In general, however, applications of force field analysis have been static. There has been little emphasis on time or on the possibility of causal forces interacting and changing in the course of an event.

A model of competing propensities would extend Lewinian force field analysis in several ways. First, the concept of focal achievement applies to outcomes that are not goals, such as someone dying from a disease, and to situations that do not involve intentions at all, such as a storm destroying a building. Second, the focus of the competitive model is on extended causal episodes. Third, the competitive model attributes inherent uncertainty to causal systems and describes causal episodes in terms of propensities that may change and interact.

Psychology – or Philosophy?

The present study occupies a somewhat uncomfortable middle ground between psychology and philosophy. We have attempted to identify the conditions under which a particular class of counterfactual assertions would be considered true, or appropriate, and we have introduced a notion of propensity to account for these observations. The questions we addressed are similar to those modern philosophers often raise: Philosophical analyses of counterfactuals, for example, focus on the truth conditions or assertability conditions for counterfactual conditionals. Furthermore, some elements of the method are similar: Persuasive philosophical arguments commonly draw on compelling examples that evoke strong shared intuitions. Although the final product of philosophical analysis often has the form of a formal deductive system, induction from intuitions about particular examples is clearly an important part of philosophical endeavor. However, there are important differences between the aims and assumptions of the two disciplines. Philosophers try to understand causality, probability, or counterfactual conditionals, whereas psychologists try to understand how people think about these topics. These different aims have important consequences in

the attitude toward logical consistency: Understanding a matter involves imposing a consistent logical structure on it, but the study of human thinking should neither assume nor impose consistency on its subject matter.

There is a large and interesting philosophical literature on counterfactuals (e.g., Adams, 1976; Goodman, 1954; Lewis, 1973, 1979; Nute, 1980; Pollock, 1976; Skyrms, 1980; Stalnaker, 1968).[4] After developing our notions of causal episodes and changing propensities, we encountered similar ideas in Kvart's treatment of counterfactuals and in his later work on causality (Kvart, 1986, 1989). Kvart (1986) described the truth conditions for counterfactual conditionals on the basis of causal processes diverging from actual historical processes at a particular point in time. He introduced a notion of causal paths, explicated by reference to conditional probabilities changing over time. Kvart also emphasized that the commonsense view of the world is nondeterministic, involving a concept of an open future. As might be expected in a philosophical analysis, Kvart treated counterfactuals as objects of thought, not as constructions of the mind. He also had recourse to formal notions of probability and to formal constraints on causal paths, which we have avoided.

Psychologists have drawn most heavily on the tools and concepts of logical and philosophical analysis in studies of deductive reasoning (Braine, 1978; Johnson-Laird, 1983; Rips, 1990). The costs of such borrowing could be high in studies of causality, probability, and counterfactuals. The intensity of current philosophical debate regarding these topics suggests the existence of compelling but mutually inconsistent intuitions. The concepts that have been developed in attempts to resolve these inconsistencies are sometimes quite remote from the naive categories of thought with which psychologists are concerned. Just as an understanding of naive physics may benefit more from acquaintance with Aristotelian physics than with the modern variety, psychological studies of causality, probability, and counterfactuals may do well to avoid exaggerated dependence on the categories of modern philosophical thought.

The dominant approach to causality in psychology, perhaps reflecting a similar dominance in philosophy, treats causation as a particular relationship of dependency between events – expressed by necessary or sufficient conditions or by increased conditional probabilities (Einhorn & Hogarth, 1986; Kelley, 1967; Mackie, 1974). There is another view, however, which treats causality as a directly perceived link between events or as an emergent property of a patterned sequence of events. The main sources of this approach to causality in psychology are still the classic works by Michotte (1946) and Heider and Simmel (1944), which, respectively, explored variations on the themes of spatiotemporal contiguity and of schemas of intentional action. Ducasse (1969) has developed a philosophical analysis that draws on similar intuitions. The notion of propensity that has been presented here belongs to this tradition of research in causality.

In our use of the term, the representation of propensity is inherently causal, and inherently predictive, much like the perception of an object in motion (Freyd & Finke, 1984). Our emphasis on event cues to propensity deliberately straddled the standard distinction between causes and effects as well as the distinction between causal force and probability. Is there a justification for a concept that blurs accepted distinctions between important categories of thought? There may be. We have described propensity as a perceived attribute with objective reference, much like the perceived length of a line or the perceived distance of an object. Even in the case of lengths and distances, the crude correspondence of the dimensions of percepts to the dimensions of physical description of the world does not guarantee correspondence of the geometries that describe the space people perceive and the space in which they move. The more general point is that the mental representations of events and their relations may not correspond to any logical analysis of causality or probability, and that intuitions about these matters may not be internally consistent. The student of lay intuitions faces a problem that is familiar to cultural anthropologists: How does one make sense of a system of thought without imposing alien categories on it?

Notes

1 The importance of the word *almost* as an indication of cognitively and emotionally relevant alternatives to outcomes that actually materialized was pointed out by Heider (1958, pp. 141–144), who drew attention to an instructive passage in Henry Fielding's *Tom Jones* (1749/1975, Vol. 2, p. 691); see also Hofstadter (1979, pp. 634–643).

2 The number in parentheses refers to the number of respondents answering the question. In later examples, results will only be reported for the two extreme categories of response.

3 Kvart (1986) has offered a treatment for a broad class of counterfactual conditionals in which causality is explicated by probabilities that change over time.

4 Skyrms (1980) has a treatment of counterfactual conditionals that relies on what he calls "prior propensities." However, the meaning of his term more closely resembles our usage of dispositions.

References

Adams, E. W. (1976). Prior probabilities and counterfactual conditionals. In W. L. Harper and C. A. Hooker (Eds.), *Foundations of probability theory, statistical inference, and statistical theories of science* (Vol. 1, pp. 1–21). Dordrecht, Holland: Reidel.

Ajzen, I. (1977). Intuitive theories of events and the effects of base-rate information on prediction. *Journal of Personality and Social Psychology 35*, 303–314.

Bar-Hillel, M. (1990). Back to base rates. In R. M. Hogarth (Ed.), *Insights in decision making: A tribute to Hillel J. Einhorn* (pp. 200–216). Chicago: University of Chicago Press.

Black, J. B., and Bower, G. H. (1979). Episodes as chunks in narrative memory. *Journal of Verbal Learning and Verbal Behavior, 18*, 187–198.

Braine, M. D. S. (1978). On the relation between the natural logic of reasoning and standard logic. *Psychological Review, 85*, 1–21.

Ducasse, C. J. (1969). *Causation and the types of necessity*. New York: Dover.

Einhorn, H., and Hogarth, R. (1986). Judging probable cause. *Psychological Bulletin, 99*, 3–19.

Fielding, H. (1975). *The History of Tom Jones, a foundling* (Vol. 2). Oxford, England: Wesleyan University Press/Oxford University Press. (Original work published 1749.)

Fischhoff, B. (1975). Hindsight ≠ foresight: The effect of outcome knowledge on judgment under uncertainty. *Journal of Experimental Psychology: Human Perception and Performance, 1*, 288–299.

Fischhoff, B. (1982). For those condemned to study the past. In D. Kahneman, P. Slovic, and A. Tversky (Eds.), *Judgment under uncertainty: Heuristics and biases* (pp. 422–444). Cambridge, England: Cambridge University Press.

Freyd, J., and Finke, R. (1984). Representational momentum. *Journal of Experimental Psychology: Learning, Memory and Cognition, 10*, 126–132.

Gigerenzer, G., Hell, W., and Blank, H. (1988). Presentation and content: The use of base rates as a continuous variable. *Journal of Experimental Psychology: Human Perception and Performance, 14*, 513–525.

Gilovich, T., Vallone, R., and Tversky, A. (1985). The hot hand in basketball: On the misperception of random sequences. *Cognitive Psychology, 17*, 295–314.

Goodman, N. (1954). *Fact, fiction and forecast* (1st ed.). London: Athlone Press.

Goodman, N. (1983). *Fact, fiction, and forecast* (4th ed.). Cambridge, MA: Harvard University Press.

Hart, H. L. A., and Honore, A. M. (1959). *Causation in the law*. London: Oxford University Press.

Heider, F. (1958). *The psychology of interpersonal relations*. New York: Wiley.

Heider, F., and Simmel, M. (1944). An experimental study of apparent behavior. *American Journal of Psychology, 57*, 243–259.

Hofstadter, D. (1979). *Gödel, Escher, Bach: An eternal golden braid*. New York: Basic Books.

Johnson, J. T. (1986). The knowledge of what might have been: Affective and attributional consequences of near outcomes. *Personality and Social Psychology Bulletin, 12*, 51–62.

Johnson, J. T., Ogawa, K. H., Delforge, A., and Early, D. (1989). Causal primacy and comparative fault: The effect of position in a causal chain on judgments of legal responsibility. *Personality and Social Psychology, 15*, 161–174.

Johnson, M. K. (1988). Discriminating the origin of information. In T. F. Oltmanns and B. A. Maher (Eds.), *Delusional beliefs: Interdisciplinary perspectives* (pp. 34–65). New York: Wiley.

Johnson-Laird, P. N. (1983). *Mental models: Towards a cognitive science of language, inference, and consciousness*. Cambridge, MA: Harvard University Press.

Kahneman, D., and Miller, D. T. (1986). Norm theory: Comparing reality to its alternatives. *Psychological Review, 93*, 136–153.

Kahneman, D., Slovic, P., and Tversky, A. (Eds.). (1982). *Judgment under uncertainty: Heuristics and biases*. New York: Cambridge University Press.

Kahneman, D., and Tversky, A. (1973). On the psychology of prediction. *Psychological Review, 80*, 237–251.

Kahneman, D., and Tversky, A. (1982a). The simulation heuristic. In D. Kahneman, P. Slovic, and A. Tversky (Eds.), *Judgment under uncertainty: Heuristics and biases* (pp. 201–208). New York: Cambridge University Press.

Kahneman, D., and Tversky, A. (1982b). Variants of uncertainty. *Cognition, 11*, 143–157.

Kelley, H. H. (1967). Attribution theory in social psychology. In D. Levine (Ed.), *Nebraska Symposium on Motivation* (Vol. 15, pp. 192–240). Lincoln: University of Nebraska Press.

Keren, G., and Wagenaar, W. A. (1985). On the psychology of playing blackjack: Normative and descriptive considerations with implications for decision theory. *Journal of Experimental Psychology: General, 114*, 133–158.

Kintsch, W., and van Dijk, T. A. (1978). Toward a model of text comprehension and production. *Psychological Review, 85*, 363–384.

Kvart, I. (1986). *A theory of counterfactuals*. Indianapolis: Hackett.

Kvart, I. (1989). *Causal independence*. Unpublished manuscript.

Lakoff, G. (1987). *Women, fire, and dangerous things: What categories reveal about the mind*. Chicago: University of Chicago Press.

Lakoff, G., and Johnson, M. (1980). *Metaphors we live by*. Chicago: University of Chicago Press.

Landman, J. (1987). Regret and elation following action and inaction. *Personality and Social Psychology Bulletin, 13*, 524–536.

Lewin, K. (1936). *Principles of topological psychology* (F. Heider & G. M. Heider, Trans). New York: McGraw-Hill.

Lewis, D. (1973). *Counterfactuals*. Cambridge, MA: Harvard University Press.

Lewis, D. (1979). Counterfactual dependence and time's arrow. *Noûs, 13*, 455–476.

Lyons, J. (1977). *Semantics, Volume 2*. Cambridge, England: Cambridge University Press.

Mackie, J. L. (1974). *The cement of the universe: A study of causation*. Oxford, England: Clarendon Press (Oxford University Press).

Michotte, A. E. (1946). *La perception de la causalité* [The perception of causality]. Louvain, Belgium: University of Louvain Publications.

Miller, D. T., and Gunasegaram, S. (1990). Temporal order and the perceived mutability of events: Implications for blame assignment. *Journal of Personality and Social Psychology, 59*, 1111–1118.

Miller, D. T., Turnbull, W., and McFarland, C. (1990). Counterfactual thinking and social perception: Thinking about what might have been. In M. Zanna (Ed.), *Advances in experimental social psychology* (Vol. 23, pp. 305–331). Orlando, FL: Academic Press.

Miller, G. A., and Johnson-Laird, P. L. (1976). *Language and perception*. Cambridge, England: Cambridge University Press.

Nute, D. (1980). *Topics in conditional logic*. Boston: Reidel.

Pennington, N., and Hastie, R. (1988). Explanation-based decision making: Effects of memory structure on judgment. *Journal of Experimental Psychology: Learning, Memory and Cognition, 14*, 521–533.

Pollock, J. L. (1976). *Subjunctive reasoning*. Dordrecht, Holland: Reidel.

Read, S. J. (1987). Constructing causal scenarios: A knowledge structure approach to causal reasoning. *Journal of Personality and Social Psychology, 52*, 288–302.

Rips, L. (1990). Reasoning. *Annual Review of Psychology, 41*, 321–353.

Rumelhart, D. E. (1977). Understanding and summarizing brief stories. In D. Laberge and J. Samuels (Eds.), *Basic processes in reading, perception and comprehension* (pp. 265–303). Hillsdale, NJ: Erlbaum.

Schank, R. C. (1975). The structure of episodes in memory. In D. G. Bobrow and A. Collins (Eds.), *Representation and understanding: Studies in cognitive science* (pp. 237–272). New York: Academic Press.

Schank, R. C., and Abelson, R. P. (1977). *Scripts, plans, goals, and understanding.* Hillsdale, NJ: Erlbaum.

Shafer, G. (1976). *A mathematical theory of evidence.* Princeton, NJ: Princeton University Press.

Skyrms, B. (1980). The prior propensity account of subjunctive conditionals. In W. L. Harper, R. Stalnaker, and G. Pearce (Eds.), *Ifs: Conditionals, belief, decision, chance and time* (Vol. 1, pp. 125–162). Dordrecht, Holland: Reidel.

Stalnaker, R. C. (1968). A theory of conditionals. In N. Rescher (Ed.), *Studies in logical theory: American Philosophical Quarterly monograph series 2* (pp. 98–112). Oxford, England: Blackwell.

Talmy, L. (1981, May). *Force images.* Paper presented at the Conference on Language and Mental Imagery, University of California, Berkeley.

Talmy, L. (1983). How language structures space. In H. Pick & L. Acredolo (Eds.), *Spatial orientation: Theory, research, and application* (pp. 219–282). New York: Plenum Press.

Trabasso, T., Secco, T., and van den Broek, P. (1984). Causal cohesion and story coherence. In H. Mandl, N. L. Stein, and T. Trabasso (Eds.), *Learning and comprehension of text* (pp. 83–111). Hillsdale, NJ: Erlbaum.

Tversky, A., and Kahneman, D. (1980). Causal schemas in judgments under uncertainty. In M. Fishbein (Ed.), *Progress in social psychology* (Vol. 1, pp. 153–160). Hillsdale, NJ: Erlbaum.

Tversky, A., and Kahneman, D. (1982). Evidential impact of base rates. In D. Kahneman, P. Slovic, and A. Tversky (Eds.), *Judgment under uncertainty: Heuristics and biases* (pp. 201–208). New York: Cambridge University Press.

Vendler, Z. (1967). *Linguistics in philosophy.* Ithaca, NY: Cornell University Press.

Wells, G. L., and Gavanski, I. (1989). Mental simulation of causality. *Journal of Personality and Social Psychology, 56,* 161–169.

Wells, G. L., Taylor, B. R., and Turtle, J. W. (1987). The undoing of scenarios. *Journal of Personality and Social Psychology, 53,* 421–430.

Section 8: Argumentation

Chapter 32: The Layout of Arguments

STEPHEN EDELSTON TOULMIN

An argument is like an organism. It has both a gross, anatomical structure and a finer, as-it-were physiological one. When set out explicitly in all its detail, it may occupy a number of printed pages or take perhaps a quarter of an hour to deliver; and within this time or space one can distinguish the main phases marking the progress of the argument from the initial statement of an unsettled problem to the final presentation of a conclusion. These main phases will each of them occupy some minutes or paragraphs, and represent the chief anatomical units of the argument – its 'organs', so to speak. But within each paragraph, when one gets down to the level of individual sentences, a finer structure can be recognised, and this is the structure with which logicians have mainly concerned themselves. It is at this physiological level that the idea of logical form has been introduced, and here that the validity of our arguments has ultimately to be established or refuted.

The time has come to change the focus of our inquiry, and to concentrate on this finer level. Yet we cannot afford to forget what we have learned by our study of the grosser anatomy of arguments, for here as with organisms the detailed physiology proves most intelligible when expounded against a background of coarser anatomical distinctions. Physiological processes are interesting not least for the part they play in maintaining the functions of the major organs in which they take place; and micro-arguments (as one may christen them) need to be looked at from time to time with one eye on the macro-arguments in which they figure; since the precise manner in which we phrase them and set them out, to mention only

the least important thing, may be affected by the role they have to play in the larger context.

In the inquiry which follows, we shall be studying the operation of arguments sentence by sentence, in order to see how their validity or invalidity is connected with the manner of laying them out, and what relevance this connection has to the traditional notion of 'logical form'. Certainly the same argument may be set out in quite a number of different forms, and some of these patterns of analysis will be more candid than others – some of them, that is, will show the validity or invalidity of an argument more clearly than others, and make more explicit the grounds it relies on and the bearing of these on the conclusion. How, then, should we lay an argument out, if we want to show the sources of its validity? And in what sense does the acceptability or unacceptability of arguments depend upon their 'formal' merits and defects?

We have before us two rival models, one mathematical, the other jurisprudential. Is the logical form of a valid argument something quasi-geometrical, comparable to the shape of a triangle or the parallelism of two straight lines? Or alternatively, is it something procedural: is a formally valid argument one *in proper form*, as lawyers would say, rather than one laid out in a tidy and simple *geometrical* form? Or does the notion of logical form somehow combine both these aspects, so that to lay an argument out in proper form necessarily requires the adoption of a particular geometrical layout? If this last answer is the right one, it at once creates a further problem for us: to see how and why proper procedure demands the adoption of simple geometrical shape, and how that shape guarantees in

Reproduced with permission from Toulmin, S. E. (1958). *The Uses of Argument* (Chapter 3). Cambridge, UK: Cambridge University Press.

its turn the validity of our procedures. Supposing valid arguments can be cast in a geometrically tidy form, how does this help to make them any the more cogent?

These are the problems to be studied in the present inquiry. If we can see our way to unravelling them, their solution will be of some importance – particularly for a proper understanding of logic. But to begin with we must go cautiously, and steer clear of the philosophical issues on which we shall hope later to throw some light, concentrating for the moment on questions of a most prosaic and straightforward kind. Keeping our eyes on the categories of applied logic – on the practical business of argumentation, that is, and the notions it requires us to employ – we must ask what features a logically candid layout of arguments will need to have. The establishment of conclusions raises a number of issues of different sorts, and a practical layout will make allowance for these differences: our first question is – what are these issues, and how can we do justice to them all in subjecting our arguments to rational assessment?

Two last remarks may be made by way of introduction, the first of them simply adding one more question to our agenda. Ever since Aristotle it has been customary, when analysing the micro-structure of arguments, to set them out in a very simple manner: they have been presented three propositions at a time, 'minor premiss; major premiss; *so* conclusion'. The question now arises, whether this standard form is sufficiently elaborate or candid. Simplicity is of course a merit, but may it not in this case have been bought too dearly? Can we properly classify all the elements in our arguments under the three headings, 'major premiss', 'minor premiss', and 'conclusion', or are these categories misleadingly few in number? Is there even enough similarity between major and minor premisses for them usefully to be yoked together by the single name of 'premiss'?

Light is thrown on these questions by the analogy with jurisprudence. This would naturally lead us to adopt a layout of greater complexity than has been customary, for the questions we are asking here are, once again, more general versions of questions already familiar in jurisprudence, and in that more specialised field a whole battery of distinctions has grown up. 'What different sorts of propositions', a legal philosopher will ask, 'are uttered in the course of a law-case, and in what different ways can such propositions bear on the soundness of a legal claim?' This has always been and still is a central question for the student of jurisprudence, and we soon find that the nature of a legal process can be properly understood only if we draw a large number of distinctions. Legal utterances have many distinct functions. Statements of claim, evidence of identification, testimony about events in dispute, interpretations of a statute or discussions of its validity, claims to exemption from the application of a law, pleas in extenuation, verdicts, sentences: all these different classes of proposition have their parts to play in the legal process, and the differences between them are in practice far from trifling. When we turn from the special case of the law to consider rational arguments in general, we are faced at once by the question whether these must not be analysed in terms of an equally complex set of categories. If we are to set our arguments out with complete logical candour, and understand properly the nature of 'the logical process', surely we shall need to employ a pattern of argument no less sophisticated than is required in the law.

The Pattern of an Argument: Data and Warrants

'What, then, is involved in establishing conclusions by the production of arguments?' Can we, by considering this question in a general form, build up from scratch a pattern of analysis which will do justice to all the distinctions which proper procedure forces upon us? That is the problem facing us.

Let it be supposed that we make an assertion, and commit ourselves thereby to the claim which any assertion necessarily involves. If this claim is challenged, we must be able to establish it – that is, make it good, and show that it was justifiable. How is this to be done? Unless the assertion was made quite wildly and irresponsibly, we shall normally have some facts to which we can point in its support: if the claim is challenged, it is up to us to appeal to these facts, and present them as the foundation upon which our claim is based. Of course we may not get the challenger even to agree about the correctness of these facts, and in that case we have to clear his objection out of the way by a preliminary argument: only when this prior issue or 'lemma', as geometers would call it, has been dealt with, are we in a position to return to the original argument. But this complication we need only mention: supposing the lemma to have been disposed of, our question is how to set the original argument out most fully and explicitly. 'Harry's hair is not black', we assert. What have we got to go on? we are asked.

Our personal knowledge that it is in fact red: that is our datum, the ground which we produce as support for the original assertion. Petersen, we may say, will not be a Roman Catholic: why? We base our claim on the knowledge that he is a Swede, which makes it very unlikely that he will be a Roman Catholic. Wilkinson, asserts the prosecutor in Court, has committed an offence against the Road Traffic Acts: in support of this claim, two policemen are prepared to testify that they timed him driving at 45 m.p.h. in a built-up area. In each case, an original assertion is supported by producing other facts bearing on it.

We already have, therefore, one distinction to start with: between the *claim* or conclusion whose merits we are seeking to establish (C) and the facts we appeal to as a foundation for the claim – what I shall refer to as our *data* (D). If our challenger's question is, 'What have you got to go on?', producing the data or information on which the claim is based may serve to answer him; but this is only one of the ways in which our conclusion may be challenged. Even after we have produced our data, we may find ourselves being asked further questions of another kind. We may now be required not to add more factual information to that which we have already provided, but rather to indicate the bearing on our conclusion of the data already produced. Colloquially, the question may now be, not 'What have you got to go on?', but 'How do you get there?'. To present a particular set of data as the basis for some specified conclusion commits us to a certain *step*; and the question is now one about the nature and justification of this step.

Supposing we encounter this fresh challenge, we must bring forward not further data, for about these the same query may immediately be raised again, but propositions of a rather different kind: rules, principles, inference-licences or what you will, instead of additional items of information. Our task is no longer to strengthen the ground on which our argument is constructed, but is rather to show that, taking these data as a starting point, the step to the original claim or conclusion is an appropriate and legitimate one. At this point, therefore, what are needed are general, hypothetical statements, which can act as bridges, and authorise the sort of step to which our particular argument commits us. These may normally be written very briefly (in the form 'If D, then C'); but, for candour's sake, they can profitably be expanded, and made more explicit: 'Data such as D entitle one to draw conclusions, or make claims, such as C',

or alternatively 'Given data D, one may take it that C.'

Propositions of this kind I shall call *warrants* (W); to distinguish them from both conclusions and data. (These 'warrants', it will be observed, correspond to the practical standards or canons of argument referred to in our earlier essays.) To pursue our previous examples: the knowledge that Harry's hair is red, entitles us to set aside any suggestion that it is black, on account of the warrant, 'If anything is red, it will not also be black.' (The very triviality of this warrant is connected with the fact that we are concerned here as much with a counter-assertion as with an argument.) The fact that Petersen is a Swede is directly relevant to the question of his religious denomination for, as we should probably put it, 'A Swede can be taken almost certainly not to be a Roman Catholic.' (The step involved here is not trivial, so the warrant is not self-authenticating.) Likewise in the third case: our warrant will now be some such statement as that 'A man who is proved to have driven at more than 30 m.p.h. in a built-up area can be found to have committed an offence against the Road Traffic Acts.'

The question will at once be asked, how absolute is this distinction between data, on the one hand, and warrants, on the other. Will it always be clear whether a man who challenges an assertion is calling for the production of his adversary's data, or for the warrants authorising his steps? Can one, in other words, draw any sharp distinction between the force of the two questions, 'What have you got to go on?' and 'How do you get there?'? By grammatical tests alone, the distinction may appear far from absolute, and the same English sentence may serve a double function: it may be uttered, that is, in one situation to convey a piece of information, in another to authorise a step in an argument, and even perhaps in some contexts to do both these things at once. (All these possibilities will be illustrated before too long.) For the moment, the important thing is not to be too cut-and-dried in our treatment of the subject, nor to commit ourselves in advance to a rigid terminology. At any rate we shall find it possible in *some* situations to distinguish clearly two different logical functions; and the nature of this distinction is hinted at if one contrasts the two sentences, 'Whenever A, one *has found* that B' and 'Whenever A, one *may take it* that B.'

We now have the terms we need to compose the first skeleton of a pattern for analysing arguments. We may symbolise the relation between the data and the claim in support of which they are produced by an arrow, and indicate the authority for taking the step from one to the other by writing the warrant immediately below the arrow:

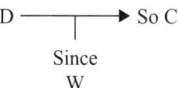

Or, to give an example:

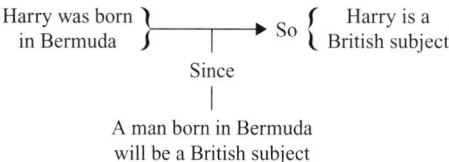

As this pattern makes clear, the explicit appeal in this argument goes directly back from the claim to the data relied on as foundation: the warrant is, in a sense, incidental and explanatory, its task being simply to register explicitly the legitimacy of the step involved and to refer it back to the larger class of steps whose legitimacy is being presupposed.

This is one of the reasons for distinguishing between data and warrants: data are appealed to explicitly, warrants implicitly. In addition, one may remark that warrants are general, certifying the soundness of *all* arguments of the appropriate type, and have accordingly to be established in quite a different way from the facts we produce as data. This distinction, between data and warrants, is similar to the distinction drawn in the law-courts between questions of fact and questions of law, and the legal distinction is indeed a special case of the more general one – we may argue, for instance, that a man whom we know to have been born in Bermuda is presumably a British subject, simply because the relevant laws give us a warrant to draw this conclusion.

One more general point in passing: unless, in any particular field of argument, we are prepared to work with warrants of *some* kind, it will become impossible in that field to subject arguments to rational assessment. The data we cite if a claim is challenged depend on the warrants we are prepared to operate with in that field, and the warrants to which we commit ourselves are implicit in the particular steps from data to claims we are prepared to take and to admit. But supposing a man rejects all warrants whatever authorising (say) steps from data

about the present and past to conclusions about the future, then for him rational prediction will become impossible; and many philosophers have in fact denied the possibility of rational prediction just because they thought they could discredit equally the claims of all past-to-future warrants.

The skeleton of a pattern which we have obtained so far is only a beginning. Further questions may now arise, to which we must pay attention. Warrants are of different kinds, and may confer different degrees of force on the conclusions they justify. Some warrants authorise us to accept a claim unequivocally, given the appropriate data – these warrants entitle us in suitable cases to qualify our conclusion with the adverb 'necessarily'; others authorise us to make the step from data to conclusion either tentatively, or else subject to conditions, exceptions, or qualifications – in these cases other modal qualifiers, such as 'probably' and 'presumably', are in place. It may not be sufficient, therefore, simply to specify our data, warrant and claim: we may need to add some explicit reference to the degree of force which our data confer on our claim in virtue of our warrant. In a word, we may have to put in a *qualifier*. Again, it is often necessary in the law-courts, not just to appeal to a given statute or common-law doctrine, but to discuss explicitly the extent to which this particular law fits the case under consideration, whether it must inevitably be applied in this particular case, or whether special facts may make the case an exception to the rule or one in which the law can be applied only subject to certain qualifications.

If we are to take account of these features of our argument also, our pattern will become more complex. Modal qualifiers (Q) and conditions of exception or rebuttal (R) are distinct both from data and from warrants, and need to be given separate places in our layout. Just as a warrant (W) is itself neither a datum (D) nor a claim (C), since it implies in itself something about both D and C – namely, that the step from the one to the other is legitimate; so, in turn, Q and R are themselves distinct from W, since they comment implicitly on the bearing of W on this step – qualifiers (Q) indicating the strength conferred by the warrant on this step, conditions of rebuttal (R) indicating circumstances in which the general authority of the warrant would have to be set aside. To mark these further distinctions, we may write the qualifier (Q) immediately beside the conclusion which it qualifies (C), and the exceptional conditions which might be capable of defeating or rebutting the warranted conclusion (R) immediately below the qualifier.

To illustrate: our claim that Harry is a British subject may normally be defended by appeal to the information that he was born in Bermuda, for this datum lends support to our conclusion on account of the warrants implicit in the British Nationality Acts; but the argument is not by itself conclusive in the absence of assurances about his parentage and about his not having changed his nationality since birth. What our information does do is to establish that the conclusion holds good 'presumably', and subject to the appropriate provisos. The argument now assumes the form:

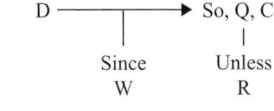

i.e.

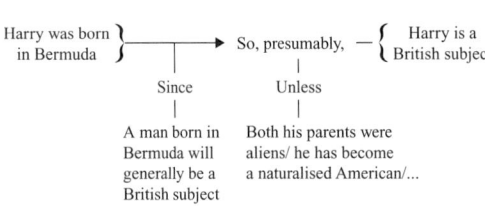

We must remark, in addition, on two further distinctions. The first is that between a statement of a warrant, and statements about its applicability – between 'A man born in Bermuda will be British', and 'This presumption holds good provided his parents were not both aliens, etc.' The distinction is relevant not only to the law of the land, but also for an understanding of scientific laws or 'laws of nature': it is important, indeed, in all cases where the application of a law may be subject to exceptions, or where a warrant can be supported by pointing to a general correlation only, and not to an absolutely invariable one. We can distinguish also two purposes which may be served by the production of additional facts: these can serve as further data, or they can be cited to confirm or rebut the applicability of a warrant. Thus, the fact that Harry was born in Bermuda and the fact that his parents were not aliens are both of them directly relevant to the question of his present nationality; but they are relevant in different ways. The one fact is a datum, which by itself establishes a presumption of British nationality; the other fact, by setting aside one possible rebuttal, tends to confirm the presumption thereby created.

One particular problem about applicability we shall have to discuss more fully later: when we set out a piece of applied mathematics, in which some system of mathematical relations is used to throw light on a question of (say) physics, the correctness of the calculations will be one thing, their appropriateness to the problem in hand may be quite another. So the question 'Is this calculation mathematically impeccable?' may be a very different one from the question 'Is this the relevant calculation?' Here too, the applicability of a particular warrant is one question: the result we shall get from applying the warrant is another matter, and in asking about the *correctness* of the result we may have to inquire into both these things independently.

The Pattern of an Argument: Backing Our Warrants

One last distinction, which we have already touched on in passing, must be discussed at some length. In addition to the question whether or on what conditions a warrant is applicable in a *particular* case, we may be asked why *in general* this warrant should be accepted as having authority. In defending a claim, that is, we may produce our data, our warrant, and the relevant qualifications and conditions, and yet find that we have still not satisfied our challenger; for he may be dubious not only about this particular argument but about the more general question whether the warrant (W) is acceptable at all. Presuming the general acceptability of this warrant (he may allow) our argument would no doubt be impeccable – if D-ish facts really do suffice as backing for C-ish claims, all well and good. But does not that warrant in its turn rest on something else? Challenging a particular claim may in this way lead on to challenging, more generally, the legitimacy of a whole range of arguments. 'You presume that a man born in Bermuda can be taken to be a British subject,' he may say, 'but why do you think that?' Standing behind our warrants, as this example reminds us, there will normally be other assurances, without which the warrants themselves would possess neither authority nor currency – these other things we may refer to as the *backing* (B) of the warrants. This 'backing' of our warrants is something which we shall have to scrutinise very carefully: its precise relations to our data, claims, warrants, and conditions of rebuttal deserve some clarification, for confusion at this point can lead to trouble later.

We shall have to notice particularly how the sort of backing called for by our warrants varies from one field of argument to another. The *form* of argument we employ in different fields

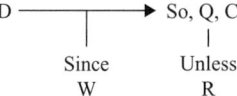

need not vary very much as between fields. 'A whale will be a mammal', 'A Bermudan will be a Briton', 'A Saudi Arabian will be a Muslim': here are three different warrants to which we might appeal in the course of a practical argument, each of which can justify the same sort of straightforward step from a datum to a conclusion. We might add for variety examples of even more diverse sorts, taken from moral, mathematical or psychological fields. But the moment we start asking about the *backing* which a warrant relies on in each field, great differences begin to appear: the kind of backing we must point to if we are to establish its authority will change greatly as we move from one field of argument to another. 'A whale will be (i.e. *is classifiable as*) a mammal', 'A Bermudan will be (*in the eyes of the law*) a Briton', 'A Saudi Arabian will be (*found to be*) a Muslim' – the words in parentheses indicate what these differences are. One warrant is defended by relating it to a system of taxonomical classification, another by appealing to the statutes governing the nationality of people born in the British colonies, the third by referring to the statistics which record how religious beliefs are distributed among people of different nationalities. We can for the moment leave open the more contentious question, how we establish our warrants in the fields of morals, mathematics and psychology: for the moment all we are trying to show is the *variability* or *field dependence* of the backing needed to establish our warrants.

We can make room for this additional element in our argumentpattern by writing it below the bare statement of the warrant for which it serves as backing (B):

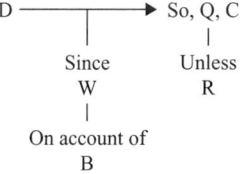

This form may not be final, but it will be complex enough for the purpose of our present discussions. To take a particular example: in support of the claim (C) that Harry is a British subject, we appeal to the datum (D) that he was born in Bermuda, and the warrant can then be stated in the form, 'A man born in Bermuda may be taken to be a British subject': since, however, questions of nationality are always subject to qualifications and conditions, we shall have to insert a qualifying 'presumably' (Q) in front of the conclusion, and note the possibility that our conclusion may be rebutted in case (R) it turns out that both his parents were aliens or he has since become a naturalised American. Finally, in case the warrant itself is challenged, its backing can be put in: this will record the terms and the dates of enactment of the Acts of Parliament and other legal provisions governing the nationality of persons born in the British colonies. The result will be an argument set out as follows:

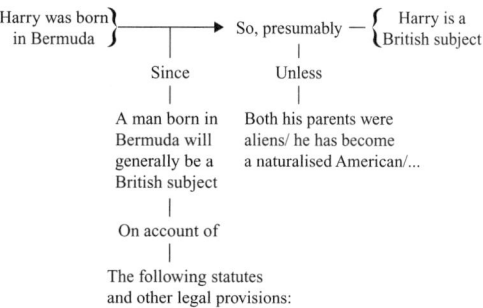

In what ways does the backing of warrants differ from the other elements in our arguments? To begin with the differences between B and W: statements of warrants, we saw, are hypothetical, bridgelike statements, but the backing for warrants can be expressed in the form of categorical statements of fact quite as well as can the data appealed to in direct support of our conclusions. So long as our statements reflect these functional differences explicitly, there is no danger of confusing the backing (B) for a warrant with the warrant itself (W): such confusions arise only when these differences are disguised by our forms of expression. In our present example, at any rate, there need be no difficulty. The fact that the relevant statutes have been validly passed into law, and contain the provisions they do, can be ascertained simply by going to the records of the parliamentary proceedings concerned and to the relevant volumes in the books of statute law: the resulting discovery, that such-and-such a statute enacted on such-and-such a date contains a provision specifying that people born in the British colonies of suitable parentage shall be entitled to British citizenship, is a straightforward statement of fact. On the other hand, the warrant which we apply *in virtue of* the statute containing this provision is logically of a very different character – 'If a man was born in a British colony, he *may be presumed to be* British.' Though the facts about the statute may provide all the backing required by this warrant, the explicit statement of the warrant itself is more than a repetition of these facts: it is a general *moral* of a practical character, about the ways in which we can safely argue in view of these facts.

We can also distinguish backing (B) from data (D). Though the data we appeal to in an argument and the backing lending authority to our warrants may alike be stated as straightforward matters-of-fact, the roles which these statements play in our argument are decidedly different. Data of some kind must be produced, if there is to be an argument there at all: a bare conclusion, without any data produced in its support, is no argument. But the backing of the warrants we invoke need not be made explicit – at any rate to begin with: the warrants may be conceded without challenge, and their backing left understood. Indeed, if we demanded the credentials of all warrants at sight and never let one pass unchallenged, argument could scarcely begin. Jones puts forward an argument invoking warrant W_1, and Smith challenges that warrant; Jones is obliged, as a lemma, to produce another argument in the hope of establishing the acceptability of the first warrant, but in the course of this lemma employs a second warrant W_2; Smith challenges the credentials of this second warrant in turn; and so the game goes on.

Some warrants must be accepted provisionally without further challenge, if argument is to be open to us in the field in question: we should not even know what sort of data were of the slightest relevance to a conclusion, if we had not at least a provisional idea of the warrants acceptable in the situation confronting us. The existence of considerations such as would establish the acceptability of the most reliable warrants is something we are entitled to take for granted.

Finally, a word about the ways in which B differs from Q and R: these are too obvious to need expanding upon, since the grounds for regarding a warrant as generally acceptable are clearly one thing, the force which the warrant lends to a conclusion another, and the sorts of exceptional circumstance which may in particular cases rebut the presumptions the warrant creates a third. They correspond, in our example, to the three statements, (i) that the statutes about British nationality *have in fact* been validly passed into law, and say this: ... , (ii) that Harry *may be presumed* to be a British subject, and (iii)

that Harry, having recently become a naturalised American, *is no longer covered* by these statutes.

One incidental point should be made, about the interpretation to be put upon the symbols in our pattern of argument: this may throw light on a slightly puzzling example which we came across when discussing Kneale's views on probability. Consider the arrow joining D and C. It may seem natural to suggest at first that this arrow should be read as 'so' in one direction and as 'because' in the other. Other interpretations are however possible. As we saw earlier, the step from the information that Jones has Bright's Disease to the conclusion that he cannot be expected to live to eighty does not reverse perfectly: we find it natural enough to say, 'Jones cannot be expected to live to eighty, *because* he has Bright's Disease', but the fuller statement, 'Jones cannot be expected to live to eighty, *because* the probability of his living that long is low, *because* he has Bright's Disease', strikes us as cumbrous and artificial, for it puts in an extra step which is trivial and unnecessary. On the other hand, we do not mind saying, 'Jones has Bright's Disease, *so* the chances of his living to eighty are slight, *so* he cannot be expected to live that long', for the last clause is (so to speak) an *inter alia* clause – it states one of the many particular morals one can draw from the middle clause, which tells us his general expectation of life.

So also in our present case: reading along the arrow from right to left or from left to right we can normally say both 'C, because D' and 'D, so C'. But it may sometimes happen that some more general conclusion than C may be warranted, given D: where this is so, we shall often find it natural to write, not only 'D, so C', but also 'D, so C', so C', C' being the more general conclusion warranted in view of data D, from which in turn we infer *inter alia* that C. Where this is the case, our 'so' and 'because' are no longer reversible: if we now read the argument backwards the statement we get – 'C, because C', because D' – is again more cumbrous than the situation really requires.

Ambiguities in the Syllogism

The time has come to compare the distinctions we have found of practical importance in the layout and criticism of arguments with those which have traditionally been made in books, on the theory of logic: let us start by seeing how our present distinctions apply to the syllogism or syllogistic argument. For the purposes of our present argument we can confine our attention to one of the many forms of syllogism – that represented by the time-honoured example:

Socrates is a man;

All men are mortal;

So Socrates is mortal.

This type of syllogism has certain special features. The first premiss is 'singular' and refers to a particular individual, while the second premiss alone is 'universal'. Aristotle himself was, of course, much concerned with syllogisms in which both the premisses were universal, since to his mind many of the arguments within scientific theory must be expected to be of this sort. But we are interested primarily in arguments by which general propositions are applied to justify particular conclusions about individuals; so this initial limitation will be convenient. Many of the conclusions we reach will, in any case, have an obvious application – *mutatis mutandis* – to syllogisms of other types. We can begin by asking the question 'What corresponds in the syllogism to our distinction between data, warrant, and backing?' If we press this question, we shall find that the apparently innocent forms used in syllogistic arguments turn out to have a hidden complexity. This internal complexity is comparable with that we observed in the case of modally-qualified conclusions: here, as before, we shall be obliged to disentangle two distinct things – the force of universal premisses, when regarded as warrants, and the backing on which they depend for their authority.

In order to bring these points clearly to light, let us keep in view not only the two universal premisses on which logicians normally concentrate – 'All A's are B's' and 'No A's are B's' – but also two other forms of statement which we probably have just as much occasion to use in practice – 'Almost all A's are B's' and 'Scarcely any A's are B's,' The internal complexity of such statements can be illustrated first, and most clearly, in the latter cases.

Consider, for instance, the statement, 'Scarcely any Swedes are Roman Catholics.' This statement can have two distinct aspects: both of them are liable to be operative at once when the statement figures in an argument, but they can nevertheless be distinguished. To begin with, it may serve as a simple statistical report: in that case, it can equally well be written in the fuller form, 'The proportion of Swedes who are Roman Catholics is less than (say) 2%' – to which we may add a parenthetical reference to the source of our information, '(According to the tables in *Whittaker's Almanac)*'. Alternatively, the same statement may serve as a genuine inference-warrant: in that case, it will be natural to expand it rather differently, so as to obtain the more candid statement, 'A Swede can be taken almost certainly not to be a Roman Catholic.'

So long as we look at the single sentence 'Scarcely any Swedes are Roman Catholics' by itself, this distinction may appear trifling enough: but if we apply it to the analysis of an argument in which this appears as one premiss, we obtain results of some significance. So let us construct an argument of quasi-syllogistic form, in which this statement figures in the position of a 'major premiss'. This argument could be, for instance, the following:

Petersen is a Swede;

Scarcely any Swedes are Roman Catholics;

So, almost certainly, Petersen is not a Roman Catholic.

The conclusion of this argument is only tentative, but in other respects the argument is exactly like a syllogism.

As we have seen, the second of these statements can be expanded in each of two ways, so that it becomes either, 'The proportion of Swedes who are Roman Catholics is less than 2%', or else, 'A Swede can be taken almost certainly not to be a Roman Catholic.' Let us now see what happens if we substitute each of these two expanded versions in turn for the second of our three original statements. In one case we obtain the argument:

Petersen is a Swede;

A Swede can be taken almost certainly not to be a Roman Catholic;

So, almost certainly, Petersen is not a Roman Catholic.

Here the successive lines correspond in our terminology to the statement of a datum (D), a warrant (W), and a conclusion (C). On the other hand, if we make the alternative substitution, we obtain:

Petersen is a Swede;

The proportion of Roman Catholic Swedes is less than 2%;

So, almost certainly, Petersen is not a Roman Catholic.

In this case we again have the same datum and conclusion, but the second line now states the backing (B) for the warrant (W), which is itself left unstated.

For tidiness' sake, we may now be tempted to abbreviate these two expanded versions. If we do so, we can obtain respectively the two arguments:

(D) Petersen is a Swede;

(W) A Swede is almost certainly not a Roman Catholic;

So, (C) Petersen is almost certainly not a Roman Catholic:

and,

(D) Petersen is a Swede;

(B) The proportion of Roman Catholic Swedes is minute;

So, (C) Petersen is almost certainly not a Roman Catholic.

The relevance of our distinction to the traditional conception of 'formal validity' should already be becoming apparent, and we shall return to the subject shortly.

Turning to the form 'No A's are B's' (e.g. 'No Swedes are Roman Catholics'), we can make a similar distinction. This form of statement also can be employed in two alternative ways, either as a statistical report, or as an inference-warrant. It can serve simply to report a statistician's discovery – say, that the proportion of Roman Catholic Swedes is in fact zero; or alternatively it can serve to justify the drawing of conclusions in argument, becoming equivalent to the explicit statement, 'A Swede can be taken certainly not to be a Roman Catholic.' Corresponding interpretations are again open to us if we look at an argument which includes our sample statement as the universal premiss. Consider the argument:

Petersen is a Swede;

No Swedes are Roman Catholics;

So, certainly, Petersen is not a Roman Catholic.

This can be understood in two ways: we may write it in the form:

Petersen is a Swede;

The proportion of Roman Catholic Swedes is zero;

So, certainly, Petersen is not a Roman Catholic,

or alternatively in the form:

Petersen is a Swede;

A Swede is certainly not a Roman Catholic;

So, certainly, Petersen is not a Roman Catholic.

Here again the first formulation amounts, in our terminology, to putting the argument in the form 'D, B, so C'; while the second formulation is equivalent to putting it in the form 'D, W, so C'. So, whether we are concerned with a 'scarcely any . . .' argument or a 'no . . .' argument, the customary form of expression will tend in either case to conceal from us the distinction between an inference-warrant and its backing. The same will be true in the case of 'all' and 'nearly all': there, too, the distinction between saying 'Every, or nearly every single *A has been found* to be a B' and saying 'An A *can be taken*, certainly or almost certainly, to be a B' is concealed by the over-simple form of words 'All A's are B's.' A crucial difference in practical function can in this way pass unmarked and unnoticed.

Our own more complex pattern of analysis, by contrast, avoids this defect. It leaves no room for ambiguity: entirely separate places are left in the pattern for a warrant and for the backing upon which its authority depends. For instance, our 'scarcely any . . .' argument will have to be set out in the following way:

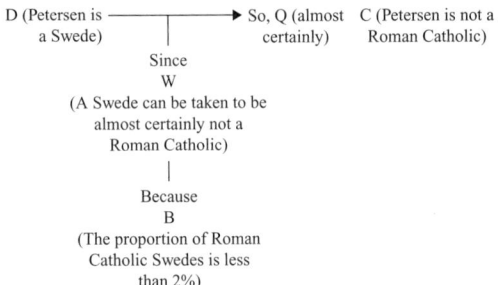

Corresponding transcriptions will be needed for arguments of the other three types.

When we are theorising about the syllogism, in which a central part is played by propositions of the forms 'All A's are B's' and 'No A's are B's', it will accordingly be as well to bear this distinction in mind. The form of statement 'All A's are B's' is as it stands deceptively simple: it may have in use both the force of a warrant and the factual content of its backing, two aspects which we can bring out by expanding it in different ways. Sometimes it may be used, standing alone, in only one of these two ways at once;

but often enough, especially in arguments, we make the single statement do both jobs at once and gloss over, for brevity's sake, the transition from backing to warrant – from the factual information we are presupposing to the inference-licence which that information justifies us in employing. The practical economy of this habit may be obvious; but for philosophical purposes it leaves the effective structure of our arguments insufficiently candid.

There is a clear parallel between the complexity of 'all . . .' statements and that of modal statements. As before, the *force* of the statements is invariant for all fields of argument. When we consider this aspect of the statements, the form 'All A's are B's' may always be replaced by the form 'An A can certainly be taken to be a B': this will be true regardless of the field, holding good equally of 'All Swedes are Roman Catholics', 'All those born in British colonies are entitled to British citizenship', 'All whales are mammals', and 'All lying is reprehensible' – in each case, the general statement will serve as a warrant authorising an argument of precisely the same form, D → C, whether the step goes from 'Harry was born in Bermuda' to 'Harry is a British citizen' or from 'Wilkinson told a lie' to 'Wilkinson acted reprehensibly.' Nor should there be any mystery about the nature of the step from D to C, since the whole *force* of the general statement 'All A's are B's', as so understood, is to authorise just this sort of step.

By contrast, the kind of *grounds* or *backing* supporting a warrant of this form will depend on the field of argument: here the parallel with modal statements is maintained. From this point of view, the important thing is the factual content, not the force of 'all . . .' statements. Though a warrant of the form 'An A can certainly be taken to be a B' must hold good in any field in virtue of *some* facts, the actual sort of facts in virtue of which any warrant will have currency and authority will vary according to the field of argument within which that warrant operates; so, when we expand the simple form 'All A's are B's' in order to make explicit the nature of the backing it is used to express, the expansion we must make will also depend upon the field with which we are concerned. In one case, the statement will become 'The proportion of A's found to be B's is 100%'; in another, 'A's are ruled by statute to count unconditionally as B's'; in a third, 'The class of B's includes taxonomically the entire class of A's'; and in a fourth, 'The practice of doing A leads to the following intolerable consequences, etc.' Yet, despite

the striking differences between them, all these elaborate propositions are expressed on occasion in the compact and simple form 'All A's are B's.'

Similar distinctions can be made in the case of the forms, 'Nearly all A's are B's', 'Scarcely any A's are B's', and 'No A's are B's.' Used to express warrants, these differ from 'All A's are B's' in only one respect, that where before we wrote 'certainly' we must now write 'almost certainly', 'almost certainly not' or 'certainly not'. Likewise, when we are using them to state not warrants but backing: in a statistical case we shall simply have to replace '100%' by (say) 'at least 95%', 'less than 5%' or 'zero'; in the case of a statute replace 'unconditionally' by 'unless exceptional conditions hold', 'only in exceptional circumstances' or 'in no circumstances whatever'; and in a taxonomical case replace 'the entirety of the class of A's' by 'all but a small sub-class . . .', 'only a small subclass . . .' or 'no part of . . .'. Once we have filled out the skeletal forms 'all . . .' and 'no . . .' in this way, the field-dependence of the backing for our warrants is as clear as it could be.

The Notion of 'Universal Premisses'

The full implications of the distinction between force and backing, as applied to propositions of the form 'All A's are B's', will become clear only after one further distinction has been introduced – that between 'analytic' and 'substantial' arguments. This cannot be done immediately, so for the moment all we can do is to hint at ways in which the traditional way of setting out arguments – in the form of two premisses followed by a conclusion – may be misleading.

Most obviously, this pattern of analysis is liable to create an exaggerated appearance of uniformity as between arguments in different fields, but what is probably as important is its power of disguising also the great differences between the things traditionally classed together as 'premisses'. Consider again examples of our standard type, in which a particular conclusion is justified by appeal to a particular datum about an individual – the singular, minor premiss – taken together with a general piece of information serving as warrant and/or backing – the universal, major premiss. So long as we interpret universal premisses as expressing not warrants but their backing, both major and minor premisses are at any rate categorical and factual: in this respect, the information that not a single Swede is recorded as being a Roman Catholic is on a par with the information that Karl Henrik Petersen is a Swede. Even so, the different roles played in practical argument by one's data and by the backing for one's warrants make it rather unfortunate to label them alike 'premisses'. But supposing we adopt the alternative interpretation of our major premisses, treating them instead as warrants, the differences between major and minor premisses are even more striking. A 'singular premiss' expresses a piece of information *from* which we are drawing a conclusion, a 'universal premiss' now expresses, not a piece of information at all, but a guarantee *in accordance with* which we can safely take the step from our datum to our conclusion. Such a guarantee, for all its backing, will be neither factual nor categorical but rather hypothetical and permissive. Once again, the two-fold distinction between 'premisses' and 'conclusion' appears insufficiently complex and, to do justice to the situation, one needs to adopt in its place at least the fourfold distinction between 'datum', 'conclusion', 'warrant' and 'backing'.

One way in which the distinction between the various possible interpretations of the 'universal premiss' may prove important to logicians can be illustrated by referring to an old logical puzzle. The question has often been debated, whether the form of statement 'All A's are B's' has or has not any existential implications: whether, that is, its use commits one to the belief that some A's do exist. Statements of the form 'Some A's are B's' have given rise to no such difficulty, for the use of this latter form always implies the existence of some A's, but the form 'All A's are B's' seems to be more ambiguous. It has been argued, for instance, that such a statement as 'All club-footed men have difficulty in walking' need not be taken as implying the existence of any club-footed men: this is a general truth, it is said, which would remain equally true even though, for once in a while, there were no living men having club feet, and it would not suddenly cease to be true that club-footedness made walking difficult just because the last club-footed man had been freed of his deformity by a skilful surgeon. Yet this leaves us uncomfortable: has our assertion then no existential force? Surely, we feel, club-footed men must at any rate *have* existed if we are to be able to make this assertion at all?

This conundrum illustrates very well the weaknesses of the term 'universal premiss'. Suppose that we rely on the traditional mode of analysis of arguments:

Jack is club-footed;

All club-footed men have difficulty in walking;

So, Jack has difficulty in walking.

For so long as we do, the present difficulty will be liable to recur, since this pattern of analysis leaves it unclear whether the general statement 'All . . .' is to be construed as a permissive inference warrant or as a factual report of our observations. Is it to be construed as meaning 'A club-footed man will (i.e. may be expected to) have difficulty in walking', or as meaning 'Every club-footed man of whom we have records had (i.e. was found to have) difficulty in walking'? We are not bound, except by long habit, to employ the form 'All A's are B's', with all the ambiguities it involves. We are at liberty to scrap it in favour of forms of expression which are more explicit, even if more cumbersome; and if we make this change, the problem about existential implications will simply no longer trouble us. The statement 'Every club-footed man of whom we have records . . .' implies, of course, that there have been at any rate *some* club-footed men, since otherwise we should have no records to refer to; while the warrant 'A club-footed man will have difficulty in walking', equally of course, leaves the existential question open. We can truthfully say that club-footedness would be a handicap to any pedestrian, even if we knew that at this moment everyone was lying on his back and nobody was so deformed. We are therefore not compelled to answer as it stands the question whether 'All A's are B's' has existential implications: certainly we can refuse a clear Yes or No. Some of the statements which logicians represent in this rather crude form do have such implications; others do not. No entirely general answer can be given to the question, for what determines whether there are or are not existential implications in any particular case is not the form of statement itself, but rather the practical use to which this form is put on that occasion.

Can we say then that the form 'All A's are B's' has existential implications when used to express the backing of a warrant, but not when used to express the warrant itself? Even this way of putting the point turns out to be too neat. For the other thing which excessive reliance on the form 'All A's are B's' tends to conceal from us is the different sorts of backing which our general beliefs may require, and these differences are relevant here. No doubt the statement that every club-footed man of whom we have any record found his deformity a handicap in walking, which we have here cited as backing, implies that there have been some such people; but we can back the same warrant by appeal to considerations of other kinds as well, e.g. by arguments explaining from anatomical principles in what way club-footedness may be expected to lead to disability – just how this shape of foot will prove a handicap. In these theoretical terms we could discuss the disabilities which would result from any kind of deformity we cared to imagine, including ones which nobody is known ever to have had: this sort of backing accordingly leaves the existential question open.

Again, if we consider warrants of other types, we find plenty of cases in which the backing for a warrant has, as it stands, no existential implication. This may be true, for instance, in the case of warrants backed by statutory provisions: legislation may refer to persons or situations which have yet to be – for instance, to all married women who will reach the age of 70 after 1 January 1984 – or alternatively to classes of persons none of whom may ever exist, such as men found guilty on separate occasions of ten different murders. Statutes referring to people of these types can provide backing for inference-warrants entitling us to take all kinds of steps in argument, without either the warrants or their backing implying anything about the existence of such people at all. To sum up: if we pay closer attention to the differences between warrants and backing, and between different sorts of backing for one and the same warrant, and between the backing for warrants of different sorts, and if we refuse to focus our attention hypnotically on the traditional form 'All A's are B's', we can not only come to see *that* sometimes 'All A's are B's', does have existential implications and sometimes not, but furthermore begin to understand *why* this should be so.

Once one has become accustomed to expanding statements of the form 'All A's are B's', and replacing them, as occasion requires, by explicit warrants or explicit statements of backing, one will find it a puzzle that logicians have been wedded to this form of statement for so long. The reasons for this will concern us in a later essay: for the moment, we may remark that they have done so only at the expense of impoverishing our language and disregarding a large number of clues to the proper solutions of their conundrums. For the form 'All A's are B's' occurs in practical argument much less than one would suppose from logic textbooks: indeed, a great deal of effort has to be expended in order to train students in ways of rephrasing in this special form the idiomatic statements to which they are already accustomed, thereby making these idiomatic utterances apparently amenable to traditional syllogistic analysis. There is no need, in complaining of this, to argue that idiom is sacrosanct, or provides by itself understanding of a kind we could not have had before. Nevertheless, in our normal ways of expressing ourselves, one will find many points of idiom which can serve as very definite clues, and are capable in this case of leading us in the right direction.

Where the logician has in the past cramped all general statements into his predetermined form, practical speech has habitually employed a dozen different forms – 'Every single A is a B', 'Each A is a B', 'An A will be a B', 'A's are generally B's' and 'The A is a B' being only a selection. By contrasting these idioms, instead of ignoring them or insisting that they all fall into line, logicians would long ago have been led on to the distinctions we have found crucial. The contrast between 'Every A' and 'Not a single A', on the one hand, and 'Any A' or 'An A', on the other, points one immediately towards the distinction between statistical reports and the warrants for which they can be the backing. The differences between warrants in different fields are also reflected in idiom. A biologist would hardly ever utter the words 'All whales are mammals'; though sentences such as 'Whales are mammals' or 'The whale is a mammal' might quite naturally come from his lips or his pen. Warrants are one thing, backing another; backing by enumerative observation is one thing, backing by taxonomic classification another; and our choices of idiom, though perhaps subtle, reflect these differences fairly exactly.

Even in so remote a field as philosophical ethics, some hoary problems have been generated in just this way. Practice forces us to recognise that general ethical truths can aspire at best to hold good in the absence of effective counter-claims: conflicts of duty are an inescapable feature of the moral life. Where logic demands the form '*All* lying is reprehensible' or '*All* promise-keeping is right', idiom therefore replies 'Lying is reprehensible' and 'Promisekeeping is right.' The logician's 'all' imports unfortunate expectations, which in practice are bound on occasion to be disappointed. Even the most general warrants in ethical arguments are yet liable in unusual situations to suffer exceptions, and so at strongest can authorise only presumptive conclusions. If we insist on the 'all', conflicts of duties land us in paradox, and much of moral theory is concerned with getting us out of this morass. Few people insist on trying to put into practice the consequences of insisting on the extra 'all', for to do so one must resort to desperate measures: it can be done only by adopting an eccentric moral position, such as absolute pacifism, in which one principle and one alone is admitted to be genuinely universal, and this principle is defended through thick and thin, in the face of all the conflicts and counter-claims which would normally qualify its application. The road from nice points about logic and idiom to the most difficult problems of conduct is not, after all, such a long one.

The Notion of Formal Validity

The chief morals of this study of practical argument will be our concern in the final pair of essays. But there is one topic – the one from which this present essay began – about which we are already in a position to say something: namely, the idea of 'logical form', and the doctrines which attempt to explain the validity of arguments in terms of this notion of form. It is sometimes argued, for instance, that the validity of syllogistic arguments is a consequence of the fact that the conclusions of these arguments are simply 'formal transformations' of their premisses. If the information we start from, as expressed in the major and minor premisses, leads to the conclusion it does by a valid inference, that (it is said) is because the conclusion results simply from shuffling the parts of the premisses and rearranging them in a new pattern. In drawing the inference, we re-order the given elements, and the formal relations between these elements as they appear, first in the premisses and then in the conclusion, somehow or other assure for us the validity of the inference which we make.

How does this doctrine look, if we now make our central distinction between the two aspects of the statement-form 'All A's are B's'? Consider an argument of the form:

X is an A;

All A's are B's;

So X is a B.

If we expand the universal premiss of this argument as a warrant, it becomes 'Any A can certainly be taken to be a B' or, more briefly, 'An A is certainly a B.' Substituting this in the argument, we obtain:

X is an A;

An A is certainly a B;

So X is certainly a B.

When the argument is put in this way, the parts of the conclusion are manifestly the same as the parts of the premisses, and the conclusion can be obtained simply by shuffling the parts of the premisses and rearranging them. If that is what is meant by saying that the argument has the appropriate 'logical form', and that it is valid on account of that fact, then this may be said to be a 'formally valid' argument. Yet one thing must be noticed straight away: provided that the correct warrant is employed, any argument can be expressed in the form 'Data; warrant; so conclusion' and so become formally valid. By suitable choice of phrasing, that is, any such argument can be so expressed that its validity is apparent simply from its form: this is true equally, whatever the field of the argument – it makes no difference if the universal premiss is 'All multiples of 2 are even', 'All lies are reprehensible' or 'All whales are mammals.' Any such premiss can be written as an unconditional warrant, 'An A is certainly a B', and used in a formally valid inference; or, to put the point less misleadingly, can be used in an inference which is so set out that its validity becomes formally manifest.

On the other hand, if we substitute the backing for the warrant, i.e. interpret the universal premiss in the other way, there will no longer be any room for applying the idea of formal validity to our argument. An argument of the form 'Data; backing; so conclusion' may, for practical purposes, be entirely in order. We should accept without hesitation the argument:

Petersen is a Swede;

The recorded proportion of Roman Catholic Swedes is zero;

So, certainly, Petersen is not a Roman Catholic.

But there can no longer be any pretence that the soundness of this argument is a consequence of any formal properties of its constituent expressions. Apart from anything else, the elements of the conclusion and premisses are not the same: the step therefore involves more than shuffling and re-ordering. For that matter, of course, the validity of the (D; W; so C) argument was not really a *consequence* of its formal properties either, but at any rate in that case one could state the argument in a particularly tidy form. Now this can no longer be done: a (D; B; so C) argument will not be formally valid. Once we bring into the open the backing on which (in the last resort) the soundness of our arguments depends, the suggestion that validity is to be explained in terms of 'formal properties', in any geometrical sense, loses its plausibility.

This discussion of formal validity can throw some light on another point of idiom: one in which the customary usage of arguers again parts company with logical tradition. The point arises in the following way. Suppose we contrast what may be called 'warrant-using' arguments with 'warrant-establishing' ones. The first class will include, among others, all those in which a single datum is relied on to establish a conclusion by appeal to some warrant whose acceptability is being taken for granted – examples are 'Harry was born in Bermuda, so presumably (people born in the colonies being entitled to British citizenship) Harry is a British citizen', 'Jack told a lie, so presumably (lying being generally reprehensible) Jack behaved in a reprehensible way', and 'Petersen is a Swede, so presumably (scarcely any Swedes being Roman Catholics) Petersen is not a Roman Catholic' Warrant-establishing arguments will be, by contrast, such arguments as one might find in a scientific paper, in which the acceptability of a novel warrant is made clear by applying it successively in a number of cases in which both 'data' and 'conclusion' have been independently verified. In this type of argument the warrant, not the conclusion, is novel, and so on trial.

Professor Gilbert Ryle has compared the steps involved in these two types of argument with, respectively, the taking of a journey along a railway already built and the building of a fresh railway: he has argued persuasively that only the first class of arguments should be referred to as 'inferences', on the ground that the essential element of innovation in the latter class cannot be made the subject of rules and that the notion of inference essentially involves the possibility of 'rules of inference'.

The point of idiom to be noticed here is this: that the distinction we have marked by the unwieldy terms 'warrant-using' and 'warrant-establishing' is commonly indicated in practice by the word 'deductive', its affiliates and their opposites. Outside the study the family of words, 'deduce', 'deductive', and 'deduction', is applied to arguments from many fields; all that is required is that these arguments shall be warrant-using ones, applying established warrants to fresh data to derive new conclusions. It makes no difference to the propriety of these terms that the step from D to C will in some cases involve a transition of logical type – that it is, for instance, a step from information about the past to a prediction about the future.

Sherlock Holmes, at any rate, never hesitated to say that he had *deduced*, e.g., that a man was recently in East Sussex from the colour and texture of the fragments of soil he left upon the study carpet; and in this he spoke like a character from real life. An astronomer would say, equally readily, that he had *deduced* when a future eclipse would occur from the present and past positions and motions of the heavenly bodies involved. As Ryle implies, the meaning of the word 'deduce' is effectively the same as that of 'infer'; so that, wherever there are established warrants or set procedures of computation by which to pass from data to a conclusion, there we may properly speak of 'deductions'. A regular prediction, made in accordance with the standard equations of stellar dynamics, is in this sense an unquestionable deduction; and so long as Sherlock Holmes also is capable of producing sound, well-backed warrants to justify his steps, we can allow that he too has been making deductions – unless one has just been reading a textbook of formal logic. The protestations of another sleuth that Sherlock Holmes was in error, in taking for deductions arguments which were really inductive, will strike one as hollow and mistaken.

The other side of this coin is also worth a glance: namely, the way in which the word 'induction' can be used to refer to warrant-establishing arguments. Sir Isaac Newton, for instance, regularly speaks of 'rendering a proposition general by induction': by this he turns out to mean 'using our observations of regularities and correlations as the backing for a novel warrant'. We begin, he explains, by establishing that a particular relation holds in a certain number of cases, and then, 'rendering it general by induction', we continue to apply it to fresh examples for so long as we can successfully do so: if we get into trouble as a result, he says, we are to find ways of rendering the general statement 'liable to exceptions', i.e. to discover the special circumstances in which the presumptions established by the warrant are liable to rebuttal. A general statement in physical theory, as Newton reminds us, must be construed not as a statistical report about the behaviour of a very large number of objects, but rather as an open warrant or principle of computation: it is established by testing it in sample situations where both data and conclusion are independently known, then rendered general by induction, and finally applied as a rule of deduction in fresh situations to derive novel conclusions from our data.

In many treatises on formal logic, on the other hand, the term deduction is reserved for arguments in which the data and backing positively entail the conclusion – in which, that is to say, to state all the data and backing and yet to deny the conclusion would land one in a positive inconsistency or contradiction. This is, of course, an ideal of deduction which no astronomer's prediction could hope to approach; and if that is what formal logicians are going to demand of any 'deduction', it is no wonder they are unwilling to call such computations by that name. Yet the astronomers are unwilling to change their habits: they have been calling their elaborate mathematical demonstrations 'deductions' for a very long time, and they use the term to mark a perfectly genuine and consistent distinction.

What are we to make of this conflict of usage? Ought we to allow any argument to count as a deduction which applies an established warrant, or must we demand in addition that it should be backed by a positive entailment? This question we are not yet ready to determine. All we can do at the moment is register the fact that at this point customary idiom outside the study tends to deviate from the professional usage of logicians. As we shall see, this particular deviation is only one aspect of a larger one, which will concern us throughout a large part of our fourth essay and whose nature will become clearer when we have studied one final distinction. To that distinction, between 'analytic' and 'substantial' arguments, we must now turn.

Analytic and Substantial Arguments

This distinction is best approached by way of a preamble. We remarked some way back that an argument expressed in the form 'Datum; warrant; so conclusion' can be set out in a formally valid manner, regardless of the field to which it belongs; but this could never be done, it appeared, for arguments of the form 'Datum; backing for warrant; so conclusion'. To return to our stock example: if we are given information about Harry's birthplace, we may be able to draw a conclusion about his nationality, and defend it with a formally valid argument of the form (D; W; so C). But the warrant we apply in this formally valid argument rests in turn for its authority on facts about the enactment and pro-

visions of certain statutes, and we can therefore write out the argument in the alternative form (D; B; so C), i.e.:

Harry was born in Bermuda;

The relevant statutes ($W_1 \ldots$) provide that people born in the colonies of British parents are entitled to British citizenship;

So, presumably, Harry is a British citizen.

When we choose this form, there is no question of claiming that the validity of the argument is evident simply from the formal relations between the three statements in it. Stating the backing for our warrant in such a case inevitably involves mentioning Acts of Parliament and the like, and these references destroy the formal elegance of the argument. In other fields, too, explicitly mentioning the backing for our warrant – whether this takes the form of statistical reports, appeals to the results of experiments, or references to taxonomical systems – will prevent us from writing the argument so that its validity shall be manifest from its formal properties alone.

As a general rule, therefore, we can set out in a formally valid manner arguments of the form 'D; W; so C' alone: arguments of the form 'D; B; so C' cannot be so expressed. There is, however, one rather special class of arguments which appears at first sight to break this general rule, and these we shall in due course christen *analytic* arguments. As an illustration we may take the following:

Anne is one of Jack's sisters;

All Jack's sisters have red hair;

So, Anne has red hair.

Arguments of this type have had a special place in the history of logic, and we shall have to pay close attention to them: it has not always been recognised how rare, in practice, arguments having their special characteristics are.

As a first move, let us expand this argument as we have already done those of other types. Writing the major premiss as a statement of backing, we obtain:

Anne is one of Jack's sisters;

Each one of Jack's sisters has (been checked individually to have) red hair;

So, Anne has red hair.

Alternatively, writing warrant in place of backing, we have:

Anne is one of Jack's sisters;

Any sister of Jack's will (i.e. may be taken to) have red hair;

So, Anne has red hair.

This argument is exceptional in the following respect. If each one of the girls has been checked individually to have red hair, then Anne's hair-colour has been specifically checked in the process. In this case, accordingly, the backing of our warrant includes explicitly the information which we are presenting as our conclusion: indeed, one might very well replace the word 'so' before the conclusion by the phrase 'in other words', or 'that is to say'. In such a case, to accept the datum and the backing is *thereby* to accept implicitly the conclusion also; if we string datum, backing and conclusion together to form a single sentence, we end up with an actual tautology – 'Anne is one of Jack's sisters and each one of Jack's sisters has red hair *and also* Anne has red hair.' So, for once, not only the (D; W; so C) argument but also the (D; B; so C) argument can – it appears – be stated in a formally valid manner.

Most of the arguments we have practical occasion to make use of are, one need hardly say, not of this type. We make claims about the future, and back them by reference to our experience of how things have gone in the past; we make assertions about a man's feelings, or about his legal status, and back them by references to his utterances and gestures, or to his place of birth and to the statutes about nationality; we adopt moral positions, and pass aesthetic judgements, and declare support for scientific theories or political causes, in each case producing as grounds for our conclusion statements of quite other logical types than the conclusion itself. Whenever we do any of these things, there can be no question of the conclusion's being regarded as a mere restatement in other words of something already stated implicitly in the datum and the backing: though the argument may be formally valid when expressed in the form 'Datum; warrant; so conclusion', the step we take in passing to the conclusion from the information we have to rely on – datum and backing together – is a substantial one. In most of our arguments, therefore, the statement obtained by writing 'Datum; backing; *and also* conclusion' will be far from a tautology – obvi-

ous it may be, where the legitimacy of the step involved is transparent, but tautological it will not.

In what follows, I shall call arguments of these two types respectively *substantial* and *analytic*. An argument from D to C will be called analytic if and only if the backing for the warrant authorising it includes, explicitly or implicitly, the information conveyed in the conclusion itself. Where this is so, the statement 'D, B, and also C' will, as a rule, be tautological. (This rule is, however, subject to some exceptions which we shall study shortly.) Where the backing for the warrant does not contain the information conveyed in the conclusion, the statement 'D, B, and also C' will never be a tautology, and the argument will be a substantial one.

The need for some distinction of this general sort is obvious enough, and certain aspects of it have forced themselves on the attention of logicians, yet its implications have never been consistently worked out. This task has been neglected for at least two reasons. To begin with, the internal complexity of statements of the form 'All A's are B's' helps to conceal the full difference between analytic and substantial arguments. Unless we go to the trouble of expanding these statements, so that it becomes manifest whether they are to be understood as stating warrants or the backing for warrants, we overlook the great variety of arguments susceptible of presentation in the traditional syllogistic form: we have to bring out the distinction between backing and warrant explicitly in any particular case if we are to be certain what sort of argument we are concerned with on that occasion. In the second place, it has not been recognised how exceptional genuinely analytic arguments are, and how difficult it is to produce an argument which will be analytic past all question: if logicians had recognised these facts, they might have been less ready to treat analytic arguments as a model which other types of argument were to emulate.

Even our chosen example, about the colour of Anne's hair, may easily slip out of the analytic into the substantial class. If the backing for our step from datum, 'Anne is Jack's sister', to conclusion, 'Anne has red hair', is just the information that each of Jack's sisters has *in the past* been observed to have red hair, then – one might argue – the argument is a substantial one even as it stands. After all, dyeing is not unknown. So ought we not to rewrite the argument in such a way as to bring out its substantial character openly? On this interpretation the argument will become:

Datum – Anne is one of Jack's sisters;

Backing – All Jack's sisters have previously been observed to have red hair;

Conclusion – So, presumably, Anne now has red hair.

The warrant relied on, for which the backing is here stated, will be of the form, 'Any sister of Jack's may be taken to have red hair': for the reasons given, this warrant can be regarded as establishing no more than a presumption:

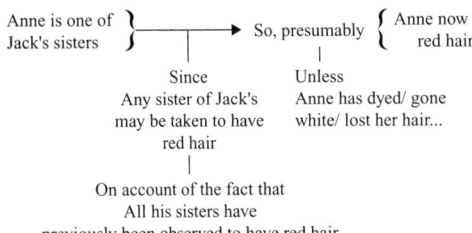

It seems, then, that I can defend my conclusion about Anne's hair with an unquestionably analytic argument only if at this very moment I have all of Jack's sisters in sight, and so can back my warrant with the assurance that every one of Jack's sisters has red hair at this moment. But, in such a situation, what need is there of an *argument* to establish the colour of Anne's hair? And of what relevance is the other sisters' hair-colour? The thing to do now is use one's eyes, not hunt up a chain of reasoning. If the purpose of an argument is to establish conclusions about which we are not entirely confident by relating them back to other information about which we have greater assurance, it begins to be a little doubtful whether any genuine, practical argument could *ever* be properly analytic.

Mathematical arguments alone seem entirely safe: given the assurance that every sequence of six or more integers between 1 and 100 contains at least one prime number, and also the information that none of the numbers from 62 up to 66 is a prime, I can thankfully conclude that the number 67 is a prime; and that is an argument whose validity neither time nor the flux of change can call in question. This unique character of mathematical arguments is significant. Pure mathematics is possibly the only intellectual activity whose problems and solutions are 'above time'. A mathematical problem is not a quandary; its solution has no time-limit; it involves no steps of substance. As a model argument for formal logi-

cians to analyse, it may be seducingly elegant, but it could hardly be less representative.

The Peculiarities of Analytic Arguments

For the rest of this essay, two chief tasks remain. First, we must clarify a little further the special characteristics of analytic arguments: after that, we must contrast the distinction between analytic and substantial arguments with three other distinctions whose importance we have already seen:

(I)   that between formally valid arguments and those which are not formally valid,

(II) that between warrant-using and warrant-establishing arguments,

(III) that between arguments leading to necessary conclusions and those leading only to probable conclusions.

As to the nature of analytic arguments themselves, two things need to be discussed. To begin with we must ask upon what foundation arguments of this type ultimately depend for their validity: after that, we must go on to reconsider the criteria provisionally suggested for distinguishing analytic arguments from others – for the 'tautology test' turns out, after all, to involve unsuspected difficulties.

To see how the first question arises, one should first recall how much less sharply than usual, in the case of analytic arguments, we can distinguish between data and warrant-backing – between the information we argue *from*, and the information which lends authority to the warrants we argue *in accordance with*: so far as it concerns the conclusion that Anne has red hair, the information that Anne is Jack's sister has, at first sight, the same sort of bearing as the information that every one of Jack's sisters has red hair. This similarity may lead us to construe both pieces of information as data, and if we do so the question may be raised, 'What warrant authorises us to pass from these two premises jointly to the required conclusion?' Surely we cannot get from *any* set of data to a conclusion without *some* warrant; so what warrant can we produce to justify our inference in this case? This is the problem, and we can tackle it in only two ways: either we must accept the question, and produce a warrant, or alternatively we must reject the question in the form in which it stands, and insist on sending it back for rephrasing. (It is arguable, for instance, that we have a perfectly good warrant for passing from the *first* datum to the conclusion, and that the second piece of information is the backing for that warrant.) For the moment, however, let us consider this problem in the form in which it arises here.

The first thing to notice about this problem is the fact that it is completely general. So long as one is arguing only from Anne's being Jack's sister to her having red hair, the question what warrant authorises our inference is a *particular* question, relevant only to this argument and a few others; but if one asks, what warrant authorises us to pass from the information *both* that Anne is Jack's sister *and* that every single one of Jack's sisters has red hair to the conclusion that Anne has red hair, that question is nowhere near so restricted a question, since it can arise in exactly the same form for all arguments of this type, whatever their explicit subject-matter. The answer to be given must therefore be equally general, and stated in such a way as to apply equally to all such arguments. What warrant, then, are we to say does authorise this particular step? The attempts to answer this question satisfactorily have been prolonged and inconclusive, and we cannot follow them through here: several different principles of a wholly general character have been put forward as the implied warrant for steps of this kind – the 'Principle of the Syllogism', the 'Dictum de Omni et Nullo', and others. But, quite apart from the respective merits of their rival answers, philosophers have not even been agreed about *how* such general principles really authorise us to argue as we do. What sort of a statement is (say) the Principle of the Syllogism? – that is the first question needing attention.

There is a temptation to say that any principle validating all syllogisms alike must be understood as a statement about the meanings of our words – an implicit analysis of such preeminently logical words as 'all' and 'some'. One consequence of this view, which we shall scrutinise in essay IV of *The Uses of Argument*, has been the growth of a rather limited doctrine about the nature and scope of logic. If the only principles of inference properly so-called are statements about the meanings of our words, then (some have argued) it is misleading to apply the title of inferring-rules to other sorts of general statement also, which are concerned with matters of substance and not simply with the meanings of our words: as a result, the whole notion of inference-warrants, as set out in this essay, has been pushed aside as confused.

Now we may agree that there is not an exact parallel between the Principle of the Syllogism

and those other sorts of argument-governing rules we have given the name of 'warrant', and yet feel that this conclusion goes too far. Without questioning at the moment the need for some Principle of the Syllogism, we may yet object to its being called a statement *about* the meanings of our words: why should we not see in it, rather, a warrant of a kind that holds good *in virtue of* the meanings of our words? This is an improvement on the previous formulation in at least one respect, for it leaves us free to say that other warrants – those we argue in accordance with outside the analytic field – hold good in virtue of other sorts of consideration. Legal principles hold good in virtue of statutory enactments and judicial precedents, the scientist's laws of nature in virtue of the experiments and observations by which they were established, and so on. In all fields, the force of our warrants is to authorise the step from certain types of data to certain types of conclusions, but, after all we have seen about the field-dependence of the criteria we employ in the practical business of argument, it is only natural to expect that inference-warrants in different fields should need establishing by quite different sorts of procedure.

Accordingly, there seems room for an accommodation – for us to accept the Principle of the Syllogism as the warrant of all analytic syllogisms, while retaining other kinds of general statement as warrants for arguments of other types. Yet there remains something paradoxical about admitting the need for a Principle of the Syllogism at all. With arguments of all other kinds, a man who is given the data and the conclusion and who understands perfectly well what he is told may yet need to have explained to him the authority for the step from one to the other. 'I understand what your evidence is, and I understand what conclusion you draw from it,' he may say, 'but I don't see *how* you get there.' The task of the warrant is to meet his need: in order to satisfy him we have to explain what is our warrant, and if necessary show on what backing it depends, and until we have done this it is still open to him to challenge our argument. With analytic arguments, on the other hand, this sort of situation is hardly conceivable: one is tempted to say of analytic arguments (as of analytic statements) that anyone who understands them must acknowledge their legitimacy. If a man does not see the legitimacy of an analytic step in any particular case, we shall not help him much by proffering him any principle so general as the Principle of the Syllogism.

The suggestion that this principle really does a job for us, by serving as the warrant for all syllogistic arguments, is therefore implausible. Certainly, if it *is* to be regarded as a warrant, it is a warrant which requires no backing: this much is conceded by Aristotle in the fourth book of the *Metaphysics*, where he goes out of his way to reject any demand that the law of non-contradiction should be *proved* – he recognises that no backing we could produce would add anything to the strength of the principle, and that all we need do in its defence is to challenge a critic to produce a meaningful objection to it.

Let us therefore try following the alternative course: let us reject the request for a warrant to lend authority to all analytic syllogisms, insisting instead that one premiss of every such syllogism provides all the warrant we need. The information that *every* one of Jack's sisters has red hair, we may say, serves as backing for the warrant that *any* of his sisters may be taken to have hair of that colour, and it is this limited warrant which takes us from our initial information about Anne's being Jack's sister to the conclusion about her hair-colour: 'that's just analytic!' Our task is now to define more carefully what exactly here is 'just analytic', and to work out clearer tests than we have stated so far for recognising whether an argument is an analytic or a substantial one.

Three different tests suggest themselves, and their merits we must now consider. First, there is the *tautology* test: in an analytic syllogism with an 'all' in the major premiss, the data and backing positively entail the conclusion, so that we can write 'D, B, or *in other words* C', confident that in stating the conclusion we shall simply be repeating something already stated in the backing. The question is whether this is true of *all* analytic arguments: I shall argue that it is not. Secondly, there is the *verification* test: must verifying the backing implicitly relied on in an argument *ipso facto* involve checking the truth of the conclusion? This does not universally lead to the same result as the first test, and will prove to be a more satisfactory criterion. Finally, there is the test of *self-evidence*: once a man has had data, backing and conclusion explained to him, can he still raise genuine questions about the validity of the argument? This might at first seem to amount to the same as the first test but, as we shall see, it corresponds in practice more nearly to the second.

One type of example can be mentioned straight away in which the tautology criterion leads to difficulties. This is the 'quasi-syllogism', discussed earlier, in which the universal quantifiers 'all' and 'no' are replaced by the more restrictive ones 'nearly all' and 'scarcely any'. As an instance, we may take the argument:

Petersen is a Swede;

Scarcely any Swedes are Roman Catholics;

So, almost certainly, Petersen is not a Roman Catholic.

This argument differs from the corresponding 'no' argument –

Petersen is a Swede;

No Swedes are Roman Catholics;

So, certainly, Petersen is not a Roman Catholic –

only in relying on a weaker warrant and so ending in a more tentative conclusion. (Written explicitly as warrants the universal premisses are, respectively, 'A Swede can almost certainly be taken not to be a Roman Catholic' and 'A Swede can certainly be taken not to be a Roman Catholic'.)

The validity of the argument is in each case manifest, and by the test of self-evidence both should be classed as analytic arguments. If we imagine a man to challenge the 'scarcely any' argument, and to demand further backing to show its validity, his request will be no more intelligible than it would be in the case of the 'no' argument: he might ask in the first case to have the *conclusion* more firmly grounded, seeing that so long as we know only that scarcely any Swedes are Roman Catholics the possibility of any particular Swede's being of that persuasion is not ruled out past all question, but the *validity* of both arguments is surely not open to doubt. If he fails to see the force of either argument, there is little more we can do for him; and if he presents the same data and warrant-backing in support of the negated conclusion, the result will in either case be not just implausible but incomprehensible:

Petersen is a Swede;

The proportion of Roman Catholic Swedes is less than 5%/zero;

So, almost certainly/certainly, Petersen *is* a Roman Catholic.

By the test of self-evidence, then, the 'scarcely any' and 'nearly all' arguments have as much right to be classed as analytic as have the 'all' and 'no' arguments.

But if we allow this parallel, how far do our other tests for recognising analytic arguments fit? In checking the backing for our warrant, we asked, would we *ipso facto* check the conclusion of our arguments? (This we called the verification test.) Alternatively, if we wrote down our data and backing, and added the words 'and also C' – C being our conclusion – would the result be a tautology? Traditional syllogisms satisfy all our criteria equally well. Checking exhaustively that the proportion of Roman Catholic Swedes is zero of course involves checking what Petersen's religion is; while in addition the statement, 'Petersen is a Swede, and the proportion of Roman Catholic Swedes is zero, and also Petersen is not a Roman Catholic', can reasonably be called tautological. But when we look at quasi-syllogisms, we find the tautology test no longer applicable.

The verification test still fits the new cases, though it applies in a slightly Pickwickian manner: in checking exhaustively that the proportion of Roman Catholic Swedes was (say) less than 5% we should *ipso facto* check what Petersen's religion was – whether it was actually Roman Catholicism or not. On the other hand, the statement, 'Petersen is a Swede and the proportion of Roman Catholic Swedes is less than 5%, and also Petersen is not a Roman Catholic', is no longer tautological: it is, rather, genuinely informative, since the conclusion locates Petersen definitely in the 95% majority. Even if we insert the modal qualifier 'almost certainly' in the conclusion, the resulting statement is not tautological either – 'Petersen is a Swede, the proportion of Roman Catholic Swedes is less than 5%, and also, almost certainly, Petersen is not a Roman Catholic.'

As a result, when we look for a general criterion to mark off analytic arguments from others, the verification test will enable us to classify quasi-syllogisms along with traditional syllogisms in a way the tautology test will not. We shall therefore class an argument as analytic if, and only if, it satisfies that criterion – if, that is, checking the backing of the warrant involves *ipso facto* checking the truth or falsity of the conclusion – and we shall do this whether a knowledge of the full backing would in fact verify the conclusion or falsify it.

At this point, two comments are needed about Petersen's case. Once we do have access to the complete backing, we shall of course no longer be entitled to rely simply on the bare percentage of the statistician's tables and our original argument will no longer be in place.

We must base our argument about the likelihood of Petersen's being a Roman Catholic on *all* the relevant information we can get: if we in fact possess the detailed census returns, the only proper procedure is to look Petersen up by name, and find out the answer for certain. Secondly, the statement, 'Petersen is a Swede and the proportion of Roman Catholic Swedes is very low, and Petersen is almost certainly not a Roman Catholic', *would* be entirely tautological if one could properly *define* 'certainty' and 'probability' directly in terms of proportions and frequency. But to do this, as we saw, would mean ignoring the practical function of the term 'probability' and its cognates as modal qualifiers. It would also lead to paradox: as things stand, a man can say with perfect propriety, 'Petersen is a Swede and the proportion of Roman Catholic Swedes is very low, and yet Petersen is almost certainly a Roman Catholic' – he will be entitled to say this, for instance, if he knows something further about Petersen which places him very probably in the Roman Catholic minority – whereas, if the original statement were a tautology, this new statement would be bound to be a self-contradiction.

One cannot, then, characterise analytic arguments as arguments in which the statement 'D, B and also C' is a tautology: in some cases at least, this criterion fails to serve our purposes. This helps to explain one further philosophical doctrine – that even analytic syllogisms are not valid in virtue of the meanings of words alone, and that failure to understand such an argument is a sign, not of linguistic incompetence, but rather of a 'defect of reason'. Suppose we tell a man that Petersen is a Swede, and that the proportion of Roman Catholic Swedes is either zero or very low; 'so', we conclude, 'Petersen is certainly – or almost certainly – not a Roman Catholic'. He fails to follow us: what then are we to say about him? If the tautology test were adequate, this would show that he did not really understand the meanings of all the words we had employed: if we give up the tautology view, this explanation is no longer open to us. Now we must say, rather, that he is blind to, i.e. fails to see the force of, the argument. Indeed what else can we say? This is not an explanation: it is a bare statement of the fact. He just does not follow the step, and the ability to follow such arguments is, surely, one of the *basic* rational competences.

This observation can throw some light on the true status of the Principle of the Syllogism. That principle, I suggested, enters logic when the second premiss of an analytic syllogism is misinterpreted as stating a datum instead of a warrant or its backing, and the argument is thereupon (apparently) left without any authorising warrant. The Principle of the Syllogism is then held out to us as somehow showing the *ultimate* foundation for the validity of *all* syllogistic arguments.

When considering arguments in other fields, we may again find ourselves going through this same sequence of steps. Suppose we begin by mistaking the backing of our warrant for an additional set of data; having done this, we shall appear to be arguing straight from data to conclusion, without our step's having any authority; and this lack will be found to affect, not just one, but every argument in the field concerned. To fill these fresh gaps, further completely general principles will now need to be invoked: one basic principle to lie behind all scientific predictions, another to lie behind all properly grounded moral judgements, and so on. (This is a topic which we need mention here only in passing, since we shall have to return to it in essay V of *The Uses of Argument*.) Now, if the ability to follow valid syllogisms and quasi-syllogisms can best be described as a basic rational competence, and is not really explained in terms of linguistic ability or incompetence, perhaps there will be nothing more to be said in other cases either. The ability to follow simple predictive arguments, whose warrants are backed by sufficiently wide and relevant experience, may just have to be recognised as another simple rational skill, which most men possess but which is lacking in some mental defectives; and for other fields, other basic skills. Could this be said for arguments in all fields whatever? Is the ability to follow, and see the force of simple moral arguments (say), also such a skill? Or simple aesthetic arguments? Or simple theological arguments? . . . At this point we come directly up against the fundamental philosophical issue: whether all fields of argument alike are open to rational discussion, and whether the Court of Reason is competent to adjudicate equally, whatever the type of problem under discussion.

Some Crucial Distinctions

One major task remains for us to perform in this essay: we have to distinguish the division of arguments into analytic and substantial from three or four other possible modes of division. The dangers resulting from confusing these distinctions, and still more from running them together, are serious and can be avoided only with care.

To begin with, the division into analytic and substantial arguments does not correspond at all exactly to the division into *formally valid* arguments and others. An argument in any field whatever *may* be expressed in a formally valid manner, provided that the warrant is formulated explicitly as a warrant and authorises precisely the sort of inference in question: this explains how mathematical computations can be formally valid, even when the data argued from are entirely past and present observations and the conclusion argued to is a prediction about the future. On the other hand, an argument may be analytic, and yet not be expressed in a formally valid way: this is the case, for instance, when an analytic argument is written out with the backing of the warrant cited in place of the warrant itself.

Nor does the distinction between analytic and substantial arguments correspond, either, to that between *warrant-using* and *warrant-establishing* arguments. In a very few cases, warrant-establishing arguments can be stated in a form which is formally valid: thus the argument, 'Jack has three sisters; the first has red hair, the second has red hair, the third has red hair; so all Jack's sisters have red hair', might be said to be at once warrant-establishing, formally valid and analytic. But, by and large, these characteristics vary independently. There can be warrant-using and warrant-establishing arguments both in the analytic field, and in other, substantial fields of argument, and one cannot seriously hope to make the two distinctions cut along one and the same line.

Again, it has sometimes been thought that one could mark off a specially 'logical' class of arguments by reference to the *sorts of words* appearing in them. In some arguments, for instance, the words 'all' and 'some' play a crucial part, and such arguments as these deserve separate consideration. But if we do mark them off from others, we must immediately observe that the division which results corresponds no more closely than the previous two to the division between analytic arguments and substantial ones. Not all arguments are analytic in which the word 'all' appears in the major premiss or warrant: this will be so only in cases where the process of establishing the warrant would involve *ipso facto* checking the truth of the conclusion now to be inferred with its aid, and we do not restrict our use of 'all' to such cases. The task of identifying analytic arguments cannot therefore be performed by looking for key words like 'all' and 'some': it can be done only by looking at the nature of the problem under investigation, and the manner in which we establish the warrants relevant to its solution.

These three distinctions can be recognised easily enough. The fourth and last distinction is at once the most contentious and the most important. Dividing arguments into analytic and substantial is not the same, I shall argue, as dividing them into arguments whose conclusions can be inferred *necessarily* or *certainly* and those whose conclusions can be inferred only *possibly* or with *probability*. As we saw when discussing modal qualifiers, there are some arguments in which the warrant authorises the step from D to C unambiguously, and others in which the step is authorised only tentatively, conditionally or with qualifications. This division is marked in practice by the words 'necessary' or 'conclusive' on the one hand, and 'tentative', 'probable', 'provisional', or 'conditional' on the other, and it is quite independent of the division into analytic arguments and substantial ones. Yet often enough logical theorists have attempted to run these two distinctions together, identifying analytic arguments with necessary or conclusive ones, and substantial arguments with tentative, probable, or inconclusive ones. The crucial question is whether this conflation can be justified, or whether, rather, we do not have occasion in practice to classify some arguments as at once substantial *and* conclusive, or as both analytic *and* tentative.

If we pay attention to the manner in which these categories are employed in the practical business of arguing, we shall discover plenty of occasions for making use of these seeming cross-classifications. For instance, a great many of the warrants in accordance with which we argue in the explanatory sciences authorise us to draw a conclusion unambiguously and unequivocally. The arguments they figure in are, accordingly, both substantial and conclusive, and scientists who make use of such arguments do not hesitate to round them off with the words ' . . . so necessarily C'. Arguments of this kind are commonly met with in applied mathematics, as when, using the methods of geometrical optics, one calculates from the height of a wall and the angle of elevation of the sun how deep a shadow the wall will cast on level ground when the sun is shining directly on to it – if told that the wall is 6 ft. high and the sun at an angle of 30 degrees, a physicist will happily say that the shadow *must* have a depth of ten and a half feet.

In his *Philosophical Essay on Probabilities*, Laplace draws explicit attention to this class of substantial-yet-conclusive arguments: 'In the applications of mathematical analysis to physics,' he says, 'the results have all the certainty of facts,'[1] and he contrasts them with those arguments in which statistics are relied on, and whose conclusions are no more than probable. It is significant that he draws his distinction in just the manner he does. By applying the Newtonian system of mechanics to a problem in stellar dynamics, he reminds us we are normally led, not to a whole battery of possible predictions each with a greater or lesser expectation of eventual confirmation, but to one single, unambiguous and unequivocal solution. If we are prepared to acknowledge that Newtonian mechanics is sufficiently well established for the purpose of the problem in hand, then we must accept this particular conclusion as following necessarily from our original data.

The point can be put more strongly: given the present standing of the theory, we are entitled to dispute the necessity of the conclusion only if we are prepared to challenge the adequacy or relevance of Newtonian dynamics. This means, not just pointing out that arguments in planetary dynamics are substantial ones (so that their soundness can be questioned *without contradiction*), but showing that they are *in fact* unreliable; i.e. attacking Newtonian dynamics on its own ground. Unless we are prepared to carry through this challenge, with all that it involves, the astronomer is entitled to ignore our objections and to claim that, for his purposes, the theory provides a unique and uniquely reliable answer to his questions. An answer obtained by these methods certainly *must* be the answer, he will say, for it is the answer to which a correctly performed calculation in accordance with well-established procedures necessarily leads us.

Nor do we find these substantial-yet-conclusive arguments in the more elaborate and technical sciences alone. When Sherlock Holmes says to Watson, 'So you see, my dear Watson, it *could only* have been Joseph Harrison who stole the Naval Treaty', or 'I concluded that the thief *must* be somebody living in the house', he does not mean that he can produce an analytic argument to establish his conclusion: he means rather that, by other-than-analytic standards and by appeal to other-than-analytic warrants, the evidence admits of this conclusion alone.

How widely this point of view deviates from that of many formal logicians, we shall see in essay IV of *The Uses of Argument*. For them it is a commonplace that no argument can be both substantial and conclusive: only the conclusions of analytic arguments, they claim, can properly be classified as necessary, and the conclusions of substantial arguments – however well established and securely based the warrants relied on in reaching them – can never be more than highly probable. Why do they embrace this conclusion? Well, they explain, one can always imagine circumstances in which we might be forced to reconsider any substantial warrant: however well established any theory may appear at the moment, it makes sense to talk of future experiences forcing us to revise it, and so long as that remains the case – as in the nature of things it always must do – it will be presumptuous of us to call any conclusion reached in this way a necessary one. We could escape from this quandary only if the idea of our having to reconsider our inference-warrant gave rise to a positive contradiction, and this could never happen except with an analytic argument, whose warrant was backed not by experience but by an entailment.

If we have occasion to recognise in practice a class of arguments which are at once substantial and conclusive, so also do we recognise a class of analytic arguments with tentative or qualified conclusions. Quasi-syllogisms once more provide a good example. As is clear from their very wording, these arguments are not absolutely conclusive: all they entitle us to infer is (say) that Petersen is *almost certainly*, or *probably*, *not* a Roman Catholic. At the same time, we must accept these arguments as analytic for two reasons: they satisfy our primary criterion of analyticity – the backing for the warrant employed including an implicit reference to the fact we are interested in inferring, even though we ourselves do not possess all the detailed backing; and further, the validity of such arguments must be evident as they stand, or not at all – if a man asks about a quasi-syllogism, 'Does it really follow? Is this really a legitimate inference?', we shall be as much at a loss to understand him as we should had he queried a genuine syllogism. One thing alone seems at first to count against calling quasi-syllogistic arguments analytic: the fact that data and backing taken together are, by linguistic standards, consistent with the negation of the conclusion – there is, as we saw, no positive contradiction in the supposition of Petersen's being a Swede, scarcely any Swedes being Roman Catholic, and yet Petersen's being a Roman Catholic. But then, how could one expect any *positive* contradiction here? The whole point of the qualifier 'probably' is to avoid any positive commitments, and this is its understood effect, whether it appears

in an isolated statement or in the conclusion of an argument, and whether that argument is substantial or analytic. So here we have a *prima facie* case of an argument which is analytic without being conclusive.

At this point one objection may be pressed, as follows: 'Granted that quasi-syllogistic arguments are analytic, they nevertheless do not provide the example you require. You claim that they are tentative, but you succeed in giving this impression only by suppressing some of the essential data. If you were to state explicitly all the information needed for such arguments as these to be valid, it would become clear that they are not really tentative at all, but are as conclusive as one could ask.' What sort of information might one say was being suppressed? And would it, if brought to light, remove all inconclusiveness from these arguments? Two suggestions must be considered. Quasi-syllogistic arguments, it might be said, are valid only if we can add the datum, (a), ' . . . and we know nothing else relevant about Petersen' – given this extra datum, the argument turns into an analytic one, leading necessarily to the conclusion that the likelihood of Petersen's being a Roman Catholic is small. Or alternatively, it may be argued, we must insert the additional datum, (b), ' . . . and Petersen is a random Swede' – making this additional datum explicit, we shall see that a quasi-syllogistic argument is really a conclusive argument in disguise.

We cannot meet this objection by a straight denial, but only by restating it in a way which removes its force. It must of course be conceded that quasi-syllogisms can properly be advanced only if the initial data from which we argue state all that we know of relevance to the question at issue: if they represent no more than a part of our relevant knowledge, we shall be required to argue not categorically but hypothetically – 'Given only the information that Petersen is a Swede, we might conclude that the chances of his being a Roman Catholic were slight . . . '. But does this mean that the statement, (a), was an essential item in our data, which we should never have omitted? Surely this statement is not so much a statement *of* a datum as a statement *about the nature of* our data: it would naturally appear, not as part of our answer to the question, 'What have you got to go on?', but rather as a comment which we might add subsequently, after having stated (say) the solitary fact about Petersen's nationality.

The objection that we have omitted the information, (b), that Petersen is a random Swede (or a Swede taken at random) can be turned in a similar way. The information that he was a red-haired Swede, or a dark-complexioned Swede, or a Finnish-speaking Swede, could be called an 'extra fact' about him, and might possibly affect, in one way or another, our expectations about his religious beliefs. But the information that he was a *random* Swede is not like this at all. It is not a further fact about him which might be relevant to our expectations; it is at most a second-order comment on our previous information, indicating that, for all we know, we are entitled to presume about Petersen anything which established generalities about Swedes would suggest. So, once again, the so-called additional datum, (*b*), turns out to be not so much a datum as a passing comment about the applicability to this particular man of a warrant based only on statistical generalities.

The division of arguments into analytic and substantial is, therefore, entirely distinct from that into conclusive (necessary) and tentative (probable) arguments. Analytic arguments can be conclusive or tentative, and conclusive ones analytic or substantial. At once, one terminological precaution becomes urgent: we must renounce the common habit of using the adverb 'necessarily' interchangeably with the adverb 'deductively' – where this is used to mean 'analytically'. For where a substantial argument leads to an unequivocal conclusion, we are entitled to use the form 'D, so necessarily. C', despite the fact that the relation between data, backing and conclusion is not analytic; and where an analytic argument leads to a tentative conclusion, we cannot strictly say any longer that the conclusion follows 'necessarily' – only that it follows analytically. Once we fall into the way of identifying 'analytically' and 'necessarily', we shall end up by having to conclude an argument with the paradoxical words, ' . . . so Petersen is necessarily probably not a Roman Catholic', or even, ' . . . so Petersen is necessarily necessarily not a Roman Catholic'. Perhaps, indeed, it would be better to scrap the words 'deductively' and 'necessarily' entirely, and to replace them either by 'analytically' or by 'unequivocally' according to the needs of the example.

The Perils of Simplicity

This essay has been deliberately restricted to prosaic studies of the different sorts of criticism to which our micro-arguments are subject, and to building up a pattern of analysis sufficiently complex to do justice to the most obvious dif-ferences between these forms of criticism. Much of this distinction-making would be tedious if we were not looking ahead to a point where the distinctions would prove of philosophical importance. So, in this concluding section, we can afford not only to look back over the ground which we have covered, but also to glance ahead to see the sort of value which these distinctions will have, and which will give a point to these laborious preliminaries.

We began from a question about 'logical form'. This had two aspects: there was the question, what relevance the geometrical tidiness sought in traditional analyses of the syllogism could have for a man trying to tell sound arguments from unsound ones; and there was the further question whether, in any event, the traditional pattern for analysing micro-arguments – 'Minor Premiss, Major Premiss, so Conclusion' – was complex enough to reflect all the distinctions forced upon us in the actual practice of argument-assessment. We tackled the latter question first, with an eye to the example of jurisprudence. Philosophers studying the logic of legal arguments have long since been forced to classify their propositions into many more than three types, and, keeping our eyes on the actual practice of argument, we found ourselves obliged to follow them along the same road. There are in practical argument a good half-dozen functions to be performed by different sorts of proposition: once this is recognised, it becomes necessary to distinguish, not just between premisses and conclusions, but between claims, data, warrants, modal qualifiers, conditions of rebuttal, statements about the applicability or inapplicability of warrants, and others.

These distinctions will not be particularly novel to those who have studied explicitly the logic of special types of practical argument: the topic of exceptions or conditions of rebuttal, for instance – which were labelled (R) in our pattern of analysis – has been discussed by Professor H. L. A. Hart under the title of 'defeasibility', and he has shown its relevance not only to the jurisprudential study of contract but also to philosophical theories about free-will and responsibility. (It is probably no accident that he reached these results while working in the borderland between jurisprudence and philosophy.) Traces of the distinction can be discerned even in the writings of some who remain wedded to the traditions of formal logic. Sir David Ross, for example, has discussed the same topic of rebuttals, especially in the field of ethics. He recognises that in practice we are compelled to allow exceptions to all moral rules, if only because any man recognising more than one rule is liable on occasion to find two of his rules pointing in different directions; but, being committed to the traditional pattern of argument-analysis, he has no category of presumptive arguments, or of rebuttals (R), in terms of which to account for this necessity. He gets around this by continuing to construe moral rules of action as major premises, but criticising the manner in which they are normally phrased. If we are to be logical, he claims, all our moral rules should have the words *prima facie* added to them: in the absence of these words, he can see no strict possibility of admitting any exceptions.

We accordingly found it more natural to look for parallels between logic and jurisprudence than for parallels between logic and geometry: a clearly analysed argument is as much one in which the formalities of rational assessment are clearly set out and which is couched 'in proper form', as one which has been presented in a tidy geometrical shape. Granted, there is a large class of valid arguments which can be expressed in the neat form, 'Data; Warrant; so Conclusion', the warrant serving precisely as the bridge required to make the transition from data to conclusion; but to call such an argument formally valid is to say only something about the manner in which it has been phrased, and tells us nothing about the *reasons for* its validity. These reasons are to be understood only when we turn to consider the *backing* of the warrant invoked.

The traditional pattern of analysis, I suggested, has two serious defects. It is always liable to lead us, as it leads Sir David Ross, to pay too little attention to the differences between the different modes of criticism to which arguments are subject – to the differences, for instance, between warrants (W) and rebuttals (R). Particular premises commonly express our data; whereas universal premises may express either warrants or the backing for warrants, and when they are stated in the form 'All A's are B's' it will often be entirely obscure just which function they are to be understood as performing. The consequences of this obscurity can be grave, as we shall see later, particularly when we allow for the other defect of the traditional pattern – the effect it has of obscuring the differences between different fields of argument, and the sorts of warrant and backing appropriate to these different fields.

One central distinction we studied at some length: that between the field of analytic arguments, which in practice are somewhat rare, and those other fields of argument, which can be grouped together under the title of substantial arguments, as logicians discovered early on, the field of analytic arguments is particularly simple; certain complexities which inevitably afflict substantial arguments need never trouble one in the case of analytic ones; and when the warrant of an analytic argument is expressed in the form 'All A's are B's', the whole argument can be laid out in the traditional pattern without harm resulting – for once in a while, the distinction between our data and the backing of our warrant ceases to be of serious importance. This simplicity is very attractive, and the theory of analytic arguments with universal major premises was therefore seized on and developed with enthusiasm by logicians of many generations.

Simplicity, however, has its perils. It is one thing to choose as one's first object of theoretical study the type of argument open to analysis in the simplest terms. But it would be quite another to treat this type of argument as a paradigm and to demand that arguments in other fields should conform to its standards regardless, or, to build up from a study of the simplest forms of argument alone a set of categories intended for application to arguments of all sorts: one must at any rate begin by inquiring carefully how far the artificial simplicity of one's chosen model results in these logical categories also being artificially simple. The sorts of risks one runs otherwise are obvious enough. Distinctions which all happen to cut along the same line for the simplest arguments may need to be handled quite separately in the general case; if we forget this, and our new-found logical categories yield paradoxical results when applied to more complex arguments, we may be tempted to put these results down to defects in the arguments instead of in our categories; and we may end up by thinking that, for some regrettable reason hidden deep in the nature of things, only our original, peculiarly simple arguments are capable of attaining to the ideal of validity.

At this point, these perils can be hinted at only in entirely general terms. In the last two essays in this book, I shall make it my business to show more precisely how they have affected the actual results obtained, first by formal logicians, and then by philosophers working in the field of epistemology. The development of logical theory, I shall argue, began historically with the study of a rather special class of arguments – namely, the class of unequivocal, analytic, formally valid arguments with a universal statement as 'major premiss'. Arguments in this class are exceptional in four different ways, which together make them a bad example for general study. To begin with, the use of the form 'All A's are B's' in the major premiss conceals the distinction between an inference-warrant and the statement of its backing. Secondly, with this class of arguments alone the distinction between our data and our warrant-backing ceases to be of serious importance. (These first two factors between them can lead one to overlook the functional differences between data, warrants, and the backing of warrants; and so to put them on a level and label them all alike as 'premisses'.) In the third place, arguments of this chosen type being analytic, the procedure for verifying the backing in each case involves *ipso facto* verifying the conclusion; while since they are, in the fourth place, unequivocal also, it becomes impossible to accept the data and backing and yet deny the conclusion, without positively contradicting oneself. These special characteristics of their first chosen class of arguments have been interpreted by logicians as signs of special merit; other classes of argument, they have felt, are deficient in so far as they fail to display all the characteristic merits of the paradigm class; and the distinctions which in this first case alone all cut along one and the same line

are identified and treated as a single distinction. The divisions of arguments into analytic and substantial, into warrant-using and warrant-establishing, into conclusive and tentative, and into formally valid and not formally valid: these are regimented for purposes of theory into a single distinction, and the pair of terms 'deductive' and 'inductive', which in practice – as we saw – is used to mark only the second of the four distinctions, is attached equally to all four.

This vast initial oversimplification marks the traditional beginning of much in logical theory. Many of the current problems in the logical tradition spring from adopting the analytic paradigm-argument as a standard by comparison with which all other arguments can be criticised. But analyticity is one thing, formal validity is another; and neither of these is a universal criterion of necessity, still less of the soundness of our arguments. Analytic arguments are a special case, and we are laying up trouble for ourselves, both in logic and in epistemology, if we treat them as anything else. That, at any rate, is the claim I hope to make good in the two essays which follow.

Note

1   Ch. III, 'Third Principle'.

Chapter 33: The Skills of Argument

DEANNA KUHN

Introduction

Scope of the Investigation

The investigation to be described focuses on an individual's thinking processes, and as such it relates most directly to the sizable psychological literature on thinking and reasoning. Yet the work also addresses issues that are prominent in a number of other disciplines.

From a philosophical perspective, the present work relates to an increasing interest shown by philosophers in the nature and logic of natural language argumentation (Walton, 1989). As already mentioned, philosophers of education such as Scheffler (1965) have noted the importance of reflective thinking about thought, but their ideas have not been connected explicitly to the analysis of argumentation. Here we offer those with philosophical interests an analysis of elementary argumentive reasoning that is grounded in empirical data about the competencies and incompetencies that people exhibit in their argumentive reasoning about everyday topics.

From a language perspective, the present work relates to a growing area of research within discourse analysis pertaining to discourse that is argumentive (Grimshaw, 1990). What are the unique features that characterize argumentive in contrast to other kinds of discourse? Although it does not investigate social discourse directly, the research presented here, focused on the cognitive prerequisites of competent argument, offers some insight regarding the language of argument.

From sociological and political perspectives, the present work is relevant to a growing under-standing of the complex interrelations that exist between individual and sociological processes (Dowd, 1990). Political scientists have for some time been interested in the political development of individuals, but they no longer treat this development simply as a process of socialization and are showing increasing attention to the cognitive underpinnings of political participation (Allen, 1989). In chapter 10 of *The Skills of Argument*, we consider the implications of our findings with respect to people's capacity for participation in the political processes involved in a democratic society.

From a psychological perspective, the present work relates directly to a number of issues that are salient in the current research literature. Most prominent among them are (a) the nature of informal reasoning and its relation to formal reasoning (Galotti, 1989), (b) the domain generality versus domain specificity of cognitive skills, (c) the development of reasoning skills, and (d) sex differences in cognitive abilities. Our findings will be considered in relation to each of these issues.

Finally, as has already been noted, a major interest has developed among educators in the teaching of thinking. The present work bears direct relevance to these efforts, and its educational implications will be considered in some detail in the concluding chapter.

Design of the Research Interview

Participants in the investigation were interviewed individually in two sessions taking place from one to several days apart. Sessions varied in length from 45 to 90 minutes and were recorded and transcribed for subsequent analysis. The interviews took place at various locations, but always in an environment familiar to the participant – his or her school, workplace, or home. Financial compensation of $20 was provided for each participant. In some cases, this compensation was given to the school or group to which the participant belonged and in others it was given to the individual.

At the beginning of the interview, we explained to the subject that the purpose of the project was to help us understand people's views about urban social problems. The major part of the interview consisted of eliciting and probing the subject's reasoning regarding three topics. The initial question for each topic elicited the subject's theories regarding the cause of the phenomenon:

What causes prisoners to return to crime after they're released?

What causes children to fail in school?

What causes unemployment?

These three topics were chosen from a larger group that had been pretested with a previous sample. They were chosen as ones people are likely to have occasion to think and talk about and ones about which people are able and willing to make causal inferences without a large base of technical knowledge. They nevertheless involve phenomena the true causal structure of which is complex and uncertain. These topics were also chosen as ones that represent a range with respect to the degree of personal knowledge a subject is likely to have. All subjects had been to school and, in the case of most of the older subjects, had been parents of children in school, making the school topic the one for which personal knowledge was likely to be greatest. Few, in contrast, were likely to have personal knowledge regarding the reasons for engaging in criminal activity, and unemployment was most likely to be intermediate in this respect. As reported in chapter 7 of *The Skills of Argument*, subjects' self-reports of the extent of their knowledge about the three topics (in response to the question "How much would you say that you know about this topic, compared to the average person?") corroborate this ordering. Differences in performance across topics can thus be examined in light of these at least self-reported knowledge differences. (We did not undertake to measure knowledge directly.)

After a subject offered his of her theory regarding the cause of the phenomenon, the interviewer inquired how the subject came to hold this view. The interviewer then proceeded to the most important part of the interview, in which the subject was asked to justify the theory by providing supporting evidence. The key question was "How do you know that this is the cause?" The initial question was followed by several probes, for example, "If you were trying to convince someone else that your view is right, what *evidence* would you give to try to show this?" (The complete interview protocol is presented in appendix 1 of *The Skills of Argument*.)

In the next segment of the interview, the subject was asked to generate an opposing position: "Suppose now that someone disagreed with your view that this is the cause. What might *they* say to show that you were wrong?" This question sometimes elicited a counterargument with respect to the subject's theory and sometimes an alternative theory. In either case, the subject was asked for a rebuttal: "What could you say to show that this other person was wrong?" If subjects' initial responses did not entail an alternative theory, they were subsequently asked for one, so as to assess all subjects' ability to generate an alternative theory. If the subject was unable to generate an alternative theory, the interviewer proposed one and asked the subject to rebut it.

In the remaining part of the interview for each topic, the subject was asked for a remedy – "Is there any one important thing which, if it could be done, would lessen prisoners' returning to crime (school failure; unemployment)?" – as a way of assessing the consistency of the subject's causal theory, that is, whether the recommended remedy was consistent with the proposed cause. The interviewer ended with a series of questions that addressed subjects' epistemological reflections on their own thinking, for example, "How sure are you about what causes___?" and "Do experts know for sure what causes___?". Three final questions elicited ratings of how much subjects felt they knew about the topic compared with the average person, how important the topic was to society as a whole, and how much the topic mattered to the subject personally (the latter two relative to a list of other topics provided for comparison).

The main part of the second session involved the evaluation of evidence presented by the interviewer for two of the topics, crime and school failure. For this reason, the main interview for these two topics occurred during the first session, so as to separate it from the evidence evaluation phase. (Counterbalancing the presentation order of these two topics within the first session established that the order itself did not affect responses.) The second session began with the main interview for the unemployment topic, followed by the evidence evaluation for the crime and school topics. Two kinds of evidence were presented for each of the two topics. What we label *underdetermined* evidence is in effect nonevidence. A scenario was presented describing a main character who exhibited the phenomenon (school failure or return to crime), but no real evidence was given regarding the cause. Subjects were thus left to draw on their own causal theories to account for the character's behavior. In the case of *overdetermined* evidence, in contrast, evidence was presented to suggest each of three different broad causes of the phenomenon, each advocated by an authority figure. Hence, if the evidence was valid and all causes were operating, the outcome could be regarded as overdetermined. Because all three co-occurred with outcome, however, whether one, two, or all three were in fact causal was indeterminate. Following their evaluation of the evidence, subjects were also asked several epistemological questions regarding certainty and influence of the evidence on their own thinking.

Participants

MAIN SAMPLE

Our aim was to interview a cross section of average people across the life span. We chose four age intervals to sample – teens, 20s (19–29), 40s (40–49), and 60s (60–69). All of the teenaged participants were ninth-graders and therefore in the age range of 14 to 15. This was the youngest age at which an extended verbal interview seemed feasible. We might have extended the range upward even beyond the 60s but decided to postpone any work with the very old, given the special methodological issues it raises.

In addition to age, two other subject variables warrant, close attention – sex and education level, both variables that in previous research have been suggested to have some bearing on reasoning ability. Within each of the four age groups, participants were therefore selected from two education levels – referred to in subsequent chapters as *college* and *noncollege* – and within each education level the two sexes were equally represented. Ten people of each sex within each age group and education level participated. The number of participants in each of the four age groups was thus 40, with a total of 160 participants in the main sample.

The teenaged participants came from four New York City high schools. Those in the higher education group came from two private schools that served primarily a middle- to upper-middle-class population, with more than 90% of students going on to four-year colleges. Those in the lower education group came from two parochial schools (one girls' and one boys') serving a lower-to lower-middle-class population. Though most finished high school, 60% of students from these schools did not go on to further education; the other 40% typically enrolled in junior colleges or vocational schools. The racial composition of all of the schools was mixed black, Hispanic, Asian, and white, though the proportion of blacks and Hispanics was slightly higher in the parochial schools.

Participants in their 20s came from two schools. Those in the higher education group were university students in their junior or senior years. Those in the lower education group were students at a combined business training institute and beauty school in New York City. Students in this school were required to possess a high school diploma or to earn a certificate of equivalency concurrently with their vocational training. The racial composition was mixed black, Hispanic, Asian, and white in both schools, though the proportion of blacks and Hispanics was higher at the business institute.

The female participants in their 40s of both education levels were either attendees at a YWCA job reentry program or employees at 2 suburban junior high school (where they worked primarily in administrative positions). Male participants in their 40s of both education levels came from the suburban neighborhood in which one of the interviewers lived and were solicited through personal contacts. They were of varied occupations. In the case of both sexes, assignment to education group was based on each participant's own report. Participants categorized in the higher education group had completed at least 2 years of college (and most had completed college). Those in the lower education group had completed at least the 10th grade (though almost all had completed high school); none had attended college. Racial composition was mixed black, Hispanic, and white in roughly equal proportion in both education groups.

Participants in their 60s were members of a YMCA social group in a middle-class neighborhood in New York City. All were retired and had previously worked in a range of occupations. All were white. Assignment to education group was again based on each participant's own report.

Participants categorized in the higher education group had completed at least 2 years of college. Those in the lower education group had completed at least the 10th grade; none had attended college.

Evidence to Support Theories

To justify adequately an assertion that one has made is in some sense the heart of argumentative reasoning. An inability to answer the "How do you know?" question suggests that the assertion should not have been made. In subsequent chapters of *The Skills of Argument*, a case will be made that there are other aspects of argumentative reasoning that warrant close attention as well, but first it is essential to take a very close look at the arguments people offer to support the theories they espouse.

After subjects present their causal theories, the second segment of the interview for each of the three topics begins with the question, "How do you know that this is the cause____?" A number of probes follow, encouraging the subject to expand and become more specific, for example, "If you were trying to convince someone else that your view [that this is the cause] is right, what *evidence* [verbal emphasis] would you give to try to show this?" (See appendix 1 in *The Skills of Argument* for full sequence of probes.) Probing ends with the question, "Is there anything someone could say or do to *prove* [verbal emphasis] that this is what causes____?" (If the answer is yes, the subject is asked to describe what it would be; if the answer is no, the subject is asked to explain why not.)

Subjects' responses to the request for evidence cover a very wide range. Not all or even a majority of responses, it turns out, fall into the category that we shall define as genuine evidence. The most prevalent response is of a type we term *pseudoevidence;* a third, smaller category of responses we term nonevidence. In this chapter, we first describe and give examples of these three forms of evidence. Next, we examine frequencies of occurrence of each of the types of evidence, overall and in relation to the major subject variables of age, education level, and sex. [...] We begin with genuine evidence, so as to provide a standard against which less successful responses can be compared.

Genuine Evidence

School failure, repeated crime, and unemployment are problems of such complexity that even experts are unable to offer definitive evidence regarding their causes. What kinds of evidence could we expect lay people with no special knowledge or interest in the topics to generate? The evidence we categorize here as genuine is by no means conclusive, nor compelling, nor even necessarily high-quality evidence. The criteria adopted for genuine evidence, rather, are simply that it (a) be distinguishable from description of the causal sequence itself and (b) bear on its correctness. The importance of the first criterion will become more apparent when we examine responses in the pseudoevidence category, in which this differentiation is absent.

The genuine evidence that subjects generate takes a wide range of forms. We begin with what is by far the most frequent form, covariation evidence, and then proceed to a description of less common forms. Genuine evidence is typically produced only in response to one or two of the interviewer's probes, usually those toward the end of the probe sequence, as the requests for evidence become more specific. In most of the following examples, for the sake of brevity, only that segment of a subject's response in which genuine evidence is generated is excerpted. [...] Examples are limited to the school and crime topics, and subjects are identified in parentheses by their age group (T, 20, 40, 60), education group (C, N), sex (m, f), and topic (s, c).

COVARIATION EVIDENCE

The most common forms of genuine evidence show some reliance on the presence of covariation between alleged causal antecedent and outcome as support for the theory that the antecedent causes the outcome. Such evidence, in addition to being distinguishable from description of the causal sequence itself, as previously noted, is also characterized by some differentiation between antecedent and outcome, in contrast to the embedding of antecedent and outcome in a narrative scenario that we shall see is characteristic of pseudoevidence. Differentiation of antecedent and outcome makes it possible for variation in the antecedent to be related to variation in the outcome.

Correspondence. We begin with the weakest form of covariation evidence – evidence that does no more than note a correspondence, or co-occurrence, of antecedent and outcome. The subject who provides the first example offers such evidence only in response to the final probe. He initially identifies emotional distress from problems at home as the cause of school failure:

> (20Cms) (*Is there anything someone could say or do to* prove *that this is the cause?*) Just looking at their performance and just looking at their problems. (*How do you mean exactly?*) I mean by . . . well, if someone makes a study of cases of students where failures, dropouts . . . students who drop out of school . . . and sees where they have family problems, perhaps that would be solid evidence to prove what I believe.

The next example is similar. The cause the subject identifies initially is lack of parental support:

> (40Cms) (*Is there anything someone could say or do to* prove *that this is the cause?*) Well, I think they can look at kids that are failing in school and see if the parent or parents are doing their job. (*What do you think they would find out?*) Well, I think they would find that the parents weren't there. They weren't behind the kids.

The evidence offered in the two preceding examples is clearly minimal. In both cases, however, the antecedent is distinct from the outcome, and there is an attempt to establish that there is a correspondence between the two, even though the idea of this correspondence is not developed in explicit, quantitative terms. [. . .]

Covariation. In this category, the idea of covariation becomes explicit. The two features that differentiate responses in this category from those in the correspondence category are some sense of (a) comparison and (b) quantification. Instances that represent one level of the antecedent are compared with those that represent another; the comparison is with respect to incidence of the outcome. In the first example, the subject begins with a response like those of the correspondence type but then, when asked about proof, adds the features of comparison and quantification. The cause the subject identifies is unemployment:

> (40Nmc) (*Is there anything further you could say to help show that this is the cause?*) I think just the fact that people that have criminal records as a whole – there are exceptions to the rule – but as a whole don't seem to land any type of a decent job, any type of job whatsoever that has any kind of security. (*Is there*

anything someone could say or do to prove *that this is the cause?*) I think if they just check past records, they could prove that, as a whole, anyone that has a criminal record . . . should be able to prove that, as a whole, they don't make out as well as people without any kind of a record.

The quantification in the preceding example remains implicit, deriving from the comparison of the two groups. In the following example, in contrast, the quantification is explicit. The cause is again unemployment:

> (TCmc) (*If you were trying to convince someone else that your view is right, what* evidence *would you give to try to show this?*) You could probably take a survey and find out the percentage of people who get jobs who have been convicts. I'm sure it's very low [. . .]

Correlated Change. Though it is usually present in the case of a causal relationship, covariation of course does not establish causality, because there may exist additional factors that also covary with antecedent and outcome and therefore have the status of potential causes. For this reason, a stronger form of evidence for a causal relationship is one in which *change* in the antecedent co-occurs with change in the outcome. Co-occurrence of change increases the likelihood that change in one factor is responsible for the change in the other. For example, the following subject identifies lack of motivation as a cause and cites as evidence the following single-case instance:

> (60Cms) (*If you were trying to convince someone else that your view is right, what* evidence *would you give to try to show this?*) Well, I had a son who was very science involved, you know, involved scientifically. He loved science, you know, and he didn't think . . . he didn't think like things like . . . what was that, social studies, or whatever it was, that he did poorly in. He just didn't like it, and I had to have a long talk with him. After, I don't know if he failed or got a bad mark or got a low mark or whatever it was, I had a very long talk with him and that, and by constantly getting after him. I had him do his homework in that subject in front of me. I had to do it with him. I had to show . . . I was trying to show him what's good about it, cause I knew it was motivation. He just didn't care for it. And by trying to make it more interesting to him

I think he must have picked that up, because he started doing better. So to me that's proof enough in that particular thing. Now if there are other cases, I simply don't remember, but I don't... it seems to me it's very obvious.

Both the preceding and following examples illustrate that, like covariation evidence, the correlated change form of evidence often originates in personal experience. In the preceding case, in fact, the evidence does not extend beyond the single instance involving the subject and his son that is described. The evidence offered by the following subject is based on a larger number of instances. The cause is problems at home:

(60Nfs) (*How do you know that this is the cause?*) My husband was a teacher, and he had a class of emotionally disturbed children. It was something new they were trying at the time, and all the problem children from all the different grades came into his class, and he had to cope with each one at each level. Nine out of ten children have problems at home. There were children who were shifted from one foster home to another. There were parents where there was illness and the mother was paying too much attention to the father and not enough to the child. Drinking problems. There were problems. These were the problems. These were the problem children. (*Is there anything further you could say to help show that what you've said is correct?*) When their problems were resolved, many of the children left that class environment and went back to their original classes and did very well. So, that in itself shows that it was the problems that were at home.

Though this subject needs prompting from the interviewer to complete her argument, the form the argument takes is clear [...]

EVIDENCE EXTERNAL TO THE CAUSAL SEQUENCE
In all three subtypes in the covariation category of genuine evidence – correspondence, covariation, and correlated change – the function of the evidence is to establish existence of a link between an antecedent and outcome. In the external evidence category of genuine evidence, the subject goes beyond the antecedent and outcome themselves to invoke some additional, external factor. The presence of this additional actor serves as evidence supporting the claim that the antecedent actor is both present and operating to produce the outcome. The follow-

ing is an example. The cause identified initially by the subject is return to the same environment:

(20Cfc) (*Is there anything further you could say to help show that this is the cause?*) Perhaps if older brothers and sisters, or peers, or people close to prisoners, have been in prison before, that might show that this is the sort of environment that one was brought up in and knows and can easily return to.

The criminal record of siblings or peers is a factor external to the causal sequence, but if it is present, it supports the claim that poor environment is a factor that is present in the case of a prisoner returning to crime. Thus, implicit in responses of the external evidence form is the claim of covariation. But the subject goes beyond merely asserting the covariation and offers some additional evidence to support its existence [...]

Negative External Evidence (Counterfactual Arguments). Two final examples in the external evidence category illustrate the special case in which the subject claims that some factor external to the causal sequence is absent, rather than present, as was the case in the preceding examples. These cases are worthy of mention because they involve counterfactual reasoning, and there is evidence in the research literature on formal reasoning indicating that reasoning involving counterfactuals is considerably more difficult than reasoning based on positive cases. In the first example, failure of prison to rehabilitate is the cause the subject identifies initially:

(40Nmc) (*How do you know that this is the cause?*) Their habit patterns. All outward appearances in every case that I have known or even heard of has not changed. If they had had their head properly shrunk, everything about them would have changed... from their haircut right on through.

The structure of the argument in this case appears to be that if prisoners had been rehabilitated (i.e., the causal antecedent were absent), not only would the outcome (return to crime) be absent, but an additional external factor that would be present is change in other physical or psychological aspects of the prisoner's makeup. The reasoning, however, is counterfactual: Presence of the external factor would negate the presence and hence operation of the causal antecedent; the external factor, however, is *not* present, and it therefore follows that the causal antecedent is present (the prisoner has not been rehabilitated), and this causal antecedent can be expected to lead to the outcome (return to crime).

In the second example, the cause identified is the same, failure of prison to rehabilitate:

(40Cfc) (*Is there anything someone could say or do to* prove *that this is the cause?*) If the statistics showed even half were successful... in other words, that they finished their term in prison and could go out and ... being successful meaning that they would attain a way of life, a way of living... that there would be something for them outside of crime... I think is the only proof that I could see.

Again, the argument is counterfactual: If some prisoners were to make a successful adjustment ("attain a way of life"), it would negate the presence and hence operation of the causal antecedent (failure of prison to rehabilitate). But the subject implies that this is not the case, hence supporting the causal sequence she has identified.

INDIRECT EVIDENCE

In this final category of genuine evidence are included four forms of evidence that bear only in an indirect way on the correctness of the causal sequence identified by the subject. Direct evidence is actual or potential factual information that, if correct, supports (though does not prove) the existence of a causal link between the specified antecedent and the outcome. In the category of indirect evidence, we include those forms of evidence that might make the causal sequence more likely to be true, though not providing data directly related to it.

Analogy (Particular to Particular). Analogy is probably the most familiar form of argument in this category, one that cognitive psychologists believe plays an important role in many kinds of thinking and problem solving. In the present context, argument by analogy consists of a mapping of the alleged causal sequence from the domain in which it actually occurs onto a new domain. Because it is shown to operate similarly in the new domain, its operation in the domain under discussion is rendered more likely.

In the first example, the subject himself identifies his reasoning as analogical. The cause he identifies initially is familiarity with criminal life:

(20Cmc) (*How do you know that this is the cause?*) Well, take an example by analogy. A college student goes to college. He'll be in an atmosphere of learning, and from there he'll either go on to a job or further his education. During these four years he's preparing for another part of his life, another few years. A prisoner, on the other hand, will be in an environment of criminals. That's all they probably talk about. That's all they have in common to talk about. I'm sure they're not talking about Plato when they're in prison. So, it's on their mind.

The analogy this subject draws between the college student and criminal is extended across multiple elements. As college prepares students for what they will do when they leave college, so prison prepares criminals for what they will do when they leave this institution. While in their respective institutions, both college students and prisoners exist in an "atmosphere," of learning in one case, crime in the other.

The content of the next example is similar, but the analogy is not as fully elaborated. The cause again is familiarity with criminal life:

(20Cmc) (*How do you know that this is the cause?*) I think if you look at it in terms of, well, an occupation, whether crime could be an occupation or not... most people generally stay in an occupation their whole life, and it's very hard for them to change [...]

Assumption (General to Particular). Indirect evidence of this type is like analogy in the respect that there occurs a mapping from one domain to another. In the case of analogy, this mapping is from one particular domain to another particular domain. In the present case, in contrast, the mapping is from general to particular. The reasoning is based on a broad assertion, or assumption, typically about "human nature." The causal theory with respect to the topic under discussion then becomes a particular case subsumed under the more general proposition, with the alleged truth of the general proposition serving as support for correctness in the more particular case. If the assumption is correct, the causal theory pertaining to the particular case is more likely to be correct. Following are examples for the crime topic. In the first example, the cause the subject identifies is return to the same environment:

(20Cmc) (*What causes prisoners to return to crime after they're released?*) Human beings are very much creatures of habit, and I don't think that there's such a habit as committing a crime, but everything that leads up to committing a crime is probably habit. (*How do you know that this is the cause?*) I'm not certain, but it just seems pretty obvious from all the other spheres of life, people are so set in their ways.

In the second example, the cause is desire for material rewards:

(20Cmc) (*Is there anything someone could say or do to* prove *that this is the cause?*) Yes. They could say that people that don't have things...I mean, everybody wants things, especially in this country. This is a consumer society. People want to accumulate things, and that's not true of everywhere. People just want basic things, and if you don't have them, and you don't know how to get them, then, you can take them.

In the third example, the cause is emotional problems originating in childhood:

(TCfc) (*How do you know that this is the cause?*) Well, I know that children need love from their parents, and if they're neglected, they can feel hostile towards people. So, they'll...I guess they'll feel hatred towards people in general, because they were never cared for. So, I think that a broken home accounts for a lot of the hatred and the, you know, harsh feelings which cause murder and these other crimes.

In each of these cases, a general proposition is advanced that is meant to apply to a far broader range of instances than prisoners returning to crime – in these cases, to humans in general, or at least at entire culture. If the proposition is assumed, then the phenomenon under discussion is merely a particular case to which it applies, and the alleged causal antecedent by implication is present (and hence serves as at least a potential cause): If everyone behaves according to habit, so do criminals; if everyone wants to accumulate material things, so do criminals. The particular outcomes in the specific case of criminals remain, perhaps, to be spelled out, but the argument derives its force from the underlying general assumption.

Discounting (Elimination of Alternatives). A third form of indirect evidence is evidence against an alternative causal theory that the subject introduces. While the discounting of an alternative theory does not of course by itself establish that the theory advocated by the sub-

ject is correct, discounting is an important form of reasoning, for it indicates that the subject is contemplating the likely truth of the causal theory *relative to others*, an important capacity that we explore in chapter 4 of *The Skills of Argument*. Discounting sometimes stands by itself as the only form of evidence the subject offers and sometimes is offered in addition to another form of evidence that more directly supports the causal theory the subject advocates.

The first example is from a subject who begins with evidence to support the causal theory he has identified, problems at home, and then offers evidence discounting an alternative theory, intelligence:

(TCms) (*How do you know that this is the cause?*) For the most part the kids who get much lower grades, I know, have problems at home, and the kids...well, I find that kids who have normal families get the average grades for the most part, and the kids who have abnormal families get extremely high or extremely low. Well, that's obviously because of changes...either someone gets stronger or they get weaker from problems at home. (*If you were trying to convince someone else that your view is right, what evidence would you give to try to show this?*) Well, as compared with intelligence, you know, saying it's more important than that. It's just simply that a lot of intelligent kids do fail in certain classes in certain times, and certainly not consistently. You know, someone fails one class this year and gets an A in the same class the next year. (*What does this show?*) Well, that probably means something is...well, there's obviously going to be a difference, and since you can pretty much assume that the kid didn't get a lot smarter suddenly, and even without, you know, often without it [intelligence] they fail classes, and sometimes they get a tutor, sometimes they don't. Even if they don't sometimes, they still get a better grade, a lot better. So, it's not necessarily intelligence that's important [...]

Partial Discounting. A final form of indirect evidence we term *partial discounting* because it does not completely discredit the alternative causal theory. Instead, the factor is discounted at one level or end of its range, while its operation at the other end is left unspecified. Like the full discounting previously described, it is significant in that it reflects the subject's consideration of alternative theories. In the following example, the causal theory the subject identifies is lack of motivation:

> (TCms) (*Is there anything someone could say or do to* prove *that this is the cause?*) Some people just have lower IQs, you could say that some people tend to have lower IQs than other people. It's just the way it's going to be. Like some people are smarter than others. (*What does that show?*) Well, that some people can be realy genius, one hundred seventy IQ, and just not care. So even if you're smart, it doesn't mean like you're going to not fail, because that's the way it works.

This subject notes that intelligence will not covary with outcome, specifically high intelligence can co-occur with failure, in cases in which the subject's preferred cause, lack of motivation (not caring) is operating. In this case, the preferred cause overrides the alternative one. The subject's assertion does not, however, completely discount the alternative cause, for it leaves unspecified what would happen in the reverse case in which motivation is high but intelligence low. If in this case the intelligence factor overrides the motivation factor (yielding failure), then both high intelligence and high motivation are required for success, and the intelligence factor has been only partially discounted (as it has no effect in the case of a low level of the motivation factory) [. . .]

Pseudoevidence

Though, we do not attempt a precise ordering of them, the forms of genuine evidence that have been described cover a very wide range, and it would seem likely that every subject would produce at least one of them as a means of supporting a causal theory. In fact, as we shall report in detail, for each of the three topics less than half of our subjects produce any genuine evidence at all. We thus go on now to examine other forms of responses subjects make to the request for evidence to support their theories.

By far the most prevalent is what we term *pseudoevidence*. Characterized most simply, pseudoevidence takes the form of a scenario, or script, depicting how the phenomenon might occur. The scripts observed in the present work are often expressed in general terms. Sometimes, however, they consist of one or two specific instances in terms of which the script is described. In this respect, our use of the term *script* is broader than its characteristic use by cognitive psychologists to refer to a generalized

description of a sequence of events (covering a range of specific instances). In the present case, description, either in the form of one or two specific instances or in more general, summary form, serves to show how the events depicted might plausibly lead to the outcome. Pseudoevidence can thus be thought of as evidence by illustration.

The defining characteristic that distinguishes pseudoevidence from genuine evidence is that, in contrast to the latter, pseudoevidence cannot be sharply distinguished from description of the causal sequence itself. In offering pseudoevidence, subjects may elaborate their initial depictions of the sequence generated in response to the interviewer's elicitation of the causal theory. But responses to the question "What causes____?" do not differ sharply from responses to the questions "How do you know that this is so?" or "What evidence would you give to try to show this?"

GENERALIZED SCRIPTS

We begin with scripts that take a more generalized form. The following subject, who in the initial segment of the interview identifies problems at home, specifically divorce, as cause, provides an example of a simple, minimally elaborated script, not clearly distinguishable from specification of the cause itself. In this and several of the examples to follow, subjects' responses are quoted in their entirety, in order to provide a fuller sense of the subjects' approaches to evidence:

> (TNms) (*How do you know that this is the cause?*) Well, it's like mostly when the mother and father are divorced they can, have psychological problems, you know, and they can't actually function in school. (*Just to be sure I understand, can you explain exactly how this shows that problems at home are the cause?*) Well, the kid, like, concentrates on how he's going to keep his mother and father together. He can't really concentrate on schoolwork. (*If you were trying to convince someone else that your view that this is the cause is right, what evidence would you give to try to show this?*) Well, let's see, I would take some kids maybe if their mother and father get divorced and show how it affects them mentally, you know. It makes them less alert in class. (*Can you be very specific, and tell me some particular facts you could mention to try to convince the person?*) Sometimes they have editorials in newspapers or on TV, you know, and maybe it could be a friend

of yours that it happens to. (*Is there anything further you could say to help show that what you've said is correct?*) Not at the moment. (*Is there anything someone could say or do to prove that this is what causes children to fail in school?*) Yes. It could be, you know, partly, they could be the persons that have problems at home, and can't really handle it [...]

Narrative Scripts. Sometimes scripts have an even stronger narrative character. The following subject, for example, initially specifies as the cause that the family does not provide support that would enable the prisoner to readjust to life outside prison:

(TNfc) (*How do you know that this is the cause?*) Cause sometimes when the wife is ... wants to marry him or something, she don't expect him to do things – raping, robbing – because, you know, like if a family has money problems, you have to try to find a job, or do a part-time job to get money. (*Just to be sure I understand, can you explain exactly how this shows that this is the cause?*) Well, when he gets out, he goes ... he knows where he still lives and he knows that she's still living there, and he knocks on the door, and she says, "Who are you?" He'll say, "Well, I'm your husband." She will say, "Well, my husband wasn't in prison." And she's gone and left him, and she's going to say, "You're not my husband; my husband wouldn't do such a thing." And she won't want him.

(*If you were trying to convince someone else that your view that this is the cause is right, what evidence would you give to try to show this?*) Well, I would get somebody that was in prison and tell them how prison is like. And he would see the difference of prisoners and him[self]. Prison is something on the dark side of life, instead of being outside in the world where he could see everything. (*Can you be very specific, and tell me some particular facts you could mention to try to convince the person?*) Well, when the prison ... like when he gets out, let's say, and the wife is having a ... has another husband, like, and she probably gets divorced while he's in prison, cause sometimes they do that, and he comes back and he don't know nothing about it. She's going to say, "Well, since you was in prison for two or three years, I couldn't wait for you." So, he would be neglected, and he would feel bad because he don't have nobody else to go to. And that's it ... they go back to crime. (*Is there anything further you could say to help show that what you've said is correct?*) Well, my uncle, since he knows. Eight years he was dealing in drugs and everything. He went into prison. When he came out, his wife had two kids. And she didn't want him anymore, because he was in prison. And she said, "If I marry somebody to love me and everything, he was not supposed to go out there and steal or deal with drugs. He was supposed to stay in one place, get himself a job, you know, take care of the family." But he didn't do that, so now he's in prison.

(*Is there anything someone could say or do to prove that this is what causes prisoners to return to crime?*) Yes, it is sometimes, cause the man feels hurt because if he loves somebody, and he was in prison, the other person should have the same love for him.

Though the preceding script derives from a specific instance known to the subject and is clearly driven by its narrative elements, the causal scenario remains at least a coherent, plausible account of a course of events that might lead a prisoner to return to crime. In this respect, the pseudoevidence successfully serves its function. In other cases, however, it is not entirely successful in even this respect. The script may take on such a life of its own that it becomes to some degree detached from the causal theory in connection with which it is intended to function as evidence [...]

Shifts from Cause to Consequence. The following example illustrates another way in which scripts sometimes go astray. Rather than retaining focus on the causal question, the subject drifts from the cause of the phenomenon to its consequences and, in this case, fails to differentiate cause and remedy. The subject initially identifies not wanting to study as cause.

(TNms) (*How do you know that this is the cause?*) Alright, if you, like, when they get homework they go home and just drop their books and go outside. (*If you were trying to convince someone else that your view that this is the cause is correct, what evidence would you give to try to show this?*) I'd just try to, try my best, you know, to make them want to study. (*Question repeated.*) Tell them that, just put a little lie into it, you know, tell him if he don't study, how will it be? They won't get a job or education. (*Can you be very specific, and tell me some particular facts you could mention* to try to convince someone that not wanting to study is the cause of failing in school?) Okay, thinking about it, how will it look if they, when they get old enough, have to go for like an interview. (Is there anything further you could say to help show that what you've said is correct?) Or they have to like go to the store; they have to count money. If you go into any kind of business, when it's time to go to college.... When you play any sports you're supposed to know how to read, to understand the rules.

The subject's response in this case is consistent with his causal theory, but the focus is only minimally on depicting the causal sequence leading to the outcome. Instead, the subject's focus turns to the (negative) consequences of the outcome, which, if pointed out, the subject claims, might lead to remedy. Once the subject's focus shifts, the interviewer's attempts to bring him back to the question of cause are not successful.

SCRIPTS IN THE FORM OF SPECIFIC INSTANCES

Most subjects' pseudoevidence scripts are not as severely undermined by lack of focus on the causal sequence itself as are those of the preceding few subjects. The more common way in which the force of a script may be diminished is by restriction to one or two specific instances. A generalized script depicts a causal sequence as the general case, with the implication that what is being described is what usually happens. If, instead, only one or two specific instances are described, the power of the script in depicting how the phenomenon normally occurs is reduced. Implicit in the subject's response is the claim that these specific instances illustrate how the phenomenon occurs generally, but this claim neither is made explicit nor is any justification offered for it.

We turn now to some examples of scripts that are conveyed in terms of specific instances, rather than in generalized form. The two types cannot be sharply divided, however, and there are numerous cases that are intermediate between the two, as the following subject's response reflects. The cause is a combination of laziness (7) and peer pressure (15). The subject begins with specific instances:

(TNms) (How do you know that this is the cause?) Cause I see it around me, you know. I have friends who fail. They figure it's the right thing to do, and, you know, they just get lazy or want to hang out with their friends.

In response to the next probe, however, this subject proceeds to a generalized script that embodies the specific instances he has described:

(If you were trying to convince someone else that your view is correct, what evidence would you give to try to show this?) Like I said, you know, just take a person, for example, and like say he has a number of friends, and like the majority of his friends are failing, so he decides to do what they do, and maybe he could be lazy, or that could right there be peer pressure, cause they have to follow their friends in order to be in with the crowd.

In contrast to the preceding example, scripts frequently remain in the form of specific instances known to the subject [...]

SCRIPTS AS (UNFALSIFIABLE) ILLUSTRATION

In sum, at their most minimal, scripts simply illustrate a causal sequence. At their best, they elaborate the sequence in a way that enhances its plausibility. While the generalized form is arguably superior, the difference between scripts presented in generalized form and those embodied in specific examples from the subject's experience appears to be a surface rather than a deep one. In both cases, the scenarios subjects describe are likely to derive from experiences that they have had personally or that are known to them, and the scenario is seen as sufficient to account for the phenomenon. Subjects who generate pseudoevidence may differ, then, only in whether they choose to portray the script in specific or general form and, as one of the excerpts we examined showed, a subject may shift from one form to the other in the course of presenting a script.

Thus, whether in a generalized or specific form, pseudoevidence scripts serve the function of depicting how the phenomenon might occur, and we earlier characterized them as evidence by illustration, or example. Comments made by a number of subjects in fact explicitly equate evidence with examples:

(20Cfc) (Is there anything someone could say or do to prove that what you've said is what causes prisoners to return to crime?) You mean can I give you an example? (Question repeated.) Okay, I can give you an example ... [subject proceeds with an example].

Or:

(40Nfs) (Is there anything someone could say or do to prove that this is the cause?) I'm running into difficulty here. (*Why is that?*) To think of another reason why... how you could prove it besides giving examples, or... ask them about their own experiences. You could ask children if you have them available, or you could ask the person. (*The person who had this view?*) Yes. (*What would that show?*) Maybe you could somehow get them to give an example.

In fact, subjects often see examples not just as evidence but as proof for their theories, as the following response shows:

TCfs) (*If you were trying to convince someone else that your view is right, what evidence would you give to try to show this?*) Well, I could give examples of people I heard about that it happened to, and I could ask them questions about what they've seen in their own classes. (*Just to be sure I understand, can you explain exactly how this would show that this is the cause?*) Because if I could give examples, they couldn't disprove my examples since they really happened. (*Is there anything further you could say to help snow that what you've said is correct?*) I could ask them if it ever happened to themselves. (*What would that show?*) Well, then, if it did, it would prove it very well.

In other words, because the examples are proved, the theory is proved, suggesting again that examples *are* the evidence [...]

Nonevidence

We turn finally to examples from a much smaller group of subjects who offer neither genuine evidence nor pseudoevidence to support their theories. The category we term *nonevidence* covers a range of responses in which subjects (a) imply that evidence is unnecessary or irrelevant, (b) make assertions not connected to a causal theory, or (c) cite the phenomenon itself as evidence regarding its cause. While some subjects claim evidence to be unnecessary or irrelevant, it is notable that no subjects claim that they are *unable* to provide evidence – that they believe what they do but are unable to say why. All subjects offer some form of answer to questions about evidence.

EVIDENCE AS UNNECESSARY
We begin with subjects who treat evidence as unnecessary. The following subject explicitly claims that evidence is irrelevant:

(40Nfs) (*If you were trying to convince someone else that your view is right, what evidence would you give to try to show this?*) I would not try to give any evidence. I only... when it comes to kids, I work by my good instinct, and I would say there are sometimes parents who are totally tuned into their children will know more than the professional. If you live with your child, day in and day out, and if you can stand outside that circle and be objective, As well as subjective when you must be, you know what's happening. Sometimes being here you can analyze and know exactly what's going on more than someone who knows book theory, cause sometimes book theory is garbage. (*Is there anything someone could say or do to* prove *that what you've said is what causes school failure.*) I would go by my life experience. Everybody has life experience. I'm not trying to push my views on anyone else. I think my views are very liberal. That's what gets me through. But, no, I'm not going to go toe-to-toe with anyone. It's not important to me.

In contrast to the preceding subject, who emphasizes instinct or intuition as an alternative to evidence, subjects who claim that evidence is unnecessary more commonly subscribe to a simple *argument by telling*, as the following response illustrates:

(20Nfc) (*If you were trying to convince someone else that your view is right, what evidence would you give to try to show this?*) I wouldn't really give them evidence. I would just try to convince them that that was the reason why. (*How would you do that?*) I'd keep at it, you know, keep telling them that, yes, this is the reason, this is the reason. If it ends up that he doesn't believe me, or whatever, it ends right there [...]

EVIDENCE UNCONNECTED TO A THEORY
Subjects whose responses fall into a second category of nonevidence make reference to specific content relevant to the topic, but the content is not linked to a causal theory. The similarity between the stance taken by many of these subjects and the argument-by-telling stance of subjects in the preceding category is clear:

(TCmc) (*If you were trying to convince someone else that your view is right, what evidence would you give to try to show this?*) Well, I'd look up in books to see what percentage of people did crimes, just to get the percentage, and then

I'd check out the seriousness of the crime. I might see what type of crime it was. And, I don't know, I might if possible, try to get in to meet the people. I mean just through information, I mean give him more facts and more facts. To back up the facts I'd give him more facts. I think I could convince someone.

Again, further probing suggests that this subject has no more specific idea that would take him beyond this *argument-by-facts* stance – an idea of exactly how these "facts" could be connected to the causal theory in question:

> (*Is there anything further you could say to help show that what you've said is correct?*) Well, I could try logic, uh . . . reason it through.

Is it possible that responses in the nonevidence category like the ones quoted thus far simply reflect the fact that the subjects do not possess the content knowledge that would enable them to put any flesh on the general "facts," "talk," and "telling" that they invoke. Although it cannot be ruled out as a contributing factor, this explanation rendered less likely by the fact that many responses classified as nonevidence are in fact rich in specific content. Rather than lack of content knowledge, the problem seems to be one of connecting content (whether rich or minimal) to a causal theory, so that the content bears on the theory [. . .]

EFFECT AS EVIDENCE OF ITS CAUSE

The most prevalent and in many ways most striking type of nonevidence is that in which the subject simply restates the phenomenon. In doing so, the subject makes it clear that the existence of the phenomenon itself is sufficient evidence that it is produced by the cause the subject invokes. We cite several examples. In the first, the cause the subject has identified is poor nutrition:

> (20Nms) (*If you were trying to convince someone else that your view is right, what evidence would you give to try to show this?*) The points that they get in school. The grades that they get in school to show . . . (*What would that show?*) That they are lacking something in their body. That the kids who were failing lack something in their body.

The following is a parallel example for the crime topic. The cause is desire to return to prison:

> (40Nfc) (*If you were trying to convince someone else that your view is right, what evidence*

> *would you give to try to show this?*) Just things you read about in the paper and hear in the news. (*Can you be very specific, and tell me particular facts you could mention to try to convince the person?*) Well, like when people do repeated . . . keep repeating the same crime, keep being put back, and coming out. They've never learned their lesson. It doesn't bother them. So that would show that maybe they'd rather . . . they'd be happier there [. . .]

Quantitative Results

CLASSIFICATION INTO EVIDENCE CATEGORIES

In analyzing subjects' responses to the evidence segment of the interview, each unit of evidence presented by the subject is classified into one of the categories that have been described. A unit is taken to be a complete idea. On average, these are two to three sentences long. Most often, one unit occurs in response to each of the interviewer's probes, though sometimes more than one occurs. Each unit is assigned to one of the evidence categories described in this chapter. Subsequent analysis is based on which of the categories are represented in the subject's total response. Details regarding interrater reliability are given in appendix 2 of *The Skills of Argument*.

As reflected in a number of the examples that have been presented, a subject's response often spans more than one of the three major categories. In the most common combination, the subject initially offers pseudoevidence and then, in response to the interviewer's probes, proceeds to give one or more forms of genuine evidence. Other subjects, in contrast, do not proceed beyond pseudoevidence. Nonevidence most often proceeds to or alternates with pseudoevidence. For the crime topic, only 5 of the 160 subjects never go beyond nonevidence. Corresponding numbers for the unemployment and school topics are 2 and 3 subjects, respectively (with subjects distributed across age, education, and sex groupings.)

Hence, the most important contrast is between subjects who offer some genuine evidence and those who never proceed beyond pseudoevidence or nonevidence. As shown in table 1, less than half of subjects overall give genuine evidence for each of the topics. Topic differences are slight but consistent with prediction: Subjects reason best on the topic for which they are most likely to have personal knowledge (school failure) and least well on the topic for which they are least likely to have personal knowledge (return to crime). While percentages

Table 1: Percentages of Subjects Generating Genuine Evidence

	Crime	Unemployment	School
Age group			
Teens	33	38	38
20s	43	43	58
40s	48	53	55
60s	33	28	40
Education group			
Noncollege	16	28	29
College	61	53	66
Total group	39	40	48

are slightly higher for the two middle age groups, age group differences are not significant, nor are percentages by sex (not shown). Percentages of subjects offering genuine evidence by education level, in contrast, differ significantly. A summary of statistical tests is contained in appendix 3.[1]

Among those subjects who produce some genuine evidence, the majority produce only one of the nine individual subtypes described earlier (three subtypes of covariation evidence, two of external evidence, and four of indirect evidence). A sizable minority, however, produce two subtypes, and a few subjects three or more. Mean numbers of different subtypes produced by a subject are 1.40 for the crime topic, 1.36 for the unemployment topic, and 1.45 for the school topic. These means are only slightly (nonsignificantly) lower for noncollege subjects (1.31–1.38 across topics) than college subjects (1.41–1.51 across topics) and likewise do not differ by age group or sex. Thus, subjects who produce genuine evidence do not differ in the number of different kinds of evidence they produce.

With what frequencies do the various types of genuine evidence appear? Percentages in table 2 are based on the different types of genuine evidence appearing in a subject's response. As seen there, genuine evidence most often falls into the covariation category and next most often into the indirect evidence category. These percentages do not differ significantly by education

Table 2: Percentages of Genuine Evidence in Different Categories

	Crime	Unemployment	School
Covariation	36	51	67
External	26	24	08
Indirect	38	25	25

level, sex, or age group. A difference across topics is reflected in table 2, however, with covariation evidence becoming more likely for topics for which subjects are more likely to have personal knowledge. Covariation evidence is more direct and straightforward than external or indirect evidence, and subjects apparently prefer it when they are able to provide it.

Frequencies of the three types of covariation evidence (correspondence, covariation, and correlated change) vary across the three topics but occur in roughly equal proportion overall. Certain content is apparently more conducive to certain forms of argument, with correspondence evidence more frequent for the unemployment topic, covariation evidence for the school topic, and correlated change evidence for the crime topic. Within the external evidence category, the simple positive form is much more common, with only four instances of the negative (counterfactual) form appearing overall. Within the indirect evidence category, there is likewise variation across topics, but overall 17% of instances are of the analogy form, 33% of the assumption form, 32% of the full discounting, and 18% of the partial discounting form.

PERCEIVED STRENGTH OF EVIDENCE

In chapter 7 of *The Skills of Argument*, we look extensively at subjects' reflections on their reasoning. One of these findings, however, warrants mention here, and that is the strength subjects attribute to the evidence they generate. The interviewer's final probe in the evidence segment of the interview, "Is there anything someone could say or do to *prove* (verbal emphasis) that this is what causes___?", yields an index of whether the subject sees the evidence offered as proving the correctness of the causal theory. Subjects who offer evidence in response to this probe, or who reiterate evidence given previously, are categorized as regarding their evidence as proof, while subjects who reply no (regardless of the nature of the accompanying justification) are categorized as not regarding the evidence they have offered as proof.

The figures in this respect are striking not only in their absolute level, but because they are independent of the actual quality of evidence. Of subjects generating genuine evidence, only 14–18% (across topics) *do not* regard the evidence they offer as sufficient to prove the theory's correctness. Despite the inferior character of their evidence, of subjects generating only nonevidence or pseudoevidence, these figures are comparable: Only 19–22% do *not* regard the evidence they offer as sufficient to prove the theory's correctness. The remaining roughly 80% of subjects regard their evidence as proof of the correctness of their causal theories, irrespective of the actual quality of this evidence.

Conclusions: The Limits of Pseudoevidence

The findings presented in this chapter reflect both the competence and lack of competence that people display in justifying the causal theories they hold. The majority of people do not appear able to make realistic appraisals of the strength of the evidence they generate. Yet the various forms of genuine evidence that have been described are all reasonable, valid forms of evidence that can be invoked to support a causal theory, whether or not in individual cases they constitute strong enough evidence to be persuasive. The present results show that many average people without any particular expertise either in scientific reasoning or in the topic domains being considered are able to invoke these forms of evidence as a means of argument for their beliefs. This finding, and the particular forms of evidence that are identified, are important in their own right, as we discuss further in chapter 10 of *The Skills of Argument*.

Yet the major finding of this chapter is the prevalence of pseudoevidence. Pseudoevidence is perceived by subjects who rely on it to be as powerful as is genuine evidence as a means of establishing the correctness of causal theories. What basis do we have for claiming the inferiority of pseudoevidence to genuine evidence? At their best, we observed, pseudoevidence scripts serve to establish or enhance the intuitive *plausibility* of a causal theory by portraying how the causal sequence occurs. Genuine evidence, in contrast, bears on the *correctness* of a causal theory – on establishing that it in fact operates and produces the observed instances of the outcome (although a few of the forms of genuine evidence that we have observed, notably analogy, may also contribute to enhancing the plausibility of a causal theory).

The plausibility involved in pseudoevidence has to do with *mechanism*, the means by which a cause produces an effect, as aspect of causal thinking that has received a good deal of attention by researchers studying causal reasoning, as we note further in Chapter 10 of *The Skills of Argument*. Might not we, then, simply regard pseudoevidence and genuine evidence as reflecting alternative explanatory preferences or styles?

The difference is a more fundamental one than that of style. Genuine evidence can be regarded as superior to pseudoevidence on the grounds that it is more definitive. First, plausibility is neither a necessary nor a sufficient condition for the correctness of a causal theory. Often, in the history of science, causal theories that initially appear very implausible have been proved correct, and, likewise, highly plausible theories have been disconfirmed. Second, a causal relationship between two factors can be demonstrated in the absence of any plausible theory whatsoever to connect them. Again, in the history of science, there are many cases of a causal relationship being demonstrated in the absence of an understanding of the mechanism connecting cause and effect (e.g., when a substance is found beneficial in treating a disease in the absence of an understanding of how it achieves its effect).

"Good" pseudoevidence, then, might heighten our interest in testing a causal theory, but it cannot tell us whether the theory is correct. Since physical and mental limitations permit us to explore only some theories and not others, the former function is not trivial. Yet it represents only the beginning, not the totality, of a rigorous investigation of cause.

Even more fundamentally, pseudoevidence must be regarded not as evidence at all, but as part of the theory. In proposing their theories, it is reasonable to assume that all of our subjects envisioned some mechanism whereby the alleged cause produces the effect. When, in offering pseudoevidence, they elaborate the description of this mechanism, they are elaborating the theory, not providing any evidence of its correctness. Again, even the most plausible theories may be wrong. Consonant with this claim, we noted that there is typically little differentiation between the pseudoevidence a subject offers and the subject's statement of the theory itself. Both portray a scenario of "how it happens." Genuine evidence, in contrast, is differentiated from the theory and bears on its correctness [. . .]

Raising the possibility that the theory is not correct introduces the adversarial or argumentative, framework that dominates the interview. In this framework, the limitations of pseudoevidence are brought into even sharper focus. The elicitation of evidence begins with the straightforward "How do you know?" question. Plausibility, or mechanism, is conceivably relevant to the matter of how one knows that an antecedent is the cause of an outcome, and, as we saw, subjects often begin their discussion of evidence in this vein. The interviewer goes on, however, to invoke a hypothetical other, one who later will be explicitly characterized as "disagree[ing] with your view." The task confronting subjects, then, becomes one not just of explaining how they know, but of indicating what they would say to convince the hypothetical other ("To convince someone else that your view is right..."). It is implicit in the set of questions that, unlike the subject, the hypothetical other does *not* know that this is the cause and may in fact hold a different view. An explicit mode of argument is thus called for, one that may include plausibility but must go beyond it.

As we have seen, some subjects do go on to exhibit this argumentive skill, offering evidence to support the claim that the alleged cause does operate to produce the outcome. Others, in contrast, never go beyond pseudoevidence accounts of how the cause might produce the outcome [...]

Note

1   Because, as noted in above, the pattern of significant education differences and absence of differences by age group or sex is very consistent across all of our findings, we do not under-

take more complex statistical analyses of subject variables in interaction with one another, in particular of the comparability of education differences within sex and age groups, which, in any case, samples sizes are not large enough to judge with any certainty. Except where otherwise noted, however, inspection shows education differences to be comparable within sex and age groups.

References

Allen, G. (1989). Introduction. Special-topic section: Children's political socialization and cognition. *Human Development*, *32*, 1–4.

Dowd, J. (1990). Ever since Durkheim: The socialization of human development. *Human Development*, *33*, 138–59.

Galotti, K. (1989). Approaches to studying formal and everyday reasoning. *Psychological Bulletin*, *105*, 331–51.

Grimshaw, A. (Ed.) (1990). *Conflict talk: Sociolinguistic investigations of arguments in conversations*. Cambridge University Press.

Scheffler, I. (1965). *Conditions of knowledge: An introduction to epistemology and education*. Chicago: University of Chicago Press.

Walton, D. (1989). *Informal logic: A handbook for critical argumentation*. Cambridge University Press.

Chapter 34: Reasoning and Conversation

LANCE J. RIPS

This article focuses on the nature of informal arguments, provides a model of these interactions, and reports experiments that test the model. In many arguments, people try to convince others of the truth of a claim (or the worthiness of an action), or they try to evaluate the believability of others' claims. In the following dialogue, for example, Ann tries to convince Bill of the claim in Line la:

(1) a. Ann: There's no place on campus to get a good cup of coffee.
     b. Bill: What makes you say that?
     c. Ann: I've tried all the coffee shops on campus and none has good coffee.
     d. Bill: You haven't tried the new coffee shop in Garrett, I bet.
     e. Ann: I have too: I was there just yesterday.
     f. Bill: Also, coffee shops aren't the only source of coffee on campus – maybe you can get good coffee in one of the cafeterias.
     g. Ann: All of the campus coffee comes from the same supplier.
     a. Bill: Okay, I guess you're right about that.

This is the type of informal argument that we explore here, and these arguments occur in many everyday contexts, including debates on medical treatments (ten Have, 1995), courtroom interactions (Riley, Hollihan, & Freadhoff, 1987), political controversies (Elster, 1995; Homer-Dixon & Karapin, 1989), class discussions (Cavalli-Sforza, Lesgold, & Weiner, 1992; Chinn, 1995), scientific exchanges (Vicedo, 1991), negotiations within organizations or work groups (Coulson & Flor, 1994; Firth, 1995), marital dis-agreements (Gottman, 1979), conflicts between children (Eisenberg & Garvey, 1981; Miller, Danaher, & Forbes, 1986), and many other social contexts (e.g., Hewitt, Duchan, & Segal, 1993; Schiffrin, 1984). They occur in traditional cultures, as well as in our own (Hutchins, 1980; Starr, 1978). And they appear in literary forms, prominently in plays, from Sophocles to Shaw.

Not every verbal dispute is an informal argument. Name-calling, exchanging demands, and exchanging threats, for example, do not have evaluating claims as a goal, and I'll use *argumentation* when necessary to distinguish informal arguments in the intended sense from other verbal encounters.[1] Argumentation is a way to manage conflicts between points of view – one that appeals to the merits of the case, the reasonableness of certain conclusions. One can evaluate argumentation in terms of the practical goals of the participants, for example, in convincing others of their claims or refuting others' claims (Hamblin, 1970). However, one can also evaluate argumentation in terms of its potential for promoting true beliefs (Goldman, 1994) or advancing understanding of an issue (Wright, 1995).

In the first part of this article, I briefly review prior approaches to argumentation in order to situate the theory to be proposed here. The central idea of the current theory is that an argument consists of a claim by one participant and a critical response by another, where the response can itself embed further claims and responses. The second part of the article defines this argument structure. In the third part, I set out a theory of how participants negotiate commitment to the claims that arise in the argument. I propose that commitment depends on the types of responses

Reproduced with permission from Rips, L. (1998) Reasoning and conversation. *Psychological Review*, 105, 411–441.

(a)

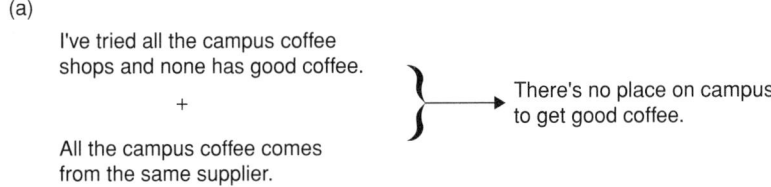

I've tried all the campus coffee shops and none has good coffee.

+

All the campus coffee comes from the same supplier.

There's no place on campus to get good coffee.

(b)

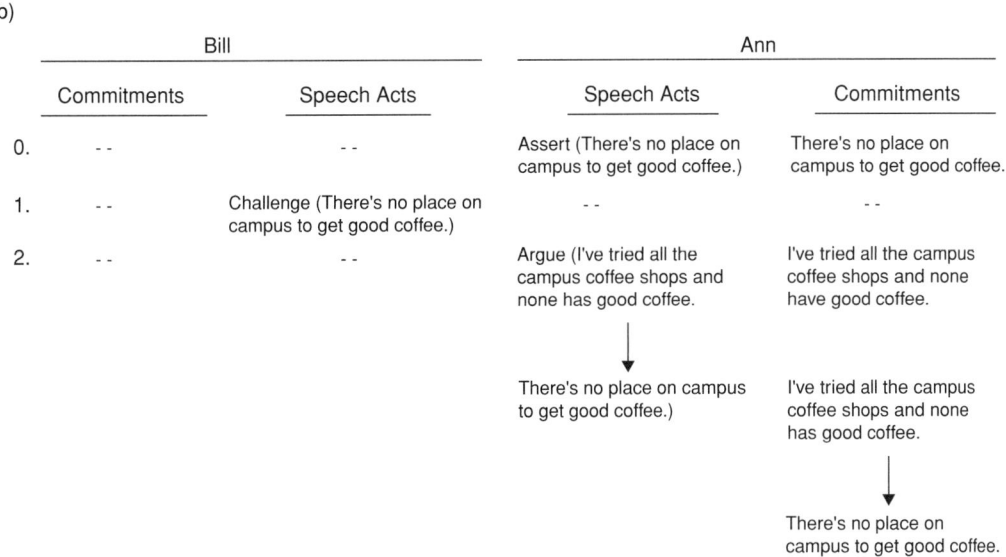

Bill		Ann	
Commitments	Speech Acts	Speech Acts	Commitments
0. - -	- -	Assert (There's no place on campus to get good coffee.)	There's no place on campus to get good coffee.
1. - -	Challenge (There's no place on campus to get good coffee.)	- -	- -
2. - -	- -	Argue (I've tried all the campus coffee shops and none has good coffee.	I've tried all the campus coffee shops and none have good coffee.
		↓	
		There's no place on campus to get good coffee.)	I've tried all the campus coffee shops and none has good coffee.
			↓
			There's no place on campus to get good coffee.

Figure 1. Partial representations of Argument 1, according to (a) a system of Fisher's (1988) and (b) a dialogue-game model by Walton and Krabbe (1995).

that participants offer (e.g., challenges, rebuttals, and acceptances), and I give a formal account of how commitment changes. Section 4 discusses tests of the model in experiments in which people read arguments and decide which characters in the argument are committed to each claim and which character has greater burden of proof. Finally, in the last section, I consider an alternative connectionist theory and draw further conclusions about the current theory.

Argumentation as Reason Giving versus Argumentation as Dialogue

The present theory unites two strands of earlier work on argumentation. One traditional perspective emphasizes the support that one statement lends another. The support might be the strong deductive connection that occurs when the supported statement must be true whenever the supporting statement is true. However, statements also gain support in nondeductive ways when the supporting statement makes the supported one more likely. Support

can accrue through plausible reasoning (Collins & Michalski, 1989), probabilistic reasoning (Jeffrey, 1965), heuristics (Kahneman & Tversky, 1984), and other strategies.

We can picture the support among an argument's statements as a network with links running from basic statements that are taken as given to the argument's main conclusion (e.g., Fisher, 1988; Thomas, 1973; Toulmin, Rieke, & Janik, 1979). Each link indicates a reason for its supported statement; so the structure consists of statements partially ordered by the support or reason relation. A link might be marked in the text of the argument by an adverbial connective, such as *because*, *thus*, or *hence* (Grosz, Pollack, & Sidner, 1989; Reichman-Adar, 1984; Schiffrin, 1987).

As an example of how this type of theory works, Figure 1a gives a reconstruction of Ann's argument 1, according to Fisher's (1988) system. The diagram shows that Ann's claims in Lines 1c and 1g provide support for her main conclusion in Line 1a. That is, the fact that none of the campus coffee shops has good coffee, together with the fact that all of the campus coffee comes from the same supplier, supports her case that there is no place on campus to get good coffee. The bracket and plus sign in the diagram indicate that the two bracketed sentences *jointly* imply the conclusion. The notation derives from logic systems with similar display formats (e.g., Gentzen, 1935/1969), but in Fisher's system the arrows do not necessarily denote a valid relationship. Instead, the arrows show the support that the arguer intended, as determined by an analysis of the discourse. Whether the sentences at the base of the arrow actually provide (deductive or inductive) support for the conclusion is also a matter for analysis and depends on "appropriate standards of evidence or appropriate standards of what is possible" (Fisher, 1988, p. 27).

The diagram in Figure 1a gives a reasonable picture of Ann's central argument, but it leaves out much of what transpires in Argument 1. Bill explicitly challenges some of Ann's assertions, leading her to elaborate her reasons; however, these challenges do not appear in the figure. It is possible to adapt schemes like Fisher's to include challenges and criticisms, but the diagramming conventions become complicated and ad hoc. Moreover, the dialogue itself has a sequential, orderly character that is lost in Figure 1a, which focuses solely on the support relation. Ann's assertions are reactions to Bill's probes, and it is difficult to capture this interactional aspect of the reasoning in simple premise-to-conclusion links.

To get around some of these limitations, a second tradition views argumentation as a conversational or "dialectical" exchange. Informal arguments, like other conversations, take place under tacit agreements to cooperate in order to advance the discussion (Grice, 1989; Lewis, 1979; Sperber Wilson, 1986). Participants obviously disagree about specific points, but no argument is possible unless they cooperate on how the interaction should proceed (Schiffrin, 1985; van Eemeren, Grootendorst, Jackson, & Jacobs, 1993). In conducting the argument, the participants assume that there are certain relevant beliefs that they mutually accept as part of the participants' *common ground* (Clark & Schaefer, 1989). There are also relevant beliefs that one participant accepts, but that others either reject or are uncertain about, for otherwise there would be little point in the argument. Thus, a participant's goal might be to establish a belief as part of common ground by showing that it follows from other mutual beliefs. Opponents, in turn, may attempt to

make the belief a mutually rejected one. In carrying out these goals, the participants engage in a variety of dialogue moves, loosely analogous to moves in a game. Formal theories along these lines appear in the work of Hamblin (1970), Mackenzie (1979, 1984), Pilkington, Hartley, Hintze, and Moore (1992), Rescher (1977), and Walton and Krabbe (1995). Jackson and Jacobs (1980), Muntigl and Turnbull (1998), Resnick, Salmon, Zeitz, Wathen, and Holowchak (1993), and van Eemeren, Grootendorst, and their colleagues (e.g., van Eemeren, et al., 1993; van Eemeren, Grootendorst, & Snoeck Henkemans, 1996, Chap. 11) have developed more informal, discourse-based approaches to argumentative dialogues along similar lines.

In Walton and Krabbe's (1995) system for *permissive persuasion dialogues*, for example, the dialogue game consists of two players who take turns making concessions, retractions, arguments, and challenges. The goal of the game is for "each party to get each of its initial assertions conceded by its adversary and ... to get the other party to retract its initial assertions, or at least some of them" (p. 135). A set of rules govern the commitments of the participants and limit the range of conversational moves they can make at each turn in the dialogue. Figure 1b shows the first part of Argument 1, as Walton and Krabbe's (1995) model might represent it (cf. their Figure 4.6, p. 144). The first two columns of the figure record the statements to which Bill is committed (none in this segment of the dialogue) and the speech acts he performs in each of his turns in the game; the last two columns record Ann's speech acts and commitments. The numbered rows indicate the sequence of turns. Officially, the game begins with preparatory moves in which each participant makes initial assertions and concessions. In Argument 1 the only such assertion is Ann's claim that there's no place on campus to get good coffee, and this automatically becomes a commitment of hers. According to the rules of the game, Bill's first move must either concede or challenge this assertion, and he challenges it in row 1 of the figure. The rules also specify that Ann must offer an argument for the challenged assertion in her very next move. Although Ann's actual response in Argument 1 is simply her statement about having tried all the coffee shops, we can view this as a truncated argument that could be expanded as: *I've tried all the coffee shops on campus, and none has good coffee; therefore, there's no place on campus to get good coffee.* This argument appears in Ann's speech act column. The rules dictate that the premise of the argument and the implication itself become Ann's commitments, as shown in the fourth column.

It is difficult to continue the description of Argument 1 in this fashion because of limitations of the Walton-Krabbe system. Bill's comment in Line 1d that Ann hasn't tried the Garrett coffee shop is a challenge to Ann to defend her previous claim, but it is also an assertion in its own right. It can be attacked in turn, as Ann proceeds to do in 1e. It is possible to regard Bill's comment as the beginning of a new dialogue game that has Line 1d as its basic assertion, but within the Walton-Krabbe system there would then be no way to record the fact that this statement also criticizes what went before. In general, the dialogue-game framework makes it difficult to represent the embedded or recursive structure of support that is often typical of argumentation. Nearly any statement that is introduced into an argument can itself become the argument's focus and generate additional justification and criticism.

In the present article, I describe a theory that adheres to the conversational approach in describing argumentation as a series of moves or speech acts by two or more people as they attempt to determine what to believe. But, in addition, it introduces a set of recursive rules that make it clear, for example, how attacks can become the subject of counterattacks, as in Argument 1. Unlike many conversational approaches, these rules generate an explicit, global structure for an argument that displays the reasons and critiques for each claim. The participants' commitment to the claims is defined over this structure. That is, the theory views an argument as being more than a sequence of moves in a game, and it represents the relation among the moves in terms of support, as in the structural tradition. The theory attempts in this way to unite previous work in cognitive psychology, philosophy, and linguistics in order to understand the nature of argumentation.

Although the theory depicts argumentation as occurring between two participants, the results are also relevant to individual deliberation and reasoning. As many investigators have remarked, people's skill and fairness in reasoning depends on their considering multiple sides of an issue and avoiding bias in evaluating claims (e.g., Baron, 1991, 1995; Perkins, Farady, & Bushey, 1991; Voss, Blais, Means, Greene, & Ahwesh, 1986; Voss & Means, 1991). Reasoning, in this sense, is often a process of internal argumentation in which a person considers the potential challenges, refutations, and justifications of an initial position (e.g., Billig, 1987; Ford, 1994; Kuhn, 1991); Hintikka (1984) traces this idea to Plato and Peirce. Sophisticated arguments in the humanities and social sciences, for example, usually take the form of an alternating sequence of claims, justifications, and potential counterclaims. Similarly, recent theories of individual decision making depict choice as a matter of internally weighing arguments for and against the options (Curley, Browne, Smith, & Benson, 1995; Hogarth & Kunreuther, 1995; Shafir, Simonson, & Tversky, 1993). Thus, describing multiperson argumentation may aid in analyzing single-person reasoning and in improving thinking and decision making.

Clearly, argumentation is not the only way to settle disagreements or to gain new knowledge. Other methods may be more appropriate for certain purposes or for certain individuals (see, e.g., Clinchy, 1989). Nevertheless, argumentation is an important tool for understanding, and it deserves closer attention from cognitive psychology than it has received. The goal of the present article is to provide a starting point for a rigorous theory of argumentation that goes beyond the somewhat unsystematic treatment common in textbooks in informal logic and critical thinking.

Argumentation Structure

According to the present theory, arguments are sequences of critical reactions to a claim. Suppose, for example, that Ann utters Line 1a, there's no place on campus to get a good cup of coffee. Making this claim is not only a way to express a personal conviction, but also a way to get Bill to adopt the same belief. Unless Ann and Bill are simply engaged in small talk, Ann initially thinks Bill may not believe Line 1a; otherwise, she has little reason for stating it. By asserting 1a, Ann expects to get Bill to state his relevant beliefs, probably in the hope that Bill will affirm it. If all goes smoothly, Bill will accept Line 1a, either on the basis of his prior conviction or on Ann's authority, and 1a will then be part of these participants' common ground. Phrases such as "You're right about that," "That's true," and "I agree" accept the previous assertion and end the issue. We can refer to these phrases as *accepters* (similar to Resnick et al.'s, 1993, concessions), and the final line in Argument 1 is of this type. Arguments arise, however, when the listener doesn't immediately accept the initial claim. In the sample dialogue, instead of accepting Line 1a at the outset, Bill delays until he explores its support.

Rules for Argument Structure

This section surveys some possible reactions to claims and attempts to show how they fit together and lend structure to an argument. What sorts of conversational moves do arguments contain? Faced with claim 1a, Bill has a number of options in addition to agreeing with it. First, if he is uncertain whether he should believe the claim, he can ask for reasons. For example, Bill can ask, "What makes you say that?" as he does in Line 1b, or ask some similar question (e.g., "Why?" or "How come?"). This challenges Ann to justify her original claim by asserting reasons in its favor. Her response in Line 1c (i.e., *I've tried all the coffee shops on campus and none has good coffee*) justifies the claim by citing evidence. However, clarifying or explaining the original claim can also justify it in some contexts (Brem & Rips, 1995; Ranney, Schank, Hoadley, & Neff, 1994). Note that Ann's 1c is itself a claim and is open to requests for justification, just as was 1a. Thus, arguments allow embedding and repeating of the participants' moves, as we saw earlier.

Bill's question in Line 1b probes the reasons for 1a, but he could also ask for the point of the statement (i.e., the conclusion that the statement supports). If Bill suspects that Line 1a was uttered with a motive, as a step leading to a further claim, he could ask Ann where she was going:

(2)   Bill: {So (what)? | What's the point? | What do you say that for?}

Bill's 1b seeks justification for the previous statement, whereas the questions in 2 seek the conclusion toward which it is headed. (Some questions, such as "Why do you say that?" seem appropriate for both purposes; see Graesser & Person, 1994; Zwicky & Zwicky, 1973, for related distinctions.) Although the justification in Line 1c appropriately answers 1b, it cannot easily answer 2, except perhaps to clarify or to paraphrase the original claim. Instead, 3 more naturally follows 2:

(3)   Ann: I've decided to open my own coffee shop in Swift Hall.

To distinguish sequences such as 1b–1c from those such as 2–3, we can call the former pair a *justification query* and a *justification* and the latter pair a *conclusion query* and a *conclusion*.

Instead of asking for a justification or a conclusion, Bill could attempt to refute Ann's claim. In responding to 1c, for example, Bill attacks the claim directly by offering the counterclaim in 1d that Ann has not tried the new coffee shop in Garrett. Like 1a and 1c, 1d is a claim in its own right and is subject to the same types of replies. Ann could challenge 1d by asking for a justification, or she could attempt to refute 1d by making her own counterclaim, as she does in 1e. Pollock (1989) called statements like 1d–1f *defeaters*, because their aim is to defeat an earlier piece of the argument. Pollock distinguished between *rebutting defeaters*, such as 1d and 1e, that directly conflict with an earlier claim, and *undercutting defeaters*, such as 1f, that attack the relation between a claim and its support (see, also, Flowers et al., 1982). For example, in Line 1f, Bill attempts to undercut the relation between 1c and 1a by noting that coffee shops are not the only place on campus for coffee. According to Bill, Ann's statement that all the coffee shops have bad coffee does not sufficiently support her claim that there's no good coffee on campus.

Claims, challenges, defeaters, and accepters give arguments their structure. It is possible to depict this structure in a number of ways, using rules, schemas (Rumelhart & Norman, 1988), superstructures (van Dijk and Kintsch, 1983), context spaces (Reichman-Adar, 1984), discourse spaces (Allen, 1995), or similar representations. These formats have different advantages, but for present purposes the differences between them are not crucial. For simplicity in representing arguments, I adopt simple rewrite rules for dialogues, leaving open the possibility that extending the theory may require more complex representations. In the examples given here, the claims, challenges, and other moves correspond directly to text in the dialogue, with possibly more than one move per speaking turn. In naturally occurring arguments, however, participants may leave some of these items implicit.

The rules in Table 1, then, summarize the possibilities discussed so far. Each of these rules means that the discourse component on the left decomposes into those on the right, as in other rewrite rules. However, the plus signs in Rules A, C, and others indicate not only the order of the components, but also a change of turn from one speaker to another. Thus, Rule A means that an argument consists of a claim by the first participant (indicated by the subscript 1) followed by a response by the second participant (subscript 2). An asterisk following a component indicates that

Table 1: Structural Rules for Two-Person Argumentation

A. Argument → {Claim$_1$ + Response$_2^*$ | Claim$_1$ + Ø$_2$}^{a}

B. Response$_2$ → {Challenge$_2$ | Rebutting Defeater$_2$ | Accepter$_2$}^{a}

C. Subargument$_i$ → {Claim$_i$ + Subresponse$_{3-i}^*$ | Claim$_i$ + Ø$_{3-i}$}^{a}

D. Subresponse$_i$ → {Challenge$_i$ | Rebutting Defeater$_i$ | Undercutting Defeater$_i$ | Accepter$_i$}^{a}

E. Challenge$_i$ → {Justification Query$_i$ + Justification$_{3-i}^*$ | Justification Query$_i$ + Ø$_{3-i}$ | Conclusion Query$_i$ + Conclusion$_{3-i}^*$ | Conclusion Query$_i$ + Ø$_{3-i}$}^{a}

F. Justification Query$_i$ → {Why? | Why do you think so? | How come?| ... }

G. Conclusion Query$_i$ → {So? | What's the point? | What do you say that for?| ... }

H. Justification$_i$ → Subargument$_i$

I. Conclusion$_i$ → Subargument$_i$

J. Rebutting Defeater$_i$ → Subargument$_i$

K. Undercutting Defeater$_i$ → Subargument$_i$

L. Accepter$_i$ → {That's right | You're right about that | I agree| ... }

Note. Subscripts on constituents indicate the first speaker ($i = 1$) or the second speaker ($i = 2$). The expression $3 - i$ indicates a change of speaker (if $i = 1$, then $3 - i = 2$; if $i = 2$, then $3 - i = 1$). Asterisks denote possible repetition of the same constituent.

^{a} Accepters and null responses (Ø) can appear only on the right-most branch of the lowest argument or subargument that dominates them.

the constituent can be repeated. Thus, after the first participant's claim, the second participant can produce more than one response (e.g., several attempts to defeat the original claim). Bracketed items separated by vertical bars, as in A–G, are alternative constituents, only one of which can be selected on a given turn. For example, Rule B stipulates that a response can consist of a challenge, a rebutting defeater, or an accepter. The rules in Table 1 are not exhaustive because it is possible to analyze some of the categories in more detail.[2] The present rules, however, provide a working hypothesis that will allow us to test their accuracy.

As an example of how these rules operate, Figure 2 shows the structure they generate for Argument 1. (I have omitted subscripts for the participants because the participants' names appear at the terminal nodes.) Ann's statement 1a is the argument's initial claim, and the rest of the argument is a response to that claim. Within this response, Ann's justification in 1c is an embedded claim that elicits an embedded response from Bill (in this case, a rebutting defeater). The argument could be continued through repeated application of the same rules.[3]

Some Advantages of the Structural Rules

Argumentation does not normally occur in isolation, but as part of larger interactions. It is unlikely for this reason that the rules in Table 1 are mentally isolated from the more general procedures people use in coping with conversation. People's ability to understand argumen-

tation shades into their ability to understand instructions, excuses, and other discourse types. Nonetheless, the rules in Table 1 possess an internal structure that may give rise to consistent impressions and modes of response. The concept of argumentation is thus like many other concepts (e.g., *tree, shrub*) that exhibit coherence despite close connections to other categories. The systematic patterns that occur in arguments make them a reasonable topic of theorizing.

One advantage of these rules is that they illuminate the two-sidedness of arguments by means of the claim-response pairings in Rules A and C. In this respect, the current theory is similar to that of Jackson and Jacobs (1980). In their approach, argumentation is based on a speech-act pair (e.g., a proposal and a refusal) in which the second act of the pair indicates some type of disagreement. The rest of the argument is an attempt to manage this conflict. The rules in Table 1 generalize and formalize this idea. Every claim implies the possibility of a response, so every claim is subject to challenge and criticism. Justifications and defeaters are themselves claims and have responses like any other.

Within this framework, participants can fail to respond to a specific claim, either because their response is preempted by another participant or because they choose to return to an earlier point in the dialogue. Within the context of an argument, however, these skipped responses are meaningful; they are "official silences" that arguers and onlookers can interpret (Schegloff, 1972). Rules A, C, and E provide for these skipped responses, representing them by means

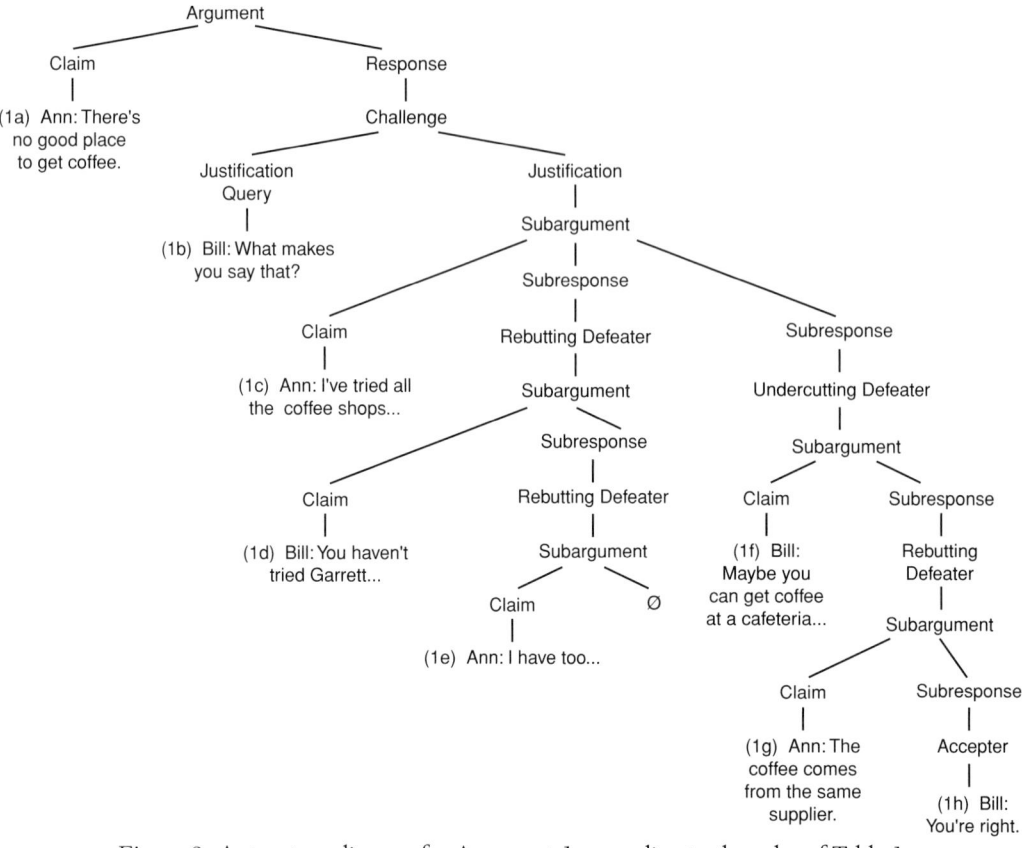

Figure 2. A structure diagram for Argument 1, according to the rules of Table 1.

of the null symbol (∅). An example of a skipped response occurs at 1f in the sample dialogue: Instead of responding directly to Ann's claim that she was in the Garrett coffee shop, Bill backs up to re-attack her justification in 1c. Participants often preface these jumping-back points by phrases such as *anyway, besides, in any case, at any rate, in any event*, and similar markers (Grosz et al., 1989; Reichman-Adar, 1984). Skipped responses also mean that a single conversational turn can contain more than one terminal constituent in the argument structure. In place of 1g, for example, Ann could have said, *All the campus coffee comes from the same supplier; and besides, I've tried the coffee at the cafeterias, too.* Ann would thus be preempting Bill's response to her claim about the supplier. She hurries on to give a second defeater to 1f without giving Bill a chance to respond to her first defeater.

The representation also distinguishes the different lines of argument as separate branches in the structure. For example, Bill makes two different attacks on 1c (i.e., that Ann hasn't tried all the coffee shops and that coffee shops aren't the only places for coffee), and these two lines

appear as two branches in Figure 2. The rules are compatible, too, with different styles of argumentation. More combative styles are likely to exhibit many rebutting defeaters and challenges; more conciliatory styles would exhibit more accepters.

Some Limitations of the Structural Theory

The rules in Table 1 describe some ways arguments develop. The present claim is that people hearing or reading an argument extract some structure analogous to the one these rules generate, but, of course, they get more out of an argument than the bare structure. In the following parts of this article, I take up two additional aspects of argumentation: information about which participants are committed to which claims and which participant has greater burden of proof. However, there are other aspects that the theory does not address. First, the justification and defeater categories in Table 1 capture the way participants publicly position their utterances within the argument, but they do not convey how successful these attempts are.

Some justifications and defeaters are obviously stronger and more convincing than others, but the participants and the audience would have to evaluate this by independent means. The structural rules may be preliminary to such an evaluation because understanding the role of an utterance in the argument is fundamental to assessing it. But the rules don't by themselves decide the assessment. (The limitation here is similar to that of the support links in Fisher's theory, discussed earlier.)

Second, challenges and defeaters in arguments are potentially embarrassing to participants and so add an emotionally threatening element. It is often in the interest of both participants to maintain each other's dignity or "face," and for this reason they may couch their responses in ways that preserve the other's self-esteem (Brown & Levinson, 1987). For example, instead of Bill's forthright 1d, he could hedge by saying "I wonder whether you've tried the new coffee shop in Garrett" or "Have you heard about the new coffee shop in Garrett?" These aspects of politeness and tact are important elements in argumentation (Muntigl & Turnbull, 1998), but the present theory does not treat them because they belong to a much wider class of conversational settings, including invitations, requests, advice giving, and many others.

Third, the rules in Table 1 are limited to two-sided argumentation. Some issues have more than two sides, of course. A group may have to decide which of many possible actions to take to achieve a goal, with each action having its own advocates. In the present article, I develop the two-sided case as a starting point, leaving to further work the task of generalizing to more than two speakers.

It should also be clear that the rules do not describe the strategies participants use to generate their contributions to a debate. Although the rules in Table 1 are part of the knowledge they employ in planning their conversational moves, participants choose these moves on the basis of many background factors, including their knowledge of the argument's subject matter, their memory of previous conversations, and their judgment of whether a retort is likely to offend their opponent. I mention a few of the issues concerning argument production at the end of this chapter, but the theory aims to account for argument comprehension. A related point is that people may sometimes organize their arguments around some global attitude (e.g., support or opposition to a general point of view) that does not appear in the dialogue as a specific claim. These attitudes then impose a more abstract structure on the argument than the one I describe here. Although the Table 1 rules don't represent these global attitudes, there is no reason to think the rules conflict with them.

Finally, because a number of investigators have criticized the use of rewrite rules in describing the structure of stories, one should consider whether the same criticisms apply here (see Black & Wilensky, 1979, and Garnham, 1983, for critiques of story grammars, and Rumelhart, 1980, for a response). Many of the criticisms have focused on the difficulty of using these grammars to parse a story in initial comprehension. Because the story grammars' categories (e.g., *setting* or *resolution*) can contain an unlimited number of possible texts, comprehenders have to understand the content of the text before they can assign it to the appropriate category. This reverses the order of operations in traditional theories of comprehension, where people first extract grammatical structure and then use the structure to interpret the text. Whatever problems this poses for story grammars, however, the present theory is not intended as a parser for arguments. The rules of Table 1 describe the structure that people uncover in thinking about an argument, and they presuppose many lower-level abilities in understanding its sentences initially. Although the rules may help guide interpretation by allowing people to anticipate upcoming segments of the argument, they are obviously only one part of the text comprehension process. (See Cohen, 1990, for suggestions on parsing onesided arguments.) Similarly, the point of the present rules is not to distinguish between "grammatical" and "ungrammatical" arguments, but to describe one dimension along which arguments can vary. It seems uncontroversial that people recognize justifications, accepters, and defeaters as components of arguments, and the rewrite rules state generalizations about how arguments configure these components.

An Application to Trial Proceedings

The rules in Table 1 specify the types of conversational moves that make up the core of argumentation, and it is easy to use the rules to construct dialogues, such as Argument 1, that appear to be well-formed arguments. It is another question, however, whether the rules also pick out instances of argumentation that occur in natural contexts. Can the rules distinguish arguments from other types

Table 2: Two Excerpts from the Simpson Civil Trial That Served as Stimulus Passages

---

Passage 1

Mr. Petrocelli:	Well, Your Honor, for the record, I want to say I think the comments of Mr. Baker were not warranted.
The Court:	I'm not concerned with Mr. Baker's comment.
Mr. Petrocelli:	This a public proceeding. I don't think he has any right making those comments and talking about referring matters to the State Bar. Maybe we ought to talk about Mr. Taft, his colleague.
The Court:	Mr. Petrocelli, Mr. Baker, as you know, I'm not influenced by any of this personality interchange. I've always wanted counsel to desist from that. I will continue to ask counsel to desist from that. I made no complaints about whatever things you want to say about me. I could only make a record. And I'm going to deny the motion because I think it's untimely. I think you had ample opportunity to make the effort to make the correction, and it's too late.

Passage 2

Mr. Blasier:	Tell you what Dr. Gerdes is going to say, if you like. [Pause in proceedings for the Court to review document.]
The Court:	Okay, go ahead.
Mr. Blasier:	He is also going to testify that those results in 30 and 31 are not valid because of the – the extraneous alleles, which showed up in the positive controls; that because of those alleles showing up where they're not supposed to be, that those whole – that whole series of tests is invalidated.
The Court:	By whom? Tests by whom?
Mr. Blasier:	All of them by DOJ. I'm sorry. I think it's DOJ on 30 and 31; that they had extraneous alleles on the positive controls. He's also going to testify that Bundy drop 52 shows evidence of contamination, as well, with an extra 1.3 allele as a result of possible cross-contamination at the crime scene.

---

of conversations (e.g., advice giving or permission seeking) in the form they take in ordinary speech? One source of evidence comes from a recent analysis by Muntigl and Turnbull (1998) of naturally occurring arguments among family members and among university students. The types of exchanges that Muntigl and Turnbull identified bear a close correspondence to the categories in Table 1. Their irrelevancy claims (e.g., "You're straying off the topic") are similar to undercutting defeaters, challenges to justification queries, and contradictions (e.g., "I don't hate him") to rebutting defeaters. (Muntigl & Turnbull also recognize a category of counterclaims [e.g., "Yeah but it's still not what I like"], which might be analyzed as an accepter followed by a defeater for an earlier claim.) This convergence between categories provides independent support for the Table 1 rules.

Further support for the rules comes from two-person interactions that occur in trial transcripts. Obviously, legal proceedings contain many argumentative exchanges, but they also contain other kinds of interaction, such as petitions to the judge. Thus, it is possible to ask whether the rules in Table 1 describe (independently identified) arguments rather than nonar-

guments in the proceedings. As a way of exploring this issue, 20 excerpts were selected from the O. J. Simpson civil trial because the complete transcript is readily available in digital form.[4] The excerpts were dialogues from sidebar discussions (either between the judge and a lawyer or between two lawyers) that took place near the middle of the trial (between December 3 and December 11, 1996). Each excerpt conformed to the following constraints: (a) It consisted of at least four consecutive speaking turns, two each from the two participants; (b) the participants' statements were addressed to each other (rather than to a third party); and (c) no single turn contained more than nine sentences. The last constraint was intended to eliminate long speeches that a participant had prepared prior to the time of the dialogue. The 20 excerpts were random selections from the dialogues that met these restrictions. The length of the passages varied from 4 to 20 turns (31 to 425 words). Table 2 shows two examples that illustrate the range of the dialogues.

These trial excerpts contain many sorts of conversational moves, including queries of fact (e.g., "Tests by whom?"), requests for permission ("Then let us lead as well, Your Honor"), offers ("Tell you what Dr. Gerdes is going to say, if you like"), refusals ("I'm inclined not to permit him to testify unless he's subject to a deposition"), grantings of requests ("Okay, go ahead"), and many others. Some of these speech acts can occasion an argument (e.g., a refusal can lead to an argument about its fairness) or can be embedded in an argument (e.g., questions of fact can occur when one participant is trying to understand another's position), but are not part of the arguments, according to the current theory. In order to predict whether an excerpt is an argument, it is necessary to find a way to separate these extraneous speech acts from those of the rules in Table 1 because the theory holds the latter to be constitutive of argumentation. For the sake of objectivity and simplicity, two assistants independently classified each turn according to whether it contained an explicit phrase indicating that it was a defeater (e.g., the phrases " ... is irrelevant," " ... is meaningless," "No, it's ... [rather than –]," "No, it's not ... [it's –]," etc.), a justification query (e.g., "Why assume ... ?," "Why is ... relevant?," "Why is ... reasonable/unreasonable?"), or a conclusion query (e.g., "Where is ... leading?," etc.). These categories are the ones from Table 1 that are most easily identified and most representative of arguments; thus, they should provide a rough index of the character of the excerpt.[5] The Spearman correlation between the number of such categories that the two assistants identified was .75 across passages ($df = 18, p < .001$). For example, both assistants marked each exchange as a defeater in the first passage in Table 2. Both also marked the fourth exchange of the second passage as a query. (One assistant also marked the second exchange as a query, presumably on the grounds that it elicits an explanation from the attorney.)

The theory predicts that the larger the number of these Table 1 categories, the more likely it is that the passage will appear to be an argument. As a test of this prediction, 27 Northwestern University undergraduates read the same 20 excerpts and rated how typical each was of conversational argumentation. They made their ratings on an 11-point scale, with 0 defined as *very atypical* and 10 defined as *very typical*. As examples of their decisions, they gave the first passage in Table 2 a mean rating of 7.0, and the second a rating of 4.1. In line with the hypothesis, the Spearman correlation between their mean typicality rating and the mean number of argument categories in a passage was .70 ($df = 18$, $p < .001$). Of course, coding of the excerpts takes

into account only one aspect of the Table 1 rules; so, at best, it provides only a partial test of the present framework. More stringent tests appear later. Nevertheless, it provides a hint that the framework is pertinent to arguments as they occur in everyday contexts.

Principles of Commitment

One reason that argument structure is important is that it defines which claims become part of common ground and, hence, which issues get settled during an argument. In order to understand this process, I focus on how participants publicly commit themselves to a claim because if both participants are publicly committed to the same claim, that claim becomes part of common ground. (See Bly, 1993, for the notion of a negotiated common ground.) Once a participant's claim is admitted to common ground, then that participant can use it to support other points. By the same token, the greater the number of the participant's claims that are still under contention, the greater his or her burden of proof in the argument, other things being equal.

In this section of the article, I develop a theory of how participants commit themselves to claims and how they retract commitment. This theory then generates predictions for experiments in which subjects judge the commitments of speakers.[6] The central notion is that when people read or hear an argument they keep a running mental record of the participants' commitments. For this purpose, they maintain mental *commitment stores or commitment tags*, a notion that originates in formal theories of argumentation (Hamblin, 1970). In the present model, the commitment tags are mental representations that record for each claim C and participant S, whether S accepts C, rejects C, or is neutral with respect to C at the current stage of the debate. The commitment tags will typically change during the debate, as participants accept and reject each others' assertions. In this theory, conventions or principles governing argumentation determine how people tag claims on the basis of the structure of Table 1.

The first subsection presents some principles governing commitment and shows how they apply to Argument 1. The strategy is to describe a set of principles that has certain ideal properties, properties that push participants toward agreeing with each other on which claims they should accept or reject. I discuss these ideal properties in the second subsection, and Appendix A [of Rips, 1998] contains proofs that they hold. It is obvious, however, that real arguments do not always end in consensus. Sometimes we recognize that one participant accepts and the other rejects a claim; sometimes we see that one participant is neutral about a claim (and the other nonneutral) when the debate ends. We can model these residual disagreements by identifying within the ideal set certain principles that people do not always employ. Failure to apply these principles thus provides obstacles to agreement. This theory, called the *commitment change* model, is taken up in the third subsection, and the rest of the article tests some of its implications.

Clearly, participants may have many private beliefs about an issue that may or may not surface during a debate. In this article, I concentrate on public commitments, not because private ones are unimportant, but because the focus is on how an audience comes to understand arguments that others put forth. From the point of view of someone listening to an argument, the publicly established commitments are usually the main sources of evidence about the participants' positions.

Some Principles of Commitment

Table 3 lists some hypothetical principles that might determine commitment. These principles are rules that people may follow as they listen to or read an argument, and they distill possible inferences that people might use in deciding who is committed to which claims. The rules constitute an idea about what one is entitled to conclude about the commitments, based on participants' explicit statements of agreement (or disagreement) and tacit knowledge of argumentation strategies. Taken together, these rules have properties of completeness or closure (as later sections show). The rules lead to agreement among participants, and for this reason, they can be considered ideal or "normative." There are other normative considerations, however, that these rules do not necessarily fulfill. For example, they may or may not reliably promote true beliefs or provide deeper understanding of an issue.

The most obvious rules (and probably the ones most likely to be obeyed in comprehension) are the *assertion principle* and the *acceptance principle*, listed at the top of Table 3. According to the assertion principle, participants commit themselves to their own claims when they assert them. For example, Ann commits herself to Line 1a by virtue of asserting it at the beginning of

the dialogue, and 1a would therefore be tagged as one of Ann's commitments. The same goes for the claims in 1c to 1g. The assertion principle follows simply from what it means to make an assertion. Although there are special devices that allow participants to withhold commitment from some of their own statements (e.g., by saying that they are assuming something "for the sake of the argument" or that they are playing "devil's advocate"), these cases have to be marked as hypothetical. A second, equally obvious, principle is that when a participant explicitly accepts a claim (via Rule L of Table 1), then the participant is committed to the opponent's last claim. Thus, Bill commits himself to Ann's claim 1g at the end of the sample argument because of his accepter in 1h, and 1g therefore becomes part of common ground. This is the acceptance principle in the table.

More interestingly, some of the rules imply that accepting a lower claim in the argument structure can also affect whether higher claims become part of common ground. (The experiments later in this article test this assumption.) Suppose, for example, that in 1d Bill were to accept Ann's justification, instead of trying to defeat it. That is, instead of saying "You haven't tried the new coffee shop...," he simply says "Okay, you're right." Accepting the justification means that Ann's second claim ("I've tried all the coffee shops on campus...") becomes common ground by the acceptance and assertion principles, but what of Ann's original claim 1a ("There's no place on campus to get a good cup of coffee")? If the argument ends at this point, then it seems that Bill has implicitly accepted the original claim by virtue of accepting its justification. So both of Ann's previous claims would then be part of common ground. If the argument continues, however, then it is possible for Bill to ward off committing himself to the original claim by attempting to defeat it on other grounds. This suggests that, in informal reasoning, commitment to a justification implies default commitment to the justified claim, and justification principle (a) in Table 3 states this policy. A participant can later reverse this commitment, however, by defeating the claim directly or undercutting the relation between it and the justification, as other principles in the table make clear. Table 3 also contains a parallel conclusion principle for arguments resulting from Rule I of Table 1.

Accepting a defeater can also have implications for commitment to higher claims. An example occurs at the end of Argument 1. Ann's

Table 3: Some Principles of Commitment in Two-Person Arguments

Assertion Principle
   A participant who asserts a claim accepts that claim.[a,b,c]
Acceptance Principle
   A participant who utters an accepter (e.g., "I agree") accepts the previous claim.[a,b,c]
Rebutting Principles

(a) A participant who accepts a rebutting defeater to a claim rejects that claim, unless the defeater is undercut for the participant (see undercutting principle [a]).[a,b,c,d]
(b) A participant who rejects a rebutting defeater to a claim accepts that claim.[c,e]

Justification Principles

(a) A participant who accepts a justification for a claim accepts that claim, unless the justification is undercut for the participant (see undercutting principle [a]).[a,b,c,d]
(b) A participant who rejects a justification for a claim rejects that claim.[a,b,c,d]
(c) A participant who passes up the chance to respond to a justification query for a claim rejects that claim. In these circumstances, the participant uttering the justification query also rejects the claim.[b,c,d]

Conclusion Principles

(a) A participant who accepts a claim that directly supports a conclusion accepts that conclusion, unless the conclusion is undercut for the participant (see undercutting principle [a]).[d]
(b) A participant who rejects a claim that directly supports a conclusion rejects that conclusion.[e]

Undercutting Principles

(a) A justification, conclusion, rebutting, or undercutting defeater is undercut for a participant if the claim is followed by an odd-numbered string of undercutting defeaters that the participant accepts.[a,b,c,d]
(b) A participant who accepts an undercutting defeater accepts the supporting claim (justification, rebutting defeater, undercutting defeater, or claim supporting a conclusion) of the undercut pair.[a,b,c,d]
(c) A participant who accepts an undercutting defeater for a justification (conclusion) rejects the justified claim (conclusion), unless the defeater is undercut for the participant (see undercutting principle [a]).[a,b,c,d]
(d) A participant who accepts an undercutting defeater for a rebutting defeater accepts the claim against which the rebutting defeater was aimed, unless the undercutting defeater is itself undercut for the participant (see undercutting principle [a]).[c,e]
(e) A participant who rejects an undercutting defeater for a justification (conclusion) accepts the justified claim (conclusion).[c]
(f) A participant who rejects an undercutting defeater for a rebutting defeater rejects the claim against which the rebutting defeater was aimed.[e]

Skipped-Response Principle
   A participant who passes up the opportunity to respond to a claim accepts that claim.[b,c,e]

---

[a] Received empirical support in either Experiment 1 or Experiment 2.
[b] These principles are required for the determination theorem (Appendix A in Rips, 1998).
[c] These principles are required for the mutual determination theorem (Appendix A in Rips, 1998).
[d] These principles are the moderate items for model fitting.
[e] These principles are the liberal items for model fitting.

---

final claim ("All of the campus coffee comes from the same supplier") is a rebutting defeater for Bill's prior assertion in 1f, "... maybe you can get good coffee in one of the cafeterias," and this implies that Ann rejects 1f. Rebutting principle (a) in the table makes this explicit by requiring participants who accept a rebutting defeater to reject the defeated claim. Notice that this same principle also applies to Bill when he agrees in the final line to Ann's last claim. At this point,

Bill is agreeing to a defeater for his own prior assertion, and this puts him in a position where he must also back off that assertion. The upshot is that, at the end of the dialogue, Ann and Bill mutually reject 1f by rebutting principle (a) and mutually accept 1g, by the assertion and acceptance principles.

Conservative versus liberal commitment. The commitment principles seem straightforward so far, but there is a grey area where intuitions may differ. At one extreme, people could view almost any conversational move as changing the speaker's commitment to earlier claims, and one can write commitment principles that implement that policy. The effect would be that commitment to an individual claim would fluctuate rapidly during a debate. We call this approach a *liberal* policy toward commitment. At the opposite extreme, a *conservative* commitment policy would make a speaker's commitment to a claim less likely to change on the basis of later conversational moves. Speakers would tend to retain their initial positions toward a claim through subsequent exchanges.

The following sections develop and test models of argumentation based on both conservative and liberal policies. For the moment, however, the commitment principles will be formulated in a way that reflects the liberal view. The conservative view omits some of the principles in question, thus preserving the status of the participants' commitment prior to the conversational move.[7] Liberal policies often reflect inferences based on participants' choice of strategies, inferences that conservatives don't gamble on.

The difference between liberal and conservative commitment policies comes into focus when a participant ignores an opportunity to respond. Sometimes a participant preempts another's response by rushing to make a further point, and in such situations the second participant's silence clearly does not imply either acceptance or rejection. Sometimes, however, a participant deliberately passes up the chance to respond. For example, as we noticed earlier, Bill chooses not to respond directly to Ann's claim 1e (i.e., her assertion that she was just in the Garrett coffee shop), and instead he returns at 1f to attack an earlier point. This leaves the empty response ($\emptyset$) that appears in Figure 2. Formal models of dialectical argument (Hamblin, 1970; Mackenzie, 1979; Rescher, 1977;

Walton & Krabbe, 1995) all adopt the liberal stance that any such failure to respond immediately to a claim is a concession: Because Bill does not respond to 1e, he is automatically committed to it. For example, Walton and Krabbe's (1995) model of permissive persuasion dialogues (PPD) requires that

> If a party makes an assertion, the other party, in the very next move, is to make clear its position with respect to that assertion (unless this assertion is already among the latter party's concessions or has already been challenged); that is, it should either challenge or concede the new assertion.... [This principle] stipulates that in PPD unchallenged assertions count as conceded. We do not see any reason to admit a middle position. If you do not want to concede something, just challenge it. (p. 137)

A similar skipped-response principle appears in Table 3, but it is not obvious that this principle applies in a blanket way to everyday arguments. (The experiments in the following part of the chapter provide evidence that conservative participants do not follow it.)

An example of commitment change in arguments. We can summarize the commitment principles of Table 3 in terms of our running example. Figure 3 illustrates the way in which Ann's and Bill's commitments change as Argument 1 unfolds. In this figure, commitment tags for each claim (the shaded boxes) appear next to the argument structure, and labels at the top of the tag identify the claim it represents. Each tag is in tabular form (as a kind of score card) with the first column containing Ann's commitments for the claim and the second column containing Bill's. The individual entries indicate whether each participant accepts the claim (+), rejects the claim (−), or remains neutral (blank). The rows show how commitments for the claim

---

Figure 3. An illustration of changes of commitment in Argument 1, according to the rules of Table 3. Panel (a) represents commitment changes that occur during the first five lines of the argument; Panel (b) represents changes that occur in the last three lines. Each of the shaded boxes (commitment tags) within the figure indicates whether Ann and Bill accept (+), reject (−), or are neutral (blank) about the adjacent claim. The first column of a box represents Ann's commitments; the second column represents Bill's. The rows of each box show how commitments for the claim change as the argument progresses. The first row gives Ann's and Bill's commitments when the claim is first uttered, the second row shows their commitments to the claim when a later part of the dialogue next alters one of the commitments, and so on. The last row in the box shows Ann and Bill's commitments at the end of the argument. The arrows between the boxes indicate how commitment to later claims affects commitment to earlier ones. The name of the rule that produces this change labels the arrow. (See Table 3 for a description of these rules.)

(a)

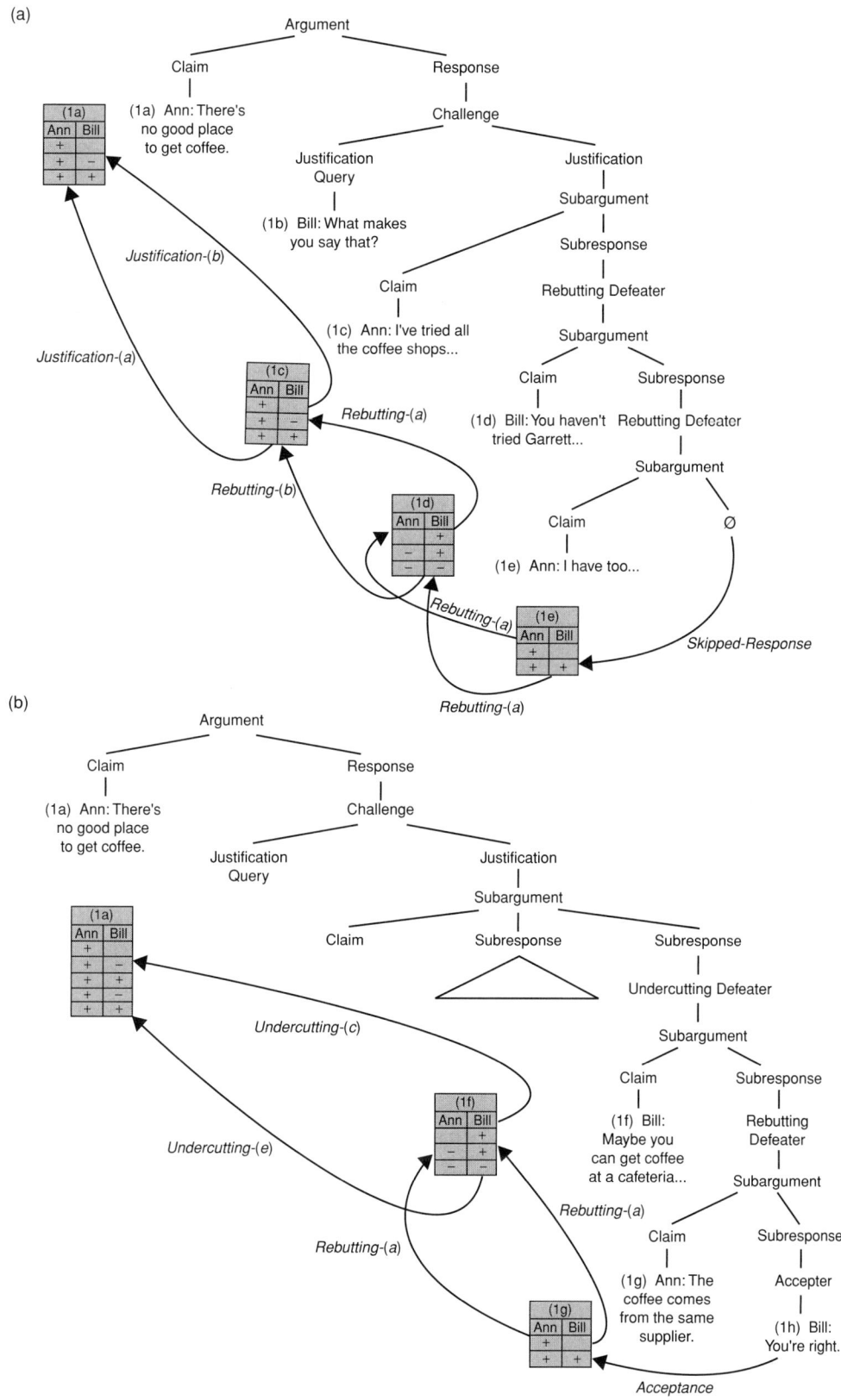

(b)

change at successive stages of the argument: The first row of each box shows Ann's and Bill's commitments at the point at which the claim is first uttered; the second row shows their commitments to the same claim when a later exchange in the dialogue alters one of the commitments. The final row in the box shows Ann's and Bill's commitment to the claim at the end of the argument. The arrows between the boxes show how commitment to later claims affects commitment to earlier ones. For example, an arrow from a plus entry for Ann in a lower box to a minus entry for her in an upper box means that her acceptance of the lower claim implies her rejection of the upper claim, according to one of the Table 3 rules. The name of the rule in question labels the arrow.

To see how this notation works, consider the box at the upper left corner of Figure 3a, which represents commitments for claim 1a (i.e., that there's no place on campus to get good coffee). When Ann first makes this claim, she accepts it (by the assertion principle), and Bill is neutral about it. The first row of the box represents this with a plus sign in Ann's column and a blank in Bill's. As the dialogue progresses, Ann justifies this claim ("I've tried all the coffee shops . . . "), and Bill attacks Ann's justification ("You haven't tried the coffee shop in Garrett . . . "). By justification principle (b) in Table 3, Bill's rejection of the justification entails his rejection of the justified claim 1a itself. This latter rejection appears in the second row of the upper-left box as a minus sign in Bill's column. The arrow pointing to this entry means that his rejection of 1c (the minus sign at the base of the arrow) is what causes his rejection of 1a (the minus sign at the head of the arrow). The label *Justification-(b)* indicates the relevant principle for this change. Because Ann is still committed to 1a, Ann's column in the second row retains the plus sign.

A little later in the argument, Bill skips a response to Ann's claim 1e that she has tried the Garrett coffee shop. This sets off a complicated chain reaction: First, skipping the response tacitly concedes 1e by the skipped response rule (see the plus sign under Bill's column in the box for 1e). Second, conceding 1e forces Bill to retract his own assertion that Ann hasn't tried Garrett, as shown by the minus sign in Bill's column in the 1d box. Third, retracting 1d means Bill must accept 1c, which 1d was originally supposed to defeat. And, finally, accepting 1c causes Bill to accept 1a because 1c justifies it. The third row of the 1a box represents this realignment, where both participants accept 1a. The remain-

ing boxes in Figure 3a show in a similar way the changes in commitments to claims 1c, 1d, and 1e.

Panel a in Figure 3 shows the commitment changes in the first part of the argument (through Line 1e), using the full set of rules in Table 3. The remaining changes for Lines 1f through 1h appear in Figure 3b.[8] At the end of Argument 1, Ann and Bill mutually accept 1a, 1c, 1e, and 1g, and mutually reject 1d and 1f. Ann has a clear advantage here because all her claims have become mutually accepted, whereas all Bill's claims are mutually rejected at the conclusion of the dialogue. These commitment tags are, no doubt, subject to memory limitations: If there are many claims and many participants, people may lose track of which participants are committed to which claims. This can interfere with people's ability to follow an argument. The experiments reported here, however, attempt to minimize memory difficulties by allowing subjects to review the argument text.

As this example hints, tracing the kinematics of commitment can pose some intricate cognitive problems. Initially disputed claims can become accepted or retracted on the basis of later moves in the dialogue, when supporting and defeating claims are themselves accepted or retracted.

A Theory of Commitment in Arguments

The commitment principles of Table 3 provide a type of evaluation for informal arguments that bears similarities to the semantic evaluation of arguments in formal logic (Tarski, 1936/1956) and formal linguistics (Chierchia & McConnell-Ginet, 1990). Formal semantics specifies conditions, under which individual sentences are true or false in particular situations. It then defines a formal argument as valid just in case the conclusion of the argument is true in all situations in which the premises are true. In the present endeavor, we are not concerned with determining the truth of claims or the overall validity of an argument, but we can look at conditions under which the argument's participants end up committed (positively or negatively) to its claims and conditions under which they agree in their commitment. This provides a type of consensus analog to truth. In this subsection we develop some of the formal properties of the Table 3 commitment principles. As we noted earlier, however, some of these principles must be relaxed when we attempt to model real argumentation, a task that we discuss in the subsection that follows.

The purpose of developing the formal properties of the full set of rules is to see in what ways people can fall short of achieving full consensus in an argument.

Determination of arguments. Consider an argument between two participants. A claim in such an argument is *determined* if each participant either accepts or rejects the claim. Thus, a claim will be *undetermined* only if one or both participants are neutral about it (i.e., neither accept nor reject it). A claim is *mutually determined* if the participants both accept or both reject the claim. By extension, an entire argument structure is determined if each claim in it is determined; similarly, an argument structure is mutually determined if each claim in it is mutually determined. In a mutually determined argument, some claims can be mutually accepted while others are mutually rejected; however, no claim can be accepted by one participant and rejected by the other. All mutually determined claims are determined claims, and all mutually determined arguments are determined arguments, by these definitions. At the end of Argument 1, for example, the argument is mutually determined (and, hence, determined), because as Figure 3 shows, the participants ultimately concur in accepting or rejecting each claim. One question, then, is under what general conditions is an argument necessarily determined or mutually determined.

The liberal principles in Table 3 tend to make informal arguments determined ones, but they do not quite suffice to do so. First, as noted earlier, if a participant preempts the response of his or her opponent, then there is no way to tell whether the opponent accepts or rejects the first claim. (For example, if Ann asserts that there is no good coffee and then, without allowing Bill a chance to reply, goes on to make another claim, we don't interpret the absence of Bill's response as acquiescence to the statement about coffee.) Second, arguments that contain conclusion queries can sometimes be undetermined, even under the full set of principles in Table 3. For example, consider Argument 4, which begins with a claim and a conclusion query:

(4)   Ann: There's no place on campus to get a good cup of coffee.
       Bill: What do you say that for?
       Ann: . . .

If Ann simply ends the argument at this point by ignoring Bill's question, should Bill reject her claim? Ann's failure to supply a conclusion that follows from her claim does not seem to be a reason for rejecting the claim and provides no reason at all for accepting it. Similar problems surround accepted conclusions. Third, whether a participant accepts or rejects a claim depends on how we combine the different responses to that claim. Because a participant can give more than one response to a claim according to the Table 1 rules, it is possible that the participant will accept the claim in a first response and will reject it in a second. A participant is typically credited with the commitment that he or she adopts last; later responses take precedence over earlier ones. The discussion in the previous subsection used this policy implicitly, and it seems the most natural one for everyday arguments. An alternative policy is to average earlier responses with later ones; but if responses can cancel in determining commitment, then participants can end an argument neither accepting nor rejecting a claim.

With these three exceptions, however, the Table 3 principles yield determined arguments. Appendix A [in Rips, 1998] proves that if an argument (a) contains no conclusion queries, (b) contains no preempted responses, and (c) assigns commitment on the basis of the last principle that applies to a claim, then the argument is determined. The commitment principles necessary for determination are noted in Table 3.

Mutual determination of arguments. Under this regime, arguments still need not be *mutually* determined. Exceptions occur when a claim that the participants have come to reject is then accepted by one of them. At the end of the bizarre dialogue in Argument 5, for example, Ann would reject and Bill would accept Ann's first claim:

(5)   Ann: There's no place on campus to get a good cup of coffee.
       Bill: No, you can get good coffee at Garrett.
       Ann: Okay, you're right about that.
       Bill: And you're right, too, that there's no place on campus to get a good cup of coffee.

What seems strange about this case is not that Bill changes his mind about Ann's first claim: Arguments must allow participants to change their position, for otherwise there would be little reason for them to attempt to convince each other. Also, Argument 5 is structurally sound because the Table 1 rules will generate it. Rather, what is odd is that Bill spontaneously accepts a claim that he has just attacked without Ann giving any further support for it. If these situations are eliminated, then the rules in Table 3 imply that arguments are mutually determined. I will label these exceptions by saying that a participant *resurrects* a claim if he or she accepts a claim that the opponent asserted and now rejects. Appendix A [of Rips, 1998] proves that if an argument contains no resurrected claims and also obeys the conditions mentioned in the preceding paragraph, the argument is mutually determined. (A few additional principles from Table 3 are necessary for this result beyond those needed for proof of determination, and these are noted in Table 3.)

The import of the proof can be summarized in the following way: No matter how many times participants disagree within a line of argument, eventually that line must come to an end. The end could come through an accepter or it could come through silence (a skipped response), but because the skipped response principle equates these options, the line always ends in agreement. The remaining rules propagate the agreement to higher levels of the argument. Thus, within the confines of the rules of Table 1, participants lack a way to perpetuate a disagreement. The ability to "agree to disagree" calls for a metacognitive skill that goes beyond what these rules supply.[9]

A Probabilistic Model of Commitment

The commitment principles in Table 3 make for consensus. But, on intuitive grounds, arguments are not always mutually determined, even when they follow the structure of Table 1. Sometimes participants are left at the end of an argument disagreeing about whether a claim should be accepted or rejected. Sometimes a participant is left in a neutral state about a claim, neither accepting nor rejecting it; so the argument as a whole is not determined, much less mutually determined. Because the goal of this article is to account for people's comprehension of arguments in a realistic fashion, I will explore the way actual comprehension differs from the Table 3 ideal. This subsection formulates a probabilistic model that adapts Table 3 to allow disagreement and to account for empirical data.

Modeling conservatives, moderates, and liberals. The Table 3 principles as a group make for an extremely liberal policy toward commitment in which participants switch their attitude toward claims whenever any hint about this appears in the debate. Relaxing some of these principles would allow people to adopt a more inertial, conservative policy and would allow initial differences in their positions to remain in force at the end of an argument.

Suppose, in particular, that people adopt one of three possible views about commitment – a conservative, a moderate, or a liberal view – that differ in how many of the commitment principles they accept. Conservatives recognize only the strongest, most obvious forms of evidence for change of commitment; moderates recognize somewhat wider forms of evidence; and liberals the widest, most inferential forms. Thus, conservatives adopt only a minimal number of principles from Table 3, moderates a slightly larger subset, and liberals the full set of principles. Empirical judgments about whether a participant in an argument is committed to some claim will then reflect the proportion of conservatives, moderates, and liberals among the population.

Of the items in Table 3, the assertion and acceptance principles seem unavoidable in any rational exchange, and they must be part of even the most conservative policy. Similarly, conservatives must also recognize that if one participant directly attacks another's claim, then in some cases the first participant rejects that claim (see rebutting principle [a]). It is not so obvious, however, that people *always* interpret rebutting defeaters as entailing rejection of the defeated claim. It is possible to hold that if a participant accepts a claim and later comes to accept a defeater for it, then the participant could still cling to his or her original commitment. (Evidence for this appears in connection with the second study reported later.) A *restricted* version of rebutting principle (a) allows for this possibility: It specifies that if a participant accepts a rebutting defeater for a claim, then he or she rejects that claim, provided that this participant has not yet taken a stand on the claim. Thus, the conservative position adopts only the assertion and the acceptance principles, along with restricted rebutting (a), and we can refer to these items as *conservative* principles. They have the effect that participants always remain committed to their own claims and never accept others' claims except by explicitly uttering an accepter. In the case of Argument 1, this conservative policy means that Ann accepts her own claims 1a, 1c, 1e, and 1g at the end of the argument and rejects Bill's 1d and 1f, which she attacks directly. Bill would accept his own 1d and 1f, would remain neutral about Ann's 1a and 1e, would reject her 1c, and would accept Ann's claim 1g because of the accepter in the final line.

A moderate policy would allow participants to convince each other by successfully supporting or defeating claims. Accepting a rebutting defeater for a claim, accepting support for a claim, or undercutting a justification or defeater can all change a participant's commitments, according to this moderate position. The principles that implement such changes are rebutting principle (a) in its unrestricted form, justification principle (a), conclusion principle (a), and undercutting principle (a), and we refer to these as *moderate* principles in what follows. Moderate participants adopt these principles (along with assertion and acceptance). As a result, these participants would judge that Bill rejects 1f in Argument 1, because this follows from unrestricted rebutting (a). For the remaining claims, however the participants' commitments will be the same as the conservative view, described earlier.

The liberal view adds the remaining principles: rebutting (b), justification (b)–(c), conclusion (b), undercutting (b)–(f), and skipped response. We've seen the effect of these principles in Figure 3: Ann and Bill should both accept 1a, 1c, 1e, and 1g and reject 1d and 1f. These *liberal* principles have the status of closure rules that force commitment whenever this is possible, as Appendix A [in Rips, 1998] demonstrates. They lead participants to take the same stand (acceptance or rejection) toward each claim.

Predictions about commitment. The following part of this article reports experiments in which subjects read arguments and decided which of the arguments' participants were committed to each claim. The data from the experiments include the proportion of subjects who said that Participant S accepts Claim C, the proportion who said that S rejects C, and the proportion who said that S is neutral about C. To predict these proportions, the present commitment change model assumes that they reflect a mixture of responses from different groups of subjects. Liberal, moderate, and conservative groups respond according to the principles defined earlier. As in nearly all experiments, however, some subjects probably failed to follow instructions and responded to the questions on a random basis through lack of motivation, lack of attention, or other factors. These inattentive subjects constitute a fourth group. Let p_c represent the proportion of conservatives, p_m the proportion of moderates, and p_l the proportion of liberals in the subject sample. The remaining proportion $(1 - p_c - p_m - p_l)$ are the random responders.

To predict responses to questions about whether an individual speaker is committed to a specific claim, we must determine separately whether liberal, moderate, and conservative subjects will view the speaker as accepting, rejecting, or remaining neutral toward it. As an exam-

ple of how these assumptions operate, consider Ann's claim 1a in Argument 1. As we saw earlier, Ann commits herself to this claim (by the assertion principle) when she utters it, and none of the Table 3 principles change that commitment. Because conservatives, moderates, and liberals all subscribe to the assertion principle, all three groups should view Ann as committed to 1a at the conclusion of the argument. The only subjects who could view Ann as neutral about or as rejecting 1a are the inattentive ones. Because these subjects respond randomly, a third of them should say that Ann accepts 1a, a third that she rejects it, and a third that she is neutral about it. If we write $P(S,C,+)$ for the overall proportion of subjects who say that speaker S accepts claim C, $P(S,C,-)$ for the proportion who say that S rejects C, and $P(S,C,0)$ for the proportion who say that S is neutral about C, then Equations 1, 2, and 3 give the predictions about Ann's commitment to 1a at the end of the argument:

$$P(\text{Ann}, 1a, +) = p_c + p_m + p_l$$
$$+ .33(1 - p_c - p_m - p_l). \quad (1)$$
$$P(\text{Ann}, 1a, 0) = .33(1 - p_c - p_m - p_l). \quad (2)$$
$$P(\text{Ann}, 1a, -) = .33(1 - p_c - p_m - p_l). \quad (3)$$

The final term in each of these equations (i.e., .33 $[1 - p_c - p_m - p_l]$) represents chance responses from the inattentive subjects.

Predictions about Bill's commitments to 1a are more complicated, both because there are more points at which he can change his mind and because they have more long-range effects. Figure 3 shows that Bill is initially neutral about 1a, rejects it as the result of his defeaters, and finally accepts it when he agrees with Ann at the end of the dialogue. Liberal subjects apply all the commitment principles responsible for these changes, so they should see Bill as accepting 1a at the end of the argument. Conservative and moderate subjects, however, fail to apply some of the principles in the chain, leading them to see Bill as neutral toward 1a. None of the principles they adopt cause them to see Bill as changing his initial neutral stance. Using the earlier notation, Equations 4, 5, and 6 give the predictions about Bill's commitment to 1a:

$$P(\text{Bill}, 1a, +) = p_l + .33(1 - p_c - p_m - p_l). \quad (4)$$
$$P(\text{Bill}, 1a, 0) = p_m + p_c$$
$$+ .33(1 - p_c - p_m - p_l). \quad (5)$$
$$P(\text{Bill}, 1a, -) = .33(1 - p_c - p_m - p_l). \quad (6)$$

Table 4: Sample Arguments from Experiment 1

One-Branch Argument	*Two-Branch Argument*	*Three-Branch Argument*
1. Bob: The El is the best form of transportation around here.	1. Bob: The El is the best form of transportation around here.	1. Bob: The El is the best form of transportation around here.
2. Fran: Why do you say that?	2. Fran: Why do you say that?	2. Fran: Why do you say that?
3. Bob: It's fast and goes wherever you might have to go.	3. Bob: It's fast and goes wherever you might have to go.	3. Bob: It's fast and goes wherever you might have to go.
4. Fran: The El isn't that fast. It takes a long time to get downtown from Evanston.	4. Fran: It doesn't go to Hyde Park.	4. Fran: [That's true, but] the El stops are in dangerous areas.
5. Bob: It's not that long – an hour at the most.	5. Bob: It goes to Hyde Park; I was just there the other day.	5. Bob: The El stops are relatively safe, if you ask me.
6. Fran: The length of time is a lot longer, since you wait at Howard while switching trains.	6. Fran: [Okay, that's true, but] the El also doesn't go to within walking distance of some places downtown.	6. Fran: [Well, I guess that's true, too, but] it is really inconvenient to change trains at Howard.
7. Bob: Look, I go downtown 4 days a week to work, and I have never had to wait more than five minutes.	7. Bob: Look, I go downtown 4 days a week, and I have never had to walk more than 4 blocks to my destination.	7. Bob: How can you say that – there is usually a train waiting there to board.
8. Fran: I have heard that it can take as long as a half hour at Howard until the next train comes.	8. Fran: [I guess that's true, too, but] the El also does not go to Oak River.	8. Fran: [All right, you've convinced me, but] the Metra is a much better alternative in all areas of concern.
9. Bob: Okay, you're right about that.	9. Bob: Okay, you're right about that.	9. Bob: Okay, you're right about that.

Note. Material in square brackets appeared only in explicit versions of arguments. The remaining material appeared in both explicit and implicit versions.

Predictions for Ann's and Bill's commitment to other lines and at other points in the argument can be derived in a similar way.

Empirical Implications

The commitment change model makes a number of predictions about the way people comprehend arguments. This section reports three studies that test these predictions. The first examines how people decide whether a given participant is committed to a claim, and it allows a direct test of the model against subjects' judgments. The second experiment examines the difference between rebutting and undercutting defeaters, and the third investigates the effect the commitment principles have on subjects' judgments of burden of proof.

Experiment 1: Argument Structure and Commitment

To follow an argument, people need to identify those claims to which each participant is committed. The commitment change model pro-

vides a way to predict the likelihood that they will recognize each claim as one that a participant in an argument accepts, rejects, or is neutral about. These predictions can be assessed by fitting them explicitly to subjects' judgments about a set of stimulus arguments.

In addition to global quantitative predictions, we can use the same arguments to test two of the specific rules in Table 3: rebutting principle (a) and the skipped response rule. To see how this can be done, consider the three sample arguments in Table 4. All three arguments begin with a claim, a justification query, and a justification, and then proceed with a series of rebutting defeaters. The arguments always end with the first speaker uttering an accepter. In the first one-branch argument, each participant tries in turn to rebut the opponent's preceding claim. In the two- and three-branch arguments, however, the second speaker gives up on the initial line of argument and returns to attack one of the earlier points in a new way. This happens twice in the two-branch arguments at Lines 6 and 8, and three times in the three-branch arguments at Lines 4, 6, and 8. In the two-branch dialogue, for example, Fran decides at Line 6 not to pursue the issue of whether the El goes to Hyde Park and instead attacks Bob's claim about the El going everywhere ("The El also doesn't go to within walking distance of some places downtown"). (For the moment, ignore the material in square brackets; I will return to it later.)

This difference in the structure of the arguments allows a test of the rebutting principle. Notice that Bob's final accepter in Line 9 has different implications for commitment in the three arguments. In all arguments, what Bob accepts is Fran's rebutting defeater in Line 8, but Line 8 is directed toward different claims in these arguments. Fran's defeater attacks Line 7 in the one-branch arguments, Line 3 in the two-branch arguments, and Line 1 in the three-branch arguments. Thus, if subjects adhere to rebutting principle (a) in its unrestricted version, they should recognize that Bob has to retract these lines, producing a different pattern of judgment about Bob's commitments across the three arguments.

A second aspect of these arguments gives us a direct test of the skipped response principle. When Fran returns to an earlier point in the two- and three-branch arguments, she is passing up the opportunity of responding to Bob's preceding claim. For example, Fran skips a response to Bob's claim (in Line 5 of the two-branch argument) that the El goes to Hyde Park. If subjects follow the skipped response rule, they should therefore see Fran as implicitly conceding Line 5. To check this, we can compare subjects' responses here to those from a similar argument in which Fran explicitly concedes Line 5 before going on. In the *explicit* version of the argument, Fran says "Okay, that's true, but..." before returning to the earlier point. If subjects subscribe to the skipped response principle, they should decide that Fran accepts Bob's previous claim in both the explicit and the *implicit* versions. If they don't subscribe to it, they should decide that Fran is neutral about Bob's claim in the implicit version, but that she accepts the claim in the explicit one. The text in square-brackets in Table 4 is the material added to the implicit version to produce the explicit version of the same argument.

Method

In a test of these predictions, subjects read a series of arguments (in the form of dialogues between two characters) and selected those claims to which each character was committed. The arguments were about everyday issues, such as whether animal rights activists are too outspoken or whether the El is the best form of transportation in Chicago. There were 12 such topics, and the topics were rotated through six different argument types. These varied in both the number of branches in the argument structure (one, two, or three branches) and the presence or absence of skipped responses (points at which a participant fails to respond directly to the preceding claim). Figure 4 shows the three different structures in abbreviated form. (I have omitted intermediate nodes in the diagrams where they are predictable from other information in the trees.) The implicit versions of the two- and three-branch arguments contained skipped responses at the points marked by a Ø in the figure. The explicit arguments contained accepters (e.g., "Okay, you're right but...") in place of the Øs. All arguments, however, contained the same number of claims and the same number of speaking turns.

In this experiment, 48 subjects read explicit versions of the arguments, and 48 read implicit versions. (The explicit/implicit difference affects only the two- and three-branch arguments; there are no skipped responses in the one-branch items. Thus, all subjects saw the same one-branch arguments.) Each subject saw one-, two-, and three-branch arguments on different trials. The topics of these arguments varied for a given subject, but across subjects the topics appeared equally often in the three argument types. Subjects read the arguments in a booklet, containing one argument per page. The argument lines were numbered as in Table 4. At the bottom of each page was a response form that asked subjects to decide for each claim whether, at the end of the argument, the first speaker was "committed to the statement" or was "never committed or is no longer committed" to the statement. Subjects made a similar choice for the second speaker. The instructions stressed that subjects were to base their decisions on what the characters publicly declare in the dialogue and not on any private beliefs that the characters might harbor. The critical arguments appeared in the booklets intermixed with nine filler arguments of a variety of forms. The arguments' order varied so that each argument appeared equally often in each serial position in the booklet across subjects. All subjects were introductory psychology students at Northwestern University.

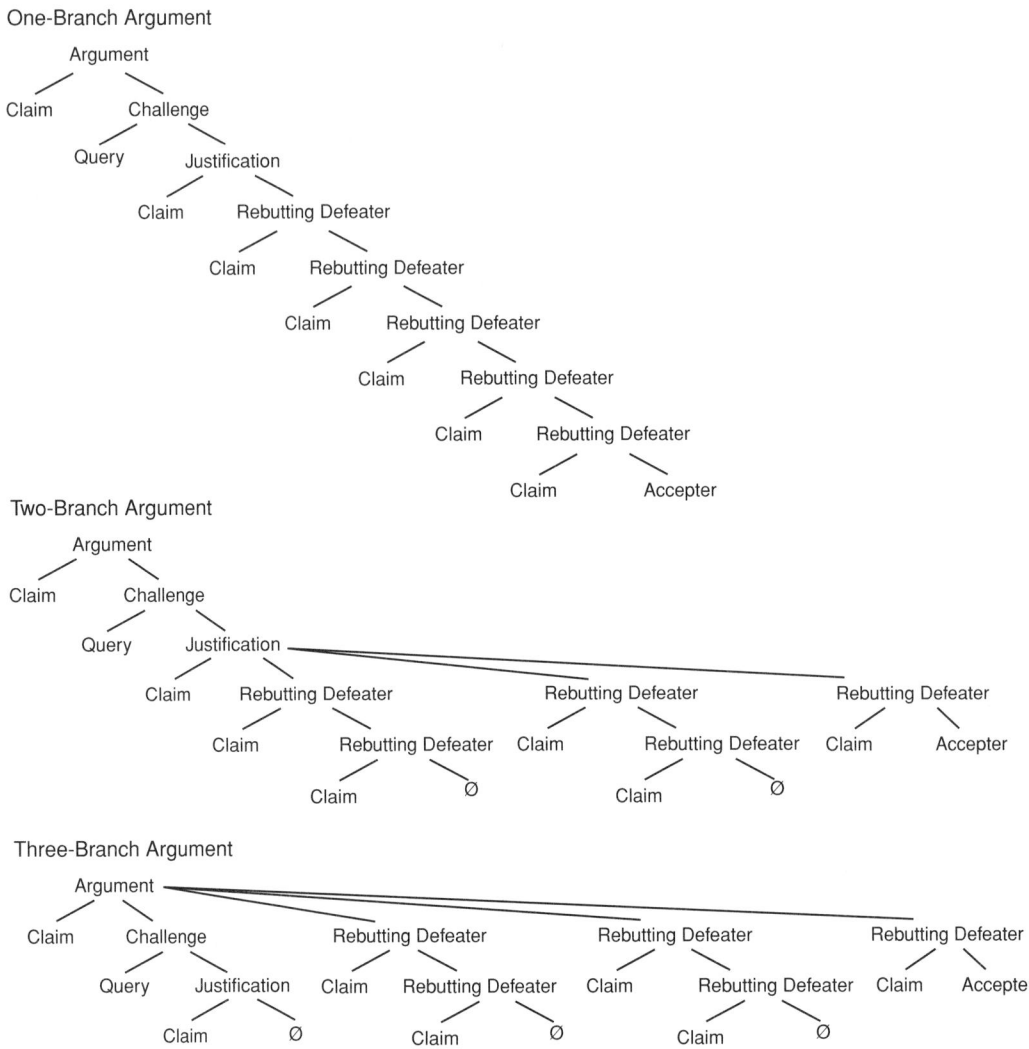

Figure 4. Structure diagrams for the three argument types that served as stimuli in the first and third studies.

Results on the Rebutting and Skipped Response Principles

The data from Experiment 1 consist of the proportion of subjects who judged that each participant was committed to the individual claims. In evaluating these results, let's look first at the qualitative predictions, then at the quantitative ones. As mentioned earlier, rebutting principle (a) in its unrestricted form predicts different patterns of commitment in the three argument structures. The first speaker's accepter in Line 9 implies that he or she should retract Line 7 in the one-branch arguments, Line 3 in the two-branch arguments, and Line 1 in the three-branch arguments (see Figure 4). Table 5 gives

the data relevant to this prediction. The cells represent the proportion of trials on which subjects judged that the first speaker was committed to Lines 1, 3, and 7 in each of the three argument structures. In terms of the sample arguments in Table 4, for example, the first row of Table 5 corresponds to the proportions of subjects who said that Bob was committed to Line 1 ("The El is the best form of transportation . . . "), Line 3 ("It's fast and goes wherever you might have to go"), and Line 7 ("I have never had to wait more than five minutes . . . ") in the one-branch arguments. Similarly, the second row corresponds to the first speaker's commitment to Lines 1, 3, and 7 in the two-branch arguments, and the third row to the first speaker's commitment to Lines 1, 3, and 7

Table 5: Proportion of Subjects Who Judged That Speaker 1 Was "Committed" to Lines 1, 3, and 7 in the Arguments

	Line Number		
Argument Structure	1	3	7
One-branch	.938	.906	.667
Two-branch	.947	.800	.884
Three-branch	.823	.926	.927

Note. n = 96. Rows of the table refer to the one-, two-, and three-branch arguments shown in Figure 4.

in the three-branch arguments. (The tabled proportions, of course, include all argument topics, not just the sample.)

The diagonal cells in Table 5 running from the lower left to the upper right represent those lines that the first speaker should retract, according to (unrestricted) rebutting principle (a). Thus, the first speaker should be less committed to these items than to the remaining entries in the table, and the data confirm this prediction. The overall proportion of committed responses for these to-be-retracted lines is .763; for the remaining lines .921. The interaction between argument structure and line is significant by a repeated-measures analysis for categorical data, $\chi^2 (4, N = 94) = 33.04, p < .001$ (Agresti, 1990, chap. 11; Koch, Landis, Freeman, Freeman, & Lehnen, 1977). The effect appears larger for the one-branch arguments than for the two- or three-branch arguments, probably because the to-be-retracted line, its rebutting defeater, and the accepter appear together in the one-branch items (in Lines 7, 8, and 9). In the other structures, the retracted line is separated from the defeater and its accepter. Notice that the proportion of committed responses, for the retracted lines is still fairly high. According to the model, this is due to the presence of conservative subjects (see the later discussion of model fitting).

Although the results in Table 5 lend support to rebutting principle (a), other data from this experiment tend to disconfirm the skipped response principle. The difference between the implicit and the explicit arguments indicates that subjects do not process skipped responses in the same way as accepters, contrary to the formal models by Hamblin (1970), Rescher (1977), Walton and Krabbe (1995), and others mentioned earlier. Consider first the implicit argu-

ments – the ones containing skipped responses. The first speaker's Lines 5 and 7 in the implicit two-branch arguments and Lines 3, 5, and 7 in the implicit three-branch arguments all appear just before a skipped response by the second speaker (see Table 4). If a skipped response is equivalent to an accepter, then subjects should judge that the second speaker is committed to these five lines. However, the overall proportion of committed responses for Speaker 2 is only .200 for these items. The explicit arguments (accepters replace skipped responses) produced a very different outcome. In these arguments, the same lines appear just before the accepter ("That's true, but . . . "), and the proportion of committed responses for these items jumps to .680.[10] Thus, subjects clearly do not see these arguments, as equivalent.

Model fitting. Equations similar to those in Equations 1 through 6 can provide quantitative predictions for these data. For this purpose, assume that subjects respond "committed" if they think that the participant in the argument accepted the claim and respond "uncommitted or never committed" if they think the participant was neutral about or rejected the claim. Figures 5 and 6 plot the proportion of these committed responses separately for each structure and participant. Figure 5 contains the data for the one-branch arguments and for implicit versions of the two- and three-branch arguments. (The results for one-branch arguments combine the responses from the two groups of subjects.) Figure 6 plots the data for the explicit versions of the two- and three-branch arguments.

A nonlinear least-squares procedure fit the model to all 70 points in Figures 5 and 6, optimizing the values of the three parameters p_c, p_m, and p_l. The resulting estimates showed a large proportion of conservative responses ($p_c = .49$), a smaller proportion of moderate responses ($p_m = .15$), and a tiny proportion of liberal responses ($p_l = .03$). The latter value suggests that the model could achieve nearly equivalent accuracy on the assumption that there were no liberal responders. To test this assumption, one can compare the fits of the three-parameter model to a simpler two-parameter version in which p_l is set to 0. A likelihood ratio test (Bates & Watts, 1988) found no significant difference in the fit of the two models, $F(1, 67) < 1$. Further reduction in the number of parameters, however, did result in lack of fit. If p_m is also set to 0, the likelihood ratio test is $F(1, 68) = 19.29, p < .001$. We can therefore adopt the two-parameter

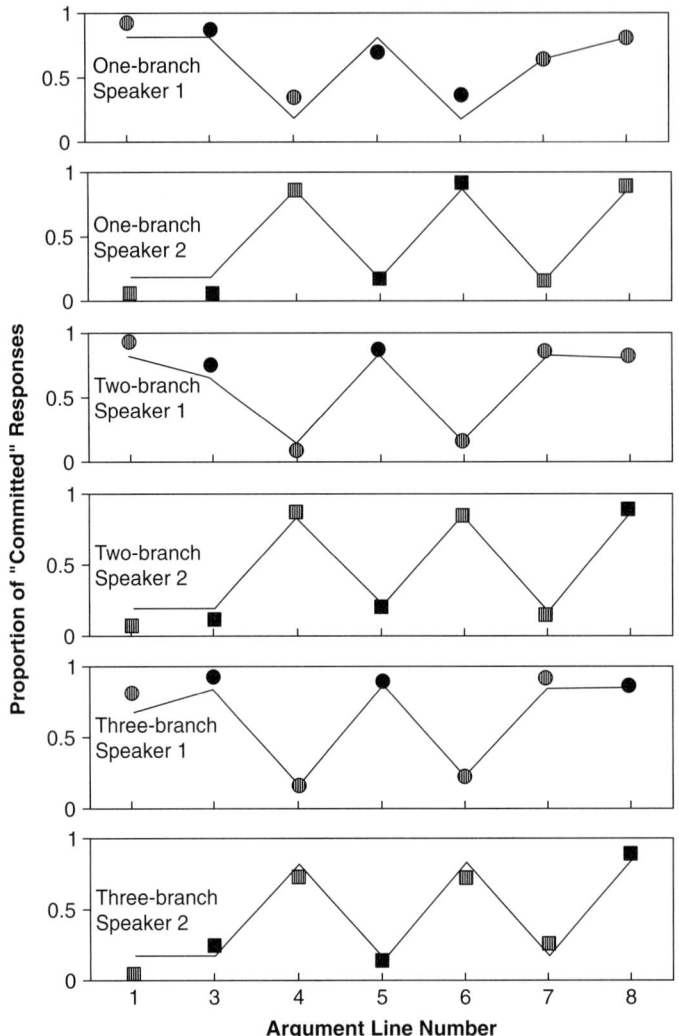

Figure 5. Observed responses (points) and predicted responses (lines) from implicit arguments in Experiment 1. The y axis shows proportion of trials in which subjects identified the speakers as committed to each claim. The top two panels provide data from the one-branch arguments, the middle two panels from the two-branch arguments, and the bottom two panels from the three-branch arguments. Panels 1, 3, and 5 show commitments of first speaker (circles); Panels 2, 4, and 6 show commitments of second speaker (squares).

model in which $p_c = .49$ and $p_m = .17$. These estimates accord with the qualitative findings in that there is little evidence for the skipped response principle (a liberal rule) but significant effects for unrestricted rebutting (a) (a moderate rule). R^2 for this model is .89 and root mean square deviation (RMSD) is .106.

The predictions from this two-parameter model appear as solid lines in Figures 5 and 6. Two main types of deviation appear in the figures. First, subjects' responses tend to be more extreme (closer to 0 or 1) than predicted for the first two claims. The prominence of these two claims at the beginning of the argument may help subjects keep their status straight; commitments to later claims may be cloudier for subjects because of the rapid changes that take place in the debate. Second, Figure 6 reveals that although the model generally predicts the correct shape of the distributions for the explicit arguments, it overpredicts the committed responses for the second speaker and

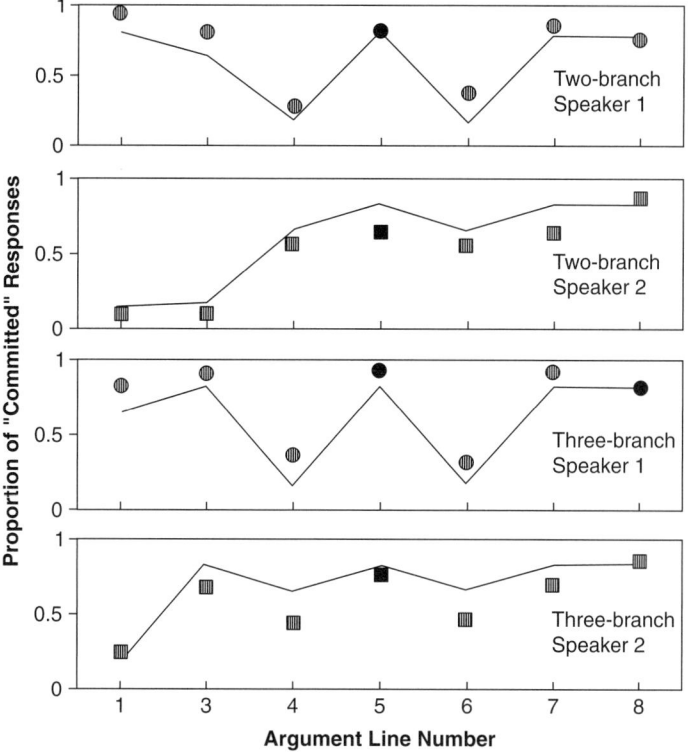

Figure 6. Observed responses (points) and predicted responses (lines) from
explicit arguments in Experiment 1. The y axis shows proportion of trials
subjects identified the speakers as committed to each claim. The top two
panels provide data from the two-branch arguments, and the bottom two
panels from the three-branch arguments. Panels 1 and 3 show commitments
of first speaker (circles); Panels 2 and 4 show commitments of second
speaker (squares).

underpredicts those of the first speaker. One
possible reason for this is that the second speaker
tends to concede points explicitly as soon as they
are attacked in these arguments, whereas the first
speaker makes a concession only in the final line.
This may create a global impression – not captured by the model – that the second speaker is
uncertain about, and therefore less committed
to, the topic of the argument, relative to the first
speaker. In line with this hypothesis, lack of fit
is somewhat greater for the three-branch arguments (where the second speaker makes three
concessions) than in the two-branch arguments
(where the second speaker makes two concessions).

Individual differences. The model assumes that
(apart from the inattentive subjects) individuals
adopt a conservative or a moderate stance and
respond to each argument on this basis. Thus,
it should be possible to classify subjects as conservatives or moderates from the data. For these

arguments, conservatives and moderates differ
in their responses when a character in the dialogue accepts a defeater for one of his or her
own earlier claims and is therefore faced with
retracting that claim. Moderates believe that the
character retracts the claim because they subscribe to the unrestricted rebutting principle (a),
whereas conservatives believe that the character
remains committed to the claim because they
subscribe to the restricted rebutting principle.
In the explicit arguments, this situation occurs in
seven places (e.g., for Speaker 1 with respect to
Line 7 in the one-branch arguments, for Speaker
2 with respect to Line 4 in the two-branch arguments, etc.); thus, these are the places to look
for individual differences.

It is possible to check on these individual
differences by applying cluster analysis to the
subjects' responses to these seven critical lines.
The clusters may be blurred, both because of
the presence of inattentive subjects and because

errors can occasionally affect the responses of even a card-carrying conservative or moderate; nevertheless, the analysis should recover clusters corresponding roughly to the conservative and the moderate groups if the commitment change model is correct. For these purposes, the analysis used the 48 subjects in the explicit condition and computed a measure of similarity between each pair of subjects. (The implicit condition contains a smaller number of items that distinguish conservatives and moderates, and for this reason the analysis omitted the subjects in that condition.) The similarity measure gave each pair of subjects a score of 1 if they agreed in their responses to all seven critical items, a score of 6/7 if they agreed on six, a score of 5/7 if they agreed on five, . . . , and a score of 0 if they agreed on none. This set of scores then provided input to a clustering routine, Johnson's (1967) hierarchical clustering scheme (HCS). HCS has the advantage of producing hierarchical clusters based on nonmetric assumptions. The present analysis used HCS's maximum or complete linkage option, which generally yields more compact and interpretable clusters than the program's other methods. The output revealed two main clusters of subjects, differing as expected in their tendency to see the arguments' characters as committed or not committed to their own earlier claims. The larger cluster contained 34 subjects who usually judged the characters as committed to the seven critical lines. The mean number of committed responses for this group was 5.0 of 7. The smaller cluster contained the remaining 14 subjects, with an average of only 2.4 committed responses per subject ($W^* = 4.34$, $p < .0001$, by a Wilcoxon two-sample test). This division into more conservative and more moderate groups is not a necessary result of the scoring or clustering procedures because they could equally well pick out clusters based on subjects' responses to the first or second character, to the one-branch versus two- or three-branch arguments, or to many other factors. Thus, the analysis lends further support to the present framework.

Experiment 2: Rebutting versus Undercutting Defeaters

The arguments in Table 4 all contained rebutting defeaters, but the theory also allows a participant to use undercutting defeaters to weaken an opponent's case. As the commitment principles make clear, the difference between these two kinds of defeaters has implications for which claims the participant accepts and rejects. For example, consider the two dialogues in Argument 6 and 7:

(6) a. Bob: Giordano's has the best pizza in Chicago.
b. Fran: Why do you say that?
c. Bob: It has incredible stuffed pizza.
d. Fran: The stuffed pizza at Giordano's isn't all that great – the stuffed pizza is too greasy and that makes the crust soggy.
e. Bob: Okay, you're right about that.

(7) a. Bob: Giordano's has the best pizza in Chicago.
b. Fran: Why do you say that?
c. Bob: It has incredible stuffed pizza.
d. Fran: The quality of their stuffed pizza doesn't mean that they have the all around best pizza – their thin crust isn't good at all.
e. Bob: Okay, you're right about that.

These arguments are identical, except for their fourth line. On one hand, Fran's rebutting defeater in 6d implies that she rejects Bob's justification in the preceding line. On the other hand, her undercutting defeater in 7d does not imply that she rejects 7c: The undercutting defeater attacks the relation between 7c and 7a, not the acceptability of 7c itself. We would therefore predict that subjects would be more likely to say that Fran rejects 6c than that she rejects 7c. More interesting, the same is true of Bob's commitments. Because he accepts the rebutting defeater for 6c, he should reject that claim, according to unrestricted rebutting principle (a). However, accepting an undercutting defeater does not oblige him to retract 7c.

This distinction between defeaters isn't always available in earlier models of argumentation. For example, Rescher's (1977) theory assumes that

> moves of the form X/Y [i.e., X normally obtains when Y does] are always "correct" in the setting of a disputation; that the disputants cannot make . . . erroneous claims regarding purely evidential relationships. We thus exclude the prospect of incorrect contentions about the merely probative issue of what constitutes evidence for what. Accordingly, the disputing parties can avoid addressing themselves to the proprieties of the reasoning and need only attend to issues of substance in the development of the argumentation. (p. 8)

Table 6: Observed and Predicted Proportion of Trials on Which Subjects Judged That Speaker 1 and Speaker 2 Accepted, Rejected, or Were Neutral about the Argument's Claims

| | Argument Line | | | | | | | | |
| | Line 1 | | | Line 3 | | | Line 4 | | |
Speaker	Acc.	Neut.	Reject	Acc.	Neut.	Reject	Acc.	Neut.	Reject
				Rebutting defeaters					
Speaker 1									
Obs.	.594	.208	.198	.344	.177	.479	.865	.104	.031
Pred.	.585	.066	.349	.400	.066	.534	.870	.066	.064
Speaker 2									
Obs.	.031	.667	.302	.031	.073	.896	.896	.042	.062
Pred.	.064	.587	.349	.064	.066	.870	.870	.066	.064
				Undercutting defeaters					
Speaker 1									
Obs.	.468	.281	.250	.896	.083	.021	.812	.125	.062
Pred.	.585	.066	.349	.870	.066	.064	.870	.066	.064
Speaker 2									
Obs.	.000	.542	.458	.427	.354	.218	.917	.010	.073
Pred.	.064	.587	.349	.349	.587	.064	.870	.066	.064

Note. Acc. = accept; Neut. = neutral; Obs. = observed; Pred. = predicted. See Arguments 6 and 7 in the text for arguments with rebutting defeaters and undercutting defeaters.

It is therefore worth investigating whether people recognize the distinction between an attack on earlier claims and an attack on reasoning.

Method

As a test of whether people are sensitive to this difference, subjects read a set of arguments and decided for each claim, whether the participants in the argument: (a) accepted the claim, (b) rejected the claim, or (c) neither accepted nor rejected it. Subjects made separate judgments for each character, as in the preceding experiment. We used a three choice response, rather than the committed/not committed format from the earlier study, because the predicted difference between rebutting and undercutting defeaters depends partly on whether participants reject a claim, as opposed to being merely neutral about it. With the exception of these response options, however, the procedure was like that of the first study. The stimulus items were similar to Arguments 6 and 7 in having a justification followed by either a rebutting or an undercutting defeater, followed by an accepter. We created pairs of arguments, such as Arguments 6 and 7, for each of the 12 topics we used in the earlier study. Each subject received only one argument from each pair, but an equal number of the two basic argument types (arguments with rebutting defeaters and arguments

with undercutting defeaters). Thirty-two introductory psychology students participated in the study.

Results on Types of Defeaters

Table 6 shows the response distributions from these subjects for arguments with rebutting defeaters (at the top) and arguments with undercutting defeaters (bottom). The distributions for the first and fourth lines of the arguments – corresponding to Lines 6a and 7a and 6d and 7d – are fairly similar across the two argument types. The distribution for the third line, however, changes radically. Subjects are less apt to say that the characters accept Line 3 when it is followed by a rebutting defeater than by an undercutting defeater. (Compare the accept responses for Line 3 in the arguments with rebutting defeaters to those for undercutting defeaters.) This result is what one would expect from the difference between the commitment rules for the two defeater types. This difference produced a significant interaction between line of the argument (first, third, or fourth) and argument type (rebutting vs. undercutting), $\chi^2(4, N = 32) = 65.71$, $p < .001$ (Agresti, 1990, chap. 11; Koch et al., 1977).

Many more subjects said that the second speaker rejected Line 3 than that the first speaker rejected Line 3 in the rebutting arguments (see

Table 6). For example, about half the subjects said that Bob rejects his own claim 6c by the end of the argument, whereas nearly all agreed that Fran rejects 6c. This is consistent with our treatment of rebutting principle (a). Conservatives adhere to the restricted version of this principle, and they thus apply rebutting (a) to a claim only if a speaker hasn't previously taken a positive or negative stand on it. Once the speaker is committed (i.e., nonneutral), however, that position locks in for conservatives. In Argument 6, for example, Bob commits himself to the position that Giordano's has incredible stuffed pizza by asserting it in 6c, and conservatives believe this is the position he maintains. However, Fran's initial response to it in 6d is an attack, which conservatives view as rejecting 6c. The presence of conservative responses therefore accounts for the asymmetry in the data.

Model fitting. The commitment change model produces a good fit to the proportions of accepted and of rejected responses (a total of 24 data points). (The neutral responses add no further information because the proportion of neutral + accepted + rejected responses equals 1 for each line and speaker.) R^2 for these items is .958 and $RMSD = .069$. The predicted values from the model appear under the observed values in Table 6 (predictions for neutral responses were calculated by subtraction). Parameter values for the proportion of conservative and moderate subjects are roughly similar to those of the earlier study. Here, $p_c = .34$ and $p_m = .18$, compared with .49 and .17 in the preceding experiment. However, this study produced a larger proportion of liberal subjects, $p_l = .28$, compared with a near-zero value earlier. The model needs a larger proportion of liberals because many subjects view the speakers as rejecting the initial claim in the arguments with undercutting defeaters. Undercutting principle (c) is responsible for this rejection, a principle that is currently assumed to be a liberal one. Two other liberal principles help account for aspects of the data: Undercutting principle (b) for the proportion of accepted responses by Speaker 2 in undercutting arguments, and justification principle (b) for rejected responses by both speakers in rebutting arguments. It is possible, of course, that these principles should be reclassified as moderate, but it is also possible that other features of the experiment encouraged liberal responding. For example, the relatively short arguments may have played a role: Liberals have to compute many more changes in commitment than conservatives. Longer arguments, such as those in the pre-

ceding study, may therefore discourage liberal responding.

In sum, the results of this study suggest that people discern the difference between an attack on an earlier assertion and an attack on its support. The ability to capture this difference allows the present system to describe a wider range of arguments than can models like Rescher's (1977). However, the fact that people can recognize the distinction doesn't imply that people are equally able to produce such attacks in their own arguments. Claims are more salient than interclaim relations, and it may therefore be easier to formulate objections to claims (i.e., rebutting defeaters) than objections to the claims' support (undercutting defeaters). Evidence along these lines comes from a recent study by Shaw (1996), who asked subjects to provide objections to arguments from newspapers, magazines, and textbooks. The subjects' objections contained a larger proportion of rebutting defeaters than undercutting defeaters across all arguments.

Experiment 3: Burden of Proof

In legal terminology, *burden of proof* has technical meanings having to do with which party is obliged to produce evidence relevant to some decision (Wigmore, 1935). But there is also a more informal sense, discussed by Whately (1855), in which the person with the burden of proof is the one who has most to do to support his or her position (see Gaskins, 1992, for a discussion). Burden of proof determines the default winner of the argument if no further support is offered. It's likely that many factors influence people's perception of burden of proof, including, of course, how sensible the individual claims are. If a participant makes an outlandish claim, then that will increase the person's burden of proof, all else being equal. In the present context, however, we are interested in how argument structure and commitment contribute to burden of proof, in a way that goes beyond the plausibility of the independent claims.

We have seen that the commitment principles of Table 3 determine which claims become mutually accepted during the course of an argument, and mutual acceptance should predict systematic shifts in perceived burden of proof. If a claim becomes mutually accepted, then the participant who offered it need no longer defend it. Because there are fewer claims that the participant must now establish, his or her burden will be lighter. By contrast, a claim that is mutually rejected or *open* (i.e., not mutually determined) can increase a participant's burden. The participant must find new ways to support claims that are currently under contention and new ways to shore up previous points when currently supporting claims fail. The theory should therefore predict that the smaller the number of mutually accepted claims and the larger the number of mutually rejected or open claims, the greater the burden of proof.

To check this prediction, consider the arguments with rebutting defeaters from the first study (see Figure 4 and Table 4). In the explicit versions of the arguments, the second speaker accepts no claims in the one-branch arguments, accepts two claims in the two-branch arguments, and accepts three claims in the three-branch arguments. The first speaker accepts one claim in each of the three argument types. The second speaker's concessions mean that the conceded claim is mutually accepted, and this should decrease the first speaker's burden of proof. Subjects should therefore perceive the first speaker's burden decreasing from one-branch to two-branch to three-branch structures. In the implicit version of the arguments, the second speaker never accepts a claim outright; this speaker's concessions (if any) occur only through skipped responses. The second speaker again accepts one claim in each argument type in Line 9. Thus, if subjects ignore the skipped response principle (as seems likely, based on Experiment 1), burden of proof for the two speakers should be approximately constant across the three implicit argument types. If subjects adopt the skipped response principle, the results for implicit arguments should be identical to those for explicit ones. Other aspects of the argument do not alter the balance of accepted to nonaccepted claims across the different structures and, hence, do not affect these predictions.

Method

During the experiment, subjects decided which of the two characters in the dialogues had the greater burden of proof and rated their confidence in their decision. The stimulus arguments were the same as in the first experiment, as was the general procedure. The main change was that, after reading an argument, the subjects were to decide "which character has the most to do in order to prove that he or she is right." The words "had most to do" appeared as a proxy for "burden of proof" to avoid confusing subjects about the legal connotations of the latter

Table 7: Mean Signed Confidence That the First Speaker Has Burden of Proof (−10 to 10 Scale)

Version	Argument Structure		
	One-Branch	Two-Branch	Three-Branch
Explicit	4.31	1.39	0.35
Implicit	2.31	2.27	1.43

Note. $n = 48$.

term. To record their answer, subjects checked one of two boxes, each labeled with the name of one of the two speakers (e.g., *Fran* and *Bob* in the case of the Table 4 arguments). They then rated their confidence on a 0-to-10-point scale, where 0 was marked *not at all confident* and 10 was marked *completely confident*. Forty-eight subjects read implicit arguments and an equal number read explicit arguments. Half the subjects in each group saw the check boxes listed with the first speaker first; the remaining subjects saw the second speaker listed first.

Results

To analyze these results, we calculated signed confidence ratings by multiplying each rating by $+1$ if the subject said that Speaker 1 had greater burden of proof and by -1 if the subject said that Speaker 2 had the greater burden. Thus, numbers near $+10$ indicate great conviction that Speaker 1 has the burden, and numbers near -10 indicate great conviction that Speaker 2 has the burden. Table 7 displays the mean ratings, according to the number of branches in the argument and whether the argument was implicit or explicit. (On 6 of 288 trials, subjects failed to mark their choice of speaker or failed to rate their confidence. These data were replaced by the mean of the relevant condition for purposes of analysis.)

Note first the predicted decrease in Speaker 1's burden for explicit arguments, a difference of 3.96 scale points between the one- and the three-branch structures. The implicit arguments show a smaller decrease, 0.88 points. The overall difference is significant by an analysis of variance, $F(2, 188) = 3.26$, $p < .05$. The interaction with argument version (explicit vs. implicit) was not significant, $F(2, 188) = 1.63$, $p > .10$. However, when examined separately, the decrease for the explicit version is significant, $F(2, 94) = 4.28$, $p < .05$, whereas the decrease for the implicit version is not, $F(2, 94) < 1$.[11]

Table 7 also shows a second important fact about burden of proof: Subjects tend to see the first speaker as saddled with the burden in all six conditions. If subjects believed that the first and second speaker had the same burden across trials, the grand mean in Table 7 would be 0. In fact, the mean of the signed ratings is 2.05, significantly greater than 0, $t(95) = 4.36$, $p < .001$. This goes along with the results of several earlier experiments (Bailenson & Rips, 1996), using arguments of a variety of types. In these studies, the person making the first claim typically had greater burden of proof. We have called this effect *antiprimacy* because the first claim places its speaker at a disadvantage. In some of Bailenson and Rips's experiments, the first speaker is not the speaker making the first claim: The argument could begin with a question or with material that is irrelevant to the upcoming debate. What matters in these arguments is not the first speaker, but the first claimant, presumably because the first claim takes a stand on an issue that sets the agenda for the rest of the discussion.[12]

Implications and Extensions

The goals of the present article have been to construct a theory of two-person arguments and to use the model to predict some of these arguments' empirical properties. The model consists of two layers: a structural layer that defines the conversational moves that take place in arguments and a commitment layer that determines which claims participants in the argument accept or reject. The structural layer specifies the arrangement of claims, challenges, justifications, and defeaters, as well as their interrelations in the debate. The main idea behind this layer is that arguments are built recursively from claim-response pairs: Each new assertion by a participant implies the possibility of a critical response by an opponent. Because the response can itself be a claim, this pattern can generate complex embedded structures, such as the ones in Figures 2 and 4.

The commitment layer is defined over the argument's structure. Rules of commitment determine whether a participant publicly accepts, rejects, or is neutral about a claim, based on the participant's conversational moves. Participants can accept a claim directly by asserting it or by explicitly agreeing to it (e.g., by saying "That's right"), and they can accept a claim indirectly by agreeing to one of its justifications. Participants can also reject a claim directly by issuing a rebutting defeater or indirectly by agreeing to an opponent's defeater. The aim has been to trace participants' public commitments, and the theory focuses on how an audience perceives what transpires during an argument. However, the commitment principles also define the tools participants can use to convey commitments they hold privately, as discussed later.

The experimental studies suggest that people perceive commitment as changing rather gradually in the course of a debate. Although people believe that commitments can change, there are limits to the changes they countenance. In the context of our stimulus arguments, they did not view failing to respond to a claim as a concession. Similarly, they did not view rejecting a rebuttal to a claim as equivalent to accepting it. This attitude toward commitment change allows people to see some arguments as necessarily incomplete, in the sense that some of an argument's claims remain essentially unresolved at the end of the discussion. The experimental results also show that people discriminate between attacks on claims and attacks on the justification or support relation that holds between claims. The principles, of commitment change that receive empirical support in Experiment 1 or Experiment 2 are noted in Table 3. Of the remaining principles, Experiment 1 tested skipped response directly and rebutting (b) indirectly, but obtained no support for them. The rest of the principles have yet to be tested.

The results also suggest that the structural and commitment layers contribute to the audience's perception of burden of proof. People believe that the participant who makes the first substantive claim acquires the burden of proof, but that this burden can be reduced or eliminated if the opponent concedes other claims. In general, the findings suggest that the model proposed here can provide the beginnings of a systematic, theoretical account of argumentative reasoning. In this final section, I consider some additional questions about the nature of argumentation by exploring issues surrounding argument production and by comparing the model to a connectionist alternative.

Argument Generation

The present model is a theory of how people comprehend arguments that they read or hear, but we assume that some of its tenets also apply to active participants. Participants in an argument must also have information about its structure in order to contribute in appropriate ways.

They need to understand the sequence of conversational moves that precedes their own next move, and they need to recognize which earlier claims have been accepted or rejected by their opponents. Contributing to an argument, however, also involves knowledge that goes beyond what our theory supplies. It's useful to consider the nature of this additional knowledge, because doing so clarifies some limits on the theory and some possibilities for extending it.

The commitments discussed here are ones the participants trade publicly in the debate; however, individual participants also have access to their own private stock of beliefs and opinions (those that Walton & Krabbe, 1995, call *dark-side commitments*). It is obvious that participants don't volunteer claims at random, but instead use their prior beliefs to determine their best next response. Their purpose may be to convince an opponent of the correctness of one of these prior beliefs, and they may draw on other prior beliefs to supply it with justifications. Moreover, participants may have hypotheses about their opponent's unstated beliefs and can select their conversational moves to capitalize on these opinions. Thus, beliefs provide constraints on what participants assert during an argument and on what they are likely to accept. These underlying beliefs may vary, even within the context of persuasive dialogues. Argumentation can convey new information or help formulate a new position, not just inveigle concessions from an opponent. For that reason, a realistic theory of argument production has to allow for adoption of new beliefs and for use of these beliefs in later parts of the debate.

Producing arguments also means devising strategies for fulfilling the aims of the argument. In part, this entails following the claim-response pairings that the argument structure dictates. Challenges, for example, should be followed by justifications; defeaters by challenges or counterdefeaters. These are rules of argument "etiquette" or good conduct (Cavalli-Sforza et al., 1992; van Eemeren et al., 1996, chap. 11). There must be additional strategies, however, for furthering the participants' goals. This is the traditional domain of rhetoric, the study of methods for tailoring arguments to specific audiences to improve their effectiveness. Rhetorical strategies can produce "an organized chain of arguments about *this* subject for *this* audience that will bridge the gap between what you believed when you came and what I want you to believe when you depart" (Booth, 1967, p. 10 [italics in original]). Participants' choice of a rhetorical

strategy will depend in part on their representations of their opponents' beliefs because it is to the participants' advantage to show that the opinion they are advocating follows from the opponents' own point of view (Perelman, 1982).

Research on persuasion in social psychology is relevant to the study of strategy choice because this research has examined factors that make for more convincing messages (see McGuire, 1985, for a review). Most of these experiments, however, have concentrated on the effects of one-sided arguments that the experimenter presents, rather than two-sided arguments in which the subjects produce their own line of reasoning. This focus on preformulated messages is probably due to the methodological difficulties associated with studying interactive contexts, but the result is that we currently have little empirical knowledge about how people choose to argue when they are confronted with an opponent who can parry their remarks. The hope is that the present model can contribute to research on persuasion by defining a more interactive framework within which we can formulate specific hypotheses about argument strategies.

Comparison with Connectionist Approaches

I noted earlier that models of informal reasoning have usually focused either on the support relation that unites individual premises and conclusions or on participants' moves in formalized argument games. The first type of model is difficult to extend to contexts that include challenges and criticisms; the second type tends to ignore the embedded structure that informal arguments often have. To capture both the structural and conversational aspects, some recent theories have studied naturally occurring arguments, with a view both to the justification and criticism in which participants engage (e.g., Muntigl & Turnbull, 1998; van Eemeren et al., 1993; Resnick et al., 1993). The present theory is similar to those in this third class, though it proposes structural rules (Table 1) and commitment rules (Table 3) that are more explicit than those usually appearing in these frameworks.

The current stock of theories, however, do not exhaust the potentially valuable approaches in this area. It might be possible, for example, to capture some of the back and forth of argumentation in another manner by modeling commitment as excitation or inhibition within a connectionist framework. The purpose of exploring this framework here is not so much to set it up as

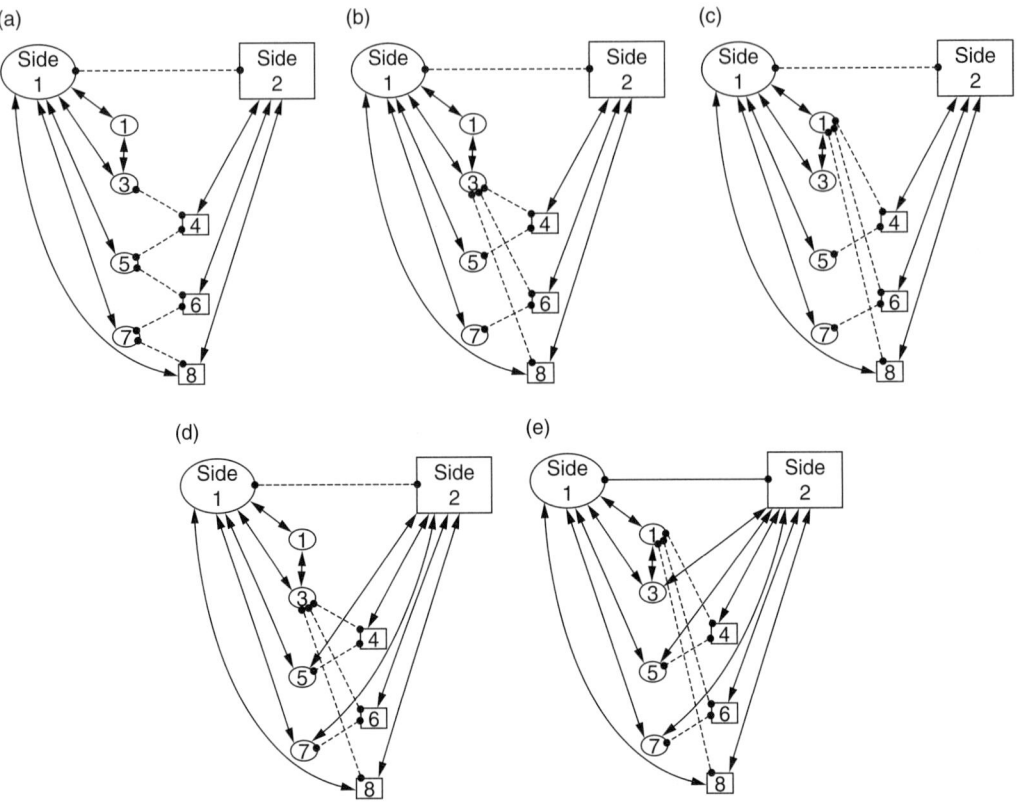

Figure 7. Connectionist networks corresponding to (a) one-branch arguments, (b) implicit two-branch arguments, (c) implicit three-branch arguments, (d) explicit two-branch arguments, and (e) explicit three-branch arguments. Small numbered units represent individual claims; large units represent the two sides or participants in the debate. Solid lines are excitatory connections; dashed lines are inhibitory connections.

a rival to the rule-based theory, but to see which aspects of argumentation are best suited to each approach.

Consider a (local) connectionist network for the arguments in Table 4 in which each claim appears as an individual node or unit. One way of hooking up networks for these arguments appears in Figure 7, where the networks on the top represent one-, two-, and three-branch arguments in their implicit versions, and the networks on the bottom represent the explicit versions of the two- and three-branch items. For clarity, the figure shows the claims of the first speaker as rounded nodes and the claims of the second speaker as square nodes, although the two types of nodes are treated identically in the model. If one claim provides support for another, an excitatory link (solid line) connects the unit representing the first claim to the unit representing the second. Likewise, if one claim provides a rebutting defeater for another, an inhibitory link

(dashed line) connects the first to the second. I assume for the time being that excitation or inhibition can spread in either direction across a link.[13]

One can also associate with each claim-unit a level of activation that varies from some maximum value ($+1$) when the claim has greatest support to some minimum value (-1) when its negation has greatest support. Activation of a unit can thus represent the degree of commitment that resides in each claim, with positive numbers being degrees of acceptance and negative numbers degrees of rejection. Of course, the commitment that one participant has invested in a claim will generally differ from the commitment of another participant, as shown earlier. In order to represent this difference, one can include units that correspond to each participant or "side" of the debate. These side-units (larger nodes at the top of the diagrams in Figure 7) have excitatory connections to the claims that the participant asserts or agrees to, and the side units connect to each other through inhibitory links. Separate runs of the model can then obtain the commitments of each participant by activating that participant's side (i.e., clamping the side-unit at 1) and seeing how activation spreads over the claims. Activation of all units (claims and sides) is adjusted at each cycle as a function of the net level of excitation and inhibition flowing into them, as in Thagard's (1989) ECHO model of explanatory coherence or other models of hypothesis competition (see Rumelhart, Hinton, & McClelland, 1986).

How well does the model of Figure 7 do in predicting the commitment data of our first study? Simulation of the model obviously depends on the weights of the excitatory and inhibitory connections. For simplicity, the model assumes that all excitatory connections have the same weight, w^+, and all inhibitory connections have the same weight, w^-. A nonlinear least-squares procedure was used to estimate these parameters, as in the earlier studies. Details of the model-fitting appear in Appendix B [in Rips, 1998]. R^2 over all 70 data points is .85 and RMSD $= .126$, slightly inferior to the comparable figures for the earlier model (.89 and .105, respectively). The obtained value for the excitation parameter w^+ is .15 and the value for the inhibition parameter w^- is $-.10$.

The predictions show that the connectionist model does quite well in fitting the middle lines of the arguments, but exhibits some deviations for the last claim (Line 8), especially for Speaker 1. For this line, the predicted commitment score is markedly less than the obtained proportions. Speaker 1 concedes this claim outright in Line 9; so this speaker's commitment should be high, as subjects affirmed in our first study (see Figures 5 and 6). However, connections from other units keep activation relatively low at Line 8 and prohibit the model from accurately accounting for the data.

There may, of course, be other network implementations whose predictions improve on the version considered here.[14] For example, it is likely one could get better fits by individually weighting the links in Figure 7, by adding new links, or by increasing the number of parameters. In general, the network approach has the advantage of simplicity in treating commitment in a unified way. However, the commitment-rule approach has the advantage of greater explicitness in explaining how commitment is determined. It also has the advantage of distinguishing in a straightforward way between rebutting defeaters and undercutting defeaters, which are more difficult to represent in a connectionist network. It may prove useful in future research to build a theory that merges these advantages: It seems feasible, for example, to construct a two-stage model in which commitment rules decide initially where the excitatory and inhibitory links should appear; in the second stage, activation could then determine the degree or strength of commitment. Such a model could resemble older network theories (e.g., Anderson, 1983) or more recent hybrid systems (e.g., Sun, 1995).

Conclusion

In traditional studies of reasoning in psychology, subjects usually inspect a group of premises, such as *All grizzlies are mammals* and *Fred is a grizzly*, and then generate a conclusion that is supposed to follow from them (or evaluate a conclusion that the experimenter proposes). Investigators have followed this procedure, both in studying deductively valid arguments and inductively strong ones (e.g., Osherson, Smith, Wilkie, Lopez, & Shafir, 1990; Rips, 1975). This focus on premise-conclusion arguments is an important analytic tool that isolates the way in which one set of statements transmits support to another. Human reasoning, however, takes place in more extended contexts than one-step (and one-sided) arguments, as many critics have pointed out. An individual reasoning step can sometimes be construed as a transition from premises to a conclusion, but in the larger context the premises are rarely held constant. Nearly any claim that's introduced into the discussion is subject to potential justification. Moreover, extended reasoning often occurs between multiple agents. Agents can demand further support for another's assertions or can criticize those assertions. Multiple agents are obvious in external debates and discussions, such as our stimulus examples; but we can also think of many internal deliberations as including multiple mental agents advocating rival positions.

Although investigators have recognized the pervasiveness of multiple-step, multiple-sided reasoning, there have been relatively few psychological proposals about its internal structure. The present suggestion is that a more adequate theory of reasoning should consider individual claims in relation to a larger, varied set of potential responses. Claims can link to others, not just through inductive and deductive support, but also through adversarial challenges and critiques. These critiques in turn create the possibility of further bondings and prompt extended webs of inferences. The model proposed here exhibits some of these potential relations.

Notes

1 Intermediate cases include formal debates and adversary arguments (Flowers, McGuire, & Birnbaum, 1982) in which the participants don't attempt to convince their opponents of the truth of their position. Nevertheless, the participants in such encounters do appeal to reasons in supporting their own positions and in attacking those of their adversary. These debates appear to be addressed to an actual or to an ideal audience that is evaluating the rival claims. As such, they have much the same structure as the argumentation considered here.

2 As mentioned earlier, it is possible to make more fine-grained distinctions among types of justifications, separating explanations, evidence, and clarifications (see Brem & Rips, 1995). Similarly, one could divide rebutting defeaters into those that are direct contradictions of previous statements (e.g., "The coffee in Garrett is great." "No, it's not.") from more guarded attacks ("Do you go there much?"). One might also distinguish rebutting defeaters based on fact versus opinion. These distinctions are important ones to pursue in further work on argumentation especially because they may affect the strength of a participant's case (see Farley & Freeman, 1995). The present theory concentrates, however, on the large-scale structure.

3 Table 1 distinguishes two types of responses, Responses and Subresponses, for technical reasons: Because undercutting defeaters can only occur in the context of justifications, conclusions, or (superordinate) defeaters, the rules must separate these contexts from others. Subresponses represent the context where undercutting defeaters can occur. Thus, after the topmost level of the argument, the structure is fully recursive, allowing subarguments to be embedded in subresponses ad infinitum. The left-to-right ordering of constituents in the rules are intended to correspond to the chronological sequence of the dialogue. This means that the rules allow a speaker to return to an earlier point in the current branch of the tree in order to start a new branch, but they prohibit a speaker from returning to an earlier branch. It is unclear whether this restriction is violated in arguments, but to accommodate such backward moves, the rules could be revised to include a separate index for the order of the contribution.

4 One location for an online copy of the civil proceedings is http://cnn.com/US/OJ/simpson.civil.trial/.

5 Other categories from Table 1 depend more heavily on context and are more difficult to code. For example, whether a sentence such as "I've tried all the coffee shops on campus" is a justification, as in Argument 1, or a simple statement of fact depends on what precedes it in the discourse. Some of this discourse context was not available in the excerpts because of the way the samples were selected. This partly motivated the focus on explicit defeaters and justification queries.

6 In this article, I use *participants* or *speakers* to refer to the characters in the stimulus dialogue and *subjects* to refer to people taking part in the experiment.

7 The conservative approach to commitment is related to the conservative theory of epistemology that Harman (1986) has advocated. According to this approach, people are justified in continuing to maintain their current beliefs, even when they are unable to remember their reasons for originally believing them. Only positive reasons to doubt current beliefs are grounds for changing them.

8 For example, the upper left box in Figure 3b shows further changes of commitment to 1a that take place during Lines 1f to 1h of the argument. Bill's undercutting defeater in 1f means that he rejects 1a, due to undercutting principle (c); so the fourth row of the box contains a negative sign for Bill. At the end of the argument, though, Bill explicitly accepts Ann's rebutting defeater for 1f, and he must therefore retract it. Because 1f was supposed to undercut justification for 1a, Bill ends up reaccepting 1a by undercutting principle (c). The last row of the upper left box shows the state at the end of the argument with both Ann and Bill subscribing to 1a.

9 It is possible, of course, to write a set of rules in which a rebutting defeater would end a line of argument. However, such rules would not capture the intuition that rebutting defeaters ("That's not true!") always seem to imply the possibility of further rebuttal ("It is true!") rather than an end to debate. For this reason, the Table 1 rules specify that responses (possibly skipped responses) follow defeaters.

10 Still, although skipped responses are not as powerful as accepters, they may increase the second speaker's perceived commitment to the preceding claim, relative to a more neutral baseline. For example, Lines 5 and 7 in the two-branch arguments are followed by Speaker 2's skipped responses, whereas Line 1 is followed by a query from the same speaker. If skipped responses increase perceived commitment, we should expect higher scores for 5 and 7 than for

1. There is a small, marginally significant trend in this direction, with proportion of committed responses equal to .163 for the fifth and seventh lines and .065 for the first line, χ^2 (2, N = 48) = 4.80, p =.09. In general, though, the small size of this difference suggests that few of our subjects applied the more liberal commitment principles. It is also possible that people might follow the skipped response principle in special contexts. For instance, if an initial claim is obviously strong, then skipping a response to the claim might appear as a concession. This possibility needs to be tested, but note that some of the skipped claims in the stimulus arguments do seem quite strong (see Table 4) and yet did not produce a significant effect.

11 One anomaly in the data is the difference in the first column of Table 7. The one-branch arguments were identical for the implicit and explicit groups because no skipped responses occurred within these items. The difference between them may be due to subjects in the two groups normalizing their responses on the rating scale.

12 The first speaker had a female name and the second had a male name in five of the stimulus arguments, whereas these positions were reversed in the remaining seven arguments; hence it is possible to test after the fact whether subjects assigned greater burden to the female or to the male. For this purpose, the confidence ratings were rescored so that +10 indicated high confidence that the female speaker had the greater burden of proof and −10 indicated high confidence that the male speaker had the greater burden. Mean confidence was −0.46 (i.e., in the direction of greater burden on the male), but was not reliably different from 0, $t(95)$ = −1.08, p =.28. Although there is no evidence here for gender bias, it is certainly possible that such effects depend on interactions with other factors, such as the content of the argument or the gender of the subjects, factors that were not controlled (see, e.g., Carli, 1990).

13 The postmortem in the text suggests that it might be possible to reduce the model's misprediction by rethinking the nature of the links in Figure 7. In the simulations just reported, excitation or inhibition from earlier lines in the argument can flow to later lines. This accords with ECHO in which all links are bidirectional, but it may be unrealistic for the present arguments. Arguments unfold sequentially in a way that may give precedence to later responses. Indeed, this is an assumption of my initial theory (see A Theory of Commitment in Arguments section and the right branch condition in Appendix A of Rips, 1998). If excitation and inhibition can flow only from later lines to earlier ones, this would avoid part of the inhibition that suppresses the activation of Line 8. Unfortunately, however, further simulations suggest that chang-

ing the model in this way produces other deficiencies. These simulations removed the interclaim connections in Figure 7 that pointed from earlier claims to later ones. (Connections to and connections between side-units remained bidirectional.) The degree of fit for this revised version was about the same as the original connectionist model (R^2 = .85 and RMSD = .122). Although the revision succeeded in reducing the discrepancy for Line 8, it increased the lack of fit for Speaker 2 in the explicit arguments. Predictions for Lines 4 and 6, in particular, were too large by 26 percentage points in the two-branch arguments and by 37 percentage points in the three-branch arguments. In the model, Lines 1 and 3 receive some indirect excitation from side 2 through Lines 5, 7, 8, and the side 1 unit, as Figure 7 illustrates. Activation at Line 1 or 3 can exert an inhibitory force on Lines 4 and 6 in the original connectionist model, due to the backward connections. Removing these connections in the revised model increases activation at Lines 4 and 6 and results in the overpredictions at these points.

14 Ibid.

References

Agresti, A. (1990). *Categorical data analysis.* New York: Wiley.

Allen, J. (1995). *Natural language understanding.* Redwood City, CA: Benjamin/Cummings.

Anderson, J. R. (1983). *The architecture of cognition.* Cambridge, MA: Harvard University Press.

Bailenson, J., and Rips, L. J. (1996). Informal reasoning and burden of proof. *Applied Cognitive Psychology, 10,* S13–S16.

Baron, J. (1991). Beliefs about thinking. In J. F. Voss, D. N. Perkins, and J. W. Segal (Eds.), *Informal reasoning and education* (pp. 169–186). Hillsdale, NJ: Erlbaum.

Baron, J. (1995). Myside bias in thinking about abortion. *Thinking and Reasoning, 1,* 221–235.

Bates, D. M., and Watts, D. G. (1988). *Nonlinear regression analysis and its applications.* New York: Wiley.

Billig, M. (1987). *Arguing and thinking: A rhetorical approach to social psychology.* Cambridge, England: Cambridge University Press.

Black, J. B., and Wilensky, R. (1979). An evaluation of story grammars. *Cognitive Science, 3,* 213–230.

Bly, B. (1993). *Uncooperative language and the negotiation of meaning.* Unpublished doctoral dissertation, Stanford University.

Booth, W. C. (1967). The revival of rhetoric. In M. Steinmann, Jr. (Ed.), *New rhetorics* (pp. 2–15). New York: Scribners.

Brem, S., and Rips, L. J. (1995). Explanation and evidence in informal reasoning. *Proceedings of the*

17th Annual Conference of the Cognitive Science Society, 271–276.

Brown, P., and Levinson, S. C. (1987). *Politeness: Some universals in language usage.* Cambridge, England: Cambridge University Press.

Carli, L. L. (1990). Gender, language, and influence. *Journal of Personality and Social Psychology, 59,* 941–951.

Cavalli-Sforza, V., Lesgold, A. M., and Weiner, A. W. (1992). Strategies for contributing to collaborative arguments. *Proceedings of the 14th Annual Conference of the Cognitive Science Society,* 755–760.

Chierchia, G., and McConnell-Ginet, S. (1990). *Meaning and grammar: An introduction to semantics.* Cambridge, MA: MIT Press.

Chinn, C. A. (1995). Representing dialectical arguments. *Proceedings of the 17th Annual Conference of the Cognitive Science Society,* 544–549.

Clark, H. H., and Schaefer, E. F. (1989). Contributing to discourse. *Cognitive Science, 13,* 259–294.

Clinchy, B. M. (1989). The development of thoughtfulness in college women. *American Behavioral Scientist, 32,* 647–657.

Cohen, R. (1990). A processing model for the analysis of one-way arguments in discourse. *Argumentation, 4,* 431–446.

Collins, A., and Michalski, R. (1989). A logic of plausible reasoning: A core theory. *Cognitive Science, 13,* 1–50.

Coulson, S., and Flor, N. V. (1994). Rational choice and framing devices: Argumentation and computer programming. *Proceedings of the 16th Annual Conference of the Cognitive Science Society,* 219–224.

Curley, S. P., Browne, G. J., Smith, G. F., and Benson, P. G. (1995). Arguments in practical reasoning underlying constructed probability responses. *Journal of Behavioral Decision Making, 8,* 1–20.

Eisenberg, A. R., and Garvey, C. (1981). Children's use of verbal strategies in resolving conflicts. *Discourse Processes, 4,* 149–170.

Elster, J. (1995). Strategic uses of argument. In K. J. Arrow, R. H. Mnookin, L. Ross, A. Tversky, and R. B. Wilson (Eds.), *Barriers to conflict resolution* (pp. 237–257). New York: Norton.

Farley, A. M., and Freeman, K. (1995). *Burden of proof in legal argumentation* (Tech. Rep. No. CIS-TR-95-11). Eugene: University of Oregon, Department of Computer and Information Science.

Firth, A. (1995). "Accounts" in negotiation discourse: A single-case analysis. *Journal of Pragmatics, 23,* 199–226.

Fisher, A. (1988). *The logic of real arguments.* Cambridge, England: Cambridge University Press.

Flowers, M., McGuire, R., and Birnbaum, L. (1982). Adversary arguments and the logic of personal attacks. In W. G. Lehnert and M. H. Ringle (Eds.), *Strategies for natural language processing* (pp. 275–294). Hillsdale, NJ: Erlbaum.

Ford, C. E. (1994). Dialogic aspects of talk and writing: *Because* on the interactive-edited continuum. *Text, 14,* 531–554.

Garnham, A. (1983). What's wrong with story grammars? *Cognition, 15,* 145–154.

Gaskins, R. H. (1992). *Burden of proof in modern discourse.* New Haven, CT: Yale University Press.

Gentzen, G. (1969). Investigations into logical deduction. In M. E. Szabo (Ed.), *The collected papers of Gerhard Gentzen.* (Original work published 1935.)

Goldman, A. I. (1994). Argumentation and social epistemology. *Journal of Philosophy, 91,* 27–49.

Gottman, J. M. (1979). *Marital interaction: Experimental investigations.* New York: Academic Press.

Graesser, A. C., and Person, N. K. (1994). Question asking during tutoring. *American Educational Research Journal, 31,* 104–137.

Grice, H. P. (1989). Logic and conversation. In *Studies in the way of words* (pp. 1–143). Cambridge, MA: Harvard University Press.

Grosz, B. J., Pollack, M. E., and Sidner, C. L. (1989). Discourse. In M. I. Posner (Ed.), *Foundations of cognitive science* (pp. 437–468). Cambridge, MA: MIT Press.

Hamblin, C. L. (1970). *Fallacies.* London: Methuen.

Harman, G. (1986). *Change in view: Principles of reasoning.* Cambridge, MA: MIT Press.

Hewitt, L. E., Duchan, J. F., and Segal, E. M. (1993). Structure and function of verbal conflicts among adults with mental retardation. *Discourse Processes, 16,* 525–543.

Hintikka, J. (1984). Questioning as a philosophical method. In J. H. Fetzer (Ed.), *Principles of philosophical reasoning* (pp. 25–43). Totowa, NJ: Rowman & Allanheld.

Hogarth, R. M., and Kunreuther, H. (1995). Decision making under ignorance: Arguing with yourself. *Journal of Risk and Uncertainty, 10,* 15–36.

Homer-Dixon, T. F., and Karapin, R. S. (1989). Graphical argument analysis: A new approach to understanding arguments, applied to a debate about the window of vulnerability. *International Studies Quarterly, 33,* 389–410.

Hutchins, E. (1980). *Culture and inference: A Trobriand case study.* Cambridge, MA: Harvard University Press.

Jackson, S., and Jacobs, S. (1980). The structure of conversational argument: Pragmatic bases for the enthymeme. *Quarterly Journal of Speech, 66,* 251–265.

Jeffrey, R. C. (1965). *The logic of decision.* New York: McGraw-Hill.

Johnson, S. C. (1967). Hierarchical clustering schemes. *Psychometrika, 32,* 241–254.

Kahneman, D., and Tversky, A. (1984). Choices, values, and frames. *American Psychologist, 39,* 341–350.

Koch, G. G., Landis, J. R., Freeman, J. L., Freeman, D. H., and Lehnen, R. G. (1977). A general methodology for the analysis of experiments with repeated measurement of categorical data. *Biometrics, 33,* 133–158.

Kuhn, D. (1991). *The skills of argument.* Cambridge, England: Cambridge University Press.

Lewis, D. (1979). Score keeping in a language game. *Journal of Philosophical Logic, 8,* 339–359.

Mackenzie, J. D. (1979). Question-begging in non-cumulative systems. *Journal of Philosophical Logic, 8,* 117–133.

Mackenzie, J. D. (1984). Begging the question in dialogue. *Australasian Journal of Philosophy, 62,* 174–181.

McGuire, W. J. (1985). Attitudes and attitude change. In G. Lindzey and E. Aronson (Eds.), *Handbook of social psychology* (Vol. 2, pp. 233–346). New York: Random House.

Miller, P. M., Danaher, D. L., and Forbes, D. (1986). Sex-related strategies for coping with interpersonal conflict in children aged five and seven. *Developmental Psychology, 22,* 543–548.

Muntigl, P., and Turnbull, W. (1998). Conversational structure and face-work in arguing. *Journal of Pragmatics, 29,* 225–256.

Osherson, D. N., Smith, E. E., Wilkie, O., Lopez, A., and Shafir, E. (1990). Category-based induction. *Psychological Review, 97,* 185–200.

Perelman, C. (1982). *The realm of rhetoric.* Notre Dame, IN: University of Notre Dame Press.

Perkins, D. N., Farady, M., and Bushey, B. (1991). Everyday reasoning and the roots of intelligence. In J. F. Voss, D. N. Perkins, and J. W. Segal (Eds.), *Informal reasoning and education* (pp. 83–105). Hillsdale, NJ: Erlbaum.

Pilkington, R. M., Hartley, J. R., Hintze, D., and Moore, D. J. (1992). Learning to argue and arguing to learn: An interface for computer-based dialogue games. *Journal of Artificial Intelligence in Education, 3,* 275–295.

Pollock, J. (1989). *How to build a person.* Cambridge, MA: MIT Press.

Ranney, M., Schank, P., Hoadley, C., and Neff, J. (1994). "I know one when I see one": How (much) do hypotheses differ from evidence? *Proceedings of the 5th ASIA SAG/C Classification Research Workshop,* 139–155.

Reichman-Adar, R. (1984). Extended person-machine interface. *Artificial Intelligence, 22,* 157–218.

Rescher, N. (1977). *Dialectics: A controversy-oriented approach to the theory of knowledge.* Albany: State University of New York Press.

Resnick, L. B., Salmon, M., Zeitz, C. M., Wathen, S. H., and Holowchak, M. (1993). Reasoning in conversation. *Cognition and Instruction, 11,* 347–364.

Riley, P., Hollihan, T. A., and Freadhoff, K. D. (1987). Argument in law: The special case of the small claims court. In F. H. van Eemeren, R. Grootendorst, J. A. Blair, and C. A. Willard (Eds.), *Argumentation: Analysis and practices* (pp. 142–151). Dordrecht, The Netherlands: Foris.

Rips, L. J. (1975). Inductive judgments about natural categories. *Journal of Verbal Learning and Verbal Behavior, 14,* 665–681.

Rips, L. J. (1998). Reasoning and conversation. *Psychological Review, 105,* 411–441.

Rumelhart, D. E. (1980). On evaluating story grammars. *Cognitive Science, 4,* 313–316.

Rumelhart, D. E., Hinton, G. E., and McClelland, J. L. (1986). A general framework for parallel distributed processing. In D. E. Rumelhart and J. L. McClelland (Eds.), *Parallel distributed processing* (Vol. 1, pp. 45–76). Cambridge, MA: MIT Press.

Rumelhart, D. E., and Norman, D. A. (1988). Representation in memory. In R. C. Atkinson, R. J. Hernstein, G. Lindzey, and R. D. Luce (Eds.), *Steven's handbook of experimental psychology* (Vol. 2, pp. 511–587). New York: Wiley.

Schegloff, E. A. (1972). Sequencing in conversational openings. In J. J. Gumperz and D. Hymes (Eds.), *Directions in sociolinguistics* (pp. 346–380). New York: Holt, Rinehart & Winston.

Schiffrin, D. (1984). Jewish argument as sociability. *Language in Society, 13,* 311–335.

Schiffrin, D. (1985). Everyday argument: The organization of diversity in talk. In T. A. van Dijk (Ed.), *Handbook of discourse analysis* (Vol. 3, pp. 35–46). Orlando, FL: Academic Press.

Schiffrin, D. (1987). *Discourse markers.* Cambridge, England: Cambridge University Press.

Shafir, E., Simonson, I., and Tversky, A. (1993). Reason-based choice. *Cognition, 49,* 11–36.

Shaw, V. F. (1996). Cognitive processes in informal reasoning. *Thinking & Reasoning, 2,* 51–80.

Sperber, D., and Wilson, D. (1986). *Relevance.* Cambridge, MA: Harvard University Press.

Starr, J. (1978). Negotiations: A pre-law stage in rural Turkish disputes. In P. H. Gulliver (Ed.), *Cross-examinations* (pp. 110–132). Leiden, Holland: Brill.

Sun, R. (1995). Robust reasoning: Integrating rule-based and similarity-based reasoning. *Artificial Intelligence, 75,* 241–295.

Tarski, A. (1956). The concept of truth in formalized languages (J. H. Woodger, Trans.). In *Logic, semantics, metamathematics* (pp. 152–278). Oxford, England: Clarendon Press. (Original work published 1936.)

ten Have, P. (1995). Disposal negotiations in general practice consultations. In A. Firth (Ed.), *The discourse of negotiations* (pp. 319–344). Tarrytown, NY: Elsevier Science.

Thagard, P. (1989). Explanatory coherence. *Behavioral and Brain Sciences, 12,* 435–502.

Thomas, S. N. (1973). *Practical reasoning in natural language.* Englewood Cliffs, NJ: Prentice Hall.

Toulmin, S. E., Rieke, R., and Janik, A. (1979). *An introduction to reasoning.* New York: Macmillan.

van Dijk, T. A., and Kintsch, W. (1983). *Strategies of discourse comprehension.* New York: Academic Press.

van Eemeren, F. H., Grootendorst, R., Jackson, S., and Jacobs, S. (1993). *Reconstructing argumentative discourse*. Tuscaloosa: University of Alabama Press.

van Eemeren, F. H., Grootendorst, R., and Snoeck Henkemans, F. (1996). *Fundamentals of argumentation theory*. Mahwah, NJ: Erlbaum.

Vicedo, M. (1991). Realism and simplicity in the Castle-East debate on the stability of the hereditary units: Rhetorical devices versus substantive methodology. *Studies in History and Philosophy of Science, 22*, 201–221.

Voss, J. F., Blais, J., Means, M. L., Greene, T. R., and Ahwesh, E. (1986). Informal reasoning and subject matter knowledge in the solving of economics problems by naive and novice individuals. *Cognition and Instruction, 3*, 269–302.

Voss, J. F., and Means, M. L. (1991). Learning to reason via instruction in argumentation. *Learning and Instruction, 1*, 337–350.

Walton, D. N., and Krabbe, E. C. W. (1995) *Commitment in dialogue*. Albany: State University of New York Press.

Whately, R. (1855). *Elements of rhetoric*. Boston: Munroe.

Wigmore, J. H. (1935). *A students' textbook of the law of evidence*. Brooklyn, NY: The Foundation Press.

Wright, L. (1995). Argument and deliberation: A plea for understanding. *Journal of Philosophy, 92*, 565–585.

Zwicky, A. M., & Zwicky, A. D. (1973). *How come* and *what for*. In B. B. Kachru, R. B. Lees, Y. Malkiel, A. Pietrangeli, and S. Saporta (Eds.), *Issues in linguistics* (pp. 923–933). Urbana: University of Illinois Press.

Section 9: Reasoning and Pragmatics

Chapter 35: Specificationism

ELIJAH MILLGRAM

During the 1970s and 1980s, various French government bodies, along with their primary contractor, Matra Transport, invested on the order of half a billion francs in a futuristic guided transportation system called Aramis.

> Aramis was...the niftiest of all, it was the programmed metro seat. The traveler merely goes to the station. He sits down, punches in the program, and opens up his newspaper. When the thing stops, he looks up, puts away his paper, and there he is, where he wanted to go. It's point-to-point, with no connections, no stops at intermediate stations.

> The ideal, for passengers, ... is what? It's not to think, not to slow down, not to transfer, and to arrive at their destination nevertheless.

That's point-to-point transportation. That's Aramis.[1]

Someone who spends a sizable portion of his weekday in rush hour traffic might well respond enthusiastically to such a description: it's a great idea, and we should build it! To which the right answer would be, of course, build *what*? What we have had described isn't yet a goal that's definite enough for anyone to start taking steps, such as having suppliers bid on a part. You first have to design it, that is, to finish deciding just what it is you want built.

The sort of thought that goes into the design phase of such a project is the *specification* of an initial, very thin description of a goal, and over the past few decades it has come in for increasing

I'm grateful to Chrisoula Andreou, Sarah Buss, Henry Richardson, Sherri Roush, Bill Talbott, and the editors of the present volume for comments on earlier drafts. Some of this material was presented to a class on Engineering Ethics at the University of Utah; thanks to the students for their constructive and critical responses, and to Margaret Battin for hosting my visits to her classroom. My commentary draws on earlier work of mine, and I'm also grateful to Blackwell Publishing for permission to reprint material from pp. 218–219 of "Williams' Argument against External Reasons," *Nous* 30(2), 1996; to MIT Press for permission for material from the Introduction to *Varieties of Practical Reasoning*; to Cambridge University Press, for material from pp. 155–156 of *Ethics Done Right*; to *The Monist*, for permission to reprint material from "Pleasure in Practical Reasoning," *The Monist* 76(3), pp. 409–412 (copyright © 1993, THE MONIST: An International Quarterly Journal of General Philosophical Inquiry, Peru, Illinois, 61354, reprinted with permission); to Harvard University Press (adapted by permission of the publisher from *Practical Induction* by Elijah Millgram, pp. 135–138, Cambridge, MA: Harvard University Press, Copyright © 1997 by the President and Fellows of Harvard College); and to Oxford University Press, for material from my review of Henry Richardson, *Practical Reasoning about Final Ends*, in *Mind* 105(419), 1996, pp. 504–506; by permission of the Mind Association. Material from "Commensurability in Perspective," *Topoi* 21(1–2), 2002, pp. 219–221 (©2002 Kluwer Academic Publishers), is used with kind permission of Springer Science and Business Media. Finally, a number of excerpts are adapted by permission of the publisher from *Aramis: Or, the Love of Technology* by Bruno Latour, translated by Catherine Porter, pp. 28–29, 54, 69–70, 89–90, 105, 112, 183–184, 238–239, Cambridge, MA: Harvard University Press, Copyright ©1996 by the President and Fellows of Harvard College.

attention on the part of philosophers who work on practical reasoning.

1

"Practical reasoning" is philosopherspeak for figuring out what to do, and is contrasted with theoretical reasoning, that is, figuring out what to believe, or what the facts are. The current debate in the field is focused on the question of what can count as a reason for action, or (a closely related question) on what patterns of inference appear in deliberation about what to do. The question is not in the first place descriptive: it is not about what sorts of cognitive activity actually lead up to decisions. (Decisions can be made for bad reasons, or no reasons at all, and still be preceded by cognitive activity.) Rather, it is advisory or commendatory: it is about what considerations legitimately *count* as reasons – *good* reasons – for action, or about what sorts of cognitive activity deserve the honorific title "reasoning." It is about what you *should* treat as a reason to do something, or, in short, it is a question about how to make up your mind, *not* about how people *do* make up their minds.

The received view in this area is instrumentalism, which has it that all practical reasoning is means-end reasoning. That is, it holds that practical reasoning consists in finding ways to attain one's goals or ends, or equivalently, to satisfy one's desires or preferences. Instrumentalism is an exclusionary position; since it holds that *only* means-end reasoning counts as practical reasoning, there is no such thing as reasoning about what one's ultimate or primary or final ends (or desires or preferences) should be in the first place.[2] On the instrumentalist view, anything that at first glance appears to be reasoning about one's final ends is not in fact *reasoning* at all, but something on a par with free association: the cognitive activity that leads up to the adoption of a final end cannot be correctly or incorrectly performed; it just *happens*, and when someone adopts an end, and it is not a means of attaining some further end he already has, we are never in a position to complain that his new end is mistaken.

Specificationism is an alternative to the instrumentalist default position. The specificationist view has it that at least some practical reasoning consists in filling in overly abstract ends (and other items as well) to arrive at richer and more concretely specified versions of those ends. Since many of our ends are simply too vague or indefinite to serve as starting points for means-

end reasoning, instrumentalist practical reasoning could not get going if one did not first further specify the overly indefinite ends; only when supplemented with the rational specification of ends is instrumental reasoning viable at all. In Musil's *The Man without Qualities*, Count Leinsdorf decides to do Something Big to celebrate the jubilee of Emperor Franz Josef, something "to put Austria in the vanguard, . . . and enable it to find its own true being again"; but that idea is not enough to go on, if one is actually *planning* the event, and much of the novel tracks the not-very-successful deliberations (and antics) of the committee put together to determine what that Something Big will be. If what I want is to write a very good paper, I am not yet in a position to do anything about it; I must first settle on a much more definite conception of what sort of paper it is I wish to write. Before searching for the means to return the patient to health, the physician must first decide whether health, in the patient's circumstances, would be a matter of prolonged life expectancy, or improved quality of life – and given the hard trade-offs, in what quality of life should be taken to consist. As Aristotle pointed out, we all want a well-lived life, but, as he famously went on to ask, what would that amount to? We may have decided that our new political party stands for the common good, but that is not yet a platform; in hashing out a platform we will be specifying a conception of what the common good is, and thus, our common end. Or, finally for now, perhaps, we want to be entertained this evening. If that is, so far, *all* we want, we aren't yet in a position to do anything about it; first, we have to settle on what kind of entertainment we're after. (Is it passive, in which case we can turn to the movie listings? Or the sort of active entertainment that might send us out for a night of clubbing?)[3]

The purpose of this chapter is first of all to present an accessible and up-to-date exposition of the current state of play in the development of this position.[4] Specificationism has encountered ongoing resistance, and I will try to show how the main objections to it have been attempts to express a single underlying concern. I'll discuss the ways in which the position has been – and might further be – developed in response to those objections. And, finally, I will argue that specificationism poses a challenge to the ways that philosophers in the analytic tradition have become accustomed to thinking both about instrumental reasoning and about rationality more generally.

2

Some methodological preliminaries are in order. A theory of practical reasoning ought to give us guidance when we are trying to decide what to do (and it ought to allow us to assess the quality of other parties' decisions). But specificationism as we have just introduced it is still too vague actually to be applied; told that part of your deliberative task is to arrive at more concrete versions of your goals, you still do not know *what it is* to go about that. Evidently, specificationism itself must first be further specified.

That is as it should be. Since the problem of how to deliberate is itself a practical problem, a solution to it must be arrived at by means that that solution – that theory of practical reasoning – itself endorses. When the theory is specificationist, we should not be surprised if it turns out that we have to arrive at that theory by specificationist means.[5]

What we're after might be with equal justice described as a better fix on the end of specifying one's ends, or a theory of how it is done correctly, or a method for doing it, or rules for doing it, or a standard for determining when one's ends have been specified properly. Evidently, the distinction between specifying goals, rules, methods, standards and so on is artificial, and we shouldn't be resting too much weight on it. I will start out by conducting the discussion in terms of ends or goals, but move onto alternative objects of specification in due course.[6]

Specifying specificationism is an especially delicate exercise. Until the view has been specified enough to be applied to this very problem, how can we tell whether one candidate specification or another is acceptable? It might seem that any argument we give for one version or another of the theory will be viciously circular.

This is the first of a series of related and progressively deeper worries that we are going to encounter about the position, and by way of postponing our engagement with them, notice that the successful specification of one's ends does not normally proceed in a vacuum, but is given traction by a terrain of live possibilities. Having already decided to go for a walk, I may need to determine what kind of a walk it will be; by choosing a direction, I determine whether it will be merely a stroll through the streets, or an occasion to commune with Nature. When I do so, I do not simply make up a more specified description of going for a walk, but rather take into account the actually available options (here, what kinds of walks are to be had by going in

different directions). The illustration is a reminder that different specifications of an end will be appropriate in different circumstances; there is no such thing as the uniquely correct specification of an end, let the circumstances be what they may.

This implies that there will be no uniquely correct specification of specificationist theory, but, rather, different versions of it shaped by (and to) the option spaces presented by particular concrete problems. Consider a social procedure for specifying ends (thus, an implicit specification of the specification of ends), and one that academics ought to find familiar. Agencies that support research may want to fund work that is original, promising, agenda-setting, and so on. This kind of end is not specific enough to guide any actual course of research (and if the agency laid out guidelines concrete enough to guide an actual course of research, it would thereby fail to be original, promising, and so on). So such agencies solicit proposals on the part of researchers, and constitute a panel whose task is to select those that are original, promising, and so on. Such a proposal amounts to a concrete specification of the agency's originally indefinite goals, and the selection process amounts to adopting one such specification (hopefully, the best). The procedure turns the choice of specification into a comparison problem.[7]

This is a workable way of disbursing research funding – and notice that it is clear enough how we would go about arguing for it, which suggests that the threatened circularity may not always be an obstacle to making up one's mind when the facts about the surrounding circumstances can be brought to bear – but it would be a terrible way to write the next chapter of your novel, or to determine the shape of an adolescent's emerging self-image, or, as we will shortly see, to solve certain sorts of engineering problem. To recap, specificationism itself needs specifying, and how a specification should proceed depends on surrounding circumstances (where that dependence allays the worry, anyway for now, that just anything goes). So the question is not: What is *the* right way to specify specificationism?

Let's serve our own purposes by adding a slight additional specification of the theory ourselves. We want specificationism to be a full-fledged alternative to the notion that all practical reasoning is means-end reasoning. But if all we have said is that specification adds content to ends, then what we have is less than the alternative we are after: Some specification of ends can, of course, be merely instrumental. To return to an earlier example, when my goal is to write a very good paper, much of the further specification that is necessary before I can actually start to write is noninstrumental (I still need a much more definite conception of what it is I want to write). When my goal is write my way through the paper I have thoroughly outlined, the point of the further specification – of the way I frame the sentences – is to serve the already fully specified goal.

The reader is warned that this distinction is almost never made in the literature, and that it is very easy to lose track of it. In particular, "constitutive" reasoning is often contrasted with instrumental reasoning; when this contrast is drawn, instrumental deliberation is typically thought of as reasoning about causal connections (to get the ball into the outfield, I have to hit it with the bat), and constitutive deliberation, as a matter of determining the parts or elements or components of something (to win the game, we must score more runs than the opposing team, and avoid being disqualified by the way we do it).[8] Both types of reasoning may be a matter of figuring out how to get something fairly definite that one already wants (e.g., winning the game), and when they are, they come under the heading of instrumental reasoning, as I am now using the term. Constitutive reasoning, when it is not simply a matter of joint constraint satisfaction (with fully specific constraints: We will turn to the possibility of underspecified constraints in due course), or helping oneself to a listing of standard constituents, may also be noninstrumental (in my sense); that is, it may amount to figuring out what one wants in the first place, rather than what is involved in getting what one already wants. Because we are interested in specificationism as an alternative to the dominant theory of practical reasoning, let's specify that the type of specification we are considering is *non*instrumental specification of ends.

Talking one's way through such a position is best done using an example that is both rich and taken from the real world. The standard illustrations (the previous section rehearsed a representative sample) tend to be either toy, or taken from ethical or moral domains. But it is probably better strategy to do one thing at a time, in this case, to investigate specificationist reasoning in a way that does not require us to cope with difficult moral questions at the same time. For this reason, industrial engineering and design, where specificationist reasoning takes you from concept to blueprints, and espe-

cially the design of novel products and technologies, seem to me to be a better testbed for this theory of practical rationality than the staple ethical and moral problems. Such cases come with a built-in advantage: Because the deliberation is institutional, rather than individual, it is often much easier to see what is going on. Institutions leave paper trails.[9]

The illustration I will use is the retrofuturistic transit system with which I began the paper. In 1987, the Aramis project was canceled, and in 1993, a postmortem by Bruno Latour, the bad boy of French philosophy of science, appeared in print.[10] I'll give enough detail for the reader to follow the thread of my argument, but if more texture – or a reality check on the claims I will be making – is needed, I recommend *Aramis, or the Love of Technology* as a fascinating afternoon's read. I'll put in place a bit more of the example now, both in order to give some of the flavor of what specification of ends looks like in a realistic case, and to make a couple of obvious but important points about it.

3

Suppose we have reached the stage at which the "programmable metro seat" consists of car-sized cars (that is, at which it is no longer being thought of as conceivably turning out to be a high-speed ski lift). If the system is to process enough passengers, these cars must be able to form trains, that is, to move together at the same velocity, with very small distances between them. Starting and stopping at stations dramatically cuts the average speed of a train, and because this version of Aramis is intended to provide dense coverage for an urban area, it would have many stations. The price paid in terms of transit time would be high. Here the decision is made that this "train" is to continue moving; its cars will slip into and leave the stream of traffic.

At this point in the process of specification, a further engineering decision is made not to manage the coupling and uncoupling of cars entering and leaving the "train" mechanically. Instead, what we would now call virtual coupling is to be used.

> The big challenge with Aramis is that the cars are autonomous; they don't touch each other, yet they work together as if they were part of a train. They have nonmaterial couplings – nothing but calculations. (54)

Because the cars are very tightly spaced, and because there is nothing physically holding the cars in place, the cars must keep their own position quite precisely. If a computer is to control the car with sufficient precision, a new sort of motor is required,

> an electric motor that doesn't involve a power transfer. You don't have a shaft or sprocket; there are no mechanical parts, except for the rotor, which is the axle. You have little notched wheels that allow very finely tuned displacements. (105)

This is a demand that is concretely specified enough to assign to a team of engineers; "the rotary... variable-reluctance motor" (104) turned out to be one of the few working devices produced by the Aramis project.

Perhaps some of these decisions could have been made differently, and something else would have been called (would have, if it had been built, *been*) Aramis. "The people carrying the ball for the project make a major decision as to what is negotiable and what isn't. Implementation, size, operation, financing, the dense network – all these are open to discussion; the mobile unit with nonmaterial couplings is not" (112). Once these decisions are made, "Aramis" is *more specified* than it had been.

Even this much is enough to allow the following remarks. First, faced with our toy introductory examples, an instrumentalist might have been inclined to respond that the problem was simply not knowing what one wants, and that is not something which calls for a novel theory of deliberation. (If you don't know *what* you want, that is *your* problem... not logic's problem.) But in this more elaborate case, it is clear that insisting that a deliberator ought to know what he wants up front, without doing anything that would count as thinking about it first, is unrealistic and unreasonable. Aramis would have had no chance at all of being a successful project unless a great deal of thought was put into determining what the fully specified goal was to be, and without such thought, there would be no reason for anyone to take the proposal seriously.[11] So we need to make room in our intellectual scheme of things for something that counts as thought of this kind.

Second, we can explain a couple of lacunae in Latour's treatment. In a postmortem of this kind, it is normal to try to answer two questions, whether the project was technically feasible, and whether it was economically viable. Latour insists on not answering either question. Whether Aramis was technically feasible would depend on what it was specified to be; obviously, some specifications would have been feasible, and others would not. (And likewise for economic viability – but I'll return to the question of Aramis's economic viability shortly.) The general point is that when we are involved in the specification of ends such questions stop having straight answers.

Third, for closely related reasons, when we are in the course of specifying ends of this sort, cost-benefit or expected-utility calculations become unavailable. These techniques have us make decisions by assessing the costs and benefits of outcomes, weighting them by the likelihood that they will occur, and choosing the outcome with highest expected value. But until we know what Aramis *is*, we cannot say what the costs or benefits or likelihoods involved in proceeding are. (Cost, benefits, and probabilities of *what?*) I will return below to a deeper relative of this problem.

4

Specificationist deliberation is meant to be a form of practical reasoning. Sarah Broadie allows that we move from less to more definite specifications of our ends, but she denies that this could be really be *reasoning*. Since the conclusions of such trains of thought have more content than their starting points, the starting points do not constrain the conclusions, and we have no way to distinguish correct specifications from incorrect specifications. The specification of an end, she argues,

> is a move from the less to the more determinate, which latter, precisely because it is more determinate, cannot be entailed by what is less so. It might seem that with suitable extra premises there could be a logically acceptable inference from the indeterminate to the determinate end. After all, there is no acceptable inference from the determinate end to the means except via additional [empirical] premises.... But... what additional premises would do the trick? (a) Factual premises, whether particular or general, would not help; nor (b) would any purely logical propositions. The addition (c) of some formal propositions about *eupraxia* [the Aristotelian end whose specification Broadie is discussing], such as that it is "self-sufficient" or "lacking in nothing," would not logically enable one to interpret the pursuit of *eupraxia* as the pursuit of *S* (where *S* is something more specific); whereas (d) inserting

a premiss that specifies *eupraxia* substantially might of course sustain the inference to a no less substantial conclusion, but only by thrusting back to an earlier stage the problem of how such propositions are obtained in the first place.[12]

It is easy to dismiss this argument too quickly. After all, Broadie is in the odd position of someone who holds that, whatever engineers were doing when they designed the ARPAnet, or the F-16, or any other innovative technology that satisfied a vague set of requirements in ingeniously new ways – or for that matter, when they ultimately failed to design Aramis – it couldn't have been *thinking*.[13] And her argument relies on more than one problematic premise, the first of which is that the more determinate cannot be inferentially extracted from the less. If the determinateness of one's starting point is not merely stipulatively linked to the determinateness of one's conclusion, we may expect to find any number of counterexamples in which determinateness increases as the inference is traversed. (Turning over several indistinct and hazy recollections of the previous day, I suddenly realize *exactly* what Sandra is up to.) Moreover, while the criterion she invokes – that if a train of thought is to be reasoning, there can be nothing in the conclusion that was not already in the premises – seems obvious to contemporary philosophers, the very opposite seemed just as obvious not so long ago. John Stuart Mill, not atypically of his time and in line with much tradition, took it for granted that a train of thought could not count as reasoning unless there was *more* to the conclusion than to the premises.[14] So the insistence that inference is conservative in this respect can look a lot like twentieth-century parochialism.

Second, Broadie takes it that the supplemental premises in a completed specificationist argument must have practical force or content – they must be evaluative, or contain operators like *should* or *ought* – and she apparently assumes that no such claim could be empirical; this is why she concludes that empirical premises cannot fill in the gaps in a specificationist train of thought.[15] But it should not be obvious that premises with practical force cannot be empirical. Suppose I am faced with a problem we have already mentioned in passing, that of deciding what would make for an entertaining evening. Mummenschanz is at the McCarter Theater, and I have not seen them, nor, I gather, anything like them, before. I have factual premises, in the form

of a friend's description ("they mime inanimate objects"), and these premises do not help. Logical and formal propositions do not help either. What I need is a premise of Broadie's type (d), one that specifies my end of being entertained substantially and in the relevant respects; we can allow knowing whether Mummenschanz will *be* entertaining to stand in for such premises here. ("Entertaining" is a so-called thick ethical concept, and has an action-guiding *should* built into it.[16])

As Broadie insists, the demand for such premises raises "the problem of how such propositions are obtained in the first place." She intends mention of the problem to have the force of a rhetorical question, for she concludes that no such premises are available. But consideration of a concrete situation in which the demand arises makes it obvious how such premises are obtained: I can go to McCarter, and discover, by observation, whether Mummenschanz is entertaining or not. In short, premises that are both empirical and evaluative (or prescriptive) are available, and the specification of ends is plausibly a form of rational deliberation that relies essentially on practical experience.[17]

Since there are more than enough places in Broadie's argument at which to dig in one's heels, why not shrug off the concern expresses? In my view, that would be a mistake. One way to see the underlying problem is as an issue of control: There are usually many ways one can make an abstract goal more concrete; what is there to make some of these right and the others wrong? To take up our main example once more, there were various ways that Aramis was reconceived over the course of its stop-and-go development. At one stage, it was an airport shuttle, Orly's version of the familiar monorail or light rail connecting the terminals. At another, it was vastly more ambitious: a network carrying four-seat cars from any point in an urban area to any other point; that is, it was a system combining the functionality of a fleet of taxis with that of a subway system. At another, it was a low-tech people mover, the sort of thing familiar from Disney's amusement parks, and meant to be installed at a Paris World's Fair. And at yet a fourth stage, Aramis had become a suburban commuter train, whose larger cars were joined in pairs – but a train that would split at junctions, with some cars going to one suburb, and the other cars to another. The different versions of Aramis were *so* different that one is left wondering whether just about *anything* would have counted as a specification of the initial goal. But in that case we would not be examining a deliberative process that could have been executed incorrectly, and so, we would not be examining a process that is to be understood as inference or reasoning.

5

Henry Richardson has taken up the challenge of showing where the added content comes from (1994). There is an additional, so-far-unmentioned reason for the specification of ends. Many of our ends conflict, but often these conflicts (whether between one's own ends or the ends of different people) can be removed by *cospecification* of the ends in question. Since the point of practical reasoning is deciding what to do, and since deciding what to do requires resolving conflicts between ends, ends are to be specified jointly so as to make them jointly achievable (and more generally, to make them cohere with one another and with other background elements of one's evaluative system). To return to one of the small-scale examples on the table, if I want to go for a walk, and I want to get exercise, and these ends conflict (how will I find time for both?), I could further specify the walk as the uphill, brisk kind, and the exercise as low-key, outdoor, not-necessarily-aerobic activity. If I do, the need to trade them off against each other is sidestepped.

(A caveat: I remarked earlier that specifications do not go ahead in a vacuum, and that there is no such thing as the correct specification of an end, regardless of surrounding circumstances. That observation holds of Richardson's further specification of specificationism. Perhaps the point is not always to resolve conflict; one might, for instance, sharpen up vague ends or rules in order to introduce conflict between them – say, in the name of brand differentiation, or as a negotiating tactic, or as a way of escalating hostilities.[18] Or, again, to develop the example we borrowed from Williams, if one of my insufficiently specified ends is to be entertained this evening, and the other is to keep a depressed, and so unentertaining friend company, I could specify my end of being entertained as being entertained passively, and keeping company as sitting side by side in silence in a dark movie theater. But even if this solution eliminates the conflict, it may raise, in some circumstances, anyway, the question of just what kind of a friend I am. Sometimes the right thing to do is to *acknowledge* a conflict, rather than to specify one's way around it.)

In introducing cospecification, I compressed into a parenthesis Richardson's insistence that it is not just ends in the mix. To see what that comes to, let's take a look at an especially problematic instance of it in the history of Aramis; the excerpt reproduced below is from interviews conducted with former RATP and Matra personnel.

[M. Berger:] "You have to understand intrinsic security. That's the underlying philosophy of the SNCF and the RATP. What it means is that, as soon as there is any sort of problem, the system goes into its most stable configuration. It shuts down. Broadly speaking, if you see the subway trains running, it's because they're authorized *not to stop*! That's all there is to it: they're always in a status of reprieve.

"As soon as this authorization stops coming through, the trains stop running. The emergency brake comes on, and everything shuts down. So everything has to be designed from A to Z – everything, the signals, the electric cables, the electronic circuits – with every possible type of breakdown in mind."

"That's why they call it *intrinsic*: it's built into the materials themselves. For example, the relays are specially designed so they'll never freeze up in a contact situation. If there's a problem, they drop back into the low position; their own weight pulls them down and they disconnect. The power of gravity is one thing you can always count on. That's the basic philosophy."

[M. Cohen:] "There was no hope for Aramis if you had to bring in the principles of intrinsic security. Not a chance."

[Interviewer:] "I thought that was the basic philosophy in transportation."

[M. Cohen:] "Not at all. An airplane doesn't have intrinsic security. Just imagine what would happen in an airplane if everything came to a halt whenever there was a minor incident! Well, people take planes, they accept the risk; this is *probabilistic* security. It was the same with Aramis. (69f)

Notice first that what must be cospecified with Aramis is a *standard* it must meet; security can be specified to be either intrinsic or probabilistic. Latour plausibly suggests that when an enterprise is large enough and innovative enough, it will not succeed unless not only the ends but the standards to be met are specified along the way. Call cospecification that restricts itself to modifying ends *narrow*; call cospecification that specifies standards, values, and so on, *wide*.[19]

Since we evidently cannot get by without wide cospecification, and since it is evidently the more problematic of the two, let's specify that the sort of specification we are interested in involves wide rather than narrow cospecification.

This is not an isolated or unique example. Recall the unanswered question of whether Aramis was economically viable. The obstacle to answering it is not just that, until we are fairly far along the process of specification, we do not know what it is that might or might not be viable. It is that the answer depends on how you specify economic viability. When we are counting up customer receipts, do we count commuters who have already paid for their monthly transit passes, and who begin using Aramis when it comes on line? Or do we just count the commuters who give up their cars and buy passes because Aramis is now available? Is a ride on Aramis valued as just another subway ride? Or does the municipality accept the idea that a more comfortable and more convenient trip is worth more? Do we count the decrease in automobile traffic? If so, how much?

Latour puts the point this way:

Every technical project has to define a type of economic calculus that makes it more profitable.

The relation between the economic calculation in camera and that in the greater Paris region is a relation to be established, to be performed, to be maintained. It is no more a given than any of the other relations. The profitability of the network and the efficiency of the rolling stock are twin notions that are negotiated and gradually realized as functions of success or failure. They follow; they do not lead. They are decided; they are not what makes it possible to decide.

And so we have a fine scientific controversy opening up within economics to determine whether "socioeconomic profitability" is acceptable or not. If politics imposes its will on the Budget Office, then the Budget Office has to take into account the calculation of passenger time and comfort, and Aramis becomes *profitable* once again. If politics hesitates, then the Budget Office imposes its own method of calculation, and Aramis goes back into the red. Aramis will survive only if it extends the scope of its network to the point where it makes humans in Paris move and modifies the usual calculation methods of the Budget Office. (183f.)

The specification of ends involves – in at least the large and important cases – cospecification of standards. And that leads us to further formulations of the objection we have been entertaining.[20]

6

If Latour is right, when the projects are large, we had better specify cospecification as wide cospecification. But that should worry us; didn't NASA famously cospecify the design for the Space Shuttle together with safety standards for the Shuttle, with results that speak for themselves? (As Stuart Russell once put it, discussing problems in robotics: "The performance standard must ultimately be externally imposed . . . particularly since, for the purposes of building useful artifacts, modification of the performance standard to flatter one's behavior does not exactly fit the bill."[21]) With enough political muscle, couldn't the accounting be made to come out any which way at all, and in that case, isn't it just a matter of politics at its most raw: the specification supported by the player with the most power wins? But then why is what we are examining a form of *inference* at all?

Let's consider two higher-resolution diagnoses of the problem, one due to Aurel Kolnai, and formulated when he kicked off the current discussion of specificationism several decades back, as well as a more recent treatment developed by Candace Vogler in the course of an argument for a position closely related to instrumentalism.

Kolnai argued that the process of specification is inevitably irrational and self-deceiving. You specify ends by reference to further ends. In so doing, you must treat the further ends as fixed, and as having fixed weights. The further ends are initially indeterminate also, and must be specified themselves in light of still further ends. The still further ends include, among others, the ends you were initially trying to specify. So the specification of the initial ends depends on the outcome of that very specification; the specification of ends generally is viciously circular.

Although this form of practical "rationality" is inevitably irrational and self-deceptive, it is going to be there come what may: the blueprints for Aramis are not going to happen by themselves. Accordingly, Kolnai depressingly labeled his conclusion the "Fundamental Paradoxy of Practice."[22]

Vogler's diagnosis is that rationality, inference, reasoning, reason, and so on are all (in the jargon of analytic metaethics) *normative* notions; or, as I put it earlier, the status of being a reason is advisory or commendatory, not merely causal. Normativity involves a contrast between doing it right and doing it wrong, and giving that contrast genuine content requires having an independent standard to which one can hold one's reasons, inferences, reasoning, and so on. Means-end reasoning provides such a standard, namely, whether your end is achieved by the means you propose to take to it. But alternatives like specification (as we have just seen) do not; the standards are mutable, and are adjusted to suit the ends on which one is working.[23]

Only means-end (or, as she calls it, "calculative") reasoning is first-class practical reasoning.[24] How then to make sense of the fact that we evidently *do* think about how our ends should be concretized and tightened up? Her answer is that the specification of ends is itself merely a means to an end, namely, the end of deciding what to do. The end of making up one's mind provides just the sort of independent standard for success or failure that seemed to be missing from the process; but then the specification of ends is just more means-end reasoning, and not an alternative to means-end reasoning.[25]

Aramis can serve not just as an illustration of these complaints, but as a reality check for them. "Nominal Aramis" – the project engineers' name for the initial thinly specified end – had been personalized point-to-point transportation; as we have seen, at the relatively early stages of the project it was conceived as a network of track carrying small (four-seat) vehicles from any point in the network to any other. Very quickly, however, as this excerpt from a further interview explains, cost considerations showed this plan to be simply not feasible.

[M. Gueguen:] "The very thing that made Aramis so different, its ace-in-the-hole, was scuttled at the start.... What costs the most in a guided-transportation system like Aramis that has an exclusive guideway? It's the infrastructure – the bridges, the tunnels, the viaducts, the tracks.... [But] cars that stop have to have a shunt line to separate them from the train. They also need room to slow down, plus a platform long enough to accommodate the number of cars, plus another shunt line so they can speed up and rejoin the train, which is running – or so Matra

was saying at the time – at about 50 kilometers an hour without stopping. Do you see?... there are actually *two* tracks almost the whole way. So even if Aramis is a narrow-gauge system, you have to carve out tunnels and make trenches for a very wide gauge! This is how an attractive advantage turns into a disadvantage. That's why the project changed shape so fast; it was impossible.

"So they said, 'Okay, PRT service is really two things: no intermediate stops, no transfers.' They kept the second, but they gave up the first..." (89)

In the face of financial pressure to make Aramis look much more like a traditional light rail system – and in fact as Aramis succumbed to the pressures, the size and seating capacity of the cars grew, first to ten persons, and eventually to twenty – no one attempted to conjure up an accounting method that would make Nominal Aramis break even. No one tried to change the "weights" of further ends so as to keep Nominal Aramis in play. While there was some wiggle room in the choice of economic and financial standards that the project had to meet, there wasn't *that* much wiggle room.

Let's return to the interview we quoted when we were discussing the specification of security standards. The second interviewee continues:

"I've finally concluded that in transportation, the only philosophy that allows a decision-maker to make a decision is intrinsic security. Not for technological reasons. When you say 'intrinsic,' it means that, if there's an accident, people can say: 'Everyone involved did everything humanly possible to provide a response for all the possible breakdowns they were able to imagine.' This way the decisionmakers are covered. They can't be blamed for anything.

"In probability theory, you say simply: 'If event x happens, and if event y then occurs, there is a risk of z in 1,000 of a fatal accident.' And this is accepted, because the probability is slight. This approach is unacceptable for a decisionmaker in the field of public transportation." (70)

The project's clients were government agencies run by public servants, and the need to keep accidents off the front page of the newspaper turned out to be a rigid constraint on the design of the system.[26] That's not to say it was enough of a constraint to obviate the need to specify standards in surprising ways. As it happened, the security standard ended up being specified in neither of the ways we have just seen. Pairs of cars were mechanically bolted together, the idea being, roughly, that if one set of brakes failed, there would always be the brakes on the second car. Here security was being specified as *redundancy*, but in a way that took into account the indefeasible political imperative. Briefly, the arguments we extracted from Kolnai and Vogler turn on the thought that, when you can cospecify the standards along with the ends for which they are standards, anything goes. But, as the evolution of Aramis teaches us, anything *doesn't* go. Now, these cases might suggest the view that mere politics (rather than the merits of the competing reasons) determines what goes and what doesn't, and I will take up that issue in a moment; first, however (not least because it is advanced in one of the more important recent discussions of practical reasoning), I want to explain why Vogler's alternative account of specification cannot be correct.

In the specification of ends, there is clearly *some* contrast between doing it right and doing it wrong. Take Aramis: if the perfume of that name, which one today finds at the cosmetics counters, turned out to be the result of the episode of specification we have been examining, we could be quite sure that something had gone wrong.[27] When it comes to practical reasoning, Vogler is committed to accounting for any such contrast in terms of the adequacy of means taken to a given end. This is why she treats the specification of ends as a means to the end of deciding what to do.

But the end of deciding what to do is too vague and indefinite an end to put one in a position to take steps toward it. Before that end can provide the accountability we have on hand, it must itself first be further specified. After all, specifying Aramis to be a perfume would give one a way of deciding what to do – one could at that point start calling the scent manufacturers – but that would not be a satisfactory specification of Nominal Aramis. To vary the example, if you are the public prosecutor, and your end is (so far, just) to deal with some criminal, not only is the end underspecified, but your further end, of deciding what to do, is also underspecified. If the former end turns out to be to deal *fairly and legally* with the criminal, then the deliberative process is identified with the operation of the judicial system. If it's to deal with him *expeditiously, decisively and permanently*, then deciding what to do is something that a handful of good old boys can do in a back room. If it's to deal with him *humanely*, you may need to move him to a different jurisdiction, where the judicial process will take a different form ... and so on. Before taking steps toward the end of deciding what to do, in such a case that end itself needs to be further specified. In short, Vogler's replacement for specificationist practical reasoning will only work if specificationist practical reasoning already works on its own.[28]

Let's return to the thought that the specification of an end wins out when the standards in play have been cospecified to make it the winner; that our examples suggest that what the standards end up being, and how much latitude there is in specifying them, is a matter of who has how much political muscle; that what it is to be a correctly specified end turns out to be no more than a matter of Lenin's "who whom"; and consequently that the specification of ends is rationalization rather than reasoning. (In this case, that Aramis died only because it lacked a sufficiently powerful patron.) Latour shows us how, in the case we have been considering, this cynical conclusion underestimates what is up for grabs in the course of wide cospecification.

Who the actors are (or, as philosophers sometimes say it nowadays, what the units of agency are) is also part of a wide cospecification. Consider two strikingly different versions of Aramis which took shape over the course of the project: The little airport shuttle, and something that might ultimately be the replacement for the subways and commuter rail lines of Paris. If Aramis turns out to be the first, it's a very small part of Matra's business; there will be a small unit inside Matra Transport that has a real stake in Aramis's existence, but Matra as a whole won't really care. (That small unit will keep having to work at convincing Matra's management that Aramis is important, that continued support is justified, and so on.) Whereas if Aramis becomes the mass transit system of the capital of France, it ends up being practically all of Matra Transport's business, in which case, Matra will just identify its interests with Aramis. Who Aramis's patron is (and how big and politically powerful it is) depends on what Aramis turns out to be.

It's easy to think that the cospecification of units of agency is only a feature of institutional deliberation, but not of practical reasoning done by individual human beings. On the contrary, people ordinarily do many things at once, and they allocate more resources to some tasks, and less to others, depending on what the task is. It is not as though there is a part of me, with fixed resources, already devoted to such-and-such a task, regardless of what it turns out to be: a part able to muscle other parts of myself into making the task happen *its* way. If gardening means having a little window box, it gets five minutes a week, and I don't care much about it; if gardening means an elaborate flower bed, I give it a few hours a week, and I'm proud enough of my flowers to care a good deal. That is, leaving the metaphor of subpersonal parts to one side, my commitment to the task depends (among other things) on how ambitious it is; although, as before, not everything is up for grabs, we often cannot explain how ambitiously the task is specified simply by appealing to my prior commitment.

7

We have seen what in restrospect look like a series of attempts to articulate a single and persistent worry about specificationism. Vogler's objection is perhaps the most revealing of them because it shows how the underlying concern depends on a presupposition widely shared by analytic philosophers: that a distinction between correct and incorrect – between doing it right and doing it wrong – requires the availability of an independent standard for correctness.

This is a very natural thought, but our discussion of specificationism has made it clear that if the specification of ends is a form of practical reasoning (thus, something to which the contrast between correct and incorrect execution can be applied), it is one for which independent standards are not going to be generally available. The observation that led Kolnai to call his version of the complaint the Fundamental Paradoxy of Practice was that we simply cannot get by without the specification (and, we have observed further, the *wide* specification) of ends. It is so fundamental, pervasive, and inevitable a feature of human deliberative practice that if we cannot make it out to be a locus of rationality, then when we make the decisions that most need to be made thoughtfully, we are really only just *pretending* to think. That is a very good reason to reconsider this part of our inherited model of rationality. Instead of throwing up our hands and rhetorically asking why, if you don't have independent standards, you couldn't just get away with *anything*, it is time to try to figure out how one could successfully use standards (for they clearly are being used in our extended example) which are *not* independent of the items to which they are to be applied.

I want to wrap up by first touching on the recently popular reflective equilibrium approach to rationality, and then returning briefly to the dispute between instrumentalists and specificationists.

The advocates of reflective equilibrium will respond to the point I have just made by telling us that it is old news. Its initial characterization in the philosophical literature – "[a] rule is amended if it yields an inference we are unwilling to accept; an inference is rejected if it violates a rule we are unwilling to amend" – treats neither rules nor the inferences they are rules for as an independent standard; each is to be modified in light of the other.[29] And it is even old news for specificationists: Richardson's treatment, for instance, explicitly appeals to it.[30]

But acknowledging the need for reasoning of this kind is not the same as having a thought-out account of how to do it, and specificationism shows us how far we are from having such an account. "Reflective equilbrium" is a new name for what was formerly called "coherence."[31] Now coherence is a vague concept; we should expect it to require specification; indeed, there are already a number of substantively different and less woolly variations on it, with indefinitely many more waiting in the wings. Reflective equilibrium has already been specified twice under its own name: once as *narrow* reflective equilibrium, in which rules and the instances that fall under them are mutually adjusted, and again as *wide* reflective equilibrium, where the elements to be coordinated include values, relevant beliefs, and even emotions.[32] That is, reflective equilibrium (or coherence) is itself underspecified, and has to undergo further specification before – or anyway, as – it is put to use: different specifications of coherence or reflective equilibrium will produce substantively different answers to first-order specification problems.[33]

As before, different enterprises will require different specifications; there is no single version of reflective equilibrium that will prove correct across the board. For instance, on the one hand, narrow reflective equilibrium is adapted from a domain for which it is obviously correct: when a linguist is trying to construct a grammar for a language, he begins by asking native informants for their linguistic intuitions about a wide range of utterances. (Is *this* one grammatical or ungrammatical? How about *that* one?) Proceeding from this data, he formulates a set of rules which largely classify the utterances as the native speakers do. When the rules and native judgments disagree, sometimes he rules in favor of the native speakers, and replaces the proposed rule with a more contoured one. And sometimes he overrules the native speakers, dismissing one utterance or another as ungrammatical. Eventually, he arrives at a set of rules that systematize his data, along, of course, with a list of the data that fail to conform to his rules.[34] On the other hand, moral philosophers who deploy reflective equilibrium have almost uniformly rejected its narrow version in favor of wide reflective equilibrium – and, let's just allow, for good reason.

One cannot merely appeal to reflective equilibrium itself to settle how reflective equilibrium is going to be specified. One reason for not going second-order at this point – that is, requiring that the specification of reflective equilibrium be in reflective equilibrium with the very elements it is supposed to bring into reflective equilibrium, and taking that to solve the problem – is that many fully appropriate specifications of the concept (such as narrow reflective equilibrium, or MDL, or the coherence concepts due to Thagard and his collaborators[35]), are not defined so as to permit reflexive application. Another is that we do not know how to exclude bizarre but self-endorsing specifications of coherence or reflective equilibrium. This is not to say that there aren't specifications of reflective equilibrium which, when brought to play in the specification of specificationist reasoning, bring you around to the right specification. And it's not to say that the circularity is necessarily vicious. It is, rather, that we don't yet understand how to talk or think our way through the mutual interplay of specification and reflective equilibrium so as to show that and how it is not vicious.

The reflective equilibrium approach may be committed to the idea that reasoning proceeds without an independent standard. But attention to the problems of specificationism shows that its advocates haven't figured out how to actually explain such reasoning. "Reflective equilibrium" is another label for the problem, rather than (so far) a solution to it. And that brings us back around to the point where our series of progressively more forcefully articulated versions of the primary objection to specificationism had led us: specificationism is philosophically important not least in that it shows us that we need to rethink our philosophical model of rationality from the ground up.

I began by introducing specificationism as an alternative to instrumentalism, and readers are likely to worry that they haven't seen a convincing refutation of the opposing view. (If you have instrumentalist leanings, you are likely to have been wondering whether cases such as Aramis can be fully accounted for by appealing to background goals and constraints, and inclined to insist that if they can't, well then, they cannot *really* have been reasoning after all.) Now, supplying a decisive refutation of instrumentalism is not part of the present agenda, for two reasons. First, the task here is describe the current state of play, and specificationists for the most part treat it as obvious that solely instrumental reasoning is a nonstarter; so they do not go out of their way to provide arguments that it is. Second, while for my own part I don't think that instrumentalism is a sustainable position, neither do I think that the best available arguments against it are specificationist.[36] Nonetheless, it does seem to me that specificationism has an occasion to bring its motivating insight to bear at the heart of the instrumentalist view, and that it is worth considering how that would go.

Instrumentalism is, once again, the idea that practical rationality is exclusively means-end rationality. But the means-end connection is one of the most mysterious notions in philosophy. Most philosophers tend to suffice with stating that a means is something one could bring about that would cause one's end; that doesn't make it any less mysterious. The academic industry engaged in analyzing causation is good evidence that causation is philosophically mysterious itself;[37] means are causes, and causes are philosophically mysterious; so means to ends are philosophically mysterious, too. Perhaps more pressingly, giving a satisfactory analysis of what it is to be a means to an end would involve explaining what makes something a *better* or *worse* means to one's end. Doing that would entail being able to give a noncircular explanation of what's wrong with Rube Goldberg machines (why they are instrumentally irrational solutions to the problems they purport to address).[38] And that's something no philosopher knows how to do.

A specificationist has available a diagnosis of this obscurity: what it is to be a means to an end is not yet sufficiently specified to serve as an anchoring concept for a theory of rationality. Just to provide a sense of what the alternatives can look like: Sometimes means are the sort of discrete sequenced steps you can represent in flow charts, and they temporally precede the ends; sometimes they are top-down adjustments to system-level variables, as when the Fed lowers the interest rate; sometimes a means consists in doing something after the fact to change the significance of an earlier event; sometimes a means is temporally posterior to the end it promotes in still other ways, as when, to move muscles in your arm that are not subject to direct voluntary control, you move your fingers; sometimes a means embeds its ends, as when one utters the phoneme "t" by uttering a syllable containing it; and the list has only just been started.[39] When one does specify the means-end relation – in different ways, of course, depending on what the practical problem is – then if one takes oneself to be specifying it correctly, one will not be in a position to insist that the honorific "practically rational" has to do only with the assessment of means-end reasoning, full stop (and not with the assessment of the specification of ends or standards). But the real point of the suggestion is not the quick refutation of instrumentalism. The more profitable and constructive use of the specificationist insight would be to organize our efforts to give concrete content to the instrumentalist's core concept. That would benefit philosophers on all sides of the debate.

Notes

1   Latour 1996: 28f. I'll give subsequent references to this book as stand-alone page numbers in the running text. Despite the now antiquated technology the project used, it is still surprisingly futuristic. See Weiss 2002.

2   The contrast here is with subsidiary ends or subgoals, adopted as means to further ends or goals; instrumentalists have no problem with these. For the sake of brevity, from here on out I won't list the alternative formulations (preferences, desires, etc.). For complications and further glosses, see the text surrounding note 8, as well as note 23, and the final section of the paper.

3   For the first example, see Musil 1996: Vol. i, 89 and *passim*. The second example is due to Allen Coates, the third and fifth to Kolnai 2001, and the last is from Williams 2001. The reading of Aristotle as a specificationist is due to Wiggins 2001; Kolnai, who takes Aristotle to be an instrumentalist, presents specificationism as an alternative to Aristotle's view.

4   The chapter will thus be an exception to the rule that philosophical essays are arguments for positions invented and endorsed by their authors: The idea is not my own, and while I think it is likely to be correct, I think the jury is (and ought to be) still out. (In my view, it clearly *is* interesting and important enough to deserve the sort of treatment I will try for here.)

5   That the form one's practical reasoning is to take is a choice, and not a matter of fact simply to be discovered, is by no means a consensus in the

field. For dissent, see Velleman 2000: esp. 229–230.

6   See Richardson 1990 for a treatment of the specification of norms or rules.

7   The technique places a great deal of reliance on the taste of the panelists, and one might worry that this is consequently not really *reasoning* after all. However, the judgments of taste occupy determinate positions in the larger structure of comparisons; they are used in the course of deliberation, but do not replace it. Moreover, those judgments may be articulated and argued about; for instance, they are importantly normally anchored to panelists' sense of the state of play in their disciplines.

8   See Schmidtz 2001: 238; Vogler 2002: 127 ff. Schmidtz contrasts "final" with "constitutive" ends; Vogler's term for constitutive but instrumental reasoning is "part-whole calculation."

    I expect that the common contrast of instrumental or means-end reasons with constitutive reasons is to be blamed on thinking that a means must be a cause, and a cause must be physically distinct from its effects. But this does not seem to me to be a useful distinction to introduce into discussions of practical deliberation.

    Philosophers are not alone in failing to mark the distinction between the two versions of constitutive reasoning; see, e.g., Newell 1990: 174ff, on "impasse resolution."

9   But we should not forget the following concern. It may be the case that institutional deliberation does – and ought to – proceed differently than practical reasoning performed by individuals. (The U.S. government deliberates by having representatives of its geographical parts assemble in Washington, where they dicker over the distribution of pork to the parts. But the right way for *you* to decide what to do is not to have your organs and limbs vote their interests.)

10 The example is in some ways a tricky one. One objection to using it is that Aramis, taken as a whole, is a *failed* case of practical reasoning: no specification was ever settled on, and the system was never built. My own reading of it is that Latour is recounting precisely that: A case of failed practical reasoning. But one might take the view that the failure was so bad that we should not really regard it as an instance of practical reasoning at all (in roughly the way we would not regard certain kinds of monkeying around in the kitchen as cooking at all). For this reason, I am going to be focusing on shorter deliberative episodes in the history of Aramis. (I'm grateful to Candace Vogler for pressing me on this point.)

    One might reply that, one's initial reactions notwithstanding, the Aramis episode is a *successful* instance of practical reasoning; after all, they ended up deciding to cancel it, and that was a decision, too. (This suggestion is due to Henry

Richardson.) But here I think we need to distinguish between the decision to sit tight that results from successful deliberation, and the kind of throwing up one's hands in confusion that results in sitting tight. Latour describes an autobiographical character engaged to do the postmortem because, after all that argument (and all that money), no one knew *what* to think.

11 A related point is that Aramis also shows that it is unrealistic to try to decompose specificationist reasoning into theoretical reasoning (i.e., reasoning about matters of fact), here, about what options are available, and an instrumentalist decision among the options. For an instrumentalist – again, a solely means-end – decision to be feasible, one has to have available goals or ends that (already) discriminate among whatever the options turn out to be. And in the specification of a project as elaborate as Aramis, it is very implausible that one starts out equipped with such ends. For a sketch of an argument supporting this last claim, see note 36.

There can be other, political reasons for not being overly definite at the outset. Latour emphasizes that studied ambiguity – underspecification – is almost always necessary, in projects the size of Aramis, for getting an effective coalition of supporters to sign on. (48)

12 Broadie 1987: 238f.

13 For a history of the specification of the ARPAnet – the ancestor of today's Internet – see Abbate 1999; for the F-16, see Fallows 1982: 95–106.

14 Mill 1967–1989: Vol. 7, 158–162.

15 Her assumption is not unusual, however; Anderson, 2005, discusses its role in the nineteenth-century psychologism debate.

16 The contrast is with "thin" concepts such as "good" and "right." Discussion of thick ethical concepts was introduced into the current philosophical literature by Williams 1985: 140f: for a survey of the literature on thick ethical concepts, see Millgram 1995; for a recent follow-up, see Putnam 2002: 34–43.

17 Testimony may of course take the place of experience, as when I am told not only that the performance is mime of such-and-such a kind, but that it is vastly entertaining. But here I rely on experience indirectly.

I have elsewhere called the view that empirical judgments can have practical content *practical empiricism*. (Millgram 2001: 16–17; for an argument in favor of the view, see Millgram 1997.). Perhaps because both practical empiricism and specificationism share the claim that one can deliberate about one's ends, I have occasionally seen the two views conflated; so here is a quick compare-and-contrast. Practical empiricism turns on the idea that you have to learn what matters from experience, using practical versions of observation and inductive arguments

from those observations. Specificationism, once again, turns on the thought that that your ends might have so little content that it would be premature to go looking for means to them, and so that a preliminary stage of adding content has to be understood as practical reasoning. As far as practical empiricism is concerned, your views about what matters could be already fully specific when they are acquired; this would allow you to skip the specification stage entirely. As far as specificationism is concerned, you could make your ends more concrete without appealing to experience at any point.

18 I owe this suggestion to Curtis Bridgeman. Richardson 1994: 20 ff., 152 f., 157, allows that coherence is not "indispensible," but does argue that it "is typically rational to pursue."

19 I'm following analogous terminology which I'll introduce later.

20 Specificationists argue among themselves about whether the position was Aristotle's (see note 3), so notice that an instance of the phenomenon we are examining – that in some cases of specificationist reasoning, the conditions for a successful specification are specified along with the solution itself – can be found in his *Nicomachean Ethics*. Aristotle takes it that everyone wants to live well, that is, to lead a happy and successful life, and his problem becomes that of specifying what such a life comes to. His *Ethics* is a sketch of the results of the deliberative exercise, or rather, of two different sets of results, since it's typical of vague or indefinite goals that you can specify them in more than one way. The contemplative life sketched in Book X and the active political life of Books I–IX are two alternative blueprints which Aristotle gets by running through the specificationist exercise twice.

Now the standards – such as "completeness" and "self-sufficiency" – that Aristotle announces a life must meet in order to count as *eudaimon* end up amounting to very different things in Books I–IX and X, respectively. For instance, in Books I–IX, being self-sufficient means having everything you need for a happy life; if the active life requires friends, as Aristotle thinks it does, part of being happy is having friends. In Book X, however, being self-sufficient means *not* needing things; the contemplative life is happy in part because someone who is thoroughly engaged in contemplation does not need any friends.

21 Russell 1989.

22 Kolnai 2001: 272 ff. There are various ways one could object to this argument as well. First, as we've seen, weighting is probably too crude a way of thinking about it. Second, circularity is not always vicious (constraint satisfaction problems containing cycles can have unique best solutions). Third, weights can be frozen into place by one's choices: Latour points out that once the Paris subway system had chosen a track gauge

incompatible with that of other train systems, and had dug tunnels for that gauge, it became very difficult indeed to reverse that decision.

23 This allows us to specify more tightly the distinction between instrumental and specificationist reasoning. On the instrumentalist view, one's goals or ends or desires together amount, at any stage of one's reasoning, to the sole standard for one's actions. So while further specifying those ends is indeed a step toward attaining those ends, because it amounts to changing the standard, it is not accepting the instrumentalist standard as is. (An analogous contrast might be that between views on which the legislature is the sole source of the law, and those on which judges, by setting precedents, are adding to the law; thus, one worry for instrumentalism is that it may be unable to reconstruct legal reasoning.)

24 Although Vogler does allow for second-class reasons that adduce the fact that an activity is pleasant, or that an action fits a pattern anchored in one's life.

25 Vogler 2002: 159–169. There are worries one might reasonably have about this move. When inductive reasoning is executed in order to arrive at an inductive conclusion, does that "in order to" make the inductive reasoning merely means-end reasoning? And if that is the wrong conclusion to draw, why should specificationist reasoning be treated any differently?

26 Although not one that had been articulated ahead of time: it was not as if the requirement that the system be safe had, at the outset, been given even this shape. Remember, we have here an administrator giving his retrospective diagnosis of what he regards as a fatal problem with the way the specification of security evolved.

27 One might suppose that there is an easy explanation at hand, namely, that Aramis was originally specified as a transit system, that a more fine-grained specification is acceptable only when it preserves the content of the thinner initial specification, and that a perfume is not a transit system. But Aramis also convincingly demonstrates that the principle this explanation invokes is false. Many quite reasonable specifications of Aramis were being explored that gave up one or another aspect of the initial description of Nominal Aramis.

Richardson 1994: 245f., accounts for this sort of flexibility by distinguishing "abstraction" (an upward move, as it were, in a taxonomic structure) from specification (the corresponding downward move), and taking abstraction to alternate with specification proper. The important point for now is that, while we can be for the moment agnostic as to how they are managed, ambitious, Aramis-scale specifications will not be successful without such adjustments. Since there is no point in focusing on a method that will not work in the cases for which we most

need it, let's specify that the specification of ends and the like be such as to allow adjustments of this kind, however in the end they turn out to be implemented.

28 A bit of experimentation confirms that, for any more specified version of the end of deciding what to do, one can come up with circumstances in which it is not sufficiently specified to proceed. We have already seen that there is no such thing as the generically correct specification of an end; rather, what the correct specifications might be depends on the concrete circumstances in which the problem arises. So it is not as though the generic end of deciding what to do might be replaced by a more specific goal that would successfully control one's specifications in any and all circumstances, and so which you could treat as the anchoring end of your instrumentally construed practical reasoning. If the detailed goals you would need to serve as a standard for the specification of your end must vary from occasion to occasion, but you cannot deliberate your way to them (because specificationist deliberation has been ruled out as a form of practical inference), then the chances of your coming up with them when and as you need them are *very* small.

Notice, for instance, that the most obvious candidate – adding "in a way that's responsible to the initial specification" to the end of deciding what to do – won't do. As before, the new goal (of deciding to do *that*) inherits all the indefiniteness of the original and underspecified goal. If the end of being entertained this evening is not specified enough to serve as a starting point for thinking about what steps to take toward it, then the end of deciding (how) to be entertained this evening is also insufficiently definite. For instance, if entertainment is understood to importantly involve a significant degree of spontaneity, then a decision process that selects a form of entertainment for the evening should not be overmethodical. But if entertainment is the sort of thing that squeezes every drop of excitement out of one's scarce and precious free time, then the planning for it had better be extremely thorough. Before the end of entertainment has been further specified, the end of deciding on that specification is also not yet specified enough for one to start taking steps toward it.

29 Goodman 1983: 64, emphasis deleted; Goodman is describing how to arrive at a reflective equilibrium between rules of inference and our judgments about particular inferences.

30 Richardson 1994: 178–90.

31 Elgin 1996: 13, 107, distinguishes the two; coherence addresses only the mutual fit of the elements of the system, whereas reflective equilibrium addresses as well the initial tenability of those commitments (or our antecedent

commitments to them). Elgin's choice of terminology is of course up to her; however, it is standard in contemporary coherentism to include ways of taking initial tenability into account. See, for instance, Thagard 1989 and Thagard and Verbeurgt 1998 for two different specifications of coherence which do this.

32 For the distinction, see Daniels 1979. For the inclusion of emotions in wide reflective equilibria, see Elgin 1996: Ch. 5; Richardson 1994: 178f. (where this partial specification of it is called "reflective sovereignty"). As before, because there are many different ways of managing such adjustments, it is not as though there will be just one way of specifying wide reflective equilibrium.

33 For an argument that one cannot simply leave one's coherence concept vague, see Millgram 2000.

34 This account of narrow reflective equilibrium brings it fairly close to yet another coherence concept, Minimum Description Length (MDL). For an introduction, see Grünwald 2005.

35 See notes 31 and 34.

36 For one of the classic objections, see Nagel 1978: 27–32; for an objection of my own, see Millgram 1997: Ch. 2.

It is not that specificationists are unable to fill out what they take to be the obvious point. For instance, against the form of instrumentalist resistance I parenthetically sketched, a specificationist might point out that the specificity of one's background goals and constraints trades off with their portability; that background goals and constraints are only plausibly available in unfamiliar choice situations if they are highly portable; thus, that they will not be specified enough to drive solely instrumental reasoning in the cases for which one most needs them.

37 For an introductory overview, see Sosa 1980.

38 For a representative sample of his work, see Goldberg 2000.

39 For discussion of the second sort of case, see Thalos 1999; for the third, see Nehamas 1985; I'm grateful to Irene Appelbaum for the last two examples. Perhaps this very lack of specificity explains why instrumentalists like Vogler have been tempted to try to reconstruct specificationist deliberation of ends as an early phase of instrumental reasoning: they sense that this is one way in which they might further specify their own inchoate core concept.

References

Abbate, J., 1999. *Inventing the Internet*. MIT Press, Cambridge, MA.

Anderson, R. L., 2005. Neo-Kantianism and the roots of anti-psychologism. *British Journal of the History of Philosophy*, 13(2), 287–323.

Broadie, S. W., 1987. The problem of practical intellect in Aristotle's ethics. In Cleary, J., editor, *Proceedings of the Boston Area Colloquium in Ancient Philosophy, Vol. III*, pages 229–252, University Press of America, Lanham, MD.

Daniels, N., 1979. Wide reflective equilibrium and theory acceptance in ethics. *Journal of Philosophy*, 76(5), 256–282.

Elgin, C., 1996. *Considered Judgment*. Princeton University Press, Princeton, NJ.

Fallows, J., 1982. *National Defense*. Vintage, New York.

Goldberg, R., 2000. *Inventions*. Simon and Schuster, New York. Edited by Maynard Frank Wolfe.

Goodman, N., 1983. *Fact, Fiction, and Forecast, Fourth Edition*. Harvard University Press, Cambridge, MA. Foreword by Hilary Putnam.

Grünwald, P., 2005. A tutorial introduction to the minimum description length principle. In Grünwald, P., Myung, I., and Pitt, M., editors, *Advances in Minimum Description Length: Theory and Applications*, MIT Press, Cambridge, MA.

Kolnai, A., 2001. Deliberation is of ends. In Millgram, 2001.

Latour, B., 1996. *Aramis, or the Love of Technology*. Harvard University Press, Cambridge, MA. Translated by Catherine Porter.

Mill, J. S., 1967–1989. *Collected Works of John Stuart Mill*. University of Toronto Press/Routledge and Kegan Paul, Toronto/London.

Millgram, E., 1995. Inhaltsreiche ethische Begriffe und die Unterscheidung zwischen Tatsachen und Werten. In Fehige, C. and Meggle, G., editors, *Zum moralischen Denken*, pages 354–388, Surhkamp, Frankfurt am Main.

Millgram, E., 1997. *Practical Induction*. Harvard University Press, Cambridge, MA.

Millgram, E., 2000. Coherence: The price of the ticket. *Journal of Philosophy*, 97(2), 82–93.

Millgram, E., editor, 2001. *Varieties of Practical Reasoning*. MIT Press, Cambridge, MA.

Musil, R., 1996. *The Man without Qualities*. Vintage International, New York. Translated and edited by Sophie Wilkins and Burton Pike.

Nagel, T., 1978. *The Possibility of Altruism*. Princeton University Press, Princeton, NJ.

Nehamas, A., 1985. *Nietzsche: Life as Literature*. Harvard University Press, Cambridge, MA.

Newell, A., 1990. *Unified Theories of Cognition*. Harvard University Press, Cambridge, MA.

Putnam, H., 2002. *The Collapse of the Fact/Value Dichotomy*. Harvard University Press, Cambridge, MA.

Richardson, H., 1990. Specifying norms as a way to resolve concrete ethical problems. *Philosophy and Public Affairs*, 19(4), 279–310.

Richardson, H., 1994. *Practical Reasoning about Final Ends*. Cambridge University Press, Cambridge.

Russell, S., 1989. Execution architectures and compilation. In *Proceedings of the Eleventh International Joint Conference on Artificial Intelligence*, Morgan Kaufmann, San Mateo, CA.

Schmidtz, D., 2001. Choosing ends. In Millgram, 2001.

Sosa, E., 1980. *Causation and Conditionals*. Oxford University Press, Oxford.

Thagard, P., 1989. Explanatory coherence. *Behavioral and Brain Sciences*, *12*, 435–467.

Thagard, P. and Verbeurgt, K., 1998. Coherence as constraint satisfaction. *Cognitive Science*, *22*(1), 1–24.

Thalos, M., 1999. Degrees of freedom: An essay on competitions between micro and macro in mechanics. *Philosophy and Phenomenological Research*, *59*(1), 1–39.

Velleman, J. D., 2000. Deciding how to decide. In *The Possibility of Practical Reason*, pages 221–243, Oxford University Press, Oxford.

Vogler, C., 2002. *Reasonably Vicious*. Harvard University Press, Cambridge, MA.

Weiss, G., 2002. Little robotic autos that can. *IEEE Spectrum*, *39*(7), 24–25.

Wiggins, D., 2001. Deliberation and practical reason. In Millgram, 2001.

Williams, B., 1985. *Ethics and the Limits of Philosophy*. Harvard University Press, Cambridge, MA.

Williams, B., 2001. Internal and external reasons (with postscript). In Millgram, 2001.

Chapter 36: Presupposition, Attention, and Why-Questions[1]

JONATHAN E. ADLER

Philosophers and psychologists share an interest in understanding the everyday activity of explaining, which I take up as it intersects pragmatics and reasoning. How does the distinction between the *focus* and the *presuppositions* of *why-questions* orient or bias answers to those questions and what are the implications for conclusions drawn of systematic errors and fallacies, particularly in how subjects respond to why-questions about chance phenomena?[2]

The pragmatics perspective is usually construed as an attempt to show that the experimenter's presentation misleads subjects with the implication that the experimenter's ascription of errors and fallacies is not warranted. Schwarz (1996), in a book extending research on pragmatic influences on experimental judgments, writes in an introductory chapter:

> Research participants...have no reason to suspect that the researcher is not a cooperative communicator and are hence likely to find meaning in the researcher's contributions.
>
> The findings reviewed in the following chapters suggest that this basic misunderstanding about the cooperative nature of the communication in research settings has contributed to some of the more puzzling findings in social and psychological research and is, in part, responsible for the less than flattering picture of human judgmental abilities that has emerged from psychological research. (1996: 5)[3]

The role of pragmatics that I explore is related, but it leads to a different, although strictly compatible, conclusion. Pragmatics contributes to explaining subjects' responses. But the contribution I follow out supports ascriptions of erroneous reasoning. I take for granted that explaining is not justifying. Unless my account of the influence of pragmatics on subjects' responses is viewed only as a contribution to explaining, not justifying, those responses, my argument will appear incoherent.

1. Why-Questions: Presupposition and Focus

Why-questions generally structure the set of answers contrastively (Dretske 1972). I might not be able to explain why I rode on the third car of the train, but I may still be able to explain why I rode on the third car *rather than* the last one (because to exit from the last one at my station you have to walk to forward cars). For a more developed example: Asking, "Why did Jim *kiss* Mary?" (with emphasis on "kiss") presupposes that Jim and Mary did something together and focuses us on Jim having kissed – rather than, say, calling, blessing, cursing, hugging – Mary. Asking instead, "Why did *Jim* kiss Mary?" presupposes that someone kissed Mary and shifts focus on Jim's having done it, rather than, say, Tom, Jane, or Tony. The response "Because that is how Jim greets his close friends" is a candidate answer to the first, but not to the second, and conversely for "Unlike the others, only Jim had the opportunity to greet Mary." If you gave the latter answer to the former question, the questioner might naturally respond, "I know that only Jim had the opportunity to greet Mary. I wanted to know why he greeted her with a kiss."

A difference in emphasis or stress is generally implicit in the formulation of the question, due to natural stress patterns (usually favoring the subject term) or to emphasis or to the operation of certain particles (e.g., "only") or to conventions such as that old information comes first. The question "Why did Jim kiss Mary?" reports the old information or norm that Jim kissed someone and then it offers the new, deviant, or surprising information that it is Mary. Semantically equivalent forms can have different focii: Why was Mary kissed by Jim – the focus is now on Jim, whereas previously it was on Mary. A difference in focus is also affected by mutual beliefs as to what is known and what is in question, which can resolve potential conflicts among the different criteria of focus. If it is mutual between speaker and hearer that someone kissed Mary, the focus will turn to Jim. So, a standard – unmarked – informative answer to a why-question will respond to its focus – why, in the original case, did Jim kiss Mary, rather than someone else; and not why Mary was kissed by Jim, rather than someone else.

The contrastive and related structuring of why-questions renders the explanatory task feasible and economical. There are an unlimited number of necessary conditions in any causal chain to an event. By presupposing most of these, focus is fixed on the few causes that make the difference between the event's occurring or not in the circumstances. Explaining the hole in the couch can be accomplished by reporting only that a lit cigarette was dropped on it, even though the burn depends on various standing conditions like the presence of oxygen. Focus-presupposition structuring is in the spirit of Grice's (1989) maxim of orderliness and the related economizing that Sperber and Wilson (1986) treat as one of the two factors which determines the relevance of a conversational contribution.

2. The Deflationary Claim and the Reformulation Strategy

Hilton (1990) and Kahneman and Miller (2002) converge on applying the pragmatics of why-questions to counterfactual reasoning, the integration of base-rates, and actor-observer asymmetries in attribution theory. The latter two are tightly connected. In accord with related research, attribution studies find that subjects tend to answer seemingly neutral questions like "Why did Jones help Smith with his move?" by citing the actor's traits (e.g., Jones is helpful), rather than because of the nature of the situation.[4] The response occurs where the background information is limited and neutral, and even in the absence of any further information at

all. Subjects' explanation by appeal to the traits of the actor – a *correspondent inference* – is held to exhibit a bias referred to as "the fundamental attribution error."

The rational model for attribution is, in simplest form, Mill's method of difference: If two otherwise similar events differ only in the presence in one of a certain factor, and if the event with that factor led to an effect (if, among viable candidate causes, omitting that factor alone fails to yield that effect), then that factor is its cause. (In its more complex and realistic form, Mill's method of difference transforms into the analysis of variance.) If many people help Smith, if the "consensus" for helping Smith is high anyway, there is nothing special about Jones's helping him. So, if the formal attribution model holds, subjects' learning that many help Smith should diminish the inference to Jones as the locus of responsibility. But the finding is that it does not significantly do so, supporting the claim of a fundamental attribution *error*.

To demonstrate the role of pragmatics in such findings, experimenters vary the formulation of a why-question or of background knowledge. If the answers subjects now provide varies with these alterations in presupposition and focus, the results are taken to weaken conclusions that subjects' responses to the original question are biased or flawed or errors. I'll call this the *deflationary* claim:

> In respect of studies . . . , the negative conclusions (of errors and worse) that have been drawn are unwarranted.

The deflationary claim is taken to follow from showing that the findings critical of subjects' judgments are strongly question-formulation dependent. Consequently, either subjects' responses are not genuine errors, given the real question communicated, or even if they are errors, they are transient or superficial, since the correct answer will be elicited by a mere reformulation of the question. (As is evident from these and other writings, Hilton holds this claim far more widely and deeply than do Kahneman and Miller.) Hilton (1990) writes:

> many biases in causal explanations may not reflect variations in underlying beliefs about causal processes, but may instead be due to the dynamics of interpersonal question-answer processes. (73)

Kahneman and Miller's (2002) norm theory is offered to explain our tendencies to belief perseverance, as well as to the fundamental attribution error. Once a norm is activated, which is "rapid and automatic," it is not subject to voluntary control:

> Any observation of behavior – even if it is discounted or discredited – increases the normality of subsequent recurrences of compatible behavior. (361)

Kahneman and Miller (2002) observe that presupposition affects *mutability* (the alterability of a situation, particularly under counterfactual suppositions): "the mutability of any aspect of a situation increases when attention is directed to it and that unattended aspects then become part of the presupposed background." (353) To illustrate that a "Why question implies that a norm has been violated" and that "A why question, then, presupposes that some state X is the case, and also implies an assertion that not-X was normal," they offer the following illustrative exchange:

Q: "Why did Joan pass this math exam?"
A: "She used the Brown textbook."

In accord with Dretske's analysis, they take the why-question to indicate that

> a particular event is surprising [Joan's passing] and requests the explanation of an *effect*, defined as a contrast between an observation and a more normal alternative [Joan's failing]. (362)

Kahneman and Miller observe that differences in the explanations provided follow upon differences in stress or emphasis. They conclude that the alteration in response justifies the deflationary claim: The difference in responses "*reflect different interpretations of an ambiguous question rather than different causal beliefs*" (364, my emphasis).

Another example that Kahneman and Miller offer is of a woman picking out causes of her husband's illness different from her doctor's, which they compare to the actor-observer asymmetries posited in attribution theory. However, the differences cannot be explained simply in those terms:

> The contrast could not be explained by differences of knowledge ... or of perceptual salience. ... It is not explained by the distinction between a state of self-consciousness and other states of consciousness. ... Nor is it compatible with the hypothesis that the focus of attention is assigned a dominant causal role ... inasmuch as the husband surely plays

> a more focal emotional role for the wife than for the physician. (365)

Rather,

> The hypothesis of the present treatment is that the same events evoke different norms in the wife and the physician of the example, and in actors and observers in other situations.

Accordingly, the conclusion they draw parallels Hilton's (1990):

> Different descriptions of the same event can appear to provide conflicting answers to the same question, when in fact they are concerned with different questions. This proposal can be subjected to a simple test: Do the observers actually disagree? A negative answer is suggested by several studies. (365)

The conclusion that the alternatively focused questions are (contrastively) different questions is crucial for the deflationary conclusion. In studies of "framing" (e.g., Tversky and Kahneman 1981) different answers to formally equivalent, though variably formulated questions (by, e.g., changing reference points or altering expressions to be stated in gains, rather than losses) are taken as evidence of suggestive, but strictly irrelevant, influences on subjects' judgments and so unsupportive of a deflationary claim.

Hilton notes that the actor-observer asymmetry of attribution theory is that

> Actors tend to explain events by reference to characteristics of the situation, whereas observers tend to explain events by reference to personal characteristics. (74)

The link between attribution theory and presupposition/focus, already touched on, is that

> an actor presupposes his or her presence as a constant background factor and asks him- or herself what is special about the situation that caused his or her behavior. In contrast, observers treat the situation as background and focus on what is special about the actor that differentiates him or her from other people in the same situation. (74)

The conjecture is that

> if the causal question is disambiguated by specifying the relevant reference class for the target event, then the actor-observer difference should disappear. This is what McGill (1989) found.

From the original question "Why did you [your best friend] choose this major?," two "disambiguations" were offered, which *overtly* direct focus:

> Why did you [your best friend] in particular choose this major? (Person focus, stimulus background)

and

> Why did you [your best friend] choose this major in particular? (Person background, stimulus focus)

The reformulations elicit from subjects the sought for answer. The central finding is similar to that reached by Kahneman and Miller:

> Consistent with the conversational model, subjects gave explanations that were relevant to the explicit focus of the question. . . . No effect of actor-observer differences were found in the presence of this explicit focus manipulation. As McGill observed, these results are consistent with the view that actor-observer differences in causal explanation are due to the implicit focus and may *not reflect differences in underlying beliefs about the true causes of behavior.* (74, my emphasis)

McGill (1989) did similar studies to explain-away asymmetries in attributions of one's success (as due to internal factors) and failure (as due to external factors).

Granted that the *reformulation strategy*, as I'll refer to it, works in Hilton (1990) and Kahneman and Miller's (2002) applications, does a presupposition-focus role always justify such a deflationary conclusion? I'll argue for a negative answer, as just hinted at: there are important cases in which a pragmatic analysis helps to explain observed biases or flaws in reasoning, rather than to explain them away.

3. Why-Questions and Chance Explanations: A Presuppositional Incompatibility

In light of this convergence to the deflationary claim, I want to look at neighboring studies, whose findings also seem affected by a presuppositional structuring of why-questions, yet which do not support a deflationary claim. I'll begin by applying the reformulation strategy found in Hilton (1990) and Kahneman and Miller (2002). The results will not be a similar alteration in subjects' judgments, I conjecture, or they would introduce confounds of their own.

In a study (Jepson, Krantz, and Nisbett 1983) of the understanding of the law of large numbers and regression by those untrained in statistics, subjects are asked to answer a set of questions for which open-ended, discursive, answers are sought on a variety of topics. I first abbreviate two on baseball batting averages:

> 1. After the first two weeks of the baseball season the leader has a batting average that is over .450. Yet, no batter ever finishes a season with a better than .450 average. What do you think is the most likely explanation for the fact that batting averages are higher early in the season? (500)

A typical answer of subjects is:

> As the season commences a player will, I think, become less motivated to impress people with a powerful bat – he is taking a sort of ho-hum attitude about it.

The favored response is anything like:

> The amount of times at bat versus the result is far greater earlier in the year than at the end of the year. . . . The more frequency he [a player] bats the clearer the truth information as to how well a batter hits. (500)

The second is suggested by Nisbett and Ross's (1980) discussion of the "sophomore slump"(164–165):

> 2. Why did [baseball] rookie Smith, who did so well his freshman year ('rookie of the year'), do so much worse his second year?

The fairly typical answers are that he was spoiled by success, that the pitchers caught on to how to throw to him, that he was exhausted after his first year and stopped training as hard, and so on. These answers are comparable to those, reported in the early work of Kahneman and Tversky (1982a). Flight instructors claimed that because criticism of their students for very bad performance was followed by better performance, and conversely for praise for very good performance, they would alter their teaching accordingly (to offer only criticism).

Contrast these candidate answers with the favored one:

> by chance alone [i.e., regression to the mean], some mediocre athletes will perform exceptionally well in their first year but perform less well in subsequent years. . . . In other words, the best explanation for a sophomore slump

is that the first year was atypical for the performer in question while the second year showed regression toward his "true" ability level or performance base line. (165)

In general, the experimenters found that

Most of these answers presumed, either tacitly or explicitly, that the sample was adequate and showed no recognition of the uncertain or probabilistic nature of events of the kind presented in the problems. (496)

However, the actual results displayed a good deal of variation. Specifically, when the problems are ones that are more readily regarded as objective and measurable, subjects are more inclined to offer statistical answers. For [1], 34 percent provided a statistical answer, and 66 percent either an "intermediate" or "deterministic" one. For the sake of brevity, I shall ignore these individual differences, despite their significance. Systematic statistical answers are correlated with higher SAT scores (Stanovich 1999). Still, when I refer to subjects answers, it will be just to the nonstatistical ones, since that represents, in brief form, the dominant finding.

The findings are explained in familiar ways as due to the use of faulty, but easy to apply, assumptions or heuristics, especially representativeness (a judgment of similarity). These assumptions or heuristics obscure the role of chance or randomness (Kahneman, Slovic, and Tversky 1982). The explanations that subjects offer, for example, that the batter became too cocky, are similar to ones that make good common sense. Performers who become conceited due to their success in a skilled demanding activity relax their efforts and then do worse.

Conversationally, the focus of the why-question for [2] is Smith's doing worse his sophomore year, rather than the same or better. The focus of the why-question for [1] is similar – why those who bat over .450 at the beginning of the season finish lower at the end, rather than around the same or better. Both why-questions seek *puzzle-reducing* explanations, rather than neutral, *information-seeking* explanations, since each implies that there is something unexpected or deviant or out of the normal about the phenomena observed.

Why-questions presuppose that an observation or phenomena *calls for explanation*. Someone's winning a fair, large lottery, however improbable, does not call for explanation, since someone had to win and each ticket had an equal chance. But if the answers of only two students to a many-question multiple choice test is the same, including the same errors, then, as so described, it calls for explanation, even if more probable as a chance occurrence than winning a lottery.[5]

The why-question automatically introduces as background a bias that what is to be explained is deviant. As Nozick (1981) observed, we ask "Why is there something rather than nothing?" treating the natural state as one of nothing existing, and something as the deviation from it. To reduce the puzzle is to explain how we moved from the latter to the former. (There is a partial parallel to our hearing asymmetrically, for example "Why is South Korea like Japan?" [Tversky 1977]. The parallel is only partial because asking "Why is there nothing rather than something?" alone presupposes a blatant falsity.)

Events or occurrences that are surprising or disturb expectations call for explanation. Is surprise or the disturbance of expectations sufficient? If I expect that the person I will meet at a conference is male because "his" name is "Tony," and it turns out that Tony is a female, I am surprised (and it disturbs my expectations). But it does not call for explanation. A call for explanation requires also that the event or occurrence is puzzling, a prominent way to surprise or to disturb expectations. A good explanation shows that the phenomena, contrary to our initial reaction, was bound to occur.

The pragmatic problem this presupposition of the why-question raises in the baseball studies is that the call for explanation is *incompatible* with the experimenters favored account. The regression or chance account explains the alteration observed only by denying the presupposition of the question that there is either significant discrepancy in early/late baseball batting averages or in a "sophomore slump"– a strikingly unexpected decline in the sophomore year of baseball players who do outstandingly well their freshman year. It is plausible that the formal incompatibility generates a psychological barrier to, or bias against, the chance or regression account, which plays a role in explaining the results. But the arguments and certainly the evidence for this conclusion are inconclusive.

The chance or regression answer is presuppositionally incompatible with any of the subjects' answers, so that a reformulation strategy like those adopted by Hilton (1990) and Kahneman and Miller (2002) is unlikely to move subjects to the sought for – chance – response. Reformulations that closely adhere to the above models by altering the location of stress include:

1a.   After the first two weeks of the baseball season, the leader has a batting average that is over .450. Yet, no batter ever finishes a season with a better than .450 average. What do you think is the most likely explanation for the fact that *batting averages* are higher early in the season?

2a.   Why did [baseball] *rookie Smith*, who did so well his freshman year ("rookie of the year"), do so much worse his second year?

Other reformulations are clearly possible to move the stress or emphasis, and so focus, elsewhere. Still, in the absence of any further context, these reformulations either do not make much sense or they are misleading. To place stress on Smith [in 2a] falsely implicates that the poorer showing is special to him, an issue to which I return below. In any case, neither of these reformulations, nor others that simply alter focus, are likely to yield a dominant shift to a regression or law of large numbers explanation. Compare them to the following heavy-handed reformulations:

1b.   After the first two weeks of the baseball season the leader has a batting average that is over .450. Yet, no batter ever finishes a season with a better than .450 average. Is this surprising? However you answer the previous question, what do you think is the most likely explanation for the fact that the average of the leading batter is so much higher early in the season than at the end?

2b.   Rookie Smith, who did so well his freshman year ("rookie of the year"), did much worse his second year.

Q: "Whether this is surprising [unexpected] or not, how do you explain it?"

These alternative questions are more promising than the previous ones [1a/2a] to impose hurdles to the subjects' standard responses, rather than an admission that one does not know. They are also likely, though much less so, to elicit the chance or regression response. However, these reformulations [1b/2b] are more intrusive and extreme than the previous ones, which merely shift focus. They attempt to neutralize key presuppositions, undermining the appropriateness

of asking the respective questions. Because of this confound and for a number of related reasons, which I pursue, even if the promise of these reformulations are empirically confirmed, they provide little support for a deflationary claim.

4. Reformulation: Light and Heavy-Handed

These last reformulations [1b/2b] do not merely generate a different focus than the original ones, they emphasize that focus, as with the studies that Hilton (1990) discusses, which depend on the overt "in particular." These heavy-handed reformulations raise doubts about the pragmatic equivalence to either the original or, more crucially, to the natural way of asking the intended question, even if unavoidable with written instructions. To make sense of the "in particular" subjects are compelled toward the desired focus. The directing of focus does not correspond to the easy and implicit way that it is normally realized, even if requiring some contrivance or awkwardness (e.g., switching to the passive voice). In the opening examples, for comparison, shifts in focus arose from minor differences in formulation or stress.

A different study helps to sharpen the concern. In a recent article, Johnson-Laird reports (2005: 201) on the following problem:

If a pilot falls from a plane without a parachute, the pilot dies. This pilot did not die, however. Why not?

Most people respond, for example, that

The plane was on the ground.

The pilot fell into a deep snow drift.

Only a minority draws the logically valid conclusion:

The pilot did not fall from the plane without a parachute.

After presenting the example, Johnson-Laird comments:

Hence, people prefer a causal explanation repudiating the first premise to a valid deduction, albeit they may presuppose that the antecedent of the conditional is true. Granted that knowledge usually takes precedence over contradictory assertions; the explanatory mechanism should dominate the ability to make deductions. (Johnson-Laird 2005: 201)

Johnson-Laird's why-not question presupposes both that the pilot did not die and crucially that his not dying calls for explanation.[6] The subjects' answers accept the latter presupposition, while a "valid conclusion" answer would reject it. Clearly, if the pilot did fall with a parachute, there is no call to explain his not dying.

One simple reformulation would alter focus by a shift in stress:

3. If a pilot falls from a plane without a parachute, the pilot dies. This pilot did not die, however. Why not?

With sufficient stress, I expect that subjects will be moved to shift their answers to the explaining-away (presupposition-rejecting) response: "The pilot did not fall from the plane without a parachute." But even if so, we are not inclined to draw a deflationary conclusion. The alteration in stress cues subjects to a conditional reading of the "if" clause, whereas subjects seem to be treating it more as a task-demanded supposition (a conditional assertion), responsive to the why-question.

The reformulation strategy is most effective for supporting a deflationary claim as the reformulation is the more minimal. The danger of heavy-handed reformulations for a deflationary end is reminiscent of the obvious difficulty that Socrates' leading questions to the slave-boy in the *Meno* (Plato 1981) pose. Socrates intends to show that the slave-boy innately knows how much one must increase the sides of a square to double its area. Socrates draws the crucial geometrical model and his questions guide the slave-boy to just the relevant observations of the model. But Socrates must claim not to be instructing the slave-boy, which is undermined by his very method.

In our main example, the presupposition of the why-question removes from candidacy a statistical answer. However, the failure of a simple reformulation strategy shows that the statistical answer is not just waiting in the wings for the right elicitation, which raises a question: If a shift in focal attention (to what?) will not elicit a statistical answer, exactly what role does presupposition play? (How do we know presupposition is actually at work in the answers subjects' offer, rather than a general distaste for statistical or chance explanations?) I address the question subsequent to setting out more of the relevant workings of presupposition.

5. Presuppositional Workings: Norms

The presupposition of the why-question of a call for explanation places a chance, statistical, or regression account in a presuppositionally rejected position. The force of presuppositional placement reflects its workings, which are now divided in two: Those due to pragmatic norms, treated in this section, and those due to psychological workings, treated in the next. In both ways, and in an extension of my previous discussion, what is presupposed – such as that the sophomore slump calls for explanation (or that it even exists) – is less available to subjects, and that lesser availability helps to explain subjects' dominant answers.

Presuppositions influence our judgments or inferences as reasons, not mere primes. In studies of dichotic listening, the hearing of one word primes or causally triggers an association that leads to the selection of a matching word from a list without an implied claim that one is the reason for the other (e.g., "basketball," "tall"). Well-known studies by Loftus (1975) and her associates help to clarify the distinction. In one study, subjects view a film. Those who are asked "Did you see the children getting on the school bus?" report having seen a school bus (unlike control groups), although none were present. Did the presupposition of the question that the children get on the school bus influence the subjects' judgment as a presupposition? The result should then be different if the experimenter had first asked "Was there a school bus present?," placing the previous presupposition now in focal position. If the presupposition of the question did play a role as a presupposition, not just as a prime, acceptance of it would be the subjects' reason for judging that they saw the children on the school bus. If, however, it functioned only as a mere prime or causal trigger, as with the dichotic listening studies, the influence should hold even if the experimenter had casually observed "I was late because a school bus got stuck in front of me." The former influence – as a reason and presupposition – should be stronger. Analogously, in the sophomore slump study, the experimenter's question "Why did Rookie Smith . . .?" provides the hearer (subject), who accommodates to it, with a reason to treat Smith's sophomore slump as calling for an explanation.

Introducing a presupposition by a question rather than an assertion is a more subtle way to influence subjects' judgments, since a question questions, it does not state. But in answering a question or accepting an assertion or even in offering a standard challenge "How do you know that p?," the hearer represents himself as endorsing the presupposition. Yet, the speaker claims the truth of what he asserts, not what he presupposes.[7]

However, the norms of presupposition, like other conversational norms, can be violated, as well as denied or challenged. S: "Even Mikey likes Life" (a breakfast cereal). H: "Why do you say 'Even Mikey'? He actually likes a lot of foods." The regular option to challenge a presupposition weakens the usual charge associated with a pragmatic approach to reasoning studies that subjects are misled.

We are familiar with challenges to why-questions by appeal to chance: "Why did the phone company give me a number that is so hard to recall, but they gave my friend Bill one that is so easy?" "There's no why to it. It's just chance." Or, if the roulette wheel comes up red six times in a row, one gambler says to the other, "The roulette wheel must be fixed to favor red. How else do you explain these outcomes?" His buddy responds, "Look, there is no 'why' about it. It's just chance. There are bound to be some runs that involve getting many reds in a row." (A similar presupposition-rejecting response would be appropriate if the friend commits a "gambler's fallacy": "It's now much more likely to come up black next."). Regression provides the basis for a closely related, though less frequent, way to challenge a why-question: "Jim's sisters are both such huge successes, how come he has not done nearly as well?" "But you cannot expect most anyone to match that stand out achievement, even a sibling."

As an implicit denial of the call for an explanation, the presupposition-rejecting response "Look, there is no 'why' to it, it's just chance" expresses our folk understanding. Although our folk understanding leaves room for chance or randomness to be involved in whole or partial explanations, they differ, as indicated, from standard presupposition-accepting ones, which remove puzzlement or perplexity or surprise, usually positing the workings of an underlying mechanism, not, effectively, the denial of one. Correspondingly, there is a conversational difference between reporting on an observation with the implication that it calls for explanation and not so implying.

In particular, only the former achieves, on its surface, relevance for the hearer. If the observa-

tion to which the why-question is directed is not surprising, the speaker lacks a mutually apparent reason to introduce his question. Speakers are expected to report only those observations or beliefs that purport to have some informational value to the hearer. Placing the presupposed fact – that the observation calls for explanation – into a focal position [1b/2b] is in tension with the expectation that reporting the observation will be informative to the hearer (subjects).[8] The why-question innocently misleads subjects to expect that a distinctive mechanism is involved in accounting for the change in performance, rather than a process that implies that the change is insignificant, since only the workings of chance.

Subjects' tacit acceptance of the presupposition (that the baseball phenomena call for a nonchance explanation) is a correlative of the unavailability of the chance account, though, as just noted, we have all had occasion to challenge that kind of presupposition. What kind of unavailability is generated by presupposition in cases like those before us? Why is it generally difficult to challenge presuppositions, though we do so when the contrary beliefs are salient? What are the (further) difficulties specific to explanatory presuppositions?

As noted above, asking someone a question presupposes that he is competent to answer it. The question itself is simply a request for information from another, so that it does not place any restraints on how the informant answers. More basically, presuppositions, especially presuppositions of a question, are difficult to challenge because they appear not to be subject to challenge. They are not asserted and so, recall, do not enter claims, which are a call on attention.

Hearers represent themselves as accepting presuppositions in accepting (or denying) the assertion. Once the hearer has accepted a presupposition, however inadvertently, which he subsequently questions (i.e., he challenges the speaker), he takes back a concession already granted. The hearer thereby admits that he wasted the speaker's time in a kind of pretense, even though misleading himself as well. The dilemma, somewhat like that for complex questions, is that hearers are generally only positioned to challenge a presupposition by accepting the assertion, and thereby the presupposition.

Another barrier to challenging a presupposition is specific to why-questions and its kin, and it is at the historical root of the discussion of presupposition: The natural reading of the why-p question is contrastive (an internal negation): "Why did Smith do so much worse his second year, *rather than the same or better?*" The implied contrastive contraries nevertheless share the presupposition that it is a fact that Smith's performance changed unexpectedly. The question then appears to exhaust the field, as if the alternative is the contradictory (an external negation), leaving no room for an option that rejects the presupposition.

A different barrier is the norm of politeness, which is a way to avoid the speaker's "losing face," and thus a way to promote cooperation (Brown and Levinson 1978). The politeness involved is the routine kind, as in stating requests as questions, which operate best as habitual or automatic. To challenge a presupposition is to challenge the speaker's entitlement to enter the assertion. In the "Emperor's New Clothes," challenging the Emperor's statements and questions ("What do you think of my robe?") threatens impoliteness in two ways, leaving aside that he is Emperor: To challenge his presupposition that he is wearing clothes is more of a rebuke than challenging the focal matter of their quality, and the more evident the falsity of what a speaker says, the harsher the challenge that calls attention to it.

Finally, presuppositions are sometimes taken for granted not because of their presumed evident truth, but because of their insignificance relative to what the speaker intends to communicate. In these cases, to deny a presupposition is either to be obtuse to the speaker's intended communicative purpose or to be a stickler. To adapt a well-known example: At a party, you and the hearer are looking in the same direction. You say of the person that you are gesturing toward, "The man drinking the martini is a spy." The actual content of this "referential use" of the presupposition that the man is drinking a martini is unimportant, so long as it succeeds at yielding attention to the intended man. If the hearer believes that the man is drinking water and he offers that belief as the basis to challenge the speaker's presupposition, he would either miss the speaker's obvious main point (that the man is a spy), or else, he is playing the stickler, whose challenge just interferes with communicative purposes.

6. Presuppositional Workings: Attention

The pragmatic and normative obstacles are presumably best enforced or learned by coming to operate as habits. Focus undermines availability by placing presuppositions in the background, diminishing the burdens on the "scarce resource" of attention (Kahneman 1973), providing an effortless mechanism to maintain the pragmatic norms. You avoid the temptation to violate a norm, if you do not notice opportunities for violation. The presupposition of a call for explanation removes a chance or regression answer from even candidacy to answer the why-questions, merely as a by-product of focus elsewhere.

The key pragmatic difference between what a speaker presupposes and what he asserts is also the key psychological difference – a speaker *claims* the truth only of what he asserts, not what he presupposes. Presuppositions are more difficult than the corresponding focal assertions to *recognize* as open to denial or to challenge than the focal assertion. Lewis (1983) extends something like Grice's cooperative principle to presuppositions:

it's not as easy as you might think to say something that will be unacceptable for lack of required presuppositions. Say something that requires a missing presupposition, and straightaway that presupposition springs into existence ... (234; for related discussion see essays 1 and 2 in Stalnaker 1999, including presupposition as mainly pragmatic and psychological, not semantic, phenomena).

In the previous example, if I assert "Even Mikey likes *Life*", and you have no reason to doubt it, as when you do not know Mikey well, then "straightaway" you accept that Mikey is antecedently unlikely to like *Life*, rather than place the burden on the speaker to provide evidence. The accommodation by hearers to speakers' presuppositions is standardly automatic and nonconscious. Nevertheless, it counts as an endorsement or commitment or some similar positive normative judgment, since the presupposition is comprehended and it goes unchallenged. Not to say "no," given the governing default norms, is to acquiesce to "yes."

The psychological operation fits with Gestalt principles for organizing a perceptual field into a foreground against an unnoticed background, which, nevertheless, serves to highlight and orient the perceiver to what is foreground. Speakers' presuppositions are to be treated as background, yet they may amount to new information for the hearer. If I say, "My guru is coming for dinner," I presuppose that I have a guru, and by so doing, I may intend to convey new information to the audience (Stalnaker 1999: 49–52).[9]

One Gestalt-like reason to expect self-other asymmetries in attribution is a difference in perceptual salience: To understand others' actions, we view the individuals as prominent against a background of circumstances, whereas the reverse is true for our own actions (the circumstances eliciting the actions is more prominent). Research on the role of attention in visual perception, as well as in verbal comprehension, shows the narrowness of attention compared to what is processed. Even Pylyshyn (2003: Ch. 4), an enemy of top-down penetration of visual perception, allows that cognition can affect early vision by selectively directing visual process. "Dichotic presentations" in tests of verbal comprehension show that information in "rejected" channels affects interpretation in the accepted channel (Lackner and Garrett 1972).

A first stop in trying to locate presuppositional inattention among research on selective perception or "inattentional blindness" (Mack and Rock 1998) is with "change blindness," in which substantial and meaningful, but nonprominent, objects are missed. They are either unseen or, more plausibly, seen but inaccessible to working memory or to reporting. Unsurprisingly, but still significantly here, more severe change blindness is found with alterations in the scene's background than in the foreground, even when the changes in the background are more extensive. Also, semantic priming can reduce change blindness (Turatto, Angrill, Mazza, Umilta, and Driver 2002). However, unlike for change blindness (or "blindsight"), presuppositional inattention escapes notice within the domain of what is comprehended and accessible.

A better model is provided by the following unremarkable vignette: About a half-hour after leaving a restaurant, I suddenly and vividly realized that I left the restaurant with the bill unsigned and my credit card on the table. I comprehended these items on the table when I was in the restaurant, otherwise I could not have so vividly recovered them from memory. The model, though better, is still very imperfect. In the studies, attention is directed toward the task and its content, whereas in the restaurant scenario there is no external or explicit directing of attention at all. The memory just pops back due, presumably, to some haphazard cue or stimulus. In this respect, the restaurant scenario is the more realistic (and the more appropriate model for evaluation of pragmatic influences). No one

is selecting information for you to comprehend, setting you a task based on that information, and eliciting an answer.

This disparity between focal attention and cognitive illusions can be obscured by comparisons between the coexistence of knowledge and perception in perceptual illusions like the Mueller-Lyer illusion (Sloman 2002). Ordinarily, although you know about the Mueller-Lyer illusion, no one tells you that right now you are looking at a Mueller-Lyer pair embedded in a natural context. When you are not given advance preparation and you are asked: What are their relative sizes? You answer that one is much larger than the other. You do not experience any conflict.

The workings of attention induced by presupposition apply to other studies, like those on base rates. But such applications suggest a conflict. In a recent article, Kahneman and Frederick (2005) observe that in the Kahneman and Tversky studies (on base rates 1982b and conjunction Tversky and Kahneman 2002), the information favoring an alternative analysis was not always presented in a "subtle" way, but in a pointed way. Yet, subjects still ignore it:

> The engineer-lawyer problem (Kahneman and Tversky, 1973) included special instructions to ensure that respondents would notice the base rates of the outcomes. The brief personality descriptions shown to respondents were reported to have been drawn from a set containing descriptions of 30 lawyers and 70 engineers (or vice versa), and respondents were asked 'What is the probability that this description belongs to one of the 30 lawyers in the sample of 100?' To the authors' surprise, base rates were largely neglected in the responses, despite their salience in the instructions. Similarly, the authors were later shocked to discover that more than 80% of undergraduates committed a conjunction error even when asked point blank whether Linda was more likely to be 'a bank teller' or 'a bank teller who is active in the feminist movement' (Tversky and Kahneman 1983). The novelty of these additional direct or 'transparent' tests was the finding that respondents continued to show the biases associated with representativeness even in the presence of strong cues pointing to the normative response. (276)

(In the section called "transparent tests" for the "Linda" conjunction study, a majority of subjects do not convert to the "bank teller" answer, though a substantial number change, when Tversky and Kahneman offer an explicit argument that every feminist bank teller is a bank teller, but not conversely [1983/2002].)

One way of expressing the compatibility of Kahneman and Frederick's (2005) claim with my proposals is that they are concerned with the explicitness of the information presented to subjects, in order to study how strong are the heuristics influencing subjects. My concern is with the organization of the information, which determines what is background (unnoticed) and focal, as well as the sources that promote this organization. (The organization would be pointless if we were Cartesian minds, where all thoughts and their components are equally in awareness.) Presuppositional inattention presumes comprehension, so that it is obviously compatible with a "transparent" presentation.

Presuppositional structuring is necessary to keep linguistic communication from demanding too much. For, at its most basic, linguistic communication is a directive to hearers to focus attention on the speaker's contribution to recover his communicative intention. To lessen the demands on attention, a good amount of what is linguistically communicated, as through implicature, is implicit. It draws on what is presupposed or placed in the background. Since its working in informing comprehension must be largely automatic and non-conscious, implicitness is easily exploited, as with the child's joke, "How many animals of each kind did Moses take on the ark?" (Erikson and Mattson 1981; Reder and Cleeremans 1990 observe that people notice the false information when "Moses" is placed in focal position, although their reformulation involves other alterations: "Was it Moses who took two animals of each kind on the ark?").

We exploit the great breadth of consciousness or attention in very different mental activities. We manipulate our focus and attention in such ordinary activities as reading literature or watching TV or movies. We make-believe, mentally bracketing our knowledge that the story is fictional to absorb ourselves psychologically and emotionally in the story. We know that whenever we need to, we can end the bracketing, although sometimes we bracket so well as to convince (deceive) ourselves. The townsfolk in 'The Emperor's New Clothes' seek to avoid the affront to the Emperor by positioning themselves not to notice that he is naked, which, of course, requires that they do already notice that he is naked. They must deceive themselves

otherwise including that they are attempting to deceive themselves.

In both the treatment of norms of presupposition and in their workings, I have noted various ways in which presuppositions strength is variable and subject to our intervention. Hilton (1990) and Kahneman and Miller (2002) do not address the strength of presuppositions or focus. I suspect it is because the workings are largely automatic and nonconscious. They then consign the operation to the broad category of "outside our control." However, while presuppositions do work that way, the possibility of challenge or denial remains as part of those workings. The treatment of presuppositions as outside our control is also misleading. The treatment obscures normative and psychological sources of resistance to challenges: Despite its normal nonconscious workings, what is presupposed by a hearer in accepting a question, garners thereby, although tacitly, his positive evaluation, as is true of the original perplexity – to deny a statement containing a presupposition is to represent oneself as endorsing it.

7. Reinforcement and Understanding: Pragmatics over Time

A central aim in the previous sections is to show that pragmatics can have a role in explaining the results on studies of reasoning – specifically, studies of explanatory reasoning about sets of events governed by the law of large numbers and regression – without that role supporting a deflationary claim, particularly one justified by a reformulation strategy. A thoroughgoing attempt to invoke pragmatics to explain away the critical import of the reasoning studies is implausible, since the results of very different experiments converge. In a range of studies, an unobtrusive reformulation strategy is not readily available or it meets with only limited success (e.g., the base rate and conjunction studies). Also, over many of these studies, Stanovich (1999) has developed insights as to systematic individual differences correlated with greater intelligence for those who provide the favored answer.

The pragmatics of why-questions imposes a barrier to recognizing an alternative (statistical) answer and to placing in focal position the assumptions informing subjects' answers. The workings, as largely appearing successful and so confirming those assumptions, reinforce a weak or poor understanding of statistical influences.

In defending these claims, I complete an answer to a dilemma for my account: If subjects do shift answers with the (b) variations, then either the pattern follows the previous examples (from Hilton [1990] and Kahneman and Miller [2002]), which supports a deflationary claim or else, it is due to the posing of "leading questions." Because the latter strongly cues subjects, it diminishes the value of the study for investigating subjects' understanding of the law of large numbers or regression. If, instead, subjects do not shift answers markedly toward a statistical one, the failing undermines the role accorded to presupposition/focus in accounting for subjects' erroneous responses.

I reject both horns. Subjects are moved away from their non-chance explanations, but not due to simple shifts of attention. The role for attention is intertwined with difficulties in understanding, rather than an alternative to it. The intertwining is a result of a regular presupposition-rejecting position for chance, statistical, or regression accounts of a phenomena.

The claim of poor understanding holds only if the scope of one's application of a rule or a principle is a facet of one's competence with that rule or principle, when there is no external interference. A decent, if informal, understanding of regression or the law of large numbers should itself cue subjects to override various intuitive or familiar solutions. There is nothing deviant when an unusually good performance is followed by a much worse one, and, in fact, the contrary is expected, as holds for extreme values in small samples. I grant that the workings of focal attention direct subjects away from a chance account, and to that extent, excuse their erroneous answers. But so what? The poor understanding remains. There is no implication, unlike for those cases where the reformulation strategy clearly succeeds and supports a deflationary claim, that merely bringing the presupposition to focal attention will elicit the statistical explanation.

Given the previous discussion of the presupposition of why-questions, I will lay out these further claims in steps that guide this closing section:

(1)   The presuppositions and related assumptions that inform and mislead subjects' judgments, even if conversationally appropriate given the why-question, are unlikely to yield predictions (expectations) that noticeably falsify or bring criti-

cal attention to these assumptions for one important reason.

(2)   A cooperative world facilitates their inferential and predictive success. Even when these assumptions misguide, they are not in a position to be targeted for the failings.

(3)   The positioning of these assumptions away from falsification or critical attention is a regular product of pragmatics, not due to a particular, labile, formulation, so it is likely to affect thought or understanding generally, not restricted to conversation.

(4)   Since the directing away from a chance explanation follows from what are presumed to be rational rules of conversation that are not conducive to clean falsification and which are not themselves recognized as playing this role [1], and the positioning is pervasive in our activities [2], there is reinforcement of the reasoning, assumptions, and pragmatics guiding subjects' answers.

(5)   Reinforcing the underlying assumptions and practice informing those answers fosters or reinforces a poor understanding of chance or probability, including an illusory sense of understanding.

Since the explanations subjects' provide as answers fail, why doesn't experience or feedback teach us otherwise, when accordingly our reasoning does fail?[10] Why doesn't faulty explanations produce errors, so that we would learn either that chance does explain (or explainaway) or that the assumption that a phenomena calls for explanation can be challenged, or that questions, particularly why-questions, bias or restrict candidate answers? Why can't the potential offense or harm to conversational practice of entering a statistical challenge be neutralized by qualification in the privacy of the mind for what it is problematic (to recognize or impolite) to assert? (For discussions of these questions, though not centering on explanation, pragmatics, and chance, see Nisbett and Ross 1980: Ch. 11; Bishop and Trout 2005: Ch. 2).

Even when assumptions lead to errors, failure is not enough to improve one's understanding. The errors must be noticeable (as errors) with the subject recognizing the source of the error. The difficulty of achieving these realizations is already indicated by the problems of attention that are consequent on the pragmatics involved, as well as the workings of belief. Falsification motivates learning only if vivid. But for the ascription of traits or responsibility, the most available source of potential falsification is the judgment of others in one's social group, not a rigorous testing ground. For the why-questions directed to the baseball disparities (early/late averages; freshman/sophomore performance), none of the candidate answers is at all likely to lead to an everyday inquiry or comparisons that would expose the failing, as in controlled studies. If a particular baseball player did do as well the next year that will hardly count as falsification of the obviously rough explanations that subjects provide. When a failure to appreciate the role of chance does impact on your actions – why did my son do so exceptionally well in school his freshman year and much less well his second – the connection with how one judges in a very different domain, like those about batting averages in baseball, is not yet illuminated or invited, unless one is antecedently motivated to generalize about the failure (to express it as a principle or to discover its causes).

A related conceptual barrier to an invitation for a statistical explanation is that subjects' (nonstatistical) answers claim completeness. Subjects present their answers, like that success made the player too cocky, so as to implicitly claim that they have fully explained the sophomore slump. Even when their correlative predictions noticeably fail, it will not implicate a chance explanation, rather than one of the competing, presupposition-accepting, explanations. The presupposition that rejects the chance account holds of each of the contrary candidate answers. In the studies presented in Hilton (1990) and Kahneman and Miller (2002), their reformulations are compatible with the basic presupposition of a why-question (of something calling for explanation because it is puzzling, deviant, unexpected, etc.). Correspondingly, subjects' answers, as responding to differently focused questions, are complementary. To refer back to the opening illustration, if you know that Jim and Mary greet each other by kissing, you learn more when you learn that among Jim, Tony, and Jane only Jim and Mary are socially close enough to greet by kissing. You now have more facets of an understanding of why Jim kissed Mary rather than not.

The prospects for noticeable falsification are weakened further according to the third claim above:

The positioning of these assumptions away from falsification or critical attention is a regular product of pragmatics . . . and a common occurrence given that conversation and explanatory interests are pervasive activities . . .

Why-questions or their cognates are common, reflecting our immense curiosity and interest in understanding (Keil and Wilson 2000).[11] Nisbett and Ross (1980) report on a study of a wide variety of conversations in which "Statements expressing or requesting causal analysis [explanations] were remarkably frequent, accounting for 15 percent, on the average, of all utterances" (184). This commonness is especially unsurprising given the interrelations of explanation and reasons: If A (e.g., to buy a ice cream cone) is X's reason to do C (e.g., to go to the ice cream store), then A explains why X went to the ice cream store. (The connection does not require the reasons to be that of an agent: The reason that the glass broke is that it fell off the counter. Then the explanation of why the glass broke is that it fell off the counter.) Under realistic conditions of a not markedly uncooperative world, there seems to be an advantage in having a workable explanation to provide guidance and confidence to act and to speak, even though (recognized) ignorance is usually much better than false belief.

In the recent survey article referred to earlier, Johnson-Laird (2005) refers to a study (with Anderson) that shows our great "propensity to explain":

The participants received pairs of sentences selected *at random* from separate stories:
John made his way to a shop that sold TV sets.
Celia had recently had her ears pierced.
In another condition, the sentences were modified to make them coreferential:
Celia made her way to a shop that sold TV sets.
She had recently had her ears pierced.

The participants' task was to explain what was going on. They readily went beyond the given information to account for what was happening. They proposed, for example, that Celia was getting reception in her earrings and wanted the TV shop to investigate, that she wanted to see some new earring on closed circuit TV, that she had won a bet by having her ears pierced and was spending the money on a TV set, and so on. Only rarely were the participants stumped for an explanation. They were almost as equally ingenious with the sentences that were not co-referential. (Johnson-Laird 2005: 201)

Why-questions motivate inquiry, a source for acquiring new beliefs. Their call for explanation satisfies on its surface the conversational expectation of relevance. However, the problematic lesson then taught is that, except where special justification is introduced, small samples, vivid cases, and uncharacteristic performances are more common as conversational contributions than the contrary (what is normal or expected or familiar). You will more readily notice and you will more readily comment to others on bad service at a favorite restaurant rather than another instance of their consistently good service.

What is communicated implicitly with these contributions is that the occurrences reported are important or significant – they are worth attending to. Yet, if a reported phenomena is really just the expected consequences of the law of large numbers or regression, it is a product of random factors of little further informative value. The bad service at this meal pales in significance compared to the underlying quality control mechanisms that provide for the otherwise unremarkable expectation of a high level of service.

The pragmatic norms render it difficult to block these implications, as we found for the various reformulation strategies ((a), (b) above). In particular, in the case of the heavy-handed (b) reformulations, the why-question secures relevance and informativeness only if the presupposed call for explanation stands. If the observation to which the why-question is directed does not call for explanation, there is loss of point for asking the hearer to explain it, as with "Why did a 3-side turn up when I rolled the die?"

For presuppositions, specifically, we should expect to run into problems of relevance since, as Grice (1989) observed, they are neither detachable (via reformulation) nor cancelable, unlike standard conversational implicatures.[12] To place stress on Smith [in 1a] falsely implicates that the poorer showing is special to him (and analogously, for stress on his sophomore year). In the [b] cases ("Is this surprising? . . . "), the attempt is to eliminate any presuppositional bias. But the cost is wordiness and a burden on comprehension, which will be construed as attempting to do more than merely shift focus, normally accomplished with little burden (Grice 1989: 27; Sperber and Wilson 1986). The reformulations (b) just introduced are odd, anyway, since if the experimenter knows that the phenomena is surprising, he should state it in the standard, briefer presuppositional form as earlier ([1] and [2]). If, however, he does not know even that it is surprising, how is it that I – the subject – am to know?

A related, but more pertinent, problem is noted above: to introduce the "Is this surprising?" question or the "whether or not it is surprising" disclaimer interferes with the aim of discovering the subjects' assumptions. It also lacks the overt relevance of the original question for raising a puzzle that a speaker is asked to resolve. (Of course, we are all familiar with institutional settings, where this presupposition fails. In schools, teachers ask students questions, where it is expected that the teacher does already know the answer. But, on this reading, the task would be a kind of pretense.)

The reinforcement role of pragmatics in supporting both a valuable conversational practice and yet, a poor understanding, answers a worry that the connection posited between presuppositional inattention and why-questions risks tautology: If you don't understand an activity (e.g., American football), you are not going to attend to – notice – an action defined by that activity, at least as so described, even if looking right at it (e.g., a strong left side tackle sweep). If your judgment (implicitly) excludes a kind of answer to a problem, isn't it self-evident that you will not attend to such a candidate answer (so described), even if right before you? (In change blindness, the converse is unsurprisingly found: the more you know of a subject, the less susceptible you are to change blindness in alterations within the domain of that subject; see Werner and Ties 2000).

There is a further, deeper concern that cannot be answered without empirical investigation.[13] Statistical explanations might be disfavored compared to more familiar mechanical ones generally, antecedent to any conversational role. Ahn et al. (1995) found that if subjects are asked to raise questions themselves to elicit information as to why an event took place (e.g., Margie did not dance the tango at the party), their questions refer much more to mechanisms (e.g., did Margie have a sore foot?), rather than to statistical ones, in particular, attributional ones about consensus (e.g., did others not dance the tango?). I already conceded that the presuppositional role posited here is not the usual kind where a different focus (via a reformulation strategy) will immediately bring a statistical explanation forward.

The additional response now available, admittedly partial and waiting on empirical testing, is that the influence of pragmatics proposed is not primarily to single cases. The influence is long term, affecting the understanding of the law of large numbers, regression, and related matters of chance in everyday circumstances, where understanding includes sensitivity to scope of application.

Although a major theme is the long-term reinforcement of poor understanding and misleading assumptions, rooted in necessities of practice, common habits, and a "cooperative" world, there is no pessimism that follows about possibilities for improvement (Jepson et al. 1983, along with the companion studies and Fong et al. 1986, are motivated by [promising] efforts to improve statistical thinking. Those with statistical knowledge were intended to be excluded from the Jepson et al. 1983 study.) Since the poor understanding is supported by a natural division between what is background and what is foreground, there is an opening for learning, whereby what has been backgrounded through presupposition is brought to attentional focus, even if not merely through reformulations.

Notes

1   Thanks to Catherine Z. Elgin Georges Rey, and Lance J. Rips for very valuable comments.

2   On the model of Geurts and van der Sandt (2004), focus generates a background, which becomes the presupposition. The presupposition-focus difference applies well beyond why-questions, e.g., "When did John come home?" focuses the hearer on the time that the presupposed fact occurred. Also, of course, not all explanatory requests take the form of why-questions and not all why-question expressions are communicated as seeking explanations, e.g., "Why do I have to tell you again to clean your room?"

3   See also Stenning and van Lambalgen 2004; Stenning et al. 2006: Ch. 3 on how pragmatics and interpretation introduce complexities in drawing conclusions from empirical studies of weaknesses in subjects' reasoning particularly in logical tasks.

4   On cross-cultural variation in attribution, see Nisbett et al. 2001.

5   Not all why-questions have this pragmatic feature. Consider a model question for introducing Plato's theory of forms as an answer: "Why is the painting, the supermodel, and the sunset all rightly called 'beautiful'?" But it is plausibly objected that this question attempts to generate a perplexity, where none exists. One traditional – nominalist – answer is simply that each one of those objects or phenomena is beautiful.

6   However, there is a difficulty: The "why not" question seems to induce a "suppose" rather than a pure "if" reading of the opening conditional.

7   The latter is tightly related to the former, on some views coindexed to it. See Geurts and van der Sandt (2004).

8   On the significance of a phenomena calling for explanation for the "stability" of an explanation, see Garfinkel 1981; White 2005.

9   For a similar observation, concluding that the requirement is that the "supposition" is noncontroversial, rather than common knowledge, see Grice 1989: 274. Even in relation to explicit questions, one's asking of a question may effectively be to enter an assertion, rather than presupposing it, e.g., "Did you hear that Johnson was fired?"

10 Bishop and Trout (2005) formulate the following ("Aristotelian") sensible principle:

    in the long run, poor reasoning tends to lead to worse outcomes than good reasoning. (20)

11 Levinson (1995) writes:

    We see design in randomness, think we can detect signals from outer space in stellar X-rays, suspect some doodles on archaeological artifacts to constitute an undiscovered code, detect hidden structure in Amazonian myths. If we are attuned to think that way, then that is perhaps further evidence for the biases of interactional intelligence: in the interactional arena, we must take all behaviour to be specifically designed to reveal its intentional source. (245)

12 The pragmatic issues of presupposition that apply here do not fall snugly under Grice's cases of a clash of maxims. Gricean clashes are always resolvable so as to facilitate realization of communicative intent, which is not so in the cases that concern us.

13 Raised by Lance J. Rips.

References

Abraham, C. (1988) "The Connection in Lay Causal Comprehension: A Return to Heider." In Hilton (1988): 145–175.

Ahn, W., Kalish, C., Medin, D., and Gelman, S. (1995) "The Role of Covariation versus Mechanism Information in Causal Attribution." *Cognition* 54: 299–352.

Bishop, M., and Trout, J. D. (2005) *Epistemology and the Psychology of Human Judgment* (Oxford: Oxford University Press).

Brown, R., and Fish, D. (1983) "The Psychological Causality Implicit in Language." *Cognition* 14: 237–273.

Brown, P., and Levinson, S. (1978) "Universals in Language Usage: Politeness Phenomena." In E. Goody, ed. *Questions and Politeness* Cambridge: Cambridge University Press: 56–311.

Donaldson, M. (1978) *Children's Minds* (New York: W. W. Norton & Co.).

Dretske, F. (1972) "Contrastive Statements." *Philosophical Review* 81: 411–437.

Erikson, T. A., and Mattson, R. E. (1981) "From Words to Meaning: A Semantic Illusion." *Journal of Verbal Learning and Verbal Behavior* 20: 540–552.

Evans, J. St. B. T., and Feeny, A. (2004) "The Role of Prior Belief in Reasoning." In Leighton and Sternberg, eds.: 78–102.

Fong, G. T., Krantz, D. H., and Nisbett, R. E. (1986) "The Effects of Statistical Training on Thinking about Everyday Problems." *Cognitive Psychology* 18: 253–292.

Funder, D. C. (1987) "Errors and Mistakes: Evaluating the Accuracy of Social Judgment." *Psychological Bulletin* 101: 75–90.

Garfinkel, A. (1981) *Forms of Explanation* (New Haven, CT: Yale University Press).

Geurts, B., and van der Sandt, R. (2004) "Interpreting Focus." *Theoretical Linguistics* 30: 1–44.

Gilovich, T., Griffin, D., and Kahneman, D. (2002) *Heuristics and Biases: The Psychology of Intuitive Judgment* (Cambridge: Cambridge University Press).

Gould, S. J. (1991) *Bully for Brontosaurus* (New York: Norton).

Grice, P. (1989) *Studies in the Way of Words* (Cambridge, MA: Harvard University Press).

Hilton, D. J. (1988) "Logic and Causal Attribution." In his *Contemporary Science and Natural Explanation*: 33–65.

———. ed. (1988) *Contemporary Science and Natural Explanation: Commonsense Conceptions of Causality* (New York: New York University Press).

———. (1990) "Conversational Processes and Causal Explanation." *Psychological Bulletin* 107: 65–81.

Holyoak, K. J., and Morrison, R. G. (2005) *The Cambridge Handbook of Thinking and Reasoning* (Cambridge: Cambridge University Press).

Jepson, C., Krantz, D. H., and Nisbett, R. E. (1983) "Inductive Reasoning: Competence or Skill?" *Behavioral and Brain Sciences* 6: 494–501.

Johnson-Laird, P. N. (2005) Mental Models and Thought. In Holyoak and Morrison, eds.: 185–208.

Kahneman. D. (1973) *Attention and Effort* (Englewood-Cliffs, NJ: Prentice Hall).

Kahneman, D., and Frederick, S. (2005) "A Model of Heuristic Judgment." In *The Cambridge Handbook of Thinking and Reasoning*: 267–293.

Kahneman, D., and Miller, D. T. (2002) "Norm Theory: Comparing Reality to Its Alternatives." In *Heuristics and Biases*, Gilovich, Griffin, and Kahneman, eds.: 348–366.

Kahneman, D. Slovic, D., and Tversky, D., eds. (1982) *Judgment under Uncertainty: Heuristics and Biases* (Cambridge: Cambridge University Press).

Kahneman, D., and Tversky, A. (1982a) "On the Psychology of Prediction." In Kahneman, Slovic, and Tversky, eds.: 48–68.

———. (1982b) "Subjective Probability: A Judgment of Representativeness." In Kahneman, Slovic, and Tversky, eds.: 32–47.

———. (1982c) "On the Study of Statistical Intuitions." In Kahneman, Slovic, and Tversky, eds.: 493–508.

Keil, F. C., and Wilson, R. A., eds. (2000) *Explanation and Cognition* (Cambridge, MA: MIT Press).

Kuhn, D. (1991) *The Skills of Argument* (Cambridge: Cambridge University Press).

Lackner, J. R., and Garret, M. F. (1972) "Resolving Ambiguity: Effects of Biasing Context in the Unattended Ear." *Cognition* 1: 359–372.

Leighton, J. P., and Sternberg, R. J., eds. (2004) *The Nature of Reasoning* (Cambridge: Cambridge University Press.

Levinson, S. C. (1995) "Interactional Biases in Human Thinking." In E. Goody, ed., *Social Intelligence and Interaction* Cambridge, UK: Cambridge University Press 221–260.

Lewis, D. (1983) "Scorekeeping in a Language-Game" in his *Philosophical Papers Vol. I* (Oxford: Oxford University Press): 233–249.

Lipton, P. (2004) *Inference to the Best Explanation*, Second Edition (London: Routledge).

Loftus, E. F. (1975) "Leading Questions and the Eyewitness Report." *Cognitive Psychology* 7: 560–572.

Mack, A., and Rock, I. (1998) *Inattentional Blindness* (Cambridge, MA: MIT Press).

McArthur, L. A. (1972) "The How and What of Why: Some Determinants and Consequences of Causal Attribution." *Journal of Personality and Social Psychology* 22: 171–193.

McGill, A. L. (1989) "Context Effects in Judgments of Causation." *Journal of Personality and Social Psychology* 57: 189–200.

Nisbett, R. E., Krantz, D. H., Jepson, C., and Kunda, Z. (2002) "The Use of Statistical Heuristics in Everyday Inductive Reasoning." In *Heuristics and Biases*, Gilovich, Griffin, and Kahneman, eds.: 510–533.

Nisbett, R. E., Peng, K., Choi, I., and Norenzayan, A. (2001) "Culture and Systems of Thought: Holistic vs. Analytic Cognition." *Psychological Review* 108: 291–310.

Nisbett, R., and Ross, L. (1980) *Human Inference: Strategies and Shortcomings of Social Judgment* (Englewood Cliffs, NJ: Prentice Hall).

Nozick, R. (1981) *Philosophical Explanations* (Cambridge, MA: Harvard University Press).

Plato (1981) *Meno* in *Five Dialogues* G. M. A. Grube, translator (Indianapolis: Hackett, 1981).

Pylyshyn, Z. (2003) *Seeing and Visualizing: It's Not What You Think.* (Cambridge, MA: MIT Press).

Reder, L. M., and Cleeremans, A. (1990) "The Role of Partial Matches in Comprehension: The Moses Illusion Revisited." In A. C. Graesser and G. H. Bower, eds., *Inferences and Text Comprehension: The Psychology of Learning and Motivation* 25 (San Diego, CA: Academic Press).

Rips, L. (2002) "Reasoning." In H. F. Pashler (Series Ed.) and D. L. Medin (Vol. Ed.), *Stevens' Handbook of Experimental Psychology: Vol. 2. Cognition* (third ed.). (New York: Wiley).

Schwarz, N. (1996) *Cognition and Communication* (Mahwah, NJ: Erlbaum).

Sloman, S. A. (2002) "Two Systems of Reasoning." In Gilovich et al.: 379–396.

Slovic, P., and Tversky, A. (1974) "Who Accepts Savage's Axioms?" *Behavioral Science* 19:271–296.

Sperber, D., and Wilson, D. (1986) *Relevance: Communication and Cognition* (Cambridge, MA: Harvard University Press).

Stalnaker, R. S. (1999) *Context and Content* (Oxford: Oxford University Press).

Stanovich, K. E. (1999) *Who Is Rational?* (Mahwah, NJ: Erlbaum).

Stanovich, K. E., and West, R. F. (1999) "Discrepancies between Normative and Descriptive Models of Decision Making and the Understanding/ Acceptance Principle." *Cognitive Psychology* 38: 349–385.

Stenning, K., and M. van Lambalgen (2004) "A Little Logic Goes a Long Way: Basing Experiment on Semantic Theory in the Cognitive Science of Conditional Reasoning." *Cognitive Science* 28 (4): 481–529.

Stenning, K., A. Lascarides, J. Calder (2006) *Introduction to Cognition and Communication* (Cambridge, MA: MIT Press).

Turnbull, W., and Slugoski, B. R. (1988) "Conversational and Linguistic Processes in Causal Attribution." In Hilton: 66–93.

Turatto, M., Angrilli, A., Mazza, V., Umilta, C., and Driver, J. (2002) "Looking without Seeing the Background Change: Electrophysiological Correlates of Change Detection During Change Blindness." *Cognition* 84: B1–B10.

Tversky, A. (1977) "Features of Similarity." *Psychological Review* 87: 327–352.

Tversky, A., and Kahneman, D. (1981) "The Framing of Decisions and the Psychology of Choice." *Science* 211: 454–458.

———. (1983/2002) "Extensional versus Intuitive Reasoning: The Conjunction Fallacy in Probability Judgment." In Gilovich, Griffin, and Kahneman, eds.: 19–48. (Original *Psychological Review* 91: 293–315.) (pp. 114–135, Chapter 6, this volume).

Werner, S., and Ties, B. (2000) "Is 'Change Blindness' Attenuated by Domain-Specific Expertise?" *Visual Cognition* 7: 163–174.

White, R. (2005) "Explanation as a Guide to Induction" *Philosophers' Imprint*, available at: www.philosophersimprint.org/005002/, 5: 1–29.

Chapter 37: Further Notes on Logic and Conversation

H. PAUL GRICE

I would like to begin by reformulating, in outline, the position which I took in an earlier article ("Logic and Conversation").[1] I was operating, provisionally, with the idea that, for a large class of utterances, the total significations of an utterance may be regarded as divisible in two different ways. First, one may distinguish, within the total signification, between what is said (in a favored sense) and what is implicated; and second, one may distinguish between what is part of the conventional force (or meaning) of the utterance and what is not. This yields three possible elements – what is said, what is conventionally implicated, and what is nonconventionally implicated – though in a given case one or more of these elements may be lacking: For example, nothing may be said, though there is something which a speaker makes as if to say. Furthermore, what is nonconventionally implicated may be (or again may not be) conversationally implicated. I have suggested a Cooperative Principle and some subordinate maxims, with regard to which I have suggested: (*i*) that they are standardly (though not invariably) observed by participants in a talk exchange; and (*ii*) that the assumptions required in order to maintain the supposition that they are being observed (or so far as is possible observed) either at the level of what is said – or failing that, at the level of what is implicated – are in systematic correspondence with nonconventional implicata of the conversational type.

Before proceeding further, I should like to make one supplementary remark. When I speak of the assumptions required in order to maintain the supposition that the cooperative principle and maxims are being observed on a given occasion, I am thinking of assumptions that are nontrivially required; I do not intend to include, for example, an assumption to the effect that some particular maxim is being observed, or is thought of by the speaker as being observed. This seemingly natural restriction has an interesting consequence with regard to Moore's "paradox." On my account, it will not be true that when I say that *p*, I conversationally implicate that I believe that *p*; for to suppose that I believe that *p* (or 'rather' think of myself as believing that *p*.) is just to suppose that I am observing the first maxim of Quality on this occasion. I think that this consequence is intuitively acceptable; it is not a natural use of language to describe one who has said that *p* as having, for example, "implied," "indicated," or "suggested" that he believes that *p*; the natural thing to say is that he has expressed (or at least purported to express) the belief that *p*. He has of course committed himself, in a certain way, to its being the case that he believes that *p*, and while this commitment is not a case of saying that he believes that *p*, it is bound up, in a special way, with saying that *p*. The nature of the connection will, I hope, become apparent when I say something about the function of the indicative mood.

In response to "Logic and Conversation," I was given in informal discussion an example which seemed to me, as far as it went, to provide a welcome kind of support for the picture I have been presenting, in that it appeared to exhibit a kind of interaction between the members of my list of maxims which I had not foreseen. Suppose that it is generally known that New York and Boston were blacked out last night, and A asks B whether C saw a particular TV program last night. It will be conversationally unobjectionable for B, who knows that C was in New

Reproduced with permission from Grice, H. P. (1978) Further notes on logic and conversation. *Syntax and Semantics*, Vol. 9. pp. 113–127. New York: Academic Press.

York, to reply, *No, he was in a blacked-out city.* B could have said that C was in New York, thereby providing a further piece of just possibly useful or interesting information, but in preferring the phrase *a blacked-out city* he was implicating (by the maxim prescribing relevance) a more appropriate piece of information, namely, why C was prevented from seeing the program. He could have provided both pieces of information by saying, e.g. *He was in New York, which was blacked out*, but the gain would have been insufficient to justify the additional conversational effort.

Rather hurriedly, at the end of "Logic and Conversation," I mentioned five features which I suggested that conversational implicatures must possess, or might be expected to possess. I was not going so far as to suggest that it was possible, in terms of some or all of these features, to devise a decisive test to settle the question whether a conversational implicature is present or not – a test, that is to say, to decide whether a given proposition *p*, which is normally part of the total signification of the utterance of a certain sentence, is on such occasions a conversational (or more generally a nonconventional) implicatum of that utterance, or is, rather, an element in the conventional meaning of the sentence in question. (I express myself loosely, but, I hope, intelligibly.) Indeed I very much doubt whether the features mentioned can be made to provide any such knock-down test, though I am sure that at least some of them are useful as providing a more or less strong prima facie case in favor of the presence of a conversational implicature. But I would say that any such case would at least have to be supported by a demonstration of the way in which what is putatively implicated could have come to be implicated (by a derivation of it from conversational principles and other data); and even this may not be sufficient to provide a decisive distinction between conversational implicature and a case in which what was originally a conversational implicature has become conventionalized.

Let us look at the features in turn. First, nondetachability. It may be remembered that I said that a conversational implicature might be expected to exhibit a fairly high degree of nondetachability insofar as the implicature was carried because of what is said, and not by virtue of the manner of expression. The implicature is nondetachable in so far as it is not possible to find another way of saying the same thing (or approximately the same thing) which simply lacks the implicature. The implicature which attaches to the word *try* exhibits this feature.

One would normally implicate that there was a failure, or some chance of failure, or that someone thinks/thought there to be some chance of failure, if one said *A tried to do x*; this implicature would also be carried if one said *A attempted to do x, A endeavored to do x*, or *A set himself to do x.*

This feature is not a necessary condition of the presence of a conversational implicature, partly because, as stated, it does not appear if the implicature depends on the manner in which what is said has been said, and it is also subject to the limitation that there may be no alternative way of saying what is said, or no way other than one which will introduce peculiarities of manner, e.g. by being artificial or long-winded.

Neither is it a sufficient condition, since the implicatures of utterances which carry presuppositions (if there are such things) (*He has left off beating his wife*) will not be detachable; and should a question arise whether a proposition implied by an utterance is entailed or conversationally implicated, in either case the implication will be nondetachable. Reliance on this feature is effective primarily for distinguishing between certain conventional implicatures and nonconventional implicatures.

Finally, cancellability. You will remember that a putative conversational implicature that *p* is explicitly cancellable if, to the form of words the utterance of which putatively implicates that *p*, it is admissible to add *but not p*, or *I do not mean to imply that p*, and it is contextually cancellable if one can find situations in which the utterance of the form of words would simply not carry the implicature. Now I think that all conversational implicatures, are cancellable, but unfortunately one cannot regard the fulfillment of a cancellability test as decisively establishing the presence of a conversational implicature. One way in which the test may fail is connected with the possibility of using a word or form of words in a loose or relaxed way. Suppose that two people are considering the purchase of a tie which both of them know to be medium green; they look at it in different lights, and say such things as *It is a light green now*, or *It has a touch of blue in it in this light.* STRICTLY (perhaps) it would be correct for them to say *It looks light green now* or *It seems to have a touch of blue in it in this light*, but it would be unnecessary to put in such qualificatory words, since both know (and know that the other knows) that there is no question of a real change of color. A similar linguistic phenomenon attends such words as *see*: If we all know that Macbeth hallucinated, we can quite safely say that Macbeth saw Banquo, even though Banquo was not there to be seen, and we should note conclude from this that an implication of the existence of the object said to be seen is not part of the conventional meaning of the word *see*, nor even (as some have done) that there is one sense of the word *see* which lacks this implication.

Let us consider this point in relation to the word *or*. Suppose that someone were to suggest that the word *or* has a single 'strong' sense, which is such that it is part of the meaning of *A or B* to say (or imply) not only (*i*) that A v B, but also (*ii*) that there is some non-truth-functional reason for accepting that A v B, i.e. that there is some reasonable (though not necessarily conclusive) argument with A v B as conclusion which does not contain one of the disjuncts as a step (does not proceed via *A* or via *B*). Now it would be easy to show that the second of the two suggested conditions is cancellable: I can say to my children at some stage in a treasure hunt, *The prize is either in the garden or in the attic. I know that because I know where I put it, but I'm not going to tell you.* Or I could just say (in the same situation) *The prize is either in the garden or in the attic*, and the situation would be sufficient to apprise the children of the fact that my reason for accepting the disjunction is that I know a particular disjunct to be true. And in neither case would I be implying that there is a non-truth-functional ground, though I am not relying on it; very likely there would not be such a ground. To this objection, the "strong" theorist (about *or*) might try the move "Ah, but when you say *A v B*, without meaning to imply the existence of a non-truth-functional ground you are using *A v B* loosely, in a relaxed way which the nature of the context of utterance makes permissible." At this point, we might (*i*) produce further cancellation cases, which were less amenable to representation as 'loose' uses, e.g. to the appearance of disjunctions as the antecedents of conditionals (*If the prize is either in the garden or in the attic, Johnny will find it first*), (*ii*) point out that to characterize a use as 'loose' carries certain consequence which are unwelcome in this case – if to say *Macbeth saw Banquo* is to speak loosely, then I speak 'under license' from other participants; if someone objects, there is at least some onus on me to speak more strictly. But not even a stickler for correct speech could complain about the utterance (in the described circumstances) of *The prize is either in the garden or in the attic.*

But the strong theorist has another obvious resource: He may say that there are two senses of the word *or*, a strong one and a weak (truth-funcunctional) one, and that all that is shown by the success of the cancellability test is that here the sense employed was the weak one. To counter this suggestion, we might proceed in one or more of the following ways.

1. We might argue that if *or* is to be supposed to possess a strong sense, then it should be possible to suppose it (*or*) to bear this sense in a reasonably wide range of linguistic settings; it ought to be possible, for example, to say *It is not the case that A or B* or *Suppose that A or B*, where what we are denying, or inviting someone to suppose, is that A or B (in the strong sense of *or*). But this, in the examples mentioned, does not seem to be possible; in anything but perhaps a very special case to say *It is not the case that A or B* seems to amount to saying that neither A nor B (that is, cannot be interpreted as based on a denial of the second condition), and to say *Suppose that A or B* seems to amount to inviting someone to suppose merely that one of the two disjuncts is true. A putative second sense of *or* should not be so restricted in regard to linguistic setting as that, and in particular should not be restricted to "unenclosed" occurrences of *A or B* – for these an alternative account (in terms of implicature) is readily available. The strong theorist might meet a part of this attack by holding that the second condition is not to be thought of as part of what is said (or entailed) by saying *A or B*, and so not as something the denial of which would justify the denial of *A or B*; it should rather be thought of as something which is conventionally implicated. And to deny *A or B* might be to implicate that there was some ground for accepting *A or B*. But he is then open to the reply that, if a model case for a word which carries a conventional implicature is *but*, then the negative form *It is not the case that A or B*, if to be thought of as involving *or* in the strong sense, should be an uncomfortable thing to say, since *It is not the case that A but B* is uncomfortable. In any case the nature of conventional implicature needs to be examined before any free use of it, for explanatory purposes, can be indulged in.

2. We might try to convince the strong theorist that if *or* is to be regarded as possessing a strong sense as well as a weak one, the strong sense should be regarded as derivative from the weak one. The support for this contention would have to be a combination of two points: (*i*) that the most natural expression of the second condition involves a use of *or* in the 'weak' sense; and even if the weak use of *or* is avoided the idea seems to be explicitly involved; it is difficult to suppose that people could use a word

so as to include in its meaning that there is evidence of a certain sort for a proposition without having a distinct notion of that for which the evidence is evidence. (*ii*) One who says that A or B, using *or* truth-functionally, could be shown in normal circumstances to implicate (conversationally) that there are non-truth-functional grounds for supposing that A v B. For to say that A or B (interpreted weakly) would be to make a weaker and so less informative statement than to say that A or to say that B, and (on the assumption, which I shall not here try to justify, that it would be of interest to an audience to know that one of the disjuncts is true) would therefore be to make a less informative statement that would be appropriate in the circumstances. So there is an implicature (provided the speaker is not opting out) that he is not in a position to make a stronger statement, and if, in conformity with the second maxim of Quality, the speaker is to be presumed to have evidence for what he says, then the speaker thinks that there are non-truth-functional grounds for accepting A or B. We might next argue that if the strong sense of *or* is derivative from the weaker sense, then it ought to conform to whatever general principles there may be which govern the generation of derivative senses. This point is particularly strong in connection with a suggestion that *or* possesses a derivative sense; for we are not particularly at home with the application of notions such as 'meaning' and 'sense' to words so nondescriptive as *or*; the difficulties we encounter here are perhaps similar to, though not so severe as, the difficulties we should encounter if asked to specify the meaning or meanings of a preposition like *to* or *in*. So I suspect that we should need to rely fairly heavily on an application to the case of *or* of whatever general principles there may be which apply to more straightforward cases and which help to determine when a derivative sense should be supposed to exist, and when it should not.

[It might be objected that whether one sense of a word is to be regarded derivative from another sense of that word should be treated as a question about the history of the language to which the word belongs. This may be so in general (though in many cases it is obvious, without historical research that one sense must be secondary to another), but if I am right in thinking that conversational principles would not allow the word *or* to be used in normal circumstances without at least an implicature of the existence of non-truth-functional grounds,

then it is difficult to see that research could contribute any information about temporal priority in this case.]

I offer one or two further reflections about the proliferation of senses.

1. I would like to propose for acceptance a principle which I might call Modified Occam's Razor (M.O.R.) *Senses are not to be multiplied beyond necessity.* Like many regulative principles, it would be a near platitude, and all would depend on what was counted as "necessity." Still, like other regulative principles, it may guide. I can think of other possible precepts which would amount to much the same. One might think, for example, of not allowing the supposition that a word has a further (and derivative) sense unless the supposition that there is such a sense does some work, explains why our understanding of a particular range of applications of the word is so easy or so sure, or accounts for the fact that some application of the word outside that range, which would have some prima facie claim to legitimacy, is in fact uncomfortable. Again one might formulate essentially the same idea by recommending that one should not suppose what a speaker would mean when he used a word in a certain range of cases to count as a special sense of the word, if it should be predictable, independently of any supposition that there is such a sense, that he would use the word (or the sentence containing it) with just that meaning. If one makes the further assumption that it is more generally feasible to strengthen one's meaning by achieving a superimposed implicature, than to make a relaxed use of an expression (and I don't know how this assumption would be justified), then Modified Occam's Razor would bring in its train the principle that one should suppose a word to have a less restrictive rather than a more restrictive meaning, where choice is possible.

What support would there be for M.O.R.? Perhaps we might look at two types of example of real or putative derivative senses. One type (unlike the case of *or*) would involve "transferred" senses; the other would involve derivative senses which are specificatory of the original senses (the proposed derivative sense of 'or' would be a special case of this kind).

a. Consider such adjectives as *loose, unfettered,* and *unbridled* in relation to a possible application to the noun *life*. (I assume that such an application of each word would not be nonderivative, or literal; that the ambiguous expression *a loose liver* would involve a nonderivative sense of *loose* if uttered e.g. by a nurse in a hospital who complained about the number of patients with loose livers, but not if uttered censoriously to describe a particular man.) It seems to me that (in the absence of any further sense for either word) one might expect to be able to mean more or less the same by *a loose life*, and *an unfettered life*; the fact that, as things are, *loose life* is tied to dissipation, whereas *unfettered life* seems quite general in meaning, suggests that perhaps *loose* does, and *unfettered* does not, have a derivative sense in this area. As for *unbridled life* (which one might perhaps have expected, prima facie, to mean much the same as *unfettered life*), the phrase is slightly uncomfortable (because *unbridled* seems to be tied to such words as *passion*, *temper*, *lust*, and so on).

b. As for words with specificatory derivative senses, there seems to be some tendency for one of two things to happen: Either the original general sense becomes obsolete (like *car*, meaning 'wheeled vehicle'), or the specificatory condition takes over; we should perhaps continue to call gramophone records *discs* even if (say) they came to be made square (provided they remained not too unlike discs, in the original sense of the word) and perhaps the word *cylinder* exemplifies the same feature. But there are words of which neither is true: an obvious example is the word *animal* (meaning [*i*] 'member of animal kingdom', [*ii*] 'beast'). There is here some sort of a parallel, in relation to M.O.R. and its variants, between *animal* and the candidate word *or*. *Animal* perhaps infringes a weak principle to the effect that a further sense should not be recognized if, *on the assumption that* the word were to have a specificatory further sense, the identity of that sense would be predictable; for it could no doubt be predicted that *if* the word *animal* were to have such a sense, it would be one in which the word did not apply to human beings. But it would seem not to be predictable (history of language apart) that anyone would *in fact* use the word *animal* to mean 'beast', whereas given a truth-functional *or* it is predictable (assuming conversational principles) that people would use *A or B* to imply the existence of non-truth-functional grounds. So, at least, so far as I can see (not far, I think), there is as yet no reason not to accept M.O.R.

2. We must of course give due (but not undue) weight to intuitions about the existence or nonexistence of putative senses of a word (how could we do without them?). Indeed if the scheme which I have been putting before

you is even proceeding in the right direction, at least some reliance must be placed on such intuitions. For in order that a nonconventional implicature should be present in a given case, my account requires that a speaker shall be able to utilize the conventional meaning of a sentence. If nonconventional implicature is built on what is said, if what is said is closely related to the conventional force of the words used, and if the presence of the implicature depends on the intentions of the speaker, or at least on his assumptions, with regard to the possibility of the nature of the implicature being worked out. then it would appear that the speaker must (in some sense or other of the word *know*) know what is the conventional force of the words which he is using. This indeed seems to lead to a sort of paradox: If we, as speakers have the requisite knowledge of the conventional meaning of sentences we employ to implicate, when uttering them, something the implication of which depends on the conventional meaning in question, how can we, as theorists have difficulty with respect to just those cases in deciding where conventional meaning ends and implicature begins? If it is true, for example, that one who says *that A or B* implicates the existence of non-truthfunctional grounds for A or B, how can there be any doubt whether the word 'or' has strong or weak sense? I hope that I can provide the answer to this question but I am not certain that I can.

3. I have briefly mentioned a further consideration bearing on the question of the admissibility of a putative sense of a word, namely, whether on the supposition that the word has that sense, there would be an adequate range of linguistic environments in which the word could be supposed to bear that sense. Failure in this respect would indicate an implicature or an idiom.

There are, I am certain, other possible principles which ought to be considered; in particular I have said nothing, or nothing explicitly, about the adequacy of substitutibility tests. But I propose to leave this particular topic at this point.

I have so far been considering questions on the following lines: (*i*) On the assumption that a word has only one conventional meaning (or only one relevant conventional meaning), how much are we to suppose to be included in that meaning? (*ii*) On the assumption that a word has at least one conventional meaning (or relevant conventional meaning), are we to say that it has one, or more than one, such meaning? In particular, are we to ascribe to it in a second sense/meaning, derivative from or dependent on a given first meaning/sense? We should consider also examples of elements in or aspects of utterances which, not being words, are candidates for conventional meaning (or significance).

Stress

Some cases of stress are clearly relevant to possession of conventional meaning, e.g. (fixed) stress on particular syllables or a word: contrast cóntent and contént. (Though we would not assign meaning to the stress itself.) I am not concerned with cases of that sort, but with the cases in which we think of a word as being stressed, and variably so: stressed on some occasions but not on others.

We might start by trying to think of stress as a purely natural way of highlighting, or making prominent, a particular word: compare putting some object (e.g. a new hat) in an obvious place in a room so that someone coming into the room will notice or pay attention to it. But there are various suggestive ways of doing this with a word: e.g. intoning it, saying it in a squeaky voice. Such methods would not just be thought unusual, they would be frowned on. They would also very likely fail to achieve the effect of highlighting just because there is an approved way of doing this. So there is a good case for regarding stress as a conventional device for highlighting. But to say this much is not to assign to stress a conventional significance or meaning; it is only to treat it as a conventional way of fulfilling a certain purpose, which is not yet established as a purpose connected with communication. But stress clearly does in fact on many occasions make a difference to the speaker's meaning; indeed it is one of the elements which help to generate implicatures. Does this fact require us to attribute any conventional meaning to stress?

In accordance with the spirit of Modified Occam's Razor, we might attribute conventional meaning to stress only if it is unavoidable. Thus we might first introduce a slight extension to the maxim enjoining relevance, making it apply not only to what is said, but to features of the means used for saying what is said. This extension will perhaps entitle us to expect that an aspect of an utterance which it is within the power of the speaker to eliminate or vary, even if it is introduced unreflectively, will have a purpose connected with what is currently being communicated; unless, of course its presence can be explained in some other way.

We might notice at least three types of context in which stress occurs which seem to invite ordering:

1.   Includes replies to "W" questions:
       (A: *Who paid the bill?* B: *Jónes did.*
       A: *What did Jones do to the cat?* B: *He kícked it.*)

and exchanges of such forms as:

A: S(α)
B: $\overline{S}(\acute{\alpha})$: S($\acute{\beta}$)

(for example:

A: *Jones paid the bill.*
B: *Jónes didn't pay the bill; Smíth paid it.*)

In such examples (*i*) stress is automatic or a matter of habit (maybe difficult to avoid) and (*ii*) we are not inclined to say that anything is meant or implicated. However, the effect is to make perspicuous elements which complete open sentences for which questions (in effect) demand completion or elements in respect of which what B is prepared to assert (or otherwise say), and what B has asserted, differ.

2. Such cases as incomplete versions of the conversational schema exemplified in the second of the above examples:

a. Without a preceding statement to the effect that Jones paid the bill says *Jónes didn't pay the bill, Smíth did.* Here, given that this sentence is to be uttered, the stress may be automatic, but the remark is not prompted by previous remark (but is volunteered), and we are inclined to say that the implicature is that someone thinks or might think that Jones did pay the bill. The maxim of relation requires that B's remark should be relevant to some thing or other, and B, by speaking as he would speak in reply to a statement that Jones paid the bill, shows that he has such a statement in mind.

b. B just says *Jónes didn't pay the bill.* B speaks as if he were about to continue as in (a); B implicates that someone (other than Jones) paid the bill.

In general, S($\acute{\alpha}$) is contrasted with the result of substituting some expression β for α, and commonly the speaker suggests that he would deny the substitute version, but there are other possibilities: e.g. *I knéw that* may be contrasted with *I believed*, and the speaker may implicate not that he would deny *I believed that p*, but that he would not confine himself to such a weaker statement (with the implicit completion *I didn't merely believe it*).

This last point has relevance to the theory of 'knowledge'. According to a certain 'strong' account of knowledge,

A knows that p =   (1) p
    (2) *A thinks that p*
    (3) *A has conclusive evidence that p*

This presents possible difficulties of a regressive nature:

1.   Does A have to know that the evidence for p is true?

2.   Does A have to know that the evidence is conclusive?

But in general the theory seems *too* strong. An examination candidate at an oral knows the date of the battle of Waterloo. He may know this without conclusive evidence; he may even have answered after hesitation (showed in the end that he knew the answer). I suggest something more like the following:

A knows that p =   (1) p
    (2) *A thinks that p*
    (3) *Some conditions placing restriction on how he came to think p* (cf. causal theory).

If I say *I know that p* then perhaps sometimes there is a nonconventional implicature of strong or conclusive evidence (not mere thinking that *p*, with *p* true)—cf. *He lóves her*. And this is not the only interpretation of stress: it can mean, 'You don't need to tell me'.

Irony

The second example of an element in, or aspect of, some utterances, with regard to which there might be some doubt whether or not it has a conventional meaning, emerges from my (too) brief characterization of irony in "Logic and Conversation". (I have profited at this point from discussion with Professor Rogers Albritton.) There was certainly something missing in the account which I gave; it seems very dubious whether A's knowledge that B has been cheated by C, that B knows that A knows that this is so, that B's remark *He is a fine friend* is to be presumed to relate to this episode, and that the remark is seemingly false (even obviously false), is enough to ensure, with reasonable certainty, that A will

suppose B to mean the negation of what he has made as if to say. A might just be baffled, or might suppose that, the despite the apparent falsity of the remark, B was meaning something like *He is, usually, a fine friend: how could he have treated me like that?* It was suggested to me that what should have been mentioned in my account was first, a familiarity with the practice of using a sentence, which would standardly mean that *p*, in order to convey that not-p (a familiarity which might be connected with a natural tendency in us to use sentences in this way), and, second, an ironical tone in which such utterances are made, and which (perhaps) conventionally signifies that they are to be taken in reverse.

This suggestion does not seem to me to remedy the difficulty. Consider the following example. A and B are walking down the street, and they both see a car with a shattered window. B says, *Look, that car has all its windows intact*. A is baffled. B says, *You didn't catch on; I was in an ironical way drawing your attention to the broken window*. The absurdity of this exchange is I think to be explained by the fact that irony is intimately connected with the expression of a feeling, attitude, or evaluation. I cannot say something ironically unless what I say is intended to reflect a hostile or derogatory judgment or a feeling such as indignation or contempt. I can for example say *What a scoundrel you are!* when I am well disposed toward you, but to say that will be playful, not ironical, and will be inappropriate unless there is some shadow of justification for a straightforward application – for example you have done something which some people (though not I) might frown upon. If when you have just performed some conspicuously disinterested action I say, *What an egotist you are! Always giving yourself the satisfaction of doing things for other people!*, I am expressing something like what might be the reaction of an extreme cynic. Whereas to say *He's a fine friend* is unlikely to involve any hint of anyone's approval.

I am also doubtful whether the suggested vehicle of signification, the ironical tone, exists as a specific tone; I suspect that an ironical tone is always a contemptuous tone, or an amused tone, or some other tone connected with one or more particular feelings or attitudes; what qualifies such a tone as ironical is that it appears, on this and other occasions, when an ironical remark is made. This question could no doubt be settled by experiment. Even if, however, there is no specifically ironical tone, it still might be suggested that a contemptuous or amused tone, when conjoined with a remark which is blatantly

772 H. PAUL GRICE

false, conventionally indicates that the remark is to be taken in reverse. But the suggestion does not seem to me to have much plausibility. While I may without any inappropriateness prefix the employment of a metaphor with *to speak metaphorically*, there would be something very strange about saying, *to speak ironically, he is a splendid fellow.* (*i*) To be ironical is, among other things, to pretend (as the etymology suggests), and while one wants the pretense to be recognized as such, to announce it as a pretense would spoil the effect. (*ii*) What is possibly more important, it might well be essential to an element's having conventional significance that it could have been the case that some quite different element should have fulfilled the same semantic purpose; that if a contemptuous tone does in fact conventionally signify in context that a remark is to be taken in reverse then it might have been the case that, e.g. a querulous tone should have been used (instead) for the same purpose. But the connection of irony with the expression of feeling seems to preclude this; if speaking ironically has to be, or at least to appear to be, the expression of a certain sort of feeling or attitude, then a tone suitable to such a feeling or attitude seems to be mandatory, at any rate for the least sophisticated examples.

Truth

It may be remembered that among the "A-philosophical" theses which I listed at the beginning of the first lecture of the series of which this article was the third was the original version of a "speech act" account of truth which Strawson put forward many years ago.[2] As I said at the time, his view, or at least the expression of it, has undergone considerable modification since then, and I am not here concerned with any but the original version of his thesis. He was influenced, I think, by three main considerations: (*i*) that the word *true* is properly, or at least primarily, to be applied to statements (what is stated), in view of the difficulties which he thought he saw in the thesis that it should be understood as applying to utterances; (*ii*) that given that the previous supposition is correct, no theory which treats truth as consisting in a relation (or correlation) between statements and facts will be satisfactory, since statements and facts cannot be allowed to be distinct items in the real world; (*iii*) Ramsey's account of truth[3] namely, that to assert that a proposition is true is to assert that proposition, is correct, so far as it goes; and (*iv*) it does not go far enough, since it omits to take

seriously the fact that we should not always be willing to tolerate the substitution of, e.g. *It is true that it is raining* for *It is raining*. So he propounded the thesis that to say of a statement that it is true is (*i*) in so far as it is to assert anything, to assert that statement and (*ii*) not merely to assert it, but to endorse, confirm, concede or reassert it (the list is not, of course, intended to be complete).

Such a theory seems to me to have at least two unattractive features, on the assumption that it was intended to give an account of the meaning (conventional significance) of the word *true*. (*i*) (A familiar type of objection) it gives no account, or no satisfactory account, of the meaning of the word *true* when it occurs in unasserted subsentences (e.g. *He thinks that it is true that . . .* or *If it is true that . . .*). (*ii*) It is open to an objection which I am inclined to think holds against Ramsey's view (of which the speech act theory is an offshoot). A theory of truth has (as Tarski noted) to provide not only for occurrences of *true* in sentences in which what is being spoken of as true is specified, but also for occurrences in sentences in which no specification is given (e.g. *The policeman's statement was true*). According to both the speech act theory, I presume, and to Ramsey's theory, at least part of what the utterer of such a sentence is doing is to assert whatever it was that the policeman stated. But the utterer may not know what that statement was; he may think that the policeman's statement was true because policemen always speak the truth, or that that policeman always speaks the truth, or that policeman in those circumstances could not but have spoken the truth. Now assertion presumably involves committing oneself, and while it is possible to commit oneself to a statement which one has not identified (I could commit myself to the contents of the Thirty-Nine articles of the Church of England, without knowing what they say), I do not think I should be properly regarded as having committed myself to the content of the policeman's statement, merely in virtue of having said that it was true. When to my surprise I learn that the policeman actually said, *Monkeys can talk*, I say (perhaps), *Well, I was wrong*, not *I withdraw that*, or *I withdraw my commitment to that*. I never was committed to it.

My sympathies lie with theories of the correspondence family, which Strawson did (and I think still does) reject, but it is not to my present purpose (nor within my capacities) to develop adequately any such theory. What I wish to do is to show that, on the assumption that a certain sort of theory of this kind is correct, then, with the aid of the apparatus discussed in "Logic and Conversation" it is possible to accommodate the linguistic phenomena which led Strawson to formulate the original version of the speech act theory. Let me assume (and hope) that it is possible to construct a theory which treats truth as (primarily) a property of utterances; to avoid confusion I shall use, to name such a property, not 'true' but 'factually satisfactory'. Let me also assume that it will be a consequence of such a theory that there will be a class K of utterances (utterances of affirmative S-P sentences) such that every member of K (*i*) *designates*[4] some item and *indicates*[4] some class (these verbs to be explained within the theory) and (*ii*) is factually satisfactory if the item belongs to the class. Let me finally assume that there could be a method of introducing a form of expression *It is true that . . .* and linking it with the notion 'factually satisfactory', a consequence of which would be that to say *It is true that Smith is happy* would be equivalent to saying that any utterance of class K which designates Smith and indicates the class of happy people is factually satisfactory (that is, any utterance which assigns Smith to the class of happy people is factually satisfactory).

If some such account of *It is true that . . .* is correct (or indeed any account which represents saying *It is true that p* as equivalent to saying something about utterances), then it is possible to deal with the linguistic facts noted by Strawson. To say *Smith is happy* is not to make a (concealed) reference to utterances of a certain sort, whereas to say *It is true that Smith is happy* is to do just that, though of course if Smith is happy it is true that Smith is happy. If I choose the

form which does make a concealed reference to utterances, and which is also the more complex form, in preference to the simpler form, it will be natural to suppose that I do so because an utterance to the effect that Smith is happy has been made by myself or someone else, or might be so made. Such speech acts as endorsing, agreeing, confirming, and conceding, which Strawson (presumably) supposed to be conventionally signalled by the use of the word *true* will be just those which, in saying in response to some remark "that's true," one would be performing (without any special signal). And supposing no one actually to have said that Smith is happy, if I say "It is true that Smith is happy" (e.g. concessively) I shall implicate that someone might say so; and I shall not select this form of words as, for example, a response to an inquiry whether Smith is happy, when I should not wish this implicature to be present.

Notes

1 "Logic and Conversation" (copyright 1975 Paul Grice). Both that paper and the present paper are excerpted from Paul Grice's William James Lectures delivered at Harvard University in 1967, which is published by Harvard University Press. The present paper appears here without substantial revision. "Logic and Conversation" was published in *Syntax and Semantics: Speech Acts*, volume 3, edited by Peter Cole and Jerry L. Morgae (New York: Academic Press, 1975).

2 P. F. Strawson, 'Truth'. *Analysis* Vol. 9, No. 6 (1949).

3 F. P. Ramsey, *The Foundations of Mathematics* (Paterson, NJ: Littlefield, Adams, & Co., 1960): pp. 142–143.

4 These verbs to be explained within the theory.

Chapter 38: The Social Context of Reasoning: Conversational Inference and Rational Judgment

DENIS J. HILTON

Most psychologists conceive of judgment and reasoning as cognitive processes, which go on "in the head" and involve intrapsychic information processing (e.g., Kahneman, Slovic, and Tversky, 1982; Nisbett and Ross, 1980). Although it is incontestable that processes of attention, memory, and inference underpin judgment and reasoning, psychologists have perhaps overlooked the extent to which these mental processes are governed by higher-level assumptions about the social context of the information to be processed. On the other hand, philosophers have in recent years drawn attention to the extent to which reasoning from ordinary language is shaped by the nature of social interaction and conversation (Austin, 1962; Grice, 1975; Hart and Honoré, 1959/1985; Mackie, 1974; Searle, 1969; Strawson, 1952). These higher-level assumptions can determine what we attend to, which memories we search, and what kinds of inference we draw.

Consider the way the word *family* can be differentially interpreted according to context and thus lead to seemingly inconsistent judgments expressed in a conversational exchange (cf. Strack, Martin, and Schwarz, 1988):

Q. How is your family?
A. Fairly well, thank you.

A married man might reply this way if he considers that his wife has recently been saddened by the loss of a close friend but that his two children are in good form. The respondent interprets *family* to mean *the wife and kids*.

Suppose, however, that a woman had asked this man about his wife and then his family. The exchange might have run as follows:

Q. How is your wife?
A. Not too good, I'm afraid.
Q. And how is your family?
A. Extremely well, thank you!

In this case, the respondent would normally feel bound to interpret *family* as *the kids* because he already gave information about his wife and did not wish to burden the questioner with redundant information that she already has. So he gives an answer about his family that is apparently inconsistent with his earlier answer to the same question, "How is your family?"

From one point of view, giving two different answers to the same question asked on different occasions may seem irrational. After all, inconsistency is usually taken as a sign of illogicality and irrationality in ordinary life (Strawson, 1952). We might therefore be tempted to conclude that our imaginary interlocutor is mentally unable to deliver a stable and consistent evaluation of his family's well-being and is therefore irrational. We might suppose, for example, that he is unable to activate the same representation of the concept *my family* on the two occasions that the question is asked because of defective or biased memory retrieval processes. This kind of argument is familiar from much research on rational judgment. Thus, irrationality is often demonstrated experimentally through producing different responses to the same question asked in different contexts, such as in the study of framing effects on risky choice (Tversky and Kahneman, 1981) and preference reversals (Payne, Bettman, and Johnson, 1992) or through question-order effects on responses in survey research (Schuman and Presser, 1981).

However, attributing irrationality to the respondent in the above case may be premature. Norms of rational communication (e.g., Grice, 1975) require a speaker to be cooperative with a hearer by not burdening him or her with redundant information. Specifically, in the case where the hearer has just been told about the health of the speaker's wife, one can argue that interlocutors are entitled to assume that the reference to *family* meant *just the kids*, rather than *the wife and kids*. This interpretation of the word *family* is conversationally rational in the context of the previous exchange about the health of the speaker's wife. The context-dependent interpretation of the word *family* would thus absolve the speaker of the charge of cognitive inconsistency. Rather, he has cooperatively and rationally altered his answers to the question as a function of the interactional context.

Recognition of conversational constraints on utterance interpretation and inference may thus have important implications for experimental psychologists. No psychological experiment or investigation takes place in a social vacuum. All experiments and surveys are forms of social interaction between the experimenter and participant, which invariably involves communication through ordinary language. Thus, survey researchers who attribute inconsistent patterns of response to questions to cognitive shortcomings, or experimental psychologists who explain patterns of judgment in terms of purely intrapersonal variables – such as memory capacity, attention factors, memory activation levels, search strategies, and judgmental heuristics – may be in danger of committing an attribution error (cf. Cheng and Novick, 1990). They may be in danger of misattributing patterns of inferential behavior to features of the person and overlooking how it is constrained by its interpersonal context.

Theories of judgment should therefore include a front-end component that determines how the incoming message is interpreted in its context. This may remove many anomalies in the interpretation of respondents' behavior. It has been a perennial problem for students of judgment and reasoning to determine whether a mistake is due to incorrect reasoning about the

information given or to the application of correct reasoning procedures to incorrect or irrelevant information that a respondent has incorporated in his or her representation of the reasoning problem (Henle, 1962; Johnson-Laird, 1983). Conversational assumptions often require one to go beyond the information explicitly given in an utterance. Thus, the final judgment may often be highly rational given the participant's use of these assumptions in forming a representation of the reasoning task.

Although many researchers have noted that widely shared assumptions about cooperative communication (Grice, 1975; Levinson, 1983) may license interpretations of the experimental task that the experimenter may not have intended, work on this topic remains fragmentary and underdeveloped in nature. On the one hand, experimental psychologists typically define a particular judgment phenomenon first and then consider how it might be analyzed from the point of view of conversational pragmatics. This practice has led to the accumulation of piecemeal knowledge about the relation between conversational pragmatics and rational inference. Thus, the conversational aspects of such diverse phenomena as the base-rate fallacy (Krosnick, Li, and Lehman, 1990; Schwarz, Strack, Hilton, and Naderer, 1991), the conjunction fallacy (Dulany and Hilton, 1991; Markus and Zajonc, 1985; Morier and Borgida, 1984; Politzer and Noveck, 1991; Tversky and Kahneman, 1983), actor-observer differences in causal explanation (Hilton, 1990a), conservation judgments (Donaldson, 1978, 1982; McGarrigle and Donaldson, 1975), and interpretation of survey questions (Schwarz and Strack, 1991; Tourangeau and Rasinski, 1988) have been for the most part considered independently of each other. In addition, articles that review several phenomena from the point of view of conversational pragmatics do not offer an integrated view of the philosophical and linguistic bases of conversational inference that would enable its relation to rational judgment to be explicated systematically (e.g., Adler, 1984; Bless, Strack, and Schwarz, 1993; Cohen, 1981; Hilton, 1990a; Macdonald, 1986; Schwarz, 1994; Shanon, 1988).

I therefore begin by reviewing some of the logical and linguistic properties of conversational inference with particular reference to the question of rationality in research on judgment and reasoning. I show how these logico–linguistic properties may be moderated by inferences about the social context of communication and particularly the hearer or respondent's attributions about the speaker or experimenter (e.g., the speaker's knowledge, intentions, and group membership). This attributional model generates predictions about the ways conversational inference may affect the representation of judgment and reasoning tasks. I apply the model to the analysis of experiments on reasoning drawn from developmental psychology, social psychology, cognitive psychology, and decision research. I show that the attributional model of conversational inference organizes phenomena found in these diversified literatures within a common framework and enables the reinterpretation of many judgment biases in terms of conversational inference processes. More important, the framework can help elucidate which biases are not susceptible of explanation in conversational terms. I conclude by discussing methodological implications for future research.

Properties of Conversational Inference

Inductive Nature of Conversational Inference

Conversational inference is itself a form of judgment under uncertainty. Hearers have to make hypotheses about the speaker's intended meaning on the basis of what is explicitly said. For example, most hearers routinely go beyond the information given in the utterance "I went to the cinema last night" to infer that the speaker meant to convey that he or she saw a film last night. The additional information conveyed in this way by the speaker is termed a *conversational implicature* (Grice, 1975). Grice argued that to understand a speaker's full meaning, the listener must understand both the meaning of the sentence itself (what is said) and what it conveys in a given context (what is implicated).

Conversational inference shares some important properties with inductive inference (Levinson, 1983). First it is ampliative, that is, the conclusion contains more information than the premises. For example, by observing that the first 1,000 carrots that I dig up are orange, I make the stronger conclusion that "All carrots are orange." The inference that the speaker went to the cinema and saw a film contains more information than the assertion that he or she just went to the cinema. Consequently, the conclusions of both conversational and inductive inference are defeasible, that is, they can be canceled by the addition of new information. Thus, just as the

conclusion that "All carrots are orange" may be canceled by digging up a 1,001st carrot that is brown, so the speaker may cancel the implicature that he or she saw a film at the cinema last night by saying, "I went to the cinema last night but couldn't get in."

Conversational inference is unlike deductive inference, where conclusions contain no new information but simply demonstrate what can be inferred from the premises, and cannot be canceled by the addition of new information. Thus, the fact that Socrates is mortal necessarily follows from the fact that Socrates is a man and all men are mortal. Nothing can be done to change this conclusion except to change the original premises.[1]

Consequently, in conversational inference – as in inductive inference – one encounters Hume's problem, namely that one can never draw correct conclusions with certainty. Just as theory is underdetermined by data, so hypotheses about the speaker's intended meaning are underdetermined by what is said. There may be an innumerable number of theories or hypotheses about intended meaning that are consistent with the data given and thus have the chance of being true. How does one decide which theory or hypothesis is best?

There are some criteria for determining the rational choice of a hypothesis in both cases. In fact, proposals made by philosophers of science and philosophers of language are broadly similar. Roughly speaking, rational inferences are those which, as well as being likely to be true, convey the most new implications for the least effort. This position is implicit in Popper's (1972) injunction that scientific hypotheses be "powerful and improbable," in Wilson and Sperber's (1985) suggestion that the relevance of an inference should be calculated in terms of the number of implications it carries for the amount of processing effort needed, and in Grice's (1975) logic of conversation.

Grice's (1975) statement of the cooperative principle underlying conversation and the conversational maxims that derive from it are detailed in the Appendix. Grice's logic of conversation describes a form of rational communication in which the maximum amount of valuable information is transmitted with the least amount of encoding and decoding effort. Although some theorists have sought to revise this approach, for example, by reducing all the maxims to a superordinate one of relevance (Sperber and Wilson, 1986), Grice's approach is adopted here because of its ability, when suitable interpreted,

Table 1: Assumed Characteristics of Message and Speaker Implied by Grice's Logic of Conversation

Assumption/Maxim of Conversation	Message Characteristics	Characteristics Attributed to Speaker
Cooperativeness	Observes four maxims (see below)	Intentional Helpful
Quality	Truth value probability	Sincerity Honesty Reliability Competence
Quantity	Informativeness	Mutual knowledge Group membership
Relation	Goal relevance	Interactional goals
Manner	Clarity	Knowledge of language

to explain a wide range of phenomena in conversational pragmatics (for more detailed discussion, see P. Brown and Levinson, 1987; Grice, 1989; Levinson, 1983, 1987; Neale, 1992). As is shown below, the cooperative principle and the subordinate maxims seem to correspond to important psychological dimensions and the tensions between them to produce important logical and linguistic consequences.

Attributional Bases of Conversational Inference

Grice's (1975) assumption of cooperativeness and the corresponding maxims of conversation depend on the hearer making certain default attributions about the speaker. In particular, the assumption of cooperativeness presupposes that utterances are produced by an intentional agent who wishes to cooperate with us and has the ability to realize this intention. I argue that each set of conversational maxims implies certain kinds of attributions about the speaker (see Table 1).

The maxims of *quality* concern the likely truth value of an utterance. Thus, if the hearer attributes properties such as sincerity, reliability, and knowledgeability to the speaker, then the hearer may well consider the probable truth value of an utterance to be high. If, on the other hand, the hearer considers the speaker to be insincere, unreliable, or unknowledgeable, then the hearer may well consider the probable truth of the utterance to be low.

The maxims of *quantity* concern the perceived informativeness of an utterance. Speakers should not burden hearers with information

they are already likely to know. What speakers and hearers take for granted may depend in part on perceptions of class membership. Competent members of western society do not need to be told why a customer who ate a good meal in a restaurant with good service left a big tip. From their own world knowledge, they are able to make the necessary bridging inferences (Clark and Haviland, 1977; Schank and Abelson, 1977). Thus, hearers often go beyond the information given in making inferences because they assume that the relevant information they are likely to know has already been omitted.

The maxim of *relation* enjoins speakers to mention information that is relevant to the goals of the interaction. Hearers are entitled to assume that any relevant information they are not likely to know has been included. They are also entitled to assume that information that has been included is relevant, otherwise why mention it? One problem for experimental research is that psychologists routinely violate this assumption by introducing information precisely because it is irrelevant to the judgment task (e.g., Nisbett, Zukier, and Lemley, 1981). If bearers (participants) continue to attribute essentially cooperative intentions to speakers (experimenters), then they are liable to be misled by the information given.

The maxims of *manner* enjoin speakers to be brief, orderly, clear, and unambiguous. The extent to which speakers can adhere to these prescriptions often depends on their command of the language. Hearers may take this into account when interpreting utterances. For example, a German tourist in England might conceivably ask a native for directions to "the

Townhouse" when he or she meant "the Town Hall." Rather than direct the tourist to the nearest renovated Georgian residence in the center of town, a cooperative hearer might attribute the speaker's unclarity to inexperience with British English and direct her or him to the Town Hall. Usually such misunderstandings in conversation can be corrected through discussion. However, such opportunities for repair do not exist in experimental and survey research. Consequently, experimenters may notice ambiguities in their response formats that are systematically reinterpreted by participants, thus leading to systematic biases in the results obtained. This seems to have been the case in much basic attribution research (Hilton, 1990b).

Although Grice (1975) formulated his maxims as injunctions to the speaker ("Be brief," "Be clear," etc.), they can also be understood as general expectations about discourse built into the comprehension processes of hearers (cf. Dulany and Hilton, 1991). I assume that these assumptions are used flexibly in utterance interpretation. For example, as Grice (1975) intended, I assume that the maxims of conversation guide utterance interpretation both when they are respected and when they are flouted. There is considerable evidence that such assumptions are used in language understanding (see Clark, 1985, 1992; Clark and Schober, 1992; Kraut and Higgins, 1984, for reviews). I do not, however, commit myself to a psycholinguistic process model that specifies how these constraints are used in comprehension (cf. Dascal, 1989; Gibbs, 1984, 1989). I simply assume that these higher-order assumptions are guided by attributions about the speaker and that they are used to choose interpretations of utterances that are rational in the conversational context.

Attribution Processes in the Interpretation of Utterances

Grice's (1975) maxims of conversation are often considered as descriptive of the rules of idealized conversations between cooperative rational hearers. However, Grice clearly considered that speakers are flexible with the maxims of conversation and indeed often flout them deliberately to create special effects such as metaphor and irony. However, when speakers flout the maxims of conversation, hearers have to *calculate* the intended implicatures by working out the speaker's intentions. This is clear from Grice's example of an unusually short letter of recommendation that violates the maxims of quantity

by not giving enough information to evaluate a job candidate properly:

> *A* is writing a testimonial about a pupil who is a candidate for a philosophy job, and his letter reads as follows: "Dear Sir, Mr. X's command of English is excellent, and his attendance at tutorials has been regular. Yours, etc." (Gloss [explanation]: *A* cannot be opting out since if he wished to be uncooperative, why write at all? He cannot be unable, through ignorance, since the man is his pupil. He must, therefore, be wishing to impart information that he is reluctant to write down, This supposition is tenable only if he thinks Mr. X is no good at philosophy. This, then, is what he is implicating.) Grice, 1975, p. 52

The calculation of implicatures clearly involves inferences about the speaker's knowledge of the topic under discussion (the pupil) and his intentions (not to be openly critical). In this example, Grice (1975) appealed to a higher-order assumption about the writer that he or she is cooperative. However, it is easy to imagine how other beliefs about the speaker would incline one to either accept or reject the proposed interpretation of the letter. For example, if one knew that the writer is normally very knowledgeable about and supportive of his pupils about whom he writes at great and glowing length, then one would certainly be inclined to accept Grice's proposed interpretation. On the other hand, if one knew that the pupil was a blunt-speaking person with ideas of his or her own and that the teacher was a rather dogmatic type, one might be inclined to consider the hypothesis that the writer has been offended by this pupil and wishes to stop him or her embarking on an academic career precisely to prevent the development of a brilliant philosophical opponent.

Such beliefs about the stable personality characteristics of actors are termed by social psychologists *dispositional attributions*. An important statement of the process of dispositional attribution by Jones and Davis (1965) bears some important resemblances to the process of utterance interpretation proposed here. Both processes begin with an action (behavioral act or utterance) that is to be explained in terms of intentions (e.g., to help or to harm) in both models. In both cases, dispositional attributions may be particularly likely to be triggered by unusual actions (e.g., socially undesirable behaviors or flouting the maxims of conversation) that may lead to inferences about the nature of the

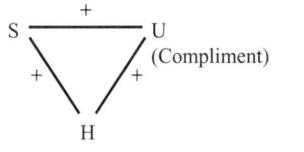 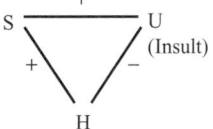

Balanced triad   Imbalanced triad

Case where the speaker   Case where the speaker
makes a compliment to a hearer   makes an insult to the hearer
who thinks the speaker likes her.   who thinks the speaker likes her.

Figure 1. Examples of balanced and imbalanced speaker-hearer-utterance relationships. S = speaker; H = hearer; U = utterance; + = positive relationship between elements; − = negative relationship between elements.

person or speaker (that they are a kind or unkind person in general). Thus, it should be of little surprise that Grice's (1975) model of utterance comprehension should be compatible with models of action attribution (Jones, 1979; Jones and Davis, 1965; Jones and McGillis, 1976), given his insistence that communication should be viewed as a form of action governed by the same general concerns of rationality as action in general.

The attributional model of utterance comprehension assumes that, all things being equal, the average hearer will assume that the average speaker is cooperative. However, if relevant evidence or beliefs are at hand, then the hearer may revise this assumption in a process of dispositional attribution. Attributional processes are particularly likely to be triggered by unexpected or undesirable events (Bohner, Bless, Schwarz, and Strack, 1988; Brown and van Kleeck, 1989; Hastie, 1984; Hilton and Slugoski, 1986; Weiner, 1985). Consequently, one may expect more attributions to be made about a speaker when he or she flouts the maxims of conversation by being untruthful, uninformative, irrelevant, and unclear than if he or she respects them by being truthful, informative, relevant, and clear. Consistent with this position, Turnbull and Smith (1985) found that neutral observers perceived a person who conveyed a defective answer as being inconsiderate and hostile and as having a negative and distant relationship with the questioner.[2]

The emphasis in classic models of dispositional attribution is a bottom-up one: The direction of inference most studied is from acts (utterances) through intentions to dispositions (Jones, 1979; Jones and Davis, 1965). In this view, information in the form of acts or utterances may lead to revision of prior beliefs about the actor or speaker. However, a reverse top-down direc-

tion of inference is also quite possible, where the observer holds strong prior beliefs about the actor, such as knowledge of his or her social category membership (Jones and McGillis, 1976). In the realm of utterance comprehension, Slugoski and Turnbull (1988) produced evidence for such top-down inference processes by showing that neutral observers revised their interpretation of literal insults and compliments in line with their knowledge of the interactants' relationship. Thus, if the interactants in question were known to hate each other, observers would reinterpret a literal compliment ("Wow, that's a great hairstyle you just got!") as a sarcastic insult ("What an awful hairstyle!"). Conversely, literal insults from friends were reinterpreted as playful banter.

The relationship among a speaker, a hearer, and an utterance can be represented as a cognitive triad (see Figure 1). According to Heider (1958), perceivers will try to ensure cognitive balance by ensuring that the signs connecting the elements of the triad multiply out positively. In Slugoski and Turnbull's (1988) experiment, the speaker or subject (S) always has a positive relationship of possession to the utterance he or she makes because he or she "owns" it. If the hearer or observer (H) believes that the speaker or subject (S) likes him or her (H), then S and H have a positive affective relationship. A compliment to the hearer or observer (H) indicates a positive relationship between H and U, resulting in three positive signs and a balanced relationship. However, if an imbalanced triad is produced when the speaker makes a literal insult to a hearer who believes the speaker likes him or her, cognitive imbalance is created due to the negative relationship between H and U. This can be reduced by changing the signs of one of the relationships. This can be achieved by (a) reinterpreting the insult as a compliment;

(b) reinterpreting the speaker's attitude to the hearer as negative rather than positive; or (c) disowning the speaker's possession of the remark ("Something got into him," "He was in a bad mood," "He didn't really mean it").

Interpreting an utterance thus requires a kind of cognitive balancing act (cf. Brown and van Kleeck, 1989). Although the previous example and Figure 1 are only schematic, they do illustrate how the hearer's perceptions of the speaker and the utterance can be reconciled according to the principles of cognitive consistency. Both top-down (revision of utterance interpretation) and bottom-up (revision of beliefs about the speaker) processes of inconsistency resolution can occur. Following research on inconsistency resolution, I speculate that weakly held beliefs will be modified more than strongly held ones (Tannenbaum, 1968). Thus, if a hearer is confident that the speaker likes the hearer, the hearer will probably change the interpretation of a literal insult to a conveyed compliment. However, if the hearer has no prior preconceptions about the speaker's attitude to the hearer, then the hearer may infer that the speaker is hostile to the hearer. This process of reinterpretation to preserve cognitive balance is consistent with Asch's (1940) demonstration of "change of meaning" effects.

The attributional model of conversational inference claims that the application of higher-order assumptions about conversation is relativized to particular characteristics known or assumed about the speaker, such as the degree of cooperativeness, friendliness, group membership, knowledge about the topic, beliefs about the hearer, and skill in the language. Consistency and coherence criteria are used to choose the speaker's most likely intended meaning and thus the most rational interpretation of an utterance.

Although the attributional model of conversational inference has been developed from Grice's (1975) characterization of the logic of conversation, its main assumptions are quite consistent with other approaches to conversational pragmatics (e.g., Allwood, 1987; Recanati, 1993; Sperber and Wilson, 1986). All share the view that conversational utterances are interpreted in the light of higher-order assumptions about the speaker's intentionality. They could therefore allow that the most rational interpretation of an utterance is the one most consistent with relevant beliefs held about the speaker. Below, I consider how beliefs about the speaker may determine the interpretation of an utterance in a routine way.

Attributions about the Speaker and the Choice of Rational Interpretations

As noted above, a major criterion for attributing rationality is consistency (Strawson, 1952). Below, I show how rational interpretations of utterances are selected because they are consistent with the conversational context and specifically with beliefs about the speaker. I begin with an example of how attributions about the speaker might guide interpretations of the quantifier *some*.

The trade-off between the maxims of quality and quantity implies that speakers should try to be as informative as possible without running the (undue) risk of being false. Consequently, the interpretations hearers choose may in large part depend on attributions they have made about the speaker's knowledge of and interests in the topic under discussion. Here's an example:

1. Some of the police officers beat up the protester.

This statement could convey one of two different implicatures. It could mean one of the following:

2. Some of the police officers beat up the protester (but the speaker knows that not all of them did).

3. Some of the police officers beat up the protester (but the speaker does not know whether all of them did).

Levinson (1983) characterized the first implicature as a K-implicature (because the speaker knows that the stronger assertion is not the case) and the second as a P-implicature (because the stronger assertion is possible, because of the speaker's lack of relevant knowledge). One may reasonably surmise that the hearer is more likely to draw the K-implicature if he or she considers the speaker to be very knowledgeable about the topic (e.g., an eyewitness who was there) than not knowledgeable (e.g., a person reporting the incident second-hand).

However, in some circumstances the hearer may not draw the K-implicature even if he or she assumes that the speaker is indeed knowledgeable about the event under discussion. Such would be the case if the speaker were a policy spokesperson at a press conference who wished to limit perceptions of police brutality in a critical public. The spokesperson may not want to tell lies, thus observing the maxim of quality, but may only commit to the weakest possible statement about police aggression that is consistent

PROCESSES   **CRITERIA OF RATIONALITY**

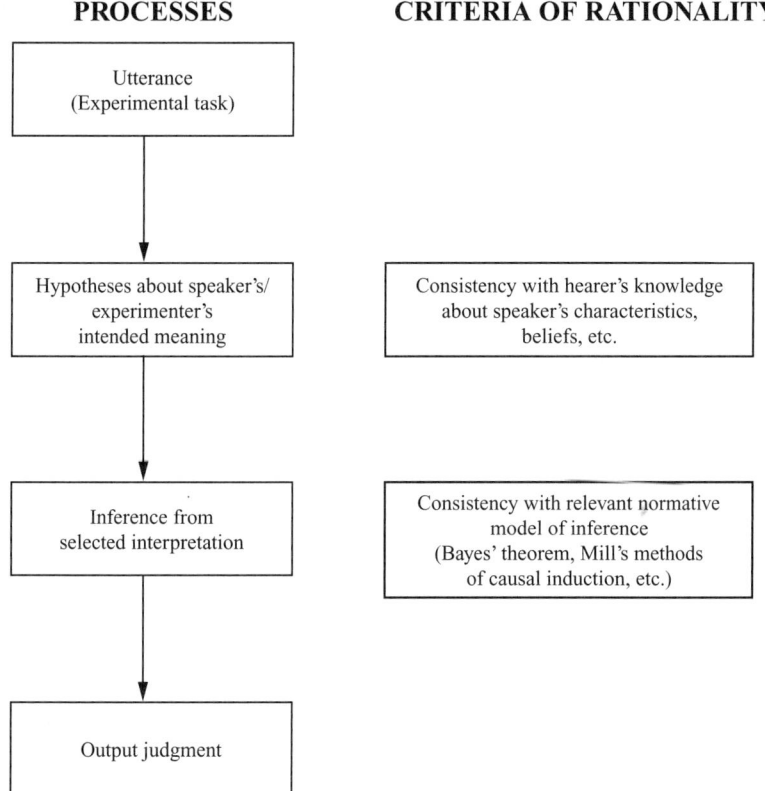

Figure 2. Two-stage resolution of uncertainty: utterance interpretation and judgment.

with evidence known to the public. If the hearer attributes noncooperativeness of this kind to the speaker, then the hearer may assume that the spokesperson may be seeking to avoid commitment to stronger statements that would be relevant but damaging to presentational goals that the police force might have.

It is not difficult to think of other factors that might affect the interpretation of such statements. For example, if the hearer knows that the speaker is a foreigner with a limited command of English and does not know such words as *a few* or *many* which the speaker might have used to specify the proportion of police involved, then the hearer might treat *some* as being vague and consistent with either a low or high proportion of police (for a further discussion of pragmatic interpretation of quantifiers, see Politzer, 1993).

Consistency in Interpretation and Reasoning

In experimental tasks, there are two major stages for arriving at a judgment from the information given, both of which require the participant to make rational choices. The first comprises the interpretation of the task by the participant. Here the participant chooses the most rational interpretation using the criterion of consistency with higher order assumptions about conversation and knowledge about the discourse context, specifically, attributions about the speaker. The second stage involves applying a normative model of reasoning to the representation formed, for example, by applying Bayes' theorem to a belief updating problem (Kahneman and Tversky, 1973), Mill's method of difference to a causal problem (Hilton and Jaspars, 1987), or laws of physics to conservation problem (Piaget and Inhelder, 1969). A schematic diagram of this two-stage process is given in Figure 2.

Most research on judgment and reasoning has focused on the second stage of rational inference. As is seen below, anomalies found in experiments on judgment and reasoning have typically been attributed to inadequate understanding of normative models of inference, such as Bayes' rule (Kahneman and Tversky, 1973),

Mill's method of difference (Hilton and Jaspars, 1987), or the laws of conservation (Piaget and Inhelder, 1969). However, less attention has been paid to the first stage of rational inference. Clearly, apparently "irrational" judgments may be due to interpretations made at the conversational inference stage.

I argue that participants enter the experimental and survey situation with prior expectations about the experimenter. Manipulating participants' perceptions of the experimenter or survey researcher's cooperativeness, intentionality, authority, and knowledge should affect the interpretations made and thus the final judgments produced. In addition, the general assumption of cooperativeness may cause information normally thought of as incidental to the experimental task – such as response scales – to be treated as relevant. These interpretations are orderly in the sense that certain patterns of conversational inference (e.g., that triggered by part-whole contrasts) can be found across a variety of experimental tasks (probability judgment, conservation, and surveys). They are rational because these interpretations seem to make the most sense given reasonable attributions about the speaker.

Next, I review evidence that supports these claims. First, this provides support for the attributional model of conversational inference by showing how information about source characteristics such as the intentionality, cooperativeness, and authority of the speaker changes output judgments. Even where task interpretations have not been directly assessed, this at least offers prima facie evidence that participants may be applying Grice's (1975) maxims of conversation to the interpretation of experimental messages. And second, in so doing, this also calls into question the classification of some of the participants' responses as errors.

Attributions about the Experimenter and Rational Inference

There is general evidence that experiments may be regarded as social interactions in which the participant's attributions about the experimenter affect his or her behavior. Social psychological research clearly suggests that participants attribute serious purposes even to patently absurd experiments (Orne, 1962). They behave in a highly cooperative manner in response to some very questionable experimental demands when they perceive the experimenter as authoritative, but they reduce this compliance when the

experimenter is perceived as lacking in authority (Milgram, 1974). In addition, it is well known that source attributes such as expertise, credibility, and prior attitude affect participants' responses to experimental attempts at belief changes (e.g., McGuire, 1969).

In addition, Singer, Hippler, and Schwarz (1992) showed that respondents to survey questionnaires may possess a certain amount of skepticism as to the researcher's trustworthiness. These researchers found, for example, that overly emphatic confidentiality assurances may lead respondents to have less faith that the confidentiality of their responses would be respected. In sum, I surmise that adult experimental participant and survey respondents are generally compliant and treat the experimenter as authoritative and cooperative, albeit with some skepticism.

Assumption of Intentionality in Conversational Inference

The most fundamental assumption we make in hearing conversation is that utterances are intentionally produced by the speaker. If they were not, there would be no basis for making judgments about the credibility, informativeness, purpose, or style of what is said on the basis of perceptions of the speaker. Unless told otherwise, respondents seem to be very resistant to attributing experimental manipulations to the operation of random or accidental processes. Respondents are very liable to perceive palpably random behavior in experiments as if they were guided by intentions. Examples are the description of the random movement of dots in a film in terms of intentional actions such as "chase" and "follow" by 49 out of 50 of Heider and Simmel's (1944) participants. Oatley and Yuill (1985) found that cues such as "jealous husband" led participants to exert considerable ingenuity in explaining why the dots in Heider and Simmel's film moved as they did. Perhaps most germane to the present issue is the behavior of naive users of Weizenbaum's (1976) ELIZA system. Although ELIZA produces some rather stereotyped examples of therapeutic discourse through the operation of an English language generator coupled with some random response selectors and a few procedures for recognizing key words, users are very prone to adopt an "intentional stance" (Dennett, 1984) to explain ELIZA's behavior and assume that ELIZA's utterances are produced by a human being (Boden, 1977).

People appear to distinguish between behavior that they are told is produced by a person or by some impersonal agent. For example, Faucheux and Moscovici (1968) showed that participants' strategies in an experimental game were affected by information indicating that their partner was a person or nature. Gibbs, Kushner, and Mills (1991) also showed that information about authorial intentions affected metaphor comprehension. Participants who were told that the metaphors they were given were produced by 20th-century poets rather than by a computer were more likely to judge them meaningful, produced more interpretations of them, and made meaningfulness judgments faster. Consequently, variables that undermine the perception that the actions performed by the experimenter are intentional, in line with the attributional model, may have critical effects on how experimental manipulations are interpreted and responded to. As is shown below, this often seems is to be the case.

Accidental and Intentional Transformations in Conservation Experiments

The procedures devised by Piaget to test children's ability to conserve quantities such as number and mass (Piaget and Inhelder, 1969) have been very widely used in developmental psychology. For purposes of exposition, one of the procedures used to test conservation of number is considered in detail. For example, a child may be shown two rows of four counters that are equal in length. The child is asked whether there is more in one row than in the other or whether they are the same. Typically, the child agrees that they are the same. The experimenter then modifies one of the rows so that the same four counters are now arranged in a longer row and repeats the question. Commonly, children younger than 7 years old will reply that there is more in the longer row. This is taken to imply that the child has failed to conserve the number of counters and perhaps has confused length with number.

However, note that the traditional Piagetian procedure involves an obviously calculated and deliberate transformation of the experimental array by the experimenter. Children may therefore have made the inference that the transformation was meant to be significant in some way. For example, the children may have recognized that the two rows still had the same number of counters, but they may have decided that the experimenter is interested in determining whether the child has recognized that the length dimension has been changed. Children may therefore have reinterpreted the question focus from number to length to give the experimental manipulation relevance (cf. Donaldson, 1982).

McGarrigle and Donaldson (1975) tested this hypothesis by effecting the transformation "accidentally." Specifically, after the child had been shown the two rows of counters and asked which one had more, a "naughty teddy" was introduced who "accidentally" disturbed the length of one of the rows in the process of "spoiling the game" (p. 343). Of course, the teddy's behavior was carefully contrived to transform the length of counters exactly as much as the experimenter did in the normal procedure. Although the transformation was objectively the same, the children's performance in the accidental condition was vastly superior to that obtained in the intentional condition. Using one criterion of conservation, 50 of the 80 children between 4 years old and 6 years old showed conservation in the accidental condition, whereas only 13 children showed conservation in the intentional condition.

This result has been replicated and extended to other Piagetian conservation procedures (for a review, see Donaldson, 1982). Moreover, it is consistent with other studies that suggest children only judge the shorter line as having more when they have been asked to make an initial judgment of whether the two lines were equal (Rose and Blank, 1974). Clearly, when the array has been transformed and the question has been asked again, children seem to experience a demand to change their response and may reinterpret the question. When children were not asked to make an initial commitment before the transformation, they were more likely to give correct answers to the question asked after the transformation.

Siegal, Waters, and Dinwiddy (1988) extended these results by investigating whether 4-, 5-, and 6-year-old children are aware of how demand effects may influence responses. They showed children a puppet doing a conservation task. In one condition, the puppet underwent the one-question procedure of Rose and Blank (1974) and in the other, the two-question procedure. They found that children attributed the incorrect responses in the two-question task to external factors (e.g., to please someone else) but attributed the same responses in the one-question task to internal factors (e.g., because they really thought it was true). Children thus seem to be aware of the role of social pressures in determining responses in such experiments.

Although Donaldson (1982) was careful to note that many nonconserving responses are still made in the accidental condition, she also noted that conventional conservation procedures seriously underestimate children's ability to conserve. In particular, many failures to conserve that have been attributed to cognitive deficits such as "perceptual domination" (Piaget and Inhelder, 1969) or "attentional deficits" (Gelman, 1969) may simply reflect the operation of generally adaptive principles of conversational inference.

Intentional and Random Presentations of Information in Base-Rate Experiments

One of the most widely known studies on decision making has been the engineers-and-lawyers problem introduced by Kahneman and Tversky (1973) and described in a *Science* article (Tversky and Kahneman, 1974). Berkeley and Humphreys (1982) found that the *Science* article was cited 227 times between 1975 and 1980, with approximately one fifth of the citations coming from sources outside of psychology, all of which used the citation to support the claim that people are poor decision makers.

Kahneman and Tversky's (1973) basic finding was that participants were more likely to rely on individuating information about the target than on base-rate information. For example, participants in some conditions were told that the target person "shows no interest in political and social issues and spends most of his free time on his many hobbies which include home carpentry, sailing, and mathematical puzzles" (p. 24). They were then presented with base-rate information indicating that the target person came from a sample of 100 people that included either 30 or 70 engineers, depending on the experimental condition. The participants predicted that the target person is probably an engineer, regardless of which base-rates they had been given. Kahneman and Tversky attributed this underuse of base-rate information to the operation of the representativeness heuristic, that is, participants based their decision about the probability that the target was an engineer on the similarity of the target to a stereotype of engineers.

However, evidence has since suggested that this phenomenon of "underuse of base-rate information" is restricted to "word problems" in which the base-rate information is presented verbally to participants in the form "30% of

the group are engineers," etc. Thus, studies that present base-rate information to participants in the form of learning trials show that participants can use base-rate information appropriately when making judgments (Christensen-Szalanski and Beach, 1982; Medin and Edelson, 1988). Other studies that have required participants to make judgments in which they have prior real-world experience or expertise also have found no tendency to underutilize base-rate information. For example, participants use their own implicit knowledge about the base-rate of diseases when judging the probability of a doctor's prediction that they will suffer from a particular illness (Wallsten, Fillenbaum, and Cox, 1986; Weber and Hilton, 1990). Doctors make appropriate adjustments for the base-rate probability of illnesses in a diagnosis task where they deploy implicit knowledge about symptom-group associations (e.g., weight loss in young girls suggests anorexia, but weight loss in old men suggests cancer) in medium-fidelity diagnosis tasks (Fox, 1980; Weber, Böckenholt, Hilton, and Wallace, 1993), whereas they fail to use explicitly presented base-rate information in a medical prognosis task presented in the form of a verbal vignette (Eddy, 1982). Consequently, participants' use of the representativeness heuristic may be governed by contextual factors, such as the assumptions that participants make about verbally presented base-rate information.

In fact, participants' use of base-rate information has been shown to be affected by various pragmatic factors. Krosnick et al. (1990) noted that participants always read individuating information first and base-rate information second in Kahneman and Tversky's (1973) procedure and other similar ones. Krosnick et al. hypothesized that the order of presentation of information may have served as a cue to participants to weight the initial information more and the later information less. Consistent with this reasoning, they found that participants used the base-rate information more when it was presented first. Krosnick et al. also took memory measures and were able to rule out the hypothesis that the greater weighting of earlier information was due to enhanced recall at the time of judgment.

If participants were indeed using order of presentation as a cue to determine the intended relevance of the information, then the significance of the cue should be invalidated if the participant believes that the cue has not been produced intentionally by the experimenter. This indeed appears to be the case. Krosnick et al. (1990) found that the order effect disappeared when participants were told that the order of presentation had been randomly determined.

Ginossar and Trope (1987, Experiment 6) presented the engineers-and-lawyers problem to participants as if the information had been generated as part of a card game. Framing the description as having been produced by a game of chance would undermine the assumption that the information was produced as part of an intentional communication. Consistent with the attributional model, they found that participants were more likely to use base-rate information in this condition.

Schwarz, Strack, et al. (1991) used a related manipulation that undermines the assumption of intentionality. They told participants that the individuating information had either been produced by a panel of psychologists or statisticians who had conducted the original set of interviews with the sample of engineers and lawyers or had been drawn randomly from the psychologists' or statisticians' files by a computer. In all cases, participants were given the personality description that is representative of an engineer and were told that there were 30 engineers in the sample of 100. When told in the psychology condition that the individuating information had been given to them by a human researcher, participants on average estimated the probability that the target was an engineer at .76, replicating Kahneman and Tversky's (1973) original findings. However, when told that the statements had been drawn at random from the psychologists' file by a computer, the participants' average estimate was .40, in line with the normative use of base-rate information.

On the other hand, in the statistics condition, participants were more likely to weight individuating information when it was drawn at random by a computer from a larger sample of descriptive information ($M = .74$) than when it was written by a nonspecified researcher ($M = .55$). One possible explanation is that random sampling is a valued procedure in a statistics framework, and therefore participants attached greater significance to the representative (i.e., randomly selected) information. Although this explanation is post hoc, it does underscore the importance of attention to participants' inferences about the particular expertise and credibility possessed by the source of information. As is shown below, explicit information about the source does indeed affect participants' judgments in this task.

Source Characteristics and the Use of Base-Rate Information

Grice's (1975) maxim of quality enjoins speakers not to say what they know to be false, or at least not to say what they lack adequate evidence for. Consequently, varying the credibility of the speaker should affect the weight attached to the speaker's messages. Ginossar and Trope (1987, Experiment 5) varied the credibility of the source of information in the engineers-and-lawyers problem. They found that participants rated the personality description as having the highest probability of being true when the source was a trained psychologist ($M = .78$), lowest when the source was a palm reader ($M = .31$), and intermediate when the source was a beginning interviewer ($M = .59$).

Although Ginossar and Trope (1987) discuss these results in the terminology of "rule activation," "accessibility," and "mismatching" (pp. 465–471), unlike Krosnick et al. (1990) they took no measures – such as salience or availability – in any of their experiments that explicitly addressed such cognitive hypotheses. Interestingly, their salience manipulations that led to greater use of base-rate information involved violations of conversational norms, either by presenting prior tasks with uninformative nondiagnostic information before the target task (Experiment 1) or by rewriting the target task in a list style uncharacteristic of normal conversational communication (Experiment 2). Consequently, their results may also be treated as just as consistent with the attributional model that suggests the weighting of individuating information is based on inferences about the Gricean quality of that information, based on perceptions of the source.

In a related vein, Zukier and Pepitone (1984, Experiment 1) enjoined their participants to either behave like clinicians or scientists in making judgments. Thus, when the task was framed as being one of "clinical judgment," participants were asked to call on their "general knowledge, sensitivity, and empathy" in understanding "the individual's personality, profession, and interests" (p. 353). Although not discussed in Gricean terms, these instructions clearly invite participants to stretch the maxim of quality and say what, in other circumstances, they might feel they lack evidence for. On the other hand, the instruction in the scientist condition to behave like "a scientist analyzing data" (p. 353) seems to enjoin participants to be strict with the maxim of quality and not to say what they lack adequate evidence for. As might be expected, the results showed that participants are more likely to weight individuating, information in the clinical condition than in the scientist condition. Interestingly, participants in the scientist condition gave lower probability estimates overall for both the stereotypic and neutral personality descriptions. This would be consistent with a general orientation toward caution and consistent with a strict application of the maxim of quality.

In sum, the above studies on the engineers-and-lawyers problem suggest that participants' use of base-rate information is governed by their assumptions about its conversational quality and relevance. When participants' assumptions about the intentionality, relevance, and quality of the information are undermined, participants tend to use base-rate information more (Ginossar and Trope 1987; Krosnick et al., 1990; Schwarz, Strack, et al., 1991; Trope and Ginossar, 1988). When, in line with the precepts of conversational inference, the participants are enjoined to go beyond the information given they weight individuating information; whereas when they are enjoined to be scientific, they stick to hard facts and figures (Zukier and Pepitone, 1984). This pattern of results suggests that participants typically enter the psychology experiment with the default assumption of conversational rationality that enjoins them to go beyond the information given in making inferences about what is required of them. More important, however, they can make inferences that correspond to scientific norms when their conversational assumptions are canceled by the context. Consequently, the production of bias in such tasks may be less attributable to cognitive factors such as representativeness (Kahneman and Tversky, 1973) or availability (Ginossar and Trope, 1987) than was first thought and may be more attributable to inferences about the social context of the experimental message that are guided by conversational assumptions. Below, I consider another example of how the operation of the representativeness heuristic may be constrained by conversational norms.

Assumed Relevance of Nondiagnostic Information: Accountability and the Activation of Conversational Norms

Although Grice's (1975) maxim of relation prescribes that speakers should include only relevant information, experimenters routinely violate this assumption by deliberately including information that is meant to be irrelevant to the task. A clear example of this is the "dilution" effect studied by Nisbett et al. (1981). They found that participants rationally used information about a target person such as IQ or an effort that is diagnostic of that person's grade point average. However, when the description of the target person included information that was not relevant to the judgment task (such as age, hair color, etc.), participants made less use of the diagnostic information. From the point of view of probability theory, there is no rational reason for this, as the diagnostic information is still as predictive when presented with nondiagnostic information as when presented alone. Nisbett et al. posited an intrapsychic explanation in terms of the representativeness heuristic due to the dilution of the diagnostic information with irrelevant nondiagnostic information, which reduced the perceived similarity of the target person to the target category (cf. Tversky and Kahneman, 1974).

However, as Tetlock and Boettger (1991) pointed out, the effect is also consistent with an explanation in terms of rational processes of conversational inference. Participants may assume that all the information that they are given, whether diagnostic or nondiagnostic, is mentioned because it is relevant. They may therefore weight all the information as diagnostic. On the assumption that nondiagnostic information is weighted negatively, the dilution effect would be observed. Such an effect would be removed if participants believed that the information had been presented without conscious design.

Tetlock and Boettger (1991) therefore presented the information to participants as having been screened for its relevance (thus activating conversational norms) or randomly sampled from a computer database (deactivation of conversational norms), with no information about the conversational relevance of the information. Half the participants were subjected to an accountability manipulation, being told that they would have to explain their decision to others when the experiment was over. This manipulation has been extremely successful in attenuating biases in judgment usually attributed to heuristics because of its presumed effect in inducing more cognitive effort (for a review, see Tetlock, 1992).

Tetlock and Boettger (1991) found that the accountability manipulation led to more use of the nondiagnostic information in the conditions where conversational norms had been activated or no information either way had been given. This is consistent with participants' belief that the nondiagnostic information must be relevant (otherwise, it would not have been mentioned), and the accountable participants' wish to perform well in the judgment task by making maximum use of information that they presume has been guaranteed by the maxim of relevance. These results replicate the findings of Tetlock and Boettger (1989) and suggest that the participants' default assumption is that conversational rules are operative in the experiment. Significantly, when conversational norms have been deactivated, participants were less likely to use the nondiagnostic information, and thus exhibit the dilution effect. Compared with nonaccountable participants in this condition, accountable participants were actually less likely to fall prey to this error, further reinforcing the view that the dilution effect is attributable to the unreciprocated respect participants have for conversational norms in this particular experimental paradigm.

Attributions of Cooperativeness and the Effect of Leading Questions

The default assumption made by Grice's (1975) model of conversational inference is that utterances are cooperatively produced. The attribution of cooperativeness to the speaker is, of course, a special case of the attribution of intention. Other intentions, including adversative ones, may also be attributed to the speaker. Children, of course, are often subjected to trick questions in testing situations by adults. Winer, Hemphill, and Craig (1988) showed that both children and adults give more nonconserving responses when the question seems to imply that conservation is not possible. Thus, the question, "When do you weigh the most, when you are standing or crouching?" seems to imply that body weight changes from one state to another. This question leads to more responses that indicate the weight changes from one state to another than when the question is asked with the tag "or do you weigh the same?" (p. 198).

Kwock and Winer (1986) explored social context variables that would lead children to reject misleading questions. Children were given classifications tasks in which they were shown a picture and asked whether it was X or Y, when in fact it was both. Thus, when shown a picture of a dog, children were asked, "Is this a dog or an animal?" When shown a picture of a black square, they were asked, "Is this black or a square?" Some children had previously been exposed to a training set in which questions fla-

grantly violated conversational norms. For example, they were shown a picture of a couch and asked, "Why is this a car?" These children were more likely to reject the misleading implication of the classification question that the object could not be both than children who had not been exposed to the questions that violated the rules of conversation. In a second experiment, Kwock and Winer found that third graders were more likely to reject the misleading implication of the question when they were asked by another third grader than by an adult.

Both children and adults are vulnerable to misleading questions. Children are less vulnerable when the questions are asked by low-credibility sources, such as other children. In addition, children's susceptibility to misleading questions decreases when they have experienced flagrantly bizarre questions asked by the adult, presumably because the credibility of the adult experimenter is then undermined (for an extensive review, see Siegal, 1991).

Conversational Inference and the Effect of Leading Questions on Memory

One of the best-known *framing* effects concerns the effect of leading questions on memory. In a classic experiment, Loftus and Palmer (1974) showed that the presuppositions loaded into questions about an automobile accident affected participants' memory about that accident. Thus, if participants were asked how fast a car was going when it *smashed* into a truck, they were more likely to give a higher estimate of the speed of the car in a subsequent memory test than if they had been asked how fast the car had been going when it *hit* the truck. These findings were consistent with other results that showed participants were inclined to accept presuppositions associated with descriptions of scenes, even when those presuppositions were not actually true of the scenes described (Hornby, 1972, 1974).

However, the effect of leading questions on memory may occur only in social settings where the cooperativeness principle is assumed to hold valid, such as psychology experiments. Participants may have assumed that the experimenter in Loftus and Palmer's (1974) study was cooperative and thus have uncritically accepted the presuppositions loaded into the question. To test this interpretation, Dodd and Bradshaw (1980) found no effect of leading questions on memory as compared with a control condition when the source was specified as a lawyer representing the defendant, although they were able to replicate the original result when the source of the leading question was the experimenter, as in Loftus and Palmer's original procedure.

Dodd and Bradshaw's (1980) results are consistent with the suggestion that when the leading question was attributed to an adversative source, such as a defending lawyer in an American court, participants suspended the assumption of cooperativeness and thus were not vulnerable to the biasing effects of leading questions. Interestingly, participants were still vulnerable to biasing effects from the recall probes about the speed of the car, which varied the descriptive cues used ("How fast was the car going when it hit/collided with/smashed"..., etc.). However, the recall probes all emanated from the same source (the experimenter) regardless of experimental condition and thus may still have been treated as guaranteed by the assumption of cooperativeness and used to infer the speed of the vehicle. Consequently, although the Loftus and Palmer (1974) results are typically discussed as demonstrating the effect of cognitive biases on memory, they may be plausibly attributed to the operation of conversational assumptions, which guide reconstructive inferences about the speed of the car. This interpretation is consistent with the findings of Strack, Schwarz, Bless, Kübler, and Wänke (1993) who showed that when participants are made aware of the priming episode, they appear to discount its influence, much in the manner suggested above. However, as Martin, Seta, and Crelia (1990) suggested, such discounting may require extra cognitive effort and therefore occur only when people are motivated by the task and have sufficient cognitive resources to allocate to it.

Given–New Contract and Mutual Knowledge

Grice's (1975) logic of conversation requires that speakers should be brief (satisfying the maxim of manner) and informative (satisfying the maxim of quantity). For this reason, speakers often do not explicitly refer to old information, treating it as given. Correspondingly, hearers are expected to focus on the new information contained in an utterance. This expectation is sometimes referred to as the *given–new contract*. Considerable evidence exists that speakers are sensitive to the mutual knowledge they share with listeners in the formulation of their utterances and that hearers are better at decoding messages from speakers with whom they share

common ground (Clark, 1985, 1992; Fussell and Krauss, 1989, 1992; Krauss and Fussell, 1991).

The given–new contract can force reinterpretations of *wholes* in the context of *parts* that they logically include. As Adler (1984) noted, children may interpret the class-inclusion questions in Piagetian conservation experiments this way: If asked the question, "Are there more primulas or are there more flowers?" children may treat *primulas* as given information and re-interpret *flowers* to mean flowers other than primulas and correspondingly answer that there are more primulas than flowers. Politzer (1993) presented experimental evidence that supports this analysis. As is shown below, this subtraction rule can explain many patterns of response that might otherwise be attributed to cognitive deficiencies, as done in Piagetian experiments.

Part–Whole Contrasts and Children's Learning of Names

The given–new contract, and the assumptions behind it, often forces contextually based interpretations of what is said. For example, Markman and Wachtel (1988) showed 3- and 4-year-old children a familiar object, such as a banana, and an unfamiliar one, such as a lemon wedge-press. Children were then asked, "Show me the *x*," where *x* was a nonsense syllable. Children almost invariably selected the unfamiliar object. Clearly, children's reasoning may be based on conversational assumptions that a cooperative experimenter would have said, "Show me the banana" if they had wanted the banana, so the unfamiliar word must refer to the unfamiliar object. Only if the adult were violating Grice's (1975) maxim of manner, and using an obscure, unknown word to refer to the banana when a well-known one (*banana*) exists, could the adult have reasonably intended the nonsense syllable to refer to the familiar object.

Markman and Wachtel (1988) extended this procedure to the study of part–whole relations. They showed children pictures of an object with a salient part. The object (e.g., a lung) was either familiar or unfamiliar to the children, whereas the part (e.g., a trachea) was always unfamiliar. When the object was unfamiliar, children tended to treat the new word (i.e., *trachea*) as referring to the whole object (i.e., *lung*). However, when children already knew the word *lung*, they were more likely to interpret the unfamiliar word *trachea* as referring to the specific part of the lung (i.e., the trachea). Clearly, the children may have been reasoning that the adults wished to be informative by Grice's (1975) maxim of quantity and asked the children to name the object that they did not know. Otherwise, this particular conversation would seem to have no point.

Subsequent research has shown conditions in which children do not follow the principle of mutual exclusivity and accept that two expressions can refer to the same object. For example, when context suggests that one word indicates a subset of another larger set (e.g., dingo dogs and dogs), children between 3 and 5 years old consider that both expressions refer to members of the lower-level category (Au and Glusman, 1990; Gelman, Wilcox, and Clark, 1989). This effect seems acceptable conversational practice: Using a more specific term to refer to a previously categorized object adds precision even though the object may have been categorized at a more general level.

Another condition in which children do not follow the assumption of mutual exclusivity is when they know that the speaker is bilingual and may use words from both languages to describe the same object. In such cases, bilingual children between 3 and 7 years old who have heard the experimenter use both languages readily accept that two words can refer to the same object, as do monolingual children between 3 and 5 years old who have been led to believe that they are going to learn words from the foreign language. Clearly, children's expectations about their interlocutor's capacities and intentions can determine whether they assume mutual exclusivity of names. For example, in a teaching or testing situation, it is still informative and relevant for the adult to teach or test for Spanish vocabulary even if the adult knows the child has the requisite English vocabulary and thus attributes two different names to the same object.

Although the nonapplication of mutual exclusivity seems very consistent with Gricean rules of inference, none of the articles cited explicitly use this approach. However, children's decisions about the rational interpretation of the referents of names can be explained in terms of the assumption that the speaker was trying to be informative. If children's successful performance in naming objects in these tasks depends on conversational assumptions, this hypothesis could be tested by performing experiments that use nonadult interlocutors for the children (e.g., naughty teddies and other children) or that explicitly signal to the children that their normal conversational assumptions should be suspended (see Kwock and Winer, 1986; for a thorough discussion of such techniques, also see Siegal, 1991).

Part–Whole Contrasts and the Interpretation of Survey Questions

Strack et al. (1988) reasoned that if a specific question precedes a general one that logically includes it, hearers interpret the general question to exclude the information already mentioned in the first question. Suppose a female survey respondent is asked about satisfaction with her life in general, she is likely to report her global satisfaction with her personal and professional life. If, however, she is asked first about her professional life and then about her life in general, she will treat life in general as referring to nonprofessional parts of her life if she wishes to respect the maxim of quantity and give her questioner new information.

Strack et al. (1988) applied this reasoning to the analysis of seemingly inconsistent responses to survey questions. In one condition, which they termed the *conversational context*, Strack et al. introduced the two questions by saying, "Now, we would like to learn about two areas of life that may be important for people's overall well-being: (a) happiness with dating, (b) happiness with life in general" (p. 434). In this condition, they hypothesized that the focus of the general question be interpreted as excluding the focus of the specific question that has been asked first. Because answers to the two questions would be based on different information, there should not be much correlation. When students were asked to rate their satisfaction with life in general after rating their satisfaction with their dating life, the correlation was very low (.26).

However, when the specific question was asked at the end of one page and the general question was asked at the beginning of the next page, Strack et al. (1988) reasoned that the two questions would not be perceived as being related and that these should be no such subtraction effect. Consistent with this reasoning, a much higher correlation (.55) was obtained for respondents' ratings of their responses to these two questions in this condition. Similar results were obtained by Schwarz, Strack, and Mai (1991).

Consequently, seemingly inconsistent responses can be explained in terms of conversational pragmatics. Also important to note is that the exclusion of the information from the preceding question (e.g., about the respondent's satisfaction with his or her marriage) from the response to the subsequent question (e.g., about satisfaction with life in general) cannot be explained in terms of priming theories. Because the information about marriage has been so recently mentioned, it should be highly available in memory and thus, according to a straightforward priming theory, have more impact on the subsequent judgment. Although cognitive accessibility may often affect salience, principles of conversational inference can override the application of the availability heuristic (cf. Strack, 1992).

Part–Whole Contrasts and the Conjunction Fallacy

Dulany and Hilton (1991) applied this logic to the analysis of Tversky and Kahneman's (1983) conjunction fallacy task. In the best-known version of this task, participants read a detailed description of a target person:

> Linda is 31 years old, single, outspoken, and very bright. She majored in philosophy. As a student she was deeply concerned with issues of discrimination and social justice, and also participated in anti-nuclear demonstrations. (p. 297)

Participants are then asked to check which one of the following two alternatives is most probable:

> Linda is a bank teller. (T)
> Linda is a bank teller and is active in the feminist movement. (T and F) (p. 297)

Tversky and Kahneman (1983) reported that 85% of the participants rated the conjunction of constituents (T and F) as more probable than the single constituent (T). This *conjunction effect* is considered a fallacy because a conjunction of two constituents cannot be more probable than one of the constituents alone. The logic of extensional sets requires that the class of people who are bank tellers and feminists be a subset of the class of people who are bank tellers. Tversky and Kahneman argued that people make this error in probability judgment because they are guided by the representativeness heuristic, which finds the conjunction (T and F) to be more similar to the *model* (i.e., the target description of Linda) than the constituent (T) alone and therefore is judged as more probable. As support of this, they noted that very few participants commit the conjunction fallacy in the *no-model* condition where minimal information about the target ("Linda is 31

years old") is presented because this fails to activate the representativeness heuristic.

Several researchers have argued from conversational principles that participants interpret "Linda is a bank teller" (T) to mean Linda is a bank teller who is not active in the feminist movement (T and not F) in this context (Morier and Borgida, 1984; Politzer and Noveck, 1991). If so, the judgment that T is more probable than T and F is no longer a fallacy because T is implicitly read as indicating another kind of conjunction, namely, T and not F. On the basis of an analysis of attribution processes in conversational inference, Dulany and Hilton (1991) sought to predict the conditions under which participants would draw the absolving interpretation of "Linda is a bank teller." They argued that the rich information given to the participant in the model condition may justify the inference that the experimenter knows a lot about the target. The participant may reason that if the experimenter knows a lot about the target, Linda, then the reason the experimenter omitted to say that Linda is active in the feminist movement is because he or she knows this not to be the case, thus conveying a K-implicature (Levinson, 1983) that Linda is not active in the feminist movement. By contrast, in the no-model condition, the participant may reason that the experimenter did not say that Linda is a bank teller because he or she does not know whether this is the case or not, thus implying the P-implicature (Levinson, 1983) that it is logically possible that Linda either may or may not be a bank teller. The P-implicature corresponds to the extensional interpretation of the constituent that would imply that the conjunction effect is indeed a logical fallacy. Dulany and Hilton found that participants did in fact draw more K-implicatures in the model condition as predicted. Thus, they were most likely to make interpretations that would absolve them of charges of fallacious reasoning in just those conditions where they were most likely to judge the conjunction as more probable than the constituent. When interpretations were controlled, Dulany and Hilton found a greatly reduced fallacy rate of 25% to 30%.[3]

Tversky and Kahneman (1983) acknowledged that participants may be interpreting T to mean T and not F and sought to deal with this problem by developing a *direct* version of the task in which the extensional nature of the conjunct was explicitly stated. Thus they asked participants to judge the probability of "Linda is a bank teller whether or not she is active in the feminist movement." However, this phrasing is also unsatisfactory as it could be reinterpreted as "Linda is a bank teller even if she is active in the feminist movement," in much the same way as "We will go to the zoo tomorrow whether or not it rains" can be interpreted as "We will go to the zoo tomorrow even if it rains. Following Grice's (1975) maxim of manner, Dulany and Hilton (1991) developed a less ambiguous version of the direct test and found less than half the conjunction fallacies obtained by Tversky and Kahneman. Thus, it seems that ambiguities in the wording used may have led Tversky and Kahneman to overestimate the number of conjunction fallacies committed.

In a closely related analysis, Politzer and Noveck (1991) showed how changes to the linguistic structure of the conjunction task that preserve its logical form also reduce error rates. In one of their problems, participants were told that Daniel was a bright high school student and were then asked to judge the probability of the following three predictions about his performance in further studies:

> Daniel entered medical school. (M)
> Daniel dropped out of medical school for lack of interest. (presupposed M and D)
> Daniel graduated from medical school. (presupposed M and G) (p. 93)

In this case, the constituent "Daniel entered medical school" is presupposed by his later dropping out or graduating. Following the conjunction rule, the implicit conjunctions should be judged as less probable than the constituent. Thirty percent of the participants did in fact judge one of the conjunctions (presupposed M and D or presupposed M and G) to be more probable than the constituent (M), thus committing the fallacy.

The Daniel problem resembles Tversky and Kahneman's (1983) Linda problem in terms of the class inclusion relations between the alternatives but differs in that these class inclusion relations are not suggested explicitly. However, it is possible to change the Daniel problem such that these relations are expressed explicitly through the connective and, as follows:

> Daniel entered medical school. (M)
> Daniel entered medical school and dropped out for lack of interest (M and D)
> Daniel entered medical school and graduated. (M and G) (p. 93)

Politzer and Noveck (1991) argued that as in the Linda problem, the use of and will force

the implicature that the constituent implies a conjunction (either M and not D or M and not G). In this explicit condition, 53% of the participants rated one the conjunctions (M and D or M and G) as more probable than the constituent (M). Politzer and Noveck thus claimed that making the inclusion relation explicit through the use of the connective and actually worsens performance, thus casting doubt on Tversky and Kahneman's (1983) claim that "people are not accustomed to the detection of nesting among events, even when the relations are clearly displayed" (p. 304). Equally, they observed that the increase in the error rate produced by the introduction of and seems to contradict Tversky and Kahneman's (1983) view that "the conjunction fallacy is not restricted to esoteric interpretations of the connective and" (p. 303).

Unlike Dulany and Hilton (1991), Politzer and Noveck (1991) did not assess how their manipulation of the explicitness of the class inclusion relation might have affected the implicature drawn from the constituent. Nevertheless, although much remains to be done to elucidate how the response alternatives used in conjunction tasks are interpreted (see Adler, 1991; Fiedler, 1988; Wolford, Taylor, and Beck, 1990, for alternative approaches), enough already seems to have been done to illustrate the value of using conversational pragmatics to analyze these issues.

Relevance of Incidental Information

Grice's (1975) maxim of relation enjoins speakers to be relevant. Speakers should not mention irrelevant information. Thus, hearers are entitled to assume that all the information given to them is relevant to the task at hand and, according to the maxim of quality, not misleading in any way. However, experimenters often include irrelevant information that may in fact be used by participants to interpret their experimental task. As is shown below, such irrelevant information may be conveyed through the kinds of dependent measures used or through interpretations of the independent variables that were not intended by the experimenter.

Relevance of Information Contained in Response Scales

Although experimenters generally use response scales to assess participants' judgments and not to influence them, there is considerable evidence that participants often use response scales as cues about the character and extent of the behavior probed (Schwarz, 1990; Wyer, 1981).

For example, the range indicated by the response scale may cue participants' interpretation of the behavior. Schwarz, Strack, Mueller, and Deutsch (1988) asked participants how often they had felt really irritated recently. One group of participants was given a scale ranging from *several times daily* to *less than once a week*, whereas other participants were given a scale ranging from *several times a year* to *less than once every three months* (p. 112). They argued that participants would use their world knowledge to decide what kind of irritations were implied by the experimenter's question. Consistent with their reasoning, participants given the former scale reported less extreme examples of irritation (e.g., having to wait for service in a restaurant). Participants given the latter scale reported more extreme examples of irritation (e.g., having a fight with one's spouse).

The numeric values assigned to points on a rating scale may also affect how a survey question is interpreted. Suppose respondents have to evaluate how successful they have been in life on an 11-point rating scale, ranging from *not at all successful* to *extremely successful*. However, the numerical labeling of the scale may influence how the question is perceived. Thus, if the 11 points on the scale are labeled from 0 to 10, respondents may interpret *not at all successful* to indicate lack of outstanding success. On the other hand, a scale ranging from −5 through 0 to 5 may lead them to interpret *not at all successful* as *extremely unsuccessful*. Accordingly, respondents may mark the absence of outstanding successes as 0 on the 0 to 10 scale, but also as 0 on the −5 to 5 scale, because they interpret −5 to mean a resounding failure rather than the absence of success. This would lead to greater use of the bottom end of the 0 to 10 scale than the −5 to 5 scale, where the bottom end would be reserved for resounding failures. Schwarz, Knäuper, et al. (1991) did indeed observe that 34% of the respondents checked the lower half of the 0 to 10 scale, whereas only 13% checked the lower half of the −5 to 5 scale. Subsequent studies also indicated that respondents were more likely to treat 2 on a 0 to 10 scale as indicating the absence of success but −4 on a −5 to 5 scale as the presence of failure, although the two scales are formally identical.

Respondents may also use response scales to decide the likely frequency of a target behavior. For example, Schwarz, Hippler, Deutsch, and Strack (1985) asked German adults to rate how frequently they watched television. Half the respondents received a scale ranging in ½-hr steps from *up to ½ hour* to *more than 2 ½ hours*, and the other half received a scale ranging from *up to 2 ½ hours* to *more than 4 ½ hours* (p. 390). Only 16% of the respondents who received the low-frequency scale reported watching television for more than 2 ½ hours, whereas 38% of the respondents who received the high-frequency scale did so. Similar effects of range of response alternatives for estimations of sexual intercourse and masturbation in dating couples exist (Schwarz and Scheuring, 1988).

Moderating Effect of Expertise on Range Effects

It might be conjectured that the effect of scale ranges on frequency estimation may reflect anchoring effects (Tversky and Kahneman, 1974). However, respondents' susceptibility to the effect of scale ranges is mediated by their knowledgeability of the topic in question. Thus, U.S. college students were least likely to be biased by scale ranges when estimating their own or a friend's frequency of watching television than when estimating the television consumption of a typical undergraduate. Moreover, college students who are high on private self-consciousness (Fenigstein, Scheier, and Buss, 1975) are less likely to be influenced by scale ranges than students low on private self-consciousness. This is consistent with the view that high-on-private-self-consciousness individuals, who reflect more about the nature of their behavior, are more likely to know how often they watch television (Schwarz et al., 1985).

Comparable results were obtained by Joyce and Biddle (1981). They showed that trained accountants were not subject to anchoring effects on an auditing task when they themselves generated the anchors. Self-generated anchors cannot provide information about the experimenter's estimate of the frequency of a behavior in the target population. However, trained accountants were still susceptible to anchoring effects on tasks when the experimenter provided the anchors (Joyce and Biddle, 1981).

Similar results were obtained by Sanbonmatsu, Kardes, and Herr (1992), who showed that expertise moderated the effects of incomplete information on preference judgments. Respondents were presented either with four or eight statements about a camera that were uniformly positive (e.g., "The Brand A camera is lighter and more compact than most other

35-mm cameras"). The respondents had been classified as possessing either high, medium, or low knowledge about cameras. Expertise had no effect on preference when the amount of information given was large. However, when the amount of information given was small, high-knowledge respondents were significantly less positive in their evaluations. Presumably, low- and medium-knowledge respondents considered the range of relevant information given to be complete, whether they received four or eight items of information. However, high-knowledge respondents who received four items of information presumably recognized that information about important dimensions of judgment was missing. In the absence of explicitly positive statements about dimensions known by the experts to be relevant, they may have implicitly presumed relatively negative attributes on these dimensions. This would have resulted in the more negative evaluation reported. Sanbonmatsu et al. suggested that these findings are inconsistent with the predictions of the anchoring and adjustment hypothesis, which would predict that the effect of set size on favorability of impressions should generalize across all respondents, regardless of expertise.

In sum, experimental results suggest that when respondents do not have direct access to the frequency information required, they use the frequency range provided by the experimenter to estimate the likely frequency of a behavior in the population, which they then use to calculate their response, for example, their position on that scale. Respondents seem to be guided by a strategy of guessing on the basis of the response scales that had been provided by a cooperative experimenter who did not wish to mislead the respondent about the likely range of responses in the population studied. Cognitive explanations based on anchoring and adjustment cannot explain why self-provided anchors are ineffective, why experimenter-provided anchors are most effective in domains about which the respondent knows little, or why set size effects on preference judgment are most pronounced for experts.

Relevance of the Range and Phrasing of Response Sets: A Reexamination of Attribution Experiments

It is often claimed that respondents underuse consensus information, a form of base-rate information referring to how other people would have behaved in the target situation (Alloy

and Tabachnik, 1984; Higgins and Bargh, 1987; Kassin, 1979; McArthur, 1972, 1976; Nisbett and Borgida, 1975; Nisbett, Borgida, Crandall, and Reed, 1976; Ross and Fletcher, 1985). One reason for this claim is that in an influential study, McArthur found little influence of consensus information on attributions. However, Hilton (1990b) suggested that this pattern may be the result of methodological artifacts. One factor of key importance is McArthur's failure to specify interactional attributions in her response format. In such studies, respondents are given a target event such as "Sue is afraid of the dog" and three items of covariation information: consensus, indicating covariation of the target behavior over other persons (whether other people are afraid of the dog); distinctiveness, indicating covariation of the target behavior over other stimuli (whether Sue is afraid of other dogs); and consistency, indicating covariation of the target behavior over other times (whether Sue has been afraid of this dog on other occasions). A representative information pattern that respondents might receive in such studies is the low-consensus, high-distinctiveness, low-consistency information configuration below:

Sue is afraid of the dog.
Hardly anyone else is afraid of the dog.
Sue is afraid of hardly any other dog.
In the past, Sue has hardly ever been afraid of this dog.

In McArthur's (1972, 1976) original tests of Kelley's (1967) model, respondents were given main effect attributions to the person, stimulus, or circumstances to select or were asked to write any interactional attributions in a space provided.

Please circle the cause of the event.
    a. Something about Sue caused her to be afraid of the dog.
    b. Something about the dog caused her to be afraid of it.
    c. Something about the circumstances caused Sue to be afraid of the dog.
    d. Some combination of these causes. (please write your answer in the space below)

The attribution predicted by the application of Mill's (1872/1973) method of difference is the combination of the person, the stimulus, and the circumstances (Jaspars, Hewstone, and Fincham, 1983). However, McArthur (1972, 1976) found a strong preference to attribute this configuration to a single effect, the circumstances (cf. Orvis, Cunningham, and Kelley, 1975).

This attributional pattern could reflect a bias produced by the response set. This set of response alternatives, in combination with the use of the ambiguous term *the circumstances*, may have caused respondents not to make predicted interactional attributions to combinations of factors (e.g., the person and stimulus and the occasion). Respondents may have taken the lack of interactional attributions explicitly specified in the response format as a cue not to produce them and may have also used *the circumstances* to indicate interactional attributions. This supposition is supported by results obtained by studies that used a full set of response alternatives:

Please circle the cause of the event.
  a. Something about Sue caused her to be afraid of the dog.
  b. Something about the dog caused her to be afraid of it.
  c. Something about the circumstances caused Sue to be afraid of the dog.
  d. Some combination of Sue and the dog caused her to be afraid of it.
  e. Some combination of Sue and the circumstances caused her to be afraid of the dog.
  f. Some combination of the dog and the circumstances caused Sue to be afraid of it.
  g. Some combination of Sue, the dog, and the circumstances caused her to be afraid of it.

With this format, the most favored response is the predicted interactional attribution to the combination of the person, the stimulus, and the circumstances (Jaspars, 1983). More generally, studies that did give a full range of interactional attributions in the response format found 61% (Jaspars, 1983) and 47% (Hilton and Jaspars, 1987) interactional attributions, whereas studies that did not use such response formats found only 37% (McArthur, 1972) and 35% (Hewstone and Jaspars, 1983) interactional attributions. Thus, the data collected by McArthur may have been systematically biased (Hilton, 1990b). Studies that used full-response formats show the predicted effect of consensus information on person attribution (Cheng and Novick, 1990; Försterling, 1989; Hilton and Jaspars, 1987; Iacobucci and McGill, 1990; Jaspars, 1983). Consequently, the original finding that consensus information is underused may be attributable to methodological problems, in part caused by

how respondents interpreted the response sets that they were given (Hilton, 1990b).

Another explanation for the apparent underuse of consensus information may have been the failure of earlier research to take into account the role of respondents' pragmatic presuppositions about event base rates in causal inference (Cheng and Novick, 1990; Försterling, 1989). In addition, actor – observer differences (Jones and Nisbett, 1972) and success – failure asymmetries in explanation (Weiner et al., 1972) are amenable to explanation in terms of pragmatic question focus (McGill, 1989). Interested readers are referred to Hilton (1990a, 1991) for a detailed discussion.

Pragmatic Inferences and Stimulus Vocabulary Choice

Some pragmatic phenomena are not determined by inferences about the speaker's intended meaning derived through application of Grice's (1975) principles (Levinson, 1983). These include inferences about focus determined through *pragmatic particles*. Pragmatic particles – such as *but, few, a few, occasionally*, and *seldom* – conventionally determine the interpretation of words with which they are conjoined, as well as having truth values that determine their own range of applicability. For example, *seldom* and *occasionally* indicate approximately the same frequency of occurrence of a behavior and thus have the same truth values. However, although similar in semantic terms, they have different pragmatic properties. Thus, they focus attention on different aspects of the behavior (Moxey and Sanford, 1987). If one is asked to explain why John seldom walks the dog, one is apt to come up with reasons for the nonoccurrence of the behavior (e.g., because he is always busy), whereas if one is asked to explain why he occasionally walks the dog, one tends to give reasons that account for the occurrence of the behavior (e.g., because he likes the exercise).

Experimental psychologists and survey researchers who are not aware of the functions of pragmatic particles are liable to produce unintended effects or to misattribute effects that they obtain. An example can be found in the stimulus material used by Kahneman and Miller (1986) to test norm theory. Kahneman and Miller argued that unusual events are more likely to activate counterfactual alternatives in which the nonoccurrence of the target event is brought to mind. However, if an experimenter describes an event as *seldom* rather than *occasionally* happening, then this would serve as a cue to the respondent to focus on why the event did not happen rather than why it did happen, regardless of the actual normality of the event. Such is the case in one of the stimulus passages used by Kahneman and Miller: "On the day of the accident, Mr. Jones left the office earlier than usual, to attend to some household chores at his wife's request. He drove home along his regular route. Mr. Jones occasionally chose to drive along the shore, to enjoy the view on exceptionally clear days, but that day was just average" (p. 143). Hence, one cannot be sure whether the effects obtained (e.g., events undone by counterfactual reasoning) are attributable to the normality of the events described or to the focus indicated by the experimenter's choice of temporal quantifier.

A related effect may be the *forbid–allow* asymmetry studied by Hippler and Schwarz (1986). Forbidding something and not allowing something appear to be semantically similar; they would seem to be true of the same kind of event. However, survey respondents are much more likely to agree, for example, that peepshows should not be allowed than that they should be forbidden (Hippler and Schwarz, 1986). Although it is not altogether clear why the forbid–allow asymmetry should exist, it is clear that seemingly irrelevant changes in phrasing that appear to preserve the literal meaning of the target stimulus, nevertheless, change the meaning conveyed to the respondent.

Transparency of Reference and Use of Base-Rate Information

Grice's (1975) maxim of manner exhorts speakers to be clear and unambiguous. Using methods similar to those of Dulany and Hilton (1991), Macchi (1991) showed that respondents use base-rate information in response to questions that clarify the nature of the judgment required. In one of Macchi's experimental tasks, adapted from the suicide problem of Tversky and Kahneman (1980), respondents were informed that 80% of a population of young adults were married, whereas 20% were single. They were also told that the percentage of deaths is three times higher among single individuals than among married individuals. Macchi suggested that the phrasing "three times higher" is ambiguous between the percentage of all suicides (implying that 75% of deaths are singles, whereas 25% are marrieds) and the percentage among singles as opposed to the per-

centage among marrieds. It is an empirical question as to the interpretation that is more likely to be preferred here and a normative question for the rules of conversation to decide which is more rational. In any case, respondents' median response (3:1) is entirely consistent with the former interpretation. Thus, respondents appear not to use the base-rate information about the proportion of marrieds and singles in the population in making their judgments.

Noting that this effect may be due to a misunderstanding, Macchi (1991) rephrased this item of information as "30% of single individuals and 10% of married individuals commit suicide" (p. 9), which has the merit of being unambiguous, clear, and coherent with the manner of describing the base-rate information, which was also expressed in percentage. In this condition, respondents used the base-rate information appropriately.

Macchi (1991) also showed that similar changes in discourse structure that add no information but simply clarify the relationship between supersets and subsets produce similar variations in use of base-rate information in Tversky and Kahneman's (1980) suicide problem. In particular, she showed that the manipulation of causal relevance that induced use of base-rate information may have done so because it manipulated discourse structure by explicitly mentioning both the superset (young adults) and the subset (suicides) in the same question. A similar superset–subset phrasing of a logically similar but noncausal problem involving books and paperbacks likewise induced use of base-rate information, whereas a question that referred explicitly to the subset but not to the superset did not induce corresponding use of base-rate information. As has been noted above with other paradigms, an effect (the use of base-rate information) may have been misattributed to a cognitive factor (causal relevance) when in fact it is attributable to discourse processes.

Implications of Conversational Inference for the Attribution of Rationality

The larger issue addressed in this review has been the attribution of rationality or irrationality to human judgments. I have argued that in many cases judgments that have been or could be considered irrational may in fact be considered rational if prior processes of conversational inference are taken into account. These shape the representation of the task used by the experimental or survey respondent. Moreover, these processes of conversational inference are not ad hoc or defective in some way but reflect the rationality of social interaction and communication, where trade-offs have to be made, for example, between explicitness and economy in communication. Consequently, as in everyday communication, respondents may transform the information given explicitly by the experimenter by adding information they assume to be relevant but omitted by a cooperative experimenter who assumed that such information was implicitly shared. Alternatively, they may assume that all the information given by the experimenter must be relevant, otherwise why mention it? Or, they may assume that the order in which the information is presented indicates its degree of importance or relevance to the judgment task.

In each case, the respondent goes beyond the information given (or intended to be given) by the experimenter. Such departures from the explicit reasoning task may not be so much the result of an individual's failure to apply normative rules of inference properly to the information given (the cognitive bias explanation) but to the socially skilled application of shared rules of message interpretation (the conversational inference interpretation). These rules of inference have a quite general application. Thus, undermining the assumption of intentionality reduces biases in such diverse tasks as Piagetian conservation tasks, the engineers-and-lawyers task of Tversky and Kahneman (1974), and the leading questions paradigm of Loftus and Palmer (1974). Another example is the similar kinds of experimental demands created by juxtaposing questions comparing specific and general quantities in tasks involving conservation, object naming, probability judgments, and survey judgments of life satisfaction. Conversational inference thus has general features that emerge in a wide range of tasks.

In particular, I have argued that two important features of conversational inferences are their ampliativeness and their defeasibility. Like good inductions, good conversational inferences go beyond the information given and can be corrected by empirical evidence. However, these general properties of conversational inference are in direct conflict with basic assumptions of much judgment research, as is discussed below.

particular ways and be justified in adding extra premises that seem to be relevant in interpreting what is said. The inductive nature of conversational inference poses a general problem for the metaphysical assumptions of workers interested in assessing errors in human judgment. This is because such workers normally assume that the correct answer can be determined by applying a normative model to the explicitly given data set, such as Bayes' rule for probabilistic inference tasks (Tversky and Kahneman, 1974) or the assumption of reversibility of logical operations for conservation tasks (Inhelder and Piaget, 1958).

In the negative rationality perspective (Rommetveit, 1978), errors are defined by deviations from the predictions of the normative model. The inference task is thus essentially deductive in nature; given the premises, the correct answer can be deduced. However, according to conversational inference, it is rational to add to, elaborate, or reinterpret the information given, subject to Gricean assumptions. Consequently, the overall experimental task of forming a representation of the information given and of reasoning from that representation also becomes inductive in nature. In assessing the overall rationality of the participant's response, the experimenter has to take the rationality of his or her interpretation of the task into account, as well as the rationality of his or her reasoning processes.

The inductive nature of conversational inference suggests that many of the experimental results that have been attributed to faulty reasoning may be reinterpreted as being due to rational interpretations of experimenter-given information. However, the attributional model of conversational inference does not imply that respondents never make bona fide errors of reasoning. Rather, better specification of these inference processes should enable researchers to identify cases in which mistakes may be attributable to conversationally guided interpretations of the judgment task, as opposed to cases in which mistakes are due to genuine errors of reasoning. Below, I consider how the present framework can help classify errors more clearly, by either explicitly controlling respondents' assumptions about the conversational relevance of information or assessing the representations built on the basis of such assumptions.

Implications of Conversational Inference for the Thesis of Negative Rationality

According to the logic of conversation, respondents may interpret what is said to them in

Controlling for Conversational Inference: Methodological Implications

The present framework suggests that the interpretation of experimenter-given information should be systematically investigated and controlled for in experimental and survey research. Although the research reported in this review gives support to the attributional model of conversational inference, much of it was not conducted with this model in mind and therefore did not examine variables that would enable a full test of the model. Below, I suggest some general methodological procedures that can aid in this task.

First, as suggested by the attributional model of conversational inference, assumptions about the source of a message can be manipulated or otherwise controlled. For example, the basic assumption of conversational inference that the source is intentional can be undermined by persuading the respondent that the information provided has been randomly generated (e.g., by computer) or has been generated by the respondent (e.g., through the respondent's own search efforts).

Second, even where the source is intentional, the respondent's perception of the reliability of the source may be affected by the cooperativeness or knowledgeability of the source. As argued above (e.g., Dulany and Hilton, 1991), the inference that what is left unsaid did not in fact happen because it would otherwise have been mentioned by a cooperative and knowledgeable speaker rests on attributions about the speaker. These attributions can be measured and manipulated. For example, the intuition that a witness who gives more details is more credible (although precise descriptions must necessarily have less chance of being true than vague ones, see Macdonald, 1986) may rest on the assumption that detailed testimony indicates a clear mind, attentiveness, and first-hand experience of the event in question. However, where detailed testimony indicates unreliability (e.g., when it seems improbable that any witness could form a coherent and detailed impression of the scene, for example, in the seconds after the assassination of President John F. Kennedy), it may be perceived as less probable than a fleeting description of the scene. Such questions are open to empirical verification.

Third, key words should be checked for conventional implicatures. Words such as *but* and *although* suggest an adversative relation between items of information and signal the experimenter's expectancies. Likewise, quantifiers such as *a few* and *few*, and adverbs such as *occasionally* and *seldom*, signal the speaker's focus of interest (e.g., on reasons for doing or not doing, respectively). Although words signaling

conventional implicatures are few (Grice, 1968), they are frequently used. Consequently, where their use may signal the experimenter's hypothesis, they should be suppressed, or alternatively, dual versions of the task should be created that signal both the hypothesis and its contrary (e.g., the use of *occasionally* in tests of the norm theory, Kahneman and Miller, 1986, p. 143). For example, Krosnick et al. (1990) made use of this technique in comparing the effects of *but* and *although* on the integration of base-rate and diagnostic information.

Fourth, experimenters need to be fully sensitive to conversational implicatures. For example, Tversky and Kahneman (1983) were quite aware of conversational explanations of the conjunction fallacy and tried to rebut these with a direct phrasing of the conjunction. However, their extensional phrasing "Linda is a bank teller whether or not she is a feminist" (the intended meaning is "bank teller and either feminist or not a feminist") can be rationally understood as "Linda is a bank teller even if she is a feminist" (the conveyed meaning is "bank teller and feminist"), just as the everyday phrase "Let's go to the zoo whether or not it rains" conveys "Let's go to the zoo even if it does rain." Such examples suggest that even those psychologists sensitive to conversational processes may benefit from a deeper consideration of the nature of conversational implicature (cf. Adler, 1991).

Fifth, respondents' interpretations of experimenter-given information can be checked by either multiple-choice check methods or analysis of open-ended protocols (e.g., Dulany and Hilton, 1991; Macchi, 1991). Of course, to be effective, the coding of such data needs to be in terms of categories that can be justified on theoretical grounds.

Sixth, the production of open-ended responses may be controlled by explicitly instructing respondents to maximize the maxim of either quality or quantity. Such variation in instructions has been shown to affect respondents' verbal protocols (Fiedler, Semin, and Bolten, 1989) and may be a useful technique in exploring respondents' representations of their task. For example, respondents may be more likely to include inferred conversational implicatures in a verbal protocol when told to be as informative as possible, but less so if instructed to stick as close as possible to the truth.

Seventh, researchers need to test for evidence supporting the implication of any nonconversational variables they hypothesize as causing a pattern of judgment. For example, theorists have sometimes made claims about the role of cognitive variables in judgment such as salience (Trope and Ginossar, 1988) or causal relevance (Tversky and Kahneman, 1980), without collecting relevant recall, recognition, and belief measures. That they have not felt the need to do so perhaps testifies to a perception shared by editors and reviewers that a plausible alternative position does not exist. In the future, more studies should include measures that test for the operation of both cognitive biases and conversational inference processes.

Eighth, if changes with age in performance on various reasoning tasks are due to development of conversational inference strategies, then such changes should appear simultaneously on several tasks. For example, if young children's failure in the conservation task and their use of the mutual exclusivity assumption in word learning are both dependent on their assumption that the experimenter is respecting the given–new contract, then an ability to recognize that the given–new contract is not being respected should lead to simultaneous changes on both tasks.

Finally, data should be sought that distinguishes conversational and cognitive bias explanations. For example, Bar-Hillel and Neter (1993) reported an experiment in which monetary incentives failed to remove a misinterpretation of a reasoning task (cf. Wolford et al., 1990). However, it is not clear why increasing the financial stakes in an experiment should cause respondents to abandon an interpretation that is pragmatically correct and rational. Recall that Tetlock and Boettger (1991) manipulated their respondents' conversational interpretations of the judgment task by undermining the respondents' assumption of intentionality. Respondents then rejected or used nondiagnostic information on the basis of its perceived conversational relevance. Then they found that accountability manipulations, which, like monetary incentives, should accentuate the value of getting a right answer, simply amplified the effect of conversational relevance, suggesting that incentives simply made respondents adhere more strongly to the answer that seemed conversationally rational. Incentives are not going to make respondents drop a conversationally rational interpretation in favor of a less plausible one in the context.

The above issue highlights a difference between the conversational inference approach to rationality and others that argue that a larger context than the experiment should be taken into account in establishing rational judgment. For example, one approach has been to accept that heuristics or logically suboptimal rules of thumb are used, but they are used flexibly and rationally with an eye to the costs and benefits of accurate inference and are thus normative (Payne, Bettman, and Johnson, 1993). However, when the decision is important, respondents use more accurate but resource-expensive strategies. Like Tetlock's (1992) accountability approach, this perspective therefore predicts that performance becomes more accurate where the decision outcomes become more important. However, as noted above, the conversational inference approach does not predict that increased incentives lead respondents to change an interpretation that seems rational in the context.

A clear list of criteria and methods for specifying and controlling conversational inference will also enable conversational absolutions of errors to be distinguished from others. For example, Fiedler (1988) showed a dramatic reduction in Tversky and Kahneman's (1983) conjunction effect by framing the task in terms of frequencies rather than probabilities. If the frequentistic frame changed the way respondents interpreted the task (cf. Dulany and Hilton, 1991), then this effect could fairly be considered conversational, if not then another presumably cognitive bias explanation of this improved performance should be considered.

In some cases, investigators have used multiple methods to evaluate claims about biases. For example, in a variant of the engineer-and-lawyer study, Kahneman and Tversky (1973) not only gave respondents personality descriptions and then asked them to estimate the probability that the person described would major in a number of subjects but also to give the base rate of people majoring in that subject. They found that respondents underused their own base-rate information – an error that cannot be attributed to conversational inference processes as defined in this article. Although underuse of base-rate information may occur in certain conditions, this should not be taken as invalidating the current perspective. Understanding how the conversational factors reviewed earlier, such as source characteristics, information order, and question-phrasing, influence use of base-rate information help us better understand when its underuse is truly due to cognitive shortcomings rather than to communicational factors.

Controlling for Conversational Inference in the Identification of Errors of Reasoning

It may therefore be that many patterns of judgment that have been classified as errors appear quite rational when systematic and normal processes of conversational inference are taken into account. However, the approach also allows us to deem as irrational errors that cannot be explained by processes of conversational inference. For example, Tversky and Kahneman (1974) reported that numerical anchors produced randomly by a roulette wheel biased subsequent estimates of the number of African countries in the United Nations. Because randomness prevents the attribution of intentionality to the number given as an anchor, such an effect can only be the result of a cognitive bias. Likewise, Tetlock's (1985) finding that anchoring effects are reduced by making respondents accountable for their judgments are consistent with the heuristics view that the effect can be reduced with incentives inducing more cognitive effort.

However, other effects attributable to anchoring with insufficient adjustment may in fact be the result of conversational factors (e.g., a tendency to treat early information as more important) if presented in conversational form (e.g., Krosnick et al., 1990). For example, R. Brown (1986) gave an insightful analysis of Asch's (1946) impression formation paradigm that suggests that both the primacy and centrality effects can be attributed to the operation of a principle of information gain consistent with that of the maxim of quantity. According to R. Brown, traits that come later in a description of a person's character (e.g., kind) are likely to have less effect if they are redundant with earlier traits (e.g., honest) that are used to predict them. For this primacy effect to be classified as nonconversational in nature, for example, it should be shown to be reduced by accountability instructions (Tetlock, 1985) and also to occur in conditions where respondents have been made to believe that the information was presented in random order.

Conclusions

Judgments about the intended meaning of utterances are themselves judgments under uncertainty. The likely intended meaning is likely to be affected by the hearer's perceptions about the speaker. The implication for psychological experiments on rationality is that respondents' answers may not deviate from what might be expected from a normative model because of an individual's cognitive shortcomings, but because of the application of consensually shared rules of conversational inference.

Like previous work on experimental demand effects, the attributional model of conversational inference predicts that source characteristics affect the experimental respondent's performance. However, previous work on source effects has focused on how respondents comply with experimental demands, for example, by detecting the experimenter's hypothesis and producing the desired behavior (Orne, 1962; Rosenthal and Rubin, 1978). The present approach focuses on how respondents deviate from the judgments predicted by the normative model considered relevant by the experimenter by using rules of conversational inference very different than those assumed by the experimenter.

Understanding conversational inference may help clarify the question as to which normative model is appropriate in a given situation. Thus, various writers have addressed the question of whether the experimental tasks used are truly representative of real-life decision tasks (e.g., Funder, 1987; Hogarth, 1981; Tetlock, 1985). Sometimes it can be suggested that an alternative normative model of judgment can describe respondents' patterns of reasoning, as when Cohen (1979) suggested a Baconian model of judgment as an alternative to the Bayesian model used by Tversky and Kahneman (1974). One advantage of the conversational framework is, of course, that it can help identify how responses reflect one reasoning process more so than another by better specifying the implicit premises that the respondent derives from the information explicitly given. For example, Hilton (1990a, 1991) showed how laypeople's causal attributions can be seen to follow a normative model of causal inference, namely, the analysis of variance, when the role of presupposed knowledge in completing the data matrix necessary for the computation of an analysis of variance or its equivalent is taken into account.

Recognition of the conversational context of the psychology experiment thus may enable researchers to better recognize the rationality of respondents' judgments. However, it is also important to recognize how processes of conversational inference may produce errors in real-world settings. This could happen in several ways. First, hearers may be inaccurate in their perceptions of speakers, thus causing them to misinterpret utterances. Athough this is a common source of miscommunication, it may be that some errors in social perception are systematic. For example, Fussell and Krauss (1992) suggested that hearers overestimate the mutual knowledge they share with speakers because of the false consensus effect. Second, as Levinson (1995) suggested, many reasoning heuristics may have evolved because they are adaptive in contexts of social interaction. For example, the expectation that errors of interpretation will be quickly repaired may be correct when we are interacting with a human being but incorrect when managing a complex system such as an aircraft, a nuclear power plant, or an economy. The evolutionary adaptiveness of such an expectation to a conversational setting may explain why people are so bad at dealing with lagged feedback in other settings.

Recognition of linguistic and conversational factors may also have practical implications for facilitating statistical reasoning. Presentations of numerical information in terms of frequencies rather than probabilities (Fiedler, 1988) or that make set – superset relations clear (Macchi, 1991) are likely to facilitate correct understanding of statistical problems. Clearly, newspapers and other media should take advantage of this.

Thus, the attributional model of conversational inference introduces a social dimension to the study of reasoning and inference. It suggests that no utterance is depersonalized, that all messages have a source, and that reasoning and inference processes typically operate on socially communicated information. However, it does by no means deny the importance of cognitive processes. Rather, it argues that the processes of inference, reasoning, and understanding are shaped by interpersonal assumptions, even in supposedly neutral settings such as the laboratory experiment or survey questionnaire. As such it offers a view of social cognition other than the application of cognitive psychology to the understanding of how information is processed about social objects, important though this enterprise is (see Fiske and Taylor, 1991, for a review). Instead, by locating reasoning and inference processes in communicative settings, the attributional model of conversational inference offers another view of social cognition, namely, the social psychology of higher mental processes.

Appendix: Grice's (1975) Cooperative Principle and the Maxims of Conversation

The Cooperative Principle

Make your contribution such as is required, at the stage at which it occurs, by the accepted purpose or direction of the talk exchange in which you are engaged.

The Maxims of Quality

Try to make your contribution one that you believe to be true, specifically:

(a)   Do not say what you believe to be false.

(b)   Do not say that for which you lack adequate evidence.

The Maxims of Quantity

(a)   Make your contribution as informative as is required for the current purposes of the exchange.

(b)   Do not make your contribution more informative than is required.

The Maxim of Relation

Make your contributions relevant.

The Maxims of Manner

(a)   Avoid obscurity.

(b)   Avoid ambiguity.

(c)   Be brief.

(d)   Be orderly.

Notes

1   Sperber and Wilson (1986), while acknowledging the importance of inductive inference in comprehension, also considered that deductive inference plays an important role.

2   Grice (1989) himself was quite categorical about the centrality of attribution in the calculation of implicatures and indeed in his last writings defined implicatures in terms of attributed mental states: "Implicatures are thought of as arising in the following way; an implicatum (factual or imperatival) is the content of that psychological state or attitude which needs to be attributed to a speaker to secure one or another of the following results: (a) that a violation on his

part of conversational maxim is in the circumstances justifiable, at least in his eyes, or (b) that what appears to be a violation by him of a converstional maxim is only a seeming, not a real violation; the spirit, though perhaps not the letter, of the maxim is respected" (p. 370).

3 Dulany and Hilton (1991) also studied empirical possibility implicatures, such as "Linda is a bank teller who is probably active in the feminist movement." They also treat these as interpretations that absolve conjunction effects of being fallacies.

References

Adler, J. E. (1984). Abstraction is uncooperative. *Journal for the Theory of Social Behaviour, 14*, 165–181.

Adler, J. E. (1991). An optimist's pessimism: Conversation and conjunction. *Poznan Studies in the Philosophy of the Sciences and the Humanities: Probability and Rationality* [special ed.], *21*, 251–282.

Alloy, L. B., and Tabachnik, N. (1984). Assessment of covariation by humans and animals: The joint influence of prior expectations and current situational information. *Psychological Review, 91*, 112–149.

Allwood, J. (1987). Linguistic communication as action and cooperation. *Gothenburg Monographs in Linguistics* (2nd ed.).

Asch, S. E. (1940). Studies in the principles of judgments and attitudes: II. Determinants of judgments by group and by ego standards. *Journal of Social Psychology, 12*, 433–465.

Asch, S. E. (1946). Forming impressions of personality. *Journal of Abnormal and Social Psychology, 41*, 258–290.

Au, T. K., and Glusman, M. (1990). The principle of mutual exclusivity in word learning: To honor or not to honor? *Child Development, 61*, 1474–1490.

Austin, J. L. (1962). *How to do things with words.* Oxford, England: Clarendon Press.

Bar-Hillel, M., and Neter, E. (1993). How alike is it? Versus how likely is it?: A disjunction fallacy in probability judgments. *Journal of Personality and Social Psychology, 65*, 1119–1131.

Berkeley, D., and Humphreys, P. (1982). Structuring decision problems and the "bias heuristic." *Acta Psychologica, 50*, 201–252.

Bless, H., Strack, F., and Schwarz, N. (1993). The informative functions of research procedures: Bias and the logic of conversation. *European Journal of Social Psychology, 23*, 149–165.

Boden, M. A. (1977). *Artificial intelligence and natural man.* Brighton, England: Harvester Press.

Bohner, G., Bless, H., Schwarz, N., and Strack, F. (1988). What triggers causal attributions? The impact of valence and subjective probability. *European Journal of Social Psychology, 18*, 335–345.

Brown, P., and Levinson, S. C. (1987). *Politeness: Some universals in language usage.* Cambridge, England: Cambridge University Press.

Brown, R. (1986). *Social psychology* (2nd ed.). New York: Free Press.

Brown, R., and van Kleeck, R. (1989). Enough said: Three principles of explanation. *Journal of Personality and Social Psychology, 57*, 590–614.

Cheng, P. W., and Novick, L. R. (1990). A probabilistic contrast model of causal induction. *Journal of Personality and Social Psychology, 58*, 545–567.

Christensen-Szalanski, J. J., and Beach, L. R. (1982). Experience and the base-rate fallacy. *Organizational Behavior and Human Performance, 29*, 270–278.

Clark, H. H. (1985). Language use and language users. In G. Lindzey and E. Aronson (Eds.), *Handbook of social psychology Vol. II. Special fields and applications* (3rd ed., pp. 179–231). New York: Random House.

Clark, H. H. (1992). *Arenas of language use.* Chicago: University of Chicago Press.

Clark, H. H., and Haviland, S. E. (1977). Comprehension and the given–new contract. In R. O. Freedle (Ed.), *Discourse production and comprehension* (pp. 1–40). Norwood, NJ: Ablex.

Clark, H. H., and Schober, M. F. (1992). Asking questions and influencing answers. In J. M. Tanur (Ed.), *Questions about questions: Inquiries into the cognitive bases of surveys* (pp. 15–48). New York: Russell Sage Foundation.

Cohen, L. J. (1979). On the psychology of prediction: Whose is the fallacy? *Cognition, 8*, 385–407.

Cohen, L. J. (1981). Can human irrationality be experimentally demonstrated? *Behavioral and Brain Sciences, 4*, 317–330.

Dascal, M. (1989). On the roles of context and literal meaning in understanding. *Cognitive Science, 13*, 253–257.

Dennett, D. L. (1984). *Elbow room: The varieties of free-will worth having.* Cambridge, MA: Bradford Books/MIT Press.

Dodd, D. H., and Bradshaw, J. M. (1980). Leading questions and memory: Pragmatic constraints. *Journal of Verbal Learning and Memory, 19*, 695–704.

Donaldson, M. (1978). *Children's minds.* London: Fontana.

Donaldson, M. (1982). Conservation: What is the question? *British Journal of Psychology, 73*, 199–207.

Dulany, D. L., and Hilton, D. J. (1991). Conversational implicature, conscious representation, and the conjunction fallacy. *Social Cognition, 9*, 85–100.

Eddy, D. (1982). Probabilistic reasoning in clinical medicine: Problems and opportunities. In D. E. Kahneman, P. Slovic, and A. Tversky (Eds.),

Judgment under uncertainty: Heuristics and biases (pp. 249–267). Cambridge, England: Cambridge University Press.

Faucheux, C., and Moscovici, S. (1968). Self-esteem and exploitative behavior in a game against chance and nature. *Journal of Personality and Social Psychology, 8,* 83–88.

Fenigstein, A., Scheier, M. F., and Buss, A. H. (1975). Public and private self-consciousness: Assessment and theory. *Journal of Consulting and Clinical Psychology, 43,* 522–527.

Fiedler, K. (1988). The dependence of the conjunction fallacy on subtle linguistic factors. *Psychological Research, 50,* 123–129.

Fiedler, K., Semin, G. K., and Bolten, S. (1989). Language use and reification of social information: Top-down and bottom-up processing in person cognition. *European Journal of Social Psychology, 19,* 271–295.

Fiske, S. T., and Taylor, S. E. (1991). *Social cognition* (2nd ed.). New York: McGraw-Hill.

Försterling, F. (1989). Models of covariation and attribution: How do they relate to the analogy of analysis of variance? *Journal of Personality and Social Psychology, 57,* 615–625.

Fox, J. (1980). Making decisions under the influence of memory. *Psychological Review, 87,* 190–211.

Funder, D. C. (1987). Errors and mistakes: Evaluating the accuracy of social judgment. *Psychological Bulletin, 101,* 75–90.

Fussell, S. R., and Krauss, R. M. (1989). The effects of intended audience on message production and comprehension: Reference in a common ground framework. *Journal of Experimental Social Psychology, 25,* 203–219.

Fussell, S. R., and Krauss, R. M. (1992). Coordination of knowledge in communication: Effects of speakers' assumptions about what others know. *Journal of Personality and Social Psychology, 62,* 378–391.

Gelman, R. (1969). Conservation acquisition: A problem of learning to attend to relevant attributes. *Journal of Experimental Child Psychology, 7,* 67–87.

Gelman, S. A., Wilcox, S. A., and Clark, E. V. (1989). Conceptual and lexical hierarchies in young children. *Cognitive Development, 4,* 309–326.

Gibbs, R. W. (1984). Literal meaning and psychological theory. *Cognitive Science, 8,* 275–304.

Gibbs, R. W. (1989). Understanding and literal meaning. *Cognitive Science, 13,* 243–251.

Gibbs, R. W., Kushner, J. M., and Mills, W. R. (1991). Authorial intentions and metaphor comprehension. *Journal of Psycholinguistic Research, 20,* 11–30.

Ginossar, Z., and Trope, Y. (1987). Problem solving in judgment under uncertainty. *Journal of Personality and Social Psychology, 52,* 464–474.

Grice, H. P. (1968). Utterer's meaning, sentence-meaning and word-meaning. *Foundations of Language, 4,* 225–242.

Grice, H. P. (1975). Logic and conversation. In P. Cole and J. L. Morgan (Eds.), *Syntax and semantics 3: Speech acts* (pp. 41–58). San Diego, CA: Academic Press.

Grice, H. P. (1989). *Studies in the way of words.* Cambridge, MA: Harvard University Press.

Hart, H. L. A., and Honoré, T. (1985). *Causation in the law* (2nd ed.). Oxford, England: Clarendon Press. (Original work published 1959.)

Hastie, R. (1984). Causes and effects of causal attribution. *Journal of Personality and Social Psychology, 46,* 44–56.

Heider, F. (1958). *The psychology of interpersonal relations.* New York: Wiley.

Heider, F., and Simmel, M. (1944). An experimental study of apparent behavior. *American Journal of Psychology, 57,* 243–259.

Henle, M. (1962). On the relation between logic and thinking. *Psychological Review, 69,* 366–378.

Hewstone, M. R. C., and Jaspars, J. M. F. (1983). A re-examination of the roles of consensus, consistency and distinctiveness: Kelley's cube revisited. *British Journal of Social Psychology, 22,* 41–50.

Higgins, E. T., and Bargh, J. A. (1987). Social cognition and social perception. *Annual Review of Psychology, 38,* 369–425.

Hilton, D. J. (1990a). Conversational processes and causal explanation. *Psychological Bulletin, 107,* 65–81.

Hilton, D. J. (1990b). *Formal models of causal attribution: Conceptual, methodological, and empirical issues.* Unpublished manuscript.

Hilton, D. J. (1991). A conversational model of causal explanation. In W. Stroebe and M. Hewstone (Eds.), *European review of social psychology* (pp. 51–81). Chichester, England: Wiley.

Hilton, D. J., and Jaspars, J. M. F. (1987). The explanation of occurrences and non-occurrences: A test of the inductive logic model of causal attribution. *British Journal of Social Psychology, 26,* 189–201.

Hilton, D. J., and Slugoski, B. R. (1986). Knowledge-based causal attribution: The abnormal conditions focus model. *Psychological Review, 93,* 75–88.

Hippler, H. J., and Schwarz, N. (1986). Not forbidding isn't allowing: The cognitive basis of the forbid–allow asymmetry. *Public Opinion Quarterly, 50,* 87–96.

Hogarth, R. M. (1981). Beyond discrete biases: Functional and dysfunctional aspects of judgmental heuristics. *Psychological Bulletin, 90,* 197–217.

Hornby, P. A. (1972). The psychological subject and predicate. *Cognitive Psychology, 3,* 612–642.

Hornby, P. A. (1974). Surface structure and presupposition. *Journal of Verbal Learning and Verbal Behavior, 13,* 530–538.

Iacobucci, D., and McGill, A. L. (1990). Analysis of attribution data: Theory testing and effects estimation. *Journal of Personality and Social Psychology, 59,* 426–441.

Inhelder, B., and Piaget, J. (1958). *The growth of logical thinking from childhood to adolescence*. New York: Basic Books.

Jaspars, J. M. F. (1983). The process of attribution in common-sense. In M. R. C. Hewstone (Ed.), *Attribution theory: Social and functional extensions* (pp. 28–44). Oxford, England: Basil Blackwell.

Jaspars, J. M. F., Hewstone, M. R. C., and Fincham, F. D. (1983). Attribution theory and research: The state of the art. In J. M. F. Jaspars, F. D. Fincham, and M. R. C. Hewstone (Eds.), *Attribution theory: Conceptual, developmental and social dimensions* (pp. 3–26). London: Academic Press.

Johnson-Laird, P. N. (1983). *Mental models*. Cambridge, England: Cambridge University Press.

Jones, E. E. (1979). The rocky road from acts to dispositions. *American Psychologist, 34,* 107–117.

Jones, E. E., and Davis, K. E. (1965). From acts to dispositions: The attribution process in person perception. In L. Berkowitz (Ed.), *Advances in experimental social psychology* (Vol. 2, pp. 219–266). San Diego, CA: Academic Press.

Jones, E. E., and McGillis, D. (1976). Correspondent inferences and the attribution cube: A comparative reappraisal. In J. H. Harvey, W. J. Ickes, and R. F. Kidd (Eds.), *New directions in attribution research* (Vol. 1, pp. 389–420). Hillsdale, NJ: Erlbaum.

Jones, E. E., and Nisbett, R. E. (1972). The actor and the observer: Divergent perspectives of the causes of behavior. In E. E. Jones, D. E. Kanouse, H. H. Kelley, R. E. Nisbett, S. Valins, and B. Weiner (Eds.), *Attribution: Perceiving the causes of behavior* (pp. 79–94). Morristown, NJ: General Learning Press.

Joyce, E. J., and Biddle, G. C. (1981). Anchoring and adjustment in probabilistic inference in auditing. *Journal of Accounting Research, 19,* 120–145.

Kahneman, D. A., and Miller, D. T. (1986). Norm theory: Comparing reality to its alternatives. *Psychological Review, 93,* 136–153.

Kahneman, D., Slovic, P., and Tversky, A. (Eds.). (1982). *Judgement under uncertainty: Heuristics and biases*. Cambridge, England: Cambridge University Press.

Kahneman, D., and Tversky, A. (1973). On the psychology of prediction. *Psychological Review, 80,* 237–251.

Kassin, S. M. (1979). Consensus information, prediction, and causal attribution: A review of the literature and issues. *Journal of Personality and Social Psychology, 37,* 1966–1981.

Kelley, H. H. (1967). Attribution theory in social psychology. In D. Levine (Ed.), *Nebraska Symposium on Motivation* (pp. 192–241). Lincoln: University of Nebraska Press.

Krauss, R. M., and Fussell, S. R. (1991). Perspective-taking in communication: Representations of others' knowledge in reference. *Social Cognition, 9,* 2–24.

Kraut, R. E., and Higgins, E. T. (1984). Communication and social cognition. In R. S. Wyer and T. K. Srull (Eds.), *Handbook of social cognition*. Hillsdale, NJ: Erlbaum.

Krosnick, J. A., Li, F., and Lehman, D. R. (1990). Conversational conventions, order of information acquisition, and the effect of base-rates and individuating information on social judgments. *Journal of Personality and Social Psychology, 59,* 1140–1152.

Kwock, M. S., and Winer, G. A. (1986). Overcoming leading questions: Effects of psychosocial task variables. *Journal of Educational Psychology, 78,* 289–293.

Levinson, S. C. (1983). *Pragmatics*. Cambridge, England: Cambridge University Press.

Levinson, S. C. (1987). Minimization and conversational inference. In J. Verschueren and M. Bertuccelli-Papi (Eds.), *The pragmatic perspective: Selected papers from the 1985 International Pragmatics Conference* (pp. 61–129). Amsterdam; John Benjamins.

Levinson, S. C. (1995). Interactional biases in human thinking. In E. Goody (Ed.), *Social intelligence and interaction*. Cambridge, MA: Cambridge University Press, 221–260.

Loftus, E. F., and Palmer, J. C. (1974). Reconstruction of automobile destruction. *Journal of Verbal Learning and Verbal Behavior, 13,* 585–589.

Macchi, L. (1991). *Base rate use in probabilistic reasoning*. Paper presented at the Subjective Probability, Utility and Decision Making Conference, Fribourg, Germany.

Macdonald, R. R. (1986). Credible conceptions and implausible probabilities. *British Journal of Mathematical and Statistical Psychology, 39,* 15–27.

Mackie, J. L. (1974). *The cement of the universe*. London: Oxford University Press.

Markman, E. M., and Wachtel, G. F. (1988). Children's use of mutual exclusivity to constrain the meanings of words. *Cognitive Psychology, 20,* 121–157.

Markus, H., and Zajonc, R. B. (1985). Cognitive theories in social psychology. In G. Lindzey and E. Aronson (Eds.), *Handbook of social psychology* (3rd ed., Vol. 1, pp. 137–230). New York: Random House.

Martin, L. L., Seta, J. J., and Crelia, R. A. (1990). Assimilation and contrast as a function of people's willingness and ability to expend effort in forming an impression. *Journal of Personality and Social Psychology, 59,* 27–37.

McArthur, L. A. (1972). The how and what of why: Some determinants and consequences of causal attributions. *Journal of Personality and Social Psychology, 22,* 171–193.

McArthur, L. A. (1976). The lesser influence of consensus than distinctiveness information. The person-thing hypothesis. *Journal of Personality and Social Psychology, 33*(6), 733–742.

McGarrigle, J., and Donaldson, M. (1975). Conservation accidents. *Cognition, 3,* 341–350.

McGill, A. L. (1989). Context effects in judgments of causation. *Journal of Personality and Social Psychology, 57,* 189–200.

McGuire, W. J. (1969). The nature of attitudes and attitude change. In G. Lindzey and E. Aronson (Eds.), *Handbook of social psychology* (2nd ed., Vol. 3, pp. 136–314). Reading, MA: Addison Wesley.

Medin, D. L., and Edelson, S. M. (1988). Problem structure and the use of base-rate information from experience. *Journal of Experimental Psychology: General, 117,* 68–85.

Milgram, S. (1974). *Obedience to authority.* New York: Harper and Row.

Mill, J. S. (1973). A system of logic (8th ed.). In J. M. Robson (Ed.), *Collected works of John Stuart Mill* (Vols. 7 and 8). Toronto, Canada: University of Toronto Press. (Original work published 1872.)

Morier, D. M., and Borgida, E. (1984). The conjunction fallacy: A task specific phenomenon? *Personality and Social Psychology Bulletin, 10,* 243–252.

Moxey, L., and Sanford, A. J. (1987). Quantifiers and focus. *Journal of Semantics, 5,* 189–206.

Neale, S. (1992). Paul Grice and the philosophy of language. *Linguistics and Philosophy, 15,* 509–559.

Nisbett, R. E., and Borgida, E. (1975). Attribution and the psychology of prediction. *Journal of Personality and Social Psychology, 32,* 932–943.

Nisbett, R. E., Borgida, E., Crandall, R., and Reed, H. (1976). Popular induction: Information is not necessarily informative. In J. S. Carroll and J. W. Payne (Eds.), *Cognition and social behavior.* Hillsdale, NJ: Erlbaum.

Nisbett, R. E., and Ross, L. (1980). *Human inference: Strategies and shortcomings of social judgment.* Englewood Cliffs, NJ: Prentice-Hall.

Nisbett, R. E., Zukier, H., and Lemley, R. H. (1981). The dilution effect: Nondiagnostic information. *Cognitive Psychology, 13,* 248–277.

Oatley, K., and Yuill, N. (1985). Perception of personal and interpersonal action in a cartoon film. *British Journal of Social Psychology, 24,* 115–124.

Orne, M. T. (1962). On the social psychology of the psychological experiment: With particular reference to demand characteristics and their implications. *American Psychologist, 17,* 776–783.

Orvis, B. R., Cunningham, J. D., and Kelley, H. H. (1975). A closer examination of causal inference: The roles of consensus, distinctiveness, and consistency information. *Journal of Personality and Social Psychology, 32,* 605–616.

Payne, J. W., Bettman, J. R., and Johnson, E. J. (1992). Behavioral decision theory: A constructive processing perspective. *Annual Review of Psychology, 43,* 87–131.

Payne, J. W., Bettman, J. R., and Johnson, E. J. (1993). *The adaptive decision-maker.* Cambridge, England: Cambridge University Press.

Piaget, J., and Inhelder, B. (1969). *The psychology of the child.* London: Routledge and Kegan Paul.

Politzer, G. (1993). *La psychologie du raisonnement: Lois de la pragmatique et logique formelle* [The psychology of reasoning: Pragmatic laws and formal logic]. Thesis for the Doctorat d'Etat ès Lettres et Sciences Humaines. University of Paris VIII.

Politzer, G., and Noveck, I. (1991). Are conjunction rule violations the result of conversational rule violations? *Journal of Psycholinguistic Research, 20,* 83–102.

Popper, K. R. (1972). *Objective knowledge.* London: Oxford University Press.

Recanati, F. (1993). *Direct reference: From language to thought.* Oxford, England: Basil Blackwell.

Rommetveit, R. (1978). On Piagetian cognitive operations, semantic competence, and message-structure in adult – child communication. In I. Markova (Ed.), *The social context of language* (pp. 113–150). Chichester, England: Wiley.

Rose, S. A., and Blank, M. (1974). The potency of context in children's cognition: An illustration through conservation. *Child Development, 45,* 499–502.

Rosenthal, R., and Rubin, D. B. (1978). Interpersonal expectancy effects: The first 345 studies. *Behavioral and Brain Sciences, 3,* 377–415.

Ross, M., and Fletcher, G. J. O. (1985). Attribution and social perception. In G. Lindzey and E. Aronson (Eds.), *Handbook of social psychology: Vol. 2. Special fields and applications* (pp. 73–122). New York: Random House.

Sanbonmatsu, D. M., Kardes, F. R., and Herr, P. M. (1992). The role of prior knowledge and missing information in multiattribute evaluation. *Organizational Behavior and Human Decision Processes, 51,* 76–91.

Schank, R. C., and Abelson, R. P. (1977). *Scripts, plans, goals and understanding: An enquiry into human knowledge structures.* Hillsdale, NJ: Erlbaum.

Schuman, H., and Presser, S. (1981). *Questions and answers in attitude surveys: Experiments on question form, wording, and context.* New York: Academic Press.

Schwarz, N. (1990). Assessing frequency reports of mundane behaviors: Contributions of cognitive psychology to questionnaire construction. In C. Hendrick and M. S. Clark (Eds.), *Review of personality and social psychology: Vol. 2. Research methods in personality and social psychology* (pp. 98–119). Beverly Hills, CA: Sage.

Schwarz, N. (1994). Judgment in a social context: Biases, shortcomings, and the logic of conversation. In M. P. Zanna (Ed.), *Advances in experimental social psychology* (Vol. 26, pp. 123–162), San Diego, CA: Academic Press.

Schwarz, N., Hippler, H. J., Deutsch, B., and Strack, F. (1985). Response categories: Effects on behavioral reports and comparative judgments. *Public Opinion Quarterly, 49,* 388–395.

Schwarz, N., Knäuper, B., Hippler, H. J., Noelle-Neumann, E., and Clark, F. (1991). Rating scales: Numeric values may change the meaning of scale labels. *Public Opinion Quarterly, 55,* 570–582.

Schwarz, N., and Scheuring, B. (1988). Judgments of relationship satisfaction: Inter- and intraindividual comparisons as a function of questionnaire structure. *European Journal of Social Psychology, 18,* 485–496.

Schwarz, N., and Strack, F. (1991). Context effects in attitude surveys: Applying cognitive theory to social research. In W. Stroebe and M. Hewstone (Eds.), *European review of social psychology* (pp. 31–50). Chichester, England: Wiley.

Schwarz, N., Strack, F., Hilton, D. J., and Naderer, G. (1991). Base-rates, representativeness, and the logic of conversation. *Social Cognition, 9,* 67–84.

Schwarz, N., Strack, F., and Mai, H.-P. (1991). Assimilation and contrast effects in part–whole question sequences: A conversational-logic analysis. *Public Opinion Quarterly, 55,* 3–23.

Schwarz, N., Strack, F., Mueller, G., and Deutsch, B. (1988). The range of response alternatives may determine the meaning of the question. *Social Cognition, 6,* 107–117.

Searle, J. R. (1969). *Speech acts: An essay in the philosophy of language.* Cambridge, England: Cambridge University Press.

Shanon, B. (1988). Semantic representation of meaning: A critique. *Psychological Bulletin, 104,* 70–83.

Siegal, M. (1991). *Knowing children: Experiments in conversation and cognition.* Hillsdale, NJ: Erlbaum.

Siegal, M., Waters, L. J., and Dinwiddy, L. S. (1988). Misleading children: Causal attributions for inconsistency under repeated questioning. *Journal of Experimental Child Psychology, 45,* 438–456.

Singer, E., Hippler, H. J., and Schwarz, N. (1992). Confidentiality assurances in surveys: Reassurance or threat? *International Journal of Public Opinion Research, 4,* 256–268.

Slugoski, B. R., and Turnbull, W. M. (1988). Cruel to be kind and kind to be cruel: Sarcasm, banter, and social relations. *Journal of Language and Social Psychology, 7,* 101–121.

Sperber, D., and Wilson, D. (1986). *Relevance: Communication and cognition.* Oxford, England: Basil Blackwell.

Strack, F. (1992). "Order effects" in survey research: Activative and informative functions of preceding questions. In N. Schwarz and S. Sudman (Eds.), *Order effects in social and psychological research* (pp. 23–34). New York: Springer-Verlag.

Strack, F., Martin, L. L., and Schwarz, N. (1988). Priming and communication: Social determinants of information use in judgments of life satisfaction. *European Journal of Social Psychology, 18,* 429–442.

Strack, F., Schwarz, N., Bless, H., Kübler, A., and Wänke, M. (1993). Awareness of the influence as a determinant of assimilation versus contrast. *European Journal of Social Psychology, 23,* 53–62.

Strawson, P. F. (1952). *Introduction to logical theory.* London: Methuen.

Tannenbaum, P. H. (1968). The congruity principle: Retrospective reflections and current research. In R. P. Abelson, E. Aronson, W. J. McGuire, T. M. Newcomb, M. J. Rosenberg, and P. H. Tannenbaum (Eds.), *Theories of cognitive consistency: A sourcebook* (pp. 52–72). Chicago: Rand McNally.

Tetlock, P. E. (1985). Accountability: The neglected social context of judgment and choice. *Research in Organizational Behavior, 7,* 297–332.

Tetlock, P. E. (1992). The impact of accountability on judgment and choice: Toward a social contingency model. In M. P. Zanna (Ed.), *Advances in experimental social psychology* (Vol. 25, pp. 331–376). New York: Academic Press.

Tetlock, P. E., and Boettger, R. (1989). Accountability: A social magnifier of the dilution effect. *Journal of Personality and Social Psychology, 57,* 388–398.

Tetlock, P. E., and Boettger, R. (1991). *Accountability amplifies the status quo effect when changes create victims.* Unpublished manuscript. University of California, Berkeley.

Tourangeau, R., and Rasinski, K. (1988). Cognitive processes underlying context effects in attitude measurement. *Psychological Bulletin, 103,* 299–314.

Trope, Y., and Ginossar, Z. (1988). On the use of statistical and non-statistical knowledge: A problem-solving approach. In D. Bar-Tal and A. Kruglanski (Eds.), *The social psychology of knowledge* (pp. 209–230). Cambridge, England: Cambridge University Press.

Turnbull, W. M., and Smith, E. E. (1985). *Attribution and conversation: Comprehending uncooperative question-answer exchanges.* Unpublished manuscript.

Tversky, A., and Kahneman, D. (1974, September). Judgment under uncertainty: Heuristics and biases. *Science, 185,* 1124–1131.

Tversky, A., and Kahneman, D. (1980). Causal schemas in judgments under uncertainty. In M. Fishbein (Ed.), *Progress in social psychology* (Vol. 1). Hillsdale, NJ: Erlbaum.

Tversky, A., and Kahneman, D. (1981, January). The framing of decisions and the psychology of choice. *Science, 211,* 453–458.

Tversky, A., and Kahneman, D. (1983). Extensional versus intuitive reasoning: The conjunction fallacy in probability judgment. *Psychological Review, 90,* 293–315.

Wallsten, T. S., Fillenbaum, S., and Cox, J. A. (1986). Base-rate effects on the interpretations of probability and frequency expressions. *Journal of Memory and Language, 25,* 571–587.

Weber, E. U., Böckenholt, U., Hilton, D. J., and Wallace, B. (1993). Determinants of diagnostic generation: Effects of information, base rates, and experience. *Journal of Experimental Psychology: Learning, Memory, and Cognition, 19,* 1151–1164.

Weber, E. U., and Hilton, D. J. (1990). Contextual effects in the interpretations of probability words: Perceived base rate and severity of events. *Journal of Experimental Psychology: Human Perception and Performance, 16,* 781–789.

Weiner, B. (1985). "Spontaneous" causal thinking. *Psychological Bulletin, 97,* 74–84.

Weiner, B., Frieze, I., Kukla, A., Reed, I., Rest, S. A., and Rosenbaum, R. M. (1972). Perceiving the causes of success and failure. In E. E. Jones, D. E. Kanouse, H. H. Kelley, R. E. Nisbett, S. Valins, and B. Weiner (Eds.), *Attribution: Perceiving the causes of behavior* (pp. 95–120). Morristown, NJ: General Learning Press.

Weizenbaum, J. (1976). *Computer power and human reason.* San Francisco: Freeman.

Wilson, D., and Sperber, D. (1985). On choosing the context for utterance interpretation. In J. Allwood and E. Hjelmquist (Eds.), *Foregrounding background* (pp. 51–64). Lund, Sweden: Doxa.

Winer, G. A., Hemphill, J., and Craig, R. K. (1988). The effect of misleading questions in promoting nonconservation responses in children and adults. *Developmental Psychology, 24,* 197–202.

Wolford, G., Taylor, H. A., and Beck, J. R. (1990). The conjunction fallacy? *Memory and Cognition, 18,* 47–53.

Wyer, R. S. (1981). An information-processing perspective on social attribution. In J. H. Harvey, W. Ickes, and R. F. Kidd (Eds.), *New directions in attribution research* (Vol. 3, pp. 359–403). Hillsdale, NJ: Erlbaum.

Zukier, H., and Pepitone, A. (1984). Social roles and strategies in prediction: Some determinants of the use of base-rate information. *Journal of Personality and Social Psychology, 47,* 349–360.

Section 10: Domain-Specific, Goal-Based, and Evolutionary Approaches

---

Chapter 39: Domain-Specific Knowledge and Conceptual Change

SUSAN CAREY AND ELIZABETH SPELKE

Overview

We argue that human reasoning is guided by a collection of innate domain-specific systems of knowledge. Each system is characterized by a set of core principles that define the entities covered by the domain and support reasoning about those entities. Learning, on this view, consists of an enrichment of the core principles, plus their entrenchment, along with the entrenchment of the ontology they determine. In these domains, then, we would expect cross-cultural universality: cognitive universals akin to language universals.

However, there is one crucial disanalogy to language. The history of science and mathematics demonstrates that conceptual change in cognitive domains is both possible and actual. Conceptual change involves overriding core principles, creating new principles, and creating new ontological types. We sketch one potential mechanism underlying conceptual change and motivate a central empirical problem for cognitive anthropology: To what extent is there cross-cultural universality in the domains covered by innate systems of knowledge?

Domain-Specific Cognition

The notion of domain-specific cognition to be pursued here is articulated most clearly by Chomsky (1980a). Humans are endowed with domain-specific systems of knowledge such as

knowledge of language, knowledge of physical objects, and knowledge of number. Each system of knowledge applies to a distinct set of entities and phenomena. For example, knowledge of language applies to sentences and their constituents; knowledge of physical objects applies to macroscopic material bodies and their behavior; knowledge of number applies to sets and to mathematical operations such as addition. More deeply, each system of knowledge is organized around a distinct body of core principles. For language, these are the principles of universal grammar; for physical objects, the principles might include Newton's axioms and the principles of continuity and solidity; for number, they might include the principles of one–one correspondence and succession.

This notion of domain specificity provides a basis for determining, and distinguishing among, the domains of human knowledge: Two systems of knowledge are distinct just in case they center on distinct principles. For example, if knowledge of language and knowledge of number were found to center on the same core principles, psychologists should conclude that they constitute a single system of knowledge, despite the many obvious differences between the abilities that knowledge of language and knowledge of number support. Indeed, Chomsky (1980b) has suggested that language and number are connected in this way. This notion similarly provides a basis for distinguishing the genuine cognitive domains

---

from more trivial collection of beliefs: Only genuine domains are characterized by distinct sets
of core principles. In particular, reasoning about
material bodies, about persons and about sets
may well depend on distinct systems of knowledge of physics, psychology, and number. In contrast, reasoning about billiard balls, about bricks,
and about plates probably depends on a single
knowledge system: The core principles underlying reasoning about one of these collections of
objects probably apply to the other collections
as well (Carey, 1985).

Domain-Specific Perception

If human reasoning depends on domain-specific
knowledge systems, then reasoners face a crucial
task: They must single out the entities to which
each system of knowledge applies. For example,
a well-developed system of knowledge of psychology is useless unless a reasoner can determine when he or she is faced with a person.
Similarly, systems of knowledge of physics and
number can function only insofar as a reasoner
can single out material bodies and sets. The
mechanisms that single out such entities need
not be (and never are) flawless: It is sufficient
for the reasoner to pick out some of the persons, some of the material bodies, and the like.
Without some mechanisms for singling out entities within a domain, however, reasoning cannot proceed. A domain-specific reasoner cannot
simply ask of some part of the layout, "How
does this thing behave?" The reasoner also must
ask, "What kind of thing is this?" (see Wiggins,
1980).

We will call the processes that single out
material bodies, persons and sets *domain-specific
perception*. These processes may not be perceptual, however in a narrow sense. Most of the processes studied in psychophysics, sensor physiology, and computational vision do not function
to single out the entities about which one reasons but rather they function to construct representations of the continuous surrounding surface
layout. Vision, for example, appears to culminate in representations of the distances, orientations, colors, textures, and motions of light-
reflecting surfaces (Gibson, 1950; Marr, 1982).
These representations are not sufficient for the
operation of domain-specific reasoning. To reason about material bodies, one must carve the
surface layout into unitary, bounded, and persisting things (Spelke, 1988). To reason about
number, one must represent a collection of bod-

ies, surfaces, or other entities as a set (Gelman
& Gallistel, 1978; also see Shipley & Shepperson, 1990; Wynn, 1992). To reason about human
action and mental life, one must represent a portion of the surface layout as a sentient, purposive
being. The processes that culminate in such representations are our focus here.

There are two general ways in which the
task of apprehending the entities in a domain
could be accomplished: Domain-specific perception either could depend on principles that
are distinct from the principles guiding domain-
specific reasoning, or domain-specific perception
and reasoning could depend on a single set of
principles. Consider, for example, the domain of
reasoning about human action and experience.
It is possible that perceivers single out human
beings by virtue of a face-recognizer, a voice-
recognizer, a gait-recognizer, and the like. Whenever the perceiver is confronted by eyes, hair,
and other features in the proper configuration,
his or her face-recognizer would signal the presence of a person. This signal would then trigger the operation of the processes of psychological reasoning, whereby the actions of the
person are understood in terms of the person's
goals and feelings. On this view, apprehending persons and reasoning about human actions
depends on distinct principles: principles governing the physical arrangement of eyes, noses,
and so forth, on one hand, and principles concerning the relation among purposes, perceptions, and the like, on the other. Psychological
reasoning would proceed appropriately, because
the mechanisms that embody these distinct principles would be suitably linked together.

Alternatively, perceivers may single out persons by analyzing the behavior of entities, asking whether an entity's behavior appears to be
directed to some goal, to be guided by perceptions of its environment, to be colored by emotions, and so on. Entities would be perceived as
persons insofar as their behavior was consistent
with such an analysis. On the second account,
processes of perceiving and reasoning about psychological beings are intimately connected: They
are guided by the same system of knowledge.

In human infancy, we suggest, perception
and reasoning are guided by a single knowledge
system in at least three domains: physics, psychology, and number. We begin with the case
of physics by reviewing the findings of studies
of object perception and physical reasoning in
infancy (see Spelke, 1990, or Spelke & Van de
Walle, 1999, for a more extensive review).

Perceiving and Reasoning about Physical Objects

Research on object perception provides evidence that young infants can perceive the unity, boundaries, complete shapes, and persistence of objects under some conditions. Object perception appears to depend on amodal mechanisms that divide the surface layout into bodies in accordance with a small number of principles, each of which reflects constraints on object motion.

Consider first young infants' perception of the unity of a visible object. Experiments using preferential looking methods, which rely on infants' well-documented tendency to look longer at displays that they perceive to be novel, provide evidence that infants as young as 3 months of age perceive a three-dimensional object presented against a uniform background as a connected body that will maintain its connectedness as it moves. For example, infants who were familiarized with a cohesive object subsequently looked longer at the outcome of an event in which the object broke in two than at the outcome of an event in which the object moved as a whole (Spelke, Breinlinger, & Jacobson, 1992). Infants' preference for the former outcome reliably exceeded that of infants in a baseline condition who viewed the same outcome displays with no preceding events. The experiment provides evidence that infants perceived the original object as a connected body that should maintain its connectedness over motion.

Further experiments focusing on infants' preferential looking or object-directed reaching provide evidence that young infants perceive the distinctness of adjacent objects if the objects undergo different rigid motions (Hofsten & Spelke, 1985; Spelke, Hofsten, & Kestenbaum, 1989). Infants also perceive the distinctness of stationary objects if the objects are spatially separated: Spatially separated objects are perceived as distinct units even if they are separated only in depth such that the gap between them is not directly visible (von Hofsten & Spelke, 1985; Kestenbaum, Termine, & Spelke, 1987; Spelke, von Hofsten, & Kestenbaum, 1989).

The above findings suggest that infants perceive objects in accord with two constraints on object motion. First, objects are connected bodies that maintain their connectedness as they move: Two spatially separated objects, or two adjacent objects that slide with respect to one another, are therefore perceived as distinct. Second, objects are not connected to other objects and retain their separateness as they move: Two stationary and adjacent objects, lacking any spatially or spatiotemporally specified boundary, are therefore perceived as one connected body. These two constraints can be captured by a single *principle of cohesion*: Surfaces in the layout lie on a single object if and only if they are connected.

Now consider infants' perception of the unity of an object whose ends are visible or tangible but whose center is hidden. Four-month-old infants have been familiarized with such an object and then presented with a fully visible complete object or with two objects separated by a gap where the original object had been hidden. If infants perceived the original object as a connected body, then they should look longer at the two-object test display, relative to infants in a baseline condition who viewed the same test displays with no previous familiarization.

Such experiments provide evidence that 4-month-old infants perceive a visible, center-occluded object as a connected body if the ends of the object undergo a common rigid motion (Kellman & Spelke, 1983; Slater, Morison, Somers, Mattock, Brown, & Taylor, 1990; Craton & Baillargeon, personal communication, 1991). Rigid motion in any direction, including motion in depth, specifies the connectedness of the object (Kellman, Spelke, & Short, 1986); a pattern of common retinal displacement in the absence of true motion does not (Kellman, Gleitman, & Spelke, 1987). Studies in the haptic mode provide evidence that infants perceive the unity of objects whose ends are tangible under the same conditions as they perceive the unity of objects whose ends are visible (Streri & Spelke, 1988, 1989; Streri, Spelke, & Rameix 1992). Infants aged $4\frac{1}{2}$ months held the two ends of a haptic assembly in their two hands, without visual or haptic access to the full assembly. They perceived the assembly as one connected body when the ends moved together and as two spatially separated bodies when the ends moved independently.

The findings of these studies suggest that infants perceive objects in accordance with two further constraints on object motion. First, surfaces move together only if they are in contact: The two rigidly moving ends of a center-occluded visible object or of a haptic assembly are therefore connected. Second, surfaces move independently only if they are spatially separated: Two independently movable seen or felt objects are therefore separated by a gap. These two constraints can be encompassed by a single *principle of contact*: Surfaces move together if and only if they are in contact.

Finally, consider infants' perception of objects that move fully out of view. Experiments using visual preference methods provide evidence that young infants perceive the persisting identity or distinctness of objects over successive encounters in accordance with the principle of contact (discussed earlier) and the principle of continuity: An object moves on exactly one connected path over space and time. First, Van de Walle and Spelke (1993) presented infants with an object that moved back and forth behind an occluder such that its two ends were visible in immediate succession but never simultaneously: The left side of the object moved behind the occluder until the object was fully hidden, and then the right side of the object began to appear from behind the opposite side, moving at the same speed and on the same path. Subsequent looking preferences between nonoccluded complete and broken displays provided evidence that the infants perceived the object as a connected body, in accordance with the contact principle. Second, Spelke and Kestenbaum (1986) and Xu and Carey (1992) presented infants with events in which an object moved out of view behind the first of two spatially separated occluders, and after a pause an object moved into view from behind the second occluder. Subsequent visual preferences between fully visible one- and two-object displays provided evidence that infants perceived two objects in this event in accordance with the continuity principle: Because no object appeared between the two screens, the object moving on the left must have been distinct from that on the right.

In summary, young infants appear to perceive objects in accordance with the principles of cohesion, contact, and continuity. We now consider whether infants respect these principles when they reason about objects that move from view.

A variety of experiments provide evidence that young infants represent the existence of an object that moves from view and make certain inferences about the object's continued motion (e.g., Baillargeon, 1986; Leslie, 1991; Spelke, Breinlinger, Macomber, & Jacobson, 1992). These experiments have used preferential looking methods to assess infants' reactions to an "invisible displacement task" (Piaget, 1954), in which an object moves from view and infants must infer its further motion. The experiments

provide evidence that infants make some, but not all, of the inferences about object motion made by older children and adults. A consideration of infants' successes and failures may thus shed light on the principles guiding infants' inferences.

Experiments from three laboratories offer evidence that infants' inferences accord with two constraints on object motion: continuity (objects move only on connected paths), and solidity (objects move only on unobstructed paths, such that two objects never occupy the same place at the same time) (Baillargeon, 1986; Leslie, 1991; Spelke et al., 1992). In one experiment (Spelke et al., 1992, Exp. 1), 4-month-old infants first were familiarized with an event in which a ball fell behind a screen on an open stage and was revealed on the stage floor. Then a second surface was placed above the stage floor and a test sequence was presented in which the ball fell behind the screen, and the screen was raised to reveal the ball at rest either on the upper surface or on the lower surface. The latter position was inconsistent with the continuity and solidity constraints, because the ball could reach the lower surface only by jumping discontinuously over or by passing through the upper surface. Infants looked longer at the inconsistent than at the consistent test outcome. Their preference for the inconsistent outcome reliably exceeded the preferences of infants in a separate control condition, who viewed the same outcome displays preceded by consistent events. The experiment therefore provides evidence that 4-month-old infants infer that a hidden object will move on a connected and unobstructed path, in accordance with the continuity and solidity constraints. Further experiments provide evidence for the same ability at ages ranging from $2\frac{1}{2}$ months to 10 months, with a variety of displays and events (e.g., Baillargeon, 1986; Baillargeon, Graber, DeVos, & Black, 1990; Leslie, 1991; Spelke et al., 1992).

The continuity and solidity constraints are closely related: Whereas the continuity constraint dictates that an object must move on at least one connected path (i.e., the path of an object can contain no gaps), the solidity constraint dictates that an object must move on at most one connected path (i.e., the paths of two objects cannot intersect in space and time). Both constraints therefore can be captured by the principle of continuity: An object traces exactly one connected path.

Additional experiments provide evidence that infants infer that a hidden object will move in accordance with the principles of cohesion and contact. Carey, Klatt, and Schlaffer (1992) tested 8-month-old infants with events in which one object was lowered, raised, and lowered again behind a screen, and then the screen was raised to reveal one or two objects on the display floor. Infants looked longer at the two-object event, relative to the length of infants' looks in a baseline control experiment. The experiment provided evidence that infants inferred that the object would move in accordance with the cohesion principle: Unlike nonsolid substances (which were tested in other experiments), moving objects do not leave parts of themselves behind. Ball (1973) familiarized infants with an event in which one object moved out of view behind a screen and then a second object, which was initially half visible and stationary, moved fully into view. Then infants were tested with nonoccluded displays in which the first object either came into contact with the second object or stopped short of the second object. Infants looked longer at the no-contact event, relative to baseline controls. The experiment provides evidence that the infants inferred that the first object contacted the second object, in accordance with the contact principle (for further evidence, see Leslie, 1988).

In summary, infants appear to infer that hidden objects will move in accordance with the principles of cohesion, contact, and continuity. These are the same principles that guide infants' perception of the unity, boundaries, and persistence of the objects they see and feel. A single system of knowledge therefore appears to underlie object perception and physical reasoning in infancy. We now ask briefly whether a single system of knowledge also guides infants' perception and reasoning in the domains of psychology and number.

Perceiving and Reasoning about Persons

The system of knowledge guiding reasoning about human action and mental life is currently a subject of much study and some debate (see Astington, Harris, & Olson, 1988; Leslie, 1987; Perner, 1991; Wellman, 1990). Central to our understanding of other human beings, however, appears to be the notion that people are sentient beings who choose their actions (see Wellman, 1990, for a discussion). If this notion is central to reasoning about human action, then the system of knowledge of psychology is distinct from that of physics. We must ask, therefore, how reasoners single out a person as an entity in the domain of their psychological reasoning.

Babies appear to have an innate representation of the structure of the human face; this representation allows neonates to direct attention to faces that move across the field of view (see Johnson & Morton, 1991, for a review). Perhaps babies use that representation to identify people as entities expected to be capable of perceptions and purposive action. Evidence from a number of sources suggests this is not the case: Infants, children, and adults identify animate, sentient beings by taking account of their actions, not by analyzing their surface appearance.

Consider first young children's reactions to dolls. Many young children are delighted by dolls, with whom they engage in rich pretend interactions. At no age, however, do children appear to be led by dolls' human features to treat dolls as animate, sentient beings (R. Gelman, 1990; R. Gelman, Spelke, & Meck, 1983). Even infants respond differently to dolls and to living faces: A stationary doll's faces is an object of interest or delight, whereas a stationary human face, seen under similar circumstances, can evoke fear or aversion (Tronick, 1982). In addition, young infants appear to respond to object the lack any clearly animate features (e.g., mobiles) as animate and social beings, if the behavior of those objects approximates the behavior of a responsive social agent. These findings, and other findings with adults (Heider & Simmel, 1944), suggest that children and adults use some principles of their intuitive psychology not only to reason about persons but also to persive persons as persons (for more detailed expositions of this view, see R. Gelman, 1990, and Premack, 1990).[1]

Perceiving and Reasoning about Number

The origin and the nature of knowledge of number has been a topic of philosophical debate at least since Hume (e.g., Kitcher, 1983). Psychological research on infants (e.g., Wynn, 1992) and animals (see Gallistel, 1990, for a review) strongly supports the existence of innate knowledge of number that includes core principles of one-to-one correspondence and succession (every number has a unique successor, Gallistel & R. Gelman, 1992). If this view is correct, then number would appear to be a domain of knowledge distinct from physics or psychology. How do reasoners single out the entities in this domain, apprehending sets and their numerosity?

A controversy exists concerning the relations between perceiving and reasoning about small sets. On one view, perception of small sets depends on a special pattern-recognition process, "subitizing," whereas perception of large sets depends on a counting process (Klahr & Wallace, 1973; Davis & Pérusse 1988). The principles of operation of the subitizing process are unknown, but they are believed to be distinct from the principles governing numerical reasoning. On a different view (Gallistel, 1990; Gallistel & R. Gelman, 1992), sets of all sizes are enumerated by a counting process. Proponents of both views agree that the principles at the core of the counting process include one-to-one correspondence and succession, and that these principles underline not only counting but also the operations of spontaneous arithmetic.

In our terms, the difference between these two views of the process of enumerating small sets is exactly the difference between the thesis that a single system of knowledge underlies number perception and numerical reasoning, and the thesis that distinct systems underlie these abilities. Note that on both views, a single set of principles is thought to enable humans to perceive and reason about large sets.

In summary, domain-specific reasoning and domain-specific perception appear to depend on a single system of knowledge in the domains of physics, psychology, and number (at least for large sets). We now ask how knowledge grows and changes in these domains.

Cognitive Development

It is natural to suppose that humans learn about the world by observing it. We learn that bodies fall by watching them fall; we learn that insults make people angry by watching people react to insults; we learn that $2 + 2 = 4$ by observing two sets of two things combine into one set of four things. Variants of this thesis may be offered. Children may learn through active manipulation (releasing or throwing objects, hitting people, combining sets), or by social interaction (tossing balls around, participating in social exchanges, playing number games).

If any of these proposals is correct, then children and adults will learn only about the things they perceive. A child who cannot perceive any object that falls, any person who is moved to anger, or any sets of two things that combine into a set of four things, will never learn about these entities, however much he or she observes, manipulates, or communicates about the surrounding layout. Perception limits the development of knowledge.

The consequences of this limit depend on the relation between the principles governing perception and those governing reasoning. If perception and reasoning are guided by distinct principles, experience may overturn the original principles governing reasoning. For example, suppose that perception of persons depends on a face-recognizer, whereas initial reasoning about persons depends on notions that action is internally generated in accordance with perceptions and feelings. Encountering a doll, the child would perceive a person. The behavior of this person, however, would not appear to result from choices but from the blind operation of the laws of mechanics. Because the doll must be admitted to the class of persons (we are assuming that the face-recognizer, not the psychological reasoner, makes this decision), the child is now in a position to learn that his or her initial psychology is false: Not all persons are purposive, sentient beings. With increased exposure to dolls, stuffed animals, portraits, and the like, this learning will grow and be extended. Learning will therefore bring changes to the child's initial system of knowledge.

If the same system of knowledge guides perception and reasoning, in contrast, it would seem that children *cannot* learn, by observing the world, that their initial system of knowledge is false. For example, suppose that both perception and reasoning about persons are guided by the notion that people are sentient and purposive. When children encounter an entity that looks like a human being but does not engage in self-generated action, they will not conclude that their notion of person is false but rather that this entity does not fall within the domain of their psychology: It is not a person.

In any domain in which perception and reasoning depend on the same system of knowledge, learning from observation, from action, or from social interchange will tend to preserve the initial system of knowledge. Knowledge will grow by a process of enrichment, whereby core principles become further entrenched. The initial system of knowledge will not be overthrown by any process of induction from experience, because only objects that conform to that system are available to be experienced. Cognitive development will result in the enrichment of knowledge around unchanging core principles.

Some aspects of mature, commonsense reasoning appear to support the view that knowledge of physical objects, persons, and number develops by enrichment. In the domain of physics, principles such as cohesion, contact, and continuity appear to be central to mature intuitions about object persistence (see Hirsch, 1982) and object motion (see Spelke, 1991, for discussion). In the domain of psychology, the notion that people choose their actions appears to be deeply ingrained in mature common-sense reasoning (Wellman, 1990). Finally, in the domain of number, Gallistel and R. Gelman (1992) argue that the most intuitive mature conceptions of number are those that derive from the principles of one-to-one correspondence and succession.

Nevertheless, this reasoning leads to a contradiction. Conceptual change in the domains of physics, psychology, and number is not only possible but actual. In the history of science and mathematics, it has occurred with the development of Newtonian and quantum mechanics, with the attempt to construct a purely behavioristic or mechanistic psychology, and with the discovery of rational, real, and complex numbers. In each of these cases, the development of science has led to the construction of new principles and to the abandonment of principles that formerly were central to knowledge in the domain. In each of these cases, new types of entities were discovered or posited. The existence of conceptual change in science challenges the view that knowledge develops by enrichment around a constant core, and it raises the possibility that there are no cognitive universals: no core principles of reasoning that are immune to cultural variation.

Conceptual Change

The nature and existence of conceptual change has been extensively analyzed and debated since Feyerabend (1962) and Kuhn (1962) independently adopted the mathematical term "incommensurability" (no common meature) to refer to mutually untranslatable theoretical languages (see Suppe, 1977, for a comprehensive critique of the early Kuhn/Feyerabend positions). These debates have led to a softening of Kuhn's and Feyerabend's early claims. In particular, current analyses of conceptual change in science deny that the meanings of all terms in a theory change when some do, that theories completely determine evidence and therefore are unfalsifiable, or that theory change is akin to religious conversion. These analyses nevertheless hold that the core insight of the Kuhn/Feyerabend early work stands: The history of science is marked by transitions across which students of the same phenomena speak incommensurable languages.

Carey (1991) summarizes the recent analyses of conceptual change that have been offered by philosophers of science (Kitcher, 1988; Kuhn, 1982; see also Hacking, 1993; Nersessian, 1992) and by cognitive scientists (Thagard, 1988; see also Chi, 1992; Vosniadou & Brewer, 1992). Conceptual change consists of conceptual differentiations, such that the undifferentiated parent concept plays no role in subsequent theories (Carey, 1991; Kuhn, 1977), and of the creation of new ontological categories (Thagard, 1988; Chi, 1992). Conceptual change involves change in the core principles that define the entities in a domain and govern reasoning about those entities. It brings the emergence of new principles, incommensurable with the old, which carve the world at different joints.

Cognitive Science and the History of Science

Some doubt the relevance of historical analyses of conceptual change to cognitive science and especially to cognitive development. Scientific reasoning and concepts, one might argue, are different from ordinary reasoning and concepts. Only the former undergo changes in core principles.

We consider it a serious empirical question as to whether the core concepts of commonsense reasoning are subject to change. Whatever answer one gives to this question, however, the existence of conceptual change in science challenges the argument for enrichment given above. If the development of domain-specific reasoning is constrained by domain-specific perception, and if the same system of knowledge underlies both reasoning and perception, then no person at any level of expertise is in a position to learn that his or her initial system of knowledge is false. This argument applies to any perceiver and reasoner, whether human or animal, layperson or scientist. The existence of conceptual change in domain-specific core knowledge presents a serious counterexample to the argument for enrichment and needs to be explained (Carey, 1991).

Those who emphasize the differences between intuitive theories and explicit scientific theories often imply that those differences in themselves *explain* conceptual change. In particular, the community of scientists, the self-reflective nature of explicit theory construction, and the instructional institutions that create scientists may be engines of conceptual change (e.g., Spelke, 1991). We grant that developed science differs from intuitive knowledge in these three ways. Nonetheless, communication among scientists, reflection, and instruction do not in themselves provide a mechanism for conceptual change.

First, processes that occur within an interactive community of scientists cannot, in themselves, bring about conceptual change, because the interactions within a scientific community can only be as effective as the conceptions of its individual members permit. Communication between scientists succeeds only insofar as two scientists can single out the same things to talk about (see Kuhn, 1962). The arguments against the possibility of conceptual change therefore apply to the community of scientists as well as to the individual scientist.

Next, consider the possibility that reasoners use "disciplined reflection" to revise conceptions within a domain. Many have argued that metacognitive abilities enable human intelligence to extend itself beyond its initial limits (e.g., Rozin, 1976; Sperber, 1994). By itself, however, reflection can do nothing to extricate developing conceptions from the self-perpetuating cycle described above. We as humans can only reflect on the entities we perceive. If our initial conceptions determine those entities then we will be able to reflect only on entities whose behavior accords with our initial conceptions. Reflection by itself will not produce conceptual change.

Finally, instructional institutions that create scientists cannot in themselves account for conceptual change, for two reasons. First, instruction cannot account for individual discovery or invention. Second, instruction, like all communication, is limited by the student's ability to apprehend the objects to which it applies. If a student is not able to apprehend the entities in a to-be-learned theory, he or she may mouth the correct words but will assign to them meanings licensed by his or her own concepts (see the science misconceptions literature reviewed in Carey, 1986, and Vosniadou, 1994).

In sum, we do not dispute that Western science is a social process, the product of self-reflective, metaconceptually sophisticated adults, and that systematic instruction is required to form these adults. These facts, however, do not provide an account of conceptual change. We require such an account: an explanation of how a reasoner can move beyond the core principles in a system of knowledge. Once such an account is provided, we may ask how it tempers the generalization that knowledge develops by enrichment around a constant core.

Mechanisms of Conceptual Change

Mappings across Domains

The formal reflections of scientists provide one source of evidence concerning the processes of conceptual change. We begin with the reflections of the physicist, historian, and philosopher of science, Pierre Duhem. Duhem (1949) suggested that scientific physics is not built directly upon commonsense understanding of physical phenomena but depends instead on translations between the language of ordinary experience and the language of mathematics. According to Duhem, the objects of science are not concrete material bodies but numbers. To provide explanations for physical phenomena, physicists first translate from a physical to a mathematical description of the world, and then they look for generalizations and regularities in the mathematical description. These generalizations, when translated back into the language of everyday objects, are the physicist's laws.

In our terms, scientists who effect a translation from physics to mathematics are using their innately given system of knowledge of number to shed light on phenomena in the domain of their innately given system of knowledge of physics. Scientists do this by devising and using systems of measurement to create *mappings* between the objects in the first system (numbers) and those in the second (bodies).[2] Once a mapping is created, the scientists can use conceptions of number to reason about physical objects. They therefore may escape the constraints imposed by the core principles of physical reasoning. In effect, the mapping from physics to number creates a new perceptual system for the domain of physics, centering not on the principles of cohesion, contact, and continuity but on the principles of one-to-one correspondence, succession, and the like. The entities picked out by this new perceptual system need not be commensurable with those picked out by the old.

Duhem focuses exclusively on the construction of a translation, or mapping, from physics to mathematics. Conceptual change may occur as well through mappings across other domains. In particular, conceptual changes in science appear to have resulted from the construction and use of mappings from psychology to physics. By viewing animals and people as complex machines, mechanistic biology and mechanistic psychology aim to explain animal and human action in terms of physical principles. We return to these conceptual changes below.

How do scientists construct mappings across domains? Science's informal documents (lab notebooks, journals) provide an excellent source of data concerning this process. Recently, cognitive scientists as well as historians and philosophers of science have begun to mine this source (e.g., Gruber, 1974, on Darwin; Nersessian, 1992, on Maxwell; Tweney, 1991, on Faraday). Nersessian (1992) concentrates on two interconnected pairs of processes that recur in historical cases of conceptual change: (1) the use of physical analogy, and (2) the construction of thought experiments and limiting case analyses. These processes serve both to reveal tensions and inadequacies within a system of knowledge and to restructure that system through the construction of mappings across knowledge domains.

Physical Analogies

Nersessian's analysis of Maxwell's use of physical analogies provides a worked example of the productive use of such mappings in the process of conceptual change. According to Nersessian, Maxwell himself used the term "physical analogy" in explaining his method. A physical analogy exploits a set of mathematical relationships as they are embodied in a source domain so as to analyze a target domain about which there is only partial knowledge. In Maxwell's case, the source domain was fluid mechanics as an embodiment of the mathematics of continuum mechanics, and the target domain was electromagnetism. By constructing the analogy between these two areas of physics, Maxwell was able ultimately to construct an effective mathematical theory of electromagnetism.

Nersessian notes several important lessons from this case study. First, the analogy from fluid mechanics to electromagnetism did real inferential work: Important mistakes in Maxwell's first characterization of the electromagnetic field are traceable to points at which this analogy breaks down. Second, the process of constructing mappings across domains is difficult: Each mapping must be explored and tested in depth to determine its usefulness. Third, "imagistic representations" play an important part in constructing the mapping from physics to number. They express mathematical relationships in a directly comprehensible way and thus serve as a good bridge between domains. Fourth, the process of constructing a mapping across domains is not one of transferring the relations from source domain to target in one fell swoop by plug-

ging in and testing values. Rather, a scientist explores different possible mappings from the source domain onto the target domain, imposing different conceptualizations of the target domain in so doing. Finally, the mapping thus created can produce conceptual change in both domains. By using the Newtonian mathematics of continuum mechanics to understand electromagnetic fields, Maxwell constructed a mathematics of greater generality than that of his source domain (Nersessian, 1992).

Thought Experiments and Limiting Case Analyses

Another modeling activity is the construction of thought experiments, including limiting case analyses. Philosophers of science have often discussed how (or whether) thought experiments can be *experimental*: Can they have empirical content even though they involve no data? Kuhn (1977), analyzing a thought experiment that figured in the process by which Galileo differentiated instantaneous velocity from average velocity, argued that one function of thought experiments is to show that current concepts cannot apply to the world without contradiction. Nersessian (1992) extended Kuhn's analysis arguing that thought experiments involve mental model simulations, which are part of the source of their empirical content.

Nersessian's example is Galileo's famous thought experiment showing that heavier objects do not fall faster than lighter ones. Galileo imagined two objects, a large heavy one and a small light one, in free fall. According to Aristotelian and scholastic physics, the heavier object should fall faster. He then imagined joining the two objects with an extremely thin rod, creating a composite object. This thought experiment suggests two contradictory outcomes: (1) The composite object is heavier still and therefore should fall even faster, and (2) the slower speed of the smaller object should impede the speed of the larger object, so the composite object should fall more slowly! Galileo went on to construct a limiting case analysis concerning the medium in which objects fall to resolve the contradiction. He concluded that in a vacuum, objects of any weight will fall at the same speed. This thought experiment and limiting case analysis played a role in constructing a differentiated, extensive conception of weight. That conception, in turn, depends on the mathematical distinction between a sum and an average.[3]

Conceptual Change and Cognitive Universals

If processes such as those discussed by Nersessian are necessary components of the engine for conceptual change, we can account for the plausibility of the intuition that conceptual change results from the cooperative activity of a scientific community, from reflection, and from instruction. Galileo, Maxwell, Faraday, Einstein, and Darwin left writings, diaries, and notebooks showing that they used the heuristic processes Nersessian describes, and that they were fully conscious of doing so. They used these processes in the context of a self-reflective understanding of the goal of constructing new scientific theories. When one constructs a mapping across domains for the first time, one never knows how useful or deceptive it will prove to be. Thought experiments, physical analogies, and limiting case analyses serve as devices to communicate new conceptualizations to the scientific community, but these new conceptualizations will be adopted only insofar as they provide resolutions to standing puzzles and promote a productive research program. The jury is the social institutions of science.

But do heuristic processes of the kind Nersessian describes, and the mappings that result from them, also occur outside of developed science? Do they bring conceptual change to lay adults and children, creating cultural differences in core knowledge systems? The evidence considered thus far is consistent with three different hypotheses concerning conceptual change outside of science, each with different consequences for the existence of cross-cultural cognitive universals.

According to the *strong universality hypothesis*, only metaconceptually sophisticated scientists can overturn the core principles that innately determine ontology and reasoning. If this hypothesis is true, then the intuitive theories of people in all cultures will be enriched versions of those innate principles. The core principles of commonsense reasoning will be universal.

According to the *weak universality hypothesis*, children and lay adults can overturn innate, core principles of reasoning, but only through experience in a culture with a developed science. The source of conceptual change is the assimilation by children of the conceptions of the adults around them as those conceptions are expressed in adult language, in the measurement devices and technology of the culture, and in systematic instruction in school. And the source of the lay adult's conceptions, in turn, is the cultural assimilation of conceptual changes *originally* made by metaconceptually sophisticated scientists. If the weak universality hypothesis is true, then the intuitive knowledge systems of all cultures will share a common innate core, except in the case of cultures with a developed science.

According to the *no universality hypothesis*, the processes of conceptual change observed in scientists also occur spontaneously in children and lay adults. Although infants the world over share a set of initial systems of knowledge, those systems are spontaneously overturned over the course of development and learning, as children and adults construct, explore, and adopt mappings across knowledge systems. Because of the diversity of the potential mappings across domains, it is unlikely that the knowledge systems of members of different cultures will share a common core.

In the rest of this chapter, we turn to evidence bearing on these hypotheses. Rather than rely on cross-cultural data, we will examine a population that stands outside the cultural institutions of science and that lacks metaconceptual awareness of theory construction and choice: American children. Even though children do not engage in the social process of explicit theory construction and are not self-reflective theorizers, there is ample empirical evidence for conceptual change in childhood. Conceptual change occurs both spontaneously, as the child masters the language and the intuitive knowledge systems of the adult culture, and also as the result of systematic instruction in school. The existence of conceptual change in childhood militates against the strong universality hypothesis.

Conceptual Change in Childhood

Number

The preschool child's concept of number is the *positive integer* (see R. Gelman, 1991), as defined by the core principles of one-to-one correspondence and succession. This core notion changes early in the child's school years as the child constructs the concept of *0* (Wellman & Miller, 1986), the concept of *infinity* (in the form of a realization that there is no highest number; R. Gelman & Evans, 1981), and the concept of *rational number* (R. Gelman, 1991), and as the child becomes explicitly aware of the core principles defining number and thereby becomes able to reason about conservation of number (see R. Gelman & Gallistel, 1978, for a review).

It could be argued that the construction of 0 and *no highest number* involve change in the concept of number, as both changes begin to separate number from counting. Moreover, the construction of the concept of *rational number* brings an even deeper conceptual change. Coming to see .5 or 1/3 as numbers requires abandoning the identification of number with counting, abandoning the successor principle, and constructing a new understanding of division (as a different operation from repeated subtraction). The new principles that jointly determine what constitutes a number and that govern reasoning with numbers include closure under division, construed in this new way.

R. Gelman (1991) suggested that changing conceptions of number depend in part on the construction of mappings between number and physical objects (as the child learns measurement) and on the construction of mappings between number and geometry (via devices such as the number line). Children's ability to benefit from these mappings suggests that the strong universality thesis is false for the domain of number. It is not clear, however, whether children or adults would spontaneously devise measurement devices or construct number lines in the absence of a developed science and mathematics. The weak universality hypothesis and the no universality hypothesis are both consistent with the above studies.

Biology and Psychology

The principles determining the entities of the earliest psychology – capacity for self-generated motion and attention and contingent reaction to surrounding events – actually determine the ontological kind *animal*, not just *person*. For this reason, Carey (1985) speculated that young children's intuitive biology is not differentiated from their intuitive psychology. Her claim that 4-year-olds do not have an autonomous domain of intuitive biology has come under much scrutiny (e.g., Inagaki & Hatano, 1988; Springer & Keil, 1989; Wellman & Gelman, 1992). Regardless of whether preschool children should be granted an autonomous biology, however, it is clear that their understanding of biological phenomena differs radically from that of older children. In Hatano and Inagaki's (1987) terms, children progress from a vitalistic biology to a mechanistic biology.

Much of the evidence for this conceptual change was reviewed in Carey (1985, 1988): Evidence for the differentiation of the concepts *dead* and *inanimate*, for a change in the status of *person* as *animal*, and for the coalescence of the concepts *animal* and *plant* into a new concept, *living thing*. To that evidence, Keil and his colleagues have added many new phenomena suggesting conceptual change over these years (Keil, 1989; Springer & Keil, 1989). Keil's data serve two important purposes: They provide information concerning the precise characterization of the preschool child's initial biological concepts, and they provide evidence for conceptual change in the concept of *animal* and perhaps the concept of *person*.

Take Keil's transformation studies. Preschool children believe that a skunk can be turned into a raccoon through surgery; by age 9 (and earlier in some studies), children believe that the animal resulting from such a transformation is still a skunk that just looks like a raccoon (Keil, 1989). Preschool children do not think, however, that anything that looks like raccoon is a raccoon: A skunk wearing a raccoon costume and pictured to look identical to a raccoon is judged to be a skunk (Keil, 1989). Similarly a dog with all its insides removed (the blood and bones and stuff like that) is judged not to be a dog any more (Gelman & Wellman, 1991). These data suggest that to preschool children, the core of the notion of *animal kind* includes bodily structure: It is not enough to look just like an animal (e.g., a stuffed dog) or a particular kind of animal (e.g., a raccoon-costumed skunk), in order for an entity to be an animal or a particular kind of animal. Rather, the body of the entity must have the right structure, including internal structure. But these data also show that 9-year-olds have constructed a deeper notion of how that bodily structure must come to be: For 4- to 6-year-olds, surgery will do it; for 9-year-olds, bodily structure must result from a natural growth process. We take this developmental difference to reflect changes in the principles that define the entities in the domain of biology: By age 9, aspects of the life cycle have become part of the core principles. Changes of this sort are typical of historical cases of conceptual change (Kitcher, 1988).[4]

That this change actually reflects conceptual change rather than enrichment is further shown by changes in children's understanding of why children resemble their parents. Both Springer and Keil (1989) and Gelman and Wellman (1991) claim that preschool children understand that babies (including animal babies) inherit an innate potential from their parents to develop certain traits rather than others. However, their data do not establish that the preschool child has an understanding of the *biological* inheritance of properties.

We take an understanding of inheritance of properties to include, at a minimum, two essential components. First, children resemble their parents: Black parents tend to have black children, blue-eyed parents are more likely to have blue-eyed children than are brown-eyed parents, dogs have baby dogs rather than baby cats, and so on. Second, the *mechanism* underlying this resemblance crucially involves birth. There are many ways children may come to resemble their parents: Curly-haired parents may have curly-haired children because they give them permanents; prejudiced parents may have prejudiced children because they taught them to be so. Such mechanisms are not part of a biological process of inheritance of properties. To be credited with a biological concept of inheritance, children need not understand anything like a genetic mechanism, but they must distinguish the process underlying family resemblance from mechanical or psychological processes. At a minimum, children should realize that the process through which an animal originates – birth – is crucially involved in the process through which animals come to have their specific characteristics.

Without doubt, preschool children understand that offspring resemble their parents. Springer (1992) told 4- to 8-year-olds that a pictured animal had an unusual property (e.g., this horse has hair inside its ears) and then probed for projection of the property to a physically similar horse, described as a friend who is unrelated to the target, and to a physically dissimilar horse, described as the target's baby. At all ages, the property was projected more to the baby than to the friend. This important result confirms the mounting evidence that preschool children are not appearance-bound (S. Gelman, Coley, & Gottfried, 1994) and establishes the family resemblance component of a belief in inheritance of properties. However, because Springer did not probe the mechanism responsible for inheritance, his study does not bear on the second component. Springer distinguished what he considers a biological relationship (parentage) from a social relationship (friendship), but, as Carey (1985, 1988) points out, parentage is also a social relationship. At a minimum, one would like to see biological parentage distinguished from adoptive parentage.

The same issue arises with respect to the data of Springer and Keil (1989). Four- to seven-

year-old children, plus adults, were told that both parents have a particular atypical property (e.g., pink rather than the usual red hearts) and were asked whether an offspring would have that property. They manipulated further information about the unusual property (whether the parents were born with the property or acquired it in an accident, whether the property was internal or external to the body, and whether the property had "biological" functional consequences).[5] Two important results emerged. First, only adults based their judgments solely on information about how the parents acquired the property: That is, only adults related birth to inheritance. In one study, 7-year-olds were beginning to take this variable into account. Second, even preschool children made systematic judgments, influenced by whether or not the property was described as having biological consequences. From this result, Springer and Keil concluded that preschoolers have a biological concept of inheritance, but that it is different from the adult's concept. Again, a comparison between natural parentage and adoptive parentage is necessary to determine whether preschoolers' concept of inheritance goes beyond an understanding of family resemblance.

S. Gelman and Wellman (1991) specifically contrasted nature versus nurture. For example, they asked whether a cow, Edith, who had been separated from other cows at birth and raised with pigs, would (1) moo or oink and (2) have a straight or curly tail. Even 4-year-olds judged that Edith would moo and have a straight tail. But the story asserts that Edith is a cow, in spite of having been raised in the company of pigs. There is a wealth of evidence, much of it from Gelman herself (S. Gelman, Coley, & Gottfried, 1994), that preschoolers take category membership as predictive of category-relevant properties, even in the face of conflicting information. Furthermore, the task does not stress that the baby cow is raised in a pig family, a child among other children who are pigs. S. Gelman and Wellman also posed a story about a seed from an apple, planted in a flower pot, and found that by age 5, children judged it would come up an apple rather than a flower. This scenario contrasts environment (in the company of flowers) with parentage (seed from an apple) and confirms Springer's (1992) finding that *family* resemblance is crucial. The experiment does not provide evidence, however for an understanding of biological inheritance and a differentiation between biological and adoptive parentage.

Solomon, Johnson, Zaitchik, and Carey (1993) have carried out several studies contrasting adoptive with biological parentage. For example, a story is told about a (tall) shepherd whose son is taken at birth to be adopted by a (short) king and raised as the prince. The child is then asked whether the boy, when he grows up, will be tall like the shepherd or short like the king. Adults project physical properties such as height on the basis of biological parentage. This pattern does not begin to emerge until age 7: the age at which Springer and Keil (1989) begin to see the effect of information as to whether the property of the parent was inborn or acquired. As of now, there is no evidence that preschoolers have a conception of biological inheritance that goes beyond expectations of resemblance between parents and their offspring.

These data are consistent with those reviewed in Carey (1985), indicating changes in children's understanding of reproduction during the early school years. Preschool children do not take reproduction as one of the core principles defining animals and governing inferences about them. By age 10, in contrast, knowledge of reproduction begins to organize children's understanding of animals, as reflected both in the beginning understanding of inheritance and as reflected in judgments of what makes a skunk a skunk (Keil, 1989). This change is part of the construction of the new ontological category, *living thing*, which includes plants as well as animals (Carey, 1985). New core principles and new entities in the domain are hallmarks of conceptual change.

How do these fundamental changes in children's concept of *animal* bear on children's innate concept of *person*? Does the notion of a person as a sentient, freely acting being change once children begin to construct a mechanistic biology? If so, how does this change come about, if the principles at the center of the initial concept of person underlie not only psychological reasoning but also perception of persons?

Although answers to these questions are far from clear, we offer the following observations. First, biological concepts appear to exert some influence on mature, commonsense psychology. For example, Western adults are inclined to consider the living descendant of two persons as a person, even if that person lacks all capacity to act (e.g., while sleeping or in a coma). Adults also are inclined to deny personhood to apes, dolphins, and parrots, however impressive their behavioral accomplishments. *Person* is, at least in part, a species concept (see, e.g., Wiggins, 1980).

Second, the initial conception of a person as a freely acting, sentient being remains a powerful part of Western adults' commonsense understanding of human action, surviving in uneasy coexistence with the later-developing biological conception. Tensions between these conceptions can be found not only in scientific psychology and philosophy of mind but also in everyday life, as current debates over abortion, criminal responsibility, and other topics demonstrate.

Finally, note that the development of mechanistic biology and mechanistic psychology depend in part on the construction of mappings across the domains of psychology and physics. The research reviewed above provides evidence that the construction of these mappings is a difficult and extended process. Insofar as it succeeds, however, there arises the possibility for conceptual change. A person may be viewed not only as a free agent but also as a complex machine and a member of a living kind (see Gentner & Grudin, 1985, for a historical analysis of changes in metaphors for the mind over 90 years of scientific psychology).

Studies of American children's changing biological and psychological conceptions cast doubt on the strong universality hypothesis, but they do not distinguish between the weak and the no universality hypotheses. To explore the conjecture that conceptual change in biology and psychology requires a developed scientific tradition, we need empirical studies of the intuitive biological and psychological theories held by children and adults in a wide range of cultures. Atran (1990) finds evidence for cross-cultural universality of folk taxonomies in biology but does not review research on folk explanations of biological phenomena: disease, reproduction, inheritance, and the functions of body parts. To our knowledge, the only work exploiting recent methodologies to diagnose intuitive biological conceptions is that of Jeyifous (1986), building on the work of Keil (1989). Jeyifous's results suggest that the developing conceptions of biology sketched in this section occur in cultures isolated from Western biological thought. For example, unschooled rural Yoruba children shift from the judgment that an operated-upon raccoon has become a skunk to the judgment that it is still a raccoon at about the same age as their American counterparts. If this shift reflects conceptual change, then Jeyifous's finding suggests two conclusions. First, conceptual change does not require developed scientific institutions. Even though Yoruba biology differs greatly from intuitive American biology, both involve a notion of animal kind that is deeper than bodily structure, whereas the preschool child's biology (in both cultures) does not. Second, even though conceptual change is seen in both cultures, cross-cultural universality is still observed. Of course, whether intuitive Yoruba biology is commensurable with intuitive American biology is an open empirical question.

Matter and Physical Objects

We have suggested that objects, for babies, are defined by the principles of cohesion, continuity, and contact: Objects are coherent solids that maintain their boundaries as they move along spatiotemporally continuous paths, and that act upon each other only on contact. There are tensions in the baby's application of these principles, however, and these tensions may provide the seeds for future conceptual change. The principles do not apply equally well to persons (who commonly appear to violate the contact principle, while behaving in accord with the principles of cohesion and continuity). Similarly, nonsolid substances such as liquids, gels, and powders obey the principle of continuity (e.g., sand cannot pass through solid barriers) but not the principle of cohesion (e.g., sand can disperse and coalesce as it moves). Although innate principles determine an ontology for the child, they do not define entirely nonoverlapping sets of entities. How do children conceptualize the entities in the overlapping sections of their ontological universe, and how do their conceptions change with development and experience? We focus here on changing conceptions of nonsolid substances and on emerging conceptions of *matter*.

The distinction between objects and nonsolid substances is very salient to young children. Objects are typically quantified as individuals, whereas nonsolid substances are typically not quantified as individuals. This quantificational distinction is marked as the count/mass distinction in the syntax of many of the world's languages, and it conditions 2-year-old children's hypotheses about word meaning (Soja, Carey, & Spelke, 1991). But do young children appreciate that both objects and nonsolid substances are material?

Four-year-old children treat both objects and nonsolid substances as subject to the continuity principle: They judge that it is impossible for water to fill a box if the box is already filled by a steel block of the same dimensions (Carey, 1991). Moreover, 3- and 4-year-olds distinguish objects from ideas, dreams, and images on the basis of two properties that are relevant to the distinction between material and immaterial entities: objective perceptual access and causal interaction with other material entities (Estes, Wellman, & Woolley, 1989). Children's abilities to distinguish some material entities (i.e., objects) from some immaterial entities (i.e., ideas) on the basis of some properties that for adults are part of the core of the distinction between material and immaterial entities does not show, however, that children draw a material/immaterial distinction. Rather, children might draw a distinction between objects and mental entities, or between real and imaginary entities, on the basis of these properties. Two types of further information are required before we attribute a material/immaterial distinction to the child: We need to probe more widely the entities that fall under the distinction, and we need to analyze the explanatory work the distinction does for the child, in relation to the explanatory work that the material/immaterial distinction does for adults.

Carey (1991) presents such an investigation and concludes that preschool and early elementary-aged children *do* draw a material/immaterial distinction. The child's concept of matter, however, is incommensurable with that of the adult. Conceptual change in the years from 4 to 12 involves each of the interrelated concepts of *matter, kind of stuff, weight, density,* and *air.* The analysis includes two examples of initially undifferentiated concepts that are incommensurable with adult concepts: *weight/density* and *air/nothing.*[6] The principles that pick out material entities and guide reasoning about them for preschool children include the principle that a given region of space can be occupied by only one portion of matter at a time (the continuity principle), the principle that material entities are publicly observable, and the principle that material entities interact causally with each other (the contact principle). Unlike adults, the young child does not take weight to be a core property of matter. This is seen by the judgment that heat, light, and electricity are "made of some kind stuff," just like cars, trees, and animals and unlike ideas and dreams. More strikingly, weight is viewed as an accidental property of prototypical material entities. For example, most children up through age 10 judge that a pea-sized piece of styrofoam, although material, weighs nothing at all. Weight therefore is not a necessary property of entities judged material.

Because weight is not a necessary property of material entities, it cannot provide a measure of amount of matter. Like the Greeks (Jammer, 1961), young children have no measure of matter (Piaget & Inhelder, 1941; Carey, 1991). For young children, weight (an extensive magnitude) is not differentiated from density (an intensive magnitude) and therefore cannot be an extensive property of matter (Carey, 1991; Smith, Carey, & Wiser, 1985). Children know that if object A weighs 250 grams and if object B weighs less than A, then object B will weigh less than 250 grams. But the same children are perfectly happy to judge that object A can be broken into 10 pieces, each of which weighs 0 grams!

Finally, preschool children, and roughly half of our sample of 6- to 10-year-olds, have not constructed a model of matter as continuous and homogeneous. Asked to imagine cutting a piece of steel in half repeatedly, they claim one finally will arrive at a piece that is so small that it no longer occupies space, and also that one will arrive at a piece of steel in which one could (in principle) see all the steel: There would be no more steel inside. The other half of the elementary schoolchildren, and all the 12-year-olds, judged that steel is continuous, homogeneous, and infinitely divisible: No matter how small the piece, it would still occupy space and would have more steel inside it. (By age 12, in spite of science education, most children have constructed a continuous model of matter.) The continuous model of matter supports the distinction between weight and density, providing the possibility that weight may become one of the core properties of material entities.

How do children come to reconceptualize matter and material objects? Mappings between the domains of physics and number, constructed through the processes described by Nersessian, appear to play a role in this process. Carol Smith and her collaborators (e.g., Smith, Snir, & Grosslight, 1992; Smith, Grosslight, Macklin, & Davis, 1993) have explored the use of physical analogies to drive 11- to 13-year-olds' reconceptualization of matter, especially the differentiation of weight from density and the construction of weight as an extensive quantity. The ideas are tested in the arena of science education. The curriculum that Smith et al. have developed centers around computer implemented, interactive visual models that serve to represent the mathematics of intensive and extensive quantities. For example, in one model, weight is represented by the number of dots, volume by the number of boxes of a fixed size, and density by the number of dots per box. Students first work with the models, exploring the mathematical relations between the extensive and intensive quantities internal to the models. Then students work on mapping the models to the material world, by exploring such phenomena as the constant ratios of size to weight within each material and the laws of floating and sinking. This mapping is slow and difficult: Without having differentiated weight from density, students cannot readily succeed in mapping number of dots per box to density, rather than to absolute weight or to some other physical variable.

To facilitate this mapping, Smith et al. use the physical analogy of dissolving sugar in water as a source domain (in which sweetness is the intensive quantity and amounts of sugar and water are the extensive quantities) as well as the visual model of the intensive quantity (dot crowdedness). The visual model embodies the mathematics of extensive and intensive quantities, and serves as a bridge between mathematical representations and the target domain. As did Maxwell, students explore the analogy in a piecemeal manner, over time. When they encounter the phenomenon of thermal expansion and attempt to model it, they must change the model (material kinds do not have constant densities). This process consolidates and extends their understanding of the mathematics of intensive and extensive quantities, and it contributes to change in their concept of matter. It results in a mapping between physics and mathematics that gives rise to a new core concept: *quantity of matter.*

Smith et al. also employ thought experiments and limiting case analyses in their curricular intervention. Here we provide one example of a limiting case analysis (concretely exemplified rather than part of a thought experiment). Students who lack an extensive concept of weight maintain that a single grain of rice weighs nothing at all. As a classroom exercise, teams of students discover how many grains of rice placed on one edge of a playing card balanced on a thick fulcrum cause it to topple (around 50). They are asked to explain why the card fell. (Most say, "the rice was heavy.") Then the playing card is balanced on a thinner fulcrum, such that 10 grains of rice suffice, and again students explain that the rice was heavy enough to topple the card. Then the card is balanced on a very very thin fulcrum, and a single grain of rice placed on its edge causes it to fall. Students are asked to reconsider whether a single grain of rice weighs a tiny amount or nothing at all. Seven-year-olds are unmoved by this experience; they insist that the single grain of rice weighs nothing. A classroom of 10- or 11-year-olds presents a completely different picture. First, they are very interested in the experiment, and a lively discussion ensues, pitting those who now think that a grain of rice weighs a tiny amount against those who still maintain it weighs nothing. In every class observed thus far, the proponents of the former view have spontaneously produced two arguments: (1) a sensitivity of the measuring device argument and (2) the argument that a single grain of rice must weigh something, because if it weighed 0 grams, then 50 grains of rice would weigh 0 grams as well.

Note that these two arguments depend on the mapping from physical objects to number: It is only in the realm of mathematics that repeated division of a positive quantity always yields a positive quantity, and that repeated addition of 0 always yields 0. In the realm of physics, in contrast, every physical interaction has a threshold. Repeated division of an object always results, eventually, in objects that are too small to be detected by any given physical device. Moreover, a collection of objects, each of which falls below the threshold of a given device, may well be detectable by the device. Like the Aristotelian physicists discussed by Jammer (1961, see note 3), 7-year-old children who resist Smith's limiting case analysis and continue to insist that a single grain of rice weighs nothing are not necessarily irrational. Rather, they may be reasoning consistently within the domain of perceivable objects and outside the domain of number. Smith's limiting case analysis forms part of the process of constructing a mapping between weight and number and fosters the development of an extensive concept of weight. It does not, however, guarantee that the mapping will be constructed and used.

Smith et al. (1993) recently documented that their model-based curriculum, including thought experiments and limiting case analyses, is more effective in inducing conceptual change than is a control curriculum that does not involve these heuristics. Wiser (1988) has obtained similar results from the use of physical analogy in inducing conceptual change in high school students' thermal concepts, especially the differentiation of heat and temperature.

These results support Duhem's and Nersessian's proposals concerning the mechanisms effecting conceptual change. In addition, they reveal that meta-conceptually unsophisticated individuals, who are not part of the social process of scientific theory building, can use the heuristics that scientists use to effect conceptual change. The success of these curricula suggests that conceptual change in childhood is the same sort of process as is conceptual change in the history of science. Studies of conceptual change in physics provide evidence against the strong universality hypothesis.

As in the case of number and psychology, however, the weak universality hypothesis is left untouched. Smith's students did not spontaneously explore the mapping between number and weight, and they did not invent the physical analogy, the thought experiments, or the limiting case analyses. These were constructed to be instructional aids by adults who understood the students' conceptions of matter and who knew what conceptual change they wanted to effect. This demonstration therefore leaves open the possibility that only metaconceptually aware theory builders invent thought experiments, limiting case analyses, and physical analogies in order to construct and use mappings between different knowledge domains.

In summary, studies of conceptual change in childhood show the strong universality hypothesis to be false. Children and adults, like scientists can bring about changes in their core, domain-specific systems of knowledge by constructing and using mappings across those systems. These studies weaken the expectation of cross-cultural cognitive universals, even in domains supported by innate principles. The personal qualities of mature scientists and the cultural institutions of science are not necessary for conceptual change. Psychologists and anthropologists therefore cannot expect that intuitive theories held by lay people the world over will be enriched versions of the innate principles in these domains.

Conclusions

Studies of conceptual change, both in the history of science and in childhood, suggest that human reasoners go beyond the principles at the core of their initial systems of knowledge. Reasoners do this, in part by constructing mappings across different knowledge domains. Because the possibilities for mapping across different domains of knowledge are vast, there is little reason to expect, a priori, that all adults in all cultures will have commensurable conceptions, even in those domains where humans are endowed with systems of knowledge whose principles both determine the entties of the domain and support reasoning about those entities.

Still, we do not know whether children or adults spontaneously construct mappings across domains, by means of such heuristics as those described above, in the process of developing systems of culturally constructed knowledge. In the absence of developed science, does cognitive development in all cultures require conceptual change, such that the conceptual systems of the members of distinct cultures are incommensurable with the innately given systems? And does the cultural construction of knowledge in these domains lead to intuitive theories across different cultures that are incommensurable with each other? We offer these two related questions as *the* central problems for cognitive anthropology. At least they are the questions we would most like to have answered.

Notes

1   Some researchers take the wide-ranging changes, at about age 4, in children's abilities to reason about false beliefs, about the appearance–reality distinction, and about certain perspective-taking tasks as evidence for conceptual change in the child's theory of mind (e.g., Perner, 1991). Others maintain that the mature psychological conception of a person is an enriched version of the 2-year-old's conception (e.g., Wellman, 1990; Fodor, 1992). We do not take sides in this debate but note that researchers on both sides hold that the child, even the baby, attributes to people the capacity for self-generated action, for contingent reactions to the baby's own reactions, and for attention to entities in the world. The later development of representational theories of mind would appear to preserve this core conception of people as sentient and purposive beings.

2   Competing views of analogical reasoning within cognitive science (e.g., Gentner, 1989; Holyoak & Thagard, 1989; Carbonell, 1986) flesh out the details of how such mappings are constructed and used.

3   Galileo's thought experiment reveals that the Aristotelian concept of *weight* is undifferentiated between an extensive quantity (the weight of the composite object is additive) and an intensive quantity (the weight of the composite object is an average). According to Jammer (1961), Aristotle's concept of weight was in fact undifferentiated in this way. Indeed, Aristotle considered a version of Galileo's thought experiment and drew the conclusion that the composite object would fall faster, because the weight of any given piece of substance was a function of the totality of which it was part: Both the small

and the large object would be heavier when they became part of a single object! Galileo's thought experiment therefore leads to no contradiction within Aristotelian physics. Thought experiments, like any experiments, depend upon current conceptualizations and do not guarantee conceptual change.

4   This deepening continues beyond age 10; ten-year-olds judge that a skunk, accidentally given an injection of a chemical shortly after birth, which caused it to grow into an animal that looks just like a raccoon, has indeed become a raccoon; adults judge it will continue to be a skunk (Keil, 1989).

5   Springer and Keil (1989) offer no analysis of what constitutes a "biological" functional consequence and include such examples as "has stretched out eyes which make it easier to see their enemies."

6   For example, all 4-year-olds and roughly half of the 6- to 10-year-olds maintained that the box mentioned here could contain both the steel block and an equal volume of air at the same time, "because air isn't anything." The same children also asserted that we need air to breathe, that the wind is made of air, that there is no air in outer space or on the moon. In a different interview of 6-year-olds, in which air had not been mentioned, about one quarter of the children posited air as the material of which dreams and ideas are made!

References

Astington, J. W., Harris, P. L., & Olson, D. R. (Eds.). (1988). *Developing theories of mind*. New York: Cambridge University Press.

Atran, S. (1990). *Cognitive foundations of natural history*. Cambridge: Cambridge University Press.

Baillargeon, R. (1986). Representing the existence and the location of hidden objects: Object permanence in 6- and 8-month-old infants. *Cognition, 23*, 21–41.

Baillargeon, R., Graber, M., DeVos, J., & Black, J. C. (1990). Why do young infants fail to search for hidden objects? *Cognition, 36*, 255–284.

Ball, W. A. (1973, April). The perception of causality in the infant. Paper presented at the Society for Research in Child Development, Philadelphia, PA.

Carbonell, J. (1986). Derivational analogy: A theory of reconstructive problem solving and expertise acquisition. In R. Michalski, J. Carbonell, & T. Mitchell (Eds.), *Machine learning: An artificial intelligence approach* (pp. 371–392). Los Altos, CA: Morgan Kaufmann.

Carey, S. (1985). *Conceptual change in childhood*. Cambridge, MA: Bradford/MIT Press.

Carey, S. (1986). Cognitive science and science education. *American Psychologist, 41*, 1123–1130.

Carey, S. (1988). Conceptual differences between children and adults. *Mind and Language*, 3, 167–181.

Carey, S. (1991). Knowledge acquisition: Enrichment or conceptual change? In S. Carey & R. Gelman (Eds.), *Epigenesis of mind: Studies in biology and cognition*. Hillsdale, NJ: Erlbaum.

Carey, S., Klatt, L., & Schlaffer, M. (1992). Infants' representations of objects and nonsolid substances. Unpublished manuscript, MIT.

Chi, M. T. H. (1992). Conceptual change within and across ontological categories: Examples from learning and discovery in science. In R. N. Giere (Ed.), *Cognitive models of science. Minnesota Studies in the Philosophy of Science*, 15, 129–186. Minneapolis: University of Minnesota Press.

Chomsky, N. (1980a). *Rules and representations*. New York: Columbia University Press.

Chomsky, N. (1980b). Rules and representations. *Behavioral and Brain Sciences*, 3, 1–61.

Davis, H., & Pérusse, R. (1988). Numerical competence in animals: Definitional issues, current evidence, and a new research agenda. *Behavioral and Brain Sciences*, 11, 561–615.

Duhem, P. (1949). *The aim and structure of physical theory*. Princeton, NJ: Princeton University Press.

Estes, D., Wellman, N. M., & Woolley, J. D. (1989). Children's understanding of mental phenomena. In H. Reese (Ed.), *Advances in child development and behavior* (pp. 41–87). New York: Academic Press.

Feyerabend, P. (1962). Explanation, reduction, empiricism. In H. Feigl & G. Maxwell (Eds.), *Minnesota Studies in the Philosophy of Science*, 3, 41–87. Minneapolis: University of Minnesota Press.

Fodor, J. (1992). A theory of the child's theory of mind. *Cognition*, 44, 283–296.

Gallistel, C. R. (1990). *The organization of learning*. Cambridge, MA: Bradford/MIT Press.

Gallistel, C. R., & Gelman, R. (1992). Preverbal and verbal counting and computation. *Cognition*, 44, 43–74.

Gelman, R. (1990). First principles organize attention to and learning about relevant data: Number and the animate–inanimate distinction as examples. *Cognitive Science*, 14, 79–106.

Gelman, R. (1991). Epigenetic foundations of knowledge structures: Initial and transcendent constructions. In S. Carey & R. Gelman (Eds.), *The epigenesis of mind: Essays on biology and cognition* (pp. 293–322). Hillsdale, NJ: Erlbaum.

Gelman, R., & Evans, R. (1981). Understanding infinity: A beginning inquiry Paper presented at the Society for Research in Child Development, Boston, MA.

Gelman, R., & Gallistel, C. R. (1978). *The child's understanding of number*. Cambridge, MA: Harvard University Press.

Gelman, R., Spelke, E. S., & Meck, E. (1983). What preschoolers know about animate and inanimate objects. In D. Rogers & I. A. Sloboda (Eds.), *The acquisition of symbolic skills*. New York: Plenum.

Gelman, S. A., Coley, J. D., & Gottfried, G. M. (1994). Essentialist beliefs in children: The acquisition of concepts and theories. In L. A. Hirschfeld & S. A. Gelman, eds., 341–365.

Gelman, S. A., & Wellman, H. M. (1991). Insides and essences: Early understandings of the nonobvious. *Cognition*, 38, 213–244.

Gentner, D. (1989). The mechanisms of analogical learning. In S. Vosniadou & A. Ortony (Eds.), *Similarity and analogical reasoning* (pp. 200–241). Cambridge: Cambridge University Press.

Gentner, D., & Grudin, J. (1985). The evolution of mental metaphors in psychology: A 90-year retrospective. *American Psychologist*, 40, 181–192.

Gibson, J. J. (1950). *The perception of the visual world*. Boston: Houghton-Mifflin.

Gruber, H. E. (1974). *Darwin on man: A psychological study of scientific creativity*. New York: E. P. Dutton.

Hacking, I. (1993). Working in a new world: The taxonomic solution. In P. Horwich & J. Thomson (Eds.), *World changes*. Cambridge, MA: MIT Press.

Hatano, G., & Inagaki, K. (1987). Everyday biology and school biology: How do they interact? *The Quarterly Newsletter of the Laboratory of Comparative Human Cognition*, 9, 120–128.

Heider, F., & Simmel, M. (1944). An experimental study of apparent behavior. *American Journal of Psychology*, 57, 243–259.

Hirsch, E. (1982). *The concept of identity*. New York: Oxford University Press.

Hirschfeld, L. A. and Gelman, S. A. eds. (1994). *Mapping the Mind* (Cambridge: Cambridge University Press).

Hofsten, C. von, & Spelke, E. S. (1985). Object perception and object-directed reaching in infancy. *Journal of Experimental Psychology: General*, 114, 198–212.

Holyoak, K., & Thagard, P. (1989). Analogical mapping by constraint satisfaction: A computational theory. *Cognitive Science*, 13, 295–356.

Inagaki, K., & Hatano, G. (1988). Young children's understanding of the mind–body distinction. Paper presented at the Meeting of the American Educational Research Association, New Orleans.

Jammer, M. (1961). *Concepts of mass*. Cambridge, MA: Harvard University Press.

Jeyifous, S. (1986). *Atimodemo: Semantic conceptual development among the Yoruba*. Doctoral dissertation, Cornell University.

Johnson, M. H., & Morton, J. (1991). *Biology and cognitive development: The case of face recognition*. Oxford: Blackwell.

Keil, F. C. (1989). *Concepts, kinds, and cognitive development*. Cambridge, MA: MIT Press.

Kellman, P. J., Gleitman, H., & Spelke, E. S. (1987). Object and observer motion in the perception of objects by infants. *Journal of Experimental Psychology: Human Perception and Performance, 13*, 586–593.

Kellman, P. J., & Spelke, E. S. (1983). Perception of partly occluded objects in infancy. *Cognitive Psychology, 15*, 483–524.

Kellman, P. J., Spelke, E. S., & Short, K. (1986). Infant perception of object unity from translatory motion in depth and vertical translation. *Child Development, 57*, 72–86.

Kestenbaum, R., Termine, N., & Spelke, E. S. (1987). Perception of objects and object boundaries by three-month-old infants. *British Journal of Developmental Psychology, 5*, 367–383.

Kitcher, P. (1983). *The nature of mathematical knowledge.* Oxford: Oxford University Press.

Kitcher, P. (1988). The child as parent of the scientist. *Mind and Language, 3*, 217–228.

Klahr, D., & Wallace, J. G. (1973). The role of quantification operators in the development of conservation. *Cognitive Psychology, 4*, 301–327.

Kuhn, T. S. (1962). *The structure of scientific revolutions.* Chicago: University of Chicago Press.

Kuhn, T. S. (1977). A function for thought experiments. In T. S. Kuhn (Ed.), *The essential tension.* Chicago: University of Chicago Press.

Kuhn, T. S. (1982). Commensurability, comparability, communicability *PSA, 1982 2* (pp. 669–688). East Lansing, MI: Philosophy of Science Association.

Leslie, A. M. (1987). Pretense and representation: The origins of "Theory of mind." *Psychological Review, 94*, 412–426.

Leslie, A. M. (1988). The necessity of illusion: Perception and thought in infancy. In L. Weiskrantz (Ed.), *Thought and language* (pp. 185–210). Oxford: Oxford University Press.

Leslie, A. M. (1991, April). Infants' understanding of invisible displacement. Paper presented at the Society for Research in Child Development, Seattle, WA.

Marr, D. (1982). *Vision.* San Francisco, CA: Freeman.

Nersessian, N. J. (1992). How do scientists think? Capturing the dynamics of conceptual change in science. In R. N. Giere (Ed.), *Cognitive models of science, Minnesota Studies in the Philosophy of Science, 15*, 3–44. Minneapolis: University of Minnesota Press.

Perner, J. (1991). *Understanding the representational mind.* Cambridge, MA. Bradford/MIT Press.

Piaget, J. (1954). *The construction of reality in the child.* New York: Basic Books.

Piaget, J., & Inhelder, B. (1941). *Le development des quantites chez l'enfant.* Neufchatel: Delchaux et Niestle.

Premack, D. (1990). The infant's theory of self-propelled objects. *Cognition, 36*(1), 1–16.

Roan, P. (1976). The evolution of intelligence and access to the cognitive inconscious. *Progress in Psychobiology and Physiological Psychology, 6*, 245–279.

Shipley, E. F., & Shepperson, B. (1990). Countable entities: Developmental changes. *Cognition, 34*, 109–136.

Slater, A., Morison, V., Somers, M., Mattock, A., Brown, E., & Taylor, D. (1990). Newborn and older infants' perception of partly occluded objects. *Infant Behavior and Development, 13*, 33–49.

Smith, C., Carey, S., & Wiser, M. (1985). On differentiation: A case study of the development of the concepts of size, weight, and density. *Cognition, 21*, 177–237.

Smith, C., Grosslight, L., Macklin, D., & Davis, H. (1993). A comparison of IPS and a parallel model-based curriculum in producing conceptual change. Paper presented at the American Educational Research Association, [city of conference].

Smith, C., Snir, Y., & Grosslight, L. (1992). Using conceptual models to facilitate conceptual change: The case of weight and density. *Cognition and Instruction, 9*, 221–283.

Soja, N., Carey, S., & Spelke, E. (1991). Ontological constraints on early word meanings. *Cognition, 38*, 179–211.

Solomon, G., Johnson, S., Zaitchik, D., & Carey, S. (1993). The young child's conception of inheritance. Paper presented at the Society for Research in Child Development, New Orleans.

Spelke, E. S. (1988). Where perceiving ends and thinking begins: The apprehension of objects in infancy. In A. Yonas (Ed.), *Perceptual development in infancy. Minnesota Symposium on Child Psychology, 20*, 191–234. Hillsdale, NJ: Erlbaum.

Spelke, E. S. (1990). Principles of object perception. *Cognitive Science, 14*, 29–56.

Spelke, E. S. (1991). Physical knowledge in infancy: Reflections on Piaget's theory. In S. Carey & R. Gelman (Eds.), *Epigenesis of mind: Studies in biology and cognition.* Hillsdale, NJ: Erlbaum.

Spelke, E. S., Breinlinger, K., & Jacobson, K. (1992). Gestalt relations and object perception in infancy. Unpublished manuscript, Cornell University.

Spelke, E. S., Breinlinger, K., Macomber, J., & Jacobson, K. (1992). Origins of knowledge. *Psychological Review, 99*, 605–632.

Spelke, E. S., Hofsten, C. von, & Kestenbaum, R. (1989). Object perception and object-directed reaching in infancy: Interaction of spatial and kinetic information for object boundaries. *Developmental Psychology, 25*, 185–196.

Spelke, E. S., & Kestenbaum, R. (1986). Les origines du concept d'objet. *Psychologie Francaise, 31*, 67–72.

Spelke, E. S., & Van de Walle, G. (1999). Perceiving and reasoning about objects: Insights from infants. In N. Eilan, W. Brewer, & R. McCarthy (Eds). *Spatial Representation.* Oxford: Basil Blackwell. 132–161.

Sperber, D. (1994). Epidemiology of representations: The modularity of thought and the epidemiology of representations. In L. A. Hirschfeld & S. A. Gelman, eds., 39–47.

Springer, K. (1992). Children's beliefs about the biological implications of kinship. *Child Development, 63,* 950–959.

Springer, K., & Keil, F. C. (1989). On the development of biologically specific beliefs: The case of inheritance. *Child Development, 60,* 637–648.

Streri, A., & Spelke, E. S. (1988). Haptic perception of objects in infancy. *Cognitive Psychology, 20,* 1–23.

Streri, A., & Spelke, E. S. (1989). Effects of motion and figural goodness on haptic object perception in infancy. *Child Development, 60,* 1111–1125.

Streri, A., Spelke, E. S., & Rameix, E. (1992). *Modality-specific and amodal aspects of object perception in infancy: The case of active touch.* Unpublished manuscript.

Suppe, F. (1977). *The structure of scientific theories.* Urbana: University of Illinois Press.

Thagard, P. (1988). *Conceptual revolutions.* Princeton, NJ: Princeton University Press.

Tronick, E. (1982). *Social interchange in infancy.* Baltimore, MD: University Park Press.

Tweney, R. D. (1991). Faraday's notebooks: The active organization of creative science. *Physics Education, 26,* 301.

Van de Walle, G. A., & Spelke, E. S. (1993). Integration of information over time: Infants' perception of partly occluded objects. Poster presented at the Society for Research in Child Development, New Orleans, LA.

Vosniadro, S. (1994). Universal and culture-specific properties of children's mental models of the earth. In Hirschfeld & Gelman, eds., 412–430.

Vosniadou, S., & Brewer, W. F. (1992). Mental models of the earth: A study of conceptual change in childhood. *Cognitive Psychology, 24,* 535–585.

Wellman, H. M. (1990). *The child's theory of mind.* Cambridge, MA: Bradford/MIT Press.

Wellman, H. M., & Gelman, S. A. (1992). Cognitive development: Foundational theories of core domains. *Annual Review of Psychology, 43,* 337–375.

Wellman, H. M., & Miller, K. F. (1986). The development of understanding of the concept of the number zero, 3–7 year-olds. *British Journal of Developmental Psychology, 4,* 31–42.

Wiggins, D. (1980). *Sameness and substance.* Cambridge, MA: Harward University Press.

Wiser (1988). Can models foster conceptual change? The case of heat and temperature. Harvard University: Educational Technology Center Technical Report.

Wynn, K. (1992). Addition and subtraction by human infants. *Nature, 358,* 749.

Xu, F., & Carey, S. (1992). Infants' concept of numerical identity. Paper presented at the Boston University Language Acquisition Conference.

Chapter 40: Pragmatic Reasoning Schemas

PATRICIA W. CHENG AND KEITH J. HOLYOAK

Reasoning fallacies are apparent in discourse and behavior. Their causes, however, have been as mysterious and elusive as the fallacies themselves are evident. A classic debate among both philosophers and psychologists concerns whether apparent fallacies directly reflect errors in the deductive process or indirectly reflect changes in the interpretation of the material from which one reasons. According to the latter view, "fallacies" in fact stem from interpretational changes such as the addition or omission of premises. It has been claimed that if such changes are taken into account, adults in fact reason in accord with formal logic (Henle, 1962). The above view assumes two components in the reasoning process: a deductive component that has context-free, syntactic rules comparable to those in formal logic and an interpretative component that maps statements in natural language onto syntactic rules in the deductive component.

Despite abundant evidence for such interpretational changes (e.g., Fillenbaum, 1975, 1976; Geis & Zwicky, 1971), they in fact cannot fully account for typical patterns of errors produced by college students in deductive reasoning tasks (see Evans, 1982, for a review). Some of these patterns are inconsistent with any logical interpretation of the materials. One such line of evidence is based on Wason's (1966) selection task. In this task, subjects are informed that they will be shown cards that have numbers on one side and letters on the other, and are given a rule such as, "If a card has a vowel on one side, then it has an even number on the other." Subjects are then presented with four cards, which might show an "A," a "B," a "4," and a "7" and are asked to indicate all and only those cards that must be turned over to determine whether the rule is

true or false. The correct answer in this example is to turn over the cards showing "A" and "7." More generally, the rule used in such problems is a conditional, *if p then q*, and the relevant cases are *p* and *not-q*. When presented in an "abstract" form, such as in the above example, typically less than 10% of college students produce the above answer. Subjects also rarely select in accord with a biconditional interpretation of the rule (i.e., *p if and only if q*), which requires that all four cards be turned over. Instead they often select patterns that are irreconcilable with any logical interpretation, such as "A" and "4" (i.e., *p* and *q*). One of the errors in the above answer is omission of the card showing "7," indicating a failure to see the equivalence of a conditional statement and its contrapositive (i.e., "If a card does not have an even number on one side, then it does not have a vowel on the other"). Such systematic errors suggest that typical college students do commit fallacies due to errors in the deductive process, at least with "abstract" materials.

Although subjects typically fail to reason correctly with "abstract" materials, they nonetheless seem capable of doing so with materials that have been characterized as "concrete," "realistic," or "thematic" (e.g., Johnson-Laird, Legrenzi, & Legrenzi, 1972; Wason & Shapiro, 1971). Reasoning performance has sometimes been shown to dramatically improve when the selection task is recast in such contexts (see Evans, 1982, Griggs, 1983, and Wason, 1983, for reviews). Johnson-Laird et al., for example, asked their subjects to pretend that they were postal workers sorting letters, and had to determine whether rules such as, "If a letter is sealed, then it has a 5d stamp on it," were violated. The problem was cast in the frame of a selection task. The

Reproduced with permission from Cheng, P. W., and Holyoak, K. J. (1985) Pragmatic reasoning schemas. *Cognitive Psychology*, 17, 391–416.

percentage of correct responses for this version was 81. In sharp contrast, only 15% of the same subjects produced the correct response when given the "card" version mentioned earlier.

Despite these and other positive results, however, the search for thematic facilitation has also been fraught with failures to replicate. To illustrate, although the postal rule problem mentioned above produced facilitation for British subjects in the 1972 study by Johnson-Laird et al., it produced no facilitation at all for American subjects studied by Griggs and Cox (1982). Golding (1981) found that the postal rule problem produced facilitation for older British subjects who were familiar with a similar but now defunct postal regulation imposed by the British post office, but not for younger British subjects who were not as familiar with this rule. The pattern of replications suggested to some that the source of facilitation was prior experience with a rule, particularly prior experience with counterexamples to the rule. It has been argued that subjects familiar with the postal rule do well because the falsifying instance – a sealed but understamped envelope – would be available immediately in the subjects' memory, prompting them to inspect the sealed envelope (p) and the understamped envelope ($not\text{-}q$). Faced with the mass of evidence indicating illogical reasoning, several psychologists have recently hypothesized that people typically are not able to use rules of inference to reason, but instead use their memory of domain-specific experiences (e.g., Griggs & Cox, 1982; Manktelow & Evans, 1979; Reich & Ruth, 1982).

The syntactic view has not been abandoned by all, however. Various theorists have proposed *natural logics* which specify repertoires of inferential rules that people untutored in formal logic naturally use (Braine, 1978; Braine, Reiser, & Rumain, 1984; Johnson-Laird, 1975; Osherson, 1975; Rips, 1983). With respect to the connective *if-then*, every one of these repertoires proposed include modus ponens. Only one includes modus tollens (Osherson, 1975); however, others include reductio ad absurdum (an inference method which can be used to derive indirectly the same conclusion as follows from tollens) for some or all people (Braine, 1978; Braine et al., 1984; Johnson-Laird, 1975; Rips, 1983).

A different approach, which can be viewed as an attempt to merge the extreme positions represented by specific knowledge and abstract syntactic rules, has been taken by Johnson-Laird (1982, 1983). He proposed that people possess a set of procedures for "modeling" the relations in deductive reasoning problems so as to reach conclusions about possible states of affairs given the current model of relations among elements. In Johnson-Laird's theory, mental models are constructed using both general linguistic strategies for interpreting logical terms such as quantifiers and specific knowledge retrieved from memory. The modeling procedures themselves are formal and domain independent. Although Johnson-Laird's theory differs from other accounts of reasoning in its performance aspects, it does not introduce novel types of knowledge structures.

Critique of Two Current Theories

To recapitulate, the view that people typically reason in accord with formal logic has been overwhelmingly refuted by evidence based on experiments in conditional reasoning. In its place, two major views have been proposed: the specific-experience view and the natural-logic view. We find neither of these views entirely convincing. The inadequacies of each are discussed in turn.

The specific-experience view faces two difficulties. First, remembered counterexamples do not always facilitate performance. In a series of four experiments, Manktelow and Evans (1979) failed to observe facilitation with conditional rules for which subjects were likely to have experienced counterexamples. The rules were arbitrary combinations of foods and drinks, such as, "If I eat haddock then I drink gin." It should be noted that although the particular combinations used were arbitrary, the general idea of selecting drinks based on the selection of food would presumably be familiar to most people, as would the foods and drinks themselves. A further problem with the above hypothesis is that prior experience does not seem to be required for facilitation: A version of the selection problem developed by D'Andrade (1982) involves an assistant at a department store who has to check sales receipts to ensure that receipts exceeding a certain value were initialed at the back by a section manager. Few subjects would be expected to have a counterexample to this rule readily available in memory. Yet the problem has reliably produced facilitation. Thus experience with a specific rule appears to be neither necessary nor sufficient to yield facilitation.

A further problem with the specific memory approach is that subjects are prone to different types of errors on different types of problems. Reich and Ruth (1982) reported that with "symbolic" problems subjects tended to match the terms mentioned in the rule with those provided in the cards (disregarding negatives associated with those terms), whereas with "realistic" problems they tended to verify the rule (i.e., selecting p and q). These two patterns of errors can be explained by neither the specific-experience approach nor the natural-logic approach.

The natural-logic view (as well as the syntactic view in general) assumes that when the invitation to infer the converse is taken into account, rules associated with the connective *if-then* are general across contexts. This assumption implies that any variation in performance that is logically unrelated to the invitation to infer the converse, such as the different patterns of errors just mentioned, either falls outside the scope of the theory, or contradicts it. Another type of variation in performance that is logically unrelated to the invitation to infer the converse is variation in the frequency of selecting the *not-q* case in a selection task. The natural logic view, by positing that some subjects do not have reductio or modus tollens available, can explain some subjects' failure to select *not-q*. This view cannot, however, explain why the same subjects who fail to select *not-q* in one context do select it in other contexts.

These problems, and others that are raised in the General Discussion, beset any theory of conditional reasoning that assumes context-free inference rules associated with *if-then*. Therefore, a different approach seems warranted.

Pragmatic Reasoning Schemas

Our own approach is based on a type of knowledge structure qualitatively different from those postulated by other theories of deductive reasoning. We propose that people often reason using neither syntactic, context-free rules of inference, nor memory of specific experiences. Rather, they reason using abstract knowledge structures induced from ordinary life experiences, such as "permissions," "obligations," and "causations." Such knowledge structures are termed *pragmatic reasoning schemas*. A pragmatic reasoning schema consists of a set of generalized, context-sensitive rules which, unlike purely syntactic rules, are defined in terms of classes of goals (such as taking desirable actions or making predictions about possible future events) and relationships to these goals (such as cause and effect or precondition and allowable action). Although context-sensitive, the rules that comprise pragmatic schemas may extend beyond the scope of purely syntactic rules of logic, because they will serve to interpret "nonlogical" terms such

as *cause* and *predict* as well as terms treated by formal logic, such as *if-then* and *only-if.*

Although a syntactically based reasoning system tells us which inferences are valid, it does not tell us which inferences are useful among the potentially many that are valid. Consider, for example, the contrapositive transformation of the material conditional. Given the statement, "If two particles have like electrical charges, then they repel each other," a logic-based reasoning system lets us infer the potentially useful conclusion, "If two particles do not repel each other, then they don't have like electrical charges." In contrast, given the statement, "If I have a headache, then I should take some aspirin," the same rule will produce the inference, "If it's not the case that I should take some aspirin, then I don't have a headache," which is hardly ever a useful inference to make. More generally, the fact that a problem exists creates the goal of finding a remedy for it; however, the absence of the need for a remedy does not create the goal of inferring the absence of a problem. Since people do not seem to make this type of useless inference, it seems that pragmatic goals must guide the process of inference.

Our theoretical framework assumes that the role of prior experience in facilitation is in the induction and evocation of certain types of schemas. Not all schemas are facilitating, as becomes clear below. Some schemas lead to responses that correspond more closely than others with those that follow from the material conditional in formal logic. Performance as evaluated by the standard of formal logic depends on what type of schema is evoked, or whether any schema is evoked at all.

An arbitrary rule, being unrelated to typical life experiences, will not reliably evoke any reasoning schemas. Subjects confronted with such a rule may attempt to interpret it in terms of a reasoning schema. Failing that, they would have to draw upon their knowledge of formal reasoning to arrive at a correct solution. Only a small percentage of college students apparently know the material conditional or can derive the contrapositive or modus tollens using reductio ad absurdum. Failing either, some might draw on some nonlogical strategy such as matching, as observed by Reich and Ruth (1982) and Manktelow and Evans (1979), among others.

In contrast, some rules evoke schemas with structures that yield the same solutions as the material conditional (under circumstances explicated below). In particular, most of the thematic problems that have yielded facilitation fit a *permission* schema. The permission schema describes a type of regulation in which taking a particular action requires satisfaction of a certain precondition.

In standard propositional logic the deductive rules pertaining to *if-then* specify syntactic patterns based on the components *if, then, not,* and *only if.* For example, one rule states that *if p then q* is equivalent to *if not-q then not-p,* where the symbols *p* and *q* represent any statements. The permission schema, in contrast, contains no context-free symbols such as *p* and *q* above. Instead the inference patterns include as components the concepts of possibility, necessity, an action to be taken, and a precondition to be satisfied. (The deontic concepts of possibility and necessity are typically expressed in English by the modals *can* and *must,* respectively, and various synonyms, such as *may* and *is required to.*)

The core of the permission schema can be succinctly summarized in four production rules, each of which specifies one of the four possible antecedent situations, assuming the occurrence or nonoccurence of the action and the precondition:

Rule 1: If the action is to be taken, then the precondition must be satisfied.

Rule 2: If the action is not to be taken, then the precondition need not be satisfied.

Rule 3: If the precondition is satisfied, then the action may be taken.

Rule 4: If the precondition is not satisfied, then the action must not be taken.

To understand when and why the permission schema facilitates selection performance, compare the above rules to the four possible inference patterns of the material conditional. When a situation or problem evokes a permission schema, the entire set of rules comprising the schema becomes available. Suppose the conditional rule in a given selection problem is in the form of Rule 1, such as "If one is to drink alcohol, then one must be over eighteen." Rule 1 has the same effect as modus ponens. Rule 2, because it indicates that the precondition is irrelevant if the action is not taken (the precondition need not be satisfied, but may be anyway), effectively blocks the fallacy of Denying the Antecedent. Similarly, Rule 3 indicates that if the precondition is satisfied, then the action is allowed but not dictated, thus blocking the fallacy of Affirming the Consequent. Finally, Rule 4 explicitly states that failure to satisfy the precondition precludes taking the action, an inference pattern corresponding to the contrapositive. A rule corresponding to the contrapositive is thus available directly, rather than requiring an indirect derivation by means of reductio ad absurdum. In sum, when a conditional statement in the form of Rule 1 evokes a permission schema, the solution derivable from the permission schema matches that required by the material conditional. Hence, the permission schema should be facilitative.

This does not imply that the permission schema is equivalent to the material conditional in standard propositional logic. The permission schema is context-sensitive. In addition, as is discussed further in Experiment 3, the permission schema is directly related to deontic concepts such as *must* and *may* that cannot be expressed in standard propositional logic. Furthermore, the rules attached to reasoning schemas are often useful heuristics rather than strictly valid inferences. For example, Rule 3 above does not logically follow from Rule 1, since it could yield a false conclusion if the precondition is necessary but not sufficient to render the action permissible (e.g., if a drinking law required drinkers to be both over 18 and free of recent drunk driving violations, then the inference "If a person is over eighteen, then he or she may drink alcohol" would not hold). Because reasoning schemas are not restricted to strictly valid rules, our approach is not equivalent to any proposed formal or natural logic of the conditional.

Not all conditional reasoning schemas suggest the same solution to selection problems as does formal logic. A *causal* schema, for example, will sometimes invite an assumption of the converse of a given conditional statement. (Assumption of the converse is to be distinguished here from the biconditional, which includes assumption of both the converse and its contrapositive.) A conditional, *if p then q,* interpreted in the context of a causal schema may be represented as "If ⟨cause⟩, then ⟨effect⟩." To the degree that only a single cause is perceived, the effect may be treated as evidence for concluding the presence or prior existence of the cause, yielding an inference in the opposite direction, "If ⟨evidence⟩, then ⟨conclusion⟩." Since events are sometimes perceived as having a single cause, problems evoking a causal schema are more likely to lead to the fallacy of Affirming the Consequent than problems evoking a permission schema.

Alternative reasoning schemas may account for reported variations in performance on the selection task. As noted earlier, Reich and Ruth (1982) found that "realistic" sentences such as, "If a fruit is yellow, then it is ripe," tended to lead to verification (selecting p and q), whereas arbitrary "symbolic" problems tended to lead to a matching strategy (also Manktelow & Evans, 1979). It seems that there may be a general "covariation" schema, which can be applied to any situation in which two situations or events are for some reason expected to co-occur, as in Reich and Ruth's "realistic" sentences. The covariation schema, like the causal schema, can be expected to invite an assumption of the converse of a given conditional statement and would lead to selection of p and q, the pattern observed for Reich and Ruth's "realistic" sentences. Arbitrary rules, being unrelated to real-life experiences, may fail to evoke even a covariation schema for some subjects, so that these subjects must resort to an entirely nonlogical strategy. It is therefore possible that evocation of different reasoning schemas can account for variations in performance even among problems in which none of the dominant response patterns are consistent with formal logic.

To summarize, we suggest that many inference schemas are pragmatic in nature, with the purposes of the set of rules being salient features of each schema. Because these purposes differ between schemas, they may serve to discriminate between types of schemas at the interpretative stage. Regulations such as permissions and obligations are imposed typically by an authority to achieve some social purpose. In contrast, causal rules are not imposed by an authority, but simply serve to generate useful predictions about transitions between environmental states. Thus the purposes of the schemas are of different natures. As we see in Experiment 1, provision of the purpose of a regulation constitutes a major cue for evocation of the permission schema.

We propose that people typically make inferences based on pragmatic reasoning schemas. Whereas the logic approach assumes that an interpretative component maps statements onto particular context-free syntactic inference rules comprising the deductive component, the schema approach assumes that the interpretative component maps statements onto a particular set of context-sensitive rules attached to the relevant schema. Such schemas vary in their degree of correspondence with the material conditional. The experiments reported below were designed to provide direct tests of the schema hypothesis.

Experiment 1

According to the schema hypothesis, failure on selection problems is due to failure to evoke a schema that corresponds well with the conditional in formal logic. A possible explanation for the conflicting results obtained with the envelope problem (discussed earlier) is that subjects who have had experience with the postal rule (or one that is highly similar to it) understand the rule in terms of a permission – one is permitted to seal an envelope only if it carries a certain amount of postage. In contrast, subjects who have not had any experience with such rules perceive it as being arbitrary. If people in fact reason using pragmatic reasoning schemas, then it may be possible to improve performance by evoking a facilitating schema, such as the permission schema, without providing subjects with experience on specific rules.

In the present experiment we attempted to evoke a permission schema by providing a rationale for conditional rules that may otherwise appear arbitrary. Two versions of each of two thematic problems were administered to groups of college students: a version with a rationale and a version without it. If provision of a rationale succeeds in evoking a permission schema, then performance should generally be better in the rationale than in the no-rationale condition. The two thematic problems were the envelope problem mentioned earlier, involving the rule: "If an envelope is sealed, then it must have a 20 cent stamp"; and a "cholera" problem, involving the rule: "If a passenger's form says 'Entering' on one side, then the other side must include 'cholera'."

In addition to varying the inclusion of a rationale, we also varied subjects' prior experience with a rule by using subjects in Michigan and in Hong Kong. Whereas subjects in Michigan were not familiar with the postal rule, since no similar rule had been in effect in the United States, subjects in Hong Kong were familiar with it, since a similar rule was in effect until about 6 months before the experiment was run. Few of the subjects in either location would be expected to have had experience with the cholera rule. In general, those who have had experience with the rules should be able to perceive them as permissions, even though they may appear arbitrary to other subjects. The schema hypothesis therefore predicts that for the no-rationale condition only subjects in Hong Kong given the envelope problem would do well, but for the rationale condition subjects in both Hong Kong and Michigan would do well on both thematic problems.

In contrast, the syntactic view predicts that performance would be similar across all conditions, since the forms of the conditional statements were identical in the rationale and no-rationale versions for subjects in both places. Even allowing for differences in the tendency to invite the converse assumption, the syntactic view would still predict that the frequency of selecting the *not-q* case would be constant across conditions. The domain-specificity view also predicts that the rationale should have no effect. However, it predicts that the performance of Hong Kong subjects on the envelope problem should be superior to performance in all other conditions, since Hong Kong subjects alone were familiar with the postal rule.

Method

Subjects. Eighty-two students who were enrolled in an introductory psychology course at the Chinese University of Hong Kong participated in the experiment as partial fulfillment of the course requirement. Eighty-eight students at the University of Michigan participated in the experiment for the same reason. None of the participants had had any prior experience with the selection task.

Procedure. Subjects at each location were randomly assigned to two equal-sized groups. Each subject received one version of each of two thematic problems: a rationale version of one problem, and a no-rationale version of the other problem. Half of the subjects at each location received the rationale version of a problem, and the other half received the no-rationale version of the same problem. Subjects were run in groups of 8 to 10. All subjects were told to think carefully and solve the problems as best they could. To ensure that subjects arrived at the best answer they were capable of, they were allowed as much time as they needed, and were also allowed to make corrections. Subjects were encouraged to write brief explanations of their responses. As mentioned earlier, the two problems were the envelope problem and the cholera problem. The envelope problem preceded the cholera problem. For the Hong Kong subjects, who were bilingual, the rule in each problem was stated in both English and Chinese.

Materials. The no-rationale version of the envelope problem stated, "You are a postal clerk working in some foreign country. Part of your job is to go through letters to check the postage. The country's postal regulation requires that *if a letter is sealed, then it must carry a 20-cent stamp.* In order to check that the regulation is followed, which of the following four envelopes would you turn over? Turn over only those that you need to check to be sure."

The above paragraph was followed by drawings of four envelopes, one carrying a 20-cent stamp, a second carrying a 10-cent stamp, a third one labeled "back of sealed envelope," and a fourth one labeled "back of unsealed envelope."

The rationale version of the envelope problem was identical to the no-rationale version, except that the conditional rule (underscored) was immediately followed by the sentences: "The rationale for this regulation is to increase profit from personal mail, which is nearly always sealed. Sealed letters are defined as personal and must therefore carry more postage than unsealed letters."

The no-rationale version of the cholera problem stated "You are an immigration officer at the International Airport in Manila, capital of the Philippines. Among the documents you have to check is a sheet called Form H. One side of this form indicates whether the passenger is entering the country or in transit, while the other side of the form lists names of tropical diseases. You have to make sure that *if the form says 'ENTERING' on one side, then the other side includes cholera among the list of diseases.* Which of the following forms would you have to turn over to check? Indicate only those that you need to check to be sure." The above paragraph was followed by drawings of four cards. One of them carried the word "TRANSIT," another carried the word "ENTERING," a third listed "cholera, typhoid, hepatitis," and a fourth listed "typhoid, hepatitis."

The rationale version of the cholera problem was identical to the no-rationale version except that instead of saying that the form listed names of tropical diseases, it said that the form listed inoculations the passenger had had in the past 6 months. In addition, the conditional rule (underscored) was followed by the sentence. "This is to ensure that entering passengers are protected against the disease."

Results

Figure 1 presents the percentage of subjects who solved the selection problem in each condition.

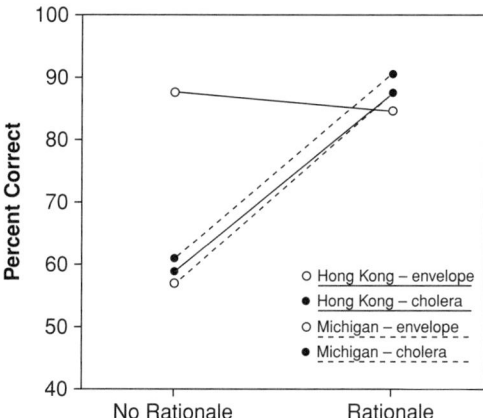

Figure 1. Percentage of subjects who solved the selection task correctly in each condition as a function of provision of a rationale (Experiment 1).

The pattern of results was precisely as predicted by the schema hypothesis. The rationale versions produced uniformly high success rates for subjects at both locations for both thematic problems, whereas the no-rationale versions produced a high success rate only for the envelope problem with Hong Kong subjects. The difference in frequency of correct solutions as a function of provision of a rationale was tested using the χ^2 statistic for each problem and subject group. Except for the envelope problem with the Hong Kong subjects, for whom the rationale was redundant as predicted, all conditions produced a significantly higher success rate for the rationale versions ($p < .01$ for each of the 3 location-problem conditions). The frequency of successfully selecting the not-q case reflects the same pattern of performance as the frequency of solving the entire problem correctly.

Performance levels for the no-rationale groups were higher in the present experiment than in other studies using subjects lacking experience with similar rules (Griggs & Cox, 1982). It is difficult to interpret such differences in absolute performance levels across subject populations. It may be that our subjects were sometimes able to provide their own implicit rationales for the stated rules even when none were provided by the experimenter. Our procedure of allowing for corrections might also have contributed to the higher performance level.

The results of Experiment 1 provide clear support for the schema hypothesis. Since experience on the given domains did not differ between the rationale and the no-rationale

groups, the effect of the rationales cannot be due to the amount of specific experience. And since the syntactic form of the if-then rules remained constant across all conditions, the effect of the rationales cannot be accounted for by the syntactic view either.

Experiment 2

It might be argued that since the rationales in Experiment 1 were not content free, their introduction might have changed the nature of the relevant experience brought to bear on the problems. For example, although specific experience with the postal rule per se was not affected by introduction of the rationale, the idea of increasing profit – probably familiar to most subjects – may have prompted subjects to check envelopes carrying relatively small amounts of postage to ensure that they did not unduly reduce profit. Similarly, the idea of protection against a disease may prompt subjects to check passengers unprotected against it. In both cases, the rationales may encourage checking the not-q case, the omission of which is a frequent error in selection problems. The relevant experience evoked by the rationales would extend beyond the specific conditional statements, but would nonetheless be content specific.

To provide clearcut evidence for abstract schemas that are not bound to any domain-specific content, we tested performance on a selection problem that described a permission situation abstractly, with no reference to any concrete content. Subjects were asked to check regulations that have the general form, "If one is to take action 'A,' then one must first satisfy precondition 'P.'" To demonstrate that concreteness of the if-then rule, in the absence of a facilitating schema such as a permission, does not lead to logically correct responses, subjects were also tested on an arbitrary "card" version of the selection problem involving a rule specifying concrete entities.

Method

Subjects. Forty-four University of Michigan undergraduates enrolled in psychology courses volunteered for the experiment. None of the students had had any previous experience with the selection paradigm.

Materials. Each subject was given two selection problems. One was an abstract description of a permission, stating, "Suppose you are an authority checking whether or not people are obeying certain regulations. The regulations all have the general form, "If one is to take action 'A,' then one must first satisfy precondition 'P.'" In other words, in order to be permitted to do "A," one must first have fulfilled prerequisite "P." The cards below contain information on four people one side of the card indicates whether or not a person has taken action "A," the other indicates whether or not the same individual has fulfilled precondition "P." In order to check that a certain regulation is being followed, which of the cards below would you turn over? Turn over only those that you need to check to be sure."

The above instructions were followed by drawings of four cards stating the four possible cases: "has taken action A," "has not taken action A," "has fulfilled precondition P," and "has not fulfilled precondition P."

The other problem involved an arbitrary card rule stating, "Below are four cards. Every card has a letter on one side and a number on the other. Your task is to decide which of the cards you need to turn over in order to find out whether or not a certain rule is being followed. The rule is: If a card has an 'A' on one side, then it must have a '4' on the other side. Turn over only those cards that you need to check to be sure." Although this rule has often been labeled "abstract" in the literature, we would like to call attention to the distinction between the arbitrariness of the relation and the abstractness of the entities involved in the rule (Wason & Shapiro, 1971). The above rule specifies an arbitrary relation between specific, concrete entities.

Drawings of four cards followed, showing four possible cases: "A," "B," "4," and "7." To more closely match the syntactic form of the cases in the permission problem, cases that negated terms in the if-then rule were so indicated explicitly. The card showing "7" carried the caption "i.e., not '4,'" and the card showing "B" carried the caption "i.e., not 'A.'" In addition, the modal must was included in the arbitrary version of the rule to match the syntactic form of the permission rule.

Procedure. Subjects were given the same general instructions for solving the problems as in Experiment 1, except that they were not allowed to change answers on a previous problem. Subjects were run in small groups. The ordering of the two problems was counterbalanced across subjects. The four cases to be selected in each problem were either ordered p, not-p, q, not-q, or the reverse. Each subject received a different ordering of the cases in each problem. The

ordering of the cases was counterbalanced across problems.

Results and Discussion

In order to assess performance on the permission and card problems independently of any transfer from one to the other, an analysis was performed on data from just the first problem solved by each subject. Although the permission problem was more abstract than the card problem, 61% of the subjects solved the permission problem correctly, whereas only 19% solved the card problem correctly, $\chi^2(1) = 7.76, p < .01$. Since the permission problem made no reference to any domain-specific content, and the syntactic form of the if-then rules was matched across the permission and card problems, superior performance on the permission problem provides strong evidence for the existence of an abstract permission schema.

The effect of the ordering of the two problems did not approach significance; however, the card problem was more often solved correctly when it followed the permission problem (39%) than when it preceded it (19%), suggesting possible positive transfer. In contrast, the permission problem was less often solved correctly when it followed the card problem (48%) than when it preceded it (61%), suggesting possible negative transfer. Collapsing over the two orders of the problems, 55% of the subjects solved the permission problem correctly, whereas only 30% of the same subjects solved the card problem correctly. This difference was significant when tested with a binomial test of symmetry ($p = .01$). The order of the four alternative choices had no significant effect on the frequency of solving a problem correctly. The frequency of successfully selecting the not-q case reflects the same pattern of performance as the frequency of solving the entire problem correctly.

Experiment 3

The knowledge contained in the permission schema should affect performance in other tasks besides the selection paradigm. For example, since rules in the schema govern and aid the rephrasing of sentences from if-then into only-if form and vice versa, such rephrasings of permission statements should follow certain consistent patterns, some of which correspond well with formal logic. In contrast, since transformations of arbitrary conditional statements are not guided by any rule that corresponds well with formal logic, performance on such rephrasings should be no different from chance.

According to standard logic a conditional of the form *if p then q* is equivalent to *p only if q*, in the sense that the two statements have identical truth tables. As Evans (1977) has noted, the *only-if* form stresses the necessity of the consequent – i.e., the fact that *q* must hold in order for *p* to be the case. The *only-if* form is thus closely related to the contrapositive of the *if-then* form (i.e., *if not-q then not-p*), which also emphasizes the necessity of *q*.

Because people do not in general use an inference rule equivalent to the contrapositive, we would expect them to have great difficulty in rephrasing between *if-then* and *only-if* forms for arbitrary statements (Braine, 1978). There will be no rules to help them decide whether a statement in the form *if p then q* should be rephrased into *p only if q* or its converse, *q only if p* (and vice versa).

In contrast, such rephrasings of permission statements should follow certain consistent patterns. Consider the following two possible rephrasings into *only-if* form of an *if-then* permission statement, "If the action is to be taken, then the precondition must be satisfied":

(5)   The action is to be taken only if the precondition is satisfied.

(6)   The precondition must be satisfied only if the action is to be taken.

Although only (5) is a valid rephrasing ((6) would be false if there were some other reason for the precondition being necessary), both are plausible inferences. Nonetheless, (5) is a more natural and direct inference than (6). A possible reason is that a statement in the form *p only if q* carries the connotation that *q* is necessary for *p* as well as prior to it in time (Evans, 1977; Evans & Newstead, 1977), both aspects of which are central to what it means to constitute a precondition or prerequisite. Hence, the form is highly compatible with the content in Statement (5), whereas Statement (6) carries the implication that taking the action is the prerequisite for the necessity of satisfying the precondition, which is a very circuitous way of saying, "If the action is not to be taken, then the precondition need not be satisfied." There seems to be no natural way of stating a permission in an *only-if* form in which the precondition precedes the action. It follows that subjects are more likely to produce Statement (5) than Statement (6) (or corresponding variants) when asked to phrase a per-

mission statement in an *only-if* form. Since (5) is the strictly valid inference, it follows that subjects will appear to follow the dictates of formal logic in rephrasing a permission statement from *if-then* into *only-if* form.

Such a difference in naturalness will not guide the rephrasing of permission statements in the reverse direction, from *only-if* form as in (5) into *if-then* form. Either the action or the precondition can be the antecedent of a permission statement in an *if-then* form without any awkwardness. Rules 1 and 3 of the permission schema described in the introduction are examples of the two orderings,

(1)   If the action is to be taken, then the precondition must be satisfied.

(3)   If the precondition is satisfied, then the action may be taken.

According to formal logic only (1) is a valid rephrasing of (5) (with the caveat that a deontic logic is required to account for the introduction of *must* in (1); see below); as noted in the introduction, (3) could be false if the stated precondition were necessary but not sufficient for the action. Nonetheless, both (1) and (3) are pragmatically plausible and natural inferences in most permission contexts. We therefore do not expect any difference in subjects' propensity to produce the two forms of *if-then* sentences in our rephrasing task. It follows that for permission statements, subjects' rephrasings will appear to follow the dictates of formal logic more closely when the direction is from *if-then* into *only-if* form rather than vice versa. This asymmetry is only apparent, however, in that the entire predicted response pattern follows from the nature of the information contained in the permission schema.

The schema hypothesis also generates predictions about the introduction of modals into rephrasings. The concept of permission is based on the deontic concepts of "possibility" and "necessity." The modals that express these concepts allow inference patterns beyond the scope of standard propositional logic. For example, applying a rule of standard propositional logic to the permission statement, "A customer is to drink an alcoholic beverage only if she is at least eighteen," we obtain the supposedly equivalent statement, "If a customer is to drink an alcoholic beverage, then she is at least eighteen." However, this rephrasing is quite unnatural because it tends to be interpreted as a claim that drinking an alcoholic beverage *causes* the person to be 18. To maintain the sense of permission, it is much more natural to introduce the modal *must* into the consequent: "If a customer is to drink an alcoholic beverage, then she *must* be at least eighteen." In contrast, introduction of the modal is not dictated for arbitrary statements, which are not interpreted deontically. For example, the statement, "A card has an 'A' on one side only if it has a '4' on the other" can be rephrased as, "If a card has an 'A' on one side, then it has a '4' on the other." In this case introduction of *must* ("then it *must* have a '4' on the other") is unnecessary, since the original statement has no deontic implications. Accordingly, the schema hypothesis predicts that *must* will be introduced in rephrasing from *only-if* to *if-then* form for permission statements but not for arbitrary statements.

Similarly, *can* or its synonyms will be introduced in rephrasing from *if-then* to *only-if* form more often for permission than for arbitrary statements. For example, the alcohol rule discussed in the last paragraph is more naturally stated as, "A customer *can* drink alcohol only if she is at least eighteen," rather than, "A customer drinks alcohol only if she is at least eighteen." The modal *can*, or its synonyms such as *may, is to,* or *is allowed to,* serves to retain the sense of a social regulation. In contrast, arbitrary statements do not require any modal (e.g., "A card has an 'A' on one side only if it has a '4' on the other").

Method

Subjects. Fifty-two undergraduates at the University of Michigan, none of whom had prior experience with the selection task, served as subjects.

Procedure. All subjects received four problems, two based on permission statements and two on arbitrary statements. One statement of each type was presented in *if-then* form and one in *only-if* form. For each statement subjects first performed the standard selection task and then attempted to rephrase the statement into an alternative form (i.e., *if-then* into *only-if* or vice versa).

Materials. In addition to the usual selection-task instructions, the first page of the booklet given to subjects explained that *if-then* statements can be rephrased into *only-if* form and vice versa. An arbitrary statement was used as an example: "If the tablecloth is brown, then the wall is white" corresponds to "The tablecloth is brown only if the wall is white."

The two permission statements were the "cholera" rule used in Experiment 1 (the ratio-

Table 1: Percentage Correct on Selection Task (Experiment 3)

Given Form	Rule Type		Mean
	Permission	Arbitrary	
If-then	67	17	42
Only-if	56	4	30
Mean	62	11	

nale version), and the "alcohol" rule used above as an example. The arbitrary statements were the card problem and a "bird" problem, which in *if-then* form involved the statement, "If a bird has a purple spot underneath each wing, then it must build nests on the ground." As this example illustrates, all statements included *must* in their *if-then* forms in order to equate the syntactic structure of the permission and arbitrary statements.[1]

Each problem was presented on a separate page of the booklet. The selection task was presented at the top of each page. The basic statement was then repeated below, and subjects were asked to write the equivalent rephrasing in either *if-then* or *only-if* form. Which statements were presented in which form, and the order of the problems, were counterbalanced across subjects.

Results and Discussion

Selection task. Table 1 presents the percentage of subjects who gave logically correct responses in the selection task as a function of the type of rule (permission and arbitrary) and the form of the rule (*if-then* or *only-if*). The data were analyzed using analysis of variance. We will report the results collapsed across the two problems of each type, since the overall pattern held for the individual problems.

As Table 1 indicates, subjects were far more accurate in choosing the two correct alternatives, *p* and *not-q*, for permission statements (62%) than for arbitrary statements (11%), $F(1, 51) = 131$, $p < .001$. This result is of course predicted by the hypothesis that people are able to apply a specialized schema to reason about permission statements. In addition, performance was more accurate, when the rules were stated in *if-then* rather than *only-if* form, $F(1, 51) = 5.22$, $p < .05$. These two factors, the type and form of the rule, did not significantly interact.

Rephrasing. According to the schema hypothesis, modals should be systematically introduced

Table 2: Percentage "Correct" Rephrasings, Including and Excluding Modals (Experiment 3)

Given Form	Permission			Arbitrary		
	Modal	No Modal	Total	Modal	No Modal	Total
If-then	42[a]	29	71	4[a]	33	37
Only-if	31[b]	11	42	6[b]	42	48

[a] *Can p only if q.*
[b] *If p then must q.*

into rephrased permission statements to preserve their deontic sense, whereas modals will not be introduced into arbitrary statements. Moreover, whereas permission statements of the form *if p then must q* should be readily rephrased into the form *p only if q* (or *can p only if q*), permission statements of the form *p only if q* would likely be rephrased into two modal forms: *if p then must q* or *If q then can p.* Only the first of the two modal forms is a strictly valid inference from the original statement.

Table 2 reports the percentage of subjects who rephrased rules of each type and form into forms in which *p* was ordered before *q*, with or without the inclusion of modals. This ordering of *p* and *q* corresponds to that dictated by formal logic, and hence will be referred to as "correct," although we emphasize that within our schema framework certain forms that reverse the order of *p* and *q* also constitute pragmatically appropriate inferences. Two transformations form a statement in the form *if p then q* were scored as correct: *p only if q* (no modal) and *can p only if q* (with modal). Similarly, two transformations from a statement in the form *p only if q* were scored as correct: *If p then q* (no modal) and *if p then must q* (with modal). A response was thus scored as correct if the propositions *p* and *q* were placed as the antecedent and the consequent, regardless of the insertion or omission of the appropriate modal. Since there are only two possible permutations of *p* and *q*, subjects would be expected to achieve 50% accuracy if they ordered the propositions randomly.

As Table 2 indicates, the rephrasing results were entirely in accord with the schema hypothesis. Arbitrary statements in either the *if-then* or the *only-if* form were not rephrased correctly with a frequency significantly different from the chance level of 50%. The interaction between the form of the given statement (*if-then* versus *only-if*) and its content (permission versus arbitrary) was highly significant, $F(1, 51) = 19.2$, $p < .001$. Permission state-

ments in *if-then* form were rephrased correctly significantly more often than arbitrary *if-then* statements, $F(1, 51) = 21.6$, $p < .001$, whereas permission statements in *only-if* form were not rephrased correctly more often than arbitrary statements.[2] As predicted, *only-if* permission statements were often rephrased into the alternative form *if q then can p.* This alternative rephrasing was produced in 38% of the cases for *only-if* permission statements versus only 2% of the *only-if* arbitrary statements.

The data in Table 2 also reveal that among the correct rephrasings, modals tended to be introduced for permission but not for arbitrary statements. For *if-then* permission statements there was a nonsignificant tendency to introduce *can* or a synonym (i.e., *can p only if q*) more often than not, whereas for *if-then* arbitrary statements the correct rephrasings were much more likely to omit any modal, $\chi^2(1) = 11.8$, $p < .001$. Similarly, for *only-if* permission statements correct rephrasings included a modal (i.e., *if p then must q*) more often than not, $\chi^2(1) = 4.55$, $p < .05$, whereas for *only-if* arbitrary statements correct rephrasings more often omitted any modal, $\chi^2(1) = 14.4$, $p < .001$. Thus for both correct and incorrect rephrasings, modals were consistently inserted into transformations of permission statements but not of arbitrary statements.

General Discussion

The present results support the view that people typically reason using schematic knowledge structures that can be distinguished both from representations of specific experiences and from context-free syntactic inference rules. In Experiment 1, a rationale designed to evoke a permission schema facilitated performance on selection problems for which subjects lacked specific experience. Indeed, provision of a rationale raised performance to the same level of accuracy as did prior experience with the rule. Neither the specific-experience view nor the syntactic view can account for the observed performance pattern.

Experiment 2 demonstrated that a selection problem based on an abstract statement of a permission rule, totally devoid of concrete content, produced substantially more accurate performance than did an arbitrary rule. This result is damaging to both the syntactic and the specific-experience view. Finally, Experiment 3 provided evidence that evocation of a permission schema affects not only performance on the selection task, but also how subjects rephrased sentences from *if-then* into *only-if* forms and vice versa. In particular, statements in the form *if p then q* were rephrased into the form *p only if q* much more frequently for permission than for arbitrary statements, and rephrasings of permission statements produced a pattern of introduction of modals (*must, can*) totally unlike that observed for arbitrary conditional statements that lack a deontic context. Again, neither of the alternative views can account for the observed pattern of results.

Comparison with Other Approaches

Our results thus speak strongly for the existence of pragmatic schemas; the findings are inexplicable according to either the specific-experience view or the syntactic view. Nonetheless, our findings need not be interpreted as evidence against the very possibility of the two extreme modes of reasoning. It is conceivable that alternative knowledge structures relevant to deductive reasoning coexist within a population and even within an individual. Cheng, Holyoak, Nisbett, and Oliver (1985) propose a possible set of relations between logical rules, specific experience, and pragmatic schemas. Although the three levels of knowledge structures may coexist, the apparent priority of the pragmatic level in reasoning has important implications for attempts to alter performance on reasoning tasks by direct instruction. Cheng et al. (1985) compared the impact on selection-task performance of purely formal logic training with that of training based on a pragmatic schema for obligation. They found that purely formal training was quite ineffectual, whereas instruction in the nature of obligations improved performance on a range of conditional rules that could be interpreted as expressing obligations.

Other theorists have suggested that schemas (Rumelhart, 1980; Wason, 1983) or scenarios (Pollard, 1982) play a role in deductive reasoning; however, previous discussions have said little about the types and nature of the information that might be included in such schemas or scenarios. One suggestion related to the present proposal is that performance on the selection task is facilitated if subjects are oriented toward checking for violations, rather than testing a hypothesis (see Griggs, 1983; Yachanin & Tweney, 1982). The core of the permission schema, as well as of similar schemas for other types of regulations, indeed consists of procedural knowledge for assessing whether a type of rule is being followed or violated. However, the schema approach predicts that violation checking will only lead to accurate performance if the problem evokes a schema specifying those situations that in fact constitute violations. Asking subjects to check for violations in an otherwise arbitrary problem would not suffice, as Griggs (1984) and Yachanin (1985) have shown. In addition, the pattern of selections will only correspond to that required by formal logic if the schema yields the same solution as does the formal conditional. Although the permission schema does so when the given *if-then* statement is in the form of Rule 1, other regulation schemas have a different structure. For example, many obligations are pragmatically biconditional. Thus the rule, "If a child has reached age six, then he or she must enter school" may be given an "if and only if" interpretation, in which case the pattern of choices on a selection task will not correspond to that specified by the formal conditional, even if the subject checks for violations.

It is also clear from the results of Experiment 3 that the impact of the permission schema on performance is broader than simply encouraging violation checking. The rephrasing results indicate that evocation of the schema has consequences for a linguistic task involving declarative knowledge. Even if such declarative knowledge is derived from more basic procedural knowledge, performance on the linguistic task certainly goes beyond what could be described as orientation toward violation checking.

We do not claim, however, that all variations in performance on reasoning problems can be accounted for solely in terms of variations in the reasoning schemas evoked by different problems. For example, Wason and Green (1984) demonstrated that more accurate performance is observed when the selection task is simplified by only offering the subject alternatives based on the consequent (i.e., *q* and *not-q*), omitting those based on the antecedent. Wason and Green also found that subjects were more accurate when the rule related properties of a unitary object (e.g., "If the figure on the card is a triangle then it has been colored red"), rather than properties of disjoint objects (e.g., "All the triangles have a red patch above them"). The positive effects of such task manipulations are most likely due to decreases in the overall cognitive load imposed by the task.

Causal Schemas and Linguistic Anomalies

Although this chapter dealt most directly with the permission schema, we expect that a number of other schemas are used to reason about conditional rules. We have already mentioned schemas for obligations. An obligation is very similar to a permission except that the temporal direction is reversed. In a permission, performing an action requires satisfaction of a precondition, whereas in an obligation, a certain situation requires execution of a subsequent action.

Outside of the realm of social regulations, the concept of "causation" appears to correspond to a family of reasoning schemas (Kelley, 1972, 1973). There are very likely several subtypes of causal schemas, varying on such basic dimensions as whether the causal relation is deterministic or probabilistic and whether single or multiple causes are believed to produce the effect. In addition, as we noted earlier, schemas relating causes and their effects are closely related to schemas for "evidence" (e.g., an observed effect is evidence for the operation of its known cause).

Schematic knowledge about causation and evidence can account for anomalies sometimes created by the contrapositive transformation (which changes statements in the form *if p then q* into the form *if not-q then not-p*). Note the transformations of the following two sentences:

(7) If the bomb explodes, then everyone will die.

(8) If one takes proper care of a plant, then it grows.

They result in the following pragmatically anomalous contrapositives:

(7a) If not everyone will die, then the bomb does not explode.

(8a) If a plant does not grow, then one does not take proper care of it.

In contrast, the transformations of the following two sentences,

(9) If there is smoke, then there is fire.

(10) If one has been inoculated against cholera, then one is immune to it.

result in meaningful contrapositives:

(9a) If there is no fire, then there is no smoke.

(10a) If one is not immune to cholera, then one has not been inoculated against it.

No syntactic interpretation of the connective *if-then* in terms of either standard or natural logic can account for the difference in acceptability between (7a) and (8a) on the one hand, and (9a) and (10a) on the other.[3] The temporal direction of *if-then* statements hypothesized by Evans and Newstead (1977) – although a factor in determining acceptability, as we shall see – also cannot fully account for the difference. Sentences (10) and (10a), for example, are both acceptable, despite the antecedent and the consequent being ordered temporally in opposite directions.

But let us consider the transformations in terms of pragmatic knowledge about causation, which could be represented by rules attached to a causal schema. The contrapositive transformation reverses the antecedent and the consequent of a conditional. The inference, "If ⟨cause⟩, then ⟨effect⟩," in a causal schema has the contrapositive, "If ⟨absence of effect⟩, then ⟨absence of cause⟩," where the absence of the effect serves as evidence for concluding the absence of the cause. The above two conditionals have a common temporal restriction involving the relative temporal order of cause and effect. When the cause and the effect are temporally ordered by world knowledge, as in Sentences (7), (8), and (10), the event interpreted as the cause (or its absence) must temporally precede the effect (or its absence). Notice that this temporal restriction hinges on the semantic content of the events, regardless of which event is logically the antecedent or the consequent. Whereas the antecedent should be prior to the consequent in the conditional, "If ⟨cause⟩, then ⟨effect⟩," the consequent should be prior to the antecedent in the conditional, "If ⟨evidence: absence of effect⟩, then ⟨conclusion: absence of cause⟩."

If the temporal order of a causal relation expressed in a conditional sentence violates the above restriction, the sentence will sound anomalous. This may occur in the contrapositive transformation of conditionals in which the antecedent and consequent are not temporally ordered by tense. In such cases, the *if-then* frame imposes a forward temporal direction on them

(Evans & Beck, 1981; Evans & Newstead, 1977). Thus, the meaningful temporal order in Sentence (8), "If one takes proper care of a plant, then it grows," becomes anomalously reversed upon transformation into Sentence (8a), "If the plant does not grow, then one does not take proper care of it." Sentence (8a) suggests that the plant's lack of growth (the supposed effect) precedes one's failure to take proper care of it (the supposed cause). A similar anomalous reversal occurs in Sentence (7a). Notice that the anomalousness of Sentence (7a) disappears when the priority of the absence of the cause (the consequent) is specified by tense: "If not everyone will die, then the bomb is not exploding."

The remaining examples do not violate the above restriction. In the case of Sentence (9), "If there is smoke, then there is fire," both tense and world knowledge indicate that the evidence and conclusion are continuous and contemporaneous states. Since the events are contemporaneous, the contrapositive transformation causes no change in the temporal order, therefore yielding a meaningful Sentence in (9a). Sentence (10a), "If one is not immune to cholera, then one has not been inoculated against it," also does not violate the temporal restriction mentioned above, despite the events being temporally ordered by world knowledge. In this case explicit tense markers indicate that the conclusion temporally precedes the evidence, rendering the sentence meaningful.

The above examples illustrate how pragmatic knowledge of causation can account for the differing effects of the contrapositive transformation. It is not the case that p must occur prior to q for statements in the form if p then q in order to be acceptable. Rather, when the conditional expresses a temporally ordered causal relation, p must occur prior to q if p expresses the cause (or its absence), and the reverse if p expresses the effect (or its absence). This restriction does not apply when the events are contemporaneous. And as noted earlier, different temporal restrictions apply if an if-then statement is interpreted in terms of a noncausal schema such as permission or obligation (also see Cheng et al., 1985).

Conclusion

In this chapter, we have applied the concept of pragmatic reasoning schemas to explain three different types of phenomena: the complex patterns of performance observed in Wason's selection task, patterns of rephrasing between state-

ments in if-then and only-if forms (including introduction of modals), and linguistic anomalies involving the contrapositive transformation of certain causal statements. Our theoretical approach has other potential directions for development. In other work (Cheng et al., 1985), we have interpreted the effects of alternative methods of training on deductive reasoning in terms of the pragmatic-schema hypothesis.

Another direction that bears mention because of its perennial interest is the relationship between reasoning and language. Our approach to reasoning implies that the schematic structures that guide everyday reasoning are primarily the products of induction from recurring experience with classes of goal-related situations. Reasoning rules are fundamentally based on our pragmatic interpretations of situations, rather than on the syntactic interpretation of sentences. Our view thus diverges from the Whorfian hypothesis that thought is shaped by the language one speaks, particularly, it has been argued (Bloom, 1981), for such abstract concepts as the conditional. The results of Experiment 1 (as well as of the experiment mentioned in Footnote 2) in fact provide suggestive evidence in favor of our position. The Hong Kong subjects received conditional rules in Chinese, a language which (unlike English) has distinct colloquial connectives corresponding to the concepts if and if and only if (ruguo jui and ruguo cai, respectively). A Whorfian might suppose that these expressions would allow Chinese speakers to distinguish more readily between these two confusable senses of if-then, and therefore perform more accurately on selection problems. However, no such advantage was detected in our experiments. Although these null results are far from conclusive, there is certainly no convincing evidence that cross-linguistic syntactic differences in expression of conditionals have any impact on reasoning performance (Au, 1983; Cheng, 1985). Our framework implies that if reasoning performance is found to vary across populations, the explanation will lie not in linguistic differences, but rather in cultural differences regarding pragmatically important goals and situations.

Notes

1 In a further experiment we compared selection-task performance for an arbitrary rule (the card problem) with or without must in the consequent. Performance did not differ across the alternative versions.

2 In an earlier experiment, essentially the same pattern of results for rephrasing from *if-then* into *only-if* forms was obtained with subjects at the Chinese University of Hong Kong.

3 The anomalousness of (7a) and (8a) can be avoided by changes of tense. For example (7a) can be changed into "If not everyone dies, then the bomb did not explode." Such adjustments, however, still cannot circumvent the issue of *differences* in acceptability, which can simply be rephrased as: Why do some contrapositive transformations require tense adjustment whereas others do not?

References

Au, T. K. (1983). Chinese and English counterfactuals: The Sapir–Whorf hypothesis revisited. *Cognition*, **15**, 155–187.

Bloom, A. (1981). *The linguistic shaping of thought: A study in the impact of language on thinking in China and the West*. Hillsdale, NJ: Erlbaum.

Braine, M. D. S. (1978). On the relation between the natural logic of reasoning and standard logic. *Psychological Review*, **85**, 1–21.

Braine, M. D. S., Reiser, B. J., & Rumain, B. (1984). Some empirical justification for a theory of natural propositional logic. In G. H. Bower (Ed.), *The psychology of learning and motivation* (Vol. 18). New York: Academic Press.

Cheng, P. W. (1985). Pictures of ghosts: A critique of Alfred Bloom's *The linguistic shaping of thought*. *American Anthropologist*, **87**, 917–922.

Cheng, P. W., Holyoak, K. J., Nisbett, R. E., & Oliver, L. M. (1986). *Cognitive Psychology*, **18**, 293–328.

D'Andrade, R. (1982, April). *Reason versus logic*. Paper presented at the Symposium on the Ecology of Cognition: Biological, Cultural, and Historical Perspectives, Greensboro, NC.

Evans, J. St. B. T. (1977). Linguistic factors in reasoning. *Quarterly Journal of Experimental Psychology*, **29**, 297–306.

Evans, J. St. B. T. (1982). *The psychology of deductive reasoning*. London: Routledge & Kegan Paul.

Evans, J. St. B. T., & Beck, M. A. (1981). Directionality and temporal factors in conditional reasoning. *Current Psychological Research*, **1**, 111–120.

Evans, J. St. B. T., & Newstead, S. E. (1977). Language and reasoning: A study of temporal factors. *Cognition*, **8**, 387–390.

Fillenbaum, S. (1975). If: Some uses. *Psychological Research*, **37**, 245–260.

Fillenbaum, S. (1976). Inducements: On phrasing and logic of conditional promises, threats and warnings. *Psychological Research*, **38**, 231–250.

Geis, M. C., & Zwicky, A. M. (1971). On invited inferences. *Linguistic Inquiry*, **2**, 561–566.

Golding, E. (1981). *The effect of past experience on problem solving*. Paper presented at the Annual Conference of the British Psychological Society, Surrey University.

Griggs, R. A. (1983). The role of problem content in the selection task and in the THOG problem. In J. St. B. T. Evans (Ed.), *Thinking and reasoning: Psychological approaches*. London: Routledge & Kegan Paul.

Griggs, R. A. (1984). Memory cueing and instructional effects on Wason's selection task. *Current Psychological Research and Reviews*.

Griggs, R. A., & Cox, J. R. (1982). The elusive thematic-materials effect in Wason's selection task. *British Journal of Psychology*, **73**, 407–420.

Henle, M. (1962). On the relation between logic and thinking. *Psychological Review*, **69**, 366–378.

Johnson-Laird, P. N. (1975). Models of deduction. In R. J. Falmagne (Ed.), *Reasoning: Representation and process*. New York: Wiley.

Johnson-Laird, P. N. (1982). Ninth Bartlett memorial lecture: Thinking as a skill. *Quarterly Journal of Experimental Psychology*, **34A**, 1–29.

Johnson-Laird, P. N. (1983). *Mental models*. Cambridge, MA: Harvard Univ. Press.

Johnson-Laird, P. N., Legrenzi, P., & Legrenzi, S. M. (1972). Reasoning and a sense of reality. *British Journal of Psychology*, **63**, 395–400.

Kelley, H. H. (1972). Causal schemata and the attribution process. In E. E. Jones et al. (Eds.), *Attribution: Perceiving the causes of behavior*. Morristown, NJ: General Learning Press.

Kelley, H. H. (1973). The process of causal attribution. *American Psychologist*, **78**, 107–128.

Manktelow, K. I., & Evans, J. St. B. T. (1979). Facilitation of reasoning by realism: Effect or non-effect? *British Journal of Psychology*, **70**, 477–488.

Osherson, D. (1975). Logic and models of logical thinking. In R. J. Falmagne (Ed.), *Reasoning: Representation and process*. New York: Wiley.

Pollard, P. (1982). Human reasoning: Some possible effects of availability. *Cognition*, **12**, 65–96.

Reich, S. S., & Ruth, P. (1982). Wason's selection task: Verification, falsification and matching. *British Journal of Psychology*, **73**, 395–405.

Rips, L. J. (1983). Cognitive processes in propositional reasoning. *Psychological Review*, **90**, 38–71.

Rips, L. J., & Conrad, F. G. (1983). Individual differences in deduction. *Cognition and Brain Theory*, **6**, 259–285.

Rumelhart, D. E. (1980). Schemata. The building blocks of cognition. In R. J. Spiro, B. C. Bruce, & W. F. Brewer (Eds.), *Theoretical issues in reading comprehension*. Hillsdale, NJ: Erlbaum.

Wason, P. C. (1966). Reasoning. In B. M. Foss (Ed.), *New horizons in psychology* (Vol. 1). Harmondsworth: Penguin.

Wason, P. C. (1983). Realism and rationality in the selection task. In J. St. B. T. Evans (Ed.)., *Thinking and reasoning: Psychological approaches*. London: Routledge & Kegan Paul.

842   PATRICIA W. CHENG AND KEITH J. HOLYOAK

Wason, P. C., & Green, D. W. (1984). Reasoning and mental representation. *Quarterly Journal of Experimental Psychology*, **36A**, 597–610.

Wason, P. C., & Shapiro, D. (1971). Natural and contrived experience in a reasoning problem. *Quarterly Journal of Experimental Psychology*, **23**, 63–71.

Yachanin, S. A. (1985). *Facilitation in Wason's selection task: Content and instruction*. Unpublished manuscript. Lake Erie College.

Yachanin, S. A., & Tweney, R. D. (1982). The effect of thematic content on cognitive strategies in the four-card selection task. *Bulletin of the Psychonomic Society*, **19**, 87–90.

Chapter 41: Beyond Intuition and Instinct Blindness: Toward an Evolutionarily Rigorous Cognitive Science

LEDA COSMIDES AND JOHN TOOBY

Nothing in biology makes sense except in the light of evolution.

Theodosius Dobzhansky

Is it not reasonable to anticipate that our understanding of the human mind would be aided greatly by knowing the purpose for which it was designed?

George C. Williams

The cognitive sciences have reached a pivotal point in their development. We now have the opportunity to take our place in the far larger and more exacting scientific landscape that includes the rest of the modern biological sciences. Every day, research of immediate and direct relevance to our own is being generated in evolutionary biology, behavioral ecology, developmental biology, genetics, paleontology, population biology, and neuroscience. In turn, many of these fields are finding it necessary to use concepts and research from the cognitive sciences.

But to benefit from knowledge generated in these collateral fields, we will have to learn how to use biological facts and principles in theory formation and experimental design. This means shedding certain concepts and prejudices inherited from parochial parent traditions: the obsessive search for a cognitive architecture that is general purpose and initially content-free; the excessive reliance on results derived from artificial "intellectual" tasks; the idea that the field's scope is limited to the study of "higher" mental processes; and a long list of false dichotomies reflecting premodern biological thought – evolved/learned, evolved/developed, innate/learned, genetic/environmental, biological/social, biological/cultural, emotion/cognition, animal/human. Most importantly, cognitive scientists will have to abandon the functional agnosticism that is endemic to the field (Tooby & Cosmides, 1992).

The biological and cognitive sciences dovetail elegantly because in evolved systems – such as the human brain – there is a causal relationship between the adaptive problems a species encountered during its evolution and the design of its phenotypic structures. Indeed, a theoretical synthesis between the two fields seems inevitable, because evolutionary biologists investigate and inventory the set of adaptive information-processing problems the brain evolved to solve, and cognitive scientists investigate the design of the circuits or mechanisms that evolved to solve them. In fact, the cognitive subfields that already recognize and exploit this relationship between function and structure, such as visual perception, have made the most rapid empirical progress. These areas succeed because they are guided by (1) theories of adaptive function, (2) detailed analyses of the tasks each mechanism was designed by evolution to solve, and (3) the recognition that these tasks are usually solved by cognitive machinery that is highly functionally specialized. We believe the study of central processes can be revitalized by applying the same adaptationist program. But for this to happen, cognitive scientists

Reproduced with permission from Cosmides, L., and Tooby, J. (1994) Beyond intuition and instinct blindness: Toward an evolutionarily rigorous cognitive science. *Cognition*, 50, 41–77.

will have to replace the intuitive, folk psychological notions that now dominate the field with evolutionarily rigorous theories of function.

It is exactly this reluctance to consider function that is the central impediment to the emergence of a biologically sophisticated cognitive science. Surprisingly, a few cognitive scientists have tried to ground their dismissal of functional reasoning in biology itself. The claim that natural selection is too constrained by other factors to organize organisms very functionally has indeed been made by a small number of biologists (e.g., Gould & Lewontin, 1979). However, this argument has been empirically falsified so regularly and comprehensively that it is now taken seriously only by research communities too far outside of evolutionary biology to be acquainted with its primary literature (Clutton-Brock & Harvey, 1979; Daly & Wilson, 1983; Dawkins, 1982, 1986; Krebs & Davies, 1987; Williams, 1966; Williams & Nesse, 1991).[1] Other cognitive scientists take a less ideological, more agnostic stance; most never think about function at all.

As a result, cognitive psychology has been conducted as if Darwin never lived. Most cognitive scientists proceed without any clear notion of what "function" means for biological structures like the brain, or what the explicit analysis of function could teach them. Indeed, many cognitive scientists think that theories of adaptive function are an explanatory luxury – fanciful, unfalsifiable speculations that one indulges in at the end of a project, after the hard work of experimentation has been done.

But theories of adaptive function are not a luxury. They are an indispensable methodological tool, crucial to the future development of cognitive psychology. Atheoretical approaches will not suffice – a random stroll through hypothesis space will not allow you to distinguish figure from ground in a complex system. To isolate a functionally organized mechanism within a complex system, you need a theory of what function that mechanism was designed to perform.

This article is intended as an overview of the role we believe theories of adaptive function should play in cognitive psychology. We will briefly explain why they are important, where exactly they fit into a research program, how they bear on cognitive and neural theories, and what orthodoxies they call into question. (For a more complete and detailed argument, see Tooby & Cosmides, 1992.)

I. Function Determines Structure

Explanation and Discovery in the Cognitive Sciences

> . . . trying to understand perception by studying only neurons is like trying to understand bird flight by studying only feathers: it just cannot be done. In order to understand bird flight, we have to understand aerodynamics; only then do the structure of feathers and the different shapes of birds' wings make sense. (Marr, 1982, p. 27)

David Marr developed a general explanatory system for the cognitive sciences that is much cited but rarely applied. His three-level system applies to any device that processes information – a calculator, a cash register, a television, a computer, a brain. It is based on the following observations:

(1) Information-processing devices are designed to solve problems.

(2) They solve problems by virtue of their structure.

(3) Hence to explain the structure of a device, you need to know
     (a) *what* problem it was designed to solve, and
     (b) *why* it was designed to solve that problem and not some other one.

In other words, you need to develop a task analysis of the problem, or what Marr called a *computational theory* (Marr, 1982). Knowing the physical structure of a cognitive device and the information-processing program realized by that structure is not enough. For human-made artifacts and biological systems, form follows function. The physical structure is there because it embodies a set of programs; the programs are there because they solve a particular problem. A computational theory specifies what that problem is and why there is a device to solve it. It specifies the *function* of an information-processing device. Marr felt that the computational theory is the most important and the most neglected level of explanation in the cognitive sciences.

This functional level of explanation has not been neglected in the biological sciences, however, because it is essential for understanding how natural selection designs organisms. An

Table 1: Three Levels at Which Any Machine Carrying Out an Information-Processing Task Must Be Understood (from Marr, 1982, p. 25)

1. Computational theory
   What is the goal of the computation, why is it appropriate, and what is the logic of the strategy by which it can be carried out?
2. Representation and algorithm
   How can this computational theory be implemented? In particular, what is the representation for the input and output, and what is the algorithm for the transformation?
3. Hardware implementation
   How can the representation and algorithm be realized physically?

In evolutionary biology:
Explanations at the level of the computational theory are called *ultimate* level explanations.
Explanations at the level of representations and algorithm, or at the level of hardware implementation, are called *proximate* levels of explanation.

---

organism's phenotypic structure can be thought of as a collection of "design features" – micromachines, such as the functional components of the eye or liver. Over evolutionary time, new design features are added or discarded from the species' design because of their consequences. A design feature will cause its own spread over generations if it has the consequence of solving adaptive problems: cross-generationally recurrent problems whose solution promotes reproduction, such as detecting predators or detoxifying poisons. Natural selection is a feedback process that "chooses" among alternative designs on the basis of how well they function. By selecting designs on the basis of how well they solve adaptive problems, this process engineers a tight fit between the function of a device and its structure.[2] To understand this causal relationship, biologists had to develop a theoretical vocabulary that distinguishes between structure and function. Marr's computational theory is a functional level of explanation that corresponds roughly to what biologists refer to as the "ultimate" or "functional" explanation of a phenotypic structure.

A computational theory defines what problem the device solves and why it solves it; theories about programs and their physical substrate specify *how* the device solves the problem. "How" questions – questions about programs and hardware – currently dominate the research agenda in the cognitive sciences. Answering such questions is extremely difficult, and most cognitive scientists realize that groping in the dark is not a productive research strategy. Many see the need for a reliable source of theoretical guidance. The question is, what form should it take?

Why Ask Why? – or – How to Ask How

It is currently fashionable to think that the findings of neuroscience will eventually place strong constraints on theory formation at the cognitive level. Undoubtedly they will. But extreme partisans of this position believe neural constraints will be *sufficient* for developing cognitive theories. In this view, once we know enough about the properties of neurons, neurotransmitters and cellular development, figuring out what cognitive programs the human mind contains will become a trivial task.

This cannot be true. Consider the fact that there are birds that migrate by the stars, bats that echolocate, bees that compute the variance of flower patches, spiders that spin webs, humans that speak, ants that farm, lions that hunt in teams, cheetahs that hunt alone, monogamous gibbons, polyandrous seahorses, polygynous gorillas ... There are millions of animal species on earth, each with a different set of cognitive programs. *The same basic neural tissue embodies all of these programs*, and it could support many others as well. Facts about the properties of neurons, neurotransmitters, and cellular development cannot tell you which of these millions of programs the human mind contains.

Even if all neural activity is the expression of a uniform process at the cellular level, it is the arrangement of neurons – into birdsong templates or web-spinning programs – that matters. The idea that low-level neuroscience will generate a self-sufficient cognitive theory is a physicalist expression of the ethologically naive associationist/empiricist doctrine that all animal brains are essentially the same.

Table 2: Why Cash Registers Add (Adapted from Marr, 1982, pp. 22–23)

Rules Defining Addition	*Rules Governing Social Exchange in a Supermarket*
1. There is a unique element, "zero"; Adding zero has no effect: $2 + 0 = 2$	1. If you buy nothing, it should cost you nothing; and buying nothing and something should cost the same as buying just the something. (The rules for zero.)
2. Commutativity: $(2 + 3) = (3 + 2) = 5$	2. The order in which goods are presented to the cashier should not affect the total. (Commutativity.)
3. Associativity: $(2 + 3) + 4 = 2 + (3 + 4)$	3. Arranging the goods into two piles and paying for each pile separately should not affect the total amount you pay. (Associativity; the basic operation for combining prices.)
4. Each number has a unique inverse that when added to the number gives zero: $2 + (-2) = 0$	4. If you buy an item and then return it for a refund, your total expenditure should be zero. (Inverses.)

In fact, as David Marr put it, a program's structure "depends more upon the computational problems that have to be solved than upon the particular hardware in which their solutions are implemented" (1982, p. 27). In other words, knowing *what* and *why* places strong constraints on theories of *how*.

For this reason, a computational theory of function is not an explanatory luxury. It is an essential tool for discovery in the cognitive and neural sciences. A theory of function may not determine a program's structure uniquely, but it reduces the number of possibilities to an empirically manageable number. Task demands radically constrain the range of possible solutions; consequently, very few cognitive programs are capable of solving any given adaptive problem. By developing a careful task analysis of an information-processing problem, you can vastly simplify the empirical search for the cognitive program that solves it. And once that program has been identified, it becomes straightforward to develop clinical tests that will target its neural basis.

To figure out how the mind works, cognitive scientists will need to know what problems our cognitive and neural mechanisms were designed to solve.

Beyond Intuition: How to Build a Computational Theory

To illustrate the notion of a computational theory, Marr asks us to consider the what and why of a cash register at a check-out counter in a grocery store. We know the what of a cash register: it adds numbers. Addition is an operation that maps pairs of numbers onto single numbers, and

it has certain abstract properties, such as commutativity and associativity (see Table 2). How the addition is accomplished is quite irrelevant: any set of representations and algorithms that satisfy these abstract constraints will do. The input to the cash register is prices, which are represented by numbers. To compute a final bill, the cash register adds these numbers together. That's the what.

But *why* was the cash register designed to add the prices of each item? Why not multiply them together, or subtract the price of each item from 100? According to Marr, "the reason is that the rules we *intuitively feel to be appropriate* for combining the individual prices in fact define the mathematical operation of addition" (p. 22, emphasis added). He formulates these intuitive rules as a series of constraints on how prices should be combined when people exchange money for goods, then shows that these constraints map directly onto those that define addition (see Table 2). On this view, cash registers were designed to add because addition is the mathematical operation that realizes the constraints on buying and selling that our intuitions deem appropriate. Other mathematical operations are inappropriate because they violate these intuitions; for example, if the cash register subtracted each price from 100, the more goods you chose the less you would pay – and whenever you chose more than $100 of goods, the store would pay *you*.

In this particular example, the buck stopped at intuition. But it shouldn't. Our intuitions are produced by the human brain, an information-processing device that was designed by the evolutionary process. To discover the structure of the brain, you need to know *what* problems it was designed to solve and *why* it was designed to solve those problems rather than some other ones. In other words, you need to ask the same questions of the brain as you would of the cash register.

Cognitive science is the study of the design of minds, regardless of their origin. Cognitive psychology is the study of the design of minds that were produced by the evolutionary process. Evolution produced the what, and evolutionary biology is the study of why.

Most cognitive scientists know this. What they don't yet know is that understanding the evolutionary process can bring the architecture of the mind into sharper relief. For biological systems, the nature of the designer carries implications for the nature of the design.

The brain can process information because it contains complex neural circuits that are functionally organized. The only component of the evolutionary process that can build complex structures that are functionally organized is natural selection. And the only kind of problems that natural selection can build complexly organized structures for solving are adaptive problems, where "adaptive" has a very precise, narrow technical meaning (Dawkins, 1986; Pinker & Bloom, 1990; Tooby & Cosmides, 1990a, 1992; Williams, 1966). Bearing this in mind, let's consider the *source* of Marr's intuitions about the cash register.

Buying food at a grocery store is a form of social exchange – cooperation between two or more individuals for mutual benefit. The adaptive problems that arise when individuals engage in this form of cooperation have constituted a long-enduring selection pressure on the hominid line. Paleoanthropological evidence indicates that social exchange extends back at least 2 million years in the human line, and the fact that social exchange exists in some of our primate cousins suggests that it may be even more ancient than that. It is exactly the kind of problem that selection can build cognitive mechanisms for solving.

Social exchange is not a recent cultural invention, like writing, yam cultivation, or computer programming; if it were, one would expect to find evidence of its having one or several points of origin, of its having spread by contact, and of its being extremely elaborated in some cultures and absent in others. But its distribution does not fit this pattern. Social exchange is both universal and highly elaborated across human cultures, presenting itself in many forms: reciprocal gift-

giving, food-sharing, marketing-pricing, and so on (Cosmides & Tooby, 1992; Fiske, 1991). It is an ancient, pervasive and central part of human social life.

In evolutionary biology, researchers such as George Williams, Robert Trivers, W. D. Hamilton, and Robert Axelrod have explored constraints on the evolution of social exchange using game theory, modeling it as a repeated Prisoner's Dilemma. These analyses have turned up a number of important features of this adaptive problem, a crucial one being that social exchange cannot evolve in a species unless individuals have some means of detecting individuals who cheat and excluding them from future interactions (e.g., Axelrod, 1984; Axelrod & Hamilton, 1981; Boyd, 1988; Trivers, 1971). One can think of this as an *evolvability constraint*. Selection cannot construct mechanisms in any species – including humans – that systematically violate such constraints. Behavior is generated by computational mechanisms. If a species engages in social exchange behavior, then it does so by virtue of computational mechanisms that satisfy the evolvability constraints that characterize this adaptive problem.

Behavioral ecologists have used these constraints on the evolution of social exchange to build computational theories of this adaptive problem – theories of what and why. These theories have provided a principled basis for generating hypotheses about the phenotypic design of mechanisms that generate social exchange in a variety of species. They spotlight design features that any cognitive program capable of solving this adaptive problem must have. By cataloging these design features, animal behavior researchers were able to look for – and discover – previously unknown aspects of the psychology of social exchange in species from chimpanzees, baboons and vervets to vampire bats and hermaphroditic coral-reef fish (e.g., Cheney & Seyfarth, 1990; de Waal & Luttrell, 1988; Fischer, 1988; Smuts, 1986; Wilkinson, 1988, 1990).

This research strategy has been successful for a very simple reason: *very few cognitive programs satisfy the evolvability constraints for social exchange*. If a species engages in this behavior (and not all do), then its cognitive architecture must contain one of these programs.

In our own species, social exchange is a universal, species-typical trait with a long evolutionary history. We have strong and cross-culturally reliable intuitions about how this form of cooperation should be conducted, which arise in the absence of any explicit instruction (Cosmides & Tooby, 1992; Fiske, 1991). In developing his computational theory of the cash register – a tool used in social exchange – David Marr was consulting these deep human intuitions.[3]

From these facts, we can deduce that the human cognitive architecture contains programs that satisfy the evolvability constraints for social exchange. As cognitive scientists, we should be able to specify *what* rules govern human behavior in this domain, and *why* we humans reliably develop circuits that embody these rules rather than others. In other words, we should be able to develop a computational theory of the organic information-processing device that governs social exchange in humans.

Since Marr, cognitive scientists have become familiar with the notion of developing computational theories to study perception and language, but the notion that one can develop computational theories to study the information-processing devices that give rise to social behavior is still quite alien. Yet some of the most important adaptive problems our ancestors had to solve involved navigating the social world, and some of the best work in evolutionary biology is devoted to analyzing constraints on the evolution of mechanisms that solve these problems. In fact, these evolutionary analyses may be the *only* source of constraints available for developing computational theories of social cognition.

Principles of Organic Design

The field of evolutionary biology summarizes our knowledge of the engineering principles that govern the design of organisms. As a source of theoretical guidance about organic design, functionalism has an unparalleled historical track record. As Ernst Mayr notes, "The adaptationist question, 'What is the function of a given structure or organ?' has been for centuries the basis for every advance in physiology" (1983, p. 328).

Attention to function can advance the cognitive sciences as well. Aside from those properties acquired by chance or imposed by engineering constraint, the mind consists of a set of information-processing circuits that were designed by natural selection to solve adaptive problems that our hunter-gatherer ancestors faced generation after generation.[4] If we know what these problems were, we can seek mechanisms that are well engineered for solving them.

The exploration and definition of these adaptive problems is a major activity of evolutionary biologists. By combining results derived from mathematical modeling, comparative studies, behavioral ecology, paleoanthropology and other fields, evolutionary biologists try to identify what problems the mind was designed to solve and why it was designed to solve those problems rather than some other ones. In other words, evolutionary biologists explore exactly those questions that Marr argued were essential for developing computational theories of adaptive information-processing problems.

Computional theories address *what* and *why*, but because there are multiple ways of achieving any solution, experiments are needed to establish *how*. But the more precisely you can define the goal of processing – the more tightly you can constrain what would count as a solution – the more clearly you can see what a mechanism capable of producing that solution would have to look like. The more constraints you can discover, the more the field of possible solutions is narrowed, and the more you can concentrate your experimental efforts on discriminating between viable hypotheses.

A technological analogy may make this clearer. It is difficult to figure out the design of the object I'm now thinking about if all you know is that it is a machine (toaster? airplane? supercollider?). But the answer becomes progressively clearer as I add functional constraints: (1) it is well designed for entertainment (movie projector, TV, CD player?); it was not designed to project images (nothing with a screen); it is well designed for playing taped music (stereo or Walkman); it was designed to be easily portable during exercise (Walkman).

Knowing the object is well engineered for solving these problems provides powerful clues about its functional design features that can guide research. Never having seen one, you would know that it must contain a device that converts magnetic patterns into sound waves; a place to insert the tape; an outer shell no smaller than a tape, but no larger than necessary to perform the transduction; and so on.

Guessing at random would have taken forever. Information about features that have no impact on the machine's function would not have helped much either (e.g., its color, the number of scratches). Because functionally neutral features are free to vary, information about them does little to narrow your search.

Functional information helps because it narrowly specifies the outcome to be produced. The smaller the class of entities capable of producing that outcome, the more useful functional

Table 3: Evolutionary Biology Provides Constraints from Which Computational Theories of Adaptive Information-Processing Problems Can Be Built

To build a computational theory, you need to answer two questions:
1. What is the adaptive problem?
2. What information would have been available in ancestral environments for solving it?

Some sources of constraints
1. More precise definition of Marr's "goal" of processing that is appropriate to evolved (as opposed to artificial) information-processing systems
2. Game-theoretic models of the dynamics of natural selection (e.g., kin selection, Prisoner's Dilemma and cooperation – particularly useful for analysis of cognitive mechanisms responsible for social behavior)
3. Evolvability constraints: can a design with properties X, Y, and Z evolve, or would it have been selected out by alternative designs with different properties? (i.e., does the design represent an evolutionary stable strategy? – related to point 2)
4. Hunter-gatherer studies and paleoanthropology – source of information about the environmental background against which our cognitive architecture evolved. (Information that is present now may not have been present then, and vice versa.)
5. Studies of the algorithms and representations whereby other animals solve the same adaptive problem. (These will sometimes be the same, sometimes different.)

information is. This means (1) narrow definitions of outcomes are more useful than broad ones (tape player versus entertainment device), and (2) functional information is most useful when there are only a few ways of producing an outcome (Walkman versus paperweight; seeing versus scratching).

Narrow definitions of function are a powerful methodological tool for discovering the design features of any complex problem-solving device, including the human mind. Yet the definition of function that guides most research on the mind (it "processes information") is so broad that it applies even to a Walkman.

It is possible to create detailed theories of adaptive function. This is because natural selection is only capable of producing certain kinds of designs: designs that promoted their own reproduction in past environments. This rule of organic design sounds too general to be of any help. But when it is applied to real species in actual environments, this deceptively simple constraint radically limits what counts as an adaptive problem and, therefore, narrows the field of possible solutions. Table 3 lists some principles of organic design that cognitive psychologists could be using, but aren't.

Doing experiments is like playing "20 questions" with nature, and evolutionary biology gives you an advantage in this game: it tells you what questions are most worth asking, and what the answer will probably look like. It provides constraints – functional and otherwise – from which computational theories of adaptive information-processing problems can be built.

Taking Function Seriously

We know the cognitive science that intuition has wrought. It is more difficult, however, to know how our intuitions might have blinded us. What cognitive systems, if any, are we *not* seeing? How would evolutionary functionalism transform the science of mind?

Textbooks in psychology are organized according to a folk psychological categorization of mechanisms: "attention", "memory", "reasoning", "learning". In contrast, textbooks in evolutionary biology and behavioral ecology are organized according to adaptive problems: foraging (hunting and gathering), kinship, predator defense, resource competition, cooperation, aggression, parental care, dominance and status, inbreeding avoidance, courtship, mateship maintenance, trade-offs between mating effort and parenting effort, mating system, sexual conflict, paternity uncertainty and sexual jealousy, signaling and communication, navigation, habitat selection, and so on.

Textbooks in evolutionary biology are organized according to adaptive problems because these are the only problems that selection can build mechanisms for solving. Textbooks in behavioral ecology are organized according to adaptive problems because circuits that are functionally specialized for solving these problems have been found in species after species. No less should prove true of humans. Twenty-first-century textbooks on human cognition will probably be organized similarly.

Fortunately, behavioral ecologists and evolutionary biologists have already created a library of sophisticated models of the selection pressures, strategies and trade-offs that characterize these very fundamental adaptive problems, which they use in studying processes of attention, memory, reasoning and learning in non-humans. Which model is applicable for a given species depends on certain key life-history parameters. Findings from paleoanthropology, hunter-gatherer archaeology, and studies of living hunter-gatherer populations locate humans in this theoretical landscape by filling in the critical parameter values. Ancestral hominids were ground-living primates; omnivores, exposed to a wide variety of plant toxins and having a sexual division of labor between hunting and gathering; mammals with altricial young, long periods of biparental investment in offspring, enduring male–female mateships, and an extended period of physiologically obligatory female investment in pregnancy and lactation. They were a long-lived, low-fecundity species in which variance in male reproductive success was higher than variance in female reproductive success. They lived in small nomadic kin-based bands of perhaps 20–100; they would rarely (if ever) have seen more than 1000 people at one time; they had little opportunity to store provisions for the future; they engaged in cooperative hunting, defense and aggressive coalitions; they made tools and engaged in extensive amounts of cooperative reciprocation; they were vulnerable to a large variety of parasites and pathogens. When these parameters are combined with formal models from evolutionary biology and behavioral ecology, a reasonably consistent picture of ancestral life begins to appear (e.g., Tooby & DeVore, 1987).

In this picture, the adaptive problems posed by social life loom large. Most of these are characterized by strict evolvability constraints, which could only be satisfied by cognitive programs that are *specialized* for reasoning about the social world. This suggests that our evolved mental architecture contains a large and intricate "faculty" of social cognition (Brothers, 1990; Cosmides & Tooby, 1992; Fiske, 1991; Jackendoff, 1992). Yet despite its importance, very little work in the cognitive sciences has been devoted to looking for cognitive mechanisms that are specialized for reasoning about the social world. Nor have cognitive neuroscientists been looking for dissociations among different forms of social reasoning, or between social reasoning and other cognitive functions. The work on autism as a neurological impairment of a "theory of mind" module is a very notable – and very successful –

exception (e.g., Baron-Cohen, Leslie, & Frith, 1985; Frith, 1989; Leslie, 1987).

There are many reasons for the neglect of these topics in the study of humans (see Tooby & Cosmides, 1992), but a primary one is that cognitive scientists have been relying on their intuitions for hypotheses rather than asking themselves what kind of problems the mind was designed by evolution to solve. By using evolutionary biology to remind ourselves of the types of problems hominids faced across hundreds of thousands of generations, we can escape the narrow conceptual cage imposed on us by our intuitions and folk psychology. This is not a minor point: if you don't think a thing exists, you won't take the steps necessary to find it. By having the preliminary map that an evolutionary perspective provides, we can find our way out into the vast, barely explored areas of the human cognitive architecture.

II. Computational Theories Derived from Evolutionary Biology Suggest that the Mind is Riddled with Functionally Specialized Circuits

During most of this century, research in psychology and the other biobehavioral and social sciences has been dominated by the assumptions of what we have elsewhere called the Standard Social Science Model (SSSM) (Tooby & Cosmides, 1992). This model's fundamental premise is that the evolved architecture of the human mind is comprised mainly of cognitive processes that are content-free, few in number and general purpose. These general-purpose mechanisms fly under names such as "learning", "induction", "imitation", "reasoning" and "the capacity for culture", and are thought to explain nearly every human phenomenon. Their structure is rarely specified by more than a wave of the hand.

In this view, the same mechanisms are thought to govern how one acquires a language and a gender identity, an aversion to incest and an appreciation for vistas, a desire for friends and a fear of spiders – indeed, nearly every thought and feeling of which humans are capable. By definition, these empiricist mechanisms have no inherent content built into their procedures, they are not designed to construct certain mental contents more readily than others, and they have no features specialized for processing particular kinds of content over others. In other words, they are assumed to operate uniformly, no matter what content, subject matter or domain of life experience they are operating on. (For this reason, such procedures are described as *content-independent, domain-general* or *content-free*). The premise that these mechanisms have no content to impart is what leads to the doctrine central to the modern behavioral and social sciences: that all of our particular mental content originated in the social and physical world and entered through perception. As Aquinas put this empiricist tenet a millennium ago, "There is nothing in the intellect that was not first in the senses."

As we will discuss, this view of central processes is difficult to reconcile with modern evolutionary biology.

The Weakness of Content-Independent Architectures

To some it may seem as if an evolutionary perspective supports the case that our cognitive architecture consists primarily of powerful, general-purpose problem-solvers – inference engines that embody the content-free normative theories of mathematics and logic. After all, wouldn't an organism be better equipped and better adapted if it could solve a more general class of problems over a narrower class?

This empiricist view is difficult to reconcile with evolutionary principles for a simple reason: content-free, general-purpose problem-solving mechanisms are extraordinarily weak – or even inert – compared to specialized ones. Every computational system – living or artificial – must somehow solve the frame problem (e.g., Pylyshyn, 1987). Most artificial intelligence programs have domain-specific knowledge and procedures that do this (even those that are called "general purpose"). A program equipped solely with domain-general procedures can do nothing unless the human programmer solves the frame problem for it: either by artificially constraining the problem space or by supplying the program – by fiat – with pre-existing knowledge bases ("innate" knowledge) that it could not have acquired on its own, with or without connections to a perceptual system.

However, to be a viable hypothesis about our cognitive architecture, a proposed design must pass a solvability test. It must, in principle, be able to solve problems humans are known to be able to solve. At a minimum, any proposed cognitive architecture had to produce sufficiently self-reproductive behavior in ancestral environments – we know this because all living species have been able to reproduce themselves in an unbroken chain up to the present. While arti-

ficial intelligence programs struggle to recognize and manipulate coke cans, naturally intelligent programs situated in organisms successfully negotiate through lifetimes full of biotic antagonists – predators, conspecific competitors, self-defending food items, parasites, even siblings. At the same time, these naturally intelligent programs solve a large series of intricate problems in the project of assembling a sufficient number of replacement individuals: offspring. Just as a hypothesized set of cognitive mechanisms underlying language must be able to account for the facts of human linguistic behavior, so too must any hypothetical domain-general cognitive architecture reliably generate solutions to all of the problems that were necessary for survival and reproduction in the Pleistocene. For humans and most other species, this is a remarkably diverse, highly structured and very complex set of problems.

If it can be shown that there are essential adaptive problems that humans must have been able to solve in order to have propagated and that domain-general mechanisms cannot solve them, then the domain-general hypothesis fails. We think there is a very large number of such problems, including inclusive fitness regulation, mate choice, nutritional regulation, foraging, navigation, incest avoidance, sexual jealousy, predator avoidance, social exchange – at a minimum, any kind of information-processing problem that involves motivation, and many others as well. We have developed this argument in detail elsewhere (Cosmides & Tooby, 1987, 1994; Tooby & Cosmides, 1990a, 1992), so we won't belabor it here. Instead, we will simply summarize a few of the relevant points.

(1) *The "Stoppit" problem.* There is a Gary Larson cartoon about an "all-purpose" product called "Stoppit". When sprayed from an aerosol can, Stoppit stops faucet drips, taxis, cigarette smoking, crying babies and charging elephants. An "all-purpose" cognitive program is no more feasible for an analogous reason: *what counts as adaptive behavior differs markedly from domain to domain.* An architecture equipped only with content-independent mechanisms must succeed at survival and reproduction by applying the same procedures to every adaptive problem. But there is no domain-general criterion of success or failure that correlates with fitness (e.g., what counts as a "good" mate has little in common with a "good" lunch or a "good" brother). Because what counts as the wrong thing to do differs from one class of problems to the next, there must be as many domain-specific

subsystems as there are domains in which the definitions of successful behavioral outcomes are incommensurate.

(2) *Combinatorial explosion.* Combinatorial explosion paralyzes even moderately domain-general systems when encountering real-world complexity. As generality is increased by adding new dimensions to a problem space or new branch points to a decision tree the computational load increases with catastrophic rapidity. A content-independent, specialization-free architecture contains no rules of relevance, procedural knowledge or privileged hypotheses, and so could not solve any biological problem of routine complexity in the amount of time an organism has to solve it (for discussion see, for example, Carey, 1985; Gallistel, Brown, Carey, Gelman, & Keil, 1991; Keil, 1989; Markman, 1989; Tooby & Cosmides, 1992). The question is not "How much specialization does a general purpose system require?" but rather "How many degrees of freedom can a system *tolerate* – even a specialized, highly targeted one – and still compute decisions in useful, real-world time?" Combinatorics guarantee that real systems can only tolerate a small number. (Hence this problem cannot be solved by placing a few "constraints" on a general system.)

(3) *Clueless environments.* Content-free architectures are limited to knowing what can be validly derived by general processes from perceptual information. This sharply limits the range of problems they can solve: when the environment is clueless, the mechanism will be too. Domain-specific mechanisms are not limited in this way. They can be constructed to embody clues that fill in the blanks when perceptual evidence is lacking or difficult to obtain.

Consider the following adaptive problem. All plants foods contain an array of toxins. Ones that your liver metabolizes with ease sometimes harm a developing embryo. This subtle statistical relationship between the environment, eating behavior and fitness is ontogenetically "invisible": it cannot be observed or induced via general-purpose processes on the basis of perceptual evidence.[5] It can, however, be "observed" phylogenetically, by natural selection, because selection does not work by inference or simulation. Natural selection "counts up" the actual results of alternative designs operating in the real world, over millions of individuals, over thousands of generations, and weights these alternatives by the statistical distribution of their consequences: those design features that statistically lead to the best available outcome

are retained. In this sense it is omniscient – it is not limited to what could be validly deduced by one individual, based on a short period of experience, it is not limited to what is locally perceivable, and it is not confused by spurious local correlations. As a result, it can build circuits – like those that regulate food choice during pregnancy – which embody privileged hypotheses that reflect and exploit these virtually unobservable relationships in the world. For example, the embryo/toxin problem is solved by a set of functionally specialized mechanisms that adjust the threshold on the mother's normal food aversion system (Profet, 1992). They lower it when the embryo is most at risk – thereby causing the food aversions, nausea and vomiting of early pregnancy – and raise it when caloric intake becomes a priority. As a result, the mother avoids ordinarily palatable foods when they would threaten the embryo: she responds adaptively to an ontogenetically invisible relationship. Functionally specialized designs allow organisms to solve a broad range of otherwise unsolvable adaptive problems. (For discussion of this design principle, see Cosmides & Tooby, 1987, 1994; Shepard, 1981, 1987; Tooby & Cosmides, 1990a.)

In sum, architectures that do not come factory-equipped with sufficiently rich sets of content-specific machinery fail the solvability test. They could not have evolved, survived or propagated because they are incapable of solving even routine adaptive problems (Cosmides & Tooby, 1987, 1994; Tooby & Cosmides, 1992).

Natural Selection, Efficiency and Functional Specialization

Some researchers accept the conclusion that the human mind cannot consist solely of content-independent machinery, but nevertheless continue to believe that the mind needs very little content-specific organization to function. They believe that the preponderance of mental processes are content-independent and general purpose. Moreover, they believe that the correct null hypothesis – the parsimonious, prudent scientific stance – is to posit as few functionally specialized mechanisms as possible.

This stance ignores what is now known about the nature of the evolutionary process and the types of functional organization that it produces. Natural selection is a relentlessly hill-climbing process which tends to replace relatively less efficient designs with ones that perform better. Hence, in deciding which of two alternative designs is more likely to have evolved, their comparative performance on ancestral adaptive problems is the appropriate standard to use. Given this standard, positing a preponderance of general-purpose machinery is neither prudent nor parsimonious.[6] General-purpose mechanisms can't solve most adaptive problems at all, and in those few cases where one could, a specialized mechanism is likely to solve it more efficiently. The reason why is quite straightforward.

A general engineering principle is that the same machine is rarely capable of solving two different problems equally well. We have both cork-screws and cups because each solves a particular problem better than the other. It would be extremely difficult to open a bottle of wine with a cup or to drink from a cork-screw.

This same principle applies to the design of the human body. The heart is elegantly designed for pumping blood, but it is not good at detoxifying poisons; the liver is specialized for detoxifying poisons, but it cannot function as a pump. Pumping blood throughout the body and detoxifying poisons are two very different problems: consequently, the human body has a different machine for solving each of them. In biology, machines like these – ones that are specialized and functionally distinct – are called *adaptive specializations* (Rozin, 1976). Specialization of design is natural selection's signature and its most common result (Williams, 1966).[7] In fact, the more important the adaptive problem, the more intensely natural selection tends to specialize and improve the performance of the mechanism for solving it.

There is no reason to believe that the human brain and mind are any exception. The cognitive programs that govern how you choose a mate should differ from those that govern how you choose your dinner. Different information-processing problems usually have different solutions. Implementing different solutions requires different, functionally distinct mechanisms (Sherry & Schacter, 1987). Speed, reliability and efficiency can be engineered into specialized mechanisms, because they do not need to engineer a compromise between mutually incompatible task demands: a jack of all trades – assuming one is possible at all – is necessarily a master of none. For this reason, one should expect the evolved architecture of the human mind to include many functionally distinct *cognitive* adaptive specializations.

And it does. For example, the learning mechanisms that govern language acquisition are different from those that govern the acquisition of food aversions, and both of these are different from the learning mechanisms that govern the acquisition of snake phobias (e.g., Cook, Hodes, & Lang, 1986; Cook & Mineka, 1989; Garcia, 1990; Mineka & Cook, 1988; Pinker, 1994; Ohman, Dimberg, & Ost, 1985; Ohman, Eriksson, & Olofsson, 1975). These adaptive specializations are *domain-specific*: the specialized design features that make them good at solving the problems that arise in one domain (avoiding venomous snakes) make them bad at solving the problems that arise in another (inducing a grammar). They are also *content-dependent*: they are activated by different kinds of content (speech versus screams), and their procedures are designed to accept different kinds of content as input (sentences versus snakes). A mind that applied relatively general-purpose reasoning circuits to all these problems, regardless of their content, would be a very clumsy problem-solver. But flexibility and efficiency of thought and action can be achieved by a mind that contains a battery of special-purpose circuits. The mind is probably more like a Swiss army knife than an all-purpose blade: competent in so many situations because it has a large number of components – bottle opener, corkscrew, knife, toothpick, scissors – each of which is well designed for solving a different problem.

The functional architecture of the mind was designed by natural selection; natural selection is a hill-climbing process which produces mechanisms that solve adaptive problems well; a specialized design is usually able to solve a problem better than a more generalized one. It is unlikely that a process with these properties would design central processes that are general purpose and content-free. Consequently, one's default assumption should be that the architecture of the human mind is saturated with adaptive specializations.

How to Find a Needle in a Haystack

The human brain is the most complex system scientists have ever tried to understand; identifying its components is enormously difficult. The more functionally integrated circuits it contains, the more difficult it will be to isolate and map any one of them. Looking for a functionally integrated mechanism within a multimodular mind is like looking for a needle in a haystack. The odds you'll find one are low unless you can radically narrow the search space. Marr's central insight was that you could do this by developing computational theories of the problems these mechanisms were designed to solve – for the human brain, the adaptive problems our hunter-gatherer ancestors faced.

The only behavioral scientists who still derive their hypotheses from intuition and folk psychology, rather than an evolutionary based theory, are those who study humans.[8] The empirical advantages of using evolutionary biology to develop computational theories of adaptive problems have already been amply demonstrated in the study of non-human minds (e.g., Gallistel, 1990; Gould, 1982; Krebs & Davies, 1987; Real, 1991). We wanted to demonstrate its utility in studying the human mind. We thought an effective way of doing this would be to use an evolutionarily derived computational theory to discover cognitive mechanisms whose existence no one had previously suspected. Because most cognitive scientists still think of central processes as content-independent, we thought it would be particularly interesting to demonstrate the existence of central processes that are functionally specialized and content-dependent: domain-specific reasoning mechanisms.

Toward this end, we have conducted an experimental research program over the last 10 years, exploring the hypothesis that the human mind contains specialized circuits designed for reasoning about adaptive problems posed by the social world of our ancestors: social exchange, threat, coalitional action, mate choice, and so on. We initially focused on social exchange because (1) the evolutionary theory is clear and well developed, (2) the relevant selection pressures are strong, (3) paleoanthropological evidence suggests that hominids have been engaging in it for millions of years – more than enough time for selection to shape specialized mechanisms – and (4) humans in all cultures engage in social exchange. By starting with an adaptive problem hunter-gatherers are known to have faced, we could proceed to design experiments to test for associated cognitive specializations.

The evolutionary analysis of social exchange parallels the economist's concept of trade. Sometimes known as "reciprocal altruism", social exchange is an "I'll scratch your back if you scratch mine" principle (for evolutionary analyses see, for example, Axelrod, 1984; Axelrod & Hamilton, 1981; Boyd, 1988; Trivers, 1971; Williams, 1966.). Using evolvability constraints that biologists had already identified (some involving the Prisoners' Dilemma), we developed a computational theory of the information-processing problems that arise in this domain (Cosmides, 1985; Cosmides & Tooby, 1989). This gave us a principled basis for generating detailed hypotheses about the design of the circuits that generate social exchange in humans. Some of the design features we predicted are listed in Table 4.

For example, mathematical analyses had established cheater detection as a crucial adaptive problem. Circuits that generate social exchange will be selected out unless they allow individuals to detect those who fail to reciprocate favors – cheaters. This evolvability constraint led us directly to the hypothesis that humans might have evolved inference procedures that are specialized for detecting cheaters. We tested this hypothesis using the Wason selection task, which had originally been developed as a test of logical reasoning (Wason, 1966; Wason & Johnson-Laird, 1972).

A large literature already existed showing that people are not very good at detecting logical violations of "if–then" rules in Wason selection tasks, even when these rules deal with familiar content drawn from everyday life (e.g., Manktelow & Evans, 1979; Wason, 1983). For example, suppose you are skeptical when an astrologer tells you, "If a person is a Leo, then that person is brave," and you want to prove him wrong. In looking for exceptions to this rule, you will probably investigate people who you know are Leos, to see whether they are brave. Many people also have the impulse to investigate people who are brave, to see if they are Leos. Yet investigating brave people would be a waste of time; the astrologer said that all Leos are brave – not that all brave people are Leos – so finding a brave Virgo would prove nothing. And, if you are like most people, you probably won't realize that you need to investigate cowards. Yet a coward who turns out to be a Leo would represent a violation of the rule.

If your mind had reasoning circuits specialized for detecting logical violations of rules, it would be immediately obvious to you that you should investigate Leos and cowards. But it is not intuitively obvious to most subjects. In general, fewer than 10% of subjects spontaneously realize this. Despite claims for the power of culture and "learning", even formal training in logical reasoning does little to boost performance (e.g., Cheng, Holyoak, Nisbett, & Oliver, 1986; Wason & Johnson-Laird, 1972).

However, we found that people who ordinarily cannot detect violations of "if–then" rules

Table 4: Reasoning About Social Exchange: Evidence of Special Design[a]

(a) The Following Design Features Were Predicted and Found	(b) The Following By-Product Hypotheses Were Empirically Eliminated
1. The algorithms governing reasoning about social contracts operate even in unfamiliar situations.	1. Familiarity cannot explain the social contract effect.
2. The definition of cheating that they embody depends on one's perspective.	2. It is not the case that social contract content merely facilitates the application of the rules of inference of the propositional calculus.
3. They are just as good at computing the cost–benefit representation of a social contract from the perspective of one party as from the perspective of another.	3. Social contract content does not merely "afford" clear thinking.
4. They embody implicational procedures specified by the computational theory.	4. Permission schema theory cannot explain the social contract effect; in other words, application of a generalized deontic logic cannot explain the results.
5. They include inference procedures specialized for cheater detection.	5. It is not the case that any problem involving payoffs will elicit the detection of violations.
6. Their cheater detection procedures cannot detect violations of social contracts that do not correspond to cheating.	
7. They do not include altruist detection procedures.	
8. They cannot operate so as to detect cheaters unless the rule has been assigned the cost–benefit representation of a social contract.	

[a] To show that an aspect of the phenotype is an adaptation to perform a particular function, one must show that it is particularly well designed for performing that function, and that it cannot be better explained as a by-product of some other adaptation or physical law.

can do so easily and accurately when that violation represents cheating in a situation of social exchange. This is a situation in which one is entitled to a benefit only if one has fulfilled a requirement (e.g., "If you are to eat these cookies, then you must first fix your bed" or "If you are to eat cassava root, then you must have a tattoo on your face"). In these situations, the adaptively correct answer is immediately obvious to almost all subjects, who commonly experience a "pop out" effect. No formal training is needed. Whenever the content of a problem asks subjects to look for cheaters on a social exchange – even when the situation described is culturally unfamiliar and even bizarre – subjects experience the problem as simple to solve, and their performance jumps dramatically. Seventy to 90% of subjects get it right, the highest performance ever found for a task of this kind.

From a domain-general, formal view, investigating people eating cassava root and people without tattoos is logically equivalent to investigating Leos and cowards. But everywhere it has been tested, people do not treat social exchange problems as equivalent to other kinds of rea-

soning problems. Their minds distinguish social exchange contents, and apply domain-specific, content-dependent rules of inference that are adaptively appropriate only to that task. (For a review of the relevant experiments, see Cosmides & Tooby, 1992. For more detailed descriptions, see Cosmides, 1985, 1989; Cosmides & Tooby, 1989; Gigerenzer & Hug, 1992.)

We think that the goal of cognitive research should be to recover, out of carefully designed experimental studies, high-resolution "maps" of the intricate mechanisms that collectively constitute the cognitive architecture. Our evolutionarily derived computational theory of social exchange allowed us to construct experiments capable of detecting, isolating and mapping out previously unknown cognitive procedures. It led us to predict a large number of design features in advance – features that no one was looking for and that most of our colleagues thought were outlandish (Cosmides & Tooby, 1989). Experimental tests have confirmed the presence of all the predicted design features that have been tested for so far. Those design features that have been tested and confirmed are listed in Table 4, along with the alternative by-product hypotheses that we and our colleagues have eliminated. So far, no known theory invoking general-purpose cognitive processes has been able to explain the very precise and unique pattern of data that experiments like these have generated. The data seem best explained by the hypothesis that humans reliably develop circuits that are complexly specialized for reasoning about reciprocal social interactions.

Parallel lines of investigation have already identified two other domain-specialized reasoning mechanisms: one for reasoning about aggressive threats and one for reasoning about protection from hazards (e.g., Manktelow & Over, 1990; Tooby & Cosmides, 1989). We are now designing clinical tests to identify the neural basis for these mechanisms. By studying patient populations with autism and other neurological impairments of social cognition, we should be able to see whether dissociations occur along the fracture lines that our various computational theories suggest.

Reasoning Instincts

In our view, a large range of reasoning problems (like the astrological one) are difficult because (1) their content is not drawn from a domain for which humans evolved functionally specialized reasoning circuits, and (2) we lack the content-independent circuits necessary for performing certain logical operations ("logical reasoning"). In contrast, social exchange problems are easy because we do have evolved circuits specialized for reasoning about that important, evolutionarily long-enduring problem in social cognition. The inferences necessary for detecting cheaters are obvious to humans for the same reason that the inferences necessary for echolocation are obvious to a bat.

Instincts are often thought of as the polar opposite of reasoning. Non-human animals are widely believed to act through "instinct", while humans "gave up instincts" to become "the rational animal". But the reasoning circuits we have been investigating are complexly structured for solving a specific type of adaptive problem, they reliably develop in all normal human beings, they develop without any conscious effort and in the absence of any formal instruction, they are applied without any conscious awareness of their underlying logic, and they are distinct from more general abilities to process information or to behave intelligently. In other words, they have all the hallmarks of what one usually thinks of as

an "instinct" (Pinker, 1994). Consequently, one can think of these specialized circuits as *reasoning instincts*. They make certain kinds of inferences just as easy, effortless and "natural" to us as humans, as spinning a web is to a spider or dead-reckoning is to a desert ant.

Three decades of research in cognitive psychology, evolutionary biology and neuroscience have shown that the central premise of the SSSM – that the mind is general purpose and content-free – is fundamentally misconceived. An alternative framework – sometimes called evolutionary psychology – is beginning to replace it (Tooby & Cosmides, 1992). According to this view, the evolved architecture of the human mind is full of specialized reasoning circuits and regulatory mechanisms that organize the way we interpret experience, construct knowledge and make decisions. These circuits inject certain recurrent concepts and motivations into our mental life, and they provide universal frames of meaning that allow us to understand the actions and intentions of others. Beneath the level of surface variability, all humans share certain views and assumptions about the nature of the world and human action by virtue of these universal reasoning circuits (Atran, 1990; Boyer, 1994; Brown, 1991; Carey & Gelman, 1991; Gelman & Hirschfeld, 1994; Keil, 1989; Leslie, 1987; Markman, 1990; Spelke, 1990; Sperber, 1985, 1990, 1994; Symons, 1979; Tooby & Cosmides, 1992).

III. Intuition is a Misleading Source of Hypotheses Because Functionally Specialized Mechanisms Create "Instinct Blindness"; Computational Theories are Lenses that Correct for Instinct Blindness

Intuitions About Cognition: The Limitations of an Atheoretical Approach

The adaptationist view of a multimodular mind was common at the turn of the century. Early experimental psychologists, such as William James and William McDougall, thought the mind is a collection of "faculties" or "instincts" that direct learning, reasoning and action (James, 1890; McDougall, 1908). These faculties were thought to embody sophisticated information-processing procedures that were domain-specific. In James's view, human behavior is so much more flexibly intelligent than that of other animals because we have *more* instincts than they do – not fewer (James, 1890).

The vocabulary may be archaic, but the model is modern. With every new discovery, it becomes more apparent that the evolved architecture of the human mind is densely multimodular – that it consists of an enormous collection of circuits, each specialized for performing a particular adaptive function. The study of perception and language has provided the most conspicuous examples, but evidence for the existence of learning instincts (Marler, 1991) and reasoning instincts is pouring in from all corners of the cognitive sciences (for examples, see Atran, 1990; Barkow, Cosmides, & Tooby, 1992; Baron-Cohen, Leslie, & Frith, 1985; A. Brown, 1990; D. E. Brown, 1991; Carey & Gelman, 1991; Cosmides & Tooby, in press; Daly & Wilson, 1988, 1994; Frith, 1989; Gelman & Hirschfeld, 1994; Gigerenzer, Hoffrage, & Kleinbolting, 1991; Leslie, 1988; Pinker, 1994; Rozin, 1976; Spelke, 1988; Sperber, 1994; Symons, 1979; Wilson & Daly, 1992; Wynn, 1992).

In spite of this consistent pattern, however, most cognitive scientists balk at the model of a brain crowded with specialized inference engines. Even Fodor, who has championed the case for modular processes, takes the traditional view that "central" processes are general purpose (Fodor, 1983). The notion that learning and reasoning are like perception and language – the complex product of a large collection of functionally specialized circuits – is deeply at war with our intuitions.

But so is the inherent indeterminacy in the position of electrons. It is uncomfortable but scientifically necessary to accept that common sense is the faculty that tells us the world is flat.[9] Our intuitions may feel authoritative and irresistibly compelling, and they may lead us to dismiss many ideas as ridiculous. But they are, nevertheless, an untrustworthy guide to the reality of subatomic particles or the evolved structure of the human mind.

In the case of central processes, we think human intuition is not merely untrustworthy: it is systematically misleading. Well-designed reasoning instincts should be invisible to our intuitions, even as they generate them – no more accessible to consciousness than retinal cells and line detectors, but just as important in creating our perception of the world.

Intuitively, we are all naive realists, experiencing the world as already parsed into objects, relationships, goals, foods, dangers, humans, words, sentences, social groups, motives, artifacts, animals, smiles, glares, relevances and saliences, the known and the obvious. This automatically manufactured universe, input as toy worlds into computers, seems like it could almost be tractable by that perennially elusive collection of general-purpose algorithms cognitive scientists keep expecting to find. But to produce this simplified world that we effortlessly experience, a vast sea of computational problems are being silently solved, out of awareness, by a host of functionally integrated circuits. These reasoning instincts are powerful inference engines, whose automatic, non-conscious operation creates our seamless experience of the world. The sense of clarity and self-evidence they generate is so potent it is difficult to see that the computational problems they solve even exist. As a result, we incorrectly locate the computationally manufactured simplicity that we experience as a natural property of the external world – as the pristine state of nature, not requiring any explanation or research.

Thus the "naturalness" of certain inferences acts to obstruct the discovery of the mechanisms that produced them. Cognitive instincts create problems for cognitive scientists. Precisely because they work so well – because they process information so effortlessly and automatically – we tend to be blind to their existence. Not suspecting they exist, we do not conduct research programs to find them.

To see that they exist, you need to envision an alternative conceptual universe. But these dedicated circuits structure our thought so powerfully that it can be difficult to imagine how things could be otherwise. As William James wrote:

It takes . . . a mind debauched by learning to carry the process of making the natural seem strange, so far as to ask for the *why* of any instinctive human act. To the metaphysician alone can such questions occur as: why do we smile, when pleased, and not scowl? Why are we unable to talk to a crowd as we talk to a single friend? Why does a particular maiden turn our wits so upside-down? The common man can only say, *Of course* we smile, *of course* our heart palpitates at the sight of the crowd, *of course* we love the maiden, that beautiful soul clad in that perfect form, so palpably and flagrantly made for all eternity to be loved!

And so, probably, does each animal feel about the particular things it tends to do in the presence of particular objects. . . . To the lion it is the lioness which is made to be loved; to the bear, the she-bear. To the broody hen the notion would probably seems monstrous

Table 5: Inferences that Violate a Grammar of Social Reasoning

(a)
I want to help him because he has helped me so often in the past.
I don't want to help him because whenever I'm in trouble he refuses to help me.
*I want to help him because whenever I'm in trouble he refuses to help me.
*I don't want to help him because he has helped me so often in the past.

(b)
I love my daughter. If you hurt her, I'll kill you.
*I love my daughter. If you hurt her, I'll kiss you.

(c)
If I help you now, then you must promise to help me.
*If I help you now, then you must promise to never help me.

(d)
He gave her something expecting nothing in return; she was touched.
*He gave her something expecting nothing in return; she was enraged.

(e)
She paid $5 for the book because the book was more valuable to her than $5.
*She paid $5 for the book because the book was less valuable to her than $5.

that there should be a creature in the world to whom a nestful of eggs was not the utterly fascinating and precious and never-to-be-too-much-sat-upon object which it is to her. (James, 1890)

For exactly this reason, intuition is an unreliable guide to points of interest in the human mind. Functionally specialized reasoning circuits will make certain inferences intuitive – so "natural" that there doesn't seem to be any phenomenon that is in need of explanation.

Consider, for example, sentences (1) and (2):

(1) If he's the victim of an unlucky tragedy, then we should pitch in to help him out.

(2) If he spends his time loafing and living off of others, then he doesn't deserve our help.

The inferences they express seem perfectly natural; there seems to be nothing to explain. They may not always be applicable, but they are perfectly intelligible.

But consider sentences (3) and (4):

*(3) If he's the victim of an unlucky tragedy, then he doesn't deserve our help.

*(4) If he spends his time loafing and living off of others, then we should pitch in to help him out.

Sentences (3) and (4) sound eccentric in a way that (1) and (2) do not. Yet they involve no *logical* contradictions. The inferences they embody seem to violate a grammar of social reasoning –

in much the same way that "Alice might slowly" violates the grammar of English but "Alice might come" does not (Cosmides, 1985; Cosmides & Tooby, 1989, 1992). If so, then one needs to look for a reasoning device that can reliably generate (1) and (2) without also generating (3) and (4).

Realizing that *not* generating (3) and (4) is a design feature of the mechanism is tricky, however. Precisely because the device in question does not spontaneously generate inferences like (3) and (4), we rarely notice their absence or feel the need to explain it. And that is the root of the problem. There is a complex pattern to the inferences we generate, but seeing it requires a contrast between figure and ground; the geometry of a snowflake disappears against a white background. "Unnatural" inferences form the high contrast background necessary to see the complex geometry of the inferences that we do spontaneously generate. Yet these "unnatural" inferences are exactly the ones we don't produce. Without this background, the pattern can't be seen. As a result, we look neither for the pattern, nor for the mechanisms that generate it. And no one guesses that our central processes instantiate domain-specific grammars every bit as rich as that of a natural language (for more examples, see Table 5).

Hidden Grammars

In the study of language, a grammar is defined as a finite set of rules that is capable of generating all the sentences of a language without generating any non-sentences; a sentence is defined as a string of words that members of a linguistic community would judge as well formed. In the study of reasoning, a grammar is a finite set of rules that can generate all appropriate inferences while not simultaneously generating inappropriate ones. If it is a grammar of social reasoning, then these inferences are about the domain of social motivation and behavior; an "inappropriate" inference is defined as one that members of a social community would judge as incomprehensible or nonsensical.[10]

The cornerstone of any computational theory of the problem of language acquisition is the specification of a grammar. Discovering the grammar of a human language is so difficult, however, that there is an entire field – linguistics – devoted to the task. The task is difficult precisely because our linguistic inferences are generated by a "language instinct" (Pinker, 1994). One thing this set of specialized circuits can do is distinguish grammatical from ungrammatical sentences. But the rules that generate sentences – the grammar itself – operate effortlessly and automatically, hidden from our conscious awareness. Indeed, these complex rules are so opaque that just 40 years ago most linguists thought each human language – English, Chinese, Setswana – had a completely different grammar. Only recently have these grammars been recognized as minor variants on a Universal Grammar (UG): an invariant set of rules embodied in the brains of all human beings who are not neurologically impaired (Chomsky, 1980; Pinker, 1994).[11]

Universal grammars of social reasoning are invisible to cognitive scientists now for the same reason that UG was invisible to linguists for such a long time. The fact that the internal operations of the computational machinery in question are automatic and unconscious is a contributing factor; but the causes of invisibility go even deeper.

Instinct Blindness

UG is a small corner of hypothesis space; there are an indefinitely large number of grammars that are *not* variants of UG. To explain the fact that all natural languages fall within the bounds of UG, one must first realize that UG exists. To realize that it exists, one must realize that there are alternative grammars.

But this last step is where our imagination stumbles. The language instinct structures our thought so powerfully that alternative grammars are difficult to imagine. This is not an incidental feature of the language instinct; it is the language acquisition device's (LAD) principal adaptive function.[12] Any set of utterances a child hears is consistent with an infinite number of possible grammars, but only one of them is the grammar of its native language. A content-free learning mechanism would be forever lost in hypothesis space. The LAD is an adaptation to combinatorial explosion: by restricting the child's grammatical imagination to a very small subset of hypothesis space – hypotheses consistent with the principles of UG – it makes language acquisition possible. Its function is to generate grammatical inferences consistent with UG *without simultaneously* generating inconsistent ones. To do this, the LAD's structure must make alternative grammars literally unimaginable (at least by the language faculty).

This is good for the child learning language, but bad for the cognitive scientist, who needs to imagine these unimaginable grammars. Forming the plural through mirror reversal – so that the plural of "cat" is "tac" – is a rule in an alternative grammar. No child considers this possibility; the LAD cannot generate this rule. The cognitive scientist needs to know this, however, in order to characterize UG and produce a correct theory of the LAD's cognitive structure. UG is *what*, an algorithm is *how*. A proposed algorithm can be ruled out, for example, if formal analyses reveal that it produces both the mirror reverse rule and the "add 's' to a stem" rule.

Alternative grammars – and hence Universal Grammar – were difficult to discover because circuits designed to generate only a small subset of all grammatical inferences in the child also do so in the linguist. This property of the language instinct is crucial to its adaptive function. But it caused a form of theoretical blindness in linguists, which obstructed the discovery of UG and of the language instinct itself. One can think of this phenomenon as *instinct blindness*.

Discovering a grammar of social reasoning is likely to prove just as difficult as discovering the grammar of a language, and for exactly the same reasons. Yet there is no field, parallel to linguistics, that is devoted to this task; indeed, very few individuals even recognize the need for such a grammar, let alone such a field (for exceptions, see Cosmides, 1985; Cosmides & Tooby, 1989, 1992; Fiske, 1991; Jackendoff, 1992).

Our intuitions blind us not only to the existence of instincts, but to their complexity. The phenomenal experience of an activity as "easy" or "natural" often leads scientists to assume that the processes that give rise to it are simple.

Legend has it that in the early days of artificial intelligence, Marvin Minsky assigned the development of machine vision to a graduate student as a summer project. This illusion of simplicity hampered vision research for years:

> ... in the 1960s almost no one realized that machine vision was difficult. The field had to go through [a series of fiascoes] before it was at last realized that here were some problems that had to be taken seriously. The reason for this misperception is that we humans are ourselves so good at vision. (Marr, 1982, p. 16)

Phenomenally, seeing seems simple. It is effortless, automatic, reliable, fast, unconscious and requires no explicit instruction. But seeing is effortless, automatic, reliable, fast, and unconscious precisely because there is a vast array of complex, dedicated computational machinery that makes this possible.

Most cognitive scientists don't realize it, but they are grossly underestimating the complexity of our central processes. To find someone beautiful, to fall in love, to feel jealous, to experience moral outrage, to fear disease, to reciprocate a favor, to initiate an attack, to deduce a tool's function from its shape – and a myriad other cognitive accomplishments – can seem as simple and automatic and effortless as opening your eyes and seeing. But this apparent simplicity is possible only because there is a vast array of complex computational machinery supporting and regulating these activities, the human cognitive architecture probably embodies a large number of domain-specific "grammars", targeting not just the domain of social life, but also disease, botany, tool-making, animal behavior, foraging and many other situations that our hunter-gatherer ancestors had to cope with on a regular basis.

Research on the computational machinery responsible for these kinds of inferences, choices and preferences – especially the social ones – is almost totally absent in the cognitive sciences. This is a remarkable omission, from an evolutionary point of view. Instinct blindness is one culprit; extreme and unfounded claims about cultural relativity is another (e.g., Brown, 1991; Sperber, 1982; Tooby & Cosmides, 1992).

Anthropological Malpractice

As a result of the rhetoric of anthropologists, most cognitive researchers have, as part of their standard intellectual furniture, a confidence that cultural relativity is an empirically established

finding of wide applicability (see discussion of the Standard Social Science Model in Tooby & Cosmides, 1992). Consequently, most scientists harbor the incorrect impression that there is no "Universal Grammar" of social reasoning to be discovered. According to this view, a grammar of social reasoning might exist in each culture, but these grammars will differ dramatically and capriciously from one culture to the next. In its most extreme form, the relativist position holds that the grammars of different cultures are utterly incommensurate – that there is no transformation that can map the rules of one onto the rules of another. If so, then these rules cannot be expressions of an underlying UG of social reasoning.

Among anthropologists, however, cultural relativism is an interpretation imposed as an article of faith – not a conclusion based on scientific data (Brown, 1991; Sperber, 1982; Tooby & Cosmides, 1992).[13] Indeed, Maurice Bloch, a prominent member of the field, has complained that it is the "professional malpractice of anthropologists to exaggerate the exotic character of other cultures" (Bloch, 1977). To some degree, this is a self-legitimizing institutional pressure: why go long distances to study things that could be studied at home (Brown, 1991)? More importantly, however, anthropologists are just as oblivious to what is universally natural for the human mind as the rest of us. Their attention is drawn to what differs from culture to culture, not what is absent from all cultures or what differs from species to species. Drawing on their cognitive instincts, they understand, automatically and without reflection, much of what happens in other cultures. They know they can work out exchanges without language, or see a smile, a shared look, or an aggressive gesture and infer its meaning and its referent. Indeed, they operate within a huge set of implicit panhuman assumptions that allow them to decode the residue of human life that does differ from place to place (Sperber, 1982; Tooby & Cosmides, 1992).

The notion of universal human reasoning instincts – including social reasoning instincts – is completely compatible with the ethnographic record. It is more than empirically reasonable; it is a logical necessity, for the reasons discussed above. Indeed, without universal reasoning instincts, the acquisition of one's "culture" would be literally impossible, because one wouldn't be able to infer which representations, out of the infinite universe of possibilities, existed in the minds of other members of the culture (Boyer, 1994; Chomsky, 1980; Sperber, 1985, 1990; Tooby & Cosmides, 1992).

Instinct blindness is a side-effect of any instinct whose function is to generate some inferences or behaviors without simultaneously generating others. This is a very general property of instincts, because combinatorial explosion is a very general selection pressure (for discussion, see Tooby & Cosmides, 1992). The fact that human instincts are difficult for human minds to discover is a side-effect of their adaptive function.

Many aspects of the human mind can't be seen by the naked "I" – by intuition unaided by theory. A good theory rips away the veil of naturalness and familiarity that our own minds create, exposing computational problems whose existence we never even imagined. The cognitive sciences need theoretical guidance that is grounded in something beyond intuition. Otherwise, we're flying blind.

Corrective Lenses

There are various ways of overcoming instinct blindness. One of the most common is the study of non-human minds that differ profoundly from our own – animal minds and electronic minds, broody hens and AI programs. Linguists were awakened to the existence of alternative grammars by the creation of computer "languages", which are not variants of UG. These languages "made the natural seem strange", inspiring linguists to generate even stranger grammars. To do this, they had to escape the confines of their intuitions, which they did through the use of mathematical logic and the theory of computation. In William James's terms, they debauched their minds with learning.

The study of animal behavior is another time-honored method for debauching the mind – the one used by William James himself. Hermaphroditic worms, colonies of ant sisters who come in three "genders" (sterile workers, soldiers, queens), male langur monkeys who commit systematic infanticide when they join a troop, flies who are attracted to the smell of dung, polyandrous jacanas who mate with a male after breaking the eggs he was incubating for a rival female, fish who change sex when the composition of their social group changes, female praying mantises who eat their mate's head while copulating with him – other animals engage in behaviors that truly are exotic by human standards. Human cultural variation is trivial in comparison. Observing behaviors

caused by alternative instincts jars us into recognizing the specificity and multiplicity of our own instincts.

Observations like these tell us what we are not, but not what we are. That's why theoretical biology is so important. It provides positive theories of what kinds of cognitive programs we should expect to find in species that evolved under various ecological conditions: theories of what and why. Evolutionary biology's formal theories are powerful lenses that correct for instinct blindness. In their focus, the intricate outlines of the mind's design stand out in sharp relief.

Notes

1 Similar results emerge from the cognitive sciences. Although artificial intelligence researchers have been working for decades on computer vision, object recognition, color constancy, speech recognition and comprehension, and many other evolved competences of humans, naturally selected computational systems still far outperform artificial systems on the adaptive problems they evolved to solve – on those rare occasions when artificial systems can solve the assigned tasks at all. In short, natural selection is known to produce cognitive machinery of an intricate functionality as yet unmatched by the deliberate application of modern engineering. This is a far more definable standard than "optimality" – where many anti-adaptationist arguments go awry. There are an uncountable number of changes that could conceivably be introduced into the design of organisms and, consequently, the state space of potential organic designs is infinitely large and infinitely dimensioned. Thus, there is no way of defining an "optimal" point in it, much less "measuring" how closely evolution brings organisms to it. However, when definable engineering standards of functionality are applied, adaptations can be shown to be very functionally designed for solving *adaptive* problems.

2 All traits that comprise species-typical designs can be partitioned into adaptations, which are present because they were selected for, by-products, which are present because they are causally coupled to traits that were selected for, and noise, which was injected by the stochastic components of evolution. Like other machines, only narrowly defined aspects of organisms fit together into functional systems: most of the system is incidental to the functional properties. Unfortunately, some have misrepresented the well-supported claim that selection organizes organisms very functionally as the obviously

false claim that all traits of organisms are functional – something no sensible evolutionary biologist would ever maintain. Nevertheless, cognitive scientists need to recognize that while not everything in the designs of organisms is the product of selection, all complex functional organization is (Dawkins, 1986; Pinker & Bloom, 1990; Tooby & Cosmides, 1990a, 1990b, 1992; Williams, 1966, 1985).

3   Had Marr known about the importance of cheating in evolutionary analyses of social exchange, he might have been able to understand other features of the cash register as well. Most cash registers have anti-cheating devices. Cash drawers lock until a new set of prices is punched in; two rolls of tape keep track of transactions (one is for the customer; the other rolls into an inaccessible place in the cash register, preventing the clerk from altering the totals to match the amount of cash in the drawer); and so on.

4   Our ancestors spent the last 2 million years as Pleistocene hunter-gatherers (and several hundred million years before that as one kind of forager or another). The few thousand years since the scattered appearance of agriculture is a short stretch, in evolutionary terms (less than 1% of the past 2 million years). Complex designs – ones requiring the coordinated assembly of many novel, functionally integrated features – are built up slowly, change by change, subject to the constraint that each new design feature must solve an adaptive problem better than the previous design (the vertebrate eye is an example). For these and other reasons, it is unlikely that our species evolved complex adaptations even to agriculture, let alone to post-industrial society (for discussion, see Dawkins, 1982; Tooby & Cosmides, 1990a, 1990b).

5   Women ingest thousands of plant toxins every day; embryos self-abort for many reasons; early term abortions are often undetectable; the best trade-off between calories consumed and risk of teratogenesis is obscure.

6   Parsimony applies to number of principles, not number of entities – physicists posit a small number of laws, not a small number of elements, molecules or stellar bodies. Epicycle upon epicycle would have to be added on to evolutionary theory to create a model in which less efficient designs frequently outcompeted more efficient ones.

7   There are strict standards of evidence that must be met before a design feature can be considered an adaptation for performing function X. (1) The design feature must be species-typical; (2) function X must be an *adaptive* problem (i.e., a cross-generationally recurrent problem whose solution would have promoted the design feature's own reproduction); (3) the design feature must reliably develop (in the appropriate morphs) given the developmental circumstances that characterized its environment of evolutionary adaptedness; and, most importantly, (4) it must be shown that the design feature is particularly *well designed for performing function X*, and that it cannot be better explained as a by-product of some other adaptation or physical law. Contrary to popular belief, the following forms of "evidence" are *not* relevant: (1) showing that the design feature has a high heritability; (2) showing that variations in the environment do not affect its development; (3) showing that "learning" plays no role in its development. (Criteria for frequency-dependent adaptations differ. For refinements and complications, see Dawkins, 1982, 1986; Symons, 1992; Tooby & Cosmides, 1992b, 1992; and, especially, Williams, 1966, 1985).

8   For a detailed analysis of the common arguments against the application of evolutionary biology to the study of the human mind, see Tooby and Cosmides (1992).

9   This should not be surprising. Our intuitions were designed to generate adaptive behavior in Pleistocene hunter-gatherers, not useful theories for physicists and cognitive scientists.

10 The similarities between a grammar of language and a grammar of social reasoning run even deeper. Context can make a seemingly ungrammatical sentence grammatical. To pick a standard linguistic example, "The horse raced past the barn fell" seems ungrammatical when "raced" is categorized as the main verb of the sentence, but grammatical if the context indicates that there are two horses. "Fell" is then *recategorized* as the main verb, and "raced" as a passive verb within a prepositional phrase. Context can have the same effect on statements that seem socially ungrammatical. "I'll give you $1000 for your gum wrapper" seems eccentric – ungrammatical – because gum wrappers are considered worthless. It violates a grammatical constraint of social contract theory: that (benefit to offerer) > (cost to offerer) (Cosmides & Tooby, 1989). To become grammatical, the context must cause the violated constraint to be satisfied. For example, recategorizing the gum wrapper as something extremely valuable (potentially justifying the $1000 payment) would do this: the statement seems sensible if you are told that the speaker is a spy who knows the gum wrapper has a microdot with the key for breaking an enemy code.

11 The term "innate" means different things to different scientific communities, but no person who uses the term means "immune to every environmental perturbation". UG is innate in the following sense: its intricate internal organization is the product of our species' genetic

endowment in the same way that the internal organization of the eye is. Its neurological development is buffered against most naturally occurring variations in the physical and social environment. Certain environmental conditions are necessary to trigger the development of UG, but these conditions are not the source of its internal organization. As a result, all normal human beings raised in reasonably normal environments develop the same UG (e.g., Pinker, 1994). For an extensive discussion of how natural selection structures the relationships among genotype, phenotype and environment in development, see Tooby and Cosmides (1992).

12 As a side-effect, it can also solve problems that played no causal role in its selective history. For example, the LAD was not designed to support writing, but its properties made the design and spread of this cultural invention possible.

13 For a history and discussion of how unsupported relativist claims gained widespread acceptance in the social sciences, see Brown (1991) and Tooby and Cosmides (1992).

References

Atran, S. (1990). *The cognitive foundations of natural history*. New York: Cambridge University Press.

Axelrod, R. (1984). *The evolution of cooperation*. New York: Basic Books.

Axelrod, R., & Hamilton, W. D. (1981). The evolution of cooperation. *Science*, **211**, 1390–1396.

Barkow, J., Cosmides, L., & Tooby, J. (Eds.) (1992). *The adapted mind: Evolutionary psychology and the generation of culture*. New York: Oxford University Press.

Baron-Cohen, S., Leslie, A., & Frith, U. (1985). Does the autistic child have a "theory of mind"? *Cognition*, **21**, 37–46.

Bloch, M. (1977). The past and the present in the present. *Man*, **12**, 278–292.

Boyd, R. (1988). Is the repeated prisoner's dilemma a good model of reciprocal altruism? *Ethology and Sociobiology*, **9**, 211–222.

Boyer, P. (1994). *The naturalness of religious ideas*. Berkeley: University of California Press.

Brothers, I. (1990). The social brain: A project for integrating primate behavior and neurophysiology in a new domain. *Concepts in Neuroscience*, **9**, 27–51.

Brown, A. (1990). Domain-specific principles affect learning and transfer in children. *Cognitive Science*, **14**, 107–133.

Brown, D. E. (1991). *Human universals*. New York: McGraw-Hill.

Carey, S. (1985). Constraints on semantic development. In J. Mehler & R. Fox (Eds.), *Neonate cognition* (pp. 381–398). Hillsdale, NJ: Erlbaum.

Carey, S., & Gelman, R. (Eds.) (1991). *The epigenesis of mind*. Hillsdale, NJ: Erlbaum.

Cheney, D. L., & Seyfarth, R. (1990). *How monkeys see the world*. Chicago: University of Chicago Press.

Cheng, P., Holyoak, K., Nisbett, R., & Oliver, L. (1986). Pragmatic versus syntactic approaches to training deductive reasoning. *Cognitive Psychology*, **18**, 293–328.

Chomsky, N. (1980). *Rules and representations*. New York: Columbia University Press.

Clutton-Brock, T. H., & Harvey, P. (1979). Comparison and adaptation. *Proceedings of the Royal Society, London B*, **205**, 547–565.

Cook, E. W., III, Hodes, R. L., & Lang, P. J. (1986). Preparedness and phobia: Effects of stimulus content on human visceral conditioning. *Journal of Abnormal Psychology*, **95**, 195–207.

Cook, M., & Mineka, S. (1989). Observational conditioning of fear to fear-relevant versus fear-irrelevant stimuli in rhesus monkeys. *Journal of Abnormal Psychology*, **98**, 448–459.

Cosmides, L. (1985). Deduction or Darwinian algorithms? An explanation of the "elusive" content effect on the Wason selection task. Doctoral dissertation. Department of Psychology. Harvard University. University Microfilms #86-02206.

Cosmides, L. (1989). The logic of social exchange: Has natural selection shaped how humans reason? Studies with the Wason selection task. *Cognition*, **31**, 187–276.

Cosmides, L., & Tooby, J. (1987). From evolution to behavior: Evolutionary psychology as the missing link. In J. Dupre (Ed.), *The latest on the best: Essays on evolution and optimality*. Cambridge, MA: MIT Press.

Cosmides, L., & Tooby, J. (1992). Evolutionary psychology and the generation of culture, Part II. Case study: A computational theory of social exchange. *Ethology and Sociobiology*, **10**, 51–97.

Cosmides, L., & Tooby, J. (1992). Cognitive adaptations for social exchange. In J. Barkow, L. Cosmides, & J. Tooby (Eds.). *The adapted mind: Evolutionary psychology and the generation of culture*. New York: Oxford University Press.

Cosmides, L., & Tooby, J. (1994). Origins of domain specificity: The evolution of functional organization. In S. Gelman & L. Hirschfeld (Eds.). *Mapping the mind: Domain specificity in cognition and culture*. New York: Cambridge University Press.

Cosmides, L., & Tooby, J. (1996). Are humans good intuitive statisticians after all? Rethinking some conclusions of the literature on judgment under uncertainty. *Cognition*, **58**, 1–73.

Daly, M., & Wilson, M. (1983). *Sex, evolution and behavior*. Boston: Wadsworth.

Daly, M., & Wilson, M. (1988). *Homicide*, Hawthorne, NY: Aldine de Gruyter.

Daly, M., & Wilson, M. (1994). Discriminative parental solicitude and the relevance of evolutionary models to the analysis of motivational systems. In M. Gazzaniga (Ed.), *The cognitive neurosciences.* Cambridge, MA: MIT Press.

Dawkins, R. (1982). *The extended phenotype.* Oxford: W. H. Freeman.

Dawkins, R. (1986). *The blind watchmaker.* New York: Norton.

de Waal, F. B. M., & Luttrell, L. M. (1988). Mechanisms of social reciprocity in three primate species: Symmetrical relationship characteristics or cognition? *Ethology and Sociobiology, 9,* 101–118.

Fischer, E. A. (1988). Simultaneous hermaphroditism, tit-for-tat, and the evolutionary stability of social systems. *Ethology and Sociobiology, 9,* 119–136.

Fiske, A. P. (1991). *Structures of social life: The four elementary forms of human relations.* New York: Free Press.

Fodor, J. A. (1983). *The modularity of mind.* Cambridge, MA: MIT Press.

Frith, U. (1989). *Autism: Explaining the enigma.* Oxford: Blackwell.

Gallistel, C. R. (1990). *The organization of learning.* Cambridge, MA: MIT Press.

Gallistel, C. R., Brown, A. L., Carey, S., Gelman, R., & Keil, F. C. (1991). Lessons from animal learning for the study of cognitive development. In S. Carey & R. Gelman (Eds.), *The epigenesis of mind.* Hillsdale, NJ: Erlbaum.

Garcia, J. (1990). Learning without memory. *Journal of Cognitive Neuroscience, 2,* 287–305.

Gelman, S., & Hirschfeld, L. (Eds.) (1994). *Mapping the mind: Domain specificity in cognition and culture.* New York: Cambridge University Press.

Gigerenzer, G., Hoffrage, U., & Kleinbolting, H. (1991). Probabilistic mental models: A Brunswikean theory of confidence. *Psychological Review, 98,* 506–528.

Gigerenzer, G., & Hug, K. (1992). Domain-specific reasoning: Social contracts, cheating and perspective change. *Cognition, 43,* 127–171.

Gould, J. L. (1982). *Ethology: The mechanisms and evolution of behavior.* New York: Norton.

Gould, S. J., & Lewontin, R. C. (1979). The spandrels of San Marco and the Panglossian paradigm: A critique of the adaptationist programme. *Proceedings of the Royal Society, London B, 205,* 581–598.

Jackendoff, R. (1992). *Languages of the mind.* Cambridge, MA: MIT Press.

James, W. (1890). *Principles of psychology.* New York: Henry Holt.

Keil, F. C. (1989). *Concepts, kinds, and cognitive development.* Cambridge, MA: MIT Press.

Krebs, J. R., & Davies, N. B. (1987). *An introduction to behavioural ecology.* Oxford: Blackwell Scientific Publications.

Leslie, A. M. (1987). Pretense and representation: The origins of "theory of mind". *Psychological Review, 94,* 412–426.

Leslie, A. M. (1988). The necessity of illusion: Perception and thought in infancy. In L. Weiskrantz (Ed.), *Thought without language* (pp. 185–210). Oxford: Clarendon Press.

Manktelow, K. I., & Evans, J. St.B. T. (1979). Facilitation of reasoning by realism: Effect or non-effect? *British Journal of Psychology, 70,* 477–488.

Manktelow, K. I., & Over, D. E. (1990). Deontic thought and the selection task. In K. J. Gilhooly, M. T. G. Keane, R. H. Logie, & G. Erdos (Eds.), *Lines of thinking* (Vol. 1). Chichester: Wiley.

Markman, E. M. (1989). *Categorization and naming in children: Problems of induction.* Cambridge, MA: MIT Press.

Markman, E. (1990). Constraints children place on word meanings. *Cognitive Science, 14,* 57–77.

Marler, P. (1991). The instinct to learn. In S. Carey & R. Gelman (Eds.), *The epigenesis of mind.* Hillsdale, NJ: Erlbaum.

Marr, D. (1982). *Vision: A computational investigation into the human representation and processing of visual information.* San Francisco: Freeman.

Mayr, E. (1983). How to carry out the adaptationist program? *The American Naturalist, 121,* 324–334.

McDougall, W. (1908/1916). *Introduction to social psychology.* Boston: John W. Luce.

Mineka, S., & Cook, M. (1988). Social learning and the acquisition of snake fear in monkeys. In T. R. Zentall & B. G. Galef (Eds.), *Social learning: Psychological and biological perspectives* (pp. 51–73). Hillsdale, NJ: Erlbaum.

Ohman, A., Dimberg, U., & Ost, L. G. (1985). Biological constraints on the fear response. In S. Reiss & R. Bootsin (Eds.), *Theoretical issues in behavior therapy* (pp. 123–175). New York: Academic Press.

Ohman, A., Eriksson, A., & Olofsson, A. (1975). One-trial learning and superior resistance to extinction of autonomic responses conditioned to potentially phobic stimuli. *Journal of Comparative and Physiological Psychology, 88,* 619–627.

Pinker, S. (1994). *The language instinct.* New York: Morrow.

Pinker, S., & Bloom, P. (1990). Natural language and natural selection. *Behavioral and Brain Sciences, 13,* 707–727.

Profet, M. (1992). Pregnancy sickness as adaptation: A deterrent to maternal ingestion of teratogens. In J. Barkow, L. Cosmides, & J. Tooby (Eds.), *The adapted mind: Evolutionary psychology and the generation of culture.* New York: Oxford University Press.

Pylyshyn, Z. W. (Ed.) (1987). *The robot's dilemma: The frame problem in artificial intelligence,* Norwood, NJ: Ablex.

Real, L. A. (1991). Animal choice behavior and the evolution of cognitive architecture. *Science, 253,* 980–986.

Rozin, P. (1976). The evolution of intelligence and access to the cognitive unconscious. In J. M. Sprague & A. N. Epstein (Eds.), *Progress in psychobiology and physiological psychology*. New York: Academic Press.

Shepard, R. N. (1981). Psychophysical complementarity. In M. Kubovy & J. Pomerantz (Eds.), *Perceptual organization*. Hillsdale, NJ: Erlbaum.

Shepard, R. N. (1987). Evolution of a mesh between principles of the mind and regularities of the world. In J. Dupre (Ed.), *The latest on the best: Essays on evolution and optimality*. Cambridge, MA: MIT Press.

Sherry, D. F., & Schacter, D. L. (1987). The evolution of multiple memory systems. *Psychological Review, 94*, 439–454.

Smuts, B. (1986). *Sex and friendship in baboons*. Hawthorne: Aldine.

Spelke, E. S. (1988). The origins of physical knowledge. In L. Weiskrantz (Ed.), *Thought without language* (pp. 168–184). Oxford: Clarendon Press.

Spelke, E. (1990). Principles of object perception. *Cognitive Science, 14*, 29–56.

Sperber, D. (1975). *Rethinking symbolism*, transl. Alice Morton. Cambridge, UK: Cambridge University Press.

Sperber, D. (1982). *On anthropological knowledge*, Cambridge, UK: Cambridge University Press.

Sperber, D. (1985). Anthropology and psychology: Towards an epidemiology of representations. *Man (N. S.), 20*, 73–89.

Sperber, D. (1990). The epidemiology of beliefs. In C. Fraser & G. Geskell (Eds.), *Psychological studies of widespread beliefs*. Oxford: Clarendon Press.

Sperber, D. (1994). The modularity of thought and the epidemiology of representations. In S. Gelman & L. Hirschfeld (Eds.), *Mapping the mind: Domain specificity in cognition and culture*, New York: Cambridge University Press.

Symons, D. (1979). *The evolution of human sexuality*. New York: Oxford University Press.

Symons, D. (1992). On the use and misuse of Darwinism in the study of human behavior. In J. Barkow, L. Cosmides, & J. Tooby (Eds.), *The adapted mind: Evolutionary psychology and the generation of culture*. New York: Oxford University Press.

Tooby, J., & Cosmides, L. (1989). The logic of threat: Evidence for another cognitive adaptation? Paper presented at the Human Behavior and Evolution Society, Evanston, IL.

Tooby, J., & Cosmides, L. (1990a). The past explains the present: Emotional adaptations and the structure of ancestral environments. *Ethology and Sociobiology, 11*, 375–424.

Tooby, J., & Cosmides, L. (1990b). On the universality of human nature and the uniqueness of the individual: The role of genetics and adaptation. *Journal of Personality, 58*, 17–67.

Tooby, J., & Cosmides, L. (1992). The psychological foundations of culture. In J. Barkow, L. Cosmides, & J. Tooby (Eds.), *The adapted mind: Evolutionary psychology and the generation of culture*. New York: Oxford University Press.

Tooby J., & DeVore, I. (1987). The reconstruction of hominid behavioral evolution through strategic modeling. In W. Kinzey (Ed.), *Primate models of hominid behavior*. New York: SUNY Press.

Trivers, R. L. (1971). The evolution of reciprocal altruism. *Quarterly Review of Biology, 46*, 35–57.

Wason, P. (1966). Reasoning. In B. M. Foss (Ed.), *New horizons in psychology*. Harmondsworth: Penguin.

Wason, P. (1983). Realism and rationality in the selection task. In J. St. B. T. Evans (Ed.), *Thinking and reasoning: Psychological approaches*. London: Routledge & Kegan Paul.

Wason, P., & Johnson-Laird, P. N. (1972). *Psychology of reasoning: Structure and content*. London: Batsford.

Wilkinson, G. S. (1988). Reciprocal altruism in bats and other mammals. *Ethology and Sociobiology, 9*, 85–100.

Wilkinson, G. S. (1990). Food sharing in vampire bats. *Scientific American*, February, 76–82.

Williams, G. C. (1966). *Adaptation and natural selection: A critique of some current evolutionary thought*. Princeton: Princeton University Press.

Williams, G. C. (1985). A defense of reductionism in evolutionary biology. *Oxford surveys in evolutionary biology, 2*, 1–27.

Williams, G. C., & Nesse, R. M. (1991). The dawn of Darwinian medicine. *Quarterly Review of Biology, 66*, 1–22.

Wilson, M., & Daly, M. (1992). The man who mistook his wife for a chattel. In J. Barkow, L. Cosmides, & J. Tooby (Eds.), *The adapted mind: Evolutionary psychology and the generation of culture*. New York: Oxford University Press.

Wynn, K. (1992). Addition and subtraction by human infants. *Nature, 358*, 749–750.

Chapter 42: Use or Misuse of the Selection Task? Rejoinder to Fiddick, Cosmides, and Tooby

DAN SPERBER AND VITTORIO GIROTTO

1. Introduction

Why has Wason's selection task (Wason, 1966)[1] been, for almost 40 years, so extensively used in psychology of reasoning? Because it has a simple, logically compelling solution, and yet, in most versions, most participants fail to solve it. Philosophers have seen this as highly relevant evidence in assessing human rationality (e.g., Stein, 1996). Psychologists have found ways of improving participants' performance, in particular by changing the narrative content of the task, and have offered various interpretations of these results. Selection task data have thus been garnered in support of various general claims about human reasoning.

In particular, Leda Cosmides, John Tooby, and their collaborators have, over the past 20 years, performed a variety of original selection task experiments to establish the existence of evolved domain-specific reasoning mechanisms. Their most famous, best developed hypothesis concerns the existence of a "social contract algorithm," one subcomponent of which is a cheater detection device (Cosmides, 1989; Cosmides & Tooby, 1989, 1992, 1997; Fiddick, Cosmides, & Tooby, 2000). They define a social contract as a situation in which one party is obligated to satisfy a requirement in order to be entitled to receive a benefit from another party, and they define cheating as the taking of the benefit without satisfying the requirement. A social contract situation can be depicted in a selection task by means of cards representing on one side whether or not the benefit has been taken and on the other side whether or not the requirement has

been satisfied. A cheater detection device should favor the selection of the "benefit taken" and of the "requirement not satisfied" cards, either of which could turn out to correspond to a case of cheating. This is indeed what a majority of participants select in the social contract situations used in the experiments of Cosmides, Tooby, and their collaborators. The selection task thus seems to provide crucial data in favor of the evolutionary psychology approach of which Tooby and Cosmides have been the most articulate exponents.

Although many researchers clearly believe that the selection task provides appropriate evidence for general claims about human reasoning, no such claim has ever been accepted by the scientific community on the basis of such evidence. Rather, what seems to drive the continuous production of selection task experiments is that their interpretations can be endlessly contested by means of further experiments with the task. This in itself would be reason enough to question the reasonableness of the proliferation of research based on the selection task of which the work of Cosmides, Tooby, and their collaborators is a striking example. Moreover, Sperber, Cara, and Girotto (1995) (henceforth SCG) have put forward an analysis of the task itself that casts principled doubts on its scientific utility.

SCG argued that, in the selection task, relevance-guided comprehension mechanisms tend to pre-empt the use of whatever domain-general or domain-specific reasoning mechanisms people are endowed with.[2] In support of this claim, they showed how to manipulate relevance factors in descriptive versions of the task so as to elicit more than 50% correct responses (a rate of success normally found with deontic rather than descriptive versions). Girotto, Kemmelmeir, Sperber, and van der Henst (2001) provided further evidence by manipulating relevance factors in deontic versions so as to elicit more than 80% incorrect responses (a rate of failure normally found with descriptive rather than deontic versions). The only challenge to SCG purporting to contain counterevidence has been Fiddick et al. (2000) (henceforth FCT). What we aim to do here is rebut FCT's central theoretical argument (what they call the "principle of pre-emptive specificity") and demonstrate a methodological flaw in their experimental evidence. We hope that this will be enough to vindicate and indeed reinforce our earlier warnings against basing any important claim in the psychology of reasoning on Wason selection task data (other issues raised by FCT are discussed in Sperber & Girotto, in press; see also Atran, 2000).

1.1. Comprehension, Reasoning, and the Order of Pre-emption

According to most modern pragmatics, comprehension is an inferential process that takes as input an utterance and contextual information, and that produces as output an interpretation of the speaker's meaning. Comprehension is an attribution of a mental state to the speaker, a form of mind-reading. According to relevance theory in particular, this comprehension process consists of developing an interpretation that satisfies the expectation of relevance raised by the utterance itself. This process is specific to comprehension. If mind-reading is viewed as a module of the human mind, then comprehension can be viewed as a sub-module (Sperber, 2000; Sperber & Wilson, 2002). Cheater detection too is presented by FCT as a sub-module of the social contract algorithm. Let us accept, for the sake of discussion, that the normally developed human mind is equipped with both a comprehension mechanism and a cheater detection mechanism. What happens when participants in an experiment are verbally presented with a selection task involving a social contract, that is, with an input that could, in principle, activate both the comprehension and the cheater detection mechanisms? This is where SCG and FCT give almost diametrically opposed answers.

SCG argued that, in Wason's selection task, pragmatic comprehension mechanisms tend to pre-empt the use of whatever domain-general or domain-specific reasoning mechanisms people may be endowed with (and this is what makes the selection task an inappropriate tool to study reasoning). FCT claim on the contrary that the more specialized mechanism will pre-empt the less specialized mechanism and in particular cheater detection will pre-empt inferential comprehension.

FCT's (p. 24) main argument is this: "a well-engineered problem-solving system should deploy, to the extent possible, the most specialized problem-solving machinery that is activated by the problem at hand, because on average, it will be more knowledgeable than the alternative, more general problem-solvers that also apply [...] This principle of cognitive design – what we will call the *principle of pre-emptive specificity* – should be expressed in design features throughout the cognitive architecture. It applies to the problems herein. Social contract algorithms and hazard management algorithms are more content-specialized than relevance mechanisms, whose domain is all content that arrives via communication from an agent." While this argument has obvious merits, it ignores essential design factors. Some mechanisms accept as input the output of other mechanisms. Whatever their relative degree of specialization, the receiver mechanism cannot prevent the feeder mechanism from performing its operations. In fact, without the output of the feeder mechanism, the receiver mechanism would have no input to process.

In order to recognize a verbally presented reasoning problem, whatever the domain-general or domain-specific reasoning mechanism they may ultimately bring to bear on its solution, participants must first comprehend the text of the problem and, for this, use their comprehension mechanism. According to relevance theory, comprehending a text involves grasping its intended relevance, and this involves a meaning construction process that often goes beyond or away from strict literal meaning. With standard reasoning problems, participants are presented with verbal premises and are explicitly asked to infer or evaluate conclusions. Their understanding of the premises may be biased by comprehension factors (for a review, see Evans, Newstead, & Byrne, 1993; for illustrations, e.g. Begg & Harris, 1982; Politzer, 1990), but, at least, it is clear that they must engage in a reasoning effort, over and above comprehension proper.

The selection task is not a standard reasoning problem. Participants are not asked to reason from premises to conclusions, and they are not even told that the question they are asked can best be answered by making use of deductive reasoning. Participants are just asked to evaluate the relevance of one part of the problem (the cards) to another part of the problem (the conditional rule). What SCG argued is that the intuitions of relevance arrived at in the process of comprehending a selection task problem provide what looks like an intuitive solution to the problem itself. So, it is not just that comprehension will take place anyhow. It is that, in the particular case of the selection task, there is no incentive, for most participants, to engage in further active reasoning of either a general or a domain-specific kind, in order to find the solution to the problem.

Our answer to FCT is therefore, firstly, that there is no way that a cheater detection mechanism could pre-empt a comprehension mechanism in the processing of a selection task problem, since, anyhow, the problem must first be comprehended. Secondly, the comprehension mechanism automatically provides what looks like a solution to the selection task. It may well – and does for a majority of participants – pre-empt any further reasoning processes.

1.2. Distinguishing the Wason Selection Task from the FCT Selection Task

As SCG (p. 42) pointed out, a number of past experiments with deontic tasks (e.g. Cosmides, 1989; Light, Girotto, & Legrenzi, 1990; Manktelow & Over, 1991) suffered from a methodological defect. Participants were simultaneously asked, not one, but two questions: the standard Wason task question of whether the conditional rule had been obeyed or violated and the direct question of whether some cheating had taken place (or worse, they were asked just the question about cheating). Answering correctly the first question is performing successfully on Wason's selection task, but answering correctly the second question is not: it demonstrates just the ability to identify a cheater on the basis of the information provided in the problem narrative. FCT (p. 15) themselves point out the difference. They write: "Note that the definition of cheating *does not map onto the logical definition of violation* (the latter being a true antecedent paired with a false consequent). Cheating is a content-dependent concept: there must be an illicitly taken *benefit*. This, and only this, counts as cheating. Logical categories and definitions of viola-

tion form an orthogonal representational dimension." This should make them wary of using as evidence data obtained with the two questions, that of cheating and that of violation posed simultaneously.

For instance, in one of the problems used in Experiments 2 and 4 in Cosmides (1989), participants were asked "Did Big Kiku get away with cheating any of these four men [a question directly about cheating]? Indicate only those card(s) you definitely need to turn over to see if Big Kiku has broken his word to any of these four men [an indirect question about the respect or violation of the conditional rule uttered by Big Kiku]" (Cosmides, 1989, p. 265). This kind of formulation suggests that both questions have the same correct answer and, in fact, in Cosmides' Experiment 2, where the conditional rule was Big Kiku's statement: "if you get a tattoo on your face, then I'll give you cassava root," they do. Big Kiku got away with cheating a man just in case Big Kiku did not do what he said he would do. This correct answer was given by 71% of the participants, but there is no way to decide whether they based their response on the first question ("Did Big Kiku get away with cheating?"), or the second (is it the case that "Big Kiku has broken his word?"), or paid attention to both questions.

In Experiment 4, however, the conditional rule was "switched" to "If I give you cassava root, then you must get a tattoo on your face" (Cosmides, 1989, p. 217). This time, to begin with, both questions become harder to interpret. Strictly understood, Big Kiku's word expresses not a conditional contractual promise (i.e., a commitment to do something conditional on the other party's action), but a requirement that the other party do something (see Legrenzi, Politzer, & Girotto, 1996). Therefore, Big Kiku is not in a position to either cheat or break his word. However – as has long been known in pragmatics (Geis & Zwicky, 1971) – many conditional statements and in particular conditional promises are commonly understood as implying their converse (see e.g. Fillenbaum, 1975; Newstead, Ellis, Evans, & Dennis, 1997). Here Big Kiku's statement can be understood as implying that, if his interlocutor got a tattoo, then he would give him cassava root, making sense of the narrative and of the ideas that Big Kiku might cheat. At this point, of course, the question about cheating, and the Wason task question about whether the conditional rule was violated or not have different answers (that is, if the conditional rule is strictly understood). The correct answer to the Wason task question would be, as always, to select the P and not-Q cards, whereas the correct answer to the cheating question would be to select the not-P and Q cards, which 75% of the participants in Cosmides (1989) did. She took this to show that people use a cheater detection Darwinian algorithm to solve such a Wason selection task. We suggest that this shows that participants answered the cheating question and not the Wason task question, or that they reinterpreted Big Kiku's statement as meaning its converse (in which case both questions result in the same answer).

What is it that makes the Wason task question significantly different from the question about cheating? The Wason task question is about the truth or falsity (in the descriptive versions) or the respect or violation (in the deontic versions) of a conditional rule. The only fail-safe way of answering it involves applying conditional reasoning to four hypothetical cases. The cheating question is not a conditional reasoning question but a categorization question. As explained in detail by Cosmides and her collaborators, cheating is commonly understood as the co-occurrence of the taking of a benefit and the failure to fulfill a requirement, in particular of paying a cost. It is, in other terms, characterized by the conjunction of these two features. In order to answer the cheating question, then, all that participants have to do is select the cards that exhibit one of these two features (and that might have the other characteristic feature on the other side).

More generally, one could devise a categorization task that would use material similar to that used in the Wason selection task, and in particular cards exhibiting one of two possible values for a pair of traits (e.g., *benefit taken* vs. *benefit not taken*, and *requirement fulfilled* vs. *requirement not fulfilled*; or *flying vehicle* vs. *non-flying vehicle*, and *has an engine* vs. *does not have an engine*). Out of the four possible combinations of such trait values, one and only one would determine a given category. For instance the combination *benefit taken + requirement not fulfilled* would determine the category of cheaters, or the combination *flying vehicle + does not have an engine* would determine the category of gliders. Participants would then be asked which of the four cards could turn out to represent an instance of the category. This is what FCT have actually done, devising a task that is superficially similar to the Wason selection task, but that tests for a different cognitive capacity. As we indicated above, in order to distinguish it from the gen-

uine Wason task – something that FCT totally failed to do – we will call this categorization task the "FCT selection task." When both the Wason and the FCT questions are posed in the same problem, as in the Big Kiku example, we speak of a Wason/FCT task.

Is there any reason to think that the FCT selection task is of particular psychological interest? Should we expect people to generally fail at the FCT task, as they do with the Wason task, and to succeed when the material used activates domain-specific evolved mechanisms? We believe not. The FCT task is quite trivial. As we will show, participants perform it without difficulty, even with totally artificial material. It looks interesting only when it is confused with the Wason task, and used without adequate control conditions. As with the Wason selection task, the FCT selection task is inadequate to test the interesting Cosmides (1989) hypothesis that humans are endowed with an evolved mental module to reason about social contracts, or other similar evolutionary psychology hypotheses.

2. Experiment 1

The goal of our first experiment was to check whether the FCT selection task is, as we claimed, trivially easy. Can individuals, if asked to do so, correctly select the cards that might represent an instance not just of cheating, but of any category defined by the combination of a positive and a negative trait?

We devised three conditions: a first condition where the relevant category was explicitly that of cheating defined by the combination of "cost paid" and "benefit not received"; a second condition, with material strictly parallel to the first condition but where the relevant category was an arbitrary one called "Wason's selection" defined by the combination of "food item" and "non-Italian"; and a third condition where the relevant category was that of a glider. Whereas, in the two former conditions, the relevant categories were explicitly defined as the combination of a positive and a negative trait, participants did not receive the definition of "glider." In this experiment, we were comparing a condition of a kind assumed by FCT to provide evidence for the existence of an evolved mental cheating detector, with two conditions where what had to be "detected" was either a made-up arbitrary category, or an ordinary language category of no evolutionary significance and the relevant properties of which were not even mentioned in the text. We predicted that participants would do well in all conditions.

2.1. Method

2.1.1. PARTICIPANTS

A total of 100 humanities undergraduates at Trieste University (Italy) participated in the experiment voluntarily. They were randomly assigned to one of three groups: "look for cheater," "look for Wason's selection," and "look for glider."

2.1.2. PROCEDURE AND MATERIALS

The study was carried out in Italian with native speakers of the language. The participants were tested in groups, but they worked on the problems individually, at their own pace. In the "look for cheater" condition, the problem read as follows:

Paolo often buys things through the Internet, but he is fearful of being cheated. For each order, he fills a card. On one side of the card, he indicates whether he has received the item ordered. On the other side of the card, he indicates whether he has paid for the item ordered.
Paolo puts in a box labeled "Risk of cheating" the cards indicating that he has paid for the item and has not received the item.
Below are four cards, each of which represents a different order. Two cards show the side that indicates whether Paolo has received the item ordered. The two other cards show the side that indicates whether Paolo has paid for the item.

7th December 2000:	14th December 2000:
Item paid for	Item not paid for

29th October 2000:	21st November 2000:
Item received	Item not received

Indicate only the card or cards you definitely need to turn over to see whether, among these cards, there are some cards that Paolo should put in the "Risk of cheating" box.

In the "look for Wason's selection" condition, the problem read as follows:

Paolo often buys things through the Internet. For each order, he fills a card. On one side of the card, he indicates whether the item ord-

ered is food. On the other side of the card, he indicates whether the item ordered is Italian. Paolo puts in a box labeled "Wason's selection" the cards indicating a food item that is not Italian.
Below you find four cards, each of which represents a different order. Two cards show the side that indicates whether the items ordered are food or not. The two other cards show the side that indicates whether the items are Italian or not.

7th December 2000:	14th December 2000:
Food item	Non food item

29th October 2000:	21st November 2000:
Italian item	Non Italian item

Indicate only the card or the cards you definitely need to turn over to see whether, among these cards, there are some cards that Paolo should put in the "Wason's selection" box.

In the "look for gliders" condition, the problem read as follows:

Paolo collects pictures of vehicles. For each vehicle, he fills a card. On one side, he indicates where the vehicle movements take place. On the other side, he indicates whether the vehicle has an engine or not.
Paolo puts in a box labeled "Gliders" the cards representing a glider. Below are four cards, each of which represents a different vehicle. Two cards show the side that indicates where the vehicle movements take place. The two other cards show the side that indicates whether the vehicle has an engine or not.

Vehicle 15	Vehicle 8
Where does it move? In the air	Where does it move? On rails

Vehicle 34	Vehicle 27
Does it have an engine? Yes	Does it have an engine? No

Indicate only the card or cards you definitely need to turn over to see whether, among these cards, there are some cards that Paolo should put in the "Gliders" box.

Table 1: Percentage of the Selection Patterns in the Three Conditions of Experiment 1

	Condition (N)		
Pattern	Look for Cheater (35)	Look for Wason (35)	Look for Glider (30)
P, not-Q	68	91	73
P	6	3	–
P, Q	–	–	13
Not-Q	20	–	10
Not-P, Q	–	3	3
P, not-P, not-Q	6	–	–
All	–	3	–

2.2. Results and Discussion

Table 1 reports the percentages of the selection patterns obtained in the three conditions. As predicted, participants performed well in all conditions. In particular, in the condition in which they were required to look, not for cheaters, but for the arbitrary category of Wason's selection, 91% of them selected the cards corresponding to the P and not-Q features. This rate of correct performance is significantly higher than the one (68%) obtained in the "look for cheater" condition ($\chi^2(1, N = 70) = 4.37, p < 0.05$), and marginally higher than in the "look for glider" condition ($\chi^2(1, N = 65) = 2.7, p < 0.10$).

The fact that the participants' performance is lower in the "look for glider" than in the "look for Wason's selection" condition is readily explained by the fact that the two defining traits of a "Wason's selection" were mentioned in the text of the problem, whereas participants had to know and remember that a glider is a vehicle that moves in air without an engine. This interpretation was confirmed by a replication of the "look for glider" condition, in which we asked participants (20 humanities undergraduates at Trieste University) to justify their selections. The rate of correct performance (65%) was similar to the one obtained in the previous "look for glider" condition, and significantly lower than the one obtained in the "look for Wason" condition ($\chi^2(1, N = 55) = 4.33, p < 0.05$). All but one participant who failed selected only the P card ("vehicle moving on air"). All of them explained that they did not select the not-Q card ("engineless vehicle") because they were not sure whether a glider has an engine or not. Presumably, then, if we had mentioned in the text of the problem the two defining traits of

the relevant category, the performance in the "look for glider" condition would have been higher.

On the other hand, the fact that the participants' performance is lower in the "look for cheater" than in the "look for Wason's selection" condition and is similar to that in the "look for glider" condition is somewhat puzzling, since in the "cheater" condition the two defining traits *were* mentioned. Whatever the explanation of this less-than-perfect performance in the "look for cheater" condition, and whatever the remedies that could be found to improve this performance, the fact remains that, in an FCT task, cheaters are not more easily detected than arbitrary items such as Wason's selections, or items devoid of evolutionary significance such as gliders. As we predicted, participants did well in all three conditions. We would expect participants to do well with any category whatsoever, provided that they knew or were told its defining traits.

3. Experiment 2

Experiment 1 showed that the FCT selection task is trivially easy, and therefore is quite unlike the Wason selection task, in spite of being modeled on it. In their Experiment 1, FCT argue that, in the Wason selection task, people do not reason from the logical form expressed in the conditional rule, as shown by the fact that they perform as well when the logical connective "if...then" is removed. From a pragmatic point of view, we would anyhow agree that logical connectives are not necessary for people to give a conditional interpretation to a text or dialogue. For instance in a dialogue such as:

Child: I want to go out and play!
Mother: You must put on your coat!

the mother's reply is normally understood as meaning implicitly: *If* you want to go out and play, *then* you must put on your coat. The logical form of an utterance need not be wholly explicit, and there is no reason why a proper Wason selection task could not be performed with an implicit rather than an explicit conditional rule. This, however, was not FCT's point.

FCT assumed that if people, in a task describing a social exchange, performed equally well with or without an explicit conditional, this showed that they didn't reason on the conditional logical form, but just on the "logic of social exchange." However, FCT used as evidence not a Wason selection task but an FCT selection task. We would argue that the conditional form, whether it is implicitly retrieved by the participants or not, is anyhow irrelevant to successful performance of an FCT selection task. More specifically, FCT asked participants to indicate the cards they had to turn over "to see whether any of these people [represented by the cards] have cheated you." They compared two conditions, one where the exchange was explicitly described in conditional form, the other where it was not. Since this is an FCT task, we would have predicted that participants would perform equally well in both conditions, as indeed they did. Our claim is that when people are explicitly instructed to identify possible cheaters, they have no problem understanding the instruction and following it. FCT do not consider this simple possibility and argue that when people recognize an exchange situation, and moreover adopt the perspective of one of the two parties to the exchange, then they automatically look for cheaters. If FCT are so confident that this is so, it is hard to understand why they mar their experimental evidence by explicitly asking participants to look for cheaters.

To help decide whether people look for cheaters because they are asked to look for cheaters, or because they are asked to reason about an exchange situation, we performed an FCT experiment with two conditions replicating FCT's own and two other conditions identical in every point, except that participants were not asked to look for instances of cheating, but for instances of exchange. If it is the exchange situation that triggers the selection of the P and not-Q cards representing a possible instance of cheating, then this modification should have little or no effect. If, as we claim, participants in an FCT task trivially do just what they are asked to do, then we should expect participants in the new conditions to select the P and Q cards, which represent possible instances of exchange, more often than the P and not-Q cards, which represent possible instance of cheating.

3.1. Method

3.1.1. PARTICIPANTS

The participants were 120 humanities undergraduates from Trieste University. They were randomly assigned to one of four equal-sized groups: "look for exchange (conditional)," "look for exchange (want)," "look for cheater (conditional)," and "look for cheater (want)" ($N = 30$).

3.1.2. PROCEDURE AND MATERIALS

The same procedure as in Experiment 1 was used. Each participant had to solve one problem. The "look for cheater (conditional)" and "look for cheater (want)" conditions replicated, respectively, the "conditional" and "want" problems of FCT Experiment 1. They read as follows:

> You are a South American farmer. At the end of the harvest you find you have more potatoes than you need so you pack up some of them and travel to the neighboring village. When you get to the village four different people approach you, and though you don't speak the same dialect, you recognize that each of them is telling you:
> "If you give me some potatoes, then I will give you some corn." [conditional version] "I want some potatoes." You, in turn, know a little bit of their dialect, and tell them "I want some corn." [want version]
> The cards below represent four people who approached you. One side of the cards tells whether or not you gave the person any potatoes and the other side of the cards tells whether or not that person gave you any corn.

You gave this person potatoes	You gave this person nothing
This person gave you corn	This person gave you nothing

> Indicate only the card or the cards you definitely need to turn over to see whether any of these people have cheated you.

The "look for exchange (conditional)" and "look for exchange (want)" conditions presented exactly the same problems, except that the final instruction read as follows:

> Indicate only the card or the cards you definitely need to turn over to see whether any of these people have made an exchange with you.

3.2. Results and Discussion

Table 2 presents the percentages of the main selection patterns in the four versions. In both "look for cheater" conditions, the most frequently selected pattern was the correct P and not-Q pattern. In the want version, the proportion of participants who made such a selection

Table 2: Percentage of the Main Selection Patterns in the Four Conditions of Experiment 2 ($N = 30$)

	Condition			
Pattern	Look for Cheater (Conditional)	Look for Cheater (Want)	Look for Exchange (Conditional)	Look for Exchange (Want)
P, not-Q	33	43	10	0
P, Q	7	13	33	53
P	30	10	30	20
Not-Q	13	17	13	0
Other[a]	17	17	13	27

[a] Each of the patterns indicated in the "Other" cells was produced by fewer than four participants.

was similar to the one obtained in FCT's study (43% vs. 50%, respectively), and significantly higher than the one obtained in the corresponding "look for exchange" condition, in which no participant made this selection ($\chi^2(1, N = 60) = 14.14, p < 0.001$). In the conditional version, however, our participants made this selection less often than FCT's ones (33% vs. 66%, respectively). We have no confident explanation for this failure to replicate their results. As we predicted, in both "look for exchange" conditions the most frequently selected pattern was the correct P and Q pattern. Participants produced more such P and Q selections than in the "look for cheater" conditions (conditional versions: $\chi^2(1, N = 60) = 5.10, p < 0.05$; want versions: $\chi^2(1, N = 60) = 9.07, p < 0.01$).

These results confirm our main claim that, in an FCT task, people do as they are told and, in particular, look for a cheater when they are told to do so, just as they look for an exchange when this is what they are told to do. They disconfirm FCT's claim that when people recognize a situation as an exchange and moreover take the perspective of a party, they automatically look for cheaters.

4. Conclusion

Let us be quite clear: nothing we have said and none of the evidence we have mustered implies that the Cosmides (1989) hypothesis about the existence of a specific competence to deal with social exchanges is wrong. What we have tried to show is that this hypothesis, in spite of having been at the center of heated debates in the past 12 years, has not yet been properly experimentally tested, since almost all the evidence is based on the Wason or the FCT selection task, which are inappropriate for this purpose, or on

a mixed Wason/FCT task, which is methodologically unsound. Incidentally, using patients with brain lesions (see Adolphs, 1999) with Wason or FCT selection tasks to test hypotheses about specialized mechanisms for social information processing is just further and more costly use of an inappropriate methodology. In no ways does this constitute independent evidence for the claims based on standard uses of the tasks. There is a variety of methods by means of which Cosmides' hypothesis might be seriously tested (see Sperber & Girotto, in press). Experimenting with the Wason or the FCT selection task is not one of them.

More generally, much of the work done with the selection task should be considered a sunk cost in the history of the psychology of reasoning and further investments of research effort and journal pages in uses of the task should be discouraged.

Notes

1   In the Wason selection task, participants are presented with a conditional rule of the form: If an item has the feature P, then it has the feature Q (descriptive versions) or If an item has the feature P, then it should have the feature Q (deontic versions), and with four cards representing individual items. Only half of the information these four cards contain is visible, showing that the four items represented have respectively the P, not-P, Q, and not-Q feature (the cards are accordingly called the P, not-P, Q, and not-Q cards). The full information can be made visible by turning over the card in order to find out whether or not the P and not-P cards also have feature Q, and whether or not the Q and not-Q cards also have feature P. Participants are asked which cards it is necessary to turn over to determine whether the rule is true or false (descriptive version) or obeyed or disobeyed

(deontic versions). Since, as far as these four cards are concerned, the rule is true (or obeyed) unless there are cards combining the P and the not-Q features, the logically correct selection is that of the P and the not-Q cards, either of which could turn out to provide a counterexample to (or a violation of) the rule.

2   See also Evans (1989) for an earlier and different relevance-based account of the task, and Sperber and Wilson (1995) for relevance theory.

References

Adolphs, R. (1999). Social cognition and the human brain. *Trends in Cognitive Sciences, 3*, 469–479.

Atran, S. (2000). A cheater-detection module? Dubious interpretations of the Wason selection task and logic. *Evolution and Cognition, 7*, 187–193.

Begg, I., & Harris, G. (1982). On the interpretation of syllogisms. *Journal of Verbal Learning and Verbal Behavior, 21*, 595–620.

Cosmides, L. (1989). The logic of social exchange: has natural selection shaped how humans reason? Studies with the Wason selection task. *Cognition, 31*, 187–276.

Cosmides, L., & Tooby, J. (1989). Evolutionary psychology and the generation of culture, Part II. Case study: a computational theory of social exchange. *Ethology & Sociobiology, 10*, 51–97.

Cosmides, L., & Tooby, J. (1992). Cognitive adaptations for social exchange. In J. Barkow, L. Cosmides, & J. Tooby (Eds.), *The adapted mind: evolutionary psychology and the generation of culture* (pp. 163–228). New York: Oxford University Press.

Cosmides, L., & Tooby, J. (1997). Dissecting the computational architecture of social inference mechanisms. *Characterizing human psychological adaptations. Ciba Foundation symposium #208* (pp. 132–156). Chichester: Wiley.

Evans, J. St. B. T. (1989). *Bias in human reasoning: causes and consequences.* Hillsdale, NJ: Erlbaum.

Evans, J. St. B. T., Newstead, S. R., & Byrne, R. M. J. (1993). *Human reasoning: The psychology of deduction.* Hove, UK: Erlbaum.

Fiddick, L., Cosmides, L., & Tooby, J. (2000). No interpretation without representation: the role of domain-specific representations in the Wason selection task. *Cognition, 77*, 1–79.

Fillenbaum, S. (1975). If: some uses. *Psychological Research, 37*, 245–260.

Geis, M. C., & Zwicky, A. M. (1971). On invited inferences. *Linguistic Inquiry, 2*, 561–566.

Girotto, V., Kemmelmeir, M., Sperber, D., & van der Henst, J. B. (2001). Inept reasoners or pragmatic virtuosos? Relevance and the deontic selection task. *Cognition, 81*, 69–76.

Legrenzi, P., Politzer, G., & Girotto, V. (1996). Contract proposals: a sketch of a grammar. *Theory and Psychology, 6*, 247–265.

Light, P. H., Girotto, V., & Legrenzi, P. (1990). Children's reasoning on conditional promises and permissions. *Cognitive Development, 5*, 369–383.

Manktelow, K. I., & Over, D. E. (1991). Social rules and utilities in reasoning with deontic conditionals. *Cognition, 39*, 85–105.

Newstead, S. R., Ellis, M. C., Evans, J. St. B. T., & Dennis, J. (1997). Conditional reasoning with realistic material. *Thinking and Reasoning, 3*, 49–76.

Politzer, G. (1990). Immediate deduction between quantified sentences. In K. J. Gilhooly, M. T. G. Keane, R. H. Logie, & G. Erdos (Eds.), *Lines of thinking: reflections on the psychology of thought.* London: Wiley.

Sperber, D. (2000). Metarepresentations in an evolutionary perspective. In D. Sperber (Ed.), *Metarepresentations* (pp. 117–137). New York: Oxford University Press.

Sperber, D., Cara, F., & Girotto, V. (1995). Relevance theory explains the selection task. *Cognition, 52*, 3–39.

Sperber, D., & Girotto, V. (in press). Does the selection task detect cheater detection? In J. Fitness & K. Sterelny (Eds.), *New directions in evolutionary psychology. Macquarie monographs in cognitive science.* Hove, UK: Psychology Press.

Sperber, D., & Wilson, D. (1995). *Relevance: communication and cognition* (2nd ed.). Oxford: Blackwell.

Sperber, D., & Wilson, D. (2002). Pragmatics, modularity and mind-reading. *Mind and Language, 17*, 3–23.

Stein, E. (1996). *Without good reason: The rationality debate in philosophy and cognitive science.* Oxford: Clarendon Press.

Wason, P. C. (1966). Reasoning. In B. M. Foss (Ed.), *New horizons in psychology.* Harmondsworth: Penguin.

Chapter 43: Why We Are So Good at Catching Cheaters

JERRY A. FODOR

There is robust experimental evidence that Ss who are required to check whether P→Q regularly overlook the relevance of ~Qs. So, Ss asked to verify (1), though they routinely want to know what the under-18s are drinking, only rarely remember to ask the non-Coke drinkers whether they are under 18 (Wason 1966).

(1) If someone is under 18 (s)he is drinking Coke.

(2) It's required that if someone is under 18 (s)he drinks Coke.[1]

By contrast, Ss who are told that (2) is a regulation and asked to check whether everyone is in compliance reliably remember to ask anyone not drinking Coke how old (s)he is. It appears that what sort of drinking is going on is somehow more salient if you're evaluating (2) than if you're evaluating (1). Why on earth is that?

One explanation, recently widely bruited, is that we are innately equipped with special, domain-specific, modular mechanisms for cheater detection, and that these mechanisms are better at their job than the other circuits we use for coping with hypotheticals. (See Cosmides and Tooby [1992] and references therein.) The reason we have this high-performance equipment available, it is further explained, is that it would have been useful for us to have it back when we were heavily into hunting and gathering. (A similar theory would account for our uncanny innate ability to navigate according to the earth's magnetic field – *such* a comfort if you're driving home late from a hunt or a gather – except that we haven't got one.) This putative selectional explanation of the data about cheater detection is among the very

small number of flagship results that are supposed to provide experimental support for a neo-Darwinian account of the evolution of cognition. So it's of some polemical significance whether it can be sustained.

In fact, there would seem to be a perfectly plausible, if less imaginative, synchronic explanation of the asymmetry between (1) and (2). The key, I think, is the following intuition, which you are hereby encouraged to share: (1) asserts that there's a conditional relation between *P* and *Q* (namely, that Q is true if *P* is). *P* is thus one of the relata between which (1) says that this conditional relation obtains (the other being, of course, Q). By contrast, what (2) prohibits isn't anything conditional at all. Rather, (2) categorically prohibits Q, though, to be sure, it imposes its categorical ban on Q only in case that *P*. It's thus the whole symbol "*P*→Q" that expresses what is asserted by (1). But it's only the "Q" part that expresses what is prohibited by (2). All *P* does in (2) is determine *on whom the prohibition falls*. If this intuition about the parsing of (2) is correct, then it's hardly surprising that Ss who fail to see non-Coke drinkers as ipso facto prospective falsifiers of (1), are perfectly able to see non-Coke drinkers as ipso facto prospective violators of (2). It is, to repeat, precisely non-Coke drinking that (2) prohibits.

So the mystery about cheater detecting vanishes if we can make it plausible that, whereas in some sense (1) is about its being the case that if *P* then Q, (2) is about Q's being mandatory. And it is, in fact, plausible that (1) and (2) differ in just this way. That they do so is built into a difference between the logic of indicative and deontic conditionals; that is, between conditionals that assert truths and those that impose obligations.

Here's a sketch of an argument showing that, whereas it's common ground that "if P then Q" asserts $P \rightarrow Q$, "it's required that if P then Q" requires Q rather than $P \rightarrow Q$.[2]

I.   Assume, for reductio, that "it's required that if P then Q" is equivalent to *required* $(P \rightarrow Q)$.

II.   Assume (*required* $P \rightarrow Q$) & $\sim Q$

III. The inference scheme $((A$ & (*required* $A \rightarrow B)) \rightarrow$ (*required* B) is valid. (If it weren't, *Sam is under 18* & (*required* (*if under 18* $\rightarrow$ *drinks coke*)) wouldn't entail *required* (*Sam drinks coke*).)

IV.   *Required* $(P \rightarrow Q)$ $\rightarrow$ *required* $(\sim Q \rightarrow \sim P)$. Contraposition is valid in the scope of "*required.*" ("*Required A*" is closed under A's entailments.)

V. $(\sim Q$ & (*required* $(\sim Q \rightarrow \sim P)) \rightarrow$ *required* $\sim P)$ (by *iii* and *iv*, putting $\sim Q$ for A, and putting *required* $\sim Q \rightarrow \sim P$ for *required* $A \rightarrow B$). This says that if it's required that $P \rightarrow Q$, and it's the case that $\sim Q$, then it's required that $\sim P$.

But (see below) there are counterexamples to (v), so the argument that leads to it must be unsound. And, since the only tendentious premise the argument employs is (i), it follows that we should not read "it's required that if P then Q" as *required* $(P \rightarrow Q)$.

Here's a case where (ii)–(iv) are true but (v) is false.[3] Suppose everyone under 18 is obliged to drink Coke. Then if Sam is under 18, he is prohibited from drinking whiskey. But *it does not follow* that if Sam is drinking whiskey, he is then obliged to be over 18. In fact, Sam *can't* be obliged to be over 18 because he can't be obliged to do *anything* that he is unable to do. And with Sam, as with the rest of us, there's nothing much that he can do about how old he is (in, alas, either direction). I conclude that Authority cannot mandate the conditional (Sam drinks Coke if he is under 18). The only course it can coherently pursue, having taken note of Sam's being under 18, is to mandate categorically that he drink Coke.

So, then, we have an argument that, although *it's true that if $P \rightarrow Q$ is*, as it were, really about $P \rightarrow Q$ being true, *it's required that $P \rightarrow Q$ isn't* really about $P \rightarrow Q$ being required. *It's required that $P \rightarrow Q$ is about Q being required* (in a certain case; viz., in the case that P). Since Ss know all this, they hear (2) as *mandating Coke drinking* (in a certain case, viz., when the drinker is

under 18); and since they hear (2) as mandating Coke drinking, they see, straight off, that if (2) is being flouted, whiskey drinkers are among the likely suspects.[4] That they do see this straight off should hardly be surprising; if the mandate is "drink only Coke," whiskey drinkers are *on the face of it* not in compliance (though, as a lawyer might say, the ones over 18 have secured a variance).[5]

You can assert that $P \rightarrow Q$ or you can assert that Q, whichever you prefer. But since you can't *require* that $P \rightarrow Q$, you likewise can't *cheat* on $P \rightarrow Q$; the best you can do is cheat on Q in case it's the case that P. But that $\sim Q$s may be cheating on Q should, on anybody's story, be more obvious than that $\sim Q$s may contradict $P \rightarrow Q$ since, on any reasonable way of counting, $\sim (Q \& \sim Q)$ is more obvious than $((P \rightarrow Q) \& \sim Q) \rightarrow \sim P$. It's plausibly these logical truisms, and not whatever it was that happened to Granny and Gramps on their way to the savannah, that explain why we are so good at detecting cheaters (compared, anyhow, with how bad we are on the standard Wason task).

The received view has it that cheater detection data show that we reason about sentences like (1) and (2) *with different parts of our minds*. The present proposal, not nearly so glamorous, is that we reason about sentences like (1) and (2) *along different inferential routes*. We could hardly do otherwise, considering the structural disanalogies between them that I've just been expounding. In effect, I claim that much, quite possibly all, of the putative experimental evidence for a cheater detection effect on the Wason task conflates the distinction *reasoning with the Law of Contraposition/reasoning with the Law of Contradiction* with the distinction *reasoning about indicative conditionals/reasoning about deontic conditionals*; and is therefore null and void.

Methodological moral: When subjects appear to behave peculiarly in an experimental task, this is not infrequently because they are sensitive to a materials variable that the experimenter has failed to notice.[6]

Notes

1   "*P*" and "*Q*" correspond, respectively, to "someone is under 18" and "(s)he drinks/is drinking coke." The examples may seem less forced if you add "(rather than whiskey)" as a codicil throughout, and stipulate that "drinks whiskey iff doesn't drink Coke" is true of everybody involved.

2 For the record: I think what's in the text is an ok argument and that it does indeed strongly suggest that *P* doesn't belong to the content of what's required in "it's required that if *P* then Q." But explaining the cheater detection effect in the Wason task, which is the main point of the discussion, doesn't actually need this argument to be sound. All it needs is the truth of the conclusion, namely, that Q is what is required by "it's required that if *P* then Q."

3 That (v) is invalid doesn't, of course, mean that every inference of that form is unsound. Inferences of an invalid form may nonetheless be sound in light of entailments carried by the *non*logical vocabulary. I'm grateful to Alan Leslie for examples like: "if you borrow my trumpet, you should give me some tomatoes," from which it does follow that if you don't give me the tomatoes, you shouldn't borrow my trumpet. I take it, however, that it's the meaning of "borrow," rather than the logic of conditional deontic inferences per se, that supports contraposition in such cases. Compare "if I sell you my trumpet, you should be grateful," from which it doesn't follow that if you're not grateful I ought not sell you my trumpet.

4 The other likely suspects being, of course, drinkers who are under 18. Unsurprisingly, *Ss* evaluating sentences like (1) in the Wason selection task practically always understand that the *P*-card is germane. (The *P*-card is the one that asserts the antecedent of the hypothetical to be verified.) *S* contemplates modus ponens on "If you're under 18, you're required to drink Coke"; so, if you're under 18, *S* wants to know what you're drinking.

5 I have, however, encountered an evolutionary psychology enthusiast who did find surprising my claim that if *Ss* construe deontic conditionals in the way I've suggested, then they should see "straight off" that whiskey drinkers are potential violators of "if you're under 18, drink Coke." He held, indeed, that if they did so, that would be as much in need of explanation as the original finding that the Wason task is easier in the cheater-detection version. If he was right, then of course my labor's been in vain; I've only explained one mystery by invoking another. But I suspect him of a merely tactical bemusement. Imagine an experiment in which *S* is told about a party where some are drinking and some are not. *S* is offered for verification "at this party, they are drinking only Coke" and asked whom he'd prefer to interview, the drinkers or the others. Which do you suppose he'll choose?

6 Many thanks to David Rosenthal for helping me to sort out all this stuff. He does *P*s and Qs much better than I do.

References

Cosmides, L., & Tooby, J. (1992). *The Adapted Mind*. Oxford, UK: Oxford University Press.

Wason, P. (1966). "Reasoning." In D. W. Foss (ed.), *New Horizons in Psychology*. London: Penguin Books.

Chapter 44: The Modularity of Mind: An Essay on Faculty Psychology

JERRY A. FODOR

A Functional Taxonomy of Cognitive Mechanisms

I want to argue that the current best candidates for treatment as *modular* cognitive systems share a certain functional role in the mental life of organisms; the discussion in this section is largely devoted to saying which functional role that is. As often happens in playing cognitive science, it is helpful to characterize the functions of psychological systems by analogy to the organization of idealized computing machines. So, I commence with a brief digression in the direction of computers.

When philosophers of mind think about computers, it is often Turing machines that they are thinking about. And this is understandable. If there is an interesting analogy between minds qua minds and computers qua computers, it ought to be possible to couch it as an analogy between minds and Turing machines, since a Turing machine is, in a certain sense, as general as any kind of computer can be. More precisely: if, as many of us now suppose, minds are essentially symbol-manipulating devices, it ought to be useful to think of minds on the Turing-machine model since Turing machines are (again "in a certain sense") as general as any symbol-manipulating device can be.

However, as we have already had reason to observe, Turing machines are also very simple devices; their functional architecture is exhaustively surveyed when we have mentioned a small number of interacting subsystems (tape, scanner, printer, and executive) and a small inventory of primitive machine operations (stop, start, move

the tape, read the tape, change state, print). Moreover – and this is the point of present concern – Turing machines are *closed* computational systems; the sole determinants of their computations are the current machine state, the tape configuration, and the program, the rest of the world being quite irrelevant to the character of their performance; whereas, of course, organisms are forever exchanging information with their environments, and much of their psychological structure is constituted of mechanisms which function to mediate such exchanges. If, therefore, we are to start with anything like Turing machines as models in cognitive psychology, we must think of them as embedded in a matrix of subsidiary systems which affect their computations in ways that are responsive to the flow of environmental events. The function of these subsidiary systems is to provide the central machine with information about the world; information expressed by mental symbols in whatever format cognitive processes demand of the representations that they apply to.

I pause to note that the format constraint on the subsidiary systems is vital. *Any* mechanism whose states covary with environmental ones can be thought of as registering information about the world; and, given the satisfaction of certain further conditions, the output of such systems can reasonably be thought of as *representations* of the environmental states with which they covary. (See Dretske, 1981; Stampe, 1977; Fodor, 1987.) But if cognitive processors are *computational* systems, they have access to such information solely in virtue of the *form* of

---

the representations in which it is couched. Computational processes are, by definition, *syntactic*; a device which makes information available to such processes is therefore responsible for its format as well as its quality. If, for example, we think of such a device as writing on the tape of a Turing machine, then it must write *in a language that the machine can understand* (more precisely, in the language in which the machine computes). Or, to put it in a psychological-sounding way, if we think of the perceptual mechanisms as analogous to such devices, then we are saying that *what perception must do is to so represent the world as to make it accessible to thought*. The condition on appropriateness of format is by way of emphasizing that not every representation of the world will do for this purpose.

I wish that I knew what to call the "subsidiary systems" that perform this function. Here are some possibilities that I have considered and – with varying degrees of reluctance – decided to reject:

– 'Perceptual systems' would be the obvious choice except that, as we shall presently see, perception is not the only psychological mechanism that functions to present the world to thought, and I would like a term broad enough to embrace them all. Moreover, as will also become apparent, there are important reasons for not viewing the subsidiary systems as effecting the fixation of belief. By contrast, perception is a mechanism of belief fixation par excellence: the normal consequence of a perceptual transaction is the acquisition of a perceptual belief. (Having entered this caveat, I shall nevertheless often speak of the subsidiary systems as mechanisms of perceptual analysis. For most purposes it is harmless to do so and it does simplify the exposition.)

– I have sometimes thought of calling these subsidiary systems 'compilers', thereby stressing that their output consists of representations that are accessible to relatively central computational processes. But that way of talking leads to difficulties too. Real compilers are functions from programs onto programs, programs themselves being (approximately) sequences of instructions. But not much of what perception makes available to thought is plausibly viewed as a program. Indeed, it is partly the attempt to force perceptual information into that mold which engenders procedural semantics, the identification of perceptual categories with action schemes, and other such aberrations of theory. (For discussion, see Fodor, 1981, chapter 8.)

– One could try calling them 'transducers' except that, on at least one usual under-

standing (see Lowenstein, 1960), transducers are analog systems that take proximal stimulations onto more or less precisely covarying neural signals. Mechanisms of transduction are thus *contrasted* with computational mechanisms: whereas the latter may perform quite complicated, inference-like transformations, the former are supposed – at least ideally – to preserve the informational content of their inputs, altering *only* the format in which the information is displayed. We shall see, however, that representations at the interface between (what I have been calling) 'subsidiary' and 'central' systems exhibit levels of encoding that are quite abstractly related to the play of proximal stimulation.

Pylyshyn and I (1981) have called these subsidiary systems 'compiled transducers', using the 'compiled' part to indicate that they have an internal computational structure and the 'transducer' part to indicate that they exhibit a certain sort of informational encapsulation that will presently loom large in this discussion. I think that usage is all right given the explication, but it admittedly hasn't much to do with the conventional import of these terms and thus probably produces as much confusion as it avoids.

It is, perhaps, not surprising that computer theory provides no way of talking that does precisely the job I want to do. Computers generally interface with their environments *via some human being* (which is what makes them computers rather than robots). The programmer thus takes on the function of the subsidiary computational systems that I have been struggling to describe – viz., by providing the machine with information about the world in a form in which the machine can use it. Surprising or not, however, it is a considerable nuisance. Ingenuity having failed me completely, I propose to call them variously 'input systems', or 'input analyzers' or, sometimes, 'interface systems'. At least this terminology emphasizes that they operate relatively early on. I rely on the reader to keep it in mind, however, that input systems are *post*-transductive mechanisms according to my usage. Also that switches from one of the epithets to another usually signify no more than a yen for stylistic variation.

So, then, we are to have a trichotomous functional taxonomy of psychological processes; a taxonomy which distinguishes transducers, input systems, and central processors, with the flow of input information becoming accessible to these mechanisms in about that order. These categories are intended to be exclusive but not, of course, to exhaust the types of psychological mechanisms that a theory of cognition might have reason to postulate. Since the trichotomy is not exhaustive, it is left wide open that there may be modular systems that do not subserve any of these functions. Among the obvious candidates would be systems involved in the motor integration of such behaviors as speech and locomotion. It would please me if the kinds of arguments that I shall give for the modularity of input systems proved to have application to motor systems as well. But I don't propose to investigate that possibility here.

Input systems function to get information into the central processors; specifically, they mediate between transducer outputs and central cognitive mechanisms by encoding the mental representations which provide domains for the operations of the latter. This does not mean, however, that input systems *translate* from the representations that transducers afford into representations in the central code. On the contrary, translation preserves informational content and, as I remarked above, the computations that input systems perform typically do not. Whereas transducer outputs are most naturally interpreted as specifying the distribution of stimulations at the 'surfaces' (as it were) of the organism, the input systems deliver representations that are most naturally interpreted as characterizing the arrangement of *things in the world*. Input analyzers are thus inference-performing systems within the usual limitations of that metaphor. Specifically, the inferences at issue have as their 'premises' transduced representations of proximal stimulus configurations, and as their 'conclusions' representations of the character and distribution of distal objects.

It is hard to see how a computer could fail to exhibit mechanisms of transduction if it is to interface with the world at all. But it is perfectly possible to imagine a machine whose computations are appropriately sensitive to environmental events but which does *not* exhibit a functional distinction between input systems and central systems. Roughly, endorsing this computational architecture is tantamount to insisting upon a perception/cognition distinction. It is tantamount to claiming that a certain class of computational problems of 'object identification' (or, more correctly, a class of computational problems whose solutions consist in the recovery of certain proprietary descriptions of objects) has been 'detached' from the domain of cognition at large and handed over to functionally distinguishable psychological mechanisms. Perceptual

analysis is, according to this model, not, strictly speaking, a species of thought. (The reader is again reminded, however, that the identification of input processing with perceptual analysis is itself only approximate. This will all presently sort itself out; I promise.)

Given the possibility in principle that the perceptual mechanisms could be continuous with the higher cognitive processes, one is tempted to ask what the point of a trichotomous functional architecture could be. What, teleologically speaking, might it buy for an organism that has transducers and central cognitive processors to have input analyzers as well? I think there probably *is* an answer to this question: Implicit in the trichotomous architecture is the isolation of perceptual analysis from certain effects of background belief and set; and, as we shall see, this has implications for both the speed and the objectivity of perceptual integration. It bears emphasis, however, that putting the teleological issues in the way I just did involves some fairly dubious evolutionary assumptions. To suppose that the issue is *Why, given that there are central processors, should there be input systems as well?* is to take for granted that the former should be viewed as philogenetically prior to the latter. However, an equally plausible story might have it the other way 'round – viz., that input analyzers, with their (as I shall argue) relatively rigid domain specificity and automaticity of functioning, are the aboriginal prototypes of inference-making psychological systems. Cognitive evolution would thus have been in the direction of gradually freeing certain sorts of problem-solving systems from the constraints under which input analyzers labor – hence of producing, as a relatively late achievement, the comparatively domain-free inferential capacities which apparently mediate the higher flights of cognition. (See Rozin, 1976, where the plausibility of this picture of cognitive phylogeny is impressively defended.)

In any event, the justification for postulating a functionally individuated class of input analyzers distinct from central cognitive mechanisms must finally rest on two sorts of evidence: I have to show that there are interesting things that the input analyzers have in common; and I have to show that there are interesting respects in which they differ from cognitive processes at large. The second of these burdens will be taken up in [the third part of this chapter]. For now, I am going to argue that the functionally specified class *input system* does pick out a "natural kind" for purposes of psychological theory construction; that there are, in fact, lots of interesting things to say about the common properties of the mechanisms that mediate input analysis.

There is, however, one more preliminary point to make before getting down to that business. To claim that the functional category *input system* picks out a natural kind is to endorse an eccentric taxonomy of cognitive processes. Eyebrows should commence to be raised starting here. For, if you ask "which *are* the psychological mechanisms that can plausibly be thought of as functioning to provide information about the distal environment in a format appropriate for central processing?" the answer would seem to be "the perceptual systems *plus language.*" And this is, from the point of view of traditional ways of carving things up, an odd category.

The traditional taxonomy goes something like this: perception (vision, audition, or whatever) on the one side, and thought-and-language (the representational processes) on the other. Now, the representational character of language is self-evident, and I don't doubt the theoretical importance of the representational character of thought. (On the contrary, I think that it is *the* essential fact that an adequate theory of the propositional attitudes would have to account for. (See Fodor, 1981, chapter 7.)) But we're not, of course, committed to there being only one right way of assigning psychological mechanisms to functional classes. The present claim is that, for purposes of assessing the issues about modularity, a rather different taxonomy proves illuminating.

Well then, what precisely *is* the functional similarity between language mechanisms and perceptual mechanisms in virtue of which both count as 'input systems'? There is, of course, the obvious point that utterances (e.g., sentence tokens) are themselves objects to be perceptually identified, just as mountains, teacups, and four-alarm fires are. Understanding a token sentence presumably involves assigning it a structural description, this being part and parcel of computing a token-to-type relation; and that is precisely the sort of function we would expect an input system to perform. However, in stressing the functional analogy between language and perception, I have something more in mind than the fact that understanding utterances is itself a typical perceptual process.

I've said that input systems function to interpret transduced information and to make it available to central processes; and that, in the normal case, what they provide will be information about the "layout" (to borrow a term of

Gibson's) of distal stimuli. How might such a system work? Heaven knows there are few harder questions; but I assume that, in the case of perception, the answer must include some such story as the following. The character of transducer outputs is determined, in some lawful way, by the character of impinging energy at the transducer surface; and the character of the energy at the transducer surface is itself lawfully determined by the character of the distal layout. Because there are regularities of this latter sort, it is possible to infer properties of the distal layout from corresponding properties of the transducer output. Input analyzers are devices which perform inferences of this sort.

A useful example is Ullman's (1979) algorithm for inferring "form from motion" in visual perception. Under assumptions (e.g., of rigidity) that distal stimuli usually satisfy, a specific sequence of transformations of the energy distributions at the retina will be reliably interpretable as having been caused by (and hence as specifying) the spatial displacement of a distal object of determinate three-dimensional shape. A device that has access to the transducer outputs can infer this shape by executing Ullman's (or some equivalent) algorithm. I assume that performing such computations is precisely the function of input systems, Ullman's case being unusual primarily in the univocality with which the premises of the perceptual inference warrant its conclusion.

Now about language: Just as patterns of visual energy arriving at the retina are correlated, in a complicated but regular way, with certain properties of distal layouts, so too are the patterns of auditory energy that excite the tympanic membrane in speech exchanges. With, of course, this vital difference: What underwrites the correlation between visual stimulations and distal layouts are (roughly) the laws of light reflectance. Whereas, what underwrites the correlation between token utterances and distal layouts is (roughly) a convention of truth-telling. In the root case, the convention is that we say of x that it is F only if x is F. Because that convention holds, it is possible to infer from what one hears said to the way that the world is.[1]

Of course, in neither the linguistic nor the perceptual case is the information so provided infallible. The world often isn't the way it looks to be or the way that people say it is. But, equally of course, input systems don't have to deliver apodictic truths in order to deliver quite useful information. And, anyhow, *the operation of the input systems should not be identified with the fixation of belief.* What we *believe* depends on the evaluation of how things look, or are said to be, *in light of background information* about (inter alia) how good the seeing is or how trustworthy the source. Fixation of belief is *just* the sort of thing I have in mind as a typical *central* process.

So much, then, for the similarity of function between the linguistic and the perceptual systems: both serve to get information about the world into a format appropriate for access by such central processes as mediate the fixation of belief. But now, is there anything to be said for exploiting this analogy? What, from the point of view of psychological theory, do we gain by postulating a functional class of perceptual-and-linguistic processes? Clearly, the proof of this pudding is *entirely* in the eating. I'm about to argue that, if we undertake to build a psychology that acknowledges this functional class as a natural kind, we discover that the processes we have grouped together do indeed have many interesting properties in common – properties the possession of which is not entailed by their functional homogeneity. (I take it that that is what a natural kind is: a class of phenomena that have many scientifically interesting properties in common over and above whatever properties define the class.) In the present case, what the input systems have in common besides their functional similarities can be summarized in a phrase: *input systems are modules.* A fortiori, they share those properties that are characteristic of vertical faculties. Input systems are – or so I'll argue – what Gall was right about.

What follows is the elaboration of that claim, together with an occasional glimpse at the state of the evidence. I should say at the outset that not every psychologist would agree with me about what the state of the evidence is. I am arguing well in advance of (and, in some places, a little in the face of) the currently received views. So, perhaps one should take this exercise as in part a thought experiment: I'll be trying to say what you might expect the data to look like if the modularity story is true of input systems; and I'll claim that, insofar as any facts are known, they seem to be generally compatible with such expectations.

Input Systems as Modules

The modularity of the input systems consists in their possession of most or all of the properties now to be enumerated. If there are other psychological systems which possess most or all of these properties then, of course, they are modular too.

It is, however, a main thesis of this work that the properties in virtue of which input systems are modular are ones which, in general, central cognitive processes do not share.

Input Systems are Domain Specific

Let's start with this: how many input systems are there? The discussion thus far might be construed so as to suggest an answer somewhere in the vicinity of six – viz., one for each of the traditional sensory/perceptual 'modes' (hearing, sight, touch, taste, smell) and one more for language. This is *not*, however, the intended doctrine; what is proposed is something much more in the spirit of Gall's bumps. I imagine that within (and, quite possibly, across)[2] the traditional modes, there are highly specialized computational mechanisms in the business of generating hypotheses about the distal sources of proximal stimulations. The specialization of these mechanisms consists in constraints either on the range of information they can access in the course of projecting such hypotheses, or in the range of distal properties they can project such hypotheses about, or, most usually, on both.

Candidates might include, in the case of vision, mechanisms for color perception, for the analysis of shape, and for the analysis of three-dimensional spatial relations.[3] They might also include quite narrowly task-specific 'higher level' systems concerned with the visual guidance of bodily motions or with the recognition of faces of conspecifics. Candidates in audition might include computational systems that assign grammatical descriptions to token utterances; or ones that detect the melodic or rhythmic structure of acoustic arrays; or, for that matter, ones that mediate the recognition of the *voices* of conspecifics. There is, in fact, some evidence for the domain specificity of several of the systems just enumerated, but I suggest the examples primarily by way of indicating the levels of grain which input systems might be modularized.

What, then, are the arguments for the domain specificity of input systems? To begin with, there is a sense in which input systems are ipso facto domain specific in a way in which computational systems at large are not. This is, however, quite uninteresting, a merely semantic point. Suppose, for example, that the function of the mechanisms of visual perception is to map transduced patterns of retinal excitation onto formulas of some central computational code. Then it follows trivially that their computational domain *qua mechanisms of visual perception* is specific to the class of possible retinal outputs. Correspondingly, if what the language-processing mechanisms do is pair utterance tokens with central formulas, then their computational domains *qua mechanisms of language processing*, must be whatever encodings of utterances the auditory transducer produce. In similar boring fashion, the psychological mechanism that mediate the perception of cows are ipso facto domain specific *qua mechanisms of cow perception*.

From such truisms, it goes without saying, nothing useful follows. In particular, the modularity of a system cannot be inferred from this trivial kind of domain specificity. It is, for example, entirely compatible, with the cow specificity of cow perception that the recognition of cows should be mediated by precisely the same mechanisms that effect the perception of language, or of earth quakes, or of three-masted brigantines. For example, all four could perfectly well be accomplished by one and the same set of horizontal faculties. The interesting notion of domain specificity, by contrast, is Gall's idea that there are distinct psychological mechanisms – *vertical* faculties – corresponding to distinct stimulus domains. It is this latter claim that's now at issue.

Evidence for the domain specificity of an input analyzer can be of a variety of different sorts. Just occasionally the argument is quite direct and the demonstrations correspondingly dramatic. For example, there are results owing to investigators at the Haskins Laboratories which strongly suggest the domain specificity of the perceptual systems that effect the phonetic analysis of speech. The claim is that these mechanisms are different from those which effect the perceptual analysis of auditory nonspeech, and the experiments show that how a signal sounds to the hearer does depend, in rather startling ways, on whether the acoustic context indicates that the stimulus is an utterance. Roughly, the very same signal that is heard as the onset of a consonant when the context specifies that the stimulus is speech is heard as a "whistle" or "glide" when it is isolated from the speech stream. The rather strong implication is that the computational systems that come into play in the perceptual analysis of speech are distinctive in that they operate *only* upon acoustic signals that are taken to be utterances. (See Liberman et al., 1967; for further discussion, see Fodor, Bever, and Garrett, 1974.)

The Haskins experiments demonstrate the domain specificity of an input analyzer by showing that only a relatively restricted class of stim-

ulations can throw the switch that turns it on. There are, however, other kinds of empirical arguments that can lead to the same sort of conclusions. One that has done quite a lot of work for cognitive scientists goes like this: If you have an *eccentric* stimulus domain – one in which perceptual analysis requires a body of information whose character and content is specific to that domain – then it is plausible that psychological processes defined over that domain may be carried out by relatively special purpose computational systems. All things being equal, the plausibility of this speculation is about proportional to the eccentricity of the domain.

Comparing perceiving cows with perceiving sentences will help to show what's going on here. I really have no idea how cow perception works, but let's follow the fashions and suppose, for purposes of discussion, that we use some sort of prototype-plus-similarity-metric. That is, the perceptual recognition of cows is effected by some mechanism which provides solutions for computational problems of the form: how similar – how 'close' – is the distal stimulus to a prototypical cow? My point is that if that's the way it's done, then cow perception might be mediated by much the same mechanisms that operate in a large variety of other perceptual domains as well – in fact, in any domain that is organized around prototypes. This is because we can imagine a quite general computational system which, given a specification of a prototype and a similarity metric for an arbitrary domain of percepts, will then compute the relevant distance relations in that domain. It seems plausible, that is to say, that procedures for estimating the distance between an input and a perceptual prototype should have pretty much the same computational structure wherever they are encountered.

It is, however, most unlikely that the perceptual recognition of sentences should be mediated by such procedures, and that is because sentence tokens constitute a set of highly eccentric stimuli: All the available evidence suggests that the computations which sentence recognizers perform must be closely tuned to a complex of stimulus properties that is quite specific to sentences. Roughly, the idea is that the structure of the sentence recognition system is responsive to universal properties of language and hence that the system works only in domains which exhibit these properties.

I take it that this story is by now pretty well known. The argument goes like this: Consider the class of *nomologically possible human languages*. There is evidence that this class constitutes quite a small subset of the logically possible linguistic systems. In particular, the nomologically possible human languages include only the ones that satisfy a set of (contingent) generalizations known as the 'linguistic universals.' One way to find out something about what linguistic universals there are is by examining and comparing *actual* human languages (French, English, Urdu, or whatever) with an eye to determining which properties they have in common. Much work in linguistics over the last twenty-five years or so has pursued this strategy, and a variety of candidate linguistic universals have been proposed, both in phonology and in syntax.

It seems quite unlikely that the existence of these universals is merely fortuitous, or that they can be explained by appeal to historical affinities among the languages that share them or by appeal to whatever pragmatic factors may operate to shape communication systems. (By pragmatic factors, I mean ones that involve general properties of communication exchanges as such, including the utilities of the partners to the exchanges. So, for example, Putnam (1961) once suggested that there are grammatical transformations because communicative efficiency is served by the deletion of redundant portions of messages, etc.) The obvious alternative to such accounts is to assume that the universals represent biases of a species-specific language-learning system, and a number of proposals have been made about how, in detail, such systems might be pretuned. It is assumed, according to all these accounts, that the language-learning mechanisms 'know about' the universals and operate only in domains in which the universals are satisfied. (For a review, see Pinker, 1979.)

Parity of argument suggests that a similar story should hold for the mechanisms of language *perception*. In particular, the perceptual system involved is presumed to have access to information about how the universals are realized in the language it applies to. The upshot of this line of thought is that the perceptual system for a language comes to be viewed as containing quite an elaborate theory of the objects in its domain; perhaps a theory couched in the form of a grammar of the language. Correspondingly, the process of perceptual recognition is viewed as the application of that theory to the analysis of current inputs. (For some recent work on the parsing of natural language, see Marcus, 1977; Kaplan and Bresnan, 1982; and Frazier and Fodor, 1978. All these otherwise quite different approaches share the methodological framework just outlined.)

To come to the moral: Since the satisfaction of the universals is supposed to be a property that distinguishes sentences from other stimulus domains, the more elaborate and complex the theory of universals comes to be the more eccentric the stimulus domain for sentence recognition. And, as we remarked above, the more eccentric a stimulus domain, the more plausible the speculation that it is computed by a special-purpose mechanism. It is, in particular, very hard to see how a device which classifies stimuli in respect of distance from a prototype could be recruited for purposes of sentence recognition. The computational question in sentence recognition seems to be not "How far to the nearest prototype?" but rather "How does the theory of the language apply to the analysis of the stimulus now at hand?"

There are probably quite a lot of kinds of relatively eccentric stimulus domains – ones whose perceptual analysis requires information that is highly specific to the domain in question. The organization of sentence perception around syntactic and phonological information does not exhaust the examples even in the case of language. So, for a further example, it is often and plausibly proposed that the processes that mediate phone recognition must have access to an internal model of the physical structure of the vocal apparatus. The argument is that a variety of constancies in speech perception seem to have precisely the effect of undoing garble that its inertial properties produce when the vocal mechanism responds to the phonetic intentions of the speaker. If this hypothesis is correct, then phone recognition is quite closely tuned to the mechanisms of speech production (see note 2). Once again, highly tuned computations are suggestive of special-purpose processors. Analogous points could be made in other perceptual modes. Faces are favorite candidates for eccentric stimuli (see Yin, 1969, 1970; Carey, 1978); and as I mentioned above, Ullman's work has made it seem plausible that the visual recognition of three-dimensional form is accomplished by systems that are tuned to the eccentricities of special classes of rigid spatial transformations.

From our point of view, the crucial question in all such examples is: how good is the inference from the eccentricity of the stimulus domain to the specificity of the corresponding psychological mechanisms? I am, in fact, not boundlessly enthusiastic about such inferences; they are clearly a long way from apodictic. Chess playing, for example, exploits a vast amount of eccentric information, but nobody wants to postulate a chess faculty. (Well, *almost* nobody. It is of some interest that recent progress in the artificial intelligence of chess has been achieved largely by employing specialized hardware. And, for what it's worth, chess is notably one of those cognitive capacities which breeds prodigies; so it is a candidate for modularity by Gall's criteria if not by mine.) Suffice it, for the present to suggest that it is probably characteristic of many modular systems that they operate in eccentric domains, since a likely motive for modularizing a system is that the computations it performs are idiosyncratic. But the converse inference – from the eccentricity of the domain to the modularity of the system – is warranted by nothing stronger than the maxim: specialized systems for specialized tasks. The most transparent situation is thus the one where you have a mechanism that computes an eccentric domain and is also modular by independent criteria; the eccentricity of the domain rationalizes the modularity of the processor and the modularity of the processor goes some way towards explaining how the efficient computation of eccentric domains is possible.

The Operation of Input Systems is Mandatory

You can't help hearing an utterance of a sentence (in a language you know) as an utterance of a sentence, and you can't help seeing a visual array as consisting of objects distributed in three-dimensional space. Similarly, mutatis mutandis, for the other perceptual modes: you can't, for instance, help feeling what you run your fingers over as the surface of an object.[4] Marslen-Wilson and Tyler (1981), discussing word recognition, remark that "... even when subjects are asked to focus their attention on the acoustic-phonetic properties of the input, they do not seem to be able to avoid identifying the words involved.... This implies that the kind of processing operations observable in spoken-word recognition are mediated by automatic processes which are obligatorily applied..." (p. 327).

The fact that input systems are apparently constrained to apply whenever they can apply is, when one thinks of it, rather remarkable. There is every reason to believe that, in the general case, the computational relations that input systems mediate – roughly, the relations between transducer outputs and percepts – are quite remote. For example, on all current theories, it requires elaborate processing to get you from the representation of a proximal stimulus that the retina provides to a representation of the distal stimuli as an array of objects in space.[5] Yet we apparently have no choice but to take up this computational burden whenever it is offered. In short, the operation of the input systems appears to be, in this respect, inflexibly insensitive to the character of one's utilities. You can't hear speech as noise *even if you would prefer to*.

What you can do, of course, is choose not to hear it at all – viz., not attend.[6] In the interesting cases – where this is achieved without deactivating a transducer (e.g., by sticking your fingers in your ears) – the strategy that works best is rather tortuous: one avoids attending to x by deciding to concentrate on y, thereby taking advantage of the difficulty of concentrating on more than one thing at a time. It may be that, when this strategy is successful, the unattended input system does indeed get selectively 'switched off', in which case there is a somewhat pickwickian sense in which voluntary control over the operation of an input system is circuitously achieved. Or it may be that the unattended input systems continue to operate but lose their access to some central processes (e.g., to those that mediate storage and report). The latter account is favored, at least for the case of language perception, in light of a fair number of results which seem to show relatively high-level processing of the unattended channel in dichotic listening tasks (Lackner and Garrett, 1973; Corteen and Wood, 1972; Lewis, 1970). But since the experimental results in this area are not univocal perhaps the most conservative claim is this: input analysis is mandatory in that it provides the *only* route by which transducer output can gain access to central processes; if transduced information is to affect thought at all, it must do so via the computations that input systems perform.

I suppose one has to enter a minor caveat. Painters, or so I'm told, learn a little to undo the perceptual constancies and thus to see the world in something like the terms that the retina must deliver – as a two-dimensional spread of color discontinuities varying over time. And it is alleged that phoneticians can be taught to hear their language as something like a sound-stream – viz., as something like what the spikes in the auditory nerves presumably encode. (Though, as a matter of fact, the empirical evidence that phoneticians are actually able to do this is equivocal; see, for example, Lieberman, 1965.) But I doubt that we should take these highly skilled phenomenological reductions very seriously as counterexamples to the generalization that input processes are manda-tory. For one thing, precisely because they *are* highly skilled, they may tell us very little about the character of normal perceptual processing. Moreover, it is tendentious – and quite possibly wrong – to think of what painters and phoneti-cians learn to do as getting access to, as it were, raw transducer output. An at least equally plau-sible story is that what they learn is how to 'cor-rect' perceptually interpreted representations in ways that compensate for constancy effects. On this latter view, "seeing the visual field" or "hear-ing the speech stream" are *super*sophisticated perceptual achievements. I don't know which of these stories is the right one, but the issue is clearly empirical and oughtn't to be prejudged.

Anyhow, barring the specialized achieve-ments of painters and phoneticians, one simply cannot see the world under its retinal projection and one has practically no access to the acoustics of utterances in languages that one speaks. (You all know what Swedish and Chinese sound like; what does *English* sound like?) In this respect (and in other respects too, or so I'll presently argue) the input mechanisms approximate the condition often ascribed to reflexes: they are automatically triggered by the stimuli that they apply to. And this is true for both the language comprehension mechanisms and the perceptual systems traditionally so-called.

It is perhaps unnecessary to remark that it does *not* seem to be true for nonperceptual cog-nitive processes. We have only the narrowest of options about how the objects of perception shall be represented, but we have all the leeway in the world as to how we shall represent the objects of *thought*; outside perception, the way that one deploys one's cognitive resources, is, in general, rationally subservient to one's utilities. Here are some exercises that you can do if you choose: think of *Hamlet* as a revenge play; as a typical product of Mannerist sensibility; as a pot-boiler; as an unlikely vehicle for Greta Garbo. Think of sixteen different ways of using a brick. Think of an utterance of "All Gaul is divided into three parts" as an acoustic object. Now try *hearing* an utterance of "All Gaul is divided into three parts" as an acoustic object. Notice the difference.

No doubt there are *some* limits to the free-dom that one enjoys in rationally manipulat-ing the representational capacities of thought. If, indeed, the Freudians are right, more of the direction of thought is mandatory – not to say obsessional – than the uninitiated might suppose. But the quantitative difference surely

seems to be there. There is, as the computer peo-ple would put it, "executive control" over cen-tral representational capacities; and intellectual sophistication consists, in some part, in being able to exert that control in a manner conducive to the satisfaction of one's goals – in ways, in short, that seem likely to get you somewhere. By contrast, perceptual processes apparently apply willy-nilly in disregard of one's immediate con-cerns. "I couldn't help hearing what you said" is one of those clichés which, often enough, expresses a literal truth; and it is what is *said* that one can't help hearing, not just what is *uttered*.

There is Only Limited Central Access to the Mental Representations That Input Systems Compute

It is worth distinguishing the claim that input operations are mandatory (you can't but hear an utterance of a sentence *as* an utterance of a sentence) from the claim that what might be called 'interlevels' of input representation are, typically, relatively inaccessible to consciousness. Not only must you hear an utterance of a sen-tence as such, but, to a first approximation, you can hear it *only* that way.

What makes this consideration interesting is that, according to all standard theories, the com-putations that input systems perform typically proceed via the assignment of a number of inter-mediate analyses of the proximal stimulation. Sentence comprehension, for example, involves not only acoustic encoding but also the recov-ery of phonetic and lexical content and syntactic form. Apparently an analogous picture applies in the case of vision, where the recognition of a distal array as, say, a-bottle-on-a-table-in-the-corner-of-the-room proceeds via the recovery of a series of preliminary representations (in terms of visual frequencies and primal sketches inter alia. For a review of recent thinking about interlevels of visual representation, see Zucker, 1981).

The present point is that the subject doesn't have equal access to all of these ascending lev-els of representation – not at least if we take the criterion of accessibility to be the avail-ability for explicit report of the information that these representations encode. Indeed, as I remarked above, the lowest levels (the ones that correspond most closely to transducer out-puts) appear to be completely *in*accessible for all intents and purposes. The rule seems to be that, even if perceptual processing goes from 'bottom to top' (each level of representation of a stimulus computed being more abstractly related to transducer outputs than the one that immediately preceded), still *access* goes from top down (the further you get from transducer outputs, the more accessible the representations recovered are to central cognitive systems that presumably mediate conscious report).

A plausible first approximation might be that only such representations as constitute the *final* consequences of input processing are fully and freely available to the cognitive processes that eventuate in the voluntary determination of overt behavior. This arrangement of accessibility relations is reasonable enough assuming, on the one hand, that the computational capacities of central cognitive systems are not inexhaustible in their ability to attend to impinging information and, on the other, that it is the relatively abstract products of input-processing that encode most of the news that we are likely to want to know. I said in [the previous] section that the operation of input systems is relatively insensitive to the subject's utilities. By contrast, according to this account, the architectural arrangements that govern exchanges of information between input systems and other mechanisms of cognition do reflect aspects of the organism's standing concerns.

The generalization about the relative inaccessibility of intermediate levels of input analysis is pretty rough, but all sorts of anecdotal and experimental considerations suggest that something of the sort is going on. A well known psychological party trick goes like this:

E: Please look at your watch and tell me the time.
S: (Does so.)
E: Now tell me, without looking again, what is the shape of the numerals on your watch face?
S: (Stumped, evinces bafflement and awe.) (See Morton, 1967)

The point is that visual information which specifies the shape of the numerals must be registered when one reads one's watch, but from the point of view of access to later report, that information doesn't take. One recalls, as it were, pure position with no shape in the position occupied. There are analogous anecdotes to the effect that it is often hard to remember whether somebody you have just been talking to has a beard (or a moustache, or wears glasses). Yet visual information that specifies a beard must be registered and processed whenever you recognize a bearded face. More anecdote: Almost nobody can tell you how the letters and numbers are grouped on a telephone dial, though you use this information whenever you make a phone call. And Nickerson and Adams (1979) have shown that not only are subjects unable to describe a Lincoln penny accurately, they also can't pick out an accurate drawing from ones that get it grossly wrong.

There are quite similar phenomena in the case of language, where it is easy to show that details of syntax (or of the choice of vocabulary) are lost within moments of hearing an utterance, only the gist being retained. (Which did I just say was rapidly lost? Was it the syntactic details or the details of syntax?) Yet it is inconceivable that such information is not registered somewhere in the comprehension process and, within limits, it is possible to enhance its recovery by the manipulation of instructional variables. (For edifying experiments, see Sachs, 1967; Wanner, 1968.)

These sorts of examples make it seem plausible that the relative inaccessibility of lower levels of input analysis is at least in part a matter of how priorities are allocated in the transfer of representations from relatively short- to relatively long-term memory.[7] The idea would be that only quite high-level representations are stored, earlier ones being discarded as soon as subsystems of the input analyzer get the goodness out of them. Or, more precisely, intermediate input representations, when not discarded, are retained only at special cost in memory or attention, the existence of such charges-for-internal-access being itself a prototypical feature of modular systems.

This is, no doubt, part of the story. Witness the fact that in tasks which minimize memory demands by requiring comparison of *simultaneously* presented stimuli, responses that are sensitive to stimulus properties specified at relatively low levels of representation are frequently *faster* than responses to properties of the sort that high-level representations mark. Here, then, the ordering of relative accessibility reverses the top-to-bottom picture proposed above. It may be worth a digression to review some relevant findings.

The classical experimental paradigm is owing to Posner (1978). S's are required to respond 'yes' to visually presented letter pairs when they are *either* font identical (t,t; T,T) *or* alphabetically identical (t,T; T,t). The finding is that when letters in a pair are presented *simultaneously*, response to alphabetically identical pairs that are also font identical is faster than response to pairs that are identical alphabetically but not in font. This effect diminishes asymptotically with increase in the interstimulus interval when the letters are presented *sequentially*.

A plausible (though not mandatory) interpretation is that the representation that specifies the physical shape of the impinging stimulus is computed earlier than representations that specify its alphabetic value. (At a minimum, *some* shape information must be registered prior to alphabetic value, since alphabetic value depends upon shape.) In any event, the fact that representations of shape can drive voluntary responses suggests that they must be available to central processes at *some* point in the course of S's interaction with the stimulus. And this suggests, in turn, that the inaccessibility of font- as compared with alphabetic-information over the relatively long term must be a matter of how memory is deployed rather than of the intrinsic opacity of low-level representations to high-level processes. It looks as though, in these cases, the relative unavailability of lower levels of input analysis is primarily a matter of the way that the subsystems of the input processors interface with memory systems. It is less a matter of information being unconscious than of its being unrecalled. (See also Crowder and Morton, 1969.)

It is unlikely, however, that this is the whole story about the inaccessibility of interlevels of input analysis. For one thing, as was remarked above, some very low levels of stimulus representation appear to be absolutely inaccessible to report. It is, to all intents and purposes (i.e., short of extensive training of the subject) impossible to elicit voluntary responses that are selectively sensitive to subphonetic linguistic distinctions (or, in the case of vision, to parameters of the retinal projection of distal objects) even though we have excellent theoretical grounds for supposing that such information must be registered somewhere in the course of linguistic (/visual) processing. And not *just* theoretical grounds: *we can often show that aspects of the subject's behavior are sensitive to the information that he can't report.*

For example, a famous result on the psychophysics of speech argues that utterances of syllables may be indistinguishable despite very substantial differences in their acoustic structure *so long as these differences are subphonetic.* When, however, quantitatively identical acoustic differences happen to be, as, linguists say, 'contrastive' – i.e., when they mark distinctions between phones – they will be quite discriminable to the subject; as distinguishable, say, as "ba" is from "pa". It appears, in short, that there is a perceptual constancy at work which determines, in a wide range of cases, that only such acoustic differences as have linguistic value are accessible to the hearer in discrimination tasks. (See Liberman, et al., 1967.) What is equally striking, however, is that these 'inaccessible' differences *do affect reaction times*. Suppose a/a and a/b are utterance pairs such that the members of the first pair are literally acoustically identical and the members of the second differ only in *non*contrastive acoustic properties – i.e., the acoustic distinction between a and b is subphonetic. As we have seen, it is possible to choose such properties so that the members of the a/b pair are perceptually indistinguishable (as are, of course, the members of the pair a/a). Even so, in such cases reaction times to make the 'same' judgment for the a/a pair are reliably faster than reaction times to make the 'same' judgment for the a/b pair. (Pisoni and Tash, 1974.) The subject can't report – and presumably can't hear – the difference between signal a and signal b, but his behavior is sensitive to it all the same.

These kinds of cases are legion in studies of the constancies, and this fact bears discussion. The *typical* function of the constancies is to engender perceptual similarity in the face of the variability of proximal stimulation. Proximal variation is very often misleading; the world is, in general, considerably more stable than are its projections onto the surfaces of transducers. Constancies correct for this, so that in general percepts correspond to distal layouts *better than* proximal stimuli do. But, of course, the work of the constancies would be undone unless the central systems which run behavior were required largely to ignore the representations which encode *un*connected proximal information. The obvious architectural solution is to allow central systems to access information engendered by proximal stimulation only *after* it has been run through the input analyzers. Which is to say that central processes should have free access only to the *outputs* of perceptual processors, interlevels of perceptual processing being correspondingly opaque to higher cognitive systems. This, I'm claiming, is the architecture that we in fact do find.

There appears, in short, to be a generalization to state about input systems as such. Input analysis typically involves *mediated* mappings from transducer outputs onto percepts – mappings that are effected via the computation of interlevels of representation of the impinging stimulus. These intermediate representations are sometimes absolutely inaccessible to central processes, or, in many cases, they are accessible at a price: you can get at them, but only by imposing special demands upon memory or attention. Or, to put it another way: To a first approximation, input systems can be freely queried by memory and other central systems only in respect of *one* of the levels of representation that they compute; and the level that defines this interface is, in general, the one that is most abstractly related to transduced representations. This claim, if true, is substantive; and if, as I believe, it holds for input systems at large, then that is another reason to believe that the construct *input system* subsumes a natural kind.

Input Systems are Fast

Identifying sentences and visual arrays are among the fastest of our psychological processes. It is a little hard to quantify this claim because of unclarities about the individuation of mental activities. (What precisely are the boundaries of the processes to be compared? For example, where does sentence (/scene) *recognition* stop and more central activities take over? [. . .]) Still, granting the imprecision, there are more than enough facts around to shape one's theoretical intuitions.

Among the simplest of voluntary responses are two-choice reactions (push the button if the *left*-hand light goes on). The demands that this task imposes upon the cognitive capacities are minimal, and a practiced subject can respond reliably at latencies on the low side of a quarter of a second. It thus bears thinking about that the recovery of semantic content from a spoken sentence can occur at speeds quite comparable to those achieved in the two-choice reaction paradigm. In particular, appreciable numbers of subjects can 'shadow' continuous speech with a quarter-second latency (shadowing is repeating what you hear as you hear it) and, contrary to some of the original reports, there is now good evidence that such 'fast shadowers' understand what they repeat. (See Marslen-Wilson, 1973.) Considering the amount of processing that must go on in sentence comprehension (unless all our current theories are *totally* wrongheaded), this finding is mind-boggling. And, mind-boggling or otherwise, it is clear that shadowing latency is an extremely conservative measure of the speed of comprehension. Since shadowing requires *repeating* what one is hearing, the 250 msec. of lag between stimulus and response includes not only the time required for the perceptual analysis of the message, but also the time required for the subject's integration of his verbalization.

In fact, it may be that the phenomenon of fast shadowing shows that the efficiency of language processing comes very close to achieving theoretical limits. Since the syllabic rate of normal speech is about 4 per second, the observed 250 msec. latency is compatible with the suggestion that fast shadowers are processing speech in syllable-length units – i.e., that the initiation of the shadower's response is commenced upon the identification of each syllable-length input. Now, work in the psychoacoustics of speech makes it look quite likely that the syllable is the shortest linguistic unit that *can* be reliably identified in the speech stream (see Liberman et al., 1967). Apparently, the acoustic realizations of shorter linguistic forms (like phones) exhibit such extreme context dependence as to make them unidentifiable on a unit-by-unit basis. Only at the level of the syllable do we begin to find stretches of wave form whose acoustic properties are at all reliably related to their linguistic values. If this is so, then it suggests the following profoundly depressing possibility: the responses of fast shadowers lag a syllable behind the stimulus *not* because a quarter second is the upper bound on the speed of the mental processes that mediate language comprehension, but rather because, if the subject were to go any faster, he would overrun the ability of the speech stream to signal linguistic distinctions.[8]

In the attempt to estimate the speed of computation of visual processing, problems of quantification are considerably more severe. On the one hand, the stimulus is not usually spread out in time, so it's hard to determine how much of the input the subject registers before initiating his identificatory response. And, on the other hand, we don't have a taxonomy of visual stimuli comparable to the classification of utterance tokens into linguistic types. Since the question what type a linguistic token belongs to is a great deal clearer than the corresponding question for visual arrays, it is even less obvious in vision than in speech what sort of response should count as indicating that a given array has been identified.

For all of which there is good reason to believe that given a motivated decision about how to quantify the observations, the facts about visual perception would prove quite as appalling as those about language. For example, in one study by Haber (1980), subjects were exposed to 2,560 photographic slides of randomly chosen natural scenes, each slide being exposed for an interval of 10 seconds. Performance on recognition recall (ability to correctly identify a test slide as one that had been seen previously) approached 90 percent one hour after the original exposure. Haber remarks that the results "suggest that recognition of pictures is essentially perfect." Recent work by Potter (personal communication) indicates that 10 seconds of exposure is actually a great deal more than subjects need to effect a perceptual encoding of the stimulus adequate to mediate this near-perfect performance. According to Potter, S's performance in the Haber paradigm asymptotes at an exposure interval of about 2 seconds per slide.

There are some other results of Potter's (1975) that make the point still more graphically. S is shown a sequence of slides of magazine photographs, the rate of presentation of the slides being the experimentally manipulated variable. Prior to each sequence, S is provided with a brief description of an object or event that may appear in one or another slide – e.g., a boat, two men drinking beer, etc. S is to attend to the slides, responding when he sees one that satisfies the description. Under these conditions, S's respond with better than 70 percent accuracy when each slide is exposed for 125 msec. Accuracy asymptotes (at around 96 percent) at exposure times of 167 msec, per slide. It is of some interest that S's are as good at this task as they are at recognition recall (i.e., at making the global judgment that a given slide is one that they have seen before).

Two first-blush morals should be drawn from such findings about the computational efficiency of input processes. First, it contrasts with the relative slowness of paradigmatic central processes like problem-solving; and, second, it is presumably no accident that these very fast psychological processes are mandatory.

The first point is, I suppose, intuitively obvious: one can, and often does, spend hours thinking about a problem in philosophy or chess, though there is no reason to suppose that the computational complexity of these problems is greater than that of the ones that are routinely solved effortlessly in the course of perceptual processing. Indeed, the puzzle about input analysis is precisely that the computational complexity of the problem to be solved doesn't seem to predict the difficulty of solving it; or, rather, if it does, the difference between a 'hard' problem and an 'easy' one is measured not in months but in milliseconds. This dissimilarity between perception and thought is surely so adequately robust that it is unlikely to be an artifact of the way that we individuate cognitive achievements. It is only in trick cases, of the sorts that psychologists devise in experimental laboratories, that the perceptual analysis of an utterance or a visual scene is other than effectively instan-

taneous. What goes on when you parse a standard psycholinguistic poser like "the horse raced past the barn fell" is, almost certainly, *not* the same sort of processing that mediates sentence recognition in the normal case. They even *feel* different.

Second, it may well be that processes of input analysis are fast *because* they are mandatory. Because these processes are automatic, you save computation (hence time) that would otherwise have to be devoted to deciding whether, and how, they ought to be performed. Compare: eyeblink is a fast response *because* it is a reflex – i.e., because you don't have to *decide* whether to blink your eye when someone jabs a finger at it. Automatic responses are, in a certain sense, deeply unintelligent; of the whole range of computational (and, eventually, behavioral) options available to the organism, only a stereotyped subset is brought into play. But what you save by indulging in this sort of stupidity is *not having to make up your mind*, and making your mind up takes time. Reflexes, whatever their limitations, are not in jeopardy of being sicklied o'er with the pale cast of thought. Nor are input processes, according to the present analysis.

There is, however, more than this to be said about the speed of input processes. We'll return to the matter shortly.

Input Systems are Informationally Encapsulated

Some of the claims that I'm now about to make are in dispute among psychologists, but I shall make them anyway because I think that they are true. I shall run the discussion in this section largely in terms of language, though, as usual, it is intended that the morals should hold for input systems at large.

I remarked above that, almost certainly, understanding an utterance involves establishing its analysis at several different levels of representation: phonetic, phonological, lexical, syntactic; and so forth. Now, in principle, information about the probable structure of the stimulus at any of these levels could be brought to bear upon the recovery of its analysis at any of the others. Indeed, in principle *any* information available to the hearer, including meteorological information, astrological information, or – rather more plausibly – information about the speaker's probable communicative intentions could be brought to bear at any point in the comprehension process. In particular, it is entirely possible that, in the course of computing a structural description, information that is specified only at relatively high levels of representation should be 'fed back' to determine analyses at relatively lower levels.[9] But though this is possible in principle, the burden of my argument is going to be that the operations of input systems are in certain respects unaffected by such feedback.

I want to emphasize the 'in certain respects'. For there exist, in the psychological literature, dramatic illustrations of the effects of information feedback upon some input operations. Consider, for example, the 'phoneme restoration effect' (Warren, 1970). You make a tape recording of a word (as it might be, the word "legislature") and you splice out one of the speech sounds (as it might be, the 's'), which you then replace with a tape recording of a cough. The acoustic structure of the resultant signal is thus /legi(cough)lature/ But what a subject will *hear* when you play the tape to him is an utterance of /legislature/ with a cough 'in the background'. It surely seems that what is going on here is that the perceived phonetic constituency of the utterance is determined not just by the transduced information (not just by information specified at *sub*-phonetic levels of analysis) but also by higher-level information about the probable lexical representation of the utterance (i.e., by the subject's guess that the intended utterance was probably /legislature/).

It is not difficult to imagine how this sort of feedback might be achieved. Perhaps, when the stimulus is noisy, the subject's mental lexicon is searched for a 'best match' to however much of the phonetic content of the utterance has been securely identified. In effect, the lexicon is queried by the instruction 'Find an entry some ten phones long, of which the initial phone sequence is /legi/ and the terminal sequence is /lature/.' The reply to this query constitutes the lexical analysis under which the input is heard.

Apparently rather similar phenomena occur in the case of visual scotoma (where neurological disorders produce a 'hole' in the subject's visual field). The evidence is that scotoma can mask quite a lot of the visual input without creating a phenomenal blind spot for the subject. What happens is presumably that information about higher-level redundancies is fed back to 'fill in' the missing sensory information. Some such process also presumably accounts for one's inability to 'see' one's retinal blind spot.

These sorts of considerations have led some psychologists (and many theorists in AI) to pro-pose relentlessly top-down models of input analysis, in which the perceptual encoding of a stimulus is determined largely by the subject's (conscious or unconscious) beliefs and expectations, and hardly at all by the stimulus information that transducers provide. Extreme examples of such feedback-oriented approaches can be found in Schank's account of language comprehension, in Neisser's early theorizing about vision, and in 'analysis by synthesis' approaches to sentence parsing. Indeed, a sentimental attachment to what are known generically as 'New Look' accounts of perception (Bruner, 1957) is pervasive in the cognitive science community. It will, however, be a main moral of this discussion that the involvement of certain sorts of feedback in the operation of input systems would be incompatible with their modularity, at least as I propose to construe the modularity thesis. One or other of these doctrines will have to go.

In the long run, which one goes will be a question of how the data turn out. Indeed, a great deal of the empirical interest of the modularity thesis lies in the fact that the experimental predictions it makes tend to be diametrically opposed to the ones that New Look approaches license. But experiments to one side, there are some prima facie reasons for doubting that the computations that input systems perform could have anything like unlimited access to high-level expectations or beliefs. These considerations suggest that even if there are *some* perceptual mechanisms whose operations are extensively subject to feedback, there must be others that compute the structure of a percept largely, perhaps solely, in isolation from background information.

For one thing, there is the widely noted persistence of many perceptual illusions (e.g., the Ames room, the phi phenomenon, the Muller-Lyer illusion in vision; the phoneme restoration and click displacement effects in speech) even in defiance of the subject's explicit knowledge that the percept is illusory. The very same subject who can tell you that the Muller-Lyer arrows are identical in length, who indeed has seen them measured, still finds one looking longer than the other. In such cases it is hard to see an alternative to the view that at least *some* of the background information at the subject's disposal is inaccessible to at least some of his perceptual mechanisms.

An old psychological puzzle provides a further example of this kind. When you move your head, or your eyes, the flow of images across the retina may be identical to what it would be were the head and eyes to remain stationary while the scene moves. So: why don't we experience apparent motion when we move our eyes? Most psychologists now accept one or other version of the "corollary discharge" answer to this problem. According to this story, the neural centers which initiate head and eye motions communicate with the input analyzer in charge of interpreting visual stimulations (see Bizzi, 1968). Because the latter system knows what the former is up to, it is able to discount alterations in the retinal flow that are due to the motions of the receptive organs.

Well, the point of interest for us is that this visual-motor system is informationally encapsulated. Witness the fact that, if you (gently) push your eyeball with your finger (as opposed to moving it in the usual way: by an exercise of the will), you *do* get apparent motion. Consider the moral: when you voluntarily move your eyeball with your finger, you certainly are possessed of the information that it's your eye (and not the visual scene) that is moving. This knowledge is absolutely explicit; if I ask you, you can *say* what's going on. But this explicit information, available to you for (e.g.) report, is *not* available to the analyzer in charge of the perceptual integration of your retinal stimulations. That system has access to corollary discharges from the motor center *and to no other information that you possess*. Modularity with a vengeance.

We've been surveying first blush considerations which suggest that at least some input analyzers are encapsulated with respect to at least some sorts of feedback. The next of these is a point of principle: feedback works only to the extent that the information which perception supplies is redundant; and it is possible to perceptually analyze arbitrarily unredundant stimulus arrays. This point is spectacularly obvious in the case of language. If I write "I keep a giraffe in my pocket," you are able to understand me despite the fact that, on even the most inflationary construal of the notion of context, there is nothing in the context of the inscription that would have enabled you to predict either its form or its content. In short, feedback is effective only to the extent that, *prior* to the analysis of the stimulus, the perceiver knows quite a lot about what the stimulus is going to be like. Whereas, the *point* of perception is, surely, that it lets us find out how the world is even when the world is some way that we *don't* expect it to be. The teleology of perceptual capacities presupposes a considerably-less-than-omniscient-organism; they'd be no use to

God. If you already *know* how things are, why look to *see* how things are?[10]

So: The perceptual analysis of *un*anticipated stimulus layouts (in language and elsewhere) is possible only to the extent that (a) the output of the transducer is insensitive to the beliefs/expectations of the organism; and (b) the input analyzers are adequate to compute a representation of the stimulus from the information that the transducers supply. This is to say that the perception of novelty depends on bottom-to-top perceptual mechanisms.

There is a variety of ways of putting this point, which is, I think, among the most important for understanding the character of the input systems. Pylyshyn (1980) speaks of the "cognitive impenetrability" of perception, meaning that the output of the perceptual systems is largely insensitive to what the perceiver presumes or desires. Pylyshyn's point is that a condition for the *reliability* of perception, at least for a fallible organism, is that it generally sees what's there, not what it wants or expects to be there. Organisms that don't do so become deceased.

Here is another terminology for framing these issues about the direction of information flow in perceptual analysis: Suppose that the organism is given the problem of determining the analysis of a stimulus at a certain level of representation – e.g., the problem of determining which sequence of words a given utterance encodes. Since, in the general case, transducer outputs underdetermine perceptual analyses,[11] we can think of the solution of such problems as involving processes of nondemonstrative inference. In particular, we can think of each input system as a computational mechanism which projects and confirms a certain class of hypotheses on the basis of a certain body of data. In the present example, the available hypotheses are the word sequences that can be constructed from entries in the subject's mental lexicon, and the perceptual problem is to determine which of these sequences provides the right analysis of the currently impinging utterance token. The mechanism which solves the problem is, in effect, the realization of a *confirmation function*: it's a mapping which associates with each pair of a lexical hypothesis and some acoustic datum a value which expresses the degree of confirmation that the latter bestows upon the former. (And similarly, mutatis mutandis, for the nondemonstrative inferences that the other input analyzers effect.) I emphasize that construing the situation this way involves no commitment to a detailed theory of the operation of perceptual systems. *Any* nondemonstrative inference can be viewed as the projection and confirmation of a hypothesis, and I take it that perceptual inferences must in general be nondemonstrative, since their underdetermination by sensory data is not in serious dispute.

Looked at this way, the claim that input systems are informationally encapsulated is equivalent to the claim that the data that can bear on the confirmation of perceptual hypotheses includes, in the general case, considerably less than the organism may know. That is, the confirmation function for input systems does not have access to all of the information that the organism internally represents; there are restrictions upon the allocation of internally represented information to input processes.

Talking about the direction of information flow in psychological processes and talking about restrictions upon the allocation of information to such processes are thus two ways of talking about the same thing. If, for example, we say that the flow of information in language comprehension runs directly from the determination of the phonetic structure of an utterance to the determination of its lexical content, then we are saying that only phonetic information is available to whatever mechanism decides the level of confirmation of perceptual hypotheses about lexical structure. On that account, such mechanisms are encapsulated with respect to *non*phonetic information; they have no access to such information; not even if it is *internally represented, accessible to other cognitive processes* (i.e., to cognitive processes other than the assignment of lexical analyses to phone sequences) and *germane* in the sense that if it *were* brought to bear in lexical analysis, it would affect the confirmation levels of perceptual hypotheses about lexical structure.

I put the issue of informational encapsulation in terms of constraints on the data available for hypothesis confirmation because doing so will help us later, when we come to compare input systems with central cognitive processes. Suffice it to say, for the moment, that this formulation suggests another possible reason why input systems are so fast. We remarked above that the computations that input systems perform are mandatory, and that their being so saves time that would otherwise have to be used in executive decision-making. We now add that input systems are bull-headed and that this, too, makes for speed. The point is this: to the extent that input systems are informationally encapsulated, of all the information that might *in principle* bear

upon a problem of perceptual analysis only a portion (perhaps only quite a small and stereotyped portion) is actually admitted for consideration. This is to say that speed is purchased for input systems by permitting them to ignore lots of the facts. Ignoring the facts is not, of course, a good recipe for problem-solving in the general case. But then, as we have seen, input systems don't function in the *general* case. Rather, they function to provide very special kinds of representations of very specialized inputs (to pair transduced representations with formulas in the domains of central processes). What operates in the general case, and what is sensitive, at least in principle, to *everything* that the organism knows, are the central processes themselves. Of which more later.

I should add that these reflections upon the value of bull-headedness do not, as one might suppose, entirely depend upon assumptions about the speed of memory search. Consider an example. Ogden Nash once offered the following splendidly sane advice: "If you're called by a panther/don't anther." Roughly, we want the perceptual identification of panthers to be very fast and to err, if at all, only on the side of false positives. If there is a body of information that must be deployed in such perceptual identifications, then we would prefer not to have to recover that information from a large memory, assuming that the speed of access varies inversely with the amount of information that the memory contains. This is a way of saying that we do not, on that assumption, want to have to access panther-identification information from the (presumably *very* large) central storage in which representations of background-information-at-large are generally supposed to live. Which is in turn to say that we don't want the input analyzer that mediates panther identification to communicate with the central store on the assumption that large memories are searched slowly.

Suppose, however, that random access to a memory is *insensitive* to its size. *Even so* panther-identification (and, mutatis mutandis, other processes of input analysis) had better be insensitive to much of what one knows. Suppose that we can get at *everything* we know about panthers *very* fast. We still have the problem of deciding, for each such piece of information retrieved from memory, *how much inductive confirmation it bestows upon the hypothesis that the presently observed black-splotch-in-the-visual-field is a panther.* The point is that in the rush and scramble of panther identification, there are many things I know about panthers whose bearing on the likely pantherhood of the present stimulus *I do not wish to have to consider*. As, for example, that my grandmother abhors panthers; that every panther bears some distant relation to my Siamese cat Jerrold J.; that there are no panthers on Mars; that there is an Ogden Nash poem about panthers . . . etc. Nor is this all; for, in fact, the property of being 'about panthers' is not one that can be surefootedly relied upon. Given enough context, practically everything I know can be construed as panther related; and, *I do not want to have to consider everything I know* in the course of perceptual panther identification. In short, the point of the informational encapsulation of input processes is not – or not solely – to reduce the memory space that must be searched to find information that is perceptually relevant. The primary point is to so restrict the number of *confirmation relations* that need to be estimated as to make perceptual identifications fast. (I am indebted to Scott Fahlman for raising questions that provoked the last two paragraphs.)[12]

The informational encapsulation of the input systems is, or so I shall argue, the essence of their modularity. It's also the essence of the analogy between the input systems and reflexes; reflexes are informationally encapsulated with bells on.

Suppose that you and I have known each other for many a long year (we were boys together, say) and you have come fully to appreciate the excellence of my character. In particular, you have come to know perfectly well that under no conceivable circumstances would I stick my finger in your eye. Suppose that this belief of yours is both explicit and deeply felt. You would, in fact, go to the wall for it. Still, if I jab my finger near enough to your eyes, and fast enough, you'll blink. To say, as we did above, that the blink reflex is mandatory is to say, inter alia, that it has no access to what you know about my character or, for that matter, to any other of your beliefs, utilities and expectations. For this reason the blink reflex is often produced when sober reflection would show it to be uncalled for; like panther-spotting, it is prepared to trade false positive for speed.

That is what it is like for a psychological system to be informationally encapsulated. If you now imagine a system that is encapsulated in the way that reflexes are, but also computational in a way that reflexes are not, you will have some idea of what I'm proposing that input systems are like.

It is worth emphasizing that being modular in this sense is not quite the same thing as being autonomous in the sense that Gall had in mind. For Gall, if I read him right, the claim that the vertical faculties are autonomous was practically equivalent to the claim that there are no horizontal faculties for them to share. Musical aptitude, for example, is autonomous *in that* judging musical ideas shares no cognitive mechanisms with judging mathematical ideas; remembering music shares no cognitive mechanisms with remembering faces; perceiving music shares no cognitive mechanisms with perceiving speech; and so forth.

Now, it is unclear to what extent the input systems are autonomous *in that* sense. We do know, for example, that there are systematic relations between the amount of computational strain that decoding a sentence places on the language handling systems and the subject's ability to perform simultaneous nonlinguistic tasks quickly and accurately. 'Phoneme monitor' (Foss, 1969) techniques, and others, can be used to measure such interactions, and the results suggest a picture that is now widely accepted among cognitive psychologists: Mental processes often compete for access to resources variously characterized as attention, short-term memory, or work space; and the result of allocating such resources to one of the competing processes is a decrement in the performance of the others. How general this sort of interaction is is unclear in the present state of the art (for contrary cases, suggesting isolated work spaces for visual imagery on the one hand and verbal recall on the other, see Brooks, 1968). In any event, where such competition does obtain, it is a counterexample to autonomy in what I am taking to be Gall's understanding of that notion.[13]

On the other hand, we can think of autonomy in a rather different way from Gall's – viz., in terms of informational encapsulation. So, instead of asking what access language processes (e.g.) have to *computational resources* that other systems also share, we can ask what access they have to the *information* that is available to other systems. If we do look at things this way, then the question "how much autonomy?" is the same question as "how much constraint on information flow?" In a nutshell: one way that a system can be autonomous is by being encapsulated, by not having access to facts that other systems know about. I am claiming that, whether or not the input systems are autonomous in Gall's sense, they are, to an interesting degree, autonomous in this informational sense.

However, I have not yet given any arguments (except some impressionistic ones) to show that the input systems actually are informationally encapsulated. In fact, I propose to do something considerably more modest: I want to suggest some caveats that ought to be, but frequently aren't, observed in interpreting the sorts of data that have usually been alleged in support of the contrary view. I think that many of the considerations that have seemed to suggest that input processes are cognitively penetrable – that they are importantly affected by the subject's belief about context, or his background information, or his utilities – are, in fact, equivocal or downright misleading. I shall therefore propose several ground rules for evaluating claims about the cognitive penetrability of input systems; and I'll suggest that, when these rules are enforced, the evidence for 'New Look' approaches to perception begins to seem not impressive. My impulse in all this is precisely analogous to what Marr and Poggio say motivates their work on vision: "... to examine ways of squeezing the last ounce of information from an image before taking recourse to the descending influence of high-level interpretation on early processing" (1977, pp. 475–476).

(a) Nobody doubts that the information that input systems provide must somehow be reconciled with the subject's background knowledge. We sometimes know that the world can't really be the way that it looks, and such cases may legitimately be described as the correction of input analyses by top-down information flow. (This, ultimately, is the reason for refusing to identify input analysis with perception. The point of perception is the fixation of belief, and the fixation of belief is a *conservative* process – one that is sensitive, in a variety of ways, to what the perceiver already knows. Input analysis may be informationally encapsulated, but perception surely is not.) However, to demonstrate that sort of interaction between input analyses and background knowledge is not, in and of itelf, tantamount to demonstrating the cognitive penetrability of the former; you need also to show that the locus of the top-down effect is *internal* to the input system. That is, you need to show that the information fed back interacts with interlevels of input-processing and not merely with the final results of such processing. The penetrability of a system is, by definition, its susceptibility to top-down effects at stages *prior* to its production of output.

I stress this point because it seems quite possible that input systems specify only relatively shallow levels of representation (see section [III.6 of the original work]). For example,

it is quite possible that the perceptual representation delivered for a token sentence specifies little more than the type to which the token belongs (and hence does *not* specify such information as the speech act potential of the token, still less the speech act performed by the tokening). If this is so, then data showing effects of the hearer's background information on, e.g., his estimates of the speaker's communicative intentions would *not* constitute evidence for the cognitive penetration of the presumptive language-comprehension module; by hypothesis, the computations involved in making such estimates would not be among those that the language-comprehension module *per se* performs. Similarly, mutatis mutandis, in the case of vision. There is a great deal of evidence for context effects upon certain aspects of visual object recognition. But such evidence counts for nothing in the present discussion unless there is independent reason to believe that these aspects of object recognition are part of visual input analysis. Perhaps the input system for vision specifies the stimulus only in terms of "primal sketches" for whose cognitive impenetrability there is, by the way, some nontrivial evidence. (See Marr and Nishihara (1978).) The problem of assessing the degree of informational encapsulation of input systems is thus not independent of the problem of determining how such systems are individuated and what sorts of representations constitute their outputs. I shall return to the latter issue presently; for the moment, I'm just issuing caveats.

(b) Evidence for the cognitive penetrability of some computational mechanism that does what input systems do is not, in and of itself, evidence for the cognitive penetrability of input systems.

To see what is at issue here, consider some of the kinds of findings that have been taken as decisively exhibiting the effects of background expectations upon language perception. A well known way of estimating such expectations is the use of the so-called Cloze procedure. Roughly, S is presented with the first n words of a sentence and is asked to complete the fragment. Favored completions (as, for example, "salt" in the case of the fragment "I have the pepper, but would you please pass the——") are said to be "high Cloze" and are assumed to indicate what the subject would expect a speaker to say next if he had just uttered a token of the fragment. An obvious generalization allows the estimation of the Cloze value at each point in a sentence, thereby permitting experiments in which the average Cloze value of the stimulus sentences is a manipulated variable.

It is quite easy to show that relative Cloze value affects S's performance on a number of experimental tasks, and it is reasonable to infer from such demonstrations that whatever mechanisms mediate the performance of these tasks must have access to S's expectations about what speakers are likely to say, hence not just to the 'stimulus' (e.g., acoustic) properties of the linguistic token under analysis. (For an early review of the literature on redundancy effects in sentence processing, see Miller and Isard, 1963.) So, for example, it can be shown that the accuracy of S's perception of sentences heard under masking noise is intimately related to the average Cloze value of the sentences: high Cloze sentences can be understood under conditions of greater distortion than the perception of low Cloze sentences tolerates. (Similarly, high Cloze sentences are, in general, more easily remembered than low Cloze sentences; recognition thresholds for words that are high Cloze in a context are lower than those for words that are low Cloze in that context; and so forth.)

The trouble with such demonstrations, however, is that although they show that there exist *some* language-handling processes that have access to the hearer's expectations about what is likely to be said, they do *not* show that the input systems enjoy such access. For example, it might be argued that, in situations where the stimulus is acoustically degraded, the subject is, in effect, encouraged to guess the identity of the material that he can't hear. (Similarly, mutatis mutandis, in memory experiments where a reasonable strategy for the subject is to guess at such of the material as he can't recall.) Not surprisingly, in such circumstances, the subject's background information comes into play with measurable effect. The question, however, is whether the psychological mechanisms deployed in the slow, relatively painful, highly attentional process of reconstructing noisy or otherwise degraded linguistic stimuli are the same mechanisms which mediate the automatic and fluent processes of normal speech perception.

That this question is not merely frivolous is manifested by results such as those of Fishler and Bloom (1980). Using a task in which sentences are presented in clear they found only a marginal effect of high Cloze on the recognition of test words, and such effects vanished entirely when the stimuli were presented at high rates. (High presentation rates presumably discour-

age guessing; guessing takes time.) By contrast, words that are 'semantically anomalous' in context showed considerable inhibition in comparison with neutral controls. This last finding is of interest because it suggests that at least some of the effects of sentence context in speech recognition must be, as psychologists sometimes put it, 'post-perceptual'. In our terminology, these processes must operate *after* the input system has provided a (tentative) analysis of the lexical content of the stimulus. The point is that even if the facilitation of redundant items is mediated by predictive, expectation-driven mechanisms, the inhibition of contextually anomalous items cannot be. It is arguable that, in the course of speech perception, one is forever making such predictions as that 'pepper' will occur in 'salt and——'; but surely one can't also be forever predicting that 'dog', 'tomorrow', and all the other anomalous expressions will *not* occur there.[14] The moral is: some processes which eventuate in perceptual identifications are, doubtless, cognitively penetrated. But this is compatible with the informational encapsulation of the input systems themselves. Some traditional enthusiasm for context-driven perceptual models may have been prompted by confusion on this point.

(c) The claim that input systems are informationally encapsulated must be very carefully distinguished from the claim that there is top-down information flow *within* these systems. These issues are very often run together, with consequent exaggeration of the well-groundedness of the case against encapsulation.

Consider, once again, the phoneme restoration effect. Setting aside the general caution that experiments with distorted stimuli provide dubious grounds for inferences about speech perception in clear, phoneme restoration provides considerable prima facie evidence that phone identification has access to what the subject knows about the lexical inventory of his language. If this interpretation is correct, then phoneme restoration illustrates top-down information flow in speech perception. It does *not*, however, illustrate the cognitive penetrability of the language input system. To show that that system is penetrable (hence informationally unencapsulated), you would have to show that its processes have access to information that is not specified at any of the levels of representation that the language input system computes; for example, that it has generalized access to what the hearer knows about the probable beliefs and intentions of his interlocutors. If, by contrast, the 'background information' deployed in phoneme restoration is simply the hearer's knowledge of the words in his language, then that counts as top-down flow within the language module; on any remotely plausible account, the knowledge of a language includes knowledge of its lexicon.

The most recent work in phoneme restoration makes this point with considerable force. Samuel (1981) has shown that both information about the lexical inventory and 'semantic' information supplied by sentential context affect the magnitude of the phoneme restoration effect. Specifically, you get more restoration in words than in (phonologically possible) nonwords, and you get more restoration when a word is predictable in sentence context than when the context is neutral. This looks like the penetration of phone recognition by both lexical and 'background' information, but the appearance is misleading. In fact, Samuel's data suggest that, of the two effects, *only the former* is strictly perceptual, the latter operating in consequence of a response bias to report predictable words as intact. (Detection theoretically: the word/nonword difference affects d', whereas the neutral context/predictive context difference affects β.) As Samuel points out, the amount of restoration is inversely proportional to S's ability to distinguish the stimulus word with a phone missing from an undistorted token of the same type; and, on Samuel's data, this discrimination is actually *better* for items that are highly predictable in context than for items that aren't. Another case, in short, where what had been taken to be an example of context-driven prediction in perception is, in fact, an effect of the biasing of post-perceptual decision processes.

The importance of distinguishing cognitive penetration from intramodular effects can be seen in many other cases where predictive analysis in perception is demonstrable. It is, for example, probable (though harder to show than one might have supposed) that top-down processes are involved in the identification of the surface constituent structure of sentences (see Wright, 1982). For example, it appears that the identification of nouns is selectively facilitated in contexts like T A ——, the identification of verbs is selectively facilitated in contexts like T N ——, and so forth. Such facilitation indicates that the procedures for assigning lexical items to form classes have access to information about the general conditions upon the well-formedness of constituent structure trees.

Now, it is a question of considerable theoretical interest whether, and to what extent, predictive analysis plays a role in parsing; but this issue must be sharply distinguished from the question whether the parser is informationally encapsulated. Counterexamples to encapsulation must exhibit the sensitivity of the parser to information that is not specified internal to the language-recognition module, and constraints on syntactic well-formedness are paradigms of information that does *not* satisfy this condition. The issue is currently a topic of intensive experimental and theoretical inquiry; but as things stand I know of no convincing evidence that syntactic parsing is ever guided by the subject's appreciation of semantic context or of 'real world' background. Perhaps this is not surprising; there are, in general, so many syntactically different ways of saying the same thing that even if context allowed you to estimate the *content* of what is about to be said, that information wouldn't much increase your ability to predict its *form*.[15]

These questions about where the interacting information comes from (whether it comes from inside or outside the input system) take on a special salience in light of the following consideration: it is possible to imagine ways in which mechanisms *internal* to a module might contrive to, as it were, mimic effects of cognitive penetration. The operation of such mechanisms might thus invite overestimations of the extent to which the module has access to the organism's general informational resources. To see how this might occur, let's return to the question of contextual facilitation of word recognition; traditionally a parade case for New Look theorizing, but increasingly an area in which the data are coming to seem equivocal.

Here are the bare bones of an ingenious experiment of David Swinney's (1979; for further, quite similar, results, see Tanenhaus, Leiman, and Seidenberg, 1979). The subject listens to a stimulus sentence along the lines of "Because he was afraid of electronic surveillance, the spy carefully searched the room for bugs." Now, we know from previous research that the response latencies for 'bugs' (say, in a word/nonword decision task) will be faster in this context, where it is relatively predictable, than in a neutral context where it is acceptable but relatively low Cloze. This seems to be – and is traditionally taken to be – the sort of result which demonstrates how expectations based upon an intelligent appreciation of sentential context can guide lexical access; the subject predicts 'bugs' before he hears the word. His responses are correspondingly accelerated whenever his prediction proves true. Hence, cognitive penetration of lexical access.

You can, or so it seems, gild this lily. Suppose that, instead of measuring reaction time for word/nonword decisions on 'bugs', you simultaneously present (flashed on a screen that the subject can see) a different word belonging to the same (as one used to say) 'semantic field' (e.g., 'microphones'). If the top-down story is right in supposing that the subject is using semantic/background information to predict lexical content, then 'microphones' is as good a prediction in context as 'bugs' is, so you might expect that 'microphones', too, will exhibit facilitation as compared with a neutral context. And so it proves to do. Cognitive penetration of lexical access with bells on, or so it would appear.

But the appearance is misleading. For Swinney's data show that if you test with 'insects' instead of 'microphones', you get the same result: facilitation as compared with a neutral context. Consider what this means. 'Bugs' has two paraphrases: 'microphones' and 'insects'. But though only one of these is contextually relevant, *both are contextually facilitated*. This looks a lot less like the intelligent use of contextual/background information to guide lexical access. What it looks like instead is some sort of associative relation among lexical forms (between, say, 'spy' and 'bug'); a relation pitched at a level of representation sufficiently superficial to be *in*sensitive to the semantic content of the items involved. This possibility is important for the following reason: If facilitation is mediated by merely interlexical relations (and not by the interaction of background information with the semantic content of the item and its context), then the information that is exploited to produce the facilitation can be represented *in the lexicon*; hence *internal to the language recognition module*. And if that is right, then contextual facilitation of lexical access is *not* an argument for the cognitive penetration of the module. It makes a difference, as I remarked above, where the penetrating information comes from.

Let's follow this just a little further. Suppose the mental lexicon is a sort of connected graph, with lexical items at the nodes and with paths from each item to several others. We can think of accessing an item in the lexicon as, in effect, exciting the corresponding node; and we can assume that one of the consequences of accessing a node is that excitation spreads along the path-

ways that lead from it. Assume, finally, that when excitation spreads through a portion of the lexical network, response thresholds for the excited nodes are correspondingly lowered. Accessing a given lexical item will thus decrease the response times for items to which it is connected. (This picture is familiar from the work of, among others, Morton, 1969, and Collins and Loftus, 1975; for relevant experimental evidence, see Meyer and Schvaneveldt, 1971.)

The point of the model-building is to suggest how mechanisms internal to the language processor could mimic the effects that cognitive penetration would produce if the latter indeed occurred. In the present example, what mimics the background knowledge that (roughly) spies have to do with bugs is the existence of a connection betweeen the node assigned to the word 'spy' and the node assigned to the word 'bug'. Facilitation of 'bug' in spy contexts is affected by the excitation of such intralexical connections.

Why should these intralexical connections exist? Surely not just in order to lead psychologists to overestimate the cognitive penetrability of language-processing. In fact, if one works the other way 'round and assumes that the input systems are encapsulated, one might think of the mimicry of penetration as a way that the input processors contrive to make the best of their informational isolation. Presumably, what encapsulation buys is speed; and, as we remarked above, it buys speed at the price of unintelligence. It would, one supposes, take a lot of time to make reliable decisions about whether there is the kind of relation between spies and bugs that makes it on balance likely that the current token of 'spy' will be followed by a token of 'bug'. But that is precisely the kind of decision that the subject would have to make if the contextual facilitation of lexical access were indeed an effect of background knowledge interacting with the semantic content of the context. The present suggestion is that no such intelligent evaluation of the options takes place; there is merely a brute facilitation of the recognition of 'bug' consequent upon the recognition of 'spy'. The condition of this brute facilitation buying anything is that it should be possible, with reasonable accuracy, to mimic what one knows about connectedness *in the world* by establishing corresponding connections among entries in the mental lexicon. In effect, the strategy is to use the structure of interlexical connections to mimic the structure of knowledge. The mimicry won't be precise (a route from 'spy' to 'insect' will be generated as a by-product of the route from 'spy' to 'bug'). But there's no reason to doubt that it may produce savings over all.

Since we are indulging speculations, we might as well indulge this one: It is a standing mystery in psychology why there should be interlexical associations at all; why subjects should exhibit a reliable and robust disposition to associate 'salt' with 'pepper', 'cat' with 'dog', 'mother' with 'father', and so forth. In the heyday of associationism, of course, such facts seemed quite *un*mysterious; they were, indeed, the stuff of which the mental life was supposed to be made. On one account the utterance of a sentence was taken to be a chained response, and associations among lexical items were what held the links together. According to still earlier tradition, the postulation of associative connections between Ideas was to be the mechanism for reconstructing the notion of degree of belief. None of this seems plausible now, however. Belief is a matter (not of association but) of *judgment*; sentence production is a matter (not of association but) of *planning*. So, what on earth are associations *for*?

The present suggestion is that associations are the means whereby stupid processing systems manage to behave as though they were smart ones. In particular, interlexical associations are the means whereby the language processor is enabled to act as though it knows that spies have to do with bugs (whereas, in fact, it knows no such thing). The idea is that, just as the tradition supposed, terms for things frequently connected in experience become themselves connected in the lexicon. Such connection is *not* knowledge; it is not even judgment. It is simply the mechanism of the contextual adjustment of response thresholds. Or, to put the matter somewhat metaphysically, the formation of interlexical connections buys the synchronic encapsulation of the language processor at the price of its cognitive penetrability *across time*. The information one has about how things are related in the world is inaccessible to modulate lexical access; that is what the encapsulation of the language processor implies. But one's experience of the relations of things in the world does affect the structure of the lexical network – viz., by instituting connections among lexical nodes. If the present line of speculation is correct, these connections have a real, if modest, role to play in the facilitation of the perceptual analysis of speech. The traditional, fundamental, and decisive objection to association is that it is too stupid a relation

to form the basis of a mental life. But stupidity, when not indulged in to excess, is a virtue in fast, peripheral processes; which is exactly what I have been supposing input processes to be.

I am not quite claiming that all the putative effects of information about background (context, etc.) on sentence recognition are artifacts of connections in the lexical network (though, as a matter of fact, such experimental attempts as I've seen to demonstrate a residual effect of context after interlexical/associative factors are controlled for strike me as not persuasive). I am claiming only that the possibility of such artifacts contaminates quite a lot of the evidence that is standardly alleged. The undoubted fact that "semantically" coherent text is relatively easy to process does not, in and of itself, demonstrate that the input system for language has access to what the organism knows about how the world coheres. Such experimental evidence as supported early enthusiasms for massively top-down perceptual models was, I think, sexy but inconclusive; and the possibility of a modular treatment of input processes provides motivation for its reconsideration. The situation would seem to be paradigmatically Kuhnian: the data look different to a jaundiced eye.

Consider the provenance of New Look theorizing. Cognitive psychologists in the '40s and '50s were faced with the proposal that perception is *literally* reflexive; for example, that the theory of perception is reducible without residue to the theory of discriminative operant response. It was natural and admirable in such circumstances to stress the 'intelligence' of perceptual integration. However, in retrospect it seems that the intelligence of perceptual integration may have been seriously misconstrued by those who were most its partisans.

In the ideal condition – one approached more frequently in the textbooks than *in rerum naturae*, to be sure – reflexes have two salient properties. They are computationally simple (the stimulus is "directly connected" to the response), and they are informationally encapsulated (see above). I'm suggesting that New Look theories failed to distinguish these properties. They thus assumed, wrongly, that the disanalogy between perceptual and reflexive processes consisted in the capacity of the former to access and exploit background information. From the point of view of the modularity thesis, this is a case of the right intuition leading to the wrong claim. Input systems *are* computationally elaborated. Their typical function is to perform inference-like operations on representations of impinging stimuli. Processes of input analysis are thus unlike reflexes in respect of the character and complexity of the operations that they perform. But this is quite compatible with reflexes and input processes being similar in respect of their informational encapsulation; in this latter respect, both of them contrast with "central processes" – problem-solving and the like – of which cognitive penetrability is perhaps the most salient feature, or so I shall argue below. To see that informational encapsulation and computational elaboration are compatible properties, it is only necessary to bear in mind that unencapsulation is the exploitation of information from outside a system; a computationally elaborated sytem can thus be encapsulated if it stores the information that its computations exploit. Encapsulation is a matter of foreign affairs; computational elaboration begins at home.

It may be useful to summarize this discussion of the informational encapsulation of input systems by comparing it with some recent, and very interesting, suggestions owing to the philosopher Stephen Stich (1978). Stich's discussion explores the difference between belief and the epistemic relation that is alleged to hold between, for example, speaker/hearers and the grammar of their native language (the relation that Chomsky calls 'cognizing'). Stich supposes, for purposes of argument, that the empirical evidence shows that speakers *in some sense* 'know' the grammar of their native language; his goal is to say something about what that sense is.

Let us call the epistemic relation that a native speaker has to the grammar of his language *subdoxastic* belief.[16] Stich suggests that there are two respects in which subdoxastic beliefs differ from beliefs strictly so-called. In the first place, as practically everybody has emphasized, subdoxastic beliefs are *unconscious*. But, Stich adds, subdoxastic beliefs are also typically "inferentially unintegrated." The easiest way to understand what Stich means by this is to consider one of his examples.

> If a linguist believes a certain generalization to the effect that no transformation rule exhibits a certain characteristic, and if he comes to (nonsubdoxastically) believe a given transformation which violates the generalization, he may well infer that the generalization is false. But merely having the rule stored (in the way that we are assuming all speakers of the language do) does not enable the linguist to draw

the inference. . . . Suppose that for some putative rule, you have come to believe that if r then Chomsky is seriously mistaken. Suppose further that, as it happens, r is in fact among the rules stored by your language processing mechanism. The belief along with the subdoxastic state will not lead to the belief that Chomsky is seriously mistaken. By contrast, if you believe (perhaps even mistakenly) that r, then the belief that Chomsky is seriously mistaken is likely to be inferred. [pp. 508–509]

Or, as Stich puts the argument at another point, "It is characteristic of beliefs that they generate further beliefs via inference. What is more, beliefs are inferentially promiscuous. Provided with a suitable set of supplementary beliefs, almost any belief can play a role in the inference to any other. . . . (However) subdoxastic states, as contrasted with beliefs, are largely inferentially isolated from the large body of inferentially integrated beliefs to which a subject has (conscious) access."

Now, as Stich clearly sees, the proposal that subdoxastic states are typically both unconscious and inferentially unintegrated raises a question – viz., *Why should these two properties co-occur?* Why should it be, to put it in my terminology, that subdoxastic states are typically encapsulated with respect to the processes which affect the inferential integration of beliefs?

Notice that there is a kind of encapsulation that follows from unconsciousness: an unconscious belief cannot play a role as a premise in the sort of reasoning that goes on in the conscious drawing of inferences. Stich is, however, urging something more interesting than this trivial truth. Stich's claim is that subdoxastic beliefs are largely inaccessible even to *un*conscious mental processes of belief fixation. If this claim is true, the question does indeed arise why it should be so.

I want to suggest, however, that the question doesn't arise because, as a matter of act, subdoxastic beliefs are not in general encapsulated; or, to put it more precisely, they are not in general encapsulated *qua* subdoxastic. Consider, as counterexamples, one's subdoxastic views about inductive and deductive warrant; for example, one's subdoxastic acquiescence in the rule of *modus ponens*. On the sort of psychological theory that Stich has in mind, subdoxastic knowledge of such principles must be accessible to practically all mental processes, since practically all inferential processes exploit them in one way or another. One's subdoxastic beliefs about validity and confirmation are thus quite unlike one's subdoxastic beliefs about the rules of grammar; though both are unconscious, the former are paradigms of promiscuous and un-encapsulated mental states. So the connection between unconsciousness and encapsulation cannot be *intrinsic*.

Nevertheless, I think that Stich is onto something important. For, though much unconscious information must be widely accessible to processes of fixation of belief, it is quite true that very many of the examples of unconscious beliefs for which there is currently good empirical evidence are encapsulated. This is because most of our current cognitive science is the science of input systems, and, as we have seen, *informational encapsulation is arguably a pervasive feature of such systems*. Input systems typically do not exchange subdoxastic information with central processes or with one another.

Stich almost sees this point. He says that "subdoxastic states occur in a variety of separate, special purpose cognitive systems" (p. 508). True enough; but they must also occur in integrated, general purpose systems (in what I'm calling "central" systems), assuming that much of the fixation of belief is both unconscious and subserved by inferential mechanisms of that kind. The point is: subdoxastic states are informationally encapsulated *only* insofar as they are states of special purpose systems (e.g., states of input analyzers). Practically all psychologically interesting cognitive states are unconscious; but it is only the beliefs accessible to modules that are subdoxastic by the second of Stich's criteria as well.

Central Systems

Vertical faculties are domain specific (by definition) and modular (by hypothesis). So the questions we now want to ask can be put like this: *Are there psychological processes that can plausibly be assumed to cut across cognitive domains?* And, if there are, is there reason to suppose that such processes are subserved by nonmodular (e.g., informationally unencapsulated) mechanisms?

The answer to the first of these questions is, I suppose, reasonably clear. Even if input systems are domain specific, there must be some cognitive mechanisms that are not. The general form of the argument goes back at least to Aristotle: *the representations that input systems deliver have to interface somewhere, and the computational mechanisms that effect the interface*

must ipso facto have access to information from more than one cognitive domain. Consider:

(a) We have repeatedly distinguished between what the input systems compute and what the organism (consciously or subdoxastically) believes. Part of the point of this distinction is that input systems, being informationally encapsulated, typically compute representations of the distal layout on the basis of less information about the distal layout than the organism has available. Such representations want correction in light of background knowledge (e.g., information in memory) and of the simultaneous results of input analysis in other domains (see Aristotle on the 'common sense'). Call the process of arriving at such corrected representations "the fixation of perceptual belief." To a first approximation, we can assume that the mechanisms that effect this process work like this: they look simultaneously at the representations delivered by the various input systems and at the information currently in memory, and they arrive at a best (i.e., best available) hypothesis about how the world must be, given these various sorts of data.[17] But if there are mechanisms that fix perceptual belief, and if they work in anything like this way, then these mechanisms are not domain specific. Indeed, the point of having them is precisely to ensure that, wherever possible, what the organism believes is determined by all the information it has access to, regardless of which cognitive domains this information is drawn from.

(b) We use language (inter alia) to communicate our views on how the world is. But this use of language is possible only if the mechanisms that mediate the production of speech have access to what we see (or hear, or remember, or think) that the world is like. Since, by assumption, such mechanisms effect an interface among vertical faculties, they cannot themselves be domain specific. More precisely, they must at least be *less* domain specific than the vertical faculties are.[18]

(c) One aspect of the 'impenetrability' of the input systems is, we assumed, their insensitivity to the utilities of the organism. This assumption was required in part to explain the *veridicality* of perception given that the world doesn't always prove to be the way that we would prefer it to be. However, an interface between perception and utilities must take place *somewhere* if we are to use the information that input systems deliver in order to determine how we ought to act. (Decision theories are, to all intents and purposes, models of the structure of this interface. The point is, roughly, that wishful seeing is avoided by requiring interactions with utilities to occur *after* – not *during* – perceptual integration.) So, again, the moral seems to be that there must be some mechanisms which cross the domains that input systems establish.

For these and other similar reasons, I assume that there must be relatively nondenominational (i.e., domain-*in*specific) psychological systems which operate, inter alia, to exploit the information that input systems provide. Following the tradition, I shall call these "central" systems, and I will assume that it is the operation of these sorts of systems that people have in mind when they talk, pretheoretically, of such mental processes as thought and problem-solving. Central systems may be domain specific in *some* sense – we will consider this when we get to the issues about 'epistemic boundedness' – but at least they aren't domain specific in the way that input systems are. The interesting question about the central systems is whether, being nondenominational, they are also non-modular in other respects as well. That is, whether the central systems fail to exhibit the galaxy of properties that lead us to think of the input systems as a natural kind – the properties enumerated in [the previous section].

Briefly, my argument is going to be this: we have seen that much of what is typical of the input systems is more or less directly a product of their informational encapsulation. By contrast, I'll claim that central systems are, in important respects, *un*encapsulated, and that it is primarily for this reason that they are not plausibly viewed as modular. Notice that I am not going to be arguing for a tautology. It is perfectly possible, in point of logic, that a system which is *not* domain specific might nevertheless be encapsulated. Roughly, domain specificity has to do with the range of questions for which a device provides answers (the range of inputs for which it computes analyses); whereas encapsulation has to do with the range of information that the device consults in deciding what answers to provide. A system could thus be domain specific but unencapsulated (it answers a relatively narrow range of questions but in doing so it uses whatever it knows); and a system could be nondenominational but encapsulated (it will give some answer to any question; but it gives its answers off the top of its head – i.e., by reference to less than all the relevant information). If, in short, it is true that only domain-specific systems are encapsulated, then that truth is interesting. Perhaps it goes without saying that I am not about to demonstrate this putative truth. I am, however, about to explore it.

So much for what I'm going to be arguing *for*. Now a little about the strategy of the argument. The fact is that there is practically no direct evidence, pro or con, on the question whether central systems are modular. No doubt it is possible to achieve some gross factoring of "intelligence" into "verbal" versus "mathematical/spatial" capacities; and no doubt there is something to the idea of a corresponding hemispheric specialization. But such dichotomies are *very* gross and may themselves be confounded with the modularity of the input systems – that is to say, they give very little evidence for the existence of domain-specific (to say nothing of modular) systems other than the ones that subserve the functions of perceptual and linguistic analysis.

When you run out of direct evidence, you might just as well try arguing from analogies, and that is what I propose to do. I have been assuming that the typical function of central systems is the fixation of belief (perceptual or otherwise) by nondemonstrative inference. Central systems look at what the input systems deliver, and they look at what is in memory, and they use this information to constrain the computation of 'best hypotheses' about what the world is like. These processes are, of course, largely unconscious, and very little is known about their operation. However, it seems reasonable enough that something can be inferred about them from what we know about *explicit* processes of nondemonstrative inference – viz., from what we know about empirical inference in science. So, here is how I am going to proceed. First, I'll suggest that scientific confirmation – the nondemonstrative fixation of belief in science – is typically unencapsulated. I'll then argue that if, pursuing the analogy, we assume that the central psychological systems are also unencapsulated, we get a picture of those systems that is, anyhow, not radically implausible given such information about them as is currently available.

The nondemonstrative fixation of belief in science has two properties which, though widely acknowledged, have not (so far as I know) yet been named. I shall name them: confirmation in science is *isotropic* and it is *Quineian*. It is notoriously hard to give anything approaching a rigorous account of what being isotropic and Quineian amounts to, but it is easy enough to convey the intuitions.

By saying that confirmation is isotropic, I mean that the facts relevant to the confirmation of a scientific hypothesis may be drawn from anywhere in the field of previously established empirical (or, of course, demonstrative) truths. Crudely: everything that the scientist knows is, in principle, relevant to determining what else he ought to believe. In principle, our botany constrains our astronomy, if only we could think of ways to make them connect.

As is usual in a methodological inquiry, it is possible to consider the isotropy of confirmation either normatively (as a principle to which we believe that rational inductive practice *ought* to conform) or sociologically (as a principle which working scientists actually adhere to in assessing the degree of confirmation of their theories). In neither case, however, should we view the isotropy of confirmation as merely gratuitous – or, to use a term of Rorty's (1979) as merely "optional." If isotropic confirmation 'partially defines the language game that scientists play' (remember when we used to talk that way?), that is because of a profound conviction – partly metaphysical and partly epistemological – to which scientists implicitly subscribe: the world is a connected causal system *and we don't know how the connections are arranged*. Because we don't, we must be prepared to abandon previous estimates of confirmational relevance as our scientific theories change. The points of all this is: confirmational isotropy is a reasonable property for nondemonstrative inference to have because the goal of nondemonstrative inference is to determine the truth about a causal mechanism – the world – of whose workings we are arbitrarily ignorant. That is why our institution of scientific confirmation is isotropic, and it is why it is plausible to suppose that what psychologists call "problem-solving" (i.e., nondemonstrative inference in the service of individual fixation of belief) is probably isotropic too.

The isotropy of scientific confirmation has sometimes been denied, but never, I think, very convincingly. For example, according to some historians it was part of the Aristotelian strategy against Galileo to claim that no data other than observations of the movements of astronomical objects could, in principle, be relevant to the

(dis)confirmation of the geocentric theory. Telescopic observations of the phases of Venus were thus ruled irrelevant a priori. In notably similar spirit, some linguists have recently claimed that no data except certain specified kinds of facts about the intuitions of native speakers could, in principle, be relevant to the (dis)confirmation of grammatical theories. Experimental observations from psycholinguistics are thus ruled irrelevant a priori. However, this sort of methodology seems a lot like special pleading: you tend to get it precisely when cherished theories are in trouble from prima facie disconfirming data. Moreover, it often comports with Conventionalist construals of the theories so defended. That is, theories for which nonisotropic confirmation is claimed are often viewed, even by their proponents, as merely mechanisms for making predictions; what is alleged in their favor is predictive adequacy rather than correspondence to the world. (Viewed from our perspective, nonisotropic confirmation is, to that extent, not a procedure for fixation of belief, since, on the Conventionalist construal, the predictive adequacy of a theory is *not* a reason for believing that the theory is *true*.)

One final thought on the isotropy issue. We are interested in isotropic systems because such systems are ipso facto unencapsulated. We are interested in scientific confirmation because (a) there is every reason to suppose that it is isotropic; (b) there is every reason to suppose that it is a process fundamentally similar to the fixation of belief; and (c) it is perhaps the only "global", unencapsulated, holistic cognitive process about which anything is known that's worth reporting. For all that, scientific *confirmation* is probably not the best place to look if you want to see cognitive isotropy writ large. The best place to look, at least if one is willing to trust the anecdotes, is scientific *discovery*.

What the anecdotes say about scientific discovery – and they say it with a considerable show of univocality (see, e.g., papers in Ortony, 1979) – is that some sort of 'analogical reasoning' often plays a central role. It seems to me that we are thoroughly in the dark here, so I don't propose to push this point very hard. But it really does look as though there have been frequent examples in the history of science where the structure of theories in a new subject area has been borrowed from, or at least suggested by, theories *in situ* in some quite different domain: what's known about the flow of water gets borrowed to model the flow of electricity; what's known about the structure of the solar system gets borrowed to model the structure of the atom; what's known about the behavior of the market gets borrowed to model the process of natural selection, which in turn gets borrowed to model the shaping of operant responses. And so forth. The point about all this is that "analogical reasoning" would seem to be isotropy in the purest form: a process which depends precisely upon the transfer of information among cognitive domains previously assumed to be mutually irrelevant. By definition, encapsulated systems do not reason analogically.

I want to suggest two morals before I leave this point. The first is that the closer we get to what we are pretheoretically inclined to think of as the 'higher,' 'more intelligent', less reflexive, less routine exercises of cognitive capacities, the more such global properties as isotropy tend to show up. I doubt that this is an accident. I suspect that it is precisely its possession of such global properties that we have in mind when we think of a cognitive process as paradigmatically intelligent. The second moral preshadows a point that I shall jump up and down about further on. It is striking that, while everybody thinks that analogical reasoning is an important ingredient in all sorts of cognitive achievements that we prize, nobody knows anything about how it works; not even in the dim, in-a-glass-darkly sort of way in which there are some ideas about how confirmation works. I don't think that this is an accident either. In fact, I should like to propose a generalization; one which I fondly hope will some day come to be known as 'Fodor's First Law of the Nonexistence of Cognitive Science'. It goes like this: the more global (e.g., the more isotropic) a cognitive process is, the less anybody understands it. Very global processes, like analogical reasoning, aren't understood at all. More about such matters in the last part of this discussion.

By saying that scientific confirmation is Quineian, I mean that the degree of confirmation assigned to any given hypothesis is sensitive to properties of the entire belief system; as it were, the shape of our whole science bears on the epistemic status of each scientific hypothesis. Notice that being Quineian and being isotropic are not the same properties, though they are intimately related. For example, if scientific confirmation is isotropic, it is quite possible that some fact about photosynthesis in algae should be relevant to the confirmation of some hypothesis in astrophysics ("the universe in a grain of sand" and all that). But the point about being Quineian is that we might have two astrophysical theories, both of which make the same predictions about algae and about everything else that we can think of to test, but such that one of the theories is better confirmed than the other – e.g., on grounds of such considerations as simplicity, plausibility, or conservatism. The point is that simplicity, plausibility, and conservatism are properties that theories have in virtue of their relation to the whole structure of scientific beliefs *taken collectively*. A measure of conservatism or simplicity would be a metric over *global* properties of belief systems.

Consider, by way of a simple example, Goodman's original (1954) treatment of the notion of projectability. We know that two hypotheses that are equivalent in respect of all the available data may nevertheless differ in their level of confirmation depending on which is the more projectable. Now, according to Goodman's treatment, the projectability of a hypothesis is inherited (at least in part) from the projectability of its vocabulary, and the projectability of an item of scientific vocabulary is determined by the (weighted?) frequency with which that item *has been projected* in previously successful scientific theories. So, the whole history of past projections contributes to determining the projectability of any given hypothesis on Goodman's account, and the projectability of a hypothesis (partially) determines its level of confirmation. Similarly with such notions as simplicity, conservatism, and the rest if only we knew how to measure them.

The idea that scientific confirmation is Quineian is by no means untendentious. On the contrary, it was a legacy of traditional philosophy of science – one of the "dogmas of Empiricism" (Quine, 1953) that there must be *semantic* connections between each theory statement and some data statements. That is, each hypothesis about "unobservables" must *entail* some predictions about observables, such entailments holding in virtue of the meanings of the theoretical terms that the hypotheses contain.[19] The effect of postulating such connections would be to determine a priori that certain data would disconfirm certain hypotheses, *whatever the shape of the rest of one's science might be*. For, of course, if H entails O, the discovery that –O would entail that –H. To that extent, the (dis)confirmation of H by –O is independent of global features of the belief system that H and O belong to. To postulate meaning relations between data statements and theory statements is thus to treat confirmation as a *local* phenomenon rather than a global one.

I emphasize this consideration because analogous semantic proposals can readily be found in the psychological literature. For example, in the sorts of cognitive theories espoused by, say, Bruner or Vygotsky (and, more recently, in the work of the "procedural" semanticists), it is taken for granted that there must be connections of meaning between 'concepts' and 'percepts'. Basically, according to such theories, concepts are recipes for sorting stimuli into categories. Each recipe specifies a (more or less determinate) galaxy of tests that one can perform to effect a sorting, and each stimulus category is identified with a (more or less determinate) set of outcomes of the tests. To put the idea crudely but near enough for present purposes, there's a rule that you can test for *dog* by finding out if a thing barks, and the claim is that this rule is constitutive (though not, of course, exhaustive) of the concept *dog*. Since it is alleged to be a *conceptual* truth that whether it barks is relevant to whether it's a dog, it follows that the confirmation relation between "a thing is a dog" and "it barks" is insensitive to global properties of one's belief system. So considerations of theoretical simplicity etc. *could* not, even in principle, lead to the conclusion that whether it barks is *ir*relevant to whether it's a dog. To embrace that conclusion would be to change the concept.

This sort of example makes it clear how closely related being Quineian and being isotropic are. Since, on the view just scouted, it is a matter of *meaning* that barking is relevant to dogness, it is not possible to discover on empirical grounds that one was wrong about that relevancy relation. But isotropy is the principle that *any* fact may turn out to be (ir)relevant to the confirmation of any other. The Bruner-Vygotsky-procedural semantics line is thus incompatible with the isotropy of confirmation as well as with its Quineianness.

In saying that confirmation is isotropic and Quineian, I am thus consciously disagreeing with major traditions in the philosophy of science and in cognitive psychology. Nevertheless, I shall take it for granted that scientific confirmation is Quineian and isotropic. (Those who wish to see the arguments should refer to such classic papers in the modern philosophy of science as Quine, 1953, and Putnam, 1962.) Moreover, since I am committed to relying upon the analogy between scientific confirmation and psychological fixation of belief, I shall take it for granted that the latter must be Quineian and isotropic too, hence that the Bruner-Vygotsky-procedural semantics tradition in cognitive psychology must

be mistaken. I propose, at this point, to be both explicit and emphatic. The argument is that the central processes which mediate the fixation of belief are typically processes of rational nondemonstrative inference and that, since processes of rational nondemonstrative inference are Quineian and isotropic, so too are central processes. In particular, the theory of such processes must be consonant with the principle that the level of acceptance of any belief is sensitive to the level of acceptance of any other and to global properties of the field of beliefs taken collectively.

Given these assumptions, I have now got two things to do: I need to show that this picture of the central processes is broadly incompatible with the assumption that they are modular, and I need to show that it is a picture that has some plausibility independent of the putative analogy between cognitive psychology and the philosophy of science.

I take it that the first of these claims is relatively uncontroversial. We argued that modularity is fundamentally a matter of informational encapsulation and, of course, informationally encapsulated is precisely what Quineian/isotropic systems are not. When we discussed input systems, we thought of them as mechanisms for projecting and confirming hypotheses. And we remarked that, viewed that way, the informational encapsulation of such systems is tantamount to a constraint on the confirmation metrics that they employ; the confirmation metric of an encapsulated system is allowed to 'look at' only a certain restricted class of data in determining which hypothesis to accept. If, in particular, the flow of information through such a system is literally bottom-to-top, then its informational encapsulation consists in the fact that the ith-level hypotheses are (dis)confirmed solely by reference to lower-than-ith level representations. And even if the flow of data is unconstrained *within* a module, encapsulation implies constraints upon the access of intramodular processes to extramodular information sources. Whereas, by contrast, isotropy is by definition the property that a system has when it can look at anything it knows about in the course of determining the confirmation levels of hypotheses. So, in general, the more isotropic a confirmation metric is, the more heterogeneous the provenance of the data that it accepts as relevant to constraining its decisions. Scientific confirmation is isotropic in the limit in this respect; it provides a model of what the nonmodular fixation of belief is like.

Similarly with being Quineian. Quineian confirmation metrics are ipso facto sensitive to global properties of belief systems. Now, an informationally encapsulated system *could*, strictly speaking, nevertheless be Quineian. Simplicity, for example, could constrain confirmation even in a system which computes its simplicity scores over some arbitrarily selected subset of beliefs. But this is mere niggling about the letter. In spirit, global criteria for the evaluation of hypotheses comport most naturally with isotropic principles for the relevance of evidence. Indeed, it is only on the assumption that the selection of evidence is isotropic that considerations of simplicity (and other such global properties of hypotheses) are *rational* determinants of belief. It is epistemically interesting that H & T is a simpler theory than -H & T where H is a hypothesis to be evaluated and T is the rest of what one believes. But there is no interest in the analogous consideration where T is some *arbitrarily delimited* subset of one's beliefs. Where relevance is non-isotropic, assessments of relative simplicity can be gerrymandered to favor any hypothesis one likes. This is one of the reasons why the operation of (by assumption informationally encapsulated) input systems should not be identified with the fixation of perceptual belief; not, at least, by those who wish to view the fixation of perceptual belief as by and large a rational process.

So it seems clear that isotropic/Quineian systems are ipso facto unencapsulated; and if unencapsulated, then presumably nonmodular. Or rather, since this is all a matter of degree, we had best say that *to the extent that* a system is Quineian and isotropic, it is also nonmodular. If, in short, isotropic and Quineian considerations are especially pressing in determining the course of the computations that central systems perform, it should follow that these systems differ in their computational character from the vertical faculties.

We are coming close to what we started out to find: an overall taxonomy of cognitive systems. According to the present proposal, there are, at a minimum, two families of such systems: modules (which are, relatively, domain specific and encapsulated) and central processes (which are, relatively, domain neutral and isotropic/Quineian). We have suggested that the characteristic function of modular cognitive systems is input analysis and that the characteristic function of central processes is the fixation of belief. If this is right, then we have three ways of taxonomizing cognitive processes which prove to be coextensive:

FUNCTIONAL TAXONOMY: input analysis versus fixation of belief
TAXONOMY BY SUBJECT MATTER: domain specific versus domain neutral
TAXONOMY BY COMPUTATIONAL CHARACTER: encapsulated versus Quineian/isotropic

I repeat that this coextension, if it holds at all, holds contingently. Nothing in point of logic stops one from imagining that these categories cross-classify the cognitive systems. If they do not, then that is a fact about the structure of the mind. Indeed, it is a *deep* fact about the structure of the mind.

All of which would be considerably more impressive if there were better evidence for the view of central processes that I have been proposing. Thus far, that account rests entirely on the analogy between psychological processes of belief fixation and a certain story about the character of scientific confirmation. There is very little that I can do about this, given the current underdeveloped state of psychological theories of thought and problem-solving. For what it's worth, however, I want to suggest two considerations that seem relevant and promising.

The first is that the difficulties we encounter when we try to construct theories of central processes are just the sort we would expect to encounter if such processes are, in essential respects, Quineian/isotropic rather than encapsulated. The crux in the construction of such theories is that there seems to be no way to delimit the sorts of informational resources which may affect, or be affected by, central processes of problem-solving. We can't, that is to say, plausibly view the fixation of belief as effected by computations over bounded, local information structures. A graphic example of this sort of difficulty arises in AI, where it has come to be known as the "frame problem" (i.e., the problem of putting a "frame" around the set of beliefs that may need to be revised in light of specified newly available information. Cf. the discussion in McCarthy and Hayes, 1969, from which the following example is drawn).

To see what's going on, suppose you were interested in constructing a robot capable of coping with routine tasks in familiar human environments. In particular, the robot is presented with the job of phoning Mary and finding out whether she will be late for dinner. Let's assume that the robot 'knows' it can get Mary's number by consulting the directory. So it looks up Mary's number and proceeds to dial. So far, so good. But now, notice that commencing to dial has all sorts of direct and indirect effects on the state of the world (including, of course, the internal state of the robot), and some of these effects are ones that the device needs to keep in mind for the guidance of its future actions and expectations. For example, when the dialing commences, the phone ceases to be free to outside calls; the robot's fingers (or whatever) undergo appropriate alterations of spatial location; the dial tone cuts off and gets replaced by beeps; something happens in a computer at Murray Hill; and so forth. Some (but, in principle, not all) such consequences are ones that the robot must be designed to monitor since they are relevant to "updating" beliefs upon which it may eventually come to act. Well, *which* consequences? The problem has at least the following components. The robot must be able to identify, with reasonable accuracy, those of its previous beliefs whose truth values may be expected to alter as a result of its current activities; and it must have access to systems that do whatever computing is involved in effecting the alterations.

Notice that, unless these circuits are arranged correctly, things can go absurdly wrong. Suppose that, having consulted the directory, the robot has determined that Mary's number is 222–2222, which number it commences to dial, pursuant to instructions previously received. But now it occurs to the machine that *one of the beliefs that may need updating in consequence of its having commenced dialing is its (recently acquired) belief about Mary's telephone number.* So, of course, it stops dialing and goes and looks up Mary's telephone number (again). Repeat, *da capo,* as many times as may amuse you. Clearly, we have here all the makings of a computational trap. Unless the robot can be assured that some of its beliefs are invariant under some of its actions, it will never get to *do* anything.

How, then, does the machine's program determine which beliefs the robot ought to reevaluate given that it has embarked upon some or other course of action? What makes this problem so hard is precisely that it seems unlikely that any *local* solution will do the job. For example, the following truths appear to be self-evident: First, that there is no fixed set of beliefs such that, for any action, those and only those beliefs are the ones that require reconsideration. (That is, which beliefs are up for grabs depends inti-

mately upon which actions are performed and upon the context of the performances. There are *some* – indeed, indefinitely many – actions which, if performed, *should* lead one to consider the possibility that Mary's telephone number has changed in consequence.) Second, new beliefs don't come docketed with information about which old beliefs they ought to affect. On the contrary, we are forever being surprised by the implications of what we know, including, of course, what we know about the actions we perform. Third, the set of beliefs apt for reconsideration cannot be determined by reference to the recency of their acquisition, or by reference to their generality, or by reference to merely semantic relations between the contents of the beliefs and the description under which the action is performed . . . etc. Should any of these propositions seem *less* than self-evident, consider the special case of the frame problem where the robot is a mechanical scientist and the action performed is an experiment. Here the question 'which of my beliefs ought I to reconsider given the possible consequences of my action' is transparently equivalent to the question "What, in general, is the optimal adjustment of my beliefs to my experiences?" This is, of course, exactly the question that a theory of confirmation is supposed to answer; and, as we have been at pains to notice, confirmation is not a relation reconstructible by reference to local properties of hypotheses or of the data that bear upon them.

I am suggesting that, as soon as we begin to look at cognitive processes other than input analysis – in particular, at central processes of nondemonstrative fixation of belief – we run into problems that have a quite characteristic property. They seem to involve isotropic and Quineian computations; computations that are, in one or other respect, sensitive to the whole belief system. This is exactly what one would expect on the assumption that nondemonstrative fixation of belief really is quite like scientific confirmation, and that scientific confirmation is itself characteristically Quineian and isotropic. In this respect, it seems to me, the frame problem is paradigmatic, and in this respect the seriousness of the frame problem has not been adequately appreciated.

For example, Raphael (1971) comments as follows: "(An intelligent robot) will have to be able to carry out tasks. Since a task generally involves some change in the world, it must be able to update its model (of the world) so it remains as accurate during and after the performance of a task as it was before. Moreover, it must be able to *plan* how to carry out a task, and this planning process usually requires keeping 'in mind' simultaneously a variety of possible actions and corresponding models of hypothetical worlds that would result from those actions. The bookkeeping problems involved with keeping track of these hypothetical worlds account for much of the difficulty of the frame problem" (p. 159). This makes it look as though the problem is primarily (a) how to notate the possible worlds and (b) how to keep track of the *demonstrative* consequences of changing state descriptions. But the deeper problem, surely, is to keep track of the *non*demonstrative consequences. Slightly more precisely, the problem is, given an arbitrary belief world W and a new state description 'a is F', what is the appropriate successor belief world W'? What ought the device to believe, given that it used to believe W and now believes that a is F? But this isn't just a bookkeeping problem; it is the general problem of inductive confirmation.[20]

So far as I can tell, the usual assumption about the frame problem in AI is that it is somehow to be solved 'heuristically'. The idea is that, while nondemonstrative confirmation (and hence, presumably, the psychology of belief fixation) is isotropic and Quinean *in principle*, still, given a particular hypothesis, there are, in practice, heuristic procedures for determining the range of effects its acceptance can have on the rest of one's beliefs. Since these procedures are by assumption merely heuristic, they may be assumed to be local – i.e., to be sensitive to less than the whole of the belief systems to which they apply. Something like this may indeed be true; there is certainly considerable evidence for heuristic short-cutting in belief fixation, deriving both from studies of the psychology of problem-solving (for a recent review, see Nisbett and Ross, 1980) and from the sociology of science (Kuhn, 1970). In such cases, it is possible to show how potentially relevant considerations are often systematically ignored, or distorted, or misconstrued in favor of relatively local (and, of course, highly fallible) problem-solving strategies. Perhaps a bundle of such heuristics, properly coordinated and rapidly deployed, would suffice to make the central processes of a robot as Quinean and isotropic as yours, or mine, or the practicing scientist's ever actually succeed in being. Since there are, at present, no serious proposals about what heuristics might belong to such a bundle, it seems hardly worth arguing the point.

Still, I am going to argue it a little.

There are those who hold that ideas recently evolved in AI – such notion as, e.g., those of 'frame' (see Minsky, 1975)[21] or 'script' (see Schank and Abelson, 1975) – will illuminate the problems about the globality of belief fixation since they do, in a certain sense, provide for placing a frame around the body of information that gets called when a given sort of problem is encountered. (For a discussion that runs along these optimistic lines, see Thagard, 1980.) It seems to me, however, that the appearance of progress here is entirely illusory – a prime case of confusing a notation with a theory.

If there were a principled solution to the frame problem, then no doubt that solution could be expressed as a constraint on the scripts, or frames, to which a given process of induction has access. But, lacking such a solution, there is simply no content to the idea that only the information represented in the frame (/script) that a problem elicits is computationally available for solving the problem. For one thing, since there are precisely no constraints on the individuation of frames (/scripts), *any* two pieces of information can belong to the same frame (/script) at the discretion of the programmer. This is just a way of saying that the solution of the frame problem can be accommodated to the frame (/script) notation *whatever that solution turns out to be*. Which is just another of saying that the notation does not constrain the solution. Second, it is a widely advertised property of frames (/scripts) that they can cross-reference to one another. The frame for Socrates says, among other things, 'see Plato' . . . and so forth. There is no reason to doubt that, in any developed model, the system of cross-referencing would imply a graph in which there is a route (of greater or lesser length) from each point to any other. But now we have the frame problem all over again, in the form: Which such paths should actually be traversed in a given case of problem-solving, and what should bound the length of the trip? All that has happened is that, instead of thinking of the frame problem as an issue in the logic of confirmation, we are now invited to think of it as an issue in the theory of executive control (a change which there is, by the way, no reason to assume is for the better). More of this presently.

For now, let's summarize the major line of argument. If we assume that central processes are Quinean and isotropic, then we ought to predict that certain kinds of problems will emerge when we try to construct psychological theories which simulate such processes or

THE MODULARITY OF MIND: AN ESSAY ON FACULTY PSYCHOLOGY

otherwise explain them; specifically, we should predict problems that involve the characterization of nonlocal computational mechanisms. By contrast, such problems should not loom large for theories of psychological modules. Since, by assumption, modular systems are informationally encapsulated, it follows that the computations they perform are relatively local. It seems to me that these predictions are in reasonably good accord with the way that the problems of cognitive science have in fact matured: the input systems appear to be primarily stimulus driven, hence to exploit computational processes that are relatively insensitive to the general structure of the organism's belief system. Whereas, when we turn to the fixation of belief, we get a complex of problems that appear to be intractable precisely because they concern mental processes that aren't local. Of these, the frame problem is, as we have seen, a microcosm.

I have been marshaling considerations in favor of the view that central processes are Quineian/isotropic. That is what the analogy to scientific confirmation suggests that they ought to be, and the structure of the problems that arise in attempts to model central processes is quite compatible with that view of them. I now add that the view of central processes as computationally global can perhaps claim some degree of neurological plausibility. The picture of the brain that it suggests is a reasonably decent first approximation to the kind of brain that it appears we actually have.

When we discussed input analyzers, I commented on the natural connection between informational encapsulation and fixed neural architecture. Roughly, standing restrictions on information flow imply the option of hardwiring. If, in the extreme case, system B is required to take note of information from system A and is allowed to take note of information from nowhere else, you might as well build your brain with a permanent neuroanatomical connection from A to B. It is, in short, reasonable to expect biases in the distribution of information to mental processes to show up as structural biases in neural architecture.

Consider, by contrast, Quineian/isotropic systems, where more or less any subsystem may want to talk to any other at more or less any time. In this case, you'd expect the corresponding neuroanatomy to be relatively diffuse. At the limit, you might as well have a random net, with each computational subsystem connected, directly or indirectly, with every other; a kind of wiring in which you get a minimum of sta-

ble correspondence between neuroanatomical form and psychological function. The point is that in Quineian/isotropic systems, it may be *unstable, instantaneous* connectivity that counts. Instead of hardwiring, you get a connectivity that changes from moment to moment as dictated by the interaction between the program that is being executed and the structure of the task in hand. The moral would seem to be that computational isotropy comports naturally with neural isotropy (with what Lashley called "equipotentiality" of neural structure) in much the same way that informational encapsulation comports naturally with the elaboration of neural hardwiring.

So, if input analysis is modular and thought is Quineian/isotropic, you might expect a kind of brain in which there is stable neural architecture associated with perception-and-language but not with thought. And, I suggest, this seems to be pretty much what we in fact find. There is, as I remarked above, quite a lot that can be said about the neural specificity of the perceptual and linguistic mechanisms: at worst we can enumerate in some detail the parts of the brain that handle them; and at best we can exhibit characteristic neural architecture in the areas where these functions are performed. And then there are the rest of the higher brain systems (cf. what used to be called "association cortex"), in which neural connectivity appears to go every which way and the form/function correspondence appears to be minimal. There is some historical irony in all this. Gall argued from a (vertical) faculty psychology to the macroscopic differentiation of the brain. Flourens, his archantagonist, argued from the unity of the Cartesian ego to the brain's equipotentiality (see Bynum, 1976.). The present suggestion is that they were *both* right.[22]

I am, heaven knows, not about to set up as an expert on neuropsychology, and I am painfully aware how impressionistic this all is. But while we're collecting impressions, I think the following one is striking. A recent issue of *Scientific American* (September, 1979) was devoted to the brain. Its table of contents is quite as interesting as the papers it contains. There are, as you might expect, articles that cover the neuropsychology of language and of the perceptual mechanisms. But there is nothing on the neuropsychology of thought – presumably because nothing is known about the neuropsychology of thought. I am suggesting that there is a good reason why nothing is known about it – namely, that there is nothing *to* know about it. You get form/function correspondence for the modular processes (specifically, for the input systems); but, in the case of central processes, you get an approximation to universal connectivity, hence no stable neural architecture to write *Scientific American* articles about.

To put these claims in a nutshell: there are *no* content-specific central processes for the performance of which correspondingly specific neural structures have been identified. Everything we now know is compatible with the claim that central problem-solving is subserved by equipotential neural mechanisms. This is precisely what you would expect if you assume that the central cognitive processes are largely Quineian and isotropic.

Notes

1 Strictly speaking, I suppose, a convention must be something one can adhere to if one chooses; so perhaps the principle at issue is not "Say only what is true" but rather "Say only what you believe." General adherence to the latter injunction will license inferences from utterances to how the world is, given the assumption (which is, anyhow, in all sorts of ways epistemologically indispensable) that much of what people believe is true.

2 The "McGurk effect" provides fairly clear evidence for cross-modal linkages in at least one input system for the modularity of which there is independent evidence. McGurk has demonstrated that what are, to all intents and purposes, hallucinatory speech sounds can be induced when the subject is presented with a visual display of a speaker making vocal gestures appropriate to the production of those sounds. The suggestion is that (within, presumably, narrowly defined limits) mechanisms of phonetic analysis can be activated by – and can apply to – *either* accoustic or visual stimuli. (See McGurk and MacDonald, 1976). It is of central importance to realize that the McGurk effect – though cross-modal – is itself domain specific – viz., specific to language. A motion picture of a bouncing ball does not induce bump, bump, bump hallucinations. (I am indebted to Professor Alvin Liberman both for bringing McGurk's results to my attention and for his illuminating comments on their implications.)

3 Generally speaking, the more peripheral a mechanism is in the process of perceptual analysis – the earlier it operates, for example – the better candidate for modularity it is likely to be. In the limit, it is untendentious – even traditional – to view the functioning of psychophysical (/sensory) mechanisms as largely autonomous with respect to central processes and largely parallel with respect to one another. There is recent,

striking evidence owing to Treisman and her colleagues that the detection of such stimulus "features" as shape and color is typically parallel, preattentive, and *prior* to the identification of the object in which the features, as it were, inhere: "...features are registered early, automatically, and in parallel across the visual field, while objects are identified separately only at a later stage, which requires focused attention" (Treisman and Gelade, 1980, p. 98). There is analogous evidence for the modularity of phonetic feature detectors that operate in speech perception (see Eimas and Corbet, 1973), though its interpretation is less than univocal (see Ganong, 1977).

4 I won't, in general, have much to say about input processes other than those involved in vision and language, since these are by far the areas in which the available psychology is most developed. But I hope, and believe, that the points I'll be making apply pretty well to all of the perceptual mechanisms.

5 Strictly speaking, I suppose I should say that this is true according to all current non-Gibsonian accounts. For reasons given elsewhere, however (see Fodor and Pylyshyn, 1981), I am deeply unmoved by the Gibsonian claim to have devised a noncomputational theory of perception. I propose simply to ignore it in this discussion.

6 Also, given that you hear it as speech, you may have some (surely very limited) options as to which speech you hear it as. For a demonstration of instructional effects in phone recognition, see Carden, Levitt, Jusczyk, and Walley (1981). In somewhat similar fashion: it's hard to see the Necker cube in anything but three-dimensional projection; but you do have some control over which three-dimensional projection you see.

7 Pedantic footnote: To the best of my knowlege, the suggestion that what seems to be the inaccessibility of information to *consciousness* is in fact just its inaccessibility to *recall* was first made by William James in the *Principles of Psychology*. James, in his enthusiasm, takes this claim to be quite general. If he'd been right, then the specific inaccessibility of intermediate input representations to report would be a relatively uninteresting epiphenomenon of the subject's allocation of memory resources. However, as we shall see, James's story won't wash; there is clearly more to unconsciousness than he supposed.

8 A similar moral is suggested by studies of 'compressed' speech, in which signals presented at input rates much in excess of normal are apparently quite intelligible so long as the increased speed is not achieved at the price of acoustic degradation of the signal. (See Foulke, 1971.)

9 A sufficient, but not a necessary, condition for the level of representation *n* being 'higher' than

the level of representation *m* is that the entities specified at *n* contain the entities specified at *m* as constituents (in the way that words have syllables as constituents, for example). It would be nice if there proved to be a well-ordering of the interlevels of representation computed by each input system, but nothing in the present discussion depends on assuming that this is so. Still less is there reason to assume, in cases where the computations that a system performs are affected by data fed into it from outside, that the exogenous information can always be ordered, with respect to abstractness, relative to the levels of representation that the system computes. I shall conform to the prevalent usage in which *all* effects of background beliefs and expectations in perceptual processing are described as the feedback of information from 'higher levels'. But it is far from clear that either 'higher' or 'level' should be taken very seriously when so employed.

10 A corollary consideration is that, if the argument for expectation-driven processes in perception is to be made on teleological grounds, their putative advantages must be carefully weighed against their likely costs. In cases where the environment does *not* exhibit the expected redundancy, the typical effect of predictive error will be to *interfere with* the correct analysis (see Posner, 1978). It is thus by no means a trivial matter to show – even in cases like langue processing where quantitative estimates of redundancy can, in some respects, be achieved – that the balance of payoffs favors predictive mechanisms over ones that are data driven. (See Gough, Alford, and Haley-Wilcox, 1978.)

11 That is, perceptual categories are not, in general, *definable* in terms of transducer outputs; phenomenalists, operationalists, Gibsonians, and procedural semanticists to the contrary notwithstanding. (See Fodor, 1981, chap. 7; Fodor and Pylyshyn, 1981.)

12 A plausible inference from this discussion is that lots of information to which input analyzers do have access must be stored twice; once internal to the input analyzers and once in the (putative) central memory where it is accessible to nonmodular cognitive processes. This seems natural enough: when you learn about English syntax (e.g., in a linguistics course), what you are learning is something that, in some sense, you already knew. See the discussion of 'subdoxastic' belief at the end of this section.

13 It might be suggested that the impressive consideration is not that there is sometimes measurable competition between input systems, but that the decrements in performance that such competition produces are so small. Given the amount of processing that each must involve, the very fact that we can speak and see at the same time is,

arguably, enough to vindicate Gall. But nobody knows what the null hypothesis would look like here, and given the impossibility of serious quantitative estimates, I don't propose to press the point.

14 Recent experiments increasingly suggest that the effects of contextual variables upon the identification of words in sentences are far more fragile than psychologists of the top-down persuasion used to suppose. For example, if you ask a subject to decide, at his best speed, whether a stimulus item is a word (i.e., as opposed to a phonologically licit nonsense syllable), then he will be faster for a word that is highly predictable in context than for that same word in a neutral context. In effect, 'salt' is faster in 'pepper and——' than in 'cheese and——'. This makes it look as though contextual predictability is facilitating 'lexical decision' and is just the sort of result that is grist for the New Look psychologist's mill. It turns out, however, that if you compare reaction times for a highly-predictable-in-context word with reaction times for that same word *in isolation*, you find no facilitation at all when the Cloze probability of the former stimulus is less than 90 percent (Fishler and Bloom, 1979). It appears, in light of such findings, that previous claims for the cognitive penetration of lexical access by contextual information may have been considerably exaggerated. At best, the phenomenon seems to be sensitive to the choice of experimental paradigm and of baseline.

15 A proposal currently in the air is to split the difference between strictly encapsulated parsers and contextually driven ones, as follows: semantic information is never used to predict syntactic structure, but a line of analysis on which the parser is engaged can be aborted whenever it produces structures that resist contextual integration. Boxologically, this means that the parser feeds information freely to the context analyzer, but all that the context analyzer is allowed to say to the parser is either 'yes' (continue with the present line of analysis) or 'no' (try something else, I can't fit what you're giving me to the context). What the context analyzer is *prohibited* from doing is telling the parser *which* line of analysis it ought to try next – i.e., semantic information can't be used predictively to guide the parse. (For a discussion of this model, see Crain and Steedman, 1981.) All the results I know on context effects in parsing are compatible with this account; I'm inclined to bet (small denominations) that something of the sort will prove to be true.

16 Stich himself speaks not of subdoxastic beliefs but of subdoxastic *states*, not only to avoid etymological solecism, but also to emphasize that the subdoxastic lacks some of belief's paradigm properties. Granting Stich's point, the present

terminology is nonetheless convenient and I shall adhere to it.

17 This is, of course, an idealization; decisions about what to believe (subdoxastically or otherwise) do not, in general, succeed in making the optimal use of the available data. This consideration does not, however, affect the present point, which is just that such decisions must, of necessity, be sensitive to information from many different sources.

18 There is an assumption underlying this line of argument which the reader may not wish to grant: that the mechanisms that interface between vertical faculties have to be *computational* rather than, as one might say, merely mechanical. Old views of how language connects with perception (e.g., percepts are pictures and words are their associates) implicitly deny this assumption. It seems to me, however, that anyone who thinks seriously about what must be involved in deciding (e.g.) how to say what we see will accept the plausibility of the view that the mental processes that are implicated must be both computational and of formidable complexity.

19 Stronger versions had it that each theory statement must be logically equivalent to some (finite?) conjunction of observation statements. For a sophisticated review of this literature, see Glymour, 1980. Glymour takes exception to some aspects of the Quinean account of confirmation, but not for reasons that need concern us here.

20 It is often proposed (see, e.g., McCarthy, 1980) that a logic capable of coping with the frame problem will have to be 'nonmonotonic'. (Roughly, a logic is monotonic when the addition of new postulates does *not* reduce the set of previously derivable theorems; nonmonotonic otherwise.) The point is that new beliefs don't just get *added on* to the old set; rather, old beliefs are variously altered to accommodate the new ones. This is, however, hardly surprising on the analysis of the frame problem proposed in the text. For, on that account, the frame problem is not distinguishable from the problem of nondemonstrative confirmation, and confirmation relations are themselves typically nonmonotonic. For example, the availability of a new datum may necessitate the assignment of new confirmation levels to indefinitely many previously accepted hypotheses. Hence, if we think of the confirmation system as formalized, indefinitely many previously derivable formulas of the form 'the level of H is L' may become nontheorems whenever new data become available.

21 Since there is no particular relation between *the frame problem* and *frames-cum*-data structures, the nomenclature in this area could hardly be more confusing.

22 The localization dispute didn't, of course, end with Gall and Flourens. For a useful, brief survey of its relatively modern history (since Wernicke), see Eggert (1977). It is of some interest – in passing – that Wernicke, committed localizationalist though he was in respect of the language mechanisms, held that only "primary functions … can be referred to specific areas. … All processes which exceed these primary functions (such as the synthesis of various perceptions into concepts and the complex functions such as thought and consciousness) are dependent upon the fiber bundles connecting different areas of the cortex" (p. 92). Barring the associationism, Wernicke's picture is not very different from the one that we've been developing here.

References

Bizzi, E. (1968), Discharge of Frontal Eye Field Neurons during Saccadic and Following Eye Movements in Unanesthetized Monkeys, *Experimental Brain Research*, 6:69–80.

Brooks, L. (1968), Spatial And Verbal Components of the Act of Recall, *Canadian Journal of Psychology*, 22:349–368.

Bruner, J. (1957), On Perceptual Readiness, *Psychological Review*, 64:123–152.

Bynum, W. (1976), Varieties of Cartesian Experience in Early Nineteenth Century Neurophysiology, in S. Spicker and H. Engelhardt, *Philosophical Dimensions of the Neuro-Medical Sciences*, Dodrecht, Reidel.

Carden, G., Levitt, A., Jusczyk, P., and Walley, A. (1981), Evidence for Phonetic Processing of Cues to Place of Articulation: Perceived Manner Affects Perceived Place, *Perception and Psychophysics*, 29 1:26–36.

Carey, S. (1978), A Case Study: Face Recognition, in E. Walker (ed.), *Explorations in the Biology of Language*, Cambridge, Mass., MIT Press.

Collins, A., and Loftus, E. (1975), A Spreading-Activation Theory of Semantic Processing, *Psychological Review*, 82:407–428.

Corteen, R., and Wood, B. (1972), Autonomic Responses to Shock-Associated Words in an Unattended Channel, *Journal of Experimental Psychology*, 94:308–313.

Crain, S., and Steedman, M. (1981), On Not Being Led Up the Garden Path: The Use of Context by the Psychological Parser, Paper presented at the Sloan Conference on Human Parsing, University of Texas, Austin.

Crowder, R., and Morton, J. (1969), Precategorical Acoustic Storage (PAS), *Perception and Psychophysics*, 5:365–373.

Dretske, F. (1981), *Knowledge and the Flow of Information*, Cambridge, Mass., MIT Press.

Eggert, G. (1977), *Wernicke's Works on Aphasia: A Sourcebook and Review*, The Hague, Mouton.

Eimas, P., and Corbit, J. (1973), Selective Adaptation of Linguistic Feature Detectors, *Cognitive Psychology*, 4:99–109.

Fishler, I., and Bloom, P. (1980), "Rapid Processing of the Meaning of Sentences," *Memory and Cognition*, 8:216–225.

Fodor, J. (1987) Psychosemantics, or: Where Do Truth Conditions Come From?

Fodor, J., Bever, T., and Garrett, M. (1974), *The Psychology of Language*, New York, McGraw-Hill.

Fodor, J., and Pylyshyn, Z. (1981), How Direct Is Visual Perception? *Cognition*, 9:139–196.

Foss, D. (1969), Decision Processes during Sentence Comprehension: Effects of Lexical Item Difficulty and Position upon Decision Times, *Journal of Verbal Learning and Verbal Behavior*, 8:457–462.

Foulke, E. (1971), The Perception of Time Compressed Speech, in D. Horton and J. Jenkins (eds.), *The Perception of Language*, Ohio, Charles E. Merrill.

Frazier, L., and Fodor, J. D. (1978), The Sausage Machine: A New Two-Stage Parsing Model, *Cognition*, 6:291–325.

Ganong, W. (1977), Selective Adaptation and Speech Perception, Ph.D. thesis, M.I.T.

Glymour, C. (1980), *Theory and Evidence*, Princeton, Princeton University Press.

Goodman, N. (1954), *Fact, Fiction, and Forecast*, University of London, Athlone Press.

Gough, P., Alford, J., and Halley-Wilcox, P. (1978), Words and Contexts, unpublished ms presented at the National Reading Conference, St. Petersburg Beach, Fla., November 1978.

Haber, R. (1980), How We Remember What We See, in R. and R. Atkinson (eds.), *Mind and Behavior, Readings from Scientific American*, San Francisco, W. H. Freeman.

Kaplan, R., and Bresnan J. (1982), Lexical Functional Grammar: A Formal System for Grammatical Representation, in J. Bresnan (ed.), *The Mental Representation of Grammatical Relations*, Cambridge, Mass., MIT Press.

Kuhn, T. (1970), *The Structure of Scientific Revolutions*, 2d ed., Chicago, University of Chicago Press.

Lackner, J., and Garrett, M. (1973), Resolving Ambiguity; Effects of Biasing Context in the Unattended Ear, *Cognition*, 1:359–372.

Lewis, J. (1970), Semantic Processing of Unattended Messages Using Dichotic Listening, *Journal of Experimental Psychology*, 85:225–228.

Liberman, A., Cooper, F., Shankweiler, D., and Studdert-Kennedy, M. (1967), The Perception of the Speech Code, *Psychological Review*, 74:431–461.

Lieberman, P. (1965), On the Acoustic Basis of the Perception of Intonation by Linguists, *Word*, 21:40–54.

Loewenstein, W. (1960), Biological Transducers, *Scientific American*. Also in *Perception: Mechanisms and Models: Readings from Scientific American* (1972), San Francisco, Freeman.

Marcus, M. (1977), A Theory of Syntactic Recognition for Natural Language, Ph.D. thesis, M.I.T.

Marr, D., and Nishihara, H. (1978), Visual Information Processing: Artificial Intelligence and the Sensorium of Sight, *Technology Review*, October, 28–49.

Marr, D., and Poggio, T. (1977), From Understanding Computation to Understanding Neural Circuitry, *Neurosciences Research Progress Bulletin*, 15:470–488.

Marslen-Wilson, W. (1973), Speech Shadowing and Speech Perception, Ph.D. thesis, M.I.T.

Marslen-Wilson, W., and Tyler, L. (1981), Central Processes in Speech Understanding, *Philosophical Transactions of the Royal Society*, B 295:317–322.

McCarthy, J. (1980), Circumscription – A Form of Non-Monotonic Reasoning, *Artificial Intelligence*, 13:27–39.

McCarthy, J., and Hayes, P. (1969), Some Philosophical Problems from the Standpoint of Artificial Intelligence, in B. Meltzer and D. Mitchie (eds.), *Machine Intelligence*, 4, New York, American Elsevier.

McGurk, H., and Macdonald, J. (1976), Hearing Lips and Seeing Voices, *Nature*, 264:746–748.

Meyer, D., and Schvaneveldt, R. (1971), Facilitation in Recognizing Pairs of Words: Evidence of a Dependence between Retrieval Operations, *Journal of Experimental Psychology*, 90:227–234.

Miller, G., and Isard, S. (1963), Some Perceptual Consequences of Linguistic Rules, *Journal of Verbal Learning and Verbal Behavior*, 2:217–228.

Minsky, M. (1975), A Framework for Representing Knowledge, in P. Winston (ed.), *The Psychology of Computer Vision*, New York, McGraw Hill.

Morton, J. (1967), A Singular Lack of Incidental Learning, *Nature*, 215:203–204.

Morton, J. (1969), The Interaction of Information in Word Recognition, *Psychological Review*, 76:165–178.

Nickerson, R., and Adams, M. (1979), Long-Term Memory for a Common Object, *Cognitive Psychology*, 11:287–307.

Nisbett, R., and Ross, L. (1980), *Human Inference: Strategies and Shortcomings of Social Judgment*, Englewood Cliffs, NJ, Prentice-Hall.

Ortony, A. (ed.) (1979), *Metaphor and Thought*, Cambridge, England, Cambridge University Press.

Pinker, S. (1979), Formal Model of Language Learning *Cognition*, 7:217–283.

Pisoni, D., and Tash, J. (1974), Reaction Times to Comparisons within and across Phonetic Categories, *Perception and Psychophysics*, 15:285–290.

Posner, M. (1978). *Chronometric Studies of Mind*, Hillsdale, N.J., Lawrence Erlbaum Associates.

Potter, M. (1975), Meaning in Visual Search, *Science*, 187:965–966.

Putnam, H. (1961), Some Issues in the Theory of Grammar, in R. Jakobsen (ed.), *Proceedings of the Twelfth Symposium of Applied Mathematics: Structure of Language and Its Mathematical Aspects*, Providence, R.I., American Mathematical Society.

Putnam, H. (1962), The Analytic and the Synthetic in H. Feigl and G. Maxwell (eds.), *Minnesota Studies in the Philosophy of Science*, III, Minneapolis, University of Minnesota Press.

Pylyshyn, Z. (1980), Computation and Cognition: Issues in the Foundations of Cognitive Science, *Behavioral and Brain Sciences*, 3:111–132.

Quine, W. (1953), Two Dogmas of Empiricism, in *From a Logical Point of View*, Cambridge, Mass., Harvard University Press.

Raphael, B. (1971), The Frame Problem in Problem-Solving Systems, in N. Findler and B. Metzler (eds.), *Artificial Intelligence and Heuristic Programming*, Edinburgh, Edinburgh University Press.

Rozin, P. (1976), The Evolution of Intelligence and Access to the Cognitive Unconscious, in *Progress in Psychobiology and Physiological Psychology*, Vol. 6, New York, Academic Press.

Rorty, R. (1979), *Philosophy and the Mirror of Nature*, Princeton, Princeton University Press.

Sachs, J. (1967), Recognition Memory for Syntactic and Semantic Aspects of Connected Discourse, *Perception and Psychophysics*, 2:437–442.

Samuel, A. (1981), Phoneme Restoration: Insights from a New Methodology, *Journal of Experimental Psychology: General*, 110:474–494.

Schank, R., and Abelson, R. (1975), Scripts, Plans and Knowledge, *Proceedings of the Fourth International Joint Conference on Artificial Intelligence*, Tbilisi. Re-published in P. Johnson-Laird and P. Wason, *Thinking*, Cambridge, England, Cambridge University Press, 1977.

Stampe, D. (1977), Toward a Causal Theory of Linguistic Representation, *Midwest Studies in Philosophy*, 2:42–63.

Stich, S. (1978), Beliefs and Subdoxastic States, *Philosophy of Science*, 45:499–518.

Swinney, D. (1979), Lexical Access during Sentence Comprehension: (Re)consideration of Context Effects, *Journal of Verbal Learning and Verbal Behavior*, 18:645–660.

Tanenhaus, M., Leiman, J., and Seidenberg, M. (1979), Evidence for Multiple Stages in the Processing of Ambiguous Words in Syntactic Contexts, *Journal of Verbal Learning and Verbal Behavior*, 18:427–441.

Thagard, P. (1980), Scientific Theories as Frame Systems, unpublished ms, University of Michigan, Dearborn.

Treisman, A., and Gelade, G. (1980), A Feature-Integration Theory of Attention, *Cognitive Psychology*, 12:97–136.

Ullman, S. (1979), *The Interpretation of Visual Motion*, Cambridge, Mass., MIT Press.

Wanner, E. (1968), On Remembering, Forgetting, and Understanding Sentences: A Study of the Deep Structure Hypothesis, Ph.D. thesis, Harvard University.

Warren, R. (1970), Perceptual Restoration of Missing Speech Sounds, *Science*, 167:392–393.

Wright, B. (1982), Syntactic Effects from Lexical Decision in Sentences: Implications for Human Parsing, Ph.D. thesis, M.I.T.

Yin, R. (1969), Looking at Upside-Down Faces, *Journal of Experimental Psychology*, 81:141–145.

Yin, R. (1970), Face Recognition by Brain Injured Patients: A Dissociable Ability? *Neuropsychologia*, 8:395–402.

Zucker, S. (1981), Computer Vision and Human Perception, Technical report 81–10, Computer Vision and Graphics Laboratory, McGill University.

Chapter 45: Commitment[1]

BRIAN SKYRMS

Modular Rationality

In Stanley Kubrick's 1963 film, *Dr. Strangelove, or How I Learned to Stop Worrying and Love the Bomb*,[2] the USSR has built a doomsday machine – a device that, when triggered by an enemy attack or when tampered with in any way, will set off a nuclear explosion potent enough to destroy all human life. The doomsday machine is designed to be set off by tampering, not to guard it from the enemy but to guard it from its builders having second thoughts. For surely if there were an attack, it would be better for the USSR to suffer the effects of the attack than to suffer the combined effects of the attack and the doomsday machine. After an attack, if they could, they would disable the doomsday machine. And if their enemies could anticipate this, the doomsday machine would lose its power to deter aggression. For this reason, the commitment to retaliate had been built into the doomsday machine. Deterrence requires that all this be known. There is a memorable scene in the film in which Peter Sellers as Dr. Strangelove shouts over the hotline: "You fools! A doomsday machine isn't any good if you don't tell anyone you have it!"

Hollywood is not that far from Santa Monica, where cold war strategies were analyzed at the RAND Corporation. Hermann Kahn reports a typical beginning to a discussion of the policy of massive retaliation:

One Gedanken experiment that I have used many times and in many variations over the last twenty-five or thirty years begins with the statement: "Let us assume that the president of the United States has just been informed that a multimegaton bomb has been dropped on New York City. What do you think that he would do?" When this was first asked in the mid-1950s, the usual answer was "Press every button for launching nuclear forces and go home." The dialogue between the audience and myself continued more or less as follows:

Kahn: What happens next?
Audience: The Soviets do the same!
Kahn: And then what happens?
Audience: Nothing. Both sides have been destroyed.
Kahn: Why then did the American President do this?

A general rethinking of the issue would follow, and the audience would conclude that perhaps the president should not launch an immediate all-out retaliatory attack.[3]

In his story, Kahn has led his audience to the point at which the policy of massive retaliation and the supposed equilibrium in deterrence by mutually assured destruction begins to unravel. They have begun to see that the policy is based on a threat that would not be rational to carry out if one were called upon to do so.

The fundamental insight is not new. My friend Bill Harper likes to use Puccini's opera *Gianni Schicchi*[4] as an illustration.[5] The plot is based on an old story; the title character can be found in Dante's *Inferno*.[6] Buoso Donati has died and his will leaves his fortune to a monastery. His relatives call in a noted mimic, Gianni Schicchi. After first explaining the severe penalties for tampering with a will, which include having one's hand cut off, he offers to impersonate Buoso on his deathbed and dictate a new will to a

Reproduced with permission from Skyrms, B. (1996). *Evolution of the Social Contract* (chapter 2). Cambridge, UK: Cambridge University Press.

notary. The relatives accept, but on the occasion Schicchi names himself rather than the relatives as the heir. At this juncture, the relatives have no recourse but to remain silent, for to expose Schicchi would be to expose themselves.[7]

There is a clear folk moral here. A strategy that includes a threat that would not be in the agent's interest to carry out were she called upon to do so, and which she would have the option of not carrying out, is a defective strategy. The point is not really confined to threats. In a credible contingency plan for a situation in which an agent faces a sequence of choices, her plan should specify a *rational* choice at each choice point, relative to her situation at that choice point. Such a contingency plan exhibits *modular rationality* in that it is made up of modules that specify rational choices for the constituent decisions.

Kahn led his audiences into a realization that *peace by mutually assured destruction* is a doctrine that fails the test of modular rationality. Building a doomsday machine preempts the question of modular rationality by removing a choice point. In strategic interactions where the agents' contingency plans and continuing rationality are common knowledge, folk wisdom tells us that modular rationality of strategies is a necessary condition for a credible equilibrium.

It should come as no surprise that this principle is also to be found in contemporary game theory. In 1965, Reinhard Selten[8] argues that a credible equilibrium in a game should be *subgame perfect*. That is to say that the players' strategies restricted to any subgame should be an equilibrium of that subgame. The mutually assured destruction equilibrium, MAD, is not subgame perfect because the decision problem in which country A has been attacked and must decide for or against mutual destruction counts as a (degenerate) subgame, and in the subgame, MAD prescribes a non-optimal, non-equilibrium action. Subgame imperfect equilibria always reflect failures of modular rationality, but some failures of modular rationality do not show up in subgames in this way.[9] Modularity rationality is the fundamental general principle.[10]

Empirical Justice

To say that a principle is part of folk wisdom is not the same as to say that it is part of common practice. Experiments devised to test bargaining theory have been interpreted to show that modular rationality is routinely violated in practice.

In 1982, Güth, Schmittberger, and Schwartze investigated behavior in a bargaining game that brings the question of modular rationality into play. [. . . There] is a good – here a sum of German marks – to be divided. But now player one – the ultimatum giver – gets to make an opening proposal and player two can only accept or reject the offer. If player two rejects the offer, neither player gets anything; otherwise player one gets what he proposes and player two gets what is left. This game is known as *The Ultimatum Game* or *Take It or Leave It*!

Under the assumption that utility here is equal to money, this game has an infinite number of game theoretic equilibria. A version of fair division is one of them. If player one has a strategy of proposing equal division, and player two has a strategy of accepting an offer of at least half, but rejecting any offer of less, the players are at a Nash equilibrium of the game – that is to say, for each player that given the other player's strategy, she is doing as well as possible. But there are also similar Nash equilibria in which the split is 40 percent–60 percent, 10 percent–90 percent, or whatever you please.

Most of these equilibria, however, fail the Gianni Schicchi test. Supposing that player two prefers more to less and acts on her preferences, she will not carry out the threat to refuse a positive offer less than 50 percent (or 40 percent or . . .). If the threat is not credible, player one need not worry about it and would do better asking for more. We are left with a subgame perfect equilibrium in which player one offers player two one pfennig and proposes to keep the rest, and player two the strategy of accepting one pfennig but rejecting an offer of nothing. But this modular-rational behavior is not what the experimenters find.

Güth, Schmittberger, and Schwarze tried the ultimatum game on graduate students in economics at the University of Cologne.[11] A round of twenty-one games was played. A week later, the experiment was repeated with different random matching of subjects. The modular-rational equilibrium behavior described above was not played in any of these games. In the first experiment, the most frequent offer[12] was equal division. Other subjects in the role of player one tried to exploit their strategic advantage a bit, but not to the point of claiming almost all of the money. The mean demand was just under 2/3. In two cases, quite greedy demands[13] were rejected. When the same subjects played the game again after having a week to think about it, the ultimatum givers were slightly more greedy with a mean demand of 69% and more of those asked to "take it or leave it" left it, with 6 offers declined. One subject attempted to implement our modular-rational solution by demanding 4.99 out of 5 marks but that offer was rejected (as were three offers that would have left player two with only 1 mark).[14]

The pattern of most naive subjects making an offer at an equal split or close to it, when in the role of player one, and punishing low offers at their own expense by rejection as player two has been widely observed. Roth, Prasnikar, Okuno-Fujiwara, and Zamir[15] ran ultimatum game experiments at their respective universities in the United States, Yugoslavia, Japan and Israel. The experimenters were interested in the effect of learning when subjects repeatedly played the game over ten rounds. (In the context of a somewhat different bargaining game, Binmore, Shaked, and Sutton[16] had suggested that learning from experience would turn "fairmen" into modular-rational "gamesmen".) In all countries the modal initial offer was an even split, and a substantial number of low offers were rejected. In round ten, this is still true in the United States and Yugoslavia but the modal offer in Israel has fallen to 40 percent. In Japan, there are modes at 40 percent and 45 percent. In some cases, experience has led to an attempt to exploit the strategic advantage of the first move, but nowhere are the experienced players close to being gamesmen. A 60–40 split is closer to 50–50 than to 99–1. One might speculate whether 100 or 1,000 rounds would have moved the players close to subgame perfect equilibrium behavior. However that may be, we want to focus here on the initial behavior exhibited by naive subjects. Why do they do it?

It will come as no surprise that the most widely suggested hypothesis is simply that many subjects, rather than maximizing their expected monetary payoff, are implementing norms of fairness. It is important to keep in mind that these must include not only norms for making fair offers in the role of player one, but also norms for punishing unfair offers in the role of player two – provided the cost of punishment is not too high. None of the punishers is risking having his hands cut off. None is launching all ICBMs. But many are willing to give up a dollar or two to punish a greedy proposer who wanted eight or nine.

Richard Thaler chooses the ultimatum game as the subject for the initial article in a series on anomalies in economics – an anomaly being "an empirical result which requires implausible assumptions to explain within the rational choice paradigm." But we have a clear violation of the rational choice paradigm here only on the assumption that, for these subjects, utility = income. From the standpoint of rational choice theory, the subjects' utility functions are up to them. There is no principled reason why norms of fairness cannot be reflected in their utilities in such a way as to make their actions consistent with the theory of rational choice.[17]

Appeal to norms of fairness, however, hardly constitutes an explanation in itself. Why do we have such norms? Where do they come from? If they are modeled as factors in a subjective utility function, how do such utility functions come to be so widespread? An explanation might be attempted at the psychological level. Here it may be natural to appeal to the phenomenon of generalization. The sequential problem of dividing a cake in ultimatum bargaining may not seem to subjects much different than the problem where claims are simultaneous and submitted independently. In the latter case, fair division is a perfectly acceptable game theoretic solution. Perhaps subjects generalize from the simultaneous case to the sequential case. That would explain the equal-split offers on the part of player one, but leave unexplained the rejection of low offers on the part of player two. Perhaps punishing behavior could be explained by generalization from some different context. But even if that were the case, we would still be left with the evolutionary question: Why have norms of fairness not been eliminated by the process of evolution? An increase in income of real goods usually translates into an increase in evolutionary fitness.[18] How then could norms of fairness, of the kind observed in the ultimatum game, have evolved?

Evolution of an Anomaly

Of course, generalization can play a role in evolutionary theory. Just as an organ that evolves for one function may be used for another, so a behavioral rule that evolves in the context of one sort of encounter may well be triggered by a similar encounter. Ultimatum game behavior did not evolve solely in a context of ultimatum games. Nevertheless, it may be instructive to build and study a model in which it does. We will see that under favorable conditions, standard evolutionary game dynamics allows the anomalous behavior observed in experiments to evolve.

Table 1: Rule-Based Strategies

	If Player One	If Player Two
S1: Gamesman	Demand 9	Accept All
S2	Demand 9	Reject All
S3	Demand 9	Accept 5, Reject 9
S4: Mad Dog	Demand 9	Accept 9, Reject 5
S5: Easy Rider	Demand 5	Accept All
S6	Demand 5	Reject All
S7: Fairman	Demand 5	Accept 5, Reject 9
S8	Demand 5	Accept 9, Reject 5

We will begin with a simplified ultimatum game, in which each player has only two choices. The cake is divided into ten pieces, and player one can either demand five pieces or nine pieces. Player two either accepts or rejects the proposal as before.[19] We will analyze this game within the context of standard evolutionary game theory.

First, we have to determine the evolutionary strategies at issue in this game. Player one has only two strategies: Demand 9; Demand 5. Player two has four strategies, as evolution must tell her what to do in each contingency. Her strategies are: Accept All; Reject All; Accept if 5 is demanded, but Reject if 9 is demanded; Accept if 9 is demanded but Reject if 5 is demanded.

Next we have to decide between two evolutionary stories. According to the first story, there are two different populations: The Proposers and the Disposers. Those who take the role of player one come from the proposers and those who take the role of player two come from the disposers. According to the second story, there is one population, and individuals from that population sometimes play one role and sometimes another. The two-population model has recently been investigated by Binmore, Gale, and Samuelson (1995). They reach the conclusion that, under certain conditions regarding relative amounts of "noise" in the two populations, the anomalous behavior can evolve. This raises the question whether that behavior can evolve in a single population. The single-population story, after all, seems more relevant to the phenomena under discussion. Here each individual must have as a strategy a rule that tells her what to do in each role, so there are now eight strategies to consider. The strategies are listed in Table 1. I have given names to strategies that are of special interest. In particular, we have two strategies on which most of the game theoretical literature is focused: S1 = Gamesman and S7 = Fairman. (Note that

"reject 9" means "reject a demand by the first player for 9" or equivalently "reject an offer of 1 to you.") The role of the other two named strategies will emerge in the following discussion.

We assume that individuals are randomly paired from the population; that the decision as to which individual is to play which role is made at random; and that the payoffs are in terms of evolutionary fitness. Because a strategy determines what a player will do in each role, we can now calculate the expected fitness for any of the eight strategies that results from an encounter with any of the eight strategies.[20] The assumption of random pairing from a large population, together with the payoffs being in terms of fitness, leads to the replicator dynamics of evolutionary game theory. You can program your computer to simulate this dynamics and observe how populations with various proportions of these strategies will evolve.

Suppose we start with a population with equal proportions of the strategies. Fairmen (S7) go extinct and Gamesmen (S1) persist. But Gamesmen do not take over the entire population. Rather, the population evolves to a polymorphic state composed of about 87 percent Gamesmen and about 13 percent Mad Dogs. The surprise here is the persistence of the rather odd strategy, Mad Dog, which rejects fair offers and accepts unfair ones. Mad Dogs do worse against S5, S6, S7, and S8 than Gamesmen do, but S5, S6, S7, and S8 die off more rapidly than Mad Dogs. When they are extinct, and only greedy first moves are made, Mad Dogs do exactly as well as Gamesmen.

Not every initial mixed population, however, will lead to the extinction of Fairmen. Suppose we start with 30 percent of the population using the Fairman strategy S7 with the remaining strategies having equal proportions of the rest of the population. Then Gamesmen, Mad Dogs, and several other types are driven to extinction. The dynamics carries the population to a state composed of about 64 percent Fairmen and about 36 percent Easy Riders. Let us try a somewhat more plausible initial point, where the population proportions of S1-S8 are, respectively, <.32, .02, .10, .02, .10, .02, .40, .02>. The replicator dynamics carries this population to a state of 56.5 percent Fairmen and 43.5 percent Easy Riders.[21] Again, the "anomalous" Fairman strategy has survived.

Again, it is accompanied by Easy Rider. This is a strategy which makes fair offers but accepts all offers. It free rides on Fairman during the period it takes to drive the greedy S1–S4 to extinction.

As long as some of these greedy strategies are around, Easy Riders do strictly better than Fairmen; but when greedy strategies have been driven to extinction, Fairmen and Easy Riders do exactly as well as each other.

Notice that it is also true that, in the scenario where Gamesmen and Mad Dogs win out, the Gamesmen are free riding on the Mad Dogs in exactly the same way during the extinction of those who make fair offers. It is not usual to think of punishing those who make fair offers, but this is exactly what Mad Dogs do. Gamesmen do strictly better than Mad Dogs as long as there are some fair offer makers in the population, and exactly as well as Mad Dogs when the fair offer makers have gone extinct. In the terminology of game theory, the "free rider" in each of the scenarios *weakly dominates* its partner. That is to say that it does better against some strategies, but worse against none. One interesting thing about the replicator dynamics is that it need not carry weakly dominated strategies, such as our "anomalous" Fairman strategy, to extinction.[22]

This is closely related to the fact that the replicator dynamics need not respect modular rationality.[23] Fairman is not modular rational because, if confronted with an unfair offer, it requires choosing a payoff of 0 rather than 1. If Fairman is modified by reversing just that choice, we get a strategy that weakly dominates it, Easy Rider. Some types of inductive learning rules do eliminate weakly dominated strategies. It is the special kind of dynamics induced by replication that allows the evolution of strategies that are not modular rational.[24]

In this ultimatum game, when we choose the initial conditions at random, the evolutionary dynamics *always* carries us to a polymorphism that includes weakly dominated, modular-irrational strategies. We either get some Fairmen or some Mad Dogs. The same is true if we analyze the evolutionary dynamics of this ultimatum game when played between two populations. This is not evident from the paper of Binmore, Gale, and Samuelson only because they do not admit Mad Dog as a possible strategy. If you put it in, you find Gamesman-Mad Dog polymorphisms just as in the one-population model. Our general conclusion does not depend on having only two possible demands in our game. If you allow more possible demands, you typically end up with a more complicated polymorphism that contains several weakly dominated, modular-irrational strategies.[25] As we increase the options, the evolutionary dynamics generates a richer set of anomalies.

The Trembling Hand

There is another aspect of modular rationality that we have yet to explore. To introduce it, we return to *The Divine Comedy*. In the *Paradiso*, Dante explains how imperfection arises in the sublunar realm:

> If the wax were exactly worked and the heavens were at the heights of their power, the light of the whole seal would be apparent. But nature always gives it defectively, like an artist who in the practice of his art has a hand that trembles.[26]

Failures of execution are a problem even for God. Although the Divine plan is perfect, the imperfection of the matter on which it is imposed persists. If God's strategies cannot be executed without mistakes, how can we ignore the possibility of mistakes in the execution of human strategies? This raises a problem for the theology of commitment.

As Selten showed, strategies that fail to be modular rational are not robust with respect to considerations of the "trembling hand." For an illustration, let us return to *Dr. Strangelove*. Suppose that you build a doomsday machine and the other side follows a policy of not attacking but, as in the film, an insane field commander attacks anyway. Then you will suffer from the execution of that part of your policy that failed the test of modular rationality. If one factors in some small probability of attack by computer or human error, building a perfect doomsday machine would no longer be optimal. It would be better to construct one that doesn't work. The point is quite general for strategic situations of the kind under consideration. Robustness of a strategic equilibrium with respect to considerations of the trembling hand implies that equilibrium passes the test of modular rationality.[27]

How does this apply in the ultimatum game? In a population of Fairmen it would be a "mistake" to make a greedy offer, but if those mistakes are made Easy Riders do strictly better than Fairmen. Should we worry about the trembling hand when we think about the evolution of strategies in the ultimatum game? Indeed we should, for evolution involves its own kind of trembles. Evolution is the result of the interplay of two processes: variation and differential reproduction. The replicator dynamics we used in the last section models only differential reproduction. What about variation?

In a species like ours that reproduces sexually, there are two sources of variation: mutation and recombination. In a species that reproduces asexually all variation is due to mutation. Mutations are rare and only make a significant contribution in the long run. Sexual reproduction vastly increases the amount of variation. There is a Mendelian shuffling of the genome at the conception of each individual. Consequently, sex speeds up the process of evolution.[28] Cultural evolution has its own kinds of recombination and mutation.

Recombination

In evolutionary game theory there has been considerable recent interest in modeling mutation,[29] but less attention has been paid to recombination.[30] The theme of recombination has been pursued in computer science by John Holland and his students under the appellation "genetic algorithms."[31] Replication is governed by success, judged by some standards appropriate to the problem. Recombination is implemented by "crossover." Once in a while, the code for programs is cut into two pieces, and the first and last pieces are swapped between programs, creating new programs. Most of these new programs will be useless and will die out due to the dynamics of replication. But over many cycles, useful programs are created. The most successful applications of the genetic algorithm approach have been to problems of optimization against a fixed environment. How should the idea of recombination be applied in the context of game theory?

How one cuts and recombines depends on how one parses the underlying structure. In the kind of extensive games that we have been considering, the strategies have a natural structure. We can use this structure, and implement recombination at the level of strategy substructures rather than at the level of strings in some programming language. Thus the strategy: *If player one demand 9; If player two accept a demand of 5 but reject a demand of 9* has as large substrategies: *If player one demand 9* and *If player two then accept a demand of 5 but reject a demand of 9* and as smaller substrategies: *If player two and confronted with a demand of 5 accept it* and *If player two and confronted with a demand of 9 reject it.* The idea to cut and recombine at the level of strategy substructures is put forward in the context of sequential decision problems by John Koza,[32] in his book on genetic programming. It is applied to the computer modeling of games by Peter Danielson.[33] Related techniques are used in Axelrod's[34] latest work on iterated

Prisoner's Dilemma. I do not want to explore any of these models in detail here, but rather to make a general point about the kind of variation they introduce.

Let us return to the ultimatum game and to the polymorphic equilibrium states discussed in the last section. What is the effect of the trembling hand in the form of recombination on these equilibria? Consider the state of 64 percent Fairmen and 36 percent Easy Riders. Both strategies demand 5. So recombination between them can only produce a strategy that demands 5. Both accept a demand of 5, so recombination between them can only produce a strategy that accepts a demand of 5. Recombination between Fairmen and Easy Riders can only produce Fairmen and Easy Riders. Likewise, recombination will not introduce any new strategies into a population of only Gamesmen and Mad Dogs.

This contrasts with a population composed of players playing S3 and S8. First, notice that each of these strategies does badly against itself but better against the other. If only these two strategies are represented in the population, the replicator dynamics carries the population to a polymorphic equilibrium state where 70 percent of the population plays S3 and 30 percent plays S8. Next, notice that S3 and S8 each have three minimal modules, which are:

S3:	S8:
Demand 9	Demand 5
If 9 demanded, reject	If 9 demanded, accept
If 5 demanded, accept	If 5 demanded, reject

Any of the eight possible strategies can arise from S3 and S8 by recombination. But now against a population consisting of almost all S3 and S8, Gamesmen do better than S3 and Easy Riders do better than S8, so even a little bit of recombination causes the S3–S8 equilibrium to unravel.

The variation introduced here by recombination is a rather special kind of variation. Some population equilibria of the process of differential reproduction represented by the replicator dynamics are more robust to a bit of recombination than others. In particular, the persistence of the weakly dominated and modular-irrational Fairmen strategy is quite consistent with this version of Mother Nature's trembling hand.

Mutation

Mutation is a different process. Unlike recombination, mutation can take any strategy into any other. There is no reason to suppose, however, that every transformation is equiprobable.

Depending on how the mutation mechanism works, some transformations may be more probable than others. We will assume, however, that all transformations have positive probability, so that over the long run no strategy remains extinct. It might seem, at first glance, that weakly dominated strategies could not survive forever in such an environment. Those strategies against which the dominating strategies do better keep popping up, so that differential reproduction must favor the dominating strategies. Is it not simply a matter of time before the dominating strategies take over?

This conclusion may seem plausible, but it does not follow from the stated assumptions. It is correct that the play against mutant strategies of all kinds must give the dominating strategy some reproductive advantage over the dominated one. But it is quite possible that, at the same time, the mutation process creates enough extra individuals using the dominated strategy to counterbalance this effect. Whether these small pressures balance each other or not depends on the proportions of the population playing various strategies, on the mutation rate and on the transition probabilities for mutations.[35] There are values for these parameters for which Fairman–Easy Rider polymorphisms persist and for which Gamesman–Mad Dog polymorphisms do. But the Gamesman–Mad Dog polymorphisms do have more modest requirements: And in some plausible scenarios, Easy Riders slowly take over more and more of a Fairman–Easy Rider polymorphism until greedy strategies can profitably invade by exploiting the Easy Rider's accommodating nature.

Could strategies that fail the Gianni Schicchi test survive the trembling hand of evolution? The evolutionary process incorporates two kinds of variation, neither of which corresponds exactly to the metaphor of the trembling hand. Recombination and mutation do not create a mere momentary lapse in behavior, but rather a new individual playing a new strategy. Thus they alter not only the distribution of behaviors determining average fitness, but also the composition of the population. They do so in different ways, with mutation making possible transitions of a type not possible with recombination, but doing so on a much longer time scale. Neither source of variation is guaranteed to eliminate strategies that are not modular rational. Recombination might not even make those strategies that exploit the defect. Mutation introduces all strategies and exploits all defects, although the effect may be very small. However it may also have a

dynamic effect favorable to the strategy in question that counterbalances the weak selection pressure against it. Evolution does not respect modular rationality.

The Theology of Commitment

Folk wisdom recognizes that there can be a conflict between commitment and modular rationality. This happens when an agent commits to a strategy like massive retaliation, which would not be in the agent's interest to carry out if the contingency arose. Nevertheless, we find what appear to be violations of modular rationality in experiments, and we find the persistence of such behavior to be consistent with simple models of the evolutionary process. Should we simply conclude that we have here the evolution of irrationality?

Two philosophers, David Gauthier and Edward McClennen, have taken the opposite point of view – that where commitment conflicts with modular rationality, it is committed behavior that should be called rational. The concept of modular rationality is to be relegated to the intellectual junk pile. This is McLennen's doctrine of "resolute choice"[36] and (part of) Gauthier's doctrine of "constrained maximization."[37] In opposition to both folk wisdom and game theory, McClennen and Gauthier are promulgating a new theology of commitment.

This movement to "reform" rationality is supported by a consistency argument and an ulterior motive. The consistency argument is put as a question: *Would it not be inconsistent to judge it optimal to have a disposition and yet to judge it suboptimal to carry out the act specified by that disposition?* The ulterior motive is the possibility of deriving ethics from the bare postulates of rational behavior.

Suppose you take it to be rational to build a doomsday machine for its deterrent effect, and you build one and announce it. The other side launches a first strike. If the doomsday machine works, you have no choice, but it malfunctions. You now have a choice of whether to launch all missiles. You decide not to. Are you inconsistent? I do not see an inconsistency. The judgment not to launch all missiles was made in a different state than the judgment that it was optimal to construct the doomsday machine. The decision against massive retaliation was made with the knowledge that a first strike had indeed been launched. The decision to build the doomsday machine was made without that knowledge and in the belief that building the machine would prevent the first strike. There is nothing very surprising here, and certainly no inconsistency.

Suppose Buoso's relatives had written a letter to be opened if the will came out wrong and let Schicchi know about it. Suppose that, without Schicchi's knowledge, the letter was accidentally destroyed. Suppose that Schicchi names himself as heir anyway – for whatever reason. Would the relatives then be *irrational* not to have their hands cut off in order to carry out their threat? Here I find myself more comfortable with folk wisdom than with philosophical innovation.[38]

Now for the ulterior motive. Let me start with some history. In 1980 John Harsanyi wrote an important paper on *rule utilitarianism*. Harsanyi argued that the moral behavior of rule utilitarians can be gotten from two assumptions:

1. They play a cooperative game in normal form. In choosing a strategy, they solve the *constrained maximization*[39] problem of choosing rules that maximizes social utility subject to the constraint that everyone chooses the same rules.

2. They commit to these rules and follow them no matter what.

Rule utilitarianism is in many ways an attractive ethical position. Rule utilitarians cooperate to their mutual benefit in situations in which *act utilitarians* do not. Harsanyi argues that rule utilitarians can make sense of rights and obligations in a way that act utilitarians cannot.

If you could build 1 and 2 into the meaning of individual rationality, you could derive morality from rationality! Something like this is, I believe, what both Gauthier and McClennen have in mind. The first thing to say about the ulterior motive is that it *is* an ulterior motive. The project of deriving morality from rationality loses much of its interest when it becomes clear that the first step of the derivation is a redefinition of rationality. The second thing to say is that it is not so clear that commitment, by itself, always leads to a kind of behavior that is morally desirable. The examples we have already discussed illustrate this point. Robert Frank[40] uses the feud between the Hatfield and McCoy families as an opening illustration of a book whose theme is commitment. Commitment can lead to endless chains of retribution. As a model illustration, consider a strategy that has gotten remarkably good press recently – that of Tit-for-Tat in repeated Prisoner's Dilemma. On each round, each player can either cooperate or defect.

Tit-for-tat begins by cooperating and then does to the other player whatever the other did to him in the last round. Suppose both players adopt a strategy of Tit-for-tat and both players know it, but that at some point one player "trembles" and defects by mistake. The other player will punish him in the next round, and he will punish the other player in the subsequent round, and so on ad infinitum.[41] In this situation each of these players would be better off doing what was necessary to restore mutual cooperation. They are not acting in accordance with modular rationality.[42] Moral and political philosophers should be aware of the dark side of commitment.

Of course whether we look on the dark side or the sunny side of commitment has little to do with the substantive issue of the relation of rationality to commitment. Rationality is not just a word to play with. There is a *theory* of rational decision, due to Ramsey, de Finetti, and Savage, which is an important part of our intellectual heritage. The theory shows that an agent who has a rich, coherent system of choice-dispositions can be endowed with subjective utilities and subjective probabilities such that choice maximizes expected utility. Suppose we are really talking about such an agent's subjective expected utility. A strategy that is not modular rational in these terms is just one that in certain circumstances would require such a rational agent to choose what she would not choose. Credible implementation requires removing the possibility of choice – as when one builds the Doomsday Machine.

If expected utility theory is kept in mind, the idea of modifying the normative theory by somehow building in commitment appears quixotic. Instead of tilting at subjected expected utility theory, moral theorists could more profitably study the conditions under which moral behavior is consistent with it. This is possible when sympathy and justice are reflected in an agent's utilities and when these operate through good habits, whose maintenance carries high utility for her.[43]

It is also clear that there is a large gap between the results of ultimatum game experiments and the falsification of subjective expected utility as a descriptive theory. Some players may like to make fair offers and to punish those who don't make fair offers. Why shouldn't they? Who presumes to tell them that utility should equal monetary income? Considerations of fairness could be reflected in utilities.[44]

In contrast with subjective expected utility theory, both evolution and experimentation share an interest in tangible income. It is for this reason that evolutionary dynamics has some relevance to experimental results. We have seen that strategies that are not modular rational in payoffs in evolutionary fitness may evolve. It remains to be seen how useful it is to conceptualize these strategies within the framework of subjective expected utility theory. If they are treated in this way, one could think of evolution as generating bounds on utility functions for the species. The alchemy of the endocrine system and the emotions can be thought of as a powerful tool in this work.[45] There is no conflict between subjective utility theory and David Hume's famous rejoinder to Spinoza: "Reason is and ought to be the slave of the passions."

Modularity in Evolution and in Choice

Evolution may – if the conditions are right – favor commitment over modular rationality. Mixed populations that include individuals using strategies that are not modular rational in Darwinian fitness can evolve according to the replicator dynamics. They may not be eliminated in the long run even when we take into account the variation due to both recombination and mutation. We should not be surprised to observe some modest implementation of such strategies, as we do in the ultimatum game experiments.

These strategies need not even fail the test of modular rationality in the subject's own terms, providing we construe the subject's own utility function according to Davidson's principle of charity: "Charity in interpreting the words and thoughts of others is unavoidable in another direction as well: just as we must maximize agreement, or risk not making sense of what the alien is talking about, so we must maximize the self-consistency that we attribute to him, on pain of not understanding him."[46] A pragmatic version of the principle would urge charity in interpreting the *acts* of others so as to maximize coherence.

However, the process of implementing strategies drawn from a stock of evolved behaviors is a process that introduces its own complications. A choice situation may fall under more than one rule, and then which rule that chooser invokes to characterize or "frame" the situation becomes crucial. Thus, in the ultimatum game, player two could see it as a situation in which she was being offered a choice between $2 or nothing and apply the rule "More is better" or could see it as an ultimatum game in which the other player was trying to take unfair advantage and apply the rule "Don't accede to unfair offers in the ultimatum game." Both descriptions correctly characterize the situation, but the rules conflict.

The evolution of behavior itself has a modular aspect. It is not possible to have evolved a special rule for every decision situation. Complex problems have to be solved by combining behavioral modules that have evolved separately. The stock of available modules may be rich enough to generate ambiguity in the characterization of the problem. All sorts of cues[47] may be relevant to how the ambiguity is resolved, and different resolutions may lead to different decisions.[48] Even if we leave aside the inevitable confusions and errors, we should not be surprised to find a wide range of behavior in situations like the ultimatum game.

The considerations brought forward in this chapter do not pretend to be a full evolutionary explanation of the fairness effect. Rather, we raise the prior question as to how it might be possible for such behavior to survive in the struggle for existence. In the ultimatum game, this becomes the question of whether a strategy of commitment that fails the test of modular rationality can persist. It can. Evolution does not respect modular rationality.

Notes

1 More technical details regarding this chapter may be found in my forthcoming "Evolution of an Anomaly."
2 Screenplay by Stanley Kubrick, Peter George, and Terry Southern.
3 Kahn (1984), p. 59.
4 Premier performance at the Metropolitan Opera, Dec. 14, 1918.
5 See Harper (1991).
6 Dante, *Paradiso*, Canto XXX.
7 If the relatives had devised a doomsday machine – perhaps a letter in the hands of a suitable third party to be delivered to the authorities just in case they are not named as heirs – and if Schicchi had known about it, then he would have had no recourse but to abide by his agreement.
8 Selten (1965).
9 For examples, see Selten (1975).
10 This is the position taken by Kreps and Wilson (1982). Modular rationality is the same as their "sequential rationality."
11 The students were not familiar with game theory. Forty-two students were divided equally into player one and player two groups. Subjects did not know which member of the other group they were matched against. The amount to be distributed ranged from 4 to 10 marks.

12 Seven of 21 games.

13 Demands of all of 4 marks and of 4.80 of 6 marks.

14 Subsequently, a third experiment was performed in which 37 new subjects were asked to play both roles in the game by submitting a proposal as player one, and a minimal acceptable share as player two. Notice that *this is not an ultimatum game*. Player one does not deliver an ultimatum, and player two does not decide after receiving one. Rather, they simultaneously make actions that determine their payoffs [...]. The questions of modular rationality and of subgame perfection do not arise. The same point applies to the experiments of Kahneman, Knetsch, and Thaler (1986). However the considerations of weak dominance and the trembling hand raised in this chapter are relevant to these games.

15 Roth, Prasnikar, Okuno-Fujiwara, and Zamir (1991).

16 Binmore, Shaked, and Sutton (1985).

17 For an attempt to account for the experimental literature on the ultimatum game in this way, see Bolton (1991). On the other hand, there is already a large body of other experimental literature that raises much more fundamental problems for the descriptive validity of expected utility theory. Against this background, one might try to model the experimental results directly in terms of systems of normative rules of behavior. For this approach, see Güth (1988) and Güth and Teitz (1990).

18 It is sometimes objected that rich families now have fewer children than poor families. The comment is directed toward biological evolution rather than cultural evolution. Even there the objection can hardly be taken seriously. Does the objector imagine yuppie *Homo erectus* driving BMWs on the savannah? Through most of evolutionary time, payoff in real goods means the difference between nutrition and starvation, and it correlates very well with Darwinian fitness.

19 A variant of this simplified game was used in an experiment by Kahneman, Knetsch, and Thaler (1986).

20 Here is the resulting fitness matrix:

	S1	S2	S3	S4	S5	S6	S7	S8
S1	5	.5	.5	5	7	2.5	2.5	7
S2	4.5	0	0	4.5	4.5	0	0	4.5
S3	4.5	0	0	4.5	7	2.5	2.5	7
S4	5	.5	.5	5	4.5	0	0	4.5
S5	3	.5	3	.5	5	2.5	5	2.5
S6	2.5	0	2.5	0	2.5	0	2.5	0
S7	2.5	0	2.5	0	5	2.5	5	2.5
S8	3	.5	3	.5	2.5	0	2.5	0

21 This state is dynamically stable in the replicator dynamics – that is to say, that any state close to it remains close to it. But it is not asymptotically stable. It is not true that any state close to it is carried to it by the dynamics. It is not evolutionarily stable in the sense of Maynard Smith and Price (1973).

22 That replicator dynamics need not eliminate weakly dominated strategies was, to my knowledge, first noted in Samuelson (1988).

23 They are equivalent in the kind of game under discussion here. It is an extensive form two-person game in which each person has exactly one move. See van Damme (1987).

24 See Samuelson (1988) and Skyrms (1991).

25 William Harms (1994) has investigated a game in which one may demand .2, .4, .6, .8, or 1.0 of the pie. Choosing initial population proportions at random, most of the runs (408 of 500) ended up at populations that demand .8, with a polymorphism in the response strategies that accept that demand.

26 Dante, *Paradiso*, Canto XIII. The whole passage is an exposition of Aristotelian doctrine.

27 The idea is formally introduced into game theory by Selten (1975) in the concept of a (trembling hand) perfect equilibrium, and elaborated by Myerson (1978) in his more stringent concept of a proper equilibrium. Every proper equilibrium is perfect and every perfect equilibrium uses only undominated strategies. An equilibrium in hardwired (committed) strategies that is robust to trembles in the sense of Myerson's proper equilibrium is modular rational in the sense of Kreps and Wilson's "sequential equilibrium" and Selten's "subgame perfect equilibrium." For details, see van Damme (1987).

28 There is a large literature on the question of how recombination itself evolved. For a sampling of important work, see Muller (1932, 1964), Maynard Smith (1978), and Hamilton (1980).

29 Starting with the seminal paper of Foster and Young (1990).

30 There are two studies that incorporate recombination into the dynamics: Robert Axelrod (1992), a political scientist, and Peter Danielson (1992), a philosopher. There are also recombination models in Hofbauer and Sigmund (1988).

31 See Holland (1975).

32 Koza (1992).

33 Danielson (1992).

34 Axelrod (1997).

35 Notice that, even if the transition probabilities are taken to be all equal, mutation may favor the dominated strategy in a given state of the population. Consider the equilibrium of the replicator dynamics with $\mathrm{pr}(S1) = .948$ and $\mathrm{pr}(S4) = .052$. If a transition in either direction is equally likely, mutation will turn many more S1s into S4s than conversely.

36 McClennen (1990).

37 Gauthier (1986); but see Gauthier (1990) for second thoughts.

38 For philosophical defense of folk wisdom, see Kavka (1978, 1983a, 1983b, 1987) and Lewis (1984).
39 Harsanyi's terminology.
40 Frank (1988).
41 Or until another tremble either has them both cooperate and sets them right or has them both defect and sets them on a path of unrelieved vengeance.
42 Thus Tit-for-Tat against Tit-for-Tat is not a subgame perfect equilibrium in repeated Prisoner's Dilemma.
43 See the discussion of Good Habits in chapter 6 of my 1990 book.
44 As in the model proposed by Bolton (1991).
45 As Hirshliefer and Frank point out.
46 From "Truth and Meaning" (1967), reprinted in Davidson (1984), p. 27. In the introduction, Davidson attributes the basic idea to Neil Wilson and points out that Quine, in *Word and Object*, applies the principle to logical constants.
47 Including the importance of what is at stake.
48 This is the approach I would take to the Dictator game of Kahneman, Knetsch, and Thaler (1986). Here the subjects were psychology students at Cornell University. Each subject was asked to divide $20 between herself and an anonymous student in the same class. She could choose either $18 for herself and $2 to the other participant or an even split. There was no possibility of rejection of the offer by the recipient. Some subjects may have seen the dictator game as tantamount to an ultimatum game played against a player who accepts all offers. If such a subject had a generous strategy for the ultimatum game, she might simply apply that and choose an even split. If such a subject had a greedy strategy for the ultimatum game, she would choose the $18. Some subjects may have framed the problem as simply a choice between $18 and $10. In fact, 76 percent of the students divided the money equally. These striking results for the dictator game are somewhat controversial. Other investigators find much lower proportions of subjects offering an equal split in the dictator game. See Forsythe, Horowitz, Savin, and Sefton (1988) and Hoffman, McCabe, Shachat, and Smith (1991). The magnitude of the "fairness factor" is controversial, but its existence is not. That robust phenomenon is consistent with the approach advocated here.

References

Axelrod, R. (1994). "The Evolution of Strategies in the Iterated Prisoner's Dilemma." Forthcoming in *The Dynamics of Norms*. Ed. Bicchieri, C., Jeffrey, R., and Skyrms, B. New York: Cambridge University Press, 199–220.

Binmore, K., Gale, J., and Samuelson, L. (1995). "Learning to Be Imperfect: The Ultimatum Game." *Games and Economic Behavior* 8:56–90.

Binmore, K., Shaked, A., and Sutton, J. (1985). "Testing Non-Cooperative Bargaining Theory: A Preliminary Study." *American Economic Review* 75:178–80.

Bolton, G. (1991). "A Comparative Model for Bargaining: Theory and Evidence." *American Economic Review* 81:96–136.

Danielson, P. (1992). *Artificial Morality: Virtuous Robots for Virtual Games*. London: Routledge & Kegan Paul.

Davidson, D. (1984). *Inquiries into Truth and Interpretation*. Oxford: Oxford University Press (Clarendon Press).

Forsythe, R., Horowitz, J., Savin, N., and Sefton, M. (1988). "Replicability, Fairness and Pay in Experiments with Simple Bargaining Games." Working paper, University of Iowa, Iowa City.

Foster, D., and Young, P. (1990). "Stochastic Evolutionary Game Dynamics." *Theoretical Population Biology* 38:219–32.

Frank, R. (1988). *Passions Within Reason*. New York: Norton.

Gauthier, D. (1986). *Morals by Agreement*. Oxford: Oxford University Press (Clarendon Press).

Gauthier, D. (1990). *Moral Dealing: Contract, Ethics and Reason*. Ithaca, N.Y.: Cornell University Press.

Güth, W. (1988). "On the Behavioral Approach to Distributive Justice – A Theoretical and Experimental Investigation." In *Applied Behavioral Economics*. Vol. 2. Ed. S. Maital, pp. 703–17. New York: New York University Press.

Güth, W., Schmittberger, R., and Schwarze, B. (1982). "An Experimental Analysis of Ultimatum Bargaining." *Journal of Economic Behavior and Organization* 3:367–88.

Güth, W., and Tietz, R. (1990). "Ultimatum Bargaining Behavior: A Survey and Comparison of Experimental Results." *Journal of Economic Psychology* 11:417–49.

Hamilton, W. D. (1980). "Sex Versus Non-Sex Versus Parasite." *Oikos* 35:282–90.

Harms, W. (1994). "Discrete Replicator Dynamics for the Ultimatum Game with Mutation and Recombination" Technical report, University of California, Irvine.

Harper, W. (1991). "Ratifiability and Refinements in Two-Person Noncooperative Games." In *Foundations of Game Theory: Issues and Advances*, ed. Bacharach, M., and Hurley, S., pp. 263–93. Oxford: Blackwell Publisher.

Harsanyi, J. (1980). "Rule Utilitarianism, Rights, Obligations and the Theory of Rational Behavior." *Theory and Decision* 12:115–33.

Hirshliefer, J. (1987). "On the Emotions as Guarantors of Threats and Promises." In *The Latest on* the Best: Essays on Evolution and Optimality, ed. Dupré, J. Cambridge, Mass.: MIT Press.

Hofbauer, J., and Sigmund, K. (1988). The Theory of Evolution and Dynamical Systems. New York: Cambridge University Press.

Hoffman, E., McCabe, K., Shachat, K., and Smith, V. (1994). "Preferences, Property Rights and Anonymity in Bargaining Games." Games and Economic Behavior 7:346–80.

Holland, J. (1975). Adaptation in Natural and Artificial Systems. Ann Arbor: University of Michigan Press.

Kahn, H. (1984). Thinking About the Unthinkable in the 1980s. New York: Simon & Schuster.

Kahneman, D., Knetsch, J., and Thaler, R. (1986). "Fairness and the Assumptions of Economics." Journal of Business 59:8285–8300. Reprinted in Rational Choice: The Contrast Between Economics and Psychology, ed. Hogarth, R. M., and Reder, M., pp. 101–16. Chicago: University of Chicago Press.

Kavka, G. (1978). "Some Paradoxes of Deterrence." Journal of Philosophy 75:285–302.

Kavka, G. (1983a). "Hobbes' War of All Against All." Ethics 93:291–310.

Kavka, G. (1983b). "The Toxin Puzzle." Analysis 43:33–6.

Kavka, G. (1987). Paradoxes of Nuclear Deterrence. New York: Cambridge University Press.

Koza, J. (1992). Genetic Programming: On the Programming of Computers by Natural Selection. Cambridge, Mass.: MIT Press.

Kreps, D., and Wilson, D. (1982). "Sequential Equilibria." Econometrica 50:863–94.

Lewis, D. (1984). "Devil's Bargains and the Real World." In The Security Gamble, ed. MacLean, D., pp. 141–54. Totowa, N.J.: Rowman & Allenheld.

Maynard Smith, J. (1978). The Evolution of Sex. New York: Cambridge University Press.

Maynard Smith, J., and Price, G. R. (1973). "The Logic of Animal Conflict." Nature 146:15–18.

McClennen, E. (1990). Rationality and Dynamic Choice: Foundational Explorations. New York: Cambridge University Press.

Muller, H. (1932). "Some Genetic Aspects of Sex." American Naturalist 66:118–38.

Muller, H. (1964). "The Relation of Recombination to Mutational Advance." Mutation Research 1: 2–9.

Myerson, R. B. (1978). "Refinements of the Nash Equilibrium Concept." International Journal of Game Theory 7:73–80.

Ramsey, F. P. (1931). The Foundations of Mathematics and Other Essays. New York: Harcourt Brace.

Roth, A., Prasnikar, V., Okuno-Fujiwara, M., and Zamir, S. (1991). "Bargaining and Market Behavior in Jerusalem, Ljubljana, Pittsburgh and Tokyo: An Experimental Study." American Economic Review 81:68–95.

Samuelson, L. (1988). "Evolutionary Foundations of Solution Concepts for Finite Two-Player Normal Form Games." In Proceedings of the Second Conference on Theoretical Aspects of Reasoning About Knowledge, ed. Vardi, M., pp. 211–26. Los Altos, Calif.: Morgan Kaufmann.

Savage, L. J. (1954). The Foundations of Statistics. New York: Wiley.

Selten, R. (1965). "Spieltheoretische Behandlung eines Oligopolmodells mit Nachfragetragheit." Zeitschrift fur die gesamte Staatswissenschaft 121:301–24, 667–89.

Selten, R. (1975). "Reexamination of the Perfectness Concept of Equilibrium in Extensive Games." International Journal of Game Theory 4:25–55.

Skyrms, B. (1991). The Dynamics of Rational Deliberation. Cambridge, Mass.: Harvard University Press.

Thaler, R. (1988). "Anomalies: The Ultimatum Game." Journal of Economic Perspectives 2:195–206.

van Damme, E. (1987). Stability and Perfection of Nash Equilibria. Berlin: Springer.

Chapter 46: Evolution of Inference

BRIAN SKYRMS

Philosophical Skepticism

Jean-Jacques Rousseau begins his discussion of the origin of language in *A Discourse on Inequality* by toying with a paradox:

> [A] substitution of voice for gesture can only have been made by common consent, something rather difficult to put into effect by men whose crude organs had not yet been exercised; something indeed, even more difficult to conceive of having happened in the first place, for such a unanimous agreement would need to be proposed, which means that speech seems to be absolutely necessary to establish the use of speech.[1]

Rousseau moves on without taking the problem seriously, but the paradox echoes through modern philosophy of language. How can we explain the genesis of speech without presupposing speech, reference without presupposing reference, meaning without presupposing meaning? A version of this paradox forms the basis of Quine's attack on the logical empiricist doctrine that logic derives its warrant from conventions of meaning – that logical truths are true and logical inferences are valid by virtue of such conventions. Quine raised the general skeptical question of how conventions of language could be established without preexisting language, as well as calling attention to more specific skeptical circularities. If conventions of logic are set up by explicit definitions, or by axioms, must we not presuppose logic to unpack those conventions?

Convention According to David Lewis

David Lewis (1969) sought to answer these skeptical doubts within a game theoretical framework in his book *Convention*. This account contains fundamental new insights, and I regard it as a major advance in the theory of meaning. Lewis sees a convention as being a special kind of strict Nash equilibrium in a game that models the relevant social interaction. To say that a convention is a Nash equilibrium is to say that if an individual deviates from a convention that others observe, he is no better off for that. To say that it is a *strict* Nash equilibrium is to say that he is actually worse off. To this, Lewis adds the additional requirement that an individual unilateral deviation makes *everyone* involved in the social interaction worse off, so that it is in the common interest to avoid such deviations.

A theory of convention must answer two fundamental questions: How do we arrive at conventions? And by virtue of what considerations do conventions remain in force? Within Lewis's game-theoretic setting, these questions become, respectively, the problems of *equilibrium selection* and *equilibrium maintenance*.

On the face of it, the second problem may seem to have a trivial solution – the equilibrium is maintained because it is an equilibrium! No one has an incentive to deviate. In fact, since it is a strict equilibrium, everyone has an incentive not to deviate. This is part of the answer, but Lewis shows that this is not the whole answer.

There is an incentive to avoid unilateral deviation, but, for example, if you expect me to deviate, you might believe you would be better off

---

deviating as well. And if I believe that you have such beliefs, I may expect you to deviate and by virtue of such expectations deviate myself. It is when I believe that others will not deviate that I must judge deviation to be against my own interest. The self-reinforcing character of a strict Nash equilibrium must be backed by a hierarchy of appropriate interacting expectations.

These considerations lead to Lewis's introduction of the concept of *common knowledge*. A proposition, P, is common knowledge among a group of agents if each of them knows that P, and each of them knows that each of them knows that P, and so forth for all finite levels. To the requirement that a convention must be the appropriate kind of strict Nash equilibrium, he adds the additional requirement that it be backed by the appropriate kind of common knowledge. The game being played must be common knowledge to the players, along with the fact that their actions are jointly at the equilibrium of the game that constitutes the convention.

Considerations of common knowledge are thus at the center of Lewis's theory of equilibrium maintenance. What about equilibrium selection? A convention is typically an equilibrium in an interaction, which admits many different equilibria. That is what makes conventions conventional. An alternative equilibrium might have done as well. How, then, do the agents involved come to coordinate on one of the many possible equilibria involved? Lewis, following Thomas Schelling, identifies three factors that may affect equilibrium selection: prior agreement, precedent and salience. A *salient* equilibrium (Schelling's focal equilibrium) is one that "stands out" to the agents involved for some reason or another. Salience is a psychological property, and the causes of salience are not restricted in any way. Prior agreement and precedent can be viewed as special sources of salience.

Lewis's Signaling Games

Lewis discusses the conventionality of meaning in the context of signaling games.[2] We suppose that one player, the Sender, comes into possession of some private knowledge about the world and wishes to share it with another player, the Receiver, who could use that knowledge to make a more informed decision. The decision has payoff implications for both Sender and Receiver, and their interests in this decision are common, which is why both wish the decision to be an informed one.

The Sender has a number of potential messages or signals that he can send to the Receiver to convey that information, the only hitch being that the "messages" have no preexisting meaning. The model that Lewis considers has an equal number of states of the world, S, messages, M, and acts, A. The payoffs for both players make the game a game of common interest. For example, where the number of states, messages, and acts is three, we might have payoffs

	Act 1	Act 2	Act 3
State 1	1,1	0,0	0,0
State 2	0,0	1,1	0,0
State 3	0,0	0,0	1,1

(where payoffs are entered as sender payoff, receiver payoff). We will assume in this example that states are equiprobable.

A *Sender's strategy* in this game is a rule that associates each state with a message to be sent in that state; a *Receiver's strategy* associates each message with an act to be taken if the message has been received. Sender's strategy and Receiver's strategy taken together associate an act taken by the Receiver with each state of the world. If, for every state, the act taken is optimal for that state, the combination of Sender's strategy and Receiver's strategy is called a *signaling system*. For example, for three states, messages, and acts, the following is an example of a signaling system:

Sender's Strategy	Receiver's Strategy
$S_1 \to M_1$	$M_1 \to A_1$
$S_2 \to M_2$	$M_2 \to A_2$
$S_3 \to M_3$	$M_3 \to A_3$

It is evident, however, that this is not the only signaling system for this game. If we take it, and permute the messages in any way, we get another equally good signaling system, for example:

Sender's Strategy	Receiver's Strategy
$S_1 \to M_3$	$M_3 \to A_1$
$S_2 \to M_1$	$M_1 \to A_2$
$S_3 \to M_2$	$M_2 \to A_3$

Thus, the meaning of a message is a function of which signaling system is operative. Meaning emerges from social interaction.

Signaling systems are clearly Nash equilibria of the sender-receiver game. They are not the only Nash equilibria of the game. There are totally noncommunicative equilibria, where the Sender always sends the same message and the

Receiver performs the same action regardless of the message received, such as

Sender's Strategy	Receiver's Strategy
$S_1 \rightarrow M_1$	$M_3 \rightarrow A_2$
$S_2 \rightarrow M_1$	$M_1 \rightarrow A_2$
$S_3 \rightarrow M_1$	$M_2 \rightarrow A_2$

This is an equilibrium, no matter how inefficient it is, since neither player can improve a payoff by unilaterally switching strategies. There are equilibria in which partial information is transmitted, such as

Sender's Strategy	Receiver's Strategy
$S_1 \rightarrow M_1$	$M_1 \rightarrow A_1$
$S_2 \rightarrow M_1$	$M_2 \rightarrow A_1$
$S_3 \rightarrow M_3$	$M_3 \rightarrow A_3$

These games contain many equilibria, some of which are signaling systems and some of which are not.

But signaling systems are special. They are not only Nash equilibria but also strict Nash equilibria. (And they are the kind of strict Nash equilibria that are *conventions* in Lewis's general theory of convention.) The other non–signaling system equilibria do not come up to these standards. Unilaterally changing a potential response to an unsent message, or unilaterally changing the circumstance in which you send a message that will be ignored, is of no consequence. It does not make one better off, but it does not make one worse off either. So signaling systems are conventions, and the only conventions, in the kind of sender-receiver game that has been described.[3]

Lewis's account is a fundamental advance in the philosophy of meaning. It focuses attention on social interaction and information transmission. And it provides an account of how conventions of meaning can be maintained. Still, it does not appear that Lewis's account has completely answered the skeptical doubts with which we began.

Where did all the common knowledge come from? The skeptic is certainly entitled to ask for the origin of the common knowledge invoked by the account of equilibrium maintenance. And the skeptic can also ask for a noncircular account of equilibrium selection for equilibria that constitute conventions of meaning. Prior agreement and precedent can hardly be invoked to explain the genesis of meaningful signals. And where is the salience in Lewis's models of signaling games? All signaling system equilibria are equally good. None seems especially salient. Per-haps some sort of salience extrinsic to the model might get us off the ground, but we lack any explicit theory of such salience.

Bacteria Do It

Wait a minute! Before we let ourselves become too confused by philosophical skepticism, we should remember that bacteria have developed and maintain effective signaling systems. They do this without benefit of common knowledge, intentionality, or rational choice. Perhaps we have not been looking at the problem in the right way.

In fact, signaling systems are ubiquitous at all levels of biological organization.[4] The honeybee has a signaling system that successfully encodes and transmits information regarding the location and quality of a food source. Birds use signals for warning, indicating territory, and mating. The species-specific alarm calls of the vervet monkeys, which are the focus of D. Cheney and R. M. Seyfarth's delightful book *How Monkeys See the World*, give us a particularly nice example. Vervets are prey to three main kinds of predator: leopards, snakes, and eagles. For each there is a different alarm call, and each alarm call elicits a different action, appropriate to the type of predator that triggers the call. The situation is remarkably close to that modeled in a Lewis sender-receiver game. Other nonprimate species, such as meerkats and some birds, also instantiate a similar game structure in their alarm calls.

Let us see what happens if we approach Lewis signaling games from the point of view of the evolutionary process – presupposing nothing that could not in principle apply at the level of bacteria, or below. If we start in this way we do not cut ourselves off from the rest of the biological world, and the theory can be augmented as appropriate when applied to organisms with intelligence, knowledge, intentionality, or rationality.

Evolution

J. Maynard Smith and G. Price (1973) introduced a notion of equilibrium maintenance into evolutionary theory, that of an *evolutionarily stable strategy*. The leading idea is that an evolutionarily stable strategy must be able to resist invasion by a small number of mutants. Applying this in a plain-vanilla, large-population, random-encounter evolutionary model, this yields the definition of Maynard Smith and G. Parker

(1976) – in a population playing the strategy, either the natives do better against themselves than a mutant, or both do equally well against the natives, but the natives do better against the mutant.

Suppose we have a species in which an individual sometimes finds herself or himself in the role of Sender, sometimes in the role of Receiver. Individuals have "strategies" (or rules or routines) that determine how they play the game in each role. Suppose that a population consists of individuals who all have the same strategy, which is a signaling system in a Lewis signaling game. If you consider potential mutations to other strategies in the game, you will see that a signaling system is here an evolutionarily stable strategy.

If we look for evolutionarily stable strategies of the signaling game other than signaling systems, we find that they do not exist. The other Nash equilibria of the game correspond to strategies that fail the test of evolutionary stability. For example, consider a population with the noninformative strategy of always sending the same signal, regardless of the state observed, and always taking the same act, regardless of the signal received. That population can be invaded by a mutant playing a signaling system. When playing against natives, both types do equally badly. But when playing against mutants, mutants rather than natives do the best.[5] Evolutionary stability gives a qualitative account of equilibrium maintenance with no presuppositions of common knowledge or rationality.

But how do we get to a particular equilibrium in the first place? We find one attractive suggestion in a remarkable passage from Darwin's (1898) *Descent of Man*:

> Since monkeys certainly understand much that is said to them by man, and when wild, utter signal cries of danger to their fellows; and since fowls give distinct warnings for danger on the ground, or in the sky from hawks (both, as well as a third cry, intelligible to dogs), may not an unusually wise ape-like animal have imitated the growl of a beast of prey, and thus have told his fellow-monkeys the nature of the expected danger? This would have been the first step in the formation of language.[6]

Darwin knows of species-specific alarm calls. Modern studies support his remarks about the alarm calls of fowl.[7] He knows that one species may be able to use the information in another species' alarm call. Cheney and Seyfarth found that vervets use the information in the alarm calls of the Superb starling. Darwin also has a hypothesis about the genesis of animal signaling.

Darwin's hypothesis is that the crucial determinant of the signaling system selected is *natural salience*. The prey imitate the natural sounds of the predator to communicate the presence of the predator to their fellows. The only problem with this suggestion is that there seems to be no empirical evidence in support of it. For other kinds of animal signals, such as threat displays, natural salience provides a plausible explanation for the origin of the signal. Baring of teeth in dogs retains its natural salience. But species-specific alarm calls do not resemble the sounds made by the type of predator that they indicate. Of course, it is still possible that they began in the way suggested by Darwin, and that the course of evolution so modified them that their origins are no longer discernible. But in the absence of evidence to this effect, we are led to ask whether signaling systems could evolve without benefit of natural salience.

We can approach this question by applying a simple model of large-population, random-mixing differential reproduction, *replicator dynamics*,[8] to a Lewis sender-receiver game. We can let all kinds of combinations of Sender and Receiver strategies arise in the population, and run the replicator dynamics. Signaling systems *always* evolve. This can be shown both by computer simulation, and – in simple cases – analytically.[9]

The signaling system that evolves is not always the same. Each possible signaling system evolves for some initial population proportions. But the equilibria that are not signaling systems never evolve. The reason for this is that they are dynamically unstable. Only signaling systems are attractors in the evolutionary dynamics.

If natural salience had been present at the start of the process, it could have had the effect of constraining initial conditions so as to fall within the basin of attraction of a "natural signaling system." In the absence of natural salience, where meaning is purely conventional, signaling systems arise spontaneously, but which signaling system is selected depends on the vagaries of the initial stages of the evolutionary process.

Evolutionary dynamics has provided a remedy for our skepticism. We have an account of the spontaneous emergence of signaling systems that does not require preexisting common knowledge, agreement, precedent, or salience.

Learning

Is the point confined to strictly evolutionary settings? Adam Smith (1761), in *Considerations Concerning the First Formation of Languages*, suggested a different approach:

> Two savages, who had never been taught to speak, but had been bred up remote from the societies of men, would naturally begin to form that language by which they would endeavor to make their mutual wants intelligible to each other, by uttering certain sounds, whenever they meant to denote certain objects.[10]

Smith is suggesting that, given the proper incentives, signaling systems can arise naturally from the dynamics of *learning*.

It is not feasible to carry out Smith's thought experiment exactly, but A. Blume, D. V. deJong, Y.-G. Kim, and G. B. Sprinkle (2001) saw whether undergraduates at the University of Iowa would spontaneously learn to play some signaling system in a Sender-Receiver game of the kind discussed by Lewis. They take extraordinary precautions to exclude natural salience from the experimental setting. Sender and Receiver communicate to each other over a computer network. The messages available to the Sender are the asterisk and the pound sign, {*,#}. These are identified to the players as possible messages on their computer screens. The order in which they appear on a given player's screen is chosen at random to control for the possibility that order of presentation might function as the operative salience cue. Then players repeatedly play a Lewis signaling game. They are kept informed of the history of play of the group. Under these conditions, the players rapidly learn to coordinate on one signaling system or another.

The result might be expected, because the qualitative dynamical behavior of the replicator dynamics that explain evolutionary emergence of signaling systems is shared by a wide range of adaptive dynamics.[11] In Lewis signaling games, which are games of common interest, evolutionary dynamics, learning dynamics, and almost any reasonable sort of adaptive dynamics lead to successful coordination on a signaling system equilibrium. In the absence of natural salience, which signaling system emerges depends on the vicissitudes of initial conditions and chance aspects of the process. But some signaling system does

evolve because signaling systems are powerful attractors in the dynamics, and other Nash equilibria of the game are dynamically unstable.

Logic?

The dynamics of evolution and learning show us how signaling systems can emerge spontaneously. The skeptical questions concerning equilibrium selection and equilibrium maintenance are completely answered by the dynamical approach. But we should remember that the thrust of Quine's skepticism was directed at conventionalist accounts of logic. And although our account of the dynamics of Lewis signaling games has given us an account of the emergence of a kind of meaning, it has not given us an account of logical truth or logical inference based on that meaning.

Pursuit of such a theory would have to take on some of the complexity of thought that I have deliberately excluded from the basic model. We are still very far from an account of the evolution of logic, and I do not have any general account to offer here. I would like only to indicate a few small steps that we can take in the desired direction.

Proto-Truth Functions

As a first step, I propose that we modify Lewis signaling games to allow for the possibility that the Sender's observation gives less than perfect information about the relevant state of the world. For example, suppose that a vervet Sender could sometimes determine the exact kind of predator, but sometimes tell only that it is a leopard or a snake.

It may well be that the optimal evasive action, given that a leopard or snake is present, is different from either the optimal act for leopard or the optimal act for snake. One would not want to stumble on the snake while running for the nearest tree to escape the leopard. One would not want to draw a leopard's attention by standing up straight and scanning the ground for snakes.[12] A new message should not be hard to come by. (In fact, vervets that have migrated to new localities where they are faced with new predators that call for new evasive action have developed new messages and the appropriate signaling system.)[13]

So we now have a model with four types of knowledge that Senders may have, four messages, and four states with a common interest payoff structure as before. Then, the evolutionary (or learning) dynamics is no different than the one we would have if we had four predators, four messages, and four appropriate evasive actions in the original setting. The story is the same. A signaling system will emerge with signals for eagle, snake, leopard, and *leopard or snake*. The last signal I call a *proto-truth function*. The truth function "or" is a sentence connective which forms a compound sentence that is true just in case at least one of its constituent simple sentences is true. The last signal need not be a complex sentence with meaningful parts, one of which is the truth function "or," but one way of giving its meaning is as such a truth function.[14]

More generally, we can modify the Lewis model by letting nature decide randomly the specificity with which the Sender can identify the state of nature.[15] Then, given the appropriate common interest structure, we have the conditions for the emergence of a rich signaling system with lots of proto-truth functional signals.

We are now well out of the vervets' league, and perhaps into the province of "an unusually wise ape-like animal," but I will continue to frame my example in terms of the vervets for the sake of narrational continuity. Our Sender may now have proto-truth functional signals for both "snake or leopard" and for "not-leopard."

Inference

Now I would like to complicate the model a little more. Most of the time, one member of the troop detects a predator, gives the alarm call appropriate to his or her state of knowledge, and everything goes as in the last section. This predominant scenario is sufficiently frequent to fix a signaling system, which includes proto-truth functions.

Occasionally, two members of the troop detect a predator at the same time, and both give alarm calls. Sometimes they both have maximally specific information, and both give the alarm call for the specific predator. Sometimes, however, they will have complementary imprecise information as, for example, when one signals *snake or leopard* and the other signals *not-leopard*.

Since the Senders detect the presence of a predator independently and at approximately the same time, they just use their strategies in the signaling game of the last section. What do the Receivers do? Initially, some will do one thing and some will do another. Those who take the evasive action appropriate to snakes will, on average, fare better than those who don't. Over time, evolution, learning, or any reasonable adaptive dynamics will fix this behavior. Here we have a kind of evolution of inference, where the inference is based on the kind of meaning explicated by Lewis signaling games.

The setting need not be the Amboseli forest preserve, and the signaling game need not involve alarm calls. The essential points are that a signaling system evolves for communicating partial information, that the Receiver may get multiple signals encoding various pieces of information, and that it is in the common interest of Sender and Receiver that the latter takes the action that is optimal in light of all the information received. When these conditions are realized, adaptive dynamics favors the emergence of inference.

Notes

1   Rousseau (1984: 94).
2   A more general model of sender-receiver games was introduced and analyzed by Crawford and Sobel (1982).
3   This striking result depends to a certain extent on the modeling decision to make the number of states, messages, and actions equal. Suppose that we add a fourth message to our three-state, three-act game and extend a signaling system equilibrium of the original game by extending the Receiver's strategy to take act 1 if message 4 were received. According to the Sender's strategy, message 4 is never sent, so what the Receiver would do if she received that message is of no consequence. Thus, we do not have a strict equilibrium, and we do not have a Lewis convention of the game with the enlarged message space. This is perhaps not as serious a difficulty as it may at first seem. Let us bracket these concerns for now. We will return to this matter later in a different context.
4   See, for instance, Hauser (1997) and England et al. (1999).
5   This striking conclusion, like Lewis's result that signaling systems are conventions, depends on our modeling assumption that the number of states, messages, and acts are equal. If we add some extra messages to the model, then signaling systems will not be evolutionarily stable strategies in the sense of Maynard Smith and Parker. The reason, as before, is that we can consider a mutant whose strategy specifies a different strategy to a message that is never sent. Such a mutant will not be eliminated. The difficulty, however, does not seem so serious, since the mutant *behaves* just like the native in sending signals and in reacting to signals actually sent. We can shift our attention to classes of behaviorally

equivalent strategies and consider evolutionarily stable classes as ones such that in a population using members of that class, any mutant strategy outside the class will be eliminated. Then the connection between evolutionary stability and signaling systems can be recaptured. The interested reader can find this worked out in Wärneryd (1993).

6 Darwin, *Descent of Man*, 87.
7 Evans et al. (1994).
8 Taylor and Jonker (1978); Schuster and Sigmund (1983).
9 Skyrms (1999).
10 Smith, *Considerations*, 201.
11 See Skyrms (1999).
12 Vervets run out on branches where the leopard cannot follow.
13 Kavanaugh (1980); Cheney and Seyfarth (1990).
14 There are, of course, other ways of giving its meaning, such as terrestrial predator.
15 Nature chooses a random information partition, and the Sender is informed only of the cell that contains the actual situation.

References

Blume, A., DeJong, D. V., Kim, Y.-G., and Sprinkle, G. B. (2001) "Evolution of Communication with Partial Common Interest." *Games, and Economic Behavior* 37: 79–120.

Cheney, D., and Seyfarth, R. M. (1990) *How Monkeys See the World: Inside the Mind of Another Species*. Chicago: University of Chicago Press.

Crawford, V., and Sobel, J. (1982) "Strategic Information Transmission." *Econometrica* 50: 1431–1451.

Darwin, C. (1882) *The Descent of Man and Selection in Relation to Sex*. 2nd. ed. New York: D. Appleton.

England, R. R., Hobbs, G., Bainton, N. J., and Roberts, D. McL. (1999) *Microbial Signalling and Communication*. Cambridge: Cambridge University Press.

Evans, C. S., Evans, C. L., and Marler, P. (1994) "On the Meaning of Alarm Calls: Functional Reference in an Avian Vocal System." *Animal Behavior* 73: 23–38.

Hauser, M. D. (1997) *The Evolution of Communication*. Cambridge, Mass.: MIT Press.

Kavanaugh, M. (1980) "Invasion of the Forest by an African Savannah Monkey: Behavioral Adaptations." *Behavior* 73: 238–260.

Lewis, D. K. (1969) *Convention: A Philosophical Study*. Oxford: Blackwell.

Maynard Smith, J., and Parker, G. (1976) "The Logic of Asymmetric Contests." *Animal Behavior* 24: 159–179.

Maynard Smith, J., and Price, G. (1973) "The Logic of Animal Conflicts." *Nature* 246: 15–18.

Rousseau, J. (1984) *A Discourse on Inequality*. Trans. M. Cranston. New York: Penguin Books.

Schelling, T. (1960) *The Strategy of Conflict*. Cambridge, Mass.: Harvard University Press.

Schuster, P., and Sigmund, K. (1983) "Replicator Dynamics." *Journal of Theoretical Biology* 100: 535–538.

Skyrms, B. (1999) "Stability and Explanatory Significance of Some Simple Evolutionary Models." *Philosophy of Science* 67: 94–113.

Skyrms, B. (2000) "Evolution of Inference." In *Dynamics of Human and Primate Societies*. Ed. T. Kohler and G. Gumerman. New York: Oxford University Press, 77–88.

Smith, A. (1761) "Considerations Concerning the First Formation of Languages." Reprinted in *Lectures on Rhetoric and Belles Lettres*. Ed. J. C. Bryce (1983). Oxford: Oxford University Press, 201–226.

Taylor, P., and Jonker, L. (1978) "Evolutionarily Stable Strategies and Game Dynamics." *Mathematical Biosciences* 40: 145–156.

Wärneryd, K. (1993) "Cheap Talk, Coordination and Evolutionary Stability." *Games and Economic Behavior* 5: 532–546.

Section 11: Reasoning and Cultures

Chapter 47: Reasoning across Cultures

RUSSELL C. BURNETT AND DOUGLAS L. MEDIN

In 1931, A. R. Luria traveled to rural Uzbekistan with a question: Is thinking influenced by the social and cultural environment? The fieldwork he did there (Luria 1976) was likely the first attempt to answer this question using methods of experimental psychology. Rural folk in Uzbekistan were at that time in the midst of a socioeconomic transition that involved, among other things, the collectivization of agriculture and the growth of schools and literacy. Luria saw in this a natural experiment. He found groups of participants with different levels of involvement in this transition – including different levels of schooling and literacy – and gave them a variety of cognitive tasks. Some of these were designed to elicit deductive inferences from premises like "precious metals don't rust" and "gold is a precious metal." Luria found that subjects with no formal schooling often balked at such problems, rejecting the premises and saying, for example, that "one can speak only of what one has seen." In contrast, subjects who had been to school were more likely to use the hypothetical premises to draw conclusions (e.g., "gold doesn't rust") with no obvious basis in personal experience. Luria also exercised some experimental control, manipulating whether the content of an argument was familiar or unfamiliar to participants. Participants who had not been to school treated the two kinds of content differently, drawing conclusions from premises more often when the content was familiar than when it was unfamiliar. Schooled participants tended to reason from the premises regardless of content.

We revisit Luria's work because it illustrates two challenges in comparative cultural research. First, there is the natural confounding of numerous factors that might constitute "culture," and various other factors besides. Luria favored the theory that literacy enables "verbal-logical" reasoning, but his groups differed in countless other ways, including general schooling, "practical activities," "modes of communication," "cultural outlooks," "access to a technological culture," "social relations," and "life principles" (Luria 1976: 15). Which of these, or what other factors, caused the groups to respond differently? Second, even if the practical problem of confounding could be solved (and nature may sometimes disentangle such factors for us), there is a theoretical problem: Which factors should be understood as constituting culture? Or should culture be thought of as an irreducible construct, something that would remain even after one has controlled for "practical activities," "social relations," and so on? Any empirical demonstration of cultural differences presupposes some definition, however vague, of culture, but without a suitably specific theory of culture comparative research has no basis for causal analysis and is capable of little more than cataloging phenomena or disproving their universality.

In evidence of these difficulties, there has been a good deal of disagreement over which social or cultural factors were responsible for the group difference Luria (1976) observed. Cole and Scribner (1974) suggested that this difference was due not to literacy but to schooling or involvement in "complex acts of social planning." This interpretation found some support in work by Scribner and Cole (1981), who capitalized on a partial disentangling of literacy and schooling among the Vai, a people of Liberia who employed a system of writing apart from formal education. Yet Scribner and Cole's own findings have been interpreted as due to literacy, where literacy is defined in functional context (e.g., literacy for formal education; Greenfield 1983). Distinguishing between these theories would require finding a case of formal schooling without literacy, which seems unlikely.

The cognitive causes of the group difference are also unclear. Cole and Scribner (1974) argued against a qualitative difference in methods of reasoning: "There is no evidence for different *kinds* of reasoning processes such as the old classic theories alleged – we have no evidence for a 'primitive' logic" (p. 170). Scribner (1977) proposed that schooling promotes a shift from an "empirical bias," or a bias to draw on personal experience, to a more "theoretical" approach to reasoning that allows greater use of hypothetical premises. More recently, Dias, Roazzi, and Harris (2005) found that whereas both schooled and unschooled participants could be prompted to reason from unfamiliar premises (by a suggestion that the premises described a distant planet), there was a persistent gap between schooled and unschooled participants, as in Luria's studies. This suggests that reasoning from novel or hypothetical information does not require schooling, but also that schooling (or one of its correlates) does promote something like a stable orientation or stance that facilitates such reasoning (see also Harris 2000).

In this chapter we will review recent research on reasoning and culture that differs from Luria's (1976) work in an important respect. Whereas Luria's probes were designed to elicit abstract reasoning, guided by content-free principles like class inclusion and entailment, the work we will describe focuses on reasoning that makes greater use of a knowledge base. We will suggest that culture-related variations in knowledge are an important source of differences in reasoning. Of course, differences attributable to the mere presence or absence of relevant knowledge might be fairly uninteresting from a theoretical point of view. Our story will be more interesting. We will suggest that knowledge is often organized according to culture-related framework theories or expectations and that graded differences in the organization or accessibility of knowledge are reflected in reasoning.

That culture influences reasoning by way of such things as framework theories and expectations is consistent with the epidemiological view of culture, or the idea that culture can be understood as socially distributed mental representations, as well as expressions of these representations and behaviors associated with them in given ecological contexts (Atran, Medin, and Ross, 2005; Sperber 1996). The epidemiological approach leads naturally to treating within-culture variation not as noise, but rather as important information that may be used to identify paths of cultural transmission and relevant correlates of within- and between-culture differences (Medin, Ross, and Cox 2006). To be sure, we are far from a full understanding of the sources of the kinds of representations we will describe in this chapter and the modes by which they are transmitted – we will return to this topic later. Nonetheless, the work reviewed in this chapter benefits from a theory of culture that is specific enough to move us beyond a simple catalog of group differences in reasoning, to hypotheses about proximal causes of these differences in individual minds.

We begin with a distinction that is slippery but still useful. Reasoning can be a tool for understanding cultural differences, or cultural comparisons can be a tool for understanding reasoning. As an example of the former, Choi, Nisbett, and Smith (1997) investigated the suggestion that Westerners (undergraduates at a university in the United States) are more likely to encode examples into categories than Easterners (undergraduates at a Korean university) by giving participants inductive reasoning tests where they might spontaneously generate categories, according to the similarity-coverage model of Osherson, Smith, Wilkie, López, and Shafir (1990). We will describe this model in a moment, but for now the point is that the reasoning task was used as a tool to make observations about a cultural difference in propensity for categorizing. As an example of the latter, López, Atran, Coley, Medin, and Smith (1997) gave Itza' Maya agroforesters and University of Michigan undergraduates the same sorts of reasoning probes as a test of the generality of the similarity-coverage model. They failed to find evidence for one of the reasoning phenomena predicted by the model, and in this way the cross-cultural comparison revealed something about the limits of the model.

Of course, no strict principle distinguishes these two types of studies. Choi et al. (1997) were also, implicitly or explicitly, testing the generality of the similarity-coverage model, and a different pattern of results could have led to changes in the model. Furthermore, as we have said, an observed cultural difference tells us little about reasoning if we do not understand the source of the difference. Nonetheless, the distinction is important for present purposes, because our focus will be on what comparative research tells us about theories of reasoning and not vice versa.

We will focus on two kinds of reasoning. The first is inductive reasoning about categories and their properties (what is often called category-based induction), especially in the biological domain. Cultural research has shown the importance of framework theories and the organization of knowledge to this kind of reasoning. The second is causal reasoning, where interesting cross-cultural research is being done and where, at the same time, a promising new body of theory has been adopted by cognitive scientists. In this case, the cross-cultural findings and their implications are less clear, but we can begin to see how they might inform the new theory. In trading breadth for depth, we will not discuss some other kinds of reasoning that have been topics of recent cross-cultural research. For recent reviews of other research on culture and cognition, see Cohen (2001); Medin and Atran (2004); Medin, Unsworth, and Hirschfeld (2007); Nisbett and Norenzayan (2002); and Norenzayan and Heine (2005).

Inductive Generalization of Properties over Categories

One form of reasoning studied extensively in cultural research involves the inductive generalization of properties over objects or, more typically, over categories of objects. A fisherman who learns that brown trout are affected by a certain disease might infer, with some degree of confidence, that rainbow trout, or all trout, or catfish, or fish in rivers, or even all fish are affected by this disease. Each of these inferences can be thought of as an argument in which the premise doesn't guarantee the truth of the conclusion but provides some support for it. From this perspective, understanding knowledge generalization involves understanding how reasoners judge the support that a premise like "brown trout have a certain disease" lends to a conclusion like "rainbow trout have this disease."

Reasoning from Similarity and Taxonomic Relationships

Rips (1975) gave undergraduates at Stanford University premises like "all of the robins on an island have a certain disease" and asked them to judge what proportion of, say, the geese on the island are affected by the disease. It was found that judgments were well explained as a function of two constructs. The first was the similarity between the premise category and the conclusion category (the similarity between robins and geese); all else equal, diseases associated with robins generalized to sparrows more strongly than to geese. The second construct was the typicality of the premise category with respect to a

salient category that included both the premise and the conclusion (the typicality of robins with respect to the bird category); for generalizing to other birds, robins were a better premise category than were geese, all else equal. As Rips noted, participants reasoned as if they expected the novel property (the disease) to be distributed over categories in a way that mirrored the distributions of known properties. That robins and sparrows are similar is a consequence (or restatement) of the fact that they share many known properties, and because they share many known properties they are likely to share a novel one, too.

These ideas were elaborated by Osherson et al. (1990) in their *similarity-coverage model.* Consider the following inferences, each of which involves projecting a novel property from a specific category to a more general, inclusive category.

Sparrows have a certain enzyme; therefore, all birds have it.   (1)

Penguins have a certain enzyme; therefore, all birds have it.   (2)

Osherson et al. and many others have found a *typicality effect* in inferences like these. Sparrows are deemed more typical of birds than are penguins, and (1) is deemed a stronger inference than (2). The similarity-coverage model explains this effect and others as due to (a) similarities among categories and (b) the degree to which small categories "cover" inclusive categories. (1) is better than (2) because sparrows provide better coverage of the bird category, in the sense that they have higher average similarity to other birds. The model also predicts the *similarity effect* found by Rips (1975), in which similar kinds are better bases for inferences about each other than are dissimilar kinds, and a *diversity effect*, in which multiple kinds jointly form a better basis for inferences about an inclusive category if they are more dissimilar and therefore more diverse (less redundant) in their coverage. For example:

Robins and sparrows have a certain enzyme; therefore, all birds have it.   (3)

Robins and hawks have a certain enzyme; therefore, all birds have it.   (4)

According to the similarity-coverage model, (4) is better than (3) because robins and hawks are more diverse in their coverage of the bird category than are robins and sparrows.

The similarity-coverage model, like Rips's (1975) account, assumes two kinds of knowledge: (a) knowledge of similarity relationships among categories and (b) knowledge of class-inclusion relationships – for example, knowledge that bird is the relevant category that includes robins and geese, so that robin's coverage of the bird category (or the average similarity of robins to other birds, or the typicality of robins with respect to the bird category) can be assessed. Another well-known model, Sloman's (1993) *feature-based model*, does away with the latter component and works just on the similarities between premises and conclusions. This buys some flexibility, as the model applies even in domains that lack clear class-inclusion relationships, but the driving principle is the same: A novel property is likely to cluster with known properties, so categories are likely to share a novel property to the extent that they are similar in their known properties. This model makes many of the same predictions as the similarity-coverage model, including typicality, similarity, and diversity effects.

Insofar as these models work on the general assumption that novel properties mirror known properties, they are *similarity-based*.[1] Studies of cognitive psychology's standard participants (undergraduates at research universities) have found that similarity-based reasoning – including the similarity, typicality, and diversity effects – is quite robust (López et al. 1997; Osherson et al. 1990; Rips 1975; Sloman 1993; and many others).

Studies of culture and expertise have revealed a very different picture. First, reasoners with even moderate knowledge of the domain often employ other strategies; only research subjects with impoverished knowledge consistently reason in line with the similarity-based models. Second, even among reasoners with equal knowledge of the domain, cultural differences in the organization of this knowledge may influence the strategies that are used. Third, even when reasoning is similarity based, culture-related beliefs or theories may influence how broadly properties are generalized from different premise categories. In the sections that follow, we first describe these findings in some detail and then explore their implications for models of reasoning.

A Focus on Biology

Before proceeding, we should explain that most studies of this sort of reasoning have focused on biology. Participants are usually asked to generalize properties like a disease, an enzyme, or "sesamoid bones" over kinds of animals. Biology is an especially informative domain for several reasons. First, it is a domain in which all cultures have some knowledge, and so it constitutes a common ground for cultural comparisons. Second, as a domain, biology has an abstract structure that all cultures seem to recognize (Atran 1998; Berlin 1992; Medin and Atran 2004). This abstract structure involves clusters of properties that travel together (for example, things that have wings tend to fly, to build nests, and so on) and are distributed systematically through downward-branching taxonomies in which nonoverlapping categories are nested under higher-level categories. Importantly, and not accidentally, this structure is just what is required by the similarity-coverage model. Clusters of co-occurring properties tend to provide clear similarity relationships among categories, and taxonomies yield clear class-inclusion relationships. Note also that the mere fact of property clustering fits the very principle behind similarity-based reasoning: All else equal, a novel property is likely to be distributed along with known properties. Since what the feature-based model requires is just a subset of what is required by the similarity-coverage model (namely, similarity relationships among categories), the abstract structure of the biological domain suits it, as well. In short, if similarity-based models apply anywhere, they should apply in biology. Moreover, since the understood structure of biology is largely invariant across cultures, these models tend to predict invariance in reasoning.

Third, however, biological entities are often the objects of people's goals, theories, beliefs, and practices. If reasoning is sensitive to such factors, then we might expect differences in these factors to be reflected in reasoning. Fourth, biology is an information-rich domain where a lot is hidden even from experts, and so there is room for biases or framework theories to guide the interpretation of experience (Keil 1995; Keil, Levin, Richman, and Gutheil 1999), highlight certain types of information over others, and promote certain inferences over others. In short, people's relationships with plants and animals often involve many of the factors that one might take to constitute or be related to culture. Focusing on biology allows us to test hypotheses about whether and how such factors influence reasoning.

To begin to see how the complexity of biology might play into reasoning, consider that not all of the properties that one might want to reason about participate in the abstract similarity-based structure of the domain, and that similarity-based reasoning might therefore work better for some properties than for others (cf. Heit and Rubinstein 1994). If one interprets the abstract domain structure as a consequence of progressive speciation via natural selection, then similarity-based reasoning should tend to work for properties that "load" heavily on genes. Other properties are likely to be distributed in ways that are less closely related, or perhaps completely unrelated, to the similarity-and-taxonomy structure of the domain. Take, for example, diseases, which have been used as novel properties in many studies. Some diseases may have little basis in genes or innate potential. Whether an organism or a population is affected by such a disease may have mostly to do with whether it is exposed to a pathogen, and intrinsic susceptibility to the pathogen may be relatively independent of genes, at least in the population of organisms under consideration. (Of course, many other diseases are species-specific.) Other properties might have some basis in innate potential, but it might also be clear that these properties don't travel with other large bundles of features. For example, flying-related properties in bats do not generalize outward through taxonomic space or its associated similarity space very well. Simply put, there is reason to expect that similarity-based models work only for certain properties. Indeed, Osherson et al. (1990) emphasized that the similarity-coverage model is meant to apply to "blank" properties, or properties for which the reasoner has little prior knowledge about their distribution. In practice, experimenters have tended to use properties, like "sesamoid bones," that have a "biological flavor" (Rips 2001) and more than a hint of genes or innate potential.

Reasoning from Causal-Ecological Knowledge

The first finding from studies of culture and expertise is that even in biology, with its structure involving similarity and taxonomic relationships, reasoners often prefer inductive strategies that have little to do with this structure – that is, strategies that are not similarity based at all. Knowledgeable reasoners often prefer to project properties like diseases and enzymes on the basis of specific causal mechanisms by which these properties might have arisen in both the premise and the conclusion, and these causal mechanisms often involve ecological interactions between members of the different categories. For example, in judging which of two kinds of trees was more likely to share a disease with all other trees, three different groups of Chicago-area tree experts preferred the tree with wider geographic distribution or greater intrinsic susceptibility to disease (Proffitt, Coley, and Medin 2000). In the former case, the idea is that trees with wider geographic distribution have greater potential to pass the disease to other species. In the latter case, the rationale is that the disease will spread more easily among trees of the susceptible species, which renders the disease widely distributed and more likely to spread to other species. These experts tended not to invoke similarity or taxonomic strategies.

Similarly, in reasoning about diseases and enzymes (or "little things inside") in birds, both North American birdwatchers and Itza' Maya farmers in Guatemala tended to base their inferences on causal-ecological interactions, often focusing on geographic distribution (Bailenson, Shum, Atran, Medin, and Coley 2002). They tended to prefer, as premises, birds that were rich in known ecological associations with other birds. Similarly, in a study that involved reasoning about diseases among mammals, Itza' Maya tended to focus on geographic range and ecological diversity (López et al. 1997).

In a recent study, conducted in collaboration with Norbert Ross, we asked fishermen of two cultural groups in northern Wisconsin to reason about diseases and enzymes in fish. Most of the probes lent themselves to reasoning by typicality, similarity, or diversity. For example, in one item river shiners were said to have one enzyme (or disease), and sunfish another. Participants were asked which enzyme was more likely to be found in (or which disease was more likely to affect) smallmouth bass. Sunfish are more similar to smallmouth bass than are river shiners, and in taxonomies reported by members of the same populations (including many of the same participants) smallmouth bass tended to be closer to sunfish than to river shiners. Similarity-based reasoning thus predicts that sunfish are the better premise. Nonetheless, a great majority of participants chose river shiners and explained this choice by saying either that smallmouth bass eat river shiners or that smallmouth bass and river shiners are found in the same waters. More generally, over twenty items, participants tended to focus on ecological interactions or associations through which the novel property might be transmitted among fish. In many cases, participants reasoned upward through the food chain from premise to conclusion; that is, they chose the premise fish that was more likely to transmit the property to the conclusion fish by being eaten (for a similar result, see Shafto and Coley 2003). But food chain knowledge was used in other ways, too. Participants sometimes reasoned downward through the food-chain, choosing the premise that was more likely to have "caught" the property by eating the conclusion fish. In still other cases, participants chose the premise that shared with the conclusion a common food source, the idea being that both fish might have gotten the property from this source. Overall, only 9 percent of inferences were based on similarity and/or taxonomic relationships. Fully 90 percent were based on transmission of the property through ecological interactions (Burnett, Medin, and Ross 2004).

These various groups of participants differ in many ways, of course, and we will turn to cultural differences in a moment. For now, a reasonable generalization is that participants with normal levels of experience with plants and animals often invoke causal knowledge and reason about the mechanisms by which properties might come to be distributed in different ways across categories. For properties like diseases and enzymes (even enzymes), these causal mechanisms often involve ecological interactions that are more or less unrelated to the similarity-and-taxonomy structure of the domain.

Flexibility in Reasoning

The above findings on causal-ecological reasoning notwithstanding, knowledgeable reasoners almost surely prefer similarity-based strategies for properties that (they believe) participate in the similarity-based structure of the domain. What knowledge provides is flexibility, in the form of a variety of strategies that allow the reasoner to project different properties in different ways. In evidence of this flexibility, Shafto and Coley (2003) found that whereas fishermen projected diseases according to food chain relations among marine animals, they projected more abstract or ambiguous properties like "a property called sarca" among the same animals according to similarity or taxonomic relatedness, as did domain novices.

Even novices show some flexibility when stimuli tap their knowledge. Using ecological contrasts that even undergraduates often know (e.g., jungle creatures versus desert creatures), Shafto, Coley, and Baldwin (2005) found that,

against a background preference for reasoning according to taxonomic relatedness, undergraduates showed a tendency to distinguish between properties, such that participants with greater knowledge of the ecological groups were more likely to project diseases and toxins, but not abstract properties like "a property called sarca," among ecologically related animals. (For other examples of relative novices basing inferences on causal considerations instead of, or in addition to, similarity, see Gelman and Markman 1986; Hadjichristidis, Sloman, Stevenson, and Over 2004; Heit and Rubinstein 1994; and Ross and Murphy 1999. For reviews, see Heit 2000 and Rips 2001.)

An interesting question is how reasoning by causal mechanisms or ecological interactions relates to similarity-based reasoning. On the one hand, there are reasons to think of similarity-based reasoning as simpler or more basic. Similarity and taxonomic relationships are often available even to extreme novices. They seem to be at the core of folk/biological knowledge, robust even under devolution in knowledge (Medin and Atran 2004). Furthermore, reasoners who employ ecological knowledge under normal conditions may abandon this knowledge and fall back on similarity under time pressure (Shafto et al. 2005; see also Coley, Shafto, Stepanova, and Baraff 2005).

On the other hand, causal reasoning and similarity-based reasoning are not mutually exclusive, and reasoning based on similarity and taxonomic relatedness may itself involve or interact with causal considerations. Hadjichristidis et al. (2004) found that similarity had a greater influence on inference when the property in question was more causally central to the category in which it appeared (i.e., when more of the category's other properties depended on it).[2] This suggests that similarity-based reasoning is invoked to the degree that causal considerations support it – that is, to the degree that the property in question is involved in the causal mechanisms that give rise to the similarity-and-taxonomy structure of the domain in the first place.

Or consider a related task: inferring whether an individual category member has some property that is associated with the category. Rehder and Burnett (2005) found that inferences were stronger when the individual was known to have other category-associated features. Importantly, results suggested that this was not because the known features made the individual a better or more typical member of the category, as a similarity-based account might suggest, but because they indicated that the individual possessed some underlying cause or causes of the category's other features. Although known features did tend to boost the individual's typicality, their importance for reasoning lay not in this, but in their relevance to causal considerations.

Of course, this point is meaningful only if people do actually have beliefs about causal structure even in cases where they appear to invoke similarity-based strategies. Other work has suggested that they often do. Even young children and domain novices have intuitions about what properties, or what kinds of properties, of biological organisms are due to intrinsic causes or innate potential (Keil, Smith, Simons, and Levin 1998; Medin and Atran 2004). As for the finding that reasoners fall back on similarity under time pressure, this effect has been most clearly demonstrated in relative novices (Shafto et al. 2005), and it is possible that more knowledgeable reasoners are often as fluent with causal strategies as with similarity.

In general and in short, it is difficult to distinguish (a) true similarity-based reasoning from (b) causal reasoning based on causes that participate in the similarity-and-taxonomy structure of the domain. For example, consider two interpretations of Shafto and Coley's (2003) finding that fishermen reason (as if) from similarity or taxonomic relatedness for properties like "sarca" but from foodchain relationships for diseases. One possibility is that, given an ambiguous or abstract property, these experts fell back on similarity-based reasoning as a default strategy. The other is that these experts assumed that ambiguous properties were causally related to innate potential – for example, properties grounded in genes – and projected them accordingly. As Rips (2001) observed, studies showing that relative novices override similarity in cases where causal considerations provide better bases for reasoning (e.g., Gelman and Markman 1986; Heit and Rubinstein 1994; Ross and Murphy 1999) suggest that, even in novices, inferences consistent with similarity may conceal an influence of causal considerations.

Cultural Factors

We have explained the first of three findings: Knowledgeable reasoners use similarity and taxonomic relationships only some of the time; even for properties like enzymes, which are plausibly related to the similarity-and-taxonomy structure of the domain, knowledgeable reasoners

often invoke causal-ecological strategies instead. In itself this finding concerns the importance of the reasoner's knowledge base, but it also sets the stage for culture. We turn now to two ways in which cultural factors might influence reasoning.

DIFFERENCES IN ORGANIZATION OR ACCESSIBILITY OF KNOWLEDGE

Knowledgeable reasoners often have many bases for generalization available to them. Causal-ecological reasoning is not one strategy but rather a potentially large set of strategies that draw on various causal mechanisms and ecological interactions known by the reasoner. In generalizing diseases, reasoners with knowledge of trees sometimes prefer premise categories with great geographic range or ecological diversity, the idea being that widely or diversely distributed trees will have greater opportunity to transmit the disease to other trees. Sometimes they prefer premises with greater intrinsic susceptibility to disease; here the rationale is that the disease will spread more easily among trees of the susceptible kind, which renders the disease widely distributed and more likely to spread to other kinds. Sometimes they seem to go in the opposite direction, preferring a premise with greater intrinsic resistance to diseases, the idea being that the disease itself must be highly infectious if it managed to spread to an intrinsically resistant kind of tree. Of course, such reasoners also have similarity-based strategies available to them.

Cultural beliefs, values, goals, and attitudes might influence the contents of a person's knowledge base by constraining the practices that he or she undertakes with respect to plants and animals. If a group abhorred trout and avoided catching or touching them, then members of this group would likely know less about trout than if they regarded trout as ideal or desirable. Here we focus on a somewhat more interesting possibility: that even among reasoners with the same knowledge, cultural factors may influence how this knowledge is organized, or the relative accessibility of different pieces of the knowledge base (e.g., Hong, Morris, Chiu, and Martinez 2000; Medin, Ross, Atran, Burnett, and Blok 2002; Medin, Ross, Atran, Cox, Coley, Proffitt, and Blok 2006). Differences in organization or accessibility may, in turn, be reflected in how reasoning strategies are derived from the knowledge base. That is, a single knowledge base may be organized so as to make different reasoning strategies more or less fluent (see also Higgins 1996). In what follows we will first describe recent studies of cultural differences in the organization or accessibility of folkbiological knowledge and then consider how these differences play into reasoning.

One way of assessing organization of knowledge is to ask participants to sort biological kinds into hierarchies that have the structure characteristic of folkbiological taxonomies. The participant is presented with a set of cards. On each card is printed the name of a kind (e.g., "rainbow trout"), and the participant is asked to sort these kinds into groups "that go together by nature." This instruction is accompanied by telling informants that they should create groups that make sense to them. After this initial sort, the participant is given opportunities to join these groups into progressively more inclusive categories, and then to split the groups into progressively smaller, more specific categories. The result is a downward-branching hierarchy of biological kinds.

This task has revealed differences among various groups of participants in various subdomains of biology (e.g., Bailenson et al. 2002; López et al. 1997; Medin, Lynch, Coley, and Atran 1997; Proffitt et al. 2000; Shafto and Coley 2003). One recent study is especially interesting in that it has shown cultural differences in the organization of knowledge that cannot be reduced to differences in raw experience or practices, but rather seem to arise from differences in what might be called framework theories (Medin, Ross, Atran et al. 2006). This case involves fishermen of two groups in northern Wisconsin: Native American Menominee Indians and a nearby majority-culture (European-American) community. These groups allow a close comparison because they are similar in many ways. They fish in similar waters and are familiar with the same fish. Though they do differ slightly in some of their practices – for example, Menominee put somewhat more emphasis on fishing for food (versus for sport) and are less likely to practice catch and release – these differences in themselves have small, if any, consequences for knowledge acquired through experience.

Whereas these groups showed substantial overall agreement in their sortings of local fish, they also showed some reliable differences. Multidimensional scaling revealed that Menominee sorts, but not majority-culture sorts, tended to express a dimension related to habitat or ecological niche. This difference was also evident in participants' explanations of their sorts. Majority-culture participants gave many taxo-nomic or morphological justifications such as "bass" and few ecological justifications such as "lake fish" or "fish you find in cool, fast-moving water." In contrast, Menominee participants gave fewer taxonomic or morphological justifications and more ecological ones. In short, Menominee participants seem to organize their knowledge somewhat more around ecological considerations, whereas majority-culture participants seem to focus more on taxonomic and morphological characteristics of fish. This was also reflected in a "species interactions" task, where participants were asked to say how various kinds of fish affect one another. In this task, Menominee participants reported more causal interactions among kinds of fish than did majority-culture participants (Medin, Ross, Atran et al. 2006).

Just as these differences in organization cannot be explained by group differences in practices, neither can they be explained by differences in mere possession of knowledge. When members of the same groups were asked to sort fish according to ecological relatedness, there were no significant group differences. Likewise, when the stimuli used in the "species interactions" task were pared down so that participants spent more time thinking about each response, group differences disappeared (Medin, Ross, Atran et al. 2006). In short, it is not that Menominee participants know more ecological relations; rather, ecological relations seem to play a greater role in organizing their knowledge of fish and are more accessible. The differential importance of ecological relations in organizing knowledge of biological kinds has also been seen in studies with other cultural groups (e.g., Atran et al. 1999, 2002; López et al. 1997).

A significant challenge is to understand how these differences arise. Ross, Medin, Coley, and Atran (2003) reported parallel differences between young rural Euro-American children and young Menominee children – Menominee children were more likely to give ecological justifications on a reasoning task – and so the difference in emphasis on ecological relationships seems to be present early. One possibility is that the mediating factor is cultural differences in skeletal principles or framework theories. Several Menominee participants commented that "every fish has a role to play," and in the "species interaction" task several Menominee participants made explicit mention of the idea that, in general, any two fish are likely to affect each other somehow. In interviews, majority-culture parents often said that they wanted their children to learn to take care of nature, whereas Menominee parents said they wanted their children to see themselves as part of nature (Bang, Medin, Unsworth, and Townsend 2005). Such ideas might function like framework theories to guide the interpretation of experience, but just how this happens remains a challenging question.

Are differences in organization or accessibility of knowledge reflected in reasoning? One fairly direct way of addressing this question is to measure reasoning and organization of knowledge separately and compare the results. López et al. (1997) asked Itza' Maya farmers in Guatemala and undergraduates at the University of Michigan to both sort and reason about mammals. Not surprisingly, the groups differed in their sorts. Itza' tended to draw finer distinctions among mammals based on more detailed knowledge of morphology, behavior, and ecological associations. Some of the reasoning probes tapped specific differences in the two groups' sorts, and in these cases the groups diverged in reasoning in ways that mirrored their differences in sorting. For example, in their sorts the undergraduates tended to group foxes with dogs, whereas the Itza' grouped foxes with cats. Both groups were given a forced-choice reasoning item in which foxes were said to have some disease, and the task was to generalize this disease to either dogs or cats. Consistent with their respective sorts, undergraduates preferred dogs, and Itza' preferred cats. In short, each group presumably used its relevant knowledge, and the knowledge differences led to group differences in induction. Also, as we have seen, there is some evidence of a relationship between reasoning and organization of knowledge among Menominee and majority-culture participants in Wisconsin, although in this case the relevant pieces of evidence come from different age groups. In sorting, Menominee adults tend to emphasize ecological relationships more than do majority-culture adults. In reasoning, Menominee children invoke ecological mechanisms more than do majority-culture children.

The previous method is correlational, and it would be nice to show the influence of accessibility on reasoning by controlled experimentation. Accessibility itself is difficult to manipulate (it is unclear how to prime, say, ecological relations without introducing a task demand to use these relations in reasoning), but an indirect way to get at accessibility is to manipulate the amount of time the reasoner has to access knowledge. Shafto et al. (2005) observed that undergraduate participants knew certain ecological associations (e.g., jungle animals, desert animals) but, when forced to choose between ecological and taxonomic relations, tended to generalize novel properties according to taxonomic relatedness. (This was true even for diseases.) To test whether this was due to poor accessibility of ecological relations, they ran speeded and unspeeded versions of another task, in which undergraduates did show evidence of reasoning from the ecological relations. In this task a novel property was attributed to a premise category (e.g., tigers) and the participant rated the likelihood that the property was also present in a conclusion category (e.g., anacondas). In the unspeeded version of the task, ratings were highest for taxonomically related animals, intermediate for ecologically related animals, and lowest for animals that had no close taxonomic or ecological relation. Under time pressure, however, ratings for ecologically related animals dropped to roughly equal those given to unrelated animals. Ratings given to taxonomically related animals were unaffected. This is consistent with the idea that graded differences in accessibility are reflected in reasoning; present but relatively inaccessible knowledge is sometimes invoked in reasoning but in a way that is sensitive to processing costs (Shafto et al. 2005; see also Coley et al. 2005).

In this case, the relevant distinction was between similarity-based reasoning and causal-ecological reasoning, but causal-ecological reasoning consists of a potentially large set of strategies that draw on various causal mechanisms and ecological interactions known by the reasoner. Do different kinds of causal-ecological knowledge vary in accessibility, and are these variations reflected in reasoning? Bailenson et al. (2002) found that in reasoning U.S. experts relied on geographic distribution, whereas Itza' used specific causal-ecological interactions as well as geographic distribution. It remains to be seen whether this difference reflects knowledge accessibility.

ASYMMETRIES AND OTHER DIFFERENCES IN BREADTH OF GENERALIZATION

Similarity-based reasoning itself is subject to variability in how broadly one generalizes from a given premise category. Similarity and taxonomic relationships specify ordinal relationships among categories – a property should generalize outward like a ripple through similarity space or through the taxonomy – but these ordinal relationships do not in themselves say how far the ripple should travel.

Breadth of generalization has been a focus of developmental research since Carey (1985) argued that young children's understanding of biology is organized around humans. She gave children a reasoning task in which a novel property was said to be true of one biological kind (e.g., "Humans have a little green thing inside them called an omentum") and the child was asked whether that property was true of other biological kinds (e.g., "Do you think that dogs also have an omentum?"). Her participants tended to treat humans as a privileged base for inferences. In general, inferences from humans to nonhuman biological kinds were stronger than (a) from these same nonhuman kinds to humans and (b) from nonhuman kinds to other nonhuman kinds. In some cases this meant that children violated similarity; inferences from humans to bugs were stronger than from bees to bugs. In short, reasoning was anthropocentric.

One interpretation is that Carey's (1985) participants – mostly urban children – knew more about humans than about other kinds, and that better known or more richly represented categories are better premises for generalization. In support of this interpretation, Inagaki (1990) compared two groups of urban children, one group who had raised goldfish at home and another group who had not. Children who had raised goldfish were more likely to draw inferences from both goldfish and humans than were children who had not raised goldfish; the latter group reasoned more like Carey's participants, treating humans as a uniquely privileged premise category. Likewise, Atran et al. (2001) studied Yukatek Maya children and adults in southern Mexico and found no evidence of systematic anthropocentrism. Instead they found a pattern of age- and gender-related differences that were consistent with familiarity effects. For example, girls knew less about the peccary than did boys and also treated the peccary as a weaker premise category. In related work, Tarlowski (2006) has demonstrated that children's patterns of inductive generalization are influenced both by urban versus rural status and by parents' knowledge of the domain.

The finding that better-known kinds make for better premises is problematic but not fatal for the similarity-based models; they can accommodate the finding but have trouble explaining it. For example, the similarity-coverage model can handle the finding by (a) putting much greater weight on the coverage component (e.g., the

degree to which "human" covers "living thing") than on the similarity component (e.g., the similarity of "human" to "bug") and (b) assuming that the representations of the various categories are such that the privileged premise category ("human") covers the relevant inclusive category ("living thing") better than do other, nonprivileged categories. Still, the model provides no reason why coverage should be weighted so much more heavily than similarity (Rips, 2001).

A bigger problem comes from recent cross-cultural work which suggests that richness of knowledge of the premise category is not all that matters. Ross et al. (2003; see also Medin and Atran 2004) studied three groups of children: Menominee children in rural Wisconsin, majority-culture children in rural Wisconsin, and majority-culture children in (urban) Boston. Rural children of both cultural groups have similar levels of experience with animals and plants, and so if amount of knowledge were the only strong determinant of breadth of generalization, then we would expect these two groups to be similar. However, Ross et al. found different developmental trajectories in all three groups.

The rural majority-culture children treated humans as a privileged base at an early age; this anthropocentrism waned with age. When they declined to generalize from nonhuman animals to humans, children in this group (at all ages) often explained that "people aren't animals." In contrast, Menominee children showed no reliable anthropocentrism at any age. Also, they showed less differentiation between "higher" animals and "lower" animals when generalizing from humans, as if humans are intimately related to all other animals.[3] In interpreting this finding, Medin and Atran (2004) note that "the Menominee origin myth has people coming from the bear, and even the youngest children are familiar with the animal-based clan system. In short, there is cultural support for a symmetrical relation between humans and other animals" (p. 967).

Interpreting asymmetries is difficult. Medin and Waxman (2007) propose that they often reflect not just richness of knowledge of the premise kind but also the distinctive features of both premise and conclusion kinds and also the higher-level categories that these kinds belong to. In many cases the properties and higher-level categories of the *conclusion* kind seem to matter more than properties and categories of the *premise* kind. Thus, when children fail to generalize a property of peccaries to a target like humans, this may be not because peccaries are unfamiliar or atypical but rather because humans have distinctive properties that limit generalization to them. In other cases, asymmetries may be due to ecological reasoning, where some kinds are seen as more active ecological agents than others. Until we have a better understanding of the cognitive mechanisms that underlie asymmetries, interpretations should be made with caution. For now, a reasonable conclusion is that at least some asymmetries are due to (culture-related) knowledge of the properties of the relevant kinds and also to (culture-related) tendencies to think of certain kinds as belonging to certain higher-level categories (e.g., a tendency to think of humans as a kind of animal or as a kind distinct from other animals; Anggoro, Waxman, and Medin 2005). Such tendencies are problematic for the similarity-based models.

Implications for Models of Reasoning

To summarize, cross-cultural and other studies have revealed the following.

(1)   Reasoners with domain knowledge flexibly invoke a variety of strategies – including, but not limited to, the similarity-based strategies described by the similarity-coverage model (Osherson et al. 1990) and the feature-based model (Sloman 1993).

(2)   Reasoning favors causal knowledge. Of course, the strategies we have called causal-ecological involve causal knowledge directly (e.g., reasoning about how a property might be transmitted through ecological interactions), and knowledgeable reasoners seem to prefer these to similarity-based strategies even for properties that might plausibly be generalized according to similarity (e.g., enzymes). But even similarity-based reasoning might sometimes involve causal considerations indirectly. Although it may sometimes serve as a mere fallback or default strategy, at other times similarity is invoked just because the property in question is understood to be involved in the causal mechanisms that underlie the similarity-and-taxonomy structure of the domain (Hadjichristidis et al. 2004; Rips 2001).

(3)   Taxonomic relations matter, and they may differ, at least in salience, across cultures. For example, some cultures do not have a superordinate term for animals, and cultures that do have such a term do not always include humans in it (see Anggoro et al. 2005, for evidence and implications). This may mean that, for example, generalization from a given premise category will be broader when the superordinate category that supports broad generalization is more salient (say, because it is named rather than covert).

(4)   When various similarity-based and causal-ecological strategies are available to the reasoner, which strategy is invoked depends in part upon the organization or relative accessibility of different pieces of the reasoner's knowledge base (e.g., Shafto et al. 2005). Or, to put it differently, a single knowledge base can be organized in different ways that render different reasoning strategies more or less fluent. The organization of the knowledge base, in turn, is sensitive not just to the practices or experiences through which people acquire domain knowledge but also to cultural milieu (perhaps in the form of framework theories) (e.g., Medin et al. 2002; Medin, Ross, Atran et al. 2006).

(5)   Even similarity-based reasoning, which one might expect to be well constrained by the intrinsic structure of the domain (taxonomic relationships, clusters of related features, and so on), is sensitive to cultural milieu. Even at early ages, cultural beliefs or framework theories seem to influence how broadly reasoners generalize from different premise categories (Ross et al. 2003; see also Medin and Atran 2004).

What are the implications of these findings for models of reasoning? That reasoners often abandon similarity in favor of causal-ecological strategies (findings 1, 2, and 4) represents a serious limitation of the similarity-coverage and feature-based models, because they seem to predict that similarity-based reasoning will be universal. Of course, one might argue that these models are only meant to apply to truly blank properties – that is, properties for which the reasoner has absolutely no prior belief about their distribution – and that people with some domain knowledge interpret almost any property in such a way that, functionally, it is not blank. There are two problems with this counterargument. One is that it restricts the applicability of such models to the point of irrelevance. The second is that it is not the case that knowledgeable reasoners never show similarity-based reasoning; rather, similarity-based reasoning is one strategy among many.

Indeed, the similarity-based models seem to emerge from this analysis as good accounts of one strategy that is invoked when knowledge is sparse or when the reasoner believes that the property in question is related to other properties that determine the similarity-and-taxonomy structure of the domain. Still, how can models of reasoning handle findings 1, 2, and 4? We turn now to three alternative theories, each of which addresses some part of these findings.

McDonald, Samuels, and Rispoli (1996) presented a *hypothesis-assessment model* of inductive reasoning. On this model, generalization of properties over categories can be viewed as a form of hypothesis assessment in which the conclusion is the relevant hypothesis and the premise is some evidence for this hypothesis. A general prediction of this model is that inferences will be sensitive to the same sorts of factors that influence hypothesis assessment in other contexts – especially the number of competing hypotheses. McDonald et al. provide support for this prediction by asking people to generate hypotheses or explanations and showing that confidence in inferences decreases when there are competing hypotheses (i.e., other candidates for a conclusion category). The hypothesis-assessment model places no constraints on the hypotheses or explanations that a reasoner might consider, and so in principle it is consistent with a variety of strategies (finding 1). However, it has trouble with finding 2, in that it gives no special status to causal factors. As for knowledge accessibility (finding 4), the model as initially described has little to say, but McDonald et al. discussed this. In their data, judgments of argument strength seemed to be sensitive to how accessible the corresponding conclusion categories were (as measured by the number of participants who, given the premises, spontaneously generated the conclusion category). McDonald et al. noted that adding accessibility to the model as a predictor would be reasonable, given that the influence of accessibility on hypothesis strength has been shown in other contexts.

Heit (1998, 2000) proposed a *Bayesian model* that works more or less as follows. If the task is to generalize a novel property from cows to sheep, then various known properties of cows and sheep are called to mind. Of these, some are likely shared by cows and sheep, and others

distinctive to cows. From the numbers of properties that are shared and distinctive, the reasoner computes the likelihood that the novel property belongs to one group or the other. (If known properties tend to be shared, then it's likely that the novel property is shared. If known properties tend to be distinctive, then it's likely that the novel property is distinctive.) To the extent that the novel property is likely to belong to the shared group, the inference from cows to sheep is strong. In one important respect, this model is like the similarity-based models (and especially the feature-based model): It works on the assumption that the novel property is associated with known properties, and larger clusters of known properties carry more weight in reasoning. Yet the Bayesian model allows flexibility in just which of the known properties of sheep and cows are considered. In this way the model explains, for example, Heit and Rubinstein's (1994) finding that anatomical properties were generalized according to animals' anatomical similarity, whereas behavioral properties were generalized according to behavioral similarity. On the Bayesian model, this is because a novel anatomical property calls to mind known anatomical properties, and these dominate in the inference process. In contrast, a novel behavioral property calls to mind known behavioral properties.

Because the Bayesian model is similarity based (i.e., works on the assumption that the novel property is associated with known properties), it has trouble with findings 1 and (especially) 2. As for finding 4, the Bayesian model allows that different bits of knowledge are called to mind in different contexts, and this can be seen as reflecting context-specific differences in knowledge accessibility. Still, the model's ability to account for finding 4 in this way is limited. First, it relies on an independent theory to explain which bits of knowledge – that is, which known properties of the premise and conclusion categories – are called to mind. Second, and more importantly, the relevant bits of knowledge are always known properties of the premise and conclusion categories; they are not causal mechanisms by which properties are acquired or transmitted. This is another way of saying what has already been said, namely, that the model is similarity based and does not predict causal-ecological reasoning.[4]

A theory better suited to finding 4 is the *relevance framework* outlined by Medin, Coley, Storms, and Hayes (2003). One way to motivate this framework is to consider some responses that a tree expert gave to Proffitt et al. (2000). The expert was given probes such as the following: "Suppose we know that river birch get disease X and that white oaks get disease Y. Which disease do you think is more likely to affect all trees?" In this case, the expert said disease X, noting that river birches are very susceptible to disease (so that "if one gets it they all get it"). The very next probe involved the gingko tree, and the expert chose the disease associated with it as more likely to affect all trees on the grounds that "gingkos are so resistant to disease that if they get it, it must be a very powerful disease." He then said that he felt as if he had just contradicted himself, but that nonetheless these seemed like the right answers.

Normatively, this expert's answers do not represent a contradiction. Instead, he appeared to be using the information that was most salient and accessible to guide his reasoning (birches are notoriously susceptible to, and gingkos notoriously resistant to, diseases). Simply put, the expert was using the knowledge that he considered most relevant. Medin et al. (2003) suggested that Sperber and Wilson's (1986) relevance theory provides a good framework for understanding these and related patterns of responding. One motivation for this view is the fact that experiments take place in a social context and participants reasonably infer that the experimenter is being relevant and informative with respect to the inductive argument forms (cf. Grice 1975). Furthermore, this view leads to a number of novel predictions that contrast with those of other models.

In relevance theory, relevance is seen as a property of inputs to cognitive processes:

An input is relevant to an individual at a certain time if processing this input yields cognitive effects. Examples of cognitive effects are the revision of previous beliefs, or the derivation of contextual conclusions, that is, conclusions that follow from the input taken together with previously available information. Such revisions or conclusions are particularly relevant when they answer questions that the individual had in mind (or in an experimental situation, was presented with).... Everything else being equal, the greater the cognitive effects achieved by processing an input, the greater its relevance. On the other hand, the greater the effort involved in processing an input, the lower the relevance.... One implication of the definition of relevance in terms of effect and

effort is that salient information, everything else being equal, has greater relevance, given that accessing it requires less effort. (Van der Henst, Sperber, and Politzer 2002: 4)

In support of this approach, Medin et al. (2003) experimentally manipulated effort and effect to determine whether they have the sorts of consequences predicted by relevance theory. Undergraduates contrast with experts in having little background knowledge to bring to bear on these sorts of reasoning tasks, and consequently it is not surprising that they rely heavily on more abstract reasoning strategies. In their studies with undergraduates, Medin et al. were able to identify accessible background knowledge to bring out the effect side of relevance and manipulated the premise and conclusion categories to show consequences on the effort side. As an example of the former, they found that the argument "bananas have enzyme X, therefore monkeys have Enzyme X" was rated stronger than the argument "mice have enzyme X, therefore monkeys have Enzyme X." In this case-relevant background knowledge that monkeys like bananas leads to a violation of similarity.

As an example of varying effort, Medin et al. (2003) showed that undergraduates rate the inductive strength of the argument "grass has enzyme Y, therefore humans have enzyme Y" to be less strong than the argument "grass has enzyme Y, therefore cows and humans have enzyme Y." (The arguments were not juxtaposed but rather were used in a between-subjects design.) In this case, the data yield a "conclusion conjunction fallacy" since, normatively, the former argument's conclusion cannot be less likely than the conclusion of the latter argument. From a relevance perspective, the addition of cows to the conclusion made it easier for the participants to access a sensible causal pathway between grass and humans.

In other conditions, Medin et al. demonstrated premise nonmonotonicity, that is, a drop in argument strength with the addition of premises. For example, "white oaks get disease X, therefore sugar maples do" was rated stronger than "white oaks, red oaks, and burr oaks get disease X, therefore sugar maples do." In this case the idea is that multiple premises involving oaks make "oaks" salient and relevant and reinforce the idea that disease X is specific to oaks.

Of the other models we have described, the relevance framework is most closely related to the hypothesis-assessment model, in that one could see the relevance framework as a basis for predicting which hypotheses people will tend to generate. Importantly, due to its emphasis on effort, the relevance theory explains differences due to knowledge accessibility (finding 4) in a natural way: Greater accessibility means less effort, and more accessible pieces of knowledge are therefore favored in reasoning. We readily concede that relevance theory seems vague, especially in relation to computational models like the similarity-coverage model. But a theory must also be judged on its ability to generate novel predictions, and relevance theory fares well by this standard.

Although there are numerous other studies looking at inductive reasoning in a cultural context, their primary focus is on induction informing culture rather than vice versa. We now turn to a more speculative consideration of how culture may inform theories of causal reasoning.

Culture and Causal Reasoning

Psychologists have recently begun to explore a theory of learning and reasoning about systems of causal relationships. At the same time, crosscultural work has revealed ways in which reasoning is guided by abstract expectations or understandings of causal structure. Both lines of work are young (consequently, this section will be shorter and more speculative than the previous one), yet both are far enough along that we can begin to see tensions between them and ways in which the cultural research might inform the new theory.

Causal Bayes Net Theory

The use of causal knowledge to predict and control events is a form of reasoning that is ubiquitous both in everyday life and in more formal contexts like science and medicine. Causal knowledge enables us to discern with some precision whether, or to what degree, variables are relevant to predictions about one another, or to interventions to control one another. When we know causal relationships, we tend to base our predictions on factors that are causally relevant, and to focus our interventions on factors that will in fact transmit influence to the things we wish to control. For example, if we knew that two variables X and Y were associated just because they had a common cause C, and if we wanted to make a prediction about Y, we would rather base this prediction on C than on X. If we wished to exercise control over Y by manipulating one

of the other variables, we would manipulate C, not X.

A detailed account of how causal knowledge can be used to make predictions and exercise control has been developed in philosophy, statistics, and computer science (Pearl 2000; Spirtes, Glymour, and Scheines 2000) and is known as causal Bayes net theory, or causal graphical model theory. There has recently been a good deal of interest in using this theory as a basis of psychological accounts (e.g., Glymour 2001; Gopnik et al. 2004; Lagnado and Sloman 2004; Rehder and Hastie 2001; Sloman and Lagnado 2005; Steyvers, Tenenbaum, Wagenmakers, and Blum 2003; Waldmann and Martignon 1998). Briefly, causal Bayes net theory specifies mappings between causation and correlation (where we use *correlation* broadly, to refer to statistical relationship of any form). Causal knowledge is represented as graphs in which variables (events, states, and so on) appear as nodes, and causal relationships as directed links between nodes. The heavy explanatory work is done by a principle called the *causal Markov assumption*: Any variable is uncorrelated with, or statistically independent of, all variables that are not its descendants in causal structure – that is, not its direct or indirect effects – conditional on its immediate cause(s).

Given a causal graph, the Markov assumption says just which variables are relevant to any instance of prediction or control. For example, suppose that a certain virus, V, causes two symptoms, A and B, by different mechanisms. In graphical form: $A \leftarrow V \rightarrow B$. According to the Markov assumption, A and B should be correlated in general but uncorrelated conditional on V, that is, when V is controlled for. (Neither is a descendant of the other, and each has V as its sole immediate cause.) A reasoner who respects the Markov assumption should treat A as predictive of B except when there is information about V, in which case a prediction about B should be based on V alone. If it is known that a patient has (or does not have) the virus, then the appearance of symptom A should not be predictive of the appearance of B. Interventions to control variables are represented as surgeries on graphs (Pearl 2000), in which the links leading into an intervened-upon variable are broken, and the intervention itself becomes the sole cause of the variable. The Markov assumption can then be applied to determine how relevance flows through the new graph. For example, intervening to control symptom B (by means of a perfectly effective drug, say) breaks the influence of the virus V on this symptom; consequently, B is no longer predictive of V or A.

The causation-correlation mappings specified by the Markov assumption can also be applied in the other direction, to learn causal models from correlational evidence. If X and Y are correlated in general but uncorrelated when Z is controlled for, then, given a few additional assumptions, there are three ways in which these variables might be related: $X \to Z \to Y$, $X \leftarrow Z \leftarrow Y$, and $X \leftarrow Z \to Y$. Other models, like $Z \to X \to Y$, can be ruled out. Though the details are beyond the scope of this chapter, causal Bayes net theory also provides leverage for understanding some seemingly more complicated tasks, including (a) learning causal models by intervening to manipulate variables and (b) inferring the presence of hidden causes.[5]

Several features of causal Bayes net theory are pertinent:

(1) The theory requires that causal knowledge be *complete*, in two respects. First, there can be no unknown cause of any combination of known variables; this requirement has been called *causal sufficiency* (Spirtes et al. 2000). Second, there can be no unknown paths of influence between variables. If causal knowledge is not complete in these ways, then the Markov assumption does not apply. To see why, suppose there were an unknown common cause of symptoms A and B that did not act via the virus V, or an unknown path of influence between A and B (perhaps A promotes B independently of their joint dependence on V). In these cases A and B would be relevant to predictions about one another (and perhaps to interventions to control one another) even conditional on V.

(2) Causal knowledge is *concrete*, in two senses. First, causal graphs are made of relationships among specific variables, by which we mean variables encoded with enough specificity to map onto the events and states that we make predictions about, base predictions on, manipulate, and so on. There is (as yet) no place in the formalism for more abstract notions about what *kinds* of variables might be related or relevant to one another. Second, the mechanisms underlying causal relationships must often be understood in some detail if causal knowledge is to be properly complete (Hausman and Woodward 1999). For example, in cases of a single cause with multiple effects, it is often difficult to tell whether the effects come about by truly distinct mechanisms or by way of a single unseen mechanism. If virus V gave rise to symptoms A and B by way of a single hidden variable (say, lack of a certain enzyme), then A and B would have an unknown common cause, completeness would be violated, and the Markov assumption would not apply. Such arrangements have been called *interactive forks* (Salmon 1984; on the failure of the Markov assumption to apply in these cases, see Sober 1988).

(3) There are two general approaches to learning causal models from correlational evidence: (a) a bottom-up or "constraint-based" approach, in which learning is primarily a matter of using the causation-correlation mappings specified by the Markov assumption to work backwards, from patterns of correlation to causal models consistent with these patterns (e.g., Spirtes et al. 2000); and (b) a top-down Bayesian approach, in which learning begins with a set of candidate causal models and evaluates these models for their likelihood of having generated the correlational evidence (e.g., Heckerman, Meek, and Cooper 1999). The bottom-up view ties causal structure closely to the correlational input. This view suggests that, in cases where causal knowledge is acquired from correlational evidence, there should be little cultural variation in the understood causal structure of the world (unless, of course, there is corresponding variation in the correlational evidence available to learners in different cultures). If there *were* cultural variation in the interpretation of correlational evidence, this would favor the top-down approach, where culture-related expectations of causal structure might guide the construction of the initial set of candidate structures.

Culture-Related Understandings of Causation

Recent cross-cultural research suggests that causal reasoning is often guided by abstract expectations or understandings of the causal structure of the world. Consider the theory that Easterners and Westerners have holistic and analytic theories, respectively, about causation

(Nisbett 2003; Nisbett, Peng, Choi, and Noren-zayan 2001). The idea is that Westerners (roughly, Europeans and European Americans) think of the world as partitioned into causally unrelated objects. When reasoning about the behavior of an object, they tend to look for causes in the intrinsic disposition or attributes of the object itself (e.g., an object falls to earth because of its weight). In contrast, Easterners (roughly, east and central Asians) are thought to have a more holistic view of the causal structure of the world, which can be characterized (or perhaps caricaturized) as "everything affects everything else." They tend to consider multiple, perhaps interactive causes and, when reasoning about the behavior of an object, to look outside of the object to situational or environmental influences (e.g., an object falls because of an external force) (Choi, Nisbett, and Norenzayan 1999; Morris and Peng 1994; Nisbett 2003; Nisbett et al. 2001; Peng and Knowles 2003).

The evidence for this view is mostly in the social domain (for a review, see Choi et al. 1999). Miller (1984) found that, in explaining a person's behavior, participants in India invoked more contextual or situational factors than did Americans, who spoke to a greater extent about the person's disposition. Similarly, Morris and Peng (1994) asked graduate students to explain the behavior of a murderer and found that Americans favored dispositional factors and Chinese situational factors. These findings have been echoed in studies of attributions made in print by American and Chinese journalists (Lee, Hallahan, and Herzog 1996; Morris and Peng 1994). When asked to explain the behavior of a cartoon fish which moved in various ways relative to a group of other fish, Americans showed a greater tendency than did Chinese to rate internal causes as more important than the other fish (Morris and Peng 1994).

Predictions in other domains have found less support. Morris and Peng (1994) asked participants about the causes of movements of physical objects (in animated depictions). Participants were asked to rate the relative importance of internal and external causes. This revealed only one difference between American and Chinese participants, and it was in the direction opposite what one might have predicted. Given an animated depiction of an "entraining" event in which one object collides with another and then continues on its path, pushing the second object before it, Americans seemed to favor external over internal causes for the second object's motion, whereas Chinese showed no preference.

Ji, Peng, and Nisbett (2000) used a contingency learning task in which the goal was to judge the strength of a relationship between which of two abstract shapes appeared on the left side of a screen and which of two other shapes appeared on the right. Whereas there were differences in the judgments made by American and Chinese participants, these differences can be explained largely as reflecting a group difference in response bias.[6]

Peng and Knowles (2003) found some suggestive differences in how American and Chinese participants explained abstract, seemingly physical events. When participants' explanations were classified as either dispositional (e.g., referring to a target object's weight or composition) or contextual (e.g., referring to another object or a surrounding medium), American college students showed a bias, relative to Chinese college students, toward dispositional explanations on a few items. Still, this trend was not statistically reliable over the whole set of items, and large differences between items suggest that a considerable part of the story is yet unexplained.

Our belief is that there is something right about the idea that cultures differ in understandings of causal structure, but that these understandings have sometimes been theorized too abstractly.[7] They are probably bound up with beliefs, habits, goals, and ideals in particular domains. On this view, the robust findings in the social domain are the result not of domain-general stances like holism but of more specific theories of personal behavior and social interaction. Such theories were measured directly by Norenzayan, Choi, and Nisbett (2002), who asked Korean and American participants to rate their agreement with each of three general explanations of human behavior: a dispositional theory, a situational theory, and an interactionist theory (according to which dispositional and situational factors interact to yield behavior). Compared to Americans, Koreans reported reliably greater agreement with situationism in two studies and with interactionism in one. We suspect that theories at this level of abstraction are likely guides of causal reasoning.[8]

Research in folkbiology has revealed other cases in which cultural groups seem to differ in (domain-specific) understandings of causal structure. This work involves the "species interaction" task described earlier. Atran et al. (1999, 2002) asked participants in three cultural groups in Guatemala to say whether and how various kinds of plants and animals affect each other. It was found that the groups differed in the numbers of interactions they reported and, in particular, in the numbers of helpful effects of animals on plants. In short, the groups seemed to have different understandings of the kinds of causal relationships in the ecosystem. As we noted earlier, Medin, Ross, Atran et al. (2006) found that Menominee and majority-culture fishermen in Wisconsin also have different views of causal structure, such that reciprocal relationships among fish are more salient to Menominee participants. Informally, Menominee participants have sometimes articulated framework theories of causal interaction like "every fish has a role to play" and "all in all, living things affect each other."

In sum, cross-cultural research suggests that causal reasoning is often guided by understandings of causal structure that are more abstract than causal Bayes nets (although probably not as abstract as domain-general stances like holism). It is too early to say just what these understandings are – perhaps they are skeletal framework theories (Keil 2003a, 2003b) or "causal grammars" (Tenenbaum, Griffiths, and Niyogi 2007) – but in at least some cases they seem to vary along a dimension that runs from *autonomy* (things in a domain tend not to affect each other) to *influence* (things tend to affect each other).

Bringing the Cultural Research to Bear on Causal Bayes Net Theory

These two lines of work are young, and the tasks they involve are quite different – for example, learning whether a certain object causes a machine to light up (Gopnik et al. 2004) versus explaining a murder (Morris and Peng 1994). Yet we can begin to see tensions between them that are similar to the tensions between similarity-based models of inductive reasoning and cross-cultural research on reasoning about plants and animals.

Recall that the principal way in which causal Bayes net theory explains prediction and control is to specify the relevance of variables to one another, based on their relative positions in causal structure. It does this by applying a general principle, the causal Markov assumption, to causal models that are complete and concrete. There are no representational tools for accommodating abstract beliefs about relevance in a domain, and the Markov assumption fails if causal knowledge is incomplete in certain ways. These limitations should be taken seriously in building psychological accounts of reasoning on causal Bayes net theory, because

natural causal knowledge, knowledge that supports reasoning, is often abstract and incomplete (Keil 2003b; Rozenblit and Keil 2002). Indeed, it is often abstract and incomplete in just the ways that invalidate the causal Markov assumption (interactive forks, etc.; Hausman and Woodward 1999). In these cases (and they may be the norm), the lack of complete, concrete knowledge makes room for abstract understandings of relevance and causal relatedness to guide learning and reasoning. Cultural research shows that learning and reasoning are indeed guided by abstract expectations – and, more specifically, expectations that may vary along a continuum from autonomy to influence.

Expectations of autonomy are roughly consistent with the causal Markov assumption, which has the form "variables are irrelevant to one another unless proven otherwise." Proving otherwise requires knowing just how variables are related in a complete, concrete causal graph, with the result that relevance is assigned to variables conservatively. In contrast, expectations of influence seem to run against the Markov assumption, as they assign relevance more liberally. For a reasoner who knows the model $A \rightarrow B \rightarrow C$, the causal Markov assumption dictates that a prediction about C, given information about A and B, should be based on B alone. But if this reasoner has an expectation of influence, then their prediction might be based also on A. This can be seen as allowing for the possibility that A and C are related in some unknown way. We know of no cross-cultural research on this question, but within-culture work has shown that both undergraduates and domain experts do tend to deviate from the Markov assumption in this way (Burnett 2005; Rehder and Burnett 2005). There is also some tentative evidence that scientists in different fields override the causal Markov assumption to different degrees, consistent with abstract expectations in their respective fields (Burnett 2004). The clear prediction for cultural comparisons is that reasoners with a greater expectation of influence in a given domain will go farther in assigning relevance or predictive value to variables which, according to the causal Markov assumption, should be irrelevant or nonpredictive. We might make similar predictions about active intervention. Consider again a reasoner who knows the model $A \rightarrow B \rightarrow C$. If B is manipulated as a way of controlling C, the Markov assumption says there is no additional benefit to manipulating A. Reasoners with an expectation of influence might see additional benefit and, when given the option, might manipulate A as well as B in order to control C.

Cultural research also has implications for the learning of causal systems from correlational evidence. In the bottom-up or constraint-based approach, where learning is driven mainly by the Markov assumption, there is no room for abstract expectations of influence or autonomy. Furthermore, because an infinity of causal structures involving latent variables are (according to the Markov assumption) consistent with any pattern of correlational evidence, the bottom-up approach requires additional assumptions that favor causal structures that are parsimonious in some respect(s) (e.g., having the fewest latent variables). Cultural research suggests that learning is guided by abstract expectations about causal structures in different domains, and this argues in favor of the top-down approach, where abstract knowledge may influence the causal models that a learner considers (e.g., Tenenbaum and Griffiths 2003; Tenenbaum et al. 2007). Furthermore, when expectations favor influence instead of autonomy, learning may deviate from the parsimony assumptions used in the bottom-up approach. Learners with expectations of influence may infer causal structures that are more than minimally elaborate, perhaps with more latent variables than are necessary to account for observed correlations.

Conclusion

In both of the cases we have discussed, models have been proposed which ground reasoning in concrete knowledge. In the case of inductive reasoning about biological properties, the similarity-based models explain reasoning in terms of that aspect of the domain that is most readily detected: clusters of correlated features and the taxonomies that form around these clusters. In the case of causal reasoning, causal Bayes net theory explains reasoning (i.e., prediction and control) in terms of graphical models of causal systems that are complete and concrete. In both cases, one can imagine how the relevant knowledge might be acquired by an individual learner exploring the world independently of any cultural influence.

In both cases, cultural research suggests that reasoning is guided by more abstract knowledge that is less constrained by the observable structure of the world and more culturally variable. Reasoning about biological properties draws preferentially on an aspect of the domain that is less easily detected than feature clusters

and taxonomies, namely, causal mechanisms by which properties arise and by which properties are transmitted among categories. Furthermore, the knowledge base that supports reasoning – which may include feature clusters, taxonomic relationships, causal-ecological relationships, and more – may be organized according to different framework theories, so as to render different kinds of knowledge more or less accessible. These differences are reflected in reasoning. As for causal reasoning, in at least some domains it draws not only on concrete knowledge but also on abstract theories or expectations of causal structure.

This is not to say that framework theories and expectations of the kinds described in this chapter are the only paths through which culture influences reasoning. It is possible, for example, that cultural factors sometimes promote certain modes of reasoning over others. Furthermore, some cultural differences related to reasoning – for example, differences in typicality among members of biological categories – seem better explained by ideals and goals than by theories and expectations (Burnett, Medin, Ross, and Blok 2005; Lynch, Coley, and Medin 2000).

Given that we take the proximal mechanisms of culture to be cognitive constructs like theories and expectations, one might wonder what is to be gained by studying culture itself. There are several things to be gained. First, in many cases it would be difficult or impossible to identify the relevant cognitive constructs without knowing their sources in culture. Second, the cognitive constructs that depend on culture may be stable or entrenched in ways that cannot be mimicked or modified in laboratory experiments. Finally, the cultural sources of cognitive constructs are interesting in their own right, especially if one wants to predict reasoning in real-world settings.

We have said little about what exactly the operative theories and expectations are, beyond suggesting that they are somewhat domain specific – like the theories of human behavior described by Norenzayan et al. (2002) and the idea that "every fish has a role to play," mentioned by some Menominee fishermen (Medin et al. 2002). We have said even less about how they are acquired and transmitted. Possibilities include imitation, inference from other people's behavior, explicit communication of abstract principles (e.g., one Menominee participant explained his bias to see interactions among species by saying that his grandmother had taught him that all living things affect each other), explicit communication of more concrete facts from which principles can be abstracted, communication of goals and ideals that lead indirectly to differences in knowledge, and so on. As an example of the work that can be done in this area, Atran et al. (2002) employed social network analysis to trace the transmission of mental models of the ecosystem among members of different cultural groups in Guatemala. As this work illustrates, collaboration between psychology and anthropology has the potential to reveal determinants of reasoning that are neither easily detected in the structure of the world nor easily identified without considering the cultural milieus in which individual minds develop and function.

Notes

1   Heit (1998, 2000) has proposed a Bayesian model of inductive reasoning based on this same idea. The Bayesian model, however, is somewhat more flexible in its application of the idea that novel properties mirror known properties – as we will discuss later.
2   Hadjichristidis et al. distinguish between causal structure and more generic "dependency structure" and draw their conclusions about the latter, but for simplicity we focus here on causal structure.
3   Another finding of Ross et al. (2003) and Atran et al. (2001) was that some groups of children – especially Yukatek Maya and Menominee children – showed causal-ecological reasoning even at early ages. Since our focus here is on breadth of generalization by similarity and/or taxonomic relationships, we have disregarded causal-ecological generalizations in our description of the data.
4   One might suggest that the Bayesian model handles causal-ecological strategies by computing probabilities over just those properties that are associated with a certain ecological interaction, but here the activation of just those properties is doing most of the explanatory work, and this requires an independent theory. Furthermore, this method of mimicking causal-ecological reasoning is limited to cases where the premise and conclusion categories share some property (e.g., habitat) that can serve as a proxy for the relevant causal mechanism – for example, an inference from one river fish to another might be predicted if "lives in rivers" is called to mind as a shared property – but it is difficult to imagine what shared property might mimic an inference that cows get a property from grass by eating it.
5   For applications of these ideas to psychology, see: on reasoning about interventions, Sloman and Lagnado (2005), Waldmann and Hagmayer

(2005); on learning causal models by intervention, Gopnik et al. (2004), Lagnado and Sloman (2004), Steyvers et al. (2003); on inferring hidden variables, Gopnik et al. (2004), Kushnir, Gopnik, Schulz, and Danks (2003).
6   Ji et al. also reported that Americans but not Chinese showed a primacy effect, in which the judged strength of the relationship was more sensitive to cases presented early in the learning phase than to those presented later. This might have been due to a group difference in level of engagement in the task.
7   As a consequence, the mapping between an abstract principle and a particular task typically involves a series of assumptions, often implicit, that themselves may not be straightforward.
8   To illustrate how theories and goals might vary by domain, a Korean colleague has suggested that Korean explanations of mental illness or deviant behavior might actually be less holistic than American explanations, precisely because social interconnectedness is valued in Korean culture. A holistic explanation (e.g., society drove him mad) would implicate society, and to avoid this Koreans might prefer analytic explanations (e.g., bad traits or genes).

References

Anggoro, F., Waxman, S., & Medin, D. (2005). The effect of naming practices on children's understanding of living things. *Proceedings of the 27th Annual Conference of the Cognitive Science Society*.

Atran, S. (1998). Folk biology and the anthropology of science: Cognitive universals and cultural particulars. *Behavioral and Brain Sciences, 21*, 547–609.

Atran, S., Medin, D., Lynch, E., Vapnarsky, V., Ucan Ek', E., & Sousa, P. (2001). Folkbiology doesn't come from folk psychology: Evidence from Yukatek Maya in cross-cultural perspective. *Journal of Cognition and Culture, 1*, 3–42.

Atran, S., Medin, D. L., & Ross, N. O. (2005). The cultural mind: Environmental decision making and cultural modeling within and across populations. *Psychological Review, 112*, 744–776.

Atran, S., Medin, D., Ross, N., Lynch, E., Coley, J., Ucan Ek', E., & Vapnarsky, V. (1999). Folk ecology and commons management in the Maya Lowlands. *Proceedings of the National Academy of Sciences of the United States of America, 96*, 7598–7603.

Atran, S., Medin, D., Ross, N., Lynch, E., Vapnarsky, V., Ek', E. U., Coley, J., Timura, C., & Baran, M. (2002). Folk ecology, cultural epidemiology, and the spirit of the commons: A garden experiment in the Maya lowlands, 1991–2001. *Current Anthropology, 43*, 421–441.

Bailenson, J. N., Shum, M. S., Atran, S., Medin, D. L., & Coley, J. D. (2002). A bird's eye view:

Biological categorization and reasoning within and across cultures. *Cognition, 84,* 1–53.

Bang, M., Medin, D., Unsworth, S., & Townsend, J. (2005, April). *Cultural models of nature and their relevance to science education.* Paper presented at the annual meeting of the American Educational Research Association, Montreal.

Berlin, B. (1992). *Ethnobiological classification: Principles of categorization of plants and animals in traditional societies.* Princeton, NJ: Princeton University Press.

Burnett, R. C. (2004). *Inference from complex causal models.* Unpublished doctoral dissertation, Northwestern University.

Burnett, R. C. (2005). Close does count: Evidence of a proximity effect in inference from causal knowledge. *Proceedings of the 27th Annual Conference of the Cognitive Science Society.*

Burnett, R. C., Medin, D. L., & Ross, N. O. (2004). *Experts don't reason about fish out of water: Fishermen's inductive reasoning is based on causal-ecological relations* [Contribution to festschrift for Edward E. Smith]. Available in PsycEXTRA.

Burnett, R. C., Medin, D. L., Ross, N. O., & Blok, S. V. (2005). Ideal is typical. *Canadian Journal of Experimental Psychology, 59,* 5–10.

Carey, S. (1985). *Conceptual change in childhood.* Cambridge, MA: MIT Press.

Choi, I., Nisbett, R. E., & Norenzayan, A. (1999). Causal attribution across cultures: Variation and universality. *Psychological Bulletin, 125,* 47–63.

Choi, I., Nisbett, R. E., & Smith, E. E. (1997). Culture, category salience, and inductive reasoning. *Cognition, 65,* 15–32.

Cohen, D. (2001). Cultural variation: Considerations and implications. *Psychological Bulletin, 127,* 451–471.

Cole, M., & Scribner, S. (1974). *Culture and thought: A psychological introduction.* New York: John Wiley & Sons.

Coley, J. D., Shafto, P., Stepanova, O., & Baraff, E. (2005). Knowledge and category-based induction. In W. Ahn, R. L. Goldstone, B. C. Love, A. B. Markman, & P. Wolff (Eds.), *Categorization inside and outside the laboratory: Essays in honor of Douglas L. Medin.* Washington, DC: American Psychological Association.

Dias, M., Roazzi, A., & Harris, P. L. (2005). Reasoning from unfamiliar premises: A study with unschooled adults. *Psychological Science, 16,* 550–554.

Gelman, S. A., & Markman, E. M. (1986). Categories and induction in young children. *Cognition, 23,* 183–209.

Glymour, C. (2001). *The mind's arrows: Bayes nets and graphical causal models in psychology.* Cambridge, MA: MIT Press.

Gopnik, A., Glymour, C., Sobel, D. M., Schulz, L. E., Kushnir, T., & Danks, D. (2004). A theory of causal learning in children: Causal maps and Bayes nets. *Psychological Review, 111,* 3–32.

Greenfield, P. M. (1983). Review of the book *The psychology of literacy. Harvard Educational Review, 53,* 216–220.

Grice, H. P. (1975). Logic and conversation. In P. Cole & J. L. Morgan (Eds.), *Syntax and semantics: Vol. 3. Speech acts* (pp. 41–58). New York: Academic Press.

Hadjichristidis, C., Sloman, S., Stevenson, R., & Over, D. (2004). Feature centrality and property induction. *Cognitive Science, 28,* 45–74.

Harris, P. L. (2000). *The work of the imagination.* Oxford: Blackwell.

Hausman, D. M., & Woodward, J. (1999). Independence, invariance and the Causal Markov Condition. *British Journal for the Philosophy of Science, 50,* 521–583.

Heckerman, D., Meek, C., & Cooper, G. (1999). A Bayesian approach to causal discovery. In C. Glymour & G. F. Cooper (Eds.)., *Computation, causation, and discovery* (pp. 141–165). Menlo Park, CA: AAAI Press.

Heit, E. (1998). A Bayesian analysis of some forms of inductive reasoning. In M. Oaksford & N. Chater (Eds.), *Rational models of cognition* (pp. 248–274). Oxford: Oxford University Press.

Heit, E. (2000). Properties of inductive reasoning. *Psychonomic Bulletin & Review, 7,* 569–592.

Heit, E., & Rubinstein, J. (1994). Similarity and property effects in inductive reasoning. *Journal of Experimental Psychology: Learning, Memory, and Cognition, 20,* 411–422.

Higgins, E. (1996). Knowledge activation: Accessibility, applicability, and salience. In E. Higgins & A. Kruglanski (Eds.), *Social psychology: Handbook of basic principles* (pp. 133–168). New York: Guilford.

Hong, Y., Morris, M. W., Chiu, C., & Martinez, V. B. (2000). Multicultural minds. *American Psychologist, 55,* 709–720.

Inagaki, K. (1990). The effects of raising animals on children's biological knowledge. *British Journal of Developmental Psychology, 8,* 119–129.

Ji, L.-J., Peng, K., & Nisbett, R. E. (2000). Culture, control, and perception of relationships in the environment. *Journal of Personality and Social Psychology, 78,* 943–955.

Keil, F. C. (1995). The growth of causal understandings of natural kinds. In D. Sperber, D. Premack, & A. J. Premack (Eds.), *Causal cognition: A multidisciplinary debate* (pp. 234–262). New York: Oxford University Press.

Keil, F. C. (2003a). Categorisation, causation, and the limits of understanding. *Language and Cognitive Processes, 18,* 663–692.

Keil, F. C. (2003b). Folkscience: Coarse interpretations of a complex reality. *Trends in Cognitive Sciences, 7,* 368–373.

Keil, F. C., Levin, D. T., Richman, B. A., & Gutheil, G. (1999). Mechanism and explanation in the development of biological thought: The case of disease. In D. L. Medin & S. Atran (Eds.), *Folkbiology* (pp. 285–319). Cambridge, MA: MIT Press.

Keil, F. C., Smith, W. C., Simons, D. J., & Levin, D. T. (1998). Two dogmas of conceptual empiricism: Implications for hybrid models of the structure of knowledge. *Cognition, 65*, 103–135.

Kushnir, T., Gopnik, A., Schulz, L., & Danks, D. (2003). Inferring hidden causes. *Proceedings of the 25th annual conference of the Cognitive Science Society.*

Lagnado, D. A., & Sloman, S. (2004). The advantage of timely intervention. *Journal of Experimental Psychology: Learning, Memory, and Cognition, 30*, 856–876.

Lee, F., Hallahan, M., & Herzog, T. (1996). Explaining real-life events: How culture and domain shape attributions. *Personality and Social Psychology Bulletin, 22*, 732–741.

López, A., Atran, S., Coley, J. D., Medin, D. L., & Smith, E. E. (1997). The tree of life: Universal and cultural features of folkbiological taxonomies and inductions. *Cognitive Psychology, 32*, 251–295.

Luria, A. R. (1976). *Cognitive development: Its cultural and social foundations* (M. Lopez-Morillas & L. Solotaroff, trans.; M. Cole, ed.). Cambridge, MA: Harvard University Press.

Lynch, E. B., Coley, J. D., & Medin, D. L. (2000). Tall is typical: Central tendency, ideal dimensions, and graded category structure among tree experts and novices. *Memory & Cognition, 28*, 41–50.

McDonald, J., Samuels, M., & Rispoli, J. (1996). A hypothesis-assessment model of categorical argument strength. *Cognition, 59*, 199–217.

Medin, D. L., & Atran, S. (2004). The native mind: Biological categorization and reasoning in development and across cultures. *Psychological Review, 111*, 960–983.

Medin, D. L., Coley, J. D., Storms, G., & Hayes, B. K. (2003). A relevance theory of induction. *Psychonomic Bulletin & Review, 10*, 517–532.

Medin, D. L., Lynch, E. B., Coley, J. D., & Atran, S. (1997). Categorization and reasoning among tree experts: Do all roads lead to Rome? *Cognitive Psychology, 32*, 49–96.

Medin, D. L., Ross, N. O., Atran, S., Cox, D., Coley, J., Proffitt, J. B., & Blok, S. (2006). Folkbiology of freshwater fish. *Cognition, 99*, 237–273.

Medin, D. L., Ross, N., Atran, S., Burnett, R. C., & Blok, S. V. (2002). Categorization and reasoning in relation to culture and expertise. In B. Ross (Ed.), *The psychology of learning and motivation: Advances in research and theory* (Vol. 41, pp. 1–41). New York: Academic Press.

Medin, D. L., Ross, N. O. & Cox, D. G. (2006). *Culture and resource conflict: Why meanings matter.* New York: Russell Sage Foundation.

Medin, D. L., Unsworth, S. J., & Hirschfeld, L. (2007). Culture, categorization and reasoning. In S. Kitayama & D. Cohen (Eds.), *Handbook of cultural psychology.* New York: Guilford.

Medin, D. L., & Waxman, S. R. (2007). Interpreting asymmetries of projection in children's inductive reasoning. In A. Feeney & E. Heit (Eds.), *Inductive reasoning.* New York: Cambridge University Press.

Miller, J. G. (1984). Culture and the development of everyday social explanation. *Journal of Personality and Social Psychology, 46*, 961–978.

Morris, M. W., & Peng, K. (1994). Culture and cause: American and Chinese attributions for social and physical events. *Journal of Personality and Social Psychology, 67*, 949–971.

Nisbett, R. E. (2003). *The geography of thought: How Asians and Westerners think differently . . . and why.* New York: Free Press.

Nisbett, R. E., & Norenzayan, A. (2002). Culture and cognition. In D. Medin (Ed.), *Stevens' handbook of experimental psychology: Vol. 2. Memory and cognitive processes* (3rd ed.; H. Pashler, editor-in-chief) (pp. 561–597). New York: John Wiley & Sons.

Nisbett, R. E., Peng, K., Choi, I., & Norenzayan, A. (2001). Culture and systems of thought: Holistic versus analytic cognition. *Psychological Review, 108*, 291–310.

Norenzayan, A., Choi, I., & Nisbett, R. E. (2002). Cultural similarities and differences in social inference: Evidence from behavioral predictions and lay theories of behavior. *Personality and Social Psychology Bulletin, 28*, 109–120.

Norenzayan, A., & Heine, S. J. (2005). Psychological universals: What are they and how can we know? *Psychological Bulletin, 131*, 763–784.

Osherson, D. N., Smith, E. E., Wilkie, O., López, A., & Shafir, E. (1990). Category-based induction. *Psychological Review, 97*, 185–200.

Pearl, J. (2000). *Causality: Models, reasoning, and inference.* Cambridge: Cambridge University Press.

Peng, K., & Knowles, E. D. (2003). Culture, education, and the attribution of physical causality. *Personality and Social Psychology Bulletin, 29*, 1272–1284.

Proffitt, J. B., Coley, J. D., & Medin, D. L. (2000). Expertise and category-based induction. *Journal of Experimental Psychology: Learning, Memory and Cognition, 26*, 811–828.

Rehder, B., & Burnett, R. C. (2005). Feature inference and the causal structure of categories. *Cognitive Psychology, 50*, 264–314.

Rehder, B., & Hastie, R. (2001). Causal knowledge and categories: The effects of causal beliefs on categorization, induction, and similarity. *Journal of Experimental Psychology: General, 130*, 323–360.

Rips, L. J. (1975). Inductive judgments about natural categories. *Journal of Verbal Learning and Verbal Behavior, 14*, 665–681.

Rips, L. J. (2001). Necessity and natural categories. *Psychological Bulletin, 127,* 827–852.

Ross, B. H., & Murphy, G. L. (1999). Food for thought. *Cognitive Psychology, 38,* 495–553.

Ross, N., Medin, D., Coley, J. D., & Atran, S. (2003). Cultural and experiential differences in the development of folkbiological induction. *Cognitive Development, 18,* 25–47.

Rozenblit, L., & Keil, F. (2002). The misunderstood limits of folk science: An illusion of explanatory depth. *Cognitive Science, 26,* 521–562.

Salmon, W. (1984). *Scientific explanation and the causal structure of the world.* Princeton, NJ: Princeton University Press.

Scribner, S. (1977). Modes of thinking and ways of speaking: Culture and logic reconsidered. In P. N. Johnson-Laird & P. C. Wason (Eds.), *Thinking: Readings in cognitive science* (pp. 483–500). New York: Cambridge University Press.

Scribner, S., & Cole, M. (1981). *The psychology of literacy.* Cambridge, MA: Harvard University Press.

Shafto, P., & Coley, J. D. (2003). Development of categorization and reasoning in the natural world: Novices to experts, naive similarity to ecological knowledge. *Journal of Experimental Psychology: Learning, Memory, and Cognition, 29,* 641–649.

Shafto, P., Coley, J. D., & Baldwin, D. (2005). *Knowledge-based induction: A matter of availability.* Manuscript submitted for publication.

Sloman, S. A. (1993). Feature-based induction. *Cognitive Psychology, 25,* 231–280.

Sloman, S. A., & Lagnado, D. A. (2005). Do we "do"? *Cognitive Science, 29,* 5–39.

Sober, E. (1988). The principle of the common cause. In J. H. Fetzer (Ed.), *Probability and causality: Essays in honor of Wesley C. Salmon* (pp. 211–228). Dordrecht, Holland: Reidel.

Sperber, D. (1996). *Explaining culture: A naturalistic approach.* Oxford: Blackwell.

Sperber, D., & Wilson, D. (1986). *Relevance: Communication and cognition.* Oxford: Blackwell.

Spirtes, P., Glymour, C., & Scheines, R. (2000). *Causation, prediction, and search* (2nd ed.). Cambridge, MA: MIT Press.

Steyvers, M., Tenenbaum, J. B., Wagenmakers, E.-J., & Blum, B. (2003). Inferring causal networks from observations and interventions. *Cognitive Science, 27,* 453–489.

Tarlowski, A. (2006). If it's an animal it has axons: Experience and culture in preschool children's reasoning about animates. *Cognitive Development, 21,* 249–265.

Tenenbaum, J. B., & Griffiths, T. L. (2003). Theory-based causal inference. In S. Becker, S. Thrun, & K. Obermayer (Eds.), *Advances in Neural Information Processing Systems 15.* Cambridge, MA: MIT Press.

Tenenbaum, J. B., Griffiths, T. L., & Niyogi, S. (2007). Intuitive theories as grammars for causal inference. In A. Gopnik & L. Schulz (Eds.), *Causal learning: Psychology, philosophy, and computation.* New York: Oxford University Press.

Van der Henst, J.-B., Sperber, D., & Politzer, G. (2002). When is a conclusion worth deriving? A relevance-based analysis of indeterminate relational problems. *Thinking & Reasoning, 8,* 1–20.

Waldmann, M. R., & Hagmayer, Y. (2005). Seeing versus doing: Two modes of accessing causal knowledge. *Journal of Experimental Psychology: Learning, Memory, and Cognition, 31,* 216–227.

Waldmann, M. R., & Martignon, L. (1998). A Bayesian network model of causal learning. *Proceedings of the 20th Annual Conference of the Cognitive Science Society.*

Chapter 48: Culture and Systems of Thought: Holistic versus Analytic Cognition

RICHARD E. NISBETT, KAIPING PENG, INCHEOL CHOI, AND ARA NORENZAYAN

The British empiricist philosophers of the 18th and 19th centuries, including Locke, Hume, and Mill, wrote about cognitive processes as if they were the same for all normal adults. This assumption of universality was adopted by mainstream psychology of the 20th century, where it has been predominant from the earliest treatment of cognitive psychology by Piaget, to mid-century learning theorists, to modern cognitive science. The assumption of universality was probably strengthened by the analogy to the computer, which has been implicit and often explicit for the past 30 years (Block, 1995; Shweder, 1991). Brain equals hardware, inferential rules and data processing procedures equal the universal software, and output equals belief and behavior, which can, of course, be radically different given the different inputs possible for different individuals and groups. "Basic" processes such as categorization, learning, inductive and deductive inference, and causal reasoning are generally presumed to be the same among all human groups.

It appears, however, that fairly marked differences in knowledge about and use of inferential rules exist even among educated adults. Work by Nisbett and his colleagues (Larrick, Nisbett, & Morgan, 1993; Nisbett, 1993; Nisbett, Fong, Lehman, & Cheng, 1987; Smith, Langston, & Nisbett, 1992) shows that people can learn statistical, probabilistic, methodological, logical, deontic, cost-benefit, and other quite abstract rule systems and categorization proce-

dures, and that training can affect their reasoning about everyday life events and even their behavior. Significant effects can be obtained not merely by extensive training in formal courses but sometimes even by brief instruction in the laboratory. Given that inferential rules and cognitive processes appear to be malleable even for adults within a given society, it should not be surprising if it turned out to be the case that members of markedly different cultures, socialized from birth into different world views and habits of thought, might differ even more dramatically in their cognitive processes.

In this article, we argue that the considerable social differences that exist among different cultures affect not only their beliefs about specific aspects of the world but also (a) their naive metaphysical[1] systems at a deep level, (b) their tacit epistemologies,[2] and (c) even the nature of their cognitive processes – the ways by which they know the world. More specifically, we put forward the following propositions, which we develop in more detail later.

1. Social organization directs attention to some aspects of the field at the expense of others.

2. What is attended to influences metaphysics, that is, beliefs about the nature of the world and about causality.

3. Metaphysics guides tacit epistemology, that is, beliefs about what it is important

Reproduced with permission from Nisbett, R. E., Peng, K., Choi, I., and Norenzayan, A. (2001) Culture and systems of thought: Holistic versus analytic cognition. *Psychological Review*, 108, 291–310.

to know and how knowledge can be obtained.

4. Epistemology dictates the development and application of some cognitive processes at the expense of others.

5. Social organization and social practices can directly affect the plausibility of metaphysical assumptions, such as whether causality should be regarded as residing in the field versus the object.

6. Social organization and social practices can influence directly the development and use of cognitive processes such as dialectical versus logical ones.

First, we review evidence that we find to be a convincing example of the contention that societies can differ markedly in their systems of thought. This evidence concerns a comparison of the societies, philosophical orientations, and scientific outlooks of two highly sophisticated cultures: those of ancient China and Greece. We summarize the views of many historians, philosophers of science, and ethnographers indicating that the two societies differed in marked ways both socially and cognitively, and that the social and cognitive differences were related. We next present a general proposal concerning the relation between social factors and cognition based on an examination of social life and cognitive procedures in the ancient world, deriving a number of quite specific predictions from that formulation. We then present a review of evidence regarding these predictions that comes mostly from our recent research comparing modern individuals raised in societies influenced by ancient Chinese thought with people raised in societies influenced by ancient Greek thought. This research shows that, to a remarkable extent, the social and cognitive differences that scholars have reported about ancient China and Greece find their counterparts among contemporary peoples. Moreover, these are not mere parameter differences, but in many cases differences that are quantitatively very large and even qualitatively distinct. Finally, we speculate on the origins of differences in systems of thought, sketch an analysis of the factors that might sustain "sociocognitive homeostatic systems" over millennia, and present a consideration of the implications of our findings for claims about cognitive universality and for the traditional distinction between cognitive content and cognitive process.

Ancient Greek and Chinese Society

From roughly the 8th to the 3rd century B.C., many civilizations made great strides in philosophical and moral thought and in scientific and technological endeavors, notably Persia, India, the Middle East, China, and Greece. We will examine the differences between the two civilizations that were most distant from one another and probably influenced one another the least: those of Greece and China. In addition, the influence each of these civilizations has had on the modern world is particularly great. Greek civilization gave rise to European civilization and post-Columbian American civilization, and Chinese civilization gave rise to the civilizations of East Asia, including Japan and Korea, and also greatly influenced Southeast Asia.

The Ancient Greeks and Personal Agency

One of the most remarkable characteristics of the ancient Greeks (Jonians and Athenians in particular) was the location of power in the individual. Ordinary people developed a sense of personal agency that had no counterpart among the other ancient civilizations. Indeed, one definition of happiness for the Greeks was "the exercise of vital powers along lines of excellence in a life affording them scope" (Hamilton, 1930/1973, p. 25). Though the Greeks believed in the influence of the gods, "divine intervention and independent human action" were seen to work together (Knox, 1990, p. 39). The daily lives of the Greeks were imbued with a sense of choice and an absence of social constraint that were unparalleled in the ancient world. "The idea of the Athenian state was a union of individuals free to develop their own powers and live in their own way, obedient only to the laws they passed themselves and could criticize and change at will" (Hamilton, p. 144).

Related to the Greek sense of personal freedom is their tradition of debate, which was already well established at least by the time of Homer in the 8th century (Galtung, 1981; Lloyd, 1990; Nakamura, 1964/1985). Homer emphasizes repeatedly that, next to being a capable warrior, the most important skill for a man to have was that of the debater. Even ordinary people participated in the debate of the marketplace and the political assembly and could challenge even a king (Cromer, 1993, p. 65).

An aspect of Greek civilization that had a great effect on posterity was their sense of curiosity about the world and the presumption that it could be understood by the discovery of rules (Lloyd, 1991; Toulmin & Goodfield, 1961, p. 62). The Greeks speculated about the nature of the objects and events around them and created causal models of them. The construction of these models was done by categorizing objects and events and generating rules about them for the purpose of systematic description, prediction, and explanation. This characterized their advances in, some have said invention of, the fields of physics, astronomy, axiomatic geometry, formal logic, rational philosophy, natural history, history, and ethnography. Whereas many great ancient civilizations, including the earlier Mesopotamian and Egyptian and the later Mayan, made systematic observations in many scientific domains, only the Greeks attempted to model such observations in terms of presumed underlying physical causes (Cromer, 1993; Kane, 2000; Lin, 1936, p. 84; Toulmin & Goodfield, 1961).

The Ancient Chinese and Harmony

The ancient Chinese provide a particularly valuable contrast to the Greeks. The Chinese counterpart to the Greek sense of personal agency was a sense of reciprocal social obligation or collective agency. The Chinese felt that individuals are part of a closely knit collectivity, whether a family or a village, and that the behavior of the individual should be guided by the expectations of the group. The chief moral system of China, Confucianism, was essentially an elaboration of the obligations that obtained between emperor and subject, parent and child, husband and wife, older brother and younger brother, and between friend and friend. Chinese society made the individual feel very much a part of a large, complex, and generally benign social organism in which prescriptive role relations were a guide to ethical conduct (Lin, 1936; Munro, 1985). Individual rights were construed as one's "share" of the rights of the community as a whole. "[R]ole fulfillment in a hierarchical system ... [took] priority over most other goods" (Munro, p. 19).

Such an emphasis on collective agency resulted in the Chinese valuing in-group *harmony*, "as when the occupants of a social group ... perform their functions and do not transgress the boundaries of duty or expectations that accompany those functions" (Munro, 1985, pp. 20–21). Within the social group, any form of confrontation, such as debate, was discouraged. Though there was a time, called the period of

the "hundred schools" of 600–200 B.C., during which debate, among philosophers at least, did occur (Yang, 1988), "[t]here never developed a 'spirit of controversial language' nor a 'tradition of free public debate'" (Becker, 1986, p. 78). "In philosophy, in medicine, and elsewhere there is criticism of other points of view ... [b]ut the Chinese generally conceded far more readily than did the Greeks, that other opinions had something to be said for them" (Lloyd, 1990, p. 550). So far from debate being encouraged in a society with such values, one person could not contradict another without fear of making an enemy (Cromer, 1993, pp. 73–74), and to "be involved in a lawsuit was *ipso facto* ignominious" (Lin, 1936).

Chinese civilization was technologically far advanced beyond that of the Greeks. The Chinese have been credited with the original or independent invention of irrigation systems, ink, porcelain, the magnetic compass, stirrups, the wheelbarrow, deep drilling, the Pascal triangle, pound-locks on canals, fore-and-aft sailing, watertight compartments, the stempost rudder, the paddle-wheel boat, quantitative cartography, immunization techniques, astronomical observations of novae, seismographs, and acoustics (Logan, 1986, p. 51). Many of these technological achievements were in place at a time when the Greeks had none.

But most experts hold that these advances should not be regarded as the result of scientific theory and investigation (Cromer, 1993; Kane, 2000; Logan, 1986). Instead, they are reflective of a Chinese genius for practicality (Nakamura, 1964/1985, p. 189). "In Confucianism there was no thought of *knowing* that did not entail some consequence for action" (Munro, 1969, p. 55; see also On, 1996). The Chinese did not make formal models of the natural world but rather proceeded by intuition and empiricism. Indeed, it has been maintained that the Chinese never developed a concept corresponding to the laws of nature for the sufficient reason that they did not have a concept of "nature" as distinct from human or spiritual entities (Fung, 1983, p. 55; Lloyd, 1991; Logan, 1986, p. 50; Munro, 1969; Zhou, 1990).

Chinese and Greek Science, Mathematics, and Philosophy

The social–psychological aspects of ancient Greek and Chinese life had correspondences in the systems of thought of the two cultures. Their metaphysical beliefs were reflections of their social existences. And their tacit epistemologies in turn seem to have reflected their different metaphysical beliefs. These resulted in very great differences between Greece and China in their approaches to scientific, mathematical, and philosophical questions.

The cognitive differences between ancient Chinese and Greeks can be loosely grouped under the heading of holistic versus analytic thought (Nisbett, 1998; Peng & Nisbett, 1999). We define holistic thought as involving an orientation to the context or field as a whole, including attention to relationships between a focal object and the field, and a preference for explaining and predicting events on the basis of such relationships. Holistic approaches rely on experience-based knowledge rather than on abstract logic and are dialectical, meaning that there is an emphasis on change, a recognition of contradiction and of the need for multiple perspectives, and a search for the "Middle Way" between opposing propositions. We define analytic thought as involving detachment of the object from its context, a tendency to focus on attributes of the object to assign it to categories, and a preference for using rules about the categories to explain and predict the object's behavior. Inferences rest in part on the practice of decontextualizing structure from content, the use of formal logic, and avoidance of contradiction.

The distinction between holistic and analytic thought rests on a long tradition of theory about reasoning beginning with James and Piaget and continuing to the present. Holistic thought is associative, and its computations reflect similarity and contiguity. Analytic thought recruits symbolic representational systems, and its computations reflect rule structure. Sloman (1996) has recently reviewed evidence for this distinction in the cognitive realm. Witkin and his colleagues (Witkin, Dyk, Faterson, Goodenough, & Karp, 1974; Witkin et al., 1954) have made a similar distinction in the perceptual realm between "field dependence" and "field independence." Our definition encompasses both reasoning aspects and perceptual aspects of the distinction as well as the belief systems that underlie those differences.

Historians and philosophers of science have identified a number of important differences between the Greeks and the Chinese that fit under the definitions above.

CONTINUITY VERSUS DISCRETENESS

A fundamental intellectual difference between the Chinese and the Greeks was that

the Chinese held the "view that the world is a collection of overlapping and interpenetrating stuffs or substances.... [This contrasts] with the traditional Platonic philosophical picture of objects which are understood as individuals or particulars which instantiate or 'have' properties" (Hansen, 1983, p. 30) that are themselves universals (e.g., "whiteness," "hardness"). This profound difference in metaphysics had many ramifications. Most fundamentally, the Greeks, unlike the Chinese, were inclined to see the world as a collection of discrete objects which could be categorized by reference to some subset of universal properties that characterized the object. Thus although the Greeks debated whether matter was best understood as waves or particles, the Chinese seem never to have had any doubt about the continuous nature of matter (Needham, 1962, p. 1).

FIELD VERSUS OBJECT

Since the Chinese were oriented toward continuities and relationships, the individual object was "not a primary conceptual starting point" (Moser, 1996, p. 31). Instead, "parts exist only within wholes, to which they have inseparable relations" (Munro, 1985, p. 17). The Greeks, in contrast, were inclined to focus primarily on the central object and its attributes (Hansen, 1983, p. 31). This tendency likely contributed to the Greeks' lack of understanding of the fundamental nature of causality in the physical domain. Aristotle explained a stone's falling through the air as being due to the stone having the property of "gravity" and explained a piece of wood's floating on the surface of water as being due to the wood having the property of "levity." The Chinese, in contrast, recognized that all events are due to the operation of a field of forces. They had knowledge of magnetism and acoustic resonance, for example, and knew the correct explanation for the behavior of the tides (Needham, 1962, p. 60).

RELATIONSHIPS AND SIMILARITIES VERSUS CATEGORIES AND RULES

A consequence of their assumptions about continuity and the importance of the field is that the Chinese were concerned with relationships among objects and events (Zhang, 1985). In contrast, the Greeks were more inclined to focus on the categories and rules that would help them to understand the behavior of the object independent of its context (Nakamura, 1964/1985, pp. 185–186). The Chinese were convinced of the fundamental relatedness of all things and the consequent alteration of objects and events by the context in which they were located. It is only the whole that exists; and the parts are linked relationally, like "the ropes in a net" (Munro, 1985). Thus any attempt to categorize objects with precision would not have seemed a terribly important epistemic goal (Chan, 1967; Logan, 1986, p. 122; Moser, 1996, p. 116).[3]

The relationship view versus the rule stance is well illustrated by the difference between the holistic approach to medicine characteristic of the Chinese and the effort to find effective rules and treatment principles in the West. Surgery was common in the West from a very early period because the idea that some part of the body could be malfunctioning was a natural one to the analytic mind. But the idea of surgery was "heretical to ancient Chinese medical tradition, which taught that good health depended on the balance and flow of natural forces throughout the body" (Hadingham, 1994, p. 77).

DIALECTICS VERSUS FOUNDATIONAL PRINCIPLES AND LOGIC

The Chinese seem not to have been motivated to seek first principles underlying their mathematical procedures or scientific assumptions, and, except for the brief "Mohist" period from the end of the 4th to the end of the 3rd century B.C., "the Chinese did not develop any formal systems of logic [or] anything like ... an Aristotelian syllogism" (Liu, 1974). Indeed, there was an absence "not only of formal logical systems, but indeed of a principle of contradiction" (Becker, 1986, p. 83). It is noteworthy that the Indians did have a strong logical tradition, but the Chinese translations of their texts were full of errors and misunderstandings (Becker, p. 84). It has been argued that the lack of interest in logic accounts for why, although Chinese advances in algebra and arithmetic were substantial, the Chinese made little progress in geometry where proofs rely on formal logic, especially the notion of contradiction (Lloyd, 1990, p. 119; Logan, 1986, p. 48; Needham, 1962, p. 1). (Algebra did not become deductive until the 12th century; Cromer, 1993, p. 89.)

In place of logic, the Chinese developed a dialectic (Lloyd, 1990, p. 119), which involves reconciling, transcending, or even accepting apparent contradictions. In the Chinese intellectual tradition, there is no necessary incompatibility between the belief that A and not A both have merit. Indeed, in the spirit of the Tao or yin-yang principle, A can actually imply that not A is also the case – the opposite of a state of

affairs can exist simultaneously with the state of affairs itself (Chang, 1939; Mao, 1937/1962). It is this belief that lies behind much of Chinese thought designed to find the "Middle Way" between extremes – accepting that two parties to a quarrel can both have right on their side or that two opposing propositions can both contain some truth. The Chinese dialectic includes notions resembling the Hegelian dialectic of thesis–antithesis–synthesis and finds its counterpart in modern "post-formal operations" in the Piagetian tradition – for example, understanding of part-whole relations, reciprocal relations, contextual relativism, and self-modifying systems (Baltes & Staudinger, 1993; Basseches, 1984; Riegel, 1973).

EXPERIENCE-BASED KNOWLEDGE VERSUS ABSTRACT ANALYSIS

"The Chinese ... sought intuitive instantaneous understanding through direct perception" (Nakamura, 1964/1985, p. 171). This resulted in a focus on particular instances and concrete cases in Chinese thought (Fung, 1983; Lloyd, 1990; Nakamura, p. 171). Many Greeks favored the epistemology of logic and abstract principles, and many Greek philosophers, especially Plato and his followers, actually viewed concrete perception and direct experiential knowledge as unreliable and incomplete at best, and downright misleading at worst. Thus they were prepared to reject the evidence of the senses when it conflicted with reason (Lloyd, p. 118).

Ironically, important as the Greek discovery of formal logic was for the development of science, it also impeded it in many ways. After the 6th-century Ionian period, the empirical tradition in Greek science was greatly weakened. It was countered by the conviction on the part of many philosophers that it ought to be possible to understand things through reason alone, without recourse to the senses (Logan, 1986, pp. 114–115). Importantly, there never developed in Greece the critical concept of zero, which is needed for an Arabic-style place number system as well as for algebra. Zero was rejected as an impossibility on the grounds that nonbeing is logically self-contradictory (Logan, p. 115)! Eventual Western understanding of zero, infinity, and infinitesimals required a detour to the East.

Sociocognitive Systems

It is possible to derive the intellectual differences between the ancient Greek and Chinese approaches to science and philosophy – their differing metaphysics and epistemology – from their differing social psychological attributes. And, more generally, it is possible to build a psychological theory from the historical evidence. We now return to the points sketched in the introduction concerning the links from social organization to cognitive process. We believe that social organization affects cognitive processes in two basic ways: indirectly by focusing attention on different parts of the environment and directly by making some kinds of social communication patterns more acceptable than others.

From Attention to Cognitive Processes

SOCIAL ORGANIZATION, ATTENTION, AND NAIVE METAPHYSICS

If one lives in a complex social world with many role relations, one's attention is likely to be directed outside oneself and toward the social field. The Chinese habit of attending to the social environment might have carried over to the environment in general, allowing, for example, for the discovery of the relevance of the field in understanding physical events. As Markus and Kitayama (1991) put it, "If one perceives oneself as embedded within a larger context of which one is an interdependent part, it is likely that other objects or events will be perceived in a similar way" (p. 246). Attention to the field should foster attempts to understand relations among objects and events in the field and should encourage explanation of events in terms of the relationship between the object and the field. Similarly, the world might naturally seem continuous and interpenetrating to people who view themselves as part of a larger whole and who are motivated to maintain harmony within it.

On the other hand, if one lives in a world with fewer and less significant social relations and role constraints, it may be possible to attend primarily to the object and one's goals with respect to it. The object's properties may thus be salient, and one may be encouraged to use those properties to develop categories and rules that presumably govern the object's behavior. The belief that one knows the rules governing the object's behavior might encourage exclusive focus on the object for explanation and might encourage the belief that the world is a place that is controllable through one's own actions. Moreover, the world is likely to be perceived as discrete and discontinuous by those who regard themselves as fully distinct and autonomous entities having limited connections to others and possessing the ability to act autonomously.

NAIVE METAPHYSICS AND TACIT EPISTEMOLOGY

Beliefs about the nature of the world can be expected to influence tacit epistemologies or beliefs about how to get knowledge. If the world is a place where relations among objects and events are crucial in determining outcomes, then it will seem important to be able to see all the important elements in the field, to see relations among objects, and to see the relation between the parts and the whole. If the world is a place where the behavior of objects is governed by rules and the categories to which they apply, then it is crucial to be able to isolate the object from its context, to infer category membership of the object from its properties, and to infer how rules apply to categories.

TACIT EPISTEMOLOGY AND COGNITIVE PROCESSES

If it seems important to see relations in the field, then perceptual habits such as deep processing of the environment and covariation-detection skills could be expected to develop as well as cognitive habits such as explaining events with reference to the field. If it is important to find out the object's properties and the categories to which it belongs, then perceptual habits such as decontextualization of the object from the field and cognitive habits such as explaining the object's behavior in terms of the categories and rules that apply to it could be expected to develop. Such differential cognitive habits would, of course, be expected to become largely automatic and unconscious, just as the underlying naive epistemology would be expected to be largely beyond the reach of conscious awareness.

From Social Organization to Cognitive Processes

Social organization can influence cognitive processes without mediation by metaphysical beliefs. Dialectics and logic can both be seen as cognitive tools developed to deal with social conflict. People whose social existence is based on harmony would not be expected to develop a tradition of confrontation or debate. On the contrary, their intellectual goals when confronted with a contradiction in views might be oriented toward resolving the contradiction, transcending it, or finding a "Middle Way" – in short, to exercise a dialectical approach. In contrast, people who are free to contend with their fellows

might be expected to develop rules for the conduct of debate, including the principle of non-
contradiction and formal logic (Becker, 1986;
Cromer, 1993; Lloyd, 1990, pp. 8–9). Several
commentators have maintained that the Greeks
brought to the pursuit of science essentially the
same principles of rhetoric that governed debate
in the marketplace.

> Science, in this view, is an extension of
> rhetoric. It was invented in Greece, and only
> in Greece, because the Greek institution
> of the public assembly attached great pres-
> tige to debating skill.... A geometric proof
> is ... the ultimate rhetorical form. (Cromer,
> 1993, p. 144)

The exact psychological processes by which
social organization influences metaphysical
beliefs, or metaphysical beliefs affect epistemology, or epistemology governs the development of
particular processes cannot, of course, be known
at this time. This is true in part because all of
these elements are in homeostatic balance, and
there is reciprocal influence among all of them.
Despite this, it is fruitful to identify the kinds
of social practices that tend to be found in conjunction with particular cognitive processes, and
we will describe some important ones later. We
will also speculate about the ways that the social
practices might operate to sustain the cognitive
processes.

Contemporary Cognitive Differences?

If the differences in the nature of social life
between East and West have been maintained,
and if the original differences in cognitive orientations were due to the social psychological ones,
then cognitive differences might also be found
today and not just among the intelligentsia.

There is substantial evidence that the
social psychological differences characteristic of
ancient China and Greece do in fact persist.
China and other East Asian societies remain collectivist and oriented toward the group, whereas
America and other European-influenced societies are more individualist in orientation.[4] For
reviews and general treatments of these differences, see Bond (1996), Fiske, Kitayama,
Markus, and Nisbett (1998), Hofstede (1980),
Hsu (1981), Markus and Kitayama (1991),
Nakamura (1964/1985), and Triandis (1972,
1995). As the psychologist L.-H. Chiu (1972)
put it:

> Chinese are situation-centered. They are
> obliged to be sensitive to their environ-
> ment. Americans are individual-centered.
> They expect their environment to be sensi-
> tive to them. Thus, Chinese tend to assume
> a passive attitude while Americans tend to
> possess an active and conquering attitude in
> dealing with their environment. (p. 236)

> [The American] orientation may inhibit
> the development of a tendency to perceive
> objects in the environmental context in terms
> of relationships or interdependence. On the
> other hand, the Chinese child learns very
> early to view the world as based on a net-
> work of relationships; he is *socio-oriented*, or
> *situation-centered*. (p. 241)

If the social differences have persisted, and
if we are correct in believing that social factors
influence metaphysics, epistemology, and ultimately cognitive processes, then several interrelated predictions can be made concerning cognitive differences between contemporary societies
that have been influenced by China and those
that have been influenced by Greece.

ATTENTION

We believe that attention to the social environment is what underlay ancient Chinese attention to the field in general and accounts in part
for metaphysical beliefs such as their recognition of the principle of action at a distance.
If this notion is correct, we might find that
contemporary Easterners and Westerners attend
to different aspects of the environment. East
Asians would be expected to attend more to
the field than European Americans, who would
be expected to attend more to a salient target
object. Process implications follow: East Asians
should be more accurate at covariation detection
than Americans are, that is, the perception of
relationships within the field. East Asians should
also be more field dependent (Witkin, Dyk et al.,
1974); that is, they should find it more difficult
than Americans to isolate and analyze an object
while ignoring the field in which it is embedded.

CONTROL

If a belief in personal agency underlay Greek
curiosity and the invention of science, then
Americans might be expected to perceive more
control in a given situation than do East Asians
and to benefit more from being given control.
They might also be more subject to the illusion of control (Langer, 1975), that is, a greater

expectation of success when the self is involved in interaction with the object – even when that interaction could not logically have an effect on the outcome.

EXPLANATION

If East Asians continue to have a metaphysical commitment to the notion that the whole context is relevant for a causal assessment of outcomes, we should find that their explanations of events invoke situational factors more frequently than do those of Americans. East Asians would be expected to explain events, both social and physical, with respect to the field – that is, contexts and situations – more than Americans would, and Americans would be expected to explain events more with respect to a target object and its properties. Thus Americans would be expected to be more prone to the fundamental attribution error – the tendency to attribute behavior to dispositions of the person and to slight the role of situations and contexts (Ross, 1977).

PREDICTION AND "POSTDICTION"

We are proposing that East Asians have always lived in a complex world in which many relevant factors are important to a consideration of outcomes. Thus their predictions about events might cast a wider net among potential causal candidates. They might also be expected to be less surprised by any given outcome because of their ready ability to find some explanation for it in the complex of potentially relevant factors. If explanations come to mind very easily for Asians, we might find that they are more susceptible to hindsight bias, the tendency to regard events as having been inevitable in retrospect (Fischhoff, 1975).

RELATIONSHIPS AND SIMILARITIES VERSUS RULES AND CATEGORIES

If Easterners are oriented toward the field, we would expect that they would organize their worlds in terms of relationships among events in the environment. More concretely, East Asians would be expected to group objects and events on the basis of functional relationships and part–whole relationships; for example, "A is a part of B." Americans, in contrast, would be expected to group objects more on the basis of category membership; for example, "A and B are both Xs." Other predictions include the expectations that Americans might learn rule-based categories more readily than East Asians do and

that Americans might rely more on categories for purposes of deduction and induction.

LOGIC VERSUS EXPERIENTIAL KNOWLEDGE

If the scant role played by logic in the history of East Asian mathematics, science, and philosophy has resonance in the thought processes of ordinary people today, and if the sympathy for formal approaches remains in the West, East Asians might be expected to rely more on prior beliefs and experience-based strategies when evaluating the convincingness of formal arguments than do Americans. We might also find that East Asians would be heavily influenced by prior beliefs in judging the soundness of formal arguments. Americans should be more capable of ignoring prior beliefs and setting aside experience in favor of reasoning based on logical rules.

DIALECTICS VERSUS THE LAW OF NONCONTRADICTION

If harmony remains the watchword in social relations for East Asians, and if social needs influence intellectual stances, East Asians would be expected to seek compromise solutions to problems, to prefer arguments based on principles of holism and continuity, and to try to reconcile or transcend seeming contradictions. If the debater's concern about contradiction continues to affect Western approaches to problems, Americans should be more inclined to reject one or both of two propositions that could be construed as contradicting one another.

As we will see, there is support for each of these hypotheses. In our review, we will not provide details about samples of participants in particular studies. Suffice it to say that we find supportive evidence whether the East Asians studied are ethnic Chinese, Koreans, or Japanese and whether they are living in their own countries or living as foreign students at U.S. universities and whether materials for East Asians are in English or translated into their native languages. Though most of the participants in research to date are students, there is also supportive evidence for nonstudents. It is entirely possible, of course, that there are significant differences among the various East Asian populations with respect to some of the issues we discuss. Certainly there are substantial social and cultural differences, some of which might plausibly affect cognitive processes. It should also be noted that the great majority of people of European culture who have been studied are Americans, and North Americans may well differ more from East Asians than do Europeans or Latin Americans.

Attention and Control

Work by Meyer and Kieras and their colleagues (Meyer, 1995; Meyer & Kieras, 1997a, 1997b, 1999) suggests that allocation of attention is highly malleable and subject to learned strategic adjustments such that perceptual "bottlenecks" can be ameliorated. Work by Rogoff and her colleagues (Chavajay & Rogoff, 2000; Rogoff, Mistry, Göncü, & Mosier, 1993) indicates that people in some cultures attend to a much wider range of events simultaneously than do people in other cultures. Thus East Asians might be capable of attending to both the object and the field, and to a wider range of objects in the field, than are Americans. We might also expect that, if Westerners attend to the object more, and if they believe that they understand the rules influencing the object's behavior, they might have a greater belief in the controllability of the object than is characteristic of Asians. Several implications follow from these considerations: (a) Easterners should see wholes where Westerners see parts; (b) Easterners should more easily see relationships among elements in the field but (c) find it more difficult to differentiate an object when it is embedded in the field; and (d) Westerners' perceptions and behavior should be more influenced by the belief that they have control over the object or environment.

HOLISTIC VERSUS ANALYTIC
RORSCHACH RESPONSES

In an early study by Abel and Hsu (1949), Rorschach cards were presented to European Americans and Chinese Americans. The investigators found that their Chinese American participants were more likely than their European American counterparts to give so-called "whole-card" responses, in which all aspects of the card, or its Gestalt as a whole, was the basis of the response. Their European American participants were more likely to give "part" responses, in which only a single aspect of the card was the basis of the response.

ATTENTION TO THE FIELD

Masuda and Nisbett (2001) presented realistic animated scenes of fish and other underwater objects to Japanese and Americans and asked them to report what they had seen. The first statement by American participants usually referred to the focal fish ("there was what looked like a trout swimming to the right"), whereas the first statement by Japanese participants usually referred to background elements ("there was a lake or pond"). Although Americans and Japanese were equally likely to mention details about the focal fish, Japanese participants made about 70% more statements about background aspects of the environment. In addition, Japanese participants made about twice as many statements concerning relations involving inanimate aspects of the environment ("the big fish swam past the gray seaweed"). In a subsequent recognition task, Japanese performance was harmed by showing the focal fish with the wrong background, indicating that the perception of the object had been "bound" (Chalfonte & Johnson, 1996) to the field in which it had appeared. In contrast, American recognition of the object was unaffected by the wrong background.

A similar "binding" result was obtained by Hedden and his colleagues (Hedden et al., 2000; Park, Nisbett, & Hedden, 1999). They asked their Chinese and American participants to look at a series of cards having a word printed either on a background of social stimuli (e.g., people at a market) or on no background. The words were unrelated to the pictures. Then participants were asked to recall as many words as they could. Chinese, but not Americans, recalled words better if they had been presented on the background, indicating that recall of the background served as a retrieval cue for the word for them.

DETECTION OF COVARIATION

Ji, Peng, and Nisbett (2000) examined ability to detect covariation among environmental stimuli. Chinese and American participants were asked to judge the degree of association between arbitrary figures. On the left side of a computer screen, one of the two arbitrary figures was shown – for example, a schematic medal or a schematic light bulb. Immediately following that, on the right of the screen, one of another two figures was shown – for example, either a pointing finger or a schematic coin. Actual covariation between figures on the left and those on the right ranged from the equivalent of a correlation of .00 to one of .60. Chinese participants reported a greater degree of covariation than did American participants and were more confident about their covariation judgments. Their confidence judgments were also better calibrated with actual covariation. In addition, as Yates and Curley (1996) found, American participants showed a strong primacy effect, making predictions about future covariations that were much more influenced by the first pairings they had seen than by the overall degree of covariation to which they had been exposed. Chinese participants, in contrast, showed no primacy effect at all, making predictions about future covariation that were based on the overall covariation they had actually seen.

FIELD DEPENDENCE

Because of their habit of decontextualization and analysis, Americans should find it easier to separate an object from the field in which it is embedded than should East Asians. To examine this possibility, Ji and her colleagues (2000) examined the performance of East Asians and Americans (matched for SAT math score) on the Rod and Frame Test of Witkin and his colleagues (Witkin et al., 1954). In this task, the participant looks into a rectangular box framing a rod that sits inside it. The task is to report when the rod appears to be vertical. Field dependence is indicated by the degree to which judgments about the position of the rod are influenced by the position of the frame. Ji and colleagues found that East Asian participants made more errors on the test than did American participants. East Asian participants were also less confident about the accuracy of their performance than were American participants.[5]

(ILLUSION OF) CONTROL

It seems likely that if Americans believe they have control over events, they might pay more attention to them. Moreover, control is sufficiently important that people often fail to distinguish between objectively controllable events and uncontrollable ones. This "illusion of control" was defined by Langer (1975) as being an expectancy of personal success higher than the objective probability would warrant. The illusion of control can actually result in improvement of some cognitive functions for Americans. For example, participants were found to perform better on routine tasks when they believed mistakenly that they could control a loud noise that occurred periodically during the tasks (Glass & Singer, 1973). Some cross-cultural work suggests that East Asians may not be so susceptible to this illusion. Yamagushi, Gelfand, Miguno, and

Zemba (1997) found that American males were more optimistic in a condition in which they had an illusion of personal control over the environment, whereas American females and Japanese of both genders were not.

As these considerations would suggest, both the covariation detection findings and the field dependence findings just discussed were affected by manipulations intended to give participants a sense of control. In one condition of the covariation-detection task, participants were allowed to push a button to control which stimulus was presented on the left, and they could also control the intertrial interval. Whereas this manipulation could have no effect on the degree of covariation, Americans who were given "control" in this fashion tended to see more covariation and express more confidence in their judgments about covariation, whereas Chinese participants showed the opposite tendencies. Moreover, control actually impaired the calibration of Chinese judgments, whereas this was not true for Americans. Similarly, in the Rod and Frame task, when participants were allowed to control the movement of the rod, the accuracy of American males improved whereas that of the other groups did not. Finally, the confidence of both American males and American females was greater when they had control over the rod, and this was not true for East Asians of either gender.

Thus the attention of East Asians appears to be directed more toward the field as a whole and that of Americans more toward the object. East Asians found it easier to see relationships in the environment but found more difficulty in separating object from field. In addition, Americans and East Asians were affected quite differently by control or the illusion of it: Americans' performance improved and their confidence increased with control, whereas that of East Asians did not.

Explanation and Prediction

It seems reasonable to assume that people attribute causality to the events they attend to. If Westerners attend to the object, we would expect them to attribute causality to the object. If East Asians attend to the field and the object's relations with the field, it seems likely that they would be more inclined to attribute causality to context and situations. Each of these expectations is supported by a substantial amount of evidence.

Dispositions Versus Contexts in Explanation

CAUSAL ATTRIBUTION AND PREDICTION

One of the best established findings in cognitive social psychology concerns the so-called "correspondence bias" (Gilbert & Malone, 1995) or "fundamental attribution error" (FAE; Ross, 1977) – the tendency to see behavior as a product of the actor's dispositions and to ignore important situational determinants of the behavior. If it is really the case that East Asians are more oriented toward contextual factors than are European Americans, then we might expect that they would be less subject to the FAE. I. Choi, Nisbett, and Norenzayan (1999; Norenzayan, Choi, & Nisbett, 1999) have recently reviewed research supporting this contention.

Work by Miller (1984) initially suggested that the FAE might indeed be more characteristic of Western culture than of other cultures. She found that whereas Americans explained another person's behavior predominantly in terms of traits, (e.g., recklessness or kindness), Hindu Indians explained comparable behaviors in terms of social roles, obligations, the physical environment, and other contextual factors. A similar demonstration by Morris and Peng (Morris, Nisbett, & Peng, 1995; Morris & Peng, 1994) showed that causal explanations by Americans of events such as mass murders focused almost wholly on the presumed mental instability and other negative dispositions of the murderers, whereas accounts by Chinese of the same events speculated on situational, contextual, and even societal factors that might have been at work. Lee, Hallahan, and Herzog (1996) found that sports editorial writers in Hong Kong focused on contextual explanations of sports events, whereas American sports writers were more likely to prefer explanations involving the dispositions of individual team members. Norenzayan, Choi, and Nisbett (2001) found that Korean participants were more responsive to contextual factors when making predictions about how people in general would be expected to behave in a given situation and, much more than did American subjects, made use of their beliefs about situational power when making predictions about the behavior of a particular individual. Cha and Nam (1985) also found Koreans to make far more use of situationally relevant information when making causal attributions than Americans did.

Importantly, Norenzayan et al. (2001) found that Koreans and Americans were able to articulate metatheories of behavior that accorded with their explanations and predictions. Koreans endorsed situational and interactional theories more than did Americans. The East Asian focus on the field and the American focus on the object can be apparent even when the East Asian attributions are dispositional in nature. Menon, Morris, Chiu, and Hong (1999) have found that East Asian dispositional explanations of events (e.g., scandals in organizations) were more likely than those of Americans to refer to *group* dispositions.

The different forms of preferred explanation apparently extend beyond social events. Morris and Peng (1994) and Hong, Chiu, and Kung (1997) showed participants cartoon displays of fish moving in relation to one another in various ways. Chinese participants were more likely to see the behavior of the individual fish as being produced by external factors than Americans were, and American participants were more inclined to see the behavior as being produced by internal ones. Peng and Nisbett (2000) have shown that the physical theories of contemporary Chinese and Americans reflect those of their respective scientific predecessors two-and-a-half millennia ago. For ambiguous physical events involving phenomena that appeared to be hydrodynamic, aerodynamic, or magnetic, Chinese were more likely to refer to the field when giving explanations (e.g., "the ball is more buoyant than the water") than Americans were. (For less ambiguous, lever and "billiard ball" events, the explanations of Americans and Chinese were almost identical.) Thus the attributional differences probably should not be regarded as mere belief differences about local aspects of the world, but rather as deep metaphysical differences not limited to rules about particular domains specifically taught by the culture.

ATTITUDE ATTRIBUTION PARADIGM

One of the first experimental demonstrations of the fundamental attribution error was by Jones and Harris (1967). Participants read an essay, either supporting or opposing some position on an important social question of the day, that allegedly had been written by another student. It was made clear to participants in a "No Choice" condition that the target had no choice about which side to take in the essay. For example, the target had been required to write an essay in favor of Castro's Cuba for a political science exam. Although normatively this information might be expected to eliminate any assumption that the essay reflected anything about the actual beliefs of the target, participants who read the "Pro" essay reported believing that its writer was probably much more in favor of the question than did participants who read the "Con" essay.

I. Choi and Nisbett (I. Choi, 1998; I. Choi & Nisbett, 1998) duplicated the basic conditions of the Jones and Harris study and added a condition in which, before making judgments about the target's attitude, participants were required to write an essay themselves and allowed no choice about which side to take. It was made clear to participants that the target had been through the same procedure they themselves had been. The American participants in this condition made inferences about the target's attitude that were as strong as those made by participants in the standard "No Choice" condition. Korean participants, in contrast, made much less extreme inferences than did Korean participants in the standard "No Choice" condition. Thus Korean participants, presumably by virtue of seeing the role that the situation played in their own behavior, recognized its power and made attributions about others accordingly. Similar sensitivity to situational constraints in attitude attribution was obtained with Japanese participants by Masuda and Kitayama (Kitayama & Masuda, 1997; Masuda, 1996).

Holistic Prediction and Postdiction

Attention to the field would appear to have clear advantages for explanation of events, inasmuch as it allows for avoidance of the fundamental attribution error. But attention to a broad range of factors might mean that any event can be readily explained – perhaps too readily explained. If a host of factors is attended to, and if naive metaphysics and tacit epistemology support the view that multiple, interactive factors are usually operative in a given outcome, then any outcome may seem to be understandable, even inevitable, after the fact. And indeed, I. Choi, Dalal, and Kim-Prieto (2000) have shown that Koreans regard a larger number of factors as potentially relevant to explaining a given event. They gave European American, Asian American, and Korean participants a detective story and listed a large number of facts. Participants were asked to indicate which of the facts were irrelevant to solving the mystery. Koreans reported believing that far fewer facts were irrelevant than did European Americans. Asian Americans were intermediate between the other two groups.

HINDSIGHT BIAS

An advantage of the more simplistic, rule-based stance of the Westerner may be that surprise is a frequent event. Post hoc explanations may be relatively difficult to generate, and epistemic curiosity may be piqued. The curiosity, in turn, may provoke a search for new, possibly superior models to explain events. In contrast, if Eastern theories about the world are less focused, and a wide range of factors are presumed to be potentially relevant to any given outcome, it may be harder to recognize that a particular outcome could not have been predicted. Hindsight bias (Fischhoff, 1975), or the tendency to assume that one knew all along that a given outcome was likely, might therefore be greater for Easterners.

These notions were tested in a series of experiments by I. Choi and Nisbett (I. Choi, 1998; I. Choi & Nisbett, 2000). One study presented a scenario based on the "Good Samaritan" experiment of Darley and Batson (1973). Participants were told about one particular young seminary student, who, they were assured, was a very kind and religious person. He was headed across campus to deliver a sermon and along the way he encountered a man lying in a doorway asking for help. Participants were also told that the seminarian was late to deliver his sermon. In Condition A, where participants did not know what the target had done, they were asked what they thought was the probability that the target would help and how surprised they would be if they were to find out that he had not helped. Both Koreans and Americans reported about an 80% probability that the target would help and indicated they would be quite surprised if he did not. In Condition B, participants were told the target had helped the victim, and in Condition C they were told he had not helped the victim. Participants in these conditions were asked what they believed they *would* have regarded as the probability that the target would have helped – if, in fact, they had not been told what he did – and also how surprised they were by his actual behavior. Again, both Koreans and Americans in Condition B indicated they would have thought the probability of helping was about 80%, and both groups reported no surprise that he did help. Americans in Condition C, where the target unexpectedly did not help the victim, also reported that they would have thought the probability was about 80% that the target would have helped and reported a great deal of surprise that he did not do so. In contrast, Koreans in Condition C reported that they would have thought the probability was only about 50% that the target would have helped and reported little surprise that he did not. Thus Americans experienced surprise where Koreans did not, and Koreans showed a very pronounced hindsight bias, indicating that they thought they knew something all along which in fact they did not.

INFLUENCE OF ALTERNATIVE POSSIBILITIES ON SURPRISE AT OUTCOMES

An additional study by I. Choi and Nisbett (2000) indicates that Easterners are not as surprised by unanticipated outcomes as Americans are. We would expect Westerners to regard a scientific finding as more likely if they had previously been presented only with a theory that would lead them to expect that finding than if they had also been presented in addition with a theory that would lead them to expect the opposite. On the other hand, if Koreans are in the habit of regarding outcomes as inevitable, then we would not necessarily expect them to be much more surprised when presented with two opposing theories than when presented only with the theory predicting the actual outcome. And, indeed, this is what was found. Americans reported being more surprised when presented with two strongly competing hypotheses, whereas Koreans were no more surprised when presented with two opposing hypotheses than when presented with only one.

SURPRISE WHEN AN "OUTCOME" IS FOUND NOT TO BE TRUE

In a final study, I. Choi and Nisbett (2000) showed that Koreans expressed little surprise even when an outcome literally contradicted another outcome they had just read about. Participants read either that scientific research had shown that more-optimistic people have better mental health or that more-realistic people do. Participants rated how surprising they found this result to be. Then, under a ruse, the experimenter "discovered" that the materials they had read were mistaken, due to a printing error, and that it was the opposite hypothesis that had been supported. Apologetically, he asked the participants if they would fill out the materials again. Americans reported substantial surprise if they read that it was the less plausible, "realism" hypothesis that, after all, was the correct one. Koreans reported much less surprise than Americans.[6]

The results support the view that East Asians have complicated but underspecified theories about the world that leave them insufficiently surprised by outcomes that differ from those that are anticipated. Thus, we would maintain that the same cognitive predispositions that make Asians less prone to the fundamental attribution error leave them prey to the hindsight bias and may also reduce their epistemic curiosity.

Relationships and Similarities Versus Rules and Categories

If Westerners attribute causality primarily to objects, it seems likely that they do so on the basis of rules that they presume to govern the behavior of objects. Rules, in turn, are of value to the extent that they apply over a large number and specifiable type of objects, that is, to a category. Thus rules and categories would be expected to be a major basis of organizing events for Westerners. If Easterners attribute causality primarily to the field, then it is relationships between the object and the field, and relationships among events in the field, that might serve as the basis of organization. There is a good deal of evidence supporting these expectations.

RELATIONSHIPS VERSUS CATEGORIES AS THE BASIS FOR GROUPING

Chiu (1972) gave items consisting of three pictures of human, vehicle, furniture, tool, or food categories to American and Chinese children. Children were asked "to choose any two of the three objects in a set which were alike or went together and to state the reason for the choice" (p. 237). The dominant style of the Chinese children was "relational-contextual." For example, shown a picture of a man, a woman, and a child, the Chinese children were likely to group the woman and child together because "the mother takes care of the baby." In contrast, American children were much more likely to group objects on the basis of category membership or shared features, for example, to group the man and the woman because "they are both adults."

RELATIONSHIPS VERSUS CATEGORIES AS THE BASIS FOR JUDGMENTS OF ASSOCIATION

Ji and Nisbett (Ji, 2001; Ji & Nisbett, 2001) obtained the same results as Chiu did with adult Chinese and American college students, who were tested in their native languages. They asked participants to indicate which of two objects out of three, described verbally, were most closely related. In all cases, two of the objects shared some kind of relationship, either functional (e.g., pencil and notebook) or contextual (e.g., sky and sunshine) and also shared a category (e.g., notebook and magazine) or some feature that would allow them to be categorized together (e.g., sunshine and brightness). Chinese were more likely to group on the basis of relationships, and Americans were more likely to group on the basis of categories or shared object features. Participants were asked to justify their groupings and Chinese were found to be more likely to offer relationships as the justification ("the sun is in the sky"), whereas Americans were more likely to offer category membership as the justification ("the sun and the sky are both in the heavens").

FAMILY RESEMBLANCE VERSUS RULES AS THE BASIS FOR JUDGMENTS OF SIMILARITY

Norenzayan, Nisbett, Smith, and Kim (2000; Norenzayan, 1999) presented East Asians (Chinese and Koreans), Asian Americans, and European Americans with a series of stimuli on a computer screen in which a simple target object appeared beneath two groups of four similar objects. The groups were always constructed so that the use of a family resemblance strategy and the use of a rule strategy led to different responses (Kemler-Nelson, 1984). The objects in one group had a close family resemblance to one another and to the target object, whereas the objects in the other group did not share a close resemblance with the target object. Instead, the objects of the second group were all describable by a unidimensional, deterministic rule; for example, they all had a curved stem (vs. a straight stem), and the rule was also applicable to the target object. Participants were asked to indicate to which group the target object was most similar. A majority of East Asian participants picked the "family resemblance" group, whereas a majority of the European American participants picked the "rule" group. Asian Americans showed intermediate reasoning, having equal preferences for the rule group and the family resemblance group.

CATEGORIES AND INDUCTION

Osherson, Smith, Wilkie, Lopez, and Shafir (1990) have proposed a theory of inductive inference from categories, which holds that people's willingness to generalize is in part a function of the extent to which premise categories "cover" the lowest level category that includes all premise categories. Thus, when people are told that lions and giraffes have a particular property, they are more willing to infer that rabbits have the property than when they are told that lions and tigers have the property (since lions and giraffes provide more coverage of the category *mammal* than do lions and tigers). Work by I. Choi, Nisbett, and Smith (1997) indicates that Koreans make less use of categories for purposes of inductive inference than do Americans. For example, they were less influenced than Americans by coverage of the category – unless the category was made salient in some way. In one manipulation, the category was mentioned in the conclusion (i.e., participants made an inference about "mammals" rather than "rabbits"). This manipulation had no effect on Americans but increased the degree to which Koreans relied on the category. Thus categories are apparently less spontaneously salient for Koreans and, hence, are less available for guiding generalizations.

CATEGORY LEARNING

If East Asians are relatively unlikely to use explicit rules for assigning attributes to objects and objects to categories, then it might be more difficult for them to learn how to classify objects by applying rule systems. Work by Norenzayan et al. (2000) suggests this is the case. Adopting a paradigm of Allen and Brooks (1991), they presented East Asians, Asian Americans, and European Americans with cartoon animals on a computer screen and told them that some of the animals were from Venus and some were from Saturn. Participants in an exemplar-based categorization condition were asked simply to observe a series of animals and make guesses, with feedback, about the category to which each belonged. Other participants were assigned to a rule condition and went through a formal, rule-based category learning procedure. They were told to pay attention to five different properties of the animals – curly tail, knobby antennas, and so forth – and were told that if the animal had any three of these properties it was from Venus; otherwise, it was from Saturn.

Asian and American participants performed equally well at the exemplar-based categorization task with respect both to errors and to speed of response. But in the rule condition, East Asian participants' response times were slower than those of Americans. Most tellingly, when the test trial in the rule condition presented an animal that met the formal rule criteria for a given category but more closely resembled an animal in the other category – thus placing rule-based and memory-based categorizations in conflict – Asians made more errors of classification than did Americans. (They did not make more errors when the test animal more closely resembled an instance of the category of which it was also a member in terms of the formal rule, and thus either a rule-based decision or an exemplar-based decision would yield the right answer.) Asian Americans' performance was almost identical to that of European Americans for both speed and accuracy.

Thus the results of several studies indicate that East Asians rely less on rules and categories and more on relationships and similarities in organizing their worlds than do Americans. East Asians preferred to group objects on the basis of relationships and similarity, whereas Americans were more likely to group objects on the basis of categories and rules. Americans were more likely to rely spontaneously on categories for purposes of inductive reasoning than were East Asians and found it easier to learn and use rule-based categories.

Formal Logic Versus Experiential Knowledge

There is a long Western tradition – from the ancient Greeks, to the medieval Scholastics, to the propositional logic theoreticians of the late 19th and early 20th centuries – of analyzing argument structure apart from content and of reasoning on the basis of the underlying abstract propositions alone. Such a tradition has never been common in the East, where instead there has been an explicit disapproval of such decontextualizing practices and an emphasis on the appropriateness of plausibility and sense experience in evaluating propositions. Several studies suggest that East Asians do indeed rely less on formal logic and more on experiential knowledge in reasoning than do Americans – at any rate when logic and experience are in conflict.

TYPICALITY VERSUS LOGIC

Consider the following two deductive arguments. Is one more convincing than the other?

1. All birds have ulnar arteries.
Therefore, all eagles have ulnar arteries.

2. All birds have ulnar arteries.
Therefore, all penguins have ulnar arteries.

One way to measure the extent to which people spontaneously rely on formal logic versus experiential knowledge in reasoning is to examine how they project properties (the "blank" property "ulnar arteries" in the above example) from superordinate categories (birds) to subordinate categories (eagles, penguins). Notice that the two arguments have identical premises, but their conclusions vary in the typicality of the exemplar. (Eagles are more typical birds than penguins.) Reasoners who apply logic would "see" the implicit middle premises of each argument ("All eagles are birds," and "all penguins are birds"). Such reasoners would find both deductive valid arguments equally convincing. But people often find typical arguments to be more convincing than atypical ones (Sloman, 1993).

Norenzayan and colleagues (2000) asked Korean, Asian American, and European American participants to evaluate the convincingness of a series of such arguments. The responses of participants who received only typical arguments were compared with those who received only atypical arguments. As expected, Koreans showed a large typicality effect, being more convinced by typical than by atypical arguments. European Americans, in contrast, were equally convinced by typical and atypical arguments. Asian Americans' responses were in between those of European Americans and Koreans. (When an experimental manipulation was introduced that increased the salience of the typicality information, all three groups showed the typicality effect to the same extent.)

KNOWLEDGE VERSUS LOGIC

In another study, Norenzayan and colleagues (2000) presented participants with syllogisms that were either valid or invalid and that had conclusions that were either plausible or implausible. In addition, some arguments were presented in abstract form with no content. Korean and American university students were instructed to evaluate the logical validity of each argument and decide whether the conclusion followed from the premises. Results showed that, overall, there was an effect of logic as well as of knowledge, consistent with past research. Thus, participants correctly judged valid arguments to be more valid than invalid ones, and incorrectly judged arguments with plausible conclusions to be more valid than arguments with implausible conclusions. As predicted, Korean participants showed a stronger "belief bias" for valid arguments than did American students, being more inclined to judge valid arguments as invalid if they had implausible conclusions. Importantly, this difference cannot be attributed to cultural differences in the ability to reason logically, since both cultural groups showed equal performance on the abstract items. Rather, the results indicate that when logical structure conflicts with everyday belief, American students are more willing to set aside empirical belief in favor of logic than are Korean students.

Dialectics Versus the Law of Noncontradiction

Peng and Nisbett (Peng, 1997; Peng & Nisbett, 1999) have maintained that East Asians do not have the same commitment to avoiding the appearance of contradiction as do Westerners. Examples of rules about contradiction that have played a central role in the Western intellectual tradition include the following:

1. *The law of identity*: A = A. A thing is identical to itself.

2. *The law of noncontradiction*: A ≠ not-A. No statement can be both true and false.

3. *The law of the excluded middle*: Any statement is either true or false.

Following the proposals of many philosophers of both the East and the West (e.g., Liu, 1974; Needham, 1962, 1978; Zhang & Chen, 1991), Peng and Nisbett argued that there is a tradition in Eastern philosophy that is opposed at its roots to the formal logic tradition, namely the dialectical approach. So-called "naive dialecticism" resembles the dialectic of Hegel and Marx inasmuch as it sometimes involves the creation of a synthesis from a thesis and antithesis. But more commonly it involves transcending, accepting, or even insisting on the contradiction among premises (Huff, 1993; Liu, 1974; Lloyd, 1990; Needham, 1962; Zhang & Chen, 1991; Zhou, 1990). Peng and Nisbett (1999) characterized dialecticism in terms of three principles.

1. *The principle of change*: Reality is a process that is not static but rather is dynamic and changeable. A thing need not be identical to itself at all because of the fluid nature of reality.

2. *The principle of contradiction*: Partly because change is constant, contradiction is constant. Thus old and new, good and bad, exist in the same object or event and indeed depend on one another for their existence.

3. *The principle of relationship or holism*: Because of constant change and contradiction, nothing either in human life or in nature is isolated and independent, but instead everything is related. It follows that attempting to isolate elements of some larger whole can only be misleading.

These principles are, of course, not altogether alien to Western epistemology of either the naive or the professional sort. Indeed, Western developmental psychologists (Baltes & Staudinger, 1993; Basseches, 1980, 1984; Riegel, 1973) have argued that such "post-formal" principles are learned in late adolescence and early adulthood to one degree or another by Westerners and that "wisdom" consists in part of being able to supplement the use of formal operations with a more holistic, dialectical approach to problems. But evidence we now present indicates that Western reliance on dialectical principles is weaker than that of Easterners, and Western reliance on the foundational principles of formal logic, especially the principle of noncontradiction, is stronger.

DIALECTICAL RESOLUTION OF SOCIAL CONTRADICTIONS

Peng and Nisbett (Peng, 1997; Peng & Nisbett, 1999) presented Chinese and American students with contradictions drawn from everyday life. For example, they were asked to analyze a conflict between mothers and their daughters and between having fun and going to school. American responses tended to come down in favor of one side or the other ("mothers should respect daughters' independence"). Chinese responses were more likely to find a "Middle Way," which found merit and fault on both sides and attempted to reconcile the contradiction ("both the mothers and the daughters have failed to understand each other").

DIALECTICISM AND PREFERRED ARGUMENT FORM

Peng and Nisbett (Peng, 1997; Peng & Nisbett, 1999) gave Chinese and American participants, all of whom were graduate students in the natural sciences, two different types of arguments for each of two different propositions and asked them to indicate which argument they preferred. In each case, one of the arguments was a logical one involving contradiction and one was a dialectical one. Thus, in one problem, two arguments for the existence of God were pitted against one another. One was a variant of the so-called "cosmological" or "first cause" argument. It holds that because everything must have a cause, this creates an infinite regression of cause and effect unless there is a primary cause by an infinite being. The dialectical argument applied the principle of holism, stating that when two people see the same object, such as a cup, from different perspectives, one person sees some aspects of the cup, and the other sees other aspects. But there must be a God above all individual perspectives who sees the truth about the object. Americans preferred the argument based on noncontradiction in each case, and Chinese preferred the dialectic one.

JUDGMENTS ABOUT CONTRADICTORY PROPOSITIONS

One of the strongest implications of the notion that Westerners adhere to a logical analysis of problems is that, when presented with apparently contradictory propositions, they should be inclined to reject one in favor of the other. Easterners, on the other hand, committed to the principle of the Middle Way, might be inclined to embrace both propositions, finding them each to have merit. In one study, Peng and Nisbett (1999) presented participants with either one proposition or two propositions that were, if not outright contradictions, at least very different and on the surface unlikely to both be true. The propositions were presented in the form of social science studies. For example, one proposition was: "A survey found that older inmates are more likely to be ones who are serving long sentences because they have committed severely violent crimes. The authors concluded that they should be held in prison even in the case of a prison population crisis." Its counterpart was: "A report on the prison overcrowding issue suggests that older inmates are less likely to commit new crimes. Therefore, if there is a prison population crisis, they should be released first."

Participants read about one of these studies (A or B) or both (A and B) and rated their plausibility. In the case of all five issues presented, Chinese and American participants agreed on which of the two was the more plausible. In the A and B condition, Americans judged the plausibility of the more plausible proposition as greater than did Americans who read only the more plausible assertion by itself. Thus Americans actually found a contradicted assertion to be more plausible than the same proposition when not contradicted, a normatively dubious

tendency that indicates that they felt substantial pressure to resolve the contradiction by buttressing their prior beliefs. (This finding is reminiscent of one by Lord, Ross, & Lepper [1979], who found that when people read about two different studies, one supporting their view on capital punishment and one opposing it, they were more convinced of their initial position than if they had not read about any studies.) In contrast, Chinese participants in the A and B condition resolved the contradiction between the two propositions by finding them to be equally plausible, as if they felt obligated to find merit in both the conflicting propositions. They actually found the less plausible proposition to have more merit when it had been contradicted than when it had not – also a normatively dubious inference but utterly different in kind from that of the Americans.

PERSUASION BY STRONG VERSUS WEAK ARGUMENTS

If Westerners respond to apparent contradiction by trying to decide which side is correct, but Easterners respond by yielding points to both sides, then the two groups might respond differently to arguments against an initially held position. Westerners might increase their confidence in their initial position when presented with a weak argument, whereas Easterners might decrease their confidence. This is what was found by Davis and her colleagues (Davis, 2000; Davis, Nisbett, & Schwarz, 2000). They presented groups of Korean, Asian American, and European American participants with a set of strong arguments in favor of funding a particular scientific project. They presented another group with the same set of strong "pro" arguments and an additional set of weak arguments against funding the project. Korean and American participants were equally in favor of funding the project when presented with just the strong "pro" arguments, but the two groups behaved in qualitatively different ways when presented additionally with weak "anti" arguments. Koreans were more unfavorable when weak "anti" arguments were added. But Americans were actually more favorable toward funding the project when presented with the additional weak "anti" arguments than when presented with no "anti" arguments – behavior that is normatively quite suspect.

JUSTIFICATION OF CHOICE

The Western preference for principle-guided decisions and the Eastern preference for the

"Middle Way" appears to apply also for actual choice behavior. Briley, Morris, and Simonson (2000) studied the consumer choices of East Asians and European Americans. All choices were among a triad of objects that differed on two dimensions. Object A was superior to both Object B and C on one dimension, and Object C was superior to both Object A and B on the other dimension. Object B was always intermediate between A and C on both dimensions. On average, across the range of choices, Americans and East Asians in a control condition were about equally likely to choose intermediate Object B. In an experimental condition, Briley et al. had participants give reasons for their choice. They anticipated that this would prompt Americans to look for a simple rule that would justify a given choice (e.g., "RAM is more important than hard drive space") but would prompt people of Asian culture to seek a compromise ("both RAM and hard drive space are important"). This is what was found. Americans in the justification condition moved to a preference for one of the extreme objects whose choice could be justified with reference to a simple rule, whereas Asian culture participants moved to a preference for the compromise object. Justifications given by participants were consistent with their choices, with Americans being more likely to give rule-based justifications and Chinese being more likely to give compromise-based justifications.

Thus, there is substantial evidence to indicate that Easterners are not concerned with contradiction in the same way as are Westerners. They have a greater preference for compromise solutions and holistic arguments; they are more willing to endorse apparently contradictory arguments; and they are more willing to move their beliefs in the direction of an argument, even when it is a weak one. Finally, when asked to justify their choices, they seem to move to a compromise, "Middle Way," instead of referring to a dominating principle. It should be noted that the greater adherence to the principle of noncontradiction on the part of Americans seems to produce no guarantee against normatively questionable inferences. On the contrary, their adherence to the principle of noncontradiction may sometimes cause them to become more extreme in their judgments under conditions in which the evidence indicates they should become less extreme. This tendency mirrors complaints about hyperlogical Western habits of mind often expressed by philosophers and social critics (Korzybyski, 1933/1994;

Lin, 1936; Liu, 1974; Nagashima, 1973; Saul, 1992).

Creating and Sustaining Systems of Thought

What produced the differences in ancient times? What sustains them today? These are matters of speculation, of course, so we will confine our response to brief considerations, especially for the first, historical question.

The Origin of Sociocognitive Systems

The explanation for the cognitive differences that we prefer is a distally materialistic but proximally social one that we have put together from the arguments of scholars in a large number of disciplines (Barry, Child, & Bacon, 1959; Berry, 1976; Cromer, 1993; Nakamura, 1964/1985; Needham, 1954; Whiting & Child, 1953; Whiting & Whiting, 1975; Witkin & Berry, 1975).

Chinese civilization was based on agriculture, which entailed that substantial cooperation with neighbors was necessary to carry out economic activities in an effective way. This is especially true of the rice agriculture common in the south of China. China was organized at the level of the large state very early on, and society was complex and hierarchical: The king and later the Emperor and the bureaucracy were ever-present controlling factors in the lives of individual Chinese. Harmony and social order were thus central to Chinese society. Social scientists since Marx have observed that economic and social arrangements such as these are generally associated with "collectivist" or "interdependent" social orientations as distinguished from "individualistic" or "independent" social orientations that are characteristic of societies with economies based on hunting, fishing, trading, or the modern market economy.

In marked contrast to all the other great civilizations of the ancient world, the Greek economy was not completely dependent on agriculture. The Greek ecology conspired against an agrarian base, consisting as it does mostly of mountains descending to the sea. This sort of ecology was more suited to herding and fishing than to large-scale agriculture. The sense of personal agency that characterized the Greeks could have been the natural response to the genuine freedom that they experienced in their less socially complex society.

The politically decentralized Greek cities also provided great scope of action as compared to

Chinese cities. Greeks who wished to leave one city for another were free to do so: The sea provided an escape route for dissidents. In addition, Greeks were involved in trade at one of the crossroads of the world. Thus they would have had plenty to pique their curiosity and much to discuss. The nature of social relations meant that debate would have posed few interpersonal risks, and the authority structure of the city state was too weak to prevent the free expression of opinion. Indeed for Athens and other city states debate was an integral part of the political system.

Speculative as it is, this view has the virtue that it at least is consistent with the economic changes that preceded the Renaissance, namely, the reduced reliance on agriculture and the rise of relatively independent city-states with economies based on crafts and trade. During the Renaissance, the West recapitulated some of the Greek social forms and intellectual traditions, including the rediscovery of science. The invention of the printing press greatly enhanced the conditions of freedom of thought. Ironically, though the Chinese invented movable type before the Europeans did, it was suppressed in China, on the quite correct grounds that the authority of the government would be undermined by it.

Some research by Witkin and his colleagues gives credence to the notion that stronger social networks might produce a more holistic orientation to the world. Berry and Witkin (Berry, 1967, 1976; Witkin & Berry, 1975) showed that farmers in a number of societies are more field dependent than hunters, herders, or industrialized peoples. Witkin and his colleagues (Adevai, Silverman, & McGough, 1970; Dershowitz, 1971; Meizlik, 1973) found that Orthodox Jewish boys, whose families and communities require strict observance of a variety of social rules, were more field dependent than were secular Jewish boys, who in turn were more field dependent than Protestant boys. These differences held even when general intelligence was controlled for. Moreover, individual differences in social orientation within a culture apparently are associated with field dependence. Americans who are more interested in social activities and in dealing with other people are more field dependent (even when intelligence is controlled) than are people with less social interest (Witkin & Goodenough, 1977; Witkin, Price-Williams, et al., 1974).

Finally, Kühnen, Hannover, and Schubert (2000) were able to prime field dependence

on the Embedded Figures Test by a variety of techniques intended to make participants temporarily more collectivist in their orientations. For example, they asked participants to think about what they had in common with family and friends (vs. asking them to think about how they differed from family and friends). The results confirmed that a collectivist prime led to more field dependence.

Sociocognitive Systems in Homeostasis

Mere inertia would not result in contemporary differences in the way people think. We propose that systems of thought exist in homeostasis with the social practices that surround them. We will describe a number of ways in which the social practices and cognitive processes could support or "prime" one another (Y.-y. Hong, Morris, Chiu, & Benet-Martinez, 2000).

HOLISTIC VERSUS ANALYTIC PRACTICES

1. The practice of fêng shui for choosing building sites (even Hong Kong skyscrapers) may encourage the idea that the factors affecting outcomes are extraordinarily complex and interactive, which in turn encourages the search for relationships in the field. This may be contrasted with more atomistic and rule-based approaches to problem-solving characteristic of the West. Consider, for example, the nature of approaches to self-help in the West: "The Three Steps to a Comfortable Retirement" or "Six Ways to Increase Your Word Power."

2. Employees in the top one third of the Japanese economy are rotated among their company's divisions frequently, to be able to see the company's operations from as many viewpoints as possible. A graduate of a top university would be expected to work in the factory for the first year or two of employment and might actually represent union employees to the company (Hampden-Turner & Trompenaars, 1993).

3. The West, beginning in the 18th century and continuing at an increasingly rapid pace into the 20th century, introduced "modularity" – that is, uniform, atomistic, and interchangeable design and production (Shore, 1996). From the introduction of piece good manufacture in English cottages to Henry Ford's production line

to the chain restaurant, the West – and America in particular – remain the chief innovators and consumers of modular production and products.

4. The most popular game of intellectuals in the East is Go and the most popular in the West is chess. Xia (1997) and Campbell (1983) have pointed out that Go is more complex and holistic than chess, the analytic game par excellence. Go boards have 19 × 19 spaces whereas chess boards have 8 × 8 spaces. Go pieces have more variation in possible moves than do chess pieces, which must adhere to a fixed set of rules for movement. Hence, moves in Go are more difficult to predict. The appropriate strategy for Go has been termed dialectic in that the "competition between the black and white is a well calculated trade-off.... It is not wise to be greedy and overplay" (Xia, 1997).

ARGUMENT, DEBATE, AND RHETORIC

1. In daily life, East Asians strive to maintain harmony. Ohbuchi and Takahasi (1994) asked Japanese and American businesspeople how they dealt with conflict with their fellow managers. Twice as many Japanese as American respondents reported using avoidance as a means of dealing with a conflict of views, and three times as many Americans as Japanese reported attempting to use persuasion.

2. Decision processes in boardrooms and executive councils in Japan are designed to avoid conflicts. Meetings often consist of nothing more than the ratification of consensus among members obtained by the leader prior to the meeting.

3. Western educators often complain that their Asian students do not participate in class discussions and that they do not follow the requirements of rhetoric in their writings – for example, statement of principles and assumptions, derivations, hypotheses, evidence, argumentation, conclusion. Neither their culture nor their prior educational experience has prepared them for the canonical rhetoric forms that are taken for granted in the West. (See Tweed & Lehman, 2000, for a review.)

4. Galtung (1981) has described the intellectual styles of academics from different cultures. The Anglo-American style "fosters and encourages debate and discourse... and pluralism is an overriding value" (pp. 823–824). In contrast, for the Japanese, *the first rule would be not to harm pre-established social relations*" (p. 825).

LAW AND CONTRACTS

1. Although the ancient Chinese had a complex legal system, it was in general not codified in the way it was in the West (Logan, 1986). Today, courts of law are relatively rare in the East, and there is a marked preference for solving conflicts on the basis of the particulars of a specific case and by negotiation through a middleman (Leung & Morris, 2001).

2. Easterners and Westerners have fundamentally different understandings of the nature of contracts. In the West, a contract is unalterable; in the East, a contract is continually renegotiable in the light of changed circumstances (Hampden-Turner & Trompenaars, 1993). This drastic difference of view has often resulted in conflict and bitterness between Eastern and Western negotiators.

RELIGION

1. Some scholars have contended that Christianity has far stronger theological concerns than other religions have, finding it "necessary to formulate elaborately precise statements about the abstract qualities and relations of gods and humans" (Dyson, 1998, p. 8).

2. Religions in East Asia have long been characterized by their interpenetrating and blending qualities. Societies and individuals readily incorporate aspects of several different religions into their worldviews. In contrast, for Christians, there is a strong tendency toward insistence on doctrinal purity. This sometimes results in religious wars in the West, a rarity in East Asia.

LANGUAGE AND WRITING

Perhaps the most pervasive and important of all practices that operate to sustain the cognitive differences are those having to do with language and writing. Indeed, some scholars, notably Logan (1986), have tried to make the case that most of the cognitive differences we have discussed are due primarily to differences in language and writing systems.

1. The basic writing system of Chinese and
    other East Asian languages has been essen-
    tially pictographic. It can be maintained
    that the Western alphabet is more atom-
    istic and analytic by nature and "is a nat-
    ural tool for classifying and served as a
    paradigm for codified law, scientific clas-
    sification, and standardized weights and
    measures" (Logan, p. 55).

2. The actual grammar of Indo-European
    languages encourages thinking of the
    world as being composed of atom-
    istic building blocks, whereas East Asian
    languages encourage thinking of the
    world as continuous and interpenetrating.
    "[R]ather than one-many, the Chinese lan-
    guage motivates a part-whole dichotomy"
    (Hansen, 1983, p. vii).

3. East Asian languages are highly contex-
    tual in every sense. Because of their mul-
    tiple meanings, words must be under-
    stood in the context of sentences. Because
    of the minimal nature of syntax in
    Sinitic languages, context is important
    to understanding sentences (Freeman &
    Habermann, 1996). In contrast, Heath
    (1982) has shown that language social-
    ization for middle-class American chil-
    dren quite deliberately decontextualizes
    language. Parents try to make words under-
    standable independent of verbal context
    and utterances understandable indepen-
    dent of situational context.

4. Although Western toddlers learn nouns
    (i.e., words referring to objects) at a much
    more rapid rate than they learn verbs
    (i.e., words referring to relationships), the
    reverse appears to be true for Chinese
    (Tardif, 1996) and Koreans (S. Choi &
    Gopnik, 1995). Moreover, Western tod-
    dlers hear more noun phrases from their
    mothers, whereas East Asian children hear
    more verbs (Fernald & Morikawa, 1993;
    Tardif, Shatz, & Naigles, 1997).

5. "Generic" noun phrases – that is, those ref-
    erring to categories and kinds (e.g., "birds,"
    "tools," as opposed to exemplars such as
    "sparrow," "hammer") – are more com-
    mon for English speakers than for Chi-
    nese speakers (Gelman & Tardif, 1998),
    perhaps because Western languages mark
    in a more explicit way whether a generic
    interpretation of an utterance is the cor-
    rect one (Lucy, 1992).

6. Consistent with the above findings about
    category usage, Ji and Nisbett (Ji, 2001;
    Ji & Nisbett, 2001) found that English-
    speaking Chinese used relationships more
    and categories less when they grouped
    words in Chinese than when they did so
    in English.

Thus there are some good reasons to believe
that social practices and cognitive ones maintain
each other in a state of equilibrium. Cognitive
practices may be highly stable because of their
embeddedness in larger systems of beliefs and
social practices.

Implications for Psychology

Magnitude of Effects

The cognitive differences we have discussed vary
in size, but it is important to note that many of
them are unusually large, whether the standard is
the magnitude of mean or proportion differences
(often on the order of 2:1, 3:1, or higher) or
effect size (often well in excess of 1.00).

But, in fact, most of the differences we
have reported are not merely large. The East
Asians and the Americans responded in qualitatively different ways to the same stimulus situation in study after study. For example, American participants showed large primacy effects
in judgments about covariation, whereas Chinese participants showed none. "Control" tended
to increase the degree of covariation seen and
the self-reported accuracy of Americans but
tended to have the opposite effect on Chinese,
and "control" increased the accuracy and confidence of American participants for the Rod
and Frame test but had no effect for Chinese participants (Ji et al., 2000). Similarly,
Cha and Nam (1985) and Norenzayan, Choi,
and Nisbett (2001) found that Koreans were
greatly influenced in their causal attributions
by the sort of situational information that has
no effect for Americans. I. Choi and Nisbett
(2000) found that Koreans showed large hindsight bias effects under conditions where Americans showed none. Peng and Nisbett (1999)
found that Americans responded to contradiction by polarizing their beliefs, whereas Chinese
responded by moderating their beliefs. Qualitative differences, with Americans responding
in one way and East Asians in another, were
found in other studies by Briley et al. (2000),
I. Choi and Nisbett (1998), Davis et al. (2000),
Norenzayan et al. (2000), and Peng and Nisbett

(1999). These qualitative differences indicate that literally different cognitive processes are often invoked by East Asians and Westerners dealing with the same problem.

Universality

The assumption of universality of cognitive processes lies deep in the psychological tradition. We believe that the results discussed here force consideration of the possibility that an indefinitely large number of presumably "basic" cognitive processes may be highly malleable. When psychologists perform experiments on "categorization," "inductive inference," "logical reasoning," or "attributional processes," it does not normally occur to them that their data may apply only rather locally, to people raised in a tradition of European culture. They are, of course, prepared for parameter differences, but parameter differences between populations on the order of 3:1 or more provide an occasion for wondering about universality. It is no exaggeration to state that qualitative differences between populations preempt any claim to universality – unless there is reason to believe that experimental procedures are not comparable across groups.

Just how great the cultural differences can be is unclear at this point, of course. Moreover, although we have looked at tasks that measure important perceptual and cognitive variables, we have no way of knowing what population these variables were selected from. It is possible that the particular variables we have examined exhibit cultural differences that are substantially greater than the differences that might be found in other tasks that are equally good measures of the conceptual variables. But it is equally – if not more – probable that investigators have not been uncannily insightful at this early stage of research and that there are variables and measures that would show even larger differences than the ones we have examined. Moreover, the participant populations, consisting mostly of college students, would be expected to be more similar to one another than to more representative members of their parent populations.

Fixedness of Cognitive Content

It is ironic that, just as our evidence indicates that some cognitive processes are highly susceptible to cultural influence, other investigators are providing evidence that some cognitive content may not be very susceptible to cultural influence. Naive theories of mechanics

and physics (Baillargeon, 1995; Carey & Spelke, 1994; Leslie, 1982; Spelke, 1988, 1990), naive theories of biology (Atran, 1990, 1995; Berlin, 1992; Berlin, Breedlove, & Raven, 1973; Gelman, 1988) and naive theory of mind (Asch, 1952; D'Andrade, 1987; Leslie, 1994; Wellman, 1990) appear so early and are apparently so widespread that it seems quite likely that at least some aspects of them are largely innate and resistant to social modification. Theories of causality – both highly general ones having to do with temporal sequence and spatial contiguity (Seligman, 1970), as well as highly specific ones, such as the link that all omnivorous mammals are likely to make between distinctive-tasting food and gastrointestinal illness experienced many hours later (Garcia, McGowan, Ervin, & Koelling, 1968) – are clearly a part of the organism's biologically given cognitive equipment. Hirschfeld (1996) has argued that "essentialist" beliefs about the nature of the social world are universal, and Sperber (1985) and Boyer (1993) have argued that even religious conceptions such as spirits and superhuman agents are remarkably similar from one culture to another. As Sperber (1996) has written, the human mind is equipped with a set of cognitive properties that make it easier or harder to think certain kinds of thoughts.

Thus, it appears that the assumption that cognitive content is learned and indefinitely malleable and the assumption that cognitive processes are universally the same and biologically fixed may both be quite wrong. Some important content may be universal and part of our biologically given equipment, and some important processes may be highly alterable. The continued existence on the planet of widely different social and intellectual traditions offers an opportunity to learn a great deal more about the fixedness and malleability of both content and process.

The Inseparability of Process and Content

Our theoretical position is at the same time less radical and more radical than the assertion that basic processes differ across cultures. We are urging the view that metaphysics, epistemology, and cognitive processes exist in mutually dependent and reinforcing systems of thought, such that a given stimulus situation often triggers quite different processes in one culture than in another. Thus it is not possible to make a sharp distinction between cognitive process and cognitive content. Content in the form of metaphysical beliefs about the nature of the world determines tacit epistemology. Tacit epistemology in turn dictates the cognitive procedures that people use for solving particular problems.

People who believe that knowledge about objects is normally both necessary and sufficient for understanding their behavior will believe it is important to find the appropriate categories that apply to the object and the appropriate rules that apply to the categories. The search for categories and rules will dictate particular ways of organizing knowledge as well as procedures for obtaining new knowledge about rules. Such practices in turn are aided by a reliance on formal logic, especially including attention to the specter of contradiction that undermines beliefs about the validity of rules. Abstractions will be a goal because categories and rules will seem to be useful just to the extent that they have wide applicability and because it can be easier to apply formal logic to abstractions than to concrete objects.

Similar points can be made about people who believe that causality is a complex function of multiple factors operating on an object in a field. Complexity indicates dynamism and constant change. A belief in change and instability will tend to make the habits of categorization and of search for universal rules about objects seem dubiously relevant. Rather, an attempt to see the interrelatedness of events will seem important. Contradiction will seem inevitable, since change is constant, and opposing factors always coexist. A concern with concrete objects and events will seem to be more useful than will a search for abstractions. Logic will not be allowed to overrule sensory experience or common sense.

Thus, without saying that Easterners are unable to make use of categorization or that Westerners are unable to detect covariation, we can see that the differences between cultures can still be very great: (a) The circumstances that prompt the use of one process versus another will differ substantially across cultures; (b) the frequencies with which the very most basic cognitive processes are used will differ greatly; (c) consequently, the degree and nature of expertise in the use of particular cognitive processes will differ; and (d) tacit or even explicit normative standards for thought will differ across cultures (Stich, 1990).

Claude Lévi-Strauss, the great French anthropologist, proposed that, in their attempts to solve the problems of daily life, people might be regarded as bricoleurs – handymen with their bags of cognitive tools. Pursuing this metaphor, we may say that even if all cultures possessed essentially the same basic cognitive processes as their tools, the tools of choice for the same problem may habitually be very different. People may differ markedly in their beliefs about whether a problem is one requiring use of a wrench or pliers, in their skill in using the two types of tools, and in the location of particular tools at the top or the bottom of the tool kit. Moreover, members of different cultures may not see the same stimulus situation as a problem in need of repair. A seeming contradiction is a problem for Westerners but may not be for Easterners. Indeed, as some of the perceptual work we have reviewed indicates, the different focus of attention of Easterners and Westerners indicates that they may sometimes not be seeing the same stimulus situation at all – even when their heads are immobilized at a fixed distance away from a computer screen.

Another way that cognitive processes can differ is that cultures may construct composite cognitive tools out of the basic universal toolkit, thereby performing acts of elaborate cognitive engineering, as Dennett's (1995) characterization of culture as a "crane-making crane" (p. 338) suggests. Modern statistical, methodological, and cost-benefit rules provide examples of such crane-produced cranes. Nothing like them existed prior to the 17th century, when they were constructed in the West on the basis of rule-based empirical observation, mathematics, and formal logic, and there is great variation among members of Western society today in the degree of understanding and use of these rules. Similar points may be made about the transformation of the ancient Chinese notions about yin and yang into more sophisticated dialectical notions about change, moderation, relativism, and the necessity of multiple viewpoints.

The psychological ideas that our position most closely resembles are those in the tradition of Vygotsky (1978, 1987; e.g., Cole, 1995; Cole & Scribner, 1974; Hutchins, 1995; Lave, 1988; Luria, 1931; Rogoff, 1990), which insists that thought always occurs in a pragmatic problem setting, including the cultural assumptions that are brought to the task. This view, recently referred to as the "situated cognition" view, has been defined by Resnick as the assumption that "the tools of thought . . . embody a culture's intellectual history. . . . Tools have theories built into them, and users accept these theories – albeit unknowingly – when they use these tools" (Resnick, 1994, pp. 476–477).

The particular cognitive orientations we have been discussing have endured for millennia. One of the questions that intrigues us most concerns what it might take to seriously disturb the homeostasis of one of these historically rooted systems of thought. It is not hard to introduce Westerners to cost-benefit rules; these rules can affect their reasoning and their behavior and leave them fully accepted members of their communities. It is far from clear that it would be so easy to introduce East Asians to that rule system, that it would leave members who adopted the rule system so fully accepted by their communities or that it would leave unscathed the sociocognitive homeostasis of their societies if the rule system were to be widely adopted. There seems to be one quite interesting case of resistance to change of a homeostatic system. The introduction of the highly individualistic economic element of capitalism into Japan 130 years ago appears to have had far less effect on either social practices or, as our research indicates, cognitive processes, than might have been anticipated.

It is clear from some of the work summarized in this article that Asians move radically in an American direction after a generation or less in the United States. But it might be a mistake to extrapolate from these facts and assume that it would be an easy matter to teach one culture's tools to individuals in another without total immersion in that culture. It is far from clear that, using normal pedagogical techniques, Americans could be given many of the advantages of a dialectical stance or that East Asians could be taught to experience surprise at outcomes when surprise is warranted.

We hope we have persuaded the reader that the cognitive processes triggered by a given situation may not be so universal as generally supposed, or so divorced from content, or so independent of the particular character of thought that distinguishes one human group from another. Two decades ago, Richard E. Nisbett wrote a book with Lee Ross entitled, modestly, *Human Inference* (Nisbett & Ross, 1980). Roy D'Andrade, a distinguished cognitive anthropologist, read the book and told Richard Nisbett he thought it was a "good ethnography." The author was shocked and dismayed. But we now wholeheartedly agree with D'Andrade's contention about the limits of research conducted in a single culture. Psychologists who choose not to do cross-cultural psychology may have chosen to be ethnographers instead.

Notes

1   We use the philosopher's term *metaphysics* rather than *ontology*, which is a more common term for psychologists to use to describe theories about the nature of the world, because we wish to convey concerns with very general notions about the nature of causality and reality, as well as the relationships between substance and attribute, fact and value.

2   We use the term *epistemology* to refer to peoples' theory of knowledge, including what counts as knowledge, the degree to which different kinds of knowledge are certain, and the presumed relation between the knower and the object that is known. This definition is probably congenial to both psychologists and philosophers.

3   At any rate, the Chinese were not much interested in constructing rigorous classifications of a sort that could make possible scientific rule construction (Atran, 1995).

4   We do not wish to imply that Eastern and Western societies have been marked continuously by the sorts of differences found in ancient times. The West during the Middle Ages was similar economically and socially to ancient China in many ways, and one would never characterize the feudal period as being notably individualistic. In contrast, in various periods in China, especially during the late 2nd century to the early 4th century A.D., there were substantial strains of individualism (Yu, 1985). It was probably not until the late Medieval Period that the West began to return to levels of individualism characteristic of ancient Greece. Since that time, however, the West has continued on an ever more individualist trajectory while the East in general has not. It is also important to note that there are marked differences even today within both the societies that we are labeling collectivist and those that we are labeling individualist. While acknowledging these differences, we agree with the mainstream view of historians, ethnographers, sociologists, and cultural psychologists that there are nonetheless broad and deep differences between East and West with respect to the collectivist-individualist dimension.

5   Several studies compared the field dependence of East Asians and Westerners using Witkin's Embedded Figures Test (EFT), in which a small figure is shown to participants and they are then asked to find it in a larger, more complicated figure. Typically no difference is found or a slight difference is found favoring East Asians (Bagley, 1995; Huang & Chao, 1995). As Bagley has pointed out, however, this result is ambiguous, because the figures used in the test resemble the characters in Chinese and other East Asian writing systems. To examine if, indeed, writing systems might be responsible for the

lesser field dependence of East Asians examined using the EFT, Kühnen, Hannover, Röder, et al. (2000) compared various Western populations with Malaysians – a highly collectivist East Asian population that, however, has a Latin writing system – and found the Malaysians substantially more field dependent than any of the other three groups.

6 When shown only one hypothesis, Koreans and Americans regarded the "optimism" hypothesis as equally likely and the two groups also regarded the "realism" hypothesis as equally likely. Neither Americans nor Koreans expressed much surprise when the more plausible hypothesis replaced the less plausible one.

References

Abel, T. M., & Hsu, F. I. (1949). Some aspects of personality of Chinese as revealed by the Rorschach Test. *Journal of Projective Techniques, 13,* 285–301.

Adevai, G., Silverman, A. J., & McGough, W. E. (1970). Ethnic differences in perceptual testing. *International Journal of Social Psychiatry, 16,* 237–239.

Allen, S. W., & Brooks, L. R. (1991). Specializing in the operation of an explicit rule. *Journal of Experimental Psychology: General, 120,* 3–19.

Asch, S. (1952). *Social psychology.* Englewood Cliffs, NJ: Prentice Hall.

Atran, S. (1990). *Cognitive foundations of natural history.* New York: Cambridge University Press.

Atran, S. (1995). Causal constraints on categories and categorical constraints on biological reasoning across cultures. In D. Sperber, D. Premack, & A. J. Premack (Eds.), *Causal cognition: A multidisciplinary debate* (pp. 205–233). Oxford, England: Oxford University Press.

Bagley, C. (1995). Field independence in children in group-oriented cultures: Comparisons from China, Japan, and North America. *The Journal of Social Psychology, 135,* 523–525.

Baillargeon, R. (1995). Physical reasoning in infancy. In M. S. Gazzaniga (Ed.), *The cognitive neurosciences* (pp. 181–204). Cambridge, MA: MIT Press.

Baltes, P. B., & Staudinger, U. M. (1993). The search for a psychology of wisdom. *Current Directions in Psychological Science, 2,* 75–80.

Barry, H., Child, I., & Bacon, M. (1959). Relation of child training to subsistence economy. *American Anthropologist, 61,* 51–63.

Basseches, M. (1980). Dialectical schemata: A framework for the empirical study of the development of dialectical thinking. *Human Development, 23,* 400–421.

Basseches, M. (1984). *Dialectical thinking and adult development.* Norwood, NJ: Ablex.

Becker, C. B. (1986). Reasons for the lack of argumentation and debate in the Far East. *International Journal of Intercultural Relations, 10,* 75–92.

Berlin, B. (1992). *Ethnobiological classification: Principles of categorization of plants and animals in traditional societies.* Princeton, NJ: Princeton University Press.

Berlin, B., Breedlove, D., & Raven, P. (1973). General principles of classification and nomenclature in folk biology. *American Anthropologist, 74,* 214–242.

Berry, J. W. (1967). Independence and conformity in subsistence-level societies. *Journal of Personality and Social Psychology, 7,* 415–418.

Berry, J. W. (1976). *Human ecology and cognitive style: Comparative studies in cultural and psychological adaptation.* New York: Sage/Halsted.

Block, N. (1995). The mind as the software of the brain. In E. E. Smith & D. N. Osherson (Eds.), *Thinking: An invitation to cognitive science* (pp. 377–425). Cambridge, MA: MIT Press.

Bond, M. H. (1996). Chinese values. In M. H. Bond (Ed.), *Handbook of Chinese psychology* (pp. 208–226). Hong Kong, China: Oxford University Press.

Boyer, P. (1993). *The naturalness of religious ideas.* Berkeley: University of California Press.

Briley, D. A., Morris, M., & Simonson, I. (2000). Reasons as carriers of culture: Dynamic versus dispositional models of cultural influence on decision making. *Journal of Consumer Research, 27,* 157–178.

Campbell, J. A. (1983). Go: Introduction. In M. A. Bramer (Ed.), *Computer game playing* (pp. 136–140). Chicester, England: Ellis Horwood.

Carey, S., & Spelke, E. (1994). Domain-specific knowledge and conceptual change. In L. A. Hirschfeld & S. A. Gelman (Eds.), *Mapping the mind: Domain specificity in cognition and culture* (pp. 169–200). Cambridge, England: Cambridge University Press.

Cha, J.-H., & Nam, K. D. (1985). A test of Kelley's cube theory of attribution: A cross-cultural replication of McArthur's study. *Korean Social Science Journal, 12,* 151–180.

Chalfonte, B. L., & Johnson, M. K. (1996). Feature memory and binding in young and older adults. *Memory & Cognition, 24,* 403–416.

Chan, W.-T. (1967). The story of Chinese philosophy. In C. A. Moore (Ed.), *The Chinese mind: Essentials of Chinese philosophy and culture* (pp. 245–257). Honolulu, HI: East-West Center Press.

Chang, T.-S. (1939). A Chinese philosopher's theory of knowledge. *Yen-ching Journal of Social Studies, 11*(2).

Chavajay, P., & Rogoff, B. (2000). *Cultural variation in management of attention by children and their caregivers.* Unpublished manuscript. University of California at Santa Cruz.

Chiu, L.-H. (1972). A cross-cultural comparison of cognitive styles in Chinese and American children. *International Journal of Psychology, 7,* 235–242.

Choi, I. (1998). *The cultural psychology of surprise: Holistic theories, contradiction, and epistemic curiosity.* Unpublished doctoral dissertation, University of Michigan.

Choi, I., Dalal, R., & Kim-Prieto, C. (2000). *Information search in causal attribution: Analytic vs. holistic.* Unpublished manuscript, University of Illinois.

Choi, I., & Nisbett, R. E. (1998). Situational salience and cultural differences in the correspondence bias and in the actor-observer bias. *Personality and Social Psychology Bulletin, 24,* 949–960.

Choi, I., & Nisbett, R. E. (2000). The cultural psychology of surprise: Holistic theories and recognition of contradiction. *Journal of Personality and Social Psychology, 79,* 890–905.

Choi, I., Nisbett, R. E., & Norenzayan, A. (1999). Causal attribution across cultures: Variation and universality. *Psychological Bulletin, 125,* 47–63.

Choi, I., Nisbett, R. E., & Smith, E. E. (1997). Culture, categorization and inductive reasoning. *Cognition, 65,* 15–32.

Choi, S., & Gopnik, A. (1995). Early acquisition of verbs in Korean: A cross-linguistic study. *Journal of Child Language, 22,* 497–529.

Cole, M. (1995). Socio-cultural-historical psychology: Some general remarks and a proposal for a new kind of cultural-genetic methodology. In J. V. Wertsch, P. D. Rio, & A. Alvarez (Eds.), *Sociocultural studies of mind* (pp. 113–144). Cambridge, England: Cambridge University Press.

Cole, M., & Scribner, S. (1974). *Culture and thought: A psychological introduction.* New York: Wiley.

Cromer, A. (1993). *Uncommon sense: The heretical nature of science.* New York: Oxford University Press.

D'Andrade, R. (1987). A folk model of the mind. In D. Holland & N. Quinn (Eds.), *Cultural models in language and thought* (pp. 112–148). New York: Cambridge University Press.

Darley, J. M., & Batson, C. D. (1973). From Jerusalem to Jericho: A study of situational and dispositional variables in helping behavior. *Journal of Personality and Social Psychology, 27,* 100–119.

Davis, M. (2000). *Responses to weak argument on the part of Asians and Americans.* University of Michigan, Ann Arbor.

Davis, M., Nisbett, R. E., & Schwarz, N. (2000). *Responses to weak arguments by Asians and Americans.* Ann Arbor: University of Michigan.

Dennett, D. C. (1995). *Darwin's dangerous idea: Evolution and meanings of life.* New York: Simon & Schuster.

Dershowitz, Z. (1971). Jewish subcultural patterns and psychological differentiation. *International Journal of Psychology, 6,* 223–231.

Dyson, F. J. (1998, May 28). Is God in the lab? *New York Review of Books,* 8–10.

Fernald, A., & Morikawa, H. (1993). Common themes and cultural variations in Japanese and American mothers' speech to infants. *Child Development, 64,* 637–656.

Fischhoff, B. (1975). Hindsight/foresight: The effect of outcome knowledge on judgment under uncertainty. *Journal of Experimental Psychology: Human Perception and Performance, 1,* 288–299.

Fiske, A. P., Kitayama, S., Markus, H. R., & Nisbett, R. E. (1998). The cultural matrix of social psychology. In D. T. Gilbert, S. T. Fiske, & G. Lindzey (Eds.), *Handbook of social psychology* (4th ed., pp. 915–981). Boston: McGraw-Hill.

Freeman, N. H., & Habermann, G. M. (1996). Linguistic socialization: A Chinese perspective. In M. H. Bond (Ed.), *The handbook of Chinese psychology* (pp. 79–92), Oxford, England: Oxford University Press.

Fung, Y. (1983). *A history of Chinese philosophy* (D. Bodde, Trans.) (Vol. 1–2). Princeton, NJ: Princeton University Press.

Galtung, J. (1981). Structure, culture, and intellectual style: An essay comparing saxonic, teutonic, gallic and nipponic approaches. *Social Science Information, 20,* 817–856.

Garcia, J., McGowan, B. K., Ervin, F., & Koelling, R. (1968). Cues: Their relative effectiveness as reinforcers. *Science, 160,* 794–795.

Gelman, S. A. (1988). The development of induction within natural kind and artifact categories. *Cognitive Psychology, 20,* 65–95.

Gelman, S. A., & Tardif, T. (1998). A cross-linguistic comparison of generic noun phrases in English and Mandarin. *Cognition, 66,* 215–248.

Gilbert, D. T., & Malone, P. S. (1995). The correspondence bias. *Psychological Bulletin, 117,* 21–38.

Glass, D. C., & Singer, J. E. (1973). Experimental studies of uncontrollable and unpredictable noise. *Representative Research in Psychology, 4,* 165–183.

Hadingham, E. (1994). The mummies of Xinjiang. *Discover, 15,* 68–77.

Hamilton, E. (1973). *The Greek way.* New York: Avon. (Original work published 1930)

Hampden-Turner, C., & Trompenaars, A. (1993). *The seven cultures of capitalism: Value systems for creating wealth in the United States, Japan, Germany, France, Britain, Sweden, and the Netherlands.* New York: Doubleday.

Hansen, C. (1983). *Language and logic in ancient China.* Ann Arbor: University of Michigan Press.

Heath, S. B. (1982). What no bedtime story means: Narrative skills at home and school. *Language in Society, 11,* 49–79.

Hedden, T., Ji, L., Jing, Q., Jiao, S., Yao, C., Nisbett, R. E., & Park, D. C. (2000, April). *Culture and age differences in recognition memory for social dimensions.* Paper presented at the Cognitive Aging Conference, Atlanta, GA.

Hirschfeld, L. (1996). *Race in the making: Cognition, culture, and the child's construction of human kinds.* Cambridge, MA: MIT Press.

Hofstede, G. (1980). *Culture's consequences: International differences in work-related values.* Beverley Hills, CA: Sage.

Hong, Y., Chiu, C., & Kung, T. (1997). Bringing culture out in front: Effects of cultural meaning system activation on social cognition. In K. Leung, Y. Kashima, U. Kim, & S. Yamaguchi (Eds.), *Progress in Asian social psychology* (Vol. 1, pp. 135–146). Singapore: Wiley.

Hong, Y.-y., Morris, M. W., Chiu, C.-y., & Benet-Martinez, V. (2000). Multicultural minds: A dynamic constructivist approach to culture and cognition. *American Psychologist, 55,* 709–720.

Hsu, F. L. K. (1981). *Americans and Chinese: Passage to differences.* Honolulu: University of Hawaii Press.

Huang, J., & Chao, L. (1995). Chinese and American students' perceptual styles of field independence versus field dependence. *Perceptual and Motor Skills, 80,* 232–234.

Huff, T. E. (1993). *The rise of early modern science: Islam, China, and the West.* Cambridge, England: Cambridge University Press.

Hutchins, E. (1995). *Cognition in the wild.* Cambridge, MA: MIT Press.

Ji, L. (2001). *Culture, language and relationships vs. categories in cognition.* Unpublished doctoral dissertation, University of Michigan, Ann Arbor.

Ji, L., & Nisbett, R. E. (2001). *Culture, language and categories.* Unpublished manuscript, University of Michigan.

Ji, L., Peng, K., & Nisbett, R. E. (2000). Culture, control, and perception of relationships in the environment. *Journal of Personality and Social Psychology, 78,* 943–955.

Jones, E. E., & Harris, V. A. (1967). The attribution of attitudes. *Journal of Experimental Social Psychology, 3,* 1–24.

Kane, G. (2000). *Culture and science.* Unpublished manuscript, University of Michigan.

Kemler-Nelson, D. G. (1984). The effect of intention on what concepts are acquired. *Journal of Verbal Learning and Verbal Behavior, 23,* 734–759.

Kitayama, S., & Masuda, T. (1997). *Shaiaiteki ninshiki no bunkateki baikai model: taiousei bias no bunkashinrigakuteki kentou.* [Cultural psychology of social inference: The correspondence bias in Japan]. In K. Kashiwagi, S. Kitayama, & H. Azuma (Eds.), *Bunkashinrigaju: riron to jisho* [*Cultural psychology: Theory and evidence*] (pp. 109–127). Tokyo: University of Tokyo Press.

Knox, B. (1990). *Introduction to Homer's The Iliad* (Robert Fagles, Trans.). St. Paul, MN: Penguin-High Bridge.

Korzybyski, A. (1994). *Science and sanity: An introduction to non-Aristotelian systems and general semantics.* Englewood, NJ: Institute of General Semantics. (Original work published 1933)

Kühnen, U., Hannover, B., Röder, U., Schubert, B., Shah, A. A., & Zakaria, S. (2000). *Cross-cultural variations in identifying embedded figures: Comparisons from the US, Germany, Russia and Malaysia.* Unpublished manuscript, University of Michigan.

Kühnen, U., Hannover, B., & Schubert, B. (2000). *Procedural consequences of semantic priming: The role of self-knowledge for context-bounded versus context-independent modes of thinking.* Unpublished manuscript, University of Michigan.

Langer, E. (1975). The illusion of control. *Journal of Personality and Social Psychology, 32,* 311–328.

Larrick, R. P., Nisbett, R. E., & Morgan, J. N. (1993). Who uses the cost-benefit rules of choice? Implications for the normative status of microeconomic theory. *Organizational Behavior and Human Decision Processes, 56,* 331–347.

Lave, J. (1988). *Cognition in practice: Mind, mathematics, and culture in everyday life.* New York: Cambridge University Press.

Lee, F., Hallahan, M., & Herzog, T. (1996). Explaining real life events: How culture and domain shape attributions. *Personality and Social Psychology Bulletin, 22,* 732–741.

Leslie, A. M. (1982). The perception of causality in infants. *Perception, 11,* 173–186.

Leslie, A. M. (1994). ToMM, ToBY, and agency: Core architecture and domain specificity. In L. A. Hirschfeld & S. A. Gelman (Eds.), *Mapping the mind: Domain specificity in cognition and culture.* Cambridge, England: Cambridge University Press.

Leung, K., & Morris, M. W. (2001). Justice through the lens of culture and ethnicity. In J. Sanders & V. L. Hamilton (Eds.), *Handbook of law and social science: Justice.* (pp. 343–377) New York: Plenum Press.

Lin, Y. (1936). *My country and my people.* London: William Heinemann.

Liu, S. H. (1974). The use of analogy and symbolism in traditional Chinese philosophy. *Journal of Chinese Philosophy, 1,* 313–338.

Lloyd, G. E. R. (1990). *Demystifying mentalities.* New York: Cambridge University Press.

Lloyd, G. E. R. (1991). The invention of nature. In G. E. R. Lloyd (Ed.), *Methods and problems in Greek Science* (pp. 417–434). Cambridge, England: Cambridge University Press.

Logan, R. F. (1986). *The alphabet effect.* New York: Morrow.

Lord, C., Ross, L., & Lepper, M. (1979). Biased assimilation and attitude polarization: The effects of prior theories on subsequently considered evidence. *Journal of Personality and Social Psychology, 37,* 2098–2109.

Lucy, J. A. (1992). *Language diversity and thought: A reformulation of the linguistic relativity hypothesis.* New York: Cambridge University Press.

Luria, A. R. (1931). Psychological expedition to Central Asia. *Science, 74,* 383–384.

Mao, T.-T. (1962). *Four essays on philosophy.* Beijing, China: People's Press. (Original work published 1937)

Markus, H. R., & Kitayama, S. (1991). Culture and the self: Implications for cognition, emotion, and motivation. *Psychological Review, 98,* 224–253.

Masuda, T. (1996). *Bunkashinrigakutekuteki approach niyoru tashakou-dousuiron process soikou: correspondence bisas no hunensei no kento.* [Rethinking the inference process about the other's behavior from a cultural psychogical approach.] Kyoto, Japan: Kyoto University.

Masuda, T., & Nisbett, R. E. (2001). *Culture and attention to object vs. field.* Unpublished manuscript, University of Michigan.

Meizlik, F. (1973). *Study of the effect of sex and cultural variables on field independence/dependence in a Jewish sub-culture.* Unpublished master's thesis, City University of New York.

Menon, T., Morris, M. W., Chiu, C.-y., & Hong, Y.-y. (1999). Culture and the construal of agency: Attribution to individual versus group dispositions. *Journal of Personality & Social Psychology, 76,* 701–717.

Meyer, D. E. (1995). Adaptive executive control: Flexible multiple-task performance without pervasive immutable response-selection bottlenecks. *Acta Psychologica, 90,* 163–190.

Meyer, D. E., & Kieras, D. E. (1997a). A computational theory of executive cognitive processes and multiple-task performance: I. Basic mechanisms. *Psychological Review, 104,* 3–65.

Meyer, D. E., & Kieras, D. E. (1997b). A computational theory of executive cognitive processes and multiple-task performance: II. Accounts of psychological refractory-period phenomena. *Psychological Review, 104,* 749–791.

Meyer, D. E., & Kieras, D. E. (1999). Precis to a practical unified theory of cognition and action: Some lessons from EPIC computational models of human multiple-task performance. In D. Gopher (Ed.), *Attention and performance XVII: Cognitive regulation of performance: Interaction of theory and application* (Vol. 17–88). Cambridge, MA: MIT Press.

Miller, J. G. (1984). Culture and the development of everyday social explanation. *Journal of Personality and Social Psychology, 46,* 961–978.

Morris, M., Nisbett, R. E., & Peng, K. (1995). Causal understanding across domains and cultures. In D. Sperber, D. Premack, & A. J. Premack (Eds.), *Causal cognition: A multidisciplinary debate* (pp. 577–612). Oxford, England: Oxford University Press.

Morris, M. W., & Peng, K. (1994). Culture and cause: American and Chinese attributions for social and physical events. *Journal of Personality and Social Psychology, 67,* 949–971.

Moser, D. J. (1996). *Abstract thinking and thought in ancient Chinese and early Greek.* Unpublished doctoral dissertation, University of Michigan, Ann Arbor.

Munro, D. J. (1969). *The concept of man in early China.* Stanford, CA: Stanford University Press.

Munro, D. J. (1985). Introduction. In D. Munro (Ed.), *Individualism and holism: Studies in Confucian and Taoist values* (pp. 1–34). Ann Arbor: Center for Chinese Studies, University of Michigan.

Nagashima, N. (1973). A reversed world: Or is it? In R. Horton & R. Finnegan (Eds.), *Modes of thought* (pp. 187–213). London: Faber and Faber.

Nakamura, H. (1985). *Ways of thinking of eastern peoples.* Honolulu: University of Hawaii Press. (Original work published 1964)

Needham, J. (1954). *Science and civilisation in China* (Vol. 1). Cambridge, England: Cambridge University Press.

Needham, J. (1962). *Science and civilisation in China. Vol. 4: Physics and physical technology.* Cambridge, England: Cambridge University Press.

Needham, J. (1978). *The history of Chinese science and technology.* Chiu-lung, China: Chung Hua Shu Chu. (Original work published 1962)

Nisbett, R. E. (1993). *Rules for reasoning.* Hillsdale, NJ: Erlbaum.

Nisbett, R. E. (1998). Essence and accident. In J. Cooper & J. Darley (Eds.), *Attribution processes, person perception, and social interaction: The legacy of Ned Jones* (pp. 169–200). Washington, DC: American Psychological Association.

Nisbett, R. E., Fong, G. T., Lehman, D. R., & Cheng, P. W. (1987). Teaching reasoning. *Science, 238,* 625–631.

Nisbett, R. E., & Ross, L. D. (1980). *Human inference: Strategies and shortcomings of social judgment.* Englewood Cliffs, NJ: Prentice Hall.

Norenzayan, A. (1999). *Rule-based and experience-based thinking: The cognitive consequences of intellectual traditions.* Unpublished doctoral dissertation, University of Michigan.

Norenzayan, A., Choi, I., & Nisbett, R. E. (1999). Eastern and western perceptions of causality for social behavior: Lay theories about personalities and social situations. In D. Prentice & D. Miller (Eds.), *Cultural divides: Understanding and overcoming group conflict* (pp. 239–272). New York: Sage.

Norenzayan, A., Choi, I., & Nisbett, R. E. (2001). *Eastern and Western folk psychology and the prediction of behavior.* Unpublished manuscript, University of Illinois.

Norenzayan, A., Nisbett, R. E., Smith, E. E., & Kim, B. J. (2000). *Rules vs. similarity as a basis for reasoning and judgment in East and West.* Unpublished manuscript, University of Illinois.

Ohbuchi, K. I., & Takahashi, Y. (1994). Cultural styles of conflict management in Japanese and

Americans: Passivity, covertness, and effectiveness of strategies. *Journal of Applied Psychology, 24*, 1345–1366.

On, L. W. (1996). The cultural context for Chinese learners: Conceptions of learning in the Confucian tradition. In D. A. Watkins & J. B. Biggs (Eds.), *The Chinese learner: Cultural, psychological, and contextual influences* (pp. 142–156). Hong Kong, China: Comparative Education.

Osherson, D. N., Smith, E. E., Wilkie, O., Lopez, A., & Shafir, E. (1990). Category-based induction. *Psychological Review, 97*, 185–200.

Park, D. C., Nisbett, R. E., & Hedden, T. (1999). Culture, cognition, and aging. *Journal of Gerontology, 54B*, 75–84.

Peng, K. (1997). *Naive dialecticism and its effects on reasoning and judgment about contradiction.* Unpublished doctoral dissertation, University of Michigan.

Peng, K., & Nisbett, R. E. (1999). Culture, dialectics, and reasoning about contradiction. *American Psychologist, 54*, 741–754.

Peng, K., & Nisbett, R. E. (2000). *Cross-cultural similarities and differences in the understanding of physical causality.* Unpublished manuscript, University of California, Berkeley.

Resnick, L. B. (1994). Situated rationalism: Biological and social preparation for learning. In L. A. Hirschfeld & S. A. Gelman (Eds.), *Mapping the mind: Domain specificity in cognition and culture* (pp. 474–494). Cambridge, England: Cambridge University Press.

Riegel, K. F. (1973). Dialectical operations: The final period of cognitive development. *Human Development, 18*, 430–443.

Rogoff, B. (1990). *Apprenticeship in thinking: Cognitive development in social context.* New York: Oxford University Press.

Rogoff, B., Mistry, J., Göncü, A., & Mosier, C. (1993). Guided participation in cultural activity by toddlers and caregivers. *Monographs of the Society for Research in Child Development, 58* (236).

Ross, L. (1977). The intuitive psychologist and his shortcomings. In L. Berkowitz (Ed.), *Advances in experimental social psychology* (Vol. 10, pp. 173–220). New York: Academic Press.

Saul, J. R. (1992). *Voltaire's bastards: The dictatorship of reason in the West.* New York: Random House.

Seligman, M. E. P. (1970). On the generality of the laws of learning. *Psychological Review, 77*, 127–190.

Shore, B. (1996). *Culture in mind: Cognition, culture and the problem of meaning.* New York: Oxford University Press.

Shweder, R. A. (1991). Cultural psychology: What is it? In R. A. Shweder (Ed.), *Thinking through cultures: Expeditions in cultural psychology* (pp. 73–110). Cambridge, MA: Harvard University Press.

Sloman, S. (1993). Feature-based induction. *Cognitive Psychology, 25*, 231–280.

Sloman, S. (1996). The empirical case for two systems of reasoning. *Psychological Bulletin, 119*, 30–52.

Smith, E. E., Langston, C., & Nisbett, R. E. (1992). The case for rules in reasoning. *Cognition, 16*, 1–40.

Spelke, E. S. (1988). Where perceiving ends and thinking begins: The apprehension of objects in infancy. In A. Yonas (Ed.), *Perceptual development in infancy. Minnesota Symposium on Child Psychology* (Vol. 20, pp. 191–234). Hillsdale, NJ: Erlbaum.

Spelke, E. S. (1990). Principles of object perception. *Cognitive Science, 14*, 29–56.

Sperber, D. (1985). Anthropology and psychology: Towards an epidemiology of representations (The Malinowski Memorial Lecture 1984). *Man (N.S.), 20*, 73–89.

Sperber, D. (1996). *Explaining culture: A naturalistic approach.* Cambridge, MA: Blackwell.

Stich, S. (1990). *The fragmentation of reason.* Cambridge, MA: MIT Press.

Tardif, T. (1996). Nouns are not always learned before verbs: Evidence from Mandarin-speakers early vocabularies. *Developmental Psychology, 32*, 492–504.

Tardif, T., Shatz, M., & Naigles, L. (1997). Caregiver speech and children's use of nouns versus verbs: A comparison of English, Italian and Mandarin. *Journal of Child Language, 24*, 535–565.

Toulmin, S., & Goodfield, J. (1961). *The fabric of the heavens: The development of astronomy and physics.* New York: Harper and Row.

Triandis, H. C. (1972). *The analysis of subjective culture.* New York: Wiley.

Triandis, H. C. (1995). *Individualism and collectivism.* Boulder, CO: Westview Press.

Tweed, R. G., & Lehman, D. (2000). *Learning considered within a cultural context: Confucian and Socratic approaches.* Unpublished manuscript, University of British Columbia, Vancouver, Canada.

Vygotsky, L. S. (1978). *Mind in society: The development of higher psychological processes.* Cambridge, MA: Harvard University Press.

Vygotsky, L. S. (1987). *The collected works of L. S. Vygotsky* (J. S. Bruner, Trans.). New York: Plenum Press.

Wellman, H. M. (1990). *The child's theory of mind.* Cambridge, MA: MIT Press.

Whiting, B. B., & Whiting, J. W. M. (1975). *Children of six cultures: A psycho-cultural analysis.* Cambridge, MA: Harvard University Press.

Whiting, J. W. M., & Child, I. L. (1953). Child training and personality: A cross-cultural study. New Haven, CT: Yale University Press.

Witkin, H. A., & Berry, J. W. (1975). Psychological differentiation in cross-cultural perspective. *Journal of Cross Cultural Psychology, 6*, 4–87.

Witkin, H. A., Dyk, R. B., Faterson, H. F., Goodenough, D. R., & Karp, S. A. (1974). *Psychological differentiation*. Potomac, MD: Erlbaum.

Witkin, H. A., & Goodenough, D. R. (1977). Field dependence and interpersonal behavior. *Psychological Bulletin, 84*, 661–689.

Witkin, H. A., Lewis, H. B., Hertzman, M., Machover, K., Meissner, P. B., & Karp, S. A. (1954). *Personality through perception*. New York: Harper.

Witkin, H. A., Price-Williams, D., Bertini, M., Christiansen, B., Oltman, P. K., Ramirez, M., & Van Meel, J. (1974). Social conformity and psychological differentiation. *International Journal of Psychology, 9*, 11–29.

Xia, C. (1997). *Decision-making factors in Go expertise*. Unpublished doctoral dissertation, New Mexico State University, Las Cruces.

Yamagushi, S., Gelfand, M., Mizuno, M., & Zemba, Y. (1997). *Illusion of collective control or illusion of personal control: Biased judgment about a chance event in Japan and the U.S.* Paper presented at the Second Conference of the Asian Association of Social Psychology, Kyoto, Japan.

Yang, S. (1988). *History of Chinese thoughts on logic*. Ganshu, China: People's Press of Ganshu.

Yates, J. F., & Curley, S. P. (1996). Contingency judgment: Primacy effects and attention decrement. *Acta Psychologica, 62*, 293–302.

Yu, Y.-s. (1985). Individualism and the Neo-Taoist movement in Wei-Chin China. In D. Munro (Ed.), *Individualism and holism: Studies in Confucian and Taoist values* (pp. 121–156). Ann Arbor: Center for Chinese Studies, University of Michigan.

Zhang, D. L. (1985). The concept of "Tian Ren He Yi" in Chinese philosophy. *Beijing University Journal, 1*, 8.

Zhang, D. L., & Chen, Z. Y. (1991). *Zhongguo Siwei Pianxiang (The orientation of Chinese thinking)*. Beijing: Social Science Press.

Zhou, G. X. (1990). *Chinese traditional philosophy*. Beijing: Beijing Normal University Press.

Chapter 49: On the Very Idea of a Conceptual Scheme

DONALD DAVIDSON

Philosophers of many persuasions are prone to talk of conceptual schemes. Conceptual schemes, we are told, are ways of organizing experience; they are systems of categories that give form to the data of sensation; they are points of view from which individuals, cultures, or periods survey the passing scene. There may be no translating from one scheme to another, in which case the beliefs, desires, hopes and bits of knowledge that characterize one person have no true counterparts for the subscriber to another scheme. Reality itself is relative to a scheme: what counts as real in one system may not in another.

Even those thinkers who are certain there is only one conceptual scheme are in the sway of the scheme concept; even monotheists have religion. And when someone sets out to describe "our conceptual scheme," his homey task assumes, if we take him literally, that there might be rival systems.

Conceptual relativism is a heady and exotic doctrine, or would be if we could make good sense of it. The trouble is, as so often in philosophy, it is hard to improve intelligibility while retaining the excitement. At any rate that is what I shall argue.

We are encouraged to imagine we understand massive conceptual change or profound contrasts by legitimate examples of a familiar sort. Sometimes an idea, like that of simultaneity as defined in relativity theory, is so important that with its addition a whole department of science takes on a new look. Sometimes revisions in the list of sentences held true in a discipline are so central that we may feel that the terms involved have changed their meanings. Languages that have evolved in distant times or places may differ extensively in their resources for dealing with one or another range of phenomena. What comes easily in one language may come hard in another, and this difference may echo significant dissimilarities in style and value.

But examples like these, impressive as they occasionally are, are not so extreme but that the changes and the contrasts can be explained and described using the equipment of a single language. Whorf, wanting to demonstrate that Hopi incorporates a metaphysics so alien to ours that Hopi and English cannot, as he puts it, "be calibrated," uses English to convey the contents of sample Hopi sentences.[1] Kuhn is brilliant at saying what things were like before the revolution using – what else? – our post-revolutionary idiom.[2] Quine gives us a feel for the "pre-individuative phase in the evolution of our conceptual scheme,"[3] while Bergson tells us where we can go to get a view of a mountain undistorted by one or another provincial perspective.

The dominant metaphor of conceptual relativism, that of differing points of view, seems to betray an underlying paradox. Different points of view make sense, but only if there is a common coordinate system on which to plot them; yet the existence of a common system belies the claim of dramatic incomparability. What we need, it seems to me, is some idea of the considerations that set the limits to conceptual contrast. There are extreme suppositions that founder on paradox or contradiction; there are modest examples we have no trouble understanding. What determines where we cross from the merely strange or novel to the absurd?

We may accept the doctrine that associates having a language with having a conceptual

Reproduced with permission from Davidson, D. (1973–1974) On the very idea of a conceptual scheme. *Proceedings and addresses of the American Philosophical Association*, 47, 5–20.

scheme. The relation may be supposed to be this: if conceptual schemes differ, so do languages. But speakers of different languages may share a conceptual scheme provided there is a way of translating one language into the other. Studying the criteria of translation is therefore a way of focussing on criteria of identity for conceptual schemes. If conceptual schemes aren't associated with languages in this way, the original problem is needlessly doubled, for then we would have to imagine the mind, with its ordinary categories, operating with a language with *its* organizing structure. Under the circumstances we would certainly want to ask who is to be master.

Alternatively, there is the idea that *any* language distorts reality, which implies that it is only wordlessly if at all that the mind comes to grips with things as they really are. This is to conceive language as an inert (though necessarily distorting) medium independent of the human agencies that employ it; a view of language that surely cannot be maintained. Yet if the mind can grapple without distortion with the real, the mind itself must be without categories and concepts. This featureless self is familiar from theories in quite different parts of the philosophical landscape. There are, for example, theories that make freedom consist in decisions taken apart from all desires, habits and dispositions of the agent; and theories of knowledge that suggest that the mind can observe the totality of its own perceptions and ideas. In each case, the mind is divorced from the traits that constitute it; a familiar enough conclusion to certain lines of reasoning, as I said, but one that should always persuade us to reject the premises.

We may identify conceptual schemes with languages, then, or better, allowing for the possibility that more than one language may express the same scheme, sets of intertranslatable languages. Languages we will not think of as separable from souls; speaking a language is not a trait a man can lose while retaining the power of thought. So there is no chance that someone can take up a vantage point for comparing conceptual schemes by temporarily shedding his own. Can we then say that two people have different conceptual schemes if they speak languages that fail of intertranslatability?

In what follows I consider two kinds of case that might be expected to arise: complete, and partial, failures of translatability. There would be complete failure if no significant range of sentences in one language could be translated into the other; there would be partial failure if some range could be translated and some range could

not (I shall neglect possible asymmetries.) My strategy will be to argue that we cannot make sense of total failure, and then to examine more briefly cases of partial failure.

First, then, the purported cases of complete failure. It is tempting to take a very short line indeed: nothing, it may be said, could count as evidence that some form of activity could not be interpreted in our language that was not at the same time evidence that that form of activity was not speech behavior. If this were right, we probably ought to hold that a form of activity that cannot be interpreted as language in our language is not speech behavior. Putting matters this way is unsatisfactory, however, for it comes to little more than making translatability into a familiar tongue a criterion of languagehood. As fiat, the thesis lacks the appeal of self-evidence; if it is a truth, as I think it is, it should emerge as the conclusion of an argument.

The credibility of the position is improved by reflection on the close relations between language and the attribution of attitudes such as belief, desire and intention. On the one hand, it is clear that speech requires a multitude of finely discriminated intentions and beliefs. A person who asserts that perseverance keeps honor bright must, for example, represent himself as believing that perseverance keeps honor bright, and he must intend to represent himself as believing it. On the other hand, it seems unlikely that we can intelligibly attribute attitudes as complex as these to a speaker unless we can translate his words into ours. There can be no doubt that the relation between being able to translate someone's language and being able to describe his attitudes is very close. Still, until we can say more about *what* this relation is, the case against untranslatable languages remains obscure.

It is sometimes thought that translatability into a familiar language, say English, cannot be a criterion of languagehood on the grounds that the relation of translatability is not transitive. The idea is that some language, say Saturnian, may be translatable into English, and some further language, like Plutonian, may be translatable into Saturnian, while Plutonian is not translatable into English. Enough translatable differences may add up to an untranslatable one. By imagining a sequence of languages, each close enough to the one before to be acceptably translated into it, we can imagine a language so different from English as to resist totally translation into it. Corresponding to this distant language would be a system of concepts altogether alien to us.

This exercise does not, I think, introduce any new element into the discussion. For we should have to ask how we recognized that what the Saturnian was doing was *translating* Plutonian (or anything else). The Saturnian speaker might tell us that that was what he was doing or rather, we might for a moment assume that that was what he was telling us. But then it would occur to us to wonder whether our translations of Saturnian were correct.

According to Kuhn, scientists operating in different scientific traditions (within different "paradigms") "live in different worlds."[4] Strawson's *The Bounds of Sense* begins with the remark that "It is possible to imagine kinds of worlds very different from the world as we know it."[5] Since there is at most one world, these pluralities are metaphorical or merely imagined. The metaphors are, however, not at all the same. Strawson invites us to imagine possible nonactual worlds, worlds that might be described, using our present language, by redistributing truth values over sentences in various systematic ways. The clarity of the contrasts between worlds in this case depends on supposing our scheme of concepts, our descriptive resources, to remain fixed. Kuhn, on the other hand, wants us to think of different observers of the same world who come to it with incommensurable systems of concepts. Strawson's many imagined worlds are seen (or heard) – anyway described – from the same point of view; Kuhn's one world is seen from different points of view. It is the second metaphor we want to work on.

The first metaphor requires a distinction within language of concept and content: using a fixed system of concepts (words with fixed meanings) we describe alternative universes. Some sentences will be true simply because of the concepts or meanings involved, others because of the way of the world. In describing possible worlds, we play with sentences of the second kind only.

The second metaphor suggests instead a dualism of quite a different sort, a dualism of total scheme (or language) and uninterpreted content. Adherence to the second dualism, while not inconsistent with adherence to the first, may be encouraged by attacks on the first. Here is how it may work.

To give up the analytic-synthetic distinction as basic to the understanding of language is to give up the idea that we can clearly distinguish between theory and language. Meaning, as we might loosely use the word, is contaminated by

theory, by what is held to be true. Feyerabend puts it this way:

> Our argument against meaning invariance is simple and clear. It proceeds from the fact that usually some of the principles involved in the determinations of the meanings of older theories or points of view are inconsistent with the new ... theories. It points out that it is natural to resolve this contradiction by eliminating the troublesome ... older principles, and to replace them by principles, or theorems, of a new ... theory. And it concludes by showing that such a procedure will also lead to the elimination of the old meanings.[6]

We may now seem to have a formula for generating distinct conceptual schemes. We get a new out of an old scheme when the speakers of a language come to accept as true an important range of sentences they previously took to be false (and, of course, vice versa). We must not describe this change simply as a matter of their coming to view old falsehoods as truths, for a truth is a proposition, and what they come to accept, in accepting a sentence as true, is not the same thing that they rejected when formerly they held the sentence to be false. A change has come over the meaning of the sentence because it now belongs to a new language.

This picture of how new (perhaps better) schemes result from new and better science is very much the picture philosophers of science, like Putnam and Feyerabend, and historians of science, like Kuhn, have painted for us. A related idea emerges in the suggestion of some other philosophers, that we could improve our conceptual lot if we were to tune our language to an improved science. Thus both Quine and Smart, in somewhat different ways, regretfully admit that our present ways of talking make a serious science of behavior impossible. (Wittgenstein and Ryle have said similar things without regret.) The cure, Quine and Smart think, is to change how we talk. Smart advocates (and predicts) the change in order to put us on the scientifically straight path of materialism; Quine is more concerned to clear the way for a purely extensional language. (Perhaps I should add that I think our *present* scheme and language are best understood as extensional and materialist.)

If we were to follow this advice, I do not myself think science or understanding would be advanced, though possibly morals would. But the present question is only whether, if such changes were to take place, we should be justified in calling them alterations in the basic conceptual apparatus. The difficulty in so calling them is easy to appreciate. Suppose that in my office of Minister of Scientific Language I want the new man to stop using words that refer, say, to emotions, feelings, thoughts and intentions, and to talk instead of the physiological states and happenings that are assumed to be more or less identical with the mental riff and raff. How do I tell whether my advice has been heeded if the new man speaks a new language? For all I know, the shiny new phrases, though stolen from the old language in which they refer to physiological stirrings, may in his mouth play the role of the messy old mental concepts.

The key phrase is: for all I know. What is clear is that retention of some or all of the old vocabulary in itself provides no basis for judging the new scheme to be the same as, or different from, the old. So what sounded at first like a thrilling discovery – that truth is relative to a conceptual scheme – has not so far been shown to be anything more than the pedestrian and familiar fact that the truth of a sentence is relative to (among other things) the language to which it belongs. Instead of living in different worlds, Kuhn's scientists may, like those who need Webster's dictionary, be only words apart.

Giving up the analytic-synthetic distinction has not proven a help in making sense of conceptual relativism. The analytic-synthetic distinction is however explained in terms of something that may serve to buttress conceptual relativism, namely the idea of empirical content. The dualism of the synthetic and the analytic is a dualism of sentences some of which are true (or false) both because of what they mean and because of their empirical content, while others are true (or false) by virtue of meaning alone, having no empirical content. If we give up the dualism, we abandon the conception of meaning that goes with it, but we do not have to abandon the idea of empirical content: we can hold, if we want, that *all* sentences have empirical content. Empirical content is in turn explained by reference to the facts, the world, experience, sensation, the totality of sensory stimuli, or something similar. Meanings gave us a way to talk about categories, the organizing structure of language, and so on; but it is possible, as we have seen, to give up meanings and analyticity while retaining the idea of language as embodying a conceptual scheme. Thus in place of the dualism of the analytic-synthetic we get the dualism of conceptual scheme and empirical content. The new dualism is the foundation of an empiricism shorn of the untenable dogmas of

the analytic-synthetic distinction and reductionism – shorn, that is, of the unworkable idea that we can uniquely allocate empirical content sentence by sentence.

I want to urge that this second dualism of scheme and content, of organizing system and something waiting to be organized, cannot be made intelligible and defensible. It is itself a dogma of empiricism, the third dogma. The third, and perhaps the last, for if we give it up it is not clear that there is anything distinctive left to call empiricism.

The scheme-content dualism has been formulated in many ways. Here are some examples. The first comes from Whorf, elaborating on a theme of Sapir's. Whorf says that:

> . . . language produces an organization of experience. We are inclined to think of language simply as a technique of expression, and not to realize that language first of all is a classification and arrangement of the stream of sensory experience which results in a certain world-order . . . In other words, language does in a cruder but also in a broader and more versatile way the same thing that science does . . . We are thus introduced to a new principle of relativity, which holds that all observers are not led by the same physical evidence to the same picture of the universe, unless their linguistic backgrounds are similar, or can in some way be calibrated.[7]

Here we have all the required elements: language as the organizing force, not to be distinguished clearly from science; what is organized, referred to variously as "experience," "the stream of sensory experience," and "physical evidence"; and finally, the failure of intertranslatability ("calibration"). The failure of intertranslatability is a necessary condition for difference of conceptual schemes; the common relation to experience or the evidence is what is supposed to help us make sense of the claim that it is languages or schemes that are under consideration when translation fails. It is essential to this idea that there be something neutral and common that lies outside all schemes. This common something cannot, of course, be the *subject matter* of contrasting languages, or translation would be possible. Thus Kuhn has recently written:

> Philosophers have now abandoned hope of finding a pure sense-datum language . . . but many of them continue to assume that theories can be compared by recourse to a

basic vocabulary consisting entirely of words which are attached to nature in ways that are unproblematic and, to the extent necessary independent of theory... Feyerabend and I have argued at length that no such vocabulary is available. In the transition from one theory to the next words change their meanings or conditions of applicability in subtle ways. Though most of the same signs are used before and after a revolution – e.g. force, mass, element, compound, cell – the ways in which some of them attach to nature has somehow changed. Successive theories are thus, we say, incommensurable.[8]

"Incommensurable" is, of course, Kuhn and Feyerabend's word for "not intertranslatable." The neutral content waiting to be organized is supplied by nature.

Feyerabend himself suggests that we may compare contrasting schemes by "choosing a point of view outside the system or the language." He hopes we can do this because "there is still human experience as an actually existing process"[9] independent of all schemes.

The same, or similar, thoughts are expressed by Quine in many passages: "The totality of our so-called knowledge or beliefs... is a man-made fabric which impinges on experience only along the edges...;"[10] "...total science is like a field of force whose boundary conditions are experience";[11] "As an empiricist I... think of the conceptual scheme of science as a tool... for predicting future experience in the light of past experience."[12] And again:

> We persist in breaking reality down somehow into a multiplicity of identifiable and discriminable objects... We talk so inveterately of objects that to say we do so seems almost to say nothing at all; for how else is there to talk? It is hard to say how else there is to talk, not because our objectifying pattern is an invariably trait of human nature, but because we are bound to adapt any alien pattern to our own in the very process of understanding or translating the alien sentences.[13]

The test of difference remains failure or difficulty of translation: "... to speak of that remote medium as radically different from ours is to say no more than that the translations do not come smoothly."[14] Yet the roughness may be so great that the alien has an "as yet unimagined pattern beyond individuation."[15]

The idea is then that something is a language, and associated with a conceptual scheme,

whether we can translate it or not, if it stands in a certain relation (predicting, organizing, facing or fitting) to experience (nature, reality, sensory promptings). The problem is to say what the relation is, and to be clearer about the entities related.

The images and metaphors fall into two main groups: conceptual schemes (languages) either *organize* something, or they *fit* it (as in "he warps his scientific heritage to fit his... sensory promptings"[16] The first group contains also *systematize, divide up* (the stream of experience); further examples of the second group are *predict, account for, face* (the tribunal of experience). As for the entities that get organized, or which the scheme must fit, I think again we may detect two main ideas; either it is reality (the universe, the world, nature), or it is experience (the passing show, surface irritations, sensory promptings, sense data, the given).

We cannot attach a clear meaning to the notion of organizing a single object (the world, nature etc.) unless that object is understood to contain or consist in other objects. Someone who sets out to organize a closet arranges the things in it. If you are told not to organize the shoes and shirts, but the closet itself, you would be bewildered. How would you organize the Pacific Ocean? Straighten out its shores, perhaps, or relocate its islands, or destroy its fish.

A language may contain simple predicates whose extensions are matched by no simple predicates, or even by any predicates at all, in some other language. What enables us to make this point in particular cases is an ontology common to the two languages, with concepts that individuate the same objects. We can be clear about breakdowns in translation when they are local enough, for a background of generally successful translation provides what is needed to make the failures intelligible. But we were after larger game: we wanted to make sense of there being a language we could not translate at all. Or, to put the point differently, we were looking for a criterion of languagehood that did not depend on, or entail, translatability into a familiar idiom. I suggest that the image of organizing the closet of nature will not supply such a criterion.

How about the other kind of object, experience? Can we think of a language organizing *it*? Much the same difficulties recur. The notion of organization applies only to pluralities. But whatever plurality we take experience to consist in – events like losing a button or stubbing a toe, having a sensation of warmth or hearing an oboe – we will have to individuate according to familiar principles. A language that organizes *such* entities must be a language very like our own.

Experience (and its classmates like surface irritations, sensations and sense data) also makes another and more obvious trouble for the organizing idea. For how could something count as a language that organized *only* experiences, sensations, surface irritations or sense data? Surely knives and forks, railroads and mountains, cabbages and kingdoms also need organizing.

This last remark will no doubt sound inappropriate as a response to the claim that a conceptual scheme is a way of coping with sensory experience; and I agree that it is. But what was under consideration was the idea of *organizing* experience, not the idea of *coping with* (or fitting or facing) experience. The reply was apropos of the former, not the latter, concept. So now let's see whether we can do better with the second idea.

When we turn from talk of organization to talk of fitting we turn our attention from the referential apparatus of language – predicates, quantifiers, variables and singular terms – to whole sentences. It is sentences that predict (or are used to predict), sentences that cope or deal with things, that fit our sensory promptings, that can be compared or confronted with the evidence. It is sentences also that face the tribunal of experience, though of course they must face it together.

The proposal is not that experiences, sense data, surface irritations or sensory promptings are the sole subject matter of language. There is, it is true, the theory that talk about brick houses on Elm Street is ultimately to be construed as being about sense data or perceptions, but such reductionistic views are only extreme, and implausible, versions of the general position we are considering. The general position is that sensory experience provides all the *evidence* for the acceptance of sentences (where sentences may include whole theories). A sentence or theory fits our sensory promptings, successfully faces the tribunal of experience, predicts future experience, or copes with the pattern of our surface irritations, provided it is borne out by the evidence.

In the common course of affairs, a theory may be borne out by the available evidence and yet be false. But what is in view here is not just actually available evidence; it is the totality of possible sensory evidence past, present and future. We do not need to pause to contemplate what this might mean. The point is that for a theory to fit or face up to the totality of possible sensory evidence is for that theory to be true. If a theory quantifies over physical objects, numbers or sets, what it says about these entities is true provided the theory as a whole fits the sensory evidence. One can see how, from this point of view, such entities might be called posits. It is reasonable to call something a posit if it can be contrasted with something that is not. Here the something that is not is sensory experience – at least that is the idea.

The trouble is that the notion of fitting the totality of experience, like the notions of fitting the facts, or being true to the facts, adds nothing intelligible to the simple concept of being true. To speak of sensory experience rather than the evidence, or just the facts, expresses a view about the source or nature of evidence, but it does not add a new entity to the universe against which to test conceptual schemes. The totality of sensory evidence is what we want provided it is all the evidence there is; and all the evidence there is is just what it takes to make our sentences or theories true. Nothing, however, no *thing*, makes sentences and theories true: not experience, not surface irritations, not the world, can make a sentence true. *That* experience takes a certain course, that our skin is warmed or punctured, that the universe is finite, these facts, if we like to talk that way, make sentences and theories true. But this point is put better without mention of facts. The sentence "My skin is warm" is true if and only if my skin is warm. Here there is no reference to a fact, a world, an experience, or a piece of evidence.[17]

Our attempt to characterize languages or conceptual schemes in terms of the notion of fitting some entity has come down, then, to the simple thought that something is an acceptable conceptual scheme or theory if it is true. Perhaps we better say *largely* true in order to allow sharers of a scheme to differ on details. And the criterion of a conceptual scheme different from our own now becomes: largely true but not translatable. The question whether this is a useful criterion is just the question how well we understand the notion of truth, as applied to language, independent of the notion of translation. The answer is, I think, that we do not understand it independently at all.

We recognize sentences like "'Snow is white' is true if and only if snow is white" to be trivially true. Yet the totality of such English sentences uniquely determines the extension of the concept of truth for English. Tarski generalized this observation and made it a test of theories of truth: according to Tarski's Convention T, a satisfactory theory of truth for a language L must entail, for every sentence s of L, a theorem of the form "s is true if and only if p" where "s" is replaced by a description of s and "p" by s itself if L is English, and by a translation of s into English if L is not English.[18] This isn't, of course, a definition of truth, and it doesn't hint that there is a single definition or theory that applies to languages generally. Nevertheless, Convention T suggests, though it cannot state, an important feature common to all the specialized concepts of truth. It succeeds in doing this by making essential use of the notion of translation into a language we know. Since Convention T embodies our best intuition as to how the concept of truth is used, there does not seem to be much hope for a test that a conceptual scheme is radically different from ours if that test depends on the assumption that we can divorce the notion of truth from that of translation.

Neither a fixed stock of meanings, nor a theory-neutral reality, can provide, then, a ground for comparison of conceptual schemes. It would be a mistake to look further for such a ground if by that we mean something conceived as common to incommensurable schemes. In abandoning this search, we abandon the attempt to make sense of the metaphor of a single space within which each scheme has a position and provides a point of view.

I turn now to the more modest approach: the idea of partial rather than total failure of translation. This introduces the possibility of making changes and contrasts in conceptual schemes intelligible by reference to the common part. What we need is a theory of translation or interpretation that makes no assumptions about shared meanings, concepts or beliefs.

The interdependence of belief and meaning springs from the interdependence of two aspects of the interpretation of speech behavior: the attribution of beliefs and the interpretation of sentences. We remarked before that we can afford to associate conceptual schemes with languages because of these dependencies. Now we can put the point in a somewhat sharper way. Allow that a man's speech cannot be interpreted without knowing a good deal about what he believes (and intends and wants), and that fine distinctions between beliefs are impossible without understood speech; how then are we to interpret speech or intelligibly to attribute beliefs and other attitudes? Clearly we must have a theory that simultaneously accounts for attitudes and interprets speech – a theory that rests on evidence which assumes neither.

I suggest, following Quine, that we may without circularity or unwarranted assumptions accept certain very general attitudes towards sentences as the basic evidence for a theory of radical interpretation. For the sake of the present discussion at least we may depend on the attitude of accepting as true, directed at sentences, as the crucial notion. (A more full-blooded theory would look to other attitudes towards sentences as well, such as wishing true, wondering whether true, intending to make true, and so on). Attitudes are indeed involved here, but the fact that the main issue is not begged can be seen from this: if we merely know that someone holds a certain sentence to be true, we know neither what he means by the sentence nor what belief his holding it true represents. His holding the sentence true is thus the vector of two forces: the problem of interpretation is to abstract from the evidence a workable theory of meaning and an acceptable theory of belief.

The way this problem is solved is best appreciated from undramatic examples. If you see a ketch sailing by and your companion says, "Look at that handsome yawl," you may be faced with a problem of interpretation. One natural possibility is that your friend has mistaken a ketch for a yawl, and has formed a false belief. But if his vision is good and his line of sight favorable it is even more plausible that he does not use the word "yawl" quite as you do, and has made no mistake at all about the position of the jigger on the passing yacht. We do this sort of off the cuff interpretation all the time, deciding in favor of reinterpretation of words in order to preserve a reasonable theory of belief. As philosophers we are peculiarly tolerant of systematic malapropism, and practised at interpreting the result. The process is that of constructing a viable theory of belief and meaning from sentences held true.

Such examples emphasize the interpretation of anomalous details against a background of common beliefs and a going method of translation. But the principles involved must be the same in less trivial cases. What matters is this: if all we know is what sentences a speaker holds true, and we cannot assume that his language is our own, then we cannot take even a first step towards interpretation without knowing or assuming a great deal about the speaker's beliefs. Since knowledge of beliefs comes only with the ability to interpret words, the only possibility at the start is to assume general agreement on beliefs. We get a first approximation to a finished theory by assigning to sentences of a speaker conditions of truth that actually obtain (in our own opinion) just when the speaker holds those sentences true. The guiding policy is to do this as far as possible, subject to considerations of simplicity, hunches about the effects of social conditioning, and of course our common sense, or scientific, knowledge of explicable error.

The method is not designed to eliminate disagreement, nor can it; its purpose is to make meaningful disagreement possible, and this depends entirely on a foundation – *some* foundation – in agreement. The agreement may take the form of widespread sharing of sentences held true by speakers of "the same language," or agreement in the large mediated by a theory of truth contrived by an interpreter for speakers of another language.

Since charity is not an option, but a condition of having a workable theory, it is meaningless to suggest that we might fall into massive error by endorsing it. Until we have successfully established a systematic correlation of sentences held true with sentences held true, there are no mistakes to make. Charity is forced on us; whether we like it or not, if we want to understand others, we must count them right in most matters. If we can produce a theory that reconciles charity and the formal conditions for a theory, we have done all that could be done to ensure communication. Nothing more is possible, and nothing more is needed.

We make maximum sense of the words and thoughts of others when we interpret in a way that optimizes agreement (this includes room, as we said, for explicable error, i.e. differences of opinion). Where does this leave the case for conceptual relativism? The answer is, I think, that we must say much the same thing about differences in conceptual scheme as we say about differences in belief: we improve the clarity and bite of declarations of difference, whether of scheme or opinion, by enlarging the basis of shared (translatable) language or of shared opinion. Indeed, no clear line between the cases can be made out. If we choose to translate some alien sentence rejected by its speakers by a sentence to which we are strongly attached on a community basis, we may be tempted to call this a difference in schemes; if we decide to accommodate the evidence in other ways, it may be more natural to speak of a difference of opinion. But when others think differently from us,

no general principle, or appeal to evidence, can force us to decide that the difference lies in our beliefs rather than in our concepts.

We must conclude, I think, that the attempt to give a solid meaning to the idea of conceptual relativism, and hence to the idea of a conceptual scheme, fares no better when based on partial failure of translation than when based on total failure. Given the underlying methodology of interpretation, we could not be in a position to judge that others had concepts or beliefs radically different from our own.

It would be wrong to summarize by saying we have shown how communication is possible between people who have different schemes, a way that works without need of what there cannot be, namely a neutral ground, or a common coordinate system. For we have found no intelligible basis on which it can be said that schemes are different. It would be equally wrong to announce the glorious news that all mankind – all speakers of language, at least – share a common scheme and ontology. For if we cannot intelligibly say that schemes are different, neither can we intelligibly say that they are one.

In giving up dependence on the concept of an uninterpreted reality, something outside all schemes and science, we do not relinquish the notion of objective truth – quite the contrary. Given the dogma of a dualism of scheme and reality, we get conceptual relativity, and truth relative to a scheme. Without the dogma, this kind of relativity goes by the board. Of course truth of sentences remains relative to language, but that is as objective as can be. In giving up the dualism of scheme and world, we do not give up the world, but reestablish unmediated touch with the familiar objects whose antics make our sentences and opinions true or false.

Notes

1 B. L. Whorf, "The Punctual and Segmentative Aspects of Verbs in Hopi", in *Language, Thought and Reality: Selected Writings of Benjamin Lee Whorf*, ed. J. B. Carroll. MIT Press, Cambridge, MA, 1956.

2 T. S. Kuhn, *The Structure of Scientific Revolutions*. University of Chicago Press, Chicago, 1962.

3 W. V. Kuhn, "Speaking of Objects" *Ontological Relativity and Other Essays*. Columbia University Press, New York 1969.

4 T. S. Kuhn, *The structure of scientific revolutions*, p. 134.

5 Peter Strawson, *The Bounds of Sense*, London, 1966, p. 15.

6   Paul Feyerabend, "Explanation, Reduction, and Empiricism," in *Scientific Explanation, Space, and Time: Minnesota Studies in the Philosophy of Science*, Vol. III, Minneapolis, 1962, p. 82.

7   Benjamin Lee Whorf, *Language, Thought and Reality: Selected Writings of Benjamin Lee Whorf*, ed. J. B. Carroll, MIT Press, Cambridge, MA. 1956, p. 55.

8   Thomas Kuhn, "Reflection on my Critics" in *Criticism and the Growth of Knowledge*, eds. I. Lakatos and A. Musgrave, Cambridge, 1970, pp. 266, 267.

9   Paul Feyerabend, "Problems of Empiricism," in *Beyond the Edge of Certainty*. ed. R. G. Colodny, Englewood Cliffs, New Jersey, 1965, p. 214.

10 W. V. O. Quine, "Two Dogmas of Empiricism," reprinted in *From a Logical Point of View*, 2nd edition, Cambridge, Mass., 1961, p. 42.

11 *Ibid.*

12 *Ibid.*, p. 44.

13 W. V. O. Quine, "Speaking of Objects," reprinted in *Ontological Relativity and Other Essays*, New York, 1969, p. 1.

14 *Ibid.*, p. 25.

15 *Ibid.*, p. 24.

16 "Two Dogmas of Empiricism," p. 46.

17 These remarks are defended in my "True to the Facts," *The Journal of Philosophy*, Vol. 66 (1969), pp. 748–764.

18 Alfred Tarski, "The Concept of Truth in Formalized Languages," in *Logic, Semantics, Metamathematics*, Oxford, 1956.

Chapter 50: The Truth in Relativism

BERNARD WILLIAMS

This chapter tries to place certain issues in the discussion of relativism, rather than to deal with any one of them thoroughly. It is concerned with any kind of relativism, in the sense that the questions raised are ones that should be asked with regard to relativistic views in any area, whether it be the world-views of different cultures, shifts in scientific paradigms, or differences of ethical outlook. A machinery is introduced which is intended to apply quite generally. But the only area in which I want to claim that there is truth in relativism is the area of ethical relativism. This does not mean that I here try to argue against its truth in any other area, nor do I try to pursue any of the numerous issues involved in delimiting the ethical from other areas.

1. Conditions of the Problem

(a) There have to be two or more *systems of belief* (Ss) which are to some extent self-contained. No very heavy weight is put on the propositional implications of the term 'belief', nor, still less, is it implied that all relevant differences between such systems (let 'S1', 'S2', stand for examples from now on) can be adequately expressed in propositional differences: the extent to which this is so will differ with different sorts of examples. Any application of this structure will involve some degree of idealisation, with regard to the coherence and homogeneity of an S. There is more than one way in which these characteristics may be imposed, however, and difference in these affects the way (perhaps, the sense) in which the resultant S is an idealisation.

The characteristics may be involved in the very identification of the Ss: thus two synchronously competing scientific theories may be picked out in part in terms of what bodies of beliefs hang together. But even in this case the Ss will not just be intellectual items constructed from the outside on the basis of the harmony of their content: there will in fact be bodies of scientists working within these theories (or research programmes) and seeking to impose coherence on them. If failures in imposing coherence were to be regarded as *a priori* impossible, the structure of description in terms of various Ss would lose a great deal of explanatory value.

In the case of alien cultures, the identification of an S may be effected initially through other features (geographical isolation and internal interaction of a group of persons), and the coherence of the S operate rather as an ideal limit for the understanding of the group's beliefs. This idea is in fact problematical, at least if taken as indicative of understanding in any objective sense: one comprehensible, and surely plausible, hypothesis is that no group of human beings will have a belief system which is fully coherent. The demand operates, nevertheless, as a constraint on theory-construction about the group, since the data will even more radically underdetermine theory if room is left for indeterminate amounts of incoherence within the S that theory constructs.

The problems of relativism concern communication between S1 and S2, or between them and some third party, and, in particular, issues of preference between them. It is worth noticing that quite a lot is taken for granted in the construction of the problem-situation already, in the application of the idea of there being a plurality of different Ss. Thus it is presupposed that persons within each S can understand other persons within that S; also that persons

Reproduced with permission from Williams, B. (1981) The truth in relativism. *Moral Luck*. Cambridge, UK: Cambridge University Press, pp. 132–43.

receive information in certain ways and not others, are acculturated in certain ways, etc. It may be that some forms of relativism can be shown to be false by reference to these presuppositions themselves: not on the ground (which would prove nothing) that the *genesis* of ideas such as 'a culture', like that of 'relativism' itself, lies in a certain sort of culture, but on the ground that the *application* of a notion such as 'a culture' presupposes the instantiation in the subject-matter of a whole set of relations which can be adequately expressed at all only via the concepts of one culture rather than another (e.g., certain notions of causality). Any relativism which denied the non-relative validity of concepts involved in setting up its problem at all, would be refuted. This aspect of the matter has received some attention;[1] I shall not try to take it further here.

(b) $S1$ and $S2$ have to be *exclusive of one another*. That this should in some sense be so is a necessary condition of the problems arising to which relativism is supposed to provide an answer; indeed, it can itself be seen as a condition of identifying $S1$ and $S2$, in any sense relevant to those problems. Suppose for example that two putative Ss constituted merely the history or geography of two different times or places: then evidently they are not Ss in the sense of the problem, because they can merely be conjoined.

A much harder question, however, is raised by asking what are the (most general) conditions of two Ss excluding one another. The most straightforward case is that in which $S1$ and $S2$ have conflicting consequences, a condition which I shall first take in the form of requiring that there be some yes/no question to which consequence $C1$ of $S1$ answers 'yes' and consequence $C2$ of $S2$ answers 'no'. Under this condition, $S1$ and $S2$ have to be (at least in the respect in question) *comparable*.

The questions to which relativism is supposed to give an answer may be raised by the case of conflicting consequences, but relativism will not stay around as an answer to them unless something else is also true, namely that the answering of a yes/no question of this sort in one way rather than the other does not constrain either the holder of $S1$ or the holder of $S2$ to abandon respectively the positions characteristic of $S1$ and $S2$ (and of the difference between them). If this further condition does not hold, there will be a straightforward decision procedure between $S1$ and $S2$, and relativism will have been banished. In the scientific case, the possibility of this condition holding, granted that $C1$ and $C2$ are consequences of $S1$ and $S2$, lies in the possibility that the consequence follows from the system only using material peripheral to the system and to its most characteristic positions: the situation is the much-discussed one in which theory is underdetermined by observation.

However, if theory is radically underdetermined by observation, can it be required that Ss are even to this modest degree comparable? Thus, in the spirit of one fashionable line of argument, if every observation statement is theory-laden, and all theory-ladenness displays meaning-variance, then it is unclear how there can be one yes/no question which stands in the required relation to $S1$ and $S2$. Here it is important to see how little is implied by there being conflicting consequences of $S1$ and $S2$. All that is required is that there be *some* description of a possible outcome, which description is acceptable to both $S1$ and $S2$, and in terms of which a univocal yes/no question can be formed: it may well be that there are other descriptions of what is (in some sense) the same event which are non-comparable. If this minimal requirement is not satisfied, severe problems are likely to follow, particularly in the case of scientific theories, for the original description of the Ss. We lose control on the notion of observation, concerning which it is said that it underdetermines theory; and we lose the descriptions of certain passages in the history of science which are the subject and in some part the motivation of these accounts (roughly it looks as though not only the choice of a replacement paradigm, but the occasion of that choice, might emerge as entirely socially determined, as though a chief determinant of the alteration of scientific theory were boredom).

However it may be with scientific theories, it would be unwise to exclude the possibility of systems so disparate that they were not, in terms of conflicting consequences, comparable at all. Some social anthropologists have given accounts of the Ss of traditional (pre-scientific) societies in terms which seem to imply that they are quite incommensurable with the Ss of modern, scientific, societies. I shall not go into the question of whether such accounts could be true.[2] The issue is rather, if such accounts were true, what content could be left to the idea that the traditional and the scientific Ss were exclusive of one another – as surely everyone, including these social anthropologists, would say that they were. Here it looks as though the only thing to be said is that, in ways which need to be analysed, it is impossible to live within both Ss. Accepting this vague idea, we can indeed continue to use, at a different level, the language of conflicting consequences, since if it is impossible to live within both S1 and S2, then the consequences of (holding) S1 include actions, practices, etc. which are incompatible with those which are consequences of (holding) S2.

I do not take this to be a very illuminating assimilation, since the variation required in the interpretation of 'consequence' remains unexplained. But it does harmlessly help to handle a wider range of cases without constant qualification; and it does, more than that, positively bring out one thing – that even in this limiting case (which I shall call that of *incommensurable exclusivity*), there has to be something which can be identified as the *locus* of exclusivity, and hence the Ss are not entirely incommensurable. This locus will be that of the actions or practices which are the consequences of living within S1 and S2. Another light will be shed on them when we turn, next, to broadly ethical cases.

In ethical cases (taken in a broad sense), the conditions of conflict come out, obviously enough, differently from the form they take with, for instance, scientific theories. The simplest case is that of conflict between answers which are given to yes/no questions which are practical questions, questions about whether to do a certain thing. Now such a question might be a general, or type, action question, asking whether a certain type of thing was to be done in a certain type of situation. In this case, the relevant formulation is that it is possible for S1 to answer 'yes' to such a question while S2 answers 'no' to it; this is parallel to two theories yielding conflicting predictions, but without the question yet being raised of one or the other actually being borne out in fact. We get a structure resembling the occurrence of an actual observation only when we move to the idea of a particular token action question, as asked by a particular agent in a particular situation. Here the practical question *gets answered* in actual fact, and this occurrence of course trivially satisfies the conditions: the fact that a given question gets answered in this sense in a way which conflicts with, say, the consequence if S1 does not constrain a holder of S1 to abandon his position (he may say that the agent was wrong so to decide). What actually is done trivially underdetermines systems of belief about what ought to be done.

Action decisions are not the only possible site of conflicting consequences in the ethical case: various forms of approval, sentiment, etc. can equally come into it. With these, but also with action-descriptions, difficulties can, once more,

arise about the satisfaction of the comparability condition. This condition is easily satisfied under a theory such as Hare's, which is strongly analogous to a positivist philosophy of science, in regarding an ethical outlook or value system (theory) as consisting of a set of principles (laws) whose content is totally characterised by what imperatives (predictions) they generate. But on any more complex view, very severe problems of comparability arise. Here again, we can appeal to the weak requirement which was made in the theory case: that there be some description of the action (say) in terms of which a univocal yes/no question can be formulated. Thus it is certainly true and important that marriage to two persons in a polygamous society is not the same state or action as bigamy in a monogamous society, nor is human sacrifice the same action as murder in the course of armed robbery. But there may well be descriptions such that a univocal yes/no question can be formed for each of these examples, and S1 and S2 differ in their answers. There can be, that is to say, system-based conflict. Two persons can be in a situation of conflict, in which they give opposed answers to the same question of action or approval, and they can be motivated to this by their value system (that is to exclude quarrels inspired by motivations themselves not sanctioned by the value system).

The line I have sketched for describing cases (if there are any) of incommensurable exclusivity implies that for every pair of Ss which are incommensurably exclusive, there must be some action, practice, etc., which under some agreed description will be a locus of disagreement between the holders of the Ss. If this condition is not met, it is unclear what room is left for the notion of exclusivity at all, and hence for the problems of relativism.

2. Variation and Confrontation

With regard to a given kind of S, there can be both diachronic and synchronic variation. In the history and philosophy of science, anthropology, etc., there is room for a great deal of discussion about the interrelations of and the limitations of these kinds of variation. There is for instance the question whether certain synchronic variations represent certain diachronic ones, i.e., whether certain cultural variations in one place are survivals of what was an earlier culture elsewhere (do the Hottentots have a Stone Age culture?). Again, the definition of a certain class of Ss can limit variation: thus the range within which something can count as a *scientific theory* is a well-known matter of dispute, as is the question whether the use of such restrictions to delimit what is counted as diachronic variation (to constitute, that is, a history *of science*) is merely a matter of *ex post facto* evaluation. (The matter takes on a different aspect with respect to synchronic variation at the present time, in view of the existence of a unified and institutionalized international scientific culture.)

In many, if not all, cases of diachronic variation, it is an important fact that a later S involves consciousness of at least its neighbouring predecessor (though not necessarily, of course, in terms which the predecessor, or again S's successors, would assent to). There are very important issues at this point about the writing of 'objective' cultural history, but I do not intend to take them on. In fact, I propose from this point on to ignore cases in which S2 arises in a way which involves some conscious relation with S1, and to consider only those in which mutual awareness can be regarded as, in principle, a development independent of the existence of S1 and S2. While this simplification is a drastic one, it will do for present purposes.

Under this simplification, let us now consider some possible relations, or lack of them, between S1 and S2. There is, first, the primitive situation in which S1 and S2 exist in ignorance of one another. After that, there are cases in which at least one of S1 and S2 encounters the other: either directly, in the case in which persons who hold one of the Ss encounter persons who hold the other, or indirectly, when persons holding one merely learn of the other.

Some such encounters, I shall call *real confrontations* (the term 'confrontation' is not meant to carry all the implications it has in contemporary politics). For any S, there has to be something which counts as assenting to that S, fully accepting it or living within it – whatever it is, in each sort of case, for an S of that sort to be *somebody's* S. I shall call this relation in general 'holding'. There is a real confrontation between S1 and S2 at a given time if there is a group at that time for whom each of S1 and S2 is a real option. This includes, but is not confined to, the case of a group which already holds S1 or S2, for whom the question is one of whether to *go over* to the other S. We shall come back shortly to the question of what a 'real option' is.

Contrasted with this situation is that of *notional confrontation*.[3] Notional confrontation resembles real confrontation in that there are persons who are aware of S1 and S2, and aware of their differences; it differs from it in that at least

one of S1 and S2 do not present a real option to them. S1 and S2 can of course be in both real and notional confrontation, but not with respect to the same persons at the same time. S1 and S2 can be in notional confrontation without ever having been in real confrontation: no one may come to know of both S1 and S2 until at least one of them has ceased to present real options. Again, S1 and S2 can be in real confrontation without ever being in notional confrontation: no one may ever think of one of them after the hour of its struggle (presumably unsuccessful) with the other.

What is it for an S to be a real option? In accordance with the starting-point that Ss belong to groups (which is not to deny that they are held by individuals, but to assert that they are held by individuals in ways which require description and explanation by reference to the group), the idea of a real option is meant to be a social notion. S2 is a real option for a group if either it is their S or it is possible for them to go over to S2; where going over to S2 involves, first, that it is possible for them to live within, or hold, S2 and retain their hold on reality, and, second, to the extent that rational comparison between S2 and their present outlook is possible, they could acknowledge their transition to S2 in the light of such comparison.[4] Both these conditions use concepts which imply that whether a given S is a real option to a given group at a given time is, to some extent at least, a matter of degree: this consequence is not unwelcome.

Something must be said in explanation of each of these conditions. Let me take the second first. The purpose of this is to ensure that the question of whether an S is a real option is not just (granted the satisfaction of the first condition) a matter of such things as the state of psychological technology. We do not want to say that an eccentric scientific theory is a real option for a group of scientists because they could be drugged or operated upon in such a way that they emerged believing it. To the extent that S1 and S2 are comparable, do expose themselves to experiment which can tend to favour one over the other, etc., these methods of assessment are what are to count in the consideration of the accessibility of S2 from S1. Whether something is a real option is a social question, but one rooted in as much rationality as is available on the given type of issue.

In the limiting case of incommensurable exclusivity, this condition will have virtually no effect. There will be little room in such a case for anything except conversion. But even conversion had better be something which can be lived sanely, and this is the force of the first condition. To speak of people who have accepted S2 'retaining their hold on reality' is to imply such things as that it is possible for S2 to become their S, and for them to live within S2, without their engaging in extensive self-deception, falling into paranoia, and such things. The extent to which that is so depends in turn, to some degree, on what features of their existing social situation are held constant under the assumption of their going over to S2. Thus S2 may not be realistically possible for a group granted features of their present social situation, but it might be if those features were changed. The question of whether S2 is, after all, a real option for them then involves the question of whether those features could be changed.

It is neither a necessary nor a sufficient condition of an S's being a real option for a group that they think that it is a real option. It is not a sufficient condition, because they may be ill-informed, unimaginative, un-self-aware or optimistic about what it would be like for them to try to live within that S (and this may not be just a personal, but a social or political mistake). It is not a necessary condition, because they may not have realised what possibilities going over to that S would offer them: the psychology of conversion of course relates to this matter. I regard the question of whether a given S is a real option for a given group at a given time as basically an objective question. Of course, people may differ about such questions as what is included under 'a hold on reality', and also, notoriously, about what degree of rational comparability can be displayed by Ss of a given kind. In terms of the present structure, such disagreements may well affect what range of Ss those people will regard as real options, for themselves or others.

In this sense many Ss which have been held are not real options now. The life of a Greek Bronze Age chief, or a mediaeval Samurai, and the outlooks that go with those, are not real options for us: there is no way of living them. This is not to say that reflection on those value-systems may not provide inspiration for thoughts about elements missing from modern life, but there is no way of taking on those Ss. Even Utopian projects among a small band of enthusiasts could not reproduce *that* life. Still more, the project of re-enacting it on a societal scale in the context of actual modern industrial life would involve one of those social or political mistakes, in fact a vast illusion. The prospect of removing the conditions of modern industrial life alto-

gether is something else again – another, though different, impossibility.

In this connexion it is important that there are asymmetrically related options. Some version of modern technological life and its outlooks has become a real option for members of some traditional societies, but their life is not, despite the passionate nostalgia of many, a real option for us. The theories one has about the nature and extent of such asymmetries (which Hegelians would ground in asymmetries of both history and consciousness) affect one's views about the objective possibilities of radical social and political action.

3. Relativism

Suppose that we are in real confrontation with some S. Then there will be some vocabulary of appraisal – 'true–false', 'right–wrong', 'acceptable–unacceptable' etc. – which will be deployed, and essentially deployed, in thought and speech about this confrontation. The ways in which it is deployed, and the considerations it is geared into, will of course differ with the type of S in question – for instance, with the degree of comparability that obtains between Ss of this type. Whatever these differences, in speaking of a 'vocabulary of appraisal', I refer only to those expressions which can *at least* be used to express one's own acceptance or rejection of an S or an element of an S. Such a vocabulary is essentially deployed in reflective thought within situations of real confrontation, since in reflection one has to be able to think, and articulate one's feelings, about the different Ss which are a real option for one, and to organise what is to be said in favour or against a given S becoming one's own. Since Ss are things held or accepted, not just conformed to, what has to be said in favour of or against a given S must have some footing in the appraisal of its content.

We can also use this vocabulary about Ss which stand in merely notional confrontation with our own. For some types of S, however, the life of the vocabulary is largely confined to cases of real confrontation, and the more remote a given S is from being a real option for us, the less substantial seems the question of whether it is 'true', 'right', etc. While the vocabulary can no doubt be applied without linguistic impropriety, there is so little to this use, so little of what gives content to the appraisals in the context of real confrontation, that we can say that for a reflective person the question of appraisal does not genuinely arise for such a type of S when it is standing in purely notional confrontation.

We can register that the S in question is not ours, and that it is not a real option for us. There is indeed quite a lot we can say about it, and relevantly to our concerns. Thus certain features of an alien way of life, for instance, can stand to us symbolically as emblems of conduct and character to which we have certain attitudes in our own society, in much the same way, indeed, as we can treat works of fiction. The socially and historically remote has always been an important object of self-critical and self-encouraging fantasy. But from the standpoint I am now considering, to raise seriously questions in the vocabulary of appraisal about this culture considered as a concrete historical reality will not be possible for a reflective person. In the case of such Ss, to stand in merely notional confrontation is to lack the relation to our concerns which alone gives any point or substance to appraisal. With them, the only real questions of appraisal are about real options.

To think that the standpoint I have just sketched is the appropriate standpoint towards a given type of Ss is, in a recognizable sense, to hold a relativistic view of such Ss. Relativism, with regard to a given type of S, is the view that for one whose S stands in purely notional confrontation with such an S, questions of appraisal of it do not genuinely arise. This form of relativism, unlike most others,[5] is coherent. The truth in relativism – which I shall state, not argue for – is that for ethical outlooks at least this standpoint is correct.

This form of relativism (as a structure – its application to any particular type of S will always of course be a further question) is coherent because unlike most other forms it manages, in the distinction between real and notional confrontation, to cohere with two propositions both of which are true. The first is that we must have a form of thought not relativized to our own existing S for thinking about other Ss which may be of concern to us, and to express those concerns. The second is that we can nevertheless recognize that there can be many Ss which are related to our concerns too distantly for our judgments to have any grip on them, while admitting that other persons' judgment might get a grip on them, namely, those for whom they were a real option.

Most traditional forms of relativism have paid insufficient respect to the first of these propositions. The simplest form merely seeks to relativize the vocabulary of appraisal, into such phrases as 'true for us', 'true for them'. It is well known that these formulations do not work, and in particular cannot represent the basic use of the vocabulary in real confrontations. This view could be said to reduce the entire vocabulary of appraisal to expressions for the description of confrontation. Related to this is the view in ethics which I have elsewhere[6] called 'vulgar relativism', the view which combines a relativistic account of the meaning or content of ethical terms with a non-relativistic principle of toleration. This view is not hard to refute; it was perhaps worth discussing, since it is widely held, but to dispose of it certainly does not take us very far. We can perhaps now see that view more clearly. What vulgar relativism tries to do is to treat real confrontations like notional confrontations, with the result that it either denies that there are any real confrontations at all, or else brings to bear on them a principle which is inadequate to solve them, and is so because while it looks like a principle for deciding between real options, it is really an expression of the impossibility or pointlessness of choosing between unreal options.

Opposed to these kinds of views is that which represents the use of the vocabulary of appraisal as solely that of expressing (not stating) that an S is or is not the speaker's own. For such a view (consider for example the pure redundancy or 'speech-act' view of 'true') the issues which have concerned relativists evaporate – there is no way of expressing them. But equally, what has rightly concerned relativists evaporates, and we lose hold on the second truth which the present account is designed to accommodate. The distinction among Ss, between that which is and those which are not the speaker's own, is by no means the most significant in this area. The assumption that it is, is something that the discarded forms of relativism, and the evaporating view which apparently stands opposed to them, have in common.

With those types of S for which relativism is not true, it is not that there is no distinction between real and notional confrontations, but that questions of appraisal genuinely arise even for Ss in notional confrontation. But if that is so, then the status of those Ss will reveal itself also in the relevant criteria for distinguishing real and notional confrontations, the considerations that go into determining that a given S is or is not a real option for a given group at a given time. This is important for the case of scientific theories. Phlogiston theory is, I take it, not now a real option, but I doubt that this just means that to try to live the life of a convinced phlogiston theorist in the contemporary Royal Society is as incoherent an enterprise as to try to live the life of a Teutonic knight in 1930s Nuremberg. One reason that phlogiston theory is not a real option is that it cannot be squared with a lot that we know to be true.

These considerations, if pursued, would lead us to the subject of realism. One necessary (but not sufficient) condition of there being the kind of truth I have tried to explain in relativism as applied to ethics, is that ethical realism is false, and there is nothing for ethical Ss to be true of – though there are things for them to be true to, which is why many options are unreal. But scientific realism could be true, and if it is, relativism for scientific theories must be false.

Notes

1   See *e.g.*, Steven Lukes, 'Some Problems about Rationality', *European Journal of Sociology* 8 (1967), reprinted in B. R. Wilson ed., *Rationality*, Oxford, 1970; and 'On the Social Determination of Truth', in R. Horton and R. Finnegan eds., *Modes of Thought*, London, 1973.

2   For an illuminating discussion, see Robin Horton, 'Lévy-Bruhl, Durkheim and the Scientific Revolution', in Horton and Finnegan eds. *op cit*.

3   The terminology of 'real' and 'notional' was suggested by Newman's *Grammar of Assent*.

4   'They' does not mean 'each and every one of them': the problem is a familiar one in the description of social phenomena. There are other difficulties which will have to be overlooked, connected with the very simple use made of the notion of a group – *e.g.*, that it ignores the case of persons who could adopt a different S if they belonged to a different group.

5   For a different kind of relativist view which avoids the standard errors, see Gilbert Harman, 'Moral Relativism Defended', *Philosophical Review* 84 (1975), pp. 3–22.

6   *Morality* (Harmondsworth, 1972), ch. 3.

Section 12: Biology, Emotions, and Reasoning

Chapter 51: Logic and Biology: Emotional Inference and Emotions in Reasoning

RONALD DE SOUSA

The unrefined and sluggish mind
of Homo Javanensis
Could only treat of things concrete
and present to the senses

W. V. Quine

Tropisms and Transitions: Some Leading Questions

Before planning and reasoning, there were tropisms. Tropisms have functions and make use of information detected, but they don't, I assume, involve any actual reasoning. Somewhere along the course of evolution, and at some time in any one of us on the way from zygote to adult, some forms of detection became beliefs, and some tropisms turned into reasoned desires. And at some stage – perhaps, if Quine is right, with *Homo javanensis* – we became adept at processing information, that yet fell short of the power to abstract and generalize. What selective pressures can we then suppose to have effected in our brains, since then, the innovations required to bring us the capacity for fully abstract and general reasoning?

I take for granted that reasoning is something we do; that much or most of what we do is influenced by emotion; that psychology is interested in everything we do; and that psychology is a branch of biology. These breezy premises raise a number of questions.

1. What kind of connection might there be between biology and rationality?

2. More specifically, how does the normativity of logic relate to its biological origins? Is there not, in the very idea of such a connection, something akin to the naturalistic fallacy?

3. If our capacity for inference is in part a legacy of natural selection, are there specific emotional mechanisms that serve to influence reasoning at the proximate level?

4. If so, what is the connection between those means by which our inferences are policed by our emotions, and the formalisms that govern careful reasoning in science and mathematics?

I shall not address these questions directly. By the end of this chapter, however, I hope to have gleaned enough to warrant saying a little about each. On the way there, here is the route I shall follow.

I will begin with prima facie distinctions among strategic, epistemic and axiological domains of rationality. The domains soon merge at the edges, and the role of emotions in adjudicating border disputes turns out to be both crucial and equivocal, because of the emotions' ability to function as both cause and effect in all three domains. In addition, emotions are ubiquitous in both of what I shall call the mind's "two tracks": Some emotions were shaped by natural selection long before the invention of language, but the elicitors and very identity of many emotions now commonly rest essentially on explicit linguistic function. In practice, for example, the "feeling of rightness" plays an indispensable role in our assessment of certain basic inferential forms as acceptable or unacceptable. But a striking characteristic of such inferential forms is that they apparently do not, at least in their prelinguistic form, reflect any truly topic-neutral power of logic. That comes only with the contribution of explicit linguistic formulations of logical rules, and even then the best we can say about our capacities in that department is that they are uneven. This throws some light, I shall suggest, on the "rationality wars" that have pitted "pessimists" about human rationality against both "optimists" and "meliorists." From those considerations, I will turn to a sampling of cases where inferences appear to affected not merely by prelinguistic but actually by subpersonal processes, including, in some cases, what appear to be very directly chemical factors affecting belief, desire, or emotion as they affect our disposition to get from one belief to another.

Kinds of Emotional Rationality

A plausible first approach to rationality distinguishes three forms or domains of its application: the *epistemic*, which aims at maximizing true beliefs and minimizing false ones (neither suffices alone, and no easy formula guarantees both); the *strategic* or practical, which aims at success in action in the light of goals and desires; and the *axiological*, which aims at appropriateness of evaluative emotional response. A running theme in the history of philosophy has consisted in attempts by each of the first two to subsume the other. Socrates famously asserted that the true explanation for bad choices invariably lay with a lack of knowledge. That claim rested on the dubious premise that everyone desires the same thing, namely the Good. From that, Socrates inferred that wrong choices reflect not ill-will, but misinformation. If we remove the dubious premise, we can still make a case: If strategic irrationality consists in adopting a counterproductive course of action, it seems reasonable to presume that its counterproductive nature was not known. When I act, I must in some sense believe my action to be the best available. That belief (which doesn't necessarily exclude a simultaneous contrary belief) may be false or irrationally acquired. From that vantage point, epistemic rationality subsumes the strategic.

By contrast, there is a considerable literature on the "ethics" of belief (Adler 2002). And while opinions differ as to whether believing can be done at will, the whole discussion presupposes that it is at least sometimes something that is *done*. As such it must be subject to considerations of strategic rationality (Levi 1967). Viewed thus, the strategic subsumes the epistemic.

Common cases in which the two clash involve self-deception that serve the agent's short- or long-term interests. Self-deception is a good

thing, it is sometimes claimed, when it contributes to self-confidence, encourages effort, or keeps crippling realizations out of consciousness (Taylor 1989).[1] Emotions standardly play a determining role in self-deception, but they need not enter into the reasoning that motivates it. In some grander styles of self-deception, as advocated by Pascal with his famous wager, or in William James's plea for faith (James 1979) as against Clifford's insistence on the requirement of "adequate evidence" (Clifford 1886), emotions only come in at the implementation stage, once self-deception has been chosen by a dispassionate argument as a maximizing policy.

To see this, let us focus on Pascal. Ignoring theological subtleties,[2] Pascal's wager can be succinctly characterized in Baycsian terms:

> *The expected utility of believing in God is the weighted sum of the utility of living a life of relative deprivation, followed by eternal bliss, and that of living a life of deprivation followed by nothing. The weights are the probability that God (as conceived by the particular theology in question) actually exists and its converse. Even if the probability of God's existence is tiny (but still finite), the resulting expected utilities – respectively positive and negative – are infinitely large.*

It is important to note that while this argument deals with probabilities or Bayesian beliefs, it treats believing or disbelieving themselves as actions. Their expected desirabilities are determined in the same way as that of other actions in terms of their consequences weighted by their likelihoods. And while something like religious terror may well have motivated Pascal's invention of the wager, the argument itself is not overtly driven by emotion. On the contrary, it is a pure calculation of costs and benefits, intended to counter what might be thought of as the greater prima facie emotional weight of the temptation of present earthly pleasures. It is only when Pascal goes on to give advice about how to implement the goal of believing against evidence that he counsels habit-forming behavior, which might in turn bring the emotional tone of conviction. So he seems well aware that concentrating on the expected utilities figuring in the calculation would be ineffectual in changing belief.

But surely, the epistemologist will claim, considerations about heavenly bliss and hellish torment are not relevant to the issue of truth. Truth is by definition the formal object of belief, and therefore the standard of a belief's correctness; and only evidence is relevant to truth (Adler

1999: 268). Therefore, treating practical considerations as bearing on the rationality of belief is simple confusion.

Against this, however, Pascal can insist that the purity of truth can't have been an original virtue of belief. It had to be distilled, as it were, from the soup of overall benefit. Knowing the truth is useful in general, to be sure, but it is hasty to think that practical pursuits will massively fail if concern for truth is not paramount. Indeed, it seems to be strategically rational to lie a certain proportion of the time, both at the level of conscious policy and at the level of phylogenetic strategies. Mimetism, in which the markings of one species have in effect been selected to get a "free ride" on the toxicity of another similar-looking species, is effectively deception at the species level (Sober 1994). Furthermore, as Chris Stephens (2001) as shown, while believing what is true is a good idea in general, there are cases – aptly captured in the slogan "Better safe than sorry," when a signal is wrongly interpreted as indicating the presence of a predator – where the best policy may systematically result in acting on falsehoods as often as on truths.[3]

In short, the value of truth – telling it, or believing it – should not be exaggerated, and it is only in a context in which one has already agreed to take the purity of epistemic norms for granted that Pascal's wager can be ruled inappropriate.

What then does distinguish those contexts in which epistemic norms are primary, from those which call for more pragmatic criteria?

This question, as I have argued elsewhere, calls for a meta-level judgment of appropriate value: sometimes a value is purely epistemic, at other times, broadly practical. Since that judgment arbitrates between the epistemic and the strategic, neither mode of rationality can make it without begging the question. When each side accuses the other of an ignoratio elenchi, the decision between them will inevitably depend on how much one *cares* about one and the other. Emotional endorsement is the only ultimate arbiter of the appropriateness of a standard of rationality (de Sousa 2003).

But if emotions are – in any sense, however perverse – to lord it over logic, what can that mean for the validity of logic? Although an arbitrator is not a dictator, and arbitration is called for only in very special circumstances, it would be paradoxical if the faculty we are accustomed to think most disruptive of Reason were crucially to contribute to the determination of reasons. To resolve that paradox, we should note that at some point in the articulation of the most basic procedural rules, considerations of normative correctness must merge with certain factual necessities. Correct inference, at the most basic level, consists in the regular functioning of basic psychological mechanisms constrained by the power of social sanctions over individuals.

In a moment, I shall adduce a striking example of the depth of that power, not merely over individual emotions, but over the content of perception. (See "Six Paradigms," later in this chapter.) But it must be acknowledged at the outset that social pressure is sometimes – indeed, perhaps *often* – deplorably wrongheaded. If the power of social influence results from nothing but the random parasitism of memes, this line of thought is unpromising. The key to doing better lies in acknowledging something deeper than social pressure: an original evolutionary basis for some of the "intuitive" judgments that are codified in social consensus.

Evolution and Rational Inference

The need to posit innate predispositions to certain forms of information could be made out with reference to concept acquisition, to classical induction, and to Nelson Goodman's "new" problem of induction (Goodman 1983). But let me illustrate with reference to a narrow and uncontroversial level of rationality: the rationality of logical inference. Clearly, making valid inferences is something we can study to do more effectively but, as famously demonstrated in Plato's *Meno*, it is also something that we know "instinctively." Meno's slave may not know geometry, and he is ever ready to hazard thoughtless answers, but when confronted directly with the consequences of his suggestions he can recognize them as right or wrong – something he could never do with merely empirical information. Similarly, whatever our level of logical sophistication, there are inferences of which we recognize the validity, others which we immediately see as invalid. That fact is no lucky accident. Unless we spontaneously recognized the validity of some basic pattern of inference, such as Modus Ponens or Modus Tollens,[4] no instruction manual could save our inferences from sinking into logical quicksand. That is the lesson Lewis Carroll's story of Achilles and the Tortoise: if we required every applicable rule of inference to be written down as a premise, we would need another rule to tell that the inference was an instance of it, and so on forever. The simplest inference would require us to endorse an infinite number of finite steps (Carroll 1895).

So it's no mystery that at the most elementary level, the gap closes up between what we do naturally and what valid logical rules prescribe. What does remain unexplained by this, however, is *how* this happy harmony might have come to be preestablished.

This problem is made the more acute, as Mohan Matthen has pointed out, by the fact that most philosophers have given up on the hope of establishing a type-type identity between contentful mental states and neurological ones. So how are we to explain the lucky fact that the causal powers of belief states reflect the logical relations between the propositions believed? If assenting to p, assenting to $(p \rightarrow q)$, and assenting to q are merely token identical to the neurological states that implement them, how does it happen that the conjunction of the first two states tend to cause the third? Perhaps those states are somehow tagged with the right syntactic markers in the brain. But if so, we still need to "show why syntax parallels semantics" (Matthen 1989: 563). He then argues that we have "no choice" about adopting some sort of evolutionary explanation (p. 564), appealing to the now standard notion of an evolutionary function, as arising from selection for some characteristic performance (Millikan 1993). Specifically, Matthen suggests,

> we might have a special state that has *if p then q* as content, without its being a special purpose state that brings the q state into being whenever the p state occurs. Such a conditional state would depend for its effectiveness on the existence of higher level modules that were able to execute the logic of conditionals. (Matthen 1989: 567)

This suggestion raises three questions. The first is whether an evolved mechanism such as the one Matthen envisages could be prelinguistic. The second is about the role of emotion in the processes in question. The third, which I shall refer to as the *problem of scope*, is whether the mechanisms in question are sufficiently general to cover the full range of possible inferences.

To address the first question, we should first note that logic aspires to operate on topic-neutral form. It presupposes abstraction, requiring some form of representation that is devoid of specific reference. But it is hard to see how a prelinguistic representation might have the required generality. Hence, it may be more promising to reject the question, on the supposition that organisms that do not have language

don't actually ever *need* topic-neutral mechanisms. It may be, as Peter Carruthers among others has suggested, that among the specific virtues of language, is the capacity to bridge and connect information derived from encapsulated prelinguistic modules. On that view, language holds the monopoly on the capacity for abstract or topic neutral reasoning (Carruthers 2002).

This idea fits in with much evidence for a two-tiered organization of our cognitive faculties, a "two-track mind." Track One comprises relatively modular response patterns. The more abstract, language-bound patterns of Track two sometimes supersede the others, but often both remain in competition. Prima facie, it would seem that simply in virtue of involving older structures in the brain, emotions might play an important role in the former but not in the latter. In an early formulation of the hypothesis that brain structures originating at different stages of evolution have overlapping functions, Paul MacLean (1975) identified the limbic system as implicated in both emotional functions and cognitive ones; but only the cortex is involved in language capacity. More recent versions of the view are less cut-and-dried, but there is accumulating evidence for the basic hypothesis of the existence of two systems of mental processing, grounded in structures set up both by evolution and learning on the one hand, and involving explicit linguistic processing on the other. The two systems sometimes compete in generating beliefs, wants, and plans. The idea has appeared many times in psychology (Evans 2003), and its consequences have been most thoroughly explored by Keith Stanovich (2004), who lists twenty-three versions of it. His own version lists "automaticity, modularity, and heuristic processing" as the features characteristic of Track one, while Track two is described as "rule-based, often language based, computationally expensive" (Stanovich 2004: 34–36).

All this suggests, in answer to my second question, that, insofar as emotions can be attributed to beings without language, they belong primarily in Track one. But the two-track mind hypothesis is not committed to drawing the line by opposing the phylogenetic origins of the faculties involved to those that arise by learning, including language learning. Many emotions require language for their full specification, and language reaches deep into the emotional brain. This is obvious from a glance at the power of political rhetoric. Equally obvious, however, is the fact that the emotional power of political rhetoric doesn't work by stimulating our capacity for logical inference. Instead, such uses of language proceed by triggering what George Lakoff calls "frames" and what I have called "paradigm scenarios" (Lakoff 2002; de Sousa 1987). Frames and paradigm scenarios are fundamentally emotional in their mode of operation, and tend to wrest control from logical reasoning altogether.

The Rationality Debate

It may be objected that the best-known examples of systematic irrationality involve word problems, as detailed by (Kahneman, Slovic, and Tversky 1982), do not appear to involve emotions. How does this square with the idea that the irrationality is explained in part by emotional aspects of the two-track mind?

Let's look at how this question might apply to one of the best known cases, the Wason test. In the classic version of this, subjects are shown four cards, showing 3, D, 7, K. They are told that all cards have a letter on one side and a number on the other, and they are asked what cards must be turned over to verify that *if a card has D on one side it has 3 on other*. Most people get this wrong, in a puzzling variety of ways. Yet most people can easily solve a problem about how to make sure that underage customers are not drinking alcohol. This latter problem has the same abstract form: in either case, the question can be represented abstractly as requiring verification of a statement of the form "if *p* then *q*," where the possible moves comprise turning over a *p* card, a $\sim p$, a *q*, or a $\sim q$. Given that falsification of "if *p* then *q*" is secured iff *p* &$\sim q$ is true, it should be clear that the actions required are turning over just the *p* and the $\sim q$ cards. In the case of the drinking problem, that means inspecting the ID of those drinking beer and checking the drinks of those without ID. In the abstract card version, it means turning over the D and the 7. Why does the former seem so much easier than the latter? And what does it have to do with the use of language?

There have been a number of attempts to reject the head the problem off at the pass. One recent argument is made by Jerry Fodor, who denies the basic assumption that the two versions of the problem have the same logical form. Fodor notes that in cheater detection, the subject is charged with conditionally enforcing an imperative, whereas the card-turning version requires verification of a conditional statement (Fodor 2000: 101–104). To be sure, checking on *q* just in case *p* is not the same task as checking the truth of *if p then q*. The former task requires nothing unless p is true. But that accounts only for one typical mistake, which consists in checking only the *p* card.[5] But Fodor's ingenious attempt to pry the two tasks apart is a red herring. For among the vast number of variant experiments to which the Wason test has been submitted, some cases that could be represented as requirements or permissions fail to yield a majority of correct judgments, unless they specifically involve possible violations due to cheating (Cosmides and Tooby 1992: 199–205). Consensus on a clear diagnosis is still lacking; what is clear, however, is that a number of different content-dependent factors appear to be involved in determining whether problems of the same abstract form are more or less easily solved. The difficulty of accessing and applying the purely abstract schema is well established.

We can draw two morals, which at first blush appear somewhat inconsistent. First, that we are sometimes poor at reasoning about abstract problems, compared to our ability to deal with some of their specific concrete instantiations; second, that when we insist on applying formal rules of inference strictly, we can get it right and convincingly expose the error. So is explicit reasoning systematically irrational or not? What seems to be happening in the Wason test is that when the question is posed, it commonly fails to trigger the truth-table for the material conditional even when that schema has been studied in formal logic class. Lacking the clue that will route it to the cheater-detection schema, subjects fall back on some more accessible course, such as attending to the cards mentioned in the problem ("matching bias"), leading to the choice of turning over 3 and D, or confusing "if" with the biconditional. If an emotion is involved, it might come under the heading of intellectual sloth. An abstract word problem requires an analytical Track Two strategy, and that is harder to access if some familiar and more easily available schema appears ready to hand.

Topic-neutrality is a defining characteristic of logic, in which arguments can be assessed independently of the reference of their terms. It is closely related to the idea of universality: for if validity can be assessed without regard to subject matter, then nothing is in principle beyond our comprehension. Yet one might reasonably doubt whether the capacities we now have, even when boosted by language, are able to span topics far removed from those likely to be treated by, or useful to, "the unrefined and sluggish mind of homo Javanensis." That is the problem of scope: are there inherent limits to our mental capacities that forever bar us from understanding some things? This idea has taken many forms. Here is a generic version: *Our mental capacities have evolved under the selective pressure of a limited range of practical problems; so we have no good reasons to trust them when we venture beyond that restricted range into theoretical speculation.* The Whorf hypothesis – that a specific language may be equipped to express only a specific range of thoughts (Whorf 1973) – and Colin McGinn's "mysterian" suggestion that there might be an intrinsic limit to the capacity of the mind to understand itself (McGinn 1982), are well-known variants of the scope problem. But its classic formulation comes from Descartes:

> For the proper purpose of the sensory perceptions given me by nature is simply to inform the mind of what is beneficial or harmful. . . . I misuse them by treating them as reliable touchstones for immediate judgments about the essential nature of the bodies located outside us. (*Med. VI*)

The very precision of Descartes' version of the problem hints at a solution. The answer to the problem of scope lies not in the senses alone, but in our capacity to link sensory data to scientific models and thereby to mathematics. The possibility of discovering or constructing advanced mathematical structures cannot have evolved *as such*. Our remote ancestors are unlikely to have left significantly more offspring on the basis of abilities that could only have been manifested in the past two thousand years. The capacity to think about higher mathematics has to be what Gould called a spandrel or an exaptation (Gould and Lewontin 1979). But then what Eugene Wigner has called "the unreasonable effectiveness of mathematics in the natural sciences" (Wigner 1960) becomes a telling piece of evidence. The success of mathematics in solving problems that have nothing to do with immediate survival, coupled with its applicability in the construction of entirely new technological devices, affords credible support for the view that mathematical inference gives us some access to an objective world. Mathematics and science, however, do not (despite an apparent exception taken up in the next section) progress far without language. This leaves us free to suppose that while our prelinguistic ancestors and cousins mastered an abundance of modular inferences based on analogue computation and applicable in specific domains, they could not manipulate topic-neutral abstractions embodied in digital systems of representation.

That the first track deals in analogue computing, while the second track is the domain of digital representation is strikingly confirmed by work on non verbal counting and calculation in animals and infants, which suggests that animals are capable of primitive forms of ordering, adding, subtracting, and even some forms of multiplication and division (Gallistel and Gelman 2000; Gelman and Cordes 2001). Unsurprisingly, however, there is no evidence for a prelinguistic domain-neutral representation system.

The topic-neutrality of language does not solve the problem of scope. It tells us nothing about the completeness of the potential knowledge to which we could give linguistic expression. The mysterians might still be right about the ultimate limits of knowledge.[6] But it does lead us to expect a dichotomy between the range of problems that can be expressed and solved in the explicit language of science and mathematics, and those that are best approached in terms of the "intuitive" methods of Track One. The problem of the role of emotions in reasoning is particularly acute here, because it is obviously at the level most relevant to the activities and needs of our ancestors in the environment of evolutionary adaptation (EEA) that emotions are most likely to have preempted, or set up effective precursors to, explicit rational thought. As triggers to fast, prereflective and relatively organized responses to urgent situations, emotions are most likely to be involved in the inferential and decision-making shortcuts that were, at least in the EEA, highly cost-effective if not always such as to guarantee correct answers. That would place them in the domain of Track One. By the same token, emotions are notoriously likely to block rational analysis. They can get in the way of the sort of calculation that might be required to devise more elaborate solutions to problems different in nature from those typically encountered in their contexts of adaptation. By contrast, Antonio Damasio (1999) has described neurological evidence that brain lesions in the frontal lobes, by affecting patients' capacity for normal emotional responses, result in profound disruptions of practical rationality even while leaving unimpaired the ability to solve Track Two problems on the analytical and verbal level. Just why that is, Damasio leaves unclear; but we can speculate that the emotions are crucial to rational decision making in several ways. They routinely control the agenda of practical reasoning by modifying the salience of different aspects of life situations; they narrow down to manageable size the unmanageable vastness of our options at any given moment of choice; and they may incline us to one side or another of alternatives that promise comparable expected utilities but different levels of risk (de Sousa 1987). They may also be essential to our ability to commit ourselves to stick with policies that affect our long-term interests (Ainslie 2001). Furthermore, specifically "epistemic" emotions such as wonder, doubt, curiosity, surprise, or the "feeling of rightness" spur the quest for analytic rigor typical of Track two processing.

It is in that light, I suggest, that we should view the "rationality wars" that have opposed, in recent decades, "pessimists" against "Panglossians" about human rationality. These terms are those of Keith Stanovich (2004). Among the pessimists are the contributors (Kahneman, Slovic, and Tversky 1982), who take themselves to have demonstrated a number of ways in which human reasoning is systematically flawed. The best-known Panglossians are the contributors to Gigerenzer, Todd, and ABC Research Group (1999) and Gigerenzer and Selten (2001), who argue that the examples exploited by Tversky, Kahneman, and their colleagues are either artifacts of misleading test conditions, or instances of "fast and frugal" strategies, fine-tuned by natural selection, which are actually superior to those methods thought by the pessimists to embody rational thought.[7] Against both, Stanovich presents himself as a "meliorist," advocating an acknowledgment of the shortcomings of ancient and particularly of nonverbal strategies of decision and reasoning, followed by the careful cultivation of improved methods of explicit reasoning that take advantage of the sophisticated language developed for logic, mathematics, and science. This approach is grounded in the acknowledgment of our two-track minds. But the meliorist attitude mustn't be interpreted as placing emotions exclusively in the first track, nor as requiring that they should play no role in reasoning. On the contrary, that role is deep and pervasive, and by no means limited to the preverbal strategies that might have been selected for us in the course of the EEA.

The difficulty most subjects have in solving abstract word problems such as the Wason test is slight compared to those observed long ago by Aleksander Luriia in conversations with illiterate Russian peasants. What impeded his subjects from performing simple Modus Ponens seemed to be an inability to focus on just the suppositions embodied in the premises of an argument. They always brought more information to the problem than was contained in the problem they were asked to consider. This prevented them from marshaling the information expressed in the premise of the argument. When presented with *There are no camels in Germany; The city of B. is in Germany, Are there camels there or not?* some subjects reasoned that there probably were camels there if B was a large city, and if not, it was because it was too crowded. When asked for what "didn't belong," or was "not alike" in the list of words *saw, hammer, hatchet,* and *log,* one response was: "They all work together and chop the log." When Luriia persisted in trying to get them to attend to the fact that all except logs can be called "tools," the informant replies:

> Yes, you could, except a log isn't a tool. Still, the way we look at it, the log has to be here. Otherwise, what good are the others?[8]

Luriia noted that his informants were apparently incapable of repeating the problems put to them. And yet, as Wilson (unpublished) comments:

> An untutored peasant will be perfectly clear in practice that if milk is healthy for humans and this is milk it is healthy for humans, and that if something looks like ordinary milk but is fatal to humans it is not ordinary milk. But she may not be able to repeat the corresponding syllogism or to draw the right inference on command.

It seems that the problems, when stated in words, trigger neither verbal schemata nor situational ones. Luriia's account doesn't allow us to judge whether emotions play a role in these difficulties; but it seems to me that it does suggest the power of what (Lakoff 2002) calls "frames" and I have called "paradigm scenarios": Basic narratives reminiscent of situations and responses experienced in early age, that remain significant in someone's life, and that typically evoke tendencies to specific sequences of action. The triggering of such a scenario seems to me sufficient, in many circumstances, to warrant speaking of emotion. But it is not entirely clear whether the triggering of such a frame or scenario should be construed as necessarily involving an emotion or not.

Six Paradigms

To try to cast a little light on this question, I shall presently turn to five examples of reasoning or inference in which emotion is somehow involved, but where its exact role is hard to define. They are cases where we can observe, if not quite understand, the role that subpersonal factors, including chemical agents commonly implicated in emotional states, affect in a surprisingly direct way what we would otherwise regard as inferences driven solely by considerations of validity or evidence. But first, a reminder that nonverbal proto-reasoning is ubiquitous, but that in many forms it needn't involve emotion in any way.

Animal Computation

In the sort of skilled physical activity that we share with other animals, subpersonal computation plays an indispensable role. This does not explicitly involve emotions. A cartoon by Harry Hargreaves, published in *Punch* in 1960, summed this up rather well. A kingfisher looks down at a fish in the water, and the caption records its thoughts: "target in sector 3; speed, 2 knots; angle of deflection, 25°. . . . Who'd be a kingfisher?" Apart from the explicit form of the bird's thought, Hargreaves's cartoon is highly realistic about animals' powers of computation. Studies of ant navigation show that desert ants track their distance from home by means of some sophisticated way of measuring the horizontal ground distance they have traveled even when their actual path involved a hilly journey of greater absolute length (Wohlgemuth, Ronacher, and Wehner 2001). Pharaoh ants appear equally ingenious in their method of reorienting themselves to their nests. They rely on an ability to identify the angle of branching paths out from their nests, typically 60° when facing the nest, but 120° when going the other way (Jackson, Holcombe, and Ratnieks 2004). But such capacities are by no means confined to "lower" species. Humans playing tennis – or more exactly their brains – solve complicated and efficient Bayesian equations, involving both acquired expectations and fast updating of feedback information (Körding and Wolpert 2004). This is done at the subpersonal level, and achieves a precision that couldn't possibly be attained by anyone attempting to solve the problem explicitly without the aid of sophisticated computers. These cases illustrate First Track processing at its most impressive, involving neither explicit reasoning nor emotion, yet producing highly accurate results. Such feats make it irresistible to postulate sophisticated computing mechanisms working at the subpersonal level, deep beneath the level of any consciousness or explicit formulation.

Unlike these first examples, which are intended merely as reminders of the vast terrain of subpersonal "inference" involved in the ordinary physical motions of humans and other animals, the next series of examples all involve emotion.

The Capgras Syndrome

The first involves the emotion of *feel of familiarity*, or rather a stubborn feeling of *unfamiliarity* that resists ordinary recognition. Typical patients afflicted with the Capgras syndrome persist in believing that a person close to them – wife, or father – is an impostor.[9]

According to Ramachandran, the best explanation for this strange disorder is that a direct link normally exists between the facial recognition mechanism and the areas controlling the appropriate emotional responses (particularly the amygdala). The sight of a close relative – a parent, in the case of Ramachandran's patient Arthur – normally triggers an affective response, which is itself subject to a "familiarity" evaluation. In Arthur's case, the direct link to the area in charge of generating the affective response is missing. As a result, the affective response to his father is not produced. This sets up a incongruity between the strictly cognitive familiarity check that applies to the face and the missing familiarity check applied to the expected affective response. The Capgras delusion can then be construed as the conclusion of a perfectly reasonable inference (though of course one that is neither conscious nor explicit): *I get a characteristic thrill when my father appears; I'm not getting that now; therefore the person before me is not my father.* By contrast, *he looks exactly like my father. Therefore he is an impostor, a stranger who looks just like my father.* This hypothesis is particularly neat in its capacity to explain why it is that the "impostor" delusion occurs only with persons to whom the person is close: typically parents or spouses. It doesn't occur with mere acquaintances, because in most cases of recognition a more or less indifferent emotional reaction is normal, not aberrant. (It also doesn't normally occur over the telephone, which doesn't implicate the same pathways of facial recognition.) If something like this is correct, it would imply that the emotional aspect of recognition is subject to an independent familiarity marker. Where the person recognized is both familiar and affectively significant, both markers are involved in the required ID check.

Two things are worth noting about this case. First, although we can make sense of it by construing it as a kind of inference, it is not experienced as an inference but as intuitive conviction. Second, while the "feeling of rightness" acts as a marker, it doesn't present itself as a marker of correct inference *as such*. There are other cases, such as obsessive-compulsive disorder (OCD), however, where the feeling of rightness does just that.

Obsessive-Compulsive Disorder

OCD affects specifically not the sense of familiarity but the feeling of "rightness" itself. OCD may be seen as resulting from some sort of disconnection of the normal emotion of rightness in relation to recent memory of having taken necessary precautions. The relevant emotions here would be specifically *epistemic* emotions. As Chris Hookway has pointed out, epistemic emotions have been almost wholly neglected in the literature but constitute an extremely important aspect of our ability rationally to reason our way to new beliefs. If I didn't experience *doubt*, I wouldn't launch on an inquiry in the first place. If I didn't have the feeling of *rightness* about an inference, I wouldn't rely on it. If I didn't have the feeling of *conviction* about a conclusion, I wouldn't infer it (Hookway 1998). The patient suffering from OCD lacks some of those normal feelings. OCD has traditionally been taken to be a neurotic syndrome calling for psychoanalytic diagnosis and therapy. But the fact that some of these cases are apparently capable of clearing up under the influence of a targeted drug such as Prozac (Kramer 1993) suggests that this apparent complexity is an illusion. As in the case to which I turn in the next paragraph, it seems that the feeling of rightness is an emotion can be triggered or at least facilitated by a simple chemical agent, and in turn determine the presence or absence of conviction in a particular proposition.

The Chemistry of Trust

In a recent article in *Nature* widely reported in the press, researchers at the University of Zurich have shown that "intranasal administration of oxytocin, a neuropeptide that plays a key role in social attachment and affiliation in non-human mammals, causes a substantial increase in trust among humans" (Kosfeld, Heinrichs, Zak et al. 2005). Their results also support the conclusion that "the effect of oxytocin on trust is not due to a general increase in the readiness to bear risks. On the contrary, oxytocin specifically affects an individual's willingness to accept social risks arising through interpersonal interactions" (ibid.). The experimental setup in each run of the experiment involved two subjects, an "investor" and a "trustee." Both received twelve monetary units, and each unit invested by the investor was tripled by the experimenter. Thus if the investor handed over all of his twelve units, the trustee now had forty-eight, comprising his original twelve plus the tripled investment. He could then return any amount to the investor.

Trust is a nice bridge emotion between the strictly epistemic and the strategic; for it inclines us to believe identifiable propositions – in this case, the proposition that investment in this particular trustee would prove profitable for the investor – but only in the context of a transaction envisaged with a person. A *specific* acceptance of *social* risk was ingeniously distinguished from a *generic* increase in risk tolerance. This was done by comparing the original setup with a situation in which the investor was told that a computer, not a person, would determine what return if any the investor would get. In that situation, the oxytocin had no significant effect. This seems to show that oxytocin didn't simply shift the estimate of risk down a notch; rather, it worked specifically on the emotional component of trust. Another significant control contrasted the effects of oxytocin on the investor with its effect on the trustee: The latter was nil. This showed that the causal factor responsible for the effect wasn't a general increase in benevolence or good feeling. For that would presumably also have led to larger returns from the trustees.

The authors note that there is substantial independent evidence "that oxytocin promotes prosocial approach behaviour by inhibiting defensive behaviours" (p. 675). In the light of this known effect of oxytocin on social approach in other mammals, they tend to minimize its specific effect on belief: "the investors given oxytocin show more trusting behaviour but do not hold significantly different beliefs about the trustworthiness of others." That is paradoxical, if we assume that in either case the behavior of the investor follows a roughly Bayesian strategy. It can be partly though not wholly explained, according to the authors, by appealing to an evaluative rather than a strictly cognitive appraisal: what the chemical has done is help the investors "overcome their betrayal aversion in social interactions." Still, the *consequence* of the diminished "betrayal aversion" is equivalent to a change in the probability measure of the expectation of return. So we have here a kind of primitive, purely causal case of direct biological influence over a process that is, we might say, functionally equivalent to an inference, even though no explicit inference is made.

If we represent the process in question as a Bayesian calculation,

$$V = \sum_{i=1}^{n} (P_i \times V_i)$$

the fact that the estimate of risk [p] is not directly affected suggests that "betrayal anxiety" feeds into the desirability factor [v] rather than the probability estimate [p]. Yet there is no explicit inference. We have only the behavioral upshot to go on. So we can think of the emotion as feeding into the practical inference without necessarily assuming that such an "inference" can, like an explicit Bayesian argument, be split into "belief" and "desire" components. Insofar as the Bayesian model fits, however, emotion seems to be targeting the desirability rather than the belief component.

In any case, as might be expected, the effect of the oxytocin is not determining. It may contribute to a Svengali effect, but cannot guarantee its success and could hardly be credited with one all by itself. (Specifically, the median amount entrusted by investors who had absorbed oxytocin was 25 percent higher than those sprayed with a placebo.) So what needs to be made more precise is the nature of the relation between that sort of direct chemical influence on inference, on the one hand, and the influence that common sense attributes to other emotions in cases of bona fide valid inference, on the other.

Cognitive Foraging

One more illustration of the surprisingly direct influence of emotional chemistry on inference is worth noting. In a recent issue of *Nature*, Jonathan Cohen and Gary Aston-Jones (2005) look at some findings by Angela Yu and Peter Dayan (2005) on the application to science of the trade-off between exploration and exploitation. Exploitation of known resources is safe but likely to yield diminishing returns. By contrast, giving up well-trodden paths for the sake of exploration may yield a jackpot of discovery, but is inherently risky.

That trade-off is well known to students of foraging. An ant faced with an established path may either follow it, in the expectation of finding food where many others have already found it, or else strike out in an unexplored direction. The latter option is risky but will pay off, if not for the individual at least for the colony, when the

original sources of food are exhausted (Johnson 2003). This is a good example, then, of a mechanism first instantiated at the most basic level of foraging decisions. What is surprising is that it can be directly applied in the context of sophisticated scientific cognitive strategies, where it appears still to be controlled by a combination of chemical triggers.

Subjectively, the tension between the relative security of "normal science" and the excitement of a potentially fruitful paradigm shift is experienced as an urbane sort of struggle between fear and greed. What Yu and Dayan found is that the balance between the tendency to explore and the tendency to exploit in the cognitive domain are apparently regulated in part by specific neuromodulators, controlling, respectively, the kind of uncertainty that arises from the bearing of a signal and the kind of uncertainty that arises from the reliability of the signal:

Acetylcholine signals expected uncertainty, coming from known unreliability of predictive cues within a context. Norepinephrine signals unexpected uncertainty, as when unsignaled switches produce strongly unexpected observations. These uncertainty signals interact to enable optimal inference and learning in noisy and changeable environments. This formulation is consistent with a wealth of physiological, pharmacological, and behavioral data implicating acetylcholine and norepinephrine in specific aspects of a range of cognitive processes (Yu and Dayan 2005: 681).

They go on to remark that there seem to be "a class of attentional cueing tasks that involve both neuromodulators and shows how their interactions may be part-antagonistic, part-synergistic" (ibid.). And of course those sorts of situations are typically experienced, in humans, as giving rise to emotional states: the "fear" of risk; the "lure" of the unknown; the "disappointment" generated by scientific prospects that don't pan out. What Yu and Dayan's discovery seems to be telling us, is that a chemical mechanism underlies, in part, both the phenomenology of emotion and the process of what we assume to be high-level decision making. What they don't tell us, which raises an intriguing question, is just what relationship there is between those two aspects of brain chemistry and their felt and functional consequences in the subjective experience of the quest for invention and discovery.

The Emotional Price of Nonconformism

In some famous experiments on the power of social conformism done in the 1950s, Solomon Asch had found that when asked to make a judgment of a visual quantity, some 40 percent of subjects went along with the false judgment of stooges posing as fellow subjects (Asch 1962). In a new variant on these experiments, a group of researchers explored "the potency of social pressure in inducing conformity, how information that originates from humans, versus inanimate sources, alters either perception or decision making and the neural basis for such changes" (Berns, Chappelow, Zink et al. 2005: 250). Here again, there are intriguing questions about the role of emotion, and about the precise locus of the inference to the wrong conclusion. Using fMRI data, Berns et al. found a "highly suggestive . . . lack of concomitant activity changes in more frontal areas," where one might have expected activity if the subject's judgment had resulted from a decision to override one's own judgment in favour of that of the majority. The surprising aspect of their findings is that no special cognitive activity was detected in the cortex of those who conformed to others' false opinion. Instead, "the effects of social conformity are exerted on the very same brain regions that perform the task." In other words, far from being an inference required by the need to resolve cognitive dissonance ("So many others can't be wrong, I must revise my verdict"), the influence of others' judgments seems to act *directly on perception*. The distorting effect of conformity did not require any calculation of costs and benefits: it was those who saw and stood up for an independent truth who endured emotional cost. This finding is as intriguing as it is discouraging, for the emotions involved (though the authors make no attempt to pinpoint these in our repertoire of normal emotions) do not seem to be among those that we would spontaneously label "epistemic emotions."

Skeptical Concluding Remarks

The mere activation of neuromodulating chemicals, as instantiated in the findings I have sketched, can't be assimilated to the presence of an emotion. One reason for this is that emotions are phenomena that belong to the *personal* level; the activation of neuromodulators is a *subpersonal* phenomenon. Some of what we are learning about the involvement of specific parts or functions of the brain in reasoning, illustrated above, implicates just such subpersonal factors,

but it is not clear to what extent we are justified in inferring, from the fact that some of the same chemical factors are involved in emotion, that emotions, as commonly conceived, are involved in reasoning. Nevertheless, I shall risk some tentative answers to my leading questions.

1. WHAT KIND OF CONNECTION MIGHT THERE BE BETWEEN BIOLOGY AND RATIONALITY?

Social pressure alone won't suffice to guarantee the normative correctness of our inclinations to draw inference. A sort of core of basic procedures – perhaps including Modus Ponens – had to be installed by natural selection, in the sense that we have a native disposition to effect transitions from one belief to another in accordance with such principles in specific domains. Thus far, only Track One processes need be involved. But when these transitions are codified by rules of language, logic, or mathematics, we can see them in their full generality as well as provide an explicit and conclusive argument for their validity. In practice, however, commonly used inference patterns do not necessarily become more reliable. The reason is that the fit between the "native" dispositions to acquire beliefs and their implementation in explicit language is not itself part of that system of mechanisms on which natural selection has put its certificate of warranty.

2. IS THERE NOT, IN THE VERY SUGGESTION THAT THERE MIGHT BE A CONNECTION BETWEEN LOGIC AND BIOLOGY, SOMETHING AKIN TO THE NATURALISTIC FALLACY?

There is a prima facie presumption of functionality to any heritable disposition the complexity of which makes it unlikely to be accidental. But it is crucial to remember that what's been put in place by natural selection, however useful to our ancestors in the EEA, may be not be worthy now of any evaluative endorsement. Justification can't be infallibly grounded. It has to run in circles, the capacity of which to inspire respect depends directly on their size. Ultimately, we trust our epistemic emotions to tell us when the circle is big enough for comfort. In that way, Track Two's analytic mechanisms must submit to the judgment of emotions.

3. IF OUR CAPACITY FOR INFERENCE IS INDEED IN PART A FRUIT OF NATURAL SELECTION, ARE THERE SPECIFIC EMOTIONAL MECHANISMS THAT SERVE TO GUIDE OUR INFERENCE AT THE PROXIMATE LEVEL?

The surprising lesson to be learned from the samples that I have cited from recent psychological and brain research is that in some cases a relatively abstract inference is triggered by what appears to be a fairly simple chemical agent. It would obviously be greatly exaggerated to conclude from the Zurich experiments that trust was simply triggered by oxytocin, or from those of Yu and Dayan that strategic research decisions were determined by noradrenaline. But these experiments are part of an accumulating body of evidence that suggests that emotional factors, more obviously linked to noncortical brain and hormonal activities, are important to our judgments of what inferences are or are not acceptable.

4. WHAT IS THE CONNECTION BETWEEN THOSE MEANS BY WHICH OUR INFERENCES ARE POLICED BY EMOTIONS, AND THE FORMALISMS THAT GUIDE OUR MOST CAREFUL EXPLICIT INFERENCES IN SCIENCE AND MATHEMATICS?

To answer this question, I have suggested that we must take seriously the two-track hypothesis: We are endowed with two only partly connected and sometimes conflicting levels of processing. Emotions are involved in both; and while it is not surprising to find their role in Track One processes closely tied to the effects of various subpersonal factors, including neuromodulators, what is more surprising is that such factors also appear to be implicated in Track Two reasoning.

In the final analysis, the increasing precision of our understanding of the brain mechanisms underlying the actual and the normatively correct practices studied by psychology and epistemology may blur the image I have sought to sketch. The idea that one should be able to distinguish specific contributions of emotion to inference, and indeed that there is always a clear answer to the question of what inferences have been drawn, presupposes that we can set out clear lines of demarcation between the mind's two tracks, between emotional and merely evaluative determinants of decision making, and between the influence that brain chemicals exert on reasoning and the effects they have on emotions. But the fine-grained picture, when it emerges, may overwrite the lines drawn in the sand by the presuppositions of our questions.

Notes

1 I am grateful to Julie Kirsch for this reference.
2 Ignore, in particular, the fact that the choice of a faith is not a binary one, so that whichever sect one joins, one risks the fate promised by all the others to those who deny the True Faith.
3 As the editors of this volume have pointed out to me, it could be claimed that the belief embedded in the higher level of caution need not be the falsehood that "this is a tiger," but the truth that "this is sufficiently tiger-like not to be worth the risk." But since the belief is bundled into the behavior, it's not clear what evidence could justify one attribution rather than the other. In any case, however the behavior is interpreted, the "better safe than sorry" policy, typically sacrifices high expected utility for a drastic reduction of risk. In the perspective of evolution, that makes it, by definition, a losing strategy in the long run.
4 These two patterns are not necessarily on a par as a matter of psychological fact. The point made here, like the point made in the *Meno*, holds a priori: It is that unless some patterns of transition are built into the architecture of the brain, no process of reasoning can get going. What those patterns are is an empirical question: In theory – and sometimes in practice – they might include *believe what you are told*.
5 Intriguingly, this mistake is more common among mathematicians, who are much less likely to make the mistake often made by other subjects, which is to turn over both the D and the 3 (Inglis 2005).
6 My late Hegelian colleague Emil Fackenheim, puffing on his pipe in the Common Room in the days when North American philosophers were not yet not prosecuted for that egregious crime, once enunciated this Deep Thought: "The aim of philosophy is to find the limits of knowledge . . . " (puff) " . . . and then transcend them."
7 A recent best-selling book takes a similar line, although radically downplaying the role of emotion (Gladwell 2005).
8 (Luriia 1976: 58–59). I'm indebted to Catherine Wilson for the reference and a discussion in an unpublished talk to the Canadian Philosophical Association (Wilson 2000).
9 See Ramachandran and Blakeslee 1998; Pacherie 2005; Mangan 2001. The next two paragraphs draw from my comments on Mangan's paper in the same online issue of *Psyche*.

References

Adler, J. E. 1999. The ethics of belief: Off the wrong track. *Midwestern Studies in Philosophy* 23:267–285.

———. 2002. *Belief's own ethics*. Cambridge, MA: MIT Press.

Ainslie, G. 2001. *Breakdown of will*. Cambridge: Cambridge University Press.

Asch, S. 1962. *Social Psychology*. Englewood Cliffs, NJ: Prentice Hall.

Berns, G. S., et al. 2005. Neurobiological correlates of social conformity and independence during mental rotation. *Biological Psychiatry*, 58(3): 245–253.

Carroll, L. 1895. What the Tortoise said to Achilles. *Mind* 4:278–80. Available at http://www.ditext.com/carroll/tortoise.html.

Carruthers, P. 2002. The cognitive functions of language. *Behavioral and Brain Sciences* 25(6):657–674; 705–710.

Clifford, W. K. 1886. The ethics of belief. In *Lectures and essays (2nd ed.)*, ed. L. Stephen and F. Pollock. London: Macmillan.

Cohen, J. D., and G. Aston-Jones. 2005. Decision amid uncertainty. *Nature* 436 (28 July):471–472.

Cosmides, L., and J. Tooby. 1992. Cognitive adaptations for social exchange. In *The adapted mind: Evolutionary psychology and the generation of culture*, ed. J. H. Barkow, L. Cosmides, and J. Tooby, 163–228. Oxford: Oxford University Press.

Damasio, A. R. 1999. *The feeling of what happens: Body and emotion in the making of consciousness.* New York, San Diego, London: Harcourt Brace.

de Sousa, R. 1987. *The rationality of emotion.* Cambridge, MA: MIT Press.

———. 2003. Paradoxical emotions. In *Weakness of will and practical irrationality*, ed. S. Stroud and C. Tappolet, 274–297. Oxford and New York: Oxford University Press.

Evans, J. S. B. T. 2003. In two minds: Dual process accounts of reasoning. *Trends in Cognitive Science* 7(10):454–459.

Fodor, J. 2000. *The mind doesn't work that way: The scope and limits of computational psychology.* Cambridge, MA: Bradford/MIT Press.

Gallistel, C., and R. Gelman. 2000. Non-verbal numerical cognition: From reals to integers. *Trends in Cognitive Sciences* 4(2):59–65.

Gelman, R., and S. Cordes. 2001. Counting in animals and humans. In *Language, brain, and cognitive development: Essays in honor of Jacques Mehler*, E. Dupoux, 279–301. Cambridge, MA: MIT Press.

Gigerenzer, G., and R. Selten, eds. 2001. *Bounded Rationality*, 320. Cambridge, MA: MIT Press.

Gigerenzer, G., P. Todd, and ABC Research Group. 1999. *Simple heuristics that make us smart.* New York: Oxford University Press.

Gladwell, M. 2005. *Blink: The power of thinking without thinking.* New York: Little, Brown.

Goodman, N. 1983. *Fact, fiction, and forecast*, fourth ed. Cambridge, MA: Harvard University Press.

Gould, S. J., and R. L. Lewontin. 1979. The spandrels of San Marco and the Panglossian paradigm: A critique of the adaptationist programme. *Proceedings of the Royal Society of London* B 205:581–598.

Hookway, C. 1998. Doubt: Affective states and the regulation of inquiry. *Canadian Journal of Philosophy, Supplementary Volume* 24:203–26.

Jackson, D. E., M. Holcombe, and F. L. Ratnieks. 2004. Trail geometry gives polarity to ant foraging networks. *Nature* 432:907–909.

James, W. 1979. The will to believe. In *The will to believe: And other essay in popular philosophy*, ed. F. H. Burkhardt. Cambridge, MA: Harvard University Press.

Johnson, S. 2001. *Emergence: The connected lives of ants, brains, cities, and software.* New York: Scribner.

Kahneman, D., P. Slovic, and A. Tversky, eds. 1982. *Judgment under uncertainty: Heuristics and biases.* Cambridge and New York: Cambridge University Press.

Kosfeld, M., et al. 2005. Oxytocin increases trust in humans. *Nature* 435(2), 2 June:673–676.

Körding, K., and D. M. Wolpert. 2004. Bayesian integration in sensorimotor learning. *Nature* 427(6971), 1915 January:244–247.

Kramer, P. D. 1993. *Listening to Prozac: A psychiatrist explores antidepressant drugs and the remaking of the self.* London, New York: Penguin Books.

Lakoff, G. 2002. *Moral politics: How liberals and conservatives think.* Chicago: University of Chicago Press.

Levi, I. 1967. *Gambling with Truth.* New York: Alfred A. Knopf.

Luriia, A. R. 1976. *Cognitive development: Its cultural and social foundations.* Cambridge, MA: Harvard University Press.

MacLean, P. D. 1975. Sensory and perceptive factors in emotional functions of the triune brain. In *Emotions: Their parameters and measurement*, ed. L. Levi. New York: Raven Press.

Mangan, B. 2001. Sensation's ghost: The non-sensory "fringe" of consciousness. *Psyche* 7. Available at: http://psyche.cs.monash.edu.au/v7/psyche-7-18-mangan.html.

Matthen, M. 1989. Intentional parallelism and the two-level structure of evolutionary theory. In *Issues in evolutionary epistemology*, K. Hahlweg and C. A. Hooker (eds.), 559–69. Albany, NY: SUNY Press.

McGinn, C. 1982. *The character of mind.* Oxford: Oxford University Press.

Millikan, R. 1993. *White Queen psychology and other essays for Alice.* Cambridge, MA: MIT Press.

Pacherie, E. 2008. Perception, emotions and delusions: The case of the Capgras delusion. In *Delusions and self-deception: Affective influences on belief formation.* T. Baynes and J. Fernandez (eds.), Hove, UK: Psychology Press.

Sober, E. 1994. The primacy of truth-telling and the evolution of lying. In *From a biological point of view: Essays in evolutionary biology.* Cambridge Studies in Philosophy and Biology, 71–92. Cambridge: Cambridge University Press.

Stanovich, K. 2004. *The robot's rebellion: Finding meaning in the age of Darwin.* Chicago: Chicago University Press.

Stephens, C. 2001. When is it selectively advantageous to have true beliefs? Sandwiching the better safe than sorry argument. *Philosophical Studies* 105:161–189.

Taylor, S. 1989. *Positive illusions: Creative self-deception and the healthy mind*. New York: Basic Books.

Whorf, B. L. 1973. *Language, thought, and reality*. Ed. J. B. Carroll. Foreword by S. Chase. Cambridge, MA: MIT Press.

Wigner, E. P. 1960. The unreasonable effectiveness of mathematics in the natural sciences. *Communications in Pure and Applied Mathematics* 13:1–14.

Wilson, C. Unpublished. "Human rationality" as a misplaced composite: A response to the controversy between optimists and pessimists. Canadian Philosophical Association. Edmonton, May 2000.

Wohlgemuth, S., B. Ronacher, and R. Wehner. 2001. Ant odometry in the third dimension. *Nature* 411:795–798.

Yu, A. P., and P. Dayan. 2005. Uncertainty, neuromodulation, and attention. *Neuron* 46:681–692.

Chapter 52: Distinct Brain Loci in Deductive versus Probabilistic Reasoning

DANIEL N. OSHERSON, DANIELA PERANI, STEFANO CAPPA,
TATIANA SCHNUR, FRANCO GRASSI, AND FERRUCCIO FAZIO

Introduction

Normative theories of reasoning distinguish two kinds of persuasive arguments depending on the inferential connection between premises and conclusion. If the truth of an argument's premises guarantee that of its conclusion, the argument is called *valid*, whereas if the premises merely enhance the plausibility of the conclusion, the argument is *probabilistically strong*. Human intuition about validity and probability is limited to inferences of moderate size and reveals systematic imperfections even when applied to simple cases. Nonetheless, starting from adolescence both forms of reasoning are recognizable approximations to their normative counterparts [3, 6, 11].

What is the psychological relation between deductive and probabilistic reasoning? One influential theory conceives both kinds of reasoning as involving the manipulation of 'mental models'. In this view, an argument is evaluated by constructing alternative models of its premises, where each model is a representation of potential circumstances that would render the premises true. The argument is then judged to be probabilistically strong in case a large proportion of the models generated for the premises render the conclusion true as well; the intuition of validity arises from the limiting case in which this proportion reaches one. Within epistemology, such an account of the relation between validity and probability was proposed by Wittgenstein [[41], §5.15], and followed up by de Finetti [9] and

others. A psychological version of the same idea has recently been proposed by Johnson-Laird [23], where it receives detailed and persuasive defense.[1] Moreover, the same theory has been claimed to predict right hemispheric predominance in the manipulation of mental models (see [24, 40]). Johnson-Laird writes: "The model theory also makes a critical prediction about the role of the cerebral hemispheres in reasoning. As Whitaker *et al.* [40] first pointed out, the construction of models is likely to depend on the right hemisphere". The mental models perspective on reasoning thus leads to the following theses:

(1) The brain structures responsible for deductive and probabilistic reasoning are largely the same.

(2) The brain structures responsible for deductive reasoning are predominantly right hemispheric.

Of course, it follows from identity theses (1) and (2) that:

(3) The brain structures responsible for deductive and probabilistic reasoning are both predominantly right hemispheric.

Opposing theories conceive deduction as based on mental rules specific to logic [5] and thus envision no particular relation between deductive and probabilistic reasoning. Mental rules for

Reproduced with permission from Osherson, D., Perani, D., Cappa, S., Schnur, T., Grassi, F., and Fazio, F. (1995) Distinct brain loci in deductive versus probabilistic reasoning. *Neuropsychologia*, 36, 369–376.

Table 1: Sample Arguments: A Is Valid, B Invalid, C Has Anomalous Content

(A)   None of the bakers play chess.
        Some of the chess players listen to opera.
        Some of the opera listeners are not bakers.

(B)   Some of the computer programmers play the piano.
        No one who plays the piano watches soccer matches.
        Some computer programmers watch soccer matches.

(C)   All the engineers own a computer.
        None of the engineers has been to school.
        All the people who own computers are married.

B was used for test, and thus evaluated on separate occasions for validity, probability and anomaly.

---

deduction are thought to analyze and transform certain kinds of linguistic structures, namely, the logical forms of sentences. Consequently, such theories would place deductive reasoning in areas involved with linguistic processing, thus principally in the left hemisphere.[2] It can thus be seen that rule theories suggest the following contrast with thesis (2):

(4)   The brain structures responsible for deductive reasoning are predominantly left hemispheric.

To clarify the empirical status of the foregoing claims, we used positron emission tomography (PET) to examine brain activation during three kinds of reasoning tasks. The three tasks will be called 'logic', 'probability' and 'meaning'. In the logic task, subjects were asked to distinguish valid from invalid arguments. Arguments in the probability and meaning tasks had the same layout as in the logic task, but none were valid. For probability, subjects were asked whether the conclusion had a greater chance of being true than false, supposing the truth of the premises. The meaning task required subjects to examine premises and conclusion individually and determine whether any had anomalous content; it served as a baseline condition since no more than sentence comprehension was involved. As explained below, stimulus presentation was arranged so that during PET scanning identical arguments were evaluated either for validity, probability or anomaly. Sample arguments are presented in Table 1.

Methods

Subjects

Ten right-handed males aged 21–25 years, and recruited from local universities, served as subjects. All claimed to have little or no training in formal logic. The protocol was approved by the Ethics Committee of the San Raffaele Hospital, where the experiment was performed. Subjects provided written consent to participate.

Experimental Tasks

Each of the logic, probability and meaning tasks consisted of four arguments, the first two called 'warm-up', the last two 'test'. The warm-up arguments in a given task varied with respect to possession of the target property (validity, probability or anomaly), and differed across tasks. For example, the warm-up task for logic consisted of one valid and one invalid argument, ordered randomly. Validity is an objective property of arguments, so there was no difficulty distinguishing valid from invalid. Our choice of anomalous statements similarly left little doubt about how to characterize arguments along this dimension. On the other hand, probability is more subjective, so an attempt was made on purely intuitive grounds to select (invalid) arguments that varied in probability.

In contrast to warm-up, the test arguments for all three tasks were identical, namely, a pair of invalid arguments with no anomalous content. Thus, the mental activity required to solve test problems depended only on the kind of reasoning engaged, and practiced during warm-up; the stimuli were identical for the three tasks at the moment of data acquisition. We constructed two other sets of tasks of the same design, using different arguments. The three sets of stimuli yield nine tasks, namely, three each for logic, probability and meaning.

The procedure consisted of a 30-min training session followed by PET scanning within 24 hr. The training session explained the character of the three kinds of reasoning tasks, stated that all arguments concerned a small town in northeastern Italy, and gave examples (no argument figuring in training appeared later among the experimental stimuli). For the PET session, the nine tasks were individually randomized for each subject with the constraint that successive tasks always differ (for example, two logic tasks could not be given successively). The four arguments of a given task were presented sequentially, each for 25 sec with no interstimulus interval. They appeared in the center of a 36-cm video monitor placed 60 cm from the subject's eyes. Relevant instructions from the training session were repeated prior to each task in order to ensure that the subject evaluated the succeeding four arguments in terms of the appropriate distinction (valid/invalid, probable/improbable or anomalous/normal). Subjects studied each argument silently, and made no response during the 100 sec of the task. Warm-up stimuli were evaluated for the 50 sec prior to PET acquisition. Then, without alerting the subject, PET scanning began with the first test argument and continued for the 50 sec required to complete the task. The monitor was then blanked, and the subject closed his eyes for 20 sec (this allowed completion of PET acquisition). Subsequently, the four arguments of the task were re-presented and the subject was asked to indicate the evaluation he had made of each argument during its initial presentation. This part of the procedure lasted around 2 min, and was extended to a 10-min pause between tasks (thereby allowing radioactivity to decay to the baseline level).

PET Method and Data Analysis

Subjects were studied in the supine position using a PET tomograph GE-Advance (General Electric Medical System, Milwaukee, WI, U.S.A.) with collimating septa retracted [10]. The system has 18 rings allowing 35 transaxial images with a slice thickness of 4.25 mm, covering an axial field of view of 15.2 cm. Transmission data were acquired using a pair of rotating pin sources filled with ^{68}Ge (10mCi/pin). A filtered back-projection algorithm was employed for image reconstruction, on a 128×128 matrix with pixel size 1.9 mm, using a Hanning filter (cut-off 4 mm width) in the transaxial plane, and a ramp filter (cut-off 8.5 mm) in the axial direction. Regional cerebral blood flow (rCBF) was measured by recording the distribution of radioactivity following intravenous bolus injection of 5 mCi of ^{15}O-H$_2$O through a forearm cannula [15, 28]. The integrated counts, collected for 70 sec, starting 20 sec after injection, were used as an index of rCBF. Image manipulation and statistical analysis were performed in MATLAB 4.2 (Math Works, Natick, MA, U.S.A.) using statistical parametric mapping (SPM95, Wellcome Department of Cognitive Neurology, London, U.K.). Individual PET data were oriented along the intercommisural

line and transformed into a standard stereotactic space. Global differences in cerebral blood flow were covaried out for all voxels and comparisons across conditions were made using t statistics with appropriate linear contrasts, and then converted to Z-scores [17, 18]. Only regional activations significant at $P < 0.001$ (thresholding SPM $Z > 3.09$) were considered.

Results

Task Performance

We first consider whether subjects remained focussed on the tasks during PET scanning. The brief period allotted for the evaluation of arguments combined with the long interscan interval was expected to promote mental concentration during PET acquisition, and subjects subsequently reported no difficulty in this regard. The subjects' accurate performance on the logic arguments confirms the focussed character of their thought. They averaged 83% correct responses to the logic problems, with range 67–100%. This level of accuracy is equal to that of college students evaluating syllogisms without time stress [[34], pp. 232–234]. For the probability arguments there are no objectively correct answers. That the subjects were able to sustain their attention on the task is nonetheless suggested by their concordant judgment, reflected in a Kuder–Richardson reliability coefficient of 0.87. (Exactly half of the 12 arguments figuring in the probability tasks were judged 'probable' by a majority of subjects.)

PET Data Analysis

Table 2 reports the activation foci and the Z-scores found in the comparison between each experimental condition (logic and probability taken separately) versus the baseline meaning task. The table also shows the foci for the meaning task when compared to the two reasoning conditions pooled. The foci are identified via their stereotactic coordinates, measured in millimeters, relative to the anterior–posterior commissure, corresponding to the Talairach and Tournoux atlas [38].

Consider first the comparison with meaning when the logic and probability tasks are taken separately. We found common foci of activation in the left frontal mesial cortex (dorsal frontal gyrus, BA 6), right and left cerebellar hemisphere, and vermis. We also found common activations for the two reasoning tasks in subcortical

Table 2: Coordinates and Z-Scores for Regions Showing Differential Activation during Logical and Probabilistic Reasoning Compared to the Meaning Task

Region	Coordinates			Z-score
	x	y	z	
Logic vs Meaning				
L dorsal frontal gyrus (BA 6)	−16	2	52	4.29
L cuneus (BA 18)	−10	−86	24	3.57
L thalamus	−10	−16	12	3.37
R caudate	16	2	20	3.91
R thalamus	10	−26	4	3.50
R cerebellum	4	−80	−32	4.54
L cerebellum	4	−74	−36	3.52
Vermis	−2	−64	−16	3.71
Probability vs Meaning				
L dorsal frontal gyrus (BA 6)	−14	−2	48	3.71
L ant. cingulate gyrus (BA 24/32)	−2	14	32	3.41
L thalamus	−16	−16	20	4.02
R mid frontal gyrus (BA 10)	26	40	16	3.64
R caudate nucleus	8	14	8	3.15
R cerebellum	6	−84	−28	4.65
L cerebellum	−6	−64	−36	3.39
Vermis	0	−68	−16	3.41
Meaning vs Logic + Probability				
L temporal pole (BA 38)	−32	8	−28	4.76
L fusiform gyrus (BA 37)	−40	−36	−8	3.73
L sup. frontal gyrus (BA 9)	−14	46	32	3.61
L mid temporal gyrus (BA 21/22)	−46	−30	4	3.25
L inf. temporal gyrus (BA 20)	−40	−8	−24	3.22
R inf. frontal gyrus (BA 45)	48	28	12	4.18
R inf. frontal gyrus (BA 47)	48	18	−4	4.12
R temporal pole (BA 38)	48	8	8	3.80
R inf. temporal gyrus (BA 20)	50	−14	−24	3.80
R mid temporal gyrus (BA 21)	50	−8	−16	3.75
R sup. temporal gyrus (BA 22)	54	−2	0	3.49
R/L orbitofrontal cortex (BA 11)	0	40	−20	3.99

Coordinates are in millimeter relative to the anterior–posterior commissure, corresponding to the Talairach and Tournoux atlas [38]. SPM $P < 0.001$ throughout.

structures, namely, the left thalamus and right caudate. A distinctive focus of activation for the logic task was found in the left cuneus (BA 18), whereas a distinctive focus for probability appeared in the left anterior cingulate gyrus (BA 24/32).

Now let us consider the activation foci found for the meaning task when compared to the pooled data from the two experimental conditions. The comparison reveals bilateral foci of activation in the temporal poles (BA 38), inferior and middle temporal gyri (BA 20, 21), and in the orbital frontal cortex (BA 11). In addition, there were activations in the superior frontal (BA 9) and fusiform (BA 37) gyri of the left hemi-

sphere, and in the inferior frontal (BA 45, 47) and superior temporal (BA 22) gyri of the right hemisphere.

Table 3 shows the stereotactic coordinates and Z-scores of the activation foci found in direct comparisons of the two experimental conditions (logic and probabilistic reasoning). The same foci are shown in Figure 1. In probabilistic reasoning we found activations in the right insula and in the left prefontal cortex, specifically, in the middle (BA 10) and the superior frontal (BA 8) gyri. In contrast, deductive reasoning activated the right anterior cingulate gyrus (BA 24/32) and a set of posterior brain regions, prevalently in the right hemisphere, namely: right

Table 3: Coordinates and Z-Scores for Regions Showing Differential Activation
during Logical versus Probabilistic Reasoning

	Coordinates			
Region	x	y	z	Z-score
Probability vs Logic				
R insula	26	28	16	3.34
L mid frontal gyrus (BA 10)	−40	48	16	3.88
L sup. frontal gyrus (BA 8)	−12	24	44	3.33
Logic vs Probability				
R cingulate gyrus (BA 24/32)	8	38	0	4.18
R sup. parietal lobule (BA 7)	30	−76	40	4.06
R precuneus (BA 7)	8	−76	48	3.45
R mid occipital gyrus (BA 19)	46	−76	−4	3.38
R thalamus	14	−28	12	3.36
R sup. occipital gyrus (BA 19)	22	−80	24	3.31
L cuneus (BA 18)	−2	−94	24	3.72
L precuneus (BA 7)	−10	−80	44	3.53

Coordinates are in millimeter relative to the anterior–posterior commissure, corresponding to
the Talairach and Tournoux atlas [38]. SPM $P < 0.001$ throughout.

superior parietal lobule (BA 7), right superior
and middle occipital gyri (BA 19), right thalamus, left and right precuneus (BA 7), and left
cuneus (BA 18).[3]

Discussion

The principal result of this study is the difference in brain activity associated with probabilistic and deductive reasoning (Table 3). We discuss these differences first, and then turn to
the differences between the reasoning tasks and
the baseline condition. When we write 'X compared to Y' we refer to the activation observed
in the performance of task X that is observed
at a significantly lower level in the performance
of task Y.

Probability Compared to Deduction

Compared to deductive reasoning, the probability task produced activation in the left

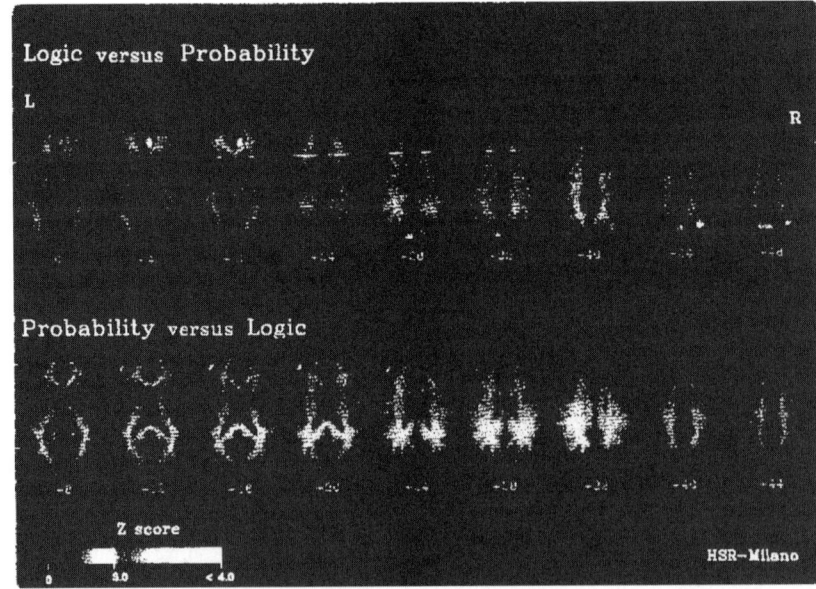

Figure 1. Activation foci in the direct comparison of logic and probability
tasks, superimposed over a magnetic resonance imaging atlas.

dorsolateral frontal cortex (BA 8 and 10), as well as in the right insular cortex. Studies with brain-damaged patients help to explain these findings, even though none appears to have considered probabilistic reasoning *per se*. In a study by Smith and Milner [37], 24 abstract figures were presented various numbers of times to patients with focal cortical ablations for treatment of epilepsy. The subjects were asked to estimate the frequency of appearance of each figure. Only patients with left or right mediolateral frontal corticectomy were impaired, while subjects with temporal and temporo-hippocampal lesions performed comparably to controls. Given that the frontal ablation patients performed normally in recognizing the figures, their disorder was considered to reflect an inability to estimate relative frequency. Since relative frequency is a principal source of information about probability [19], the frontal ablation patients can thus be considered impaired in at least one aspect of probabilistic thought. Another task that may be related to probabilistic reasoning is 'cognitive estimation'. It has been shown that, compared to retro-rolandic damage, frontal lesions on either side of the cortex disturb answers to questions such as 'how fast do race horses gallop?' [35]. In a related study of focal cortical ablations it was found that patients with dorsolateral frontal lesions made more errors in pricing objects (such as a car, a TV set, etc.) than patients with temporal and temporo-hippocampal lesions [36]. Both cognitive estimation and pricing require the selection of a value along a continuous dimension. Chance is likewise a continuous dimension, so determining the probability of a statement might require similar skills. Overall, the foregoing studies provide reason to believe that the dorsolateral frontal cortex is involved in the kind of judgment requested in our probability task.

Deduction Compared to Probability

The prevalent frontal pattern of activation found with probabilistic reasoning can be contrasted with the foci associated with deductive reasoning on identical arguments. For deductive reasoning, the activation was predominantly posterior and bilateral, with a right-side prevalence. There was involvement of the associative visual areas (cuneus, precuneus, middle and superior occipital gyri), as well as the right superior parietal lobule and thalamus. A considerable literature – involving both neuropsychological investigations [39] and PET procedures [8, 21, 22, 27] – implicates these areas in visuo-spatial processing, including form discrimination and imaginative operations. A relationship between visuo-spatial operations and syllogistic reasoning is suggested by the fact that syllogistic reasoning protocols from naive subjects often involve spatial diagrams resembling Euler circles; the remaining subjects typically connect selected terms of the premises, often using arrows [14]. Both strategies have a geometrical character that would be expected to require visuo-spatial processing. Further evidence comes from clinical and PET studies of deductive reasoning involving spatial–relational terms, like 'taller than'. A study by Caramazza *et al.* [7] reported right brain-damaged, non-aphasic subjects to have difficulty with verbal reasoning tasks involving antonymic contrast ('taller than A but shorter than C'). The findings suggest reliance for such reasoning on visuo-imaginative strategies, involving the right hemisphere. A recent PET study using similar tasks showed significant activation of the right lateral and mesial parietal cortex during reasoning, compared to control conditions in which reasoning could not be initiated [2].

The only significant anterior activation found for logic compared to probability was in the right anterior cingulate cortex. The activation of this area has frequently been observed in PET experiments, and related to attentional processes, in particular to selective or divided attention [8, 29]. In the work of Posner and Petersen [33], the anterior cingulate is conceived as a component of the 'anterior attentional system', devoted to executive control. One aspect of this control function is thought to be the integration of linguistic and spatial processing [32]. Its relative increase in activation during deductive reasoning could thus be due to the greater involvement of spatial processing in logic compared to probability (both tasks obviously presuppose a linguistic component).

The comparisons discussed to this point allow tentative evaluation of the theses formulated in the introductory section. Our data cast doubt on thesis (1), and favor thesis (2) over thesis (4). In other words, the brain structures responsible for deductive and probabilistic reasoning appear to be substantially distinct; moreover, deductive reasoning activates sites predominantly in the right rather than left hemisphere.

Reasoning Compared to Anomaly Detection

Comparison of each reasoning task with the baseline condition (requiring only reading for meaning) revealed common activation in the left medial frontal cortex (area 6), the cerebellum and in several subcortical structures. Cerebellar activation was particularly extensive. The foregoing structures have been shown to be activated in verbal working memory tasks [12, 30], and are considered to reflect articulatory rehearsal [1]. Cerebellar activation has also been implicated in the manipulation of transient, non-verbal information [26].

The activation of the foregoing structures is consistent with the character of our two reasoning tasks, which require the integration of information in separate premises, and thus probably entail continuous rehearsal of sentences. Indeed, the role of working memory in syllogistic reasoning has been documented via an interference paradigm [20]. In contrast, the meaning task can be performed without integrating information across sentences, since each sentence may be examined separately for anomaly. It is thus likely that the meaning task requires no verbal rehearsal. The activation found in comparing the reasoning tasks with the baseline condition may therefore be explained in terms of the differential requirements for verbal rehearsal in reasoning compared to anomaly detection.

Anomaly Detection Compared to Reasoning

The reverse subtraction (reading for meaning vs reasoning) was associated with activation in a widespread network of cortical areas in both hemispheres. The areas of activation in the left hemisphere included most of the classical perisylvian language areas, as well as the temporal pole. These foci have been shown in PET studies to be involved in processing prose passages [13, 31]. Similar patterns of activation in homologous contralateral hemispheric areas have been reported for comprehending metaphors [4] and 'theory of mind' stories [13].

In summary, the present results suggest that reasoning about syllogisms engages distinct brain mechanisms, depending on the intention to evaluate them deductively versus probabilistically. Likewise, reading the same syllogisms merely for meaning involves a pattern of cortical activation distinct from that obtained during reasoning.

Notes

1   For algorithmic simulation of the mental steps presumed to underlie the construction of mental models, see [[25], p. 171 ff.].

2   Computer simulation of one version of a mental rule theory is provided in [[34], Ch. 3].

3   Principal component analysis [16] of the PET dataset yielded highly similar profiles between tasks belonging to the same kind of reasoning. In particular, the first component (45% of the variance) cleanly separates the neural sites subserving the six reasoning tasks (three each for logic and probability) from the sites subserving the three anomaly detection tasks. The second component (19% of the variance) separates the neural sites for probability from those for logic. This suggests uniform brain activation across each of the three tasks used to induce deductive reasoning, and similarly for probability and anomaly.

References

1. Baddeley, A. D., *Working Memory*. Oxford University Press, Oxford, 1992.
2. Baker, S. C., Dolan, R. J. and Frith, C. D., The functional anatomy of logic: a PET study of inferential reasoning. *NeuroImage*, 1996, **3**, S218.
3. Baron, J., *Thinking and Deciding*, 2nd edn. Cambridge University Press, Cambridge, 1994.
4. Bottini, G., Corcoran, R., Sterzi, R., Paulesu, E., Schenone, P., Scarpa, P., Frackowiak, R. S. J. and Frith, C. D., The role of the right hemisphere in the interpretation of figurative aspects of language. *Brain*, 1994, **117**, 1241–1253.
5. Braine, M. D. S., On the relation between the natural logic of reasoning and standard logic. *Psychological Review*, 1978, **85**, 1–21.
6. Braine, M. D. S., The 'natural logic' approach to reasoning. In *Reasoning, Necessity, and Logic: Developmental Perspectives*, ed. W. F. Overton. Erlbaum, Hillsdale, NJ, 1990.
7. Caramazza, A., Gordon, J., Zurif, E. B. and De Luca, D. Right hemispheric damage and verbal problem solving behavior. *Brain and Language*, 1976, **3**, 41–46.
8. Corbetta, M., Miezin, F. M., Dobmeyer, S., Shulman, G. L. and Petersen, S. E., Selective and divided attention during visual discriminations of shape, color, and speed: functional anatomy by positron emission tomography. *Journal of Neuroscience*, 1991, **11**, 2383–2402.
9. De Finetti, B., Foresight: its logical laws and its subjective sources. In *Studies in Subjective Probability*, ed. H. Kyburg and H. Smokler. Wiley, New York, 1964.
10. DeGrado, T. R., Turkington, T. G., Williams, J. J., Stearns, C. W., Hoffman, J. M. and Coleman, R. E., Performance characteristics of a whole-body PET scanner. *Journal of Nuclear Medicine*, 1994, **35**, 1398–1406.
11. Evans, J. St. B. T., *Bias in Human Reasoning*. Erlbaum, Hillsdale, NJ, 1989.
12. Fiez, J. A., Raife, E. A., Balota, D. A., Schwarz, J. P., Raichle, M. E. and Petersen, S. E., A positron emission tomography study of the short-term maintenance of verbal information. *Journal of Neuroscience*, 1996, **16**, 808–822.

13. Fletcher, P. C., Happé, F., Frith, U., Baker, S. C., Dolan, R. J., Frackowiak, R. S. J. and Frith, C. D., Other minds in the brain: a functional imaging study of "theory of mind" in story comprehension. *Cognition*, 1995, **57**, 109–128.

14. Ford, M., Two modes of mental representation and problem solution in syllogistic reasoning. *Cognition*, 1995, **54**, 1–71.

15. Fox, P. and Mintun, M., Noninvasive functional brain mapping by change-distribution analysis of averaged PET images of $H_2{}^{15}O$ tissue activity. *Journal of Nuclear Medicine*, 1989, **30**, 141–149.

16. Friston, K. J., Frith, C. D., Liddle, P. F. and Frackowiak, R. S. J., The principal component analysis of large (PET) data sets. *Journal of Cerebral Blood Flow and Metabolism*, 1993, **13**, 5–14.

17. Friston, K. J., Ashburner, J., Poline, J. B., Frith, C. D., Heather, J. D. and Frackowiak, R. S. J., Spatial registration and normalization of images. *Human Brain Mapping*, 1995, **2**, 165–168.

18. Friston, K. J., Holmes, A. P., Worsley, K. J., Poline, J. B., Frith, C. and Frackowiak, R. S. J., Statistical parameter maps in functional imaging: a general linear approach. *Human Brain Mapping*, 1995, **2**, 189–210.

19. Gigerenzer, G. and Murray, D. J., *Cognition as Intuitive Statistics*. Erlbaum, Hillsdale, NJ, 1987.

20. Gilhooly, K. J., Logie, R. H., Wetherick, N. E. and Wynn, V., Working memory and strategies in syllogistic-reasoning tasks. *Memory and Cognition*, 1993, **21**, 115–124.

21. Haxby, J. V., Grady, C. L., Horwitz, B., Ungerleider, L. G., Mishkin, M., Carson, R. E., Herscovitch, P., Schapiro, M. B. and Rapoport, S. I., Dissociation of object and spatial visual processing pathways in human extrastriate cortex. *Proceedings of the National Academy of Science, U.S.A.*, 1991, **88**, 1621–1625.

22. Hirsch, J., DeLaPaz, R. L., Relkin, R. N., Victor, J., Kim, K., Li, T., Borden, P., Rubin, N. and Shapley, R., Illusory contours activate specific regions in human visual cortex: evidence from functional magnetic resonance imaging. *Proceedings of the National Academy of Science, U.S.A.*, 1995, **92**, 6469–6473.

23. Johnson-Laird, P. N., Mental models and probabilistic thinking. *Cognition*, 1995, **50**, 171–191.

24. Johnson-Laird, P. N., Mental models, deductive reasoning, and the brain. In *The Cognitive Neurosciences*, ed. M. S. Gazzaniga. MIT Press, Cambridge, MA, 1995, pp. 999–1008.

25. Johnson-Laird, P. N. and Byrne, R. M. J., *Deduction*. Erlbaum, Hillsdale, NJ, 1991.

26. Kim, S.-G., Ugurbil, K. and Strick, P. L., Activation of cerebellar output nucleus during cognitive processing. *Science*, 1994, **265**, 949–951.

27. Kosslyn, S. M., Thompson, W. L., Kim, I. J. and Alpert, N. M., Topographic representations of mental images in primary visual cortex. *Nature*, 1995, **378**, 496–498.

28. Mazziotta, J. C., Huang, S. C., Phelps, M. E., Carson, R. E., Donald, N. S. and Mahoney, K., A non-invasive positron computed tomography technique using oxygen-15 labelled water for the evaluation of neurobehavioral task batteries. *Journal of Cerebral Blood Flow Metabolism*, 1985, **5**, 70–78.

29. Pardo, J. V., Pardo, J. P., Janer, K. W. and Raichle, M. E., The anterior cingulate cortex mediates processing selection in the Stroop attentional conflict paradigm. *Proceedings of the National Academy of Science, U.S.A.*, 1990, **87**, 256–259.

30. Paulesu, E., Frith, C. D. and Frackowiak, R. S. J., The neural correlates of the verbal component of working memory. *Nature*, 1993, **362**, 342–345.

31. Perani, D., Dehaene, S., Grassi, F., Cappa, S. F., Dupoux, E., Fazio, F. and Mehler, J., Brain processing of native and foreign languages. *NeuroReport*, 1996, **55**, 99–101.

32. Posner, M. I., Attention in cognitive neuroscience: an overview. In *The Cognitive Neurosciences*, ed. M. S. Gazzaniga. MIT Press, Cambridge, MA, 1995, pp. 615–624.

33. Posner, M. I. and Petersen, S. E., The attention system of the human brain. *Annual Review of Neuroscience*, 1990, **13**, 25–42.

34. Rips, L., *The Psychology of Proof*. MIT Press, Cambridge, MA, 1994.

35. Shallice, T. and Evans, M. C., The involvement of the frontal lobe in cognitive estimation. *Cortex*, 1978, **14**, 294–303.

36. Smith, M. A. and Milner, B., Estimation of frequency of occurrence of abstract designs after frontal or temporal lobectomy. *Neuropsychologia*, 1988, **26**, 297–306.

37. Smith, M. A. and Milner, B., Differential effects of frontal lobe lesions on cognitive estimation and spatial memory. *Neuropsychologia*, 1984, **22**, 697–705.

38. Talairach, J. and Tournoux, P., *Co-planar Stereotaxic Atlas of the Human Brain*. Thieme, New York, 1988.

39. Warrington, E. K. and McCarthy, R. A., *Cognitive Neuropsychology*. Academic Press, New York, 1992.

40. Whitaker, H., Savary, F., Markovits, H. and Grou, C., Inference deficits after brain damage. INS Meeting, San Antonio, 1991.

41. Wittgenstein, L., *Tractatus Logico-Philosophicus*. Routledge & Kegan Paul, London, 1961. German edition published in 1921.

Chapter 53: The Emotional Dog and Its Rational Tail: A Social Intuitionist Approach to Moral Judgment

JONATHAN HAIDT

Julie and Mark are brother and sister. They are traveling together in France on summer vacation from college. One night they are staying alone in a cabin near the beach. They decide that it would be interesting and fun if they tried making love. At the very least it would be a new experience for each of them. Julie was already taking birth control pills, but Mark uses a condom too, just to be safe. They both enjoy making love, but they decide not to do it again. They keep that night as a special secret, which makes them feel even closer to each other. What do you think about that? Was it OK for them to make love?

Most people who hear the above story immediately say that it was wrong for the siblings to make love, and they then begin searching for reasons (Haidt, Bjorklund, & Murphy, 2000). They point out the dangers of inbreeding, only to remember that Julie and Mark used two forms of birth control. They argue that Julie and Mark will be hurt, perhaps emotionally, even though the story makes it clear that no harm befell them. Eventually, many people say something like, "I don't know, I can't explain it, I just know it's wrong." But what model of moral judgment allows a person to know that something is wrong without knowing why?

Moral psychology has long been dominated by rationalist models of moral judgment (Figure 1). Rationalist approaches in philosophy stress "the power of a priori reason to grasp substantial truths about the world" (Williams, 1967, p. 69). Rationalist approaches in moral psychology, by extension, say that moral knowledge and moral judgment are reached primarily by a process of reasoning and reflection (Kohlberg, 1969; Piaget, 1932/1965; Turiel, 1983). Moral emotions such as sympathy may sometimes be inputs to the reasoning process, but moral emotions are not the direct causes of moral judgments. In rationalist models, one briefly becomes a judge, weighing issues of harm, rights, justice, and fairness, before passing judgment on Julie and Mark. If no condemning evidence is found, no condemnation is issued.

This article reviews evidence against rationalist models and proposes an alternative: the social intuitionist model (Figure 2). Intuitionism in philosophy refers to the view that there are moral truths and that when people grasp these truths they do so not by a process of ratiocination and reflection but rather by a process more akin to perception, in which one "just sees without argument that they are and must be true" (Harrison, 1967, p. 72). Thomas Jefferson's declaration that certain truths are "self-evident" is an example of ethical intuitionism. Intuitionist approaches in moral psychology, by extension, say that moral intuitions (including moral emotions) come first and directly cause moral judgments (Haidt, 2003; Kagan, 1984; Shweder & Haidt, 1993; J. Q. Wilson, 1993). Moral intuition is a kind of cognition, but it is not a kind of reasoning.

The social part of the social intuitionist model proposes that moral judgment should be studied as an interpersonal process. Moral reasoning is usually an ex post facto process used to influence the intuitions (and hence judgments) of other people. In the social intuitionist model,

Reproduced with permission from Haidt, J. (1995). The emotional dog and its rational tail: A social intuitionist approach to moral judgment. *Psychological Review*, 108, 814–834.

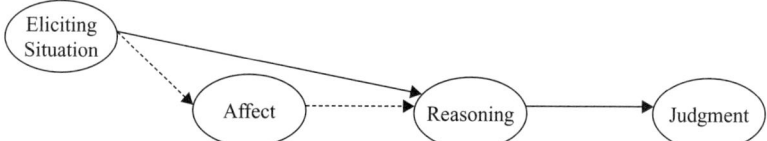

Figure 1. The rationalist model of moral judgment. Moral affects such as sympathy may sometimes be inputs to moral reasoning.

one feels a quick flash of revulsion at the thought of incest and one knows intuitively that something is wrong. Then, when faced with a social demand for a verbal justification, one becomes a lawyer trying to build a case rather than a judge searching for the truth. One puts forth argument after argument, never wavering in the conviction that Julie and Mark were wrong, even after one's last argument has been shot down. In the social intuitionist model, it becomes plausible to say, "I don't know, I can't explain it, I just know it's wrong."

The article begins with a brief review of the history of rationalism in philosophy and psychology. It then describes the social intuitionist model and recent relevant findings from a variety of fields. These findings offer four reasons for doubting the causality of reasoning in moral judgment: (a) There are two cognitive processes at work – reasoning and intuition – and the reasoning process has been overemphasized; (b) reasoning is often motivated; (c) the reasoning process constructs post hoc justifications, yet we experience the illusion of objective reasoning;

and (d) moral action covaries with moral emotion more than with moral reasoning. Because much of this evidence is drawn from research outside of the domain of moral judgment, the social intuitionist model is presented here only as a plausible alternative approach to moral psychology, not as an established fact. The article therefore concludes with suggestions for future research and for ways of integrating the findings and insights of rationalism and intuitionism.

It must be stressed at the outset that the social intuitionist model is an antirationalist model only in one limited sense: It says that moral reasoning is rarely the direct cause of moral judgment. That is a descriptive claim, about how moral judgments are actually made. It is not a normative or prescriptive claim, about how moral judgments ought to be made. Baron (1998) has demonstrated that people following their moral intuitions often bring about nonoptimal or even disastrous consequences in matters of public policy, public health, and the tort system. A correct understanding of the intuitive basis of moral judgment may therefore be useful

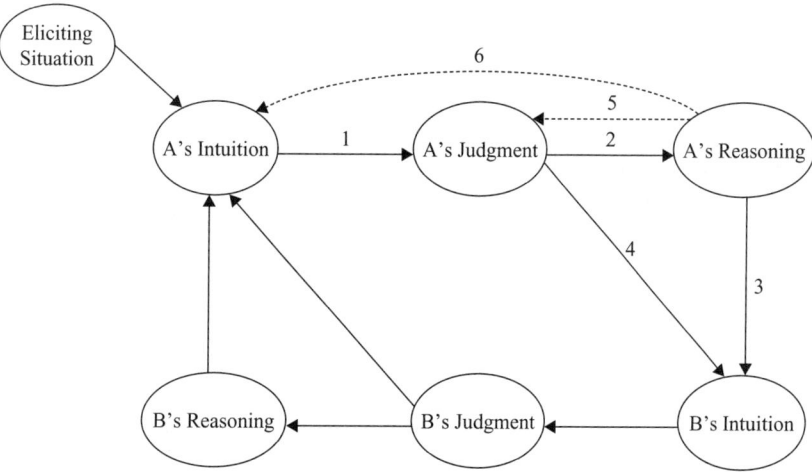

Figure 2. The social intuitionist model of moral judgment. The numbered links, drawn for Person A only, are (1) the intuitive judgment link, (2) the post hoc reasoning link, (3) the reasoned persuasion link, and (4) the social persuasion link. Two additional links are hypothesized to occur less frequently: (5) the reasoned judgment link and (6) the private reflection link.

in helping decision makers avoid mistakes and in helping educators design programs (and environments) to improve the quality of moral judgment and behavior.

Philosophy and the Worship of Reason

Philosophers have frequently written about the conflict between reason and emotion as a conflict between divinity and animality. Plato's *Timaeus* (4th century B.C./1949) presents a charming myth in which the gods first created human heads, with their divine cargo of reason, and then found themselves forced to create seething, passionate bodies to help the heads move around in the world. The drama of human moral life was the struggle of the heads to control the bodies by channeling the bodies' passions toward virtuous ends. The stoic philosophers took an even dimmer view of the emotions, seeing them as conceptual errors that bound one to the material world and therefore to a life of misery (R. C. Solomon, 1993). Medieval Christian philosophers similarly denigrated the emotions because of their link to desire and hence to sin. The 17th century's continental rationalists (e.g., Leibniz, Descartes) worshiped reason as much as Plato had, hoping to model all of philosophy on the deductive method developed by Euclid.

In the 18th century, however, English and Scottish philosophers (e.g., Shaftesbury, Hutcheson, Hume, and Smith) began discussing alternatives to rationalism. They argued that people have a built-in moral sense that creates pleasurable feelings of approval toward benevolent acts and corresponding feelings of disapproval toward evil and vice. David Hume in particular proposed that moral judgments are similar in form to aesthetic judgments: They are derived from sentiment, not reason, and we attain moral knowledge by an "immediate feeling and finer internal sense," not by a "chain of argument and induction" (Hume, 1777/1960, p. 2). His most radical statement of this position was that "we speak not strictly and philosophically when we talk of the combat of passion and of reason. Reason is, and ought only to be the slave of the passions, and can never pretend to any other office than to serve and obey them"[1] (Hume, 1739–1740/1969, p. 462).

The thrust of Hume's attack on rationalism was that reason alone cannot accomplish the magnificent role it has been given since Plato. Hume saw reason as a tool used by the mind to obtain and process information about events in the world or about relations among objects.

Reason can let us infer that a particular action will lead to the death of many innocent people, but unless we care about those people, unless we have some *sentiment* that values human life, reason alone cannot advise against taking the action. Hume argued that a person in full possession of reason yet lacking moral sentiment would have difficulty choosing any ends or goals to pursue and would look like what we now call a psychopath (Cleckley, 1955; Hume, 1777/1960).

Hume's emotivist approach to ethics was not well received by philosophers. Kant's (1785/1959) rationalist ethical theory[2] was created as an attempt to refute Hume, and Kant has had a much larger impact than Hume on modern moral philosophers (e.g., R. M. Hare, 1981; Rawls, 1971), many of whom have followed Kant in attempting to deduce a foundation for ethics from the meaning of rationality itself.

Psychology and the Focus on Reasoning

Psychologists, however, freed themselves from the worship of reason in the late 19th century, when they abandoned the armchair and went into the laboratory. Until the cognitive revolution of the 1960s, the major schools of psychology did not see reason as the master of anything, and their views on morality were compatible with Hume's emphasis on emotions. Freud (1900/1976) saw people's judgments as driven by unconscious motives and feelings, which are then rationalized with publicly acceptable reasons. The behaviorists also saw moral reasoning as epiphenomenal in the production of moral behavior, explaining morality as the acts that a society happens to reward or punish (Skinner, 1971).

Kohlberg and the Cognitive Revolution

But then came Lawrence Kohlberg. Kohlberg's work was a sustained attack on "irrational emotive theories" (1971, p. 188), and his cognitive–developmental theory was an important part of the cognitive revolution. Kohlberg built on Piaget's (1932/1965) pioneering work, developing an interviewing method that was suitable for use with adults as well as children. Kohlberg presented participants with dilemmas in which moral and nonmoral claims were present on both sides, and he then looked to see how people resolved the conflicts. In his best-known dilemma, a man named Heinz must decide whether he should break into a druggist's shop to steal a drug that may save the life of his dying wife. Kohlberg found a six-level progression of increasing sophistication in how people handled such dilemmas. He claimed that children start as egoists, judging actions by the good or bad consequences they bring to the self, but as children's cognitive abilities expand they develop the ability to "role-take," or see a situation from other people's perspectives. The experience of role-taking drives the child on to the less egocentric and more powerful conventional and then post-conventional levels of moral reasoning.

Kohlberg's focus was on development, but he often addressed the question of mechanism. He consistently endorsed a rationalist and somewhat Platonic model in which affect may be taken into account by reason (as in Figure 1) but in which reasoning ultimately makes the decisions:

> We are claiming...that the moral force in personality is cognitive. Affective forces are involved in moral decisions, but affect is neither moral nor immoral. When the affective arousal is channeled into moral directions, it is moral; when it is not so channeled, it is not. The moral channeling mechanisms themselves are cognitive. (Kohlberg, 1971, pp. 230–231)

Kohlberg was quite explicit that the cognitive mechanisms he discussed involved conscious, language-based thinking. He was interested in the phenomenology of moral reasoning, and he described one of the pillars of his approach as the assumption that "moral reasoning is the conscious process of using ordinary moral language" (Kohlberg, Levine, & Hewer, 1983, p. 69).

After Kohlberg

Kohlberg trained or inspired most of the leading researchers in moral psychology today (see chapters in Kurtines & Gewirtz, 1991; Lapsley, 1996). Rationalism still rules, and there appears to be a consensus that morality lives within the individual mind as a traitlike cognitive attainment, a set of knowledge structures about moral standards that children create for themselves in the course of their everyday reasoning (see Darley, 1993).

The social interactionist perspective (Nucci & Turiel, 1978; Turiel, 1983, 1998; Turiel, Killen, & Helwig, 1987), one of the most widely used approaches at present, can serve as an illustrative model. This research is based on a method developed by Nucci and Turiel (1978) in which children are interviewed about rule violations. After giving an initial judgment, the child is asked to respond to a series of probe questions designed to assess how the child thinks about the rule in question (e.g., if there were no rule, would the action be OK? Could the rule be changed?). Participants are also asked to provide justifications of their judgments.

In the social interactionist model, people are said to think about the consequences of an action before determining whether the action is a moral violation. Actions that lead to injustice, to harm, or to the violation of rights are recognized as falling within the moral domain and are treated differently from other kinds of rule violations. Rules prohibiting moral violations are judged, even by young children, to be universally applicable and unalterable. Actions that involve no injustice, harm, or rights violations are treated as violations of social conventions (involving locally agreed on uniformities of behavior within social systems) or as personal issues (areas of individual prerogative).

Researchers in this tradition are sensitive to how moral development occurs in a social context, driven forward by children's interactions with peers in such contexts as taking turns, sharing, harming, and responding to harm. This emphasis on social interaction is in harmony with the social part of the social intuitionist model and is not a source of contention in the present article. The central source of contention, and the focus of the present article concerns the causal role of reflective, conscious reasoning.

Questioning the Causality of Reasoning

People undeniably engage in moral reasoning. But does the evidence really show that such reasoning is the cause, rather than the consequence, of moral judgment? Turiel, Hildebrandt, and Wainryb (1991) examined young adults' reasoning about issues of abortion, homosexuality, pornography, and incest. They found that people who judged the actions to be moral violations also talked about harmful consequences, whereas people who thought the actions were not wrong generally cited no harmful consequences. Turiel et al. (1991) interpreted these findings as showing the importance of "informational assumptions"; for example, people who thought that life begins at conception were generally opposed to abortion, whereas people who thought that life begins later were generally not opposed to abortion. In making this interpretation, however, Turiel et al. made a jump from correlation to causation. The correlation they found between judgment and supporting belief does not necessarily mean that the belief caused the judgment. An intuitionist interpretation is just as plausible: The anti-abortion judgment (a gut feeling that abortion is bad) causes the belief that life begins at conception (an ex post facto rationalization of the gut feeling).

Haidt, Koller, and Dias (1993) found evidence for such an intuitionist interpretation. They examined American and Brazilian responses to actions that were offensive yet harmless, such as eating one's dead pet dog, cleaning one's toilet with the national flag, or eating a chicken carcass one has just used for masturbation. The stories were carefully constructed so that no plausible harm could be found, and most participants directly stated that nobody was hurt by the actions in question, yet participants still usually said the actions were wrong, and universally wrong. They frequently made statements such as, "It's just wrong to have sex with a chicken." Furthermore, their affective reactions to the stories (statements that it would bother them to witness the action) were better predictors of their moral judgments than were their claims about harmful consequences. Haidt and Hersh (2001) found the same thing when they interviewed conservatives and liberals about sexual morality issues, including homosexuality, incest, and unusual forms of masturbation. For both groups, affective reactions were good predictors of judgment, whereas perceptions of harmfulness were not. Haidt and Hersh also found that participants were often "morally dumbfounded" (Haidt et al., 2000); that is, they would stutter, laugh, and express surprise at their inability to find supporting reasons, yet they would not change their initial judgments of condemnation.

It seems, then, that for affectively charged events such as incest and other taboo violations, an intuitionist model may be more plausible than a rationalist model. But can an intuitionist model handle the entire range of moral judgment? Can it accommodate the findings from rationalist research programs while also explaining new phenomena and leading to new and testable predictions? The social intuitionist model may be able to do so.

The Social Intuitionist Model

The central claim of the social intuitionist model is that moral judgment is caused by quick moral intuitions and is followed (when needed) by slow, ex post facto moral reasoning. Clear definitions of moral judgment, moral intuition, and moral reasoning are therefore needed.

Moral Judgment

Moral philosophers have long struggled to distinguish moral judgments from other kinds of judgments (e.g., aesthetics, skill, or personal taste). Rather than seeking a formal definition that lists the necessary and sufficient features of a moral judgment, the present article takes a more empirical approach, starting from a behavioral fact about human beings: that in every society, people talk about and evaluate the actions of other people, and these evaluations have consequences for future interactions (Boehm, 1999). Many of these evaluations occur against the backdrop of specific cultural practices, in which one praises or criticizes the skills or talents of an individual (e.g., "she is a daring chef"). However, an important subset of these evaluations are made with respect to virtues or goods that are applied to everyone in the society (e.g., fairness, honesty, or piety in some cultures), or to everyone in a certain social category (e.g., chastity for young women in some cultures or generosity for lineage heads). These virtues are obligatory in that everyone (within the relevant categories) is expected to strive to attain them. People who fail to embody these virtues or whose actions betray a lack of respect for them are subject to criticism, ostracism, or some other punishment. It is this subset of evaluations that is at issue in the present article. (For more on moral goods, see Ross, 1930; Shweder & Haidt, 1993.)

Moral judgments are therefore defined as evaluations (good vs. bad) of the actions or character of a person that are made with respect to a set of virtues held to be obligatory by a culture or subculture. This definition is left broad intentionally to allow a large gray area of marginally moral judgments. For example, "eating a low-fat diet" may not qualify as a moral virtue for most philosophers, yet in health-conscious subcultures, people who eat cheeseburgers and milkshakes are seen as morally inferior to those who eat salad and chicken (Stein & Nemeroff, 1995).

Moral Reasoning

Everyday moral reasoners are sometimes said to be like scientists, who learn by forming and testing hypotheses, who build working models of the social world as they interact with it, and

Table 1: General Features of the Two Systems

The Intuitive System	*The Reasoning System*
Fast and effortless	Slow and effortful
Process is unintentional and runs automatically	Process is intentional and controllable
Process is inaccessible; only results enter awareness	Process is consciously accessible and viewable
Does not demand attentional resources	Demands attentional resources, which are limited
Parallel distributed processing	Serial processing
Pattern matching; thought is metaphorical, holistic	Symbol manipulation; thought is truth preserving, analytical
Common to all mammals	Unique to humans over age 2 and perhaps some language-trained apes
Context dependent	Context independent
Platform dependent (depends on the brain and body that houses it)	Platform independent (the process can be transported to any rule following organism or machine)

Note. These contrasts are discussed in Bruner (1986), Chaiken (1980), Epstein (1994), Freud (1900/1976), Margolis (1987), Metcalfe and Mischel (1999), Petty and Cacioppo (1986), Posner and Snyder (1975), Pyszczynski and Greenberg (1987), Reber (1993), Wegner (1994), T. D. Wilson (2002), and Zajonc (1980).

who consult these models when making moral judgments (Turiel, 1983). A key feature of the scientist metaphor is that judgment is a kind of inference made in several steps. The reasoner searches for relevant evidence, weighs evidence, coordinates evidence with theories, and reaches a decision (Kuhn, 1989; Nisbett & Ross, 1980). Some of these steps may be performed unconsciously and any of the steps may be subject to biases and errors, but a key part of the definition of reasoning is that it has steps, at least a few of which are performed consciously. Galotti (1989), in her definition of everyday reasoning, specifically excludes "any one-step mental processes" such as sudden flashes of insight, gut reactions, or other forms of "momentary intuitive response" (p. 333).

Building on Galotti (1989), *moral reasoning* can now be defined as conscious mental activity that consists of transforming given information about people in order to reach a moral judgment. To say that moral reasoning is a conscious process means that the process is intentional, effortful, and controllable and that the reasoner is aware that it is going on (Bargh, 1994).

Moral Intuition

Commentators on intuition have generally stressed the fact that a judgment, solution, or other conclusion appears suddenly and effortlessly in consciousness, without any awareness by the person of the mental processes that led to the

outcome (Bastick, 1982; Simon, 1992). Bruner (1960) said that intuition does not advance in careful steps; rather, it involves "manoeuvres based seemingly on an implicit perception of the total problem. The thinker arrives at an answer, which may be right or wrong, with little if any awareness of the process by which he reached it" (p. 57). It must be stressed that the contrast of intuition and reasoning is not the contrast of emotion and cognition. Intuition, reasoning, and the appraisals contained in emotions (Frijda, 1986; Lazarus, 1991) are all forms of cognition. Rather, the words *intuition* and *reasoning* are intended to capture the contrast made by dozens of philosophers and psychologists between two kinds of cognition. The most important distinctions (see Table 1) are that intuition occurs quickly, effortlessly, and automatically, such that the outcome but not the process is accessible to consciousness, whereas reasoning occurs more slowly, requires some effort, and involves at least some steps that are accessible to consciousness.

Building on Bastick (1982), Bruner (1960), Simon (1992), and others, *moral intuition* can be defined as the sudden appearance in consciousness of a moral judgment, including an affective valence (good–bad, like–dislike), without any conscious awareness of having gone through steps of searching, weighing evidence, or inferring a conclusion. Moral intuition is therefore the psychological process that the Scottish philosophers talked about, a process akin to aesthetic judgment: One sees or hears about a social event and one instantly feels approval or disapproval.

The Links in the Model

The social intuitionist model is composed of four principal links or processes, shown as solid arrows in Figure 2. The existence of each link is well established by prior research in some domains of judgment, although not necessarily in the domain of moral judgment. The model is therefore presented as a proposal to spur thinking and new research on moral judgment.

1. THE INTUITIVE JUDGMENT LINK

The model proposes that moral judgments appear in consciousness automatically and effortlessly as the result of moral intuitions. Examples of this link in nonmoral cognition include Zajonc's (1980) demonstrations that affectively valenced evaluations are made ubiquitously and rapidly, before any conscious processing has taken place. More recent examples include findings that much of social cognition operates automatically and implicitly (Bargh & Chartrand, 1999; Greenwald & Banaji, 1995).

2. THE POST HOC REASONING LINK

The model proposes that moral reasoning is an effortful process, engaged in after a moral judgment is made, in which a person searches for arguments that will support an already-made judgment. Nisbett and Wilson (1977) demonstrated such post hoc reasoning for causal explanations. Kuhn (1991), Kunda (1990), and Perkins, Farady, and Bushey (1991) found that everyday reasoning is heavily marred by the biased search only for reasons that support one's already-stated hypothesis.

3. THE REASONED PERSUASION LINK

The model proposes that moral reasoning is produced and sent forth verbally to justify one's already-made moral judgment to others. Such reasoning can sometimes affect other people, although moral discussions and arguments are notorious for the rarity with which persuasion takes place. Because moral positions always have an affective component to them, it is hypothesized that reasoned persuasion works not by providing logically compelling arguments but by triggering new affectively valenced intuitions in the listener. The importance of using affective persuasion to change affectively based attitudes has been demonstrated by Edwards and von Hippel (1995) and by Shavitt (1990).

4. THE SOCIAL PERSUASION LINK

Because people are highly attuned to the emergence of group norms, the model proposes that the mere fact that friends, allies, and acquaintances have made a moral judgment exerts a direct influence on others, even if no reasoned persuasion is used. Such social forces may elicit only outward conformity (Asch, 1956), but in many cases people's privately held judgments are directly shaped by the judgments of others (Berger & Luckman, 1967; Davis & Rusbult, 2001; Newcomb, 1943; Sherif, 1935).

These four links form the core of the social intuitionist model. The core of the model gives moral reasoning a causal role in moral judgment but only when reasoning runs through other people. It is hypothesized that people rarely override their initial intuitive judgments just by reasoning privately to themselves because reasoning is rarely used to question one's own attitudes or beliefs (see the motivated reasoning problem, below).

However, people are capable of engaging in private moral reasoning, and many people can point to times in their lives when they changed their minds on a moral issue just from mulling the matter over by themselves. Although some of these cases may be illusions (see the post hoc reasoning problem, below), other cases may be real, particularly among philosophers, one of the few groups that has been found to reason well (Kuhn, 1991). The full social intuitionist model therefore includes two ways in which private reasoning can shape moral judgments.

5. THE REASONED JUDGMENT LINK

People may at times reason their way to a judgment by sheer force of logic, overriding their initial intuition. In such cases reasoning truly is causal and cannot be said to be the "slave of the passions." However, such reasoning is hypothesized to be rare, occurring primarily in cases in which the initial intuition is weak and processing capacity is high. In cases where the reasoned judgment conflicts with a strong intuitive judgment, a person usually has a "dual attitude" (T. D. Wilson, Lindsey, & Schooler, 2000) in which the reasoned judgment may be expressed verbally yet the intuitive judgment continues to exist under the surface.

6. THE PRIVATE REFLECTION LINK

In the course of thinking about a situation a person may spontaneously activate a new intuition that contradicts the initial intuitive judgment. The most widely discussed method of triggering new intuitions is role-taking (Selman, 1971). Simply by putting oneself into the shoes of another person, one may instantly feel pain, sympathy, or other vicarious emotional responses. This is one of the principal pathways of moral reflection according to Piaget (1932/1965), Kohlberg (1969, 1971), and other cognitive developmentalists. A person comes to see an issue or dilemma from more than one side and thereby experiences multiple competing intuitions. The final judgment may be determined either by going with the strongest intuition or by allowing reason to choose among the alternatives on the basis of the conscious application of a rule or principle. This pathway amounts to having an inner dialogue with oneself (Tappan, 1997), obviating the need for a discourse partner.

Rationalist models focus on Links 5 and 6. In the social intuitionist model, in contrast, moral judgment consists primarily of Links 1–4, although the model allows that Links 5 and 6 may sometimes contribute (such as during a formal moral judgment interview). The next section of this article reviews four problems for rationalist models. For each problem, a social intuitionist reinterpretation of the evidence is offered, relying primarily on Links 1–4.

Four Reasons to Doubt the Causal Importance of Reason

1. The Dual Process Problem: There Is a Ubiquitous and Under-studied Intuitive Process at Work

It is now widely accepted in social and cognitive psychology that two processing systems are often at work when a person makes judgments or solves problems (see Table 1; see also Chaiken & Trope, 1999). Because these two systems typically run in parallel and are capable of reaching differing conclusions, these models are usually called *dual process* models. Dual process models have thus far had little impact on moral judgment research because most researchers have focused their efforts on understanding the reasoning process (but see Eisenberg, Shea, Carlo, & Knight, 1991; Gibbs, 1991). There is evidence, however, that moral judgment works like other kinds of judgment, in which most of the action is in the intuitive process.

AUTOMATIC EVALUATION

Affective evaluation occurs so quickly, automatically, and pervasively that it is generally

thought to be an integral part of perception. Zajonc (1980) synthesized findings from a variety of fields to create a modern version of Wundt's (1897/1969) affective primacy theory, in which he argued that feeling and thought are to some extent separate systems with separate biological bases. The affective system has primacy in every sense: It came first in phylogeny, it emerges first in ontogeny, it is triggered more quickly in real-time judgments, and it is more powerful and irrevocable when the two systems yield conflicting judgments (see also Reber, 1993). Research on the automatic evaluation effect confirms that very brief or even subliminal presentations of affectively valenced words (Bargh, Chaiken, Raymond, & Hymes, 1996; Fazio, Sanbonmatsu, Powell, & Kardes, 1986), facial expressions (Murphy & Zajonc, 1993), and photographs of people and animals (Hermans, De Houwer, & Eelen, 1994) alter the time it takes to evaluate a target object presented immediately afterward, indicating that affective processing is at work within a quarter second of stimulus presentation.

AUTOMATIC MORAL JUDGMENT

Moral judgments typically involve more complex social stimuli than the simple words and visual objects used in automatic evaluation studies. Could moral judgments be made automatically as well? The emerging view in social cognition is that *most* of our behaviors and judgments are in fact made automatically (i.e., without intention, effort, or awareness of process; Bargh, 1994; Bargh & Chartrand, 1999; Greenwald & Banaji, 1995).

The literature most relevant to moral judgment is the literature on attitudes, where a central question has been how people form attitudes about other people. The evidence indicates that attitude formation is better described as a set of automatic processes than as a process of deliberation and reflection about the traits of a person. People form first impressions at first sight (Albright, Kenny, & Malloy, 1988), and the impressions that they form from observing a "thin slice" of behavior (as little as 5 s) are almost identical to the impressions they form from much longer and more leisurely observation and deliberation (Ambady & Rosenthal, 1992). These first impressions alter subsequent evaluations, creating a halo effect (Thorndike, 1920), in which positive evaluations of nonmoral traits such as attractiveness lead to beliefs that a person possesses corresponding moral traits such as kindness and good character (Dion,

Berscheid, & Walster, 1972). People also categorize other people instantly and automatically,
applying stereotypes that often include morally
evaluated traits (e.g., aggressiveness for African
Americans; Devine, 1989). All of these findings
illustrate the operation of the intuitive judgment
link (Link 1 in Figure 2), in which the perception of a person or an event leads instantly and
automatically to a moral judgment without any
conscious reflection or reasoning.

Another illustration of automatic moral judgment can be seen in the literature on persuasion.
Moral discourse in its natural setting is often a
kind of persuasion, in which one person tells others about an event and tries to recruit them to
her reading of the event. According to Chaiken's
(1987) heuristic–systematic model of persuasion, people are guided in part by the "principle
of least effort." Because people have limited cognitive resources, and because heuristic processing is easy and adequate for most tasks, heuristic processing (the intuitive process) is generally
used unless there is a special need to engage in
systematic processing (see also Simon, 1967).
A particularly important heuristic for the study
of moral judgment is the "I agree with people I
like" heuristic (Chaiken, 1980). If your friend is
telling you how Robert mistreated her, there is
little need for you to think systematically about
the good reasons Robert might have had. The
mere fact that your friend has made a judgment
affects your own intuitions directly, illustrating
the social persuasion link (Link 4). Only if the
agreement heuristic leads to other conflicts (e.g.,
if Robert is a friend of yours) will your sufficiency
threshold be raised above your actual level of
confidence, triggering effortful systematic processing (Links 5 and 6) to close the gap.

However, the social intuitionist model posits
that moral reasoning is usually done interperson-
ally rather than privately. If Robert is in fact a
friend of yours, then you and your friend might
present arguments to each other (Link 3, the
reasoned persuasion link) in the hope of triggering new intuitions, getting the other to see
Robert's actions in a better or worse light. Moral
discussions can then be modeled as a repeated
cycle through Links 1, 2, and 3 in Person A,
then in Person B, then in Person A, and so on.
Link 4 would exert a constant pressure toward
agreement if the two parties were friends and a
constant pressure against agreement if the two
parties disliked each other. If at least one of
the parties began without a strong initial intuition, then some degree of convergence would
be likely. Davis and Rusbult (2001) recently doc-

umented this convergence process, which they
called *attitude alignment*. However, if both parties began with strongly felt opposing intuitions
(as in a debate over abortion), then reasoned
persuasion would be likely to have little effect,
except that the post hoc reasoning triggered in
the other person could lead to even greater disagreement, a process labeled "attitude polarization" by Lord, Ross, and Lepper (1979).

Petty and Cacioppo's (1986) elaboration–
likelihood model gives a similar reading of the
standard moral judgment discussion. If you feel
a strong identification with the source of the persuasive message (your friend), and you have no
conflict motivating elaborated thinking, then a
peripheral process is sufficient to lead to an attitude shift, a judgment that Robert is evil. However, if the person talking to you is a stranger
(a research psychologist) who challenges your
judgment at every turn ("What if Heinz didn't
love his wife, should he still steal the drug?"),
then you will be forced to engage in extensive effortful, verbal, central processing. Standard moral judgment interviews may therefore
create an unnaturally reasoned form of moral
judgment, leading to the erroneous conclusion
that moral judgment is primarily a reasoning process. Also, because forcing people to introspect
to find reasons for their attitudes can change
those attitudes temporarily (T. D. Wilson et al.,
2000; T. D. Wilson & Schooler, 1991), standard moral judgment interviews might not even
provide a valid measure of people's real moral
beliefs. (See also Schooler, Fiore, & Brandimonte,
1997, on the impairments caused by forcing people to verbalize what they know intuitively.)

THE SOCIAL INTUITIONIST SOLUTION

The social intuitionist model is fully compatible with modern dual process theories. Like
those theories, the model posits that the intuitive
process is the default process, handling everyday moral judgments in a rapid, easy, and holistic way. It is primarily when intuitions conflict,
or when the social situation demands thorough
examination of all facets of a scenario, that the
reasoning process is called upon. Reasoning can
occur privately (Links 5 and 6), and such solitary moral reasoning may be common among
philosophers and among those who have a high
need for cognition (Cacioppo & Petty, 1982).
Yet ever since Plato wrote his *Dialogues*, philosophers have recognized that moral reasoning naturally occurs in a social setting, between people
who can challenge each other's arguments and
trigger new intuitions (Links 3 and 4). The social

intuitionist model avoids the traditional focus on conscious private reasoning and draws attention to the role of moral intuitions, and of other people, in shaping moral judgments.

2. The Motivated Reasoning Problem: The Reasoning Process Is More Like a Lawyer Defending a Client Than a Judge or Scientist Seeking Truth

It appears, then, that a dual process model may be appropriate for a theory of moral judgment. If so, then the relationship between the two processes must be specified. Is the reasoning process the "smarter" but more cognitively expensive process, called in whenever the intuitive process is unable to solve a problem cheaply? Or is the relationship one of master and servant, as Hume suggested, in which reason's main job is to formulate arguments that support one's intuitive conclusions? Research on both motivated reasoning and everyday reasoning suggests that the post hoc reasoning link (Link 2) is more important than the reasoned judgment and private reflection links (Links 5 and 6).

Two major classes of motives have been shown to bias and direct reasoning. The first class can be called *relatedness motives*, for it includes concerns about impression management and smooth interaction with other people. The second class can be called *coherence motives*, for it includes a variety of defensive mechanisms triggered by cognitive dissonance and threats to the validity of one's cultural worldview.

RELATEDNESS MOTIVES

From an evolutionary perspective, it would be strange if our moral judgment machinery was designed principally for accuracy, with no concern for the disastrous effects of periodically siding with our enemies and against our friends. Studies of attitudes, person perception, and persuasion show that desires for harmony and agreement do indeed have strong biasing effects on judgments. Chaiken and her colleagues incorporated *impression motivation* into the heuristic–systematic model, which is described as "the desire to hold attitudes and beliefs that will satisfy current social goals" (Chen & Chaiken, 1999, p. 78). Chen, Shechter, and Chaiken (1996) found that people who expected to discuss an issue with a partner whose views were known expressed initial attitudes, before the interaction, that were shifted toward those of their anticipated partner. More broadly, Darley and Berscheid (1967) found that people rate a

description of a person's personality as more likable if they expect to interact with the person than if they do not expect to interact.

The existence of motivations to agree with our friends and allies means that we can be directly affected by their judgments (the social persuasion link). The mere fact that your friend expresses a moral judgment against X is often sufficient to cause in you a critical attitude toward X. Such direct influence, circumventing reasoning entirely, fits with Chartrand and Bargh's (1999) recent demonstration of the "chameleon effect," in which people unconsciously mimic the postures, mannerisms, and facial expressions of their interaction partners. Chartrand and Bargh found that such automatic mimicry is socially adaptive, for people who are "in sync" with another person are liked better by that person.

COHERENCE MOTIVES

Psychologists since Freud have argued that people construct views of themselves and of the world and that they experience potentially crippling anxiety when these constructions are threatened (Moskowitz, Skurnik, & Galinsky, 1999). Research on cognitive dissonance (Festinger, 1957; Wicklund & Brehm, 1976) showed just how readily people change their thinking and beliefs to avoid the threat of internal contradictions. More recently, Chaiken, Giner-Sorolla, and Chen (1996) defined *defense motivation* as "the desire to hold attitudes and beliefs that are congruent with existing self-definitional attitudes and beliefs" (p. 557). Self-definitional attitudes include values and moral commitments. When defense motivation is triggered, both heuristic and systematic thinking work to preserve self-definitional attitudes.

The biasing effects of defense motivation can be seen in studies that challenge participants' moral and political ideology. Lord et al. (1979) found that students with strong opinions about the death penalty, when exposed to research evidence on both sides of the issue, accepted evidence supporting their prior belief uncritically while subjecting opposing evidence to much greater scrutiny. Lerner's (1965) "just world" hypothesis stated that people have a need to believe that they live in a world where people generally get what they deserve. People who suffer for no reason are a threat to this belief, so participants adjusted their moral judgments, derogating or blaming innocent victims (Lerner & Miller, 1978). Tetlock, Kristel, Elson, Green, and Lerner (2000) found that people's willingness to use relevant baserate information, or to engage in counterfactual thinking, depended on whether or not their "sacred values" were threatened by doing so. In all of these examples, reasoning is used to defend prior moral commitments.

Moral judgments are also affected by the defensive motivations of terror management (S. Solomon, Greenberg, & Pyszczynski, 1991). When people are asked to think about their own deaths, they appear to suppress a generalized fear of mortality by clinging more tightly to their cultural worldview. Death-primed participants then shift their moral judgments to defend that worldview. They mete out harsher punishment to violators of cultural values, and they give bigger rewards to people who behaved morally (Rosenblatt, Greenberg, Solomon, Pyszczynski, & Lyon, 1989). Death-primed participants have more negative attitudes toward those who do not fully share their worldview (e.g., Jews; Greenberg et al., 1990). From a terror-management perspective, moral judgment is a special kind of judgment, because moral judgments always implicate the cultural worldview. It is plausible to say, "I don't like asparagus, but I don't care if you eat it." It is not plausible to say, "I think human life is sacred, but I don't care if you kill him."

MECHANISMS OF BIAS

Studies of everyday reasoning reveal the mechanisms by which relatedness and coherence motivations make people act like lawyers. Kuhn (1991) found that most people have difficulty understanding what evidence is, and when pressed to give evidence in support of their theories they generally give anecdotes or illustrative examples instead. Furthermore, people show a strong tendency to search for anecdotes and other "evidence" exclusively on their preferred side of an issue, a pattern that has been called the "my-side bias" (Baron, 1995; Perkins et al., 1991). Once people find supporting evidence, even a single piece of bad evidence, they often stop the search, since they have a "makes-sense epistemology" (Perkins, Allen, & Hafner, 1983) in which the goal of thinking is not to reach the most accurate conclusion but to find the first conclusion that hangs together well and that fits with one's important prior beliefs.

Research in social cognition also indicates that people often behave like "intuitive lawyers" rather than "intuitive scientists" (Baumeister & Newman, 1994). Kunda's (1990) review of "motivated reasoning" concludes that "directional goals" (motivations to reach a preor-

dained conclusion) work primarily by causing a biased search in memory for supporting evidence only. However, Pyszczynski and Greenberg (1987) proposed a more comprehensive "biased hypothesis testing" model, in which self-serving motives bias each stage of the hypothesis-testing sequence, including the selection of initial hypotheses, the generation of inferences, the search for evidence, the evaluation of evidence, and the amount of evidence needed before one is willing to make an inference. Research on the "confirmatory bias" (Snyder & Swan, 1978) shows that people do not always seek to confirm their initial hypothesis; sometimes they ask the right questions to get at the truth (Higgins & Bargh, 1987; Trope & Bassok, 1983). However, such demonstrations of truth seeking always involve hypotheses that the participant has no need to defend (e.g., "the person you are about to meet is an extrovert"). When hypotheses involve one's moral commitments (e.g., "the death penalty does not deter murder"), the empirical findings generally show bias and motivated reasoning (Kuhn, 1989; Lord et al., 1979).

This review is not intended to imply that people are stupid or irrational. It is intended to demonstrate that the roots of human intelligence, rationality, and ethical sophistication should not be sought in our ability to search for and evaluate evidence in an open and unbiased way. Rather than following the ancient Greeks in worshiping reason, we should instead look for the roots of human intelligence, rationality, and virtue in what the mind does best: perception, intuition, and other mental operations that are quick, effortless, and generally quite accurate (Gigerenzer & Goldstein, 1996; Margolis, 1987).

THE SOCIAL INTUITIONIST SOLUTION

The reasoning process in moral judgment may be capable of working objectively under very limited circumstances: when the person has adequate time and processing capacity, a motivation to be accurate, no a priori judgment to defend or justify, and when no relatedness or coherence motivations are triggered (Forgas, 1995; Wegner & Bargh, 1998). Such circumstances may be found in moral judgment studies using hypothetical and unemotional dilemmas. Rationalist research methods may therefore *create* an unusual and nonrepresentative kind of moral judgment. However, in real judgment situations, such as when people are gossiping or arguing, relatedness motives are always at work.

THE EMOTIONAL DOG AND ITS RATIONAL TAIL 1035

If more shocking or threatening issues are being judged, such as abortion, euthanasia, or consensual incest, then coherence motives also will be at work. Under these more realistic circumstances, moral reasoning is not left free to search for truth but is likely to be hired out like a lawyer by various motives, employed only to seek confirmation of preordained conclusions.

3. The Post Hoc Problem: The Reasoning Process Readily Constructs Justifications of Intuitive Judgments, Causing the Illusion of Objective Reasoning

When people are asked to explain the causes of their judgments and actions, they frequently cite factors that could not have mattered and fail to recognize factors that did matter. Nisbett and Schachter (1966), for example, asked participants to take electric shocks, either with or without a placebo pill that was said to produce the same symptoms as electric shock. Participants in the pill condition apparently attributed their heart palpitations and butterflies in the stomach to the pill and were able to take four times as much shock as those who had no such misattribution available for their symptoms. However, when the placebo condition participants were asked if they had made such an attribution, only 25% of them said that they had. The remaining participants denied that they had thought about the pill and instead made up a variety of explanations for their greater shock tolerance, such as, "Well, I used to build radios and stuff when I was 13 or 14, and maybe I got used to electric shock" (Nisbett & Wilson, 1977, p. 237).

Nisbett and Wilson (1977) interpreted such causal explanations as post hoc constructions. When asked to explain their behaviors, people engage in an effortful search that may feel like a kind of introspection. However, what people are searching for is not a memory of the actual cognitive processes that caused their behaviors, because these processes are not accessible to consciousness. Rather, people are searching for plausible theories about why they might have done what they did. People turn first to a "pool of culturally supplied explanations for behavior," which Nisbett and Wilson (1977) refer to as "a priori causal theories" (p. 248). When asked why he enjoyed a party, a person turns first to his cultural knowledge about why people enjoy parties, chooses a reason, and then searches for evidence that the reason was applicable. The search is likely to be a one-sided search of mem-

ory for supporting evidence only (Kunda, 1990; Pyszczynski & Greenberg, 1987).

Additional illustrations of post hoc causal reasoning can be found in studies in which hypnosis (Zimbardo, LaBerge, & Butler, 1993) and subliminal presentation (Kunst-Wilson & Zajonc, 1980) were used to make people perform actions. When asked to explain their actions or choices, people readily made up reasons that sounded plausible but were false. Split-brain patients show this effect in its most dramatic form. When the left hand, guided by the right brain, performs an action, the verbal centers in the left brain readily make up stories to explain it (Gazzaniga, Bogen, & Sperry, 1962). The language centers are so skilled at making up post hoc causal explanations that Gazzaniga (1985) speaks of an "interpreter" module. He argues that behavior is usually produced by mental modules to which consciousness has no access but that the interpreter module provides a running commentary anyway, constantly generating hypotheses to explain why the self might have performed any particular behavior.

POST HOC MORAL REASONING

The idea that people generate causal explanations out of a priori causal theories is easily extended into the moral domain. In a moral judgment interview, a participant is asked to decide whether an action is right or wrong and is then asked to explain why she thinks so. However, if people have no access to the processes behind their automatic initial evaluations then how do they go about providing justifications? They do so by consulting their a priori moral theories. A priori moral theories can be defined as a pool of culturally supplied norms for evaluating and criticizing the behavior of others. A priori moral theories provide acceptable reasons for praise and blame (e.g., "unprovoked harm is bad"; "people should strive to live up to God's commandments"). Because the justifications that people give are closely related to the moral judgments that they make, prior researchers have assumed that the justificatory reasons caused the judgments. But if people lack access to their automatic judgment processes then the reverse causal path becomes more plausible.

If this reverse path is common, then the enormous literature on moral reasoning can be reinterpreted as a kind of ethnography of the a priori moral theories held by various communities[3] and age groups. Kohlberg's (1969) studies demonstrate that young children in many cultures hold the a priori moral theory that "acts that get punished are wrong; acts that get rewarded are good" (Stages 1 and 2), but they soon advance to the theory that "acts that others approve of are good; acts that others condemn are bad" (Stage 3). If such statements were the rules that children really used to evaluate actions, then children at Stages 1 and 2 would conclude that actions that are not punished must not be bad, yet Turiel (1983) has shown that young children do not believe this. They say that harmful acts, such as hitting and pulling hair, are wrong whether they are punished or not. They even say that such acts would be wrong if adults ordered them to be done (Damon, 1977; Laupa & Turiel, 1986). Thus, when a child offers the Stage 1 statement that "it's wrong because she'll get punished," the child is not introspecting on the reasoning that led to his condemnation; he is just giving a reason that sounds plausible, perhaps a reason he himself has heard from adults ("if you do that, I will punish you").

THE ILLUSIONS OF MORAL JUDGMENT

If moral reasoning is generally a post hoc construction intended to justify automatic moral intuitions, then our moral life is plagued by two illusions. The first illusion can be called the *wag-the-dog illusion*: We believe that our own moral judgment (the dog) is driven by our own moral reasoning (the tail). The second illusion can be called the *wag-the-other-dog's-tail illusion*: In a moral argument, we expect the successful rebuttal of an opponent's arguments to change the opponent's mind. Such a belief is like thinking that forcing a dog's tail to wag by moving it with your hand will make the dog happy.

The wag-the-dog illusion follows directly from the mechanics of the reasoning process described above. Pyszczynski and Greenberg (1987) point out that by going through all the steps of hypothesis testing, even though every step can be biased by self-serving motivations, people can maintain an "illusion of objectivity" about the way they think. The wag-the-dog illusion may therefore be one of the mechanisms underlying naive realism (Griffin & Ross, 1991; Robinson, Keltner, Ward, & Ross, 1995), the finding that people think that they see the world as it is whereas their opponents in a moral dispute are biased by ideology and self-interest.

The bitterness, futility, and self-righteousness of most moral arguments can now be explicated. In a debate about abortion, politics, consensual incest, or what my friend did to your friend, both sides believe that their positions are based on reasoning about the facts and issues involved (the wag-the-dog illusion). Both sides present what they take to be excellent arguments in support of their positions. Both sides expect the other side to be responsive to such reasons (the wag-the-other-dog's-tail illusion). When the other side fails to be affected by such good reasons, each side concludes that the other side must be closed minded or insincere. In this way the culture wars over issues such as homosexuality and abortion can generate morally motivated players on both sides who believe that their opponents are not morally motivated (Haidt & Hersh, 2001; Robinson et al., 1995).

THE SOCIAL INTUITIONIST SOLUTION

People have quick and automatic moral intuitions, and when called on to justify these intuitions they generate post hoc justifications out of a priori moral theories. They do not realize that they are doing this, so they fall prey to two illusions. Moral arguments are therefore like shadow-boxing matches: Each contestant lands heavy blows to the opponent's shadow, then wonders why she doesn't fall down. Thus, moral reasoning may have little persuasive power in conflict situations, but the social intuitionist model says that moral reasoning can be effective in influencing people before a conflict arises. Words and ideas do affect friends, allies, and even strangers by means of the reasoned-persuasion link. If one can get the other person to see the issue in a new way, perhaps by reframing a problem to trigger new intuitions, then one can influence others with one's words. Martin Luther King Jr.'s "I Have a Dream" speech was remarkably effective in this task, using metaphors and visual images more than propositional logic to get White Americans to see and thus feel that racial segregation was unjust and un-American (see Lakoff, 1996, on the role of metaphor in political persuasion).

4. The Action Problem: Moral Action Covaries with Moral Emotion More Than with Moral Reasoning

The analysis thus far has focused on moral judgment, not moral behavior, but the debate between rationalism and intuitionism can also be carried out using moral action as the dependent variable. There is a literature that directly examines the relationship between moral reasoning and moral action, and there is a literature that examines what happens when moral reasoning and moral emotions become dissociated (in the case of psychopaths).

The weak link between moral reasoning and moral action. In a major review of the literature on moral cognition and action, Blasi (1980) concluded that "moral reasoning and moral action are statistically related" (p. 37). But what is the nature of this relationship? Blasi was careful to state that the connection between moral reasoning ability and moral behavior is only a correlation, although later authors in the cognitive developmental tradition read the relationship as causal, stating that higher levels of moral reasoning cause better moral behavior (e.g. Lapsley, 1996). Blasi's review, however, raised the possibility that a third variable caused both better reasoning and better behavior: intelligence. Blasi found that IQ was consistently related to honesty, and he concluded that future investigators must do a better job of controlling for IQ. Kohlberg (1969) reported that scores on his moral judgment interviews correlated with measures of IQ in the .30–.50 range. Rest (1979) reported correlations of .20–.50 between IQ and his Defining Issues Test (DIT).

Intelligence may also be related to better moral behavior by a pathway that does not run through better moral reasoning. Metcalfe and Mischel (1999) proposed a dual process model of willpower in which two separate but interacting systems govern human behavior in the face of temptation. The "hot" system is specialized for quick emotional processing and makes heavy use of amygdala-based memory. The "cool" system is specialized for complex spatiotemporal and episodic representation and thought. It relies on hippocampal memory and frontal lobe planning and inhibition areas. It can block the impulses of the hot system, but it develops later in life, making childhood and adolescence seem like a long struggle to overcome impulsiveness and gain self-control. This theory was proposed in part to explain the astonishing finding that the number of seconds preschoolers were able to delay choosing an immediate small reward (one marshmallow) in favor of a later, bigger reward (two marshmallows) was a powerful predictor of adolescent social and cognitive competence measured about 13 years later, including SAT scores and the ability to exert self-control in frustrating situations (Shoda, Mischel, & Peake, 1990).

The correlation that Blasi (1980) found between moral reasoning and moral behavior may therefore be explained by a third variable, the strength of the cool system. Children start off with limited ability to resist temptation, but as the hippocampus and frontal cortex finish their development, children become more able to inhibit impulsive behaviors. Some children start off with a more effective cool system (Kochanska, Murray, Jacques, Koenig, & Vandegeest, 1996) because of better or faster frontal cortex development. Frontal cortex development makes these children smarter, and they therefore perform better on measures of moral reasoning, but their improved moral behavior comes more from their greater self-regulatory abilities than from their greater moral reasoning abilities. The development of the cool system does not represent the triumph of reasoning over emotion; rather, Metcalfe and Mischel (1999, p. 16) see the successful development and integration of the cool system as an essential feature of emotional intelligence.

This reinterpretation is supported by the fact that moral reasoning ability, in Blasi's (1980) review, was most predictive of negative morality – refraining from delinquent behavior. Criminologists have consistently found an inverse relationship between criminality and IQ. Even after correcting for socioeconomic status, the difference between delinquent and nondelinquent adolescent populations is approximately 8 IQ points (Hirschi & Hindelang, 1977). However, the story for positive morality – directly helping others – is less clear. Blasi found some support for the claim that high scorers on Kohlberg's and Rest's scales were more likely to help other people, but more recent studies have raised doubts. Hart and Fegley (1995) and Colby and Damon (1992) both compared highly prosocial moral exemplars with nonexemplars and found that the groups did not differ in their moral reasoning ability assessed by Kohlbergian techniques. A recent review of evidence supporting the utility of the DIT described three studies that showed a relationship between DIT scores and negative moral behaviors but none showing a relationship between DIT scores and positive morality (Thoma, Narvaez, Rest, & Derryberry, 1999).

The relationship between moral reasoning ability and moral behavior therefore appears to be weak and inconsistent once intelligence is partialed out. Emotional and self-regulatory factors seem to be more powerful determinants of actual behavior (Mischel & Mischel, 1976).

THE STRONG LINK BETWEEN MORAL EMOTIONS
AND MORAL ACTION

Further evidence that moral reasoning matters less than moral emotions comes from the study of psychopaths. Cleckley's (1955) case studies present chilling portraits of people in whom reasoning has become dissociated from moral emotions. Cleckley characterizes psychopaths as having good intelligence and a lack of delusions or irrational thinking. Psychopaths know the rules of social behavior and they understand the harmful consequences of their actions for others. They simply do not care about those consequences. Cleckley's psychopaths show a general poverty of major affective reactions, particularly those that would be triggered by the suffering of others (remorse, sympathy), condemnation by others (shame, embarrassment), or attachment to others (love, grief). (See R. D. Hare, 1993, for a more recent discussion of the emotional deficit.) Psychopaths can steal from their friends, dismember live animals, and even murder their parents to collect insurance benefits without showing any trace of remorse or, when caught, of shame. The very existence of the psychopath illustrates Hume's statement that "'tis not contrary to reason to prefer the destruction of the whole world to the scratching of my little finger" (1739–1740/1969, p. 461). It is not contrary to reason to kill your parents for money unless it is also contrary to sentiment.

Several lines of research are converging on the conclusion that psychopaths and people with antisocial personality disorder differ from normal people in the operation of the frontal cortex. Mednick, Pollock, Volavka, and Gabrielli (1982) reviewed studies of electroencephalogram differences between criminals and noncriminals and concluded that the bulk of the research points to differences in the *anterior regions* of the *brain*. More recent studies using positron emission tomography techniques have narrowed the location of interest to the prefrontal cortex (Raine, 1997). Samples of aggressive offenders show reduced metabolic activity in this area, relative to controls (Raine et al., 1994).

The importance of the prefrontal cortex for moral behavior has been most fully explored by Damasio and his colleagues, who have found a consistent pattern of changes associated with damage to the ventromedial area of the prefrontal cortex (VMPFC, the area behind the bridge of the nose). Patients with damage restricted to the VMPFC show no reduction in their reasoning abilities. They retain full knowledge of moral rules and social conventions, and they show normal abilities to solve logic problems, financial problems, and even hypothetical moral dilemmas (Damasio, 1994). When faced with real decisions, however, they perform disas-

trously, showing poor judgment, indecisiveness, and what appears to be irrational behavior.

Damasio and his colleagues have demonstrated that the central deficit resulting from destruction of the VMPFC is the loss of emotional responsiveness to the world in general and to one's behavioral choices in particular. When shown pictures that arouse strong skin conductance responses in undamaged people (nudity, mutilation, people dying), individuals with VMPFC damage show no response (Damasio, Tranel, & Damasio, 1990), mirroring the lack of autonomic responsiveness of psychopaths (R. D. Hare & Quinn, 1971). The patients know that the images should affect them, but they report feeling nothing. Damasio refers to this pattern of affect loss combined with intact reasoning as "acquired sociopathy." Patients with acquired sociopathy do not generally become moral monsters, perhaps because they have a lifetime of normal emotional learning and habit formation behind them. They do, however, become much less concerned with following social norms, and they sometimes show outrageous and antisocial behavior, as in the case of Phineas Gage (Damasio, 1994). If we imagine a child growing up without a normal VMPFC, who never in his life felt the stings of shame and embarrassment or the pain of emotional loss or empathic distress, then it becomes almost possible to understand the otherwise incomprehensible behavior of Cleckley's psychopaths. With no moral sentiments to motivate and constrain them, they simply do not care about the pain they cause and the lives they ruin.[4]

EMOTIONS LEAD TO ALTRUISM

If reasoning ability is not sufficient to motivate moral action, then what is? Batson and his colleagues have developed the *empathy–altruism hypothesis*, which states that empathy aroused by the perception of someone's suffering evokes an altruistic motivation directed toward the ultimate goal of reducing the suffering (Batson, 1987; see also Hoffman, 1982). Batson, O'Quinn, Fulty, Vanderplass, and Isen (1983) found that participants who experienced empathy while watching a woman receiving (fake) electric shocks generally volunteered to take the shocks in her place, even when they were given the option of leaving the scene. Participants who experienced only nonempathic personal distress about the woman's plight volunteered to trade places with her only when they thought they would have to continue watching the woman receive the shocks. Participants in the first group seemed to be genuinely motivated to help the distressed woman, not to relieve their own distress.

Cialdini and his colleagues have challenged the empathy–altruism hypothesis, using a variety of experimental designs to show that other motives can often explain seemingly altruistic behavior (Cialdini et al., 1987). Throughout this long debate, however, both sides have consistently agreed that people are often motivated to help others and that the mechanisms involved in this helping are primarily affective, including empathy as well as reflexive distress, sadness, guilt, and shame (Cialdini, 1991).

THE SOCIAL INTUITIONIST SOLUTION

It is easier to study verbal reasoning than it is to study emotions and intuitions, but reasoning may be the tail wagged by the dog. The dog itself may turn out to be moral intuitions and emotions such as empathy and love (for positive morality) and shame, guilt, and remorse, along with emotional self-regulation abilities (for negative morality; see Haidt, in press, for a review and taxonomy of the moral emotions). A dog's tail is worth studying because dogs use their tails so frequently for communication. Similarly, moral reasoning is worth studying because people use moral reasoning so frequently for communication. To really understand how human morality works, however, it may be advisable to shift attention away from the study of moral reasoning and toward the study of intuitive and emotional processes.

The Mechanism of Intuition

Because intuition is the heart of the social intuitionist model, more must be said about exactly how intuitive moral judgments are made (Link 1). Recent work on the importance of bodily experience, as represented in the mind, makes such an account possible.

Gut Feelings in the Mind

The somatic marker hypothesis (Damasio, 1994) states that experiences in the world normally trigger emotional experiences that involve bodily changes and feelings. Once the brain is properly tuned up by repeated experiences of such emotional conditioning (e.g., Pavlov, 1927), the brain areas that monitor these bodily changes begin to respond whenever a similar situation arises. It is then no longer necessary for the rest of the body to be involved. At that point, the mere

thought of a particular action becomes sufficient to trigger an "as if" response in the brain, in which the person experiences in a weaker form the same bodily feelings that she would experience if she performed the action. The critical job of the VMPFC is to integrate these feelings, or "somatic markers," with the person's other knowledge and planning functions so that the brain can decide quickly on a response. Damasio's work fits well with research in social psychology on the "affect as information" hypothesis, which demonstrates that people frequently rely on their moods and momentary flashes of feeling as guides when making judgments and decisions (Clore, Schwarz, & Conway, 1994; Loewenstein, Weber, Hsee, & Welch, 2001; Schwarz & Clore, 1983; see also an fMRI finding that such flashes help explain people's varying responses to philosophical moral dilemmas in Greene, Sommerville, Nystrom, Darley, & Cohen, 2001).

Two recent studies have directly manipulated moral judgments by manipulating somatic markers. Batson, Engel, and Fridell (1999) used false physiological feedback to tell participants about their emotional reactions when listening to stories in which the values of either freedom or equality were threatened. When later asked to choose which value should be selected as a theme for a weeklong program of events at their university, participants were more likely to choose the value for which they thought they had shown a stronger visceral reaction. Wheatley and Haidt (2001) manipulated somatic markers even more directly. Highly hypnotizable participants were given the suggestion, under hypnosis, that they would feel a pang of disgust when they saw either the word *take* or the word *often*. Participants were then asked to read and make moral judgments about six stories that were designed to elicit mild to moderate disgust, each of which contained either the word *take* or the word *often*. Participants made higher ratings of both disgust and moral condemnation about the stories containing their hypnotic disgust word. This study was designed to directly manipulate the intuitive judgment link (Link 1), and it demonstrates that artificially increasing the strength of a gut feeling increases the strength of the resulting moral judgment.

Metaphor and Embodiment

Whereas Damasio focuses on the role of the autonomic nervous system in thinking, Lakoff and Johnson (1999; Lakoff, 1987) have shown how the entire range of physical and emotional experience may underlie our "embodied cognition." By analyzing how people think and talk about love, politics, morality, and other issues, they have shown that nearly all complex thought relies on metaphors, drawn mostly from our experience as physical creatures. For example, because we all have experience with foods that are easily contaminated, we come to equate purity and cleanliness with goodness in the physical domain. We learn from experience that pure substances are quickly contaminated (e.g., by mold, dust, or insects) when not guarded and that once contaminated, it is often difficult to purify them again. These experiences in the physical world then form the basis (in many cultures) of conceptual schemes about moral purity – for example, that children start off in a state of purity and innocence but can be corrupted by a single exposure to sex, violence, drugs, homosexuality, or the devil (Haidt, Rozin, McCauley, & Imada, 1997; Rozin, Haidt, & McCauley, 2000). Some losses of purity can be rectified with great difficulty (e.g., exorcism after exposure to the devil), and others cannot be rectified at all (e.g., the loss of virginity).

Moral intuition, then, appears to be the automatic output of an underlying, largely unconscious set of interlinked moral concepts. These concepts may have some innate basis (to be discussed shortly), which is then built up largely by metaphorical extensions from physical experience. Metaphors have entailments, and much of moral argument and persuasion involves trying to get the other person to apply the right metaphor. If Saddam Hussein is Hitler, it follows that he must be stopped. But if Iraq is Vietnam, it follows that the United States should not become involved (Spellman & Holyoak, 1992). Such arguments are indeed a form of reasoning, but they are reasons designed to trigger intuitions in the listener.

The Origin of Intuitions

Perhaps because moral norms vary by culture, class, and historical era, psychologists have generally assumed that morality is learned in childhood, and they have set out to discover how morality gets from outside the child to inside. The social intuitionist model takes a different view. It proposes that morality, like language, is a major evolutionary adaptation for an intensely social species, built into multiple regions of the brain and body, that is better described as emergent than as learned yet that requires input and shaping from a particular culture. Moral intu-

itions are therefore both innate and enculturated. The present section describes the ways in which moral intuitions are innate; the next section describes the ways in which they are shaped by culture during development.

Primate Protomorality

Darwin (1874/1998) believed that the human moral sense grew out of the social instincts of other animals, and modern primatological research supports him. All species can be said to follow *descriptive* rules for behavior with conspecifics, but it is primarily the primates that show signs of *prescriptive* rules, which de Waal (1991) defines as rules that individuals "have learned to respect because of active reinforcement by others" (p. 338). Chimpanzee groups develop and enforce norms for mating, for playing with or touching infants, and for many other forms of interaction. When one individual violates these norms, others will sometimes look to or even get the attention of the individual whose interests have been violated, who may then take action to punish the transgressor (de Waal, 1991). De Waal's work indicates that prescriptive behavioral norms can emerge and be understood and enforced by chimpanzees without the benefit of language or language-based reasoning. Language may greatly increase the human use of norms, but the cognitive and emotional machinery of norm creation and norm enforcement was available long before language existed.

It appears, furthermore, that this machinery has been carried forward into the human mind. Alan Fiske (1991, 1992) has identified four underlying models of social cognition that seem to be at work in all human cultures. His first three models fit closely with descriptions of other primates. Fiske's first model, *communal sharing*, involves the linkage of kindness, kinship, and empathic concern for close others that de Waal describes both for chimpanzees (de Waal, 1996) and for bonobos (de Waal & Lanting, 1997). Fiske's second model, *authority ranking*, describes the ways that power and rank regulate access to resources but also obligate superiors to protect their subordinates. Such mutual obligations are clear among chimpanzees (de Waal, 1982; Goodall, 1986). Fiske's third model, *equality matching*, involves the double-edged reciprocal altruism first described by Trivers (1971). Most apes and many monkeys seem remarkably adept at remembering and repaying both favors and slights (de Waal, 1982,

1996). The only model that seems to be uniquely human is Fiske's fourth model, *market pricing*, in which ratio values of goods and services must be computed and aggregated across transactions (Haslam, 1997). Given so many close parallels between the social lives of humans and chimpanzees, the burden of proof must fall on those who want to argue for discontinuity – that is, that human morality arose ex nihilo when we developed the ability to speak and reason.

The above considerations are not meant to imply that chimpanzees have morality or that humans are just chimps with post hoc reasoning skills. There is indeed a moral Rubicon that only Homo sapiens appears to have crossed: widespread third-party norm enforcement. Chimpanzee norms generally work at the level of private relationships, where the individual that has been harmed is the one that takes punitive action. Human societies, in contrast, are marked by a constant and vigorous discussion of norms and norm violators and by a willingness to expend individual or community resources to inflict punishment, even by those who were not harmed by the violator (Boehm, 1999). Dunbar (1996) has even proposed that language evolved primarily to fulfill the need for gossip. Only with language is it possible to keep track of who did what to whom, who is in, who is out, who can be trusted, and who should be avoided. Although the evolution of language and intelligence may have been driven by the Machiavellian benefits they gave to individuals (Byrne & Whiten, 1988), the combination of language and a full theory of mind (Premack & Premack, 1995) made it possible for large groups of non-kin to reap the benefits of cooperation by monitoring each other's behavior (with gossip), shunning or punishing cheaters, and rewarding team players.

The social intuitionist model fits with this view of the functions of language by including two interpersonal links. Once morality is located in a group's efforts to solve cooperation and commitment problems (Darwin, 1874/1998; Frank, 1988), it becomes clear that individuals must use language to influence others while simultaneously being at least somewhat open to interpersonal influence as specific norms, values, or judgments spread through a community. A group of judges independently seeking truth is unlikely to reach an effective consensus, but a group of people linked together in a large web of mutual influence (an extension of Figure 2 to multiple parties) may eventually settle into a stable configuration, in the same way that a connectionist network reaches a stable equilibrium after several iterations.

The Externalization of Intuitions

If many moral intuitions (e.g., sympathy, reciprocity, and loyalty) are partially built in by evolution, then the most important developmental question about intuitions is not, "How do they get into the child?" but rather, "How do they get out?" Fiske (1991) argues that social development should be thought of partly as a process of *externalization*, in which innate cognitive models manifest themselves as a part of normal maturation. He reviews evidence (e.g., Damon, 1975) showing that the four models emerge during development in an invariant sequence: communal sharing in infancy, authority ranking by age 3, equality matching around age 4, and market pricing during middle or late childhood. This is the same sequence in which the models appear to have emerged phylogenetically in the mammalian and primate lineages.

The contrast between internalization and externalization is particularly clear for equality matching. Western parents often try to get their young children to share and to play fairly. If moral development were a matter of gradual internalization, or even of reward and punishment, then children's adherence to principles of fairness would show a gradual increase throughout early childhood. Instead, Fiske (1991) argues that children seem relatively insensitive to issues of fairness until around the age of 4, at which point concerns about fairness burst forth and are overgeneralized to social situations in which they were never encouraged and in which they are often inappropriate. This pattern of sudden similarly timed emergence with overgeneralization suggests the maturation of an endogenous ability rather than the learning of a set of cultural norms. Only after the cognitive model has externalized itself can it be shaped and refined by cultural norms about when and how it should be used.

The Development of Intuitions

Even if moral intuitions are partially innate, children somehow end up with a morality that is unique to their culture or group. There are at least three related processes by which cultures modify, enhance, or suppress the emergence of moral intuitions to create a specific morality: by selective loss, by immersion in custom complexes, and by peer socialization.

The Selective Loss of Intuitions

The acquisition of phonology provides a useful analogy for the acquisition of morality. Children are born with the ability to distinguish among hundreds of phonemes, but after a few years of exposure to a specific language they lose the ability to make some unexercised phoneme contrasts (Werker & Tees, 1984). Likewise, Ruth Benedict (1934/1959) suggested, we can imagine a great "arc of culture" on which are arrayed all the possible aspects of human functioning. "A culture that capitalized even a considerable proportion of these would be as unintelligible as a language that used all the clicks, all the glottal stops, all the labials" (Benedict, 1934/1959, p. 24).

Similarly, a culture that emphasized all of the moral intuitions that the human mind is prepared to experience would risk paralysis as every action triggered multiple conflicting intuitions. Cultures seem instead to specialize in a subset of human moral potential. For example, Shweder's theory of the "big three" moral ethics (Shweder, Much, Mahapatra, & Park, 1997; see also Jensen, 1997) proposes that moral "goods" (i.e., culturally shared beliefs about what is morally admirable and valuable) generally cluster into three complexes, or ethics, which cultures embrace to varying degrees: the ethic of autonomy (focusing on goods that protect the autonomous individual, such as rights, freedom of choice, and personal welfare), the ethic of community (focusing on goods that protect families, nations, and other collectivities, such as loyalty, duty, honor, respectfulness, modesty, and self-control), and the ethic of divinity (focusing on goods that protect the spiritual self, such as piety and physical and mental purity). A child is born prepared to develop moral intuitions in all three ethics, but her local cultural environment generally stresses only one or two of the ethics. Intuitions within culturally supported ethics become sharper and more chronically accessible (Higgins, 1996), whereas intuitions within unsupported ethics become weaker and less accessible. Such "maintenance-loss" models have been documented in other areas of human higher cognition. It seems to be a design feature of mammalian brains that much of neural development is "experience expectant" (Black, Jones, Nelson, & Greenough, 1998). That is, there are developmentally timed periods of high neural plasticity, as though the brain "expected" certain types of experience to be present at a certain time to guide its final wiring.

Such sensitive periods are well documented in the development of sensory systems (Hubel & Wiesel, 1970) and language (Johnson & Newport, 1989). Huttenlocher (1994) reports that most synapse selection and elimination in the human cerebral cortex occurs in the first few years but that in the prefrontal cortex the period of plasticity is greatly delayed. Synapse selection in the prefrontal cortex starts later, accelerates in late childhood, and then tails off in adolescence (see also Spear, 2000). Because the prefrontal cortex is the brain area most frequently implicated in moral judgment and behavior (Damasio et al., 1990; Raine, 1997), this suggests that if there is a sensitive period for moral learning it is likely to be later in childhood than psychoanalysts and most American parents suppose. But how exactly does a culture choose and emphasize a subset of the available intuitions?

Immersion in Custom Complexes

The *custom complex* has recently been proposed as the key construct for understanding development within a cultural context (Shweder et al., 1998). The custom complex was originally defined by Whiting and Child (1953) as consisting of "a customary practice and . . . the beliefs, values, sanctions, rules, motives and satisfactions associated with it" (p. 27). The custom complex captures the idea that cultural knowledge is far more than a set of inherited beliefs about the right and wrong ways of doing things. Cultural knowledge is a complex web of explicit and implicit, sensory and propositional, affective, cognitive, and motoric knowledge (D'Andrade, 1984; Shore, 1996).

Custom complexes are easily found in the moral socialization of children. For example, in Orissa, India, many spaces and objects are structured by rules of purity and pollution. Foreigners and dogs may be allowed near the entrance to a temple complex, but only worshipers who have properly bathed may be allowed into the central courtyard (Mahapatra, 1981). In the inner sanctum, where the deity sits, only the Brahmin priest is permitted to enter. Private homes have a similar structure, with zones of high purity (the kitchen and the room where the household deity is kept) and zones of lower purity. The human body has a similar structure, in which the head is the zone of highest purity and the feet are highly polluting.

Children in Orissa constantly encounter spaces and bodies structured by purity, and they learn to respect the dividing lines. They learn when to remove their shoes and how to use their heads and feet in a symbolic language of deference (as when one touches one's head to the feet of a highly respected person). They develop an intuitive sense that purity and impurity must be kept apart. By participating in these interlinked custom complexes, an Oriya child's physical embodiment comes to include experiences of purity and pollution. When such children later encounter the intellectual content of the ethics of divinity (e.g., ideas of sacredness, asceticism, and transcendence), their minds and bodies are already prepared to accept these ideas, and their truth feels self-evident (see Lakoff, 1987).

American children, in contrast, are immersed in a different set of practices regarding space and the body, supported by a different ideology. When an American adult later travels in Orissa, he may know how rules of purity and pollution govern the use of space, but he knows these things only in a shallow, factual, consciously accessible way; he does not know these things in the deep cognitive, affective, motoric way that a properly enculturated Oriya knows them.

Fiske (1999) reviewed evidence in anthropology that children are taught surprisingly little in most cultures and that they acquire most of their cultural knowledge and expertise by observing and then imitating the practices of older children and adults (see also Bandura & Walters, 1963, on imitation and social learning). Fiske argued that anthropologists have generally underestimated the importance of motor schemas and implicit knowledge, relying instead on the verbal reports of informants as their primary source of ethnographic data. In other words, there is an asymmetry between how culture gets into children and how it gets out to anthropologists. Cultural knowledge gets in largely through nonverbal and nonconscious means, but it gets out through conscious verbal communication. This asymmetry brings the Nisbett and Wilson (1977) problem straight into the heart of anthropology: "Informants pressed to explain practices that they themselves learned by observation, imitation, and participation *generally have to make up concepts* that have very tenuous, often imaginary relations with the manner in which the informants themselves actually acquired or generate the actions in question" (Fiske, 1999, p. 1; emphasis added).

The importance of practice, repetition, and physical movement for the tuning up of cultural intuitions is further demonstrated by Lieberman's (2000) recent review of the neural substrates of intuition. Lieberman finds that social

learning uses some of the same circuits in the basal ganglia that motoric learning does, causing many social skills to become rapid and automatic, like well-learned motor sequences. Social skills and judgmental processes that are learned gradually and implicitly then operate unconsciously, projecting their results into consciousness, where they are experienced as intuitions arising from nowhere (see also Reber, 1993, on implicit learning and Clark, 1999, on the underestimated role of the body in cognition).

The implication of these findings for moral psychology is that moral intuitions are developed and shaped as children behave, imitate, and otherwise take part in the practices and custom complexes of their culture. Participation in custom complexes in this way provides a cultural "front end" for Damasio's (1994) somatic marker hypothesis, and for Lakoff's (1987) embodied cognition. Even though people in all cultures have more or less the same bodies, they have different embodiments, and therefore they end up with different minds.

Peer Socialization

The social intuitionist model presents people as intensely social creatures whose moral judgments are strongly shaped by the judgments of those around them. But whose judgments have the strongest effects on children? Harris (1995) pointed out that children's task in late childhood and adolescence is not to become like their parents but to fit into their peer group, for it is among peers that alliances must be formed and prestige garnered. She therefore proposed a group socialization theory in which children acquire their culture – including moral values – from their peers, just as they acquire their phonology (i.e., children of immigrants copy the accent of their peers, not of their parents).

Harris's (1995) emphasis on peers receives support from a study by Minoura (1992) of Japanese children who spent a few years in California when their fathers were transferred to the United States for work. Minoura found that there was a sensitive period for culture learning between the ages of 9 and 15. When children spent a few years in the United States during this period, they developed American ways of interacting with friends and American ways of feeling about problems in interactions. A few years spent in America before that period led to shallower, nonemotional learning about norms and left no lasting effects. A few years spent in America after the age of 15 led to puzzlement and culture shock but to little change in the self. These later arrivals, like their parents, knew and could state explicitly the American norms for interpersonal behavior, friendship, and self-promotion, yet these norms did not become internalized. The norms never came to be automatic or to feel self-evidently valid, as intuitive knowledge would be if acquired during the sensitive period.

Putting together all of the developmental theories and findings presented above yields the following expansion of the social intuitionist model: Moral development is primarily a matter of the maturation and cultural shaping of endogenous intuitions. People can acquire explicit propositional knowledge about right and wrong in adulthood, but it is primarily through participation in custom complexes (Shweder et al., 1998) involving sensory, motor, and other forms of implicit knowledge (Fiske, 1999; Lieberman, 2000; Shore, 1996) shared with one's peers during the sensitive period of late childhood and adolescence (Harris, 1995; Huttenlocher, 1994; Minoura, 1992) that one comes to feel, physically and emotionally (Damasio, 1994; Lakoff & Johnson, 1999), the self-evident truth of moral propositions.

Integrating Rationalism and Intuitionism

The debate between rationalism and intuitionism is an old one, but the divide between the two approaches may not be unbridgeable. Both sides agree that people have emotions and intuitions, engage in reasoning, and are influenced by each other. The challenge, then, is to specify how these processes fit together. Rationalist models do this by focusing on reasoning and then discussing the other processes in terms of their effects on reasoning. Emotions matter because they can be inputs to reasoning. Social settings and social interactions matter because they encourage or retard the development of reasoning, in part by providing or blocking opportunities for role-taking. However, if researchers want to get at the heart of the process, the place where most of the variance is located, they should focus on moral reasoning.

The social intuitionist model proposes a very different arrangement, one that fully integrates reasoning, emotion, intuition, and social influence. The discussion thus far may have given the impression that the model dismisses reasoning as post hoc rationalization (Link 2). However, it must be stressed that four of the six links in

the model are reasoning links, and three of these links (Links 3, 5, and 6) are hypothesized to have real causal effects on moral judgment.

Link 3, the reasoned persuasion link, says that people's (ex post facto) moral reasoning can have a causal effect – on *other people's* intuitions. In the social intuitionist view, moral judgment is not just a single act that occurs in a single person's mind but is an ongoing process, often spread out over time and over multiple people. Reasons and arguments can circulate and affect people, even if individuals rarely engage in private moral reasoning for themselves.

Link 6, the reflective judgment link, allows that people may sometimes engage in private moral reasoning for themselves, particularly when their initial intuitions conflict. Abortion may feel wrong to many people when they think about the fetus but right when their attention shifts to the woman. When competing intuitions are evenly matched, the judgment system becomes deadlocked and the "master" (in Hume's metaphor) falls silent. Under such circumstances one may go through repeated cycles of Links 6, 1, and 2, using reasoning and intuition together to break the deadlock. That is, if one consciously examines a dilemma, focusing in turn on each party involved, various intuitions will be triggered (Link 6), leading to various contradictory judgments (Link 1). Reasoning can then be used to construct a case to support each judgment (Link 2). If reasoning more successfully builds a case for one of the judgments than for the others, the judgment will begin to feel right and there will be less temptation (and ability) to consider additional points of view. This is an account of how a "makes sense" epistemology (Perkins et al., 1983) may become a "feels right" ethic. We use conscious reflection to mull over a problem until one side feels right. Then we stop.

Link 5, the reasoned judgment link, recognizes that a person could, in principle, simply reason her way to a judgment that contradicts her initial intuition. The literature on everyday reasoning (Kuhn, 1991) suggests that such an ability may be common only among philosophers, who have been extensively trained and socialized to follow reasoning even to very disturbing conclusions (as in the case of Socrates or the more recent work of Peter Singer [1994]), but the fact that there are at least a few people among us who can reach such conclusions on their own and then argue for them eloquently (Link 3) means that pure moral reasoning can play a causal role in the moral life of a society.

If the social intuitionist model is correct as a description of human moral judgment, it may be possible to use the model to get reasoning and intuition working more effectively together in real moral judgments. One approach would be to directly teach moral thinking and reasoning skills, thereby encouraging people to use Links 5 and 6 more often. However, attempts to directly teach thinking and reasoning in a classroom setting generally show little transfer to activities outside of the classroom (Nickerson, 1994), and because moral judgment involves "hotter" topics than are usually dealt with in courses that attempt to teach thinking and reasoning, the degree of transfer is likely to be even smaller.

A more intuitionist approach is to treat moral judgment style as an aspect of culture and to try to create a culture that fosters a more balanced, reflective, and fair-minded style of judgment. The "just community" schools that Kohlberg created in the 1970s (Power, Higgins, & Kohlberg, 1989) appear to do just that. By making high school students create their own rules, enforce their own discipline, and vote on numerous policies, Kohlberg created an environment where students enacted democracy. By putting students and teachers on an equal footing (all had just one vote; all used first names only; all sat in a circle on the floor at community meetings), Kohlberg created an environment where students and teachers enacted equality. Years of such implicit learning, coupled with explicit discussion, should gradually tune up intuitions (Fiske, 1999; Lieberman, 2000) about justice, rights, and fairness, leading perhaps to an automatic tendency to look at problems from multiple perspectives. By creating a community in which moral talk was ubiquitous (Link 3, reasoned persuasion) and in which adults modeled good moral thinking, Kohlberg may well have strengthened his students' tendency to use Link 6 (private reflection) on their own. (See Baron, 2000, for more on how cultural beliefs and practices about thinking can help or hinder good thinking.)

The social intuitionist model also offers more general advice for improving moral judgment. If the principal difficulty in objective moral reasoning is the biased search for evidence (Kunda, 1990; Perkins et al., 1991), then people should take advantage of the social persuasion link (Link 4) and get other people to help them improve their reasoning. By seeking out discourse partners who are respected for their wisdom and open-mindedness, and by talking about the evidence, justifications, and mitigating factors involved in a potential moral violation, people can help trigger a variety of conflicting intuitions in each other. If more conflicting intuitions are triggered, the final judgment is likely to be more nuanced and ultimately more reasonable.

The social intuitionist model, therefore, is not an antirationalist model. It is a model about the complex and dynamic ways that intuition, reasoning, and social influences interact to produce moral judgment.

Testing the Social Intuitionist Model

The social intuitionist model is more complex and comprehensive than most rationalist models. Is the extra complexity necessary? Does the model do a better job of explaining and illuminating human moral life? That is a question that future research must decide. At least three kinds of research may shed light on the relative merits of the model.

1. Interfering with reasoning. If reasoning is a slow and effortful process that demands attentional resources, whereas intuition is fast, effortless, and undemanding (see Table 1), then manipulations that interfere with reasoning during a moral judgment interview should affect the quality of the post hoc reasoning produced without affecting the quality of the initial judgment. Rationalist models, in contrast, predict that the quality and speed of a judgment should be heavily dependent on one's reasoning ability.

2. Ecological variation. This article has suggested that standard moral judgment interviews represent unique and ecologically suspect settings in which a variety of factors conspire to maximize the amount and quality of reasoning. If this is true, then the reasoning produced in such interviews is consistent both with rationalist models and with the private reflection loop of the social intuitionist model (Links 1, 2, and 6). However, as the conditions of the interview are gradually changed to increase ecological validity, the social intuitionist model predicts that the reasoning produced should become recognizably post hoc. Alterations that would increase ecological validity include using real (rather than hypothetical) stories, asking about people known to the participant, working questions into a normal conversation (not a formal interview), and conducting the conversation in front of other people (not alone in a private room). Post hoc reasoning can be recognized by three features: (a) attempts to change facts about the story or to introduce new and tangential concerns, (b) a lack of responsiveness of the judgment to large changes in the facts of the story, and (c) a longer delay between the time the evaluation is made and the time that the first substantive reason is produced.

3. *Consilience.* Edward O. Wilson (1998) resurrected the term *consilience* to refer to the degree to which facts and theories link up across disciplines to create a common groundwork of explanation. He argued that theories that contribute to the unification of the sciences should be preferred to those that contribute to their fragmentation. The present article has tried to show that the social intuitionist model easily links findings in social and developmental psychology to recent findings and theories in neuroscience, primatology, and anthropology, but perhaps a similar case can be made for rationalist models. The debate between rationalism and intuitionism, now over 200 years old, is not just a debate between specific models; it is a debate between perspectives on the human mind. All of the disciplines that study the mind should contribute to the debate.

Conclusion

Rationalist models made sense in the 1960s and 1970s. The cognitive revolution had opened up new ways of thinking about morality and moral development, and it was surely an advance to think about moral judgment as a form of information processing. But times have changed. Now we know (again) that most of cognition occurs automatically and outside of consciousness (Bargh & Chartrand, 1999) and that people cannot tell us how they really reached a judgment (Nisbett & Wilson, 1977). Now we know that the brain is a connectionist system that tunes up slowly but is then able to evaluate complex situations quickly (Bechtel & Abrahamsen, 1991). Now we know that emotions are not as irrational (Frank, 1988), that reasoning is not as reliable (Kahneman & Tversky, 1984), and that animals are not as amoral (de Waal, 1996) as we thought in the 1970s. The time may be right, therefore, to take another look at Hume's perverse thesis: that moral emotions and intuitions drive moral reasoning, just as surely as a dog wags its tail.

Notes

1 This is one of Hume's most radical statements, taken from his first book, *A Treatise of Human Nature.* His more mature work, *An Enquiry Con-*

cerning the Principles of Morals, raises reason from a slave to a respected assistant of the moral sense, yet it maintains the basic position that "the ultimate ends of human actions can never...be accounted for by reason, but recommend themselves entirely to the sentiments and affections of mankind" (1777/1960, p. 131).

2 Kant responded to Hume's skepticism about the powers of reason. He argued that any rational agent could and should figure out the morally correct thing to do by applying the categorical imperative: "I should never act in such a way that I could not also will that my maxim should be a universal law" (1785/1959, p. 18).

3 An ironic example of an a priori moral theory used in a post hoc way is found in Miller's (1999) recent review of the norm of self-interest. Americans strongly embrace the theory that people act, and ought to act, primarily out of self-interest. Americans therefore frequently make up self-interest explanations for their attitudes, votes, and charitable actions, even in cases where they appear to be acting against their self-interest (see also Baron, 1997).

4 In fact, two of the only such children ever studied sound uncannily like Cleckley's psychopaths (Anderson, Bechara, Damasio, Tranel, & Damasio, 1999). See also Grandin's (1995) discussion of how the emotional deficits of autism made it difficult for her to understand many social and moral rules, although her feelings of empathy, particularly for animals, and her feelings of social anxiety appear to have been a sufficient foundation for a moral compass.

References

Albright, L., Kenny, D. A., & Malloy, T. E. (1988). Consensus in personality judgments at zero acquaintance. *Journal of Personality and Social Psychology, 55,* 387–395.

Ambady, N., & Rosenthal, R. (1992). Thin slices of expressive behavior as predictors of interpersonal consequences: A meta-analysis. *Psychological Bulletin, 111,* 256–274.

Anderson, S. W., Bechara, A., Damasio, H., Tranel, D., & Damasio, A. R. (1999). Impairment of social and moral behavior related to early damage in human prefrontal cortex. *Nature Neuroscience, 2,* 1032–1037.

Asch, S. (1956). Studies of independence and conformity: A minority of one against a unanimous majority. *Psychological Monographs, 70*(9, Whole No. 416).

Bandura, A., & Walters, R. (1963). *Social learning and personality development.* New York: Holt, Rinehart & Winston.

Bargh, J. (1994). The four horsemen of automaticity: Awareness, efficiency, intention, and control in social cognition. In J. R. S. Wyer & T. K. Srull

(Eds.), *Handbook of social cognition* (2nd ed., pp. 1–40). Hillsdale, NJ: Erlbaum.

Bargh, J. A., Chaiken, S., Raymond, P., & Hymes, C. (1996). The automatic evaluation effect: Unconditionally automatic activation with a pronunciation task. *Journal of Experimental Social Psychology, 32*, 185–210.

Bargh, J. A., & Chartrand, T. L. (1999). The unbearable automaticity of being. *American Psychologist, 54*, 462–479.

Baron, J. (1995). Myside bias in thinking about abortion. *Thinking and Reasoning, 1*, 221–235.

Baron, J. (1997). The illusion of morality as self-interest. *Psychological Science, 8*, 330–335.

Baron, J. (1998). *Judgment misguided: Intuition and error in public decision making.* New York: Oxford University Press.

Baron, J. (2000). *Thinking and deciding* (3rd ed.). Cambridge, England: Cambridge University Press.

Bastick, T. (1982). *Intuition: How we think and act.* Chichester, England: Wiley.

Batson, C. D. (1987). Prosocial motivation: Is it ever truly altruistic? *Advances in Experimental Social Psychology, 20*, 65–122.

Batson, C. D., Engel, C. L., & Fridell, S. R. (1999). Value judgments: Testing the somatic-marker hypothesis using false physiological feedback. *Personality and Social Psychology Bulletin, 25*, 1021–1032.

Batson, C. D., O'Quinn, K., Fulty, J., Vanderplass, M., & Isen, A. M. (1983). Influence of self-reported distress and empathy on egoistic versus altruistic motivation to help. *Journal of Personality and Social Psychology, 45*, 706–718.

Baumeister, R. F., & Newman, L. S. (1994). Self-regulation of cognitive inference and decision processes. *Personality and Social Psychology Bulletin, 20*, 3–19.

Bechtel, W., & Abrahamsen, A. (1991). *Connectionism and the mind: An introduction to parallel processing in networks.* Cambridge, MA: Blackwell.

Benedict, R. (1959). *Patterns of culture.* Boston: Houghton Mifflin. (Original work published in 1934.)

Berger, P. L., & Luckman, T. (1967). *The social construction of reality.* New York: Doubleday.

Black, J. E., Jones, T. A., Nelson, C. A., & Greenough, W. T. (1998). Neuronal plasticity and the developing brain. In N. E. Alessi, J. T. Coyle, S. I. Harrison, & S. Eth (Eds.), *Handbook of child and adolescent psychiatry* (pp. 31–53). New York: Wiley.

Blasi, A. (1980). Bridging moral cognition and moral action: A critical review of the literature. *Psychological Bulletin, 88*, 1–45.

Boehm, C. (1999). *Hierarchy in the forest: The evolution of egalitarian behavior.* Cambridge, MA: Harvard University Press.

Bruner, J. S. (1960). *The process of education.* Cambridge, MA: Harvard University Press.

Bruner, J. S. (1986). *Actual minds, possible worlds.* Cambridge, MA: Harvard University Press.

Byrne, R., & Whiten, A. (Eds.). (1988). *Machiavellian intelligence.* London: Oxford University Press.

Cacioppo, J. T., & Petty, R. E. (1982). The need for cognition. *Journal of Personality and Social Psychology, 42*, 116–131.

Chaiken, S. (1980). Heuristic versus systematic information processing and the use of source versus message cues in persuasion. *Journal of Personality and Social Psychology, 39*, 752–766.

Chaiken, S. (1987). The heuristic model of persuasion. In M. P. Zanna, J. M. Olson, & C. P. Herman (Eds.), *Social influence: The Ontario symposium* (pp. 3–39). Hillsdale, NJ: Erlbaum.

Chaiken, S., Giner-Sorolla, R., & Chen, S. (1996). Beyond accuracy: Defense and impression motives in heuristic and systematic information processing. In P. M. Gollwitzer & J. A. Bargh (Eds.), *The psychology of action: Linking cognition and motivation to behavior* (pp. 553–578). New York: Guilford Press.

Chaiken, S., & Trope, Y. (Eds.). (1999). *Dual process theories in social psychology.* New York: Guilford Press.

Chartrand, T. L., & Bargh, J. A. (1999). The chameleon effect: The perception–behavior link and social interaction. *Journal of Personality and Social Psychology, 76*, 893–910.

Chen, S., & Chaiken, S. (1999). The heuristic–systematic model in its broader context. In S. Chaiken & Y. Trope (Eds.), *Dual process theories in social psychology* (pp. 73–96). New York: Guilford Press.

Chen, S., Shechter, D., & Chaiken, S. (1996). Getting at the truth or getting along: Accuracy- versus impression-motivated heuristic and systematic processing. *Journal of Personality and Social Psychology, 71*, 262–275.

Cialdini, R. B. (1991). Altruism or egoism? That is (still) the question. *Psychological Inquiry, 2*, 124–126.

Cialdini, R., Schaller, M., Houlihan, D., Arps, K., Fultz, J., & Beaman, A. (1987). Empathy-based helping: Is it selflessly or selfishly motivated? *Journal of Personality and Social Psychology, 52*, 749–758.

Clark, A. (1999). *Being there: Putting brain, body, and world together again.* Cambridge, MA: MIT Press.

Cleckley, H. (1955). *The mask of sanity.* St. Louis, MO: C. V. Mosby.

Clore, G. L., Schwarz, N., & Conway, M. (1994). Affective causes and consequences of social information processing. In R. S. Wyer & T. K. Srull (Eds.), *Handbook of social cognition* (pp. 323–417). Hillsdale, NJ: Erlbaum.

Colby, A., & Damon, W. (1992). *Some do care: Contemporary lives of moral commitment.* New York: Free Press.

Damasio, A. (1994). *Descartes' error: Emotion, reason, and the human brain.* New York: Putnam.

Damasio, A. R., Tranel, D., & Damasio, H. (1990). Individuals with sociopathic behavior caused by frontal damage fail to respond autonomically to social stimuli. *Behavioral Brain Research, 41*, 81–94.

Damon, W. (1975). Early conceptions of positive justice as related to the development of logical operations. *Child Development, 46*, 301–312.

Damon, W. (1977). *The social world of the child.* San Francisco: Jossey-Bass.

D'Andrade, R. G. (1984). Cultural meaning systems. In R. A. Shweder & R. A. LeVine (Eds.), *Culture theory* (pp. 88–119). Cambridge, England: Cambridge University Press.

Darley, J. (1993). Research on morality: Possible approaches, actual approaches. *Psychological Science, 4*, 353–357.

Darley, J. M., & Berscheid, E. (1967). Increased liking as a result of anticipation of personal contact. *Human Relations, 20*, 29–40.

Darwin, C. (1998). *The descent of man.* Amherst, NY: Prometheus Books. (Original work published 1874.)

Davis, J. L., & Rusbult, C. E. (2001). Attitude alignment in close relationships. *Journal of Personality and Social Psychology, 81*, 65–84.

de Waal, F. (1982). *Chimpanzee politics.* New York: Harper & Row.

de Waal, F. (1991). The chimpanzee's sense of social regularity and its relation to the human sense of justice. *American Behavioral Scientist, 34*, 335–349.

de Waal, F. (1996). *Good natured: The origins of right and wrong in humans and other animals.* Cambridge, MA: Harvard University Press.

de Waal, F., & Lanting, F. (1997). *Bonobo: The forgotten ape.* Berkeley: University of California Press.

Devine, P. G. (1989). Stereotypes and prejudice: Their automatic and controlled components. *Journal of Personality and Social Psychology, 56*, 5–18.

Dion, K., Berscheid, E., & Walster, E. (1972). What is beautiful is good. *Journal of Personality and Social Psychology, 24*, 207–213.

Dunbar, R. (1996). *Grooming, gossip, and the evolution of language.* Cambridge, MA: Harvard University Press.

Edwards, K., & von Hippel, W. (1995). Hearts and minds: The priority of affective versus cognitive factors in person perception. *Personality and Social Psychology Bulletin, 21*, 996–1011.

Eisenberg, N., Shea, C. L., Carlo, G., & Knight, G. P. (1991). Empathy-related responding and cognition: A "chicken and the egg" dilemma. In W. M. Kurtines & J. L. Gewirtz (Eds.), *Handbook of moral behavior and development: Vol. 1. Theory* (pp. 63–88). Hillsdale, NJ: Erlbaum.

Epstein, S. (1994). Integration of the cognitive and the psychodynamic unconscious. *American Psychologist, 49*, 709–724.

Fazio, R. H., Sanbonmatsu, D. M., Powell, M. C., & Kardes, F. R. (1986). On the automatic evaluation of attitudes. *Journal of Personality and Social Psychology, 50*, 229–238.

Festinger, L. (1957). *A theory of cognitive dissonance.* Stanford, CA: Stanford University Press.

Fiske, A. P. (1991). *Structures of social life.* New York: Free Press.

Fiske, A. P. (1992). Four elementary forms of sociality: Framework for a unified theory of social relations. *Psychological Review, 99*, 689–723.

Fiske, A. P. (1999). *Learning culture the way informants do: Observing, imitating, and participating.* Unpublished manuscript, University of California, Los Angeles.

Forgas, J. P. (1995). Mood and judgment: The affect infusion model (AIM). *Psychological Bulletin, 117*, 39–66.

Frank, R. (1988). *Passions within reason: The strategic role of the emotions.* New York: Norton.

Freud, S. (1976). *The interpretation of dreams* (J. Strachey, Trans.). New York: Norton. (Original work published 1900).

Frijda, N. (1986). *The emotions.* Cambridge, England: Cambridge University Press.

Galotti, K. M. (1989). Approaches to studying formal and everyday reasoning. *Psychological Bulletin, 105*, 331–351.

Gazzaniga, M. S. (1985). *The social brain.* New York: Basic Books.

Gazzaniga, M. S., Bogen, J. E., & Sperry, R. W. (1962). Some functional effects of sectioning the cerebral commissures in man. *Proceedings of the National Academy of Sciences, USA, 48*, 1765–1769.

Gibbs, J. C. (1991). Toward an integration of Kohlberg's and Hoffman's theories of morality. In W. M. Kurtines & J. L. Gewirtz (Eds.), *Handbook of moral behavior and development: Vol. 1. Advances in theory, research, and application* (pp. 183–222). Hillsdale, NJ: Erlbaum.

Gigerenzer, G., & Goldstein, D. G. (1996). Reasoning the fast and frugal way: Models of bounded rationality. *Psychological Review, 103*, 650–669.

Goodall, J. (1986). *The chimpanzees of Gombe: Patterns of behavior.* Cambridge, MA: Belknap Press of Harvard University Press.

Grandin, T. (1995). *Thinking in pictures: And other reports from my life with autism.* New York: Doubleday.

Greenberg, J., Pyszczynski, T., Solomon, S., Rosenblatt, A. V. M., Kirkland, S., & Lyon, D. (1990). Evidence for terror management theory II: The effects of mortality salience on reactions to those who threaten or bolster the cultural worldview. *Journal of Personality and Social Psychology, 58*, 308–318.

Greene, J. D., Sommerville, R. B., Nystrom, L. E., Darley, J. M., & Cohen, J. D. (2001). An fMRI study of emotional engagement in moral judgment. *Science, 293,* 2105–2108.

Greenwald, A. G., & Banaji, M. R. (1995). Implicit social cognition. *Psychological Review, 102,* 4–27.

Griffin, D. W., & Ross, L. (1991). Subjective construal, social inference, and human misunderstanding. *Advances in Experimental Social Psychology, 24,* 319–359.

Haidt, J. (2001). The moral emotions. In R. J. Davidson, K. Scherer, & H. H. Goldsmith (Eds.), *Handbook of affective sciences* (pp. 852–870). Oxford, England: Oxford University Press.

Haidt, J., Bjorklund, F., & Murphy, S. (2000). *Moral dumbfounding: When intuition finds no reason.* Unpublished manuscript, University of Virginia.

Haidt, J., & Hersh, M. (2001). Sexual morality: The cultures and reasons of liberals and conservatives. *Journal of Applied Social Psychology, 31,* 191–221.

Haidt, J., Koller, S., & Dias, M. (1993). Affect, culture, and morality, or is it wrong to eat your dog? *Journal of Personality and Social Psychology, 65,* 613–628.

Haidt, J., Rozin, P., McCauley, C. R., & Imada, S. (1997). Body, psyche, and culture: The relationship between disgust and morality. *Psychology and Developing Societies, 9,* 107–131.

Hare, R. D. (1993). *Without conscience.* New York: Pocket Books.

Hare, R. D., & Quinn, M. J. (1971). Psychopathy and autonomic conditioning. *Journal of Abnormal Psychology, 77,* 223–235.

Hare, R. M. (1981). *Moral thinking: Its levels, method, and point.* London: Oxford University Press.

Harris, J. R. (1995). Where is the child's environment? A group socialization theory of development. *Psychological Review, 102,* 458–489.

Harrison, J. (1967). Ethical objectivism. In P. Edwards (Ed.), *The encyclopedia of philosophy* (Vols. 3–4, pp. 71–75). New York: Macmillan.

Hart, D., & Fegley, S. (1995). Prosocial behavior and caring in adolescence: Relations to self-understanding and social judgment. *Child Development, 66,* 1346–1359.

Haslam, N. (1997). Four grammars for primate social relations. In J. A. Simpson & D. T. Kenrick (Eds.), *Evolutionary social psychology* (pp. 297–316). Mahwah, NJ: Erlbaum.

Hermans, D., De Houwer, J., & Eelen, P. (1994). The affective priming effect: Automatic evaluation of evaluative information in memory. *Cognition and Emotion, 8,* 515–533.

Higgins, E. T. (1996). Knowledge activation: Accessibility, applicability, and salience. In E. T. Higgins & A. W. Kruglanski (Eds.), *Social psychology: Handbook of basic principles* (pp. 133–168). New York: Guilford Press.

Higgins, E. T., & Bargh, J. A. (1987). Social cognition and social perception. *Annual Review of Psychology, 38,* 369–425.

Hirschi, T., & Hindelang, M. J. (1977). Intelligence and delinquency: A revisionist view. *American Sociological Review, 42,* 571–587.

Hoffman, M. L. (1982). Development of prosocial motivation: Empathy and guilt. In N. Eisenberg (Ed.), *The development of prosocial behavior* (pp. 218–231). New York: Academic Press.

Hubel, D. H., & Wiesel, T. N. (1970). The period of susceptibility to the physiological effects of unilateral eye closure. *Journal of Physiology, 206,* 419–436.

Hume, D. (1960). *An enquiry concerning the principles of morals.* La Salle, IL: Open Court. (Original work published 1777.)

Hume, D. (1969). *A treatise of human nature.* London: Penguin. (Original work published 1739–1740.)

Huttenlocher, P. R. (1994). Synaptogenesis, synapse elimination, and neural plasticity in human cerebral cortex. In C. A. Nelson (Ed.), *Threats to optimal development: Integrating biological, psychological, and social risk factors. The Minnesota Symposia on Child Development, Vol. 27* (pp. 35–54). Hillsdale, NJ: Erlbaum.

Jensen, L. A. (1997). Different worldviews, different morals: America's culture war divide. *Human Development, 40,* 323–344.

Johnson, J. S., & Newport, E. L. (1989). Critical period effects in second language learning: The influence of maturational state on the acquisition of English as a second language. *Cognitive Psychology, 21,* 60–99.

Kagan, J. (1984). *The nature of the child.* New York: Basic Books.

Kahneman, D., & Tversky, A. (1984). Choices, values, and frames. *American Psychologist, 39,* 341–350.

Kant, I. (1959). *Foundation of the metaphysics of morals* (L. W. Beck, Trans.). Indianapolis, IN: Bobbs-Merrill. (Original work published 1785.)

Kochanska, G., Murray, K., Jacques, T. Y., Koenig, A. L., & Vandegeest, K. A. (1996). Inhibitory control in young children and its role in emerging internalization. *Child Development, 67,* 490–507.

Kohlberg, L. (1969). Stage and sequence: The cognitive–developmental approach to socialization. In D. A. Goslin (Ed.), *Handbook of socialization theory and research* (pp. 347–480). Chicago: Rand McNally.

Kohlberg, L. (1971). From is to ought: How to commit the naturalistic fallacy and get away with it in the study of moral development. In T. Mischel (Ed.), *Cognitive development and epistemology* (pp. 151–235). New York: Academic Press.

Kohlberg, L., Levine, C., & Hewer, A. (1983). *Moral stages: A current formulation and a response to critics.* Basel, Switzerland: Karger.

Kuhn, D. (1989). Children and adults as intuitive scientists. *Psychological Review, 96,* 674–689.

Kuhn, D. (1991). *The skills of argument*. Cambridge, England: Cambridge University Press.

Kunda, Z. (1990). The case for motivated reasoning. *Psychological Bulletin, 108*, 480–498.

Kunst-Wilson, W. R., & Zajonc, R. B. (1980). Affective discrimination of stimuli that cannot be recognized. *Science, 207*, 557–558.

Kurtines, W. M., & Gewirtz, J. L. (Eds.). (1991). *Handbook of moral behavior and development* (Vols. 1–3). Hillsdale, NJ: Erlbaum.

Lakoff, G. (1987). *Women, fire, and dangerous things*. Chicago: University of Chicago Press.

Lakoff, G. (1996). *Moral politics: What conservatives know that liberals don't*. Chicago: University of Chicago Press.

Lakoff, G., & Johnson, M. (1999). *Philosophy in the flesh*. New York: Basic Books.

Lapsley, D. K. (1996). *Moral psychology*. Boulder, CO: Westview.

Laupa, M., & Turiel, E. (1986). Children's conceptions of adult and peer authority. *Child Development, 57*, 405–412.

Lazarus, R. S. (1991). *Emotion and adaptation*. New York: Oxford University Press.

Lemer, M. J. (1965). Evaluation of performance as a function of performer's reward and attractiveness. *Journal of Personality and Social Psychology, 1*, 355–360.

Lerner, M. J., & Miller, D. T. (1978). Just world research and the attribution process: Looking back and ahead. *Psychological Bulletin, 85*, 1030–1051.

Lieberman, M. D. (2000). Intuition: A social cognitive neuroscience approach. *Psychological Bulletin, 126*, 109–137.

Loewenstein, G. F., Weber, E. U., Hsee, C. K., & Welch, E. S. (2001). Risk as feelings. *Psychological Bulletin, 127*, 267–286.

Lord, C. G., Ross, L., & Lepper, M. R. (1979). Biased assimilation and attitude polarization: The effects of prior theories on subsequently considered evidence. *Journal of Personality and Social Psychology, 37*, 2098–2109.

Mahapatra, M. (1981). *Traditional structure and change in an Orissan temple*. Calcutta, India: Punthi Pustak.

Margolis, H. (1987). *Patterns, thinking, and cognition*. Chicago: University of Chicago Press.

Mednick, S. A., Pollock, V., Volavka, J., & Gabrielli, W. F. (1982). Biology and violence. In M. Wolfgang & N. A. Weiner (Eds.), *Criminal violence* (pp. 21–80). Beverly Hills: Sage.

Metcalfe, J., & Mischel, W. (1999). A hot/cool-system analysis of delay of gratification: Dynamics of willpower. *Psychological Review, 106*, 3–19.

Miller, D. T. (1999). The norm of self-interest. *American Psychologist, 54*, 1053–1060.

Mischel, W., & Mischel, H. N. (1976). A cognitive social-learning approach to morality and self-regulation. In T. Lickona (Ed.), *Moral develop-*

ment and behavior: Theory, research, and social issues (pp. 84–107). New York: Holt, Rinehart & Winston.

Minoura, Y. (1992). A sensitive period for the incorporation of a cultural meaning system: A study of Japanese children growing up in the United States. *Ethos, 20*, 304–339.

Moskowitz, G. B., Skurnik, I., & Galinsky, A. D. (1999). The history of dual process notions, and the future of pre-conscious control. In S. Chaiken & Y. Trope (Eds.), *Dual process theories in social psychology* (pp. 12–36). New York: Guilford Press.

Murphy, S. T., & Zajonc, R. B. (1993). Affect, cognition, and awareness: Affective priming with optimal and suboptimal stimulus exposures. *Journal of Personality and Social Psychology, 64*, 723–729.

Newcomb, T. M. (1943). *Personality and social change: Attitude formation in a student community*. New York: Dryden.

Nickerson, R. S. (1994). The teaching of thinking and problem solving. In R. J. Sternberg (Ed.), *Thinking and problem solving* (pp. 409–449). San Diego, CA: Academic Press.

Nisbett, R., & Ross, L. (1980). *Human inference: Strategies and shortcomings of social judgment*. Englewood Cliffs, NJ: Prentice Hall.

Nisbett, R. E., & Schacter, S. (1966). Cognitive manipulation of pain. *Journal of Experimental Social Psychology, 2*, 227–236.

Nisbett, R. E., & Wilson, T. D. (1977). Telling more than we can know: Verbal reports on mental processes. *Psychological Review, 84*, 231–259.

Nucci, L., & Turiel, E. (1978). Social interactions and the development of social concepts in preschool children. *Child Development, 49*, 400–407.

Pavlov, I. (1927). *Conditioned reflexes*. Oxford, England: Oxford University Press.

Perkins, D. N., Allen, R., & Hafner, J. (1983). Difficulties in everyday reasoning. In W. Maxwell (Ed.), *Thinking: The frontier expands* (pp. 177–189). Hillsdale, NJ: Erlbaum.

Perkins, D. N., Farady, M., & Bushey, B. (1991). Everyday reasoning and the roots of intelligence. In J. F. Voss, D. N. Perkins, & J. W. Segal (Eds.), *Informal reasoning and education* (pp. 83–105). Hillsdale, NJ: Erlbaum.

Petty, R. E., & Cacioppo, J. T. (1986). The elaboration likelihood model of persuasion. In L. Berkowitz (Ed.), *Advances in experimental social psychology* (pp. 123–205). New York: Academic Press.

Piaget, J. (1965). *The moral judgement of the child* (M. Gabain, Trans.). New York: Free Press. (Original work published 1932.)

Plato. (1949). *Timaeus* (B. Jowen, Trans.). Indianapolis, IN: Bobbs-Merrill. (Original work published 4th century B.C.)

Posner, M. I., & Snyder, C. R. R. (1975). Attention and cognitive control. In R. L. Solso (Ed.),

Information processing and cognition: The Loyola Symposium (pp. 55–85). Hillsdale, NJ: Erlbaum.

Power, F. C., Higgins, A., & Kohlberg, L. (1989). *Lawrence Kohlberg's approach to moral education.* New York: Columbia University Press.

Premack, D., & Premack, A. J. (1995). Origins of human social competence. In M. S. Gazzaniga (Ed.), *The cognitive neurosciences* (pp. 205–218). Cambridge, MA: MIT Press.

Pyszczynski, T., & Greenberg, J. (1987). Toward in integration of cognitive and motivational perspectives on social inference: A biased hypothesis-testing model. *Advances in Experimental Social Psychology, 20,* 297–340.

Raine, A. (1997). Antisocial behavior and psychophysiology: A biosocial perspective and a prefrontal dysfunction hypothesis. In D. M. Stoff, J. Breiling, & J. D. Maser (Eds.), *Handbook of antisocial behavior* (pp. 289–304). New York: Wiley.

Raine, A., Buchsbaum, M. S., Stanley, J., Lottenberg, S., Abel, L., & Stoddard, J. (1994). Selective reductions in pre-frontal glucose metabolism in murderers. *Biological Psychiatry, 36,* 365–373.

Rawls, J. (1971). *A theory of justice.* Cambridge, MA: Harvard University Press.

Reber, A. S. (1993). *Implicit learning and tacit knowledge: An essay on the cognitive unconscious.* New York: Oxford University Press.

Rest, J. R. (1979). *Development in judging moral issues.* Minneapolis: University of Minnesota Press.

Robinson, R. J., Keltner, D., Ward, A., & Ross, L. (1995). Actual versus assumed differences in construal: "Naive realism" in intergroup perception and conflict. *Journal of Personality and Social Psychology, 68,* 404–417.

Rosenblatt, A., Greenberg, J., Solomon, S., Pyszczynski, T., & Lyon, D. (1989). Evidence for terror management theory: I. The effects of mortality salience on reactions to those who violate or uphold cultural values. *Journal of Personality and Social Psychology, 57,* 681–690.

Ross, W. D. (1930). *The right and the good.* London: Oxford University Press.

Rozin, P., Haidt, J., & McCauley, C. R. (2000). Disgust. In M. Lewis & J. M. Haviland-Jones (Eds.), *Handbook of emotions* (2nd ed., pp. 637–653). New York: Guilford Press.

Schooler, J. W., Fiore, S. M., & Brandimonte, M. A. (1997). At a loss from words: Verbal overshadowing of perceptual memories. *The Psychology of Learning and Motivation, 37,* 291–340.

Schwarz, N., & Clore, G. L. (1983). Mood, misattribution, and judgments of well-being: Information and directive functions of affective states. *Journal of Personality and Social Psychology, 45,* 513–523.

Selman, R. (1971). The relation of role taking to the development of moral judgment in children. *Child Development, 42,* 79–91.

Shavitt, S. (1990). The role of attitude objects in attitude formation. *Journal of Experimental Social Psychology, 26,* 124–148.

Sherif, M. (1935). A study of some social factors in perception. *Archives of Psychology, 27*(187).

Shoda, Y., Mischel, W., & Peake, P. K. (1990). Predicting adolescent cognitive and self-regulatory competencies from preschool delay of gratification: Identifying diagnostic conditions. *Developmental Psychology, 26,* 978–986.

Shore, B. (1996). *Culture in mind: Cognition, culture, and the problem of meaning.* New York: Oxford University Press.

Shweder, R. A., Goodnow, J., Hatano, G., LeVine, R. A., Markus, H., & Miller, P. (1998). The cultural psychology of development: One mind, many mentalities. In W. Damon (Series Ed.) & R. M. Lerner (Vol. Ed.), *Handbook of child psychology: Vol. 1. Theoretical models of human development* (5th ed., pp. 865–937). New York: Wiley.

Shweder, R. A., & Haidt, J. (1993). The future of moral psychology: Truth, intuition, and the pluralist way. *Psychological Science, 4,* 360–365.

Shweder, R. A., Much, N. C., Mahapatra, M., & Park, L. (1997). The "big three" of morality (autonomy, community, and divinity), and the "big three" explanations of suffering. In A. Brandt & P. Rozin (Eds.), *Morality and Health* (pp. 119–169). New York: Routledge.

Simon, H. A. (1967). Motivational and emotional controls of cognition. *Psychological Review, 74,* 29–39.

Simon, H. A. (1992). What is an "explanation" of behavior? *Psychological Science, 3,* 150–161.

Singer, P. (1994). *Rethinking life and death.* New York: St. Martin's Press.

Skinner, B. F. (1971). *Beyond freedom and dignity.* New York: Knopf.

Snyder, M., & Swann, W. B. (1978). Hypothesis testing processes in social interaction. *Journal of Personality and Social Psychology, 36,* 1202–1212.

Solomon, R. C. (1993). The philosophy of emotions. In M. Lewis & J. Haviland (Eds.), *Handbook of emotions* (pp. 3–15). New York: Guilford Press.

Solomon, S., Greenberg, J., & Pyszczynski, T. (1991). A terror management theory of social behavior. In M. Zanna (Ed.), *Advances in experimental social psychology* (pp. 93–159). San Diego, CA: Academic Press.

Spear, L. P. (2000). Neurobehavioral changes in adolescence. *Current Directions in Psychological Science, 9,* 111–114.

Spellman, B. A., & Holyoak, K. J. (1992). If Saddam is Hitler then who is George Bush? Analogical mapping between systems of social roles. *Journal of Personality and Social Psychology, 62,* 913–933.

Stein, R., & Nemeroff, C. J. (1995). Moral overtones of food: Judgments of others based on what they eat. *Personality and Social Psychology Bulletin, 21,* 480–490.

Tappan, M. (1997). Language, culture, and moral development: A Vygotskian perspective. *Developmental Review, 17,* 78–100.

Tetlock, P. E., Kristel, O. V., Elson, B., Green, M., & Lerner, J. (2000). The psychology of the unthinkable: Taboo trade-offs, forbidden base rates, and heretical counterfactuals. *Journal of Personality and Social Psychology, 78,* 853–870.

Thoma, S. J., Narvaez, D., Rest, J., & Derryberry, P. (1999). Does moral judgment development reduce to political attitudes or verbal ability? Evidence using the defining issues test. *Educational Psychology Review, 11,* 325–341.

Thorndike, E. L. (1920). A constant error in psychological ratings. *Journal of Applied Psychology, 4,* 25–29.

Trivers, R. L. (1971). The evolution of reciprocal altruism. *Quarterly Review of Biology, 46,* 35–57.

Trope, Y., & Bassok, M. (1983). Information-gathering strategies in hypothesis-testing. *Journal of Experimental Social Psychology, 19,* 560–576.

Turiel, E. (1983). *The development of social knowledge: Morality and convention.* Cambridge, England: Cambridge University Press.

Turiel, E. (1998). The development of morality. In W. Damon (Series Ed.) & N. Eisenberg (Vol. Ed.), *Handbook of child psychology: Vol. 3. Social, emotional, and personality development* (5th ed., pp. 863–932). New York: Wiley.

Turiel, E., Hildebrandt, C., & Wainryb, C. (1991). Judging social issues: Difficulties, inconsistencies, and consistencies. *Monographs of the Society for Research in Child Development, 56,* 1–103.

Turiel, E., Killen, M., & Helwig, C. C. (1987). Morality: Its structure, function, and vagaries. In J. Kagan & S. Lamb (Eds.), *The emergence of morality in young children* (pp. 155–243). Chicago: University of Chicago Press.

Wegner, D. (1994). Ironic processes of mental control. *Psychological Review, 101,* 34–52.

Wegner, D., & Bargh, J. (1998). Control and automaticity in social life. In D. T. Gilbert, S. T. Fiske, & G. Lindzey (Eds.), *Handbook of social psychology* (4th ed., pp. 446–496). New York: McGraw-Hill.

Werker, J., & Tees, R. (1984). Cross-language speech perception: Evidence for perceptual reorganization during the first year of life. *Infant Behavior and Development, 7,* 49–63.

Wheatley, T., & Haidt, J. (2001). *Hypnotically induced disgust makes moral judgments more severe.* Manuscript in preparation, University of Virginia.

Whiting, J., & Child, I. (1953). *Child training and personality.* New Haven, CT: Yale University Press.

Wicklund, R. A., & Brehm, J. W. (1976). *Perspectives on cognitive dissonance.* Hillsdale, NJ: Erlbaum.

Williams, B. (1967). Rationalism. In P. Edwards (Ed.), *The encyclopedia of philosophy* (Vols. 7–8, pp. 69–75). New York: Macmillan.

Wilson, E. O. (1998). *Consilience: The unity of knowledge.* New York: Knopf.

Wilson, J. Q. (1993). *The moral sense.* New York: Free Press.

Wilson, T. D. (2002). *Strangers to ourselves: Self-insight and the adaptive unconscious.* Cambridge, MA: Harvard University Press.

Wilson, T. D., Lindsey, S., & Schooler, T. (2000). A model of dual attitudes. *Psychological Review, 107,* 101–126.

Wilson, T. D., & Schooler, J. W. (1991). Thinking too much: Introspection can reduce the quality of preferences and decisions. *Journal of Personality and Social Psychology, 60,* 181–192.

Wundt, W. (1969). *Outlines of psychology* (C. H. Judd, Trans.). St Clair Shores, MI: Scholarly Press. (Original work published in 1897.)

Zajonc, R. B. (1980). Feeling and thinking: Preferences need no inferences. *American Psychologist, 35,* 151–175.

Zimbardo, P. G., LaBerge, S., & Butler, L. D. (1993). Psychophysiological consequences of unexplained arousal: A posthypnotic suggestion paradigm. *Journal of Abnormal Psychology, 102,* 466–473.

Index